CENSUS

OF THE

STATE OF NEW-YORK,

FOR

1855;

TAKEN IN PURSUANCE OF ARTICLE THIRD OF THE CONSTITUTION OF THE STATE, AND OF CHAPTER SIXTY-FOUR OF THE LAWS OF 1855.

PREPARED FROM THE ORIGINAL RETURNS,

UNDER THE DIRECTION OF HON. JOEL T. HEADLEY, SECRETARY OF STATE,

BY FRANKLIN B. HOUGH, SUPERINTENDENT OF THE CENSUS.

ALBANY:
PRINTED BY CHARLES VAN BENTHUYSEN.
1857.

PREFACE.

In submitting the present Census to the State, I would remark, that the delay in its appearance has grown out of the immense amount of labor bestowed on the work. The clerk force employed since the returns were received, in the summer of 1855, has been equal to the steady labor of one man for twenty consecutive years. The present is the first Census ever taken by the State of New-York, in which the work of preparing the results was executed in the office of the Secretary of State. Heretofore the returns of each town were summed up by the persons taking the enumeration, and transmitted to the county clerks, by whom summaries were prepared for their respective counties. These were sent to the Secretary's Office and published, without revision, and with no further care than the preparation of a general recapitulation for the State. Experience has shown that when labor of this kind is done in detailed portions, by persons who have no consultation upon doubtful points, different constructions will be placed on the same subjects, and hence when the results are brought together, the whole will lack that completeness, clearness of arrangement, and symmetry which constitute its great value.

To illustrate the growth of the State, the results of all previous censuses are inserted in the introduction. The tables giving the total population of each town, at each census since 1790, with the date of erection, and name of town from which taken, will be found to embrace an amount of historical information of much value in studying the rapid development of our numbers and resources. Diagrams are introduced to illustrate the changes which time has wrought upon the population of different sections of the State, and their mutual relations, so that with a single glance they can be understood far better than by any elaborate description, or detailed statement. As the value of statistics in a great degree consists in the facility they furnish of being compared with others, the arrangement of the present Census has been carefully planned to this end, while new modes of classification have been introduced to meet the probable wants in future comparisons. It will be seen that the statistics cover more ground than ever before attempted in an American census, and in some respects are more complete than any in Europe. There are some deficiencies and inaccuracies which cannot be avoided. It is to be regretted, that a census planned on so broad and comprehensive a scale, could not have been kept out of party strife. The marshals have always been appointed by the supervisor and town clerk, who would select men least obnoxious to the inhabitants, and of sufficient intelligence to comprehend their duties. Taking these appointments away from their localities, and bestowing them on the Secretary of State, and for partizan purposes, wrought two evils. In the first place, it rendered it impossible to get as good marshals as could have been obtained in the ordinary way; for however anxious the Secretary may be to perform his duty, it is not to be expected that one man can appoint one thousand seven hundred and forty-four men, (the number actually employed,) in the various towns in the State, and not get some very incompetent persons. In the second place, there is always more or less reluctance, among a portion of our population, to answer the minute inquiries required of the marshal. This reluctance and indifference were increased by the animosity created by the passage of the act transferring the appointing power, so that in many cases answers were refused, or given without any regard to their accuracy.

The Census was taken under my predecessor, Mr. Leavenworth, and although feeling to the fullest extent the importance of the work, and endeavoring to secure the most complete returns, he could not remedy these evils. Especially could he have no control over the feeling of hatred engendered by witnessing the attempted prostitution of so great and valuable a work to political ends. It is the more to be regretted because it may be a long time before the State will have an officer who will take the comprehensive views that my predecessor did, and lay out the work on so broad a scale, while it will be next to impossible to find another person so well qualified, in every respect, to perform the duty of compiling and arranging, as the recent superintendent, Dr. Hough. The whole merit of this work belongs to him, and he has brought to it an energy, industry, comprehensiveness of views, and a careful study which reflect the highest honor on himself, and have enabled him to furnish a model Census report for the country.

J. T. HEADLEY,

Secretary of State.

CONTENTS.

INTRODUCTION.

In presenting the results of the census of the State of New-York for the year 1855, it may be proper, before giving a statement of the instructions under which it was taken, and the deductions which may be drawn from its returns, to offer a concise summary of previous enumerations, and trace the progressive increase of our population through a series of years.

Although the wants of government, have from remote periods suggested in almost every country the necessity of some authentic summary of their social condition and industrial wealth, it is but recently that attention has been directed to the importance of publishing these results; hence comparisons extending back beyond a quarter of a century, must necessarily be reduced to a few general heads of inquiry, which the exigencies of war or the requirements of revenue or representation made indispensable. Detailed classifications of ages, professions, origin, mortality and other items now expected in an official census, and considered so essential to the civil economist, the philanthropist and the statesman, may be regarded as originating in the present century. The effect of moral and political causes, in modifying the relative proportions of these social elements, or varying the average term of human life, can only be determined by the future study of accumulated series of these facts.

The want of data for the administration of the affairs of her American colonies, led the English government, at an early period, to direct an enumeration of their inhabitants; and these censuses were repeated at irregular intervals until near the period of the revolution, affording more definite information within the limited field they embraced, than is possessed in relation to England itself during the same period. Upon the organization of an independent government in New-York in 1777, a provision was inserted in the constitution, requiring a septennial census of electors, which before the revision of 1822 had been extended, to include the whole population; and this requirement, with a change of the interval, has been continued till the present time; affording, it is believed, the first instance in which a regular periodical census was established by government. The example of New-York was followed in framing the constitution of the United States in 1787, but not until two censuses had been taken by our national government, was a similar measure adopted in Great Britain. It is gratifying to observe that the practice thus begun, has been followed by nearly every civilized country on the globe, and that at each succeeding period, a progressive improvement has been observed in the extent of their inquiries and in the arrangement of the results.

Colonial Censuses: From the first agricultural settlement of New Netherlands by the Dutch, in 1623, until after its conquest by the English in 1664, but few memoranda are preserved, affording a definite knowledge of the population of the colony, or its growth between different intervals. The spread of settlements was prevented and their population repeatedly reduced by Indian hostilities, while the uncertainty and disputes respecting boundaries with the neighboring colonies, had an unfavorable effect, by discouraging immigration.

In 1628 Manhattan island contained 270 souls, all told,* and in 1643, from four to five hundred men, while Albany, at the latter date, contained about one hundred inhabitants.†

In 1645 the Manhattan settlement contained "scarcely one hundred men besides traders;‡ and at the beginning of Governor Stuyvesant's administration in 1647, there were estimated to be but about 250, or at most 300 men able to bear arms.§ Under the sound and liberal policy adopted by this governor, the colony began to flourish, and a survey made by Captain De Koninck in 1656, showed that New Amsterdam contained 120 houses, and 1,000 souls,|| and in 1658 the colony numbered over 6,000. When surrendered to the English in 1664, the province was estimated to contain full 10,000, and the city 1,500 inhabitants.¶ In September, 1673, the population of New-York was estimated at 6,000.**

The first attempt towards procuring a census of the colony after its occupation by the English, appears to have been made in 1686, in pursuance of a request from the committee of trade in the province of New-York. Governor Dongan, with the advice of his council, on the 4th of October of that year, directed the sheriffs in each county to report on or before the 1st of April ensuing, the military strength, number of

* Brodhead's Hist. of N. Y. i., p. 183. † Ib. p. 373. ‡ Ib. p. 410. § Hol. Doc. xi.; Brodhead's Hist. i., p. 465. || Br. Hist. 623. ¶ Ib. 734.

** Vanderkemp's Trans. from Dutch Rec. xxiii., 311. There appears to be much uncertainty in respect to this estimate, which is apparently too large for the city at that time, and certainly too small for the whole colony.

inhabitants and merchants, English or foreigners, servants and slaves, and what number of marriages, christenings and burials had occurred in each county within seven years, together with inquiries in reference to quit rents, revenues, escheats, forfeitures, duties, &c.; the names of patentees under the crown, and the rents due from each throughout the colony.* Only scattered portions of the results of this census are preserved in the Secretary's office.†

The war between England and France (1689-1697,) seriously affected the growth of the colony of New York, and induced numbers to leave for places less liable to molestation from the enemy in Canada, and their Indian allies. On the 3rd of May, 1697, Governor Fletcher issued an order for a full enumeration of the inhabitants of the city and county of Albany, and the number of families and individuals that had removed since the beginning of the war, or who had been killed or taken captive. The result of this inquiry was as follows:

	Men	Women	Children	Total
In 1689,········	662 men,	340 women,	1,014 children;	total, 2,016.
In 1697,········	382 "	262 "	805 "	" 1,449.
Decrease, ·······	280 "	78 "	209 "	" 567.

This diminution of the population was from the following causes:‡

	Men	Women	Children	Total
Departed,················	142 men,	68 women,	209 children;	total, 419.
Taken prisoners, ·········	16 "	························		" 16.
Killed by the enemy,·····	84 "	························		" 84.
Died, ····················	38 "	························		" 38.

In 1698, a full census of the province was taken by the high sheriffs and justices of the peace in the several counties, by order of Governor Bellomont, with the following result:

Census of 1698.§

COUNTIES.	Men.	Women.	Children.	Negroes.	Total.
Albany,................................	380	270	803	23	1,476
Dutchess and Ulster,...................	248	111	869	156	1,384
Kings, ...	308	332	1,081	296	2,017
New-York, ...	1,019	1,057	2,161	700	4,937
Orange, ...	29	31	140	19	219
Queens, ...	1,465	1,350	551	199	3,565
Richmond, ...	328	208	118	73	727
Suffolk,...............................	973	1,024	124	558	2,679
Westchester, ...	316	294	307	146	1,063
Total, ...	5,066	4,677	6,154	2,170	18,067

In 1703, Lord Cornbury, then governor of New-York, issued an order to the sheriffs to take an enumeration of the inhabitants within each county, distinguishing by age, sex and color, the result of which was as follows:

Census of 1703.||

COUNTIES.	Males from 16 to 60.	Females.	Male children.	Female children.	Male negroes.	Female negroes.	Male negro children.	Female negro children.	All above 60.	Total.**
Albany,......................	510	385	515	605	83	53	36	28	58	2,273
Kings, ...	345	304	433	487	135	75	72	61	....	1,912
New-York, ...	813	1,009	934	989	102	288	131	109	....	4,375
Orange, ...	49	40	57	84	13	7	7	6	5	268
Queens, ...	952	753	1,093	1,170	117	114	98	95	¶	4,392
Richmond, ...	176	140	42	49	60	32	4	1	....	504
Suffolk, ...	787	756	818	797	60	52	38	38	¶	3,346
Ulster,......................	383	305	436	357	63	36	31	15	23	1,649
Westchester, ...	472	469	382	386	74	45	50	29	39	1,946
Total, ...	4,487	4,161	4,710	4,924	707	702	467	382	125	20,665

* New-York Colonial MSS. xxxiv.

† *Albany Co.*, on the 27th of March, 1687, reported the following: 1,058 males, 928 females; 107 male and 50 female negroes; 8 companies of foot, 369; 1 troop of horse, 54; 8 merchants, 202 male, and 130 female christenings, and 199 burials during the seven years preceding. (N. Y. Col. MSS. xxxv.)

Jamaica, Queens Co., reported 32 marriages, 82 christenings, and 33 burials within the seven preceding years. (Ib.)

Newtown, Queens Co., reported (March 30, 1687) 28 marriages, and 35 burials; one company of foot, 125; 265 children, 31 servants, and 49 slaves. (Ib.)

Huntington, Suffolk Co., reported (Dec. 16, 1686), 60 families, 204 males, 158 females; 3 male and 3 female negroes; 72, militia; 11 marriages, and 15 deaths. (N. Y. Col. MSS. xxxiii.)

Southampton, Suffolk Co., reported a population of 786, 142 soldiers, 175 marriages, christenings and burials. (Ib.)

Southold, Suffolk Co., reported 114 families, 231 white males, 300 white females; 14 male and 10 female negroes; 129 militia, including 16 troopers; 151 births, 44 marriages and 72 deaths. (Ib.)

‡ See Colonial History of New-York, iv., pp. 338 and 420.

§ Colonial History of New-York, iv. p. 420.

|| New-York Colonial MSS., vol. xlviii.

¶ Included in first column.

** In a subsequent communication to the Lords of Trade in 1712 (Colonial Hist. of New-York, v., p. 339,) the totals of the census of 1703 are quoted differently from those in the above table. There are no means for determining whether this difference arose from a subsequent correction of errors, or from mistakes in copying. As given in the latter the totals were as follows: New-York, 4,436; Kings, 1,915; Richmond, 503; Orange, 268; Westchester, 1,946; Queens, 4,392; Suffolk, 3,346; Albany, 2,273; Ulster and Dutchess, 1,669.

The next official census of New-York was taken by order of Governor Hunter, in 1712,* upon the receipt of a communication from the Lords of Trade, inquiring into the affairs of the province.† At a council held March 20th of that year, it was "ordered that the justices of the peace, do cause an exact account to be taken, with all possible speed, of the number of inhabitants of their respective counties, and that the secretary send to each county a form of such account."‡

The returns of the census thus ordered are imperfect, "the people being deterred by a simple superstition, and observation *that the sickness followed upon the last numbering of the people*."§ So far as can be compiled from the original returns,‖ the results were as follows:

Partial Census of 1712.

COUNTIES.	WHITES.						SLAVES.				Total.
	Males under 16.	Males between 16 and 60.	Males over 60.	Females under 16.	Females 16 to 60.	Females over 60.	Males under 16.	Males over 16.	Females under 16.	Females over 16	
Kings,¶	....	....	....	....	....	....	....	....	....	....	1,925
New-York,	1,197	1,062	60	1,182	1,268	97	155	321	179	320	5,841
Orange,	105	98	4	82	91	5	9	21	11	12	438
Richmond,	....	....	....	....	....	....	....	....	....	....	1,279
Suffolk,	1,092	929	114	1,044	926	64	26	116	32	70	4,413
Westchester,	672	560	75	577	539	62	72	127	62	72	2,818
Total,	3,066	2,649	253	2,885	2,824	228	262	585	284	474	16,714

Returns from Albany, Dutchess, and Ulster counties were not received until 1714, and were as follows:**

Partial Census of 1714.

COUNTIES.	WHITES.						SLAVES.				Total
	Males under 16	Males between 16 and 60.	Males over 60.	Females under 16.	Females between 16 and 60.	Females over 60.	Males under 16.	Males over 16.	Females under 16.	Females over 16.	
Albany,	753	688	54	651	676	49	98	155	83	122	3,329
Dutchess,	120	89	11	98	97	1	6	12	4	7	445
Ulster,	450	424	44	427	406	36	68	148	39	78	2,120

A census of the colony of New-York was subsequently taken in the years, 1723, 1731, 1737, 1746, 1749 1756, and 1771. The results of these several enumerations were as follows:

Census of 1723.††

COUNTIES.	WHITES.					NEGROES AND OTHER SLAVES.					Total.
	Men.	Women.	Male children.	Female children.	Total of white persons.	Men.	Women.	Male children.	Female children.	Total negroes and other slaves.	
Albany,	1,512	1.408	1,404	1,369	5,693	307	200	146	155	808	6,501
Dutchess,	276	237	259	268	1,040	22	14	2	5	43	1,083
Kings,	490	476	414	394	1,774	171	123	83	67	444	2,218
New-York,	1,460	1,726	1,352	1,348	5,886	408	476	220	258	1,362	7,248
Orange,	309	245	304	239	1,097	45	29	42	31	147	1,244
Queens,	1,568	1,599	1,530	1,371	6,068	393	294	228	208	1,123	7,191
Richmond,	335	320	305	291	1,251	101	63	49	42	255	1,506
Suffolk,	1,441	1,348	1,321	1,156	5,266	357	367	197	54	975	6,241
Ulster,	642	453	563	600	2,357	227	126	119	94	566	2,923
Westchester,	1,050	951	1,048	912	3,961	155	118	92	83	448	4,409
Total,	9.083	8.763	8.500	8,047	34,393	2,186	1,810	1,178	997	6,171	40,564

Census of 1731.‡‡

COUNTIES.	WHITES.				BLACKS.				Total.
	Males over 10 years.	Females over 10 years.	Males under 10 years	Females under 10 years.	Males over 10 years	Females over 10 years.	Males under 10 years.	Females under 10 years.	
Albany,	2,481	1,255	2,352	1,212	568	185	346	174	8,573
Dutchess,	573	481	263	298	591	32	13	8	2,259
Kings,	629	518	243	268	205	146	65	76	2,150
New-York,	2,628	2,250	1,143	1,024	599	607	186	185	8,622
Orange,	627	537	325	299	85	47	19	33	1,972
Queens,	2,239	2,175	1,178	1,139	476	363	226	199	7.995
Richmond,	423	571	263	256	111	98	51	44	1,817
Suffolk,	2,144	1,130	2,845	955	239	83	196	83	7,675
Ulster,	990	814	577	515	321	196	124	91	3,728
Westchester,	1,879	1,701	1,054	707	269	96	176	151	6,033
Total,	14,613	11,532	10,243	6,673	3,464	1,853	1,402	1,044	50,824

* A census of Ulster county was taken in 1710, with the following result: Males under 16, 421; males between 16 and 60, 384; males over 60, 43, females under 16, 409; females between 16 and 60, 388; females over 60, 36; male slaves under 16, 84; male slaves over 16, 137; female slaves under 16, 37; female slaves over 16, 66; total, 2,005. (New-York Col MSS. lii.)

† Dated October 26, 1711. See Colonial Hist. of New-York, v., p. 282.

‡ Council Minutes, xi., p. 68.

§ Colonial History of New-York, v., p. 339.

‖ New-York Colonial MSS., vol. lvii. Secretary's office

¶ Colonial Hist. of New York, v., p. 339

** New-York Colonial MSS., vol. lix.

†† Colonial History, v., p. 702.

‡‡ Colonial History, v., p. 929.

Census of 1737.*

COUNTIES.	WHITES.				BLACKS.				Total.
	Males above 10.	Females above 10.	Males under 10.	Females under 10.	Males above 10.	Females above 10.	Males under 10.	Females under 10.	
Albany,	3, 209	2, 995	1, 463	1, 384	714	496	223	197	10, 681
Dutchess,	940	860	710	646	161	42	37	22	3, 418
Kings,	654	631	235	264	210	169	84	101	2, 348
New-York,	3, 253	3, 568	1, 088	1, 036	674	609	229	207	10, 664
Orange,	860	753	501	433	125	95	38	35	2, 840
Queens,	2, 407	2, 290	1, 395	1, 656	460	370	254	227	9, 059
Richmond,	488	497	289	266	132	112	52	53	1, 889
Suffolk,	2, 297	2, 353	1, 175	1, 008	393	307	203	187	7, 923
Ulster,	1, 175	1, 681	541	601	378	260	124	110	4, 870
Westchester	2, 110	1, 890	950	944	304	254	153	140	6, 745
Total,	17, 393	17, 518	8, 347	8, 238	3, 551	2, 714	1, 397	1, 279	60, 437

Census of 1746.†

COUNTIES.	WHITES.					BLACKS.					Total.
	Males under 16.	Males 16 and under 60.	Males above 60.	Females under 16.	Females above 16.	Males under 16.	Males 16 and under 60.	Males above 60.	Females under 16	Females above 16.	
Albany,	......	......	......	......	......	......	......	......	......	......	......
Dutchess,	2, 200	2, 056	200	2, 100	1, 750	106	160	26	108	100	8, 806
Kings,	350	435	71	366	464	140	167	32	154	152	2, 331
New-York,	2, 117	2, 097	149	2, 013	2, 897	419	645	76	735	569	11, 717
Orange,	536	763	67	871	721	82	99	34	51	44	3, 268
Queens,	1, 946	1, 826	233	2, 077	1, 914	365	466	61	391	361	9, 640
Richmond,	445	376	35	421	414	92	88	13	95	94	2, 073
Suffolk,	1, 887	1, 835	226	1, 891	2, 016	329	393	52	315	310	9, 254
Ulster,	1, 022	1, 044	116	972	1, 000	244	321	43	229	264	5, 265
Westchester,	2 435	2, 090	303	2, 095	1, 640	187	180	27	138	140	9, 235
Total,	12, 938	12, 522	1, 400	12, 806	12, 816	1, 964	2, 529	364	2, 216	2, 034	61, 589

Census of 1749.‡

COUNTIES.	WHITES.						BLACKS.						Total.
	Males under 16.	Males 16 and under 60.	Males above 60	Females under 16.	Females 16 and upwards	Total whites.	Males under 16.	Males 16 and under 60.	Males above 60	Females under 16.	Females 16 and upwards	Total blacks.	
Albany,	2, 249	2, 359	322	2, 137	2, 087	9, 154	309	424	48	334	365	1, 480	10, 634
Dutchess,	1, 970	1, 820	160	1, 790	1, 751	7, 491	103	155	21	63	79	421	7, 912
Kings,	288	437	62	322	391	1, 500	232	244	21	137	149	783	2, 283
New-York,	2, 346	2, 765	183	2, 364	3, 268	10, 926	460	610	41	556	701	2, 368	13, 294
Orange,	1, 061	856	66	992	899	3, 874	62	95	16	84	103	360	4, 234
Queens,	1, 630	1, 508	151	1, 550	1, 778	6, 617	300	386	43	245	349	1, 323	7, 940
Richmond,	431	420	36	424	434	1, 745	88	110	20	93	98	409	2, 154
Suffolk,	2, 058	1, 863	248	1, 960	1, 969	8, 098	305	355	41	292	293	1, 286	9, 384
Ulster,	913	992	110	810	979	3, 804	217	301	50	198	240	1, 006	4, 810
Westchester,	2, 511	2, 312	228	2, 263	2, 233	9, 547	303	270	66	238	279	1, 156	10, 703
Total,	15, 457	15, 332	1, 566	14, 612	15, 789	62, 756	2, 379	2, 950	367	2, 240	2, 656	10, 592	73, 348

Census of 1756.§

COUNTIES.	WHITES.						BLACKS.						Total.
	Males under 16.	Males 16 and under 60	Males above 60	Females under 16.	Females 16 and upwards.	Total whites.	Males under 16.	Males 16 and under 60.	Males 60 and upwards.	Females under 16	Females 16 and upwards.	Total blacks.	
Albany,	3, 474	3, 795	456	3, 234	3, 846	14, 805	658	786	76.	496	603	2, 619	17, 424
Dutchess,	3, 910	2, 873	203	3, 530	2, 782	13, 298	211	270	53	163	162	859	14, 157
Kings,	417	467	84	358	536	1, 862	212	214	21	201	197	845	2, 707
New-York,	2, 260	2, 308	174	2, 359	3, 667	10, 768	468	604	68	443	695	2, 278	13, 046
Orange,	1, 213	1, 088	74	1, 083	998	4, 456	103	116	24	93	94	430	4, 886
Queens,	1, 960	2, 147	253	1, 892	2, 365	8, 617	581	563	55	500	470	2, 169	10, 786
Richmond,	344	411	107	334	471	1, 667	145	92	30	97	101	465	2. 132
Suffolk,	2, 283	2, 141	221	2, 265	2, 335	9, 245	278	297	40	194	236	1, 045	10, 290
Ulster,	1, 655	1, 687	156	1, 489	1, 618	6, 605	328	437	49	326	360	1, 500	8, 105
Westchester,	3, 153	2, 908	1, 039	2, 440	2, 379	11, 919	296	418	77	267	280	1, 338	13, 257
Total,	20, 669	19, 825	2, 767	18, 984	20, 997	83, 242	3, 280	3, 797	493	2, 780	3, 198	13, 548	96, 790

* Colonial History of New-York, vi., p. 133. The original returns are found in N. Y. Col. MSS., lxxii.

† Ib., vi., p. 392.

‡ Ib., vi., p. 550. Governor Clinton remarked of this census, that it was difficult to obtain satisfactory returns, as there were no means allowed for paying for the service. (Col. Hist. of N. Y., vi., p. 500.)

§ London Doc., xliv., p. 123.

There was no census of New-York, taken after the above until 1771,* during which interval an unparaleled increase of population was observed. The reasons assigned for this growth, were, the high price of labor, and the abundance and cheapness of land fit for cultivation, which by increasing the means of subsistence, afforded strong additional incitements to early marriages. The proportion of births to the population was said to much exceed that in Europe, and it was computed that the colonies doubled their inhabitants by natural increase in twenty years. In addition to the causes above cited, a very prominent source of prosperity was derived from the conquest of Canada in 1760, which, by removing all danger of Indian hostilities, allowed the frontiers to expand without obstruction, and induced large immigrations for the settlement of the immense grants which were procured during this period. Many of these grants were conditioned to their occupation by a certain number of families within seven years, or other definite time, which led to energetic measures for immigration and settlement.

Census of 1771.†

COUNTIES.	WHITES.						BLACKS.						Total.
	Males under 16.	Males 16 and under 60.	Males above 60.	Females under 16.	Females 16 and upwards.	Total whites.	Males under 16.	Males 16 and under 60	Males above 60.	Females under 16.	Females 16 and upwards.	Total blacks.	
Albany,	9,740	9,822	1,136	9,086	9,045	38,829	876	1,100	250	671	980	3,877	42,706
Dutchess,	5,721	4,687	384	5,413	4,839	21,044	299	417	34	282	328	1,360	22,404
Kings,	548	644	76	513	680	2,461	297	287	22	261	295	1,162	3,623
New-York,	3,720	5,083	280	3,779	5,864	18,726	568	890	42	552	1,085	3,137	21,862
Orange,	2,651	2,297	167	2,191	2,124	9,430	162	184	22	120	174	662	10,092
Queens,	1,253	2,083	950	2,126	2,332	8,744	374	511	271	545	534	2,235	10,980
Richmond,	616	438	96	508	595	2,253	177	152	22	106	137	594	2,847
Suffolk,	2,731	2,834	347	2,658	3,106	11,676	350	389	59	320	334	1,452	13,128
Ulster,	2,835	3,023	262	2,601	3,275	11,996	518	516	57	422	441	1,954	13,950
Westchester,	3,813	5,204	549	3,483	5,266	18,315	793	916	68	766	887	3,430	21,745
Total within present limits of New-York,	33,628	36,115	4,247	32,358	37,126	143,474	4,414	5,362	847	4,045	5,195	19,863	163,337
Cumberland,‡	1,071	1,002	59	941	862	3,935	....	6	1	3	2	12	3,947
Gloucester,‡	178	185	8	193	151	715	2	4	....	1	....	7	722
General total,	34,877	37,302	4,314	33,492	38,139	148,124	4,416	5,372	848	4,049	5,197	19,882	168,006

The estimated population in 1774 was 161,098 whites, and 21,149 blacks, making a total of 182,247. (Lond. Doc., xliv.)

Comparative Results of Colonial Censuses.

YEARS.	Total population	INCREASE.		TOTAL BY SEXES.				PERCENTAGE OF COLORS AND SEXES.							
		Total increase.	Annual rate per cent.	Whites.		Blacks.		Whites.		Blacks.		Whites	Blacks.	Males	Females.
				Male.	Female.	Male.	Female	Male	Female	Male	Female.				
1698	18,067	....	....	8,143§	7,754§	2,170		45.1	42.9	12.0		88.0	12.0	51.1	48.9
1703	20,665	2,598	2.87	9,322	9,085	1,174	1,084	45.1	43.9	5.7	5.3	89.0	11.0	50.8	49.2
1723	40,564	19,899	4.81	17,583	16,810	3,364	2,807	43.4	41.4	8.3	6.9	84.8	15.2	51.7	48.3
1731	50,824	10,260	3.16	24,856	18,205	4,866	2,897	48.9	35.8	9.5	5.8	84.7	15.3	58.4	41.6
1737	60,437	9,613	3.15	25,740	25,756	4,948	3,993	42.6	42.6	8.2	6.6	85.2	14.8	50.8	49.2
1746	61,589	1,152	0.21	26,860	25,622	4,857	4,250	43.6	41.6	7.9	6.9	85.2	14.8	51.5	48.5
1749	73,348	11,759	6.36	32,355	30,401	5,696	4,896	44.1	41.4	7.8	6.7	85.5	14.5	51.9	48.1
1756	96,790	23,442	4.57	43,261	39,981	7,570	5,978	44.7	41.3	7.8	6.2	86.0	14.0	52.5	47.5
1771	163,337	66,547	4.59	73,990	69,484	10,623	9,240	45.3	42.5	6.5	5.7	87.8	12.2	51.8	48.2

Censuses of the Revolutionary Period: To ascertain the quotas of men and means necessary to maintain the war with Great Britain, the Continental Congress, in 1775,‖ directed an enumeration of inhabitants in the several colonies. In pursuance of this order, the Provincial Congress of New-York, on the 22d of May, 1776, ordered letters to be addressed to the committees of each county in the colony, requesting them to appoint proper persons for taking the enumeration, according to the following form. A fragment only of this census is preserved in the Secretary's office,¶ the summary of which is here given:

* Doc. Hist. N. Y., 8vo., i., p. 763. † London Documents, xliv., p. 144.

‡ Within the present limits of Vermont.

§ The number of white children not being designated by sexes, is equally divided in forming the above estimate.

‖ *Resolved*, That it be recommended to the general assemblies, conventions or councils, or committees of safety of the respective colonies, to ascertain, by the most impartial and effectual means in their power, the number of inhabitants in each respective colony, taking care that the lists be authenticated by the oaths of the several persons who shall be intrusted with this service; and that the said assemblies, conventions, councils, or committees of safety, do respectively lay before this Congress a return of the number of inhabitants of their respective colonies, as soon as the same shall be procured. (Journal of Congress, Dec. 26, 1775.)

¶ Volume lettered, "Military Committee, vol. 25,—1775, 1776, 1777, 1778," where the names of the heads of families of the above are given.

Partial Census of 1776.

PARTS OF SUFFOLK COUNTY.	WHITE MALES			WHITE FEMALES.		NEGROES MALE AND FEMALE.	
	Above 50 years of age	Above 16 and under 50 years.	Under 16 years of age	Above 16 years of age.	Under 16 years of age.	Above 16 years of age	Under 16 years of age.
Shelter Island,	10	29	29	40	32	21	12
Brookhaven,	123	391	498	546	473	68	74
Manor of St. George and Patentship of Moritches,*	19	43	73	76	81	50	34
Eastern district of Southampton,	75	290	318	407	340	68	35
Western " " population 700,	....	....	....	....	....	....	....
Islip,	19	64	84	88	60	33	27
East Hampton,	69	249	297	341	294	45	22
Smithtown,	35	109	141	156	118	91	70

A clause in the ninth Article of Confederation, enumerated among the powers of Congress, the right "to agree upon the number of land forces, and to make requisitions from each State for its quota, in proportion to the number of white inhabitants in each State." Under this authority, Congress, by a resolution of Dec. 11, 1781, recommended another enumeration, which was ordered by an act of the New-York Legislature of March 20, 1782.†

This act required the county sheriffs, to direct the constables of the several wards, cities and towns, to take the number of white inhabitants within their several districts, distinguishing age and sex, as on the former occasion, and specifying the number that had been driven from their usual place of abode by the incursions of the enemy. The form prescribed was as follows. The returns of Ulster county, and so much of Westchester as was not within the range of the enemy, are also given:

Partial Census of 1782.

COUNTIES.	NUMBER OF WHITE INHABITANTS.					REFUGEES FROM THEIR USUAL PLACE OF ABODE BY REASON OF INCURSIONS OF ENEMY.				
	Males,			Females.		Males.			Females.	
	Under 16 years of age.	Above 16 and under 60	Above 60 years of age.	Under 16 years of age	Above 16 years of age	Under 16 years of age.	Above 16 and under 60.	Above 60 years of age.	Under 16 years of age.	Above 16 years of age.
Ulster,‡	4,133	3,534	401	3.543	3,941	313	253	36	309	294
Part of Westchester,§	1,785	1,154	126	1,472	1,741	199	275	13	293	272

The results of other counties are not known.

On the 18th of April, 1783, the Continental Congress decided upon a change in the eighth Article of Confederation, in reference to the expenses for the common defence or public welfare, previously charged to the several States, in proportion to the value of land granted to or surveyed for individuals. By this change these expenses were made payable by the States, "in proportion to the whole number of white and other free citizens, and inhabitants of every age, sex and condition, including those bound to servitude for a term of years, and three fifths of all other persons not comprehended in the foregoing description, except Indians not paying taxes in each State; which number shall be triennially taken and transmitted to the United States in Congress assembled, in such mode as they shall direct and appoint."||

The first and only census that appears to have been taken in New-York under this arrangement, was ordered by an act of Feb. 18, 1786, with the following results:

Census of 1786.¶

COUNTIES.	WHITES.					SLAVES		Indians who pay taxes.	Total.
	Males under 16 years.	Males above 16 and under 60 years.	Males above 60 years.	Females under 16 years	Females above 16 years.	Males negroes	Female negroes.		
Albany,	17,703	15,866	1,364	16,644	16,093	2,335	2,355	....	72,360
Dutchess,	8,209	6,973	628	7,700	7,481	830	815	....	32,636
Kings,	542	776	66	519	766	695	622	....	3,986
Montgomery,	3,564	3,487	342	3.844	3,415	217	188	....	15,057
New-York,	4,360	5,742	399	4,260	6,746	896	1,207	4	23,614
Orange,	3,382	3,182	247	3,206	3,187	442	416	....	14,062
Queens,	2,441	2,717	295	2,308	3,140	1,160	1,023	....	13,084
Richmond,	616	622	43	540	638	369	324	....	3,152
Suffolk,	2,917	3,141	334	2,700	3,633	567	501	....	13,793
Ulster,	4,971	4,792	464	4,381	4,865	1,353	1,309	8	22,143
Washington,	1,130	1,152	58	1,118	983	8	7	....	4,456
Westchester,	4,972	4,477	491	4,546	4,818	649	601	....	20,554
Total,	54.807	52,927	4,731	51,766	55,765	9,521	9,368	12	238,897

* Moritches, in the present town of Brookhaven, Suffolk county.
† See folio ed. Laws of New-York, 5th Session, p. 219.
‡ Documentary History, iii., p. 958. § Ib., p. 996.
|| Journals of Continental Congress, viii., p. 188.
¶ Recorded in Secretary's Office, Deeds, xxii., p. 35.

Electoral Censuses : In accordance with the requirements of the first State constitution,* there were taken, between the close of the revolution and the revision of 1821, six several State censuses of electors, each of which was made the basis of a reapportionment of senatorial and assembly districts. Separate acts were passed for taking these enumerations, and the returns were printed in the legislative journals of the following year.

In 1814, the occasion was improved by obtaining a very general classification by age and sex, and the total number of whites, free blacks and slaves. In 1821, the first attempt was made in the State census to obtain statistics of agriculture and manufactures.

These inquiries were limited to a few general subjects, and the results will be given in their proper connection.

Summary of the several State Electoral Censuses.

COUNTIES.	1790.				1795.				1801.			
	Electors owning freeholds.		Electors not freeholders but renting tenements of annual value of 40s.	Other electors.†	Electors owning freeholds.		Electors not freeholders but renting tenements of annual value of 40s	Other electors.†	Electors owning freeholds.		Electors not freeholders renting tenements of annual value of 40s.	Other electors.†
	Worth £100 and over.	Worth from £20 to £100.			Worth £100 and over.	Worth from £20 to £100.			Worth £100 and over.	Worth from £20 to £100		
Albany,	3,967	5,122	4,030	45	3,264	439	2,311	73	3,248	286	1,476	19
Allegany,	......	......	......	......	......	......	......	......	......	......	......	......
Broome,	......	......	......	......	......	......	......	......	......	......	......	......
Cattaraugus,	......	......	......	......	......	......	......	......	......	......	......	......
Cayuga,	......	......	......	......	......	......	......	......	1,718	278	953	......
Chautauque,	......	......	......	......	......	......	......	......	......	......	......	......
Chenango,	......	......	......	......	......	......	......	......	2,131	528	417	......
Clinton,	......	......	......	......	336	22	266	......	444	97	220	......
Columbia,	2,070	2,534	964	......	2,534	283	743	......	2,582	136	1,091	......
Cortland,	......	......	......	......	......	......	......	......	......	......	......	......
Delaware,	......	......	......	......	......	......	......	......	984	124	421	......
Dutchess,	2,413	2,780	1,115	......	3,236	316	2,461	......	3,648	202	2,227	......
Erie,	......	......	......	......	......	......	......	......	......	......	......	......
Essex,	......	......	......	......	......	......	......	......	334	34	286	......
Franklin,	......	......	......	......	......	......	......	......	......	......	......	......
Genesee,	......	......	......	......	......	......	......	......	......	......	......	......
Greene,	......	......	......	......	......	......	......	......	1,215	94	438	......
Herkimer,	......	......	......	......	2,478	510	1,173	......	1,397	151	857	......
Jefferson,	......	......	......	......	......	......	......	......	......	......	......	......
Kings,	357	376	148	......	417	22	168	......	491	7	244	......
Lewis,	......	......	......	......	......	......	......	......	......	......	......	......
Livingston,	......	......	......	......	......	......	......	......	......	......	......	......
Madison,	......	......	......	......	......	......	......	......	......	......	......	......
Monroe,	......	......	......	......	......	......	......	......	......	......	......	......
Montgomery,	1,479	2,069	1,583	......	1,985	293	1,101	......	2,827	164	1,262	......
New-York,	1,209	1,221	2,661	93	2,144	10	4,948	170	2,332	19	5,693	44
Niagara,	......	......	......	......	......	......	......	......	......	......	......	......
Oneida,	......	......	......	......	......	......	......	......	2,353	506	904	......
Onondaga,	......	......	......	......	847	155	323	......	1,060	149	452	......
Ontario,	......	......	......	......	1,040	103	110	......	1,691	247	923	......
Orange,	941	1,149	584	......	1,392	172	534	......	2,271	115	1,079	......
Oswego,	......	......	......	......	......	......	......	......	......	......	......	......
Otsego,	......	......	......	......	2,038	382	817	......	2.390	316	968	......
Putnam,	......	......	......	......	......	......	......	......	......	......	......	......
Queens,	1,274	1,397	438	......	1,372	303	557	......	1,059	158	558	......
Rensselaer,	......	......	......	......	1,960	413	1,217	......	2,796	242	1,246	......
Richmond,	298	274	109	......	335	21	132	......	417	33	136	......
Rockland,	......	......	......	......	......	......	......	......	599	59	166	......
St. Lawrence,	......	......	......	......	......	......	......	......	......	......	......	......
Saratoga,	......	......	......	......	1,978	258	1,034	......	2,423	286	855	......
Schenectady,	......	......	......	......	......	......	......	......	......	......	......	......
Schoharie,	......	......	......	......	......	......	......	......	812	127	831	......
Seneca,	......	......	......	......	......	......	......	......	......	......	......	......
Steuben,	......	......	......	......	......	......	......	......	181	21	133	......
Suffolk,	1,511	1,827	242	......	1,907	302	400	......	2,219	245	469	......
Sullivan,	......	......	......	......	......	......	......	......	......	......	......	......
Tioga,	......	......	......	......	552	109	504	......	644	56	465	......
Tompkins,	......	......	......	......	......	......	......	......	......	......	......	......
Ulster,	1,610	1,885	1,096	......	2,650	373	1,406	......	1,889	226	885	......
Warren,	......	......	......	......	......	......	......	......	......	......	......	......
Washington,	799	1,059	514	......	1,886	196	1,288	......	2,839	208	1,801	......
Westchester,	1,441	1,732	1,130	......	1,987	151	1,105	......	2,464	150	1,066	......
Total,	19,369	23,425	14.674	138	36,338	4,838	22.598	243	52,058	5,264	28,522	63

* The provision in the constitution of 1777 for a census of electors was as follows:

"That as soon after the expiration of seven years, subsequent to the termination of the present war, as may be, a census of the electors and inhabitants of this State shall be taken, under the direction of the legislature. And if on such census it shall appear that the number of representatives in Assembly from the said counties is not justly proportioned to the number of electors in the said counties respectively, that the legislature do adjust and apportion the same by that rule. And further, that once in every seven years after the taking of the said first census, a just account of the electors resident in each county shall be taken; and if it shall thereupon appear that the number of electors in any county shall have increased or diminished one or more seventieth parts of the whole number of electors, which on the first census shall be found in this State, the number of representatives for such county shall be increased or diminished accordingly; that is to say, one representative for every seventieth part, as aforesaid."

Sec. xii. also directs a census for apportionment of senate districts.

† Electors who were freemen in New-York on the 14th day of October, 1775, and in Albany on the 20th day of April, 1777.

Summary of the several State Electoral Censuses.—(Continued.)

COUNTIES.	1807. Electors owning freeholds. Worth £100 and over.	1807. Electors owning freeholds. Worth from £20 to £100.	1807. Electors not freeholders but renting tenements of annual value of 40s.	1807. Other electors.*	1814. Electors owning freeholds. Worth £100 and over.	1814. Electors owning freeholds. Worth from £20 to £100.	1814. Electors not freeholders but renting tenements of annual value of 40s.	1814. Other electors.*	1821. Electors owning freeholds. Worth $250 and over.	1821. Electors owning freeholds. Worth from $50 to $250.	1821. Electors not freeholders but renting tenements of annual value of $5.	1821. †
Albany,	3,745	178	2,156	26	3,069	106	2,301	......	2,128	148	2,534	1,687
Allegany,	66	....	278	......	135	11	473	......	325	66	1,292	439
Broome,	583	78	487	......	917	84	528	......	1,123	164	1,071	638
Cattaraugus,	....	....	....	......	....	....	....	......	147	59	477	272
Cayuga,	2,236	338	1,123	......	3,180	286	2,060	......	3,215	302	2,399	1,438
Chautauque,	....	....	....	......	430	115	95	......	629	137	1,141	988
Chenango,	1,570	333	841	......	1,961	140	1,651	......	2,318	239	1,593	1,509
Clinton,	688	87	583	......	635	28	630	......	822	56	787	400
Columbia,	2,968	91	1,466	......	3,232	119	1,966	......	3,180	154	3,414	1,559
Cortland,	....	....	....	......	1,042	122	376	......	1,575	180	756	766
Delaware,	1,498	160	806	......	1,928	181	1,018	......	1,935	391	1,285	1,355
Dutchess,	4,191	179	2,382	......	3,782	151	2,751	......	3,578	246	2,932	1,873
Erie,	....	....	....	......	....	....	....	......	871	104	1,690	684
Essex,	517	214	510	......	621	71	874	......	770	91	1,030	679
Franklin,	....	....	....	......	183	17	252	......	331	72	502	265
Genesee,	477	128	1,318	......	745	43	3,197	......	1,813	223	4,052	2,242
Greene,	1,643	101	711	......	1,867	69	925	......	1,947	130	1,378	1,030
Herkimer,	1,722	55	1,197	......	2,020	71	1,347	......	2,800	132	1,716	1,132
Jefferson,	835	239	914	......	1,039	107	1,641	......	1,880	185	3,037	2,094
Kings,	584	5	408	......	695	23	507	......	743	33	769	534
Lewis,	574	72	450	......	614	71	499	......	740	34	617	330
Livingston,	....	....	....	......	....	....	....	......	1,086	112	1,722	636
Madison,	2,220	246	521	......	2,508	126	1,378	......	2,730	277	1,667	1,155
Monroe,	....	....	....	......	....	....	....	......	1,737	58	2,718	1,196
Montgomery,	3,512	220	1,484	......	4,166	163	2,108	......	3,399	327	2,025	1,334
New-York,	3,000	20	9,334	62	3,141	17	10,763	20	3,881	17	12,761	3,266
Niagara,	....	....	....	......	418	78	955	......	276	16	689	716
Oneida,	3,501	357	1,550	......	4,088	304	2,524	......	4,300	322	2,660	2,071
Onondaga,	2,331	227	1,134	......	2,748	201	1,729	......	3,624	411	2,442	1 678
Ontario,	2,806	297	1,786	......	4,499	312	4,285	......	4,399	365	4,638	2,052
Orange,	2,583	123	1,109	......	3,081	152	1,787	......	3,081	135	1,830	1,789
Oswego,	....	....	....	......	....	....	....	......	675	61	1,156	634
Otsego,	3,254	378	1,228	......	3,746	151	2,505	......	4,110	386	2,570	1,264
Putnam,	....	....	....	......	857	43	599	......	866	82	570	369
Queens,	1,891	178	638	......	2,065	153	992	......	2,080	254	814	1,067
Rensselaer,	3,103	123	1,502	......	3,426	136	2,362	......	3,746	171	2,618	1,503
Richmond,	513	45	153	......	584	41	199	......	600	73	253	258
Rockland,	766	65	153	......	838	63	245	......	817	59	298	341
St. Lawrence,	616	151	93	......	880	175	401	......	1,163	458	1,070	932
Saratoga,	2,997	139	1,290	......	3,275	87	1,758	......	3,154	204	2,039	1,306
Schenectady,	....	....	....	......	1,043	51	751	......	1,061	119	756	542
Schoharie,	1,468	146	783	......	1,850	185	1,209	......	2,071	251	1,314	832
Seneca,	912	110	582	......	1,768	151	1,351	......	1,763	115	1,522	1,092
Steuben,	250	23	647	......	538	46	1,247	......	902	104	2,080	955
Suffolk,	2,610	142	507	......	2,898	168	643	......	2,827	283	798	1,063
Sullivan,	....	....	....	......	643	23	381	......	649	111	616	322
Tioga,	485	39	565	......	702	45	842	......	994	171	1,110	1,198
Tompkins,	....	....	....	......	....	....	....	......	1,527	141	1,063	1,206
Ulster,	2,498	253	1,100	......	2,727	239	1,223	......	2,655	257	1,484	1,084
Warren,	....	....	....	......	699	58	564	......	502	95	567	258
Washington,	3,289	164	1,585	......	3,434	111	1,942	......	3,195	224	2,260	1,372
Westchester,	2,657	96	906	......	2,773	137	1,380	......	2,760	180	1,453	1,473
Total,	71,159	5,800	44,330	88	87,491	5,231	59,104	20	100,490	8,985	93,035	56,877

Comparative Results of the several State Electoral Censuses.

YEARS.	Electors owning freeholds worth $250 and over. Number.	Increase.	Percentage. Of all electors.	Percentage. Of total estimated population.	Electors owning freeholds worth from $50 to $250. Number.	Increase or decrease.	Percentage. Of all electors.	Percentage. Of total estimated population.	Electors not freeholders, but renting tenements of annual value of $5. Number.	Increase.	Percentage. Of all electors.	Percentage. Of total estimated population.	Other electors. Number.	Increase or decrease.	Percentage. Of all electors.	Percentage. Of total estimated population.	Total electors of all classes. Number	Increase.	Percentage of estimated population.
1790	19,369	....	33.4	6.06	23,425	....	40.7	7.34	14,674	....	25.5	4.59	138	....	0.4	0.04	57,606	....	18.03
1795	36,338	16,969	56.8	7.84	4,838	‡18,587	7.5	1.04	22 598	7,824	35.3	4.87	243	§105	0.4	0.03	64,017	6,411	13.78
1801	52,058	15,720	60·6	8.33	5,264	§426	6.0	0.84	28,522	5,924	33.2	4.56	63	‡180	0.2	0.01	85,907	21,890	13.74
1807	71,159	19,101	58.6	8.37	5,800	§536	4.8	0.68	44,330	15,808	36.5	5.21	88	§25	0.1	0.01	121,289	35,382	14.27
1814	87,491	16,332	57.6	8.43	5,231	‡569	3.4	0.54	59,104	14,774	38.9	5.69	20	‡68	0.1	0.01	151,846	30,557	14.66
1821	100,490	12,992	38.7	7.17	8,985	§3,754	3.4	0.64	93,035	33,931	35.9	6.65	......	....	....	....	202,510	50,677	14.76

* Electors who were freemen in New-York on the 14th day of October, 1775, and in Albany on the 20th day of April, 1777.

† Free male inhabitants, who were citizens of the State, of the age of 21 years or upwards, who were not possessed of freeholds, and who did not rent tenements of the yearly value of $5, but who had been actually rated and paid taxes to this State, or who had been enrolled in the militia or in a uniform company of this State, and served therein, either as an officer or private, or who had done service in any other way which by law exempts from taxation or military duty, or who had been rated, and actually paid highway taxes by commutation or by labor This class became voters the next year; see page xlii.

‡ Decrease. § Increase.

The State census of 1790, included besides electors, the classes embraced in the following table. No returns were received from Clinton and Ontario counties:

State Census of 1790.

COUNTIES.	Males.	Females.	Slaves.	Total.
Albany,	37, 310	34, 112	3, 771	75, 193
Columbia,	13, 357	12, 650	1, 638	27, 545
Dutchess,	20, 445	19, 919	1, 871	42, 235
Kings,	1, 556	1, 396	1, 471	4, 423
Montgomery,	13, 850	12, 182	574	26, 606
New-York,	13, 330	14, 429	2, 263	30, 022
Orange,	8, 119	7, 654	904	16, 677
Queens,	6, 025	6, 163	2, 197	14, 385
Richmond,	1, 596	1, 531	801	3, 928
Suffolk,	7, 546	7, 421	1, 127	16, 094
Ulster,	12, 208	11, 306	2, 876	26, 390
Washington,	6, 876	6, 468	44	13, 388
Westchester,	10, 830	10, 512	1, 398	22, 741
Total,	152, 949	145, 749	20, 935	319, 627

Slaves: Near the close of the last century, measures were taken for the gradual abolition of slavery in New-York, and on the 31st of March, 1817, an act was passed declaring that every child born of a slave after July 4, 1799, should be free, if a male, at 28, and if a female, at 25 years of age. Every child born after the passage of this act was to become free at the age of 21, and measures were adopted for the education of children held in service, and for prohibiting the importation and exportation of slaves. The following table gives the number reported as slaves in this State by the several censuses. The census of 1855 returned one aged slave in Putnam county:

Slaves.

COUNTIES.	1790.	1800.	1810.	1814.	1820.	1830.	1840.
Albany,	3, 924	1, 808	772	470	413	2	
Allegany,			21	13	17		
Broome,			23	24	25		
Cattaraugus,					2		
Cayuga,		53	75	54	48		
Chautauque,				5	3	1	
Chenango,		16	13	26	7	3	
Clinton,	17	58	29	2	2		
Columbia,	1, 623	1. 471	879	698	721		
Cortland,				2	1		
Delaware,		16	55	34	56		
Dutchess,	1, 856	1, 609	1, 262	1, 005	772		
Essex,				7	3		
Franklin,			3				
Genesee,			11	10	35		
Greene,		520	367	404	134		
Hamilton,					1		
Herkimer,		61	64	75	72		
Jefferson,				30	5		
Kings,	1, 432	1, 479	1, 118	943	879		3
Lewis,			4	8			
Madison,			35	22	10		
Montgomery,	588	466	712	519	349	26	
New-York,	2, 369	2, 868	1, 686	920	518		
Niagara,			8	10	15		
Oneida,		50	81	55	9	15	
Onondaga,		11	50	49	59		
Ontario,	11	57	212	203			
Orange,	966	1, 145	966	666	1, 125		
Otsego,		48	74	72	16		
Putnam,				45	49		1
Queens,	2, 309	1, 528	809	630	559		
Rensselaer,		890	750	561	433		
Richmond,	759	675	437	343	532		
Rockland,		551	316	218	124		
St. Lawrence,			5	9	8		
Saratoga,		358	107	252	123		
Schenectady,			318	260	102		
Schoharie,		354	316	405	302		
Seneca,			101	63	84		
Steuben,		22	87	76	46		
Suffolk,	1, 098	886	413	339	323		
Sullivan,			43	24	69		
Tioga,		17	61	20	104		
Tompkins,					6		
Ulster,	2, 906	2, 257	1, 437	1, 192	1, 523		
Warren,				14	7		
Washington,	47	80	315	138	150	8	
Westchester,	1, 419	1, 259	982	565	205		
Total,	21, 324	20, 613	15, 017	11, 480	10, 046	55	4

National and State Censuses: The constitution of the United States,* directs an enumeration to be made at intervals of ten years, as the basis of apportionment of representatives in Congress, and under this authority censuses have been taken in 1790, 1800, 1810, 1820, 1830, 1840 and 1850. The constitutions of the State of New-York of 1821† and 1846‡, provided that censuses should also be taken at the like intervals and for a similar purpose, in the years ending in 5, and the present is the fourth that has been taken under this authority.

The National census was conducted under the direction of the Secretary of State, until the formation of the Department of the Interior, when it was made a subordinate branch of that office. The statistics were obtained by the marshals of the district courts, and special deputies appointed by them. Several months were usually devoted to the labor, and the returns thus obtained are subject to all the errors arising from changes and removals during the time the marshals were employed.

The State census previous to 1855, was taken by persons appointed by town officers, and their labors transmitted to the several county clerks for summary. The reports of the county clerks were transmitted to the Secretary of State, and published with a general summary for the State.

The following table contains the aggregate results, and most of the deductions that may be drawn from the statistics of population contained in these returns.

* Art. I., sec. 2. † Art. I., sec. 6. ‡ Art. III., sec. 4.

Population of New-York.—Comparative Results of National and State Censuses.

	NATIONAL CENSUSES.			Electoral State census	National census.	State census	National census.	State census.	National census.	State census.	National census	State census.
	1790.	1800.	1810.	1814.	1820.	1825.‡	1830.	1835.	1840	1845.	1850.	1855.
Total population of the State of New-York of all classes,	340, 120	586, 756	959, 049	1, 035, 910	1, 372, 812	1, 616, 458	1, 918, 608	2, 174, 517	2, 428, 921	2, 604, 495	3, 097, 394	3, 466, 212
Males, do,	....	....	....	....	698, 097	822, 897	972, 920	1, 102, 658	1, 231, 170	1, 311, 362	1, 567, 941	1, 727, 650
Females, do,	....	....	....	....	674, 014	793, 561	940, 086	1, 071, 859	1, 197, 751	1, 293, 153	1, 529, 453	1, 738, 562
Excess of males, do,	....	....	....	....	24, 083	29, 336	32, 834	30, 799	33, 419	18, 209	38, 488	....
,, females, do,	....	....	....	....	....	....	....	....	....	....	....	10, 912
Percentage of males,	....	....	....	....	50.85	50.91	50.72	50.71	50.68	50.35	50.62	49.84
,, females,	....	....	....	....	49.15	49.09	49.28	49.29	49.32	49.65	49.38	50.16
Increase between the different censuses, do,	....	246, 636	372, 293	76, 861	336, 902	243, 646	302, 150	255, 909	254, 404	175, 574	492, 899	368, 818
Annual rate per cent of this increase, do,	....	7.25	6.35	2.00	5.42	3.55	3.73	2.66	2.34	1.44	3.79	2.38
Percentage of population of New-York to that of the United States,	8.69	11.05	13.11	....	14.24	....	14.91	....	14.21	....	13.35	....
WHITES.*												
Total number	314, 142	556, 039	918, 699	997, 816	1, 332, 744	1, 576, 459	1, 873, 663	2, 130, 169	2, 378, 890	2, 559, 148	3, 048, 325	3, 420, 926
Percentage to total population,	92.36	94.76	95.79	96.32	97.08	97.52	97.66	97.96	97.94	98.26	98.43	98.66
Males.												
Total number,	161, 822	297, 452	474, 281	500, 812	679, 551	....	951, 441	....	1, 207, 357	....	1, 544, 489	1, 706, 273
Percentage to total population,	47.51	50.71	49.45	48.34	49.50	....	49.59	....	49.71	....	49.84	49.23
Ages.												
Under 1 year,	....	....	....	....	....	....	....	....	....	....	38, 090	51, 440
1 year and under 5,	....	....	....	....	....	....	....	....	....	....	162, 659	186, 368
5 years " 10,	....	....	....	....	....	....	137, 071	....	158, 107	....	187, 834	198, 742
10 " " 15,	....	....	....	....	....	....	118, 523	....	139, 752	....	170, 053	189, 239
15 " " 20,	....	....	....	....	....	....	101, 712	....	130, 094	....	157, 151	170, 015
20 " " 25,	....	....	....	....	....	....	....	....	....	....	....	168, 114
25 " " 30,	....	....	....	....	....	....	....	....	....	....	....	158, 547
30 " " 35,	....	....	....	....	....	....	....	....	....	....	....	140, 355
35 " " 40,	....	....	....	....	....	....	....	....	....	....	....	111, 489
40 " " 45,	....	....	....	....	....	....	....	....	....	....	....	93, 297
45 " " 50,	....	....	....	....	....	....	....	....	....	....	....	72, 949
50 " " 60,	....	....	....	....	....	....	40, 503	....	54, 975	....	85, 440	100, 985
60 " " 70,	....	....	....	....	....	....	23, 909	....	30, 869	....	45, 927	53, 825
70 " " 80,	....	....	....	....	....	....	10, 034	....	14, 694	....	19, 947	22, 462
80 " " 90,	....	....	....	....	....	....	2, 561	....	3, 984	....	5, 709	5, 919
90 " " 100,	....	....	....	....	....	....	255	....	379	....	618	702
100 years and upwards,	....	....	....	....	....	....	35	....	56	....	33	41
Under 5 years,	....	....	....	....	....	....	158, 077	....	187, 730	....	200, 749	237, 808
20 years and under 30,	....	....	....	....	....	....	176, 754	....	230, 981	....	308, 816	326, 661
30 " " 40,	....	....	....	....	....	....	113, 136	....	158, 194	....	216, 542	251, 844
40 " " 50,	....	....	....	....	....	....	68, 871	....	97, 542	....	144, 462	166, 246
Under 16 years,	78, 122	154, 640	239, 635	....	326, 905	....	....	....	....	....	....	....
16 years and upwards,	83, 700	142, 812	234, 646	....	352, 646	....	....	....	....	....	....	....
Under 10 years,	....	100, 367	165. 933	....	222, 608	....	95, 148	....	....	....	....	....
10 years and under 16,	....	54, 273	73, 702	....	104 297	....	....	....	....	....	....	....
16 " " 26,	....	49, 275	85, 779	....	132, 753	....	....	....	....	....	....	....
26 " " 45,	....	61, 594	94, 882	....	138, 634	....	....	....	....	....	....	....
45 years and upwards,	....	31, 943	53, 985	58, 088	81, 259	....	....	....	....	....	....	....
Under 18 years,	....	....	....	283, 371	....	....	....	....	....	....	....	....
18 years and under 45,	....	....	....	159, 353	....	....	....	....	....	....	....	....
Females.												
Total number,	152, 320	258, 857	444, 418	497, 004	653, 193	....	916, 620	....	1, 171, 533	....	1, 503, 836	1, 714, 653
Percentage to total population,	44.85	44.05	46.34	47.98	47.58	....	48.07	....	48.23	....	48.59	49.43
Ages.												
Under 1 year,	....	....	....	....	....	....	....	....	....	....	37, 126	51, 082
1 year and under 5,	....	....	....	....	....	....	....	....	....	....	159, 831	182, 729
5 years " 10,	....	....	....	....	....	....	133, 084	....	154, 525	....	184, 305	195, 639
10 " " 15,	....	....	....	....	....	....	115, 166	....	134, 977	....	167, 472	185, 252
15 " " 20,	....	....	....	....	....	....	105, 196	....	137, 414	....	171, 592	188, 927
20 " " 25,	....	....	....	....	....	....	....	....	....	....	....	195, 100
25 " " 30,	....	....	....	....	....	....	....	....	....	....	....	166, 530
30 " " 35,	....	....	....	....	....	....	....	....	....	....	....	134, 234
35 " " 40,	....	....	....	....	....	....	....	....	....	....	....	103, 409
40 " " 45,	....	....	....	....	....	....	....	....	....	....	....	86, 960
45 " " 50,	....	....	....	....	....	....	....	....	....	....	....	65, 453
50 " " 60,	....	....	....	....	....	....	38, 344	....	53, 496	....	78, 911	95, 817
60 " " 70,	....	....	....	....	....	....	22 589	....	30, 190	....	43, 920	54, 215
70 " " 80,	....	....	....	....	....	....	9, 645	....	14, 281	....	19, 264	22, 555
80 " " 90,	....	....	....	....	....	....	2, 673	....	4, 152	....	5, 877	6, 339
90 " " 100,	....	....	....	....	....	....	304	....	522	....	713	847
100 years and upwards,	....	....	....	....	....	....	17	....	25	....	29	50
Under 5 years,	....	....	....	....	....	....	151, 868	....	180, 769	....	196, 957	233, 811
20 years and under 30,	....	....	....	....	....	....	168, 897	....	227, 137	....	308, 392	361, 630
30 " " 40,	....	....	....	....	....	....	104, 522	....	143, 882	....	197, 332	237, 643
40 " " 50,	....	....	....	....	....	....	64, 315	....	90, 163	....	128, 561	152, 413
Under 16 years,	....	125, 349	226, 756	....	318, 417	....	....	....	....	....	....	....
16 years and upwards,	....	133, 238	217, 662	....	334, 776	....	....	....	....	....	....	....
Under 10 years,	....	35, 473	157, 945	....	216, 513	....	....	....	....	....	....	....
10 years and under 16,	....	39, 876	68, 811	....	101, 904	....	....	....	....	....	....	....
16 " " 26,	....	48, 176	85, 139	....	132, 492	....	....	....	....	....	....	....

* Free whites. † Under 5 years of age.
‡ The ages of whites and colored were not classified separately in 1825, 1835, 1845 and 1855.

Population of New-York.—Comparative Results of National and State Censuses.—(Continued.)

	NATIONAL CENSUSES.			Electoral State census	National census.	State. census.	National census.	State census.	National census.	State census.	National census.	State census.
	1790	1800.	1810.	1814.	1820.	1825 *	1830.	1835.	1840.	1845.	1850.	1855.
26 years and under 45, ..	....	56, 411	85, 805	....	129, 899	....	....	....	....	....	....	....
45 years and upwards, ..	....	28, 651	46, 718	55, 103	72, 385	....	....	....	....	....	....	....
Under 18 years, ...	....	....	....	269, 266	....	....	....	....	....	....	....	....
18 years and under 45, ..	....	....	....	172, 635	....	....	....	....	....	....	....	....
Married under 45 years,.	....	....	....	....	....	200, 481	....	283, 230	....	230, 216	....	....
Unmarried under 16 yr's,	....	....	....	....	....	361, 824	....	456, 224	....	490, 709	....	....
Unmarried between 16 and 45 years,........	....	....	....	....	....	135, 391	....	195, 499	....	161, 334	....	....
FREE COLORED PERSONS.												
Total number,..........	4, 654	10, 374	25, 333	26, 614	29, 980	....	44, 870	....	50, 027	....	49, 069	45, 286
Percentage to total population,...............	1.36	1.77	2.62	2.57	2.18	....	2.34	....	2.06	....	1.57	1.34
Males.												
Total number,..........	....	....	....	....	13, 458	....	21, 466	....	23, 809	....	23, 452	21, 377
Percentage to total population,.............	....	....	....	....	0.92	....	1.12	....	0.99	....	0.83	.61
Ages.												
Under 1 year, ...	....	....	....	....	....	....	....	....	....	....	582	....
1 year and under 5, ..	....	....	....	....	....	....	....	....	....	....	2, 213	....
5 years " 10, ..	....	....	....	....	....	....	....	....	....	....	2, 666	....
10 " " 15, ..	....	....	....	....	....	....	....	....	....	....	2, 507	....
15 " " 20, ..	....	....	....	....	....	....	....	....	....	....	2, 045	....
20 " " 30, ..	....	....	....	....	....	....	....	....	....	....	4, 556	....
30 " " 40, ..	....	....	....	....	....	....	....	....	....	....	3, 719	....
40 " " 50, ..	....	....	....	....	....	....	....	....	....	....	2, 619	....
50 " " 60, ..	....	....	....	....	....	....	....	....	....	....	1, 432	....
60 " " 70, ..	....	....	....	....	....	....	....	....	....	....	702	....
70 " " 80, ..	....	....	....	....	....	....	....	....	....	....	268	....
80 " " 90, ..	....	....	....	....	....	....	....	....	....	....	100	....
90 " " 100, ..	....	....	....	....	....	....	....	....	....	....	24	....
100 years and upwards, .	....	....	....	....	....	....	19	....	23	....	12	....
Under 10 years, ...	....	....	....	....	....	....	5, 643	....	6, 008	....	....	....
10 years and under 24, ..	....	....	....	....	....	....	6, 094	....	6, 370	....	....	....
24 " " 36, ..	....	....	....	....	....	....	4, 860	....	5, 711	....	....	....
36 " " 55, ..	....	....	....	....	....	....	3, 492	....	4, 221	....	....	....
55 " " 100, ..	....	....	....	....	....	....	1, 358	....	1, 476	....	....	....
Under 14 years, ...	....	....	....	....	5, 197	....	....	....	....	....	....	....
14 years and under 26, ..	....	....	....	....	3, 011	....	....	....	....	....	....	....
26 " " 45, ..	....	....	....	....	3, 347	....	....	....	....	....	....	....
45 years and upwards, ..	....	....	....	....	1, 903	....	....	....	....	....	....	....
Females.												
Total number,..........	....	....	....	....	15, 821	....	23, 404	....	26, 218	....	25, 617	23, 909
Percentage to total population, ...	....	....	....	....	1.26	....	1.22	....	1.07	....	.74	0.73
Ages.												
Under 1 year,.........	....	....	....	....	....	....	....	....	....	....	539	....
1 year and under 5, ..	....	....	....	....	....	....	....	....	....	....	2, 390	....
5 years " 10, ..	....	....	....	....	....	....	....	....	....	....	2, 800	....
10 " " 15, ..	....	....	....	....	....	....	....	....	....	....	2, 619	....
15 " " 20, ..	....	....	....	....	....	....	....	....	....	....	2, 541	....
20 " " 30, ..	....	....	....	....	....	....	....	....	....	....	5, 280	....
30 " " 40, ..	....	....	....	....	....	....	....	....	....	....	3, 719	....
40 " " 50, ..	....	....	....	....	....	....	....	....	....	....	2, 635	....
50 " " 60, ..	....	....	....	....	....	....	....	....	....	....	1, 476	....
60 " " 70, ..	....	....	....	....	....	....	....	....	....	....	820	....
70 " " 80, ..	....	....	....	....	....	....	....	....	....	....	355	....
80 " " 90, ..	....	....	....	....	....	....	....	....	....	....	171	....
90 " " 100, ..	....	....	....	....	....	....	....	....	....	....	44	....
100 years and upwards, .	....	....	....	....	....	....	54	....	44	....	14	....
Under 10 years,.......	....	....	....	....	....	....	5, 509	....	6, 032	....	....	....
10 years and under 24, ..	....	....	....	....	....	....	6, 843	....	6, 951	....	....	....
24 " " 36, ..	....	....	....	....	....	....	5, 504	....	6, 809	....	....	....
36 " " 55, ..	....	....	....	....	....	....	3, 780	....	4, 454	....	....	....
55 " " 100, ..	....	....	....	....	....	....	1, 714	....	1, 928	....	....	....
Under 14 years, ...	....	....	....	....	5, 342	....	....	....	....	....	....	....
14 years and under 26, ..	....	....	....	....	4, 195	....	....	....	....	....	....	....
26 " " 45, ..	....	....	....	....	4, 126	....	....	....	....	....	....	....
45 years and upwards, ..	....	....	....	....	2, 158	....	....	....	....	....	....	....
SLAVES.												
Total number,..........	21, 324	20, 343	15, 017	11, 480	10, 088	....	75	....	....	....	....	....
Percentage to total population,...............	6.28	3.47	1.59	1.11	0.74	....	0.004	....	....	....	....	....
Males												
Total number,..........	....	....	....	....	5, 088	....	13	....	....	....	....	....
Percentage to total population,..............	....	....	....	....	0.40	....	....	....	....	....	....	....
Ages.												
Under 10 years, ...	....	....	....	....	....	....	5	....	1	....	....	....
10 years and under 24, ..	....	....	....	....	....	....	6	....	2	....	....	....
24 " " 36, ..	....	....	....	....	....	....	....	....	....	....	....	....
36 " " 55, ..	....	....	....	....	....	....	1	....	....	....	....	....
55 " " 100, ..	....	....	....	....	....	....	....	....	1	....	....	....
100 years and upwards, .	....	....	....	....	....	....	....	....	....	....	....	....
Under 14 years, ...	....	....	....	....	1, 861	....	....	....	....	....	....	....
14 years and under 26, ..	....	....	....	....	1, 624	....	....	....	....	....	....	....

* The ages of whites and colored were not classified separately in 1825, | 1835, 1845 and 1855.

Population of New-York.—Comparative Result of National and State Censuses.—(Continued.)

	NATIONAL CENSUSES.			Electoral State census.	National census.	State census	National census.	State census.	National census.	State census.	National census.	State census.
	1790.	1800.	1810.	1814.	1820.	1825 *	1830.	1835.	1840.	1845.	1850.	1855.
26 years and under 45,					932							
45 years and upwards,					671							
Females.												
Total number,					5,000		62					
Percentage to total population,					0.34							
Ages.												
Under 10 years,							23					
10 years and under 24,							12					
24 " " 36,							17					
36 " " 55,							3					
55 " " 100,							6					
100 years and upwards,							1					
Under 14 years,					1,544							
14 years and under 26,					1,579							
26 " " 45,					1,065							
45 years and upwards,					812							
VOTERS.												
Total number,	57,608			151,846		296,132		422,034		539,379		652,322
Percentage to total population,	16.93			14.65		18.32		19.41		20.32		18.01
Percentage to total white male population,	18.31			15.22		18.78		19.81		21.08		19.07
Native,												516,745
Percentage to total number of voters,												70.02
Naturalized,												135,577
Percentage to total number of voters,												29.98
ALIENS.												
Total number,						40,430	52,488	82,319		153,717		632,746
Percentage to total population,						2.50	3.04	3.79		5.89		18.54
PERSONS OF COLOR.												
Not taxed,						38,770		42,836		42,321		35,956
Percentage to total population,						2.39		1.91		1.60		1.03
Who are taxed,						931		934		2,025		9,330
Percentage to total population,						0.09		0.04		0.08		0.27
PAUPERS.												
Total number,						5,610		6,821		8,909		
Percentage to total population,						0.34		0.31		0.32		
MILITARY DUTY.												
White males between 18 and 45 liable to,						180,645		201,901		228,292		
Percentage of above to total population,						11.16		9.26		8.32		
Do to total white male population,						11.46		9.48		8.76		
DEAF AND DUMB.												
Total number,						645	928	933	1,107	1,082	1,263	1,422
Percentage to total population,						0.039	0.048	0.043	0.045	0.042	0.048	0.41
Males.												
Total number,						289		330		417	699	785
Ages.												
Under 10 years,						68		108				88
10 years and under 25,						221		222				321
Under 12 years,										127		
12 years and under 25,										290		
Females.												
Total number,						280		360		392	564	637
Ages.												
Under 10 years,						67		83				48
10 years and under 25,						213		277				254
Under 12 years,										109		
12 years and under 25,										283		
Whites.—Ages.												
Under 14 years,							277		269			
14 years and under 25,							310		362			
25 years and upwards,							255		408			
Slaves and Colored—Ages.												
Under 14 years,							17		68			
14 years and under 25,							14					
25 years and upwards,							12					
Whose friends are unable to educate and support them,						141		278		487		

* The ages of whites and colored were not classified separately in 1825, 1835, 1845 and 1855.

Population of New-York.—Comparative Results of National and State Censuses.—(Continued).

	NATIONAL CENSUSES.			Electoral State census	National census.	State. census.	National census.	State census.	National census.	State census.	National census.	State census.
	1790	1800.	1810.	1814.	1820.	1825.	1830.	1835.	1840.	1845.	1850.	1855.
Whose friends are able to educate and support them,	....	....	....	....	....	387	....	541	....	329	....	....
Slaves and free colored,	....	....	....	....	....	....	43	....	....	....	7	....
BLIND.												
Total number,	....	....	....	....	....	....	642	889	875	877	1, 181	1, 136
Percentage to total population,	....	....	....	....	....	....	0.32	0.049	0.036	0.034	0.038	0.038
Males.												
Total number,	....	....	....	....	....	....	....	....	....	....	711	682
Ages.												
Under 8 years,	....	....	....	....	....	....	....	....	....	33	....	....
8 years and under 25,	....	....	....	....	....	....	....	....	....	148	....	....
Under 10 years,	....	....	....	....	....	....	....	38	....	....	....	20
10 years and under 25,	....	....	....	....	....	....	....	80	....	....	....	139
Females.												
Total number,	....	....	....	....	....	....	....	....	....	....	470	454
Ages.												
Under 8 years,	....	....	....	....	....	....	....	....	....	41	....	....
8 years and under 25,	....	....	....	....	....	....	....	....	....	110	....	....
Under 10 years,	....	....	....	....	....	....	....	29	....	....	....	22
10 years and under 25,	....	....	....	....	....	....	....	70	....	....	....	121
Whose friends are unable to educate and support them,	....	....	....	....	....	....	....	270	....	167	....	....
Do, who are able,	....	....	....	....	....	....	....	426	....	165	....	....
Slaves and free colored,	....	....	....	....	....	....	82	....	91	....	....	....
INSANE.												
Total number,	....	....	....	....	....	†819	....	‡2, 051	*2, 146	2, 168	2, 521	2, 742
Percentage to total population,	....	....	....	....	....	0.051	....	0.094	....	0.083	0.081	0.079
Males.												
Total number,	....	....	....	....	....	410	....	475	....	1, 011	1, 220	1, 215
Ages.												
Under 21 years,	....	....	....	....	....	33	....	40	....	65	....	....
21 years and upwards,	....	....	....	....	....	373	....	435	....	946	....	....
Females.												
Total number,	....	....	....	....	....	383	....	582	....	1, 134	1, 301	5, 527
Ages.												
Under 21 years,	....	....	....	....	....	27	....	54	....	49	....	....
21 years and upwards,	....	....	....	....	....	356	....	528	....	1, 085	....	....
Supported by charity,	....	....	....	....	....	184	....	382	*683	1, 116	....	....
In lunatic asylums,	....	....	....	....	....	....	....	....	....	1, 228	....	....
Not supported by public or private charity,	....	....	....	....	....	263	....	312	*10, 463	787	....	....
Born in State of New-York,	....	....	....	....	....	....	....	....	....	....	1, 388	....
Born in other States of the United States,	....	....	....	....	....	....	....	....	....	....	1, 778	....
Born in foreign countries,	....	....	....	....	....	....	....	....	....	....	642	....
Birthplace unknown,	....	....	....	....	....	....	....	....	....	....	101	....
Free colored (included in foregoing),	....	....	....	....	....	....	....	....	*194	....	34	....
IDIOTIC.												
Total number,	....	....	....	....	....	1, 421	....	1, 484	*	1, 620	1, 665	1, 812
Percentage to total population,	....	....	....	....	....	0.087	....	0.067	....	0.062	0.054	0.052
Males.												
Total number,	....	....	....	....	....	733	....	794	....	912	970	1, 002
Ages.												
Under 21 years,	....	....	....	....	....	336	....	344	....	373	....	....
21 years and upwards,	....	....	....	....	....	397	....	450	....	539	....	....
Females.												
Total number,	....	....	....	....	....	643	....	689	....	703	695	810
Ages.												
Under 21 years,	....	....	....	....	....	321	....	305	....	315	....	....
21 years and upwards,	....	....	....	....	....	322	....	384	....	388	....	....
Supported by charity,	....	....	....	....	....	442	....	514	....	334	....	....
" by friends,	....	....	....	....	....	459	....	549	....	1, 286	....	....
MARRIAGES.												
Total number the year previous,	....	....	....	....	....	11, 553	....	15, 535	....	27, 783	§15, 732	21, 106
BIRTHS.												
Total number the year previous,	....	....	....	....	....	61, 383	....	77, 244	....	89, 755	‖76, 337	†102. 522
Males, total number,	....	....	....	....	....	31, 514	....	39, 839	....	46, 817	38, 672	50, 440
Females, total number,	....	....	....	....	....	29, 869	....	37, 405	....	42, 938	37, 639	51, 082
DEATHS.												
Total number the year previous,	....	....	....	....	....	22, 544	....	32, 766	....	36, 284	45, 584	46, 297
Males, total number,	....	....	....	....	....	12, 525	....	17, 486	....	18, 722	....	24, 980
Females, total number,	....	....	....	....	....	10, 019	....	15, 280	....	17, 562	....	21. 317

* The insane and idiotic were reported together in 1840.
† 24 confined in jails for offences or safe keeping.
‡ 59 confined in jails for offences or safe keeping.

§ The census of 1850 reported 31,465 persons married within the year.
‖ Includes of those born, only the number living June 1. All of the above returns of births are much less than the true number.

Comparative Population of Towns and Counties at different Periods.

The date and origin of the several towns, cities and counties, are given in the following table, together with their population at the several periods indicated in the headings of the columns. The towns are here distributed among the counties as they now exist, without reference to the counties in which they were embraced at the time of taking the several censuses.

With the exception of the minor changes arising from the subdivision of towns, and the transfer of parts of towns to other counties, the table exhibits a connected view of the successive changes in population, which these several sections of the State have undergone since 1790. The first recapitulation by counties exhibits the actual population then existing within the district now embraced within their several boundaries. The second presents the population of each county, as it existed at the time each census was taken.

ALBANY COUNTY.

CITIES & TOWNS.	When formed	FROM WHAT TAKEN.	1790.	1800.	1810	1814.	1820.	1825.	1830.	1835.	1840.	1845.	1850.	1855.
Albany city:														
1st ward,		(Ancient wards),		2, 808		3, 201	3, 330	4, 251	6, 857	7, 638	9, 809	3, 712	6, 177	8, 038
2d ward,		(Ancient wards),		1, 471		2, 796	2, 943	4, 247	6, 263	5, 742	6, 855	3, 676	4, 001	4, 518
3d ward,		(Ancient wards),		1, 010		1, 435	2, 035	1, 666	2, 011	3, 845	4, 137	5, 053	4, 617	4, 667
4th ward,		(Ancient wards),				2, 591	2, 815	3, 943	5, 872	6, 365	7, 244	4, 759	4, 758	4, 492
5th ward,	1815	Town of Colonie,					1, 507	1, 864	3, 206	4, 519	5, 676	3, 129	2, 929	3 016
6th ward,	1841	3d and 5th wards,										3, 661	3, 798	3, 460
7th ward,	1841	5th ward,										3, 532	5, 244	6, 006
8th ward,	1841	5th ward,										4, 001	6, 269	7, 467
9th ward,	1841	2d ward,										5, 204	6, 332	7, 343
10th ward,	1841	1st ward,										4, 412	6, 638	8, 326
Total Albany city,			3, 498	5, 289	10, 762	†11680	12, 630	15, 971	24, 209	28, 109	33, 721	42, 139	50, 763	57, 333
Berne,	1795	Rensselaerville,		3, 486	‡5, 136	4, 447	5, 531	3, 509	3, 607	3, 956	3, 740	3, 667	3, 441	3, 206
Bethlehem,	1793	Watervliet,		3, 733	4, 430	4, 325	5, 114	5, 643	6, 082	3, 103	3, 238	3, 315	4, 102	5, 151
Coeymans,	1791	Watervliet,		3, 095	3, 574	3, 272	2, 872	2, 666	2, 723	2, 957	2. 978	3, 050	3, 050	2, 963
Guilderland,	1803	Watervliet,			2, 466	2, 264	2, 270	2, 428	2, 742	2, 803	2, 790	2, 995	3, 279	3, 188
Knox,	1822	Berne,						2, 222	2, 189	2, 262	2, 143	2, 161	2, 021	1, 888
New Scotland,	1832	Bethlehem,								3, 130	2, 912	3, 288	3, 459	3, 327
Rensserlaerville,	1790	Watervliet,	2, 771	4, 560	5, 928	5, 333	3, 435	3, 462	3, 685	3, 507	3, 705	3, 589	3, 629	3, 088
Watervliet,	1788		7, 419	4, 992	2, 365	2, 564	2, 806	3, 574	4, 962	6, 961	10, 141	11, 209	14, 675	20, 889
Westerlo,	1815	Coeymans and Rensselaerville,					3, 458	3, 346	3, 321	3, 074	3, 096	2, 927	2, 860	2, 648
Total,			*13717	25, 155	34, 661	33, 885	38, 116	42, 821	53, 520	59, 762	68, 593	77. 268	93, 279	103681

ALLEGANY COUNTY.

CITIES & TOWNS.	When formed	FROM WHAT TAKEN.	1790.	1800.	1810	1814.	1820.	1825.	1830.	1835.	1840.	1845.	1850.	1855.
Alfred,	1808	Angelica,			273	458	1, 701	1, 160	1, 476	1, 903	1, 630	1, 625	2, 679	1, 707
Allen,	1823	Angelica,						726	898	1, 089	867	906	955	1, 026
Alma,	1854	Willing,												412
Almond,	1821	Alfred,						1, 378	1, 804	2, 059	1, 434	1, 735	1, 914	1, 952
Amity,	1830	Angelica and Scio,							872	1, 280	1, 354	1, 485	1, 792	2, 655
Andover,	1824	Independence,						404	598	708	848	1, 070	1, 476	1, 775
Angelica,	1805	Leicester,			439	555	1, 510	1, 008	998	1, 502	1, 257	1, 329	1, 592	1, 832
Belfast,	1824	Caneadea,						560	743	1, 035	1, 646	1, 417	1, 679	2, 130
Birdsall,	1829	Allen and Almond,							543	573	328	475	597	838
Bolivar,	1825	Friendship,						303	449	752	408	517	708	985
Burns,	1826	Ossian,							702	936	867	924	943	1, 087
Caneadea,	1808	Angelica,			515	924	696	550	780	1, 046	1, 633	1, 167	1, 477	2, 400
Centreville,	1819	Pike,					421	763	1, 195	1, 426	1, 513	1, 436	1, 441	1, 349
Clarksville,	1835	Cuba,								252	326	443	668	781
Cuba,	1822	Friendship,						670	1, 059	1, 478	1, 768	1, 585	2, 243	2, 116
Friendship,	1815	Caneadea,					662	1, 129	1, 502	1, 764	1, 244	1, 401	1, 675	1, 838
Genesee,	1830	Cuba,							219	470	578	659	672	895
Granger,	1838	Grove,									1, 064	1, 178	1, 309	1, 218
Grove,	1827	Nunda,							1, 388	1, 663	623	843	1, 154	1, 118
Hume,	1822	Pike,						607	951	1, 523	2, 303	1, 980	2, 159	2 094
Independence,	1821	Alfred,						570	877	1, 189	1, 440	1, 679	1, 701	1, 136
New Hudson,	1825	Rushford,						377	655	1, 065	1, 502	1, 290	1, 433	1, 451
Ossian,	1808	Angelica,			216	270	921	1, 419	812	940	938	953	1, 283	1, 313
Rushford,	1816	Caneadea,					609	803	1, 115	1, 520	1, 512	1, 769	1, 816	1, 995
Scio,	1823	Angelica,						757	602	1, 122	1, 156	1, 356	1, 922	3, 184
West Almond,	1833	Angelica, Alfred and Almond,									808	875	976	972
Willing,	1851	Independence and Scio,												1, 127
Wirt,	1838	Bolivar and Friendship,									1, 207	1, 305	1, 544	1, 524
Total,					1, 443	2, 207	6, 520	13, 184	20, 238	27, 295	30, 254	31, 402	37, 808	42, 910

BROOME COUNTY.

CITIES & TOWNS.	When formed	FROM WHAT TAKEN.	1790.	1800.	1810	1814.	1820.	1825.	1830.	1835.	1840.	1845.	1850.	1855.
Barker,	1831	Lisle,								1, 150	1, 259	1, 379	1, 456	1, 324
Chenango,	1791		45	1, 149	1, 360	1, 495	2, 626	2, 782	3, 730	5, 441	5, 465	6, 602	8, 734	13, 128
Colesville,	1821	Windsor,						1, 774	2, 387	2, 230	2, 528	2, 829	3, 061	3, 135
Conklin,	1824	Chenango,						635	906	1, 142	1, 475	1, 869	2, 232	2, 539
Lisle,	1801	Union,		660	2, 144	2, 420	3, 083	3, 615	4, 378	1, 413	1, 560	1, 657	1, 680	1, 815
Maine,	1848	Union,											1, 843	1, 979
Nanticoke,	1831	Lisle,								295	400	479	576	819
Sanford,	1821	Windsor,						692	931	1, 143	1, 173	1, 618	2, 508	3, 060
Triangle,	1831	Lisle,								1. 669	1, 692	1, 749	1, 728	1, 784
Union,	1791			921	998	1, 284	2, 037	1, 674	2, 121	2. 415	3, 165	3. 519	2, 143	2, 463
Vestal,	1823	Union,						794	946	1, 124	1, 253	1, 017	2. 054	1, 967
Windsor,	1807	Chenango,			1, 979	2. 224	3, 354	1, 927	2, 180	2, 168	2, 368	2, 408	2, 645	2, 637
Total,			45	2, 730	6, 481	7, 423	11, 100	13, 893	17, 579	20, 190	22, 3:8	25. 808	30, 660	36. 650

* Including 29 residing on islands not within the corporate limits of towns.

† Including 1,657 in the town of Colonie, soon after annexed to the city.

‡ Including 1,406 in the town of Colonie.

Comparative Population of Towns and Counties at different Periods.—(Continued.)

CATTARAUGUS COUNTY.

CITIES & TOWNS	When formed.	FROM WHAT TAKEN.	1790.	1800	1810.	1814.	1820	1825.	1830.	1835.	1840	1845.	1850.	1855
Allegany,	1831	Great Valley,								809	530	621	1,037	1,583
Ashford,	1824	Ellicottville,						275	631	1,201	1,469	1,376	1,658	1,913
Bucktooth,	1854	Little Valley,												453
Carrolton,	1842	Great Valley,										193	515	511
Cold Spring,	1827	Napoli,						443			673	602	591	664
Connewango,	1823	Little Valley,						1,105	1,712	1,166	1,317	1,224	1,408	1,345
Dayton,	1835	Perrysburgh,								1,114	946	1,007	1,448	1,139
East Otto,	1854	Otto,												1,228
Ellicottville,	1820	Ischua (afterwards Franklinville),						380	626	941	1,084	1,211	1,725	1,838
Farmersville,	1821	Ischua, " "						636	1,005	1,164	1,294	1,462	1,554	1,443
Franklinville,	1812	Olean,				261	1,453	523	903	1,330	1,293	1,439	1,706	1,686
Freedom,	1820	Ischua (afterwards Franklinville),						935	1,505	1,835	1,831	1,478	1,652	1,443
Great Valley,	1818	Olean,					271	378	647	613	852	756	1,638	1,198
Hinsdale,	1820	Olean,						383	919	1,543	1,937	1,910	1,302	2,129
Humphrey,	1826	Burton,									444	591	824	759
Ischua,	1846	Hinsdale,											906	1,103
Leon,	1832	Connewango,								1,139	1,326	1,194	1,340	1,330
Little Valley,	1818	Perry,					484	462	336	610	700	780	1,383	801
Lyndon,	1829	Franklinville,							271	539	628	819	1,092	1,123
Machias,	1827	Yorkshire,							735	1,025	1,085	1,243	1,342	1,366
Mansfield,	1830	Little Valley,							378	720	942	962	1,057	1,125
Napoli,	1823	Little Valley,							852	1,379	1,145	1,119	1,233	1,222
New Albion,	1830	Little Valley,							380	848	1,016	1,199	1,633	1,562
Olean,	1808				458	276	1,047	404	561	830	638	550	899	1,611
Otto,	1823	Perrysburgh,						601	1,224	1,731	2,133	1,110	2,267	1,094
Perrysburgh,	1814	Olean & Ischua (after'ds Franklinv'e,)					835	1,262	2,440	1,549	1,660	1,642	1,861	1,456
Persia,	1835	Perrysburgh,								898	892	1,086	1,955	1,204
Portville,	1837	Olean,									462	585	747	1,164
Randolph,	1826	Connewango,							776	938	1,283	1,300	1,606	1,723
South Valley,	1847	Cold Spring and Randolph,											561	586
Yorkshire,	1820	Ischua,						856	823	1,066	1,292	1,740	2,010	1,728
Total,					458	537	4,090	8,643	16,724	24,986	28,872	30,169	38,950	*39530

CAYUGA COUNTY.

CITIES & TOWNS	When formed.	FROM WHAT TAKEN.	1790.	1800	1810.	1814.	1820	1825.	1830.	1835.	1840	1845.	1850.	1855
Auburn:								2,982	4,486	5,368	5,626	6,171		
1st ward,	1848	Town of Auburn,												2,404
2nd ward,	1848	Town of Auburn,												1,922
3d ward,	1848	Town of Auburn,												1,985
4th ward,	1848	Town of Auburn,												3,165
Total Aub'rn city,													9,548	9,476
Aurelius,	1789	Batavia,		3,312	4,642	5,955	7,923	2,289	2,767	2,771	2,645	2,504	2,831	2,574
Brutus,	1802	Aurelius,			2,030	2,624	3,579	4,098	1,827	1,991	2,044	3,263	3,046	2,807
Cato,	1802	Aurelius,			1,075	1,770	4,021	1,407	1,782	2,214	2,380	2,312	2,247	2,252
Conquest,	1821	Cato,						1,069	1,507	1,782	1,911	1,921	1,863	1,872
Fleming,	1823	Aurelius,						1,507	1,461	1,363	1,317	1,187	1,193	1,164
Genoa,	1789			3,553	5,425	5,876	2,585	2,756	2,768	2,721	2,593	2,426	2,503	2.352
Ira,	1821	Cayuga,						1,778	2,199	2,187	2,283	2,121	2,110	2,133
Ledyard,	1823	Scipio,						2,280	2,427	2,373	2,143	2,095	2,043	1,976
Locke,	1802	Milton,			2,388	3,002	2,559	2,925	3,310	1,752	1,654	1,528	1,478	1,293
Mentz,	1802	Aurelius,			1,207	1,996	3,010	3,472	4,143	3,986	4,215	4.288	5,239	5,058
Moravia,	1833	Sempronius,								1,756	2,010	1,785	1,876	1,819
Niles,	1833	Sempronius,								2,197	2,234	2,153	2,053	1,912
Owasco,	1802	Aurelius,			496	1,072	1,290	1,326	1,350	1,278	1,319	1,277	1,254	1,303
Scipio,	1794			3,147	7,100	7,583	8,105	2,702	2,691	2,523	2,255	2,136	2,135	1,895
Sempronius,	1799	Scipio,		805	3,137	3,471	5,033	5,371	5,705	1,280	1,304	1,314	1,266	1,269
Sennett,	1827	Brutus,							2,297	2,009	2,060	2,033	2,347	2,082
Springport,	1823	Aurelius and Scipio,						1,607	1,528	1,829	1.890	1,832	2,041	2,171
Sterling,	1812	Cato,				260	792	1,081	1,436	2,001	2,533	2,732	2,808	3,024
Summer Hill,	1831	Locke,								1,432	1,446	1,324	1,251	1,184
Venice,	1823	Scipio,						2,530	2,445	2,238	2,105	2,000	2,028	1,939
Victory,	1821	Cato,						1,563	1,819	2,091	2,391	2,261	2,298	2,016
Total,				10,817	29.843	33,609	38,897	42,743	47,948	49,202	50,338	49.663	55,458	53,571

CHAUTAUQUE COUNTY.

CITIES & TOWNS	When formed.	FROM WHAT TAKEN.	1790.	1800	1810.	1814.	1820	1825.	1830.	1835.	1840	1845.	1850.	1855
Arkwright,	1829	Pomfret and Villenova,							926	1,293	1,418	1,295	1,283	1,110
Busti,	1823	Ellicott and Harmony,						1,187	1,680	2,079	1,894	1,923	1,990	1,920
Carroll,	1825	Ellicott,							1,015	1,414	1,649	1,725	1,833	1,408
Charlotte,	1829	Gerry,							886	1,208	1,428	1.428	1,718	1,672
Chautauque,	1804	Batavia,			1,039	1,073	2,519	1,423	2,442	3,119	2,980	2,809	2,622	2,591
Cherry Creek,	1829	Ellington,							574	923	1,141	1,100	1,311	1,226
Clymer,	1821	Chautauque,						304	567	843	909	979	1,127	1,164
Ellery,	1821	Chautauque,						1,207	2,002	2,395	2,242	2,134	2,104	1,865
Ellicott,	1812	Pomfret,				565	1,462	1,653	2,101	2,355	2,571	3,176	3,523	3,935
Ellington,	1824	Gerry,						824	1,279	1,773	1,725	1,832	2,001	1,930
French Creek,	1829	Clymer,							420	553	621	647	725	766
Gerry,	1812	Pomfret,				172	947	1,157	1,110	1,339	1,288	1,344	1,332	1,258
Hanover,	1812	Pomfret,				559	2,217	2,620	2,614	3,520	3,998	3,718	5,144	4,101
Harmony,	1816	Chautauque,					845	926	1,989	2,915	3,340	3,431	3,749	3,443
Kiantone,	1853	Carroll,												490

* Exclusive of Indians.

Comparative Population of Towns and Counties at different Periods.—(Continued).

CHAUTAUQUE COUNTY.—(Continued.)

CITIES & TOWNS.	When formed.	FROM WHAT TAKEN.	1790.	1800.	1810.	1814.	1820.	1825.	1830.	1835.	1840.	1845.	1850.	1855.
Mina,	1824	Clymer,						558	1, 388	798	871	882	996	1, 036
Poland,	1832	Ellicott,								916	1, 087	1, 015	1, 174	1, 325
Pomfret,	1808	Chautauque,			1, 342	1, 093	2, 306	3, 188	3, 386	4, 041	4, 566	4, 286	4, 483	9, 157
Portland,	1813	Chautauque,				797	1, 162	1, 989	1, 771	2, 181	2, 136	1, 966	1, 905	1, 936
Ripley,	1817	Portland,					1, 111	1, 821	1, 647	2, 023	2, 197	1, 938	1, 732	1, 703
Sheridan,	1827	Pomfret and Hanover,							1, 666	1, 919	1, 883	1, 592	2, 173	1, 591
Sherman,	1832	Mina,								830	1, 099	1, 131	1, 292	1, 314
Stockton,	1821	Chautauque,						927	1, 605	1, 943	2, 078	1, 780	1, 640	1, 688
Villenova,	1823	Hanover,						855	1, 126	1, 453	1, 655	1, 531	1, 536	1, 413
Westfield,	1829	Portland and Ripley,							2, 477	3, 036	3, 199	2, 886	3, 100	3, 338
Total,					2, 381	4, 259	12, 568	20, 639	34, 671	44, 869	47, 975	46, 548	50, 493	53, 380

CHEMUNG COUNTY.

CITIES & TOWNS.	When formed.	FROM WHAT TAKEN.	1790.	1800.	1810.	1814.	1820.	1825.	1830.	1835.	1840.	1845.	1850.	1855.
Big Flats,	1822	Elmira,						826	1, 149	1, 238	1, 375	1, 421	1, 709	1, 852
Catlin,	1823	Catharines,						1, 105	2, 015	2, 356	1, 119	1, 247	1, 474	1, 518
Chemung,	1789		2, 391	515	683	728	1, 327	1, 150	1, 461	2, 231	2, 377	2, 575	2, 673	2, 785
Elmira,	1792	Chemung,		1, 333	2, 169	2, 387	2, 945	1, 915	2, 892	3, 879	4, 791	5, 898	8, 166	8, 486
Erin,	1822	Chemung,						643	975	1, 099	1, 441	1, 581	1, 833	1, 190
Horseheads,	1854	Elmira,												2, 648
Southport,	1822	Elmira,						1, 114	1, 454	1, 711	2, 101	2, 539	3, 184	4, 479
Van Etten,	1854	Erin and Cayuta,												1, 522
Veteran,	1823	Catharines,						1, 258	1, 616	1, 925	2, 279	2, 481	2, 698	2, 807
Total,			2, 391	1, 848	2, 852	3, 115	4, 272	8, 011	11, 562	14, 439	15, 483	17, 742	21, 737	27, 288

CHENANGO COUNTY.

CITIES & TOWNS.	When formed.	FROM WHAT TAKEN.	1790.	1800.	1810.	1814.	1820.	1825.	1830.	1835.	1840.	1845.	1850.	1855.
Bainbridge,	1791			939	1, 604	2, 065	2, 290	2, 772	3, 038	3, 010	3, 324	3, 081	3, 338	3, 377
Columbus,	1805	Brookfield,			1, 386	1, 512	1, 805	1, 723	1, 661	1, 656	1, 561	1, 461	1, 381	1, 331
Coventry,	1806	Greene,			861	1, 053	1, 431	1, 485	1, 576	1, 603	1, 681	1, 765	1, 677	1, 684
German,	1806	De Ruyter,			1, 529	1, 945	2, 675	1, 498	884	886	965	947	903	806
Greene,	1798	Union and Jericho,		655	1, 285	1, 635	2, 590	2, 628	2, 962	4, 096	3, 462	3, 965	3, 763	3, 717
Guilford,	1813	Oxford,				1, 817	2, 175	2, 393	2, 636	2, 703	2, 827	2, 787	2, 600	2, 552
Lincklaen,	1823	German,						1, 527	1, 425	1, 014	1, 249	1, 172	1, 196	1, 331
Macdonough,	1816	Preston,					789	1, 044	1, 232	1, 425	1, 369	1, 514	1, 522	1, 417
New Berlin,	1807	Norwich,			1, 657	1, 842	2, 366	2, 511	2, 680	2, 967	3, 086	2, 704	2, 562	2, 507
North Norwich,	1849	Norwich,											1, 172	1, 126
Norwich,	1793	Jericho and Union,		2, 219	2, 748	2, 917	2, 257	3, 349	3, 619	3, 807	4, 145	4, 269	3, 615	4, 109
Otselic,	1817	German,					526	968	1, 236	1, 439	1, 621	1, 483	1, 800	1, 721
Oxford,	1793	Jericho and Union,		1, 405	3, 010	1, 691	2, 313	2, 801	2, 943	3, 765	3, 179	3, 059	3, 227	3, 116
Pharsalia,	1806	Norwich,			482	550	873	895	1, 011	1, 170	1, 213	1, 209	1, 185	1, 152
Pitcher,	1827	German and Lincklaen,							1, 214	1, 533	1, 562	1, 501	1, 403	1, 281
Plymouth,	1806	Norwich,			1, 269	1, 169	1, 496	1, 591	1, 609	1, 563	1, 625	1, 476	1, 551	1, 541
Preston,	1806	Norwich,			1, 007	1, 116	1, 092	1, 224	1, 213	1, 126	1, 117	1, 059	1, 082	1, 044
Sherburne,	1795	Paris,		1, 282	2, 521	2, 607	2, 590	2, 493	2, 601	3, 108	2, 791	2, 680	2, 623	2, 776
Smithville,	1808	Greene,			1, 005	1, 209	1, 553	1, 733	1, 839	1, 885	1, 762	1, 794	1, 771	1, 661
Smyrna,	1808	Sherburne,			1, 340	1, 093	1, 390	1, 580	1, 859	2, 026	2, 246	1, 944	1, 940	1, 866
Total,				6, 500	21, 704	24, 221	31, 215	34, 215	37, 238	40, 762	40, 785	39, 900	40, 311	30, 915

CLINTON COUNTY.

CITIES & TOWNS.	When formed.	FROM WHAT TAKEN.	1790.	1800.	1810.	1814.	1820.	1825.	1830.	1835.	1840.	1845.	1850.	1855.
Au Sable,	1839	Peru,									3, 222	3, 976	4, 492	3, 803
Beekmantown,	1820	Plattsburgh,					1, 343	1, 511	2, 391	2, 263	2, 769	3, 078	3, 384	2, 933
Black Brook,	1839	Peru,									1, 064	1, 598	2, 525	3, 025
Champlain,	1788		578	1, 169	1, 210	942	1, 618	1, 824	2, 456	2, 691	3, 632	4, 050	5, 067	6, 197
Chazy,	1804	Champlain,			1, 466	1, 404	2, 313	2, 396	3, 097	3, 023	3, 584	3, 571	4, 324	4, 462
Clinton,	1845	Ellenburgh,										833	1, 436	1, 371
Dannemora,	1854	Beekmantown,												723
Ellenburgh,	1830	Mooers,								645	1, 171	902	1, 504	1, 751
Mooers,	1804	Champlain,			301	272	567	743	1, 222	1, 137	1, 703	2, 207	3, 365	3, 622
Peru,	1792	Plattsburgh and Willsborough,		1, 347	1, 923	1, 755	2, 710	3, 996	4, 949	5, 796	3, 134	3, 273	3, 640	3, 522
Plattsburgh,	1785		458	1, 400	3, 102	3, 390	3, 519	3, 753	4, 913	4, 426	6, 416	6, 095	5, 618	6, 080
Saranac,	1824	Plattsburgh,						263	316	761	1, 462	1, 695	2, 582	3, 058
Schuyler's Falls,	1848	Plattsburgh,											2, 110	1, 937
Total,			1, 036	3, 916	8, 802	7, 764	12, 070	14, 486	19, 344	20, 742	28, 157	31, 278	40, 047	42, 482

COLUMBIA COUNTY.

CITIES & TOWNS.	When formed.	FROM WHAT TAKEN.	1790.	1800.	1810.	1814.	1820.	1825.	1830.	1835.	1840.	1845.	1850.	1855.
Ancram,	1803	Livingston,			2, 471	2, 161	3, 147	3, 126	1, 533	1, 617	1, 770	1, 705	1, 569	1, 801
Austerlitz,	1818	Canaan, Chatham and Hillsdale,					2, 355	2, 247	2, 245	2, 092	2, 091	1, 812	1, 873	1, 619
Canaan,	1788	King's District,	6, 692	5, 195	4, 941	4, 850	2, 079	2, 048	2, 063	2, 042	1, 957	1, 973	1, 941	1, 946
Chatham,	1795	Canaan and Kinderhook,		3, 716	3, 381	3, 658	3, 372	3, 522	3, 538	3, 469	3, 662	3, 570	3, 839	4, 023
Claverack,	1788		3, 262	4, 414	3, 593	3, 824	2, 813	2, 970	3, 000	2, 840	3, 056	2, 934	3, 208	3, 363
Clermont,	1787	Manor of Livingston,	867	1, 142	1, 090	1, 013	1, 164	1, 146	1, 203	1, 166	1, 231	1, 131	1, 130	1, 058
Copake,	1824	Taghkanick,						1, 639	1, 676	1, 616	1, 505	1, 607	1, 652	1, 620
Gallatin,	1830	Ancram,							1, 588	1, 655	1, 644	1, 676	1, 586	1, 517
Germantown,	1788	German or East Camp,	516	736	690	737	891	920	967	979	969	991	1, 023	1, 131
Ghent,	1818	Claverack, Kinderhook and Chatham,					2, 379	2, 290	2, 783	2, 375	2, 558	2, 417	2, 293	2, 537
Greenport,	1837	Hudson city,									1, 161	1, 182	1, 300	1, 383
Hillsdale,	1788		4, 556	4, 702	4, 182	4, 212	2, 511	2, 389	2, 446	2, 266	2, 470	2, 374	2, 123	2, 194

Comparative Population of Towns and Counties at different Periods.—(Continued.)

COLUMBIA COUNTY.—(Continued.)

CITIES & TOWNS	When formed.	FROM WHAT TAKEN.	1790.	1800.	1810.	1814.	1820	1825.	1830.	1835.	1840.	1845.	1850.	1855
Hudson city:														
1st ward, ...	1785	Claverack,						2,789		2,914	2,854	2,640	2,936	1,460
2nd ward, ...	1785	Claverack,						2,215		2,617	2,818	3,017	3,350	1,675
3rd ward, ...	1854	1st and 2nd wards,												1,764
4th ward, ...	1854	1st and 2nd wards,												1,821
Total Huds'n city,			2,584	3,664	4,048	4,725	5,310	5,004	5,392	5,531	5,672	5,657	6,286	6,720
Kinderhook, ...	1788		4,661	4,348	3,709	4,221	3,963	2,471	2,706	2,831	3,512	3,679	3,970	3,864
Livingston,......	1788		4,594	7,405	1,651	1,437	1,938	1,988	2,087	2,206	2,119	2,083	2,020	2,064
New Lebanon, ...	1818	Canaan,					2,808	2,628	2,695	2,713	2,536	2,282	2,300	2,329
Stockport, ...	1833	Ghent and Stuyvesant,								1,023	1,815	1,661	1,655	1,621
Stuyvesant, ...	1823	Kinderhook,						1,889	2,331	1,736	1,779	1,718	1,766	1,937
Taghkanick,.....	1803	Livingston,			2,634	3,141	3,600	1,693	1,654	1,589	1,674	1,524	1,539	1,665
Total, ...			27,732	35,322	32,390	33,979	38,330	37,970	39,907	40,746	43,252	41,976	43,073	44,391

CORTLAND COUNTY.

CITIES & TOWNS	When formed.	FROM WHAT TAKEN.	1790.	1800.	1810.	1814.	1820	1825.	1830.	1835.	1840.	1845.	1850.	1855
Cincinnatus,.....	1804	Solon,			1,525	1,614	885	1,057	1,308	1,180	1,301	1,195	1,206	1,119
Cortlandville, ...	1829	Homer,							3,673	3,715	3,799	4,111	4,203	4,329
Freetown,......	1818	Cincinnatus,					663	877	1,051	962	950	925	1,035	955
Harford, ...	1845	Virgil,											949	926
Homer, ...	1794			612	2,975	4,046	5,504	6,128	3,307	3,584	3,572	3,602	3,836	3,785
Lapeer, ...	1845	Virgil,											822	750
Marathon, ...	1818	Cincinnatus,					807	873	895	986	1,063	1,080	1,149	1,341
Preble, ...	1808	Tully,			1,179	1,311	1,257	1,327	1,435	1,408	1,247	1,325	1,312	1,219
Scott, ...	1815	Preble,					775	1,006	1,452	1,504	1,332	1,368	1,290	1,293
Solon, ...	1798	Homer,		370	1,263	717	1,262	1,781	2,033	2,103	2,311	2,426	1,150	1,057
Taylor, ...	1849	Solon,											1.232	1,201
Truxton, ...	1808	Fabius,			1,031	1,768	2,956	3,325	3,885	3,712	3,658	3,587	3,623	3,444
Virgil,..........	1804	Homer,			906	1,437	2,411	3,317	3,912	4,291	4,502	4,541	2,410	2,231
Willett,.........	1818	Cincinnatus,					437	580	840	723	872	921	923	925
Total, ...				982	8,879	10,893	16,507	20.271	23.791	24,168	24,607	25,081	25,140	24,575

DELAWARE COUNTY.

CITIES & TOWNS	When formed.	FROM WHAT TAKEN.	1790.	1800.	1810.	1814.	1820	1825.	1830.	1835.	1840.	1845.	1850.	1855
Andes, ...	1819	Middletown,					1,378	1,808	1,860	2,109	2,176	2,440	2,672	2,536
Bovina,.........	1820	Delhi, Stamford and Middletown,					1,267	1,248	1,348	1,412	1,403	1,436	1,316	1,224
Colchester, ...	1792	Middletown,		1,207	885	888	1,064	1,153	1,424	1,516	1,567	1,858	2,184	2,360
Davenport,......	1817	Kortright and Middletown,					1,384	1,661	1,778	2,052	2,052	2,143	2,305	2,233
Delhi, ...	1798	Middletown, Kortright and Walton,		820	2,396	2,374	2,285	2,654	2,114	2,363	2,554	2,665	2,909	2,711
Franklin, ...	1792	Harpersfield,		1,390	1,708	2,051	2,481	2.397	2,786	2,951	3,025	3,007	3,087	3,186
Hamden,........	1825	Walton and Delhi,							1,230	1,349	1,469	1,767	1,919	1,881
Hancock, ...	1806	Colchester,			578	596	525	649	766	895	1,026	1,208	1,798	2,512
Harpersfield, ...	1788		1.726	1,007	1,691	1,694	1,884	1,952	1,976	1,741	1,708	1.569	1,613	1,480
Kortright, ...	1793			1,513	2,993	3,079	2,548	2,766	2,870	2,531	2.441	2,211	2,181	2,013
Masonville, ...	1811	Sidney,				621	719	851	1,145	1,278	1,420	1,383	1,550	1,543
Meredith, ...	1800	Franklin and Kortright,		213	726	769	1,375	1.521	1,666	1,603	1,640	1,678	1,634	1,503
Middletown,.....	1789	Rochester and Woodstock,	1,019	1,064	2,318	2,360	1,949	2,115	2,383	2,487	2,608	2.695	3,005	2,946
Roxbury, ...	1799	Stamford,		936	1.892	1,974	2.488	2.944	3,234	2,856	3,013	3,121	2,853	2,533
Sidney, ...	1801	Franklin,			1,388	834	1,107	1,137	1,410	1,597	1,732	1,759	1,807	1,797
Stamford, ...	1792			924	1,658	1,747	1,495	1,595	1,597	1,747	1,681	1,715	1,708	1.597
Tompkins, ...	1806	Walton,			869	987	1,206	1,547	1,774	1,951	2,035	2,261	3,022	3,290
Walton, ...	1797	Franklin,		1,154	1,211	1,316	1,432	1,567	1,663	1,754	1,846	2,074	2,271	2,404
Total, ...			2.745	10,228	20,303	21,290	26,587	20.565	33,024	34,192	35.396	36,990	39,834	39,749

DUTCHESS COUNTY.

CITIES & TOWNS	When formed.	FROM WHAT TAKEN.	1790.	1800.	1810.	1814.	1820	1825.	1830.	1835.	1840.	1845.	1850.	1855
Amenia, ...	1788		3,078	2,978	3,083	2,988	3,114	2,167	2,389	2,138	2,179	2,076	2,229	2,199
Beekman, ...	1788		3,597	3,756	3,980	4,360	4,257	2,808	1,584	1,447	1,400	1,432	1,386	1,379
Clinton, ...	1786	Charlotte and Rhinebeck precincts,	4,607	5,208	5,471	6,790	6,611	2,069	2,130	1,919	1.830	1,816	1,795	1,840
Dover,..........	1807	Pawling,			2,146	2,062	2,193	2,198	2,198	1,981	2,000	1,944	2,146	1,925
East Fishkill,....	1849	Fishkill,											2,610	2,612
Fishkill, ...	1788		5,941	6,168	6,984	7,510	8,203	6,916	8,292	9,623	10.437	10,651	9,240	8,764
Hyde Park, ...	1821	Clinton,						2,415	2,554	2,368	2,364	2,477	2,425	2,480
La Grange,......	1821	Beekman and Fishkill,						2,415	2,044	1,927	1,851	1,834	1,941	1,852
Milan,..........	1818	North East,					1,797	1,769	1,886	1,813	1,725	1,744	1,764	1,630
North East, ...	1788		3,401	3,252	3,487	3,451	2,037	1,596	1,689	1,495	1,385	1,436	1,555	1,757
Pawling, ...	1788		4,330	4,269	1,756	1,704	1,804	1,691	1.705	1,565	1,571	1.626	1,720	1,792
Pine Plains, ...	1823	North East,						1,421	1,502	1,355	1,334	1,499	1,416	1,453
Pleasant Valley, .	1821	Clinton,						2,506	2,419	2,245	2,219	2,142	2,226	1.853
Poughkeepsie, ...	1788		2,529	3,246	4,669	5,673	5,726	5,935	7,222	8,529	10,006	11,791	13,944	3,110
P'ghkeepsie city:														
1st ward,.....	1854	Town of Poughkeepsie,												4,099
2nd ward,.....	1854	Town of Poughkeepsie,												2,663
3rd ward,.....	1854	Town of Poughkeepsie,												3,461
4th ward,.....	1854	Town of Poughkeepsie,												2,540
Total P'ghkeepsie,														12.763
Redhook, ...	1812	Rhinebeck,				2.395	2,714	2,798	2,983	2,824	2.829	3,085	3,264	3.750
Rhinebeck, ...	1788		3,662	4.022	4,425	2,805	2,729	2,735	2,938	2,624	2,659	2,989	2,816	3,065
Stanford, ...	1793	Washington,		2,344	2,335	2,546	2,518	2.463	2,521	2,358	2,278	2,301	2,158	2,201
Union Vale, ...	1827	Beekman & Freedom (now La Grange),							1,833	1,596	1,498	1,484	1,552	1,463
Washington, ...	1788		5,189	2,666	2,854	1,423	2,882	2,796	3,036	2,897	2,833	2,797	2,805	2,740
Total, ...			36.334	37,909	41,190	43,707	46,615	46,698	50,926	50,704	52,398	55,124	58,002	60,635

Comparative Population of Towns and Counties at different Periods.—(Continued.)

ERIE COUNTY.

CITIES & TOWNS.	When formed.	FROM WHAT TAKEN.	1790.	1800.	1810.	1814.	1820.	1825.	1830.	1835.	1840.	1845.	1850.	1855.
Alden,	1823	Clarence,						793	1,258	1,969	1,984	2,187	2,520	2,404
Amherst,	1818	Buffalo,					768	1,308	2,485	3,376	2,451	3,133	4,153	5,118
Aurora,	1804				2,028	1,178	1,285	1,727	2,423	2,967	2,908	3,010	3,435	3,665
Black Rock,	1839	Buffalo city, to which it was re-annexed in 1853,									3,625	4,883	7,508	
Boston,	1817	Eden,					686	992	1,521	1,825	1,745	1,779	1,872	1,769
Brandt,	1839	Collins and Evans,									1,088	987	1,028	1,093
Buffalo:					1,508	1,060	2,095	5,141	8,668					
1st ward,	1832									4,838	3,531	7,107	7,341	7,994
2d ward,	1832									2,805	3,400	5,877	8,529	5,882
3d ward,	1832									1,909	1,829	3,511	5,072	4,293
4th ward,	1832									3,407	5,483	9,061	15,709	8,000
5th ward,	1832									2,702	3,970	4,217	5,607	8,759
6th ward,	1853													7,354
7th ward,	1853													7,804
8th ward,	1853													5,404
9th ward,	1853													5,625
10th ward,	1853													5,238
11th ward,	1853													3,314
12th ward,	1853													3,729
13th ward,	1853													818
Total Buffalo,										19,715	18,213	29,773	42 261	74,214
Chictawauga,	1839	Amherst,									1,137	2,029	3,042	2,526
Clarence,	1808	Willink (now Aurora).			1,131	1,670	3,278	2,465	3,360	2,239	2,271	2,497	2,727	3,253
Colden,	1827	Holland,							464	788	1,088	1,086	1,344	1,381
Collins,	1821	Concord,						1,627	2,123	4,025	4,257	3,969	4,001	*2,025
Concord,	1812	Willink (now Aurora),				739	2,786	1,460	1,895	2,658	3,021	3,132	3,242	2,805
East Hamburgh,	1850	Hamburgh,												1,946
Eden,	1812	Willink (now Aurora),				519	1,065	862	1,086	2,093	2,174	2,213	2,494	2,426
Evans,	1821	Eden,						770	1,185	2,638	1,807	1,859	2,182	2,252
Grand Island,	1852	Tonawanda,												838
Hamburgh,	1812	Willink (now Aurora),				1,035	2,034	2,661	3,351	4,126	3,727	4,252	5,219	3,037
Holland,	1818	Willink, " "					768	1,001	1,071	1,166	1,242	1,355	1,315	1,321
Lancaster,	1833	Clarence,								2,009	2,083	2,737	3,794	5,489
Marilla,	1853	Alden and Wales,												1,377
Newstead,	1804	Batavia,						1,375	1,926	2,383	2,653	2,610	2,899	2,987
North Collins,	1852	Collins,												1,859
Sardinia,	1821	Concord,						951	1,453	1,633	1,743	1,600	1,761	1,765
Tonawanda,	1836	Buffalo,									1,261	1,634	2,072	2,569
Wales,	1818	Willink (now Aurora),					903	1,183	1,470	1,984	1,987	1,910	2,124	1,689
West Seneca,	1851	Hamburgh, East Hamburgh, Chictawauga and Lancaster,												2,523
Total,					4,667	6,201	10.834	24,316	35,719	57,594	62,465	78,635	100993	132831*

ESSEX COUNTY.

CITIES & TOWNS.	When formed.	FROM WHAT TAKEN.	1790.	1800.	1810.	1814.	1820.	1825.	1830.	1835.	1840.	1845.	1850.	1855.
Chesterfield,	1802	Willsborough,			630	547	667	1,154	1,671	2,083	2,716	3,022	4,171	3,327
Crown Point,	1786		203	941	1,182	1,194	1,522	1,728	2,041	2,189	2,212	2,261	2,378	2,216
Elizabethtown,	1798	Crown Point,		899	1,360	1,412	889	1,029	1,015	856	1,061	1,194	1,635	1,402
Essex,	1805	Willsborough,			1,173	1,015	1,225	1,288	1,543	1,529	1,681	1,720	2,351	2,115
Jay,	1798	Willsborough,		601	1,056	1,273	1,647	1,216	1,629	1,732	2,258	2,431	2,688	2,850
Keene,	1808	Elizabethtown and Jay,			642	596	605	707	787	700	730	809	756	774
Lewis,	1805	Willsborough,			548	621	779	1,101	1,305	1,358	1,505	1,681	2,058	1,803
Minerva,	1817	Schroon,					271	371	358	335	455	496	586	767
Moriah,	1808	Crown Point and Elizabethtown,			574	602	842	1,251	1,742	2,293	2,595	2,807	3,065	3,120
Newcomb,	1828	Minerva and Moriah,							62	46	74	126	277	226
North Elba,	1849	Keene,											210	301
North Hudson,	1848	Moriah,											561	519
St. Armand,	1844	Wilmington,										129	210	289
Schroon,	1804	Crown Point,			690	869	888	1,190	1,614	1,723	1,660	1,705	2,031	2,085
Ticonderoga,	1804	Crown Point,			179	1,222	1,493	1,833	1,996	2,080	2,169	2,309	2,669	2,125
Westport,	1815	Elizabethtown,					1,095	1,322	1,513	1,724	1,932	2,094	2,352	2,041
Willsborough,	1788		375	1,716	655	598	888	1,166	1,316	1,253	1,658	1,424	1,932	1,675
Wilmington,	1821	Jay,						637	695	798	928	894	1,218	904
Total,			578	4,157	9,477	9,949	12,811	15,993	19. 287	20,699	23. 634	25,102	31,148	28,539

FRANKLIN COUNTY.

CITIES & TOWNS.	When formed.	FROM WHAT TAKEN.	1790.	1800.	1810.	1814.	1820.	1825.	1830.	1835.	1840.	1845.	1850.	1855.
Bangor,	1812	Dickinson,				252	370	910	1,076	1,035	1,289	1,606	2,159	2,154
Bellmont,	1833	Chateaugay,								382	472	510	660	873
Bombay,	1833	Fort Covington,								1,357	1,446	1,667	1,963	*2,319
Brandon,	1828	Bangor,							316	417	531	578	590	728
Burke,	1844	Chateaugay,										1,285	2,477	1,900
Chateaugay,	1799	Champlain,		443	625	407	828	1,384	2,016	2,039	2,824	1,952	3,728	2,676
Constable,	1807	Harrison (now Malone),			916	989	637	1,016	693	724	1,122	1,177	1,447	1,443
Dickinson,	1808	Harrison, " "			411	185	495	899	446	597	1,005	1,074	1,119	1,255
Duane,	1828	Malone,							247	237	324	178	222	325
Fort Covington,	1817	Constable,					979	2,136	2,901	1,665	2,094	2,369	2,641	2,559
Franklin,	1836	Bellmont,									192	361	724	947
Harrietstown,	1841	Duane,										129	181	306
Malone,	1805	Chateaugay,			767	735	1,130	1,633	2,207	2,589	3,229	3,634	4,550	5,186
Moira,	1828	Dickinson,							791	798	962	1,013	1,340	1,459
Westville,	1829	Constable,							619	661	1,028	1,159	1,301	1,354
Total,				443	2,719	2,568	4,439	7,978	11,312	12,501	16,518	18,692	25,102	*25897

* Exclusive of Indians.

Comparative Population of Towns and Counties at different Periods.—(Continued).

FULTON COUNTY.

TIES & TOWNS.	When formed	FROM WHAT TAKEN.	1790.	1800.	1810.	1814.	1820.	1825.	1830.	1835.	1840.	1845.	1850.	1855.
ecker,	1831	Johnstown,								332	346	267	510	904
oadalbin,	1793	Caughnawaga (changed to Broadalbin, Johnstown, and Amsterdam, 1793,	with Amsterdam.	1133	2,238	2,369	2,428	2,400	2,655	2,721	2,738	2,358	2,476	2,646
roga,	1842	Bleecker, Stratford and Johnstown,										342	589	714
phrata,	1827	Palatine,							1,902	2,146	2,009	2,085	2,079	2,183
ohnstown,	1793	Caughnawaga (see note above),	with Amsterdam.	3932	6,225	6,373	6,527	7,359	7,700	7,557	5,409	5,408	6,131	7,912
ayfield,	1793	Caughnawaga, " "		876	2,065	1,704	2,025	2,439	2,609	2,908	2,615	2,397	2,429	2,393
orthampton,	1799	Broadalbin,		990	1,474	1,346	1,291	1,344	1,380	1,369	1,526	1,377	1,701	1,943
ppenheim,	1808	Palatine,			2,693	2,380	3,045	3,025	3,654	3,927	2,169	2,388	2,315	2,412
erth,	1838	Amsterdam,									738	1,214	1,140	1,131
tratford,	1805	Palatine,			353	319	407	439	551	637	500	743	801	1,046
Total,				6,931	15,048	14,491	15,723	17,006	20,451	21,597	18,049	18,579	20,171	23,284

GENESEE COUNTY.

Towns	When formed	From what taken	1790	1800	1810	1814	1820	1825	1830	1835	1840	1845	1850	1855
labama,	1826	Pembroke and Shelby,							819	1,638	1,798	1,800	2,054	2,194
lexander,	1812	Batavia,				975	1,496	1,893	2,331	2,487	2,242	1,994	1,927	1,798
atavia,	1802				3,660	2,384	2,597	3,353	4,264	4,430	4,219	4,384	4,461	5,304
ergen,	1812	Batavia,				1,157	2,438	1,342	1,508	1,519	1,832	1,822	1,897	1,800
ethany,	1812	Batavia,				1,194	1,691	2,088	2,374	2,532	2,286	2,051	1,904	1,879
yron,	1820	Bergen,					1,767	1,720	1,936	1,953	1,907	1,807	1,566	1,641
arien,	1832	Pembroke,								2,621	2,406	2,212	2,084	2,176
lba,	1820	Batavia,					1,333	1,770	2,678	3,134	3,161	1,950	1,772	1,869
e Roy,	1812	Caledonia,				2,457	2,611	2,973	3,902	4,239	4,323	3,352	3,473	4,206
akfield,	1842	Elba,										1,360	1,457	1,510
avilion,	1841	Covington,										1,834	1,640	1,758
embroke,	1812	Batavia,				1,268	2,576	3,153	3,828	2,029	1,970	2,140	2,279	2,844
tafford,	1820	Batavia and Le Roy,					2,069	2,416	2,368	2,563	2,561	2,139	1,974	2,055
Total,					3,660	9,435	18,578	20,708	26,008	29,145	28,705	28,845	28,488	31,532

GREENE COUNTY.

Towns	When formed	From what taken	1790	1800	1810	1814	1820	1825	1830	1835	1840	1845	1850	1855
shland,	1848	Windham,											1,290	1,139
thens,	1815	Catskill and Coxsackie,					2,030	2,038	2,425	2,673	2,387	2,593	2,986	2,870
airo,	1803	Catskill, Coxsackie and Freehold, (now Durham),			2,035	2,071	2,353	2,642	2,912	2,861	2,862	2,812	2,831	2,557
atskill,	1788		1,980	2,408	4,245	4,480	3,510	4,085	4,861	5,179	5,339	5,458	5,454	5,710
oxsackie,	1788		3,406	4,676	4,047	2,570	2,355	3,028	3,373	3,364	3,539	3,799	3,741	3,682
Durham,	1790	Coxsackie,	1,822	3,812	2,944	2,753	2,979	3,180	3,039	2,954	2,813	2,613	2,600	2,540
reenville,	1803	Coxsackie and Freehold,			2,304	2,196	2,374	2,404	2,566	2,313	2,338	2,261	2,242	2,173
alcott,	1851	Lexington,												474
unter,	1814	Greenland,				621	1,025	1,467	1,960	2,024	2,019	2,433	1,849	1,594
ewett,	1849	Lexington and Hunter,											1,452	1,129
exington,	1813	Windham,				1,292	1,798	2,221	2,548	2,598	2,813	2,902	2,263	1,595
New Baltimore,	1811	Coxsackie,				1,984	2,036	2,171	2,370	2,395	2,306	2,347	2,381	2,402
Prattsville,	1833	Windham,								1,469	1,613	2,069	1,989	1,588
Windham,	1798	Woodstock,		1,688	3,961	2,243	2,536	2,993	3,471	2,343	2,417	2,670	2,048	1,684
Total,			7,208	12,584	19,536	20,210	22,996	26,229	29,525	30,173	30,446	31,957	33,126	31,137

HAMILTON COUNTY.

Towns	When formed	From what taken	1790	1800	1810	1814	1820	1825	1830	1835	1840	1845	1850	1855
Arietta,	1836	Lake Pleasant,									209	114	108	149
Gilman,	1839	Wells,									98	95	101	90
Hope,	1818	Wells,					608	696	719	768	711	648	789	822
Lake Pleasant,	1812	Johnstown,				215	312	235	266	336	296	296	305	300
Long Lake,	1837	Wells, Lake Pleasant, Arietta and Morehouse,									59	72	157	139
Morehouse,	1835	Lake Pleasant,								119	199	211	242	275
Wells,	1805	Mayfield and Northampton,			465	341	331	365	340	431	365	446	486	768
Total,					465	556	1,251	1,296	1,325	1,654	1,907	1,882	2,188	2,543

HERKIMER COUNTY.

Towns	When formed	From what taken	1790	1800	1810	1814	1820	1825	1830	1835	1840	1845	1850	1855
Columbia,	1812	Warren,				1,870	2,051	2,180	2,181	1,983	2,129	2,126	2,000	1,831
Danube,	1817	Minden,					3,183	3,275	1,724	1,651	1,960	1,693	1,730	1,791
Fairfield,	1796	Norway,		2,065	2,705	2,275	2,610	2,535	2,266	2,062	1,836	1,662	1,646	1,493
Frankfort,	1796	German Flats,		946	1,314	1,294	1,860	2,148	2,620	2,670	3,096	3,082	3,023	3,217
German Flats,	1788		1,307	1,637	2,228	2,327	2,665	3,065	2,466	2,715	3,245	3,237	3,578	3,855
Herkimer,	1788		1,525	2,634	2,743	2,887	3,055	3,198	2,486	2,710	2,369	2,379	2,601	2,866
Litchfield,	1796	German Flats,		1,976	2,533	2,299	1,729	1,701	1,750	1,620	1,672	1,677	1,676	1,582
Little Falls,	1829	Herkimer, Fairfield and Germ'n Flats,							2,539	3,147	3,881	4,244	4,855	4,930
Manheim,	1797	Palatine,		1,037	1,444	1,608	1,777	1,841	1,937	2,095	2,095	1,872	1,902	1,672
Newport,	1806	Herkimer, Fairfield, Norway and Schuyler,			1,605	1,415	1,746	1,811	1,863	1,955	2,020	2,112	2,125	2,015

* Exclusive of Indians.

Comparative Population of Towns and Counties at different Periods.—(Continued.)

HERKIMER COUNTY.—(Continued.)

CITIES & TOWNS.	When formed.	FROM WHAT TAKEN.	1790.	1800	1810.	1814.	1820	1825.	1830.	1835.	1840.	1845.	1850	1855.
Norway,	1792	Herkimer,		1,913	1,466	1,365	1,612	1,168	1,151	1,131	1,046	1,079	1,052	1.059
Ohio,	1823	Norway,						515	713	698	692	763	1,051	1.087
Russia,	1806	Norway,			1,381	1,429	1,685	2,174	2,458	2,313	2,298	2,439	2,349	2.288
Salisbury,	1797	Palatine,		716	1,252	1,280	1,438	1,779	1,999	1,974	1,859	1,860	2,035	2,306
Schuyler,	1792	Herkimer,		963	2,107	1,507	1,837	1,936	2,074	2,153	1,798	1,824	1,696	1,690
Stark,	1828	Danube,							1,781	1,581	1,766	1.775	1,576	1,478
Warren,	1796	German Flats,		2,445	3,964	2,169	2,013	2.077	2,084	2,004	2,003	1,952	1,756	1,741
Wilmurt,	1836	Russia & West Brunswick (now Ohio),									60	89	112	268
Winfield,	1816	Litchfield, Richfield, and Plainfield,					1,715	1,637	1,778	1,739	1,652	1,559	1,481	1,397
Total,			2,827	16,332	24.742	23,725	31,017	33,040	35,870	36,201	37,477	37.424	38,244	38,566

JEFFERSON COUNTY.

CITIES & TOWNS.	When formed.	FROM WHAT TAKEN.	1790.	1800	1810.	1814.	1820	1825.	1830.	1835.	1840.	1845.	1850	1855.
Adams,	1802	Mexico,			1,386	1,693	2,467	2,415	2,995	2,970	2,966	3,055	3,106	3,105
Alexandria,	1821	Brownville and Le Ray,						1,543	1,522	2,701	3,475	3,711	3,178	3,353
Antwerp,	1810	Le Ray,				303	1,319	2,257	2,411	2,614	3,109	3,380	3,665	3,763
Brownville,	1802	Leyden,			1,660	1,937	3,990	2,580	2,928	2,890	3,968	4,380	4,282	3,589
Cape Vincent,	1849	Lyme,											3,044	3,375
Champion,	1800	Mexico,		143	1,481	1,691	2,080	2,028	2,342	2,490	2,206	2,146	2,085	1,946
Clayton,	1833	Orleans and Lyme,								3,344	3,990	4,682	4,191	4,232
Ellisburgh,	1803	Mexico,			1,715	2,325	3,531	4,733	5,292	5,029	5,349	5,531	5,524	5,339
Henderson,	1806	Ellisburgh,			1,138	1,402	1,919	2,074	2,428	2,270	2,480	2,345	2,239	2,139
Hounsfield,	1806	Watertown,			943	1,386	3,429	2,769	3,415	3,558	4,146	3,917	4,136	3,221
Le Ray,	1806	Brownville,			1,149	1,121	2,944	2,556	3,419	3,668	3,721	3,853	3,654	3,203
Lorraine,	1804	Mexico,			812	810	1,112	1,400	1,727	1,615	1,699	1,640	1,511	1,470
Lyme,	1818	Brownville,					1,724	2,565	2,873	2,816	5,472	6,018	2,919	2,563
Orleans,	1821	Brownville,						3,544	3,091	2,044	3,001	3,047	3,265	2,806
Pamelia,	1819	Brownville,					1,342	1,988	2,273	2,322	2,104	2,254	2,528	2,511
Philadelphia,	1821	Le Ray,						826	1,167	1,616	1,888	1,942	1,915	1,743
Rodman,	1804	Adams,			1,277	1,484	1,735	1,719	1,901	1,698	1,702	1,694	1,784	1,752
Rutland,	1802	Watertown,			1,738	1,694	1,946	2,102	2,339	2,111	2,090	2,148	2,265	1,977
Theresa,	1841	Alexandria,										2,109	2,342	2,278
Watertown,	1800	Mexico,		119	1,841	2,458	2,766	3,425	4,768	4,279	5,027	5,433	7,201	7,557
Wilna,	1819	Le Ray and Leyden,					261	648	1,126	1,602	2,053	2,591	2,714	2,993
Worth,	1848	Lorraine,											326	474
Total,				262	15,140	18,564	32,952	41,650	48,493	53,088	60,984	64.999	68,153	65,420

KINGS COUNTY.

CITIES & TOWNS.	When formed.	FROM WHAT TAKEN.	1790.	1800	1810.	1814.	1820	1825.	1830.	1835.	1840.	1845.	1850	1855.
Brooklyn:			1,603	2,378	4,402	3,805	7,175	10,791	†15394					
1st ward,	1834	Village and town of Brooklyn,								1,523	2,148	4,622	6,062	6,441
2nd ward,	1834	Village and town of Brooklyn,								4,674	5,447	6,903	9,357	8,383
3rd ward,	1834	Village and town of Brooklyn,								2,764	3,834	5,936	8,749	8,900
4th ward,	1834	Village and town of Brooklyn,								5,724	6,827	8,819	11,032	12,282
5th ward,	1834	Village and town of Brooklyn,								4,510	7,415	9,419	13,682	16,352
6th ward,	1834	Town of Brooklyn,								2,139	4,043	10,651	11,536	18,490
7th ward,	1834	Town of Brooklyn,								2,042	4,521	9,958	6,371	12,523
8th ward,	1834	Town of Brooklyn,								487	944	1,369	2,585	5,318
9th ward,	1834	Town of Brooklyn,								666	1,054	1,897	3,261	9,133
10th ward,	1850												11,782	21,749
11th ward,	1850												12,421	22,213
12th ward,	1854													6,990
13th ward,	1854	Williamsburgh until 1854,									*5,094	*11338	*30780	14,044
14th ward,	1854	Williamsburgh until 1854,												12,414
15th ward,	1854	Williamsburgh until 1854,												6,559
16th ward,	1854	Williamsburgh until 1854,												15,350
17th ward,	1854	Bushwick until 1854,	540	656	798	759	930	958	‡1,620	*3,325	*1,295	*1,857	*3,139	5,508
18th ward,	1854	Bushwick until 1854,												2,601
Total Brooklyn,										24,529	36,233	59,574	96,838	205250
Flatbush,	1788		941	946	1,159	1,062	1,027	1,049	1,143	1,537	2,099	2,225	3,177	3,280
Flatlands,	1788		423	493	517	507	512	491	596	684	810	936	1,155	1,578
Gravesend,	1788		426	489	520	552	534	408	565	695	799	898	1,064	1,256
New Lots,	1852	Flatbush,											2,129	2.261
New Utrecht,	1788		562	778	907	970	1,009	982	1,217	1.287	1,283	1,863	39,780	2,730
Total,			4,495	5.740	8,303	7.655	11,187	14.679	20,535	32,057	47,613	78,691	138882	216355

LEWIS COUNTY.

CITIES & TOWNS.	When formed.	FROM WHAT TAKEN.	1790.	1800	1810.	1814.	1820	1825.	1830.	1835.	1840.	1845.	1850	1855.
Croghan,	1841	Watson and Diana,										1,014	1,135	1,531
Denmark,	1807	Harrisburgh,			§	1,495	1,745	1,989	2,370	2,522	2,388	2,551	2,824	2,381
Diana,	1830	Watson,							309	449	883	793	970	1,177
Greig,	1828	Watson,							662	538	592	880	1,074	1,203
Harrisburgh,	1803	Lowville, Champion and Mexico,			§	399	520	722	712	803	850	986	1,367	1,240
High Market,	1852	West Turin,												1.125
Lewis,	1852	West Turin and Leyden,												1.157
Leyden,	1797	Steuben,		622	§	871	1.203	1,156	1,502	1,687	2,438	1,941	2,253	1,856
Lowville,	1800	Mexico,		300	§	1,604	1,943	2,107	2,334	2,097	2,047	2,167	2,377	2,144

* Not included in the city of Brooklyn.
† The five wards of Brooklyn contained 12,406, the township 2,988.
‡ Williamsburgh and Bushwick.
§ Population of towns not reported separately.

Comparative Population of Towns and Counties at different Periods.—(Continued.)

LEWIS COUNTY.—(Continued.)

Cities & Towns	When formed.	From what taken.	1790.	1800	1810.	1814.	1820	1825.	1830.	1835.	1840	1845.	1850.	1855
Martinsburgh,	1803	Turin,			*	997	1,497	1,950	2,382	2,288	2,272	2,408	2,677	2,489
Montague,	1850	West Turin,												571
New Bremen,	1848	Watson and Croghan,											1,510	1,647
Osceola,	1844	West Turin,										213	412	513
Pinckney,	1808	Harris'n (now Rodm'n) & Harrisb'gh,			*	404	507	664	763	796	907	996	1,208	1,039
Turin,	1800	Mexico,		440	*	1,078	1,812	2,388	1,661	1,907	1,704	1,882	1,826	1,748
Watson,	1821	Leyden,						693	909	1,163	1,707	2,763	1,138	930
West Turin,	1830	Turin,							1,635	1,843	2,042	1,624	3,793	2,478
Total,				1,362	6,433	6,848	9,227	11,669	15,239	16,093	17,830	20,218	24,564	25,229

LIVINGSTON COUNTY.

Cities & Towns	When formed.	From what taken.	1790.	1800	1810.	1814.	1820	1825.	1830.	1835.	1840	1845.	1850.	1855
Avon,	1789			535	1,880	2,336	1,933	2,301	2,372	2,754	2,999	2,450	2,809	2,694
Caledonia,	1802				2,288	2,228	2,645	1,466	1,618	1,677	1,987	1,758	1,804	1,991
Conesus,	1819	Livonia and Groveland,					1,288	1,356	1,690	1,690	1,654	1,579	1,418	1,413
Geneseo,	1789			348	894	1,286	1,598	2,202	2,675	2,714	2,892	2,613	2,958	2,883
Groveland,	1789					1,137	1,273	1,551	1,703	1,715	2,000	1,759	1,724	1,610
Leicester,	1802				917	1,142	1,331	1,772	2,042	2,135	2,415	2,287	2,142	2,076
Lima,	1789			1,060	1,474	1,758	1,963	1,775	1,764	2,227	2,176	2,158	2,433	1,670
Livonia,	1808	Pittstown,			1,187	1,406	2,427	2,417	2,665	2,659	2,719	2,695	2,627	2,635
Mount Morris,	1818	Leicester,					1,002	1,896	2,534	3,499	4,576	4,293	4,531	4,042
North Dansville,	1846	Sparta,											4,377	3,481
Nunda,	1808	Angelica,			499	1,090	1,188	2,871	1,291	2,031	2,637	2,528	3,128	2,887
Portage,	1827	Nunda,							1,839	2,560	4,721	2,668	2,478	1,569
Sparta,	1789			505	1,387	798	1,475	3,289	3,777	4,507	5,841	5,944	1,372	1,233
Spring Water,	1816	Sparta and Naples,					1,154	1,659	2,253	2,567	2,832	2,761	2,670	2,481
West Sparta,	1846	Sparta,											1,619	1,496
York,	1819	Caledonia and Leicester,					1,729	2,176	2,630	2,948	3,049	2,896	2,785	2,782
Total,				2,448	10,526	13,181	21,006	26,731	27,729	35,683	42,498	38,389	40,875	37,943

MADISON COUNTY.

Cities & Towns	When formed.	From what taken.	1790.	1800	1810.	1814.	1820	1825.	1830.	1835.	1840	1845.	1850.	1855
Brookfield,	1795	Paris,		1,973	4,024	3,760	4,240	4,284	4,367	3,950	3,695	3,623	3,585	3,770
Cazenovia,	1795	Whitestown and Paris,		3,080	3,151	3,341	3,909	3,860	4,344	4,647	4,153	4,675	4,812	4,495
De Ruyter,	1798	Cazenovia,		310	1,503	1,522	1,214	1,419	1,447	1,562	1,799	1,829	1,931	1,920
Eaton,	1807	Hamilton,			2,263	2,231	3,021	3,215	3,559	3,758	3,409	3,444	3,944	4,061
Fenner,	1823	Cazenovia and Smithfield,						1,933	2,017	1,972	1,997	1,833	1,690	1,622
Georgetown,	1815	De Ruyter,					824	1,044	1,094	1,177	1,130	1,386	1,411	1,442
Hamilton,	1795	Paris,		2,673	2,220	2,428	2,681	2,931	3,220	4,022	3,738	3,878	3,599	3,737
Lebanon,	1807	Hamilton,			1,634	1,694	1,940	2,059	2,249	2,337	1,794	1,867	1,709	1,661
Lenox,	1809	Sullivan,			1,734	2,349	3,360	4,326	5,039	5,314	5,440	5,931	7,507	7,800
Madison,	1807	Hamilton,			2,229	2,373	2,420	2,488	2,544	3,655	2,344	2,313	2,405	2,483
Nelson,	1807	Cazenovia,			1,763	2,070	2,329	2,404	2,445	2,231	2,100	1,976	1,965	1,876
Smithfield,	1807	Cazenovia,			2,651	2,611	3,338	2,553	2,636	2,750	1,699	1,629	1,669	1,514
Stockbridge,	1836	Vernon, Augusta, Smithfield & Lenox,									2,320	2,215	2,081	2,052
Sullivan,	1803	Cazenovia,			1,974	1,897	2,932	3,130	4,077	4,366	4,390	4,388	4,764	5,253
Total,				8,036	25,144	26,276	32,208	35,646	39,038	41,741	40,008	40,987	43,072	†43687

MONROE COUNTY.

Cities & Towns	When formed.	From what taken.	1790.	1800	1810.	1814.	1820	1825.	1830.	1835.	1840	1845.	1850.	1855
Brighton,	1819	Smallwood and Penfield,		‡414	‡2,860	673	1,972	4,375	3,128	2,883	2,336	2,290	3,117	3,323
Chili,	1822	Riga,						1,827	2,010	1,951	2,174	2,043	2,247	2,203
Clarkson,	1819	Murray,					1,612	2,620	3,249	3,836	3,486	4,207	4,555	2,177
Gates,	1802			778	464	638	2,643	4,191	1,631	1,447	1,728	1,822	2,005	2,347
Greece,	1822	Gates,						1,547	2,571	3,265	3,669	3,818	4,219	4,487
Henrietta,	1819	Pittsford,					2,181	2,145	2,322	2,215	2,085	2,219	2,513	2,144
Irondequoit,	1839	Brighton,									1,252	1,461	2,397	3,234
Mendon,	1812	Bloomfield,				1,353	2,012	2,777	3,029	3,404	3,435	3,243	3,353	3,015
Ogden,	1817	Parma,					1,435	1,922	2,399	2,434	2,404	2,560	2,598	3,080
Parma,	1801	Northampton (now Gates),			495	1,041	1,342	1,910	2,639	2,995	2,652	2,740	2,947	2,783
Penfield,	1810	Boyle (afterw'ds Brighton & Pittsford)				1,874	3,244	4,117	4,474	4,905	2,842	2,937	3,185	3,030
Perrinton,	1812	Boyle, " " "				821	1,664	2,190	2,183	2,203	2,513	2,636	2,891	3,175
Pittsford,	1814	Smallwood (changed to Brighton and Pittsford),				2,222	1,582	1,758	1,831	1,969	1,983	1,860	2,061	2,133
Riga,	1808	Northampton,			864	1,736	3,139	1,745	1,907	1,905	1,984	1,985	2,159	2,025
Rochester city:														
1st ward,	1834	Towns of Brighton and Gates,							1,654	2,272	2,816	3,002	3,053	2,225
2nd ward,	1834	Towns of Brighton and Gates,							2,082	3,314	4,685	2,768	3,630	3,656
3rd ward,	1834	Towns of Brighton and Gates,							2,353	2,892	4,203	3,730	4,491	4,386
4th ward,	1834	Towns of Brighton and Gates,							1,677	3,013	3,832	2,828	3,511	3,323
5th ward,	1834	Towns of Brighton and Gates,							1,441	2,913	4,655	4,121	3,705	4,376
6th ward,	1844											3,984	7,061	5,391
7th ward,	1844											1,861	3,336	4,619
8th ward,	1844											1,975	2,920	3,951
9th ward,	1844											2,696	4,696	7,218
10th ward,	1852													4,732
Total Rochester,									§9,207	14,404	20,191	26,965	36,403	43,877

* Population of towns not reported separately.
† Exclusive of Indians.
‡ Northfield, afterwards Boyle, now Brighton and Penfield.
§ Village of Rochester.

Comparative Population of Towns and Counties at different Periods.—(Continued).

MONROE COUNTY.—(CONTINUED).

CITIES & TOWNS.	When formed.	FROM WHAT TAKEN.	1790.	1800.	1810.	1814.	1820.	1825.	1830.	1835.	1840	1845.	1850.	1855.
Rush,	1818	Avon,					1,701	1,929	2,098	2,026	1,929	1,798	2,015	1,750
Sweden,	1813	Murray,				820	2,761	2,327	2,937	3,559	3,133	3,179	3,623	3,967
Union,	1852	Clarkson,												2,369
Webster,	1840	Penfield,									2,235	2,725	2,446	2,388
Wheatland,	1821	Caledonia,						1,728	2,240	2,684	2,871	2,311	2,916	2,816
Total,				1,192	4,683	11,178	27,288	39,108	49,855	58,085	64,902	70,899	87,650	96,324

MONTGOMERY COUNTY.

CITIES & TOWNS.	When formed.	FROM WHAT TAKEN.	1790.	1800.	1810.	1814.	1820.	1825.	1830.	1835.	1840	1845.	1850.	1855.
Amsterdam,	1793	Caughnawaga (see note to Broadalbin)	4,261	1 064	3,039	3,028	3,171	3,207	3,356	4,109	5,334	3,581	4,128	4,012
Canajoharie,	1788		6,156	2,266	4,010	3,907	4,677	3,664	4,347	4,671	5,146	4,988	4,097	4,022
Charleston,	1793	Mohawk (changed to Florida and Charleston,)	4,440	2,001	5,282	5,154	5,365	2,102	2,148	2,124	2,103	1,995	2,216	1,899
Florida,	1793	Mohawk (ditto),		1,238	2,777	2,297	2,743	2,689	2,851	2,896	5,214	3,172	3,571	3,154
Glen,	1823	Charleston,						1,975	2,451	2,612	3,678	2,718	3,043	2,956
Minden,	1798	Canajoharie,		2,929	4,788	4,838	1,954	2,085	2,619	2,902	3,507	3,322	4,623	4,671
Mohawk,	1837	Johnstown,									3,112	2,752	3,095	3,077
Palatine,	1788		3,404	3,517	3,111	3,481	3,936	4,072	2,742	2,876	2,823	2,695	2,856	2,525
Root,	1823	Canajoharie and Charleston,						2,806	2,750	2,918	2,979	2,804	2,736	2,748
St. Johnsville,	1838	Oppenheim,									1,923	1,616	1,627	1,744
Total,			18,261	13,015	23,007	22,705	21,846	22,600	23,264	25,108	35,818	29,643	31,992	30,808

NEW-YORK COUNTY.

CITIES & TOWNS.	When formed.	FROM WHAT TAKEN.	1790.	1800.	1810.	1814.	1820.	1825.	1830.	1835.	1840	1845.	1850.	1855.
New-York city:*														
1st ward,				4,320	7,941	7,630	12,085	9,929	11,331	10,380	10,629	12,230	19,754	13,486
2d ward,				5,167	8,493	7,439	8,214	9,315	8,203	7,549	6,394	6,962	6,665	3,249
3d ward,				6,449	7,426	7,495	9,201	10,801	9,599	10,884	11,581	11,900	10,355	7,909
4th ward,				6,935	10,226	9,856	10,736	12,240	12,705	11,439	15,770	21,000	23,250	22,895
5th ward,				9,148	14,744	14,523	12,421	15,093	17,722	18,495	19,159	20,362	22,686	21,617
6th ward,				13,076	11,286	11,821	13,309	20,061	13,570	14,827	17,198	19,343	24,698	25,562
7th ward,	1791			15,394	12,120	10,886	13,006	14,192	15,873	21,481	22,982	25,556	32,690	34,422
8th ward,	1803				9,128	10,702	13,766	24,285	20,729	28,570	29,073	30,900	34,612	34,052
9th ward,	1803				4,719	4,343	11,162	10,956	17,333	20,618	24,795	30,907	40,657	39,982
10th ward,	1808	7th ward,			10,290	10,824	17,806	23,932	16,438	20,929	29,026	20,993	23,316	26,378
11th ward,	1825							7,344	14,915	26,845	17,053	27,259	43,758	52,979
12th ward,	1825							7,938	11,808	24,437	11,652	13,378	10,451	17,656
13th ward,	1827	10th ward,							12,598	17,130	18,517	22,411	28,246	26,597
14th ward,	1827	6th and 8th wards,							14,288	17,306	20,235	21,103	25,196	24,754
15th ward,	1832	9th ward,								13,202	17,755	19,422	22,564	24,046
16th ward,	1836	12th ward,									22,723	40,350	52,882	39,823
17th ward,	1837	11th ward,									18,619	27,147	43,766	59,548
18th ward,	1846	16th ward,											31,546	39,415
19th ward,	1850	12th ward,											18,465	17,866
20th ward,	1851	16th ward,												47,055
21st ward,	1853	18th ward,												27,914
22d ward,	1853	19th ward,												22,605
Total,			33,131	60,489	96,373	95,519	123706	166086	197112	268089	312710	371223	515547	629810

NIAGARA COUNTY.

CITIES & TOWNS.	When formed.	FROM WHAT TAKEN.	1790.	1800.	1810.	1814.	1820.	1825.	1830.	1835.	1840	1845.	1850.	1855.
Cambria,	1808	Willink (now Aurora),			1,465	586	1,134	1,239	1,712	2,070	2,099	2,224	2,366	2,216
Hartland,	1812	Cambria,				350	1,448	1,415	1,584	2,195	2,350	2,674	3,028	3,033
Lewiston,	1818	Cambria,					869	1,255	1,528	2,302	2,533	2,540	2,924	3,260
Lockport,	1824	Royalton and Cambria,						3,007	3,823	6,092	9,125	9,314	12,323	13,386
Newfane,	1824	Wilson, Hartland and Somerset,						919	1,450	2,148	2,372	2,795	3,271	3,164
Niagara,	1812	Cambria,				192	484	1,807	1,401	2,013	1,277	1,468	1,951	5,457
Pendleton,	1827	Niagara,							572	1,069	1,098	1,285	2,166	1,826
Porter,	1812	Cambria,				148	850	925	1,490	1,838	2,177	2,303	2,455	2,643
Royalton,	1817	Hartland,					1,849	2,458	3,138	3,397	3,549	3,773	4,024	4,930
Somerset,	1823	Hartland,						569	871	1,730	1,742	2,037	2,154	1,923
Wheatfield,	1836	Niagara,									1,057	1,793	2,659	3,152
Wilson,	1818	Porter,					688	475	913	1,636	1,753	2,344	2,955	3,292
Total,					1,465	1,276	7,322	14,069	18,482	26,490	31,132	34,550	42,276	†48282

ONEIDA COUNTY.

CITIES & TOWNS.	When formed.	FROM WHAT TAKEN.	1790.	1800.	1810.	1814.	1820.	1825.	1830.	1835.	1840	1845.	1850.	1855.
Annsville,	1823	Lee, Florence, Camden and Vienna,						1,161	1,481	1,352	1,765	2,192	2,686	2,715
Augusta,	1798	Whitestown,		1,598	2,004	2,377	2,771	2,911	3,058	3,347	275	2,117	2,271	2,383
Ava,	1846	Boonville,											1,037	1,242
Boonville,	1805	Leyden,			393	812	1,294	2,071	2,746	3,012	5,519	3,653	3,306	4,424
Bridgewater,	1797	Sangerfield,		1,061	1,170	1,322	1,533	1,525	1,608	1,449	1,418	1,351	1,315	1,203
Camden,	1799	Mexico,		384	1,132	1,340	1,772	1,598	1,945	2,114	2,331	2,434	2,820	2,900
Deerfield,	1798	Schuyler,		1,048	1,232	1,921	2,346	3,331	4,182	2,536	3,120	2,347	2,287	2,257
Florence,	1805	Camden,			396	394	640	678	964	1,106	1,259	1,994	2,575	2,812
Floyd,	1796	Steuben,		767	970	1,324	1,498	1,557	1,699	1,795	1,742	1,592	1,495	1,443

* New-York was divided into six wards in 1683.

† Exclusive of Indians.

Comparative Population of Towns and Counties at different Periods.—(Continued.)

ONEIDA COUNTY.—(CONTINUED.)

CITIES & TOWNS.	When formed	FROM WHAT TAKEN.	1790.	1800.	1810.	1814.	1820.	1825	1830.	1835.	1840.	1845.	1850.	1855.
Kirkland,	1827	Paris,							2, 505	3, 497	2, 984	3, 014	3, 421	3, 809
Lee,	1811	Western,				1, 724	2, 186	2, 077	2, 514	2, 618	2, 936	2, 963	3, 033	3, 020
Marcy,	1832	Deerfield,								1, 730	1, 799	1, 769	1, 857	1, 767
Marshall,	1829	Kirkland,							1, 908	2, 579	2, 251	2. 148	2, 115	2, 147
New Hartford,	1827	Whitestown,							3, 599	3, 909	3, 819	4, 043	4, 847	4, 517
Paris,	1792	Whitestown,		4, 721	5, 418	6, 535	6, 707	6, 810	2, 765	2, 849	2, 844	3, 097	4, 283	3, 695
Remsen,	1798	Norway,		254	489	655	912	1, 070	1, 400	1, 498	1, 638	1, 903	2, 407	2, 684
Rome,	1796	Steuben,		1, 479	2, 003	3, 069	3, 569	3, 531	4, 360	4, 505	5, 680	5, 955	7, 918	10, 720
Sangerfield,	1795	Paris,		1, 144	1, 324	1, 917	2, 911	1, 986	2, 272	2, 242	2, 551	2, 272	2. 371	2, 424
Steuben,	1792	Whitestown,		552	1, 105	1, 082	1, 461	1, 674	2, 094	2, 159	1, 993	1, 924	1, 744	1, 592
Trenton,	1797	Schuyler,		624	1, 548	2, 128	2, 617	2, 233	3, 221	3, 220	3, 178	3, 543	3, 540	3, 987
Utica,							2, 972	5, 040	8, 323					
1st ward,										1, 633	1, 738	1, 574		1, 443
2d ward,	1832									1, 755	2, 392	1, 963		2, 799
3d ward,	1832									2, 731	3, 781	3, 490		2, 111
4th ward,	1832									4, 064	4, 871	5, 163		4, 827
5th ward,	1832													5, 380
6th ward,	1849													4, 609
Total Utica city,										10, 183	12, 782	12, 190	17, 565	22, 169
Vernon,	1802	Westmoreland and Augusta,			1, 519	2, 308	2, 707	2, 807	3, 045	2, 827	3, 043	3, 074	3, 093	3, 005
Verona,	1802	Westmoreland,			1, 014	1, 987	2, 447	2. 845	3, 739	4, 155	4, 504	4. 942	5, 570	6, 923
Vienna,	1807	Camden,			454	547	1, 307	1, 479	1, 766	2, 172	2, 530	2, 867	3, 393	3, 248
Western,	1797	Steuben,		1, 453	*2, 416	1, 557	2, 237	2, 190	2, 419	2, 502	3, 488	2, 523	2, 516	2, 546
Westmoreland,	1792	Whitestown,		1, 542	1, 135	2, 480	2, 791	3. 270	3, 303	3, 140	3, 105	3, 072	3 291	3, 279
Whitestown,	1788		1, 891	4, 212	4, 912	5, 148	5, 219	6, 003	4, 410	5, 022	5, 156	5, 797	6. 810	4. 838
Total,			1. 891	20. 839	30, 634	45, 627	50, 997	57, 847	71, 326	77, 518	85, 310	84, 776	99, 566	107749

ONONDAGA COUNTY.

CITIES & TOWNS.	When formed	FROM WHAT TAKEN.	1790.	1800.	1810.	1814.	1820.	1825	1830.	1835.	1840.	1845.	1850.	1855.
Camillus,	1799	Marcellus,		336	2, 378	3, 377	5, 791	7, 108	2, 518	3, 006	3, 957	2, 976	3, 105	2. 740
Cicero,	1807	Lysander,			252	452	1, 303	2, 462	1, 808	2, 191	2, 464	2. 651	2, 980	3, 388
Clay,	1827	Cicero,							2, 095	2, 538	2, 852	2, 789	3, 402	3. 326
De Witt,	1835	Manlius,								2, 716	2, 802	2, 876	3, 302	2, 985
Elbridge,	1829	Camillus,							3, 357	3, 599	4, 647	3, 829	3, 924	4, 561
Fabius,	1798			844	1, 865	1, 785	2, 494	2, 596	3, 070	2, 852	2, 562	2, 529	2. 410	2, 256
Geddes,	1848	Salina,											2, 011	2, 066
La Fayette,	1825	Pompey,							2, 560	2, 592	2, 600	2, 527	2. 533	2, 340
Lysander,	1794			121	624	921	1, 723	2, 279	3, 228	2, 838	4, 306	4, 506	5, 833	5, 060
Manlius,	1794			899	3, 127	4, 241	5, 372	6, 005	7, 375	5, 594	5. 509	5, 602	6, 298	6, 228
Marcellus,	1794			909	4, 725	5, 306	6, 503	7, 045	2, 625	2, 456	2, 726	2, 649	2, 759	2, 547
Onondaga,	1798	Marcellus, Pompey and Manlius,		893	3, 745	4, 179	5, 552	5. 888	5, 668	4, 789	5. 658	5, 142	5, 694	5. 400
Otisco,	1806	Pompey, Marcellus and Tully,			759	1, 325	1. 726	1, 862	1, 938	1, 863	1. 906	1, 701	1, 804	1, 725
Pompey,	1789			2, 432	5, 669	5, 770	6, 701	6, 517	4, 812	4, 521	4, 371	4, 112	4. 006	3, 770
Salina,	1809	Manlius and Onondaga,			1, 259	1, 241	1, 814	3, 833	6. 929	7, 793	11, 013	15, 804	2, 142	2, 580
Skaneateles,	1830	Marcellus,							3 812	3, 575	3, 981	3, 827	4, 081	3, 976
Spafford,	1811	Tully,				598	1, 294	1, 450	2, 647	2, 404	1, 873	1, 977	1, 903	1, 816
Syracuse city:														
1st ward,	1847	Town of Salina,											4, 514	3, 597
2d ward,	1847												7, 629	3. 437
3d ward,	1847												4, 654	2, 260
4th ward,	1847												5, 474	4, 167
5th ward,	1853													2, 063
6th ward,	1853													3, 256
7th ward,	1853													4. 165
8th ward,	1853													2, 162
Total Syracuse,													22, 271	25, 107
Tully,	1803	Fabius,			1, 092	825	1, 194	1, 390	1, 640	1, 618	1, 663	1, 621	1, 559	1, 619
Van Buren,	1829	Camillus,							2, 890	2, 963	3, 021	3, 057	3, 873	3, 085
Total,				6, 434	25, 495	30, 020	41. 467	48, 435	58, 973	60, 908	67, 911	70, 175	85, 890	†86575

ONTARIO COUNTY.

CITIES & TOWNS.	When formed	FROM WHAT TAKEN.	1790.	1800.	1810.	1814.	1820.	1825	1830.	1835.	1840.	1845.	1850.	1855.
Bristol,	1789		?	751	1, 540	1, 868	2, 429	2. 717	2. 953	3, 005	1. 953	1, 801	1, 733	1, 715
Canadice,	1829	Richmond,							1, 379	1, 515	1, 341	1, 179	1, 075	977
Canandaigua,	1789		?	1, 153	2, 387	3, 643	4, 680	4, 297	5, 162	5, 452	5, 652	5, 627	6, 143	6, 480
East Bloomfield,	1789		?	1, 940	4, 525	3, 232	3, 621	3, 702	3, 861	1, 952	1. 986	2, 015	2, 262	2. 168
Farmington,	1789		?	633	1, 908	2. 281	4, 214	1, 773	1, 773	1, 843	2, 122	2, 062	1. 876	1, 950
Gorham,	1789		?	476	2, 869	3, 516	3, 991	2, 957	2, 981	2. 684	2, 779	2, 663	2, 645	2, 380
Hopewell,	1822	Gorham,						2, 158	2, 193	2, 058	1, 976	2, 068	1, 923	1, 783
Manchester,	1821	Farmington,						2, 658	2, 811	2. 655	2. 912	2, 657	2, 940	3, 009
Naples,	1789		?	259	637	1, 128	1, 038	1, 376	1, 941	2. 156	2, 345	2, 270	2. 376	2, 118
Phelps,	1789		?	1, 097	3, 408	4. 385	5, 668	4, 740	4, 876	4, 786	5, 563	5, 375	5, 542	5, 293
Richmond,	1789		?	635	1, 382	1, 908	2. 765	3. 033	1, 876	1, 786	1, 937	1, 732	1, 852	1, 493
Seneca,	1789		?	1, 522	3, 432	3, 681	4, 802	5, 847	6, 207	6, 608	7, 073	7, 911	8, 505	8, 298
South Bristol,	1838	Bristol,									1, 375	1, 211	1, 129	1, 179
Victor,	1812	Bloomfield,				1, 170	2, 084	2, 164	2, 270	2. 265	2 393	2, 225	2, 230	2, 208
West Bloomfield,	1833	Bloomfield,								2, 075	2, 094	1, 796	1, 698	1, 621
Total,			1, 075	8. 466	22, 088	26, 812	35, 292	37, 422	40, 280	40, 870	43, 501	42, 592	43, 929	42, 672

* Lee and Western.

† Exclusive of Indians.

Comparative Population of Towns and Counties at different Periods.—(Continued).

ORANGE COUNTY.

CITIES & TOWNS.	When formed.	FROM WHAT TAKEN.	1790.	1800.	1810.	1814.	1820	1825.	1830.	1835.	1840.	1845.	1850.	1855.
Blooming Grove,	1799	Cornwall,	......	1,611	1,759	1,622	2,219	2,258	2,099	2,001	2,396	1,962	2,184	2,184
Chester,	1845	Goshen, Warwick, Blooming Grove and Monroe,	......	......	......	......	......	......	......	......	......	1,744	1,641	1,696
Cornwall,	1788	....	4,225	1,648	1,769	1,830	3,020	3,020	3,486	3,289	3,925	3,854	4,471	4,578
Crawford,	1823	Montgomery,	......	......	......	......	......	2,018	2,019	2,007	2,075	2,072	1,912	2,000
Deerpark,	1798	Mamakating,	......	955	1,230	1,189	1,340	963	1,167	1,329	1,607	2,012	4,032	5,504
Goshen,	1788	....	2,448	2,563	3,155	3,054	3,441	3,022	3,361	2,967	3,889	3,232	3,149	3,213
Greenville,	1853	Minisink,	......	......	......	......	......	......	......	......	......	......	......	1,218
Hamptonburgh,	1830	Goshen, Blooming Grove, Montgomery, New Windsor and Walkill,	......	......	......	......	......	......	1,365	1,319	1,379	1,399	1,343	1,303
Minisink,	1788	....	2,215	3,584	4,005	3,947	5,053	4,710	4,979	4,439	5,093	5,258	4,972	1,295
Monroe,	1799	Cornwall,	......	2,116	2,570	2,686	2,969	3,186	3,671	3,712	3,914	3,935	4,280	4,551
Montgomery,	1788	....	3,563	4,206	4,710	4,677	5,541	3,712	3,885	4,016	4,100	4,020	3,933	3,792
Mount Hope,	1825	Walkill, Minisink and Deerpark,	......	......	......	......	......	1,457	1,535	1,484	1,565	1,600	1 512	1,735
Newburgh,	1788	....	2,365	3,258	4,627	5,107	5,812	6,168	6,424	7,683	8,933	9,001	11,415	12,773
New Windsor,	1788	....	1,819	2,001	2,331	2,175	2,425	2,255	2,310	2,460	2,482	2,474	2,457	2,555
Walkill,	1788	....	2,571	3,592	4,213	4,290	4,887	4,328	4,056	3,714	4,268	4,968	4,942	5,415
Warwick,	1788	....	3,603	3,834	3,978	4,331	4,506	4,635	5,009	4,676	5,113	4,696	4,902	4,987
Wawayanda,	1849	Minisink,	......	......	......	......	......	......	......	......	......	......	......	2,069
Total,	.....	....	22,809	29,368	34,347	34,908	41,213	41,732	45,366	45,096	50,739	52,227	57,145	60,868

ORLEANS COUNTY.

CITIES & TOWNS.	When formed.	FROM WHAT TAKEN.	1790.	1800.	1810.	1814.	1820	1825.	1830.	1835.	1840.	1845.	1850.	1855.
Barre,	1818	Gaines,	......	......	......	......	......	3,681	4,768	5,182	5,539	5,614	6,437	6,797
Carlton,	1825	Gaines and Ridgeway,	......	......	......	......	......	709	1,222	2,080	2,275	2,471	2,809	2,329
Clarendon,	1821	Sweden,	......	......	......	......	......	1,912	1,893	1,842	2,251	1,893	1,809	1,749
Gaines,	1816	Ridgeway,	......	......	......	......	1,134	1,607	1,833	2,230	2 268	2,479	2,722	2,532
Kendall,	1837	Murray,	......	......	......	......	......	......	......	......	1,692	1,914	2,289	1,884
Murray,	1808	Northampton,	......	......	1,164	843	1,561	2,202	2,790	3,592	2,675	2,496	2,520	2,876
Ridgeway,	1812	Batavia,	......	......	......	681	1,496	1,310	1,972	3,349	3,554	3,943	4,591	5,226
Shelby,	1818	Ridgeway,	......	......	......	......	1,158	1,969	1,879	2,440	2,643	2,663	3,082	3,046
Yates,	1822	Ridgeway,	......	......	......	......	......	1,070	1,375	2,178	2,230	2,372	2,242	1,996
Total,	.....	....	......	......	1,164	1,524	5,349	14,460	17,732	22,893	25,127	25,845	28,501	28,435

OSWEGO COUNTY.

CITIES & TOWNS.	When formed.	FROM WHAT TAKEN.	1790.	1800.	1810.	1814.	1820	1825.	1830.	1835.	1840.	1845.	1850.	1855.
Albion,	1825	Richland,	......	......	......	......	......	371	669	945	1,503	1,644	2,010	2,212
Amboy,	1830	Williamstown,	......	......	......	......	......	......	669	767	1,070	988	1,132	1,172
Boylston,	1828	Orwell,	......	......	......	......	......	......	388	368	481	538	661	815
Constantia,	1808	Mexico,	......	......	153	267	767	1,355	1,193	1,967	1,476	1,705	2,495	3,355
Granby,	1818	Hannibal,	......	......	......	......	555	932	1,423	2,049	2,385	2,741	3,368	3,747
Hannibal,	1806	Lysander,	......	......	692	781	935	1,340	1,794	2,204	2,269	2,534	2,857	3,028
Hastings,	1825	Constantia,	......	......	......	......	......	......	1,494	1,828	1,983	2,113	2,920	3,069
Mexico,	1792	Whitestown,	......	241	845	504	1,590	2,408	2,681	3,138	3,729	3,768	4,221	4,022
New Haven,	1813	Mexico,	......	......	......	447	899	1,218	1,426	1,551	1,738	1,707	2,015	2,012
Orwell,	1817	Oswego,	......	......	......	......	488	741	501	679	808	1,016	1,106	1,258
Oswego,	1818	Hannibal,	......	......	......	......	992	1,182	2,703	4,902	4,665	6,048	2,445	2,760
Oswego city:														
1st ward,	1848	Towns of Oswego and Scriba,	......	......	......	......	......	......	......	......	......	......	......	4,143
2nd ward,	1848		......	......	......	......	......	......	......	......	......	......	......	2,839
3rd ward,	1848		......	......	......	......	......	......	......	......	......	......	......	4,254
4th ward,	1848		......	......	......	......	......	......	......	......	......	......	......	4,580
Total Oswego city	.....	....	......	......	......	......	......	......	......	......	......	......	12,205	15,816
Palermo,	1832	Volney,	......	......	......	......	......	......	......	1,655	1,928	1,906	2,053	2,023
Parish,	1828	Mexico,	......	......	......	......	......	......	968	1,295	1,543	1,456	1,799	1,675
Redfield,	1800	Mexico,	......	107	362	334	336	295	341	412	507	584	752	798
Richland,	1807	Williamstown,	......	......	947	1,460	2,728	1,989	2,733	3,461	4,050	3,758	4,079	4,012
Sandy Creek,	1825	Richland,	......	......	......	......	......	1,615	1,839	2,100	2,420	2,257	2,456	2,273
Schroeppel,	1832	Volney,	......	......	......	......	......	......	......	1,191	2,098	2,516	3,258	3,747
Scriba,	1811	Fredericksburgh (now Volney),	......	......	328	447	741	1,071	2,073	4,180	4,051	5,495	2,738	2,958
Volney,	1806	Mexico,	......	......		560	1,691	2,372	3,618	2,895	3,155	3,895	5,310	6,476
West Monroe,	1839	Constantia,	......	......	......	......	......	......	......	......	918	990	1,197	1,217
Williamstown,	1804	Mexico,	......	......	562	582	652	986	606	658	842	782	1,121	953
Total,	.....	....	......	348	3,889	5,382	12,374	17,875	27,119	38,245	43,619	48,441	62,198	69,398

OTSEGO COUNTY.

CITIES & TOWNS.	When formed.	FROM WHAT TAKEN.	1790.	1800.	1810.	1814.	1820	1825.	1830.	1835.	1840.	1845.	1850.	1855.
Burlington,	1792	Otsego,	......	2,380	3,196	2,374	2,457	2,281	2,459	2,227	2,154	1,998	1,835	1,808
Butternuts,	1796	Unadilla,	......	1,388	3,181	3,277	3,601	3,766	3,991	4,323	4,057	4,179	1,928	2,029
Cherry Valley,	1791	Canajoharie,	......	1,550	2,775	3,053	3,684	3,874	4,098	3,876	3,923	4,125	4,186	2,540
Decatur,	1808	Worcester,	......	......	902	819	908	1,061	1,110	975	1,071	975	927	913
Edmeston,	1808	Burlington,	......	......	1,317	1,355	1,841	1,960	2,087	2,044	1,907	1,820	1,885	1,783
Exeter,	1799	Richfield,	......	712	1,418	1,421	1,430	1,588	1,690	1,462	1,423	1,487	1,526	1,540
Hartwick,	1802	Otsego,	......	......	2,002	2,107	2,579	2,625	2,772	2,586	2,490	2,482	2,352	2,220
Laurens,	1810	Otego,	......	......	......	1,873	2,074	2,148	2,231	2,235	2,173	2,208	2,168	2,106
Maryland,	1808	Worcester,	......	......	1,106	1,314	1,439	1,749	1,834	2,015	2,085	2,128	2,152	2,177
Middlefield,	1797	Cherry Valley,	......	1,044	2,003	2,234	2,579	2,832	3,323	3,163	3,319	3,196	3,131	3,071
Milford,	1796	Unadilla,	......	711	2,025	2,239	2,505	2,842	3,025	2,112	2,095	2,385	2,227	2,329
Morris,	1849	Butternuts,	......	......	......	......	......	......	......	......	......	......	2,155	2,038
New Lisbon,	1806	Pittsfield,	......	......	1,982	2,020	2,221	2,085	2,232	2,008	1,909	1,872	1,773	1,792
Oneonta,	1796	Unadilla,	1,702	4,224	2,512	1,150	1,416	1,527	1,149	1,762	1,936	1,928	1,902	2,167
Otego,	1822	Franklin and Unadilla,	......	......	......	......	......	1,031	1,757	2,123	1,919	1,922	1,792	1,8[illegible]

Comparative Population of Towns and Counties at different Periods.—Continued.

OTSEGO COUNTY.—(Continued).

CITIES & TOWNS.	When formed.	FROM WHAT TAKEN.	1790.	1800.	1810	1814.	1820	1825.	1830.	1835.	1840	1845.	1850.	1855.
Otsego,	1788		......	1,362	3,810	3,871	4,186	3,917	4,363	4,276	4,120	4.320	3,901	4,334
Pittsfield,	1797	Burlington,	......	1,206	745	749	830	908	1,006	1.318	1,395	1,730	1,591	1,656
Plainfield,	1799	Richfield,	......	1,005	2,122	1,940	1,611	1,636	1,626	1,530	1,450	1,458	1,450	1,281
Richfield,	1792	Otsego,	......	1,405	2,079	2,365	1,772	1,893	1,752	1,673	1,680	1,641	1,502	1,543
Roseboom,	1854	Cherry Valley,	......	......	......	......	......	......	......	......	......	......	......	1,887
Springfield,	1797	Cherry Valley,	......	1,586	1,846	1,961	2,065	2,572	2,816	2,548	2,382	2,356	2,322	2,463
Unadilla,	1792	Otsego,	......	828	1,426	1,829	2.194	1,905	2,313	2,415	2,272	2,505	2,463	2,722
Westford,	1808	Worcester,	......	......	1,215	1,336	1,526	1,488	1,645	1,547	1,478	1,500	1,423	1,371
Worcester,	1797	Cherry Valley,	......	2,235	1,140	1,300	1,938	2,210	2,093	2,210	2,390	2,294	2,047	2,115
Total,			1,702	21,636	38,802	40,587	44,856	47,898	51,372	50,428	49,628	50,509	48,638	49,735

PUTNAM COUNTY.

CITIES & TOWNS.	When formed.	FROM WHAT TAKEN.	1790.	1800.	1810	1814.	1820	1825.	1830.	1835.	1840	1845.	1850.	1855.
Carmel,	1795	Frederickstown (now Kent,)	......	1,979	2,020	1,763	2,247	2,192	2,371	2,163	2,263	2.389	2,442	2,406
Kent,	1788		5.932	1,661	1,811	1,119	1,801	1,794	1,931	1,661	1,830	1.729	1,557	1,539
Patterson,	1795	Frederickstown (Kent) and South East Town (South East),	......	1,546	1,446	1,557	1,578	1,572	1,539	1,347	1,349	1,289	1,371	1,422
Phillipstown,	1788		2,079	2,754	3,129	3.144	3,733	4,418	4,761	4,562	3,814	4,209	5,063	4,809
Putnam Valley,	1839	Phillipstown,	......	......	......	......	......	......	......	......	1,659	1,598	1,629	1,573
South East,	1795	Frede ickstown (Kent), and South East Town (South East),	921	1,956	1,887	1,770	1,909	1,890	2,036	1,818	1,910	2,044	2,079	2,185
Total,			8,932	9,896	10,293	9,353	11,268	11,866	12,628	11,551	12.825	13,258	14.138	13,934

QUEENS COUNTY.

CITIES & TOWNS.	When formed.	FROM WHAT TAKEN.	1790.	1800.	1810	1814.	1820	1825.	1830.	1835.	1840	1845.	1850.	1855.
Flushing,	1788		1,607	1,818	2,230	2,271	......	2,325	2,820	3,643	4,124	3,918	5,376	7,970
Hempstead,	1788		3,828	4,141	5,084	5,223	......	5,295	6,215	6,654	7,609	8.269	8,811	10,477
Jamaica,	1788		1,675	1,661	2,110	1,880	......	2,401	2,376	2.885	3,781	3,883	4,247	5,632
Newtown,	1788		2,111	2,312	2.437	2,472	......	2,478	2,610	3,505	5,054	5,521	7,208	4,694
North Hempstead,	1788		2,696	2,413	2,750	2,881	......	2.827	3,091	3,360	3,891	3,897	4,291	9,446
Oyster Bay,	1788		4,097	4,548	4,725	4,542	......	5,005	5,348	5,083	5,865	6,361	6,900	8,047
Total,			16.014	16.893	19.336	19.269	*21519	20,331	22,460	25,130	30,324	31,849	36,833	46,266

RENSSEEAER COUNTY.

CITIES & TOWNS.	When formed.	FROM WHAT TAKEN.	1790.	1800.	1810	1814.	1820	1825.	1830.	1835.	1840	1845.	1850.	1855.
Berlin,	1806	Petersburgh, Schodack and Stephentown,	......	......	3,012	1,955	1,986	1,989	2,019	1,757	1,794	1,845	2,005	2,167
Brunswick,	1807	Troy,	......	......	2,302	2,233	2,318	2,478	2,575	2,679	3,051	2,855	3,146	3,101
Clinton,	1855	Greenbush,	......	......	......	......	......	......	......	......	......	......	......	1,606
Grafton,	1807	Troy and Petersburgh,	......	......	1,410	1,378	1,611	1,593	1,681	1,682	2,019	1,905	2,033	1,888
Greenbush,	1795	Rensselaerwyck (changed to Greenbush and Schodack,)	8,318	3.472	4.458	2.396	2,764	2,914	3.216	3,345	3,701	4,182	4,945	3,303
Hoosick,	1788		3,035	3,141	3,117	2,907	3.373	3,481	3,584	3,325	3,539	3,576	3,724	4,120
Lansingburgh,	1807	Troy and Petersburgh,	......	......	1,658	1,599	2,035	2,423	2,663	2,268	3,330	3,982	5.752	5,700
Nassau,	1806	Petersb'gh, Stephentown & Schodack,	......	......	2,501	2,747	2,873	2,935	3,255	3,227	3,236	3,104	3,261	3,000
North Greenbush,	1855	Greenbush,	......	......	......	......	......	......	......	......	......	......	......	1,812
Petersburgh,	1791	Stephentown,	......	4,412	2,039	1,761	2,248	2,088	2,011	1,950	1,901	1,876	1,908	1,663
Pittstown,	1788		2,447	3,483	3,692	3,108	3,772	3,746	3,702	3,919	3,784	3,628	3,732	3,602
Poestenkill,	1848	Sand Lake,	......	......	......	......	......	......	......	......	......	......	2,092	1,878
Sand Lake,	1812	Greenbush and Berlin,	......	......	......	3,293	3,302	3,426	3,650	3,840	4,303	4,291	2.559	2,588
Schaghticoke,	1788		1,833	2,355	2,492	2,847	2,522	2,924	3,002	3,243	3,389	3,091	3,290	3,303
Schodack,	1795	Rensselaerwyck (see note to Greenbush),	See Greenbush	3688	3,166	3,128	3,493	3,506	3,794	3,793	4,125	3,740	3,500	3,837
Stephentown,	1784	Eastern district of Rensselaer Manor,	6,795	4,968	2.567	2,640	2,592	2,703	2,716	2,528	2,753	2,548	2,622	2,397
Troy,			......	4,926	3,895	4,841	......	......	......	......	......	......	......	......
1st ward,	1816	Town of Troy,	......	......	......	......	......	2,036	2.593	3,837	3,234	3,405	4,032	4,232
2d ward,	1816	Town of Troy,	......	......	......	......	......	1,951	2,865	3,593	3,778	3,888	4,284	4,257
3d ward,	1816	Town of Troy,	......	......	......	......	......	1,209	1,435	2.451	2,774	2,701	2,794	2,394
4th ward,	1816	Town of Troy,	......	......	......	......	......	1,885	3,344	5,447	3,557	3,720	4.054	4,122
5th ward,	1816	Town of Troy,	......	......	......	......	......	376	739	683	800	1,067	1,818	2.375
6th ward,	1816	Town of Troy,	......	......	......	......	......	402	575	948	1,326	1,981	4,139	2,599
7th ward,	1837		......	......	......	......	......	......	......	......	3,037	3,754	4.923	3,700
8th ward,	1837		......	......	......	......	......	......	......	......	828	1,193	2,741	3,876
9th ward,	1851	6th ward,	......	......	......	......	......	......	......	......	......	......	......	3,339
10th ward,	1851	7th ward,	......	......	......	......	......	......	......	......	......	......	......	2,375
Total Troy city,			......	......	......	......	5,264	7,859	11,551	16,959	19,334	21,709	28,785	33,269
Total,			22.428	30,442	36.309	36,833	40,153	44,065	49.424	55.515	60,259	62,338	73,363	79,234

RICHMOND COUNTY.

CITIES & TOWNS.	When formed.	FROM WHAT TAKEN.	1790.	1800.	1810	1814.	1820	1825.	1830.	1835.	1840	1845.	1850.	1855.
Castleton,	1788		805	1.056	1.301	1,348	1,527	1,786	2,216	2,868	4,275	5,203	5,389	8,252
Northfield,	1788		1,024	1,377	1,595	1,710	1,980	1,984	2,162	2,297	2,745	3,343	4,020	4,187
Southfield,	1788		855	932	1,007	998	1.012	719	971	845	1,619	2,631	2,709	5,449
Westfield,	1788		1,151	1,198	1,444	1,446	1,616	1,443	1,773	1,681	2,326	2,497	2,943	3,501
Total,			3,835	4,563	5,347	5,502	6,135	5,932	7,082	7,691	10,965	13,673	15,061	21,389

* Aggregate of the county only given.

Comparative Population of Towns and Counties at different Periods.—(Continued).

ROCKLAND COUNTY.

CITIES & TOWNS.	When formed.	FROM WHAT TAKEN.	1790.	1800.	1810.	1814.	1820.	1825.	1830.	1835.	1840.	1845.	1850.	1855.
Clarkstown,	1791	Haverstraw,		1,806	1,996	1,962	1,808	2,075	2,298	2,176	2,533	2,797	3,111	3,512
Haverstraw,	1788		4,826	1,229	1,866	1,851	2,700	2,026	2,306	2,865	3,449	4,806	5,855	6,747
Orangetown,	1788		1,175	1,337	1,583	1,518	2,257	1,536	1,947	2,079	2,771	3,227	4,769	5,838
Ramapo,	1791	Haverstraw,		1,981	2,313	2,486	2,072	2,379	2,837	2,576	3,222	2,911	3,197	3,414
Total,			6,001	6,353	7,758	7,817	8,837	8,016	9,388	9,696	11,975	13,741	16,962	19,511

ST. LAWRENCE COUNTY.

CITIES & TOWNS.	When formed.	FROM WHAT TAKEN.	1790.	1800.	1810.	1814.	1820.	1825.	1830.	1835.	1840.	1845.	1850.	1855.
Brasher,	1825	Massena,						401	826	929	2,118	2,218	2,582	2,968
Canton,	1805	Lisbon,		*24	699	815	1,337	1,898	2,439	2,412	3,465	4,035	4,683	4,995
Colton,	1843	Parishville,										466	506	1,040
De Kalb,	1806	Oswegatchie,			541	487	709	766	1,268	1,200	1,531	1,723	2,389	2,676
De Peyster,	1825	Oswegatchie and De Kalb,						787	813	788	1,074	1,138	906	1,663
Edwards,	1827	Fowler,							633	739	956	1,064	1,023	1,180
Fine,	1844	Russell and Pierrepont,										243	293	316
Fowler,	1816	Rossie and Russell,					605	1,671	1,447	1,571	1,752	1,840	1,813	1,620
Gouverneur,	1810	Oswegatchie,			224	862	765	1,267	1,430	1,796	2,538	2,600	2,783	2,856
Hammond,	1827	Rossie and Morristown,							767	1,327	1,845	1,911	1,819	1,875
Hermon,	1830	De Kalb and Edwards,							668	870	1,271	1,580	1,690	1,648
Hopkinton,	1805	Massena,			372	453	581	884	827	910	1,147	1,435	1,476	1,554
Lawrence,	1828	Hopkinton and Brasher,							1,097	1,241	1,845	1,970	2,214	2,365
Lisbon,	1801			*135	820	626	930	1,474	1,891	2,411	3,508	4,376	5,295	5,109
Louisville,	1810	Massena,		13		235	831	864	1,076	1,315	1,693	1,970	2,054	2,120
Macomb,	1841	Gouverneur and Morristown,										1 113	1,197	1,466
Madrid,	1802	Lisbon,		*13	1,420	1,184	1,930	2,639	3,459	4,069	4,511	4,376	4,856	4,862
Massena,	1802			*102	955	384	944	1,701	2,068	2,288	2,726	2,798	2,870	2,701
Morristown,	1821	Oswegatchie,					†827	1,723	1,600	2,339	2,809	2,328	2,274	2,111
Norfolk,	1823	Louisville and Stockholm,						755	1,039	1,373	1,728	1,544	1,753	1,804
Oswegatchie,	1802	Lisbon,		*159	1,245	789	1,661	3,133	3,993	4,656	5,719	6,414	7,756	10,060
Parishville,	1818	Hopkinton,				273	594	959	1,477	1,657	2,250	2,090	2,132	2,114
Pierrepont,	1818	Russell,					235	558	749	922	1,430	1,450	1,459	1,834
Pitcairn,	1836	Fowler,									396	553	503	531
Potsdam,	1806	Madrid,			928	1,317	1,911	3,112	3,661	3,810	4,473	4,856	5,349	6,631
Rossie,	1813	Russell,				368	869	1,074	641	722	1,553	1,386	1,471	1,480
Russell,	1807	Hopkinton,			394		486	480	541	655	1,373	1,499	1,808	2,108
Stockholm,	1806	Massena,		*8	307	459	822	1,449	1,944	2,047	2,995	3,293	3,661	3,790
Total,				454	7.885	8,252	16,037	27,595	36,354	42,047	56,706	62,354	68,617	74,977

SARATOGA COUNTY.

CITIES & TOWNS.	When formed.	FROM WHAT TAKEN.	1790.	1800.	1810.	1814.	1820.	1825.	1830.	1835.	1840.	1845.	1850.	1855.
Ballston,	1788		7,333	2,099	1,155	2,106	2,407	1,852	2,113	2,001	2,044	2,072	2,269	2,20[illegible]
Charlton,	1792	Balston,		1,746	1,946	1,907	1,953	1,912	2,023	1,981	1,933	1,787	1,902	1,701
Clifton Park,	1828	Half Moon,							2,494	2,282	2,719	2,421	2,868	2,917
Corinth,	1818	Hadley,					1,490	1,341	1,412	1,261	1,365	1,363	1,501	1,534
Day,	1819	Edinburgh and Hadley,					571	790	758	829	942	992	1,045	1,079
Edinburgh,	1801	Providence,			1,319	1,324	1,469	1,590	1,571	1,447	1,458	1,413	1,336	1,318
Galway,	1792	Ballston,		2,310	2,705	2,521	2,579	2,505	2,710	2,638	2,412	2.385	2,158	2,441
Greenfield,	1793	Saratoga and Wilton,		3,073	3,087	3,054	3,024	3,298	3,144	2,927	2,803	2,744	2,890	2,842
Hadley,	1801	Greenfield and Northumberland,			1,725	1,005	798	943	829	862	865	842	1,003	1,172
Halfmoon,	1788		3,602	3,851	5,292	5,123	4,024	4,232	2,042	2,146	2,631	2,331	2,788	3,315
Malta,	1802	Stillwater,			1,438	1,410	1,518	1,518	1,517	1,386	1,457	1,324	1,349	1.236
Milton,	1792	Ballston,		2,146	2,763	2,899	2,796	2,746	2,079	3,020	3,166	3,607	4,220	4,669
Moreau,	1805	Northumberland,			1,347	1,378	1,549	1,613	1,690	1,502	1,576	1,701	1,834	2,166
Northumberland,	1798	Saratoga,		2,007	2,041	1,946	1,279	1,042	1,606	1,547	1,672	1,599	1,775	1,668
Providence,	1796	Galway,		1,888	1,694	634	1,515	1,582	1,579	1,497	1,507	1,436	1,458	1,368
Saratoga,	1788		3,071	2,491	3,183	3,254	2,233	2,010	2,461	2,435	2,624	2,755	3,492	2,832
Saratoga Springs,	1819	Saratoga,					1,909	2,054	2,204	2,438	3,384	4,276	4,650	6,307
Stillwater,	1788		3,071	2,872	2,492	2,578	2,821	2,552	2,601	2,565	2,733	2,807	2,967	2,963
Waterford,	1816	Half Moon,					1,184	1,323	1,473	1,998	1,824	2,248	2,683	3,249
Wilton,	1818	Northumberland,					1,293	1,392	1,373	1,250	1,438	1,374	1,458	1,401
Total,			17,077	24,483	33,147	31,139	36,052	36,295	38,679	38,012	40,553	41,477	45,646	49,379

SCHENECTADY COUNTY.

CITIES & TOWNS.	When formed.	FROM WHAT TAKEN.	1790.	1800.	1810.	1814.	1820.	1825.	1830.	1835.	1840.	1845.	1850.	1855.
Duanesburgh,	1788	Schenectady,	1,470	2,787	3,052	2,968	3,510	3,384	2,837	3,281	3,357	3,287	3,464	3,119
Glenville,	1820	Schenectady,					2,514	2,373	2,497	3,027	3,038	2,984	3,409	3,153
Niskayuna,	1809	Watervliet,			424	388	516	506	452	565	693	644	783	1,120
Princetown,	1798	Schenectady,		812	826	713	1,073	1,042	812	975	1,201	950	1,031	956
Rotterdam,	1820	Schenectady,					1,529	1,503	1,481	2,110	2,284	2,210	2,446	2,835
Schenectady city:	1798													
1st ward,				1,331	1,376	1,780	1,809	1,581	1,818	2,300	1,509	1,318		1,544
2d ward,				1,304	1,477	1,809	2,130	2,487	2,450	3,972	1,557	1,502		1,530
3d ward,				1,025	994	1,366					1,242	1,218		1,951
4th ward,				1,629	2,056	2,179					2,476	2,517		3,364
Total Schenectady			‡4,228	5,289	5,903	7,134	3,939	4,068	4,268	6,272	6,784	6,555	8,920	8,389
Total,			5,698	8,888	10,205	11,203	13,081	12.876	12,347	16,230	17,387	16,630	20,054	19,572

* In unorganized townships of the above names.
† Township of Hague.

‡ Of these 3,472 were south of the Mohawk.

Comparative Population of Towns and Counties at different Periods.—(Continued.)

SCHOHARIE COUNTY.

ITIES & TOWNS.	When formed	FROM WHAT TAKEN.	1790.	1800.	1810.	1814.	1820.	1825	1830.	1835.	1840	1845.	1850.	1855.
lenheim, ...	1797	....	......	783	1, 319	1, 379	1, 826	1, 879	2, 271	2, 366	2, 725	2, 685	1, 314	1, 351
roome.	1797	Lisle, ...	......	1, 078	1, 942	2, 130	2, 680	3, 111	3, 133	3, 342	2, 404	2, 572	2, 268	2, 138
arlisle, ...	1807	Cobleskill and Sharon, ...	......	......	1, 231	1, 300	1, 583	1, 638	1, 748	1, 743	1, 850	1, 819	1, 817	1, 723
obleskill, ...	1797	Schoharie, ...	......	1, 765	2, 494	2, 768	2, 440	2, 765	2, 988	3, 261	3, 583	3, 618	2, 229	2, 208
onesville, ...	1836	Broome and Durham, ...	......	......	......	......	......	......	......	......	1, 621	1, 637	1, 582	1, 407
sperance, ...	1846	Schoharie, ...	......	......	......	......	......	......	......	......	......	......	1, 428	1, 370
ulton, ...	1828	Middleburgh, ...	......	......	......	......	......	......	1, 604	1, 758	2, 147	2, 319	2, 566	2, 817
ilboa, ...	1848	Broome and Blenheim, ...	......	......	......	......	......	......	......	......	......	......	3, 024	2, 657
efferson, ...	1803	Blenheim, ...	......	......	1, 740	1, 813	1, 573	1, 669	1, 743	1, 851	2, 033	1, 870	1, 748	1, 688
liddleburgh, ...	1797	Schoharie, ...	......	1, 831	3, 236	3, 188	3, 782	4, 551	3, 278	3, 139	3, 843	3, 922	2, 967	3, 075
ichmondville, ..	1845	Cobleskill, ...	......	......	......	......	......	......	......	......	......	......	1, 666	2, 027
choharie, ...	1788	....	2, 073	1, 696	3, 232	3, 419	3, 820	4, 499	5, 157	5, 066	5, 534	5, 477	2, 588	2, 869
eward, ...	1840	Sharon, ...	......	......	......	......	......	......	......	......	2, 088	2, 214	2, 203	1, 925
haron, ...	1797	Schoharie, ...	......	2, 655	3, 751	3, 326	3, 982	4, 214	4, 247	4, 363	2 520	2, 387	2, 632	2, 716
ummit, ...	1819	Cobleskill and Jefferson, ...	......	......	......	......	1, 468	1, 600	1, 733	1, 619	2, 010	1, 968	1, 800	1, 890
right, ...	1846	Schoharie, ...	......	......	......	......	......	......	......	......	......	......	1, 716	1, 658
Total, ...	......	....	2, 073	9, 808	18, 945	19, 323	23, 154	25, 926	27, 902	28, 508	32, 358	32, 488	33, 548	33, 519

SCHUYLER COUNTY.

			1790.	1800.	1810.	1814.	1820.	1825	1830.	1835.	1840	1845.	1850.	1855.
atharines, ...	1798	Newtown (now Elmira), ...	......	266	836	1, 206	2, 478	1. 424	2, 062	2, 261	2, 424	2, 611	3, 096	3, 517
ayuta, ...	1811	Spencer, ...	......	......	......	......	......	528	641	765	835	1, 001	1, 035	618
ix, ...	1835	Catlin, ...	......	......	......	......	......	......	......	......	1, 990	2, 335	2, 953	2, 884
lector, ...	1802	Ovid, ...	......	......	1, 563	2, 208	4, 012	4, 957	5, 212	5, 663	5, 652	5, 904	6, 052	5, 629
range, ...	1813	Wayne, ...	......	......	......	384	912	1, 780	2, 391	2, 724	1, 824	1, 756	2, 055	2, 483
eading, ...	1806	Frederickstown, (now Wayne), ...	......	......	1, 210	1, 754	3, 009	3, 431	1, 568	1, 644	1, 541	1, 555	1, 434	1, 453
yrone, ...	1822	Wayne, ...	......	......	......	......	......	1, 653	1, 880	2, 106	2, 122	2, 165	1, 894	2, 194
Total, ...	......	....	......	266	3, 609	5, 552	10, 411	13, 773	13, 754	15, 163	16, 388	17, 327	18, 519	18, 777

SENECA COUNTY.

			1790.	1800.	1810.	1814.	1820.	1825	1830.	1835.	1840	1845.	1850.	1855.
overt, ...	1817	Ovid, ...	......	......	......	......	3, 439	3, 833	1, 791	1, 615	1, 563	2, 398	2, 253	2, 230
ayette, ...	1800	Romulus, ...	......	863	1. 754	2, 210	2, 869	3, 140	3, 216	3, 461	3, 731	3, 781	3, 786	3, 370
unius, ...	1803	Washington (now Fayette), ...	......	......	2, 251	3, 189	5, 113	6, 213	1, 581	1, 517	1, 594	1, 606	1, 516	1, 415
odi, ...	1826	Covert, ...	......	......	......	......	......	......	1, 786	1, 772	2, 236	2, 246	2, 269	2, 018
vid, ...	1794	....	......	2, 169	4, 535	5, 407	2, 654	2, 856	2, 756	2, 997	2, 721	2, 129	2, 248	2, 274
omulus, ...	1794	....	......	1, 025	2, 766	3, 129	3, 698	4, 127	2, 089	1, 793	2, 235	1, 894	2, 050	1, 879
eneca Falls, ...	1829	Junius, ...	......	......	......	......	......	......	2, 603	3, 786	4, 281	3, 997	4, 296	4, 984
yre, ...	1826	Junius, ...	......	......	......	......	......	......	1, 482	1, 527	1, 506	1, 304	1, 356	1, 419
arick, ...	1830	Romulus, ...	......	......	......	......	......	......	1, 890	1, 950	1, 971	1, 983	1, 852	1, 723
Waterloo, ...	1829	Junius, ...	......	......	......	......	......	......	1, 847	2, 209	3, 036	3, 634	3, 795	4, 046
Total, ...	......	....	......	4, 057	11, 306	13, 935	17, 773	20, 169	21, 041	22, 627	24, 874	24, 972	25, 441	25, 358

STEUBEN COUNTY.

			1790.	1800.	1810.	1814.	1820.	1825	1830.	1835.	1840	1845.	1850.	1855.
Addison, ...	1796	....	......	174	369	466	652	544	944	1, 388	1, 920	2, 432	3, 721	3, 156
Avoca, ...	1843	Bath, Cohocton and Wheeler, ...	......	......	......	......	......	......	......	......	......	1, 668	1, 574	1, 786
Bath, ...	1796	....	......	452	1, 036	1, 625	2, 578	2, 422	3, 387	4, 100	4, 915	4, 976	6, 185	6, 031
Bradford, ...	1836	Jersey (now Orange), ...	......	......	......	......	......	......	......	......	1, 547	1, 715	2, 010	1, 285
Cameron, ...	1822	Addison, ...	......	......	......	......	......	553	924	1, 224	1, 359	1, 189	1, 701	1, 835
Campbell, ...	1831	Hornby, ...	......	......	......	......	......	......	......	842	852	957	1, 175	1, 542
Canisteo, ...	1796	....	......	510	656	430	891	604	619	780	941	1, 170	2, 030	1, 985
Caton, ...	1839	Painted Post,.	......	......	......	......	......	......	......	......	797	1, 051	1, 214	1, 585
Cohocton, ...	1812	Bath and Dansville, ...	......	......	......	746	1, 560	2, 143	2, 544	2, 855	2, 965	2, 656	1, 993	2, 242
Corning, ...	1796	(Formerly Painted Post), ...	......	262	954	1, 097	2, 088	2, 646	974	1, 619	1, 674	2, 521	4, 372	6, 334
Dansville, ...	1796	....	......	......	666	526	1, 565	1, 489	1, 726	2, 558	2, 725	2, 910	2, 545	2, 160
Erwin, ...	1826	Painted Post (now Corning,).	......	......	......	......	......	......	795	1, 089	785	1, 033	1, 435	1, 819
Fremont, ...	1854	Hornellsville, Dansville, Wayland and Howard, ...	......	......	......	......	......	......	......	......	......	......	......	1, 119
Greenwood, ...	1827	Troupsburgh and Canisteo, ...	......	......	......	......	......	......	899	1, 140	1, 138	903	1, 185	1, 224
Hartsville, ...	1844	Hornellsville, ...	......	......	......	......	......	......	......	......	......	759	854	1, 110
Hornby, ...	1826	Painted Post (now Corning), ...	......	......	......	......	......	......	1, 365	972	1, 048	1, 294	1, 314	1, 410
Hornellsville, ...	1820	Canisteo, ...	......	......	......	......	......	834	1, 572	1, 850	2, 121	1, 761	2, 637	3, 843
Howard, ...	1812	Bath and Dansville, ...	......	......	......	366	1, 140	1, 703	2, 464	3, 037	3, 247	2, 989	3, 244	2, 669
Jasper, ...	1827	Troupsburgh and Canisteo, ...	......	......	......	......	......	......	657	984	1, 187	1, 384	1, 749	1, 768
Lindley, ...	1837	Erwin, ...	......	......	......	......	......	......	......	......	638	639	686	704
Prattsburgh, ...	1813	Pultney, ...	......	132	......	615	1, 377	1, 865	2, 402	2, 557	2, 455	2, 503	2, 786	2, 582
Pultney, ...	1808	Bath, ...	......	......	1, 038	799	1. 162	1, 501	1, 724	1, 822	1, 784	1, 800	1, 815	1, 560
Thurston, ...	1844	Cameron, ...	......	......	......	......	......	......	......	......	......	576	726	925
Troupsburgh, ...	1808	Middletown and Canisteo, ...	......	......	292	421	650	1, 265	666	876	1, 171	1, 498	1, 754	1, 979
Urbana, ...	1822	Bath, ...	......	......	......	......	......	966	1, 288	1, 642	1, 884	2, 046	2, 079	1, 938
Wayland, ...	1848	Cohocton and Dansville, ...	......	......	......	......	......	......	......	......	......	......	2, 067	2, 651
Wayne, ...	1796	....	......	258	1, 025	1, 892	3, 607	865	1, 172	1, 350	1, 377	908	1, 347	928
West Union, ...	1845	Greenwood, ...	......	......	......	......	......	......	......	......	......	539	,950	1, 211
Wheeler, ...	1820	Bath and Prattsburgh, ...	......	......	......	......	798	882	1, 389	1, 604	1, 294	1, 204	1, 471	1, 376
Woodhull, ...	1828	Troupsburgh and Addison, ...	......	......	......	......	......	......	501	672	827	1, 122	1, 769	2, 205
Total, ...	......	....	.....	1, 788	6, 036	8, 983	18, 068	20, 282	28, 012	34, 961	40, 651	46, 203	58, 388	62, 965

Comparative Population of Towns and Counties at different Periods.—(Continued.)

SUFFOLK COUNTY.

CITIES & TOWNS	When formed.	FROM WHAT TAKEN.	1790.	1800	1810.	1814.	1820	1825.	1830.	1835.	1840.	1845.	1850.	1855.
Brookhaven,	1788		3, 224	4, 022	4, 176	4, 790	5, 218	5, 393	6, 095	6, 866	7, 050	7, 461	8, 595	9, 696
Easthampton,	1788		1, 497	1, 549	1, 484	1, 449	1, 646	1, 556	1, 668	1, 819	2, 076	2, 155	2, 122	2, 145
Huntington,	1788		3, 260	3, 894	4, 424	3, 946	4, 935	4, 540	5, 582	5, 498	6, 562	6, 746	7, 481	8, 142
Islip,	1788		609	958	885	1, 074	1, 156	1, 344	1, 653	1, 528	1, 909	2, 098	2, 602	3, 282
River Head,	1792	Southold,		1, 498	1, 711	1, 753	1, 857	1, 816	2, 016	2, 138	2, 449	2, 373	2, 540	2, 734
Shelter Island,	1788		201	260	329	379	389	349	330	334	379	446	386	483
Smithtown,	1788		1, 022	1, 413	1, 592	1, 771	1, 874	1, 677	1, 686	1, 580	1, 932	1, 897	1, 972	2, 087
Southampton,	1788		3, 408	3, 670	3, 899	3, 527	4, 229	4, 561	4, 850	5, 275	6, 205	7, 212	6, 501	6, 821
Southhold,	1788		3, 219	2, 200	2, 613	2, 679	2, 968	2, 459	2, 900	3, 236	3, 907	4, 191	4, 723	5, 676
Total,			16, 440	19, 464	21, 113	21, 368	24, 272	23, 695	26, 780	28, 274	32, 469	34, 579	36, 922	41, 066

SULLIVAN COUNTY.

CITIES & TOWNS	When formed.	FROM WHAT TAKEN.	1790.	1800	1810.	1814.	1820	1825.	1830.	1835.	1840.	1845.	1850.	1855.
Bethel,	1809	Lumberland,			737	795	1, 096	1, 337	1, 192	1, 247	1, 483	1, 509	2, 087	2, 611
Cochecton,	1828	Bethel,							438	528	622	896	1, 981	3, 071
Collicoon,	1842	Liberty,										605	1, 671	2, 092
Fallsburgh,	1826	Thompson and Neversink,							1, 173	1, 533	1, 782	2, 370	2, 626	3, 029
Forrestburgh,	1837	Thompson,									433	477	715	839
Fremont,	1851	Collikoon,												1, 301
Highland,	1853	Lumberland,												865
Liberty,	1807	Lumberland,			419	422	851	970	1, 277	1, 331	1, 569	1, 889	2, 612	2, 866
Lumberland,	1798	Mamakating,		733	525	596	569	610	953	1, 179	1, 205	1, 607	2, 635	902
Mamakating,	1788		1, 763	1, 631	1, 865	1, 585	2, 702	2, 704	3, 070	3, 115	3, 418	3, 514	4, 107	4, 084
Neversink,	1798	Rochester,		858	953	1, 056	1, 380	1, 679	1, 257	1, 380	1, 681	1, 965	2, 281	2, 180
Rockland,	1809	Neversink,			309	290	405	554	547	744	826	1, 070	1, 175	1, 272
Thompson,	1803	Mamakating,			1, 300	1, 489	1, 897	2, 519	2, 457	2, 698	2, 610	2, 825	3, 198	3, 550
Tusten,	1853	Lumberland,												825
Total,			1, 763	3, 222	6, 108	6, 233	8, 900	10, 373	12, 364	13, 755	15, 629	18, 727	25, 088	29, 487

TIOGA COUNTY.

CITIES & TOWNS	When formed.	FROM WHAT TAKEN.	1790.	1800	1810.	1814.	1820	1825.	1830.	1835.	1840.	1845.	1850.	1855.
Barton,	1824	Tioga,						585	982	1, 469	2, 324	2, 847	3, 522	3, 842
Berkshire,	1808	Tioga,			792	1, 059	1, 502	1, 404	1, 711	964	956	878	1, 049	1, 068
Candor,	1811	Spencer,				1, 098	1, 655	2, 021	2, 656	2, 710	3, 370	3, 422	3, 433	3, 894
Newark,	1823	Berkshire,						801	1, 027	1, 385	1, 616	1, 728	1, 983	1, 945
Nichols,	1824	Tioga,						951	1, 284	1, 641	1, 986	1, 924	1, 905	1, 871
Owego,	1791			1, 284	1, 083	1, 099	1, 741	2, 260	3, 076	4, 089	5, 340	6, 104	7, 159	8, 328
Rich ord,	1831	Berkshire,								882	939	1, 093	1, 208	1, 182
Spencer,	1806	Owego,			3, 128	670	1, 252	975	1, 278	1, 407	1, 532	1, 682	1, 782	1, 805
Tioga,	1800	Union,		750	857	1, 262	1, 816	991	1, 411	1, 987	2, 464	2, 778	2, 839	3, 027
Total,				2, 034	5, 860	5, 188	7, 966	9, 988	13, 425	16, 534	20, 527	22, 456	24, 880	26, 962

TOMPKINS COUNTY.

CITIES & TOWNS	When formed.	FROM WHAT TAKEN.	1790.	1800	1810.	1814.	1820	1825.	1830.	1835.	1840.	1845.	1850.	1855.
Caroline,	1811	Spencer,				905	1, 608	2, 128	2, 633	2, 581	2, 457	2, 534	2, 537	2. 466
Danby,	1811	Spencer,				1, 200	2, 001	2, 372	2, 481	2, 473	2. 570	2, 494	2, 411	2, 331
Dryden,	1803	Ulysses,			1, 893	2, 545	3, 951	4, 822	5, 206	5, 851	5, 446	5, 230	5, 122	5, 003
Enfield,	1821	Ulysses,						2, 000	2, 332	2, 240	2, 340	2, 283	2, 117	1, 912
Groton,	1817	Locke,					2, 742	3, 458	3, 597	3, 512	3, 618	3, 353	3, 342	3, 404
Ithaca,	1821	Ulysses,						3, 621	5, 270	5, 556	5, 650	6, 055	6, 909	7, 153
Lansing,	1817	Genoa,					3, 631	4, 158	4. 020	3, 592	3, 672	3, 463	3, 318	3, 256
Newfield,	1811	Spencer,				982	1, 889	2, 392	2, 664	3, 296	3, 567	3. 665	3, 816	2, 800
Ulysses,	1799			927	3, 260	4, 184	6, 345	3, 000	3, 130	3, 244	2, 976	3, 187	3, 122	3, 191
Total,				927	5, 153	9, 816	22, 167	27, 951	31, 333	32, 345	32, 296	32, 264	32, 694	31, 516

ULSTER COUNTY.

CITIES & TOWNS	When formed.	FROM WHAT TAKEN.	1790.	1800	1810.	1814.	1820	1825.	1830.	1835.	1840.	1845.	1850.	1855.
Denning,	1849	Shandaken,											447	692
Esopus,	1811	Kingston,				1, 163	2, 063	1, 520	1, 770	1, 626	1, 939	2, 655	2, 900	4, 287
Gardiner,	1853	Shawangunk, New Paltz & Rochester,												1, 923
Hurley,	1788		847	1, 159	1, 333	1, 246	1, 352	1, 283	1, 408	1, 519	2, 201	1, 487	2, 003	2, 115
Kingston,	1788		3, 929	4, 615	5, 760	2, 898	2, 956	3, 010	4, 170	4, 057	5, 824	6, 508	10, 232	13, 974
Lloyd,	1845	New Paltz,										2, 035	2. 035	2, 192
Marbletown,	1788		2. 190	2, 847	3, 363	3, 392	3, 809	2, 879	3, 223	3, 269	3, 813	3, 143	3, 839	3, 727
Marlborough,	1788		2, 241	1. 656	1, 964	2, 148	2, 248	2, 364	2, 273	2, 434	2, 523	2, 429	2, 406	2. 668
New Paltz,	1788		2, 309	3, 255	3, 999	4, 027	4, 612	4, 704	5, 098	5, 480	5, 408	2, 818	2, 729	2, 021
Olive,	1823	Marbletown, Hurley and Shandaken,						1, 520	1, 636	1, 793	2, 023	2, 225	2, 710	2, 924
Plattekill,	1800	Marlborough,		1, 625	1, 936	1, 912	2, 139	2, 058	2, 044	2, 008	2, 125	2, 131	1, 998	1, 932
Rochester,	1788		1, 628	2, 423	1, 882	1, 717	1, 811	2, 227	2, 420	2, 665	2, 674	2, 688	3, 174	3, 475
Rosendale,	1844	Hurley, Marbletown and New Paltz,										1, 802	2, 418	2, 572
Saugerties,	1811	Kingston,				2, 206	2. 699	2, 664	3, 747	4, 942	6, 216	6, 529	8, 041	9, 318
Shandaken,	1804	Woodstock,			1. 002	842	1, 043	960	966	1, 263	1, 455	1, 981	2, 307	2, 452
Shawangunk,	1788		2, 128	2, 809	3, 062	2, 963	4, 612	3, 589	3, 681	3, 690	3, 886	4, 011	4, 036	2, 631
Wawarsing,	1806	Rochester,			1, 325	1, 198	3, 372	1, 964	2, 738	3, 735	4. 044	4, 922	6, 459	7, 227
Woodstock,	1787		1, 025	1, 244	950	716	1, 317	1, 273	1, 376	1, 479	1, 691	1, 542	1, 650	1, 806
Total,			16, 297	21, 633	26. 576	26. 428	30, 934	32, 015	36, 550	39, 960	45. 822	48, 907	59, 384	67, 936

Comparative Population of Towns and Counties at different Periods.—Continued

WARREN COUNTY.

CITIES & TOWNS.	When formed.	FROM WHAT TAKEN.	1790.	1800.	1810.	1814.	1820	1825.	1830.	1835.	1840.	1845.	1850.	1855.
Bolton,	1799	Thurman (afterwards Athol and Warrensburgh),	......	959	726	877	1,087	1,226	1,467	1,496	937	1,110	1,147	1,167
Caldwell,	1810	Queensbury, Bolton and Thurman,	......	......	560	672	723	885	797	640	693	725	752	880
Chester,	1799	Thurman,	......	508	937	988	1,013	1,231	1,284	1,361	1,633	1,608	1,850	1,936
Hague,	1807	Bolton,	......	......	398	440	514	618	721	769	610	617	717	615
Horicon,	1838	Bolton and Hague,	......	......	......	......	......	......	......	......	659	840	1,152	1,246
Johnsburgh,	1805	Thurman (see note to Bolton),	......	......	651	485	727	933	985	1,016	1,139	1,297	1,503	1,983
Luzerne,	1792	Queensbury,	......	591	1,015	1,284	1,430	1,315	1,362	1,387	1,284	1,380	1,300	1,286
Queensbury,	1786	......	1,080	1,435	1,948	1,731	2,433	2,759	3,080	3,088	3,789	4,442	5,314	6,438
Stony Creek,	1852	Athol,	......	......	......	......	......	} 809	909	987	1,210	1,342	1,590	{ 913
Thurman,	1852	Athol (first erected in 1792),	......	1,332	1,330	519	570	}						{ 1259
Warrensburgh,	1813	Thurman,	......	......	......	842	956	1,130	1,191	1,290	1,468	1,547	1,874	1,946
Total,	......	......	1,080	4,825	7,565	7,838	9,453	10,906	11,796	12,034	13,422	14,908	17,199	19,669

WASHINGTON COUNTY.

CITIES & TOWNS.	When formed.	FROM WHAT TAKEN.	1790.	1800.	1810.	1814.	1820	1825.	1830.	1835.	1840.	1845.	1850.	1855.
Argyle,	1786	......	2,341	4,597	3,813	3,962	2,811	3,025	3,450	3,013	3,111	3,241	3,274	3,244
Cambridge,	1788	......	4,996	6,187	6,730	6,599	2,491	2,163	2,325	2,105	2,005	2,175	2,593	2,304
Dresden,	1822	Putnam,	......	......	......	......	......	532	495	659	679	674	674	735
Easton,	1789	Stillwater and Saratoga,	2,539	3,069	3,253	3,253	3,051	3,211	3,758	2,908	2,988	2,825	3,225	3,012
Fort Ann,	1788	......	2,103	2,502	3,100	1,840	2,911	3,020	3,200	3,242	3,559	3,380	3,383	3,544
Fort Edward,	1818	Argyle,	......	......	......	......	1,631	1,642	1,816	1,784	1,726	1,711	2,328	2,964
Granville,	1786	......	2,240	3,175	3,717	3,863	3,727	3,543	3,881	3,862	3,846	3,500	3,434	3,363
Greenwich,	1803	Argyle,	......	......	2,752	3,138	3,197	3,134	3,847	3,363	3,382	3,681	3,803	3,888
Hampton,	1786	......	463	700	820	861	963	940	1,069	933	972	871	899	846
Hartford,	1793	Westfield (now Fort Ann),	......	2,108	2,389	2,466	2,493	2,537	2,420	2,223	2,164	2,094	2,051	2,196
Hebron,	1786	......	1,703	2,528	2,436	2,737	2,754	2,705	2,686	2,469	2,498	2,359	2,548	2,549
Jackson,	1815	Cambridge,	......	......	......	......	2,004	1,817	2,057	1,739	1,730	1,815	2,129	1,770
Kingsbury,	1786	......	1,120	1,651	2,272	2,216	2,203	2,359	2,606	2,426	2,773	2,796	3,032	3,364
Putnam,	1806	Westfield,	......	......	499	453	892	768	718	731	784	783	753	724
Salem,	1786	......	2,186	2,861	2,833	2.955	2,985	3,028	2,972	2,982	2,855	2,588	2,904	2,925
White Creek,	1815	Cambridge,	......	......	......	......	2,377	2,316	2,446	2,111	2,195	2,107	2,994	2,439
Whitehall,	1786	......	806	1,604	2,110	2,016	2,341	2,540	2,889	3,076	3,813	3,954	4,726	4,538
Total,	......	......	20,497	30,982	36,724	36,359	38,831	39,280	42,635	39,326	41,080	40,554	44,750	44,405

WAYNE COUNTY.

CITIES & TOWNS.	When formed.	FROM WHAT TAKEN.	1790.	1800.	1810.	1814.	1820	1825.	1830.	1835.	1840.	1845.	1850.	1855.
Arcadia,	1825	Lyons,	......	......	......	......	......	3,479	3,901	4,099	4,980	4,979	5,145	5,516
Butler,	1826	Wolcott,	......	......	......	......	......	......	1,764	2,160	2,271	2,258	2,272	2,225
Galen,	1812	Junius,	......	......	......	1,074	2,979	2,935	3,631	3,775	4 234	4,438	4,609	5.181
Huron,	1826	Wolcott,	......	......	......	......	......	......	1,082	1,831	1,943	1,909	1,966	1,881
Lyons,	1811	Sodus,	......	......	......	2,102	3,972	3,068	3,603	4,013	4,302	4,267	4,925	5,205
Macedon,	1823	Palmyra,	......	......	......	......	......	1,903	1,989	2,190	2,396	2,359	2,384	2,434
Marion,	1825	Williamson,	......	......	......	......	......	......	1,967	2,043	1,903	1,869	1,839	1,937
Ontario,	1807	Williamson,	......	......	814	1,391	2,233	2,732	1,585	1,626	1,889	1,906	2,246	2,323
Palmyra,	1789	......	......	994	2,187	2,964	3,724	2,613	3,427	3,326	3,549	3,542	3,893	4,115
Rose,	1826	Wolcott,	......	......	......	......	......	......	1,641	1,715	2,038	2,060	2,264	2,114
Savannah,	1824	Galen,	......	......	......	......	......	452	886	1,324	1,718	1,803	1,700	1,762
Sodus,	1789	......	......	416	1,957	965	2,013	2,496	3,528	4,079	4,472	4,565	4,598	4,538
Walworth,	1829	Ontario,	......	......	......	......	......	......	1,753	1,798	1,734	1,575	1,981	1,964
Williamson,	1802	Sodus,	......	......	1,137	1,560	2,521	3,190	1,801	2,017	2,147	2,139	2,381	2,552
Wolcott,	1807	Junius,	......	......	480	1,164	2 867	3,893	1,085	1,792	2,481	2,826	2,751	3,013
Total,	......	......	......	1,410	6,575	11,220	20,309	26.761	33,643	37,788	42,057	42,515	44,953	46,760

WESTCHESTER COUNTY.

CITIES & TOWNS.	When formed.	FROM WHAT TAKEN.	1790.	1800.	1810.	1814.	1820	1825.	1830.	1835.	1840.	1845.	1850.	1855.
Bedford,	1788	......	2,470	2,404	2,374	2,287	2,432	2,508	2,750	2,735	2,822	2,725	3,207	3,464
Cortlandt,	1788	......	1,932	2,752	3,054	2,477	3,421	3,385	3,840	3,994	5,592	6,738	7,758	8,468
East Chester,	1788	......	740	738	1,039	942	1,021	931	1,030	1,168	1,502	1,369	1,769	4,715
Greenburgh,	1788	......	1,400	1,581	1,862	1,792	2,064	2,001	2,195	2,606	3,361	3,205	4,291	6,435
Harrison,	1788	......	1,004	855	1,119	825	994	999	1,085	1,016	1,139	1,039	1,262	1,271
Lewisboro,	1788	......	1,453	1,696	1,566	1,458	1,429	1,504	1,537	1,470	1,619	1,541	1,608	1,775
Mamaroneck,	1788	......	452	503	496	797	878	1,032	838	882	1,416	780	928	1,068
Mount Pleasant,	1788	......	1,924	2,744	3,119	2,802	3,684	3,799	4,932	5,568	7,307	2,778	3,323	3,677
New Castle,	1791	North Castle,	......	1,468	1,291	1,243	1,368	1,367	1,336	1,406	1,529	1,495	1,800	1,762
New Rochelle,	1788	......	692	943	996	992	1,135	1,201	1,274	1,261	1,816	1,977	2,458	3,101
North Castle,	1788	......	2,478	1,168	1,366	1,220	1,480	1,543	1,653	1,789	2,058	2,010	2,189	2,415
North Salem,	1788	......	1,058	1,155	1,204	1,033	1,165	1,195	1,276	1,178	1,161	1,228	1,335	1,528
Ossining,	1845	Mount Pleasant,	......	......	......	......	......	......	......	......	......	3,312	4,939	5,758
Pelham,	1788	......	199	234	267	182	283	265	334	255	789	486	577	833
Poundridge,	1788	......	1,062	1,266	1,249	913	1,357	1,414	1,437	1,426	1,407	1,727	1,486	1,439
Rye,	1788	......	986	1,074	1,278	1,185	1,342	1,303	1,602	1,607	1,803	2,180	2,584	3,468
Scarsdale,	1788	......	281	258	259	292	329	321	317	329	255	341	342	445
Somers,	1788	......	1,297	1,578	1,782	1,783	1,841	1,896	1,997	1,900	2,082	1,761	1,722	1,744
Westchester,	1788	......	1,336	1,377	1,969	1,345	2,162	2,163	2,362	3,044	4,154	5,052	2,492	3,464
West Farms,	1846	Westchester,	......	......	......	......	......	......	......	......	......	......	4,436	12,436
White Plains,	1788	......	505	571	603	670	675	638	759	1,064	1,087	1,155	1,414	1.512
Yonkers,	1788	......	1,125	1,176	1,365	954	1,586	1,621	1,761	1,879	2,968	2,517	4,160	7,554
Yorktown,	1788	......	1,609	1,806	1,924	1,175	1,992	2,045	2,141	2,212	2,819	2,278	2,773	2,346
Total,	......	......	24,003	27,347	30,272	26.367	32,638	33,131	36.456	38,789	48.686	47,394	58,262	80,678

Comparative Population of Towns and Counties at different Periods.—(Continued).

WYOMING COUNTY.

CITIES & TOWNS.	When formed.	FROM WHAT TAKEN.	1790.	1800.	1810.	1814.	1820.	1825.	1830.	1835	1840.	1845.	1850.	1855.
Attica,	1811	Sheldon,	......	......	......	1,373	1,519	1,915	2,492	2,581	2,710	2,382	2,363	2,679
Bennington,	1818	Sheldon,	......	......	......	......	796	1,463	2,224	2,676	2,368	2,104	2,406	2,555
Castile,	1821	Perry,	......	......	......	......	......	1,592	2,269	2,536	2,833	2,526	2,446	2,343
China,	1818	Sheldon,	......	......	......	......	780	1,466	2,387	1,279	1,437	1,643	1,961	2,108
Covington,	1817	Le Roy and Perry,	......	......	......	......	2,144	2,444	2,716	2,514	2,438	1,427	1,385	1,330
Eagle,	1823	Pike,	......	......	......	......	......	577	892	1,149	1,187	1,314	1,381	1,390
Gainesville,	1814	Warsaw,	......	......	......	586	1,088	1,482	1,934	2,097	2,367	1,897	1,760	1,753
Genesee Falls,	1846	Pike and Portage,	......	......	......	......	......	......	......	......	......	......	1,222	1,098
Java,	1832	China,	......	......	......	......	......	......	......	1,972	2,331	2,331	2,245	2,295
Middlebury,	1812	Warsaw,	......	......	......	914	1,782	2,086	2,416	2,518	2,445	2,022	1,799	1,787
Orangeville,	1816	Attica,	......	......	......	......	1,556	1,202	1,525	1,791	1,949	1,410	1,438	1,441
Perry,	1814	Leicester,	......	......	......	690	2,317	2,396	2,792	2,984	3,082	2,952	2,832	2,560
Pike,	1818	Nunda,	......	......	......	......	1,622	1,532	2,016	2,179	2,176	2,172	2,003	1,887
Sheldon,	1808	Batavia,	......	......	1,419	962	887	1,248	1,731	2,186	2,353	2,435	2,527	2,666
Warsaw,	1808	Batavia,	......	......	1,317	886	1,658	2,089	2,474	2,686	2,841	2,659	2,624	2,794
Wethersfield,	1823	Orangeville,	......	......	......	......	......	815	1,179	1,623	1,728	1,417	1,489	1,462
Total,	......	......	......	......	2,736	5.411	16,149	22,307	29,047	32,771	34,245	30,691	31,981	32,148

YATES COUNTY.

CITIES & TOWNS.	When formed.	FROM WHAT TAKEN.	1790.	1800.	1810.	1814.	1820.	1825.	1830.	1835	1840.	1845.	1850.	1855.
Barrington,	1822	Wayne,	......	......	......	......	......	2,099	1,854	1,937	1,868	1,783	1,550	1,504
Benton,	1803	Jerusalem,	......	......	3,339	3,403	3,357	3,730	3,957	3,851	3,911	3,681	3,456	2,500
Italy,	1815	Naples,	......	......	......	......	728	995	1,092	1,245	1,634	1,698	1,627	1,506
Jerusalem,	1789	......	......	1,219	450	776	1,610	2,050	2,783	2,843	2,935	2,710	2,912	2,797
Middlesex,	1789	......	......	483	1,078	1,255	2,718	3,161	3,428	1,440	1,439	1,433	1,385	1,303
Milo,	1818	Benton,	......	......	......	......	2,612	3,278	3,610	3,824	3,986	4,559	4,791	4,304
Potter,	1832	Starkey,	......	......	......	......	......	......	......	2,256	2,245	2,374	2,194	2,148
Starkey,	1824	Reading,	......	......	......	......	......	......	2,285	2,400	2,426	2,539	2,675	2,428
Torrey,	1851	Benton and Milo,	......	......	......	......	......	......	......	......	......	......	......	1,320
Total,	......	......	......	1,702	4,867	5,434	18,025	15,313	19,009	19,796	20,444	20,777	20,590	19,812

Recapitulation.

COUNTIES.	When organized.	FROM WHAT TAKEN.	1790.	1800.	1810.	1814.	1820.	1825.	1830.	1835.	1840	1845.	1850.	1855.
Albany, ...	1683	An original county, ...	13, 717	25, 155	34, 661	33, 885	38, 116	42, 821	53, 520	59, 762	68, 593	77, 268	93, 279	103, 681
Allegany, ...	1806	Genesee, ...	......	......	1, 443	2, 207	6, 520	13, 184	20. 238	27, 295	30, 254	31, 402	37, 808	42, 910
Broome, ...	1806	Tioga, ...	45	2, 730	6, 481	7, 423	11, 100	13, 893	17, 579	20, 190	22, 338	25, 808	30, 660	36, 650
Cattaraugus, .	1808	Genesee, ...	......	......	458	537	4, 090	6, 643	16, 724	24, 986	28, 872	30, 169	38, 950	39, 530
Cayuga, ...	1799	Onondaga, ...	......	10, 817	29, 843	33. 609	38, 897	42, 743	47, 948	49, 202	50, 338	49, 663	55, 458	53, 571
Chautauque, ..	1808	Genesee, ...	......	......	2, 381	4, 259	12, 568	20, 639	34, 671	44, 869	47, 976	46. 548	50, 493	53, 380
Chemung, ...	1836	Tioga, ...	2, 391	1, 848	2, 852	3, 115	4, 272	8, 011	11, 562	14, 439	15, 483	17, 742	21, 737	27, 288
Chenango, ...	1798	Tioga and Herkimer, ...	......	6, 500	21, 704	24, 221	31, 215	34, 215	37, 238	40, 762	40, 785	39, 900	40, 311	39, 915
Clinton, ...	1788	Albany, ...	1, 036	3, 916	8, 802	7, 764	12, 070	14, 486	19, 344	20, 742	28, 157	31, 278	40, 047	42, 482
Columbia, ...	1786	Albany, ...	27, 732	35, 322	32, 390	33, 979	38, 330	37, 970	39, 907	40, 746	43, 252	41, 976	43, 073	44, 341
Cortland, ...	1808	Onondaga, ...	......	982	8, 879	10, 893	16, 507	20, 271	23, 791	24, 168	24, 607	25, 081	25, 140	24, 575
Delaware, ...	1797	Otsego and Ulster, ...	2, 745	10, 228	20, 303	21, 290	26, 587	29, 565	33, 024	34, 192	35, 396	36, 990	39, 834	39, 749
Dutchess, ...	1683	An original county, ...	36, 334	37, 909	41, 190	43, 707	46, 615	46, 698	50, 926	50, 704	52, 398	55, 124	58, 992	60, 635
Erie, ...	1821	Niagara, ...	......	......	4, 667	6, 201	10, 834	24, 316	35, 719	57, 594	62, 465	78, 635	100, 993	132, 331
Essex, ...	1799	Clinton, ...	578	4, 157	9. 477	9, 949	12, 811	15, 993	19, 287	20, 699	23, 634	25, 102	31, 148	28, 539
Franklin, ...	1808	Clinton, ...	......	443	2, 719	2, 568	4, 439	7, 978	11, 312	12, 501	16, 518	18, 692	25, 102	25, 897
Fulton, ...	1838	Montgomery, ...	......	6, 931	15, 048	14, 491	15, 723	17, 006	20, 451	21, 597	18, 049	18, 579	20, 171	23, 284
Genesee, ...	1802	Ontario, ...	......	......	3, 660	9, 435	18, 578	20, 708	26, 008	29, 145	28, 705	28, 845	28, 488	31, 532
Greene, ...	1800	Albany and Ulster, ...	7, 208	12, 584	19, 536	20, 210	22, 996	26, 229	29, 525	30, 173	30, 446	31, 957	33, 126	31, 137
Hamilton, ...	1816	Montgomery, ...	......	......	465	556	1, 251	1, 296	1, 325	1, 654	1, 907	1, 882	2, 188	2, 543
Herkimer, ...	1791	Montgomery, ...	2, 827	16, 332	24, 742	23, 725	31, 017	33, 040	35, 870	36, 201	37, 477	37, 424	38, 244	38, 566
Jefferson, ...	1805	Oneida, ...	......	262	15, 140	18, 564	32, 952	41, 650	48, 493	53, 088	60, 984	64. 999	68, 153	65, 420
Kings.	1683	An original county, ...	4, 495	5, 740	8. 303	7, 655	11, 187	14, 679	20, 535	32, 057	47, 613	78, 691	138, 882	216, 355
Lewis, ...	1805	Oneida, ...	......	1, 362	6, 433	6, 848	9, 227	11, 669	15, 239	16, 093	17, 830	20, 218	24, 564	25, 229
Livingston, ...	1821	Genesee and Ontario, ...	......	2, 448	10. 526	13, 181	21. 006	26, 731	27, 729	35, 683	42. 498	38, 389	40, 875	37, 943
Madison, ...	1806	Chenango, ...	......	8, 036	25, 141	26, 276	32, 208	35, 646	39, 038	41, 741	40, 008	40, 987	43, 072	43, 687
Monroe, ...	1821	Genesee and Ontario, ...	......	1, 192	4, 683	11, 178	27, 288	39, 108	49, 855	58, 085	64, 902	70, 899	87, 650	96, 324
Montgomery, ..	1772	Albany, ...	18, 261	13, 015	23, 007	22, 705	21, 846	22, 600	23, 264	25, 108	35, 818	24, 643	31, 992	30. 808
New-York, ...	1683	An original county, ...	33, 131	60, 489	96, 373	95, 519	123, 706	166, 086	197, 112	268, 089	312, 710	371, 223	515, 547	629, 810
Niagara, ...	1808	Genesee, ...	......	......	1, 465	1, 276	7, 322	14, 069	18, 482	26, 490	31, 132	34. 550	42. 276	48, 282
Oneida, ...	1798	Herkimer, ...	1, 891	20, 839	30, 634	45, 627	50, 997	57, 847	71, 326	77, 518	85, 310	84, 776	99, 566	107, 749
Onondaga, ...	1794	Herkimer, ...	......	6, 434	25, 495	30, 020	41, 467	48, 435	58, 973	60, 908	67, 911	70, 175	85, 890	86, 575
Ontario, ...	1789	Montgomery, ...	1, 075	8, 466	22, 088	22, 812	35, 292	37, 422	40, 288	40, 870	43, 501	42, 592	43, 929	42, 672
Orange, ...	1683	An original county, ...	22, 809	29, 368	34, 347	34, 908	41, 213	41, 732	45, 366	45, 096	50, 739	52, 227	57, 145	60, 868
Orleans, ...	1824	Genesee, ...	......	......	1, 164	1, 524	5, 349	14, 460	17, 732	22, 893	25. 127	25, 845	28, 501	28, 435
Oswego, ...	1816	Oneida and Onondaga, ...	......	348	3, 889	5, 382	12, 374	17, 875	27, 119	38, 245	43, 619	48, 441	62, 198	69, 398
Otsego, ...	1791	Montgomery, ...	1, 702	21, 636	38, 802	41, 587	44, 856	47, 898	51, 372	50, 428	49, 628	50, 509	48, 638	49, 735
Putnam, ...	1812	Dutchess, ...	8, 932	9, 836	10, 293	9, 353	11, 268	11, 866	12, 628	11, 550	12, 825	13, 258	14, 138	13, 934
Queens, ...	1683	An original county, ...	16, 014	16, 893	19, 336	19, 239	21, 519	20, 331	22, 460	25, 130	30, 324	31, 849	36, 833	46, 266
Rensselaer, ...	1791	Albany, ...	22, 428	30, 442	36. 309	36, 833	40, 153	44, 065	49, 424	55, 515	60, 259	62, 338	73, 363	79, 234
Richmond, ...	1683	An original county, ...	3, 835	4, 563	5, 347	5. 502	6, 135	5, 932	7, 082	7, 691	10, 965	13, 673	15, 061	21, 389
Rockland, ...	1798	Orange, ...	6, 001	6, 353	7, 758	7, 817	8, 837	8, 016	9, 388	9, 696	11, 975	13, 741	16, 962	19, 511
St. Lawrence, ..	1802	Clinton, ...	......	454	7, 885	8, 252	16, 037	27. 595	36, 354	42, 047	56, 706	62, 354	68, 617	74, 977
Saratoga, ...	1791	Albany, ...	17, 077	24, 483	33, 147	31, 139	36, 052	36, 295	38, 679	38, 012	40, 553	41, 477	45, 646	49, 379
Schenectady, .	1809	Albany, ...	5, 698	8. 888	10. 205	11, 203	13. 681	12, 876	12, 347	16, 230	17. 387	16, 630	20, 054	19, 572
Schoharie, ...	1795	Albany and Otsego, ...	2, 073	9, 808	18, 945	19, 323	23, 154	25, 926	27, 902	28, 508	32, 358	32, 488	33, 548	33, 519
Schuyler, ...	1854	Chemung, Steuben and Tompkins, ...	......	266	3 609	5, 552	10, 411	13, 773	13, 754	15, 163	16. 388	17, 327	18, 519	18, 777
Seneca, ...	1804	Cayuga, ...	......	4, 057	11, 306	13, 935	17, 773	20, 169	21, 041	22, 627	24, 874	24, 972	25, 441	25, 358
Steuben, ...	1796	Ontario, ...	......	1, 788	6, 036	8, 983	18, 068	20. 282	28, 012	34. 961	40. 651	46, 203	58, 388	59, 099
Suffolk, ...	1683	An original county, ...	16. 440	19, 464	21, 113	21, 368	24, 272	23, 695	26, 780	28, 274	32, 460	34, 579	36, 922	41, 066
Sullivan, ...	1809	Ulster, ...	1, 763	3. 222	6, 108	6, 233	8, 900	10, 373	12, 364	13, 755	15, 629	18, 727	25, 088	29, 487
Tioga, ...	1791	Montgomery, ...	......	2, 034	5, 860	5, 188	7. 966	9, 988	13, 425	16, 534	20, 527	22, 456	24, 880	26, 962
Tompkins, ...	1817	Cayuga and Seneca, ...	......	927	5, 153	9, 816	22, 167	27, 951	31, 333	32, 345	32, 296	32, 264	32, 694	31, 516
Ulster, ...	1683	An original county, ...	16, 297	21, 633	26, 576	26, 428	30, 934	32, 015	36, 550	39, 960	45, 822	48. 907	59, 384	67, 936
Warren, ...	1813	Washington, ...	1, 080	4, 825	7, 565	7, 838	9, 453	10, 906	11, 796	12, 034	13, 422	14, 908	17, 199	19, 669
Washington, ..	1772	Albany, ...	20, 497	30, 982	36, 724	36, 359	38, 831	39, 280	42, 635	39, 326	41, 080	40, 554	44, 750	44, 405
Wayne, ...	1823	Ontario and Seneca, ...	......	1, 410	6, 575	11, 220	20, 309	26, 761	33, 643	37, 788	42, 057	42, 515	44, 953	46, 760
Westchester, ..	1683	An original county, ...	24, 003	27, 347	30, 272	26, 367	32, 638	33, 131	36, 456	38, 789	48, 686	47, 394	58, 263	80, 678
Wyoming, ...	1841	Genesee, ...	......	......	2, 736	5, 411	16, 149	22, 307	29, 047	32, 771	34, 245	30, 691	31, 981	32, 148
Yates, ...	1823	Ontario, ...	......	1, 702	4, 867	5, 434	18, 025	15, 313	19, 009	19, 796	20, 444	20, 777	20, 590	19, 812
Total, ...	....	....	340120	588603	961888	1035910	1372812	1614458	1913131	2174517	2428921	2604495	3097394	3466212

Population of the several Counties at the Time of taking each Census.

COUNTIES.	1700	1800.	1810.	1814.	1820.	1825	1830.	1835.	1840.	1845.	1850.	1855.
Albany,	75, 736	34, 043	34, 661	33, 885	38, 116	42, 821	53, 520	59, 762	68, 593	77, 268	93, 279	103, 681
Allegany,			1, 942	3, 834	9, 330	18, 164	26, 276	35, 214	40, 975	40, 084	37, 808	42, 910
Broome,			8, 130	9, 581	14, 343	13, 893	17, 579	20, 190	22, 338	25, 808	30, 660	36, 650
Cattaraugus,			458		4, 090	8, 643	16, 724	24, 986	28, 872	30, 169	38, 950	39. 530
Cayuga,		15, 871	29, 843	37, 318	38, 897	42, 743	47, 948	49, 202	50, 338	49, 663	55, 458	53, 571
Chautauque,			2, 381	4, 259	12, 568	20, 640	34, 671	44, 869	47, 975	46, 548	50, 493	53, 380
Chemung,									20, 732	23, 689	28, 821	27, 288
Chenango,		15, 666	21, 704	24, 221	31, 215	34, 215	37, 238	40, 762	40, 785	39, 900	40, 311	39, 915
Clinton,	1, 614	8, 514	8, 002	7, 764	12, 070	14, 486	19, 344	20, 742	28, 157	31, 278	40, 047	42, 482
Columbia,	27, 732	35, 322	32, 390	33, 979	38, 330	37, 970	39, 907	40, 746	43, 252	41, 976	43, 073	44, 391
Cortland,			8, 869	10, 893	16, 507	20, 271	23, 791	24, 168	24, 607	25, 081	25, 140	24, 575
Delaware,		10, 228	20, 303	21, 290	26, 587	29, 565	33, 024	34, 192	35, 396	36, 990	39, 834	39, 749
Dutchess,	45, 266	49, 775	51, 363	43, 708	46, 615	46, 698	50, 926	50, 704	52, 398	55, 124	58, 992	60, 635
Erie,						24, 316	35, 719	57, 594	62, 465	78, 635	100, 993	132, 331
Essex,		*	9, 477	9, 949	12, 811	15, 993	19, 287	20, 699	23, 634	25, 102	31, 148	28, 539
Franklin,			2, 617	2, 568	4, 439	7, 978	11, 312	12, 501	16, 518	18, 692	25, 102	25, 477
Fulton,									18, 049	18, 579	20, 171	23, 284
Genesee,			12, 588	23, 975	58, 093	40, 905	52, 147	58, 588	59, 587	28, 845	28, 488	31, 034
Greene,		12, 584	19, 536	20, 211	22, 996	26, 229	29, 525	30, 173	30, 446	31, 957	33, 126	31, 137
Hamilton,					1, 251	†	1, 325	†	1, 907	1, 882	2, 188	2, 543
Herkimer,		14, 479	22, 046	20, 837	31, 017	33, 040	35, 870	36, 201	37, 477	37, 424	38, 244	38, 566
Jefferson,			15, 140	18, 564	32, 952	41, 650	48, 493	53, 088	60, 984	64, 999	68, 153	65, 420
Kings,	4, 495	5, 740	8, 303	7, 655	11, 187	14, 679	20, 535	32, 057	47, 613	78, 691	138, 882	216, 229
Lewis,			6, 433	6, 848	9, 227	11, 669	15, 239	16, 093	17, 830	20, 218	24, 564	25, 229
Livingston,						23, 860	27, 729	31, 092	35, 140	33, 193	40, 875	37, 943
Madison,			25, 144	26, 276	32, 208	35, 646	39, 038	41, 741	40, 008	40, 987	43, 072	43, 687
Monroe,						39, 108	49, 855	58, 085	64, 902	70, 899	87, 650	96, 324
Montgomery,	28, 848	21, 700	41, 214	40, 640	37, 569	40, 902	43, 715	48, 359	35, 818	29, 643	31, 992	30, 808
New-York,	33, 131	60, 489	96, 373	95, 519	123, 706	166, 086	197, 112	270, 089	312, 710	371, 223	515, 547	629, 904
Niagara,			8, 971	7, 477	22, 990	14, 069	18, 482	26, 490	31, 132	34, 550	42, 276	48, 282
Oneida,		22, 047	33, 792	45, 228	50, 997	57, 847	71, 326	77, 518	85, 310	84, 776	99, 566	107, 749
Onondaga,		7, 406	25, 987	30, 801	41, 467	48, 435	58, 973	60, 908	67, 911	70, 175	85, 890	86, 575
Ontario,	1, 075	15, 218	42, 032	56, 892	88, 267	37, 422	40, 288	40, 870	43, 501	42, 592	43, 929	42, 672
Orange,	18, 492	29, 345	34, 347	34, 908	41, 213	41, 732	45, 366	45, 096	50, 739	52, 227	57, 145	60, 868
Orleans,						14, 460	17, 732	22, 893	25, 127	25, 845	28, 501	28, 435
Oswego,					12, 374	17, 875	27, 119	38, 245	43, 619	48, 441	62, 198	69, 398
Otsego,		21. 636	38, 802	40, 587	44, 856	47, 898	51, 372	50, 428	49, 628	50, 509	48, 638	49, 735
Putnam,				9, 353	11, 268	11, 866	12, 628	11, 551	12, 825	13, 258	14, 138	13, 934
Queens,	16, 014	16, 893	19, 336	19, 269	21, 519	20, 331	22, 460	25, 130	30, 324	31, 849	36, 833	46, 266
Rensselaer,		30, 442	36, 309	36, 833	40, 153	44, 065	49, 424	55, 515	60, 259	62, 338	73, 363	79, 234
Richmond,	3, 835	4, 563	5, 347	5, 502	6, 135	5, 932	7, 082	7, 691	10, 965	13, 673	15, 061	21, 389
Rockland,		6, 353	7, 758	7, 817	8, 837	8, 016	9, 388	9, 696	11, 975	13. 741	16, 962	19, 511
St. Lawrence,			7, 885	8, 252	16, 037	27, 595	36, 354	42, 047	56, 706	62, 354	68, 617	74, 977
Saratoga,		24, 483	33, 147	31, 139	36, 052	36, 295	38, 679	38, 012	40, 553	41, 477	45, 646	49, 379
Schenectady,			10, 201	11, 203	13, 081	12, 876	12, 347	16, 230	17, 387	16, 630	20, 054	19, 572
Schoharie,		9, 808	18, 945	19, 323	23, 154	25, 926	27, 902	28, 508	32, 358	32, 488	33, 548	33, 519
Schuyler,												18, 777
Seneca,			16, 609	21, 401	23, 619	20, 169	21, 041	22, 627	24, 879	24, 972	25, 441	25, 358
Steuben,		1, 788	7, 246	11, 121	21, 989	29, 245	33, 851	41, 435	46, 138	51, 679	63, 771	62, 965
Suffolk,	16, 440	19, 464	21, 113	21, 368	24, 272	23, 695	26, 780	28, 274	32, 469	34, 579	36, 922	40, 906
Sullivan,			6, 108	6, 233	8, 900	10, 373	12, 364	13, 755	15, 629	18, 727	25, 088	29, 487
Tioga,		6, 889	7, 899	10, 438	19, 971	19, 951	27, 690	33, 999	20, 527	22, 456	24, 880	26, 962
Tompkins,					20, 681	32, 908	36, 545	38, 008	37, 948	38, 168	38, 746	31, 516
Ulster,	29, 397	24, 855	26, 576	26, 428	30, 934	32, 015	36, 550	39, 960	45, 822	49, 907	59, 384	67, 936
Warren,				7, 838	9, 453	10, 906	11, 796	12, 034	13, 422	14, 908	17, 199	19, 669
Washington,	14, 042	35, 574	44, 289	36, 359	38, 831	39, 280	42, 635	39, 326	41, 080	40, 554	44, 750	44, 405
Wayne,						26, 761	33, 643	37, 788	42, 057	42, 515	44, 953	46, 760
Westchester,	24, 003	27, 428	30, 272	26, 367	32, 638	33, 131	36, 456	38, 790	48, 686	47, 578	58, 263	80, 678
Wyoming,										27, 205	31, 981	32, 140
Yates,						13, 214	19, 009	19, 796	20, 444	20, 777	20, 590	19, 812
Total,	340, 120	588, 603	961, 888	1, 035. 910	1, 372, 812	1. 614, 456	1. 913, 131	2, 174, 517	2, 428, 921	2, 604, 495	3, 097, 394	3, 466, 212

* Reported with Clinton.

† Reported with Montgomery

Proportional Increase of Population: The following table, derived from the summary given on page xxxiii, shows the number of persons to every 1,000 now living, who were reported by the several censuses since 1790. The inequalities of growth and relative changes, which have occurred in the population of the several counties, are thus brought into one view upon a uniform scale, and the effects of causes tending to promote or retard the growth of different sections, are shown to advantage. For example: in Tompkins county, to every 1,000 persons now living, there were in 1800, 23; in 1810, 164; in 1814, 311; in 1820, 703; in 1825, 887; in 1830, 994; in 1835, 1,023; in 1840, 1,024; in 1845, 1,024; and in 1850, 1,037. The rapid increase of this county before 1825, and almost stationary condition since, presents a remarkable contrast with Kings county, which has acquired nearly two-thirds of its population within the last ten years.

As a further illustration of comparative increase between similar periods, the proportional numbers in the United States and in several foreign countries and large cities are added. In preparing these numbers, where the years for taking the enumerations or the intervals between them were different, the increase is assumed to be uniform between each, and the numbers corresponding to the years given in the table were taken.

YEARS.	COUNTIES.																	
	Albany.	Allegany	Broome.	Cat'gus.	Cayuga.	Chau'que	Chem'g.	Che'go.	Clinton.	Col'mbia	Cortland	Del'wre.	Dutch'ss	Erie.	Essex.	Fr'nklin.	Fulton.	Genesee.
1790, ...	132	......	1	......	......	......	88	......	24	603	......	68	603	......	20	......	......	......
1800, ...	242	......	74	......	202	......	68	163	92	795	98	257	626	......	146	16	298	......
1810, ...	334	33	177	11	557	44	103	543	207	729	361	511	683	35	332	105	690	116
1814, ...	327	51	203	14	627	79	114	607	182	765	443	536	721	47	348	98	623	298
1820, ...	367	152	303	103	726	234	156	789	284	863	671	668	769	82	448	171	676	588
1825, ...	413	307	379	219	798	387	293	857	341	858	824	743	770	189	560	307	730	657
1830, ...	516	472	479	423	894	649	424	934	455	876	968	831	839	288	675	436	878	825
1835, ...	576	636	551	639	918	841	502	1,021	488	917	983	860	836	435	728	483	927	924
1840, ...	661	705	609	734	939	898	567	1,022	662	974	1,003	888	864	472	824	634	774	913
1845, ...	745	731	704	763	903	872	639	1,000	736	945	1,020	936	909	594	879	722	797	915
1850, ...	890	881	837	985	1,035	946	796	1,009	943	973	1,023	1,002	973	876	1,092	977	866	903
1855, ...	1,000	1.000	1,000	1,000	1,000	1,000	1,000	1.000	1,000	1,000	1,000	1,000	1,000	1.000	1,000	1,000	1,000	1,000

YEARS.	COUNTIES.																	
	Greene	Hamilt'n	H'rk'm'r	Jeffers'n.	Kings.	Lewis.	Liv'gst'n	Madison	Monroe.	Mont'ry.	N.-Y.	Niagara	Oneida.	On'nd'ga	Ontario	Orange.	Orleans	Oswego.
1790, ...	231	......	73	......	21	......	......	......	......	593	52	......	18	......	25	374	......	......
1800, ...	404	......	424	40	26	54	64	184	12	425	96	......	193	75	198	484	......	5
1810, ...	627	182	642	231	38	255	278	575	41	746	156	30	284	294	515	564	41	56
1814, ...	649	218	615	283	35	257	347	601	116	737	151	26	423	346	534	573	54	77
1820, ...	738	492	804	504	51	365	554	737	282	709	196	151	473	478	827	677	188	178
1825, ...	842	509	856	637	68	462	704	814	406	734	263	291	536	559	877	686	321	258
1830, ...	948	521	930	741	95	608	731	894	518	755	328	383	661	681	944	745	635	397
1835, ...	969	650	938	811	148	677	914	956	602	815	425	532	719	703	958	749	805	551
1840, ...	978	749	972	931	220	706	1,120	917	674	1,163	496	645	791	784	1,066	833	883	628
1845, ...	1,026	740	970	994	363	801	1,012	939	736	800	589	716	787	810	998	858	909	698
1850, ...	1,064	860	992	1,042	642	974	1,077	989	909	1,038	818	876	923	992	1,029	939	1,002	894
1855, ...	1,000	1.000	1,000	1,000	1,000	1,000	1,000	1,000	1,000	1,000	1,000	1,000	1,000	1,000	1,000	1,000	1,000	1,000

YEARS.	COUNTIES.																	
	Otsego	Putnam	Queens.	Rens'ler.	Richm'd.	Rockl'nd	St Law.	Sarat'ga	Sche'dy.	Scho'rie.	Sch'yler	Seneca.	Steuben	Suffolk	Sullivan	Tioga.	T'mpk'ns	Ulster.
1790.	34	641	346	283	179	307	......	366	290	62	......	......	......	400	59	......	......	238
1800, ...	435	710	349	383	213	325	66	536	454	292	14	159	30	474	100	75	23	318
1810, ...	780	739	418	459	246	397	105	671	521	565	195	445	104	514	204	217	164	390
1814, ...	816	671	417	465	259	401	110	630	572	576	301	549	152	523	208	193	311	388
1820, ...	902	808	465	518	287	453	214	730	668	691	554	701	304	591	302	295	703	455
1825, ...	963	851	439	569	277	410	369	735	657	773	728	795	339	577	352	370	887	471
1830, ...	1,033	906	486	624	331	481	485	784	637	832	727	829	474	652	419	494	994	538
1835, ...	1,014	803	543	701	359	497	568	769	852	851	807	892	592	688	466	613	1,023	587
1840, ...	998	902	655	761	512	613	756	821	891	965	873	981	688	790	564	761	1,024	673
1845, ...	1,015	927	688	786	635	704	831	839	852	968	913	984	782	842	635	816	1,024	702
1850, ...	978	1,014	796	948	704	869	915	924	1,024	1,001	986	1,003	971	899	851	923	1,037	864
1855.	1,000	1,000	1,000	1,000	1,000	1,000	1.000	1,000	1,000	1,000	1,000	1,000	1,000	1,000	1,000	1,000	1,000	1,000

YEARS.	COUNTIES.						State of New York.	United States	OTHER COUNTRIES.				CITIES.					
	Warren	Wash-ington.	Wayne.	West-chester.	Wyom-ing.	Yates			England & Wales	Scotland	Great Britain	France.	London	Paris.	New York	Brookl'n	Albany	Buffalo.
1790, ...	55	462	......	297	......	......	96	149	......	......	......	......	......	......	52	10	61	......
1800, ...	242	698	30	339	......	86	169	202	......	......	......	......	......	......	96	14	91	......
1810, ...	384	827	140	375	53	245	277	274	536	596	566	818	488	576	156	25	187	......
1814, ...	394	819	239	326	168	274	298	312	586	642	603	828	507	595	151	22	203	......
1820, ...	488	874	434	404	502	909	394	369	637	688	658	844	536	638	196	39	220	28
1825, ...	551	884	572	416	694	773	467	429	684	743	708	869	594	711	263	57	279	69
1830, ...	599	960	702	451	878	959	556	489	732	798	758	898	653	734	328	82	422	118
1835, ...	616	885	820	481	1,019	999	627	569	784	840	810	926	706	758	425	119	490	265
1840, ...	682	925	899	603	1.065	1,032	701	649	836	883	863	947	759	883	496	176	588	245
1845, ...	756	913	909	587	954	1,048	751	765	891	928	905	076	838	979	589	250	735	401
1850, ...	874	1,003	961	722	963	1,039	860	881	946	973	947	992	918	1,000	818	471	885	589
1855.	1,000	1,000	1,000	1.000	1,000	1,000	1.000	1,000	1,000	1,000	1,000	1,000	1.000	1.000	1,000	1,000	1,000	1,000

Sexes: A reference to the numbers of males and females, as given by successive censuses of this State, will show an excess of the former, at each period before 1855, when a greater number of the latter were reported. The several national censuses have uniformly shown an excess of males in the white population, in the general aggregate, and in all of the States, excepting Connecticut, Delaware, Massachusetts, New Hampshire, North Carolina, Rhode Island, Vermont, and the district of Columbia. In Connecticut, Massachusetts and Rhode Island the females have uniformly outnumbered the males. In New Hampshire, since 1790, in North Carolina since 1820, in Vermont in 1820, in Delaware in 1840, and in the district of Columbia since 1810, the same has been observed. In general, the excess of males is greatest in newly settled States, where the population is mostly made up of emigrants from other States or from foreign countries, among whom the male sex uniformly preponderates.* As the inducement for immigration ceases, or is diverted to other quarters, the disproportion of the sexes becomes less, until it assumes the condition now observed in this State and New England, and that which exists in nearly every country in Europe.† It is a well established fact, that there are born more males than females, the percentage of the former in Europe being over 51 in 100. The proportion is observed to vary in different countries and periods.

The relative number of the sexes, is found to change between different ages. The following comparisons will serve to illustrate this point.

Proportion of Females to every 100 *Males at different Periods of Life.*§

COUNTRIES.	Years.	All Ages.	Under 20 years.	20 and under 40.	40 and under 60	60 and under 80.	80 and under 100.
State of New-York,	†1830	96.625	98.033	94.319	93.860	94.968	105.105
" "	†1840	97.285	98.528	95.334	94.109	97.823	106.336
" "	1850	97.552	100.745	96.456	89.800	96.282	105.422
" "	1855	100.631	100.983	103.763	92.899	100.633	109.216
United States,	†1830	97.038	96.959	95.153	97.057	98.339	111.279
" "	†1840	96.459	97.167	92.905	94.318	99.842	111.552
" "	1850	95.916	98.221	91.417	90.231	98.131	110.436
Great Britain,‡	1821	102.968	98.419	107.765	104.874	110.438	125.769
" "	1841	103.769	99.497	106.319	105.948	115.196	134.139
" "	1851	103.363	98.856	105.291	105.628	118.115	141.636
England and Wales,	1821	102.112	98.274	106.668	102.688	108.399	125.339
" "	1841	103.015	99.544	105.154	104.122	113.095	131.573
" "	1851	102.674	99.047	104.233	103.834	115.616	138.235
Scotland,	1821	107.826	99.167	114.281	117.784	121.416	126,357
"	1841	108.102	99.085	113.163	117.615	128.228	145.002
"	1851	107.378	97.595	111.638	117.016	134.649	158.629
Islands in the British seas,	1821	106.472	100.690	103.562	114.811	137.271	169.630
" "	1841	111.052	102.383	117.664	114.310	125.101	209.063
" "	1851	110.265	100.947	115.684	118.002	123.744	175.263

A comparison of the relative number of the sexes in the several counties of this State, as given on pages 16, 17, will show an excess of one per cent, or more, of males, in Allegany, Cattaraugus, Cayuga, Erie, Essex, Genesee, Hamilton, Herkimer, Montgomery, Niagara, Orleans, Oswego, Rockland, Steuben, Sullivan, Ulster, Warren, and Wayne counties. An excess of females is noticed in Albany, Columbia, Dutchess,

* Of the immigrants from foreign countries during 36¼ years preceding Dec. 31, 1855, 2,713,931 were males and 1,720,205 females; a proportion of 158 to 100. (*Bromwell's History of Immigration into the United States*, p. 175.)

† The number of males to every 100 females in European countries, at different periods, is given in the following table, from Guillard's *Elements de Statistique Humaine*, p. 137.

COUNTRIES.	Years.	Males to every 100 females.	COUNTRIES	Years.	Males to every 100 females.	COUNTRIES.	Years.	Males to every 100 females.
Sweden,	1757	89·12	Netherlands,	1840	95·51	Saxony,	1834	94·18
"	1763	90·10	Belgium,	1830	91·67	"	1840	94·34
"	1825	92·10	"	1846	99·53	"	1849	94·81
"	1830	92·37	France,	1763	92·82	Baden,	1834	94·88
"	1840	93·05	"	1792	100·00	Wurtemberg,	1833	94·74
Canton of Zurich,	1764	103·38	"	1800	94·55	"	1840	96·45
The Thirteen Cantons,	1770	96·58	"	1820	94·15	"	1850	96·53
Canton of Berne,	1784	93·48	"	1840	97·37	Bavaria,	1846	95·48
Switzerland,	1837	98·12	"	1850	98·99	"	1849	94·98
"	1850	97·56	Prussia,	1819	98·91	"	1852	95·88
Norway,	1835	95·88	"	1843	99·62	Russia,	1850	95·92
Denmark,	1840	97·47	"	1849	99·94	Savoy,	1838	95·96
England,	1810	97·51	Austria,	1830–37	94·20	Roman States,	1827	98·31
"	1820	97·80	"	1840–46	94·86	Sicily,	1831	97·50
"	1830	97·24	"	1851	99·45	Spain,	1799	98·43
"	1840	97·02	Hanover,	1842	98·98	Portugal,	1801	93·86
"	1850	97·32	"	1848	99·07	Tuscany,	1832	103·58
Wales,	1840	98·03	Hesse-Cassel,	1840	96·97	"	1846	104·36
"	1850	100·16	Hesse-Darmstadt,	1849	97·62	Sardinia,	1848	100·56
Netherlands,	1830	95·46						

† The ages of whites only were specified in the above.

‡ This and the following are from the British census of 1851, Part II., vol I., page xxv.

§ The percentage of males and females of each five years to the age of 50, and of ten years above that age, is given on pages 54, 55 of this volume.

Kings, and New-York counties. The proportion is nearly equal in Chemung, Chenango, Fulton, Greene, Oneida, Ontario, Putnam, Queens, Schoharie, Schuyler, Seneca, Suffolk, Tompkins, Westchester and Yates. The greatest inequality of the sexes is observed in cities and large villages. In each of the cities of the State, excepting Buffalo, Oswego and Syracuse, the number of females exceeds the males, in proportions varying from 1 in 14, to 1 in 86, the average being 1 in 30.*

Ages: A reference to the summaries already given, will show that the ages when capable of military service, with males, and the productive period with females, were made the original bases of classification. A subdivision into terms of five years to twenty, and of ten years above that age, was employed in 1830 and 1840; and in 1850 a separate class was made for those under one year of age. In the present census, there was required the specific age of each person, and these returns have been grouped by sexes into periods of five years up to the age of fifty, and of ten years above that age.

It has been found, that in obtaining the ages of each person by the census, there is a tendency to report the nearest round number instead of the precise age, and the classifications by single years made in some of the latest European censuses, show conspicuously the practical error thus occasioned. In reality, the total number actually living of different ages, at a given time, is greatest in early life, and the numbers become less each year till the extreme period is reached. But the numbers of the census, by single years, show a constant fluctuation and irregularity. The division into periods of five years is found to equalize this inequality and present the numbers in an order approaching that actually existing. This subject is best illustrated by a diagram, which, with an explanation, will be found in the appendix.

The number of each sex of the different groups of ages, reduced to the percentage of the total population is shown by the following table, which includes, besides the results of New-York, those of the United States, Canada, Great Britain and Belgium.

Percentages of Sexes and at different Ages.

COUNTRIES.	YEARS.	Under 5.		5 and under 10		10 and under 15.		15 and under 20.		20 and under 30		30 and under 40.		40 and under 50.	
		Male.	Female.	Male.	Female.	Male.	Female.	Male.	Female.	Male.	Female.	Male.	Female.	Male.	Female.
New-York (whites),	1830	8·46	8·13	7·34	7·12	6·35	6·17	5·45	5·61	9·46	9·04	6·04	5·60	3·69	3·44
" "	1840	7·89	7·60	6·65	6·50	5·87	5·67	5·47	5·78	9·71	9·55	6·66	6·05	4·10	3·79
" "	1850	6·48	6·35	6·06	5·95	5·49	5·40	5·07	5·54	9·97	9·95	6·99	6·37	4·66	4·15
" (colored),	1850	0·18	0·17	0·73	0·77	0·86	0·90	0·80	0·84	0·66	0·82	·137	·170	·120	·126
" (total),	1850	6·66	6·52	6·79	6·72	6·35	6·30	5·87	6·38	10·63	10·77	7·13	6·54	4·78	4·28
" "	1855	6·85	6·74	5·73	5·64	5·46	5·35	4·91	5·45	9·43	10·44	7·28	6·78	4·79	4·39
United States (whites),	1830	9·24	8·76	7·42	7·13	6·36	6·07	5·44	5·66	9·09	8·73	5·63	5·28	3·50	3·39
" " "	1840	8·96	8·48	7·22	6·96	6·20	5·90	5·33	5·58	9·32	8·84	6·11	5·49	3·78	3·54
" " "	1850	7·53	7·29	7·03	6·81	6·27	5·91	5·33	5·59	9·56	8·99	6·59	5·78	4·29	3·83
Canada,	1851	9·26	8·97	6·69	7·08	6·29	5·89	5·79	5·08	8·54	8·43	5·58	5·28	3·95	3·39
Great Britain,	1851	6·57	6·51	5·88	5·82	5·42	5·31	4·90	4·99	8·22	9·24	6·32	6·77	4·78	5·04
Belgium,	1846	5·86	5·78	5·52	5·39	4·99	4·78	4·55	4·44	8·36	8·26	6·82	6·70	6·03	5·77

COUNTRIES.	YEARS.	50 and under 60.		60 and under 70.		70 and under 80.		80 and under 90.		90 and under 100.	
		Male.	Female.	Male.	Female.	Male.	Female.	Male.	Female.	Male.	Female.
New-York (whites),	1830	2·17	2·05	1·28	1·20	0·54	0·52	0·14	0·15	0·01	0·02
" "	1840	2·32	2·25	1·30	1·27	0·61	0·60	0·16	0·17	0·01	0·02
" "	1850	2·76	2·54	1·46	1·41	0·64	0·62	0·18	0·19	0·02	0·02
" (colored),	1850	·084	·085	·046	·045	·022	·026	·008	·011	·003	·005
" (total),	1850	2·84	2·62	1·51	1·45	0·66	0·65	0·19	0·20	0·02	0·02
" "	1855	2·91	2·76	1·55	1·56	0·65	0·65	0·17	0·18	0·02	0·02
United States (whites),	1830	2.18	2·12	1·28	1·25	0·55	0·55	0·15	0·17	0·02	0·02
" " "	1840	2·22	2·15	1·23	1·22	0·57	0·57	0·15	0·17	0·02	0·02
" " "	1850	2·55	2·36	1·35	1·31	1·57	0·57	0·16	0·17	0·02	0·02
Canada,	1851	2·53	2·90	1·34	1·07	0·55	0·43	0·14	0·12	0·02	0·02
Great Britain,	1851	3·32	3·57	2·09	2·42	0·99	1·22	0·26	0·36	......	......
Belgium,	1846	3·59	4·22	2·54	2·95	1·26	1·43	0·32	0·39	0·02	0.03

* A recent statistical writer notices some remarkable instances of this inequality. After mentioning the prominent causes of the difference, as wars, emigration, insalubrious occupations, irregular habits, the perils of navigation, mining, &c., he adds, "We may appreciate the extent of these influences, in observing that in 1810 the females exceeded the males by a fifth in Austria, and that in 1819 they were nearly double in Vienna. The least disparity between the sexes is found to exist in Russia and in Spain. Its mean term appears to be a twentieth, and we may commonly admit that in the States of Europe the proportion will not vary far from 21 females to 20 males." (*Elemens de Statistique, par A. Moreau de Jonnes*, p. 309.)

In most large cities, the number of males is considerably less in proportion than in the rural districts, but to this there are some singular exceptions. The following comparative numbers of the sexes in London and Paris illustrate this fact:

LONDON.

	Males.	Females.	Excess of females
1801,	437,571	521,292	83,721
1811,	517,783	621,032	103,249
1821,	641,221	737,726	96,505
1831,	766,727	888,267	121,540
1841,	912,020	1,036,397	124,377
1851,	1,106,558	1,255,678	149,120

PARIS.

	Males.	Females.	Excess of males.	Excess of females
1801,	262,888	284,868	......	21,980
1806,	278,665	301,944	......	23,279
1821,	350,955	363,011	......	12,056
1831,	376,084	398,254	......	22,170
1836,	459,526	449,600	9,926	......
1841,	480,898	454,363	26,535	......
1846,	543,496	510,401	33,095	......
1851,	532,313	520,949	11,364	......

The disproportion of the sexes in Paris is explained in the official returns, by the large number of young men attracted thither by the secondary, superior, and special seminaries of learning, the crowd of unmarried artificers drawn from the departments and even from foreign countries, and the numerous laborers upon public and private works. The excess of the male sex would have been considerably greater but for the number of female domestics, which in 1851 were about 48,000 to 20,000 males.

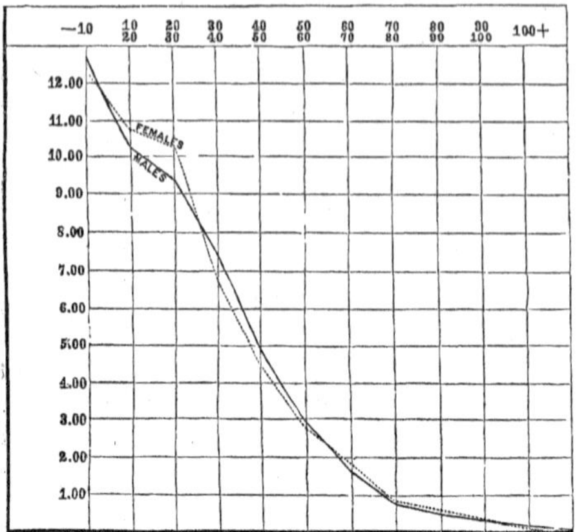

Comparative Percentage of the Sexes, 1855.

The relative proportion of males and females at different ages in the State of New-York in 1855, is represented in the accompanying cut, in which the numbers on the side, show the percentage to the total population, and those at the top the ages. A diagram, giving the actual, instead of the relative numbers of different ages, would exhibit a corresponding curvature. This change in the proportion of the sexes at different periods of life, has been observed in all countries where statistics have been obtained. While this number of males is uniformly greater in childhood, there is usually observed among those of more advanced age, an excess of the female sex.

The extreme period of life reported in the present census was 120 years, and the number 100 years old and upwards, (exclusive of Indians, of which there is much uncertainty) was 92.* The number of this class reported in several censuses of this and other countries has been as follows:

Persons 100 Years Old and Upwards.

COUNTRIES.	Years.	Males	Females	Total.	Percen. total pop.	COUNTRIES.	Years.	Males.	Females.	Total.	Percen. total po
New-York, ...	1830	54	71	125	0·0065	Canada, ...	1851	31	27	58	0·0031
New-York, ...	1840	79	69	148	0·0061	Great Britain, ...	1821	111	215	326	0·0023
New-York, ...	1850	45	43	88	0·0028	Great Britain, ...	1841	128	225	353	0·0019
New-York, ...	1855	41	50	91	0·0026	Great Britain, ...	1851	111	208	319	0·0015
United States, ...	1830	301	238	539	0·0051	France, ...	1851	102	180	282	0·0008
United States, ...	1840	476	316	792	0·0055	Belgium, ...	1846	14	17	31	0·0007
United States, ...	1850	357	430	787	0·0040						

* The interest usually attached to these cases of extreme longevity, is deemed sufficient to warrant the insertion of the following details:

Persons reported as One Hundred Years of Age or upwards.

Names.	Age.	Residence.	Place of birth.	Names.	Age.	Residence.	Place of birth.
Catharine Colenburgh, ...	100	Bethlehem, Albany co.,...	Schoharie co.	Edney Tenant (female),...	100	Rome, Oneida co.,........	Connecticut.
C. Burt (female),.........	103	Hinsdale, Cattaraugus co.,	Ireland.	Robert Flanagan,.........	100	Utica, “	Ireland.
Harry Hughs (colored,) ..	102	Aurelius, Cayuga co., ...	N.-Y. city.	John Sixbury, ...	100	Lysander, Onondaga co.,..	M’tgomery c
Jane Hufftailing, ...	100	Brutus, “	....	Elizabeth Scouton,........	110	Syracuse, Onondaga co., ..	Connecticut.
John O’Bryan (Indian), ..	103	“ “	Mas’chusetts.	James Smith, ...	100	Gorham, Ontario co.,.....	Columbia co
H. Barber (female), ...	104	Catlin, Chemung co., ...	Connecticut.	Thomas Mason, ...	100	Seneca, “	Penns’lvania
Peter Rhinehart, ...	104	Horseheads, “	Schoharie co.	Minto Cosin (colored fem.)	105	Newburgh, Orange co., ...	Maryland.
Bernard Casey, ...	100	Smithville, Chenango co.,.	Ireland.	Gideon Bentley, ...	105	Constantia, Oswego co., ..	Rhode Island
Rene Frazier, ...	107	Ansable, Clinton co., ...	France.	Peter Rosell, ...	101	Oswego, “ ..	N.-Y. city.
Jacob Oakley (colored),...	100	Beekmantown, Clinton co.,	Long Island.	Susanna Cole,...........	100	Carmel, Putnam co., ...	Putnam co.
Mary Wood, ...	100	Champlain, “	Canada.	Jane Johnson, ...	110	“ “	Westchester.
Margaret Berry, ...	106	Taylor, Cortland co.,.....	Mas’chusetts.	Prince Cornwall (colored),	103	Kent, “	“
Currance Bostwick, ...	102	Franklin, Delaware co.,...	Connecticut.	Charles Mayhew, ...	100	Jamaica, Queens co., ...	Queens co.
David Crispell, ...	100	Sidney, “ ...	Dutchess co.,	Anna Baldwin, ...	100	North Hempstead, do., ...	“
Thomas Carr (colored),...	100	Dover, Dutchess co., ...	“	Michael Onderdonk, ...	100	“ “ ...	“
John Smyth,.............	102	Milan, “	Westchester.	Hannah Campbell,........	100	Brunswick, Rensselaer co.,	Rensselaer c
Catharine Hoag,..........	100	Amherst, Erie co., ...	Germany.	Thomas Decker,..........	100	Northfield, Richmond co.,	Richmond c
Margaret Fraly, ...	100	Buffalo, “	Ireland.	Harry Bosseau,...........	103	Canton, St. Lawrence co.,.	Canada.
Lydia Hawkins (colored),..	100	“ “	Maryland.	Samuel Andrews,.........	100	Colton, “	Connecticut.
Adam Philips,............	100	Clarence, “	France.	Peter Sebattus, ...	100	“ “	Vermont.
Peter Demo, ..., ...	105	Dickinson, Franklin co., ..	Canada.	Edmond Dundon,.........	104	Madrid, “	Ireland.
Rosette Colware, ...	100	Malone, “ ..	“	Biddy Anderson.	106	Oswegatchie, “	“
Mary Cawger,............	100	“ “ ..	“	Susan Wadsworth,........	120	“ “	Connecticut.
Solomon Hill, ...	101	Elba, Genesee co.,........	....	Joseph Wood,............	104	“ “	France.
Hannah Piersons,.........	105	Pavillion, ,, ...	Connecticut.	John Carter, ...	104	Galway, Saratoga co., ...	Ulster co.
Catharine Shafee, ...	106	Cairo, Greene co.,........	Columbia co.	Clary Shafer (colored),....	100	Schoharie, Schoharie co., .	Schoharie c
Thomas Smith, ...	104	Columbia, Herkimer co.,..	....	Enos Marshall, senior, ...	100	Covert, Seneca co., ...	Dutchess co.
Sarah Munn (colored), ...	104	German Flats, “ ..	Schoharie co.	Samuel Preston (colored),.	100	Lodi, “	Connecticut.
David Wright (colored), ..	106	Pamelia, Jefferson co.,....	....	Rhoda Tucker (colored), ..	100	Brookhaven, Suffolk co., ..	Suffolk co.
Hannah Halbert, ...	100	Wilna, “	....	Frederick Shaff, ...	102	Berkshire, Tioga co., ...	Dutchess co.
H. Bolton, ...	101	Brooklyn, Kings co., ...	England,....	Henry Taylor (colored), ..	100	Lansing, Tompkins co.,...	....
Maria Cumming, ...	100	“ “	N.-Y. city.	Nancy Goodwen, ...	102	Hurley, Ulster co.,.......	Connecticut.
David Davis,.............	101	“ “	New Jersey.	Hannah Austin, ...	100	Queensbury, Warren co., .	Dutchess co.
Mary Hohen, ...	101	“ “	Ireland.	Jack Pain (colored),......	100	“ “	Africa,.....
Sarah Keenan, ...	100	“ “	“	Lydia Church, ...	101	Argyle, Washington co., ..	W’hingt’n c
Catharine Dunn,..........	101	Nunda, Livingston co., ...	Penns’lvania	George McGregor, ...	103	Sodus, Wayne co., ...	Scotland.
Cynthia Milliman, ...	100	Springwater, “ ...	Mas’chusetts.	Christian Romer, ...	102	Greenburgh, Westchester,	Westchester
John Doxtater (Indian), ..	100	Lenox, Madison co,,......	Oneida co.	Elizabeth Lawrence, ...	100	New Rochelle, “	Queens co.
Abigal Wood, ...	102	Sweden, Monroe co., ...	Connecticut.	Job Minot,...............	102	Rye, “	Westchester
David Smith,.............	101	Union, “	Mas’chusetts.	Sarah Peterson (colored), .	101	Somers, “	Putnam co.
Johanna Bethune, ...	100	New-York city,..........	Scotland.	“ Old Mingo” (colored), ..	100	Torrey, Yates co,,........	Virginia.
Mary Dinan,.............	100	“ “	Ireland.				
Elenor Hanavan, ...	109	“ “	....	INDIANS.			
Margaret Mackay, ...	100	“ “	Ireland.	Philip Curry, ...	100	Allegany Reservation, ...	C taraugus c
Mary Paris,..............	105	“ “	Portugal.	Governor Blacksnake, ...	107	“ (Head chief), ...	Ontario co.
Rose Ridgely, ...	103	“ “	Ireland.	Philip Benjockety,........	101	Cattaraugus Reservation, .	....
Maria Roberts, ...	111	“ “	N.Y city.	Young Jackson’s mother,..	100	“ “	....
Betty Smith,.............	100	“ “	Ireland.	Mrs. Green,..............	104	Tonawanda, ...	Lit. Beardst’
Mary Wright (colored),...	100	“ “	Richmond co.	Isaac Doctor’s grandmoth’r,	100	“	Squaukie hil
Ellen Farrar, ...	100	“ “	Ireland.	Mrs. Taylor, ...	101	“	Canada.

The number of persons of extreme age in a given country, is found to be but an uncertain indication of the general average of human life. France, has a greater relative number than England by one-third, of persons between sixty and seventy years, and in the next period of ten years, it maintains this superiority, but above the age of eighty, the proportion rapidly decreases, and centennarians become rare, in the same country which has carried life through maturity to a period fixed as the usual limit of man's years. In Great Britain, we notice a considerable diversity in the different kingdoms. While in Ireland, the number of births is relatively much greater, at the age of forty, the number living in Scotland and England is proportionably higher. In the former, the number between forty and fifty is but a thirteenth, while in the latter it is an eleventh, of the whole population. Between seventy and eighty, England and Scotland count double the relative number of Ireland, and from eighty to ninety, triple the proportion, but above that age, the latter gains in relative numbers, and exhibits as many centennarians as Scotland, and many more than England.

Place of Birth: No inquiries into the nativities of our population were made until the census of 1845, when there were reported as born, in

	Number.	Per cent.		Number.	Per cent.
State of New-York,	1,894,278 or	72·73	Great Britain and its possessions,	277,890	10·67
New England States	228,881	8·78	France,	10,619	0·41
Other States and Territories of the United States,	83,642	3·31	Germany,	49,558	1·90
Mexico and South America,	977	0·04	Other European countries,	8,222	0·32
			Nativities not reported,	50,428	1·93

In 1850, the deputy marshals were required to enter the name of the State or Territory, or of the government, in which each person was born. In condensing these returns, only the following was ascertained concerning this State:

		Per cent.			Per cent.
Born in the State of New-York,	2,092,076 or	68·63	Born in foreign countries,	655,224	21·49
Born in other States and Territories of the United States,	296,754	9·74	Nativities not reported,	4,271	0·14

In the present census, there was required the county, if in this State, the State or Territory if in the United States, or the foreign country in which each person was born. In classifying these returns, we have deemed it proper to give them all the detail which they admitted, as well to show by its origin the general character of our population, as to afford a full and ample means of comparison in the future.

In communities where, from interest or necessity, there are few changes of residence, and the sons as, of course, follow the callings of their fathers, local peculiarities of language and customs will arise, which, strengthened by habit and early associations, will cling tenaciously to their inhabitants through life. Where numbers from the same section settle in a new locality, their former peculiarities are preserved, and thus we often see reproduced in our State, in miniature, the local customs of New England or of Europe. The concentration of our people in cities and large towns, adds additional interest to this inquiry, by showing the course of the migration that is constantly going on, and the directions which the human current takes in its unceasing fluctuations. The distribution of population, and its tendency to concentrate in cities, appears to be governed by general laws, like those which regulate the centralization of trade and wealth in localities which natural facilities or artificial lines of communication may indicate. While the growth of commercial and manufacturing towns is much greater than the natural increase by births, some of the rural districts exhibit no growth whatever; the field of enterprise offered by the one, having no definite limit, while in the other, the capacity for profitable accommodation, is in some sections of our State already reached. An extended generalization of the kind we have offered, will show the origin of this excess of growth in the one case, and explain the stationary condition in the other, by showing what becomes of their increase. The migratory habits of our people have been often remarked by foreigners, and a comparison of results obtained in this country and in Europe, would show a wide contrast in the relative permanence of the population.*

The tendency of our emigration is *westward*, as is most strikingly shown by comparing the origin of the population of almost any county in the eastern with one in the western part of the State. The following are examples:

In Steuben, born in Otsego,	1,173	In Otsego, born in Steuben,	23
Livingston, born in Washington,	353	Washington, born in Livingston,	8
Jefferson, born in Montgomery,	1,502	Montgomery, born in Jefferson,	55
Genesee, born in Herkimer,	104	Herkimer, born in Genesee,	15

* The national census of 1850, showed in several of the older States, as North Carolina, South Carolina, Virginia, Maryland and Pennsylvania, a percentage of 95, 92, 90, 78 and 79 respectively, of free population, as born in the States of their residence, while in the newer States of Wisconsin, Iowa, and California, the percentage was 17, 21, and 8. The British census of 1851 shows that of the people of Great Britain 82 per cent were born in England and Wales; 13 per cent in Scotland; 3·5 per cent in Ireland; 0·6 per cent in the islands of the British seas; 0·2 per cent in the British colonies; and 0·3 per cent in foreign States. (*Compendium of U. S. Census*, 1850:—*British Census*, 1851, Part II., vol. I., p. ci.)

The number and percentage of our population in 1855, born in the several sections of the Union, and in foreign countries, are as follows:

Origin of the Population of New-York.

	Number	Percent.		Number	Percent.
New-York,..................	2,222,321	64·077	Southern States,............	13,124	0·378
Connecticut,................	63,691	1·863	Ohio,........................	5,256	0·151
Massachusetts, ...	57,086	1·648	Michigan, ...	3,413	0·098
Vermont,...................	54,266	1·565	Illinois,......................	1,255	0·036
New Hampshire,............	14,941	0·431	Wisconsin,..................	1,163	0·033
Rhode Island,..............	11,737	0·339	Indiana, ...	606	0·017
Maine, ...	5,818	0·168	Other States,...............	183	0·005
New England States,........	207,539	6·014	United States,...............	2,528,444	72·903
New Jersey,.................	40,391	1·164	At sea and unknown, ...	17,749	0·512
Pennsylvania, ...:..........	31,472	0·907	Foreign countries, ...	922,019	26·585

The relative numbers of our population born in foreign countries, having over 100 emigrants in the State compared with the total immigration into the United States during 36¼ years as shown by official data,* are contained in the following table:

Relative Number of Foreign Immigrants.

Foreign countries in the order of their emigrants living in New-York, June 1. 1855.	Total immigration into United States in 36¼ years.		Residing in New-York, June 1, 1855.		Foreign countries in the order of their emigrants living in New-York, June 1, 1855.	Total immigration into the United States in 36¼ years.		Residing in New-York, June 1, 1855.	
	Number.	Percentage of total immigration.	Number	Percentage of total population.		Number.	Percentage of total immigration.	Number.	Percentage of total population.
Ireland,..................	§747, 930	17·754	469, 753	13·549	Sweden, ...	‡29. 441	0·694	1, 472	0·042
Germany, ...	1, 206, 087	28·630	218, 997	6·314	Italy,....................	7, 185	0·171	1, 231	0·036
England,.................	§207, 492	4·925	102, 286	2·949	Austria, ...	¶	....	1, 197	0·034
Canada, ...	†91, 699	2·177	47, 842	1·379	New Brunswick, ...	†	....	766	0·022
Scotland, ...	§34, 559	0·820	27, 523	0·794	Denmark, ...	3, 059	0·073	583	0·017
France,..................	188, 725	4·482	18, 366	0·529	Spain,...................	11, 251	0·267	570	0·017
Wales, ...	§4, 782	0·114	8, 557	0·246	Norway,................	‡	....	537	0·016
Prussia, ...	35, 995	0·854	6, 352	0·183	Belgium,................	6, 991	0·166	454	0·013
Holland,.................	17. 583	0·417	4, 214	0·124	Newfoundland, ...	†	....	398	0·011
Switzerland, ...	31, 725	0·738	3, 948	0·114	South America,..........	5, 440	0·129	296	0·008
Poland, ...	1, 318	0·031	1, 880	0·054	Portugal, ...	6, 049	0·144	291	0·008
West Indies, ...	35, 317	0·838	1, 846	0·053	Russia, ...	938	0·022	256	0·007
Nova Scotia,.............	†	....	1, 602	0·046	Mexico, ...	15, 969	0·379	119	0·003

Civil Condition: Previous censuses in New-York, afford no data for comparison with the present, under this head. The following table shows the relative numbers of the various classes implied in this inquiry, in New-York, Canada, and several European Countries:

Percentages of the Various Civil Conditions.

COUNTRIES.	Years	Single.	Married.	Widowers.	Widows.	COUNTRIES.	Years.	Single.	Married.	Widowers.	Widows.
New-York, all classes,......	1855	60·08	36·15	1·02	2·75	Great Britain, males,**.....	1851	63·08	33·17	3.75	....
Canada, "	1851	66·66	30·81	0·94	1·59	Great Britain, females,**...	1851	60·35	32·24	....	7·41
England, "	1821	60·00	33·00	....	....	Belgium, all classes, ...	1846	63·91	30·49	1·97	3·63
England & Wales, males,*..	1851	62·50	33·69	3·80	....	France, males,**	1851	56·04	39·26	4·70	....
England & Wales, females,*..	1851	59·79	32·97	....	7·24	France, females,**	1851	51·99	38·63	....	9·38
Scotland, males,*..........	1851	66·77	29·83	3·40	....	Denmark, all classes,.......	1834	62·00	33·00	....	6·4
Scotland, females,*........	1851	63·71	27·91	....	8·38	Spain "	1803	55·00	38·00	....	6·9
Isles of the Brit. seas, m's.**.	1851	63·12	33·44	3·44	....	Sweden & Finl'd, all classes,	1809	50·00	34·00	....	6·1
Isles of the Brit. seas, fem.**.	1851	60·97	30·93	....	9·06	Switzerland, "	1827	56·00	35·00	....	7·8

The relative proportion of married persons to the total population, is observed in Europe to vary from, nearly half, as in France before the revolution, to somewhat more than a quarter. There is usually observed a greater number of unmarried males than females, and the number of widows is uniformly about twice as great as that of widowers. The widows number 1 to every 8 or 9 females, in France and England, and 1 to every 11 or 12 in Sweden and Spain; while of widowers there is found 1 to every 18 males in France, 1 to every 21 in Spain, 1 to every 22 in Paris, and 1 to every 33 in England and Sweden.†† In this State, the proportion of the former is 1 to 18 females, and of the latter 1 to 49 males. It is yet to be determined what changes occur in this country between different periods in the relative proportion of these numbers.‡‡ A reference to page 202 will in some degree explain the disproportion of the widowed, by

* See *Bromwell's History of Immigration to the United States*, p. 16. The period embraced in the work cited extends from Sept. 30, 1819, to Sept. 31, 1855. The total number of immigrants was 4,212,624.

† British America, the provinces not specified.

‡ Sweden and Norway reported together.

§ In addition to the above 1,346,682, or 32·015 per cent were born in Great Britain, the division not designated.

¶ Included in Germany.

** Percentage of the sex.

†† *Elemens de Statistique, par A Moreau de Jonnes*, p. 334.

‡‡ The percentages of the various classes have varied in France as follows:

	1789.	1801.	1806.	1821.	1831.	1836.	1841.	1851.
Single, both sexes,..	48·	53·	54·	55·	56·	56·	55·	54·
Married, " ..	46·	...	38·	38·	40·	36·	36·	38·
Widowed, " ..	7·5	...	6·7	6·8	6·8	6·8	6·9	5·5

—*Ibid*, (p. 336).

showing a remarkable difference between the number of each sex married within the year. The number of widows in this class is only about half as great as of widowers, being the reverse of the existing proportions, as given on page 16.

Professions and Occupations: In 1840 the number of persons in New-York employed in mining was 1,898; in agriculture 455,954; in commerce 28,468; in manufactures and trades 173,193; in navigating the ocean 5,511; in navigating canals, lakes and rivers 10,167; in learned professions and as engineers 14,111.

In 1845 there were reported 253,292 farmers, 20,758 merchants, 13,088 mechanics, 3,549 attorneys, 4,399 clergymen, with an aggregate salary of $1,531,287, and 4,610 physicians and surgeons.

In 1850 there were reported 312,697 engaged in commerce, trade, manufactures, mechanic arts and mining, 313,980 in agriculture, 196,613 in labor not agricultural, 1,462 in the army, 23,242 in sea and river navigation, 14,258 in law, medicine and divinity; 11,104 in other pursuits requiring education; 4,985 in government civil service, 6,324 as domestic servants, and 3,628 in other occupations.

In 1855 the professions and occupations have been reduced to the classification found on pages 178 to 195. Most statistics in this particular inquiry are defective, from their not also exhibiting the number of persons of all classes dependent upon the several occupations for their support. If an additional column were provided for showing this item, we might arrive at very interesting results, which are now left to conjecture and vague estimates.

*Families and Dwellings:** The following table exhibits the number of families and dwellings in New-York in 1850 and 1855, compared with those in the United States in 1850, and in Canada in 1851:

---

* A "dwelling" was defined in the instructions for taking the present census, as "a separate inhabited tenement, having one or more families under one roof. Where several tenements are in one block with walls, either of brick or wood, to divide them, having separate entrances, they are each to be numbered as separate houses, but when not so divided, they are to be numbered as one house. If a house is used partly for a store, shop, office or other purpose, and partly for a dwelling house, it is to be numbered as a dwelling house, but where used for lodging only, it is not. Hotels, poorhouses, garrisons, hospitals, asylums, jails, penitentiaries, houses of refuge and other similar institutions, are each to be numbered as a dwelling house."

The returns were not sufficiently definite to give the number of boats and vessels used as dwellings.

The term "family" was defined to mean "either one person living separately in a house, or part of a house, and providing for him or herself; or several persons living together in a house or part of a house upon one common means of support, and separately from others in similar circumstances. A widow living alone, and separately providing for herself, or two hundred individuals, living together, and provided for by a common head, should each be numbered as one family. The resident inmates of a hotel, jail, prison, garrison, hospital, poorhouse, asylum, house of refuge or other similar institution, should be considered as one family." *Instructions*, page 16. A similar definition was given in 1850.

The following is a list of several of the larger institutions in the city of New-York, that were reported together, as families, under the above rule. The number of inmates in the asylums for the deaf and dumb, blind and insane, are reported elsewhere in connection with these subjects.

The *American Female Guardian Society and Home of the Friendless*, (East Thirtieth-street, between Fourth and Madison-avenues, N. Y.), reported 10 officers, teachers and servants, and 89 inmates, of whom 40 were boys and 49 girls. The ages of these children were as follows: 2 one, 2 two, 4 three, 6 four, 8 five, 11 six, 13 seven, 7 eight, 10 nine, 5 ten, 2 eleven, 8 twelve, 6 thirteen, 2 fourteen and 2 fifteen.

The Asylum of the *Association for the Benefit of Colored Orphans*, (Fifth-avenue, between Forty-third and Forty-fourth-streets), reported 157 boys and 87 girls. They were of the following ages: 1 two, 7 three, 5 four, 18 five, 17 six, 25 seven, 25 eight, 44 nine, 37 ten, 30 eleven, 19 twelve, 9 thirteen, 5 fourteen and 2 fifteen.

A building in the second election district of the Nineteenth Ward, hired as a temporary use of the *Asylum for Juvenile Delinquents*, was reported as having (besides officers and servants) 215 inmates under 17 years of age, of whom 47 were girls.

The *Asylum for the Relief of Respectable Aged and Indigent Females*, (East Twentieth-street), reported 87 inmates, of whom 1 was under 60 years of age, 31 between 60 and 70, 38 between 70 and 80, 12 between 80 and 90, and five over 90 All but 21 were reported as widows.

The population of *Blackwell's Island* was reported as 2,960, of whom 43 (21 males and 22 females) were returned as wardens and other officers and their families; 387 (252 males and 135 females) as inmates of the penitentiary; 263 (56 males and 207 females) as inmates of the hospital; 866 (304 males and 562 females) as inmates of the alms-house; 514 (413 males and 471 females) as inmates of the workhouse; and 517 (225 males and 292 females) as inmates of the lunatic asylum.

The *Colored Home*, (Nineteenth Ward), reported 257 inmates, of whom 85 were males and 162 females. Of the former, 13 were under ten years of age, 12 between 10 and 20, 16 between 20 and 30, 12 between 30 and 40, 6 between 40 and 50, 5 between 50 and 60, 12 between 60 and 70, 7 between 70 and 80 and 2 between 80 and 90. Of the females, 22 were under 10, 5 between 10 and 20, 31 between 20 and 30, 31 between 30 and 40, 13 between 40 and 50, 15 between 50 and 60, 25 between 60 and 70, 11 between 70 and 80, 6 between 80 and 90, 1 between 90 and 100, and 1, 100 years of age.

The nativity of all of these was reported as New-York, excepting 50 of other States and 10 of foreign countries.

The *Episcopal Orphan's Home* (Ninth Ward), reported 66 inmates, (39 boys and 27 girls), of the following ages, viz.:—5 four, 7 five, 9 six, 9 seven, 14 eight, 9 nine, 13 ten, 6 eleven, and 5 twelve years.

The *Five Points Mission*, reported 38 boarders.

The *Five Points House of Industry*, reported 98 inmates.

The *House of Mercy, or Magdalen Asylum* (Twelfth Ward), reported 11 inmates, who were females between the ages of 14 and 20.

Institution of Mercy (Fourteenth Ward), 103 females.

A *Jewish Hospital* (Twentieth Ward), reported 19 employees and inmates.

The *Leake and Watts Orphan Asylum* (Manhattanville, between Ninth and Tenth-avenues and 111th and 112th-streets), reported 26 persons in the family of the superintendent and attendants, and 200 inmates (145 boys and 55 girls) of the following ages: –3 three, 4 four, 5 five, 4 six, 10 seven, 17 eight, 16 nine, 34 ten, 31 eleven, 26 twelve, 28 thirteen, 13 fourteen, 8 fifteen and 1 sixteen years.

The *Magdalen Female Benevolent Society*, (Eighty-eighth and Eighty-ninth-streets, Fourth and Fifth-avenues), reported 21 inmates.

The *Methodist Episcopal Ladies' Union Aid Society for Indigent Females* (No. 14 Horatio-street, N. Y.), reported 26 inmates.

The *New-York County Jail*, reported 10 male prisoners.

The *New-York Hospital*, reported 56 officers and attendants (39 males and 17 females), and 232 patients, of whom 39 were females.

The *New-York Orphan Asylum* (Seventy-first-street and Bloomingdale-road), reported 204 inmates, of whom 126 were boys and 78 girls, of the following ages:—3 under one year, 3 one, 2 three, 3 four, 4 five, 9 six, 10 seven, 14 eight, 41 nine, 24 ten, 18 eleven, 28 twelve, 17 thirteen, 12 fourteen, 9 fifteen, 3 sixteen, 1 seventeen, 1 twenty one and 2 unknown.

The *New-York Roman Catholic Orphan Asylum for Boys* (Fifth-avenue, between Fifty-first and Fifty-second-streets), under the care of 18 sisters of charity, reported 383 pupils, of whom 4 were four years of age, 11 five, 23 six, 37 seven, 55 eight, 65 nine, 58 ten, 58 eleven, 41 twelve, 22 thirteen, 4 fourteen, 2 fifteen, 2 sixteen and 1 seventeen.

The *Protestant Half Orphan Asylum* (Fifteenth Ward), reported 191 children between 4 and 12 years of age, of whom 100 were boys and 91 girls.

Randall's Island.—The House of Refuge on Randall's Island reported 442 inmates, of whom 373 were males and 69 females. The ages of the males were as follows: 1 eight, 3 nine, 5 ten, 17 eleven, 26 twelve, 45 thirteen, 73 fourteen, 82 fifteen, 54 sixteen, 22 seventeen, 16 eighteen, 3 nineteen, and the remainder not given. Of the females the ages were as follows:—1 eleven, 5 twelve, 4 thirteen, 7 fourteen, 7 fifteen, 13 sixteen, 8 seventeen, 4 eighteen, 15 not given and the remainder twenty or upwards.

Ward D Refuge on Randall's Island reported 100 inmates. There were in addition 464 inmates of the institutions on the island, of which less definite particulars were given, as many had been discharged between the 1st of June (to which the census referred) and the time of obtaining the statistics. The marshal remarked in a note, that the difficulty of obtaining accurate data arose from the frequent discharge from and return to the institutions of the same persons. The returns of the census somewhat overrun the number officially reported.

The Nursery on Randall's Island reported 112 officers and attendants, including the family of the warden, and 1,001 inmates, of whom 644 were boys and 357 girls. The ages of the boys were as follows:—1 one, 18 two, 41 three, 62 four, 58 five, 68 six, 77 seven, 86 eight, 59 nine, 53 ten, 43 eleven, 24 twelve, 12 thirteen, 10 fourteen, 24 fifteen, 6 sixteen and 4 seventeen years. The ages of the girls were 3 one, 11 two, 34 three, 38 four, 34 five, 35 six, 39 seven, 34 eight, 32 nine, 26 ten, 17 eleven, 11 twelve, 11 thirteen, 12 fourteen, 13 fifteen, 5 seventeen, 1 eighteen, and 1 twenty years.

A Roman Catholic Boarding School (Second District, Fourteenth Ward), reported 266 inmates, of whom 245 were scholars, all females. Another in Twelfth Ward reported 75 boys.

F

COUNTRIES.	Years	DWELLINGS. Number.	DWELLINGS. Average number of persons in each.	FAMILIES. Number.	FAMILIES. Average number of persons in each
New-York, ...	1850	473,936	6·53	566,869	5·46
New-York, ...	1855	522,325	6·64	663,124	5·23
United States (whites and free colored),..	1850	3,362,337	5·94	3,598,195	5·55
Canada, ...	1851	....	....	293,667	6·27

The actual and relative number, and the average value of dwellings of different kinds, as reported in the present census, are shown in the following table. The details of these, by towns and counties, are given on pages 229 to 246:

Kind.	Number.	Relative percentage to total number.	Average value.
Stone, ...	7,536	1·44	$6,997
Brick, ...	57,450	10·97	5,500
Framed, ...	397,638	76·49	785
Logs, ...	33,092	6·35	46
Other,*	22,240	4·25	234
Total, ...	517,956†	100	Average, $1,351

If the number of married persons be considered as equally divided between the sexes, the resulting half is found to be 36,617 less than the reported number of families. In most countries, where the facts have been obtained, it is observed that the number of wives, at any time, somewhat exceeds that of husbands, chiefly from the absence of the latter in other countries. The term "family," in the census, must therefore imply other than the ordinary association of husband, wife, children and other inmates, in at least the number of instances denoted by the above excess.

Twins: The marshals who reported the present census, almost invariably entered the names of the children in each family in the order of their ages. This afforded an opportunity of noting the number of twins under the age of 20, living with their parents at the date of the census. Although this inquiry was not contemplated, and no instructions were given respecting it, the data thus accidentally offered were improved in ascertaining the number of this class, viz.:

Pairs of twins, under 20 years of age, both males, ...	2,388
" " " both females, ...	2,380
" " " male and female, ...	1,548
Total, ...	6,316

Four cases of triplets, all females, were noticed.

Voters and Aliens: These classes possess an inverse relation to each other, the percentage of one increasing as the other diminishes. Neither are governed by causes similar to those which regulate the relative proportions of the several ages, sexes, and civil conditions of the population, and both are closely dependant upon the definition given them by law.

In each of the Constitutions of New-York, the qualifications of voters have been specified, and their number required to be obtained periodically by the census. The results of these enumerations, previous to 1821 have been already given.‡ Of the number denominated electors, only those owning freeholds, worth £100 or $250 either by their own right or that of their wives, were entitled to vote for Governor, Lieutenant-Governor and Senators, the remainder being restricted to the privilege of voting for Members of Assembly and Congress, and for local officers.

The elective franchise was further extended by the Constitution of 1821, to all white males of the age of 21, who paid taxes or performed military duty, or who were by law exempt from taxes or military service.|| In 1826, the constitution was amended by abolishing the property qualification of white voters,¶

St. Catharine's Convent (Fourteenth Ward), 38 females.

The *Sacred Heart Institution* (Twelfth Ward), reported 225 inmates, all females.

The *Sisters of Charity of the St. Vincent Academy* (Twelfth Ward), reported 70 inmates, exclusive of servants.

Theological Seminary (Third District, Fifteenth Ward), 180 inmates, of whom 174 were young men.

The *Ward's Island Emigrants' Refuge and Hospital*, reported a population of 2,157, of whom 211 (110 males and 101 females) were employed as officers, nurses, servants, and their families, the remainder 3; Portugal and Switzerland, each 2; Hungary and Holland, each 1; the remainder not known.

* This class includes temporary dwellings, shantees, huts, plank, board, block and other houses not belonging in the other classes.

† Of 4,268 no particulars were given.

(899 males and 1,048 females), being inmates of the various establishments on the island, under the supervision of the Commissioners of Emigration. The nativities of these inmates were as follows:—Ireland, 1,948; Germany, 537; United States, 233 (mostly young children); England, 50; France, 8; Bohemia, 7; Sweden, 6; Belgium, 5; Scotland,

‡ Pages ix and x.

|| See Constitution of 1821, Art. ii., §1, and act of April 17, 1822. Taxes might be either in money upon property or poll taxes due in labor upon the highways. By an act passed April 4, 1823, the property qualification was extended to tenants paying taxes, and special enactments were repeatedly made for the relief of the inhabitants of certain districts, in which most of the land was held by contract.

¶ The popular vote upon this amendment was 127,077 for, to 3,215 against the extension of the elective franchise.

and in 1845, the property qualification for office previously existing was also abolished.* The admission of aliens to the privileges of citizenship is regulated by Congress, and the requirements have been several times changed.†

Comparative Number and Percentage of Voters and Aliens under the late and present Constitution.

COUNTIES.	NUMBER.								PERCENTAGE TO POPULATION IN EACH COUNTY.							
	VOTERS				ALIENS.				VOTERS.				ALIENS.‡			
	1825.	1835.	1845.	1855.	1825.	1835.	1845	1855.	1825.	1835.	1845.	1855.	1825.	1835.	1845.	1855.
Albany, ...	7,592	10,941	15,878	18,616	996	3,381	7,258	20,282	17·73	18·30	20·55	17 95	2·32	5·66	9·39	19·56
Allegany, ...	3,826	7,013	8,754	9,884	78	143	379	2,032	28·71	25·89	27·87	23·04	0·59	0·52	1·21	4·73
Broome, ...	2,770	4,102	5,814	8,282	84	426	200	2,056	19·92	20·31	22·53	22·59	0·60	2·11	0·77	5·61
Cattaraugus, ...	1,826	5,030	6,588	8,637	15	141	281	2,645	27·49	20·12	21·43	21·85	0·22	0·57	0·93	6·69
Cayuga, ...	8,000	10,058	11,140	11,526	201	548	778	4,863	18·71	20·44	22·43	21·56	0·45	1·11	1·56	9·07
Chautauque, ...	4,243	9,012	10,159	11,912	195	400	432	4,795	20·56	20·07	21·86	22·31	0·94	0·87	0·93	8·98
Chemung, ...	....	....	5,191	5,859	......	......	187	1,991	......	......	21·91	21·52	......	......	0·79	7·29
Chenango, ...	6,610	8,681	9,393	9,700	79	1,170	221	977	19·32	21·29	23·54	24·30	0·23	2·87	0,55	2·44
Clinton, ...	2,417	3,304	5,306	6,374	1,505	1,996	4,056	8,404	16·09	15·92	16·96	19·57	10·38	9·62	12·07	19·78
Columbia, ...	6,941	8,534	9,444	9,412	422	553	756	3,800	18·28	20·94	22·49	21·19	1·11	1·36	1·80	8·56
Cortland, ...	3,752	5,057	5,741	5,902	31	85	140	704	18·51	20·92	22·89	24·50	0 15	0·35	0·55	2·86
Delaware, ...	5,575	6,875	8,190	9,065	558	475	633	1,532	18·85	20·18	22·14	22·80	1·88	1·38	1·71	3·88
Dutchess, ...	8,957	10,611	12,149	12,498	495	960	1,507	6,861	19·16	20·93	22·04	20·60	1·06	1·89	2·72	11·31
Erie, ...	4,945	9,974	14,631	21,743	798	5,172	8,874	37,274	20·33	17·31	18·66	16·42	3·28	8·98	11·28	28·17
Essex, ...	3,158	4,157	5,286	5,652	363	625	1,551	2,994	19·73	20·08	21·06	19·79	2·27	3·02	6·14	10·49
Franklin, ...	1,575	2,083	3,356	4.462	451	1,009	2,054	3,739	19·74	16·65	17·95	17·50	5·65	8·04	10.98	10·75
Fulton, ...	....	....	4,203	5,066	......	......	208	1,559	......	......	22·62	21·96	......	......	1·12	6·69
Genesee, ...	8,170	11,808	6,509	6,477	164	978	627	4,107	19·47	20·15	22.55	20·87	0·41	1·67	2·17	13·21
Greene, ...	5,027	6,257	6,884	6,952	235	633	695	1,522	19·20	20·73	21·54	22·32	0·89	2·09	2·24	4·89
Hamilton,§.......	....	....	428	599	......	......	50	168	......	......	22·74	23·11	......	......	2·65	6·61
Herkimer, ...	6,190	7,699	8,552	8,578	270	1,024	797	3,955	18·73	21·28	22·85	22·23	0·82	2·82	2·13	10·09
Jefferson, ...	8,153	10,498	13,772	14,206	1,030	1,712	2,049	5,377	19·57	19·77	21·19	21·71	2·47	3·23	3·15	8·21
Kings, ...	2,039	5,107	12,896	32,627	850	3,414	13,998	65,536	13·21	15·93	16·39	15·07	5·79	10·65	17·79	30·29
Lewis, ...	2,248	3,161	4,287	5,284	160	604	1,011	2,751	19,27	19·64	21·20	20·94	1·37	3·76	5·00	10·90
Livingston, ...	4,694	6,486	7.300	8,136	310	544	713	4,329	19,67	20·86	21·99	21 44	1·97	1·78	2·15	11·41
Madison, ...	6,843	8,757	9,615	9,974	250	1,653	627	3,232	19,11	20·98	23·46	22·82	0·70	3·96	1·53	7·39
Monroe, ...	7,606	11,151	14,231	17.272	1,060	2,484	6,505	22,837	19,43	19·19	20·07	17·92	2·78	4·28	9·24	22·67
Montgomery, ...	8,821	9,932	6,592	6,786	276	1,285	594	2,688	21·59	20·53	22·23	21·99	0·67	2·65	2·04	8·72
New-York, ...	18.283	43,091	63.927	88,877	18,826	27,669	60,946	232,678	11·00	15·95	17·22	14·11	11·33	10·24	16·14	36·93
Niagara, ...	2,776	5,000	6,784	8,257	1,274	973	2,793	10,327	19·73	18·87	19·63	16·95	9·05	3·67	8,08	21·31
Oneida, ...	10.689	14,426	17,435	20,946	1,922	4,196	5,325	18,472	18·47	18·60	20·56	19·43	3·32	5·41	6·28	17·15
Onondaga, ...	9,452	12.409	15,812	16,933	364	1,323	2,133	13,549	19·51	20·37	22·53	19·56	0·78	2·17	3·04	15·64
Ontario, ...	7,373	8,334	9,405	9,147	275	697	1,169	4,757	19·70	20·39	22·07	21·43	0·73	1·71	2·73	11·14
Orange, ...	7.524	8,873	10,590	11,301	939	1,265	1,299	7,955	18·02	19·67	20·25	18·57	2·24	2·87	2·49	13·07
Orleans, ...	3.034	4,696	5,759	5,704	57	333	305	3,813	20·98	20·51	22·24	20·10	0·31	1·45	1·17	13·39
Oswego, ...	3.547	7,467	10 310	14.609	135	1,381	1,265	7,372	19·84	19·53	21·28	21·09	0·75	3·61	2·61	10·48
Otsego, ...	9,006	10,434	11,745	12,177	272	534	475	1,640	18·80	20·69	23·25	24·48	0·57	1·06	0·94	3·29
Putnam, ...	2,362	2,409	3,009	3,037	122	67	222	1.215	23·83	21·72	22·69	21·80	1·02	0·58	1·64	8·71
Queens, ...	3,838	4,797	6,168	8,187	131	636	1,356	8,618	18·87	19·88	19·37	17·68	0·64	2·53	4·26	18·65
Rensselaer, ...	8,586	11,019	13,437	14,933	570	2,081	2,608	14,921	19·48	19·85	21·55	18·85	1·29	3·74	4·18	18·93
Richmond, ...	1,112	1,476	2,608	3,795	48	294	753	5,078	18·73	19·19	19·08	17·74	0·81	3·83	5·51	23·74
Rockland, ...	1,713	2,076	2,772	3,580	17	280	1,039	3,457	21·37	21·41	20·17	18 34	0·21	2·89	7·56	17·72
St. Lawrence, ...	5.272	7.234	11 885	13,984	1,489	2,459	3,432	9,915	19·10	17·24	19·07	18·65	5·39	5·85	5·50	13·22
Saratoga, ...	7,140	8,011	9,582	10,377	308	861	860	5,748	19·39	21·07	23·34	21·02	0·85	2·26	2·07	11·64
Schenectady, ...	2,382	3,290	3,365	3.790	199	728	442	2,943	18·49	20·27	21·85	19·36	1·54	4·41	2·66	15·03
Schoharie, ...	4,890	5,781	7,053	7,376	70	101	141	874	18·86	20·28	21·71	22·00	0·29	3·54	0·44	2·67
Schuyler, ...	....	....	....	4,377	......	......	....	587	......	......	......	23·30	......	......	......	3·12
Seneca, ...	3,765	4,690	5,459	5,395	84	323	464	2,153	18·66	20·73	21·86	21·27	0·41	1·48	1·86	8·49
Steuben, ...	5,532	8,177	11,212	14,151	249	267	564	8,605	18·88	19·73	21·69	22·47	0·85	0·60	1·09	5·72
Suffolk, ...	4,623	6,034	7.767	7,939	44	225	740	3,083	19·51	21·34	22·47	18·40	0·14	0·12	2·14	7·53
Sullivan, ...	2.138	2,903	4.019	5.727	238	219	520	3,606	20·61	21·14	21·46	19·43	2·29	1·71	2·79	12·23
Tioga, ...	3,965	7,110	4.933	6,181	78	143	148	979	19·87	20·91	21·97	22·92	0·39	0·23	0·68	3·63
Tompkins, ...	6,308	7.809	8,668	7.456	73	256	334	1,160	19·17	20·54	22·80	23·63	0·22	0·19	0·87	3·68
Ulster, ...	6.119	8.313	10,546	13,097	213	659	1,529	9,487	19·11	20·80	21·13	18·68	0·66	0·53	3·06	13·95
Warren, ...	2.208	2,544	3,373	4,165	74	104	158	1,643	20·24	21·14	22·62	21·17	0·69	0·61	1·05	8·35
Washington, ...	7,532	8,181	9,203	9.355	620	924	1,042	4,822	19·20	20·80	22·69	21·06	1 57	1·57	2·56	10·86
Wayne, ...	5.110	7.496	9,348	10,205	324	684	1,023	4.767	19·09	19·83	21·98	21·81	1·21	0·85	2·41	10·19
Westchester, ...	6,252	7,772	9,858	14.245	496	1,047	2,491	16,741	18·87	20·04	20·08	17·65	1·49	1·22	5·24	20·75
Wyoming, ...	....	....	5,767	7,064	......	......	805	2,827	......	......	21·42	21·96	......	......	3·09	8·93
Yates, ...	2,623	3,894	4,822	4.474	53	165	157	942	19·85	19·61	23·21	21·57	0·40	0·83	0·75	4·60
Total, ...	296.132	422.034	539,379	652.322	40,430	82,319	153,717	632,746	18·31	19·77	20·71	19·18	2.44	3·83	7·52	18·54

* The popular vote for amending the constitution, by abrogating the property qualification for office, was—for the amendment, 114,900; against the amendment, 3,901.

In adopting the constitution of 1846, the question of extending an equal right of suffrage to free blacks was submitted to the popular vote and decided against, by a vote of 223,834 to 85,306.

The existing qualifications of voters are, to white males of the age of 21 years, citizenship at least 10 days, a residence in the State of one year, in the county of four months, and in the election district of thirty days. To persons of color, the possession of a freehold, worth $250 is also required. Persons convicted of bribery, larceny, or of any infamous crime, lose their right of voting until expressly restored by pardon of the governor, and those concerned in betting upon elections, lose their right of voting at such elections —*Constitution*, art. ii., sec. 1, 2.

In the schedules for obtaining this census, columns were provided for noting the native and naturalized voters and aliens, by a mark opposite the name. In condensing the returns, the age, sex and place of birth were assumed as correct, and entries inconsistent with these were corrected to agree with them. The following were the principal errors committed by the marshals:—1. Persons under age, or females, marked in column of voters. 2. Natives of United States marked as aliens or naturalized voters. 3. Natives of foreign countries marked as native voters. 4. The head of the family marked as alien, and his wife and minor children of foreign birth not marked. 5. The head of the family marked as naturalized, and his wife and minor children of foreign birth as alien. Of these, No. 1 were stricken from the list of voters; of No. 2, the aliens were stricken out, and the naturalized voters carried to the column of native voters; No. 3 were carried to the column of naturalized voters; No 4 were marked as all alien; and No. 5 were stricken from the column of aliens.

In other and less frequent cases, as that of children of citizens born in foreign countries, &c., such corrections were made as the definition of aliens and voters by existing statutes, appeared to warrant.

‡ In comparing the percentage of this class to the total population at different times, there will be observed an inequality and apparent inconsistency, which is not so much due to corresponding differences in number, as to imperfection of the returns, and the absence of system in reducing them to a general result. Judging from the original reports of the present census, there is no department of its inquiry in which there was more need of careful revision, or greater necessity for the application of uniform rules for its arrangement. By strictly applying the legal definitions to every case of manifest inconsistency and error, it is believed that the present census affords a very close approximation to the actual numbers of these classes at the date to which it refers.

§ Reported with Montgomery in 1825 and 1835.

Students: Students in colleges, academies or schools, when absent from the families to which they belonged, were in the present census directed to be enumerated as if at home; but if such students had no other home, they were to be counted as members of the family in which they boarded. Students belonging to families in this State, but attending school or college out of the State, were to be enumerated as if at home, but if residing out of the State and attending temporarily within it, they were not included. A separate return of the number attending common and private schools, academies and colleges, was not required in the present census, because the official reports made annually to the Superintendent of Public Instruction and to the Regents of the University, were deemed sufficient to afford these data. Former census returns have shown the following statistics under this head:

In 1840, universities and colleges, 12, students, 1,285; academies and grammar schools, 505, students, 34,715; primary and common schools, 10,593, scholars, 502,367; scholars at public charge, 27,075.

Educational Statistics of the Census of 1845.

Educational Institutions.	Number.	Cost of buildings.	Cost of other improvements.	Cost of real estate
Colleges,	10	$505,000	$119,350	$781,500
Academies,	163	743,104	110,040	137,814
Female Seminaries,	55	205,601	14,753	64,840
Other incorporated institutions,	22	420,800	22,555	191,720
Normal schools,	2	2,000	2,000	10,000
Common schools,	10,707	2,997,155	135,362	606,605
Private schools,	1,569	312,137	43,206	191,759

The number of pupils on the teachers' lists, in common schools, was 463,069, and the average attendance was 291,595. The number of children attending private and select schools was 44,783.

Educational Statistics of the Census of 1850.

EDUCATIONAL INSTITUTIONS.	Number.	Teachers.	Pupils.	ANNUAL INCOME.				
				Endowment	Taxation.	Public funds.	Other sources.	Total.
Colleges, New-York,	18	174	2, 673	$29, 567	....	$12, 855	$105, 836	$148, 258
" United States,	239	1, 678	27, 821	466, 614	$15, 485	194, 249	1, 288, 080	1, 964, 428
Public schools, New-York,	11, 580	13, 965	675, 221	20, 426	756, 693	564, 104	131, 434	1, 472, 657
" United States,	80, 978	91, 966	3, 354, 011	182, 594	4, 653, 816	2, 552, 402	2, 141, 450	9, 529, 542
Academies & priv. schools, New-York	887	3, 136	49, 328	23, 185	4, 812	46, 465	735, 870	810, 332
" " U. S.,	6, 085	12. 260	263, 096	288, 855	14, 202	115, 724	4, 225, 433	4, 644, 214

Number Attending School During the Year Previous to 1850.

	WHITES.			FREE COLORED.			TOTAL.		
	Males.	Females.	Total.	Males.	Females.	Total.	Native.	Foreign.	Aggregate.
State of New-York,	356, 602	331, 272	687, 894	2, 840	2, 607	5, 447	644, 087	49, 234	693, 321
United States,	2 146, 432	1, 916, 614	4, 063, 046	13, 864	12, 597	26, 461	3, 942, 087	147, 426	4, 089, 507

Professional Schools in New-York in 1850.

	Number.	Number of professors.	Number of students
Theological,	7	21	256
Medical,	4	31	692
Law,	1	3	50

In preparing the present census, an inquiry was instituted with the view of ascertaining the number of students from other States attending colleges in the State of New-York, and the number from New-York, attending in other States. Returns were received from 15 colleges and professional schools in New England, 16 in New-York, 3 in New Jersey, 8 in Pennsylvania, 37 in the Southern States, and 23 in the Western States, in all 102.* The following table exhibits the results of this inquiry in the principal colleges of the New England and other neighboring States, and the general aggregates of others. These numbers were in most cases derived from the published catalogues of the several colleges for the year ending in the summer of 1855. In medical schools, at which two courses of lectures are delivered during the year, the numbers of students attending the spring course of 1855, were taken.

* The American Almanac affords the following statistics of colleges in the United States since 1830, at intervals of five years. Medical and theological students were not included in the number, and only such colleges as gave the number of their undergraduates are embraced in the table:

Years.	Colleges.	Undergraduates.
1830,	35	3, 941
1835,	56	5, 548
1840,	88	9, 224
1845,	103	10, 038
1850,	118	10, 780
1855,	116	11, 731

Students in Colleges and Professional Schools of other States in 1854-5

COLLEGES AND PROFESSIONAL SCHOOLS.	Whole number of Students except in the preparatory departments.	Students in professional and scientific departments.		Undergraduates in college course.	
		From New-York	F'm other States.	From New-York.	F'm other States.
Bowdoin College, Maine,	245	....	66	1	176
Waterville College, Maine,	91	....	....	....	91
Dartmouth College, New Hampshire,	353	3	97	6	245
Middlebury College, Vermont,	80	....	....	12	66
University of Vermont, Vermont,	130	4	20	12	84
Vermont Medical College, Vermont,	44	3	40	....	....
Harvard University, Massachusetts,	661	19	288	24	313
Amherst College, Massachusetts,	254	3	14	39	197
Berkshire Medical College, Massachusetts,	44	11	32	....	....
Williams College, Massachusetts,	231	....	....	81	150
Brown's University, Rhode Island,	252	....	....	26	224
Yale College, Connecticut,	605	24	121	102	340
Trinity College, Connecticut,	77	....	....	13	62
Wesleyan University, Connecticut,	123	....	....	38	84
College of New Jersey, New Jersey,	247	....	....	32	210
Rutgers College, New Jersey,	109	....	....	40	65
Burlington College, New Jersey,	10	....	....	....	10
Pennsylvania College, Pennsylvania,	88	....	....	....	87
University of Pennsylvania, Pennsylvania,	567	8	451	....	89
University of Lewisburgh, Pennsylvania,	60	....	15	....	45
Jefferson College (Cannonsburgh), Pennsylvania,	182	....	....	....	180
" (med. dep., Phila.), Pennsylvania,	565	9	544	....	....
Alleghany College, Pennsylvania,	102	....	....	4	97
Lafayette College, Pennsylvania,	100	....	....	5	95
Dickinson College, Pennsylvania,	130	....	....	1	129
Thirty-seven colleges in Southern and South-Western States,*	4,850	7	1,381	9	3,355
Twenty-three colleges in Western States,†	2,089	‡36	822	§34	1,178

Students in Colleges in New-York, 1854-5.

COLLEGES AND PROFESSIONAL SCHOOLS.	Total number of students.	HOME RESIDENCES OF STUDENTS.					
		New-York.	New England.	New Jersey, Pa., and Delaware.	Southern & south-western States	Western States.	Foreign countries.
Albany Law School,	45	32	10	....	....	3	....
" Medical College,	91	62	15	2	4	4	4
Buffalo Medical College,	38	27	1	1	....	2	7
College of Physicians and Surgeons, New-York,	182	109	21	24	6	7	15
Columbia College, New-York,	167	154	....	10	3	....	....
Genesee College, Lima,	82	65	1	3	1	2	10
Hamilton College, Clinton,	158	136	2	4	5	10	1
Hobart Free College, Geneva,	98	83	1	4	....	8	2
Madison University, Hamilton,	159	88	22	13	4*	27	5
New-York Medical College,	116	62	22	1	15	6	10
New-York University,‖	80	65	....	....	....	....	....
" " Medical Department,	388	217	21	34	85	12	19
St. John's College, Fordham,	162	91	4	1	11	2	53
Union College, Schenectady,	300	217	31	26	11	12	3
University of Rochester,	116	93	6	4	2	7	4
Total,	2,182	1,501	157	127	147	102	133

Deaf and Dumb, Blind, Insane and Idiotic: Inquiries into the numbers of these unfortunate classes, with specifications of sex, age, and dependance upon public or private support, were made in the State censuses of 1825, 1835, and 1845, as well as in the national censuses of 1830, 1840 and 1850, extending, however, in the latter only to the whites, excepting in 1850, when the free colored class was included. In the present census, in addition to the usual inquiries, the cause of the infirmity, if known, was required to be noted, and the marshals were particularly directed to use the utmost care in procuring accurate intelligence on this point.¶

* Delaware College, in Del.; Mt. St. Mary's College, College of St. James, Washington College, Medical Dep. University of Maryland, in Maryland; Georgetown College and Columbia College in Dist. Columbia; Roanoke College, William and Mary's College, Richmond College; Randolph Macon College, Emory and Henry College, Virginia; Mil. Inst., Univ. of Virginia, and Prot. Episc. Sem., Fairfax co., in Virginia; Univ. of North Carolina, and Wake Forest College in N. C.; South Carolina College, and Med. Coll. of South Carolina, in S. C.; Franklin College, Oglethorpe University, Emory College, Mercer University and Medical College of Georgia, in Ga.; University of Alabama, in Al.; St. Peter's and St. Paul's College, and Centennary College of La.; Jackson's College, Cumberland University, Union University, Franklin College, and Univ. of Nashville, in Tennessee; Centre College, St. Joseph's College, Kentucky Mil. Inst.; Georgetown College, and Med. Dep. University of Louisville, in Kentucky.

† Ohio Wesleyan University, Marietta College, Kenyon College, Denison University, Wittenberg College, Ohio University, Miami University, Western Reserve College, Do. Med. Dep. Cleveland, Oberlin College, Antioch College, and Urbana University in Ohio; University of Michigan, in Michigan; Franklin College and Wabash College, in Ind.; Shurtleff College, Knox College, and Rush Med. Col., in Ill.; Beloit College, in Wis.; Missouri University, St. Louis Med. Col., and Concordia Coll. in Mo.

‡ Of these 26 were in the University of Michigan, 5 in Oberlin College, 3 in Western Reserve Med. College, and 2 in the Rush Med. College.

§ Of these 5 were in the University of Michigan, 22 in Oberlin College, 5 in Antioch College, and 2 in Concordia College.

‖ The number of students from different States not ascertained.

¶ The following instructions were given for obtaining the statistics of these classes:

"A person is to be noted as deaf and dumb who was born without the sense of hearing, and, consequently, has not acquired the use of speech, or who lost the sense of hearing before the faculty of speech had been acquired.

If a person is mute from disease, or any cause other than deafness from childhood, no entry is to be made in the schedules. In like manner, if a person has become deaf from age, or disease, no notice thereof should be made, unless the loss of hearing occurred in early childhood, as above stated; in which case, such person may be entered as deaf and dumb, and a note, referring to the margin or bottom of the page, may be made, stating the cause, if known. This fact, taken in connection with the age, would afford a knowledge as to whether such person is a proper subject of instruction, and entitled to the privileges of a special institution for the

From difficulties apparently inherent to our mode of taking the census, these returns exhibit less detail and reliability than is desirable, although they compare very nearly in results with those of other enumerations. It remains for future investigation to discover the influences of locality, elevation, salubrity, density of population, hereditary tendency and other causes, upon the development of these maladies, and the practicability of diminishing their prevalence by a modification of the causes.

The numerical proportion of these classes to the whole population, in different countries and at different times, has been made the subject of careful examination both by individual writers and in official reports.*

The following table exhibits the relative proportions of each of these classes in this State and in the United States, as given by the several censuses since 1825:

Number of the Total Population to each Person who is Deaf and Dumb, Blind, Insane, and Idiotic.

STATE OF NEW-YORK.	Deaf and Dumb.	Blind.	Insane.	Idiotic.
Census of 1825,	2,503	....	1,971	1,135
" 1835,	2,331	2,446	2,249	1,464
" 1840,	2,184	2,517	†1,036	†....
" 1845,	2,407	2,969	1,201	1,755
" 1850,	2,452	2,623	1,229	1,798
" 1855,	2,431	3,051	1,264	1,972
UNITED STATES—WHITES.				
Census of 1830,	1,965	2,652	....	....
" 1840,	2,124	2,825	969	*....
" 1850,	2,140	2,451	1,305	1,372

Instances occur in which a complication of maladies exists, leading to erroneous returns, as inability to speak from paralysis or idiocy, reported as deaf and dumb, and other cases in which a more careful inquiry would show that the malady was but partial, or acquired at an advanced age, and consequently not a proper subject of entry in the returns.‡

European statistics of the blind, show the greatest relative number of this class in cities, and the least in rural districts. The proportion to the whole population in different countries has been estimated as follows: in Ireland, 1 to 864; in the low flat portions of Belgium, Hanover, Saxony, Prussia, Lombardy and Denmark, 1 to 950; the more elevated portions of Saxony, Prussia and other German States, 1 to 1,340; in the mountainous parts of Switzerland and Sardinia, 1 to 1,500; and in Norway, 1 to 482.

The delicacy attending inquiries relating to the insane and idiotic, has hitherto prevented us from obtaining reliable statistics concerning them, particularly in large cities, where the proportion as reported is so very much below that of the rural districts, that it is impossible to ascribe the difference to any other cause than the entire omission of great numbers. Idiots have frequently been reported as deaf and dumb, being often mentioned in popular language as such, and the infinite degrees and varieties under which the infirmity appears, renders it impossible to decide in many cases, even when the facts are known, whether

---

education of deaf mutes. When deafness occurs in middle life or old age, it is like many other infirmities, a serious personal inconvenience, but does not generally disqualify a person from his accustomed employment, or render him sooner chargeable to the public, if poor.

If a person be blind, the fact should be written; and, if the cause is known, it should be stated in a note in the margin. Partial blindness, or a loss of of one eye only, should not be noted.

Insanity exists in every degree, from a slight aberration of mind on some particular subject to raving madness; and the marshals may find it difficult at times to decide whether or not a person should be classed with the insane. In general, if a person is reputed to be erratic on some particular subject, yet attends regularly to his business, and provides for his family, without evincing to an ordinary observer special symptoms of insanity, he should not be entered as insane. This subject is left to the discretion of the marshals, who, in most cases, will be able from the facts before them, to draw a just inference. If insane persons are in asylums, poor-houses or similar institutions, they should only be enumerated at such institutions, and not in the families to which they belong when at home.

Idiots should be, in like manner, enumerated in the place where they resided on the first day of June; whether in families, or in institutions devoted wholly or in part to their support.

In general, a person capable of self support, and the transaction of ordinary business, should not be classed with the idiotic, although his grade of intellect may be below the general average. In no case should dementia from old age be so entered, unless it has existed through life. It is a matter of especial interest to ascertain the number of the idiotic below the age of twelve years, as many of such are capable of a useful degree of education; and the marshals are requested to take especial care in enumerating all of this class, notwithstanding the delicacy attending inquiries of this kind. A proper discretion, and explanation of the objects of the inquiry, will generally secure the requisite information. If the cause of the infirmity be known, it may be entered in the margin.

In some cases it may be difficult to distinguish between a passive insanity, or dementia, and idiocy. In cases of doubt, the opinion of physicians should be consulted."—*Instructions*, p. 22.

* See a pamphlet on Statistics of the Deaf and Dumb, 1852, by Dr. H. P. Peet; also Compendium of U. S. Census, 1850, p. 113; Census of Ireland, 1851, Part III., p. 2, &c. Dr. Sauveur, in 1835, commenced an examination of the statistics of the deaf, dumb, and blind, which was published by the Belgian government in 1847. See "Bulletin de la Commission Centrale de Statisque," tome iii.

According to the best information that can be obtained, the proportion of deaf mutes to the whole population in Europe is as 1 to 1,593. The duchies of Luxembourg and Wurtemburg, and the kingdoms of Tuscany, Bavaria, Belgium, and Holland have the fewest, while Sardinia, Norway, and parts of Switzerland have the greatest proportion, the average being 1 to 2,209 in the former, and 1 in 642 in the latter. In Ireland, 1 in every 1,573 is born deaf and dumb. (Census of Ireland, 1851, Part III., pp. 8, 9.)

† The insane and idiotic were classed together in this census.

‡ In the following tables, 169 were returned in 1855 as "only deaf," 71 as "only dumb," 1 as "also blind and idiotic" 7 as "also idiotic," 2 as "also blind," and two cases of the deaf and dumb as "hereditary." Congenital deafness is said to be more prevalent in rural districts, and that acquired by accident or disease, in crowded cities and towns. The usual proportion of males and females among the deaf and dumb is 100 to 74·5.

persons should be returned as idiotic or insane, or neither.* Persons insane on a particular subject, yet managing their business, or feeble-minded to a degree approaching idiocy, yet capable of self support by their labor, were probably not reported by the majority of marshals in either of these censuses.

Comparative Numbers of the Deaf and Dumb, Blind, Insane, and Idiotic, in the several counties, as shown by different censuses.

COUNTIES.	DEAF AND DUMB					BLIND.				INSANE.					IDIOTIC.			
	1825.	1835.	1840.	1845.	1855	1835.	1840.	1845.	1855	1825.	1835.	†1840.	1845.	1855.	1825.	1835.	1845.	1855.
Albany,	24	27	11	36	18	25	15	26	25	20	42	17	40	46	44	45	54	46
Allegany,	8	21	8	17	18	12	11	14	11	5	10	20	8	20	22	38	14	46
Broome,	5	11	13	13	18	1	5	7	5	6	6	15	18	32	17	9	28	35
Cattaraugus,	7	19	18	13	21	7	9	17	16	6	9	31	16	31	4	18	21	26
Cayuga,	25	20	18	18	17	15	28	20	14	18	16	57	36	39	68	53	52	45
Chautauque,	8	15	16	11	14	9	23	12	11	2	17	51	26	21	19	22	30	38
Chemung,	.....	.....	1	6	8	......	4	6	5	......	......	13	14	11	......	......	11	11
Chenango,	6	16	7	17	17	7	6	22	19	10	19	50	33	34	33	37	34	46
Clinton,	12	17	12	5	20	17	7	6	18	6	10	4	9	18	12	11	19	28
Columbia,	12	17	19	17	20	20	15	12	11	18	61	106	60	34	53	34	35	28
Cortland,	4	12	3	5	7	4	7	8	13	5	10	27	16	25	15	23	19	34
Delaware,	11	19	17	14	18	26	23	12	6	12	18	50	16	29	38	34	29	25
Dutchess,	8	16	7	10	19	26	4	14	15	22	22	57	39	43	49	33	30	17
Erie,	9	11	19	18	35	13	24	24	32	9	15	45	62	66	13	32	33	43
Essex,	4	7	11	12	7	8	7	7	10	1	10	34	21	15	11	20	12	21
Franklin,	5	8	5	12	15	8	5	7	15	6	10	11	5	17	5	9	12	20
Fulton,	.....	.....	10	12	12	......	15	11	10	......	......	18	18	20	......	......	17	20
Genesee,	17	22	31	11	16	14	16	7	9	12	20	44	10	30	29	29	24	35
Greene,	15	10	13	13	11	20	5	17	8	15	26	29	18	27	34	30	25	27
Hamilton,	.....	.....	2	2	......	......	......	......	......	......	......	......	1	1	......	......	2	4
Herkimer,	12	14	45	14	21	11	36	20	26	15	29	79	27	37	48	35	26	36
Jefferson,	18	33	28	28	41	15	16	18	28	13	25	52	32	62	31	29	56	66
Kings,	.....	8	9	15	45	8	11	27	44	6	3	35	49	16	4	7	14	27
Lewis,	5	5	9	11	8	9	21	9	7	6	6	32	10	21	9	4	21	36
Livingston,	6	9	12	16	13	12	34	15	9	5	14	45	9	14	17	19	25	13
Madison,	12	15	16	23	27	14	19	16	18	15	14	56	36	43	23	15	35	41
Monroe,	8	24	28	25	27	26	52	37	30	8	9	46	33	56	23	29	45	30
Montgomery,	55	47	33	37	26	23	8	17	14	38	17	34	20	14	77	63	27	21
New-York,	56	177	250	254	411	106	144	80	316	193	176	201	539	655	46	34	47	52
Niagara,	5	7	13	7	11	9	3	5	14	2	4	19	12	25	13	15	19	24
Oneida,	19	33	26	30	48	41	47	29	42	17	38	121	327	‡517	46	48	50	56
Onondaga,	14	21	20	18	24	26	30	32	28	18	20	72	33	22	29	43	39	40
Ontario,	16	8	16	13	21	19	21	14	10	17	10	46	11	26	36	37	30	32
Orange,	17	26	17	14	18	25	20	17	14	32	43	54	29	42	47	27	38	36
Orleans,	8	9	10	6	13	5	8	11	4	2	6	26	4	10	8	15	28	11
Oswego,	1	20	20	25	33	12	8	13	24	11	10	8	21	41	9	28	32	62
Otsego,	26	30	35	21	24	19	17	20	18	24	36	77	48	54	46	27	62	60
Putnam,	2	6	......	3	5	5	1	3	2	4	6	16	6	5	9	18	12	13
Queens,	9	15	10	10	21	17	8	1	9	12	6	32	35	46	13	20	19	8
Rensselaer,	13	19	17	17	19	25	10	19	13	30	30	40	38	42	26	28	30	32
Richmond,	.....	.....	1	1	3	6	14	7	12	2	5	1	11	12	4	8	4	2
Rockland,	.....	5	18	5	7	9	4	3	2	......	2	4	5	7	9	7	9	16
St. Lawrence,	10	16	24	25	26	19	17	24	23	12	16	48	27	39	21	25	46	51
Saratoga,	13	12	23	12	18	19	26	23	13	23	18	52	38	35	41	35	45	43
Schenectady,	4	17	7	12	7	15	2	8	8	9	6	8	6	8	7	21	15	16
Schoharie,	14	11	11	16	9	11	5	19	9	10	12	21	17	7	31	25	32	19
Schuyler,	.....	.....	......	......	4	......	......	......	4	......	......	......	......	10	......	......	......	24
Seneca,	4	5	6	3	5	7	8	8	8	6	9	18	18	19	12	16	16	18
Steuben,	14	20	19	20	21	12	13	14	7	12	22	26	16	28	26	44	28	29
Suffolk,	7	18	19	12	12	14	18	11	6	13	24	38	29	26	21	32	22	13
Sullivan,	1	2	3	3	8	3	7	7	7	1	3	19	6	11	12	11	23	20
Tioga,	2	8	11	12	11	4	23	6	13	6	11	32	14	16	22	20	19	13
Tompkins,	17	16	9	12	6	14	8	1	5	10	13	38	18	28	21	27	29	43
Ulster,	19	25	13	21	26	18	12	29	21	16	19	32	33	23	41	47	49	28
Warren,	4	7	3	4	9	4	1	3	1	1	4	4	15	10	6	2	14	12
Washington,	25	20	12	20	22	25	16	15	12	35	39	70	50	44	48	36	24	44
Wayne,	23	41	39	31	21	19	24	17	15	6	12	61	26	22	16	21	22	36
Westchester,	4	7	30	9	14	18	18	15	20	26	10	83	23	56	40	28	29	41
Wyoming,	.....	.....	......	7	17	......	......	5	11	......	......	......	15	21	......	......	16	30
Yates,	2	9	9	8	9	13	6	5	16	......	9	15	16	13	17	21	23	23
Total,	645	933	1,112	1,082	1,422	889	965	877	1,136	819	967	2,340	2,168	2,742	1,421	1,484	1,620	1,812

Owners of Land: This class was defined to include those holding land by deed, contract, or perpetual lease. The number thus reported was 361,013, or 10·41 per cent of the total population. There are no previous returns in this State which afford data for comparison.

* The Irish census of 1851, gave in that country the proportion of 1 lunatic to every 1,291 inhabitants, and 1 idiot to every 1,336 of the whole population. Of the former there were 100 males to 102·72 females, and of the latter, 100 males to 84·62 females.

† Including the idiotic.

‡ The New-York State Lunatic Asylum at Utica reported 472 patients, and 103 other persons, including the superintendent and his family. Of the former 246 were males, and 226 females. The ages of the male patients were as follows: Under 20, 6; between 20 and 30, 63; between 30 and 40, 68; between 40 and 50, 43; between 50 and 60, 27; over 60, 12; unknown, 27. The ages of the female patients were: Under 20, 6; between 20 and 30, 67; between 30 and 40, 61; between 40 and 50, 44; between 50 and 60, 30; over 60, 11; unknown, 7.

Table showing the Numbers living in New-York in 1855 *of each Sex over Twenty-one Years of Age who cannot Read and Write, with their Place of Birth.*

COUNTIES.	NATIVE COUNTRIES. United States.		England.		Scotland.		Ireland.		France.		Germany.		Switzerland.		Other European countries.		Canada.		Total number over 21 who cannot read or write.		Total number over 21 who can read but not write.	
	Male.	Fem.	Male.	Fem.	Male.	Fem.	Male.	Fem.	Male.	Fem.	Male.	Fem.	Male	Fem	Male	Fem.	Male.	Fem.	Male.	Fem.	Male.	Fem.
Albany,	228	200	30	23	5	5	935	1,531	11	1	32	32	....	....	7	7	95	89	1,343	1,888	566	1,399
Allegany,	142	93	9	3	....	....	143	135	....	....	1	4	1	....	....	....	4	1	300	236	96	98
Broome,	125	80	4	2	2	....	190	202	....	....	3	2	....	....	1	....	....	....	325	286	100	123
Cattaraugus,	99	54	11	....	....	....	149	167	3	1	3	3	....	....	....	....	3	3	268	228	90	97
Cayuga,	198	98	27	13	4	1	214	219	1	1	23	7	2	3	8	6	39	26	516	374	271	235
Chautauque,	97	57	30	18	....	....	186	260	2	....	18	26	1	....	13	23	12	6	359	390	115	177
Chemung,	146	76	6	1	....	1	174	248	1	2	10	7	2	....	....	....	1	....	340	335	95	136
Chenango,	97	66	6	1	....	....	45	54	1	....	1	1	....	....	....	....	1	....	151	122	40	57
Clinton,	291	157	30	13	1	3	433	428	6	....	7	....	....	....	1	1	1,768	1,310	2,537	1,912	222	255
Columbia,	370	306	10	2	1	....	174	181	....	....	4	1	....	....	9	3	6	2	574	495	190	330
Cortland,	81	55	5	1	....	....	50	52	....	....	....	....	....	....	....	....	1	....	137	108	40	55
Delaware,	156	69	1	....	1	1	24	29	....	....	1	....	....	....	....	....	....	1	183	100	93	126
Dutchess,	459	420	20	15	2	2	283	347	1	....	6	4	....	....	4	....	3	1	778	789	423	559
Erie,	142	80	60	30	4	3	500	850	42	52	161	210	1	8	40	40	59	33	1,008	1,307	493	1,093
Essex,	89	45	10	5	3	1	159	130	3	....	1	....	....	....	2	....	447	259	714	440	120	125
Franklin,	61	30	10	3	1	2	186	143	2	....	....	....	....	....	....	....	492	393	752	571	73	99
Fulton,	219	146	8	5	1	....	50	61	1	1	16	17	1	....	....	....	3	2	299	232	118	213
Genesee,	36	17	37	12	....	....	169	148	2	....	3	2	....	....	....	1	5	4	250	186	65	89
Greene,	213	149	1	1	....	....	77	65	....	....	4	3	....	....	....	1	1	1	296	220	130	76
Hamilton,	26	10	....	1	....	....	7	3	1	....	....	....	....	....	2	....	3	....	39	14	18	19
Herkimer,	156	132	13	3	....	....	141	129	1	....	18	10	....	....	....	....	4	1	333	275	99	135
Jefferson,	140	70	31	11	1	....	163	162	13	18	5	5	....	....	2	1	217	152	572	419	141	240
Kings,	438	525	60	64	9	10	2,304	4,645	25	33	287	462	1	1	22	21	11	6	3,157	5,767	1,420	4,123
Lewis,	89	42	22	11	....	....	191	204	37	34	23	16	4	1	2	....	26	20	328	394	124	231
Livingston,	57	41	10	7	....	1	121	128	....	....	2	3	....	....	1	1	3	1	194	182	71	128
Madison,	194	108	72	28	2	2	202	190	3	....	12	9	1	....	4	2	10	9	500	348	166	216
Monroe,	90	61	53	29	4	1	800	753	6	3	63	70	3	8	23	20	66	52	1,108	997	374	660
Montgomery,	199	200	8	5	....	1	84	88	1	1	19	14	....	....	2	1	1	1	314	311	97	217
New-York,	1,108	955	97	162	20	41	6,383	14,995	43	56	597	856	3	6	260	223	25	28	8,536	17,322	4,229	10,063
Niagara,	82	40	54	21	....	1	328	328	4	2	24	32	2	1	1	1	35	20	530	446	213	315
Oneida,	310	240	180	130	4	2	975	880	22	20	120	104	4	2	12	3	32	22	1,659	1,403	567	952
Onondaga,*	233	134	91	34	5	3	678	668	12	5	54	54	2	1	4	6	43	40	1,163	987	331	498
Ontario,	126	66	40	18	....	....	148	160	....	2	2	2	1	....	1	1	2	1	320	250	109	153
Orange,	342	276	3	6	....	....	286	288	2	18	14	1	1	3	....	....	1	....	649	592	245	281
Orleans,	25	13	85	53	....	1	354	179	1	....	8	5	1	....	2	....	6	3	482	254	57	65
Oswego,	226	131	46	17	....	3	454	479	23	28	6	1	1	1	4	....	217	141	977	801	255	393
Otsego,	272	161	23	17	....	....	39	48	....	1	2	....	....	....	....	....	4	2	340	229	126	208
Putnam,	129	100	...	2	....	....	82	108	1	....	2	....	....	....	....	....	1	....	215	210	54	106
Queens,	432	351	11	7	1	4	314	414	1	1	24	21	....	....	3	1	1	2	787	801	282	525
Rensselaer,	275	240	33	30	4	1	932	1,257	5	4	37	34	1	....	4	4	113	106	1,404	1,676	562	990
Richmond,	83	33	2	....	1	...	55	68	....	....	1	....	1	1	....	....	....	....	143	102	47	76
Rockland,	252	177	5	4	....	....	280	235	....	....	12	9	....	....	1	2	2	1	552	428	101	187
St. Lawrence,	203	143	70	26	5	6	452	427	11	4	1	1	....	....	2	1	533	387	1,277	995	246	344
Saratoga,	179	125	18	12	2	2	398	480	....	....	3	2	....	....	1	1	28	20	629	642	181	271
Schenectady,	79	67	4	1	....	....	43	60	1	2	5	5	1	....	2	....	....	....	133	136	86	147
Schoharie,	326	220	2	2	....	1	24	16	....	....	4	3	1	....	....	....	2	....	359	242	148	279
Schuyler,	88	57	10	6	1	....	26	30	....	....	....	....	....	....	....	....	....	1	125	94	79	110
Seneca,	37	40	5	1	....	1	133	138	....	....	7	1	....	....	....	1	1	....	183	182	76	102
Steuben,	258	150	7	3	....	....	188	220	2	....	14	15	....	....	3	5	2	3	474	396	195	248
Suffolk,	171	136	14	3	....	....	160	175	....	....	4	3	....	....	8	5	2	....	359	322	69	127
Sullivan,	198	110	4	2	....	....	142	152	2	....	11	24	2	1	....	1	3	3	362	293	161	221
Tioga,	193	89	3	1	....	....	68	72	3	2	2	1	....	....	....	....	2	....	271	165	85	103
Tompkins,	124	62	11	6	1	....	23	44	....	....	....	....	....	....	....	....	....	....	159	112	36	62
Ulster,	789	547	17	13	1	....	784	686	2	1	77	69	....	....	3	3	4	1	1,677	1,320	360	558
Warren,	92	47	3	....	....	....	87	64	....	....	1	1	....	....	....	....	36	17	219	129	31	36
Washington,	123	63	8	4	....	....	306	273	....	....	1	....	....	....	....	....	155	97	593	437	211	309
Wayne,	144	76	50	24	....	....	184	138	2	1	10	12	1	....	10	8	5	3	406	262	132	172
Westchester,	472	344	32	17	4	1	1,031	1,160	2	2	29	26	....	....	8	....	2	....	1,580	1,550	518	886
Wyoming,	48	34	5	6	1	....	67	75	3	....	10	12	....	....	....	1	3	1	137	129	47	67
Yates,	71	53	9	5	....	1	66	71	....	1	....	....	....	....	1	2	....	1	147	134	48	68
Total,	12 128	8667	1526	949	91	102	23,644	35.941	305	297	1.805	2,202	39	37	473	397	4,541	3,272	44,522	51.967	15.737	30,332

* Nativities of 83 of those who cannot read and write not given.

Adults who cannot Read and Write: The censuses of 1840, 1850, and 1855, give the following results under this head:

	1840.		1850.		1855.
	New-York	United States	New-York.	United States.	New-York.
Whites over 20 who cannot read and write,	44,452	549,693	91,293	962,898	....
Percentage to total white population	1.87	3.87	2.99	4.92	....
do to whites over 20 years of age,	3.83	8.53	5.66	10.93	....
White males over 20 who cannot read and write,	....	....	39,178	389,664	....
White females over 20 who cannot read and write,	....	....	52,115	573,234	....
Colored males over 20 who cannot read and write,	....	....	3,387	40,722	....
Colored females over 20 who cannot read and write,	....	....	4,042	49,800	....
Persons of all classes over 21 who cannot read and write,	....	....	....	....	*96,489
Percentage to total population	....	....	....	....	2.78
do to total population, over 21 years,	....	....	....	....	4.95
Males,	....	....	....	....	44,491
Females,	....	....	....	....	51,925
Persons over 21 who can read but not write,	....	....	....	....	46,070
Percentage to total population,	....	....	....	....	1.33
do to total population over 21 years,	....	....	....	....	2.39
Of native birth over 20 who cannot read and write,	....	....	30,670	858,306	....
Percentage to total illiterate,	....	....	31.07	89.13	....
Of foreign birth over 20 who cannot read and write,	....	....	68,052	195,114	....
Percentage to total illiterate,	....	....	68.93	10.87	....
Of native birth over 21 who cannot read and write,	....	....	....	....	20,795
Percentage to total illiterate,	....	....	....	....	21.55
Of foreign birth over 21 who cannot read and write,	....	....	....	....	75,694
Percentage to total illiterate,	....	....	....	....	78.45

Marriages: The ages of the parties, and the time and place of each marriage that occurred within the State during the year preceding June 1, 1855, were required to be returned in the present census. Marriages within the State, of parties not residing therein, were not reported. In reducing these details to the tabular form given on page 200, 201, 202, all marriages occurring in a different county from that where the parties answering the inquiry resided, were transferred to those counties where the marriage was held, and all marriages out of the State by parties living within it, (as occasionally returned) were omitted.

The impracticability of obtaining reliable statistics on this subject by the census, is quite as apparent as in that of deaths. While the number of marriages during the year in New-York city is returned as only 2,852, the official report of the city inspector for the corresponding months, gave the number as 5,308. In rural districts, the number will often be found very nearly equal to the true number, but probably in no instance, was an accurate return of a county made. An act enforcing the immediate report of every marriage to some proper local officer, by the persons legally authorized to officiate, appears to offer the only means of attaining valuable statistics on this subject.

Deaths during the year ending June 1, 1855: The marshals were charged in taking this census, to ascertain and report the number of deaths that had occurred in their several districts during the preceding year with the age, sex, color, civil condition, month in which the death occurred, (specifying the day of the month, if by an epidemic,) native country, and trade or occupation of the deceased, with the disease or cause of death. In pursuance of this requirement 46,434 deaths were reported.

From difficulties necessarily attending the plan of taking a census, in which the inquiries are seldom made professional men, and often answered by persons who know little or nothing of the cause, and often less of the time of death, age, and other circumstances of the deceased, the returns of these statistics, particularly from cities, where no official registration is maintained, are found to possess little or no value as showing the absolute number dying. They may, however, afford an approximate knowledge of the relative number of deaths from different causes, and a comparative means of judging the extent and prevalence of epidemics, and the peculiar influences of localities in modifying the action of disease.

It is only by means of a careful system of registration that we can expect to arrive at precise statistics of mortality, and it is earnestly hoped that the example of other States will be followed by New-York, and that the existing but neglected statutes on the registration of births, deaths, and marriages, will be so modified as to extend to the whole State the system now in operation in New-York city.

In classifying these returns, it was deemed inexpedient to give that minuteness of specification with which a portion of them were made, for the reason, that the greater number of marshals employed generic terms to denote the cause of death; as for example, the term "cancer," to express that which some specified by naming the tissue or organ affected, and using the various technical terms by which the varieties of this disease are known. A considerable number of deaths must occur, in which the cause is unknown. In many instances, from the absence of professional opinion, the removal of friends, and other causes, the persons furnishing the general information were unable to give all the required details. The list of cases in which the cause of death was unknown, has been somewhat increased, by neglecting a few slight and trivial diseases given as a cause of death, and a small number in which the terms used were unintelligible.

* Of 70 of these the sex was not reported, which explains the discrepancy between this number and the sum of those in the following table.

A comparison of the following tables with those of the mortality statistics of the United States Census of 1850, shows that the number of deaths reported by the latter was 1 to every 67.9 of the living, or 1.47 per cent of the whole population, while in the present census it is 1 to 74.4, or 1.34 per cent. Both of these ratios are undoubtedly too low. The registration reports of Belgium from 1841 to 1850, inclusive, containing the statistics of 1,057,262 deaths, give a ratio for the whole period, of 1 death to every 40.6 living, or 2.45 per cent; those of England from 1838 to 1850, inclusive, give the mean annual ratio of mortality, as 2.3 per cent, and other European countries for shorter periods in still greater proportions. From difference of climate, social condition, and other circumstances, the relative mortality of this country might be supposed to vary from that of Europe, but no analogy would justify the inference that the actual difference is as great as these returns appear to indicate. The near agreement of the results of the Federal and State censuses, affords additional ground for the belief, that accuracy in regard to mortality statistics is not attainable by the methods used in obtaining a census, or by any other than that above suggested.*

The classification commonly used in English and American registration reports,† has been followed

* A comparison of the statistics of deaths in New-York city, obtained by this census with the official returns of the city inspector, will amply confirm the above statement. The number of deaths from all causes annually since 1803 therein reported, were as follows:

YEARS.	City reports.	YEARS.	City reports.	Census.	YEARS.	City reports.	Census.	YEARS.	City reports.	Census.
1804, ...	2,125	1817, ...	2,527	....	1830, ...	5,537	....	1843, ...	8,693	....
1805, ...	2,344	1818, ...	3,265	....	1831, ...	6,363	....	1844, ...	8,875	....
1806, ...	2,235	1819, ...	3,176	....	1832, ...	10,359	....	1845, ...	10,948	6,293
1807, ...	2,312	1820, ...	3,515	....	1833, ...	5,746	....	1846, ...	11,318	....
1808, ...	2,014	1821, ...	3,542	....	1834, ...	9,082	....	1847, ...	15,778	....
1809, ...	2,108	1822, ...	3,231	....	1835, ...	7,082	5,925	1848, ...	15,919	....
1810, ...	2,167	1823, ...	3,444	....	1836, ...	8,009	....	1849, ...	23,783	....
1811, ...	2,524	1824, ...	4,341	....	1837, ...	8,732	....	1850, ...	16,978	11,883
1812, ...	2,553	1825, ...	5,018	3,239	1838, ...	8,053	....	1851, ...	22,024	....
1813, ...	2,283	1826, ...	4,973	....	1839, ...	7,953	....	1852, ...	21,601	....
1814, ...	1,977	1827, ...	5,181	....	1840, ...	8,474	....	1853, ...	22,702	....
1815, ...	2,507	1828, ...	5,181	....	1841, ...	9,115	....	1854, ...	28,568	....
1816, ...	2,739	1829, ...	5,094	....	1842, ...	9,176	....	1855, ...	23,042	11,022

† A brief enumeration of the reputed causes of death, and a list of the synonyms under which they were reported, will assist the reader in understanding the following tables:

By this arrangement, all diseases are divided into ZYMOTIC, or those supposed to depend upon a specific cause, whether endemic, epidemic, or contagious; and SPORADIC, or those spontaneously occurring, independent of local, transmitted, or prevailing influences. These are subdivided into classes, depending upon the character of disease, or the organs affected. In the following classification, all after the first class are of the Sporadic division, and the list of diseases or causes under each, is accompanied by an enumeration of the synonyms under which they were reported, and such remarks as appeared necessary to a full understanding of the subject.

CLASS I.—ZYMOTIC DISEASES.

Cholera.—Asiatic cholera, malignant cholera, cholera asphyxia, epidemic cholera.
Cholera infantum.
Cholera morbus.
Croup.—Cynanche maligna, cynanche trachealis, hives, diptheritic croup, angina trachealis, angina membranacea, membranous croup. It is placed in this class because other reports have so arranged it, although properly not a zymotic disease.
Diarrhœa.—Flux of the bowels, summer complaint, chronic diarrhœa.
Dysentery.—Camp distemper, bloody dysentery, chronic dysentery, malignant dysentery.
Epidemic, not otherwise specified.
Erysipelas.—Malignant erysipelas, erysipelas gangrenosum.
Fever, not otherwise specified, with continued fever, synochal fever, &c.
Bilious fever.
Intermittent fever.—Fever and ague.
Remittent fever.—Bilious remittent fever, &c.
Typhus fever.—Typhoid fever, congestive fever, low fever, nervous fever, ship fever, &c.
Yellow fever.—The few cases reported under this name are of doubtful character.
Hooping cough.—Chin cough.
Hydrophobia.
Influenza.
Measles.—Rubeola, rubeola maligna.
Mumps.—Parotitis.
Purulent Infection —Purulent cellulitis.
Scald Head.—Tinea capitis.
Scarlet Fever.—Scarlatina, scarlatina maligna, scarlet rash.
Small Pox.—Variola.
Syphilis.—Hereditary syphilis, venereal disease.
Thrush.—Spruc.

CLASS II.—DISEASES OF UNCERTAIN OR VARIABLE SEAT.

Abscess.
Atrophy.
Boils.
Cancers, of every locality. Carcinoma, schirrus, fungus hæmatoides, medullary sarcoma, &c.
Debility.—Weakness, decay, decline, exhaustion, inanition, asthenia, exhaustion of vital power, general debility, general weakness, &c.
Dropsy, of every locality excepting the brain and heart.—Anasarca, hydrothorax, ascites, &c.
Fistula.
Gangrene.—Mortification.
Gout.
Hæmorrhage, from every cause not otherwise specified.
Inflammation, not otherwise specified.
Malformation.—Cyanosis, spina bifida, &c.
Marasmus.—Tabes mesenterica, consumption of bowels.
Rickets.
Scrofula.—Scrofulous cachexy.
Tumor, of every kind and seat not otherwise specified
Ulcer, of every locality and variety.—Phagedenic ulcers.

CLASS III.—DISEASES OF THE BRAIN AND NERVOUS SYSTEM.

Amaurosis.
Apoplexy.—Bursting of blood vessels.
Disease of Brain, not otherwise specified
Congestion of Brain.
Dropsy of Brain.—Hydrocephalus, water on brain, St. Vitus's dance.
Inflammation of Brain.—Meningitis, cerebritis, arachnitis.
Chorœa.—St. Vitus's dance.
Convulsions.—Spasms, cramps, fits.
Delirium tremens.—Mania a potu.
Epilepsy.—Falling sickness.
Insanity.—Lunacy.
Nervous Diseases.—Neuralgia, nervous debility.
Paralysis.—Hemiplegia, paraplegia, palsy, numb palsy, lead palsy, general paralysis.
Sun stroke.—Coup de soleil
Tetanus.—Lock-jaw, trismus neonatorum.

CLASS IV.—DISEASES OF THE RESPIRATORY ORGANS.

Asthma.—Phthisic.
Bronchitis.—Chronic bronchitis, capillary bronchitis.
Catarrh.
Consumption.—Phthisis, phthisis pulmonalis, pulmonary consumption, tuberculosis, quick consumption, &c.
Laryngitis.
Congestion of Lungs.
Hæmorrhage from lungs.—Bleeding at lungs
Inflammation of lungs.—Pulmonitis, pneumonia, peripneumonia.
Pleurisy.—Pleuritis.
Quinsey.
Trachitis.

CLASS V.—DISEASES OF THE CIRCULATIVE ORGANS.

Anæmia.
Aneurism.
Angina pectoris.
Disease of Heart, not otherwise specified.
Dropsy of heart.

employed in the ensuing tables, with such modifications as seemed necessary to adapt it to the condensed summary which the returns rendered expedient.

The following table exhibits the percentage of deaths at the several ages and in different seasons:

Ages and Seasons.	Males.	Females.	Total.
Under five years, ...	19.17	16.55	35.72
Five years and under fifteen,...............	4.43	3.94	8.37
Fifteen years and under forty-five,.........	14.79	14.05	28.84
Forty-five years and upwards,..............	13.95	10.45	24.40
Age unknown, ...	1.69	0.98	2.67
Spring, ...	.....	.....	27.5
Summer,..................................	.....	.....	27.6
Autumn,..................................	.....	.....	22.7
Winter, ...	.....	.....	22.2

The number and percentage of deaths ascribed to the several classes of causes, were as follows:

Classes	Number.	Percentage.	Classes.	Number.	Percentage.
Zymotic diseases,....................	14,373	30.93	Diseases of generative organs,......	437	0.94
Diseases of uncertain or variable seat,	3,164	6.81	Diseases of locomotive organs, ...	314	0.69
Diseases of brain and nervous system,	5,572	11.99	Diseases of integumentive organs ..	4	0.08
Diseases of respiratory organs, ...	10,846	23.36	Old age, ...	1,486	3.20
Diseases of circulative organs,......	1,003	2.15	External causes,....................	2,135	4.59
Diseases of digestive organs, ...	2,237	4.82	Premature birth,....................	329	0.71
Diseases of urinary organs,..........	262	0.56	Unknown, ...	3,813	8.21

Agricultural Statistics.—The earliest attempt to collect the agricultural statistics of New-York, was made in 1821. The number of acres of improved land, and the number of neat cattle, horses and sheep were then returned, together with a few branches of manufactures that will be hereafter noticed. In 1825 and 1835 the same inquiries, with the addition of swine to the list of domestic animals, were required.

Enlargement of heart.
Inflammation of heart.—Carditis, endocarditis, pericarditis.
Hydræmia.
Phlebitis.

CLASS VI.—DISEASES OF THE DIGESTIVE ORGANS.

Inflammation of Bowels.—Enteritis, muco-enteritis, peritonitis.
Intussusception of Bowels.
Perforation of Bowels.
Stricture of Bowels.
Colic.—Bilious colic.
Colic.—Painters' colic.
Constipation.
Dyspepsia.—Indigestion.
Gastritis.—Inflammation of stomach.
Hæmorrhoids.—Piles.
Hernia.—of every variety.
Jaundice.—Black jaundice, yellow jaundice.
Liver Disease of, not otherwise specified.—Liver complaint.
Cirrhosis of liver.
Congestion of liver.
Hypertrophy of liver.
Inflammation of liver.
Hypertrophy of Spleen.
Inflammation of Spleen.
Starvation.
Disease of Stomach.—Softening of stomach, hœmatemesis, &c.
Teething.—Dentition, irritation from teething, &c.
Disease of Throat.—Sore throat and other diseases not otherwise specified.
Worms.

CLASS VII.—DISEASES OF THE URINARY ORGANS.

Albuminaria.—Bright's disease, morbus Brightii, granular disease of kidneys.
Cystitis.—Inflammation of bladder.
Diabetes.
Gravel.—Stone.
Infiltration of Urine.
Disease of Kidney not otherwise specified.
Inflammation of Kidney.
Rupture of Bladder.
Strangury.
Stricture.

CLASS VIII.—DISEASES OF THE GENERATIVE ORGANS AND CHILD BIRTH.

Amenorrhœa.
Child Birth.
Chlorosis.
Leucorrhœa.
Menorrhagia.
Miscarriage.—Abortion.
Ovarian Disease.
Phlegmasia Dolens.—Milk Leg.
Puerperal Fever.—Childbed fever, puerperal peritonitis.
Uterine Disease.—Uteritis.
Uterine Hemorrhage.—Flooding.

CLASS IX.—DISEASES OF THE LOCOMOTIVE ORGANS AND OSSEOUS SYSTEM.

Disease of bone, caries, necrosis, caries of vertebræ, fever sore, softening of bones, &c.
Dry Gangrene.—Gangrena senilis. Mortification of feet.
Hip Disease.—Coxalgia, sciatica, &c.
Rheumatism.
Spinal Disease.
Synovitis.—Chronic synovitis.

CLASS X.—DISEASES OF THE INTEGUMENTARY SYSTEM.

Carbuncles.
Eruption, not otherwise specified.

CLASS XI.—OLD AGE.

CLASS XII.—EXTERNAL CAUSES.

Accident, of every kind not otherwise specified.
Asphyxia, from every cause not otherwise specified.
Burned.
Camphene accident.
Cold.
Crushed.
Drinking cold water.
Drowned.
Executed.
Exposure.
Falls.
Fright.
Frozen.
Grief.
Intemperance.
Lightning.
Murder, homicide, &c.
Neglect.
Overheated.
Poison of every kind except in suicide.
Railroad accidents of every kind.
Scalded.
Smothered, suffocated
Strangled.
Suicide, of every variety.

CLASS XIII.—PREMATURE BIRTH AND STILL BORN.

In 1840, the number of horses, mules, cattle, sheep and swine, and the value of poultry were ascertained. The number of bushels of wheat, barley, oats, rye, buckwheat and corn, the pounds of wool, hops, and wax, the bushels of potatoes, the tons of hay and of hemp and flax, the pounds of sugar made, and cords of wood sold, the value of the products of the dairy, orchard, and market garden, the gallons of wine made, and the number of men employed, and capital invested in nurseries, were also ascertained.

In 1845, to the above inquiries in reference to live stock and amount of product of the cereal grains and root crops, was added the amount of land devoted to each separate crop. The censuses of 1850 and 1855 adopted similar inquiries, in addition to which, the latter provided for the return of unenumerated articles of farm produce, and the amount, kind, and value of special manures employed. The following comparative summaries exhibit the results of these several enumerations.

Summary of Agricultural Returns in New-York, as shown by successive Censuses

	Electoral State Census. 1821	State Census. 1825	State Census. 1835.	National Census. 1840.	State Census. 1845	National Census. 1850.	State Census. 1855.
Acres of land,*						19,119,084	26,758,183½
" improved,	5,717,494	7,160,967	9,655,426		11,757,276	12,408,964	13,657,490¾
" unimproved,						6,710,120	13,100,692⅝
Farms, total number,						170,621	231,740
Cash value of farms,						$554,546,842	$799,355,367
" stock,						$73,570,496	$103,776,053
" tools and implements,						$22,084,926	$26,927,502
Acres ploughed the year previous,							3,377,471
Acres in fallow the year previous,							506,030⅜
Acres in pasture the year previous,							4,984,114½
Meadow, acres,							3,384,440¾
Tons of hay,				3,127,047		3,728,797	3,256,948½
Bushels of grass seed,						96,493	120,866⅝
Spring wheat, acres sown,							194,346⅜
Bushels harvested,							2,033,353
Winter wheat, acres sown,							601,141½
Bushels harvested,							7,059,049¼
Wheat of both kinds, acres sown,					1,013,665		795,487⅝
Bushels harvested,				12,286,418	13,391,770	13,121,498	9,092,402¼
Oats, acres sown,					1,026,915		1,349,384¼
Bushels harvested,				20,675,847	26,323,051	26,552,814	27,015,296
Rye, acres sown,					317,099		281,714⅞
Bushels harvested,				2,979,323	2,966,322	4,148,182	3,039,438
Barley, acres sown,					192,503		212,608⅛
Bushels harvested,				2,520,068	3,108,704	3,585,059	3,563,540
Buckwheat acres sown,					255,495		293,233¼
Bushels harvested,				2,287,885	3,634,679	3,183,955	2,481,079¼
Indian corn, acres planted,					595,134		917,601
Bushels harvested,				10,972,286	14,722,114	17,858,400	19,290,691⅛
Potatoes, acres planted,					255,762		220,575¾
Bushels harvested,				30,123,614	23,653,418	15,398,368	15,191,852⅛
Peas, acres sown,					117,379		48,154¾
Bushels harvested,					1,761,503	†	705,967⅝
Beans, acres planted,					16,231		16,917⅝
Bushels harvested,					162,187	†	244,079
Turnips, acres sown,					15,322		7,584¼
Bushels harvested,					1,350,332		985,522½
Flax, acres sown,				‡	46,089		11,764
Pounds of lint,					2,896,000	§940,500	4,907,556⅛
Bushels of seed,						57,963	87,093½
Hemp, acres sown,				‡			3⅜
Tons of hemp,						§4	¾
Hops, acres planted,				447,250			9,481¾
Pounds harvested						2,536,299	7,192,254
Tobacco, acres planted,				744			786½
Pounds harvested,						83,189	946,502½
Apple orchards, bushels of apples,							13,668,830¾
Barrels of cider,				$1,701,935		1,761,950	273,639
Orchards, value of products,							
Market gardens, acres cultivated,				499,126		912,047	12,590⅞
Value of products,				10,048,109		10,357,484	1,138,682
Maple sugar, pounds made,						56,539	4,935,815¾
Molasses, gallons made,				6,799			85,091½
Wine, gallons made,						9,172	18,181¾
Honey, pounds collected,				52,795		} 1,755,830	2,557,876
Wax, pounds collected,				1,735¾			138,033¼
Silk, pounds of cocoons raised,					¶	1,774	267½
Neat cattle, total number,	1,215,049	1,513,421	1,885,771	1,911,244	2,072,330	1,877,639	2,105,465
Under 1 year old,					334,456	} 767,406	311,474
Over 1 year old,					1,709,479		††577,887
Working oxen,						178,909	144,597
Cows,					‖999,490	‖931,324	1,068,427
Cattle killed for beef,						**	225,338
Butter, number of pounds,					79,501,733	79,766,094	90,293,073½
Cheese, number of pounds,					36,744,976	49,741,413	38,944,249¾
Milk, gallons sold to market,							20,957,861
Dairy products, total value,				10,496,021			

* The area of the State, according to Burr's Atlas, is 28,297,142 acres. In 1855, 28,059,994 acres were assessed. The aggregate assessed value of real estate in 1855 was $1,107,272,715.

† The amount of peas and beans in 1850 was reported at 741,546 bush.

‡ Tons of flax and hemp, 1840, 1,030⅝.

§ In addition to this there were reported 1,130⅝ tons of flax and hemp.

¶ Pounds of raw silk manufactured from cocoons, 1,439.

‖ Number of cows milked.

** Value of animals slaughtered 1850, $13,573,884.

†† Number of neat cattle over one year old, exclusive of working oxen and cows.

Agricultural Returns—(*Continued.*)

	Electoral State Census. 1821	State Census. 1825.	State Census. 1835.	National Census 1840.	State Census. 1845	National Census. 1850.	State Census. 1855.
Horses,	262, 623	349, 628	524, 895	} 474, 543	{ 505, 155	447, 014	579, 715
Mules,	....	....	....		{	963	2, 254
Swine, total number,	....	1, 467, 573	1, 554, 358	1, 900, 065	1, 584, 344	1, 018, 252	1, 069. 792
Under 6 months,	....	....	....	....	....	....	530, 176
Over 6 months,	....	....	....	....	....	....	539, 616
Sheep,	2, 147, 351	3, 496, 539	4, 261, 765	5, 118, 777	*6, 443, 855	3, 453, 241	3, 217, 024
Wool, pounds shorn,	....	....	....	9, 845, 295	13, 864. 828	10, 171, 301	9, 231, 959¼
Number of fleeces,	....	....	....	....	4, 607, 012	....	2, 630, 203
Poultry, value of,	....	....	....	$1, 153, 413	....	$1, 280, 333	....
Value sold year previous,	....	....	....	....	....	....	$1, 071, 598
Eggs, value, sold the year previous,	....	....	....	....	....	....	$1, 360, 673
Nurseries, number of men employed,	....	....	....	525	....	....	....
Value of products,	....	....	....	258, 558	....	....	....
Miscellaneous products, total value,	....	....	....	....	....	....	$1, 421, 750
Cords of wood sold the year previous,	....	....	....	1, 058, 923	....	1, 058, 923	....

In obtaining the present census, the agricultural inquiries were directed to be made of the person in charge of each farm, or if removed, of those having the best means of information.†

* Of this number 1,870,728 were under one year old; 4,505,369 over one year old, and 67,758 age not stated.

† The instructions that were given for obtaining information under the several heads of agricultural statistics were in substance as follows:

Acres improved, to include all land reclaimed from a state of nature, deducting highways, lakes, and ponds of water, when latter exceeded ten acres in area.

Acres unimproved, to include all woodlands, uncultivated swamps and marshes, and lakes, and ponds of water over ten acres in area, if considered private property. Unimproved village and city lots, unless cultivated, were not to be returned.

Cash value of farms, to include the value of the whole farm, including buildings and improvements, as well as wild or unimproved lands. In making this estimate, reference was to be had to the price the farm would ordinarily bring, if sold, and without reference to its assessed value.

Cash value of stock, to be ascertained with reference to the current price of property of this kind in the vicinity on the first day of June, 1855. It would, of course, depend upon nearness to market, and other circumstances

Cash value of tools and implements.—All machinery used for agricultural purposes only, as cider mills and presses, steam or other power, and machinery for threshing, sawing, churning, &c., fixtures for making maple sugar, vehicles, and the tools, machines, and implements of farm labor generally, were directed to be included under this head. Pleasure carriages were not included.

Acres plowed the year previous.—In this column were entered the number of acres plowed in the spring of 1854, for spring sowing and planting, but not the number plowed for the sowing of winter grain in the fall, after producing a spring crop.

Acres in fallow the year previous.—This column was to include no part of the land entered in the last preceding column.

Acres in pasture the year previous.—This included only enclosed pastures. Highways, fallow, and land entered as unimproved were not embraced.

Acres in meadow, to include the amount of land reserved for mowing grass or clover. As the season to which the census referred was one of unusual drouth, in some sections, cases might occur in which land so kept was not mowed; still, if so reserved, it was to be entered as meadow. Some misunderstanding occurred with a few marshals at an early stage of the census, by applying to the term "meadow," the English definition, of a *flat intervale* not necessarily mown, but perhaps planted or sown. The term as used in this country is, it is believed, applied as directed in the instructions, to all land mown for hay.

Tons of hay.—As farmers seldom weigh the hay they collect for their own use, this inquiry in most cases was expected to be merely an approximation, estimated with reference to bulk, extent of meadow, and amount of stock supported through the winter.

Bushels of grass seed.—This included the aggregate amount of grass seed specially harvested, or screened, from grain the year preceding. The seed of timothy, or herds grass, (*Phleum pratense*), is believed to have been almost exclusively referred to under this head. Clover, lucerne, and other seeds of plants not gramineæ, raised for feeding stock, were not entered in this column, but in the columns for unenumerated articles of farm produce.

Acres of spring wheat sown, and bushels harvested.—These referred to the season of 1854, in which this crop was unusually short.

Acres of winter wheat sown, and bushels harvested.—These referred to the crop sown in 1853, and harvested in the summer of 1854. The acres sown, were directed to be entered whether harvested or not. In some instances the crop was so injured by drouth and insects as not to be worth the labor of gathering.

Acres and bushels of oats, rye, (both winter and spring), barley, buckwheat, corn, potatoes, peas, beans, turnips and flax.—These all referred to the crop of 1854, and were mostly considerably below the average of common years.

Pounds of lint.—Large crops, for the manufacture of cordage, were occasionally reported in tons. Care was taken in summing these returns to reduce them uniformly to pounds.

Acres and quantity of hemp, hops and tobacco, bushels of apples, and barrels of cider.—These also referred to the yield of 1854.

Acres of market gardens cultivated, and value of product.—No account was taken in this census of the products of small gardens for domestic use, but only of those devoted to the raising of culinary vegetables for market. The aggregate value raised in 1854, without specification of items, was required.

Pounds of maple sugar, and gallons of molasses.—These quantities referred to the spring of 1855.

Gallons of wine made.—This related to wine made from grapes in 1854. Currant and other wines were reported under the head of unenumerated articles of farm produce.

Pounds of honey and wax collected in 1854, both from wild and domestic bees. The relative quantities of these products could not, in many instances, be ascertained, on account of the honey being sold in the comb.

Silk, pounds of cocoons.—The quantity referred to 1854, and was much less than that indicated by previous censuses.

Unenumerated articles of farm produce.—Columns were provided for entering under this head the kind, quantity, and value of every crop made a special subject of cultivation, and for which no other place was assigned. A summary of products thus returned is given on pages 324-26.

Domestic animals, as specified in the agricultural returns of this census, referred to June 1, 1855. An attempt was made to obtain the number of cows milked, the number milked for butter, for cheese, and for the milk market, but it was found impracticable to derive useful results from this arrangement, on account of the uncertainty often arising as to which class they were to be assigned. In the same dairy butter and cheese are often made from the milk of the same cows. The percentage of cows not milked is probably small. There is reason to believe that the number of horses and cows kept by villagers, who own no land, is reported too small. The number of sheep is reported, in many cases, different from the number of fleeces and quantity of wool shorn. This apparent inconsistency arises from the former referring to 1855, and the latter to 1854.

Value of poultry and eggs sold.—These inquiries referred to the year preceding June 1, 1855.

Special manures.—The kind, quantity and value of special manures, purchased and used on farms, was directed to be entered in the agricultural schedule, and the results of this inquiry are given on page 327. The term "special manure," was defined to include guano, gypsum, poudrette, saline compounds, and other substances prepared and sold as fertilizing agents, aside from those ordinarily produced upon farms. Of the latter no return was made. In many instances, two or more of these were so reported together that they could not be separated, and sometimes the value only was given. These were classed under the general term "miscellaneous," without further specification.

It will be remembered that the returns of crops, as given in the present census, are those of 1854, which year was characterized by an unusual drought.* With the expectation that these results would fall short of the average of common years, and present an incorrect view of the agricultural capabilities of our soil, unless associated with data, showing the cause and extent of the deficiency, a blank was furnished to each marshal for entering the relative yield of the several field crops, as compared with favorable seasons, and the cause of failure, if existing. This was to be determined from his own observation, and by inquiry of those best informed upon the subject. The results given on pages 245—326, are those actually observed, without reference to relative quantity. The aggregate opinions thus obtained are scarcely capable of reduction into definite form, from the very unequal field of observation of the different marshals, and the failure of many to make reports on this subject where there was a manifest occasion. Of the 1,744 marshals appointed to collect the materials of this census, about 1,450 made returns of agricultural statistics, the remainder being in cities and large villages. The principal cause of failure was drought, and its extent was estimated as follows:

CROPS.	Total number of marshals reporting relative yield.	AMOUNT REPORTED.					
		Usual yield.	Three-fourths the usual yield.	Two-thirds the usual yield.	One-half the usual yield.	One-third the usual yield.	One-fourth or less of the usual yield.
Spring wheat,	800	86	142	112	288	69	103
Winter wheat,	519	50	74	59	129	55	159
Rye,	800	147	180	154	204	58	57
Oats,	1,279	45	201	216	479	160	178
Barley,	872	74	193	155	283	68	99
Peas,	688	61	85	76	239	80	147
Beans,	622	57	67	57	214	54	173
Corn,	1,181	99	218	211	401	117	135
Buckwheat,	1,159	25	60	42	276	108	648
Potatoes,	1,176	74	153	114	446	148	311
Turnips,	529	88	67	33	169	21	151
Flax,	146	39	20	14	43	5	25
Hemp,	19	5	1	5	6	....	2
Hops,	149	61	45	15	15	2	11
Tobacco,	40	12	8	6	8	3	3
Apples,	905	230	93	69	212	55	247
Market gardens,	153	18	24	25	45	17	24
Meadows,	1,190	80	216	248	451	111	84
Butter dairies,	1,091	119	564	285	88	10	25
Cheese dairies,	513	54	260	122	50	8	19

In addition to the above, there were reported failures from other causes, as insects, worms, blight, winter and spring kill, rust, hail, frost, storms and running fires, either singly or combined with each other, and with drought. These causes operate more or less every year in some part of the State, and their influence upon the crops of 1854 cannot therefore be considered as affecting the average yield, except so far as they were aggravated by the drought. The relative influence of these causes were as follows:

* The following table shows the total depth of rain in inches and hundredths, reported as falling at several stations within the State, during part of the year, by which it appears that the amount was unusually great in April, and considerably less than the common average in July and August. The greater amounts for June at Clinton, Mexico and Rochester, and for July at Oxford, appear to have been from local showers. The general mean for the whole State during twenty-five years, taken from the official reports of academies to the Regents of the University, is added for convenience of comparison:

PLACES OF OBSERVATION & YEARS.		DEPTH OF RAIN.					
		April.	May.	June.	July.	Aug.	Sept.
Albany, Albany county,	1854,	6·82	1·79	2·96	3·35	0·62	3·87
Clinton, Oneida county,	1854,	8·19	2·70	4·81	2·76	2·60	3·92
Elmira, Chemung county,	1854,	6·09	2·86	5·09	3·12	1·16	3·25
Flatbush, Kings county,	1854,	11·36	5·34	2·17	1·69	0·85	3·22
Geneva, Ontario county,	1854,	5·20	2·21	2·48	0·89	0·77	3·27
Homer, Cortland county,	1854,	5·84	2·33	3·31	2·19	2·19	3·71
Jamaica, Queens county,	1854,	11·19	6·25	1·33	2·51	1·26	3·22
Liberty, Sullivan county,	1854,	6·70	5·55	2·37	2·42	0·92	3·21
Mexico, Oswego county,	1854,	4·51	3·06	4·56	2·92	1·72	4·84
New-York city,	1854,	10·11	4·28	2·29	2·81	1·06	4·15
Oxford, Chenango county,	1854,	7·11	3·22	2·10	4·04	2·08	4·77
Plattsburgh, Clinton county,	1854,	2·29	1·45	2·95	0·99	0·39	3·81
Rochester, Monroe county,	1854,	2·43	2·15	5·47	0·25	1·82	5·18
White Plains, Westchester co.,	1854,	8·20	5·10	1·80	3·02	0·40	5·40
Mean of the above,	1854,	6·85	3·45	3·11	2·35	1·27	3·99
Mean quantity in 1826,		1·99	0·81	7·02	3·12	2·21	2·88
" " 1827,		3·72	2·81	3·48	3·70	4·08	4·00
" " 1828.		2·41	3·28	3·74	5·69	3·20	5·29
" " 1829,		3·62	2·48	3·30	3·16	3·12	3·01
" " 1830,		1·95	3·74	6·15	4·15	1·55	2·63

YEARS	DEPTH OF RAIN.					
	April	May.	June.	July.	Aug.	Sept.
Mean quantity in 1831,	4·10	2·71	3·91	4·42	3·81	3·54
" " 1832,	2·39	3·15	1·72	4·00	5·37	2·7[illegible]
" " 1833,	1·31	5·56	3·24	4·41	3·29	2·98
" " 1834,	2·72	3·26	4·29	3·38	1·74	2·97
" " 1835,	4·03	1·90	4·76	3·61	3·90	1·8[illegible]
" " 1836,	2·24	3·42	4·59	2·58	1·87	2·5[illegible]
" " 1837,	1·85	4·21	4·39	3·69	5·12	2·0[illegible]
" " 1838,	1·49	4·34	4·28	2·44	3·51	3·4[illegible]
" " 1839,	2·42	3·79	4·11	3·92	2·43	2·6[illegible]
" " 1840,	3·40	3·15	3·20	3·13	3·49	3·1[illegible]
" " 1841,	3·55	1·98	2·79	2·65	2·65	3·2[illegible]
" " 1842,	2·90	2·33	3·68	4·18	3·43	5·3[illegible]
" " 1843,	2·84	1·90	4·37	2·99	4·35	3·6[illegible]
" " 1844,	1·37	4·85	2·85	4·63	2·99	1·8[illegible]
" " 1845,	2·29	2·52	2·89	2·74	1·92	3·6[illegible]
" " 1846,	1·14	3·92	2·63	4·25	2·78	2·1[illegible]
" " 1847,	1·79	2·09	3·83	3·15	2·99	5·1[illegible]
" " 1848,	1·02	4·95	3·37	4·91	2·45	2·5[illegible]
" " 1849,	1·34	4·11	2·39	1·13	3·75	1·8[illegible]
" " 1850,	2·15	2·51	2·98	5·80	3·63	4·6[illegible]
Mean quantity of 25 years, 1825–50,	2·53	2·31	3·75	3·59	2·99	3·1[illegible]

Spring wheat, three-fourths of the usual yield, 16; two-thirds, 18; one-half, 56; one-third, 23; one-fourth and less, 38.

Winter wheat, three-fourths, 39; two-thirds, 39; one-half, 105; one-third, 93; one-fourth and less, 252.

Rye, three-fourths, 35; two-thirds, 15; one-half, 35; one-third, 5; one-fourth and less, 5.

Oats, three-fourths, 9; two-thirds, 13; one-half, 27; one-third, 14; one-fourth and less, 10.

Barley, three-fourths, 9; two-thirds, 6; one-half, 12; one-third, 2; one-fourth and less, 7.

Peas, three-fourths, 2; two-thirds, 5; one-half, 15; one-third, 2; one-fourth and less, 7.

Beans, three-fourths, 4; two-thirds, 1; one-half, 5; one-fourth and less, 2.

Corn, three-fourths, 27; two-thirds, 24; one-half, 39; one-third, 13; one-fourth and less, 16.

Buckwheat, three-fourths, 1; two-thirds, 5; one-half, 21; one-third, 7; one-fourth and less, 38.

Potatoes, three-fourths, 3; two-thirds, 2; one-half, 25; one-third, 6; one-fourth and less, 18.

Turnips, two-thirds, 1; one-half, 5; one-third, 1; one-fourth and less, 4.

Hops, three-fourths, 1; two-thirds, 2; one-half, 1; one-fourth, 2.

Tobacco, three-fourths, 1.

Apples, three-fourths, 9; two-thirds, 15; one-half, 57; one-third, 15; one-fourth or less, 62.

Market Gardens, three-fourths, 1; one-half, 1; one-third, 1; one-fourth, 1.

Meadows, three-fourths, 5; two-thirds, 11; one-half 24; one-third 2; one-fourth and less, 4.

Cheese dairies, three-fourths, 1; one-fourth, 1.

Domestic Manufactures—The several State censuses since 1821 have reported the number of yards of cloth of different kinds made in families, with the following results:

CLOTHS MANUFACTURED THE YEAR PREVIOUS	1821.	1825.	1835.	1845.	1855 *
Fulled cloth, number of yards,	1,958,712	2,918,233	2,183,951	1,664,366	198,203
Flannel and other woolen cloths not fulled, number of yards,	2,451,107	3,468,001	2,790,069	2,650,116	379,922½
Linen, cotton and other thin cloths, number of yards,	5,635,985	8,079,992	3,799,953	2,775,657	350,550

The remarkable decrease of these products of home industry finds a ready explanation in the corresponding increase of cloth manufacture by machinery. The cheapness and superiority of fabrics thus produced, appear to indicate a further and much greater reduction of this class of domestic manufactures. With the view of ascertaining the amount of other articles made in families, columns were provided in the present census for entering the kind, quantity, and value of such products of household manufacture as had been made for sale only, but not of those for use in the family where made. The results of these returns are given on page 328. From the entire absence of entries under this head in the reports of many marshals, it is probable that the statistics of domestic manufactures of this census are below the actual quantity.

Manufactures: No department of a census presents so many difficulties, or is accompanied by circumstances so much tending to impair the correctness of results, as that relating to manufactures. Amidst the infinite diversity of details, and unlimited amount of combinations and varieties, in the absence of authentic and definite figures, showing the amount and value of raw materials and products, in the unwillingness frequently expressed to giving this key to prosperity or loss in business, in the constant recourse to memory for data which, although offered with honest intentions, may differ widely from the true facts, and in the disposition sometimes shown to under state the results of the manufacture, with the view of avoiding taxation or rivalry, on the one hand, or of creating a fictitious credit or reputation by exaggerating the extent of their transactions on the other—we find abundant cause to doubt the exactness with which these returns are made, and to question the soundness of positive deductions that may be drawn from them.

In classifying the returns of manufactures, cases of great difficulty and doubt will often occur, and in none more so than where several distinct kinds of business are carried on by the same person or company, often under the same roof, and so blended together that it is impossible to analyze them, and refer each to its proper place in the classification adopted. There is, however, in an inquiry extended over a large territory, something like a compensating tendency in the balancing of extremes, the under statements of one being raised by the over estimates of others; and although in everything but number of establishments, the returns may differ somewhat from the actual facts, the statistics of manufactures obtained by the census, may be regarded as useful approximations, and as valuable for comparison with one another. Whatever imperfections they may contain, there is no indication that in general, one section is better represented

* The following directions were given for obtaining these statistics: "These inquiries should be made for the year ending June 1, 1855, and include the quantities of the above cloths woven by hand in families, although the carding, spinning, dyeing, and dressing may have been done elsewhere. * * * The quantity is to include the whole amount made, whether sold or consumed in the family."—*Instructions*, p. 32.

than another, or that the errors of one census would relatively vary from those of another obtained at a different time, under similar instructions. This opinion needs to be qualified by the general remark, most amply warranted by an examination of the original schedules, that the census throughout, is taken with more care in the rural districts than in cities. In the former case, those appointed as marshals were personally acquainted with the greater number of the inhabitants of their districts, and more or less informed of the general character and extent of business of each,* while in cities and large towns the marshals were mostly left to rely upon the answers which parties interested might be willing to give to his questions. In several instances, in the latter case, no schedule of manufactures was returned, and in a few others, the marshals reported that no information could be obtained under this head.

It may in general terms be remarked, that the tendency to understate the aggregate amount of manufactures, prevails in every census in which an attempt is made to obtain the value of materials used and products sold, for, while no establishments would be reported that did not exist, numbers that transacted an extensive business might be omitted or but partially reported.

In the census of 1810 the first attempt was made to collect industrial statistics along with the returns of population. The results of this census in New-York, not comparing with those which follow, will be here given separately†.

Statistics of Manufactures in 1810.

Cotton goods made in families, &c., yards.,	216, 013
Averaged at 32c. per yard,	$69, 124 16
Manufacturing establishments,	26
Flaxen goods, in families, &c., yards.,	5, 372, 645
Averaged at 37½c. per yard,	$2, 014, 742
Blended and unnamed cloths and stuffs, yards.,	180, 659
Averaged at 35c. per yard,	$63, 231
Tow cloth, yards,	21, 721
Averaged at 30c. per yard,	$6. 516
Woolen goods in families, &c., yards.,	3, 257, 812
Averaged at 87½c. per pound,	$2, 850, 585
Thread, runs (all in Rensselaer county),	43, 680
Value,	$7, 644
Looms, number,	33, 069
Carding machines, number,	413
Pounds carded,	1, 881, 596
Averaged at 50c. per pound,	$940, 798
Fulling mills, number,	427
Yards fulled,	1, 811, 065
Averaged at $1.25 per yard,	$2, 263, 756
Spindles, number,	12, 293
Hatteries, number,	124
Hats, number made,	104, 014
Averaged at $2.50 each,	$260, 035
Blast furnaces, number,	11
Air furnaces, number,	10
Iron, tons made,	3, 359
1,306 tons, averaged at $120, and 2,053 tons at $100 p. ton,	$362, 020
Bloomeries, number,	7
Tons of iron made,	212
Average value of iron, at $100 per ton,	$21, 200
Forges, number,	48
Tons of iron made,	1, 684
Average value of iron, at $100 per ton,	$168, 400
Trip hammers, number,	49
Rolling and slitting mills, number,	1
Tons of iron used,	230
Value of iron,	$33, 120
Naileries, number,	44
Pounds of nails made,	2, 292 960
Average value, 12c. per pound,	$275, 155
Tanneries, number,	867
Hides tanned,	151, 165
Calf skins tanned,	210, 445
Sheepskins tanned,	61, 618
Average value, hides $4 25, calf skins $1 12, sheepskins $1.15,	$1, 079, 742
Morocco, dozen of skins dressed,	13, 083
Average value $1.40 per skin,	$219, 800
Oil mills, for linseed oils,	28
Oil, gallons made,	33, 427
Averaged at $1.25 per gallon,	$41, 784
Distilleries, number,	591
Gallons distilled,	2, 107, 243
Averaged at 80c. per gallon,	$1, 685, 794
Breweries, number,	42
Gallons brewed,	2, 004, 504
Averaged at 17c. per gallon,	$340, 767
Sugar refineries, number (in New-York city,)	10
Pounds refined,	2, 411, 742
Valued at	$420, 706
Paper mills, number,	28
Reams made,	77, 756
Averaged at $3 per ream,	233, 268
Glass works, number,	4
Square feet made,	3, 805, 000
Averaged at 17c. per square foot,	$608, 800
Tobacco and snuff mills, number,	2
Pounds of tobacco,	200, 000
Pounds of snuff,	26, 000
Value of tobacco and snuff,	45, 200
Rope walks, number,	18
Tons of cordage made,	1, 345
Averaged at $400 per ton,	538, 000
Chocolate mills, number	1
Pounds made,	30, 000
Value,	$8, 550
Gunpowder mills, number,	2
Pounds made (at one),	26, 000
Averaged at 40c. per pound,	$10, 400

The aggregate of the foregoing in the United States was not given, which prevents a ready comparison of the statistics of New-York with those of the Union.

In the national census of 1820, the name and nature of the articles manufactured, their market value, the kind, quantity, and cost of raw materials annually consumed, the number of men, women, boys and girls employed, the whole quantity and kind of machinery, and the quantity in operation, the amount of capital invested, the sum paid annually for wages, the amount of contingent expenses, and general observations respecting each distinct branch of manufactures, were required to be reported by the marshals. These were classified under the above heads alphabetically, by counties, but no general summaries by states, or even of columns, was given; and from the values returned being in many instances pro rata, instead of by totals, it is impossible to represent concisely the results of this enumeration.‡

* With the express design of obtaining persons having this acquaintance with the districts to which they were appointed, the act under which the present census was taken, required one or more marshals, "who shall have been resident at least one year previous," to be appointed in each ward or town. A still further subdivision among competent enumerators would undoubtedly have enhanced the accuracy of the returns.

† These returns were classified by Mr. Tench Coxe, of Philadelphia, and although they contained many inconsistencies, this gentleman was able to arrive at an approximate estimate of the results.

‡ The Digest of the accounts of manufacturing establishments returned with the census of 1820, were prepared and printed under a resolution of Congress, approved March 30, 1822, after the population statistics had been published.

The defective and unsatisfactory result of this census appears to have prevented any attempt from being made in 1830 to procure, with the census, any industrial statistics whatever.

In January, 1832, Congress, by resolution,* directed the Secretary of the Treasury to report such statistics of manufactures as he might be able to procure, with the view of modifying the tariff, in accordance with which, a circular was issued February 5th, of that year, directed to leading manufacturers, and requesting answers on thirty-five specific inquiries, bearing upon the interests and prosperity of their business, their relative profit and loss, the influence of foreign competition, and of restrictions by way of duties, at home and abroad, upon their several branches of manufacture. The answers from New-York were limited to facts concerning cotton and woolen goods, iron and salt.†

The statistics thus obtained are here given in the aggregate. Those of cotton were collected by Mr. Richard P. Hartt, of Troy, in the latter part of 1831 and early part of 1832, by corresponding with the proprietors and agents of factories; and those of iron by Mr. Peter Townsend, of New-York, from a personal examination during the year 1831. These statistics were generally very full except those of woolen factories, furnished by Peter H. Schenck, of New-York, which were incomplete. The results of this inquiry were as follows:

Cotton Factories, 1831-2.

Mills, total number,‡	112
Capital employed,	$3,671,500
Spindles, total number,	157,316
Looms, total number,	3,673
Yarn, pounds sold annually,	1,867,790
Cloth, yards made annually,	21,010,920
Persons employed, males,	1,246
" females,	3,684
" males, between 12 and 16 years,	323
" number under 12 years,	466
Persons dependent for support,	12,954
Cotton, pounds used annually,	7,961,670
Sizing, pounds of starch,	23,007
" pounds of flour,	292,704
Fuel, cords of wood,	7,038
' tons of coal,	493
Oil, gallons used,	35,323
Value of unenumerated articles,	$20,900

Woolen Factories, 1831.§

Capital, including stock and goods,	$895,377
Persons employed,	1,203
Wages,	$160,000
Wool, pounds used,	1,158,797
" value of,	$402,659
Goods manufactured, value of,	$832,003
Broadcloths, yards of,	274,308
Kerseymere, yards of,	151,682
Flannels and baizes, yards of,	485,381
Satinets, yards of,	470,970
Cassinets, kerseys, and narrow cloth,	11,148
Carpeting,	6,000

Iron Manufacture, 1828 to 1830.

	1828.	1829.	1830.
Blast Furnaces.‖			
Pig iron, tons,	3,737	3,980	4,453
Castings, tons,	2,133	2,334	2,263
Wood, cords used,	60,743	63,969	63,215
Men employed,	951	1,014	1,092
Persons dependent,	3,259	3,459	3,622
Horses and cattle employed,	692	730	772
Refining Forges.¶			
Bar iron, tons,	651	630	644
Wood, cords used,	6,760	6,563	6,710
Men employed,	93	95	108
Persons dependent,	342	364	396
Horses and cattle employed,	59	59	59
*Bloomeries.***			
Bar iron, tons,	3,555	3,759	3,767
Wood, cords used,	54,862	58,303	58,353
Men employed,	1,161	1,232	1,259
Persons dependent,	3,619	3,822	3,837
Horses and cattle employed,	798	480	842

Salt Manufacture.††

Manufactories of fine salt,	135
Cost of erections for,	$250,000
Coarse salt fields, (200 acres),	6
Cost of erections,	$25,000
Total investment of every kind,	$430,000
Capital invested in coarse salt manufacture,	$150,000

The national census of 1840, directed inquiries into the statistics of mines, agriculture, horticulture, commerce, fisheries, products of the forest and manufactures, which gave the following results in the State of New-York and the United States:‡‡

* On the 19th of January, 1832, Mr. Adams, from the committee on manufactures, offered a resolution "that the Secretary of the Treasury be directed to obtain information as to the quantities and kinds of the several articles manufactured in the United States during the year, particularly those of iron, cotton, wool, hemp, and sugar, and the cost thereof; and also the quantities and cost of similar articles imported from abroad, during the same year; and that he lay the same before this House as early as may be during the present session of Congress, together with such information as he may deem material, and such suggestions as he may think useful, with a view to the adjustment of the tariff, after the payment of the public debt." This resolution was agreed to the same day.—*Congressional Debates*, viii., Part II., 1585.

† Executive Documents, 1st session 22d Cong., No. 308, vol. ii., p. 1 to 133.

‡ Of these 1 was in Cayuga, 1 in Chenango, 2 in Clinton, 7 in Columbia, 12 in Dutchess, 1 in Franklin, 5 in Herkimer, 3 in Jefferson, 3 in Madison, 2 in Monroe, 20 in Oneida, 2 in Onondaga, 3 in Orange, 11 in Otsego, 15 in Rensselaer, 1 in Rockland, 4 in Saratoga, 1 in Schenectady, 1 in Seneca, 1 in Suffolk, 3 in Tompkins, 3 in Ulster, 5 in Washington, and 5 in Westchester county.

§ This return included 34 of the large woolen establishments of the 202 reported as existing in 1832. The greater part of these were engaged in manufacturing to a limited extent only, and depending principally upon "custom work" for their business.

‖ Including returns from 23 establishments, of which 2 were in Clinton, 1 in Columbia, 1 in Dutchess, 2 in Essex, 2 in Herkimer, 1 in Jefferson, 5 in Oneida, 2 in Ontario, 3 in Orange, 1 in Oswego, 1 in Putnam, 1 in St. Lawrence, and 1 in Wayne county.

¶ Embraced returns from 6 forges, of which 1 was in Columbia, 1 in Jefferson, 1 in Orange, and 3 in Rockland county.

** Embracing returns from 40 establishments, of which 8 were in Clinton, 2 in Essex, 2 in Franklin; 1 in Herkimer, 1 in Oneida, 1 in Putnam, 4 in St. Lawrence, 1 in Washington, and 1 in Warren county. Returns were also received from 109 cupolas and air furnaces, 9 nail factories and rolling mills, and 2 forges for making anchors.

†† The statistics of this manufacture are reported annually to the Legislature. The reports of the Superintendent of the Salt Springs contain summaries of the quantities of salt made annually through a series of many years.

‡‡ The summaries of agriculture and horticulture have been given elsewhere. Only such headings of inquiry as appear in the returns of New-York are given in the following summary.

	New-York	United States.
Mines.		
Iron, cast iron furnaces,	186	804
Tons produced,	29,088	286,903
Bar, bloomeries, forges & rolling mills,	120	795
Fuel, tons consumed,	123,677	1,528,110
Men employed in mines,	3,456	30,497
Capital invested,	$2,103,418	20,432,131
Lead, smelting houses,	9	120
Pounds produced,	670,000	31,239,453
Men employed,	333	1,017
Capital invested,	$221,000	1,346,756
Other metals, value produced,	$84,564	370,614
Men employed,	119	728
Capital invested,	$42,930	238,980
Salt, bushels produced.*	2,864,718	....
Granite, marble, and other stone, value,	$1,541,480	3,695,884
Men employed,	3,649	7,859
Capital invested,	$1,002,555	2,540,159
Commerce.		
Commercial houses in foreign trade,	469	1,108
Commission houses,	1,044	2,881
Capital invested,	49,583,001	119,295,367
Retail dry goods, grocery and other stores,	12,207	57,565
Capital invested,	$42,135,795	250,301,799
Lumber yards and trade,	414	1,793
Capital invested,	$2,694,170	9,848,307
Men employed,	9,592	35,963
Internal transportation, men employed,	7,593	17,594
Butchers, packers, &c., men employed,	804	4,808
Capital invested,	$2,833,916	11,526,950
Fisheries.		
Fish, quintals of, smoked or dried,	5	773,947
Barrels, pickled fish,	22,224	472,359½
Gallons, spermaceti oil,	400,251	4,764,708
Gallons, whale and other fish oil,	1,269,541	7,536,778
Whalebone, value of, and other productions of fisheries,	$344,665	1,153,234
Men employed,	1,228	36,584
Capital invested,	$949,250	16,429,620
Products of the Forest.		
Lumber produced, value of,	3,891,302	12,943,507
Tar, pitch, turpentine & rosin, barrels of,	402	619,106
Pot and pearl ashes, tons of,	7,613¾	15,935½
Skins and furs, value produced,	15,556	1,065,869
Ginseng and all other productions of the forest, value,	$143,332	526,580
Men employed,	4,664	22,042
Manufactures.		
Machinery, value manufactured,	$2,895,517	10,980,581
Men employed,	3,631	13,001
Hardware and cutlery, value made,	$1,566,974	6,451,967
Men employed	962	5,492
Cannon cast,	112	274
Small arms made,	8,308	88,073
Men employed upon cannon & small arms,	203	1,744
Precious metals, value manufactured,	$1,106,203	4,734,960
Men employed,	708	1,556
Various metals, value manufactured,	$2,456,792	9,779,442
Men employed,	1,713	6,677
Granite, marble, &c., value manufactured,	$966,220	2,442,950
Men employed,	1,447	3,734
Bricks and lime, value manufactured,	$1,198,527	9,736,945
Men employed,	3,160	22,807
Capital invested in preceding manufactu's,	$4,563,188	20,620,869
Wool, fulling mills, number of,	890	2,585
Woolen manufactories,	323	1,420
Value of manufactured goods,	$3,537,337	20,696,999
Persons employed,	4,636	21,342
Capital invested,	$3,469,349	15,765,124
Cotton, manufactories of,	117	1,240
Spindles, number of,	211,659	2,284,631
Dyeing and printing establishments,	12	129
Value of manufactured goods,	$3,640,237	46,350,453
Persons employed,	7,407	72,119
Capital invested,	$4,900,772	51,102,359
Silk, pounds of reeled, thrown, or other silks made,	377⅜	15,745½
Value of the above,	$2,415	119,814
Males employed,	35	246
Females and children employed,	66	521
Capital invested,	$8,034	274,374
Flax, value of manufactures,	$46,429	322,205
Persons employed,	90	1,628
Capital invested,	$15,000	208,087
Mixed manufactures, value,	$1,497,067	6,545,503
Persons employed,	2,005	15,905
Capital invested,	$675,953	4,368,991
Tobacco, value of manufactures,	$831,570	5,819.568
Persons employed,	669	8,384
Capital invested,	$395,530	3,437,191
Hats and caps, value made,	$2,914,117	8,704,342

	New-York.	United States.
Straw bonnets, value made,	$160,248	1,476,505
Persons employed,	3,880	20,176
Capital invested,	$1,676,559	4,485,300
Tanneries number of,	1,216	8,229
Sides of sole leather tanned,	1,252,890	3,463,611
Sides of upper leather tanned,	827,993	3,781,868
Men employed,	5,579	26,018
Capital invested,	$3,907,348	15,650,929
All other manufactories of leather, saddleries, &c.,	2,849	17,136
Value of manufactures,	$6,232,924	33,134,403
Capital invested,	$2,743,765	12,881,262
Soap, pounds made,	11,939,834	49,820,497
Tallow candles, pounds made,	4,029,783	17,904,507
Spermaceti and wax candles, pounds,	353,000	2,936,951
Men employed,	489	5.641
Capital invested,	$618,875	2,757,273
Distilleries, number of,	212	10,30
Gallons distilled,	11,973,815	41,402,627
Breweries, number of,	83	40
Gallons brewed,	6,059,122	23,267,73
Men employed,	1,486	12,22
Capital invested,	$3,107,066	9,147,36
Powder mills, number,	8	13
Pounds made,	1,185,000	8,977,34
Men employed,	41	49
Capital invested,	$81,500	875,87
Drugs, medicine, paint, dyes, &c., value,	$877,816	4,151,89
Turpentine and varnish, value,	$431,467	660,82
Persons employed,	677	1,84
Capital invested,	$1,267,835	4,507,67
Glass houses, number of,	13	8
Glass cutting establishments,	11	3
Men employed,	498	3,23
Value of manufactures in looking glass,	$411,371	2,890,29
Capital invested,	$204,700	2,084,10
Potteries, number of,	47	65
Value of manufactures,	$159,292	1.104,82
Men employed,	197	1,61
Capital invested,	$88,450	551,43
Sugar refineries, number of,	7	4
Value of produce,	$385,000	3,250,70
Chocolate, value manufactured,	$5,000	79,90
Confectionary, value made,	$386,142	1,143,96
Men employed,	416	1,35
Capital invested,	$474,656	1,769,57
Paper manufactories,	77	42
Value of products,	$673,121	5,641,49
Value of all other manufactures of paper, playing cards, &c.,	$89,637	511,59
Men employed,	749	4,72
Capital invested,	$703,550	4,745,2
Printing offices, number,	321	1,55
Binderies, number,	107	44
Daily newspapers,	34	1
Weekly newspapers,	198	1,14
Semi-weekly and tri-weekly newspapers,	13	1
Periodicals,	57	2
Men employed,	3,231	11,5
Capital invested,	$1,876,540	5,873,8
Cordage, number of rope walks,	46	3
Value of products,	$792,910	4,078,3
Men employed,	597	4,4
Capital invested,	$242,180	2,465,5
Musical instruments, value made,	$472,910	923,9
Men employed,	438	9
Capital invested,	$408,775	734,3
Carriages and wagons, value made,	$2,364,461	10,897,8
Men employed,	4,710	21,9
Capital invested,	$1,485,023	5,551,6
Mills: Flouring mills, number of,	338	4,3
Barrels of flour made,	1,861,385	7,404,5
Grist mills, number of,	1,750	23,6
Saw mills, number of,	6,356	31,6
Oil mills, number of,	63	8
Value of manufactures,	$16,953,280	76,545,2
Men employed,	10,807	60,7
Capital invested,	$14,648,814	65,858,4
Ships and vessels, value of, built,	$797,317	7,016,0
Furniture, value made,	$1,971,776	7,016,0
Men employed,	3,660	18,0
Capital invested,	$1,610,810	6 989,9
Houses, brick and stone built,	1,233	8,4
Wooden built,	5,198	45,6
Men employed,	16,768	85,5
Value of buildings built,	$7,265,849	41,917,4
Value of all other manufactures,	$9,615,206	34,785,3
Capital invested,	$6,078,507	25,019,7
Total capital invested in manufactures,	$55,252,779	267,726,5

* From the report of the superintendent of salt springs.

The national census of 1850 directed inquiries to be made into all the products of industry, including the name of the corporation, company, or individual, the name of the business or manufacture, capital invested in real and personal estate, quantity, kind, and value of raw materials used, and ot manufactured products, the kind of motive power, machinery, structure or resource,* and number of hands employed, with their wages. In compiling the results of that census, only a few generalizations were made, embracing the aggregate product of manufactures, mining, and the mechanic arts, and special summaries of cotton, woolen, iron, and salt manufactures, distilleries, breweries, and fisheries. All kinds of mercantile, commercial, or trading business, where no special article was produced or manufactured, but which were confined to dealing and exchange of articles of merchandize, or manufacture, were *expressly excepted.* The general results of the census in New-York, aud in the United States, so far as published, were as follows:

	New-York	United States.
Manufactures, Mining, and Mechanic Arts.		
Individuals and establishments,	23,553	121,855
Capital invested,	$99,904,405	$527,209,193
Raw materials used,	134,655,674	554,655,038
Hands employed—Males,	147,737	719,479
Females,	51,612	225,512
Annual wages,	49,131,000	229,736,377
Annual product, value of,	237,597,249	1,013,336,463
Per cent. profit,	53.86	43.43
Cotton manufactures.		
Establishments,	86	1,094
Capital invested,	4,176,920	74,500,931
Raw materials used—Bales cotton,	37,778	641,240
Tons of coal,	1,539	121,099
Raw materials, value of,	1,985.973	34,835,056
Hands employed—Males,	2.632	33,150
Females,	3,688	59,136
Average monthly wages—Male,	18 32	...
Female,	9 38	...
Annual product, value of,	3,591,989	61,869,184
Woolen manufactures.		
Establishments,	249	1,559
Capital invested,	4,459,370	28,118,650
Raw materials used—Pounds of wool,	12,538,786	70,862,829
Tons of coal,	...	46,370
Raw materials, value of,	3,838,292	25,755,991
Hands employed—Males,	4,262	22,678
Females,	2,412	16,574
Average monthly wages—Male,	19 97	...
Female,	11 76	...
Annual products, value of,	7,030,604	43,207,545
Manufactures of pig iron.		
Establishments,	18	377
Capital invested,	605,000	17,346,425
Raw materials used—Tons of ore,	46,385	1,579,318
" value of,	321,027	7,005,289
Hands employed—Males,	505	20,298
Females,	...	150
Average monthly wages—Males,	25,000	...
Annual product—Tons of pig iron,	23,022	565,755
Other products,	12,800	259,700
Value of,	597,920	12,748,727

	New-York.	United States.
Manufactures of iron castings.		
Establishments,	323	1,391
Capital invested,	$4,622,482	$17,416,361
Raw materials used—Tons of pig iron,	108,945	345,553
T'ns of old met'l,	3,212	11,416
Fuel, &c.,	2,393,768	10,346,265
Hands employed—Males,	5,925	23,541
Average monthly wages—Males,	27 49	...
Annual product, value of,	5,921,980	25,108,155
Manufactures of wrought iron.		
Establishments,	81	552
Capital invested,	1,871,650	17,033,279
Value of raw materials,	2,305,441	13,524,777
Hands employed—Males,	2,130	16,110
Females,	...	138
Average monthly wages—Males,	28 91	...
Annual product, value of,	3,758,547	22,629,271
Distilleries and breweries.		
Establishments,	189	1,217
Capital invested,	2,585,900	8,507,574
Raw materials used—Bush. of barley,	2,062,250	3,787,195
Bushels of corn,	1,647,266	11,067,761
Bushels of rye,	909,067	2,143,927
Men employed,	1,676	6,140
Quanity produced—Barrels ale, &c.,	644,700	1,179,495
Gal's whisk'y and high wines,	9,231,700	41,364,224
Gallons of rum,	2,488,800	6,500,500
Fisheries.		
Number,	26	1,384
Capital invested,	482,100	8,966,044
Value of raw materials used,	...	99,681
Men employed,	583	20,704
Entire monthly wages,	11,862	371,599
Annual product, value of,	484,345	10,000,182
Manufactures of salt.		
Establishments,	192	340
Capital invested,	819,950	2,640,885
Value of raw materials used,	631,955	1,051,425
Hands employed—Males,	873	2,699
Females,	...	87
Average yearly wages—Male,	299,376	744,432
Female,	...	9,792
Annual product—Bushels,	4,500,000	9,763,840
" value of,	998,315	2,222,745

The Electoral State census of 1821, and the State censuses of 1825, 1835, and 1845, embraced statistics of a few of the leading manufactures of the State, which in the first two cases included only the number of establishments, and in the others, the value of raw materials and manufactured products. These returns, compared with those of 1855, were as follows:

* These were defined to include, 1st, *motive power*, as water, steam, horse, wind, or otherwise; 2d, *machinery*, as number of spindles, looms, presses, mills, and runs of stones; saw mills and number of saws, or other appropriate amount of the kind and quantity of machinery; 3d, *structure, or resource*, as furnaces, number of fires; bloomeries, number of fires; stone quarries, mines, ships, vessels, boats used for fishing, &c. *Instructions for taking Seventh Census*, p. 24.

MANUFACTURES.	1821.	1825.	1835.			1845.§			1855.		
	No. of est'blish-ments	No. of est'blish-ments.	No. of est'blish-ments.	Value of raw materials used.	Value of manufac-tured products.	No. of est'blish-ments.	Value of raw materials used.	Value of manufac-tured products	No. of est'blish-ments.	Value of raw materials used.	Value of manu-factured products.
Grist mills, ...	2, 132	2, 264	2, 051	$17, 687, 009	$20, 140, 435	1, 984	$18, 580, 372	$22, 794, 474	1, 475	$42, 345, 756	$51, 531 358
Saw mills,............	4, 304	5. 195	6, 948	3, 651, 153	6, 881, 055	7, 406	4, 210, 713	7, 577, 154	4, 946	7, 286, 197	14, 655, 103
Oil mills,............	139	121	71	214, 812	275, 574	87	1, 360, 074	1, 695, 025	27	1, 092, 420	1, 316, 627
Fulling mills,.........	991	1, 222	965	1, 994, 491	2, 894, 096	740	1, 125, 539	1, 660. 881	} 264	174, 344	250, 552
Carding machines, ...	1, 233	1, 584	1, 061	2, 179, 414	2, 651, 638	820	1, 416, 904	1, 678, 320			
Cotton factories,*	*	76	111	1, 630, 352	3, 030, 709	118	1, 132, 702	2, 877, 500	86	2, 492, 531	4, 621, 133
Woolen factories,†	*	189	234	1, 450, 825	2, 433, 192	345	2, 877, 804	4, 281, 257	184	2, 054, 882	3, 392, 207
Iron works, ...	107	170	293	2, 366, 065	4, 349, 949	500	4, 451, 674,	8, 402, 586	¶	....	....
Trip hammers, ...	172	164	141	168, 896	363, 581	156	284, 360	586, 328	¶	....	....
Distilleries,...........	1, 057	1, 129	337	2, 278, 420	3, 098, 042	221	3, 162, 586	4, 222, 154	88	6, 267, 824	8, 681, 061
Asheries,.............	1, 226	2, 105	693	434, 394	726, 414	738	613, 516	909, 194	68	113, 327	165, 302
Glass factories, ...	......	......	13	163, 312	448, 559	15	115, 200	378, 700	21	302, 628	980, 500
Rope factories,........	......	......	63	664, 394	980, 083	79	659, 413	918, 540	29	1, 550, 624	2, 448, 798
Chain cable factories,..	......	......	2	20, 871	28, 625	1	2, 500	5, 000	......	....	....
Oil cloth factories,...	......	......	24	63, 119	95, 646	24	167, 992	270, 260	17	353, 889	544, 250
Dyeing & printing fac.,	......	......	15	1, 999, 000	2, 465, 600	18	1, 497, 038	2, 086, 986	16	61, 959	195, 624
Clover mills, ...	......	......	69	95 693	100, 025	115	107, 803	124, 567	10	17, 563	20, 430
Paper mills, ...	......	......	70	358, 857	685, 784	82	369, 966	702, 505	109	1, 511, 724	2, 813. 147
Tanneries, ...	......	......	412	3, 563, 593	5, 598, 626	1, 414	4, 052, 949	6, 585, 006	863	9, 670, 386	15, 642. 383
Breweries, ...	......	......	94	916, 252	1. 381, 446	102	805, 797	1, 313, 273	128	2, 698, 389	4, 448, 352

The present census directed nearly the same inquiries to be made in relation to manufactures as that of 1850,** and in reducing these returns, an effort has been made to exhibit the results of each branch of industry with as much detail and accuracy as the data would admit. In cases where the value of raw materials, or products, were omitted, while the quantities were given, the deficiency has been supplied by estimating the amount at the rates reported by establishments similarly circumstanced. Denominations of

* Cotton and woolen factories, 184.

† Yards of cotton cloth manufactured in 1835, 24,175,357; in 1845, 31,234,633.

‡ Yards of woolen cloth manufactured in 1835, 6,626,058; in 1845, 4,916,998. Yards of cotton and woolen manufacture in 1835, 686,203; in 1845, 1,592,899.

§ Number of incorporated manufactories, 71; number not incorporated, 1,608.

‖ Chiefly reported under other heads.

¶ Reported under several heads, as iron manufacture, furnaces, forges, &c. It is uncertain how far these would compare with former returns.

** The following Instructions, in relation to manufactures, were given to the marshals charged with reporting the present census:

"*Industry other than Agriculture and Domestic Manufactures.*—This schedule is designed to contain the products of industry, (excepting agriculture and domestic manufacture) of each producer or establishment. Should any one object, on the ground of not wishing to expose the nature of his business, the marshal should state that it is not desired to elicit any information, which will be used or published as concerning the operations of any individual or company. The individual facts are confidentially imparted and received, and will only be published as part of a great body of similiar facts, from which it will be impossible to abstract or distinguish those of single firms or corporations. Small mechanical operations, not pursued as a regular employment but incidentally followed, and producing less than $500 worth of product annually, should not be entered by the marshals. All kinds of mercantile, commercial, or trading business, where no specific article is produced or manufactured, but which are limited to dealing and exchange of merchandise, or manufacture, are not to be included in this schedule. If an establishment consists of several mills, or branches of manufacture, or is carried on in several different places in the same marshal's district, but for the same concern, it is to be considered as one, being owned by one individual or company. Where the same concern has branches in the districts of different marshals, they are to be enumerated in the district in which they are located.

Name of person or company owning the Shop, Factory, Mine, Quarry, or other object of Industry.—In this column, insert the name of the individual, firm, or corporation, owning or conducting the business.

Name of Business or Manufacture.—As many lines in this column are to be filled, as there are distinct branches of manufacture carried on.

Capital invested in Real Estate.—In this column insert the present value of the premises, considered with reference to location and surrounding advantages, and without reference to original cost. It is intended to represent the price for which the property might be sold in the ordinary course of business, and not the assessed value, which is unequal in the several counties and towns of the State, and generally below the price for which it could be sold.

Capital invested in Tools and Machinery.—In this column enter the present value, without reference to first cost, of the tools and machinery employed in the business or manufacture.

Quantity, kind and value of Raw Materials.—In these columns insert the aggregate quantity, kind and value of the articles used in the manufacture, including fuel used in generating steam power, or otherwise. Where several important items enter into the account, they should be separately stated, using as many lines for that purpose as may be necessary. An article produced at one establishment may be the raw material at another, as the ore is the product of the mine, and the raw material at the furnace. The pig iron, which is the article produced at the latter, is the raw material at the forge for the manufacturing of bar iron, and the latter the raw materal of the blacksmith, or the machinist. So in almost every kind of manufacture, a material has to pass through many processes of different establishments before it reaches its ultimate use. The object of the census in this schedule being to ascertain the aggregate value of labor aided by machinery, there will generally be no difficulty in filling these columns. In quarrying, mining, and similar business, no raw materials being used, these columns will be blank.

Quantity, Kind, and Value of manufactured Product.—In these columns enter the aggregate of the several distinct classes of manufacture, using as many lines as are requisite. It is not necessary that these entries generally should range on the same horizontal lines with those in the three preceding columns, but the first one should be on the same line with the name of the person or company. The remarks under the preceding head concerning what are relatively raw materials and manufactured products apply to this. By *Quantity* is meant the usual mode and terms of expressing weights, measures or amount, as pounds of tallow, bales of cotton, reams of paper, tons or bushels of coal, barrels or bushels of salt, &c. The initials of the term used should be written after the figures representing the quantity, as *B.* for bales, *Bush.* for bushels, *Bl.* for barrel, &c. By *Kind* is intended to include the name of the articles used or produced. Where different articles of the same class are manufactured, a general term should be used, as "cutlery," "hollow ware," "furniture," "glass ware," &c., but where the manufacture is limited to a single article, it should be specified, as "knives," "kettles," "chairs," "window glass," &c. The *Value*, of the whole amount of each article, whose kind and quantity are given, should be entered in the aggregate for the year ending June 1, 1855, to which date all inquiries in schedule No. III. should refer.

The value of raw materials, as well as of the manufactured product, is to be estimated at the place of manufacture, and will include the cost of transportation of the former to where used, but not of the latter to the market.

Kind of Motive Power.—In this column write "steam," "water," "horse power," &c., as the case may be. Where more than one kind of power is employed, each should be entered. As hand power is more or less used in connection with machinery, it is not to be specified, unless forming the only or principal motive power of looms, printing presses or other machinery.

Persons employed.—In these columns enter the average number of persons engaged in the manufacture or business, including agents, overseers clerks and employees of every class, directly and principally employed, but not those transiently engaged for brief periods. If the nature of the business is such that it cannot be carried on throughout the year, but only for a season, the average number of persons engaged in such season is to be entered.

Wages exclusive of Board.—In these columns insert the average wages, reduced to months, of persons employed. Where different rates are paid, those only of persons of the most numerous class are to be included, without reference to the compensation of agents, overseers or officers charged with the superintendence of the business. It is designed to get the average earnings of the laboring classes, in the several departments of industry throughout the State. Where board is included in the rate of wages, the rate of board should be added to that of the wages, so as to make the latter in all cases equal to what would be paid to employees, who paid their board out of their earnings. The object of the inquiry being, to arrive at the *cost of labor*, care should be taken to get uniformity in results, which can only be obtained by observing the above rule. In these columns include the individual labor of a producer working on his own account, whose productions are separately enumerated."—*Instructions*, page 33.

different kinds were reduced to the one most frequently used in the business, or manufacture, and technical denominations, of special or limited application, were exchanged for those more generally known.

In selecting a plan of arrangement, difficulties were found to attend every method that was examined, on account of the mixed and doubtful character of many manufactures as reported. The system used in classifying mechanical, and other inventions at the national Patent Office, with slight changes, appeared to be attended with fewer objections than any other, and was adopted. In general theory, this makes the character of the thing produced, or end accomplished, the basis of arrangement; and requires that not only the manufacture itself, but that also of the tools, machines, or implements by which the result is attained, should be placed together. Manufactures of parts of machines, or other articles, when made a distinct and separate business, have been usually placed separately, but in such manner, that their aggregate may be included under their appropriate general heads. The subdivisions of classes are arranged alphabetically under each, and only such towns and cities as reported the manufactures in question, are named in the summary. The absence of the name of a town or city, therefore, indicates that nothing was reported under the head to which the table relates.

CHURCHES.

In the census of 1845, inquiries were directed to be made with reference to the number and cost of church edifices, and the cost of other real estate owned by religious societies. In 1850 there were reported the number of church edifices, their capacity for accommodation, and the amount of property belonging to each.

In the present census, the value of church and lot, and of other real estate, the number capable of seating, usual attendance, membership and salaries of clergy, were required to be reported from each religious society owning a church edifice. As this inquiry did not extend to societies worshipping in school-houses, or other places of secular use, these returns, if made with rigorous precision, would fail to afford full statistics of religious worship in the State. They will therefore be received with due allowance for these omissions.

The comparative synopsis given on page 478, presents the aggregate results of the three enumerations above mentioned, and affords the data for the following deductions:

	1845.	1850.	1855
Average value of churches,	$3,979	$5,089	$6,200
" accommodation,	....	501	421
Percentage of accommodation to total population,	....	61.83	61.73
" attendance to total poplation,	....	....	32.41
" membership to total population,	....	....	20.23
Average number of inhabitants to each church,	636	743	683

To further illustrate this subject, an effort was made during the preparation of this volume, to obtain concise summaries of the principal religious denominations of the State, as reported and claimed in their several official registers. These statistics, although procured through the medium of their regular ecclesiastical organizations, are often avowedly imperfect, but so far as relates to the subdivision of the State, and the general results, they may be received as useful approximations, comparable, at least, with one another. The summaries thus obtained do not include all of the denominations of the State, as several do not publish registers, and from others no answers to our inquiries were received.

Baptists.—The official report of the Regular Baptists, for 1855,* gave in the United States, 537 Associations, 10,774 churches, 6,935 ordained ministers, 833 licentiates, 62,966 as baptized in 1855, and 869,462 members. There were in the State of New-York 44 Associations, 848 churches, 754 ordained ministers, 105 licentiates, and 87,479 members. The following is a list of the several Associations: *Black River, Broome and Tioga, Buffalo, Canisteo River, Cattaraugus, Cayuga, Chemung River, Chenango, Cortland, Deposit, Dutchess, Erie, Essex and Champlain, Franklin, Genesee, Genesee River, Harmony, Hudson River N., Hudson River S., Lake George, Livingston, Madison, Mohawk River, Monroe, New-York, Niagara, Oneida, Onondaga, Ontario, Orleans, Oswego, Otsego, Rensselaerville, St. Lawrence, Saratoga, Seneca, Stephentown, Steuben, Union, Washington, Wayne, Worcester, Yates,* and a new Association from Franklin 1854.

Free Will Baptists.—This denomination divides the United States into 28 yearly meetings, embracing 1,168 churches, 929 ordained preachers, 151 licensed preachers, and 49,684, communicants.† These yearly meetings are subdivided into 130 quarterly meetings, which often include parts of adjacent states. The State of New-York is divided into the *Holland Purchase, Genesee, Susquehanna, New-York and*

* *The American Baptist Almanac* for 1857, p. 47. In addition to the numbers above reported, there were in the British Provinces and the West Indies 17 Associations, 450 churches, 325 ordained ministers, 38 licentiates, 3,550 added in 1855 by baptism, and a total of 63,215 members.

† See *The Free Will Baptist Register* for 1857, p. 78.

Pennsylvania, St. Lawrence, Union, and *Central New-York* Yearly Meetings, of which the third and fourth extend into Pennsylvania. These embrace 29 Quarterly Meetings, 225 churches, 173 ordained preachers, 94 licensed preachers, and 8,506 communicants. The number of these in Pennsylvania cannot be determined with certainty.

Of other denominations of Baptists, separate statistics of the State of New-York were not obtained.*

Christian Connection.—The Christian sect divides the State into the *New-York Eastern, New-York Central, New-York Western, Northern or Black River,* and *Tioga River* Christian Conferences, each having distinct boundaries.

Congregational Churches.—There were reported in the official statistics of this denomination for 1855, in the United States, 2,449 churches, 1,843 ministers, and 207,608 members. Of these, there were in New-York, 390 churches, 259 ministers, and 11,443 members.† In some instances, it is probable, the census marshals reported churches belonging to this order as Presbyterian; for, of the number above given, 131 churches and 89 ministers were connected with Presbytery, and the distinction between them consists rather in form of church government, than difference of creed.

The General Association of New-York, in 1856, included the following Associations, viz: *Oneida, Black River, Essex, St. Lawrence, Western New-York, Long Island, New-York and Brooklyn, Ontario, Susquehanna, Albany, and Puritan of Wyoming and Allegany.*‡

Disciples of Christ.—This denomination in 1855, reported in the State of New-York, 28 churches, and 2,015 members.§ The "New-York State Convention," embraces, besides these, one church in Connecticut, and three in Vermont.

Evangelical Lutheran.—This church comprises in the United States, 34 synods, nearly 1,000 ministers, and about 1,900 congregations. The State of New-York embraces the *Synod of New-York,* formed in 1785, and having 48 ministers and 41 congregations; the *Hartwick Synod,* formed in 1830, and having 24 ministers, and 29 congregations; the *Franckean Synod,* formed in 1838, and having 21 ministers and 31 congregations; and the *Synod of Buffalo,* formed in 1839, and having 12 ministers and 13 congregations. The last two synods are not in connection with the General Synod.‖ These synods do not have definite boundaries, but overlap each other, and in some instances extend into other states.

Friends.—This denomination, nearly thirty years since, became divided, and have since been known as "Hicksite," and "Orthodox" Friends.

The former, have a General Meeting for the United States and Canada, and six Yearly Meetings, embracing extensive districts. Of these, the "New-York," and the "Genesee" Yearly Meetings, include the State of New-York, and parts of adjacent territory. They are subdivided into Quarterly Meetings, which are again divided into Monthly and Preparatory Meetings. The New-York Yearly Meeting consists of the *Westbury, Purchase, Nine Partners, Stanford, Easton, Saratoga, Duanesburgh,* and *Shrewsbury and Rahway* Quarterly Meetings, of which the latter is in New Jersey. The Genesee Yearly Meeting is subdivided into the *Farmington,* and *Scipio* Quarterly, and the *Canada,* and *Pelham,* Half-Yearly Meetings.

The corresponding statistics of the Orthodox branch of Friends have not been obtained.

Methodist Episcopal Church.—This church divides the United States into 39 Conferences, which often include parts of different states. They are subdivided into Districts and Circuits. The official minutes of 1855 show the following statistics in the United States:¶ Members, 692,255; probationers, 107,176; total, 799,431. Increase in preceding year 16,073; per cent. of increase, 2.1. Total number of traveling preachers, 5,408, and of local preachers, 6,610. Raised during the year for missions, $197,973.

Of these numbers, there were in the State of New-York about 117,000 members, 21,000 probationers, and 920 local preachers. The State was divided into Conferences and Districts, as follows:

---

* *The American Baptist Almanac* for 1857, gives of these the following totals for North America:

	Associations.	Churches.	Ordained ministers.	Licentiates.	Baptized in 1855	Total number.
Anti-Mission [Old School] Baptists in United States,..........	155	1,720	825	....	1,560	58,000
Free Will Baptists,..........	....	1,173	1,107	....	....	49,809
General Baptists,..........	....	18	16	....	....	2,300
Seventh-Day Baptists,..........	....	67	70	17	....	7,000
Church of God,..........	....	275	132	....	....	13,750
Disciples,..........	....	2,400	1,500	....	....	180,000
Tunkers,..........	....	150	200	....	....	8,000
Mennonites,..........	....	300	250	....	....	36,000

† *American Congregational Year Book* for 1855, p. 67.

‡ *Minutes of the General Association of New-York* for 1856, p. 28

§ *Minutes of the N. Y. State Convention of the Disciples of Christ,* 1856, p. 6. The denomination is sometimes known as "Campbellite," from the Rev. Alexander Campbell, the founder.

‖ *The Lutheran Almanac* for 1855, p. 21.

¶ *Minutes of the Annual Conferences of the Methodist Episcopal Church* for 1855, p. 667. The above general statistics do not include the M. E. Church South, which, according to the Methodist Almanac, for 1856, (p. 40), embraces 1,943 traveling, 150 superannuated, and 4,359 local preachers, and 596,852 church members.

:k *River Conference.*—Districts of Rome, Syracuse, Oswego, Adams, Watertown, Ogdensburgh and Potsdam.

? Conference, (mostly in Ohio and Pennsylvania).—District of Fredonia, in New-York.

t Genesee Conference.—Districts of Geneva, Rochester, West Rochester, Bath, Corning, Elmira, and Troy.

esee Conference.—Districts of Buffalo, Niagara, Genesee, Wyoming, and Olean.

)-York Conference.—Districts of Poughkeepsie, Rhinebeck, Prattsville, Monticello, N. Y. German Mission, Rochester, and German Mission.

)-York East Conference.—Districts of New-York, (E. Dist.), Long Island, and two others in Connecticut.

ida Conference.—Districts of Oneida, Otsego, Chenango, Cortland, Auburn, and Cazenovia.

y Conference.—Districts of Troy, Albany, Saratoga, Plattsburgh, and three others in Vermont.

oming Conference, (mostly in Pennsylvania).—Districts of Binghamton and Owego, mostly in New-York.

)f other denominations of Methodists, their own statistics were not procured.

'resbyterian Church.—The two divisions of this church, known as Old School, and New School sbyterians, subdivide the State of New-York as follows:*

School.—Synods of *Albany, Buffalo,* and *New-York.*

Albany Synod comprises the Presbyteries of Londonderry, Troy, Albany, Columbia, and Mohawk, of which the first named is entirely within the New England States.

Buffalo Synod comprises the Presbyteries of Ogdensburgh, Genesee River, Buffalo City, Michigan, and Rochester City, of which the fourth is within the states of Michigan and Iowa.

New-York Synod comprises the Presbyteries of Hudson, North River, Bedford, Long Island, New-York, New-York 2d, Canton, Ningpo, and Connecticut. Several members of the New-York Presbytery, and all of those of the last three, are without the limits of this State.

v School.—Synods of *Albany, Utica, Geneva, Susquehanna, Genesee,* and *New-York and New Jersey.*

Albany Synod comprises the Presbyteries of Champlain, Troy, Albany, Columbia and Catskill.

Utica Synod comprises those of St. Lawrence, Watertown, Oswego, and Utica.

Geneva Synod comprises those of Onondaga, Cayuga, Geneva, Cortland, Tioga, Bath, Chemung, Ithaca and Pennsylvania, the latter mostly without the limits of this State

Susquehanna Synod comprises those of Otsego, Chenango, and Delaware.

Genesee Synod comprises those of Genesee, Ontario, Rochester, Niagara, Buffalo, and Angelica

New-York and New Jersey Synod comprises those of Hudson, North River, Long Island, New-York 3d, New-York 4th, Brooklyn, Newark, Rockaway, Montrose, and San Francisco, the last four beyond the limits of this State.

The reports made to the respective General Assemblies of the two divisions of this church for 1855,)w the following statistics of each Synod:

SYNODS.	OLD SCHOOL.			SYNODS.	NEW SCHOOL.		
	Number of ministers.	Number of churches	Number of communicants.		Number of ministers	Number of churches	Number of communicants.
ɒany,	90	64	8,064	Albany,	78	66	9,043
ffalo,	56	61	4,998	Utica,	69	77	7,453
w-York,	163	116	15,568	Geneva,	104	92	10,344
				Onondaga,†	91	76	8,256
Total New-York,	309	241	28,630	Susquehanna,	47	46	4,699
				Genesee,	116	126	14,447
Total United States,	2,261	3,079	231,404	New-York and New Jersey,	218	156	23,179
				Total United States,	1,567	1,659	143,029

Associate Presbyterian Church.—This church in New-York forms a part of the "*Associate Synod of North merica,*" which, from the official report of 1855,‡ contains 20 Presbyteries, 164 ministers, 21 licentiates, 7 congregations, 9,648 families, and 21,588 members. They contributed for various missionary and nevolent purposes within the year $10,729.77.

The State of New-York is divided by uncertain boundaries into the Synods of *Albany, Cambridge,* (1st and), and *New-York,* the most of which extend into neighboring states.

Of other denominations of Presbyterians, their own statistics were not procured.

Protestant Episcopal Church.—The United States are divided by this church into 30 Dioceses, embracing 821 parishes, 1,768 clergymen, and 107,560 communicants. The State of New-York comprises two oceses; that of *New-York,* having 264 parishes, 304 clergy, and 4,871 communicants; and that of *'estern New-York,* having 151 parishes, 118 clergy, and 1,489 communicants.§

* The statistics of the first division of this church are derived from e *Presbyterian Family Almanac* for 1856, p. 16, and of the second, m the *American Presbyterian Almanac* for 1856, p. 24.

† Recently formed.

‡ *Evangelical Repository,* vol. xiv., p. 139.

§ See *The Church Almanac* for 1856, p. 48.

The Diocese of New-York embraces that part of the State east of the east lines of Broome, Chenango, Madison, Oneida, Lewis, and Jefferson counties.

The Diocese of Western New-York includes all west of the east line of the above mentioned counties.

Reformed Protestant Dutch Church.—The "General Synod of the Reformed Protestant Dutch Church in North America," is subdivided into the *Particular Synod of New-York*, composed of 16 Classes, and the *Particular Synod of Albany*, of 14 Classes. Of these 19 Classes are embraced in the State of New-York, partly in New Jersey, and the remainder in New Jersey, Pennsylvania, Illinois, Michigan, Wisconsin, Holland and India. The following synopsis is compiled from the official summary of 1855:* Churches, 364; ministers, 348; families, 29,278, total of congregations, 130,120; communicants, 38,927. Amount contributed for religious and benevolent purposes, $77,999.46.

Of the above there were in New-York 260 churches, 259 ministers, 21,027 families, 97,553 total of congregations, and 38,927 communicants.

Roman Catholic Churches.—The United States are divided by Catholics into 9 Provinces, 2 Apostolic Vicarates, and 41 Dioceses.† These include 1,824 churches, 7 archbishops, 33 bishops, 1,704 priests, and population of 1,745,000, besides 7 dioceses of which the population was not reported.

The State of New-York comprises four Dioceses. The *Diocese of Brooklyn* embraces the counties on Long Island, and reports 24 churches, 11 other stations, 30 clergymen in the ministry, and 14 clerical students. Its Catholic population is not stated.

The *Arch-Diocese of New-York* includes the remainder of the State south of the 42 deg. of N. Lat., and reports 47 churches, 30 other stations, 82 clergymen in the ministry, 26 clergymen otherwise employed, 51 clerical students, and a Catholic population of 280,000.

The *Diocese of Albany* embraces that part of the State north of the last mentioned, and east of the east lines of Cayuga, Tompkins, and Tioga counties. It reports 87 churches, 50 other stations, 74 clergymen in the ministry, and 15 clerical students. Population not stated.

The *Diocese of Buffalo* comprises the remainder of the State, and reports 100 churches, 78 clergymen in the ministry, 10 clerical students, and 100,000 Catholic population.

Shakers, or the "United Society of Believers," sometimes known as the "Millennial Church." There are 18 societies of this sect in the United States, numbering about 6,000 members. Each society is usually divided into several large families, and their property is held in common.

Unitarians.—The number of churches of this denomination reported in the census, exceeds that claimed in the official Register for 1855, probably from some being thus returned who should be properly classed with the Christian Connection, or with Universalists, with portions of which they have much resemblance.

There were in 1855, 279 clergymen and 249 societies of Unitarians in the United States. Of the latter 11 were in New-York. There were about 30 associations and societies for religious, charitable, or educational purposes, and 8 periodicals.

Universalists.—The "New-York State Convention," of this denomination, embraces 16 associations, 2[illegible] societies, 178 meeting houses, and 128 preachers. The number of members and societies is not given.§

SCHOOL HOUSES.

A deficiency of other means for obtaining the number, condition, and value of District School Houses, led to the insertion of a blank in the census for this purpose. From the returns it appears that there were 11,137 School Houses in the State, viz:

	Number.	Per cent.	Condition.		Per cent.
Stone,	601	5.4	Very good,	195	1.7
Brick,	738	6.6	Good,	6,181	55.5
Framed,	9,238	83.0	Ordinary,	447	4.0
Logs,	313	2.8	Poor,	3,626	32.6
Plank,	247	2.2	Very poor,	688	6.2

UNINCORPORATED LITERARY AND BENEVOLENT INSTITUTIONS.

As there existed no means for ascertaining the number and value of these institutions, an inquiry was inserted in the census blanks of 1855, for obtaining information concerning them. The returns are as follows:

* *The Acts and Proceedings of the General Synod of the Reformed Protestant Dutch Church*, 1855, p. 572.

† See *The Metropolitan Catholic Almanac and Laity's Directory* for 1855, p. 289, &c.

‡ See the *Unitarian Congregational Register* for 1855, p. 43.

§ The above information concerning this society was communicated by the Rev. Wm. S. Balch, of New-York.

DESCRIPTION.	Number.	Value of real estate
Parochial schools, chiefly Roman Catholic, and Protestant Episcopal,	40	$156,950
Select schools, private seminaries, and schools not reported as belonging to religious societies,	68	301,988
Halls of Masons, Odd Fellows, Rechabites, &c.,	18	11,290
Lyceums, and halls for lectures, &c.,	5	21,950
Asylums, and private benevolent societies,	6	39,000
Mission houses, and Sabbath schools,	4	5,000
Ladies' benevolent societies,	7	3,655
Library Association,	1	100
Total,	149	$539,933

INNS, STORES, AND GROCERIES.

Returns having been made under these heads in 1845, it was deemed proper to obtain data for comparison in the present census. The result was as follows:

	1845.	1855.
Hotels, inns, and taverns,	5,813	6,025
Wholesale stores,	2,540	4,836
Retail stores,	12,257	22,607
Groceries,	5,860	10,421

NEWSPAPERS AND OTHER PERIODICALS.

The marshals appointed to take this census, were directed to learn by inquiry of the publishers, and report, the name of each newspaper and other periodical published in their several districts, the names of the editors and publishers, the object to which devoted, date of establishment, subscription price, circulation, and intervals of publication; and to forward to the Secretary's office a specimen number of each periodical so reported. The returns of this class of statistics were generally quite full, excepting from the city of New-York, where, from frequent changes, the issue of journals having an ephemeral object, and terminating with the causes that produced them, the difficulty of procuring data of those published in foreign languages, and those representing a narrow and special interest or subject, and therefore not generally known, and from other difficulties, which could not be remedied, these literary statistics were much less definite than from other counties. To indicate the relative sizes of newspapers, the copies returned as specimens have been measured, and the size and form of the sheets are noted in the published tables. In some cases no information on the subject could be procured from data in the census office. In classifying these publications, daily papers, and editions made up from them, are first given, *each being regarded as a separate paper*, then weekly, semi-monthly, monthly, quarterly, and annual periodicals, in the alphabetical order of their principal titles, without reference to their form, or the objects to which they are devoted. At the end of the list is a recapitulation by counties, with a summary of the circulation of each class. It is highly probable that the actual circulation of the periodicals of the State exceeds the number here reported, but no data exist for ascertaining the probable amount. All of the newspapers whose sizes are given in the following list, and most of the other periodicals of the State were collected, and have been bound in a uniform series of eleven volumes, for the State Library.

The earliest newspaper in New-York, was the "New-York Gazette," which was commenced October 16th, 1725, and printed weekly. Other papers were commenced as follows: "New-York Weekly Journal," by John Peter Zenger, October 5th, 1733; "New-York Gazette or Weekly Post Boy," by James Parker, January 174$\frac{2}{3}$; "New-York Evening Post," by Henry De Forrest, before 1746; "New-York Gazette," by William Weyman, February 16th, 1759, and down to the period of the Revolution about half a dozen others.

In 1775 there were 4 papers printed in New-York, viz: New-York Mercury, New-York Journal, New-York Gazetteer, and Albany Post Boy. In 1810 there were 66 papers printed in the State, with an aggregate annual circulation of 4,139,200 sheets.* In 1828 there were 161 newspapers and periodicals,* and in 1832 the number printed in New-York city was 64, and in the State 258. The number and circulation was thus estimated in the "New-York Annual Register" for that year: Dailies, 13, (average 1,400), 5,623,800; semi-weeklies, 12, (average 1,600), 1,996,800; weeklies, 33, 2,912,000; semi-monthlies, 372,000; and monthlies, 324,000. Total estimated number of copies, 16,028,600.

In 1834 there were reported 267 periodicals, viz: 21 dailies, 16 semi-weeklies, 208 weeklies, 9 semi-monthlies, and 13 monthlies. The average circulation of the 10 large dailies in New-York city was then estimated at about 1,700 each.

* Compendium of U. S. Census, 1850; quoted from *American Almanac*, 1830, and an early issue of the National Intelligencer. See also *Williams' Register*, 1832, 1834; *Amercian Almanac*, 1835; *Thomas' History of Printing*, *Munsell's Typography*, &c *Jeffersonian*, [Newspaper, Albany, 1839], p. 407, where the details for that year are given by counties.

On the 1st of January, 1839, there were 307 periodicals published in the State, of which 186 were political—83 being for and 104 against the administration party. 31 were religious, 10 philanthropic, 26 daily, 2 tri-weekly, 16 semi-weekly, 206 weekly, 7 semi-monthly, and 26 monthly. There were published in New-York city 15 dailies, 1 tri-weekly, 10 semi-weekly, 38 weekly, 3 semi-monthly, 16 monthly, and 5 quarterly papers and Magazines.

The census of 1840 reported 34 dailies, 198 weeklies, 13 semi and tri-weeklies, and 57 other periodicals in the State.

The census of 1850 reported the following:

PAPERS.	Number.	Number of copies printed annually.	CHARACTER OF PAPERS.	Number.	Number of copies printed annually.
Dailies,	51	63, 928, 685	Literary and miscellaneous,	101	18, 449, 016
Tri-weeklies,	8	776, 100	Neutral and independent,	15	37, 317, 010
Semi-weeklies,	13	3, 116, 360	Political,	263	45, 463, 015
Weeklies,	308	39, 205, 920	Religious,	37	12, 438, 432
Semi-monthlies,	9	1, 704, 000	Scientific,	12	1, 718, 000
Monthlies,	36	6, 629, 808			
Quarterlies,	3	24, 600	Aggregate,	428	115, 385, 473
Aggregate,	428	115, 385, 473			

The results of the census of 1855 are given on page 480 to 497. Of the 671 periodicals of all classes, the circulation of 138 was not given. If these be estimated at the same rates as those reported, the result will be as follows:

CLASSES.	CIRCULATION REPORTED.		Circulation not reported.	Estimated annual number printed.	Estimated number of copies printed at each edition.
	Number.	Total annual number printed.			
Dailies,	62	97, 901, 079	11	115, 270, 288	5, 045
Tri-weeklies,	10	1, 310, 400	3	1, 703, 520	840
Semi-weeklies,	10	4, 199, 312	6	7, 718, 899	4, 038
Weeklies,	359	67, 305, 680	52	77, 054, 692	3, 605
Semi-monthlies,	10	6, 879, 600	8	12, 383, 280	26, 460
Monthlies,	64	15, 451, 800	49	27, 282, 066	20, 119
Quarterlies,	11	127, 800	5	185, 890	2, 904
Semi-annuals,	2	22, 000	....	22, 000	5, 500
Annuals,	12	96, 950	4	129, 267	8, 080
Total,	540	193, 294, 621	138	241, 749, 902	....

Indian Census: The act of 1855, under which the present census was taken, required the appointment of marshals to enumerate the several Indian tribes of the State. The persons thus appointed were: For the Oneidas and Onondagas, Nathaniel T. Strong; for the St. Regis, Franklin B. Hough; for the Allegany Reservation, Marius B. Pierce; for the Tuscarora Reservation, William Mount Pleasant; and for the Cattaraugus and Tonawanda Reservations, Nicholson H. Parker. The latter failing to enumerate the Tonawandas, David E. E. Mix was appointed. The statistics of the Shinecock tribe were reported by the marshal for East Hampton, within whose district they were embraced.

The numbers embraced within the Indian census in the appendix are exclusive of those included in the body of the census.

CENSUS OF THE STATE OF NEW-YORK,

FOR THE YEAR 1855.

POPULATION.

CLASSIFICATION BY SEX, COLOR, CIVIL CONDITION, ETC.

ALBANY COUNTY.

CITIES AND TOWNS.	Total population.	WHITES.		COLORED PERSONS.			CIVIL CONDITION.				VOTERS.		Aliens.	Number of families.	Owners of land.	Over 21 who cannot read or write.	Over 21 who can read but not write.
		Males.	Females.	Males.	Females.	No. not taxed.	Single.	Married.	Widowers.	Widows	Native.	Naturalized.					
Albany city: 1st ward,	8, 038	4, 027	3, 922	35	54	83	4, 622	3, 087	69	260	226	780	2, 796	1, 721	321	436	125
2d ward,	4, 518	2, 167	2, 322	8	21	20	2, 730	1, 586	21	181	417	412	937	481	213	170	152
3d ward,	4, 667	2, 179	2, 442	20	26	20	2, 952	1, 526	35	154	524	381	883	408	170	81	31
4th ward,	4, 492	2, 146	3, 313	10	23	27	3, 001	1, 402	63	206	666	282	941	509	257	104	29
5th ward,	3, 016	1, 384	1, 606	14	12	17	1, 970	714	31	121	328	152	804	444	107	65	47
6th ward,	3, 460	1, 526	1, 933	1	......	......	2, 289	1, 066	18	87	377	173	761	441	123	17	31
7th ward,	6, 006	3, 017	2, 978	7	4	10	3, 600	2, 142	66	198	476	607	1, 310	539	235	406	333
8th ward,	7, 467	3, 514	3, 859	39	55	52	4, 573	2, 557	72	265	562	733	1, 257	1, 514	402	279	63
9th ward,	7, 343	3, 539	3, 695	51	58	57	4, 409	2, 616	53	265	660	502	2, 044	942	302	30	10
10th ward,	8, 326	3, 888	4, 265	89	84	128	5, 460	2, 443	76	347	824	540	1, 611	1, 542	637	144	148
Total Albany, ...	57, 333	27, 387	29, 335	274	337	409	35, 606	19, 139	504	2, 084	5, 060	4, 562	13, 344	8, 536	2, 767	1, 732	974
Bern, ...	3, 206	1, 578	1, 627	......	1	......	1, 901	1, 182	32	91	687	42	60	574	475	45	62
Bethlehem, ...	5, 151	2, 594	2, 450	52	55	82	3, 194	1, 799	51	107	683	161	1, 160	981	476	34	16
Coeymans, ...	2, 963	1, 459	1, 445	27	32	57	1, 768	1, 077	30	88	631	31	227	554	343	57	3
Guilderland, ...	3, 188	1, 572	1, 588	15	13	15	1, 952	1, 109	39	88	656	51	229	564	411	69	65
Knox, ...	1, 888	939	949	......	......	......	1, 123	692	21	52	461	7	25	344	312	17	15
New Scotland, ...	3, 327	1, 674	1, 640	6	7	9	2, 438	786	34	69	735	20	116	613	263	42	29
Rensselaerville, ...	3, 088	1, 506	1, 580	1	1	1	1, 756	1, 197	41	94	752	21	57	582	466	28	38
Watervliet, ...	20, 889	10, 241	10, 635	5	8	9	12, 758	7, 241	197	693	2, 134	1, 283	4, 990	2, 736	1, 525	1, 198	744
Westerlo, ...	2, 648	1, 324	1, 319	3	2	4	1, 531	1, 001	27	89	635	4	74	499	440	9	19
Total, ...	103, 681	50, 274	52, 568	383	456	586	64, 027	35, 223	976	3 455	12, 434	6, 182	20, 282	15, 983	7, 478	3, 231	1, 965

ALLEGANY COUNTY.

CITIES AND TOWNS.	Total population.	Whites: Males.	Whites: Females.	Colored: Males.	Colored: Females.	No. not taxed.	Single.	Married.	Widowers.	Widows	Native.	Naturalized.	Aliens.	Number of families.	Owners of land.	Over 21 who cannot read or write.	Over 21 who can read but not write.
Alfred, ...	1, 707	859	848	......	......	......	925	694	44	44	401	10	43	372	328	31	33
Allen, ...	1, 026	518	508	......	......	......	604	399	4	19	212	14	37	203	173	9	......
Alma, ...	412	243	169	......	......	......	246	160	4	2	91	4	46	74	37	3	10
Almond, ...	1, 952	987	952	6	7	13	1, 146	737	19	50	452	18	49	384	323	35	......
Amity, ...	2, 655	1, 331	1, 313	8	3	8	1, 524	1, 071	25	45	589	44	136	522	384	54	51
Andover, ...	1, 775	907	868	......	......	......	1, 064	648	24	39	322	30	161	340	285	40	......
Angelica, ...	1, 832	925	895	4	8	11	1, 132	645	20	35	346	49	187	330	254	23	3
Belfast, ...	2. 130	1, 077	1, 052	......	1	1	1, 268	812	14	36	406	41	122	414	266	83	22
Birdsall, ...	838	452	386	......	......	......	522	299	10	7	154	31	23	156	126	5	......
Bolivar, ...	985	503	482	......	......	......	586	382	7	10	223	7	18	195	155	1	......
Burns, ...	1, 087	566	521	......	......	......	670	395	11	11	242	8	74	211	165	7	1
Caneadea, ...	2, 400	1, 225	1, 146	12	17	24	1, 466	884	10	40	482	34	162	493	272	2	......
Centreville, ...	1, 349	674	075	......	......	......	801	504	18	26	293	31	69	254	242	7	......
Clarksville, ...	781	421	360	......	......	......	449	313	4	10	189	4	7	164	140	11	......
Cuba, ...	2, 116	1, 116	990	4	6	9	1, 220	844	12	40	471	22	166	421	330	22	1
Friendship, ...	1, 838	900	938	......	......	......	1, 014	753	20	51	433	20	82	386	331	42	......
Genesee, ...	895	446	445	3	1	4	528	343	9	15	199	2	21	175	154	3	......
Granger, ...	1, 218	630	588	......	......	......	719	466	11	22	239	54	19	265	196	5	......
Grove, ...	1, 118	594	523	1	......	......	686	412	7	13	217	36	49	285	185	8	3
Hume, ...	2, 094	1, 069	1, 021	1	3	4	1, 182	841	18	53	466	20	72	428	295	27	9
Independence, ...	1, 136	585	551	......	......	......	656	454	14	12	260	7	19	227	218	9	8
New Hudson, ...	1, 451	750	700	1	......	1	855	550	13	33	314	8	45	274	246	11	......
Ossian, ...	1, 313	711	602	......	......	......	812	467	17	17	277	32	42	250	179	1	5
Rushford, ...	1, 995	999	983	6	7	10	1, 128	794	24	49	494	19	61	404	372	9	5
Scio, ...	3, 184	1, 625	1, 506	32	21	5	1, 848	1, 275	21	40	675	49	257	639	415	39	27
West Almond, ...	972	508	462	......	2	......	573	374	6	19	230	8	17	194	94	21	......
Willing, ...	1, 127	587	538	......	2	......	660	431	15	21	219	9	36	225	203	23	16
Wirt, ...	1, 524	783	716	14	11	......	891	601	9	23	375	2	5	299	285	5	......
Total, ...	42, 910	21, 991	20, 738	92	89	90	25, 165	16, 553	410	782	9, 271	613	2, 032	8, 584	6, 653	536	194

BROOME COUNTY.

CITIES AND TOWNS.	Total population.	Whites: Males.	Whites: Females.	Colored: Males.	Colored: Females.	No. not taxed.	Single.	Married.	Widowers.	Widows	Native.	Naturalized.	Aliens.	Number of families.	Owners of land.	Over 21 who cannot read or write.	Over 21 who can read but not write.
Barker, ...	1, 324	637	684	2	1	......	803	475	15	31	311	9	37	257	234	......	......
Chenango, ...	13, 128	6, 438	6, 310	188	192	250	8, 186	4, 547	111	284	2, 382	326	1, 384	2, 305	1, 352	366	93
Colesville, ...	3, 135	1, 613	1, 521	......	1	1	1, 709	1, 249	22	65	769	15	25	644	550	27	24
Conklin, ...	2, 539	1, 329	1, 188	11	11	8	1, 506	956	32	45	525	32	147	483	403	44	12
Lisle, ...	1, 815	925	890	......	......	......	1, 058	696	16	45	458	8	21	376	382	7	......
Maine, ...	1, 979	1, 005	964	3	7	9	1, 120	801	15	43	446	29	25	406	355	11	4
Nanticoke, ...	819	425	393	1	......	......	507	294	3	15	177	8	16	160	129	7	......
Sanford, ...	3, 060	1, 583	1, 430	21	26	43	1, 843	1, 130	29	58	629	49	249	559	434	79	68
Triangle, ...	1, 784	909	868	3	4	4	1, 082	642	15	45	428	3	43	374	283	3	......
Union, ...	2, 463	1, 239	1, 181	20	23	42	1, 435	953	22	53	549	17	69	498	383	56	5
Vestal, ...	1, 967	997	970	......	......	......	1, 248	663	15	41	420	11	9	370	363	......	......
Windsor, ...	2, 637	1, 336	1, 300	1	......	......	1, 516	1, 053	18	50	666	16	31	530	480	11	17
Total, ...	36, 650	18. 436	17, 699	250	265	366	22, 113	13, 459	313	775	7, 760	522	2, 056	6, 962	5, 348	611	223

CATTARAUGUS COUNTY.

CITIES AND TOWNS.	Total population.	WHITES.		COLORED PERSONS.			CIVIL CONDITION.				VOTERS.		Aliens.	Number of families.	Owners of land.	Over 21 who cannot read or write.	Over 21 who can read but…
		Males.	Females.	Males.	Females.	No. not taxed.	Single.	Married.	Widowers.	Widows.	Native.	Naturalized.					
Allegany,	1, 583	820	763	......	......	......	919	629	15	20	314	26	206	303	228	9	
Ashford,	1, 913	957	943	9	4	5	1, 082	782	21	28	372	32	188	389	337	30	
Bucktooth,	453	244	209	......	......	......	261	184	2	6	89	5	49	69	38	19	...
Carrolton,	511	256	255	......	......	......	318	182	3	8	84	22	27	89	59	10	
Cold Spring,	664	351	313	......	......	......	419	236	3	6	136	7	18	119	80	9	
Connewango,	1, 345	674	671	......	......	......	793	531	7	14	316	6	2	275	228	3	...
Dayton,	1, 139	581	558	......	......	......	608	437	12	22	245	7	40	226	157	9	
East Otto,	1, 228	604	624	......	......	......	701	489	9	29	262	9	53	242	227	13	
Ellicottville,	1, 838	915	909	6	8	14	1, 147	650	16	25	275	73	198	343	152	42	
Farmersville,	1, 443	761	682	......	......	......	873	528	13	29	306	14	87	267	244	5	
Franklinville,	1, 686	845	841	......	......	......	987	640	13	46	357	49	57	334	348	5	
Freedom,	1, 443	743	700	......	......	......	821	580	11	31	245	82	120	300	261	13	
Great Valley,	1, 198	608	590	......	......	......	693	463	13	29	226	30	119	236	183	12	
Hinsdale,	2, 129	1, 099	1, 030	......	......	......	1, 234	841	15	39	330	18	480	434	229	165	
Humphrey,	759	395	364	......	......	......	450	294	6	9	160	19	25	151	130	5	
Ischua,	1, 103	585	518	......	......	......	596	496	8	3	226	13	75	204	167	5	...
Leon,	1, 330	682	648	......	......	......	789	509	8	24	302	4	25	264	283	14	
Little Valley,	801	415	382	2	2	......	437	344	7	13	160	18	24	160	142	26	...
Lyndon,	1, 123	593	530	......	......	......	640	449	8	26	201	48	34	220	220	3	
Machias,	1, 366	669	697	......	......	......	853	492	7	14	276	9	66	226	210	2	...
Mansfield,	1, 125	575	549	1	......	......	644	450	9	22	253	15	43	257	185	8	
Napoli,	1, 222	589	633	......	......	......	704	487	8	23	297	......	6	243	231	2	
New Albion,	1, 562	799	763	......	......	......	916	614	7	25	338	15	51	310	241	10	
Olean,	1, 611	808	749	31	23	15	952	611	15	33	307	21	260	310	223	14	
Otto,	1, 094	563	531	......	......	......	635	420	11	28	261	8	43	213	189	1	...
Perrysburgh,	1, 456	723	728	4	1	1	845	552	22	37	330	2	70	288	248	11	
Persia,	1, 204	614	579	6	5	......	721	460	7	16	227	11	83	185	240	6	
Portville,	1, 164	610	554	......	......	......	709	427	13	15	276	21	34	213	173	11	
Randolph,	1, 723	842	881	......	......	......	1, 049	631	8	35	343	10	103	327	226	10	...
South Valley,	586	322	264	......	......	......	363	207	4	12	122	6	41	111	72	4	
Yorkshire,	1, 728	897	804	13	14	27	1, 016	677	16	19	385	16	18	338	312	20	...
Total,	39, 530	20, 139	19, 262	72	57	62	23, 235	15, 292	317	686	8, 021	616	2, 645	7, 646	6, 263	496	

CAYUGA COUNTY.

CITIES AND TOWNS.	Total population.	Whites, Males.	Whites, Females.	Colored, Males.	Colored, Females.	No. not taxed.	Single.	Married.	Widowers.	Widows.	Voters, Native.	Voters, Naturalized.	Aliens.	Number of families.	Owners of land.	Over 21 who cannot read or write.	Over 21 who can read but…
Auburn city, 1st ward,	2, 404	1, 111	1, 250	15	28	24	1, 389	909	14	92	339	92	370	487	337	75	
2d ward,	1.922	875	1, 000	20	27	30	1, 340	516	14	52	319	68	347	352	266	57	
*3d ward,	1, 985	914	1, 031	16	24	23	1, 180	702	23	80	325	82	331	289	205	47	
4th ward,	3, 165	1, 823	1, 289	45	8	11	1, 838	1, 213	42	72	326	127	413	516	314	169	
Total Auburn,	9, 476	4, 723	4, 570	96	87	88	5, 747	3, 340	93	296	1, 309	369	1, 461	1, 644	1, 122	348	
Aurelius,	2, 574	1, 359	1, 200	8	7	14	1, 622	840	32	80	476	79	360	511	360	37	
Brutus,	2, 807	1, 457	1, 322	9	19	15	1, 737	979	24	67	474	40	421	409	335	8	...
Cato,	2, 252	1, 164	1, 088	......	......	......	1, 310	871	20	51	512	20	102	455	323	15	
Conquest,	1, 872	968	903	......	1	1	1, 075	739	13	45	433	15	68	314	280	29	
Fleming,	1, 164	604	560	......	......	......	699	435	10	20	257	16	143	226	216	19	...
Genoa,	2, 352	1, 147	1, 201	3	1	4	1, 374	891	31	56	568	15	119	489	363	14	
Ira,	2, 133	1, 061	1, 066	3	3	......	1, 214	849	15	55	491	10	92	432	342	27	
Ledyard,	1, 976	965	960	29	22	25	1, 194	698	23	61	384	29	246	393	266	33	
Locke,	1, 293	636	657	......	......	......	762	486	10	35	300	8	12	265	208	8	
Mentz,	5, 058	2, 617	2, 393	20	28	36	2, 968	1, 908	46	136	986	91	542	794	694	205	
Moravia,	1, 819	904	912	2	1	1	1, 056	703	20	40	383	10	56	361	250	16	
Niles,	1, 912	973	939	......	......	......	1, 078	776	16	42	482	12	38	319	279	8	...
Owasco,	1, 303	627	652	9	15	12	801	449	16	37	257	16	151	258	275	27	
Scipio,	1, 895	963	930	2	......	2	1, 153	689	11	42	403	24	130	370	258	13	
Sempronius,	1, 269	614	655	......	......	......	722	492	15	40	317	7	18	258	258	10	
Sennett,	2, 082	1, 049	1, 024	5	4	7	1, 268	749	21	44	380	35	284	389	298	10	...
Springport,	2, 171	1, 155	998	12	6	15	1, 367	729	24	51	366	55	295	399	282	6	...
Sterling,	3, 024	1, 541	1 483	......	......	......	1, 912	1, 045	25	42	607	65	152	579	492	31	...
Summer Hill,	1, 184	606	578	......	......	......	660	486	11	27	292	10	1	256	127	3	...
Venice,	1, 939	1, 002	929	5	3	......	1, 177	692	17	53	443	28	131	389	306	16	
Victory,	2, 016	1, 025	991	......	......	......	1, 170	805	7	34	436	16	41	413	327	7	...
Total,	53, 571	27, 160	26, 011	203	197	220	32, 066	19, 651	500	1, 354	10, 556	970	4, 863	9, 923	7, 661	890	

* An unofficial enumeration of this ward gave 123 more names than the above.

CHAUTAUQUE COUNTY.

CITIES AND TOWNS.	Total population.	Whites, Males.	Whites, Females.	Colored, Males.	Colored, Females.	No. not taxed.	Single.	Married.	Widowers.	Widows.	Voters, Native.	Voters, Naturalized.	Aliens.	Number of families.	Owners of land.	Over 21 who cannot read or write.	Over 21 who can read but…
Arkwright,	1, 110	561	549	......	......	......	670	411	12	17	241	4	31	205	187	9	
Busti,	1, 920	937	977	3	3	......	1, 091	763	24	42	420	29	108	375	339	5	
Carroll,	1, 408	698	710	......	......	......	827	539	12	30	317	3	45	278	274	4	...
Charlotte,	1, 672	845	827	......	......	......	961	660	13	38	341	44	40	337	327	13	
Chautauque,	2, 591	1, 320	1, 267	4	......	......	1, 492	1, 008	32	59	564	51	152	521	418	32	
Cherry Creek,	1, 226	632	594	......	......	......	666	514	11	35	308	4	26	258	234	2	
Clymer,	1, 164	607	557	......	......	......	671	463	12	18	213	28	128	216	211	14	
Ellery,	1, 865	972	893	......	......	......	1, 088	724	21	32	477	4	43	355	327	7	
Ellicott,	3, 935	1, 955	1, 949	16	15	15	2, 340	1, 495	25	75	789	53	296	757	409	42	
Ellington,	1, 930	972	958	......	......	......	1, 097	770	18	45	473	5	7	407	364	1	...
French Creek,	766	400	366	......	......	......	425	318	7	16	171	6	28	153	146	3	
Gerry,	1, 258	634	620	1	3	4	726	508	9	15	300	6	17	253	211	5	
Hanover,	4, 101	2, 053	2, 041	4	3	6	2, 382	1, 578	49	92	832	61	303	815	641	40	
Harmony,	3, 443	1, 742	1, 701	......	......	......	1, 919	1, 413	25	86	820	17	117	707	621	11	
Kiantone,	490	257	233	......	......	......	270	199	3	18	118	3	35	96	91	......	...
Mina,	1, 036	522	514	......	......	......	617	381	10	28	189	36	70	200	192	1	
Poland,	1, 325	701	618	1	5	......	781	509	13	22	291	8	43	245	206	......	...
Pomfret,	9, 157	4, 733	4, 383	21	20	10	5, 340	3, 529	92	196	1, 545	207	2, 353	1, 841	1, 046	463	
Portland,	1, 936	978	958	......	......	......	1, 102	777	17	40	426	18	146	373	303	16	
Ripley,	1, 703	852	851	......	......	......	1, 018	623	19	43	314	37	133	331	281	41	
Sheridan,	1, 591	763	828	......	......	......	891	629	20	51	338	25	122	335	295	12	
Sherman,	1, 314	652	662	......	......	......	725	556	11	22	260	28	57	274	240	5	
Stockton,	1, 688	869	819	......	......	......	922	708	23	35	410	5	45	350	319	3	...

CHAUTAUQUE COUNTY.—(Continued.)

Cities and towns.	Total population.	Whites.		Colored persons.			Civil condition.				Voters.		Aliens.	Number of families.	Owners of land.	Over 21 who cannot read or write.	Over 21 who can read but not write.
		Males.	Females	Males.	Females	No. not taxed.	Single.	Married.	Widowers.	Widows.	Native.	Naturalized.					
Villenova,	1,413	721	692	......	......	......	752	621	13	27	339	5	31	315	264	6	4
Westfield,	3,338	1,670	1,658	5	5	10	1,968	1,246	42	82	642	87	419	569	582	14	5
Total,	53,380	27,046	26,225	55	54	45	30,741	20,942	533	1,164	11,138	774	4,795	10,566	8,528	749	292

CHEMUNG COUNTY.

Cities and towns.	Total population.	Whites.		Colored persons.			Civil condition.				Voters.		Aliens.	Number of families.	Owners of land.	Over 21 who cannot read or write.	Over 21 who can read but not write.
		Males.	Females	Males.	Females	No. not taxed.	Single.	Married.	Widowers.	Widows.	Native.	Naturalized.					
Big Flats,	1,853	924	919	5	5	......	1,184	615	17	37	380	23	102	353	203	56	21
Catlin,	1,518	757	757	2	2	......	957	533	10	18	301	9	25	300	245	1	......
Chemung,	2,785	1,433	1,346	4	2	1	1,735	970	25	55	572	20	56	498	386	20	12
Elmira,	8,486	3,965	4,178	172	171	217	5,084	3,090	67	245	1,546	236	1,211	1,589	1,023	331	144
Erin,	1,190	603	584	1	2	......	728	445	6	11	272	6	1	231	232	......	......
Horseheads,	2,648	1,344	1,284	12	8	12	1,712	885	20	31	534	35	144	467	314	14	......
Southport,	4,479	2,253	2,168	32	26	47	2,739	1,610	40	90	849	59	404	869	578	172	5
Van Etten,	1,522	781	741	......	......	......	950	544	12	16	342	2	4	281	268	16	7
Veteran,	2,807	1,413	1,375	10	9	18	1,608	1,083	45	71	636	37	44	568	416	65	42
Total,	27,288	13,473	13,352	238	225	295	16,697	9,775	242	574	5,432	427	1,991	5.156	3,665	675	231

CHENANGO COUNTY.

Cities and towns.	Total population.	Whites.		Colored persons.			Civil condition.				Voters.		Aliens.	Number of families.	Owners of land.	Over 21 who cannot read or write.	Over 21 who can read but not write.
		Males.	Females	Males.	Females	No. not taxed.	Single.	Married.	Widowers.	Widows.	Native.	Naturalized.					
Bainbridge,	3,377	1,681	1,684	7	5	6	1,957	1,285	41	94	843	11	38	643	555	22	2
Columbus,	1,331	670	661	......	......	......	730	551	18	32	353	10	17	292	238	1	......
Coventry,	1,684	841	842	1	......	1	941	676	25	42	431	7	20	357	214	12	15
German,	806	406	400	......	......	......	505	284	4	13	176	10	6	146	133	9	12
Greene,	3,717	1,865	1,823	15	14	23	2,175	1,421	40	81	859	45	69	743	528	54	......
Guilford,	2,552	1,272	1,276	......	4	4	1,436	1,034	19	63	620	9	65	524	443	6	1
Lincklaen,	1,131	549	582	......	......	......	683	435	5	8	243	13	14	219	194	......	......
Macdonough,	1,417	700	715	1	1	......	817	555	17	28	336	7	20	282	252	......	......
New Berlin,	2,507	1,212	1,276	12	7	2	1,394	1,012	33	68	591	20	61	524	354	19	......
North Norwich,	1,126	584	541	1	......	1	653	432	19	22	264	2	34	235	194	4	2
Norwich,	4,109	1,965	2,068	40	36	53	2,483	1,489	53	84	890	54	197	822	583	9	9
Otselic,	1,721	887	834	......	......	......	965	703	16	37	409	10	4	360	277	12	13
Oxford,	3,116	1,492	1,576	27	21	9	1,802	1,205	18	91	715	35	102	636	521	14	3
Pharsalia,	1,152	594	558	......	......	......	687	434	7	24	263	7	11	218	209	5	......
Pitcher,	1,281	652	629	......	......	......	722	510	13	36	319	6	4	315	260	6	1
Plymouth,	1,541	767	767	2	5	7	825	663	14	39	379	10	12	577	503	21	18
Preston,	1,044	511	532	1	......	......	604	395	11	34	253	11	26	483	279	26	8
Sherburne,	2,776	1,360	1,403	7	6	5	1,554	1,102	30	90	613	47	131	392	297	50	11
Smithville,	1,661	837	824	......	......	......	1,038	560	12	51	318	50	111	198	175	2	......
Smyrna,	1,866	920	945	......	1	1	1,067	723	20	56	447	14	35	270	226	1	2
Total,	39,915	19,765	19,936	114	100	112	23,038	15,469	415	993	9,322	378	977	8,236	6,435	273	97

CLINTON COUNTY.

Cities and towns.	Total population.	Whites.		Colored persons.			Civil condition.				Voters.		Aliens.	Number of families.	Owners of land.	Over 21 who cannot read or write.	Over 21 who can read but not write.
		Males.	Females	Males.	Females	No. not taxed.	Single.	Married.	Widowers.	Widows.	Native.	Naturalized.					
Au Sable,	3,803	1,851	1,946	3	3	6	2,444	1,263	31	65	357	191	732	655	257	393	53
Beekmantown,	2,933	1,456	1,437	24	16	25	1,858	964	36	75	352	163	400	482	425	208	32
Black Brook,	3,025	1,557	1,468	......	......	......	1,896	1,087	18	24	232	98	793	541	192	463	75
Champlain,	6,197	3,079	3,113	1	4	5	3,971	2,081	52	93	517	205	1,714	1,052	373	787	65
Chazy,	4,462	2,222	2,222	11	7	17	2,781	1,572	35	74	568	176	586	809	575	372	13
Clinton,	1,371	709	662	......	......	......	912	449	4	6	38	138	336	248	157	242	7
Dannemora,*	723	476	222	25	......	25	440	268	12	3	79	22	146	84	62	24	1
Ellenburgh,	1,751	906	843	1	1	1	1,054	659	12	26	278	65	174	348	231	104	22
Mooers,	3,622	1,818	1,802	1	1	2	2,274	1,258	32	58	340	201	823	630	492	316	4
Peru,	3,520	1,784	1,727	4	5	9	2,381	1,039	30	70	482	132	478	635	441	243	49
Plattsburgh,	6,080	2,992	3,077	6	5	......	3,883	2,062	40	95	664	245	1,421	984	642	668	133
Saranac,	3,058	1,649	1,397	7	5	2	1,956	1,044	23	35	291	185	574	533	362	458	63
Schuyler's Falls,	1,937	974	962	......	1	1	1,238	646	18	35	266	89	227	344	272	171	60
Total,	42,482	21,473	20,878	83	48	93	27,088	14,392	343	659	4,464	1,910	8,401	7,345	4,481	4,449	577

* 258 in Clinton Prison.

COLUMBIA COUNTY.

Cities and towns.	Total population.	Whites.		Colored persons.			Civil condition.				Voters.		Aliens.	Number of families.	Owners of land.	Over 21 who cannot read or write.	Over 21 who can read but not write.
		Males.	Females	Males.	Females	No. not taxed.	Single.	Married.	Widowers.	Widows.	Native.	Naturalized.					
Ancram,	1,801	929	871	......	1	1	1,209	528	16	48	407	10	99	323	171	20	10
Austerlitz,	1,618	761	784	35	38	65	938	610	20	50	368	7	85	354	228	17	5
Canaan,	1,946	967	932	22	25	37	1,312	557	24	53	414	30	196	426	235	62	35
Chatham,	4,023	1,948	1,901	82	92	145	2,397	1,501	35	90	809	65	456	821	460	98	46
Claverack,	3,363	1,637	1,689	17	20	23	2,032	1,199	37	95	729	59	220	519	444	59	......
Clermont,	1,058	533	518	5	2	7	699	306	18	35	242	3	47	183	136	18	6
Copake,	1,620	832	774	6	8	14	981	582	18	39	338	14	101	269	180	18	9
Gallatin,	1,517	775	736	3	3	4	949	522	15	31	349	6	14	272	166	35	7
Germantown,	1,131	565	543	8	15	16	732	359	12	28	225	4	70	193	132	39	......
Ghent,	2,537	1,219	1,197	53	68	119	1,530	904	43	60	462	68	307	471	237	20	7
Greenport,	1,383	662	681	23	17	7	887	448	20	28	243	40	141	242	146	10	2
Hillsdale,	2,194	1,098	1,085	3	8	11	1,312	816	20	46	511	11	72	366	273	9	4
Hudson city, 1st ward,	1,460	690	749	7	14	12	906	484	11	59	224	34	258	281	95	13	6
2d ward,	1,675	743	836	41	55	65	951	652	15	57	135	60	300	370	95	99	40
3d ward,	1,764	808	938	5	13	14	1,102	578	19	65	348	35	132	333	153	16	3
4th ward,	1,821	755	913	71	82	95	1,055	684	13	69	256	79	151	381	157	71	64
Total Hudson,	6,720	2,996	3,436	124	164	186	4,014	2,398	58	250	963	208	841	1,365	500	199	113
Kinderhook,	3,864	1,732	1,969	68	95	158	2,456	1,267	34	107	696	82	360	743	161	70	18
Livingston,	2,064	1,017	1,032	8	7	15	1,298	687	18	61	459	23	78	370	204	122	99
New Lebanon,	2,329	1,142	1,170	9	8	4	1,521	695	44	69	493	29	245	370	291	42	18
Stockport,	1,621	757	817	19	28	41	1,030	527	18	46	240	63	211	304	125	34	6
Stuyvesant,	1,937	803	879	81	84	151	1,197	652	25	53	342	33	238	354	287	69	28
Taghkanic	1,665	826	834	2	3	4	1,042	568	20	35	357	10	19	291	178	128	107
Total,	44,391	21,289	21,848	568	686	1,008	27,536	15,126	495	1,224	8,647	765	3,800	8,236	4,554	1,069	520

CORTLAND COUNTY.

CITIES AND TOWNS.	Total population.	WHITES.		COLORED PERSONS.			CIVIL CONDITION.				VOTERS.		Aliens.	Number of families.	Owners of land.	Over 21 who cannot read or write.	Over 21 who can read but not write.
		Males.	Females.	Males.	Females.	No. not taxed.	Single.	Married.	Widowers.	Widows.	Native.	Naturalized.					
Cincinnatus,	1, 119	551	568	......	......	......	635	454	5	25	299	5	13	247	179	7	6
Cortlandville,	4, 329	2, 115	2, 194	12	8	9	2, 477	1, 691	47	114	1, 009	56	133	879	749	51	10
Freetown,	955	484	471	......	......	......	553	378	9	15	216	13	15	137	164	5	3
Harford,	926	477	449	......	......	......	520	368	10	28	208	3	10	190	168	13	13
Homer,	3, 785	1, 806	1, 976	1	2	2	2, 246	1, 405	36	98	831	52	164	477	573	23	3
Lapeer,	750	383	367	......	......	......	432	294	9	15	189	4	2	149	133	4	2
Marathon,	1, 341	686	655	......	......	......	770	539	6	26	306	4	66	275	214	22	8
Preble,	1, 219	614	604	......	1	......	717	467	9	26	296	22	40	268	212	17	16
Scott,	1, 293	669	621	1	2	1	779	465	13	36	319	6	28	259	225	7	1
Solon,	1, 057	549	508	......	......	......	603	425	6	23	225	32	22	206	188	17	10
Taylor,	1, 201	615	586	......	......	......	726	426	10	39	267	8	2	232	221	18	......
Truxton,	3, 444	1, 736	1, 708	......	......	......	2, 041	1, 299	34	70	732	59	194	765	601	25	11
Virgil,	2, 231	1, 093	1, 137	1	......	1	1, 290	866	12	63	501	19	9	456	410	25	12
Willet,	925	464	461	......	......	......	529	359	13	24	217	4	6	182	175	11	......
Total,	24, 575	12, 242	12, 305	15	13	13	14, 318	9, 436	219	602	5, 615	287	704	4, 722	4, 212	245	95

DELAWARE COUNTY.

CITIES AND TOWNS.	Total population.	Whites: Males.	Whites: Females.	Colored: Males.	Colored: Females.	No. not taxed.	Single.	Married.	Widowers.	Widows.	Native.	Naturalized.	Aliens.	Number of families.	Owners of land.	Over 21 who cannot read or write.	Over 21 who can read but not write.
Andes,	2, 536	1, 333	1, 195	4	4	5	1, 629	822	27	58	395	169	144	441	365	19	10
Bovina,	1, 224	638	586	......	......	......	802	374	15	33	194	81	89	220	183	......	......
Colchester,	2, 360	1, 229	1, 115	8	8	7	1, 494	806	29	31	518	41	96	427	376	53	56
Davenport,	2, 233	1, 111	1, 115	2	5	5	1, 348	817	24	44	482	36	4	422	279	4	......
Delhi,	2, 711	1, 316	1, 358	19	18	29	1, 702	910	21	78	405	122	151	489	409	29	7
Franklin,	3, 186	1, 581	1, 604	......	1	1	1, 794	1, 286	37	69	743	44	45	651	557	10	8
Hamden,	1, 881	941	915	16	9	8	1, 157	648	29	47	305	84	91	360	307	7	10
Hancock,	2, 512	1, 334	1, 176	1	1	2	1, 581	885	13	33	465	52	318	456	204	11	......
Harpersfield,	1, 480	720	754	2	4	6	865	562	16	37	351	25	36	298	283	4	9
Kortright,	2, 013	958	1, 055	......	......	......	1, 219	721	25	48	381	63	81	389	330	7	2
Masonville,	1, 543	800	742	1	......	1	926	567	10	40	361	6	17	294	307	4	7
Meredith,	1, 503	738	765	......	......	......	897	562	14	30	299	56	49	316	273	14	7
Middletown,	2, 946	1, 488	1, 455	2	1	3	1, 816	1, 053	28	49	588	45	117	575	370	53	84
Roxbury,	2, 533	1, 269	1, 252	7	*5	12	1, 598	850	23	62	541	36	60	473	277	7	2
Sidney,	1, 797	920	877	......	......	......	1, 037	710	12	38	427	12	24	373	299	......	......
Stamford,	1, 597	776	812	4	5	9	955	572	20	50	345	31	51	322	249	......	......
Tompkins,	3, 290	1, 659	1, 602	12	17	26	1, 966	1, 237	25	62	719	59	114	653	539	51	12
Walton,	2, 404	1, 188	1, 178	14	24	37	1, 403	915	28	58	558	26	45	491	398	10	5
Total,	39, 749	19, 999	19, 556	92	102	151	24, 189	14, 297	396	867	8. 077	988	1, 532	7, 650	6, 005	283	219

* One female colored person, aged 77, reported a slave.

DUTCHESS COUNTY.

CITIES AND TOWNS.	Total population.	Whites: Males.	Whites: Females.	Colored: Males.	Colored: Females.	No. not taxed.	Single.	Married.	Widowers.	Widows.	Native.	Naturalized.	Aliens.	Number of families.	Owners of land.	Over 21 who cannot read or write.	Over 21 who can read but not write.
Amenia,	2, 199	1, 047	1, 091	33	28	50	1, 465	650	16	68	435	20	280	409	250	62	74
Beekman,	1, 379	636	651	42	50	91	751	559	19	50	295	13	80	269	169	58	45
Clinton,	1, 840	936	895	4	5	9	1, 071	689	25	55	450	19	75	390	282	42	37
Dover,	1, 925	962	944	9	10	14	1, 163	701	21	40	432	25	175	282	161	69	33
East Fishkill,	2, 619	1, 230	1, 266	59	64	87	1, 627	911	22	56	521	22	203	495	239	135	71
Fishkill,	8, 764	4, 057	4, 301	187	219	346	5, 438	2, 938	108	280	1, 382	246	1, 251	1, 602	568	351	255
Hyde Park,	2, 480	1, 186	1, 215	33	46	60	1, 487	841	50	102	443	37	382	207	238	56	33
La Grange,	1, 852	867	912	37	36	62	1, 118	639	35	60	404	34	88	360	235	28	32
Milan,	1, 630	790	801	22	17	19	956	602	26	46	404	8	31	330	231	50	26
North East,	1, 757	852	864	23	18	41	1, 064	629	28	36	341	9	148	336	193	11	......
Pawling,	1, 792	889	887	6	10	15	1, 025	685	26	56	413	16	95	361	280	106	82
Pine Plains,	1, 453	740	682	14	17	23	917	471	17	48	364	9	77	272	150	25	......
Pleasant Valley,	1, 853	897	920	18	18	36	1, 118	684	23	28	423	42	60	269	362	......	......
Poughkeepsie,	3, 110	1, 517	1, 532	32	29	58	1, 977	1, 033	28	72	471	105	528	495	256	17	......
Poughkeepsie city:																	
1st ward,	4, 099	1, 922	2, 145	10	22	32	3, 107	763	54	175	422	291	834	843	297	136	14
2d ward,	2, 663	1, 106	1, 369	86	102	133	1, 443	1, 049	31	140	390	87	342	452	262	125	6
3d ward,	3, 461	1, 649	1, 721	45	46	70	2, 436	875	20	130	387	216	615	695	186	18	......
4th ward,	2, 540	1, 095	1, 398	23	24	38	975	1, 465	10	90	369	61	373	446	188	8	1
Total Poughkeepsie,	12, 763	5, 772	6, 633	164	194	273	7, 961	4, 152	115	535	1, 568	655	2, 164	2, 436	933	287	22
Red Hook,	3, 750	1, 841	1, 799	54	56	33	2, 310	1, 310	40	90	657	54	399	701	292	114	
Rhinebeck,	3, 065	1, 491	1, 491	36	47	55	1, 809	1, 097	51	108	658	47	330	611	335	75	4
Stanford,	2, 201	1, 089	1, 062	18	32	48	1, 332	796	30	43	497	17	150	446	301	50	2
Union Vale,	1, 463	712	725	15	11	24	903	515	12	33	337	13	70	300	204	......	......
Washington,	2, 740	1, 267	1, 357	54	62	106	1, 711	898	48	83	599	13	275	510	305	31	
Total,	60, 635	28, 778	30, 028	860	969	1, 450	37, 203	20, 800	740	1, 892	11, 094	1, 404	6, 861	10, 081	5, 984	1, 567	98

ERIE COUNTY.

CITIES AND TOWNS.	Total population.	Whites: Males.	Whites: Females.	Colored: Males.	Colored: Females.	No. not taxed.	Single.	Married.	Widowers.	Widows.	Native.	Naturalized.	Aliens.	Number of families.	Owners of land.	Over 21 who cannot read or write.	Over 21 who can read but not write.
Alden,	2, 404	1, 230	1, 174	......	......	......	1, 399	919	26	60	340	115	501	469	395	......	......
Amherst,	5, 118	2, 561	2, 550	4	3	6	3, 103	1, 850	52	113	321	421	1, 368	1, 016	727	106	[illegible]
Aurora,	3, 665	1, 868	1, 789	4	4	6	2, 054	1, 456	62	93	696	114	490	759	578	68	[illegible]
Boston,	1, 769	908	861	......	......	......	1, 072	627	29	41	223	131	188	311	298	3	......
Brandt,	1, 093	570	523	......	......	......	615	440	13	25	235	13	85	211	169	14	......
Buffalo city, 1st ward,	7, 994	4, 233	3, 748	5	8	10	4, 678	2, 961	86	269	343	805	3, 272	1, 625	438	608	4
2d ward,	5, 882	2, 765	3, 068	14	35	19	3, 659	1, 981	40	202	892	248	1, 468	918	488	69	[illegible]
3d ward,	4, 293	2, 208	2, 035	26	24	9	2, 396	1, 730	54	113	344	331	1, 227	940	288	122	[illegible]
4th ward,	8, 000	3, 897	3, 879	105	119	222	4, 735	2, 907	94	264	408	726	2, 722	1, 631	602	15	[illegible]
5th ward,	8, 759	4, 415	4, 193	74	77	136	4, 986	3, 545	69	159	244	906	3, 030	1, 877	951	57	
6th ward,	7, 354	3, 698	3, 476	91	89	114	3, 950	3, 173	63	168	41	643	3, 473	1, 741	775	245	1
7th ward,	7, 804	4, 015	3, 759	18	12	18	4, 425	3, 141	86	152	121	825	3, 268	1, 777	853	68	2
8th ward,	5, 404	2, 824	2, 566	12	2	2	3, 332	1, 878	34	160	225	490	2. 289	961	297	340	3
9th ward,	5, 625	2, 641	2, 949	20	15	17	3, 639	1, 755	45	186	839	300	1, 243	868	388	19	
10th ward,	5, 238	2, 372	2, 852	5	9	8	3, 302	1, 733	31	172	512	317	1, 378	928	330	29	

ERIE COUNTY.—(CONTINUED.)

CITIES AND TOWNS.	Total population.	WHITES.		COLORED PERSONS.			CIVIL CONDITION.				VOTERS.		Aliens.	Number of families.	Owners of land.	Over 21 who cannot read or write.	Over 21 who can read but not write.
		Males.	Females.	Males.	Females.	No. not taxed.	Single.	Married.	Widowers.	Widows.	Native.	Naturalized.					
Buffalo city, 11th ward,	3, 314	1, 651	1, 663				1, 999	1, 200	34	81	248	267	988	637	372	70	12
12th ward,	3, 729	2, 025	1, 686	12	6	3	2, 363	1, 263	43	60	190	321	1, 392	656	326	88	18
13th ward,	818	432	380	3	3	1	492	311	7	8	50	49	336	156	45	7	1
Total Buffalo, ...	74, 214	37, 176	36, 254	385	399	559	43, 956	27, 578	686	1, 994	4, 457	6, 228	26, 086	14, 715	6, 153	1, 737	1, 236
Chictawaga,	2, 526	1, 313	1, 212	1			1, 534	923	25	44	115	229	812	497	365	69	16
Clarence,	3, 253	1, 694	1, 556	1	2		1, 930	1, 239	37	47	431	139	746	630	459	30	10
Colden,	1, 381	709	672				792	552	19	18	241	43	118	283	286	4	1
Collins,	2, 025	1, 008	1, 010	5	2		1, 172	794	25	34	438	16	104	408	287	18	3
Concord,	2, 805	1, 408	1, 394	1	2	1	1, 613	1, 101	29	62	798	47	333	535	527	9	5
East Hamburgh,	1, 946	1, 012	934				1, 112	764	30	40	348	41	431	388	330	3	
Eden,	2, 426	1, 241	1, 185				1, 426	898	34	68	273	205	336	470	414	7	1
Evans,	2, 252	1, 194	1, 058				1, 286	887	23	56	439	35	276	463	384	38	9
Grand Island,	838	478	353	5	2	2	500	318	12	8	92	29	339	173	90	62	64
Hamburgh,	3, 037	1, 615	1, 418	2	2	3	1, 843	1, 105	33	56	310	117	874	564	385	3	1
Holland,	1, 321	690	629	1	1		769	518	10	24	274	15	58	255	260	6	
Lancaster,	5, 489	2, 851	2, 633	3	2	1	3, 186	2, 129	60	114	356	475	1, 727	1, 080	794	23	
Marilla,	1, 377	701	669	3	4		786	542	14	35	268	24	126	294	257	4	
Newstead,	2, 987	1, 576	1, 411				1, 744	1, 149	30	64	544	68	305	595	486	1	
North Collins,	1, 859	964	895				1, 085	723	18	33	283	96	218	367	340	7	13
Sardinia,	1, 765	888	876		1		1, 013	694	15	43	417	26	48	369	328		
Tonawanda,	2, 569	1, 381	1, 176	4	8	6	1, 501	988	33	47	189	233	680	507	323	78	132
Wales,	1, 689	870	819				995	628	19	47	327	41	106	341	329	17	9
West Seneca,	2, 523	1, 328	1, 188	5	2	3	1, 601	819	36	67	79	348	919	493	602	8	
Total,	132, 331	67, 234	64, 239	424	434	587	78, 087	49, 641	1, 370	3, 233	12, 494	9, 249	37, 274	26, 193	15, 566	2, 315	1, 586

ESSEX COUNTY.

CITIES AND TOWNS.	Total population.	Whites: Males.	Whites: Females.	Colored: Males.	Colored: Females.	Colored: No. not taxed.	Single.	Married.	Widowers.	Widows.	Voters: Native.	Voters: Naturalized.	Aliens.	Number of families.	Owners of land.	Over 21 who cannot read or write.	Over 21 who can read but not write.
Chesterfield,	3, 327	1, 657	1, 661	4	5		2, 060	1, 171	25	71	336	148	470	636	288	235	26
Crown Point,	2, 216	1, 160	1, 043	7	6		1, 259	891	23	43	535	10	64	435	297	34	29
Elizabethtown,	1, 402	723	658	11	10	13	865	493	15	29	278	42	98	252	175	45	18
Essex,	2, 115	1, 039	1, 070	3	3	6	1, 325	724	17	49	331	71	274	358	195	94	15
Jay,	2, 850	1, 455	1, 389	3	3		1, 906	861	23	60	459	84	288	501	292	43	
Keene,	774	386	388				458	288	5	23	146	20	30	155	128	5	8
Lewis,	1, 803	934	869				1, 147	611	22	23	336	39	169	325	251	54	5
Minerva,	767	403	364				460	278	8	21	119	58	48	148	133	2	2
Moriah,	3, 120	1, 587	1, 530	3		3	1, 930	1, 079	34	77	446	160	453	592	317	216	54
Newcomb,	226	130	96				140	82		4	40	11	34	39	21	15	6
North Elba,	301	150	110	25	16	3	171	123	5	2	72	9	5	60	61	2	1
North Hudson,	519	275	244				334	168	13	4	87	5	81	79	41	43	10
St. Armand,	289	151	130	4	4	2	176	107	2	4	63	1	13	58	42		
Schroon,	2, 085	1, 145	940				1, 282	744	31	28	420	25	273	378	284	75	21
Ticonderoga,	2, 125	1, 071	1, 053	1			1, 244	809	27	45	415	43	212	435	197	83	24
Westport,	2, 041	1, 029	988	15	9	17	1, 317	669	14	41	331	33	251	408	207	88	15
Willsborough,	1, 675	840	831	2	2	4	920	713	17	25	296	18	205	312	212	100	10
Wilmington,	904	435	469				589	300	6	9	147	18	26	168	112	20	1
Total,	28, 539	14, 570	13, 833	78	58	48	17, 583	10, 111	287	558	4, 857	795	2, 994	5, 339	3, 253	1, 154	245

FRANKLIN COUNTY.

CITIES AND TOWNS.	Total population.	Whites: Males.	Whites: Females.	Colored: Males.	Colored: Females.	Colored: No. not taxed.	Single.	Married.	Widowers.	Widows.	Voters: Native.	Voters: Naturalized.	Aliens.	Number of families.	Owners of land.	Over 21 who cannot read or write.	Over 21 who can read but not write.
Bangor,	2, 154	1, 101	1, 053				1, 277	825	18	34	306	71	272	421	335	105	6
Bellmont,	873	462	409	1	1	1	550	310	4	9	131	40	49	62	135	33	
Bombay,	2, 312	1, 168	1, 144				1, 508	749	14	41	193	137	490	377	229	205	9
Brandon,	728	361	367				424	289	4	11	144	31	25	141	228	65	
Burke,	1, 900	957	943				1, 230	621	18	31	279	97	153	339	278	4	
Chateaugay,	2, 676	1, 344	1, 332				1, 744	883	16	33	302	130	303	440	283	78	
Constable,	1, 443	746	697				1, 047	386	5	5	155	87	228	259	198	69	
Dickinson,	1, 255	654	601				747	480	2	17	256	24	59	241	230	14	1
Duane,	325	171	154				213	107	4	1	50	11	26	44	43	1	
Fort Covington,	2, 559	1, 252	1, 307				1, 615	882	15	47	290	88	634	448	312	203	
Franklin,	947	499	438	4	6		597	331	7	12	124	70	91	169	136	51	20
Harrietstown,	306	158	148				177	127	2		59	11	7	66	56	14	
Malone,	5, 186	2, 595	2, 586	3	2	3	3, 214	1, 823	44	105	647	211	1, 054	943	653	376	101
Moira,	1, 459	747	712				875	543	13	28	264	21	158	295	203	30	4
Westville,	1, 354	704	650				861	459	8	26	185	48	190	247	223	75	31
Total,	25, 477	12, 919	12, 541	8	0	4	16, 079	8, 824	174	400	3, 385	1, 077	3, 739	4. 492	3, 542	1, 323	172

FULTON COUNTY.

CITIES AND TOWNS.	Total population.	Whites: Males.	Whites: Females.	Colored: Males.	Colored: Females.	Colored: No. not taxed.	Single.	Married.	Widowers.	Widows.	Voters: Native.	Voters: Naturalized.	Aliens.	Number of families.	Owners of land.	Over 21 who cannot read or write.	Over 21 who can read but not write.
Bleecker,	904	473	419	6	6	3	531	346	13	14	83	58	251	182	150	35	23
Broadalbin,	2, 640	1, 245	1, 394	3	4	7	1, 495	1, 044	33	74	556	58	69	559	397	39	31
Caroga,	714	360	320	18	16	10	418	283	10	3	120	23	68	142	83	15	1
Ephrata,	2, 183	1, 116	1, 062	1	4	5	1, 320	798	24	41	478	15	77	393	288	177	93
Johnstown,	7, 912	3, 802	4, 050	27	33	39	4, 843	2, 738	82	249	1, 541	170	659	1, 500	748	91	34
Mayfield,	2, 393	1, 160	1, 212	10	11	21	1, 397	904	27	65	467	38	95	503	358	20	33
Northampton,	1, 943	979	959	4	1	5	1, 120	760	18	45	413	12	104	406	286	7	
Oppenheim,	2, 412	1, 241	1, 155	9	7	15	1, 451	902	16	43	541	28	31	450	369	89	115
Perth,	1, 131	569	562				731	352	14	34	198	38	118	214	169	31	
Stratford,	1, 046	550	496				600	416	13	17	204	25	87	211	148	27	1
Total,	23, 284	11, 495	11, 629	78	82	105	13, 906	8, 543	250	585	4, 601	465	1, 559	4, 560	2, 996	531	331

GENESEE COUNTY.

CITIES AND TOWNS.	Total population.	Whites: Males.	Whites: Females.	Colored: Males.	Colored: Females.	Colored: No. not taxed.	Single.	Married.	Widowers.	Widows.	Voters: Native.	Voters: Naturalized.	Aliens.	Number of families.	Owners of land.	Over 21 who cannot read or write.	Over 21 who can read but not write.
Alabama,	2, 194	1, 148	1, 025	11	10	1	1, 286	834	31	43	420	45	229	436	315	34	9
Alexander,	1, 798	911	887				1, 020	700	35	43	403	21	235	378	268	15	5
Batavia,	5, 304	2, 636	2, 633	17	18	6	3, 203	1, 916	55	130	672	151	710	990	723	167	49
Bergen,	1, 800	900	890	5	5		1, 008	724	18	50	351	51	188	363	303	27	27

GENESEE COUNTY.—(CONTINUED.)

CITIES AND TOWNS.	Total population.	WHITES.		COLORED PERSONS.			CIVIL CONDITION.				VOTERS.		Aliens.	Number of families.	Owners of land.	Over 21 who cannot read or write.	Over 21 who can read but not write.
		Males.	Females.	Males.	Females.	No. not taxed.	Single.	Married.	Widowers.	Widows.	Native.	Naturalized.					
Bethany,	1, 879	925	954	...	...	...	1, 035	752	20	72	408	17	184	382	327	29	8
Byron,	1, 641	843	797	...	1	...	940	647	16	38	354	16	129	329	272	36	26
Darien,	2, 176	1, 112	1, 064	...	...	...	1, 225	861	29	61	476	35	291	435	362	20	5
Elba,	1, 869	959	910	...	...	...	1, 044	757	16	52	402	25	240	384	251	8	...
Le Roy,	4, 206	2, 108	2, 079	9	10	10	2, 505	1, 529	50	122	787	103	740	532	511	58	25
Oakfield,	1, 510	817	693	...	...	...	929	543	14	24	276	32	245	279	178	...	...
Pavilion,	1, 758	915	843	...	...	...	1, 014	681	18	45	381	18	194	333	280	...	...
Pembroke,	2, 844	1, 432	1, 412	...	...	...	1, 620	1, 135	34	55	583	53	216	566	452	22	...
Stafford,	2, 055	1, 073	982	...	...	...	1, 229	753	20	53	322	75	506	385	186	20	...
Total,	31, 034	15, 779	15, 169	42	44	17	18, 058	11, 832	356	788	5, 835	642	4, 107	5, 792	4, 428	436	154

GREENE COUNTY.

CITIES AND TOWNS.	Total population.	Whites Males.	Whites Females.	Colored Males.	Colored Females.	No. not taxed.	Single.	Married.	Widowers.	Widows.	Native.	Naturalized.	Aliens.	Number of families.	Owners of land.	Over 21 who cannot read or write.	Over 21 who can read but not write.
Ashland,	1, 139	554	584	1	...	1	648	456	15	20	256	15	18	235	140	12	...
Athens,	2, 870	1, 382	1, 310	88	90	76	1, 858	937	20	55	577	157	159	551	343	163	77
Cairo,	2, 557	1, 278	1, 255	12	12	18	1, 616	829	33	79	588	21	50	478	341	26	1
Catskill,	5, 710	2, 725	2, 785	87	113	171	3, 615	1, 890	20	185	1, 070	90	552	1, 094	544	38	8
Coxsackie,	3, 682	1, 758	1, 660	133	131	192	2, 207	1, 333	32	110	724	42	224	603	432	107	47
Durham,	2, 540	1, 230	1, 288	9	13	11	1, 462	978	25	75	604	14	48	491	393	8	3
Greenville,	2, 173	1, 083	1, 077	5	8	12	1, 307	785	25	56	493	5	91	450	342	12	6
Halcott,	474	246	228	...	...	...	298	162	9	5	105	1	6	89	79	1	...
Hunter,	1, 594	829	755	4	6	9	1, 030	523	12	29	249	64	88	276	207	40	5
Jewett,	1, 129	578	551	...	...	...	580	524	4	21	257	9	2	220	176	29	4
Lexington,	1, 595	786	806	2	1	3	979	580	9	27	349	14	17	217	235	...	...
New Baltimore,	2, 402	1, 211	1, 112	37	42	41	1, 472	856	20	54	496	20	166	455	306	37	26
Prattsville,	1, 588	739	834	7	8	11	994	539	10	45	284	18	70	290	225	42	29
Windham,	1, 684	804	877	3	...	...	949	677	21	37	409	21	31	258	188	1	...
Total,	31, 137	15, 203	15, 122	388	424	545	19, 015	11, 069	255	798	6, 461	491	1 522	5, 707	3, 951	516	206

HAMILTON COUNTY.

CITIES AND TOWNS.	Total population.	Whites Males.	Whites Females.	Colored Males.	Colored Females.	No. not taxed.	Single.	Married.	Widowers.	Widows.	Native.	Naturalized.	Aliens.	Number of families.	Owners of land.	Over 21 who cannot read or write.	Over 21 who can read but not write.
Arietta,	149	77	72	...	...	...	79	66	2	2	43	3	...	32	18	3	...
Gilman,	90	52	38	...	...	...	57	32	...	1	24	2	5	21	19	...	...
Hope,	822	451	371	...	...	...	488	319	6	9	166	20	51	148	116	8	13
Lake Pleasant,	300	162	138	...	...	...	184	110	3	3	74	2	1	53	33	...	2
Long Lake,	139	71	68	...	...	...	78	57	2	2	28	...	3	29	22	2	2
Morehouse,	275	147	128	...	...	...	149	119	1	6	22	32	63	59	51	5	2
Wells,	768	428	336	2	2	4	451	293	9	15	165	18	45	146	93	35	18
Total,	2, 543	1, 388	1, 151	2	2	4	1, 486	996	23	38	522	77	168	488	352	53	37

HERKIMER COUNTY.

CITIES AND TOWNS.	Total population.	Whites Males.	Whites Females.	Colored Males.	Colored Females.	No. not taxed.	Single.	Married.	Widowers.	Widows.	Native.	Naturalized.	Aliens.	Number of families.	Owners of land.	Over 21 who cannot read or write.	Over 21 who can read but not write.
Columbia,	1, 831	939	887	3	2	2	1, 125	622	33	51	453	3	67	397	304	10	9
Danube,	1, 791	986	802	1	2	1	1, 143	593	16	39	334	42	265	296	188	73	22
Fairfield,	1, 493	743	741	3	6	...	898	541	22	32	314	9	180	265	440	42	...
Frankfort,	3, 217	1, 637	1, 576	2	2	...	1, 954	1, 171	29	63	557	83	345	648	407	26	4
German Flats,	3, 855	1, 974	1, 862	9	10	1	2, 263	1, 462	48	82	775	107	337	783	506	78	49
Herkimer,	2, 866	1, 434	1, 411	13	8	8	1, 759	976	36	95	542	56	339	487	303	31	...
Litchfield,	1, 582	826	751	3	2	5	933	581	27	41	307	50	188	319	207	6	11
Little Falls,	4, 930	2, 401	2, 477	23	29	47	3, 026	1, 707	50	147	856	196	612	922	413	67	4
Manheim,	1, 672	858	814	...	...	...	1, 030	598	13	31	325	39	167	315	207	10	1
Newport,	2, 015	976	1, 008	19	12	12	1, 170	760	22	63	405	37	196	407	283	39	19
Norway,	1, 059	535	524	...	...	...	623	392	17	27	224	18	98	207	150	18	9
Ohio,	1, 087	582	505	...	...	...	672	382	8	25	188	31	135	191	185	23	35
Russia,	2, 288	1, 174	1, 112	1	1	...	1, 379	822	33	54	475	38	236	448	374	13	6
Salisbury,	2, 306	1, 204	1, 102	...	...	...	1, 008	1, 229	24	45	457	44	246	466	336	56	36
Schuyler,	1, 690	842	848	...	...	...	1, 003	607	20	60	328	58	217	317	196	35	7
Stark,	1, 478	743	733	1	1	1	802	628	21	27	358	12	107	303	224	10	...
Warren,	1, 741	885	843	5	8	3	1, 031	629	22	59	465	11	69	297	281	52	22
Wilmurt,	268	180	88	...	...	...	178	81	8	1	41	9	71	42	29	4	...
Winfield,	1, 397	688	703	3	3	...	800	549	11	37	307	24	80	286	186	15	...
Total,	38, 566	19, 607	18, 787	86	86	80	22, 797	14, 330	460	979	7, 711	867	3, 955	7, 396	5, 219	608	234

JEFFERSON COUNTY.

CITIES AND TOWNS.	Total population.	Whites Males.	Whites Females.	Colored Males.	Colored Females.	No. not taxed.	Single.	Married.	Widowers.	Widows.	Native.	Naturalized.	Aliens.	Number of families.	Owners of land.	Over 21 who cannot read or write.	Over 21 who can read but not write.
Adams,	3, 105	1, 502	1, 603	...	...	...	1, 684	1, 300	34	87	763	30	160	653	524	23	14
Alexandria,	3, 353	1, 711	1, 620	13	9	9	2, 020	1, 255	28	50	576	88	320	623	369	80	47
Antwerp,	3, 763	1, 961	1, 801	1	...	1	2, 287	1, 350	47	79	754	77	430	675	574	51	12
Brownville,	3, 589	1, 767	1, 806	6	10	15	2, 095	1, 368	27	99	689	69	248	697	360	11	...
Cape Vincent,	3, 375	1, 711	1, 663	1	...	1	2, 038	1, 240	32	65	452	209	479	639	463	65	41
Champion,	1, 946	970	962	7	7	14	1, 096	782	25	43	474	19	42	402	315	11	4
Clayton,	4, 232	2, 125	2, 070	17	20	22	2, 553	1, 587	26	66	699	86	485	772	581	159	25
Ellisburgh,	5, 339	2, 677	2, 662	...	...	...	3, 004	2, 121	59	155	1, 260	17	215	1, 034	831	22	9
Henderson,	2, 139	1, 090	1, 048	1	...	1	1, 238	833	27	41	489	20	93	419	322	6	...
Hounsfield,	3, 221	1, 629	1, 571	12	9	15	1, 895	1, 185	44	97	597	106	220	646	443	30	2
Le Ray,	3, 203	1, 664	1, 536	2	1	3	1, 872	1, 210	42	79	659	74	186	635	515	86	38
Lorraine,	1, 470	778	675	9	8	3	853	580	9	28	281	20	44	297	230	11	...
Lyme,	2, 563	1, 294	1, 266	...	3	3	1, 522	958	27	56	556	25	96	554	325	21	10
Orleans,	2, 806	1, 438	1, 368	...	...	...	1, 676	1, 039	28	63	525	67	197	537	436	14	6
Pamelia,	2, 511	1, 278	1, 224	6	3	9	1, 523	892	28	68	442	55	265	442	223	94	12
Philadelphia,	1, 743	898	845	...	...	...	1, 018	670	22	33	369	47	78	335	267	5	2
Rodman,	1, 752	882	870	...	...	...	958	725	21	48	432	8	54	363	319	5	7
Rutland,	1, 977	961	1, 016	...	...	...	1, 077	813	30	57	460	18	143	400	383	50	15
Theresa,	2, 278	1, 148	1, 129	...	1	1	1, 359	860	19	40	479	40	38	418	390	3	...
Watertown,	7, 557	3, 619	3, 889	20	29	40	4, 528	2,724	69	236	1, 117	236	1, 376	1, 387	687	154	101
Wilna,	3, 024	1, 555	1, 467	1	1	2	1, 760	1, 169	35	60	602	113	196	598	416	79	25
Worth,	474	238	236	...	...	...	255	210	...	9	95	12	12	103	90	11	11
Total,	65, 420	32, 896	32, 327	96	101	139	38. 311	24, 871	679	1, 559	12, 770	1. 436	5, 377	12. 629	9, 063	991	381

KINGS COUNTY.

CITIES AND TOWNS.	Total population.	WHITES.		COLORED PERSONS.			CIVIL CONDITION.				VOTERS.		Aliens.	Number of families.	Owners of land.	Over 21 who cannot read or write.	Over 21 who can read but not write.
		Males.	Females.	Males.	Females.	No. not taxed.	Single.	Married.	Widowers.	Widows.	Native.	Naturalized.					
Brooklyn City:																	
1st ward,	6, 441	2, 962	3, 431	15	33	36	4, 077	2, 058	101	205	579	347	2, 445	1, 132	329	228	180
2d ward,	8, 383	3, 945	4, 316	50	72	96	5, 078	2, 892	94	319	584	713	2, 640	1, 752	215	461	407
3d ward,	8, 900	3, 691	5, 135	24	50	71	5, 961	2, 533	94	312	1, 356	271	2, 583	1, 214	444	254	238
4th ward,	12, 282	5, 329	6, 460	197	296	394	7, 808	3, 924	150	400	1, 519	595	3, 047	2, 202	592	209	142
5th ward,	16, 352	7, 925	8, 193	94	140	195	9, 601	6, 014	149	588	1, 107	1, 496	4, 612	3, 541	459	788	528
6th ward,	18, 490	8, 463	9, 969	18	40	47	10, 054	7, 689	170	577	1, 468	1, 029	7, 464	3, 605	532	802	792
7th ward,	12, 523	5, 914	6, 517	34	58	63	7, 737	4, 450	92	244	1, 003	1, 034	2, 710	2, 558	729	123	21
8th ward,	5, 318	2, 664	2, 563	49	42	58	3, 071	2, 037	76	134	369	436	1, 605	1, 099	385	345	249
9th ward,	9, 133	4, 273	4, 291	282	287	370	5, 185	3, 645	93	210	459	781	2, 801	1, 988	1, 380	857	371
10th ward,	21, 749	9, 943	11, 645	63	98	122	13, 699	7, 227	219	604	1, 832	1, 410	6, 919	4, 337	1, 099	901	768
11th ward,	22, 213	10, 072	11, 472	295	374	607	13, 279	7, 947	243	744	2, 360	1, 417	5, 151	4, 442	1, 293	850	463
12th ward,	6, 990	3, 509	3, 474	3	4	6	3, 828	2, 868	86	208	162	634	3, 082	1, 595	234	461	342
13th ward,	14, 044	6, 331	7, 558	55	100	96	8, 738	4, 766	96	444	1, 828	583	2, 943	2, 684	946	188	144
14th ward,	12, 414	6, 052	6, 162	89	111	99	7, 160	4, 717	136	401	814	1, 072	3, 323	2, 697	305	393	135
15th ward,	6, 559	3, 145	3, 299	50	65	115	3, 777	2, 548	43	191	473	469	1, 649	1, 364	310	240	93
16th ward,	15, 350	7, 351	7, 322	298	379	559	7, 998	6, 891	143	318	358	1, 163	7, 318	3, 677	930	764	267
17th ward,	5, 508	2, 696	2, 798	8	6	5	3, 206	2, 184	35	83	652	344	1, 176	1, 132	467	163	114
18th ward,	2, 601	1, 234	1, 358	6	3	1	1, 619	921	15	46	220	209	637	419	238	124	69
Total Brooklyn, .	205, 250	95, 499	105,963	1, 630	2, 158	2, 940	121 876	75, 311	2, 035	6, 028	17, 143	14, 003	62, 105	41, 438	10, 887	8, 151	5, 323
Flatbush, ...	3, 280	1, 448	1, 600	111	121	199	2, 228	771	106	175	217	68	1, 264	308	162	383	158
Flatlands, ...	1, 578	816	653	63	46	63	1, 042	491	14	31	206	40	314	258	172	170	......
Gravesend, ...	1, 256	566	523	98	69	144	785	417	16	38	189	22	253	226	127	78	......
New Lots, ...	2, 261	1, 159	1, 054	22	26	44	1, 320	862	27	52	229	134	719	444	285	31	16
New Utrecht, ...	2, 730	1, 364	1, 230	71	65	136	1, 782	845	23	80	293	83	881	459	239	111	46
Total, ...	216, 355	100,852	111,023	1, 995	2, 485	3, 526	129,038	78, 697	2, 221	6, 404	18, 277	14. 350	65. 536	43, 133	11, 872	8, 924	5, 543

LEWIS COUNTY.

CITIES AND TOWNS.	Total population.	Whites: Males.	Whites: Females.	Colored: Males.	Colored: Females.	No. not taxed.	Single.	Married.	Widowers.	Widows.	Voters: Native.	Voters: Naturalized.	Aliens.	Number of families.	Owners of land.	Over 21 who cannot read or write.	Over 21 who can read but not write.
Croghan, ...	1, 531	823	699	6	3	2	914	574	20	23	82	126	530	300	296	121	48
Denmark, ...	2, 381	1, 159	1, 218	3	1	3	1, 338	941	37	65	532	52	155	489	430	52	16
Diana, ...	1, 177	530	647	......	......	......	693	454	12	18	193	38	105	227	190	47	10
Greig, ...	1, 203	660	543	......	......	......	680	503	10	10	264	25	78	245	192	18	19
Harrisburgh, ...	1, 240	658	577	3	2	5	745	466	13	16	228	67	77	243	113	47	33
High Market, ...	1, 125	593	532	......	......	......	770	333	5	17	47	161	144	182	189	133	56
Lewis, ...	1, 157	600	557	......	......	......	685	442	14	16	80	85	359	225	219	5	......
Leyden, ...	1, 856	923	927	3	3	......	1, 038	742	27	49	347	85	107	399	277	54	......
Lowville, ...	2, 144	1, 041	1, 093	7	3	9	1, 240	817	34	53	458	37	207	421	342	35	......
Martinsburgh, ...	2, 489	1, 160	1, 323	4	2	5	1, 482	937	17	53	471	68	154	429	393	49	11
Montague, ...	571	312	259	......	......	......	335	228	3	5	100	12	85	118	120	22	13
New Bremen, ...	1, 647	864	783	......	......	......	986	628	13	20	120	138	356	313	300	13	103
Osceola, ...	513	261	252	......	......	......	294	210	1	8	58	51	29	110	107	26	22
Pinckney, ...	1, 039	546	493	......	......	......	573	442	9	15	253	9	25	232	207	......	......
Turin, ...	1, 748	841	906	......	1	......	1, 029	675	13	31	372	44	96	349	287	15	10
Watson, ...	930	508	422	......	......	......	549	348	11	22	190	18	35	183	185	45	......
West Turin, ...	2, 478	1, 294	1, 182	1	1	......	1, 526	868	35	49	264	209	209	462	251	40	14
Total, ...	25, 229	12, 773	12, 413	27	16	24	14, 877	9, 608	274	470	4, 059	1, 225	2. 751	4, 927	4, 098	722	355

LIVINGSTON COUNTY.

CITIES AND TOWNS.	Total population.	Whites: Males.	Whites: Females.	Colored: Males.	Colored: Females.	No. not taxed.	Single.	Married.	Widowers.	Widows.	Voters: Native.	Voters: Naturalized.	Aliens.	Number of families.	Owners of land.	Over 21 who cannot read or write.	Over 21 who can read but not write.
Avon, ...	2, 694	1, 336	1, 329	16	13	29	1, 731	866	31	66	483	72	429	483	344	5	......
Caledonia, ...	1, 991	1, 059	923	4	5	......	1, 315	590	25	61	266	103	532	346	242	64	19
Conesus, ...	1, 413	718	695	......	......	......	852	517	21	23	313	7	102	300	184	8	......
Geneseo, ...	2, 883	1, 451	1, 384	20	28	32	1, 920	854	38	71	484	92	453	505	338	21	5
Groveland, ...	1, 610	800	810	......	......	......	1, 069	481	21	39	294	24	149	272	177	12	......
Leicester, ...	2, 076	1, 005	1, 030	21	20	22	1, 280	723	26	47	428	30	222	330	239	5	......
Lima, ...	2, 670	1, 311	1, 334	13	12	25	1, 609	974	21	66	479	83	396	227	381	31	9
Livonia, ...	2, 635	1, 301	1, 333	......	1	1	1, 607	932	28	68	601	31	236	498	455	10	5
Mount Morris, ...	4, 042	2, 036	1, 987	9	10	10	2, 394	1, 510	43	95	750	79	400	790	506	74	52
North Dansville, ...	3, 481	1, 657	1, 821	1	2	3	2, 047	1, 298	25	111	511	170	405	711	457	61	24
Nunda, ...	2, 887	1, 420	1, 458	5	4	9	1, 681	1, 105	22	79	568	59	181	403	430	10	......
Portage, ...	1, 569	787	782	......	......	......	893	616	17	43	318	43	149	313	430	1	1
Sparta, ...	1, 233	626	607	......	......	......	761	428	6	38	295	19	63	141	217	18	34
Springwater, ...	2, 481	1, 291	1, 183	5	2	1	1, 475	938	31	37	581	18	48	482	355	10	3
West Sparta, ...	1, 496	770	719	4	3	......	924	530	13	29	308	32	56	283	192	18	9
York, ...	2, 782	1, 429	1, 342	5	6	2	1, 763	891	34	94	496	99	508	587	381	28	38
Total, ...	37, 943	18, 997	18, 737	103	106	134	23, 321	13, 253	402	967	7, 175	961	4, 329	6, 671	5, 328	376	199

MADISON COUNTY.

CITIES AND TOWNS.	Total population.	Whites: Males.	Whites: Females.	Colored: Males.	Colored: Females.	No. not taxed.	Single.	Married.	Widowers.	Widows.	Voters: Native.	Voters: Naturalized.	Aliens.	Number of families.	Owners of land.	Over 21 who cannot read or write.	Over 21 who can read but not write.
Brookfield, ...	3, 770	1, 877	1, 865	14	14	25	2, 109	1, 521	38	102	935	14	135	788	631	21	9
Cazenovia, ...	4, 495	2, 149	2, 318	13	15	18	2, 449	1, 841	62	143	933	81	296	975	746	93	37
De Ruyter, ...	1, 921	973	948	......	......	......	1, 096	754	24	47	427	10	39	379	309	3	......
Baton, ...	4, 061	2, 002	2, 036	12	11	18	2, 376	1, 514	49	122	814	45	526	799	557	55	7
Fenner, ...	1, 622	780	814	11	17	27	943	608	16	55	353	12	60	327	291	23	11
Georgetown, ...	1, 442	724	711	4	3	7	755	639	17	31	340	14	11	333	264	4	......
Hamilton, ...	3, 737	1, 840	1, 882	7	8	11	2, 064	1, 495	59	119	913	32	192	795	575	28	......
Lebanon, ...	1, 661	834	816	6	5	4	928	664	23	46	371	17	51	344	256	15	......
Lenox, ...	7, 800	3, 992	3, 740	29	39	49	4, 584	2, 944	95	177	1, 541	212	778	1, 512	858	364	210
Madison, ...	2, 483	1, 221	1, 259	1	2	3	1, 411	978	30	64	532	25	175	541	355	22	......
Nelson, ...	1, 876	966	909	1	......	1	1, 078	703	33	62	409	31	148	194	351	22	33
Smithfield, ...	1, 514	724	710	34	40	55	901	559	18	36	318	18	47	314	184	1	......
Stockbridge, ...	2, 052	1, 029	1, 006	8	9	8	1, 223	740	34	55	410	21	172	217	298	43	......
Sullivan, ...	5, 253	2, 753	2, 478	11	11	12	3, 054	1, 998	64	137	1, 011	136	002	1, 026	674	154	75
Total, ...	43, 687	21, 864	21, 498	151	174	238	24, 971	16, 958	562	1, 196	9, 316	658	3, 232	8, 544	6, 349	848	382

MONROE COUNTY.

CITIES AND TOWNS.	Total population.	WHITES. Males.	WHITES. Females.	COLORED PERSONS. Males.	COLORED PERSONS. Females.	COLORED PERSONS. No. not taxed.	CIVIL CONDITION. Single.	CIVIL CONDITION. Married.	CIVIL CONDITION. Widowers.	CIVIL CONDITION. Widows.	VOTERS. Native.	VOTERS. Naturalized.	Aliens.	Number of families.	Owners of land.	Over 21 who cannot read or write.	Over 21 who can read but not write.
Brighton,	3, 323	1, 777	1, 544	.....	2	2	2, 179	1, 034	35	75	377	141	1, 026	532	291	188	47
Chili,	2, 203	1, 131	1, 070	.....	2	1	1, 316	823	16	48	335	91	395	400	318	57	14
Clarkson,	2, 177	1, 107	1, 070	.....	.....	.....	1, 299	804	19	55	414	53	367	415	291	41	3
Gates,	2, 347	1, 219	1, 126	2	.....	2	1, 378	899	22	48	250	165	524	459	296	39	15
Greece,	4, 487	2, 317	2, 157	6	7	8	2, 672	1, 642	58	115	946	191	1, 009	852	589	181	48
Henrietta,	2, 144	1, 103	1, 039	2	.....	1	1, 275	809	13	47	381	58	406	357	300	11	9
Irondequoit,	3, 234	1, 658	1, 573	2	1	1	1, 969	1, 197	19	49	196	260	1, 036	614	460	43	30
Mendon,	3, 015	1, 518	1, 485	7	5	1	1, 764	1, 146	25	80	599	64	413	594	444	22	.....
Ogden,	3, 080	1, 602	1, 475	2	1	.....	1, 817	1, 145	41	77	512	108	638	585	464	121	11
Parma,	2, 783	1, 401	1, 375	3	4	4	1, 583	1, 094	37	69	577	43	221	556	453	69	56
Penfield,	3, 031	1, 544	1, 486	.....	1	.....	1, 756	1, 184	25	66	577	82	464	612	434	55	27
Perrington,	3, 175	1, 656	1, 511	5	3	2	1, 898	1, 183	28	66	575	77	549	647	433	48	.....
Pittsford,	2, 133	1, 123	1, 010	.....	.....	.....	1, 270	769	35	59	314	80	549	412	315	91	10
Riga,	2, 025	1, 048	975	2	.....	1	1, 251	709	19	46	307	52	479	385	202	50	.....
Rochester city,																	
1st ward,	2, 225	1, 052	1, 173	.....	.....	.....	1, 409	722	16	78	309	129	539	371	178	41	15
2d ward,	3, 656	1, 774	1, 872	4	6	6	2, 181	1, 246	52	177	493	175	1, 059	633	330	124	135
3d ward,	4, 386	1, 988	2, 233	77	88	117	2, 644	1, 508	47	187	487	259	1, 015	873	444	167	186
4th ward,	3, 323	1, 598	1, 715	5	5	10	1, 998	1, 145	44	136	442	207	822	624	349	20	19
5th ward,	4, 376	2, 184	2, 188	4	.....	.....	2, 703	1, 488	42	143	353	201	1, 348	827	519	144	21
6th ward,	5, 391	2, 712	2, 668	3	8	.....	2, 955	2, 239	63	134	312	328	2, 225	1, 144	606	26	12
7th ward,	4, 619	2, 250	2, 302	30	37	23	2, 645	1, 787	43	144	437	312	1, 194	929	612	28	33
8th ward,	3, 951	1, 906	1, 982	31	32	31	2, 431	1, 397	33	90	251	358	1, 012	789	521	57	45
9th ward,	7, 218	3, 737	3, 455	20	6	18	4, 409	2, 565	60	184	350	574	2, 178	1, 379	1, 394	175	131
10th ward,	4, 732	2, 298	2, 419	9	6	.....	2, 792	1, 789	31	120	391	362	1, 309	988	631	12	13
Total Rochester,	43, 877	21, 499	22, 007	183	188	205	26, 167	15, 886	431	1, 393	3, 825	2, 905	12, 701	8, 557	5, 584	794	610
Rush,	1, 750	889	861	.....	.....	.....	1, 049	625	30	46	315	18	375	318	215	22	16
Sweden,	3, 967	1, 968	1, 973	14	12	16	2, 252	1, 533	50	132	717	105	681	523	523	152	90
Union,	2, 369	1, 251	1, 113	2	3	5	1, 431	862	30	46	458	40	122	444	323	17	5
Webster,	2, 388	1, 216	1, 143	12	17	13	1, 359	937	33	59	521	31	218	518	333	20	12
Wheatland,	2, 816	1, 439	1, 376	.....	1	.....	1, 762	932	37	85	360	132	664	503	283	84	31
Total,	96, 324	48, 466	47, 369	242	247	262	57, 447	35, 213	1, 003	2, 661	12, 576	4, 696	22, 837	18, 283	12, 551	2, 105	1, 034

MONTGOMERY COUNTY.

CITIES AND TOWNS.	Total population.	WHITES. Males.	WHITES. Females.	COLORED PERSONS. Males.	COLORED PERSONS. Females.	COLORED PERSONS. No. not taxed.	CIVIL CONDITION. Single.	CIVIL CONDITION. Married.	CIVIL CONDITION. Widowers.	CIVIL CONDITION. Widows.	VOTERS. Native.	VOTERS. Naturalized.	Aliens.	Number of families.	Owners of land.	Over 21 who cannot read or write.	Over 21 who can read but not write.
Amsterdam,	4, 012	1, 948	2, 021	21	22	40	2, 373	1, 463	46	130	736	121	383	500	188	39	14
Canajoharie,	4, 022	1, 996	1, 915	58	53	59	2, 460	1, 409	47	106	689	116	353	673	391	116	24
Charleston,	1, 899	950	946	2	1	3	1, 124	696	29	50	477	12	22	385	249	45	71
Florida,	3, 154	1, 616	1, 507	16	15	28	1, 897	1, 100	46	111	639	81	481	512	395	102	49
Glen,	2, 956	1, 528	1, 402	14	12	26	1, 827	1, 015	38	76	599	69	194	556	304	37	6
Minden,	4, 671	2. 378	2, 240	23	30	37	3, 445	1, 096	35	95	918	102	406	850	565	75	75
Mohawk,	3, 077	1, 519	1, 458	48	52	86	1, 263	1, 635	67	112	572	73	263	560	348	80	.....
Palatine,	2, 525	1, 285	1, 230	6	4	9	1, 535	899	31	60	530	54	187	428	349	55	38
Root,	2, 748	1, 470	1, 265	6	7	13	1, 687	973	27	61	561	25	264	519	309	38	10
St. Johnsville,	1, 744	895	838	8	3	11	1, 040	648	20	36	390	22	135	327	208	38	27
Total,	30, 808	15, 585	14, 822	202	199	312	18, 651	10, 934	386	837	6, 111	675	2, 688	5, 310	3, 306	625	314

NEW-YORK COUNTY.

CITIES AND TOWNS.	Total population.	WHITES. Males.	WHITES. Females.	COLORED PERSONS. Males.	COLORED PERSONS. Females.	COLORED PERSONS. No. not taxed.	CIVIL CONDITION. Single.	CIVIL CONDITION. Married.	CIVIL CONDITION. Widowers.	CIVIL CONDITION. Widows.	VOTERS. Native.	VOTERS. Naturalized.	Aliens.	Number of families.	Owners of land.	Over 21 who cannot read or write.	Over 21 who can read but not write.
New-York City:																	
1st ward,	13, 486	7, 019	6, 420	27	20	43	7, 882	5, 042	141	421	570	1, 425	6, 062	2, 646	302	1, 063	340
2d ward,	3, 249	1, 929	1, 244	43	33	64	2, 365	704	78	102	500	290	1, 384	434	79	164	51
3d ward,	7, 909	4, 786	2, 970	109	44	140	5, 766	1, 838	105	200	2, 069	694	2, 765	1, 012	279	793	133
4th ward,	22, 895	11, 898	10, 896	64	37	80	14, 375	7, 519	215	786	922	2, 459	10, 785	4, 732	159	1, 684	518
5th ward,	21, 617	9, 679	9, 869	932	1, 137	1, 842	12, 657	7, 540	327	1, 093	1, 962	1, 471	7, 462	4, 233	432	875	518
6th ward,	25, 562	12, 862	12, 055	282	363	550	15, 709	8, 586	224	1, 043	686	2, 263	13, 010	5, 241	288	2, 829	699
7th ward,	34, 422	16, 437	17, 747	111	127	190	18, 859	14, 386	247	930	2, 767	2, 649	12, 344	6, 811	718	1, 650	659
8th ward,	34, 052	14, 821	16, 730	1, 031	1, 470	2, 444	20, 685	11, 240	476	1, 651	2, 992	1, 910	10, 783	7, 066	863	1, 394	757
9th ward,	39, 982	18, 356	21, 202	168	256	378	24, 081	13, 887	369	1, 645	5, 133	1, 976	9, 346	7, 745	1, 287	821	639
10th ward,	26, 378	12, 824	13, 280	104	170	255	16, 112	9, 030	272	964	2, 160	1, 476	10, 218	5, 825	450	200	154
11th ward,	52, 979	25, 921	26, 748	141	169	285	32, 659	18, 585	382	1, 353	2, 763	3, 612	21, 237	11, 893	798	1, 002	3, 647
12th ward,	17, 656	8, 737	8, 725	102	92	147	12, 436	4, 792	87	341	957	787	7, 864	2, 335	602	875	377
13th ward,	26, 597	12, 899	13, 162	241	295	536	16, 144	9, 761	122	570	2, 120	1, 852	8, 784	6, 040	270	799	255
14th ward,	24, 754	11, 445	12, 403	398	508	716	15, 837	7, 661	173	1, 083	1, 246	1, 954	10, 275	5, 143	258	846	273
15th ward,	24, 046	9, 914	13, 332	293	507	740	15, 911	6, 590	288	1, 257	3, 091	1, 292	7, 406	3, 690	1, 192	816	570
16th ward,	39, 823	18, 054	21, 383	143	243	353	24, 321	13, 958	273	1, 271	3, 350	2, 173	13, 495	8, 125	1, 028	1, 518	1, 245
17th ward,	59, 548	28, 140	31, 051	142	215	348	34, 648	22, 238	486	2, 176	3, 229	3, 689	26, 780	12, 708	857	2, 458	1, 094
18th ward,	*39, 509	17, 419	21, 850	78	162	231	23, 831	13, 661	361	1, 656	2, 774	2, 345	15, 677	7, 551	1, 730	1, 235	625
19th ward,	17, 866	8, 594	8, 615	317	340	646	11, 246	5, 475	350	795	1, 022	1, 460	6, 507	2, 796	522	1, 638	516
20th ward,	47, 055	22, 329	24, 172	223	331	519	27, 876	17, 298	366	1, 515	2. 437	3, 045	14, 441	10, 178	1, 025	1, 253	424
21st ward,	27, 914	12, 770	15, 021	47	76	119	17, 503	9, 170	299	942	2, 262	1, 993	8, 136	5, 451	995	947	541
22d ward,	22, 605	11, 037	11, 319	120	129	181	12, 531	8, 770	253	1, 051	1, 161	1, 889	8, 027	4, 903	650	998	257
Total,	629, 904	297870	320194	5, 116	6, 724	10, 807	383434	217731	5, 894	22, 845	46, 173	42, 704	232678	126558	14, 784	25, 858	14, 292

* From an error not discovered until after publication, the Preliminary Report on this Census, contained 94 less in this ward, which affected the total of the city and whole State to that amount.

NIAGARA COUNTY.

CITIES AND TOWNS.	Total population.	WHITES. Males.	WHITES. Females.	COLORED PERSONS. Males.	COLORED PERSONS. Females.	COLORED PERSONS. No. not taxed.	CIVIL CONDITION. Single.	CIVIL CONDITION. Married.	CIVIL CONDITION. Widowers.	CIVIL CONDITION. Widows.	VOTERS. Native.	VOTERS. Naturalized.	Aliens.	Number of families.	Owners of land.	Over 21 who cannot read or write.	Over 21 who can read but not write.
Cambria,	2, 216	1, 124	1, 091	1	.....	1	1, 364	792	22	38	361	27	298	407	287	3	.....
Hartland,	3, 033	1, 524	1, 504	3	2	5	1, 715	1, 215	32	71	590	75	332	642	523	78	65
Lewiston,	3, 260	1, 650	1, 585	15	10	20	2, 046	1, 095	31	88	290	90	975	581	280	54	25
Lockport,	13, 386	6, 563	6, 623	112	88	137	8, 149	4, 747	168	322	1, 589	654	3, 092	2, 286	1, 613	396	239
Newfane,	3, 164	1, 641	1, 523	.....	.....	.....	1, 910	1, 152	35	67	611	62	188	619	340	20	3
Niagara,	5, 457	2, 808	2, 504	105	40	128	3, 397	1, 880	58	122	527	89	2, 220	967	439	209	46
Pendleton,	1, 826	972	854	.....	.....	.....	1, 095	672	14	45	237	119	303	359	272	51	69
Porter,	2, 643	1, 362	1, 280	.....	1	1	1, 668	874	32	69	412	98	461	484	336	80	20
Royalton,	4, 930	2, 597	2, 331	1	1	2	3, 016	1, 762	46	106	763	96	1, 107	931	600	29	30
Somerset,	1, 923	952	971	.....	.....	.....	1, 152	714	19	38	357	14	154	378	275	3	1

NIAGARA COUNTY.—(Continued.)

CITIES AND TOWNS.	Total population.	WHITES.		COLORED PERSONS.			CIVIL CONDITION.				VOTERS.		Aliens.	Number of families.	Owners of land.	Over 21 who cannot read or write.	Over 21 who can read but not write.
		Males.	Females.	Males.	Females.	No. not taxed.	Single.	Married.	Widowers.	Widows.	Native.	Naturalized.					
Wheatfield, ...	3, 152	1, 630	1, 504	11	7	18	1, 798	1, 259	41	54	196	305	886	675	522	17	1
Wilson, ...	3, 292	1, 736	1, 551	3	2	5	1, 995	1, 193	34	70	621	74	311	622	492	36	29
Total, ...	48, 282	24, 559	23, 321	251	151	317	29, 305	17, 355	532	1, 090	6, 554	1, 703	10, 327	8, 951	5, 979	976	528

ONEIDA COUNTY.

CITIES AND TOWNS.	Total population.	Whites: Males.	Whites: Females.	Colored: Males.	Colored: Females.	No. not taxed.	Single.	Married.	Widowers.	Widows.	Native.	Naturalized.	Aliens.	Number of families.	Owners of land.	Over 21 who cannot read or write.	Over 21 who can read but not write.
Annsville, ...	2, 715	1, 380	1, 335	......	......	......	1, 660	985	19	51	439	115	259	521	415	104	5
Augusta, ...	2, 383	1, 178	1, 195	5	5	10	1, 397	903	25	58	476	49	182	480	378	32	8
Ava, ...	1, 242	668	572	2	......	2	749	458	14	21	185	74	139	229	207	22	27
Boonville, ...	4, 424	2, 355	2, 068	......	1	1	2, 664	1 638	50	72	703	250	606	823	560	169	90
Bridgewater, ...	1, 203	615	588	......	......	......	708	450	14	31	253	28	136	257	191	13	18
Camden, ...	2, 900	1, 418	1, 460	13	9	16	1, 616	1, 156	26	102	590	98	152	606	522	18	......
Deerfield, ...	2, 257	1, 148	1, 108	1	......	1	1, 351	833	21	52	269	156	464	421	292	84	24
Florence, ...	2, 812	1, 435	1, 348	16	13	7	1, 763	971	33	45	280	219	336	539	417	274	22
Floyd, ...	1, 443	725	718	......	......	......	870	529	15	29	210	87	158	285	195	17	9
Kirkland, ...	3, 809	1, 856	1, 924	9	20	29	2, 211	1, 414	46	138	594	138	731	728	522	127	76
Lee, ...	3, 020	1, 519	1, 481	14	6	1	1, 661	1, 242	38	79	600	60	197	595	481	33	35
Marcy, ...	1, 767	916	851	......	......	......	1, 083	639	21	24	194	130	376	355	281	29	124
Marshall, ...	2, 147	1, 085	1, 034	10	18	15	1, 241	815	29	62	379	85	230	431	325	41	5
New Hartford, ...	4, 517	2, 123	2, 375	9	10	12	2, 756	1, 553	62	146	545	227	842	827	418	71	113
Paris, ...	3, 695	1, 818	1, 865	7	5	7	2, 117	1, 443	49	86	706	110	402	768	481	31	11
Remsen, ...	2, 684	1, 423	1, 261	......	......	......	1, 677	915	40	52	342	242	388	505	365	93	40
Rome, ...	10, 720	5, 366	5, 195	83	76	146	6, 453	3, 895	114	258	1, 354	598	2, 263	2, 032	848	446	266
Sangerfield, ...	2, 424	1, 198	1, 193	18	15	20	1, 371	960	27	66	478	47	480	491	340	36	37
Steuben, ...	1, 592	827	765	......	......	......	999	547	23	23	240	113	186	307	246	68	100
Trenton, ...	3, 987	2, 076	1, 908	2	1	3	2, 472	1, 362	61	92	619	181	758	734	527	14	......
Utica city: 1st ward,	1, 443	702	738	2	1	3	882	486	25	50	209	116	342	230	143	67	39
2d ward,	2, 799	1, 376	1, 409	7	7	3	1, 710	938	41	110	234	202	961	532	209	9	18
3d ward,	3, 111	1, 387	1, 706	11	7	18	1, 959	1, 047	20	85	389	170	653	557	283	40	25
4th ward,	4, 827	2, 239	2, 482	47	59	81	2, 950	1, 595	76	206	583	315	1, 101	1, 063	569	190	88
5th ward,	5, 380	2, 554	2, 803	11	12	6	3, 219	1, 948	44	169	384	474	1, 447	1, 108	623	171	34
6th ward,	4, 609	2, 206	2, 397	6	......	......	2, 717	1, 671	69	152	213	379	1, 321	849	346	73	77
Total Utica, ...	22, 169	10, 464	11, 535	84	86	111	13, 437	7, 685	275	772	2, 012	1, 656	5, 825	4, 339	2, 173	550	281
Vernon, ...	3, 005	1, 519	1, 476	5	5	9	1, 824	1, 073	19	89	537	86	405	619	329	86	23
Verona, ...	6, 923	3, 702	3, 204	10	7	17	4, 120	2, 558	82	163	1, 011	314	1, 286	1, 350	882	325	29
Vienna, ...	3, 248	1, 684	1, 562	1	1	2	1, 925	1, 230	23	70	614	105	154	662	453	60	29
Western, ...	2, 546	1, 269	1, 248	17	12	15	1, 525	944	25	52	504	97	184	490	325	83	58
Westmoreland, ...	3, 279	1, 613	1, 663	2	1	3	1, 884	1, 266	34	95	547	147	458	675	503	114	29
Whitestown, ...	4, 838	2, 279	2, 543	10	6	16	3, 084	1, 507	56	191	591	262	875	1, 106	340	122	60
Total, ...	107, 749	53, 659	53, 475	318	297	443	64, 618	38, 971	1, 241	2, 919	15, 272	5, 674	18, 472	21, 175	13, 016	3, 062	1, 519

ONONDAGA COUNTY.

CITIES AND TOWNS.	Total population.	Whites: Males.	Whites: Females.	Colored: Males.	Colored: Females.	No. not taxed.	Single.	Married.	Widowers.	Widows.	Native.	Naturalized.	Aliens.	Number of families.	Owners of land.	Over 21 who cannot read or write.	Over 21 who can read but not write.
Camillus, ...	2, 740	1, 399	1, 332	2	7	......	1, 634	999	24	83	527	54	351	535	328	97	39
Cicero, ...	3, 388	1, 774	1, 600	6	8	6	1, 923	1, 357	42	66	734	57	311	689	529	97	26
Clay, ...	3, 326	1, 761	1, 564	1	......	1	1, 892	1, 355	30	49	695	56	273	576	511	57	64
De Witt, ...	2, 985	1, 552	1, 417	10	6	11	1, 788	1, 092	34	71	524	70	546	599	422	106	16
Elbridge, ...	4, 561	2, 248	2, 268	25	20	31	2, 655	1, 737	41	128	853	90	449	884	445	94	37
Fabius, ...	2, 256	1, 125	1, 127	3	1	......	1, 264	922	20	50	512	4	170	438	375	2	1
Geddes, ...	2, 066	1, 108	944	8	6	8	1, 221	765	23	57	256	128	445	384	157	139	58
La Fayette, ...	2, 340	1, 213	1, 126	1	......	1	1, 352	912	25	51	487	10	167	473	365	55	7
Lysander, ...	5, 060	2, 023	2, 307	19	21	40	2, 938	1, 967	57	98	1, 013	76	427	997	654	110	32
Manlius, ...	6, 228	3, 110	3, 107	6	5	11	3, 812	2, 219	55	142	754	176	779	1, 404	764	85	31
Marcellus, ...	2, 547	1, 258	1, 289	......	......	......	1, 481	972	23	71	485	53	275	517	394	64	8
Onondaga, ...	5, 400	2, 748	2, 574	45	33	32	3, 353	1, 863	62	122	901	133	909	901	856	211	20
Otisco, ...	1, 725	830	895	......	......	......	981	686	21	37	358	15	197	361	298	11	16
Pompey, ...	3, 770	1, 864	1, 900	3	3	3	2, 096	1, 523	43	108	831	34	308	584	538	63	17
Salina, ...	2, 580	1, 377	1, 201	......	2	......	1, 528	987	28	37	309	137	580	497	274	50	15
Skaneateles, ...	3, 976	2, 002	1, 967	3	4	2	2, 323	1, 530	36	87	619	153	744	745	445	78	43
Spafford, ...	1, 816	894	922	......	......	......	1, 028	725	18	45	423	16	84	369	271	25	17
Syracuse city:																	
1st ward,	3, 597	1, 789	1, 792	11	5	16	2, 117	1, 342	23	115	344	307	871	714	440	114	38
2d ward,	3, 437	1, 870	1, 521	23	23	22	2, 138	1, 192	37	70	91	377	1, 006	717	397	25	......
3d ward,	2, 260	1, 163	1, 091	4	2	4	1, 451	732	15	62	327	179	575	375	183	140	67
4th ward,	4, 167	2, 030	2, 073	31	33	49	2, 450	1, 587	35	95	394	260	1, 182	848	477	143	67
5th ward,	2, 063	1.039	1, 023	......	1	......	1, 181	824	8	50	185	137	603	436	263	156	95
6th ward,	3, 256	1, 625	1, 630	......	1	......	2, 043	1, 090	31	92	620	121	645	541	279	17	6
7th ward,	4, 165	1, 960	2, 168	16	21	13	2, 430	1, 563	35	137	396	214	919	827	477	151	55
8th ward,	2, 162	1, 017	1, 064	33	48	31	1, 282	779	27	74	276	82	391	423	200	19	18
Total Syracuse, ..	25, 107	12, 493	12, 362	118	134	135	15, 092	9, 109	211	695	2, 633	1, 677	6, 192	4, 881	2, 716	765	346
Tully, ...	1, 619	806	812	......	1	......	992	583	14	30	343	25	92	352	289	11	13
Van Buren, ...	3, 085	1, 598	1, 486	......	1	......	1, 787	1, 189	27	82	658	54	250	612	426	30	14
Total, ...	86, 575	43, 783	42, 290	250	252	281	51, 140	32. 492	834	2, 109	13, 915	3, 018	13, 549	16, 798	11, 057	2, 150	829

ONTARIO COUNTY.

CITIES AND TOWNS.	Total population.	Whites: Males.	Whites: Females.	Colored: Males.	Colored: Females.	No. not taxed.	Single.	Married.	Widowers.	Widows.	Native.	Naturalized.	Aliens.	Number of families.	Owners of land.	Over 21 who cannot read or write.	Over 21 who can read but not write.
Bristol, ...	1, 715	862	853	......	......	......	969	673	25	48	410	15	86	397	316	12	14
Canadice, ...	977	491	486	......	......	......	583	367	9	18	229	7	19	185	163	19	......
Canandaigua, ...	6, 480	3, 110	3, 240	56	74	46	3, 819	2, 407	74	180	1, 088	208	1, 092	1, 184	767	115	9
East Bloomfield, ...	2, 168	1, 111	1, 045	6	6	12	1, 305	770	20	64	417	42	321	406	339	69	25
Farmington, ...	1, 950	994	949	4	3	5	1, 195	662	40	53	392	26	273	368	309	26	16
Gorham, ...	2, 380	1, 182	1, 191	3	4	7	1, 396	886	33	65	514	45	162	455	388	6	3
Hopewell, ...	1, 783	901	868	9	5	14	1, 069	632	17	65	370	35	151	321	237	24	1
Manchester, ...	3, 009	1, 520	1, 442	21	26	12	1, 780	1, 117	29	83	621	43	280	569	349	31	11
Naples, ...	2, 118	1, 083	1, 029	5	1	6	1, 255	792	22	49	459	6	20	409	346	28	26

ONTARIO COUNTY.—(Continued.)

Cities and towns.	Total population.	Whites.		Colored persons.			Civil condition.				Voters.		Aliens.	Number of families.	Owners of land.	Over 21 who cannot read or write.	Over 21 who can read but not write
		Males.	Females.	Males.	Females.	No. not taxed.	Single	Married.	Widowers.	Widows.	Native.	Naturalized.					
Phelps,	5,293	2,672	2,574	22	25	24	3,091	2,020	47	135	1,115	56	485	1,014	761	92	4[cut off]
Richmond,	1,493	759	721	8	7	13	893	554	13	33	317	15	200	291	206	......	.....
Seneca,	8,298	3,911	4,087	122	178	206	4,971	2,912	96	319	1,314	261	1,134	1,589	909	74	5[cut off]
South Bristol,	1,179	614	565	......	......	......	678	456	17	28	271	10	27	241	202	15	
Victor,	2,208	1,153	1,055	......	......	......	1,283	851	26	48	476	38	261	426	295	31	2
West Bloomfield,	1,621	819	801	1	......	1	957	595	13	56	330	17	246	325	258	28	2
Total,	42,672	21,182	20,906	255	329	346	25,244	15,694	490	1,244	8,323	824	4,757	8,180	5,845	570	26

ORANGE COUNTY.

Cities and towns.	Total population.	Whites, males.	Whites, females.	Colored, males.	Colored, females.	No. not taxed.	Single	Married.	Widowers.	Widows.	Native.	Naturalized.	Aliens.	Number of families.	Owners of land.	Over 21 who cannot read or write.	Over 21 who can read but not write
Blooming Grove,	2,184	1,034	1,035	60	55	97	1,368	720	24	72	385	44	254	389	211	5	
Chester,	1,696	790	819	51	36	80	1,062	565	15	54	308	23	160	310	189	38	
Cornwall,	4,578	2,393	2,124	27	34	58	2,913	1,502	35	128	737	141	874	808	401	159	
Crawford,	2,000	929	1,016	30	25	50	1,298	617	25	60	415	22	147	356	221	15	
Deerpark,	5,504	2,861	2,472	85	86	148	3,438	1,909	61	96	885	119	1,020	972	449	107	
Goshen,	3,213	1,453	1,554	113	93	195	2,135	953	33	92	511	48	379	529	226	128	
Greenville,	1,218	605	610	1	2	2	721	442	11	34	242	8	16	233	140	2	
Hamptonburgh,	1,303	587	591	75	50	109	853	370	25	55	246	7	122	223	141	52	
Minisink,	1,295	623	642	12	18	30	815	447	8	35	272	8	52	242	161	12	
Monroe,	4,551	2,374	2,165	6	6	9	2,954	1,492	32	73	696	89	404	812	290	87	
Montgomery,	3,792	1,711	1,871	109	101	181	2,367	1,222	50	153	640	67	487	715	380	45	
Mount Hope,	1,735	844	860	13	18	27	1,015	641	18	61	346	28	137	363	220	35	
Newburgh,	12,773	5,913	6,435	209	216	341	7,951	4,256	111	455	1,502	498	2,641	2,443	630	136	
New Windsor,	2,555	1,224	1,230	54	47	82	1,670	776	37	72	376	103	419	444	216	68	
Wallkill,	5,415	2,556	2,706	80	73	135	3,433	1,766	58	158	1,003	99	531	1,040	622	119	
Warwick,	4,987	2,352	2,367	136	132	227	3,125	1,680	49	133	992	44	191	930	477	193	
Wawaganda,	2,069	960	1,014	47	48	84	1,282	696	24	67	378	19	121	377	172	40	
Total,	60,868	29,209	29,511	1,108	1,040	1,855	38,400	20,054	616	1,798	9,934	1,367	7,955	11,186	5,146	1,241	5[cut off]

ORLEANS COUNTY.

Cities and towns.	Total population.	Whites, males.	Whites, females.	Colored, males.	Colored, females.	No. not taxed.	Single	Married.	Widowers.	Widows.	Native.	Naturalized.	Aliens.	Number of families.	Owners of land.	Over 21 who cannot read or write.	Over 21 who can read but not write
Barre,	6,797	3,410	3,350	18	19	7	4,034	2,566	52	145	1,283	236	886	1,142	888	115	
Carlton,	2,329	1,232	1,094	1	2	......	1,323	933	24	49	516	17	161	466	364	......	
Clarendon,	1,749	912	826	6	5	5	986	701	23	39	360	16	101	350	258	14	
Gaines,	2,532	1,336	1,189	3	4	7	1,485	976	26	45	490	41	381	493	322	86	....
Kendall,	1,884	975	909	......	......	......	1,111	727	23	23	358	29	94	381	306	......	....
Murray,	2,876	1,469	1,400	1	6	1	1,692	1,101	26	57	485	85	405	552	391	113	
Ridgeway,	5,226	2,767	2,414	26	19	23	3,140	1,900	56	130	683	81	1,244	977	779	311	
Shelby,	3,046	1,593	1,453	......	......	......	1,775	1,193	23	55	545	65	406	205	395	85	
Yates,	1,996	1,023	973	......	......	......	1,136	790	12	58	385	29	135	427	322	12	
Total,	28,435	14,717	13,608	55	55	43	16,682	10,887	265	601	5,105	599	3,813	4,993	4,025	736	1[cut off]

OSWEGO COUNTY.

Cities and towns.	Total population.	Whites, males.	Whites, females.	Colored, males.	Colored, females.	No. not taxed.	Single	Married.	Widowers.	Widows.	Native.	Naturalized.	Aliens.	Number of families.	Owners of land.	Over 21 who cannot read or write.	Over 21 who can read but not write
Albion,	2,212	1,147	1,065	......	......	......	1,271	886	18	37	306	35	65	435	375	30	
Amboy,	1,172	636	536	......	......	......	699	436	11	26	227	49	51	222	190	9	....
Boylston,	815	424	391	......	......	......	480	322	7	6	177	12	6	146	145	7	....
Constantia,	3,355	1,571	1,744	20	20	5	2,018	1,251	38	48	647	125	246	632	442	48	
Granby,	3,747	1,961	1,779	2	5	7	2,188	1,451	35	73	679	53	405	767	458	13	
Hannibal,	3,028	1,552	1,472	3	1	2	1,680	1,252	31	65	693	37	123	639	511	52	
Hastings,	3,069	1,607	1,458	3	1	3	1,796	1,184	41	48	633	77	110	608	505	60	
Mexico,	4,022	2,014	2,005	1	2	1	2,304	1,565	48	105	876	66	177	831	743	57	
New Haven,	2,012	1,009	1,001	2	......	2	1,123	822	17	50	454	27	66	433	344	2	
Orwell,	1,258	668	589	1	......	1	709	513	13	23	302	10	14	260	232	......	...
Oswego,	2,760	1,420	1,324	8	8	10	1,566	1,136	11	47	495	66	294	545	293	113	
Oswego city:																	
1st ward,	4,143	2,015	2,098	15	15	13	2,369	1,590	50	134	483	231	1,209	674	403	59	
2d ward,	2,839	1,484	1,323	20	12	19	1,653	1,095	26	65	245	218	796	548	293	236	
3d ward,	4,254	2,153	2,048	25	28	20	2,532	1,589	48	85	376	264	1,158	864	533	326	
4th ward,	4,580	2,297	2,258	13	12	25	2,721	1,713	34	112	405	298	981	876	542	236	
Total Oswego,	15,816	7,949	7,727	73	67	77	9,275	5,987	158	396	1,599	1,011	4,144	2,962	1,771	857	
Palermo,	2,023	1,046	973	2	2	......	1,085	866	26	46	508	20	42	457	277	27	
Parish,	1,675	875	800	......	......	......	950	680	18	27	370	34	31	337	295	10	
Redfield,	798	452	346	......	......	......	509	282	7	......	163	19	27	158	139	13	
Richland,	4,012	2,078	1,932	1	1	2	2,323	1,558	39	92	870	49	150	677	520	19	
Sandy Creek,	2,273	1,175	1,097	......	1	1	1,311	892	19	51	552	9	44	488	337	11	...
Scroeppel,	3,747	1,914	1,791	23	19	41	2,234	1,428	23	62	726	50	286	756	443	102	
Scriba,	2,958	1,534	1,412	5	7	......	1,698	1,173	37	50	580	91	170	587	532	99	
Volney,	6,476	3,324	3,071	41	40	54	3,685	2,605	60	126	1,261	131	809	1,343	855	210	...
West Monroe,	1,217	627	581	4	5	9	724	457	9	27	242	43	73	241	204	17	
Williamstown,	953	490	463	......	......	......	557	365	14	17	216	19	39	187	170	22	
Total,	69,398	35,473	33,557	189	179	215	40,185	27,111	680	1,422	12,576	2,033	7,372	13,711	9,781	1,778	

OTSEGO COUNTY.

Cities and towns.	Total population.	Whites, males.	Whites, females.	Colored, males.	Colored, females.	No. not taxed.	Single	Married.	Widowers.	Widows.	Native.	Naturalized.	Aliens.	Number of families.	Owners of land.	Over 21 who cannot read or write.	Over 21 who can read but not write
Burlington,	1,808	893	910	3	2	......	1,033	688	24	63	387	29	87	370	292	15	
Butternuts,	2,029	1,001	1,020	5	3	6	1,087	845	32	65	475	31	100	435	262	25	
Cherry Valley,	2,540	1,365	1,172	2	1	3	1,575	857	43	65	496	73	130	285	332	7	
Decatur,	913	475	438	......	......	......	546	345	12	10	219	......	3	181	159	10	
Edmeston,	1,783	887	894	1	1	2	983	725	20	55	461	6	24	384	291	13	..
Exeter,	1,540	757	782	......	1	1	874	594	20	52	355	7	60	305	238	9	
Hartwick,	2,220	1,038	1,182	......	......	......	1,256	869	29	66	489	6	33	601	245	2	
Laurens,	2,106	1,029	1,077	......	......	......	1,171	853	17	65	507	13	10	446	346	21	
Maryland,	2,177	1,099	1,073	3	2	4	1,278	820	31	48	524	14	70	432	339	37	

OTSEGO COUNTY.—(Continued.)

CITIES AND TOWNS.	Total population.	WHITES. Males.	WHITES. Females.	COLORED PERSONS. Males.	COLORED PERSONS. Females.	COLORED PERSONS. No. not taxed.	CIVIL CONDITION. Single.	CIVIL CONDITION. Married.	CIVIL CONDITION. Widowers.	CIVIL CONDITION. Widows.	VOTERS. Native.	VOTERS. Naturalized.	Aliens.	Number of families.	Owners of land.	Over 21 who cannot read or write.	Over 21 who can read but not write.
Middlefield,	3 071	1, 552	1, 506	6	7	10	1, 788	1, 177	40	66	690	69	115	571	446	60	43
Milford,	2, 329	1, 150	1, 169	6	4	10	1, 285	954	26	64	580	15	15	483	372	38	7
Morris,	2, 038	994	1, 033	7	4	5	1, 107	846	29	56	466	22	62	434	312	11	7
New Lisbon,	1, 792	882	910	......	......	......	1, 011	708	25	48	404	34	41	373	300	......	......
Oneonta,	2, 167	1, 100	1, 058	5	4	9	1, 215	865	24	63	527	5	23	440	327	40	3
Otego,	1, 850	914	936	......	......	......	1, 009	769	22	50	510	9	3	394	336	20	7
Otsego,	4, 334	2, 089	2, 193	26	26	47	2, 517	1, 602	53	162	940	82	279	825	529	30	9
Pittsfield,	1, 656	798	849	7	2	......	957	637	30	32	387	21	29	345	268	19	4
Plainfield,	1, 281	637	631	4	9	5	683	549	13	36	323	11	81	280	230	10	1
Richfield,	1, 543	771	736	20	16	33	854	624	27	38	385	21	83	312	259	35	39
Roseboom,	1, 887	948	935	1	3	......	1, 107	726	11	43	444	16	16	373	295	62	74
Springfield,	2, 463	1, 232	1, 222	3	6	9	1, 436	923	26	78	514	41	220	611	351	59	57
Unadilla,	2, 722	1, 386	1, 316	7	13	11	1, 573	1, 052	33	64	695	12	89	533	453	15	9
Westford,	1, 371	678	693	......	......	......	727	601	10	33	357	6	16	314	293	5	......
Worcester,	2, 115	1, 051	1, 057	4	3	3	1, 227	820	18	50	468	31	51	411	322	26	19
Total,	49, 735	24, 726	24, 792	110	107	158	28, 299	19, 449	615	1, 372	11, 603	574	1, 640	10, 138	7, 597	569	334

PUTNAM COUNTY.

CITIES AND TOWNS.	Total population.	WHITES. Males.	WHITES. Females.	COLORED PERSONS. Males.	COLORED PERSONS. Females.	COLORED PERSONS. No. not taxed.	CIVIL CONDITION. Single.	CIVIL CONDITION. Married.	CIVIL CONDITION. Widowers.	CIVIL CONDITION. Widows.	VOTERS. Native.	VOTERS. Naturalized.	Aliens.	Number of families.	Owners of land.	Over 21 who cannot read or write.	Over 21 who can read but not write.
Carmel,	2, 406	1, 153	1, 225	16	12	28	1, 395	894	32	85	554	9	162	483	345	16	14
Kent,	1, 539	754	781	1	3	4	911	557	23	48	352	11	26	308	225	133	50
Patterson,	1, 422	689	709	13	11	22	792	560	14	56	338	7	103	302	204	13	13
Philipstown,	4, 809	2, 424	2, 381	3	1	4	2, 928	1, 693	51	137	711	197	646	932	433	225	78
Putnam Valley,	1, 573	826	746	......	1	1	998	508	24	43	356	......	38	312	264	......	......
South East,	2, 185	1, 052	1, 065	39	29	54	1, 298	758	28	101	495	7	240	409	268	38	5
Total,	13, 934	6, 898	6, 907	72	57	113	8, 322	4, 970	172	470	2. 806	231	1, 215	2, 746	1, 739	425	160

QUEENS COUNTY.

CITIES AND TOWNS.	Total population.	WHITES. Males.	WHITES. Females.	COLORED PERSONS. Males.	COLORED PERSONS. Females.	COLORED PERSONS. No. not taxed.	CIVIL CONDITION. Single.	CIVIL CONDITION. Married.	CIVIL CONDITION. Widowers.	CIVIL CONDITION. Widows.	VOTERS. Native.	VOTERS. Naturalized.	Aliens.	Number of families.	Owners of land.	Over 21 who cannot read or write.	Over 21 who can read but not write.
Flushing,	7, 970	3, 699	3, 734	260	277	441	4, 834	2, 865	74	197	781	444	1, 943	1, 500	657	338	154
Hempstead,	10, 477	5, 053	5, 031	211	182	292	6, 330	3, 801	86	260	2, 000	243	686	2, 051	1, 409	151	35
Jamaica,	5, 632	2, 632	2, 661	164	175	274	3, 543	1, 884	66	139	867	175	1, 033	1, 005	640	124	69
North Hempstead,	4, 694	1, 992	1, 991	339	372	631	2, 857	1, 620	61	156	761	45	731	904	434	317	183
Newtown,	9, 446	4, 549	4, 603	134	160	205	5, 843	3, 239	107	257	861	507	3, 024	1, 766	914	384	244
Oyster Bay,	8, 047	3, 731	3, 540	378	398	695	4, 864	2. 820	112	251	1, 344	159	1, 201	1, 456	994	274	122
Total,	46, 266	21, 656	21, 560	1, 486	1, 564	2, 538	28, 271	16, 229	506	1, 260	6, 614	1, 573	8, 618	8, 682	5, 048	1, 588	807

RENSSELAER COUNTY.

CITIES AND TOWNS.	Total population.	WHITES. Males.	WHITES. Females.	COLORED PERSONS. Males.	COLORED PERSONS. Females.	COLORED PERSONS. No. not taxed.	CIVIL CONDITION. Single.	CIVIL CONDITION. Married.	CIVIL CONDITION. Widowers.	CIVIL CONDITION. Widows.	VOTERS. Native.	VOTERS. Naturalized.	Aliens.	Number of families.	Owners of land.	Over 21 who cannot read or write.	Over 21 who can read but not write.
Berlin,	2, 167	1, 088	1, 078	1	......	1	1, 200	877	29	61	407	47	260	455	289	22	15
Brunswick,	3, 101	1, 527	1, 567	6	1	5	1, 858	1, 109	51	83	637	43	377	570	370	48	50
Clinton,	1, 606	821	759	8	18	26	991	565	21	29	244	52	344	227	131	15	......
Grafton,	1, 888	962	926	......	......	......	1, 109	710	21	48	389	16	71	370	254	42	9
Greenbush,	3, 303	1, 622	1, 639	20	22	28	1, 833	1, 328	49	93	422	236	619	709	299	219	71
Hoosick,	4, 120	1, 998	2, 059	31	32	29	2, 476	1, 476	48	120	764	71	646	736	327	180	43
Lansingburgh,	5, 700	2, 636	2, 939	61	64	111	3, 551	1, 874	54	221	655	311	1, 066	1, 120	391	86	103
Nassau,	3, 000	1, 465	1, 527	5	3	8	1, 727	1, 148	39	86	332	37	283	587	423	21	22
North Greenburgh,	1, 812	892	905	9	6	5	1, 068	675	19	50	650	30	164	358	137	16	12
Petersburgh,	1, 663	804	852	5	2	7	954	646	19	44	370	13	106	313	192	14	23
Pittstown,	3, 602	1, 746	1, 825	16	15	29	2, 147	1, 286	47	122	717	72	366	707	497	106	78
Poestenkill,	1, 878	965	913	......	......	......	1, 111	702	18	47	355	32	226	403	223	30	1
Sand Lake,	2, 588	1, 245	1, 331	6	6	6	1, 497	995	29	67	485	51	350	522	291	89	58
Schaghticoke,	3, 303	1, 651	1, 637	9	6	15	2, 073	1, 105	37	88	506	78	616	608	318	162	47
Schodack,	3, 837	1, 944	1, 831	34	28	38	2, 235	1, 445	54	103	760	62	606	757	512	112	72
Stephentown,	2, 397	1, 183	1, 204	5	5	6	1, 386	941	17	53	536	21	85	481	323	15	......
Troy City: 1st ward,	4, 232	1, 937	2, 101	91	103	172	2, 439	1, 526	52	215	422	308	1, 167	843	176	275	121
2d ward,	4, 257	1, 967	2, 170	52	68	112	2, 662	1, 392	40	163	512	225	1, 049	797	169	91	61
3d ward,	2, 394	1, 064	1, 251	37	42	63	1, 503	743	34	114	429	90	512	426	141	124	78
4th ward,	4, 122	1, 875	2, 218	12	17	25	2, 494	1, 366	57	205	547	210	797	811	221	215	73
5th ward,	2, 375	1, 168	1, 205	1	1	2	1, 581	689	21	84	232	188	403	411	96	7	......
6th ward,	2, 599	1, 376	1, 219	3	1	2	1, 608	895	32	64	204	176	812	469	12	189	107
7th ward,	3, 700	1, 839	1, 855	2	4	6	2, 127	1, 404	41	128	395	264	845	796	92	223	......
8th ward,	3, 876	1, 862	1, 995	8	11	12	2, 355	1, 360	24	137	233	248	1, 419	752	194	245	177
9th ward,	3, 339	1, 767	1, 564	3	5	1	1, 912	1, 315	23	89	110	306	1, 246	684	238	403	218
10th ward,	2, 675	1, 153	1, 213	6	3	8	1, 339	934	25	77	309	124	486	506	143	131	113
Total Troy,	33, 269	16, 008	16, 791	215	255	403	20, 020	11, 624	349	1, 276	3, 393	2, 139	8, 736	6, 495	1, 482	1, 903	948
Total,	79, 234	38, 557	39, 783	431	463	717	47, 236	28, 506	901	2, 591	11, 622	3, 311	14 921	15 418	6, 459	3, 080	1, 552

RICHMOND COUNTY.

CITIES AND TOWNS.	Total population.	WHITES. Males.	WHITES. Females.	COLORED PERSONS. Males.	COLORED PERSONS. Females.	COLORED PERSONS. No. not taxed.	CIVIL CONDITION. Single.	CIVIL CONDITION. Married.	CIVIL CONDITION. Widowers.	CIVIL CONDITION. Widows.	VOTERS. Native.	VOTERS. Naturalized.	Aliens.	Number of families.	Owners of land.	Over 21 who cannot read or write.	Over 21 who can read but not write.
Castleton,	8, 252	4, 068	4, 113	34	37	68	5, 390	2, 580	56	226	795	669	2, 274	1, 447	623	45	8
Northfield,	4, 187	2, 026	2, 081	38	42	76	2, 504	1, 480	51	152	684	109	673	939	518	134	75
Southfield,	5, 449	2, 534	2, 664	120	131	188	3, 367	1, 845	57	180	425	467	1, 667	1, 003	473	30	16
Westfield,	3, 501	1, 665	1 648	84	104	155	2, 224	1, 148	45	84	537	109	464	667	473	36	24
Total,	21, 389	10, 293	10, 506	276	314	487	13, 485	7, 053	209	642	2, 441	1, 354	5, 078	4, 056	2, 087	245	123

ROCKLAND COUNTY.

CITIES AND TOWNS.	Total population.	WHITES. Males.	WHITES. Females.	COLORED PERSONS. Males.	COLORED PERSONS. Females.	COLORED PERSONS. No. not taxed.	CIVIL CONDITION. Single.	CIVIL CONDITION. Married.	CIVIL CONDITION. Widowers.	CIVIL CONDITION. Widows.	VOTERS. Native.	VOTERS. Naturalized.	Aliens.	Number of families.	Owners of land.	Over 21 who cannot read or write.	Over 21 who can read but not write.
Clarkstown,	3, 512	1, 762	1, 611	69	70	136	2, 000	1, 387	46	79	630	79	522	743	498	106	40
Haverstraw,	6, 747	3, 691	3, 012	15	29	3	4, 159	2, 382	55	151	870	236	1, 690	1, 263	348	530	171
Orangetown,	5, 838	2, 789	2, 816	106	127	209	3, 261	2, 281	67	229	929	151	993	1, 210	568	247	44
Ramapo,	3, 414	1, 686	1, 647	37	44	55	2, 059	1, 231	40	84	664	21	252	644	400	97	33
Total,	19, 511	9, 928	9, 086	227	270	403	11, 479	7, 281	208	543	3, 093	487	3, 457	3, 860	1, 814	980	288

ST. LAWRENCE COUNTY.

CITIES AND TOWNS.	Total population.	WHITES.		COLORED PERSONS.			CIVIL CONDITION.				VOTERS.		Aliens.	Number of families.	Owners of land.	Over 21 who cannot read or write.	Over 21 who can read but not write.
		Males.	Females	Males.	Females.	No. not taxed.	Single.	Married.	Widowers.	Widows	Native.	Naturalized.					
Brasher,	2, 968	1, 514	1, 453	.....	1	1	1, 924	978	21	45	310	98	524	507	435	247	7
Canton,	4, 995	2, 497	2, 498	.....	.....	.....	2, 981	1, 831	60	123	889	112	525	880	806	119	4
Colton,	1, 040	545	494	1	.....	1	604	429	5	2	199	20	75	212	140	3	.....
De Kalb,	2, 676	1, 360	1, 315	.....	1	1	1, 603	997	32	44	471	55	279	511	319	31	1
De Peyster,	1, 163	599	564	.....	.....	.....	725	409	11	18	180	47	105	196	153	11	.....
Edwards,	1, 180	625	555	.....	.....	.....	722	427	11	20	212	51	29	210	211	1	
Fine,	316	172	144	.....	.....	.....	193	114	3	6	58	1	19	57	56	7	
Fowler,	1, 620	814	806	.....	.....	.....	949	633	13	25	351	24	28	303	241	4	
Gouverneur,	2, 856	1, 402	1, 447	4	3	7	1, 741	1, 046	21	48	513	47	238	512	399	40	1
Hammond,	1, 875	970	905	.....	.....	.....	1, 199	612	29	35	245	105	210	320	112	2	.....
Hermon,	1, 648	854	794	.....	.....	.....	986	626	14	22	338	9	56	305	244	8	
Hopkinton,	1, 554	775	779	.....	.....	.....	905	602	13	34	319	13	72	267	241	29	.....
Lawrence,	2, 365	1, 226	1, 139	.....	.....	.....	1, 362	946	17	40	469	53	154	473	407	20	
Lisbon,	5, 109	2, 603	2, 469	19	18	32	3, 257	1, 691	55	106	488	283	895	905	761	163	6
Louisville,	2, 120	1, 080	1, 028	7	5	12	1, 348	700	20	52	268	95	312	356	338	72	.....
Macomb,	1, 466	749	717	.....	.....	.....	925	519	10	12	176	57	186	124	221	39	3
Madrid,	4, 862	2, 435	2, 427	.....	.....	.....	3, 097	1, 582	57	126	456	330	678	877	736	121	6
Massena,	2, 701	1, 334	1, 359	7	1	5	1, 703	896	36	66	422	57	322	468	341	226	2
Morristown,	2, 111	1, 049	1, 062	.....	.....	.....	1, 264	778	29	40	367	84	209	399	281	20	4
Norfolk,	1, 804	880	915	2	7	1	1, 047	690	21	46	338	35	210	350	310	43	.....
Oswegatchie,	10, 060	5, 023	5, 012	10	15	25	6, 436	3, 333	69	222	875	407	3, 165	1, 474	1, 096	675	12
Parishville,	2, 114	1, 054	1, 060	.....	.....	.....	1, 196	870	19	29	479	31	102	395	404	36	
Pierrepont,	1, 834	906	928	.....	.....	.....	1, 064	730	12	28	384	27	94	347	309	25	
Pitcairn,	531	269	262	.....	.....	.....	315	204	5	7	117	7	7	106	89	3	.....
Potsdam,	6, 631	3, 328	3, 302	.....	1	1	3, 955	2, 477	66	133	1, 308	156	835	1, 191	1, 015	239	2
Rossie,	1, 480	752	728	.....	.....	.....	944	489	17	30	181	76	223	314	153	58	2
Russell,	2, 108	1, 115	993	.....	.....	.....	1, 358	719	12	19	392	43	103	392	262	4	.....
Stockholm,	3, 790	1, 954	1, 836	.....	.....	.....	2, 228	1, 437	51	74	810	46	260	726	610	26	.....
Total,	74, 977	37, 884	36, 991	50	52	86	46, 031	26, 765	729	1, 452	11, 615	2, 369	9, 915	13, 177	10, 690	2, 272	59

SARATOGA COUNTY.

CITIES AND TOWNS.	Total population.	Whites: Males.	Whites: Females.	Colored: Males.	Colored: Females.	No. not taxed.	Single.	Married.	Widowers.	Widows.	Voters: Native.	Voters: Naturalized.	Aliens.	Number of families.	Owners of land.	Over 21 who cannot read or write.	Over 21 who can read but not write.
Ballston,	2, 201	1, 052	1, 135	6	8	14	1, 326	781	22	72	390	59	227	435	343	44	.....
Charlton,	1, 701	835	851	7	8	15	1,042	591	19	49	309	44	164	326	214	3	.....
Clifton Park,	2, 917	1, 475	1, 390	27	25	36	1, 746	1, 064	30	77	570	49	397	577	424	34	
Corinth,	1, 534	780	753	1	.....	1	875	610	16	33	320	8	91	317	131	30	.....
Day,	1, 079	560	519	.....	.....	.....	646	406	7	20	203	3	10	198	144	10	
Edinburgh,	1, 318	626	685	3	4	7	755	527	17	19	299	9	13	283	283	2	.....
Galway,	2, 441	1, 208	1, 230	.....	3	3	1, 424	922	27	68	509	59	205	504	401	10	.....
Greenfield,	2, 842	1, 423	1, 399	9	11	18	1, 524	1, 175	51	92	684	38	177	613	425	39	
Hadley,	1, 172	626	546	.....	.....	.....	686	461	7	18	176	22	198	222	112	66	.....
Half Moon,	3, 315	1, 657	1, 655	2	1	1	2, 046	1, 184	18	67	507	57	538	603	231	123	
Malta,	1, 236	611	619	4	2	6	690	482	26	38	299	9	100	257	222	47	
Milton,	4, 669	2, 202	2, 324	59	84	127	2, 779	1, 693	46	151	847	143	491	225	261	63	
Moreau,	2, 166	1, 066	1, 074	13	13	14	1, 316	766	26	58	439	28	225	401	264	81	
Northumberland,	1, 668	852	795	8	13	11	970	620	37	41	380	33	91	312	244	87	
Providence,	1, 368	678	690	.....	.....	.....	800	531	20	17	316	9	46	295	196	.....	.....
Saratoga,	3, 832	1, 810	1, 992	12	18	29	2, 377	1, 281	41	133	679	85	523	701	374	97	
Saratoga Springs,	6, 307	2, 866	3, 237	85	119	167	3, 653	2, 343	81	230	1, 082	181	1, 189	1, 239	694	227	1
Stillwater,	2, 963	2, 445	1, 470	23	25	48	1, 764	1, 076	37	86	556	35	437	590	313	132	
Waterford,	3, 249	1, 551	1, 658	18	22	37	2, 025	1, 096	31	97	447	143	592	605	226	140	
Wilton,	1, 401	678	714	4	5	5	807	534	27	33	334	17	34	281	233	36	
Total,	49, 379	24, 001	24, 736	281	361	539	29, 251	18, 143	586	1, 399	9, 346	1, 031	5, 748	8, 984	5, 735	1, 271	4

SCHENECTADY COUNTY.

CITIES AND TOWNS.	Total population.	Whites: Males.	Whites: Females.	Colored: Males.	Colored: Females.	No. not taxed.	Single.	Married.	Widowers.	Widows.	Voters: Native.	Voters: Naturalized.	Aliens.	Number of families.	Owners of land.	Over 21 who cannot read or write.	Over 21 who can read but not write.
Duanesburgh,	3, 119	1, 547	1, 558	9	5	14	1, 886	1, 091	44	98	640	57	119	395	596	27	
Glenville,	3, 153	1, 651	1, 475	15	12	10	1, 955	1, 078	37	83	573	70	358	417	700	44	
Niskayuna,	1, 120	580	531	4	5	9	659	414	16	31	200	36	160	118	217	34	
Princetown,	956	495	459	1	1	.....	541	390	12	13	160	7	61	120	172	1	.....
Rotterdam,	2, 835	1, 491	1, 259	46	39	22	1, 760	1, 000	32	43	450	72	592	293	492	10	
Schenectady City:																	
1st ward,	1, 544	662	854	9	19	28	952	498	18	76	197	59	284	104	321	53	
2d ward,	1, 530	711	814	2	3	5	890	542	17	81	230	66	297	112	336	8	
3d ward,	1, 951	921	957	32	41	50	1, 125	729	20	77	165	149	487	138	301	28	
4th ward,	3, 364	1, 643	1, 653	32	36	42	2, 022	1, 162	60	120	518	141	585	256	648	64	
Total Schenectady,	8, 389	3, 937	4, 278	75	99	125	4, 989	2, 931	115	354	1, 110	415	1, 653	610	1, 606	153	1
Total,	19, 572	9, 701	9, 560	150	161	180	11, 790	6, 904	256	622	3, 133	657	2, 943	1, 953	3, 783	269	[illegible]

SCHOHARIE COUNTY.

CITIES AND TOWNS.	Total population.	Whites: Males.	Whites: Females.	Colored: Males.	Colored: Females.	No. not taxed.	Single.	Married.	Widowers.	Widows.	Voters: Native.	Voters: Naturalized.	Aliens.	Number of families.	Owners of land.	Over 21 who cannot read or write.	Over 21 who can read but not write.
Blenheim,	1, 351	678	658	8	7	11	827	486	11	27	278	12	57	245	186	15	...
Broome,	2, 138	1, 071	1, 067	.....	.....	.....	1, 265	820	24	29	489	7	22	427	270	46	
Carlisle,	1, 723	872	849	1	1	2	1, 031	634	9	49	410	7	36	326	276	27	
Cobleskill,	2, 208	1, 092	1, 105	4	7	7	1, 261	875	24	48	470	18	91	401	335	6	...
Conesville,	1, 407	700	707	.....	.....	.....	816	541	13	37	304	6	4	292	215	15	
Esperance,	1, 370	629	714	14	13	27	845	473	10	42	293	9	75	262	177	29	
Fulton,	2, 817	1, 439	1, 359	11	8	13	1, 694	1, 049	27	47	624	14	17	530	402	133	
Gilboa,	2, 657	1, 303	1, 347	3	4	2	1, 638	954	23	42	547	23	75	526	322	50	
Jefferson,	1, 688	820	868	.....	.....	.....	991	651	12	34	356	8	8	321	252	3	...
Middleburgh,	3, 075	1, 582	1, 420	39	34	66	1, 921	1, 078	18	58	621	18	110	547	363	4	
Richmondville,	2, 027	1, 019	991	9	8	13	1, 204	758	19	46	435	9	52	378	291	45	
Schoharie,	2, 869	1, 321	1, 343	108	97	200	1, 742	1, 019	29	79	528	48	147	495	310	161	
Seward,	1, 925	953	957	9	6	7	1, 144	726	15	40	430	6	42	335	247	6	...
Sharon,	2, 716	1, 335	1, 323	25	33	36	1, 616	1, 009	19	72	597	19	81	489	424	8	...
Summit,	1, 890	940	949	.....	1	1	1, 372	471	11	36	411	10	31	374	268	.....	.....
Wright,	1, 658	841	811	2	4	6	972	628	18	40	360	9	26	310	236	53	
Total,	33, 519	16, 595	16, 468	233	223	391	20, 339	12, 172	282	726	7, 153	223	874	6, 258	4, 574	601	

SCHUYLER COUNTY.

CITIES AND TOWNS.	Total population.	WHITES. Males.	WHITES. Females.	COLORED PERSONS. Males.	COLORED PERSONS. Females.	COLORED PERSONS. No. not taxed.	CIVIL CONDITION. Single.	CIVIL CONDITION. Married.	CIVIL CONDITION. Widowers.	CIVIL CONDITION. Widows.	VOTERS. Native.	VOTERS. Naturalized.	Aliens.	Number of families.	Owners of land.	Over 21 who cannot read or write.	Over 21 who can read but not write.
Catharines,	3,517	1,747	1,741	14	15	20	2,097	1,308	30	82	794	34	183	593	421	32	20
Cayuta,	618	324	294	......	......	......	367	231	7	13	149	5	1	119	130	7	3
Dix,	2,884	1,440	1,432	7	5	6	1,727	1,077	27	53	635	35	78	574	454	19	16
Hector,	5,629	2,788	2,819	13	9	9	3,366	2,050	53	160	1,258	35	159	1,102	988	85	74
Orange,	2,483	1,249	1,226	7	1	......	1,482	927	17	57	524	33	79	483	374	25	......
Reading,	1,452	733	714	3	2	5	874	522	17	39	315	23	44	277	237	10	......
Tyrone,	2,194	1,083	1,111	......	......	......	1,274	854	22	44	515	22	43	429	342	41	76
Total,	18,777	9,364	9,337	44	32	40	11,187	6,969	173	448	4,190	187	587	3,577	2,946	219	189

SENECA COUNTY.

CITIES AND TOWNS.	Total population.	WHITES. Males.	WHITES. Females.	COLORED PERSONS. Males.	COLORED PERSONS. Females.	COLORED PERSONS. No. not taxed.	CIVIL CONDITION. Single.	CIVIL CONDITION. Married.	CIVIL CONDITION. Widowers.	CIVIL CONDITION. Widows.	VOTERS. Native.	VOTERS. Naturalized.	Aliens.	Number of families.	Owners of land.	Over 21 who cannot read or write.	Over 21 who can read but not write.
Covert,	2,230	1,141	1,078	5	6	1	1,355	799	26	50	453	31	180	432	351	35	17
Fayette,	3,370	1,704	1,658	4	4	8	1,896	1,329	44	101	692	25	277	653	491	39	28
Junius,	1,415	710	699	3	3	6	801	562	18	34	297	15	109	295	228	19	9
Lodi,	2,018	1,010	997	6	5	1	1,323	616	30	49	445	16	90	402	298	9	7
Ovid,	2,274	1,083	1,163	15	13	15	1,389	794	21	70	433	24	174	439	374	64	37
Romulus,	1,879	979	898	......	2	2	1,177	645	17	40	400	2	164	360	251	67	23
Seneca Falls,	4,984	2,500	2,458	11	15	4	3,259	1,574	54	97	899	136	466	956	619	97	55
Tyre,	1,419	717	702	......	......	......	744	628	19	28	314	7	44	283	212	1	......
Varick,	1,723	853	860	5	5	6	1,042	634	16	31	393	10	27	343	271	1	......
Waterloo,	4,046	1,933	2,047	31	35	34	2,454	1,451	32	109	619	184	622	781	526	33	2
Total,	25,358	12,630	12,560	80	88	77	15,440	9,032	277	609	4,945	450	2,153	4,944	3,621	365	178

STEUBEN COUNTY.

CITIES AND TOWNS.	Total population.	WHITES. Males.	WHITES. Females.	COLORED PERSONS. Males.	COLORED PERSONS. Females.	COLORED PERSONS. No. not taxed.	CIVIL CONDITION. Single.	CIVIL CONDITION. Married.	CIVIL CONDITION. Widowers.	CIVIL CONDITION. Widows.	VOTERS. Native.	VOTERS. Naturalized.	Aliens.	Number of families.	Owners of land.	Over 21 who cannot read or write.	Over 21 who can read but not write.
Addison,	3,156	1,594	1,550	8	4	6	1,950	1,130	24	52	648	45	125	565	236	1	4
Avoca,	1,786	926	860	......	......	......	1,083	676	11	16	424	19	47	359	286	8	......
Bath,	6,031	2,963	2,936	64	68	75	3,744	2,084	64	139	1,179	144	322	984	860	92	36
Bradford,	1,285	630	623	12	20	24	811	445	9	20	284	3	3	245	189	3	2
Cameron,	1,835	916	919	......	......	......	1,116	674	16	29	393	14	51	343	288	24	22
Campbell,	1,542	815	725	1	1	2	927	578	11	26	348	16	63	292	226	23	25
Canisteo,	1,985	1,057	926	1	1	2	1,243	700	18	24	449	21	65	372	271	17	27
Caton,	1,585	835	744	2	4	......	975	578	10	22	341	11	55	291	267	15	19
Cohocton,	2,242	1,113	1,112	13	4	12	1,308	874	17	43	437	33	156	444	297	1	......
Corning,	6,334	3,233	3,030	42	29	57	3,794	2,368	39	133	1,476	178	880	1,160	514	180	6
Dansville,	2,160	1,077	1,083	......	......	......	1,316	782	18	44	374	64	102	413	287	5	4
Erwin,	1,819	929	865	15	10	9	1,115	665	15	24	335	36	223	339	174	59	52
Fremont,	1,119	569	545	2	3	5	639	446	7	27	258	7	7	233	210	25	......
Greenwood,	1,224	622	602	......	......	......	742	447	13	22	219	20	83	237	233	18	19
Hartsville,	1,110	584	526	......	......	......	668	421	6	15	249	6	30	212	177	9	2
Hornby,	1,410	756	654	......	......	......	869	491	19	31	308	10	49	274	239	3	......
Hornellsville,	3,843	1,931	1,880	19	13	18	2,233	1,489	41	80	792	69	474	744	477	102	68
Howard,	2,669	1,365	1,302	......	2	2	1,652	935	28	54	545	36	103	512	458	9	7
Jasper,	1,768	881	887	......	......	......	1,089	637	10	32	384	10	16	344	299	33	34
Lindley,	704	363	328	6	7	9	415	272	5	12	140	4	43	143	59	12	......
Prattsburgh,	2,582	1,276	1,254	25	27	37	1,516	987	24	55	588	17	91	536	440	24	6
Pultney,	1,560	752	808	......	......	......	890	629	13	28	364	16	4	309	275	14	......
Thurston,	925	479	444	1	1	......	574	340	1	10	189	10	13	177	157	8	2
Troupsburgh,	1,979	1,042	937	......	......	......	1,224	717	14	24	428	13	8	373	322	25	10
Urbana,	1,938	965	971	1	1	2	1,191	691	21	35	419	26	30	363	288	27	29
Wayland,	2,651	1,344	1,307	......	......	......	1,650	934	20	47	312	138	428	462	332	18	......
Wayne,	928	467	461	......	......	......	549	349	6	24	215	8	6	183	143	16	11
West Union,	1,214	617	597	......	......	......	738	447	10	19	199	39	98	233	215	68	32
Wheeler,	1,376	716	659	1	......	1	833	519	8	16	324	15	7	256	197	18	14
Woodhull,	2,205	1,159	1,046	......	......	......	1,353	814	14	24	498	4	23	425	294	13	12
Total,	62,965	81,076	30,581	213	195	261	38,207	23,119	512	1,127	13,119	1,032	3,605	11,823	8,710	870	443

SUFFOLK COUNTY.

CITIES AND TOWNS.	Total population.	WHITES. Males.	WHITES. Females.	COLORED PERSONS. Males.	COLORED PERSONS. Females.	COLORED PERSONS. No. not taxed.	CIVIL CONDITION. Single.	CIVIL CONDITION. Married.	CIVIL CONDITION. Widowers.	CIVIL CONDITION. Widows.	VOTERS. Native.	VOTERS. Naturalized.	Aliens.	Number of families.	Owners of land.	Over 21 who cannot read or write.	Over 21 who can read but not write.
Brookhaven,	9,696	4,531	4,699	230	236	397	5,795	3,508	111	282	1,706	92	524	1,970	1,431	70	24
Easthampton,	2,145	979	987	71	108	106	1,253	777	40	75	456	37	93	431	317	18	7
Huntington,	8,142	3,930	3,784	223	205	400	4,893	2,888	101	260	1,102	102	672	1,584	1,068	197	38
Islip,	3,282	1,609	1,538	67	68	132	1,961	1,220	32	69	561	60	480	673	418	64	34
Riverhead,	2,734	1,344	1,342	25	23	42	1,595	1,041	23	75	575	22	140	555	519	20	3
Shelter Island,	483	223	244	10	6	16	293	170	4	16	93	1	33	96	70	3	......
Smithtown,	2,087	940	945	97	105	201	1,249	721	37	80	343	33	192	410	242	128	19
Southampton,	6,661	3,196	3,213	129	123	211	4,129	2,147	68	317	1,397	51	365	1,356	1,064	142	63
Southold,	5,676	2,790	2,724	75	87	100	3,229	2,178	55	214	1,239	69	584	1,129	964	39	8
Total,	40,906	19,542	19,476	927	961	1,605	24,397	14,650	471	1,388	7,472	467	3,083	8,204	6,093	681	196

SULLIVAN COUNTY.

CITIES AND TOWNS.	Total population.	WHITES. Males.	WHITES. Females.	COLORED PERSONS. Males.	COLORED PERSONS. Females.	COLORED PERSONS. No. not taxed.	CIVIL CONDITION. Single.	CIVIL CONDITION. Married.	CIVIL CONDITION. Widowers.	CIVIL CONDITION. Widows.	VOTERS. Native.	VOTERS. Naturalized.	Aliens.	Number of families.	Owners of land.	Over 21 who cannot read or write.	Over 21 who can read but not write.
Bethel,	2,611	1,360	1,249	2	......	......	1,689	868	14	40	304	102	347	486	301	5	6
Cochecton,	3,071	1,639	1,430	1	1	2	1,895	1,109	33	34	295	199	759	550	411	43	16
Collikoon,	2,092	1,117	974	1	......	1	1,300	756	14	22	195	186	463	416	328	50	31
Fallsburgh,	3,029	1,579	1,438	7	5	12	1,872	1,071	40	46	555	85	258	590	414	159	46
Forrestburgh,	839	466	367	2	4	6	526	295	11	7	146	36	120	140	83	52	42
Fremont,	1,301	726	571	3	1	......	778	497	13	13	147	71	313	245	184	7	10
Highland,	865	454	411	......	......	......	547	301	5	12	146	10	119	158	112	26	13
Liberty,	2,866	1,474	1,387	3	2	5	1,719	1,064	39	44	558	88	158	532	472	82	71
Lumberland,	902	497	405	......	......	......	567	318	4	13	121	35	155	162	115	28	24
Mamakating,	4,084	2,080	1,946	30	28	48	2,450	1,462	53	119	807	64	294	793	511	128	62
Neversink,	2,180	1,136	1,044	......	......	......	1,355	762	25	38	413	42	88	420	318	......	......
Rockland,	1,272	674	598	......	......	......	780	462	12	18	259	22	47	237	204	34	51
Thompson,	3,550	1,791	1,739	10	10	20	2,189	1,245	37	79	632	82	281	630	514	38	8
Tusten,	825	439	386	......	......	......	518	307	......	......	103	24	201	158	103	3	2
Total,	29,487	15,432	13,945	59	51	94	18,185	10,517	300	485	4,681	1,046	3,606	5,517	4,070	655	382

TIOGA COUNTY.

CITIES AND TOWNS.	Total population.	WHITES.		COLORED PERSONS.			CIVIL CONDITION.				VOTERS.		Aliens.	Number of families.	Owners of land.	Over 21 who cannot read or write.	Over 21 who can read but
		Males.	Females.	Males.	Females.	No. not taxed.	Single.	Married.	Widowers.	Widows.	Native.	Naturalized.					
Barton,	3,842	1,848	1,942	28	24	26	2,371	1,356	37	78	792	28	98	775	553	37	
Berkshire,	1,068	531	533	2	2	......	594	430	15	29	265	2	47	219	213	8	
Candor,	3,894	1,990	1,891	7	6	10	2,191	1,580	32	91	880	43	74	787	624	77	
Newark,	1,945	983	962	......	......	......	1,085	800	22	38	467	29	88	403	365	35	
Nichols,	1,871	931	918	14	8	11	1,207	644	11	9	377	17	21	347	170	79	
Owego,	8,328	4,169	4,064	54	41	66	5,052	3,030	78	168	1,763	120	534	1,376	1,115	178	
Richford,	1,182	590	575	8	9	13	661	495	10	16	274	1	25	242	189	4	......
Spencer,	1,805	910	893	1	1	2	1,019	730	20	36	435	9	14	379	328	7	
Tioga,	3,027	1,534	1,468	16	9	5	1,841	1,126	17	43	633	46	78	579	369	11	......
Total,	26,962	13,486	13,246	130	100	133	16,021	10,191	242	508	5,886	295	979	5,107	3,926	436	

TOMPKINS COUNTY.

CITIES AND TOWNS.	Total population.	Whites: Males.	Whites: Females.	Colored: Males.	Colored: Females.	No. not taxed.	Single.	Married.	Widowers.	Widows.	Voters: Native.	Voters: Naturalized.	Aliens.	Number of families.	Owners of land.	Over 21 who cannot read or write.	Over 21 who can read but
Caroline,	2,466	1,241	1,206	9	10	3	1,409	959	29	69	584	23	27	496	456	19	......
Danby,	2,331	1,179	1,147	3	2	3	1,324	922	28	57	593	9	23	488	424	9	
Dryden,	5,003	2,497	2,506	......	......	......	2,905	1,932	55	111	1,193	50	70	1,035	918	71	
Enfield,	1,912	941	969	1	1	......	1,221	630	19	42	442	8	53	392	331	26	......
Groton,	3,404	1,721	1,683	......	......	......	1,883	1,401	28	92	818	28	46	733	486	14	
Ithaca,	7,153	3,405	3,579	80	89	116	4,221	2,658	63	211	1,404	135	602	1,322	812	58	
Lansing,	3,256	1,624	1,615	12	5	10	1,938	1,205	22	91	760	7	102	643	414	1	......
Newfield,	2,800	1,440	1,360	......	......	......	1,646	1,060	31	63	648	28	21	571	482	35	
Ulysses,	3,191	1,542	1,612	24	13	26	1,881	1,181	39	90	702	24	216	626	442	38	
Total,	31,516	15,590	15,677	129	120	158	18,428	11,948	314	826	7,144	312	1,160	6,306	4,765	271	

ULSTER COUNTY.

CITIES AND TOWNS.	Total population.	Whites: Males.	Whites: Females.	Colored: Males.	Colored: Females.	No. not taxed.	Single.	Married.	Widowers.	Widows.	Voters: Native.	Voters: Naturalized.	Aliens.	Number of families.	Owners of land.	Over 21 who cannot read or write.	Over 21 who can read but
Denning,	692	381	307	4	......	4	422	263	2	5	152	9	42	131	86	......	......
Esopus,	4,287	2,242	2,022	10	13	21	2,529	1,630	38	90	626	137	926	837	505	220	
Gardiner,	1,923	895	898	59	71	99	1,171	677	24	51	399	15	120	354	249	102	
Hurley,	2,115	1,066	969	28	52	69	1,306	740	24	45	347	33	300	395	181	60	
Kingston,	13,974	7,019	6,664	133	158	217	8,245	4,918	197	614	1,515	641	3,936	2,773	746	1,030	
Lloyd,	2,192	1,093	1,073	13	13	19	1,320	778	29	65	470	25	130	428	269	73	
Marbletown,	3,727	1,779	1,723	108	117	161	2,244	1,337	44	102	754	29	172	699	639	233	
Marbleborough,	2,668	1,267	1,327	35	39	72	1,671	874	27	96	530	32	197	514	255	46	
New Paltz,	2,021	971	962	38	50	82	1,328	605	33	55	383	8	192	326	252	97	
Olive,	2,924	1,480	1,409	16	19	34	1,819	1,012	31	62	611	34	163	591	367	199	
Plattekill,	1,932	955	933	26	18	41	1,200	655	21	56	399	18	95	369	255	32	
Rochester,	3,475	1,740	1,672	28	35	56	2,226	1,154	29	66	742	25	89	641	391	145	
Rosendale,	2,572	1,317	1,222	16	17	31	1,512	978	33	49	378	87	485	491	163	67	
Saugerties,	9,318	4,753	4,439	59	67	74	5,606	3,344	100	268	1,384	406	1,510	1,788	1,020	468	
Shandaken,	2,452	1,293	1,151	5	3	2	1,507	884	24	37	463	67	156	454	266	45	
Shawangunk,	2,631	1,[illegible]53	1,299	40	39	72	1,662	891	52	26	589	24	72	484	316	70	
Wawarsing,	7,227	3,691	3,470	38	28	44	4,36[illegible]	2,695	42	124	1,109	253	850	1,436	716	60	
Woodstock,	1,806	887	888	19	12	21	1,104	647	18	37	381	22	52	340	218	50	
Total,	67,936	34,082	32,428	675	751	1,119	41,238	24,082	768	1,848	11,232	1,865	9,487	13,051	6,894	2,997	

WARREN COUNTY.

CITIES AND TOWNS.	Total population.	Whites: Males.	Whites: Females.	Colored: Males.	Colored: Females.	No. not taxed.	Single.	Married.	Widowers.	Widows.	Voters: Native.	Voters: Naturalized.	Aliens.	Number of families.	Owners of land.	Over 21 who cannot read or write.	Over 21 who can read but
Bolton,	1,167	625	542	......	......	......	685	441	13	28	285	5	2	232	196	5	
Caldwell,	880	451	428	1	......	1	555	305	11	9	190	4	25	170	138	......	......
Chester,	1,936	993	943	......	......	......	1,126	734	29	47	456	36	97	385	353	12	
Hague,	615	303	302	6	4	......	422	172	6	15	117	9	15	110	67	15	
Horicon,	1,246	678	568	......	......	......	740	487	11	8	252	16	68	335	175	25	......
Johnsburgh,	1,983	1,059	924	......	......	......	1,218	746	10	9	368	35	143	396	293	49	
Luzerne,	1,286	666	620	......	......	......	737	510	19	20	291	16	90	265	208	20	......
Queensbury,	6,438	3,207	3,164	30	37	34	3,760	2,439	59	180	1,134	176	900	1,294	848	86	
Stony Creek,	913	491	422	......	......	......	546	353	9	5	157	13	106	180	123	60	......
Thurman,	1,259	687	572	......	......	......	774	448	11	26	212	11	118	247	168	47	......
Warrensburgh,	1,946	987	957	......	2	2	1,210	681	16	39	325	57	79	365	238	29	
Total,	19,669	10,147	9,442	37	43	37	11,773	7,316	194	386	3,787	378	1,643	3,979	2,807	348	

WASHINGTON COUNTY.

CITIES AND TOWNS.	Total population.	Whites: Males.	Whites: Females.	Colored: Males.	Colored: Females.	No. not taxed.	Single.	Married.	Widowers.	Widows.	Voters: Native.	Voters: Naturalized.	Aliens.	Number of families.	Owners of land.	Over 21 who cannot read or write.	Over 21 who can read but
Argyle,	3,244	1,609	1,624	4	7	8	2,040	1,067	53	84	600	113	366	608	484	25	
Cambridge	2,304	1,132	1,172	......	......	......	1,362	857	23	62	444	43	235	459	286	4	
Dresden,	735	387	348	......	......	......	424	304	2	5	157	3	66	150	100	17	
Easton,	3,012	1,472	1,516	10	14	15	1,717	1,160	44	91	623	47	311	614	397	82	
Fort Ann,	3,544	1,833	1,693	12	6	18	2,124	1,311	34	75	655	71	278	695	327	106	
Fort Edward,	2,964	1,530	1,434	......	......	......	1,841	1,010	36	77	553	95	352	528	350	83	
Granville,	3,363	1,710	1,652	......	1	......	2,084	1,145	55	79	637	38	535	660	469	118	
Greenwich,	3,888	1,940	1,911	19	18	32	2,263	1,461	61	103	907	65	317	790	473	84	
Hampton,	846	428	416	1	1	2	508	315	5	18	145	6	105	161	106	7	......
Hartford,	2,196	1,132	1,064	......	......	......	1,314	804	30	48	44	58	200	416	345	27	
Hebron,	2,549	1,283	1,266	......	......	......	1,505	964	26	54	534	36	266	530	379	10	......
Jackson,	1,770	897	854	9	10	16	1,104	588	26	52	357	34	175	335	242	33	
Kingsbury,	3,364	1,720	1,615	16	13	29	2,049	1,190	35	90	654	139	334	626	464	90	
Putnam,	724	378	346	......	......	......	480	221	10	13	122	29	42	129	101	8	
Salem,	2,925	1,450	1,453	11	11	17	1,778	1,024	39	84	656	52	262	561	410	25	
White Creek,	2,439	1,245	1,173	12	9	14	1,454	890	41	54	510	39	243	586	325	60	
Whitehall,	4,538	2,283	2,219	16	20	16	2,612	1,712	56	158	750	139	735	893	472	251	
Total,	44,405	22,429	21,756	110	110	167	26,659	16,023	576	1,147	8,348	1,007	4,822	8,741	5,730	1,030	

WAYNE COUNTY.

CITIES AND TOWNS.	Total population.	WHITES.		COLORED PERSONS.			CIVIL CONDITION.				VOTERS.		Aliens.	Number of families.	Owners of land.	Over 21 who cannot read or write.	Over 21 who can read but not write.
		Males.	Females.	Males.	Females.	No. not taxed.	Single.	Married.	Widowers.	Widows.	Native.	Naturalized.					
Arcadia	5,516	2,822	2,671	10	13	15	3,109	2,179	69	159	1,122	126	523	1,102	796	85	86
Butler	2,225	1,125	1,098	1	1	2	1,317	834	17	57	503	6	51	438	360	12	
Galen	5,181	2,684	2,458	22	17	37	3,131	1,850	57	143	856	151	739	995	490	182	6
Huron	1,881	969	887	16	9	19	1,064	764	17	36	413	41	49	384	315	21	1
Lyons	5,205	2,594	2,587	10	14	17	3,041	1,959	66	139	830	239	848	978	676	77	35
Macedon	2,434	1,243	1,178	6	7	5	1,371	962	33	68	509	41	333	493	366	38	24
Marion	1,937	985	952				1,020	831	17	69	450	32	163	419	366	17	8
Ontario	2,323	1,220	1,098	2	3		1,348	921	17	37	489	59	212	466	371	26	29
Palmyra	4,115	2,045	2,028	17	25	33	2,342	1,546	92	135	757	107	602	846	527	71	60
Rose	2,114	1,080	1,027	4	3	7	1,246	821	6	41	414	24	145	419	329	34	4
Savannah	1,762	947	806	4	5	2	1,061	666	13	22	355	24	115	349	212	27	12
Sodus	4,538	2,304	2,178	27	29	43	2,566	1,806	60	106	905	109	323	932	777	28	22
Walworth	1,964	991	973				1,138	765	18	43	387	41	201	417	347	12	14
Williamson	2,552	1,301	1,251				1,399	1,063	38	52	447	102	364	529	428	10	3
Wolcott	3,013	1,535	1,478				1,760	1,172	22	59	646	20	99	609	484	28	
Total	46,760	23,845	22,670	119	126	180	26,913	18,139	542	1,166	9,083	1,122	4,767	9,376	6,844	668	304

WESTCHESTER COUNTY.

CITIES AND TOWNS.	Total population.	Whites Males.	Whites Females.	Colored Males.	Colored Females.	No. not taxed.	Single.	Married.	Widowers.	Widows.	Voters Native.	Naturalized.	Aliens.	Number of families.	Owners of land.	Over 21 who cannot read or write.	Over 21 who can read but not write.
Bedford	3,464	1,651	1,706	55	52	106	2,137	1,179	55	93	699	13	316	674	464	56	26
Cortlandt	8,468	4,444	3,916	56	52	93	5,425	2,703	90	250	1,260	198	1,769	1,576	679	709	86
East Chester	4,715	2,391	2,240	34	50	83	2,753	1,788	57	117	399	330	1,461	935	597	177	69
Greenburgh	6,435	3,048	3,283	45	59	58	4,046	2,161	56	172	899	208	1,563	1,192	624	168	82
Harrison	1,271	522	574	89	86	162	761	446	21	43	205	7	160	240	152	64	35
Lewisboro	1,775	887	886	2		2	991	714	24	46	440	6	95	385	288	27	10
Mamaroneck	1,068	496	510	29	33	62	605	407	10	46	163	31	250	226	81	54	13
Mount Pleasant	3,677	1,756	1,866	27	28	32	2,171	1,342	50	114	635	106	571	704	259	249	79
Newcastle	1,762	851	852	28	31	32	1,044	662	16	40	363	15	199	345	220	15	6
New Rochelle	3,101	1,396	1,517	93	95	122	1,848	1,134	23	96	385	137	713	607	100	104	59
North Castle	2,415	1,153	1,162	60	40	87	1,452	869	25	69	494	16	167	467	277	54	52
North Salem	1,528	722	772	14	20	34	974	480	19	55	339	19	137	318	188	19	27
Ossining	5,758	3,024	2,525	149	60	175	3,577	1,935	66	180	732	142	1,462	900	615	323	267
Pelham	833	383	434	8	8	16	576	228	11	18	104	26	202	122	78	7	2
Poundridge	1,439	708	726	1	4	5	821	539	24	55	324	7	34	313	250	26	1
Rye	3,468	1,585	1,745	66	72	124	2,169	1,149	35	115	530	97	643	666	411	69	37
Searsdale	445	193	224	12	16	28	286	138	10	11	67	15	87	74	45	5	
Somers	1,744	846	863	13	22	35	1,120	564	22	38	286	7	185	316	157	64	47
Westchester	3,464	1,713	1,668	35	48	68	2,229	1,105	35	95	295	251	913	582	303	226	168
West Farms	12,436	6,134	6,216	39	47	45	7,568	4,422	103	343	985	1,067	3,012	2,419	1,445	284	204
White Plains	1,512	694	784	23	11	34	995	466	13	38	225	44	246	262	90	36	
Yonkers	7,554	3,631	3,793	64	66	115	4,595	2,657	86	216	856	312	2,336	1,436	568	327	97
Yorktown	2,346	1,111	1,149	45	41	62	1,379	866	30	71	493	13	220	466	324	67	37
Total	80,678	39,339	39,411	987	941	1,580	49,522	27,954	881	2,321	11,178	3,067	16,741	15,225	8,215	3,130	1,404

WYOMING COUNTY.

CITIES AND TOWNS.	Total population.	Whites Males.	Whites Females.	Colored Males.	Colored Females.	No. not taxed.	Single.	Married.	Widowers.	Widows.	Voters Native.	Naturalized.	Aliens.	Number of families.	Owners of land.	Over 21 who cannot read or write.	Over 21 who can read but not write.
Attica	2,679	1,325	1,350	2	2	4	1,517	1,080	20	62	460	27	556	540	406	5	
Bennington	2,555	1,301	1,254				1,456	1,029	24	46	389	132	371	545	493	16	5
Castile	2,343	1,185	1,158				1,309	952	27	55	531	33	122	408	374	22	21
China	2,108	1,051	1,057				1,275	793	11	29	353	99	126	389	316	18	
Covington	1,330	670	660				776	493	18	43	246	30	161	255	216	6	
Eagle	1,390	733	657				802	560	8	20	319	26	57	283	215	10	1
Gainesville	1,753	874	862	10	7	17	1,002	686	24	41	408	10	92	361	312	8	2
Genesee Falls	1,098	559	538	1		1	647	410	7	34	226	22	93	225	145	28	7
Java	2,295	1,187	1,108				1,399	825	23	48	345	156	95	422	383	54	30
Middlebury	1,787	904	883				1,004	722	19	42	418	2	119	376	323	8	1
Orangeville	1,441	730	711				815	562	20	44	263	50	132	244	231	33	25
Perry	2,560	1,251	1,306	2	1	3	1,450	1,004	29	77	588	43	142	532	384	17	5
Pike	1,887	930	957				1,064	743	25	55	434	15	80	370	280	5	4
Sheldon	2,666	1,347	1,319				1,588	993	33	52	261	220	426	519	432	9	4
Warsaw	2,794	1,391	1,399	2	2	3	1,697	993	28	76	578	39	198	525	452	5	
Wethersfield	1,462	734	728				839	590	12	21	317	24	57	291	246	22	9
Total	32,148	16,172	15,947	17	12	28	18,640	12,435	328	745	6,136	928	2,827	6,285	5,208	266	114

YATES COUNTY.

CITIES AND TOWNS.	Total population.	Whites Males.	Whites Females.	Colored Males.	Colored Females.	No. not taxed.	Single.	Married.	Widowers.	Widows.	Voters Native.	Naturalized.	Aliens.	Number of families.	Owners of land.	Over 21 who cannot read or write.	Over 21 who can read but not write.
Barrington	1,504	760	744				841	616	10	37	361	4	7	216	223	8	
Benton	2,500	1,273	1,220	6	1	7	1,434	963	22	81	505	32	160	504	355	55	9
Italy	1,506	783	723				900	550	21	35	276	11	60	289	250	5	4
Jerusalem	2,797	1,433	1,349	6	9	7	1,616	1,070	33	78	609	30	142	552	456	64	68
Middlesex	1,305	642	663				751	501	9	44	295	1	40	263	223	11	10
Milo	4,304	2,056	2,197	20	31	19	2,472	1,632	37	163	940	66	242	610	530	86	18
Potter	2,148	1,080	1,061	3	4	7	1,287	770	32	59	420	25	153	402	346	14	
Starkey	2,428	1,191	1,237				1,413	963	19	33	583	12	72	527	316	32	3
Torrey	1,320	637	666	10	7	2	755	513	19	33	296	8	66	258	185	6	4
Total	19,812	9,855	9,860	45	52	42	11,469	7,578	202	563	4,285	189	942	3,621	2,884	281	116

RECAPITULATION OF POPULATION, COLORS, SEXES, CIVIL CONDITION, &c.

COUNTIES.	Total population.	WHITES.		COLORED PERSONS.			CIVIL CONDITION.				VOTERS.		Aliens.	Number of families.	Owners of land.	Over 21 who cannot read or write.	Over 21 who can read but
		Males.	Females.	Males.	Females.	No. not taxed.	Single.	Married.	Widowers.	Widows	Native.	Naturalized.					
Albany,.....	103, 681	50, 274	52. 568	383	456	586	64, 027	35, 223	976	3, 455	12, 434	6, 182	20, 282	15, 983	7, 478	3, 231	1,
Allegany, ...	42, 910	21, 991	20, 738	92	89	90	25, 165	16, 553	410	782	9, 271	613	2, 032	8, 584	6, 653	536	
Broome, ...	36, 650	18, 436	17, 699	250	265	366	22, 103	13, 459	313	775	7, 760	522	2, 056	6, 962	5, 348	611	
Cattaraugus,.	39, 530	20, 139	19, 262	72	57	62	23, 235	15, 292	317	686	8, 021	616	2, 645	7, 646	6, 263	496	
Cayuga,.....	53, 571	27, 160	26, 011	203	197	220	32, 066	19, 651	500	1, 354	10, 556	970	4, 863	9, 923	7, 661	890	
Chautauque,.	53, 380	27, 046	26, 225	55	54	45	30, 741	20, 942	533	1, 164	11, 138	774	4, 795	10, 566	8, 528	749	
Chemung, ...	27, 288	13, 473	13, 352	238	225	295	16, 697	9, 775	242	574	5, 432	427	1, 991	5, 156	3, 665	675	
Chenango,...	39, 915	19, 765	19, 936	114	100	112	23, 038	15, 469	415	993	9, 322	378	977	8, 236	6, 435	273	
Clinton,.....	42, 482	21, 473	20, 878	83	48	93	27, 088	14, 392	343	659	4, 464	1, 910	8, 404	7, 345	4, 481	4, 449	
Columbia, ...	44, 391	21, 289	21, 848	568	686	1, 008	27, 536	15, 126	495	1, 234	8, 647	765	3, 800	8, 236	4, 554	1, 069	
Cortland, ...	24, 575	J2, 242	12, 305	15	13	13	14, 318	9, 436	219	602	5, 615	287	704	4, 722	4, 212	245	
Delaware, ...	39, 749	19, 999	19, 556	92	102	151	24, 189	14, 297	396	867	8, 077	988	1, 532	7, 650	6, 005	283	
Dutchess, ...	60, 635	28, 778	30, 028	860	969	1, 450	37, 203	20, 800	740	1, 892	11, 094	1, 404	6, 861	10, 081	5, 984	1, 567	
Erie,........	132, 331	67, 234	64, 239	424	434	587	78, 087	49, 641	1, 370	3, 233	12, 494	9, 249	37, 274	26, 193	15, 566	2, 315	1,
Essex, ...	28, 539	14, 570	13, 833	78	58	48	17, 583	10, 111	287	558	4, 857	795	2, 994	5, 339	3, 253	1, 154	
Franklin, ...	25, 477	12, 919	12, 541	8	9	4	16, 079	8, 824	174	400	3, 385	1, 077	3, 739	4, 492	3, 542	1, 323	
Fulton, ...	23, 284	11, 495	11, 629	78	82	105	13, 906	8, 543	250	585	4, 601	465	1, 559	4, 560	2, 996	531	
Genesee, ...	31, 034	15, 779	15, 169	42	44	17	18, 058	11, 832	356	788	5, 835	642	4, 107	5, 792	4, 428	436	
Greene, ...	31, 137	15, 203	15, 122	388	424	545	19, 015	11, 069	255	798	6, 461	491	1, 522	5, 707	3, 951	516	
Hamilton, ...	2, 543	1, 388	1, 151	2	2	4	1, 486	996	23	38	522	77	168	488	352	53	
Herkimer, ...	38, 566	19, 607	18, 787	86	86	80	22, 797	14, 330	460	979	7, 711	867	3, 955	7, 396	5, 219	608	
Jefferson, ...	65, 420	32, 896	32, 327	96	101	139	38, 311	24, 871	679	1, 559	12, 770	1, 436	5, 377	12, 629	9, 063	991	
Kings, ...	216, 355	100, 852	111, 023	1, 995	2, 485	3, 526	129, 033	78, 697	2, 221	6, 404	18, 277	14, 350	65, 536	43, 133	11, 872	8, 924	5,
Lewis, ...	25, 229	12, 773	12, 413	27	16	24	14, 877	9, 608	274	470	4, 059	1, 225	2, 751	4, 927	4, 098	722	
Livingston, ..	37, 943	18, 997	18, 737	103	106	134	23, 321	13, 253	402	967	7, 175	961	4, 329	6, 671	5, 328	376	
Madison, ...	43, 687	21, 864	21, 498	151	174	238	24, 971	16, 958	562	1, 196	9, 316	658	3, 232	8, 544	6, 349	848	
Monroe, ...	96, 324	48, 466	47, 369	242	247	262	57, 447	35, 213	1, 003	2, 661	12, 576	4, 696	22, 837	18, 283	12, 551	2, 105	1,
Montgomery,	30, 808	15, 585	14, 822	202	199	312	18, 651	10, 934	386	837	6, 111	675	2, 688	5, 310	3, 306	625	
New-York, ..	629, 904	297, 870	320, 194	5, 116	6, 724	10, 807	383, 434	217, 731	5, 894	22, 845	46, 173	42, 704	232,678	126,558	14, 784	25, 858	14,
Niagara, ...	48, 282	24, 559	23, 321	251	151	317	29, 305	17, 355	532	1, 090	6, 554	1, 703	10, 327	8, 951	5, 979	976	
Oneida, ...	107, 749	53, 659	53, 475	318	297	443	64, 618	38, 971	1, 241	2, 919	15, 272	5, 674	18, 472	21, 175	13, 016	3, 062	1,
Onondaga, ..	86, 575	43, 783	42, 290	250	252	281	51, 140	32, 492	834	2, 109	13, 915	3, 018	13, 549	16, 798	11, 057	2, 150	
Ontario, ...	42, 672	21, 182	20, 906	255	329	346	25, 244	15, 694	490	1, 244	8, 323	824	4, 757	8, 180	5, 845	570	
Orange, ...	60, 868	29, 209	29, 511	1, 108	1, 040	1, 855	38, 400	20, 054	616	1, 798	9, 934	1, 367	7, 955	11, 186	5, 146	1, 241	
Orleans, ...	28, 435	14, 717	13, 608	55	55	43	16, 682	10, 887	265	601	5, 105	599	3, 813	4, 993	4, 025	736	
Oswego, ...	69, 398	35, 473	33, 557	189	179	215	40, 185	27, 111	680	1, 422	12, 576	2, 033	7, 372	13, 711	9, 781	1, 778	
Otsego, ...	49, 735	24, 726	24, 792	110	107	158	28, 299	19, 449	615	1, 372	11, 603	574	1, 640	10, 138	7, 597	569	
Putnam, ...	13, 934	6, 898	6, 907	72	57	113	8, 322	4, 970	172	470	2, 806	231	1, 215	2, 746	1, 739	425	
Queens, ...	46. 266	21, 656	21, 560	1, 486	1, 564	2, 538	28, 271	16, 229	506	1, 260	6, 614	1, 573	8, 618	8, 682	5, 048	1, 588	
Rensselaer, ..	79, 234	38, 557	39, 783	431	463	717	47, 236	28, 506	901	2, 591	11, 622	3, 311	14, 921	15, 418	6, 459	3, 080	1,
Richmond, ..	21, 389	10, 293	10, 506	276	314	487	13, 485	7, 053	209	642	2, 441	1, 354	5, 078	4, 056	2, 087	245	
Rockland, ...	19, 511	9, 928	9, 086	227	270	403	11, 479	7, 281	208	543	3, 093	487	3, 457	3, 860	1, 814	980	
St. Lawrence,	74, 977	37, 884	36, 991	50	52	86	46, 031	26, 765	729	1, 452	11, 615	2, 369	9, 915	13, 177	10, 690	2, 272	
Saratoga, ...	49, 379	24, 001	24, 736	281	361	539	29, 251	18, 143	586	1, 399	9, 346	1, 031	5, 748	8, 984	5, 735	1, 271	
Schenectady,	19, 572	9, 701	9, 560	150	161	180	11, 790	6, 904	256	622	3, 133	657	2, 943	1, 953	3, 783	269	
Schoharie, ...	33, 519	16, 595	16, 468	233	223	391	20, 339	12, 172	282	726	7, 153	223	874	6, 258	4, 574	601	
Schuyler, ...	18, 777	9, 364	9, 337	44	32	40	11, 187	6, 969	173	448	4, 190	187	587	3, 577	2, 946	219	
Seneca, ...	25, 358	12, 630	12, 560	80	88	77	15, 440	9, 032	277	609	4, 945	450	2, 153	4, 944	3, 621	365	
Steuben, ...	62, 965	31, 976	30, 581	213	195	261	38, 207	23, 119	512	1, 127	13, 119	1, 032	3, 605	11, 823	8, 710	870	
Suffolk, ...	40, 906	19, 542	19, 476	927	961	1, 605	24, 397	14, 650	471	1, 388	7, 472	467	3, 083	8, 204	6, 093	681	
Sullivan, ...	29, 487	15, 432	13, 945	59	51	94	18, 185	10, 517	300	485	4, 681	1, 046	3, 606	5, 517	4, 070	655	
Tioga, ...	26, 962	13 486	13, 246	130	100	133	16, 021	10, 191	242	508	5, 886	295	979	5, 107	3, 926	436	
Tompkins, ..	31, 516	15, 590	15, 677	129	120	158	18, 428	11, 948	314	826	7, 144	312	1, 160	6, 306	4, 765	271	
Ulster, ...	67, 936	34, 082	32, 428	675	751	1, 119	41, 238	24, 082	768	1, 848	11, 232	1, 865	9, 487	13, 051	6, 894	2, 997	
Warren, ...	19, 669	10, 147	9, 442	37	43	37	11, 773	7, 316	194	386	3, 787	378	1, 643	3, 979	2, 807	348	
Washington,.	44, 405	22, 429	21, 756	110	110	167	26, 659	16, 023	576	1, 147	8, 348	1, 007	4, 822	8, 741	5, 730	1, 030	
Wayne, ...	46, 760	23, 845	22, 670	119	126	180	26, 913	18, 139	542	1, 166	9, 083	1, 122	4, 767	9, 376	6, 844	668	
Westchester, .	80, 678	39, 339	39, 411	987	941	1, 580	49, 522	27, 954	881	2, 321	11, 178	3, 067	16, 741	15, 225	8, 215	3, 130	1
Wyoming, ..	32, 148	16, 172	15, 947	17	12	28	18, 640	12, 435	328	745	6, 136	928	2, 827	6, 285	5, 208	266	
Yates, ...	19, 812	9, 855	9, 860	45	52	42	11, 469	7, 578	202	563	4, 285	189	942	3, 621	2, 884	281	
Total, ...	3,466.212	1,706,273	1,714 653	21.377	23, 909	35, 956	2,082.618	1,253,015	35, 397	95, 182	516,745	135,577	682,746	663.124	361,018	96, 489	46

PERCENTAGE OF THE FOREGOING CLASSES TO THE TOTAL POPULATION IN EACH COUNTY.

COUNTIES.	WHITES.		COLORED PERSONS.		TOTAL.		CIVIL CONDITION.				VOTERS.		Aliens.	Owners of land.	Over 21 who cannot read or write.	Over 21 who can read but not write.
	Males.	Females	Males.	Females.	Males.	Females.	Single.	Married.	Widowers.	Widows	Native.	Naturalized.				
Albany,	48.49	50.66	0.37	0.48	48.86	51.14	61.75	33.97	0.95	3.33	11.99	5.96	19.56	7.21	3.11	1.89
Allegany,	51.25	48.33	0.21	0.21	51.46	48.54	58.66	38.58	0.95	1.81	21.61	1.43	4.73	15.51	1.25	0.42
Broome,	50.30	48.29	0.68	0.73	50.98	49.02	60·33	36.72	0.89	2.06	21.17	1.42	5.61	14.59	1.66	0.61
Cattaraugus,	50.95	48.73	0.18	0.14	51.13	48.87	58.77	38.68	0.31	0.24	20.29	1.56	6.69	15.84	1.25	1.47
Cayuga,	50.70	48.56	0.38	0.36	51.08	48.92	59.85	36.68	0.95	2.52	19.75	1.81	9.07	14.31	1.66	0.94
Chautauque,	50.67	49.13	0.10	0.10	50.77	49.23	57.59	39.23	1.00	2.18	20.86	1.45	8.98	15.97	1.40	0.55
Chemung,	49.37	48.93	0.87	0.83	50.24	49.76	61.18	35.82	0.87	2.13	19.96	1.56	7.29	13.43	2.47	0.85
Chenango,	49.52	49.94	0.29	0.25	49.81	50.19	57.72	38.75	1.09	2.41	23.35	0.95	2.44	16.10	0.68	0.24
Clinton,	50.54	49.14	0.19	0.03	50.73	49.17	63.76	33.88	0.81	1.55	15.08	4.49	19.78	10.54	10.47	1.35
Columbia,	47.73	49.21	1.28	1.78	49.01	50.99	62.03	34.07	1.12	2.78	19.47	1.72	8.56	10.25	2.41	1.17
Cortland,	49.81	50.07	0.06	0.06	49.87	50.13	58.26	38.39	0.90	2.45	22.84	1.66	2.86	17.14	0.99	0·38
Delaware,	50.31	49.19	0.23	0.27	50.54	49.46	60.85	35.96	1.01	2.18	20.32	2.48	·3.88	15.10	0.71	0.55
Dutchess,	47.46	49.52	1.41	1.61	48.87	51.13	61.35	34.30	1.23	3.12	18.29	2.31	11.31	9.86	2.58	1.62
Erie,	50.81	48.54	0.32	0.33	51.13	48.87	59.01	37.51	1.04	2.44	9.44	6.98	28.17	11.79	1.75	1.19
Essex,	51.05	48.47	0.27	0.21	51.32	48.68	61.60	35.43	1.02	1.95	17.02	2.78	10.49	11.39	4.04	0.86
Franklin,	50.77	49.21	0.01	0.01	50.78	49.22	63.11	34.63	0.69	1.57	13.28	4.22	10.75	13.90	5.19	0.67
Fulton,	49.37	49.91	0.34	0.38	49.71	50.25	59.72	36.69	1.10	2.49	19.97	1.99	6.69	12.86	2.28	1.42
Genesee,	50.87	48.88	0.13	0.12	51.00	49.00	58.19	38.13	1.15	2.53	18.80	2.07	13.21	14.26	1.40	0.49
Greene,	48.83	48.42	1.24	1.51	50.07	49.93	61.06	35.54	0.84	2.56	20.75	1.57	4.89	12.69	1.66	0.12
Hamilton,	54.57	45.25	0.09	0.09	54.66	45.34	58.43	39.15	0.93	1.49	20.13	2.98	6.61	13.84	2.08	1.49
Herkimer,	50.84	48.72	0.22	0.22	51.06	48.94	59.11	37.15	1.21	2.53	19.99	2.24	10.09	13.50	1.83	0.60
Jefferson,	50.28	49.41	0.15	0.16	50.43	49.57	58.56	38.01	1.05	2.38	19.52	2.19	8.21	13.86	1.52	0.51
Kings,	46.61	51.31	0.92	1.16	47.53	52.47	59.64	36.37	1.03	2.96	8.44	6.63	30.29	5.48	4.12	2.56
Lewis,	50.63	49.21	0.10	0.06	50.73	49.27	58.93	38.08	1.13	1.86	16.09	4.85	10.90	15.94	2.85	1.41
Livingston,	50.06	49.38	0.27	0.29	50.33	49.67	61.46	34.93	1.06	2.55	18.91	2.53	11.41	14.04	0.99	0.52
Madison,	50.05	49.21	0.34	0.40	50.39	49.61	57.46	38.82	0.99	2.73	21.32	1.50	7.39	14.53	1.94	0.87
Monroe,	50.31	49.17	0.25	0.27	50.56	49.44	59.64	36.55	1.05	2.76	13.05	4.87	22.67	13.03	2.18	1.07
Montgomery,	50.58	48.11	0.66	0.65	51.24	48.76	60.54	35.49	1.26	2.71	19.80	2.19	8.72	10.69	2.02	1.02
New-York,	47.29	50.83	0.81	1.07	48.10	51.90	60.92	34.41	1.04	3.63	7.33	6.78	36.93	2.34	4.10	2.27
Niagara,	50.86	48.30	0.52	0.32	51.38	48.62	60.69	35.94	1.11	2.26	13.42	3.53	21.31	12.31	2.02	1.74
Oneida,	49.80	49.62	0.30	0.28	50.10	49.90	59.97	36.17	1.15	2.71	14.17	5.26	17.15	12.07	2.84	1.41
Onondaga,	50.57	48.85	0.29	0.29	50.86	49.14	59.07	37.52	0.98	2.43	16.07	3.49	15.64	12.77	2.49	0.96
Ontario,	49.63	48.99	0.59	0.79	50.22	49.78	59.15	36.79	1.15	2.91	19.50	1.93	11.14	13.69	1.34	0.61
Orange,	47.99	48.48	1.82	1.71	49.81	50.19	63.08	32.95	1.03	2.94	16.32	2.25	13.07	8.45	2.04	0.86
Orleans,	51.05	47.85	0.55	0.55	51.60	48.40	58.86	38.28	0.75	2.11	17.94	2.16	13.39	14.15	2.59	0.43
Oswego,	51.19	48.35	0.27	0.19	51.46	48.54	57.90	39.06	0.99	2.05	18.13	2.96	10.48	13.95	2.56	0.93
Otsego,	49.72	49.84	0.23	0.21	49.95	50.05	56.89	39.10	1.26	2.76	23.33	1.15	3.29	15.27	1.14	0.67
Putnam,	49.49	49.57	0.52	0.42	50.01	49.99	59.73	35.67	1.88	2.72	20.14	1.66	8.71	12.49	3.05	1.15
Queens,	46.81	46.60	3.21	3.38	50.02	49.98	61.10	35.05	1.13	2.72	14.29	3.39	18.65	10.91	3.43	1.72
Rensselaer,	48.66	50.21	0.54	0.59	49.20	50.80	59.62	35.98	1.14	3.26	14.67	4.18	18.83	8.15	3.89	1.96
Richmond,	48.12	49.11	1.29	1.48	49.41	50.59	63.04	32.98	0.97	3.01	11.41	6.33	23.74	9.76	1.15	0.58
Rockland,	50.88	46.63	1.11	1.38	51.99	48.01	58.83	37.32	1.07	2.78	15.85	2.49	17.72	9.29	5.02	1.47
St. Lawrence,	50.53	49.33	0.07	0.07	50.60	49.40	61.39	35.69	0.98	1.94	15.49	3.16	13.22	14.25	3.03	0.79
Saratoga,	48.60	50.09	0.56	0.75	49.16	50.84	59.24	36.74	1.19	2.83	18.93	2.09	11.64	11.72	2.57	0.92
Schenectady,	49.56	48.84	0.77	0.83	50.33	49.67	60.24	35.22	1.35	3.19	16.01	3.35	15.03	14.23	1.33	1.19
Schoharie,	49.51	49.13	0.69	0.67	50.20	49.80	60.61	36.32	0.91	2.16	21.34	0.66	2.67	13.64	1.79	1.30
Schuyler,	49.87	49.72	0.23	0.18	50.10	49.90	59.57	37.13	0.92	2.38	22.31	0.99	3.12	15.69	1.16	1.01
Seneca,	49.81	49.53	0.31	0.35	50.12	49.88	60.89	35.62	1.09	2.40	19.50	1.77	8.49	14.29	1.43	0.71
Steuben,	50.78	48.56	0.34	0.32	51.12	48.88	60.68	36.71	0.90	1.71	20.83	1.64	5.72	13.83	1.38	0.71
Suffolk,	47.77	47.61	2.26	2.36	50.03	49.97	59.07	35.81	1.13	3.39	18.26	1.14	7.53	14.61	1.42	0.48
Sullivan,	52.33	47.25	0.22	0.20	52.55	47.45	61.66	35.66	1.04	1.64	15.88	3.55	12.23	13.80	2.22	1.29
Tioga,	50.02	49.13	0.48	0.37	50.50	49.50	59.42	37.79	0.91	1.88	21.83	1.09	3.63	14.56	1.62	0.79
Tompkins,	49.46	49.74	0.41	0.39	49.87	50.13	58.44	37.91	1.09	2.58	22.64	0.99	3.68	15.12	0.86	0.31
Ulster,	50.17	47.73	0.98	1.12	51.15	48.85	60.70	35.45	1.10	2.75	16.53	2·15	13.95	10.15	4.41	1.35
Warren,	51.59	47.91	0.19	0.31	51.78	48.22	59.85	37.19	0.99	1.97	19.25	1.92	8.35	14.27	1.77	0.34
Washington,	50.51	48.99	0.25	0.25	50·76	49.24	60.03	36.08	1.31	2.58	18.79	2.27	10.86	12.94	2.32	1.17
Wayne,	51.00	48.49	0.23	0.28	51.23	48.77	57.55	38.79	1.17	2.49	19.42	2.39	10.19	14.64	1.43	0.65
Westchester,	48.76	48.84	1.23	1.17	49.99	50.01	61.38	34.65	1.01	2.88	13.85	3.80	20.75	10.18	3.88	1.74
Wyoming,	50.30	49.61	0.05	0.04	50.35	49.65	57.98	38.68	1.02	2.32	19.08	2.88	8.93	16.40	0.83	0.35
Yates,	49.75	49.76	0.23	0.26	49.98	50.02	57.90	38.22	1.02	2.85	21.62	0.95	4.60	14.55	1.42	0.59
Mean,	49.23	49.47	0.61	0.69	49.84	50.16	60.08	36.15	1.02	2.75	14.90	3.91	18.54	10.41	2.78	1.32

POPULATION OF VILLAGES.

[The Instructions for taking this Census, had the following directions for noting the population of villages:

"In cases where incorporated villages occur entirely in an election district, the marshal should take care to make such memoranda at the beginning and end of the enumeration, as will enable him to add up the number of inhabitants within the incorporated limits. These he should add up and enter on the last page, in the space designated 'Remarks.' If an incorporated village lies partly in other election districts, or in two or more towns or counties, state the fact in the entry, and give the number of such district, if in the same town, or the name of such towns and counties, other than his own, in which such village is located, *but give only the population of the part which is in the district he is enumerating.* These parts being added together at this office, will give the aggregate population of the villages.

There are many villages of considerable size, which have never been incorporated, and, consequently, have no definite limits. In all cases where such a village has a well established name, by which it is known in the country around, the marshal should enter its population in the 'Remarks,' on the last page, using his own discretion in deciding the limits of the villages, and stating, if the fact, that it is situated partly in two or more districts, whose numbers or names he should give."

The neglect of noting, in many instances, the beginning and end of villages, in the returns, has prevented us from entering in the following list, many of considerable size, and may, in some cases, have occasioned erroneous entries. In a few instances the population of a part of a village is recorded, with explanatory notes, or a mark of interrogation, denoting the omission of a part.]

Names of Villages.	Towns.	Counties.	Population.
Abbott's Corners,	Hamburgh,	Erie,	145
Acabonac,	East Hampton,	Suffolk,	70
Acra,	Cairo,	Greene,	50
Adams,	Adams,	Jefferson,	963
Adams Centre,	Adams,	Jefferson,	242
Akron,	Newstead,	Erie,	462
Alabama Centre,	Alabama,	Genesee,	166
Albion,	Barre,	Orleans,	3, 776
Alden,	Alden,	Erie,	285
Alexander,	Alexander,	Genesee,	345
Alexandria,	Ticonderoga,	Essex,	125
Alfred Centre,	Alfred,	Allegany,	177
Altay,	Tyrone,	Schuyler,	144
Amaganset,	East Hampton,	Suffolk,	270
Amboy,	Camillus,	Onondaga,	170
Ames,	Canajoharie,	Montgomery,	204
Amity,	Huntington,	Suffolk,	304
Amsterdam,	Amsterdam,	Montgomery,	2, 044
Andes,	Andes,	Delaware,	350
Andover,	Andover,	Allegany,	374
Angelica,	Angelica,	Allegany,	846
Antwerp,	Antwerp,	Jefferson,	621
Apalachia,	Owego,	Tioga,	200
Apulia,	Fabius,	Onondaga,	140
Arcade,	China,	Wyoming,	637
Argusville,	Carlisle, 61 Sharon, ?	Schoharie,	?
Argyle,	Argyle,	Washington,	373
Arnoldton,	Esopus,	Ulster,	150
Ashland,	Ashland,	Greene,	400
Ashville,	Harmony,	Chautauque,	247
Astoria,	Newtown,	Queens,	*2, 971
Athens,	Athens,	Greene,	1, 747
Attica,	Attica,	Wyoming,	1, 184
Augusta Centre,	Augusta,	Oneida,	100
Auriesville,	Glen,	Montgomery,	170
Aurora,	Ledyard,	Cayuga,	459
Austerlitz,	Austerlitz,	Columbia,	150
Avoca,	Avoca,	Steuben,	301
Avon,	Avon,	Livingston,	879
Babylon,	Huntington,	Suffolk,	470
Bainbridge,	Bainbridge,	Chenango,	350
Baker's Bridge,	Alfred,	Allegany,	134
Bald Mountain,	Greenwich,	Washington,	225
Baldwinsville,	Van Buren, 560 Lysander, 1, 115	Onondaga,	1, 675
Ballston Spa,	Ballston, 344 Milton, 1, 941	Saratoga,	2, 285
Barcelonia,	Westfield,	Chautauque,	169
Barrytown,	Red Hook,	Dutchess,	250
Batavia,	Batavia,	Genesee,	2, 868
Bath,	Bath,	Steuben,	2, 012
Battenville,	Greenwich,	Washington,	175
Beanville,	Willing,	Allegany,	61
Belfast,	Belfast,	Allegany,	801
Belgium,	Clay,	Onondaga,	190
Belle Isle,	Camillus,	Onondaga,	140
Belleville,	Ellisburgh,	Jefferson,	363

Names of Villages.	Towns.	Counties.	Population
Bellona,	Benton,	Yates,	205
Bellport,	Brookhaven,	Suffolk,	383
Bellvale,	Warwick,	Orange,	192
Belmont,	Amity,	Allegany,	763
Belvidere,	Amity,	Allegany,	181
Berietown,	Fayette, 77 Varick, 51	Seneca,	128
Berlin,	Berlin,	Rensselaer,	326
Bernhard's Bay,	Constantia,	Oswego,	360
Beyersville,	West Sparta,	Livingston,	61
Big Flats,	Big Flatts,	Chemung,	180
Binghamton,	†Chenango,	Broome,	8, 818
Black River,	Le Ray, 92 Rutland, 125	Jefferson,	217
Blockville,	Harmony,	Chautauque,	118
Blood's Corners,	Cohocton,	Steuben,	150
Bloomingburgh,	Mamakating,	Sullivan,	365
Bloomville,	Kortright,	Delaware,	184
Bolivar,	Bolivar,	Allegany,	157
Bombay Corners,	Bombay	Franklin,	48
Boonville,	Boonville,	Oneida,	1, 000
Boquet,	Essex,	Essex,	253
Borodino,	Spafford,	Onondaga,	202
Boston Corner,	Ancram,	Columbia,	83
Bowmansville,	Lancaster,	Erie,	196
Bradford,	Bradford,	Steuben,	260
Braman's Corners,	Duanesburgh,	Schenectady,	82
Brasher Iron Works	Brasher,	St. Lawrence,	100
Brasher Falls,	Brasher,	St. Lawrence,	257
Breakaben,	Fulton,	Schoharie,	200
Brewerton,	Cicero, 421 Hastings, 200(?)	Onondaga, Oswego,	621(?)
Brewster's Station,	South East,	Putnam,	176
Bridgeport,	Seneca Falls,	Seneca,	145
Bridgewater,	Bridgewater,	Oneida,	306
Brockport,	Sweden,	Monroe,	2, 143
Bronx,	Westchester,	Westchester,	400
Brownville,	Brownville,	Jefferson,	621
Brushland,	Bovina,	Delaware,	183
Brunswick,	Shawangunk,	Ulster,	75
Burdett,	Hector,	Schuyler,	360
Burlingham,	Mamakating,	Sullivan,	130
Burlington Green,	Burlington,	Otsego,	118
Burtonville,	Charleston,	Montgomery,	154
Bushnell's Basin,	Perrinton,	Monroe,	252
Buskirk's Bridge,	Hoosick,	Rensselaer,	125
Busti Corners,	Busti,	Chautauque,	201
Buttermilk Falls,	Cornwall,	Orange,	307
Cadiz,	Franklinville,	Cattaraugus,	165
Cairo,	Cairo,	Greene,	353
Caledonia,	Caledonia,	Livingston,	623
Camden,	Camden,	Oneida,	862
Camillus,	Camillus,	Onondaga,	552
Canajoharie,	Canajoharie,	Montgomery,	1, 500
Canandaigua,	Canandaigua,	Ontario,	4, 154
Canasaraga,	Sullivan,	Madison,	185
Canastota,	Lenox,	Madison,	1, 081
Cannonsville,	Tompkins,	Delaware,	325

* Village population of second district only, that of the other districts not having been returned separately. † Erected into the town of Binghamton since the census was taken.

Names of Villages.	Towns.	County.	Population.
noga,	Fayette,	Seneca,	197
nterbury,	Cornwall,	Orange,	428
nton,	Van Buren,	Onondaga,	188
nton,	Canton,	St. Lawrence,	1, 029
pe Vincent,	Cape Vincent,	Jefferson,	1, 026
rlisle,	Carlisle,	Schoharie,	107
rmel,	Carmel,	Putnam,	391
rthage,	Wilna,	Jefferson,	785
ryville,	Oakfield,	Genesee,	500
sadaga,	Stockton,	Chautauque,	151
stile,	Castile,	Wyoming,	682
stle Creek,	Chenango,	Broome,	185
stleton,	Schodack,	Rensselaer,	431
ato,	Cato, ? Ira, 243	Cayuga,	?
atskill,	Catskill,	Greene,	2, 520
aughnawaga,	Mohawk,	Montgomery,	217
ayuga,	Aurelius,	Cayuga,	400
azenovia,	Cazenovia,	Madison,	1, 177
edarville,	Columbia, 70 Litchfield, 75	Herkimer,	145
entrefield,	Canandaigua,	Ontario,	111
entreport,	Huntington,	Suffolk,	142
entre Village,	Colesville,	Broome,	147
entreville,	Portland,	Chautauque,	233
entreville,	Clay,	Onondago,	111
hampion,	Champion,	Jefferson,	118
hamplain,	Champlain,	Clinton,	1, 473
haseville,	Maryland,	Otsego,	170
hateaugay,	Chateaugay,	Franklin,	359
hatham,	Chatham,	Columbia,	214
hatham Centre,	Chatham,	Columbia,	127
hatham 4 Corners,	Chatham,	Columbia,	697
haumont,	Lyme,	Jefferson,	306
hazy,	Chazy,	Clinton,	326
henango Forks,	Barker, 287 Chenango, 127 Greene, 92	Broome, Broome, Chenango,	506
herry Creek,	Cherry Creek,	Chautauque,	240
herry Valley,	Cherry Valley,	Otsego,	933
hester,	Chester,	Orange,	704
hestertown,	Chester,	Warren,	246
hesterville,	Westerlo,	Albany,	196
hittenango,	Sullivan,	Madison,	916
hurchville,	Riga,	Monroe,	450
icero,	Cicero,	Onondaga,	242
incinnatus,	Cincinnatus,	Cortland,	290
larence Hollow,	Clarence,	Erie,	400
larkson,	Clarkson,	Monroe,	325
larksville,	New Scotland,	Albany,	211
larksville,	Aurelius,	Cayuga,	300
larksville,	Brookfield,	Madison,	578
larksville,	Middlefield,	Otsego,	260
laverack,	Claverack,	Columbia,	496
layton,	Clayton,	Jefferson,	896
layville,	Paris,	Oneida,	817
leveland,	Constantia,	Oswego,	1, 005
lermont,	Clermont,	Columbia,	155
lifton,	Chili,	Monroe,	201
lifton Spa,	Manchester,	Ontario,	340
Clinton,	Kirkland,	Oneida,	1, 174
Clintonville,	Ausable,	Clinton,	855
Clockville,	Lenox,	Madison,	279
Clyde,	Galen,	Wayne,	1, 856
Clymer,	Clymer,	Chautauque,	110
Cobleskill,	Cobleskill,	Schoharie,	364
Cochecton,	Cochecton,	Sullivan,	269
Cochecton Centre,	Cochecton,	Sullivan,	209
Coeymans Landing,	Coeymans,	Albany,	640
Cohocton,	Cohocton,	Steuben,	200
Cohoes,	Watervliet,	Albany,	6, 106
Cold Brook,	Russia,	Herkimer,	218
Cold Spring,	Phillipstown,	Putnam,	2, 237
Cold Spring,	Huntington,	Suffolk,	602
Colicoon Depot,	Cochecton,	Sullivan,	207
Collinsville,	West Turin,	Lewis,	200?
Colosse,	Mexico,	Oswego,	119
Colton,	Colton,	St. Lawrence,	379
Columbia Centre,	Columbia,	Herkimer,	98
Columbusville,	Newtown,	Queens,	375
Comac,	Huntington,	Suffolk,	121
Constableville,	West Turin,	Lewis,	472
Constantia,	Constantia,	Oswego,	600
Cooper's Plains,	Erwin,	Steuben,	293
Cooperstown,	Otsego,	Otsego,	....
Copenhagen,	Denmark,	Lewis,	505
Corning,	Corning,	Steuben,	3, 626
Cornwall Landing,	Cornwall,	Orange,	615
Cortland Village,	Cortlandville,	Cortland,	2, 117
Covington Centre,	Covington,	Wyoming,	82
Cowlesville,	Bennington,	Wyoming,	206
Coxsackie,	Coxsackie,	Greene,	1, 800
Crane's Village,	Amsterdam,	Montgomery,	92
Crescent,	Half-Moon,	Saratoga,	593
Croton,	Franklin,	Delaware,	200
Cuba,	Cuba,	Allegany,	816

Name of Village.	Towns.	County.	Population
Cummingville,	North Dansville,	Livingston,	119
Cuyler,	Truxton,	Cortland,	112
Cuylerville,	Leicester,	Livingston,	354
Dansville,	North Dansville,	Livingston,	2, 879
Davenport,	Davenport,	Delaware,	95
Davenport Centre,	Davenport,	Delaware,	125
Deansville,	Marshall,	Oneida,	185
Decatur,	Decatur,	Otsego,	120
De Kalb,	DeKalb,	St. Lawrence,	116
Delanti,	Stockton,	Chautauque,	180
Delhi,	Delhi,	Delaware,	919
Delphi,	Pompey,	Onondaga,	219
Delta,	Lee, 228 Western, ?	Oneida,	?
Depauville,	Clayton,	Jefferson,	386
Deposit,	Sanford, 656 Tompkins, 593	Broome, Delaware,	1, 249
De Ruyter,	De Ruyter,	Madison,	727
De Wittville,	Chautauque,	Chautauque,	133
Dexter,	Brownville,	Jefferson,	429
Dexterville,	Ellicott,	Chautauque,	275
Dobbs Ferry,	Greensburgh,	Westchester,	1, 040
Dover Plains,	Dover,	Dutchess,	375
Downsville,	Colchester,	Delaware,	206
Dryden,	Dryden,	Tompkins,	522
Dundee,	Starkey,	Yates,	732
Dunkirk,	Pomfret,	Chautauque,	4, 754
Durhamville,	Verona, 800 Lenox, 234	Oneida, Madison,	1, 034
Eagle Harbor,	Gaines, 509 Barre, 130	Orleans,	639
Earlville,	Sherburne, 208 Hamilton, 233	Chenango, Madison,	441
East Aurora,	Aurora,	Erie,	360
East Bloomfield,	East Bloomfield,	Ontario,	590
East Chatham C'tre,	Chatham,	Columbia,	245
East Chester,	East Chester,	Westchester,	551
East Durham,	Durham,	Greene,	70
East Greene,	Greene,	Chenango,	158
East Henrietta,	Henrietta,	Monroe,	181
East Marion,	Southold,	Suffolk,	300
East Mount Vernon,	East Chester,	Westchester,	275
East New-York,	New Lots,	Kings,	1, 000
Eaton,	Eaton,	Madison,	510
Ebenezer,	West Seneca, 993 Lancaster, ?	Erie,	?
Eddytown,	Starkey,	Yates,	123
Edmeston Centre,	Edmeston,	Otsego,	275
Edwards,	Edwards,	St. Lawrence,	350
Elbridge,	Elbridge,	Onondaga,	630
Elizabethtown,	Elizabethtown,	Essex,	440
Ellenburgh Corners,	Ellenburgh,	Clinton,	125
Ellicottville,	Ellicottville,	Cattaraugus,	695
Ellington,	Ellington,	Chautauque,	487
Ellisburgh,	Ellisburgh,	Jefferson,	230
Elmira,	Elmira, 7,173 Southport, 1,135	Chemung,	8, 308
Ephratah,	Ephratah,	Fulton,	359
Erieville,	Nelson,	Madison,	191
Esperance,	Esperance,	Schoharie,	322
Essex,	Essex,	Essex,	601
Etna,	Dryden,	Tompkins,	230
Euclid,	Clay,	Onondaga,	140
Evans Mills,	Le Ray,	Jefferson,	410
Exeter Centre,	Exeter,	Otsego,	106
Fabius,	Fabius,	Onondaga,	472
Factoryville,	Barton,	Tioga,	180
Fairport,	Perrinton,	Monroe,	685
Fairville,	Arcadia,	Wayne,	159
Farmersville,	Covert,	Seneca,	350
Farmingdale,	Oyster Bay,	Queens,	230
Farmington,	Farmington,	Ontario,	206
Fayetteville,	Manlius,	Onondaga,	1, 376
Felt's Mills,	Rutland,	Jefferson,	200
Fentonville,	Carroll,	Chautauque,	100
Fergusonville,	Davenport,	Delaware,	125
Fillmore,	Hume,	Allegany,	372
Fish House,	Northampton,	Fulton,	210
Fishkill Landing,	Fishkill,	Dutchess,	1, 100
Flemingville,	Owego,	Tioga,	100
Flushing,	Flushing,	Queens,	3. 488
Fluvanna,	Ellicott,	Chautauque,	75
Fonda,	Mohawk,	Montgomery,	687
Fonda's Bush,	Broadalbin,	Fulton,	651
Forge,	Cairo,	Greene,	100
Forestville,	Hanover,	Chautauque,	540
Fort Ann,	Fort Ann,	Washington,	608
Fort Covington,	Fort Covington,	Fulton,	894
Fort Edward,	Fort Edward,	Washington,	1, 565
Fort Hunter,	Florida,	Montgomery,	261
Fort Miller,	Fort Edward,	Washington,	225
Fort Plain,	Minden,	Montgomery,	1, 502
Fowlerville,	York,	Livingston,	369
Frankfort,	Frankfort,	Herkimer,	1, 150
Franklin,	Franklin,	Delaware,	490
Franklinton,	Broome,	Schoharie,	100

Name of Villages.	Towns.	Counties.	Population.
Franklinville,	Franklinville,	Cattaraugus,	370
Fredonia,	Pomfret,	Chautauque,	2, 004
Freerville,	Esopus,	Ulster,	180
Fremont Centre,	Fremont,	Sullivan,	141
Frewsburgh,	Carroll,	Chautauque,	400
Friendship,	Friendship,	Allegany,	163
Fulton,	Volney,	Oswego,	3, 192
Fultonville,	Glen,	Montgomery,	850
Gaines,	Gaies,	Orleans,	342
Gansevoort,	Northumberland,	Saratoga,	162
Gardnersville,	Seward,	Schoharie,	84
Garrattsville,	New Lisbon,	Otsego,	192
Gasport,	Royalton,	Niagara,	273
Geddes,	Geddes,	Onondaga,	950
Geneva,	Seneca,	Ontario,	5, 057
Genoa,	Genoa,	Cayuga,	300
Georgetown,	Georgetown,	Madison,	280
Gibson,	Corning,	Steuben,	428
Gilbertsville,	Butternuts,	Otsego,	442
Gilboa,	Gilboa,	Schoharie,	566
Glasshouse,	Sand Lake,	Rensselaer,	200
Glen,	Glen,	Montgomery,	218
Glens Falls,	Queensbury,	Warren,	3, 420
Gloversville,	Johnstown,	Fulton,	1, 965
Gorham,	Gorham,	Ontario,	310
Gouverneur,	Gouverneur,	St. Lawrence,	785
Gowanda,	{ Persia, 520 { Collins, 388	Cattaraugus, } Erie, }	858
Graniteville,	Northfield,	Richmond,	481
Grangerville,	Saratoga,	Saratoga,	90
Granville,	Granville,	Washington,	425
Great Bend,	Champion,	Jefferson,	106
Greenbush,	Greenbush,	Rensselaer,	3, 303
Greene,	Greene,	Chenango,	814
Greenfield Centre,	Greenfield,	Saratoga,	85
Green Island,	Watervliet,	Albany,	1, 324
Greenport,	Southold,	Suffolk,	1, 665
Green River,	Hillsdale,	Columbia,	60
Groesbeck,	Bethlehem,	Albany,	1, 232
Grosvenor's Corners	Carlisle,	Schoharie,	48
Groton,	Groton,	Tompkins,	587
Guilford,	Guilford,	Chenango,	263
Harlemville,	Hillsdale,	Columbia,	225
Hageman's Mills,	Amsterdam,	Montgomery,	124
Hallsport,	Willing,	Allegany,	64
Halsey Valley,	Tioga,	Tioga,	100
Hamden,	Hamden,	Delaware,	191
Hamilton,	Hamilton,	Madison,	1, 448
Hamlet,	Villenova,	Chautauque,	181
Hammondsport,	Urbana,	Steuben,	560
Hampton,	Westmoreland,	Oneida,	400
Hancock,	Hancock,	Delaware,	502
Harpersfield Centre,	Harpersfield,	Delaware,	83
Harpersville,	Colesville,	Broome,	230
Harrowsburgh,	Tusten,	Sullivan,	277
Hartfield,	Chautauque,	Chautauque,	123
Hartford,	Hartford,	Washington,	300
Havana,	{ Catharines, 1, 241 } { Dix, 49 }	Schuyler,	1, 290
Hastings,	Greenburg,	Westchester,	1, 135
Hawkinsville,	Boonville,	Oneida,	339
Hawversville,	Broome,	Schoharie,	150
Hecla,	Westmoreland,	Oneida,	130
Helena,	Brasher,	St. Lawrence,	100
Hemlock Lake,	Livonia,	Livingston,	319
Hempstead,	Hempstead,	Queens,	1, 486
Hemrods,	Milo,	Yates,	78
Henderson,	Henderson,	Jefferson,	404
Hensonville,	Windham,	Greene,	124
Herkimer,	Herkimer,	Herkimer,	1, 371
Hermon,	Hermon,	St. Lawrence,	346
Hervelton,	Oswegatchie	St. Lawrence,	300
Higginsville,	Verona,	Oneida,	172
Hindsburgh,	Murray,	Orleans,	167
Hinkleyville,	Parma,	Monroe,	64
Hillsdale,	Hillsdale,	Columbia,	225
Hinsdale,	Hinsdale,	Cattaraugus,	255
Hobart,	Stamford,	Delaware,	391
Hogansburgh,	Bombay,	Franklin,	246
Holland Patent,	Trenton,	Oneida,	353
Holley,	Murray,	Orleans,	614
Homer,	Homer,	Cortland,	1, 625
Honeoye,	Richmond,	Ontario,	244
Hoosick Falls,	Hoosick,	Rensselaer,	1, 200
Hornellsville,	Hornellsville,	Steuben,	1, 519
Horseheads,	Horseheads,	Chemung,	1, 000
Houseville,	Turin,	Lewis	90
Howard,	Howard,	Steuben,	143?
Hughsonville,	Fishkill,	Dutchess,	245
Hulberton,	Murray,	Orleans,	278
Hume,	Hume,	Allegany,	271
Hunter,	Hunter,	Greene,	393
Huntersland,	Middleburgh,	Schoharie,	101
Huntington,	Huntington,	Suffolk,	1, 328
Hurley,	Hurley,	Ulster,	160
Hyde Park,	Hyde Park,	Dutchess,	692

Name of Villages.	Towns.	Counties.	Population.
Hyndsville,	Seward,	Schoharie,	143
Ilion,	German Flats,	Herkimer,	813
Ira,	Ira,	Cayuga,	145
Irving,	Hanover,	Chautauque,	404
Irvington,	Greenburgh,	Westchester,	599
Ithaca,	Ithaca,	Tompkins,	4, 908
Jacksonsburgh,	Little Falls,	Herkimer,	206
Jacksonville,	Coxsackie,	Greene,	48
Jamaica,	Jamaica,	Queens,	2, 817
Jamesport,	Riverhead,	Suffolk,	148
Jamestown,	Ellicott,	Chautauque,	1, 625
Jamesville,	De Witt,	Onondaga,	270
Jasper,	Jasper,	Steuben,	222
Jeddo,	Ridgeway,	Orleans,	124
Jeffersonville,	{ Colicoon, 305 } { Cochecton, 128 }	Sullivan,	433
Johnson's Creek,	Hartland,	Niagara,	114
Johnstown,	Johnstown,	Fulton,	1, 661
Jordan,	Elbridge,	Onondaga,	1, 331
Jordanville,	Warren,	Herkimer,	125
Joy,	Sodus,	Wayne,	72
Keeseville,	{ Ausable, 1,199 { Chesterfield, 1,370	Clinton, } Essex, }	2, 569
Kensico,	North Castle,	Westchester,	10[illegible]
Kenwood,	Bethlehem,	Albany,	27[illegible]
Kidder's Ferry,	Ovid,	Seneca,	16[illegible]
Kinderhook,	Kinderhook,	Columbia,	1, 07[illegible]
Kingsbury,	Johnstown,	Fulton,	30[illegible]
Kingston,	Kingston,	Ulster,	3, 97[illegible]
Knowlesville,	Ridgeway,	Orleans,	49[illegible]
Knox Corners,	Augusta,	Oneida,	20[illegible]
Knoxville,	Corning,	Steuben,	62[illegible]
Knoxville,	Stockbridge,	Madison,	13[illegible]
Kysorville,	West Sparta,	Livingston,	7[illegible]
Lackawack,		Ulster,	14[illegible]
Lafargeville,	Orleans,	Jefferson,	29[illegible]
Lafayetteville,	Milan,	Dutchess,	11[illegible]
Lakeland,	Islip,	Suffolk,	21[illegible]
Lakeport,	Sullivan,	Madison,	18[illegible]
Lakeville,	Greenwich,	Washington,	15[illegible]
Lancaster,	Lancaster,	Erie,	1,25[illegible]
Lansingburgh,	Lansingburgh,	Rensselaer,	2d dist } 2,73[illegible]
Lansingville,	Hamden,	Delaware,	11[illegible]
Laona,	Pomfret,	Chautauque,	40[illegible]
Laurens,	Laurens,	Otsego,	72[illegible]
Lawrenceville,	Lawrence,	St. Lawrence,	20[illegible]
Lebanon Springs,	New Lebanon,	Columbia,	27[illegible]
Leeds,	Catskill,	Greene,	45[illegible]
Leonardsville,	{ Brookfield, 331 { Plainfield, 35	Madison, Otsego,	36[illegible]
Le Raysville,	Le Ray,	Jefferson,	13[illegible]
Le Roy,	Le Roy,	Genesee,	2, 08[illegible]
Levanna,	Ledyard,	Cayuga,	10[illegible]
Lewis,	Lewis,	Essex,	13[illegible]
Lewiston,	Lewiston,	Niagara,	1, 01[illegible]
Lewisville,	Morris,	Otsego,	50[illegible]
Leyden Hill,	Leyden,	Lewis,	4[illegible]
Liberty,	Liberty,	Sullivan,	36[illegible]
Limerick,	Brownville,	Jefferson,	5[illegible]
Lisle, (upper vil'ge)	Triangle,	Broome,	13[illegible]
Little Falls,	{ Little Falls, 3,804 } { Manheim, 168 } { Danube, 12? }	Herkimer,	3,984
Little Lakes,	Warren,	Herkimer,	11[illegible]
Liverpool,	Salina,	Onondaga,	67[illegible]
Livingstonville,	Broome,	Schoharie,	1[illegible]
Livonia,	Livonia,	Livingston,	40[illegible]
Lockport,	Lockport,	Niagara,	8, 9[illegible]
Lodi,	Lodi,	Seneca,	3[illegible]
Logan	Hector,	Schuyler,	[illegible]
Lower Falls,	Ticonderoga,	Essex,	3[illegible]
Lowville,	Lowville,	Lewis,	9[illegible]
Luzerne,	Luzerne,	Warren,	2[illegible]
Lyndonville,	Yates,	Orleans,	24[illegible]
Lyons,	Lyons,	Wayne,	3, 2[illegible]
Lysander,	Lysander,	Onondaga,	2[illegible]
McConnellsville,	Vienna,	Oneida,	1[illegible]
Macdonough,	Macdonough,	Chenango,	1[illegible]
McGrawville,	Cortlandville,	Cortland,	5[illegible]
Madison,	Madison,	Madison,	3[illegible]
Maine,	Maine,	Broome,	2[illegible]
Malden,	Chatham,	Columbia,	1[illegible]
Malden,	Saugerties,	Ulster,	3[illegible]
Malone,	Malone,	Franklin,	1, 9[illegible]
Manchester,	{ Manchester, 346 } { Phelps, 28 }	Ontario,	37[illegible]
Manlius,	Manlius,	Onondaga,	9[illegible]
Mannsville,	Ellisburgh,	Jefferson,	3[illegible]
Marathon,	Marathon,	Cortland,	5[illegible]
Marcellus,	Marcellus,	Onondaga,	3[illegible]
Marcellus Falls,	Marcellus,	Onondaga,	2[illegible]
Mariaville,	Duanesburgh,	Schenectady,	1[illegible]
Marilla,	Marilla,	Erie,	2[illegible]
Mariners' Harbor,	Northfield,	Richmond,	1, 1[illegible]
Marion,	Marion,	Wayne,	3[illegible]
Martinsburgh,	Martinsburgh,	Lewis,	2[illegible]

Name of Villages.	Towns.	County.	Population.
sonville,	Masonville,	Delaware,	234
ssena,	Massena,	St. Lawrence,	310
ssena Springs,	Massena,	St. Lawrence,	120
tteawan,	Fishkill,	Dutchess,	1, 476
yfield Corners,	Mayfield,	Fulton,	600
yville,	Chautauque,	Chautauque,	501
chanicsville,	Stillwater, 616 Half Moon, 495	Saratoga,	1, 111
chanicsville,	Oakfield,	Genesee,	168
cklenburgh,	Hector,	Schuyler,	338
dina,	Ridgeway, 1,915 Shelby, 189	Orleans,	2, 104
lville,	Huntington,	Suffolk,	108
ridian,	Cato,	Cayuga,	360
xico,	Mexico,	Oswego,	948
ddle Granville,	Granville,	Washington,	439
ddleport,	Hartland, 103 Royalton, 586	Niagara,	689
ddleport,	Wawarsing,	Ulster,	208
ddletown,	Walkill,	Orange,	1, 873
ddletown,	Half-Moon,	Saratoga,	230
ddleville,	Newport,	Herkimer,	295
ddleville	Newtown,	Queens,	250
an,	Locke,	Cayuga,	180
es' Tannery,	Fremont,	Sullivan,	102
lers' Place,	Brookhaven,	Suffolk,	197
lport,	Veteran,	Chemung,	706
ltown,	Southeast,	Putnam,	167
o Centre,	Milo,	Yates,	150
naville,	Florida,	Montgomery,	95
netto,	Oswego,	Oswego,	150
dern Times,	Islip,	Suffolk,	85
hawk,	German Flats,	Herkimer,	1, 355
nroe,	Monroe,	Orange,	266
ntezuma,	Mentz,	Cayuga,	650
ntgomery,	Montgomery,	Orange,	760
nterey,	Orange,	Schuyler,	301
nticello,	Richfield,	Otsego,	139
nticello,	Thompson,	Sullivan,	629
rganville,	Stafford,	Genesee,	200
riah,	Moriah,	Essex,	275
rley,	Canton,	St. Lawrence,	350
rrissania,	West Farms,*	Westchester,	2, 587
rristown,	Morristown,	St. Lawrence,	254
rrisville,	Eaton,	Madison,	715
scow,	Leicester,	Livingston,	320
tt Haven,	West Farms,	Westchester,	843
ttville,	Skaneateles,	Onondaga,	250
unt Hope,	Mount Hope,	Orange,	120
unt Kisco,	Bedford,	Westchester,	200
unt Morris,	Mount Morris,	Livingston,	1, 851
unt Pleasant,	Greenfield,	Saratoga,	140
unt Sinai,	Brookhaven,	Suffolk,	276
unt Upton,	Guilford,	Chenango,	190
unt Vernon,	East Chester,	Westchester,	1, 661
mford,	Wheatland,	Monroe,	535
nnsville,	Stockbridge,	Madison,	287
yersville,	Red Hook,	Dutchess,	500
ples,	Naples,	Ontario,	700
poneck,	Wawarsing,	Ulster,	700
ssau,	Nassau,	Rensselaer,	299
avarino,	Onondaga,	Onondaga,	115
ealy's Hollow,	Seward,	Schoharie,	65
elson,	Nelson,	Madison,	146
ew Albion,	New Albion,	Cattaraugas,	95
ewark,	Arcadia,	Wayne,	2, 042
ew Baltimore,	New Baltimore,	Greene,	709
ew Berlin,	New Berlin,	Chenango,	740
ew Bremen,	New Bremen,	Lewis,	200
ewburgh,	Newburgh,	Orange,	9, 256
ew Carthage,	Fishkill,	Dutchess,	146
ew Centreville,	Albion,	Oswego,	154
ew Concord,	Chatham,	Columbia,	109
ew Hamburgh,	Poughkeepsie,	Dutchess,	339
ew Hartford,	New Hartford,	Oneida,	892
ewkirkville,	Caroga,	Fulton,	150
ew London,	Verona,	Oneida,	668
ewport,	Newport,	Herkimer,	671
ew Rochelle,	New Rochelle,	Westchester,	2, 000
ew Salem,	New Scotland,	Albany,	134
ew Scotland,	New Scotland,	Albany,	67
ew Sweden,	Ausable,	Clinton,	150
ewtownville,	Newtown,	Queens,	375
ew Woodstock,	Cazenovia,	Madison,	273
iagara City,	Niagara,	Niagara,	1, 365
iagara Falls,	Niagara,	Niagara,	2, 976
icholville,	Lawrence,	St. Lawrence,	200
orth Bay,	Vienna,	Oneida,	300
orth Brookfield,	Brookfield,	Madison,	275
orth Chatham,	Chatham,	Columbia,	179
orth Granville,	Granville,	Washington,	220
orth Hector,	Hector,	Schuyler,	114
orth Hoosick,	Hoosick,	Rensselaer,	175
orth Lawrence,	Lawrence,	St. Lawrence,	215
orthport,	Huntington,	Suffolk,	430

* Erected into the town of Morrissania since the census was taken.

Name of Villages.	Towns.	County.	Population.
Northumberland,	Northumberland,	Saratoga,	118
Northville,	Northampton,	Fulton,	450
Northville,	Genoa,	Cayuga,	200
North White Creek,	White Creek,	Washington,	652
Norwich,	Norwich,	Chenango,	2, 430
Nunda,	Nunda,	Livingston,	1, 125
Nyack,	Orangetown,	Rockland,	1, 458
Oak Hill,	Durham,	Greene,	320
Oak Orchard,	Ridgeway,	Orleans,	136
Ogdensburgh,	Oswegatchie,	St. Lawrence,	7, 057
Olean,	Olean,	Cattaraugus,	994
Omar,	Orleans,	Jefferson,	100
Oneida,	Lenox,	Madison,	1, 713
Oneida Castle,	Lenox, 62 Vernon, 275	Madison,	337
Oneida Community,	Lenox,	Madison,	170
Oneida Valley,	Lenox,	Madison,	143
Oneonta,	Oneonta,	Otsego,	678
Onondaga Valley,	Onondaga,	Onondago,	385
Oppenheim Centre,	Oppenheim,	Fulton,	59
Oramel,	Canedea,	Allegany,	733
Oran,	Pompey,	Onondaga,	82
Orangeport,	Royalton,	Niagara,	224
Oriskany,	Whitestown,	Oneida,	701
Oriskany Falls,	Augusta, 711 Marshall, ?	Oneida,	?
Orleans,	Phelps,	Ontario,	218
Orville,	De Witt,	Onondaga,	158
Oswego Falls,	Granby,	Oswego,	703
Otego,	Otego,	Otsego,	331
Otisville,	Mount Hope,	Orange,	309
Otselic,	Otselic,	Chenango,	100
Owego,	Owego,	Tioga,	3, 041
Ox Bow,	Antwerp,	Jefferson,	240
Oxford,	Oxford,	Chenango,	1, 218
Oyster Bay,	Oyster Bay,	Queens,	900
Page's Corners,	Warren,	Herkimer,	82
Painted Post,	Erwin,	Steuben,	777
Palmyra,	Palmyra,	Wayne,	2, 310
Panama,	Harmony,	Chautauque,	500
Parishville,	Parishville,	St. Lawrence,	236
Parma Centre,	Parma,	Monroe,	109
Parma Corners,	Parma,	Monroe,	116
Patchogue,	Brookhaven,	Suffolk,	1, 562
Pavillion,	Pavillion,	Genesee,	216
Pavillion Centre,	Pavillion,	Genesee,	80
Pekin,	Lewiston,	Niagara,	73
Peekskill,	Cortlandt,	Westchester,	3, 538
Penfield,	Penfield,	Monroe,	560
Penn Yan,	Milo, 2,114 Benton, 163	Yates,	2, 277
Pentaquit,	Islip,	Suffolk,	292
Peoria,	Covington,	Wyoming,	74
Perkins' Corners,	Conquest,	Cayuga,	130
Perry,	Hector,	Schuyler,	120
Perry,	Perry,	Wyoming,	935
Peru,	Peru,	Clinton,	504
Peterboro',	Smithfield,	Madison,	350
Phelps,	Phelps,	Ontario,	1, 278
Philadelphia,	Philadelphia,	Jefferson,	275
Phillipsport,	Mamakating,	Sullivan,	294
Phœnix,	Schrœppel,	Oswego,	1, 164
Piermont,	Orangetown,	Rockland,	2, 204
Pierrepont Manor,	Ellisburgh,	Jefferson,	255
Pike,	Pike,	Wyoming,	581
Pike Pond,	Cochecton,	Sullivan,	188
Pine Bush,	Crawford,	Orange,	120
Pine Hill,	Elba,	Genesee,	400
Pine Plains,	Pine Plains,	Dutchess,	382
Pineville,	Albion,	Oswego,	144
Pittsford,	Pittsford,	Monroe,	702
Plainfield Centre,	Plainfield,	Otsego,	25
Plainville,	Lysander,	Onondaga,	218
Plattsburg,	Plattsburgh,	Clinton,	2, 926
Pleasant Plains,	Westfield,	Richmond,	200
Pleasant Valley,	Pleasant Valley,	Dutchess,	500
Pleasant Valley,	Oriskany,	Oneida,	272
Pleasantville,	Mount Pleasant,	Westchester,	358
Plymouth,	Plymouth,	Chenango,	150
Poestenkill,	Poestenkill,	Rensselaer,	300
Poland,	Russia,	Herkimer,	179
Pompey,	Pompey,	Onondaga,	270
Pope's Corners,	Northumberland,	Saratoga,	137
Pope's Mills,	Macomb,	St. Lawrence,	56
Portageville,	Genesee Falls,	Wyoming,	561
Port Benjamin,	Wawarsing,	Ulster,	206
Port Byron,	Mentz,	Cayuga,	1, 669
Port Chester,	Rye,	Westchester,	1, 695
Port Crane,	Chenango,†	Broome,	193
Port Ewan,	Esopus,	Ulster,	1, 300
Porter's Corners,	Greenfield,	Saratoga,	65
Port Henry,	Moriah,	Essex,	503
Port Jackson,	Florida,	Montgomery,	369
Port Jefferson,	Brookhaven,	Suffolk,	1, 247
Port Jervis,	Deerpark,	Orange,	3, 023

† Erected into the town of Port Crane since the census was taken.

Name of Villages.	Towns.	Counties.	Population.
Port Leyden,	Leyden,	Lewis,	192
Port Richmond,	Northfield,	Richmond,	1,429
Portville,	Portville,	Cattaraugus,	287
Potsdam,	Potsdam,	St. Lawrence,	*2,123
Potterville,	Chester,	Warren,	126
Prattsville,	Prattsville,	Greene,	617
Prattville,	Mexico,	Oswego,	55
Preble,	Preble,	Cortland,	199
Preston Corners,	Preston,	Chenango,	105
Pulaski,	Richland,	Oswego,	1,168
Quincy,	Ripley,	Chautauque,	289
Ransomville,	Porter,	Niagara,	195
Rapids,	Champlain,	Clinton,	300
Red Creek,	Wolcott,	Wayne,	400
Red Falls,	Prattsville,	Greene,	231
Red Hook,	Red Hook,	Dutchess,	‖625
Redwood,	Alexandria,	Jefferson,	429
Remsen,	Remsen, 510 Trenton, ?	Oneida,	?
Remy's Mills,	Champlain,	Clinton,	400
Rensselaerville,	Rensselaerville,	Albany,	561
Reynolds' Basin,	Royalton,	Niagara,	132
Reynoldsville,	Hector,	Schuyler,	117
Rhinebeck,	Rhinebeck,	Dutchess,	1,051
Richfield Springs,	Richfield,	Otsego,	368
Richmondville,	Richmondville,	Schoharie,	370
Richville,	De Kalb,	St. Lawrence,	250
Ridgeway,	Ridgeway,	Orleans,	64
Riverhead,	Riverhead, 723 Southampton, 90	Suffolk,	813
Roanoke,	Stafford,	Genesee,	115
Rock City,	Milan,	Dutchess,	84
Rochdale,	Poughkeepsie,	Dutchess,	163
Rockland Lake,	Clarkstown,	Rockland,	430
Rockwood,	Ephratah,	Fulton,	196
Rocky Point,	Brookhaven,	Suffolk,	132
Rodman,	Rodman,	Jefferson,	300
Rogersville,	South Dansville,	Steuben,	200
Rome,	Rome,	Oneida,	7,083
Romulusville,	Varick, 114 Romulus, ?	Seneca,	?
Rondout,	Kingston,	Ulster,	5,978
Roseboom,	Roseboom,	Otsego,	111
Rosendale,	Rosendale,	Ulster,	450
Rose Valley,	Rose,	Wayne,	218
Rossville,	Westfield,	Richmond,	300
Roslyn,	North Hempstead,	Queens,	592
Rossie,	Rossie,	St. Lawrence,	214
Rouse's Point,	Champlain,	Clinton,	1,769
Roxbury,	Roxbury,	Delaware,	232
Royalton,	Royalton,	Niagara,	168
Rushford,	Rushford,	Allegany,	654
Rushville,	Potter, 408 Gorham, 175	Yates, Ontario,	583
Russell,	Russell,	St. Lawrence,	250
Russia,	Russia,	Herkimer,	140
Rutledge,	Conewango,	Cattaraugus,	100
Rye,	Rye,	Westchester,	300
Sacketts Harbor,	Hounsfield,	Jefferson,	994
Sag Harbor,	Southampton, 2,041 Easthampton, 735	Suffolk,	2,776
St. Johnsville,	St. Johnsville,	Montgomery,	648
St. Regis,	Bombay,	Franklin,	¶200
Salem,	Salem,	Washington,	832
Salem,	Portland,	Chautauque,	258
Salisbury,	Blooming Grove, 221 Cornwall, 20	Orange,	241
Salisbury Centre,	Salisbury,	Herkimer,	319
Salt Springville,	Cherry Valley,	Otsego,	70
Sand Bank,	Albion,	Oswego,	313
Sand Lake,	Sand Lake,	Rensselaer,	300
Sandusky,	Freedom,	Cattaraugus,	175
Sandy Hill,	Kingsbury,	Washington,	1,260
Saratoga Springs,	Saratoga Springs,	Saratoga,	5,129
Saugerties,	Saugerties,	Ulster,	3,334
Sauquoit,	Paris,	Oneida,	690
Savona,	Bath,	Steuben,	232
Sayville,	Islip,	Suffolk,	822
Schaghticoke Point,	Schaghticoke,	Rensselaer,	1,148
Schaghticoke,	Schaghticoke,	Rensselaer,	889
Schenevus,	Maryland,	Otsego,	383
Schodack Landing,	Schodack,	Rensselaer,	250
Schoharie,	Schoharie,	Schoharie,	806
Schroon,	Schroon,	Essex,	192
Schuyler Lake,	Exeter,	Otsego,	280
Schuylerville,	Westchester,	Westchester,	300
Schuylerville,	Saratoga,	Saratoga,	1,184
Scio,	Amity, 77 Scio, 419	Allegany,	496
Scipio Centre,	Scipio,	Cayuga,	80
Scipioville,	Scipio,	Cayuga,	80
Scotch Bush,	Florida,	Montgomery,	48
Scotia,	Glenville,	Schenectady,	266
Scott Centre,	Scott,	Cortland,	294
Scottsville,	Wheatland,	Monroe,	925

Name of Villages.	Towns.	Counties.	Population.
Searsburgh,	Hector,	Schuyler,	66
Seneca Falls,	Seneca Falls,	Seneca,	‡2,125
Setauket,	Brookhaven,	Suffolk,	1,136
Shaker Village,	New Lebanon,	Columbia,	392
Sharon Springs,	Sharon,	Schoharie,	230
Sheldrake,	Ovid,	Seneca,	168
Sherburne,	Sherburne,	Chenango,	1,140
Sherman,	Sherman,	Chautauque,	401
Sherwood's Corners	Scipio,	Cayuga,	80
Shushan,	Salem, Jackson,	Washington,	300
Sidney Plains,	Sidney,	Delaware,	80
Siloam,	Smithfield,	Madison,	60
Silver Creek,	Hanover,	Chautauque,	652
Sinclairville,	Charlotte,	Chautauque,	450
Sing Sing,	Osining,	Westchester,	1,440
Skaneateles,	Skaneateles,	Onondaga,	1,200
Sliter's Corners,	Sand Lake,	Rensselaer,	106
Sloansville,	Esperance,	Schoharie,	252
Sloatsburgh,	Ramapo,	Rockland,	180
Smithboro,	Tioga,	Tioga,	230
Smithville,	Alabama,	Genesee,	147
Smithville,	Adams, 116 Henderson, 92	Jefferson,	218
Smithville Flats,	Smithville,	Chenango,	315
Smyrna,	Smyrna,	Chenango,	320
Somerville,	Rossie,	St. Lawrence,	98
South Bainbridge,	Bainbridge,	Chenango,	270
South Cairo,	Cairo,	Greene,	50
South Cortland.	Cortlandville,	Cortland,	161
Southeast Centre,	Southeast,	Putnam,	144
South Glens Falls,	Moreau,	Saratoga,	513
South Granville,	Granville,	Washington,	111
South New Berlin,	New Berlin,	Chenango,	§285
South Onondaga,	Onondaga,	Onondaga,	290
South Otselic,	Otselic,	Chenango,	225
South Trenton,	Trenton,	Oneida,	204
South Valley,	Roseboom,	Otsego,	175
South Waterloo,	Fayette,	Seneca,	597
South Westerlo,	Westerlo,	Albany,	72
Speedsville,	Caroline,	Tompkins,	159
Spencerport,	Ogden,	Monroe,	578
Spencertown,	Austerlitz,	Columbia,	225
Spring Brook,	Aurora,	Erie,	300
Springville,	Concord,	Erie,	953
Stafford,	Stafford,	Genesee,	350
Stamford,	Stamford,	Delaware,	185
Starkville,	Stark,	Herkimer,	190
Sterlingville,	Philadelphia,	Jefferson,	316
Sterling Works,	Warwick,	Orange,	305
Stillwater,	Stillwater,	Saratoga,	552
Stittsville,	Marcy, 41 Trenton, 223	Oneida,	264
Stone Mills,	Orleans,	Jefferson,	115
Stony Brook,	Brookhaven, 542 Smithtown, ?	Suffolk,	?
Strattonport,	Flushing,	Queens,	1,150
Sullivanville,	Veteran,	Chemung,	155
Summer Hill,	Summer Hill,	Cayuga,	115
Talcottville,	Leyden,	Lewis,	50
Theresa Falls,	Theresa,	Jefferson,	559
Three Mile Bay,	Lyme,	Jefferson,	295
Three River Point,	Clay,	Onondaga,	54
Throopsville,	Mentz,	Cayuga,	160
Thurmansville,	Collikoon,	Sullivan,	126
Tonawanda,	Tonawanda, 1,257 Wheatfield, ?	Erie, Niagara,	?
Tottenville,	Westfield,	Richmond,	600
Triangle,	Triangle,	Broome,	175
Tribes Hill,	Mohawk, 212 Amsterdam, 115	Montgomery,	327
Trumansburgh,	Ulysses,	Tompkins,	1,052
Truxton,	Truxton,	Cortland,	257
Tully,	Tully,	Onondaga,	246
Turin,	Turin,	Lewis,	438
Tuscarora,	Mount Morris,	Livingston,	194
Tyrone,	Tyrone,	Schuyler,	160
Ulsterville,	Shawangunk,	Ulster,	75
Unadilla,	Unadilla,	Otsego,	795
Unadilla Forks,	Brookfield, 17 Plainfield, 236	Madison, Otsego,	253
Union,	Union,	Broome,	520
Union Corners,	West Sparta, 29 Mount Morris, ?	Livingston,	?
Union Place,	New Lots,	Kings,	500
Union Springs,	Springport,	Cayuga,	1,118
Union Village,	Easton, 285 Greenwich, 888	Washington,	1,173
Unionville,	Parma,	Monroe,	145
Unionville,	Mount Pleasant,	Westchester,	97
Upper Nyack,	Clarkstown,	Rockland,	208
Upper Redhook,	Redhook,	Dutchess,	175
Van Hornsville,	Stark,	Herkimer,	228
Varna,	Dryden,	Tompkins,	170
Vernon,	Vernon,	Oneida,	330

* In first and fourth election districts. † South village, 625. ‡ In first election district. § Portion in Otsego county. ‖ Second district.

¶ The greater part of the Indian village of St. Regis lies north of the Provincial line. The Canada census of 1851 showed a population of 1,069 in that part of the village lying in Canada.

Name of Villages.	Towns.	County.	Population.
rnon Valley, ...	Huntington, ...	Suffolk, ...	100
rplanck's, ...	Cortlandt, ...	Westchester, ...	1, 456
rsailles, ...	Perrysburgh, ...	Cattaraugus, ...	274
ctory Mills, ...	Saratoga, ...	Saratoga, ...	729
enna, ...	Vienna, ...	Oneida,.	110
rgil, ...	Virgil, ...	Cortland, ...	206
addington, ...	Madrid, ...	St. Lawrence, ...	705
alden, ...	Montgomery, ...	Orange, ...	641
alton, ...	Walton, ...	Delaware, ...	430
alworth, ...	Walworth, ...	Wayne, ...	230
appenger Falls, ..	Fishkill, ... 1,139; Poughkeepsie, 680	Dutchess, ...	1, 819
ardville, ...	Bergen, ...	Genesee, ...	443
arrensburgh, ...	Warrensburgh, ...	Warren, ...	700
arsaw, ...	Warsaw, ...	Wyoming, ...	1, 200
arwick, ...	Warwick, ...	Orange, ...	358
ashingtonville, ..	Blooming Grove, ...	Orange, ...	369
ashingtonville, ..	Sandy Creek, ...	Oswego, ...	423
aterford, ...	Waterford, ...	Saratoga, ...	3, 083
aterloo, ...	Waterloo, ...	Seneca, ...	3, 050
aterport, ...	Carlton, ...	Orleans, ...	184
aterville, ...	Marshall, ... 159; Sangerfield, ... 950	Oneida, ...	1, 109
atertown, ...	Watertown, ...	Jefferson, ...	5, 873
ater Valley, ...	Hamburgh, ...	Erie, ...	202
atkins, ...	Reading, ... 210; Dix, ... 874	Schuyler, ...	1, 084
averly, ...	Otto, ...	Cattaraugus, ...	277
averly, ...	Barton, ...	Tioga, ...	1, 067
ayne, ...	Tyrone, ... 87; Wayne, ... ?	Schuyler, ...; Steuben, ...	?
ebster, ...	Webster, ...	Monroe, ...	310
eedsport, ...	Brutus, ...	Cayuga, ...	1, 226
egatchie, ...	Rossie, ...	St. Lawrence, ...	170
ellsburgh, ...	Southport, ...	Chemung, ...	365
ellsville, ...	Scio,*	Allegany, ...	1, 286
est Branch, ...	Lee, ...	Oneida, ...	180
est Burlington, ..	Burlington, ...	Otsego, ...	143
est Carthage, ...	Champion, ...	Jefferson, ...	199
est Chazy, ...	Chazy, ...	Clinton, ...	281
estchester, ...	Westchester, ...	Westchester, ...	1, 000
est Davenport, ..	Davenport, ...	Delaware, ...	90
est Dresden, ...	Torrey, ...	Yates, ...	365
est Dryden, ...	Dryden, ...	Tompkins, ...	93
est Hebron, ...	Hebron, ...	Washington, ...	146
estern, ...	Tyrone, ...	Schuyler, ...	177
esternville, ...	Western, ...	Oneida, ...	287

Name of Villages.	Towns.	County.	Population.
West Exeter, ...	Exeter, ...	Otsego, ...	100
Westfield, ...	Westfield, ...	Chautauque, ...	1, 433
Westford, ...	Westford, ...	Otsego, ...	181
West Granville, ...	Granville, ...	Washington, ...	100
West Martinsburgh,	Martinsburgh, ...	Lewis, ...	164
West Mount Vernon	East Chester, ...	Westchester, ...	630
Westport, ...	Westport, ...	Essex, ...	456
West Sand Lake, ..	Sand Lake, ...	Rensselaer, ...	306
West Troy, ...	Watervleit, ...	Albany, ...	8, 306
West Vienna, ...	Vienna, ...	Oneida, ...	140
West Walworth, ..	Walworth, ...	Wayne, ...	115
West Winfield, ...	Winfield, ...	Herkimer, ...	381
Whallonsburgh, ...	Essex, ...	Essex, ...	221
Wheatville, ...	Alabama, ...	Genesee, ...	93
White Creek, ...	White Creek, ...	Washington, ...	207
Whitehall, ...	Whitehall, ...	Washington, ...	3, 225
Whitesboro, ...	Whitestown, ...	Oneida, ...	953
White's Corners, ..	Hamburgh, ...	Erie, ...	609
Whitestone, ...	Flushing, ...	Queens, ...	630
Whitesville, ...	Independence, ...	Allegany, ...	220
Whitesville, ...	Rodman, ...	Jefferson, ...	53
Whitney's Point, ..	Triangle, ...	Broome, ...	205
Willett, ...	Willett, ...	Cortland, ...	120
Williamsville, ...	Amherst, ...	Erie, ...	1, 166
Williamstown Mills,	Williamstown, ...	Oswego, ...	240
Willink, ...	Aurora, ...	Erie, ...	365
Willsborough Falls,	Willsborough, ...	Essex, ...	300
Wilson, ...	Wilson, ...	Niagara, ...	666
Windham Centre, ..	Windham, ...	Greene, ...	350
Windsor Village, ..	Windsor, ...	Broome, ...	339
Winfieldville, ...	Newtown, ...	Queens, ...	400
Wolcott, ...	Butler, ... ?; Wolcott, ... 566	Wayne, ...	?
Wolcottville, ...	Royalton, ...	Niagara, ...	319
Woodhull, ...	Woodhull, ...	Steuben, ...	215
Woodville, ...	West Sparta, ...	Livingston, ...	130
Woodville, ...	Brookhaven, ...	Suffolk, ...	104
Woodville, ...	Ellisburgh, ...	Jefferson, ...	180
Wurtsboro, ...	Mamakating, ...	Sullivan, ...	492
Wynantville, ...	Newtown, ...	Queens, ...	180
Wyoming, ...	Middlebury, ...	Wyoming, ...	378
Yates Centre, ...	Yates, ...	Orleans, ...	191
Yonkers, ...	Yonkers, ...	Westchester, ...	4, 710
York Centre, ...	York, ...	Livingston, ...	321
Youngstown, ...	Porter, ...	Niagara, ...	768
Youngsville, ...	Colicoon, ...	Sullivan, ...	128
Zoar, ...	Rodman, ...	Jefferson, ...	82

* The town of Wellsville has been erected since the census was taken.

CLASSIFICATION BY AGE AND SEX.

ALBANY COUNTY.

TOWNS.	Under 1. Males.	Under 1. Females.	1 and under 5. Males.	1 and under 5. Females.	5 and under 10. Males.	5 and under 10. Females.	10 and under 15. Males.	10 and under 15. Females.	15 and under 20. Males.	15 and under 20. Females.	20 and under 25. Males.	20 and under 25. Females.	25 and under 30. Males.	25 and under 30. Females.	30 and under 35. Males.	30 and under 35. Females.
Albany city: 1st ward,	156	149	497	536	527	528	403	412	352	345	344	363	371	343	353	338
2d ward,	74	69	244	273	278	240	237	242	226	269	221	289	196	221	166	180
3d ward,	67	67	221	241	260	259	221	231	203	310	231	338	225	261	189	189
4th ward,	38	54	197	175	199	184	187	188	230	292	274	369	251	251	198	203
5th ward,	35	27	111	96	108	114	119	141	143	261	172	227	155	200	135	118
6th ward,	14	26	165	178	152	150	145	182	170	260	160	287	161	199	139	161
7th ward,	127	117	382	361	335	400	312	278	264	264	266	305	321	314	275	257
8th ward,	125	122	337	421	467	448	416	436	357	420	295	413	317	342	306	339
9th ward,	121	97	423	394	457	474	439	408	333	391	307	371	311	338	268	330
10th ward,	97	124	426	450	588	534	485	470	422	523	300	416	283	421	341	346
Total Albany,	854	852	3,003	3,125	3,371	3,331	3,024	2,988	2,700	3,335	2,570	3,378	2,591	2,890	2,370	2,461
Bern,	38	29	165	165	210	186	197	199	190	193	114	162	113	128	105	87
Bethlehem,	88	76	274	283	283	291	288	285	258	274	236	258	268	219	196	17[illegible]
Coeymans,	43	44	155	154	167	157	148	173	148	162	136	131	135	108	113	108
Guilderland,	39	55	173	163	201	192	189	176	130	142	167	142	117	105	116	11[illegible]
Knox,	19	26	96	76	111	107	109	109	109	112	70	86	67	60	42	69
New Scotland,	43	40	185	187	219	203	191	206	179	179	160	164	125	133	123	10[illegible]
Rensselaerville,	16	32	127	117	161	176	201	161	162	177	133	149	98	139	82	9[illegible]
Watervliet,	342	310	1,173	1,108	1,196	1,221	1,201	1,170	954	1,234	936	1,148	900	977	831	80[illegible]
Westerlo,	35	29	122	104	138	147	142	124	157	153	123	115	101	105	83	8[illegible]
Total,	1,517	1,493	5,473	5,482	6,057	6,011	5,690	5,591	4,987	5,961	4,645	5,733	4,524	4,864	4,060	4,09[illegible]

ALLEGANY COUNTY.

TOWNS.	Under 1. Males.	Under 1. Females.	1 and under 5. Males.	1 and under 5. Females.	5 and under 10. Males.	5 and under 10. Females.	10 and under 15. Males.	10 and under 15. Females.	15 and under 20. Males.	15 and under 20. Females.	20 and under 25. Males.	20 and under 25. Females.	25 and under 30. Males.	25 and under 30. Females.	30 and under 35. Males.	30 and under 35. Females.
Alfred,	24	29	98	95	96	118	93	98	82	88	84	78	93	73	61	5[illegible]
Allen,	12	11	53	62	69	68	67	72	62	48	44	46	42	36	29	3[illegible]
Alma,	7	12	26	18	29	26	25	14	28	21	41	20	27	17	17	1[illegible]
Almond,	15	31	112	101	131	121	126	105	96	121	105	116	97	67	75	8[illegible]
Amity,	38	46	161	125	156	158	147	139	135	136	143	122	132	127	94	18[illegible]
Andover,	29	28	100	118	150	107	115	107	71	101	72	74	60	68	69	6[illegible]
Angelica,	28	20	82	99	100	107	95	111	120	107	93	78	76	98	58	5[illegible]
Belfast,	29	24	121	133	153	153	125	132	106	110	88	81	83	73	80	8[illegible]
Birdsall,	18	15	67	44	65	54	51	58	36	41	34	27	24	36	31	2[illegible]
Bolivar,	12	22	44	61	70	73	57	56	58	51	49	41	46	42	45	4[illegible]
Burns,	19	13	57	65	72	62	62	62	62	56	56	49	52	46	46	3[illegible]
Caneadea,	25	41	144	144	182	164	142	130	121	137	129	112	94	102	99	7[illegible]
Centreville,	14	8	64	72	83	85	82	77	70	86	59	63	49	47	46	3[illegible]
Clarksville,	14	17	52	50	58	41	55	45	35	30	43	46	36	25	25	2[illegible]
Cuba,	26	16	93	94	135	112	129	135	133	111	101	99	91	65	77	7[illegible]
Friendship,	18	16	85	87	94	126	122	109	88	104	81	75	83	78	63	6[illegible]
Genesee,	11	14	51	48	60	67	53	62	49	49	44	42	37	37	33	3[illegible]
Granger,	19	11	61	49	77	81	88	72	63	73	54	54	45	41	37	3[illegible]
Grove,	19	20	70	64	84	78	78	71	54	58	55	38	55	37	34	4[illegible]
Hume,	20	29	101	98	130	124	131	127	127	106	106	103	74	63	77	8[illegible]
Independence,	12	17	62	54	55	76	80	57	76	64	45	60	54	43	45	3[illegible]
New Hudson,	16	21	72	80	99	72	93	85	82	81	77	70	52	46	48	4[illegible]
Ossian,	16	15	85	65	78	86	98	69	77	72	69	56	55	55	49	4[illegible]
Rushford,	29	23	107	86	108	106	103	115	105	116	98	116	89	88	77	7[illegible]
Scio,	54	49	187	191	201	209	166	159	168	172	163	188	175	150	137	10[illegible]
West Almond,	18	18	56	45	56	58	57	54	64	63	60	45	32	31	27	2[illegible]
Willing,	17	19	68	71	77	83	70	69	72	48	45	45	48	41	38	3[illegible]
Wirt,	18	13	85	77	95	89	108	89	87	75	70	69	66	68	54	5[illegible]
Total	577	598	2,364	2,296	2,763	2,704	2,618	2,479	2,327	2,325	2,108	2,013	1,867	1,700	1,571	1,56[illegible]

BROOME COUNTY.

TOWNS.	Under 1. Males.	Under 1. Females.	1 and under 5. Males.	1 and under 5. Females.	5 and under 10. Males.	5 and under 10. Females.	10 and under 15. Males.	10 and under 15. Females.	15 and under 20. Males.	15 and under 20. Females.	20 and under 25. Males.	20 and under 25. Females.	25 and under 30. Males.	25 and under 30. Females.	30 and under 35. Males.	30 and under 35. Females.
Barker,	15	26	59	59	71	70	76	68	76	93	68	73	52	54	41	[illegible]
Chenango,	178	163	697	685	755	756	799	795	711	812	707	771	618	539	473	47[illegible]
Colesville,	38	34	166	159	195	202	216	170	176	157	120	143	118	117	116	11[illegible]
Conklin,	40	42	170	140	154	135	180	143	142	132	114	127	112	115	93	[illegible]
Lisle,	20	20	107	83	103	110	91	102	95	92	88	66	62	61	60	7[illegible]
Maine,	25	24	125	105	136	134	124	118	114	90	84	82	78	69	60	[illegible]
Nanticoke,	14	11	47	54	38	61	64	55	57	39	47	42	43	23	20	[illegible]
Sanford,	52	34	190	165	190	200	171	186	153	157	155	152	155	126	133	[illegible]
Triangle,	16	18	91	91	111	99	118	102	107	103	77	90	76	61	63	[illegible]
Union,	26	31	164	123	168	170	139	140	128	125	100	120	84	83	89	[illegible]
Vestal,	15	29	113	116	154	146	131	124	114	95	75	62	60	95	69	[illegible]
Windsor,	35	30	185	178	179	176	153	151	125	123	124	125	127	124	129	11[illegible]
Total,	474	462	2,114	1,958	2,254	2.259	2,262	2,154	1,998	2,018	1,759	1,853	1,585	1,467	1,346	1,31[illegible]

CATTARAUGUS COUNTY.

TOWNS.	Under 1. Males.	Under 1. Females.	1 and under 5. Males.	1 and under 5. Females.	5 and under 10. Males.	5 and under 10. Females.	10 and under 15. Males.	10 and under 15. Females.	15 and under 20. Males.	15 and under 20. Females.	20 and under 25. Males.	20 and under 25. Females.	25 and under 30. Males.	25 and under 30. Females.	30 and under 35. Males.	30 and under 35. Females.
Allegany,	28	31	96	98	91	89	96	95	76	86	79	78	89	75	61	[illegible]
Ashford,	30	35	103	129	137	121	107	109	105	94	72	88	81	76	70	[illegible]
Bucktooth,	7	11	32	30	37	30	33	20	15	14	20	15	24	20	16	[illegible]
Carrolton,	16	10	37	29	41	34	31	28	26	26	26	23	14	28	19	[illegible]
Cold Spring,	10	11	40	42	51	41	45	39	28	33	32	31	23	21	27	[illegible]
Connewango,	22	18	50	68	77	80	86	85	70	87	58	62	57	55	45	[illegible]
Dayton,	18	20	65	74	84	77	78	54	52	60	48	59	48	48	42	[illegible]
East Otto,	17	27	69	64	68	73	79	84	69	65	49	68	46	47	42	[illegible]
Ellicottville,	31	32	115	109	115	128	94	101	92	90	73	100	77	79	70	[illegible]
Farmersville,	24	23	71	74	98	93	96	72	91	78	71	55	51	50	35	[illegible]
Franklinville,	23	23	106	83	94	113	96	103	82	101	83	80	64	64	60	[illegible]
Freedom,	17	25	75	68	95	80	87	66	80	71	68	78	58	62	55	[illegible]
Great Valley,	20	23	74	83	74	71	63	64	60	65	45	59	60	52	46	[illegible]

ALBANY COUNTY.—(Continued.)

TOWNS.	35 and under 40.		40 and under 45.		45 and under 50.		50 and under 60.		60 and under 70.		70 and under 80.		80 and under 90.		90 and under 100.		100 and upwards		Ages unknown.
	Males	Females.	Males.	Females	Males.	Males.	Males.	Females	Males.	Females	Males.	Females	Males	Fems	Males	Fems.	Males	Fems	
any City: 1st ward,	264	262	253	253	149	129	213	180	71	82	20	28	7	8	1	1	....	....	40
2d ward,	138	135	120	128	101	88	98	114	40	64	14	14	9	3	....	1	....	....	26
3d ward,	136	132	149	139	89	62	116	125	49	56	10	23	10	12	1	1	....	....	44
4th ward,	144	134	125	132	82	80	130	148	63	77	24	35	7	8	2	2	....	....	9
5th ward,	113	83	80	93	56	48	64	80	29	43	20	20	3	6	....	1	....	....	115
6th ward,	93	136	92	103	62	62	100	95	45	53	10	22	5	6	1	1	....	....	25
7th ward,	205	156	168	147	98	71	121	147	57	71	21	22	3	3	1	....	....	....	137
8th ward,	264	214	202	205	128	136	161	196	66	95	31	45	4	5	....	....	....	....	154
9th ward,	234	249	210	210	162	151	196	194	79	83	26	36	5	9	1	....	....	....	36
10th ward,	310	322	261	220	168	142	182	207	81	107	21	51	11	14	1	2	....	....	......
Total Albany, ...	1,901	1,823	1,660	1,630	1,095	969	1,381	1,486	580	731	197	296	64	74	8	9	....	....	586
rn, ...	81	77	70	82	63	79	118	116	59	67	25	27	13	15	1	....	....	....	33
thlehem, ...	182	139	145	120	114	115	155	136	87	67	41	39	10	6	....	2	....	1	38
eymans, ...	96	94	73	66	67	47	85	91	63	69	27	35	6	13	....	1	....	....	48
ilderland, ...	99	192	81	70	88	60	104	91	43	55	32	33	7	9	1	3	....	....	......
ox, ...	66	56	42	43	42	41	77	79	46	43	25	22	11	7	2	1	....	....	17
w Scotland, ...	97	81	81	80	70	62	106	108	58	52	34	33	4	11	2	....	....	....	5
nsselaerville, ...	96	91	85	71	57	93	138	127	75	85	36	32	14	7	1	....	....	....	56
atervliet, ...	677	639	593	528	404	379	422	478	238	267	82	99	22	21	1	2	....	....	521
esterlo, ...	88	81	58	64	53	68	107	112	68	80	25	34	8	9	3	1	....	....	29
Total, ...	3,383	3,273	2,888	2,754	2,053	1,913	2,693	2,824	1,317	1,516	524	650	159	172	19	19	....	1	1,333

ALLEGANY COUNTY.—(Continued.)

TOWNS.	35 and under 40.		40 and under 45.		45 and under 50.		50 and under 60.		60 and under 70.		70 and under 80.		80 and under 90.		90 and under 100.		100 and upwards		Ages unknown.
	Males	Females.	Males.	Females	Males.	Males.	Males.	Females	Males.	Females	Males.	Females	Males	Fems	Males	Fems.	Males	Fems	
fred, ...	59	51	41	42	32	28	49	48	35	34	11	8	1	5	....	....	....	....	......
len, ...	27	30	29	14	26	28	30	25	19	19	8	13	1	2	....	....	....	....	......
ma, ...	18	7	6	1	4	4	10	7	3	2	1	......	....	....	....	1	....	....	1
mond, ...	52	43	46	56	43	26	50	47	29	29	12	13	3	2	1	....	....	....	......
nity, ...	87	73	63	55	40	39	84	73	37	25	14	13	7	3	1	1	....	....	......
ndover, ...	59	50	46	52	39	20	48	42	32	26	10	7	1	4	1	1	....	....	8
ngelica, ...	78	59	39	37	44	30	63	57	27	24	20	14	6	1	....	2	....	....	......
lfast, ...	77	71	51	53	44	36	63	50	34	37	16	12	6	4	1	1	....	....	......
rdsall, ...	29	15	19	20	23	15	27	15	19	10	4	4	1	3	1	....	....	....	6
olivar, ...	26	31	29	13	18	20	28	19	16	10	3	1	1	....	....	....	....	....	2
irns, ...	25	33	27	21	17	26	43	27	21	18	7	8	....	....	....	....	....	....	......
neadea, ...	71	72	63	47	57	48	76	58	21	21	9	8	4	2	....	1	....	....	......
entreville, ...	36	58	40	37	30	19	46	47	34	24	9	9	7	5	1	1	....	....	6
arksville, ...	33	13	15	23	20	15	19	19	14	6	2	4	....	3	....	....	....	....	......
iba, ...	82	71	57	61	50	32	95	65	25	30	14	19	4	2	1	....	....	....	15
iendship, ...	62	64	38	44	40	32	57	67	35	36	20	16	2	6	1	....	....	....	23
enesee, ...	28	28	30	13	13	10	22	18	14	14	2	2	1	2	....	1	....	....	3
ranger, ...	44	40	28	27	17	23	56	42	27	24	11	9	3	2	....	1	....	....	......
rove, ...	39	25	27	12	15	24	34	32	18	13	13	4	....	....	....	1	....	....	4
ume, ...	68	69	55	43	46	47	70	63	50	53	12	12	3	3	....	1	....	....	......
idependence, ...	22	36	29	24	30	25	42	33	22	16	10	7	1	2	....	....	....	....	1
ew Hudson, ...	29	39	36	38	33	33	68	43	28	29	14	11	3	6	....	1	....	....	3
ssian, ...	37	28	31	34	30	16	45	35	26	22	9	4	4	4	2	....	....	....	......
ushford, ...	64	64	45	42	49	38	73	79	35	29	17	10	6	4	....	....	....	....	......
cio, ...	105	74	81	67	62	31	81	70	40	29	12	10	5	2	....	....	....	....	38
Vest Almond, ...	19	24	16	25	34	21	33	32	17	8	9	5	3	1	....	....	....	....	15
Villing, ...	26	35	33	19	25	23	36	27	13	10	6	5	....	....	....	....	....	....	26
Virt, ...	46	27	22	27	35	30	57	59	23	20	16	13	7	3	....	1	....	....	16
Total, ...	1,348	1,230	1,042	947	916	739	1,405	1,199	714	618	291	241	80	71	10	14	....	....	167

BROOME COUNTY.—(Continued.)

TOWNS.	35 and under 40.		40 and under 45.		45 and under 50.		50 and under 60.		60 and under 70.		70 and under 80.		80 and under 90.		90 and under 100.		100 and upwards		Ages unknown.
	Males	Females.	Males.	Females	Males.	Males.	Males.	Females	Males.	Females	Males.	Females	Males	Fems	Males	Fems.	Males	Fems	
Barker, ...	38	39	24	26	31	37	42	53	29	21	11	14	5	4	1	....	....	....	......
Chenango, ...	418	365	364	345	271	257	321	264	170	153	84	62	24	20	7	12	....	....	61
Colesville, ...	94	87	85	71	63	72	118	102	67	58	28	23	11	9	2	....	....	....	......
Conklin, ...	69	55	73	44	48	44	75	76	48	37	20	13	2	6	....	....	....	....	......
Lisle, ...	58	54	55	54	57	40	40	70	51	30	18	22	8	2	....	2	....	....	22
Maine, ...	52	59	54	50	54	42	67	74	11	32	17	16	5	6	1	1	....	....	3
Nanticoke, ...	17	16	19	22	15	15	19	19	17	5	5	3	....	....	....	....	....	....	6
Sanford, ...	90	85	87	65	55	46	76	66	53	40	20	14	2	....	....	....	....	....	44
Triangle, ...	59	58	32	33	34	42	75	60	28	35	15	13	4	4	2	....	....	....	8
Union, ...	63	56	76	85	68	49	66	65	48	42	30	15	4	2	4	1	....	....	4
Vestal, ...	57	59	60	50	45	34	65	55	30	29	8	15	4	6	....	....	....	....	2
Windsor, ...	80	90	57	50	30	29	55	51	44	40	9	11	1	1	1	....	....	....	7
Total, ...	1,095	1,023	986	895	771	707	1,019	955	596	522	265	221	70	60	18	16	....	....	157

CATTARAUGUS COUNTY.—(Continued.)

TOWNS.	35 and under 40.		40 and under 45.		45 and under 50.		50 and under 60.		60 and under 70.		70 and under 80.		80 and under 90.		90 and under 100.		100 and upwards		Ages unknown.
	Males	Females.	Males.	Females	Males.	Males.	Males.	Females	Males.	Females	Males.	Females	Males	Fems	Males	Fems.	Males	Fems	
Allegany, ...	41	33	47	34	30	26	54	44	21	14	5	6	3	4	....	....	....	....	6
Ashford, ...	50	56	39	45	49	33	67	58	34	34	17	13	2	1	....	....	....	....	6
Bucktooth, ...	14	20	15	13	11	8	12	7	5	6	2	......	1	....	....	....	....	....	....
Carrolton, ...	12	9	6	14	9	11	12	20	4	3	......	1	3	....	....	....	....	....	....
Cold Spring, ...	23	16	12	14	15	10	17	12	6	3	1	1	....	2	....	....	....	....	41
Conewango, ...	44	27	32	30	34	36	48	46	26	20	13	13	6	5	2	1	....	....	7
Dayton, ...	39	36	29	17	21	18	33	29	18	20	5	4	1	2	....	1	....	....	......
East Otto, ...	36	39	28	26	28	25	36	38	25	22	11	10	2	1	....	....	....	....	......
Ellicottville, ...	61	56	54	44	40	29	53	50	29	22	10	7	2	2	1	....	....	....	6
Farmersville, ...	45	40	35	31	39	26	49	49	33	26	15	10	4	4	1	2	....	....	6
Franklinville, ...	70	50	29	41	35	30	56	52	34	33	9	13	2	2	....	....	....	....	4
Freedom, ...	40	31	34	32	19	35	63	56	34	26	11	14	6	1	1	1	....	....	......
Great Valley, ...	38	26	36	21	25	24	36	28	20	11	7	15	4	2	....	....	....	....	......

CATTARAUGUS COUNTY.—(Continued.)

TOWNS.	Under 1.		1 and under 5.		5 and under 10.		10 and under 15.		15 and under 20.		20 and under 25.		25 and under 30.		30 and under 35.	
	Males.	Females.	Males.	Females.	Males.	Females.	Males.	Females.	Males.	Females.	Males.	Females.	Males.	Females.	Males.	Females.
Hinsdale,	54	40	151	141	145	138	123	108	87	99	88	106	91	88	96	85
Humphrey,	17	7	40	45	50	56	54	47	37	41	30	30	33	24	26	23
Ischua,	17	15	59	64	72	71	82	72	68	50	58	48	40	31	42	37
Leon,	12	14	62	81	81	76	80	76	81	64	55	57	54	52	45	40
Little Valley,	15	12	47	43	53	40	53	50	34	39	28	35	41	38	19	27
Lyndon,	23	10	71	60	83	73	77	75	52	42	36	41	49	43	37	42
Machias,	17	15	83	81	85	102	84	91	72	61	51	64	47	56	54	44
Mansfield,	10	8	70	54	79	60	70	86	53	57	48	60	40	32	38	43
Napoli,	14	16	69	68	70	91	58	68	67	79	61	49	50	37	46	37
New Albion,	23	26	88	85	104	105	100	96	90	73	73	79	80	61	50	49
Olean,	30	22	102	71	81	107	94	92	83	91	94	84	74	72	83	61
Otto,	11	14	52	52	73	61	68	66	58	68	69	49	35	44	33	34
Perrysburgh,	14	16	60	66	78	93	78	87	91	91	72	82	67	62	48	45
Persia,	17	12	75	58	79	82	85	67	47	71	55	49	48	55	37	33
Portville,	19	26	67	65	83	78	64	62	51	56	75	54	52	57	44	31
Randolph,	26	29	84	92	104	111	109	107	81	116	84	101	71	81	74	54
South Valley,	11	7	39	35	48	39	38	34	31	28	32	26	34	29	27	18
Yorkshire,	20	18	99	84	141	117	125	96	89	82	55	78	61	61	66	46
Total,	613	596	2,251	2,196	2,571	2,530	2,433	2,300	2,018	2,078	1,788	1,888	1,659	1,600	1,453	1,270

CAYUGA COUNTY.

TOWNS.	Under 1. Males.	Under 1. Females.	1–5 Males.	1–5 Females.	5–10 Males.	5–10 Females.	10–15 Males.	10–15 Females.	15–20 Males.	15–20 Females.	20–25 Males.	20–25 Females.	25–30 Males.	25–30 Females.	30–35 Males.	30–35 Females.
Auburn city, 1st ward,	43	38	156	120	155	144	129	137	103	151	78	124	81	127	80	103
2d ward,	22	28	96	102	104	99	86	106	84	126	82	110	85	91	69	86
3d ward,	18	24	102	88	94	131	96	108	101	115	88	126	82	105	84	89
4th ward,	47	39	136	164	170	144	148	136	108	113	204	113	204	123	188	111
Total Auburn,	130	129	490	474	523	518	459	487	396	505	452	473	452	446	421	389
Aurelius,	35	27	122	117	164	135	161	147	134	148	137	130	125	129	104	100
Brutus,	30	32	156	159	158	152	132	126	137	142	145	123	128	123	140	117
Cato,	28	24	126	105	122	130	144	128	130	124	133	120	105	99	70	78
Conquest,	35	23	95	101	127	101	111	103	107	100	87	98	81	72	71	55
Fleming,	15	10	55	55	55	60	50	61	76	51	67	51	55	56	40	47
Genoa,	30	21	91	101	112	128	101	112	125	122	125	138	87	111	88	82
Ira,	18	21	112	114	115	107	118	137	130	123	98	105	74	75	82	84
Ledyard,	29	28	96	80	131	98	115	106	94	105	72	91	66	81	71	73
Locke,	15	18	58	62	85	80	78	89	65	75	57	55	37	45	29	47
Mentz,	63	67	303	247	301	279	251	284	270	243	244	240	219	193	206	189
Moravia,	35	22	85	94	105	109	95	96	80	81	70	73	65	65	70	70
Niles,	24	20	93	90	107	103	113	106	101	97	93	90	98	97	55	54
Owasco,	15	19	58	63	85	88	78	75	65	68	57	55	37	40	29	28
Scipio,	28	25	105	102	105	101	96	90	112	109	98	97	76	78	72	70
Sempronius,	13	18	54	62	80	80	77	89	65	76	51	54	36	46	29	48
Sennett,	27	25	96	98	121	117	115	114	117	115	88	86	72	73	77	75
Springport,	37	31	108	104	97	94	209	121	106	99	110	103	119	103	88	83
Sterling,	41	30	118	111	234	216	194	190	182	178	128	130	102	97	70	68
Summer Hill,	17	17	50	51	74	72	65	66	68	65	57	56	47	49	47	48
Venice,	31	26	86	81	116	114	114	110	90	87	107	103	87	80	56	45
Victory,	30	27	104	100	120	116	137	135	120	119	88	85	74	72	60	57
Total,	726	660	2,661	2,571	3,137	2,998	3,013	2,972	2,770	2,832	2,564	2,556	2,242	2,230	1,975	1,907

CHAUTAUQUE COUNTY.

TOWNS.	Under 1. Males.	Under 1. Females.	1–5 Males.	1–5 Females.	5–10 Males.	5–10 Females.	10–15 Males.	10–15 Females.	15–20 Males.	15–20 Females.	20–25 Males.	20–25 Females.	25–30 Males.	25–30 Females.	30–35 Males.	30–35 Females.
Arkwright,	10	11	58	51	68	74	66	70	75	84	49	37	39	37	29	37
Busti,	23	25	97	101	118	129	111	124	96	118	85	96	59	57	68	79
Carroll,	19	19	76	77	90	99	86	89	71	79	56	79	64	52	52	51
Charlotte,	33	18	89	71	109	106	92	105	85	88	60	70	70	77	52	62
Chautauque,	32	23	131	119	145	145	148	144	148	148	129	137	105	87	81	85
Cherry Creek,	13	11	66	52	69	59	68	81	70	55	54	70	57	44	46	38
Clymer,	15	12	78	65	70	65	77	62	68	69	41	48	47	47	46	33
Ellery,	24	17	87	92	112	102	117	102	105	106	119	91	80	79	53	45
Ellicott,	58	46	193	206	246	241	233	217	215	238	174	237	166	176	151	129
Ellington,	20	23	97	88	127	100	123	117	100	128	82	90	70	66	56	66
French Creek,	9	13	45	44	62	51	51	37	39	39	26	39	30	28	31	23
Gerry,	20	17	63	62	70	77	70	84	68	70	56	56	50	48	38	38
Hanover,	62	40	194	199	257	255	223	232	206	260	189	188	175	172	153	153
Harmony,	38	33	160	177	224	212	196	196	200	179	164	193	135	116	105	114
Kiantone,	8	7	34	24	22	21	23	18	26	33	29	21	29	26	25	16
Mina,	16	18	58	62	74	68	62	62	54	61	44	36	31	34	31	36
Poland,	23	21	80	78	102	76	91	75	77	65	47	64	48	53	48	44
Pomfret,	145	136	519	488	476	478	482	453	431	483	492	508	578	498	438	358
Portland,	35	24	97	96	105	103	122	118	96	106	94	101	87	74	65	66
Ripley,	26	24	106	96	112	90	99	109	79	102	68	74	62	69	53	64
Sheridan,	25	25	72	102	90	80	70	78	71	98	78	71	69	83	64	69
Sherman,	27	16	63	47	97	92	67	84	61	75	55	67	60	62	38	44
Stockton,	13	12	83	75	84	101	109	97	92	86	96	73	63	67	59	55
Villenova,	25	17	68	67	93	92	84	72	69	73	63	66	61	60	52	51
Westfield,	37	57	143	161	168	164	189	193	194	202	185	156	129	150	124	124
Total,	756	665	2,757	2,700	3,190	3,080	3,059	3,019	2,796	3,045	2,535	2,668	2,364	2,262	1,958	1,880

CHEMUNG COUNTY.

TOWNS.	Under 1. Males.	Under 1. Females.	1–5 Males.	1–5 Females.	5–10 Males.	5–10 Females.	10–15 Males.	10–15 Females.	15–20 Males.	15–20 Females.	20–25 Males.	20–25 Females.	25–30 Males.	25–30 Females.	30–35 Males.	30–35 Females.
Big Flats,	21	30	90	120	124	130	108	117	98	88	92	82	83	83	70	55
Catlin,	18	27	92	87	92	116	116	88	66	96	67	68	62	55	47	58
Chemung,	31	43	166	152	210	184	192	164	149	159	121	122	114	119	83	85
Elmira,	141	119	462	452	494	462	401	444	377	517	391	544	451	458	402	369
Erin,	13	19	76	91	88	74	73	67	58	68	48	51	70	30	28	27

CATTARAUGUS COUNTY.—(CONTINUED.)

TOWNS.	35 and under 40.		40 and under 45.		45 and under 50.		50 and under 60.		60 and under 70.		70 and under 80.		80 and under 90.		90 and under 100.		100 and upwards		Ages unknown.
	Males	Females.	Males.	Females	Males.	Females.	Males.	Females	Males.	Females	Males.	Females	Males	Fems	Males	Fems.	Males	Fems	
Hinsdale,	55	65	71	56	37	34	64	46	28	14	9	7	....	2	....	....	....	1	......
Humphrey,	20	21	13	16	20	14	31	21	18	9	5	6	....	4	....	....	....	....	1
Ischua,	17	27	29	18	23	22	43	37	24	15	10	8	1	1	....	....	....	....	2
Leon,	38	38	27	28	26	35	63	40	31	21	17	13	5	6	....	1	....	....	11
Little Valley,	29	17	22	21	12	15	31	24	21	14	6	5	1	....	....	....	....	....	9
Lyndon,	31	25	34	24	32	31	35	31	20	18	11	10	....	3	....	....	....	....	4
Machias,	34	45	32	44	29	22	42	36	18	21	15	9	3	3	....	1	....	....	5
Mansfield,	39	28	25	31	34	29	36	27	15	21	15	11	2	1	....	....	....	....	3
Napoli,	23	38	25	38	32	33	45	44	15	18	10	12	3	4	1	....	....	....	1
New Albion,	43	42	24	34	35	42	50	38	28	20	7	9	....	....	....	1	....	....	7
Olean,	58	51	35	37	42	34	35	17	13	14	5	8	....	2	....	....	....	....	19
Otto,	30	31	24	25	37	26	38	32	24	15	8	10	3	4	....	....	....	....	......
Perrysburgh,	47	38	24	30	43	37	53	45	33	22	13	10	6	5	....	....	....	....	......
Persia,	45	44	30	30	37	23	29	25	17	18	14	9	....	2	....	....	....	....	11
Portville,	35	41	30	26	25	11	36	22	15	14	6	6	2	2	....	....	....	....	9
Randolph,	31	40	37	29	49	29	54	55	24	24	13	9	1	3	....	....	....	....	1
South Valley,	22	17	8	7	16	8	6	10	7	3	1	1	....	1	1	....	....	....	2
Yorkshire,	62	48	36	45	37	38	63	52	39	36	10	11	4	4	....	....	....	....	5
Total,	1,172	1,095	922	901	921	794	1,290	1,091	679	557	281	261	67	73	7	8	....	1	166

CAYUGA COUNTY.—(CONTINUED.)

TOWNS.	35 and under 40. Males	Females	40 and under 45. Males	Females	45 and under 50. Males	Females	50 and under 60. Males	Females	60 and under 70. Males	Females	70 and under 80. Males	Females	80 and under 90. Males	Fems	90 and under 100. Males	Fems	100 and upwards Males	Fems	Ages unknown.
Auburn city, 1st ward,	75	81	64	82	60	58	59	60	29	33	9	16	4	2	1	1	....	....	1
2d ward,	68	78	47	58	45	47	58	59	25	18	15	17	7	2	1	1	....	....	......
3d ward,	77	69	64	59	44	36	44	56	28	36	6	8	....	2	....	1	....	....	4
4th ward,	178	83	162	68	101	54	135	65	56	46	15	20	2	3	....	1	....	....	28
Total Auburn, ...	398	311	337	267	250	195	296	240	138	133	45	61	13	9	2	4	....	....	33
Aurelius,	86	65	67	55	55	81	98	41	50	21	21	6	3	3	1	....	1	1	5
Brutus,	120	72	92	75	61	55	93	85	47	39	17	29	7	8	....	1	1	....	4
Cato,	65	60	53	46	52	40	71	78	42	35	17	16	6	5	....	....	....	....	......
Conquest,	48	50	46	56	47	40	63	59	30	30	11	10	6	4	....	2	....	....	3
Fleming,	40	36	24	31	25	16	44	47	35	25	15	9	4	1	....	....	....	....	8
Genoa,	70	72	61	55	70	61	105	109	56	55	18	18	9	13	....	2	....	....	4
Ira,	66	53	47	58	44	40	84	69	52	58	17	17	4	4	1	1	....	....	5
Ledyard,	60	70	68	52	36	39	70	71	52	56	30	19	2	9	....	2	....	....	4
Locke,	45	38	45	40	39	19	48	47	19	27	12	10	2	3	1	....	....	....	3
Mentz,	174	155	138	134	128	97	159	142	108	83	45	46	20	12	2	2	....	....	14
Moravia,	55	55	46	49	49	49	63	63	40	42	.30	30	15	12	2	2	....	....	2
Niles,	61	62	42	40	52	49	66	64	45	42	16	15	4	4	....	2	....	....	7
Owasco,	45	49	44	47	39	44	48	48	18	17	13	16	2	3	1	2	....	....	7
Scipio,	67	62	33	35	38	40	60	56	39	34	24	21	8	7	1	1	....	....	5
Sempronius,	45	37	40	41	39	18	48	48	19	26	12	8	2	2	1	....	....	....	5
Sennett,	58	55	55	52	45	46	91	86	61	57	24	21	6	6	....	....	....	....	3
Springport,	67	60	62	55	56	51	48	45	39	34	16	14	1	2	....	1	....	....	8
Sterling,	84	86	100	104	90	86	82	85	74	60	32	30	6	7	1	1	....	....	7
Summer Hill,	30	28	29	27	25	26	47	27	28	29	11	9	8	6	....	....	....	....	5
Venice,	63	58	46	42	45	40	80	74	44	40	26	22	12	8	1	....	....	....	5
Victory,	63	60	51	48	42	46	58	54	46	43	22	20	7	6	....	....	....	....	6
Total,	1,810	1,594	1,526	1,409	1,327	1,178	1,822	1,638	1,082	986	474	447	147	134	14	23	2	1	143

CHAUTAUQUE COUNTY.—(CONTINUED.)

TOWNS.	35 and under 40. Males	Females	40 and under 45. Males	Females	45 and under 50. Males	Females	50 and under 60. Males	Females	60 and under 70. Males	Females	70 and under 80. Males	Females	80 and under 90. Males	Fems	90 and under 100. Males	Fems	100 and upwards Males	Fems	Ages unknown.
Arkwright,	28	30	22	24	32	31	49	34	22	12	5	9	3	2	1	1	....	....	10
Busti,	45	45	44	52	52	30	56	47	59	56	18	16	6	4	1	....	....	....	3
Carroll,	42	44	28	31	26	23	55	35	24	25	6	5	1	1	1	2	....	....	......
Charlotte,	67	49	33	39	42	37	62	45	35	45	11	14	3	....	....	....	....	....	3
Chautauque,	76	75	57	64	69	58	100	84	65	58	29	23	4	12	....	....	....	....	10
Cherry Creek,	34	32	25	32	31	27	52	50	30	27	11	12	1	1	....	....	....	....	8
Clymer,	23	35	34	30	32	26	45	41	20	15	10	6	1	2	....	1	....	....	......
Ellery,	51	53	34	51	43	45	74	59	51	36	14	10	7	4	....	1	....	....	1
Ellicott,	121	104	100	102	86	73	127	103	56	43	20	21	5	7	1	1	....	....	39
Ellington,	55	59	44	44	51	34	69	83	42	38	24	13	9	4	....	2	....	....	6
French Creek,	28	26	23	14	12	17	20	20	12	10	8	3	1	3	....	....	....	....	2
Gerry,	30	35	34	34	32	26	54	36	30	25	15	12	3	1	....	....	....	....	4
Hanover,	137	110	93	118	94	83	134	120	87	68	35	31	11	7	....	1	....	....	14
Harmony,	106	93	72	86	94	93	134	122	72	56	33	27	6	3	1	1	....	....	2
Kiantone,	14	13	7	6	5	9	17	22	14	13	3	3	1	1	....	....	....	....	......
Mina,	32	33	24	17	24	22	39	31	20	17	10	11	1	3	....	1	....		4
Poland,	33	41	32	33	35	15	48	35	20	14	13	7	1	2	1	....	....	....	3
Pomfret,	307	248	257	187	173	179	247	222	137	102	61	54	5	8	4	1	....	....	2
Portland,	50	69	60	39	36	32	69	72	42	42	18	16	2	....	....	....	....	....	......
Ripley,	39	40	45	42	45	45	72	56	27	29	11	7	7	5	....	....	....	....	......
Sheridan,	51	44	39	43	32	25	53	57	32	35	14	15	3	3	....	....	....	....	......
Sherman,	41	39	28	30	28	31	52	42	21	21	7	6	2	....	1	....	....	....	10
Stockton,	50	61	40	34	46	47	62	57	54	32	14	16	3	6	....	....	....	....	1
Villenova,	38	34	29	37	29	32	64	53	27	23	15	13	3	1	....	....	....	....	2
Westfield,	91	72	78	91	76	92	138	107	82	55	35	33	4	4	....	....	....	....	4
Total,	1,589	1,484	1,282	1,280	1,225	1,132	1,892	1,633	1,081	897	440	383	93	84	11	12	....	....	128

CHEMUNG COUNTY.—(CONTINUED.)

TOWNS.	35 and under 40. Males	Females	40 and under 45. Males	Females	45 and under 50. Males	Females	50 and under 60. Males	Females	60 and under 70. Males	Females	70 and under 80. Males	Females	80 and under 90. Males	Fems	90 and under 100. Males	Fems	100 and upwards Males	Fems	Ages unknown.
Big Flats,	61	50	42	44	38	36	44	44	35	29	12	5	2	6	1	....	....	....	13
Catlin,	45	29	40	39	30	31	48	34	22	21	10	0	2	1	....	....	....	1	4
Chemung,	80	71	60	65	62	40	81	69	59	48	17	16	6	7	2	....	....	....	8
Elmira,	294	275	252	223	160	141	179	193	88	93	30	40	5	10	2	1	....	....	16
Erin,	24	33	31	26	26	27	38	34	21	18	7	6	2	4	....	....	....	....	3

CHEMUNG COUNTY.

TOWNS.	Under 1.		1 and under 5.		5 and under 10.		10 and under 15.		15 and under 20.		20 and under 25.		25 and under 30.		30 and under 35.	
	Males.	Females.	Males.	Females.	Males.	Females.	Males.	Females.	Males.	Females.	Males.	Females.	Males.	Females.	Males.	Females.
Horseheads,	33	35	128	155	168	146	132	138	148	160	152	146	123	114	116	92
Southport,	74	79	279	269	293	265	256	264	216	236	222	226	203	220	189	143
Van Etten,	14	24	93	90	123	110	95	96	84	84	66	65	53	59	50	45
Veteran,	46	47	155	150	178	178	152	160	143	138	139	122	125	140	115	100
Total,	391	423	1,541	1,566	1,770	1,665	1,525	1,538	1,339	1,546	1,298	1,426	1,284	1,287	1,100	974

CHENANGO COUNTY.

TOWNS.	Under 1.		1 and under 5.		5 and under 10.		10 and under 15.		15 and under 20.		20 and under 25.		25 and under 30.		30 and under 35.	
	Males.	Females.	Males.	Females.	Males.	Females.	Males.	Females.	Males.	Females.	Males.	Females.	Males.	Females.	Males.	Females.
Bainbridge,	16	18	184	185	212	208	205	207	163	169	132	133	109	112	127	123
Columbus,	9	8	63	64	48	47	77	75	72	73	71	70	47	45	36	35
Coventry,	22	20	75	78	100	102	88	86	90	92	76	75	52	53	67	68
German,	20	7	42	45	46	48	53	52	44	45	25	23	39	41	25	26
Greene,	54	50	175	179	222	214	213	208	176	173	159	164	135	128	143	140
Guilford,	28	27	103	110	149	127	138	146	116	138	127	130	111	99	101	100
Lincklaen,	17	16	62	65	69	72	71	73	63	66	47	51	25	29	31	33
Macdonough,	17	9	78	79	80	97	87	83	73	86	65	75	52	43	46	53
New Berlin,	30	26	115	118	140	122	129	149	129	150	102	143	91	87	80	104
North Norwich,	11	8	66	51	75	70	72	60	49	62	66	41	34	48	29	49
Norwich,	48	44	176	179	195	216	194	209	210	254	206	246	209	226	166	153
Otselic,	27	18	81	97	114	105	112	97	94	78	82	71	58	73	62	55
Oxford,	33	33	135	156	170	174	177	160	137	169	156	164	122	112	104	118
Pharsalia,	17	15	62	54	66	72	74	72	70	74	61	42	44	41	40	41
Pitcher,	15	16	71	43	75	69	83	69	75	59	55	63	45	50	39	40
Plymouth,	12	21	68	69	91	92	104	91	85	84	55	70	58	59	54	54
Preston,	8	6	46	44	57	65	48	61	52	45	46	41	38	53	37	37
Sherburne,	37	26	124	125	169	158	152	146	135	140	118	115	88	125	96	98
Smithville,	24	18	87	73	101	108	89	97	102	99	86	83	54	60	56	47
Smyrna,	21	19	80	77	107	106	119	108	85	104	77	83	68	64	59	78
Total,	466	405	1,893	1,801	2,286	2,272	2,285	2,249	2,020	2,160	1,812	1,883	1,479	1,548	1,398	1,452

CLINTON COUNTY.

TOWNS.	Under 1.		1 and under 5.		5 and under 10.		10 and under 15.		15 and under 20.		20 and under 25.		25 and under 30.		30 and under 35.	
	Males.	Females.	Males.	Females.	Males.	Females.	Males.	Females.	Males.	Females.	Males.	Females.	Males.	Females.	Males.	Females.
Au Sable,	57	53	243	238	279	279	247	288	199	226	150	173	114	146	106	112
Beekmantown,	31	40	157	177	236	195	202	204	176	163	109	135	96	84	85	72
Black Brook,	66	72	231	252	247	238	178	177	143	137	115	127	123	114	122	98
Champlain,	107	131	388	414	472	428	406	399	285	364	247	311	220	217	198	184
Chazy,	71	73	292	286	348	309	291	322	217	228	171	197	150	155	128	127
Clinton,	19	29	104	89	122	127	102	89	75	62	40	41	36	44	35	32
Dannemora,	......	1	40	40	38	30	30	23	53	23	88	27	69	23	49	19
Ellenburgh,	25	32	114	103	132	138	120	108	96	83	82	82	74	58	49	46
Mooers,	51	54	245	255	291	278	224	233	196	191	128	145	132	162	109	95
Peru,	56	54	228	212	260	248	246	230	171	192	164	159	115	106	108	104
Plattsburgh,	88	107	396	389	406	405	365	367	302	343	282	363	208	253	206	196
Saranac,	60	42	268	196	235	220	199	196	165	146	142	127	123	110	99	80
Schuyler's Falls,	23	26	108	106	142	134	123	138	120	118	89	88	62	59	45	52
Total,	654	714	2,814	2,757	3,208	3,029	2,733	2,774	2,198	2,276	1,807	1,975	1,522	1,531	1,339	1,217

COLUMBIA COUNTY.

TOWNS.	Under 1.		1 and under 5.		5 and under 10.		10 and under 15.		15 and under 20.		20 and under 25.		25 and under 30.		30 and under 35.	
	Males.	Females.	Males.	Females.	Males.	Females.	Males.	Females.	Males.	Females.	Males.	Females.	Males.	Females.	Males.	Females.
Ancram,	24	13	83	97	107	109	141	108	100	86	93	103	70	52	68	67
Austerlitz,	19	16	85	73	87	87	105	93	69	78	50	69	46	47	42	69
Canaan,	23	32	103	83	95	105	105	84	77	91	95	71	72	71	70	69
Chatham,	60	45	195	169	238	200	195	210	184	205	178	196	163	188	180	154
Claverack,	23	33	161	150	194	182	192	194	186	196	164	156	144	167	95	124
Clermont,	7	12	44	55	62	48	73	57	66	54	47	54	48	40	42	45
Copake,	20	28	88	77	95	98	117	56	82	84	70	83	66	69	76	52
Gallatin,	21	21	94	100	88	93	113	85	83	78	65	58	53	54	43	46
Germantown,	15	15	58	64	66	69	80	65	60	73	59	52	42	45	35	29
Ghent,	31	39	142	109	141	134	118	145	112	120	138	146	123	98	91	95
Greenport,	23	19	83	76	80	83	78	76	74	70	60	75	53	60	45	50
Hillsdale,	21	24	113	100	138	135	132	118	107	128	87	88	74	69	86	93
Hudson city, 1st ward,	23	21	83	64	65	63	73	71	75	94	69	89	63	77	60	50
2d ward,	26	28	86	89	89	115	82	111	75	78	80	68	64	84	61	67
3d ward,	17	16	84	79	90	91	92	121	85	116	88	111	65	76	55	65
4th ward,	27	28	104	106	98	113	103	103	75	94	60	119	62	91	53	76
Total Hudson,	93	93	357	338	342	382	350	406	310	382	297	387	254	328	229	258
Kinderhook,	43	43	158	191	212	216	222	211	184	239	184	242	133	177	127	136
Livingston,	35	30	94	121	114	131	139	118	107	130	97	88	88	82	64	58
New Lebanon,	23	20	99	91	122	119	146	102	132	126	93	109	78	70	74	84
Stockport,	25	29	78	93	85	89	109	109	71	108	80	92	61	65	57	52
Stuyvesant,	21	27	106	94	134	115	114	102	88	98	89	118	83	77	62	69
Taghkanic	22	26	94	98	124	110	112	126	86	92	61	74	50	66	63	62
Total,	549	565	2,235	2,179	2,524	2,505	2,641	2,495	2,178	2,438	2,007	2,261	1,701	1,825	1,549	1,612

CORTLAND COUNTY

TOWNS.	Under 1.		1 and under 5.		5 and under 10.		10 and under 15.		15 and under 20.		20 and under 25.		25 and under 30.		30 and under 35.	
	Males.	Females.	Males.	Females.	Males.	Females.	Males.	Females.	Males.	Females.	Males.	Females.	Males.	Females.	Males.	Females.
Cincinnatus,	13	9	47	52	50	61	62	65	65	69	59	40	40	43	35	44
Cortlandville,	49	33	209	179	239	208	228	220	201	282	200	239	190	196	141	166
Freetown,	13	13	49	54	66	60	62	61	51	47	41	44	29	34	31	32
Harford,	15	11	50	45	57	53	66	52	50	60	43	49	34	3	39	31
Homer,	32	45	160	140	203	195	186	202	210	242	185	209	120	142	127	152
Lapeer,	9	5	47	38	36	58	54	27	27	49	42	31	38	31	21	27
Marathon,	22	17	89	69	72	89	85	66	55	68	58	71	65	56	55	51
Preble,	17	16	50	53	63	61	66	65	59	63	59	54	54	55	42	49

CHEMUNG COUNTY.—(CONTINUED.)

TOWNS.	35 and under 40.		40 and under 45.		45 and under 50.		50 and under 60.		60 and under 70.		70 and under 80.		80 and under 90.		90 and under 100.		100 and upwards		Ages unknown.
	Males.	Females.	Males.	Females.	Males.	Females	Males.	Females	Males.	Females	Males.	Females.	Males	Fems	Males	Fems	Males	Fems	
Horseheads, ...	64	69	63	64	62	47	89	66	42	37	23	13	4	2	....	....	1	....	16
Southport, ...	138	121	109	101	85	81	116	103	79	60	21	17	5	7	1	....	....	....	1
Van Etten, ...	50	45	41	31	37	28	39	36	21	22	13	4	2	2	....	....	....	....	......
Veteran, ...	76	66	83	68	57	62	83	86	47	41	20	17	4	7	1	1	....	....	.....
Total, ...	832	759	721	661	557	493	717	665	414	369	153	124	32	40	7	2	1	1	61

CHENANGO COUNTY.—(CONTINUED.)

TOWNS.	35 and under 40.		40 and under 45.		45 and under 50.		50 and under 60.		60 and under 70.		70 and under 80.		80 and under 90.		90 and under 100.		100 and upwards		Ages unknown.
	Males.	Females.	Males.	Females.	Males.	Females	Males.	Females	Males.	Females	Males.	Females.	Males	Fems	Males	Fems	Males	Fems	
Bainbridge, ...	92	94	83	82	79	76	144	142	82	81	34	35	17	18	2	1	....	....	12
Columbus, ...	41	40	39	38	31	32	67	65	27	28	30	29	11	10	1	1	....	....	1
Coventry, ...	62	61	39	38	44	46	50	51	45	44	23	22	4	3	3	2	....	....	3
German, ...	19	18	17	18	15	16	23	22	19	20	17	18	1	1	1	....	....	....	......
Greene, ...	125	127	115	109	90	86	133	122	69	67	43	48	18	15	2	1	....	....	14
Guilford, ...	83	68	66	82	66	55	100	101	55	58	19	31	9	5	....	3	....	....	1
Lincklaen, ...	34	38	15	15	31	31	48	52	22	24	10	12	....	1	....	....	....	....	8
Macdonough, ...	41	35	34	31	22	35	58	47	29	28	17	13	2	2	....	....	....	....	......
New Berlin, ...	88	84	65	79	66	58	99	75	47	48	32	25	9	11	2	3	....	....	1
North Norwich, ...	35	36	33	27	27	21	38	26	27	30	17	11	5	1	....	....	....	....	1
Norwich, ...	139	129	86	98	106	94	133	129	78	81	44	41	10	5	....	....	....	....	5
Otselic, ...	54	50	36	32	38	37	75	77	34	22	13	16	7	3	....	1	....	....	2
Oxford, ...	79	99	88	97	95	89	100	116	70	66	37	31	13	10	1	....	....	....	5
Pharsalia, ...	26	23	24	29	26	23	45	31	19	29	17	9	3	2	....	1	....	....	......
Pitcher, ...	27	41	40	33	32	34	46	62	30	26	12	14	7	9	....	1	....	....	......
Plymouth, ...	37	44	45	45	42	35	59	50	28	30	24	23	6	5	1	....	....	....	......
Preston, ...	32	29	27	36	36	24	37	41	26	24	18	14	4	8	....	4	....	....	......
Sherburne, ...	87	100	81	79	77	78	89	104	67	69	36	34	8	11	....	1	1	....	3
Smithville, ...	50	58	49	37	33	43	58	55	26	23	17	17	4	6	1	....	....	....	......
Smyrna, ...	66	69	42	50	51	44	65	76	46	36	25	25	9	7	....	....	....	....	......
Total, ...	1,217	1,243	1,024	1,055	1,007	957	1,467	1,444	846	834	485	468	147	133	14	19	1	....	56

CLINTON COUNTY.—(CONTINUED.)

TOWNS.	35 and under 40.		40 and under 45.		45 and under 50.		50 and under 60.		60 and under 70.		70 and under 80.		80 and under 90.		90 and under 100.		100 and upwards		Ages unknown.
	Males.	Females.	Males.	Females.	Males.	Females	Males.	Females	Males.	Females	Males.	Females.	Males	Fems	Males	Fems	Males	Fems	
Au Sable, ...	90	102	104	79	82	72	108	101	57	46	17	20	2	5	....	2	....	1	5
Beekmantown, ...	60	76	66	72	58	55	106	100	59	48	25	23	10	8	3	1	1	....	......
Black Brook, ...	77	82	84	57	65	38	67	50	25	16	12	5	1	4	....	1	....	....	1
Champlain, ...	176	165	149	131	121	103	152	131	99	90	44	33	8	8	....	....	....	1	15
Chazy, ...	127	128	78	98	84	70	144	114	89	81	34	36	8	3	....	1	....	....	2
Clinton, ...	26	23	24	32	30	28	49	35	29	18	15	9	....	....	....	....	....	....	7
Dannemora, ...	37	9	29	9	25	8	28	9	10	1	3	1	....	....	....	....	....	....	1
Ellenburgh, ...	50	47	36	38	40	35	53	43	24	25	10	4	2	1	....	1	....	....	......
Mooers, ...	93	84	88	83	58	57	104	75	65	57	25	29	8	5	2	....	....	....	......
Peru, ...	91	102	73	86	82	68	88	88	72	45	25	28	5	10	3	....	....	....	1
Plattsburg, ...	148	172	131	111	107	107	196	155	106	73	46	29	7	9	1	1	....	....	5
Saranac, ...	95	84	80	66	57	43	78	43	38	34	15	8	....	4	....	....	....	....	5
Schuyler's Falls, ...	48	48	38	44	41	42	63	63	45	30	21	11	6	2	....	2	....	....	......
Total, ...	1,118	1,122	980	906	850	726	1,236	1,007	718	564	292	236	57	59	9	9	1	2	42

COLUMBIA COUNTY.—(CONTINUED.)

TOWNS.	35 and under 40.		40 and under 45.		45 and under 50.		50 and under 60.		60 and under 70.		70 and under 80.		80 and under 90.		90 and under 100.		100 and upwards		Ages unknown.
	Males.	Females.	Males.	Females.	Males.	Females	Males.	Females	Males.	Females	Males.	Females.	Males	Fems	Males	Fems	Males	Fems	
Ancram, ...	40	49	52	37	46	45	60	55	24	35	15	12	4	4	1	....	....	....	1
Austerlitz, ...	43	55	54	44	43	40	81	67	42	43	24	29	6	8	....	3	....	....	1
Canaan, ...	72	61	60	63	54	43	71	81	53	58	28	32	9	12	2	1	....	....	......
Chatham, ...	140	134	118	100	95	97	159	149	71	86	32	32	16	20	2	4	....	....	8
Claverack, ...	115	106	90	88	72	80	116	112	63	77	33	39	6	5	....	....	....	....	......
Clermont, ...	30	24	32	29	15	29	27	39	30	26	11	5	4	3	....	....	....	....	......
Copake, ...	57	39	44	43	43	29	39	40	21	34	15	16	2	3	....	....	....	....	1
Gallatin, ...	57	52	35	35	32	27	44	42	28	26	17	15	4	6	1	1	....	....	......
Germantown, ...	39	33	28	23	21	27	46	33	14	13	8	14	2	3	....	....	....	....	......
Ghent, ...	74	67	64	66	54	56	88	103	48	50	33	22	10	11	1	....	....	....	8
Greenport, ...	44	43	25	29	24	25	50	39	21	29	17	16	4	4	....	....	....	....	8
Hillsdale, ...	64	75	74	62	57	53	77	69	43	57	20	17	7	5	1	....	....	....	......
Hudson city, 1st ward,	29	40	42	42	32	39	42	59	26	34	11	16	3	3	....	1	....	....	1
2d ward,	46	58	60	56	41	37	42	48	21	36	6	9	3	5	1	....	....	....	3
3d ward,	58	60	50	51	38	48	55	60	26	35	6	17	4	5	....	....	....	....	......
4th ward,	66	57	41	48	34	46	54	49	35	42	11	18	2	4	1	1	....	....	......
Total Hudson, ...	199	215	193	197	145	170	193	216	108	147	34	60	12	17	2	2	....	....	4
Kinderhook, ...	106	136	128	115	74	83	126	157	75	77	20	27	5	11	....	1	....	....	5
Livingston, ...	61	55	44	49	55	44	68	70	42	38	17	18	....	5	....	....	....	....	2
New Lebanon, ...	58	79	71	74	56	65	92	97	57	73	42	44	8	24	....	....	....	....	1
Stockport, ...	35	41	34	40	36	42	64	48	22	27	9	7	6	2	....	....	....	....	5
Stuyvesant, ...	61	60	44	53	58	28	60	66	28	25	18	22	8	8	....	1	....	....	......
Taghkanic, ...	55	52	51	26	32	21	30	34	28	31	15	13	3	3	2	3	....	....	......
Total, ...	1,350	1,376	1,241	1,173	1,012	1,004	1,491	1,517	821	952	408	440	116	154	12	16	....	....	44

CORTLAND COUNTY.—(CONTINUED.)

TOWNS.	35 and under 40.		40 and under 45.		45 and under 50.		50 and under 60.		60 and under 70.		70 and under 80.		80 and under 90.		90 and under 100.		100 and upwards		Ages unknown.
	Males.	Females.	Males.	Females.	Males.	Females	Males.	Females	Males.	Females	Males.	Females.	Males	Fems	Males	Fems	Males	Fems	
Cincinnatus, ...	27	40	36	30	25	25	40	43	31	29	15	12	5	4	1	....	....	....	2
Cortlandville, ...	137	151	121	123	105	89	130	148	98	93	56	56	19	12	1	3	....	....	7
Freetown, ...	32	30	21	24	25	18	41	31	9	14	11	7	3	2	....	....	....	....	......
Harford, ...	26	20	20	23	21	17	29	27	16	15	8	8	3	3	....	....	....	....	......
Homer, ...	96	112	97	113	105	109	134	145	92	97	39	53	10	20	2	2	....	....	3
Lapeer, ...	24	17	16	23	14	16	28	25	16	13	10	5	1	1	....	1	....	....	......
Marathon, ...	38	36	36	31	34	33	40	31	18	24	17	10	2	3	....	....	....	....	......
Preble, ...	52	44	35	32	24	26	43	41	29	30	16	14	3	2	2	....	....	....	......

CORTLAND COUNTY.—(Continued.)

TOWNS.	Under 1.		1 and under 5.		5 and under 10.		10 and under 15.		15 and under 20.		20 and under 25.		25 and under 30.		30 and under 35.	
	Males.	Females	Males.	Females	Males.	Females	Males.	Females.	Males.	Females	Males.	Females.	Males.	Females.	Males	Females.
Scott,	15	12	73	58	76	80	74	80	77	57	61	56	59	40	46	45
Solon,	21	10	56	45	55	46	75	71	68	64	53	54	29	32	34	31
Taylor,	13	17	79	57	74	73	80	74	66	61	49	44	43	52	32	39
Truxton,	56	48	193	190	216	230	200	198	164	166	140	166	151	135	111	111
Virgil,	31	23	117	114	143	136	120	137	119	133	92	93	61	87	96	73
Willet,	13	15	54	57	47	55	64	51	48	44	44	49	30	39	40	30
Total,	319	274	1. 273	1, 151	1, 397	1, 405	1, 422	1, 369	1, 260	1, 405	1, 126	1, 199	943	977	850	881

DELAWARE COUNTY.

TOWNS.	Under 1. Males.	Under 1. Females	1 and under 5. Males.	1 and under 5. Females	5 and under 10. Males.	5 and under 10. Females	10 and under 15. Males.	10 and under 15. Females.	15 and under 20. Males.	15 and under 20. Females	20 and under 25. Males.	20 and under 25. Females.	25 and under 30. Males.	25 and under 30. Females.	30 and under 35. Males	30 and under 35. Females.
Andes,	38	23	176	137	181	159	171	172	146	148	120	110	100	101	85	73
Bovina,	18	9	72	48	70	66	78	79	85	70	63	63	44	42	39	44
Colchester,	34	39	152	128	164	169	134	148	133	123	109	104	118	96	92	61
Davenport,	19	21	117	116	153	146	121	155	119	131	116	92	88	89	90	82
Delhi,	38	24	136	125	176	164	163	143	134	172	121	133	90	106	76	87
Franklin,	43	40	161	146	186	168	167	164	162	177	126	163	121	117	113	130
Hamden,	27	24	114	92	134	133	124	120	91	100	76	71	71	68	57	57
Hancock,	46	45	181	152	177	173	146	136	113	111	113	136	149	99	112	82
Harpersfield,	13	24	65	58	78	83	82	90	83	84	75	76	66	56	46	55
Kortright,	18	23	108	98	104	122	103	118	93	123	91	102	69	87	72	62
Masonville,	21	19	94	81	99	91	108	84	74	85	89	67	56	65	57	49
Meredith,	11	26	82	73	83	98	98	81	74	83	51	55	53	64	49	62
Middletown,	47	57	183	178	201	205	191	180	142	155	111	149	120	114	100	71
Roxbury,	34	26	124	103	158	161	165	125	153	143	103	129	87	113	83	87
Sidney,	14	15	88	80	102	106	128	114	94	88	88	77	69	75	72	69
Stamford,	17	13	87	66	77	99	101	82	67	79	68	85	53	58	51	56
Tompkins,	34	45	204	214	212	204	209	108	169	158	161	165	125	145	127	126
Walton,	36	33	135	121	127	135	150	128	123	137	93	118	90	81	74	85
Total,	508	506	2, 279	2, 016	2, 482	2. 482	2, 439	2, 207	2, 055	2, 167	1, 774	1, 895	1, 569	1, 576	1, 395	1, 338

DUTCHESS COUNTY.

TOWNS.	Under 1. Males.	Under 1. Females	1 and under 5. Males.	1 and under 5. Females	5 and under 10. Males.	5 and under 10. Females	10 and under 15. Males.	10 and under 15. Females.	15 and under 20. Males.	15 and under 20. Females	20 and under 25. Males.	20 and under 25. Females.	25 and under 30. Males.	25 and under 30. Females.	30 and under 35. Males	30 and under 35. Females.
Amenia,	31	26	111	101	94	124	102	116	102	112	120	105	121	101	80	89
Beekman,	17	17	65	71	81	78	84	56	65	79	54	66	43	46	41	57
Clinton,	27	15	104	82	89	98	110	90	99	80	87	95	65	80	71	67
Dover,	27	14	83	94	105	101	94	108	90	104	105	102	83	71	80	78
East Fishkill,	47	36	123	157	151	131	119	149	143	148	129	150	112	99	96	99
Fishkill,	104	111	456	449	484	494	514	464	470	532	414	509	313	377	302	336
Hyde Park,	47	34	130	124	128	142	127	122	111	133	118	131	103	114	91	103
La Grange,	12	15	78	85	124	98	106	104	84	96	67	95	51	79	57	86
Milan,	21	21	78	90	91	74	99	87	69	84	79	80	55	52	42	65
North East,	22	32	73	69	96	106	99	99	87	108	88	101	80	66	81	66
Pawling,	32	23	90	90	98	105	107	91	81	93	86	83	74	82	71	65
Pine Plains,	13	15	81	51	85	72	87	81	64	77	65	73	65	64	58	48
Pleasant Valley,	17	15	73	82	104	102	113	84	89	100	70	93	60	82	62	82
Poughkeepsie,	26	38	166	164	181	151	216	183	154	178	137	159	101	123	104	129
Poughkeepsie city:																
1st ward,	82	68	232	239	228	244	195	218	170	218	157	231	180	220	182	174
2d ward,	50	25	120	114	138	159	141	128	115	182	84	196	122	172	86	109
3d ward,	65	47	200	219	234	195	218	206	168	163	108	146	125	162	125	129
4th ward,	25	35	117	94	125	133	134	158	127	178	110	184	81	107	79	109
Total Poughkeepsie,	222	175	669	666	725	731	688	710	580	741	459	757	508	661	472	521
Red Hook,	56	52	212	199	211	229	222	178	184	183	164	191	161	155	160	148
Rhinebeck,	44	32	120	142	166	139	157	143	152	178	149	171	131	138	124	106
Stanford,	22	26	115	101	108	111	114	111	108	116	118	116	93	87	78	76
Union Vale,	14	11	63	72	92	89	87	83	67	69	67	64	53	57	53	70
Washington,	32	38	89	153	125	153	155	138	133	154	158	148	104	117	87	105
Total,	833	746	2, 979	3. 042	3. 338	3. 328	3, 400	3. 197	2. 932	3, 365	2, 734	3. 289	2, 376	2, 651	2. 210	2, 396

ERIE COUNTY.

TOWNS.	Under 1. Males.	Under 1. Females	1 and under 5. Males.	1 and under 5. Females	5 and under 10. Males.	5 and under 10. Females	10 and under 15. Males.	10 and under 15. Females.	15 and under 20. Males.	15 and under 20. Females	20 and under 25. Males.	20 and under 25. Females.	25 and under 30. Males.	25 and under 30. Females.	30 and under 35. Males	30 and under 35. Females.
Alden,	40	39	122	148	150	156	130	124	123	127	105	95	99	98	117	83
Amherst,	77	100	351	354	328	383	295	316	228	219	187	218	183	177	194	176
Aurora,	64	58	197	213	213	211	219	189	160	191	159	174	161	131	138	122
Boston,	30	23	108	89	116	133	124	124	96	98	65	55	61	62	56	53
Brandt,	15	13	54	69	62	58	74	47	71	60	55	49	44	37	34	40
Buffalo city, 1st ward,	181	187	488	521	414	405	353	357	381	342	539	465	589	445	446	355
2d ward,	68	85	234	233	246	283	273	299	267	522	444	520	346	315	225	234
3d ward,	90	61	250	249	274	275	224	219	217	209	189	238	267	236	231	155
4th ward,	135	137	472	465	439	474	395	404	413	448	420	457	410	437	374	326
5th ward,	173	196	637	645	567	499	428	431	371	312	335	405	462	472	495	411
6th ward,	207	200	524	507	520	426	350	363	249	203	238	317	356	407	405	322
7th ward,	169	192	596	571	544	464	421	363	267	296	272	292	325	385	395	328
8th ward,	95	107	279	327	286	280	269	286	279	291	383	308	357	244	260	229
9th ward,	68	59	223	245	250	260	262	312	311	445	364	482	279	333	236	218
10th ward,	82	59	290	287	310	297	254	301	243	411	196	384	219	310	204	235
11th ward,	52	56	210	230	198	187	180	182	160	187	143	174	141	147	158	141
12th ward,	64	85	235	215	256	237	204	163	157	147	201	164	216	156	200	154
13th ward,	14	14	52	54	47	61	48	43	36	30	40	37	41	30	44	35
Total Buffalo,	1, 398	1, 438	4, 490	4, 549	4, 351	4, 148	3, 661	3, 723	3, 351	3, 843	3, 764	4, 243	4, 008	3, 917	3, 673	3, 143
Chictawauga,	46	52	178	170	186	166	167	128	108	110	87	75	81	88	86	93
Clarence,	46	59	204	181	208	179	192	202	172	186	157	140	159	134	119	114
Colden,	19	18	63	78	76	93	100	91	84	63	73	58	40	48	50	35
Collins,	28	20	85	102	125	132	123	128	124	131	103	106	76	80	63	63

CORTLAND COUNTY.—(CONTINUED.)

TOWNS.	35 and under 40.		40 and under 45.		45 and under 50.		50 and under 60.		60 and under 70.		70 and under 80.		80 and under 90.		90 and under 100.		100 and upwards.		Ages unknown.
	Males.	Females.	Males.	Females.	Males.	Females.	Males.	Females.	Males.	Females.	Males.	Females.	Males.	Fems.	Males.	Fems.	Males.	Fems.	
Scott,	42	38	29	27	24	30	44	53	36	31	12	11	2	4	....	1	....	....	......
Solon,	22	29	26	27	36	29	38	40	18	15	12	8	5	6	1	1	....	....	......
Taylor,	32	23	24	19	30	33	43	52	30	16	16	11	4	12	....	2	....	1	11
Truxton,	99	95	81	86	74	57	112	102	78	79	35	22	10	9	10	9	....	....	3
Virgil,	46	64	54	50	57	56	80	82	51	52	21	24	5	10	....	1	....	....	......
Willet,	32	22	14	23	22	15	21	27	23	20	9	11	3	3	....	....	....	....	......
Total,	705	721	610	631	596	553	823	847	545	528	277	252	81	91	17	20	....	1	26

DELAWARE COUNTY.—(CONTINUED.)

TOWNS.	35 and under 40.		40 and under 45.		45 and under 50.		50 and under 60.		60 and under 70.		70 and under 80.		80 and under 90.		90 and under 100.		100 and upwards.		Ages unknown.
	Males.	Females.	Males.	Females.	Males.	Females.	Males.	Females.	Males.	Females.	Males.	Females.	Males.	Fems.	Males.	Fems.	Males.	Fems.	
Andes,	64	56	64	56	48	37	66	68	37	38	34	16	6	4	1	....	....	....	1
Bovina,	26	27	37	28	27	24	41	48	17	18	18	16	3	4	....	....	....	....	......
Colchester,	65	73	61	48	42	36	65	57	44	27	20	12	3	1	1	1	....	....	......
Davenport,	61	70	50	51	54	42	56	72	35	29	28	22	3	2	1	....	....	....	2
Delhi,	79	106	63	68	68	60	105	92	48	64	20	26	9	5	2	1	....	....	7
Franklin,	105	110	78	76	73	65	97	117	94	83	42	39	13	5	....	2	....	1	2
Hamden,	64	66	41	31	38	34	62	71	35	30	21	17	2	10	....	....	....	....	......
Hancock,	82	56	52	56	50	41	65	53	28	24	13	11	7	2	....	....	....	....	1
Harpersfield,	38	38	23	30	32	33	65	73	36	40	14	13	6	5	....	....	....	....	......
Kortright,	59	60	49	52	40	55	66	79	43	42	33	28	9	3	1	1	....	....	......
Masonville,	41	40	28	34	45	29	40	49	28	29	16	18	5	2	....	....	....	....	......
Meredith,	53	47	41	40	33	36	44	40	43	42	19	14	2	3	2	1	....	....	......
Middletown,	92	90	76	61	69	53	81	81	45	41	23	13	7	7	1	....	....	....	2
Roxbury,	80	71	60	65	60	66	86	85	50	51	20	29	11	1	2	2	....	....	......
Sidney,	44	49	47	47	46	45	73	60	30	33	20	12	3	6	....	1	1	....	1
Stamford,	47	53	54	47	30	42	69	67	36	45	19	16	2	8	....	....	....	....	3
Tompkins,	109	78	81	68	76	70	87	83	43	59	25	20	9	5	....	....	....	....	1
Walton,	58	63	54	63	65	56	93	87	59	54	32	30	9	5	....	3	....	....	7
Total,	1,167	1,153	959	921	896	824	1,261	1,282	751	749	417	352	109	78	11	12	1	1	27

DUTCHESS COUNTY.—(CONTINUED.)

TOWNS.	35 and under 40.		40 and under 45.		45 and under 50.		50 and under 60.		60 and under 70.		70 and under 80.		80 and under 90.		90 and under 100.		100 and upwards.		Ages unknown.
	Males.	Females.	Males.	Females.	Males.	Females.	Males.	Females.	Males.	Females.	Males.	Females.	Males.	Fems.	Males.	Fems.	Males.	Fems.	
Amenia,	63	68	64	70	58	42	68	71	40	47	13	35	7	7	....	1	....	....	10
Beekman,	46	52	38	34	35	33	56	58	35	28	14	20	3	5	1	1	....	....	......
Clinton,	54	60	53	54	52	32	62	61	45	56	19	21	3	8	....	1	....	....	......
Dover,	56	56	59	54	47	31	79	71	35	41	25	23	2	5	....	1	1	....	......
East Fishkill,	81	64	70	66	49	35	89	108	53	51	19	20	7	10	2	....	....	....	6
Fishkill,	235	297	220	214	214	204	298	302	139	145	59	62	14	19	3	4	....	....	6
Hyde Park,	79	78	69	65	52	58	81	68	46	46	32	28	5	12	....	3	....	....	......
La Grange,	68	65	51	52	43	44	83	61	64	41	12	18	3	7	1	2	....	....	......
Milan,	66	43	40	35	36	39	58	68	51	49	19	28	7	2	....	....	1	....	1
North East,	56	47	35	40	39	34	56	62	36	27	22	16	5	6	....	3	....	....	......
Pawling,	53	49	44	51	44	48	50	51	37	36	23	25	5	5	....	....	....	....	......
Pine Plains,	48	50	50	33	35	36	51	46	34	35	10	13	4	5	....	....	....	....	4
Pleasant Valley,	58	57	50	55	44	47	96	71	47	48	21	17	11	3	....	....	....	....	......
Poughkeepsie,	102	99	81	93	89	54	111	95	60	56	17	34	3	5	....	....	....	....	1
Poughkeepsie city:																			
1st ward,	121	148	124	123	90	67	91	120	59	70	19	21	2	5	....	1	....	....	......
2d ward,	81	85	54	73	60	56	81	90	42	50	11	19	6	12	1	1	....	....	......
3d ward,	120	146	111	112	89	59	82	99	33	60	10	20	5	3	1	1	....	....	......
4th ward,	76	94	64	83	53	73	78	93	31	52	15	23	3	5	....	....	....	....	1
Total Poughkeepsie,	398	473	353	391	292	255	332	402	165	232	55	83	16	25	2	3	....	....	1
Red Hook,	122	103	103	87	70	80	116	125	56	72	39	42	9	9	....	2	....	....	1
Rhinebeck,	101	98	70	83	82	76	113	109	68	75	43	43	7	4	....	1	....	....	......
Stanford,	69	85	56	60	57	47	87	85	55	41	22	23	5	9	....	....	....	....	......
Union Vale,	53	49	48	31	39	33	51	43	26	37	11	20	3	6	....	2	....	....	......
Washington,	98	86	63	56	75	64	90	100	63	61	39	35	9	10	1	1	....	....	......
Total,	1,906	1,979	1,617	1,624	1,461	1,292	2,027	2,057	1,155	1,224	514	606	128	162	10	25	2	....	30

ERIE COUNTY.—(CONTINUED.)

TOWNS.	35 and under 40.		40 and under 45.		45 and under 50.		50 and under 60.		60 and under 70.		70 and under 80.		80 and under 90.		90 and under 100.		100 and upwards.		Ages unknown.
	Males.	Females.	Males.	Females.	Males.	Females.	Males.	Females.	Males.	Females.	Males.	Females.	Males.	Fems.	Males.	Fems.	Males.	Fems.	
Alden,	73	53	57	45	46	58	81	86	62	42	23	13	2	7	....	....	....	....	......
Amherst,	180	143	150	111	115	99	161	134	92	91	25	26	2	1	....	1	....	1	......
Aurora,	116	112	99	97	86	77	131	116	78	65	44	32	7	4	....	1	....	....	......
Boston,	53	61	37	35	41	37	64	45	36	28	16	15	4	3	1	....	....	....	......
Brandt,	26	27	32	29	25	23	36	37	30	26	7	6	5	2	....	....	....	....	......
Buffalo city: 1st ward,	290	193	222	169	111	97	130	137	54	55	18	17	4	4	1	2	....	1	21
2d ward,	194	193	174	119	127	84	113	128	44	51	10	21	2	11	....	....	....	....	17
3d ward,	152	126	118	78	68	69	99	91	33	35	17	13	4	5	....	....	....	....	1
4th ward,	286	236	200	192	164	118	194	171	71	90	22	38	7	3	....	1	....	1	......
5th ward,	328	296	236	212	164	121	161	154	66	64	20	15	3	2	....	....	....	....	78
6th ward,	298	262	222	171	149	123	184	160	64	82	21	20	2	2	....	....	....	....	......
7th ward,	334	277	234	194	163	127	196	176	85	81	28	19	3	4	1	....	....	....	2
8th ward,	199	165	175	140	87	57	107	79	35	39	10	14	2	1	....	....	....	....	14
9th ward,	192	188	158	142	119	87	135	115	48	51	13	22	3	5	....	....	....	....	......
10th ward,	178	178	136	127	95	78	111	103	42	57	15	27	2	7	....	....	....	....	......
11th ward,	124	98	87	85	75	56	81	69	30	39	12	9	....	3	....	....	....	....	......
12th ward,	138	102	115	70	64	52	116	78	54	43	16	21	1	5	....	....	....	....	......
13th ward,	29	25	25	23	24	15	23	11	8	2	3	3	1	....	....	....	....	....	......
Total Buffalo,	2,742	2,339	2,102	1,722	1,410	1,084	1,650	1,472	634	689	205	239	34	52	2	3	....	2	133
Chictawauga,	78	78	85	66	63	50	92	80	42	37	25	16	....	3	....	....	....	....	......
Clarence,	81	83	82	64	77	54	102	91	65	41	21	24	7	4	2	2	1	....	......
Colden,	34	49	36	39	28	32	59	32	29	21	12	8	5	3	....	....	....	....	5
Collins,	64	54	42	49	40	37	69	61	48	38	18	7	4	4	....	....	....	....	1

ERIE COUNTY.

TOWNS.	Under 1.		1 and under 5.		5 and under 10.		10 and under 15.		15 and under 20.		20 and under 25.		25 and under 30.		30 and under 35.	
	Males.	Females	Males.	Females	Males.	Females	Males.	Females	Males.	Females	Males.	Females.	Males.	Females	Males.	Females.
Concord,	44	23	161	140	184	176	175	175	116	138	129	150	84	102	86	101
East Hamburgh,	26	29	91	90	95	112	113	90	108	110	95	95	108	95	94	75
Eden,	41	17	134	133	167	170	139	145	129	116	91	82	79	98	84	88
Evans,	40	26	123	111	135	115	145	133	130	108	114	103	92	80	91	79
Grand Island,	8	15	49	56	46	41	40	35	35	19	58	50	65	44	60	36
Hamburgh,	60	54	192	165	189	175	162	164	162	144	159	143	117	133	116	81
Holland,	21	15	82	90	98	76	82	68	77	59	36	73	61	40	33	43
Lancaster,	120	104	368	381	341	345	288	265	246	225	240	256	264	223	269	207
Marilla,	21	17	70	82	85	91	85	70	82	69	58	60	58	59	60	43
Newstead,	46	39	186	154	175	174	183	180	171	139	154	158	128	99	111	103
North Collins,	32	22	115	90	132	124	106	116	98	102	86	70	67	73	62	54
Sardinia,	25	22	85	105	98	105	101	90	101	87	80	81	72	81	74	59
Tonawanda,	46	42	186	149	174	160	138	141	123	121	109	105	140	121	103	89
Wales,	22	24	107	79	105	109	104	102	94	83	67	77	62	74	65	46
West Seneca,	28	37	113	128	123	143	134	103	133	110	112	93	131	108	125	97
Total,	2,343	2,306	7,914	7,906	7,962	7,774	7,080	6,949	6,322	6,658	6,343	6,809	6,440	6,202	5,963	5,123

ESSEX COUNTY.

TOWNS.	Under 1. Males.	Under 1. Females	1 and under 5. Males.	1 and under 5. Females	5 and under 10. Males.	5 and under 10. Females	10 and under 15. Males.	10 and under 15. Females	15 and under 20. Males.	15 and under 20. Females	20 and under 25. Males.	20 and under 25. Females.	25 and under 30. Males.	25 and under 30. Females	30 and under 35. Males.	30 and under 35. Females.
Chesterfield,	51	67	220	183	224	223	200	199	174	183	147	162	100	135	109	121
Crown Point,	28	27	122	112	143	128	132	129	123	97	98	100	94	80	85	86
Elizabethtown,	20	16	62	89	90	90	90	81	91	72	79	64	64	51	41	34
Essex,	28	35	120	129	156	136	118	140	105	110	103	110	80	89	62	69
Jay,	29	41	197	195	221	205	193	171	144	142	130	148	87	97	97	75
Keene,	11	12	43	49	63	55	51	54	33	40	24	25	24	22	28	30
Lewis,	21	23	102	87	138	114	110	123	106	114	80	68	61	53	48	38
Minerva,	15	17	57	53	45	44	42	43	35	39	37	31	41	26	28	24
Moriah,	49	56	210	204	207	199	171	179	138	152	146	131	132	127	133	117
Newcomb,	4	5	21	15	20	15	10	8	8	7	13	11	19	12	11	10
North Elba,	6	3	24	13	18	15	16	22	12	13	26	11	13	9	11	7
North Hudson,	9	9	44	33	35	47	32	36	24	30	36	12	16	20	16	17
St. Armand,	1	......	22	15	17	26	17	17	20	16	19	9	12	12	9	6
Schroon,	43	32	125	91	131	143	120	114	108	99	145	109	112	70	73	61
Ticonderoga,	22	33	130	103	133	160	123	126	110	117	81	89	92	71	73	56
Westport,	32	28	124	110	139	138	125	121	109	107	82	98	72	73	59	64
Willsborough,	22	23	93	89	119	118	101	87	87	103	68	91	63	59	47	59
Wilmington,	14	7	58	66	71	71	64	72	36	57	28	38	22	35	26	30
Total,	405	434	1,774	1,636	1,970	1,927	1,715	1,722	1,463	1,498	1,342	1,307	1,104	1,041	956	904

FRANKLIN COUNTY.

TOWNS.	Under 1. Males.	Under 1. Females	1 and under 5. Males.	1 and under 5. Females	5 and under 10. Males.	5 and under 10. Females	10 and under 15. Males.	10 and under 15. Females	15 and under 20. Males.	15 and under 20. Females	20 and under 25. Males.	20 and under 25. Females.	25 and under 30. Males.	25 and under 30. Females	30 and under 35. Males.	30 and under 35. Females.
Bangor,	41	38	149	136	150	143	130	120	124	97	72	98	80	93	74	70
Bellmont,	16	18	71	46	66	64	61	51	42	47	40	37	31	37	26	21
Bombay,	44	34	152	145	195	161	154	154	122	143	89	109	79	76	61	65
Brandon,	12	10	44	38	39	58	46	46	32	33	26	33	31	28	18	17
Burke,	21	26	129	125	146	130	126	122	94	113	78	80	51	63	63	57
Chateaugay,	46	51	161	183	200	190	186	191	148	155	102	96	83	94	72	76
Constable,	18	9	90	89	101	96	108	84	77	80	60	67	47	49	41	47
Dickinson,	18	7	70	88	90	91	82	75	68	55	66	53	50	44	35	35
Duane,	3	6	23	20	25	23	18	21	13	19	18	18	15	13	14	11
Fort Covington,	30	32	149	161	182	165	164	173	144	183	115	136	67	88	68	67
Franklin,	16	20	65	65	64	71	73	49	45	46	47	32	45	37	36	26
Harrietstown,	6	8	22	29	29	20	12	16	9	16	8	16	21	10	7	9
Malone,	81	71	333	313	360	355	334	320	284	291	206	223	180	213	137	165
Moira,	17	25	91	67	107	91	71	92	61	63	73	67	57	58	43	44
Westville,	26	17	97	85	103	88	101	91	71	66	48	52	34	41	34	41
Total,	395	372	1,646	1,590	1,857	1,746	1,666	1,605	1,334	1,407	1,048	1,117	871	944	729	751

FULTON COUNTY.

TOWNS.	Under 1. Males.	Under 1. Females	1 and under 5. Males.	1 and under 5. Females	5 and under 10. Males.	5 and under 10. Females	10 and under 15. Males.	10 and under 15. Females	15 and under 20. Males.	15 and under 20. Females	20 and under 25. Males.	20 and under 25. Females.	25 and under 30. Males.	25 and under 30. Females	30 and under 35. Males.	30 and under 35. Females.
Bleecker,	18	26	73	53	52	64	53	46	32	38	33	39	52	35	48	30
Broadalbin,	31	36	134	148	148	162	144	161	119	126	89	110	79	110	75	102
Caroga,	7	13	46	47	63	49	44	41	28	31	36	27	32	29	25	21
Ephrata,	34	25	131	120	143	126	151	150	111	127	92	95	87	89	77	72
Johnstown,	100	106	388	411	440	425	428	446	414	496	442	490	362	392	291	297
Mayfield,	29	34	123	107	143	131	137	134	123	135	89	123	87	112	85	81
Northampton,	30	25	118	89	122	118	112	110	93	100	85	107	70	77	63	58
Oppenheim,	34	43	138	137	170	162	160	140	133	119	124	110	104	85	63	51
Perth,	10	10	54	43	68	68	70	86	76	62	51	43	41	40	28	35
Stratford,	19	20	74	62	64	71	72	50	44	52	52	45	46	40	43	29
Total,	312	338	1,279	1,217	1,413	1,376	1,371	1,364	1,173	1,286	1,093	1,189	960	1,009	798	776

GENESEE COUNTY.

TOWNS.	Under 1. Males.	Under 1. Females	1 and under 5. Males.	1 and under 5. Females	5 and under 10. Males.	5 and under 10. Females	10 and under 15. Males.	10 and under 15. Females	15 and under 20. Males.	15 and under 20. Females	20 and under 25. Males.	20 and under 25. Females.	25 and under 30. Males.	25 and under 30. Females	30 and under 35. Males.	30 and under 35. Females.
Alabama,	24	30	112	95	124	132	125	120	149	116	132	97	106	102	74	72
Alexander,	22	19	83	72	71	93	90	97	100	109	100	98	81	72	72	65
Batavia,	73	75	291	280	285	271	255	288	281	287	285	292	253	265	202	190
Bergen,	22	22	81	90	94	83	104	85	96	112	90	93	81	88	66	69
Bethany,	24	21	78	68	96	97	94	112	94	98	102	79	77	89	64	79
Byron,	21	18	75	79	85	95	71	71	92	98	106	92	92	76	64	53
Darien,	25	35	98	104	115	96	109	108	122	130	102	110	94	72	79	69
Elba,	35	19	77	70	80	94	104	105	101	110	112	88	77	73	75	69
Le Roy,	55	54	203	191	210	216	194	183	222	241	239	249	210	207	182	165
Oakfield,	17	24	84	60	93	82	90	75	85	79	95	85	81	54	54	52

ERIE COUNTY.—(Continued.)

TOWNS.	35 and under 40.		40 and under 45.		45 and under 50.		50 and under 60.		60 and under 70.		70 and under 80.		80 and under 90.		90 and under 100.		100 and upwards		Ages unknown.
	Males	Females.	Males.	Females	Males.	Females	Males.	Females	Males.	Females	Males.	Females.	Males	Fems	Males	Fems	Males	Fems	
Concord,	89	83	72	75	54	52	112	94	66	52	25	28	8	5	3	....	....	....	3
East Hamburgh,	52	43	44	45	41	40	81	60	36	39	20	10	7	1	1	....	....	....	......
Eden,	77	70	63	40	43	42	80	100	80	64	28	14	5	6	1	....	....	....	......
Evans,	68	62	52	59	46	53	83	61	43	49	24	15	5	3	3	....	....	....	1
Grand Island,	41	14	24	14	19	14	27	11	8	4	3	2	....	....	....	....	....	....	......
Hamburgh,	110	74	89	80	56	45	98	92	63	45	35	18	5	3	1	2	....	....	5
Holland,	58	40	35	37	25	20	40	44	29	18	11	6	3	1	....	....	....	....	......
Lancaster,	180	167	143	111	102	81	174	147	96	85	26	26	5	2	1	....	....	....	1
Marilla,	43	31	24	39	29	27	52	50	30	24	6	8	....	3	1	....	....	....	......
Newstead,	102	78	75	68	62	57	103	76	65	59	11	16	3	2	1	4	....	....	5
North Collins,	49	39	35	47	45	33	69	66	49	40	14	18	4	1	1	....	....	....	......
Sardinia,	53	52	35	46	42	27	54	65	46	39	18	10	4	5	....	1	....	....	2
Tonawanda,	103	73	78	49	51	38	78	54	36	29	14	13	3	....	....	....	....	....	3
Wales,	56	67	42	29	36	27	55	59	41	30	11	11	3	1	....	1	....	....	......
West Seneca,	104	89	76	70	72	59	104	92	54	50	22	11	2	1	....	....	....	....	......
Total,	4,632	3,981	3.609	3,066	2,644	2,166	3,655	3,225	1,858	1,705	664	592	127	117	18	15	1	3	159

ESSEX COUNTY.—(Continued.)

TOWNS.	35 and under 40.		40 and under 45.		45 and under 50.		50 and under 60.		60 and under 70.		70 and under 80.		80 and under 90.		90 and under 100.		100 and upwards		Ages unknown.
	Males	Females.	Males.	Females	Males.	Females	Males.	Females	Males.	Females	Males.	Females.	Males	Fems	Males	Fems	Males	Fems	
Chesterfield,	101	89	78	69	60	54	119	97	55	63	15	16	5	4	1	1	....	....	2
Crown Point,	75	68	43	48	70	35	69	64	60	52	16	20	8	2	1	1	....	....	......
Elizabethtown,	39	39	33	29	29	29	44	33	34	30	14	7	4	4	....	....	....	....	......
Essex,	41	49	49	45	44	42	69	58	40	36	17	16	9	8	1	1	....	....	......
Jay,	66	65	78	61	48	47	94	76	47	46	21	15	6	8	....	....	....	....	......
Keene,	23	23	18	14	16	12	22	25	22	13	6	7	2	3	....	1	....	....	3
Lewis,	54	50	37	50	42	40	70	55	36	29	20	17	9	6	....	....	....	....	2
Minerva,	20	18	26	11	18	15	22	22	11	14	6	5	....	2	....	....	....	....	......
Moriah,	98	93	86	59	67	60	75	67	44	61	26	22	7	2	1	1	....	....	......
Newcomb,	6	1	3	2	5	4	5	4	1	2	2	1	1	....	....	....	....	....	......
North Elba,	14	12	11	5	7	4	6	8	7	1	4	2	....	1	....	....	....	....	......
North Hudson,	12	10	13	4	11	12	14	9	8	4	1	1	3	....	1	....	....	....	......
St. Armand,	7	9	3	4	7	8	13	8	5	4	3	......	....	....	....	....	....	....	......
Schroon,	65	61	49	38	45	33	77	53	25	19	17	14	9	3	1	....	....	....	......
Ticonderoga,	56	80	56	49	58	46	67	67	47	36	16	9	5	10	3	1	....	....	......
Westport,	66	49	49	46	43	48	73	50	45	46	20	13	6	6	....	....	....	....	......
Willsborough,	48	38	34	34	36	35	62	51	36	24	17	15	8	5	....	....	....	....	3
Wilmington,	24	13	22	17	13	21	33	20	18	16	3	4	2	2	1	....	....	....	......
Total,	815	767	688	585	619	545	934	767	541	496	224	184	84	66	10	6	....	....	10

FRANKLIN COUNTY.—(Continued.)

TOWNS.	35 and under 40.		40 and under 45.		45 and under 50.		50 and under 60.		60 and under 70.		70 and under 80.		80 and under 90.		90 and under 100.		100 and upwards		Ages unknown.
	Males	Females.	Males.	Females	Males.	Females	Males.	Females	Males.	Females	Males.	Females.	Males	Fems	Males	Fems	Males	Fems	
Bangor,	57	62	40	37	43	38	71	77	53	32	12	9	3	3	1	....	....	....	1
Bellmont,	24	20	17	20	21	15	31	20	14	13	3	1	....	....	....	....	....	....	......
Bombay,	34	46	46	49	47	45	79	52	42	42	29	13	1	8	....	2	....	....	1
Brandon,	16	24	23	18	22	17	31	24	14	12	4	5	3	4	....	....	....	....	......
Burke,	50	62	37	37	42	33	59	50	42	29	16	11	3	4	....	1	....	....	......
Chateaugay,	85	59	46	55	60	53	66	77	59	35	23	12	5	4	1	1	....	....	1
Constable,	38	24	33	38	28	28	55	46	35	26	12	10	2	4	1	....	....	....	......
Dickinson,	36	24	17	22	31	28	53	55	24	17	9	6	4	1	....	....	1	....	......
Duane,	7	6	7	4	5	4	16	6	3	3	3	......	....	....	....	....	....	....	1
Fort Covington,	59	61	53	57	57	52	82	70	52	42	23	16	6	4	....	....	....	....	1
Franklin,	21	22	24	28	25	12	28	22	12	13	2	1	....	....	....	....	....	....	......
Harrietstown,	11	4	6	5	7	6	10	6	3	1	4	3	2	....	....	....	....	....	......
Malone,	128	140	123	134	136	107	154	144	84	60	41	35	12	8	2	2	....	2	8
Moira,	45	47	26	35	36	23	60	55	39	23	10	9	3	4	1	....	....	....	16
Westville,	40	43	28	32	27	20	42	33	35	28	15	11	4	1	....	....	....	....	......
Total,	651	644	526	571	587	481	837	737	511	376	206	142	48	45	6	6	1	2	29

FULTON COUNTY.—(Continued.)

TOWNS.	35 and under 40.		40 and under 45.		45 and under 50.		50 and under 60.		60 and under 70.		70 and under 80.		80 and under 90.		90 and under 100.		100 and upwards		Ages unknown.
	Males	Females.	Males.	Females	Males.	Females	Males.	Females	Males.	Females	Males.	Females.	Males	Fems	Males	Fems	Males	Fems	
Bleecker,	33	29	29	13	23	18	20	14	11	17	2	3	....	....	....	....	....	....	......
Broadalbin,	65	73	77	74	62	70	113	111	62	71	34	32	13	12	2	1	....	....	......
Caroga,	23	23	20	17	15	14	18	11	14	9	5	3	2	1	....	....	....	....	......
Ephrata,	61	49	56	42	39	40	59	71	48	41	21	14	5	4	2	1	....	....	......
Johnstown,	234	257	186	176	146	144	217	219	116	126	49	69	15	23	1	4	....	....	2
Mayfield,	61	64	63	62	42	50	95	105	52	47	22	29	9	5	....	1	....	....	13
Northampton,	58	49	45	51	46	43	75	67	38	32	17	24	9	9	1	....	....	....	2
Oppenheim,	50	53	64	53	55	70	91	68	40	48	17	13	6	7	1	2	....	....	1
Perth,	32	30	30	32	25	28	41	35	22	33	17	11	3	5	1	1	....	....	......
Stratford,	24	31	33	20	18	21	29	23	17	19	9	8	5	3	1	....	....	....	2
Total,	641	658	603	540	471	498	758	724	420	443	193	206	67	69	9	10	....	....	20

GENESEE COUNTY.—(Continued.)

TOWNS.	35 and under 40.		40 and under 45.		45 and under 50.		50 and under 60.		60 and under 70.		70 and under 80.		80 and under 90.		90 and under 100.		100 and upwards		Ages unknown.
	Males	Females.	Males.	Females	Males.	Females	Males.	Females	Males.	Females	Males.	Females.	Males	Fems	Males	Fems	Males	Fems	
Alabama,	71	57	49	51	53	49	80	68	38	26	16	17	5	3	....	....	....	....	1
Alexander,	55	47	42	45	37	40	77	68	56	42	21	18	4	2	....	....	....	....	......
Batavia,	183	158	116	145	108	87	171	162	106	90	26	34	5	12	3	....	....	....	25
Bergen,	57	53	45	35	44	45	64	59	36	43	22	10	3	6	....	2	....	....	......
Bethany,	62	54	57	54	39	54	70	66	52	58	21	17	3	5	1	1	....	....	3
Byron,	53	45	35	34	30	42	57	56	36	24	15	14	1	1	....	....	....	....	1
Darien,	72	65	68	66	52	46	94	80	50	60	24	18	7	5	1	....	....	....	......
Elba,	50	52	41	38	55	51	81	80	47	38	18	17	4	5	1	....	1	....	1
Le Roy,	129	141	119	101	79	84	134	130	92	88	41	31	6	7	....	1	....	....	2
Oakfield,	46	44	38	35	26	23	59	47	31	21	6	4	2	1	....	....	....	....	17

GENESEE COUNTY.

TOWNS.	Under 1.		1 and under 5.		5 and under 10.		10 and under 15.		15 and under 20.		20 and under 25.		25 and under 30.		30 and under 35.	
	Males.	Females.	Males.	Females.	Males.	Females.	Males.	Females.	Males.	Females.	Males.	Females.	Males.	Females.	Males.	Females.
Pavillion,	20	14	80	62	95	79	99	78	106	102	98	91	90	84	62	69
Pembroke,	43	40	133	162	168	177	178	170	138	136	122	136	112	113	101	103
Stafford,	28	24	118	115	119	122	107	112	113	91	120	102	92	76	87	67
Total,	409	395	1,513	1,448	1,635	1,637	1,620	1,604	1,699	1,709	1,703	1,612	1,446	1,371	1,182	1,122

GREENE COUNTY.

TOWNS.	Under 1. Males.	Under 1. Females.	1–5 Males.	1–5 Females.	5–10 Males.	5–10 Females.	10–15 Males.	10–15 Females.	15–20 Males.	15–20 Females.	20–25 Males.	20–25 Females.	25–30 Males.	25–30 Females.	30–35 Males.	30–35 Females.
Ashland,	.....	.....	75	78	84	74	57	56	40	66	48	65	47	55	48	44
Athens,	44	57	163	155	183	172	171	181	147	123	152	136	122	120	99	92
Cairo,	32	16	112	107	133	134	159	159	136	158	114	100	103	87	75	78
Catskill,	75	73	315	266	323	349	308	296	255	309	269	323	237	266	222	219
Coxsackie,	52	46	190	182	244	175	234	211	199	208	193	188	164	152	108	121
Durham,	30	31	108	130	143	142	143	129	133	141	107	109	83	90	84	102
Greenville,	16	26	110	91	118	111	137	135	136	90	105	110	68	86	71	85
Halcott,	5	13	29	26	24	35	39	22	31	26	31	25	20	22	11	11
Hunter,	27	22	104	97	123	128	122	98	95	78	59	70	43	39	35	54
Jewett,	13	15	66	53	72	78	79	74	63	62	52	50	29	27	29	41
Lexington,	23	25	86	92	115	105	100	116	74	62	59	81	61	64	50	58
New Baltimore,	24	38	145	113	150	114	160	124	128	128	138	114	92	95	72	85
Prattsville,	16	21	86	88	94	115	108	103	80	110	59	88	48	39	39	54
Windham,	21	23	73	75	109	126	81	91	72	105	52	74	76	83	70	54
Total,	378	406	1,662	1,553	1,915	1,858	1,898	1,795	1,589	1,666	1,438	1,533	1,193	1,225	1,013	1,098

HAMILTON COUNTY.

TOWNS.	Under 1. Males.	Under 1. Females.	1–5 Males.	1–5 Females.	5–10 Males.	5–10 Females.	10–15 Males.	10–15 Females.	15–20 Males.	15–20 Females.	20–25 Males.	20–25 Females.	25–30 Males.	25–30 Females.	30–35 Males.	30–35 Females.
Arietta,	.....	3	11	9	5	10	7	12	8	7	6	7	8	5	8	3
Gilman,	2	2	5	3	8	5	3	5	5	5	5	4	4	3	6	3
Hope,	13	12	54	49	52	62	61	41	48	36	51	35	41	33	23	13
Lake Pleasant,	4	8	15	19	18	13	25	19	20	15	15	13	18	10	5	5
Long Lake,	2	3	6	16	10	9	13	3	6	5	4	9	6	5	3	3
Morehouse,	6	3	17	17	15	22	16	12	14	6	12	13	14	7	7	6
Wells,	13	8	50	55	52	39	55	36	41	33	39	38	44	16	28	35
Total,	40	39	158	168	160	160	180	128	142	107	132	119	135	79	80	68

HERKIMER COUNTY.

TOWNS.	Under 1. Males.	Under 1. Females.	1–5 Males.	1–5 Females.	5–10 Males.	5–10 Females.	10–15 Males.	10–15 Females.	15–20 Males.	15–20 Females.	20–25 Males.	20–25 Females.	25–30 Males.	25–30 Females.	30–35 Males.	30–35 Females.
Columbia,	19	10	80	83	106	95	125	91	98	100	86	95	81	63	60	68
Danube,	20	20	77	78	107	90	110	95	92	87	138	105	106	78	84	49
Fairfield,	12	11	66	59	62	69	78	65	82	94	92	89	68	80	52	45
Frankfort,	45	34	168	174	202	202	192	200	178	160	145	140	121	135	105	116
German Flats,	42	55	200	188	242	235	216	194	192	182	185	194	180	168	152	145
Herkimer,	34	25	131	135	165	160	154	158	172	170	142	165	110	118	118	87
Litchfield,	24	17	65	70	105	90	101	75	87	72	78	62	45	65	52	55
Little Falls,	53	68	236	244	300	270	277	288	252	282	275	320	196	215	193	182
Manheim,	20	27	91	80	84	95	90	110	78	95	96	68	76	80	63	69
Newport,	31	36	98	90	111	100	106	108	102	110	89	112	79	80	77	90
Norway,	16	13	54	57	54	68	62	52	54	58	46	48	64	38	40	52
Ohio,	12	17	73	68	92	58	70	72	64	48	41	41	36	31	32	31
Russia,	27	20	110	107	114	128	126	145	129	122	115	117	120	71	79	82
Salisbury,	39	34	146	134	138	125	138	120	118	120	111	110	105	97	91	70
Schuyler,	17	26	98	77	90	100	75	104	82	104	101	88	88	74	63	54
Stark,	22	17	71	80	71	75	76	70	70	82	77	97	72	59	56	55
Warren,	17	15	66	63	89	77	102	93	85	94	86	91	84	69	70	58
Wilmurt,	7	3	17	14	18	12	16	6	16	10	33	8	19	10	18	8
Winfield,	15	12	60	65	73	72	73	73	77	85	68	64	59	57	40	40
Total,	472	460	1,907	1,866	2,223	2,121	2,187	2,119	2,028	2,075	2,004	2,014	1,709	1,588	1,445	1,356

JEFFERSON COUNTY.

TOWNS.	Under 1. Males.	Under 1. Females.	1–5 Males.	1–5 Females.	5–10 Males.	5–10 Females.	10–15 Males.	10–15 Females.	15–20 Males.	15–20 Females.	20–25 Males.	20–25 Females.	25–30 Males.	25–30 Females.	30–35 Males.	30–35 Females.
Adams,	27	42	127	123	176	180	154	180	137	194	157	174	106	124	112	114
Alexandria,	48	51	205	191	257	230	225	220	186	170	129	172	128	112	101	104
Antwerp,	41	40	214	200	220	240	239	194	220	222	206	201	165	145	143	129
Brownville,	34	47	175	150	217	235	258	196	200	250	168	174	106	154	101	114
Cape Vincent,	50	44	210	183	225	230	207	196	160	211	135	150	143	131	104	106
Champion,	21	21	93	80	112	89	113	103	102	109	73	93	63	72	65	66
Clayton,	66	44	244	209	290	277	285	267	220	289	200	206	146	148	135	136
Ellisburgh,	65	60	276	253	297	292	300	302	295	293	214	275	239	219	196	199
Henderson,	31	21	107	104	142	119	142	123	115	136	83	100	92	81	80	80
Hounsfield,	42	32	172	145	215	178	195	200	187	177	129	156	107	128	94	98
Le Ray,	45	25	183	136	200	184	179	180	203	176	145	157	119	123	97	102
Lorraine,	23	20	101	64	102	77	92	75	97	71	65	68	41	65	57	39
Lyme,	36	37	115	141	163	169	172	136	141	162	124	128	105	108	84	67
Orleans,	36	31	166	176	192	177	183	181	155	134	113	113	93	93	98	97
Pamelia,	39	17	147	124	165	132	143	122	134	145	93	158	97	105	96	95
Philadelphia,	27	25	104	89	113	94	89	104	88	88	71	74	80	74	54	62
Rodman,	12	11	93	73	99	87	87	101	96	96	73	93	73	79	71	64
Rutland,	21	23	86	78	93	101	98	105	113	124	82	98	73	94	71	70
Theresa,	23	28	132	126	147	157	142	154	118	105	101	88	85	87	67	78
Watertown,	90	94	380	368	427	399	380	389	377	514	356	505	335	386	291	296
Wilna,	50	27	184	153	195	181	172	182	138	182	153	146	115	115	107	102
Worth,	10	8	28	28	28	30	28	24	25	18	11	24	22	24	19	18
Total,	837	748	3,542	3,194	4,075	3,858	3,883	3,734	3,507	3,866	2,881	3,353	2,533	2,667	2,243	2,236

GENESEE COUNTY.—(Continued.)

TOWNS.	35 and under 40.		40 and under 45.		45 and under 50.		50 and under 60.		60 and under 70.		70 and under 80.		80 and under 90.		90 and under 100.		100 and upwards		Ages unknown.
	Males.	Females.	Males.	Females	Males.	Females	Males.	Females	Males.	Females	Males.	Females	Males	Fems	Males	Fems	Males	Fems	
Pavillion,	53	58	41	44	30	27	55	66	59	49	19	12	5	4	1	3	....	1	2
Pembroke,	105	78	68	62	70	60	92	94	66	56	29	16	6	7	....	....	....	....	3
Stafford,	63	64	42	49	54	45	73	57	36	29	13	21	8	6	....	2	....	....	......
Total,	989	916	761	759	686	653	1,107	1,033	705	624	271	229	59	64	7	9	1	1	55

GREENE COUNTY.—(Continued.)

TOWNS.	35 and under 40.		40 and under 45.		45 and under 50.		50 and under 60.		60 and under 70.		70 and under 80.		80 and under 90.		90 and under 100.		100 and upwards		Ages unknown.
	Males.	Females.	Males.	Females	Males.	Females	Males.	Females	Males.	Females	Males.	Females	Males	Fems	Males	Fems	Males	Fems	
Ashland,	29	24	37	31	18	28	41	36	14	15	10	10	6	2	1	....	....	....	......
Athens,	83	65	73	65	55	57	101	92	51	51	17	22	6	10	2	2	....	....	1
Cairo,	67	80	67	63	67	62	94	94	73	80	40	33	14	13	3	2	....	1	1
Catskill,	199	181	155	154	119	108	193	181	95	116	38	45	6	11	....	1	....	....	3
Coxsackie,	121	104	91	95	80	97	116	114	60	52	33	34	5	11	....	1	....	....	1
Durham,	83	87	71	69	60	60	86	102	71	66	29	35	8	7	....	1	....	....	......
Greenville,	63	73	45	62	53	49	90	98	44	40	22	22	9	7	....	....	....	....	1
Halcott,	10	9	9	9	14	7	15	16	7	2	......	4	....	1	1	....	....	....	......
Hunter,	43	40	36	38	43	22	59	40	31	17	8	12	....	2	1	1	....	....	7
Jewett,	35	34	31	24	26	20	31	41	41	24	10	7	1	1	....	....	....	....	......
Lexington,	52	46	43	37	30	33	53	44	27	24	11	15	3	5	....	....	....	....	1
New Baltimore,	73	63	61	77	63	47	73	72	41	47	19	28	9	7	....	2	....	....	......
Prattsville,	50	52	34	48	38	39	49	47	29	23	14	12	2	3	....	....	....	....	......
Windham,	53	52	38	32	37	36	61	68	43	31	9	20	11	6	1	1	....	....	......
Total,	961	910	791	804	703	665	1,062	1,045	627	588	260	299	80	86	9	11	....	1	15

HAMILTON COUNTY.—(Continued.)

TOWNS.	35 and under 40.		40 and under 45.		45 and under 50.		50 and under 60.		60 and under 70.		70 and under 80.		80 and under 90.		90 and under 100.		100 and upwards		Ages unknown.
	Males.	Females.	Males.	Females	Males.	Females	Males.	Females	Males.	Females	Males.	Females	Males	Fems	Males	Fems	Males	Fems	
Arietta,	5	4	3	2	4	1	7	7	4	......	1	2	....	....	....	....	....	....	......
Gilman,	3	1	2	1	2	2	2	2	4	......	......	2	1	....	....	....	....	....	......
Hope,	20	26	20	11	16	16	28	16	19	14	5	6	....	1	....	....	....	....	......
Lake Pleasant,	7	5	6	6	4	3	16	10	2	5	5	7	2	....	....	....	....	....	......
Long Lake,	5	5	2	2	4	1	6	4	3	2	1	1	....	....	....	....	....	....	......
Morehouse,	7	4	7	7	14	9	9	11	6	7	3	1	....	1	....	....	....	....	2
Wells,	26	17	22	12	20	8	21	20	13	15	3	4	2	2	1	....	....	....	......
Total,	73	62	62	41	64	40	89	70	51	43	18	23	5	4	1	....	....	....	2

HERKIMER COUNTY.—(Continued.)

TOWNS.	35 and under 40.		40 and under 45.		45 and under 50.		50 and under 60.		60 and under 70.		70 and under 80.		80 and under 90.		90 and under 100.		100 and upwards		Ages unknown.
	Males.	Females.	Males.	Females	Males.	Females	Males.	Females	Males.	Females	Males.	Females	Males	Fems	Males	Fems	Males	Fems	
Columbia,	59	57	49	44	36	41	78	70	42	47	14	15	7	10	1	....	1	....	......
Danube,	58	41	50	28	32	35	72	60	28	29	9	7	3	2	1	....	....	....	......
Fairfield,	41	43	38	31	25	34	60	70	27	26	22	25	18	4	....	....	....	....	5
Frankport,	104	78	94	84	88	68	101	108	56	52	21	18	10	7	1	....	....	....	10
German Flats,	153	120	126	105	96	81	110	102	51	62	26	28	5	10	....	....	....	1	9
Herkimer,	83	87	80	68	68	68	93	85	53	48	28	30	13	11	3	3	....	....	1
Litchfield,	62	50	52	48	44	34	53	54	36	28	17	24	8	9	....	....	....	....	......
Little Falls,	170	171	136	114	108	105	125	133	73	75	27	22	4	9	....	2	....	....	5
Manheim,	42	46	36	40	28	34	65	59	26	36	12	13	6	5	1	1	....	....	......
Newport,	75	61	43	51	44	34	60	81	54	45	21	15	5	6	....	1	....	....	......
Norway,	22	32	28	25	20	21	42	31	15	15	15	12	3	1	....	....	....	....	1
Ohio,	40	30	26	32	34	22	31	25	19	20	11	8	1	2	....	....	....	....	......
Russia,	67	71	68	57	60	42	82	85	41	39	25	24	11	2	....	1	....	....	1
Salisbury,	64	58	55	47	53	59	75	70	46	33	19	21	6	4	....	....	....	....	......
Schuyler,	57	48	42	29	28	29	48	60	41	38	8	11	3	5	1	1	....	....	......
Stark,	54	47	40	31	31	24	44	35	39	46	11	9	10	6	....	1	....	....	......
Warren,	57	49	31	51	40	40	76	75	52	49	23	20	11	7	1	....	....	....	......
Wilmurt,	8	4	9	2	4	2	8	6	2	2	5	1	....	....	....	....	....	....	......
Winfield,	42	48	36	43	39	39	59	51	25	26	22	26	3	5	....	....	....	....	......
Total,	1,258	1,141	1,039	930	878	812	1,282	1,260	726	716	336	329	127	105	9	10	1	1	32

JEFFERSON COUNTY.—(Continued.)

TOWNS.	35 and under 40.		40 and under 45.		45 and under 50.		50 and under 60.		60 and under 70.		70 and under 80.		80 and under 90.		90 and under 100.		100 and upwards		Ages unknown.
	Males.	Females.	Males.	Females	Males.	Females	Males.	Females	Males.	Females	Males.	Females	Males	Fems	Males	Fems	Males	Fems	
Adams,	106	92	77	86	90	74	104	113	84	66	38	31	7	8	....	1	....	....	1
Alexandria,	96	96	89	72	77	68	88	80	61	41	27	17	7	5	....	....	....	....	......
Antwerp,	101	102	84	68	75	75	150	105	71	47	22	25	10	8	1	....	....	....	......
Brownville,	97	96	99	92	92	86	106	118	75	62	34	32	8	9	....	....	....	....	4
Cape Vincent,	87	84	66	75	88	67	132	105	73	56	22	17	6	6	2	2	....	....	2
Champion,	55	62	44	56	49	53	73	71	69	53	32	31	12	9	1	1	....	....	......
Clayton,	105	107	108	102	101	89	126	114	81	70	28	24	6	8	1	....	....	....	......
Ellisburgh,	165	170	138	138	123	113	169	172	121	108	66	59	10	9	3	....	....	....	......
Henderson,	54	65	58	51	40	41	69	70	48	28	23	19	7	7	....	3	....	....	......
Houndsfield,	93	86	78	85	75	77	123	105	72	69	47	36	12	8	....	....	....	....	......
Le Ray,	79	92	79	79	87	73	111	102	90	72	37	30	9	4	....	....	....	....	5
Lorraine,	33	36	31	33	26	33	59	55	38	24	16	17	4	5	1	1	....	....	1
Lyme,	82	75	68	53	46	45	89	75	37	48	26	19	6	4	....	....	....	....	2
Orleans,	84	78	63	58	62	61	89	79	66	55	29	21	8	13	....	1	....	....	1
Pamelia,	65	64	72	72	51	39	87	73	58	50	30	20	5	8	1	3	1	....	......
Philadelphia,	66	63	38	31	37	25	72	60	40	35	16	12	2	7	....	2	....	....	1
Rodman,	62	59	53	48	35	38	53	51	37	37	31	27	7	5	....	1	....	....	......
Rutland,	54	61	53	51	51	51	62	82	60	45	33	28	11	4	....	1	....	....	......
Theresa,	72	54	58	73	60	50	71	73	46	33	19	14	4	8	1	2	....	....	2
Watertown,	273	228	184	214	150	152	209	198	117	103	53	55	10	15	1	1	....	....	7
Wilna,	77	78	80	77	68	52	101	90	78	57	30	22	8	3	....	....	....	1	......
Worth,	11	9	17	11	11	13	15	18	10	7	3	3	....	1	....	....	....	....	......
Total,	1,917	1,857	1,637	1,625	1,494	1,375	2,158	2,009	1,432	1,166	662	559	159	154	12	19	1	1	26

KINGS COUNTY.

TOWNS.	Under 1. Males.	Under 1. Females	1 and under 5. Males.	1 and under 5. Females	5 and under 10. Males.	5 and under 10. Females	10 and under 15. Males.	10 and under 15. Females	15 and under 20. Males.	15 and under 20. Females	20 and under 25. Males.	20 and under 25. Females.	25 and under 30. Males.	25 and under 30. Females	30 and under 35. Males.	30 and under 35. Females.
Brooklyn City:																
1st ward, ...	68	52	316	349	309	336	277	281	283	362	346	588	378	477	276	328
2d ward, ...	132	163	440	481	420	458	401	440	350	477	470	596	456	513	400	345
3d ward, ...	89	90	341	329	310	391	350	400	387	635	445	1, 026	427	684	308	476
4th ward, ...	158	159	508	541	523	636	570	594	603	823	692	1, 083	618	802	458	552
5th ward, ...	329	334	993	954	938	847	823	828	720	851	821	1, 053	862	928	732	719
6th ward, ...	324	322	964	981	866	925	779	837	764	1, 162	924	1, 626	1, 021	1, 360	913	884
7th ward, ...	196	194	808	759	761	785	680	753	488	708	444	753	573	702	579	558
8th ward, ...	84	78	363	325	325	315	280	257	229	262	242	280	259	307	253	234
9th ward, ...	156	138	527	548	565	594	523	523	400	399	319	431	414	458	445	422
10th ward, ...	361	348	1, 186	1, 226	1, 142	1, 156	1, 012	1, 118	914	1, 247	1, 023	1, 743	992	1, 374	965	1, 082
11th ward, ...	363	341	1, 185	1, 222	1, 288	1, 314	1, 106	1, 159	983	1, 362	1, 032	1, 540	1, 017	1, 311	846	928
12th ward, ...	186	175	473	489	394	427	346	305	242	233	294	347	402	422	418	404
13th ward, ...	199	211	773	709	757	747	688	773	641	1, 026	606	1, 117	603	819	563	657
14th ward, ...	161	171	872	835	732	753	649	683	487	594	570	651	624	708	671	600
15th ward, ...	79	72	417	400	425	430	345	389	276	355	264	332	288	357	294	270
16th ward, ...	385	357	998	974	881	939	688	718	551	597	568	723	808	889	907	793
17th ward, ...	93	112	356	370	320	342	264	273	186	252	240	335	326	351	288	247
18th ward, ...	36	37	165	164	160	105	125	143	103	148	115	138	108	152	117	103
Total Brooklyn, ...	3, 399	3, 354	11, 685	11, 656	11, 116	11, 590	9, 906	10, 474	8, 607	11, 493	9, 415	14, 362	10, 176	12, 614	9, 433	9, 602
Flatbush, ...	47	41	114	130	185	152	152	133	124	165	162	257	155	201	152	172
Flatlands, ...	18	9	25	20	80	80	115	95	91	75	76	72	76	68	81	60
Gravesend, ...	17	15	56	50	51	50	75	62	68	76	82	76	67	50	51	37
New Lots, ...	40	34	136	125	123	127	120	100	103	97	116	135	116	107	103	90
New Utrecht, ...	35	33	116	130	129	117	145	132	125	137	224	182	180	141	143	110
Total, ...	3, 556	3, 486	12, 132	12, 111	11, 684	12, 116	10, 513	10, 996	9, 118	12, 043	10, 075	15, 084	10, 770	13, 181	9, 963	10, 071

LEWIS COUNTY.

TOWNS.	Under 1. Males.	Under 1. Females	1 and under 5. Males.	1 and under 5. Females	5 and under 10. Males.	5 and under 10. Females	10 and under 15. Males.	10 and under 15. Females	15 and under 20. Males.	15 and under 20. Females	20 and under 25. Males.	20 and under 25. Females.	25 and under 30. Males.	25 and under 30. Females	30 and under 35. Males.	30 and under 35. Females.
Croghan, ...	21	22	105	95	112	101	109	81	95	59	46	51	52	50	59	42
Denmark, ...	30	28	114	104	122	140	118	132	121	129	87	125	100	109	82	79
Diana, ...	23	20	87	69	88	78	82	54	71	54	44	61	50	39	36	34
Greig, ...	22	13	71	63	80	56	82	60	69	68	65	55	55	49	53	43
Harrisburgh, ...	11	19	77	73	81	66	88	65	76	61	58	71	44	39	48	45
High Market, ...	16	15	77	78	86	91	100	88	60	43	51	33	39	33	26	23
Lewis, ...	26	15	71	85	84	77	60	76	50	51	52	47	48	41	42	34
Leyden, ...	19	19	78	90	110	113	122	105	81	103	87	79	70	71	57	61
Lowville, ...	17	22	92	92	118	110	102	110	106	122	127	150	86	93	74	86
Martinsburgh, ...	22	33	140	135	152	195	139	160	121	145	117	122	73	85	85	86
Montague, ...	10	12	41	43	47	39	44	31	25	18	16	14	24	20	29	16
New Bremen, ...	37	26	116	92	131	114	99	102	78	79	51	60	63	54	46	46
Osceola, ...	13	9	23	33	36	29	39	40	26	26	12	18	20	18	18	15
Pinckney, ...	12	11	70	50	67	72	69	48	48	50	43	45	44	41	43	45
Turin, ...	16	25	96	74	124	97	113	95	91	94	74	92	77	63	50	59
Watson, ...	3	4	50	53	67	54	79	46	63	45	39	35	37	27	27	37
West Turin, ...	44	40	159	154	164	161	176	141	122	114	100	105	100	72	81	92
Total, ...	342	333	1, 467	1, 383	1, 669	1, 593	1, 621	1, 434	1, 303	1, 261	1, 069	1, 163	982	904	856	843

LIVINGSTON COUNTY.

TOWNS.	Under 1. Males.	Under 1. Females	1 and under 5. Males.	1 and under 5. Females	5 and under 10. Males.	5 and under 10. Females	10 and under 15. Males.	10 and under 15. Females	15 and under 20. Males.	15 and under 20. Females	20 and under 25. Males.	20 and under 25. Females.	25 and under 30. Males.	25 and under 30. Females	30 and under 35. Males.	30 and under 35. Females.
Avon, ...	27	33	115	137	146	132	126	133	146	180	197	182	140	126	92	77
Caledonia, ...	29	34	108	92	81	95	96	87	111	87	133	131	133	98	103	68
Conesus, ...	24	15	65	76	80	79	73	89	91	83	77	68	58	66	56	55
Geneseo, ...	33	28	151	135	152	147	163	144	171	183	169	183	128	117	98	101
Groveland, ...	22	28	90	72	93	89	87	92	86	106	74	84	79	63	52	55
Leicester, ...	24	29	81	97	97	124	113	121	124	122	108	123	109	100	76	72
Lima, ...	24	18	144	126	121	145	137	138	147	159	139	153	124	122	99	106
Livonia, ...	26	34	128	129	119	140	140	157	149	157	159	140	114	121	83	96
Mount Morris, ...	54	41	208	197	219	222	239	238	249	214	188	223	179	142	115	145
North Dansville, ...	48	63	208	203	217	234	191	223	156	192	126	169	131	139	140	172
Nunda, ...	30	28	152	125	169	178	169	202	152	158	136	138	101	123	85	88
Portage, ...	19	29	106	79	99	86	79	87	61	93	74	66	62	78	49	60
Sparta, ...	11	10	62	63	58	71	65	59	78	76	78	72	58	45	38	40
Springwater, ...	29	22	142	163	182	139	150	148	149	135	112	101	99	98	97	77
West Sparta, ...	30	27	85	74	114	101	85	82	83	78	56	66	67	73	67	46
York, ...	25	30	122	106	148	153	148	134	171	159	181	156	154	132	84	80
Total, ...	455	469	1, 967	1, 874	2, 095	2, 135	2, 061	2, 134	2, 124	2, 182	2, 007	2, 055	1, 736	1, 643	1, 334	1, 338

MADISON COUNTY.

TOWNS.	Under 1. Males.	Under 1. Females	1 and under 5. Males.	1 and under 5. Females	5 and under 10. Males.	5 and under 10. Females	10 and under 15. Males.	10 and under 15. Females	15 and under 20. Males.	15 and under 20. Females	20 and under 25. Males.	20 and under 25. Females.	25 and under 30. Males.	25 and under 30. Females	30 and under 35. Males.	30 and under 35. Females.
Brookfield, ...	43	47	171	172	177	200	233	208	197	211	203	196	151	153	117	130
Cazenovia, ...	55	49	192	207	247	234	248	261	216	233	185	238	149	190	155	167
De Ruyter, ...	20	17	96	88	131	103	119	109	86	109	88	100	78	77	45	54
Eaton, ...	53	55	206	178	210	216	192	210	213	238	184	226	171	175	160	167
Fenner, ...	19	25	78	82	84	89	95	105	86	89	72	68	58	59	44	62
Georgetown, ...	11	21	65	80	90	84	84	75	64	73	63	64	67	60	44	45
Hamilton, ...	28	39	159	144	190	179	209	189	146	204	184	227	162	162	149	119
Lebanon, ...	25	23	76	74	91	93	88	99	85	83	82	86	71	64	53	37
Lenox, ...	101	126	445	370	417	456	478	407	376	450	414	370	352	323	267	244
Madison, ...	26	29	127	119	149	135	117	131	120	148	115	126	84	101	86	83
Nelson, ...	26	21	83	82	118	98	120	106	106	82	79	89	71	55	45	60
Smithfield, ...	14	21	75	89	91	82	103	80	95	94	60	72	52	54	46	47
Stockbridge, ...	22	28	103	113	138	110	129	124	110	126	90	82	72	76	64	72
Sullivan, ...	76	67	301	299	320	288	303	268	267	254	281	278	269	219	204	188
Total, ...	519	568	2, 177	2. 097	2, 453	2. 367	2. 518	2. 372	2. 167	2, 394	2. 100	2, 222	1, 807	1, 768	1, 479	1, 475

KINGS COUNTY.—(Continued.)

TOWNS.	35 and under 40.		40 and under 45.		45 and under 50.		50 and under 60.		60 and under 70.		70 and under 80.		80 and under 90.		90 and under 100.		100 and upwards		Ages unknown.
	Males.	Females.	Males.	Females.	Males.	Females	Males.	Females	Males.	Females	Males.	Females.	Males	Fems	Males	Fems	Males	Fems	
Brooklyn City:																			
1st ward,	239	216	203	168	107	89	111	115	46	60	13	29	2	10	2	....	....	....	5
2d ward,	267	251	232	197	136	117	184	199	69	98	12	29	5	7	....	2	....	....	36
3d ward,	303	306	240	255	177	169	225	241	82	117	21	43	5	15	....	1	....	....	12
4th ward,	423	401	318	354	225	198	260	327	119	194	43	66	5	25	1	1	....	....	2
5th ward,	497	484	446	428	289	239	372	403	140	176	40	68	7	18	3	....	....	....	10
6th ward,	643	558	499	451	274	242	326	384	134	189	33	51	6	24	....	....	....	....	24
7th ward,	431	388	329	326	258	204	255	261	109	125	30	46	6	6	....	6	....	....	2
8th ward,	196	160	195	139	114	89	121	96	42	46	8	14	1	3	1	....	....	....	......
9th ward,	353	331	336	291	193	134	198	184	95	81	24	28	6	11	....	2	....	2	2
10th ward,	718	713	611	577	380	317	419	449	162	238	72	82	15	29	1	....	....	....	77
11th ward,	798	719	626	610	403	370	460	491	170	292	40	113	6	24	....	7	1	....	86
12th ward,	264	230	222	179	107	70	118	126	28	50	14	16	4	4	....	....	....	....	1
13th ward,	463	454	400	367	234	224	296	302	112	160	31	75	11	13	....	....	....	....	13
14th ward,	449	368	328	298	222	144	231	255	85	134	37	53	4	8	1	2	1	....	33
15th ward,	242	233	213	175	119	106	146	140	46	70	22	23	2	7	....	....	....	....	22
16th ward,	602	552	474	398	319	248	316	335	115	134	28	34	5	7	....	....	....	1	6
17th ward,	204	152	168	110	80	69	117	113	36	51	13	14	3	5	....	....	....	....	18
18th ward,	76	83	68	60	50	44	83	55	22	30	9	6	2	3	....	....	....	....	1
Total Brooklyn,..	7,168	6,599	5,908	5,383	3,687	3,073	4,238	4,476	1,612	2,245	490	790	95	219	9	21	2	3	350
Flatbush, ...	115	108	72	89	81	65	107	105	54	61	23	25	13	10	1	5	....	....	4
Flatlands, ...	90	56	57	45	40	36	42	20	55	40	22	11	10	10	1	2	....	....	......
Gravesend, ...	41	45	44	30	36	25	44	41	21	16	10	16	1	3	....	....	....	....	......
New Lots, ...	100	69	67	54	47	41	78	52	27	34	5	10	....	4	....	1	....	....	......
New Utrecht, ...	97	70	65	90	61	50	74	66	28	25	12	9	1	3	....	....	....	....	......
Total, ...	7,611	6,947	6,213	5,691	3,952	3,290	4,583	4,760	1,797	2,421	562	861	120	249	11	29	2	3	354

LEWIS COUNTY.—(Continued.)

TOWNS.	35 and under 40. Males.	Females.	40 and under 45. Males.	Females.	45 and under 50. Males.	Females	50 and under 60. Males.	Females	60 and under 70. Males.	Females	70 and under 80. Males.	Females.	80 and under 90. Males	Fems	90 and under 100. Males	Fems	100 and upwards Males	Fems	Ages unknown.
Croghan, ...	45	40	33	44	42	32	69	45	32	27	8	10	1	....	....	....	....	....	3
Denmark, ...	68	69	63	62	66	62	91	90	59	56	35	27	6	6	....	....	....	....	1
Diana, ...	39	17	32	24	24	24	47	33	21	17	3	5	1	....	....	....	....	....	......
Greig, ...	35	33	27	17	13	19	50	35	28	23	9	8	1	1	....	....	....	....	......
Harrisburgh,.........	40	34	38	20	21	24	46	34	20	20	10	5	3	3	....	....	....	....	......
High Market, ...	27	31	30	32	20	13	41	31	13	15	6	5	1	1	....	....	....	....	......
Lewis, ...	40	28	35	32	27	28	32	22	20	14	10	3	2	3	1	1	....	....	......
Leyden, ...	60	55	55	56	43	46	74	62	40	41	22	24	8	5	....	....	....	....	......
Lowville, ...	63	70	61	50	37	52	78	68	44	44	32	19	11	7	....	1	....	....	......
Martinsburgh, ...	57	86	59	61	40	61	92	86	36	41	20	22	11	7	....	....	....	....	......
Montague, ...	24	16	12	18	20	10	9	15	9	3	1	3	1	1	....	....	....	....	......
New Bremen, ...	54	42	49	39	33	35	63	53	29	20	9	20	6	1	....	....	....	....	......
Osceola, ...	19	14	10	8	9	15	21	16	14	8	1	2	....	1	....	....	....	....	......
Pinckney, ...	39	24	26	28	17	22	37	31	16	19	12	3	2	4	1	....	....	....	......
Turin,................	68	48	29	40	38	40	75	67	32	27	15	15	7	5	....	....	....	....	2
Watson,..............	33	25	34	20	20	26	32	23	17	18	5	5	2	4	....	....	....	....	......
West Turin, ...	70	64	62	56	59	43	81	71	47	43	25	20	5	6	....	1	....	....	......
Total, ...	781	696	655	607	529	552	938	782	477	436	223	196	68	55	2	3	....	....	6

LIVINGSTON COUNTY.—(Continued.)

TOWNS.	35 and under 40. Males.	Females.	40 and under 45. Males.	Females.	45 and under 50. Males.	Females	50 and under 60. Males.	Females	60 and under 70. Males.	Females	70 and under 80. Males.	Females.	80 and under 90. Males	Fems	90 and under 100. Males	Fems	100 and upwards Males	Fems	Ages unknown.
Avon, ...	83	72	70	69	50	52	84	81	52	42	20	21	4	5	....	....	....	....	......
Caledonia, ...	76	58	52	32	35	32	47	53	35	40	15	14	9	....	7	....	....	....	......
Conesus, ...	40	30	26	40	23	15	50	44	26	19	16	12	2	3	....	....	....	....	2
Geneseo, ...	91	99	73	66	58	52	88	84	50	45	32	18	7	6	....	1	....	....	10
Groveland,...........	46	64	47	35	33	31	42	46	28	20	10	14	2	5	....	....	....	....	......
Leicester, ...	68	52	47	48	34	29	69	60	60	57	16	10	....	6	....	....	....	....	......
Lima, ...	84	89	74	69	59	50	105	96	47	48	13	21	7	5	....	....	....	....	1
Livonia, ...	83	74	63	59	65	54	84	80	52	66	29	22	10	1	....	....	....	....	1
Mount Morris, ...	125	128	97	119	105	88	147	142	71	64	31	20	6	8	....	1	....	....	17
North Dansville,......	110	96	91	94	72	53	80	105	65	57	20	13	3	7	....	....	....	....	3
Nunda,...............	78	75	70	91	79	69	119	95	49	54	25	25	4	8	2	....	....	1	8
Portage, ...	55	55	40	23	35	31	53	55	41	30	6	6	7	2	1	1	....	....	......
Sparta, ...	29	35	28	28	28	27	48	41	35	25	7	10	3	5	....	....	....	....	......
Springwater, ...	69	64	53	45	62	65	76	64	50	38	23	20	3	4	....	1	....	1	......
West Sparta,.........	34	33	26	34	29	32	51	36	25	27	18	10	4	2	....	1	....	....	......
York, ...	67	73	70	81	55	65	115	89	60	53	19	31	10	4	1	1	....	....	5
Total, ...	1,138	1,097	927	933	832	745	1,258	1,171	746	691	309	267	81	71	11	6	....	2	49

MADISON COUNTY.—(Continued.)

TOWNS.	35 and under 40. Males.	Females.	40 and under 45. Males.	Females.	45 and under 50. Males.	Females	50 and under 60. Males.	Females	60 and under 70. Males.	Females	70 and under 80. Males.	Females.	80 and under 90. Males	Fems	90 and under 100. Males	Fems	100 and upwards Males	Fems	Ages unknown.
Brookfield, ...	126	108	128	93	78	77	121	133	72	85	56	51	17	12	....	1	....	....	3
Cazenovia, ...	148	152	114	134	114	126	183	162	82	98	48	64	24	16	1	2	....	....	1
De Ruyter, ...	67	64	48	46	45	49	76	71	37	33	27	23	8	5	....	....	....	....	2
Eaton,................	137	123	121	107	96	90	135	138	66	73	42	38	10	7	3	1	....	....	20
Fenner, ...	60	43	29	47	37	36	59	63	42	37	19	22	8	3	1	1	....	....	......
Georgetown, ...	55	48	39	35	34	35	69	61	24	16	12	11	5	4	....	....	....	....	4
Hamilton, ...	116	141	116	99	95	100	145	132	77	99	44	42	16	11	4	1	....	....	9
Lebanon, ...	56	59	47	53	39	33	65	57	32	27	15	24	13	9	....	....	....	....	2
Lenox, ...	269	251	216	188	198	168	286	223	124	130	58	55	16	16	....	1	....	1	4
Madison, ...	71	86	76	75	56	53	95	84	50	50	38	25	8	15	....	1	....	....	1
Nelson,..............	64	65	63	60	33	50	72	78	42	33	30	23	14	4	1	3	....	....	......
Smithfield,...........	40	41	32	43	35	42	63	49	25	24	23	14	3	3	1	....	....	....	1
Stockbridge, ...	61	67	55	55	46	27	71	63	45	46	24	21	5	3	2	2	....	....	......
Sullivan, ...	170	140	152	123	130	93	146	146	81	70	50	41	8	10	3	4	....	....	4
Total, ...	1,443	1,388	1,236	1,158	1,036	979	1,586	1,460	799	821	486	454	155	118	16	17	....	1	51

MONROE COUNTY.

TOWNS.	Under 1.		1 and under 5.		5 and under 10.		10 and under 15.		15 and under 20.		20 and under 25.		25 and under 30.		30 and under 35.	
	Males.	Females.	Males.	Females.	Males.	Females.	Males.	Females.	Males.	Females.	Males.	Females.	Males.	Females.	Males.	Females.
Brighton,	48	46	161	145	193	150	148	160	165	181	193	172	204	150	111	110
Chili,	35	23	122	130	143	130	124	120	107	115	114	105	104	103	83	68
Clarkson,	28	21	109	110	118	118	121	137	117	109	112	98	85	102	98	82
Gates,	46	35	131	125	154	134	149	144	107	107	113	99	101	90	72	75
Greece,	63	63	251	266	271	258	269	263	230	223	221	221	195	184	171	138
Henrietta,	24	17	119	109	101	119	119	104	115	113	127	114	101	95	83	81
Irondequoit,	54	69	225	210	234	241	192	170	148	148	114	121	117	102	120	133
Mendon,	32	37	150	134	149	163	175	157	154	159	167	162	134	134	103	110
Ogden,	39	35	163	167	152	133	148	156	150	165	191	177	176	138	138	120
Parma,	40	30	145	157	152	180	168	150	143	146	128	123	117	132	97	85
Penfield,	41	26	161	148	181	180	179	187	162	183	154	137	111	125	104	109
Perrington,	37	38	140	148	156	158	170	157	181	199	193	144	165	128	136	123
Pittsford,	27	24	118	113	116	112	100	104	112	103	121	105	103	90	103	84
Riga,	19	21	99	92	127	115	111	121	124	119	108	94	96	87	79	76
Rochester city:																
1st ward,	27	33	76	95	79	91	110	116	100	170	155	177	132	132	92	103
2d ward,	44	56	178	163	167	189	162	212	199	230	273	271	219	216	149	112
3d ward,	66	67	237	216	245	239	243	246	190	279	194	298	181	230	153	150
4th ward,	48	46	141	155	174	157	133	180	154	214	199	263	180	170	146	139
5th ward,	61	76	267	237	239	248	239	225	198	242	247	281	223	229	190	169
6th ward,	122	132	354	334	302	300	239	239	212	263	254	325	317	306	287	226
7th ward,	78	87	256	274	301	265	262	253	208	231	177	212	189	244	198	203
8th ward,	56	74	248	253	231	275	229	236	197	215	166	178	166	186	156	140
9th ward,	154	131	478	463	456	445	543	433	422	337	297	326	303	312	293	250
10th ward,	73	65	298	300	304	318	249	264	184	249	201	271	225	221	224	210
Total Rochester,	729	767	2, 533	2, 490	2, 498	2, 527	2, 409	2, 404	2, 064	2, 430	2, 163	2, 602	2, 135	2, 246	1, 888	1, 702
Rush,	24	23	97	104	89	99	93	96	83	86	117	97	76	67	74	64
Sweden,	50	59	201	193	168	194	175	200	201	240	247	239	194	186	215	157
Union,	41	31	112	140	161	158	161	153	166	94	105	100	101	101	75	74
Webster,	31	20	127	107	145	129	124	144	135	131	115	119	101	103	82	77
Wheatland,	37	42	143	153	148	142	159	161	147	136	165	155	129	137	125	92
Total,	1, 445	1, 427	5, 307	5, 241	5, 456	5, 440	5, 294	5, 288	4, 811	5, 187	4, 968	5, 184	4, 545	4, 500	3, 957	3, 560

MONTGOMERY COUNTY.

TOWNS.	Under 1. Males.	Under 1. Females.	1–5 Males.	1–5 Females.	5–10 Males.	5–10 Females.	10–15 Males.	10–15 Females.	15–20 Males.	15–20 Females.	20–25 Males.	20–25 Females.	25–30 Males.	25–30 Females.	30–35 Males.	30–35 Females.
Amsterdam,	46	58	216	179	226	217	230	251	203	227	152	203	159	172	129	134
Canajoharie,	72	53	229	210	255	248	241	194	222	253	197	213	153	154	149	134
Charleston,	22	23	100	89	100	118	90	109	109	93	93	79	83	86	53	64
Florida,	46	41	171	156	172	170	193	181	197	162	145	146	143	125	116	119
Glen,	50	41	136	145	186	173	147	158	156	144	170	152	157	118	111	109
Minden,	64	63	259	194	297	271	268	289	267	272	224	239	207	172	160	158
Mohawk,	41	42	154	177	191	152	188	193	164	180	157	158	148	136	119	100
Palatine,	33	33	130	131	164	152	155	153	132	146	114	119	112	104	90	68
Root,	40	38	137	153	164	147	171	139	152	124	151	137	149	117	122	76
St. Johnsville,	31	22	83	98	117	99	87	92	102	92	88	94	81	82	83	56
Total,	445	414	1, 615	1, 532	1, 872	1, 747	1, 770	1, 759	1, 704	1, 693	1, 491	1, 540	1, 392	1, 266	1, 132	1, 018

NEW-YORK COUNTY.

TOWNS.	Under 1. Males.	Under 1. Females.	1–5 Males.	1–5 Females.	5–10 Males.	5–10 Females.	10–15 Males.	10–15 Females.	15–20 Males.	15–20 Females.	20–25 Males.	20–25 Females.	25–30 Males.	25–30 Females.	30–35 Males.	30–35 Females.
New-York City:																
1st ward,	245	248	735	688	571	525	560	562	599	592	842	894	964	877	821	741
2d ward,	28	27	80	88	72	80	107	88	244	158	404	267	332	173	231	140
3d ward,	68	68	200	187	175	187	187	189	503	411	1, 002	634	969	456	644	274
4th ward,	388	426	1, 123	990	918	916	970	789	1, 085	1, 091	1, 588	1, 740	1, 634	1, 557	1, 416	1, 147
5th ward,	315	312	906	1, 004	856	897	795	819	885	1, 169	1. 303	1, 678	1, 467	1, 517	1, 300	1, 141
6th ward,	428	446	1, 291	1, 244	1, 134	1, 061	1,.116	984	1, 139	1, 240	1, 635	1, 723	1, 629	1, 627	1, 406	1, 236
7th ward,	554	607	1, 868	1, 949	1, 564	1, 580	1, 454	1, 510	1, 536	1, 829	1, 755	2, 530	2, 051	2, 301	1, 747	1, 616
8th ward,	518	514	1, 631	1, 687	1, 436	1, 482	1, 226	1, 430	1, 421	1, 962	1, 842	2, 841	2, 074	2, 391	1, 799	1, 715
9th ward,	649	610	2, 051	1, 959	1, 928	1, 947	1, 782	1, 863	1, 725	2, 543	2, 102	3, 079	2, 056	2, 603	1, 792	1, 811
10th ward,	419	508	1, 360	1, 287	1, 194	1, 211	1, 031	1, 162	1, 222	1, 516	1, 649	1, 988	1, 730	1, 784	1, 523	1, 209
11th ward,	1, 182	1, 353	3, 119	2, 783	2, 756	2, 695	2, 596	2 578	2, 313	2, 741	2, 644	3, 198	3, 051	3, 163	2, 756	2, 426
12th ward,	328	367	883	838	1, 231	973	1, 144	847	833	949	811	1, 115	796	1, 033	719	793
13th ward,	473	527	1, 448	1, 359	1, 293	1, 304	1, 237	1, 304	1, 238	1, 417	1, 451	1, 641	1, 532	1, 519	1, 353	1, 192
14th ward,	397	371	1, 249	1, 278	1, 158	1, 257	999	1, 151	1, 094	1, 404	1, 413	1. 888	1, 481	1, 592	1, 328	1, 204
15th ward,	237	177	796	852	929	991	951	1, 074	974	1, 839	1, 106	2, 427	1, 231	1, 860	1, 038	1, 324
16th ward,	715	775	2, 093	2, 137	1, 972	2, 038	1, 830	1, 904	1, 658	2, 369	1, 817	3, 050	1, 975	2, 624	1, 815	1, 947
17th ward,	1, 066	1, 191	3, 226	3, 317	2, 871	2, 825	2, 617	2, 525	2, 532	3, 222	3, 019	4, 429	3, 536	4, 103	3, 075	2, 792
18th ward,	632	618	2, 007	2, 149	1, 837	1, 849	1, 723	1, 855	1, 506	2, 258	1, 692	3, 346	1, 907	3, 017	1, 790	2, 121
19th ward,	270	283	890	854	1, 063	827	1, 097	815	798	893	780	1, 089	847	1, 109	892	905
20th ward,	986	957	2, 927	2. 982	2, 571	2, 594	2, 198	2, 360	1, 830	2, 436	1, 970	3, 006	2, 422	2, 893	2, 435	2, 283
21st ward,	478	514	1, 509	1, 601	1, 390	1, 425	1, 212	1, 284	1, 038	1, 596	1, 247	2, 198	1, 385	1, 947	1, 356	1, 498
22d ward,	400	436	1, 432	1, 410	1, 368	1, 337	1, 268	1, 146	865	1, 161	868	1, 260	1, 104	1, 272	1, 126	1, 042
Total,	10. 776	11, 335	32. 824	32. 643	30, 287	30, 001	28, 100	28, 239	27, 038	34, 796	32. 940	46, 021	36, 173	41, 418	32, 362	30, 557

NIAGARA COUNTY.

TOWNS.	Under 1. Males.	Under 1. Females.	1–5 Males.	1–5 Females.	5–10 Males.	5–10 Females.	10–15 Males.	10–15 Females.	15–20 Males.	15–20 Females.	20–25 Males.	20–25 Females.	25–30 Males.	25–30 Females.	30–35 Males.	30–35 Females.
Cambria,	20	26	116	132	149	129	122	144	140	130	105	95	88	90	87	86
Hartland,	39	46	178	178	155	167	184	175	154	168	144	140	119	110	120	106
Lewiston,	61	56	208	177	198	194	185	186	172	198	164	185	132	144	137	95
Lockport,	204	191	744	724	782	842	750	848	651	816	624	681	575	561	529	507
Newfane,	42	36	157	169	193	200	226	168	190	183	156	163	133	113	99	98
Niagara,	81	114	364	269	274	264	239	261	234	284	389	382	421	311	329	219
Pendleton,	33	26	118	103	126	138	118	101	103	76	88	74	77	73	65	46
Porter,	26	35	145	142	176	179	184	148	132	161	153	128	104	104	93	88
Royalton,	67	82	255	279	286	247	273	288	276	258	289	222	246	195	197	164

MONROE COUNTY.—(CONTINUED.)

TOWNS.	35 and under 40. Males	Females	40 and under 45. Males	Females	45 and under 50. Males	Females	50 and under 60. Males	Females	60 and under 70. Males	Females	70 and under 80. Males	Females	80 and under 90. Males	Fems	90 and under 100. Males	Fems	100 and upwards. Males	Fems	Ages unknown.
Brighton,	114	93	111	95	81	74	130	95	65	54	32	18	5	3	....	....	....	...	16
Chili,	73	65	57	48	39	47	75	64	37	34	13	16	5	4	....	....	....	....	......
Clarkson,	69	74	53	43	50	39	78	63	47	53	14	15	8	6	....	....	....	....	......
Gates,	73	62	59	66	50	54	101	77	41	41	22	15	1	2	1	....	....	....	......
Greece,	159	134	117	100	111	88	148	112	87	76	23	29	5	7	....	....	....	....	4
Henrietta,	62	57	61	47	35	39	73	68	56	49	20	21	6	4	....	....	....	....	5
Irondequoit,	108	99	107	92	68	48	86	75	64	51	18	9	3	4	....	....	....	....	4
Mendon,	101	98	75	74	67	62	112	105	72	61	24	19	7	13	....	1	....	....	4
Ogden,	99	79	73	74	68	60	108	85	61	59	29	23	9	4	....	1	....	....	......
Parma,	87	88	67	57	70	57	103	97	56	53	26	22	5	1	....	....	....	....	1
Penfield,	95	92	91	77	72	60	103	95	60	40	23	21	5	4	1	1	....	....	3
Perrinton,	112	107	88	77	89	63	109	88	58	53	23	21	3	7	1	1	....	....	2
Pittsford,	80	66	61	52	41	40	74	65	44	37	18	14	5	....	....	....	....	....	1
Riga,	76	63	56	48	35	31	64	59	41	34	12	12	3	3	....	....	....	....	......
Rochester city:																			
1st ward,	87	68	59	54	52	48	53	53	23	17	7	9	....	2	....	....	....	....	5
2d ward,	111	122	90	92	61	65	87	85	23	47	14	13	1	4	....	....	....	....	1
3d ward,	133	151	119	130	98	94	127	145	59	54	18	18	1	2	....	1	....	....	2
4th ward,	126	106	83	77	67	69	84	82	43	50	21	9	3	3	....	....	....	....	1
5th ward,	160	124	115	116	84	67	90	86	35	48	10	10	6	5	....	....	....	....	49
6th ward,	192	166	134	115	95	74	132	122	54	57	19	16	2	1	....	....	....	....	......
7th ward,	161	152	132	127	105	91	142	116	53	65	13	12	2	4	1	....	....	....	5
8th ward,	120	117	116	100	77	75	113	107	46	41	16	13	....	3	....	1	....	....	......
9th ward,	232	205	190	191	145	95	148	157	66	82	25	28	3	6	1	....	....	....	1
10th ward,	165	173	113	102	101	76	108	101	43	53	14	15	3	4	....	....	....	....	5
Total Rochester,	1,487	1,384	1,151	1,104	885	754	1,084	1,054	445	514	157	143	21	34	2	2	....	....	69
Rush,	52	46	38	50	27	38	68	51	23	23	11	13	7	4	....	....	....	....	......
Sweden,	126	136	105	88	75	67	120	129	74	73	20	18	10	5	1	....	....	1	......
Union,	81	65	57	51	47	39	78	62	49	28	15	12	3	7	....	....	1	....	1
Webster,	65	64	72	58	69	51	89	81	43	57	23	13	3	5	2	1	....	....	2
Wheatland,	96	83	65	67	59	50	86	83	55	49	20	13	3	12	1	1	....	....	2
Total,	3.215	2,955	2,564	2,368	2,048	1,761	2,889	2,608	1,478	1,439	543	467	117	129	9	8	1	1	114

MONTGOMERY COUNTY.—(CONTINUED.)

TOWNS.	35 and under 40. Males	Females	40 and under 45. Males	Females	45 and under 50. Males	Females	50 and under 60. Males	Females	60 and under 70. Males	Females	70 and under 80. Males	Females	80 and under 90. Males	Fems	90 and under 100. Males	Fems	100 and upwards. Males	Fems	Ages unknown.
Amsterdam,	107	145	119	113	109	90	146	126	83	78	33	36	8	11	....	1	....	....	5
Canajoharie,	112	117	92	91	102	69	128	114	68	78	21	27	7	9	2	....	....	....	8
Charleston,	67	55	49	51	45	37	58	72	40	41	23	23	18	7	2	....	....	....	......
Florida,	108	90	79	86	62	63	109	90	53	50	30	37	4	7	2	1	....	....	......
Glen,	90	91	86	65	77	59	94	77	45	48	24	25	12	7	1	2	....	....	......
Minden,	140	128	136	123	116	106	140	128	75	83	38	33	10	10	....	1	....	....	......
Mohawk,	91	65	88	74	70	58	88	91	44	53	17	25	6	4	....	2	....	....	1
Palatine,	78	85	55	46	51	44	91	78	59	48	20	15	7	11	....	1	....	....	......
Root,	86	71	66	74	59	55	99	74	41	44	23	18	5	5	....	....	....	....	11
St. Johnsville,	56	42	40	41	35	34	49	38	32	34	16	13	2	1	....	1	....	....	3
Total,	935	889	810	764	726	615	1,002	888	540	557	245	252	79	72	7	9	....	....	28

NEW-YORK COUNTY.—(CONTINUED.)

TOWNS.	35 and under 40. Males	Females	40 and under 45. Males	Females	45 and under 50. Males	Females	50 and under 60. Males	Females	60 and under 70. Males	Females	70 and under 80. Males	Females	80 and under 90. Males	Fems	90 and under 100. Males	Fems	100 and upwards. Males	Fems	Ages unknown.
New-York City:																			
1st ward,	545	368	497	400	217	162	297	247	97	101	32	24	3	4	....	....	....	1	27
2d ward,	151	68	126	76	66	34	85	47	35	26	8	4	....	1	....	....	....	....	......
3d ward,	411	179	310	161	169	79	178	106	47	50	24	12	7	18	1	2	....	1	......
4th ward,	920	617	737	609	413	290	507	435	159	211	44	44	0	13	1	2	....	2	107
5th ward,	830	682	718	612	450	348	502	466	186	238	59	84	10	32	4	6	....	1	25
6th ward,	972	779	830	714	472	400	572	517	223	260	52	40	13	20	8	5	....	....	346
7th ward,	1,150	1,002	997	930	662	585	720	784	331	452	96	135	29	38	2	4	....	2	52
8th ward,	1,275	1,133	934	1,015	597	522	685	795	294	467	73	169	26	44	3	15	....	....	34
9th ward,	1,286	1,296	996	1,009	696	720	898	1,099	348	571	123	216	23	62	4	6	....	1	128
10th ward,	1,006	806	643	628	403	393	502	485	173	284	57	118	16	22	....	....	....	1	48
11th ward,	1,690	1,753	1,370	1,387	952	976	1,061	1,022	409	501	115	146	13	33	1	2	....	1	193
12th ward,	520	477	465	408	317	288	416	348	180	202	48	75	11	28	1	3	....	....	209
13th ward,	914	888	777	690	467	542	611	648	245	315	84	90	15	14	2	....	....	....	7
14th ward,	859	762	680	656	404	397	510	572	211	281	42	74	12	18	2	3	....	....	7
15th ward,	782	842	699	784	487	491	568	676	263	332	76	136	28	31	....	3	....	....	42
16th ward,	1,270	1,287	1,052	1,083	676	664	830	980	351	481	92	187	17	53	5	5	....	....	71
17th ward,	1,956	1,872	1,541	1,495	914	994	1,172	1,481	539	726	148	213	29	45	3	4	....	....	70
18th ward,	1,267	1,396	1,181	1,187	691	583	793	848	286	472	105	191	28	31	....	10	....	....	133
19th ward,	627	611	566	440	332	290	422	417	230	255	62	100	18	30	2	4	....	....	48
20th ward,	1,672	1,486	1,330	1,203	751	711	948	922	369	465	90	136	16	26	5	7	....	....	68
21st ward,	1,027	905	818	699	478	434	556	547	234	289	48	96	10	24	2	3	....	....	67
22d ward,	859	714	750	603	404	338	486	431	151	215	56	58	15	20	3	5	....	....	2
Total,	21,992	19,923	18,016	16,789	11,018	10,241	13,319	13,873	5,361	7,194	1.534	2,348	345	607	49	89	....	10	1,684

NIAGARA COUNTY.—(CONTINUED.)

TOWNS.	35 and under 40. Males	Females	40 and under 45. Males	Females	45 and under 50. Males	Females	50 and under 60. Males	Females	60 and under 70. Males	Females	70 and under 80. Males	Females	80 and under 90. Males	Fems	90 and under 100. Males	Fems	100 and upwards. Males	Fems	Ages unknown.
Cambria,	46	59	56	39	49	45	71	56	48	38	18	16	10	4	....	....	....	....	2
Hartland,	82	82	75	75	85	58	94	103	71	68	23	27	2	1	2	2	....	....	......
Lewiston,	81	88	87	70	70	54	85	76	46	41	17	21	7	7	....	....	....	....	3
Lockport,	433	412	407	325	301	252	385	317	187	171	82	52	15	6	2	2	....	....	8
Fewfane,	109	87	60	74	81	65	100	78	70	62	24	19	....	5	....	2	....	....	2
Niagara,	183	129	144	106	84	59	117	87	33	36	13	17	5	4	2	1	....	....	2
Pendleton,	63	47	42	48	35	36	66	49	22	25	14	10	2	2	....	....	....	....	......
Porter,	88	67	68	57	53	52	72	59	43	39	19	14	6	6	....	2	....	....	......
Royalton,	173	145	145	109	104	98	164	130	85	77	31	28	6	8	....	....	....	....	3

NIAGARA COUNTY.—(Continued.)

TOWNS.	Under 1. Males.	Under 1. Females.	1 and under 5. Males.	1 and under 5. Females	5 and under 10. Males.	5 and under 10. Females	10 and under 15. Males.	10 and under 15. Females	15 and under 20. Males.	15 and under 20. Females	20 and under 25. Males.	20 and under 25. Females.	25 and under 30. Males.	25 and under 30. Females	30 and under 35. Males.	30 and under 35. Females
Somerset,	20	25	93	110	107	121	105	120	123	101	97	101	66	72	63	6
Wheatfield,	64	51	222	212	241	219	171	155	118	142	119	106	108	114	126	11
Wilson,	53	52	210	163	225	203	219	196	172	178	182	156	137	124	124	10
Total,	710	740	2,810	2,658	2,912	2,903	2,776	2,790	2,465	2,695	2,510	2,433	2,206	2,011	1,969	1,68

ONEIDA COUNTY.

TOWNS.	Under 1. Males.	Under 1. Females.	1 and under 5. Males.	1 and under 5. Females	5 and under 10. Males.	5 and under 10. Females	10 and under 15. Males.	10 and under 15. Females	15 and under 20. Males.	15 and under 20. Females	20 and under 25. Males.	20 and under 25. Females.	25 and under 30. Males.	25 and under 30. Females	30 and under 35. Males.	30 and under 35. Females
Annsville,	34	43	149	151	185	178	171	174	155	150	115	117	96	95	103	7
Augusta,	28	28	107	121	145	139	158	130	126	129	108	123	92	85	63	8
Ava,	30	21	81	75	81	66	87	73	59	58	54	62	62	45	44	3
Boonville,	58	68	238	250	279	251	257	240	243	231	248	209	216	171	191	14
Bridgewater,	13	11	56	50	70	44	71	60	63	65	50	55	51	44	33	3
Camden,	42	28	150	144	166	175	169	170	147	159	113	134	111	101	97	10
Deerfield,	25	33	118	107	130	124	128	109	115	142	123	111	84	89	80	6
Florence,	36	49	149	136	192	229	216	197	169	148	132	100	93	79	59	6
Floyd,	17	12	63	75	86	81	84	78	85	84	63	74	49	59	46	4
Kirkland,	52	56	187	156	204	190	177	211	194	232	181	224	155	152	164	16
Lee,	41	33	170	147	164	195	194	190	183	159	125	134	102	104	95	9
Marcy,	19	21	82	80	119	112	124	95	96	84	78	76	55	60	46	5
Marshall,	28	19	112	115	125	111	105	109	123	120	102	106	94	84	69	5
New Hartford,	61	61	203	210	239	230	275	270	229	320	188	270	169	192	129	14
Paris,	50	52	170	206	210	204	210	185	173	206	175	175	146	166	150	14
Remsen,	39	12	160	171	152	175	166	153	151	147	148	112	127	97	100	7
Rome,	176	165	594	569	603	642	549	539	483	505	566	620	518	536	524	45
Sangerfield,	35	25	120	115	125	135	125	136	119	106	121	139	114	111	98	8
Steuben,	21	19	72	71	83	74	95	84	78	99	82	76	57	56	72	5
Trenton,	64	49	203	184	217	204	214	204	215	204	194	181	188	203	153	12
Utica city: 1st ward,	17	18	55	62	61	67	52	74	86	92	113	122	82	71	65	5
2d ward,	31	43	123	132	137	139	168	160	161	145	138	180	139	118	105	10
3d ward,	32	32	153	146	184	157	144	167	151	238	126	237	142	207	122	14
4th ward,	61	71	234	236	268	270	228	287	228	298	258	343	221	244	188	17
5th ward,	89	106	310	335	300	337	276	290	243	279	241	314	239	272	205	22
6th ward,	60	88	229	246	264	263	208	232	169	224	197	259	196	250	194	21
Total Utica,	290	358	1,104	1,157	1,214	1,233	1,076	1,210	1,038	1,276	1,073	1,455	1,019	1,162	879	91
Vernon,	34	35	162	138	195	154	159	156	164	155	138	137	98	105	100	12
Verona,	118	104	356	370	402	360	375	379	366	301	383	340	349	275	298	22
Vienna,	48	41	175	160	213	185	203	206	194	184	149	137	121	107	117	10
Western,	39	20	125	131	143	155	137	155	127	129	138	141	118	105	81	7
Westmoreland,	45	44	170	145	179	189	175	190	157	178	150	152	116	127	110	12
Whitestown,	55	54	224	186	276	265	307	283	232	319	230	300	164	220	134	17
Total,	1,498	1,461	5,500	5,420	6,197	6,100	6,007	5,986	5,484	5,890	5,227	5,760	4,564	4,630	4,035	3,85

ONONDAGA COUNTY.

TOWNS.	Under 1. Males.	Under 1. Females.	1 and under 5. Males.	1 and under 5. Females	5 and under 10. Males.	5 and under 10. Females	10 and under 15. Males.	10 and under 15. Females	15 and under 20. Males.	15 and under 20. Females	20 and under 25. Males.	20 and under 25. Females.	25 and under 30. Males.	25 and under 30. Females	30 and under 35. Males.	30 and under 35. Females
Camillus,	35	32	161	140	171	154	155	156	127	150	148	149	131	126	122	10
Cicero,	46	48	169	184	236	196	218	180	171	196	176	134	149	146	130	10
Clay,	53	42	185	170	215	201	205	185	182	167	163	167	165	134	97	10
De Witt,	25	32	176	140	173	167	173	178	154	174	177	145	130	125	115	8
Elbridge,	66	72	210	237	252	287	239	248	264	249	251	270	225	206	166	15
Fabius,	24	29	116	102	125	121	136	121	123	143	98	107	80	81	74	7
Geddes,	27	33	122	116	122	102	141	102	93	98	119	93	109	91	84	7
La Fayette,	23	22	99	125	146	118	121	112	117	113	124	126	109	93	98	7
Lysander,	73	71	276	284	300	295	280	280	307	278	268	261	246	189	164	14
Manlius,	96	82	347	318	357	358	348	355	284	391	320	328	292	237	212	21
Marcellus,	34	35	117	123	154	143	143	150	127	131	113	135	111	111	80	8
Onondaga,	48	68	274	261	289	275	326	293	323	296	273	238	201	213	190	19
Otisco,	20	22	65	88	87	111	91	106	97	95	80	79	57	63	49	7
Pompey,	42	36	176	162	195	208	212	198	201	208	184	185	145	151	127	12
Salina,	38	40	154	154	158	156	148	147	130	113	139	129	138	105	114	8
Skaneateles,	47	59	207	191	244	221	223	193	203	216	189	196	161	192	163	14
Spafford,	25	24	80	97	96	103	91	98	103	95	84	86	74	88	71	6
Syracuse city: 1st ward,	69	80	206	242	210	228	180	187	139	156	189	194	182	162	162	13
2d ward,	74	64	223	200	221	202	194	168	199	126	172	157	187	150	171	12
3d ward,	39	40	116	120	112	131	96	102	102	106	154	126	157	146	118	9
4th ward,	76	86	232	241	250	255	233	198	201	221	173	240	209	226	177	17
5th ward,	50	46	138	144	117	117	94	87	80	100	101	122	127	128	122	8
6th ward,	49	27	127	119	148	122	119	134	157	230	262	277	199	212	148	13
7th ward,	69	65	251	241	231	255	181	202	184	255	188	273	166	230	168	17
8th ward,	30	31	109	115	171	142	130	126	96	135	92	107	82	116	81	10
Total Syracuse,	456	439	1,402	1,422	1,460	1,452	1,227	1,204	1,158	1,329	1,331	1,496	1,309	1,370	1,147	1,02
Tully,	16	23	56	88	105	92	91	83	86	81	74	77	68	71	59	6
Van Buren,	49	39	137	138	190	175	189	170	180	180	163	152	150	117	117	9
Total,	1,243	1,248	4,529	4,540	5,075	4,935	4,757	4,559	4,430	4,703	4,474	4,553	4,050	3,909	3,379	3,06

ONTARIO COUNTY.

TOWNS.	Under 1. Males.	Under 1. Females.	1 and under 5. Males.	1 and under 5. Females	5 and under 10. Males.	5 and under 10. Females	10 and under 15. Males.	10 and under 15. Females	15 and under 20. Males.	15 and under 20. Females	20 and under 25. Males.	20 and under 25. Females.	25 and under 30. Males.	25 and under 30. Females	30 and under 35. Males.	30 and under 35. Females
Bristol,	28	20	76	81	99	100	81	94	96	89	88	89	81	71	56	6
Canadice,	12	13	64	66	67	56	60	65	37	42	40	37	35	51	46	4
Canandaigua,	76	59	320	349	385	353	311	341	308	365	290	370	305	322	235	25
East Bloomfield,	33	24	110	90	108	113	102	122	154	127	126	119	102	91	80	6
Farmington,	12	24	95	100	99	99	93	94	133	119	126	112	91	89	79	7
Gorham,	20	38	108	118	125	130	135	124	135	122	115	118	106	85	80	9
Hopewell,	11	18	84	72	98	78	104	98	98	106	89	83	78	87	74	6
Manchester,	39	35	143	153	189	184	179	157	180	165	153	133	126	102	96	10

NIAGARA COUNTY.—(Continued.)

TOWNS	35 and under 40. Males.	Females	40 and under 45. Males.	Females	45 and under 50. Males.	Females	50 and under 60. Males.	Females	60 and under 70. Males.	Females	70 and under 80. Males	Females	80 and under 90. Males	Fems	90 and under 100. Males	Fems	100 and upwards Males	Fems	Ages unknown.
Somerset,	50	51	47	64	50	35	78	63	39	28	11	13	3	3	....	....	....	....	......
Wheatfield,	107	96	99	84	86	61	116	85	48	55	13	17	3	3	....	....	....	....,	......
Wilson,	95	105	89	69	63	58	99	80	48	40	19	24	2	2	2	....	....	....	1
Total,	1,510	1,368	1,319	1,126	1,070	873	1,447	1,183	740	680	284	258	61	51	8.	9	....	....	21

ONEIDA COUNTY.—(Continued.)

TOWNS	35 and under 40. Males.	Females	40 and under 45. Males.	Females	45 and under 50. Males.	Females	50 and under 60. Males.	Females	60 and under 70. Males.	Females	70 and under 80. Males	Females	80 and under 90. Males	Fems	90 and under 100. Males	Fems	100 and upwards Males	Fems	Ages unknown.
Annsville,	79	78	63	67	66	59	98	77	42	41	21	22	2	4	1	....	....	....	......
Augusta,	75	76	66	65	59	55	77	87	38	40	28	24	12	10	....	....	....	....	1
Ava,	35	28	35	24	29	20	40	26	17	25	11	8	5	4	....	....	....	....	......
Boonville,	147	118	118	94	101	86	145	125	71	54	35	19	7	6	1	1	....	....	3
Bridgewater,	24	39	34	36	39	34	55	59	26	35	20	16	8	6	1	....	....	....	1
Camden,	77	92	74	75	73	77	116	103	56	58	31	35	8	12	1	1	....	....	......
Deerfield,	71	61	63	53	48	47	82	84	48	52	23	22	9	7	2	1	....	....	......
Florence,	58	62	84	90	87	69	84	65	67	44	17	16	7	9	1	....	....	....	2
Floyd,	45	36	37	45	28	29	65	47	37	38	16	12	4	6	....	2	....	....	......
Kirkland,	130	101	93	90	77	101	128	124	70	77	36	44	12	15	3	1	....	....	5
Lee,	85	101	80	80	95	57	91	86	70	72	26	28	11	9	1	1	....	....	......
Marcy,	47	50	49	53	47	44	98	66	34	35	17	16	5	7	....	....	....	....	......
Marshall,	77	69	55	56	57	58	83	80	39	36	16	22	10	7	....	1	....	....	......
New Hartford	120	152	106	132	126	116	137	137	90	93	40	36	16	14	4	4	....	....	1
Paris,	110	108	84	80	97	94	134	141	76	67	31	29	9	6	....	2	....	....	3
Remsen,	61	66	67	61	77	56	86	61	57	40	17	28	12	2	1	1	....	....	2
Rome,	363	281	313	275	218	173	307	287	138	145	67	64	13	13	....	3	....	1	17
Sangerfield,	75	77	57	56	55	56	85	76	53	55	21	29	9	7	1	2	....	....	5
Steuben,	47	35	36	32	36	38	68	69	52	44	22	10	3	3	3	1	....	....	......
Trenton,	116	118	119	95	91	79	134	112	100	85	52	50	16	11	....	....	....	....	10
Utica city: 1st ward,	51	48	41	36	13	24	34	34	24	26	8	9	2	3	....	....	....	....	......
2d ward,	89	96	82	71	63	66	95	91	29	52	17	13	5	5	....	....	1	....	......
3d ward,	87	94	54	68	58	60	86	101	48	49	11	12	....	....	....	....	....	....	3
4th ward,	152	164	112	117	104	102	123	109	78	80	22	30	9	9	....	3	....	....	......
5th ward,	182	160	142	130	84	98	154	167	70	65	24	29	4	4	....	....	....	....	5
6th ward,	190	147	142	141	118	111	144	133	48	55	23	22	3	5	....	....	....	....	34
Total Utica,	751	709	573	563	440	461	636	635	297	327	105	115	23	26	....	3	1	....	42
Vernon,	96	94	80	87	79	72	115	116	63	67	33	30	7	6	....	2	....	....	1
Verona,	254	171	218	165	156	120	225	204	103	107	48	56	18	13	5	2	....	....	57
Vienna,	83	104	97	91	92	64	98	86	53	63	32	28	7	4	....	1	....	....	5
Western,	79	86	64	52	65	54	86	78	50	53	30	21	3	7	1	....	....	....	......
Westmoreland,	85	96	83	85	75	81	122	125	88	81	41	32	13	7	2	1	....	....	8
Whitestown,	125	149	130	142	116	131	149	157	83	88	42	54	12	17	3	....	....	....	14
Total,	3,315	3,157	2,878	2,744	2,529	2,331	3,544	3,313	1,918	1,922	878	872	261	238	31	30	1	1	177

ONONDAGA COUNTY.—(Continued.)

TOWNS	35 and under 40. Males.	Females	40 and under 45. Males.	Females	45 and under 50. Males.	Females	50 and under 60. Males.	Females	60 and under 70. Males.	Females	70 and under 80. Males	Females	80 and under 90. Males	Fems	90 and under 100. Males	Fems	100 and upwards Males	Fems	Ages unknown.
Camillus,	67	69	66	61	57	50	75	72	54	51	22	23	8	6	1	....	....	....	1
Cicero,	100	93	87	78	78	64	130	93	60	56	26	28	4	9	....	....	....	....	1
Clay,	126	100	87	59	78	66	119	90	70	54	12	19	3	7	1	....	....	....	1
De Witt,	74	83	91	74	72	54	122	108	52	45	19	11	7	4	2	1	....	....	.....́
Elbridge,	131	123	119	115	110	92	140	105	57	85	33	39	8	4	1	....	....	....	1
Fabius,	66	70	56	62	52	49	85	92	51	41	28	20	12	11	2	3	....	....	......
Geddes,	66	62	55	40	59	45	69	60	31	29	12	7	5	1	2	....	....	....	......
La Fayette,	72	62	62	50	52	58	94	93	51	49	31	18	8	6	....	1	....	....	12
Lysander,	160	146	127	121	111	99	107	139	112	79	40	29	9	3	....	1	1	....	1
Manlius,	165	173	169	155	158	128	106	203	111	108	44	38	15	13	1	2	....	....	8
Marcellus,	80	74	61	73	62	46	82	76	50	65	26	24	10	12	1	....	....	....	10
Onondaga,	143	170	179	128	134	129	201	178	124	99	67	46	16	15	2	3	....	....	4
Otisco,	54	40	43	43	42	52	77	68	30	34	29	16	8	7	....	....	....	....	2
Pompey,	107	135	96	110	95	87	145	130	79	92	47	57	16	17	....	3	....	....	3
Salina,	95	82	75	55	58	41	86	57	29	32	9	9	3	....	....	....	....	....	6
Skaneateles,	134	133	101	113	81	84	123	118	82	68	87	37	10	7	....	1	....	....	1
Spafford,	58	58	43	48	37	35	54	57	42	41	28	20	8	8	....	....	....	....	......
Syracuse city: 1st ward,	138	127	102	77	73	53	82	97	43	43	20	16	4	1	....	1	....	....	......
2d ward,	126	87	110	85	73	51	97	82	39	40	7	6	....	1	....	....	....	....	1
3d ward,	88	70	73	51	38	28	46	46	19	20	6	11	1	2	1	....	....	....	3
4th ward,	146	121	102	100	87	78	105	102	49	43	13	14	4	3	2	....	....	....	5
5th ward,	65	56	47	42	26	25	46	39	21	21	4	12	1	1	....	....	....	....	......
6th ward,	121	108	89	77	71	53	78	65	27	38	6	17	1	2	....	....	....	....	35
7th ward,	126	156	141	97	96	73	75	90	42	53	9	16	3	4	....	....	....	....	50
8th ward,	84	71	55	52	38	33	45	50	26	25	11	7	....	1	....	....	....	1	......
Total Syracuse,	894	796	719	581	502	394	574	571	266	283	76	99	14	15	3	1	....	1	94
Tully,	51	53	54	44	36	27	54	61	36	39	18	7	2	4	....	1	....	....	......
Van Buren,	83	95	78	79	64	68	108	99	63	54	26	20	1	6	....	....	....	....	......
Total,	2,726	2,617	2,368	2,089	1,938	1,668	2,700	2,470	1,450	1,404	630	567	167	155	16	17	1	1	145

ONTARIO COUNTY.—(Continued.)

TOWNS	35 and under 40. Males.	Females	40 and under 45. Males.	Females	45 and under 50. Males.	Females	50 and under 60. Males.	Females	60 and under 70. Males.	Females	70 and under 80. Males	Females	80 and under 90. Males	Fems	90 and under 100. Males	Fems	100 and upwards Males	Fems	Ages unknown.
Bristol,	60	59	41	35	36	39	65	50	31	38	19	16	4	6	1	1	....	....	......
Canadice,	31	10	18	16	17	18	29	31	23	20	10	5	2	2	....	....	....	....	......
Canandaigua,	240	211	184	166	124	141	190	203	131	113	51	50	11	15	....	2	....	....	8
East Bloomfield,	63	67	45	52	54	51	79	74	37	32	13	18	10	10	1	....	....	....	......
Farmington,	51	49	44	40	43	42	62	49	44	40	18	20	7	2	1	....	....	....	......
Gorham,	70	82	72	58	47	60	87	88	51	45	25	25	5	6	....	2	1	....	7
Hopewell,	64	62	46	44	40	31	58	59	36	43	25	21	5	5	....	....	....	....	......
Manchester,	68	107	97	87	83	58	109	95	48	45	20	37	9	7	....	....	....	....	3

ONTARIO COUNTY.

TOWNS.	Under 1.		1 and under 5.		5 and under 10.		10 and under 15.		15 and under 20.		20 and under 25.		25 and under 30.		30 and under 35.	
	Males.	Females.	Males.	Females	Males.	Females	Males.	Females.	Males.	Females	Males.	Females	Males.	Females	Males.	Females.
Naples,	29	40	115	111	150	145	132	116	125	107	87	87	86	91	66	71
Phelps,	67	59	255	243	333	302	343	288	276	283	248	275	197	193	165	180
Richmond,	18	12	82	67	71	64	100	89	80	93	79	88	62	58	50	49
Seneca,	79	82	360	386	434	415	443	452	431	491	402	505	339	373	314	333
South Bristol,	10	17	70	62	87	81	84	69	65	54	40	45	39	49	38	32
Victor,	31	22	113	104	126	117	122	122	117	132	115	108	96	83	81	89
West Bloomfield,	19	25	79	65	83	80	100	72	98	76	77	99	67	59	50	74
Total,	484	488	2,074	2,067	2,454	2,322	2.389	2,303	2,333	2,371	2,075	2,268	1,810	1,804	1,510	1,581

ORANGE COUNTY.

TOWNS.	Under 1.		1 and under 5.		5 and under 10.		10 and under 15.		15 and under 20.		20 and under 25.		25 and under 30.		30 and under 35.	
	Males.	Females.	Males.	Females	Males.	Females	Males.	Females.	Males.	Females	Males.	Females	Males.	Females	Males.	Females.
Blooming Grove,	27	26	99	104	128	109	120	109	137	130	113	136	93	99	79	63
Chester,	22	17	92	89	88	103	104	84	91	100	82	100	70	74	65	54
Cornwall,	83	60	259	240	265	250	234	253	254	212	340	235	245	205	198	171
Crawford,	23	23	94	110	104	120	113	113	105	126	96	104	75	74	66	81
Deerpark,	110	102	349	313	328	325	282	263	276	277	347	308	337	272	300	222
Goshen,	40	42	153	164	183	175	176	152	166	173	134	185	117	165	122	130
Greenville,	12	15	60	62	85	67	78	69	69	77	61	56	41	41	32	45
Hamptonburgh,	13	12	62	50	65	54	88	77	81	86	60	83	64	47	41	47
Minisink,	20	18	76	69	84	78	79	78	57	88	55	58	52	51	44	40
Monroe,	49	39	305	285	313	337	290	269	243	229	227	197	177	169	174	129
Montgomery,	33	47	160	182	220	200	214	191	207	225	168	191	141	142	107	150
Mount Hope,	36	24	89	84	98	107	94	89	82	99	84	86	66	79	75	68
Newburgh,	180	178	685	653	740	724	720	657	640	744	590	849	525	647	462	495
New Windsor,	33	40	125	110	120	125	145	135	165	157	120	164	108	104	73	78
Walkill,	60	57	224	269	289	272	306	322	288	313	284	312	225	249	182	195
Warwick,	66	55	260	270	335	320	290	297	255	302	237	248	172	195	170	150
Wawayanda,	23	24	117	112	143	122	121	131	101	123	79	107	60	80	70	73
Total,	830	779	3,209	3,166	3,588	3,488	3,454	3,289	3,217	3,461	3,077	3,419	2.568	2,693	2,260	2.191

ORLEANS COUNTY.

TOWNS.	Under 1.		1 and under 5.		5 and under 10.		10 and under 15.		15 and under 20.		20 and under 25.		25 and under 30.		30 and under 35.	
	Males.	Females.	Males.	Females	Males.	Females	Males.	Females.	Males.	Females	Males.	Females	Males.	Females	Males.	Females.
Barre,	83	76	321	289	349	368	355	372	381	430	376	386	303	295	247	234
Carlton,	36	24	127	111	154	142	159	114	131	119	107	126	108	97	88	74
Clarendon,	25	27	70	82	109	96	120	74	102	105	96	71	72	83	54	65
Gaines,	35	22	129	111	144	138	148	119	149	147	147	113	99	107	97	93
Kendall,	21	8	84	82	136	115	118	122	109	113	71	71	65	86	69	64
Murray,	32	36	122	152	174	168	140	171	155	139	168	125	129	119	123	96
Ridgeway,	63	76	243	232	279	255	280	279	310	285	345	272	277	210	210	196
Shelby,	39	39	162	145	181	201	182	157	175	173	160	126	140	126	124	88
Yates,	30	34	111	77	132	109	113	114	111	106	96	92	79	84	67	70
Total,	364	342	1,369	1,281	1,658	1,592	1,615	1,522	1,623	1,617	1,566	1,382	1,272	1.207	1,079	980

OSWEGO COUNTY.

TOWNS.	Under 1.		1 and under 5.		5 and under 10.		10 and under 15.		15 and under 20.		20 and under 25.		25 and under 30.		30 and under 35.	
	Males.	Females.	Males.	Females	Males.	Females	Males.	Females.	Males.	Females	Males.	Females	Males.	Females	Males.	Females.
Albion,	20	33	120	125	145	128	135	152	135	108	131	103	85	78	70	66
Amboy,	16	18	68	70	93	71	76	60	77	53	60	40	50	44	36	38
Boylston,	11	6	64	62	58	67	55	37	40	39	35	31	21	32	27	28
Constantia,	66	42	219	185	232	229	190	193	171	183	198	155	166	126	123	118
Granby,	50	64	231	203	245	206	230	182	187	192	190	190	155	168	158	138
Hannibal,	49	47	175	142	176	193	180	182	168	148	140	137	111	121	99	99
Hastings,	39	36	176	173	208	187	203	177	167	196	150	140	147	110	106	85
Mexico,	62	54	204	179	225	223	247	225	205	219	181	227	151	151	112	120
New Haven,	21	42	89	117	127	114	116	114	103	85	84	94	92	80	63	66
Orwell,	21	15	73	64	101	70	64	87	79	57	51	56	68	56	43	43
Oswego,	47	37	146	145	186	185	159	167	146	143	140	118	121	100	108	89
Oswego city:																
1st ward,	64	80	201	234	239	226	209	197	201	281	255	294	231	222	182	166
2d ward,	62	65	169	170	177	159	163	127	143	125	158	150	159	161	129	107
3d ward,	87	84	278	257	267	214	209	199	182	247	224	259	223	209	207	167
4th ward,	88	90	305	279	303	265	239	245	207	249	197	246	238	232	181	183
Total Oswego,	301	319	953	940	986	864	820	768	733	902	834	949	851	824	699	623
Palermo,	40	39	98	93	108	98	128	103	103	111	104	97	91	76	60	63
Parish,	25	20	99	96	96	100	111	95	99	92	69	62	66	56	63	60
Redfield,	18	8	51	24	73	52	63	43	47	30	30	27	24	28	17	28
Richland,	52	47	232	176	268	248	254	233	210	223	195	205	147	150	146	131
Sandy Creek,	59	56	98	109	127	113	157	128	138	112	104	109	75	83	67	71
Schroeppel,	74	65	210	229	255	264	232	211	178	157	175	180	166	162	151	128
Scriba,	44	49	172	155	169	193	209	158	165	181	150	119	113	98	97	101
Volney,	90	95	378	348	371	359	377	348	370	352	320	370	321	260	269	247
West Monroe,	19	26	61	61	94	79	82	76	64	58	53	54	47	32	36	36
Williamstown,	23	15	51	48	54	61	56	47	51	42	40	46	30	43	24	33
Total,	1,147	1,133	3,968	3,744	4,397	4,104	4,144	3,786	3,636	3,683	3,434	3,509	3,098	2,878	2,574	2,411

OTSEGO COUNTY.

TOWNS.	Under 1.		1 and under 5.		5 and under 10.		10 and under 15.		15 and under 20.		20 and under 25.		25 and under 30.		30 and under 35.	
	Males.	Females.	Males.	Females	Males.	Females	Males.	Females.	Males.	Females	Males.	Females	Males.	Females	Males.	Females.
Burlington,	18	29	83	82	106	100	97	99	105	106	85	82	53	75	66	59
Butternuts,	32	27	93	105	95	106	109	88	98	94	86	110	102	97	72	59
Cherry Valley,	36	45	125	130	155	142	145	124	155	145	126	128	110	102	110	91
Decatur,	11	16	54	46	54	52	54	44	53	54	41	34	31	39	32	35
Edmeston,	26	18	84	98	88	89	109	88	80	93	86	86	83	85	54	53
Exeter,	17	30	73	93	99	76	81	87	75	85	60	68	52	56	57	53
Hartwick,	22	38	90	107	112	138	134	136	112	135	88	87	66	97	64	92
Laurens,	36	33	77	77	124	111	115	124	122	122	84	116	79	86	59	69

ONTARIO COUNTY.—(CONTINUED.)

TOWNS.	35 and under 40. Males	35 and under 40. Females	40 and under 45. Males	40 and under 45. Females	45 and under 50. Males	45 and under 50. Females	50 and under 60. Males	50 and under 60. Females	60 and under 70. Males	60 and under 70. Females	70 and under 80. Males	70 and under 80. Females	80 and under 90. Males	80 and under 90. Fems	90 and under 100. Males	90 and under 100. Fems	100 and upwards. Males	100 and upwards. Fems	Ages unknown.
Naples,	76	52	45	46	53	41	59	63	44	40	17	13	3	4	....	1	....	....	3
Phelps,	183	178	160	140	130	110	160	159	110	122	50	45	13	7	1	2	....	....	16
Richmond,	40	40	34	49	32	32	59	42	32	28	15	14	11	3	....	....	....	....	......
Seneca,	279	239	211	214	168	198	315	312	156	145	70	96	26	21	2	2	1	....	4
South Bristol,	36	35	31	23	33	30	32	33	31	20	16	10	....	4	2	1	....	....	......
Victor,	79	60	72	52	52	30	79	77	42	39	21	15	4	4	1	....	....	....	3
West Bloomfield,	49	56	39	32	34	42	68	53	38	35	13	20	4	3	1	1	....	....	4
Total,	1,389	1,316	1,139	1,054	946	923	1,451	1,388	854	805	383	405	114	99	10	12	2	....	48

ORANGE COUNTY.—(CONTINUED.)

TOWNS.	35–40 Males	35–40 Females	40–45 Males	40–45 Females	45–50 Males	45–50 Females	50–60 Males	50–60 Females	60–70 Males	60–70 Females	70–80 Males	70–80 Females	80–90 Males	80–90 Fems	90–100 Males	90–100 Fems	100 up Males	100 up Fems	Ages unknown.
Blooming Grove,	58	59	52	44	41	48	80	82	39	51	20	24	5	5	....	....	....	....	4
Chester,	55	54	47	49	32	33	56	51	27	25	6	18	1	4	....	....	....	....	3
Cornwall,	152	138	101	96	84	75	103	113	63	77	29	20	4	9	....	1	....	....	9
Crawford,	60	61	46	43	44	49	70	70	43	44	19	17	1	5	....	1	....	....	......
Deerpark,	170	143	145	99	99	77	114	86	51	44	27	17	4	4	....	2	....	....	11
Goshen,	105	89	88	82	76	61	110	112	62	68	29	33	3	8	....	1	....	....	9
Greenville,	36	38	29	31	19	24	34	43	38	30	10	11	1	3	....	....	....	....	1
Hamptonburgh,	38	43	38	25	28	25	43	48	22	28	15	9	1	2	....	2	....	....	6
Minisink,	40	43	45	34	15	25	34	41	21	22	11	6	....	4	....	....	....	....	7
Monroe,	134	119	101	105	115	75	128	97	86	80	23	18	3	7	1	1	....	....	26
Montgomery,	118	126	104	121	83	83	139	163	86	89	31	52	8	5	....	4	....	....	2
Mount Hope,	56	51	49	47	30	34	48	58	34	38	11	9	4	3	....	1	....	....	2
Newburgh,	392	392	334	355	248	254	352	389	165	204	63	82	23	23	1	1	....	1	5
New Windsor,	81	88	76	68	67	55	98	82	45	55	11	9	10	5	1	1	....	....	1
Walkill,	188	164	128	153	128	125	185	169	85	124	45	42	10	9	....	1	....	....	12
Warwick,	135	121	112	104	124	116	172	167	95	95	49	45	15	11	....	2	....	....	2
Wawayanda,	58	63	63	53	36	32	75	66	28	43	21	25	6	8	3	....	....	....	3
Total,	1,876	1,792	1,558	1,509	1,269	1,191	1,841	1,837	990	1,117	420	437	99	115	6	18	....	1	103

ORLEANS COUNTY.—(CONTINUED.)

TOWNS.	35–40 Males	35–40 Females	40–45 Males	40–45 Females	45–50 Males	45–50 Females	50–60 Males	50–60 Females	60–70 Males	60–70 Females	70–80 Males	70–80 Females	80–90 Males	80–90 Fems	90–100 Males	90–100 Fems	100 up Males	100 up Fems	Ages unknown.
Barre,	209	201	196	156	153	147	249	250	154	110	44	38	8	13	....	1	....	....	3
Carlton,	74	69	49	66	70	46	73	63	45	28	9	9	1	6	....	2	....	....	2
Clarendon,	55	45	49	35	43	45	61	55	40	29	14	12	7	5	2	1	....	....	......
Gaines,	86	76	67	62	64	51	99	90	54	42	14	19	6	3	1	....	....	....	......
Kendall,	64	56	55	42	29	36	79	57	51	39	13	13	9	5	2	....	....	....	......
Murray,	87	82	82	74	66	59	93	102	69	53	22	24	4	3	1	....	....	....	6
Ridgeway,	205	132	140	131	125	94	190	166	91	66	28	33	5	5	2	1	....	....	......
Shelby,	90	95	80	75	76	65	93	60	60	75	27	20	3	8	1	....	....	....	......
Yates,	58	61	43	45	55	47	62	66	41	49	22	11	3	8	....	....	....	....	......
Total,	928	817	761	686	681	590	999	909	605	491	193	179	46	56	9	5	....	....	11

OSWEGO COUNTY.—(CONTINUED.)

TOWNS.	35–40 Males	35–40 Females	40–45 Males	40–45 Females	45–50 Males	45–50 Females	50–60 Males	50–60 Females	60–70 Males	60–70 Females	70–80 Males	70–80 Females	80–90 Males	80–90 Fems	90–100 Males	90–100 Fems	100 up Males	100 up Fems	Ages unknown.
Albion,	67	51	45	59	52	45	90	67	36	29	12	13	3	8	1	....	....	....	......
Amboy,	31	19	20	21	25	21	51	50	25	22	6	7	2	2	....	....	....	....	......
Boylston,	26	25	24	20	21	16	15	11	17	14	10	3	....	....	....	....	....	....	......
Constantia,	120	94	81	59	82	57	82	65	40	37	16	18	3	3	1	....	1	....	......
Granby,	119	112	84	49	72	72	129	110	62	56	23	28	10	6	9	7	....	....	10
Hannibal,	79	60	82	87	89	68	106	98	65	48	26	33	8	1	2	....	....	....	......
Hastings,	97	85	81	77	61	54	88	71	60	46	21	20	6	2	....	....	....	....	......
Mexico,	109	127	106	115	124	94	150	151	86	73	39	37	12	12	2	....	....	....	......
New Haven,	57	49	40	44	41	37	94	82	52	44	25	26	4	4	....	1	....	....	5
Orwell,	40	27	25	23	25	21	43	39	26	17	6	8	2	6	....	....	....	....	2
Oswego,	77	75	73	60	52	56	90	82	60	47	16	17	4	8	1	1	....	....	4
Oswego City:																			
1st ward,	117	119	96	96	92	54	95	99	35	34	9	8	3	2	....	....	....	....	2
2d ward,	110	75	68	65	66	42	52	49	26	27	15	11	1	....	1	1	....	....	6
3d ward,	116	99	106	98	104	67	115	82	37	42	16	45	7	4	....	1	....	....	2
4th ward,	159	117	101	96	89	90	122	95	44	57	20	16	3	3	2	2	1	....	16
Total Oswego,	502	410	371	355	351	253	384	325	142	160	60	80	14	9	3	4	1	....	26
Palermo,	57	64	62	49	44	56	81	65	39	33	24	22	6	6	1	....	....	....	2
Parish,	53	43	37	33	36	38	59	60	44	30	18	15	....	....	....	....	....	....	......
Redfield,	27	29	26	25	26	12	21	22	17	10	8	7	4	1	....	....	....	....	......
Richland,	123	118	106	94	97	81	119	111	94	72	25	29	7	7	2	3	....	....	7
Sandy Creek,	63	52	68	55	49	54	80	82	51	43	33	26	3	4	1	1	....	....	2
Schroeppel,	145	125	90	94	84	51	109	81	47	37	14	20	6	6	1	....	....	....	......
Scriba,	80	75	64	65	84	55	108	94	55	51	20	20	8	5	....	....	....	....	1
Volney,	200	164	186	174	140	111	202	161	93	75	38	37	10	10	....	....	....	....	......
West Monroe,	49	33	26	26	25	25	51	36	24	22	8	15	1	5	....	....	....	....	2
Williamstown,	36	23	22	20	29	22	36	37	28	23	6	1	4	2	....	....	....	....	......
Total,	2,148	1,869	1,719	1,604	1,609	1,299	2,188	1,900	1,163	989	454	482	117	107	24	17	2	....	61

OTSEGO COUNTY.—(CONTINUED.)

TOWNS.	35–40 Males	35–40 Females	40–45 Males	40–45 Females	45–50 Males	45–50 Females	50–60 Males	50–60 Females	60–70 Males	60–70 Females	70–80 Males	70–80 Females	80–90 Males	80–90 Fems	90–100 Males	90–100 Fems	100 up Males	100 up Fems	Ages unknown.
Burlington,	48	44	52	54	38	40	74	74	41	36	17	20	12	11	1	1	....	....	......
Butternuts,	57	66	40	38	46	54	88	88	49	51	26	26	10	9	3	4	....	....	1
Cherry Valley,	90	61	53	46	68	31	94	73	55	33	28	14	9	3	3	4	....	....	6
Decatur,	33	32	29	16	21	21	35	26	15	13	6	8	6	2	....	....	....	....	......
Edmeston,	52	61	52	49	54	43	65	74	33	32	13	20	8	6	1	....	....	....	......
Exeter,	44	40	46	41	44	43	55	57	28	25	15	20	8	7	1	1	....	....	3
Hartwick,	77	76	62	63	50	60	77	77	42	43	33	24	8	9	1	....	....	....	......
Laurens,	54	63	54	54	49	59	92	84	41	47	39	28	3	5	1	1	....	....	......

OTSEGO COUNTY.

TOWNS.	Under 1. Males.	Under 1. Females	1 and under 5. Males.	1 and under 5. Females	5 and under 10. Males.	5 and under 10. Females	10 and under 15. Males.	10 and under 15. Females	15 and under 20. Males.	15 and under 20. Females	20 and under 25. Males.	20 and under 25. Females	25 and under 30. Males.	25 and under 30. Females	30 and under 35. Males.	30 and under 35. Females.
Maryland,	29	39	95	107	116	126	136	133	135	108	109	99	80	82	85	73
Middlefield,	29	30	134	145	168	166	190	176	183	166	137	136	128	131	92	95
Milford,	28	44	113	118	108	129	127	114	148	125	109	146	90	89	78	77
Morris,	33	27	117	80	117	120	106	102	98	109	78	97	68	98	70	74
New Lisbon,	21	32	89	75	89	101	106	73	102	93	79	107	68	64	48	72
Oneonta,	28	40	122	110	129	95	127	115	122	103	94	117	96	90	91	95
Otego,	27	35	84	94	82	91	91	112	94	78	102	90	79	79	68	61
Otsego,	78	82	197	176	204	237	200	221	226	235	242	231	182	211	150	162
Pittsfield,	19	26	78	94	105	103	92	102	75	74	60	72	59	72	64	59
Plainfield,	22	24	52	60	67	69	61	73	66	68	45	58	59	41	53	47
Richfield,	21	19	71	52	74	63	77	80	79	81	86	85	68	76	56	53
Roseboom,	23	23	93	90	115	123	139	102	92	124	92	85	68	69	61	67
Springfield,	37	40	109	109	119	128	149	114	136	147	147	128	117	100	82	84
Unadilla,	46	38	125	125	169	142	141	149	148	149	135	129	108	108	100	82
Westford,	16	21	63	60	86	64	71	70	59	78	53	73	63	61	57	61
Worcester,	28	34	118	113	123	123	120	105	106	115	115	110	72	88	70	77
Total,	683	790	2, 339	2, 346	2, 704	2, 694	2, 777	2, 631	2, 669	2 687	2, 339	2, 474	1, 981	2, 096	1, 739	1, 750

PUTNAM COUNTY.

TOWNS.	Under 1. Males.	Under 1. Females	1 and under 5. Males.	1 and under 5. Females	5 and under 10. Males.	5 and under 10. Females	10 and under 15. Males.	10 and under 15. Females	15 and under 20. Males.	15 and under 20. Females	20 and under 25. Males.	20 and under 25. Females	25 and under 30. Males.	25 and under 30. Females	30 and under 35. Males.	30 and under 35. Females.
Carmel,	34	15	117	109	115	131	124	134	114	120	94	128	95	116	85	87
Kent,	25	17	83	91	92	111	96	83	61	79	66	68	58	68	49	49
Patterson,	20	11	63	49	75	56	71	59	65	90	80	98	58	51	50	62
Philipstown,	81	96	315	285	288	300	294	286	222	227	241	220	190	195	165	195
Putnam Valley,	25	19	98	75	99	85	100	105	96	78	66	74	56	57	50	43
South East,	23	30	95	98	113	94	100	98	114	117	141	152	110	95	92	75
Total,	208	188	771	707	782	777	785	765	672	711	688	740	567	582	491	511

QUEENS COUNTY.

TOWNS.	Under 1. Males.	Under 1. Females	1 and under 5. Males.	1 and under 5. Females	5 and under 10. Males.	5 and under 10. Females	10 and under 15. Males.	10 and under 15. Females	15 and under 20. Males.	15 and under 20. Females	20 and under 25. Males.	20 and under 25. Females	25 and under 30. Males.	25 and under 30. Females	30 and under 35. Males.	30 and under 35. Females.
Flushing,	131	139	456	442	395	433	410	406	329	385	389	434	368	398	402	384
Hempstead,	168	131	551	537	644	653	654	624	520	547	447	514	393	410	332	321
Jamaica	62	68	248	303	292	304	308	322	242	263	329	332	254	237	276	255
Newtown,	145	154	509	533	545	564	439	486	359	439	447	530	466	534	455	407
North Hempstead,	71	72	205	210	254	251	245	260	223	264	230	252	219	189	183	174
Oyster Bay,	112	104	399	391	453	389	458	411	401	448	384	419	327	303	288	290
Total,	689	668	2, 368	2, 416	2, 583	2, 594	2, 514	2, 509	2, 074	2, 346	2, 226	2, 481	2, 027	2, 071	1, 936	1, 831

RENSSELAER COUNTY.

TOWNS.	Under 1. Males.	Under 1. Females	1 and under 5. Males.	1 and under 5. Females	5 and under 10. Males.	5 and under 10. Females	10 and under 15. Males.	10 and under 15. Females	15 and under 20. Males.	15 and under 20. Females	20 and under 25. Males.	20 and under 25. Females	25 and under 30. Males.	25 and under 30. Females	30 and under 35. Males.	30 and under 35. Females.
Berlin,	26	31	126	117	132	130	126	118	105	97	88	83	83	83	64	98
Brunswick,	31	52	134	150	149	159	174	180	167	178	152	170	126	127	121	108
Clinton,	15	25	88	65	93	82	89	74	78	96	83	84	82	71	62	54
Grafton,	22	28	134	114	134	119	121	124	95	103	53	78	74	70	66	48
Greenbush,	68	76	215	223	176	203	142	160	98	151	146	160	189	175	170	158
Hoosick,	48	43	215	215	215	235	230	252	211	256	238	224	156	187	160	117
Lansingburgh,	86	94	308	300	340	355	329	325	266	346	261	339	190	233	230	239
Nassau,	40	29	145	118	168	186	175	167	156	165	128	141	89	142	95	99
North Greenburgh,	28	18	92	96	94	90	83	107	86	102	90	100	86	85	73	65
Petersburgh,	16	21	96	79	93	94	86	99	88	118	62	76	63	76	50	45
Pittstown,	39	44	172	173	186	216	185	198	176	206	154	177	146	160	147	148
Poestenkill,	32	25	109	128	127	121	92	102	79	77	93	85	100	81	71	68
Sand Lake,	36	30	119	144	149	178	142	166	113	128	101	131	94	83	82	92
Schaghticoke,	47	42	159	165	197	177	191	207	176	194	171	160	132	136	115	125
Schodack,	49	42	202	161	195	176	193	196	227	219	204	193	149	152	136	135
Stephentown,	17	35	103	116	159	132	120	140	140	118	95	123	78	106	84	69
Troy City: 1st ward,	76	72	204	229	210	209	205	200	184	228	227	272	217	228	201	198
2d ward,	75	55	218	172	192	218	206	207	218	272	234	344	233	239	171	209
3d ward,	15	14	72	96	91	89	96	102	117	155	172	252	115	146	101	97
4th ward,	51	58	190	195	204	208	208	237	176	287	227	319	192	229	173	160
5th ward,	26	20	142	150	137	129	139	147	116	145	117	121	112	125	83	84
6th ward,	47	43	178	162	186	162	148	139	102	106	129	131	119	130	140	105
7th ward,	68	74	222	167	226	190	190	191	175	204	164	207	187	228	143	167
8th ward,	90	71	236	227	221	232	225	221	150	204	180	252	195	229	164	169
9th ward,	78	78	245	227	209	222	189	153	141	107	163	145	182	153	181	170
10th ward,	46	44	132	142	133	168	136	126	102	115	90	132	135	129	116	105
Total Troy,	572	529	1, 839	1, 767	1, 809	1, 827	1, 742	1, 723	1, 481	1, 823	1, 703	2, 175	1, 687	1, 836	1, 473	1, 464
Total,	1, 172	1. 164	4, 256	4, 131	4, 416	4, 480	4, 220	4, 338	3, 742	4, 377	3, 822	4, 499	3, 524	3, 803	3, 199	3, 132

RICHMOND COUNTY.

TOWNS.	Under 1. Males.	Under 1. Females	1 and under 5. Males.	1 and under 5. Females	5 and under 10. Males.	5 and under 10. Females	10 and under 15. Males.	10 and under 15. Females	15 and under 20. Males.	15 and under 20. Females	20 and under 25. Males.	20 and under 25. Females	25 and under 30. Males.	25 and under 30. Females	30 and under 35. Males.	30 and under 35. Females.
Castleton,	129	96	438	439	444	457	400	414	365	433	349	535	359	451	312	332
Northfield,	48	60	246	231	242	238	232	227	204	242	189	223	189	172	142	173
Southfield,	81	98	298	285	281	268	235	261	202	310	299	394	277	318	271	247
Westfield,	42	65	180	150	186	197	223	188	175	206	158	180	149	153	140	124
Total,	300	319	1, 162	1, 105	1, 153	1, 160	1, 090	1, 090	946	1, 191	995	1, 332	974	1, 094	865	876

OTSEGO COUNTY.—(CONTINUED.)

TOWNS.	35 and under 40.		40 and under 45.		45 and under 50.		50 and under 60.		60 and under 70.		70 and under 80.		80 and under 90.		90 and under 100.		100 and upwards.		Ages unknown.
	Males.	Females	Males.	Females	Males.	Females	Males.	Females	Males.	Females	Males.	Females	Males	Fems	Males	Fems	Males	Fems	
aryland,	60	64	58	50	49	47	71	64	50	53	22	25	7	4	....	1	....	....	......
iddlefield,	75	84	92	103	100	80	102	108	72	51	44	32	10	8	2	2	....	....	......
lford,	69	55	59	51	55	47	83	90	59	58	21	21	6	4	2	2	....	....	2
orris,	63	63	52	51	44	54	76	77	38	43	26	26	10	15	2	1	....	....	3
ew Lisbon,	55	56	43	54	50	49	64	61	39	41	23	24	6	8	....	....	....	....	......
neonta,	70	66	51	50	49	44	67	68	40	41	14	23	4	4	1	1	....	....	......
ego,	51	55	53	57	44	37	66	79	42	46	25	16	5	6	1	....	....	....	......
sego,	140	129	125	130	100	96	128	153	86	95	41	42	9	19	1	....	....	....	6
ttsfield,	48	59	41	43	33	46	66	58	32	29	25	11	8	3	....	....	....	....	......
ainfield,	44	35	37	39	42	33	40	44	26	27	16	12	7	8	....	....	....	....	6
chfield,	45	40	33	40	39	36	69	73	38	35	21	11	13	8	1	....	....	....	......
oseboom,	57	52	37	44	52	39	58	62	31	36	24	18	7	4	....	....	....	....	......
pringfield,	67	71	68	59	39	60	77	85	55	60	24	32	8	11	....	1	....	....	......
nadilla,	75	75	68	80	76	64	102	92	57	61	29	23	9	7	1	2	....	....	7
estford,	52	39	30	34	19	17	53	58	43	38	9	14	4	5	....	....	....	....	......
orcester,	69	58	45	51	55	34	52	74	55	57	21	15	6	5	....	....	....	....	1
Total,	1, 495	1. 444	1, 280	1, 297	1, 216	1, 134	1, 754	1, 799	1, 067	1, 051	562	505	183	171	, 22	21	....	....	35

PUTNAM COUNTY.—(CONTINUED.)

TOWNS.	35-40 Males	35-40 Females	40-45 Males	40-45 Females	45-50 Males	45-50 Females	50-60 Males	50-60 Females	60-70 Males	60-70 Females	70-80 Males	70-80 Females	80-90 Males	80-90 Fems	90-100 Males	90-100 Fems	100+ Males	100+ Fems	Ages unknown
armel,	75	84	61	61	62	61	93	95	61	55	35	28	4	10	....	1	....	2	......
ent,	32	38	41	33	36	31	52	57	37	35	21	14	4	7	1	1	1	....	2
atterson,	51	34	41	40	25	37	49	61	31	46	20	18	2	7	1	1	....	....	......
hillipstown,	163	140	123	132	94	73	143	130	82	71	19	23	5	6	2	3	....	....	......
utnam Valley,	39	34	50	34	31	31	46	47	41	42	25	19	3	3	1	1	....	....	......
outh East,	56	60	50	53	39	43	77	79	43	60	27	29	7	5	....	4	....	....	6
Total,	416	390	366	353	287	276	460	469	295	309	147	131	25	38	5	11	1	2	8

QUEENS COUNTY.—(CONTINUED.)

TOWNS.	35-40 Males	35-40 Females	40-45 Males	40-45 Females	45-50 Males	45-50 Females	50-60 Males	50-60 Females	60-70 Males	60-70 Females	70-80 Males	70-80 Females	80-90 Males	80-90 Fems	90-100 Males	90-100 Fems	100+ Males	100+ Fems	Ages unknown
Flushing,	293	273	264	226	174	135	204	182	100	122	28	38	10	14	1	....	....	....	5
empstead,	337	303	279	265	251	212	342	347	227	212	91	96	23	35	5	6	....	....	......
amaica,	183	178	158	134	128	107	166	160	91	105	49	46	7	19	2	1	1	....	2
ewtown,	320	310	347	253	206	130	284	228	112	129	40	44	6	18	3	4	....	....	......
orth Hempstead,	142	159	139	115	107	108	162	144	93	101	38	44	14	13	1	3	1	1	7
yster Bay,	263	240	212	212	200	164	299	254	178	190	96	82	27	29	2	8	....	....	14
Total,	1, 538	1, 463	1, 399	1, 205	1, 066	856	1, 457	1, 315	801	859	342	350	87	128	14	22	2	1	28

RENSSELAER COUNTY.—(CONTINUED.)

TOWNS.	35-40 Males	35-40 Females	40-45 Males	40-45 Females	45-50 Males	45-50 Females	50-60 Males	50-60 Females	60-70 Males	60-70 Females	70-80 Males	70-80 Females	80-90 Males	80-90 Fems	90-100 Males	90-100 Fems	100+ Males	100+ Fems	Ages unknown
erlin,	70	75	61	45	58	47	75	83	47	42	19	22	6	7	3	....	....	....	......
runswick,	106	94	105	89	59	57	108	106	63	58	30	30	7	7	....	1	....	1	2
linton,	50	57	37	33	38	36	65	48	31	32	13	14	5	6	....	....	....	....	......
rafton,	55	49	38	34	40	49	79	55	28	34	15	15	7	6	1	....	....	....	......
reenbush,	139	107	114	79	68	51	77	61	32	41	7	13	1	3	....	....	....	....	......
oosick,	116	139	116	99	97	96	133	114	62	77	24	31	6	6	....	....	....	....	2
ansingburgh,	185	209	143	74	103	111	148	137	65	90	30	39	13	10	....	2	....	....	......
assau,	86	116	85	176	68	69	118	113	72	56	35	39	6	10	4	4	....	....	......
orth Greenburgh,	65	57	49	42	54	42	56	49	24	35	19	19	1	3	1	1	....	....	......
etersburgh,	41	53	45	44	31	28	78	71	28	25	22	17	10	8	....	....	....	....	......
ittstown,	135	109	106	81	71	69	129	134	72	76	39	39	8	9	2	1	....	....	......
oestenkill,	62	51	44	44	47	37	58	47	29	29	17	13	5	5	....	....	....	....	......
and Lake,	75	79	101	65	58	63	97	89	50	50	29	32	5	6	....	1	....	....	......
chaghticoke,	103	100	101	88	70	65	105	101	62	56	24	22	6	2	1	3	....	....	......
chodack,	120	105	114	123	101	92	151	135	79	80	39	37	14	10	2	2	....	....	4
tephentown,	74	63	59	75	55	52	99	91	59	54	36	29	9	6	....	....	....	....	1
Troy City: 1st ward,	129	129	135	132	76	89	106	122	35	60	19	24	4	11	....	1	....	....	......
2d ward,	127	120	117	119	66	65	102	140	42	50	16	22	1	4	....	1	....	....	2
3d ward,	84	84	58	68	51	53	60	76	34	28	6	14	5	5	....	....	....	....	38
4th ward,	109	146	92	105	94	95	104	104	50	67	14	15	3	9	....	1	....	....	......
5th ward,	92	91	63	60	51	38	42	51	22	30	11	10	1	3	....	1	....	....	16
6th ward,	105	70	70	55	57	35	54	57	35	15	8	7	1	3	....	....	....	....	......
7th ward,	126	112	91	93	89	73	95	85	39	41	12	12	4	4	....	....	....	....	21
8th ward,	125	113	96	92	72	51	84	84	25	36	7	16	....	9	....	....	....	....	......
9th ward,	118	99	113	85	51	33	65	59	23	25	10	9	2	3	....	....	....	....	1
10th ward,	78	65	61	57	45	39	51	59	26	22	6	11	1	1	1	1	....	....	......
Total Troy,	1, 093	1, 029	896	866	652	571	763	837	331	374	109	140	22	52	1	5	....	....	78
Total,	2, 575	2, 492	2, 214	2, 057	1, 670	1, 535	2, 339	2, 271	1, 134	1, 209	507	551	126	156	15	20	....	1	87

RICHMOND COUNTY.—(CONTINUED.)

TOWNS.	35-40 Males	35-40 Females	40-45 Males	40-45 Females	45-50 Males	45-50 Females	50-60 Males	50-60 Females	60-70 Males	60-70 Females	70-80 Males	70-80 Females	80-90 Males	80-90 Fems	90-100 Males	90-100 Fems	100+ Males	100+ Fems	Ages unknown
Castleton,	283	260	271	240	211	153	259	182	165	102	98	33	13	11	4	2	....	....	3
Northfield,	140	150	119	108	97	82	122	105	65	80	21	26	7	4	....	2	1	....	......
Southfield,	212	150	179	149	89	81	134	119	60	69	27	34	5	10	....	1	....	....	5
Westfield,	102	107	98	89	74	68	122	105	79	69	23	32	7	5	....	1	....	....	4
Total,	737	607	667	595	471	384	637	511	369	320	169	125	32	30	4	6	1	....	12

ROCKLAND COUNTY.

TOWNS.	Under 1.		1 and under 5.		5 and under 10.		10 and under 15.		15 and under 20.		20 and under 25.		25 and under 30.		30 and under 35.	
	Males.	Females.	Males.	Females.	Males.	Females	Males.	Females.	Males.	Females	Males.	Females.	Males.	Females	Males.	Females.
Clarkstown,	52	45	206	190	192	180	195	161	175	179	145	175	145	150	135	116
Haverstraw,	139	111	463	405	404	351	367	349	360	296	487	327	406	350	334	257
Orangetown,	107	87	309	365	331	328	290	286	271	286	282	323	287	268	251	229
Ramapo,	52	47	167	183	205	219	225	180	170	204	165	151	102	109	135	114
Total,	350	290	1, 145	1, 143	1, 132	1, 078	1, 077	976	976	965	1, 079	976	940	877	855	716

ST. LAWRENCE COUNTY.

TOWNS.	Under 1.		1 and under 5.		5 and under 10.		10 and under 15.		15 and under 20.		20 and under 25.		25 and under 30.		30 and under 35.	
	Males.	Females.	Males.	Females.	Males.	Females	Males.	Females.	Males.	Females	Males.	Females.	Males.	Females	Males.	Females.
Brasher,	43	50	215	189	218	225	201	199	176	159	114	124	97	109	97	92
Canton,	63	57	286	287	345	287	309	267	223	257	191	280	180	225	185	186
Colton,	13	15	65	73	94	65	55	65	49	39	44	51	33	39	46	46
De Kalb,	42	37	182	175	175	187	153	150	150	152	108	122	100	105	102	76
De Peyster,	11	20	64	59	97	75	68	61	56	64	58	68	42	43	43	34
Edwards,	20	25	75	55	87	79	80	70	67	79	61	45	37	40	48	35
Fine,	4	4	25	24	30	18	25	20	15	15	16	13	12	8	5	8
Fowler,	25	22	92	94	116	110	102	97	78	87	65	94	46	60	55	39
Gouverneur,	28	45	161	174	186	165	200	176	139	175	110	166	108	107	97	82
Hammond,	32	33	110	93	125	122	132	109	108	103	88	104	75	59	60	68
Hermon,	27	18	104	97	114	116	129	97	73	99	82	74	51	56	53	43
Hopkinton,	18	25	90	88	100	96	90	83	78	89	65	71	59	55	51	51
Lawrence,	31	38	148	123	160	134	144	149	142	110	93	107	80	77	82	76
Lisbon,	78	80	334	295	387	360	380	313	257	292	202	227	147	149	147	158
Louisville,	36	29	126	139	147	150	150	118	140	111	72	92	72	77	67	76
Macomb,	29	29	117	113	119	135	101	87	66	66	45	58	47	55	53	47
Madrid,	50	60	270	231	291	326	322	276	275	283	221	285	183	189	130	134
Massena,	36	43	149	172	188	180	190	162	148	146	106	144	80	113	71	69
Morristown,	34	25	105	110	131	122	134	140	105	133	100	115	82	67	54	71
Norfolk,	22	24	85	95	105	111	100	110	105	102	81	101	75	75	53	60
Oswegatchie,	160	165	590	568	672	620	642	562	503	636	481	642	419	427	329	316
Parishville,	28	40	108	113	133	131	121	137	101	106	84	97	83	89	58	72
Pierrepont,	19	40	90	113	123	120	104	111	104	89	73	78	66	65	65	75
Pitcairn,	8	8	32	34	35	39	35	39	25	34	23	29	29	12	18	10
Potsdam,	68	82	339	352	406	336	334	379	353	387	372	368	300	340	241	222
Rossie,	15	20	93	79	105	108	95	104	90	71	70	84	53	51	38	49
Russell,	31	20	150	115	149	142	134	114	119	107	83	99	80	88	80	64
Stockholm,	64	47	256	179	244	244	237	217	178	202	168	163	149	159	116	117
Total,	1, 035	1, 101	4, 461	4, 239	5, 082	4, 803	4, 767	4, 412	3, 923	4, 193	3, 276	3, 901	2, 785	2, 939	2, 444	2, 376

SARATOGA COUNTY.

TOWNS.	Under 1.		1 and under 5.		5 and under 10.		10 and under 15.		15 and under 20.		20 and under 25.		25 and under 30.		30 and under 35.	
	Males.	Females.	Males.	Females.	Males.	Females	Males.	Females.	Males.	Females	Males.	Females.	Males.	Females	Males.	Females.
Ballston,	35	38	98	93	128	114	113	119	125	121	76	120	77	88	63	68
Charlton,	6	11	71	72	98	73	115	102	108	101	63	79	45	58	49	54
Clifton Park,	44	44	164	164	164	171	175	145	130	124	139	124	122	131	146	111
Corinth,	22	22	79	79	95	95	92	94	86	76	64	66	49	45	58	63
Day,	23	17	69	66	80	73	74	65	53	64	55	52	34	25	35	26
Edinburgh,	6	18	59	86	77	82	81	76	66	62	60	72	38	52	44	41
Galway,	31	31	102	107	142	131	135	124	118	120	98	110	83	92	85	100
Greenfield,	32	43	146	139	153	142	152	143	128	129	126	130	105	111	74	91
Hadley,	25	22	81	74	76	65	78	70	49	48	48	44	53	55	50	46
Half Moon,	34	31	179	169	177	171	153	194	155	188	167	169	149	148	119	118
Malta,	37	45	58	68	79	69	77	59	46	46	38	38	55	39	38	60
Milton,	81	67	232	236	283	278	226	260	221	235	199	235	189	226	165	196
Moreau,	29	38	109	127	131	150	122	126	115	117	112	99	82	87	83	69
Northumberland,	27	16	87	69	107	94	84	100	90	83	78	71	67	72	44	52
Providence,	8	10	74	66	100	87	94	83	50	74	42	58	45	54	39	55
Saratoga,	61	44	189	168	211	218	210	203	170	251	165	233	147	187	132	135
Saratoga Springs,	85	87	285	288	310	319	284	326	285	370	320	396	275	347	246	300
Stillwater,	34	28	161	152	163	162	148	169	146	156	143	170	110	125	115	109
Waterford,	50	44	168	196	201	188	178	177	147	188	148	179	133	168	143	134
Wilton,	21	12	52	60	83	91	72	97	64	73	59	60	38	41	46	43
Total,	691	668	2, 463	2, 479	2, 858	2, 773	2, 663	2, 732	2, 352	2, 626	2, 200	2, 505	1, 896	2, 151	1, 774	1, 871

SCHENECTADY COUNTY.

TOWNS.	Under 1.		1 and under 5.		5 and under 10.		10 and under 15.		15 and under 20.		20 and under 25.		25 and under 30.		30 and under 35.	
	Males.	Females.	Males.	Females.	Males.	Females	Males.	Females.	Males.	Females	Males.	Females.	Males.	Females	Males.	Females.
Duanesburgh,	31	34	138	160	209	176	212	202	169	165	139	140	96	111	92	105
Glenville,	42	28	188	148	196	192	186	169	188	153	156	157	127	118	112	97
Niskayuna,	15	12	58	58	65	72	63	60	52	50	53	46	50	40	46	40
Princetown,	14	7	66	52	50	60	57	61	54	43	40	36	35	30	43	32
Rotterdam,	25	37	175	141	177	180	162	143	138	132	155	118	150	120	129	101
Schenectady City:																
1st ward,	15	26	76	81	82	82	66	90	73	87	64	103	53	83	46	54
2d ward,	24	19	73	75	69	69	63	67	76	99	74	102	65	88	64	60
3d ward,	33	36	117	119	101	119	92	86	103	96	85	109	106	105	80	75
4th ward,	48	47	171	167	209	180	178	170	151	198	184	190	145	170	118	134
Total Schenectady,	120	128	437	442	461	450	399	413	403	480	407	504	369	446	308	323
Total,	247	246	1, 062	1, 001	1, 158	1, 130	1, 079	1, 048	1, 004	1, 023	950	1, 001	827	865	730	698

SCHOHARIE COUNTY.

TOWNS.	Under 1.		1 and under 5.		5 and under 10.		10 and under 15.		15 and under 20.		20 and under 25.		25 and under 30.		30 and under 35.	
	Males.	Females.	Males.	Females.	Males.	Females	Males.	Females.	Males.	Females	Males.	Females.	Males.	Females	Males.	Females.
Blenheim,	31	15	84	95	73	89	86	83	74	78	56	50	48	52	51	42
Broome,,	29	30	116	117	143	163	143	132	123	137	58	91	80	71	69	62
Carlisle,	20	23	98	88	117	96	111	92	81	98	74	73	59	55	62	57
Cobleskill,	34	26	114	110	133	145	136	136	115	120	85	103	93	93	84	75
Conesville,	26	22	56	62	83	84	74	73	63	70	57	60	59	58	49	49

ROCKLAND COUNTY.—(CONTINUED.)

TOWNS.	35 and under 40. Males	35 and under 40. Females	40 and under 45. Males	40 and under 45. Females	45 and under 50. Males	45 and under 50. Females	50 and under 60. Males	50 and under 60. Females	60 and under 70. Males	60 and under 70. Females	70 and under 80. Males	70 and under 80. Females	80 and under 90. Males	80 and under 90. Fems	90 and under 100. Males	90 and under 100. Fems	100 and upwards. Males	100 and upwards. Fems	Ages unknown.
Clarkstown,	111	92	104	90	87	60	129	107	99	91	44	31	11	12	....	2	....	....	1
Haverstraw,	213	164	189	120	107	91	131	113	71	69	24	27	10	8	1	3	....	....	......
Orangetown,	192	161	162	173	129	105	139	137	93	115	44	51	6	25	2	3	....	....	1
Ramapo,	93	80	79	87	78	64	118	127	85	74	34	36	14	14	1	2	....	....	......
Total,	609	497	534	470	401	320	517	484	348	349	146	145	41	59	4	10	....	....	2

ST. LAWRENCE COUNTY.—(CONTINUED.)

TOWNS.	35 and under 40. Males	35 and under 40. Females	40 and under 45. Males	40 and under 45. Females	45 and under 50. Males	45 and under 50. Females	50 and under 60. Males	50 and under 60. Females	60 and under 70. Males	60 and under 70. Females	70 and under 80. Males	70 and under 80. Females	80 and under 90. Males	80 and under 90. Fems	90 and under 100. Males	90 and under 100. Fems	100 and upwards. Males	100 and upwards. Fems	Ages unknown.
Brasher,	80	80	68	59	52	47	93	69	46	42	10	7	3	1	....	1	....	....	2
Canton,	147	155	128	133	120	96	156	123	108	99	47	37	12	8	....	1	1	....	1
Colton,	42	21	32	28	26	15	23	18	12	14	8	3	1	2	....	....	2	....	1
De Kalb,	67	65	56	53	56	53	80	64	64	46	19	23	5	7	1	1	....	....	......
De Peyster,	27	24	32	21	18	15	43	40	24	25	12	10	3	5	....	....	....	....	1
Edwards,	24	30	23	18	25	15	37	33	30	22	9	8	2	....	....	1	....	....	......
Fine,	4	6	8	5	7	8	9	9	7	3	4	2	1	1	....	....	....	....	......
Fowler,	47	47	43	36	35	37	61	32	28	30	15	14	3	2	1	2	....	....	5
Gouverneur,	73	78	64	78	62	65	81	65	64	49	26	23	7	2	....	....	....	....	......
Hammond,	43	32	37	47	43	36	69	49	28	24	14	21	6	5	....	....	....	....	......
Hermon,	51	52	32	39	31	33	64	38	28	17	8	12	7	3	....	....	....	....	......
Hopkinton,	31	48	42	37	44	33	53	59	38	28	14	11	2	5	....	....	....	....	......
Lawrence,	60	69	58	57	62	65	94	71	39	42	23	14	10	7	....	....	....	....	......
Lisbon,	123	123	132	136	119	93	182	154	95	68	30	25	8	11	....	3	....	....	1
Louisville,	71	52	48	46	45	37	59	55	39	34	13	12	2	5	....	....	....	....	......
Macomb,	43	26	32	24	21	27	45	28	23	17	7	4	1	1	....	....	....	....	......
Madrid,	135	137	114	114	91	80	162	170	127	97	50	30	12	12	....	2	1	....	2
Massena,	79	73	49	51	59	52	89	75	57	53	27	20	10	6	....	1	....	....	3
Morristown,	43	50	45	50	54	48	75	69	49	40	26	16	6	5	1	1	....	....	5
Norfolk,	51	46	35	36	43	39	68	60	38	37	14	18	4	7	3	1	....	....	......
Oswegatchie,	289	259	269	215	151	169	270	228	137	129	48	55	13	14	4	4	1	2	71
Parishville,	59	47	48	52	49	37	99	73	45	46	27	18	8	2	3	....	....	....	......
Pierrepont,	53	46	43	46	27	40	61	46	45	40	18	16	5	3	....	....	....	....	......
Pitcairn,	6	11	13	11	13	9	21	15	9	8	2	2	....	1	....	....	....	....	......
Potsdam,	205	181	153	151	133	121	204	198	158	121	50	52	9	6	1	4	....	....	5
Rossie,	46	43	33	25	25	29	53	37	21	17	12	10	2	1	1	....	....	....	......
Russell,	43	48	49	37	39	43	81	63	48	35	20	15	8	2	....	....	....	....	2
Stockholm,	121	120	71	63	69	86	149	136	86	62	37	28	8	10	1	2	....	....	1
Total,	2,063	1,969	1,752	1,668	1,529	1,428	2,481	2,077	1,493	1,245	590	506	158	134	16	24	5	2	100

SARATOGA COUNTY.—(CONTINUED.)

TOWNS.	35 and under 40. Males	35 and under 40. Females	40 and under 45. Males	40 and under 45. Females	45 and under 50. Males	45 and under 50. Females	50 and under 60. Males	50 and under 60. Females	60 and under 70. Males	60 and under 70. Females	70 and under 80. Males	70 and under 80. Females	80 and under 90. Males	80 and under 90. Fems	90 and under 100. Males	90 and under 100. Fems	100 and upwards. Males	100 and upwards. Fems	Ages unknown.
Ballston,	58	71	62	62	62	59	81	94	47	51	25	37	8	7	....	1	....	....	......
Charlton,	46	45	51	58	53	54	69	72	43	39	15	28	9	11	1	1	....	...	1
Clifton Park,	100	96	96	74	67	63	78	83	46	49	29	30	2	4	....	2	....	....	......
Corinth,	48	36	42	57	38	28	55	37	25	27	19	23	9	5	....	....	....	....	......
Day,	24	32	28	21	16	18	33	21	17	23	13	13	1	1	2	....	....	....	5
Edinburgh,	32	41	28	35	28	34	57	44	33	24	16	18	3	2	1	1	....	....	1
Galway,	77	67	66	87	69	58	102	102	57	57	29	33	10	11	3	3	1	....	......
Greenfield,	88	101	89	64	71	73	122	110	88	67	42	46	15	20	1	1	....	....	......
Hadley,	36	29	42	19	26	23	33	30	21	12	7	3	1	6	....	....	....	....	......
Half Moon,	115	100	110	76	64	89	109	92	52	60	28	30	5	4	....	3	....	....	57
Malta,	39	44	37	33	59	56	25	32	22	27	5	5	....	....	....	....	....	....	......
Milton,	150	136	127	117	99	93	150	165	93	99	31	48	15	15	....	2	....	....	......
Moreau,	68	67	49	40	39	41	65	65	49	45	17	12	7	3	2	1	....	....	......
Northumberland,	45	50	49	45	43	32	56	57	44	34	23	21	11	6	....	....	....	....	11
Providence,	43	41	43	34	28	23	53	43	32	31	18	19	7	10	2	2	....	....	......
Saratoga,	110	119	109	113	82	85	121	144	72	74	34	24	8	11	1	1	....	....	......
Saratoga Springs,	183	223	212	217	133	128	193	196	96	110	35	41	8	6	1	....	....	....	2
Stillwater,	101	95	92	92	71	56	101	87	55	59	24	25	3	7	....	1	....	....	3
Waterford,	99	111	108	88	61	51	68	82	37	40	23	22	4	5	....	....	....	....	8
Wilton,	48	49	45	44	33	36	49	50	33	42	18	16	15	5	6	....	....	....	......
Total,	1,510	1,553	1,485	1,376	1,142	1,100	1,620	1,606	962	970	451	494	141	139	20	19	1	....	88

SCHENECTADY COUNTY.—(CONTINUED.)

TOWNS.	35 and under 40. Males	35 and under 40. Females	40 and under 45. Males	40 and under 45. Females	45 and under 50. Males	45 and under 50. Females	50 and under 60. Males	50 and under 60. Females	60 and under 70. Males	60 and under 70. Females	70 and under 80. Males	70 and under 80. Females	80 and under 90. Males	80 and under 90. Fems	90 and under 100. Males	90 and under 100. Fems	100 and upwards. Males	100 and upwards. Fems	Ages unknown.
Duanesburgh,	89	81	78	77	75	76	124	120	61	62	28	40	14	14	1	....	....	....	......
Glenville,	102	88	87	72	70	66	104	90	64	56	24	40	12	8	3	2	....	....	8
Niskayuna,	47	35	30	26	26	25	41	40	24	18	11	9	3	3	....	2	....	....	......
Princetown,	26	29	32	24	24	24	19	26	18	23	9	10	7	2	1	1	....	....	1
Rotterdam,	113	70	79	62	68	62	88	67	44	42	23	21	5	6	2	....	....	....	......
Schenectady City:																			
1st ward,	48	49	39	59	46	30	32	58	19	36	8	24	2	5	....	1	....	....	7
2d ward,	56	46	39	44	41	41	38	54	21	30	8	15	2	8	....	....	....	....	......
3d ward,	69	58	48	54	29	31	55	54	25	33	8	16	2	6	....	1	....	....	......
4th ward,	124	93	91	87	75	59	101	116	50	53	20	14	5	8	....	1	....	....	7
Total Schenectady,	297	246	217	244	191	161	226	282	115	152	44	69	11	27	....	3	....	....	14
Total,	674	549	523	505	454	414	602	625	326	353	139	189	52	60	7	8	....	....	23

SCHOHARIE COUNTY.—(CONTINUED.)

TOWNS.	35 and under 40. Males	35 and under 40. Females	40 and under 45. Males	40 and under 45. Females	45 and under 50. Males	45 and under 50. Females	50 and under 60. Males	50 and under 60. Females	60 and under 70. Males	60 and under 70. Females	70 and under 80. Males	70 and under 80. Females	80 and under 90. Males	80 and under 90. Fems	90 and under 100. Males	90 and under 100. Fems	100 and upwards. Males	100 and upwards. Fems	Ages unknown.
Blenheim,	37	36	46	28	21	21	45	38	21	28	9	8	4	2	....	....	....	....	......
Broome,	57	63	71	61	56	30	58	55	42	42	19	10	5	3	1	....	....	....	1
Carlisle,	58	56	29	43	44	42	60	56	34	38	20	21	6	12	....	....	....	....	......
Cobleskill,	68	65	54	44	45	55	70	78	43	34	19	19	2	7	....	....	....	....	3
Conesville,	39	52	37	32	40	38	48	53	31	30	28	15	8	7	1	1	....	....	2

SCHOHARIE COUNTY.

TOWNS.	Under 1.		1 and under 5.		5 and under 10.		10 and under 15.		15 and under 20.		20 and under 25.		25 and under 30.		30 and under 35.	
	Males.	Females	Males.	Females	Males.	Females	Males.	Females	Males.	Females	Males.	Females	Males.	Females	Males.	Females.
Esperance,	19	18	52	59	83	92	81	90	70	67	47	69	37	61	42	52
Fulton,	32	51	198	165	205	217	180	154	148	132	99	127	115	111	106	84
Gilboa,	26	40	164	148	175	176	161	210	144	129	104	122	86	89	83	77
Jefferson,	25	33	100	117	93	92	101	109	84	80	92	80	40	64	59	71
Middleburgh,	51	39	190	164	235	199	210	170	150	151	156	122	117	139	98	91
Richmondville,	28	17	112	115	143	127	127	127	98	105	87	86	85	76	77	79
Schoharie,	44	31	170	153	183	169	150	186	158	162	134	142	113	123	97	89
Seward,	16	21	90	87	118	112	131	133	123	120	96	117	66	58	58	66
Sharon,	37	27	130	141	194	160	158	160	140	155	137	125	92	105	91	91
Summit,	32	35	111	99	114	105	118	100	107	97	83	99	79	88	60	79
Wright,	20	19	112	90	103	107	105	102	94	86	63	60	63	62	52	60
Total,	470	447	1, 897	1, 810	2, 195	2, 133	2, 072	2, 057	1, 772	1, 787	1, 428	1, 526	1, 232	1, 305	1, 138	1, 124

SCHUYLER COUNTY.

TOWNS.	Under 1. Males.	Under 1. Females	1 and under 5. Males.	1 and under 5. Females	5 and under 10. Males.	5 and under 10. Females	10 and under 15. Males.	10 and under 15. Females	15 and under 20. Males.	15 and under 20. Females	20 and under 25. Males.	20 and under 25. Females	25 and under 30. Males.	25 and under 30. Females	30 and under 35. Males.	30 and under 35. Females.
Catharines,	46	47	183	168	200	234	204	199	194	203	169	172	148	167	147	121
Cayuta,	9	5	35	33	43	40	44	32	31	33	29	34	26	19	19	20
Dix,	41	35	149	145	187	183	182	208	138	137	119	144	112	123	113	100
Hector,	67	68	269	267	332	332	353	354	304	337	278	255	220	238	183	189
Orange,	32	29	121	120	170	173	169	142	147	151	103	103	95	84	71	79
Reading,	22	15	66	57	98	81	88	91	88	81	73	76	33	58	63	54
Tyrone,	17	30	93	105	123	125	130	145	134	127	114	120	85	95	70	72
Total,	234	229	916	895	1, 153	1, 168	1, 170	1, 171	1, 036	1, 069	885	904	719	784	666	635

SENECA COUNTY.

TOWNS.	Under 1. Males.	Under 1. Females	1 and under 5. Males.	1 and under 5. Females	5 and under 10. Males.	5 and under 10. Females	10 and under 15. Males.	10 and under 15. Females	15 and under 20. Males.	15 and under 20. Females	20 and under 25. Males.	20 and under 25. Females	25 and under 30. Males.	25 and under 30. Females	30 and under 35. Males.	30 and under 35. Females.
Covert,	36	23	119	132	132	117	131	116	136	109	90	100	97	87	78	83
Fayette,	41	36	163	167	215	215	211	195	199	170	165	175	128	150	106	125
Junius,	17	21	54	79	87	79	81	68	88	80	58	69	72	65	50	48
Lodi,	33	14	109	94	132	107	114	125	107	122	80	115	60	69	74	72
Ovid,	29	32	102	136	127	136	142	137	126	117	91	140	75	94	97	80
Romulus,	25	20	100	80	141	110	129	121	92	91	94	95	72	70	53	57
Seneca Falls,	57	78	269	265	284	293	285	299	236	277	274	253	245	241	190	189
Tyre,	23	20	78	70	79	89	79	88	76	79	67	74	47	52	49	39
Varick,	13	23	99	87	98	107	115	100	87	96	76	82	61	75	71	67
Waterloo,	55	45	206	220	242	251	225	244	193	246	172	218	166	196	136	154
Total,	329	312	1, 299	1, 330	1, 537	1, 504	1, 512	1, 493	1, 340	1, 387	1, 167	1, 321	1, 023	1, 099	904	914

STEUBEN COUNTY.

TOWNS.	Under 1. Males.	Under 1. Females	1 and under 5. Males.	1 and under 5. Females	5 and under 10. Males.	5 and under 10. Females	10 and under 15. Males.	10 and under 15. Females	15 and under 20. Males.	15 and under 20. Females	20 and under 25. Males.	20 and under 25. Females	25 and under 30. Males.	25 and under 30. Females	30 and under 35. Males.	30 and under 35. Females.
Addison,	29	36	197	207	210	195	189	178	153	206	166	174	151	122	104	111
Avoca,	22	22	90	78	117	102	112	99	111	107	87	89	73	80	56	46
Bath,	85	74	316	356	396	367	365	382	319	380	294	307	250	227	201	195
Bradford,	24	16	65	99	87	97	85	87	71	63	62	55	52	49	34	31
Cameron,	33	40	108	130	144	118	106	125	73	99	78	89	81	63	63	71
Campbell,	26	16	93	85	109	90	88	93	83	87	90	64	73	65	51	46
Canisteo,	35	15	125	118	154	126	125	134	103	103	98	115	91	61	67	68
Caton,	28	21	99	104	112	105	114	85	85	77	73	70	65	73	63	49
Cohocton,	29	16	148	149	133	144	135	127	106	124	102	100	80	101	109	81
Corning,	87	83	409	375	383	416	331	314	265	357	375	330	357	318	323	229
Dansville,	29	28	117	142	117	135	135	131	119	115	66	72	48	53	121	101
Erwin,	38	34	102	115	116	113	103	95	101	96	95	99	108	89	75	75
Fremont,	15	14	71	64	66	77	80	63	62	56	45	57	46	44	35	46
Greenwood,	18	22	80	75	82	87	72	83	63	56	57	60	45	51	40	36
Hartsville,	21	15	76	81	75	71	78	71	54	55	59	42	45	49	41	30
Hornby,	27	10	89	79	108	90	94	84	85	72	54	62	62	47	52	48
Hornellsville,	64	66	208	238	219	248	187	175	167	220	252	227	231	199	185	152
Howard,	35	33	150	162	189	198	184	167	141	155	122	102	97	97	80	80
Jasper,	27	34	109	104	113	138	114	122	84	96	83	71	73	62	50	47
Lindley,	11	7	47	46	53	45	39	40	37	28	30	32	39	34	18	32
Prattsburgh,	36	35	134	124	154	162	178	159	124	140	107	138	108	92	93	94
Pultney,	8	12	77	72	84	105	96	87	81	106	67	90	60	65	59	44
Thurston,	12	7	58	62	52	64	84	56	50	53	37	38	37	27	30	30
Troupsburgh,	43	27	120	110	138	131	145	117	114	121	88	82	93	76	66	56
Urbana,	26	21	113	96	130	121	110	129	99	115	89	101	88	100	76	68
Wayland,	51	45	154	175	202	197	177	183	118	122	107	112	114	93	86	76
Wayne,	16	9	45	39	65	57	60	60	48	62	44	49	43	39	32	23
West Union,	26	27	85	97	85	90	80	67	56	66	45	48	49	44	53	33
Wheeler,	22	19	73	67	86	86	85	103	91	79	70	56	58	35	34	46
Woodhull,	41	39	146	136	158	165	147	119	119	120	99	85	88	85	81	79
Total,	964	843	3, 704	3, 785	4, 137	4, 140	3, 898	3, 735	3, 182	3, 536	3, 041	3, 016	2, 805	2, 540	2, 378	2, 123

SUFFOLK COUNTY.

TOWNS.	Under 1. Males.	Under 1. Females	1 and under 5. Males.	1 and under 5. Females	5 and under 10. Males.	5 and under 10. Females	10 and under 15. Males.	10 and under 15. Females	15 and under 20. Males.	15 and under 20. Females	20 and under 25. Males.	20 and under 25. Females	25 and under 30. Males.	25 and under 30. Females	30 and under 35. Males.	30 and under 35. Females.
Brookhaven,	129	139	477	535	536	617	614	613	477	509	436	471	378	366	335	311
Easthampton,	22	16	85	92	111	97	129	120	102	112	93	93	75	81	65	76
Huntington,	96	83	366	410	490	438	512	448	482	444	409	372	289	327	269	298
Islip,	42	51	199	206	202	213	196	164	171	159	120	144	150	137	133	116
Riverhead,	49	39	119	115	145	165	181	163	144	171	117	145	106	96	83	75
Shelter Island,	9	7	17	23	22	18	35	38	24	22	21	28	25	15	13	15
Smithtown,	25	25	93	101	115	116	136	131	121	110	84	100	62	79	63	67
Southampton,	94	85	302	310	342	375	487	356	356	344	281	283	231	243	224	227
Southold,	74	75	230	247	260	260	326	278	315	307	324	316	245	205	216	203
Total,	540	520	1, 888	2, 039	2, 223	2, 299	2, 616	2, 311	2, 192	2, 178	1, 885	1, 952	1, 561	1, 549	1, 401	1, 388

OTSEGO COUNTY.—(Continued.)

TOWNS.	35 and under 40.		40 and under 45.		45 and under 50.		50 and under 60.		60 and under 70.		70 and under 80.		80 and under 90.		90 and under 100.		100 and upwards.		Ages unknown.
	Males.	Females	Males.	Females	Males.	Females.	Males.	Females	Males.	Females	Males.	Females	Males	Fems.	Males	Fems	Males	Fems.	
Esperance, ...	48	56	48	40	31	27	38	39	33	40	11	10	3	7	....	....	....	....	......
Fulton, ...	85	71	68	63	38	40	92	77	55	49	22	19	7	5	....	2	....	....	......
Gilboa, ...	70	63	64	60	60	68	75	82	60	54	29	25	4	3	....	2	....	....	4
Jefferson, ...	40	30	37	41	30	37	60	58	30	38	22	13	6	3	1	2	....	....	......
Middleburgh, ...	89	71	86	52	56	65	89	96	64	65	23	21	3	5	2	2	....	....	4
Richmondville, ...	65	59	37	45	38	35	69	67	35	39	25	16	2	5	....	1	....	....	......
Schoharie, ...	80	84	71	73	57	51	89	87	50	58	26	25	5	6	2	....	....	....	......
Seward, ...	50	45	48	53	37	41	69	57	36	30	16	22	8	1	....	....	....	1	......
Sharon, ...	85	90	77	81	58	63	80	64	52	50	22	29	5	14	1	1	....	....	1
Summit, ...	50	50	45	48	42	49	50	55	36	29	11	13	1	3	1	1	....	....	......
Wright, ...	43	52	42	40	34	31	48	44	41	34	16	20	5	7	2	....	....	....	1
Total, ...	964	943	860	804	687	693	1, 040	1, 006	663	658	318	286	74	90	11	12	....	1	16

SCHUYLER COUNTY.—(Continued.)

TOWNS.	35 and under 40.		40 and under 45.		45 and under 50.		50 and under 60.		60 and under 70.		70 and under 80.		80 and under 90.		90 and under 100.		100 and upwards.		Ages unknown.
	Males.	Females	Males.	Females	Males.	Females.	Males.	Females	Males.	Females	Males.	Females	Males	Fems.	Males	Fems	Males	Fems.	
Catharines, ...	113	99	87	86	69	68	130	109	45	55	19	20	6	8	1	....	....	....	......
Cayuta, ...	19	14	14	20	13	15	23	12	8	10	9	6	2	....	....	1	....	....	......
Dix, ...	93	95	81	63	56	63	104	90	49	26	17	21	4	4	1	....	....	....	1
Hector, ...	165	169	154	139	126	142	181	165	103	110	43	43	22	17	....	3	....	....	1
Orange, ...	68	82	66	57	52	62	84	69	53	48	17	18	7	7	....	....	....	....	4
Reading, ...	43	39	32	39	29	33	58	51	26	27	11	11	5	3	1	....	....	....	......
Tyrone, ...	72	70	50	46	42	45	69	60	54	46	25	16	4	9	1	....	....	....	......
Total, ...	573	568	484	450	387	428	649	556	338	322	141	135	50	48	4	4	....	....	6

SENECA COUNTY.—(Continued.)

TOWNS.	35 and under 40.		40 and under 45.		45 and under 50.		50 and under 60.		60 and under 70.		70 and under 80.		80 and under 90.		90 and under 100.		100 and upwards.		Ages unknown.
	Males.	Females	Males.	Females	Males.	Females.	Males.	Females	Males.	Females	Males.	Females	Males	Fems.	Males	Fems	Males	Fems.	
Covert, ...	73	72	67	60	57	43	69	82	36	37	19	18	5	3	....	....	1	....	2
Fayette, ...	113	90	91	75	79	78	109	96	55	60	26	23	8	6	....	....	....	....	1
Junius, ...	39	34	32	28	29	28	51	57	34	30	13	11	6	3	....	....	....	....	3
Lodi, ...	59	76	49	46	51	31	63	62	49	39	24	22	10	8	....	....	1	....	1
Ovid, ...	77	64	51	53	57	45	61	68	34	45	23	26	5	2	....	....	....	....	2
Romulus, ...	51	52	57	46	51	46	58	61	27	27	23	17	6	7	....	....	....	....	......
Seneca Falls, ...	157	141	136	112	124	91	138	138	76	62	20	25	7	6	....	....	....	....	16
Tyre, ...	43	47	34	27	38	26	49	48	33	25	15	14	6	4	....	....	....	....	1
Varick, ...	40	45	37	40	44	34	69	51	33	37	14	19	1	2	....	....	....	....	......
Waterloo, ...	136	121	112	106	89	72	118	117	84	60	23	23	5	8	1	1	....	....	1
Total, ...	788	742	666	593	619	494	785	780	461	422	200	198	59	49	1	1	2	....	27

STEUBEN COUNTY.—(Continued.)

TOWNS.	35 and under 40.		40 and under 45.		45 and under 50.		50 and under 60.		60 and under 70.		70 and under 80.		80 and under 90.		90 and under 100.		100 and upwards.		Ages unknown.
	Males.	Females	Males.	Females	Males.	Females.	Males.	Females	Males.	Females	Males.	Females	Males	Fems.	Males	Fems	Males	Fems.	
Addison, ...	104	83	80	71	59	55	96	58	47	33	14	13	3	6	....	4	....	....	2
Avoca, ...	57	46	37	48	45	36	57	50	40	37	21	15	1	5	....	....	....	....	......
Bath, ...	179	164	133	133	129	106	208	187	82	75	50	46	19	5	1	....	....	....	......
Bradford, ...	34	38	31	36	27	19	38	25	24	21	7	7	1	....	....	....	....	....	......
Cameron, ...	50	46	45	29	36	25	45	48	27	25	13	3	5	2	....	1	....	....	14
Campbell, ...	45	34	39	37	26	31	51	46	31	24	7	7	3	1	....	....	....	....	1
Canisteo, ...	66	47	54	46	58	23	42	40	22	17	13	8	1	2	....	....	....	....	8
Caton, ...	39	34	37	31	35	25	55	47	19	17	11	8	2	1	....	1	....	....	......
Cohocton, ...	58	76	47	48	59	41	64	61	37	28	13	13	4	5	....	2	....	....	2
Corning, ...	199	179	137	115	124	90	139	114	57	67	31	20	6	9	2	1	....	....	92
Dansville, ...	90	93	39	44	69	43	59	67	44	38	17	18	6	2	....	1	....	....	1
Erwin, ...	55	42	45	34	31	31	47	30	14	13	11	6	....	1	....	2	....	....	3
Fremont, ...	30	25	26	16	20	22	44	41	23	17	5	5	1	....	....	1	....	....	2
Greenwood, ...	46	25	32	28	19	21	36	35	19	17	8	5	4	1	....	....	....	....	1
Hartsville, ...	27	27	15	16	25	16	46	32	16	15	5	6	1	....	....	....	....	....	......
Hornby, ...	50	38	28	24	19	26	47	40	29	21	8	11	2	1	1	1	....	....	1
Hornellsville, ...	108	93	88	81	75	63	98	72	49	51	16	8	3	....	....	....	....	....	......
Howard, ...	83	74	71	58	53	40	85	85	51	31	16	16	7	4	1	....	....	....	2
Jasper, ...	55	47	43	50	33	28	47	37	28	31	20	19	2	....	....	....	....	....	1
Lindley, ...	22	13	17	13	16	12	24	19	11	9	3	3	1	2	1	....	....	....	......
Prattsburgh, ...	90	75	49	53	49	59	95	84	53	41	20	17	7	6	....	....	....	....	6
Pultney, ...	36	42	39	43	28	39	57	50	39	32	13	13	5	6	....	....	....	....	5
Thurston, ...	21	28	17	17	23	19	37	30	14	7	5	5	3	2	....	....	....	....	......
Troupsburgh, ...	46	50	49	49	39	26	58	41	25	34	16	10	2	3	....	....	....	....	4
Urbana, ...	50	43	40	39	34	41	62	48	33	34	11	11	4	5	....	....	....	....	1
Wayland, ...	73	80	59	56	51	31	86	77	46	38	17	12	3	9	....	....	....	....	1
Wayne, ...	27	24	16	27	18	19	30	29	16	12	5	8	2	2	....	1	....	....	1
West Union, ...	30	39	29	25	20	20	34	21	18	9	4	8	3	2	....	1	....	....	......
Wheeler, ...	46	33	33	29	34	30	45	44	28	20	8	10	4	2	....	....	....	....	......
Woodhull, ...	66	55	57	47	34	31	67	53	39	21	15	9	2	1	....	1	....	....	......
Total, ...	1, 882	1, 693	1, 432	1, 343	1, 288	1, 068	1. 899	1, 611	981	835	403	340	107	85	6	17	....	....	148

SUFFOLK COUNTY.—(Continued.)

TOWNS.	35 and under 40.		40 and under 45.		45 and under 50.		50 and under 60.		60 and under 70.		70 and under 80.		80 and under 90.		90 and under 100.		100 and upwards.		Ages unknown.
	Males.	Females	Males.	Females	Males.	Females.	Males.	Females	Males.	Females	Males.	Females	Males	Fems.	Males	Fems	Males	Fems.	
Brookhaven, ...	283	286	258	268	213	190	300	296	207	209	84	78	20	31	1	2	....	1	26
Easthampton, ...	58	67	76	66	65	62	86	97	42	72	32	29	8	5	1	3	....	....	7
Huntington, ...	242	229	230	212	182	161	309	270	170	168	71	89	25	24	2	3	....	....	16
Islip, ...	120	106	84	78	71	63	104	86	55	56	22	21	6	6	1	....	....	....	......
Riverhead, ...	82	69	80	82	73	48	99	103	58	48	27	37	6	9	....	....	....	....	......
Shelter Island, ...	10	14	14	17	18	10	8	21	9	12	6	9	2	1	....	....	....	....	......
Smithtown, ...	49	58	74	48	51	43	78	75	52	56	24	24	7	14	....	1	....	....	5
Southampton, ...	191	200	183	203	184	177	227	224	132	181	71	99	15	21	....	3	....	....	10
Southold, ...	196	177	152	148	137	142	216	202	107	148	53	68	8	28	1	4	....	....	8
Total, ...	1, 231	1, 206	1, 151	1, 122	994	896	1, 427	1, 380	832	950	390	454	97	139	6	16	....	1	72

SULLIVAN COUNTY.

TOWNS.	Under 1.		1 and under 5.		5 and under 10.		10 and under 15.		15 and under 20.		20 and under 25.		25 and under 30.		30 and under 35.	
	Males.	Females.	Males.	Females.	Males.	Females.	Males.	Females.	Males.	Females.	Males.	Females.	Males.	Females.	Males.	Females.
Bethel,	41	28	178	180	185	170	156	149	153	138	109	127	101	78	102	81
Cochecton,	65	56	195	237	218	188	193	160	145	130	143	138	142	103	138	105
Collikoon,	33	37	171	148	128	142	114	110	95	74	98	80	100	80	103	90
Fallsburgh,	64	47	172	180	229	225	189	183	140	148	158	130	122	100	104	107
Forrestburgh,	8	20	60	43	59	54	47	55	45	37	62	39	40	27	42	22
Fremont,	30	19	90	75	89	95	67	71	74	35	72	45	69	55	62	45
Highland,	15	11	67	57	47	66	54	46	53	48	43	35	24	25	39	24
Liberty,	53	44	193	188	189	185	169	164	139	147	127	141	115	124	106	94
Lumberland,	16	19	63	57	65	50	71	47	43	44	38	27	41	37	43	26
Mamakating,	70	52	237	219	262	252	255	237	218	200	188	194	176	152	128	139
Neversink,	26	23	148	150	156	140	139	130	122	105	97	105	76	70	77	75
Rockland,	21	24	90	78	73	92	79	82	74	51	64	60	63	48	50	35
Thompson,	38	50	211	190	215	230	223	230	184	195	148	160	124	125	124	120
Tusten,	14	12	67	60	47	47	46	44	36	36	40	38	37	43	35	20
Total,	494	442	1,942	1,862	1,962	1,936	1,802	1,708	1,521	1,388	1,387	1,319	1,230	1,067	1,153	983

TIOGA COUNTY.

TOWNS.	Under 1.		1 and under 5.		5 and under 10.		10 and under 15.		15 and under 20.		20 and under 25.		25 and under 30.		30 and under 35.	
	Males.	Females.	Males.	Females.	Males.	Females.	Males.	Females.	Males.	Females.	Males.	Females.	Males.	Females.	Males.	Females.
Barton,	45	51	209	231	213	282	245	239	201	224	171	181	120	153	141	141
Berkshire,	14	10	54	46	50	59	56	53	61	54	54	61	48	49	37	36
Candor,	64	36	219	168	216	255	244	247	208	199	191	170	142	142	131	137
Newark,	18	22	88	89	104	114	113	115	105	89	91	94	76	76	68	75
Nichols,	16	22	95	92	108	135	138	106	126	128	84	77	66	69	66	53
Owego,	92	105	420	424	493	516	494	496	504	506	430	427	356	367	292	279
Richford,	17	14	78	62	68	81	63	79	66	57	53	55	47	38	23	39
Spencer,	19	19	85	89	109	111	119	110	101	94	73	81	64	76	57	60
Tioga,	39	50	151	143	183	192	214	200	175	167	158	129	110	128	104	97
Total,	324	329	1,399	1,344	1,544	1,745	1,686	1,645	1.547	1,518	1,305	1,275	1,029	1,098	919	917

TOMPKINS COUNTY.

TOWNS.	Under 1.		1 and under 5.		5 and under 10.		10 and under 15.		15 and under 20.		20 and under 25.		25 and under 30.		30 and under 35.	
	Males.	Females.	Males.	Females.	Males.	Females.	Males.	Females.	Males.	Females.	Males.	Females.	Males.	Females.	Males.	Females.
Caroline,	41	19	98	120	157	149	162	132	127	145	114	121	95	100	86	88
Danby,	38	30	103	103	140	131	134	137	123	115	115	106	88	90	79	85
Dryden,	76	56	263	233	270	291	255	313	275	292	210	244	204	218	169	150
Enfield,	20	18	76	87	106	118	100	114	114	134	84	92	80	79	65	57
Groton,	38	32	171	148	199	180	182	190	199	190	164	173	144	147	132	127
Ithaca,	90	89	365	310	399	410	373	397	348	458	363	421	308	343	295	313
Lansing,	43	36	162	158	196	203	192	186	176	175	155	145	131	131	118	117
Newfield,	37	29	152	135	181	172	182	180	164	144	109	123	109	103	100	92
Ulysses,	35	50	147	154	181	170	186	172	158	185	139	176	129	144	106	109
Total,	418	359	1,537	1,448	1,829	1,824	1,766	1,821	1,684	1,838	1,453	1,601	1,288	1,355	1,150	1,138

ULSTER COUNTY.

TOWNS.	Under 1.		1 and under 5.		5 and under 10.		10 and under 15.		15 and under 20.		20 and under 25.		25 and under 30.		30 and under 35.	
	Males.	Females.	Males.	Females.	Males.	Females.	Males.	Females.	Males.	Females.	Males.	Females.	Males.	Females.	Males.	Females.
Denning,	8	12	50	41	55	41	47	44	32	39	50	28	32	29	29	19
Esopus,	69	68	248	259	275	221	229	216	214	210	228	226	208	200	209	151
Gardiner,	23	24	100	116	101	126	129	118	94	86	102	90	71	78	62	69
Hurley,	33	34	135	143	112	116	137	136	85	111	106	92	121	78	76	67
Kingston,	274	263	837	847	804	743	682	715	643	690	723	779	803	729	691	568
Lloyd,	23	37	126	121	147	131	140	107	89	127	103	114	106	111	81	76
Marbletown,	71	55	229	197	242	264	243	216	185	194	168	172	122	130	117	113
Marlborough,	33	42	134	149	178	150	145	159	134	130	120	131	110	110	90	104
New Paltz,	30	22	131	108	95	128	118	110	110	102	84	99	70	86	74	66
Olive,	50	33	172	172	167	206	181	174	152	176	152	132	131	109	118	94
Plattekill,	28	22	102	99	133	100	112	116	110	108	79	93	76	80	62	53
Rochester,	58	57	205	185	240	240	235	217	161	196	173	166	135	126	115	86
Rosendale,	57	57	141	159	166	157	137	132	147	128	121	111	113	120	117	83
Saugerties,	189	184	575	532	578	526	507	496	435	450	464	455	466	403	390	335
Shandaken,	38	27	170	182	168	157	149	130	115	107	144	127	126	107	80	65
Shawangunk,	27	33	131	116	140	162	180	179	118	150	111	122	99	99	79	81
Wawarsing,	116	104	477	455	487	469	444	422	352	340	324	361	301	288	309	262
Woodstock,	31	28	120	118	104	121	112	118	91	102	79	88	79	54	62	62
Total,	1,158	1,102	4,083	3,999	4,192	4,058	3,927	3,805	3,267	3,446	3,331	3,386	3,169	2,937	2,761	2,354

WARREN COUNTY.

TOWNS.	Under 1.		1 and under 5.		5 and under 10.		10 and under 15.		15 and under 20.		20 and under 25.		25 and under 30.		30 and under 35.	
	Males.	Females.	Males.	Females.	Males.	Females.	Males.	Females.	Males.	Females.	Males.	Females.	Males.	Females.	Males.	Females.
Bolton,	13	13	73	59	81	73	74	64	70	55	57	47	39	31	49	37
Caldwell,	6	12	51	36	58	66	54	62	51	38	28	48	43	26	25	22
Chester,	21	22	90	96	115	114	93	115	110	112	94	71	93	74	76	50
Hague,	5	7	33	40	47	46	39	42	33	29	19	26	24	20	14	17
Horicon,	23	35	89	91	98	67	67	78	68	46	61	50	61	52	66	40
Johnsburgh,	30	38	146	134	150	112	124	114	107	84	84	82	75	65	66	78
Luzerne,	19	21	75	65	89	75	71	75	55	69	61	68	54	50	49	32
Queensbury,	100	88	369	367	402	405	382	340	286	325	321	357	282	285	260	249
Stony Creek,	17	10	73	70	59	56	60	42	46	34	39	50	44	40	27	30
Thurman,	27	11	95	76	94	79	84	58	71	55	54	51	56	52	45	51
Warrensburgh,	29	26	122	100	147	150	104	125	109	97	78	82	68	72	56	66
Total,	290	283	1,216	1,134	1,340	1,243	1.152	1,115	1,006	944	896	932	839	767	733	672

WASHINGTON COUNTY.

TOWNS.	Under 1.		1 and under 5.		5 and under 10.		10 and under 15.		15 and under 20.		20 and under 25.		25 and under 30.		30 and under 35.	
	Males.	Females.	Males.	Females.	Males.	Females.	Males.	Females.	Males.	Females.	Males.	Females.	Males.	Females.	Males.	Females.
Argyle,	29	31	141	158	193	190	195	174	176	176	145	130	107	135	93	107
Cambridge	35	15	120	104	140	129	112	121	104	130	107	115	85	99	80	90
Dresden,	10	12	51	51	48	48	46	40	33	30	35	37	38	32	30	19
Easton,	47	41	136	155	140	165	145	178	145	137	164	167	135	122	100	98

SULLIVAN COUNTY.—(Continued.)

TOWNS.	35 and under 40.		40 and under 45.		45 and under 50.		50 and under 60.		60 and under 70.		70 and under 80.		80 and under 90.		90 and under 100.		100 and upwards		Ages unknown.
	Males	Females	Males.	Females	Males.	Females	Males.	Females.	Males.	Females.	Males.	Females.	Males	Fems	Males	Fems	Males	Fems.	
Bethel,	76	68	62	52	54	48	80	66	44	42	17	16	4	3	....	3	....	....	1
Cochecton,	107	95	85	59	63	50	89	71	49	34	6	4	1	1	....	....	....	....	......
Collikoon,	72	63	55	40	45	30	69	55	27	15	6	5	1	5	1	....	....	....	3
Fallsburgh,	96	76	87	63	72	43	67	77	47	35	30	22	8	3	1	1	....	....	......
Forrestburgh,	27	20	16	15	14	14	29	16	15	5	3	4	1	....	....	....	....	....	......
Fremont,	48	39	40	33	34	20	36	27	10	10	7	2	1	1	....	....	....	....	......
Highland,	22	20	19	26	28	18	22	16	17	14	4	4	....	1	....	....	....	....	......
Liberty,	78	59	79	65	74	52	75	62	52	40	21	21	6	3	1	....	....	....	......
Lumberland,	25	23	27	24	23	11	20	22	12	13	6	4	1	....	1	....	....	....	3
Mamakating,	137	110	108	104	93	88	131	126	73	72	29	22	2	6	1	....	....	....	3
Neversink,	69	50	46	46	42	32	69	67	44	41	19	6	4	4	2	....	....	....	......
Rockland,	32	30	29	30	28	18	29	25	27	14	11	7	2	1	2	2	....	....	1
Thompson,	114	95	105	80	89	70	119	115	67	54	24	25	15	10	....	....	....	....	1
Tusten,	29	21	28	21	19	13	22	16	16	12	2	2	1	....	....	....	....	....	1
Total,	932	769	786	658	678	507	857	761	500	401	185	144	47	38	9	6	....	....	13

TIOGA COUNTY.—(Continued.)

TOWNS.	35 M	35 F	40 M	40 F	45 M	45 F	50 M	50 F	60 M	60 F	70 M	70 F	80 M	80 F	90 M	90 F	100 M	100 F	Ages unknown.
Barton,	128	116	109	109	92	77	111	95	61	49	21	13	7	3	1	....	....	....	3
Berkshire,	31	31	19	25	18	28	48	43	24	28	10	9	6	3	2	....	1	....	......
Candor,	122	98	93	101	91	75	133	142	91	79	37	37	12	9	1	....	....	....	4
Newark,	67	57	48	56	64	40	68	73	44	42	24	14	5	6	....	....	....	....	......
Nichols,	41	56	43	45	49	40	54	54	35	34	17	12	7	2	....	....	....	....	1
Owego,	260	242	223	180	172	170	254	194	138	128	66	53	21	12	3	4	....	....	7
Richford,	34	40	39	32	22	26	51	27	23	19	10	11	4	4	....	....	....	....	......
Spencer,	56	56	56	38	46	46	58	52	38	41	27	16	2	4	....	....	....	....	2
Tioga,	87	85	75	67	73	59	83	90	68	47	19	18	8	3	2	1	....	....	2
Total,	826	781	705	653	627	561	860	770	522	467	231	183	72	46	9	5	1	....	19

TOMPKINS COUNTY.—(Continued.)

TOWNS.	35 M	35 F	40 M	40 F	45 M	45 F	50 M	50 F	60 M	60 F	70 M	70 F	80 M	80 F	90 M	90 F	100 M	100 F	Ages unknown.
Caroline,	74	72	52	59	63	50	82	79	60	53	33	19	6	5	....	4	....	....	1
Danby,	68	64	57	59	56	51	81	84	52	58	35	32	12	4	1	....	....	....	......
Dryden,	161	136	141	125	105	104	179	181	113	99	57	47	16	17	3	....	....	....	......
Enfield,	69	59	37	47	50	51	62	55	51	35	24	12	3	7	....	....	....	....	6
Groton,	104	101	76	91	84	59	118	128	73	77	28	25	7	8	....	1	....	....	8
Ithaca,	258	234	173	181	159	126	203	228	100	109	37	36	12	11	....	1	....	....	3
Lansing,	84	103	87	75	82	74	112	105	58	69	26	34	11	6	....	2	1	....	3
Newfield,	89	88	77	66	55	52	89	83	64	63	27	25	4	4	1	1	....	....	......
Ulysses,	102	102	90	83	84	68	99	101	66	74	37	27	7	8	....	2	....	....	......
Total,	1,009	959	790	786	738	635	1,025	1,044	637	637	304	257	78	70	5	11	1	....	21

ULSTER COUNTY.—(Continued.)

TOWNS.	35 M	35 F	40 M	40 F	45 M	45 F	50 M	50 F	60 M	60 F	70 M	70 F	80 M	80 F	90 M	90 F	100 M	100 F	Ages unknown.
Denning,	28	17	15	10	17	10	17	13	4	1	1	2	....	1	....	....	....	....	......
Esopus,	151	134	133	104	88	53	94	100	74	67	26	22	5	4	1	....	....	....	......
Gardiner,	56	52	53	52	43	38	64	63	42	39	11	15	3	3	....	....	....	....	......
Hurley,	73	48	52	43	43	30	57	56	38	42	19	16	3	5	....	1	....	1	6
Kingston,	503	408	424	323	241	212	322	303	133	166	59	52	9	20	1	2	....	....	5
Lloyd,	69	50	45	51	43	33	63	61	38	42	28	19	5	6	....	....	....	....	......
Marbletown,	119	122	113	84	71	77	91	96	72	81	32	30	10	7	....	1	....	....	3
Marlborough,	72	85	81	55	36	61	85	96	48	51	25	29	10	9	1	3	....	....	2
New Paltz,	65	70	56	61	46	43	63	53	38	43	24	17	3	3	2	1	....	....	......
Olive,	80	78	71	60	70	47	80	85	41	31	26	22	4	8	1	1	....	....	......
Plattekill,	53	58	50	52	35	40	76	60	34	40	22	26	7	3	2	....	....	....	1
Rochester,	96	106	79	77	68	69	113	102	54	46	27	30	9	2	....	1	....	....	1
Rosendale,	89	69	71	71	55	50	72	57	27	29	18	13	2	2	....	....	....	....	1
Saugerties,	309	266	251	217	174	159	285	250	119	148	53	65	14	18	2	2	....	....	1
Shandaken,	89	68	63	53	45	32	60	49	38	39	11	7	....	2	2	2	....	....	......
Shawangunk,	72	72	66	72	56	50	101	96	65	62	20	22	10	5	2	....	....	....	33
Wawarsing,	230	188	196	159	147	137	187	173	102	100	47	32	7	4	....	1	....	....	6
Woodstock,	50	39	35	41	35	32	49	48	44	36	13	10	1	3	1	....	....	....	......
Total,	2,204	1,930	1,854	1,585	1,313	1,173	1,879	1,761	1,011	1,063	462	429	102	105	15	15	....	1	59

WARREN COUNTY.—(Continued.)

TOWNS.	35 M	35 F	40 M	40 F	45 M	45 F	50 M	50 F	60 M	60 F	70 M	70 F	80 M	80 F	90 M	90 F	100 M	100 F	Ages unknown.
Bolton,	22	28	27	33	23	26	45	33	28	27	19	9	1	6	2	1	....	....	2
Caldwell,	27	25	21	25	23	13	28	29	19	14	14	9	4	3	....	....	....	....	......
Chester,	50	56	55	53	54	46	73	72	46	31	15	19	7	9	1	2	....	....	1
Hague,	19	13	11	12	22	14	26	19	12	9	3	9	1	3	....	....	....	....	1
Horicon,	34	21	26	26	19	11	31	31	32	15	3	5	....	....	....	....	....	....	......
Johnsburgh,	67	49	56	35	34	34	62	50	37	32	16	14	4	3	....	....	....	....	1
Luzerne,	38	36	28	34	37	27	48	32	23	27	16	7	3	2	....	....	....	....	......
Queensbury,	197	161	176	152	119	126	173	167	121	123	41	42	6	11	1	2	1	1	......
Stony Creek,	28	15	26	24	21	8	23	23	22	10	5	9	....	1	1	....	....	....	......
Thurman,	37	30	24	28	31	23	32	32	27	14	8	8	1	3	1	1	....	....	......
Warrensburgh,	55	53	56	53	49	37	63	46	29	30	17	17	5	5	....	....	....	....	......
Total,	574	487	506	475	432	365	604	534	306	332	157	148	32	46	6	6	1	1	5

WASHINGTON COUNTY.—(Continued.)

TOWNS.	35 M	35 F	40 M	40 F	45 M	45 F	50 M	50 F	60 M	60 F	70 M	70 F	80 M	80 F	90 M	90 F	100 M	100 F	Ages unknown.
Argyle,	95	92	97	112	81	76	128	114	75	83	47	28	10	23	1	1	....	1	......
Cambridge,	79	68	64	71	64	55	69	80	44	58	22	26	7	7	....	1	....	....	3
Dresden,	21	11	16	15	11	15	27	26	13	9	4	2	3	1	1	....	....	....	......
Easton,	103	76	73	81	76	75	116	114	55	71	32	36	14	13	1	1	....	....	......

WASHINGTON COUNTY.—(Continued.)

TOWNS.	Under 1.		1 and under 5.		5 and under 10.		10 and under 15.		15 and under 20.		20 and under 25.		25 and under 30.		30 and under 35.	
	Males.	Females	Males.	Females	Males.	Females	Males.	Females	Males.	Females	Males.	Females.	Males.	Females	Males.	Females.
Fort Ann	51	58	210	206	233	216	232	206	180	156	153	161	143	132	133	130
Fort Edward,	54	26	163	156	155	175	165	165	185	178	165	142	140	140	124	102
Granville,	58	40	174	156	174	175	154	180	200	169	170	179	159	155	112	125
Greenwich,	47	51	193	186	205	198	220	220	198	213	184	183	162	163	139	142
Hampton,	13	4	53	32	40	50	38	60	52	36	40	37	23	35	44	29
Hartford,	31	27	108	108	123	127	131	130	132	120	119	105	90	77	72	59
Hebron,	31	33	114	144	147	140	140	142	140	130	139	125	95	84	98	95
Jackson,	28	27	84	76	105	87	95	94	100	86	75	83	78	90	69	62
Kingsbury,	49	35	162	144	199	169	181	200	195	201	215	183	140	116	117	100
Putnam,	7	9	44	43	48	45	58	45	50	47	37	35	19	17	22	20
Salem,	38	35	114	133	139	155	170	157	168	163	136	165	142	110	117	112
White Creek,	28	36	125	108	134	119	150	130	130	125	103	120	100	106	77	78
Whitehall,	57	63	249	240	274	239	275	230	240	234	224	240	194	206	155	182
Total,	613	543	2, 241	2, 200	2, 497	2, 427	2, 507	2, 472	2, 428	2, 331	2, 211	2, 207	1, 850	1, 819	1, 582	1, 550

WAYNE COUNTY.

TOWNS.	Under 1. Males.	Under 1. Females	1–5 Males.	1–5 Females	5–10 Males.	5–10 Females	10–15 Males.	10–15 Females	15–20 Males.	15–20 Females	20–25 Males.	20–25 Females.	25–30 Males.	25–30 Females	30–35 Males.	30–35 Females.
Arcadia,	64	59	260	252	335	311	330	300	325	297	268	270	220	239	226	205
Butler,	22	25	128	118	137	132	151	130	125	132	97	94	73	100	82	67
Galen,	96	76	284	280	295	314	286	272	269	248	290	252	255	247	236	183
Huron,	16	24	97	113	142	106	117	91	98	95	86	87	76	67	67	68
Lyons,	72	102	288	260	271	307	259	276	271	279	267	294	226	244	221	201
Macedon,	26	40	110	120	138	116	127	115	124	139	146	120	120	123	99	61
Marion,	20	16	75	88	94	94	112	92	108	110	102	96	91	90	72	60
Ontario,	40	29	129	112	145	132	128	130	132	110	119	120	95	97	98	80
Palmyra,	69	58	179	195	226	209	193	207	215	231	238	240	195	210	153	147
Rose,	25	18	118	104	117	130	135	127	130	112	93	100	95	80	77	70
Savannah,	30	22	92	90	127	110	133	90	110	99	82	90	65	50	62	64
Sodus,	52	44	256	219	250	275	270	252	248	236	185	207	200	175	159	168
Walworth,	17	17	105	110	111	105	115	100	96	107	80	112	83	97	79	60
Williamson,	30	42	140	136	141	148	144	135	127	130	106	104	116	105	114	102
Wolcott,	42	45	180	164	184	200	194	169	170	160	130	147	120	119	90	111
Total,	621	617	2, 441	2, 361	2. 713	2, 689	2, 694	2, 486	2, 548	2, 485	2, 289	2, 333	2, 030	2, 043	1, 835	1, 647

WESTCHESTER COUNTY.

TOWNS.	Under 1. Males.	Under 1. Females	1–5 Males.	1–5 Females	5–10 Males.	5–10 Females	10–15 Males.	10–15 Females	15–20 Males.	15–20 Females	20–25 Males.	20–25 Females.	25–30 Males.	25–30 Females	30–35 Males.	30–35 Females.
Bedford,	36	46	153	161	205	190	197	205	210	182	168	180	120	156	107	118
Cortlandt,	135	116	474	452	505	480	455	454	426	409	514	436	498	377	374	303
Eastchester,	99	79	313	297	307	270	225	207	134	177	180	239	247	252	263	238
Greenburgh,	88	102	310	366	329	327	318	328	257	350	266	428	329	339	284	291
Harrison,	11	21	55	61	56	71	76	53	56	67	67	80	49	65	49	39
Lewisboro,	32	28	72	71	80	71	96	91	99	103	103	113	64	69	69	53
Mamaroneck,	13	24	53	51	60	45	51	46	39	57	54	63	56	57	39	39
Mount Pleasant,	52	58	188	211	195	215	232	172	170	202	143	204	148	162	119	154
Newcastle,	15	15	76	76	97	111	105	97	92	99	88	97	60	57	53	65
New Rochelle,	38	46	160	155	179	145	178	160	115	181	113	175	135	165	118	131
North Castle,	27	30	122	131	147	136	146	125	141	129	121	129	89	109	79	64
North Salem,	21	25	75	77	73	77	57	76	76	86	70	81	64	65	56	56
Ossining,	84	58	206	252	247	242	225	257	390	308	538	359	405	262	284	201
Pelham,	8	16	38	46	41	35	28	51	43	69	55	57	42	55	32	28
Poundridge,	14	17	63	66	81	84	77	92	102	84	76	64	36	42	36	42
Rye,	59	38	172	157	176	180	185	185	129	208	143	194	137	206	160	142
Scarsdale,	2	9	15	27	26	18	17	18	23	14	25	30	20	30	13	24
Somers,	29	24	80	83	92	74	95	82	102	100	86	107	62	74	51	69
Westchester,	39	47	178	180	196	221	186	192	154	172	189	191	175	156	132	146
West Farms,	217	227	799	759	782	739	689	613	516	583	445	660	507	712	587	585
White Plains,	11	10	82	77	74	72	86	79	65	79	62	103	61	83	62	63
Yonkers,	147	135	427	383	391	380	348	359	315	424	390	549	400	433	368	337
Yorktown,	34	31	108	103	119	137	138	120	127	123	107	140	72	83	91	86
Total,	1, 211	1, 202	4, 219	4, 242	4, 458	4, 320	4, 210	4, 062	3, 781	4, 206	4, 003	4, 679	3, 776	4, 009	3, 426	3, 274

WYOMING COUNTY.

TOWNS.	Under 1. Males.	Under 1. Females	1–5 Males.	1–5 Females	5–10 Males.	5–10 Females	10–15 Males.	10–15 Females	15–20 Males.	15–20 Females	20–25 Males.	20–25 Females.	25–30 Males.	25–30 Females	30–35 Males.	30–35 Females.
Attica,	31	39	140	148	151	152	149	152	126	142	115	134	111	107	101	110
Bennington,	34	30	134	148	166	156	169	145	127	116	82	115	96	90	78	80
Castile,	29	28	107	87	131	133	133	104	141	138	120	136	77	95	88	93
China,	21	11	126	121	138	147	140	141	99	113	75	98	89	85	60	66
Covington,	16	23	59	60	63	71	59	63	98	81	76	56	52	72	46	45
Eagle,	16	12	83	67	93	97	88	82	72	76	68	50	58	53	56	44
Gainesville,	19	23	88	87	95	91	109	104	100	94	80	88	57	75	62	53
Genesee Falls,	11	9	57	47	70	66	63	69	62	55	68	56	37	43	34	29
Java,	29	32	115	143	168	157	165	137	131	122	88	76	86	74	64	68
Middlebury,	16	23	71	76	93	96	99	89	102	91	92	97	75	79	75	62
Orangeville,	19	18	83	73	87	99	89	78	72	62	60	58	60	69	45	44
Perry,	28	16	99	101	131	134	143	145	152	149	120	147	98	111	78	109
Pike,	15	19	75	84	110	113	125	106	103	104	70	94	68	80	66	70
Sheldon,	49	43	171	169	191	205	174	173	114	120	97	90	77	76	69	82
Warsaw,	38	35	126	118	135	124	169	169	178	173	128	165	109	124	92	85
Wethersfield,	19	16	69	86	99	91	109	80	65	96	66	70	46	39	44	57
Total,	390	377	1, 603	1, 615	1, 921	1, 932	1. 983	1, 837	1, 742	1, 732	1, 405	1, 530	1, 196	1, 272	1, 058	1. 097

WASHINGTON COUNTY.—(Continued.)

TOWNS.	35 and under 40.		40 and under 45.		45 and under 50.		50 and under 60.		60 and under 70.		70 and under 80.		80 and under 90.		90 and under 100.		100 and upwards.		Ages unknown.
	Males.	Females.	Males.	Females.	Males.	Females.	Males.	Females.	Males.	Females.	Males.	Females.	Males.	Fems.	Males.	Fems.	Males.	Fems.	
Fort Ann,	100	77	94	98	85	65	125	87	59	71	34	26	10	10	2	....	....	....	1
Fort Edward,	101	80	63	66	63	62	86	87	38	30	23	21	....	3	....	1	....	....	5
Granville,	95	78	97	90	63	55	117	136	90	76	36	25	9	11	2	2	....	....	1
Greenwich,	123	123	125	115	90	102	150	121	76	72	32	26	13	13	2	1	....	....	......
Hampton,	21	18	17	22	21	21	33	39	21	19	10	10	2	3	1	1	....	....	1
Hartford,	59	71	52	55	55	49	76	72	54	36	22	21	8	6	....	1	....	....	......
Hebron,	81	78	62	67	60	47	88	85	58	54	20	36	10	5	....	1	....	....	......
Jackson,	61	44	40	50	43	37	71	74	32	37	19	13	5	4	....	....	....	....	1
Kingsbury,	88	93	103	84	73	84	114	112	55	60	30	34	14	12	1	1	....	....	......
Putnam,	17	14	16	19	18	21	21	18	13	7	6	6	1	....	1	....	....	....	......
Salem,	100	82	80	78	67	76	88	92	60	73	36	20	6	13	....	....	....	....	......
White Creek,	86	78	71	58	64	55	100	88	55	52	17	22	7	7	3	....	....	....	7
Whitehall,	145	133	115	108	102	95	140	137	75	79	35	36	8	4	3	1	....	....	20
Total,	1,375	1,216	1,185	1,189	1,036	990	1,549	1,482	873	887	425	388	127	135	18	12	....	1	39

WAYNE COUNTY.—(Continued.)

TOWNS.	35 and under 40. Males.	Females.	40 and under 45. Males.	Females.	45 and under 50. Males.	Females.	50 and under 60. Males.	Females.	60 and under 70. Males.	Females.	70 and under 80. Males.	Females.	80 and under 90. Males.	Fems.	90 and under 100. Males.	Fems.	100 and upwards. Males.	Fems.	Ages unknown.
Arcadia,	199	175	128	138	130	112	191	178	109	92	37	38	8	15	2	3	....	....	......
Butler,	63	61	55	60	56	46	57	58	52	49	22	20	6	6	....	1	....	....	......
Galen,	171	126	147	128	98	94	152	132	81	78	35	34	9	8	1	1	....	....	3
Huron,	54	42	49	52	44	35	69	54	48	43	13	14	8	5	1	....	....	....	......
Lyons,	198	150	134	121	110	95	143	151	100	80	36	32	5	2	1	1	....	....	8
Macedon,	72	86	52	54	57	44	93	87	49	45	22	23	7	5	2	1	....	....	11
Marion,	65	62	44	60	41	51	92	67	40	46	25	15	2	4	....	....	....	....	3
Ontario,	71	57	63	56	47	41	89	80	49	36	15	14	2	6	....	1	....	....	......
Palmyra,	140	118	112	98	94	106	148	125	66	68	21	28	11	10	1	1	....	....	3
Rose,	57	60	57	54	47	42	70	65	45	45	15	16	3	7	....	....	....	....	......
Savannah,	61	45	41	45	51	27	57	49	23	19	14	8	3	3	....	....	....	....	......
Sodus,	150	140	118	112	115	100	161	154	104	75	50	41	10	7	1	....	1	....	3
Walworth,	80	64	49	46	48	42	73	49	26	42	25	17	2	4	1	....	....	....	2
Williamson,	75	71	72	61	50	51	90	85	63	56	27	18	5	7	....	....	....	....	1
Wolcott,	85	77	84	70	75	52	102	98	55	49	19	13	5	4	....	....	....	....	......
Total,	1,541	1,334	1,205	1,155	1,063	938	1,587	1,432	910	823	376	331	86	93	10	9	1	....	34

WESTCHESTER COUNTY.—(Continued.)

TOWNS.	35 and under 40. Males.	Females.	40 and under 45. Males.	Females.	45 and under 50. Males.	Females.	50 and under 60. Males.	Females.	60 and under 70. Males.	Females.	70 and under 80. Males.	Females.	80 and under 90. Males.	Fems.	90 and under 100. Males.	Fems.	100 and upwards. Males.	Fems.	Ages unknown.
Bedford,	97	110	84	79	82	67	114	131	79	87	38	31	13	13	1	1	....	....	3
Cortland,	310	217	234	195	186	161	216	200	113	105	40	42	14	20	....	1	....	....	6
Eastchester,	224	161	135	96	84	73	118	98	58	57	29	32	4	8	2	4	....	....	5
Greenburgh,	239	189	201	198	141	113	179	150	93	108	45	36	8	11	3	....	1	....	8
Harrison,	31	30	30	27	27	25	52	65	29	27	19	18	3	10	1	....	....	....	1
Lewisboro,	47	51	49	44	37	45	63	64	33	46	34	28	10	7	1	....	....	....	2
Mamaroneck,	34	28	39	32	22	28	37	33	20	22	6	12	2	6	....	....	....	....	......
Mount Pleasant,	121	111	106	101	70	70	113	132	83	63	32	27	10	8	....	1	....	....	4
Newcastle,	48	49	55	48	43	45	82	72	42	31	15	8	6	12	2	1	....	....	......
New Rochelle,	115	102	101	88	71	76	93	102	50	56	21	19	2	8	....	2	....	1	......
North Castle,	66	75	61	58	53	60	77	77	47	43	30	21	5	11	2	3	....	....	1
North Salem,	57	45	32	39	35	37	60	56	38	47	16	13	4	7	1	3	....	....	3
Ossining,	203	145	183	137	135	111	152	140	79	77	32	27	7	8	2	1	....	....	1
Pelham,	25	23	22	21	14	11	25	15	12	10	4	5	1	....	1	....	....	....	......
Poundridge,	34	47	40	43	40	32	54	51	33	40	15	18	7	6	1	2	....	....	......
Rye,	115	105	106	111	69	63	107	124	62	58	21	32	5	8	....	2	1	....	8
Scarsdale,	18	14	9	10	8	11	10	19	9	10	8	5	1	1	....	....	....	....	1
Somers,	40	46	48	49	43	38	64	65	34	40	14	20	5	5	2	....	....	1	20
Westchester,	119	112	126	108	85	55	92	73	55	39	13	16	7	7	2	1	....	....	......
West Farms,	504	414	418	321	247	185	292	274	116	127	41	49	11	12	....	3	....	....	2
White Plains,	51	40	57	51	23	41	47	46	15	29	16	14	3	6	1	....	....	....	3
Yonkers,	260	219	213	187	138	108	162	184	88	98	34	41	11	15	2	3	....	....	5
Yorktown,	62	62	65	59	56	51	82	89	63	57	23	35	7	12	2	1	....	....	1
Total,	2,820	2,395	2,414	2,102	1,709	1,506	2,291	2,260	1,251	1,277	546	549	146	201	26	29	2	2	74

WYOMING COUNTY.—(Continued.)

TOWNS.	35 and under 40. Males.	Females.	40 and under 45. Males.	Females.	45 and under 50. Males.	Females.	50 and under 60. Males.	Females.	60 and under 70. Males.	Females.	70 and under 80. Males.	Females.	80 and under 90. Males.	Fems.	90 and under 100. Males.	Fems.	100 and upwards. Males.	Fems.	Ages unknown.
Attica,	92	72	70	64	58	57	93	90	61	54	24	23	4	7	....	1	....	....	1
Bennington,	92	74	67	75	65	64	106	78	60	62	23	15	2	5	....	....	....	....	1
Castile,	45	55	61	60	54	60	110	103	56	45	23	18	8	3	2	....	....	....	......
China,	61	49	60	59	45	53	75	60	44	35	14	14	4	5	....	....	....	....	......
Covington,	36	35	27	30	35	34	67	49	20	24	11	11	4	5	1	1	....	....	......
Eagle,	37	46	38	20	32	25	45	45	31	26	12	11	4	2	....	1	....	....	......
Gainesville,	63	60	53	46	43	31	48	49	44	49	20	17	2	2	1	....	....	....	......
Genesee Falls,	33	38	38	37	25	18	37	41	20	18	3	10	2	2	....	....	....	....	......
Java,	57	58	57	52	68	60	86	59	51	51	15	13	6	6	....	....	....	....	1
Middlebury,	62	59	49	39	32	38	62	64	50	49	22	14	2	6	1	1	....	....	1
Orangeville,	48	44	29	35	26	28	50	40	41	44	17	15	2	3	2	1	....	....	......
Perry,	79	92	62	69	63	54	98	98	66	53	22	18	12	9	2	1	....	....	1
Pike,	59	54	56	57	41	47	72	66	40	38	20	17	5	8	3	....	....	....	2
Sheldon,	78	72	63	71	66	61	104	83	66	58	23	12	4	4	1	....	....	....	......
Warsaw,	72	76	73	86	70	64	99	90	60	58	30	25	6	9	....	....	....	....	8
Wethersfield,	28	30	41	35	26	37	85	58	26	19	10	12	1	2	....	....	....	....	......
Total,	942	914	844	835	749	731	1,237	1,073	736	683	289	245	68	78	13	6	....	....	15

YATES COUNTY.

TOWNS.	Under 1.		1 and under 5.		5 and under 10.		10 and under 15.		15 and under 20.		20 and under 25.		25 and under 30.		30 and under 35.	
	Males.	Females.	Males.	Females.	Males.	Females.	Males.	Females.	Males.	Females.	Males.	Females.	Males.	Females.	Males.	Females.
Barrington,	25	15	68	75	101	80	93	85	70	99	88	69	65	73	52	60
Benton,	28	28	112	116	140	147	149	123	144	124	108	129	106	95	96	70
Italy,	19	15	90	82	116	100	104	89	73	77	68	55	49	66	48	48
Jerusalem,	35	24	171	132	167	166	175	158	135	157	128	125	113	105	100	102
Middlesex,	18	18	74	60	75	84	64	65	75	86	69	69	45	48	51	47
Milo,	30	35	212	206	240	246	244	241	213	238	184	262	170	213	159	165
Potter,	31	29	94	99	134	141	151	117	127	113	78	119	85	72	73	70
Starkey,	29	25	91	112	128	128	124	161	138	137	109	126	114	115	86	89
Torrey,	6	26	67	76	88	71	83	83	48	68	67	71	53	65	45	47
Total,	221	215	979	958	1,189	1,163	1,187	1,122	1,023	1,099	899	1,025	800	852	710	698

RECAPITULATION OF AGES AND SEXES.

COUNTIES.	Under 1.		1 and under 5.		5 and under 10.		10 and under 15.		15 and under 20.		20 and under 25.		25 and under 30.		30 and under 35.	
	Males.	Females.	Males.	Females.	Males.	Females.	Males.	Females.	Males.	Females.	Males.	Females.	Males.	Females.	Males.	Females.
Albany,	1,517	1,493	5,473	5,482	6,057	6,011	5,690	5,591	4,987	5,961	4,645	5,733	4,524	4,864	4,066	4,096
Allegany,	577	598	2,364	2,296	2,763	2,704	2,618	2,479	2,327	2,325	2,108	2,013	1,867	1,700	1,571	1,568
Broome,	474	462	2,114	1,958	2,254	2,259	2,262	2,154	1,998	2,018	1,759	1,853	1,585	1,467	1,346	1,311
Cattaraugus,	613	596	2,251	2,196	2.571	2,530	2,433	2,300	2,018	2,078	1,788	1,888	1,659	1,600	1,453	1,270
Cayuga,	726	660	2,661	2,571	3,137	2,998	3,013	2,972	2,770	2,832	2,564	2,556	2,242	2,230	1,975	1,907
Chautauque,	756	665	2,757	2,700	3,190	3,080	3,059	3,019	2,796	3,045	2,535	2,668	2 364	2,262	1,958	1,880
Chemung,	391	423	1,541	1,566	1,770	1,665	1,525	1,538	1,339	1,546	1,298	1,426	1,284	1,287	1,100	974
Chenango,	466	405	1,893	1,891	2,286	2,272	2,285	2,249	2,020	2,160	1,812	1,883	1,479	1,548	1,398	1,452
Clinton,	654	714	2,814	2,757	3,208	3,029	2,733	2,774	2,198	2,276	1,807	1,975	1,522	1,531	1,339	1,217
Columbia,	549	565	2,235	2,179	2,524	2,505	2,641	2,495	2,178	2,438	2,007	2,261	1,701	1,825	1,549	1,612
Cortland,	319	274	1,273	1,151	1,397	1,405	1,422	1,369	1,260	1,405	1,126	1,199	943	977	850	881
Delaware,	508	506	2,279	2,016	2,482	2,482	2,439	2,297	2,055	2,167	1,774	1,895	1,569	1,576	1,395	1,338
Dutchess,	833	746	2,979	3,042	3,338	3,328	3,400	3,197	2,932	3,365	2,734	3,289	2,376	2,651	2,210	2,396
Erie,	2,343	2,306	7,914	7,906	7,962	7,774	7,080	6,949	6,322	6,658	6,343	6,809	6.440	6,202	5,963	5,123
Essex,	405	434	1,774	1,636	1,970	1,927	1,715	1,722	1,463	1,498	1,342	1,307	1,104	1,041	956	904
Franklin,	395	372	1,646	1,590	1,857	1,746	1,666	1,605	1,334	1,407	1,048	1,117	871	944	729	751
Fulton,	312	338	1,279	1,217	1,413	1,376	1,371	1,364	1,173	1,286	1,093	1,189	960	1,009	798	776
Genesee,	409	395	1,513	1,448	1,635	1,637	1,620	1,604	1,699	1,709	1,703	1,612	1,446	1,371	1,182	1,122
Greene,	378	406	1,662	1,553	1,915	1,858	1,898	1,795	1,589	1,666	1,438	1,533	1,193	1,225	1,013	1,098
Hamilton,	40	39	158	168	160	160	180	128	142	107	132	119	135	79	80	68
Herkimer,	472	460	1,907	1,866	2,223	2,121	2,187	2,119	2,028	2,075	2,004	2,014	1,709	1,588	1,445	1,356
Jefferson,	837	748	3,542	3,194	4,075	3,858	3,883	3,734	3,507	3,866	2,881	3,353	2,533	2,667	2,243	2,236
Kings,	3,556	3,486	12,132	12,111	11,684	12,116	10,513	10,996	9,118	12,043	10,075	15,084	10,770	13,181	9,963	10,071
Lewis,	342	333	1,467	1,383	1,669	1,593	1,621	1,434	1,303	1,261	1,069	1,163	982	904	856	843
Livingston,	455	469	1,967	1,874	2,095	2,135	2,061	2,134	2,124	2,182	2,007	2,055	1,736	1,643	1,334	1,338
Madison,	519	568	2,177	2.097	2,453	2,367	2,518	2,372	2,167	2,394	2,100	2,222	1,807	1,768	1,479	1,475
Monroe,	1,445	1,427	5,307	5,241	5,456	5,440	5,294	5,288	4,811	5,187	4,968	5,184	4,545	4,500	3,957	3,560
Montgomery,	445	414	1,615	1,532	1,872	1,747	1,770	1,759	1,704	1,693	1,491	1,540	1,392	1,266	1,132	1,018
New-York,	10,776	11,335	32,824	32,643	30,287	30,001	28,100	28,239	27,038	34,796	32,940	46,021	36,173	41,418	32,362	30,557
Niagara,	710	740	2,810	2,658	2,912	2,903	2,776	2,790	2,465	2,695	2,510	2,433	2,206	2,011	1,969	1,686
Oneida,	1,498	1,461	5,500	5,420	6,197	6,100	6,007	5,986	5,484	5,890	5,227	5,760	4,564	4,730	4,035	3,850
Onondaga,	1,243	1,248	4,529	4,540	5,075	4,935	4,757	4,559	4,430	4,703	4,474	4,553	4,050	3,909	3,379	3,062
Ontario,	484	488	2,074	2,067	2,454	2,323	2,389	2,303	2,333	2,371	2,075	2,268	1,810	1,804	1,510	1,581
Orange,	830	779	3,209	3,166	3,588	3,488	3,454	3,289	3,217	3,461	3,077	3,419	2,568	2,693	2,260	2,191
Orleans,	364	342	1,369	1,281	1,658	1,592	1,615	1,522	1,623	1,617	1,566	1,382	1,272	1,207	1,079	980
Oswego,	1,147	1,133	3,968	3,744	4,397	4,104	4,144	3,786	3,636	3,683	3,434	3,509	3,098	2,878	2,574	2,411
Otsego,	683	790	2,339	2,346	2,704	2,694	2,777	2,631	2,669	2,687	2,339	2,474	1,981	2,096	1,739	1,750
Putnam,	208	188	771	707	782	777	785	765	672	711	688	740	567	582	491	511
Queens,	689	668	2,368	2,416	2,583	2,594	2,514	2,509	2,074	2,346	2,226	2,481	2,027	2,071	1,936	1,831
Rensselaer,	1,172	1,164	4,256	4,131	4,416	4,480	4,220	4,338	3,742	4,377	3,822	4,499	3,524	3,803	3,199	3,132
Richmond,	300	319	1,162	1,105	1,153	1,160	1,090	1,090	946	1,191	995	1,332	974	1,094	865	876
Rockland,	350	290	1,145	1,143	1,132	1,078	1,077	976	976	965	1,079	976	940	877	855	716
St. Lawrence,	1,035	1,101	4,461	4,239	5,082	4,803	4,767	4,412	3,923	4,193	3,276	3,901	2,785	2,939	2,444	2,376
Saratoga,	691	668	2,463	2,479	2,858	2,773	2,663	2,732	2,352	2,626	2,200	2,505	1,896	2,151	1,774	1,871
Schenectady,	247	246	1,062	1,001	1,158	1,130	1,079	1,048	1,004	1,023	950	1,001	827	865	730	698
Schoharie,	470	447	1,897	1,810	2,195	2,133	2,072	2,057	1,772	1,787	1,428	1,526	1,232	1,305	1,138	1,124
Schuyler,	234	229	916	895	1,153	1,168	1,170	1,171	1,036	1,069	885	904	719	784	666	635
Seneca,	329	312	1,299	1,330	1,537	1,504	1,512	1,493	1,340	1,387	1,167	1,321	1,023	1,099	904	914
Steuben,	964	843	3,704	3,785	4,137	4,140	3,898	3,735	3,182	3,536	3,041	3,016	2,805	2,540	2,378	2,123
Suffolk,	540	520	1,888	2,039	2,223	2,299	2,616	2,311	2,192	2,178	1,885	1,952	1,561	1,549	1,401	1,388
Sullivan,	494	442	1,942	1,862	1,962	1,936	1,802	1,708	1,521	1,388	1,387	1,319	1,230	1,067	1,153	983
Tioga,	324	329	1,399	1,344	1,544	1,745	1,686	1,645	1,547	1,518	1,305	1,275	1,029	1,098	919	917
Tompkins,	418	359	1,537	1.448	1,829	1,824	1.766	1.821	1,684	1,838	1,453	1,601	1,288	1,355	1,150	1,138
Ulster,	1,158	1,102	4,083	3,999	4,192	4,058	3,927	3,805	3,267	3,446	3,331	3,386	3,169	2,937	2,761	2,354
Warren,	290	283	1,216	1,134	1,340	1,243	1,152	1,115	1,006	944	896	932	839	767	733	672
Washington,	613	543	2,241	2,200	2,497	2,427	2.507	2,472	2,428	2,331	2,211	2,207	1,850	1,819	1,582	1,550
Wayne,	621	617	2,441	2,361	2,713	2,689	2,694	2,486	2,548	2,485	2,289	2,233	2,030	2,043	1,835	1,647
Westchester,	1,211	1,202	4,219	4,242	4,458	4,320	4,210	4,062	3,781	4,206	4,003	4,679	3,776	4,009	3,426	3,274
Wyoming,	390	377	1,603	1,615	1,921	1,932	1,983	1,837	1,742	1,732	1,405	1,530	1,196	1,272	1,058	1,097
Yates,	221	215	979	958	1,189	1,163	1,187	1,122	1,023	1,099	899	1,025	800	852	710	698
Total,	51,440	51,082	186,368	182.729	198.742	195,639	189,298	185,252	170,015	188,927	168,114	195,100	158,547	166,530	140,855	184,284
Percentage of each age and sex to the total population,	1.47	1.47	5.38	5.27	5.73	5 64	5.46	5.35	4.91	5.45	4.85	5.63	4.58	4.81	4.05	3.87

YATES COUNTY.—(CONTINUED.)

TOWNS.	35 and under 40.		40 and under 45.		45 and under 50.		50 and under 60.		60 and under 70.		70 and under 80.		80 and under 90.		90 and under 100.		100 and upwards		Ages unknown.
	Males.	Females	Males.	Females.	Males.	Females.	Males.	Females	Males.	Females	Males.	Females.	Males	Fems	Males	Fems	Males	Fems	
Barrington,	42	37	27	28	36	39	52	38	29	27	10	13	2	5	....	1	....	....	......
Benton,	70	85	72	62	66	59	85	91	58	50	31	31	13	11	1	....	....	....	......
Italy,	50	38	37	38	36	28	40	46	35	25	15	11	2	1	1	1	....	....	3
Jerusalem,	71	82	80	75	71	58	90	80	58	51	37	33	8	9	....	1	....	....	......
Middlesex,	32	35	27	34	28	30	43	43	33	27	6	13	2	4	....	....	....	....	......
Milo,	137	155	130	106	91	81	144	152	81	78	32	39	8	9	1	1	....	....	1
Potter,	53	72	54	42	37	33	80	84	48	41	20	15	10	7	....	2	....	....	17
Starkey,	79	77	59	76	70	58	79	73	53	35	21	19	8	6	3	....	....	....	......
Torrey,	41	48	32	23	37	30	46	32	17	19	11	9	4	4	1	1	1	....	......
Total,	575	629	518	484	472	416	659	639	412	353	183	183	57	56	7	7	1	....	21

RECAPITULATION OF AGES.—(CONTINUED.)

COUNTIES.	35 and under 40.		40 and under 45.		45 and under 50.		50 and under 60.		60 and under 70.		70 and under 80.		80 and under 90.		90 and under 100.		100 and upwards		Ages unknown.
	Males.	Females	Males.	Females	Males.	Females.	Males.	Females	Males.	Females	Males.	Females	Males	Fems	Males	Fems	Males	Fems	
Albany,	3, 383	3, 273	2, 888	2, 754	2, 053	1, 913	2, 693	2, 824	1, 317	1, 516	524	650	159	172	19	19	....	1	1, 333
Allegany,	1, 348	1, 230	1, 042	947	916	739	1, 405	1, 199	714	618	291	241	80	71	10	14	....	....	167
Broome,	1, 095	1, 023	986	895	771	707	1, 019	955	596	522	265	221	70	60	18	16	....	....	157
Cattaraugus,	1, 172	1, 095	922	901	921	794	1, 290	1, 091	679	557	281	261	67	73	7	8	....	1	166
Cayuga,	1, 810	1, 594	1, 526	1, 409	1, 327	1, 178	1, 822	1, 638	1, 082	986	474	447	147	134	14	23	2	1	143
Chautauque,	1, 589	1, 484	1, 282	1, 280	1, 225	1, 132	1, 892	1, 633	1, 081	897	440	383	93	84	11	12	....	....	128
Chemung,	832	759	721	661	557	493	717	665	414	369	153	124	32	46	7	2	1	1	61
Chenango,	1, 217	1, 243	1, 024	1, 055	1, 007	957	1, 467	1, 444	846	834	485	468	147	133	14	19	1	....	56
Clinton,	1, 118	1, 122	980	906	850	726	1, 236	1, 007	718	564	292	236	57	59	9	9	1	2	42
Columbia,	1, 350	1, 376	1, 241	1, 173	1, 012	1, 004	1, 491	1, 517	821	952	408	440	116	154	12	16	....	....	44
Cortland,	705	721	610	631	596	553	823	847	545	528	277	252	81	91	17	20	....	1	26
Delaware,	1, 167	1, 153	959	921	896	824	1, 261	1, 282	751	749	417	352	109	78	11	12	1	1	27
Dutchess,	1, 906	1, 979	1, 617	1, 624	1, 461	1, 292	2, 027	2, 057	1, 155	1, 224	514	606	128	162	10	25	2	....	30
Erie,	4, 632	3, 981	3, 609	3, 066	2, 644	2, 166	3, 655	3, 225	1, 858	1, 705	664	592	127	117	18	15	1	3	159
Essex,	815	767	688	585	619	545	934	767	541	496	224	184	84	66	10	6	....	....	10
Franklin,	651	644	526	571	587	481	837	737	511	376	206	142	48	45	6	6	1	2	29
Fulton,	641	658	603	540	471	498	758	724	420	443	193	206	67	69	9	10	....	....	20
Genesee,	989	916	761	759	686	653	1, 107	1, 033	705	624	271	229	59	64	7	9	1	1	55
Greene,	961	910	791	804	703	665	1, 062	1, 045	627	588	260	299	80	86	9	11	....	1	15
Hamilton,	73	62	62	41	64	40	89	70	51	43	18	23	5	4	1	....	....	....	2
Herkimer,	1, 258	1, 141	1, 039	930	878	812	1, 282	1, 260	726	716	336	329	127	105	9	10	1	1	32
Jefferson,	1, 917	1, 857	1, 637	1, 625	1, 494	1, 375	2, 158	2, 009	1, 432	1, 166	662	559	159	154	12	19	1	1	26
Kings,	7, 611	6, 947	6, 213	5, 691	3, 952	3, 290	4, 583	4, 760	1, 797	2, 421	562	861	120	249	11	29	2	3	354
Lewis,	781	696	655	607	529	552	938	782	477	436	223	196	68	55	2	3	....	....	6
Livingston,	1. 138	1, 097	927	933	832	745	1, 258	1, 171	746	691	309	267	81	71	11	6	....	2	49
Madison,	1, 443	1, 388	1, 236	1, 158	1, 036	979	1, 586	1, 460	799	821	486	454	155	118	16	17	....	1	51
Monroe,	3, 215	2, 955	2, 564	2, 368	2, 048	1, 761	2, 889	2, 608	1, 478	1, 439	543	467	117	129	9	8	1	1	114
Montgomery,	935	889	810	764	726	615	1, 002	888	540	557	245	252	79	72	7	9	....	....	28
New-York,	21, 992	19, 923	18, 016	16, 789	11, 018	10, 241	13, 319	13, 873	5, 361	7, 194	1, 534	2, 348	345	607	49	89	....	10	1, 684
Niagara,	1, 510	1, 368	1, 319	1, 126	1, 070	873	1, 447	1, 183	740	680	284	258	61	51	8	9	....	....	21
Oneida,	3, 315	3, 157	2, 878	2, 744	2, 529	2, 331	3, 544	3, 313	1, 918	1, 922	878	872	261	238	31	30	1	1	177
Onondaga,	2, 726	2, 617	2, 368	2, 080	1, 938	1, 668	2, 700	2, 470	1, 450	1, 404	630	567	167	155	16	17	1	1	145
Ontario,	1, 389	1, 316	1, 139	1, 054	946	923	1, 451	1, 388	854	805	383	405	114	99	10	12	2	....	48
Orange,	1, 876	1, 792	1, 558	1, 509	1, 269	1, 191	1, 841	1, 837	990	1, 117	420	437	99	115	6	18	....	1	103
Orleans,	928	817	761	686	681	590	999	909	605	491	193	179	46	56	9	5	....	....	11
Oswego,	2, 148	1, 869	1, 719	1, 604	1, 609	1, 299	2, 188	1, 900	1, 163	989	454	482	117	107	24	17	2	....	61
Otsego,	1, 495	1, 444	1, 280	1, 297	1, 216	1, 134	1, 754	1, 799	1, 067	1, 051	562	505	183	171	22	21	....	....	35
Putnam,	416	390	366	353	287	276	460	469	295	309	147	131	25	34	5	11	1	2	8
Queens,	1, 538	1, 463	1, 399	1, 205	1, 066	856	1, 457	1, 315	801	859	342	350	87	128	14	22	2	1	28
Rensselaer,	2, 575	2, 492	2, 214	2, 057	1, 670	1, 535	2, 339	2, 271	1, 134	1, 209	507	551	126	156	15	20	....	1	87
Richmond,	737	667	667	595	471	384	637	511	369	320	169	125	32	30	4	6	1	....	12
Rockland,	609	497	534	470	401	320	517	484	348	349	146	145	41	59	4	10	....	....	2
St. Lawrence,	2, 063	1, 969	1, 752	1, 668	1, 529	1, 428	2, 481	2, 077	1, 493	1, 245	590	506	158	134	16	24	5	2	100
Saratoga,	1, 510	1, 553	1, 485	1, 376	1, 142	1, 100	1, 620	1, 606	962	970	451	494	141	139	20	19	1	....	88
Schenectady,	674	549	523	505	454	414	602	625	326	353	139	189	52	60	7	8	....	....	23
Schoharie,	964	943	860	804	687	693	1, 040	1, 006	663	658	318	286	74	90	11	12	....	1	16
Schuyler,	573	568	484	450	387	428	649	556	338	322	141	135	50	48	4	4	....	....	6
Seneca,	788	742	666	593	619	494	785	780	461	422	200	198	59	49	1	1	2	....	27
Steuben,	1, 882	1, 693	1, 432	1, 34[illegible]	1, 288	1, 068	1, 899	1, 611	981	835	403	340	107	85	6	17	....	....	148
Suffolk,	1, 231	1, 206	1, 151	1, 12[illegible]	994	896	1, 427	1, 380	832	950	390	454	97	139	6	16	....	1	72
Sullivan,	932	769	786	658	678	507	857	761	500	401	185	144	47	38	9	6	....	....	13
Tioga,	826	781	705	653	627	561	860	770	521	467	231	183	72	46	9	5	1	....	19
Tompkins,	1, 009	959	790	786	738	635	1, 025	1, 044	637	637	304	257	78	70	5	11	1	....	21
Ulster,	2, 204	1, 930	1, 854	1, 585	1, 313	1, 173	1, 879	1, 761	1, 011	1, 063	462	429	102	105	15	15	....	1	59
Warren,	574	487	506	475	432	365	604	534	396	332	157	148	32	46	6	6	1	1	5
Washington,	1, 375	1, 216	1, 185	1, 189	1, 036	990	1, 549	1, 482	873	887	425	388	127	135	18	12	....	1	39
Wayne,	1, 541	1, 334	1, 205	1, 155	1, 063	938	1, 587	1, 432	910	823	376	331	86	93	10	9	1	....	34
Westchester,	2, 820	2, 395	2, 414	2, 102	1, 709	1, 506	2, 291	2, 260	1, 251	1, 277	546	549	146	201	26	29	2	2	74
Wyoming,	942	914	844	835	749	731	1, 237	1, 073	736	683	289	245	68	78	13	6	....	....	15
Yates,	575	629	518	484	472	416	659	639	412	353	183	183	57	56	7	7	1	....	21
Total,	111,489	103,409	93, 297	86, 960	72, 949	65, 453	100,985	95, 817	53, 825	54, 215	22, 462	22, 555	5,919	6,339	702	847	41	50	6, 532
Percent'e of each age & sex to total popula'n,	3.23	2.91	2.69	2.51	2.10	1.88	2.91	2.76	1, 55	1, 56	0, 65	0.65	0.17	0.18	0.02	0.02	0.01	0.01	0.19

CLASSIFICATION BY PLACE OF BIRTH.

ALBANY COUNTY.

COUNTIES OF NEW-YORK.

TOWNS.	Albany.	Allegany.	Broome.	Cattaraugus.	Cayuga.	Chautauque.	Chemung.	Chenango.	Clinton.	Columbia.	Cortland.	Delaware.	Dutchess.	Erie.	Essex.	Franklin.	Fulton.	Genesee.
Albany city:																		
1st ward,	2,865	1	......	1	1	......	......	1	1	12	......	3	35	1	1	......	......	......
2d ward,	1.969	......	1	......	......	......	1	2	4	70	......	4	28	1	1	......	2	2
3d ward,	2,196	......	1	......	......	......	......	3	5	100	1	4	19	2	6	......	9	6
4th ward,	1,878	2	1	1	2	......	4	4	4	48	3	8	41	11	4	1	3	1
5th ward,	1,310	......	......	......	5	......	1	6	3	30	......	4	8	4	4	......	2	1
6th ward,	1,796	1	......	......	8	......	3	3	1	24	1	1	21	4	7	5	5	......
7th ward,	2,627	2	2	1	5	......	3	......	9	33	......	8	43	5	2	......	3	......
8th ward,	3,500	......	......	2	1	......	......	3	10	50	......	5	48	4	1	1	7	1
9th ward,	3,330	1	1	......	5	11	......	2	3	32	3	14	31	3	2	......	......	......
10th ward,	3,927	......	3	1	3	3	1	8	7	88	1	8	80	29	2	3	7	3
Total Albany city,	25,393	7	9	6	30	14	13	32	47	487	9	59	354	64	30	10	38	14
Berne,	2,681	......	......	......	2	......	......	......	......	11	2	10	46	......	3	......	1	......
Bethlehem,	3,081	......	2	......	......	......	......	5	......	24	......	2	27	2	......	2	10	5
Coeymans,	2,160	1	......	......	3	......	1	3	......	49	......	5	55	......	1	......	......	......
Guilderland,	2,371	......	1	......	5	......	......	......	......	70	......	5	6	......	1	......	1	......
Knox,	1,579	......	3	2	......	1	......	......	1	10	1	4	18	......	1	......	......	1
New Scotland,	3,031	......	......	......	1	......	......	......	......	10	......	1	13	......	2	......	......	......
Rensselaerville,	2,119	......	2	......	1	4	......	......	1	70	2	6	112	......	......	......	1	1
Watervliet,	7,199	4	2	2	14	3	3	10	33	240	4	31	167	23	33	11	41	5
Westerlo,	1,995	......	......	......	4	......	......	......	......	38	......	3	95	......	1	......	......	......
Total,	51,614	12	19	10	60	22	17	50	82	1,009	18	126	893	89	72	23	92	26

ALLEGANY COUNTY.

TOWNS.	Albany.	Allegany.	Broome.	Cattaraugus.	Cayuga.	Chautauque.	Chemung.	Chenango.	Clinton.	Columbia.	Cortland.	Delaware.	Dutchess.	Erie.	Essex.	Franklin.	Fulton.	Genesee.
Alfred,	2	908	10	4	6	5	3	7	......	3	3	3	1	4	1	......	......	4
Allen,	......	481	......	2	15	......	......	4	......	1	12	5	8	1	......	......	......	12
Alma,	1	162	5	2	3	......	11	4	......	......	1	3	......	1	2	......	......	1
Almond,	1	918	10	6	39	1	3	21	......	7	15	12	15	4	1	......	......	9
Amity,	3	1,201	15	21	20	2	35	74	2	9	7	11	10	7	......	......	1	15
Andover,	5	810	24	3	12	1	10	18	......	3	24	7	13	1	1	......	......	4
Angelica,	7	757	5	11	21	2	7	6	......	17	8	6	2	1	......	2	......	10
Belfast,	3	952	3	17	28	6	14	13	......	1	7	5	7	4	......	......	......	24
Birdsall,	5	339	3	4	20	......	......	8	......	2	2	3	2	......	......	......	......	9
Bolivar,	2	463	3	10	15	2	6	12	......	4	33	6	5	2	......	......	......	7
Burns,	3	344	2	3	20	......	9	1	2	......	3	3	9	5	......	......	......	7
Caneadea,	11	905	8	30	21	9	29	36	......	3	5	24	11	21	1	3	3	13
Centreville,	2	612	1	47	5	1	......	6	......	4	3	3	1	8	......	1	8	7
Clarksville,	2	333	14	33	7	1	......	61	......	......	5	1	3	1	......	......	......	12
Cuba,	2	899	2	53	14	5	7	35	1	8	14	13	5	16	2	......	1	20
Friendship,	2	848	13	23	19	1	15	30	6	6	20	25	13	2	......	3	......	4
Genesee,	......	418	......	44	1	1	......	17	1	1	12	......	......	8	1	......	......	2
Granger,	......	547	1	3	27	2	......	7	2	4	......	5	4	5	1	......	1	25
Grove,	4	413	1	4	11	1	1	......	......	5	3	8	5	1	......	4	......	9
Hume,	9	862	......	15	19	11	2	17	......	3	12	20	20	16	5	1	6	32
Independence,	11	556	......	10	7	4	......	11	......	3	16	14	9	......	......	......	1	1
New Hudson,	6	866	2	37	16	7	1	12	......	2	8	11	3	5	......	4	3	3
Ossian,	4	599	......	3	31	......	......	2	......	5	4	3	4	......	......	......	......	1
Rushford,	3	824	7	88	16	7	8	11	1	2	4	12	10	21	1	4	12	18
Scio,	7	978	21	28	47	5	36	58	1	10	52	33	19	11	9	1	......	7
West Almond,	1	480	14	3	13	4	6	19	......	4	......	4	2	......	......	......	......	2
Willing,	7	458	20	6	3	4	10	30	1	1	2	9	7	1	......	......	......	7
Wirt,	5	719	1	4	18	6	8	13	......	4	48	3	11	3	1	1	......	10
Total,	108	18,652	185	514	474	88	221	533	17	112	323	252	199	149	26	24	36	275

BROOME COUNTY.

TOWNS.	Albany.	Allegany.	Broome.	Cattaraugus.	Cayuga.	Chautauque.	Chemung.	Chenango.	Clinton.	Columbia.	Cortland.	Delaware.	Dutchess.	Erie.	Essex.	Franklin.	Fulton.	Genesee.
Barker,	24	......	791	......	2	......	......	101	......	18	19	13	42	......	......	......	......	......
Chenango,	164	9	4,935	5	36	12	31	477	......	102	72	178	314	27	16	......	6	11
Colesville,	58	......	1,603	......	3	......	2	221	1	38	9	213	60	......	1	1	1	1
Conklin,	81	......	1,160	......	7	......	7	49	1	34	3	38	159	......	......	......	......	......
Lisle,	5	......	984	......	6	8	1	89	......	13	71	44	16	......	......	1	1	......
Maine,	74	2	939	1	3	......	5	36	......	10	34	21	30	......	......	......	1	2
Nanticoke,	51	......	377	......	......	......	4	24	......	18	23	15	21	......	......	......	......	......
Sanford,	64	......	1,126	......	1	2	2	104	4	41	5	509	38	......	3	......	3	......
Triangle,	11	1	877	......	......	......	......	201	......	18	73	29	36	......	1	......	......	......
Union,	10	......	1,495	1	1	......	1	31	1	30	11	26	110	......	......	......	......	1
Vestal,	62	......	1,143	......	......	......	......	15	5	5	17	9	30	......	1	......	1	......
Windsor,	19	......	1,599	1	4	......	1	59	......	18	10	86	48	......	......	......	......	1
Total,	623	12	17,029	8	63	22	54	1,407	12	345	347	1,181	904	27	22	2	12	16

CATTARAUGUS COUNTY.

TOWNS.	Albany.	Allegany.	Broome.	Cattaraugus.	Cayuga.	Chautauque.	Chemung.	Chenango.	Clinton.	Columbia.	Cortland.	Delaware.	Dutchess.	Erie.	Essex.	Franklin.	Fulton.	Genesee.
Allegany,	10	29	22	565	10	25	8	11	......	3	16	40	4	46	6	1	......	8
Ashford,	7	2	......	812	13	12	......	12	......	10	3	......	4	121	3	3	1	30
Bucktooth,	......	13	4	170	......	8	1	1	1	......	2	5	2	13	2	......	......	5
Carrolton,	4	10	5	188	3	13	......	2	......	2	1	3	......	16	2	......	......	14
Cold Spring,	1	......	......	342	1	46	......	4	......	3	5	4	5	9	1	......	......	16
Connewango,	2	10	1	606	3	111	......	15	......	2	14	2	2	22	2	2	1	39
Dayton,	4	5	17	547	12	44	1	4	......	......	2	1	2	62	......	......	......	11
East Otto,	......	1	1	584	14	12	......	4	3	3	2	......	1	51	2	1	3	35
Ellicottville,	6	17	9	953	8	10	......	9	1	3	4	12	8	46	......	......	......	16
Farmersville,	1	79	1	643	10	1	......	10	1	8	2	3	5	14	2	......	2	15
Franklinville,	5	36	3	733	8	3	......	67	2	6	12	6	7	21	......	......	......	34
Freedom,	1	32	......	522	20	4	......	8	......	7	......	4	4	43	13	......	2	19
Great Valley,	2	22	6	549	8	12	......	8	2	2	7	6	1	25	......	......	......	5

ALBANY COUNTY.—(Continued.)

TOWNS.	COUNTIES OF NEW-YORK.																	
	Greene.	Hamilton.	Herkimer.	Jefferson.	Kings.	Lewis.	Livingston.	Madison.	Monroe.	Montgomery.	New York.	Niagara.	Oneida.	Onondaga.	Ontario.	Orange.	Orleans.	Oswego.
Albany city:																		
1st ward,	25	.....	.....	3	5	.....	.....	.....	.....	13	59	.....	11	2	1	6	.....	.....
2d ward,	61	.....	10	2	1	1	.....	1	8	26	75	1	13	6	1	5	2	.....
3d ward,	47	.....	11	5	1	2	3	4	2	30	92	5	14	3	4	3	2	2
4th ward,	26	.....	5	5	5	.....	2	8	6	22	106	15	9	6	7	2	1	28
5th ward,	6	.....	15	4	7	1	.....	5	10	18	68	2	33	14	3	3	1	3
6th ward,	7	.....	2	1	4	.....	.....	4	2	19	38	1	10	2	2	3	2	1
7th ward,	23	.....	11	2	8	1	.....	.....	11	27	82	3	17	8	5	12	.....	6
8th ward,	18	1	26	13	11	2	6	5	7	29	121	1	8	4	3	12	.....	3
9th ward,	42	.....	12	12	4	.....	3	1	5	22	81	.....	15	.....	3	13	1	2
10th ward,	51	.....	17	3	10	.....	4	12	14	29	197	5	22	11	3	10	1	2
Total Albany,	306	1	109	50	56	7	18	40	65	235	919	33	152	56	31	69	10	47
Berne,	51	.....	4	.....	.....	.....	.....	.....	.....	7	9	1	2	.....	.....	2	.....	.....
Bethlehem,	27	.....	4	2	1	1	.....	.....	.....	19	18	.....	6	3	.....	3	1	.....
Coeymans,	198	.....	2	.....	1	.....	.....	1	.....	6	15	1	3	.....	.....	4	.....	.....
Guilderland,	17	.....	.....	.....	2	1	.....	1	1	23	7	.....	.....	3	2	.....	.....	.....
Knox,	6	.....	.....	.....	.....	.....	1	1	1	12	.....	.....	2	.....	.....	.....	.....	1
New Scotland,	31	.....	.....	.....	1	.....	.....	.....	1	5	2	.....	.....	2	.....	1	.....	.....
Rensselaerville,	167	1	1	1	8	.....	2	.....	.....	8	5	.....	4	1	.....	3	.....	2
Watervliet,	120	10	43	26	50	15	3	15	18	114	171	3	68	128	7	43	5	9
Westerlo,	173	.....	.....	1	1	2	.....	.....	2	9	11	2	2	1	.....	.....	2	3
Total,	1,096	12	163	80	120	26	24	58	88	438	1,157	40	239	194	40	125	18	62

ALLEGANY COUNTY.—(Continued.)

TOWNS.	Greene.	Hamilton.	Herkimer.	Jefferson.	Kings.	Lewis.	Livingston.	Madison.	Monroe.	Montgomery.	New York.	Niagara.	Oneida.	Onondaga.	Ontario.	Orange.	Orleans.	Oswego.
Alfred,	4	.....	17	6	1	2	17	50	1	1	.....	1	12	11	8	2	.....	.....
Allen,	1	.....	2	1	1	1	38	17	12	2	14	1	7	16	25	6	.....	.....
Alma,	.....	.....	.....	.....	.....	.....	7	1	5	.....	1	.....	1	1	2	1	1	.....
Almond,	2	.....	5	3	.....	1	41	13	18	10	9	.....	12	9	43	14	.....	.....
Amity,	10	.....	13	1	1	3	50	18	4	18	15	4	11	13	6	39	2	7
Andover,	.....	.....	8	5	1	2	30	34	12	2	4	3	4	15	19	6	1	1
Angelica,	15	.....	1	2	.....	.....	70	23	9	9	10	.....	15	11	42	4	1	5
Belfast,	4	.....	13	9	1	2	89	16	34	9	8	5	19	10	25	7	2	5
Birdsall,	1	.....	3	.....	.....	.....	66	6	13	.....	15	1	3	12	5	3	.....	3
Bolivar,	.....	.....	7	2	.....	.....	13	14	.....	.....	.....	.....	10	28	6	1	.....	.....
Burns,	.....	.....	1	.....	.....	.....	115	6	7	3	4	.....	2	9	21	8	6	.....
Caneadea,	4	.....	15	14	2	.....	121	25	35	14	3	21	16	30	33	6	3	.....
Centreville,	1	.....	24	10	.....	3	11	5	22	12	.....	3	21	6	5	.....	.....	2
Clarksville,	.....	.....	.....	1	.....	.....	7	24	13	2	.....	2	2	5	1	3	.....	.....
Cuba,	9	.....	16	2	.....	1	39	60	17	15	11	3	25	25	21	7	1	5
Friendship,	5	.....	17	3	.....	1	19	53	10	14	7	.....	20	18	21	5	.....	4
Genesee,	.....	.....	3	2	1	.....	10	34	1	.....	1	.....	1	2	1	5	.....	.....
Granger,	.....	.....	2	3	.....	.....	94	1	13	2	7	1	13	18	18	1	3	.....
Grove,	7	1	9	2	.....	.....	94	7	7	11	127	1	7	4	8	3	2	3
Hume,	6	.....	21	6	.....	1	84	26	24	27	4	4	16	23	30	4	3	4
Independence,	2	.....	24	3	.....	.....	16	33	1	.....	1	1	5	2	11	7	.....	3
New Hudson,	3	.....	4	.....	.....	.....	11	14	12	3	3	1	8	10	15	10	.....	1
Ossian,	1	.....	5	2	2	1	127	3	29	.....	.....	4	2	3	27	8	7	.....
Rushford,	4	.....	56	10	1	1	33	33	30	7	1	7	12	10	29	2	1	3
Scio,	19	.....	11	9	.....	1	83	43	24	13	12	4	22	30	44	16	5	8
West Almond,	2	.....	1	.....	.....	.....	16	8	3	1	12	.....	1	5	24	5	1	.....
Willing,	1	.....	4	.....	.....	.....	18	12	3	.....	7	1	15	4	11	4	.....	.....
Wirt,	6	.....	2	4	.....	.....	22	38	1	12	.....	3	12	95	8	1	.....	2
Total,	107	1	284	100	11	20	1,341	617	360	187	276	71	294	425	509	178	39	56

BROOME COUNTY.—(Continued.)

TOWNS.	Greene.	Hamilton.	Herkimer.	Jefferson.	Kings.	Lewis.	Livingston.	Madison.	Monroe.	Montgomery.	New York.	Niagara.	Oneida.	Onondaga.	Ontario.	Orange.	Orleans.	Oswego.
Barker,	7	1	.....	.....	2	.....	.....	3	3	2	4	.....	3	1	4	7	.....	.....
Chenango,	82	.....	46	12	14	6	5	93	34	73	143	7	100	99	14	191	7	10
Colesville,	45	.....	10	1	5	.....	.....	8	.....	2	4	.....	15	6	3	10	5	67
Conklin,	35	.....	4	6	1	1	.....	4	.....	24	20	.....	6	1	3	54	.....	.....
Lisle,	11	.....	15	.....	1	.....	.....	2	.....	3	3	.....	4	3	5	9	.....	25
Maine,	20	.....	2	.....	3	1	.....	1	.....	5	6	2	6	6	3	7	.....	.....
Nanticoke,	6	.....	6	.....	2	.....	1	2	2	9	2	.....	3	.....	.....	2	.....	4
Sanford,	75	.....	4	8	3	.....	1	2	.....	18	19	.....	3	5	5	35	.....	2
Triangle,	11	1	2	3	3	.....	.....	6	3	2	.....	.....	12	7	.....	11	.....	4
Union,	23	.....	.....	.....	.....	.....	.....	4	3	3	15	.....	7	5	.....	87	.....	.....
Vestal,	4	.....	6	1	.....	3	2	1	1	2	69	.....	2	8	.....	29	.....	1
Windsor,	21	.....	3	.....	.....	1	1	1	.....	10	6	.....	5	3	2	28	.....	3
Total,	340	2	98	31	34	12	10	127	46	153	291	9	166	144	39	470	12	116

CATTARAUGUS COUNTY.—(Continued.)

TOWNS.	Greene.	Hamilton.	Herkimer.	Jefferson.	Kings.	Lewis.	Livingston.	Madison.	Monroe.	Montgomery.	New York.	Niagara.	Oneida.	Onondaga.	Ontario.	Orange.	Orleans.	Oswego.
Allegany,	6	.....	5	3	.....	.....	20	5	5	10	1	3	8	50	22	9	1	2
Ashford,	1	1	159	14	.....	.....	9	11	16	60	5	2	13	5	2	1	.....	12
Bucktooth,	2	1	3	.....	.....	.....	.....	6	2	2	2	1	2	1	.....	1	1	1
Carrolton,	2	.....	3	1	.....	.....	1	13	1	2	2	3	3	5	4	.....	2	.....
Cold Spring,	4	.....	2	.....	.....	.....	2	8	7	4	2	.....	17	2	10	1	3	.....
Connewango,	6	.....	11	11	.....	1	8	25	9	21	.....	.....	24	11	15	2	7	.....
Dayton,	.....	2	2	.....	.....	.....	.....	10	5	5	.....	7	10	26	6	1	1	4
East Otto,	.....	.....	31	11	.....	.....	1	9	4	7	.....	5	38	5	1	1	3	1
Ellicottville,	1	.....	11	8	1	1	4	6	5	15	20	1	23	3	5	.....	1	5
Farmersville,	11	.....	15	4	1	10	8	12	18	5	4	4	38	6	12	1	6	2
Franklinville,	4	.....	30	4	.....	1	14	9	11	12	11	.....	10	7	13	1	.....	3
Freedom,	.....	.....	17	7	.....	5	20	12	10	5	1	7	74	2	10	1	3	.....
Great Valley,	9	.....	9	3	.....	.....	3	7	1	14	.....	1	8	12	3	5	.....	1

(Continued on page 64.)

ALBANY COUNTY.—(Continued.)

Towns.	Otsego.	Putnam.	Queens.	Rensselaer.	Richmond.	Rockland.	St. Lawrence.	Saratoga.	Schenectady.	Schoharie.	Schuyler.	Seneca.	Steuben.	Suffolk.	Sullivan.	Tioga.	Tompkins.	Ulster.
	Counties of New-York.																	
Albany city:																		
1st ward,	1	1	......	108	......	4	......	11	16	23	......	1	1	......	......	......	......	4
2d ward,	8	......	1	125	7	2	1	38	36	23	......	1	......	......	......	......	......	18
3d ward,	18	......	1	80	1	6	27	32	16	......	......	......	......	......	......	......	......	4
4th ward,	......	2	86	......	......	1	3	46	54	71	......	4	10	2	......	1	7	12
5th ward,	4	2	1	53	......	......	5	20	20	16	......	3	5	......	......	2	1	1
6th ward,	15	......	......	42	......	......	......	14	20	20	......	......	1	......	1	4	2	6
7th ward,	5	1	1	111	......	......	2	32	60	22	......	......	......	1	......	5	8	5
8th ward,	21	2	......	119	2	......	3	39	44	46	......	1	1	4	1	......	......	23
9th ward,	59	1	......	104	1	1	1	48	60	72	......	1	3	1	1	1	......	3
10th ward,	31	1	5	173	1	4	......	91	88	69	......	2	3	......	......	......	2	9
Total Albany,	162	10	95	915	12	18	42	371	414	362	......	13	24	8	3	13	20	85
Berne,	8	2	......	25	......	1	......	7	13	92	......	......	......	1	......	......	......	3
Bethlehem,	8	......	3	92	......	3	1	21	17	25	......	2	......	4	1	......	......	6
Coeymans,	2	3	3	39	2	......	......	15	5	7	......	......	1	1	......	......	......	16
Guilderland,	8	......	1	25	......	......	......	6	146	100	......	......	......	......	2	......	......	3
Knox,	2	......	......	9	......	......	1	4	39	97	......	......	......	1	1	1	......	......
New Scotland,	5	......	3	6	......	1	......	6	2	10	......	2	......	1	......	1	......	1
Rensselaerville,	14	......	1	12	......	......	......	6	3	258	......	......	......	12	1	1	2	14
Watervliet,	64	7	19	1,295	5	5	7	637	252	126	......	12	9	16	3	3	5	36
Westerlo,	17	2	......	24	......	......	......	5	3	52	......	......	2	......	......	......	......	11
Total,	290	24	125	2,442	19	28	51	1,078	894	1,129	......	29	36	44	11	19	27	175

ALLEGANY COUNTY.—(Continued.)

Towns.	Otsego.	Putnam.	Queens.	Rensselaer.	Richmond.	Rockland.	St. Lawrence.	Saratoga.	Schenectady.	Schoharie.	Schuyler.	Seneca.	Steuben.	Suffolk.	Sullivan.	Tioga.	Tompkins.	Ulster.
Alfred,	17	......	......	109	......	......	......	8	2	......	......	8	78	......	......	2	30	......
Allen,	5	1	1	5	......	......	1	9	2	2	......	10	10	......	5	1	15	1
Alma,	11	......	......	1	......	......	......	2	......	1	......	......	7	......	......	3	6	......
Almond,	17	......	......	57	......	......	......	8	......	4	......	8	144	6	......	3	24	3
Amity,	24	......	2	37	......	......	4	17	3	3	......	22	87	......	......	14	51	4
Andover,	41	5	......	36	......	1	......	4	......	2	......	13	95	......	......	7	62	5
Angelica,	17	1	......	8	......	......	......	7	......	......	......	7	35	1	1	1	28	3
Belfast,	32	......	......	3	......	1	2	13	3	6	......	16	61	......	1	10	22	......
Birdsall,	10	1	......	3	......	......	4	10	......	5	......	......	26	2	......	1	4	......
Bolivar,	59	......	......	14	......	......	4	5	......	4	......	1	47	......	......	12	10	......
Burns,	8	18	1	4	......	......	......	7	1	......	......	4	115	......	......	2	16	2
Caneadea,	33	......	1	11	......	1	3	28	15	5	......	10	51	......	7	10	19	1
Centreville,	40	1	1	2	......	......	1	9	......	1	......	5	3	......	......	......	2	1
Clarksville,	28	......	......	3	......	......	......	6	......	1	1	5	43	......	......	......	7	......
Cuba,	28	......	1	7	......	5	3	10	8	1	......	26	28	......	1	5	46	1
Friendship,	43	1	......	11	......	......	......	17	1	7	......	16	34	......	2	7	29	2
Genesee,	10	......	......	27	......	......	1	6	......	1	......	1	3	......	1	3	4	......
Granger,	16	......	......	6	......	......	14	......	1	......	......	1	10	......	......	2	1	1
Grove,	4	2	......	2	......	......	......	7	......	17	......	4	24	......	......	6	1	......
Hume,	74	......	1	6	......	......	2	15	1	4	......	2	5	1	......	2	4	......
Independence,	27	......	......	20	......	1	......	5	......	1	......	1	34	......	......	5	27	2
New Hudson,	25	......	......	1	......	......	1	5	3	1	......	11	17	1	......	......	37	1
Ossian,	7	......	......	......	......	1	3	11	2	1	......	4	48	4	1	......	3	1
Rushford,	36	......	......	2	......	......	14	8	......	2	......	11	17	......	......	3	39	......
Scio,	52	5	......	53	......	......	8	32	3	9	......	19	160	9	......	35	52	6
West Almond,	4	......	......	18	......	......	......	4	1	1	......	......	48	......	......	5	13	3
Willing,	30	1	......	13	......	......	......	4	......	2	......	......	93	......	3	17	·33	3
Wirt,	40	2	......	21	......	......	3	10	......	......	......	11	51	1	......	8	6	3
Total,	738	38	8	480	......	10	68	267	46	81	1	216	1,374	25	22	164	591	43

BROOME COUNTY.—(Continued.)

Towns.	Otsego.	Putnam.	Queens.	Rensselaer.	Richmond.	Rockland.	St. Lawrence.	Saratoga.	Schenectady.	Schoharie.	Schuyler.	Seneca.	Steuben.	Suffolk.	Sullivan.	Tioga.	Tompkins.	Ulster.
Parker,	5	2	......	8	......	......	......	4	......	20	......	......	......	......	1	1	8	13
Chenango,	236	50	14	85	......	9	10	35	65	244	......	14	39	7	42	108	101	96
Colesville,	65	1	......	34	......	......	......	17	......	122	......	2	2	3	3	13	2	16
Conklin,	31	1	......	23	1	2	......	13	25	122	......	......	5	1	13	8	9	12
Lisle,	55	8	......	4	......	......	1	......	1	22	......	5	3	2	3	29	10	......
Maine,	105	1	......	9	......	3	1	6	14	74	......	3	3	......	14	81	22	6
Nanticoke,	49	......	......	4	......	......	......	......	1	16	......	1	......	......	2	28	4	9
Sanford,	134	1	......	11	......	5	......	4	......	102	......	1	4	1	7	7	1	12
Triangle,	43	3	......	4	......	1	......	9	1	32	......	1	7	4	3	8	5	2
Union,	34	8	......	5	4	......	......	6	......	25	......	5	1	......	6	61	14	22
Vestal,	32	6	3	20	......	......	......	5	1	98	......	4	......	......	1	34	3	13
Windsor,	63	1	3	12	......	......	1	6	1	42	......	......	4	11	7	4	6	11
Total,	852	82	20	219	5	20	13	105	109	919	......	36	68	29	102	382	185	212

CATTARAUGUS COUNTY.—(Continued.)

Towns.	Otsego.	Putnam.	Queens.	Rensselaer.	Richmond.	Rockland.	St. Lawrence.	Saratoga.	Schenectady.	Schoharie.	Schuyler.	Seneca.	Steuben.	Suffolk.	Sullivan.	Tioga.	Tompkins.	Ulster.
Allegany,	23	1	1	4	......	......	1	4	3	5	......	3	14	......	1	10	23	1
Ashford,	12	......	......	5	......	......	......	10	6	3	......	......	4	......	......	3	......	......
Bucktooth,	14	......	......	......	......	......	1	2	......	7	......	1	4	......	......	1	1	......
Carrolton,	3	......	......	4	......	......	......	......	......	......	......	......	4	......	......	2	2	......
Cold Spring,	8	......	......	......	......	......	......	5	......	3	......	......	1	......	1	1	1	......
Connewango,	22	......	......	10	......	......	1	5	2	3	......	1	1	......	......	2	3	2
Dayton,	4	......	......	22	......	......	......	11	4	7	......	1	1	......	......	......	2	1
East Otto,	30	......	......	7	......	......	......	3	2	10	......	1	1	......	......	1	2	......
Ellicottville,	28	......	......	4	......	......	2	4	......	3	......	6	5	......	......	1	2	1
Farmersville,	71	......	1	2	......	......	1	15	......	3	......	4	2	......	......	1	9	......
Franklinville,	44	......	......	1	......	......	3	15	5	17	......	2	6	......	......	10	11	1
Freedom,	38	......	......	2	......	......	1	7	1	6	......	9	......	......	......	......	2	2
Great Valley,	21	......	......	4	......	......	2	5	......	8	......	1	16	......	......	1	4	......

(Continued on page 65.)

ALBANY COUNTY.—(CONTINUED.)

TOWNS.	COUNTIES OF NEW-YORK.							UNITED STATES.										
	Warren.	Washington.	Wayne.	Westchester.	Wyoming.	Yates.	New-York.	Maine.	N. Hampshire.	Vermont.	Massachusetts.	Rhode Island.	Connecticut.	New Jersey.	Pennsylvania.	Delaware.	Maryland.	District of Columbia.
Albany City:																		
1st ward,	......	16	......	2	......	2	3, 237	......	5	15	30	5	13	13	23	......	8	1
2d ward,	3	28	......	2	......	......	2, 591	1	16	30	62	7	28	19	11	......	1	1
3d ward,	6	10	2	5	......	1	2, 791	17	19	15	62	11	71	23	28	1	2	......
4th ward,	7	29	......	5	......	4	2, 613	9	22	33	128	13	74	27	18	......	2	1
5th ward,	6	17	......	4	2	2	1, 735	1	11	22	52	5	58	9	18	......	9	......
6th ward,	2	6	1	2	......	......	2, 114	1	13	17	68	3	47	8	22	......	6	......
7th ward,	3	19	2	8	......	3	3, 247	3	5	42	62	9	41	16	12	......	2	1
8th ward,	4	32	3	5	1	1	4, 254	5	7	43	76	3	56	26	21	......	9	......
9th ward,	5	18	1	5	......	......	4, 040	1	15	37	72	9	50	13	9	......	2	1
10th ward,	2	38	2	25	2	1	5, 114	8	32	60	99	12	98	38	33	......	5	......
Total Albany,	38	213	11	63	5	14	31, 736	46	145	314	711	77	536	192	195	1	46	5
Berne,	......	5	......	18	......	......	3, 007	......	5	8	18	6	21	1	4	......	......	1
Bethlehem	1	7	5	2	......	1	3, 444	1	12	16	39	5	19	2	10	......	......	1
Coeymans,	2	1	2	25	......	......	2, 633	3	2	9	10	5	18	3	1	1	......	......
Guilderland,	......	......	......	1	......	......	2, 809	......	5	9	20	2	8	4	7	......	......	......
Knox,	......	4	......	4	......	......	1, 808	1	......	2	4	......	27	2	2	......	1	......
New Scotland,	......	......	......	1	......	......	3, 140	......	......	......	8	1	10	2	......	......	......	......
Rensselaerville,	2	3	......	11	......	......	2, 862	2	1	11	18	28	44	3	3	......	......	......
Watervleit,	46	210	11	28	1	7	11, 477	45	109	351	338	44	214	84	56	3	11	1
Westerlo,	......	3	......	24	......	......	2, 488	1	......	7	17	14	21	10	1	......	......	......
Total,	89	446	29	177	6	22	65, 404	99	279	727	1, 183	182	918	303	279	5	58	8

ALLEGANY COUNTY.—(CONTINUED.)

TOWNS.	Warren.	Washington.	Wayne.	Westchester.	Wyoming.	Yates.	New-York.	Maine.	N. Hampshire.	Vermont.	Massachusetts.	Rhode Island.	Connecticut.	New Jersey.	Pennsylvania.	Delaware.	Maryland.	District of Columbia.
Alfred,	......	6	2	4	......	10	1, 373	......	7	16	18	124	41	10	29	......	......	......
Allen,	7	9	4	4	4	6	787	1	7	27	50	5	31	26	14	......	......	......
Alma,	......	1	......	......	1	1	250	36	10	3	9	1	5	......	26	......	......	......
Almond,	1	11	9	3	11	22	1, 573	......	13	24	77	28	39	25	67	......	4	......
Amity,	10	59	3	3	13	36	2, 040	49	20	71	73	17	41	43	87	5	......	1
Andover,	1	10	3	1	4	10	1, 383	1	11	21	38	23	19	17	25	......	......	......
Angelica,	1	30	7	2	25	6	1, 259	......	11	55	52	12	47	36	48	......	......	......
Belfast,	6	18	5	7	71	9	1, 628	15	14	74	34	12	35	22	57	......	1	......
Birdsall,	2	18	3	......	16	2	635	1	6	12	14	1	8	46	30	1	......	......
Bolivar,	......	10	2	1	1	5	826	12	2	14	14	13	15	6	36	......	1	......
Burns,	......	8	2	2	7	9	799	......	4	34	39	1	40	17	42	......	1	......
Caneadea,	......	16	5	2	73	8	1, 774	11	21	90	66	5	42	23	60	......	1	......
Centreville	4	18	2	......	53	2	979	1	22	103	23	5	38	6	6	......	......	......
Clarksville,	1	......	2	......	9	7	646	18	6	20	13	5	26	9	15	......	......	......
Cuba,	1	11	3	1	20	7	1, 567	2	18	72	63	10	59	34	57	......	2	......
Friendship,	2	5	12	4	12	6	1, 438	......	22	62	39	27	43	17	38	......	2	......
Genesee,	8	1	2	......	20	1	656	2	4	18	9	93	15	3	61	......	......	......
Granger,	......	21	......	......	27	5	915	19	9	39	21	4	35	7	23	......	......	......
Grove,	2	2	......	......	30	1	865	1	1	27	11	1	19	9	44	......	......	......
Hume,	......	18	14	2	139	10	1, 633	8	17	97	49	25	55	3	45	......	......	......
Independence,	......	4	......	......	1	18	898	......	11	33	16	26	33	10	66	......	......	......
New Hudson,	1	22	2	1	8	5	1, 223	1	11	48	43	9	28	24	27	......	......	......
Ossian,	......	2	6	1	24	7	1, 003	3	13	21	30	2	22	11	36	......	......	......
Rushford,	1	9	5	2	79	2	1, 519	5	36	154	70	9	48	12	21	......	......	......
Scio,	2	32	2	2	35	24	2, 207	32	22	67	42	21	80	23	109	......	2	......
West Almond,	3	74	1	3	1	9	819	......	2	22	26	8	11	23	25	......	......	......
Willing,	1	2	3	......	......	21	872	10	9	25	23	5	27	6	56	3	......	......
Wirt,	1	19	......	2	9	11	1, 259	6	4	44	27	42	56	20	34	2	......	2
Total,	55	436	99	47	693	260	32, 826	234	333	1, 293	989	534	958	483	1, 184	11	14	8

BROOME CONNTY.—(CONTINUED.)

TOWNS.	Warren.	Washington.	Wayne.	Westchester.	Wyoming.	Yates.	New-York.	Maine.	N. Hampshire.	Vermont.	Massachusetts.	Rhode Island.	Connecticut.	New Jersey.	Pennsylvania.	Delaware.	Maryland.	District of Columbia.
Barker,	......	18	3	6	......	......	1, 136	......	2	15	43	......	54	2	10	......	......	......
Chenango,	17	54	10	83	......	5	8, 655	12	48	149	401	33	413	199	655	3	35	3
Colesville,	......	17	5	15	......	2	2, 712	1	26	37	48	10	166	11	47	......	......	......
Conklin,	......	7	1	7	......	2	1, 981	1	1	8	26	10	82	78	115	3	1	......
Lisle,	2	8	......	7	......	2	1, 481	......	......	17	119	29	88	6	24	......	1	......
Maine,	1	2	......	5	......	......	1, 570	1	40	19	105	5	96	14	24	......	......	......
Nanticoke,	......	2	......	......	......	2	690	......	2	8	45	6	21	4	5	......	......	......
Sanford,	......	5	4	6	......	1	2, 388	......	6	18	45	10	58	26	155	5	1	......
Triangle,	1	3	2	6	......	1	1, 448	1	18	11	56	7	89	6	23	......	......	......
Union,	......	1	2	2	......	......	2, 061	1	11	23	53	1	61	44	57	......	2	......
Vestal,	......	3	......	3	......	1	1, 644	2	18	27	26	13	45	19	113	......	1	......
Windsor,	1	5	......	......	......	......	2, 108	......	6	27	57	7	182	15	124	......	1	......
Total,	22	125	27	140	......	16	27, 874	19	178	359	1, 024	131	1, 355	424	1, 352	11	42	3

CATTARAUGUS COUNTY.—(CONTINUED.)

TOWNS.	Warren.	Washington.	Wayne.	Westchester.	Wyoming.	Yates.	New-York.	Maine.	N. Hampshire.	Vermont.	Massachusetts.	Rhode Island.	Connecticut.	New Jersey.	Pennsylvania.	Delaware.	Maryland.	District of Columbia.
Allegany,	1	19	3	2	10	6	1, 089	7	10	45	49	3	32	6	46	......	......	......
Ashford,	2	6	1	......	10	......	1, 406	......	12	103	74	4	23	4	11	......	......	......
Bucktooth,	......	3	......	5	......	1	292	......	21	14	17	1	11	1	17	......	......	......
Carrolton,	......	3	1	......	6	......	330	2	6	14	1	......	8	2	66	......	......	......
Cold Spring,	3	4	......	......	1	......	527	8	8	19	15	......	13	2	16	......	......	......
Connewango,	......	21	......	......	9	4	1, 071	2	17	53	45	14	33	13	21	......	......	......
Dayton,	5	23	2	......	11	3	888	......	14	47	25	6	21	2	15	......	......	......
East Otto,	......	38	3	......	6	......	941	2	6	83	78	4	22	2	8	......	......	......
Ellicottville,	......	21	1	1	2	3	1, 296	2	2	38	80	8	20	......	18	......	2	......
Farmersville,	1	23	6	......	19	......	1, 112	7	15	60	45	7	39	7	12	......	......	......
Franklinville,	1	40	5	1	55	2	1, 292	2	4	46	75	10	52	7	18	......	......	......
Freedom,	......	30	5	......	34	1	991	8	24	53	38	2	23	2	8	......	......	......
Great Valley,	3	21	4	......	9	......	830	5	25	34	25	1	22	7	54	......	......	......

(Continued on page 66.)

ALBANY COUNTY.—(CONTINUED.)

TOWNS.	UNITED STATES.																	
	Virginia,	N. Carolina.	S. Carolina.	Georgia.	Florida.	Alabama.	Mississippi.	Louisiana.	Texas.	Arkansas.	Missourie.	Tennessee.	Kentucky.	Ohio.	Indiana.	Illinois.	Michigan.	Wisconsin.
Albany city:																		
1st ward,														6				
2d ward,	1	1						1			1	1	1	4	2	1		
3d ward,	3	2			1				1					10	3	1	1	
4th ward,									4				1	4		1		
5th ward,			1	1				2						2	1		1	
6th ward,	3				4			1						5			1	
7th ward,			1											2		4	3	
8th ward,	2					1		1	1	1				11	1		4	
9th ward,	10	2			1									3			3	
10th ward,	12	3					2	1			1	1	2	11	2	4	1	
Total Albany,.	31	8	2	1	6	1	2	6	6	1	2	2	4	58	9	11	14	
Berne,																		
Bethlehem,	2			1										2			2	
Coeymans,								1										
Guilderland,																		
Knox,																		
New Scotland,														1	1			
Rensselaerville,														1			2	4
Watervliet,	10	1	3	2	1		2	8			1	3	5	10	2	6	7	15
Westerlo,														2			2	
Total,	43	9	5	4	7	1	4	15	6	1	3	5	9	74	12	17	27	19

ALLEGANY COUNTY.—(CONTINUED.)

TOWNS.	Virginia,	N. Carolina.	S. Carolina.	Georgia.	Florida.	Alabama.	Mississippi.	Louisiana.	Texas.	Arkansas.	Missourie.	Tennessee.	Kentucky.	Ohio.	Indiana.	Illinois.	Michigan.	Wisconsin.
Alfred,														3			2	3
Allen,														8	1		1	
Alma,																		
Almond,														5		3	3	3
Amity,	1												5	7	1	4		2
Andover,														2	1	1	5	
Angelica,											1			3			1	2
Belfast,														7	1	1	7	1
Birdsall,														4				
Bolivar,														1			2	
Burns,																	7	2
Caneadea,	2				4									11	1	3	3	4
Centreville,											1			1	1	2		2
Clarksville,														8				
Cuba,														4		2	1	3
Friendship,										1				8	2	6	3	
Genesee,	1										1			1				
Granger,														3		1	2	
Grove,																	2	
Hume,	2													7	3	2	10	2
Independence,														1				
New Hudson,														2	1			3
Ossian,														4	2		6	1
Rushford,					1							1		5	2		10	
Scio,	1													6	4		4	1
West Almond,																	2	
Willing,														4		1	1	1
Wirt,		1												1		3	3	
Total,	7	1			5					1	3	1	5	106	20	29	75	30

BROOME COUNTY.—(CONTINUED.)

TOWNS.	Virginia,	N. Carolina.	S. Carolina.	Georgia.	Florida.	Alabama.	Mississippi.	Louisiana.	Texas.	Arkansas.	Missourie.	Tennessee.	Kentucky.	Ohio.	Indiana.	Illinois.	Michigan.	Wisconsin.
Barker,								1						1		2	1	
Chenango,	14	5	2	9		1		6					2	27	2	5	14	2
Colesville,			1											1		1	1	1
Conklin,	1	1									1			1				4
Lisle,													3	2	3	2		1
Maine,														1	1	1	1	
Nanticoke,														2				
Sanford,	1					1								1	1		1	1
Triangle,														4			3	
Union,													1	3	2			
Vestal,																		
Windsor,				1										3			1	1
Total,	16	6	3	10		2		7			1		6	46	9	11	22	10

CATTARAUGUS COUNTY.—(CONTINUED.)

TOWNS.	Virginia,	N. Carolina.	S. Carolina.	Georgia.	Florida.	Alabama.	Mississippi.	Louisiana.	Texas.	Arkansas.	Missourie.	Tennessee.	Kentucky.	Ohio.	Indiana.	Illinois.	Michigan.	Wisconsin.
Allegany,								1						5		3	3	
Ashford,	4													5		2	2	2
Bucktooth,										1				2		2		1
Carrolton,														2			1	
Cold Spring,								1						8		1	2	1
Connewango,														6		2	1	
Dayton,	1													7		4	2	2
East Otto,														1		3		1
Ellicottville,	1												1	5				
Farmersville,														3			1	2
Franklinville,		1												5	1	2	3	1
Freedom,													1	4		2	4	
Great Valley,	1													8		1	1	

(Continued on page 67.)

ALBANY COUNTY.—(Continued.)

TOWNS.	U. STATES.			Total United States.	FOREIGN COUNTRIES.													
	Iowa.	California.	Territories.		Canada.	N. Brunswick.	Nova Scotia.	N. Foundland.	West Indies.	Mexico.	S. America.	England.	Scotland.	Ireland.	Wales.	France.	Belgium.	Holland.
Albany city:																		
1st ward,				3, 356	63	1	4					159	54	2, 526	5	33		107
2d ward,				2, 780	54	2	3					160	57	1, 108	5	3	2	25
3d ward,				3, 061	24		1					204	52	1, 021	2	6		2
4th ward,				2, 951	59	1						167	75	871	5	12		27
5th ward,				1, 928	59		3		3			83	22	852	4	4		1
6th ward,				2, 313	30		1		3			109	46	849	5	7		6
7th ward,				3, 450	51	1		7	2			95	46	2, 253	1	4		
8th ward,				4, 522	117	1	2	3		1		204	94	2, 408	2	11		8
9th ward,				4, 268	56	1	2		1			343	37	906	2	30		27
10th ward,				5, 539	80		4	12	1			433	112	1, 600	23	16	9	67
Total Albany city,				24, 168	593	7	20	22	10	1		1, 957	595	14, 394	54	126	11	270
Berne,				3, 071	2							17	3	55				
Bethlehem,		2		3, 558	19	2						117	31	343		6	2	20
Coeymans,				2, 686	10							21	8	122			2	13
Guilderland,				2, 864	2				1			62	11	133	2	1		1
Knox,				1, 847	1							1		17				
New Scotland,				3, 163	7							17	6	60				
Rensselaerville,				2, 979	2		1					12	2	57		9		
Watervliet,				12, 809	665	12	3	1	1	1		858	390	5, 428	13	21	2	27
Westerlo,				2, 563								5	1	51			1	
Total,		2		69, 708	1, 301	21	24	23	12	2		3, 067	1, 047	20, 660	69	163	18	331

ALLEGANY COUNTY.—(Continued.)

TOWNS.	Iowa.	California.	Territories.	Total United States.	Canada.	N. Brunswick.	Nova Scotia.	N. Foundland.	West Indies.	Mexico.	S. America.	England.	Scotland.	Ireland.	Wales.	France.	Belgium.	Holland.
Alfred,				1, 626	2							10		43				
Allen,				953	3							31	6	13		1		
Alma,				340	8							3	1	37				
Almond,				1, 864	7							11	9	48	2			
Amity,				2, 467	11							32	3	96				
Andover,				1, 547	11							8	2	170				
Angelica,				1, 527	10		1					40	10	131				
Belfast,				1, 909	14							12	2	143				
Birdsall,				758	9							6		65				
Bolivar,				942	3							9	1	20		1		
Burns,				986	5							15	1	54				3
Cancadea,				2, 121	54		1					20	7	86	3			3
Centreville,				1, 190	3							5	3	1	136			
Clarksville,				766	6							1	1	7				
Cuba,	1			1, 895	19							18	10	148				
Friendship,				1, 708	10							8	5	103				
Genesee,				864	2							3	1	20				1
Granger,				1, 078	8							107	3	4				
Grove,				980	19							17	1	34		2		
Hume,				1, 958	13							16		79	1	1		
Independence,				1, 094	2									36				
New Hudson,				1, 420	11							1	2	10				
Ossian,	4			1, 158	55							13	4	39		1		
Rushford,				1, 893	11		1					38	1	22	18			
Scio,				2, 621	17		2					31	4	178	1			
West Almond,				938								7	1	22				
Willing,				1, 043	2							8		34	1	1		
Wirt,				1, 504	2								4	9				
Total,	5			39, 150	317		5					470	82	1, 652	162	7		7

BROOME COUNTY.—(Continued.)

TOWNS.	Iowa.	California.	Territories.	Total United States.	Canada.	N. Brunswick.	Nova Scotia.	N. Foundland.	West Indies.	Mexico.	S. America.	England.	Scotland.	Ireland.	Wales.	France.	Belgium.	Holland.
Barker,				1, 267	3							2		51				
Chenango,				10, 695	33	1	1		3			197	86	1, 645	2	5		
Colesville,				3, 063	7	1						11		34				
Conklin,				2, 314	1						1	17	49	144	1			
Lisle,				1, 776								3		28	1			
Maine,				1, 878	1		2					9	25	60				
Nanticoke,				783	1									27				5
Sanford,				2, 718	1	1						40	21	259				
Triangle,				1, 666	2				2			2	1	41				
Union,				2, 320	4							8	5	72				
Vestal,				1, 908	7							4	1	33				1
Windsor,				2, 533	2							26	3	31				
Total,				32. 921	62	3	3		5		1	319	191	2, 425	4	5		6

CATTARAUGUS COUNTY.—(Continued.)

TOWNS.	Iowa.	California.	Territories.	Total United States.	Canada.	N. Brunswick.	Nova Scotia.	N. Foundland.	West Indies.	Mexico.	S. America.	England.	Scotland.	Ireland.	Wales.	France.	Belgium.	Holland.
Allegany,				1, 299	9		1					7	4	87	4			
Ashford,			4	1, 652	5				1			4	2	9		10		
Bucktooth,				384	5							2		50				
Carrolton,				431	6							1	2	68				
Cold Spring,				621	6							16		10				
Connewango,	2			1, 278	3							6	1	19				
Dayton,				1, 036	3							13		18				
East Otto,				1, 151	13							6	1	1		5		
Ellicottville,				1, 481	20							20	6	249		4		
Farmersville,				1, 310	11							9	6	25	74			
Franklinville,				1, 519	5							21	71	58				1
Freedom,				1, 160	4							5	27	1	226			1
Great Valley,				1, 014	7							4	39	119		1		

(Continued on page 68.)

ALBANY COUNTY.—(Continued.)

FOREIGN COUNTRIES.

Towns.	Germany.	Prussia.	Austria.	Switzerland.	Italy.	Spain.	Portugal.	Poland.	Norway.	Sweden.	Russia.	Denmark.	East Indies.	Africa.	Turkey and Greece.	Islands.	Asia.	At Sea.	Unknown.
Albany city:																			
1st ward,	1, 698	2		16	1			6		5								2	
2d ward,	305	2		1	1		1	8										1	
3d ward,	274	10	1	2	1	1		2			1	1						1	
4th ward,	290	15	3	5	3			4	1		1		1				1		
5th ward,	53	3															1		
6th ward,	78	3	1		2					1		2	1					3	
7th ward,	94	1	1																
8th ward,	89					1		3			1								
9th ward,	1, 666	4																	
10th ward,	408	5		7	1		1	3		2		1						2	
Total Albany,	4, 955	45	6	31	9	2	2	26	1	8	3	4	2				2	9	
Berne,	52																		6
Bethlehem,	1, 010	24	6	2				1										4	6
Coeymans,	98			2														1	
Guilderland,	110	1																	
Knox,	21																		1
New Scotland,	70	1		2															1
Rensselaerville,	22						1					1							2
Watervliet,	568	19		24	1	1		13			2		1				4	17	8
Westerlo,	24																		3
Total,	6, 930	90	12	61	10	3	3	40	1	8	5	5	3				6	31	27

ALLEGANY COUNTY.—(Continued.)

Towns.	Germany.	Prussia.	Austria.	Switzerland.	Italy.	Spain.	Portugal.	Poland.	Norway.	Sweden.	Russia.	Denmark.	East Indies.	Africa.	Turkey and Greece.	Islands.	Asia.	At Sea.	Unknown.
Alfred,	6																		20
Allen,	19																		
Alma,	2			1															20
Almond,	8			2															1
Amity,	7																	1	38
Andover,	3																		34
Angelica,	69	1			1														42
Belfast,	5																		45
Birdsall,																			
Bolivar,																			9
Burns,	11			2															10
Caneadea,	67									1									37
Centreville,	1																		10
Clarksville,																			
Cuba,	2																	2	22
Friendship,	3																		1
Genesee,	1																		3
Granger,	10																		8
Grove,	54																		11
Hume,	2	9																	15
Independence,																			4
New Hudson,	2																		5
Ossian,	9	4																	30
Rushford,	3												1	1	1				5
Scio,	86											1							243
West Almond,				1															3
Willing,	30																		8
Wirt,	2																		3
Total,	402	14		6	1					1		1	1	1	1			3	627

BROOME COUNTY.—(Continued.)

Towns.	Germany.	Prussia.	Austria.	Switzerland.	Italy.	Spain.	Portugal.	Poland.	Norway.	Sweden.	Russia.	Denmark.	East Indies.	Africa.	Turkey and Greece.	Islands.	Asia.	At Sea.	Unknown.
Barker,	1																		
Chenango,	133	21							4	1				2				3	296
Colesville,	2																		17
Conklin,	5			1															6
Lisle,	1																		6
Maine,	1																		3
Nanticoke,	1																		2
Sanford,	13	2						2											3
Triangle,																			70
Union,	1			4															49
Vestal,																			13
Windsor,	3																		39
Total,	161	23		5				2	4	1				2				3	504

CATTARAUGUS COUNTY.—(Continued.)

Towns.	Germany.	Prussia.	Austria.	Switzerland.	Italy.	Spain.	Portugal.	Poland.	Norway.	Sweden.	Russia.	Denmark.	East Indies.	Africa.	Turkey and Greece.	Islands.	Asia.	At Sea.	Unknown.
Allegany,	142			1													1		28
Ashford,	220			6					1	1									2
Bucktooth,	6																		6
Carrolton,																		1	2
Cold Spring,																			11
Connewango,	12			1						2									23
Dayton,	24																		45
East Otto,	51																		
Ellicottville,	35			2														1	20
Farmersville,	3					1													4
Franklinville,	6			1								1							3
Freedom,																			19
Great Valley,		2			1														11

(Continued on page 69.)

CATTARAUGUS COUNTY

TOWNS	COUNTIES OF NEW-YORK.																	
	Albany.	Allegany.	Broome.	Cattaraugus.	Cayuga.	Chautauque.	Chemung.	Chenango.	Clinton.	Columbia.	Cortland.	Delaware.	Duchess.	Erie.	Essex.	Franklin.	Fulton.	Genesee.
Hinsdale,	4	82	19	681	18	9	6	33	.....	3	26	15	6	36	3	2	.....	20
Humphrey,	1	10	1	353	10	1	2	15	.....	.....	8	11	2	12	.....	.....	.....	9
Ischua,	.....	55	3	511	3	.....	6	39	.....	5	15	2	5	6	1	3	.....	3
Leon,	8	3	4	593	7	35	.....	7	3	5	5	2	9	78	6	.....	.....	17
Little Valley,	3	6	.....	333	9	10	2	4	1	8	6	1	5	27	1	.....	.....	16
Lyndon,	5	96	3	396	4	.....	3	26	.....	4	27	3	5	3	3	.....	3	8
Machias,	13	22	.....	457	27	4	2	13	2	4	8	.....	2	67	9	.....	.....	74
Mansfield,	5	2	2	501	2	19	.....	16	.....	.....	8	3	3	19	.....	.....	.....	15
Napoli,	4	12	.....	608	15	27	.....	5	.....	4	5	14	7	15	.....	.....	3	52
New Albion,	8	2	1	683	12	15	.....	4	1	9	4	.....	5	25	4	.....	1	15
Olean,	10	56	22	499	12	12	18	12	.....	3	20	12	7	23	2	1	2	10
Otto,	4	5	2	526	11	8	6	.....	.....	2	2	4	2	74	1	.....	.....	9
Perrysburgh,	8	5	20	638	6	88	1	13	2	4	2	2	15	57	2	2	3	12
Persia,	2	5	8	541	16	30	1	9	1	.....	.....	.....	4	100	1	.....	3	7
Portville,	1	114	15	409	11	3	3	24	1	12	17	8	7	6	14	.....	2	6
Randolph,	6	12	.....	507	10	103	2	21	2	2	17	1	8	19	9	1	1	30
South Valley,	1	.....	.....	207	5	126	.....	1	.....	.....	5	.....	2	3	1	.....	.....	14
Yorkshire,	4	17	1	758	10	5	.....	1	1	7	9	7	13	122	6	.....	1	29
Total,	130	760	170	16, 415	298	796	62	398	24	121	254	171	152	1, 181	96	16	28	593

CAYUGA COUNTY.

TOWNS	Albany.	Allegany.	Broome.	Cattaraugus.	Cayuga.	Chautauque.	Chemung.	Chenango.	Clinton.	Columbia.	Cortland.	Delaware.	Duchess.	Erie.	Essex.	Franklin.	Fulton.	Genesee.
Auburn city:																		
1st ward,	20	2	5	.....	971	1	.....	7	1	19	13	4	31	11	.....	.....	.....	.....
2d ward,	23	2	2	.....	771	.....	1	12	3	4	24	1	10	2	1	1	.....	.....
3d ward,	25	.....	5	.....	812	1	1	3	.....	17	15	3	18	4	.....	.....	.....	5
4th ward,	47	5	8	3	1, 072	2	3	25	.....	15	18	11	21	15	3	1	2	15
Total Auburn,	115	9	20	3	3, 626	4	5	47	4	55	70	19	80	32	4	2	2	20
Aurelius,	18	.....	6	7	1, 268	2	4	3	3	16	9	5	41	3	4	1	.....	1
Brutus,	10	.....	3	.....	1, 516	.....	4	8	6	14	9	5	30	3	1	1	3	1
Cato,	86	.....	2	1	1, 140	.....	.....	10	.....	16	3	3	32	.....	1	.....	.....	4
Conquest,	96	6	2	3	959	1	.....	7	1	72	5	18	51	.....	2	.....	.....	1
Fleming,	15	.....	1	.....	653	.....	.....	2	.....	9	12	1	14	.....	.....	.....	.....	.....
Genoa,	13	.....	5	2	1, 261	5	3	13	.....	15	13	6	36	3	.....	.....	.....	2
Ira,	131	16	.....	1	915	1	.....	28	.....	55	2	2	17	.....	.....	.....	9	1
Ledyard,	12	.....	11	.....	1, 009	.....	.....	5	6	4	29	6	54	5	.....	.....	.....	.....
Locke,	5	.....	2	4	770	.....	1	5	.....	8	33	8	21	1	.....	.....	.....	.....
Mentz,	29	1	2	.....	2, 492	4	5	14	.....	34	26	7	93	5	3	.....	3	7
Moravia,	7	2	6	.....	1, 053	6	8	15	.....	12	35	13	28	2	.....	.....	.....	.....
Niles,	3	3	.....	.....	1, 220	1	.....	2	.....	9	31	8	16	1	1	.....	1	1
Owasco,	10	1	.....	2	741	.....	.....	4	.....	.....	7	4	10	4	4	.....	.....	.....
Scipio,	21	4	2	.....	1, 107	.....	7	2	.....	2	19	8	47	.....	1	.....	2	13
Sempronius,	2	2	2	1	699	2	.....	7	.....	6	62	5	35	3	.....	.....	.....	2
Sennett,	4	.....	1	.....	954	1	.....	.....	.....	13	6	1	28	1	.....	1	7	8
Springport,	5	3	2	.....	1, 265	.....	.....	7	1	10	6	5	33	4	1	.....	10	5
Sterling,	91	4	1	.....	1, 374	4	2	5	.....	14	15	11	16	.....	7	.....	5	4
Summer Hill,	6	1	1	.....	541	.....	.....	16	.....	6	76	6	11	2	.....	.....	.....	2
Venice,	11	5	2	2	1, 126	4	.....	17	1	10	13	6	71	1	.....	.....	.....	1
Victory,	54	.....	5	.....	1, 093	1	4	1	.....	53	2	3	31	.....	3	.....	1	1
Total,	744	57	76	26	26, 782	36	43	218	22	433	483	150	795	70	32	5	43	74

CHAUTAUQUE COUNTY.

TOWNS	Albany.	Allegany.	Broome.	Cattaraugus.	Cayuga.	Chautauque.	Chemung.	Chenango.	Clinton.	Columbia.	Cortland.	Delaware.	Duchess.	Erie.	Essex.	Franklin.	Fulton.	Genesee.
Arkwright,	1	3	1	3	3	676	.....	9	.....	1	8	8	9	9	.....	.....	.....	7
Busti,	4	5	6	9	20	993	.....	19	.....	3	1	1	5	18	2	1	7	13
Carroll,	5	5	8	18	8	823	.....	5	.....	2	.....	3	5	1	3	.....	3	8
Charlotte,	3	12	.....	14	10	798	.....	18	1	3	5	6	3	14	.....	.....	.....	26
Chautauque,	4	.....	.....	4	23	1, 250	.....	23	.....	5	11	2	59	20	2	10	1	27
Cherry Creek,	1	1	2	16	2	601	.....	22	.....	2	19	5	1	20	.....	1	.....	15
Clymer,	5	3	2	4	13	500	.....	15	3	.....	2	8	4	13	12	.....	2	12
Ellery,	3	3	2	9	31	1, 123	.....	8	.....	5	1	2	14	18	.....	.....	1	7
Ellicott,	18	21	6	38	34	1, 941	6	37	2	13	9	12	9	48	29	2	.....	37
Ellington,	6	5	.....	54	26	1, 098	1	29	2	6	23	1	2	10	3	1	.....	30
French Creek,	3	5	.....	5	8	337	.....	17	.....	3	7	5	5	4	22	.....	.....	17
Gerry,	10	.....	.....	16	9	699	.....	15	.....	.....	6	1	3	8	1	.....	.....	36
Hanover,	22	20	8	138	15	1, 637	3	31	10	8	4	14	80	188	12	2	3	54
Harmony,	10	16	3	12	28	1, 830	.....	54	4	7	11	6	18	28	8	2	1	40
Kiantone,	1	7	1	7	2	251	1	2	.....	2	.....	.....	8	4	1	.....	.....	6
Mina,	4	5	.....	.....	9	500	2	4	.....	2	.....	13	1	5	1	.....	.....	9
Poland,	1	4	2	32	4	781	.....	17	1	1	2	2	4	7	13	2	.....	17
Pomfret,	29	34	29	126	32	2, 821	14	57	7	32	14	32	36	196	12	5	4	62
Portland,	11	10	2	10	10	915	.....	51	1	26	12	8	38	21	3	1	.....	13
Ripley,	9	6	.....	5	17	797	.....	8	.....	4	2	10	16	25	.....	.....	.....	3
Sheridan,	7	1	6	36	9	741	.....	9	1	7	13	22	4	24	7	2	.....	14
Sherman,	4	4	.....	6	6	651	.....	24	.....	4	18	2	6	9	8	.....	1	11
Stockton,	4	.....	.....	7	7	901	.....	8	.....	9	6	10	10	1	5	.....	.....	21
Villenova,	1	5	5	30	9	693	.....	51	1	2	3	1	10	12	1	.....	.....	10
Westfield,	13	14	2	14	15	1, 453	1	25	2	2	15	12	28	65	1	1	3	30
Total,	179	189	85	613	350	24, 810	28	558	35	149	192	186	378	768	146	30	26	525

CATTARAUGUS COUNTY.—(CONTINUED.)

TOWNS.	COUNTIES OF NEW-YORK.																	
	Greene.	Hamilton.	Herkimer.	Jefferson.	Kings.	Lewis.	Livingston.	Madison.	Monroe.	Montgomery.	New York.	Niagara.	Oneida.	Onondaga.	Ontario.	Orange.	Orleans.	Oswego.
Hinsdale,			21	6		1	11	25	19	12	11		7	24	5	4		1
Humphrey,	1		2	1			10	4		2	2		8	40	7		1	
Ischua,	1		3			1	16	6	15	4		2	3	4	10	4	4	1
Leon,	3		10	2		1	1	22	30	3	3	1	23	15	15	4	3	3
Little Valley,		2	5		1	1	2	9	8	3	6		4	7	4	7		
Lyndon,	6		18	2			11	5	7	9		1	3	10	21		1	3
Machias,	13		5	7			10	11	5	11			14	4	14	1	1	1
Mansfield,	4		36	8		3	9	9	4	6		2	7	37	1	2	1	8
Napoli,	4	1	9	1			10	11	33	2	1		7	36	16	7	2	1
New Albion,	6		7	6		2	8	23	13	32	3	6	19	78	4	2	27	4
Olean,	2		5	2	4		21	8	19	4	3	2	3	16	16	3	1	20
Otto,			14	13	2		1	4	17	20	2		9	9	8		1	5
Perrysburgh,	4		8	6		4	8	26	5	3	3	8	39	10	6	2	4	11
Persia,			5	2			5	27	7	7	5	5	8	23	5		2	2
Portville,		1	6		1		7	13	13	3			6	5	8	1		1
Randolph,	2		10	6	1		6	14	35	14	3	5	19	24	32		1	
South Valley,			1						1	1	1		2	3	2	2	2	
Yorkshire,	3		39	7			12	18	6	5	3	1	24	23	3		5	1
Total,	95	8	505	135	11	31	238	368	331	303	94	67	473	503	280	63	84	93

CAYUGA COUNTY.—(CONTINUED.)

TOWNS.	Greene.	Hamilton.	Herkimer.	Jefferson.	Kings.	Lewis.	Livingston.	Madison.	Monroe.	Montgomery.	New York.	Niagara.	Oneida.	Onondaga.	Ontario.	Orange.	Orleans.	Oswego.
Auburn city:																		
1st ward,	5	4	3	7	2		13	15	13	5	3	1	27	48	7	10	2	1
2d ward,	10		8	6	4	1	3	8	13	8	23	1	25	58	12	8		9
3d ward,	4	1	9	3	5		3	20	10	10	27	1	38	37	4	5	1	6
4th ward,	6		22	15		2	14	15	23	27	41	1	43	66	24	12	5	3
Total,	25	5	42	31	11	3	33	58	59	50	94	4	133	209	47	35	8	19
Aurelius,	8		10	1		2	25	12	12	9	16		29	67	19	11	2	2
Brutus,	13		27	4	1	9	4	4	4	24	11		11	127	2	23		16
Cato,	5		27	6		2	1	27	5	30	9	1	11	182	2	11	4	22
Conquest,	3	1	10	4	2		9	10	3	14	7	3	10	50			13	23
Fleming,	1		2	1	2		4	2	4	6	9	4	6	20	2	3		
Genoa,	10		3	9	1		1	8	1	2	20	1	17	19	3	17		1
Ira,	5		27	4		1	1	24	3	52			11	132	7	15		64
Ledyard,	5		3	3			3	10	1	10	13	2	4	14		17	1	1
Locke,	3		3		2		1	3		4	6		1	16	1	18		1
Mentz,	19	6	36	15	3	16	10	25	23	48	31	2	32	88	28	71	7	15
Moravia,	6		39	1				8	3	3	8		8	41	2	20		2
Niles,	1		41	4			8	6	1	4	7	1	5	67	2	4	1	6
Owasco,	2		2	1		1	7	2	3	12	8	1	15	54	5	14	1	4
Scipio,	17		6	3			7	7	1	3	9	2	10	18	3	2		
Sempronius,	6		12	2			1	13	1	2	3		8	37	2	22	4	7
Sennett,	3		6	3		1	2	10	3	8	3	1	15	145	5	10	1	8
Springport,	1		1	7			18	4	2	11	46	1	10	4	9	5	1	1
Sterling,	12	1	24	22		7	2	23	10	24	27		30	121		41		157
Summer Hill,	6		8	5		1		11	1	2	1		8	26	1	4		
Venice,	3		4	2	2		1	6		7	12	2	14	16	2	21		2
Victory,	5		17	5	1	1	1	5	16	30	10	1	6	47	4	17		18
Total,	159	13	350	133	25	44	139	278	156	355	350	26	394	1,500	146	381	43	369

CHAUTAUQUE COUNTY.—(CONTINUED.)

TOWNS.	Greene.	Hamilton.	Herkimer.	Jefferson.	Kings.	Lewis.	Livingston.	Madison.	Monroe.	Montgomery.	New York.	Niagara.	Oneida.	Onondaga.	Ontario.	Orange.	Orleans.	Oswego.
Arkwright,	1		23	2			1	28	5	8	1	1	23	6	10		3	1
Busti,	2		54	1	2		6	4	13	23	1		37	11	6	4		1
Carroll,			21	1	1			12	3	8	3	6	7	2	8	1		
Charlotte,			12	7		3	5	19	5	20	15	5	19	27	2	2	3	1
Chautauque,	14		40	10		4	6	28	2	14	9	3	43	10	19	8	5	11
Cherry Creek,	2		12	5			3	18	11	16		1	36	2	8		6	2
Clymer,			9	6			3	21	5	5	4		17	27	2	1	8	2
Ellery,			30	5	1		4	18	4	27		6	9	31	4	7	4	2
Ellicott,	4	1	25	6	1	4	7	40	13	16	15	13	37	37	10	21	5	5
Ellington,			27	6		1	5	44	11	40	2	3	36	18	6	1	4	1
French Creek,			3	1		4	1	9	3		1	1	16	5	2	2	2	
Gerry,	1		3	3	1	22	5	15	1	9			23	22	6	4	2	3
Hanover,	16	1	23	15		6	21	118	16	16	12	11	82	30	21	22	3	11
Harmony,			53	11		3	5	35	15	23	3	3	75	111	13	6	12	4
Kiantone,			2				1			4			3	1	2		10	
Mina,	1	7	3	2			1	3	3	8	1		19	2		2	9	3
Poland,	1		11	1			7	10	10	8		3	27	9	14	7	2	
Pomfret,	17	3	31	26		12	15	96	58	31	150	30	152	66	44	57	10	13
Portland,	15		27	7		4	4	22	7	1	9	4	56	13	7	2	1	
Ripley,	4		23	10	1		8	17	2	5	3	2	21	10	11	12	3	6
Sheridan,	4		27	1		8		46	5	3	4		49	11	11	2	4	3
Sherman,	5		12				7	12	11	18	1	2	15	12	5	7	3	1
Stockton,	2		6	3			5	24	3	7	1	5	53	30	4	1		
Villenova,	5		45	9			3	64	13	7	2	4	24	6	14	2	1	7
Westfield,	9		18	8			8	22	18	14	10	9	52	24	5	15	9	3
Totai,	103	12	540	146	7	71	131	725	237	331	247	112	931	523	234	186	109	80

CATTARAUGUS COUNTY.—(Continued.)

TOWNS	Otsego.	Putnam.	Queens.	Rensselaer.	Richmond.	Rockland.	St. Lawrence.	Saratoga.	Schenectady.	Schoharie.	Schuyler.	Seneca.	Steuben.	Suffolk.	Sullivan.	Tioga.	Tompkins.	Ulster.
	COUNTIES OF NEW-YORK.																	
Hinsdale,	7	1		4				10		3		4	40	1		8	78	2
Humphrey,	12			3				1	2			4	14		1	1	17	5
Ischua,	8			4				1		5		7	12			3	30	
Leon,	30			9			1	11		4		4	3		1	3	5	
Little Valley,	32			1			3	6		1		2	4					
Lyndon,	19	1		5			1	11	2		1	2	24	1		3	15	3
Machias,	14			5			4	14		8		8	3	2	1		6	3
Mansfield,	47			4					4	3		1	6				4	7
Napoli,	24	4		2				4		17			2		1		4	2
New Albion,	89	1		12			2	7	2	16		3	9		1	2	2	2
Olean,	14			2	1			5		2		3	32		11	9	15	2
Otto,	15			26			2	9		28			1				12	
Perrysburgh,	3	2	2	8			6	21	1	8	3	3					1	4
Persia,	9			9			2		3	1			2	4			6	3
Portville,	15			7				6	2	5		1	32			4	37	
Randolph,	18			9				9		2			13	1	4		4	3
South Valley,	2		1	2			2	9		2		1				1	1	
Yorkshire,	18			3			7	21	1	2		14	1	1		2	20	
Total,	694	10	5	180	1		42	231	40	182	4	86	257	10	22	69	319	44

CAYUGA COUNTY.—(Continued.)

TOWNS	Otsego.	Putnam.	Queens.	Rensselaer.	Richmond.	Rockland.	St. Lawrence.	Saratoga.	Schenectady.	Schoharie.	Schuyler.	Seneca.	Steuben.	Suffolk.	Sullivan.	Tioga.	Tompkins.	Ulster.
Auburn city:																		
1st ward,	11	3		15		5		13	28	3	1	11	3	1	7	4	23	8
2d ward,	25	2		17		1	1	15	7	8		9	5	2	1	8	13	11
3d ward,	18	1	4	11	1		5	19	10	3		20	3			1	15	20
4th ward,	28		1	37	1		5	31	14	11		29	9	2	3	7	32	26
Total Auburn,	82	6	5	80	2	6	11	78	59	25	1	69	20	5	11	20	83	65
Aurelius,	14	3		20				24	2	10	1	49	1			5	17	31
Brutus,	16			6			6	35	1	12		13	1			6	5	7
Cato,	15			22				46	7	20		9	1			9	1	41
Conquest,	6	1		37			2	16	3	23		5	1	1	1		6	17
Fleming,	11			10			1	11	1	5		3	1				17	2
Genoa,	16		1	15				16		2		21	8	1		7	241	12
Ira,	5		1	46		1	6	80	3	20		4	4	4		1	1	10
Ledyard,	10		12	12				23	3	3		20	3	2		7	39	1
Locke,	12		2	5		1		8		1		6	1		4	6	126	19
Mentz,	30	4		45	1	3	2	68	14	19		61	12	4		3	38	155
Moravia,	9	4	2	10				25	1	9		6	6	1	8	10	57	8
Niles,	41	1		50		10		17	2	12		6			1	2	20	27
Owasco,	3	1		7		1		14	1	7		5	2	1	1		10	25
Scipio,	10			7				14		1		4	2		2	4	22	7
Sempronius,	12			14		4	2	18	2	1				5	4	10	21	12
Sennett,	7	5	4	11		4		15	2	1		3	1		5	1	14	16
Springport,	6	1	6	22	1	2		33		4		30	1		2	1	51	3
Sterling,	12		2	9		5	5	39	28	33		20	2	3		3		19
Summer Hill,	19			5			20	5	3	4		2	5		6	3	69	9
Venice,	27	4	3	9				10	2	2		11	3		5	5	64	3
Victory,	7	1		32		2	3	44	1	12		2		1	1		8	10
Total,	370	31	38	474	4	39	58	639	135	226	2	349	75	28	51	103	910	499

CHAUTAUQUE COUNTY.—(Continued.)

TOWNS	Otsego.	Putnam.	Queens.	Rensselaer.	Richmond.	Rockland.	St. Lawrence.	Saratoga.	Schenectady.	Schoharie.	Schuyler.	Seneca.	Steuben.	Suffolk.	Sullivan.	Tioga.	Tompkins.	Ulster.
Arkwright,	27			7				5	1	4		1						
Busti,	26			26			1	10		7			1			3	12	
Carroll,	32			9			1	9	1	5		2				1	1	
Charlotte,	36			19			3	8		4		1	3	3			18	
Chautauque,	51	2	3	70			3	39	1	11		2	10	1			18	
Cherry Creek,	52			26			1	19		7		3	2		2		4	1
Clymer,	26	1		6				7	3	1		1	3	1		1		
Ellery,	33	1		79			1	55		2		3	2			2	2	
Ellicott,	77	1	32	48			6	67	2	4		3	3	5	1	7	9	5
Ellington,	26			44			5	5		1		9	1			1	26	
French Creek,	24			1			3	9		1			4	3				1
Gerry,	14	4		14			1	10		2		1	1		2		16	
Hanover,	42	3	2	44		1	9	46		28		8	7	2	2	3	9	20
Harmony,	49		1	61		1	1	32	1	2		2	8			2	40	1
Kiantone,	4	1		6				4				1	1				2	4
Mina,	30			18				3				1	2				3	
Poland,	31		1	2			1	9		3		1	3			1	4	6
Pomfret,	62		4	51	2	17	14	50	3	25		17	14	8	15	11	8	16
Portland,	29	1		6		16	2	16	1	7			4	1		1	4	10
Ripley,	45			5		1	1	17		2		8	8			6	2	1
Sheridan,	27			21		2	1	6		3				1		2	1	1
Sherman,	17	3		6		1	1	8	1	2		2	2	1				2
Stockton,	6	3		34			1	7	5	2		1					5	
Villenova,	40			7				12		11		2	1	14	1	1	1	
Westfield,	63	2		21		1	8	23	3	3		2	3	2	1	4	8	4
Total,	869	22	43	631	2	40	64	476	22	137		71	83	42	24	46	193	72

CATTARAUGUS COUNTY.—(Continued.)

TOWNS.	COUNTIES OF NEW-YORK.							UNITED STATES.										
	Warren.	Washington.	Wayne.	Westchester.	Wyoming.	Yates.	New-York.	Maine.	N. Hampshire.	Vermont.	Massachusetts.	Rhode Island.	Connecticut.	New Jersey.	Pennsylvania.	Delaware.	Maryland.	District of Columbia.
Hinsdale,	......	6	1	1	20	4	1,300	9	19	43	54	1	19	3	100	......	......	......
Humphrey,	......	9	8	......	15	1	606	......	6	25	9	7	11	2	13	......	......	......
Ischua,	......	11	......	13	1	8	834	1	3	38	41	4	8	10	54	......	......	......
Leon,	......	31	2	......	12	......	1,037	3	21	76	52	7	26	8	18	......	......	......
Little Valley,	1	6	11	2	2	2	564	6	5	34	56	7	14	4	16	......	......	......
Lyndon,	1	15	1	1	23	9	824	2	8	29	19	2	37	6	26	......	......	......
Machias,	2	20	4	5	84	1	985	1	25	66	39	5	24	6	21	1	......	......
Mansfield,	5	11	6	......	16	3	849	2	9	71	35	4	39	1	18	......	......	......
Napoli,	3	38	2	......	9	......	1,024	......	9	41	20	66	25	5	11	......	......	......
New Albion,	5	27	8	......	8	1	1,226	2	7	36	35	7	19	3	24	2	......	......
Olean,	2	4	1	9	12	4	978	30	34	35	37	5	23	20	89	......	5	......
Otto,	8	19	8	......	2	1	892	......	1	62	17	7	30	4	19	......	......	......
Perrysburgh,	5	19	......	2	7	13	1,135	2	12	96	45	6	28	5	21	......	1	......
Persia,	6	15	3	1	8	2	905	2	6	82	38	2	23	3	16	......	......	1
Portville,	11	14	......	......	54	1	1,007	1	17	36	27	13	16	7	49	......	......	......
Randolph,	2	6	1	3	10	3	911	3	22	99	45	12	28	10	34	......	......	......
South Valley,	1	1	......	......	6	......	409	3	1	13	13	1	3	6	70	......	......	......
Yorkshire,	5	25	7	3	94	2	1,367	8	28	90	94	17	21	8	12	......	1	......
Total,	73	529	94	49	555	75	28,918	120	397	1,581	1,243	233	721	166	911	3	9	1

CAYUGA COUNTY.—(Continued.)

TOWNS.	Warren.	Washington.	Wayne.	Westchester.	Wyoming.	Yates.	New-York.	Maine.	N. Hampshire.	Vermont.	Massachusetts.	Rhode Island.	Connecticut.	New Jersey.	Pennsylvania.	Delaware.	Maryland.	District of Columbia.
Auburn city:																		
1st ward,	1	9	12	45	......	9	1,463	1	13	23	81	2	46	26	14	......	......	......
2d ward,	......	9	7	11	......	3	1,209	......	12	18	56	11	69	14	14	......	......	......
3d ward,	1	20	12	7	2	12	1,278	3	14	25	46	4	63	15	12	......	1	3
4th ward,	......	26	24	10	9	5	1,895	11	11	41	80	7	50	30	44	......	7	6
Total Auburn,	2	64	55	73	11	29	5,845	15	50	107	263	24	228	85	84	......	8	9
Aurelius,	3	21	16	21	......	3	1,857	1	10	35	43	5	56	89	10	......	......	......
Brutus,	......	37	15	3	1	3	2,061	......	14	50	45	3	54	17	21	......	......	......
Cato,	......	34	20	20	......	1	1,890	1	14	42	27	4	62	36	16	......	......	......
Conquest,	1	37	80	9	6	6	1,644	......	4	26	24	6	27	16	16	......	......	......
Fleming,	1	17	2	1	......	2	858	......	3	4	40	8	27	21	10	......	1	......
Genoa,	......	9	3	23	1	2	1,868	......	8	20	51	10	96	60	66	......	......	......
Ira,	4	69	18	16	......	2	1,819	......	8	30	42	8	60	12	10	......	......	......
Ledyard,	3	16	4	17	......	3	1,400	1	5	11	65	10	54	46	44	......	2	......
Locke,	......	9	7	12	......	......	1,132	......	3	30	26	11	28	4	12	......	......	......
Mentz,	1	69	117	14	1	5	3,874	1	7	67	58	6	94	129	30	......	3	......
Moravia,	1	12	......	6	......	......	1,496	......	11	17	77	8	60	28	5	......	......	......
Niles,	......	17	6	14	......	......	1,681	......	5	9	37	11	22	49	21	......	......	......
Owasco,	......	6	12	4	......	3	1,023	......	4	5	13	3	14	30	18	......	......	......
Scipio,	......	30	1	13	2	4	1,448	1	6	24	61	14	79	24	22	......	4	......
Sempronius,	......	18	2	4	......	......	1,078	2	7	18	45	23	27	11	8	......	......	......
Sennett,	......	26	18	3	......	3	1,385	......	7	26	87	65	2	28	8	......	2	......
Springport,	1	13	3	9	2	6	1,672	......	3	23	65	8	21	69	28	......	1	......
Sterling,	......	148	103	5	1	3	2,500	16	5	40	42	7	31	23	20	......	10	......
Summer Hill,	......	7	......	6	2	......	906	......	1	20	49	6	31	15	8	......	......	......
Venice,	2	21	1	18	1	5	1,556	......	1	21	56	9	49	33	19	......	......	......
Victory,	......	51	98	6	......	3	1,717	2	6	51	35	4	54	21	7	......	2	......
Total,	19	731	581	297	28	83	40,710	40	182	676	1,251	253	1,176	846	489	......	33	9

CHAUTAUQUE COUNTY.—(Continued.)

TOWNS.	Warren.	Washington.	Wayne.	Westchester.	Wyoming.	Yates.	New-York.	Maine.	N. Hampshire.	Vermont.	Massachusetts.	Rhode Island.	Connecticut.	New Jersey.	Pennsylvania.	Delaware.	Maryland.	District of Columbia.
Arkwright,	......	6	10	1	4	......	917	6	3	35	43	7	29	2	6	......	......	......
Busti,	2	28	......	......	1	2	1,391	5	7	70	63	12	53	8	112	......	......	......
Carroll,	1	24	3	......	2	......	1,061	2	21	102	61	......	10	18	47	......	......	......
Charlotte,	......	21	15	2	9	1	1,201	2	28	57	100	11	70	8	32	......	......	......
Chautauque,	7	48	4	3	4	3	1,947	......	14	87	70	16	62	2	59	1	4	......
Cherry Creek,	2	5	2	......	9	1	966	......	23	57	59	18	26	31	4	......	......	......
Clymer,	3	13	3	......	1	......	778	......	10	54	26	7	28	2	35	......	......	......
Ellery,	13	29	11	5	1	9	1,627	1	10	52	33	14	35	4	24	......	......	......
Ellicott,	13	41	4	4	10	12	2,876	2	33	154	143	7	76	18	143	......	2	......
Ellington,	2	24	12	......	29	3	1,690	6	21	53	52	9	45	5	14	......	......	......
French Creek,	1	9	1	......	......	1	546	......	5	59	17	4	16	3	66	......	......	......
Gerry,	......	15	7	......	1	4	1,016	......	8	89	38	12	28	1	21	......	1	......
Hanover,	8	42	12	2	13	9	2,985	5	26	237	138	16	84	8	65	......	......	......
Harmony,	16	53	5	5	5	2	2,737	5	24	141	98	13	102	10	110	......	......	......
Kiantone,	......	......	......	......	......	......	339	......	6	34	19	2	10	1	23	......	......	......
Mina,	......	65	......	......	......	......	741	6	5	20	24	10	19	1	60	......	......	......
Poland,	5	8	3	......	18	......	1,096	......	13	52	40	7	13	1	19	......	2	......
Pomfret,	6	41	7	4	24	10	4,762	56	100	208	360	33	261	58	164	......	7	1
Portland,	2	32	2	2	5	1	1,453	......	24	72	54	13	51	4	39	......	......	......
Ripley,	......	37	6	......	6	2	1,187	......	8	51	17	8	62	8	121	......	4	......
Sheridan,	2	17	4	4	2	......	1,175	1	12	46	59	7	60	8	27	......	......	......
Sherman,	......	19	7	......	2	5	944	5	14	50	51	3	86	5	27	......	......	......
Stockton,	7	9	2	1	6	......	1,222	1	21	140	138	9	55	3	18	......	......	......
Villenova,	4	9	15	1	3	2	1,164	3	10	35	47	10	32	5	23	......	......	......
Westfield,	5	38	2	1	22	8	2,144	3	46	136	104	16	109	11	107	......	......	......
Total,	99	633	137	35	177	75	37,965	109	492	2,091	1,854	264	1,422	225	1,366	1	20	1

CATTARAUGUS COUNTY.—(CONTINUED.)

TOWNS.	UNITED STATES.																	
	Virginia.	N. Carolina.	S Carolina.	Georgia.	Florida.	Alabama.	Mississippi.	Louisiana.	Texas.	Arkansas.	Missouri.	Tennessee.	Kentucky.	Ohio.	Indiana.	Illinois.	Michigan.	Wisconsin.
Hinsdale,	1													1			1	
Humphrey,								1						2		2		
Ischua,														2		1	1	2
Leon,														6			1	
Little Valley,														7			4	
Lyndon,	1													11		8	4	2
Machias,														3		3	3	
Mansfield,								2						5				
Napoli,														3			2	4
New Albion,,																1		
Olean,														9	2	1	3	1
Otto,					1										1	1	3	
Perrysburgh,														1		2		2
Persia,														8	1			2
Portville,														9	1		4	2
Randolph,													1	8	2	4	4	
South Valley,	3													7				
Yorkshire,	8													5				2
Total,	20	1			1			5		1			3	148	8	45	49	27

CAYUGA COUNTY.—(CONTINUED.)

TOWNS.	Virginia.	N. Carolina.	S Carolina.	Georgia.	Florida.	Alabama.	Mississippi.	Louisiana.	Texas.	Arkansas.	Missouri.	Tennessee.	Kentucky.	Ohio.	Indiana.	Illinois.	Michigan.	Wisconsin.
Auburn city:																		
1st ward,						1			1				1	12	2	1	8	
2d ward,	3				1						1		2	5	3		8	2
3d ward,					2							2	.	9		3	3	1
4th ward,	4	2	1		1			1				1	4		2	1	4	5
Total Auburn,	7	2	1		4	1		1	1		1	3	7	26	7	5	23	8
Aurelius,								1						3	2			
Brutus,														3			3	1
Cato,	1													5		5	4	2
Conquest,														4			8	
Fleming,	2													3				
Genoa,														5			4	3
Ira,								1						5	1	1	5	3
Ledyard,														6		2	9	2
Locke,	1													4			3	1
Mentz,	1	1	1		1		1						2	2	1	5	12	2
Moravia,														9		2	3	1
Niles,														6			2	
Owasco,														2		6	5	
Scipio,	2													9		1	5	2
Sempronius,														9		4	1	
Sennett,									2					3			8	7
Springport,					1			1						4				
Sterling,	1										2					2	3	4
Summer Hill,														1		1	3	
Venice,	1									1				2		1	4	2
Victory,	1															1	2	1
Total,	17	3	2		6	1	1	4	3	1	3	3	9	111	11	36	107	39

CHAUTAUQUE COUNTY.—(CONTINUED.)

TOWNS.	Virginia.	N. Carolina.	S Carolina.	Georgia.	Florida.	Alabama.	Mississippi.	Louisiana.	Texas.	Arkansas.	Missouri.	Tennessee.	Kentucky.	Ohio.	Indiana.	Illinois.	Michigan.	Wisconsin.
Arkwright,		1												4	5	1	1	1
Busti,														6	1	4	3	1
Carroll,	1													8			1	1
Charlotte,	2												1	5	2		4	
Chautauque,	2													6	1	1	5	
Cherry Creek,													2	2		1		
Clymer,														6		1		
Ellery,														9		1	1	3
Ellicott,	7				1			1					1	22	2	1	4	5
Ellington,														10	1	3	4	3
French Creek,														4			3	1
Gerry,													1	7		2	2	
Hanover,	1			1									3	41	4	5	11	5
Harmony,													1	14	1	2	4	1
Kiantone,														3				
Mina,														7		1	1	
Poland,														3			1	
Pomfret,	9		1				1				2	3	4	84	7	14	14	13
Portland,														20		4	1	5
Ripley,	1												1	8	2	5	1	4
Sheridan,														20	1		5	2
Sherman,				2					1				1	4		3	8	
Stockton,	1													3	4	3	1	2
Villenova,														15	1	5	2	
Westfield,														36	2	7	7	3
Total,	24	1	1	3	1		1	1	1		2	3	15	347	34	64	84	50

CATTARAUGUS COUNTY.—(CONTINUED.)

TOWNS	U. STATES.			Total United States.	FOREIGN COUNTRIES.													
	Iowa.	California.	Territories.		Canada.	N. Brunswick.	Nova Scotia.	N. Foundland.	West Indies.	Mexico.	S. America.	England.	Scotland.	Ireland.	Wales.	France.	Belgium.	Holland.
Hinsdale,				1, 551	10							10	5	496				
Humphrey,				684	2							23	2	46				
Ischua,				999	4							7	5	87				
Leon,	2			1, 255	10							18	2	19	1			
Little Valley,				719	8						1	5	4	59		1		
Lyndon,				979	6							35	83	13				
Machias,				1, 182	4		2					1	22	56	3			3
Mansfield,				1, 035	4							5	1	28		3		
Napoli,				1, 210	1							5		2				
New Albion,				1, 362	9							4	1	54				
Olean,				1, 272	9							26	10	154		10		
Otto,				1, 038	10		1					4	3	13				
Perrysburgh,				1, 356	17							8		25				
Persia,				1, 089	15							10	5	48				
Portville,				1, 189	8		1					9	3	43	1			1
Randolph,				1, 183	13							20	4	75		3		
South Valley,				529	14				1			1		33				
Yorkshire,				1, 661	13		1					6		15	3	1		11
Total,	4		4	34, 629	254		6		2		1	311	309	1, 980	812	38		17

CAYUGA COUNTY.—(CONTINUED.)

TOWNS	Iowa.	California.	Territories.	Total United States.	Canada.	N. Brunswick.	Nova Scotia.	N. Foundland.	West Indies.	Mexico.	S. America.	England.	Scotland.	Ireland.	Wales.	France.	Belgium.	Holland.
Auburn city:																		
1st ward,				1, 695	8	1	1	1				97	20	298	3	2	1	
2d ward,				1, 428	4							98	35	251	1			15
3d ward,		1		1, 485	15		1					78	33	328	1	2		2
4th ward,				2, 208	50				3	1	1	92	55	559	7	12		7
Total Auburn,		1		6, 816	77	1	2	1	3	1	1	365	143	1, 436	12	16	1	24
Aurelius,				2, 112	2				1			127	30	255		1		
Brutus,				2, 272	18							62	11	353		3		
Cato,				2, 109	11							31	2	79	1			
Conquest,				1, 775	11	1						33	5	39				1
Fleming,				977	6							58	3	105				4
Genoa,				2, 191	2							47	2	106				
Ira,				2, 005	7							36		48				
Ledyard,				1, 657	10				2			147	1	135				
Locke,				1, 255	1		1					4	15	12				
Mentz,				4, 304	36		4	1				91	7	470	4	1		24
Moravia,				1, 717	13		1					17	3	32				
Niles,				1, 843	4							16	4	39				
Owasco,				1, 123	2							67	9	62				8
Scipio,				1, 702	2							48	1	127	4			
Sempronius,				1, 233	2							10	3	15				
Sennett,				1, 630	7		1					209	4	120	1			12
Springport,				1, 896	7		1					23	2	216	1			
Sterling,				2, 706	42		3					81	30	125				
Summer Hill,				1, 041	3							2	6	12				
Venice,				1, 755	7							41	3	118				
Victory,				1, 904	2							35	1	35				
Total,		1		46, 023	272	2	13	2	6	1	1	1, 550	285	3, 939	23	21	1	73

CHAUTAUQUE COUNTY.—(CONTINUED.)

TOWNS	Iowa.	California.	Territories.	Total United States.	Canada.	N. Brunswick.	Nova Scotia.	N. Foundland.	West Indies.	Mexico.	S. America.	England.	Scotland.	Ireland.	Wales.	France.	Belgium.	Holland.
Arkwright,				1, 061	1							10		2		14		3
Busti,				1, 736	2							58	6	5				
Carroll,				1, 333	5							2		8				
Charlotte,				1, 523	13							47	7	50		17		1
Chautauque,				2, 277	44	1						104	10	51				
Cherry Creek,				1, 189	4							6	3	5		8		
Clymer,				947	8							14		3				186
Ellery,				1, 814	1							10		6	1			
Ellicott,				3, 502	31							89	12	80	4	1	1	3
Ellington,				1, 912	2							2	1	5	3			
French Creek,				724	4							6	1	4	1			19
Gerry,				1, 226	9							8	2	8				
Hanover,				3, 635	65							84	32	148	8	10		6
Harmony,				3, 263	33	1						57		15				21
Kiantone,				437	3							3		15				
Mina,				895	6							50	14	19				9
Poland,				1, 247	7							24	2	20	1			1
Pomfret,			1	6, 163	29	2	4					445		1, 469	4	38		30
Portland,				1, 740	9							43	1	74	1			
Ripley,				1, 488	2							106	4	68				1
Sheridan,				1, 423	17							6	19	83	4	1		
Sherman,	1			1, 205	2							77	4					8
Stockton,				1, 621	6				1			8	7	18		1		
Villenova,				1, 352	3		1					16		9		1		
Westfield,				2, 731	28		4					180	3	318		2		1
Total,	1		1	46, 444	334	4	9		1			1, 455	128	2, 483	27	93	1	289

CATTARAUGUS COUNTY.—(CONTINUED.)

TOWNS.	FOREIGN COUNTRIES.																		
	Germany.	Prussia.	Austria.	Switzerland.	Italy.	Spain.	Portugal.	Poland.	Norway.	Sweden.	Russia.	Denmark.	East Indies.	Africa.	Turkey and Greece.	Islands.	Asia.	At Sea.	Unknown.
Hinsdale,	10																		47
Humphrey,																			2
Ischua,								1											
Leon,	5																		20
Little Valley,	2																		2
Lyndon,	5																		2
Machias,	5	9																	79
Mansfield,	25	1																	23
Napoli,																			4
New Albion,	36																	1	95
Olean,	92	3		1														1	33
Otto,	24			1															
Perrysburgh,	34																		16
Persia,	27																		10
Portville,	3					1		1											4
Randolph,	11			2															312
South Valley,	1																		7
Yorkshire,	10	1						1											5
Total,	789	16		15	1	2		3	1	3		1					1	4	835

CAYUGA COUNTY.—(CONTINUED.)

TOWNS.	Germany.	Prussia.	Austria.	Switzerland.	Italy.	Spain.	Portugal.	Poland.	Norway.	Sweden.	Russia.	Denmark.	East Indies.	Africa.	Turkey and Greece.	Islands.	Asia.	At Sea.	Unknown.
Auburn city:																			
1st ward,	91		21									1					1		162
2d ward,	81	3						4									1		1
3d ward,	19	1						4	1		1								14
4th ward,	76	17		7	1	2												2	65
Total,	267	21	21	7	1	2		8	1		1	1					2	2	242
Aurelius,	36	1																1	8
Brutus,	81		1							1								2	3
Cato,	16																		3
Conquest,	1																		6
Fleming,	5																1		5
Genoa,																			4
Ira,	21			1															15
Ledyard,	6			2															16
Locke,	1																		4
Mentz,	80	1																1	34
Moravia,	9																		27
Niles,	5																1		
Owasco,	20																		12
Scipio,	7																		4
Sempronius,	2							1											3
Sennett,	10																		88
Springport,	14																		10
Sterling,	4																		33
Summer Hill,																			120
Venice,	4							1											10
Victory,	2																		37
Total,	591	23	22	10	1	2		10	1	1	1	1					4	6	684

CHAUTAUQUE COUNTY.—(CONTINUED.)

TOWNS.	Germany.	Prussia.	Austria.	Switzerland.	Italy.	Spain.	Portugal.	Poland.	Norway.	Sweden.	Russia.	Denmark.	East Indies.	Africa.	Turkey and Greece.	Islands.	Asia.	At Sea.	Unknown.
Arkwright,	8	3																	8
Busti,	3			1						89								1	19
Carroll,				1						42									17
Charlotte,		6								6									2
Chautauque,	36			1						16								1	50
Cherry Creek,	3																		8
Clymer,										1									5
Ellery,	10									17									6
Ellicott,	18	1								150	1						1		41
Ellington,	2									3									
French Creek,	4																		3
Gerry,										5									
Hanover,	78		1	7								1				1			25
Harmony,	17			1						15									20
Kiantone,	12									12									8
Mina,	40									2							1		
Poland,				3						3									17
Pomfret,	834	15		19				20		20		4						1	60
Portland,	4			1						63									
Ripley,	14																		20
Sheridan,	29			8				1											
Sherman,	18																		
Stockton,	15			3						8									
Villenova,	17																		14
Westfield,	45									1						5		4	16
Total,	1, 207	25	1	45				21		453	1	5				6	2	7	339

CHEMUNG COUNTY.

TOWNS.	Albany.	Allegany.	Broome.	Cattaraugus.	Cayuga.	Chautauque.	Chemung.	Chenango.	Clinton.	Columbia.	Cortland.	Delaware.	Dutchess.	Erie.	Essex.	Franklin.	Fulton.	Genesee.
	COUNTIES OF NEW-YORK.																	
Big Flats,	7	1	11	2	9		839		3	5	4	30	24	1	2			
Catlin,	3	2	8		5		747	4		5	7	11	24					
Chemung,	9		27	2	14		1, 442	39	1	11	14	22	17	6	1			1
Elmira,	65	24	60	5	78	7	2, 686	9	2	13	42	85	62	12			14	12
Erin,	13	2	1				681	1		2	6	17	13				1	1
Horseheads,	34	4	5		15		1, 294	9		7	10	24	21					
Southport,	54	5	29		6	2	1, 845	54	2	8	12	86	20		2			
Van Etten,	5		4	1	8		824	6		1		14	10	2	2		6	1
Veteran,	1	3	9		11	1	1, 441	3		10	4	35	20					2
Total,	191	41	154	10	146	10	11, 799	125	8	62	99	324	211	21	7		21	17

CHENANGO COUNTY.

TOWNS.	Albany.	Allegany.	Broome.	Cattaraugus.	Cayuga.	Chautauque.	Chemung.	Chenango.	Clinton.	Columbia.	Cortland.	Delaware.	Dutchess.	Erie.	Essex.	Franklin.	Fulton.	Genesee.
Bainbridge,	33	5	112		1			1, 777	1	28	21	195	76	1	1		1	1
Columbus,	4	3	2		2			760		3	11	8	12				1	
Coventry,	16		69			1		1, 054		6	12	39	18				2	
German,	1		5	1	1			538		1	24	4	6					
Greene,	63		165		5			2, 292		29	34	73	44					3
Guilford,	17		15	2	3	5		1, 485		32	13	60	55		1		1	1
Lincklaen,	2	3	18	1	1			658		10	51	2	6				7	2
Macdonough,	2	2	6	1	1			996		11	10	22	8		2			1
New Berlin,	7	2	13	5		1		1, 323		12	10	34	13				2	1
North Norwich,	9		9	2				718		7	18	13	50				7	2
Norwich,	21		23	1	13	2		2, 352		2	55	44	31			1	7	1
Otselic,	4	3	4		1			1, 022		5	12	4	13					1
Oxford,	10	3	30	4	1			2, 088		15	4	64	41					
Pharsalia,	7	1	5			2		796		3	27	5	9					1
Pitcher,	2		10		2			799		3	67	11	7					1
Plymouth,	1		6		9			947		3	20	4	39					
Preston,			8					704		2	12	7	3	2				1
Sherburne,	17		8		4	2		1, 534			19	14	7	28			4	1
Smithville,	7		36	2	1			1, 065		5	18	33	12	2				
Smyrna,	7		11	3				1, 061		11	12	4	36	1	1			1
Total,	230	22	555	22	45	13		23, 969	1	188	450	640	486	34	5	1	32	18

CLINTON COUNTY.

TOWNS.	Albany.	Allegany.	Broome.	Cattaraugus.	Cayuga.	Chautauque.	Chemung.	Chenango.	Clinton.	Columbia.	Cortland.	Delaware.	Dutchess.	Erie.	Essex.	Franklin.	Fulton.	Genesee.
Au Sable,	4								1, 952		1		5		202	10		
Beekmantown,	6					1			1, 788				2		26	14		
Black Brook,									1, 257				3		229	30		
Champlain,	14								2, 980				10	2	49	30		1
Chazy,	1								2, 683	2			7		77	20		
Clinton,	1								562						3	44		
Dannemora,	21	1						1	237	3		1	2	9	24	10	2	
Ellenburgh,									933	5			10		39	49		
Mooers,	2							1	1, 967	2			8		46	21		
Peru,	3			3					2, 152	6			21		125	14		
Plattsburgh,	6						1	2	3, 125	8		2	20	1	109	43		1
Saranac,	4								1, 651				2		89	10	4	1
Schuyler Falls,	4								1, 175	1			4		62	15		
Total,	66	1		3		1	1	4	22, 462	27	1	3	94	12	1, 080	310	6	3

COLUMBIA COUNTY.

TOWNS.	Albany.	Allegany.	Broome.	Cattaraugus.	Cayuga.	Chautauque.	Chemung.	Chenango.	Clinton.	Columbia.	Cortland.	Delaware.	Dutchess.	Erie.	Essex.	Franklin.	Fulton.	Genesee.
Ancram,	19		5		1	2				1, 425	1	1	134					
Austerlitz,					1	1				1, 211		4	43				2	
Canaan,	25							1	1	1, 193	1	3	29	1	1	1		
Chatham,	46			1	3			2	3	2, 479		4	162	2	1		2	2
Claverack,	9									2, 689		3	69	5			2	1
Clermont,	1									862			90					
Copake,	3									1, 302		2	69	1				
Gallatin,	1							1		1, 306		1	138					5
Germantown,	2									907			30					
Ghent,	12				1					1, 837			92					
Greenport,	9									1, 042			25				1	
Hillsdale,	12	1	2		1	1		2		1, 646		4	120		1			1
Hudson City:																		
1st ward,	22							1		748		1	38	1	1			1
2d ward,	11		3		2			2		906	1	1	53					
3d ward,	25		4		1					1, 133		2	56	1			1	
4th ward,	21				1			1		1, 169	1	1	44	3			1	
Total Hudson,	79		7		4			4		3, 956	2	5	191	5	1		2	1
Kinderhook,	77		3		2			1		2. 508		8	122				4	2
Livingston,	4									1, 700			116					
New Lebanon,	33		3	2	1			9		1, 140		3	42	1	1	1		
Stockport,	14									928		5	60					
Stuyvesant,	30				1			1		1, 285			49					
Taghkanick,	5									1, 495		2	63					
Total,	381	1	20	3	15	4		21	4	30, 911	4	45	1, 644	15	5	2	13	12

CHEMUNG COUNTY.—(Continued.)

TOWNS.	COUNTIES OF NEW-YORK.																	
	Greene.	Hamilton.	Herkimer.	Jefferson.	Kings.	Lewis.	Livingston.	Madison.	Monroe.	Montgomery.	New York.	Niagara.	Oneida.	Onondaga.	Ontario.	Orange.	Orleans.	Oswego.
Big Flats,	10	.....	15	1	.....	.....	1	4	3	1	9	1	11	1	3	96	.....	.....
Catlin,	.....	.....	3	.....	.....	.....	1	3	.....	10	5	.....	6	7	3	48	2	.....
Chemung,	4	.....	2	2	.....	.....	2	4	8	3	8	1	2	2	18	310	3	8
Elmira,	42	.....	22	5	12	2	20	74	31	18	153	.....	55	52	68	390	12	19
Erin,	1	.....	1	.....	.....	.....	.....	2	1	12	2	.....	4	5	8	75	.....	.....
Horseheads,	9	.....	11	.....	.....	.....	4	9	6	5	16	1	3	5	6	266	3	5
Southport,	47	.....	2	4	1	.....	4	5	18	5	39	6	24	26	25	233	1	4
Van Etten,	1	.....	12	.....	.....	.....	.....	5	.....	7	2	.....	2	3	.....	51	.....	.....
Veteran,	1	.....	7	2	1	.....	2	8	1	29	46	4	7	19	8	127	.....	.....
Total,	115	.....	75	14	14	2	34	114	68	90	280	13	114	120	139	1,596	21	36

CHENANGO COUNTY.—(Continued.)

TOWNS.	Greene.	Hamilton.	Herkimer.	Jefferson.	Kings.	Lewis.	Livingston.	Madison.	Monroe.	Montgomery.	New York.	Niagara.	Oneida.	Onondaga.	Ontario.	Orange.	Orleans.	Oswego.
Bainbridge,	43	.....	10	.....	.....	1	2	5	1	11	16	.....	20	4	.....	11	.....	.....
Columbus,	.....	.....	12	4	1	.....	3	69	.....	8	.....	2	29	1	1	1	.....	.....
Coventry,	30	.....	1	.....	1	.....	.....	13	.....	4	7	.....	5	1	1	11	.....	.....
German,	4	.....	4	3	.....	.....	.....	9	1	25	3	.....	5	.....	.....	.....	.....	.....
Greene,	42	.....	3	4	6	.....	.....	27	3	15	3	1	14	4	2	41	.....	1
Guilford,	13	.....	13	5	.....	.....	1	22	1	1	3	1	10	3	2	30	.....	2
Lincklaen,	.....	.....	6	3	.....	.....	1	57	1	1	3	.....	6	19	7	1	.....	4
Macdonough,	6	.....	4	1	.....	.....	.....	21	2	.....	7	.....	7	1	1	2	.....	.....
New Berlin,	1	1	24	9	.....	1	.....	54	.....	5	6	.....	59	3	.....	2	.....	.....
North Norwich,	1	.....	1	.....	.....	1	.....	20	.....	1	2	.....	1	7	.....	.....	.....	.....
Norwich,	10	.....	13	1	1	5	3	73	1	6	13	.....	39	16	2	8	.....	14
Otselic,	2	.....	2	1	.....	4	.....	173	.....	16	1	.....	24	10	2	3	.....	14
Oxford,	10	.....	12	3	5	1	1	22	2	12	22	1	18	.....	1	17	.....	5
Pharsalia,	2	.....	2	2	.....	.....	.....	19	.....	1	.....	.....	10	4	.....	.....	.....	.....
Pitcher,	3	.....	.....	.....	.....	.....	.....	22	1	4	2	2	14	16	.....	.....	.....	5
Plymouth,	2	.....	18	1	.....	.....	.....	30	.....	22	2	.....	10	8	.....	.....	.....	1
Preston,	1	.....	.....	.....	.....	.....	.....	4	.....	1	1	.....	1	1	.....	3	.....	3
Sherburne,	6	.....	39	1	.....	.....	.....	211	2	11	17	1	56	11	1	.....	.....	3
Smithville,	10	.....	2	.....	1	.....	.....	8	1	.....	10	.....	1	9	.....	9	.....	5
Smyrna,	1	.....	12	7	.....	.....	2	170	.....	47	1	.....	27	10	1	1	1	.....
Total,	187	1	178	45	15	13	13	1,029	16	191	119	8	356	128	21	140	1	57

CLINTON COUNTY.—(Continued.)

TOWNS.	Greene.	Hamilton.	Herkimer.	Jefferson.	Kings.	Lewis.	Livingston.	Madison.	Monroe.	Montgomery.	New York.	Niagara.	Oneida.	Onondaga.	Ontario.	Orange.	Orleans.	Oswego.
Au Sable,	.....	.....	1	.....	.....	.....	.....	1	.....	2	9	.....	2	.....	.....	.....	.....	1
Beekmantown,	2	.....	.....	3	.....	2	.....	.....	.....	.....	10	.....	2	.....	.....	1	.....	.....
Black Brook,	.....	.....	.....	1	.....	1	.....	2	2	5	3	.....	6	2	.....	.....	.....	.....
Champlain,	.....	.....	4	3	.....	1	1	.....	1	8	7	.....	3	2	.....	.....	.....	.....
Chazy,	1	1	.....	8	.....	.....	.....	.....	.....	2	8	.....	.....	1	.....	1	1	4
Clinton,	.....	.....	.....	.....	.....	.....	.....	.....	.....	.....	4	.....	.....	1	.....	.....	.....	.....
Dannemora,	3	.....	1	1	.....	.....	.....	2	.....	2	8	.....	4	2	2	2	1	2
Ellenburgh,	.....	.....	.....	1	.....	.....	.....	.....	3	4	2	.....	3	.....	.....	.....	.....	5
Mooers,	.....	.....	.....	1	.....	.....	.....	.....	.....	.....	6	.....	1	.....	.....	.....	.....	.....
Peru,	.....	.....	6	2	1	1	.....	.....	2	.....	2	.....	1	2	.....	.....	.....	.....
Plattsburgh,	6	.....	7	2	3	2	.....	1	.....	.....	20	3	7	.....	.....	1	.....	2
Saranac,	.....	.....	3	.....	.....	.....	.....	.....	.....	2	8	2	.....	1	1	.....	.....	.....
Schuyler's Falls,	.....	.....	.....	3	.....	.....	.....	.....	1	1	2	.....	.....	.....	1	1	.....	.....
Total,	12	1	22	25	4	7	1	6	9	26	89	5	29	11	4	6	2	14

COLUMBIA COUNTY.—(Continued.)

TOWNS.	Greene.	Hamilton.	Herkimer.	Jefferson.	Kings.	Lewis.	Livingston.	Madison.	Monroe.	Montgomery.	New York.	Niagara.	Oneida.	Onondaga.	Ontario.	Orange.	Orleans.	Oswego.
Ancram,	5	.....	.....	.....	.....	.....	.....	.....	1	1	3	.....	.....	1	1	1	.....	.....
Austerlitz,	10	.....	1	3	2	.....	.....	1	.....	3	4	.....	1	.....	.....	1	.....	1
Canaan,	23	.....	4	1	8	1	.....	4	.....	2	28	.....	7	1	1	1	.....	.....
Chatham,	44	1	2	1	11	1	5	.....	1	6	51	.....	7	3	2	3	1	1
Claverack,	32	.....	6	3	6	.....	.....	1	.....	2	22	.....	2	2	2	2	.....	1
Clermont,	9	.....	.....	.....	.....	.....	.....	.....	.....	.....	20	.....	.....	.....	.....	1	.....	.....
Copake,	2	.....	.....	1	.....	.....	.....	.....	1	2	4	.....	4	.....	.....	.....	.....	.....
Gallatin,	5	.....	.....	.....	.....	.....	.....	.....	.....	.....	.....	.....	.....	.....	.....	1	.....	.....
Germantown,	15	.....	.....	.....	.....	.....	.....	.....	.....	.....	9	.....	.....	.....	.....	2	.....	.....
Ghent,	20	.....	5	.....	11	2	.....	2	.....	9	6	.....	.....	.....	.....	.....	.....	1
Greenport,	29	.....	.....	.....	5	.....	1	.....	.....	.....	22	.....	1	.....	.....	.....	.....	.....
Hillsdale,	21	.....	2	.....	.....	.....	.....	.....	.....	4	18	.....	5	1	.....	.....	.....	.....
Hudson city:																		
1st ward,	56	.....	2	.....	3	.....	.....	.....	.....	11	33	.....	2	1	.....	1	.....	.....
2d ward,	78	.....	.....	.....	3	.....	.....	1	1	2	20	.....	.....	.....	.....	5	.....	.....
3d ward,	92	.....	4	3	7	.....	.....	3	.....	6	22	.....	2	3	3	11	.....	1
4th ward,	72	.....	2	1	1	1	.....	.....	1	.....	15	.....	2	2	.....	4	.....	.....
Total Hudson,	298	.....	8	4	14	1	.....	4	2	19	90	.....	6	6	3	21	.....	1
Kinderhook,	59	.....	4	.....	6	.....	.....	2	.....	3	37	.....	6	.....	.....	13	.....	4
Livingston,	37	.....	2	.....	.....	.....	1	1	.....	3	15	.....	2	2	3	1	.....	.....
New Lebanon,	6	.....	4	6	8	.....	.....	4	1	3	42	.....	3	.....	.....	2	.....	2
Stockport,	69	.....	.....	.....	2	.....	.....	.....	4	.....	14	.....	1	3	.....	10	.....	1
Stuyvesant,	70	.....	2	.....	3	.....	.....	2	.....	.....	12	.....	6	4	1	16	1	3
Taghkanic,	8	.....	.....	.....	.....	.....	.....	.....	.....	1	8	.....	.....	.....	1	.....	.....	.....
Total,	762	1	40	19	76	5	7	21	10	58	405	.....	51	23	14	75	2	15

CHEMUNG COUNTY.—(Continued.)

TOWNS.	Counties of New-York.																	
	Otsego.	Putnam.	Queens.	Rensselaer.	Richmond.	Rockland.	St. Lawrence.	Saratoga.	Schenectady.	Schoharie.	Schuyler.	Seneca.	Steuben.	Suffolk.	Sullivan.	Tioga.	Tompkins.	Ulster.
Big Flats,	15			3		1		1	4	14	1	22	104		16	20	64	9
Catlin,	10	9		2						3		24	87		9	10	147	11
Chemung,	18	4	3	1	3	1		3		12		12	20	6	24	39	53	36
Elmira,	97	17	7	36	1	13	8	32	2	24		64	124	9	18	124	301	65
Erin,	11	2		5				7		20		3	10		8	10	87	5
Horseheads,	11		1	14		2		11	3	14	1	20	39	3	21	31	90	22
Southport,	28	4	4	11		6	4	4	1	4	60	25	54	6	25	68	151	37
Van Etten,	4	1		7		2	6	5		4	6	8	6		6	91	180	5
Veteran,	20			67		1	6	9		10	21	28	35		7	22	145	11
Total,	214	37	15	146	4	26	24	72	10	105	89	206	479	24	134	415	1,218	201

CHENANGO COUNTY.—(Continued.)

TOWNS.	Otsego.	Putnam.	Queens.	Rensselaer.	Richmond.	Rockland.	St. Lawrence.	Saratoga.	Schenectady.	Schoharie.	Schuyler.	Seneca.	Steuben.	Suffolk.	Sullivan.	Tioga.	Tompkins.	Ulster.
Bainbridge,	280	3	1	39		1		22	1	79		2	5		6	5	12	12
Columbus,	128			9			3	6	1	4		2	3				1	
Coventry,	40	1	1	7				2		19			2	4	1			
German,	27			1				2		2				1			1	
Greene,	53	12		20				6	5	21		2	10		7	10	12	28
Guilford,	236	8		5		1		9		12			4		11	7	6	3
Lincklaen,	40			32				2		3							2	
Macdonough,	19			2				7					1	1	3	2	10	
New Berlin,	411	3	1	13			2	16	3	10			3			5	5	
North Norwich,	33		2	1			2	4		9							1	
Norwich,	195	1		11				6	1	32			7		1	2	9	
Otselic,	64			25			1	9		10			3			2		
Oxford,	122	1	1	12			2	3	1	5		1	11		2	5	5	8
Pharsalia,	35							4		4			2		1	1		
Pitcher,	47	2		5				8	3								3	1
Plymouth,	20	1		2				5	2	7		1		1			2	
Preston,	20		1				1	1		6		2	3	5				1
Sherburne,	79			10				5		15					3	1	3	5
Smithville,	21			2				8		1			3	4		1	3	3
Smyrna,	48			8				11	1	5			6			1	5	1
Total,	1,918	32	7	204		2	11	136	18	244		10	63	16	35	42	80	62

CLINTON COUNTY.—(Continued.)

TOWNS.	Otsego.	Putnam.	Queens.	Rensselaer.	Richmond.	Rockland.	St. Lawrence.	Saratoga.	Schenectady.	Schoharie.	Schuyler.	Seneca.	Steuben.	Suffolk.	Sullivan.	Tioga.	Tompkins.	Ulster.
Au Sable,				15		1	24	11		1							4	
Beckmantown,				2			9	3						12				
Black Brook,				2			24	21	2				1					
Champlain,	1		2	17			26	11	6	1								
Chazy,			5	22	4	5	12	12		2				1				
Clinton,							3	1										
Dannemora,	4	1		21			11	6	4	2		1						1
Ellenburgh,				2			11	2										
Mooers,	9			2		1	23										1	
Peru,				12			12	13						2				
Plattsburgh,			9	16			16	13	3					3				
Saranac,				9			20	6										2
Schuyler Falls,				6			7	2										
Total,	14	1	16	126	4	7	198	101	15	6		1	1	18			5	3

COLUMBIA COUNTY.—(Continued.)

TOWNS.	Otsego.	Putnam.	Queens.	Rensselaer.	Richmond.	Rockland.	St. Lawrence.	Saratoga.	Schenectady.	Schoharie.	Schuyler.	Seneca.	Steuben.	Suffolk.	Sullivan.	Tioga.	Tompkins.	Ulster.
Ancram,		4		10						6								
Austerlitz,	2	2		14		1							1	5				
Canaan,	6		1	50				1	1	1					2			4
Chatham,	12		1	248				21	5	12		1		6				7
Claverack,	7	2		29				5		18					2			13
Clermont,				3						2								4
Copake,				4		1	1			1				3				
Gallatin,				4					3									
Germantown,				6						17								6
Ghent,	3			26		2		4	1	1			1					8
Greenport,	1		4	9			1	3		5				1				3
Hillsdale,	4	2	3	14		1		2		9			1	2		1		4
Hudson city:																		
1st ward,	7	2		26				5		4			1				1	6
2d ward,	1			16		1		5	1	5				1			2	19
3d ward,	11	4	1	11				2	8	10			1	9	1		2	11
4th ward,	1	1	1	17				9	2	5								9
Total Hudson,	20	7	2	70		1		21	11	24			2	10	1		5	45
Kinderhook,	4		1	217				13	6	8			2		1			19
Livingston,		1	2	17		1		1	1	9								6
New Lebanon,	9	2	2	202	1	1		9	3	3		1		1			5	1
Stockport,	1	1		52			1	7	1	8								20
Stuyvesant,	9	6		46				7	13	11					1			7
Taghkanic,	4		2	4						1							1	
Total,	82	27	18	1,025	1	8	3	94	45	136		2	7	28	7	1	11	147

CHEMUNG COUNTY.—(Continued.)

TOWNS.	Counties of New-York: Warren.	Washington.	Wayne.	Westchester.	Wyoming.	Yates.	New-York.	United States: Maine.	N. Hampshire.	Vermont.	Massachusetts.	Rhode Island.	Connecticut.	New Jersey.	Pennsylvania.	Delaware.	Maryland.	District of Columbia.
Big Flats,	1	18	1	1		14	1,403	4	8	15	15	1	29	69	106		1	
Catlin,		1	2	7		58	1,284	1	7	7	13	2	43	64	38		1	
Chemung,		5	2	11	1	2	2,239	2	6	44	15	3	41	98	198			
Elmira,	1	25	26	39	17	84	5,285	12	38	94	169	21	220	155	565		32	14
Erin,		2	1	6		3	1,029		2	13	7	4	12	70	31			
Horseheads,	2		2	7		14	2,080	2	2	15	14	3	59	83	102		2	
Southport,	3	6	1	19		24	3,114		9	34	46	19	76	120	411		6	
Van Etten,			1	10		7	1,316		2	8	14	8	23	44	89			
Veteran,	1	17	3	11		17	2,233	4	7	38	36	15	118	102	87			1
Total,	8	74	39	111	18	223	19,983	25	81	268	329	76	621	805	1,627		42	15

CHENANGO COUNTY.—(Continued.)

TOWNS.	Warren.	Washington.	Wayne.	Westchester.	Wyoming.	Yates.	New-York.	Maine.	N. Hampshire.	Vermont.	Massachusetts.	Rhode Island.	Connecticut.	New Jersey.	Pennsylvania.	Delaware.	Maryland.	District of Columbia.
Bainbridge,		8	1	27		5	2,886	2	29	109	62	26	141	7	46			
Columbus,		5					1,099		12	8	56	39	71	6				
Coventry,		5					1,373		7	26	46	3	171		14		3	
German,	5	8	1	1			684		17	7	12	7	40	2	5			
Greene,	1	14	1	25		5	3,106	1	25	49	124	11	193	3	41		2	
Guilford,	3	7	1	12	2		2,124		6	22	51	29	187	2	27		1	
Lincklaen,		5	1				954		5	8	25	43	45	1	7			
Macdonough,							1,159	1	31	16	41	42	78		2			
New Berlin,	2	17		4	1	3	2,088		5	31	75	96	88	8	5		1	1
North Norwich,	1	4	3	1			930	1	1	3	21	7	63	4	1			
Norwich,	2	17	2	1		2	3,047		21	40	102	99	249	17	20		1	
Otsego,		11	1	1			1,448	1	34	29	47	40	78	4	6			
Oxford,	1	10	1	2		1	2,586	1	10	21	70	38	130	11	9			
Pharsalia,		5					948	3	4	7	38	20	99	1	9			
Pitcher,			2				1,042		3	11	27	13	147	1	15			
Plymouth,	1	6		2			1,173	1	3	15	59	57	96	1	16			
Preston,		3		1			798	1	3	16	38	41	93	1	4			
Sherburne,	1	12	2	8			2,141		22	22	107	44	164	7	9			
Smithville,		3	1	3			1,290		7	8	41	16	70	1	7			
Smyrna,		11		1			1,526		7	12	46	102	85	1	4			
Total,	17	151	17	89	3	16	32,402	12	252	460	1,088	773	2,288	78	247		8	1

CLINTON COUNTY.—(Continued.)

TOWNS.	Warren.	Washington.	Wayne.	Westchester.	Wyoming.	Yates.	New-York.	Maine.	N. Hampshire.	Vermont.	Massachusetts.	Rhode Island.	Connecticut.	New Jersey.	Pennsylvania.	Delaware.	Maryland.	District of Columbia.
Au Sable,	8	43		1			2,298	4	46	196	31	4	18	9	5		2	
Beekmantown,	1	14					1,898	1	33	204	40	1	21	3	1			
Black Brook,	25	12					1,628	5	19	140	12		6	6	1		4	
Champlain,	1	32		1			3,214	1	31	256	88	33	29	15	13		1	
Chazy,	13	35		1			2,929	8	35	364	51	4	21	4	6			
Clinton,	4	1					624	14	5	36	3		3					
Dannemora,	1	13					406		7	62	8		5	2	2			
Ellenburgh,		5					1,074	7	29	243	27	2	10		9			
Mooers,	1	15					2,107	3	20	253	36	2	25	1	1			
Peru,	5	24					2,409	3	56	241	38	3	15	2	3		1	
Plattsburgh,	2	58	1	5			3,510	17	61	352	55	6	37	8	9	1		
Saranac,	7	9					1,832	2	41	160	26	3	9	4				
Schuyler Falls,		8					1,293	2	24	154	19	2	21	6	2			
Total,	68	269	1	8			25,222	67	407	2,661	434	60	220	60	52	1	8	

COLUMBIA COUNTY.—(Continued.)

TOWNS.	Warren.	Washington.	Wayne.	Westchester.	Wyoming.	Yates.	New-York.	Maine.	N. Hampshire.	Vermont.	Massachusetts.	Rhode Island.	Connecticut.	New Jersey.	Pennsylvania.	Delaware.	Maryland.	District of Columbia.
Ancram,		1	1				1,623			2	18		31	8	3			
Austerlitz,		4		12			1,330	1	2	3	122	3	50	4	2			
Canaan,	1	4		2			1,410	2	1	15	166	3	71	1	7			
Chatham,	1	9	4	8	1		3,183	3	2	28	126	11	72	7	8		1	
Claverack,		12	1	5		1	2,954		2	5	39	3	39	5	2			1
Clermont,							992					1	1	1	2			
Copake,		1					1,402			8	46		19		2	1	1	
Gallatin,				1			1,466			2	2		4	2	8			
Germantown,			1	7			1,002		1	1	4	5	3	8	2		1	
Ghent,		1	1	5			2,051		1	6	26	10	14	2	5		1	
Greenport,		4	1	1			1,168	1	2	1	16	1	8	7				
Hillsdale,		1	1	2	1	3	1,893	1	1	8	96	1	94		3			
Hudson city:																		
1st ward,		5		1			980	3	2	16	60	6	35	9	8			
2d ward,		2		1			1,143	2	1	7	43	3	18	13	6			
3d ward,		1	3	2		2	1,459	1	8	10	20	7	50	8	35			
4th ward,		1	1	5			1,395	4	2	6	66	5	44	13	7		4	
Total Hudson,		9	4	9		2	4,977	10	13	39	189	21	147	43	56		4	
Kinderhook,	1	4	3	2		1	3,143	6	4	8	69	18	35	9	7			
Livingston,	3	1					1,929				6	1	5	4	4			
New Lebanon,	1	8	2	8			1,579	1	9	31	250	6	74	15	23	1	1	1
Stockport,		5	1	5			1,210	1	2	4	31	11	19	4	1			
Stuyvesant,				7			1,593		4	5	15	8	7	12	4			
Taghkanic,							1,595		1		9	1	4	10	2			
Total,	7	64	20	74	2	7	36,500	26	45	166	1,230	104	697	142	141	2	9	2

CHEMUNG COUNTY.—(Continued.)

TOWNS.	UNITED STATES.																	
	Virginia.	N. Carolina.	S. Carolina.	Georgia.	Florida.	Alabama.	Mississippi.	Louisiana.	Texas.	Arkansas.	Missouri.	Tennessee.	Kentucky.	Ohio.	Indiana.	Illinois.	Michigan.	Wisconsin.
Big Flats,	......	2	......	......	......	......	......	......	......	......	......	......	......	4	2	4	1	.....
Catlin,	......	......	......	......	......	......	......	......	......	......	......	......	......	2	2	4	4	1
Chemung,	1	1	......	......	......	......	......	......	......	......	......	......	......	5	1	1	5	1
Elmira,	27	4	1	......	......	......	......	......	......	......	......	......	2	34	......	6	17	1
Erin,	......	......	......	......	......	......	......	......	......	......	......	......	......	......	......	......	......	......
Horseheads,	1	......	1	......	......	......	......	......	......	......	......	......	1	2	......	1	4	4
Southport,	7	......	......	......	......	......	......	......	......	......	......	......	2	11	......	3	7	1
Van Etten,	......	......	......	......	......	......	......	......	......	......	......	......	......	2	......	......	1	......
Veteran,	1	......	......	......	......	......	......	......	......	......	......	......	......	6	......	......	11	......
Total,	37	7	2	......	......	......	......	......	......	......	......	......	5	66	5	19	50	8

CHENANGO COUNTY.—(Continued.)

TOWNS.	Virginia.	N. Carolina.	S. Carolina.	Georgia.	Florida.	Alabama.	Mississippi.	Louisiana.	Texas.	Arkansas.	Missouri.	Tennessee.	Kentucky.	Ohio.	Indiana.	Illinois.	Michigan.	Wisconsin.
Bainbridge,	1	......	......	......	......	......	......	1	......	......	......	2	......	6	2	3	2	.....
Columbus,	......	......	......	......	......	......	......	......	......	......	......	......	......	......	......	......	1	.....
Coventry,	2	......	......	......	......	......	......	......	......	......	......	......	......	2	......	1	......	......
German,	......	......	......	......	......	......	......	......	......	......	......	......	......	1	......	......	2	......
Greene,	......	......	......	1	......	......	......	......	......	......	......	......	......	1	......	......	2	......
Guilford,	......	......	......	......	......	......	......	......	......	......	......	......	1	5	......	......	3	......
Lincklaen,	......	......	......	......	......	......	......	......	......	......	......	......	......	......	......	......	......	......
Macdonough,	......	......	......	......	......	......	......	......	......	......	......	......	......	1	......	1	3	1
New Berlin,	......	......	......	......	......	......	......	......	......	......	......	......	......	2	......	1	......	......
North Norwich,	......	......	......	......	......	......	......	......	......	......	......	......	......	3	......	2	1	1
Norwich,	3	1	......	......	......	......	......	......	......	......	......	......	......	5	......	......	3	......
Otselic,	......	......	......	......	......	......	......	......	......	......	......	......	......	1	......	1	3	......
Oxford,	......	......	......	......	......	......	1	......	......	......	......	......	......	5	......	2	......	1
Pharsalia,	......	......	......	......	......	......	......	......	......	......	......	......	......	......	......	......	......	......
Pitcher,	......	......	1	......	......	......	......	......	......	......	......	......	......	......	......	3	1	......
Plymouth,	......	......	......	......	......	......	......	1	......	......	......	......	......	1	......	1	......	3
Preston,	......	......	......	......	......	......	......	......	......	......	......	......	......	......	......	1	......	1
Sherburne,	......	5	......	......	......	......	......	......	......	......	......	......	......	1	......	4	2	3
Smithville,	......	......	......	......	......	......	......	......	......	......	......	......	......	2	......	1	......	......
Smyrna,	......	......	......	......	......	......	......	......	......	......	......	......	......	6	......	......	......	......
Total,	6	6	1	1	......	......	1	2	......	......	......	2	1	42	2	21	23	10

CLINTON COUNTY.—(Continued.)

TOWNS.	Virginia.	N. Carolina.	S. Carolina.	Georgia.	Florida.	Alabama.	Mississippi.	Louisiana.	Texas.	Arkansas.	Missouri.	Tennessee.	Kentucky.	Ohio.	Indiana.	Illinois.	Michigan.	Wisconsin.
Au Sable,	......	......	......	......	......	......	......	......	......	......	......	......	3	1	......	......	2	2
Beekmantown,	2	2	......	......	......	......	......	......	......	......	......	......	......	......	......	......	2	2
Black Brook,	......	......	1	......	......	......	......	......	......	......	......	......	......	1	......	......	1	3
Champlain,	......	......	......	1	......	......	......	......	......	......	......	......	......	4	1	4	......	......
Chazy,	1	......	......	......	......	......	5	......	......	......	......	......	......	1	......	......	......	1
Clinton,	......	......	......	......	......	......	......	......	......	......	......	......	......	......	......	......	......	......
Dannemora,	6	......	......	......	......	......	......	......	......	......	......	1	1	4	......	......	......	......
Ellenburgh,	......	......	......	......	......	......	......	......	......	......	......	......	......	2	......	1	......	......
Mooers,	......	......	......	......	......	......	......	......	......	......	......	......	......	1	......	2	1	1
Peru,	1	......	......	......	......	......	......	......	......	......	......	......	......	1	......	......	3	......
Plattsburgh,	2	......	......	......	......	......	1	......	......	......	1	......	......	5	......	1	4	2
Saranac,	......	......	......	......	......	......	......	......	......	......	......	......	......	......	......	......	......	......
Schuyler Falls,	......	......	......	......	......	......	......	......	......	......	......	......	......	1	......	1	1	......
Total,	12	2	1	1	......	......	6	......	......	......	1	1	4	21	1	9	14	11

COLUMBIA COUNTY.—(Continued.)

TOWNS.	Virginia.	N. Carolina.	S. Carolina.	Georgia.	Florida.	Alabama.	Mississippi.	Louisiana.	Texas.	Arkansas.	Missouri.	Tennessee.	Kentucky.	Ohio.	Indiana.	Illinois.	Michigan.	Wisconsin.
Ancram,	......	......	......	......	......	......	......	......	......	......	......	......	......	......	......	......	......	......
Austerlitz,	......	......	......	......	......	......	......	......	......	......	......	......	......	2	......	1	......	......
Canaan,	......	......	2	......	......	......	......	4	......	......	......	......	......	......	......	......	1	......
Chatham,	1	......	......	......	......	......	5	......	......	......	1	......	......	......	......	......	1	2
Claverack,	1	......	......	......	......	......	......	......	......	......	......	......	......	1	......	......	......	......
Clermont,	......	......	1	......	......	......	......	1	......	......	......	......	......	......	......	......	......	......
Copake,	......	......	......	......	......	......	......	......	......	......	......	......	......	......	......	......	......	......
Gallatin,	1	......	......	......	......	......	......	......	......	......	......	......	......	1	......	......	......	......
Germantown,	......	......	......	......	......	......	......	......	......	......	......	......	......	......	......	1	......	......
Ghent,	......	......	1	......	......	......	......	......	......	......	......	......	......	1	......	......	......	1
Greenport,	......	......	......	......	......	......	......	1	......	......	......	......	......	2	......	......	......	......
Hillsdale,	1	......	1	......	......	......	......	......	......	......	......	......	......	3	......	......	......	1
Hudson City:																		
1st ward,	1	......	1	......	......	......	......	......	......	......	......	......	......	1	......	......	......	......
2d ward,	1	......	......	......	......	......	......	......	......	......	......	......	......	1	......	......	......	......
3d ward,	1	......	......	......	......	......	......	......	......	......	......	......	......	......	......	......	......	......
4th ward,	3	......	......	......	......	......	......	......	......	......	......	......	......	......	......	......	2	......
Total Hudson,	6	......	1	......	......	......	......	......	......	......	......	......	......	2	......	......	2	......
Kinderhook,	......	......	......	......	......	......	......	......	......	......	......	......	......	......	......	......	......	......
Livingston,	1	......	......	......	......	......	......	1	......	......	......	......	......	2	......	......	......	......
New Lebanon,	......	......	2	......	......	......	......	......	......	......	......	......	2	9	1	2	......	......
Stockport,	......	......	......	......	......	1	......	1	......	......	......	......	......	......	......	1	......	1
Stuyvesant,	1	......	......	1	......	......	......	......	......	......	......	......	......	......	......	......	......	......
Taghkanick,	......	......	......	......	......	......	......	......	......	......	......	......	......	......	......	......	......	......
Total,	12	......	8	1	......	1	5	8	......	......	1	......	2	23	1	5	4	5

CHEMUNG COUNTY.—(CONTINUED.)

TOWNS.	U. STATES. Iowa.	California.	Territories.	Total United States.	FOREIGN COUNTRIES. Canada.	N. Brunswick.	Nova Scotia.	N. Foundland.	West Indies.	Mexico.	S. America.	England.	Scotland.	Ireland.	Wales.	France.	Belgium.	Holland.
Big Flats,				1, 664	8							31		67	2	1		
Catlin,				1, 473	1							21		15				
Chemung,				2, 661	1		1					35	1	52				
Elmira,	4			6, 701	29		2	2	3			163	46	1, 192	9	26		
Erin,				1, 168								1	7	2				
Horseheads,				2, 376	6							48	11	154	6	1		
Southport,				3, 866	9		1					85	14	370	1			
Van Etten,				1, 507	3							1	2	6				
Veteran,				2, 659	18							20	3	69		1		
Total,	4			24, 075	75		4	2	3			405	84	1, 927	18	29		

CHENANGO COUNTY.—(CONTINUED.)

TOWNS.	Iowa.	California.	Territories.	Total United States.	Canada.	N. Brunswick.	Nova Scotia.	N. Foundland.	West Indies.	Mexico.	S. America.	England.	Scotland.	Ireland.	Wales.	France.	Belgium.	Holland.
Bainbridge,		1		3, 326			2					16	2	18				
Columbus,				1, 292								12		19				
Coventry,				1, 648	1							11		15				
German,				777								1		24				
Greene,				3, 559	2							18	13	119				
Guilford,				2, 458	1							38	7	5		1		
Lincklaen,				1, 088	1							25		12				
Macdonough,				1, 376								17		18				
New Berlin,				2, 401	4				1			42	6	35	1			
North Norwich,				1, 038	1							8	1	26				
Norwich,				3, 608	6		1					57	3	157		2		
Otselic,				1, 692	3							19	2	3		1		
Oxford,				2, 885	3				1			51	1	112		1		
Pharsalia,				1, 120								7		12				
Pitcher,				1, 264	1							10		6				
Plymouth,				1, 427								6	1	16	3			
Preston,				997	3		1					7		20	1	6		
Sherburne,				2, 531	4							27	4	183		2		
Smithville,				1, 443								13	2	198				
Smyrna,				1, 789	3							32	3	19	2			
Total,		1		37, 728	33		4		2			417	45	1, 017	7	13		

CLINTON COUNTY.—(CONTINUED.)

TOWNS.	Iowa.	California.	Territories.	Total United States.	Canada.	N. Brunswick.	Nova Scotia.	N. Foundland.	West Indies.	Mexico.	S. America.	England.	Scotland.	Ireland.	Wales.	France.	Belgium.	Holland.
Au Sable,				2, 621	661		1					43	7	455	6	6		
Beekmantown,				2, 210	282							11	10	419		1		
Black Brook,				1, 827	643		1		1			37	12	497		3		
Champlain,				3, 691	1, 951	1	2					107	42	335		3	1	
Chazy,				3, 430	782	2	1					44	7	176				
Clinton,				685	373							14	3	296				
Dannemora,				504	110							18	2	67		3		
Ellenburgh,				1, 404	208		1					4	29	103				
Mooers,				2, 453	738							41	40	339		1		
Peru,				2, 776	399		1	3				40	8	287		1		
Plattsburgh,				4. 075	1, 250		5					62	7	565		7		
Saranac,				2, 077	570							41	6	350		1		
Schuyler Falls,				1, 526	197							18	1	185		1		
Total,				29, 979	8, 164	3	12	3	1			480	171	4, 074	6	27	1	

COLUMBIA COUNTY.—(CONTINUED.)

TOWNS.	Iowa.	California.	Territories.	Total United States.	Canada.	N. Brunswick.	Nova Scotia.	N. Foundland.	West Indies.	Mexico.	S. America.	England.	Scotland.	Ireland.	Wales.	France.	Belgium.	Holland.
Ancram,				1, 685	1							3	4	94		5		
Austerlitz,				1, 520	5				2			4		80				
Canaan,				1, 683	49							25	2	135	1			
Chatham,				3, 451	9				1			47	2	405		2		
Claverack,				3, 052	7				4		1	16	1	172		2		
Clermont,				999								5		35				
Copake,				1, 479								1	2	91				
Gallatin,				1, 486								1		14				
Germantown,				1, 028								7	1	36				
Ghent,				2, 119					3			13	2	252		2		
Greenport,			1	1, 208								22	14	123				
Hillsdale,				2, 103	2							14	1	58				
Hudson city:																		
1st ward,				1, 122	9				6			14	6	264	8	2		
2d ward,				1, 238	13							50	3	321		2		
3d ward,				1, 599	4		1		1			30	3	73	1	2		1
4th ward,				1, 551	7				1				2	235	1	6		
Total Hudson,				5, 510	33		1		8			94	14	893	10	12		1
Kinderhook,				3, 299	5							110	23	307		2		
Livingston,				1, 953								19	3	39		1		
New Lebanon,				2, 007	7		5	1				53	6	225				
Stockport,				1, 287	5							139	17	128		3		
Stuyvesant,				1, 650	4							47	14	177				
Taghkanick,				1, 622								2		21				
Total,			1	39, 141	127		6	1	18		1	622	106	3, 285	11	29		1

CHEMUNG COUNTY.—(Continued.)

TOWNS.	FOREIGN COUNTRIES.																		
	Germany.	Prussia.	Austria.	Switzerland.	Italy.	Spain.	Portugal.	Poland.	Norway.	Sweden.	Russia.	Denmark.	East Indies.	Africa.	Turkey and Greece.	Islands.	Asia.	At Sea.	Unknown.
Big Flats,	49																		31
Catlin,																			8
Chemung,	1									2									31
Elmira,	136	6						20	4	2							1	2	142
Erin,																			12
Horseheads,	1																		45
Southport,	86			3															44
Van Etten,	1																		2
Veteran,	13			2															22
Total,	287	6		5				20	4	4							1	2	337

CHENANGO COUNTY.—(Continued.)

TOWNS.	Germany.	Prussia.	Austria.	Switzerland.	Italy.	Spain.	Portugal.	Poland.	Norway.	Sweden.	Russia.	Denmark.	East Indies.	Africa.	Turkey and Greece.	Islands.	Asia.	At Sea.	Unknown.
Bainbridge,	13																		
Columbus,	8																		
Coventry,	9																		
German,	1																		3
Greene,	2							1											3
Guilford,	38																		4
Lincklaen,																			5
Macdonough,	5																		1
New Berlin,	2			1															14
North Norwich,	3			1															48
Norwich,	64																2		209
Otselic,																			1
Oxford,	22			4															36
Pharsalia,	4																		
Pitcher,																			
Plymouth,																			88
Preston,	8			1															
Sherburne,	14										2								9
Smithville,	2																	1	2
Smyrna,	1																		17
Total,	196			7				1			2						2	1	440

CLINTON COUNTY.—(Continued.)

TOWNS.	Germany.	Prussia.	Austria.	Switzerland.	Italy.	Spain.	Portugal.	Poland.	Norway.	Sweden.	Russia.	Denmark.	East Indies.	Africa.	Turkey and Greece.	Islands.	Asia.	At Sea.	Unknown.
Au Sable,																			3
Beekmantown,																			
Black Brook,	1																		3
Champlain,	1									1									62
Chazy,																	1		19
Clinton,																			
Dannemora,	16	1	1					1											
Ellenburgh,																		1	1
Mooers,	8																	1	1
Peru,	1	1	1																2
Plattsburgh,	25										4					4			80
Saranac,	5																	3	5
Schuyler Falls,																		3	6
Total,	57	2	2					1		1	4					4	1	8	182

COLUMBIA COUNTY.—(Continued.)

TOWNS.	Germany.	Prussia.	Austria.	Switzerland.	Italy.	Spain.	Portugal.	Poland.	Norway.	Sweden.	Russia.	Denmark.	East Indies.	Africa.	Turkey and Greece.	Islands.	Asia.	At Sea.	Unknown.
Ancram,	9																		
Austerlitz,	6			1															
Canaan,	51																		
Chatham,	99									1									6
Claverack,	107																		1
Clermont,	15					1													3
Copake,	39																		8
Gallatin,	10																		6
Germantown,	34			1															24
Ghent,	145									1									
Greenport,	16																		
Hillsdale,	13	1		1				1											
Hudson city:																			
1st ward,	17																		12
2d ward,	36													1					11
3d ward,	32	10		6				1											
4th ward,	18																		
Total Hudson,	103	10		6				1						1					23
Kinderhook,	116	1		1															
Livingston,	46	1		2															
New Lebanon,	4																		21
Stockport,	40																	1	1
Stuyvesant,	35			8													2		
Taghkanic,	19			1															
Total,	907	13		21		1		2		2				1			2	1	93

CORTLAND COUNTY.

TOWNS.	Albany.	Allegany.	Broome.	Cattaraugus.	Cayuga.	Chautauque.	Chemung.	Chenango.	Clinton.	Columbia.	Cortland.	Delaware.	Dutchess.	Erie.	Essex.	Franklin.	Fulton.	Genesee.
	COUNTIES OF NEW-YORK.																	
Cincinnatus,	7		11	1	2			99			631	11	15	1			1	
Cortlandville,	14	8	32	2	76		9	70		27	2, 219	50	27	6	4			4
Freetown,	19	1	10		3			25		4	546		8	8				
Harford,	4	1	29		16	1		19		32	436	2	7			1		4
Homer,	19	3	15	3	137	4	3	54		6	1, 872	5	27	1			2	2
Lapeer,	6		32	3			1	15		8	439	14	5					
Marathon,	2	1	108	1		1		54		19	646		7					1
Preble,	13	4	2	1	17	1		12		20	591	24	11	4			2	
Scott,	6	7	5	2	69			11		7	674	1	10	1				
Solon,	2		8		4			53	1	4	600	8	8					
Taylor,	5		5		6	1		135			608	32	4					
Truxton,	7	10	8	2	21	7		124		31	1, 749	5	19	6				4
Virgil,	17	2	11	1	28			10		18	1, 365	33	19	1	1	1		
Willet,	2	1	73		5	1		135			443	13	9					
Total,	123	38	349	16	384	16	13	816	1	176	12, 819	198	176	28	5	2	5	15

DELAWARE COUNTY.

TOWNS.	Albany.	Allegany.	Broome.	Cattaraugus.	Cayuga.	Chautauque.	Chemung.	Chenango.	Clinton.	Columbia.	Cortland.	Delaware.	Dutchess.	Erie.	Essex.	Franklin.	Fulton.	Genesee.
Andes,	11		2					1		7		1, 795	48					
Bovina,	4		2		1			1				921	9					
Colchester,	9		2		2			3		6	2	1, 761	47					
Davenport,	55			2	1			1	3	29		1, 365	19	1				
Delhi,	14		5	1	1	1		7		21		1, 874	43		1			1
Franklin,	42		4		3	1		29	1	61	3	2, 059	15		4		1	
Hamden,	11	1	2	2				5	1	15	2	1, 298	22					
Hancock,	26	1	19	1		1		4		5	1	1, 374	21					
Harpersfield,	17		2	1	13			5		8		926	14					
Kortright,	11								1	7		1, 523	39					1
Masonville,	38		20	1	1			77	2	8	11	862	18				2	
Meredith,	12	2	1				2	3		22	1	1, 077	18					1
Middletown,	37		1					2		7		2, 062	98	2	1			1
Roxbury,	18	1				1		3		18	2	1, 803	66					1
Sidney,	16	1	18					41		12	3	1, 091	16	1				1
Stamford,	2									4		1, 345	9					
Tompkins,	55		88	2	1	1		42		23	6	2, 107	41	7	1			1
Walton,	3	3	3		1	2	1	8	2	22		1, 741	20		1			1
Total,	381	9	169	10	24	7	3	232	10	275	31	26, 984	563	11	8		3	8

DUTCHESS COUNTY.

TOWNS.	Albany.	Allegany.	Broome.	Cattaraugus.	Cayuga.	Chautauque.	Chemung.	Chenango.	Clinton.	Columbia.	Cortland.	Delaware.	Dutchess.	Erie.	Essex.	Franklin.	Fulton.	Genesee.
Amenia,	2	1	2					2		38	1	1	1, 404		2		1	1
Beekman,	2				3			1		6		5	1, 048	1	1		1	
Clinton,			2		1			1		24		5	1, 569					
Dover,	5								1	25		1	1, 437					
East Fishkill,	1									4		3	1, 833		1			
Fishkill,	24			1	2		3	5		42		7	4, 974	2	1			1
Hyde Park,	8		2		1			1	1	15	2	4	1, 421					
La Grange,			1			1				2		1	1, 581	1				
Milan,	5		6							213		1	1, 248					
North East,	3		1		1	1		6		191			1, 055	1				
Pauling,	1				2					10		1	1, 439				1	1
Pine Plains,	3				2			1		224	1		960					
Pleasant Valley,										4	2	2	1, 542	3				
Poughkeepsie,	12				1	1				11		1	1, 885	1				
Poughkeepsie city:																		
1st ward,	23		1	1				1		28		6	2, 001		1		1	1
2d ward,	7				2					32		5	1, 671			1		
3d ward,	9				1					10		4	2, 001					
4th ward,	26				2	1				9	1		1, 427					
Total Poughk'e,	65		1	1	5	1		1		79	1	15	7, 100		1	1	1	1
Redhook,	10								1	332	2	5	2, 409		1			
Rhinebeck,	10		1		2					77		4	2, 199		1			1
Stanford,	12		1					1		79		6	1, 723					
Union Vale,	1							2		4	1	1	1, 220				1	
Washington,	3		1	1	1	1				13			2, 264					
Total,	167	1	18	3	21	5	3	21	3	1, 393	10	63	40, 311	9	8	1	5	5

ERIE COUNTY.

TOWNS.	Albany.	Allegany.	Broome.	Cattaraugus.	Cayuga.	Chautauque.	Chemung.	Chenango.	Clinton.	Columbia.	Cortland.	Delaware.	Dutchess.	Erie.	Essex.	Franklin.	Fulton.	Genesee.
Alden,	9	3		5	6	11		4		8	6	3	17	837	3			117
Amherst,	10	1		1	13	14	1		11	1	1	1	1	2, 265		1		9
Aurora,	11	12	2	45	45	12	1	9	2	6	6	8	19	1, 707	7			56
Boston,	2	5		3	3	2		1	1	7	2		12	972	2			4
Brandt,	17	2		5	14	40		5	3	2	4	5	8	538	1			6
Buffalo city:																		
1st ward,	39	8	2	29	11	24		9	3	2	3	4	10	2, 008	4			18
2d ward,	99	1	4	16	34	64		14	7	20	4	4	13	1, 479	4	1	3	61
3d ward,	47	2	3	10	16	11	1	9	9	6	4	4	17	1, 252	2	1	1	24
4th ward,	47	5		11	21	17		11	8	14	5	4	10	2, 522		1	3	38
5th ward,										5				1, 433				31
6th ward,	15	1		2	2	1								5, 861				13
7th ward,	8		1		10	6			2	5	1	1	10	2, 315	3			7
8th ward,	24	2		1	8	9		3	3	1		3	3	1, 310	1	2		10
9th ward,	51	3	2	15	44	31		9	3	19	5	9	23	1, 643		2		59

(Continued on page 84.)

CORTLAND COUNTY.—(Continued.)

Towns.	Counties of New-York.																	
	Greene.	Hamilton.	Herkimer.	Jefferson.	Kings.	Lewis.	Livingston.	Madison.	Monroe.	Montgomery.	New York.	Niagara.	Oneida.	Onondaga.	Ontario.	Orange.	Orleans.	Oswego.
Cincinnatus,	1	.....	3	1	2	2	.....	10	1	4	10	.....	10	2	2	8	.....	.....
Cortlandville,	37	1	40	11	2	3	5	72	11	37	23	1	55	85	5	45	2	3
Freetown,	11	.....	33	.....	1	.....	.....	8	1	11	2	1	26	8	1	17	.....	.....
Harford,	3	.....	12	.....	.....	.....	.....	6	.....	8	.....	.....	6	10	.....	3	.....	.....
Homer,	14	.....	47	10	2	2	4	62	11	25	14	2	42	138	8	20	2	7
Lapeer,	1	.....	8	1	5	.....	.....	5	2	7	.....	3	1	3	.....	9	.....	4
Marathon,	7	.....	4	.....	.....	1	1	8	.....	14	12	.....	17	21	2	27	.....	1
Preble,	72	.....	20	2	.....	5	.....	7	.....	16	.....	.....	10	110	1	7	.....	1
Scott,	7	.....	4	5	1	1	1	31	1	6	2	.....	7	105	1	2	.....	2
Solon,	1	.....	20	.....	1	.....	.....	21	.....	3	18	.....	9	12	.....	2	.....	1
Taylor,	4	.....	10	5	.....	.....	4	23	4	5	3	.....	3	13	.....	7	.....	2
Truxton,	1	.....	51	8	1	3	.....	136	1	14	13	1	33	217	1	3	1	6
Virgil,	14	.....	11	4	1	.....	1	22	1	38	2	.....	17	21	1	43	.....	6
Willet,	3	.....	1	3	.....	.....	.....	14	.....	2	6	.....	15	7	1	4	.....	.....
Total,	176	1	264	50	16	17	16	425	33	190	105	8	251	752	23	197	5	33

DELAWARE COUNTY.—(Continued.)

Towns.	Greene.	Hamilton.	Herkimer.	Jefferson.	Kings.	Lewis.	Livingston.	Madison.	Monroe.	Montgomery.	New York.	Niagara.	Oneida.	Onondaga.	Ontario.	Orange.	Orleans.	Oswego.
Andes,	18	.....	1	.....	2	.....	1	.....	1	.....	17	.....	.....	.....	.....	2	.....	.....
Bovina,	3	.....	.....	.....	.....	.....	.....	.....	.....	.....	13	1	.....	.....	.....	.....	.....	.....
Colchester,	36	.....	1	3	.....	.....	.....	.....	.....	1	24	.....	.....	1	.....	3	.....	.....
Davenport,	57	.....	1	.....	.....	1	.....	1	2	3	5	.....	2	.....	.....	1	.....	.....
Delhi,	33	.....	1	.....	2	.....	1	.....	.....	1	30	.....	5	1	1	7	.....	.....
Franklin,	42	.....	3	1	.....	2	.....	1	3	4	6	.....	5	1	1	2	1	2
Hamden,	26	.....	.....	2	.....	.....	.....	1	1	4	.....	.....	1	.....	.....	1	.....	.....
Hancock,	36	.....	.....	.....	1	.....	.....	2	.....	.....	53	.....	1	1	1	52	.....	1
Harpersfield,	33	.....	.....	.....	.....	.....	.....	2	.....	2	12	.....	2	1	1	.....	.....	.....
Kortright,	9	.....	.....	.....	.....	.....	.....	.....	.....	2	15	.....	1	.....	.....	9	.....	.....
Masonville,	48	.....	2	1	1	.....	.....	1	.....	6	.....	.....	2	4	3	2	.....	.....
Meredith,	10	.....	.....	.....	2	.....	.....	1	1	2	10	.....	1	.....	1	.....	.....	.....
Middletown,	146	.....	3	.....	.....	1	.....	.....	.....	.....	23	.....	3	1	.....	4	.....	.....
Roxbury,	159	.....	.....	.....	2	.....	.....	.....	.....	.....	8	.....	2	.....	1	2	.....	.....
Sidney,	35	.....	4	.....	1	.....	.....	6	.....	2	9	.....	13	1	.....	2	.....	.....
Stamford,	28	.....	.....	.....	.....	.....	.....	.....	.....	1	8	.....	.....	.....	.....	3	.....	.....
Tompkins,	66	.....	5	.....	.....	1	.....	3	.....	1	15	1	1	2	.....	29	.....	2
Walton,	28	.....	.....	.....	3	.....	.....	1	.....	.....	17	.....	2	.....	.....	4	.....	.....
Total,	813	.....	21	7	14	5	2	19	8	29	265	2	41	13	9	123	1	5

DUTCHESS COUNTY.—(Continued.)

Towns.	Greene.	Hamilton.	Herkimer.	Jefferson.	Kings.	Lewis.	Livingston.	Madison.	Monroe.	Montgomery.	New York.	Niagara.	Oneida.	Onondaga.	Ontario.	Orange.	Orleans.	Oswego.
Amenia,	5	1	1	1	.....	.....	.....	1	1	1	35	.....	1	.....	.....	5	.....	.....
Beekman,	3	.....	.....	2	.....	.....	.....	.....	.....	1	15	.....	2	.....	.....	4	.....	.....
Clinton,	7	.....	.....	.....	2	.....	.....	.....	.....	.....	5	1	.....	.....	.....	2	.....	.....
Dover,	3	.....	.....	.....	4	2	1	.....	1	.....	45	.....	1	.....	.....	7	.....	.....
East Fishkill,	4	.....	1	.....	5	.....	.....	.....	2	.....	24	.....	1	1	1	19	.....	.....
Fishkill,	23	.....	3	1	50	.....	.....	.....	2	1	288	.....	5	2	3	340	1	3
Hyde Park,	17	.....	.....	.....	12	.....	.....	.....	.....	.....	101	.....	1	1	.....	7	.....	1
La Grange,	3	.....	1	.....	6	.....	.....	.....	.....	.....	7	.....	1	.....	.....	2	1	.....
Milan,	6	.....	.....	3	3	.....	.....	.....	.....	2	26	.....	.....	.....	.....	1	.....	.....
North East,	3	.....	.....	2	.....	1	.....	.....	.....	.....	16	.....	.....	.....	1	4	.....	.....
Pauling,	.....	.....	.....	.....	4	1	.....	.....	.....	.....	22	.....	2	.....	.....	5	.....	4
Pine Plains,	18	.....	.....	.....	4	.....	.....	.....	1	.....	14	.....	1	1	.....	1	1	.....
Pleasant Valley,	18	.....	.....	.....	.....	.....	.....	.....	3	1	5	1	.....	.....	.....	4	.....	.....
Poughkeepsie,	6	.....	.....	.....	8	.....	.....	.....	.....	2	96	.....	4	.....	.....	26	.....	.....
Poughkeepsie city:																		
1st ward,	23	3	2	.....	24	2	.....	1	.....	.....	135	.....	5	.....	1	37	2	.....
2d ward,	18	.....	1	.....	15	.....	.....	.....	4	5	82	.....	5	1	.....	14	1	.....
3d ward,	44	3	1	.....	28	.....	.....	.....	.....	.....	41	.....	4	.....	.....	26	.....	.....
4th ward,	11	.....	1	3	10	.....	4	.....	4	1	121	.....	6	1	4	26	.....	.....
Total Po'keepsie,	96	6	5	3	77	2	4	1	8	6	379	.....	20	2	5	103	3	.....
Redhook,	21	.....	2	.....	25	.....	.....	1	1	1	94	.....	1	1	3	15	.....	1
Rhinebeck,	14	.....	.....	.....	6	.....	.....	8	.....	2	91	.....	2	2	2	11	.....	2
Stanford,	14	.....	.....	.....	.....	.....	.....	1	.....	.....	23	.....	.....	.....	.....	2	1	.....
Union Vale,	8	.....	.....	.....	2	.....	.....	.....	1	.....	16	.....	4	.....	.....	8	.....	.....
Washington,	3	.....	.....	.....	3	.....	.....	.....	2	1	16	.....	.....	2	.....	2	.....	1
Total,	272	7	13	12	211	6	5	12	22	18	1,318	2	45	12	15	568	7	12

ERIE COUNTY.—(Continued.)

Towns.	Greene.	Hamilton.	Herkimer.	Jefferson.	Kings.	Lewis.	Livingston.	Madison.	Monroe.	Montgomery.	New York.	Niagara.	Oneida.	Onondaga.	Ontario.	Orange.	Orleans.	Oswego.
Alden,	4	.....	12	3	2	3	9	17	14	3	14	15	15	11	7	8	11	.....
Amherst,	1	.....	6	6	1	2	6	21	13	5	14	70	11	3	7	.....	7	1
Aurora,	4	.....	15	5	3	2	6	24	18	29	5	5	65	14	20	4	7	3
Boston,	2	.....	5	4	1	.....	2	9	5	9	1	1	7	4	5	2	.....	1
Brandt,	3	.....	2	3	.....	.....	.....	6	1	4	.....	6	9	5	5	1	2	.....
Buffalo city:																		
1st ward,	3	1	25	14	9	.....	8	3	72	11	84	30	21	23	12	10	12	29
2d ward,	16	.....	38	23	13	2	26	19	132	46	154	55	73	52	39	21	18	12
3d ward,	8	2	10	14	.....	.....	14	11	54	18	81	19	26	27	10	8	12	28
4th ward,	2	1	15	8	2	.....	15	11	50	15	168	20	43	30	21	5	9	5
5th ward,	1	.....	.....	2	.....	.....	.....	.....	12	.....	87	.....	.....	.....	.....	.....	.....	1
6th ward,	.....	.....	.....	1	1	.....	4	.....	6	1	20	3	3	5	5	1	4	1
7th ward,	.....	.....	7	3	.....	.....	.....	.....	27	5	30	13	5	7	3	.....	.....	3
8th ward,	7	.....	15	5	8	.....	8	2	51	8	61	16	15	21	1	5	1	5
9th ward,	12	1	41	23	13	3	22	12	88	38	137	37	70	44	54	8	16	23

(Continued on page 85.)

CORTLAND COUNTY.—(Continued.)

TOWNS	COUNTIES OF NEW-YORK. Otsego.	Putnam.	Queens.	Rensselaer.	Richmond.	Rockland.	St. Lawrence	Saratoga.	Schenectady.	Schoharie.	Schuyler.	Seneca.	Steuben.	Suffolk.	Sullivan.	Tioga.	Tompkins.	Ulster.
Cincinnatus,	46			1				9		23			2				13	1
Cortlandville,	95	1		38				19	2	35		4	4	4	3	18	107	8
Freetown,	31			2		1	1	5		23		1		4		3	13	
Harford,	25			4		2	1	11	4	10		1	4	3	1	44	71	5
Homer,	79			20		3	4	16	14	21	1	1	4	1	4	4	71	16
Lapeer,	21			1		9		1	7				1	1	6	8	10	1
Marathon,	25	2		9				4	2	25		1	5	12		11	12	3
Preble,	7		3	8		1		4	5	9		1				4	6	7
Scott,	12			18		1		12		4			1		4	2	9	3
Solon,	25			11				1		18				1		1	1	1
Taylor,	78	4	1	4				11	1	1		1	4	1			6	9
Truxton,	53	3	2	47		15		12	10	3		6	2	2	9	16	3	5
Virgil,	47	1		11				6	1	7		4	8	6	22	17	94	30
Willet,	30	1		5		4	1	3		12		1	4			1		
Total,	574	12	6	179		36	7	114	46	191	1	21	39	35	49	129	416	89

DELAWARE COUNTY.—(Continued.)

TOWNS	Otsego.	Putnam.	Queens.	Rensselaer.	Richmond.	Rockland.	St. Lawrence	Saratoga.	Schenectady.	Schoharie.	Schuyler.	Seneca.	Steuben.	Suffolk.	Sullivan.	Tioga.	Tompkins.	Ulster.
Andes,	3	2		1				2	4	26			1		25			56
Bovina,	2	2						2						1	3			
Colchester,	17	23		3				1	1	16					84	2	1	37
Davenport,	202	1	5	1				2	4	88								2
Delhi,	26	2		3				2		30				3	3		1	8
Franklin,	177			10	1	1	1	11	7	62		1	2	12	1	1	5	6
Hamden,	20			5					9	38			1	1	11	1	2	8
Hancock,	31	3		1						94					65			26
Harpersfield,	50			2				2	3	194		1		1				6
Kortright,	20			6		1		1	2	20				2				6
Masonville,	119			6				20	11	45		1	10		4	2	3	8
Meredith,	32			4				3		12						1	1	8
Middletown,	6	9		9	1			3		64					6		4	158
Roxbury,	8	21		3				1		126		1		1	1		2	29
Sidney,	196			3				5		41					4	2	1	4
Stamford,	1			3				1		27			1	1				3
Tompkins,	149		7	5		6		16	2	59			1		14	1	3	33
Walton,	43	7	3	7		1	8	9	9	26			3	3	7	4	4	36
Total,	1, 102	70	15	72	2	9	9	81	52	968		4	19	25	228	14	27	434

DUTCHESS COUNTY.—(Continued.)

TOWNS	Otsego.	Putnam.	Queens.	Rensselaer.	Richmond.	Rockland.	St. Lawrence	Saratoga.	Schenectady.	Schoharie.	Schuyler.	Seneca.	Steuben.	Suffolk.	Sullivan.	Tioga.	Tompkins.	Ulster.
Amenia,	3	4	1	3			1	10		1					1		3	13
Beekman,	49	2	2					1		4		1		6	1		1	13
Clinton,		3	1	5				1	1	1				3				36
Dover,	1	11		1		1		1						1				3
East Fishkill,		304	1	1				3							7		1	35
Fishkill,	7	440	23	31	1	38	3	9		1		1	5	5	21			177
Hyde Park,	3	17	6	17				4	3	2							1	63
La Grange,	2	15	5	1		1		1				3	1	1	2			5
Milan,	2	1		10				6		1				2		2		9
North East,	1	13						5		5					2			3
Pawling,	3	116	2	8										1			1	9
Pine Plains,	1		1					10		9			1					13
Pleasant Valley,	2	12	1	1				3						1	1			30
Poughkeepsie,	4	26	6	5		4		5	3	3				2	2		1	84
Poughkeepsie city,																		
1st ward,	1	24	6	24		1		14	13	6				4	12		2	169
2d ward,	2	8	1	12		8		4	5	3			1		8			68
3d ward,		7		2		2		7		2					4		1	126
4th ward,	2	13	6	5				13	6	1				1	4			111
Total Poughk'e,	5	52	13	43		11		38	24	12			1	5	28		3	474
Red Hook,	4	1	2	7	1	1	2	5	1	9						1	1	32
Rhinebeck,	2	4	3	4		6		1	4	7					1	1		67
Stanford,		21	2	8		1		4		1								15
Union Vale,		9		1				6		1		1			2			9
Washington,	6	5	7	5		1		3						5				11
Total,	95	1, 056	76	151	2	64	6	116	36	57		6	8	32	68	4	12	1, 101

ERIE COUNTY.—(Continued.)

TOWNS	Otsego.	Putnam.	Queens.	Rensselaer.	Richmond.	Rockland.	St. Lawrence	Saratoga.	Schenectady.	Schoharie.	Schuyler.	Seneca.	Steuben.	Suffolk.	Sullivan.	Tioga.	Tompkins.	Ulster.
Alden,	10	1		10			2	5	2	5		7	1	2				1
Amherst,	4			3				5	7	11		6	3					
Aurora,	16	1		34	1		6	41		6		4	8	4			4	19
Boston,	3			2			3	15		2		1	1				2	
Brandt,	10		2	10			1	12				1					4	
Buffalo city:																		
1st ward,	3			11			16	5	12	6		6	5			3	4	1
2d ward,	20	1	1	36		2	14	33	15	3		13	13	5	2	5	18	4
3d ward,	6	3		15	2	2	8	11	20	14		2	13	1		2	7	3
4th ward,	11			14	1		7	19	8	3		4	2	7			12	
5th ward,												2						
6th ward,													1					
7th ward,	4			9			1	3	2	1		2	2		1			
8th ward,	7	1		10	3	2	14	7	4	1		4	3	1	1		5	4
9th ward,	34	3	13	47			5	29	19	8		11	7	2	2	3	9	5

(Continued on page 86.)

CORTLAND COUNTY.—(Continued.)

TOWNS.	COUNTIES OF NEW-YORK.						New-York.	UNITED STATES.										
	Warren.	Washington.	Wayne.	Westchester.	Wyoming.	Yates.		Maine.	N. Hampshire.	Vermont.	Massachusetts.	Rhode Island.	Connecticut.	New Jersey.	Pennsylvania.	Delaware.	Maryland.	District of Columbia.
Cincinnatus,	1	9		3		1	944		6	10	38	37	47	2	7			
Cortlandville,		24	5	8	2		3, 363	2	16	54	213	30	277	11	43		1	
Freetown,		23				2	853		1	6	9	5	30	5	4	6		
Harford,		3					789	8		5	36	10	33	10	12	4		
Homer,		33	10	6		4	2, 875		32	54	188	43	260	11	18	1		
Lapeer,		2				3	643	1	1	2	23	25	30	3	10			
Marathon,	1	4	3	5		1	1, 080		1	14	20	6	61	3	12	54		
Preble,		11	1	1			1, 021		9	19	19	2	51	3	4			
Scott,		18	4	2			1, 059	1	3	16	50	29	54	10	7			
Solon,		7		7			849	1	11	13	26	3	38	10	3			
Taylor,	2	8	3	2			1, 015	1	13	9	47	22	45	5	8			
Truxton,	32	2	2	1	1	16	2, 725	1	26	59	126	43	74	18	18	1		
Virgil,		5	4	12		3	1, 967	1	4	33	40	19	71	11	19			
Willet,		3		3			806		3	8	14	42	24		8	4		
Total,	36	152	32	50	3	30	19, 989	16	126	302	849	316	1, 095	102	173	70	1	

DELAWARE COUNTY.—(Continued.)

TOWNS.	Warren.	Washington.	Wayne.	Westchester.	Wyoming.	Yates.	New-York.	Maine.	N. Hampshire.	Vermont.	Massachusetts.	Rhode Island.	Connecticut.	New Jersey.	Pennsylvania.	Delaware.	Maryland.	District of Columbia.
Andes,		13		7			2, 046	1		3	19	1	12	8	2			
Bovina,		11		5			981	1			1		6	1	5			
Colchester,		3	1	20			2, 110	1	5	2	6	1	29	11	17			
Davenport,		14					1, 868		1	12	44	6	81	14				
Delhi,	1	6		13			2, 149		7	7	34	2	58	13	11			
Franklin,		7		9			2, 611	1	2	19	97	3	86	12	6			
Hamden,		1		11			1, 503		1	7	21	3	55	1	11			
Hancock,		1	1	5			1, 828		1	4	13		38	26	98			
Harpersfield,		1		1			1, 300		3	4	15	3	64	4			1	
Kortright,		37		22			1, 735	1		6	8	1	26	4	19			
Masonville,	2	1		17			1, 359		1	12	49	2	60	2	20			
Meredith,		8					1, 236		3	3	17	1	75	2	8		1	
Middletown,		1		9			2, 662	1	2	10	9	5	41	5	10			
Roxbury,		4		34			2, 318		3	5	9	5	51	10	2			
Sidney,		5	2	7			1, 543		4	17	48	4	117	2	4		1	
Stamford,		4		8			1, 449		1	3	5	1	33	1	1			
Tompkins,		5		13			2, 815	1	6	18	75	5	56	17	65			
Walton,	1	8		20			2, 062	2	5	11	28	3	174	6	12			
Total,	4	130	4	201			33, 575	9	45	143	498	46	1, 262	139	291		3	

DUTCHESS COUNTY.—(Continued.)

TOWNS.	Warren.	Washington.	Wayne.	Westchester.	Wyoming.	Yates.	New-York.	Maine.	N. Hampshire.	Vermont.	Massachusetts.	Rhode Island.	Connecticut.	New Jersey.	Pennsylvania.	Delaware.	Maryland.	District of Columbia.
Amenia,		3		6		1	1, 557			6	24	10	244	8	3		1	
Beekman,	1	2		15		2	1, 195		1		1		48	3	4			
Clinton,	3	6		28	3		1, 710				2	1	27	5				
Dover,				6			1, 558	1	3	7	15	1	106	4	2			
East Fishkill,			1	57		3	2, 313			1	2	1	28	3	6			
Fishkill,	1	10	4	115		1	6, 677	6	8	12	78	17	119	71	30		8	1
Hyde Park,		1	2	23			1, 737	2	1	4	16		34	11	7	1	2	
La Grange,							1, 645		1	4	3	3	22	16				
Milan,				5		2	1, 554				2	3	12		1		1	
North East,		2		8			1, 325			2	67		172	3	9		1	
Pawling,		1		14		1	1, 649				2	1		2	3			
Pine Plains,		1		5		1	1, 274				10		51	4	2		1	
Pleasant Valley,				32			1, 668		1		6	2	15		5			
Poughkeepsie,				27			2, 226	2	4	1	19	4	28	26	5		3	
Poughkeepsie city:																		
1st ward,	1			45			2, 621	3	5	11	36	18	71	24	11	1	2	
2d ward,		3	4	12			2, 003	6	4	19	17	8	69	14	14			
3d ward,				9			2, 332	1	1	3	17	7	30	13	5			
4th ward,	1	1	4	29			1, 855	5	9	7	27	14	70	29	9		3	
Total Po'keepsie,	2	4	8	95			8, 811	15	19	40	97	47	240	80	39	1	5	
Red Hook,		3	1	7			3, 004	3	2	4	15	4	29	15	10	2		
Rhinebeck,			5	14			2, 554	2	3	2	12	2	36	35	14		1	
Stanford,		1		16			1, 932		2		13	13	55	4	5			
Union Vale,			1	13			1, 311			5	2	2	40		5			
Washington,	2	1		13			2, 373	2	1	2	11	13	27	5	1			
Total,	9	35	22	499	3	11	48, 073	33	46	90	397	124	1, 333	295	151	4	23	1

ERIE COUNTY.—(Continued.)

TOWNS.	Warren.	Washington.	Wayne.	Westchester.	Wyoming.	Yates.	New-York.	Maine.	N. Hampshire.	Vermont.	Massachusetts.	Rhode Island.	Connecticut.	New Jersey.	Pennsylvania.	Delaware.	Maryland.	District of Columbia.
Alden,	7	12	3	2	23	2	1, 272	1	41	94	34	12	59	10	23			
Amherst,	1	2	4		1		2, 551	10	2	23	12	4	30	10	218		4	
Aurora,	2	36	14		60	5	2, 438	9	28	142	95	20	70	17	49		4	
Boston,		14		1	7		1, 125	2	2	42	44	15	21	11	8		1	
Brandt,	17	19	3	1	9	2	788		11	89	29	3	32	6	5		2	
Buffalo city:																		
1st ward,		18	14	1	6		2, 652	15	10	51	75	3	38	20	62		4	2
2d ward,	3	34	15	15	27	13	2, 867	16	27	135	212	9	184	27	53		18	1
3d ward,	2	17	17	3	17	7	1, 933	11	20	43	40	8	47	32	34		6	
4th ward,		19	13	1	14	8	3, 280	3	12	42	67	9	55	19	81		39	
5th ward,		1					3, 236	11	27	38	62	6	27	10	61		19	2
6th ward,		5	1	5			5, 962		1	4	4		3	1	45		6	3
7th ward,		2	13		1		2, 513		5	15	20	1	7	8	14		2	
8th ward,	2	11	5	3	11	2	1, 720	7	14	30	46	6	17	17	43		3	
9th ward,	4	14	28	6	13	14	2, 836	44	30	97	197	14	160	28	89		15	

(Continued on page 87.)

CORTLAND COUNTY.—(Continued.)

TOWNS.	UNITED STATES.																	
	Virginia.	N. Carolina.	S. Carolina.	Georgia.	Florida.	Alabama.	Mississippi.	Louisiana.	Texas.	Arkansas.	Missouri.	Tennessee.	Kentucky.	Ohio.	Indiana.	Illinois.	Michigan.	Wisconsin.
Cincinnatus,	1							1						2				
Cortlandville,	4	1											1	9	1	7	6	1
Freetown,														4				
Harford,	3													2			1	
Homer,				1				3										
Lapeer,														2				
Marathon,														1			1	
Preble,														3		1	3	
Scott,			1											7			3	5
Solon,																		
Taylor,														2				1
Truxton,														6		2	2	3
Virgil,	1										1						4	1
Willet,														1				
Total,	9	1	1	1				4			1		1	39	1	10	20	11

DELAWARE COUNTY.—(Continued.)

TOWNS.	Virginia.	N. Carolina.	S. Carolina.	Georgia.	Florida.	Alabama.	Mississippi.	Louisiana.	Texas.	Arkansas.	Missouri.	Tennessee.	Kentucky.	Ohio.	Indiana.	Illinois.	Michigan.	Wisconsin.
Andes,		1				1												1
Bovina,																		
Colchester,			1												2			
Davenport,														2				
Delhi,		1												5		1		
Franklin,				1										4	3			
Hamden,		2												1	2		2	
Hancock,								1	1					2	1			
Harpersfield,																		
Kortright,														1				
Masonville,														1				
Meredith,														1				
Middletown,														3	1			1
Roxbury,														4				
Sidney,														1				
Stamford,		1												1				
Tompkins,													1	1		1		
Walton,	1	4		1							1							
Total,	1	9	1	2		1		1	1		1		1	27	9	2	2	2

DUTCHESS COUNTY.—(Continued.)

TOWNS.	Virginia.	N. Carolina.	S. Carolina.	Georgia.	Florida.	Alabama.	Mississippi.	Louisiana.	Texas.	Arkansas.	Missouri.	Tennessee.	Kentucky.	Ohio.	Indiana.	Illinois.	Michigan.	Wisconsin.
Amenia,														3		1	4	
Beekman,														1				
Clinton,																		
Dover,								1										
East Fishkill,		2	1															
Fishkill,	7		3	5					1					3	1	1	7	1
Hyde Park,	2			1						1	2		2	1	3		1	
La Grange,																		
Milan,																		
North East,														1			2	
Pawling,																	1	
Pine Plains,														3				
Pleasant Valley,																		
Poughkeepsie,	1												1	1	2		3	2
Poughkeepsie city,																		
1st ward,	2		1					5						2			2	3
2d ward,		1									1	1		12				1
3d ward,	1		1											1				
4th ward,	1							11						1			3	
Total Poughk'e,	4	1	2					16			1	1		16			5	4
Red Hook,		6	4										1			5	1	
Rhinebeck,			1		1						1			3				
Stanford,														1	1			
Union Vale,																	1	
Washington,														1	3			
Total,	14	9	11	6	1			17	1	1	4	1	4	34	10	7	25	7

ERIE COUNTY.—(Continued.)

TOWNS.	Virginia.	N. Carolina.	S. Carolina.	Georgia.	Florida.	Alabama.	Mississippi.	Louisiana.	Texas.	Arkansas.	Missouri.	Tennessee.	Kentucky.	Ohio.	Indiana.	Illinois.	Michigan.	Wisconsin.
Alden,		1											3	8		2	8	4
Amherst,											1		2	10		4	5	3
Aurora,													3	15	3	3	9	
Boston,								2						9		1	1	1
Brandt,													1	9			5	
Buffalo city:																		
1st ward,	5		1	2		1		1					4	46	1	8	23	5
2d ward,	14	1	1		1		2	4		1	5		4	76	2	6	37	2
3d ward,	2		2											26			16	3
4th ward,	25	4	1	2		3		3				1	7	43	1	5	21	4
5th ward,	34	1	2	2			1	1	4		1		3	18		1	4	2
6th ward,	14		1								2		7	8		1	9	3
7th ward,	4		1	2									1	6	2		3	2
8th ward,	1					1					2	1		35	2	1	17	3
9th ward,	7	4	4	1	1	3						1	9	88	7	8	40	8

(Continued on page 88.)

CORTLAND COUNTY.—(CONTINUED.)

TOWNS.	U. STATES. Iowa.	California.	Territories.	Total United States	FOREIGN COUNTRIES. Canada.	N. Brunswick.	Nova Scotia.	N. Foundland.	West Indies.	Mexico.	S. America.	England.	Scotland.	Ireland.	Wales.	France.	Belgium.	Holland.
Cincinnatus				1, 095			1					12		8				
Cortlandville				4, 040	8	1	2		1	1		65	6	175	3			
Freetown				923								15		17				
Harford				913								4	1	2				
Homer				3, 486	20							92	18	121		2		
Lapeer				740	2									7				
Marathon				1, 253	3								1	84				
Preble				1, 135	5							24		53				
Scott				1, 245								12	1	27				
Solon				954	7							3	1	91				
Taylor				1, 168	2		2					3	3	13				
Truxton				3, 104	9		7				1	117	12	179	2			
Virgil				2, 172	2							24	6	22	1			
Willet	1			911								1	2	11				
Total	1			23, 139	58	1	12		1	1	1	372	51	810	6	2		

DELAWARE COUNTY.—(CONTINUED.)

TOWNS.	Iowa.	California.	Territories.	Total United States	Canada.	N. Brunswick.	Nova Scotia.	N. Foundland.	West Indies.	Mexico.	S. America.	England.	Scotland.	Ireland.	Wales.	France.	Belgium.	Holland.
Andes	1			2, 096	9				2			35	307	43	3			
Bovina				995	4							6	194	24				
Colchester				2, 185	1							38	60	49				
Davenport				2, 028	1							22	18	140				
Delhi				2, 288	4							34	265	93	1			
Franklin				3, 045	3		1					56	46	28				
Hamden				1, 609	2	1		1				25	186	37				
Hancock				2, 013	2	2	1					23	13	261		41		25
Harpersfield				1, 394			8					4	10	61				
Kortright				1, 801			1					32	24	147				
Masonville				1,506	3							6	4	1		1		
Meredith				1, 347								7	67	78	1			
Middletown				2, 750	3							18	57	104	2			
Roxbury				2, 407	2		1					7	24	17				
Sidney				1, 741	2		2					29	3	6				
Stamford				1, 496	2							13	22	42		1		
Tompkins				3, 061	6		3					59	22	116		1		
Walton				2, 310	1		1					17	28	45				
Total	1			36, 072	45	3	18	1	2			431	1, 350	1, 292	7	44		25

DUTCHESS COUNTY.—(CONTINUED.)

TOWNS.	Iowa.	California.	Territories.	Total United States	Canada.	N. Brunswick.	Nova Scotia.	N. Foundland.	West Indies.	Mexico.	S. America.	England.	Scotland.	Ireland.	Wales.	France.	Belgium.	Holland.
Amenia				1, 861	2							14	7	284				
Beekman				1, 253	1							9		110				
Clinton				1, 745	1							4		73		1		
Dover				1, 698			1					10	8	174				
East Fishkill				2, 357								15		211				
Fishkill				7, 057	14	2	6	1	4	3	1	449	116	970	5	23	1	
Hyde Park				1, 827	13	1			3			30	24	539		4		1
La Grange				1, 694	1							22	2	118	1	1		
Milan				1, 573	1							3	3	33				
North East				1, 582								4	6	151		6		
Pauling				1, 658	1		1					4	1	112				
Pine Plains				1, 345	1							14		78				
Pleasant Valley				1, 697								11		140				
Poughkeepsie				2, 328	2			1	1			169	48	480	1	4		
Poughkeepsie city:																		
1st ward				2, 818	17		6		1			131	71	793	1	10		
2d ward				2, 170	4		1		2			69	23	295	1	4		
3d ward				2, 412	4					1		106	17	433		6		
4th ward				2, 044	9	2	1		1	1		74	32	225		3		
Total Poughk'e				9, 444	34	2	8		4	2		380	143	1, 746	2	23		
Redhook				3, 105	3				1			39	10	400		10	1	
Rhinebeck				2, 667	3		2		1		1	42	4	251	4	3		
Stanford			2	2, 028	2							11		138		14		
Union Vale				1, 366	1							10	4	77				
Washington				2, 439								25	8	251				
Total			2	50, 724	80	5	18	2	14	5	2	1, 265	384	6, 336	13	89	2	1

ERIE COUNTY.—(CONTINUED.)

TOWNS.	Iowa.	California.	Territories.	Total United States	Canada.	N. Brunswick.	Nova Scotia.	N. Foundland.	West Indies.	Mexico.	S. America.	England.	Scotland.	Ireland.	Wales.	France.	Belgium.	Holland.
Alden				1, 572	22		10					54	5	81		135		
Amherst				2, 889	53							84	10	40	2	322	6	7
Aurora				2, 905	78		2		3			164	4	173		7	1	11
Boston				1, 285	12							34	3	40		55		
Brandt				980	8							26		26		2		
Buffalo city:																		
1st ward				3, 031	477	16	4	8	1			473	182	3, 148	22	49	1	8
2d ward				3, 713	201	9	2	2	2		2	382	83	823	5	59	1	24
3d ward				2, 223	211		1		1			237	41	714		44		22
4th ward	1			3, 728	121	2						238	66	359		673	6	54
5th ward				3, 573	134	6	6	4	2			317	26	405	10	143	2	111
6th ward				6, 077	35	2					2	46	3	13		379		49
7th ward				2, 606	56		2	1		2		148	31	172	1	455	13	19
8th ward				2, 008	248	4			1			238	118	2, 007	1	72	1	1
9th ward	1			3, 692	237	2		2	6			269	74	716	1	70		3

(Continued on page 89.)

CORTLAND COUNTY.—(Continued.)

TOWNS.	Germany.	Prussia.	Austria.	Switzerland.	Italy.	Spain.	Portugal.	Poland.	Norway.	Sweden.	Russia.	Denmark.	East Indies.	Africa.	Turkey and Greece.	Islands.	Asia.	At Sea.	Unknown.
	FOREIGN COUNTRIES.																		
Cincinnatus,																			3
Cortlandville,	9		1							3									14
Freetown,																			
Harford,	6																		
Homer,	17												4						25
Lapeer,																			1
Marathon,																			
Preble,	2																		
Scott,	1																		7
Solon,	1																		
Taylor,	2							5											3
Truxton,	13																		
Virgil,	1																		3
Willet,																			
Total,	52		1					5		3			4						56

DELAWARE COUNTY.—(Continued.)

TOWNS.	Germany.	Prussia.	Austria.	Switzerland.	Italy.	Spain.	Portugal.	Poland.	Norway.	Sweden.	Russia.	Denmark.	East Indies.	Africa.	Turkey and Greece.	Islands.	Asia.	At Sea.	Unknown.
Andes,	36			1		2			1	1									
Bovina,	1																		
Colchester,	21																		6
Davenport,	24																		
Delhi,	15							1											10
Franklin,	4			1														1	1
Hamden,	15																		5
Hancock,	74			2															55
Harpersfield,	3																		
Kortright,	2			1														1	4
Masonville,	8							1											13
Meredith,	1	1																1	
Middletown,	11			1															
Roxbury,	75																		
Sidney,	2	1																	11
Stamford,	21																		
Tompkins,	15																		7
Walton,																		1	1
Total,	328	2		6		2		2	1	1								4	113

DUTCHESS COUNTY.—(Continued.)

TOWNS.	Germany.	Prussia.	Austria.	Switzerland.	Italy.	Spain.	Portugal.	Poland.	Norway.	Sweden.	Russia.	Denmark.	East Indies.	Africa.	Turkey and Greece.	Islands.	Asia.	At Sea.	Unknown.
Amenia,	17			4															10
Beekman,	3				3														
Clinton,	15																		1
Dover,	14									1									19
East Fishkill,	29																		7
Fishkill,	97	1		7	1			1				2	2						1
Hyde Park,	31			1						2									4
La Grange,	8	1																	4
Milan,	7																		10
North East,	6			1															1
Pawling,	14																	1	
Pine Plains,	14																		1
Pleasant Valley,	4				1														
Poughkeepsie,	29			1	3			2									2	1	38
Poughkeepsie city,																			
1st ward,	240	1					1	4			1							2	2
2d ward,	89					1			1										4
3d ward,	475			2		3								1					
4th ward,	134	1	1		1			4				6							1
Total Poughk'e,	938	2	1	2	1	4	1	8	1		1	6		1				2	7
Red Hook,	89	1			1														90
Rhinebeck,	80		1		1						1								4
Stanford,				3															5
Union Vale,	4																		1
Washington,	16																		1
Total,	1,415	5	2	19	11	4	1	11	1	3	2	8	2	1			2	4	204

ERIE COUNTY.—(Continued.)

TOWNS.	Germany.	Prussia.	Austria.	Switzerland.	Italy.	Spain.	Portugal.	Poland.	Norway.	Sweden.	Russia.	Denmark.	East Indies.	Africa.	Turkey and Greece.	Islands.	Asia.	At Sea.	Unknown.
Alden,	485	19		2					3									1	15
Amherst,	1,675	10								1		1						2	16
Aurora,	276	1		3						1		1							35
Boston,	340																		
Brandt,	41	2		6															2
Buffalo city:																			
1st ward,	466	1	3	16	11		1	32	2	3	2	2						1	34
2d ward,	426	14		7	2	2		4	1		7							1	110
3d ward,	759	3		10		1			2		1							3	20
4th ward,	1,666	427	550	67	1			4	6	10	11	4		2					5
5th ward,	3,928	19		29	2			6	26	7							1		2
6th ward,		537	5	191		1	2					2						6	4
7th ward,	3,438	610	51	156	7			2	3	1	7	16		2				5	
8th ward,	629	8		6	21	1	1	12	1	3	3	5	2					6	7
9th ward,	519	4	1	1		1		6		4	3						1		13

(Continued on page 90.)

ERIE COUNTY.

TOWNS.	COUNTIES OF NEW-YORK.																	
	Albany.	Allegany.	Broome.	Cattaraugus.	Cayuga.	Chautauque.	Chemung.	Chenango.	Clinton.	Columbia.	Cortland.	Delaware.	Dutchess.	Erie.	Essex.	Franklin.	Fulton.	Genesee.
Buffalo city:																		
10th ward,	47	9	1	5	34	31	1	13	7	16	5	4	26	1, 792	1	......	......	54
11th ward,	27	1	1	4	8	8	......	2	8	3	3	3	1	1, 073	......	1	......	11
12th ward,	19	1	......	2	14	9	......	2	2	4	2	1	2	1, 024	1	......	......	10
13th ward,	2	......	......	1	1	2	......	......	......	1	......	......	1	280	......	1	......	3
Total Buffalo,..	425	33	14	96	203	213	2	72	52	96	32	37	116	23, 992	16	9	7	339
Chictawauga, ...	3	......	......	3	1	1	......	......	......	2	......	......	1	1, 035	......	......	......	14
Clarence, ...	8	8	......	4	32	1	......	3	......	8	5	5	7	1, 489	1	......	......	32
Colden, ...	5	3	......	12	3	......	......	5	18	6	......	6	6	776	......	......	......	13
Collins, ...	4	6	......	139	7	43	6	2	18	17	6	4	5	997	3	......	......	5
Concord, ...	11	11	7	117	7	20	11	7	2	18	24	13	7	1, 375	2	2	1	38
East Hamburgh, .	1	......	......	2	8	10	......	2	3	9	......	4	13	1, 029	1	......	......	4
Eden, ...	4	3	......	12	12	9	......	......	......	......	......	2	6	1, 230	4	1	......	5
Evans, ...	11	6	1	14	12	41	......	30	......	13	20	8	28	1, 045	8	2	......	9
Grand Island, ...	9	1	......	1	3	8	......	1	1	3	......	......	16	373	1	......	......	7
Hamburgh, ...	11	1	......	8	18	18	......	......	3	3	2	6	1	1, 322	4	......	2	14
Holland, ...	3	2	......	23	6	4	......	......	......	......	5	......	3	789	1	......	......	10
Lancaster, ...	15	1	4	1	9	3	3	......	......	1	6	1	3	2, 045	2	......	......	54
Marilla, ...	......	4	1	12	7	......	......	9	......	......	......	3	9	572	8	......	......	110
Newstead, ...	8	8	1	7	36	12	2	11	2	4	1	12	13	1, 318	......	......	5	186
North Collins, ...	5	......	......	13	32	9	......	2	1	7	1	2	1	1, 002	6	......	......	5
Sardinia, ...	2	8	3	83	9	10	......	3	2	8	3	14	6	813	2	1	1	57
Tonawanda, ...	9	2	1	......	15	2	......	5	2	3	1	......	4	860	5	1	......	10
Wales, ...	2	2	2	6	20	4	......	5	5	5	3	3	4	853	3	3	......	21
West Seneca, ...	......	3	1	5	6	6	......	......	1	1	......	1	......	550	1	......	......	10
Total, ...	585	125	37	617	527	493	26	176	127	228	128	138	306	49, 784	81	20	16	1, 135

ESSEX COUNTY.

TOWNS.	Albany.	Allegany.	Broome.	Cattaraugus.	Cayuga.	Chautauque.	Chemung.	Chenango.	Clinton.	Columbia.	Cortland.	Delaware.	Dutchess.	Erie.	Essex.	Franklin.	Fulton.	Genesee.
Chesterfield, ...	6	......	......	......	......	1	......	......	310	5	......	2	15	......	1, 517	8	......	1
Crown Point, ...	4	......	1	......	3	1	......	......	32	1	......	......	......	......	1, 374	4	......	......
Elizabethtown, ..	......	......	......	......	9	......	......	......	34	4	......	......	7	......	870	9	1	2
Essex, ...	......	......	......	......	......	......	......	......	125	1	......	......	8	......	1, 188	3	......	......
Jay, ...	3	......	......	......	......	......	......	......	188	......	......	......	4	......	1, 762	11	......	......
Keene, ...	7	......	......	......	......	......	......	......	22	......	......	......	2	......	479	......	......	2
Lewis, ...	3	......	......	......	1	1	......	......	79	4	......	1	3	......	1, 102	......	......	......
Minerva, ...	......	......	......	......	4	......	......	......	......	1	......	......	3	......	355	......	......	......
Moriah, ...	4	......	......	......	......	......	......	......	62	......	......	......	3	1	1, 737	2	......	1
Newcomb, ...	......	......	......	......	......	1	......	......	......	......	......	......	2	......	87	2	......	......
North Elba, ...	3	......	......	......	......	......	......	......	7	......	......	......	5	......	154	1	......	......
North Hudson, ...	1	......	......	......	......	......	......	......	28	......	......	......	......	......	287	2	1	......
St. Armand, ...	......	......	......	......	......	......	......	......	42	......	......	......	......	......	138	7	......	......
Schroon, ...	2	......	......	......	......	......	......	1	31	3	1	......	6	......	1, 159	5	1	2
Ticonderoga, ...	11	2	......	1	......	......	......	......	19	2	......	......	8	......	1, 242	4	......	......
Westport, ...	1	......	2	2	......	......	......	......	37	......	......	......	10	......	1, 223	4	......	1
Wilsborough, ...	......	......	......	......	......	5	......	......	105	7	......	......	7	......	981	1	4	......
Wilmington, ...	1	......	......	......	1	......	......	......	46	......	......	......	......	......	640	......	......	......
Total, ...	46	2	3	3	18	9	......	1	1, 167	28	1	3	83	1	16, 295	63	7	9

FRANKLIN COUNTY.

TOWNS.	Albany.	Allegany.	Broome.	Cattaraugus.	Cayuga.	Chautauque.	Chemung.	Chenango.	Clinton.	Columbia.	Cortland.	Delaware.	Dutchess.	Erie.	Essex.	Franklin.	Fulton.	Genesee.
Bangor, ...	1	......	......	......	......	......	......	......	66	1	......	......	2	......	14	1, 082	......	......
Bellmont, ...	3	......	......	......	......	......	......	2	60	2	......	2	......	......	21	456	......	1
Bombay, ...	......	......	......	......	......	......	......	......	35	......	1	1	2	......	......	1, 152	......	......
Brandon, ...	......	......	......	......	1	......	......	......	22	......	......	......	......	......	9	393	......	1
Burke, ...	......	......	......	......	1	......	......	......	80	2	......	......	7	......	19	1, 050	......	5
Chateaugay, ...	......	......	......	......	......	......	......	......	113	......	......	......	2	......	10	1, 578	......	......
Constable, ...	......	......	......	......	......	......	......	......	9	1	......	......	1	......	4	718	......	......
Dickinson, ...	1	......	......	......	......	......	1	......	16	1	......	2	......	......	40	494	......	......
Duane, ...	......	......	......	......	......	......	......	......	37	......	......	......	1	......	25	112	......	......
Fort Covington, ..	1	......	......	......	......	......	......	......	26	......	......	......	2	......	4	1, 323	......	1
Franklin, ...	1	......	1	......	......	3	......	......	140	......	......	......	......	......	105	265	......	......
Harrietstown, ...	......	......	......	......	......	......	......	......	14	......	......	......	1	......	50	115	......	......
Malone, ...	2	......	......	......	1	......	......	......	143	......	......	1	3	3	32	2, 308	1	1
Moira, ...	1	......	......	......	......	......	......	......	29	......	......	......	......	3	4	673	......	......
Westville, ...	1	......	......	......	......	......	......	......	16	......	......	......	1	......	1	709	......	......
Total, ...	11	......	1	......	3	3	1	2	806	7	1	6	22	6	338	12, 428	1	9

FULTON COUNTY.

TOWNS.	Albany.	Allegany.	Broome.	Cattaraugus.	Cayuga.	Chautauque.	Chemung.	Chenango.	Clinton.	Columbia.	Cortland.	Delaware.	Dutchess.	Erie.	Essex.	Franklin.	Fulton.	Genesee.
Bleecker, ...	37	......	......	......	2	......	......	......	......	1	1	......	3	1	......	......	319	......
Broadalbin, ...	63	......	1	......	7	1	......	1	3	20	2	2	43	1	3	......	1, 490	......
Caroga, ...	21	......	......	......	......	......	......	......	......	4	1	......	25	2	1	1	340	......
Ephrata, ...	10	......	1	......	......	......	......	......	5	......	......	......	17	......	......	......	1, 653	......
Johnstown, ...	109	1	2	3	2	......	2	1	1	56	1	8	64	2	2	1	5, 129	1
Mayfield, ...	51	......	1	......	3	3	......	......	......	30	......	3	49	1	......	......	1, 509	......
Northampton, ...	17	1	1	......	4	......	2	2	2	25	......	8	24	......	4	1	966	2
Oppenheim, ...	17	1	1	2	2	1	......	......	1	9	......	......	13	......	......	1	1, 632	1
Perth, ...	21	......	......	......	......	......	......	......	......	8	......	......	8	......	......	......	370	......
Stratford, ...	10	1	......	......	1	......	......	......	......	6	......	5	17	......	2	......	527	2
Total, ...	356	4	7	5	21	5	4	4	12	159	5	26	263	7	12	4	13, 935	6

ERIE COUNTY.—(Continued.)

TOWNS	Greene.	Hamilton.	Herkimer.	Jefferson.	Kings.	Lewis.	Livingston.	Madison.	Monroe.	Montgomery.	New York.	Niagara.	Oneida.	Onondaga.	Ontario.	Orange.	Orleans.	Oswego.
	COUNTIES OF NEW-YORK.																	
Buffalo city:																		
10th ward,	5	1	14	10	9	5	13	11	61	12	88	42	34	25	51	13	10	7
11th ward,	3	2	13	4	......	1	1	10	23	11	17	23	26	12	14	2	17	3
12th ward,	6	......	2	3	......	......	2	8	21	8	7	11	......	9	14	2	9	2
13th ward,	......	......	......	......	......	......	1	1	1	1	1	......	3	3	......	1	......	......
Total Buffalo,	63	8	180	110	55	11	114	88	598	174	935	269	319	258	224	76	108	119
Chictawauga,	6	......	1	2	......	1	1	......	6	......	3	1	2	3	1	......	......	1
Clarence,	......	......	10	3	5	......	3	4	16	4	7	81	9	14	22	3	9	2
Colden,	......	......	5	......	1	......	1	7	2	1	5	8	14	7	2	......	3	......
Collins,	2	......	1	2	1	......	3	8	6	22	9	1	14	11	8	......	6	1
Concord,	9	......	55	......	......	......	1	12	8	18	4	2	34	12	8	6	4	......
East Hamburgh,	1	......	3	3	1	......	......	1	2	6	3	1	2	5	3	2	1	1
Eden,	......	......	5	......	......	......	......	5	3	2	2	......	8	12	......	3	......	......
Evans,	8	......	4	5	1	5	9	21	12	6	15	......	26	14	13	......	4	4
Grand Island,	1	......	5	1	1	......	1	......	9	3	3	16	6	1	1	3	......	2
Hamburgh,	......	......	16	6	......	......	2	10	12	8	18	4	15	3	10	1	3	5
Holland,	......	......	6	4	......	......	9	9	2	1	......	1	3	5	8	1	......	1
Lancaster,	3	1	16	3	2	......	6	7	3	3	20	8	11	17	9	2	3	......
Marilla,	1	......	6	5	......	1	8	22	5	21	1	8	36	22	5	2	3	9
Newstead,	8	2	25	8	1	......	18	23	45	14	4	50	21	35	42	9	52	......
North Collins,	......	......	6	7	......	......	1	......	2	8	2	2	1	4	9	3	1	1
Sardinia,	1	......	31	13	......	1	6	13	18	13	1	2	25	12	14	2	9	4
Tonawanda,	......	......	17	2	1	1	5	3	25	8	23	64	15	12	6	7	8	2
Wales,	11	1	20	3	......	7	1	7	8	27	5	9	28	17	14	3	2	2
West Seneca,	1	......	1	......	2	1	3	......	2	1	1	2	4	1	6	4	2	......
Total,	129	12	453	198	78	35	215	317	835	390	1,095	626	700	502	449	142	245	159

ESSEX COUNTY.—(Continued.)

TOWNS	Greene.	Hamilton.	Herkimer.	Jefferson.	Kings.	Lewis.	Livingston.	Madison.	Monroe.	Montgomery.	New York.	Niagara.	Oneida.	Onondaga.	Ontario.	Orange.	Orleans.	Oswego.
Chesterfield,	2	......	......	......	3	......	......	1	1	3	8	......	2	......	1	......	......	......
Crown Point,	5	......	1	......	1	......	......	......	......	3	......	......	1	......	3	2	1	......
Elizabethtown,	5	......	......	2	......	......	......	......	......	1	2	......	3	......	......	......	......	......
Essex,	......	......	......	......	......	......	......	1	1	......	6	......	......	1	......	......	......	......
Jay,	1	......	......	1	......	......	3	1	......	1	6	......	2	1	......	......	......	......
Keene,	......	......	......	......	......	......	......	......	......	......	......	......	......	......	......	......	......	......
Lewis,	1	......	......	......	......	1	2	......	......	1	1	......	3	......	......	......	......	......
Minerva,	13	2	......	......	4	1	......	5	......	2	22	......	......	......	1	......	......	......
Moriah,	1	2	2	1	1	......	......	......	2	......	16	2	1	......	......	12	2	......
Newcomb,	......	12	......	......	......	......	......	......	......	6	......	......	......	......	......	......	......	......
North Elba,	1	......	......	......	1	......	......	......	......	1	......	......	......	......	......	3	......	......
North Hudson,	......	......	......	......	2	1	......	......	......	......	3	......	1	......	......	3	2	......
St. Armand,	......	......	......	......	......	......	......	......	......	......	......	......	......	......	......	......	......	......
Schroon,	1	......	......	......	1	......	......	......	......	2	2	......	2	......	......	......	1	......
Ticonderoga,	......	1	......	......	......	......	1	......	......	1	1	......	1	......	......	......	......	......
Westport,	......	......	1	......	......	......	1	......	......	......	......	......	......	3	......	......	......	......
Willsborough,	1	......	......	......	......	......	......	......	......	......	1	......	1	......	......	......	......	......
Wilmington,	......	......	1	1	......	......	......	......	......	......	......	......	......	......	......	......	......	......
Total,	31	17	5	5	13	3	7	8	4	21	68	2	17	5	4	20	6	......

FRANKLIN COUNTY.—(Continued.)

TOWNS	Greene.	Hamilton.	Herkimer.	Jefferson.	Kings.	Lewis.	Livingston.	Madison.	Monroe.	Montgomery.	New York.	Niagara.	Oneida.	Onondaga.	Ontario.	Orange.	Orleans.	Oswego.
Bangor,	......	......	3	2	......	1	......	......	1	1	1	......	......	......	......	......	......	......
Belmont,	......	......	1	1	......	......	1	2	1	......	1	......	3	1	......	......	......	1
Bombay,	......	......	3	2	1	3	......	......	5	......	6	......	1	......	......	1	2	......
Brandon,	......	......	1	......	......	......	......	......	......	......	......	......	......	......	......	......	......	......
Burke,	......	......	......	4	......	......	......	......	......	......	......	......	3	......	......	......	......	......
Chateaugay,	......	......	1	6	1	......	......	......	......	1	2	......	......	......	......	3	......	......
Constable,	......	......	......	......	......	......	......	......	4	......	1	......	1	......	......	......	......	......
Dickinson,	......	......	2	......	......	......	......	......	......	......	......	......	6	......	......	......	......	1
Duane,	......	......	......	......	......	......	......	......	......	1	......	......	......	......	......	......	......	......
Fort Covington,	......	3	1	7	6	......	......	......	......	......	......	......	1	1	......	......	1	......
Franklin,	......	......	1	......	2	1	......	......	4	......	......	......	1	......	......	2	......	......
Harristown,	......	......	......	......	......	......	......	......	......	......	......	......	......	......	......	......	......	......
Malone,	......	......	......	22	1	1	......	1	1	4	18	......	2	1	......	......	......	1
Moira,	......	......	1	7	......	......	......	2	......	......	1	1	3	......	......	......	......	6
Westville,	......	......	......	......	......	......	......	......	......	......	1	1	......	......	......	......	......	......
Total,	......	3	14	51	11	6	1	5	12	11	31	2	21	3	......	6	3	9

FULTON COUNTY.—(Continued.)

TOWNS	Greene.	Hamilton.	Herkimer.	Jefferson.	Kings.	Lewis.	Livingston.	Madison.	Monroe.	Montgomery.	New York.	Niagara.	Oneida.	Onondaga.	Ontario.	Orange.	Orleans.	Oswego.
Bleecker,	1	10	1	1	......	......	......	1	......	19	7	......	1	1	......	1	......	3
Broadalbin,	3	17	10	7	2	......	1	2	......	101	5	......	6	6	2	......	4	3
Caroga,	2	......	9	9	......	......	......	1	......	67	......	......	6	......	......	......	......	......
Ephrata,	16	1	25	13	......	1	......	4	......	186	3	......	3	1	......	1	......	......
Johnstown,	14	45	65	32	2	12	2	7	9	449	45	......	36	4	2	3	1	2
Mayfield,	14	21	14	13	2	3	......	2	1	90	8	......	17	2	1	......	2	2
Northampton,	8	91	16	2	6	......	1	1	......	17	6	......	1	6	1	3	......	4
Oppenheim,	1	1	161	22	......	2	......	2	1	175	7	......	15	......	......	1	1	......
Perth,	......	1	1	2	......	......	......	......	3	395	4	......	2	......	1	......	1	1
Stratford,	5	12	86	13	......	4	......	......	......	57	3	......	14	2	......	......	2	......
Total,	64	199	388	114	12	22	4	20	14	1,556	88	......	101	22	7	9	11	15

ERIE COUNTY.—(CONTINUED.)

TOWNS.	Otsego.	Putnam.	Queens.	Rensselaer.	Richmond.	Rockland.	St. Lawrence	Saratoga.	Schenectady.	Schoharie.	Schuyler.	Seneca.	Steuben.	Suffolk.	Sullivan.	Tioga.	Tompkins.	Ulster.
	COUNTIES OF NEW-YORK.																	
Buffalo city:																		
10th ward,	14	4		22	1		6	26	15	11		6	9	3	1	1	14	2
11th ward,	9	2	1	31			7	10	1	4		1	2			1	3	2
12th ward,	5			8		3	1	2	2	2		2	2			1	2	
13th ward,				1						2			2				1	
Total Buffalo,	113	14	15	204	7	9	79	145	98	55		53	61	19	7	16	75	21
Chictawauga,	2			7			1	1		1								
Clarence,	19	3		12			1		2	1		13	3		2			1
Colden,	6			2			3	15		2		6	1				1	4
Collins,	33			12			2	8	1	9		3	2	3		1		
Concord,	70			9			2	6	3	3		6	6	2		10	6	5
East Hamburgh,	9	2		4			10	32		1				1			1	
Eden,	23			3		1	5	5				2	3				1	2
Evans,	8	1		14			12	44		6		3	2	1	1		11	4
Grand Island,	6			3			3	3		1			2			2	2	
Hamburgh,	10	2		7			6	29	2	1		6					2	
Holland,	13			3			2	5	3	20		3					3	
Lancaster,	12		5	7				4	1	7		4	5		4	1	4	
Marilla,	7			15				27	1	6		4	7		3		1	3
Newstead,	63			28			5	15	1	12		11	8	4	1	1	10	9
North Collins,	5			4				15	1	13			3			1		
Sardinia,	15			4			2	7		3		9	7			1	5	2
Tonawanda,	6			4		2	5	4	1	8		2	6		1		1	3
Wales,	9		1	11			2	19		1		4	5	1			3	34
West Seneca,	4		4	7				1				1						1
Total,	476	24	27	419	8	12	152	463	123	174		149	134	37	19	33	136	109

ESSEX COUNTY.—(CONTINUED.)

TOWNS.	Otsego.	Putnam.	Queens.	Rensselaer.	Richmond.	Rockland.	St. Lawrence	Saratoga.	Schenectady.	Schoharie.	Schuyler.	Seneca.	Steuben.	Suffolk.	Sullivan.	Tioga.	Tompkins.	Ulster.
Chesterfield,				9			5	14	4									1
Crown Point,	1			6			13	11								1		
Elizabethtown,	1			6			11	7		1		1						3
Essex,		1		4			16	8								1		1
Jay,				14			26	5	2									
Keene,				1			5	1										
Lewis,				7			6	7		6								
Minerva,	1			8				7					2			1		
Moriah,				1			11	18	1	3							1	
Newcomb,							1	1										
North Elba,				8			5	3										3
North Hudson,				1				5										
St. Armand,				7														
Schroon,	4			6			3	15		1			1					
Ticonderoga,			3	4				12						4	1			
Westport,				11			8	9									1	1
Wilsborough,				1			4	7	1									2
Wilmington,				2			8	1										
Total,	7	1	3	96			122	131	8	11		1	3	4	1	3	2	11

FRANKLIN COUNTY.—(CONTINUED.)

TOWNS.	Otsego.	Putnam.	Queens.	Rensselaer.	Richmond.	Rockland.	St. Lawrence	Saratoga.	Schenectady.	Schoharie.	Schuyler.	Seneca.	Steuben.	Suffolk.	Sullivan.	Tioga.	Tompkins.	Ulster.
Bangor,			4	4			44											1
Bellmont,	1						11					1	1					
Bombay,				1			55											
Brandon,							7	1		1								
Burke,				1			14			3								
Chateaugay,				1			9			1				1	1			
Constable,	1						7											
Dickinson,				2			87	2										
Duane,							30		8									
Fort Covington,	1			3			40											
Franklin,				7			11	3										
Harrietstown,				6														
Malone,	8			7			78	8	5				2				1	
Moira,				1			65	1	3								1	
Westville,							11	1										
Total,	11		4	33			469	16	16	5		1	3	1	1		2	1

FULTON COUNTY.—(CONTINUED.)

TOWNS.	Otsego.	Putnam.	Queens.	Rensselaer.	Richmond.	Rockland.	St. Lawrence	Saratoga.	Schenectady.	Schoharie.	Schuyler.	Seneca.	Steuben.	Suffolk.	Sullivan.	Tioga.	Tompkins.	Ulster.
Bleecker,	5			15				29	2	3			1					5
Broadalbin,	6		2	58				265	48	22		4		1				1
Caroga,	1			1			2	20	5	29							1	1
Ephrata,	9			8			1	38	9	7			1					
Johnstown,	21		1	64			12	177	66	55		1	3	2	1			1
Mayfield,	4		1	33			5	130	19	38		3		1		2		
Northampton,	5	1	1	34			4	250	17	12		1		1				2
Oppenheim,	22			10			6	19	8	22		1				1		3
Perth,	1			8				57	27	2								3
Stratford,	14			13			2	24	9	9								
Total,	88	1	5	244			32	1,009	210	199		10	5	5	1	3	1	16

ERIE COUNTY.—(CONTINUED.)

TOWNS.	COUNTIES OF NEW-YORK.							UNITED STATES.										
	Warren.	Washington.	Wayne.	Westchester.	Wyoming.	Yates.	New-York.	Maine.	N. Hampshire.	Vermont.	Massachusetts.	Rhode Island.	Connecticut.	New Jersey.	Pennsylvania.	Delaware.	Maryland.	District of Columbia.
Buffalo city:																		
10th ward,	2	37	24	8	13	3	2, 679	10	32	69	128	15	125	20	52	.....	6	2
11th ward,	.....	9	5	1	6	.....	1, 431	2	16	41	45	1	40	16	53	.....	16	1
12th ward,	.....	3	2	.....	7	.....	1, 239	17	4	13	33	13	50	5	40	.....	.....	.....
13th ward,	.....	1	3	2	4	2	322	.....	6	6	14	.....	8	.....	6	.....	.....	.....
Total Buffalo,	13	171	140	45	119	49	32, 670	136	204	584	943	85	761	203	633	.....	134	11
Chictawauga,	.....	2	.....	.....	4	.....	1, 106	1	3	14	10	4	11	1	34	.....	1	.....
Clarence,	.....	2	3	1	.....	.....	1, 858	.....	7	38	17	4	30	17	210	.....	3	.....
Colden,	7	9	5	.....	2	.....	972	4	15	79	26	15	24	2	8	.....	.....	.....
Collins,	8	44	6	.....	6	.....	1, 495	8	13	197	64	22	18	1	23	.....	17	.....
Concord,	7	30	17	2	35	3	2, 068	5	42	135	144	24	71	8	21	.....	2	.....
East Hamburgh,	.....	43	.....	1	4	1	1, 230	2	4	52	30	8	24	34	24	.....	1	.....
Eden,	12	49	7	.....	4	.....	1, 445	.....	6	52	63	8	17	29	18	.....	.....	.....
Evans,	9	34	4	2	11	1	1, 563	5	15	107	91	6	44	10	19	.....	.....	.....
Grand Island,	.....	3	1	.....	1	.....	489	4	2	22	8	3	1	1	8	.....	1	.....
Hamburgh,	2	20	7	.....	2	3	1, 640	1	7	107	29	14	23	4	19	.....	1	1
Holland,	1	9	3	.....	44	.....	1, 005	3	48	119	18	7	15	1	2	.....	.....	.....
Lancaster,	2	5	2	4	20	2	2, 351	1	16	97	50	6	55	10	74	.....	1	.....
Marilla,	5	4	1	1	20	1	996	1	24	34	34	7	33	9	18	.....	.....	.....
Newstead,	.....	19	5	.....	14	10	2, 199	4	24	117	44	14	58	19	28	.....	1	.....
North Collins,	9	22	8	3	2	1	1, 220	1	5	67	76	14	17	6	10	.....	1	.....
Sardinia,	1	30	2	1	53	.....	1, 332	2	20	110	51	60	36	1	10	.....	.....	.....
Tonawanda,	1	9	2	2	3	1	1, 199	9	2	40	16	.....	17	23	23	.....	.....	.....
Wales,	1	6	1	1	82	2	1, 289	4	20	57	44	10	21	3	6	.....	.....	.....
West Seneca,	4	1	3	.....	2	.....	644	3	8	15	20	.....	.....	2	8	.....	.....	.....
Total,	109	595	241	67	528	83	66, 945	216	569	2, 433	1, 992	365	1, 488	438	1, 499	.....	174	12

ESSEX COUNTY.—(CONTINUED.)

TOWNS.	Warren.	Washington.	Wayne.	Westchester.	Wyoming.	Yates.	New-York.	Maine.	N. Hampshire.	Vermont.	Massachusetts.	Rhode Island.	Connecticut.	New Jersey.	Pennsylvania.	Delaware.	Maryland.	District of Columbia.
Chesterfield,	2	32	.....	.....	.....	.....	1, 953	5	50	341	28	4	16	8	16	.....	4	.....
Crown Point,	29	26	.....	2	.....	.....	1, 525	3	135	383	47	.....	24	3	.....	.....	3	.....
Elizabethtown,	4	.....	.....	.....	.....	.....	983	1	30	151	29	7	16	9	1	.....	2	.....
Essex,	1	33	1	.....	.....	.....	1, 400	9	46	218	25	2	12	13	1	.....	.....	.....
Jay,	3	17	1	.....	.....	.....	2, 052	1	56	216	47	6	12	3	2	.....	.....	.....
Keene,	2	3	.....	.....	.....	.....	524	3	52	91	15	.....	7	.....	.....	.....	.....	.....
Lewis,	1	21	1	.....	.....	.....	1, 252	1	42	190	44	4	26	2	.....	.....	.....	.....
Minerva,	52	45	.....	.....	.....	.....	528	.....	2	54	12	1	5	.....	1	.....	1	.....
Moriah,	10	44	.....	3	.....	.....	1, 944	4	45	270	41	5	18	6	5	.....	.....	.....
Newcomb,	13	1	.....	.....	.....	.....	126	.....	4	34	6	.....	3	.....	.....	.....	.....	.....
North Elba,	2	.....	.....	1	.....	.....	198	.....	14	45	8	.....	3	1	2	.....	1	.....
North Hudson,	5	7	.....	.....	.....	.....	349	.....	3	67	5	2	2	2	.....	.....	.....	.....
St. Armand,	4	6	.....	.....	.....	.....	204	.....	5	41	16	.....	3	1	.....	.....	.....	.....
Schroon,	91	36	.....	4	.....	.....	1, 381	.....	48	218	33	14	31	4	.....	.....	.....	.....
Ticonderoga,	36	85	.....	1	.....	.....	1, 440	1	37	284	41	1	26	2	1	.....	.....	.....
Westport,	6	26	.....	.....	.....	.....	1, 347	2	68	207	42	3	10	3	7	.....	1	1
Wilsborough,	1	8	.....	.....	.....	.....	1, 137	2	28	184	35	3	14	6	4	.....	.....	1
Wilmington,	.....	12	.....	.....	.....	1	714	1	21	79	12	.....	10	1	.....	.....	.....	.....
Total,	262	402	3	11	.....	1	19, 057	33	686	3, 073	486	52	238	64	40	.....	12	2

FRANKLIN COUNTY.—(CONTINUED.)

TOWNS.	Warren.	Washington.	Wayne.	Westchester.	Wyoming.	Yates.	New-York.	Maine.	N. Hampshire.	Vermont.	Massachusetts.	Rhode Island.	Connecticut.	New Jersey.	Pennsylvania.	Delaware.	Maryland.	District of Columbia.
Bangor,	.....	1	.....	.....	.....	.....	1, 234	2	50	370	39	.....	16	.....	4	.....	.....	.....
Belmont,	.....	4	.....	.....	.....	.....	577	8	40	105	9	1	3	.....	.....	.....	.....	.....
Bombay,	.....	7	.....	1	.....	.....	1, 279	.....	19	206	5	1	5	1	.....	.....	.....	.....
Brandon,	.....	.....	.....	.....	.....	.....	436	.....	29	156	16	1	2	.....	.....	.....	.....	.....
Burke,	.....	17	.....	.....	.....	.....	1, 206	1	28	264	30	.....	.....	3	.....	.....	.....	.....
Chateaugay,	1	10	.....	.....	.....	.....	1, 741	1	23	270	19	2	10	.....	.....	.....	.....	.....
Constable,	1	10	.....	.....	.....	.....	758	2	21	195	27	.....	9	.....	1	.....	.....	.....
Dickinson,	4	.....	.....	.....	.....	.....	659	4	71	385	16	5	9	.....	.....	.....	.....	.....
Duane,	.....	6	.....	.....	2	.....	222	.....	5	39	1	.....	1	.....	.....	.....	.....	.....
Fort Covington,	1	52	.....	.....	.....	.....	1, 474	5	57	177	32	1	5	1	2	.....	.....	.....
Franklin,	.....	.....	.....	.....	.....	.....	547	2	19	131	8	2	1	1	.....	.....	.....	.....
Harrietstown,	.....	.....	.....	.....	.....	.....	186	.....	7	79	2	.....	2	.....	.....	.....	.....	.....
Malone,	.....	39	1	1	.....	.....	2, 697	5	81	622	107	4	50	4	7	.....	.....	.....
Moira,	1	7	.....	1	1	.....	812	1	98	272	29	2	16	.....	2	.....	.....	.....
Westville,	.....	13	.....	.....	.....	.....	755	.....	35	197	19	2	6	.....	.....	.....	.....	.....
Total,	8	166	1	3	3	.....	14, 583	31	583	3, 468	359	21	135	10	16	.....	.....	.....

FULTON COUNTY.—(CONTINUED.)

TOWNS.	Warren.	Washington.	Wayne.	Westchester.	Wyoming.	Yates.	New-York.	Maine.	N. Hampshire.	Vermont.	Massachusetts.	Rhode Island.	Connecticut.	New Jersey.	Pennsylvania.	Delaware.	Maryland.	District of Columbia.
Bleecker,	11	17	.....	.....	.....	.....	498	1	.....	3	30	.....	2	1	1	.....	.....	.....
Broadalbin,	14	29	2	7	.....	.....	2, 265	2	7	37	34	20	76	14	5	.....	.....	.....
Caroga,	8	6	.....	1	.....	.....	564	1	6	2	16	2	7	2	6	.....	.....	.....
Ephrata,	.....	7	2	1	.....	.....	2, 023	1	1	16	11	7	7	10	.....	.....	.....	.....
Johnstown,	23	48	7	4	1	.....	6, 602	5	18	38	75	18	86	19	15	.....	1	.....
Mayfield,	4	26	.....	4	.....	1	2, 113	5	4	26	17	9	30	10	4	.....	.....	.....
Northampton,	91	34	.....	3	.....	.....	1, 618	1	7	45	69	24	46	7	4	.....	.....	.....
Oppenheim,	2	17	1	1	.....	.....	2, 183	1	28	14	39	2	31	4	4	.....	.....	.....
Perth,	.....	1	.....	1	.....	1	919	3	.....	6	2	6	17	3	1	.....	.....	.....
Stratford,	1	4	.....	2	.....	.....	847	1	5	12	16	1	21	4	1	.....	.....	.....
Total,	94	189	12	24	1	2	19, 632	21	76	199	309	89	323	74	41	.....	1	.....

ERIE COUNTY.—(CONTINUED.)

TOWNS.	UNITED STATES.																	
	Virginia.	N. Carolina	S. Carolina.	Georgia.	Florida.	Alabama.	Mississippi.	Louisiana.	Texas.	Arkansas.	Missouri.	Tennessee.	Kentucky.	Ohio.	Indiana.	Illinois.	Michigan.	Wisconsin.
Buffalo city:																		
10th ward,	2	2	3		4		7	1					2	44	5	7	23	
11th ward,								1				1		29		2	12	5
12th ward,	3													13	3		4	3
13th ward,													1	2			3	
Total Buffalo,	111	12	16	9	6	8	10	11	4	1	10	4	38	434	23	39	212	40
Chictawauga,													2	5			2	
Clarence,											2			11		1	4	
Colden,	1													2				1
Collins,	1				1									12	3	6	5	
Concord,														8			3	9
East Hamburgh,														2			7	
Eden,								1				2		3	1	1	1	1
Evans,								1						15			4	1
Grand Island,	4	1									1		2	9		2	1	
Hamburgh,	6													5			3	
Holland,														2		1		4
Lancaster,	2										1			10	2		7	1
Marilla,												1		3	1	1	3	
Newstead,														6	4			5
North Collins,														6	3		1	
Sardinia,						1					1			7	1	1		3
Tonawanda,							1						2	10		1	7	1
Wales,														9	1	2	4	3
West Seneca,	2													10		1	3	5
Total,	127	14	16	9	7	9	11	15	4	1	16	7	53	620	42	66	295	82

ESSEX COUNTY.—(CONTINUED.)

TOWNS.	Virginia.	N. Carolina	S. Carolina.	Georgia.	Florida.	Alabama.	Mississippi.	Louisiana.	Texas.	Arkansas.	Missouri.	Tennessee.	Kentucky.	Ohio.	Indiana.	Illinois.	Michigan.	Wisconsin.
Chesterfield,														1				
Crown Point,													1	1	1		2	
Elizabethtown,														1				3
Essex,												1				3		
Jay,																	3	
Keene,														1				
Lewis,														1				
Minerva,														1			1	
Moriah,			1		1									1	2		1	1
Newcomb,																		
North Elba,	1													1				
North Hudson,														1				
St. Armand,																		
Schroon,														9			4	
Ticonderoga,														1	2		1	
Westport,														1			2	3
Wilsborough,												1		1				
Wilmington,																		
Total,	1		1		1							2	1	21	5	3	14	7

FRANKLIN COUNTY.—(CONTINUED.)

TOWNS.	Virginia.	N. Carolina	S. Carolina.	Georgia.	Florida.	Alabama.	Mississippi.	Louisiana.	Texas.	Arkansas.	Missouri.	Tennessee.	Kentucky.	Ohio.	Indiana.	Illinois.	Michigan.	Wisconsin.
Bangor,														1				
Belmont,														1			1	
Bombay,																	4	
Brandon,																		
Burke,														4				
Chateaugay,																	1	
Constable,	2															3		
Dickinson,														1				
Duane,																		
Fort Covington,	1													6		1		
Franklin,														2	1			
Harrietstown,																1		
Malone,	1													4		1	4	
Moira,														5				1
Westville,																	1	
Total,	4													24	1	6	11	1

FULTON COUNTY.—(CONTINUED.)

TOWNS.	Virginia.	N. Carolina	S. Carolina.	Georgia.	Florida.	Alabama.	Mississippi.	Louisiana.	Texas.	Arkansas.	Missouri.	Tennessee.	Kentucky.	Ohio.	Indiana.	Illinois.	Michigan.	Wisconsin.
Bleecker,															1			
Broadalbin,														5	1	4	1	1
Caroga,		1																
Ephrata,																	2	
Johnstown,	4										1			6		3		2
Mayfield,																		
Northampton,																	1	
Oppenheim,			1											1				1
Perth,	3												1	4		1		
Stratford,															1			
Total,	7	1	1								1		1	16	3	8	4	4

ERIE COUNTY.—(Continued.)

TOWNS.	U. STATES. Iowa.	California.	Territories.	Total United States.	FOREIGN COUNTRIES. Canada.	N. Brunswick.	Nova Scotia.	N. Foundland.	West Indies.	Mexico.	S. America.	England.	Scotland.	Ireland.	Wales.	France.	Belgium.	Holland.
Buffalo city:																		
10th ward,	3			3, 241	165			7		1		298	79	670		99	1	16
11th ward,				1, 712	136							358	65	450		28		
12th ward,	1			1, 469	101		1		1			222	20	490	5	261		10
13th ward,				368	17							65	4	53		16		
Total Buffalo,	6			37, 441	2, 139	41	16	24	14	3	4	3, 291	792	10, 020	45	2, 348	25	317
Chictawauga,				1, 194	11							61	1	71		265		
Clarence,				2, 202	39							94	1	23		29		
Colden,				1, 149	17		1					107	2	25	1	1		
Collins,				1, 891	6		2					9		16		9	1	5
Concord,				2, 540			1					15	3	37	1	29	1	
East Hamburgh,				1, 418	21							58	2	49		8		2
Eden,				1, 648	8							21	2	5	5	22		
Evans,				1, 881	17							117	3	89		5		1
Grand Island,				559	99							41	8	60		4		21
Hamburgh,				1, 860	16	2	1					77	10	96	2	41		15
Holland,				1, 225	11						1	6	5	22		1		7
Lancaster,				2, 684	33							145	15	122	1	279	1	139
Marilla,				1, 165	23							26		63	1			
Newstead,				2, 523	30		7					92	7	88		6		1
North Collins,				1, 427	4		1					4		7		74		2
Sardinia,				1, 636	15	1						3	8	33		3		1
Tonawanda,				1, 351	90		4					38	6	217	3	311	1	7
Wales,				1, 473	8		4					48		20	2	7		
West Seneca,	1			722	37						2	117	8	131		56		
Total,	7			77, 620	2, 797	44	49	24	17	3	7	4, 732	895	11, 554	63	4, 019	36	536

ESSEX COUNTY.—(Continued.)

TOWNS.	Iowa.	California.	Territories.	Total United States.	Canada.	N. Brunswick.	Nova Scotia.	N. Foundland.	West Indies.	Mexico.	S. America.	England.	Scotland.	Ireland.	Wales.	France.	Belgium.	Holland.
Chesterfield,				2, 426	529							33	5	320		1		
Crown Point,				2, 128	34							7	18	21		2		
Elizabethtown,				1, 233	75							29	1	62		2		
Essex,				1, 730	249				1			10	6	113				
Jay,				2, 398	230	1						20	3	198				
Keene,				693	10							4		65				
Lewis,				1, 562	109							15	1	116				
Minerva,				606	10		3					5	5	130		5		
Moriah,				2, 345	153							52	7	558	1			
Newcomb,				173	31							7	1	11		2		
North Elba,				274	14							11		2				
North Hudson,				431	62							3		23				
St. Armand,				270	11							6		2				
Schroon,				1, 742	119	1						9	2	174	1	1		
Ticonderoga,				1, 837	119							20	7	142				
Westport,				1, 697	233			1				18	10	81		1		
Wilsborough,				1, 416	173							15	16	46		1		
Wilmington,				838	37							1	3	24				
Total,				23, 799	2, 198	2	3	1	1			265	85	2, 088	2	15		

FRANKLIN COUNTY.—(Continued.)

TOWNS.	Iowa.	California.	Territories.	Total United States.	Canada.	N. Brunswick.	Nova Scotia.	N. Foundland.	West Indies.	Mexico.	S. America.	England.	Scotland.	Ireland.	Wales.	France.	Belgium.	Holland.
Bangor,	2			1, 718	200							8	17	118				
Belmont,				745	60							2		66				
Bombay,	1			1, 521	534							17	1	241		1		
Brandon,				640	47	1						4	1	35				
Burke,	1			1, 537	154				1			21	19	167	1			
Chateaugay,				2, 067	304							27	28	250				
Constable,			1	1, 019	254							8	8	154				
Dickinson,				1, 150	80							2	2	19		1		
Duane,				268	27	1						11	1	17				
Fort Covington,				1,762	564							15	12	203				
Franklin,				714	79							5	1	147		1		
Harrietstown,				277	21							7			1			
Malone,				3, 587	942		1					29	16	598		4		
Moira,				1, 238	88				1			8	1	120				
Westville,				1, 015	181							8	9	140				
Total,	4		1	19, 258	3, 625	2	1		2			172	116	2, 275	2	7		

FULTON COUNTY.—(Continued.)

TOWNS.	Iowa.	California.	Territories.	Total United States.	Canada.	N. Brunswick.	Nova Scotia.	N. Foundland.	West Indies.	Mexico.	S. America.	England.	Scotland.	Ireland.	Wales.	France.	Belgium.	Holland.
Bleecker,				537	2							6		12		5		13
Broadalbin,				2, 472	3							42	39	62		2		
Caroga,				607								10	1	19		1		
Ephrata,				2, 078	4							9	9	23	1	2		
Johnstown,				6, 893	20		3					216	84	419		19	1	2
Mayfield,				2, 218	7	2						40	16	46				
Northampton,				1, 822	3		1		1			40	3	57	1			
Oppenheim,				2, 309	12							9		59		2		
Perth,				966	3							25	69	49				
Stratford,				909	3	2						5	1	55	14	3		
Total,				20, 811	57	4	4		1			402	222	801	16	34	1	15

ERIE COUNTY.—(Continued.)

TOWNS.	Germany.	Prussia.	Austria.	Switzerland.	Italy.	Spain.	Portugal.	Poland.	Norway.	Sweden.	Russia.	Denmark.	East Indies.	Africa.	Turkey and Greece.	Islands.	Asia.	At Sea.	Unknown.
	FOREIGN COUNTRIES.																		
Buffalo city:																			
10th ward,	572	35	16	5		2		1		3								4	23
11th ward,	535	5		15					6		1	1						1	1
12th ward,	1,094	12	1	26					3	1							5		7
13th ward,	267			6	1					20								1	
Total Buffalo,	14,299	1,675	627	535	45	8	4	67	50	52	35	30	2	4			7	28	226
Chictawauga,	875	21		20		3				4									
Clarence,	813	24							2	5								1	20
Colden,	65	6								1									6
Collins,	65	6		1															14
Concord,	159	7		1															11
East Hamburgh,	387									1									
Eden,	715																		
Evans,	120	2		3						1									13
Grand Island,		38		5						1			1						1
Hamburgh,	875	6	2	2	1					1									30
Holland,	43																		
Lancaster,	2,043	17		2		1					3								4
Marilla,	78									7									14
Newstead,	213	2		2								1							15
North Collins,	286	52		1															1
Sardinia,	38	5			1														21
Tonawanda,	459	38	1	32		1							1					1	8
Wales,	111	16																	
West Seneca,	1,446									1								1	2
Total,	25,907	1,947	630	615	47	13	4	67	55	76	38	33	4	4			7	34	454

ESSEX COUNTY.—(Continued.)

TOWNS.	Germany.	Prussia.	Austria.	Switzerland.	Italy.	Spain.	Portugal.	Poland.	Norway.	Sweden.	Russia.	Denmark.	East Indies.	Africa.	Turkey and Greece.	Islands.	Asia.	At Sea.	Unknown.
Chesterfield,																			13
Crown Point,																		1	5
Elizabethtown,																			
Essex,	3																		3
Jay,																			
Keene,																			2
Lewis,																			
Minerva,	2																		1
Moriah,								1								1		1	1
Newcomb,	1																		
North Elba,																			
North Hudson,																			
St. Armand,																			
Schroon,	14																		22
Ticonderoga,																			
Westport,																			
Wilsborough,																			8
Wilmington,																			1
Total,	20							1								1		2	56

FRANKLIN COUNTY.—(Continued.)

TOWNS.	Germany.	Prussia.	Austria.	Switzerland.	Italy.	Spain.	Portugal.	Poland.	Norway.	Sweden.	Russia.	Denmark.	East Indies.	Africa.	Turkey and Greece.	Islands.	Asia.	At Sea.	Unknown.
Bangor,																			3
Belmont,																			
Bombay,																			4
Brandon,																			
Burke,																			
Chateaugay,																			
Constable,																			
Dickinson,																		1	
Duane,																			
Fort Covington,																		1	2
Franklin,																			
Harrietstown,																			
Malone,	4																		5
Moira,																			3
Westville,					1														
Total,	4				1													2	17

FULTON COUNTY.—(Continued.)

TOWNS.	Germany.	Prussia.	Austria.	Switzerland.	Italy.	Spain.	Portugal.	Poland.	Norway.	Sweden.	Russia.	Denmark.	East Indies.	Africa.	Turkey and Greece.	Islands.	Asia.	At Sea.	Unknown.
Bleecker,	321	3		4															1
Broadalbin,	24	1						1											
Caroga,	68	2		1															5
Ephrata,	57																		
Johnstown,	234	6		12															3
Mayfield,	20			32														2	10
Northampton,	2			11															2
Oppenheim,	16																	1	4
Perth,	17	2																	
Stratford,	43	10																1	
Total,	802	24		60				1										4	25

GENESEE COUNTY.

TOWNS.	Albany.	Allegany.	Broome.	Cattaraugus.	Cayuga.	Chautauque.	Chemung.	Chenango.	Clinton.	Columbia.	Cortland.	Delaware.	Dutchess.	Erie.	Essex.	Franklin.	Fulton.	Genesee.
	COUNTIES OF NEW-YORK.																	
Alabama,	8	14	1	12	23	6		3		11	7	5	19	30		1	4	799
Alexander,	1	3		22	15			1	3	6	1	1	8	21		1	2	740
Batavia,	26	10	2	18	29	6	2	12	1	26	10	17	28	59	3		2	2, 044
Bergen,	2	5	1	3	21			1		14	1		12	4	1	1		719
Bethany,	6	7		6	23	4		8	1	8		4	6	10	2	1	2	877
Byron,	8	1		4	16	7		1	1	11		6	4	5		2	1	758
Darien,	6	2		9	15	15		4	7	17	1	2	18	103	1		3	838
Elba,	5	3		2	10	2		7	1	16		2	21	16	1	1		791
Le Roy,	25	19	4	10	41	8	1	7		27	1	4	28	26	9		9	1, 545
Oakfield,	8	7		4	17	3		7	1	3			16	6	4	1		571
Pavilion,	3	11			16	4		2		16		2	12	7	5			764
Pembroke,	13	5	2	12	18	9		5	2	9	9	2	16	98	5		5	1, 141
Stafford,	1	1		3	9	4	3	1		5	3	2	10	6	1	5		919
Total,	112	88	10	105	253	68	6	59	17	169	33	47	198	391	32	13	28	12, 506

GREENE COUNTY.

TOWNS.	Albany.	Allegany.	Broome.	Cattaraugus.	Cayuga.	Chautauque.	Chemung.	Chenango.	Clinton.	Columbia.	Cortland.	Delaware.	Dutchess.	Erie.	Essex.	Franklin.	Fulton.	Genesee.
Ashland,	17				1				1	48		53	17					
Athens,	73		3							127	2	17	37					2
Cairo,	93		3		3			2		67		29	90					1
Catskill,	132		2		3				3	284	1	54	142	1			1	1
Coxsackie,	176		1					2		111	1	26	43		6			
Durham,	301	1	2					2	1	43	5	44	59			2		
Greenville,	286	1	1					2		49		4	59					
Halcott,	9									1		135	17					
Hunter,	19		2					1		31		18	21		1			
Jewett,	15		1		1					10	1	22	13					
Lexington,	25									41		92	33					
New Baltimore,	295	2	1					1	2	39		3	60					
Prattsville,	49		4							51		123	29					
Windham,	55		1		1	1				45		24	24		1			1
Total,	1, 545	4	21		9	1		10	7	947	10	644	644	1	8	2	1	5

HAMILTON COUNTY.

TOWNS.	Albany.	Allegany.	Broome.	Cattaraugus.	Cayuga.	Chautauque.	Chemung.	Chenango.	Clinton.	Columbia.	Cortland.	Delaware.	Dutchess.	Erie.	Essex.	Franklin.	Fulton.	Genesee.
Arietta,	1							5					1		4		9	
Gilman,								2					1		1		1	1
Hope,	5		5		2	1		4		1		1	7		2		57	
Lake Pleasant,	9												2			1	7	
Long Lake,								1							32			
Morehouse,	1				1	1							1					
Wells,	8				1	1							3	1	5		14	1
Total,	24		5		4	3		12		1		1	15	1	44	1	88	2

HERKIMER COUNTY.

TOWNS.	Albany.	Allegany.	Broome.	Cattaraugus.	Cayuga.	Chautauque.	Chemung.	Chenango.	Clinton.	Columbia.	Cortland.	Delaware.	Dutchess.	Erie.	Essex.	Franklin.	Fulton.	Genesee.
Columbia,	23				1			2		9	1		17				2	
Danube,	9				1					7		2	10				16	1
Fairfield,	9				1	2		1		3			5			2	15	
Frankfort,	20	1	4		5	3		15		18	1	1	21	3	1	1	3	1
German Flats,	12	1	3		4	7		4		9	1	1	11	4		2	10	2
Herkimer,	16				2			1		17	1	2	5		2	1	19	
Litchfield,	6	1				1		4	1	4	3		9	2			1	1
Little Falls,	55		2		7	1		6	4	11	4	10	13	4			39	1
Manheim,	18		1		2					1			7	1			58	
Newport,	9				1	1	1	3		2			4	3			24	
Norway,	1		1		1					7	11	3	7				6	
Ohio,	29									4	1	3	7				11	
Russia,	12				4					11	1	2	23	1			1	2
Salisbury,	16	1	1	8	4			3		20	3		3		4		128	1
Schuyler,	12		1	2	3			4		8	1	7	2				2	
Stark,	16	1			2					6			5				2	2
Warren,	12		1			2		1		3	2	4	9	1				1
Wilmurt,										3			1					1
Winfield,	3	2				10		10		1	2	1	7			4	2	2
Total,	278	7	14	10	38	27	1	54	5	144	32	36	166	19	7	10	339	15

JEFFERSON COUNTY.

TOWNS.	Albany.	Allegany.	Broome.	Cattaraugus.	Cayuga.	Chautauque.	Chemung.	Chenango.	Clinton.	Columbia.	Cortland.	Delaware.	Dutchess.	Erie.	Essex.	Franklin.	Fulton.	Genesee.
Adams,	9	3		2	4	3		6	2	10	7	2	9		1	1	8	4
Alexandria,	13	3			3	1		4	21	3	10		7	1	1	8	13	1
Antwerp,	14							1	13	8		1	7		4	2	3	2
Brownville,	16				3			3	6	11	1	2	13	1	2	1	11	1
Cape Vincent,	15		1		3			2	4	20	5		7		4	3	23	2
Champion,	7				2			3		5	4		8	1		1	1	1
Clayton,	14				1	1	1	2	4	4	2		4	1	3	8	2	4
Ellisburgh,	10		1	1	7	1		18	7	12	9	1	14	6	2	6	6	1
Henderson,	5				0	4		6	4	5	1	3	14	1	5	1	2	3
Hounsfield,	5				7			10	1	2	2		13	2	1	2	1	1
Le Ray,	8		3	1				2	26	18		1	12	3	11	11	19	2
Lorraine,	4		1		3			4	1	2	3		10	4			1	
Lyme,	12				11			8	5	6		12	17	2		2	63	1
Orleans,	11	1			4			3	3	6	5	2	11	1		6	9	2
Pamelia,	7					1		2	16	8			11		1	11	9	

(Continued on page 98.)

GENESEE COUNTY.—(Continued.)

TOWNS.	COUNTIES OF NEW-YORK.																	
	Greene.	Hamilton.	Herkimer.	Jefferson.	Kings.	Lewis.	Livingston.	Madison.	Monroe.	Montgomery.	New-York.	Niagara.	Oneida.	Onondaga.	Ontario.	Orange.	Orleans.	Oswego.
Alabama,	2	......	20	1	2	9	47	4	80	35	3	46	22	19	65	3	85	10
Alexander,	3	......	4	2	......	10	24	5	19	8	6	4	38	15	13	3	11	2
Batavia,	8	......	23	3	14	......	62	19	140	13	29	12	31	37	62	32	29	......
Bergen,	2	......	8	4	2	1	26	4	176	15	5	8	22	11	14	2	20	......
Bethany,	1	......	4	......	......	2	41	4	39	5	34	3	10	19	17	8	7	1
Byron,	2	......	3	8	1	......	11	15	53	4	4	6	56	7	17	......	24	......
Darien,	......	......	5	11	......	1	16	5	35	7	6	14	41	27	5	4	33	4
Elba,	10	......	6	7	......	......	26	12	61	9	2	4	41	20	22	19	33	4
Le Roy,	2	1	9	5	7	7	150	26	163	35	12	8	40	39	65	5	18	15
Oakfield,	10	......	4	2	1	......	25	7	37	38	4	5	14	5	23	4	49	2
Pavilion,	......	......	3	1	......	1	103	5	21	31	3	8	20	17	15	3	5	1
Pembroke,	11	......	9	9	1	4	59	18	95	19	6	28	20	82	28	4	30	4
Stafford,	1	......	6	4	......	1	8	10	31	7	4	4	19	6	12	......	12	1
Total,	52	1	104	57	28	36	598	134	950	226	118	150	374	304	358	87	356	44

GREENE COUNTY.—(Continued.)

TOWNS.	Greene.	Hamilton.	Herkimer.	Jefferson.	Kings.	Lewis.	Livingston.	Madison.	Monroe.	Montgomery.	New-York.	Niagara.	Oneida.	Onondaga.	Ontario.	Orange.	Orleans.	Oswego.
Ashland,	840	......	......	......	......	......	......	......	......	2	6	......	......	......	......	......	......	1
Athens,	2,138	......	1	......	9	......	......	......	......	1	35	......	3	......	......	8	1	......
Cairo,	1,840	......	1	......	1	1	......	......	......	4	16	......	......	......	......	8	......	1
Catskill,	3,574	......	3	1	9	......	1	8	......	7	16	1	2	3	......	24	1	1
Coxsackie,	2,641	......	1	......	1	......	......	1	......	3	34	......	2	5	......	5	......	5
Dunham,	1,617	......	......	1	7	1	1	1	1	2	22	......	7	......	......	4	......	......
Greenville,	1,464	......	......	......	6	......	......	......	......	9	19	......	1	1	1	1	......	......
Halcott,	270	......	......	......	......	......	3	......	......	......	......	......	......	......	......	......	......	......
Hunter,	1,013	......	......	......	2	......	......	......	......	......	29	......	2	......	1	......	4	1
Jewett,	930	......	......	......	......	......	......	1	......	......	6	......	......	......	......	......	......	......
Lexington,	1,120	......	......	......	2	......	......	......	1	......	6	......	1	......	......	2	......	......
New Baltimore,	1,594	......	2	1	5	......	1	......	......	7	18	1	6	1	......	8	......	2
Prattsville,	904	......	2	......	2	......	......	......	......	3	12	......	1	......	......	1	......	......
Windham,	1,179	......	1	1	......	......	......	......	......	......	8	......	8	......	1	1	......	......
Total,	21,124	......	11	4	44	2	6	11	2	38	227	2	33	10	3	62	6	11

HAMILTON COUNTY.—(Continued.)

TOWNS.	Greene.	Hamilton.	Herkimer.	Jefferson.	Kings.	Lewis.	Livingston.	Madison.	Monroe.	Montgomery.	New-York.	Niagara.	Oneida.	Onondaga.	Ontario.	Orange.	Orleans.	Oswego.
Arietta,	......	44	16	......	......	3	......	......	......	4	2	......	......	4	......	......	......	......
Gilman,	......	42	......	......	......	......	......	......	......	2	5	......	......	......	......	......	......	......
Hope,	3	443	1	5	......	......	1	......	1	15	......	......	......	......	......	......	2	......
Lake Pleasant,	1	191	......	......	......	......	......	......	......	9	1	......	1	......	1	3	......	......
Long Lake,	......	43	3	......	......	2	......	......	......	16	......	......	......	......	......	......	......	......
Morehouse,	3	94	7	......	......	......	......	......	......	1	15	......	2	......	......	......	......	......
Wells,	1	406	2	......	......	......	......	......	......	11	3	1	8	2	......	......	......	3
Total,	8	1,263	29	5	......	5	1	......	1	58	26	1	11	6	1	3	2	3

HERKIMER COUNTY.—(Continued.)

TOWNS.	Greene.	Hamilton.	Herkimer.	Jefferson.	Kings.	Lewis.	Livingston.	Madison.	Monroe.	Montgomery.	New-York.	Niagara.	Oneida.	Onondaga.	Ontario.	Orange.	Orleans.	Oswego.
Columbia,	1	......	1,402	8	1	......	......	3	1	39	2	......	26	1	......	......	2	3
Danube,	......	......	1,153	5	......	2	......	1	1	146	3	......	7	3	......	......	1	5
Fairfield,	2	......	937	10	2	4	......	4	......	20	......	......	35	4	......	2	......	10
Frankfort,	4	......	1,857	10	1	6	......	9	5	50	8	1	202	13	2	......	......	14
German Flats,	3	......	2,428	10	......	5	......	12	3	98	72	1	82	11	2	3	......	5
Herkimer,	11	1	1,883	15	1	9	......	6	2	51	15	1	46	10	......	1	......	7
Litchfield,	......	......	968	3	3	2	......	8	......	3	4	......	73	5	......	......	......	5
Little Falls,	6	1	2,787	24	1	11	2	21	4	192	30	......	123	23	......	14	3	8
Manheim,	6	2	1,080	9	......	......	......	5	......	110	1	......	12	8	......	......	......	2
Newport,	3	......	1,212	18	2	5	1	6	......	25	9	......	135	3	2	5	......	5
Norway,	2	......	658	10	1	8	......	......	1	13	......	......	26	3	......	......	......	6
Ohio,	7	......	571	7	3	......	......	1	......	56	6	......	29	1	6	......	......	......
Russia,	......	1	1,289	19	4	8	......	10	......	44	7	1	203	5	......	2	......	4
Salisbury,	19	12	1,174	14	1	22	......	4	3	71	14	1	56	8	1	1	......	7
Schuyler,	......	......	1,093	7	......	4	......	2	2	27	6	......	82	3	6	......	......	7
Stark,	1	......	943	2	2	......	......	......	......	152	1	......	20	1	......	......	3	2
Warren,	4	......	1,084	4	......	6	......	12	......	55	7	8	14	2	......	1	1	5
Wilmurt,	1	......	96	8	......	......	......	3	......	5	7	......	19	1	......	......	......	......
Winfield,	4	......	762	3	......	2	......	17	......	3	6	......	49	1	3	......	......	6
Total,	74	17	23,377	186	22	94	3	124	22	1,160	198	13	1,239	106	22	29	10	101

JEFFERSON COUNTY.—(Continued.)

TOWNS.	Greene.	Hamilton.	Herkimer.	Jefferson.	Kings.	Lewis.	Livingston.	Madison.	Monroe.	Montgomery.	New-York.	Niagara.	Oneida.	Onondaga.	Ontario.	Orange.	Orleans.	Oswego.
Adams,	3	......	38	1,789	1	100	1	29	2	12	2	2	118	15	1	......	......	72
Alexandria,	1	3	124	1,791	......	43	1	12	2	108	......	2	99	19	12	1	......	16
Antwerp,	......	......	88	2,111	2	69	3	8	1	26	......	......	72	16	......	3	......	6
Brownville,	2	......	110	2,243	......	34	1	8	4	141	6	2	72	10	2	1	......	22
Cape Vincent,	2	......	38	1,829	1	29	......	14	14	110	9	......	38	7	......	5	......	13
Champion,	3	......	47	1,146	......	127	......	9	2	27	2	......	66	6	......	......	1	4
Clayton,	......	......	191	2,493	......	50	1	6	3	133	5	3	74	10	2	1	1	19
Ellisburgh,	1	......	85	3,324	3	30	......	38	4	45	5	2	135	15	3	3	......	235
Henderson,	2	......	21	1,458	1	23	......	14	4	3	7	......	30	1	......	1	......	23
Hounsfield,	3	......	45	1,968	......	26	......	46	3	28	12	1	50	10	......	1	1	25
Le Ray,	3	......	244	1,867	1	39	......	8	1	74	1	1	60	2	......	......	......	12
Lorraine,	......	1	27	919	1	11	......	3	......	21	2	......	42	10	3	......	......	72
Lyme,	2	......	133	1,413	1	20	1	9	5	288	9	4	35	17	3	8	......	11
Orleans,	2	......	288	1,599	3	13	......	6	......	97	19	1	54	......	......	8	......	5
Pamelia,	1	......	86	1 368	......	24	......	4	......	146	25	3	34	8	1	......	......	17

(Continued on page 99.)

GENESEE COUNTY.—(Continued.)

TOWNS.	Otsego.	Putnam.	Queens.	Rensselaer.	Richmond.	Rockland.	St. Lawrence	Saratoga.	Schenectady.	Schoharie.	Schuyler.	Seneca.	Steuben.	Suffolk.	Sullivan.	Tioga.	Tompkins.	Ulster.
	COUNTIES OF NEW-YORK.																	
Alabama,	22	3		26		1	12	15		27		15	4	2		1	1	1
Alexander,	5			12			2	38	6	1		4	1			3		
Batavia,	44	1	2	32			3	32	2	13		11	15			4	7	5
Bergen,	9		1	6			1	20	3			5	4			1	3	7
Bethany,	7			7			1	8	9	4		3	11	1		1	3	
Byron,	20			6		1	1	6		8		5	1			1	8	
Darien,	20		1	16	2		2	22	2	4		3	7	2		1	1	4
Elba,	11	1		4			1	25		1		4	5					
Le Roy,	14	1	5	16			6	27	5	8		9	22	4	2	3	3	1
Oakfield,	5	1		6			2	5	1	1		17	1					2
Pavilion,	13			7	1		1	35	6	3		7	14			2	1	1
Pembroke,	30	1		54			2	23		8		12	3			1	4	2
Stafford,	11	1					1	5	5			1	7	9	3			
Total,	211	9	9	192	3	2	35	261	39	78		96	95	18	5	18	31	23

GREENE COUNTY.—(Continued.)

TOWNS.	Otsego.	Putnam.	Queens.	Rensselaer.	Richmond.	Rockland.	St. Lawrence	Saratoga.	Schenectady.	Schoharie.	Schuyler.	Seneca.	Steuben.	Suffolk.	Sullivan.	Tioga.	Tompkins.	Ulster.
Ashland,	15	3		9											3			
Athens,	2		2	23		2		2	1	22				3				21
Cairo,	8	3		8				8	3	44		5		4	9		1	36
Catskill,	9	5	3	23				4		88		1		3	7	2		262
Coxsackie,	14	3		27				15	6	47		1		8	1	2		22
Durham,	5	8		12				8	2	116			1		1			23
Greenville,	4	7	2	6				1		26		2		6	4	1		13
Halcott,	3																	8
Hunter,		5	2	4		1		1	1	9					5		2	108
Jewett,	6	2		8				2		7					6			5
Lexington,	7			29				2	1	18				1	5			90
New Baltimore,	4	1	4	22			1	10	11	23				2	1			10
Prattsville,	14	4	1	4		2				165				1	1	1		19
Windham,	4	5	2			1		1		39					7	1		20
Total,	95	46	16	175		6	1	54	25	604		9	1	28	50	7	3	637

HAMILTON COUNTY.—(Continued.)

TOWNS.	Otsego.	Putnam.	Queens.	Rensselaer.	Richmond.	Rockland.	St. Lawrence	Saratoga.	Schenectady.	Schoharie.	Schuyler.	Seneca.	Steuben.	Suffolk.	Sullivan.	Tioga.	Tompkins.	Ulster.
Arietta,	2			1				9	2	3								
Gilman,				1				4	2									
Hope,	1		1	17			1	45	4	10							1	2
Lake Pleasant,	2			7				19	3	2								
Long Lake,										1								
Morehouse,			2	4			2		1	13			4				1	
Wells,	7		1	31			1	31	11	12				2				
Total,	12		4	61			4	108	23	41			4	2			2	2

HERKIMER COUNTY.—(Continued.)

TOWNS.	Otsego.	Putnam.	Queens.	Rensselaer.	Richmond.	Rockland.	St. Lawrence	Saratoga.	Schenectady.	Schoharie.	Schuyler.	Seneca.	Steuben.	Suffolk.	Sullivan.	Tioga.	Tompkins.	Ulster.
Columbia,	70			14		1		17		17			2				2	
Danube,	4			14				8	1	8								7
Fairfield,	6	2		10			9	9	2	1	1		1		3		3	1
Frankfort,	32			19			5	20	5	18		1					1	
German Flats,	112		1	27			1	16	35	6			3	1		2		10
Herkimer,	30			18			21	14	10	14					3			6
Litchfield,	25	1		7			2	1		3				2				
Little Falls,	80	1	5	28	2		5	20	22	20							1	2
Manheim,	5			5		1	3	9	5	5			1				3	15
Newport,	26			19			8	13	4	3				6				1
Norway,	11			10			3	8	4	11				1	2			8
Ohio,	3			17			1	8	38	7								6
Russia,	13		1	51			1	21	29	11				5				2
Salisbury,	31	2	3	15			5	39	7	34						1	2	9
Schuyler,	6			10			1	4	1	3		1						1
Stark,	104		1	17			3		1	14		1	3					1
Warren,	186	1		21			5	8	9	20			5				1	2
Wilmurt,	2			4				2	2	11								
Winfield,	161			8				1	1	6						1		3
Total,	907	7	11	314	2	2	73	218	176	212	1	3	15	15	8	4	13	74

JEFFERSON COUNTY.—(Continued.)

TOWNS.	Otsego.	Putnam.	Queens.	Rensselaer.	Richmond.	Rockland.	St. Lawrence	Saratoga.	Schenectady.	Schoharie.	Schuyler.	Seneca.	Steuben.	Suffolk.	Sullivan.	Tioga.	Tompkins.	Ulster.
Adams,	1			144			15	27		5		1	1	2	1		5	2
Alexandria,	26			14			93	25	5	5		2						5
Antwerp,	10			7			254	29	1	2				3				
Brownville,				13			14	38		9			1			4	4	3
Cape Vincent,	13	1	2	12			19	17	6	8				5				1
Champion,	10			20			31	17		7							2	
Clayton,	16			5	2		96	35	1	4		2	1	4			1	2
Ellisburgh,	39		1	88			11	44	4	13			1				3	
Henderson,	17			8			31	11										2
Hounsfield,	8		1	22			34	27	1	5		1					1	1
Le Ray,	28			12			31	66	2	8		1						3
Lorraine,	3			11			4	8		1								1
Lyme,	35			13			8	19	5	23			1	1			2	1
Orleans,	27			11		2	33	11	2	8			1	3				4
Pamelia,	28			9			26	17		5			1					3

(Continued on page 100.)

GENESEE COUNTY.—(CONTINUED.)

TOWNS.	Warren.	Washington.	Wayne.	Westchester.	Wyoming.	Yates.	New-York.	Maine.	N. Hampshire.	Vermont.	Massachusetts.	Rhode Island.	Connecticut.	New Jersey.	Pennsylvania.	Delaware.	Maryland.	District of Columbia.
	COUNTIES OF NEW-YORK.							UNITED STATES.										
Alabama,		43	3	2	10		1,584	4	25	67	63	5	59	14	21		2	
Alexander,	1	17	1	2	120		1,205		26	69	61	2	99	6	31			
Batavia,	36	19	1	81	4	92	3,213	2	45	123	163	17	171	41	54		7	
Bergen,		8	5	5	13		1,196		6	48	58	2	123	10	21			
Bethany,		23	7	1	49		1,296	1	25	124	54	5	111	15	11		1	
Byron,	1	6	8	1	8	3	1,120		11	41	77	14	56	11	17			
Darien,	1	12	2		87	4	1,448	2	42	120	68	18	78	4	20			
Elba,		6	10	17	13	1	1,253		27	46	84	10	83	18	16			
Le Roy,	3	30	12	10	51	15	2,618	2	39	132	135	11	201	16	17	1		
Oakfield,		11	2		7	1	940		23	30	33	6	46	15	13			
Pavilion,		51	4		43	1	1,269	1	8	66	76	3	73	4	9		1	
Pembroke,		52	36	3	17	2	2,028	1	40	95	120	11	109	10	22		4	
Stafford,		6	4	1	15	1	1,169	2	18	60	70	4	56	11	6		1	
Total,	42	284	95	123	437	120	20,339	15	335	1,021	1,062	108	1,265	175	258	1	16	

GREENE COUNTY.—(CONTINUED.)

TOWNS.	Warren.	Washington.	Wayne.	Westchester.	Wyoming.	Yates.	New-York.	Maine.	N. Hampshire.	Vermont.	Massachusetts.	Rhode Island.	Connecticut.	New Jersey.	Pennsylvania.	Delaware.	Maryland.	District of Columbia.
Ashland,		1				1	1,018	2	3		8	1	50		1		2	
Athens,		1	1	13			2,550		1	7	32	2	28	15	1		4	
Cairo,			2	11			2,302	3	2	7	21	5	69	14	2		1	
Catskill,		4	1	9			4,696	1	12	13	42	17	140	33	19		3	
Coxsackie,	2			9			3,221	2	5	19	19	1	40	5	2			
Durham,			1	3			2,304	1	3	5	18	2	111	7	10			
Greenville,	1	1	1	8			1,987		1	3	10		62	5	3			
Halcott,				4			450						7		6			
Hunter,	1	4		8			1,296		1	1	19	1	28	5	6		1	
Jewett,				2			1,038			1	7	1	55	2				
Lexington,		3		2			1,481	1			18	4	42	2	1			
New Baltimore,		4	4	13			2,159		2	5	6	2	16	5	2		1	
Prattsville,		5		4			1,402		6	8	24	4	19	12	3			
Windham,	1			1			1,434		4	3	24	1	107	1				
Total,	5	23	10	87		1	27,338	10	40	72	248	41	774	106	56		12	

HAMILTON COUNTY.—(CONTINUED.)

TOWNS.	Warren.	Washington.	Wayne.	Westchester.	Wyoming.	Yates.	New-York.	Maine.	N. Hampshire.	Vermont.	Massachusetts.	Rhode Island.	Connecticut.	New Jersey.	Pennsylvania.	Delaware.	Maryland.	District of Columbia.
Arietta,	1	2		1		1	115		2	14	5	2	6					
Gilman,	5	1	1		2	3	74		1	3		1	1					
Hope,	15	5		1		1	600		2	23	34	1	4	1				
Lake Pleasant,	4	4				1	268		3	4	11	5	5					
Long Lake,	1						99			27	3		1					
Morehonse,	1					1	155				1			1				
Wells,	44	10	2	3		1	627		8	29	15	3	7	3	1			
Total,	71	22	3	5	2	8	1,998		16	100	69	12	24	5	1			

HERKIMER COUNTY.—(CONTINUED.)

TOWNS.	Warren.	Washington.	Wayne.	Westchester.	Wyoming.	Yates.	New-York.	Maine.	N. Hampshire.	Vermont.	Massachusetts.	Rhode Island.	Connecticut.	New Jersey.	Pennsylvania.	Delaware.	Maryland.	District of Columbia.
Columbia,		1		10			1,678			.6	14	6	41	5				
Danube,							1,415		2	6	7	2	9	4	1		1	
Fairfield,		12	2	11	1		1,142		1	13	33	28	42	1	3			
Frankfort,		16	1				2,398	6	10	26	54	18	69	3	13		2	
German Flats,	2	9	3	3	2		3,039	10	9	30	57	16	68	7	3		2	
Herkimer,	4	4		2			2,251	2	16	20	49	6	33	4	5		3	
Litchfield,		5	2				1,155	2	6	6	28	16	55	2	4		1	
Little Falls,	5	29	4	3			3,634	9	22	41	97	10	54	12	9			2
Manheim,		2					1,377	1	3	14	13	1	15	1	2			
Newport,		4	1				1,564	2	8	25	57	35	51	1	1		2	
Norway,		10	1				834		2	7	23	23	32					
Ohio,		5	1				828	1	2	5	27	2	5	1				
Russia,		10		4			1,802	8	4	15	47	23	56	3	3			
Salisbury,	10	16		2		2	1,778	1	14	13	46	7	96	14	10			
Schuyler,	1	5	2				1,316		4	5	17	14	14	1	3			
Stark,		1		1			1,308		1		1	2	10	4	2			
Warren,		8		4			1,509			12	31	9	65	9	3		1	
Wilmurt,		2		1			169			4	6	1		1	1			
Winfield,		4		1			1,086		6	4	45	23	57	2	3	1		
Total,	22	143	17	42	3	2	30,283	42	110	252	652	242	772	75	66	1	12	2

JEFFERSON COUNTY.—(CONTINUED.)

TOWNS.	Warren.	Washington.	Wayne.	Westchester.	Wyoming.	Yates.	New-York.	Maine.	N. Hampshire.	Vermont.	Massachusetts.	Rhode Island.	Connecticut.	New Jersey.	Pennsylvania.	Delaware.	Maryland.	District of Columbia.
Adams,	9	34		2		4	2,509	4	30	101	92	33	71	5	4			1
Alexandria,	1	18	24	4		5	2,550	2	36	118	49	9	22	18	4		1	1
Antwerp,	1	26	2				2,795	10	43	125	132	10	44	7	8			
Brownville,	8	22	1				2,846	2	43	90	81	11	55	8	18			
Cape Vincent,	2	14		1			2,299	6	19	49	40	18	25	4	2		1	
Champion,	1	16					1,577		19	65	80	10	95	1	1			
Clayton,	2	6	1	1			3,222	4	31	96	72	15	39	3	5			2
Ellisburgh,	1	37	3		1		4,306	3	34	341	177	56	82	5	3			
Henderson,	11	8	1				1,739		24	89	50	14	46	1	3			
Hounsfield,	3	20	1		1		2,392	3	37	95	81	13	94	5	11		3	
Le Ray,		8		2			2,591	1	31	80	92	13	43	6	16		1	
Lorraine,	3	10	2				1,188	2	20	17	34	6	35	4	3			
Lyme,	4	6		4		1	2,221	2	30	37	34	6	30	4	3			
Orleans,	13	7			3		2,284		24	52	39	10	28	2	12			
Pamelia,	4	11					1,887	1	10	58	54	13	38	3	7			

(Continued on page 101.)

GENESEE COUNTY.—(Continued.)

Towns.	United States.																	
	Virginia.	N. Carolina.	S. Carolina.	Georgia.	Florida.	Alabama.	Mississippi.	Louisiana.	Texas.	Arkansas.	Missouri.	Tennessee.	Kentucky.	Ohio.	Indiana.	Illinois.	Michigan.	Wisconsin.
Alabama,	2													9	2	5	4	4
Alexander,						2						1		7	1	1	11	1
Batavia,	1	3			1		2						2	15	1	5	27	
Bergen,	1		1											9		1	17	2
Bethany,								1					1	1			21	4
Byron,														6			7	
Darien,														4	1	2	4	3
Elba,														4			12	4
Le Roy,	3		2	1	2							6	2		5			7
Oakfield,	1													4			5	4
Pavilion,														3		4	8	
Pembroke,													1	8			18	6
Stafford,	1													12		1	5	1
Total,	9	3	3	1	3	2	2	1				7	6	82	10	19	139	36

GREENE COUNTY.—(Continued.)

Towns.	Virginia.	N. Carolina.	S. Carolina.	Georgia.	Florida.	Alabama.	Mississippi.	Louisiana.	Texas.	Arkansas.	Missouri.	Tennessee.	Kentucky.	Ohio.	Indiana.	Illinois.	Michigan.	Wisconsin.
Ashland,														1				
Athens,				2					2						1			
Cairo,	3																	1
Catskill,				1			1							5		2	4	2
Coxsackie,	1	1							1					2				
Durham,												1		2				
Greenville,														1			1	
Halcott,																	2	
Hunter,	1													1			1	
Jewett,	1																2	
Lexington,				1										1				
New Baltimore,	1							1								4		
Prattsville,														1		1		1
Windham,													1	3				
Total,	7	1		4			1	1	3			1	1	17	1	7	10	4

HAMILTON COUNTY.—(Continued.)

Towns.	Virginia.	N. Carolina.	S. Carolina.	Georgia.	Florida.	Alabama.	Mississippi.	Louisiana.	Texas.	Arkansas.	Missouri.	Tennessee.	Kentucky.	Ohio.	Indiana.	Illinois.	Michigan.	Wisconsin.
Arietta,																		
Gilman,																		
Hope,																		
Lake Pleasant,																		
Long Lake,																		
Morehouse,																		
Wells,																		
Total,																		

HERKIMER COUNTY.—(Continued.)

Towns.	Virginia.	N. Carolina.	S. Carolina.	Georgia.	Florida.	Alabama.	Mississippi.	Louisiana.	Texas.	Arkansas.	Missouri.	Tennessee.	Kentucky.	Ohio.	Indiana.	Illinois.	Michigan.	Wisconsin.
Columbia,														2				2
Danube,														1				
Fairfield,														5	1			1
Frankfort,	2				1									2			2	2
German Flats,	5													3		1		1
Herkimer,	2													1		2	4	
Litchfield,			1														2	1
Little Falls,	3												1	2	1	1		
Manheim,																		
Newport,	1		2											1				
Norway,														2		2	3	
Ohio,														3				
Russia,														5		1		
Salisbury,														4		1	2	1
Schuyler,																3		
Stark,														2				
Warren,	1															1	2	1
Wilmurt,																		
Winfield,																	3	
Total,	14		3		1								1	33	2	12	18	9

JEFFERSON COUNTY.—(Continued.)

Towns.	Virginia.	N. Carolina.	S. Carolina.	Georgia.	Florida.	Alabama.	Mississippi.	Louisiana.	Texas.	Arkansas.	Missouri.	Tennessee.	Kentucky.	Ohio.	Indiana.	Illinois.	Michigan.	Wisconsin.
Adams,	1			1										11	4		6	
Alexandria,														3		2	2	
Antwerp,		1					1								1	2	2	
Brownville,	1		1											2		3	8	
Cape Vincent,										1		1		5		7		6
Champion,	3													1			1	1
Clayton,	1													7		1	4	
Ellisburgh,	1								1					10	1	10	4	3
Henderson,														4				5
Hounsfield,	1		1	2							2		1	4	1	2	5	
Le Ray,														2	1		4	
Lorraine,			1											1		1	1	
Lyme,	1													4	1	1	3	3
Orleans,														8				2
Pamelia,														3	1			

(Continued on page 102.)

GENESEE COUNTY.—(Continued.)

TOWNS.	U. STATES. Iowa.	California.	Territories.	Total United States.	FOREIGN COUNTRIES. Canada.	N. Brunswick.	Nova Scotia.	N. Foundland.	West Indies.	Mexico.	S. America.	England.	Scotland.	Ireland.	Wales.	France.	Belgium.	Holland.
Alabama,				1,870	29							86	17	136		3		
Alexander,				1,523	9							38	1	42	5	16	2	
Batavia,	1			3,894	39	3	1					304	16	764	1	30		2
Bergen,				1,495	23	1						74	19	162	1			
Bethany,				1,671	19							51	7	84		7		1
Byron,				1,360	12							134	7	65		6	3	
Darien,				1,814	19							67	5	93	1	8		
Elba,				1,557	14							83	2	97		2		
Le Roy,				3,200	44		1		1			155	69	578		1		
Oakfield,				1,120	11							137	1	110				
Pavilion,				1,525	9							58	36	104		1		
Pembroke,				2,473	23							64	14	191		5		
Stafford,	1			1,418	20							472	2	90		2		
Total,	2			24,920	271	4	2		1			1,723	196	2,516	8	81	5	3

GREENE COUNTY.—(Continued.)

TOWNS.	Iowa.	California.	Territories.	Total United States.	Canada.	N. Brunswick.	Nova Scotia.	N. Foundland.	West Indies.	Mexico.	S. America.	England.	Scotland.	Ireland.	Wales.	France.	Belgium.	Holland.
Ashland,				1,086	4							2		44				
Athens,				2,645	10							30		156				
Cairo,				2,430	1							24	4	37	1	1		1
Catskill,				4,991	30		2		1		1	93	28	293	1	2		
Coxsackie,				3,319	28							14	2	293			1	4
Durham,				2,464	7							11	1	42	1			
Greenville,				2,073	1							21		50				
Halcott,				465										7				
Hunter,				1,361	2							7	1	167				
Jewett,				1,107	7							3	2	8				1
Lexington,				1,551			2					4		36		1		
New Baltimore,—				2,204	14		1					4	8	133	1			
Prattsville,				1,481								14	5	80	1	1		
Windham,				1,578	2				1			3	10	45				
Total,				28,755	106		5		2		1	230	61	1,391	5	5	1	6

HAMILTON COUNTY.—(Continued.)

TOWNS.	Iowa.	California.	Territories.	Total United States.	Canada.	N. Brunswick.	Nova Scotia.	N. Foundland.	West Indies.	Mexico.	S. America.	England.	Scotland.	Ireland.	Wales.	France.	Belgium.	Holland.
Arietta,				144									1	3				
Gilman,				80								5						
Hope,				725	4							6	15	57				
Lake Pleasant,				296	1							2						
Long Lake,				130	3									6				
Morehouse,				157								3	1	2	2	30		8
Wells,				693	9							9	1	39				
Total,				2,225	17							25	18	107	2	30		8

HERKIMER COUNTY.—(Continued.)

TOWNS.	Iowa.	California.	Territories.	Total United States.	Canada.	N. Brunswick.	Nova Scotia.	N. Foundland.	West Indies.	Mexico.	S. America.	England.	Scotland.	Ireland.	Wales.	France.	Belgium.	Holland.
Columbia,				1,754								4		26	6			
Danube,				1,448	3		1					9		260		1		
Fairfield,				1,270	3		1					50	2	129	3			
Frankfort,				2,608	4		1					140	8	202	124	16		
German Flats,			3	3,254	17							115	8	213	5	38		
Herkimer,				2,398	4							31	3	189	4	1		
Litchfield,				1,279	1				1			155	9	66	48	3		
Little Falls,				3,898	22		1	1	1			117	31	634	18	5		
Manheim,				1,427	3							16		155	4	1		
Newport,				1,750	5			1				64	14	133	41			
Norway,				928								12		103		2		
Ohio,				874	6							28	2	16	2	1		
Russia,				1,967	15							65	18	40	64	3		
Salisbury,				1,987	7	8						34		176	20	7		
Schuyler,				1,377	3		1					33	2	103	74	3		
Stark,				1,332								56	3	65				
Warren,				1,644	2							33	6	31				
Wilmurt,				182	6							19		34	12	4		
Winfield,				1,230	25		1					24	1	92	6	1		
Total,			3	32,607	126	8	6	2	2			1,005	107	2,667	431	86		

JEFFERSON COUNTY.—(Continued.)

TOWNS.	Iowa.	California.	Territories.	Total United States.	Canada.	N. Brunswick.	Nova Scotia.	N. Foundland.	West Indies.	Mexico.	S. America.	England.	Scotland.	Ireland.	Wales.	France.	Belgium.	Holland.
Adams,				2,873	63							39	5	84	8			2
Alexandria,				2,817	258							35	17	94	1	20		
Antwerp,				3,181	99							115	75	257		10		
Brownville,	1			3,171	134	2						120	11	131	1	5		
Cape Vincent,				2,482	214		1					62	14	180	2	244		
Champion,				1,856	36							18	1	26	2	5		
Clayton,				3,500	445							55	11	127	9	11		
Ellisburgh,				5,037	107							53	14	109		1		
Henderson,				1,975	64							34	9	29	1			
Hounsfield,		2		2,755	108	1	2					118	12	188	6			
Le Ray,				2,881	101							29	6	80	1	37		
Lorraine,				1,313	70							13	1	21				
Lyme,				2,380	56							37	4	60	2			
Orleans,				2,461	79							12	4	75		13		
Pamelia,				2,075	146		1					30	14	190		13		1

(Continued on page 103.)

GENESEE COUNTY.—(Continued.)

TOWNS	FOREIGN COUNTRIES																		
	Germany.	Prussia.	Austria.	Switzerland.	Italy.	Spain.	Portugal.	Poland.	Norway.	Sweden.	Russia.	Denmark.	East Indies.	Africa.	Turkey and Greece.	Islands.	Asia.	At Sea.	Unknown.
Alabama,	12	3		3														1	34
Alexander,	146			12						2									2
Batavia,	225	9		12				1										3	
Bergen,	17																		8
Bethany,	36																	1	2
Byron,	53			1															
Darien,	158	3		5						1								1	1
Elba,	102																		12
Le Roy,	123						1											1	32
Oakfield,	66			2															63
Pavilion,	14			1														1	9
Pembroke,	51			6															17
Stafford,	44			1	1														5
Total,	1,047	15		43	1		1	1		3								8	185

GREENE COUNTY.—(Continued.)

TOWNS	Germany.	Prussia.	Austria.	Switzerland.	Italy.	Spain.	Portugal.	Poland.	Norway.	Sweden.	Russia.	Denmark.	East Indies.	Africa.	Turkey and Greece.	Islands.	Asia.	At Sea.	Unknown.
Ashland,	3																		
Athens,	12			1								1							15
Cairo,	19																		39
Catskill,	240	2		7				1	1	2		3						1	11
Coxsackie,	20							1											
Durham,	11			1															2
Greenville,	27																		1
Halcott,																			2
Hunter,	46																		10
Jewett,								1											
Lexington,	1																		
New Baltimore,	37																		
Prattsville,	3	1		2															
Windham,	3									1									41
Total,	422	3		11				3	1	3		4						1	121

HAMILTON COUNTY.—(Continued.)

TOWNS	Germany.	Prussia.	Austria.	Switzerland.	Italy.	Spain.	Portugal.	Poland.	Norway.	Sweden.	Russia.	Denmark.	East Indies.	Africa.	Turkey and Greece.	Islands.	Asia.	At Sea.	Unknown.
Arietta,																			1
Gilman,	1		1																3
Hope,	14																		1
Lake Pleasant,																			1
Long Lake,																			
Morehouse,	70	1																	1
Wells,	12			3														1	1
Total,	97	1	1	3														1	8

HERKIMER COUNTY.—(Continued.)

TOWNS	Germany.	Prussia.	Austria.	Switzerland.	Italy.	Spain.	Portugal.	Poland.	Norway.	Sweden.	Russia.	Denmark.	East Indies.	Africa.	Turkey and Greece.	Islands.	Asia.	At Sea.	Unknown.
Columbia,	39																		2
Danube,	64																1		4
Fairfield,	25																		10
Frankfort,	105																		9
German Flats,	172	2																	31
Herkimer,	213	2	1															1	19
Litchfield,	5		1	1															13
Little Falls,	190	2	1	2				1											6
Manheim,	63																		3
Newport,	6																		1
Norway,	9	1																	4
Ohio,	155																		3
Russia,	88																	2	26
Salisbury,	66			1															
Schuyler,	90																		4
Stark,	9																		13
Warren,	20																		5
Wilmurt,	11																		
Winfield,	12					1												1	3
Total,	1,342	7	3	4		1		1									1	4	156

JEFFERSON COUNTY.—(Continued.)

TOWNS	Germany.	Prussia.	Austria.	Switzerland.	Italy.	Spain.	Portugal.	Poland.	Norway.	Sweden.	Russia.	Denmark.	East Indies.	Africa.	Turkey and Greece.	Islands.	Asia.	At Sea.	Unknown.
Adams,	3							1					1					1	25
Alexandria,	105							1											5
Antwerp,	6			1															19
Brownville,	8	2																	4
Cape Vincent,	166			7	1													1	1
Champion,	1			1															
Clayton,	69				1							1							3
Ellisburgh,	5							1				1					1	1	9
Henderson,	1																		26
Hounsfield,	4	1																3	23
Le Ray,	53			2														1	12
Lorraine,	1																		51
Lyme,	6			3				1											14
Orleans,	154			1														1	5
Pamelia,	35					2													5

(Continued on page 104.)

JEFFERSON COUNTY.—(Continued.)

TOWNS.	Albany.	Allegany.	Broome.	Cattaraugus.	Cayuga.	Chautauque.	Chemung.	Chenango.	Clinton.	Columbia.	Cortland.	Delaware.	Dutchess.	Erie.	Essex.	Franklin.	Fulton.	Genesee.
	COUNTIES OF NEW-YORK.																	
Philadelphia,	13		1		2			2	2	1	1	1	22	1		4	1	1
Rodman,		1			6	4		5	2	6	1	4	5		4			
Rutland,	7	1		3	2	2				1	3	6	3	2	1	2	2	
Theresa,	10		1		1			5	17		3	3	5			4		1
Watertown,	51	1	1	1	17	8		12	3	7	6	8	13	4	6	10	9	4
Wilna,	11				1			2	8	3		1	14		1		5	1
Worth,	1									1			2				2	3
Total,	243	10	9	8	85	25	1	100	145	139	63	47	221	30	47	83	190	35

KINGS COUNTY.

TOWNS.	Albany.	Allegany.	Broome.	Cattaraugus.	Cayuga.	Chautauque.	Chemung.	Chenango.	Clinton.	Columbia.	Cortland.	Delaware.	Dutchess.	Erie.	Essex.	Franklin.	Fulton.	Genesee.
Brooklyn City:																		
1st ward,	40	1			8			2	1	17	5	10	24	11			1	9
2d ward,	31		1					3	1	15		8	19	1				1
3d ward,	88		5		12	5		2		145	2	6	50	12	3			6
4th ward,	88	1	6		12	2	2	8	3	16	3	7	63	3				5
5th ward,	54	1		2	1	1		4	1	28		11	52	4	1		3	2
6th ward,	148		1		18	3	1	5	13	24	3	3	75	20	3		2	9
7th ward,	30				5			1		13	4	20	15	6			1	
8th ward,	34		3			1				11	1	5	10	1				
9th ward,	9					2				1		1	18	3				
10th ward,	171	2	5		11	4		2	8	60	6	21	111	15			2	5
11th ward,	125	1	1		6	2		6	1	68		16	129	19	10	1	8	7
12th ward,	35		1		1							3	5	4				
13th ward,	75		1		8	2		11	7	64	3	33	105	3	1		5	7
14th ward,	42				2					9	6	9	29	11	2		3	2
15th ward,	30				2			5		13		7	38	5				1
16th ward,	15				3					5		15	24	1	2			
17th ward,	20		1			1		2		13		6	55	1	2			
18th ward,	1											1	6			1		
Total Brooklyn,	1,036	6	25	2	89	23	3	51	35	502	33	182	828	120	24	2	25	54
Flatbush,	7									1			13					
Flatlands,	2									5		1	17					1
Gravesend,													3				2	
New Lots,	1									4		1	8		1		3	2
New Utrecht,	8		1							3		2	8	3				
Total,	1,054	6	26	2	89	23	3	51	35	515	33	186	877	123	25	2	30	57

LEWIS COUNTY.

TOWNS.	Albany.	Allegany.	Broome.	Cattaraugus.	Cayuga.	Chautauque.	Chemung.	Chenango.	Clinton.	Columbia.	Cortland.	Delaware.	Dutchess.	Erie.	Essex.	Franklin.	Fulton.	Genesee.
Croghan,	10								3	1						3		
Denmark,	14		1	1	3	1		1		24	4	1	33		2		11	4
Diana,		1	1	5			1			3	1	2	4			2	2	
Greig,	81						1	3	1	32	1	3	11		2		3	
Harrisburgh,	10							2		5			6			4	16	1
High Market,	12	1					1					1					1	1
Lewis,								13		1			1		1			
Leyden,	30			2					3	11		2	7	2	1		6	10
Lowville,	7	1			1			3		9			12	1	2		1	1
Martinsburgh,	7				2	1		1	1	5	1	2	6		2	3	9	
Montague,						4		3		3			2	1	1	1	7	
New Bremen,	3			3				2			6		4				2	
Osceola,	2			1	1			1										1
Pinckney,											4	1	2					
Turin,	29	1	2	1					2	25	2	1	2				2	1
Watson,	10		2			1		15	2		8	3		1		2		
West Turin,	21	1	1				1	1	1	15	1		11					
Total,	236	5	7	13	7	7	4	45	13	134	28	16	101	5	11	15	60	19

LIVINGSTON COUNTY.

TOWNS.	Albany.	Allegany.	Broome.	Cattaraugus.	Cayuga.	Chautauque.	Chemung.	Chenango.	Clinton.	Columbia.	Cortland.	Delaware.	Dutchess.	Erie.	Essex.	Franklin.	Fulton.	Genesee.
Avon,	8	12	1	2	7	2	1	7	7	5		1	52	8	4			45
Caledonia,	5	6		2	4	12		2	1	1		5	7	10			3	47
Conesus,	3	11			34			1		8	3		21	1				
Geneseo,	11	23	5	6	32	2	2	8	1	25	11	9	19	10				2
Groveland,	2	12	1	6	17	1	2		1	6	1	5	6	2	1	1		3
Leicester,	6	23	1	6	38	5		4	1	3		3	33	9	2	1	9	21
Lima,	4	22	1	3	19			10	2	17	8	4	39	27	3			33
Livonia,	11	19	1	5	68	1	6	7		14	10	4	22	10	3			24
Mount Morris,	15	88	3	11	205	2	4	13	4	16	5	17	21	6		17	6	40
North Dansville,	7	82	2	3	35	9	3	6		16	4	2	13	4	3		5	20
Nunda,	8	102	2	20	80	4		15		10	4	5	8	7	2		3	21
Portage,	1	56		2	46		5	10		5		13	11	1				10
Sparta,		13			12			1		2	1	1	1	2		2		2
Spring Water,	8	20	6	4	66	1	1	9	3	10	7	4	13	5		1	2	2
West Sparta,	3	41	5	8	45	1	12	4		2	2	1	4	6			6	3
York,	8	10	6	10	14			2		3	8	11		4			18	68
Total,	100	540	34	88	722	40	36	99	20	143	64	85	270	112	18	22	52	341

JEFFERSON COUNTY.—(Continued.)

TOWNS.	Greene.	Hamilton.	Herkimer.	Jefferson.	Kings.	Lewis.	Livingston.	Madison.	Monroe.	Montgomery.	New-York.	Niagara.	Oneida.	Onondaga.	Ontario.	Orange.	Orleans.	Oswego.
	COUNTIES OF NEW-YORK.																	
Philadelphia,			33	1,055		32		9	2	24	1		29			1		9
Rodman,	1		27	1,095		102	1	13	5	5	1		32	8				6
Rutland,	1		39	1,114		99		1		13	1		55	4		1		6
Theresa,	6		193	1,446		23		4		52	6		39	3	1	2		10
Watertown,	8		117	3,464	2	198	5	36	28	61	37	1	190	41	7	10	7	42
Wilna,	4		47	1,675	4	149		1	1	76	6		63	6		4	2	13
Worth,			27	253		12		2		12			10	5	1		1	3
Total,	45	4	2,048	37,420	20	1,253	14	280	81	1,502	156	22	1,397	213	36	50	13	641

KINGS COUNTY.—(Continued.)

TOWNS.	Greene.	Hamilton.	Herkimer.	Jefferson.	Kings.	Lewis.	Livingston.	Madison.	Monroe.	Montgomery.	New-York.	Niagara.	Oneida.	Onondaga.	Ontario.	Orange.	Orleans.	Oswego.
Brooklyn city:																		
1st ward,	10		6	1	1,497			3	5	2	642	1	16	7	5	22		2
2d ward,	7				2,342	1	4			3	915		5	2		35		
3d ward,	13	6	7	6	2,006	9	4	5	17	9	912		31	8	15	51	5	3
4th ward,	24	1	6	7	3,481	6	3	9	.12	6	1,537	2	7	5	5	71		2
5th ward,	36		1		4,735	3	3	1	2	4	1,655		7	3	1	66		6
6th ward,	23		7	1	3,162	3	3	6	9	28	2,460		19	12	11	80	3	8
7th ward,	9		1		183			4		8	2,031		5		1	59	1	
8th ward,	15		2		1,569			2	5		580	1	9	3	8	30		3
9th ward,	13			1	2,310				1		1,259		7	1		8		
10th ward,	36		20	15	5,023	1	10	17	14	17	2,663	1	52	13	15	112	2	17
11th ward,	12		6	12	6,357	1		4	14	12	2,809		49	13	4	156		3
12th ward,	1		5		1,430				1		657		4	2		8	1	
13th ward,	62		5	5	2,292		3	8	23	19	3,937	3	32	11	7	154	1	1
14th ward,	12	2	3		3,078				3	3	1,949		17			57		2
15th ward,	14			2	1,380	3		4		2	1,573		3		1	36		1
16th ward,	6				3,052		1	1	2	3	1,809	2	2	4		18		3
17th ward,	11		3	4	895	2			4	2	1,544		2	5		48		2
18th ward,				3	794			1	1		408		2			21		1
Total Brooklyn,	304	9	72	57	45,586	29	31	65	113	118	29,340	10	269	89	73	1,032	13	54
Flatbush,					930						253				1	4		
Flatlands,	2				862	1					116					3		
Gravesend,					827						49	3				2		
New Lots,			2		694			1		13	173	1		1		9		
New Utrecht,				2	1,106						170					6		
Total,	306	9	74	59	50,005	30	31	66	113	131	30,101	14	269	90	74	1,056	13	54

LEWIS COUNTY.—(Continued.)

TOWNS.	Greene.	Hamilton.	Herkimer.	Jefferson.	Kings.	Lewis.	Livingston.	Madison.	Monroe.	Montgomery.	New-York.	Niagara.	Oneida.	Onondaga.	Ontario.	Orange.	Orleans.	Oswego.
Croghan,			6	127		494	4			21	3		8	1	2			5
Denmark,	5		48	236	3	1,260		3		44	2		68	4			1	6
Diana,			11	234		413		9	1	23			24	4				3
Greig,	10	1	14	40		507	1	3	3	15	4		87		1	3		2
Harrisburgh,		1	29	73		694		1		46	1		13	4				5
High Market,	1		12	2		527		5		5	22		52	3				3
Lewis,			13	7		389		2			16		87					
Leyden,	2		42	12	5	969	2	1		9	4		117	5	1	2		9
Lowville,	5		49	97	2	1,202		5	2	66	3	1	48	9	1	1		3
Martinsburgh,	6		77	73	3	1,434		1	2	42	17	1	108	7				2
Montague,		1	18	137		158		2		13			22	1		2		13
New Bremen,		2	9	28		670		7	1	45	10		53					3
Osceola,		1	24	10		100	2	6	2	3	18		110		2	1		13
Pinckney,			35	130		723		2		5			6					
Turin,	3		34	38		1,017		8		29	5		110	3		2		5
Watson,	4	1	62	28		426		23	2	15	1	1	57	16				5
West Turin,	3		31	22	6	1,286		1		8	6		77	7		1	1	5
Total,	39	7	514	1,294	19	12,269	9	79	13	389	112	3	1,047	64	7	12	2	82

LIVINGSTON COUNTY.—(Continued.)

TOWNS.	Greene.	Hamilton.	Herkimer.	Jefferson.	Kings.	Lewis.	Livingston.	Madison.	Monroe.	Montgomery.	New-York.	Niagara.	Oneida.	Onondaga.	Ontario.	Orange.	Orleans.	Oswego.
Avon,	1		9	4	3	16	1,153	10	109	14	13	10	15	18	65	7	2	2
Caledonia,	1			2			762	1	115	49	9		6	2	9	7	4	1
Conesus,			10			5	818	9	34	5	2		10	10	25	2		
Geneseo,	1		7	1		1	1,433	7	42	15	59	3	10	12	32	1	8	
Groveland,	5	2	9	4	1		845	6	20	4	7	2	4	4	13	5	3	1
Leicester,	1		10	3			853	4	58	14	6		14	5	35	3	6	
Lima,	5		13	7	2	2	935	8	104	12	8	8	25	11	159	3	1	1
Livonia,	11	1	5	9		3	1,273	6	66	5	3	5	28	12	145	6	5	4
Mount Morris,	23		15	3	1		1,646	14	67	31	31	16	30	13	38	21	5	
North Dansville,	2		9	8	2	1	1,323	9	91	19	9	23	29	51	9	10	13	9
Nunda,	25		47	2	2		1,210	24	66	26	13		44	20	23	12	13	6
Portage,	27		12	1			613	4	12	17		1	5	8	19	4	6	1
Sparta,						1	726	2	8		1	4	3	2	11	4		
Springwater,	11	1	9		1	1	1,221	7	30	9	1	1	13	19	228	7	3	
West Sparta,	1		6	1	1		820	5	26	28	5	3	3	4	10	1	1	
York,			18	6	2	3	1,171	8	61	67	12		31	9	22	4	7	2
Total,	114	4	179	51	15	33	16,802	124	909	315	179	76	270	200	843	97	77	27

JEFFERSON COUNTY.—(CONTINUED.)

TOWNS.	Otsego.	Putnam.	Queens.	Rensselaer.	Richmond.	Rockland.	St. Lawrence	Saratoga.	Schenectady.	Schoharie.	Schuyler.	Seneca.	Steuben	Suffolk.	Sullivan.	Tioga.	Tompkins.	Ulster.
	COUNTIES OF NEW-YORK.																	
Philadelphia, ...	6	.....	.....	20	.....	.....	25	82	4	2	.....	1	1	.....	.....	.....	.....	1
Rodman, ...	9	.....	.....	24	.....	.....	14	9	2	9	.....	1	1	.....	.....	.....	5	1
Rutland, ...	6	.....	.....	8	.....	.....	42	23	.....	7	.....	.....	.....	.....	.....	.....	3	.....
Theresa, ...	46	.....	1	2	.....	.....	44	14	.....	2	.....	.....	2	.....	.....	.....	.....	.....
Watertown, ...	70	1	.....	18	.....	.....	124	58	17	23	.....	4	5	1	1	.....	7	3
Wilna, ...	13	.....	4	4	1	2	52	35	2	13	.....	1	1	1	.....	.....	.....	1
Worth, ...	11	.....	.....	2	.....	.....	6	7	.....	.....	.....	.....	.....	1	.....	.....	.....	.....
Total, ...	422	2	9	467	3	4	1, 037	619	52	159	.....	14	17	21	2	4	33	34

KINGS COUNTY.—(CONTINUED.)

TOWNS.	Otsego.	Putnam.	Queens.	Rensselaer.	Richmond.	Rockland.	St. Lawrence	Saratoga.	Schenectady.	Schoharie.	Schuyler.	Seneca.	Steuben	Suffolk.	Sullivan.	Tioga.	Tompkins.	Ulster.
Brooklyn city:																		
1st ward,	2	4	77	22	11	.....	2	4	4	1	.....	6	.....	28	.....	1	1	4
2d ward,	.....	1	59	13	9	20	.....	4	.....	1	.....	.....	.....	39	1	.....	.....	6
3d ward,	14	5	148	59	17	10	3	15	6	4	.....	5	3	35	.....	4	11	15
4th ward,	13	4	286	56	16	2	2	8	3	5	.....	4	3	142	2	4	7	31
5th ward,	3	24	283	30	23	12	1	13	3	1	.....	.....	.....	116	1	1	2	23
6th ward,	12	9	127	54	15	21	1	41	1	10	.....	13	2	29	3	2	5	18
7th ward,	.....	2	85	10	8	1	1	2	1	.....	.....	.....	1	10	.....	.....	3	15
8th ward,	.....	2	23	6	20	7	.....	4	.....	.....	.....	.....	1	9	6	3	.....	5
9th ward,	.....	1	139	.....	8	.....	.....	1	.....	.....	.....	.....	1	66	3	.....	.....	1
10th ward,	6	20	205	74	67	18	12	26	6	17	.....	15	1	139	5	1	12	20
11th ward,	12	12	690	59	43	42	4	25	10	6	.....	11	4	271	13	1	7	58
12th ward,	1	1	18	11	5	3	.....	3	.....	.....	.....	.....	.....	11	1	1	.....	7
13th ward,	8	13	251	51	43	24	2	23	14	7	.....	.....	.....	143	9	7	6	41
14th ward,	.....	5	140	10	9	1	.....	8	.....	.....	.....	3	.....	64	1	.....	.....	24
15th ward,	.....	2	86	7	5	5	3	7	.....	.....	.....	.....	2	59	.....	2	.....	15
16th ward,	.....	1	45	13	8	3	.....	2	.....	.....	.....	.....	.....	53	2	1	.....	3
17th ward,	4	7	112	22	12	15	3	4	1	.....	.....	3	.....	95	14	1	.....	22
18th ward,	.....	1	58	4	4	5	1	.....	.....	.....	.....	.....	1	12	.....	.....	1	1
Total Brooklyn,	75	114	2, 832	501	323	189	35	190	49	52	.....	60	19	1, 321	61	29	55	309
Flatbush, ...	2	.....	52	6	.....	2	.....	.....	.....	.....	.....	.....	.....	10	1	.....	.....	3
Flatlands, ...	1	2	83	2	1	2	.....	3	.....	.....	.....	.....	.....	7	.....	.....	.....	.....
Gravesend, ...	1	.....	6	3	1	.....	.....	.....	5	.....	.....	.....	.....	10	.....	.....	.....	2
New Lots, ...	.....	.....	165	1	3	3	1	1	.....	.....	.....	.....	.....	36	.....	6	1	.....
New Utrecht, ...	1	4	34	3	17	1	.....	1	.....	.....	.....	.....	.....	9	.....	.....	.....	3
Total, ...	80	120	3, 172	516	345	197	36	195	54	52	.....	60	19	1, 393	62	35	56	317

LEWIS COUNTY.—(CONTINUED.)

TOWNS.	Otsego.	Putnam.	Queens.	Rensselaer.	Richmond.	Rockland.	St. Lawrence	Saratoga.	Schenectady.	Schoharie.	Schuyler.	Seneca.	Steuben	Suffolk.	Sullivan.	Tioga.	Tompkins.	Ulster.
Croghan, ...	.....	.....	.....	.....	.....	.....	4	2	1	2	.....	.....	.....	.....	2	.....	.....	1
Denmark, ...	2	3	.....	26	.....	.....	29	9	1	9	.....	1	1	1	.....	2	.....	.....
Diana, ...	14	.....	.....	1	.....	.....	53	6	1	1	.....	.....	.....	.....	.....	.....	.....	.....
Greig, ...	24	.....	.....	40	.....	.....	2	4	2	36	.....	1	.....	.....	.....	.....	.....	.....
Harrisburgh, ...	2	.....	.....	8	.....	.....	7	3	.....	5	.....	.....	.....	.....	1	.....	.....	10
High Market, ...	.....	.....	.....	3	.....	.....	2	.....	.....	.....	.....	.....	.....	.....	.....	.....	.....	1
Lewis, ...	2	.....	.....	4	.....	.....	.....	1	.....	.....	.....	.....	.....	.....	.....	.....	.....	.....
Leyden, ...	5	.....	.....	19	.....	1	9	4	.....	3	.....	.....	.....	.....	.....	.....	.....	.....
Lowville, ...	6	1	.....	8	.....	.....	17	15	.....	7	.....	2	.....	.....	.....	.....	1	.....
Martinsburgh, ...	38	.....	.....	7	.....	.....	19	7	1	19	.....	4	.....	2	.....	.....	.....	.....
Montague, ...	2	.....	.....	1	.....	.....	10	5	.....	2	.....	.....	.....	.....	.....	.....	.....	1
New Bremen, ...	2	.....	.....	3	.....	.....	5	1	1	3	.....	.....	.....	.....	.....	.....	.....	.....
Osceola, ...	10	.....	.....	7	.....	.....	6	3	.....	8	.....	.....	.....	.....	.....	.....	.....	.....
Pinckney, ...	7	.....	.....	1	.....	.....	3	7	.....	1	.....	.....	.....	.....	.....	.....	.....	.....
Turin, ...	13	.....	.....	9	.....	.....	17	5	1	10	.....	2	.....	.....	.....	.....	.....	.....
Watson, ...	12	.....	.....	28	.....	.....	17	6	.....	5	.....	.....	1	.....	.....	.....	.....	.....
West Turin, ...	2	.....	.....	7	.....	.....	5	7	4	8	.....	.....	.....	.....	.....	.....	.....	.....
Total, ...	141	4	.....	172	.....	1	205	85	12	119	.....	10	2	3	3	2	1	13

LIVINGSTON COUNTY.—(CONTINUED.)

TOWNS.	Otsego.	Putnam.	Queens.	Rensselaer.	Richmond.	Rockland.	St. Lawrence	Saratoga.	Schenectady.	Schoharie.	Schuyler.	Seneca.	Steuben	Suffolk.	Sullivan.	Tioga.	Tompkins.	Ulster.
Avon, ...	10	3	.....	10	.....	.....	3	5	3	4	.....	8	24	.....	.....	3	.....	11
Caledonia, ...	3	.....	6	4	.....	.....	2	13	1	1	.....	16	5	.....	.....	.....	2	3
Conesus, ...	8	.....	.....	14	.....	.....	1	13	1	2	.....	7	7	2	.....	1	1	.....
Geneseo, ...	9	.....	1	8	.....	.....	1	13	.....	1	2	3	13	.....	.....	1	.....	1
Groveland, ...	10	.....	.....	24	.....	.....	.....	3	.....	5	.....	15	26	.....	.....	.....	3	.....
Leicester, ...	7	.....	.....	11	.....	.....	4	21	30	2	.....	10	24	1	1	3	1	5
Lima, ...	16	2	.....	31	.....	.....	5	11	4	4	.....	22	31	4	.....	1	10	1
Livonia, ...	9	7	.....	19	.....	1	.....	27	.....	18	2	18	23	.....	.....	2	6	7
Mount Morris, ...	5	2	1	6	.....	16	1	56	25	12	.....	31	38	1	2	2	20	3
North Dansville, .	1	1	9	3	3	.....	4	15	3	7	.....	27	182	.....	1	12	16	2
Nunda, ...	14	.....	1	20	.....	.....	3	9	22	15	.....	20	47	2	1	2	9	1
Portage, ...	6	1	.....	8	.....	.....	8	18	.....	1	.....	5	2	.....	1	1	11	1
Sparta, ...	2	.....	1	2	.....	.....	1	1	.....	.....	.....	4	30	.....	1	3	1	1
Springwater, ...	27	.....	.....	11	.....	.....	1	14	.....	6	.....	9	106	.....	1	2	9	2
West Sparta, ...	11	.....	.....	4	.....	7	.....	15	1	6	.....	4	22	.....	1	.....	4	2
York, ...	9	2	1	5	.....	.....	.....	20	13	1	.....	2	8	1	.....	.....	.....	6
Total, ...	147	18	20	180	3	24	34	254	103	85	4	201	588	11	9	33	93	46

JEFFERSON COUNTY.—(CONTINUED.)

TOWNS.	COUNTIES OF NEW-YORK.						New-York.	UNITED STATES.										
	Warren.	Washington.	Wayne.	Westchester.	Wyoming.	Yates.		Maine.	N. Hampshire.	Vermont.	Massachusetts.	Rhode Island	Connecticut.	New Jersey.	Pennsylvania.	Delaware.	Maryland.	District of Columbia.
Philadelphia, ...	4	16	1	1	......	......	1,411	2	19	44	27	5	31	7	29	......	......	......
Rodman, ...	1	19	1	......	......	......	1,430	......	16	56	59	17	81	......	1	......	......	......
Rutland, ...	1	9	1	2	......	......	1,472	10	23	87	95	13	59	1	5	......	......	......
Theresa, ...	......	13	4	3	......	......	1,966	1	32	45	67	1	23	7	4	1	......	......
Watertown, ...	1	32	5	3	1	......	4,789	7	94	185	208	15	133	22	21	......	7	......
Wilna, ...	5	14	1	......	......	1	2,252	2	24	111	86	7	55	35	18	......	......	......
Worth, ...	5	5	5	......	......	......	377	......	4	20	13	......	5	......	......	......	......	......
Total,.........	80	351	53	23	6	11	50,103	62	643	1,961	1,662	295	1,134	148	178	1	13	4

KINGS COUNTY.—(CONTINUED.)

TOWNS.	Warren.	Washington.	Wayne.	Westchester.	Wyoming.	Yates.	New-York.	Maine.	N. Hampshire.	Vermont.	Massachusetts.	Rhode Island	Connecticut.	New Jersey.	Pennsylvania.	Delaware.	Maryland.	District of Columbia.
Brooklyn city:																		
1st ward,	......	8	......	35	......	......	2,558	42	38	33	200	36	183	106	36	......	19	1
2d ward,	......	2	......	35	1	......	3,585	31	10	13	108	16	135	148	55	......	22	8
3d ward,	......	13	3	63	1	8	3,885	75	67	65	546	96	475	175	126	6	52	18
4th ward,	2	8	1	89	3	4	6,098	79	63	49	402	69	366	360	171	......	53	16
5th ward,	1	2	......	70	......	......	7,297	29	21	50	167	24	160	349	147	2	42	11
6th ward,	2	15	4	116	1	1	6,665	205	67	86	472	85	375	349	175	7	99	3
7th ward,	......	4	......	60	......	2	2,602	64	35	23	167	43	207	305	150	......	22	2
8th ward,	......	4	1	18	......	......	2,402	10	7	13	44	6	42	161	43	......	13	......
9th ward,	......	......	4	8	......	......	3,871	25	5	2	64	10	60	165	65	1	36	2
10th ward,	1	22	6	109	......	7	9,242	145	54	72	502	85	383	556	226	6	64	10
11th ward,	......	9	1	177	3	1	11,311	123	64	71	420	93	484	808	233	......	75	16
12th ward,	1	2	2	12	......	......	2,237	14	3	14	43	3	25	72	20	......	2	......
13th ward,	1	33	1	147	1	1	7,715	96	41	58	345	60	536	450	208	......	50	4
14th ward,	1	......	......	87	1	......	5,595	26	10	6	73	23	148	360	93	2	16	......
15th ward,	......	1	......	61	......	......	3,404	8	13	12	55	12	101	168	45	......	2	......
16th ward,	......	2	1	32	......	......	5,169	27	3	3	52	6	64	142	105	1	65	4
17th ward,	1	6	3	85	......	......	3,033	43	17	7	72	13	117	198	49	......	10	1
18th ward,	......	......	......	28	......	......	1,356	20	......	3	19	8	29	49	14	......	13	......
Total Brooklyn,	10	131	27	1,232	11	24	88,025	1,062	518	580	3,751	688	3,890	4,921	1,961	25	655	96
Flatbush, ...	1	1	1	3	......	......	1,511	3	2	6	14	4	20	68	15	......	7	......
Flatlands, ...	......	......	......	5	......	......	1,116	......	......	1	6	......	9	45	6	......	......	......
Gravesend, ...	......	......	......	......	......	......	914	......	......	......	5	1	2	34	......	......	1	1
New Lots, ...	......	3	1	10	......	......	1,145	1	......	4	7	2	24	40	12	......	2	......
New Utrecht, ...	......	3	......	26	......	......	1,411	3	2	11	18	3	34	91	20	......	12	2
Total,.........	11	138	29	1,276	11	24	94,122	1,069	522	602	3,801	698	3,979	5,199	2,014	25	677	99

LEWIS COUNTY.—(CONTINUED.)

TOWNS.	Warren.	Washington.	Wayne.	Westchester.	Wyoming.	Yates.	New-York.	Maine.	N. Hampshire.	Vermont.	Massachusetts.	Rhode Island	Connecticut.	New Jersey.	Pennsylvania.	Delaware.	Maryland.	District of Columbia.
Croghan, ...	......	1	......	......	......	......	701	1	2	21	14	......	6	1	1	......	1	......
Denmark, ...	......	17	1	......	......	......	1,882	2	7	52	121	8	54	2	6	......	......	......
Diana, ...	1	8	1	......	......	1	831	......	5	58	41	8	13	8	7	......	......	......
Greig, ...	......	4	6	......	......	......	948	1	8	23	26	2	15	1	......	......	......	......
Harrisburgh, ...	......	7	......	1	......	......	955	......	12	16	33	5	14	......	3	......	......	......
High Market, ...	......	......	......	......	......	......	655	......	......	1	3	1	7	......	1	......	......	......
Lewis, ...	2	1	......	1	......	......	541	......	1	10	7	4	21	......	......	......	......	......
Leyden, ...	2	3	4	......	......	1	1,305	1	11	27	56	3	153	4	3	......	......	......
Lowville, ...	......	6	1	......	......	1	1,597	......	10	37	94	11	72	5	2	......	......	......
Martinsburgh, ...	5	14	2	......	1	1	1,933	2	15	29	139	8	57	2	4	......	......	......
Montague, ...	......	......	......	......	......	......	410	......	3	15	13	8	5	1	1	......	......	......
New Bremen, ...	1	3	......	......	1	......	868	......	4	7	30	6	15	1	2	......	......	......
Osceola, ...	......	2	......	......	......	......	334	2	1	17	10	5	5	2	......	......	......	......
Pinckney, ...	......	4	......	......	......	......	931	......	......	12	26	4	20	......	......	......	......	......
Turin, ...	......	4	......	......	......	......	1,383	3	9	16	45	1	71	3	1	2	......	......
Watson, ...	2	4	7	......	......	......	767	1	14	29	14	6	15	7	2	......	......	......
West Turin, ...	......	1	......	1	......	......	1,542	2	5	13	41	2	88	6	5	......	......	......
Total,.........	13	79	22	3	2	4	17,583	15	107	383	713	82	631	43	38	2	1	......

LIVINGSTON COUNTY.—(CONTINUED.)

TOWNS.	Warren.	Washington.	Wayne.	Westchester.	Wyoming.	Yates.	New-York.	Maine.	N. Hampshire.	Vermont.	Massachusetts.	Rhode Island	Connecticut.	New Jersey.	Pennsylvania.	Delaware.	Maryland.	District of Columbia.
Avon, ...	2	10	8	2	10	16	1,745	1	10	52	63	7	103	9	32	......	......	11
Caledonia, ...	......	17	2	5	6	1	1,160	6	7	11	13	2	9	3	11	......	......	1
Conesus, ...	......	28	2	2	5	4	1,110	......	15	29	10	2	24	53	26	......	......	2
Geneseo, ...	......	10	3	......	21	7	1,892	1	10	42	59	4	87	38	60	......	......	2
Groveland, ...	......	4	1	......	9	3	1,105	......	2	13	16	2	19	69	107	......	2	1
Leicester, ...	3	24	14	2	173	1	1,514	4	18	57	56	3	71	10	45	......	......	2
Lima, ...	5	17	19	7	3	21	1,710	3	19	56	90	1	88	17	34	......	......	2
Livonia, ...	2	15	17	5	14	10	1,994	......	24	62	63	9	89	31	37	......	......	......
Mount Morris, ...	1	41	17	6	67	......	2,780	5	37	71	96	1	106	156	74	......	......	8
North Dansville, .	......	16	14	......	14	20	2,181	3	20	42	48	4	68	49	194	......	......	5
Nunda, ...	9	43	8	3	23	4	2,080	9	50	85	100	8	89	57	70	......	2	......
Portage, ...	......	21	3	8	62	6	1,053	8	14	58	36	1	75	27	15	......	......	......
Sparta, ...	......	3	2	......	1	4	856	......	3	13	10	......	4	18	206	......	......	......
Spring Water, ...	......	62	9	1	4	48	2,036	4	12	78	74	7	49	39	56	......	......	2
West Sparta, ...	......	8	4	......	8	5	1,160	......	6	14	19	3	22	50	83	......	......	1
York, ...	5	34	4	1	68	......	1,765	7	13	45	111	4	67	10	17	......	......	3
Total,.........	27	353	127	42	488	150	26,141	51	260	728	864	58	970	636	1,067	......	4	40

JEFFERSON COUNTY.—(Continued.)

Towns	United States																	
	Virginia.	N. Carolina.	S. Carolina.	Georgia.	Florida.	Alabama.	Mississippi.	Louisiana.	Texas.	Arkansas.	Missouri.	Tennessee.	Kentucky.	Ohio.	Indiana.	Illinois.	Michigan.	Wisconsin.
Philadelphia,														1				
Rodman,														6				1
Rutland,														4		1		
Theresa,	1																	
Watertown,	3	1	2		3	1					1	1		15	1	5	14	2
Wilna,			1											3		3	1	4
Worth,														1				
Total,	13	2	6	3	3	1	1		1	1	3	2	1	95	11	38	55	27

KINGS COUNTY.—(Continued.)

Towns	Virginia.	N. Carolina.	S. Carolina.	Georgia.	Florida.	Alabama.	Mississippi.	Louisiana.	Texas.	Arkansas.	Missouri.	Tennessee.	Kentucky.	Ohio.	Indiana.	Illinois.	Michigan.	Wisconsin.
Brooklyn city:																		
1st ward,	23	12			1			4			1			15	7	1	2	
2d ward,	15	16	8	3	1			7			2		1	5		4	5	3
3d ward,	50	7	16	22	4	3	7				9		4	29	8	6	7	
4th ward,	52	81	12	21	2	2	1	6	1	1	7	7	6	24	5	2	10	1
5th ward,	38	29	13	9		1		10			2	3		15	3	4		
6th ward,	59	11	23	18	4	1	4	23	3		4		19	41	3	4	26	1
7th ward,	23	19	8	5	10	1		11	2		6	5	3	31	1	3	4	1
8th ward,	9			2				3						6		2	1	1
9th ward,	98	26	6			3		8			1		2	18	3	2	7	3
10th ward,	42	12	10	29	11	14	5	14			9		14	34	3	4	5	5
11th ward,	94	56	14	10	8	7	2	14	2		6	1	5	27	6	6	7	9
12th ward,	3	7			2			1					4	4			2	
13th ward,	58	13	11	5	3	11		12	1		9	6	6	28		7	7	9
14th ward,	17	8	14	2	2	1	2	2			1	1	6	11		4	1	
15th ward,	25	2	5	8				1					1	10	1	3	1	2
16th ward,	102	8	18	2		1					5			7	1	1		
17th ward,	14	7	2						1				4	9	1		4	
18th ward,	4	2	1			1		1					2					
Total,	726	316	161	136	48	46	21	117	10	1	62	23	77	314	42	53	89	35
Flatbush,	3				1			1		1				2		1	2	
Flatlands,	1	1											1	1	3		2	
Gravesend,				1														
New Lots,	9							2					1	7	2			1
New Utrecht,	15	1		1	2			2		5	1		1	1	1	1	5	
Total,	754	318	161	138	51	46	21	122	10	7	63	23	80	325	48	55	98	36

LEWIS COUNTY.—(Continued.)

Towns	Virginia.	N. Carolina.	S. Carolina.	Georgia.	Florida.	Alabama.	Mississippi.	Louisiana.	Texas.	Arkansas.	Missouri.	Tennessee.	Kentucky.	Ohio.	Indiana.	Illinois.	Michigan.	Wisconsin.
Croghan,														2		1		
Denmark,													2	8		6	1	
Diana,																		2
Greig,													2			1		
Harrisburgh,																1		
High Market,																		
Lewis,																1	1	
Leyden,	3													3	1			1
Lowville,	1													3		4	3	1
Martinsburgh,				3										6	1		2	
Montague,																		
New Bremen,														1			2	1
Osceola,																		
Pinckney,																		
Turin,														2		1		
Watson,																	1	
West Turin,														1		1	1	
Total,	4			3									4	26	2	16	11	5

LIVINGSTON COUNTY.—(Continued.)

Towns	Virginia.	N. Carolina.	S. Carolina.	Georgia.	Florida.	Alabama.	Mississippi.	Louisiana.	Texas.	Arkansas.	Missouri.	Tennessee.	Kentucky.	Ohio.	Indiana.	Illinois.	Michigan.	Wisconsin.
Avon,	3			1	1							1		8			10	1
Caledonia,	1													9		4	2	9
Conesus,														1	1		3	2
Geneseo,	3												1	12	1	2	11	2
Groveland,	1												1	2	1		8	4
Leicester,	2			1										15	3	1	7	2
Lima,														7		1	15	3
Livonia,	1													13	4		22	1
Mount Morris,	1													8	2	1	25	1
North Dansville,				1				1						10	1	1	9	
Nunda,				1										4	1	1	14	1
Portage,							6	2						2	4		4	1
Sparta,															1		4	
Spring Water,		1												2	2		5	2
West Sparta,						1								5	1	1	4	1
York,														9		2	8	8
Total,	12	1		4	1	1	6	3				1	2	107	22	14	151	38

JEFFERSON COUNTY.—(Continued.)

TOWNS.	U. STATES. Iowa.	California.	Territories.	Total United States.	FOREIGN COUNTRIES. Canada.	N. Brunswick.	Nova Scotia.	N. Foundland.	West Indies.	Mexico.	S. America.	England.	Scotland.	Ireland.	Wales.	France.	Belgium.	Holland.
Philadelphia,				1, 576	43		1					11	2	90		5		
Rodman,				1, 667	31							10	1	34	5	3		
Rutland,				1, 770	102							17	1	64	6	4		
Theresa,				2, 148	36							34	5	36		12		
Watertown,	1			5, 531	500	1		1				182	33	1, 041	2	18		1
Wilna,				2, 602	55			1				28	6	259		9		
Worth,				420	21							7		19		2		
Total,	2	2		56, 471	2, 768	4	5	2				1, 059	246	3, 194	46	412		4

KINGS COUNTY.—(Continued.)

TOWNS.	Iowa.	California.	Territories.	Total United States.	Canada.	N. Brunswick.	Nova Scotia.	N. Foundland.	West Indies.	Mexico.	S. America.	England.	Scotland.	Ireland.	Wales.	France.	Belgium.	Holland.
Brooklyn City:																		
1st ward,				3, 318	19	8	12		9			302	118	2, 227	19	24		2
2d ward,				4, 231	24	8	21	23	7	1	2	591	163	2, 967	13	19	1	4
3d ward,				5, 758	40	7	24		44	1	15	436	107	1, 964	13	44	2	6
4th ward,	1			7, 975	82	5	16	21	22	1	1	942	173	2, 440	18	35	6	1
5th ward,				8, 434	107	6	28	9	17		1	1, 141	269	5, 629	10	11		6
6th ward,				8, 832	98	29	26	21	117	2	11	1, 116	275	6, 463	19	119	4	11
7th ward,				3, 753	36	6	21		14		3	960	132	6, 471	52	41		4
8th ward,				2, 765	14	2	3	1	16			418	108	1, 717	14	8	4	8
9th ward,				4, 489	26	1	11		10	1		528	128	2, 449	12	79		5
10th ward,	1	2		11, 569	112	27	65	55	33	1	12	1, 240	356	6, 690	8	82	2	21
11th ward,		2		13, 974	93	20	32	8	24	4	5	1, 655	214	4, 985	63	62	5	12
12th ward,				2, 456	49	2	2		3			341	68	3, 332	11	32		88
13th ward,		2		9, 751	97	25	33	1	12			909	166	2, 036	39	38	1	10
14th ward,		1		6, 425	28	7	40	1	7			702	120	4, 314	12	33	1	5
15th ward,		1		3, 884	16	4	14		3	1		426	42	870	5	26	5	14
16th ward,				5, 788	19	2	16	1	5		1	395	67	846	7	322	11	16
17th ward,				3, 602	34	28	28	1	1	3		344	88	966	20	17	5	
18th ward,				1, 522	7	1	3	2				165	4	387	3	13	2	2
Total Brooklyn,	2	8		108,526	901	188	395	144	344	15	51	12, 611	2, 598	56, 753	338	1, 005	49	215
Flatbush,				1, 664	5			2	2			169	23	1, 150	2	17		2
Flatlands,				1, 192	2	1	1					31	11	241	1	4		
Gravesend,				959					1		1	20	3	208	1	4		2
New Lots,				1, 259	5		1		1			89	15	229	6	20		
New Utrecht,			2	1, 645	4	1	4		3			91	19	727	4	8		
Total,	2	8	2	115 245	917	190	401	146	351	15	52	13, 011	2, 669	59, 308	352	1, 058	49	219

LEWIS COUNTY.—(Continued.)

TOWNS.	Iowa.	California.	Territories.	Total United States.	Canada.	N. Brunswick.	Nova Scotia.	N. Foundland.	West Indies.	Mexico.	S. America.	England.	Scotland.	Ireland.	Wales.	France.	Belgium.	Holland.
Croghan,				751	16							4		64		359		
Denmark,				2, 151	69							30	11	94	2	5		
Diana,				973	34							6	1	86		4		
Greig,				1, 027	23							14		69	27	5		
Harrisburgh,				1, 039	11							11	1	141	10	7		
High Market,				668	23							5	1	320	16	28		
Lewis,				586	1											171		
Leyden,				1, 571	18							11	6	104	48	58	1	
Lowville,				1, 840	21							15	12	63	7	50		
Martinsburgh,				2, 201	34							10	2	151	36	19		
Montague,				456	37							10		56	1	4		
New Bremen,				937	8	1								13	4	499		
Osceola,				376	2							54	20	60	1			
Pinckney,				993	3							10		32	1			
Turin,				1, 537	3							23	1	17	105	21		
Watson,				856	5							6	1	45	8	5		
West Turin,				1, 707	28							12	5	213	151	32		1
Total,				19, 669	336	1						221	61	1, 528	417	1, 267	1	1

LIVINGSTON COUNTY.—(Continued.)

TOWNS.	Iowa.	California.	Territories.	Total United States.	Canada.	N. Brunswick.	Nova Scotia.	N. Foundland.	West Indies.	Mexico.	S. America.	England.	Scotland.	Ireland.	Wales.	France.	Belgium.	Holland.
Avon,				2, 058	46		1		1			83	37	427	9			7
Caledonia,				1, 248	59							57	201	387				2
Conesus,				1, 278	5							54		43		1		
Geneseo,				2, 227	29		2		1			146	42	405		2	1	
Groveland,				1, 353	8							28	19	165	1			2
Leicester,				1, 811	12							52	22	146		2		2
Lima,				2, 046	32		3			1		66	4	448		4		
Livonia,				2, 350	21		1					34	10	202	1			
Mount Morris,	2			3, 374	48		3					82	18	427		5		
North Dansville,				2, 637	36						1	51	4	234	1	7		1
Nunda,				2, 572	33	1						46	8	115				22
Portage,				1, 306	14							33	22	178				
Sparta,	1			1, 116	8							4		58		3		
Spring Water,				2, 369	13						1	10	1	45		1		
West Sparta,				1, 371	3							9	5	75				2
York,				2, 069	32							132	160	343	2	2	2	
Total,	3			31, 185	399	1	10		2	1	2	887	553	3, 698	14	27	3	38

JEFFERSON COUNTY.—(CONTINUED.)

TOWNS	FOREIGN COUNTRIES.																		
	Germany.	Prussia.	Austria.	Switzerland.	Italy.	Spain.	Portugal.	Poland.	Norway.	Sweden.	Russia.	Denmark.	East Indies.	Africa.	Turkey and Greece.	Islands.	Asia.	At Sea.	Unknown.
Philadelphia,	13			1															1
Rodman,	1																		
Rutland,	4			3															6
Theresa,	7																		
Watertown,	140			7				3						1		1			95
Wilna,	51			2													1		10
Worth,																			5
Total,	833	3		28	2	2		7				2	1	1		1	2	8	319

KINGS COUNTY.—(CONTINUED.)

TOWNS	Germany.	Prussia.	Austria.	Switzerland.	Italy.	Spain.	Portugal.	Poland.	Norway.	Sweden.	Russia.	Denmark.	East Indies.	Africa.	Turkey and Greece.	Islands.	Asia.	At Sea.	Unknown.
Brooklyn city:																			
1st ward,	339	11	1	2	3	5	5	3	2	2						7		1	2
2d ward,	240	3	5	1	3	8		2	3	5	1	1				6		1	29
3d ward,	351	4	7	14	3	13		10	1	2	1	3					1		29
4th ward,	426	10	3	6	3	7	3	4	6	9	7	4				4		1	51
5th ward,	516	15	6	4	10	37	11	2	1	13	2	14	4			1		5	43
6th ward,	1,048	25	6	79	15	18		17	47	36	4	14		4		11		8	15
7th ward,	932	3	1	9	1	6	9	7		4	7	6						2	43
8th ward,	210	16			1	2			4			5	1				1		
9th ward,	1,292	8		5	13	12	6	1	1	15		14		2					25
10th ward,	1,200	3	4	27	9	10	6	12	17	41	18	1		1		6	4	5	112
11th ward,	723	5	9	9	5	14		6	7	23	2	11	3	4		9	2	4	221
12th ward,	536	5		9		2			18	13		14	2				2		5
13th ward,	751	4	1	4	4	8	5	4	1	10		4	3	1				2	124
14th ward,	654	10				4	14	3	3	9	1	12				4		5	
15th ward,	1,141	5		1		1		1		2		4			1	2	1	4	86
16th ward,	7,802	3		5	1	10	2	2	3	2	1	4						3	16
17th ward,	346	3	2			1		2	10	3									4
18th ward,	476	3								2	3	1	1						4
Total Brooklyn,	18,983	136	45	175	71	158	61	76	124	191	47	112	14	12	1	50	11	41	809
Flatbush,	205			1	1		1	1	1	2									32
Flatlands,	71		3	1		1		1			1								16
Gravesend,	42			1				4											10
New Lots,	624							1		1									10
New Utrecht,	187	2	1	2	8	1		4				1	1						17
Total,	20,112	138	49	180	80	160	62	87	125	194	48	113	15	12	1	50	11	41	894

LEWIS COUNTY.—(CONTINUED.)

TOWNS	Germany.	Prussia.	Austria.	Switzerland.	Italy.	Spain.	Portugal.	Poland.	Norway.	Sweden.	Russia.	Denmark.	East Indies.	Africa.	Turkey and Greece.	Islands.	Asia.	At Sea.	Unknown.
Croghan,	336																4		1
Denmark,	5	2																	8
Diana,	4	4		61				2											2
Greig,	18	7		1															12
Harrisburgh,	17			3															
High Market,	61			2															1
Lewis,	376		1	21															1
Leyden,	37	1			1														
Lowville,	95			24															17
Martinsburgh,	26			9														1	
Montague,	5																		2
New Bremen,	113	20		49															3
Osceola,																			
Pinckney,																			
Turin,	5			7															29
Watson,				1															3
West Turin,	288	12	13	5															11
Total,	1,386	46	14	183	1			2									4	1	90

LIVINGSTON COUNTY.—(CONTINUED.)

TOWNS	Germany.	Prussia.	Austria.	Switzerland.	Italy.	Spain.	Portugal.	Poland.	Norway.	Sweden.	Russia.	Denmark.	East Indies.	Africa.	Turkey and Greece.	Islands.	Asia.	At Sea.	Unknown.
Avon,	22			1														1	1
Caledonia,	19	7							2										9
Conesus,	24																		8
Geneseo,	21			5													2		
Groveland,	18		1																15
Leicester,	26																	2	1
Lima,	35																		31
Livonia,	7			1							1								7
Mount Morris,	52			3					1								1	2	26
North Dansville,	411	22	6	1														1	68
Nunda,	76	1															4		9
Portage,	9																		7
Sparta,	29	6																	9
Springwater,	37																	1	3
West Sparta,	29	1																1	
York,	24																	1	15
Total,	839	37	7	11					3		1						7	9	209

MADISON COUNTY.

TOWNS	Albany.	Allegany.	Broome.	Cattaraugus.	Cayuga.	Chautauque.	Chemung.	Chenango.	Clinton.	Columbia.	Cortland.	Delaware.	Dutchess.	Erie.	Essex.	Franklin.	Fulton.	Genesee.
	COUNTIES OF NEW-YORK																	
Brookfield,	10	12	4	8	2	20	3	160		3	31	13	3	2	2	1		7
Cazenovia,	39	7	5	1	19	4	1	64		21	63	2	32	5	2	1	5	6
De Ruyter,	5	12	2	1	9			185		21	126	2	42	2				2
Eaton,	15	6	8	4	10	4	3	116	4	22	35	17	13		5		1	2
Fenner,	13		1		1			10		6	16	7	8	2			7	3
Georgetown,	4	9	2		8			92	1	3	22	7	9	3			1	1
Hamilton,	22	2	10	6	4	1	3	244		32	18	18	7	5	1		1	5
Lebanon,	5	1	4	1	3	2	1	142		26	12	11	4					3
Lenox,	97	1	9	1	17		1	57	2	160	11	8	35	4	1	4	10	12
Madison,	6	2	6	2	1		1	54		13	8	4	6					
Nelson,	4	3	1		2	1	6	9		9	6	3	12	1			1	1
Smithfield,	8		1	5		1		12	1	3	6		5	1		1	2	
Stockbridge,	31		2	3	5	1	2	22		8	4	1	4	1			4	
Sullivan,	106	2	5	2	15	2	1	42		39	23	2	17	4	1	2	10	3
Total,	365	57	60	29	96	36	2[illegible]	1,209	8	366	381	95	197	30	12	9	42	45

MONROE COUNTY.

TOWNS	Albany.	Allegany.	Broome.	Cattaraugus.	Cayuga.	Chautauque.	Chemung.	Chenango.	Clinton.	Columbia.	Cortland.	Delaware.	Dutchess.	Erie.	Essex.	Franklin.	Fulton.	Genesee.
Brighton,	26	2		2	9			1		16	1	6	21	2	2		2	5
Chili,	6	4		3	11	8	2	4		5	7	3	9	4		2		14
Clarkson,	57	2		3	8			2		9			20	6	2		1	21
Gates,	8	2	2	2	4		3	2	1	6	9		8	7	4	1	8	11
Greece,	44	21	4	6	19		9	8	9	41	2	3	40	5	5	6		15
Henrietta,	5	3		2	11	9		4	2	18	2		17	1	5	3		15
Irondequoit,	17	2		6	13				1	25	1	1	25	6	1	1		1
Mendon,	9	8	1	4	33	3		9	5	19	8	5	83	2	2	2		14
Ogden,	16	15	1	10	20	9		5	1	8	1	4	14	7	3	2		18
Parma,	35	2	2	6	26	5		18	2	11	1	7	48	4	1	2	2	26
Penfield,	13	7		1	13	4		9		40	3	2	59	4	2		10	11
Perrington,	15	9	1	4	15	5	3	25		21	2	3	67	6	2	2	1	6
Pittsford,	6	10		1	9	1	1	4		21	2	4	23	4	2			5
Riga,	2	6	1	3	11	2		6		8	3	2	17	3	10			60
Rochester city:																		
1st ward,	5	4	2	1	20		1	10		2	2	3	15	8	1		1	17
2d ward,	24	5	4		16	1	2	8		12	7	1	37	11		5	3	25
3d ward,	44	6	4	1	24		6	4	1	16	3	4	29	12		1	2	14
4th ward,	21	2		1	34	1	3	5	5	20	2		20	11	3		1	9
5th ward,	41	7	1	1	11	1		6	4	11	2	4	21	16	1	6		14
6th ward,	21	6	1	4	29	4	2	1		10	3	5	20	13	1			22
7th ward,	42	8	5	2	29	6		6	2	6	9	3	23	18	12	3	5	16
8th ward,	29	5	4	2	16	1		3	1	3		2	3	9	1	1		13
9th ward,	25	14	4	1	23	4	7	3	6	27	9	6	20	30	5	5		12
10th ward,	32	8	1		22	3		18	5	11	9	6	33	22	4	4	23	17
Total Rochester,	284	65	26	13	224	21	21	64	24	118	46	34	221	150	28	25	35	159
Rush,	8	5	1	1	12	2		1		4	2	2	38	1	3			3
Sweden,	35	7	5	4	38	9	3	12		20	3	2	29	14	6	4	4	104
Union,	39	12		5	25			8	1	7		3	25	7	2	1		43
Webster,	4		1	2	15	3	2	6	2	87		7	25	2				4
Wheatland,	11	3	1	2	8			3	2	7		3	8	9	2	5		43
Total,	640	185	46	80	524	81	44	191	50	491	93	91	797	244	82	56	63	578

MONTGOMERY COUNTY.

TOWNS	Albany.	Allegany.	Broome.	Cattaraugus.	Cayuga.	Chautauque.	Chemung.	Chenango.	Clinton.	Columbia.	Cortland.	Delaware.	Dutchess.	Erie.	Essex.	Franklin.	Fulton.	Genesee.
Amsterdam,	135		3	2	6		1	4	3	13	1	2	22	1	5		212	2
Canajoharie,	48	4		1	4		1	2	1	19	1	3	22				9	
Charleston,	21							4		26	1		20				7	
Florida,	52	2			3				2	9	1		16				50	
Glen,	31				2			1	2	26	1	1	21				46	1
Minden,	18		1		3			7		18	1	6	18		1	1	44	
Mohawk,	44	1		1	2		1			18	1	3	10	2			162	
Palatine,	13									4			4				53	
Root,	63				2			1		20	2	1	20	1			19	1
St. Johnsville,	16		2							3		1	2	2	1		22	
Total,	441	7	6	4	22		3	19	8	156	9	17	155	6	7	1	624	4

NEW-YORK COUNTY.

TOWNS	Albany.	Allegany.	Broome.	Cattaraugus.	Cayuga.	Chautauque.	Chemung.	Chenango.	Clinton.	Columbia.	Cortland.	Delaware.	Dutchess.	Erie.	Essex.	Franklin.	Fulton.	Genesee.
New-York City:																		
1st ward,	7				4				1	1		9	3			1		
2d ward,	12		3							8		2	17	1				
3d ward,	66		5	3	10	1		9	1	52	2	8	42	24	2	3		10
4th ward,	21	1	1		2			5		7		5	21	4			1	
5th ward,	105	2	3	2	8	2	3	8	2	70	6	44	126	4	9		1	8
6th ward,	39				1			3		4	1	11	15	1				
7th ward,	94		1		4				2	27	4	19	94	8	7	1	1	1
8th ward,	250	4	3	1	7	2	5	4	3	76	4	52	235	13	4		2	3
9th ward,	235	4	3	2	8	3	2	18	5	97	4	43	501	17	5	1	3	2
10th ward,	73	1	2			1		5	1	14	1	20	48	4				10
11th ward,	09	1	6				1	2	7	50		28	184	21	9		2	2
12th ward,	84		3		2				2	30	2	8	91	1	2	1	1	3
13th ward,	64				3					49	5	24	121	1	1	1		
14th ward,	47				2					2		26	21	1	1			
15th ward,	140	3	2		9	3	2	3	2	60	4	44	126	7	5		3	1

(Continued on page 112.)

MADISON COUNTY.—(Continued.)

TOWNS.	Greene.	Hamilton.	Herkimer.	Jefferson.	Kings.	Lewis.	Livingston.	Madison.	Monroe.	Montgomery.	New-York.	Niagara.	Oneida.	Onondaga.	Ontario.	Orange.	Orleans.	Oswego.
	COUNTIES OF NEW-YORK.																	
Brookfield,	3	......	51	24	......	1	3	2, 335	8	15	7	......	201	8	......	......	5	3
Cazenovia,	5	1	54	20	4	4	3	2, 387	4	38	22	1	112	247	7	1	3	28
De Ruyter,	1	......	8	7	3	3	......	992	......	4	5	......	28	66	......	......	......	8
Eaton,	2	......	49	12	......	3	2	2, 234	4	14	3	1	181	29	5	1	1	12
Fenner,	2	2	21	2	......	2	......	1, 059	......	27	......	2	46	34	4	1	......	3
Georgetown,	10	......	15	5	......	......	......	884	......	2	2	......	46	13	1	1	1	......
Hamilton,	4	......	32	23	......	3	1	1, 983	6	27	21	......	155	23	4	......	......	7
Lebanon,	3	......	16	7	......	2	......	928	3	47	4	1	40	9	5	......	......	5
Lenox,	35	......	216	29	1	40	3	3, 508	7	235	31	5	749	203	3	8	7	54
Madison,	3	......	26	3	......	1	......	1, 555	6	3	2	......	161	13	1	1	......	3
Nelson,	1	......	7	3	1	3	2	1, 134	1	6	1	......	64	29	4	12	......	8
Smithfield,	1	......	94	8	......	......	......	963	1	16	4	2	46	25	......	......	......	11
Stockbridge,	14	......	60	4	......	3	......	1, 094	7	25	1	1	190	23	......	2	......	3
Sullivan,	11	......	138	19	1	17	2	2, 495	1	160	9	4	185	376	7	3	4	48
Total,	95	3	787	166	10	82	16	23, 551	48	619	112	17	2, 204	1, 098	41	30	21	193
MONROE COUNTY.—(Continued.)																		
Brighton,	14	3	8	3	2	2	22	10	1, 128	10	73	2	12	8	35	......	9	3
Chili,	......	......	3	15	1	......	33	10	1, 013	1	13	......	5	4	18	13	19	3
Clarkson,	2	......	5	13	......	1	12	7	928	27	5	15	20	19	29	11	42	4
Gates,	7	1	3	11	......	2	10	4	936	5	10	2	13	9	33	......	3	1
Greece,	7	......	8	43	2	8	26	5	1, 913	22	46	17	33	19	47	3	15	12
Henrietta,	......	......	21	5	......	8	28	18	986	7	12	2	18	7	16	1	9	3
Irondequoit,	3	......	6	8	2	3	7	......	1, 167	3	11	......	8	10	22	3	2	1
Mendon,	12	......	18	5	1	4	107	5	1, 293	24	10	8	1	20	161	5	6	2
Ogden,	5	......	6	13	1	2	46	7	1, 247	13	20	9	21	10	30	5	20	1
Parma,	5	......	5	14	1	5	16	19	1, 318	10	6	14	24	29	43	13	34	2
Penfield,	23	3	24	10	......	3	5	18	1, 498	28	3	6	13	15	55	3	7	12
Perrington,	13	1	24	6	2	3	9	22	1, 205	48	15	2	40	58	117	10	19	13
Pittsford,	1	......	20	4	2	1	32	9	812	10	13	3	25	14	48	6	11	......
Riga,	1	......	2	7	2	......	41	8	848	22	7	4	20	6	12	5	11	3
Rochester city:																		
1st ward,	1	......	5	4	......	......	38	6	773	6	24	11	29	12	25	3	14	......
2d ward,	10	......	20	15	6	3	26	18	1, 042	16	37	19	65	26	50	12	17	7
3d ward,	3	1	34	13	3	2	29	11	1, 654	14	63	16	37	20	35	9	20	11
4th ward,	5	......	10	16	2	2	42	9	1, 033	3	61	5	28	19	58	8	18	5
5th ward,	4	1	10	24	4	3	35	21	1, 383	11	65	6	24	25	36	6	8	7
6th ward,	5	......	18	8	2	......	24	8	1, 574	9	83	6	50	17	39	3	6	4
7th ward,	4	......	16	25	2	1	38	10	1, 627	30	13	6	41	20	48	6	17	8
8th ward,	6	......	7	18	1	5	14	5	1, 562	11	49	11	26	12	26	9	10	6
9th ward,	17	......	7	27	2	24	31	2	2, 710	21	59	15	36	25	46	21	28	30
10th ward,	8	......	23	27	3	4	34	22	1, 196	19	67	4	85	20	46	9	23	11
Total Rochest'r,	63	2	150	177	25	44	311	112	14, 554	140	521	99	421	196	409	86	161	89
Rush,	8	......	12	2	......	......	81	6	835	1	4	1	9	2	19	1	2	1
Sweden,	8	......	16	12	6	2	17	21	1, 522	24	47	18	108	26	45	21	120	9
Union,	3	......	4	20	......	......	13	5	1, 161	34	2	8	50	13	39	8	82	13
Webster,	31	......	11	7	1	1	29	7	1, 139	18	6	4	22	14	83	13	5	1
Wheatland,	6	......	19	5	5	3	98	11	1, 207	20	8	1	22	15	14	2	8	4
Total,	212	10	365	380	53	92	943	304	36, 710	467	832	215	885	494	1, 275	209	585	177
MONTGOMERY COUNTY.—(Continued.)																		
Amsterdam,	26	4	29	4	3	3	8	4	2	2, 040	32	......	40	6	6	1	1	1
Canajoharie,	4	......	59	4	1	4	2	1	......	2, 627	15	1	17	12	2	2	1	8
Charleston,	1	......	9	9	4	......	......	3	......	1, 378	4	1	......	7	1	1	2	......
Florida,	1	8	19	5	5	......	4	1	......	2, 130	8	1	12	4	......	2	......	3
Glen,	2	......	18	5	......	1	2	2	......	2, 086	14	......	9	2	......	5	1	1
Minden,	3	......	228	6	......	1	1	3	1	3, 263	23	......	25	11	1	2	4	4
Mohawk,	6	......	8	6	......	5	1	1	......	2, 086	20	......	6	2	......	8	......	......
Palatine,	6	......	40	5	......	5	2	2	......	2, 024	2	......	3	......	......	......	......	......
Root,	2	......	10	1	......	1	......	1	......	1, 850	17	1	6	13	4	1	......	......
St. Johnsville,	7	......	85	10	......	......	......	8	3	1, 224	6	......	14	1	......	2	......	......
Total,	58	12	505	55	13	20	20	26	6	20, 708	141	4	132	58	14	24	9	17
NEW-YORK COUNTY.—(Continued.)																		
New-York city:																		
1st ward,	2	......	2	2	5	1	......	......	1	7	3, 800	......	......	4	1	2	......	......
2d ward,	5	......	......	......	13	......	......	......	......	......	784	......	3	......	......	8	......	......
3d ward,	56	......	1	9	41	4	4	5	7	7	2, 308	3	31	5	1	93	......	10
4th ward,	2	......	2	4	54	......	1	......	5	......	5, 794	......	8	3	1	29	1	1
5th ward.	44	......	3	5	111	......	2	6	6	21	7, 403	4	18	2	13	268	......	9
6th ward,	5	......	......	......	45	......	......	......	4	1	6, 753	......	4	1	1	23	......	1
7th ward,	14	......	7	7	195	2	......	......	2	12	13,171	1	25	7	6	114	......	7
8th ward,	57	......	20	4	179	2	......	7	19	16	13, 519	1	27	23	4	284	......	11
9th ward,	80	6	17	10	261	3	3	4	19	25	17, 701	1	49	9	13	515	6	11
10th ward,	14	......	3	......	125	......	......	4	6	3	10, 635	1	24	3	1	88	1	......
11th ward,	29	1	5	2	259	......	1	3	3	8	19, 416	1	20	7	6	149	......	4
12th ward,	13	......	3	7	122	......	6	......	10	4	6, 364	......	15	9	3	69	1	1
13th ward,	4	......	1	6	124	......	......	......	......	7	11, 318	2	8	3	2	112	2	2
14th ward,	3	......	......	4	45	......	......	1	......	7	8, 997	......	12	1	......	23	1	3
15th ward,	14	......	14	11	76	......	3	11	8	20	9, 615	2	49	10	9	117	3	4

(Continued on page 113.)

MADISON COUNTY.—(Continued.)

TOWNS.	COUNTIES OF NEW-YORK.																	
	Otsego.	Putnam.	Queens.	Rensselaer.	Richmond.	Rockland.	St. Lawrence	Saratoga.	Schenectady.	Schoharie.	Schuyler.	Seneca.	Steuben.	Suffolk.	Sullivan.	Tioga.	Tompkins.	Ulster.
Brookfield, ...	114	2	......	25	......	1	......	8	1	12	......	......	2	......	......	......	......	......
Cazenovia, ...	36	1	......	20	......	......	1	22	4	10	......	5	11	4	1	3	16	......
De Ruyter, ...	31	......	......	32	......	......	3	16	6	3	......	......	1	......	......	......	2	5
Eaton, ...	52	......	......	27	......	......	5	16	1	12	......	2	7	......	1	3	2	......
Fenner, ...	15	......	......	8	......	......	......	15	......	6	......	1	5	......	......	......	......	......
Georgetown, ...	31	......	......	7	......	......	......	5	1	8	......	......	3	......	......	2	2	......
Hamilton, ...	58	1	......	9	......	......	4	13	13	15	......	1	4	......	6	1	2	3
Lebanon, ...	27	1	......	6	......	......	1	13	......	3	......	......	......	......	1	......	3	......
Lenox, ...	53	2	......	96	......	......	18	46	25	83	......	5	2	5	2	4	6	13
Madison, ...	17	......	......	4	......	......	3	5	......	9	......	2	......	1	1	......	6	......
Nelson, ...	11	......	......	8	......	......	1	5	3	7	......	......	1	4	1	1	3	......
Smithfield, ...	11	......	......	2	......	......	......	9	3	8	......	......	......	......	......	......	......	1
Stockbridge, ...	15	......	2	5	......	......	3	7	......	11	......	......	1	......	2	......	......	1
Sullivan, ...	44	......	......	52	......	......	10	27	7	41	......	7	3	6	1	3	2	5
Total, ...	515	7	2	301	......	1	49	207	64	228	......	23	40	20	16	17	44	28

MONROE COUNTY.—(Continued.)

TOWNS.	Otsego.	Putnam.	Queens.	Rensselaer.	Richmond.	Rockland.	St. Lawrence	Saratoga.	Schenectady.	Schoharie.	Schuyler.	Seneca.	Steuben.	Suffolk.	Sullivan.	Tioga.	Tompkins.	Ulster.
Brighton, ...	15	......	......	10	......	1	3	15	1	4	......	2	2	2	1	......	......	2
Chili, ...	3	2	......	8	......	......	9	23	......	4	......	25	9	......	......	......	5	3
Clarkson, ...	5	4	......	60	4	11	6	43	14	10	......	5	1	1	......	......	1	6
Gates, ...	1	1	1	10	3	......	9	21	6	2	......	1	5	......	......	3	......	3
Greece, ...	16	......	2	29	......	......	17	36	9	13	......	28	5	1	2	2	2	4
Henrietta, ...	15	......	......	13	......	......	1	17	1	15	......	1	2	3	3	......	3	......
Irondequoit, ...	1	3	......	11	......	......	7	12	17	8	......	8	......	2	......	2	......	......
Mendon, ...	30	5	......	34	1	......	2	27	5	4	......	10	4	3	......	3	1	17
Ogden, ...	5	1	1	27	5	1	12	18	6	6	......	10	1	......	1	1	7	1
Parma, ...	14	1	......	101	2	21	3	52	9	11	......	20	12	5	6	1	4	9
Penfield, ...	9	......	......	15	......	1	6	23	14	12	......	5	......	1	1	3	1	5
Perrington, ...	20	4	3	73	1	9	4	30	13	14	......	2	8	1	......	11	1	34
Pittsford, ...	7	1	2	41	......	......	1	16	3	2	......	3	......	2	1	......	2	6
Riga, ...	10	......	1	4	......	......	7	11	5	2	......	7	1	......	......	......	3	12
Rochester city:																		
1st ward,	5	......	......	13	3	......	1	22	18	4	......	10	7	......	1	......	3	3
2d ward,	18	2	5	36	1	1	11	19	7	7	......	21	......	......	1	4	......	8
3d ward,	10	......	......	29	......	......	15	27	12	2	......	12	13	1	......	3	6	5
4th ward,	6	3	......	28	1	2	5	32	6	8	......	9	5	......	1	1	2	1
5th ward,	12	......	......	26	......	7	16	27	5	3	......	19	10	......	2	......	5	3
6th ward,	13	......	......	11	......	1	4	17	13	3	......	13	2	......	......	1	8	1
7th ward,	15	1	2	31	......	1	6	18	2	9	......	8	5	......	......	......	7	2
8th ward,	10	......	......	13	......	1	2	19	......	1	......	5	7	1	......	2	......	1
9th ward,	11	......	3	16	......	3	15	23	13	21	......	14	8	......	......	5	4	12
10th ward,	23	4	......	27	......	1	12	36	25	9	......	18	8	......	......	10	5	12
Total Rochester,	123	10	10	230	5	17	87	240	101	67	......	129	65	2	5	26	40	48
Rush, ...	3	2	1	38	......	......	9	10	4	3	......	5	3	......	......	......	......	6
Sweden, ...	18	4	......	43	......	3	5	43	......	16	2	8	8	......	2	2	6	9
Union, ...	14	3	......	175	......	6	2	35	4	3	......	2	1	......	2	1	......	1
Webster, ...	9	1	......	34	......	......	10	28	......	10	......	3	8	......	......	3	2	5
Wheatland, ...	5	......	1	10	......	......	6	23	......	1	......	19	8	......	......	2	1	11
Total, ...	323	42	22	966	21	70	206	723	212	207	2	293	143	23	24	60	79	182

MONTGOMERY COUNTY.—(Continued.)

TOWNS.	Otsego.	Putnam.	Queens.	Rensselaer.	Richmond.	Rockland.	St. Lawrence	Saratoga.	Schenectady.	Schoharie.	Schuyler.	Seneca.	Steuben.	Suffolk.	Sullivan.	Tioga.	Tompkins.	Ulster.
Amsterdam, ...	16	......	6	41	......	......	3	186	124	31	......	2	......	2	1	......	5	2
Canajoharie, ...	104	......	......	28	......	1	......	37	47	136	......	1	......	2	......	1	2	13
Charleston, ...	24	......	......	17	......	......	......	28	58	143	......	......	......	......	......	......	......	......
Florida, ...	7	......	1	17	......	......	1	33	214	37	......	2	......	......	1	1	......	......
Glen, ...	8	1	......	20	1	......	......	24	48	54	......	2	......	......	1	......	1	4
Minden, ...	161	......	......	19	......	......	1	15	24	30	......	3	1	......	......	......	......	8
Mohawk, ...	14	......	......	23	......	......	2	22	50	21	......	3	......	1	2	......	2	5
Palatine, ...	11	......	1	3	......	......	2	8	5	4	......	......	1	......	......	1	......	7
Root, ...	16	......	......	18	......	......	......	21	49	126	......	......	2	......	......	......	3	4
St. Johnsville, ...	31	......	......	8	1	......	4	16	7	18	......	......	......	1	......	......	......	6
Total, ...	392	1	8	194	2	1	13	390	626	600	......	13	4	6	5	3	13	49

NEW-YORK COUNTY.—(Continued.)

TOWNS.	Otsego.	Putnam.	Queens.	Rensselaer.	Richmond.	Rockland.	St. Lawrence	Saratoga.	Schenectady.	Schoharie.	Schuyler.	Seneca.	Steuben.	Suffolk.	Sullivan.	Tioga.	Tompkins.	Ulster.
New-York city:																		
1st ward,	......	......	1	2	1	......	......	1	......	......	......	5	1	......	......	......	......	......
2d ward,	2	3	2	4	3	4	......	2	1	1	......	......	......	7	......	......	......	1
3d ward,	9	8	13	20	14	5	3	31	6	7	1	2	3	2	5	1	5	27
4th ward,	......	9	35	3	2	3	......	1	1	1	......	......	......	20	3	......	2	4
5th ward,	8	21	47	63	43	59	......	25	10	13	1	9	6	37	16	6	25	87
6th ward,	3	3	18	14	6	4	......	7	1	1	......	......	......	13	1	......	......	5
7th ward,	4	29	205	51	57	25	......	13	7	9	......	4	......	163	12	......	2	43
8th ward,	7	34	83	73	74	80	4	32	7	16	......	4	2	64	17	2	4	122
9th ward,	8	101	86	147	84	448	5	36	9	12	......	17	5	86	27	13	8	244
10th ward,	5	12	57	17	16	7	......	8	8	9	......	3	......	27	2	......	2	31
11th ward,	2	53	216	29	68	54	5	14	1	8	......	2	1	215	13	2	1	116
12th ward,	9	25	88	32	4	11	......	15	13	4	1	2	......	33	5	1	7	20
13th ward,	6	18	174	21	55	17	......	4	5	4	......	......	......	205	13	3	3	46
14th ward,	2	6	22	6	8	5	......	5	6	2	......	1	......	8	......	......	1	15
15th ward,	18	19	118	44	17	19	10	28	2	3	......	......	4	28	12	......	6	53

(Continued on page 114.)

MADISON COUNTY.—(Continued.)

TOWNS.	COUNTIES OF NEW-YORK.							UNITED STATES.										
	Warren.	Washington.	Wayne.	Westchester.	Wyoming.	Yates.	New-York.	Maine.	N. Hampshire.	Vermont.	Massachusetts.	Rhode Island.	Connecticut.	New Jersey.	Pennsylvania.	Delaware.	Maryland.	District of Columbia.
Brookfield,	......	9	......	2	2	......	3,118	3	10	32	55	205	154	9	5	......	......	......
Cazenovia,	3	17	2	9	1	......	3,384	4	22	53	194	49	235	18	22	......	......	7
De Ruyter,	......	7	1	......	......	......	1,641	2	16	21	46	45	58	7	5	1	......	......
Eaton,	1	12	1	3	......	1	2,964	2	27	57	186	31	153	10	26	......	1	1
Fenner,	......	4	......	6	......	......	1,339	1	4	17	59	9	81	4	6	......	......	......
Georgetown,	......	6	1	3	......	......	1,211	2	18	36	44	14	64	2	5	......	......	......
Hamilton,	......	28	1	1	1	......	2,829	7	20	49	155	58	262	6	23	......	......	1
Lebanon,	......	12	......	......	......	......	1,352	2	8	17	88	35	58	4	2	......	......	2
Lenox,	10	42	8	26	4	2	6,016	9	39	135	211	38	268	47	27	......	......	4
Madison,	8	11	......	......	......	......	1,948	2	7	29	95	61	93	1	5	......	......	......
Nelson,	......	3	......	18	......	......	1,401	1	20	46	77	27	71	10	8	......	......	......
Smithfield,	2	9	......	2	......	1	1,265	1	8	17	50	8	55	5	9	1	......	6
Stockbridge,	......	13	......	6	......	......	1,581	2	22	32	67	10	118	1	5	......	......	1
Sullivan,	1	28	6	9	2	1	4,011	2	21	60	109	17	153	6	17	......	......	1
Total,	25	201	20	85	10	5	34,060	40	242	601	1,436	607	1.823	130	165	2	1	23

MONROE COUNTY.—(Continued.)

TOWNS.	Warren.	Washington.	Wayne.	Westchester.	Wyoming.	Yates.	New-York.	Maine.	N. Hampshire.	Vermont.	Massachusetts.	Rhode Island.	Connecticut.	New Jersey.	Pennsylvania.	Delaware.	Maryland.	District of Columbia.
Brighton,	1	7	10	3	......	2	1,520	12	19	42	123	7	76	147	15	......	2	......
Chili,	......	15	......	6	2	5	1,352	6	15	19	53	4	56	41	20	......	......	......
Clarkson,	3	14	30	16	5	3	1,513	5	10	54	33	7	84	25	16	......	2	......
Gates,	......	15	7	5	3	1	1,225	2	12	59	52	8	53	5	11	......	3	......
Greece,	......	24	28	7	1	13	2,702	1	32	59	60	11	59	72	61	......	4	......
Henrietta,	......	4	14	11	3	3	1,347	1	12	56	57	5	79	10	27	......	4	......
Irondequoit,	......	10	17	9	3	10	1,476	2	6	9	33	3	26	12	7	......	......	......
Mendon,	3	21	34	8	16	12	2,129	3	16	54	79	10	68	53	10	......	3	......
Ogden,	......	37	15	16	2	7	1,770	9	82	107	78	6	109	17	7	......	3	......
Parma,	......	16	30	16	2	18	2,109	8	32	35	70	11	85	71	14	......	......	......
Penfield,	1	30	75	4	6	3	2,119	5	15	45	75	5	74	48	14	......	1	......
Perrington,	3	16	95	4	......	11	2,151	5	13	51	89	9	79	18	12	......	1	......
Pittsford,	......	11	24	13	4	2	1,245	4	12	32	49	4	45	6	8	......	......	......
Riga,	......	5	6	1	1	......	1,209	21	11	41	71	8	54	4	3	......	......	1
Rochester city:																		
1st ward,	......	6	17	2	8	3	1,169	3	21	45	79	7	61	14	4	......	1	......
2d ward,	2	17	45	6	10	3	1,774	17	48	70	132	9	63	22	19	......	11	......
3d ward,	6	30	24	8	3	3	2,355	9	28	70	109	15	117	24	35	......	27	......
4th ward,	1	16	44	7	2	3	1,645	14	24	66	86	5	107	18	36	......	4	1
5th ward,	1	1	11	12	......	4	1,984	9	18	46	86	10	64	19	44	......	8	2
6th ward,	......	18	12	......	5	4	2,124	7	19	31	70	7	64	20	31	......	......	......
7th ward,	1	14	35	28	6	5	2,303	11	38	79	87	7	107	31	26	......	10	1
8th ward,	......	2	16	3	4	5	1,963	7	16	37	37	3	68	17	9	......	5	2
9th ward,	4	10	3	5	2	10	3,484	6	34	55	59	3	41	32	21	......	3	1
10th ward,	......	18	35	7	13	8	2,090	7	32	67	69	5	92	55	58	......	6	4
Total Rochester,	15	132	242	78	53	48	20,891	90	278	566	814	71	784	252	283	......	75	11
Rush,	......	2	......	8	3	2	1,166	1	2	20	22	1	17	13	74	......	16	......
Sweden,	......	34	20	6	8	......	2,561	5	47	121	102	12	133	26	19	......	2	......
Union,	1	30	20	2	4	2	1,938	5	25	54	34	5	36	26	8	......	5	......
Webster,	......	32	109	2	6	5	1,819	3	40	63	42	6	55	39	11	......	1	......
Wheatland,	2	25	5	5	11	7	1,697	5	6	40	48	1	47	11	22	......	3	......
Total,	29	480	781	220	133	154	53,939	193	685	1,527	1,984	194	2,019	896	642	......	125	12

MONTGOMERY COUNTY.—(Continued.)

TOWNS.	Warren.	Washington.	Wayne.	Westchester.	Wyoming.	Yates.	New-York.	Maine.	N. Hampshire.	Vermont.	Massachusetts.	Rhode Island.	Connecticut.	New Jersey.	Pennsylvania.	Delaware.	Maryland.	District of Columbia.
Amsterdam,	5	21	2	12	1	......	3,082	4	13	41	58	7	51	28	10	......	......	......
Canajoharie,	1	2	2	5	4	......	3,261	5	3	11	28	11	46	14	4	......	......	1
Charleston,	6	3	......	1	......	......	1,779	......	......	4	9	9	13	36	3	......	......	......
Florida,	......	6	......	......	1	......	2,659	......	2	9	19	5	8	19	2	......	1	......
Glen,	......	2	5	......	......	......	2,451	......	1	10	22	2	17	40	24	......	......	......
Minden,	......	13	3	1	1	......	3,974	1	11	18	16	......	18	11	11	......	......	......
Mohawk,	......	9	1	1	......	......	2,550	4	2	9	16	4	16	8	14	......	1	......
Palatine,	......	1	......	1	......	......	2,208	......	1	3	1	1	3	6	2	......	3	......
Root,	1	11	1	......	......	......	2,289	......	2	6	13	4	16	22	5	......	......	......
St. Johnsville,	......	5	1	2	......	......	1,509	1	2	5	24	......	9	4	2	......	......	......
Total,	13	73	15	23	7	......	25,762	15	37	116	205	43	197	188	77	......	5	1

NEW-YORK COUNTY.—(Continued.)

TOWNS.	Warren.	Washington.	Wayne.	Westchester.	Wyoming.	Yates.	New-York.	Maine.	N. Hampshire.	Vermont.	Massachusetts.	Rhode Island.	Connecticut.	New Jersey.	Pennsylvania.	Delaware.	Maryland.	District of Columbia.
New-York city:																		
1st ward,	......	1	......	......	......	1	3,866	37	7	18	69	22	63	50	62	......	23	4
2d ward,	......	1	......	12	......	5	904	23	16	18	63	18	94	60	33	......	13	3
3d ward,	1	22	6	22	......	......	3,036	37	39	60	177	27	202	264	115	5	36	5
4th ward,	......	1	......	23	......	1	6,082	80	23	14	154	29	117	91	100	3	48	1
5th ward,	1	22	2	119	......	3	8,941	52	49	77	345	55	322	641	349	2	161	41
6th ward,	......	2	......	10	......	......	7,001	22	9	19	117	12	108	138	143	2	50	6
7th ward,	......	19	1	193	......	1	14,651	138	68	78	408	43	562	408	257	......	98	16
8th ward,	......	18	7	321	......	......	15,812	117	81	82	445	42	378	1,175	437	22	192	37
9th ward,	6	38	13	910	1	1	21,991	67	78	95	461	68	561	2,255	357	3	88	11
10th ward,	1	11	1	195	......	1	11,501	43	26	41	194	23	347	356	213	......	69	8
11th ward,	1	26	3	430	1	......	21,557	87	24	62	262	37	407	588	225	1	90	2
12th ward,	......	19	3	174	......	......	7,323	37	28	54	180	32	183	238	103	......	39	11
13th ward,	3	10	1	198	......	......	12,646	49	18	30	146	28	281	385	201	......	52	2
14th ward,	......	9	......	50	......	......	9,343	39	29	43	169	13	179	274	208	......	81	10
15th ward,	2	8	1	175	1	2	10,950	62	75	89	576	82	619	663	352	......	184	12

(Continued on page 115.)

MADISON COUNTY.—(Continued.)

TOWNS.	UNITED STATES.																	
	Virginia.	N. Carolina.	S. Carolina.	Georgia.	Florida.	Alabama.	Mississippi.	Louisiana.	Texas.	Arkansas.	Missouri.	Tennessee.	Kentucky.	Ohio.	Indiana.	Illinois.	Michigan.	Wisconsin.
Brookfield,	.....	.....	.....	.....	.....	.....	.....	.....	.....	.....	.....	.....	.....	5	.....	.....	5	2
Cazenovia,	.....	3	.....	.....	.....	3	.....	1	.....	.....	.....	.....	.....	8	.....	4	6	2
De Ruyter,	1	.....	.....	.....	.....	.....	.....	.....	.....	.....	.....	.....	.....	2	.....	5	1	1
Eaton,	1	.....	.....	.....	.....	.....	.....	.....	.....	.....	.....	.....	.....	3	1	1	5	1
Fenner,	.....	.....	.....	.....	.....	.....	.....	.....	.....	.....	.....	.....	.....	1	.....	1	2	2
Georgetown,	.....	.....	.....	.....	.....	.....	.....	.....	.....	.....	.....	.....	.....	.....	.....	.....	1	2
Hamilton,	3	1	.....	.....	.....	.....	.....	.....	.....	.....	.....	.....	2	15	.....	9	8	1
Lebanon,	.....	.....	.....	1	.....	.....	.....	.....	.....	.....	.....	.....	.....	.....	.....	1	2	.....
Lenox,	1	1	.....	.....	.....	.....	.....	2	.....	.....	.....	.....	3	11	1	3	13	4
Madison,	.....	.....	.....	.....	.....	.....	.....	.....	.....	.....	.....	.....	.....	1	.....	2	.....	3
Nelson,	.....	.....	.....	.....	.....	.....	.....	.....	.....	.....	.....	.....	.....	.....	.....	.....	5	1
Smithfield,	1	.....	1	.....	.....	.....	.....	.....	.....	.....	.....	.....	4	1	.....	.....	.....	.....
Stockbridge,	.....	.....	.....	.....	.....	.....	.....	.....	.....	.....	.....	.....	.....	2	.....	1	2	3
Sullivan,	.....	.....	.....	.....	.....	.....	.....	.....	.....	.....	.....	.....	1	10	1	.....	5	8
Total,,	7	5	1	1	.....	3	.....	3	.....	.....	.....	.....	10	59	3	27	55	30

MONROE COUNTY.—(Continued.)

TOWNS.	Virginia.	N. Carolina.	S. Carolina.	Georgia.	Florida.	Alabama.	Mississippi.	Louisiana.	Texas.	Arkansas.	Missouri.	Tennessee.	Kentucky.	Ohio.	Indiana.	Illinois.	Michigan.	Wisconsin.
Brighton,	1	1	1	.....	.....	.....	.....	.....	.....	.....	.....	.....	.....	8	7	3	16	.....
Chili,	.....	.....	.....	.....	.....	.....	.....	.....	.....	.....	.....	.....	.....	5	2	3	19	.....
Clarkson,	.....	1	.....	.....	.....	.....	.....	.....	.....	.....	.....	.....	.....	2	1	1	8	2
Gates,	.....	.....	.....	.....	.....	.....	.....	.....	.....	.....	.....	.....	.....	3	.....	1	4	1
Greece,	4	.....	.....	.....	.....	.....	.....	1	.....	.....	.....	1	.....	17	1	1	8	.....
Henrietta,	.....	.....	.....	.....	.....	.....	.....	.....	.....	.....	.....	.....	1	6	.....	5	10	2
Irondequoit,	.....	.....	.....	.....	.....	.....	.....	.....	.....	.....	.....	.....	1	13	.....	1	12	1
Mendon,	1	.....	.....	.....	.....	.....	.....	1	.....	.....	.....	.....	.....	15	1	.....	13	3
Ogden,	1	.....	.....	.....	1	.....	.....	.....	.....	.....	.....	1	.....	6	.....	.....	6	.....
Parma,	.....	.....	.....	.....	.....	.....	.....	.....	.....	.....	.....	.....	2	7	2	1	17	3
Penfield,	1	.....	.....	.....	.....	.....	.....	.....	.....	.....	.....	.....	.....	8	3	.....	13	.....
Perrington,	.....	.....	.....	1	1	.....	.....	.....	.....	.....	.....	.....	1	10	.....	1	17	2
Pittsford,	1	.....	.....	.....	.....	.....	.....	.....	.....	.....	.....	.....	.....	3	1	.....	13	.....
Riga,	.....	.....	.....	.....	1	.....	.....	.....	.....	.....	.....	.....	.....	10	.....	.....	9	3
Rochester city:																		
1st ward,	.....	.....	.....	.....	.....	.....	.....	.....	.....	.....	2	.....	3	12	2	.....	5	.....
2d ward,	6	.....	.....	.....	.....	.....	.....	.....	.....	.....	.....	.....	1	15	.....	3	8	1
3d ward,	4	.....	.....	.....	.....	2	2	1	.....	.....	.....	.....	11	13	2	.....	11	1
4th ward,	.....	3	1	.....	.....	.....	.....	.....	.....	.....	.....	.....	1	8	.....	4	10	.....
5th ward,	1	.....	.....	.....	.....	.....	6	2	.....	.....	1	.....	.....	13	.....	3	14	4
6th ward,	2	1	.....	.....	.....	.....	.....	.....	.....	.....	.....	.....	2	15	.....	.....	5	.....
7th ward,	7	3	1	.....	.....	.....	.....	.....	.....	.....	.....	.....	.....	17	.....	5	6	2
8th ward,	3	.....	.....	1	1	1	.....	.....	.....	.....	.....	1	.....	18	.....	2	6	1
9th ward,	2	.....	.....	1	.....	.....	.....	.....	1	.....	.....	.....	1	10	6	2	13	4
10th ward,	2	.....	1	.....	.....	.....	5	.....	.....	.....	.....	.....	2	26	.....	1	6	10
Total Rochest'r,	27	7	3	2	1	3	13	3	1	.....	3	1	21	147	10	20	84	23
Rush,	.....	.....	.....	.....	.....	.....	.....	.....	.....	.....	.....	.....	.....	2	2	6	6	1
Sweden,	3	1	.....	.....	.....	.....	.....	.....	.....	.....	.....	.....	2	23	4	.....	12	2
Union,	.....	.....	.....	.....	.....	.....	.....	.....	.....	.....	.....	.....	.....	3	.....	.....	9	1
Webster,	.....	.....	.....	.....	.....	.....	.....	.....	.....	.....	.....	.....	.....	3	2	3	7	.....
Wheatland,	1	.....	.....	.....	.....	.....	.....	.....	.....	.....	.....	.....	.....	1	.....	.....	4	1
Total,	40	10	4	3	4	3	13	5	1	.....	3	3	28	292	36	46	287	45

MONTGOMERY COUNTY.—(Continued.)

TOWNS.	Virginia.	N. Carolina.	S. Carolina.	Georgia.	Florida.	Alabama.	Mississippi.	Louisiana.	Texas.	Arkansas.	Missouri.	Tennessee.	Kentucky.	Ohio.	Indiana.	Illinois.	Michigan.	Wisconsin.
Amsterdam,	.....	.....	.....	1	.....	.....	.....	1	.....	.....	.....	1	.....	5	.....	1	6	.....
Canajoharie,	.....	1	.....	1	.....	.....	.....	.....	.....	.....	.....	.....	.....	6	2	2	1	1
Charleston,	.....	.....	.....	.....	.....	.....	.....	.....	.....	.....	.....	.....	.....	.....	.....	.....	.....	.....
Florida,	.....	.....	.....	.....	.....	.....	.....	.....	.....	.....	.....	.....	.....	1	.....	.....	3	.....
Glen,	.....	.....	.....	.....	.....	.....	.....	.....	.....	.....	.....	.....	.....	.....	.....	.....	.....	.....
Minden,	.....	.....	.....	.....	.....	1	.....	.....	.....	.....	.....	.....	.....	1	.....	.....	1	.....
Mohawk,	.....	.....	2	1	.....	.....	.....	1	.....	.....	.....	.....	.....	14	.....	1	1	3
Palatine,	.....	.....	.....	.....	.....	.....	.....	.....	.....	.....	.....	.....	.....	1	.....	.....	.....	1
Root,	.....	.....	1	.....	.....	.....	.....	.....	.....	.....	.....	.....	.....	.....	.....	.....	.....	3
St. Johnsville,	.....	.....	.....	.....	.....	.....	.....	.....	.....	.....	.....	.....	.....	1	.....	.....	2	.....
Total,	.....	1	3	3	.....	1	.....	2	.....	.....	.....	1	.....	29	2	4	14	8

NEW-YORK COUNTY.—(Continued.)

TOWNS.	Virginia.	N. Carolina.	S. Carolina.	Georgia.	Florida.	Alabama.	Mississippi.	Louisiana.	Texas.	Arkansas.	Missouri.	Tennessee.	Kentucky.	Ohio.	Indiana.	Illinois.	Michigan.	Wisconsin.
New-York city:																		
1st ward,	17	.....	3	2	.....	.....	.....	11	2	1	2	.....	2	1	.....	1	.....	.....
2d ward,	9	6	2	.....	.....	1	.....	1	.....	1	1	.....	1	3	.....	.....	3	.....
3d ward,	33	10	11	5	.....	1	.....	2	1	.....	.....	3	10	20	1	2	8	3
4th ward,	31	16	8	14	.....	4	1	9	1	.....	3	1	3	18	1	4	3	1
5th ward,	129	24	28	17	2	5	1	24	1	.....	2	5	10	19	2	6	7	3
6th ward,	36	13	9	16	1	.....	.....	9	.....	.....	.....	3	5	12	.....	2	1	.....
7th ward,	74	6	20	13	6	2	12	12	.....	.....	1	1	6	26	3	3	6	3
8th ward,	139	34	45	25	3	5	3	21	2	1	3	2	9	28	6	10	11	7
9th ward,	83	7	41	9	.....	15	1	22	5	.....	12	2	6	46	4	14	13	1
10th ward,	45	16	11	7	1	6	.....	3	4	.....	1	.....	11	13	2	.....	2	.....
11th ward,	61	7	15	5	2	3	.....	12	1	.....	1	.....	5	16	3	.....	3	3
12th ward,	19	4	19	16	1	2	.....	13	.....	.....	5	.....	5	21	.....	6	9	7
13th ward,	141	17	18	6	.....	3	1	1	4	.....	.....	2	.....	1	1	1	4	.....
14th ward,	75	5	13	10	1	7	1	5	.....	.....	21	1	8	10	.....	3	3	.....
15th ward,	109	17	76	43	3	11	8	36	1	1	10	4	12	67	4	11	12	4

(Continued on page 116.)

MADISON COUNTY.—(Continued.)

TOWNS.	U STATES.			Total United States.	FOREIGN COUNTRIES.													
	Iowa.	California.	Territories.		Canada.	N. Brunswick.	Nova Scotia.	N. Foundland.	West Indies.	Mexico.	S. America.	England.	Scotland.	Ireland.	Wales.	France.	Belgium.	Holland.
Brookfield,				3,603	3							35		103	11			9
Cazenovia,				4,015	9							72	3	349	27	4		2
De Ruyter,	1			1,853	3							18		38	6			
Eaton,				3,470	12							220	19	172	154	10		
Fenner,	1			1,527	1							14	3	70	7			
Georgetown,				1,399							1	35		7				
Hamilton,				3,449	10		1		2			102	8	148	7			
Lebanon,				1,572	5							17	4	31	26	4		
Lenox,				6,833	53		1					201	23	641	9	11		1
Madison,				2,247	3							141	4	48	37			
Nelson,				1,667	3							12		36	158			
Smithfield,				1,432	6							31	6	30				
Stockbridge,				1,847	1							96	4	75	9	17		
Sullivan,				4,422	32							132	16	503	16	12		
Total,	2			39,336	141		2		2		1	1,126	90	2,251	467	58		12

MONROE COUNTY.—(Continued.)

TOWNS.	Iowa.	California.	Territories.	Total United States.	Canada.	N. Brunswick.	Nova Scotia.	N. Foundland.	West Indies.	Mexico.	S. America.	England.	Scotland.	Ireland.	Wales.	France.	Belgium.	Holland.
Brighton,				2,000	82		1					192	47	571		1		37
Chili,				1,595	56							153	10	319	4	1		2
Clarkson,				1,764	49		2					94	43	178			2	4
Gates,				1,439	53	9	1					126	9	177		8		13
Greece,				3,094	110		1		1			283	19	766	3	4		5
Henrietta,	1			1,623	34	2						127	5	219	1	2		
Irondequoit,				1,602	62				1			167	17	94		45		102
Mendon,				2,459	51	1	2					111	7	314	1	1		1
Ogden,	2			2,205	62		1					171	18	558	3	2		1
Parma,				2,467	33		1					83	9	150		2		20
Penfield,				2,426	47							161	14	111	2	8		10
Perrington,				2,461	43		1					102	5	378	2	12		1
Pittsford,	2			1,425	34		1					227	4	317	3	9		1
Riga,				1,446	40	1	1					228	29	215		5		
Rochester city:																		
1st ward,				1,428	68		2					114	26	441	2	7		7
2d ward,				2,199	140	3	4		2			172	47	928	3	17		8
3d ward,	1			2,837	160				4	1		282	58	848	2	5		7
4th ward,	1			2,034	171		2				2	208	30	549		17		16
5th ward,				2,334	132	1	6		2			265	42	659	3	42		37
6th ward,				2,398	118							259	29	330	2	79	2	189
7th ward,	1			2,742	113	3	5					359	39	541	8	6	3	23
8th ward,				2,198	88		11					205	24	823		42		1
9th ward,				3,779	311	2	2		1			329	64	1,435		75		54
10th ward,	1			2,539	155	3	9					385	58	448	1	14		163
Total Rochester,	4			24,488	1,456	12	41		9	1	2	2,578	417	7,002	21	304	5	505
Rush,				1,349	6		3					31	5	158	1			3
Sweden,				3,075	83		2		1		1	152	20	501				9
Union,				2,149	59							54		68				
Webster,				2,094	31		1					83	7	26		9		1
Wheatland,				1,887	74		1					131	99	504	11	7		11
Total,	9			63,048	2,465	25	60		12	1	3	5,254	784	12,626	52	420	7	726

MONTGOMERY COUNTY.—(Continued.)

TOWNS.	Iowa.	California.	Territories.	Total United States.	Canada.	N. Brunswick.	Nova Scotia.	N. Foundland.	West Indies.	Mexico.	S. America.	England.	Scotland.	Ireland.	Wales.	France.	Belgium.	Holland.
Amsterdam,				3,309	25		1					102	95	365	4	4		1
Canajoharie,				3,398	5							62	6	111		1		4
Charleston,				1,853	5		1					11	1	17				
Florida,				2,728	9					1		59	17	284				
Glen,				2,567	4							54	10	160		1	2	2
Minden,				4,063	12							58	10	170	2	6		1
Mohawk,				2,6[illegible]7	4							49	23	215		2		
Palatine,				2,230	1							22		43		5		
Root,				2,361	1							12		302				2
St. Johnsville,				1,558	2							21	2	80		1		
Total,				26.714	68		2			1		450	164	1,747	6	20	2	10

NEW-YORK COUNTY.—(Continued.)

TOWNS.	Iowa.	California.	Territories.	Total United States.	Canada.	N. Brunswick.	Nova Scotia.	N. Foundland.	West Indies.	Mexico.	S. America.	England.	Scotland.	Ireland.	Wales.	France.	Belgium.	Holland.
New-York City:																		
1st ward,	2		2	4,267	36	3	9		7	3	1	385	72	6,207	2	137	3	17
2d ward,				1,273	12	5	2		6			147	44	1,164	4	58		
3d ward,				4,113	39	3	1		18	1	1	281	59	2,283	4	140	8	12
4th ward,				6,860	70	13	22	30	41		5	1,009	289	10,446	57	276	7	44
5th ward,		2		11,322	72	14	33	3	87	1	4	932	341	4,866	29	729	17	46
6th ward,				7,734	75	4	13	15	40	1	6	915	187	10,845	8	363	15	71
7th ward,		2		16,923	91	50	66	13	31	1	8	1,455	328	11,777	84	83	4	37
8th ward,		1		19,175	175	18	27	8	120	4	10	1,568	625	7,210	56	757	15	49
9th ward,		1		26,317	131	20	54	9	65	1	9	1,598	855	7,909	77	185	4	83
10th ward,		2		12,945	84	6	28	12	20	1	7	939	174	3,442	62	189	11	23
11th ward,		1	1	23,481	162	5	41		19	1	1	1,227	316	9,291	46	363	1	19
12th ward,	3	1		8,359	76	2	26	2	44	7	7	629	165	5,831	20	123	15	25
13th ward,		2		14,040	61	20	29	10	22	1	2	768	210	4,965	59	205	1	22
14th ward,				10,551	76	5	14	5	37			823	152	8,961	11	394	5	75
15th ward,	1	3	1	14,098	93	5	16	1	83	16	16	1,022	423	6,285	47	478	32	22

(Continued on page 117.)

MADISON COUNTY.—(Continued.)

TOWNS.	FOREIGN COUNTRIES.																		
	Germany.	Prussia.	Austria.	Switzerland.	Italy.	Spain.	Portugal.	Poland.	Norway.	Sweden.	Russia.	Denmark.	East Indies.	Africa.	Turkey and Greece.	Islands.	Asia.	At Sea.	Unknown.
Brookfield,	6																		
Cazenovia,	11			2														1	
De Ruyter,	3																		
Eaton,	2	1															1		
Fenner,																			
Georgetown,																			
Hamilton,	4																6		
Lebanon,	1			1															
Lenox,	22	2	2	1															
Madison,	3																		
Nelson,																			
Smithfield,	9																		
Stockbridge,	3																		
Sullivan,	116	1		1	1			1											
Total,	180	4	2	5	1			1									7	1	

MONROE COUNTY.—(Continued.)

TOWNS.	Germany.	Prussia.	Austria.	Switzerland.	Italy.	Spain.	Portugal.	Poland.	Norway.	Sweden.	Russia.	Denmark.	East Indies.	Africa.	Turkey and Greece.	Islands.	Asia.	At Sea.	Unknown.
Brighton,	388			4															
Chili,	61			1														1	
Clarkson,	38		1	1				1											
Gates,	502	10																	
Greece,	194	1		1	1	3												1	
Henrietta,	130			1															
Irondequoit,	1,088	5		50														1	
Mendon,	60	1		5			1												
Ogden,	56	2															1		
Parma,	15			1					2										
Penfield,	187	1		64															
Perrington,	161			8								1							
Pittsford,	109			1														2	
Riga,	43	1		13								1						2	
Rochester city:																			
1st ward,	104	1		10		1			13		1								
2d ward,	101	9		6			1		13									3	
3d ward,	169	4		3		1			2	1	1							1	
4th ward,	270	9	1	5		1		7				1							
5th ward,	813	12	2	18		1			6									1	
6th ward,	1,889	43	4	36				4	1	4							1	3	
7th ward,	763	6		2					1								1	4	
8th ward,	549			10															
9th ward,	1,136	5		19	1				1									4	
10th ward,	760	35		150			1		2	3	1	3					1	1	
Total Rochester,	6,554	124	7	259	1	4	2	11	39	8	3	4					3	17	
Rush,	174			20															
Sweden,	121	2																	
Union,	33			4					2										
Webster,	108			27		1													
Wheatland,	91																		
Total,	10,113	147	8	460	2	8	3	12	43	8	3	6					4	24	

MONTGOMERY COUNTY.—(Continued.)

TOWNS.	Germany.	Prussia.	Austria.	Switzerland.	Italy.	Spain.	Portugal.	Poland.	Norway.	Sweden.	Russia.	Denmark.	East Indies.	Africa.	Turkey and Greece.	Islands.	Asia.	At Sea.	Unknown.
Amsterdam,	47	19		1				1										1	37
Canajoharie,	397	1						2											35
Charleston,	1																		10
Florida,	28			4					6										18
Glen,	118	5		6				1											26
Minden,	315	1		1	1					1	1			1			2	3	26
Mohawk,	113											1							20
Palatine,	216		1	1															6
Root,	34		1															1	35
St. Johnsville,	78																		1
Total,	1,347	26	2	13	1			4	6	1	1	1		1			2	5	214

NEW-YORK COUNTY.—(Continued.)

TOWNS.	Germany.	Prussia.	Austria.	Switzerland.	Italy.	Spain.	Portugal.	Poland.	Norway.	Sweden.	Russia.	Denmark.	East Indies.	Africa.	Turkey and Greece.	Islands.	Asia.	At Sea.	Unknown.
New-York city:																			
1st ward,	1,979	11	1	22	11	11	2	6	68	87	3	20				1		2	113
2d ward,	344	2	1	38	7		2	1	1	5	1	1			2		1		128
3d ward,	714	16	2	21	7	9	1	7	3	4	4	4			1		3	2	148
4th ward,	2,688	95	6	118	84	35	21	114	17	73	5	56		2	5	8	36	3	360
5th ward,	2,633	64	3	122	51	17	3	30	11	15	6	5	1	3		4	3		150
6th ward,	3,590	220	30	85	357	28	55	385	5	12	23	1	1	4		6		4	464
7th ward,	2,989	95	5	16	22	25	18	59	35	100	6	80	4	1	2	9	2	3	
8th ward,	3,737	85	11	84	138	20	7	40	4	27	4	7	1	6	2	2		8	52
9th ward,	2,192	54	13	34	10	8	5	27	7	26	5	14	1	1	2	3		5	258
10th ward,	7,536	445	59	63	14	12		150	1	23	8	24	4	1	8	2	3	4	78
11th ward,	17,763	23	25	24	5	7	2	26		19	6	25	6			2		6	67
12th ward,	2,130	19	3	31	24	1	7	11	2	23	1	5		4		2	2	4	55
13th ward,	5,926	81	25	16	6	6	10	42	3	21	2	5		1	1	3		8	28
14th ward,	3,236	61	28	28	50	5	2	104	1	5	11	7	2	1	2	1		4	94
15th ward,	1,068	25	9	64	35	44	5	13	6	28	3	8	2	1	11	4	1	3	79

(Continued on page 118.)

NEW-YORK COUNTY.

TOWNS.	COUNTIES OF NEW-YORK.																	
	Albany.	Allegany.	Broome.	Cattaraugus.	Cayuga.	Chautauque.	Chemung.	Chenango.	Clinton.	Columbia.	Cortland.	Delaware.	Dutchess.	Erie.	Essex.	Franklin.	Fulton.	Genesee
New-York city:																		
16th ward,	160	2	5	......	34	5	7	3	14	117	2	29	270	21	5	3	3	7
17th ward,	129	1	7	......	14	1	1	2	3	94	11	23	137	11	3	......	......	6
18th ward,	154	3	2	5	18	7	1	2	3	85	1	49	139	21	4	3	10	9
19th ward,	35	3	4	1	......	2	2	2	1	31	1	14	55	4	4	4	1	6
20th ward,	168	1	8	1	5	......	1	7	5	67	3	38	239	17	10	2	1	11
21st ward,	147	1	8	1	11	16	......	12	3	54	5	21	165	18	4	2	19	2
22d ward,	59	......	......	......	4	......	1	4	......	40	......	9	103	4	1	......	2	2
Total, ...	2, 158	27	66	16	146	43	26	89	55	1, 035	56	526	2, 753	203	76	22	50	83

NIAGARA COUNTY.

TOWNS.	Albany.	Allegany.	Broome.	Cattaraugus.	Cayuga.	Chautauque.	Chemung.	Chenango.	Clinton.	Columbia.	Cortland.	Delaware.	Dutchess.	Erie.	Essex.	Franklin.	Fulton.	Genesee
Cambria, ...	6	4	2	1	5	2	......	2	2	18	7	1	8	20	1	......	1	13
Hartland, ...	18	1	16	6	34	6	......	7	5	30	3	8	44	23	2	1	......	66
Lewiston, ...	11	6	4	5	15	6	1	18	2	6	12	4	10	43	2	3	......	23
Lockport, ...	64	19	......	6	49	14	2	21	16	22	44	10	42	214	15	1	6	82
Newfane, ...	40	1	......	8	36	10	......	3	6	37	4	6	21	24	1	......	5	40
Niagara, ...	31	3	1	9	18	14	5	8	4	15	9	6	13	164	......	3	......	35
Pendleton, ...	2	7	......	6	1	3	......	6	......	5	7	4	......	55	2	......	......	24
Porter, ...	14	......	1	1	6	5	......	2	5	4	4	......	8	16	3	3	10	18
Royalton, ...	18	22	3	2	43	9	2	6	4	24	6	7	23	80	12	......	5	41
Somerset, ...	14	1	......	......	31	4	......	9	6	11	2	2	50	8	7	2	6	38
Wheatfield, ...	5	7	......	1	6	1	......	......	......	1	3	1	5	134	1	......	......	9
Wilson, ...	12	8	3	4	19	10	......	10	......	23	6	5	24	30	5	3	18	53
Total, ...	235	79	30	49	263	84	10	92	50	196	107	54	248	811	51	16	51	442

ONEIDA COUNTY.

TOWNS.	Albany.	Allegany.	Broome.	Cattaraugus.	Cayuga.	Chautauque.	Chemung.	Chenango.	Clinton.	Columbia.	Cortland.	Delaware.	Dutchess.	Erie.	Essex.	Franklin.	Fulton.	Genesee
Annsville, ...	46	......	......	1	6	......	1	5	2	14	6	2	13	1	3	......	3	......
Augusta, ...	11	1	3	2	7	19	......	27	1	11	14	7	5	4	1	......	4	5
Ava, ...	7	......	......	......	1	......	......	2	......	4	1	1	7	4	1	......	......	3
Boonville, ...	28	......	4	2	2	1	3	19	6	13	5	......	27	2	2	3	6	4
Bridgewater, ...	8	1	......	2	1	3	......	8	......	8	5	1	8	1	......	2	1	1
Camden, ...	53	......	4	......	4	......	......	13	1	13	1	6	11	2	1	......	......	......
Deerfield, ...	9	......	......	......	......	......	......	1	......	......	......	3	4	1	......	......	8	......
Florence, ...	71	......	......	......	2	......	......	1	......	11	10	4	3	1	......	......	1	3
Floyd, ...	16	......	......	......	1	4	......	5	......	12	1	3	7	1	......	......	......	......
Kirkland, ...	20	1	7	......	5	9	......	37	......	5	5	6	8	2	2	......	12	6
Lee, ...	17	......	......	1	9	......	......	7	......	18	1	2	41	......	......	......	1	2
Marcy, ...	8	......	......	......	......	......	......	2	......	5	2	......	5	2	2	......	3	1
Marshall, ...	4	1	4	......	1	2	......	32	......	18	7	1	4	1	2	1	2	......
New Hartford, ...	27	......	2	......	12	2	2	19	......	11	2	20	33	4	2	......	4	2
Paris, ...	14	......	1	2	7	2	......	25	......	3	10	4	13	1	......	......	3	......
Remsen, ...	8	......	......	......	1	......	......	8	2	1	......	......	5	1	1	......	25	1
Rome, ...	74	......	2	4	23	6	1	26	4	36	8	8	43	13	7	2	7	5
Sangerfield, ...	16	3	4	......	3	1	......	28	......	20	5	2	8	3	......	3	1	3
Steuben, ...	8	......	......	2	......	......	......	1	......	4	1	......	3	......	......	......	1	......
Trenton, ...	10	2	2	......	......	3	......	3	1	8	3	2	8	2	1	......	8	......
Utica city:																		
1st ward,	26	......	2	......	6	2	......	1	1	9	......	......	5	1	......	......	6	2
2d ward,	34	......	......	......	2	......	......	3	......	2	1	3	5	1	......	......	1	2
3d ward,	44	......	3	1	10	4	1	17	1	10	1	3	14	7	......	......	4	2
4th ward,	55	2	6	......	5	3	4	31	......	10	4	12	17	5	2	......	1	1
5th ward,	71	......	3	3	6	......	......	35	1	5	2	12	15	1	......	......	4	3
6th ward,	26	......	2	1	3	1	......	5	4	12	1	6	23	1	......	2	......	......
Total Utica, ...	256	2	16	5	32	10	5	92	7	48	9	36	79	16	2	2	16	10
Vernon, ...	32	......	......	......	4	1	......	12	......	17	5	4	7	......	......	......	2	6
Verona, ...	77	4	8	3	11	2	......	19	2	43	19	2	37	14	6	4	7	3
Vienna, ...	26	......	2	......	1	......	......	9	......	25	13	1	42	1	......	......	......	3
Western, ...	20	......	1	......	4	1	......	12	......	13	9	......	18	......	......	2	......	1
Westmoreland, ..	11	......	......	......	2	2	......	9	......	11	2	1	29	3	......	......	2	4
Whitestown, ...	41	5	2	1	8	6	......	29	4	28	2	4	21	......	2	3	1	3
Total, ...	918	20	62	25	147	74	12	451	30	400	146	120	489	80	35	22	118	66

ONONDAGA COUNTY.

TOWNS.	Albany.	Allegany.	Broome.	Cattaraugus.	Cayuga.	Chautauque.	Chemung.	Chenango.	Clinton.	Columbia.	Cortland.	Delaware.	Dutchess.	Erie.	Essex.	Franklin.	Fulton.	Genesee
Camillus, ...	27	2	5	......	36	......	......	12	2	14	17	......	53	1	1	......	1	2
Cicero, ...	161	......	1	1	24	3	1	10	5	27	10	5	15	8	1	......	......	1
Clay, ...	96	......	2	......	23	4	......	17	......	54	20	3	24	......	6	......	1	9
De Witt, ...	145	......	2	......	19	......	4	9	3	21	12	1	49	2	2	......	......	......
Elbridge, ...	49	1	11	1	310	1	......	8	3	8	41	21	51	2	6	2	2	1
Fabius, ...	7	1	......	6	4	......	......	32	......	16	176	1	15	6	1	......	2	3
Geddes, ...	11	......	1	2	15	......	1	10	1	7	12	......	7	3	......	......	3	1
La Fayette, ...	19	3	2	1	17	1	1	10	......	4	28	2	17	2	......	......	......	4
Lysander, ...	104	......	6	......	133	4	......	8	13	95	20	14	35	3	1	......	9	3
Manlius, ...	65	2	6	3	38	2	2	37	2	37	56	1	78	4	......	1	5	2
Marcellus, ...	9	......	3	......	48	1	......	5	......	6	20	2	58	......	......	1	......	1
Onondaga, ...	24	1	2	7	27	5	......	16	3	18	41	9	53	2	5	......	1	2
Otisco, ...	10	2	5	......	16	......	......	7	......	5	25	4	16	......	......	......	1	......
Pompey, ...	6	3	......	......	13	3	......	74	......	31	77	2	47	1	1	......	......	3
Salina, ...	30	......	2	4	15	2	......	3	1	19	17	4	15	1	......	......	......	2
Skaneateles, ...	17	2	3	1	225	3	......	10	4	6	38	6	55	2	1	......	3	8
Spafford, ...	12	3	8	......	50	1	......	9	1	11	107	5	18	5	......	......	10	1

(Continued on page 119.)

NEW-YORK COUNTY.—(CONTINUED.)

TOWNS.	Greene.	Hamilton.	Herkimer.	Jefferson.	Kings.	Lewis.	Livingston.	Madison.	Monroe.	Montgomery.	New-York.	Niagara.	Oneida.	Onondaga.	Ontario.	Orange.	Orleans.	Oswego.
	COUNTIES OF NEW-YORK.																	
New-York city:																		
16th ward,	68	......	5	10	178	3	9	8	16	40	15, 318	3	73	14	9	380	1	15
17th ward,	20	......	9	3	118	......	1	5	10	8	20, 457	2	52	8	3	143	......	8
18th ward,	37	......	13	8	198	3	1	4	12	14	13, 876	4	60	12	24	120	1	6
19th ward,	4	......	3	5	75	1	1	3	8	11	6, 691	1	20	8	11	65	3	4
20th ward,	77	......	11	14	136	2	......	10	12	22	17, 270	6	43	14	20	349	1	9
21st ward,	25	......	10	15	120	2	3	21	14	14	12, 731	2	39	16	12	125	......	7
22d ward,	21	......	2	9	76	1	5	3	......	2	8, 234	1	20	1	1	100	1	45
Total, ...	594	7	131	135	2, 556	24	40	95	162	249	232,155	35	600	160	141	3, 176	22	158

NIAGARA COUNTY.—(CONTINUED.)

TOWNS.	Greene.	Hamilton.	Herkimer.	Jefferson.	Kings.	Lewis.	Livingston.	Madison.	Monroe.	Montgomery.	New-York.	Niagara.	Oneida.	Onondaga.	Ontario.	Orange.	Orleans.	Oswego.
Cambria, ...	2	......	14	7	......	2	11	6	38	17	10	1, 055	13	14	33	2	34	4
Hartland, ...	5	......	14	18	1	7	7	23	146	25	1	1, 164	22	53	46	16	106	14
Lewiston, ...	1	......	5	23	1	......	21	10	22	......	9	1, 298	23	8	40	6	15	8
Lockport, ...	36	......	47	42	10	2	42	44	246	82	136	4, 652	114	43	102	17	134	6
Newfane, ...	12	......	15	14	6	......	12	9	68	21	10	1, 386	18	12	21	26	105	7
Niagara, ...	7	......	16	19	3	3	14	19	82	4	68	1, 191	18	40	50	18	27	6
Pendleton, ...	......	......	12	13	2	......	8	17	5	12	2	746	14	7	4	......	32	9
Porter, ...	15	......	19	18	......	4	9	8	13	7	15	1, 170	14	25	23	3	4	4
Royalton, ...	11	......	52	9	3	2	45	16	78	46	9	1, 714	39	52	56	7	119	5
Somerset, ...	12	......	9	10	......	......	7	27	60	8	3	749	21	39	25	9	85	18
Wheatfield, ...	......	......	13	2	1	......	14	7	14	5	5	1, 020	18	1	8	3	3	4
Wilson, ...	6	1	22	38	1	2	22	19	102	12	12	1, 434	31	27	18	3	67	6
Total, ...	107	1	238	213	28	22	212	205	874	239	280	17, 579	345	321	426	110	731	91

ONEIDA COUNTY.—(CONTINUED.)

TOWNS.	Greene.	Hamilton.	Herkimer.	Jefferson.	Kings.	Lewis.	Livingston.	Madison.	Monroe.	Montgomery.	New-York.	Niagara.	Oneida.	Onondaga.	Ontario.	Orange.	Orleans.	Oswego.
Annsville, ...	14	2	70	22	......	14	......	17	......	43	9	......	1, 515	19	......	......	......	25
Augusta, ...	8	3	35	12	......	5	1	229	5	22	5	......	1, 275	15	......	......	......	12
Ava, ...	1	......	33	18	......	73	1	7	3	62	11	......	593	2	......	......	......	3
Booneville, ...	3	1	286	85	1	182	......	12	9	88	15	2	2, 030	17	2	1	......	7
Bridgewater, ...	1	......	56	3	......	......	......	14	5	1	......	......	622	3	......	......	......	5
Camden, ...	19	1	68	36	......	19	......	33	2	65	10	......	1, 593	31	3	......	......	71
Deerfield, ...	......	......	154	4	......	5	1	5	4	20	9	......	1, 097	4	1	1	......	10
Florence, ...	10	......	75	12	7	13	......	16	1	40	8	......	1, 448	4	2	......	......	43
Floyd, ...	1	1	37	6	......	3	......	6	1	......	1	......	823	14	......	3	2	7
Kirkland, ...	5	......	94	14	11	17	......	75	7	21	21	1	1, 752	21	4	2	2	22
Lee, ...	4	......	43	23	......	79	......	22	2	23	5	......	1, 934	11	......	1	1	17
Marcy, ...	2	2	38	2	......	1	......	9	......	13	16	......	856	4	1	......	......	......
Marshall, ...	2	......	40	8	......	2	4	113	1	7	12	1	1, 139	7	......	1	......	10
New Hartford, ...	6	......	197	18	4	8	1	76	6	30	21	4	1, 850	9	1	7	1	25
Paris, ...	4	3	155	16	......	5	1	39	9	17	283	1	1, 720	13	1	9	2	12
Remsen, ...	1	......	80	11	2	36	......	9	......	17	32	1	1, 352	10	......	......	......	9
Rome, ...	20	2	256	128	10	157	3	81	18	123	103	3	4, 479	65	17	8	2	112
Sangerfield, ...	7	......	31	12	1	1	......	178	2	8	14	1	1, 214	11	5	1	......	13
Steuben, ...	......	......	59	4	......	2	......	4	......	24	5	......	956	3	......	1	......	2
Trenton, ...	6	......	258	16	......	16	......	11	3	16	21	1	1, 920	15	......	1	1	12
Utica city:																		
1st ward,	1	......	70	5	1	6	......	12	......	23	31	......	497	10	2	5	......	4
2d ward,	2	......	63	7	2	7	3	14	2	28	48	......	1, 000	13	2	2	1	3
3d ward,	1	1	74	13	2	8	......	32	3	25	62	2	1, 250	17	2	2	1	16
4th ward,	0	4	161	9	7	22	4	45	12	48	60	......	1, 947	20	1	8	1	18
5th ward,	5	......	130	10	6	13	3	44	5	31	94	......	1, 878	13	1	1	......	5
6th ward,	2	2	106	9	1	10	......	22	9	56	34	3	1, 579	12	......	5	......	10
Total Utica, ...	17	7	604	53	19	66	10	169	31	211	329	5	8, 151	85	8	18	3	56
Vernon, ...	6	7	86	12	1	22	1	152	2	53	17	1	1, 415	21	3	4	......	18
Verona, ...	19	......	115	61	5	47	2	152	5	104	46	3	2, 834	76	6	14	3	45
Vienna, ...	56	2	117	25	3	13	......	32	......	101	11	3	1, 661	35	2	1	3	119
Western, ...	2	......	49	17	1	24	......	10	1	69	10	......	1, 650	6	1	1	3	5
Westmoreland, ...	6	......	69	20	......	14	......	54	3	15	4	1	1, 724	9	1	4	......	14
Whitestown, ...	3	......	118	26	......	16	4	42	5	47	43	3	1, 877	23	5	9	2	37
Total, ...	223	31	3, 223	664	65	840	29	1, 567	125	1, 240	1, 061	31	49, 480	533	63	87	25	711

ONONDAGA COUNTY.—(CONTINUED.)

TOWNS.	Greene.	Hamilton.	Herkimer.	Jefferson.	Kings.	Lewis.	Livingston.	Madison.	Monroe.	Montgomery.	New-York.	Niagara.	Oneida.	Onondaga.	Ontario.	Orange.	Orleans.	Oswego.
Camillus, ...	1	......	32	6	......	2	1	31	11	82	7	2	24	1, 435	14	14	1	36
Cicero, ...	17	......	63	24	1	3	......	106	2	100	11	2	67	1, 580	2	6	1	132
Clay, ...	11	1	87	20	1	6	......	57	4	107	11	......	32	1, 670	4	1	......	105
DeWitt, ...	8	......	27	11	1	1	4	47	1	24	9	1	43	1, 479	7	16	......	21
Elbridge, ...	5	......	58	24	6	1	2	32	11	77	42	7	59	2, 027	21	51	11	45
Fabius, ...	......	......	15	6	1	......	3	82	3	22	2	1	12	1, 250	3	3	4	7
Geddes, ...	......	1	13	8	......	4	1	12	7	28	4	......	15	863	2	5	2	24
La Fayette, ...	11	......	16	2	......	2	1	31	......	10	7	2	27	1, 471	3	15	......	19
Lysander, ...	74	......	73	32	......	12	......	61	10	147	23	5	103	2, 307	12	21	3	213
Manlius, ...	6	......	105	39	......	4	3	277	5	110	33	1	84	3, 151	2	8	2	59
Marcellus, ...	5	1	12	10	3	......	1	25	1	8	8	......	19	1, 424	8	15	......	17
Onondaga, ...	6	3	33	13	3	6	2	55	9	42	18	3	36	2, 802	6	19	4	59
Otisco, ...	1	15	0	1	1	1	......	15	......	27	3	1	......	953	......	12	1	3
Pompey, ...	4	......	48	9	2	2	2	171	12	18	5	......	54	2, 094	9	0	1	17
Salina, ...	2	......	36	21	1	8	2	18	6	25	8	......	20	1, 143	2	2	1	26
Skaneateles, ...	12	......	5	5	7	......	4	20	12	28	34	......	27	1, 654	12	22	......	19
Spafford, ...	2	6	10	9	......	2	......	29	6	25	1	......	4	958	2	3	2	5

(Continued on page 120.)

NEW-YORK COUNTY.—(CONTINUED.)

TOWNS.	Otsego.	Putnam.	Queens.	Rensselaer.	Richmond.	Rockland.	St. Lawrence.	Saratoga.	Schenectady.	Schoharie.	Schuyler.	Seneca.	Steuben.	Suffolk.	Sullivan.	Tioga.	Tompkins.	Ulster.
	COUNTIES OF NEW-YORK.																	
New-York city:																		
16th ward,	23	57	109	117	46	112	10	34	27	16		4	9	74	15	2	14	133
17th ward,	1	38	77	35	49	15	4	17	9	10		4		78	5		3	32
18th ward,	12	28	65	61	56	23	4	37	20	17		3	5	80	6	2	8	95
19th ward,	6	7	20	15	13	4	5	8	6	7			4	10	3	2		30
20th ward,	12	39	78	86	88	84	8	24	26	21	1	6	1	38	10	2	7	116
21st ward,	20	51	70	76	36	17	2	16	7	7		7	1	49	7	1	8	35
22d ward,	5	28	32	57	13	33	5	7		1		2	13	11	6		8	54
Total,	162	589	1,616	973	753	1,029	65	365	172	169	4	75	55	1,248	178	37	114	1,309

NIAGARA COUNTY.—(CONTINUED.)

TOWNS.	Otsego.	Putnam.	Queens.	Rensselaer.	Richmond.	Rockland.	St. Lawrence.	Saratoga.	Schenectady.	Schoharie.	Schuyler.	Seneca.	Steuben.	Suffolk.	Sullivan.	Tioga.	Tompkins.	Ulster.
Cambria,	8	5		27		1	1	9		11		31	4		1	2	1	6
Hartland,	43	5		11			8	13	1	15		15	9		1	1	3	1
Lewiston,	9		1	17			14	14	1	10		14	5		2	3	6	3
Lockport,	61	8	4	63		2	25	58	23	51		123	10	1	2	8	28	8
Newfane,	16			16			16	24	59	31		89	6		3	1	27	2
Niagara,	7			6	3		12	23	13	5	3	11	6		2	4	6	1
Pendleton,	8			20				3	1			8					1	2
Porter,	7	2	7	7		8	14	11	1	24		44	3	6	5			2
Royalton,	20	18	4	47	1		12	64	6	10		80	9	1	3		6	1
Somerset,	15	1		13			6	25	14	11		13	3	3			8	
Wheatfield,				3			4			1		5	1		1	1		7
Wilson,	17	1	1	30			24	93	4	41		59	7	3	3		5	9
Total,	211	40	17	260	4	11	136	337	123	210	3	492	63	14	23	20	91	42

ONEIDA COUNTY.—(CONTINUED.)

TOWNS.	Otsego.	Putnam.	Queens.	Rensselaer.	Richmond.	Rockland.	St. Lawrence.	Saratoga.	Schenectady.	Schoharie.	Schuyler.	Seneca.	Steuben.	Suffolk.	Sullivan.	Tioga.	Tompkins.	Ulster.
Annsville,	29			22			8	20	11	19								9
Augusta,	21			9			1	8		11			3	1			3	
Ava,	2			20			1	4	3	4							2	1
Booneville,	34			29	1		28	20	7	36				1	1		3	3
Bridgewater,	84			7				1	3	2								1
Camden,	34			16		1		10	10	35		1	2				3	
Deerfield,	1			7			5	12	1	7	4							1
Florence,	21		1	5			3	13	1	8							1	
Floyd,				19			5	7	1			1	2					
Kirkland,	53		2	14	1	1	1	15	3	5		2		3			1	
Lee,	14			23			6	25	4	12			5	1				6
Marcy,	15		2	20			1	3	7	1		1						
Marshall,	28	2		11			1	13	3	3		1	1			2		
New Hartford,	146	1		17		2	2	11	13	46		3	3	4		3	2	
Paris,	158		1	15	2		2	15	5	30		3			1	1	6	1
Remsen,	12			5			25	4	3	2							1	1
Rome,	78			128		2	34	124	31	64		11	4	2		1	5	7
Sangerfield,	37	2		11			1	6		3		2	1					
Steuben,	1	1		2				3	3	1								
Trenton,	26		1	59				6	7	4	23		2	3	3			1
Utica city:																		
1st ward,	9			9		4	1	10	12	1							2	
2d ward,	31			4				5	1	27	6		4				2	2
3d ward,	73		2	27		1	3	19	30	13		3	7	1	1	1	5	5
4th ward,	85	1	1	69			6	21	18	20		1	2	4			6	2
5th ward,	45		1	36		1	4	9	19	6			7				1	8
6th ward,	57	1	1	12			3	7	9	28		5	1	9		1	1	4
Total Utica,	300	2	5	157		6	17	71	89	95	6	9	21	14	1	2	17	21
Vernon,	33	1		14			5	14	4					1			1	1
Verona,	63	2		135		1	13	48	11	57		3	6	5	2	1	2	6
Vienna,	38			34		1	6	30	7	48	2	3			1			2
Western,	14	1		16			4	33	2	2				5			1	6
Westmoreland,	45			38		1		16		5			2	6	4	1	1	3
Whitestown,	95		1	44	1	2	9	22	13	31		6		6	2	1	3	5
Total,	1,382	12	13	877	5	17	178	554	242	531	35	46	52	52	15	12	52	75

ONONDAGA COUNTY.—(CONTINUED.)

TOWNS.	Otsego.	Putnam.	Queens.	Rensselaer.	Richmond.	Rockland.	St. Lawrence.	Saratoga.	Schenectady.	Schoharie.	Schuyler.	Seneca.	Steuben.	Suffolk.	Sullivan.	Tioga.	Tompkins.	Ulster.
Camillus,	7	2		22		4	2	35	13	9		7	1	1	3	1	2	2
Cicero,	32	1	1	21		1	17	31	13	36		5	2					25
Clay,	37			41			3	42	4	140		1	2	1		2	7	3
De Witt,	19	1		22			1	14	3	26		1			6			10
Elbridge,	25	2	1	43		9	8	56	22	12		20	3	2	5	4	4	11
Fabius,	10			21			2	19	2	6		1	5		1		8	2
Geddes,	12	1		8		2	6	10	6	6		7	4			2	1	
La Fayette,	6		2	2		1		38	10	12	1	3	2		5		5	4
Lysander,	26	1		107			32	92	36	30		3	3	4		1	1	7
Manlius,	46			36			2	52	7	24	1	1	2	2			1	6
Marcellus,	13	7		15			4	21	7	7		1		2	1	4	1	
Onondaga,	20	2	2	22	2	3	7	47	8	6		4	16	3		7	10	11
Otisco,	31	1		24		1		26		12		2	1			2	2	
Pompey,	26	2		39		1	3	63	2	10		2	1	3	3	2	9	5
Salina,	13			29			6	14	1	5		1	5	2		2	3	
Skaneateles,	8	2	5	30		2	3	27	6	10		13	2		1	1	10	17
Spafford,	21			42				26	5	2		1	1	2			12	8

(Continued on page 121.)

NEW-YORK COUNTY.—(CONTINUED.)

TOWNS.	COUNTIES OF NEW-YORK.							UNITED STATES.										
	Warren.	Washington.	Wayne.	Westchester.	Wyoming.	Yates.	New-York.	Maine.	N. Hampshire.	Vermont.	Massachusetts.	Rhode Island	Connecticut.	New Jersey.	Pennsylvania.	Delaware.	Maryland.	District of Columbia.
New-York city:																		
16th ward,	10	35	5	439	3	3	18, 134	83	108	93	512	78	604	1, 126	374	1	98	15
17th ward,	1	8	3	386	1	5	22, 071	66	74	68	384	76	583	604	304	1	104	4
18th ward,	3	95	2	271	......	2	15, 804	76	64	73	505	83	591	565	312	4	122	10
19th ward,	2	11	6	56	1	3	7, 303	37	24	28	102	16	144	316	113	......	47	9
20th ward,	4	24	3	412	2	......	19, 672	117	60	107	380	41	360	1, 157	321	......	107	3
21st ward,	2	13	6	274	3	......	14, 373	67	52	77	354	26	410	4 9	226	1	59	15
22d ward,	1	8	1	155	4	......	9, 195	44	49	52	202	22	124	436	144	8	32	6
Total, ...	38	401	64	4, 825	17	28	262.156	1, 380	1, 001	1, 278	6, 205	873	7, 239	12, 259	4, 949	53	1, 793	231

NIAGARA COUNTY.—(CONTINUED.)

TOWNS.	Warren.	Washington.	Wayne.	Westchester.	Wyoming.	Yates.	New-York.	Maine.	N. Hampshire.	Vermont.	Massachusetts.	Rhode Island	Connecticut.	New Jersey.	Pennsylvania.	Delaware.	Maryland.	District of Columbia.
Cambria, ...	2	9	8	3	5	6	1, 495	5	12	55	43	7	35	19	92	......	2	1
Hartland, ...	4	42	24	5	13	9	2, 161	2	17	145	51	11	41	28	36	......	1	......
Lewiston, ...	1	5	3	2	2	1	1, 774	......	19	59	60	4	37	55	55	......	4	......
Lockport, ...	8	87	40	7	25	13	7, 049	21	75	313	204	37	235	97	393	......	11	......
Newfane, ...	1	29	63	4	4	2	2, 377	6	22	118	47	7	31	81	39	......	2	......
Niagara, ...	2	21	11	7	14	1	2, 081	11	31	63	162	7	53	20	126	......	21	3
Pendleton, ...	......	9	3	......	7	3	1, 070	......	6	33	23	3	28	8	48	......	1	......
Porter, ...	2	4	18	1	5	......	1, 622	5	45	84	39	3	27	44	29	......	1	......
Royalton, ...	4	61	20	11	13	7	2, 908	10	23	141	73	26	90	45	150	......	1	......
Somerset, ...	2	24	26	8	......	......	1, 445	1	11	93	39	1	51	18	11	......	2	......
Wheatfield, ...	1	3	2	1	1	1	1, 324	3	5	21	28	......	14	9	74	......	4	......
Wilson, ...	2	11	15	2	4	......	2, 387	5	35	91	49	10	54	53	37	......	......	......
Total, ...	29	305	233	51	93	43	27, 753	69	301	1, 216	818	116	696	477	1, 090	......	50	4

ONEIDA COUNTY.—(CONTINUED.)

TOWNS.	Warren.	Washington.	Wayne.	Westchester.	Wyoming.	Yates.	New-York.	Maine.	N. Hampshire.	Vermont.	Massachusetts.	Rhode Island	Connecticut.	New Jersey.	Pennsylvania.	Delaware.	Maryland.	District of Columbia.
Annsville, ...	2	26	......	......	......	......	1, 999	1	6	34	95	12	57	1	2	......	......	1
Augusta, ...	1	3	......	2	......	1	1, 813	......	16	47	71	15	120	3	6	......	......	......
Ava, ...	......	3	......	1	......	......	879	1	3	15	20	4	24	1	6	......	......	......
Booneville, ...	3	14	4	1	......	......	3, 053	5	37	31	90	21	57	11	4	......	......	......
Bridgewater, ...	......	3	2	5	......	......	868	1	6	7	22	17	88	......	1	......	......	......
Camden, ...	......	8	2	6	......	2	2, 190	2	23	42	93	5	217	2	4	......	......	......
Deerfield, ...	......	2	......	2	1	7	1, 391	1	6	14	40	10	19	4	2	......	......	......
Florence, ...	......	11	......	......	......	......	1, 850	6	23	25	68	1	43	1	2	......	......	6
Floyd, ...	......	3	1	......	......	......	994	5	5	6	32	8	40	3	2	......	......	......
Kirkland, ...	......	13	1	4	1	......	2, 314	11	7	43	127	25	186	12	8	......	2	......
Lee, ...	......	7	......	4	......	......	2, 371	1	4	32	124	21	100	12	4	......	......	......
Marcy, ...	......	1	......	2	......	......	1, 027	3	2	18	22	13	35	2	2	......	......	......
Marshall, ...	......	10	......	4	......	1	1, 507	2	1	32	62	19	90	2	4	1	1	......
New Hartford, ..	1	7	1	4	......	......	2, 713	8	6	42	88	27	154	16	7	......	......	......
Paris, ...	5	1	......	......	......	......	2, 621	17	14	20	84	49	180	6	10	......	7	......
Remsen, ...	......	8	......	5	......	......	1, 679	7	2	24	26	18	33	2	7	......	......	......
Rome, ...	3	36	15	3	3	1	6, 408	11	41	153	164	45	207	20	34	......	8	9
Sangerfield, ...	1	4	2	2	1	......	1, 672	1	11	22	77	44	101	2	3	......	2	......
Steuben, ...	......	......	......	3	......	......	1, 094	......	1	7	4	5	17	3	10	......	......	......
Trenton, ...	......	15	3	1	......	......	2, 504	4	9	30	103	14	135	11	14	......	1	......
Utica city:																		
1st ward,	......	1	3	......	......	......	780	1	7	7	27	13	26	9	3	......	1	......
2d ward,	1	5	......	3	......	......	1, 342	3	1	22	28	3	58	9	5	......	......	......
3d ward,	1	7	1	2	2	......	1, 837	9	7	29	94	27	75	17	9	......	1	......
4th ward,	......	10	1	2	......	......	2, 781	14	16	32	76	15	100	13	24	1	3	2
5th ward,	......	7	8	8	......	1	2, 561	5	10	20	51	10	62	18	20	2	2	1
6th ward,	......	6	5	6	......	......	2, 103	6	12	45	59	7	55	7	18	......	3	......
Total Utica, ...	2	42	18	21	2	1	11, 404	38	53	155	335	75	376	73	79	3	10	3
Vernon, ...	......	9	......	1	1	1	1, 997	2	12	39	125	7	168	8	10	......	......	......
Verona, ...	5	59	21	16	2	1	4, 257	13	29	78	141	42	174	44	42	......	2	......
Vienna, ...	5	22	4	8	......	1	2, 519	3	27	52	108	19	87	4	7	......	......	......
Western, ...	1	17	......	3	......	......	2, 035	1	12	14	42	5	48	3	1	......	......	......
Westmoreland, ..	1	26	......	1	......	......	2, 164	......	8	41	105	12	152	8	7	......	......	......
Whitestown, ...	1	20	3	8	1	......	2, 979	9	18	47	90	23	128	10	9	1	......	......
Total, ...	31	370	77	107	12	16	68, 302	153	382	1, 070	2, 358	556	3, 036	264	287	5	33	19

ONONDAGA COUNTY.—(CONTINUED.)

TOWNS.	Warren.	Washington.	Wayne.	Westchester.	Wyoming.	Yates.	New-York.	Maine.	N. Hampshire.	Vermont.	Massachusetts.	Rhode Island	Connecticut.	New Jersey.	Pennsylvania.	Delaware.	Maryland.	District of Columbia.
Camillus, ...	1	42	10	6	......	2	2, 044	3	6	44	48	8	64	14	19	......	2	......
Cicero, ...	......	68	2	2	......	1	2, 648	7	46	41	109	4	68	10	8	......	2	......
Clay, ...	2	30	3	7	1	7	2, 709	2	10	53	57	14	48	12	9	......	......	......
De Witt, ...	......	13	5	7	......	1	2, 098	......	11	31	39	5	87	5	3	......	4	......
Elbridge, ...	5	57	33	9	3	4	3, 335	12	9	70	116	7	110	42	6	......	3	......
Fabius, ...	......	13	2	1	2	......	1, 779	1	4	36	90	14	110	......	8	......	2	......
Geddes, ...	......	13	6	5	......	8	1, 160	5	11	37	38	3	41	10	14	......	2	......
La Fayette, ...	......	15	1	9	......	......	1, 844	2	2	43	125	2	55	7	8	......	......	......
Lysander, ...	2	84	23	38	......	3	4, 037	......	6	100	62	20	115	37	9	......	1	......
Manlius, ...	6	31	6	2	2	4	4, 461	12	29	113	139	27	187	15	9	......	1	2
Marcellus, ...	......	31	......	13	2	2	1, 842	3	4	43	75	19	128	8	1	......	3	......
Onondaga, ...	1	56	6	18	......	1	3, 587	1	16	69	117	55	218	20	16	......	......	......
Otisco, ...	1	24	1	......	1	2	1, 262	......	3	15	107	12	79	3	......	......	......	......
Pompey, ...	3	13	3	4	1	2	2, 912	3	16	52	104	14	202	5	12	......	......	......
Salina, ...	......	18	4	1	3	4	1, 547	......	13	24	36	5	40	4	3	......	2	......
Skaneateles, ...	......	29	15	12	1	2	2, 441	8	18	50	108	14	119	44	15	......	......	......
Spafford, ...	7	64	9	5	1	3	1, 514	5	6	32	46	26	44	7	7	......	......	......

(Continued on page 122.)

NEW-YORK COUNTY.—(Continued.)

TOWNS.	UNITED STATES																	
	Virginia.	N. Carolina.	S. Carolina.	Georgia.	Florida.	Alabama.	Mississippi.	Louisiana.	Texas.	Arkansas.	Missouri.	Tennessee.	Kentucky.	Ohio.	Indiana.	Illinois.	Michigan.	Wisconsin.
New-York city:																		
16th ward,	64	11	31	19	9	5	1	42	1		6	3	7	55	10	10	23	12
17th ward,	76	15	33	27	2	1	2	27	10	1	7	1	17	33	5	6	6	1
18th ward,	62	18	44	42	8	8	6	28	5		4	9	22	54	3	5	7	2
19th ward,	30	8	9	13	3	3	1	8				4	1	14	1	3	3	
20th ward,	67	9	18	10	5	2	1	22			4	5	6	43	7	2	8	3
21st ward,	48	7	32	27	6	14	2	15	3		15	1	12	61	8	8	8	2
22d ward,	29	1	7	3			2	9	2		1	3	4	14	2	2	1	4
Total,	1, 377	251	493	329	53	98	43	332	43	5	99	50	162	575	63	99	141	56

NIAGARA COUNTY.—(Continued.)

TOWNS.	Virginia.	N. Carolina.	S. Carolina.	Georgia.	Florida.	Alabama.	Mississippi.	Louisiana.	Texas.	Arkansas.	Missouri.	Tennessee.	Kentucky.	Ohio.	Indiana.	Illinois.	Michigan.	Wisconsin.
Cambria,						1	1							7		3	11	1
Hartland,														18	1	4	11	4
Lewiston,	2													3			13	3
Lockport,	25	3	2	2		1		1	1		1	8	4	67	7	6	30	11
Newfane,											1			7	1	2	12	3
Niagara,	56	2					2	1		2	1	1	6	30		7	16	5
Pendleton,	3										1			6			9	
Porter,														13		5	13	
Royalton,											1			28	1	5	20	5
Somerset,														1	2		10	2
Wheatfield,	2		1										2	7	1	2	3	
Wilson,	2													14		5	19	3
Total,	90	5	3	2		2	3	2	1	2	5	9	12	201	13	39	167	37

ONEIDA COUNTY.—(Continued.)

TOWNS.	Virginia.	N. Carolina.	S. Carolina.	Georgia.	Florida.	Alabama.	Mississippi.	Louisiana.	Texas.	Arkansas.	Missouri.	Tennessee.	Kentucky.	Ohio.	Indiana.	Illinois.	Michigan.	Wisconsin.
Annsville,											1			1			2	
Augusta,	1		1	1										3		3	4	
Ava,														1			1	
Booneville,	1		2	1										5	1		3	2
Bridgewater,							2							2			1	
Camden,	1							2						2		1	2	
Deerfield,																	1	
Florence,	1	2	1													2		
Floyd,														1		2	1	4
Kirkland,		2											1	7		2	6	2
Lee,																1		5
Marcy,														2		1		
Marshall,													1			6	5	1
New Hartford,	1						1							4		2	6	
Paris,			1										2	5		2	1	7
Remsen,																		1
Rome,	3	2	3	3								2	4	15	1	4	10	3
Sangerfield,								1						5	1	2		2
Steuben,					1											5		
Trenton,		1												5		1	4	1
Utica city:																		
1st ward,	3				1									12		1	1	
2d ward,															2			3
3d ward,		1	1		1			1			1			9			3	2
4th ward,	1	1		4	2						1			8		1	9	2
5th ward,	1							1					2	4		5	4	
6th ward,	1		1											3	2	1	2	2
Total Utica,	6	2	2	4	4			2			2		2	36	4	8	19	9
Vernon,	1		1	1										10				2
Verona,			1										5	9			10	5
Vienna,							1							4	1		1	1
Western,					1												4	2
Westmoreland,														5		4	5	1
Whitestown,				2									1	2		2	1	
Total,	15	9	12	12	6		4	5			3	2	16	124	8	48	87	48

ONONDAGA COUNTY.—(Continued.)

TOWNS.	Virginia.	N. Carolina.	S. Carolina.	Georgia.	Florida.	Alabama.	Mississippi.	Louisiana.	Texas.	Arkansas.	Missouri.	Tennessee.	Kentucky.	Ohio.	Indiana.	Illinois.	Michigan.	Wisconsin.
Camillus,	1										1			4	2	2	14	1
Cicero,														9		4	3	3
Clay,							1							2	3	3	8	
De Witt,														1		4	7	2
Elbridge,	1										1		3	7	4	3	6	8
Fabius,											1			3	3	4	1	6
Geddes,	1													4	1	2		2
La Fayette,														5			4	
Lysander,												1		17	1	4	6	2
Manlius,										1	1			15	6	7	11	6
Marcellus,														3	1	4	5	1
Onondaga,	1							3						6		1	7	1
Otisco,														1			6	
Pompey,	3		1											6	1	3	5	1
Salina,											1			7			11	
Skaneateles,	2		1				1				2			14	2	1	7	6
Spafford,														5	1	3	4	2

(Continued on page 123.)

NEW-YORK COUNTY.—(CONTINUED.)

TOWNS.	U. STATES. Iowa.	California.	Territories.	Total United States.	FOREIGN COUNTRIES. Canada.	N. Brunswick.	Nova Scotia.	N. Foundland.	West Indies.	Mexico.	S. America.	England.	Scotland.	Ireland.	Wales.	France.	Belgium.	Holland.
New-York city:																		
16th ward,		1		21, 536	180	15	38	5	94	2	16	1, 957	1, 359	11, 572	111	212	1	57
17th ward,		1		24, 610	125	14	35	8	164	2	17	1, 466	418	14, 815	62	676	11	52
18th ward,		1		18, 537	117	5	32	5	81	14	23	1, 259	400	14, 666	59	288	1	12
19th ward,	1	1		8, 242	56	8	19	2	29	1	6	610	181	6, 320	20	51	2	8
20th ward,	1	2		22, 540	161	9	21	1	56	2	12	1, 885	1, 194	12, 853	73	294	5	52
21st ward,				16, 398	88	9	18	4	50	4	18	946	263	8, 287	24	127	5	20
22d ward,	1	1		10, 400	60	1	7		7	3	1	892	432	5, 740	20	193	11	10
Total,	9	22	4	303,721	2, 040	234	551	133	1, 121	66	170	22, 713	8, 487	175.735	935	6, 321	174	756

NIAGARA COUNTY.—(CONTINUED.)

TOWNS.	Iowa.	California.	Territories.	Total United States.	Canada.	N. Brunswick.	Nova Scotia.	N. Foundland.	West Indies.	Mexico.	S. America.	England.	Scotland.	Ireland.	Wales.	France.	Belgium.	Holland.
Cambria,				1, 802	83	2	1					111	8	105		10		
Hartland,				2, 531	43							204	13	183	1	2		
Lewiston,	1			2, 089	307	1	9					114	34	524	2	7		
Lockport,				8, 608	507	4	1	6	4	3		1, 078	96	2, 214	7	48		10
Newfane,				2, 756	61	2	3					61	21	163	2	1		
Niagara,				2, 707	338	2	2		4			279	86	1, 160	1	39	1	1
Pendleton,	1			1, 240	57							38	9	119		17		
Porter,				1, 930	260	3	3		1			56	11	312	1	3	2	
Royalton,				3, 587	89		6					190	12	573		8		
Somerset,				1, 687	19				1			80	4	106	1			
Wheatfield,	3			1, 503	48	3						25	9	46		19		3
Wilson,	1			2, 765	174	1	2	1		1		96	17	137				1
Total,	6			33, 205	1, 986	18	27	7	10	4		2, 332	320	5, 642	15	154	3	15

ONEIDA COUNTY.—(CONTINUED.)

TOWNS.	Iowa.	California.	Territories.	Total United States.	Canada.	N. Brunswick.	Nova Scotia.	N. Foundland.	West Indies.	Mexico.	S. America.	England.	Scotland.	Ireland.	Wales.	France.	Belgium.	Holland.
Annsville,				2, 212	2	4						121		286	4	15		
Augusta,				2, 104	17							118		96	25	4		
Ava,				955	7							14		44	27	18		
Booneville,				3, 324	57	1	3					28	22	568	67	44		6
Bridgewater,	1			1, 016	1							6		77	95			
Camden,				2, 586	4							73	74	132	8	5		
Deerfield,				1, 488	4							86	25	184	143	82		
Florence,				2, 031	6	1						135	27	604	3	1		
Floyd,				1, 103	2							81	1	16	174	4		
Kirkland,	1			2, 756	18	2	1					182	46	603	23	14		1
Lee,				2, 675	12							40	10	64	50	39		
Marcy,				1, 127	3		4					103	9	71	263	42		3
Marshall,				1, 734	4							73	3	240	85			
New Hartford,	1			3, 076	28	1	1					483	168	419	189	27		
Paris,				3.026	13		1				1	206	28	284	90	1		
Remsen,				1, 799	33	1	1					41	9	124	537	19		
Rome,				7, 150	104		1					438	36	1, 419	181	154		
Sangerfield,				1, 946	2							172	4	198	69	2		
Steuben,				1, 147	1							6		51	365	1		
Trenton,				2, 837	17							135	18	249	456	4		3
Utica city:																		
1st ward,				892	19		1	4				79	6	312	47	3		5
2d ward,				1, 476	17				1			129	18	316	200	6		
3d ward,				2, 124	24			1	3			212	31	401	143	19		4
4th ward,				3, 106	31		3	2				499	33	697	144	18		7
5th ward,				2, 779	61		1		2			434	39	1, 236	142	99		6
6th ward,				2, 327	40							265	54	455	184	116		4
Total Utica,				12, 704	192		5	7	6			1, 648	181	3, 417	860	261		26
Vernon,				2, 383	12							297	7	209	9	27		1
Verona,				4, 852	73							158	19	805	13	140		1
Vienna,				2, 835	45	5	2					78	40	150	8	6		
Western,				2, 168	12							52	4	99	134	7		
Westmoreland,				2, 512	15			5			1	330	27	285	61	1		4
Whitestown,				3, 322	33	3	1	3				495	133	451	256	10		
Total,	3			76, 868	717	18	20	15	6		2	5, 599	891	11, 145	4, 195	928		45

ONONDAGA COUNTY.—(CONTINUED.)

TOWNS.	Iowa.	California.	Territories.	Total United States.	Canada.	N. Brunswick.	Nova Scotia.	N. Foundland.	West Indies.	Mexico.	S. America.	England.	Scotland.	Ireland.	Wales.	France.	Belgium.	Holland.
Camillus,				2, 277	38							31	7	350		2		
Cicero,	1			2, 963	48							100	5	50		20	1	
Clay,	1			2, 932	32		1					151	1	98		22		1
De Witt,				2, 297	33							230	1	271	2	19		
Elbridge,	1			3, 744	33		2					201	12	466	1	5		10
Fabius,				2, 062	8							20	2	157				
Geddes,				1, 331	52		1					69	3	474	1	12	1	
La Fayette,				2, 097	16							48	2	155	4			
Lysander,				4, 418	85	1						133	1	284	1	8		
Manlius,				5, 042	36	5	1	1				175	11	449	4	107		4
Marcellus,	1			2, 141	11		1					186	5	188		1		
Onondaga,				4, 166	69		1					304	26	720	7	7		
Otisco,				1, 488	32							67	1	90				
Pompey,				3, 340	16							60	9	330				
Salina,				1, 693	49							94	4	216		27		
Skaneateles,				2, 853	13							644	19	385	13	3		4
Spafford,				1, 702	6		1					50	1	53				

(Continued on page 124.)

NEW-YORK COUNTY.—(Continued.)

TOWNS.	FOREIGN COUNTRIES.																		
	Germany.	Prussia.	Austria.	Switzerland.	Italy.	Spain.	Portugal.	Poland.	Norway.	Sweden.	Russia.	Denmark.	East Indies.	Africa.	Turkey and Greece.	Islands.	Asia.	At Sea.	Unknown.
New-York city:																			
16th ward,	2,305	64	25	31	8	18	5	27	5	19	1	4	2		1	4	1	5	142
17th ward,	16,223	57	41	79	37	28	6	48	13	21	10	11	6		1	5		13	477
18th ward,	3,525	29	11	37	61	41	2	20	32	10	6	15	8	2		2	3	5	203
19th ward,	1,789	10	8	25	7	3	2	8	2	2		6	2	8			1	9	429
20th ward,	7,413	78	19	30	15	15	3	49	1	20	7	5	1	3		1	3	11	223
21st ward,	1,480	20	3	8	17	10	3	19	3	9		13	2		2	1	3	4	56
22d ward,	4,726	32	3	2	2		2	14	7	5	4	11				2	2		16
Total,	95,986	1,586	331	978	968	343	163	1,200	227	554	116	327	43	38	40	62	64	103	3,620

NIAGARA COUNTY.—(Continued.)

TOWNS.	Germany.	Prussia.	Austria.	Switzerland.	Italy.	Spain.	Portugal.	Poland.	Norway.	Sweden.	Russia.	Denmark.	East Indies.	Africa.	Turkey and Greece.	Islands.	Asia.	At Sea.	Unknown.
Cambria,	87	3		2				1											1
Hartland,	21								1										34
Lewiston,	103	68		1				1											
Lockport,	583	18		2				3	3	1								6	184
Newfane,	19																	2	73
Niagara,	710	51		70				1				1							4
Pendleton,	337	6																	3
Porter,	31	7		5						1		1						2	14
Royalton,	195	260		1												1		1	7
Somerset,	6																		19
Wheatfield,	418	1,067								7								3	1
Wilson,	72	2						1	2										20
Total,	2,582	1,482		81				7	6	9		2				1		14	360

ONEIDA COUNTY.—(Continued.)

TOWNS.	Germany.	Prussia.	Austria.	Switzerland.	Italy.	Spain.	Portugal.	Poland.	Norway.	Sweden.	Russia.	Denmark.	East Indies.	Africa.	Turkey and Greece.	Islands.	Asia.	At Sea.	Unknown.
Annsville,	57	5		4															5
Augusta,	16			1														1	1
Ava,	172	2		3															
Booneville,	259			27									4						14
Bridgewater,	2																		6
Camden,	14			2				2											
Deerfield,	232	5		8															
Florence,	3																		1
Floyd,	55			1															6
Kirkland,	142															3		3	15
Lee,	72	1		57															
Marcy,	130			3														2	7
Marshall,	8																		
New Hartford,	78			14															33
Paris,	39																	1	5
Remsen,	104	1		1															14
Rome,	1,151		2	20				1		1								8	54
Sangerfield,	13																		18
Steuben,	13			7															1
Trenton,	204	9		4			2											1	48
Utica city:																			
1st ward,	60			1				9									2		3
2d ward.	568	6	1					55										3	3
3d ward,	91	1		2				7					1					4	13
4th ward,	190	5		3	1			82			3							1	2
5th ward,	504	13		44	1			2									1	1	15
6th ward,	1,098	7	5	14				1		2								4	33
Total Utica,	2,511	32	6	64	2			156		2	3		1				3	13	69
Vernon,	25			3				1										1	30
Verona,	802	2		30														1	27
Vienna,	55															2			22
Western,	33			27															10
Westmoreland,	24	5		1				1										2	5
Whitestown,	88			2			1						1					3	36
Total,	6,302	62	8	279	2		3	161		3	3		6			5	3	36	427

ONONDAGA COUNTY.—(Continued.)

TOWNS.	Germany.	Prussia.	Austria.	Switzerland.	Italy.	Spain.	Portugal.	Poland.	Norway.	Sweden.	Russia.	Denmark.	East Indies.	Africa.	Turkey and Greece.	Islands.	Asia.	At Sea.	Unknown.
Camillus,	25																	1	9
Cicero,	195			3															3
Clay,	71			7															10
De Witt,	123			2															7
Elbridge,	25													1		2		1	58
Fabius,	3																		4
Geddes,	119	1		2															
La Fayette,	12																		6
Lysander,	82		1	3										1		2			40
Manlius,	358	4		8									1					2	20
Marcellus,	6																		8
Onondaga,	49												5					1	45
Otisco,	38																		
Pompey,	7																	1	7
Salina,	478	5		9														1	4
Skaneateles,	23		5	1										1					12
Spafford,	1			2															

(Continued on page 125.)

ONONDAGA COUNTY.

TOWNS.	Albany.	Allegany.	Broome.	Cattaraugus.	Cayuga.	Chautauque.	Chemung.	Chenango.	Clinton.	Columbia.	Cortland.	Delaware.	Dutchess.	Erie.	Essex.	Franklin.	Fulton.	Genesee.
	COUNTIES OF NEW-YORK.																	
Syracuse city:																		
1st ward,	20	......	1	......	9	......	1	7	3	8	6	3	6	......	3	......	......	......
2d ward,	24	1	......	......	6	......	......	1	1	2	3	......	2	1	......	1	......	......
3d ward,	22	......	1	......	23	3	2	18	1	8	28	......	12	7	......	1	1	......
4th ward,	54	1	2	1	43	......	2	15	......	13	36	1	14	10	4	......	2	2
5th ward,	32	......	3	......	14	2	......	7	......	6	6	1	10	1	1	......	......	......
6th ward,	41	......	4	......	53	8	......	24	5	10	46	7	40	3	1	1	1	3
7th ward,	54	......	3	2	16	3	......	6	1	6	31	3	26	8	......	......	2	3
8th ward,	87	......	3	2	46	1	......	15	5	3	45	2	11	7	4	......	1	3
Total Syracuse,	334	2	17	5	210	17	5	93	16	56	201	17	121	37	13	3	7	11
Tully, ...	12	......	3	1	7	......	2	13	......	5	102	2	16	......	......	2	......	2
Van Buren, ...	14	1	4	......	40	......	......	7	......	6	13	3	18	4	2	......	2	3
Total, ...	1, 152	23	83	32	1, 270	47	16	390	54	446	1, 033	102	761	83	40	9	47	59

ONTARIO COUNTY.

TOWNS.	Albany.	Allegany.	Broome.	Cattaraugus.	Cayuga.	Chautauque.	Chemung.	Chenango.	Clinton.	Columbia.	Cortland.	Delaware.	Dutchess.	Erie.	Essex.	Franklin.	Fulton.	Genesee.
Bristol, ...	6	7	2	3	15	......	2	1	......	5	2	1	17	1	......	......	......	1
Canadice, ...	......	2	......	1	24	......	......	4	......	2	1	4	8	1	......	......	......	......
Canandaigua, ...	23	17	6	3	45	5	13	18	......	6	20	11	54	11	8	2	4	19
East Bloomfield,..	7	4	3	2	17	5	1	5	1	8	2	......	13	1	2	......	3	18
Farmington, ...	10	1	......	2	23	5	1	4	2	5	1	......	47	3	2	......	2	1
Gorham, ...	23	7	2	5	14	1	1	1	2	21	1	1	14	1	1	......	2	10
Hopewell, ...	......	4	2	1	10	2	10	6	......	3	......	1	32	3	......	......	2	5
Manchester, ...	20	12	4	5	19	4	6	7	4	75	9	3	75	4	......	......	......	1
Naples, ...	4	18	......	1	22	3	5	5	......	20	5	4	14	1	2	......	2	7
Phelps, ...	35	12	10	4	61	1	3	22	......	140	7	10	74	7	1	1	7	14
Richmond, ...	10	1	1	......	31	1	......	3	1	2	2	5	7	6	......	......	2	1
Seneca, ...	92	18	6	2	68	9	46	32	1	32	14	12	62	10	1	......	2	17
South Bristol, ...	9	4	1	2	8	1	2	3	3	4	1	2	31	......	1	......	......	2
Victor, ...	5	4	1	5	19	3	1	1	......	20	......	7	21	1	......	......	2	13
West Bloomfield,.	7	4	2	3	5	4	......	1	......	4	4	......	11	7	......	2	......	13
Total, ...	251	115	40	39	381	44	91	113	14	347	69	61	480	57	18	5	28	122

ORANGE COUNTY.

TOWNS.	Albany.	Allegany.	Broome.	Cattaraugus.	Cayuga.	Chautauque.	Chemung.	Chenango.	Clinton.	Columbia.	Cortland.	Delaware.	Dutchess.	Erie.	Essex.	Franklin.	Fulton.	Genesee.
Blooming Grove,.	1	......	3	......	2	......	1	1	......	7	2	1	24	1	......	......	......	......
Chester, ...	2	......	......	......	5	......	5	3	......	3	......	3	18	......	......	......	......	......
Cornwall, ...	18	......	......	......	1	......	......	6	......	1	......	3	54	1	4	......	1	2
Crawford, ...	......	......	2	......	......	......	......	......	......	......	......	......	16	......	......	......	......	......
Deerpark, ...	13	2	13	2	6	......	9	6	......	17	2	10	55	1	......	......	......	......
Goshen, ...	3	......	1	......	6	......	2	......	1	7	3	2	13	......	......	......	......	......
Greenville, ...	1	......	......	......	......	......	......	......	......	1	......	......	11	......	......	......	......	......
Hamptonburgh,..	1	......	......	......	......	......	1	......	......	......	......	......	26	1	1	......	......	......
Minisink, ...	......	......	1	......	......	......	1	1	......	......	......	2	8	......	......	......	......	1
Monroe, ...	1	......	......	......	......	......	2	......	......	2	1	......	42	......	......	......	......	......
Montgomery, ...	6	......	2	......	1	......	......	2	......	4	......	6	75	4	......	......	......	1
Mount Hope, ...	5	2	......	......	......	......	1	1	......	1	2	......	9	......	......	......	......	......
Newburgh, ...	44	2	9	1	7	......	3	2	......	40	6	12	386	6	......	......	2	......
New Windsor, ...	4	......	......	......	1	......	......	......	......	4	......	2	89	2	......	......	......	......
Walkill, ...	17	......	2	1	......	......	4	4	1	8	8	1	79	2	......	......	......	1
Warwick, ...	......	1	......	......	......	......	3	1	......	6	......	......	22	......	2	......	......	4
Wawayanda, ...	1	......	......	......	......	......	......	......	......	1	......	1	4	......	......	......	......	......
Total, ...	117	7	33	4	29	......	32	27	2	102	24	43	931	18	7	......	3	9

ORLEANS COUNTY.

TOWNS.	Albany.	Allegany.	Broome.	Cattaraugus.	Cayuga.	Chautauque.	Chemung.	Chenango.	Clinton.	Columbia.	Cortland.	Delaware.	Dutchess.	Erie.	Essex.	Franklin.	Fulton.	Genesee.
Barre, ...	61	13	5	11	57	23	6	12	......	53	19	14	64	30	10	4	4	118
Carlton, ...	36	7	......	1	25	3	1	12	......	8	7	2	4	9	......	1	9	42
Clarendon, ...	5	2	1	2	10	7	......	14	2	11	2	2	11	5	3	1	5	116
Gaines, ...	5	10	......	4	15	1	......	13	1	11	3	2	58	5	6	3	9	42
Kendall, ...	17	1	1	......	16	......	9	7	4	8	2	......	26	6	1	4	4	25
Murray, ...	24	3	5	8	21	1	......	10	1	22	4	2	29	10	6	......	4	28
Ridgeway, ...	36	24	2	5	47	17	7	11	......	24	18	15	86	59	3	1	9	110
Shelby, ...	65	3	1	6	22	3	......	2	1	24	3	2	22	40	......	1	9	60
Yates, ...	18	2	4	1	30	......	......	3	2	11	10	7	13	2	2	2	1	35
Total, ...	267	65	19	38	243	55	23	84	11	172	68	46	313	166	31	17	54	576

OSWEGO COUNTY.

TOWNS.	Albany.	Allegany.	Broome.	Cattaraugus.	Cayuga.	Chautauque.	Chemung.	Chenango.	Clinton.	Columbia.	Cortland.	Delaware.	Dutchess.	Erie.	Essex.	Franklin.	Fulton.	Genesee.
Albion, ...	17	......	......	......	7	6	......	2	2	14	7	5	5	......	2	3	5	1
Amboy, ...	1	1	......	1	......	1	......	5	......	11	1	5	7	......	......	......	3	[illegible]
Boylston, ...	14	......	......	1	......	......	......	2	......	3	......	1	3	......	......	......	1	......
Constantia, ...	79	2	7	......	9	......	1	11	......	40	4	......	33	9	6	......	3	......
Granby, ...	51	1	3	2	110	1	......	55	7	51	11	5	28	2	3	......	2	11
Hannibal, ...	29	1	2	3	271	7	......	12	5	35	3	8	24	3	3	3	2	3
Hastings, ...	43	1	......	3	15	1	......	6	3	28	14	5	16	11	2	3	3	9
Mexico, ...	7	2	2	2	23	4	......	10	5	31	7	3	13	3	1	3	5	8
New Haven, ...	6	......	......	......	6	2	......	3	2	14	8	4	8	3	1	7	......	3
Orwell,, ...	11	......	......	......	3	2	......	1	......	16	......	11	6	1	......	......	7	3
Oswego, ...	8	2	......	1	84	......	......	3	5	12	5	3	23	1	9	10	......	......

(Continued on page 126.)

ONONDAGA COUNTY.—(CONTINUED.)

TOWNS.	COUNTIES OF NEW-YORK.																	
	Greene.	Hamilton.	Herkimer.	Jefferson.	Kings.	Lewis.	Livingston.	Madison.	Monroe.	Montgomery.	New-York.	Niagara.	Oneida.	Onondaga.	Ontario.	Orange.	Orleans.	Oswego.
Syracuse city:																		
1st ward,	2	......	17	10	......	1	1	19	......	18	13	......	31	1, 527	2	......	2	55
2d ward,	1	......	12	2	1	......	......	11	......	7	8	1	15	1, 013	1	3	2	17
3d ward,	9	......	10	6	1	2	1	50	12	17	30	......	29	681	2	3	1	12
4th ward,	7	......	21	16	3	2	5	58	29	28	34	2	86	1, 321	3	6	4	41
5th ward,	1	......	11	5	1	1	1	20	10	18	22	1	44	624	......	4	2	22
6th ward,	14	3	26	17	5	8	1	75	22	34	59	5	80	1, 036	18	6	......	57
7th ward,	8	......	30	13	1	......	1	54	11	18	23	5	40	1, 551	2	8	3	26
8th ward,	12	......	37	17	2	8	1	71	30	23	62	3	84	560	20	5	3	41
Total Syracuse,	54	3	164	86	14	22	11	358	114	163	251	17	409	8, 313	48	35	17	271
Tully, ...	14	12	15	6	......	......	......	34	......	11	7	......	12	914	2	3	......	6
Van Buren, ...	16	......	40	10	......	2	1	43	6	64	9	......	27	1, 848	2	19	......	44
Total, ...	249	42	858	342	41	78	38	1, 504	220	1, 118	403	42	1, 074	39, 336	161	276	50	1, 128

ONTARIO COUNTY.—(CONTINUED.)

TOWNS.	Greene.	Hamilton.	Herkimer.	Jefferson.	Kings.	Lewis.	Livingston.	Madison.	Monroe.	Montgomery.	New-York.	Niagara.	Oneida.	Onondaga.	Ontario.	Orange.	Orleans.	Oswego.
Bristol, ...	1	......	2	10	1	1	6	5	20	9	2	1	3	5	1, 164	5	2	2
Canadice, ...	......	1	2	5	2	......	73	......	2	2	2	......	14	10	509	11	......	1
Canandaigua, ...	12	1	17	12	12	3	60	14	70	23	121	7	36	28	2, 974	56	17	8
East Bloomfield, .	......	......	10	3	......	......	41	......	62	11	4	4	16	2	1, 085	5	1	2
Farmington, ...	19	......	13	4	1	......	10	9	52	11	10	3	11	9	932	8	3	1
Gorham, ...	15	2	15	......	1	......	13	6	10	45	8	1	10	4	1, 276	34	1	3
Hopewell, ...	1	......	......	1	......	1	20	5	22	9	10	2	14	7	952	5	8	4
Manchester, ...	6	......	18	4	3	1	13	16	34	17	5	6	19	21	1, 547	11	2	6
Naples, ...	3	......	16	4	......	6	50	16	12	7	1	2	17	12	1, 137	9	1	5
Phelps, ...	21	......	37	10	9	4	20	17	52	38	41	3	34	20	2, 441	61	9	5
Richmond, ...	1	......	1	......	1	1	58	3	17	2	4	......	4	2	788	5	1	......
Seneca, ...	13	1	37	15	19	3	23	13	41	40	121	10	44	68	3, 586	83	6	11
South Bristol, ...	2	......	1	2	1	2	44	7	19	......	2	......	4	10	661	29	......	......
Victor, ...	5	......	13	4	......	2	22	7	162	35	7	1	14	11	957	8	11	4
West Bloomfield, .	3	......	6	4	......	......	105	8	75	1	3	......	14	7	699	8	4	......
Total, ...	102	5	188	78	50	24	558	126	650	250	341	40	254	216	20, 708	338	66	52

ORANGE COUNTY.—(CONTINUED.)

TOWNS.	Greene.	Hamilton.	Herkimer.	Jefferson.	Kings.	Lewis.	Livingston.	Madison.	Monroe.	Montgomery.	New-York.	Niagara.	Oneida.	Onondaga.	Ontario.	Orange.	Orleans.	Oswego.
Blooming Grove, .	......	......	......	1	11	......	......	......	2	......	45	......	......	......	......	1, 584	......	......
Chester, ...	4	......	......	......	3	......	......	1	1	3	28	......	1	1	......	1, 262	......	......
Cornwall, ...	4	......	2	2	36	1	1	......	5	1	269	......	6	......	1	2, 260	......	2
Crawford, ...	4	......	......	......	3	......	......	......	......	......	23	......	......	......	......	1, 449	......	......
Deerpark, ...	10	......	3	......	16	......	......	3	3	2	149	4	3	......	8	2, 239	......	1
Goshen, ...	4	......	......	......	4	......	1	1	2	......	72	......	5	1	2	2, 294	......	3
Greenville, ...	......	......	......	......	......	......	......	......	......	......	5	......	......	......	......	986	......	......
Hamptonburgh, ..	1	......	......	......	......	......	......	......	......	......	16	......	......	......	......	1, 042	......	......
Minisink, ...	......	......	......	......	1	......	......	1	......	......	5	......	......	......	1	922	......	......
Monroe, ...	1	......	1	......	2	......	......	......	1	1	113	......	......	......	......	3, 304	......	......
Montgomery, ...	4	......	......	......	19	......	......	......	......	......	79	......	3	2	1	2, 584	......	......
Mount Hope, ...	1	......	......	......	6	......	......	......	......	......	8	......	......	......	1	1, 288	......	......
Newburgh, ...	32	......	3	3	44	......	......	2	3	4	463	......	4	5	5	6, 213	3	......
New Windsor, ...	......	......	1	......	6	......	......	......	1	......	58	......	......	......	......	1, 553	......	......
Walkill, ...	38	......	3	3	17	3	......	......	1	......	111	......	5	......	......	3, 701	......	1
Warwick, ...	2	......	......	5	3	......	......	......	2	1	63	......	3	......	......	3, 892	......	......
Wawayanda, ...	2	......	......	1	......	......	......	......	......	......	10	......	......	......	......	1, 549	......	......
Total, ...	107	......	13	15	171	4	2	8	21	12	1, 517	4	30	9	19	38, 122	3	7

ORLEANS COUNTY.—(CONTINUED.)

TOWNS.	Greene.	Hamilton.	Herkimer.	Jefferson.	Kings.	Lewis.	Livingston.	Madison.	Monroe.	Montgomery.	New-York.	Niagara.	Oneida.	Onondaga.	Ontario.	Orange.	Orleans.	Oswego.
Barre, ...	12	......	27	26	4	2	36	60	275	52	135	63	161	56	126	11	2, 478	17
Carlton, ...	9	......	44	11	2	3	25	25	118	33	1	17	26	31	15	8	1, 078	2
Clarendon, ...	1	......	11	15	......	......	16	6	141	22	2	13	41	34	9	4	665	......
Gaines, ...	......	......	23	11	3	......	19	12	103	10	52	32	30	13	16	6	957	10
Kendall, ...	4	......	8	4	1	......	24	3	170	7	6	6	24	8	30	2	751	8
Murray, ...	3	......	22	13	......	2	19	8	197	17	8	28	63	15	44	12	1, 040	6
Ridgeway, ...	14	......	37	20	2	3	21	32	117	58	41	123	56	72	43	18	1, 634	10
Shelby, ...	8	......	70	......	2	1	9	21	100	46	9	79	17	17	14	16	1, 200	3
Yates, ...	4	......	22	4	4	2	17	43	32	42	12	44	17	47	13	......	850	8
Total, ...	55	......	264	104	18	13	186	210	1, 253	287	266	405	435	293	310	77	10, 653	64

OSWEGO COUNTY.—(CONTINUED.)

TOWNS.	Greene.	Hamilton.	Herkimer.	Jefferson.	Kings.	Lewis.	Livingston.	Madison.	Monroe.	Montgomery.	New-York.	Niagara.	Oneida.	Onondaga.	Ontario.	Orange.	Orleans.	Oswego.
Albion, ...	8	1	157	103	2	14	3	23	1	40	2	1	178	33	2	1	......	975
Amboy, ...	3	......	115	22	......	4	......	28	......	20	5	......	80	2	......	......	......	497
Boyleston, ...	......	......	100	58	......	13	......	3	......	27	1	......	22	5	......	......	......	400
Constantia, ...	189	......	92	28	3	6	......	47	10	22	18	2	327	77	3	......	......	1, 184
Granby, ...	56	......	44	61	1	4	1	34	6	32	20	1	68	381	1	8	2	1, 357
Hannibal, ...	10	......	34	18	3	1	1	30	10	34	6	1	46	168	9	14	1	1, 246
Hastings, ...	16	......	78	38	......	2	2	144	6	47	8	......	93	433	5	......	......	1, 272
Mexico, ...	8	6	130	108	12	17	1	36	1	27	15	1	241	91	2	......	1	2, 005
New Haven, ...	7	......	73	59	......	10	1	16	4	11	5	......	138	26	3	5	......	1, 010
Orwell, ...	1	......	72	20	2	2	......	19	......	27	......	......	152	1	......	......	......	656
Oswego, ...	5	......	38	68	1	13	2	22	8	30	23	......	90	94	7	9	......	1, 200

(Continued on page 127.)

ONONDAGA COUNTY.—(Continued.)

TOWNS.	COUNTIES OF NEW-YORK.																	
	Otsego.	Putnam.	Queens.	Rensselaer.	Richmond.	Rockland.	St. Lawrence.	Saratoga.	Schenectady.	Schoharie.	Schuyler.	Seneca.	Steuben.	Suffolk.	Sullivan.	Tioga.	Tompkins.	Ulster.
Syracuse city:																		
1st ward,	8	......	1	9	1	......	13	19	1	11	......	2	4	1	......	2	8	......
2d ward,	1	1	1	5	......	......	6	6	1	......	......	......	......	......	1	......	......	......
3d ward,	14	......	......	6	1	......	3	24	9	5	......	3	1	1	......	......	5	2
4th ward,	16	......	1	13	......	......	11	31	23	17	......	17	2	1	5	......	15	12
5th ward,	7	......	1	12	......	1	2	4	22	7	......	5	1	......	......	3	1	3
6th ward,	29	......	7	28	1	2	2	27	21	14	1	12	4	4	1	2	14	1
7th ward,	7	......	......	39	......	1	11	39	......	22	......	2	2	......	1	6	6	14
8th ward,	21	......	1	30	......	......	13	14	11	2	......	3	2	......	1	2	3	16
Total Syracuse,	103	1	12	142	3	4	61	164	88	78	1	44	16	7	9	15	52	48
Tully, ...	15	......	......	15	......	2	......	16	2	8	......	3	2	4	1	2	16	......
Van Buren, ...	40	1	......	57	......	12	6	24	11	14	......	1	1	......	1	......	......	1
Total, ...	510	24	23	738	5	42	163	817	246	453	3	121	69	33	36	45	144	160

ONTARIO COUNTY.—(Continued.)

TOWNS.	Otsego.	Putnam.	Queens.	Rensselaer.	Richmond.	Rockland.	St. Lawrence.	Saratoga.	Schenectady.	Schoharie.	Schuyler.	Seneca.	Steuben.	Suffolk.	Sullivan.	Tioga.	Tompkins.	Ulster.
Bristol, ...	5	......	1	1	......	......	......	30	1	4	......	4	7	......	......	......	1	2
Canadice, ...	8	4	......	5	......	......	1	3	......	1	......	1	24	......	1	......	1	......
Canandaigua, ...	17	......	1	24	......	8	15	40	18	10	......	54	37	1	1	2	9	19
East Bloomfield, .	11	4	......	3	......	......	9	2	2	11	......	9	7	1	......	1	5	10
Farmington, ...	4	......	1	14	......	4	......	14	7	7	......	8	1	2	......	......	......	3
Gorham, ...	3	5	......	27	......	2	......	12	10	5	......	30	27	1	1	......	5	17
Hopewell, ...	3	......	......	13	......	31	......	13	4	2	......	29	7	......	1	1	15	7
Manchester, ...	8	......	......	31	......	1	1	25	3	4	......	41	5	2	1	3	2	14
Naples, ...	18	1	......	10	......	1	1	13	3	4	......	16	138	......	......	2	8	5
Phelps, ...	20	20	10	40	......	8	8	31	1	19	1	137	32	8	6	8	21	18
Richmond, ...	2	11	1	2	......	1	......	16	......	......	......	3	10	......	1	1	2	5
Seneca, ...	42	7	10	9	......	5	3	70	5	28	......	208	83	6	5	13	55	27
South Bristol, ...	12	4	1	2	......	......	......	11	......	5	......	2	21	......	2	6	2	1
Victor, ...	16	......	2	31	......	......	8	29	6	11	......	5	23	2	......	10	2	22
West Bloomfield, .	8	4	......	11	......	......	4	10	2	4	......	2	9	......	......	......	......	1
Total, ...	177	60	27	223	......	61	50	319	62	115	1	549	431	23	19	47	128	151

ORANGE COUNTY.—(Continued.)

TOWNS.	Otsego.	Putnam.	Queens.	Rensselaer.	Richmond.	Rockland.	St. Lawrence.	Saratoga.	Schenectady.	Schoharie.	Schuyler.	Seneca.	Steuben.	Suffolk.	Sullivan.	Tioga.	Tompkins.	Ulster.
Blooming Grove, .	......	3	1	......	3	9	......	3	......	......	......	5	......	12	9	......	......	44
Chester, ...	......	1	2	1	......	16	......	......	1	......	......	......	......	4	4	1	......	15
Cornwall, ...	5	118	3	4	......	51	......	7	......	4	......	1	2	7	2	......	1	68
Crawford, ...	......	5	2	......	......	1	......	......	......	......	......	......	1	1	77	......	1	187
Deerpark, ...	13	16	2	7	1	29	......	6	3	2	......	2	3	4	204	1	6	82
Goshen, ...	......	4	1	3	......	20	......	1	......	......	......	3	......	7	5	1	2	9
Greenville, ...	......	......	......	......	......	1	......	......	......	1	......	......	......	4	9	......	......	8
Hamptonburgh, ..	......	4	......	......	......	4	......	......	......	2	......	......	......	1	4	......	......	14
Minisink, ...	......	......	......	......	......	4	......	......	......	......	......	......	......	10	9	3	......	5
Monroe, ...	1	31	7	......	......	110	......	......	......	......	......	3	2	3	12	......	......	29
Montgomery, ...	2	6	7	5	1	1	......	......	1	......	......	......	......	17	20	......	2	235
Mount Hope, ...	1	3	1	......	......	5	......	......	......	2	......	......	4	4	87	3	1	14
Newburgh, ...	2	67	44	27	5	42	2	12	......	8	......	2	1	25	68	4	2	829
New Windsor, ...	1	8	7	3	......	14	......	2	......	3	......	......	......	2	1	......	......	45
Walkill, ...	1	1	10	2	......	25	......	3	......	2	......	......	2	17	215	6	4	86
Warwick, ...	3	3	5	......	......	58	......	......	......	......	......	1	......	3	9	1	2	23
Wawayanda, ...	......	1	2	......	......	1	......	......	......	......	......	1	1	2	2	3	1	3
Total, ...	29	271	94	52	10	391	2	34	5	24	......	18	16	123	737	23	22	1,090

ORLEANS COUNTY.—(Continued.)

TOWNS.	Otsego.	Putnam.	Queens.	Rensselaer.	Richmond.	Rockland.	St. Lawrence.	Saratoga.	Schenectady.	Schoharie.	Schuyler.	Seneca.	Steuben.	Suffolk.	Sullivan.	Tioga.	Tompkins.	Ulster.
Barre, ...	77	11	3	98	1	1	24	137	6	21	......	20	6	3	5	5	17	11
Carlton, ...	15	4	1	43	......	......	7	21	18	10	......	13	1	2	2	......	......	6
Clarendon, ...	16	......	......	45	......	2	1	17	......	8	......	3	6	......	......	1	3	3
Gaines, ...	16	2	1	35	1	1	4	59	7	16	......	3	6	......	2	2	3	......
Kendall, ...	9	4	3	80	......	......	2	16	8	3	......	12	3	......	......	2	7	4
Murray, ...	15	......	2	34	......	7	5	27	11	7	......	9	1	......	......	1	3	31
Ridgeway, ...	46	3	1	58	......	1	10	86	6	28	......	20	6	3	3	5	8	16
Shelby, ...	17	3	......	36	......	......	2	54	13	121	......	12	2	2	......	......	4	9
Yates, ...	11	1	......	25	......	......	1	41	5	4	......	10	2	......	2	......	29	......
Total, ...	222	28	11	454	2	12	56	458	74	218	......	102	33	10	14	16	74	80

OSWEGO COUNTY.—(Continued.)

TOWNS.	Otsego.	Putnam.	Queens.	Rensselaer.	Richmond.	Rockland.	St. Lawrence.	Saratoga.	Schenectady.	Schoharie.	Schuyler.	Seneca.	Steuben.	Suffolk.	Sullivan.	Tioga.	Tompkins.	Ulster.
Albion, ...	113	2	......	12	......	1	5	12	5	9	......	......	2	......	......	......	1	......
Amboy, ...	58	1	......	13	......	2	......	6	1	17	......	......	1	......	......	......	......	2
Boylston, ...	4	......	......	3	......	......	41	8	......	......	......	......	......	......	......	......	......	......
Constantia, ...	69	1	......	31	......	......	8	31	4	56	......	......	4	1	2	......	......	5
Granby, ...	30	1	......	68	......	1	26	52	2	13	......	4	7	......	......	1	18	2
Hannibal, ...	18	......	......	65	......	......	10	61	15	20	......	12	2	1	1	......	5	13
Hastings, ...	59	......	......	37	......	......	27	22	17	20	......	1	3	......	1	......	3	......
Mexico, ...	115	......	......	18	......	......	46	31	7	35	......	2	12	3	......	......	1	......
New Haven, ...	32	1	......	9	1	......	14	21	......	0	......	......	4	......	1	......	7	......
Orwell, ...	9	......	......	11	......	......	1	29	3	4	......	......	......	......	......	1	......	......
Oswego, ...	50	......	3	24	......	......	59	16	2	48	......	5	4	......	2	......	3	1

16

(Continued on page 128.)

ONONDAGA COUNTY.—(Continued.)

TOWNS.	COUNTIES OF NEW-YORK.							UNITED STATES.										
	Warren.	Washington.	Wayne.	Westchester.	Wyoming.	Yates.	New-York.	Maine.	N. Hampshire.	Vermont.	Massachusetts.	Rhode Island	Connecticut.	New Jersey.	Pennsylvania.	Delaware.	Maryland.	District of Columbia.
Syracuse city:																		
1st ward,	1	27	4	1	......	1	1, 879	3	13	51	54	6	87	7	8	......	......	......
2d ward,	1	5	1	......	5	......	1, 170	......	4	6	11	1	10	4	2	......	1	......
3d ward,	3	1	13	1	......	......	1, 085	8	8	17	63	4	42	16	17	......	2	......
4th ward,	1	20	5	2	......	......	2, 059	19	25	25	86	6	75	9	15	......	4	......
5th ward,	3	6	5	......	1	1	955	7	3	22	41	4	26	16	5	......	5	......
6th ward,	3	19	18	3	......	2	1, 928	7	20	39	137	15	107	20	16	......	2	1
7th ward,	7	18	9	1	2	4	2, 149	2	7	41	75	16	74	25	41	1	6	......
8th ward,	1	10	4	1	......	......	1, 349	......	9	29	43	10	54	28	9	......	......	......
Total Syracuse,	20	106	59	9	8	8	12, 574	46	89	230	510	62	475	125	113	1	20	1
Tully, ...	......	7	......	......	......	......	1, 296	......	6	18	34	11	50	3	3	......	......	......
Van Buren,......	11	41	27	1	2	......	2, 499	4	5	32	60	15	79	17	4	......	......	......
Total,.........	59	755	215	149	27	54	57, 589	114	310	1, 133	2, 020	337	2, 319	388	267	1	42	3

ONTARIO COUNTY.—(Continued.)

TOWNS.	Warren.	Washington.	Wayne.	Westchester.	Wyoming.	Yates.	New-York.	Maine.	N. Hampshire.	Vermont.	Massachusetts.	Rhode Island	Connecticut.	New Jersey.	Pennsylvania.	Delaware.	Maryland.	District of Columbia.
Bristol, ...	4	3	3	1	2	5	1, 376	......	4	17	93	11	55	6	7	......	......	......
Canadice, ...	......	3	1	......	1	54	789	......	2	17	13	3	26	71	2	......	1	......
Canandaigua, ...	1	14	73	16	4	74	4, 174	13	36	80	168	29	195	56	78	......	25	1
East Bloomfield, .	......	14	14	1	7	4	1, 453	......	8	16	84	4	98	9	8	......	1	......
Farmington,.....	......	8	75	5	2	7	1, 367	......	5	29	73	14	26	23	12	......	4	......
Gorham, ...	3	10	18	8	1	150	1, 886	1	5	19	38	4	39	41	25	......	6	......
Hopewell, ...	......	2	29	......	1	20	1, 356	3	6	21	30	4	43	33	27	......	15	......
Manchester, ...	2	20	136	......	6	24	2, 306	8	15	31	79	12	72	29	29	......	25	......
Naples, ...	7	8	4	10	......	170	1, 830	......	6	28	80	7	62	26	28	......	2	......
Phelps, ...	1	19	226	17	7	43	3, 933	16	10	53	181	8	104	174	71	......	35	1
Richmond, ...	......	5	......	1	5	20	1, 047	......	8	53	57	5	32	32	11	......	......	......
Seneca,..........	3	21	102	16	13	203	5, 492	11	24	78	142	20	147	145	163	......	43	2
South Bristol, ...	......	......	4	1	1	44	977	2	10	30	34	4	39	5	15	......	......	......
Victor,..........	......	17	28	1	3	5	1, 588	3	12	42	103	3	55	13	4	......	1	......
West Bloomfield,.	......	3	7	2	3	18	1, 092	......	20	53	48	9	73	·15	11	......	1	......
Total,.........	21	147	720	79	56	841	30, 666	57	171	567	1, 223	137	1, 066	678	491	......	159	4

ORANGE COUNTY.—(Continued.)

TOWNS.	Warren.	Washington.	Wayne.	Westchester.	Wyoming.	Yates.	New-York.	Maine.	N. Hampshire.	Vermont.	Massachusetts.	Rhode Island	Connecticut.	New Jersey.	Pennsylvania.	Delaware.	Maryland.	District of Columbia.
Blooming Grove,.	......	......	......	5	......	......	1, 780	......	......	......	3	1	12	41	11	......	1	1
Chester, ...	......	1	......	2	......	......	1, 391	......	......	1	1	......	13	63	2	......	......	......
Cornwall, ...	......	3	6	46	2	3	3, 014	26	11	13	27	7	36	81	51	......	8	3
Crawford, ...	......	......	......	11	......	......	1, 783	......	......	......	5	......	8	13	1	......	......	......
Deerpark, ...	......	2	2	23	......	5	2, 990	11	15	11	50	4	60	735	244	......	7	......
Goshen, ...	1	......	......	6	......	......	2, 490	3	1	2	6	......	21	138	19	......	3	......
Greenville, ...	......	......	2	1	......	......	1, 030	......	......	......	2	1	8	116	15	......	......	......
Hamptonburgh,..	......	......	......	1	......	......	1, 119	......	......	......	2	......	3	15	5	......	2	......
Minisink,........	......	......	......	3	......	......	978	......	......	1	2	1	10	208	23	......	......	......
Monroe,.........	......	......	1	30	......	......	3, 701	1	1	......	8	......	18	120	15	......	1	......
Montgomery, ...	......	......	......	13	......	......	3, 103	......	......	1	6	2	44	31	5	......	......	......
Mount Hope, ...	......	......	......	6	......	4	1, 460	......	......	3	6	5	13	45	19	......	......	......
Newburgh, ...	1	5	2	82	......	2	8, 539	6	11	23	79	15	165	139	53	1	19	3
New Windsor, ...	......	2	......	25	......	......	1, 834	......	2	7	33	1	22	30	5	......	......	......
Walkill, ...	......	2	......	23	......	2	4, 412	1	3	1	32	5	53	122	·48	......	1	1
Warwick, ...	......	......	......	5	......	3	4, 126	......	......	3	6	1	43	537	14	......	......	......
Wawayanda, ...	......	......	......	3	......	......	1, 589	......	1	......	3	......	5	66	6	......	1	......
Total, ...	2	15	13	285	2	19	45, 339	48	45	66	271	43	534	2, 500	536	1	43	8

ORLEANS COUNTY.—(Continued.)

TOWNS.	Warren.	Washington.	Wayne.	Westchester.	Wyoming.	Yates.	New-York.	Maine.	N. Hampshire.	Vermont.	Massachusetts.	Rhode Island	Connecticut.	New Jersey.	Pennsylvania.	Delaware.	Maryland.	District of Columbia.
Barre, ...	2	30	47	18	29	29	4, 646	6	54	196	214	18	219	41	36	......	3	1
Carlton, ...	3	34	32	3	3	2	1, 835	1	35	59	59	11	59	10	34	......	1	......
Clarendon, ...	1	20	10	......	4	4	1, 323	13	41	47	48	8	57	15	13	......	3	......
Gaines, ...	1	17	21	2	6	1	1, 691	3	37	109	60	8	80	22	16	......	1	......
Kendall, ...	8	46	18	60	3	2	1, 477	2	27	91	46	9	38	10	8	......	2	......
Murray, ...	6	32	25	9	12	5	1, 917	2	37	109	84	10	74	11	15	......	1	......
Ridgeway, ...	3	50	63	3	38	7	3, 239	8	35	145	102	21	103	43	54	......	7	......
Shelby, ...	1	17	21	3	16	1	2, 210	8	26	55	50	11	57	14	26	......	1	......
Yates, ...	8	15	25	4	3	4	1, 503	2	24	66	46	4	66	30	11	......	2	......
Total,.........	33	261	262	102	114	55	19, 841	45	316	877	709	100	753	196	213	......	21	1

OSWEGO COUNTY.—(Continued.)

TOWNS.	Warren.	Washington.	Wayne.	Westchester.	Wyoming.	Yates.	New-York.	Maine.	N. Hampshire.	Vermont.	Massachusetts.	Rhode Island	Connecticut.	New Jersey.	Pennsylvania.	Delaware.	Maryland.	District of Columbia.
Albion, ...	1	42	4	......	1	......	1, 830	1	6	72	56	17	56	6	6	......	......	......
Amboy, ...	......	7	3	......	......	......	926	......	4	10	43	8	24	......	10	......	......	......
Boylston, ...	......	7	5	......	......	......	722	1	5	16	5	2	10	......	......	......	......	......
Constantia, ...	1	8	11	4	1	......	2, 449	2	49	42	84	4	75	44	17	1	3	......
Granby, ...	7	83	11	45	......	......	2, 792	5	20	52	100	8	87	14	6	......	......	......
Hannibal, ...	8	161	65	17	......	4	2, 524	1	11	102	55	14	78	12	7	......	......	......
Hastings, ...	12	12	6	5	......	2	2, 534	5	14	55	51	12	56	14	6	......	2	......
Mexico, ...	......	64	8	1	3	......	3, 177	1	31	124	130	34	154	14	7	......	......	......
New Haven, ...	2	52	4	2	1	1	1, 596	3	12	36	71	31	88	4	8	......	......	......
Orwell, ...	......	16	3	1	......	1	1, 092	3	2	24	35	17	47	......	4	......	......	......
Oswego, ...	2	66	23	9	......	......	2, 093	3	9	40	45	36	53	4	6	......	6	......

(Continued on page 129.)

ONONDAGA COUNTY.—(Continued.)

TOWNS.	UNITED STATES.																	
	Virginia.	N. Carolina.	S. Carolina.	Georgia.	Florida.	Alabama.	Mississippi.	Louisiana.	Texas.	Arkansas.	Missouri.	Tennessee.	Kentucky.	Ohio.	Indiana.	Illinois.	Michigan.	Wisconsin.
Syracuse city:																		
1st ward,														1		4		
2d ward,											1							2
3d ward,														10		1	2	3
4th ward,	4	2									1			11	3	5	3	2
5th ward,			1											10		1	4	
6th ward,	2													18		1	6	3
7th ward,	4			1	1	1		4					3	13		2	13	2
8th ward,	5													10	1	3	1	4
Total Syracuse,	15	2	1	1	1	1		4			2		3	73	4	17	29	16
Tully,	1													3			1	1
Van Buren,														12	7		1	2
Total,	25	2	3	1	1	1	2	7		1	9	1	6	197	36	62	136	60

ONTARIO COUNTY.—(Continued.)

TOWNS.	Virginia.	N. Carolina.	S. Carolina.	Georgia.	Florida.	Alabama.	Mississippi.	Louisiana.	Texas.	Arkansas.	Missouri.	Tennessee.	Kentucky.	Ohio.	Indiana.	Illinois.	Michigan.	Wisconsin.
Bristol,														8	1		12	1
Canadice,														2			10	
Canandaigua,	7		2	2			4				2			19		2	24	3
East Bloomfield,														8	3	1	12	2
Farmington,								2						8		1	6	
Gorham,											5			9	2		3	
Hopewell,	1													5			6	
Manchester,														3		8	17	
Naples,								5						3		2	5	4
Phelps,	3										1			9	2	3	21	2
Richmond,	2													11			9	
Seneca,	18		2	2		2		8			4		2	19	3	4	17	
South Bristol,													1	3		1	8	1
Victor,	1	1												7		2	13	9
West Bloomfield,														3	2		2	1
Total,	32	1	4	4		2	4	15			12		3	117	13	24	165	23

ORANGE COUNTY.—(Continued.)

TOWNS.	Virginia.	N. Carolina.	S. Carolina.	Georgia.	Florida.	Alabama.	Mississippi.	Louisiana.	Texas.	Arkansas.	Missouri.	Tennessee.	Kentucky.	Ohio.	Indiana.	Illinois.	Michigan.	Wisconsin.
Blooming Grove,	1					1							1					
Chester,							1									3		
Cornwall,	24	14	4	15	2	7	2	8	5			12	9	19	9	1	5	1
Crawford,																		
Deerpark,				1		1					1			8		1		1
Goshen,	1		1	1							2			7		2	1	
Greenville,																		1
Hamptonburgh,														3	1			
Minisink,															5			
Monroe,																	3	1
Montgomery,	7					1								2	1	1	2	
Mount Hope,															2			
Newburgh,	17		1	7	2	3	1		1		4	3	1	4		5	2	
New Windsor,	2																	
Walkill,	3	3		2	1													
Warwick,			1	1							1					5	3	
Wawayanda,	1																	
Total,	56	17	7	27	5	13	4	8	6		8	15	11	43	18	18	16	4

ORLEANS COUNTY.—(Continued.)

TOWNS.	Virginia.	N. Carolina.	S. Carolina.	Georgia.	Florida.	Alabama.	Mississippi.	Louisiana.	Texas.	Arkansas.	Missouri.	Tennessee.	Kentucky.	Ohio.	Indiana.	Illinois.	Michigan.	Wisconsin.
Barre,	2			1			1				1	2	1	24	1	4	32	3
Carlton,	1													5			10	1
Clarendon,				1										5			9	
Gaines,	2	2			1	1								3		1	11	2
Kendall,				1										4		1	1	
Murray,											1		1	7	2	2	11	3
Ridgeway,				1							2	3	1	20	2	6	23	5
Shelby,	2			1										5		1	19	9
Yates,	1							1						5	1	3	18	
Total,	8	2		5	1	1	1	1			4	5	3	78	6	18	134	23

OSWEGO COUNTY.—(Continued.)

TOWNS.	Virginia.	N. Carolina.	S. Carolina.	Georgia.	Florida.	Alabama.	Mississippi.	Louisiana.	Texas.	Arkansas.	Missouri.	Tennessee.	Kentucky.	Ohio.	Indiana.	Illinois.	Michigan.	Wisconsin.
Albion,														3			6	2
Amboy,														2				
Boylston,														1		1	1	
Constantia,	1													7		6	1	1
Granby,											1			10			5	1
Hannibal,														10	1	3	4	6
Hastings,			1											8		2	3	6
Mexico,			1											5		1	1	6
New Haven,														3		1	5	1
Orwell,																		
Oswego,	1							1						2			10	6

(Continued on page 130.)

ONONDAGA COUNTY.—(Continued.)

TOWNS.	U. STATES.			Total United States.	FOREIGN COUNTRIES.													
	Iowa.	California.	Territories.		Canada.	N. Brunswick.	Nova Scotia.	N. Foundland.	West Indies.	Mexico.	S. America.	England.	Scotland.	Ireland.	Wales.	France.	Belgium.	Holland.
Syracuse city:																		
1st ward,				2, 113	74							58	4	990		95		
2d ward,				1, 212	17							25	10	86	1	31		
3d ward,				1, 278	39		2					61	9	662		7		3
4th ward,				2, 354	66							207	14	724	1	13		12
5th ward,				1, 100	36	1						203	17	551	9	11	1	
6th ward,		1		2, 323	46		1		4		1	186	16	433	5	10	1	
7th ward,				2, 481	80							248	16	674	13	13		17
8th ward,				1, 555	61				1			140	3	292	1	3		
Total Syracuse,		1		14, 416	419	1	3		5		1	1, 128	89	4, 412	30	183	2	32
Tully,				1, 427	1		2					57	4	70				
Van Buren,				2, 737	23	3						43	1	230				
Total,	4	1		65, 126	1, 020	10	13	1	5		1	3, 791	204	9, 457	63	416	4	51

ONTARIO COUNTY.—(Continued.)

TOWNS.	Iowa.	California.	Territories.	Total United States.	Canada.	N. Brunswick.	Nova Scotia.	N. Foundland.	West Indies.	Mexico.	S. America.	England.	Scotland.	Ireland.	Wales.	France.	Belgium.	Holland.
Bristol,				1, 591	8			4				31		78				
Canadice,				936	2							14		17				
Canandaigua,				4, 921	57							222	92	1, 024	1	9		33
East Bloomfield,				1, 707	22			1				115	2	266			1	
Farmington,				1, 570	13	1						94	27	225			1	2
Gorham,				2, 083	11							75	29	97	5	23		5
Hopewell,				1, 550	13							39	10	143	2	1		1
Manchester,				2, 634	13							120	19	161		4		2
Naples,				2, 088	5							11	3	6				
Phelps,				4, 627	19							172	19	314	5	13		1
Richmond,				1, 267								80	2	125				
Seneca,				6, 348	38	2			6			674	183	840	5	11		2
South Bristol,				1, 130	7							8	2	29				
Victor,				1, 857	21							89	2	190	1	1		
West Bloomfield,				1, 330	22		1					116	2	118				6
Total,				35, 639	251	3	1	5	6			1, 860	392	3, 633	19	62	2	52

ORANGE COUNTY.—(Continued.)

TOWNS.	Iowa.	California.	Territories.	Total United States.	Canada.	N. Brunswick.	Nova Scotia.	N. Foundland.	West Indies.	Mexico.	S. America.	England.	Scotland.	Ireland.	Wales.	France.	Belgium.	Holland.
Blooming Grove,				1, 853			1					20	4	252		1		
Chester,				1, 475	6	1						15		171				1
Cornwall,			1	3, 417	8					1	1	83	23	583	4	24	1	
Crawford,				1, 810	1							12	3	164				
Deerpark,				4, 140	7				1			96	20	766		3	1	1
Goshen,				2, 698	2			1	4			12	4	451	1	4		7
Greenville,				1, 173									1	36				
Hamptonburgh,				1, 150								13		120		2		
Minisink,				1, 228								10	1	39				
Monroe,				3, 869	2		2					63	20	510	1	1		
Montgomery,		2		3, 208	1				1			115	14	396		1		
Mount Hope,				1, 553	1							11	3	159				
Newburgh,				9, 106	22	12	12	1	2	2	4	329	196	2, 809	8	24		1
New Windsor,				1, 936	5							82	23	464		1		
Walkill,		1		4, 689	3	1	4		1			68	6	558		1		1
Warwick,				4, 741	3							47	11	174	1			
Wawayanda,				1, 672								13	2	137				
Total,		3	1	49, 718	61	14	19	2	9	3	5	989	331	7, 789	15	62	2	11

ORLEANS COUNTY.—(Continued.)

TOWNS.	Iowa.	California.	Territories.	Total United States.	Canada.	N. Brunswick.	Nova Scotia.	N. Foundland.	West Indies.	Mexico.	S. America.	England.	Scotland.	Ireland.	Wales.	France.	Belgium.	Holland.
Barre,				5, 506	97				7			465	13	591	2	8		
Carlton,				2, 121	25							113	36	27				
Clarendon,				1, 583	11							55	2	83				
Gaines,				2, 050	62				1			135	7	258				
Kendall,				1, 717	22							27	15	44	1	1	1	1
Murray,			1	2, 288	36	1		1				122	15	382	8	3		
Ridgeway,				3, 820	71		1					420	32	780	3	3		
Shelby,				2, 495	41				1			284	4	187				
Yates,				1, 783	5							118	46	34		1		
Total,			1	23, 363	370	1	1	1	9			1, 739	170	2, 386	14	16	1	1

OSWEGO COUNTY.—(Continued.)

TOWNS.	Iowa.	California.	Territories.	Total United States.	Canada.	N. Brunswick.	Nova Scotia.	N. Foundland.	West Indies.	Mexico.	S. America.	England.	Scotland.	Ireland.	Wales.	France.	Belgium.	Holland.
Albion,				2, 061	22		2					31	5	78	9	1		
Amboy,				1, 027	3							14	47	50				
Boylston,				764	15							25		3	1	1		
Constantia,				2, 786	44		5					80	16	202		18		
Granby,				3, 101	187		1		1			125	3	238		3		
Hannibal,				2, 828	52							34	11	89		1		
Hastings,				2, 769	23		1					70	4	23	1	84		1
Mexico,		1		3, 688	76		1					35	4	54		150		1
New Haven,				1, 859	46							41	4	42	2			1
Orwell,				1, 224								14	1	8	1			
Oswego,				2, 315	153							56	10	187		15		

(Continued on page 131.)

ONONDAGA COUNTY.—(Continued.)

TOWNS.	FOREIGN COUNTRIES.																		
	Germany.	Prussia.	Austria.	Switzerland.	Italy.	Spain.	Portugal.	Poland.	Norway.	Sweden.	Russia.	Denmark.	East Indies.	Africa.	Turkey and Greece.	Islands.	Asia.	At Sea.	Unknown.
Syracuse city:																			
1st ward,	252			9						1								1	
2d ward,	2,045				8													1	1
3d ward,	183			2														1	13
4th ward,	736			15				1										2	22
5th ward,	127	1		3															3
6th ward,	151	2	6	1				15						1				1	53
7th ward,	444		8	13		1		53				2						2	100
8th ward,	74			4						1		1							26
Total Syracuse,	4,012	3	14	47	8	1		69		2		3		1				8	218
Tully,	9																		49
Van Buren,	47																	1	
Total,	5,683	13	20	84	8	1		69		2		3	6	4		4		16	500

ONTARIO COUNTY.—(Continued.)

TOWNS.	Germany.	Prussia.	Austria.	Switzerland.	Italy.	Spain.	Portugal.	Poland.	Norway.	Sweden.	Russia.	Denmark.	East Indies.	Africa.	Turkey and Greece.	Islands.	Asia.	At Sea.	Unknown.
Bristol,	1																		2
Canadice,	1																		7
Canandaigua,	93	4		1	4	1			1			1						2	14
East Bloomfield,	16									1									37
Farmington,	15																	2	
Gorham,	24	1		1															26
Hopewell,	21																		3
Manchester,	48			1															7
Naples,	2																		3
Phelps,	58			19															46
Richmond,	19																		
Seneca,	122			5						2									60
South Bristol,																			3
Victor,	32	1						1										1	12
West Bloomfield,	16																		10
Total,	468	6		27	4	1		1	1	3		1						5	230

ORANGE COUNTY.—(Continued.)

TOWNS.	Germany.	Prussia.	Austria.	Switzerland.	Italy.	Spain.	Portugal.	Poland.	Norway.	Sweden.	Russia.	Denmark.	East Indies.	Africa.	Turkey and Greece.	Islands.	Asia.	At Sea.	Unknown.
Blooming Grove,	51										1								1
Chester,	21	5																	1
Cornwall,	388	8	4	4		1					5	1						1	21
Crawford,	7					1													2
Deerpark,	382	7	2	7	1			8		5		4	1						52
Goshen,	26			3															
Greenville,	7																		1
Hamptonburgh,	15			2															1
Minisink,	10																		7
Monroe,	54				1						1	1							26
Montgomery,	36			3														1	16
Mount Hope,	7																	1	
Newburgh,	214	16				1		3		1				1		2	2	1	4
New Windsor,	37			1															6
Walkill,	80			1															2
Warwick,				1															9
Wawayanda,	5																		240
Total,	1,340	36	6	22	2	3		11		6	7	6	1	1		2	2	4	389

ORLEANS COUNTY.—(Continued.)

TOWNS.	Germany.	Prussia.	Austria.	Switzerland.	Italy.	Spain.	Portugal.	Poland.	Norway.	Sweden.	Russia.	Denmark.	East Indies.	Africa.	Turkey and Greece.	Islands.	Asia.	At Sea.	Unknown.
Barre,	66	12		1						2							1		26
Carlton,																			7
Clarendon,	14																	1	
Gaines,	18																		1
Kendall,	11								30										14
Murray,	18			1															1
Ridgeway,	74			4											1			1	16
Shelby,										1									33
Yates,	1																		8
Total,	202	12		6					30	3					1		1	2	106

OSWEGO COUNTY.—(Continued.)

TOWNS.	Germany.	Prussia.	Austria.	Switzerland.	Italy.	Spain.	Portugal.	Poland.	Norway.	Sweden.	Russia.	Denmark.	East Indies.	Africa.	Turkey and Greece.	Islands.	Asia.	At Sea.	Unknown.
Albion,	3																		
Amboy,	14																		17
Boylston,																			6
Constantia,	103			1		1												2	97
Granby,	14																		74
Hannibal,	1																		12
Hastings,	63			2															28
Mexico,	10																		3
New Haven,																			17
Orwell,	10																		
Oswego,	12			1															11

(Continued on page 132.)

OSWEGO COUNTY.

TOWNS.	Albany.	Allegany.	Broome.	Cattaraugus.	Cayuga.	Chautauque.	Chemung.	Chenango.	Clinton.	Columbia.	Cortland.	Delaware.	Dutchess.	Erie.	Essex.	Franklin.	Fulton.	Genesee.
	COUNTIES OF NEW-YORK.																	
Oswego city:																		
1st ward,	30	3	2	1	45		1	6	9	13	10	6	12	7	2	6	1	3
2d ward,	16		1		26			3	1	4		3	7	7	3	2	1	
3d ward,	16				76		1	3	3	21	3	2	12	1	4		1	12
4th ward,	29		4		35	2	9	6	3	15	7	3	11	5	5	11	4	10
Total Oswego,	91	3	7	1	182	2	11	18	16	53	20	14	42	20	14	19	7	25
Palermo,	9	1	1	1	13			14		3	15	2	7		4	1		1
Parish,	12			1	5	7		10		24	1	2	8	1			2	
Redfield,	13							3		7		1					1	
Richland,	25	3	2		7	1		16	4	21	4	9	26	5	4	1	3	1
Sandy Creek,	2		1		1			2		20	1	7	8		2			
Schroeppel,	56	2		1	40		2	5	3	18	12	3	21	3	4	2	1	4
Scriba,	3				22			2	1	5	6		17	2			5	
Volney,	56	5	2	1	111	5	10	29	4	27	23	5	32	6	7	5		5
West Monroe,	14	4		1	2	2		2		14	2	3	5	4			1	1
Williamstown,	6				5			3		11		2	3				2	1
Total,	553	28	27	19	916	41	24	214	57	458	144	98	335	74	62	57	53	79

OTSEGO COUNTY.

TOWNS.	Albany.	Allegany.	Broome.	Cattaraugus.	Cayuga.	Chautauque.	Chemung.	Chenango.	Clinton.	Columbia.	Cortland.	Delaware.	Dutchess.	Erie.	Essex.	Franklin.	Fulton.	Genesee.
Burlington,	6					3		34		7	6	5	1	1			2	
Butternuts,	20	1	5		1	2		122		16	2	49	28					
Cherry Valley,	60		6	1	1	6		5		47	2	4	14				6	3
Decatur,	19							1		9	1	8	15				3	1
Edmeston,	2	1	4	1				106		1	7	3	21	1		1		1
Exeter,	3	3	1		3	1	2	14		3	2	6	7				1	1
Hartwick,	12	2	3	2	1			13		30	6	47	24					
Laurens,	27		2		5			25		8	8	62	19	1			1	1
Maryland,	71		3	1	2			3		52	2	99	40	1		1		1
Middlefield,	37	1	4	3	4			28		65		20	72				2	4
Milford,	50	5	9	1	1	2		10		47	1	57	23	1	1			1
Morris,	11		4	1		3		89		7	6	30	16					
New Lisbon,	6		2	1		4		21		6		10	9					
Oneonta,	29		9		1		2	12		15	3	193	45	1	1			1
Otego,	25		12					28		9	4	168	17		2	1	1	
Otsego,	49		6		3	6		33		27	11	30	28					3
Pittsfield,	21	4	8		3	1		119		1	1	31	19					2
Plainfield,	6	2	2		1		1	13	1	6	11		2	1				
Richfield,	8		5	1	3			12		8	3	7	10	2				3
Roseboom,	30		1					2		34		6	32					1
Springfield,	18	1	4		1	1		9		4	3	5	15				2	4
Unadilla,	36		19				2	157		52	5	229	44		4		1	1
Westford,	16		4						1	35		4	29	1				
Worcester,	110		11	1				6		24		70	26	1			4	
Total,	672	20	124	13	30	29	7	862	2	513	84	1,143	556	11	8	3	23	28

PUTNAM COUNTY.

TOWNS.	Albany.	Allegany.	Broome.	Cattaraugus.	Cayuga.	Chautauque.	Chemung.	Chenango.	Clinton.	Columbia.	Cortland.	Delaware.	Dutchess.	Erie.	Essex.	Franklin.	Fulton.	Genesee.
Carmel,	1				1					3		3	42		1			
Kent,								2				1	120					1
Patterson,	5				2			1		5		6	133		2			1
Phillipstown,	3		1			1				8		5	242					2
Putnam Valley,	1		1							2			17					
South East,	5				1					2		5	45					
Total,	15		2		4	1		3		20		20	599		3			4

QUEENS COUNTY.

TOWNS.	Albany.	Allegany.	Broome.	Cattaraugus.	Cayuga.	Chautauque.	Chemung.	Chenango.	Clinton.	Columbia.	Cortland.	Delaware.	Dutchess.	Erie.	Essex.	Franklin.	Fulton.	Genesee.
Flushing,	6				1		1			5		9	37		1			7
Hempstead,	10											1	7	1			1	
Jamaica,	9		1							7		4	26					2
Newtown,	33			1	1					6		2	53	4				1
North Hempstead,	5		1						7	5		5	24	1				
Oyster Bay,	17		1		3				4	3		1	16					1
Total,	80		3	1	5		1		11	26		22	163	6	1		1	11

RENSSELAER COUNTY.

TOWNS.	Albany.	Allegany.	Broome.	Cattaraugus.	Cayuga.	Chautauque.	Chemung.	Chenango.	Clinton.	Columbia.	Cortland.	Delaware.	Dutchess.	Erie.	Essex.	Franklin.	Fulton.	Genesee.
Berlin,	15	4	1		1			1	6	8		1	8		3			1
Brunswick,	27							1		44		1	14				2	
Clinton,	79									37			38					1
Grafton,	5	2				2				2	4		3					
Greenbush,	416				2		1	3	2	115	1	3	42	3			4	
Hoosick,	27	4			3			1	1	11	2	1	26	3	7		3	
Lansingburgh,	121				6			2	5	59	1	9	62	6	6	3	4	1
Nassau,	42	1							1	300		4	111		1			
North Greenbush,	46				1				2	30	1	2	31		1			
Petersburgh,	11				6					4	1	2	1				1	
Pittstown,	45		1		3			2	3	11			24	2	1			
Poestenkill,	10	1				1				17			10	1				
Sand Lake,	30		4							76	3	1	74	3	1		3	
Schaghticoke,	25	2			1	1		1	2	11			30		1		1	
Schodack,	147		1	1		1	2	2		77	1	1	115		1		1	
Stephentown,	9	4		1				1		93		1	18		3	1	1	

(Continued on page 133.)

OSWEGO COUNTY.—(CONTINUED.)

COUNTIES OF NEW-YORK.

TOWNS.	Greene.	Hamilton.	Herkimer.	Jefferson.	Kings.	Lewis.	Livingston.	Madison.	Monroe.	Montgomery.	New-York.	Niagara.	Oneida.	Onondaga.	Ontario.	Orange.	Orleans.	Oswego.
Oswego city:																		
1st ward,	7	.....	30	127	3	7	4	23	17	4	67	4	76	50	6	2	.....	1,395
2d ward,	3	.....	16	82	1	12	1	14	8	11	23	2	50	48	2	.....	.....	1,027
3d ward,	7	.....	33	110	2	10	4	9	3	15	55	3	75	91	3	4	1	1,429
4th ward,	9	.....	44	170	2	22	.....	47	16	14	36	11	93	54	5	.....	5	1,584
Total Oswego,	26	.....	123	489	8	51	9	93	44	44	181	20	294	243	16	6	6	5,435
Palermo,	1	.....	99	21	.....	4	1	94	1	15	1	3	114	130	1	1	.....	965
Parish,	16	.....	117	18	.....	4	1	47	5	15	1	.....	64	69	.....	.....	.....	760
Redfield,	5	.....	3	58	.....	17	.....	10	.....	17	15	1	99	.....	.....	.....	.....	272
Richland,	2	.....	115	262	1	9	3	49	1	36	13	1	191	65	6	1	3	2,080
Sandy Creek,	1	1	111	242	.....	20	2	40	.....	20	2	1	77	15	2	3	2	1,104
Schroeppel,	37	.....	172	45	3	20	2	80	5	108	8	2	118	586	8	6	.....	1,405
Scriba,	9	.....	97	87	1	15	.....	37	1	21	7	9	102	26	2	3	1	1,588
Volney,	47	.....	135	145	3	19	6	144	26	65	28	.....	265	274	3	13	10	2,723
West Monroe,	15	.....	41	17	.....	15	2	10	2	12	2	2	61	86	3	2	.....	534
Williamstown,	6	.....	34	18	.....	1	.....	10	.....	7	8	.....	106	2	.....	1	.....	422
Total,	468	8	1,980	1,985	40	261	37	1,016	131	677	369	45	2,926	2,807	73	73	26	29,090

OTSEGO COUNTY.—(CONTINUED.)

TOWNS.	Greene.	Hamilton.	Herkimer.	Jefferson.	Kings.	Lewis.	Livingston.	Madison.	Monroe.	Montgomery.	New-York.	Niagara.	Oneida.	Onondaga.	Ontario.	Orange.	Orleans.	Oswego.
Burlington,	2	.....	69	1	.....	.....	.....	17	1	14	6	.....	20	4	2	.....	.....	5
Butternuts,	14	1	10	.....	2	.....	.....	12	1	.....	6	.....	11	2	.....	3	.....	.....
Cherry Valley,	6	.....	59	1	.....	.....	1	6	.....	222	22	1	27	2	.....	1	.....	.....
Decatur,	12	.....	2	.....	.....	1	.....	.....	1	42	.....	.....	1	1	1	.....	.....	.....
Edmeston,	.....	.....	17	4	.....	.....	.....	104	.....	4	.....	.....	23	2	3	.....	.....	.....
Exeter,	1	.....	88	1	.....	.....	.....	7	.....	6	12	.....	36	.....	2	3	.....	.....
Hartwick,	2	.....	10	1	.....	3	1	4	.....	12	5	1	13	2	.....	1	.....	1
Laurens,	7	.....	5	.....	1	.....	.....	6	.....	21	9	1	5	.....	1	3	.....	1
Maryland,	59	.....	6	2	.....	.....	1	1	1	33	5	.....	9	2	.....	2	.....	.....
Middlefield,	9	.....	36	8	1	1	.....	4	.....	62	11	.....	9	4	.....	3	1	3
Milford,	21	.....	13	1	1	.....	.....	4	1	46	4	1	10	8	.....	.....	.....	.....
Morris,	12	.....	48	7	.....	4	.....	6	2	13	3	.....	17	.....	1	.....	.....	4
New Lisbon,	1	.....	8	.....	3	6	.....	5	1	4	11	.....	8	2	.....	1	.....	4
Oneonta,	29	.....	17	1	.....	4	.....	4	.....	11	24	.....	4	2	2	1	.....	3
Otego,	24	.....	3	1	2	.....	.....	6	.....	7	1	.....	6	1	.....	3	.....	.....
Otsego,	9	2	89	12	12	2	.....	15	6	59	31	6	34	6	.....	.....	.....	2
Pittsfield,	1	.....	8	.....	.....	.....	.....	19	.....	1	.....	.....	18	3	2	.....	.....	2
Plainfield,	.....	.....	59	17	.....	3	.....	88	3	6	.....	.....	52	4	.....	.....	1	3
Richfield,	3	.....	290	1	2	1	.....	21	.....	16	13	2	50	3	.....	.....	4	7
Roseboom,	4	.....	10	7	1	.....	1	2	2	114	7	.....	1	3	.....	1	.....	1
Springfield,	14	.....	209	5	2	4	.....	6	2	157	6	.....	12	6	.....	2	.....	5
Unadilla,	27	.....	9	.....	.....	2	.....	11	.....	15	15	.....	11	.....	.....	6	.....	1
Westford,	17	.....	5	3	.....	6	.....	3	.....	30	1	.....	9	1	.....	.....	.....	4
Worcester,	30	.....	6	1	1	.....	.....	8	.....	18	4	.....	6	.....	1	2	.....	.....
Total,	304	3	1,076	74	28	37	4	359	21	913	196	12	392	58	15	32	6	46

PUTNAM COUNTY.—(CONTINUED.)

TOWNS.	Greene.	Hamilton.	Herkimer.	Jefferson.	Kings.	Lewis.	Livingston.	Madison.	Monroe.	Montgomery.	New-York.	Niagara.	Oneida.	Onondaga.	Ontario.	Orange.	Orleans.	Oswego.
Carmel,	.....	.....	.....	.....	4	.....	.....	1	.....	.....	51	1	2	.....	.....	8	.....	.....
Kent,	2	.....	.....	.....	2	.....	.....	.....	.....	.....	1	.....	1	.....	.....	1	.....	.....
Patterson,	6	.....	.....	.....	3	.....	1	.....	1	.....	27	.....	.....	.....	.....	6	.....	.....
Phillipstown,	2	.....	.....	.....	5	.....	.....	.....	.....	.....	167	.....	5	1	2	184	.....	.....
Putnam Valley,	.....	.....	.....	.....	.....	.....	.....	.....	.....	.....	26	.....	.....	.....	.....	1	.....	.....
South East,	2	.....	.....	.....	8	.....	1	1	1	1	63	1	.....	.....	1	5	.....	.....
Total,	12	.....	.....	.....	22	.....	2	2	2	1	335	2	8	1	3	205	.....	.....

QUEENS COUNTY.—(CONTINUED.)

TOWNS.	Greene.	Hamilton.	Herkimer.	Jefferson.	Kings.	Lewis.	Livingston.	Madison.	Monroe.	Montgomery.	New-York.	Niagara.	Oneida.	Onondaga.	Ontario.	Orange.	Orleans.	Oswego.
Flushing,	1	.....	1	2	202	1	2	.....	5	.....	679	.....	1	1	.....	24	.....	1
Hempstead,	.....	.....	.....	2	129	1	.....	.....	.....	.....	494	.....	6	.....	.....	8	.....	.....
Jamaica,	.....	.....	4	.....	335	.....	.....	.....	1	.....	370	4	3	.....	.....	5	.....	3
Newtown,	2	.....	.....	1	356	1	1	.....	2	.....	1,122	.....	6	1	2	25	.....	2
North Hempstead,	8	1	2	2	65	.....	.....	.....	.....	4	191	.....	2	.....	.....	2	.....	.....
Oyster Bay,	2	.....	1	.....	76	.....	.....	.....	.....	4	512	.....	1	.....	.....	13	.....	.....
Total,	13	1	8	7	1,163	3	3	.....	8	8	3,368	4	19	2	2	77	.....	6

RENSSELAER COUNTY.—(CONTINUED.)

TOWNS.	Greene.	Hamilton.	Herkimer.	Jefferson.	Kings.	Lewis.	Livingston.	Madison.	Monroe.	Montgomery.	New-York.	Niagara.	Oneida.	Onondaga.	Ontario.	Orange.	Orleans.	Oswego.
Berlin,	.....	.....	5	10	1	.....	.....	3	.....	2	2	.....	2	.....	.....	2	.....	2
Brunswick,	10	.....	6	.....	1	2	2	2	4	4	9	1	9	.....	1	2	.....	.....
Clinton,	4	.....	.....	.....	2	.....	.....	.....	.....	4	7	.....	1	1	.....	.....	1	.....
Grafton,	1	.....	.....	2	1	.....	.....	.....	.....	.....	.....	1	10	.....	.....	.....	.....	.....
Greenbush,	15	.....	1	1	6	.....	3	2	1	9	48	.....	15	2	2	12	.....	3
Hoosick,	6	.....	6	5	2	1	1	9	1	7	12	.....	9	.....	.....	18	3	.....
Lansingburgh,	10	.....	11	2	10	.....	3	4	3	13	60	1	26	5	1	9	.....	4
Nassau,	20	1	2	1	1	1	.....	.....	1	7	15	.....	2	.....	1	.....	.....	2
North Greenbush,	3	1	.....	.....	2	1	1	1	1	3	13	1	5	1	1	.....	.....	1
Petersburgh,	4	.....	2	6	.....	.....	.....	.....	.....	1	.....	.....	10	4	.....	.....	.....	6
Pittstown,	3	.....	3	.....	.....	.....	.....	3	1	7	2	.....	2	4	1	3	.....	.....
Poestenkill,	2	.....	.....	.....	.....	.....	.....	.....	6	1	5	.....	1	.....	.....	1	1	.....
Sand Lake,	3	.....	1	.....	1	.....	.....	1	.....	22	2	.....	5	1	.....	.....	.....	.....
Schaghticoke,	2	.....	1	2	1	.....	.....	4	1	7	8	2	11	9	1	3	.....	.....
Schodack,	18	.....	.....	.....	7	.....	.....	2	1	6	8	.....	2	.....	1	9	2	.....
Stephentown,	11	.....	5	.....	.....	.....	2	1	.....	3	2	.....	1	4	.....	.....	.....	.....

(Continued on page 134.)

OSWEGO COUNTY.—(CONTINUED.)

TOWNS.	Otsego.	Putnam.	Queens.	Rensselaer.	Richmond.	Rockland.	St. Lawrence.	Saratoga.	Schenectady.	Schoharie.	Schuyler.	Seneca.	Steuben.	Suffolk.	Sullivan.	Tioga.	Tompkins.	Ulster.
	COUNTIES OF NEW-YORK.																	
Oswego city:																		
1st ward,	16			15			49	24	6	10		2	1		1		7	3
2d ward,	18			9			83	6	6			1	1		1		1	
3d ward,	14		7	26		1	38	19	1	16		7	5	1		2	5	1
4th ward,	49		3	25			81	27		10		5	3	3	2	8	7	4
Total,	97		10	75		1	251	76	13	36		15	10	4	4	10	20	8
Palermo,	39			8			3	10	1	33			2	1		1	3	4
Parish,	110	1		17			4	5	14	52		1	4					4
Redfield,	21			2			42	2			1		1	10		1		2
Richland,	94		1	31			12	38	2	14	1		4				7	
Sandy Creek,	16		1	69			22	20		7			1					3
Schroeppel,	34	1		17		1	24	30	3	42		3	4	1		1	8	1
Scriba,	34		1	35			45	36	2	29		4					4	
Volney,	50	4	3	57	1		71	42	9	29		19	7	9	1	2	9	5
West Monroe,	18	1		7			5	11	5	9		3						2
Williamstown,	8			42		1		8		12		1	2	5				
Total,	1,078	13	19	651	2	7	716	567	105	494	2	70	74	35	12	17	89	52

OTSEGO COUNTY.—(CONTINUED.)

TOWNS.	Otsego.	Putnam.	Queens.	Rensselaer.	Richmond.	Rockland.	St. Lawrence.	Saratoga.	Schenectady.	Schoharie.	Schuyler.	Seneca.	Steuben.	Suffolk.	Sullivan.	Tioga.	Tompkins.	Ulster.
Burlington,	1,213			12			1	11	3	5								
Butternuts,	1,209			3				4	1	8					1	1	1	6
Cherry Valley,	1,448		2	11			1	5	9	145								3
Decatur,	582			8					1	127						3		1
Edmeston,	1,197		1	6			1	1	1	7						2		
Exeter,	1,028			13				4		5			4				1	2
Hartwick,	1,711			12				1		14		1	1					1
Laurens,	1,591		1	11				7		17			1	1			3	1
Maryland,	1,363	1		15				10	6	107			1		1	1	1	1
Middlefield,	2,076			27			1	12	4	92		1	1	1		2	1	3
Milford,	1,650		1	34				10	10	92		1	3			1	1	4
Morris,	1,311			3				18	1	6		1	1			5	1	1
New Lisbon,	1,327		1	5				12	1	10			1			4	1	1
Oneonta,	1,454	2	3	26			2	7	10	63			3				2	7
Otego,	1,204			6				19	4	17			2			3		2
Otsego,	2,793	2	2	42			2	15	7	58			1	3		2	6	2
Pittsfield,	1,095			6			1	10	6	4			2		1	1		
Plainfield,	713			31				5	1	4						4		
Richfield,	714			11	2		1	6	3	12		1						
Roseboom,	1,285			6				6	7	187						1		3
Springfield,	1,390			31		1		7	5	26			1	2				5
Unadilla,	1,448		1	24			2	7	2	96		1	1	1	3	4		1
Westford,	886			16				6	1	50								
Worcester,	1,173			43				6	9	334				1				1
Total,	31,861	5	12	402	2	1	12	189	92	1,486		6	23	9	6	34	18	45

PUTNAM COUNTY.—(CONTINUED.)

TOWNS.	Otsego.	Putnam.	Queens.	Rensselaer.	Richmond.	Rockland.	St. Lawrence.	Saratoga.	Schenectady.	Schoharie.	Schuyler.	Seneca.	Steuben.	Suffolk.	Sullivan.	Tioga.	Tompkins.	Ulster.
Carmel,		1,833	2	1		4				1				7				1
Kent,		1,316							1									1
Patterson,		888	1			1									2		2	2
Phillipstown,		2,786	5	6		11								2	4		4	14
Putnam Valley,		1,367													1			
South East,	1	1,383	3	1	5	4		1				1		9		1		2
Total,	1	9,573	11	8	5	20		1	1	1		1		18	7	1	6	20

QUEENS COUNTY.—(CONTINUED.)

TOWNS.	Otsego.	Putnam.	Queens.	Rensselaer.	Richmond.	Rockland.	St. Lawrence.	Saratoga.	Schenectady.	Schoharie.	Schuyler.	Seneca.	Steuben.	Suffolk.	Sullivan.	Tioga.	Tompkins.	Ulster.
Flushing,	1	4	3,364	8	7	2								79	1		1	12
Hempstead,			8,194	9	3	1	2	1						143				1
Jamaica,	3		2,908	2	6		2	4						125	2		1	13
Newtown,	4	2	3,841	6	9	15		9				3	3	49	2		3	2
North Hempstead,		1	3,307		34	3		6	3					109		1		2
Oyster Bay,	1	1	5,204	2	15	1		8	4			2		315	2		2	
Total,	9	8	26,818	27	74	22	4	28	7			5	3	820	7	1	7	30

RENSSELAER COUNTY.—(CONTINUED.)

TOWNS.	Otsego.	Putnam.	Queens.	Rensselaer.	Richmond.	Rockland.	St. Lawrence.	Saratoga.	Schenectady.	Schoharie.	Schuyler.	Seneca.	Steuben.	Suffolk.	Sullivan.	Tioga.	Tompkins.	Ulster.
Berlin,	3			1,554			1	1		4							1	1
Brunswick,	7			2,277			1	25	13	7								4
Clinton,				903				7	6	6			1					2
Grafton,				1,620				3		1				1				
Greenbush,	14	2	2	1,106		1		42	22	39		1	1			1	1	7
Hoosick,			6	2,310		3		38	8	3			1				3	3
Lansingburgh,	3	2	3	2,799		2	4	139	8	9		2		2				9
Nassau,	8			1,974			2	17	5	9			1				3	3
North Greenbush,	2		3	1,180				11	2	9				2				3
Petersburgh,				1,270				3									1	
Pittstown,	12	1		2,479			1	58	5	3							1	2
Poestenkill,	2			1,433				16	3	9								
Sand Lake,	6			1,748				16	2	9		1						7
Schaghticoke,	7			2,041				96	4	4		1		1	3		2	2
Schodack,	7	1	2	2,237				23	16	18								5
Stephentown,	6			1,826				4	6	4								

(Continued on page 135.)

OSWEGO COUNTY.—(Continued.)

TOWNS.	COUNTIES OF NEW-YORK.							UNITED STATES.										
	Warren.	Washington.	Wayne.	Westchester.	Wyoming.	Yates.	New-York.	Maine.	N. Hampshire.	Vermont.	Massachusetts.	Rhode Island	Connecticut.	New Jersey.	Pennsylvania.	Delaware.	Maryland.	District of Columbia.
Oswego city:																		
1st ward,	6	23	18			1	2, 161	7	9	31	47	12	57	20	24		8	
2d ward,	1	15	5				1, 521	1	10	40	18	4	21	12	5		6	
3d ward,	5	28	15	6	1	2	2, 209	7	11	38	35	9	45	17	14		2	
4th ward,	1	41	10	2			2, 552	2	10	39	88	18	68	9	19			
Total Oswego,	13	107	48	8	1	3	8, 443	17	40	148	188	43	191	58	62		16	
Palermo,	13	33		2		1	1, 677	1	4	34	66	8	92		5			
Parish,		16	1	3		6	1, 428	1	4	31	44	2	46	2	2			
Redfield,	2	12	3	1			622		13	12	21	6	37	3				
Richland,		38	4	6			3, 222	4	29	175	115	24	90	4	5		2	
Sandy Creek,	1	65	3		1		1, 896		38	133	50	16	47	1	2			
Schroeppel,	3	23	8	5	1	3	2, 996	12	19	79	63	5	101	12	6		2	
Scriba,	4	57	8	1		1	2, 330	1	9	36	66	15	72	9	2		1	
Volney,	5	96	24	8		6	4, 696	8	31	117	176	40	174	22	22		1	
West Monroe,	1	14		3			938	2	13	33	29	2	25					
Williamstown,		13	6			2	748	1	6	27	35	8	24	5	1	1		
Total,	75	992	248	121	9	30	50, 731	72	369	1, 398	1, 528	352	1, 627	228	184	2	33	

OTSEGO COUNTY.—(Continued.)

TOWNS.	Warren.	Washington.	Wayne.	Westchester.	Wyoming.	Yates.	New-York.	Maine.	N. Hampshire.	Vermont.	Massachusetts.	Rhode Island	Connecticut.	New Jersey.	Pennsylvania.	Delaware.	Maryland.	District of Columbia.
Burlington,		4	1	10			1, 466	1	4	27	30	26	94	2	9			
Butternuts,		6		29			1, 577	1	5	10	53	16	175	2	17			
Cherry Valley,		11	2		1		2, 141		1	5	26	5	49	9	5			
Decatur,		5		2			847		2	13	15	1	13		6			
Edmeston,	3	14		7			1, 546		3	17	27	70	73	4	3			
Exeter,	1	3	1	3			1, 268	1	6	11	47	30	83	1	1			
Hartwick,		3		1			1, 941		1	26	66	60	66	7	2			
Laurens,	1	5	1	3			1, 862		13	27	40	53	60	5	5		1	
Maryland,		2		2			1, 908	3	7	22	52	11	47	2	9			
Middlefield,		8	3				2, 624	1	13	8	67	14	61	5	9			
Milford,		2	1	4	1		2, 134	2	2	22	49	21	42	3	4			
Morris,		4		3	1		1, 640	2	11	23	54	31	133	10	22			
New Lisbon,		5					1, 481		15	36	37	32	79	3	1			
Oneonta,		13		2			2, 008		5	10	21	14	45	8	12		3	
Otego,	4	4	1				1, 587		7	23	65	42	88	2	7			
Otsego,		13	7	5			3, 443	5	15	57	95	44	137	14	15	3		6
Pittsfield,		3	1	2		1	1, 395		7	15	41	46	47	5	10			
Plainfield,		3		6			1, 049	2	1	8	21	33	63	2	1			
Richfield,	1	6		7			1, 240	1	2	14	39	22	79	7				
Roseboom,	1					1	1, 771			4	15	2	29	8	7			
Springfield,		6	1	1		5	1, 973	2	2	12	71	7	60	12	5			
Unadilla,		2	1	14			2, 255		31	28	41	20	180	2	23		1	
Westford,		6	2	5			1, 141	1	2	7	28	6	31	5	5			
Worcester,	1	4		5		1	1, 908	1	2	20	36	5	28	3	4			
Total,	12	132	22	111	3	8	42, 205	23	157	445	1, 036	611	1, 762	121	182	3	5	6

PUTNAM COUNTY.—(Continued.)

TOWNS.	Warren.	Washington.	Wayne.	Westchester.	Wyoming.	Yates.	New-York.	Maine.	N. Hampshire.	Vermont.	Massachusetts.	Rhode Island	Connecticut.	New Jersey.	Pennsylvania.	Delaware.	Maryland.	District of Columbia.
Carmel,				187			2, 154			2	6		35	12	2		1	
Kent,				26			1, 475						15	1	1			
Patterson,		1		48		2	1, 146		1	2	3	1	136	7	1			
Philipstown,				128			3, 588	1	5	15	18	2	62	31	17		9	
Putnam Valley,				104			1, 520				1		11	2	1			
South East,		1		191			1, 745		1		10		142	8	7			
Total,		2		684		2	11, 628	1	7	19	38	3	401	61	29		10	

QUEENS COUNTY.—(Continued.)

TOWNS.	Warren.	Washington.	Wayne.	Westchester.	Wyoming.	Yates.	New-York.	Maine.	N. Hampshire.	Vermont.	Massachusetts.	Rhode Island	Connecticut.	New Jersey.	Pennsylvania.	Delaware.	Maryland.	District of Columbia.
Flushing,			4	44			4, 514	22	6	8	41	20	78	142	65		1	
Hempstead,		3		6			9, 023	7	7	6	30	7	32	35	17		1	
Jamaica,				17			3, 857	1	3	10	28	7	48	127	29		10	2
Newtown,		9	5	60		1	5, 645	6	15	15	84	25	72	145	61		14	
North Hempstead,		1		22			3, 814	3	1	8	15	5	26	51	6		1	
Oyster Bay,		1		25		1	6, 239	10	11	2	34	8	49	45	15	1	7	1
Total,		14	9	174		2	33, 092	49	43	49	232	72	305	545	193	1	34	3

RENSSELAER COUNTY.—(Continued.)

TOWNS.	Warren.	Washington.	Wayne.	Westchester.	Wyoming.	Yates.	New-York.	Maine.	N. Hampshire.	Vermont.	Massachusetts.	Rhode Island	Connecticut.	New Jersey.	Pennsylvania.	Delaware.	Maryland.	District of Columbia.
Berlin,		3					1, 646	2	3	20	62	43	10	4			1	
Brunswick,	2	14		8			2, 500		14	37	34	7	25	12	2			
Clinton,	1	3		1			1, 105	1	1	6	11	1	8	6	2			
Grafton,		6		1			1, 665		4	27	22	28	11		8			
Greenbush,	1	24		4		1	1, 981	10	21	23	92	5	25	16	7			
Hoosick,	9	189	1	1			2, 744	1	35	346	134	29	27	8	5			
Lansingburgh,	9	123	1	3			3, 565	1	27	117	120	28	59	25	11		8	2
Nassau,	3	7	2	6			2, 554	1	3	13	110	11	51	4				
North Greenbush,	1	10				2	1, 374	1	3	9	23	3	13	6			1	
Petersburgh,	3	13					1, 349	1		56	64	41	12	1	10			
Pittstown,	4	110	1	13			2, 811	4	14	108	86	24	30	10	7			
Poestenkill,	7	6		10			1, 543		4	17	16	4	14	4				
Sand Lake,		9	5	6			2, 040		13	16	29	8	28	3	1			
Schaghticoke,	8	107		1		5	2, 409	5	2	42	34	15	20	9	1			
Schodack,	1	10	2	5		1	3, 034	1		14	33	3	24	4	3			
Stephentown,		3		5			2, 015		6	9	123	32	38	1	5			

(Continued on page 136.)

OSWEGO COUNTY.—(Continued.)

TOWNS.	UNITED STATES.																	
	Virginia.	N. Carolina.	S. Carolina.	Georgia.	Florida.	Alabama.	Mississippi.	Louisiana.	Texas.	Arkansas.	Missouri.	Tennessee.	Kentucky.	Ohio.	Indiana.	Illinois.	Michigan.	Wisconsin.
Oswego city:																		
1st ward,	3	1	1	2	1								1	14	1	1	5	1
2d ward,	4				2							1		6		5	5	1
3d ward,	1							1					1	5		1	2	4
4th ward,		1												15	1	4	4	4
Total Oswego,..	8	2	1	2	3			1				1	2	40	2	11	16	10
Palermo,														3		2	4	
Parish,														2	7		4	3
Redfield,														1				
Richland,													1	3	1	4	5	7
Sandy Creek,	1		1											4			2	
Schroeppel,														9	1	3	6	4
Scriba,														7			3	1
Volney,	1												1	8		4	12	4
West Monroe,															1		2	2
Williamstown,														4			2	
Total,	12	2	4	2	3			2			1	1	4	132	13	38	92	60
OTSEGO COUNTY.—(Continued.)																		
Burlington,														1		2		
Butternuts,		1												1	1	2		
Cherry Valley,		1														1	1	2
Decatur,																		
Edmeston,														2			1	
Exeter,														4	1	1	1	1
Hartwick,																		
Laurens,	2															1	1	
Maryland,	1												9	1				
Middlefield,		1											1	1		1		1
Milford,													2			3		2
Morris,	1						1					1						1
New Lisbon,														2				1
Oneonta,	1													1				
Otego,														2			4	1
Otsego,	1		1		2				1	2				4		1	3	2
Pittsfield,																	1	
Plainfield,									1									1
Richfield,				2										1			3	1
Roseboom,															1			2
Springfield,					1									1			1	
Unadilla,														2	1	5	1	
Westford,																		
Worcester,																		2
Total,	6	3	1	2	3		1		2	2		1	12	23	4	17	17	17
PUTNAM COUNTY.—(Continued.)																		
Carmel,	3													2		1		
Kent,	1													1				
Patterson,	4			1														
Phillipstown,	4	5	2	1										3		1		
Putnam Valley,																		
South East,	1			1														
Total,	13	5	2	3										6		2		
QUEENS COUNTY.—(Continued.)																		
Flushing,	22	6	3	2	1			6					2	5		2	3	
Hempstead,	4		1		1							6						
Jamaica,		8	3	1			1	2						7				
Newtown,	13	2	4	2		1		8	1		9			5		2	4	
North Hempstead,	5	2	8		1				1				1			4	3	
Oyster Bay,	7	1	2											6	2		1	
Total,	51	19	21	5	3	1	1	16	2		9	6	3	23	2	8	11	
RENSSELAER COUNTY.—(Continued.)																		
Berlin,							1							2			2	3
Brunswick,				3														
Clinton,	1			2	1													
Grafton,														3				
Greenbush,	2												1	2		1		2
Hoosick,	2			1									1	2				
Lansingburgh,			3				1		1		2			7		2	5	1
Nassau,										1				3			1	2
North Greenbush,				2								2			1	1		
Petersburgh,																		2
Pittstown,																1		1
Poestenkill,				1														
Sand Lake,															1	3		
Schaghticoke,	2															1		
Schodack,			5	1			1							1			3	
Stephentown,																		

(Continued on page 137.)

OSWEGO COUNTY.—(Continued.)

TOWNS.	U. STATES.			Total United States.	FOREIGN COUNTRIES.													
	Iowa.	California.	Territories.		Canada.	N. Brunswick.	Nova Scotia.	N. Foundland.	West Indies.	Mexico.	S. America.	England.	Scotland.	Ireland.	Wales.	France.	Belgium.	Holland.
Oswego city:																		
1st ward,	1			2, 408	446	1	1	1	1		1	164	58	1, 004		24		
2d ward,		1		1, 663	307							85	12	656	3	11		
3d ward,				2, 403	238	3	5					180	30	1, 286	1	15		2
4th ward,				2, 834	419	1	1	5				86	24	945	5	35		
Total Oswego,	1	1		9, 308	1, 410	5	7	6	1		1	515	124	3, 891	9	85		2
Palermo,				1, 896	17							25	1	14		34		
Parish,				1, 576	13							12	8	23	6	8		
Redfield,				715	8							22	8	34	8			
Richland,				3, 691	71	1	1		2			74	5	100	10	2		1
Sandy Creek,				2, 191	16							15	1	22	9			
Schroeppel,				3, 318	65							133		152		17		
Scriba,				2, 552	134	1						45	8	182	2	7		
Volney,				5,317	335	1	3		1			177	32	484	2	7		
West Monroe,				1, 047	4							23	1	15	2	48		
Williamstown,				862	7							27	7	34	1			
Total,	1	2		56, 895	2, 701	8	21	6	5		1	1, 593	300	5, 925	63	481		6

OTSEGO COUNTY.—(Continued.)

TOWNS.	Iowa.	California.	Territories.	Total United States.	Canada.	N. Brunswick.	Nova Scotia.	N. Foundland.	West Indies.	Mexico.	S. America.	England.	Scotland.	Ireland.	Wales.	France.	Belgium.	Holland.
Burlington,				1, 662	1							48	68	12	4			
Butternuts,				1, 861	1				1			120	1	32	2			
Cherry Valley,				2, 246	6							139	13	77		2		
Decatur,				897		1						2	3					
Edmeston,				1, 746								16	2	14				
Exeter,				1, 456	1							18	2	41				
Hartwick,				2, 169	3				1			23	12	9		1		
Laurens,				2, 070	1							25		5				
Maryland,	1			2, 073	3							18	3	62				
Middlefield,				2, 807	16	1						134	20	72				1
Milford,				2, 286	2							20		9	1			
Morris,	1			1, 931	2							52	15	30	1	3		1
New Lisbon,				1, 687	3							39	45	12				
Oneonta,				2, 128	2							9	1	4				
Otego,				1, 828	1							11	2	7				
Otsego,		1		3, 852	7				6			121	27	272	4			
Pittsfield,				1, 567	1							34	21	14		1		
Plainfield,				1, 182	9							15		48	24	1		
Richfield,		1		1, 412	2							28	5	74	10	2		
Roseboom,				1, 839	4							30	3	11				
Springfield,				2, 147	3				1			125	14	148				
Unadilla,	3			2, 593	2							37	8	40				
Westford,				1, 226	3	2						14	1	10				
Worcester,				2, 009	1							17	8	77				
Total,	5	2		46, 674	74	4			9			1, 095	274	1, 080	46	10		2

PUTNAM COUNTY.—(Continued.)

TOWNS.	Iowa.	California.	Territories.	Total United States.	Canada.	N. Brunswick.	Nova Scotia.	N. Foundland.	West Indies.	Mexico.	S. America.	England.	Scotland.	Ireland.	Wales.	France.	Belgium.	Holland.
Carmel,				2, 218	3		2			1		10	3	138		11		
Kent,				1, 494	1		1					4		33	1			
Patterson,				1, 302	2						1	3	2	91				
Phillipstown,				3, 764	5	1	1		5	1		118	66	761	1	20		
Putnam Valley,				1, 535								3	2	25				
South East,				1, 915	2							16	4	210				
Total,				12, 228	13	1	4		5	2	1	154	77	1, 258	2	31		

QUEENS COUNTY.—(Continued.)

TOWNS.	Iowa.	California.	Territories.	Total United States.	Canada.	N. Brunswick.	Nova Scotia.	N. Foundland.	West Indies.	Mexico.	S. America.	England.	Scotland.	Ireland.	Wales.	France.	Belgium.	Holland.
Flushing,				4, 949	100		9		4	2	2	242	47	1, 660	11	16	1	2
Hempstead,				9, 177	3				1			208	22	547		13		1
Jamaica,				4, 144	4	1	1		11		1	161	33	746	2			9
Newtown,		1		6, 134	15	1			9	1		377	149	1, 402	4	62		3
North Hempstead,				3, 955	2		3		1	2	1	65	12	486	1	10	3	
Oyster Bay,				6, 441	9	2	2		2		1	238	31	858	1	14		1
Total,		1		34, 800	133	4	15		28	5	5	1, 291	294	5, 699	19	115	4	16

RENSSELAER COUNTY.—(Continued.)

TOWNS.	Iowa.	California.	Territories.	Total United States.	Canada.	N. Brunswick.	Nova Scotia.	N. Foundland.	West Indies.	Mexico.	S. America.	England.	Scotland.	Ireland.	Wales.	France.	Belgium.	Holland.
Berlin,				1, 799	10	1						16	1	44		1		
Brunswick,				2, 634	16							47	18	240		1		
Clinton,				1, 145	4				1			71	8	242				9
Grafton,				1, 768	14							3		39				
Greenbush,				2, 188	53	1	5					135	12	776		10		
Hoosick,				3, 335	13		1					97	11	631	1			
Lansingburgh,	4			3, 989	113	1	1				2	243	134	1, 122		8		
Nassau,	3			2, 757	6							27		110		2		
North Greenbush,				1, 439	4							38	14	118	1			
Petersburgh,				1, 536	6							2		101		1		
Pittstown,				3, 096	15		2					56	53	309	3	1		3
Poestenkill,				1, 603	16							6	4	42		3		3
Sand Lake,				2 142	5							34		70		3		1
Schaghticoke,				2, 540	30							45	26	600				
Schodack,				3, 127	30							65	15	282	1	3		9
Stephentown,				2, 229	19							3	2	92				

(Continued on page 138.)

OSWEGO COUNTY.—(Continued.)

TOWNS.	FOREIGN COUNTRIES.																		
	Germany.	Prussia.	Austria.	Switzerland.	Italy.	Spain.	Portugal.	Poland.	Norway.	Sweden.	Russia.	Denmark.	East Indies.	Africa.	Turkey and Greece.	Islands.	Asia.	At Sea.	Unknown.
Oswego city:																			
1st ward,	23	1	....	1	....	1	1	1	....	3	....	....	....	....	....	....	....	2	1
2d ward,	97	1	....	....	2	....	....	....	....	....	....	....	....	....	....	....	....	....	2
3d ward,	75	....	....	2	....	....	....	....	1	....	....	....	....	....	....	....	....	1	12
4th ward,	160	....	....	1	4	....	....	....	....	1	....	....	....	....	....	....	....	3	56
Total Oswego,	355	2	....	4	6	1	1	1	1	4	....	....	....	....	....	....	....	6	71
Palermo,	5	1	....	....	....	....	....	....	....	....	....	1	....	....	....	....	....	....	29
Parish,	18	....	....	2	1	....	....	....	....	....	....	....	....	....	....	....	....	....	8
Redfield,	....	....	....	....	....	....	....	....	....	....	....	....	....	....	....	....	....	1	2
Richland,	10	....	....	5	....	....	....	....	....	....	....	....	....	....	....	....	....	....	39
Sandy Creek,	....	....	....	....	....	....	....	....	....	....	....	....	....	....	....	....	....	....	19
Schroeppel,	56	....	....	....	....	....	1	1	....	....	....	....	....	....	....	....	....	....	4
Scriba,	20	....	....	....	....	....	....	....	....	2	....	....	1	....	....	....	....	....	4
Volney,	81	....	....	5	1	....	....	....	....	....	....	....	2	....	....	....	....	2	26
West Monroe,	54	....	....	14	....	....	....	....	....	....	....	....	....	....	....	....	....	....	9
Williamstown,	12	....	....	....	....	....	....	....	....	....	....	....	....	....	....	....	....	....	3
Total,	841	3	....	34	8	2	2	2	1	6	....	1	3	....	....	....	....	11	479

OTSEGO COUNTY.—(Continued.)

TOWNS.	Germany.	Prussia.	Austria.	Switzerland.	Italy.	Spain.	Portugal.	Poland.	Norway.	Sweden.	Russia.	Denmark.	East Indies.	Africa.	Turkey and Greece.	Islands.	Asia.	At Sea.	Unknown.
Burlington,	12	....	....	....	....	....	....	....	....	....	....	....	....	....	....	....	....	....	1
Butternuts,	3	....	....	1	....	....	....	....	....	....	....	....	....	....	....	....	1	....	6
Cherry Valley,	20	....	....	1	....	....	....	....	....	....	....	....	....	....	....	....	....	1	35
Decatur,	1	....	....	....	....	....	....	....	....	....	....	....	....	....	....	....	....	....	9
Edmeston,	2	....	....	....	....	....	....	....	....	....	....	....	....	....	....	....	....	....	3
Exeter,	12	....	....	1	....	....	....	....	....	....	....	....	....	....	....	....	....	....	9
Hartwick,	2	....	....	....	....	....	....	....	....	....	....	....	....	....	....	....	....	....	....
Laurens,	....	....	....	....	....	....	....	....	....	....	....	....	....	....	....	....	....	....	5
Maryland,	7	....	....	....	....	....	....	....	....	....	....	....	....	....	....	....	....	1	10
Middlefield,	10	....	....	....	....	....	....	....	....	....	....	....	4	....	....	....	....	....	6
Milford,	10	....	....	....	....	....	....	....	....	....	....	....	....	....	....	....	....	....	1
Morris,	3	....	....	....	....	....	....	....	....	....	....	....	....	....	....	....	....	....	....
New Lisbon,	6	....	....	....	....	....	....	....	....	....	....	....	....	....	....	....	....	....	....
Oneonta,	6	5	....	....	....	....	....	4	....	....	....	....	....	....	....	....	....	....	8
Otego,	1	....	....	....	....	....	....	....	....	....	....	....	....	....	....	....	....	....	....
Otsego,	20	....	....	....	....	....	....	....	....	....	....	....	....	....	....	....	....	1	24
Pittsfield,	....	....	....	....	....	....	....	....	....	....	....	....	....	....	....	....	....	....	18
Plainfield,	2	....	....	....	....	....	....	....	....	....	....	....	....	....	....	....	....	....	....
Richfield,	2	....	1	....	....	....	....	....	....	....	....	....	....	....	....	....	....	....	7
Roseboom,	....	....	....	....	....	....	....	....	....	....	....	....	....	....	....	....	....	....	....
Springfield,	15	....	....	....	....	....	....	....	....	....	....	....	....	....	....	....	3	....	7
Unadilla,	10	4	....	1	....	....	....	1	....	....	....	....	....	....	....	....	....	....	26
Westford,	....	....	....	....	....	....	....	....	....	....	....	....	....	....	....	....	....	....	115
Worcester,	2	....	....	....	....	....	....	....	....	....	....	....	....	....	....	....	....	....	1
Total,	146	9	1	4	....	....	....	5	....	....	....	....	4	....	....	....	4	3	291

PUTNAM COUNTY.—(Continued.)

TOWNS.	Germany.	Prussia.	Austria.	Switzerland.	Italy.	Spain.	Portugal.	Poland.	Norway.	Sweden.	Russia.	Denmark.	East Indies.	Africa.	Turkey and Greece.	Islands.	Asia.	At Sea.	Unknown.
Carmel,	9	4	....	....	....	....	....	1	....	....	....	....	....	....	....	....	....	....	6
Kent,	3	....	....	1	....	....	....	....	....	....	....	....	....	....	....	....	....	....	1
Patterson,	21	....	....	....	....	....	....	....	....	....	....	....	....	....	....	....	....	....	....
Phillipstown,	50	7	....	7	....	1	....	....	....	....	....	....	....	....	....	....	....	....	....
Putnam Valley,	7	1	....	....	....	....	....	....	....	....	....	....	....	....	....	....	....	1	....
South East,	29	....	....	....	....	....	....	....	....	4	....	....	....	....	....	....	....	....	5
Total,	119	12	....	8	....	1	....	1	....	4	....	....	....	....	....	....	....	1	12

QUEENS COUNTY.—(Continued.)

TOWNS.	Germany.	Prussia.	Austria.	Switzerland.	Italy.	Spain.	Portugal.	Poland.	Norway.	Sweden.	Russia.	Denmark.	East Indies.	Africa.	Turkey and Greece.	Islands.	Asia.	At Sea.	Unknown.
Flushing,	893	1	....	2	5	....	1	....	1	2	....	1	....	1	....	....	....	1	16
Hempstead,	398	12	4	4	....	....	....	....	....	12	....	....	....	....	....	....	....	....	75
Jamaica,	312	9	3	....	....	1	1	1	....	3	....	3	....	1	....	....	....	....	185
Newtown,	1, 246	1	8	9	4	3	....	....	1	3	....	1	....	1	....	....	1	1	10
North Hempstead,	121	1	....	3	1	....	....	3	....	1	....	....	....	....	....	1	....	....	22
Oyster Bay,	385	....	1	32	2	1	....	1	1	....	....	....	....	....	1	....	....	....	23
Total,	3, 355	24	16	50	12	5	2	5	3	21	....	5	....	3	1	1	1	2	331

RENSSELAER COUNTY.—(Continued.)

TOWNS.	Germany.	Prussia.	Austria.	Switzerland.	Italy.	Spain.	Portugal.	Poland.	Norway.	Sweden.	Russia.	Denmark.	East Indies.	Africa.	Turkey and Greece.	Islands.	Asia.	At Sea.	Unknown.
Berlin,	294	....	....	1	....	....	....	....	....	....	....	....	....	....	....	....	....	....	....
Brunswick,	130	....	....	....	3	....	....	....	....	....	....	1	....	....	....	....	....	....	11
Clinton,	122	....	....	1	....	....	....	....	....	....	....	....	....	....	....	....	....	....	3
Grafton,	57	....	....	....	....	....	....	....	....	....	....	....	....	....	....	....	....	....	4
Greenbush,	91	....	....	....	....	....	....	....	....	....	....	....	....	....	....	....	....	3	32
Hoosick,	8	1	1	....	....	....	....	....	....	....	....	....	....	....	....	....	....	....	18
Lansingburgh,	80	....	....	....	....	....	....	1	....	....	....	....	1	....	....	....	....	1	7
Nassau,	83	1	....	....	....	....	....	....	....	....	....	....	....	....	....	....	....	....	14
North Greenbush,	194	....	....	4	....	....	....	....	....	....	....	....	....	....	....	....	....	....	....
Petersburgh,	11	....	....	....	....	....	....	....	....	....	....	....	....	....	....	....	....	....	6
Pittstown,	63	1	....	....	....	....	....	....	....	....	....	....	....	....	....	....	....	....	....
Poestenkill,	189	2	1	2	....	....	....	....	....	....	....	....	....	....	....	....	....	....	1
Sand Lake,	332	....	....	....	....	....	....	....	....	....	....	....	....	....	....	....	5	1	....
Schaghticoke,	49	2	....	8	....	....	....	....	....	....	....	....	....	....	....	....	....	1	3
Schodack,	293	1	....	6	....	....	....	....	....	....	....	....	....	....	....	....	....	....	5
Stephentown,	10	....	....	7	....	....	....	....	....	....	....	....	....	....	....	....	....	....	35

(Continued on page 139.)

RENSSELAER COUNTY.

TOWNS.	COUNTIES OF NEW-YORK.																	
	Albany.	Allegany.	Broome.	Cattaraugus.	Cayuga.	Chautauque.	Chemung.	Chenango.	Clinton.	Columbia.	Cortland.	Delaware.	Dutchess.	Erie.	Essex.	Franklin.	Fulton.	Genesee.
Troy city:																		
1st ward,	100	1	...	...	1	2	...	1	10	56	...	...	22	5	10	2	4	...
2d ward,	103	1	...	1	3	2	...	...	4	68	...	3	23	...	13	1	8	2
3d ward,	58	...	...	...	1	...	...	1	6	30	1	2	26	2	14	...	...	...
4th ward,	91	...	1	2	3	...	...	3	12	57	...	4	39	1	8	...	7	5
5th ward,	21	...	...	1	...	...	...	...	...	36	...	22	16	...	3	...	1	...
6th ward,	20	...	...	...	...	...	...	...	4	3	...	...	15	...	4	...	...	...
7th ward,	98	1	1	...	2	1	...	2	...	52	4	2	27	...	9	...	9	3
8th ward,	81	...	...	...	3	...	...	1	13	42	...	1	15	4	5	...	1	...
9th ward,	67	...	...	...	1	...	...	...	9	10	...	...	19	1	1	5	1	...
10th ward,	70	2	...	...	1	...	...	2	3	26	...	2	19	3	2	...	7	...
Total Troy,	709	5	2	4	15	5	...	10	61	380	5	36	221	16	69	8	38	10
Total,	1,764	23	9	6	38	10	3	24	83	1,575	19	62	828	34	94	12	58	13

RICHMOND COUNTY.

TOWNS.	Albany.	Allegany.	Broome.	Cattaraugus.	Cayuga.	Chautauque.	Chemung.	Chenango.	Clinton.	Columbia.	Cortland.	Delaware.	Dutchess.	Erie.	Essex.	Franklin.	Fulton.	Genesee.
Castleton,	28	...	1	...	...	...	...	2	1	1	...	7	12	2	2	...	...	...
Northfield,	7	...	...	...	...	...	...	...	...	6	...	2	5	...	...	...	...	1
Southfield,	16	...	...	...	...	...	...	...	...	...	...	7	2	1	...	...	...	...
Westfield,	6	...	...	...	...	...	...	...	...	1	...	9	9	...	...	...	...	...
Total,	57	...	1	...	...	...	...	2	1	8	...	25	28	1	2	...	...	1

ROCKLAND COUNTY.

TOWNS.	Albany.	Allegany.	Broome.	Cattaraugus.	Cayuga.	Chautauque.	Chemung.	Chenango.	Clinton.	Columbia.	Cortland.	Delaware.	Dutchess.	Erie.	Essex.	Franklin.	Fulton.	Genesee.
Clarkstown,	28	...	...	...	...	...	...	...	...	3	...	5	5	...	1	...	...	...
Haverstraw,	5	...	...	...	1	...	...	1	2	1	...	37	...	1	...	...	...	...
Orangetown,	6	...	1	...	...	4	...	1	...	21	3	6	26	3	...	...	...	...
Ramapo,	3	...	4	...	1	1	1	...	1	4	1	8	11	...	...	...	...	...
Total,	42	...	5	...	2	5	1	2	3	29	4	56	42	4	1	...	...	...

ST. LAWRENCE COUNTY.

TOWNS.	Albany.	Allegany.	Broome.	Cattaraugus.	Cayuga.	Chautauque.	Chemung.	Chenango.	Clinton.	Columbia.	Cortland.	Delaware.	Dutchess.	Erie.	Essex.	Franklin.	Fulton.	Genesee.
Brasher,	...	...	...	...	1	1	...	2	33	...	...	...	1	1	16	144	...	2
Canton,	7	1	...	1	1	3	...	5	99	4	...	1	8	5	45	81	1	...
Colton,	...	...	...	...	...	...	...	...	26	...	...	...	...	1	61	38	...	6
De Kalb,	8	3	...	...	3	...	...	3	12	3	3	1	2	...	5	7	5	...
De Peyster,	2	...	...	...	...	...	...	...	3	1	1	1	...	...	10	2	4	...
Edwards,	...	...	...	...	...	...	...	2	2	...	1	...	4	...	6	...	1	...
Fine,	2	...	...	...	...	...	...	...	...	...	1	...	...	...	1	3	7	...
Fowler,	2	...	...	...	1	...	...	3	5	1	...	3	4	2	3	3	3	...
Gouverneur,	1	1	...	...	5	1	1	7	17	...	1	...	6	2	7	15	46	3
Hammond,	2	...	...	...	1	2	...	...	6	1	...	...	3	...	2	1	1	...
Hermon,	...	...	...	...	2	...	...	2	7	4	1	1	1	...	9	11	1	2
Hopkinton,	1	...	...	...	...	...	...	...	21	1	...	...	5	...	55	68	...	...
Lawrence,	...	...	...	...	...	...	...	...	80	1	...	...	2	1	117	107	...	2
Lisbon,	11	...	...	...	2	...	...	...	14	2	...	1	5	...	30	40	1	1
Louisville,	2	...	...	...	...	...	...	...	5	...	...	...	2	1	3	43	...	1
Macomb,	...	...	...	...	1	...	...	1	2	2	...	3	2	...	5	4	...	2
Madrid,	5	...	...	...	...	...	...	3	14	...	1	4	2	...	10	31	...	6
Massena,	1	...	...	1	1	...	...	...	24	1	...	1	1	1	16	63	...	...
Morristown,	8	...	...	...	...	...	...	2	3	2	...	3	4	...	...	6	10	4
Norfolk,	...	...	...	...	1	...	...	...	13	...	...	...	1	...	22	28	...	...
Oswegatchie,	50	...	2	3	8	5	2	11	33	5	5	6	18	13	19	49	14	4
Parishville,	1	...	...	...	...	1	...	1	24	...	1	1	8	...	44	52	...	...
Pierrepont,	...	...	...	...	...	...	...	2	66	...	...	...	1	...	77	26	...	1
Pitcairn,	5	...	...	...	...	1	...	...	...	...	...	...	2	1	1	1	...	...
Potsdam,	9	1	1	...	2	...	...	...	114	5	...	1	11	2	112	119	2	10
Rossie,	1	...	...	...	...	1	...	4	7	...	...	1	...	...	3	1	2	...
Russell,	5	...	...	...	2	...	...	...	24	...	...	...	2	...	15	2	...	...
Stockholm,	1	...	...	...	1	...	...	...	76	...	...	1	7	2	227	66	...	...
Total,	124	6	3	5	32	15	3	48	730	33	15	29	102	32	921	1,011	98	44

SARATOGA COUNTY.

TOWNS.	Albany.	Allegany.	Broome.	Cattaraugus.	Cayuga.	Chautauque.	Chemung.	Chenango.	Clinton.	Columbia.	Cortland.	Delaware.	Dutchess.	Erie.	Essex.	Franklin.	Fulton.	Genesee.
Ballston,	71	...	...	...	...	...	...	...	2	16	...	...	33	2	2	...	12	...
Charlton,	20	...	...	...	...	...	...	...	...	3	...	...	5	...	...	...	9	...
Clifton Park,	63	1	...	...	1	2	...	...	6	45	...	1	44	...	1	2	5	...
Corinth,	17	...	...	...	...	...	...	...	2	31	1	1	11	3	1	1	8	...
Day,	13	...	...	...	...	1	...	...	2	6	...	3	2	...	7	1	18	1
Edinburgh,	9	1	...	1	...	...	1	...	...	2	...	...	19	...	7	...	62	...
Galway,	58	...	...	...	3	...	...	1	...	33	...	2	48	...	4	...	84	1
Greenfield,	18	2	3	...	1	...	...	1	...	24	2	...	48	2	3	...	14	3
Hadley,	32	...	...	...	...	...	...	...	9	14	...	...	4	...	5	...	2	...
Halfmoon,	75	1	...	...	2	...	...	...	2	26	...	1	75	1	4	...	8	...
Malta,	20	...	...	...	1	...	...	...	1	28	1	1	56	...	2	...	...	...
Milton,	202	1	...	2	2	2	...	5	4	66	...	...	68	5	17	...	25	1
Moreau,	31	...	...	3	1	...	...	...	6	32	...	...	39	3	24	...	7	3
Northumberland,	10	...	...	1	1	1	...	2	...	27	2	2	22	...	7	1	...	...
Providence,	4	...	1	...	5	...	...	...	...	8	...	...	7	...	3	...	50	...
Saratoga,	59	...	...	...	3	1	...	1	7	35	...	...	55	2	7	6	...	...
Saratoga Springs,	101	2	4	1	7	1	...	6	24	30	2	8	71	10	22	2	21	3

(Continued on page 140.)

RENSSELAER COUNTY.—(Continued.)

TOWNS.	COUNTIES OF NEW-YORK.																	
	Greene.	Hamilton.	Herkimer.	Jefferson.	Kings.	Lewis.	Livingston.	Madison.	Monroe.	Montgomery.	New-York.	Niagara.	Oneida.	Onondaga.	Ontario.	Orange.	Orleans.	Oswego.
Troy city:																		
1st ward,	32	......	4	2	7	1	......	2	8	12	81	......	8	2	......	6	......	1
2d ward,	25	......	1	5	4	7	1	3	2	9	87	4	13	5	3	4	......	......
3d ward,	15	......	4	7	6	......	1	4	3	6	25	......	11	2	2	2	1	......
4th ward,	13	5	16	5	4	......	1	......	3	10	70	2	21	11	4	13	......	4
5th ward,	5	......	2	......	......	1	......	......	......	......	76	1	13	......	......	4	......	......
6th ward,	5	......	3	......	5	......	......	......	......	2	8	1	5	......	......	4	......	......
7th ward,	4	......	2	4	9	......	......	5	2	12	32	1	12	8	2	5	......	1
8th ward,	4	......	2	4	12	......	......	5	3	5	43	1	16	2	......	1	......	2
9th ward,	4	2	......	......	......	......	1	......	1	......	28	1	2	1	......	2	......	......
10th ward,	5	......	1	2	7	2	......	1	10	5	33	1	8	1	......	......	1	1
Total Troy,......	112	7	35	29	54	11	4	20	32	61	483	12	109	32	11	41	2	9
Total,.........	224	9	78	58	89	16	16	52	52	157	676	18	220	63	20	100	9	27

RICHMOND COUNTY.—(Continued.)

TOWNS.	Greene.	Hamilton.	Herkimer.	Jefferson.	Kings.	Lewis.	Livingston.	Madison.	Monroe.	Montgomery.	New-York.	Niagara.	Oneida.	Onondaga.	Ontario.	Orange.	Orleans.	Oswego.
Castleton,.......	6	......	......	4	67	......	......	......	2	1	900	1	4	1	9	16	......	......
Northfield,......	2	......	......	......	44	......	......	......	......	......	280	......	......	1	......	15	......	......
Southfield,......	......	......	......	1	45	......	......	......	......	......	634	......	2	......	......	2	......	7
Westfield,.......	3	......	1	......	45	......	......	......	......	......	283	......	3	......	......	16	......	......
Total,.........	11	......	1	5	201	......	......	......	2	1	2,097	1	9	2	9	49	......	7

ROCKLAND COUNTY.—(Continued.)

TOWNS.	Greene.	Hamilton.	Herkimer.	Jefferson.	Kings.	Lewis.	Livingston.	Madison.	Monroe.	Montgomery.	New-York.	Niagara.	Oneida.	Onondaga.	Ontario.	Orange.	Orleans.	Oswego.
Clarkstown,......	......	......	......	......	10	......	1	......	3	......	346	......	1	......	1	17	......	......
Haverstraw,......	4	......	6	......	8	......	......	......	......	......	299	......	1	1	3	289	......	1
Orangetown,......	9	......	2	6	31	2	1	4	5	......	395	......	6	1	1	118	......	......
Ramapo,.........	1	......	......	......	9	......	......	......	......	......	133	......	......	......	4	186	......	......
Total,.........	14	......	8	6	58	2	2	4	8	......	1,173	......	8	2	9	610	......	1

ST. LAWRENCE COUNTY.—(Continued.)

TOWNS.	Greene.	Hamilton.	Herkimer.	Jefferson.	Kings.	Lewis.	Livingston.	Madison.	Monroe.	Montgomery.	New-York.	Niagara.	Oneida.	Onondaga.	Ontario.	Orange.	Orleans.	Oswego.
Brasher,........	......	......	9	9	......	3	......	......	......	......	5	2	3	1	......	......	......	4
Canton,.........	......	......	32	190	3	51	......	7	3	17	30	8	33	2	1	3	......	1
Colton,.........	......	......	1	2	......	1	......	......	......	......	1	......	3	......	......	......	......	3
De Kalb,........	2	......	68	158	......	27	1	3	2	27	2	1	24	2	2	......	......	7
De Peyster,.....	......	......	38	15	......	3	......	......	1	14	......	......	15	3	......	......	......	2
Edwards,........	......	......	33	47	......	3	......	5	......	6	9	......	15	2	1	......	......	......
Fine,...........	1	......	4	56	......	5	......	......	......	9	......	......	5	1	......	......	......	9
Fowler,.........	......	......	63	150	......	26	......	3	......	25	5	......	16	......	......	......	3	7
Gouverneur,.....	......	......	58	250	2	50	2	10	7	21	1	2	50	7	......	2	1	4
Hammond,........	1	......	36	57	......	14	......	1	2	52	2	......	47	4	......	......	2	......
Hermon,.........	......	......	34	230	......	57	......	5	......	15	1	1	30	8	1	3	......	3
Hopkinton,......	......	......	......	11	......	1	......	......	......	......	......	......	1	......	......	......	......	......
Lawrence,.......	......	4	......	9	......	3	......	......	......	......	1	......	3	3	......	......	1	......
Lisbon,.........	......	......	18	25	......	6	......	1	6	3	2	1	10	2	......	1	......	......
Louisville,.....	......	......	......	14	......	3	......	......	3	13	......	......	......	2	2	......	1	......
Macomb,.........	1	......	23	65	......	12	2	5	1	23	......	......	6	2	1	......	......	6
Madrid,.........	1	......	10	21	2	8	......	......	3	2	4	1	2	11	......	1	2	4
Massena,........	......	......	4	12	......	1	......	1	......	1	3	1	3	......	1	2	......	......
Morristown,.....	2	......	98	42	1	10	......	......	1	170	3	......	27	2	1	1	......	......
Norfolk,........	......	......	1	......	......	5	......	......	1	1	10	......	5	1	......	......	......	......
Oswegatchie,....	6	......	57	102	1	26	3	8	17	39	38	2	58	12	9	4	1	22
Parishville,....	3	......	7	18	......	1	1	1	1	2	......	......	1	1	......	......	1	5
Pierrepont,.....	2	......	......	31	......	11	......	1	1	10	1	1	2	......	......	......	......	3
Pitcairn,.......	......	......	36	77	......	15	......	7	1	4	......	1	2	......	......	......	......	2
Potsdam,........	1	......	56	58	1	11	2	3	1	2	34	1	32	5	2	......	3	12
Rossie,.........	......	......	28	107	1	20	......	......	......	13	3	......	18	3	......	......	......	4
Russell,........	......	......	23	254	......	18	......	3	1	20	1	......	29	6	1	2	......	17
Stockholm,......	......	......	22	7	......	10	......	1	3	2	......	......	9	1	......	2	2	1
Total,.........	20	4	759	2,017	11	401	11	65	55	491	156	22	449	81	22	21	17	116

SARATOGA COUNTY.—(Continued.)

TOWNS.	Greene.	Hamilton.	Herkimer.	Jefferson.	Kings.	Lewis.	Livingston.	Madison.	Monroe.	Montgomery.	New-York.	Niagara.	Oneida.	Onondaga.	Ontario.	Orange.	Orleans.	Oswego.
Ballston,.......	4	1	1	......	2	3	2	1	2	12	10	1	1	2	......	3	......	1
Charlton,.......	......	......	......	......	......	2	......	......	......	35	6	......	......	......	1	......	......	......
Clifton Park,....	4	......	1	2	1	......	......	1	1	38	......	......	4	1	3	3	......	1
Corinth,........	......	......	2	4	......	3	......	2	......	16	7	1	4	......	1	1	......	2
Day,............	3	1	1	1	......	......	......	2	......	......	......	......	......	......	......	......	......	......
Edinburgh,......	......	14	4	5	......	......	......	......	......	23	5	......	1	1	4	......	......	......
Galway,.........	4	7	8	11	......	1	1	7	5	52	5	......	5	4	......	3	......	1
Greenfield,......	9	2	4	8	2	1	1	......	2	5	9	......	23	1	1	6	......	......
Hadley,.........	17	......	......	......	......	......	......	......	......	12	......	......	......	2	......	......	......	1
Halfmoon,.......	4	......	7	2	15	2	3	......	2	8	......	......	1	1	......	......	......	2
Malta,..........	1	2	3	......	9	......	3	......	......	4	12	......	2	2	1	4	......	......
Milton,.........	8	4	16	4	7	2	5	1	7	32	10	......	17	6	......	16	......	3
Moreau,.........	2	1	2	3	......	1	......	1	......	3	14	2	3	1	......	......	......	3
Northumberland,.	......	1	......	1	......	......	1	1	......	1	4	2	2	1	1	......	......	1
Providence,......	1	......	6	3	......	......	......	......	......	2	......	......	......	3	......	......	......	......
Saratoga,........	1	......	3	3	1	1	......	......	......	3	29	......	5	7	2	3	......	......
Saratoga Springs,	24	16	12	9	17	2	1	8	19	61	112	1	23	17	4	4	1	4

(Continued on page 141.)

RENSSELAER COUNTY.—(CONTINUED.)

TOWNS.	Otsego.	Putnam.	Queens.	Rensselaer.	Richmond.	Rockland.	St. Lawrence.	Saratoga.	Schenectady.	Schoharie.	Schuyler.	Seneca.	Steuben.	Suffolk.	Sullivan.	Tioga.	Tompkins.	Ulster.
	COUNTIES OF NEW-YORK.																	
Troy city:																		
1st ward,	2	2	6	1,765	3	....	2	48	13	5	....	1	1	2	....	....	....	6
2d ward,	8	6	6	1,696	....	....	3	68	18	9	....	1	3	2	....	....	....	5
3d ward,	....	3	1	977	....	....	1	63	9	9	....	2	1	2	1	....	....	3
4th ward,	1	....	3	1,595	1	2	5	123	20	5	....	....	....	7	....	....	1	5
5th ward,	4	1	....	1,133	....	....	5	28	4	5	....	....	....	....	....	....	....	1
6th ward,	....	....	7	1,228	....	....	....	7	3	1	....	....	....	....	....	1	....	17
7th ward,	7	2	2	1,467	....	....	....	71	10	5	....	....	1	1	....	1	2	7
8th ward,	5	1	....	1,341	....	1	2	36	7	3	....	3	1	....	6	....	1	6
9th ward,	7	....	....	1,030	....	1	1	19	12	....	....	....	....	....	....	....	....	2
10th ward,	1	....	....	1,047	....	....	1	54	3	5	....	....	....	2	1	....	....	3
Total Troy, ...	35	15	25	13,279	4	4	20	517	99	47	....	7	7	16	8	2	4	55
Total,	112	21	41	42,036	4	10	29	1,016	199	181	....	12	11	22	11	3	16	103

RICHMOND COUNTY.—(CONTINUED.)

TOWNS.	Otsego.	Putnam.	Queens.	Rensselaer.	Richmond.	Rockland.	St. Lawrence.	Saratoga.	Schenectady.	Schoharie.	Schuyler.	Seneca.	Steuben.	Suffolk.	Sullivan.	Tioga.	Tompkins.	Ulster.
Castleton,	....	1	5	2	5,089	3	....	4	4	1	....	....	....	2	....	....	2	6
Northfield,	....	4	10	....	2,645	1	4	....	....	....	....	....	....	1	....	1	....	2
Southfield,	....	2	11	....	1,494	....	....	2	....	....	....	3	....	4	....	....	....	....
Westfield,	1	....	27	....	2,156	9	....	1	....	....	....	....	....	....	....	....	....	3
Total,	1	7	53	2	11,384	13	4	7	4	1	....	3	....	7	....	1	2	11

ROCKLAND COUNTY.—(CONTINUED.)

TOWNS.	Otsego.	Putnam.	Queens.	Rensselaer.	Richmond.	Rockland.	St. Lawrence.	Saratoga.	Schenectady.	Schoharie.	Schuyler.	Seneca.	Steuben.	Suffolk.	Sullivan.	Tioga.	Tompkins.	Ulster.
Clarkstown,	....	2	1	3	....	2,285	....	1	....	1	....	....	....	5	....	1	28	....
Haverstraw,	2	33	6	2	2	3,372	....	....	....	1	....	....	....	3	7	....	4	41
Orangetown,	4	9	7	7	1	3,004	....	4	....	7	....	....	....	1	2	1	2	16
Ramapo,	....	3	....	....	....	2,236	....	5	....	1	....	....	....	1	5	....	....	13
Total,	6	47	14	12	3	10,897	....	10	....	10	....	....	....	10	14	2	34	70

ST. LAWRENCE COUNTY.—(CONTINUED.)

TOWNS.	Otsego.	Putnam.	Queens.	Rensselaer.	Richmond.	Rockland.	St. Lawrence.	Saratoga.	Schenectady.	Schoharie.	Schuyler.	Seneca.	Steuben.	Suffolk.	Sullivan.	Tioga.	Tompkins.	Ulster.
Brasher,	2	....	....	1	....	....	1,527	1	....	....	....	....	....	....	....	....	....	....
Canton,	9	....	2	4	....	....	2,747	8	3	5	....	1	....	....	....	....	1	....
Colton,	2	....	4	....	....	....	440	3	....	....	....	....	....	....	....	....	1	....
De Kalb,	14	....	1	11	....	....	1,446	9	1	3	....	....	....	....	2	....	....	1
De Peyster,	7	....	....	14	....	....	659	2	....	2	....	....	....	....	....	....	....	....
Edwards,	1	....	....	5	....	....	770	10	1	1	....	....	1	....	....	....	....	....
Fine,	1	....	....	1	....	....	141	2	....	....	....	....	....	....	....	....	....	....
Fowler,	1	....	....	4	....	....	901	35	....	1	....	....	....	....	....	....	....	....
Gouverneur,	11	....	1	5	....	....	1,441	14	3	3	....	....	....	....	....	....	....	....
Hammond,	9	....	2	6	....	....	1,022	14	3	1	....	....	....	....	....	....	....	....
Hermon,	12	....	1	13	....	....	870	9	....	1	....	....	....	2	....	....	1	....
Hopkinton,	....	....	1	2	....	....	819	3	....	....	....	....	....	....	....	....	....	....
Lawrence,	3	....	....	2	....	....	970	1	....	1	....	....	....	....	....	....	1	....
Lisbon,	4	....	....	4	....	....	2,953	8	7	3	....	....	....	1	....	....	....	....
Louisville,	....	....	....	7	....	....	1,199	1	....	2	....	....	....	....	....	....	....	....
Macomb,	11	....	....	8	....	....	870	5	2	1	....	1	....	....	....	....	....	1
Madrid,	3	3	1	10	....	....	2,794	9	4	5	....	....	....	....	....	1	....	....
Massena,	....	....	....	3	....	....	1,629	1	1	....	....	....	....	....	....	....	....	2
Morristown,	20	....	....	18	....	....	1,114	20	8	5	....	1	1	....	....	....	....	....
Norfolk,	2	....	....	....	....	....	872	....	....	....	....	....	....	2	....	....	....	....
Oswegatchie,	11	....	11	29	....	....	4,364	17	14	3	....	2	5	1	....	....	....	2
Parishville,	....	....	....	3	....	....	1,062	1	....	3	....	....	....	1	....	....	....	....
Pierrepont,	1	....	....	1	....	....	882	4	....	....	....	....	....	....	....	....	....	....
Pitcairn,	3	....	....	....	....	....	251	6	....	....	....	....	....	....	....	....	....	....
Potsdam,	....	....	....	7	....	....	3,161	11	....	....	....	....	....	....	....	1	....	....
Rossie,	1	....	....	2	....	....	785	2	....	1	....	....	....	....	1	....	....	....
Russell,	6	....	....	....	....	....	1,118	6	1	....	....	....	....	1	....	....	....	....
Stockholm,	2	....	....	2	....	....	1,919	2	....	1	....	....	4	....	....	....	....	....
Total,	136	3	24	157	....	....	38,726	204	48	42	....	5	11	8	3	2	4	6

SARATOGA COUNTY.—(CONTINUED.)

TOWNS.	Otsego.	Putnam.	Queens.	Rensselaer.	Richmond.	Rockland.	St. Lawrence.	Saratoga.	Schenectady.	Schoharie.	Schuyler.	Seneca.	Steuben.	Suffolk.	Sullivan.	Tioga.	Tompkins.	Ulster.
Ballston,	3	5	1	76	....	....	1	1,230	80	12	....	1	....	4	....	1	....	3
Charlton,	....	1	....	36	....	....	....	1,109	63	17	....	....	....	....	....	....	....	....
Clifton Park,	14	....	3	212	....	....	....	1,782	73	4	....	3	....	....	....	....	....	3
Corinth,	1	....	....	5	....	....	....	951	9	1	....	2	....	....	....	....	....	....
Day,	....	....	....	17	....	2	1	784	7	....	....	....	....	....	....	....	....	....
Edinburgh,	4	....	....	15	....	....	1	878	11	6	....	....	....	....	....	....	....	1
Galway,	....	....	....	41	....	....	5	1,402	59	7	....	....	....	....	....	....	....	9
Greenfield,	5	....	2	52	....	....	....	1,963	2	5	....	....	2	2	....	....	....	3
Hadley,	1	....	4	15	....	....	....	526	2	3	....	....	2	....	....	....	....	....
Halfmoon,	2	....	10	254	....	....	....	1,952	10	9	....	....	4	....	....	....	1	....
Malta,	....	....	....	56	....	....	....	802	5	....	....	....	....	....	....	1	....	....
Milton,	10	3	1	172	....	1	1	2,437	71	29	....	....	....	1	....	....	2	15
Moreau,	....	....	....	68	....	....	....	1,003	....	2	....	....	....	....	....	....	....	3
Northumberland,	1	....	....	64	....	....	1	1,014	1	1	....	....	....	....	....	....	....	....
Providence,	....	....	....	15	....	....	....	1,077	8	1	....	....	....	....	....	....	1	....
Saratoga,	5	3	....	191	....	....	....	2,075	....	4	....	1	....	....	....	....	....	1
Saratoga Springs,	12	1	2	248	2	1	4	2,638	58	30	....	4	1	7	3	1	4	7

(Continued on page 142.)

RENSSELAER COUNTY.—(CONTINUED.)

TOWNS.	COUNTIES OF NEW-YORK.							UNITED STATES.										
	Warren.	Washington.	Wayne.	Westchester.	Wyoming.	Yates.	New-York.	Maine.	N. Hampshire.	Vermont.	Massachusetts.	Rhode Island.	Connecticut.	New Jersey.	Pennsylvania.	Delaware.	Maryland.	District of Columbia.
Troy city:																		
1st ward,	5	35	4	8	......	......	2, 288	......	18	75	110	13	49	15	13	......	11	2
2d ward,	9	59	1	8	1	1	2, 309	5	35	109	102	8	66	17	3	......	12	......
3d ward,	12	50	3	3	......	......	1, 370	1	23	96	107	9	70	8	20	......	6	......
4th ward,	11	102	3	13	1	......	2, 313	9	54	164	135	11	55	25	20	......	2	......
5th ward,	......	17	......	2	......	......	1, 402	......	16	50	37	10	14	22	1	......	2	......
6th ward,	......	2	1	......	......	......	1, 346	5	2	12	17	2	10	15	6	......	3	......
7th ward,	9	62	6	4	1	2	1, 970	2	29	107	93	9	45	13	6	......	......	......
8th ward,	6	25	......	1	......	......	1, 711	1	20	56	77	6	36	21	12	......	3	3
9th ward,	14	10	......	1	......	......	1, 253	......	6	22	63	7	17	22	15	......	2	1
10th ward,	2	25	......	11	......	......	1, 370	12	25	72	89	19	33	11	2	......	2	......
Total Troy, ...	68	387	18	51	3	3	17, 332	35	228	763	830	94	395	169	98	......	43	6
Total, ...	117	1, 024	30	115	3	12	51, 667	63	378	1, 623	1, 823	376	790	282	160	......	53	8

RICHMOND COUNTY.—(CONTINUED.)

TOWNS.	Warren.	Washington.	Wayne.	Westchester.	Wyoming.	Yates.	New-York.	Maine.	N. Hampshire.	Vermont.	Massachusetts.	Rhode Island.	Connecticut.	New Jersey.	Pennsylvania.	Delaware.	Maryland.	District of Columbia.
Castleton, ...	......	1	......	29	......	2	6, 216	43	11	14	55	69	38	104	......	......	27	1
Northfield, ...	......	......	......	21	......	......	3, 052	3	4	5	10	3	23	145	11	......	1	......
Southfield, ...	......	5	......	8	......	......	2, 246	15	2	9	62	8	32	109	54	......	26	1
Westfield, ...	......	......	......	5	......	2	2, 580	7	2	4	17	10	22	162	16	......	59	......
Total, ...	......	6	......	63	......	4	14, 094	68	19	32	144	90	115	520	81	......	113	2

ROCKLAND COUNTY.—(CONTINUED.)

TOWNS.	Warren.	Washington.	Wayne.	Westchester.	Wyoming.	Yates.	New-York.	Maine.	N. Hampshire.	Vermont.	Massachusetts.	Rhode Island.	Connecticut.	New Jersey.	Pennsylvania.	Delaware.	Maryland.	District of Columbia.
Clarkstown, ...	......	1	......	22	......	......	2, 771	2	2	1	7	......	23	58	11	......	......	......
Haverstraw, ...	......	1	3	155	......	......	4, 292	3	......	7	23	9	50	119	33	......	5	......
Orangetown, ...	......	6	......	76	......	1	3, 800	11	45	9	90	7	57	424	48	3	......	......
Ramapo, ...	......	1	......	16	......	......	2, 649	......	......	1	13	......	4	420	9	......	3	......
Total, ...	......	9	3	269	......	1	13, 512	16	47	18	133	16	134	1, 021	101	3	8	......

ST. LAWRENCE COUNTY.—(CONTINUED.)

TOWNS.	Warren.	Washington.	Wayne.	Westchester.	Wyoming.	Yates.	New-York.	Maine.	N. Hampshire.	Vermont.	Massachusetts.	Rhode Island.	Connecticut.	New Jersey.	Pennsylvania.	Delaware.	Maryland.	District of Columbia.
Brasher, ...	......	8	......	......	2	......	1, 778	20	30	247	25	1	14	......	9	......	......	......
Canton, ...	5	32	2	......	......	......	3, 462	2	169	665	154	8	63	6	2	......	1	......
Colton, ...	5	12	......	......	......	......	610	3	33	202	26	2	8	1	......	......	......	......
De Kalb, ...	1	15	......	......	......	......	1, 885	5	40	126	138	4	36	7	5	......	......	......
De Peyster, ...	6	12	1	......	......	......	818	3	15	60	24	1	8	......	2	......	......	......
Edwards, ...	2	9	......	......	......	......	937	1	14	50	27	4	9	1	......	......	......	......
Fine, ...	......	5	......	......	......	......	254	......	4	18	13	......	3	......	1	......	......	......
Fowler, ...	......	15	......	2	......	......	1, 287	2	17	82	104	......	12	8	1	......	......	......
Gouverneur, ...	......	67	4	......	......	1	2, 130	5	15	153	96	5	51	1	3	......	......	......
Hammond, ...	1	2	......	......	......	......	1, 297	3	14	44	27	4	12	1	2	......	......	......
Hermon, ...	1	8	......	......	......	......	1,347	......	15	95	48	4	20	1	2	......	......	......
Hopkinton, ...	......	14	......	......	......	......	1, 003	1	60	302	36	2	6	1	......	......	......	......
Lawrence, ...	......	16	......	......	......	......	1, 328	2	86	594	23	4	25	......	......	......	......	......
Lisbon, ...	18	119	......	......	......	......	3, 299	3	12	142	22	3	30	9	4	......	3	......
Louisville, ...	......	6	......	......	......	......	1, 310	......	25	181	29	1	4	1	1	......	......	......
Macomb, ...	1	22	......	......	......	......	1, 086	1	10	45	8	4	4	4	1	......	......	......
Madrid, ...	......	21	1	1	......	......	3, 001	4	28	319	92	5	51	4	7	......	......	1
Massena, ...	3	11	......	1	......	......	1, 790	2	40	260	58	4	21	......	2	......	......	......
Morristown, ...	6	5	......	......	......	......	1, 598	1	17	54	29	11	15	3	1	......	......	......
Norfolk, ...	......	2	......	......	......	......	967	1	60	393	53	1	14	1	1	......	......	......
Oswegatchie, ...	2	62	3	1	......	4	5, 183	11	91	329	139	22	95	13	19	......	8	......
Parishville, ...	......	4	......	......	......	......	1, 249	7	141	435	57	12	35	1	1	......	......	......
Pierrepont, ...	9	23	3	......	......	......	1, 159	2	44	373	51	4	17	......	......	......	......	......
Pitcairn, ...	......	2	......	......	......	......	418	1	16	53	10	5	5	......	1	......	......	......
Potsdam, ...	12	12	......	1	1	......	3, 821	158	165	1, 063	194	8	82	15	3	......	......	......
Rossie, ...	1	6	......	1	......	......	1, 017	......	9	45	16	2	38	2	6	......	......	......
Russell, ...	2	15	......	......	......	......	1, 574	......	17	156	111	6	19	......	......	......	......	......
Stockholm, ...	3	9	......	......	......	......	2, 383	2	139	732	60	5	47	3	1	......	......	......
Total, ...	78	534	14	7	3	5	47, 991	240	1, 326	7, 218	1, 670	132	744	83	75	......	12	1

SARATOGA COUNTY.—(CONTINUED.)

TOWNS.	Warren.	Washington.	Wayne.	Westchester.	Wyoming.	Yates.	New-York.	Maine.	N. Hampshire.	Vermont.	Massachusetts.	Rhode Island.	Connecticut.	New Jersey.	Pennsylvania.	Delaware.	Maryland.	District of Columbia.
Ballston, ...	18	20	1	9	......	......	1, 649	2	19	35	43	2	65	11	1	......	......	......
Charlton, ...	6	23	......	......	......	1	1, 337	1	1	21	11	2	12	8	......	......	......	......
Clifton Park, ...	10	18	5	2	......	......	2, 360	3	4	20	23	2	27	7	1	......	......	......
Corinth, ...	104	30	......	1	......	......	1, 223	11	14	43	35	24	32	......	1	......	......	......
Day, ...	30	15	......	1	......	......	919	......	8	86	18	12	15	......	......	......	1	......
Edinburgh, ...	22	23	......	2	......	......	1, 122	2	6	58	49	17	30	2	1	......	......	......
Galway, ...	11	37	......	16	......	......	1, 935	4	3	38	41	9	43	15	4	......	......	......
Greenfield, ...	42	56	4	6	1	......	2, 340	2	21	54	67	51	62	1	4	......	1	......
Hadley, ...	80	22	......	......	......	......	753	3	17	68	38	2	24	1	3	......	......	......
Halfmoon, ...	17	34	......	3	1	......	2, 539	1	3	50	31	2	20	4	5	......	......	......
Malta, ...	4	24	5	3	......	......	1, 053	......	1	15	17	......	23	6	3	......	......	1
Milton, ...	20	148	3	1	1	......	3, 454	9	31	143	100	19	101	14	4	......	......	......
Moreau, ...	232	188	5	4	......	......	1, 690	......	12	94	40	12	29	5	9	......	2	......
Northumberland,.	54	123	8	4	......	2	1, 374	2	11	32	36	2	29	9	......	......	......	......
Providence, ...	8	10	......	......	1	1	1, 215	......	2	29	33	8	18	3	3	......	......	......
Saratoga, ...	49	287	6	12	......	1	2, 869	6	27	61	87	27	20	7	4	......	......	......
Saratoga Springs,	47	276	9	11	......	......	4, 016	11	77	268	187	7	77	31	20	1	8	1

(Continued on page 143.)

RENSSELAER COUNTY.—(Continued.)

TOWNS.	UNITED STATES.																	
	Virginia.	N. Carolina.	S. Carolina.	Georgia.	Florida.	Alabama.	Mississippi.	Louisiana.	Texas.	Arkansas.	Missouri.	Tennessee.	Kentucky.	Ohio.	Indiana.	Illinois.	Michigan.	Wisconsin
Troy city:																		
1st ward,	2			6	1								2	6				1
2d ward,	6		1	2	1			1					1	8	4		3	
3d ward,	5	1		1									2	3		5	4	
4th ward,													2	6		2	4	
5th ward,														1				
6th ward,	5													1		1		
7th ward,	2	1									2			6		2		1
8th ward,	2		1								1				1	1		4
9th ward,	4												1	1			1	1
10th ward,	3				1						1						2	
Total Troy, ...	29	2	2	9	3			1			4		8	32	5	11	14	7
Total, ...	36	2	10	19	4		3	1	1	1	6	2	10	52	7	20	25	18

RICHMOND COUNTY.—(Continued.)

TOWNS.	Virginia.	N. Carolina.	S. Carolina.	Georgia.	Florida.	Alabama.	Mississippi.	Louisiana.	Texas.	Arkansas.	Missouri.	Tennessee.	Kentucky.	Ohio.	Indiana.	Illinois.	Michigan.	Wisconsin
Castleton, ...	30	4	9	1	1	1	1	12		1	1			3		1	4	1
Northfield, ...	22		3					3										
Southfield, ...	17	1	3					3			3		3	1				1
Westfield, ...	20	1	4		1									5			2	
Total, ...	89	6	19	1	2	1	1	18		1	4		3	9		1	6	2

ROCKLAND COUNTY.—(Continued.)

TOWNS.	Virginia.	N. Carolina.	S. Carolina.	Georgia.	Florida.	Alabama.	Mississippi.	Louisiana.	Texas.	Arkansas.	Missouri.	Tennessee.	Kentucky.	Ohio.	Indiana.	Illinois.	Michigan.	Wisconsin
Clarkstown, ...	1																	
Haverstraw, ...	4		1												2			
Orangetown, ...	2		1					1						2	1	4		
Ramapo, ...					1								1					
Total, ...	7		2		1			1					1	2	3	4		

ST. LAWRENCE COUNTY.—(Continued.)

TOWNS.	Virginia.	N. Carolina.	S. Carolina.	Georgia.	Florida.	Alabama.	Mississippi.	Louisiana.	Texas.	Arkansas.	Missouri.	Tennessee.	Kentucky.	Ohio.	Indiana.	Illinois.	Michigan.	Wisconsin
Brasher, ...																2		
Canton, ...						1								5			1	7
Colton, ...	1													1				
De Kalb, ...														8	1			
De Peyster, ...														1				1
Edwards, ...															1			
Fine, ...														1				
Fowler, ...														5			2	
Gouverneur, ...														3		1	3	3
Hammond, ...																	1	2
Hermon, ...															1		2	
Hopkinton, ...														1			2	
Lawrence, ...														2			1	1
Lisbon, ...																2	3	
Louisville, ...																	2	1
Macomb, ...														4		1		
Madrid, ...								1						6	1		1	
Massena, ...																		1
Morristown, ...														2		1		
Norfolk, ...														1			1	1
Oswegatchie, ...	2			1	1			1			1		1	19	2	4	3	3
Parishville, ...														3		1		2
Pierrepont, ...													1	8			1	
Pitcairn, ...																		
Potsdam, ...	2							1	1					10		3	1	1
Rossie, ...														1			1	
Russell, ...																		
Stockholm, ...														3		2		3
Total, ...	5			1	1	1		3	1		1		2	84	6	17	25	26

SARATOGA COUNTY.—(Continued.)

TOWNS.	Virginia.	N. Carolina.	S. Carolina.	Georgia.	Florida.	Alabama.	Mississippi.	Louisiana.	Texas.	Arkansas.	Missouri.	Tennessee.	Kentucky.	Ohio.	Indiana.	Illinois.	Michigan.	Wisconsin
Ballston, ...					1									1		2	3	
Charlton, ...																		
Clifton Park, ...	1													2				
Corinth, ...														4	1			
Day, ...														1			2	
Edinburgh, ...																		
Galway, ...	1													2	1	1	3	2
Greenfield, ...																		
Hadley, ...														1	1		4	
Half Moon, ...		1												2			2	1
Malta, ...																	1	4
Milton, ...													1	2		2	5	
Moreau, ...								2						1		2	2	
Northumberland, .	1													1				
Providence, ...	1																	
Saratoga, ...								4						2				2
Saratoga Springs, .	10		3	2		1		5			3		3	10		8	2	2

(Continued on page 144.)

RENSSELAER COUNTY.—(Continued.)

TOWNS.	U. STATES. Iowa.	California.	Territories.	Total United States.	FOREIGN COUNTRIES. Canada.	N. Brunswick.	Nova Scotia.	N. Foundland.	West Indies.	Mexico.	S. America.	England.	Scotland.	Ireland.	Wales.	France.	Belgium.	Holland.
Troy city:																		
1st ward,				2,612	72	1	1		2		1	79	19	1,239	3	5	1	
2d ward,				2,693	66							166	44	968	1	6		4
3d ward,				1,731	26							48	11	522	2	4		
4th ward,				2,802	92		2	1	2			115	29	932			1	
5th ward,				1,555	33							218	118	358		6		15
6th ward,				1,425	126		4		1			125	97	759	18	9	3	1
7th ward,				2,288	123		1					59	41	1,094	3	2		2
8th ward,				1,956	84	2	1	1				100	36	1,638		4	2	2
9th ward,				1,416	313	1						127	62	1,299	9	21		3
10th ward,				1,642	88							81	22	482	3	1		
Total Troy,				20,120	1,023	4	9	2	5		1	1,118	479	9,291	39	58	7	27
Total,	7			57,447	1,377	7	18	2	6		3	2,006	777	14,109	45	91	7	52

RICHMOND COUNTY.—(Continued.)

TOWNS.	Iowa.	California.	Territories.	Total United States.	Canada.	N. Brunswick.	Nova Scotia.	N. Foundland.	West Indies.	Mexico.	S. America.	England.	Scotland.	Ireland.	Wales.	France.	Belgium.	Holland.
Castleton,				6,648		1	2		6	3	6	611	89	673	4	41	2	10
Northfield,				3,285	6		4		6			121	10	549	4	10	4	5
Southfield,				2,596	13	4	6		14		1	208	91	1,540	18	37		
Westfield,				2,912	5				1			74	23	382	5	9		4
Total,				15,441	24	5	12		27	3	7	1,014	213	3,144	31	97	6	19

ROCKLAND COUNTY.—(Continued.)

TOWNS.	Iowa.	California.	Territories.	Total United States.	Canada.	N. Brunswick.	Nova Scotia.	N. Foundland.	West Indies.	Mexico.	S. America.	England.	Scotland.	Ireland.	Wales.	France.	Belgium.	Holland.
Clarkstown,				2,876	2	1						57	37	243		7	2	5
Haverstraw,				4,548	14							145	40	1,371	26	5		
Orangetown,				4,505	6		10					97	29	934	5	5	2	6
Ramapo,				3,101	2		2					50	4	142	3	1		9
Total,				15,030	24	1	12					349	110	2,690	34	18	4	20

ST. LAWRENCE COUNTY.—(Continued.)

TOWNS.	Iowa.	California.	Territories.	Total United States.	Canada.	N. Brunswick.	Nova Scotia.	N. Foundland.	West Indies.	Mexico.	S. America.	England.	Scotland.	Ireland.	Wales.	France.	Belgium.	Holland.
Brasher,				2,126	367			1				16	11	442	3			
Canton,				4,546	233							71	14	41		43		
Colton,				887	90							8	4	47		4		
De Kalb,				2,255	120							77	4	186	20	1		
De Peyster,				933	39							103	4	81	2			
Edwards,				1,044	13							23	48	37		1		1
Fine,				294	2							9	3	8				
Fowler,				1,520	23							16	6	23		17		
Gouverneur,				2,469	160							53	82	63	24			
Hammond,				1,407	167		1					12	182	92	1	2		
Hermon,				1,535	35							35	8	18	6			
Hopkinton,				1,414	98							8	1	31		1		
Lawrence,				2,066	99							7	7	177				1
Lisbon,				3,532	295	5						126	93	1,045				
Louisville,				1,555	246		1					41	56	219				
Macomb,				1,168	125							86	17	69				
Madrid,				3,521	367	4	2					159	252	549		2		
Massena,				2,178	375							4	6	121				
Morristown,				1,732	132							90	43	106	1			
Norfolk,				1,494	149							19	15	97	2	2		
Oswegatchie,				5,960	1,647	11	3		1			385	133	1,790		9	1	
Parishville,				1,944	110		1					6		53				
Pierrepont,				1,660	93							6	2	60	5			
Pitcairn,				509	5							5	2	7				
Potsdam,				5,528	508	19	3		1			61	58	405		14		
Rossie,				1,137	87							34	102	117		1		
Russell,				1,883	72							42	13	62				
Stockholm,				3,380	200		1					21	2	172				
Total,				59,677	5,857	39	12	1	2			1,523	1,168	6,118	64	97	1	2

SARATOGA COUNTY.—(Continued.)

TOWNS.	Iowa.	California.	Territories.	Total United States.	Canada.	N. Brunswick.	Nova Scotia.	N. Foundland.	West Indies.	Mexico.	S. America.	England.	Scotland.	Ireland.	Wales.	France.	Belgium.	Holland.
Ballston,				1,834	7							63	7	235		1		
Charlton,				1,393								105	37	112				2
Clifton Park,				2,450	5		1				1	44	6	309		1		1
Corinth,				1,388	5							10		117		1		
Day,				1,062								2	1	6				4
Edinburgh,				1,287								2	1	25				
Galway,				2,102	4							100	37	172	3	2		1
Greenfield,				2,603	17							39	6	168	1	3		
Hadley,				915	3							10	3	231				
Halfmoon,				2,661	14	1	1					24	3	520		4		
Malta,				1,124	1							17	1	84				
Milton,				3,885	65				2			167	40	449	1	2		3
Moreau,				1,900	70	1						36	5	147		4		
Northumberland,				1,497	12				1			21	2	90				
Providence,				1,312	3							15	4	22		2		
Saratoga,				3,116	34							56	37	577				
Saratoga Springs,		1		4,754	145		2		3			144	32	1,120	4	10		2

(Continued on page 145.)

RENSSELAER COUNTY.—(CONTINUED.)

TOWNS.	FOREIGN COUNTRIES.																		
	Germany.	Prussia.	Austria.	Switzerland.	Italy.	Spain.	Portugal.	Poland.	Norway.	Sweden.	Russia.	Denmark.	East Indies.	Africa.	Turkey and Greece.	Islands.	Asia.	At Sea.	Unknown.
Troy city:																			
1st ward,	175	7		6	1			1											7
2d ward,	278	10		2				3		2		1							13
3d ward,	30			1	2														17
4th ward,	44	1						1				1					1		98
5th ward,	63																		9
6th ward,	26				1													1	3
7th ward,	53			2	2														30
8th ward,	40	1				1		1										3	4
9th ward,	63											2						5	18
10th ward,	48			1	1													2	4
Total Troy,	820	19		12	7	1		6		2		4					1	11	203
Total,	2, 826	27	2	41	10	1		7		2		5	1				6	17	342

RICHMOND COUNTY.—(CONTINUED.)

TOWNS.	Germany.	Prussia.	Austria.	Switzerland.	Italy.	Spain.	Portugal.	Poland.	Norway.	Sweden.	Russia.	Denmark.	East Indies.	Africa.	Turkey and Greece.	Islands.	Asia.	At Sea.	Unknown.
Castleton,	6	18	1	16	18	2	2	2	3	15	2	13	2		1		1	2	52
Northfield,	169		1	5															8
Southfield,	882	2		3	2		2		5	10	4	3	2				3	1	2
Westfield,	80				1					1									4
Total,	1, 137	20	2	24	21	2	4	2	8	26	6	16	4		1		4	3	66

ROCKLAND COUNTY.—(CONTINUED.)

TOWNS.	Germany.	Prussia.	Austria.	Switzerland.	Italy.	Spain.	Portugal.	Poland.	Norway.	Sweden.	Russia.	Denmark.	East Indies.	Africa.	Turkey and Greece.	Islands.	Asia.	At Sea.	Unknown.
Clarkstown,	251	10									3						1		17
Haverstraw,	570	1		15	1						1							1	9
Orangetown,	223			1				7										2	6
Ramapo,	84			2						1									13
Total,	1, 128	11		18	1			7		1	4						1	3	45

ST. LAWRENCE COUNTY.—(CONTINUED.)

TOWNS.	Germany.	Prussia.	Austria.	Switzerland.	Italy.	Spain.	Portugal.	Poland.	Norway.	Sweden.	Russia.	Denmark.	East Indies.	Africa.	Turkey and Greece.	Islands.	Asia.	At Sea.	Unknown.
Brasher,																			2
Canton,	46																		1
Colton,																			
De Kalb,	2																	2	9
De Peyster,																			1
Edwards,	1																	1	11
Fine,																			
Fowler,		9		1														1	4
Gouverneur,																			5
Hammond,	1																		10
Hermon,																			11
Hopkinton,	1																		
Lawrence,																			8
Lisbon,	2		5															2	4
Louisville,																		1	1
Macomb,								1											
Madrid,	2			1														1	2
Massena,																		2	15
Morristown,	1																		6
Norfolk,																			26
Oswegatchie,	30			1	1			1				1						3	83
Parishville,																			
Pierrepont,																			8
Pitcairn,																			3
Potsdam,	2	1						1											30
Rossie,																			2
Russell,	2			4															30
Stockholm,	2																		12
Total,	92	10	5	7	1			3				1						13	284

SARATOGA COUNTY.—(CONTINUED.)

TOWNS.	Germany.	Prussia.	Austria.	Switzerland.	Italy.	Spain.	Portugal.	Poland.	Norway.	Sweden.	Russia.	Denmark.	East Indies.	Africa.	Turkey and Greece.	Islands.	Asia.	At Sea.	Unknown.
Ballston,	31			10			1												12
Charlton,	49																		3
Clifton Park,	68			1	1														29
Corinth,	2																		11
Day,	1																		3
Edinburgh,	2																		1
Galway,	15					1												1	3
Greenfield,	3					1													1
Hadley,	4							2										1	3
Halfmoon,	86																		1
Malta,	3			5															
Milton,	46	4		1				1									3	1	
Moreau,	2																		1
Northumberland,	16	7																	22
Providence,	10																		
Saratoga,	8	3																	1
Saratoga Springs,	55		2	3									1			1			29

(Continued on page 146.)

SARATOGA COUNTY.

TOWNS.	Albany.	Allegany.	Broome.	Cattaraugus.	Cayuga.	Chautauque.	Chemung.	Chenango.	Clinton.	Columbia.	Cortland.	Delaware.	Dutchess.	Erie.	Essex.	Franklin.	Fulton.	Genesee.
	COUNTIES OF NEW-YORK.																	
Stillwater,	79		2		2	2	2	2	2	77		4	89	4	19		5	1
Waterford,	145				5	2	2		13	16		2	42	1	3	1	9	
Wilton,	13	2		2	2			1		26			37		1		3	
Total,	1,049	10	10	10	36	12	5	19	80	545	8	25	775	33	139	14	342	13

SCHENECTADY COUNTY.

TOWNS.	Albany.	Allegany.	Broome.	Cattaraugus.	Cayuga.	Chautauque.	Chemung.	Chenango.	Clinton.	Columbia.	Cortland.	Delaware.	Dutchess.	Erie.	Essex.	Franklin.	Fulton.	Genesee.
Duanesburgh,	265							1	2	34	1	5	71		1	7	5	1
Glenville,	137	1		1	1	1			2	55	1	1	17			1	8	1
Niskayuna,	136									9	1		5					
Princetown,	84								3	12			4				3	
Rotterdam,	134	1								79	2		19			1	1	
Schenectady city:																		
1st ward,	86		1					4	2	12			9				4	1
2d ward,	63		1		5		1	2	3	11			5	1	2		3	1
3d ward,	52				1					12		3	4		1		2	1
4th ward,	133	4	2	1	3			1	1	36	2	4	9	5	2		8	
Total Schenectady	334	4	4	1	9		1	7	6	71	2	7	27	6	5		17	3
Total,	1,090	6	4	2	10	1	1	8	13	260	7	13	143	6	6	9	34	5

SCHOHARIE COUNTY.

TOWNS.	Albany.	Allegany.	Broome.	Cattaraugus.	Cayuga.	Chautauque.	Chemung.	Chenango.	Clinton.	Columbia.	Cortland.	Delaware.	Dutchess.	Erie.	Essex.	Franklin.	Fulton.	Genesee.
Blenheim,	51		2		1					38		23	14		1		1	
Broome,	243							1		91		6	44				2	1
Carlisle,	73		3							26		2	27		2		1	
Cobleskill,	86				3				1	43	1	2	14					
Conesville,	105	1	2		1			1		25		20	28					
Esperance,	96		6					1	1	24			23				4	
Fulton,	250		2		2			1		78		18	20					
Gilboa,	147		4	2				2		37		76	47	1			1	2
Jefferson,	58		3		1					29		99	10					1
Middleburgh,	179		1							45	2	14	36		1			3
Richmondville,	127		1		1	2		1	1	32	2	20	24					
Schoharie,	59				4					19	2	1	9	2			4	
Seward,	59							4		14		2	17		1			
Sharon,	189		2		5			1	1	44		9	37		1			
Summit,	47					1		1	1	43		35	41			1		1
Wright,	346		3		1				1	14		1	21					
Total,	2,115	1	29	2	19	3		13	6	602	7	328	412	3	6	1	13	8

SCHUYLER COUNTY.

TOWNS.	Albany.	Allegany.	Broome.	Cattaraugus.	Cayuga.	Chautauque.	Chemung.	Chenango.	Clinton.	Columbia.	Cortland.	Delaware.	Dutchess.	Erie.	Essex.	Franklin.	Fulton.	Genesee.
Catharines,	20	5	3	1	23	2	252	25	1	6	12	38	22	6			1	1
Cayuta,	8		2		9		65	4		1		7	7					
Dix,	4	6	15	1	28		603	36	1	6	14	25	35	2	1			7
Hector,	33	21	3	5	65	2	83	31	1	36	29	93	119	3	2			7
Orange,	10	8	1		12	2	47	10		18	5	10	30	2			3	2
Reading,	5	4	2		4	2	49	6		10	6	4	26					2
Tyrone,	9	23	1	2	17	1	16	10		7	7	5	35		1			1
Total,	89	67	27	9	158	9	1,115	122	3	84	73	182	274	13	4		4	20

SENECA COUNTY.

TOWNS.	Albany.	Allegany.	Broome.	Cattaraugus.	Cayuga.	Chautauque.	Chemung.	Chenango.	Clinton.	Columbia.	Cortland.	Delaware.	Dutchess.	Erie.	Essex.	Franklin.	Fulton.	Genesee.
Covert,	7	2	12		40		2	6			9	24	39					1
Fayette,	2	2	3		60		1	3		2	3	1	16	5			1	3
Junius,	28			1	7		2	2		18	2	1	24	2		1		
Lodi,	2	1	3	1	10		8				1	11	9	2				
Ovid,	3	4	2		25		18	10		2	4	14	19	1				
Romulus,	1		4		28	3	14	8		1	1	5	15	1				
Seneca Falls,	55	7	5	2	263	2	3	12	5	16	37	7	33	6	2		1	10
Tyre,	4	2	1		49		1	5		7	1		17		2		1	1
Varick,	2	1	3		29		4	2			1	7	2	1		1		1
Waterloo,	35	3	3	6	94		1	10	4	28	5	6	43	4	1		6	7
Total,	139	22	36	10	605	5	54	58	9	74	64	76	217	22	5	2	9	23

STEUBEN COUNTY.

TOWNS.	Albany.	Allegany.	Broome.	Cattaraugus.	Cayuga.	Chautauque.	Chemung.	Chenango.	Clinton.	Columbia.	Cortland.	Delaware.	Dutchess.	Erie.	Essex.	Franklin.	Fulton.	Genesee.
Addison,	16	12	47	3	39	3	85	262	4	8	41	34	15	13	12			9
Avoca,	23	9	2		7	3	1	17	1	8	9	3	10	1			4	2
Bath,	19	30	13	3	31	6	70	50	1	25	32	38	55	12	4		2	6
Bradford,	4	3	1		9		10	7		16	4	15	17	4				
Cameron,	9	7	30		8	2	14	30		8	5	5	16	9				
Campbell,	2	11	3	3	7		63	27		2	5	17	14	4	2		1	2
Canisteo,	2	35	3	1	9	2	17	19		7	11	34	10	1	3			3
Caton,	3	10	11		28		73	82		1	7	12	6		1			3
Cohocton,	8	16	8	2	16	4	2	7		3	10	5	24	3			1	6
Corning,	49	16	99	7	60	9	195	73	2	35	35	55	55	8	7	2	1	15
Dansville,	8	53		6	14		4	8		2	3	2	2					4
Erwin,	3	11	16	2	14		58	41	9	2	8	35	13	2	5	1		2
Fremont,	4	7		5	10		1	8	1	3	4	3	2	1	1		1	1
Greenwood,	6	28			14	1	6	9		1	9	5	6	1				8
Hartsville,	1	65	1	3	13	2	9	3	3	5	20	14	5					

(Continued on page 147.)

SARATOGA COUNTY.—(Continued.)

TOWNS.	Greene.	Hamilton.	Herkimer.	Jefferson.	Kings.	Lewis.	Livingston.	Madison.	Monroe.	Montgomery.	New-York.	Niagara.	Oneida.	Onondaga.	Ontario.	Orange.	Orleans.	Oswego.
	COUNTIES OF NEW-YORK.																	
Stillwater,	5	1	8	1	9			2	5	10			6	1		4		
Waterford,	4		6	2	3		2	5	4	11	31		8	7	1	4		
Wilton,	41	1	4		2			2	1	6	7			1	2			
Total,	132	51	88	59	68	18	19	33	48	334	261	7	105	58	21	51	1	19

SCHENECTADY COUNTY.—(Continued.)

TOWNS.	Greene.	Hamilton.	Herkimer.	Jefferson.	Kings.	Lewis.	Livingston.	Madison.	Monroe.	Montgomery.	New-York.	Niagara.	Oneida.	Onondaga.	Ontario.	Orange.	Orleans.	Oswego.
Duanesburgh,	8		9	1				1	2	229	9	1	13		1	1		
Glenville,	8		2	1	2				3	136	10	1	8	4		7		2
Niskayuna,	4				2					22	9		2			1		
Princetown,				1						17								
Rotterdam,		1	4	1				2		61	9		4	4		2		
Schenectady city:																		
1st ward,	5		4	2	2			1		76	26	1	10	2		2		
2d ward,	3	1	4					2	2	30	19		9	4	2	1		2
3d ward,	9		4	3	1			1	1	34	26		15	1		1		
4th ward,	5		18	1	5	1		8	9	76	38	2	10	2	2	1	1	7
Total Schenectady	22	1	30	6	8	1		12	12	216	109	3	44	9	4	5	1	9
Total,	42	2	45	10	12	1		15	17	681	146	5	71	17	5	16	1	11

SCHOHARIE COUNTY.—(Continued.)

TOWNS.	Greene.	Hamilton.	Herkimer.	Jefferson.	Kings.	Lewis.	Livingston.	Madison.	Monroe.	Montgomery.	New-York.	Niagara.	Oneida.	Onondaga.	Ontario.	Orange.	Orleans.	Oswego.
Blenheim,	42			1					1	4	4							
Broome,	57			4						5	4	2	2			1		
Carlisle,	7		4							133	3		3	1				2
Cobleskill,	15	1	4	2	4					36	2	1	3	1		1		2
Conesville,	189		1	3						2	6		2					
Esperance,	5		2		1		3	2		125	4	1	1	2	1			
Fulton,	36	1	21		2			1		17	2	1	4	1				1
Gilboa,	125	2		3	4				1	4	4		3			6		
Jefferson,	20		1			2				3	4		1	3		2		
Middleburgh,	41		1		1					21	3			1	3	1		
Richmondville,	8		4		7			1	1	21	3	1	2				2	1
Schoharie,	6		37	1				3		214	6	1	11	4	1			4
Seward,	3		6			1		2	3	54	3		4	1	1			3
Sharon,	30		2			1				67	10		3	2		1	2	2
Summit,	21		1	5		1	1	1	2	9	3		1			2		
Wright,	18	1		1						9	2			2		3	1	1
Total,	623	5	84	20	19	5	4	10	8	724	63	7	40	18	6	17	5	16

SCHUYLER COUNTY.—(Continued.)

TOWNS.	Greene.	Hamilton.	Herkimer.	Jefferson.	Kings.	Lewis.	Livingston.	Madison.	Monroe.	Montgomery.	New-York.	Niagara.	Oneida.	Onondaga.	Ontario.	Orange.	Orleans.	Oswego.
Catharines,	12		13	3	3	2	3	6	6	10	29	3	25	20	25	71	1	4
Cayuta,			2				2	5		1	1			1	2	11		
Dix,	9		19	5	1	2	1	7	8	13	23	2	9	12	34	60		
Hector,	26	1	16		2	4	4	7	4	6	24	5	14	20	11	148	1	4
Orange,	2		7		1		3	2	2	90	12		2	5	24	68	1	5
Reading,	9		8	1			2	1	7	1	15		6	4	13	41		5
Tyrone,	6		6	1			5	3		7	4	5	9	5	14	70		1
Total,	64	1	71	10	7	8	20	31	27	128	108	15	65	67	123	469	3	19

SENECA COUNTY.—(Continued.)

TOWNS.	Greene.	Hamilton.	Herkimer.	Jefferson.	Kings.	Lewis.	Livingston.	Madison.	Monroe.	Montgomery.	New-York.	Niagara.	Oneida.	Onondaga.	Ontario.	Orange.	Orleans.	Oswego.
Covert,			2	8	8		2	9		2	1	2	2	6	2	16		1
Fayette,	2		3	1	3	1	16	2	4	9	38		16	11	64	30	1	3
Junius,	9		2				1	2	6	6	9		6	20	64	15		1
Lodi,	1		3		1		17	7		1	2		2			33		
Ovid,	1						4	3	13		28	4	2	4	3	16	3	
Romulus,	1		2				3	4	6	5	3		4	7	12	45		
Seneca Falls,	16	1	33	26	1	9	14	36	38	29	37	14	69	141	70	15		22
Tyre,	4		12	1	1	1	1	9	1	8	3		13	5	33	17	2	1
Varick,	5		1		8		10	2	2	6	1	3	1	1	7	22		
Waterloo,	7		23	8	2	11	3	11	19	19	31	4	62	54	128	28	2	4
Total,	46	1	81	44	24	22	71	85	89	85	153	27	177	249	383	237	8	32

STEUBEN COUNTY.—(Continued.)

TOWNS.	Greene.	Hamilton.	Herkimer.	Jefferson.	Kings.	Lewis.	Livingston.	Madison.	Monroe.	Montgomery.	New-York.	Niagara.	Oneida.	Onondaga.	Ontario.	Orange.	Orleans.	Oswego.
Addison,	6		9	9	3		2	15	8	6	15	1	5	10	9	32	3	8
Avoca,	6		21	2			26	2	5	355	1		5	16	27	8	1	2
Bath,	49		25	4	8		51	17	13	135	36	6	21	20	52	62	11	6
Bradford,	2		2				4	1	2	1	6		6	7	6	35	1	1
Cameron,	2		16	4			8	9	9	39	4	1	7	7	21	11	2	
Campbell,	11		8				4	4	4	13	3	2	5	10	14	17	5	4
Canisteo,	2			4	1		33	10	5	9	1	2	11	9	5	21	8	
Caton,			1	1	1			8	1	2	4	4	9	16	1	30		
Cohocton,	6		19	2			95	6	12	33	5		12	35	117	8	2	9
Corning,	15		18	25	2	3	35	40	43	30	35	1	45	58	50	91	1	25
Dansville,	2		7	1	2	1	147	5	10	18	5		11	3	23	2		3
Erwin,			10	5				7	3	13	8		11	8	7	24	1	3
Fremont,	3		36	13			19	10	4	45			2	1	10	2	1	2
Greenwood,			7		1		12	2		5	6		5	7	13	14		2
Hartsville,	1		2	1			55	10	18	1	1		8	3	11	10		1

(Continued on page 148.)

SARATOGA COUNTY.—(Continued.)

TOWNS.	COUNTIES OF NEW-YORK.																	
	Otsego.	Putnam.	Queens.	Rensselaer.	Richmond.	Rockland.	St. Lawrence.	Saratoga.	Schenectady.	Schoharie.	Schuyler.	Seneca.	Steuben.	Suffolk.	Sullivan.	Tioga.	Tompkins.	Ulster.
Stillwater,	4	.....	10	210	.....	.....	.....	1,575	7	.....	.....	.....	.....	.....	.....	.....	.....	1
Waterford,	3	1	1	260	.....	1	.....	1,357	20	12	.....	1	.....	.....	.....	.....	.....	4
Wilton,	.....	.....	.....	139	.....	.....	3	809	10	16	.....	.....	.....	.....	.....	.....	.....	.....
Total,	65	14	34	2,146	2	5	17	27,364	496	159	.....	12	9	14	3	3	8	50

SCHENECTADY COUNTY.—(Continued.)

TOWNS.	Otsego.	Putnam.	Queens.	Rensselaer.	Richmond.	Rockland.	St. Lawrence.	Saratoga.	Schenectady.	Schoharie.	Schuyler.	Seneca.	Steuben.	Suffolk.	Sullivan.	Tioga.	Tompkins.	Ulster.
Duanesburgh,	21	1	.....	40	1	.....	.....	19	1,841	168	.....	.....	.....	.....	.....	3	.....	1
Glenville,	3	.....	.....	128	.....	.....	.....	183	1,791	13	.....	1	.....	1	.....	.....	.....	3
Niskayuna,	.....	.....	.....	58	.....	.....	.....	34	559	5	.....	.....	.....	.....	.....	.....	.....	5
Princetown,	6	.....	.....	2	.....	.....	.....	4	743	.....	.....	.....	.....	.....	.....	.....	.....	.....
Rotterdam,	1	1	.....	39	.....	.....	.....	13	1,610	21	2	.....	.....	.....	.....	.....	.....	.....
Schenectady city:																		
1st ward,	1	1	.....	24	.....	.....	.....	51	761	4	.....	.....	.....	.....	.....	.....	1	3
2d ward,	2	.....	4	22	.....	.....	.....	49	718	12	.....	1	1	2	1	1	.....	1
3d ward,	4	1	.....	48	.....	.....	2	30	795	4	.....	.....	1	.....	2	.....	.....	2
4th ward,	3	2	.....	52	1	.....	.....	171	1,636	22	.....	1	.....	.....	3	1	.....	4
Total Schenectady	10	4	4	146	1	.....	2	301	3,910	42	.....	2	2	2	6	2	1	10
Total,	41	6	4	413	2	.....	2	554	10,454	249	2	3	2	3	6	5	1	19

SCHOHARIE COUNTY.—(Continued.)

TOWNS.	Otsego.	Putnam.	Queens.	Rensselaer.	Richmond.	Rockland.	St. Lawrence.	Saratoga.	Schenectady.	Schoharie.	Schuyler.	Seneca.	Steuben.	Suffolk.	Sullivan.	Tioga.	Tompkins.	Ulster.
Blenheim,	18	.....	.....	8	.....	.....	.....	1	10	993	.....	.....	.....	1	4	.....	.....	2
Broome,	11	1	.....	1	.....	1	.....	.....	2	1,546	.....	.....	2	.....	1	1	2	3
Carlisle,	14	.....	.....	26	.....	.....	.....	9	30	1,245	.....	.....	1	.....	.....	.....	.....	1
Cobleskill,	25	.....	1	23	.....	.....	3	5	19	1,741	.....	.....	1	.....	.....	.....	.....	6
Conesville,	.....	4	.....	2	.....	.....	.....	2	.....	894	.....	.....	.....	3	.....	.....	.....	17
Esperance,	8	1	.....	5	.....	.....	.....	4	103	771	.....	.....	.....	.....	.....	.....	.....	.....
Fulton,	36	.....	.....	15	.....	.....	.....	12	19	2,175	.....	.....	.....	.....	.....	1	.....	10
Gilboa,	20	.....	1	15	.....	.....	.....	5	6	1,882	.....	1	1	2	2	1	.....	23
Jefferson,	15	.....	1	19	.....	.....	.....	1	.....	1,267	.....	1	.....	10	.....	.....	.....	1
Middleburgh,	25	1	.....	7	.....	1	.....	5	15	2,376	.....	.....	.....	.....	.....	.....	.....	10
Richmondville,	74	.....	1	23	.....	1	.....	6	12	1,498	.....	.....	.....	.....	.....	.....	.....	5
Schoharie,	121	.....	.....	22	.....	.....	1	10	14	2,115	.....	3	1	.....	.....	.....	1	3
Seward,	80	.....	.....	14	.....	.....	.....	3	13	1,552	.....	.....	.....	.....	.....	.....	.....	4
Sharon,	13	.....	2	22	.....	.....	.....	9	45	1,908	.....	.....	1	.....	1	.....	.....	4
Summit,	102	.....	1	53	.....	.....	1	9	6	1,403	.....	.....	.....	1	.....	1	.....	6
Wright,	5	.....	.....	13	.....	.....	.....	2	25	1,084	.....	.....	.....	.....	.....	3	.....	5
Total,	567	7	7	268	.....	3	5	83	319	24,450	.....	5	7	17	8	7	3	100

SCHUYLER COUNTY.—(Continued.)

TOWNS.	Otsego.	Putnam.	Queens.	Rensselaer.	Richmond.	Rockland.	St. Lawrence.	Saratoga.	Schenectady.	Schoharie.	Schuyler.	Seneca.	Steuben.	Suffolk.	Sullivan.	Tioga.	Tompkins.	Ulster.
Catharines,	10	4	1	11	.....	.....	1	6	1	23	1,402	56	51	1	12	37	303	19
Cayuta,	1	1	2	.....	.....	.....	.....	.....	.....	12	251	4	12	.....	2	3	71	5
Dix,	18	8	8	.....	.....	.....	.....	14	5	6	708	59	174	1	7	25	230	23
Hector,	23	58	.....	35	1	5	1	14	1	27	3,091	286	69	10	12	24	97	70
Orange,	40	10	.....	6	2	7	.....	16	5	14	628	40	597	.....	.....	11	71	12
Reading,	6	3	.....	2	2	5	1	11	.....	.....	19	47	672	1	2	9	71	4
Tyrone,	16	9	.....	.....	.....	.....	1	5	2	3	22	66	1,177	3	.....	3	35	8
Total,	114	93	11	54	5	17	4	66	14	85	6,121	558	2,752	16	35	112	878	14

SENECA COUNTY.—(Continued.)

TOWNS.	Otsego.	Putnam.	Queens.	Rensselaer.	Richmond.	Rockland.	St. Lawrence.	Saratoga.	Schenectady.	Schoharie.	Schuyler.	Seneca.	Steuben.	Suffolk.	Sullivan.	Tioga.	Tompkins.	Ulster.
Covert,	1	16	1	6	.....	1	.....	3	.....	2	.....	1,209	12	8	4	.....	202	8
Fayette,	4	.....	8	1	1	1	.....	4	2	5	.....	2,104	8	.....	.....	4	13	6
Junius,	7	6	3	14	.....	21	1	37	.....	3	.....	668	1	.....	.....	.....	5	.....
Lodi,	4	9	.....	1	.....	14	.....	3	.....	3	.....	1,495	6	4	.....	3	32	5
Ovid,	5	2	.....	2	.....	1	.....	5	.....	2	.....	1,333	16	.....	2	6	97	6
Romulus,	8	.....	.....	1	.....	2	.....	3	.....	3	1	1,224	21	.....	.....	4	28	1
Seneca Falls,	18	3	2	15	.....	2	3	39	10	11	.....	1,995	3	2	1	4	50	14
Tyre,	3	1	2	4	.....	17	1	14	.....	13	.....	766	5	.....	1	1	2	27
Varick,	1	1	1	1	.....	3	.....	3	.....	1	.....	1,189	17	.....	.....	7	14	.....
Waterloo,	16	9	.....	22	.....	2	9	43	4	5	2	2,106	18	.....	16	6	21	43
Total,	67	47	17	67	1	64	14	154	16	48	3	14,089	107	14	24	35	464	110

STEUBEN COUNTY.—(Continued.)

TOWNS.	Otsego.	Putnam.	Queens.	Rensselaer.	Richmond.	Rockland.	St. Lawrence.	Saratoga.	Schenectady.	Schoharie.	Schuyler.	Seneca.	Steuben.	Suffolk.	Sullivan.	Tioga.	Tompkins.	Ulster.
Addison,	90	.....	.....	6	.....	.....	2	4	1	12	.....	4	1,443	1	7	20	75	3
Avoca,	20	.....	.....	5	.....	.....	1	14	.....	2	.....	5	823	.....	2	6	16	1
Bath,	75	20	5	19	.....	3	1	24	9	9	.....	42	3,288	4	2	14	109	25
Bradford,	8	5	.....	1	.....	9	.....	12	3	1	.....	21	788	1	1	2	20	6
Cameron,	42	6	.....	8	1	2	.....	7	1	7	.....	15	997	.....	.....	12	42	1
Campbell,	65	4	.....	9	.....	.....	2	15	.....	4	1	17	746	.....	3	14	22	3
Canisteo,	17	.....	.....	6	.....	.....	2	3	4	6	.....	12	1,214	.....	.....	29	56	4
Caton,	65	.....	.....	2	.....	2	.....	9	3	7	.....	11	615	.....	4	12	115	13
Cohocton,	22	2	.....	8	.....	7	1	31	1	8	.....	22	1,045	1	.....	2	8	15
Corning,	226	6	2	19	1	15	1	28	11	30	.....	48	1,993	4	15	51	306	13
Dansville,	10	.....	.....	4	.....	.....	2	14	6	2	.....	4	1,098	5	.....	1	6	6
Erwin,	21	1	.....	3	.....	2	.....	11	4	32	.....	11	733	2	1	22	30	3
Fremont,	22	.....	.....	3	.....	.....	2	15	1	2	.....	5	675	.....	.....	3	9	1
Greenwood,	4	1	1	2	.....	.....	.....	3	2	.....	.....	14	583	.....	2	1	127	7
Hartsville,	1	.....	.....	6	.....	.....	1	4	1	.....	.....	9	522	.....	.....	3	26	4

(Continued on page 149.)

SARATOGA COUNTY.—(CONTINUED.)

TOWNS.	COUNTIES OF NEW-YORK. Warren.	Washington.	Wayne.	Westchester.	Wyoming.	Yates.	New-York.	UNITED STATES. Maine.	N. Hampshire.	Vermont	Massachusetts.	Rhode Island	Connecticut.	New Jersey.	Pennsylvania.	Delaware.	Maryland.	District of Columbia.
Stillwater,	19	104		16			2, 288	2	7	30	55	14	28	8	1		1	
Waterford,	9	46	9	7	2		2, 062	4	12	44	51	4	42	5	13		4	
Wilton,	24	64	2	4			1, 225		2	44	22	11	16	3	1			
Total,	806	1, 548	57	102	6	5	37, 423	63	278	1, 233	984	227	713	140	78	1	17	2

SCHENECTADY COUNTY.—(CONTINUED.)

TOWNS.	Warren.	Washington.	Wayne.	Westchester.	Wyoming.	Yates.	New-York.	Maine.	N. Hampshire.	Vermont	Massachusetts.	Rhode Island	Connecticut.	New Jersey.	Pennsylvania.	Delaware.	Maryland.	District of Columbia.
Duanesburgh,	1	10	7	13		1	2, 795	3	2	8	28	6	22	7	4		1	
Glenville,		3	3	3			2, 543	1	1	16	21	8	12	14	3			
Niskayuna,			1	4			857	1	1	2	4	3	5	5			1	
Princetown,							879			2								
Rotterdam,	1	2		2			2, 017	1		7	9	2	10	4	4			
Schenectady city,																		
1st ward,	3	4	2	1			1, 106	2	4	6	17	5	14	1	2		2	2
2d ward,	4	9		4	1		1, 009		2	12	28	2	22	12	15		1	
3d ward,		4		4			1, 069	5	3	10	16	2	14	5	13		5	
4th ward,	3	16	3	6			2, 321	1	6	14	43	7	28	10	9		3	3
Total Schenectady	10	33	5	15	1		5, 505	8	15	42	104	16	78	28	39		11	5
Total,	12	48	16	37	1	1	14, 596	14	19	77	166	35	127	58	50		13	5

SCHOHARIE COUNTY.—(CONTINUED.)

TOWNS.	Warren.	Washington.	Wayne.	Westchester.	Wyoming.	Yates.	New-York.	Maine.	N. Hampshire.	Vermont	Massachusetts.	Rhode Island	Connecticut.	New Jersey.	Pennsylvania.	Delaware.	Maryland.	District of Columbia.
Blenheim,		2					1, 222		2		9	12	10	4	3			
Broome,		1		1		2	2, 038		4	7	10	3	27	1	3			
Carlisle,		5					1, 618		1	5	6	7	14	9				
Cobleskill,		3		4	1		2, 054		1	6	5	2	17		1			
Conesville,				3			1, 311	1	1	1	13	1	45	1	6			
Esperance,	2	5	6	2			1, 209		1	3	20	11	18	6	2			
Fulton,	1	2		1			2, 730		2	11	8	4	17	2	2			
Gilboa,		4		6			2, 440	1	7	10	29	11	28	11	1			
Jefferson,		2					1, 554			8	24	3	61	2	3		1	
Middleburgh,		2		2			2, 797		4	8	14	5	20	7	4			
Richmondville,		1		3			1, 886	1	3	9	16	1	21	1	3			
Schoharie,	5	3		1			2, 688	5	3	20	7	5	13	5				
Seward,		1	2				1, 847	1	1	3	6	3	12	2				
Sharon,	1	3		4			2, 422		2	12	9	7	14	14	12			
Summit,		2	3	6			1, 812		2	1	6		12	3				
Wright,		4		1			1, 567	1	1	9	3	4	15		3			
Total,	9	40	11	34	1	2	31, 195	10	35	113	185	79	344	68	43		1	

SCHUYLER COUNTY.—(CONTINUED.)

TOWNS.	Warren.	Washington.	Wayne.	Westchester.	Wyoming.	Yates.	New-York.	Maine.	N. Hampshire.	Vermont	Massachusetts.	Rhode Island	Connecticut.	New Jersey.	Pennsylvania.	Delaware.	Maryland.	District of Columbia.
Catharines,		8	6	20		49	2, 675	1	3	17	44	7	235	129	81		2	1
Cayuta,				1		2	495		1	4	4		22	17	24			
Dix,	2	8	3	16	1	93	2, 398	1	4	27	37	8	86	112	55		1	
Hector,		21	4	55	2	44	4, 780		15	24	45	14	106	258	102	1	1	
Orange,	5	12	4	6		150	2, 020	1	7	34	55	5	43	96	42		4	
Reading,	1	16	2	2		66	1, 175		1	13	16	4	39	53	40			
Tyrone,	4	10	5	8		188	1, 836		14	9	35	6	30	110	19			
Total,	12	75	24	108	3	502	15, 379	3	45	128	236	44	561	775	363	1	8	1

SENECA COUNTY.—(CONTINUED.)

TOWNS.	Warren.	Washington.	Wayne.	Westchester.	Wyoming.	Yates.	New-York.	Maine.	N. Hampshire.	Vermont	Massachusetts.	Rhode Island	Connecticut.	New Jersey.	Pennsylvania.	Delaware.	Maryland.	District of Columbia.
Covert,		1		9		11	1, 697		2	8		9	59	146	31		1	
Fayette,		3	15	1	1	8	2, 495	1	2	12	11	1	8	116	395		2	
Junius,	3	23	105	13		7	1, 146	3	1	12	25	8	20	37	9		3	
Lodi,			1	4		19	1, 718			3	7	1	28	112	11		4	
Ovid,		4	3	3		9	1, 679	1	3	8	22	2	24	177	41		3	
Romulus,		2	3		3	16	1, 493			3	4		18	136	38			
Seneca Falls,	3	22	70	13	9	21	3, 347	1	11	52	83	8	112	133	187			
Tyre,		22	49	32		1	1, 164	1	2	18	9	8	19	107	18		1	
Varick,			2	1		5	1, 369	1	2	3	3	1	12	148	128			
Waterloo,	6	26	59	18	2	40	3, 145	3	27	51	80	13	71	87	99		1	
Total,	12	103	307	94	15	137	19, 253	11	50	170	244	51	371	1, 199	957		15	

STEUBEN COUNTY.—(CONTINUED.)

TOWNS.	Warren.	Washington.	Wayne.	Westchester.	Wyoming.	Yates.	New-York.	Maine.	N. Hampshire.	Vermont	Massachusetts.	Rhode Island	Connecticut.	New Jersey.	Pennsylvania.	Delaware.	Maryland.	District of Columbia.
Addison,	4	6	7	1	1	30	2, 461	10	12	39	52	16	67	42	192		4	
Avoca,	2	21	5		4	18	1, 522		3	13	25	10	28	23	33		1	
Bath,	2	20	12	11	6	190	4, 803	20	20	74	57	15	109	185	146		7	1
Bradford,	3	2	4	1		101	1, 153		4	4	8	1	18	48	28		2	
Cameron,		3	4	1	3	85	1, 520		18	20	19	6	36	53	48		1	
Campbell,		7	13	3		50	1, 245	6	4	36	26	4	37	29	43			
Canisteo,		6	4	3	1	25	1, 670	4	26	17	30	4	28	26	68			
Caton,		2	2	2		5	1, 184	28	3	25	23	21	43	21	152		1	
Cohocton,		32	21	16	3	48	1, 769	8	9	23	32	5	45	28	35		1	
Corning,	10	15	21	16	1	41	4, 113	16	24	59	74	33	110	95	376		2	
Dansville,		45	8	1	4	4	1, 575	2	22	51	22	4	35	21	115		1	
Erwin,	4	9	11	1	1	37	1, 262	2	5	22	26	4	31	31	120		1	
Fremont,		47		5	1	12	1, 003	4	3	19	14	4	18	10	9			
Greenwood,	1	4	6	4	1	6	937	2	9	13	17	1	27	48	16			
Hartsville,	1	5	4	2		11	866	1	16	33	52	11	16	16	42			

(Continued on page 150.)

SARATOGA COUNTY.—(CONTINUED.)

TOWNS.	UNITED STATES.																	
	Virginia.	N. Carolina.	S. Carolina.	Georgia.	Florida.	Alabama.	Mississippi.	Louisiana.	Texas.	Arkansas.	Missouri.	Tennessee.	Kentucky.	Ohio.	Indiana.	Illinois.	Michigan.	Wisconsin.
Stillwater,	2		1	1				4					1	1				
Waterford,			1								1		1	4	1	2		
Wilton,													1					
Total,	16	1	5	3	1	1		15			4		7	34	4	17	24	11

SCHENECTADY COUNTY.—(CONTINUED.)

TOWNS.	Virginia.	N. Carolina.	S. Carolina.	Georgia.	Florida.	Alabama.	Mississippi.	Louisiana.	Texas.	Arkansas.	Missouri.	Tennessee.	Kentucky.	Ohio.	Indiana.	Illinois.	Michigan.	Wisconsin.
Duanesburgh,	2	1												6	1	2	3	
Glenville,	2							1			2			1				1
Niskayuna,						1												
Princetown,																		
Rotterdam,														2				
Schenectady city:																		
1st ward,	1													2				1
2d ward,	1					1								1		1	1	
3d ward,														1		1		
4th ward,	3	1												4		7	1	2
Total Schenectady	5	1				1								8		9	2	3
Total,	9	2				2		1			2			17	1	11	5	4

SCHOHARIE COUNTY.—(CONTINUED.)

TOWNS.	Virginia.	N. Carolina.	S. Carolina.	Georgia.	Florida.	Alabama.	Mississippi.	Louisiana.	Texas.	Arkansas.	Missouri.	Tennessee.	Kentucky.	Ohio.	Indiana.	Illinois.	Michigan.	Wisconsin.
Blenheim,	1							1										
Broome,																1	4	1
Carlisle,			2															1
Cobleskill,																		
Conesville,																	2	
Esperance,	1														1			2
Fulton,																		
Gilboa,	1						1											
Jefferson,				1				1						2				
Middleburgh,														1				
Richmondville,														2	1			3
Schoharie,														1			1	2
Seward,																		
Sharon,	1																5	2
Summit,																		1
Wright,																		1
Total,	4		2	1			1	2						6	2	1	12	13

SCHUYLER COUNTY.—(CONTINUED.)

TOWNS.	Virginia.	N. Carolina.	S. Carolina.	Georgia.	Florida.	Alabama.	Mississippi.	Louisiana.	Texas.	Arkansas.	Missouri.	Tennessee.	Kentucky.	Ohio.	Indiana.	Illinois.	Michigan.	Wisconsin.
Catharines,				1										6		2	7	1
Cayuta,														1				
Dix,														3	2	3	4	3
Hector,	2	1					1							15		1	14	1
Orange,	1													6		1	1	
Reading,														2		4	2	
Tyrone,									1					13	2		2	
Total,	3	1		1			1		1					46	4	11	30	5

SENECA COUNTY.—(CONTINUED.)

TOWNS.	Virginia.	N. Carolina.	S. Carolina.	Georgia.	Florida.	Alabama.	Mississippi.	Louisiana.	Texas.	Arkansas.	Missouri.	Tennessee.	Kentucky.	Ohio.	Indiana.	Illinois.	Michigan.	Wisconsin.
Covert,	1													2	2			2
Fayette,	1													9	1		3	
Junius,														7	1		3	
Lodi,																1	2	
Ovid,	3													2			25	1
Romulus,															1		12	3
Seneca Falls,	3							2	1			1	1	15		1	19	1
Tyre,																3	3	
Varick,														4	2		2	
Waterloo,			3									1		21	1	1	7	2
Total,	8		3					2	1			2	1	60	8	6	76	9

STEUBEN COUNTY.—(CONTINUED.)

TOWNS.	Virginia.	N. Carolina.	S. Carolina.	Georgia.	Florida.	Alabama.	Mississippi.	Louisiana.	Texas.	Arkansas.	Missouri.	Tennessee.	Kentucky.	Ohio.	Indiana.	Illinois.	Michigan.	Wisconsin.
Addison,	1		2											13			3	
Avoca,	1													1		1	1	
Bath,	5	1	1										3	10	2	8	13	2
Bradford,														3	1		3	
Cameron,	1																	1
Campbell,														3		3	3	
Canisteo,	1													1		1		
Caton,																		
Cohocton,	1										1			1	7	7	10	3
Corning,	4											1		15	2	1	5	
Dansville,														8	1		9	1
Erwin,				1									1	5		2	2	1
Fremont,														3	1	2		
Greenwood,														1			4	1
Hartsville,	1												2	5	1		2	2

(Continued on page 151.)

SARATOGA COUNTY.—(CONTINUED.)

TOWNS.	U. STATES. Iowa.	California.	Territories.	Total United States.	FOREIGN COUNTRIES. Canada.	N. Brunswick.	Nova Scotia.	N. Foundland.	West Indies.	Mexico.	S. America.	England.	Scotland.	Ireland.	Wales.	France.	Belgium.	Holland.
Stillwater,		1		2,445	20		1					90	13	377		2		
Waterford,			1	2,252	34		1					133	20	761		5		
Wilton,				1,325	13							8		40		4		
Total,		2	1	41,305	452	2	6		6		1	1,086	255	5,562	9	41		13

SCHENECTADY COUNTY.—(CONTINUED.)

TOWNS.	Iowa.	California.	Territories.	Total United States.	Canada.	N. Brunswick.	Nova Scotia.	N. Foundland.	West Indies.	Mexico.	S. America.	England.	Scotland.	Ireland.	Wales.	France.	Belgium.	Holland.
Duanesburgh,				2,891	4							55	32	94		6		
Glenville,				2,626	6	1						127	22	141	1			5
Niskayuna,				880	1							38	2	79		1		4
Princetown,				881								9	24	25				
Rotterdam,				2,056								69	20	279				1
Schenectady city:																		
1st ward,				1,165	6							51	15	137		5		2
2d ward,				1,108	6			1				66	13	171	2			5
3d ward,				1,144	10				1			140	89	466	5	4		5
4th ward,	3			2,466	12		1					95	38	290	3	13		3
Total Schenectady	3			5,883	34		1	1	1			352	155	1,064	10	22		15
Total,	3			15,217	45	1	1	1	1			650	255	1,682	11	29		25

SCHOHARIE COUNTY.—(CONTINUED.)

TOWNS.	Iowa.	California.	Territories.	Total United States.	Canada.	N. Brunswick.	Nova Scotia.	N. Foundland.	West Indies.	Mexico.	S. America.	England.	Scotland.	Ireland.	Wales.	France.	Belgium.	Holland.
Blenheim,				1 264	5		1							65				
Broome,				2,099	3							3		9				
Carlisle,				1,663	2		1					4	1	39		1		
Cobleskill,				2,086	4							17	3	53				
Conesville,				1,382	1							1		15				
Esperance,				1,274	2							25		53				
Fulton,				2,776								3		8		3		
Gilboa,				2,540	9							2	3	96				
Jefferson,				1,660										26	1			
Middleburgh,				2,860	11				1			13		73		6		
Richmondville,				1,947								13	2	28				
Schoharie,				2,750	16							9	2	77	2			4
Seward,				1,875	3							1		31				
Sharon,				2,500	2							15	2	86	1			
Summit,				1,837		1						2		27				
Wright,				1,604	2							3		28				
Total,				32,117	60	1	2		1			111	13	714	4	10		4

SCHUYLER COUNTY.—(CONTINUED.)

TOWNS.	Iowa.	California.	Territories.	Total United States.	Canada.	N. Brunswick.	Nova Scotia.	N. Foundland.	West Indies.	Mexico.	S. America.	England.	Scotland.	Ireland.	Wales.	France.	Belgium.	Holland.
Catharines,				3,212	9		1		1			58	7	146		4		
Cayuta,				568								1	4	1				
Dix,	1			2,745	10							28	4	96				
Hector,				5,381	6							64	14	148	1			
Orange,				2,316	3							36	2	119				
Reading,				1,349	5		1					4		85				
Tyrone,				2,077	1							5		76		1		
Total,	1			17,648	34		2		1			196	31	671	1	5		

SENECA COUNTY.—(CONTINUED.)

TOWNS.	Iowa.	California.	Territories.	Total United States.	Canada.	N. Brunswick.	Nova Scotia.	N. Foundland.	West Indies.	Mexico.	S. America.	England.	Scotland.	Ireland.	Wales.	France.	Belgium.	Holland.
Covert,				1,960	11							94	5	154				
Fayette,				3,057	6		1					33	20	125		8		
Junius,				1,275	6		1					74	1	31			7	
Lodi,				1,887								44	1	85				
Ovid,				1,991	4							18	1	231				1
Romulus,				1,708	1							8	4	150				
Seneca Falls,	1			3,979	20				1			151	56	679	3	4		
Tyre,				1,353	6							18	2	29		1		
Varick,				1,675	1							18	2	15				
Waterloo,				3,613	36							211	29	41				
Total,	1			22,498	91		2		1			669	121	1,540	3	13	7	1

STEUBEN COUNTY.—(CONTINUED.)

TOWNS.	Iowa.	California.	Territories.	Total United States.	Canada.	N. Brunswick.	Nova Scotia.	N. Foundland.	West Indies.	Mexico.	S. America.	England.	Scotland.	Ireland.	Wales.	France.	Belgium.	Holland.
Addison,				2,914	14	1						34	8	178	1			
Avoca,				1,662	2							9	5	41		1		
Bath,			1	5,483	24	1	1		2			60	38	368		1		
Bradford,				1,273	2							1		2				
Cameron,				1,723	8							10		64				
Campbell,				1,439	4		1					3	6	77		2		
Canisteo,				1,876	10		7					17	4	57		5		
Caton,				1,501	4	2	1					27	6	11				
Cohocton,				1,985	1							30	3	26				
Corning,	1			4,931	59							95	31	978		3		3
Dansville,				1,867			1					58	5	47		1		
Erwin,				1,516	17				2			21	13	214	1			
Fremont,				1,090	4							4		5				
Greenwood,				1,076	3							5		128				
Hartsville,				1,066	6							3		31				

19

(Continued on page 152.)

SARATOGA COUNTY.—(CONTINUED.)

TOWNS.	Germany.	Prussia.	Austria.	Switzerland.	Italy.	Spain.	Portugal.	Poland.	Norway.	Sweden.	Russia.	Denmark.	East Indies.	Africa.	Turkey and Greece.	Islands.	Asia.	At Sea.	Unknown.
	FOREIGN COUNTRIES.																		
Stillwater,	10																		5
Waterford,	25																	1	17
Wilton,	5							1											5
Total,	441	14	2	20	1	2	1	4					1			1	3	4	147

SCHENECTADY COUNTY.—(CONTINNUED.)

TOWNS.	Germany.	Prussia.	Austria.	Switzerland.	Italy.	Spain.	Portugal.	Poland.	Norway.	Sweden.	Russia.	Denmark.	East Indies.	Africa.	Turkey and Greece.	Islands.	Asia.	At Sea.	Unknown.
Duanesburgh,	18			1				1											17
Glenville,	180	39		4														1	
Niskayuna,	97	11		3															4
Princetown,	12																		5
Rotterdam,	403	4		3															
Schenectady city:																			
1st ward,	153	6		2				1										1	
2d ward,	141	9					1	3				2						2	
3d ward,	83							1										1	2
4th ward,	354	29	1	13	1			6		3		1						1	34
Total Schenectady	731	44	1	15	1		1	11		3		3						5	36
Total,	1,441	98	1	26	1		1	12		3		3						6	62

SCHOHARIE COUNTY.—(CONTINUED.)

TOWNS.	Germany.	Prussia.	Austria.	Switzerland.	Italy.	Spain.	Portugal.	Poland.	Norway.	Sweden.	Russia.	Denmark.	East Indies.	Africa.	Turkey and Greece.	Islands.	Asia.	At Sea.	Unknown.
Blenheim,	15							1											
Broome,	19																		5
Carlisle,	6							1											5
Cobleskill,	42																		3
Conesville,																			8
Esperance,	15	1																	
Fulton,	24																		3
Gilboa,	1			5															1
Jefferson,																			1
Middleburgh,	57	1																	53
Richmondville,	27		4																6
Schoharie,	8																		1
Seward,	15																		
Sharon,	108														1				1
Summit,	14		1		1			1											6
Wright,	4			1						1									15
Total,	355	2	5	6	1			3		1					1				108

SCHUYLER COUNTY.—(CONTINUED.)

TOWNS.	Germany.	Prussia.	Austria.	Switzerland.	Italy.	Spain.	Portugal.	Poland.	Norway.	Sweden.	Russia.	Denmark.	East Indies.	Africa.	Turkey and Greece.	Islands.	Asia.	At Sea.	Unknown.
Catharines,	17		1																61
Cayuta,																			44
Dix,											1								
Hector,	4																		11
Orange,																			7
Reading,	2																		6
Tyrone,																			34
Total,	23		1								1								163

SENECA COUNTY.—(CONTINUED.)

TOWNS.	Germany.	Prussia.	Austria.	Switzerland.	Italy.	Spain.	Portugal.	Poland.	Norway.	Sweden.	Russia.	Denmark.	East Indies.	Africa.	Turkey and Greece.	Islands.	Asia.	At Sea.	Unknown.
Covert,	3			1															2
Fayette,	95	1		3								1						1	19
Junius,	9																	1	10
Lodi,																			1
Ovid,	10																		18
Romulus,	5									1									2
Seneca Falls,	51							7					1						32
Tyre,	3				1														6
Varick,	8																		4
Waterloo,	110			3															3
Total,	294	1		7	1			7		1		1	1					2	97

STEUBEN COUNTY.—(CONTINUED.)

TOWNS.	Germany.	Prussia.	Austria.	Switzerland.	Italy.	Spain.	Portugal.	Poland.	Norway.	Sweden.	Russia.	Denmark.	East Indies.	Africa.	Turkey and Greece.	Islands.	Asia.	At Sea.	Unknown.
Addison,		3		1															2
Avoca,	12																		54
Bath,	48			4															1
Bradford,	1		1																5
Cameron,																			30
Campbell,	8																		2
Canisteo,	5																		4
Caton,	27				1														5
Cohocton,	167																		30
Corning,	184	17			4		5	3		6									15
Dansville,	140																		41
Erwin,	23																		12
Fremont,	4																		12
Greenwood,					1														11
Hartsville,			4																

(Continued on page 153.)

STEUBEN COUNTY.

TOWNS.	COUNTIES OF NEW-YORK.																	
	Albany.	Allegany.	Broome.	Cattaraugus.	Cayuga.	Chautauque.	Chemung.	Chenango.	Clinton.	Columbia.	Cortland.	Delaware.	Dutchess.	Erie.	Essex.	Franklin.	Fulton.	Genesee.
Hornby,	7	1	1	.....	3	1	78	13	.....	5	5	5	25	.....	.....	.....	1	4
Hornellsville,	27	171	28	12	44	12	41	58	.....	19	22	33	14	15	1	.....	1	18
Howard,	3	19	4	.....	31	1	14	16	.....	14	4	15	11	3	1	.....	4	5
Jasper,	3	5	22	1	52	3	2	62	1	2	25	14	15	2	.....	1	2	.....
Lindley,	5	5	8	.....	2	.....	26	47	1	2	10	13	3	.....	9	.....	.....	.....
Prattsburgh,	10	12	1	1	22	2	10	16	4	16	9	11	28	2	.....	.....	9	6
Pultney,	17	4	1	1	3	.....	5	5	.....	9	1	5	38	1	.....	1	.....	2
Thurston,	2	5	6	1	3	.....	15	9	.....	5	3	4	4	1	.....	.....	.....	2
Troupsburgh,	4	12	9	.....	18	1	3	144	.....	11	34	24	7	3	1	.....	.....	4
Urbana,	6	9	.....	4	6	.....	19	1	.....	6	3	3	32	.....	.....	.....	.....	1
Wayland,	1	15	2	.....	10	.....	1	.....	.....	1	13	10	9	2	.....	.....	.....	9
Wayne,	1	7	3	2	4	.....	8	2	1	3	2	2	13	1	1	.....	3	.....
West Union,	4	75	4	.....	8	1	10	14	.....	8	8	20	5	.....	.....	.....	.....	2
Wheeler,	16	3	.....	.....	4	2	6	1	.....	5	.....	5	9	2	.....	.....	.....	1
Woodhull,	4	22	39	1	5	3	30	86	.....	9	34	14	18	.....	.....	.....	.....	.....
Total,	267	678	362	58	494	58	876	1,117	28	241	376	455	481	91	48	5	30	115

SUFFOLK COUNTY.

TOWNS.	Albany.	Allegany.	Broome.	Cattaraugus.	Cayuga.	Chautauque.	Chemung.	Chenango.	Clinton.	Columbia.	Cortland.	Delaware.	Dutchess.	Erie.	Essex.	Franklin.	Fulton.	Genesee.
Brookhaven,	5	.....	5	.....	4	.....	.....	.....	2	9	.....	18	12	1	.....	.....	1	.....
Easthampton,	3	.....	.....	.....	.....	.....	.....	.....	2	.....	.....	.....	1	.....	1	.....	.....	.....
Huntington,	13	.....	.....	.....	1	1	.....	.....	.....	12	.....	7	29	2	.....	.....	.....	.....
Islip,	7	1	5	.....	.....	.....	.....	1	.....	3	.....	2	8	.....	.....	.....	.....	1
River Head,	1	1	3	.....	.....	.....	.....	.....	.....	.....	1	.....	4	2	.....	.....	.....	.....
Shelter Island,	.....	.....	.....	.....	.....	.....	.....	.....	.....	.....	.....	.....	.....	.....	1	.....	.....	.....
Smithtown,	1	.....	1	.....	.....	.....	.....	2	.....	1	.....	1	.....	1	.....	.....	.....	.....
Southampton,	2	.....	.....	.....	.....	.....	.....	.....	2	2	.....	2	6	.....	1	.....	.....	1
Southold,	6	.....	1	.....	.....	.....	.....	1	.....	5	.....	2	12	2	1	.....	.....	.....
Total,	38	2	15	.....	5	1	.....	4	6	32	1	32	72	8	4	.....	1	2

SULLIVAN COUNTY.

TOWNS.	Albany.	Allegany.	Broome.	Cattaraugus.	Cayuga.	Chautauque.	Chemung.	Chenango.	Clinton.	Columbia.	Cortland.	Delaware.	Dutchess.	Erie.	Essex.	Franklin.	Fulton.	Genesee.
Bethel,	12	.....	.....	.....	.....	.....	.....	.....	.....	1	.....	20	57	.....	.....	.....	.....	.....
Cochecton,	11	.....	7	.....	.....	.....	.....	.....	.....	11	1	54	23	.....	.....	.....	.....	.....
Collicoon,	17	.....	3	.....	.....	1	1	.....	.....	11	.....	90	11	.....	.....	.....	7	.....
Fallsburgh,	4	.....	4	.....	1	.....	.....	.....	.....	2	.....	32	78	1	.....	1	.....	1
Forrestburgh,	3	.....	.....	.....	.....	.....	.....	.....	.....	1	1	7	8	.....	.....	.....	.....	.....
Fremont,	13	.....	8	.....	.....	.....	.....	14	.....	3	1	90	13	1	.....	.....	.....	.....
Highland,	.....	.....	1	.....	8	.....	.....	1	.....	.....	.....	3	3	.....	.....	.....	.....	.....
Liberty,	18	.....	3	.....	.....	.....	.....	5	.....	7	2	60	66	1	.....	.....	.....	.....
Lumberland,	2	.....	.....	.....	.....	.....	.....	.....	.....	.....	.....	3	5	.....	.....	.....	.....	.....
Mamakating,	5	.....	5	1	2	.....	6	3	1	1	.....	7	90	.....	.....	.....	.....	.....
Neversink,	7	.....	.....	.....	.....	.....	3	1	.....	6	.....	21	35	.....	.....	.....	.....	1
Rockland,	5	1	.....	.....	.....	.....	.....	2	1	2	2	179	15	.....	.....	.....	.....	.....
Thompson,	1	.....	.....	.....	.....	2	1	.....	.....	3	.....	27	52	.....	1	.....	.....	.....
Tusten,	.....	.....	.....	.....	.....	.....	.....	.....	.....	4	.....	2	13	.....	.....	1	.....	.....
Total,	98	1	31	1	11	3	11	26	2	52	7	595	469	3	1	2	7	2

TIOGA COUNTY.

TOWNS.	Albany.	Allegany.	Broome.	Cattaraugus.	Cayuga.	Chautauque.	Chemung.	Chenango.	Clinton.	Columbia.	Cortland.	Delaware.	Dutchess.	Erie.	Essex.	Franklin.	Fulton.	Genesee.
Barton,	34	6	57	1	21	.....	109	57	.....	3	51	51	21	2	1	.....	.....	.....
Berkshire,	5	1	49	.....	7	.....	6	19	.....	7	25	8	4	2	1	.....	.....	.....
Candor,	57	1	38	3	26	1	21	41	.....	8	19	65	44	1	.....	.....	1	5
Newark,	91	1	86	.....	16	1	5	27	.....	2	26	16	12	1	.....	.....	.....	.....
Nichols,	5	.....	14	.....	.....	1	18	11	3	8	1	26	16	.....	3	.....	.....	1
Owego,	165	6	298	1	22	2	44	66	6	62	48	87	190	3	8	.....	1	3
Richford,	.....	1	26	.....	4	.....	.....	20	.....	33	91	14	10	2	3	1	.....	.....
Spencer,	15	.....	10	.....	11	.....	23	15	1	1	18	14	21	.....	4	.....	.....	1
Tioga,	53	.....	76	2	10	.....	26	34	.....	4	14	29	15	.....	1	.....	.....	1
Total,	425	16	654	7	117	5	252	290	10	128	293	310	333	11	21	1	2	11

TOMPKINS COUNTY.

TOWNS.	Albany.	Allegany.	Broome.	Cattaraugus.	Cayuga.	Chautauque.	Chemung.	Chenango.	Clinton.	Columbia.	Cortland.	Delaware.	Dutchess.	Erie.	Essex.	Franklin.	Fulton.	Genesee.
Caroline,	16	2	22	1	15	1	12	22	.....	4	44	16	80	1	.....	4	.....	6
Danby,	9	2	3	.....	40	1	20	2	2	5	10	20	92	1	3	.....	.....	1
Dryden,	12	9	34	6	110	4	5	28	.....	42	253	32	99	6	2	1	.....	1
Enfield,	1	.....	8	.....	10	1	14	2	.....	2	8	13	43	6	.....	.....	.....	.....
Groton,	13	4	14	2	275	9	9	39	.....	8	153	22	40	6	.....	.....	.....	.....
Ithaca,	44	7	33	4	123	2	64	20	2	22	56	37	74	2	2	1	.....	2
Lansing,	7	5	11	3	151	1	4	14	2	3	25	8	26	2	.....	1	.....	.....
Newfield,	14	2	4	.....	26	.....	51	8	.....	1	2	21	64	1	.....	2	.....	4
Ulysses,	13	.....	15	2	32	2	31	24	.....	4	13	65	92	1	.....	.....	.....	3
Total,	129	31	144	18	782	21	210	159	6	91	564	234	610	26	7	9	.....	17

ULSTER COUNTY.

TOWNS.	Albany.	Allegany.	Broome.	Cattaraugus.	Cayuga.	Chautauque.	Chemung.	Chenango.	Clinton.	Columbia.	Cortland.	Delaware.	Dutchess.	Erie.	Essex.	Franklin.	Fulton.	Genesee.
Denning,	6	.....	.....	.....	.....	.....	1	.....	.....	2	1	10	18	.....	.....	.....	.....	.....
Esopus,	9	.....	4	.....	1	.....	1	.....	.....	19	.....	8	105	.....	.....	.....	.....	.....
Gardiner,	3	.....	.....	.....	.....	.....	.....	.....	.....	3	.....	4	46	.....	2	.....	.....	.....
Hurley,	8	.....	.....	.....	1	.....	.....	.....	.....	6	.....	50	70	1	.....	.....	.....	.....
Kingston,	82	.....	5	.....	2	2	.....	1	2	126	4	100	387	2	4	.....	.....	.....
Lloyd,	6	.....	2	.....	2	.....	.....	.....	.....	4	.....	10	116	.....	.....	.....	.....	.....

(Continued on page 154.)

STEUBEN COUNTY.—(Continued.)

TOWNS.	Greene.	Hamilton.	Herkimer.	Jefferson.	Kings.	Lewis.	Livingston.	Madison.	Monroe.	Montgomery.	New-York.	Niagara.	Oneida.	Onondaga.	Ontario.	Orange.	Orleans.	Oswego.
	COUNTIES OF NEW-YORK.																	
Hornby,	1	1	4		2		4	4	1	53			3	11	9	17		2
Hornellsville,	9	2	11	9	1		102	64	30	11	21	4	22	16	36	22	8	19
Howard,	4		12		2		23	8	1	115	4	1	20	1	23	29	1	1
Jasper,	2		13	1			7	20		34		3	5	10	7	8		
Lindley,			2					3		1	1		4	13	3	1		1
Prattsburgh,	8	1	17	6	1	4	15	12	8	60	9	3	27	30	118	26	1	
Pultney,	10		4	2			4	6	2	3	6		9		37	14		2
Thurston,	9		22				3	3		5			2	6	11	6		1
Troupsburgh,	3		8	1		1	9	31	1	4	17		4	10	11	2		
Urbana,	8		7	3	1	1	12	3	3	5	2		11	4	14	47		
Wayland,			7	2	6		131	11	38	19	9	1	12	51	30	4	2	1
Wayne,			6					1		4	3	1	1		11	41		
West Union,	13		10				43	10	5	3	11	1	4	10	8	6		
Wheeler,	1		56			3	1	2		118	1	1	10	7	9	16		
Woodhull,	3		17	5		1	11	6	4	9	6	1	30	12	6	14		
Total,	176	4	377	100	31	14	856	330	239	1,149	220	33	327	391	699	620	48	93

SUFFOLK COUNTY.—(Continued.)

TOWNS.	Greene.	Hamilton.	Herkimer.	Jefferson.	Kings.	Lewis.	Livingston.	Madison.	Monroe.	Montgomery.	New-York.	Niagara.	Oneida.	Onondaga.	Ontario.	Orange.	Orleans.	Oswego.
Brookhaven,	16		4	2	82	1	11		2		401		10	3	2	29		2
Easthampton,	1				10						49	1	4			2		
Huntington,	15			1	170		1	3			420		9			12		
Islip,	1		1		38			1	4		213		1	4	1	6		
River Head,	2		1	1	34						48		1			11		
Shelter Island,					7						11							
Smithtown,	2		2		20						93							
Southampton,	10				40					1	195		2	1		18		
Southold,	6		4	1	62		2		2	1	224		1			26		1
Total,	53		12	5	463	1	14	4	8	2	1,654	1	28	8	3	104		3

SULLIVAN COUNTY.—(Continued.)

TOWNS.	Greene.	Hamilton.	Herkimer.	Jefferson.	Kings.	Lewis.	Livingston.	Madison.	Monroe.	Montgomery.	New-York.	Niagara.	Oneida.	Onondaga.	Ontario.	Orange.	Orleans.	Oswego.
Bethel,	60				13					3	99		2	1		139		
Cochecton,	59				5				1	1	132					48		
Collicoon,	43	1	1		3					5	125			3		40		1
Fallsburgh,	35				1						58		1	6		115		
Forrestburgh,	14				7						15					165		
Fremont,	50			1	1		1	2	1		61					29		
Highland,	2				3						18					114		
Liberty,	57			4	6				1	1	53		2		1	78		
Lumberland,					7						27				1	132		
Mamakating,	21		1		3		3			1	43		2	3	3	716		
Neversink,	29		1		3			2			7	1				25		
Rockland,	37				1				1		9	1				18		
Thompson,	44		4		11		1	1		1	74		2	3	2	250		
Tusten,	5		3		3					3	10					44		
Total,	456	1	10	5	67		5	5	4	15	731	2	9	16	7	1,913		1

TIOGA COUNTY.—(Continued.)

TOWNS.	Greene.	Hamilton.	Herkimer.	Jefferson.	Kings.	Lewis.	Livingston.	Madison.	Monroe.	Montgomery.	New-York.	Niagara.	Oneida.	Onondaga.	Ontario.	Orange.	Orleans.	Oswego.
Barton,	8		2	3	7			7	5	11	10	2		16		331		3
Berkshire,	5		2	1	1			5	1	3	7		2	11	1	8		
Candor,	37		27	2		2		18	3	26	4	1	13	7	9	99	1	2
Newark,	7		1		2			10		5	8		3	6	2	12		
Nichols,	9				2			10	1	2	8		2	4		56		
Owego,	49		12	5	10	6	2	34	19	16	70	2	28	14	25	98		4
Richford,	5		2		3			11		1	3	2	13	1		5		
Spencer,	6		5	2		1		5		8	28		1	10		30		
Tioga,	15		2	2	2		3	1	2	12	13		3	5	2	117		1
Total,	141		53	15	27	9	5	101	31	84	151	7	65	74	39	756	1	10

TOMPKINS COUNTY.—(Continued.)

TOWNS.	Greene.	Hamilton.	Herkimer.	Jefferson.	Kings.	Lewis.	Livingston.	Madison.	Monroe.	Montgomery.	New-York.	Niagara.	Oneida.	Onondaga.	Ontario.	Orange.	Orleans.	Oswego.
Caroline,	5		7		2		1	3		5	6		5	5	4	50		2
Danby,	11		2	1			1	1		7	6		2	11	2	78	1	
Dryden,	15		19	6	3	1	2	26	2	21	14	1	16	26	2	60	4	2
Enfield,	3		6	1	3		1	3	2	1	16			2	1	44		1
Groton,	10		11	1			4	21	2	3	9	3	20	72	4	23	2	1
Ithaca,	14		9	12	12	7	9	35	12	12	102	7	48	49	16	144	11	10
Lansing,			18	1			2	7	1	8	1	1	4	18		58		3
Newfield,	4			1	3		1	2	1		12	2	1	4	7	172		
Ulysses,	6		3	3			5	7	8		49	1	9	15	5	78		1
Total,	68		75	26	23	8	26	105	28	57	215	15	105	202	41	707	18	20

ULSTER COUNTY.—(Continued.)

TOWNS.	Greene.	Hamilton.	Herkimer.	Jefferson.	Kings.	Lewis.	Livingston.	Madison.	Monroe.	Montgomery.	New-York.	Niagara.	Oneida.	Onondaga.	Ontario.	Orange.	Orleans.	Oswego.
Denning,	87										7					12		
Esopus,	16				1		1		2	7	103	4		6		23	1	1
Gardiner,	9		1		1					1	13					64		
Hurley,	104				3			1		1	19		1		1	5		
Kingston,	138		4	3	12				9	6	360	1	8	4	2	100		5
Lloyd,	7				1		1		1		30				1	19		

(Continued on page 155.)

STEUBEN COUNTY.—(Continued.)

TOWNS.	COUNTIES OF NEW-YORK.																	
	Otsego.	Putnam.	Queens.	Rensselaer.	Richmond.	Rockland.	St. Lawrence.	Saratoga.	Schenectady.	Schoharie.	Schuyler.	Seneca.	Steuben.	Suffolk	Sullivan.	Tioga.	Tompkins.	Ulster.
Hornby,	45	11		4		1		5		2		15	699			6	43	3
Hornellsville,	81	11	2	18		1	3	14	9	18		24	1, 270	1	1	26	47	16
Howard,	50		5	2			1	9	2	1		18	1, 572	2	1	3	50	4
Jasper,	25	1	1	4			5	5	2	5		4	943			16	70	3
Lindley,	13				4			5	1	4		3	295			5	9	1
Prattsburgh,	7	16	1	10		3		39	7	9		20	1, 306			7	17	24
Pultney,	9	27		4				1		8		37	871	1	3	2	7	
Thurston,	11			3				3		3	20	15	476			4	24	4
Troupsburgh,	71	1	1	5				4		1		2	1, 055		1	18	13	
Urbana,	9	46		3		2	1	12		2		31	1, 167	4	1	2	8	
Wayland,	42			2				13	1	6		6	1, 157		1	3	2	3
Wayne,		27		2		2		3	1	1	1	30	539				21	1
West Union,	4	1		2			9	2		1		12	481	4	2	9	53	3
Wheeler,	6	13		62				6	1	2		8	797	1	3	2	4	3
Woodhull,	112	1		6	4	3	2	14	5	12		19	1, 072		9	17	25	4
Total,	1, 173	200	18	228	10	52	36	329	76	197	22	484	30, 263	31	59	312	1, 360	174

SUFFOLK COUNTY.—(Continued.)

TOWNS.	Otsego.	Putnam.	Queens.	Rensselaer.	Richmond.	Rockland.	St. Lawrence.	Saratoga.	Schenectady.	Schoharie.	Schuyler.	Seneca.	Steuben.	Suffolk	Sullivan.	Tioga.	Tompkins.	Ulster.
Brookhaven,		8	80	5	2	8		1		1			2	7, 900	10		1	5
Easthampton,			5					1						1, 797				
Huntington,	2	2	518	3	9		1	2		2			1	5, 613				3
Islip,	1		87	3	1	3			1	1				2, 111			2	
River Head,	1		15		2			2						2, 285				
Shelter Island,														381				
Smithtown,	1		27											1, 588		1	1	
Southampton,			22	1	4	3							1	5, 554	3			1
Southold,			54	7	1	2		4				1		4, 091	1	2		5
Total,	5	10	808	19	19	16	1	10	1	4		1	4	31, 320	14	3	4	14

SULLIVAN COUNTY.—(Continued.)

TOWNS.	Otsego.	Putnam.	Queens.	Rensselaer.	Richmond.	Rockland.	St. Lawrence.	Saratoga.	Schenectady.	Schoharie.	Schuyler.	Seneca.	Steuben.	Suffolk	Sullivan.	Tioga.	Tompkins.	Ulster.
Bethel,		4	5	4						18			3		1, 305	1	6	51
Cochecton,	4			4		6		1		62		1			1, 140	1		29
Collicoon,		1								101				2	633			28
Fallsburgh,	1		5	5		5		2		4		1		1	1, 704		1	378
Forrestburgh,						11				2					353	2		16
Fremont,	17		3	1						39			1		341			29
Highland,		2		1				1							439		2	7
Liberty,	7	20		4		19		1		56					1, 665		2	135
Lumberland,														4	369			24
Mamakating,	2	19	6	3		5				4		1	1		2,079	3	10	384
Neversink,				7		2		2		1					1, 495			234
Rockland,	2			2		6				13				1	757		3	65
Thompson,	1	16	18	3		16		2				1		2	1, 904	1	4	100
Tusten,				2											355			1
Total,	34	62	37	36		70		9		300		4	5	10	14, 539	8	28	1, 481

TIOGA COUNTY.—(Continued.)

TOWNS.	Otsego.	Putnam.	Queens.	Rensselaer.	Richmond.	Rockland.	St. Lawrence.	Saratoga.	Schenectady.	Schoharie.	Schuyler.	Seneca.	Steuben.	Suffolk	Sullivan.	Tioga.	Tompkins.	Ulster.
Barton,	50	5		8		8		8	2	15	3	12	17	2	14	1, 600	320	6
Berkshire,	20	7		1		1	2	7		6		6	3	1		429	56	3
Candor,	76	32	1	10		1		4	24	44		4	14	1	13	1, 892	345	63
Newark,	68	6		3	1	1			14	60		1		1		918	32	
Nichols,	18		3	2				37	14	28	1		1		6	1, 074	23	9
Owego,	149	17	6	61	4	7	2	63	84	178		13	19	8	16	4, 006	122	22
Richford,	31	18	5	3		1		4		4			2		2	485	88	4
Spencer,	7	2		4		1		11	2	5		2	9		2	868	247	10
Tioga,	69	8	15	6	1	1	3	14	8	32		4	4	1	2	1, 644	118	35
Total,	488	95	30	98	6	21	7	148	148	372	4	42	69	14	55	12, 916	1, 351	152

TOMPKINS COUNTY.—(Continued.)

TOWNS.	Otsego.	Putnam.	Queens.	Rensselaer.	Richmond.	Rockland.	St. Lawrence.	Saratoga.	Schenectady.	Schoharie.	Schuyler.	Seneca.	Steuben.	Suffolk	Sullivan.	Tioga.	Tompkins.	Ulster.
Caroline,	18	5	2	5	1	1		4	6	4	2	4	1		15	177	1, 338	176
Danby,	10	6		5		1		10	2	14		3	7	2	6	96	1, 359	25
Dryden,	50	4	7	86		2	5	19	7	10	4	9	12	2	7	61	3, 032	62
Enfield,	4	16	5	5		1		4		3		40	12		3	11	1, 249	10
Groton,	28	1		14				21	2	12		6	15	1	5	30	1, 774	7
Ithaca,	31	25	1	10		4		25	8	13		90	26	7	16	112	3, 752	72
Lansing,	1	2	1	10				10	1	6		13	2	1	1	24	2, 235	22
Newfield,	11	13		1		1		4	1	20		14	18		14	11	1, 849	13
Ulysses,	8	28	1	5				12	2	7	10	92	13	8		17	1, 702	13
Total,	161	100	17	141	1	10	5	109	29	89	16	371	106	21	67	539	18, 290	400

ULSTER COUNTY.—(Continued.)

TOWNS.	Otsego.	Putnam.	Queens.	Rensselaer.	Richmond.	Rockland.	St. Lawrence.	Saratoga.	Schenectady.	Schoharie.	Schuyler.	Seneca.	Steuben.	Suffolk	Sullivan.	Tioga.	Tompkins.	Ulster.
Denning,		1		1		4				168			1	5	10			273
Esopus,	2	3	1			3		6		1		6		1	20		1	2, 607
Gardiner,		24	1	1		2									5		1	1, 560
Hurley,	8		1	3		1		5	1	4				2	1		2	1, 392
Kingston,	14	15		11		10	1	20	3	30			9	3	20	1	4	6, 878
Lloyd,	1	8	5	4		4		2	1	1				1	4	2		1, 726

(Continued on page 156.)

STEUBEN COUNTY.—(Continued.)

Towns.	Counties of New-York.							United States.										
	Warren.	Washington.	Wayne.	Westchester.	Wyoming.	Yates.	New-York.	Maine.	N. Hampshire.	Vermont.	Massachusetts.	Rhode Island.	Connecticut.	New Jersey.	Pennsylvania.	Delaware.	Maryland.	District of Columbia.
Hornby,		7	1	3		17	1, 123	1	10	42	29	1	36	38	46		1	
Hornellsville,	5	12	11	4	8	49	2, 534	19	32	59	71	31	79	52	193		2	
Howard,		37	1	4	6	75	2, 233	5	5	29	35	9	50	39	44			
Jasper,	1	23	4	1		28	1, 463		68	23	35	7	23	31	57			
Lindley,	1	1		1			503	3	4	4	11	5	12	15	77		1	
Prattsburgh,		6	8	16		192	2, 193	5	2	23	49	4	89	29	28	1	1	
Pultney,		2	3	40		112	1, 319		1	2	16	3	45	90	17			
Thurston,	5	2	5	2	2	43	750	5		12	16	21	17	43	23		4	
Troupsburgh,	1	8		1	1	11	1, 571	2	13	15	31	19	36	13	198			
Urbana,		9		10		66	1, 584		3	2	24	2	22	160	31			
Wayland,		11	4	2	1	15	1, 666	2	7	23	24	1	20	13	48			
Wayne,		2	1	6		75	833			4	7		8	36	15			
West Union,	1		5	2		6	880	3	8	1	10	6	8	15	69			
Wheeler,		6	1	14		40	1, 248	2	5	7	10	1	20	22	20			
Woodhull,		4	1		2	52	1, 754	1	8	19	36	12	42	67	200		1	
Total,	41	354	167	173	46	1, 444	48, 737	151	344	713	881	261	1, 155	1, 339	2, 489	1	31	1

SUFFOLK COUNTY.—(Continued.)

Towns.	Warren.	Washington.	Wayne.	Westchester.	Wyoming.	Yates.	New-York.	Maine.	N. Hampshire.	Vermont.	Massachusetts.	Rhode Island.	Connecticut.	New Jersey.	Pennsylvania.	Delaware.	Maryland.	District of Columbia.
Brookhaven,		1	1	30			8, 677	5	2	2	28	2	99	94	29		3	
Easthampton,	1	1					1, 879	3	2	1	14	15	55	7	3		2	
Huntington,			2	44		3	6, 901	8	4	9	31	12	117	84	12		6	1
Islip,				4			2, 512	3	9	7	23	4	11	37	8		2	
River Head,				5			2, 420	3	2		16	3	33	5	14		2	
Shelter Island,				1			401				9	14	18	1			3	
Smithtown,				3			1, 748			2	19	1	20	11	8		1	
Southampton,		4		5			5, 881	4	2	7	51	19	195	51	15	2	3	
Southold,		1		33	2		4, 564	20		6	39	32	217	38	17		2	
Total,	1	7	3	125	2	3	34. 983	46	21	34	230	102	765	328	106	2	24	1

SULLIVAN COUNTY.—(Continued.)

Towns.	Warren.	Washington.	Wayne.	Westchester.	Wyoming.	Yates.	New-York.	Maine.	N. Hampshire.	Vermont.	Massachusetts.	Rhode Island.	Connecticut.	New Jersey.	Pennsylvania.	Delaware.	Maryland.	District of Columbia.
Bethel,	1	2		12			1, 819			2	20	3	72	36	39			
Cochecton,		3		15			1, 619			4	14		31	28	91			1
Collicoon,		2		16			1, 146	3		1	3	1	29	6				
Fallsburgh,		1		37			2, 485	3	1	2	3	1	69	20	9		1	
Forrestburgh,				4		1	610	4		1	7	3	11	11	13		1	
Fremont,				14			734	1		3	14	2	7	1	37			
Highland,				9			614		2		2	1	13	51	33			
Liberty,		1		50		1	2, 326			10	16	1	139	11	27			
Lumberland,				1			575	1		1			2	49	34		1	
Mamakating,				30		2	3, 466				9	2	50	55	42		2	
Neversink,				23			1 906	1		3	2	1	46	23	1			
Rockland,		2		3			1, 128		3	1	8	3	23	1	3			
Thompson,		3		82			2, 633	3		2	18	3	171	22	17		5	
Tusten,		1					447	2		1	5	9	5	23	62			
Total,	1	15		296		4	21, 508	18	6	31	121	30	668	337	408		10	1

TIOGA COUNTY.—(Continued.)

Towns.	Warren.	Washington.	Wayne.	Westchester.	Wyoming.	Yates.	New-York.	Maine.	N. Hampshire.	Vermont.	Massachusetts.	Rhode Island.	Connecticut.	New Jersey.	Pennsylvania.	Delaware.	Maryland.	District of Columbia.
Barton,		8		24		4	2, 925	13	3	32	30	8	83	147	333		3	
Berkshire,		1	1	4			729		3	8	120	6	34	12	35		1	
Candor,		16	4	27			3, 153	3	13	52	66	4	210	55	150		3	
Newark,		2	1	7			1, 455	1	7	20	153	13	85	11	62		1	
Nichols,		24		13		1	1, 455		18	16	56	1	22	48	172			
Owego,	2	43	2	24	1	12	6, 267	16	44	87	232	39	248	87	440		12	1
Richford,			1	1			900			8	96	8	46	7	18		2	
Spencer,		7		39			1, 446	1	33	23	42	1	92	32	41		1	
Tioga,	2	10		5		3	2, 430	9	9	22	35	20	85	71	152		5	
Total,	4	111	9	144	1	20	20, 760	43	130	268	830	100	905	470	1, 403		28	1

TOMPKINS COUNTY.—(Continued.)

Towns.	Warren.	Washington.	Wayne.	Westchester.	Wyoming.	Yates.	New-York.	Maine.	N. Hampshire.	Vermont.	Massachusetts.	Rhode Island.	Connecticut.	New Jersey.	Pennsylvania.	Delaware.	Maryland.	District of Columbia.
Caroline,	1	5	4	8		2	2, 120		5	19	72	4	68	29	33		1	
Danby,		13	2	16		1	1, 912	1	11	14	35	4	137	99	59		3	
Dryden,	4	19	1	7		6	4, 280	1	16	43	69	13	115	168	76		1	
Enfield,		5	2	54		5	1, 621	3	5	8	7	1	32	116	27			
Groton,		21	4	12	1	3	2, 737	3	13	58	138	9	169	68	74		1	
Ithaca,		16	7	26		5	5, 253	6	35	35	118	18	201	246	192	8	24	2
Lansing,		8		7	2	3	2, 734	8	5	8	39	2	42	105	164			
Newfield,		5	2	6		4	2, 397	2	2	25	29	3	73	84	107			
Ulysses,		3	1	17	1	6	2, 533		10	13	29	6	90	169	51		1	
Total,	5	95	23	153	4	35	25, 587	24	102	223	536	60	927	1, 084	783	8	31	2

ULSTER COUNTY.—(Continued.)

Towns.	Warren.	Washington.	Wayne.	Westchester.	Wyoming.	Yates.	New-York.	Maine.	N. Hampshire.	Vermont.	Massachusetts.	Rhode Island.	Connecticut.	New Jersey.	Pennsylvania.	Delaware.	Maryland.	District of Columbia.
Denning,		1		1			609			2	3		17	1				
Esopus,		2		16			2, 981	1		2	11	6	22	26	12		2	
Gardiner,				8			1, 749				2		1	12	1			
Hurley,				2		7	1, 700		2	2	4		16	15	2			3
Kingston,	1	4		55	2	1	8, 457	12	5	13	41	6	107	77	52		2	1
Lloyd,				24			1, 983		3	1	5		18	5	2			

(Continued on page 157.)

STEUBEN COUNTY.—(Continued.)

TOWNS.	UNITED STATES.																	
	Virginia.	N. Carolina.	S. Carolina.	Georgia.	Florida.	Alabama.	Mississippi.	Louisiana.	Texas.	Arkansas.	Missouri.	Tennessee.	Kentucky.	Ohio.	Indiana.	Illinois.	Michigan.	Wisconsin.
Hornby,															1		5	1
Hornellsville,														9	2	7	6	4
Howard,											2			6	1	2	6	6
Jasper,														1			6	
Lindley,															2			
Prattsburgh,	2						5							2	1	1	3	
Pultney,	1													6	1	3	7	1
Thurston,															1		7	
Troupsburgh,	1													5	2			
Urbana,														3	2	6	1	2
Wayland,														4		2	12	
Wayne,																	10	
West Union,														1			2	
Wheeler,	1													1			1	
Woodhull,														7	1	3	6	
Total,	20	1	3	1			5				3	1	6	114	29	49	127	25

SUFFOLK COUNTY.—(Continued.)

TOWNS.	Virginia.	N. Carolina.	S. Carolina.	Georgia.	Florida.	Alabama.	Mississippi.	Louisiana.	Texas.	Arkansas.	Missouri.	Tennessee.	Kentucky.	Ohio.	Indiana.	Illinois.	Michigan.	Wisconsin.
Brookhaven,	12	12	1					1						3		2	9	
Easthampton,	1		1										2					
Huntington,	27	2	3					1						2		3	1	
Islip,	1		2					1						12	3	5		1
River Head,														1			10	
Shelter Island,																		
Smithtown,		1		2				1										
Southampton,	2	5	3	1		1					1			3		5	3	
Southold,	6	1	1		1										1			
Total,	49	21	11	3	1	1		4			1		2	21	4	15	23	1

SULLIVAN COUNTY.

TOWNS.	Virginia.	N. Carolina.	S. Carolina.	Georgia.	Florida.	Alabama.	Mississippi.	Louisiana.	Texas.	Arkansas.	Missouri.	Tennessee.	Kentucky.	Ohio.	Indiana.	Illinois.	Michigan.	Wisconsin.
Bethel,											1			4			1	1
Cochecton,					2			1						2				
Collicoon,																		
Fallsburgh,											1			4	1	1	3	
Forrestburgh,																		
Fremont,			1										1					1
Highland,																		
Liberty,														2				
Lumberland,												1						
Mamakating,											2			3				
Neversink,																		
Rockland,														1				1
Thompson,	1	4											1	2				
Tusten,														3				
Total,	1	4	1		2			1			4	1	2	21	1	1	4	3

TIOGA COUNTY.—(Continued.)

TOWNS.	Virginia.	N. Carolina.	S. Carolina.	Georgia.	Florida.	Alabama.	Mississippi.	Louisiana.	Texas.	Arkansas.	Missouri.	Tennessee.	Kentucky.	Ohio.	Indiana.	Illinois.	Michigan.	Wisconsin.
Barton,	2	1												6	1	3	5	4
Berkshire,	1															1	1	
Candor,	2													4		1	1	2
Newark,		1												1	1		2	
Nichols,											1			2		1		
Owego,	1				1									10	1	1	13	1
Richford,	1													2			1	
Spencer,														2			2	1
Tioga,	3													5				
Total,	10	2			1						1			32	3	7	25	8

TOMPKINS COUNTY.—(Continued.)

TOWNS.	Virginia.	N. Carolina.	S. Carolina.	Georgia.	Florida.	Alabama.	Mississippi.	Louisiana.	Texas.	Arkansas.	Missouri.	Tennessee.	Kentucky.	Ohio.	Indiana.	Illinois.	Michigan.	Wisconsin.
Caroline,	4													7		1		1
Danby,														8	1	2	3	
Dryden,									1					4	4	4	7	1
Enfield,														8				
Groton,						1								5		5	3	1
Ithaca,	17						2	4					2	14		5	17	3
Lansing,														2			5	1
Newfield,	1													1			2	
Ulysses,	5							1	1					6	1	2	3	
Total,	27					1	2	5	2				2	55	6	19	40	7

ULSTER COUNTY.—(Continued.)

TOWNS.	Virginia.	N. Carolina.	S. Carolina.	Georgia.	Florida.	Alabama.	Mississippi.	Louisiana.	Texas.	Arkansas.	Missouri.	Tennessee.	Kentucky.	Ohio.	Indiana.	Illinois.	Michigan.	Wisconsin.
Denning,																		
Esopus,			1											1	1		1	1
Gardiner,	2																2	1
Hurley,														1				
Kingston,	3	1	2	2										2			1	
Lloyd,	1													5			4	

(Continued on page 158.)

STEUBEN COUNTY.—(CONTINUED.)

TOWNS.	U. STATES. Iowa.	California.	Territories.	Total United States	FOREIGN COUNTRIES. Canada.	N. Brunswick.	Nova Scotia.	N. Foundland.	West Indies.	Mexico.	S. America.	England.	Scotland.	Ireland.	Wales.	France.	Belgium.	Holland.
Hornby,				1,334	2							15	1	45				
Hornellsville,				3,100	24	1	4					75	15	471		2		
Howard,				2,472	8							8	13	147	5			
Jasper,				1,714								16	26					
Lindley,				637	1							1	1	60				
Prattsburgh,				2,438	4							59	13	51	1			
Pultney,				1,512	1							21	5	13				
Thurston,				899			1					2	2	17				
Troupsburgh,				1,906	1		2					6		21				
Urbana,				1,842	1							11	8	71				
Wayland,				1,822	4		14					7	1	16		2		
Wayne,				913								7	1	2	2	1		
West Union,				1,003	7									170				
Wheeler,				1,338								13	2	9		3		
Woodhull,				2,157	8		1					10		20				
Total,	1		1	56,489	219	5	33		4			628	207	3,340	10	21		3

SUFFOLK COUNTY.—(CONTINUED.)

TOWNS.	Iowa.	California.	Territories.	Total United States	Canada.	N. Brunswick.	Nova Scotia.	N. Foundland.	West Indies.	Mexico.	S. America.	England.	Scotland.	Ireland.	Wales.	France.	Belgium.	Holland.
Brookhaven,				8,981	7	2	2		8			164	23	319		8	5	1
Easthampton,				1,987	1				1			21	2	103				1
Huntington,		1		7,225	10	2	4		4		4	150	43	590	2	4		
Islip,	5			2,646	10	2	7		9			133	31	288	1	4	2	85
River Head,				2,509	2		1		1			50	2	121		1		
Shelter Island,				446								2	1	32				
Smithtown,				1,814								57	7	163		11	1	
Southampton,				6,255	9		2					65	10	378		4		7
Southold,				4,944	4	5	4	1	22		1	82	15	361	4	13		1
Total,	6	1		36,807	43	11	20	1	45		5	724	134	2,355	7	45	8	95

SULLIVAN COUNTY.—(CONTINUED.)

TOWNS.	Iowa.	California.	Territories.	Total United States	Canada.	N. Brunswick.	Nova Scotia.	N. Foundland.	West Indies.	Mexico.	S. America.	England.	Scotland.	Ireland.	Wales.	France.	Belgium.	Holland.
Bethel,				1,998	2				2			41	30	447				1
Cochecton,	1			1,794	2							43	7	262		5		
Collicoon,				1,189	5							17	9	95		10		
Fallsburgh,				2,604	11		3					31	2	242		7		
Forrestburgh,				661								10	1	131				
Fremont,				802	4							4	13	76		4		
Highland,				716	1							25	9	77		2		
Liberty,				2,532	1	1	2					53	12	199				
Lumberland,				664		1						22	36	77		1		
Mamakating,				3,631	4		1					77	20	306	4	1		
Neversink,				1,983			1					3	3	157		4		
Rockland,				1,172	1	1						4	8	45				
Thompson,				2,882	1	1						59	38	396	1			
Tusten,				557								14	2	75				
Total,	1			23,185	32	4	7		2			403	190	2,585	5	34		1

TIOGA COUNTY.—(CONTINUED.)

TOWNS.	Iowa.	California.	Territories.	Total United States	Canada.	N. Brunswick.	Nova Scotia.	N. Foundland.	West Indies.	Mexico.	S. America.	England.	Scotland.	Ireland.	Wales.	France.	Belgium.	Holland.
Barton,				3,599	4							34	3	100		2		
Berkshire,				951								9	2	15		2		
Candor,				3,719	15	2						43		96		2	1	
Newark,				1,813	2							12	2	47		35		1
Nichols,				1,792	7							11	1	24		1		
Owego,	1			7,502	12		1	1	1			135	15	542	3	7		
Richford,				1,089	2							10	1	17				
Spencer,				1,717	1	7						12		16				
Tioga,				2,846	1							11	14	71	1	42		
Total,	1			25,028	44	9	1	1	1			277	38	928	4	91	1	1

TOMPKINS COUNTY.—(CONTINUED.)

TOWNS.	Iowa.	California.	Territories.	Total United States	Canada.	N. Brunswick.	Nova Scotia.	N. Foundland.	West Indies.	Mexico.	S. America.	England.	Scotland.	Ireland.	Wales.	France.	Belgium.	Holland.
Caroline,	1			2,365	4		1					39	2	49		1		
Danby,				2,289	5							5		29				
Dryden,				4,803	5							24	29	125		4		1
Enfield,				1,828	4							6		67		1		
Groton,				3,285	7							10	12	69				
Ithaca,	1			6,204	22	1	2				3	197	28	553	4	4		
Lansing,				3,115	4							27	2	102		1		
Newfield,				2,726								27		44	1			
Ulysses,			2	2,923	6		4			1		97	8	139	2	1		1
Total,	2		2	29,538	57	1	7			1	3	432	81	1,177	7	12		2

ULSTER COUNTY.—(CONTINUED.)

TOWNS.	Iowa.	California.	Territories.	Total United States	Canada.	N. Brunswick.	Nova Scotia.	N. Foundland.	West Indies.	Mexico.	S. America.	England.	Scotland.	Ireland.	Wales.	France.	Belgium.	Holland.
Denning,				632	1							1		33		1		
Esopus,				3,068	18		1		3			72	28	884	3	5		
Gardiner,				1,770								13	1	105		2		
Hurley,				1,745								11	3	347				
Kingston,				8,784	18	3	4	3				162	36	3,302	2	29	1	2
Lloyd.				2,027	1		1	1				24	1	98	1	1		1

(Continued on page 153.)

STEUBEN COUNTY.—(Continued.)

FOREIGN COUNTRIES.

TOWNS.	Germany.	Prussia.	Austria.	Switzerland.	Italy.	Spain.	Portugal.	Poland.	Norway.	Sweden.	Russia.	Denmark.	East Indies.	Africa.	Turkey and Greece.	Islands.	Asia.	At Sea.	Unknown.
Hornby,	7																		6
Hornellsville,	75	1								1							1	2	71
Howard,	12			1														1	2
Jasper,	3			2															7
Lindley,	4																		
Prattsburgh,	6																		10
Pultney,	4			1															3
Thurston,				3															1
Troupsburgh,																			43
Urbana,	2																		3
Wayland,	783																	1	1
Wayne,				1													1		
West Union,	4			1															29
Wheeler,	4	1																	6
Woodhull,	1																		8
Total,	1, 524	22	5	14	6		5	3		7							2	4	414

SUFFOLK COUNTY.—(Continued.)

TOWNS.	Germany.	Prussia.	Austria.	Switzerland.	Italy.	Spain.	Portugal.	Poland.	Norway.	Sweden.	Russia.	Denmark.	East Indies.	Africa.	Turkey and Greece.	Islands.	Asia.	At Sea.	Unknown.
Brookhaven,	145	2	5	4					1			1			1			1	16
Easthampton,	23			1			1												4
Huntington,	78	1		1			2		1			1	1			3		1	15
Islip,	56	1							3	1									3
River Head,	40			3															4
Shelter Island,																			2
Smithtown,	33						1												
Southampton,	51			7		1	25	1	2							2			2
Southold,	193	14	5	2				1				1						1	2
Total,	619	18	10	18		1	29	2	7	1		3	1		1	5		3	48

SULLIVAN COUNTY.—(Continued.)

TOWNS.	Germany.	Prussia.	Austria.	Switzerland.	Italy.	Spain.	Portugal.	Poland.	Norway.	Sweden.	Russia.	Denmark.	East Indies.	Africa.	Turkey and Greece.	Islands.	Asia.	At Sea.	Unknown.
Bethel,	79			9														1	1
Cochecton,	871			86															1
Collicoon,	656	3	7	85														2	14
Fallsburgh,	125									1								1	2
Forrestburgh,	34									1									1
Fremont,	397																	1	
Highland,	33		1										1						
Liberty,	58			1															7
Lumberland,	99			1						1									
Mamakating,	23			2															15
Neversink,	27						1												1
Rockland,	26		1							8									6
Thompson,	44			1						1									126
Tusten,	177																		
Total,	2, 649	3	9	185			1			12			1					5	174

TIOGA COUNTY.—(Continued.)

TOWNS.	Germany.	Prussia.	Austria.	Switzerland.	Italy.	Spain.	Portugal.	Poland.	Norway.	Sweden.	Russia.	Denmark.	East Indies.	Africa.	Turkey and Greece.	Islands.	Asia.	At Sea.	Unknown.
Barton,	44																		56
Berkshire,	6			23															60
Candor,	3																	1	12
Newark,	15			18															
Nichols,	18					1			1										15
Owego,	32	8		4					1									2	62
Richford,	3																		60
Spencer,																	1		51
Tioga,	20																		21
Total,	141	8		45		1			2								1	3	337

TOMPKINS COUNTY.—(Continued.)

TOWNS.	Germany.	Prussia.	Austria.	Switzerland.	Italy.	Spain.	Portugal.	Poland.	Norway.	Sweden.	Russia.	Denmark.	East Indies.	Africa.	Turkey and Greece.	Islands.	Asia.	At Sea.	Unknown.
Caroline,																			5
Danby,	1																		2
Dryden,	8															1			3
Enfield,	1																		5
Groton,	1																	1	19
Ithaca,	36	4	1	2														3	89
Lansing,	2																		3
Newfield,																			2
Ulysses,	7	1																	1
Total,	56	5	1	2												1		4	129

ULSTER COUNTY.—(Continued.)

TOWNS.	Germany.	Prussia.	Austria.	Switzerland.	Italy.	Spain.	Portugal.	Poland.	Norway.	Sweden.	Russia.	Denmark.	East Indies.	Africa.	Turkey and Greece.	Islands.	Asia.	At Sea.	Unknown.
Denning,	24																		
Esopus,	201	1		1		1													1
Gardiner,	28	1		1						2									
Hurley,	9																		
Kingston,	1, 568	23		6	4			16	1	5									5
Lloyd,	35	1																	

(Continued on page 160.)

ULSTER COUNTY.

TOWNS.	COUNTIES OF NEW-YORK.																	
	Albany.	Allegany.	Broome.	Cattaraugus.	Cayuga.	Chautauque.	Chemung.	Chenango.	Clinton.	Columbia.	Cortland.	Delaware.	Dutchess.	Erie.	Essex.	Franklin.	Fulton.	Genesee.
Marbletown,	7	.....	1	.....	.....	.....	.....	1	.....	10	.....	18	30	.....	1	.....	1	.....
Marlborough,	3	.....	.....	.....	.....	5	.....	.....	.....	17	.....	2	93	.....	.....	.....	.....	.....
New Paltz,	2	.....	.....	.....	2	.....	.....	.....	.....	7	.....	.....	50	.....	.....	1	.....	.....
Olive,	22	.....	.....	.....	.....	.....	.....	.....	.....	10	.....	43	75	1	.....	.....	.....	.....
Plattekill,	1	.....	.....	.....	5	.....	3	1	.....	2	.....	1	34	.....	.....	.....	.....	.....
Rochester,	11	.....	.....	.....	.....	1	.....	.....	.....	5	.....	.....	57	.....	.....	.....	1	.....
Rosendale,	3	.....	.....	.....	1	.....	.....	3	.....	3	.....	3	21	.....	.....	.....	.....	.....
Saugerties,	102	.....	1	.....	4	.....	3	1	1	164	2	19	176	.....	3	1	1	2
Shandaken,	32	.....	2	.....	.....	.....	.....	.....	.....	20	1	224	60	4	.....	.....	.....	.....
Shawangunk	1	.....	.....	.....	.....	.....	.....	1	.....	2	.....	2	41	.....	.....	.....	1	.....
Wawarsing,	26	.....	4	.....	5	.....	2	4	.....	23	1	54	176	2	1	.....	.....	3
Woodstock,	18	.....	.....	.....	.....	.....	.....	.....	.....	89	1	13	71	.....	.....	.....	.....	.....
Total,	342	.....	19	.....	23	8	10	12	3	512	10	561	1, 626	10	11	2	4	5

WARREN COUNTY.

TOWNS.	Albany.	Allegany.	Broome.	Cattaraugus.	Cayuga.	Chautauque.	Chemung.	Chenango.	Clinton.	Columbia.	Cortland.	Delaware.	Dutchess.	Erie.	Essex.	Franklin.	Fulton.	Genesee.
Bolton,	1	.....	.....	.....	.....	.....	.....	1	1	2	1	2	2	.....	14	.....	5	.....
Caldwell,	5	.....	.....	.....	.....	.....	.....	.....	.....	2	.....	6	7	.....	10	1	1	.....
Chester,	7	.....	.....	.....	4	.....	.....	1	2	5	2	2	17	3	103	.....	.....	1
Hague,	.....	1	.....	.....	1	.....	.....	.....	4	1	.....	.....	.....	.....	77	.....	.....	.....
Horicon,	5	.....	1	.....	.....	.....	1	8	.....	.....	.....	.....	.....	.....	48	1	1	1
Johnsburgh,	3	.....	.....	1	1	.....	.....	.....	2	1	.....	.....	6	.....	35	.....	1	1
Luzerne,	2	1	.....	.....	.....	.....	1	.....	2	6	.....	2	9	.....	1	.....	.....	1
Queensbury,	60	1	5	1	2	.....	.....	3	10	24	.....	7	102	10	109	1	6	2
Stony Creek,	18	.....	.....	.....	.....	.....	.....	2	2	.....	1	.....	7	1	.....	1	3	.....
Thurman,	11	.....	.....	.....	.....	.....	.....	1	.....	2	.....	1	9	.....	2	.....	.....	.....
Warrensburgh,	10	.....	1	.....	.....	.....	.....	.....	4	2	.....	.....	10	.....	9	1	6	4
Total,	122	3	7	2	8	.....	2	16	27	45	4	20	169	14	408	5	23	10

WASHINGTON COUNTY.

TOWNS.	Albany.	Allegany.	Broome.	Cattaraugus.	Cayuga.	Chautauque.	Chemung.	Chenango.	Clinton.	Columbia.	Cortland.	Delaware.	Dutchess.	Erie.	Essex.	Franklin.	Fulton.	Genesee.
Argyle,	15	.....	1	2	6	.....	.....	.....	6	23	.....	1	16	.....	2	1	.....	1
Cambridge,	4	.....	.....	.....	.....	.....	.....	1	.....	3	.....	.....	5	.....	1	.....	1	.....
Dresden,	1	.....	3	.....	.....	.....	.....	.....	1	.....	.....	.....	3	.....	10	.....	1	.....
Easton,	33	.....	.....	.....	2	1	.....	1	10	17	1	4	37	1	1	1	.....	.....
Fort Ann,	1	.....	.....	.....	2	2	.....	.....	20	11	1	.....	.....	1	33	2	.....	2
Fort Edward,	29	5	1	.....	2	.....	.....	2	23	9	.....	8	14	.....	18	1	.....	.....
Granville,	1	1	.....	2	6	1	.....	.....	9	7	4	.....	16	1	27	2	3	1
Greenwich,	20	1	.....	.....	1	1	.....	.....	7	17	.....	5	25	2	8	.....	6	8
Hampton,	3	.....	.....	.....	.....	.....	.....	.....	2	1	1	.....	2	.....	9	.....	1	.....
Hartford,	3	1	.....	.....	6	.....	1	.....	5	8	.....	.....	2	.....	11	4	.....	1
Hebron,	2	.....	.....	.....	.....	.....	.....	1	1	5	.....	5	5	1	2	1	.....	4
Jackson,	8	.....	.....	.....	.....	.....	.....	1	.....	1	.....	2	1	.....	1	.....	.....	.....
Kingsbury,	9	.....	.....	4	7	1	.....	2	18	8	1	3	35	.....	64	3	5	1
Putnam,	2	.....	.....	.....	.....	.....	.....	.....	2	.....	.....	.....	.....	.....	15	3	1	.....
Salem,	16	1	1	.....	1	.....	.....	.....	4	4	.....	2	4	3	9	1	.....	.....
White Creek,	5	1	1	2	1	.....	.....	.....	7	3	1	3	13	.....	1	2	.....	1
Whitehall,	13	1	.....	1	2	2	.....	1	42	13	.....	.....	22	.....	75	4	1	1
Total,	165	11	7	11	36	8	1	9	157	130	9	33	200	9	287	25	19	20

WAYNE COUNTY.

TOWNS.	Albany.	Allegany.	Broome.	Cattaraugus.	Cayuga.	Chautauque.	Chemung.	Chenango.	Clinton.	Columbia.	Cortland.	Delaware.	Dutchess.	Erie.	Essex.	Franklin.	Fulton.	Genesee.
Arcadia,	40	2	1	2	41	3	2	7	5	450	4	2	110	6	2	.....	4	6
Butler,	45	3	1	3	270	.....	2	2	.....	24	4	2	31	1	.....	.....	1	6
Galen,	32	4	4	5	80	1	4	14	.....	216	14	4	71	12	2	1	12	3
Huron,	14	.....	.....	5	74	.....	.....	.....	.....	54	1	6	19	.....	1	1	.....	.....
Lyons,	27	1	5	3	67	5	1	14	3	114	12	12	85	3	1	2	1	17
Macedon,	15	.....	1	4	27	2	2	2	8	42	2	1	144	8	5	.....	3	2
Marion,	4	2	2	4	12	1	.....	4	.....	79	1	4	26	3	4	.....	.....	11
Ontario,	8	.....	3	5	19	1	1	6	6	18	1	.....	18	1	4	3	3	8
Palmyra,	36	5	1	2	24	4	4	7	1	117	6	6	132	9	1	.....	3	13
Rose,	10	1	3	4	33	.....	1	9	.....	43	4	7	68	.....	.....	2	2	4
Savannah,	36	1	.....	.....	171	.....	.....	1	.....	51	2	1	48	5	.....	.....	.....	.....
Sodus,	22	3	.....	.....	23	2	4	9	5	257	2	2	130	9	5	1	8	3
Walworth,	18	1	2	2	14	.....	.....	9	.....	52	2	1	94	3	2	.....	1	12
Williamson,	9	8	2	5	16	1	.....	7	2	43	6	.....	49	7	2	.....	2	.....
Wolcott,	51	1	.....	3	343	.....	7	20	.....	50	6	1	35	1	2	6	1	1
Total,	367	32	25	47	1, 214	20	28	111	30	1, 610	67	49	1, 060	68	31	16	41	86

WESTCHESTER COUNTY.

TOWNS.	Albany.	Allegany.	Broome.	Cattaraugus.	Cayuga.	Chautauque.	Chemung.	Chenango.	Clinton.	Columbia.	Cortland.	Delaware.	Dutchess.	Erie.	Essex.	Franklin.	Fulton.	Genesee.
Bedford,	3	.....	.....	.....	.....	.....	.....	1	.....	6	.....	1	28	.....	.....	.....	.....	1
Cortlandt,	36	.....	3	.....	2	.....	.....	2	1	13	1	15	171	4	.....	2	.....	1
East Chester,	6	.....	3	.....	1	.....	.....	2	.....	14	3	4	18	5	.....	.....	.....	.....
Greenburgh,	22	.....	1	.....	3	1	.....	.....	.....	26	2	6	52	5	.....	1	.....	.....
Harrison,	2	.....	.....	.....	.....	.....	.....	.....	.....	.....	.....	2	9	.....	.....	.....	.....	.....
Lewisboro,	3	.....	.....	.....	2	.....	.....	3	.....	2	.....	3	7	.....	.....	.....	.....	.....
Mamaroneck,	1	.....	.....	.....	.....	.....	.....	.....	.....	7	.....	1	.....	.....	.....	.....	.....	.....
Mount Pleasant,	5	.....	2	.....	1	.....	1	.....	.....	3	.....	.....	25	.....	.....	.....	.....	.....
New Castle,	5	.....	.....	.....	.....	.....	.....	.....	.....	.....	.....	1	39	.....	.....	.....	.....	1
New Rochelle,	10	.....	.....	.....	1	.....	.....	.....	.....	5	.....	.....	16	.....	.....	.....	.....	1
North Castle,	.....	.....	.....	.....	.....	.....	.....	.....	.....	.....	.....	3	11	.....	.....	.....	.....	.....
North Salem,	2	.....	1	.....	.....	.....	.....	.....	.....	6	.....	2	17	.....	.....	1	.....	1
Ossining,	52	1	.....	.....	7	.....	1	5	1	18	1	10	74	5	.....	.....	.....	2

(Continued on page 161.)

ULSTER COUNTY.—(Continued.)

TOWNS.	COUNTIES OF NEW-YORK.																	
	Greene.	Hamilton.	Herkimer.	Jefferson.	Kings.	Lewis.	Livingston.	Madison.	Monroe.	Montgomery.	New-York.	Niagara.	Oneida.	Onondaga.	Ontario.	Orange.	Orleans.	Oswego.
Marbletown,	24				9				1	3	30		4	1		21		
Marlborough,	6				4			1			85		7			136		
New Paltz,	1			2	1		1				8					20		
Olive,	89					1		1		2	24					8		
Plattekill,	6				5						29					114		1
Rochester,	48								2	1	7					28		
Rosendale,	10				2		1	1		1	10			1	1	4		
Saugerties,	462		2	1	38			2	3	6	94		5	4	1	26		3
Shandaken,	383	2	1		3				1		8		2			3		
Shawangunk,	2		2		6			1		2	29					292		
Wawarsing,	97		2	1			3		2	7	124		1	4	1	179		1
Woodstock,	63										7		1	2		4		1
Total,	1, 552	2	12	7	86	1	7	7	21	37	987	5	29	22	7	1, 058	1	12
WARREN COUNTY.—(Continued.)																		
Bolton,			1	2							1							
Caldwell,	2	4														7		
Chester,	11	1			5			2		3	17					1		1
Hague,	2							2		1								
Horicon,	7	2							1	2	1				1	9		2
Johnsburgh,	1	1	4	1	1	1		2		13			1			1	5	2
Luzerne,	1		1		1					3			2			3		1
Queensbury,	21		7		4	2		5		17	26	1	12	3		6		2
Stony Creek,	1	1	1	3		4				10	1							
Thurman,		1				2				1	3			1				
Warrensburgh,	6	2	2	3	5					2	14		1					1
Total,	52	12	16	9	16	9		11	1	52	63	1	16	4	1	27	5	9
WASHINGTON COUNTY.—(Continued.)																		
Argyle,			1		2			2			17		1			6		
Cambridge,			2	2			1		1	2	17		2	2		2		6
Dresden,			1							2	1						1	
Easton,	2		5	3	1					4	3	1	3	2		1	1	2
Fort Ann,			2	2		2	1	1	3	4	10	1	1	6		4	1	3
Fort Edward,	4		5	1	1			2	2	5	16		1	4		1		2
Granville,	1			8	1					1	13		9			1	7	
Greenwich,	2	1	10		2					9	16		5	3		3		4
Hampton,										1		1						
Hartford,		1		3			2		2	1	1		2	1	6		1	
Hebron,	1								1	1	3		2			3		
Jackson,				6						1				1		2		
Kingsbury,	6		8	2	15	1				6	18		3	3	2	4		3
Putnam,											6		1					
Salem,	5		1	2		1	4	2	3		10		7	2	1	5		4
White Creek,			1	1		2				3	10		5	4		3	1	
Whitehall,	4	1	4	4		3			2	11	8		4	1		1	1	
Total,	25	3	40	34	22	9	8	7	14	51	149	3	46	29	9	36	13	24
WAYNE COUNTY.—(Continued.)																		
Arcadia,	27		25	17	3	4	7	24	36	62	46	7	39	35	169	27	16	18
Butler,	6		22	4		1	1	23	3	11	22		31	87	11	18		20
Galen,	4	3	31	11	6	3	1	23	36	33	36	6	40	76	173	27		12
Huron,	3		8	3			1	6	13	13	1	1	13	65	35	31		10
Lyons,	6		8	7	4	3	11	16	33	50	27		46	52	145	30	12	6
Macedon,	9		16	6			7	23	104	26	15	8	26	22	158	16	4	7
Marion,	4		13	8		2	7	12	39	39	3	5	21	15	35	6	5	4
Ontario,	3		5	7		2	2	19	138	13	4	3	45	12	56	1	3	1
Palmyra,	10	1	22	24	4	3	4	15	67	34	48	5	39	28	150	35	13	9
Rose,	6	1	9	5	1	1	4	34	5	17	9	1	26	32	56	7	5	4
Savannah,	3		20	3	1	3	1	13	1	3	24		2	52	9	10		10
Sodus,	18		19	11	6	1	4	15	24	30	15		19	61	92	20	9	1
Walworth,	10		7			6	4	6	102	11	11	2	29	11	60	6	9	2
Williamson,	1		5	11	4		6	8	36	6	7		10	30	36	10	4	13
Wolcott,	11		27	16	3		1	10	4	33	17	1	27	107	16	47	1	43
Total,	121	5	237	133	32	29	61	247	631	381	285	39	413	685	1, 201	291	81	160
WESTCHESTER COUNTY.—(Continued.)																		
Bedford,	3				6				1		160	1	1	2		17		
Cortlandt,	18			3	34	1	1	3		5	384	1	8	1	3	55		
East Chester,	2	1	2	1	50			2		3	955	1	1			38	2	1
Greenburgh,	6	6			41		1		1		841	1	1		1	29	7	
Harrison,					7						85					6		
Lewisboro,					6					1	70					2		
Mamaroneck,					15						134		1			7		
Mount Pleasant,	9				9				1		245					16		2
New Castle,	2				3			1			106		3	1		2		1
New Rochelle,			3		35			1			417		5	2		20		
North Castle,					8						169		2			13		
North Salem,	1				1			1		5	43		1			7		
Ossining,	11	1	1		6			4	2	5	579		5	9	1	38		

(Continued on page 162.)

ULSTER COUNTY.—(Continued.)

TOWNS.	Otsego.	Putnam.	Queens.	Rensselaer.	Richmond.	Rockland.	St. Lawrence.	Saratoga.	Schenectady.	Schoharie.	Schuyler.	Seneca.	Steuben.	Suffolk.	Sullivan.	Tioga.	Tompkins.	Ulster.
	COUNTIES OF NEW-YORK.																	
Marbletown,	3	1	1	1					3					2	9		3	3, 281
Marlborough,		11	2	2		5		2		1		1		6	5			1, 836
New Paltz,		21	2	1		1				1			1		8			1, 652
Olive,	4	7		3		1		2		11			1		15		6	2, 303
Plattekill,	1	3	1	1		4		1		1					4		1	1, 499
Rochester,	3	15		1				3	2	2		2			10			3, 082
Rosendale,		2						2		4				1	10			1, 758
Saugerties,	3	2	17	19		12		2		39				2	5		7	5, 548
Shandaken,	3	4		13				1		32				1	8		5	1, 270
Shawangunk,		30	9					1						2	34			1, 984
Wawarsing,	5	41	2	17		4	1	5	2	13		1	4	1	342	2	3	4, 275
Woodstock,	1	2	1	23			5	2		19					1			1, 313
Total,	48	190	43	101		51	7	54	12	327		10	16	27	511	5	33	44, 237

WARREN COUNTY.—(Continued.)

TOWNS.	Otsego.	Putnam.	Queens.	Rensselaer.	Richmond.	Rockland.	St. Lawrence.	Saratoga.	Schenectady.	Schoharie.	Schuyler.	Seneca.	Steuben.	Suffolk.	Sullivan.	Tioga.	Tompkins.	Ulster.
Bolton,				7	1		1	28		1			2				1	
Caldwell,				21				26	1	2					1			
Chester,	1			12			2	29		3				1				
Hague,			1	4			4	7										
Horicon,	9			7			1	15	2								2	
Johnsburgh,	4			14			8	26	3	2							2	
Luzerne,	3			27			1	86	1									
Queensbury,	6		16	133			13	350	3	20		3	2			1	2	
Stony Creek,				5				82										
Thurman,				7				25							1			
Warrensburgh,	3			18				32	4				3			1	7	
Total,	26		17	255	1		30	706	14	28		3	7	1	2	2	14	

WASHINGTON COUNTY.—(Continued.)

TOWNS.	Otsego.	Putnam.	Queens.	Rensselaer.	Richmond.	Rockland.	St. Lawrence.	Saratoga.	Schenectady.	Schoharie.	Schuyler.	Seneca.	Steuben.	Suffolk.	Sullivan.	Tioga.	Tompkins.	Ulster.
Argyle,	1			43				25	1	2		2			5			
Cambridge,	1			148				26	5	3		1						1
Dresden,	1			3			1	4					1					
Easton,	2	1		238		1		132	5	6							1	
Fort Ann	1			41			1	28		2								2
Fort Edward,	8	1		43			3	183		6			3					1
Granville,	3		1	43			3	25	2	3						1	1	
Greenwich,				162	1		2	170	1	6		3				1		
Hampton,	1			18				6										
Hartford,	2			17			7	27	1	1		2						
Hebron,			1	22			3	16	1	2					1	2		
Jackson,	1	2		47				12	1									
Kingsbury,	2			33	1		6	98	2	2			3	1				
Putnam,			1	6				1										
Salem,	2			114	1		2	22	7	3								1
White Creek,	4	2		241			1	15	2			2				4		
Whitehall,	1	1	1	32			14	45	1	2			1					
Total,	30	7	4	1, 251	3	1	43	835	29	38		10	8	1	6	8	2	5

WAYNE COUNTY.—(Continued.)

TOWNS.	Otsego.	Putnam.	Queens.	Rensselaer.	Richmond.	Rockland.	St. Lawrence.	Saratoga.	Schenectady.	Schoharie.	Schuyler.	Seneca.	Steuben.	Suffolk.	Sullivan.	Tioga.	Tompkins.	Ulster.
Arcadia,	17	5	13	132		4	2	43	4	18		46	8	10	2		13	23
Butler,	12		1	35	1		3	78	2	10		12	9	8	1		8	1
Galen,	12	2		96	1	6	9	92	12	17		181	15	14	2	1	14	9
Huron,	5			25	1	1	16	9		10		6	13	1			4	5
Lyons,	15	11	7	70		3	6	43	12	10		53	14	5	6	4	4	7
Macedon,	6		1	22		9	4	26	18	12		11	4	5	1		2	19
Marion,	15	1		31		1		16	2	9		8	4	6	2		2	1
Ontario,	5			25	1	1	16	9		10		6	13	1			4	5
Palmyra,	8		2	43			6	34	5	11		16	5	22	1	4	5	11
Rose,	5	6		28		3	1	22	8	10		28	4	12		8	5	1
Savannah,	20	1	1	31				25	3	8		45	7	1			3	10
Sodus,	16	6	6	61		10	17	34	4	12		34	14	2		7	3	18
Walworth,	16		4	6				16	6	10		10	5		1	1	1	
Williamson,	10			39		1	5	20	2	1		6	2	2	1	1	2	4
Wolcott,	14	5		54		6	8	99	11	28		40	1	12		3	13	13
Total,	176	37	35	698	4	45	93	566	89	176		502	118	101	17	29	83	127

WESTCHESTER COUNTY.—(Continued.)

TOWNS.	Otsego.	Putnam.	Queens.	Rensselaer.	Richmond.	Rockland.	St. Lawrence.	Saratoga.	Schenectady.	Schoharie.	Schuyler.	Seneca.	Steuben.	Suffolk.	Sullivan.	Tioga.	Tompkins.	Ulster.
Bedford,		23	8	2		2	1					3	2	2	1		1	9
Cortlandt,	3	316	9	16	3	83	1	4	2				1	13	1	2	4	36
East Chester,	2	18	25	3	6	2	2	2		4		3		11	1		1	13
Greenburgh,	3	26	5	14	10	46	1	10	1	3			1	1	1			11
Harrison,		20	6	1	2	3		2					1	4	1			
Lewisboro,		31	2	1		2		2							2			2
Mamaroneck,			11			1		1					1	6	3			1
Mount Pleasant,		10	12	2	3	30	1			4				3	1			5
New Castle,		3		2		7			1			2		2	1			3
New Rochelle,	2	1	53	4	2	2		1						5				7
North Castle,		12	7	1	7	1		1								1		
North Salem,		143	1	4									1	1				5
Ossining,	2	46	76	22		29	1	14		1		2	1	10	1		3	25

(Continued on page 163.)

ULSTER COUNTY.—(CONTINUED.)

TOWNS.	COUNTIES OF NEW-YORK.							UNITED STATES.										
	Warren.	Washington.	Wayne.	Westchester.	Wyoming.	Yates.	New-York.	Maine.	N. Hampshire.	Vermont.	Massachusetts.	Rhode Island.	Connecticut.	New Jersey.	Pennsylvania.	Delaware.	Maryland.	District of Columbia.
Marbletown,		1		11			3, 478		1		1	1	14	3	4		3	
Marlborough,		1		47		1	2, 279	2	1	4	29	4	23	15	7		1	
New Paltz,				2			1, 784	3			7		6	9				
Olive,				3			2, 632	1		1	4	7	36	7	4			
Plattekill,			2	39			1, 761		2		2		8	12	10			
Rochester,			1	4			3, 286	2	1	2	2	1	10	20	9			
Rosendale,				3			1, 845		2	6	5		26	14	9			
Saugerties,		5		27			6, 815		3	10	43	10	75	43	10		4	
Shandaken,		4	3	4			2, 095			1	5	1	49		13			
Shawangunk,				15			2, 458		3	2	12	1	4	10	1			
Wawarsing,	2	10	1	89			5, 559	2		9	49	8	141	62	34			
Woodstock,	5	2	2	14			1, 665	5	2		7		24	3	12			
Total,	8	30	9	364	2	9	53. 136	28	25	55	232	45	597	334	182		12	4

WARREN COUNTY.—(CONTINUED.)

TOWNS.	Warren.	Washington.	Wayne.	Westchester.	Wyoming.	Yates.	New-York.	Maine.	N. Hampshire.	Vermont.	Massachusetts.	Rhode Island.	Connecticut.	New Jersey.	Pennsylvania.	Delaware.	Maryland.	District of Columbia.
Bolton,	805	108					988		14	77	45	13	9		2			
Caldwell,	549	98	1		2		746	1	8	47	17	7	12	1	6		1	
Chester,	1, 117	91		10			1, 454	3	10	171	50	13	48	6	1			
Hague,	285	26			1		417	1	13	109	31		6	1	3			
Horicon,	752	45					924	1	17	161	22	12	4	1				
Johnsburgh,	1, 168	177	3	5			1, 496	1	13	177	39	4	16	1	3			
Luzerne,	766	85					1, 006		18	72	28	1	14	1	1			
Queensbury,	2, 874	610	5	11	4		4, 502	14	51	331	105	19	70	10	10		2	
Stony Creek,	482	35					660	12	21	47	21	4	18	1				
Thurman,	844	49					961		16	55	25	11	24	8	4			
Warrensburgh,	1, 193	133				1	1, 478	2	59	131	25	10	16	2				
Total,	10, 835	1, 457	9	26	7	1	14, 632	35	240	1, 378	408	94	237	32	30		3	

WASHINGTON COUNTY.—(CONTINUED.)

TOWNS.	Warren.	Washington.	Wayne.	Westchester.	Wyoming.	Yates.	New-York.	Maine.	N. Hampshire.	Vermont.	Massachusetts.	Rhode Island.	Connecticut.	New Jersey.	Pennsylvania.	Delaware.	Maryland.	District of Columbia.
Argyle,	17	2, 386	5				2.590		2	24	23	4	10	9	3			
Cambridge,	11	1, 548		2			1, 799		5	70	33	31	19	5	4		5	
Dresden,	18	502					554	2	4	76	15	2	4	2				
Easton,	29	1, 842	1	1			2, 396	2	18	39	53	45	18	2	3			
Fort Ann,	85	2, 430					2, 706	5	25	256	57	16	32		8		1	
Fort Edward,	69	1, 660		1	1		2, 135	3	17	150	48	5	25	4	3			
Granville,	24	1, 897	1	3			2, 129	2	34	391	83	16	63	3	13			
Greenwich,	56	2, 488	2	5			3, 053	4	33	129	113	32	41	9	11		9	
Hampton,	1	422			6		475		11	193	23	3	17	2				
Hartford,	30	1, 476	4	3			1, 632	1	13	109	51	10	32	1	2		1	1
Hebron,	11	1, 903	1	1			2, 002	2	6	137	43	8	11	3	2			
Jackson,	3	1, 298	2				1, 390		18	59	29	4	11	4			2	
Kingsbury,	266	1, 767	9	1			2, 424	2	23	240	50	10	30	3	5		1	
Putnam,	7	513					558	1	2	56	6	1	4					
Salem,	3	1, 835	1	2	2		2, 088	3	37	317	69	9	22	2	12			
White Creek,	5	1, 296		1	1		1, 645	5	22	309	75	17	32	5	4			
Whitehall,	29	2, 365		6			2, 721	13	40	517	68	7	55	2	13			1
Total,	664	27, 628	26	26	10		32, 297	45	310	3, 072	839	220	426	56	83		19	2

WAYNE COUNTY.—(CONTINUED.)

TOWNS.	Warren.	Washington.	Wayne.	Westchester.	Wyoming.	Yates.	New-York.	Maine.	N. Hampshire.	Vermont.	Massachusetts.	Rhode Island.	Connecticut.	New Jersey.	Pennsylvania.	Delaware.	Maryland.	District of Columbia.
Arcadia,	1	43	2, 626	8		16	4, 283	32	22	66	78	13	59	82	37		7	
Butler,	1	30	1, 102	8	2		1, 979	1	7	24	39	7	69	18	8		1	
Galen,	3	81	2, 118	2	8	15	3, 716	6	7	72	44	6	72	72	51		17	1
Huron,		14	998	4			1, 490	6	9	29	64		66	30	6			
Lyons,	7	43	2, 294	7	1	13	3, 464	5	14	64	79	9	69	92	48		8	1
Macedon,	2	24	833	13	2	5	1, 739	4	9	25	66	13	46	54	6	1	7	
Marion,	1	39	932	1	1	3	1, 440	2	10	40	63	25	51	30	8			
Ontario,	6	52	1, 169	2	2	5	1, 751	2	9	39	63	13	79	32	8			
Palmyra,	4	31	1, 743	7	4	15	2, 859	10	21	44	103	11	87	50	35		5	1
Rose,	2	36	1, 045	8	1	7	1, 654	3	12	54	49	10	55	15	10		3	
Savannah,	2	17	853	3	1	5	1, 507		5	12	20	2	13	17	1		2	
Sodus,	2	59	2, 353	12	2	19	3, 521	12	14	60	92	24	63	54	36		8	1
Walworth,	2	21	861	2	4	1	1, 456	4	6	21	52	9	40	38	7		1	
Williamson,		36	1 189		2		1, 669	2	10	44	52	10	46	82	17		1	
Wolcott,	3	22	1, 302	18	2		2, 549	10	10	47	53	2	63	41	24			
Total,	36	548	21, 418	95	32	104	35, 077	99	165	641	917	154	878	707	302	1	60	4

WESTCHESTER COUNTY.—(CONTINUED.)

TOWNS.	Warren.	Washington.	Wayne.	Westchester.	Wyoming.	Yates.	New-York.	Maine.	N. Hampshire.	Vermont.	Massachusetts.	Rhode Island.	Connecticut.	New Jersey.	Pennsylvania.	Delaware.	Maryland.	District of Columbia.
Bedford,		4	1	2, 617			2, 907	1	1		14	3	151	4	10		2	
Cortlandt,		3	2	4, 750			6, 017	6	10	22	39	6	119	7[illegible]	16		2	
East Chester,	2	3	1	1, 067			2, 281	12	2	15	21	3	80	100	31		10	
Greenburgh,	1	2		2, 730			3, 920	5	5	12	55	10	92	82	31		9	1
Harrison,		1		841	1		904	2	1		9		49	8	10		1	1
Lewisboro,				1, 319			1, 460				6		183	7	1			1
Mamaroneck,			1	484			675	3	2	3	10	3	29	18	5		1	
Mount Pleasant,				2, 383			2, 773	3		1	14	4	62	18	16		1	
New Castle,				1, 295			1, 481			2	2		21	8				
New Rochelle,				1, 252			1, 847	2	4	7	27	4	83	51	28		4	3
North Castle,				1, 748			1, 984	1	3	1	6	1	100	14	0			
North Salem,				972			1, 216			5	5		113	10	2			
Ossining,	9	15		2, 481		1	3, 585	2	10	12	52	7	102	88	50		19	3

(Continued on page 164.)

ULSTER COUNTY.—(Continued.)

TOWNS.	UNITED STATES.																	
	Virginia.	N. Carolina.	S. Carolina.	Georgia.	Florida.	Alabama.	Mississippi.	Louisiana.	Texas.	Arkansas.	Missouri.	Tennessee.	Kentucky.	Ohio.	Indiana.	Illinois.	Michigan.	Wisconsin.
Marbletown,	2													1				
Marlborough,				1										3			2	1
New Paltz,														2				
Olive,														1			1	1
Plattekill,														1			1	
Rochester,																		
Rosendale,														4			1	
Saugerties,	3			2									1	2	1			
Shandaken,	1													1			2	2
Shawangunk,	1														1	1	2	1
Wawarsing,														6		1		
Woodstock,			2											1				
Total,	13	1	5	5									1	31	3	2	17	7

WARREN COUNTY.—(Continued.)

TOWNS.	Virginia.	N. Carolina.	S. Carolina.	Georgia.	Florida.	Alabama.	Mississippi.	Louisiana.	Texas.	Arkansas.	Missouri.	Tennessee.	Kentucky.	Ohio.	Indiana.	Illinois.	Michigan.	Wisconsin.
Bolton,														1		2	1	
Caldwell,								1						1				
Chester,											1			1				
Hague,																1		
Horicon,																		
Johnsburgh,														3		3	1	
Luzerne,																		
Queensbury,	1													5	1	2		3
Stony Creek,																		
Thurman,																		1
Warrensburgh,														2		1		
Total,	1							1			1			13	1	9	2	4

WASHINGTON COUNTY.—(Continued.)

TOWNS.	Virginia.	N. Carolina.	S. Carolina.	Georgia.	Florida.	Alabama.	Mississippi.	Louisiana.	Texas.	Arkansas.	Missouri.	Tennessee.	Kentucky.	Ohio.	Indiana.	Illinois.	Michigan.	Wisconsin.
Argyle,	2																	
Cambridge,				1								2		7		1		1
Dresden,														1				
Easton,	1													1			4	
Fort Ann,								1			2			3		1	1	1
Fort Edward,				1				2		2	1					1	1	
Granville,	1							1				2		2		4	2	2
Greenwich,	1									1		1		1		1		
Hampton,				3												4		
Hartford,														2			2	
Hebron,				1									1	3				
Jackson,	1															1		
Kingsbury,				1				1						3	1	2	2	
Putnam,														2			2	
Salem,	1														1			1
White Creek,											1			1			1	
Whitehall,		1			1									6		4	4	
Total,	7	1		7	1			5		3	4	5	1	32	2	19	19	5

WAYNE COUNTY.—(Continued.)

TOWNS.	Virginia.	N. Carolina.	S. Carolina.	Georgia.	Florida.	Alabama.	Mississippi.	Louisiana.	Texas.	Arkansas.	Missouri.	Tennessee.	Kentucky.	Ohio.	Indiana.	Illinois.	Michigan.	Wisconsin.
Arcadia,	2		1			3							1	15			19	4
Butler,	1													2	2		6	
Galen,	2			1	1								1	10	1	2	20	2
Huron,														6		1	2	3
Lyons,	4	2					1	3						8	2	1	9	5
Macedon,	2	1												6			21	3
Marion,														4	2	2	16	4
Ontario,					1	2						1		2		1	4	1
Palmyra,	1							2						10		5	17	2
Rose,														3			10	
Savannah,														6	1	1	4	1
Sodus,	1													7	3		16	3
Walworth,	2													4	1		9	
Williamson,	1													8			3	9
Wolcott,	1			2										10	1	2	5	3
Total,	17	3	1	3	2	5	1	5				1	2	101	13	15	161	40

WESTCHESTER COUNTY.—(Continued.)

TOWNS.	Virginia.	N. Carolina.	S. Carolina.	Georgia.	Florida.	Alabama.	Mississippi.	Louisiana.	Texas.	Arkansas.	Missouri.	Tennessee.	Kentucky.	Ohio.	Indiana.	Illinois.	Michigan.	Wisconsin.
Bedford,	1		1											1	1		1	1
Cortlandt,	3	1	5	1				3						7		2		
East Chester,	4		2	5		1		1			2		1	3				
Greenburgh,	15	1	1	9		1		5	1			1	1	7				
Harrison,	2															5	1	1
Lewisboro,	2															1		1
Mamaroneck,	2																	
Mount Pleasant,	4												1	9		3		
New Castle,	1		1											1				1
New Rochelle,	3		2	3		1		2			2			1		2	1	2
North Castle,	2				1								1	2				
North Salem,	3		1															
Ossining,	12	1	5	1	1		1	2	1		4		1	2	1	1	4	2

(Continued on page 165.)

ULSTER COUNTY.—(CONTINUED.)

TOWNS.	U. STATES. Iowa.	California.	Territories.	Total United States.	FOREIGN COUNTRIES. Canada.	N. Brunswick.	Nova Scotia.	N. Foundland.	West Indies.	Mexico.	S. America.	England.	Scotland.	Ireland.	Wales.	France.	Belgium.	Holland.
Marbletown,				3, 508	3	1						10	4	132	1	1		3
Marlborough,				2, 372	1		2		1	2		76	7	154		3	2	1
New Paltz,				1, 811				1				8	1	139				1
Olive,				2, 695	4							33	2	155	1			2
Plattekill,				1, 797			1					27	2	67		1		
Rochester,				3, 333	1							27	3	78				
Rosendale,				1, 912	1							15	8	387		4		13
Saugerties,				7, 022	10			6	2			184	19	1, 519	3	8		3
Shandaken,				2, 170	1							21	5	242		5		
Shawangunk,				2, 497			1					6	2	105				
Wawarsing,				5, 871	28		1					180	26	450		33		76
Woodstock,				1, 721	1		1					6		49				
Total,				54, 735	88	4	12	11	6	2		876	148	8, 246	11	93	3	102

WARREN COUNTY.—(CONTINUED.)

TOWNS.	Iowa.	California.	Territories.	Total United States.	Canada.	N. Brunswick.	Nova Scotia.	N. Foundland.	West Indies.	Mexico.	S. America.	England.	Scotland.	Ireland.	Wales.	France.	Belgium.	Holland.
Bolton,				1, 152	4							3	1	3				
Caldwell,				848	2							5	3	20		1		
Chester,				1, 758								40	10	100	1	1		
Hague,				582	18									10				
Horicon,				1, 142	14							4		74				
Johnsburgh,				1, 757	60							40	3	111				
Luzerne,				1, 141	19							34		76				
Queensbury,				5, 126	451	1	5					71	85	680				
Stony Creek,				784	7				5			5	2	107				
Thurman,				1, 105	6							4	9	125				
Warrensburgh,				1, 727	37							40	9	101		2		1
Total,				17, 122	618	1	5		5			246	122	1, 407	1	4		1

WASHINGTON COUNTY.—(CONTINUED.)

TOWNS.	Iowa.	California.	Territories.	Total United States.	Canada.	N. Brunswick.	Nova Scotia.	N. Foundland.	West Indies.	Mexico.	S. America.	England.	Scotland.	Ireland.	Wales.	France.	Belgium.	Holland.
Argyle,				2, 667	17							15	40	480		2		
Cambridge,				1, 983	2			1				11	18	283				
Dresden,				660	32		7					17		17				
Easton,				2, 582	18	1						24	17	353				
Fort Ann,				3, 115	118		1					20	13	264	1			
Fort Edward,	2			2, 400	155				4		2	30	20	344	2			1
Granville,				2, 748	59							13	11	347	172			
Greenwich,				3, 439	55							20	25	323				1
Hampton,				731	12							6	1	61	17			
Hartford,				1, 857	33							10	3	292	1			
Hebron,				2, 219	20							8	12	262	14			
Jackson,				1, 519	14							1	11	225				
Kingsbury,				2, 798	172		5					25	9	320				
Putnam,				632	12							6	44	30				
Salem,				2, 562	11							20	13	302	8			
White Creek,				2, 117	9							3		305	2			
Whitehall,				3, 453	425				1			38	14	547	1			
Total,	2			37, 482	1, 164	1	13	1	5		2	267	251	4, 755	218	2		2

WAYNE COUNTY.—(CONTINUED.)

TOWNS.	Iowa.	California.	Territories.	Total United States.	Canada.	N. Brunswick.	Nova Scotia.	N. Foundland.	West Indies.	Mexico.	S. America.	England.	Scotland.	Ireland.	Wales.	France.	Belgium.	Holland.
Arcadia,	2			4, 726	24	1					1	135	7	200	2	31		19
Butler,				2, 164	8							10	2	27				
Galen,				4, 104	32		4		1	1		194	6	497		21		3
Huron,				1, 712	17							66	1	20				
Lyons,				3, 888	37							204	24	266		203		2
Macedon,				2, 003	27	1					1	160	4	184		1		
Marion,				1, 697	14		1					118	6	21				43
Ontario,				2, 008	20		1					154		58		2		12
Palmyra,		1		3, 264	47		2					260	16	434		2		6
Rose,			1	1, 879	17							86		28		6		
Savannah,				1, 592	10						1	34	1	106		1		
Sodus,				3, 915	27		1					263	23	20	2	6		104
Walworth,				1, 650	20							138	7	94		2		
Williamson,				1, 954	19	1	1					171	3	14		1		350
Wolcott,			1	2, 824	16							32	2	76		1		
Total,	2	1	2	39, 380	335	3	10		1	1	3	2, 025	102	2, 045	4	277		539

WESTCHESTER COUNTY.—(CONTINUED.)

TOWNS.	Iowa.	California.	Territories.	Total United States.	Canada.	N. Brunswick.	Nova Scotia.	N. Foundland.	West Indies.	Mexico.	S. America.	England.	Scotland.	Ireland.	Wales.	France.	Belgium.	Holland.
Bedford,				3, 099	2							23	8	282	1			1
Cortlandt,				6, 334	24				2			200	30	1, 496	1	5		
East Chester,				2, 574	27						1	188	62	999	8	48		
Greenburgh,				4, 264	9	6	8		2			324	90	1, 261	18	25	3	11
Harrison,				1, 084					1			7	7	158	1			
Lewisboro,	1			1, 663								9	6	74	1			
Mamaroneck,	1			752	9		1		1			11	19	223		9		
Mount Pleasant,				2, 909	1		2	1	1			90	26	576		2		9
New Castle,				1, 518	1		1					20	5	182		1		
New Rochelle,				2, 079	0	3	7		2			110	18	662	3	5		1
North Castle,				2, 188			1	1	1			24	1	163	1			7
North Salem,				1, 355		1						10	3	138	1	2		
Ossining,				3, 968	14	4	10		9		4	269	49	1, 153	5	15	2	1

(Continued on page 166.)

ULSTER COUNTY.—(Continued.)

TOWNS.	FOREIGN COUNTRIES.																		
	Germany.	Prussia.	Austria.	Switzerland.	Italy.	Spain.	Portugal.	Poland.	Norway.	Sweden.	Russia.	Denmark.	East Indies.	Africa.	Turkey and Greece.	Islands.	Asia.	At Sea.	Unknown.
Marbletown,	58			2				1											2
Marlborough,	41		6																
New Paltz,	58			1															1
Olive,	29			2															1
Plattekill,	33			1														1	2
Rochester,	32																		1
Rosendale,	225	2		2														1	2
Saugerties,	524			5								3		1				1	8
Shandaken,	6																		2
Shawangunk	6															1			13
Wawarsing,	525	33		1				1	2										
Woodstock,	24									4									
Total,	3,426	61	6	22	4	1		18	3	11		3		1		1		3	39

WARREN COUNTY.—(Continued.)

TOWNS.	Germany.	Prussia.	Austria.	Switzerland.	Italy.	Spain.	Portugal.	Poland.	Norway.	Sweden.	Russia.	Denmark.	East Indies.	Africa.	Turkey and Greece.	Islands.	Asia.	At Sea.	Unknown.
Bolton,																			4
Caldwell,					1														
Chester,	22																	1	3
Hague,																			5
Horicon,	1															2			9
Johnsburgh,	6																	2	4
Luzerne,	1																	1	14
Queensbury,	5	7												2					5
Stony Creek,	3																		
Thurman,	1																	1	8
Warrensburgh,	13																		16
Total,	52	7			1									2		2		5	68

WASHINGTON COUNTY.—(Continued.)

TOWNS.	Germany.	Prussia.	Austria.	Switzerland.	Italy.	Spain.	Portugal.	Poland.	Norway.	Sweden.	Russia.	Denmark.	East Indies.	Africa.	Turkey and Greece.	Islands.	Asia.	At Sea.	Unknown.
Argyle,																		3	20
Cambridge,	3																		3
Dresden,																			2
Easton,	7	2																	8
Fort Ann,	2																		10
Fort Edward,	4			1															1
Granville,	8							5											
Greenwich,	19																1		5
Hampton,	11																		7
Hartford,																			
Hebron,	1																		13
Jackson,																			
Kingsbury,	9	1			1			4				1							19
Putnam,																			
Salem,	7			1															1
White Creek,	3																		
Whitehall,	5	1			2	1		4	1							1		1	43
Total,	79	4		2	3	1		13	1			1				1	1	4	132

WAYNE COUNTY.—(Continued.)

TOWNS.	Germany.	Prussia.	Austria.	Switzerland.	Italy.	Spain.	Portugal.	Poland.	Norway.	Sweden.	Russia.	Denmark.	East Indies.	Africa.	Turkey and Greece.	Islands.	Asia.	At Sea.	Unknown.
Arcadia,	342	3	1	17				1											6
Butler,	13			1															
Galen,	297			2						2								1	16
Huron,	43																2		20
Lyons,	529	5							1	1			1					1	43
Macedon,	35	2												1					15
Marion,	36		1																
Ontario,	40		1	26															1
Palmyra,	77				1														6
Rose,	75	1		1															21
Savannah,	12																		5
Sodus,	119									1	1							1	55
Walworth,	37			3															13
Williamson,	7	1		1															29
Wolcott,	14		1																47
Total,	1,676	12	4	51	1			1	1	4	1		1	1			2	3	277

WESTCHESTER COUNTY.—(Continued.)

TOWNS.	Germany.	Prussia.	Austria.	Switzerland.	Italy.	Spain.	Portugal.	Poland.	Norway.	Sweden.	Russia.	Denmark.	East Indies.	Africa.	Turkey and Greece.	Islands.	Asia.	At Sea.	Unknown.
Bedford,	41			2	1			2											2
Cortlandt,	361	2														5			8
East Chester,	776	2	1	1	9	1				3	2	1				2			10
Greenburgh,	276	113		21	1			2				1							
Harrison,	9																		4
Lewisboro,	22																		
Mamaroneck,	41			2															
Mount Pleasant,	55	2		1	1														1
New Castle,	32				1														1
New Rochelle,	195	3				1	1			2									1
North Castle,	13							1								1			13
North Salem,	15																		3
Ossining,	204	5	1	4		3	1	10		3	3	1	1	1		1	1	5	11

(Continued on page 167.)

WESTCHESTER COUNTY

TOWNS.	COUNTIES OF NEW-YORK.																	
	Albany.	Allegany.	Broome.	Cattaraugus.	Cayuga.	Chautauque	Chemung.	Chenango	Clinton.	Columbia	Cortland	Delaware.	Dutchess.	Erie.	Essex.	Franklin.	Fulton.	Genesee.
Pelham,	5												5					
Poundridge,								1		1		3	6					
Rye,	13				2		1	2	1	6		3	13	3				
Scarsdale,	1																	
Somers,	1		1		1			1		2		2	27					
Westchester,	7									2	2	2	14	2				
West Farms,	39		2		3	2		5		25	2	8	48	5	3	3	5	
White Plains,	8				3			1		3		1	8	4				1
Yonkers,	61	3	2	1	9		1	2	1	13		12	93		1			1
Yorktown,	10	1	1		3					1		9	40					
Total,	292	5	16	1	38	3	4	25	4	153	11	88	721	33	4	7	5	9

WYOMING COUNTY.

TOWNS.	Albany.	Allegany.	Broome.	Cattaraugus.	Cayuga.	Chautauque	Chemung.	Chenango	Clinton.	Columbia	Cortland	Delaware.	Dutchess.	Erie.	Essex.	Franklin.	Fulton.	Genesee.
Attica,	15	9		9	21	11	1	5		26	2	2	9	48	3		1	134
Bennington,	3	8		10	8	4		7	1	13	1	4	11	69	7	2		102
Castile,	15	16	1	19	107	8	1	6		7	3	14	61	8	1	3		7
China,	11	17		93	21	7	1	3		7	10	7	3	83	6			29
Covington,	3	7		8	34	4	2	3		3		1	5	5				70
Eagle,	19	32		34	8	1			1	1	2		4	4	2			18
Gainesville,	8	18	3	26	22	1	2	8	1	15	6	6	4	13	3			17
Genesee Falls,	2	45	1	5	17	2	4	4		1	1	2	15	13	2		4	10
Java,	12	4		9	22	4		9	14	1	2	1		57			1	31
Middlebury,	3	10	2	13	11	2		4	1	28	2	2	8	7	3	1	1	123
Orangeville,	1	8		1	11	3		11	2	6			4	28	11		1	25
Perry,	3	15		12	70	9	2	24		16	1	1	21	6	4	2	2	34
Pike,	15	96	12	16	20	2	3	6	1	1	8	5	8	11			1	23
Sheldon,	4	4		5	11			10		1		10	6	67	3			14
Warsaw,	15	11	1	3	36	13		6		14	4	10	9	25			2	89
Weathersfield,	12	6	2	2	8	2	1	9	1	5	5	3	7	26	2		4	17
Total,	141	306	22	265	427	73	17	115	22	145	47	68	175	470	47	8	17	743

YATES COUNTY.

TOWNS.	Albany.	Allegany.	Broome.	Cattaraugus.	Cayuga.	Chautauque	Chemung.	Chenango	Clinton.	Columbia	Cortland	Delaware.	Dutchess.	Erie.	Essex.	Franklin.	Fulton.	Genesee.
Barrington,	2	1			13	1	3	2	1	45	4	17	43		1			
Benton,	10	3	5	1	10	4	11	10		104		3	40	4			1	5
Italy,	4	4	1	1	14	5	5	7	3	5	7	7	12				2	4
Jerusalem,	17	12	2	3	22	2	15	5		114	1	6	85	4			2	5
Middlesex,	7	12	1	2	11		3	1		17	2	2	11	2	3			4
Milo,	29	27	6	1	47		22	15	5	87	13	25	74	9		1		11
Potter,	6	6	2		36	4	1	4		51		2	19	2			1	10
Starkey,	6	9	7		28	2	46	6		26	9	12	27	2	1		3	5
Torrey,	10	3	3		9	2	11	1		6	3	4	7		1			
Total,	91	77	27	8	190	20	117	51	9	455	39	78	318	23	6	1	9	44

WESTCHESTER COUNTY.—(Continued.)

TOWNS.	Greene.	Hamilton.	Herkimer.	Jefferson.	Kings.	Lewis.	Livingston	Madison.	Monroe.	Montgomery.	New-York.	Niagara.	Oneida.	Onondaga	Ontario.	Orange.	Orleans.	Oswego.
	COUNTIES OF NEW-YORK.																	
Pelham,	1				3						108					15		
Poundridge,	4		2		4				1		24					8		
Rye,	1				41					1	380					4		
Scarsdale,																2		
Somers,	3				4						67		2	2		4		
Westchester,	7			1	5						423		2	2		11		
West Farms,	15		7	4	193			4	1	12	2, 245		7	1		42		1
White Plains,	1			3	8				4		139		2			8		
Yonkers,	20		2	2	74			5	3	4	925	4	3	11		60	1	3
Yorktown,	1				4					2	101					4		
Total,	105	8	17	14	557	1	2	21	14	38	8, 600	8	44	31	5	408	10	8

WYOMING COUNTY.—(Continued.)

TOWNS.	Greene.	Hamilton.	Herkimer.	Jefferson.	Kings.	Lewis.	Livingston	Madison.	Monroe.	Montgomery.	New-York.	Niagara.	Oneida.	Onondaga	Ontario.	Orange.	Orleans.	Oswego.
Attica,	9		7	9		1	18	6	15	11	9	8	65	19	7	3	6	1
Bennington,	12	2	9	8			10	5	26	2	6	14	19	8	6		12	
Castile,	5		6	3	1	3	143	8	29	17	8	4	16	9	39	9	2	
China,	2	1	17	2		2	19	14	20	6	9	1	25	48	1	5	3	2
Covington,			2	3		3	68	14	12	10		6	15	8	20	9	2	4
Eagle,	8		26	6			20	16	17	28		6	37	6	1	3		1
Gainesville,	4		5	8			30	23	29	43	3	1	6	10	10	3	3	4
Genesee Falls,	2			7			107	2	16	17		4	5	16	24	1	2	
Java,	2		7	1		1	22	18	29	9	15	3	13	2	7		2	2
Middlebury,	3		4	5			21	18	19	6		4	20	14	15	3	8	1
Orangeville,	3		2	16	2	1	3	7	9	3	2	5	27	7	6		5	1
Perry,	3		19	5	1		145	12	40	5	13	15	37	19	39	13	5	9
Pike,	2		17	4	2		60	23	10	45	1	9	9	24	28	5	2	2
Sheldon,	2		12	6		3	6	12	14	2	16	5	5	11	15	2	1	1
Warsaw,	9		14	1	2		49	11	36		7	7	44	13	30	3	9	2
Weathersfield,			16	5			14	4	5	6	1	4	37	13	4	2	5	8
Total,	66	3	163	89	8	14	735	193	326	210	90	96	380	227	252	61	67	38

YATES COUNTY.—(Continued.)

TOWNS.	Greene.	Hamilton.	Herkimer.	Jefferson.	Kings.	Lewis.	Livingston	Madison.	Monroe.	Montgomery.	New-York.	Niagara.	Oneida.	Onondaga	Ontario.	Orange.	Orleans.	Oswego.
Barrington,	3		5				4	2		1	3	1	4	1	16	29		
Benton,	2		5	1		4	10	5	7	5	19	1	8	7	171	68	2	2
Italy,	7		8				12	5	2	15		1	4	4	78	25		1
Jerusalem,	3		7		1	2	5	10	4	24	22		13	30	97	70		1
Middlesex,	2	5	3	2			4	3	4	14	1	2	10	7	97	10	1	1
Milo,	5		8	9	10	2	10	24	13	14	47	3	44	28	145	78	1	10
Potter,	5		4	1			14	7	9	5	7	3	6	3	156	31		
Starkey,	7		10	8			13	6	6	10	19	13	15	5	37	75	1	1
Torrey,	2		2	2	5			5	5	5	7		8		27	14		2
Total,	36	5	52	23	16	8	72	67	50	93	125	24	112	85	824	400	5	18

WESTCHESTER COUNTY.—(Continued.)

TOWNS.	COUNTIES OF NEW-YORK.																	
	Otsego.	Putnam.	Queens.	Rensselaer.	Richmond.	Rockland	St. Lawrence.	Saratoga	Schenectady.	Schoharie.	Schuyler	Seneca.	Steuben.	Suffolk.	Sullivan.	Tioga.	Tompkins.	Ulster
Pelham,	3	3	18	1	1	2	......	5	......	......	......	......	......	18	......	......	......	......
Poundridge,	1	3	......	2	......	5	......	......	......	......	......	......	1	1	1	......	......	......
Rye,	......	10	23	4	3	6	3	4	......	......	......	......	......	6	......	......	1	2
Scarsdale,	......	2	1	......	1	......	......	......	......	......	......	......	......	......	......	......	1	......
Somers,	3	135	3	......	1	......	......	......	......	......	......	1	......	......	4	......	1	1
Westchester,	1	......	17	3	2	1	1	1	......	......	......	......	......	3	1	......	......	1
West Farms,	6	21	37	34	25	42	......	9	1	5	......	......	19	4	......	......	6	18
White Plains,	......	7	1	2	3	4	......	......	......	1	......	......	......	6	......	......	......	2
Yonkers,	3	50	22	112	12	58	......	26	3	8	......	2	1	2	4	1	......	16
Yorktown,	......	160	......	5	......	5	......	3	......	......	......	......	1	1	......	......	......	6
Total,	29	1, 040	337	235	81	331	11	85	8	26	......	13	30	99	23	4	18	163

WYOMING COUNTY.—(Continued.)

TOWNS.	Otsego.	Putnam.	Queens.	Rensselaer.	Richmond.	Rockland	St. Lawrence.	Saratoga	Schenectady.	Schoharie.	Schuyler	Seneca.	Steuben.	Suffolk.	Sullivan.	Tioga.	Tompkins.	Ulster
Attica,	26	......	......	10	......	......	1	22	1	20	......	2	8	......	2	1	4	1
Bennington,	11	......	......	4	......	2	18	6	......	1	......	5	1	......	......	......	1	2
Castile,	14	3	......	14	......	......	3	52	4	7	......	8	20	1	......	5	1	11
China,	13	......	......	6	......	......	2	4	......	7	......	5	8	......	......	1	9	1
Covington,	7	......	......	6	......	......	......	9	......	3	......	4	4	......	......	......	1	3
Eagle,	31	......	......	3	......	......	6	17	......	4	......	......	4	......	1	......	6	4
Gainesville,	12	......	......	17	......	......	1	18	1	7	......	6	6	......	......	1	2	1
Genesee Falls,	12	3	......	9	......	......	......	43	1	1	......	2	10	......	......	3	1	1
Java,	14	1	......	6	......	......	......	6	......	8	......	1	4	2	......	1	3	1
Middlebury,	22	1	......	29	......	......	......	9	4	13	......	2	......	......	1	......	2	......
Orangeville,	10	......	......	11	......	......	......	7	3	......	......	4	2	......	......	......	1	......
Perry,	33	......	......	6	......	......	1	17	1	7	......	11	4	2	1	4	13	17
Pike,	56	20	......	15	......	2	5	11	......	19	......	2	8	3	1	2	6	2
Sheldon,	4	......	......	16	......	......	......	4	......	7	......	......	3	......	......	2	2	......
Warsaw,	13	......	1	15	......	......	2	24	1	6	......	3	6	1	......	2	4	1
Weathersfield,	19	3	......	3	......	......	3	6	4	2	......	2	4	......	......	1	......	3
Total,	297	31	1	170	......	4	42	255	20	112	......	57	92	9	6	23	56	48

YATES COUNTY.—(Continued.)

TOWNS.	Otsego.	Putnam.	Queens.	Rensselaer.	Richmond.	Rockland	St. Lawrence.	Saratoga	Schenectady.	Schoharie.	Schuyler	Seneca.	Steuben.	Suffolk.	Sullivan.	Tioga.	Tompkins.	Ulster
Barrington,	9	48	1	1	......	......	......	11	......	......	1	22	105	1	......	2	26	2
Benton,	6	27	2	9	......	2	1	19	......	34	......	56	42	......	2	9	11	26
Italy,	20	......	......	6	......	......	3	18	4	7	......	10	106	4	......	......	6	6
Jerusalem,	23	20	......	11	......	......	......	41	......	11	......	26	104	1	1	3	26	2
Middlesex,	6	......	......	9	......	......	1	13	1	2	......	16	14	......	......	1	5	2
Milo,	31	8	4	15	......	2	......	18	4	13	4	104	134	10	1	13	49	4
Potter,	3	......	......	18	......	......	1	4	3	2	......	28	35	......	......	......	4	8
Starkey,	11	7	......	7	2	3	......	12	4	2	......	55	179	1	7	3	45	4
Torrey,	1	3	......	......	......	......	......	8	......	4	......	24	40	......	......	2	20	2
Total,	110	113	7	76	2	7	6	144	16	75	5	341	759	17	11	33	192	56

WESTCHESTER COUNTY.—(Continued.)

TOWNS.	COUNTIES OF NEW-YORK.							UNITED STATES.										
	Warren.	Washington.	Wayne.	Westchester.	Wyoming.	Yates.	New-York.	Maine.	N. Hampshire.	Vermont.	Massachusetts.	Rhode Island.	Connecticut.	New Jersey.	Pennsylvania.	Delaware.	Maryland.	District of Columbia.
Pelham,	......	......	......	251	......	......	439	6	......	......	3	1	31	19	11	......	5	......
Poundridge,	......	1	......	1, 175	......	......	1, 244	......	1	......	2	......	143	3	......	......	......	......
Rye,	......	......	......	1, 612	......	1	2, 146	8	5	7	47	7	319	33	20	......	7	......
Scarsdale,	......	......	......	285	......	......	301	......	1	1	2	......	3	5	6	......	2	......
Somers,	......	......	......	1, 205	......	......	1, 473	......	......	5	3	1	35	4	8	......	1	......
Westchester,	......	......	......	1, 345	......	......	1, 857	6	6	3	13	3	48	28	10	......	......	......
West Farms,	1	10	......	3, 399	......	1	6, 320	21	13	34	112	24	197	246	82	......	68	2
White Plains,	......	1	......	848	......	......	1, 072	......	......	1	14	1	46	11	......	......	3	......
Yonkers,	2	3	2	2, 372	......	......	4, 016	42	26	27	110	17	223	134	34	1	21	......
Yorktown,	......	2	3	1, 663	......	......	2, 027	......	......	2	2	......	23	14	9	......	1	1
Total,	15	45	10	38, 094	1	3	52, 035	120	90	160	568	95	2, 318	980	386	1	157	11

WYOMING COUNTY.—(Continued.)

TOWNS.	Warren.	Washington.	Wayne.	Westchester.	Wyoming.	Yates.	New-York.	Maine.	N. Hampshire.	Vermont.	Massachusetts.	Rhode Island.	Connecticut.	New Jersey.	Pennsylvania.	Delaware.	Maryland.	District of Columbia.
Attica,	6	13	3	......	1, 084	......	1, 694	3	38	60	127	1	75	8	7	......	3	......
Bennington,	1	7	1	......	1, 062	2	1, 513	1	53	74	51	20	90	4	7	......	......	......
Castile,	2	57	3	2	925	16	1, 727	2	20	130	62	11	106	22	28	......	......	......
China,	3	28	......	1	901	......	1, 464	4	16	112	58	6	48	6	18	......	1	......
Covington,	......	27	3	......	537	......	926	......	5	41	43	13	46	3	16	......	......	......
Eagle,	1	27	2	1	645	1	1, 054	1	17	88	44	6	33	1	13	......	......	......
Gainesville,	7	67	2	3	894	......	1, 380	1	7	90	67	7	43	8	11	......	......	......
Genesee Falls,	1	11	5	2	348	2	786	7	14	39	22	1	24	10	12	......	......	......
Java,	......	24	1	1	1, 137	......	1, 510	......	41	87	95	12	40	22	10	......	......	......
Middlebury,	......	26	......	1	861	......	1, 333	2	7	90	114	18	43	2	18	......	2	......
Orangeville,	4	30	......	......	741	1	1, 025	11	7	41	47	17	33	6	3	......	1	......
Perry,	......	19	4	6	1, 130	12	1, 890	5	38	136	80	7	102	22	24	......	......	......
Pike,	3	32	2	1	784	3	1, 452	1	17	119	80	4	43	4	22	......	......	......
Sheldon,	......	10	......	......	1, 176	2	1, 474	4	14	44	51	8	40	2	14	......	......	......
Warsaw,	13	104	10	......	1, 404	5	2, 090	2	46	147	65	17	94	12	12	......	1	......
Weathersfield,	6	35	2	......	790	1	1, 120	17	18	55	36	10	60	7	17	......	......	......
Total,	47	517	38	18	14, 419	45	22, 438	61	358	1, 353	1, 042	158	920	139	232	......	8	......

YATES COUNTY.—(Continued.)

TOWNS.	Warren.	Washington.	Wayne.	Westchester.	Wyoming.	Yates.	New-York.	Maine.	N. Hampshire.	Vermont.	Massachusetts.	Rhode Island.	Connecticut.	New Jersey.	Pennsylvania.	Delaware.	Maryland.	District of Columbia.
Barrington,	......	3	4	7	2	870	1, 317	......	1	8	15	13	23	41	19	......	1	......
Benton,	3	3	14	10	3	1, 199	2, 011	2	5	15	17	18	66	45	30	......	2	......
Italy,	2	12	14	3	1	763	1, 228	5	10	55	37	7	16	22	18	......	......	2
Jerusalem,	......	7	8	11	1	1, 450	2, 330	3	3	14	22	24	65	39	33	......	......	......
Middlesex,	......	6	3	1	......	750	1, 074	1	9	50	27	14	33	17	13	......	......	......
Milo,	1	13	28	9	2	2, 124	3, 414	......	23	39	58	29	122	133	103	......	5	......
Potter,	2	9	......	2	......	1, 194	1, 708	9	11	36	31	33	35	28	24	......	5	......
Starkey,	1	7	5	11	......	1, 129	1, 910	7	13	28	31	19	40	164	65	......	4	......
Torrey,	......	2	2	......	5	833	1, 090	......	2	15	20	8	20	28	13	......	3	......
Total,	9	62	78	54	14	10, 312	16, 082	27	77	260	258	165	420	517	318	......	20	2

WESTCHESTER COUNTY.—(Continued.)

TOWNS.	UNITED STATES.																	
	Virginia.	N. Carolina.	S. Carolina.	Georgia.	Florida.	Alabama.	Mississippi.	Louisiana.	Texas.	Arkansas.	Missouri.	Tennessee.	Kentucky.	Ohio.	Indiana.	Illinois.	Michigan.	Wisconsin
Pelham,	13		3	1	1		9				5	1	1	1	1			
Poundridge,														1				
Rye,	8		2	4			1	4					1	5			1	
Scarsdale,		1																
Somers,														4				
Westchester,	4	3	4	3	2	2								1	1		3	1
West Farms,	22	8	22	1		1	1		2		2	18	5	12		6	3	32
White Plains,	3		2						1				3			3	3	
Yonkers,	7	3	4	8			1	3			1			4	1	2	1	1
Yorktown,	2													1		1		
Total,	113	18	55	36	5	6	13	20	5		16	20	15	62	5	26	18	42

WYOMING COUNTY.—(Continued.)

TOWNS.	Virginia.	N. Carolina.	S. Carolina.	Georgia.	Florida.	Alabama.	Mississippi.	Louisiana.	Texas.	Arkansas.	Missouri.	Tennessee.	Kentucky.	Ohio.	Indiana.	Illinois.	Michigan.	Wisconsin
Attica,														11	1	3	4	2
Bennington,				1									1	3	1		13	1
Castile,	1	1											1	4	1	4	3	7
China,													1	3	2	2	2	1
Covington,																	16	1
Eagle,														3			4	
Gainesville,	1		1											6		4	1	3
Genesee Falls,	1													5			6	1
Java,								3						5		2	2	6
Middlebury,														6	2	3	8	
Orangeville,											1			6	1		2	2
Perry,											2			18	2	5	1	
Pike,														6	1	3	4	5
Sheldon,					1									1	1		4	6
Warsaw,	5							3						3		2	7	5
Weathersfield,														2			4	
Total,	8	1	1	1	1			6			3		3	82	12	28	81	40

YATES COUNTY.—(Continued.)

TOWNS.	Virginia.	N. Carolina.	S. Carolina.	Georgia.	Florida.	Alabama.	Mississippi.	Louisiana.	Texas.	Arkansas.	Missouri.	Tennessee.	Kentucky.	Ohio.	Indiana.	Illinois.	Michigan.	Wisconsin
Barrington,														1			5	1
Benton,	3													2		1	7	
Italy,	1													2		3	7	
Jerusalem,	2										1			2	1	1	10	
Middlesex,														6	1		12	1
Milo,	3	1											2	8	1	3	8	
Potter,	1													9	2		5	2
Starkey,	1							1						2			5	
Torrey,	2													1			4	
Total,	13	1						1			1		2	33	5	8	63	4

WESTCHESTER COUNTY.—(CONTINUED.)

TOWNS.	U. STATES.			Total United States.	FOREIGN COUNTRIES.													
	Iowa.	California.	Territories.		Canada.	N. Brunswick.	Nova Scotia.	N. Foundland.	West Indies.	Mexico.	S. America.	England.	Scotland.	Ireland.	Wales.	France.	Belgium.	Holland.
Pelham,				551	8	2	2					56	16	167				1
Poundridge,				1, 394								7		34				
Rye,				2, 625	2				1			60	21	634	1	4		
Scarsdale,				322					2			12	4	84	1			
Somers,				1, 534	2		2		1			33	1	154				
Westchester,	1			1, 999	4		3		9			219	91	973	5	24		
West Farms,		2		7, 256	83	4	16		14	2	9	863	278	2, 117	10	85		1
White Plains,				1, 163	7		3					22	12	265		3	11	4
Yonkers,				4, 687	37		7		11			388	108	1, 944	8	31		3
Yorktown,				2, 083		1	2		1			20	2	196	2		1	
Total,	3	2		57, 401	238	21	65	2	58	2	14	2, 965	857	13, 935	67	259	17	39

WYOMING COUNTY.—(CONTINUED.)

TOWNS.	Iowa.	California.	Territories.	Total United States.	Canada.	N. Brunswick.	Nova Scotia.	N. Foundland.	West Indies.	Mexico.	S. America.	England.	Scotland.	Ireland.	Wales.	France.	Belgium.	Holland.
Attica,				2, 037	8	1	1					63	3	123		74		
Bennington,				1, 833	14							56	2	21		29		
Castile,				2, 130	4	1						93	13	92				
China,				1, 744	17							7	14	275	35		4	2
Covington,				1, 110	7		1					18	20	167		2		1
Eagle,				1, 264	8	1	1					8	22	51	24			
Gainesville,				1, 630	5				1			57		46		1		
Genesee Falls,				928	20							1	2	132				
Java,				1, 835	11		1	1				18	3	367	2	6		
Middlebury,				1, 648	12							13	2	77	2	7		
Orangeville,				1, 204	5							2	2	37	6	90	10	
Perry,				2, 332	25	2	1					94	6	92		2		
Pike,				1, 761	14							29	3	38	6	2		
Sheldon,				1, 664	11							19	3	41		126	60	
Warsaw,	1			2, 512	11	2						88	1	97	7			
Weathersfield,				1, 346	10							24	2	49	3	5	8	
Total,	1			26, 978	182	7	5	1	1			590	98	1, 705	85	344	82	3

YATES COUNTY.—(CONTINUED.)

TOWNS.	Iowa.	California.	Territories.	Total United States.	Canada.	N. Brunswick.	Nova Scotia.	N. Foundland.	West Indies.	Mexico.	S. America.	England.	Scotland.	Ireland.	Wales.	France.	Belgium.	Holland.
Barrington,				1, 445		1						15		23		2		
Benton,				2, 224	13							127	12	98	2	1		
Italy,				1, 413	10							36	32	14				
Jerusalem,				2, 550	13							50	33	109		1		
Middlesex,				1, 258	8		1					13		19				
Milo,				3, 952	25							25	24	247		1		
Potter,				1, 939								29	2	35		82		
Starkey,				2, 290	10							32	4	75		1		7
Torrey,				1, 206								40	2	45				
Total				18, 277	79	1	1					367	109	665	2	88		7

WESTCHESTER COUNTY.—(CONTINUED.)

TOWNS.	FOREIGN COUNTRIES.																		
	Germany.	Prussia.	Austria.	Switzerland.	Italy.	Spain.	Portugal.	Poland.	Norway.	Sweden.	Russia.	Denmark.	East Indies.	Africa.	Turkey and Greece.	Islands.	Asia.	At Sea.	Unknown.
Pelham, ...	27			1															2
Poundridge, ...	2		1					1											
Rye, ...	106	1						1		1						1		1	9
Scarsdale, ...	20																		
Somers, ...	9			1															7
Westchester, ...	122			5										2					8
West Farms, ...	1, 604	17	1	9			4	9		7	8	19				2			7
White Plains, ...	24	3		5				1											
Yonkers, ...	243	2	1	10	1	1		3	1	6		3							58
Yorktown, ...	37																	2	
Total, ...	4, 234	150	5	62	14	6	6	30	1	22	13	25	1	3		12	1	8	145

WYOMING COUNTY.—(CONTINUED.)

TOWNS.	Germany.	Prussia.	Austria.	Switzerland.	Italy.	Spain.	Portugal.	Poland.	Norway.	Sweden.	Russia.	Denmark.	East Indies.	Africa.	Turkey and Greece.	Islands.	Asia.	At Sea.	Unknown.
Attica, ...	360	1	1	1				1											5
Bennington, ...	589	1		1															9
Castile, ...	6			1															3
China, ...	1																		9
Covington, ...	3																		1
Eagle, ...	7																		4
Gainesville, ...	2				1														10
Genesee Falls, ...																			15
Java, ...	39																		12
Middlebury, ...	12	10																	4
Orangeville, ...	77			1															7
Perry, ...	6																		
Pike, ...	22	1		1															10
Sheldon, ...	731	3		1						3									2
Warsaw, ...	58					1										1		2	14
Weathersfield, ...	10																		5
Total, ...	1, 923	16	1	6	1	1		1		3						1		2	110

YATES COUNTY.—(CONTINUED.)

TOWNS.	Germany.	Prussia.	Austria.	Switzerland.	Italy.	Spain.	Portugal.	Poland.	Norway.	Sweden.	Russia.	Denmark.	East Indies.	Africa.	Turkey and Greece.	Islands.	Asia.	At Sea.	Unknown.
Barrington, ...	3	1																	14
Benton, ...	4																		19
Italy, ...	1																		
Jerusalem, ...	1																	1	39
Middlesex, ...	6																		
Milo, ...	6			1															23
Potter, ...	37																		24
Starkey, ...	1																		8
Torrey, ...	25			2															
Total, ...	84	1		3														1	127

RECAPITULATION OF PLACE OF BIRTH.

COUNTIES.	COUNTIES OF NEW-YORK.												
	Albany.	Allegany.	Broome.	Cattaraugus	Cayuga.	Chautauque	Chemung.	Chenango.	Clinton.	Columbia.	Cortland.	Delaware.	Dutchess.
Albany,	51, 614	12	19	10	60	22	17	50	82	1, 009	18	126	893
Allegany,	108	18, 652	185	514	474	88	221	533	17	112	323	252	199
Broome,	623	12	17, 029	8	63	22	54	1, 407	12	345	347	1, 181	904
Cattaraugus,	130	760	170	16, 415	298	796	62	398	24	121	254	171	152
Cayuga,	744	57	76	26	26, 782	36	43	218	22	433	483	150	795
Chautauque,	179	189	85	613	350	24, 810	28	558	35	149	192	186	378
Chemung,	191	41	154	10	146	10	11, 799	125	8	62	99	324	211
Chenango,	230	22	555	22	45	13	....	23, 969	1	188	450	640	486
Clinton,	66	1	....	3	....	1	1	4	22, 462	27	1	3	94
Columbia,	381	1	20	3	15	4	....	21	4	30, 911	4	45	1, 644
Cortland,	123	38	349	16	384	16	13	816	1	176	12, 819	198	176
Delaware,	381	9	169	10	24	7	3	232	10	275	31	26, 984	563
Dutchess,	167	1	18	3	21	5	3	21	3	1, 393	10	63	40, 311
Erie,	585	125	37	617	527	493	26	176	127	228	128	138	306
Essex,	46	2	3	3	18	9	....	1	1, 167	28	1	3	83
Franklin,	11	....	1	....	3	3	1	2	806	7	1	6	22
Fulton,	356	4	7	5	21	5	4	4	12	159	5	26	263
Genesee,	112	88	10	105	253	68	6	59	17	169	33	47	198
Greene,	1, 545	4	21	....	9	1	....	10	7	947	10	644	644
Hamilton,	24	....	5	....	4	3	....	12	....	1	....	1	15
Herkimer,	278	7	14	10	38	27	1	54	5	144	32	36	166
Jefferson,	243	10	9	8	85	25	1	100	145	139	63	47	221
Kings,	1, 054	6	26	2	89	23	3	51	35	515	33	186	877
Lewis,	236	5	7	13	7	7	4	45	13	134	28	16	101
Livingston,	100	540	34	88	722	40	36	99	20	143	64	85	270
Madison,	365	57	60	29	96	36	22	1, 209	8	366	281	95	197
Monroe,	640	185	46	80	524	81	44	191	50	491	93	91	797
Montgomery,	441	7	6	4	22	....	3	19	8	156	9	17	155
New-York,	2, 158	27	66	16	146	43	26	89	55	1, 035	56	526	2, 753
Niagara,	235	79	30	49	263	84	10	92	50	196	107	54	248
Oneida,	918	20	62	25	147	74	12	451	30	400	146	120	489
Onondaga,	1, 152	23	83	32	1, 270	47	16	390	54	446	1, 033	102	761
Ontario,	251	115	40	39	381	44	91	113	14	347	69	61	480
Orange,	117	7	33	4	29	....	32	27	2	102	24	43	931
Orleans,	267	65	19	38	243	55	23	84	11	172	68	46	313
Oswego,	553	28	27	19	916	41	24	214	57	458	144	98	335
Otsego,	672	20	124	13	30	29	7	862	2	513	84	1, 143	556
Putnam,	15	....	2	....	4	1	....	3	....	20	....	20	599
Queens,	80	....	3	1	5	....	1	....	11	26	....	22	163
Rensselaer,	1, 764	23	9	6	38	10	3	24	83	1, 575	19	62	828
Richmond,	57	....	1	....	....	....	....	2	1	8	....	25	28
Rockland,	42	....	5	....	2	5	1	2	3	29	4	56	42
St. Lawrence,	124	6	3	5	32	15	3	48	730	33	15	29	102
Saratoga,	1, 049	10	10	10	36	12	5	19	80	545	8	25	775
Schenectady,	1, 090	6	4	2	10	1	1	8	13	260	7	13	143
Schoharie,	2, 115	1	29	2	19	3	....	13	6	602	7	328	412
Schuyler,	89	67	27	9	158	9	1, 115	122	3	84	73	182	274
Seneca,	139	22	36	10	605	5	54	58	9	74	64	76	217
Steuben,	267	678	362	58	494	58	876	1, 117	28	241	376	455	481
Suffolk,	38	2	15	....	5	1	....	4	6	32	1	32	72
Sullivan,	98	1	31	1	11	3	11	26	2	52	7	595	469
Tioga,	425	16	654	7	117	5	252	290	10	128	293	310	333
Tompkins,	129	31	144	18	782	21	210	159	6	91	564	234	610
Ulster,	342	....	19	....	23	8	10	12	3	512	10	561	1, 626
Warren,	122	3	7	2	8	....	2	16	27	45	4	20	169
Washington,	165	11	7	11	36	8	1	9	157	130	9	33	200
Wayne,	367	32	25	47	1, 214	20	28	111	30	1, 610	67	49	1, 060
Westchester,	292	5	16	1	38	3	4	25	4	153	11	88	721
Wyoming,	141	306	22	265	427	73	17	115	22	145	47	68	175
Yates,	91	77	27	8	190	20	117	51	9	455	39	78	318
Total,	76, 337	22. 516	21. 057	19, 315	38, 759	27, 349	15, 347	34, 940	26. 619	49, 347	19, 118	37, 315	67, 804

RECAPITULATION.—(Continued.)

COUNTIES.	COUNTIES OF NEW-YORK.												
	Erie.	Essex.	Franklin.	Fulton.	Genesee.	Greene.	Hamilton.	Herkimer.	Jefferson.	Kings.	Lewis.	Livingston.	Madison.
Albany,	89	72	23	92	26	1,096	12	163	80	120	26	24	58
Allegany,	149	26	24	36	275	107	1	284	100	11	20	1,341	617
Broome,	27	22	2	12	16	340	2	98	31	34	12	10	127
Cattaraugus,	1,181	96	16	28	593	95	8	505	135	11	31	238	368
Cayuga,	70	32	5	43	74	159	13	350	133	25	44	139	278
Chautauque,	768	146	30	26	525	103	12	540	146	7	71	131	725
Chemung,	21	7	....	21	17	115	....	75	14	14	2	34	114
Chenango,	34	5	1	32	18	187	1	178	45	15	13	13	1,029
Clinton,	12	1,080	310	6	3	12	1	22	25	4	7	1	6
Columbia,	15	5	2	13	12	762	1	40	19	76	5	7	21
Cortland,	28	5	2	5	15	176	1	264	50	16	17	16	425
Delaware,	11	8	....	3	8	813	....	21	7	14	5	2	19
Dutchess,	9	8	1	5	5	272	7	13	12	211	6	5	12
Erie,	49,784	81	20	16	1,135	129	12	453	198	78	35	215	317
Essex,	1	16,295	63	7	9	31	17	5	5	12	13	7	8
Franklin,	6	338	12,428	1	9	....	3	14	51	11	6	1	5
Fulton,	7	12	4	13,935	6	64	199	388	114	12	22	4	20
Genesee,	391	32	13	28	12,506	52	1	104	57	28	36	598	134
Greene,	1	8	2	1	5	21,124	....	11	4	44	2	6	11
Hamilton,	1	44	1	88	2	8	1,263	29	5	....	5	1	....
Herkimer,	19	7	10	339	15	74	17	23,377	186	22	94	3	124
Jefferson,	30	47	83	190	35	45	4	2,048	37,420	20	1,253	14	280
Kings,	123	25	2	30	57	306	9	74	59	50,005	30	31	66
Lewis,	5	11	15	60	19	39	7	514	1,294	19	12,269	9	79
Livingston,	112	18	22	52	341	114	4	179	51	15	33	16,802	124
Madison,	30	12	9	42	45	95	3	787	166	10	82	16	23,551
Monroe,	244	82	56	63	578	212	10	365	380	53	92	943	304
Montgomery,	6	7	1	624	4	58	12	504	55	13	20	20	26
New-York,	203	76	22	50	83	594	7	131	135	2,556	24	40	95
Niagara,	811	51	16	51	442	107	1	238	213	28	22	212	205
Oneida,	80	35	22	118	66	223	31	3,223	664	65	840	29	1,567
Onondaga,	83	40	9	47	59	249	42	858	342	41	78	38	1,504
Ontario,	57	18	5	28	122	102	5	188	78	50	24	558	126
Orange,	18	7	....	3	9	107	....	13	15	171	4	2	8
Orleans,	166	31	17	54	576	55	....	264	104	18	13	186	210
Oswego,	74	62	57	53	79	468	8	1,980	1,985	40	261	37	1,016
Otsego,	11	8	3	23	28	304	3	1,076	74	28	37	4	359
Putnam,	....	3	....	....	4	12	....	....	....	22	....	2	2
Queens,	6	1	....	1	11	13	1	8	7	1,163	3	3	....
Rensselaer,	34	94	12	58	13	224	9	78	58	89	16	16	52
Richmond,	1	2	....	....	1	11	....	1	5	201	....	....	....
Rockland,	4	1	....	....	....	14	....	8	6	58	2	2	4
St. Lawrence,	32	94	1,011	98	44	20	4	759	2,017	11	401	11	65
Saratoga,	33	139	14	342	13	132	51	88	59	68	18	19	33
Schenectady,	6	6	9	34	5	42	2	45	10	12	1	....	15
Schoharie,	3	6	1	13	8	623	5	84	20	19	5	4	10
Schuyler,	13	4	....	4	20	64	1	71	10	7	8	20	31
Seneca,	22	5	2	9	23	46	1	81	44	24	22	71	85
Steuben,	91	48	5	30	115	176	4	377	100	31	14	856	330
Suffolk,	8	4	....	1	2	53	....	12	5	463	1	14	4
Sullivan,	3	1	2	7	2	456	1	10	5	67	....	5	5
Tioga,	11	21	1	2	11	141	....	53	15	27	9	5	101
Tompkins,	26	7	9	....	17	68	....	75	26	23	8	26	105
Ulster,	10	11	2	4	5	1,552	2	12	7	86	1	7	7
Warren,	14	408	5	23	10	52	12	16	9	16	9	....	11
Washington,	9	287	25	19	20	25	3	40	34	22	9	8	7
Wayne,	68	31	16	41	86	121	5	237	133	32	29	61	247
Westchester,	33	4	7	5	9	105	8	17	44	557	1	2	21
Wyoming,	470	47	8	17	743	66	3	163	89	8	14	735	193
Yates,	23	6	1	9	44	36	5	52	23	16	8	72	67
Total,	55,597	20,089	14,426	16,942	19,023	32,849	1,834	41,663	47,178	56,919	16,133	23,679	35,333

RECAPITULATION.—(Continued.)

COUNTIES.	COUNTIES OF NEW-YORK.											
	Monroe.	Mo'tgom'ry	New-York.	Niagara.	Oneida.	Onondaga.	Ontario.	Orange.	Orleans.	Oswego.	Otsego.	Putnam.
Albany,	88	438	1, 157	40	239	194	40	125	18	62	290	24
Allegany,	360	187	276	71	294	425	509	178	39	56	738	38
Broome,	46	153	291	9	166	144	39	470	12	116	852	82
Cattaraugus,	331	303	94	67	473	503	280	63	84	93	694	10
Cayuga,	156	355	350	26	394	1, 500	146	381	43	369	370	31
Chautauque,	237	331	247	162	931	523	234	186	109	80	869	22
Chemung	68	90	280	13	114	120	139	1, 596	21	36	214	37
Chenango,	16	191	119	8	356	128	21	140	1	57	1, 918	32
Clinton,	9	26	89	5	29	11	4	6	2	14	14	1
Columbia,	10	58	405	....	51	23	14	75	2	15	82	27
Cortland,	33	190	305	8	251	752	23	197	5	33	574	12
Delaware,	8	29	265	2	41	13	9	123	1	5	1, 102	70
Dutchess,	22	18	1, 318	2	45	12	15	568	7	12	95	1, 056
Erie,	835	390	1, 095	626	700	502	449	142	245	159	476	24
Essex,	4	21	68	2	17	5	4	20	6	....	7	1
Franklin,	12	11	31	2	21	3	....	6	3	9	11	....
Fulton,	14	1, 556	88	....	101	22	7	9	11	15	88	1
Genesee,	950	226	118	150	374	304	358	87	356	44	211	9
Greene,	2	38	227	2	33	10	3	62	6	11	95	46
Hamilton,	1	58	26	1	11	6	1	3	2	3	12	....
Herkimer,	22	1, 160	198	13	1, 239	106	22	29	10	101	907	7
Jefferson,	81	1, 502	156	22	1, 397	213	36	50	13	641	422	2
Kings,	113	131	30, 101	14	269	90	74	1, 056	13	54	80	120
Lewis,	13	389	112	3	1, 047	64	7	12	2	82	141	4
Livingston,	909	315	179	76	270	200	843	97	77	27	147	18
Madison,	48	619	112	17	2, 204	1, 098	41	30	21	193	515	7
Monroe,	36, 710	467	832	215	885	494	1, 275	209	585	177	323	42
Montgomery,	6	20, 708	141	4	132	58	14	28	9	17	392	1
New-York,	162	249	232, 155	35	600	160	141	3, 176	22	158	162	589
Niagara,	874	239	280	17, 579	345	321	426	110	731	91	211	40
Oneida,	125	1, 240	1, 061	31	49, 480	533	63	87	25	711	1, 382	12
Onondaga,	220	1, 118	493	42	1, 074	39, 336	161	276	50	1, 128	510	24
Ontario,	650	250	341	40	254	216	20, 708	338	66	52	177	60
Orange,	21	12	1, 517	4	30	9	19	38, 122	3	7	29	271
Orleans,	1, 253	287	266	405	435	293	310	77	10, 653	64	222	28
Oswego,	131	677	369	45	2, 926	2, 807	73	73	26	29, 090	1, 078	13
Otsego,	21	913	196	12	392	58	15	32	6	46	31, 861	5
Putnam,	2	1	335	2	8	1	3	205	....	....	1	9, 573
Queens,	8	8	3, 368	4	19	2	2	77	....	6	9	8
Rensselaer,	52	157	676	18	220	63	20	100	9	27	112	21
Richmond,	2	1	2, 097	1	9	2	9	49	....	7	1	7
Rockland,	8	....	1, 173	....	8	2	9	610	....	1	6	47
St. Lawrence,	55	491	156	22	449	81	22	21	17	116	136	3
Saratoga,	48	334	261	7	105	58	21	51	1	19	65	14
Schenectady,	17	681	146	5	71	17	5	16	1	11	41	6
Schoharie,	8	724	63	7	40	18	6	17	5	16	567	7
Schuyler,	27	128	108	15	65	67	123	469	3	19	114	93
Seneca,	89	85	153	27	177	249	383	237	8	32	67	47
Steuben,	239	1, 149	220	33	327	391	699	620	48	93	1, 173	200
Suffolk,	8	2	1, 654	1	28	8	3	104	....	3	5	10
Sullivan,	4	15	731	2	9	16	7	1, 913	....	1	34	62
Tioga,	31	84	151	7	65	74	39	756	1	10	488	95
Tompkins,	28	57	215	15	105	202	41	707	18	20	161	100
Ulster,	21	37	987	5	29	22	7	1, 058	1	12	48	190
Warren,	1	52	63	1	16	4	1	27	5	9	26	....
Washington,	14	51	149	3	46	29	9	36	13	24	30	7
Wayne,	631	381	285	39	413	685	1, 201	291	81	160	176	37
Westchester,	14	38	8, 600	8	44	31	5	408	10	8	29	1, 040
Wyoming,	326	210	90	96	380	227	252	61	67	38	297	31
Yates,	50	93	125	24	112	85	824	400	5	18	110	113
Total,	46, 244	39, 724	297, 164	20, 095	70, 365	53, 590	30, 214	56, 472	13, 578	34, 478	50, 967	14, 477

RECAPITULATION.—(Continued.)

COUNTIES.	COUNTIES OF NEW-YORK.												
	Rensselaer.	Richmond.	Rockland.	St. Lawrence.	Saratoga.	Schenectady.	Schoharie.	Schuyler.	Seneca.	Steuben.	Suffolk.	Sullivan.	Tioga.
Albany,	2, 442	19	28	51	1, 078	894	1, 129	....	29	36	44	11	19
Allegany,	480	....	10	68	267	46	81	1	212	1, 374	25	22	164
Broome,	219	5	20	13	105	109	919	....	36	68	29	102	382
Cattaraugus,	180	1	....	42	231	40	182	4	86	257	10	22	69
Cayuga,	474	4	39	58	639	135	226	2	349	75	28	51	103
Chautauque,	631	2	40	64	476	22	137	....	71	83	42	24	46
Chemung,	146	4	26	24	72	10	105	89	206	479	24	134	415
Chenango,	204	....	2	11	136	18	244	....	10	63	16	35	42
Clinton,	126	4	7	198	101	15	6	....	1	1	18	....	....
Columbia,	1, 025	1	8	3	94	45	136	....	2	7	28	7	1
Cortland,	179	....	36	7	114	46	191	1	21	39	35	49	129
Delaware,	72	2	9	9	81	52	968	....	4	19	25	228	14
Dutchess,	151	2	64	6	116	36	57	....	6	8	32	68	4
Erie,	419	8	12	152	463	123	174	....	149	134	37	19	33
Essex,	96	....	....	122	131	8	11	....	1	3	4	1	3
Franklin,	33	....	....	469	16	16	5	....	1	3	1	1	....
Fulton,	244	....	....	32	1, 009	210	199	....	10	5	5	1	3
Genesee,	192	3	2	35	261	39	78	....	96	95	18	5	18
Greene,	175	....	6	1	54	25	604	....	9	1	28	50	7
Hamilton,	61	....	....	4	108	23	41	....	....	4	2	....	....
Herkimer,	314	2	2	73	218	176	212	1	3	15	15	8	4
Jefferson,	467	3	4	1, 037	619	52	159	....	14	17	21	2	4
Kings,	516	345	197	36	195	54	52	....	60	19	3	62	35
Lewis,	172	....	1	205	85	12	119	....	10	2	3	3	2
Livingston,	180	3	24	34	254	103	85	4	201	588	11	9	33
Madison,	301	....	1	49	207	64	228	....	23	40	20	16	17
Monroe,	966	21	70	206	723	212	197	2	293	151	23	24	60
Montgomery,	194	2	1	13	390	626	600	....	13	4	6	5	3
New-York,	973	753	1, 029	65	365	172	169	4	75	55	1, 248	178	37
Niagara,	260	4	11	136	337	123	210	3	492	63	14	23	20
Oneida,	877	5	17	178	554	242	531	35	46	52	52	15	12
Onondaga,	738	5	42	163	817	246	453	3	121	69	33	36	45
Ontario,	223	....	61	50	319	62	115	1	549	431	23	19	47
Orange,	52	10	391	2	34	5	24	....	18	16	123	737	23
Orleans,	454	2	12	56	458	74	218	....	102	33	10	14	16
Oswego,	651	2	7	716	567	105	494	2	70	74	35	12	17
Otsego,	402	2	1	12	189	92	1, 486	....	6	23	9	6	34
Putnam,	8	5	20	....	1	1	1	....	1	....	18	7	1
Queens,	27	74	22	4	28	7	....	....	5	3	820	7	1
Rensselaer,	42, 036	4	10	29	1, 016	199	181	....	12	11	22	11	3
Richmond,	2	11, 384	13	4	7	4	1	....	3	....	7	....	1
Rockland,	12	3	10, 897	....	10	....	10	....	....	....	10	14	2
St. Lawrence,	157	....	....	38, 726	204	48	42	....	5	11	8	3	2
Saratoga,	2, 146	2	5	17	27, 364	496	159	....	12	9	14	3	3
Schenectady,	413	2	....	2	554	10, 454	249	2	3	2	3	6	5
Schoharie,	268	....	3	5	83	319	24, 450	....	5	7	17	8	7
Schuyler,	54	5	17	4	66	14	85	6, 121	558	2, 752	16	35	112
Seneca,	67	1	64	14	154	16	48	3	14, 089	107	14	24	35
Steuben,	228	10	52	36	329	76	179	22	484	30, 263	31	59	312
Suffolk,	19	19	16	1	10	1	4	....	1	4	31, 320	14	3
Sullivan,	30	....	70	....	9	....	300	....	4	5	10	14, 539	8
Tioga,	08	6	21	7	148	148	372	4	42	69	14	55	12, 910
Tompkins,	141	1	10	5	109	29	89	16	371	106	21	07	530
Ulster,	101	....	51	7	54	12	327	....	10	16	27	511	5
Warren,	255	1	....	30	706	14	28	....	3	7	1	2	2
Washington,	1, 251	3	1	43	835	29	38	....	10	8	1	6	8
Wayne,	698	4	45	93	566	89	176	....	502	118	101	17	29
Westchester,	235	81	331	11	85	8	26	....	13	30	99	23	4
Wyoming,	170	....	4	42	255	20	112	....	57	92	9	6	23
Yates,	76	2	7	6	144	16	75	5	341	759	17	11	33
Total,	63, 787	12, 821	13, 839	43, 486	44, 620	16, 332	37, 797	6, 325	19, 926	38, 785	36, 090	17, 427	15, 915

RECAPITULATION.—(CONTINUED.)

COUNTIES.	COUNTIES OF NEW-YORK.								Total New-York.	UNITED STATES.		
	Tompkins.	Ulster.	Warren.	Washington	Wayne.	Westchester.	Wyoming.	Yates.		Maine.	N. Hampshire.	Vermont.
Albany,	27	175	89	446	29	177	6	22	64, 705	99	279	727
Allegany,	591	43	55	436	99	47	693	260	32, 826	234	333	1, 293
Broome,	185	212	22	125	27	140	....	16	27, 874	19	178	359
Cattaraugus,	319	44	73	520	94	49	555	75	28, 918	120	397	1, 581
Cayuga,	910	499	19	731	581	297	28	83	40, 720	40	182	676
Chautauque,	193	72	99	633	137	35	177	75	37, 965	109	492	2, 091
Chemung,	1, 218	201	8	74	39	111	18	223	19, 983	25	81	268
Chenango,	80	62	17	151	17	89	3	16	32, 402	12	252	460
Clinton,	5	3	68	269	1	8	....	....	25, 222	67	407	2, 661
Columbia,	11	147	7	64	20	74	2	7	36, 500	26	45	166
Cortland,	416	89	36	152	32	50	3	30	19, 989	16	126	302
Delaware,	27	434	4	130	4	201	....	....	33, 575	9	45	143
Dutchess,	12	1, 101	9	35	22	499	3	11	48, 073	33	46	90
Erie,	136	109	109	595	241	67	528	83	66, 945	216	569	2, 433
Essex,	2	11	262	402	3	11	....	1	19, 057	33	686	3, 073
Franklin,	2	1	8	166	1	3	3	....	14, 583	31	583	3, 468
Fulton,	1	16	94	189	12	24	1	2	19, 632	21	76	199
Genesee,	31	23	42	284	95	123	437	120	20, 339	15	335	1, 021
Greene,	3	637	5	23	10	87	....	1	27,338	10	40	72
Hamilton,	2	2	71	22	3	5	2	8	1, 998	....	16	100
Herkimer,	13	74	22	143	17	42	3	2	30, 283	42	110	252
Jefferson,	33	34	80	351	53	23	6	11	50, 103	62	643	1, 961
Kings,	56	317	11	138	29	1, 276	11	24	94, 122	1, 069	522	602
Lewis,	1	13	13	79	22	3	2	4	17, 583	15	107	382
Livingston,	93	46	27	353	127	42	488	150	26, 141	51	260	728
Madison,	44	28	25	201	20	85	10	5	34, 060	40	242	601
Monroe,	79	183	29	481	781	220	133	154	53, 939	193	685	1, 527
Montgomery,	13	49	13	73	15	23	7	....	25, 762	15	37	116
New-York,	114	1, 309	38	401	64	4, 825	17	28	262, 156	1, 380	1, 001	1, 278
Niagara,	91	42	29	305	233	51	93	43	27, 753	69	301	1, 212
Oneida,	52	75	31	370	77	107	12	16	68, 302	153	382	1, 070
Onondaga,	144	160	59	755	215	149	27	54	57, 589	114	310	1, 133
Ontario,	128	151	21	147	720	79	56	841	30, 666	57	171	567
Orange,	22	1, 696	2	15	13	285	2	19	45, 339	48	45	66
Orleans,	74	80	33	261	262	102	114	55	19, 841	45	316	877
Oswego,	89	52	75	992	248	121	9	30	50, 731	72	369	1, 398
Otsego,	18	45	12	132	22	111	3	8	42, 205	23	157	445
Putnam,	6	20	....	2	....	684	....	2	11, 628	1	7	19
Queens,	7	30	....	14	9	174	....	2	33, 092	49	43	49
Rensselaer,	16	103	117	1, 024	30	115	3	12	51, 667	63	378	1, 623
Richmond,	2	11	....	6	....	63	....	4	14, 094	68	19	32
Rockland,	34	70	....	9	3	269	....	1	13, 512	16	47	18
St. Lawrence,	4	6	78	534	14	7	3	5	47, 991	240	1, 326	7, 218
Saratoga,	8	50	806	1, 548	57	102	6	5	37. 423	63	278	1, 233
Schenectady,	1	19	12	48	16	37	1	1	14. 596	14	19	77
Schoharie,	3	100	9	40	11	34	1	2	31, 195	10	35	113
Schuyler,	878	141	12	75	24	108	3	592	15, 379	3	45	128
Seneca,	464	110	12	103	307	94	15	137	19, 253	11	50	170
Steuben,	1, 360	174	41	354	167	173	46	1, 444	48, 737	151	344	713
Suffolk,	4	14	1	7	3	125	2	3	34, 983	46	21	34
Sullivan,	28	1, 481	1	15	....	296	....	4	21, 508	18	6	31
Tioga,	1, 351	152	4	111	9	144	1	20	20, 760	43	130	268
Tompkins,	18, 290	400	5	95	23	153	4	35	25, 587	24	102	223
Ulster,	33	44, 237	8	30	9	364	2	9	53, 136	28	25	55
Warren,	14	....	10, 835	1, 457	9	26	7	1	14, 632	35	240	1, 378
Washington,	2	5	664	27, 628	26	26	10	....	32, 297	45	310	3, 072
Wayne,	83	127	36	548	21, 418	95	32	104	35, 077	99	165	641
Westchester,	18	163	15	45	10	38, 094	1	3	52, 035	120	90	160
Wyoming,	56	48	47	517	38	18	14, 419	45	22, 438	61	358	1, 358
Yates,	192	56	9	62	78	54	14	10, 312	16, 082	27	77	260
Total,	28, 089	55, 752	14, 329	44, 925	26, 646	50, 896	18, 022	15, 220	2, 222, 321	5, 818	14, 941	54, 266

RECAPITULATION.—(CONTINUED.)

COUNTIES.	UNITED STATES.												
	Massachusetts.	Rhode Island.	Connecticut.	New Jersey.	Pennsylvania.	Delaware.	Maryland.	District of Columbia.	Virginia	North Carolina.	South Carolina.	Georgia.	Florida.
Albany	1, 183	182	918	303	279	5	58	8	43	9	5	4	7
Allegany	989	534	958	483	1, 184	11	14	3	7	1	....	....	5
Broome	1, 024	131	1, 355	424	1, 352	11	42	3	16	6	3	10	....
Cattaraugus	1, 243	233	721	166	911	3	9	1	20	1	....	....	1
Cayuga	1, 251	253	1, 176	846	489	....	33	9	17	3	2	....	6
Chautauque	1, 854	264	1, 422	225	1, 366	1	20	1	24	1	1	3	1
Chemung	329	76	621	805	1, 627	....	42	15	37	7	2	....	....
Chenango	1, 088	773	2, 288	78	247	....	8	1	6	6	1	1	....
Clinton	434	60	220	60	52	1	8	....	12	2	1	1	....
Columbia	1, 230	104	697	142	141	2	9	2	12	....	8	1	....
Cortland	849	316	1, 095	102	173	70	1	....	9	1	1	1	....
Delaware	498	46	1, 262	139	291	....	3	....	1	9	1	2	....
Dutchess	397	124	1, 333	245	151	4	23	1	14	9	11	6	1
Erie	1, 992	365	1, 488	438	1, 499	....	174	12	127	14	16	9	7
Essex	486	52	238	64	40	....	12	2	1	....	1	....	1
Franklin	359	21	135	10	16	....	....	....	4	....	....	....	....
Fulton	309	89	323	74	41	....	1	....	7	1	1	....	....
Genesee	1, 062	108	1, 265	175	258	1	16	....	9	3	3	1	3
Greene	248	41	774	106	56	....	12	....	7	1	....	4	....
Hamilton	69	12	24	5	1	....	....	....	....	....	....	....	....
Herkimer	652	242	772	75	66	1	12	2	14	....	3	....	1
Jefferson	1, 662	295	1, 134	148	178	1	13	4	13	2	6	3	3
Kings	3, 801	698	3, 979	5, 199	2, 014	25	677	99	754	318	161	138	51
Lewis	713	82	631	43	38	2	1	....	4	....	....	3	....
Livingston	854	58	970	636	1, 067	....	40	4	12	1	....	4	1
Madison	1, 436	607	1, 823	130	165	2	23	1	7	5	1	1	....
Monroe	1, 984	194	2, 019	896	642	....	12	125	40	10	4	3	4
Montgomery	205	43	197	188	77	....	1	5	....	1	3	3	....
New-York	6, 205	873	7, 239	12, 259	4, 949	53	231	1, 793	1, 377	251	493	329	53
Niagara	818	116	696	477	1, 090	....	50	4	90	5	3	2	....
Oneida	2, 358	556	3, 036	264	287	5	33	19	15	9	12	12	6
Onondaga	2, 020	337	2, 319	388	267	1	42	3	25	2	3	1	1
Ontario	1, 223	137	1, 066	678	491	....	159	4	32	1	4	4	....
Orange	271	43	534	2, 500	536	1	43	8	56	17	7	27	5
Orleans	709	100	753	196	213	....	21	1	8	2	....	5	1
Oswego	1, 528	352	1, 627	228	184	2	33	....	12	2	4	2	3
Otsego	1, 036	611	1, 762	121	182	3	5	6	6	3	1	2	3
Putnam	38	3	401	61	29	....	10	....	13	5	2	3	....
Queens	232	72	305	545	193	1	34	3	51	19	21	5	3
Rensselaer	1, 823	376	790	282	160	....	53	8	36	2	10	19	4
Richmond	144	90	115	520	81	....	113	2	89	6	19	1	2
Rockland	133	16	134	1, 021	101	3	8	....	7	....	2	....	1
St. Lawrence	1, 670	132	744	83	75	....	12	1	5	....	....	1	1
Saratoga	984	227	713	140	78	1	17	2	16	1	5	3	1
Schenectady	166	35	127	58	50	....	13	5	9	2	....	....	....
Schoharie	185	79	344	68	43	....	1	....	4	....	2	1	....
Schuyler	236	44	561	775	363	1	8	1	3	1	....	1	....
Seneca	244	51	371	1, 199	957	....	15	....	8	....	3	....	....
Steuben	881	261	1, 155	1, 339	2, 489	1	31	1	20	1	3	1	....
Suffolk	230	102	765	328	106	2	24	1	49	21	11	3	1
Sullivan	121	30	668	337	408	....	10	1	1	4	1	....	2
Tioga	830	100	905	470	1, 403	....	28	1	10	2	....	....	1
Tompkins	536	60	927	1, 084	783	8	31	2	27	....	....	....	....
Ulster	232	45	597	334	182	....	12	4	13	1	5	5	....
Warren	408	94	237	32	30	....	3	....	1	....	....	....	....
Washington	839	220	426	56	83	....	19	2	7	1	....	7	1
Wayne	917	154	878	707	302	1	60	4	17	3	1	3	2
Westchester	568	95	2, 318	980	386	1	157	11	113	18	55	36	5
Wyoming	1, 042	158	920	139	232	....	8	....	8	1	1	1	1
Yates	258	165	420	517	318	....	20	2	13	1	....	....	....
Total	57, 086	11, 737	63, 691	40, 391	31, 472	224	2, 568	2, 187	2, 158	792	903	672	189

RECAPITULATION.—(CONTINUED.)

COUNTIES.	UNITED STATES.												
	Alabama.	Mississippi	Louisiana.	Texas.	Arkansas.	Missouri	Tennessee.	Kentucky.	Ohio.	Indiana.	Illinois.	Michigan.	Wisconsin.
Albany,	1	4	15	6	1	3	5	9	74	12	17	27	19
Allegany,	...	...	...	...	1	3	1	5	106	20	29	75	30
Broome,	2	...	7	...	...	1	...	6	46	9	11	22	10
Cattaraugus,	...	...	5	...	1	...	...	3	148	8	45	49	27
Cayuga,	1	1	4	3	1	3	3	9	111	11	36	107	39
Chautauque,	...	1	1	1	...	2	3	15	347	34	64	84	50
Chemung,	...	...	...	...	...	...	...	5	66	5	19	50	8
Chenango,	...	1	2	...	...	...	2	1	42	2	21	23	10
Clinton,	...	6	...	...	...	1	1	4	21	1	9	14	11
Columbia,	1	5	8	...	...	1	...	2	23	1	5	4	5
Cortland,	...	...	4	...	...	1	...	1	39	1	10	20	11
Delaware,	1	...	1	1	...	1	...	1	27	9	2	2	2
Dutchess,	...	...	17	1	1	4	1	4	34	10	7	25	7
Erie,	9	11	15	4	1	16	7	53	620	42	66	295	82
Essex,	...	...	...	...	...	...	2	1	21	5	3	14	7
Franklin,	...	...	...	...	...	...	...	...	24	1	6	11	1
Fulton,	...	...	...	...	...	1	...	1	16	3	8	4	4
Genesee,	2	2	1	...	...	...	7	6	82	10	19	139	36
Greene,	...	1	1	3	...	...	1	1	17	1	7	10	4
Hamilton,	...	...	...	...	...	...	...	...	...	...	...	...	...
Herkimer,	...	...	...	...	...	...	...	1	33	2	12	18	9
Jefferson,	1	1	...	1	1	3	2	1	95	11	38	55	2[illegible]
Kings,	46	21	122	10	7	63	23	80	325	48	55	98	3[illegible]
Lewis,	...	...	...	...	...	...	...	4	26	2	16	11	[illegible]
Livingston,	1	6	3	...	...	...	1	2	107	22	14	151	3[illegible]
Madison,	3	...	3	...	...	...	...	10	59	3	27	55	3[illegible]
Monroe,	3	13	5	1	...	3	3	28	292	36	46	287	4[illegible]
Montgomery,	1	...	2	...	...	...	1	...	29	2	4	14	[illegible]
New-York,	98	43	332	43	5	99	50	162	575	63	99	141	5[illegible]
Niagara,	2	3	2	1	2	5	9	12	201	13	39	167	3[illegible]
Oneida,	...	4	5	...	...	3	2	16	124	8	48	87	4[illegible]
Onondaga,	1	2	7	...	1	9	1	6	197	36	62	136	6[illegible]
Ontario,	2	4	15	...	...	12	...	3	117	13	24	165	2[illegible]
Orange,	13	4	8	6	...	8	15	11	43	18	18	16	4
Orleans,	1	1	1	...	...	4	5	3	78	6	18	134	2[illegible]
Oswego,	...	...	2	...	...	1	1	4	132	13	38	92	6[illegible]
Otsego,	...	1	...	2	2	...	1	12	23	4	17	17	1[illegible]
Putnam,	...	...	...	...	...	...	...	...	6	...	2	...	...
Queens,	1	1	16	2	...	9	6	3	23	2	8	11	...
Rensselaer,	...	3	1	1	1	6	2	10	52	7	20	25	1[illegible]
Richmond,	1	1	18	...	1	4	...	3	9	...	1	6	[illegible]
Rockland,	...	...	1	...	...	...	...	1	2	3	4	...	...
St. Lawrence,	1	...	3	1	...	1	...	2	84	6	17	25	2[illegible]
Saratoga,	1	...	15	...	...	4	...	7	34	4	17	24	1[illegible]
Schenectady,	2	...	1	...	...	2	...	...	17	1	11	5	[illegible]
Schoharie,	...	1	2	...	...	...	...	...	6	2	1	12	1[illegible]
Schuyler,	...	1	...	1	...	...	...	...	46	4	11	30	[illegible]
Seneca,	...	...	2	1	...	...	2	1	60	8	6	76	[illegible]
Steuben,	...	5	...	...	...	3	1	6	114	29	49	127	2[illegible]
Suffolk,	1	...	4	...	...	1	...	2	21	4	15	23	[illegible]
Sullivan,	...	...	1	...	...	4	1	2	21	1	1	4	[illegible]
Tioga,	...	...	...	...	...	1	...	...	32	3	7	25	[illegible]
Tompkins,	1	2	5	2	...	...	...	2	55	6	19	40	[illegible]
Ulster,	...	...	...	...	...	...	...	1	31	3	2	17	[illegible]
Warren,	...	...	1	...	...	1	...	...	13	1	9	2	4
Washington,	...	...	5	...	3	4	5	1	32	2	19	19	[illegible]
Wayne,	5	1	5	...	...	...	1	2	101	13	15	161	4[illegible]
Westchester,	6	13	20	5	...	16	20	15	62	5	26	18	4[illegible]
Wyoming,	...	...	6	...	...	3	...	3	82	12	28	81	4[illegible]
Yates,	...	...	1	...	...	1	...	2	33	5	8	63	4
Total,	208	163	695	96	29	307	185	545	5, 256	606	1, 255	3, 413	1, 163

RECAPITULATION.—(Continued.)

COUNTIES.	UNITED STATES.			Total United States.	FOREIGN COUNTRIES.							
	Iowa.	California.	Territories.		Canada.	New Brunswick.	Nova Scotia.	New Foundland.	West Indies.	Mexico.	South America.	England.
Albany,		2		70, 407	1, 301	21	24	23	12	2		3, 067
Allegany,	5			39, 150	317		5					470
Broome,				32, 921	62	3	3		5		1	319
Cattaraugus,	4		4	34, 629	254		6		2		1	311
Cayuga,		1		46, 033	272	2	13	2	6	1	1	1, 550
Chautauque,	1		1	46, 444	334	4	9		1			1, 455
Chemung,	4			24, 075	75		4	2	3			405
Chenango,		1		37, 728	33		4		2			417
Clinton,				29, 279	8, 164	3	12	3	1			480
Columbia,			1	39, 141	127		6	1	18		1	622
Cortland,	1			23, 139	58	1	12		1	1	1	372
Delaware,	1			36, 072	45	3	18	1	2			431
Dutchess,			2	50, 724	80	5	18	2	14	5	2	1, 265
Erie,	7			77, 620	2, 797	44	49	24	17	3	7	4, 732
Essex,				23, 799	2, 198	2	3	1	1			265
Franklin,	4		1	19, 258	3, 625	2	1		2			172
Fulton,				20, 811	57	4	4		1			402
Genesee,	2			24, 920	271	4	2		1			1, 723
Greene,				28, 755	106		5		2		1	230
Hamilton,				2, 225	17							25
Herkimer,			3	32, 607	126	8	6	2	2			1, 005
Jefferson,	2	2		56, 471	2, 768	4	5	2				1, 059
Kings,	2	8	2	115, 245	917	190	401	146	351	15	52	13, 011
Lewis,				19, 669	336	1						221
Livingston,	3			31, 185	399	1	10		2	1	2	887
Madison,	2			39, 336	141		2		2		1	1, 126
Monroe,	9			63, 048	2, 465	25	60		12	1	3	5, 254
Montgomery,				26, 714	68		2			1		450
New-York,	9	22	4	303, 721	2, 040	234	551	131	1, 121	66	170	22, 713
Niagara,	6			33, 205	1, 986	18	27	7	10	4		2, 332
Oneida,	3			76, 868	717	18	20	15	6		2	5, 599
Onondaga,	4	1		65, 126	1, 020	10	13	1	5		1	3, 791
Ontario,				35, 639	251	3	1	5	6			1, 860
Orange,		3	1	49, 718	61	14	19	2	9	3	5	989
Orleans,			1	23, 363	370	1	1	1	9			1, 739
Oswego,	1	2		56, 895	2. 701	8	21	6	5		1	1, 593
Otsego,	5	2		46, 674	74	4			9			1, 095
Putnam,				12, 228	13	1	4		5	2	1	154
Queens,		1		34, 800	133	4	15		28	5	5	1, 291
Rensselaer,	7			57, 447	1, 377	7	18	2	6		3	2, 006
Richmond,				15, 441	24	5	12		27	3	7	1, 014
Rockland,				15, 030	24	1	12					349
St. Lawrence,				59, 677	5, 857	39	12	1	2			1, 523
Saratoga,		2	1	41, 305	452	2	6		6		1	1, 086
Schenectady,	3			15, 217	45	1	1	1	1			650
Schoharie,				32, 117	60	1	2		1			111
Schuyler,	1			17, 648	34		2		1			196
Seneca,	1			22, 498	91		2		1			669
Steuben,	1		1	56, 489	219	5	33		4			628
Suffolk,	6	1		36, 807	43	11	20	1	45		5	721
Sullivan,	1			23, 185	32	4	7		2			403
Tioga,	1			25, 028	44	9	1	1	1			277
Tompkins,	2		2	29, 538	57	1	7			1	3	432
Ulster,				54, 735	88	4	12	11	6	2		876
Warren,				17, 122	618	1	5		5			246
Washington,	2			37, 482	1, 164	1	13	1	5		2	267
Wayne,	2	1	2	39, 380	335	3	10		1	1	3	2, 025
Westchester,	3	2		57, 401	238	21	65	2	58	2	14	2, 965
Wyoming,	1			26, 978	182	7	5	1	1			590
Yates,				18, 277	79	1	1					367
Total,	106	51	26	2, 528, 444	47, 842	766	1, 602	398	1, 846	119	296	102, 286

RECAPITULATION.—(Continued.)

COUNTIES.	FOREIGN COUNTRIES.												
	Scotland.	Ireland.	Wales.	France.	Belgium.	Holland.	Germany.	Prussia.	Austria.	Switzerland	Italy.	Spain.	Portugal.
Albany,	1, 047	21, 660	69	163	18	331	6, 930	90	12	61	10	3	3
Allegany,	82	1, 652	162	7	....	7	402	14	....	6	1	....	....
Broome,	191	2, 425	4	5	....	6	161	23	....	5	....	....	....
Cattaraugus,	309	1, 980	312	38	....	17	789	16	....	15	1	2	....
Cayuga,	285	3, 939	23	21	1	73	591	23	22	10	1	2	....
Chautauque,	128	2, 483	27	93	1	289	1, 207	25	1	45	....	....	....
Chemung,	84	1, 927	18	29	....	....	287	6	....	5	....	....	....
Chenango,	45	1, 017	7	13	....	....	196	....	....	7	....	....	....
Clinton,	174	4, 074	6	27	1	....	57	2	2	....	....	....	....
Columbia,	106	3, 285	11	29	....	1	907	13	....	21	....	1	....
Cortland,	51	810	6	2	....	....	52	....	1	....	....	....	....
Delaware,	1, 350	1, 292	7	44	....	25	328	2	....	6	....	2	....
Dutchess,	384	6, 336	13	89	2	1	1, 415	5	2	19	11	4	1
Erie,	895	11, 554	63	4, 019	36	536	25, 907	1, 947	630	615	47	13	4
Essex,	85	2, 088	2	15	....	....	20	....	....	....	....	....	....
Franklin,	116	2, 275	2	7	....	....	4	....	....	....	1	....	....
Fulton,	222	801	16	34	1	15	802	24	....	60	....	....	....
Genesee,	196	2, 516	8	81	5	3	1, 047	15	....	43	1	....	1
Greene,	61	1, 391	5	5	1	6	422	3	....	11	....	....	....
Hamilton,	18	107	2	30	....	8	97	1	1	3	....	....	....
Herkimer,	107	2, 667	431	86	....	....	1, 342	7	3	4	....	1	....
Jefferson,	246	3, 194	46	412	....	4	833	3	....	28	2	2	....
Kings,	2, 669	59, 308	352	1, 058	49	219	20, 112	138	49	180	80	160	62
Lewis,	61	1, 528	417	1, 267	1	1	1, 386	46	14	183	1	....	....
Livingston,	553	3, 698	14	27	3	38	839	37	7	11	....	....	....
Madison,	90	2, 251	467	58	....	12	180	4	2	5	1	....	....
Monroe,	784	12, 626	52	420	7	726	10, 113	147	8	460	2	8	3
Montgomery,	164	1, 747	6	20	2	10	1, 347	26	2	13	1	....	....
New-York,	8, 487	175, 735	935	6, 321	174	756	95, 986	1, 586	331	978	968	343	163
Niagara,	320	5, 642	15	154	3	15	2, 582	1, 482	....	81	....	....	....
Oneida,	891	11, 145	4, 195	928	....	45	6, 302	62	8	279	2	....	3
Onondaga,	204	9, 457	63	416	4	51	5, 683	13	20	84	8	1	....
Ontario,	392	3, 633	19	62	2	52	468	6	....	27	4	1	....
Orange,	331	7, 789	15	62	2	11	1, 340	36	6	22	2	3	....
Orleans,	170	2, 386	14	16	1	1	202	12	....	6	....	....	....
Oswego,	300	5, 925	63	481	....	6	841	3	....	34	8	2	2
Otsego,	274	1, 080	46	10	....	2	146	9	1	4	....	....	....
Putnam,	77	1, 258	2	31	....	....	119	12	....	8	....	1	....
Queens,	294	5, 699	19	115	4	16	3, 355	24	16	50	12	5	2
Rensselaer,	777	14, 109	45	91	7	52	2, 826	27	2	41	10	1	....
Richmond,	213	3, 144	31	97	6	19	1, 137	20	2	24	21	2	4
Rockland,	110	2, 690	34	18	4	20	1, 128	11	....	18	1	....	....
St. Lawrence,	1, 168	6, 118	64	97	1	2	92	10	5	7	1	....	....
Saratoga,	255	5, 562	9	41	....	13	441	14	2	20	1	2	1
Schenectady,	255	1, 682	11	29	....	25	1, 441	98	1	26	1	....	1
Schoharie,	13	714	4	10	....	4	355	2	5	6	1	....	....
Schuyler,	31	671	1	5	....	....	23	....	1	....	....	....	....
Seneca,	121	1, 540	3	13	7	1	294	1	....	7	1	....	....
Steuben,	207	3, 340	10	21	....	3	1, 524	22	5	14	6	....	5
Suffolk,	134	2, 355	7	45	8	95	619	18	10	18	....	1	29
Sullivan,	190	2, 585	5	34	....	1	2, 649	3	9	185	....	....	1
Tioga,	38	928	4	91	1	1	141	8	....	45	....	1	....
Tompkins,	81	1, 177	7	12	....	2	56	5	1	2	....	....	....
Ulster,	148	8, 246	11	93	3	102	3, 426	61	6	22	4	1	....
Warren,	122	1, 407	1	4	....	1	52	7	....	....	1	....	....
Washington,	251	4, 755	218	2	....	2	79	4	....	2	3	1	....
Wayne,	102	2, 045	4	277	....	539	1, 676	12	4	51	1	....	....
Westchester,	857	13, 935	67	259	17	39	4, 234	150	5	62	14	6	6
Wyoming,	98	1, 705	85	344	82	3	1, 923	16	1	6	1	1	....
Yates,	109	665	2	88	....	7	84	1	....	3	....	....	....
Total,	27, 523	469, 753	8, 557	18, 366	454	4, 214	218, 997	6, 352	1, 197	3, 948	1, 231	570	291

RECAPITULATION.—(CONTINUED.)

COUNTIES.	FOREIGN COUNTRIES.											
	Poland.	Norway.	Sweden.	Russia.	Denmark.	East Indies.	Africa.	Turkey and Greece	Islands.	Asia	At Sea	Unknown.
Albany,	40	1	8	5	5	3	......	......	......	6	31	27
Allegany,	......	......	1	......	1	1	1	1	1	......	3	627
Broome,	2	4	1	......	......	......	2	......	......	......	3	504
Cattaraugus,	3	1	3	......	1	......	......	......	......	1	4	835
Cayuga,	10	1	1	1	1	......	......	1	1	4	6	684
Chautauque,	21	......	453	1	5	......	......	......	2	2	7	339
Chemung,	20	4	4	......	......	......	......	......	......	1	2	337
Chenango,	1	......	......	2	......	......	......	......	......	2	1	440
Clinton,	1	......	1	4	......	......	......	......	4	1	8	182
Columbia,	2	......	2	......	......	......	1	......	......	2	1	93
Cortland,	5	......	3	......	......	4	......	......	......	......	......	56
Delaware,	2	1	1	......	......	......	......	......	......	......	4	113
Dutchess,	11	1	3	2	8	2	1	......	......	2	4	204
Erie,	67	55	76	38	33	4	4	......	......	7	34	454
Essex,	1	......	......	......	......	......	......	......	1	......	2	56
Franklin,	......	......	......	......	......	......	......	......	......	......	2	17
Fulton,	1	......	......	......	......	......	......	......	......	......	4	25
Genesee,	1	......	3	......	......	......	......	......	......	......	8	185
Greene,	3	1	3	......	4	......	......	......	......	......	1	121
Hamilton,	......	......	......	......	......	......	......	......	......	......	1	8
Herkimer,	1	......	......	......	......	......	......	......	......	1	4	156
Jefferson,	7	......	......	......	2	1	1	......	1	2	8	319
Kings,	87	125	194	48	113	15	12	1	50	11	41	894
Lewis,	2	......	......	......	......	......	......	......	......	4	1	90
Livingston,	......	3	1	......	......	......	......	......	......	7	9	209
Madison,	1	......	......	......	......	......	......	......	......	7	1	......
Monroe,	12	43	8	3	6	......	......	......	......	4	24	......
Montgomery,	4	6	1	1	1	......	1	......	......	2	5	214
New-York,	1, 200	227	554	116	327	43	38	40	62	64	103	3, 620
Niagara,	7	6	9	......	2	......	......	......	1	......	14	360
Oneida,	161	......	3	3	......	6	......	......	5	3	36	427
Onondaga,	69	......	2	......	3	6	4	......	4	......	16	500
Ontario,	1	1	3	......	1	......	......	......	......	......	5	230
Orange,	11	......	6	7	6	1	1	......	2	2	4	389
Orleans,	......	30	3	......	......	......	......	1	......	1	2	106
Oswego,	2	1	6	......	1	3	......	......	......	......	11	479
Otsego,	5	......	......	......	......	4	......	......	......	4	3	291
Putnam,	1	......	4	......	......	......	......	......	......	......	1	12
Queens,	5	3	21	......	5	......	3	1	1	1	2	331
Rensselaer,	7	......	2	......	5	1	......	......	......	6	17	342
Richmond,	2	8	26	6	16	4	......	1	......	4	3	66
Rockland,	7	......	1	4	......	......	......	......	......	1	3	45
St. Lawrence,	3	......	......	......	1	......	......	......	......	......	13	284
Saratoga,	4	......	......	......	......	1	......	......	1	3	4	147
Schenectady,	12	......	3	......	3	......	......	......	......	......	6	52
Schoharie,	3	......	1	......	......	......	......	1	......	......	......	108
Schuyler,	......	......	......	1	......	......	......	......	......	......	......	163
Seneca,	7	......	1	......	1	1	......	......	......	......	2	97
Steuben,	3	......	7	......	......	......	......	......	......	2	4	414
Suffolk,	2	7	1	......	3	1	......	1	5	......	3	48
Sullivan,	......	......	12	......	......	1	......	......	......	......	5	174
Tioga,	......	2	......	......	......	......	......	......	......	1	3	337
Tompkins,	......	......	......	......	......	......	......	......	1	......	4	129
Ulster,	18	3	11	......	3	......	1	......	1	......	3	39
Warren,	......	......	......	......	......	......	2	......	2	......	5	68
Washington,	13	1	......	......	1	......	......	......	1	1	4	132
Wayne,	1	1	4	1	......	1	1	......	......	2	3	277
Westchester,	30	1	22	13	25	1	3	......	12	1	8	145
Wyoming,	1	......	3	......	......	......	......	......	1	......	4	110
Yates,	......	......	......	......	......	......	......	......	......	......	1	127
Total,	1, 880	537	1, 472	256	583	104	76	48	159	162	511	17, 238

CLASSIFICATION BY OCCUPATIONS.

COUNTIES.	Actors.	Agents.	Agricultural implement makers	Apothecaries and druggists	Apprentices.	Architects.	Artificial flower makers.	Artists and designers.	Auctioneers.	Authors.	Axe makers.	Bakers.	Bankers.	Bank officers.	Barbers.	Bar-keepers.	Basket makers.
Albany,	26	70	9	34	87	9	3	22	5	1	148	243	13	22	79	34	23
Allegany,	.....	9	1	9	2	1	1	.....	.....	.....	1	2	4	.....	7	.....	2
Broome,	1	4	6	10	12	.....	.....	10	1	.....	.....	12	5	3	19	10	6
Cattaraugus,	.....	8	1	2	4	.....	.....	6	.....	.....	.....	5	1	.....	4	1	3
Cayuga,	1	17	9	11	15	1	.....	3	.....	.....	.....	16	.....	10	41	2	4
Chautauque,	.....	9	41	16	11	2	.....	4	.....	.....	11	14	8	5	17	5	9
Chemung,	2	13	1	11	1	1	.....	2	.....	.....	3	16	6	4	16	3	6
Chenango,	.....	3	.....	8	12	.....	.....	5	.....	.....	.....	6	4	1	5	3	3
Clinton,	.....	16	1	2	6	.....	.....	1	.....	.....	.....	5	4	1	11	.....	4
Columbia,	.....	17	5	8	16	.....	.....	5	1	2	.....	21	.....	4	12	4	1
Cortland,	.....	7	.....	4	3	.....	.....	3	.....	.....	.....	4	1	.....	4	2	3
Delaware,	.....	7	2	2	2	.....	.....	2	.....	.....	.....	3	2	3	2	1	2
Dutchess,	.....	42	7	9	16	.....	.....	4	1	1	.....	28	4	13	18	5	18
Erie,	19	130	5	22	17	12	1	24	8	1	1	190	36	14	86	14	26
Essex,	.....	8	.....	3	3	.....	.....	3	.....	.....	2	2	.....	2	2	4	8
Franklin,	.....	4	1	4	11	.....	.....	1	.....	.....	1	8	.....	2	3	1	.....
Fulton,	.....	.....	2	3	1	.....	.....	.....	.....	.....	.....	1	1	3	4	3	7
Genesee,	.....	4	3	9	1	.....	.....	8	.....	.....	.....	8	2	4	8	3	1
Greene,	.....	2	.....	3	6	.....	.....	.....	.....	.....	.....	11	1	4	9	4	3
Hamilton,	.....	.....	.....	.....	.....	.....	.....	.....	.....	.....	.....	.....	.....	.....	.....	.....	.....
Herkimer,	.....	11	2	8	12	.....	.....	5	.....	.....	6	6	6	5	13	1	2
Jefferson,	3	13	6	10	27	3	.....	3	1	.....	10	22	7	6	17	4	9
Kings,	13	307	8	230	97	51	32	82	40	7	2	789	30	104	224	50	97
Lewis,	.....	2	3	1	2	.....	.....	1	.....	.....	.....	1	3	.....	1	.....	3
Livingston,	.....	12	15	14	9	.....	.....	10	3	.....	.....	9	8	4	13	5	3
Madison,	.....	9	6	9	4	.....	.....	5	.....	1	.....	5	8	4	11	5	9
Monroe,	11	82	20	37	36	16	2	6	3	1	4	84	33	9	51	22	16
Montgomery,	.....	13	9	14	1	.....	.....	4	1	1	.....	18	4	4	11	.....	15
New-York,	231	935	7	521	591	117	190	365	112	34	.....	2,856	127	124	997	565	139
Niagara,	.....	16	2	14	4	2	.....	5	.....	.....	.....	21	7	3	16	7	6
Oneida,	.....	54	5	95	17	1	4	14	5	2	1	66	20	18	53	35	19
Onondaga,	2	26	18	39	27	7	.....	15	5	.....	1	63	7	20	36	28	17
Ontario,	.....	12	4	11	7	1	.....	6	1	2	9	13	6	5	11	6	3
Orange,	.....	27	12	27	20	5	.....	7	1	.....	.....	40	7	9	23	7	17
Orleans,	.....	8	11	3	2	.....	.....	3	.....	.....	.....	8	8	3	5	2	3
Oswego,	.....	46	.....	21	15	.....	1	12	3	.....	.....	29	13	5	24	2	6
Otsego,	.....	10	13	4	7	.....	.....	7	.....	.....	.....	1	2	4	10	2	9
Putnam,	.....	3	.....	4	19	2	.....	.....	.....	.....	.....	10	1	.....	3	1	17
Queens,	.....	16	.....	21	40	2	2	3	5	.....	.....	54	1	3	15	11	15
Rensselaer,	8	46	38	36	19	4	.....	11	3	2	15	109	6	18	34	14	18
Richmond,	1	10	.....	14	6	6	.....	2	5	1	.....	53	.....	16	11	24	3
Rockland,	.....	12	1	1	56	.....	.....	5	.....	.....	.....	17	.....	.....	5	.....	46
St. Lawrence,	1	44	13	18	7	.....	.....	2	2	.....	1	11	.....	8	12	11	3
Saratoga,	.....	28	31	9	1	1	.....	4	.....	.....	63	22	1	4	18	4	10
Schenectady,	.....	15	.....	2	.....	.....	.....	.....	1	.....	.....	.....	1	5	20	4	8
Schoharie,	.....	3	4	.....	3	.....	.....	1	.....	.....	.....	2	.....	.....	2	3	9
Schuyler,	.....	2	1	3	.....	.....	.....	.....	.....	.....	.....	2	1	2	4	1	7
Seneca,	.....	7	6	4	16	.....	.....	4	.....	.....	2	4	.....	5	11	1	4
Steuben,	.....	29	2	9	6	.....	.....	1	1	.....	.....	19	1	8	19	12	36
Suffolk,	.....	14	.....	5	81	1	.....	10	2	1	.....	16	1	.....	5	8	10
Sullivan,	.....	5	13	2	3	1	.....	.....	1	.....	.....	3	.....	1	1	5	7
Tioga,	.....	11	7	7	.....	.....	1	2	1	.....	.....	8	.....	3	11	6	10
Tompkins,	3	3	6	11	1	.....	.....	5	1	.....	.....	6	.....	5	12	6	3
Ulster,	.....	26	2	8	15	.....	.....	7	.....	.....	2	38	10	6	21	12	15
Warren,	.....	1	.....	3	.....	.....	.....	.....	.....	.....	.....	3	.....	2	5	1	3
Washington,	.....	17	7	3	6	.....	.....	4	.....	.....	.....	11	2	10	17	3	8
Wayne,	.....	3	2	10	.....	.....	.....	5	1	.....	.....	7	8	1	16	2	7
Westchester,	3	82	12	28	35	15	.....	30	6	1	.....	108	7	17	27	11	37
Wyoming,	.....	8	4	6	.....	.....	.....	1	.....	.....	.....	2	3	1	4	6	2
Yates,	.....	2	2	6	3	.....	.....	1	.....	.....	.....	5	1	2	6	1	3
Total,	325	2,340	386	1,438	1,421	261	237	751	220	58	283	5,136	432	539	2,142	987	783

COUNTIES.	Bell founders.	Bell hangers and locksmiths.	Bellows makers.	Billiard makers.	Bill posters.	Bird cage makers	Blacking makers.	Blacksmiths.	Block makers.	Boarding-house keepers.	Boat builders.	Boatmen and watermen.	Boiler makers.	Book-binders.	Booksellers and stationers.	Boot and shoe makers and dealers.	Botanists.
Albany,	4	17	1	.....	.....	.....	2	561	4	55	3	479	20	80	17	869	.....
Allegany,	.....	.....	.....	.....	.....	.....	.....	242	1	1	5	27	4	.....	2	218	.....
Broome,	.....	1	.....	.....	.....	.....	.....	196	3	7	3	126	.....	1	5	177	.....
Cattaraugus,	.....	.....	.....	.....	.....	.....	.....	160	2	1	.....	.....	.....	.....	.....	163	.....
Cayuga,	.....	.....	.....	.....	.....	.....	.....	289	9	3	10	95	2	35	4	335	.....
Chautauque,	.....	.....	.....	.....	.....	.....	.....	290	1	9	1	10	.....	5	1	298	.....
Chemung,	.....	.....	.....	.....	.....	.....	.....	156	3	.....	6	130	3	12	1	126	.....
Chenango,	.....	.....	.....	.....	.....	.....	.....	206	3	1	.....	26	.....	4	3	200	.....
Clinton,	.....	.....	.....	.....	.....	.....	.....	185	3	.....	1	10	1	1	.....	182	.....
Columbia,	.....	.....	.....	.....	.....	.....	.....	221	3	8	.....	150	.....	2	2	252	.....
Cortland,	.....	.....	.....	.....	.....	.....	.....	135	.....	.....	.....	5	.....	.....	1	159	.....
Delaware,	.....	.....	.....	.....	.....	.....	.....	183	.....	4	.....	1	.....	1	.....	183	.....
Dutchess,	.....	4	.....	.....	.....	.....	.....	292	2	17	.....	148	.....	10	2	351	.....
Erie,	3	58	3	.....	.....	.....	.....	764	12	83	27	142	41	62	7	1,050	.....
Essex,	.....	.....	.....	.....	.....	.....	.....	159	1	1	9	142	.....	.....	.....	105	.....
Franklin,	.....	.....	.....	.....	.....	.....	.....	109	.....	2	1	8	.....	.....	1	97	.....

COUNTIES.	Bell founders.	Bell hangers and locksmiths	Bellows makers.	Billiard makers.	Bill posters.	Bird-cage makers.	Blacking makers.	Blacksmiths.	Block makers.	Boarding-house keepers.	Boat builders.	Boatmen and watermen	Boiler makers.	Book binders.	Book sellers and stationers.	Boot and shoe makers and dealers.	Botanists.
Fulton,		1						111		1		4		1		117	
Genesee,								195	7	1		2		1	2	150	
Greene,								132		4	1	285				153	
Hamilton,								10								3	
Herkimer,		4					1	240		1	8	171		1	2	249	
Jefferson,								356	3	5	1	25	1	4	1	379	
Kings,		85					17	735	65	173	33	513	101	449	107	1,816	
Lewis,		1						84	1	1		4			1	102	
Livingston,								224		5	7	51	2		2	236	
Madison,								243				86		9	1	259	
Monroe,		26						618	21	31	179	147	8	18	16	878	
Montgomery,		1						165	1		4	124		1		168	
New-York,		394	18	4	5	7	12	2,611	51	1,014	99	1,004	388	1,315	239	6,745	1
Niagara,								230	4	8	7	121		3	5	235	
Oneida,		32			2			570	7	24	37	571	1	17	11	726	
Onondaga,		1		1				451	2	17	25	336	1	6	12	560	
Ontario,		1						268	4	9		61	5	2	9	243	
Orange,		2						340	1	18	12	149	16	3	2	299	
Orleans,								153	4		1	100		1	1	157	
Oswego,								303	8	15	29	383	1	5	5	338	
Otsego,								332				2		3	2	281	
Putnam,								92		3	1	2	45			133	
Queens,		4						189		16		212		1		285	
Rensselaer,	1	11						404	29	35	1	198	17	24	13	555	
Richmond,		1						80	10	8		183				86	
Rockland,								133		2		166	3		1	178	
St. Lawrence,								319		9		59		3	3	329	
Saratoga,		1						208		11		110		2	28	183	
Schenectady,								132		17	1	31	33	3	3	149	
Schoharie,								160	19	4		1				161	
Schuyler,								113	1		21	98			1	89	
Seneca,								125	6	1	19	34	2			133	
Steuben,								335			16	85	4	2	4	264	
Suffolk,								149	10	9	6	434	1	1		231	
Sullivan,								164		4	31	75				127	
Tioga,								139	1	5		1		1	2	146	
Tompkins,								172	35	1	47	138	2	6	3	169	
Ulster,								352	1	7	23	951		2	3	270	
Warren,								79	2	3	2	26	1	2	1	63	
Washington,								237	3	4		273				269	
Wayne,								226	43	2	1	129	1	2	2	265	
Westchester,		14	2					342	1	21	8	242	4	20	11	1,555	
Wyoming,								162	4			5			2	181	
Yates,								117		2	7	45			3	124	
Total,	8	659	24	5	7	7	32	16,948	391	1,680	693	9,136	708	2,121	544	24,804	1

COUNTIES.	Bottlers.	Box makers.	Brass workers.	Brewers and distillers.	Brick makers.	Bridge and dock builders.	Britannia ware makers	Brokers.	Broom makers.	Brush makers.	Builders.	Butchers.	Button makers.	Cabinet makers and dealers.	Cadets.	Calico printers.	Card makers.
Albany,		22	26	73	107		7	21	18	7	23	270		214			1
Allegany,		2		1	1							16		59			
Broome,			3		20			2	1	1	5	17		33			
Cattaraugus,		2	2	6				2	1		5	9		44			
Cayuga,				12	24			3	1		3	45		107			4
Chautauque,		2		8	9			4		2	1	34		115			
Chemung,				4	22			1		1	4	31		44			
Chenango,		1		5	9			3				17	1	52			
Clinton,					11			1	1			28		30			
Columbia,				4	11				2		14	53		49		3	
Cortland,											1	10	2	27			
Delaware,												14		38			
Dutchess,		3	10	10	128			1			1	85		147		4	
Erie,	2	12	11	126	59			19	2	8	34	325		227			
Essex,					6						1	8		19			
Franklin,					3							14		26			
Fulton,		1			7							85		24			
Genesee,				8	3				3			325		37			
Greene,				3	104				1			8		43			
Hamilton,														1			
Herkimer,		11	1	10	11				22			25		41			
Jefferson,			1	14	15	1		3			3	29		95			
Kings,	1	44	167	132	43	41		362		80	204	606	2	466			6
Lewis,		12									2	9		29		1	
Livingston,			4	12	8			2	2		1	34		76			
Madison,		3		20	6				1			31		73			
Monroe,		9	10	50	23	1		5		1	38	152	2	183			
Montgomery,		2		10	2	1		1	4		4	24		27			
New-York,	11	228	442	360	38	86	1	649	18	220	575	2,643	45	2,606		6	33
Niagara,				15	42			3	16	15	2	56		50			
Oneida,		6	8	48	68			3	1	3	17	144		221			
Onondaga,		5	6	29	49			6	1	2	8	117		107			

COUNTIES.	Bottlers.	Box makers.	Brass workers.	Brewers and distillers.	Brick makers.	Bridge and dock builders.	Britannia ware makers.	Brokers.	Broom makers.	Brush makers.	Builders.	Butchers.	Button makers.	Cabinet makers and dealers.	Cadets.	Calico printers.	Card makers.
Ontario,				29	11			1			6	43		48			
Orange,		2	1	19	228			1	3	10		90		69	201		
Orleans,				1	2			2				22		23			
Oswego,				7	21			1	1	2	13	67		97			
Otsego,				5				2	1			27		66			
Putnam,					10						1	17		9			
Queens,			2	3	9	1		12	3	2	22	63		37			
Rensselaer,		10	5	26	33	2	5	9		247	9	79	1	112			
Richmond,				12	1			47			5	33		34			
Rockland,			3	4	136			4	1		1	22		20		11	
St. Lawrence,				9	7			3		3	20	33		62			
Saratoga,				3	17						1	47		39			
Schenectady,			2	3	20			1	76		8	26		37			
Schoharie,				2	2				2			10		39			
Schuyler,					8			1				9		16			
Seneca,				19	6							22		26			
Steuben,				4	7			5			2	28		66			
Suffolk,				1	153			2		2	3	24		27			
Sullivan,				3	1						1	9		24			
Tioga,				1	7						5	15		25			
Tompkins,				4	4						6	20		53			
Ulster,				11	45					1	1	78		31			
Warren,					1							12		16			
Washington,				4	8			1				28	1	45			
Wayne,				14	9			1	1			37		65			
Westchester,		2	52	20	44	8		45		15	26	154	7	182		3	3
Wyoming,				2	2	1		1			1	15		45			
Yates,				4	6			3			4	14		33			
Total,	14	379	756	1,176	1,627	142	13	1,233	183	622	1,081	6,308	61	6,656	201	28	47

COUNTIES.	Carpenters.	Carpet makers and dealers.	Carters and draymen.	Carvers and gilders.	Case makers.	Cattle dealers.	Caulkers.	Cement makers.	Chandlers and soap makers.	Charcoal burners and dealers.	Chemists.	Chimney sweeps.	Chronometer makers.	Civil engineers.	Civil officers.	Clerks, copyists and accountants.	Clergymen.
Albany,	1,201	3	338	18			11		25	2	5	1		12	108	1,148	87
Allegany,	377		1	1			1							4	4	107	80
Broome,	414		12				1		2						8	137	67
Cattaraugus,	267								1						7	79	64
Cayuga,	633	152	18	4			5		6	2				5	18	238	89
Chautauque,	507	1	4				3		7					1	26	202	104
Chemung,	409	1	3	2			3		6	1				1	10	140	38
Chenango,	334		3											1	7	62	86
Clinton,	165		4				1			99				2	9	127	47
Columbia,	488	2	34	1		1	2		5	3				3	10	204	67
Cortland,	227								1						8	77	56
Delaware,	367														11	64	72
Dutchess,	702	15	41	16			1		2	38	2			2	14	209	88
Erie,	1,148	7	55	27			47		42		4			8	93	1,085	167
Essex,	164						1			135					5	72	31
Franklin,	143		6											1	5	60	37
Fulton,	292													1	6	61	24
Genesee,	299		2						2					1	13	98	61
Greene,	233		5				9		3						11	82	58
Hamilton,	14														3	2	1
Herkimer,	370	1	17						1	1	1			1	9	156	52
Jefferson,	665		9				6		4	5				8	34	213	116
Kings,	2,892	26	859	160			79	2	52	25	55	4		26	60	4,708	313
Lewis,	158									1				1	3	54	35
Livingston,	387		5	1					6						23	145	76
Madison,	443		3	2			1		4	1	1			2	8	136	86
Monroe,	1,148	2	63	7			5	2	25		4			25	41	668	141
Montgomery,	351	1	8						2					6	16	103	37
New-York,	6,901	52	5,338	765	32	9	378	2	317	28	84	6	4	27	316	13,897	393
Niagara,	336		8	2				1	1					4	32	272	61
Oneida,	1,394	12	48	4			9	3	9	9	1			31	51	683	174
Onondaga,	1,076	1	44	11			2	3	6	2	1			8	54	551	133
Ontario,	345		12	1				1	5		2			1	14	163	103
Orange,	665	4	48	7					22	24	7				18	298	102
Orleans,	255		4											6	18	111	54
Oswego,	681		36	3			26		3	3	1			8	37	308	112
Otsego,	570		1							1					15	129	93
Putnam,	229		5	1					1	18					5	37	25
Queens,	679	11	44	1			4		2		1	1			21	198	53
Rensselaer,	945	7	48	30			3		24	97				8	38	624	98
Richmond,	386	1	18	10			2		3	1	1			1	9	134	31
Rockland,	269		4				1		1						9	59	32
St. Lawrence,	550		30	2		2			5	8				1	23	267	110
Saratoga,	508	1	13						3		1			7	11	185	79
Schenectady,	212		23						5					7	14	137	26
Schoharie,	379		1			1								2	7	60	42
Schuyler,	215	1	1				2		1						5	37	33
Seneca,	286		16						2	1					6	89	42

COUNTIES.	Carpenters.	Carpet makers and dealers	Carters and draymen	Carvers and gilders.	Case makers.	Cattle dealers.	Caulkers.	Cement makers.	Chandlers and soap makers.	Charcoal burners and dealers.	Chemists.	Chimney sweeps.	Chronometer makers.	Civil engineers.	Civil officers.	Clerks, copyists and accountants.	Clergymen.
Steuben,	604		10				3		1						20	155	104
Suffolk,	600	6	27	1			22		2	3				1	3	117	80
Sullivan,	302						8			10					2	49	35
Tioga,	270		7						1					6	16	91	43
Tompkins,	371		3						3						13	97	52
Ulster,	698		9	1			17	249		15					28	267	68
Warren,	164						1		1					2	4	27	39
Washington,	441	4	12				2			14				3	13	171	87
Wayne,	515	1	11				1	1	2	5					14	192	83
Westchester,	1, 380	17	38	46					6	3	12			12	21	369	138
Wyoming,	240		2	1						1				3	12	75	64
Yates,	202	1					2								8	73	41
Total,	37, 475	330	7, 350	1, 125	32	13	659	264	622	556	183	12	4	249	1, 427	30, 359	4, 810

COUNTIES.	Clock makers and repairers.	Clothiers.	Cloth manufacturers not specified.	Coach and wagon makers.	Coal dealers.	Coffee, spice and mustard makers	Collectors.	Comb makers.	Confectioners.	Contractors.	Cooks.	Coopers.	Copper smiths.	Cork cutters.	Cotton manufacturers.	Custom House officers.	Cutlers.
Albany,	4	22	24	144	9		9	3	42	26	60	204	35		1	2	4
Allegany,	1	18		93			3			12	6	52					
Broome,		9		62			1		3	2	6	87	1				
Cattaraugus,		8		43			1			1		52	1				
Cayuga,	2	5	14	127			1	2	2	11	3	148	3	14			3
Chautauque,		11	1	154					1	2	1	121	1			2	
Chemung,		8	5	66			4		2	2	9	50					
Chenango,	1	7	2	101					1		1	103	1				5
Clinton,		6	2	14			1				1	30				3	
Columbia,		14		106				1	6		10	33	2		12		1
Cortland,	1	2		56					2			46					
Delaware,		18		60								48	1				
Dutchess,	2	3	1	145			2	10	13	5	27	90	1			2	43
Erie,	8	20	1	274			3	6	38	23	61	311	25		3	2	16
Essex,		50		12					2			32					
Franklin,		2		6								27				4	
Fulton,		9		35							1	43					
Genesee,	5	3		131								53					2
Greene,	2	8		59			1	6	2		2	36					
Hamilton,																	
Herkimer,	2	5	3	74					1	10	3	53	4			1	2
Jefferson,	5	14	2	104			4		4	5	2	144			6	2	
Kings,	18	79	9	116		4	45	17	106	106	92	533	54	6	6	94	31
Lewis,	1	7		40					1	4		59			1		1
Livingston,		6	1	104			1		7			102	1				1
Madison,		11	3	124			1	1		14		101					14
Monroe,	3	34	3	251			5	1	25	51	13	519	6		1		6
Montgomery,		12		58						18	10	34	1				
New-York,	79	403	6	449	123	21	94	22	704	188	755	1, 018	207	24		212	105
Niagara,	2	4		62			4		7	15	8	125				1	
Oneida,	3	20	2	244	1		2		19	33	33	184	10			1	3
Onondaga,	3	20		201	1		3		14	27	4	394	10				3
Ontario,		4		95					4	1	5	101	4				
Orange,	1	13	3	187			2	2	10	12	24	78	2		1		1
Orleans,		2	3	69			2		1	18	7	83					
Oswego,		22		95	1		4		3	7	33	698			3		
Otsego,	4	8	3	141					1			88			2		1
Putnam,	1		2	13					2		1	19					
Queens,	3	2		49			2	148	2	7	51	21	1			2	
Rensselaer,	3	13	14	120	3			2	21	9	49	126	15		1		1
Richmond,				12			6		1	11	7	16	2			5	2
Rockland,				10						2		20	7		5	1	1
St. Lawrence,	1	30		22					1	7	5	157				4	
Saratoga,	1	11	4	57			1		4	6	13	69			12		
Schenectady,			1	33			1		3	4	3	8	7				
Schoharie,	1	15		78				1				81			1		
Schuyler,		7		34						2		36		1			
Seneca,		4	3	65			5		5	9		114					
Steuben,		10	1	146			1		1	1	2	68	1			1	
Suffolk,		6	2	34					1	1	7	48	1		11		
Sullivan,		5		42					1			14					
Tioga,		13	2	61			2	1			2	60			3		
Tompkins,		11	3	97				1	6		2	62	1				
Ulster,		12	1	139			8		11	1	3	283	1		1		
Warren,	3	5		18								54					
Washington,	2	19		114			1	1	1	7	2	61			4		1
Wayne,	1	6		115						18	2	156				1	
Westchester,	1	10	1	113			2	4	7	21	94	78	2		1	6	2
Wyoming,		15		91								39					
Yates,		3	1	72							4	69	1				
Total,	164	1, 084	123	5, 637	138	25	222	229	1, 088	699	1, 424	7, 539	409	45	75	346	249

COUNTIES.	Dairymen and milk dealers.	Dealers, (not otherwise specified.)	Dentists.	Dock keepers.	Dress makers, sewers and seamstresses.	Drivers, coachmen, &c.	Drovers.	Dyers and bleachers.	Editors.	Electrotypists.	Embroiderers.	Enamelers.	Engineers.	Engravers.	Envelope makers.	Express men.	Factory operatives.
Albany,	18	6	15		767	85	8	20	23		1		138	22		22	107
Allegany,	4		4	1	24	3		1	2				22	1			
Broome,	5	1	11		92	37	5	1	4				48	4		1	1
Cattaraugus,		4	6		28	3	6		1				17			1	
Cayuga,		3	14		186	9	3	20	4				25			3	15
Chautauque,	8	6	12		176	24	19	2	1		1		39	4		7	6
Chemung,	1		6		108	4	1		4				32	3		5	1
Chenango,	3	9	13		51	20	3		3		1		2	1			
Clinton,		22	5	1	58	3	1		1				20	2		1	2
Columbia,	1	3	9		158	16	11	9					29	4			104
Cortland,		6	4		48	2	2	2	1				4	3		3	5
Delaware,		6	8		58	19	5		3				6				
Dutchess,	5	2	10	1	252	81	13	9	3				42	10		1	106
Erie,	23	14	16		385	108	19	23	19		6		207	13		23	51
Essex,		9	1		28	7							10			1	
Franklin,			4		30	3			1				2	4		1	5
Fulton,		1	5		36	5			5				1	3			
Genesee,		3	4		64	8	4		1				8				2
Greene,			5		66	11	2	1	1				9				27
Hamilton,					2												
Herkimer,		4	11		86	7	4	4	1				20			3	41
Jefferson,	1	5	9		134	8	9	1	1		4		22	2			75
Kings,	271	396	60	1	1, 734	284	19	26	52		16	1	390	188	4	78	64
Lewis,			1	3	44	8	1						6				
Livingston,			9		119	10	2		2				10	1		1	
Madison,		6	10		144	12	1	2	3		1		9	2			5
Monroe,	6	23	25		418	35	5	9	16		4		109	16		12	73
Montgomery,	2		5	29	111	3	1	3					11			2	4
New-York,	579	1, 025	194	11	7, 436	1, 741	137	163	129	10	169	2	867	403	25	169	207
Niagara,			11		87	7		1	5				58	1		3	1
Oneida,	3	17	40		483	55	9	26	13	1			99	10		7	1, 237
Onondaga,	6	12	20		265	77	15	4	9				75	5		10	18
Ontario,	4	5	14		82	7	3	1	2				22			2	
Orange,	10	4	17		298	33	5	6	5				34	5		1	56
Orleans,			7		118	1			1				21				
Oswego,	1	9	12		147	15	1		3				44	7		2	10
Otsego,	2	3	12		167	20	7	1	1				3			1	45
Putnam,	2	4	3		36	2			1				13				
Queens,	27	2	7		132	55		2	3		7		31	5		11	21
Rensselaer,	26	20	15		480	39	3	33	8		2		110	5		12	77
Richmond,	3	8	6	1	8	69		41	5				20			5	22
Rockland,	5			1	41	17		1	2				52	8		3	14
St. Lawrence,	1		9	2	98	4	1	2	6		1		40			2	1
Saratoga,		3	11		87	17		12	2				22			8	31
Schenectady,	2	3	4		94	16		3	1				33			5	4
Schoharie,		4	4		41	9	1						1	1			
Schuyler,			3		27	1	2		3				4	1			
Seneca,	1		10		72	3	1	2	1				7				3
Steuben,	2	2	9		64	3		1	1				54			2	
Suffolk,			5		213	20		1	4		2		9			1	7
Sullivan,					32	2	1						6				
Tioga,	1		9		35	13	1		4		1		25			7	
Tompkins,		8	7		82	17	2	1					15	1		1	7
Ulster,	3	1	7	3	164	13	1		5				40			1	7
Warren,					14	3	1						2				
Washington,		3	10		119	7	3	1	4				19			3	3
Wayne,	1	1	11		146	1	7				1		31				
Westchester,	22	5	11		322	161	8	33	11		1		177	24		1	11
Wyoming,			6		60	5	5	2	3				7	2			1
Yates,	1		5		82	5	4						1				
Total,	1, 050	1, 668	761	54	16, 939	3, 253	362	470	384	11	218	3	3, 180	761	29	422	2, 477

COUNTIES.	Farmers.	Farriers.	Feather dressers.	Ferrymen.	File cutters.	Fire engine makers.	Firemen.	Fish dealers.	Fishermen.	Fishing tackle makers.	Flax dressers and workers.	Fortune tellers and astrologists.	Forwarders.	Frame makers.	Fringe, tassel and gimp makers	Fruit dealers.	Furnacemen.
Albany,	5, 728	5			6		3		19				28			27	217
Allegany,	7, 364						1						2				4
Broome,	5, 851								1								9
Cattaraugus,	6, 855						1						2				10
Cayuga,	8, 223	6			1		1		20				4	1			31
Chautauque,	9, 249	2					13		31				2			1	12
Chemung,	2, 848															1	7
Chenango,	7, 457	3											3				15
Clinton,	3, 925	2					1						3				159
Columbia,	5, 260	2					4		25				5			2	12
Cortland,	4, 835	3															3
Delaware,	7, 448																3
Dutchess,	5, 591	3			35		2		58				5				34
Erie,	10, 182	7			5		17		35				51			2	19
Essex,	3, 782						2		3				1				185
Franklin,	4, 410	1															9

COUNTIES.	Farmers.	Farriers.	Feather dressers.	Ferrymen.	File cutters.	Fire engine makers.	Firemen.	Fish dealers.	Fishermen.	Fishing tackle makers.	Flax dressers and workers.	Fortune tellers and astrologists.	Forwarders.	Frame makers.	Fringe, tassel and gimp makers.	Fruit dealers.	Furnacemen.
Fulton,	2, 899				1				1		1						1
Genesee,	5, 507	1			2								1			1	17
Greene,	4, 190	2					2		13				1			2	53
Hamilton,	511								2								
Herkimer,	6, 321												5				6
Jefferson,	7, 000	2					1		20				3				34
Kings,	476	9	3		26		48	42	162		13		53	19	18	46	39
Lewis,	4, 975	3															13
Livingston,	4, 774	2			3								3				24
Madison,	7, 019	1											2				16
Monroe,	7, 957	4			3			3	11				16	1		7	89
Montgomery,	3, 131	2							1				2				12
New-York,	193	31	5	4	10	6	270	114	85	8	5	3	20	143	137	194	145
Niagara,	5, 505	1					4		7				1			1	13
Oneida,	11, 880	8			4		18		1				9			5	60
Onondaga,	9, 079	1					5		2				7			9	32
Ontario,	6, 333	6			1		3		2				1				14
Orange,	5, 455	2					2	1	12	6			1			6	17
Orleans,	4, 067	3					1		5				6				20
Oswego,	8. 667	1					4		19		1		17			5	9
Otsego,	9, 985	1							2		3		1				18
Putnam,	1, 957								1							1	2
Queens,	3, 598	1					4	2	18			1					
Rensselaer,	5, 824	3			9		8	2	20		23		4			9	50
Richmond,	574	1					1		20								
Rockland,	1, 323			1	4				5								
St. Lawrence,	11, 427			1	3												4
Saratoga,	5, 960								2		5						26
Schenectady,	2, 234	1						1			1					3	59
Schoharie,	5, 372																11
Schuyler,	3, 409				1												5
Seneca,	3, 033	1			1				2								60
Steuben,	9, 696	1							1								31
Suffolk,	3, 942	1							218								
Sullivan,	3, 616																2
Tioga,	4, 145								3								6
Tompkins,	5, 038	2							9								13
Ulster,	5, 703	3							35								7
Warren,	2, 088																1
Washington,	7, 204								3		14		7				19
Wayne,	7, 494								11				1				38
Westchester,	4, 239	21			243				76				4				95
Wyoming,	6, 328	1											3				8
Yates,	2, 794								4								9
Total,	821,930	150	8	6	358	6	416	165	965	14	66	4	274	164	155	322	1, 807

COUNTIES.	Furriers.	Gamblers.	Gardeners and florists	Gas fitters and fixture makers.	Gas makers.	Gas meter makers.	Gate keepers.	Geologists and mineralogists.	Glass cutters.	Glass makers.	Glass stainers.	Glovers.	Glue makers.	Gold beaters.	Gold and silversmiths.	Grate makers and setters.	Grindstone and millstone makers.
Albany,		3	172	19	7		9	3		1		7	5	9	21	3	
Allegany,		1	8				5								4		
Broome,		1	15		3		12								1		1
Cattaraugus,			6				2										
Cayuga,			45	1	4		12								6		1
Chautauque,			16				10			1					3		
Chemung,			23	2	2		20					1			4		
Chenango,			6				4					1			8		
Clinton,			5				1			18					4		
Columbia,			50	1	1		3						1		2		
Cortland,			4				3								2		
Delaware,			4				6								2		
Dutchess,			117	1			3								4		
Erie,	2		161	11			20			13	6		6	5	16		2
Essex,			3														
Franklin,			5									1			5		
Fulton,			2				3					102	2		3		
Genesee,			10									1			1		
Greene,			14				5						2		2		
Hamilton,															1		
Herkimer,		1	8				36								3		
Jefferson,	1		8	1	1		10			29					8		
Kings,	90	1	305	121	9		10			187	5	4	8	19	85	15	2
Lewis,										1							
Livingston,			27				17								5		
Madison,			14				15			2					6		
Monroe,	3		134	9	1		19					4			17		
Montgomery,			7				6					6			3		
New-York,	120		644	315	81	8		1	65	67	33	23	1	100	403	73	4
Niagara,			35	1	1		6			17		1			2		
Oneida,	4		97	13	3		56	1		38	4				21		4

COUNTIES.	Furriers.	Gamblers.*	Gardeners and florists.	Gas fitters and fixture makers.	Gas makers.	Gas meter makers.	Gate keepers.	Geologists and mineralogists.	Glass cutters.	Glass makers.	Glass stainers.	Glovers.	Glue makers.	Gold beaters.	Gold and silver smiths.	Grate makers and setters.	Grindstone and millstone makers.
Onondaga,			105	6	1		29			1					47		
Ontario,			21				10			1					1		
Orange,			57	1	1		9				1	2			15		
Orleans,			8				2								2		
Oswego,			38	1	3		20		14	11					3		
Otsego,			5				4						2		12		
Putnam,			11												1		
Queens,	5		240				11					2			1		
Rensselaer,			58	13	1		9		1	5		1			15	1	7
Richmond,			125				4								1		
Rockland,	1		7							1					7		
St. Lawrence,			7	1	3		2					3			6		2
Saratoga,			41	2	2		6			13						5	
Schenectady,			23		2		3			1					5		
Schoharie,			1				5								2		
Schuyler,			17				10								3		
Seneca,			20				2			1					7		
Steuben,			18	1			7			1							
Suffolk,			57		1		1			1					6		
Sullivan,			10				7								3		
Tioga,			8									2			8		
Tompkins,			22	1	2		1					2			4		
Ulster,			31	2	3		20			33			1		5		
Warren,							2										
Washington,			11				15					3					
Wayne,			22				19			17							
Westchester,			358	4			3			5	3		9	1	19	1	
Wyoming,	1		2							1					3		
Yates,			1				6								2		
Total,	227	7	3, 269	527	132	8	499	5	80	466	52	166	37	134	820	98	23

COUNTIES.	Grocers.	Gunsmiths.	Gutta percha manufacturers.	Hair cloth makers.	Hair workers.	Hame makers.	Hardware dealers.	Hat and cap makers.	Hemp dressers.	Horse dealers.	Hose makers.	Hosiers.	Hotel and inn keepers.	Hunters.	Ice dealers.	Importers.	India rubber manufacturers.
Albany,	498	12					7	99				1	122	1	3		
Allegany,	49	9					4	7					66				
Broome,	34	3					1	13					25				
Cattaraugus,	36	11						4					39				
Cayuga,	98	9				58		5	5				49				
Chautauque,	50	11					5	12		3			85	5			
Chemung,	57	8						15					26				
Chenango,	32	3				4	2	8		1			48				
Clinton,	30	4						4		1			32				
Columbia,	49	3					1	20					60		1		
Cortland,	12	3				3	1	4		1			26				
Delaware,	16	5						2					39				
Dutchess,	30	4				1		12					52		1		1
Erie,	370	13				1	6	62					108	2	6		
Essex,	17	3						1					21	2			
Franklin,	4	2											15	3			
Fulton,	11	3						2					21	1			
Genesee,	18	9					3	9					35				
Greene,	26	1					3	62	2	1			34				
Hamilton,		1												1			
Herkimer,	51	42						6					33				
Jefferson,	53	8					2	14		1			89	1			
Kings,	1, 199	30					84	406		6	4		226	1	27	131	5
Lewis,	5	3						5					27	4			
Livingston,	46	3				1	2	8		2			55				
Madison,	9	9					1	15		1			51				
Monroe,	265	9			3		11	43		4	1	1	93	1	4		
Montgomery,	106	2					1	3					50				
New-York,	4, 079	126	3	17	80		211	1, 422	4	51	1	23	709	21	91	235	57
Niagara,	104	4					10	6					63				
Oneida,	190	18			2		10	40		6			131	1	1		
Onondaga,	139	13			3	1	7	22					102	1			
Ontario,	53	9					3	12		1			34				
Orange,	78	5					4	23					85	1			
Orleans,	41	4					1	11		5			19	1			
Oswego,	110	2			1		1	9					53		1		
Otsego,	16	3					1	12		1			78				
Putnam,	7	1						10		2			4				
Queens,	67	3					2	23		1		1	46	2		7	1
Rensselaer,	208	13					2	35		2		2	86	1	10		2
Richmond,	54	3					2	24					68			25	
Rockland,	12	1						7					15		2		
St. Lawrence,	56	4					1	9		1			59	2			
Saratoga,	53	5						11					56	2			
Schenectady,	41	4					1	3		1			31		1		
Schoharie,	8	1						12					42	1			
Schuyler,	22	2						2					17				

COUNTIES.	Grocers	Gunsmiths.	Gutta percha manufacturers.	Hair cloth makers.	Hair workers.	Hame makers	Hardware dealers.	Hat and cap makers	Hemp dressers.	Horse dealers.	Hose makers.	Hosiers.	Hotel and inn keepers.	Hunters.	Ice dealers.	Importers.	India rubber manufacturers.
Seneca,	47	3					4	3					31				
Steuben,	37	9					2	9					43	1			
Suffolk,	4	3						6		1			26				
Sullivan,	10	3						1					43				
Tioga,	27	3					3	3					20				
Tompkins,	22	9					8	14					35				
Ulster,	92	3					1	12		2			96		1		
Warren,	10	4						3					18	1			
Washington,	50	1					3	13		1			32				
Wayne,	66	5					1	8		1			43				
Westchester,	142	4					12	310		5			97	2	3	11	7
Wyoming,	22	2						6					32				
Yates,	15	3					2	6					14				
Total,	9, 056	496	3	17	89	69	426	2, 928	11	102	6	28	3, 755	59	152	409	73

COUNTIES.	Ink makers.	Inspectors.	Instrument makers.	Insurance officers.	Intelligence officers.	Inventors and patentees	Iron mongers.	Iron workers.	Ivory black makers.	Ivory workers.	Japanners.	Jewellers.	Joiners.	Junk shop keepers.	Keepers and wardens of prisons, &c.	Laborers.	Lace makers.
Albany,	2	46	4	13		1	5	8				44	1		19	4, 216	17
Allegany,		5										5	88			892	
Broome,				1								10	8			477	
Cattaraugus,		1				1	1					5	59		1	643	
Cayuga,		2		8		2		1				17	14		24	1, 362	1
Chautauque,		1		4								11	184			1, 200	
Chemung,	1	1		2								9	4		2	652	
Chenango,			1								1	4	19			442	
Clinton,				1				25				2	31		34	2, 005	
Columbia,			4	3				5				9	2		1	2, 021	
Cortland,				1								6	45			250	
Delaware,				2				1				3	10		1	571	
Dutchess,		1	4	1			1	2	2			13	1		3	2, 608	1
Erie,	1	11	6	17				25	1			36	875		4	5, 367	
Fssex,							7	93				6	59		3	918	
Franklin,												1	69			254	
Fulton,				8								3	5			1, 156	
Genesee,		1						1				12	83			1, 057	
Greene,				1								4	1		2	587	
Hamilt n,																49	
Herkimer,						2						6	34		1	855	
Jefferson,				6				10				14	98			1, 045	
Kings,	7	60	36	75		3	5	76	7	1	26	333	33	101	20	7, 044	2
Lewis,				1								2	60			564	
Livingston,				1								11	40			2, 167	1
Madison,												12	41			1, 338	
Monroe,		3	6	1		1		4				34	233		7	4, 901	
Montgomery,				2								7	1		1	1, 722	
New-York,	44	129	91	103	3	20	17	256	2	2	41	1, 099	303	213	63	19, 748	35
Niagara,	2	1		2				3				17	105			2, 592	
Oneida,		1		8				15				28	93		2	4, 487	1
Onondaga,		12		5				3				37	56		7	3, 168	
Ontario,				5				2				9	65			1, 259	
Orange,		1							3			8	2		2	2. 695	
Orleans,												6	14			1, 618	
Oswego,		3		3								31	87		3	1, 976	
Otsego,		1						3				6	10			642	
Putnam,								2					1			539	
Queens,		1		5					1	1	2	8		1	3	2, 316	
Rensselaer,	3	5	10	9			3	298				17	2	2	4	3, 477	2
Richmond,		1		2				1				15		4	1	728	
Rockland,				2				6				6				423	
St. Lawrence,				4				28	1			10	150			1, 349	
Saratoga,				1								6			2	1, 293	
Schenectady,							1	6				3			2	2, 912	
Schoharie,		1										4			1	1, 613	
Schuyler,		3										4	3			174	
Seneca,												4	3			608	
Steuben,												9	28			629	
Suffolk,												7	2		1	1, 179	1
Sullivan,												1	3			1, 455	
Tioga,												8	48			692	
Tompkins,												3	16		1	502	
Ulster,				1			2	110				7			2	3, 451	
Warren,				1									4		2	520	
Washington,				5				1				12	14			1, 258	
Wayne,				2				1				13	46			1, 172	
Westchester,		4	10	7			2	4		1	3	46	9		63	4, 151	
Wyoming,	1			4								5	84		1	320	
Yates,				2								7	10		1	491	
Total,	61	295	172	319	3	30	44	990	17	5	73	2, 055	3, 256	321	284	115,800	61

COUNTIES.	Lamp-black makers.	Lamp lighters	Lamp makers.	Lapidaries.	Last makers.	Lath makers.	Laundresses.	Lawyers.	Lecturers.	Librarians.	Light house keepers.	Lime burners.	Linguists.	Lithographers.	Livery stable keepers.	Looking glass makers	Lumbermen and dealers
Albany,			1		1		70	212		4		3		1	32	7	132
Allegany,								52	1			1			9		326
Broome,								46				1			14		39
Cattaraugus,							1	33				1			1		211
Cayuga,							30	73	3			5			11	1	21
Chautauque,							4	67	1		3	1			14		35
Chemung,								46	1			2			2		85
Chenango,							2	54							7		8
Clinton,								36			1				4		26
Columbia,							8	65	1		1				2		6
Cortland,								20	6						11		7
Delaware,							2	41	1						2		101
Dutchess,							29	76				5			7		6
Erie,			4		16	2	56	196	2		2	2		8	17		132
Essex,								44			1	1			3		33
Franklin,							4	12							1		21
Fulton,								25				3			8		45
Genesee,								33							8		9
Greene,								29	6		1	3			2		26
Hamilton,																	10
Herkimer,							2	33				3			4		23
Jefferson,					10		2	68	1		7	3			13		39
Kings,			12	10	12		383	354	2		1	6	1	34	63	7	73
Lewis,					1			11							1		30
Livingston,						1	1	64				3			10		20
Madison,								43	1			3			11		10
Monroe,			5		14		35	140					1		19		36
Montgomery,							7	44	1						5		4
New-York,	1	18	29	7	26	8	2, 563	1, 112	4	1		21	8	122	191	34	156
Niagara,					1		4	41			1	4			17		62
Oneida,					8		40	147	1			2			20		118
Onondaga,					2		3	118				29		2	24	3	38
Ontario,							1	49							19		10
Orange,							12	59				2		1	18		13
Orleans,								32				1			1		8
Oswego,							13	74				1			6		88
Otsego,					5		10	52				1			4		3
Putnam,							2	13									2
Queens,							52	36							13		7
Rensselaer,	5						69	99				2			20	1	52
Richmond,							16	35						1	14		5
Rockland,							4	12									
St. Lawrence,								86			1				5		92
Saratoga,							4	54	1			3			17		65
Schenectady,							3	30									4
Schoharie,							3	39				1					
Schuyler,								18									25
Seneca,								33							7		28
Steuben,							1	51							6		196
Suffolk,							4	24			5				5		10
Sullivan,								15									125
Tioga,							2	16							2		43
Tompkins,							4	23	2			1			10		27
Ulster,							11	56			2	7			12		34
Warren,							1	12							6		49
Washington,							2	62							14		73
Wayne,							1	43			2	1			9		22
Westchester,					1		96	127			2	5		7	14		28
Wyoming,					1			36							4		7
Yates,								21				2			2		29
Total,	6	18	51	17	98	11	3, 557	4, 542	35	5	30	129	10	176	741	53	2, 933

COUNTIES.	Machinists.	Mail agents and carriers	Manufacturers, (not specified.	Map makers.	Marble dealers.	Market men and women	Masons, plasterers, bricklayers, &c.	Mat and rug makers.	Match makers.	Matrons of asylums, &c.	Mechanics, (not otherwise specified.)	Merchants.	Midwives.	Military equipment makers.	Millers.	Milliners.	Millwrights
Albany,	338	11	71		1	7	468	1	2		98	634			88	183	18
Allegany,	28		15				82		1		18	184			59	64	47
Broome,	28	2			1		133				119	200			56	50	26
Cattaraugus,	22	2	3				54		1		60	137			34	37	29
Cayuga,	151	6	17		2		192				59	176			96	99	18
Chautauque,	90	5	24		4		108				19	226			62	111	42
Chemung,	52	1	2				128	1				93			45	68	22
Chenango,	19	11	5		3		68				217	164			40	63	11
Clinton,	71	2	17				86		1		85	170			34	32	41
Columbia,	80	1	38				105				51	216			71	77	12
Cortland,	8		5		2		57				17	99			51	42	4
Delaware,	6	2	2		1		61				8	200			37	67	21
Dutchess,	171	5	75			2	205				32	385			124	67	24
Erie,	176	10	32		2		687		10		218	714	12		141	131	55
Essex,	17	1	17				56				49	112			33	31	22
Franklin,	7	1	3				35				16	88			22	19	18

COUNTIES.	Machinists.	Mail agents and carriers	Manufacturers, (not specified,)	Map makers.	Marble dealers.	Market men and women	Masons, plasterers, bricklayers, &c.	Mat and rug makers.	Match makers.	Matrons of asylums, &c.	Mechanics, (not otherwise specified)	Merchants.	Midwives.	Military equipment makers.	Millers.	Milliners.	Millwrights.
Fulton,	2		79				75				28	112			22	36	16
Genesee,	13						128				97	149			74	27	6
Greene,	19		33				54	5			32	156			53	62	18
Hamilton,	3		1								13	6			1		2
Herkimer,	52		27				99		7		79	123			53	61	20
Jefferson,	84	3	17		3		173		6		68	329			139	153	41
Kings,	556	21	111		6	111	1, 628	38	5		89	2, 649	8		37	411	22
Lewis,	3	2	8				54				22	74			25	32	13
Livingston,	56	3			1		97				40	137			86	44	9
Madison,	61		55		1		105				53	175			60	84	18
Monroe,	401	12	19		6	1	565		2		128	394	2		234	183	84
Montgomery,	15	3	6		5		78				115	162			60	44	11
New-York,	1, 714	53	182	11	13	140	3, 634	36	166	24	336	6, 001	20	5	130	1, 585	30
Niagara,	41	1	3				250				146	165			75	58	15
Oneida,	225	7	61		2	1	412	1		2	171	480	1		116	190	47
Onondaga,	122	5	22			5	365		1	6	259	342			142	123	36
Ontario,	56	7	9		1		137				1	164			101	51	14
Orange,	87	6	49				239		5		9	308	3		92	99	15
Orleans,	9	2	1				76				17	99			66	59	11
Oswego,	92	3	24				231			2	73	241			171	84	82
Otsego,	32	4	66				94		1	1	76	197			68	100	18
Putnam,	84	1	4				34				2	68			26	18	1
Queens,	76		6		1	13	174				7	187			45	25	1
Rensselaer,	301	8	85			6	330	1	2	2	119	529	1		77	108	14
Richmond,	7		8				137				9	217			12	3	
Rockland,	72		7				62				1	67			14	18	6
St. Lawrence,	40	6	9				120				74	245			79	91	63
Saratoga,	105		64				89		4		120	218			45	68	20
Schenectady,	189	2	21				63				7	120			8	52	5
Schoharie,	13	1	2		1		81				21	138			61	53	10
Schuyler,	12	1					48				2	69			42	39	17
Seneca,	97		23				67				92	107			58	54	8
Steuben,	80	3			1		154				19	230			79	65	
Suffolk,	5	2	4			7	95				9	268			41	51	
Sullivan,	1		8				55		1		3	102			24	33	8
Tioga,	25	3	1				60		1		42	88			40	28	13
Tompkins,	46		10				78				14	128			81	57	21
Ulster,	27	1	16		5		186				114	315			102	73	34
Warren,	6		4				33				22	59			15	16	7
Washington,	36	7	31				97				59	202			49	99	14
Wayne,	44	2	5		2		161				23	186			67	103	37
Westchester,	113	1	32		1	2	525		2		82	631			54	102	11
Wyoming,	14	1	7		1		72		5		51	147			55	42	18
Yates,	9		2				41				27	82			45	37	16
Total,	6, 309	231	1, 448	11	66	295	13. 781	83	223	37	3, 837	20, 664	47	5	3, 917	5, 862	1, 262

COUNTIES.	Miners.	Mineral water makers	Model makers.	Modelers.	Morocco dressers.	Moulders.	Mould makers.	Musicians.	Music dealers.	Music teachers.	Musical instrument manufacturers.	Nail makers.	Naturalists.	Needle makers.	News boys.	Nurses.	Nurserymen.
Albany,		1			26	601		27	3	15	8	16			11	36	4
Allegany,						6		21		9							1
Broome,	1					3		11		4							3
Cattaraugus,	2					9	1	3		4							1
Cayuga,		1				17		2		7							5
Chautauque,	2					17		7		7	1						2
Chemung,		3				19		2		6	3						10
Chenango,	1					7		5		4	1						
Clinton,	37					19		2		3		31				1	
Columbia,	1					34		6		5		1				9	8
Cortland,						4		1		4							
Delaware,	2					6		1		9							
Dutchess,		1				37		7		3						6	4
Erie,	5	2			8	185	2	55	3	16	30	35				17	7
Essex,	63					12		1				35					
Franklin,	1					11		1		1		1					
Fulton,	1							1		5						1	
Genesee,						14		2		8	3				1		5
Greene,	2				1	3		1		3							
Hamilton,																	
Herkimer,	2					11		4	2	3							1
Jefferson,	37	1				30		4		7	1	1				2	
Kings,	12	6			67	167		89	7	89	8	31	3		45	121	
Lewis,	10					3											
Livingston,						15		2	2	4	1						2
Madison,	1					28		5		6			1				1
Monroe,	4				1	183		6	1	38		6	1		2	9	105
Montgomery,	2					11		2		6					1	3	
New-York,	11	98	7		106	593	10	746	15	160	31	185	3		115	636	1
Niagara,					1	18		6		6	1				2		7
Oneida,	3				5	151		14	1	26	7					13	7
Onondaga,					1	22		27		17		1			5	3	9

COUNTIES.	Miners.	Mineral water makers.	Model makers.	Modelers.	Morocco dressers.	Moulders.	Mould makers.	Musicians.	Music dealers.	Music teachers.	Musical instrument manufacturers.	Nail makers.	Naturalists.	Needle makers.	News boys.	Nurses.	Nurserymen.
Ontario,		1				17		4	1	12						1	16
Orange,	122				13	27	9	35		14		1				13	5
Orleans,	2					32		3		8						1	2
Oswego,	2				10	18		4		6						1	9
Otsego,						5		5		4	27						
Putnam,	3					28										2	
Queens,	4	1	1			8		3		6		1			2	11	2
Rensselaer,					11	304	20	12	1	26		85			6	13	2
Richmond,	1	2				1		3		1	1					12	
Rockland,						2		1						1		1	
St. Lawrence,	21					41		5							1	2	1
Saratoga,	2					16		4									
Schenectady,								2				3					
Schoharie,						1				1						1	
Schuyler,	3					1		1		3							
Seneca,										5							
Steuben,									1	11	1						
Suffolk,	2					12		2		4						3	
Sullivan,										1							
Tioga,						7		1		2					2		
Tompkins,						15		2		5					1		
Ulster,	12					15		2		3					1		3
Warren,						3		2			1						
Washington,	15					18		3		3			1			2	1
Wayne,	20					22		5		8							8
Westchester,	5			1		263		15		13	5		1		2	46	7
Wyoming,	1					17		2		6							
Yates,						5				4						2	1
Total,	415	117	8	1	250	3, 114	42	1, 177	37	621	130	433	10	1	197	968	240

COUNTIES.	Occulists.	Oil cloth makers.	Oil makers.	Opticians.	Organ builders.	Ostlers.	Overseers and superintendents	Oystermen and dealers	Packers.	Paint and color makers.	Painters, glaziers and varnishers.	Paper dealers.	Paper hangers.	Paper makers.	Paper stainers.	Patent leather makers.	Patent medicine makers.
Albany,		12	2	1		35	29	8	5		399		17	24			3
Allegany,						7	2				39			2			
Broome,						18	6				65			5			
Cattaraugus,						4	1				27						
Cayuga,						11	11				132			22		1	5
Chautauque,						14	4				88			11			
Chemung,						5	1				71						
Chenango,			1			13	1				46			8			
Clinton,						1	4		3		28		1	1			
Columbia,						10	6				98			79			
Cortland,				1		4	1				36			1			
Delaware,							1				26			4			
Dutchess,						14	5				166		1	17			
Erie,	2		6	2	16	21	21				438		22				
Essex,						8	1				24			1			
Franklin,						3	1				20						
Fulton,			1			2					49			20			
Genesee,						5					73						
Greene,											36			14			
Hamilton,																	
Herkimer,			1			1	12				52			81			
Jefferson,						9	2				104			11			1
Kings,	2	38	33	9	9	75	50	28	25		1, 150	9	43	19	8	4	6
Lewis,			1			1	1				37			2			
Livingston,						6					67			20			
Madison,			1	1		5	9				97			7			1
Monroe,	2		7		1	21	29	1	2		358	1	6	35			2
Montgomery,			5			9	3				42			2			
New-York,	4	2	44	43	45	317	93	155	63	15	3, 400	9	85	75	68		22
Niagara,						9	21		1		99			10			
Oneida,	1	1	1	1	3	47	22		1		290		7	18			
Onondaga,			1			22	10	2	3		275	1	1	39			1
Ontario,	2					5			3		95			9			
Orange,		28				22	15				109			48			
Orleans,			4				5				61			4			
Oswego,	1		2			8	3	2			125		4	13			
Otsego,			1			12	5				82			14			
Putnam,						1	3				25			9			
Queens,			1	1	1	19	7	13			105		2	11			1
Rensselaer,	2	48	7	1		25	10	5			226		1	71	7	5	
Richmond,						12	9	145	1		81				2		
Rockland,			1			4		1	1	3	40			1			1
St. Lawrence,	1					16		1		1	82		1	2			
Saratoga,						10	2			1	90		1	61	1		
Schenectady,						7		1			51			3			
Schoharie,											33			7			
Schuyler,						3					33						
Seneca,						3	2				55			1			

COUNTIES.	Occulists.	Oil cloth makers.	Oil makers.	Opticians.	Organ builders.	Ostlers.	Overseers and superintendents.	Oystermen and dealers.	Packers.	Paint and color makers.	Painters, glaziers and varnishers.	Paper dealers.	Paper hangers.	Paper makers.	Paper stainers.	Patent leather makers.	Patent medicine makers.
Steuben,						5	1				74						
Suffolk,						10	4	9			75			12			
Sullivan,						1	15				15						
Tioga,						1					31						
Tompkins,		2				6					85			8			3
Ulster,						17	9				95			71			1
Warren,						1					20						
Washington,						14	5				86			28			
Wayne,						4	7		1		83						
Westchester,				3	6	43	25	87	3	1	304		4	8	1		12
Wyoming,		2				1	1				53			5			
Yates,			4			1					35						
Total,	17	133	124	63	81	948	475	458	112	21	10, 081	20	196	914	87	10	59

COUNTIES.	Pattern makers.	Pavers.	Pawn-brokers.	Pearl workers.	Pedlers.	Pen makers.	Pencil makers.	Perfumers.	Photographers and daguerreotypists.	Physicians.	Piano makers.	Pickle and preserve m.	Pilots.	Pin makers.	Pipe makers.	Plaster figure makers	Platers.
Albany,	38	39	1		221				11	174	71		23	1	4	3	22
Allegany,	3				19				4	85			1				
Broome,					27				2	68							
Cattaraugus,					10				6	74			5				
Cayuga,	6	1			32				7	114	4						1
Chautauque,	1				42				14	125			2				
Chemung,	2				25		1	1	2	52	3						1
Chenango,					23				1	77	11						1
Clinton,	6				13				1	44			1				
Columbia,	3				23				5	83	1		6				
Cortland,	1				11				3	49							
Delaware,					15				4	70							
Dutchess,	9				51				4	103	10		6	1			2
Erie,	26	10			127	1			17	218	33					5	26
Essex,	2				15					34					1		
Franklin,					9				1	29	1						
Fulton,					37				4	32							
Genesee,					21				5	75							1
Greene,					17				2	47			5				
Hamilton,					1					1							
Herkimer,	1				25				3	62							
Jefferson,					52				7	125			1				1
Kings,	50	43			189	30	7	5	28	336	42		154	1	11	6	34
Lewis,					3					42							1
Livingston,					36				1	73							1
Madison,	2				24				4	88							
Monroe,	30	29			147				13	197	17						8
Montgomery,					26				4	47							
New-York,	91	159	17	2	1, 889	22	40	26	88	1, 252	760	11	112	1	9	18	90
Niagara,	2	1			16			1	3	75	1		1				
Oneida,	24	7			216	3			16	200	8						10
Onondaga,	6	9			145				9	131	10		1				25
Ontario,	2	9			21				5	102			4				2
Orange,	4	1		2	33				15	89	16		1			3	
Orleans,					3				5	60							
Oswego,	4	2			27				4	113						4	2
Otsego,	3				30	3			5	89	2						
Putnam,	12				3				1	12	2		1				
Queens,	2	18	1		15		1		2	49	1		8				
Rensselaer,	47	7			80				11	121	16		13				13
Richmond,					5				3	17	4		16				
Rockland,					6					23	3		1				
St. Lawrence,					34	2		2	6	61	1						
Saratoga,	1				33				4	101							
Schenectady,	3	2			13				3	37	1						
Schoharie,					22				3	68	1						
Schuyler,	2				13				4	46							
Seneca,	1				28				3	49							
Steuben,	4				13				7	75	1		2				
Suffolk,					18				2	48	7		5		1		
Sullivan,		2			7					36							
Tioga,	2				14				5	49							
Tompkins,	3				25				4	61	1						
Ulster,	5				28				4	76			4				1
Warren,					4					32	4		1				
Washington,	1				50				6	76	6		3				
Wayne,	2				21				7	116							4
Westchester,	26	1	1		32				2	114	38		10	1		2	29
Wyoming,		1			39				5	69							
Yates,					7				4	39							
Total,	427	341	20	4	4, 131	61	49	35	389	6, 010	1, 076	11	387	5	26	41	269

COUNTIES.	Plate printers.	Plumbers.	Pocket book makers.	Policemen.	Polishers and burnishers	Porcelain makers.	Porters.	Port folio makers.	Portrait painters.	Post masters.	Pot and pearlash makers	Potters.	Powder makers.	Printers.	Produce dealers.	Professors.	Publishers.
Albany,		21	1	46	7		64			3		33		178	27	2	2
Allegany,										2				23	4	1	
Broome,							4			3		8		26			2
Cattaraugus,							2			1	1	5		11			
Cayuga,					4		4			3	1			73	3	3	3
Chautauque,					3		5			5				41	6	1	1
Chemung,							4							22	2		
Chenango,										5	1	4		17	1	4	
Clinton,										2				18			1
Columbia,		1			2		4							43	4		1
Cortland,							2			1		2		8	1		
Delaware,										2				14	1		
Dutchess,					11		5			4		8		42	1	12	2
Erie,		21		23	90		28			9	3	25		210	18	8	1
Essex,		3												10			
Franklin,							1			2				8	1		
Fulton,										1				3			
Genesee,										2		7		19	2		
Greene,					1					4		8	1	6	1		
Hamilton,																	
Herkimer,		1								4		1	2	20	7		
Jefferson,		2			2		1			7		3		28	9		
Kings,	11	115	30	224	40	7	575		7	7		45	1	676	85	8	43
Lewis,										1	1				1		
Livingston,							1			3				15	2		2
Madison,					5		1			4	1			22	6	7	
Monroe,		15		12	10		21			3	3	12	1	109	18	5	
Montgomery,										1		2		14		4	
New-York,	20	738	162	1, 164	357	5	3, 052	6	22	13	11	41		1, 901	225	80	74
Niagara,		1					17			6	1	2		17	4		
Oneida,		14			11		17			10	2	7		115	16	9	1
Onondaga,		2		2	8		5			6	2	10		68	14	2	2
Ontario,							6			5	1	4		23	2	1	
Orange,		8		2	8		7			2		5	1	37	1	2	2
Orleans,														21	6		
Oswego,		1		1	1		7			5	3	1		38	6	1	1
Otsego,				2			1			2				26			1
Putnam,			13											1			
Queens,		1			1		18			2				17	3		1
Rensselaer,		5		4	9		37		1	1		8	10	46	4	5	
Richmond,		3		33	2		4					1		35	1		4
Rockland,												1		7			
St. Lawrence,										3		7		23			
Saratoga,							11			5				37			
Schenectady,							1		3	1				11		7	
Schoharie,									1	2				10			
Schuyler,												4		10	4		
Seneca,			5						1	2	1	2		6	1		
Steuben,										2		1		27			
Suffolk,										3		7		23			
Sullivan,							1			1				7			
Tioga,										4		3		10	3		
Tompkins,									1	3	2	1	1	15	4	1	
Ulster,										2		3	6	30	2		
Warren,									1	1				4			
Washington,					1		4			5		7	4	16	7		
Wayne,										7		5		14	11		3
Westchester,		6	1		5		6			6		1		62	9	22	11
Wyoming,										1	2			13	2	2	2
Yates,										5		3		13	1	1	
Total,	31	958	212	1, 513	578	12	3, 916	6	37	184	36	287	27	4, 339	526	188	160

COUNTIES.	Pump makers.	Pursers.	Pyrotechnists.	Quarrymen.	Rag pickers.	Railroad employees.	Razor strop makers.	Reed makers	Refiners and assayers.	Reporters.	Restaurant keepers	Riggers	Roofers and slaters.	Rope and cord makers.	Runners.	Saddle, harness, and trunk makers	Safe makers.
Albany,			1	4	4	103					8	1	13	30	31	137	4
Allegany,						46				1						45	
Broome,						134					5					45	
Cattaraugus,						59										29	
Cayuga,			2	56		77			1					1		73	
Chautauque,				4		145									2	55	
Chemung,				1		66									1	36	
Chenango,				3										7		43	
Clinton,				1		57										39	
Columbia,				4		65					2		2			39	
Cortland,						12								1		33	
Delaware,						3										30	
Dutchess,						104					3			9		53	
Erie,			2			118				2		4	2	19	14	146	
Essex,						1										22	
Franklin,						28										16	

COUNTIES.	Pump makers.	Pursers.	Pyrotechnists.	Quarrymen.	Rag pickers.	Railroad employees.	Razor strop makers.	Reed makers.	Refiners and assayers.	Reporters.	Restaurant keepers.	Riggers.	Roofers and slaters.	Rope and cord makers.	Runners.	Saddle, harness, and trunk makers.	Safe makers
Fulton,																22	
Genesee,				4		45								1		55	
Greene,				29		3								1		26	
Hamilton,																1	
Herkimer,				2		23										51	1
Jefferson,				10		56								5		86	
Kings,	1		3	1	1	102			8	15	23	79	44	339	14	163	16
Lewis,	3													3		28	
Livingston,	2					16					2			1		60	
Madison,				1		13										67	
Monroe,			3	5	4	248					9		1	4	2	109	3
Montgomery,				3		23					3					35	
New-York,	16	10	5	52	232	523	4	13	78	36	198	361	78	121	57	884	46
Niagara,				4		32					8					50	
Oneida,					6	136		1						26		117	2
Onondaga,				42		146			2	1	3		1	1		126	
Ontario,						67							1			55	
Orange,						225								10		64	
Orleans,				1		12										32	
Oswego,	3					14					2			4	1	65	
Otsego,						1								5		78	
Putnam,						12										9	1
Queens,			1	1		12			1		1	1		19		40	
Rensselaer,				3		424		2		1	8		2	26	1	90	13
Richmond,	2				3	2				2				6	19	9	
Rockland,	2			17		87					3	2		1	5	25	
St. Lawrence,	5					87					3					67	
Saratoga,	6					62								2		30	
Schenectady,						96					4			3	1	15	
Schoharie,						2										32	
Schuyler,						2										26	
Seneca,				5		14									1	26	
Steuben,						97										55	
Suffolk,						28						16			1	24	
Sullivan,						13										17	
Tioga,						64										23	
Tompkins,				2		43	1									38	
Ulster,				640		3						4				47	
Warren,						29										15	
Washington,				113		30							27	1		61	
Wayne,						39								7		85	
Westchester,			5	23		121			1		3	1	4	8		58	2
Wyoming,						28				1				2		56	
Yates,						8										32	
Total,	40	10	22	1,031	250	4,006	5	16	91	59	288	469	175	663	150	3,895	88

COUNTIES.	Sail makers.	Sailors and mariners	Saleratus makers.	Salesmen.	Saloon keepers.	Salt makers.	Sand paper makers.	Sash and blind makers.	Saw filers.	Saw makers.	Sawyers.	Scale makers.	Scavengers.	Screw makers.	Sculptors.	Sealing wax makers.	Servants.
Albany,	7	15	1	5	46			17	6	8	29				3		1,467
Allegany,		3	2		5			7			176				1		15
Broome,		5			11			9			53						11
Cattaraugus,		5	1		1			6			131				1		29
Cayuga,	1	6		2	2			7			52				2		156
Chautauque,		137	1		10			20			59				1		29
Chemung,		1	1		5			15		3	46						13
Chenango,		7	1		2			7			39						18
Clinton,	1	64									176						214
Columbia,	3	16		1	7			6			9						333
Cortland,		1			1			12			31						16
Delaware,								2			83						2
Dutchess.		20		1	6			15			10						188
Erie,	24	429		62	69			10	3		114				1		248
Essex,		42						5			163						9
Franklin,		3			6			1			106						3
Fulton,		2									78						44
Genesee,		4		4	1			2			10						13
Greene,	2	7			1			1	1		14	1					18
Hamilton,											8						2
Herkimer,		4			2			5			26						106
Jefferson,	2	305		7	9			6			66						68
Kings,	177	1,290	1	148	56			135	8	24	84	8		3	11		4,058
Lewis,		2									55						50
Livingston,		1						5			25				2		80
Madison,		3		3				22			49				2		7
Monroe,	10	32		42	11			23	1	14	49	16			4		2,144
Montgomery,	1	3						22			91						93
New-York,	281	4,717	2	428	442	42	3	327	22	30	285	32	41	2	46	1	31,749
Niagara,		23		2	2			8			29						87
Oneida,		21	2	3	17			27		5	136	1		1			2,520
Onondaga,		12	2		32	560		8		1	87			2			2,419

COUNTIES.	Sail makers.	Sailors and mariners.	Saleratus makers.	Salesmen.	Saloon keepers.	Salt makers.	Sand paper makers.	Sash and blind makers.	Saw filers.	Saw makers.	Sawyers.	Scale makers.	Scavengers.	Screw makers.	Sculptors.	Sealing wax makers.	Servants.
Ontario,		11		2	10			6			20				4		905
Orange,		20			11			18		35	7				1		2, 140
Orleans,		3						2			10				3		387
Oswego,	10	496			15			15			152	1			1		848
Otsego,		2		1	2			16			43						592
Putnam,		7															246
Queens,	2	64			11			13			10						3, 029
Rensselaer,	4	20		1	23			14		1	49	7					2, 055
Richmond,	11	793						14									56
Rockland,		1						7									5
St. Lawrence,		48			1			14	1		46						47
Saratoga,		4						3	1		120	1					24
Schenectady,		11		2							1						18
Schoharie,		3						1			3						74
Schuyler,					1			4			66						7
Seneca,		3			3			13			13						64
Steuben,		3			16			13			317						13
Suffolk,	19	861			4			16			7						236
Sullivan,	1										53						35
Tioga,		9			6			12			90						14
Tompkins,		2						5			39						15
Ulster,	2	18			9			9			33						327
Warren,									1		96						2
Washington,	5	11						8	1		113						66
Wayne,		80		1	1						36	1					37
Westchester,		62		5	10			65		107	19	1			3		911
Wyoming,		5	1	3				5			59						1
Yates,		3			4			1			13						78
Total,	563	9, 720	15	723	871	602	3	1, 004	45	228	3, 724	69	41	8	86	1	58, 441

COUNTIES.	Sextons.	Shingle makers.	Ship carpenters, mast and spar makers	Shirt and collar makers.	Shoe peg makers.	Shot makers.	Showmen.	Silk workers.	Soldiers and military officers.	Speculators.	Spinners.	Spring makers.	Stage proprietors.	Starch makers.	Stave makers	Steel makers.	Stereotypers.
Albany,	9	1	45	5				1	1	29	95		3		1	1	2
Allegany,	1	22								3	1		2				
Broome,		1	5							4			2		1		
Cattaraugus,		32	1										1				
Cayuga,	3	2	2	1					1	9	16		4				
Chautauque,	2	7	13						1	5	5		1				
Chemung,	1	2	15							2	5						
Chenango,			2							4			2				
Clinton,		2						1						2	1		
Columbia,		1	1						3	19	60		1				
Cortland,		3							1	1	2						
Delaware,	1	1	1	1						5			2				
Dutchess,	1		19							6	36					3	
Erie,	6	6	308	6					3	10	4		6		1		2
Essex,		6	6								1		1				
Franklin,		1	1							4				3			
Fulton,		2			2						1		2		1		
Genesee,		1											1				
Greene,		2	62							9	25		2				
Hamilton,		14															
Herkimer,	1								2	2	28		1	1			
Jefferson,	1	2	76						1	8	8		3				
Kings,	16	3	875	30				7	274	23	2		8	2			13
Lewis,			2							1			1				
Livingston,	1	5	16							3			2				
Madison,			1							5	18		6		1		
Monroe,	3	6	13	1	2				1	8	9				2		1
Montgomery,		2	1							2	5						
New-York,	72	2	1, 146	267		9	15	41	78	199	13	14	29	11		3	24
Niagara,	2	10	5						2	3					2		
Oneida,				1	3				58	14			54	2			
Onondaga,	4	3	15						8	1							
Ontario,	2	1	2						1	5			3				
Orange,	1		42	2					202	1	30						
Orleans,	1		2							7							
Oswego,	3	10	148						56	3	5		3	15	1		
Otsego,		4								9	8		3				
Putnam,			1														
Queens,	4	3	40	2						2			4	3			
Rensselaer,	3		18	110					4	14	36	12	5		1		
Richmond,		1	66					18	1	2							
Rockland,			79								2					2	
St. Lawrence,		5	5							9			2		1		
Saratoga,	2	2	13	1					1	2	6		2		1		1
Schenectady,										1							
Schoharie,		4								1			1				
Schuyler,	1	9								2	1		1				
Seneca,										2	24				3		

COUNTIES.	Sextons.	Shingle makers.	Ship carpenters, mast and spar makers.	Shirt and collar makers.	Shoe peg makers.	Shot makers.	Showmen.	Silk workers.	Soldiers and military officers.	Speculators.	Spinners.	Spring makers.	Stage proprietors.	Starch makers.	Stave makers.	Steel makers.	Stereotypers.
Steuben,		4								4			1				
Suffolk,			329							1	3		5				
Sullivan,		1	21												1		
Tioga,	1	7								2							
Tompkins,		1						10		1							
Ulster,	2	1	138								11		1				
Warren,		3								5			3				
Washington,	1	4	41						3	18	1		1	1			
Wayne,		11	5						1	4					2		
Westchester,	2		50	6				3	6	7	2		4				4
Wyoming,		7	1							4			1				
Yates,				1						2							
Total,	147	217	3, 632	434	7	9	15	81	709	487	463	26	174	40	20	9	47

COUNTIES.	Stevedores.	Stewards.	Stone and marble cutters and polishers.	Store keepers.	Stove makers.	Straw workers.	Students.	Sugar refiners.	Surgeons.	Surgical instrument makers.	Surveyors.	Tailors.	Tanners, curriers and leather dealers.	Teachers.	Teamsters.	Telegraph operators.	Tinsmiths.
Albany,	2	1	136		56		47		2	3	8	1, 070	64	354	162	6	92
Allegany,			11				61				1	156	74	171	43	4	20
Broome,			22				87				6	185	110	136	31	6	32
Cattaraugus,		1	4			1	33				8	112	55	99	27	4	17
Cayuga,			17		1		66		1		1	428	45	158	31	1	39
Chautauque,			12				60				9	309	72	239	36	10	50
Chemung,			8				37				2	203	44	100	14	11	23
Chenango,			2			2	36				2	156	53	124	4		23
Clinton,			7		1		51				2	105	35	86	115		16
Columbia,			15	2	2		76				7	271	24	155	47	2	35
Cortland,			4				58				2	117	34	116	9		21
Delaware,			2				61				5	118	97	205	20		12
Dutchess,		1	8	5	2		35		1		4	288	54	201	72		59
Erie,			180	9	3		92		2		12	1, 063	187	313	100	15	157
Essex,			3				21				2	48	34	76	99		14
Franklin,			3				29		1		3	57	14	72	1	1	14
Fulton,			4				27				6	99	193	71	44		15
Genesee,			22				44		1		3	124	31	108	5	1	14
Greene,			46				27				2	141	60	115	36	1	15
Hamilton,			1									3	43	10	13		1
Herkimer,			32	3			43				6	152	111	125	23	2	26
Jefferson,			27			1	83		2		8	414	109	210	40	1	50
Kings,	109	63	543	221		23	157	7	12	12	45	2, 481	122	290	147	60	340
Lewis,			11				27				3	88	8	89	9		12
Livingston,	1	4	13				47		1		1	150	18	128	20	1	16
Madison,		1	15	2			157				6	301	41	189	38	1	32
Monroe,		3	70	7	3	9	251		2		15	858	88	281	149	11	100
Montgomery,		1	61				17				3	139	24	99	39	2	14
New-York,	158	182	1, 755	837	31	93	653	132	19	20	62	12, 609	228	1, 268	160	32	897
Niagara,			67				52				3	207	20	113	27	4	39
Oneida,		2	97	7	4		184				19	988	146	334	118	20	103
Onondaga,		4	92	3	1		126				6	488	42	250	76	3	53
Ontario,		1	6				53				1	183	5	108	40	2	32
Orange,		2	42	3	2		87		1	1	13	357	47	191	118	7	61
Orleans,			12		6		15					104	20	94	9	3	19
Oswego,		4	25	1	1		46				5	281	75	246	87	7	33
Otsego,			7				54				2	263	38	172	23		23
Putnam,			18				26					54	2	44	21	1	12
Queens,		4	16	11			64		1		5	157	2	125	2	1	78
Rensselaer,		1	55	9	33		109				9	512	98	232	210	7	70
Richmond,			18				2	1			2	79	11	36	8	1	20
Rockland,			9				7				2	88	5	36		1	25
St. Lawrence,	4	1	10				78		2		11	216	54	243	17	1	39
Saratoga,		2	19				49				1	150	29	141	28	2	21
Schenectady,			4				42				11	216	12	56	16	1	7
Schoharie,			2				43				1	147	28	159	9		18
Schuyler,							19				2	107	32	95	21	2	3
Seneca,			18				50				1	124	16	77	17		19
Steuben,			11				45				7	152	58	117	32	5	28
Suffolk,	3		8		1	1	67				1	234	7	133	8		27
Sullivan,			4				12				7	91	120	82	42	5	13
Tioga,			5				34				3	106	33	94	4		19
Tompkins,			8				42				1	148	26	124	17	3	7
Ulster,			96				44				7	326	163	154	133	1	35
Warren,			10				5				2	52	90	52	11		5
Washington,	1		34		3		112			1	5	214	36	148	62		31
Wayne,			21		1		68				6	257	45	203	17	1	49
Westchester,	2	3	314		9	1	187	4		1	13	437	30	303	108	2	87
Wyoming,			0				52				1	127	34	114	4	5	20
Yates,			5				27				1	126	20	95	6	1	8
Total,	280	281	4, 076	1, 120	160	131	4, 184	144	48	38	382	29, 236	3, 416	9, 959	2, 825	258	3, 160

COUNTIES.	Tobacconists.	Tool makers.	Toy and fancy makers and dealers.	Traders.	Trimmers.	Turners.	Turpentine makers.	Type cutters.	Type founders.	Umbrella makers.	Undertakers.	Upholsterers.	Varnish makers.	Victualers.	Vinegar makers.	Watch makers and repairers.	Watchmen.
Albany,	227	46		10	19	38			2	5	6	26	2			15	6
Allegany,	1	1		3		4						1				6	
Broome,	15				2	1						4				4	
Cattaraugus,	1			1		2										1	
Cayuga,	48	85		1		8				1	3	2		1		5	
Chautauque,	4	2				11						4				4	4
Chemung,	18	2				8	4					2					3
Chenango,	3	3		1	1	5										1	
Clinton,						1						1				1	3
Columbia,	20				10	6					1	1				9	2
Cortland,		2		1		1											
Delaware,	1	1				3								1		3	1
Dutchess,	58	4			8	22				1		3		2		11	
Erie,	126	14		7	4	71			14	5	6	57			4	49	15
Essex,				2		2											
Franklin,			1	2								7				1	
Fulton,	6	1				11										1	1
Genesee,	4			1		2					1	1				1	
Greene,	12		1		1	13						1				2	
Hamilton,																2	
Herkimer,	3	29		2	2	12				1	1	1				6	
Jefferson,	7	4		4	2	5						3				7	2
Kings,	367	12	13	13	3	84		2	45	58	36	166	7	10	11	102	98
Lewis,	1					1										3	
Livingston,	9	1			5	6										1	
Madison,	5	1		1		4				1						6	1
Monroe,	55	51		7	4	25				12	3	16	1		1	15	8
Montgomery,	3					5										2	
New-York,	1, 996	71	130	26	110	361	1	19	92	270	123	711	242	43	9	405	160
Niagara,	7	10	3	1		6						11				3	2
Oneida,	114	8	2	1	6	15				4	2	12				18	6
Onondaga,	146	6		2	15	6				2	1	11				11	1
Ontario,	4	2			6	4					2	3				3	
Orange,	54	4	2		6	5					1	2	7			15	3
Orleans,				1	8	3										2	
Oswego,	7	7		2	1	4				2	2	3				3	2
Otsego,	9	1		1	2	4						1				8	
Putnam,	2					7					1	1				2	1
Queens,	21	3	2	1	7	2				3	3	3	2			5	61
Rensselaer,	81	8	4	2	9	32				2	8	12	4			12	8
Richmond,	23		1		2	1					3	5				1	7
Rockland,	26				3	5											
St. Lawrence,	6			4		3						3					
Saratoga,	6	2	3		2	4						3				2	3
Schenectady,	15			1	8	7				1	1	3	1			1	
Schoharie,	1		2		4	1				1						3	1
Schuyler,	4															2	1
Seneca,	4			6	1	3										1	1
Steuben,	7	7			2							1				5	
Suffolk,	18			1	1					1						10	
Sullivan,	3					23										3	1
Tioga,	25					3						2				4	
Tompkins,	58	5			12	9										3	
Ulster,	37	2			6	15										7	6
Warren,	1	1			1	1										5	
Washington,	18			1	7	2						3				2	
Wayne,	2			8	4	4						2					
Westchester,	52	5			13	19			2	4	9	17	1			17	2
Wyoming,	3	1		1	5	5						1				1	2
Yates.		2			6	4										1	
Total,	3, 744	404	164	115	308	909	5	21	155	374	213	1, 106	267	57	25	813	412

COUNTIES.	Wax bleachers.	Weavers.	Whale bone workers.	Wheelwrights.	Whip makers.	White washers.	White lead makers.	Wire drawers.	Wire workers.	Wine and liquor dealers.	Window shade makers.	Wood cutters.	Wood dealers.	Wooden ware makers.	Wool carders and combers.	Wool dealers.	Woolen and worsted workers.
Albany,		490		100		5			2	7		6	3	2	78	5	
Allegany,		24		12								1				1	
Broome,		9		8		2		4				32	2	1	2		
Cattaraugus,		14		14				3				1					2
Cayuga,		98		10		3						1			13	3	61
Chautauque,		50		12						1					5	3	1
Chemung,		20		3		5						3			3		2
Chenango,		24		3						1		8			1		
Clinton,		11		57								3			3		
Columbia,		148		7	1							10			18	2	27
Cortland,		8		4										1	1		
Delaware,		17		7											3	1	
Dutchess,		185		10								1			25	1	
Erie,		58		15	4	13	2		3	7		22	7	1		8	
Essex,		3		42		1						23					2
Franklin,		26		36								1			1		3

COUNTIES.	Wax bleachers.	Weavers.	Whale bone workers.	Wheelwrights.	Whip makers.	White washers.	White lead makers.	Wire drawers.	Wire workers.	Wine and liquor dealers	Window shade makers.	Wood cutters.	Wood dealers.	Wooden ware makers.	Wool carders and combers.	Wool dealers.	Woolen and worsted workers.
Fulton,		11		9													
Genesee,		8		13						1		1			2		2
Greene,		55		4						1					14		2
Hamilton,				1													
Herkimer,		47	3	4											6		
Jefferson,		39		40	1		1					10		1	5	1	1
Kings,		69		149	5	14	11		21	92	4		18	3	1	6	4
Lewis,		5		6													1
Livingston,		10		2								12	1		2		
Madison,		79		5								7	1	1	16		1
Monroe,		43		26	16	14	1		6	12			9	3	2	5	1
Montgomery,		28		9						1					4		2
New-York,	2	589	9	308	12	148	9	7	34	619	26	8	22	23	4	4	
Niagara,		12	2	15		1				2		1	1				1
Oneida,		121	5	14		2				1		2	4		14	1	6
Onondaga,		53	1	15	3	5				1		10	3		8	1	5
Ontario,		11		17		5											1
Orange,		77	1	11	2							15			11		2
Orleans,		5	2	6	2												
Oswego,		24		6										1		1	3
Otsego,		17		13	1		1							1			1
Putnam,				5					7	2		6					
Queens,		86	29	55		3				1							4
Rensselaer,		18	64	31	4	13		1	1		1	5					1
Richmond,		2		7		20	1										
Rockland,		11		31		1			2			2			2		
St. Lawrence,		19		87								1			2		1
Saratoga,		74		29										3			3
Schenectady,		12		9									3		7	2	
Schoharie,		12		1													
Schuyler,		12		7											3		
Seneca,		47		9											10		1
Steuben,		9		1													
Suffolk,		17	6	48		1											
Sullivan,		3		3											1		
Tioga,		2		1												1	
Tompkins,		17		10		3											
Ulster,		24		32		1	20		1			1	1				
Warren,				8								8					
Washington,		23		7		1						26			2	2	6
Wayne,		7		11					2			1				1	
Westchester,		241		91		1			12			9			6		
Wyoming,		8		2								3			7		
Yates,		9															
Total,	2	3,141	122	1,498	51	262	46	15	91	749	31	240	75	41	282	49	147

DEAF AND DUMB.

COUNTIES.	Total number.	SEX.		AGES.																	
		Male.	Fem.	Under 5.		5 and under 10.		10 and under 15.		15 and under 20.		20 and under 30.		30 and under 40.		40 and under 50.		50 and under 60.		Over 60.	
				Males	Fem.	Males	Fem.	Males	Fem.	Males	Fem.	Males	Fem.	Males	Fem.	Males	Fem.	Males	Fem.	Males	Fem.
Albany,	18	12	6	....	1	1	....	3	2	2	....	2	2	1	1	....	....	2	....	1	....
Allegany,	18	10	8	....	....	....	....	4	....	1	....	3	3	1	2	....	1	1	2	....	....
Broome,	18	10	8	1	....	2	....	....	1	....	....	1	2	2	1	....	1	1	....	3	3
Cattaraugus,	21	10	11	....	....	....	1	....	3	....	1	4	3	2	....	2	2	1	1	1	....
Cayuga,	17	9	8	....	....	....	3	....	1	....	1	4	1	1	1	1	2	1	....	2	....
Chautauque,	14	9	5	....	....	....	....	1	1	2	1	3	....	1	3	1	....	....	....	1	....
Chemung,	8	5	3	....	....	....	....	....	....	....	....	3	2	1	....	1	1	....	....	....	....
Chenango,	17	6	11	....	....	....	....	....	....	....	....	1	2	1	2	2	5	1	....	1	2
Clinton,	20	7	13	1	....	1	2	1	6	....	....	1	2	1	2	1	....	....	....	1	1
Columbia,	20	12	8	....	....	....	1	1	....	1	1	1	2	2	3	4	1	3	....	....	....
Cortland,	7	5	2	....	....	....	....	1	....	....	....	2	....	1	1	....	....	1	....	1	....
Delaware,	18	10	8	....	1	....	1	1	1	1	....	1	3	5	1	....	....	1	....	1	1
Dutchess,	19	12	7	....	....	5	2	4	2	....	....	....	2	1	....	....	1	1	....	1	....
Erie,	35	21	14	....	....	4	2	2	....	2	1	5	4	3	2	3	4	2	1	....	....
Essex,	7	3	4	....	....	....	....	1	....	....	....	....	3	....	....	....	....	1	1	1	....
Franklin,	15	9	6	1	1	2	1	....	....	....	....	2	....	2	2	1	1	1	1	....	....
Fulton,	12	6	6	....	1	....	1	1	1	2	1	2	1	....	1	1	....	....	....	....	....
Genesee,	16	9	7	....	....	....	....	1	1	1	....	2	2	1	2	1	1	1	....	1	2
Greene,	11	4	7	1	....	....	....	....	....	....	....	....	1	1	3	2	3	....	....	....	....
Hamilton,	....	....	....	....	....	....	....	....	....	....	....	....	....	....	....	....	....	....	....	....	....
Herkimer,	21	11	10	....	....	....	....	....	....	1	....	3	....	....	2	3	4	1	2	3	2
Jefferson,	41	24	17	2	1	3	....	1	....	1	2	5	5	4	5	3	3	2	1	3	....
Kings,	45	21	24	....	....	3	....	1	....	2	2	4	7	5	7	3	3	2	4	1	1
Lewis,	8	3	5	....	....	....	....	....	....	....	1	1	1	1	1	....	2	....	1	....	....
Livingston,	13	5	8	....	....	....	....	....	1	....	....	....	2	1	....	1	3	1	1	2	1
Madison,	27	17	10	1	....	2	1	2	1	....	....	4	1	1	4	2	1	3	3	....	1
Monroe,	27	18	9	1	....	2	....	2	1	2	2	3	1	1	4	4	1	3	....	....	....
Montgomery,	26	12	14	....	1	1	1	....	....	1	....	2	....	2	2	5	6	....	1	1	3
New-York,*	411	228	183	4	....	11	4	59	45	84	71	44	36	9	14	10	9	5	2	2	2
Niagara,	11	8	3	....	....	2	....	1	....	....	1	2	1	1	....	1	1	....	....	1	....
Oneida,	48	27	21	1	....	3	2	1	1	3	1	6	5	1	3	1	2	5	5	6	2
Onondaga,	24	11	13	....	....	3	1	....	4	....	....	1	4	3	2	1	2	1	....	2	....
Ontario,	21	14	7	....	....	....	....	1	1	....	....	8	2	4	....	....	3	....	1	1	....
Orange,	18	11	7	....	1	1	2	....	....	3	....	....	1	4	....	2	2	1	....	....	1
Orleans,	13	8	5	....	....	....	....	1	....	1	2	1	1	1	....	1	2	....	1	2	....
Oswego,	33	15	18	....	....	3	2	2	1	....	1	2	5	2	3	4	5	1	2	....	....
Otsego,	24	13	11	....	....	1	....	1	....	....	1	3	1	2	4	3	3	3	2	....	....
Putnam,	5	5	....	....	....	....	....	....	....	....	....	4	....	1	....	....	....	....	....	....	....
Queens,	21	9	12	....	1	1	1	....	5	1	....	3	2	1	1	2	1	....	....	1	1
Rensselaer,	19	11	8	....	....	3	....	....	2	3	1	2	4	1	1	....	....	1	1	....	....
Richmond,	3	2	1	....	....	....	....	1	....	....	....	1	....	....	....	1	....	....	....	....	....
Rockland,	7	6	1	2	....	2	....	....	....	....	....	1	....	1	1	....	....	....	....	....	....
St. Lawrence,	26	13	13	2	1	3	2	3	1	2	1	2	2	1	1	....	1	....	3	....	1
Saratoga,	18	11	7	....	1	1	....	1	1	3	....	2	2	2	....	....	....	....	2	1	2
Schenectady,	7	4	3	....	....	....	....	....	....	1	....	....	1	1	....	1	....	2	....	....	1
Schoharie,	9	6	3	....	....	....	....	4	1	....	....	1	....	....	....	....	....	2	....	1	....
Schuyler,	4	....	4	....	....	....	....	....	....	....	....	....	....	....	1	....	1	....	1	....	1
Seneca,	5	3	2	....	....	....	....	....	....	....	....	1	....	1	1	1	1	....	....	....	....
Steuben,	21	13	8	....	....	....	....	2	1	....	....	4	4	4	2	1	....	1	1	1	....
Suffolk,	12	6	6	....	....	....	....	....	....	....	1	3	2	1	1	....	....	2	2	....	....
Sullivan,	8	5	3	....	....	....	....	1	....	....	....	1	1	1	1	....	....	....	....	2	1
Tioga,	11	6	5	....	....	....	....	....	....	....	....	2	1	1	1	....	1	2	1	1	1
Tompkins,	6	4	2	....	....	1	....	1	1	....	....	....	1	1	....	....	....	....	....	1	....
Ulster,	26	19	7	1	....	....	1	2	....	2	1	5	....	5	....	3	3	1	1	....	1
Warren,	9	3	6	....	1	1	1	1	....	....	....	....	1	....	1	....	2	....	....	1	....
Washington,	22	12	10	1	1	1	....	2	1	2	....	3	2	3	1	1	3	1	....	....	....
Wayne,	21	9	12	....	1	1	1	1	1	....	1	2	4	1	1	1	2	1	1	2	....
Westchester,	14	12	2	....	....	3	....	1	....	....	....	3	1	3	....	1	....	....	1	1	....
Wyoming,	17	7	10	....	....	1	1	....	....	....	1	2	....	2	3	1	1	....	3	1	1
Yates,	9	4	5	1	....	....	1	....	....	....	1	1	1	1	2	....	....	1	....	....	....
Total,	1,422	785	637	20	13	68	35	113	88	124	97	169	137	101	97	77	91	60	49	52	32

* Of these, 288 were reported as inmates of the N. Y. Institution for the Deaf and Dumb, viz: 4 male teachers, 144 male, and 133 female pupils, and 7 domestics.

The occupations of the Deaf, (for the most part Deaf-mutes,) were reported as follows:

Artist, 1; Baker, 1; Basket Maker, 1; Blacksmiths, 2; Bookbinders, 7, Brick Makers, 2; Cabinet Makers, 6; Carpenters, 9; Carter, 1; Cigar Maker, 1; Coach Maker, 1; Comb Maker, 1; Confectioner, 1; Cooper, 1; Dress Makers, 11; Embroiderer, 1; Farmers, 116; Gardener, 1; Iron Worker, 1; Laborers, 35; Laundress, 1; Lumbermen, 2; Masons, 2; Match Maker, 1; Merchant, 1; Milliner, 1; Miner, 1; Moulder, 1; Painters, 2; Pedlers, 2; Porter, 1; Printers, 3; Sawyers, 2; Servants, 11; Saddlers, 2; Shoe Makers, 22; Stonecutters, 2; Tailors, 12; Tailoresses, 11; Teachers, 4; Teamsters, 2; Turner, 1; Weavers, 3; Wheelwrights, 2.

The causes of Deafness, so far as reported, were as follows:

Catarrh and Measles, 1; Disease (not specified,) 15; Erysipelas, 1; Falls, 4; Falling into water, 2; Fever, 1; Fits, 1; Hooping cough, 2; Hydrophobia, 1; Inflammation, 1; Inflammation of Brain, 1; Injury to head, 2; Measles, 3; Mumps, 1; St. Vitus Dance, 1; Scarlet Fever, 14; Typhoid Fever, 1.

The social condition of the deaf, as reported, was as follows:—Married men, 126; Married women, 104; Widowers, 22; Widows, 21; Single, 1,149.

BLIND.

COUNTIES.	Total number.	SEX.		AGES.																	
		Males	Fem.	Under 5.		5 and under 10.		10 and under 15.		15 and under 20.		20 and under 30.		30 and under 40.		40 and under 50.		50 and under 60.		Over 60.	
				Males	Fem.	Males	Fem.	Males	Fem.	Males	Fem.	Males	Fem.	Males	Fem.	Males	Fem.	Males	Fem.	Males	Fem.
Albany,	25	12	13				2	1		1	1	1	4	5	4		1	2		2	1
Allegany,	11	8	3							1						3	1	2		2	2
Broome,	5	4	1										1			1		1		1	
Cattaraugus,	16	12	4			1		1				2	1	2	1	1		1		4	2
Cayuga,	14	5	9				1		1			1	1		1	1	1			3	4
Chautauque,	11	8	3								1	1		1	1	2		1	1	3	
Chemung,	5	4	1					1		1		1		1					1		
Chenango,	19	12	7		1				1			1		3	2	3	1	2		3	2
Clinton,	18	12	6			1	1			2		1		3	1	3	1	2	1		2
Columbia,	11	5	6													1		3		1	6
Cortland,	13	10	3					1					2	2		2		2		3	1
Delaware,	6	4	2						1									1		3	1
Dutchess,	15	7	8		1	1					1	1		1	2	1		1	1	2	3
Erie,	32	18	14			1		1	2	1		1	2	4	3	2	2	4	2	4	3
Essex,	10	10				1						1		1		2		1		4	
Franklin,	15	7	8								1		1		1	2		1		4	5
Fulton,	10	4	6									1				1	2			2	4
Genesee,	9	7	2									1		1				2		3	2
Greene,	8	7	1			1		1		1						1		1		2	1
Hamilton,																					
Herkimer,	26	13	13		1	1			2	1	1		1	2	2	1	1	2	1	6	4
Jefferson,	28	18	10			1			2			1	2			1		5	1	10	5
Kings,	44	26	18	1	2	1	1	4	1	3	1	2	1	5	4	2		3	3	5	5
Lewis,	7	3	4									1			1			2	2		1
Livingston,	9	6	3					1				2	1			2			1	1	1
Madison,	18	9	9						1					2	1	2	2	1		4	5
Monroe,	30	19	11		1	2				1	1	3		3	1	3	3	6	2	1	3
Montgomery,	14	7	7				1					1		2	1	2			2	2	3
New-York,	316	169	147	2	2	1	1	24	18	33	41	41	29	22	12	16	13	8	16	21	15
Niagara,	14	8	6		1			1				1		2	2	2	1	1		1	2
Oneida,	42	27	15			1				1	2	2	1	3	3	5	3	4	1	11	5
Onondaga,	28	20	8					1			2	2	2	4		3		3	2	7	2
Ontario,	10	6	4						1				1			1	2	1	2	2	
Orange,	14	10	4					1				1		4	2	2			1	2	1
Orleans,	4	3	1									1							1	2	
Oswego,	24	20	4			2	1	1				3	1	1		5		3	1	5	1
Otsego,	18	11	7			1	1	1				2		1	1					6	5
Putnam,	2	1	1												1					1	
Queens,	9	5	4		1			1	1						1			2		2	1
Rensselaer,	13	8	5									1	1	1		2	1	2		2	3
Richmond,	12	12												1		5		4		2	
Rockland,	2	2						1										1			
St. Lawrence,	23	11	12				1				2	1	1	4		1	3	3	2	2	3
Saratoga,	13	10	3													4	1	3		3	2
Schenectady,	8	5	3					1								2	1			2	2
Schoharie,	9	4	5					1			1	1			1		1		1	2	1
Schuyler,	4	3	1									1		1		1	1				
Seneca,	8	7	1									1		2		1		1		2	1
Steuben,	7	4	3									1	1	1			2	1		1	
Suffolk,	6	4	2									2				1			1	1	1
Sullivan,	7	4	3				1	1		1							1			1	2
Tioga,	13	10	3							1			1	2		4	1	1		2	1
Tompkins,	5	5												2		2				1	
Ulster,	21	17	4					1		1		1		3	1	4	1		2	7	
Warren,	1	1										1									
Washington,	12	7	5									1					1	1	1	5	3
Wayne,	15	9	6				1				2				1	2	1	2		5	1
Westchester,	20	11	9			1			1		1		1		2	3	1	4	1	3	2
Wyoming,	11	3	8								1			1		1	1			1	6
Yates,	16	8	8									1	3				1	1	4	6	
Total,	1,136	682	454	3	10	17	12	46	32	49	59	88	59	93	53	106	52	92	54	183	126

* Of this number, 152 were inmates of the New-York Institution for the Blind, 79 males and 73 females. Of the former, 1 was under 10; 20 between 10 and 15; 32 between 15 and 20; and 26 between 20 and 30. Of the latter, 1 was under 10; 15 between 10 and 15; 36 between 15 and 20; 19 between 20 and 30; and 2 over 30 years of age.

The *occupations* of the blind, when given, were generally those followed by the persons before the infirmity came upon them, although in several instances they are those that might be pursued with advantage by blind persons. They were as follows:

Farmers, 92; Laborers, 20; Pedlers, 12; Musicians, 11; Music Teachers, 10; Carpenters, 8; Grocers, 5; Mat Weavers, 4; Blacksmiths, 4; Basket Makers, 3; Merchants, 3; Weavers, 3; Lawyers, 2; Shoe Makers, 2; Stone Cutters, 2; Clergymen, 2; Brush Makers, 2; Wood Sawyers, 2; Physicians, 2; Book Agent, 1; Broom Maker, 1; Chair Maker, 1; City officer, 1; Collector, 1; Cooper, 1; Hatter, 1; Innkeeper, 1; Joiner, 1; Knitter, 1; Laundress, 1; Manufacturer, 1; Mason, 1; Mechanic, 1; Miner, 1; Moulder, 1; Oysterman, 1; Phrenologist, 1; Plasterer, 1; Policeman, 1; Safe Maker, 1; Sailor, 1; Ship Carpenter, 1; Shoe and Leather Dealer, 1; Silver Plater, 1; Soldier, 1; Speculator, 1; Stationer, 1; Stone Breaker, 1; Tailor, 1; Tanner, 1; Umbrella Maker, 1; Willow Worker, 1.

The *causes of blindness*, so far as reported, were as follows:

Inflammation, 77; Cataract, 26; Powder, 26; Wounds, 16; Born blind, 15; Old age, 12; Sickness, 10; Exposure, 5; Accident, 5; Amaurosis, 4; Small Pox, 4; Scrofula, 4; Mal-practice, 4; Erysipelas, 4; Scarlet Fever, 3; Study, 3; Hereditary tendency, 3; Paralysis, 2; Venereal disease, 2; Cold, 2; Brain disease, 2; Fits, 2; Blow on head, 1; Dissipation, 1; Fever, 1; Fright, 1; Measles, 1: Labor, 1; Nervous disease, 1; Poison, 1; Salt Rheum, 1; Working in iron furnace, 1.

Five were reported as also idiotic, and two as deaf.

INSANE.

COUNTIES.	Total number.	SEX.		AGES.											
		Males.	Femal's.	Under 20.		20 and under 30.		30 and under 40.		40 and under 50.		50 and under 60.		60 and upwar	
				Males.	Fem.	Males.	Fem.	Males.	Fem.	Males.	Fem.	Males.	Fem.	Males.	Fem.
Albany,	46	17	29	2	1	3	8	5	9	3	4	2	3	2	4
Allegany,	20	4	16				3	1	3		2	2	3	1	5
Broome,	32	14	18	1	1	3	1	4	7	3	7	1	1	2	1
Cattaraugus,	31	15	16	1		2	3	1	3	4	5	4	1	3	4
Cayuga,	39	15	24			1	3	1	8	8	1	2	4	3	8
Chautauque,	21	10	11	2			2	1	1	1	1	3	2	3	5
Chemung,	11	5	6		1		1		1	2	3	2		1	
Chenango,	34	12	22			1	4	4	5	4	4	3	7		2
Clinton,	18	7	11					1	2	1	2	1	4	4	3
Columbia,	34	8	26			2	3	2	7	1	6		6	3	4
Cortland,	25	12	13	1	1	4	2	3	3			2	5	2	2
Delaware,	29	12	17			3	2	2	3	2	3	2	4	3	5
Dutchess,	43	22	21		3	3	2	4	5	7	2	5	3	3	5
Erie,	66	31	35	1	4	6	8	12	11	3	8	4		5	4
Essex,	15	7	8					1	1	2	1	4	2		4
Franklin,	17	7	10			1	1			1	2	4	3	1	4
Fulton,	20	7	13				1	3	2	1	5	1	3	2	2
Genesee,	30	13	17	1		1	1	2	4	6	8	2	2	1	2
Greene,	27	14	13		1	5	1	1	2	3	4		3	5	2
Hamilton,	1	1								1					
Herkimer,	37	19	18	2		2	2	4	4	7	4	1	2	3	6
Jefferson,	62	24	38		2	5	8	3	8	4	5	5	4	7	9
Kings,	16	6	10	1	1			3	6		1	1	2	1	
Lewis,	21	8	13				1	2	4	2	3	2	1	2	4
Livingston,	14	7	7			1	1			4	2		2	2	2
Madison,	43	19	24	1		3	1	5	3	5	5	1	5	4	10
Monroe,	56	20	36	1	3	2	11	6	4	8	8	2	6	1	4
Montgomery,	14	6	8			1	1	3	3	1	3	1			1
New-York,*	655	284	371	16	24	70	137	101	93	53	66	26	25	18	26
Niagara,	25	8	17	1	1	2	4	2	1	1	5		3	2	3
Oneida,†	517	260	257	7	6	64	69	72	68	44	52	31	39	15	16
Onondaga,	22	5	17	1		1			7	2	6		1	1	3
Ontario,	26	12	14		1	2		3	8	4	2		1	3	2
Orange,	42	25	17	2		3	2	8	2	4	6	7	2	1	5
Orleans,	10	1	9					1	1		2		2		4
Oswego,	41	15	26	1	1	2	7	1	7	6	5	2	3	3	3
Otsego,	54	30	24	1		3	3	4	2	7	8	5	6	10	5
Putnam,	5	3	2			1		2			2				
Queens,	46	23	23		1		6	11	7	7	4	5	1		4
Rensselaer,	42	18	24			3	4	8	4	3	8	2	6	2	2
Richmond,	12	7	5			1	1	5	1	1	2				1
Rockland,	7	4	3					1		2	1			1	2
St. Lawrence,	39	15	24	1	1	1	4	5	5	1	6	4	5	3	3
Saratoga,	35	16	19		1	2	2	5	5	3	6	4	2	2	3
Schenectady,	8	4	4				1	2	1			1	1	1	1
Schoharie,	7	5	2				1	1			1	2		2	
Schuyler,	10	4	6					1		2	2		4	1	
Seneca,	19	7	12			1	3	3	2	1	2	1	2	1	3
Steuben,	28	7	21		1	3	3	1	4		3	2	7	1	3
Suffolk,	26	10	16	1	1	2	2		4	2	4	3		2	5
Sullivan,	11	4	7			2	1		2	1		1	3		1
Tioga,	16	3	13					1	1	1	4	1	2		6
Tompkins,	28	11	17	1		1	1	5	4	2	7		2	2	3
Ulster,	23	6	17		2	3	1	1	10	1	1	1	1		2
Warren,	10	7	3			2	2	2				2	1	1	
Washington,	44	25	19			5	3	5	3	4	4	7	4	4	5
Wayne,	22	12	10			2	1	5	1	3	2		4	2	2
Westchester,	56	31	25	1	1	7	3	8	8	8	3	3	9	4	1
Wyoming,	21	5	16		1	1	1	1	3	1	6	2	2		3
Yates,	13	6	7					1		2	3	3	1		3
Total,	2,742	1,215	1,527	47	60	233	333	340	363	250	322	172	217	146	222

* The Lunatic Asylum on Blackwell's Island, N. Y., reported 480 inmates, of whom 212 were males, and 268 females; Bloomingdale Asylum, 132 inmates, of whom 51 were males and 81 females.

† The State Lunatic Asylum, at Utica, reported 246 male and 226 female patients, the ages of 27 of the former and 7 of the latter were not reported.

In regard to the occupations of the insane there appear to have been different constructions placed upon the intentions of the inquiry, by marshals. It was desirable to arrive at the influence (if any exist) of the various employments in producing insanity, and a further advantage would have been gained, by a knowledge of the degree of education, hereditary tendency, duration of the malady, &c.: which in the absence of other data, must be left to the researches of the officers of special institutions for the insane. The occupations of the insane, so far as reported, were generally those followed by the persons in health, and as follows:

Farmers, 212; Laborers, 63; Carpenters, 16; Dress Makers, 12; Tailoresses, 12; Storekeepers, 10; Teachers, 10; Clerks, 9; Seamen and Boatmen, 9; Shoe Makers, 9; Lawyers, 8; Merchants, 8; Tailors, 7; Blacksmiths, 6; Physicians, 6; Students, 6; Masons, 5; Milliners, 5; Painters, 5; Accountants, 3; Cabinet Makers, 3; Clergymen, 3; Coach Makers, 3; Grocers, 3; Machinists, 3; Printers, 3; Pedlers, 4; Soldiers, 3; Agents, 2; Barbers, 2; Brush Makers, 2; Coopers, 3; Dentists, 2; Gate Keepers, 2; Hatters, 2; Horse Dealers, 2; Hotel Keepers, 2; House Keepers, 2; Lumbermen, 2; Servants, 2; Stone Cutters, 2; Tobacconists, 2; Weavers, 2; Apothecary, 1; Artist, 1; Bar Keeper, 1; Book Binder, 1; Butcher, 1; Chair Bottomer, 1; Chandler, 1; Chemist, 1; Civil Officer 1; Clock Maker, 1; Comb Maker, 1; Contractor, 1; Cook, 1; Editor, 1; Engineer, 1; Factory Girl, 1; Flagman, 1; Governess, 1; Lecturer, 1; Manufacturer, 1; Sculptor, 1; Ship Captain, 1; Steamboat Captain, 1; Turner, 1; Washer, 1; Wheelwright, 1.

IDIOTIC.

COUNTIES.	Total number.	SEX.		AGES.																	
		Males.	Females.	Under 5.		5 and under 10.		10 and under 15.		15 and under 20.		20 and under 30.		30 and under 40.		40 and under 50.		50 and under 60.		Over 60.	
				Males	Fem.	Males	Fem.	Males	Fem.	Males	Fem.	Males	Fem.	Males	Fem	Males	Fem.	Males	Fem.	Males	Fem.
Albany,	46	28	18			1	3	9	5	1	2	7	6	5		3	2	2			
Allegany,	46	20	26			1	2	4	1	2	4	6	8	2	3	5	2		3		3
Broome,	35	13	22			2			3	1	6	1	5	6	1	1	4	1	2	1	1
Cattaraugus,	26	18	8			1		3	1	2	2	4	4	7				1	1		
Cayuga,	45	20	25	1		1	1		3	2	3	8	5	5	7	2	4	1	2		
Chautauque,	38	21	17	1		1	4		2	4		7	6	1	3	5		1	2	1	
Chemung,	11	8	3				1			1	1	5		2	1						
Chenango,	46	24	22		2	3	2		2	3		4	5	4	5	6	3	2	2	2	1
Clinton,	28	16	12			1		2	2	2	5	7	2	2	1	2			1		1
Columbia,	28	17	11					1	4	1	2	5	1	4		1	2	2	1	3	1
Cortland,	34	17	17			3	2	2	2	1	1	6	3	4	4		4	1	1		
Delaware,	25	14	11				1	2	3	4				4	3	2	1	1	1	1	2
Dutchess,	17	9	8						1	3	2			5	2			1	2		1
Erie,	43	27	16			2		3	2	5	7	5	4	5		5	1		2	2	
Essex,	21	13	8			1		2	3	4	2	2	1	1		2	1		1	1	
Franklin,	20	10	10			2			2	2	1	4	4	2	2		1				
Fulton,	20	8	12				1	1	3		1	1	3	2	2	3			2	1	
Genesee,	35	17	18		1	2		1	2	1	2	4	2	1	6	4	3	2	1	2	1
Greene,	27	14	13	1		1	2		1	1	2	2	1	1	3	4	1	3	3	1	
Hamilton,	4	2	2			1						1	1			1					
Herkimer,	36	17	19			1	1	1	2	4	5	4	3	4	3		1		1	3	3
Jefferson,	66	38	28		1	6	5	4	1	7	4	9	7	7	5	3	3	2	2		
Kings,	27	14	13		3		2	2	3	2		3	4	3		2	1	1	1		
Lewis,	36	21	15			1	1	1	2	4	1	9	4	3	5	2		1	2		
Livingston,	13	7	6					2		3	2		2	1		1	1				1
Madison,	41	22	19		1		4	4	3	5	3	6	3	3	3	2	1	2	1		
Monroe,	30	17	13	1		2		1	5		3	5	1	4	2	2	2	2			
Montgomery,	21	12	9					3	1	1	3	4		1	2	1	2	2	1		
New-York,	52	27	25		1	2	3	2	1	5	5	7	5	2	5	3	4	1	1	3	2
Niagara,	24	10	14		1			1	1	2	7	3	2	2	1	2	1		1		
Oneida,	56	27	29			4	4	2	4	5	3	7	9	6	2	2	6	1	1		
Onondaga,	40	29	11	2		2	1	4	2	2	1	8	3	7	2	3	2	1			
Ontario,	32	16	16						2	1	1	6	7	4	3	2	1	2	1	1	1
Orange,	36	20	16			1	1	2	4	2	3	5		6	2	4	6				
Orleans,	11	4	7						2				1	1	1	2	1	1	1		1
Oswego,	62	47	15			5	2	4	3	6	2	14	4	8	1	5	2	4		1	1
Otsego,	60	31	29	1	1	3	1	6	1	4	4	4	6	7	5	2	9	2	1	2	1
Putnam,	13	8	5			1					1	3	2	2	1	1	1			1	
Queens,	8	5	3		1					2		2						1			2
Rensselaer,	32	18	14			1	1	3	5	3	3	4	5	2		2		3			
Richmond,	2	1	1							1					1						
Rockland,	16	6	10						2	1		3	2	1	1		3	1	1		1
St. Lawrence,	51	25	26				2	7	2	3	3	8	9	4	7	1	2		1	2	
Saratoga,	43	24	19		1	2	2	4	2	1	2	6	1	4	5	3	2	4	4		
Schenectady,	16	10	6			1	1			3		3	2	3	2		1				
Schoharie,	19	13	6				1	4	2	1	1	2	1	4	1	2					
Schuyler,	24	14	10			1	2	3		2	1	5	1	2	2	1	4				
Seneca,	18	13	5					1	1	2		5	4	4				1			
Steuben,	29	17	12		1			1	1	2	2	6	2	1	2	5	2	2			2
Suffolk,	13	9	4									2	1	2	1	2		3	1		1
Sullivan,	20	11	9		1	1	1	1	1	2	1	5	4			1		1	1		
Tioga,	13	10	3					1			1	6	1	1		2	1				
Tompkins,	43	24	19			1		3	1	3	3	10	3	5	3	2	6		3		
Ulster,	28	11	17					1	1			4	6	3	4	1	5			2	1
Warren,	12	8	4					2				4	3	1				1			1
Washington,	44	25	19			2		2	4	7	1	6	1	4	2	3	5		2	1	4
Wayne,	36	22	14	1		2		2	3	2	5	8	3	5	2	1		1	1		
Westchester,	41	23	18			2		5	1	4	6	4	6	5	1	1	1	1	2	1	1
Wyoming,	30	18	12			1	1	2		3	1	5	6	3	3	1	1	3			
Yates,	23	12	11				1	1		1	2	3		4	2	1	4	1		1	2
Total,	1,812	1,002	810	8	15	65	56	112	105	136	123	277	185	192	125	114	110	63	57	33	36

The causes of idiocy so far as reported, were—Epilepsy, 3; Fits, 44; Hereditary tendency, 1; Hooping cough, 1; Intemperance, 1; Injuries, 6; Measles 1 Paralysis, 1; Scarlet fever, 1; Sickness, 8; Spinal disease, 1.

MARRIAGES.

AGES OF PERSONS MARRIED.

Ages of Husbands.	AGES OF WIVES.																													
	13.	14.	15.	16.	17.	18.	19.	20.	21.	22.	23.	24.	25.	26.	27.	28.	29.	30.	31.	32.	33.	34.	35.	36.	37.	38.	39.	40.	41.	42.
15		1	1							1	1																			
16	1	4		3	1	2								1																
17		3	2	3	11	8	4	3	2	2																				
18	1	6	12	18	24	35	20	14	6	9	4	1	1	1	1								2		1	1		2		
19	1	3	38	59	73	79	91	30	25	19	11	8	5	5	1	2	3	1	2				1							
20	2	7	21	85	114	162	170	164	78	52	26	19	23	6	2	4	1	5	1				1	1		1				
21	4	13	31	85	161	258	282	257	202	113	66	37	25	19	10	12	5	5	5	1	3			1			1	1		
22	3	8	28	104	199	199	260	302	262	253	97	72	35	25	21	15	6	7	3	5	3	2	4	2	1	1	1			
23	1	6	20	68	171	251	288	266	241	219	193	75	46	32	24	10	5	9	3	4	2	1	1	1	1			1		
24		3	29	60	131	243	220	252	213	238	170	163	71	54	13	19	6	9	4	2	1	3	1	2		1	1			
25			16	49	111	182	215	248	202	224	185	149	150	52	41	26	8	19	4	7	3	3	3	3						
26		4	15	40	75	144	170	172	156	193	132	140	96	74	40	28	13	22	3	5	3	3	2			1		2		
27		2	12	20	64	76	120	131	120	135	126	99	89	62	85	34	16	14	7	6	1	1	1	4	2	3				
28		1	2	25	54	90	82	133	93	110	91	104	85	81	53	55	18	26	8	5	3	2	3	4	2	1	2	4		1
29		2	2	13	27	47	75	77	78	64	57	62	66	48	34	47	38	14	13	5	7	7	2	1	2	2	3	4		1
30		1		8	25	41	62	100	62	67	82	87	90	62	45	43	34	46	12	12	4	5	5	1	1	1		2	1	
31		1	1	4	13	16	32	34	49	34	28	29	28	33	30	27	14	12	7	12	6			1	1	2		1		
32			3	12	15	19	24	31	41	48	37	36	31	25	27	31	26	9	13	24	9	3	2		4	1	1	2	1	
33		1	1	4	4	17	16	22	23	26	27	32	29	27	17	13	16	18	8	14	12	1	5	3	1	2	1	2	2	
34			2	4	8	10	17	30	25	23	28	30	15	15	29	25	14	20	7	12	9	8	3	4		3	2	2	2	1
35			4	1	9	16	15	22	21	32	19	21	38	23	18	23	10	28	8	11	12	9	22		5	1	2	2		1
36		1	1	1	9	4	12	22	14	12	19	10	23	26	14	10	11	16	2	12	10	10	6	13	6	4	1	1		1
37			1	1	6	4	8	7	5	8	12	17	7	10	15	11	7	11	9	16	10	6	5	8	5	3	3	4	3	1
38		1		2	2	9	6	9	10	16	9	13	10	11	8	14	8	9	4	8	5	10	4	7	5	5	1	3	1	
39			1		2	5	7	6	3	11	11	7	9	10	6	7	12	4	4	8	7	5	3	3	2	6	2	3	1	2
40			1	3	3	4	8	10	6	6	14	7	16	12	19	15	9	21	8	9	9	8	18	7	7	14	1	19	4	7
41						1	1		8	2	6	4	4	5	2	3	8	8	3	5	4	4	3	5	7	2	3	5	3	
42			2			3	3	5	7	9	10	9		5	6	5	6	5	3	6	3	1	5	7	4	6	1	1	5	3
43					1		2	4	3	4	6	4	3	2	2	4	6	6	5	2	5		1	3	4	5	1	3	1	4
44				3	1	1	1	3	2	1	1	2	2	2	2	3	2		7	4	7	3	9	6	3	6	2	3	4	
45				1	1	4		2	4	2	3	4	6	1	2	4	3	6	3	2	4	6	13	2	8	2	5	6	2	4
46					1		1	1	1	3	2	3	4	8	6	3	1	4	1	6		5	7	4	5		3	4	4	1
47					1	1		1	1	3	2	2	1	1	2		2	1	2	2	1	1	4	3	4	4	4	4	2	
48					1		1	3	3	2		5			3	2	1	4	4	3	5	1	2	2		7	4	2	2	3
49			1				2	1	1	1	2		1	3	1	3	1	4	1	1	2	1	3	3	3	2	4		3	2
50			1			2	1	3	2	4	1	2	1	1	6	2	2	4	2	3		9	5	4	5	3	3	4	2	6
51										1	1	1	1	2	3	1		2		3			4	2	2	2	3	2		2
52								1			3			1	2		2	1	1	7	1	1	2	3	5	3		2	3	
53								1	1			3					1	4	1	1	5		3		2	1		1		3
54									1		1	2	1		1	1		2		2		6	1	3	1	1			4	1
55							1		1		1	2			1				3		1	6	3	3	3	2	2	3	1	1
56												1	1			1		1			2		1	1	1	3	2			3
57							1						1			1	3		3	1					1			2		2
58								2		1		1					1		1			1	2			3	4		2	1
59			1					1				2				1	2				1		1	1			1			
60													1	1		1		2		1		1	2		1	1		2	2	
61		1			1				1		1												1	2						
62										1			1				1								1	1	1			2
63																					1						1			1
64																		1	1			1				1				
65		1															1				2		1			1				
66													1			1	1		1				1				1			
67																					1							1		1
68																												1		1
69						1																							1	
70																												1		
71																													1	
72																				1							1			
73																														
74																														
75																														
76																					1									
77																														
78																														
79																														
85																												1		
	13	70	249	676	1319	1934	2227	2370	1973	1949	1485	1265	1017	746	592	507	324	380	177	228	165	137	168	120	106	109	68	103	57	56

MARRIAGES.

AGES OF PERSONS MARRIED.—(CONTINUED.)

Ages of Husbands.	AGES OF WIVES.																													
	43.	44.	45.	46.	47.	48.	49.	50.	51.	52.	53.	54.	55.	56.	57.	58.	59.	60.	61.	62.	63.	64.	65.	66.	67.	68.	69.	70.	77.	Total.
15																														4
16																														12
17																														38
18																														159
19																														457
20																														945
21													1																	1,598
22																														1,918
23			2													1														1,942
24																														1,909
25												1				1		1												1,903
26		1																												1,534
27				1			1																							1,241
28		1																												1,139
29		1		1				1																						801
30		1			1																									901
31			1																											416
32	1																													476
33	1		1		1		1						1																	349
34		1																						1						350
35		1			1									1																376
36								1																						272
37	3																													206
38		2		1																										193
39	1		1				1																							150
40	2	1	2		1	1		1																						273
41		2		2																										100
42	1	1				2	1																							125
43	2		2								1		1																	87
44	2		1	2	2	1			1																					89
45	2	1	2	1				1	1		1			1											1		1			112
46	5	1	2	2	1	1		1		1																				92
47	4	2	1		1	1		1							1															60
48	2	2		4	1	2																								71
49	1	2	1	1	2		1	2	2	1		2																		61
50	5	3	3	4		2	3	2		2			2																	104
51	2	8	1	2	1		1	1		2	1		1					1												53
52	3	1		1	1	3	1	3		1	1		1																	54
53	2	3		4		1		1	1	7	1	2																		49
54		3				3	1	2		3		3	1						1											45
55	3	1	7	1	1	4	2		2	3	2	1	1	2																64
56	1	3	2		3	4	1	1						1																33
57	2	1	2		2			1					1	1		1				1										27
58	2	1	1	1	1	2		2		3	3			1		2														38
59			2							1	1	1		2	1										1					20
60	1	1	4	2	4	2		3	1	1		1	1		1	3		1												41
61			3		1			1	1	3		1	2	1		1			1											22
62			3	1		1	2	1	2	2	2	4				1		1	1											29
63			1	1		1		1		1	2	2		1	2			3		1	1									20
64	2		1					1	2	1								1		1		1								14
65			2	1		2	2	3	1			1			1					1	1		1	1						23
66			2	2		2	1			1		1	2	1			1		2	1										22
67							1	1			1			1	2		1	1		2				1	1					15
68						2	1		1	1	2	1	2	1			1								1					15
69							1	1					1	1				1		1	1	1			1					11
70			1			1	1	1					1		1			2			1									10
71							1	1										2			1									6
72																						1			1			1		5
73														1						1	2									4
74						1								1	1		1			1										5
75								1															2				1	1		5
76	1		1								1		1			1													1	7
77																					1									1
78			1																											1
79								1																1						2
85												1																		2
	51	45	53	35	25	39	24	37	15	34	19	22	20	17	10	11	4	14	5	10	8	3	3	4	6	....	2	2	1	21.106

MARRIAGES.

NUMBER, PREVIOUS CIVIL CONDITION, AND MONTHS.

COUNTIES	Total number of marriages.	PREVIOUS CIVIL CONDITION OF PERSONS MARRIED.				MONTHS IN WHICH MARRIAGES OCCURRED.											
		Unmarried men to unmarried women.	Unmarried men to widows.	Widowers to unmarried women.	Widowers to widows.	January, 1855.	February, 1855.	March, 1855.	April, 1855.	May, 1855.	June, 1854.	July, 1854.	August, 1854.	September, 1854.	October, 1854	November, 1854	December, 1854.
Albany,	550	468	6	41	23	54	45	34	33	68	35	40	33	52	48	45	58
Allegany,	337	289	5	23	20	47	37	27	15	20	21	23	19	32	40	24	29
Broome,	215	187	1	17	10	32	17	17	16	15	8	15	18	18	25	20	14
Cattaraugus,	297	242	10	27	18	36	29	14	25	28	15	21	20	33	29	24	23
Cayuga,	382	330	11	28	13	35	47	36	35	32	27	24	13	31	31	41	30
Chautauque,	477	401	9	43	24	63	36	55	47	40	22	24	18	41	44	50	37
Chemung,	180	146	2	15	17	17	21	9	19	23	10	11	13	13	12	16	16
Chenango,	331	259	8	47	17	44	43	27	16	24	22	16	17	33	33	28	28
Clinton,	229	194	6	19	10	40	20	23	21	18	12	13	22	14	19	13	14
Columbia,	309	265	7	28	9	27	22	32	21	20	23	12	19	28	40	35	28
Cortland,	182	155	1	16	10	20	29	15	9	6	10	13	12	23	23	9	13
Delaware,	276	225	5	33	13	24	28	26	20	22	12	19	9	23	38	30	25
Dutchess,	319	262	10	39	8	36	29	20	16	26	21	21	16	29	41	43	21
Erie,	871	719	32	85	35	95	67	73	84	97	57	55	58	60	79	72	73
Essex,	191	163	7	14	7	20	14	27	15	23	9	25	10	8	16	11	13
Franklin,	177	144	7	16	10	20	10	14	12	13	12	8	17	18	21	14	18
Fulton,	213	181	3	24	5	35	17	22	13	22	4	13	10	16	17	18	26
Genesee,	213	176	3	17	17	20	11	22	19	17	8	8	10	16	36	23	22
Greene,	227	187	7	25	8	25	24	16	15	20	15	14	16	16	27	19	20
Hamilton,	20	16	.....	2	2	1	1	3	.....	3	2	1	1	3	3	2	.....
Herkimer,	278	230	4	30	14	38	26	22	30	18	21	11	10	22	38	16	26
Jefferson,	489	416	3	46	24	77	66	41	33	33	29	25	24	51	40	23	47
Kings,	907	748	42	81	36	63	63	48	87	131	86	69	44	74	81	59	43
Lewis,	142	113	3	18	8	15	18	12	8	13	7	5	4	11	15	16	18
Livingston,	246	210	2	26	8	24	23	22	16	16	18	11	6	19	36	32	23
Madison,	352	280	5	39	28	38	36	47	21	34	22	19	10	25	43	31	26
Monroe,	771	637	17	86	31	84	66	65	68	86	42	46	40	56	65	80	72
Montgomery,	179	148	4	18	9	28	25	11	11	17	11	11	10	7	15	20	13
New-York,	2,852	2,454	114	203	81	238	180	175	247	373	234	196	205	237	237	230	226
Niagara,	316	258	8	28	22	26	27	25	22	30	11	18	18	34	45	33	27
Oneida,	796	675	13	75	33	81	81	61	75	82	41	53	38	75	76	66	67
Onondaga,	555	460	13	64	18	57	48	38	47	37	32	39	31	59	57	46	63
Ontario,	299	244	5	33	17	27	35	30	16	32	16	9	14	26	37	21	36
Orange,	385	329	11	39	6	46	34	43	27	35	24	17	9	30	43	47	30
Orleans,	192	154	2	24	12	18	25	18	18	16	10	7	8	14	25	20	13
Oswego,	524	401	12	56	30	70	41	47	32	38	30	38	26	35	48	32	60
Otsego,	404	325	7	55	17	49	51	43	23	33	17	20	13	32	52	36	25
Putnam,	106	90	5	8	3	12	11	7	9	7	6	3	5	12	12	20	2
Queens,	207	155	8	16	8	17	25	13	22	12	9	10	8	16	19	18	18
Rensselaer,	527	438	15	48	26	59	52	52	35	41	36	28	26	40	43	50	64
Richmond,	66	57	2	5	2	7	3	2	4	3	9	3	8	6	7	2	12
Rockland,	68	54	5	4	5	9	4	8	6	9	4	2	3	3	4	6	10
St. Lawrence,	488	401	11	50	26	55	53	43	36	51	25	28	23	37	51	42	44
Saratoga,	349	280	11	47	11	38	16	32	29	25	19	15	17	36	56	40	26
Schenectady,	120	93	6	15	6	12	9	10	6	15	7	10	9	17	4	8	13
Schoharie,	215	183	2	25	5	26	18	27	18	4	6	14	9	25	23	31	14
Schuyler,	113	87	3	16	7	18	17	12	9	8	3	4	4	6	8	13	11
Seneca,	174	153	4	11	6	20	13	13	23	13	13	9	8	12	24	10	16
Steuben,	535	469	12	36	18	53	44	51	33	45	30	52	25	48	43	47	64
Suffolk,	281	228	7	33	13	40	24	23	20	24	21	17	9	17	24	27	35
Sullivan,	170	138	9	17	6	18	14	17	12	11	5	15	13	11	21	10	22
Tioga,	173	140	5	20	8	22	21	19	11	14	7	8	11	10	21	12	17
Tompkins,	248	198	6	36	8	34	33	27	16	16	12	10	13	15	25	27	20
Ulster,	493	437	8	27	21	61	44	42	34	51	39	29	24	35	45	43	46
Warren,	90	74	5	8	3	14	6	9	8	9	2	7	4	6	11	10	4
Washington,	301	237	6	46	12	46	23	35	26	20	15	13	16	23	30	27	27
Wayne,	345	279	13	37	16	50	26	40	13	31	18	12	9	25	36	40	45
Westchester,	382	321	6	39	16	32	34	30	37	42	37	16	18	29	38	32	37
Wyoming,	238	190	7	23	18	22	19	32	18	24	13	18	13	19	24	19	16
Yates,	179	142	4	20	13	24	17	13	18	14	10	6	9	18	19	14	17
Total,	21,551	17,935	565	2,067	927	2,359	1,918	1,817	1,675	2,050	1,342	1,299	1,145	1,780	2,163	1,893	1,903

* The discrepancy of the totals of this and the foregoing tables, arises from the omission of ages of one or both parties, in the returns of 445 marriages.

DEATHS.

CLASSIFICATION OF THE AGES AND SEXES OF THOSE DYING DURING THE YEAR ENDING JUNE 1, 1855.

COUNTIES.	Under 3 months.		3 months and under 6.		6 months and under 9.		9 months and under 12.		1 year and under 2.		2 years and under 3.		3 years and under 4.		4 years and under 5.	
	Males.	Fem.	Males.	Fem.	Males.	Fem.	Males.	Fem.	Males	Fem.	Males.	Fem.	Males.	Fem.	Males.	Fem.
Albany,	45	37	37	29	39	28	33	31	102	108	76	56	44	39	21	24
Allegany,	15	9	8	4	5	6	5	5	9	10	11	8	9	8	4	7
Broome,	9	7	7	4	3	1	5	5	10	7	8	6	6	6	3	5
Cattaraugus,	13	7	6	9	6	3	6	2	6	11	4	3	4	1	3	5
Cayuga,	12	11	4	8	4	9	5	6	24	19	12	15	6	8	6	7
Chautauque,	23	14	12	10	6	4	8	5	28	20	16	10	9	8	12	10
Chemung,	15	4	4	7	6	2	1	2	19	17	2	4	7	6	4	2
Chenango,	10	4	5	1	3	2	3	1	13	6	5	9	8	3	2	3
Clinton,	15	12	4	6	6	3	3	6	13	13	16	6	......	6	4	4
Columbia,	24	12	9	2	9	10	5	5	23	15	11	13	8	8	6	3
Cortland,	1	7	3	2	4	......	5	2	7	8	1	3	5	1	4	2
Delaware,	19	5	4	3	......	4	5	7	14	11	8	10	6	8	5	......
Dutchess,	15	17	8	5	6	14	6	6	23	22	20	17	6	13	14	6
Erie,	84	65	46	36	27	35	31	31	95	92	47	60	44	31	35	33
Essex,	5	2	4	5	1	1	4	4	13	7	6	4	1	6	2	3
Franklin,	8	9	......	4	5	1	2	1	12	7	4	5	3	3	3	1
Fulton,	11	5	2	7	10	9	8	3	12	8	11	9	4	3	3	......
Genesee,	9	10	4	7	1	2	2	2	8	3	7	6	3	2	1	3
Greene,	10	3	7	3	2	3	4	.3	9	11	3	5	3	4	5	4
Hamilton,	......	2	......	3	3	......	......	......	......	1	......	......	......	......	3	......
Herkimer,	19	9	13	8	3	5	4	2	13	13	12	4	4	8	3	5
Jefferson,	22	17	5	8	7	8	7	9	22	19	11	21	9	9	9	7
Kings,	158	143	79	76	109	105	96	76	276	262	156	126	101	72	60	61
Lewis,	6	6	3	3	1	4	2	5	7	1	6	6	7	8	8	2
Livingston,	10	9	6	3	4	1	1	1	8	10	8	5	4	4	3	2
Madison,	16	8	9	10	4	9	6	3	14	11	7	6	7	8	4	10
Monroe,	58	31	33	28	35	25	24	22	64	72	36	25	21	25	14	8
Montgomery,	10	11	3	4	7	4	6	3	5	9	11	10	6	5	5	3
New-York,	308	257	243	183	201	172	169	148	628	578	427	337	264	223	155	158
Niagara,	28	21	18	11	11	6	7	5	26	22	13	10	14	6	6	5
Oneida,	47	33	24	21	17	27	22	18	65	53	32	34	24	23	16	14
Onondaga,	23	29	14	14	13	8	13	3	54	58	25	28	20	22	14	19
Ontario,	7	13	5	6	.3	6	5	1	20	15	8	5	2	4	6	3
Orange,	20	24	5	20	22	8	6	2	45	21	22	21	15	12	11	20
Orleans,	7	7	2	2	7	1	......	1	12	10	7	2	4	5	2	5
Oswego,	37	47	15	7	5	8	7	7	46	39	25	16	11	8	17	9
Otsego,	14	10	6	4	8	3	1	1	9	15	7	12	4	12	5	2
Putnam,	3	4	3	2	2	1	1	......	9	5	6	3	2	1	2	......
Queens,	22	14	9	9	5	7	8	9	33	20	15	20	11	14	8	12
Rensselaer,	45	36	30	17	17	25	16	18	81	61	43	34	25	16	26	6
Richmond,	8	10	2	1	......	3	1	4	15	13	12	11	2	1	......	3
Rockland,	5	6	2	5	7	3	1	3	14	5	5	9	2	1	2	7
St. Lawrence,	12	10	11	11	8	7	7	3	19	22	15	27	15	8	6	6
Saratoga,	24	16	3	5	6	3	10	11	25	19	14	10	6	13	9	10
Schenectady,	7	5	4	3	8	0	2	4	12	7	9	7	4	5	......	4
Schoharie,	7	10	10	3	3	2	3	......	9	8	10	11	5	2	10	3
Schuyler,	1	4	......	5	4	6	2	2	9	8	3	5	1	5	2	1
Seneca,	2	2	......	4	5	2	4	3	12	8	5	6	4	6	5	8
Steuben,	32	20	18	6	9	14	5	10	21	32	18	9	3	7	5	3
Suffolk,	15	19	10	9	7	8	6	3	17	20	9	17	4	4	6	3
Sullivan,	7	5	3	8	6	5	2	5	6	17	11	10	8	2	5	5
Tioga,	17	10	5	3	5	1	1	3	15	14	5	8	3	4	2	1
Tompkins,	18	8	4	4	3	3	1	5	9	7	8	3	4	4	6	6
Ulster,	41	49	29	15	27	22	16	21	48	43	41	22	30	24	16	14
Warren,	8	5	5	3	1	......	1	......	6	6	4	3	1	3	6	3
Washington,	19	11	9	4	10	5	3	5	22	19	8	16	12	5	6	3
Wayne,	33	18	13	4	7	8	13	6	20	12	17	13	7	9	7	10
Westchester,	29	38	19	24	24	16	16	14	63	45	27	20	22	15	10	13
Wyoming,	6	10	1	5	3	2	4	3	12	14	14	5	5	4	1	4
Yates,	3	2	3	1	1	1	3	2	2	6	5	2	4	5	3	6
Total,	1,497	1,229	850	714	771	690	643	568	2,233	2,015	1,385	1,188	873	776	621	586

DEATHS.

CLASSIFICATION OF THE AGES AND SEXES OF THOSE DYING DURING THE YEAR ENDING JUNE 1, 1855.

COUNTIES.	5 and under 10.		10 and under 15.		15 and under 20.		20 and under 25.		25 and under 30.		30 and under 35.		35 and under 40.		40 and under 45.	
	Males.	Fem.	Males.	Fem.	Males.	Fem.	Males.	Fem.	Males.	Fem.	Males.	Fem.	Males.	Fem.	Males.	Fem.
Albany,	71	51	26	26	30	47	49	53	60	35	51	43	46	37	49	26
Allegany,	19	9	3	5	4	10	10	8	6	12	13	12	4	9	2	6
Broome,	7	5	3	5	11	9	13	11	12	3	4	9	4	3	2	4
Cattaraugus,	9	5	6	6	9	14	13	15	14	11	7	8	6	6	4	7
Cayuga,	23	20	10	6	20	20	29	23	13	19	10	10	24	13	19	10
Chautauque,	18	20	8	5	7	22	23	31	14	15	13	13	8	15	9	11
Chemung,	8	8	4	3	9	5	12	11	9	12	7	8	7	10	5	2
Chenango,	6	8	9	5	4	12	8	16	12	16	7	13	9	13	5	5
Clinton,	5	5	6	5	9	9	11	14	7	12	3	9	4	7	7	4
Columbia,	12	19	2	6	6	15	20	19	4	14	14	18	8	13	6	12
Cortland,	3	3	1	4	5	8	3	13	7	8	5	3	4	3	2	8
Delaware,	17	10	6	8	4	13	10	13	7	13	10	9	6	12	8	15
Dutchess,	20	22	20	7	11	17	27	26	30	23	13	16	18	14	15	13
Erie,	60	54	31	29	36	46	65	59	61	60	62	51	58	47	51	27
Essex,	9	6	6	3	5	9	6	11	2	5	4	4	2	15	5	4
Franklin,	3	4	1	5	5	4	5	12	2	6	6	4	5	3	3	6
Fulton,	8	11	3	4	7	5	9	4	6	9	2	8	5	......	2	3
Genesee,	11	5	4	3	5	9	11	18	16	15	4	13	7	6	3	7
Greene,	7	6	6	4	15	7	12	6	12	12	5	11	5	11	9	4
Hamilton,	1	1	1	1	2	......	......	1	......	1	......	......	1	......	1	......
Herkimer,	5	5	6	4	9	8	12	12	7	12	9	13	8	8	15	7
Jefferson,	13	17	16	10	21	28	33	25	14	22	13	22	13	10	6	13
Kings,	133	110	62	65	63	38	86	83	92	99	94	83	87	74	87	58
Lewis,	8	9	7	7	3	9	4	9	3	1	4	8	7	6	......	6
Livingston,	5	6	9	4	4	7	7	10	9	10	10	6	4	8	8	9
Madison,	13	6	7	8	8	7	24	22	10	19	10	13	10	10	9	12
Monroe,	34	26	21	16	26	37	38	25	39	39	33	35	28	38	34	29
Montgomery,	7	8	8	5	6	9	10	6	4	8	9	3	11	8	8	4
New-York,	345	256	125	99	159	163	343	290	337	313	347	269	316	194	307	155
Niagara,	20	16	11	15	8	15	28	26	16	15	14	15	15	11	15	11
Oneida,	27	39	21	29	32	41	47	49	40	44	32	36	32	20	30	35
Onondaga,	35	42	17	30	26	24	26	29	22	18	15	29	31	21	20	17
Ontario,	16	18	10	5	10	15	16	17	8	15	11	11	5	11	8	11
Orange,	30	15	17	14	21	13	38	22	24	21	24	21	15	17	20	11
Orleans,	3	7	5	6	10	6	8	9	7	10	11	7	6	6	11	3
Oswego,	20	20	15	18	18	29	24	42	26	27	19	11	14	16	12	16
Otsego,	18	10	9	4	8	16	13	27	13	20	10	17	10	6	6	10
Putnam,	2	2	3	4	2	1	3	5	4	6	8	7	5	3	6	6
Queens,	20	26	7	4	17	10	22	16	10	15	17	17	19	7	17	12
Rensselaer,	31	42	13	30	33	25	45	36	35	30	36	35	36	42	27	19
Richmond,	6	6	4	5	3	4	9	7	2	6	3	8	4	7	7	4
Rockland,	6	9	7	2	4	3	10	5	15	5	6	8	8	8	10	3
St. Lawrence,	19	16	12	13	10	14	22	39	18	24	18	14	22	19	13	9
Saratoga,	12	18	6	12	14	13	12	10	20	10	10	12	5	10	13	14
Schenectady,	6	9	6	2	9	8	7	10	6	10	7	9	14	7	10	6
Schoharie,	6	2	8	7	8	14	5	4	10	7	11	8	7	7	6	2
Schuyler,	3	2	1	4	4	9	4	11	5	9	3	7	3	4	7	3
Seneca,	10	7	3	8	7	4	8	16	2	8	5	7	4	6	4	5
Steuben,	16	5	5	10	13	18	25	14	24	10	19	10	6	13	7	11
Suffolk,	7	17	9	2	11	12	9	16	10	12	11	9	10	6	10	11
Sullivan,	14	11	13	4	7	7	9	12	7	6	2	7	2	3	7	6
Tioga,	5	6	1	2	8	7	8	10	1	14	3	10	10	10	4	2
Tompkins,	8	9	7	7	13	12	11	14	9	13	8	8	6	7	4	5
Ulster,	31	25	22	11	18	25	34	32	31	9	29	24	31	18	24	16
Warren,	4	6	3	6	3	7	6	8	......	7	1	5	2	2	1	5
Washington,	15	15	4	4	9	27	21	17	13	15	8	15	9	14	8	11
Wayne,	10	10	10	5	10	13	21	13	15	10	5	9	10	5	13	5
Westchester,	35	39	15	17	20	13	27	32	22	28	24	19	35	17	31	11
Wyoming,	16	7	6	6	20	9	16	12	7	12	4	8	9	11	4	10
Yates,	4	6	2	3	4	2	6	11	5	11	5	6	2	2	4	6
Total,	1,335	1,177	689	647	883	1,003	1,433	1,417	1,236	1,271	1,148	1,123	1,102	929	1,040	763

DEATHS.

CLASSIFICATION OF THE AGES AND SEXES OF THOSE DYING DURING THE YEAR ENDING JUNE 1, 1855.

COUNTIES.	45 and under 50.		50 and under 55.		55 and under 60.		60 and under 65.		65 and under 70.		70 and under 75.		75 and under 80.		Over 80.	
	Males.	Fem.	Males.	Fem.	Males.	Fem.	Males.	Fem.	Males.	Fem.	Males.	Fem.	Males.	Fem.	Males.	Fem.
Albany,	49	25	57	19	29	22	31	16	27	16	25	17	15	14	21	18
Allegany,	8	6	3	1	6	4	4	8	8	4	9	7	7	5	7	18
Broome,	4	3	8	1	5	3	13	4	4	3	8	2	7	3	7	6
Cattaraugus,	5	2	6	5	1	7	6	4	2	3	9	4	9	6	8	8
Cayuga,	15	9	16	9	10	5	16	12	16	11	13	10	21	13	20	13
Chautauque,	10	8	9	9	13	8	11	7	15	14	16	11	8	7	22	8
Chemung,	5	3	3	3	2	3	5	3	3	5	4	3	3	2	5	5
Chenango,	10	3	5	8	4	5	9	6	11	9	8	12	11	9	19	15
Clinton,	3	6	5	5	3	6	7	3	5	3	11	4	3	5	10	5
Columbia,	9	8	14	4	14	4	13	6	6	7	14	10	11	9	18	20
Cortland,	6	5	9	3	3	1	8	2	8	3	13	8	5	3	6	9
Delaware,	7	5	14	5	8	3	10	8	5	6	5	20	8	15	23	8
Dutchess,	17	17	19	19	13	9	17	17	14	6	14	15	17	9	19	19
Erie,	52	24	45	29	38	16	26	26	28	7	20	19	15	15	27	20
Essex,	3	3	6	3	6	4	7	4	10	5	7	3	2	6	9	8
Franklin,	4	4	5	2	4	9	4	5	5	2	1	2	5	2	4	2
Fulton,	4	7	3	4	5	8	3	4	7	3	2	6	6	2	9	9
Genesee,	2	6	9	3	7	5	7	3	13	7	6	9	8	4	11	5
Greene,	12	7	8	5	5	9	15	6	9	5	6	7	11	9	16	12
Hamilton,	......	1	......	1	......	1	......	......	......	......	1	......	......	1	......	2
Herkimer,	5	3	8	6	12	8	6	4	13	10	8	7	14	7	22	11
Jefferson,	9	10	10	8	17	15	19	19	19	16	18	7	22	10	17	18
Kings,	62	41	59	39	48	27	56	33	30	18	26	20	13	16	23	39
Lewis,	4	6	7	2	5	1	3	4	5	4	5	4	4	2	12	3
Livingston,	8	4	7	1	5	3	9	4	10	5	8	5	5	1	11	11
Madison,	6	8	12	14	13	11	16	7	10	10	13	15	4	7	18	17
Monroe,	31	20	31	16	31	19	27	19	20	19	16	13	14	13	16	15
Montgomery,	5	5	9	11	6	7	5	11	11	11	7	4	7	4	13	13
New-York,	345	111	229	107	127	67	138	72	81	61	64	67	40	49	54	70
Niagara,	15	6	14	8	11	6	12	6	9	5	4	4	7	5	16	10
Oneida,	32	25	38	24	24	17	39	27	22	19	23	19	26	17	41	40
Onondaga,	19	17	27	17	21	15	18	18	17	20	17	17	16	9	20	28
Ontario,	9	7	7	4	7	7	8	8	8	10	7	9	7	14	18	7
Orange,	17	14	20	13	8	8	14	11	21	16	19	14	14	9	25	18
Orleans,	10	8	2	3	5	2	5	6	7	5	5	7	3	2	7	7
Oswego,	8	13	15	17	13	19	18	8	18	12	10	18	11	4	25	17
Otsego,	7	5	8	10	13	14	12	8	9	12	8	12	14	6	24	27
Putnam,	4	2	3	2	5	3	2	1	6	3	7	2	4	5	5	10
Queens,	14	11	7	15	11	16	13	10	13	10	10	9	10	14	15	24
Rensselaer,	30	20	16	22	27	24	20	20	20	13	17	15	10	13	25	22
Richmond,	3	4	4	4	7	1	9	2	6	1	10	2	4	3	6	5
Rockland,	6	3	9	4	9	1	6	2	2	1	7	6	1	2	6	5
St. Lawrence,	9	7	13	11	17	7	12	14	17	10	10	15	16	12	21	24
Saratoga,	11	6	17	10	10	12	8	7	10	8	10	13	19	22	26	27
Schenectady,	5	4	7	5	1	4	4	5	7	4	7	3	3	......	7	10
Schoharie,	1	1	9	2	7	6	5	3	6	8	7	12	5	7	18	12
Schuyler,	1	3	4	4	3	1	2	1	5	2	2	4	6	6	3	4
Seneca,	3	1	2	1	5	4	7	2	8	3	8	3	3	7	14	5
Steuben,	11	10	10	6	8	9	12	8	21	7	13	12	17	13	16	10
Suffolk,	7	9	18	11	10	9	9	9	12	15	13	10	21	10	19	22
Sullivan,	9	1	9	5	3	3	6	7	5	6	5	2	7	1	8	5
Tioga,	4	2	2	6	1	5	6	5	5	15	5	6	6	5	11	6
Tompkins,	3	8	9	4	5	6	11	5	13	2	3	5	9	7	14	14
Ulster,	25	9	13	15	20	13	28	15	15	23	14	19	14	14	24	20
Warren,	3	4	3	3	1	2	4	3	1	4	1	4	5	3	7	3
Washington,	8	7	11	6	7	11	10	16	11	9	11	9	14	8	22	19
Wayne,	10	8	5	9	9	14	13	6	12	5	7	14	10	6	15	15
Westchester,	15	14	24	9	20	12	17	13	19	17	18	13	11	19	24	20
Wyoming,	4	4	6	5	10	2	6	4	11	3	7	5	4	4	9	11
Yates.	2	2	3	3	7	5	2	2	4	4	10	5	7	5	8	8
Total,	1,005	595	951	600	745	548	829	569	735	545	652	599	599	500	946	862

DEATHS.

RECAPITULATION.

COUNTIES.	Under 5 years.		5 and under 15.		15 and under 45.		Over 45.		Unknown.		General Total.		Total.
	Males.	Females.	Males.	Females.	Males.	Females.	Males.	Females.	Males.	Females.	Males.	Females.	
Albany,	397	352	97	77	285	241	254	147	19	9	1, 052	826	1, 878
Allegany,	66	57	22	14	39	57	52	53	3	4	182	185	367
Broome,	51	41	10	10	46	39	56	25	2	......	165	115	280
Cattaraugus,	48	41	15	11	53	61	46	39	1	......	163	152	315
Cayuga,	73	83	33	26	115	95	127	82	2	1	350	287	637
Chautauque,	114	81	26	25	74	107	104	72	......	......	318	285	603
Chemung,	58	44	12	11	49	48	30	27	1	......	150	130	280
Chenango,	49	29	15	13	45	75	77	67	......	......	186	184	370
Clinton,	61	56	11	10	41	55	47	37	......	1	160	159	319
Columbia,	95	68	14	25	58	91	99	68	......	1	266	253	519
Cortland,	30	25	4	7	26	43	58	34	......	......	118	109	227
Delaware,	61	48	23	18	45	75	80	70	......	1	209	212	421
Dutchess,	98	100	40	29	114	109	130	111	......	1	382	350	732
Erie,	409	383	91	83	333	290	251	156	7	1	1, 091	913	2, 004
Essex,	36	32	15	9	24	48	50	36	......	......	125	125	250
Franklin,	37	31	4	9	26	35	32	28	4	......	103	103	206
Fulton,	61	44	11	15	31	29	39	43	......	3	142	134	276
Genesee,	35	35	15	8	46	68	63	42	2	......	161	153	314
Greene,	43	36	13	10	58	51	82	60	2	......	198	157	355
Hamilton,	6	6	2	2	4	2	1	6	......	......	13	16	29
Herkimer,	71	54	11	9	60	60	88	56	2	......	232	179	411
Jefferson,	92	98	29	27	100	120	131	103	1	......	353	348	701
Kings,	1, 035	921	195	175	509	435	317	233	53	20	2, 109	1, 784	3, 893
Lewis,	40	35	15	16	21	39	45	25	......	1	121	116	237
Livingston,	44	35	14	10	42	50	63	34	2	......	165	129	294
Madison,	67	65	20	14	71	83	92	89	3	2	253	253	506
Monroe,	285	236	55	42	198	203	186	134	1	5	725	620	1, 345
Montgomery,	53	49	15	13	48	38	63	66	......	......	179	166	345
New-York,	2, 395	2, 055	470	355	1, 809	1, 384	1, 078	604	*558	*314	6, 310	4, 712	11, 022
Niagara,	123	86	31	31	96	93	88	50	4	1	342	261	603
Oneida,	247	223	48	68	213	225	245	188	2	1	755	705	1, 460
Onondaga,	176	181	52	72	140	138	155	141	2	2	525	534	1, 059
Ontario,	56	53	26	23	58	80	71	66	1	1	212	223	435
Orange,	146	128	47	29	142	105	138	103	13	2	486	367	853
Orleans,	41	33	8	13	53	41	44	40	2	1	148	128	276
Oswego,	163	141	35	38	113	141	118	108	2	......	431	428	859
Otsego,	54	59	27	14	60	96	95	94	1	......	237	263	500
Putnam,	28	16	5	6	28	28	36	28	......	......	97	78	175
Queens,	111	105	27	30	102	77	93	109	4	......	337	321	658
Rensselaer,	283	213	44	72	212	187	165	149	4	2	708	623	1, 331
Richmond,	40	46	10	11	28	36	49	22	......	......	127	115	242
Rockland,	38	39	13	11	53	32	46	24	2	......	152	106	258
St. Lawrence,	93	94	31	29	103	119	115	100	......	3	342	345	687
Saratoga,	97	87	18	30	74	69	111	105	......	1	300	292	592
Schenectady,	46	44	12	11	53	50	41	35	......	1	152	141	293
Schoharie,	57	39	14	9	47	42	58	51	2	......	178	141	319
Schuyler,	22	36	4	6	26	43	26	25	......	......	78	110	188
Seneca,	37	39	13	15	30	46	50	26	1	2	131	128	259
Steuben,	111	101	21	15	94	76	108	75	7	......	341	267	608
Suffolk,	74	83	16	19	61	66	109	95	1	......	261	263	524
Sullivan,	48	57	27	15	34	41	52	30	......	......	161	143	304
Tioga,	53	44	6	8	34	53	40	50	......	......	133	155	288
Tompkins,	53	40	15	16	51	59	67	51	......	1	186	167	353
Ulster,	248	210	53	36	167	124	153	128	1	......	622	498	1, 120
Warren,	32	23	7	12	13	34	25	26	1	1	78	96	174
Washington,	89	68	19	19	68	99	94	85	2	1	272	272	544
Wayne,	117	80	20	15	74	55	81	77	3	......	295	227	522
Westchester,	210	185	50	56	159	120	148	117	60	20	627	498	1, 125
Wyoming,	46	47	22	13	60	62	57	38	1	......	186	160	346
Yates,	24	25	6	9	26	38	43	34	......	1	99	107	206
Total,	8, 873	7. 765	2, 024	1, 824	6, 842	6, 506	6, 462	4, 817	779	405	24, 980	21, 317	46, 297

* Of these, 550 were infants.

DEATHS.

CLASSIFIED BY MONTHS AND SEASONS.

COUNTIES.	MONTHS.												TOTAL BY SEASONS.				PERCENTAGE BY SEASONS.			
	January.	February.	March.	April.	May.	June.	July.	August.	September.	October.	November.	December.	Spring.	Summer.	Autumn.	Winter.	Spring.	Summer.	Autumn.	Winter.
Albany, ...	118	162	171	130	165	104	258	267	169	136	95	101	466	629	400	381	24.8	33.9	21.3	20.0
Allegany, ...	25	28	49	41	31	32	26	31	35	26	16	21	121	89	77	74	33.5	21.9	21.3	23.3
Broome, ...	19	20	38	30	38	12	17	28	26	25	20	7	106	57	71	46	37.9	20.4	25.4	16.3
Cattaraugus, .	27	20	39	29	38	18	14	30	27	31	15	20	106	62	73	67	34.4	20.1	23.4	22.1
Cayuga, ...	66	51	73	62	73	45	42	50	57	47	38	33	208	137	142	150	32.5	21.5	22.3	23.7
Chautauque, .	38	51	70	59	65	30	44	49	54	48	29	43	194	123	131	132	33.5	21.2	22.6	22.7
Chemung, ...	19	20	28	25	19	21	22	20	26	28	22	21	72	63	86	60	26.5	23.2	28.1	22.2
Chenango, ...	32	28	45	41	35	18	28	40	33	34	20	14	121	86	87	74	32.9	23.3	23.3	20.5
Clinton, ...	22	26	40	27	43	27	26	34	20	21	15	15	110	87	56	63	34.8	27.5	17.7	20.0
Columbia, ...	39	43	69	57	56	38	25	45	37	39	37	32	182	108	113	114	35.2	20.9	21.8	22.1
Cortland, ...	21	13	31	24	26	14	11	19	19	22	10	15	81	44	51	49	36.0	19.6	22.7	21.7
Delaware, ...	30	36	56	49	37	30	21	19	44	45	25	24	142	70	114	90	34.1	16.8	27.6	21.5
Dutchess, ...	58	70	70	66	50	29	87	117	68	39	40	32	186	233	147	160	25.5	32.1	20.2	22.2
Erie, ...	126	123	132	138	163	113	280	330	233	156	92	108	433	723	481	357	21.7	36.2	24.1	18.0
Essex, ...	22	21	27	28	22	14	20	35	26	17	10	5	77	69	53	48	31.2	27.9	21.5	19.4
Franklin, ...	16	17	21	15	26	15	20	20	11	10	18	15	62	55	39	48	30.4	22.1	19.1	28.4
Fulton, ...	23	21	35	35	28	12	12	27	22	30	11	20	98	51	63	64	35.9	18.9	22.4	22.8
Genesee, ...	23	22	32	35	37	19	15	35	26	24	18	19	104	69	68	64	34.1	22.7	22.6	20.6
Greene, ...	28	19	35	27	34	23	26	56	49	23	13	22	96	105	85	69	27.0	29.6	23.9	19.5
Hamilton, ...	1	3	3	2	4	6	2	......	5	1	1	1	9	8	7	5	31.0	27.5	24.1	17.4
Herkimer, ...	38	28	36	39	42	18	39	37	35	39	26	25	117	94	100	91	29.1	24.8	24.9	21.2
Jefferson, ...	53	58	64	66	51	62	49	67	72	48	50	59	181	178	170	170	25.9	25.5	24.3	24.3
Kings, ...	241	239	340	318	287	249	532	606	354	274	205	227	945	1,387	833	707	24.4	35.8	21.5	18.3
Lewis, ...	14	29	28	24	29	12	10	23	22	12	15	18	81	45	49	61	34.3	19.1	20.7	25.9
Livingston, ...	33	26	35	27	33	12	21	21	28	21	17	20	95	54	66	79	32.3	18.3	22.4	27.0
Madison, ...	42	43	56	55	50	28	35	33	46	43	31	37	161	96	120	122	32.3	19.3	24.0	24.4
Monroe, ...	68	67	118	81	103	75	118	236	185	97	65	81	302	429	347	216	23.3	33.1	26.8	16.8
Montgomery, .	23	33	43	35	34	21	26	30	15	40	15	18	112	77	70	74	33.6	23.4	21.0	22.0
New-York, ...	897	890	964	831	961	720	1,403	1,347	874	766	570	729	2,756	3,470	2,210	2,516	25.1	31.6	20.1	23.2
Niagara, ...	36	35	43	52	34	35	78	87	77	58	24	44	129	200	159	115	21.3	33.1	26.3	19.3
Oneida, ...	113	95	127	123	138	82	151	158	141	115	109	94	388	391	365	302	26.8	27.0	25.2	21.0
Onondaga, ...	82	84	120	80	98	52	69	102	104	86	71	56	298	223	261	222	29.6	22.2	25.9	22.3
Ontario, ...	30	39	39	32	35	27	23	48	57	42	36	21	106	98	135	90	24.7	22.8	31.4	21.1
Orange, ...	59	75	106	87	88	54	59	70	68	59	55	55	281	183	182	189	33.6	21.9	21.8	22.7
Orleans, ...	13	16	25	30	30	17	24	27	25	28	17	19	85	68	70	48	31.4	25.1	25.8	17.7
Oswego, ...	65	68	81	64	80	55	70	106	98	63	64	45	225	231	225	178	26.1	26.9	25.0	22.0
Otsego, ...	38	39	76	55	39	29	24	37	44	50	30	28	170	90	124	105	34.8	18.4	25.3	21.5
Putnam, ...	18	16	10	19	16	7	14	17	20	20	11	7	45	38	51	41	25.7	21.7	29.1	23.5
Queens, ...	40	36	59	51	65	40	51	106	61	51	50	40	175	197	162	116	26.6	30.3	24.9	18.2
Rensselaer, ...	81	86	126	133	106	74	170	197	123	85	60	89	365	441	268	256	27.4	33.1	20.1	19.4
Richmond, ...	15	19	23	23	21	16	35	35	18	12	13	10	67	86	43	44	27.9	35.9	13.6	22.6
Rockland, ...	13	13	28	24	23	12	16	52	24	15	17	21	75	80	56	47	29.1	31.0	21.6	18.3
St. Lawrence, .	54	52	71	65	77	46	51	87	53	44	42	41	213	184	139	147	31.2	26.9	20.3	21.6
Saratoga, ...	46	54	55	62	57	51	53	53	45	47	40	29	174	157	132	129	29.4	26.5	22.2	21.9
Schenectady, .	15	14	26	27	21	21	40	32	33	26	19	16	74	93	78	45	25.5	32.1	26.9	15.5
Schoharie, ...	19	30	31	31	27	29	26	27	24	26	19	28	89	82	69	77	28.1	25.8	21.8	24.3
Schuyler, ...	17	20	16	19	15	13	10	14	24	12	13	14	50	37	49	51	26.6	19.8	26.2	27.4
Seneca, ...	16	20	26	33	26	18	19	15	25	13	16	22	85	52	54	58	34.1	20.9	21.6	23.4
Steuben, ...	43	50	75	64	58	53	44	36	60	39	43	34	197	133	142	127	32.9	22.2	23.9	21.0
Suffolk, ...	33	39	60	46	46	39	40	44	47	53	38	36	152	123	138	108	29.2	23.6	26.5	20.7
Sullivan, ...	26	23	39	30	30	16	16	19	34	32	13	22	99	51	79	71	33.0	17.0	26.3	23.7
Tioga, ...	19	23	26	32	31	17	9	26	32	33	19	17	89	52	84	59	31.3	18.9	29.5	20.3
Tompkins, ...	22	23	40	38	32	26	22	28	36	23	25	35	110	76	84	80	31.5	21.8	24.0	22.7
Ulster, ...	65	76	108	116	120	68	88	142	113	87	50	45	344	298	250	186	31.9	27.6	23.2	17.3
Warren, ...	21	18	20	13	17	9	18	15	12	17	6	8	50	42	35	47	28.7	24.1	20.1	27.1
Washington, .	33	48	49	72	48	39	48	52	43	38	34	37	169	139	115	118	31.2	25.6	21.2	22.0
Wayne, ...	27	51	52	48	44	21	37	61	70	52	27	32	144	119	149	110	27.5	22.7	26.6	23.2
Westchester, .	70	94	105	94	80	67	94	181	129	77	69	61	279	342	275	225	24.9	30.5	24.4	20.2
Wyoming, ...	26	31	41	27	28	23	22	31	38	33	20	24	96	76	91	81	27.9	22.1	26.4	23.6
Yates, ...	15	14	13	25	26	8	24	15	19	17	12	15	64	47	48	44	31.5	23.1	23.6	21.8
Total, ...	3,332	3,508	4,464	4,011	4,136	2.881	4,674	5,572	4,315	3,495	2,601	2,827	12,611	13,127	10,411	9,667	27.5	27.6	22.7	22.2

DEATHS.

NATIVITIES AND OCCUPATIONS OF THOSE DYING WITHIN THE YEAR ENDING JUNE 1, 1855.

COUNTIES.	NATIVITIES.			OCCUPATIONS.												
	American.	Foreign.	Unknown.	Actors.	Agents.	Agricultural implement m.	Apothecaries and druggists.	Apprentices.	Architects.	Artificial flower makers.	Artists.	Auctioneers.	Axe makers.	Bakers.	Bankers.	Bank officers.
Albany,	483	544	851	1								1	2	2		
Allegany,	153	17	197													
Broome,	128	22	130													
Cattaraugus,	161	18	136													
Cayuga,	267	52	318		1											
Chautauque,	282	52	269		1						1					
Chemung,	123	14	143													
Chenango,	175	12	183											1		
Clinton,	128	63	128				1									
Columbia,	144	34	341													
Cortland,	97	1	129													
Delaware,	156	38	227													
Dutchess,	167	112	453				1									
Erie,	485	760	759											2		
Essex,	146	26	78													
Franklin,	140	16	12				1									
Fulton,	86	14	176													
Genesee,	172	30	112			1										
Greene,	91	23	241													
Hamilton,	7	3	19													
Herkimer,	140	32	224													
Jefferson,	254	92	355											1		
Kings,	1, 341	1, 071	1, 481	1	3	1	7		2		3	1		11		
Lewis,	108	32	107													
Livingston,	105	27	162	1												
Madison,	119	32	355			1										
Monroe,	496	329	567				1									
Montgomery,	108	32	205													
New-York,	4, 362	4, 347	2, 386	3	4	11			1	3	4	1		31		1
Niagara,	142	134	429													
Oneida,	448	308	624				1				2			1		
Onondaga,	327	137	574												1	
Ontario,	164	32	239													
Orange,	204	76	556			1										
Orleans,	85	31	160												1	
Oswego,	354	106	372												1	
Otsego,	200	14	286													
Putnam,	33	9	133												1	
Queens,	198	48	269						1					1		
Rensselaer,	465	324	642		1		2									
Richmond,	118	58	66													
Rockland,	64	87	107											1		
St. Lawrence,	324	136	227													
Saratoga,	140	46	406													
Schenectady,	16	50	227					1								
Schoharie,	87	9	223													
Schuyler,	82	6	100													
Seneca,	137	15	107													
Steuben,	264	66	278											1		
Suffolk,	105	12	407					1								
Sullivan,	102	36	166								1					
Tioga,	128	13	147			2										
Tompkins,	151	11	191													
Ulster,	199	149	772											1		
Warren,	58	3	80													
Washington,	91	41	412		1											
Wayne,	246	45	231											2	1	
Westchester,	170	242	713				1									
Wyoming,	102	44	200			1		1								
Yates,	80	12	114													
Total,	15, 908	10, 145	20, 202	6	11	18	15	3	4	3	11	3	2	55	5	1

COUNTIES.	OCCUPATIONS.															
	Barbers.	Bar keepers.	Basket makers.	Bell hangers & locksmiths.	Blacking and ink makers.	Blacksmiths	Block & pump makers.	Boarding house keepers.	Boat builders.	Boatmen.	Boiler makers.	Book binders.	Book sellers.	Boot and shoe makers.	Bottlers	Box makers.
Albany,		1				6				6			1	14		
Allegany,										1						
Broome,														2		
Cattaraugus,														2		
Cayuga,	1					3				1				3		
Chautauque,						2				2				3		
Chemung,						1								4		
Chenango,		1				2							1	3		
Clinton,														2		
Columbia,										5				3		
Cortland,						1								2		
Delaware,						5								4		
Dutchess,						5				1				5		

COUNTIES.	OCCUPATIONS.															
	Barbers.	Bar keepers.	Basket makers.	Bell hangers and locksmiths.	Blacking and ink makers.	Blacksmiths.	Block and pump makers.	Boarding house keepers.	Boat builders.	Boatmen.	Boiler makers.	Book binders.	Book sellers.	Boot and shoe m.	Bottlers.	Box makers.
Erie,	3					6			1	1				24		
Essex,						3								1		
Franklin,						1								1		
Fulton,														2		
Genesee,						1	1			1				2		
Greene,	1					1				5				2		
Hamilton,																
Herkimer,						3				2				1		
Jefferson,	1	1	1			3								10		
Kings,			1			12				5		4	1	16		
Lewis,						1								2		
Livingston,						4								6		
Madison,						4				1				3		
Monroe,	1	1		1		6			1	5	1	2		21		
Montgomery,						3						1		1		
New-York,	10	3	3	7	1	34	1	1		14	4	11	7	82	1	1
Niagara,		1				4			1		1			2		
Oneida,	1					6			1		3			8		
Onondaga,			1			4			2		2	1		4		
Ontario,						1							1	2		
Orange,						5		1			4			4		
Orleans,						4	1				2			5		
Oswego,						7								2		
Otsego,						2								3		
Putnam,		1				2					3			2		
Queens,						1				1	1			4		
Rensselaer,						6		1			1			7		
Richmond,														3		
Rockland,			1			3				5				4		
St. Lawrence,						4				1				8		
Saratoga,			1			6				2				1		
Schenectady,	1					1				2				3		
Schoharie,						2								2		
Schuyler,														2		
Seneca,			1													
Steuben,						1				1				2		
Suffolk,	1					4	1			6				3		
Sullivan,						1								1		
Tioga,						1			1							
Tompkins,						2			1	2				3		
Ulster,						12			3	17				4		
Warren,														2		
Washington,						1				2				4		
Wayne,										1				14		
Westchester,						4		1		3						
Wyoming,						1										
Yates,						2				1				2		
Total,	20	9	9	8	1	194	4	4	11	94	22	19	11	322	1	1

COUNTIES.	OCCUPATIONS.															
	Brass workers.	Brewers and distillers.	Brick makers.	Britannia ware m.	Brokers.	Brush makers.	Builders.	Butchers.	Cabinet makers.	Cadets.	Carpenters.	Carpet weavers.	Carriers.	Carters.	Carvers and guilders.	Caulkers.
Albany,	1	3	2		2			4	4		15					
Allegany,									1		1					
Broome,								1			3					
Cattaraugus,									1		5					
Cayuga,									2		3					
Chautauque,									2		5					
Chemung,									1		2					
Chenango,									1		1					
Clinton,								1	1		2					
Columbia,									2		7					
Cortland,									1		2					
Delaware,											3					
Dutchess,			1					1	1		8					
Erie,		1	3			1	1	2	3		19	1				
Essex,								1			1					
Franklin,											1					
Fulton,											4					
Genesee,									1							
Greene,		1	4								1					
Hamilton,																
Herkimer,								1	1		8					
Jefferson,								2			16					
Kings,	2			1	3	1	1	17	5		28	1				2
Lewis,									1		5					
Livingston,								1			4					
Madison,									1		4					

COUNTIES	OCCUPATIONS.															
	Brass workers.	Brewers and distillers.	Brick makers.	Britannia ware m.	Brokers.	Brush makers.	Builders.	Butchers.	Cabinet m.	Cadets.	Carpenters.	Carpet weavers.	Carriers.	Carters.	Carvers and guilders.	Caulkers.
Monroe,		1					1		6		12					
Montgomery,											1					
New-York,	6	4	3		5	3	3	24	21		67			58	5	7
Niagara,								1			1				1	
Oneida,								4	3		18			1		
Onondaga,								2	1		7				1	
Ontario,											3			1		
Orange,			2					1	2	1	9		1			
Orleans,											3					
Oswego,								1	1		9					
Otsego,								1			3					
Putnam,											3					
Queens,								1			7			1		
Rensselaer,						6		2	2		9	1				
Richmond,					1						6					
Rockland,			1						1		2					
St. Lawrence,								1	1		9					
Saratoga,											5			1		
Schenectady,								3	2		2					
Schoharie,								1	2		2					
Schuyler,											1					
Seneca,		1									1					
Steuben,									1		7					
Suffolk,									1		8					
Sullivan,											6					
Tioga,											4					
Tompkins,		1						1	1		6					
Ulster,									1		16					
Warren,								1								
Washington,											10					
Wayne,		1	1						2		11					
Westchester,									3		5	2		3	1	
Wyoming,											4					
Yates,								1			1					
Total,	9	13	17	1	11	11	6	76	80	1	406	5	1	65	8	9

COUNTIES.	OCCUPATIONS.															
	Chandlers.	Charcoal burners.	Chemists.	Civil engineers.	Civil officers.	Cl'ks and accountants.	Clergymen.	Clothiers.	Coach and wagon makers	Collectors.	Comb makers.	Confectioners.	Contractors.	Cooks.	Coopers.	Coppersmiths.
Albany,					2	14	2	2			1	1	1	2	3	
Allegany,							1									1
Broome,						1						1			1	
Cattaraugus,							1								2	
Cayuga,	1			2		2			2			1			1	2
Chautauque,						1	3		1						2	
Chemung,							1		1							
Chenango,							1		1						1	
Clinton,									1							
Columbia,						1	1	1	1						2	
Cortland,									2							
Delaware,						2										
Dutchess,					1	1	4		6		1				4	
Erie,	1			1	2	7	1		2			1			7	1
Essex,		1					1									
Franklin,							1									
Fulton,						2										
Genesee,							1								1	
Greene,							3								3	
Hamilton,																
Herkimer,						1										
Jefferson,						5	2						1		1	
Kings,	1		1	2	5	40	2	1	2				2		6	1
Lewis,									1						1	
Livingston,					1		2		1						2	
Madison,						2	2		1							1
Monroe,						6			1			1		3	4	
Montgomery,						1										
New-York,			1	1	14	90	4	5	6	1		4	6	8	18	4
Niagara,					1	2										
Oneida,			1	1	1	7	3		4						1	1
Onondaga,						2	1		4						3	
Ontario,					1	1									1	
Orange,	1	1				3	2		1					1	1	1
Orleans,						1			1						1	
Oswego,						4	3		1						6	
Otsego,															1	
Putnam,							1		1							

COUNTIES.	OCCUPATIONS															
	Chandlers	Charcoal burners	Chemists	Civil engineers.	Civil officers.	Cl'ks and accountants.	Clergymen.	Clothiers.	Coach and wagon makers.	Collectors.	Comb m.	Confectioners.	Contractors.	Cooks.	Coopers.	Coppersmiths.
Queens,						3	2		2		1		1			
Rensselaer,						2	2	1	3			1	1		6	
Richmond,						4										
Rockland,																
St. Lawrence,						3									1	
Saratoga,						8	1	1	3							
Schenectady,							1		1							1
Schoharie,								1	1						2	
Schuyler,																
Seneca,							1								1	
Steuben,						1	1	1								
Suffolk,						1									1	
Sullivan,						1										
Tioga,				1					1							
Tompkins,					1	2	1		3							
Ulster,		1			1	3									2	
Warren,																
Washington,							1	2							2	
Wayne,						1	2	2	1						2	
Westchester,					2	7	1								6	
Wyoming,						1	2									
Yates,							2								3	
Total,	4	3	3	8	32	233	60	17	56	1	3	10	12	14	99	13

COUNTIES.	OCCUPATIONS.															
	Cotton manufacturers.	Cutlers.	Dairy and milkmen.	Dealers.	Dentists.	Dress makers.	Drivers.	Drovers.	Dyers and bleachers.	Editors.	Engineers.	Engravers.	Embroiderers.	Express men.	Factory hands.	Farmers.
Albany,						12					2					76
Allegany,						1										58
Broome,						4										56
Cattaraugus,																59
Cayuga,						5									1	95
Chautauque,																101
Chemung,																20
Chenango,							1							1		86
Clinton,															1	40
Columbia,						1						1			3	60
Cortland,																49
Delaware,						1										86
Dutchess,						2					1				2	65
Erie,		1				7	1		2		2				1	110
Essex,						2										39
Franklin,						1										32
Fulton,						1										31
Genesee,																69
Greene,						2		1								67
Hamilton,															1	3
Herkimer,								1							1	88
Jefferson,						1					1				1	100
Kings,				3	1	13	3			1	7	1				18
Lewis,																43
Livingston,				1		2										63
Madison,				1		4										89
Monroe,				1		9	1								3	117
Montgomery,						1										49
New-York,		2	3	9	2	85	16	3	1	1	12	1		1		20
Niagara,						1	1				2					75
Oneida,						1					2				10	145
Onondaga,																105
Ontario,					1	4		1								82
Orange,						2			1		1					102
Orleans,						2										44
Oswego,						6					1					108
Otsego,	1					1										105
Putnam,						1										23
Queens,						1						1				60
Rensselaer,						7			2		1				1	87
Richmond,									1						1	3
Rockland,											1					20
St. Lawrence,					1	3					1					125
Saratoga,													1			94
Schenectady,				1							1					25
Schoharie,						1										57
Schuyler,											1					47
Seneca,						1										42
Steuben,																112
Suffolk,						3					1					75
Sullivan,						1										38

COUNTIES.	OCCUPATIONS.															
	Cotton manufacturers.	Cutlers.	Dairy and milkmen.	Dealers.	Dentists.	Dress makers.	Drivers.	Drovers.	Dyers and bleachers.	Editors.	Engineers.	Engravers.	Embroiderers.	Express men.	Factory hands.	Farmers.
Tioga,						3										35
Tompkins,						2										61
Ulster,						4										74
Warren,																16
Washington,						2	1									62
Wayne,					1	1										75
Westchester,			1			4	1									78
Wyoming,						1										81
Yates,						1					1					31
Total,	1	3	4	16	6	207	25	6	7	2	38	4	1	2	26	3, 876

COUNTIES.	OCCUPATIONS.															
	Farriers.	Ferrymen.	File cutters.	Firemen.	Fishermen.	Forwarders.	Fruit dealers.	Furriers.	Furnacemen.	Gardeners.	Gate keepers.	Glass workers.	Glass stainers.	Glovers.	Gold beaters.	Gold and silversmiths.
Albany,	1									3						1
Allegany,																
Broome,																
Cattaraugus,																
Cayuga,										1						
Chautauque,																
Chemung,																
Chenango,																
Clinton,																
Columbia,										1						
Cortland,																
Delaware,																
Dutchess,										1						
Erie,	1									5						
Essex,																
Franklin,																1
Fulton,																
Genesee,																
Greene,										1						1
Hamilton,																
Herkimer,																
Jefferson,																
Kings,	2			1				1		3	1	2	1			1
Lewis,																
Livingston,																
Madison,																
Monroe,					1	1				1						
Montgomery,																
New-York,				6	1		2			12		2	1		12	7
Niagara,					1				1	1						
Oneida,				1							1			1		3
Onondaga,									1	2						
Ontario,																
Orange,										2						1
Orleans,									1							
Oswego,		1														
Otsego,																1
Putnam,																
Queens,																1
Rensselaer,		1			1				1							
Richmond,																
Rockland,			1													
St. Lawrence,										1						
Saratoga,										1						
Schenectady,								1								
Schoharie,																
Schuyler,																
Seneca,																
Steuben,																
Suffolk,																
Sullivan,																
Tioga,																
Tompkins,																
Ulster,																
Warren,					1											
Washington,																
Wayne,																
Westchester,					2				1	1						1
Wyoming,												1				
Yates,																
Total,	4	2	1	8	7	1	2	2	5	36	2	5	2	1	12	18

COUNTIES.	OCCUPATIONS.															
	Grocers.	Gunsmiths.	Hardware dealers	Hat and cap m	Hotel keepers.	House keepers.	Hunters.	Ice dealers.	Iron dealers.	Iron workers.	Insurance officers.	Inspectors.	Japanners.	Jewelers.	Junk shop keepers	Keepers of jails and prisons.
Albany,	6			3	2	11		1		2						
Allegany,				1		6										
Broome,				1		1										
Cattaraugus,						17										
Cayuga,	1			1	1	1										1
Chautauque,				1		23										
Chemung,																
Chenango,	1				1	12										
Clinton,					1	2				1						
Columbia,						8					1					
Cortland,						6										
Delaware,						9										
Dutchess,				3	1	20										
Erie,	6				1	8						1				
Essex,						8										
Franklin,					1	1	1			3						
Fulton,						1										
Genesee,						7										
Greene,				1		6										
Hamilton,						2										
Herkimer,			1		1											
Jefferson,				1	2	21										
Kings,	14	1		7	4	4					1	2		3		
Lewis,				1		3										
Livingston,		1			1	22										
Madison,					1	4										
Monroe,	2			1	3	21				1				1		
Montgomery,						9										
New-York,	11			25	8	58		1	1	1	1	3	2	10	5	2
Niagara,					4	16										
Oneida,	2			3	2	15										
Onondaga,	2				2	19										
Ontario,						6										
Orange,	1			2	6	17								1		
Orleans,	1					1										
Oswego,						43										
Otsego,					2	17										
Putnam,																
Queens,	1															
Rensselaer,	7			3	1	24				3						
Richmond,				1												
Rockland,						34										
St. Lawrence,	1			1	1	10										
Saratoga,	1				2	8										
Schenectady,	1					6										
Schoharie,	1				1	13										
Schuyler,				1		3										
Seneca,						10										
Steuben,				1		2										
Suffolk,					2											
Sullivan,																
Tioga,						10										
Tompkins,					19											
Ulster,	1				2	6				3						
Warren,						3										
Washington,				1	3	14				1						
Wayne,					1	21										
Westchester,	1			6		7				1			1			1
Wyoming,						19										
Yates,																
Total,	61	2	1	65	76	615	1	2	1	16	3	6	3	15	5	4

COUNTIES.	OCCUPATIONS.																
	Laborers.	Lamp makers.	Laundresses.	Lawyers.	Livery stable keepers	Lumbermen.	Machinists.	Mail agents and carriers.	Manufacturers.	Marble dealers.	Market men and women.	Masons.	Mast and spar m.	Mechanics.	Merchants.	Millers.	Milliners
Albany,	192			3	1	2						6			11		2
Allegany,	6			1											1		
Broome,	3			1								2			1		1
Cattaraugus,	7					1									1	1	1
Cayuga,	15			4			2					1		2	4		1
Chautauque,	9											1			5		1
Chemung,	4			1		1						1			1	2	
Chenango,							1	1	1			2			2	1	2
Clinton,	19				1										1		
Columbia,	12			1			1					2		2	3	1	
Cortland,	1			1								1					1
Delaware,	4			1											2	1	1
Dutchess,	43			2			1					1			4		

COUNTIES.	OCCUPATIONS.																
	Laborers.	Lamp makers.	Laundresses.	Lawyers.	Livery stable keepers.	Lumbermen.	Machinists.	Mail agents and carriers.	Manufacturers.	Marble dealers	Market men and women.	Masons.	Mast and spar m.	Mechanics.	Merchants.	Millers.	Milliners.
Erie,	100			5		1						13		3	10	5	1
Essex,	5											1		1	1		
Franklin,	1														1		2
Fulton,	5													1		1	4
Genesee,	6											1		1	1	1	
Greene,	2			2								2		1	8		
Hamilton,									1								
Herkimer,	3													2	1	1	1
Jefferson,	8			3		1	1					1			1	1	2
Kings,	144	1		6		1	2				4	23		3	25		1
Lewis,	6			1								1			1		
Livingston,	6					1	2							1	1		
Madison,	6			1			1					3		2	1	1	1
Monroe,	61			1			7					13		4	1	6	2
Montgomery,	34			1												1	
New-York,	768		3	6	1	2	17		3	1		54	2	9	42	6	10
Niagara,	29						2					6		3	4		1
Oneida,	51			1		1	1		1			7		2	12	3	1
Onondaga,	23			4	1		1					2		1	5	3	
Ontario,	8			2								1		1	5	1	2
Orange,	38			1		1						2				3	
Orleans,	7														4	1	1
Oswego,	25											4		2	9	3	
Otsego,	1						1					2		3	3	1	
Putnam,	7		1													3	
Queens,	34						1		1			2		1	4		
Rensselaer,	101		2	3		1	6		1			2		2	5		
Richmond,	5														2		
Rockland,	35						3								3		
St. Lawrence,	15			1								2			2		1
Saratoga,	4						1					2		3	2	1	1
Schenectady,	6			1			7									1	
Schoharie,	2											1			1		1
Schuyler,															1		1
Seneca,	6															2	
Steuben,	3			1		4	2								2	1	1
Suffolk,	7														2		
Sullivan,	16					5											
Tioga,	3			1		1	1							1	1		1
Tompkins,	3											2					1
Ulster,	50			4								3		2	5	1	
Warren,	11																1
Washington,												1		1	4	2	2
Wayne,	12											2		1	1	1	
Westchester,	44			1								5			5	1	1
Wyoming,	7			2			1					1			1	2	1
Yates,	3																
Total,	2,026	1	6	63	4	23	62	1	8	1	4	176	2	55	213	59	51

COUNTIES.	OCCUPATIONS.																
	Millwrights.	Miners.	Mineral water manufacturers.	Morocco dressers.	Moulders.	Musicians.	Music teachers.	Musical instrument m.	Mustard manufacturers.	Nail makers.	News boys.	Nurserymen.	Nurses.	Oil cloth manufacturers.	Oil makers and dealers.	Opticians.	Ostlers.
Albany,	1				3	1	2	3							1		3
Allegany,																	
Broome,	2																
Cattaraugus,																	
Cayuga,											1	1					
Chautauque,	3																
Chemung,																	
Chenango,	1																2
Clinton,																	
Columbia,	1	1															
Cortland,																	
Delaware,																	
Dutchess,																	
Erie,					1	2						2					1
Essex,		1															
Franklin,																	
Fulton,	1																
Genesee,																	
Greene,					1												
Hamilton,																	
Herkimer,																	
Jefferson,																	
Kings,				1		1	1		1					1			1
Lewis,	1																
Livingston,																	
Madison,																	

COUNTIES.	OCCUPATION.																
	Millwrights.	Miners.	Mineral water manufacturers	Morocco dressers.	Moulders.	Musicians.	Music teachers.	Musical instrument makers.	Mustard manufacturers.	Nail makers.	News boys.	Nurserymen.	Nurses.	Oil cloth manufacturers.	Oil makers and dealers.	Opticians	Ostlers.
Monroe,	1				1	1	1										
Montgomery,					1												
New-York,	1	1	2	1	5	8	1	1	1	1			5				4
Niagara,																	
Oneida,																	
Onondaga,																	
Ontario,																	
Orange,					2											1	
Orleans,																	
Oswego,												1					
Otsego,																	
Putnam,																	
Queens,																	
Rensselaer,	3				2												
Richmond,																	
Rockland,																	
St. Lawrence,	2	1			1												
Saratoga,																	
Schenectady,																	
Schoharie,																	
Schuyler,	1																
Seneca,																	
Steuben,																	
Suffolk,																	
Sullivan,																	
Tioga,		1															
Tompkins,	1	1															
Ulster,	2																
Warren,																	
Washington,		1															
Wayne,					1	1											
Westchester,													1				
Wyoming,																	
Yates,																	
Total,	21	7	2	2	18	14	5	4	2	1	1	4	6	1	1	1	11

COUNTIES.	OCCUPATIONS.																
	Overseers.	Oystermen.	Painters	Paper dealers.	Paper hangers.	Paper makers.	Paper stainers	Pattern makers.	Pavers.	Pedlers.	Photographers.	Physicians.	Piano manufacturers.	Pilots.	Plumbers.	Pocket book m.	Polishers.
Albany,			8					2	1	4		1			2		
Allegany,			1														
Broome,			1									3					
Cattaraugus,																	
Cayuga,			1			1					1	2					
Chautauque,												4					
Chemung,																	
Chenango,												1					
Clinton,						1											
Columbia,			3									1					
Cortland,												1					
Delaware,																	
Dutchess,			3									1					
Erie,			5									2					3
Essex,																	
Franklin,												2					
Fulton,												4					
Genesee,	1		1														
Greene,																	
Hamilton,																	
Herkimer,																	
Jefferson,						2						2					
Kings,		1	13						3	1				2			
Lewis,												5					
Livingston,																	
Madison,			1			1				1	1						
Monroe,			2			1						6					
Montgomery,			1			1						1					
New-York,		5	47	2	1		1	2	2	22	1	12	9	1	4	2	1
Niagara,			1			1				1		3					
Oneida,			4							1		6					
Onondaga,			3									4					
Ontario,																	
Orange,												1					
Orleans,																	
Oswego,			1									1					
Otsego,												2					
Putnam,																	
Queens,			2			1				1							

COUNTIES	OCCUPATIONS.																
	Overseers.	Oystermen.	Painters.	Paper dealers.	Paper hangers.	Paper makers.	Paper stainers.	Pattern makers.	Pavers.	Pedlers.	Photographers.	Physicians.	Piano manufacturers.	Pilots.	Plumbers.	Pocket book m.	Polishers.
Rensselaer,			6					2		2		5					
Richmond,																	
Rockland,																	
St. Lawrence,										1	1	3					
Saratoga,												1					
Schenectady,			1														
Schoharie,												2					
Schuyler,																	
Seneca,			1								1						
Steuben,			1									3					
Suffolk,																	
Sullivan,																	
Tioga,			1							2	2	1					
Tompkins,			2			1						2					
Ulster,												2					
Warren,																	
Washington,			2									5					
Wayne,												2					
Westchester,			6							2		1			1		
Wyoming,										1							
Yates,																	
Total,	1	6	118	2	1	10	1	6	6	39	7	92	9	3	7	2	4

COUNTIES.	OCCUPATIONS.																
	Porters	Post masters.	Pot and pearlash manufacturers	Porters.	Powder manufacturers.	Printers.	Produce dealers.	Professors.	Pubishers.	Quarrymen.	Rag pickers.	Railroad employees.	Reed makers.	Restaurant keepers.	Riggers.	Rope and cord m.	Saddlers and harness makers.
Albany,						1		1									
Allegany,																	2
Broome,						1											
Cattaraugus,																	
Cayuga,						1											2
Chautauque,						3	1					3					2
Chemung,						1						2					1
Chenango,						1											1
Clinton,						1						2					
Columbia,																	
Cortland,							1										2
Delaware,																	
Dutchess,		1															
Erie,				1		2						1				1	
Essex,																	
Franklin,												1					
Fulton,																	
Genesee,																	
Greene,												1					
Hamilton,																	
Herkimer,						1											
Jefferson,						1											
Kings,	8					9		1							3	5	
Lewis,																	
Livingston,																	1
Madison,																	
Monroe,					5							8	1				
Montgomery,																	
New-York,	19					22	3	1	5		1	8		1	6	1	10
Niagara,						1						1		1			1
Oneida,			1	2								1					3
Onondaga,	1			1			1					3					1
Ontario,						1						1					
Orange,												2					1
Orleans,										1							
Oswego,																	
Otsego,																	1
Putnam,																	
Queens,												2					
Rensselaer,					2	2					1	5					3
Richmond,																	
Rockland,																	
St. Lawrence,																	
Saratoga,												1					
Schenectady,												1					
Schoharie,	1																1
Schuyler,																	
Seneca,																	
Steuben,												1					1
Suffolk,												1					
Sullivan,																	
Tioga,																	

COUNTIES	OCCUPATIONS.																
	Porters.	Post masters.	Pot and pearlash manufacturers.	Potters.	Powder manufacturers.	Printers.	Produce dealers.	Professors.	Publishers.	Quarrymen.	Rag pickers.	Railroad employees.	Reed makers.	Restaurant keepers.	Riggers.	Rope and cord m.	Saddlers and harness makers.
Tompkins,												1					
Ulster,										7							
Warren,																	
Washington,																	
Wayne,																	
Westchester,										1		1					
Wyoming,																	
Yates,																	
Total,	29	1	1	4	7	48	6	3	5	9	2	47	1	2	9	7	33

COUNTIES.	OCCUPATIONS.																
	Sail makers.	Sailors.	Salesmen.	Saloon keepers.	Salt makers.	Sash and blind m.	Sawyer.	Sculptor.	Servants.	Sextons.	Shingle makers.	Ship carpenters.	Shirt and collar makers.	Soldiers.	Spinners.	Stage proprietors.	Stereotypists.
Albany,									27	1		2					1
Allegany,																	
Broome,				1					8			1					
Cattaraugus,							1				1						
Cayuga,		2							3						2		
Chautauque,		2							2			1					
Chemung,		2					1		1								
Chenango,		1															
Clinton,		3							11			1		1			
Columbia,																	
Cortland,																	
Delaware,		1										3					
Dutchess,		1							4								
Erie,		9					1		70								
Essex,																	
Franklin,																	
Fulton,							1		9								
Genesee,																	
Greene,									12							1	
Hamilton,																	
Herkimer,		1							4								
Jefferson,		11				2			1								
Kings,		36	1	2			3		4			6	1				1
Lewis,																	
Livingston,																	
Madison,						1			7								
Monroe,		3							6			1					
Montgomery,									1								
New-York,	4	49	1	1		2	4	1	287			19			1		
Niagara,		1					1		1	1		1					
Oneida,							1		7			1			1		
Onondaga,					1				3			1					
Ontario,		1						1	1								
Orange,						1			7			1					
Orleans,		1							1								
Oswego,		9					1										
Otsego,							1		7								
Putnam,																	
Queens,		2							2								
Rensselaer,		2		1					8			1					
Richmond,							3										
Rockland,				1			1		1			1					
St. Lawrence,									1			1					
Saratoga,																	
Schenectady,							1										
Schoharie,									9								
Schuyler,							1										
Seneca,															1		
Steuben,		1															
Suffolk,	1	26							1			4				1	
Sullivan,									2								
Tioga,						1			2								
Tompkins,																	
Ulster,									10			1					
Warren,																	
Washington,	1						2		4								
Wayne,																	
Westchester,	2								6			1					
Wyoming,									1								
Yates,																	
Total,	8	104	2	6	1	7	23	2	581	2	1	47	1	1	5	2	2

COUNTIES.	OCCUPATIONS.																
	Stevedores.	Stewards.	Stone cutters.	Straw workers.	Students.	Surgical instrument makers.	Surveyors.	Tailors.	Tanners.	Teachers.	Teamsters.	Telegraph operators.	Tinsmiths	Tobacconists.	Tool makers.	Trimmers.	Turners.
Albany,			3		5			11	4	3	6		1	4			1
Allegany,								5	2								
Broome,					1			1			1						
Cattaraugus,					2		1			5			1				
Cayuga,					1			7	2	6					1		
Chautauque,					1			1		1			1				
Chemung,								4	1	1		1					
Chenango,			1					3		5							
Clinton,								2		1							
Columbia,					2			2		3	1		1				
Cortland,					2			2		1	1						
Delaware,					4				2	1							
Dutchess,					2			3		4	1		2	2			
Erie,			4		1		1	15	1	3							
Essex,									1	3							
Franklin,																	
Fulton,																	
Genesee,								2		2							
Greene,					1			3	1								
Hamilton,			1		1												
Herkimer,								3	1	1							
Jefferson,								7	2	3							
Kings,		2	11		2		2	28	1	3			4	2			
Lewis,								3									
Livingston,								2		1							1
Madison,					1			6		2			2				
Monroe,			4		3			10	2	3	1		1	3			2
Montgomery,			1					1		1							
New-York,	3	1	25	3	6	1		81	2	13	1		7	15		1	5
Niagara,			3					5		2							
Oneida,			3					9		4	1						
Onondaga,			1					8	1	3	1		1				
Ontario,					1			1	1	2							
Orange,					2			4		1	1						
Orleans,										2							
Oswego,					2			3		4	2		2				
Otsego,								6		1							
Putnam,											1						
Queens,								2	1								1
Rensselaer,			2		1			5	1	1	2		1	1			1
Richmond,		1						2									
Rockland,										2							
St. Lawrence,					1			7		3							2
Saratoga,					1					6			1	1			
Schenectady,								2									
Schoharie,								1		1							
Schuyler,										1							
Seneca,								1	1								
Steuben,			1					3		4							
Suffolk,					2			3		4							
Sullivan,								1		2							
Tioga,								4									
Tompkins,					1			3		3							
Ulster,			2		2			10		5			2				
Warren,																	
Washington,					1			2		2						1	
Wayne,					1			2		2			1				
Westchester,			4					10			1		2	2	2		
Wyoming,								3									
Yates,			1					3		1							
Total,	3	4	67	3	50	1	4	302	27	122	21	1	30	30	3	2	13

COUNTIES.	OCCUPATIONS.																
	Type founders	Umbrella manufacturers.	Undertakers	Upholsterers.	Varnish makers.	Watchmen.	Watch makers.	Weavers.	Whalebo'e workers.	Wheelwrights.	Whip makers.	White-washers.	Wire workers.	Wine and liquor dealers	Wool carders.	Wool dealers.	Woolen & worsted workers.
Albany,				2			1	1	1								
Allegany,																	
Broome,								1									
Cattaraugus,								1									
Cayuga,				1				5									
Chautauque,																	
Chemung,																	
Chenango,																	
Clinton,								1		1							
Columbia,								1									
Cortland,																	
Delaware,								1									
Dutchess,								3									

COUNTIES.	OCCUPATIONS																
	Type founders.	Umbrella manufacturers.	Undertakers.	Upholsterers.	Varnish makers.	Watchmen.	Watch makers.	Weavers.	Whalebo'e workers.	Wheelwrights.	Whip makers.	White-washers.	Wire workers.	Wine and liquor dealers.	Wool carders.	Wool dealers.	Woolen & worsted workers.
Erie,								6					1				
Essex,								2									
Franklin,																	
Fulton,																	
Genesee,								1									1
Greene,																	
Hamilton,																	
Herkimer,								1									
Jefferson,																	
Kings,	1					1	2					1		5			
Lewis,																	
Livingston,																	
Madison,								1									
Monroe,								1					1				
Montgomery,								1									
New-York,	1	1	1	4	2	1	2	13		3			2	9		1	
Niagara,																	
Oneida,								1		1							
Onondaga,		1						1		4							
Ontario,																	
Orange,								1									
Orleans,																	
Oswego,								1			1						
Otsego,																	
Putnam,										1							
Queens,								1									
Rensselaer,						1		3							1		
Richmond,																	
Rockland,								1									
St. Lawrence,				1													
Saratoga,										2							
Schenectady,							1	1									
Schoharie,																	
Schuyler,																	
Seneca,										2							
Steuben,																	
Suffolk,								1						1			
Sullivan,										1							
Tioga,								1									
Tompkins,																	
Ulster,								4									
Warren,																	
Washington,																	
Wayne,																	
Westchester,								6		1							
Wyoming,																	
Yates,																	
Total,	2	2	1	8	2	3	6	62	1	16	1	1	4	15	1	1	1

CAUSES OF DEATHS.

COUNTIES.	Cholera.	Cholera infantum.	Cholera morbus.	Croup.	Diarrhœa	Dysentery.	Epidemic.	Erysipelas.	Fever.	Bilious fever.	Intermittent fever	Remittent fever.	Typhus fever.	Yellow fever.	Hooping cough.	Hydrophobia.	Influenza.
	ZYMOTIC DISEASES.																
Albany,	242	40	10	84	82	43		13	11	11	8	4	89	1	21		1
Allegany,	2		2	14	11	18		3	4	2	1		12		3		
Broome,	2	1		16	4	6		3	1	4		1	15	1	3		
Cattaraugus,	1	1		4	2	12		4	2	1			20		6		
Cayuga,	11	4	2	20	15	15		6	6	2	3		27		3		
Chautauque,	11	3	2	18	12	24		6	3		2		33		4		
Chemung,	1	1	1	8	3	6		6	4	8	2		21		6		
Chenango,		1	2	4	1	26		3	12	2			5		1		1
Clinton,	3	3		6	7			4	9	1			5		9		
Columbia,	9	2	1	15	2	5		5	3	3			8		9		1
Cortland,	1	1	1	7	1	13		3		1			8		2		
Delaware,		1	1	13	10	23		3	6	6			20				
Dutchess,	103	5	3	15	3	17		3	11	12	2	1	30		16		
Erie,	266	31	11	40	74	61		11	20	5	8		91	1	34	2	2
Essex,	1	2	2	2	5	9		2	2		1		5		1		
Franklin,	4			6	3	5		3	4		1		4				
Fulton,	3	2		7	2	16		2	2	2			4		5		
Genesee,	6	1	2	6	5	13		5	2	2			16		2		1
Greene,	54		2	8	4	4			2	2			18	1	6		
Hamilton,			1		2			1	1								1
Herkimer,	5	3		15	13	14		6	5	5			12				2
Jefferson,	9	1	4	22	5	5		11	11	5			17		1		
Kings,	402	119	15	134	100	147		14	26	29	22	4	58	9	67	2	
Lewis,				16	3	6		3	5	3			16				
Livingston,	4	1	1	11	6	10		5	2				14		5		1
Madison,	2	3	2	9	7	6		3	7	1			16	1	4		2
Monroe,	181	14	3	36	58	88		16	10	12	5		49		16		
Montgomery,	7		2	8	17	4		1	5	4			11		4		2
New-York,	783	236	37	383	513	413		58	44	18	21	15	296	11	161	2	1
Niagara,	156	4	5	27	17	39		5	8	2	6		36		6		
Oneida,	35	31	5	40	46	48		14	15	16	5		50		18		2
Onondaga,	32	7	3	33	35	25		5	10	5	4		36		17		1
Ontario,	1	2		5	6	36	4	5	1	1			16		4		
Orange,	8	7		28	13	45		3	3	21	1		28		17		1
Orleans,	11	4	4	1	2	5		6	5	2	2		3		4		
Oswego,	47	3	1	15	32	42	1	9	10	12	2	2	25		28		3
Otsego,	2	1	4	15	9	15		4	4	4			16		1		1
Putnam,	1	1	1	2		25		1					1				
Queens,	49	17		31	3	22		2	7	10	3		16		8		1
Rensselaer,	208	15	8	44	26	38		8	9	6	2	1	43		30		1
Richmond,	26	4		1	6	7		1		1	1		4		5		
Rockland,	50	2	1	4		16		1	3	1	2		7		12		
St. Lawrence,	51	3	3	25	15	13		6	11	2			11		1		
Saratoga,	6	5	3	18	13	14		5	6	5	4	1	17	1	2		
Schenectady,	38			6	14	5		1	2	1	1	1	4		4		
Schoharie,	3		3	14	3	7		2	4	3			6		3		
Schuyler,	1			5	2	16		3	10	2	1		18		1		
Seneca,	6	3	1	3	6	16		4	2				11		1		
Steuben,	7	2	2	16	21	10		6	3	5			37		10		
Suffolk,	11	7	3	9	3	20		4	1	17		1	13	1	19		
Sullivan,	5	4	3	3	3	37		1	3	9	2		13		4		
Tioga,	2	1		2	6	24			3	2	1		22		3		1
Tompkins,	3	2	1	3	4	12				2			10		3		
Ulster,	113	7	7	39	14	45		3	21	18			29	1	30		
Warren,	3		2	4		1		1	1				1				
Washington,	9	1	3	14	6	13			8	4		2	13		2		
Wayne,	15	3	1	15	17	70		8	7	1	4		21		9		
Westchester,	108	15	7	26	9	117		6	12	4	7	8	18	3	13		
Wyoming,	8	5		7	8	30		3	8	3			22		1		
Yates,	1	3		2	1	18		3	1				12		1		1
Total,	3, 129	635	178	1, 384	1, 310	1, 840	5	323	398	300	124	41	1, 479	31	646	6	27

COUNTIES.	Measles.	Mumps.	Purulent infection.	Scald head.	Scarlet fever.	Small pox.	Syphilis.	Thrush.	Abscess.	Atrophy.	Boils.	Cancer	Debility	Dropsy	Fistula	Gangrene.
	ZYMOTIC DISEASES.								DISEASES OF UNCERTAIN OR VARIABLE SEAT.							
Albany,	31				88	11		2	2	1		14	8	46		1
Allegany,	4				13	1			1			4	1	16		
Broome,					6				1			3		6		
Cattaraugus,	2				3	1			1			4	1	14		
Cayuga,	1				60	1			1			8		18	1	1
Chautauque,					23	4			1			9	5	24		
Chemung,	1				11	1						2	1	6		
Chenango,					6	1			2			8	2	16		
Clinton,	2				2				1			3		9		
Columbia,	5				16	1						2	5	29		
Cortland,					11							3		11		
Delaware,					14	2			1			5	2	11		
Dutchess,	1				24	1		3				4	3	22		

COUNTIES.	ZYMOTIC DISEASES.								DISEASES OF UNCERTAIN OR VARIABLE SEAT.							
	Measles.	Mumps.	Purulent infection	Scald head.	Scarlet fever.	Small pox.	Syphilis.	Thrush.	Abscess.	Atrophy.	Boils.	Cancer.	Debility.	Dropsy.	Fistula.	Gangrene.
Erie,	15				57	4	1		2		3	11	23	42		2
Essex,					6							3	2	10		
Franklin,						8						1		2		
Fulton,					12							2		11		
Genesee,	1				3	1	1					8		12		
Greene,	3				2							2		16		1
Hamilton,														2		
Herkimer,					5	1						9	1	13		
Jefferson,	7				18	1			1			14	1	25		
Kings,	67				191	22		4	4			17	25	63		
Lewis,		1			18							2		3		
Livingston,		1			5				2			5	1	6		
Madison,					10	6			4			9	1	17		
Monroe,	9				21	5						4	5	22		
Montgomery,	1				7				1			2	3	16		1
New-York,	250	3	3		467	83	21	15	27	155	1	57	179	182	2	28
Niagara,					15	5		3	1			8	1	13		2
Oneida,	20			1	38	12			1			14	4	40		1
Onondaga,	6				88	14		1	2			17	3	31		
Ontario,					11		1		1			6	7	10		1
Orange,	6	1			33	3		4				10	8	19		
Orleans,	4				8			1	2			7	2	4		
Oswego,	4				34	5			1			3	4	17		2
Otsego,				1	10				1	2		8		25		1
Putnam,	1				7							2		5		
Queens,	4				28		1	2				7	3	18		
Rensselaer,	5				35	11		3	1			9	9	27		1
Richmond,					1	2							2	27		
Rockland,	1				1	1								5		
Lawrence,	1				28	3			1			9	1	12		1
Saratoga,	4				38	1		1				4		15		1
Schenectady,	1				7			2				4		13		1
Schoharie,	3				3	2						1	2	15		1
Schuyler,					13								2	9		
Seneca,					26								2	3		
Steuben,	3				14	3		1	5			5	1	19		
Suffolk,	3				9			1	2			6	4	17		1
Sullivan,	1	1			4			1				1		5		
Tioga,	1				12	1		1				6		8		
Tompkins,	2	1			21							7	1	13		
Ulster,	10				10	3	3	5	3			8	8	38		1
Warren,					5		2					2		2		1
Washington,	1				14	1			1	1		9	2	16		
Wayne,		1			13	1		4	1			3	3	10		
Westchester,	2				47		1	3	4			10	12	31		1
Wyoming,					25				1			9	1	5		
Yates,		1			9	2			1			4	3	5		
Total,	483	10	3	2	1,706	225	31	57	81	159	4	394	354	1,147	3	50

COUNTIES.	DISEASES OF UNCERTAIN OR VARIABLE SEAT.									DISEASES OF BRAIN AND NERVOUS SYSTEM.						
	Gout.	Hemorrhage	Inflammation.	Malformation.	Marasmus.	Rickets.	Scrofula.	Tumor.	Ulcer.	Amaurosis.	Apoplexy.	Disease of brain.	Congestion of brain.	Dropsy of brain.	Inflammation of brain.	Chorea.
Albany,		3	9		15		9	1	4		6	12	14	38	30	
Allegany,		7	1				1	3			6	5	4	9	2	1
Broome,		1	4		1		1				1	1	4	6	5	
Cattaraugus,			4				2					1	6	9	9	
Cayuga,		4	2				2	2			12	3	10	15	10	
Chautauque,			3				3	1			8	2	10	17	12	
Chemung,			2		2		3	1	1		2	1	8	6	12	
Chenango,			7				2		2		3	5	1	4	5	
Clinton,			1								4			6	5	
Columbia,		5	2		1		3		1		12	2	8	15	11	
Cortland,			3		1		1		2		5	2	3	3	4	
Delaware,			12				2	2	2		5		5	4	7	
Dutchess,		1			3		3	2			19	4	9	8	11	
Erie,	9	3	15		4		5	1			14	12	7	37	36	
Essex,							1	2			1	5	2	3	4	
Franklin,											2			8		
Fulton,		1	1		1							3	5	6	13	
Genesee,		1	2				3				2	3	3	7	4	
Greene,		2					1				6	1	5	7	6	1
Hamilton,											1				1	
Herkimer,		1	3				4	1			4	1	4	13	6	
Jefferson,		1	7	1			2	2			16	5	4	15	21	
Kings,	3	7	8	1	39	1	6	2	3		20	18	89	132	49	
Lewis,			2								1	1	3	5	1	
Livingston,		2		1			3	1	1		3	2	4	6	6	
Madison,			1	1	3		5	2			8	10	2	13	13	

COUNTIES.	DISEASES OF UNCERTAIN OR VARIABLE SEAT. Gout.	Hemorrhage.	Inflammation.	Malformation.	Marasmus.	Rickets.	Scrofula.	Tumor.	Ulcer.	DISEASES OF BRAIN AND NERVOUS SYSTEM. Amaurosis.	Apoplexy.	Disease of brain.	Congestion of brain.	Dropsy of brain.	Inflammation of brain.	Chorea.
Monroe,			4	2	2		4	1			10	10	12	26	34	
Montgomery,		1					3	1	1		5	1	2	2	9	
New-York,		6	32	17	192		34	9	35	1	105	40	173	332	177	2
Niagara,			3				2		2		3	2	15	7	8	
Oneida,		1	4		5		5	2	1		12	5	31	32	20	1
Onondaga,		3	6		3		10	3	2		10	3	8	14	23	
Ontario,		1	1	3			5	3	3		6		10	15	10	
Orange,		2	2	2	1		5				18	3	10	9	21	
Orleans,		1					1		1		3		7	4	6	
Oswego,			6		1	1	9				7	2	11	11	19	
Otsego,		2	8		4	1	5		2		8	1	9	8	9	
Putnam,		1			2						2		1	3	2	
Queens,		1	5		4		1	1	1		6	2	10	8	13	
Rensselaer,		2	4	1	3		5	2			15	6	9	28	37	
Richmond,					1						1		5	5	6	
Rockland,		1	2		1		1					3	8	5	3	
St. Lawrence,			1		3	1	3				9	2	10	9	14	
Saratoga,			5				3	3	1		10	2	4	6	21	1
Schenectady,			1								6		2	11	8	
Schoharie,			2				5	2			5		3	7	22	
Schuyler,					1		1	1			2	2	3	2	5	
Seneca,			1				2		1		3		5		7	
Steuben,		1	11		1		3	2			7	2	8	7	15	
Suffolk,				1	7		2	1			7	4	4	12	11	
Sullivan,			3		1						1	1	3	3	5	
Tioga,		2					1		2		10		2	6	3	1
Tompkins,							2	2			2	2	3	9	13	2
Ulster,		4	4	1	1	1	2	1	5		8	1	7	9	30	
Warren,													1		6	
Washington,			2	1	4		2		2		9	1	7	10	13	
Wayne,		1	1				4	1	1		5	4	8	11	11	
Westchester,		1	1		12		2	1	3		12	2	17	18	23	
Wyoming,		6	2		1				2		9	3	5	3	9	
Yates,		1					1		1					2	1	
Total,	12	77	200	32	320	5	185	59	82	1	477	203	623	1,026	897	9

COUNTIES.	DISEASES OF BRAIN AND NERVOUS SYSTEM. Convulsions.	Delirium tremens.	Epilepsy.	Insanity.	Nervous disease.	Paralysis.	Sun stroke.	Tetanus.	DISEASES OF RESPIRATORY ORGANS. Asthma.	Bronchitis.	Canker.	Catarrh.	Consumption.	Laryngitis.	Congestion of lungs.	Hemorrhage from lungs.
Albany,	54	8	2	8	3	14	6		5	9		1	313	1	6	1
Allegany,	6				1	8		1		1		1	68	2	4	
Broome,	4	1	1	2		6			1				66		1	
Cattaraugus,	5		1		1	4		1		1	1	1	74		1	
Cayuga,	8	2	1	1	1	6	2		2			1	144	1	1	1
Chautauque,	9	2	1			7				1	1		137	2	10	2
Chemung,	6	4				2	3				2		58	1	2	1
Chenango,	7		2			9							100		5	1
Clinton,	5	1		1		2					1		82	1	2	
Columbia,	7		2		2	12	2		1	2			118	3	3	
Cortland,	2	1	1	3	1	6							62		2	
Delaware,	7	1			1	12					1		70	1	1	
Dutchess,	13	3		5	3	9	2			5			127	4	3	
Erie,	66	10	3	1	2	18			1	2			291	2	7	
Essex,	5					7	1			2			74			1
Franklin,	1					4							43			
Fulton,	11	1		1	1	5			1	2			51			1
Genesee,	11	1	1			5			1				78		6	
Greene,	12			1		6				1			85			
Hamilton,	1												6			
Herkimer,	15			4	1	5			1	2	1		94		8	
Jefferson,	11		2	2		8	1		1		5		173		8	1
Kings,	163	11	4	2	1	23	13	2	4	20			541	4	25	3
Lewis,	9					6						1	63			1
Livingston,	5		1			8			1				70	2	7	
Madison,	9	1			3	6			1	1			118		3	
Monroe,	16	2	1	2	1	11	1			4	1		225	1	10	3
Montgomery,	9		1			10			1				72	1	4	
New-York,	470	51	28	9	4	90	38	12	9	132	2	5	1,552	26	78	18
Niagara,	7	1	1		1	9			1	3	3	1	104	1	3	1
Oneida,	25	3	6	12	4	22		1	2	1	1		303		14	
Onondaga,	22		3		1	16	1		1	1	3	1	196		4	1
Ontario,	6		2			5			1				105		1	1
Orange,	14	2	1	6	2	11	2	2	3	5			166	2	7	1
Orleans,	6		1		1	4		1					60	1	5	
Oswego,	24	1	1	1	4	5			1	1	4		188		7	
Otsego,	14		1			7							135	1	4	
Putnam,	8	1	2			2	1						41		2	1
Queens,	13	1	2	1	1	5	2	2		4			92	2	1	

COUNTIES	D SEASES OF BRAIN AND NERVOUS SYSTEM								DISEASES OF RESPIRATORY ORGANS.							
	Convulsions.	Delirium tremens.	Epilepsy.	Insanity.	Nervous disease.	Paralysis.	Sun stroke.	Tetanus.	Asthma.	Bronchitis.	Canker.	Catarrh.	Consumption.	Laryngitis.	Congestion of lungs.	Hemorrhage from lungs.
Rensselaer,	40	5	1		3	11	2	1			2		261	2	7	2
Richmond,	4				1	4		1					50		1	
Rockland,	1			2		5	1		1	1			42		2	
St. Lawrence,	9	2	1			9				1			150	1	5	1
Saratoga,	15	2		3		14				2			143		7	
Schenectady,	5	2	1		1	7			2				61	1	2	
Schoharie,	9				1	8				5			51		2	1
Schuyler,	2				1	5				1	1		42			
Seneca,	1					5			1				65		1	
Steuben,	12		4		1	16	1		2	2	4	1	100		3	3
Suffolk,	8	1		1	1	20	1	6		1	1		100	1	9	1
Sullivan,	12		1		1	2				1			46		1	
Tioga,	7				1	4			3	2	1		59			
Tompkins,	4	1		3		3				1			87		4	1
Ulster,	28		1	2		14	3				1		178		6	4
Warren,	2					3					1		37			
Washington,	12	3	2			8	1		2	1	1		126		10	
Wayne,	10	1			2	5					2		91		13	1
Westchester,	36	1	1	1	3	15	3		1	8			149		11	1
Wyoming,	1		3		1	3							66	1	2	
Yates,	2		4		1	3							41		2	1
Total,	1,306	127	91	74	58	563	87	30	51	226	40	13	7,890	65	333	55

COUNTIES.	DISEASES OF RESPIRATORY ORGANS.				DISEASES OF CIRCULATIVE ORGANS.									DISEASES OF DIGESTIVE ORGANS.		
	Inflammation of lungs.	Pleurisy.	Quinsey.	Trachitis.	Anæmia.	Aneurism.	Angina pectoris	Disease of heart.	Dropsy of heart.	Enlargement of heart.	Inflammation of heart.	Hydræmia.	Phlebitis.	Inflammation of bowels.	Intussusception of bowels.	Perforation of bowels.
Albany,	75	4	2					22	2	3	1			33		
Allegany,	18	1						1	3					6		
Broome,	16							4	6					4		
Cattaraugus,	13							5	1	1	1			4		
Cayuga,	18	1	2					10	6					9		
Chautauque,	36	1	1					9	2					3		
Chemung,	9							2	1					4		
Chenango,	21	4						7	2					13		
Clinton,	8							3						6		
Columbia,	19	1						5		1				14		
Cortland,	6							2		1	1			5		
Delaware,	21							7	5	1				7		
Dutchess,	28	2						15	6					10		
Erie,	63	2						21	4	1	1			19		1
Essex,	9							4						4		
Franklin,	12							3						3		
Fulton,	14							8	4	1				6		
Genesee,	9							6	1					5		
Greene,	14	1						4	1	1				6		
Hamilton,																
Herkimer,	18	1						9	5					11		
Jefferson,	25	2						10	5	1				18		
Kings,	147	7						52	4	2				51		
Lewis,	7		1					5	2		1			4		
Livingston,	11							3	2					12		
Madison,	33	2						8	6	1	1			8		
Monroe,	53	5	2					21	3	6	1			21		
Montgomery,	18	2	2					24	3	1				4		
New-York,	579	47	11	7	9			177	15	17	14	11	4	141	2	3
Niagara,	20	1	1					7	3					5		
Oneida,	49	3						30	11	4	1			22		
Onondaga,	41							19	3	1				15		
Ontario,	17	1						18	1					9		
Orange,	50	6						10	2	1				22		
Orleans,	21	2						4	1					5		
Oswego,	40	5						6	4					7		
Otsego,	19	3	1	1			2	14	5					4		
Putnam,	9	1						2						5		
Queens,	22	5						9	1					10		
Rensselaer,	55	8	1					36	2	5				35		
Richmond,	7	1						8	1					7		
Rockland,	14							3						4		
St. Lawrence,	23	1				1	1	13	8					12		1
Saratoga,	25	3						9	2	1				7		
Schenectady,	8	1						4	2	2				4		
Schoharie,	7							5	2	1				10		
Schuyler,	4						1	1	1	1				1		
Seneca,	9							2	3					7		
Steuben,	34							8	3					11		
Suffolk,	15	5						5		1				6		
Sullivan,	20	1						5		2				4		
Tioga,	14							1	1					5		

COUNTIES.	DISEASES OF RESPIRATORY ORGANS.				DISEASES OF CIRCULATIVE ORGANS.									DISEASES OF DIGESTIVE ORGANS.		
	Inflammation of lungs.	Pleurisy.	Quinsey.	Trachitis.	Anæmia.	Aneurism.	Angina pectoris.	Disease of heart.	Dropsy of heart.	Enlargement of heart.	Inflammation of heart.	Hydræmia.	Phlebitis.	Inflammation of bowels.	Intussusception of bowels.	Perforation of bowels.
Tompkins,	10							8						10		
Ulster,	46	3	2					7						12		
Warren,	7	1						4	2					1		
Washington,	31	2						11	7					14		
Wayne,	16	1	1					10	1	1				4		
Westchester,	52	5						20	1					11		
Wyoming,	9	1						7		1				4		1
Yates,		1						2	2					4		
Total,	1,994	144	27	8	9	1	4	735	158	59	22	11	4	708	2	6

COUNTIES.	DISEASES OF DIGESTIVE ORGANS.															
	Stricture of bowels.	Colic.	Painter's colic.	Constipation.	Dyspepsia.	Gastritis.	Hemorrhoids.	Hernia.	Jaundice.	Disease of liver.	Cirrhosis of liver.	Congestion of liver.	Hypretrophy of liver.	Inflammation of liver.	Hypertrophy of spleen.	Inflammation of spleen.
Albany,		3	1		4		1	1	2				1	1	1	
Allegany,	1							1		1						
Broome,		3						1		2		1				
Cattaraugus,		1			2			1	2	1		1				
Cayuga,						1				4						
Chautauque,		1	1		1	2		1	3	2						
Chemung,		1			2	1	1			2						
Chenango,					1	1		1		2						
Clinton,		1						1								
Columbia,			1		2	1		1	1	3			1	1		
Cortland,					1					2						
Delaware,	2	1				1				4						
Dutchess,		3			2	2		2		3				1		
Erie,	1	4							2	2			1	2		
Essex,						1		1		3						
Franklin,										2						
Fulton,		4				1		1		1						
Genesee,						3		1	1	2						
Greene,		2				1				4						
Hamilton,																
Herkimer,						1		1	1	4			1			
Jefferson,		2			1	2				5						
Kings,		3	1			5		1	2	24			1	1		1
Lewis,					1				1					1		
Livingston,						4		1								
Madison,	1	2			2	1		1	1	5				3		
Monroe,				1			1		3	6				2		
Montgomery,						2				6			1			
New-York,	1	6	1		4	19	1	4	22	37	16		5	10		
Niagara,						1			4	3						
Oneida,		2			3	3	2	1	1	14				1		
Onondaga,		1			4	1		1	1	4			1	1	1	
Ontario,		2			1				1	4						
Orange,		1			2			2	1	7		1	1			
Orleans,		2			1					2						
Oswego,		1			1	1			2	3			1			
Otsego,		2			1	1		1		5			1			
Putnam,			1						1							
Queens,		2						1	2	4			2			
Rensselaer,		3				2	1		3	9			1			
Richmond,									1							
Rockland,								3	1	4						
St. Lawrence,		2						1	3	6				1		
Saratoga,		1						1	1	4				2		
Schenectady,					1									1		
Schoharie,		2				1				3						
Schuyler,		1			1					1				1		
Seneca,		1			2					1				2		
Steuben,						1				7				1		
Suffolk,		3			2					1						
Sullivan,		2			1											
Tioga,										2				1		
Tompkins,		1			1					4						
Ulster,		6				1	1		2	7						
Warren,	3	1								1						
Washington,						1				7						
Wayne,		3			1			1	1	5			1			
Westchester,		4	1		2		1		2	4			1			
Wyoming,		1							2	4				1		
Yates,								1		3						
Total,	9	81	7	1	47	62	9	34	70	246	16	3	20	34	2	1

COUNTIES	DISEASES OF DIGESTIVE ORGANS.					DISEASES OF URINARY ORGANS.										DIS. OF GEN O.
	Starvation.	Disease of stomach.	Teething.	Disease of throat.	Worms.	Albuminaria.	Cystitis.	Gravel.	Disease of kidneys.	Diabetis.	Inflammation of kidneys.	Infiltration of urine.	Rupture of bladder.	Strangury.	Stricture.	Amenorrhœ.
Albany,	2		41	6	2	2	1		1	1	4					3
Allegany,		1	1	1	3				3		1					
Broome,		1		2	2					1	1					
Cattaraugus,								1		2	1					
Cayuga,		1			2					2						
Chautauque,			1		2		1	1	1	2	1					
Chemung,			2	2				1								
Chenango,								1		1						
Clinton,								1								
Columbia,			3		2			2	3	1						
Cortland,			1		1				2							
Delaware,			1	2	1		1	2		3						
Dutchess,			8	3	3			3	1		1			1		
Erie,	1	1	35	9	6			2	1		1					
Essex,					3	1				2						
Franklin,			1	2	1			2								
Fulton,			2							1						
Genesee,				1	1		1	1								
Greene,			1	2					1							
Hamilton,																
Herkimer,		1	1	2			1	2								
Jefferson,			2	2	2						2					
Kings,			132	4	4			2	1	2	2					
Lewis,								1		1						
Livingston,		1			1						2					
Madison,		1						1		2						
Monroe,			30		5			2	3	2						
Montgomery,			2	3					3							
New-York,	1	7	254	28	15	36	3	3	13	4	5	1	1		2	
Niagara,		1	3		5					1						
Oneida,			6		13			1		3	2					
Onondaga,		2	9		6				3	1						
Ontario,			2	1				2	2	3						
Orange,	1		2	1					2		1					
Orleans,			1	1			1			1						
Oswego,		1	5	1	6					1						
Otsego,		3			1			4		1						
Putnam,		1														
Queens,			9	2	3				2							
Rensselaer,	1		24	2	6			2	1	1	2					
Richmond,			7	1			1									
Rockland,			4		1			2								
St. Lawrence,			1		4			5								
Saratoga,		1	2	2	3		1	2		3						
Schenectady,		1	2	2	1			1	2							
Schoharie,				1	1				1	1	3					
Schuyler,																
Seneca,					1											
Steuben,			3	4	3		1	1	4	1						
Suffolk,			6		2			1								
Sullivan,			1		1		1									
Tioga,	1	1	2	1												
Tompkins,									2	3	2					
Ulster,			4	8	1			2	1	3						
Warren,				1					2							
Washington,				4					1							
Wayne,			6	1	1			2			2					
Westchester,			9	2			1			1						
Wyoming,					1		1		1	1	1					
Yates,					1			2	2	2	1					
Total,	7	25	626	104	117	39	15	55	59	54	35	1	1	1	2	3

COUNTIES.	DISEASES OF GENERATIVE ORGANS AND CHILD BIRTH.										DISEASES OF LOCOMOTIVE ORGANS.					
	Child birth.	Chlorosis.	Leucorrhœa.	Menorrhegia.	Miscarriage.	Ovarian disease.	Phlegmesia dolens.	Puerperal fever.	Disease of uterus.	Uterine hemorrhage.	Disease of bones.	Dry gangrene.	Disease of hips.	Rheumatism.	Disease of spine.	Synovitis.
Albany,	12		1								1		2	3	5	
Allegany,	3				1			1						4	1	
Broome,	2							1							1	
Cattaraugus,	2													6	1	
Cayuga,	10							2					3	6	2	
Chautauque,	3				1			1		1		1		3	5	
Chemung,	4							1				1		1		
Chenango,	1												1	2	1	
Clinton,	3			1	1			1								
Columbia,	3							2	1							
Cortland,	1					1										
Delaware,	2							2						2	1	
Dutchess,	1				2	1					1	1			2	

COUNTIES	DISEASES OF GENERATIVE ORGANS AND CHILD BIRTH.										DISEASES OF LOCOMOTIVE ORGANS.					
	Child birth.	Chlorosis.	Leucorrhœa.	Menorrhagia.	Miscarriage.	Ovarian disease.	Phlegmasia dolens.	Puerperal fever.	Disease of uterus.	Uterine hemorrhage.	Disease of bones.	Dry gangrene.	Disease of hips.	Rheumatism.	Disease of spine.	Synovitis.
Erie,	19							1					2	6	2	
Essex,	3															
Franklin,	2					1								1	1	
Fulton,	2													2		
Genesee,	3							1							2	
Greene,	2													3	1	
Hamilton,																
Herkimer,	3												1			
Jefferson,	3													3	3	
Kings,	44							4					3	11	5	
Lewis,	2							1								
Livingston,								2						5	1	
Madison,	4							1					2	2	1	
Monroe,	15					1							1	9	3	
Montgomery,	1														2	
New-York,	53	3			3		1	24	4	3	2	4	10	21	23	
Niagara,	11				1									1	2	
Oneida,	8							2	1					2	4	
Onondaga,	4							1			1		1	7		
Ontario,	3							1		1				2	4	
Orange,	4														4	
Orleans,								2			1			1	1	
Oswego,	2				1			2				1		2	2	
Otsego,	1							1			1	1		1	1	
Putnam,	3											1		1		
Queens,	1						1							3	2	
Rensselaer,	7							4						1	3	
Richmond,	5							1							1	
Rockland,	2							1						2		
St. Lawrence,	7							4				2		3		
Saratoga,	3							1			1		1	3	1	
Schenectady,	2							1					2	1		
Schoharie,	1							2					1			
Schuyler,	1												1		1	
Seneca,								1								
Steuben,	5							3		1		1		4	3	
Suffolk,	3				1							2	1	1	1	
Sullivan,	2	1											2	3		
Tioga,	2				2			2						2		
Tompkins,	2				1			1							2	
Ulster,	8											1		8	4	
Warren,	2							1								
Washington,	6				1			3	1	1					1	
Wayne,	1			1		1		2					1	3	2	
Westchester,	5							1						4	2	
Wyoming,								1					1	1	1	
Yates,	3													1	1	
Total,	307	4	1	2	15	5	2	84	7	7	8	16	36	147	106	

COUNTIES.	DISEASES OF INTEGUMENTIVE ORG'NS		OLD AGE.	EXTERNAL CAUSES.												
	Carbuncles.	Eruption		Accident.	Asphyxia.	Burned.	Camphene accident.	Cold.	Crushed.	Drinking cold water.	Drowned.	Executed.	Exposure.	Falls.	Fright.	Frozen.
Albany,			39	15		6	1	3		1	24			11	1	
Allegany,			21	4		1		2			2			5		
Broome,			10	11		1					8					
Cattaraugus,			9	6		2			3		3			3		
Cayuga,			27	5		1					4			1		
Chautauque,			21	7		5		2			8			4		
Chemung,			5	3		5					4			2		
Chenango,			22	2		1					2			2		
Clinton,			18	13		1					3			2	1	
Columbia,			27	7							3			5		
Cortland,			10	1		1					1			2		
Delaware,			32	9		3					3			4		
Dutchess,			24	5		6	1	1			3			7		
Erie,			41	19		3	1	7			29	2		11		
Essex,			8	2		7		1			1			3		
Franklin,			4	3							3			2		
Fulton,			13	5							1			2		
Genesee,			8	13		2	1	2			2			1		
Greene,			23	4		1					2					
Hamilton,			2	2							1					
Herkimer,			28	8		2					1			1		
Jefferson,	1	1	30	7		3		3			15			6		
Kings,			75	30		3	4	6			29			13		
Lewis,			11	3		2					3			2		
Livingston,			11	4							1			2		
Madison,			15	7		1		1			5			7		

COUNTIES.	Diseases of Integumentive Org'ns.		OLD AGE.	External Causes.													
	Carbuncles.	Eruption.		Accident.	Asphyxia.	Burned.	Camphene accident.	Cold.	Crushed.	Drinking cold water.	Drowned.	Executed.	Exposure.	Falls.	Fright.	Frozen.
Monroe,			48	14		1		1			15			4		
Montgomery,			18	3				2			5			1		
New-York,	1		163	182	5	24	4	6		1	102			38		1
Niagara,			15	5		2		2			10					
Oneida,			54	15		5		1			17			2		
Onondaga,			33	18		6		2			11			2		
Ontario,			18	6		4				1	1			1		
Orange,			38	10		4					12			4		
Orleans,			9	1							1					
Oswego,			34	16		3					8			5		
Otsego,			27	4		1		1			5			2		
Putnam,			9	3							3			1		
Queens,			31	6		4					7					
Rensselaer,			42	14		4		4		1	14			10	1	
Richmond,			9	1		1	1				6					
Rockland,			8								4			1		
St. Lawrence,			45	7		2					12		1			
Saratoga,			38	7		4					6			2		
Schenectady,			12	1			1	1								
Schoharie,			20	4												
Schuyler,			5	1				1								
Seneca,			15	1							4			3		
Steuben,			23	10							5			6		
Suffolk,			35	11		2	1	2			6			2		
Sullivan,			11	7		2		1			5			2		
Tioga,			12	1							2			1		
Tompkins,			23	10		3					2			2		
Ulster,	1		40	8		3		1			24			1		1
Warren,			5	2							1			3		
Washington,			19	6		1					8			3		
Wayne,			27	2		1	2				5			1		
Westchester,			31	14		4		2			31			5		
Wyoming,			20	4		1					1			1		
Yates,			15	1							1			3		
Total,	3	1	1,486	590	5	139	17	55	3	4	495	2	1	204	3	2

COUNTIES.	External Causes.												Premature Birth and Stillborn.		Unknown.	Total.
	Grief	Intemperance.	Lightning.	Murder.	Neglect.	Over heated.	Poison.	Railroad accidents.	Scalded.	Smothered.	Strangled.	Suicide.	Premature birth.	Still born.		
Albany,		1					2	7	3	1		8	1	2	72	1,878
Allegany,		1						1	4			1		1	26	367
Broome,								8	1			1		1	21	280
Cattaraugus,								2							41	315
Cayuga,		2		1			2	3	2			5			68	637
Chautauque,		1						4	3		1	4			44	603
Chemung,								6	3			1			10	280
Chenango,		1		2	1				1			7		1	23	370
Clinton,		1							3			1		4	71	319
Columbia,		1					1	5	1			3			65	519
Cortland,								2				4			17	227
Delaware,		1	1				2	1				2		1	45	421
Dutchess,		2		2			1					1			64	732
Erie,		1	1	1			4	5	3			1		6	296	2,004
Essex,									2		2	1			31	250
Franklin,										1	1	1			23	168
Fulton,								1	2					3	28	276
Genesee,		1						2						2	27	314
Greene,							1		1	1		2		2	15	355
Hamilton,							1		1						5	29
Herkimer,		2						1	1					1	11	396
Jefferson,		2		3				1	4	3	1	2			87	701
Kings,		3		4	1		3	4	7		2		4	56	398	3,893
Lewis,				1			1								27	247
Livingston,				1			1					1		2	23	294
Madison,		1					1		1	1	1	3		2	61	506
Monroe,		6	1	1				1				2	1	7	157	1,392
Montgomery,		6						1	1			3			12	345
New-York,		11	1	20	2	4	6	19	9	11		10	43	132	457	11,095
Niagara,		3	2				3	4	2			2		2	46	705
Oneida,		2		2			1	7	3			6	2	2	103	1,380
Onondaga,		3					4	5	3	1	1				110	1,038
Ontario,							1	1	1					3	27	435
Orange,		5		3			3	14				3		2	61	872
Orleans,		1	1					1	2						35	276
Oswego,	1	1					1		3		1	1	1	1	83	832
Otsego,		2					1		1		1	1	1	1	34	500
Putnam,								2				2			14	175

COUNTIES.	EXTERNAL CAUSES.												PREMATURE BIRTH AND STILLBORN.		UNKNOWN.	TOTAL.
	Grief.	Intemperance	Lightning.	Murder.	Neglect.	Over heated.	Poison.	Railroad accidents.	Scalded.	Smothered.	Strangled.	Suicide.	Premature birth.	Stillborn.		
Queens,	......	3	......	1	......	......	......	1	2	2	......	......	......	2	92	658
Rensselaer,	......	2	......	1	......	......	3	6	3	1	......	4	2	3	112	1, 431
Richmond,	......	......	......	......	......	......	......	......	......	......	......	......	......	......	16	242
Rockland,	......	1	......	1	......	......	......	3	1	......	......	......	......	1	11	258
Lawrence,	......	1	......	......	......	......	......	......	2	1	......	4	......	2	83	687
Saratoga,	......	6	......	......	......	......	2	2	1	......	......	2	......	2	34	592
Schenectady,	......	1	......	......	......	......	......	......	......	......	......	1	......	......	23	293
Schoharie,	......	1	......	......	......	......	......	......	......	......	......	1	......	3	50	319
Schuyler,	......	......	......	......	......	......	......	......	......	......	......	1	......	......	12	188
Seneca,	......	1	1	......	......	......	1	......	......	1	......	......	3	......	24	259
Steuben,	......	1	......	......	......	......	......	5	......	1	......	1	1	6	74	608
Suffolk,	......	4	......	1	......	......	3	3	......	......	......	2	1	1	41	524
Sullivan,	......	......	......	1	......	......	......	2	......	......	......	......	......	......	46	304
Tioga,	......	......	......	......	......	......	......	......	......	......	......	......	......	......	35	288
Tompkins,	......	......	......	......	......	......	......	1	......	......	1	1	......	......	39	353
Ulster,	......	7	......	......	......	......	......	1	1	......	......	2	......	2	174	1, 120
Warren,	......	......	......	1	......	......	......	......	1	......	......	......	......	2	25	141
Washington,	......	1	......	1	......	......	......	2	1	......	......	3	......	......	71	544
Wayne,	......	4	......	......	......	......	2	5	2	2	......	1	2	1	17	522
Westchester,	......	5	......	1	......	......	2	14	2	4	......	7	......	7	51	1, 125
Wyoming,	......	1	......	......	......	......	1	1	2	......	......	3	1	......	17	346
Yates,	......	......	......	......	......	......	......	1	1	......	......	2	......	......	28	206
Total,	1	100	8	50	4	4	54	150	87	31	12	114	63	266	3, 813	46, 434

DWELLINGS.

ALBANY COUNTY.

TOWNS.	STONE.			BRICK.			FRAMED.			LOGS.			OTHER DWELLINGS.			TOTAL.		
	Total number.	No. value not given.	Value given	Total number.	No. value not given.	Value given	Total number.	No. value not given.	Value given	Total number.	No. value not given.	Value given	Total number.	No. value not given.	Value given	Total number.	No. value not given	Value given
Albany city:																		
1st ward,	....	....	....	233	....	$514, 950	429	....	$343, 986	....	....	......	2	....	......	664	....	$858, 936
2d ward,	1	....	$15, 000	296	....	809, 000	186	....	214, 100	....	....	......	....	....	......	483	....	1, 038, 100
3d ward,	....	....	....	411	....	1, 053, 300	101	....	138, 210	....	....	......	....	....	......	512	....	1, 191, 510
4th ward,	....	....	....	365	32	1, 222, 550	109	1	133, 000	....	....	......	....	....	......	498	57	1, 355, 550
5th ward,	....	....	....	342	7	1, 983, 200	59	1	158, 000	....	....	......	....	....	......	401	8	2, 141, 200
6th ward,	1	....	17, 000	352	1	1, 343, 700	78	....	120, 050	....	....	......	2	....	......	433	1	1, 480, 750
7th ward,	....	....	....	241	....	601, 200	349	....	356, 780	....	....	......	1	....	......	591	....	957, 980
8th ward,	....	....	....	241	....	554, 000	598	17	507, 956	....	....	......	....	....	......	839	17	1, 061, 956
9th ward,	9	....	351, 000	261	1	1, 112, 760	647	1	580, 240	....	....	......	....	....	......	930	15	2, 044, 000
10th ward,	....	....	....	486	....	1, 706, 200	538	....	567, 020	....	....	......	11	....	$1,180	1, 035	....	2, 274, 400
Total Albany, ...	11	....	383, 000	3, 228	41	10, 900, 860	3, 094	20	3, 119, 342	....	....	......	16	....	1, 180	6, 386	98	14, 404, 382
Berne, ...	....	....	....	1	....	400	564	4	198, 900	5	....	$58	2	....	2, 000	575	7	201, 358
Bethlehem, ...	5	....	4, 200	66	2	112, 900	721	4	359, 620	1	....	20	1	....	10	795	7	476, 750
Coeymans, ...	30	11	16, 900	35	5	54, 100	488	156	214, 415	....	....	......	....	....	......	560	179	285, 415
Guilderland, ...	3	....	2, 400	6	....	13, 200	471	4	252, 745	....	....	......	1	....	2, 000	492	15	270, 345
Knox, ...	1	...	500	1	....	1, 100	344	9	124, 285	1	....	15	1	....	2, 000	352	13	127, 900
New Scotland, ...	32	10	14, 900	4	3	2, 000	345	189	73, 645	4	3	25	....	....	......	612	432	90, 570
Rensselaerville, ...	1	....	475	6	....	6, 475	568	1	270, 915	3	....	50	3	3	......	584	7	277, 915
Watervliet, ...	2	1	800	419	34	741, 474	2, 297	87	1, 772, 474	4	4	......	7	4	400	2, 734	135	2, 515, 148
Westerlo, ...	3	....	1, 550	3	....	1, 300	493	....	178, 310	1	....	25	1	....	300	501	....	181, 485
Total, ...	88	22	424, 725	3, 769	85	11, 833, 809	9, 385	474	6, 564, 651	19	7	193	32	7	7, 890	13, 591	893	18, 831, 268

ALLEGANY COUNTY.

TOWNS.	Stone: Total number.	Stone: No. value not given.	Stone: Value given	Brick: Total number.	Brick: No. value not given.	Brick: Value given	Framed: Total number.	Framed: No. value not given.	Framed: Value given	Logs: Total number.	Logs: No. value not given.	Logs: Value given	Other: Total number.	Other: No. value not given.	Other: Value given	Total: Total number.	Total: No. value not given	Total: Value given
Alfred, ...	....	....	....	2	....	1, 400	292	....	126, 505	40	....	1, 202	9	....	162	343	....	129, 269
Allen, ...	....	....	....	......	....	....	165	....	48, 990	22	....	675	4	....	270	191	....	49, 935
Alma, ...	....	....	....	......	....	....	38	....	9, 645	16	....	4, 625	19	....	445	73	....	14, 715
Almond, ...	3	....	4, 000	1	....	1, 000	268	....	94, 595	27	....	100	48	....	70	348	1	99, 765
Amity, ...	....	....	....	......	....	....	385	2	201, 100	23	....	540	96	....	5, 430	506	4	207, 070
Andover, ...	....	....	....	......	....	....	197	1	74, 700	72	23	1, 309	57	3	3, 403	339	40	79, 412
Angelica, ...	5	....	18, 800	5	....	9, 200	266	1	153, 770	13	....	280	16	1	322	307	4	182, 372
Belfast, ...	....	....	....	1	....	1, 200	307	5	123, 000	23	1	670	83	....	1, 316	414	6	126, 186
Birdsall, ...	....	....	....	......	....	....	86	1	21, 000	58	....	1, 610	11	....	490	155	1	23, 100
Bolivar, ...	....	....	....	......	....	....	136	2	49, 560	13	1	415	40	5	805	189	8	50, 780
Burns, ...	2	....	1, 200	2	....	2, 600	155	1	44, 350	30	....	1, 385	11	....	480	201	2	50, 015
Caneadea, ...	....	....	....	1	....	200	308	1	113, 997	62	....	1, 375	76	1	1, 835	474	29	117, 407
Centreville, ...	....	....	....	......	....	....	207	3	71, 855	43	1	2, 385	5	....	500	255	4	74, 740
Clarksville, ...	....	....	....	......	....	....	115	105	6, 200	36	36	......	7	7	......	158	148	6, 200
Cuba, ...	3	....	1, 350	13	....	27, 100	320	3	185, 955	16	1	460	26	1	480	388	6	215, 345
Friendship, ...	....	....	....	......	....	....	317	1	154, 865	20	....	825	20	....	851	357	1	156, 541
Genesee, ...	....	....	....	......	....	....	164	4	70, 840	3	....	120	....	....	......	169	6	70, 960
Granger, ...	....	....	....	......	....	....	190	188	1, 800	51	50	300	3	3	......	250	247	2, 100
Grove, ...	....	....	....	......	....	....	99	....	26, 435	98	14	2, 794	15	3	275	212	22	29, 504
Hume, ...	....	....	....	......	....	....	343	50	78, 075	36	6	1, 215	43	8	620	425	67	79, 910
Independence, ...	....	....	....	1	....	600	209	1	74, 845	11	2	400	2	1	30	224	5	75, 875
New Hudson, ...	....	....	....	3	....	1, 200	212	2	71, 485	38	19	815	15	1	2, 375	275	29	75, 875
Ossian, ...	....	....	....	......	....	....	192	....	54, 200	42	....	2, 435	....	....	......	234	....	56, 635
Rushford, ...	....	....	....	......	....	....	383	....	200, 219	7	....	300	1	....	50	391	....	200, 569
Scio, ...	....	....	....	......	....	....	399	15	266, 949	42	1	980	156	1	9, 191	620	40	277, 120
West Almond, ...	....	....	....	......	....	....	150	....	48, 260	35	....	1, 370	....	....	......	185	....	49, 630
Willing, ...	....	....	....	......	....	....	152	2	35, 589	57	....	1, 180	8	2	100	218	5	36, 869
Wirt, ...	....	....	....	......	....	....	223	1	93, 077	32	....	1, 650	35	....	1, 980	291	2	96, 707
Total, ...	13	....	25, 350	29	....	44, 500	6, 287	389	2, 501, 861	966	160	31, 415	806	37	31, 480	8, 192	677	2, 634, 606

BROOME COUNTY.

TOWNS.	Stone: Total number.	Stone: No. value not given.	Stone: Value given	Brick: Total number.	Brick: No. value not given.	Brick: Value given	Framed: Total number.	Framed: No. value not given.	Framed: Value given	Logs: Total number.	Logs: No. value not given.	Logs: Value given	Other: Total number.	Other: No. value not given.	Other: Value given	Total: Total number.	Total: No. value not given	Total: Value given
Barker, ...	....	....	....	3	....	10, 000	228	....	87, 244	16	....	2, 509	9	....	2, 045	256	....	101, 798
Chenango, ...	....	....	....	66	2	377, 300	1, 697	302	1, 977, 530	97	53	2, 795	77	17	10, 395	1, 943	380	2, 368, 020
Colesville, ...	1	....	100	1	....	600	471	1	170, 840	47	8	927	85	2	28, 545	705	11	201, 012
Conklin, ...	....	....	....	2	....	3, 100	356	....	204, 800	80	....	7, 440	27	....	3, 450	465	....	218, 790
Lisle, ...	....	....	....	1	....	1, 000	335	2	136, 310	12	....	230	4	....	25	253	3	137, 565
Maine, ...	....	....	....	......	....	....	322	....	84, 645	70	....	5, 420	1	....	100	393	....	90, 165
Nanticoke, ...	1	....	100	......	....	....	130	....	33, 550	20	....	500	1	....	25	152	....	34, 175
Sanford, ...	....	....	....	......	....	....	453	....	175, 490	96	....	2, 347	6	....	107	555	....	177, 944
Triangle, ...	....	....	....	......	....	....	321	230	67, 610	12	12	......	7	6	40	340	248	67, 650
Union, ...	....	....	....	5	....	4, 300	458	2	192, 225	12	....	360	1	....	650	477	3	197, 535
Vestal, ...	....	....	....	1	1	....	323	323	....	47	47	......	7	7	......	378	378	....
Windsor, ...	2	....	800	3	....	2, 600	435	1	124, 075	51	....	1, 715	27	....	1, 570	519	1	131, 660
Total, ...	4	....	1, 000	82	3	398, 900	5, 529	861	3, 255, 219	560	120	24, 243	252	32	46, 952	6, 436	1025	3, 726, 314

CATTARAUGUS COUNTY.

TOWNS.	STONE.			BRICK.			FRAMED.			LOGS.			OTHER DWELLINGS.			TOTAL.		
	Total number.	No. value not given.	Value given	Total number.	No. value not given.	Val. given.	Total number.	No. value not given.	Val. given.	Total number.	No. value not given.	Val. given.	Total number.	No. value not given.	Val. given.	Total number.	No. value not given.	Val. given
Allegany,	....	....	....	....	....	....	196	....	$76,980	46	4	$1,185	54	1	$1,550	297	6	$79,715
Ashford	....	....	....	....	....	....	130	1	43,675	65	19	1,600	163	2	26,042	359	23	71,317
Bucktooth,	....	....	....	....	....	....	27	....	8,130	24	....	426	33	....	656	84	....	9,212
Carrolton,	....	....	....	....	....	....	41	2	10,130	16	4	430	19	13	85	81	24	10,645
Cold Spring,	....	....	....	....	....	....	62	8	15,175	29	19	325	18	5	885	110	33	16,385
Connewango,	....	....	....	....	....	....	205	10	59,271	25	15	225	33	3	8,170	267	32	67,666
Dayton,	....	....	....	....	....	....	135	....	38,660	24	....	525	57	1	6,125	217	2	45,310
East Otto,	....	....	....	2	....	$600	135	....	42,030	30	....	700	60	....	6,778	227	....	50,108
Ellicottville,	1	1	....	....	....	....	231	18	134,815	85	6	1,491	29	3	1,974	350	32	138,280
Farmersville,	....	....	....	....	....	....	196	....	74,165	58	15	1,940	11	....	1,655	265	15	77,760
Franklinville,	....	....	....	....	....	....	229	....	88,220	77	....	2,980	10	....	460	316	....	91,660
Freedom,	....	....	....	1	....	400	247	3	60,005	34	3	617	2	....	45	285	7	61,067
Great Valley,	....	....	....	....	....	....	128	....	44,180	36	....	1,295	59	3	5,069	224	4	50,544
Hinsdale,	....	....	....	....	....	....	183	....	84,333	36	....	1,110	189	....	5,919	409	1	91,362
Humphrey,	....	....	....	....	....	....	82	57	6,455	54	24	1,194	9	4	250	147	87	7,899
Ischua,	1	1	....	....	....	....	89	80	4,500	60	60	....	47	46	80	204	194	4,580
Leon,	....	....	....	....	....	....	223	167	21,160	35	34	30	1	1	....	261	204	21,190
Little Valley,	....	....	....	....	....	....	105	76	14,800	27	26	200	24	12	1,585	158	116	16,585
Lyndon,	....	....	....	....	....	....	116	....	25,430	98	....	2,495	7	....	125	225	4	28,050
Machias,	1	....	$1,200	....	....	....	190	14	35,804	4	....	125	61	1	13,780	256	15	50,909
Mansfield,	....	....	....	....	....	....	140	2	42,955	64	19	1,795	9	2	490	213	23	45,240
Napoli	....	....	....	....	....	....	170	....	54,465	26	1	1,105	33	1	5,820	229	2	61,390
New Albion,	1	....	800	1	....	2,500	167	2	65,550	55	24	910	81	19	5,455	305	45	75,215
Olean,	....	....	....	2	....	2,200	229	....	199,935	11	....	445	95	....	7,042	337	....	209,622
Otto,	....	....	....	2	....	1,600	174	....	62,885	28	....	313	7	....	212	211	....	65,010
Perrysburgh,	....	....	....	....	....	....	201	....	86,645	11	....	440	64	....	11,469	276	....	98,554
Persia,	....	....	....	....	....	....	175	....	94,991	40	....	1,190	25	....	1,525	240	....	97,706
Portville,	....	....	....	....	....	....	137	....	68,960	24	....	875	43	....	1,955	204	....	71,790
Randolph,	....	....	....	....	....	....	260	1	121,475	38	1	1,493	20	1	1,571	318	3	124,539
South Valley,	....	....	....	....	....	....	58	1	10,435	29	....	950	5	....	130	92	1	11,515
Yorkshire,	1	....	1,600	1	....	800	281	11	82,805	63	36	1,050	2	1	50	348	48	86,305
Total,	5	2	3,600	9	....	8,100	4,942	453	1,779,019	1252	310	29,459	1270	119	116952	7,515	921	1,937,130

CAYUGA COUNTY.

TOWNS.	STONE.			BRICK.			FRAMED.			LOGS.			OTHER DWELLINGS.			TOTAL.		
Auburn city:																		
1st ward,	4	....	20,600	39	....	105,000	380	....	410,215	....	....	....	....	....	....	423	....	535,815
2d ward,	2	....	8,200	65	....	283,600	231	....	311,325	....	....	....	4	....	800	302	....	603,925
3d ward,	7	2	49,500	56	3	188,900	264	10	351,050	....	....	....	3	....	1,150	345	30	590,600
4th ward,	2	....	800,800	33	....	95,300	400	....	343,356	....	....	....	9	....	2,050	444	....	1,241,506
Total Auburn,	15	2	879,100	193	3	672,800	1,275	10	1,415,946	....	....	....	16	....	4,000	1,514	30	2,971,846
Aurelius,	4	....	3,900	13	....	32,500	420	1	255,020	18	....	968	29	....	1,355	484	1	293,743
Brutus,	1	....	2,000	14	....	21,600	469	....	397,620	3	....	325	56	56	....	543	56	421,545
Cato,	5	....	8,000	8	....	10,600	340	....	172,915	54	1	3,435	20	....	3,672	429	3	198,622
Conquest,	....	....	....	2	....	6,000	280	....	107,920	63	....	2,642	15	....	545	360	....	117,107
Fleming,	3	....	7,000	6	....	15,200	213	1	167,035	1	....	25	....	....	....	223	1	189,260
Genoa,	....	....	....	....	....	....	457	7	329,631	11	4	570	4	1	750	472	12	330,951
Ira,	3	....	3,000	2	....	3,000	357	...	175,550	29	....	668	9	....	678	400	....	182,896
Ledyard,	4	1	4,000	11	....	37,200	347	....	250,200	7	....	475	....	....	....	369	1	291,875
Locke,	....	....	....	....	....	....	254	...	84,915	7	....	215	....	....	....	261	....	85,130
Mentz,	....	....	....	19	....	52,350	830	1	558,320	30	....	1,146	36	....	660	918	4	612,476
Moravia,	1	....	5,000	1	....	4,000	330	21	155,415	9	1	275	2	....	650	344	23	165,340
Niles,	....	....	....	....	....	....	375	....	201,857	10	....	315	....	....	....	385	....	202,172
Owasco,	1	....	7,000	4	....	9,700	220	3	109,715	9	1	345	5	....	125	239	4	126,885
Scipio,	1	....	1,500	10	1	13,500	352	10	168,655	6	....	180	....	....	....	369	11	183,835
Sempronius,	....	....	....	....	....	....	227	....	99,340	17	....	455	....	....	....	244	....	99,795
Sennett,	1	....	2,000	17	1	17,300	364	9	141,226	....	....	....	2	....	2,005	386	12	162,531
Springport,	26	4	48,200	18	1	31,900	308	9	270,100	11	11	....	25	25	....	392	54	350,200
Sterling,	5	....	2,950	2	....	1,100	428	20	141,348	94	12	2,864	34	2	5,030	567	38	153,292
Summer Hill,	....	....	....	....	....	....	119	1	49,575	18	....	630	117	....	37,621	254	1	87,826
Venice,	1	....	800	4	....	3,550	344	6	145,150	24	14	500	3	3	....	377	24	150,000
Victory,	2	....	3,500	1	....	700	311	5	117,640	54	....	1,500	12	....	860	386	11	124,200
Total,	73	7	977,950	325	6	933,000	9.620	104	5,515,093	475	44	17,533	385	87	57,951	10,916	286	7,501,527

CHAUTAUQUE COUNTY.

TOWNS.	STONE.			BRICK.			FRAMED.			LOGS.			OTHER DWELLINGS.			TOTAL.		
Arkwright,	....	....	....	....	....	....	182	....	58,525	14	....	260	4	....	90	202	2	58,875
Busti,	....	....	....	1	....	2,000	328	6	111,547	20	....	295	4	....	535	354	7	114,377
Carroll,	....	....	....	....	....	....	185	1	61,675	38	....	1,325	44	....	2,900	267	1	65,900
Charlotte,	....	....	....	3	....	4,400	292	....	145,030	30	....	1,570	4	....	285	329	....	151,285
Chautauque,	....	....	....	11	2	12,300	463	....	202,730	26	....	1,060	20	....	2,550	520	2	218,640
Cherry Creek,	....	....	....	....	....	....	216	1	48,990	23	....	260	7	....	97	246	1	49,347
Clymer,	....	....	....	....	....	....	183	....	59,250	36	....	781	15	....	1,187	234	....	61,218
Ellery,	....	....	....	....	....	....	294	....	101,575	47	....	1,255	5	....	310	348	2	103,140
Ellicott,	....	....	....	8	....	34,100	646	....	456,359	34	....	720	27	....	435	715	....	491,614
Ellington,	....	....	....	....	....	....	338	....	131,930	32	....	660	4	....	55	374	....	132,645
French Creek,	....	....	....	....	....	....	119	....	33,605	25	....	940	9	....	1,170	153	....	35,715
Gerry,	....	....	....	....	....	....	210	1	71,925	21	....	360	11	....	2,235	242	1	74,520
Hanover,	....	....	....	4	....	11,500	645	2	336,074	26	....	709	123	....	43,403	798	2	391,686
Harmony,	....	....	....	1	....	1,800	615	3	225,845	83	....	2,821	14	....	1,870	713	4	232,336
Kiantone,	1	....	200	....	....	....	84	....	32,975	7	....	279	4	....	305	96	....	33,759
Mina,	....	....	....	....	....	....	146	3	28,725	37	....	890	16	....	305	199	3	29,920
Poland,	....	....	....	1	....	3,000	200	10	67,900	21	11	565	12	3	420	251	41	71,885
Pomfret,	2	....	4,800	33	....	126,900	1,170	....	1,169,420	13	....	440	408	....	69,720	1,627	1	1,371,280
Portland,	4	4	....	8	6	2,600	88	26	50,250	4	4	....	29	28	350	136	71	53,200
Ripley,	....	....	....	5	....	6,100	286	1	111,280	21	3	340	7	....	200	319	4	117,920
Sheridan,	2	....	2,100	4	....	5,600	270	3	131,578	8	....	270	33	....	1,790	318	4	141,338

CHAUTAUQUE COUNTY.—(CONTINUED.)

TOWNS.	STONE.			BRICK.			FRAMED.			LOGS.			OTHER DWELLINGS.			TOTAL.		
	Total number.	No. value not given.	Value given.	Total number.	No. value not given.	Val. given.	Total number.	No. value not given.	Val. given.	Total number.	No. value not given.	Val. given.	Total number.	No. value not given.	Val. given.	Total number.	No. value not given.	Val. given.
Sherman,							232	2	$103,205	21	....	$635	14	....	$1920	268	3	$105,760
Stockton,				1	....	$1,000	311	....	116,097	22	....	300	7	....	325	343	2	117,722
Villenova,							244	....	65,875	18	....	195	28	....	4,624	290	....	70,694
Westfield,	5	....	$5,000	33	1	87,100	567	3	413,663	16	....	835	13	....	570	646	16	507,168
Total,	14	4	12,100	113	9	298,400	8,314	62	4,336,028	639	18	17,765	866	31	137651	9,988	166	4,801,944

CHEMUNG COUNTY.

TOWNS.	Stone: Total number.	No. value not given.	Value given.	Brick: Total number.	No. value not given.	Val. given.	Framed: Total number.	No. value not given.	Val. given.	Logs: Total number.	No. value not given.	Val. given.	Other: Total number.	No. value not given.	Val. given.	Total: Total number.	No. value not given.	Val. given.
Big Flats,				3	....	5,500	225	2	94,557	52	2	1,225	56	1	4,865	342	11	106,147
Catlin,							113	2	37,995	95	....	3,155	74	1	9,955	295	16	51,105
Chemung,				1	....	1,500	286	2	119,090	77	....	4,237	124	1	16,199	493	8	141,026
Elmira,	1	....	3,500	40	1	534,300	1,114	6	1,676,477	39	....	2,685	265	3	102540	1,463	14	2,319,502
Erin,							97	....	23,785	82	....	2,128	50	....	3,895	229	....	29,808
Horseheads,							330	2	244,020	25	....	840	74	....	6,705	430	3	251,565
Southport,				2	1	4,000	538	144	276,330	56	30	2,925	218	38	47,335	814	213	330,590
Van Etten,							161	....	38,935	62	....	1,505	53	....	6,475	277	1	46,915
Veteran,				1	....	1,500	400	....	190,175	28	1	700	85	....	10,002	514	1	202,377
Total,	1	....	3,500	47	2	546,800	3,264	158	2,701,364	516	33	19,400	999	44	207971	4,857	267	3,479,035

CHENANGO COUNTY.

TOWNS.	Stone: Total number.	No. value not given.	Value given.	Brick: Total number.	No. value not given.	Val. given.	Framed: Total number.	No. value not given.	Val. given.	Logs: Total number.	No. value not given.	Val. given.	Other: Total number.	No. value not given.	Val. given.	Total: Total number.	No. value not given.	Val. given.
Bainbridge,	1	....	300				611	....	278,695	6	....	310				618	....	279,305
Columbus,							241	....	87,870	2	....	100	10	....	1,000	253	....	88,970
Coventry,				1	....	1,000	318	....	125,330	10	....	250	3	....	65	333	....	126 645
German,							138	138		4	4		1	1		146	146	
Greene,	2	....	3,500	7	....	10,300	630	7	319,360	48	....	1,380	9	....	2,200	697	8	336,740
Guilford,	1	....	700				469	1	252,475	11	1	325	11	....	620	492	2	254,120
Lincklaen,							205	2	39,885	9	1	91				214	3	39,976
Macdonough,	1	....	2,000				256	2	77,788	21	....	630	1	....	200	279	2	80,618
New Berlin,	2	1	750	1	1		466	126	238,860				2	....	450	479	136	240,060
North Norwich,							206	2	45,460	4	4					210	6	45,460
Norwich,	2	....	8,000	2	....	22,000	753	2	1,169,114	1	....	500	3	....	21,250	761	2	1,220,864
Otselic,							308	....	92,725	30	....	730	1	....	50	339	....	93,505
Oxford,	3	1	900	1	1		574	219	257,875	36	27	1,435	9	4	260	629	258	260,470
Pharsalia,							186	....	56,831	23	....	449	1	....	10	210	....	57,290
Pitcher,	1	....	1,200				248	2	54,481	1	....	10				250	2	55,691
Plymouth,							290	....	87,290	6	....	70	3	2	15	299	2	87,375
Preston,	1	....	1,200				176	....	65,165	3	....	160				180	....	66,525
Sherburne,	2	....	3,100	5	....	10,100	520	3	293,080	1	....	50	4	....	310	532	3	306,640
Smithville,	3	....	3,800	2	....	2,000	280	7	130,875	19	7	445	3	1	300	311	19	137,420
Smyrna,	1	1		2	1	2,500	351	297	49,200	5	5		1	1		370	315	51,700
Total,	20	3	25,450	21	3	47,900	7,226	808	3,722,359	240	49	6,935	62	9	26,730	7,602	904	3,829,374

CLINTON COUNTY.

TOWNS.	Stone: Total number.	No. value not given.	Value given.	Brick: Total number.	No. value not given.	Val. given.	Framed: Total number.	No. value not given.	Val. given.	Logs: Total number.	No. value not given.	Val. given.	Other: Total number.	No. value not given.	Val. given.	Total: Total number.	No. value not given.	Val. given.
Au Sable,	21	....	25,300	22	....	56,700	508	....	237,665	39	....	1,705	25	....	818	616	1	322,188
Beekmantown,	16	....	12,300	62	....	49,250	247	1	85,795	143	1	7,870	15	....	1,990	483	2	157,205
Black Brook,				1	....	1,000	194	1	56,947	289	7	10,717	14	4	337	499	13	69,001
Champlain,	20	....	25,600	109	1	192,350	593	7	202,495	153	....	7,745	118	1	7,440	996	12	435,630
Chazy,	34	1	22,000	81	1	66,055	386	1	107,974	199	....	6,291	80	....	6,759	780	3	209,979
Clinton,							37	....	4,875	205	4	3,678				245	7	8.553
Dannemora,							84	....	21,330							84	....	21,330
Ellenburgh,	1	....	700	2	....	1,275	134	....	30,975	151	....	5,188	33	....	1,985	321	....	40,123
Mooers,	4	....	2,950	33	....	32,800	279	1	100,969	272	....	23,970	20	....	2,190	608	1	162,879
Peru,	17	....	16.000	19	....	15,250	410	1	122,617	146	....	3,860	13	....	1,073	606	2	158,800
Plattsburgh,	42	21	32,250	104	22	196,790	642	199	361,345	73	43	1,835	29	....	1,673	896	291	593,893
Saranac,	1	....	500	2	....	1,600	210	3	62,440	268	....	8,842	42	....	2,970	523	3	76,352
Schuyler's Falls,	7	....	7,450	25	....	22,500	235	1	76,892	50	....	1,976	19	....	622	337	2	109,440
Total,	163	22	145,950	460	24	635,570	3,959	215	1,472,319	1988	55	83,677	408	5	27,857	6,994	337	2,365,373

COLUMBIA COUNTY.

TOWNS.	Stone: Total number.	No. value not given.	Value given.	Brick: Total number.	No. value not given.	Val. given.	Framed: Total number.	No. value not given.	Val. given.	Logs: Total number.	No. value not given.	Val. given.	Other: Total number.	No. value not given.	Val. given.	Total: Total number.	No. value not given.	Val. given.
Ancram,							276	3	135,540	6	....	340				284	5	135,880
Austerlitz,							321	....	158,775							323	2	158,775
Canaan,	2	....	2,000	2	....	2,000	355	5	137,335							359	5	141,335
Chatham,	3	....	1,150	9	....	17,300	710	8	517,235				2	1	300	724	9	535,985
Claverack,	4	....	7,100	19	....	38,400	545	....	386,255							569	1	431,755
Clermont,	2	....	22,000	7	....	20,800	174	....	89,115							183	....	131,915
Copake,							262	....	119,939	3	....	95	6	....	260	271	....	120,294
Gallatin,							253	....	96,595	5	....	110	2	....	50	260	....	96,755
Germantown,	1	....	250	2	....	2,800	136	....	72,780							175	36	75,830
Ghent,	10	....	5,800	6	....	14,500	396	....	291,645							412	....	311,945
Greenport,	10	....	9,500	20	....	60,500	181	....	123,380				4	....	115	215	....	193,495
Hillsdale,	2	....	2,500	2	....	10,000	389	....	214,481				1	....	10	394	....	226,991
Hudson city:																		
1st ward,				78	2	230,200	97	....	143,725							184	11	373,925
2d ward,				42	....	91,650	159	1	143,200							202	2	234,850
3d ward,	1	....	2,500	62	....	208,500	178	....	270,600							241	....	481,606
4th ward,	2	....	7,800	69	....	186,700	197	1	107,760							200	1	302,260
Total Hudson,	3	....	10,300	251	2	717,050	631	2	755,285							895	14	1,482,635

COLUMBIA COUNTY.—(CONTINUED.)

TOWNS.	STONE.			BRICK.			FRAMED.			LOGS.			OTHER DWELLINGS.			TOTAL.		
	Total number.	No. value not given.	Val. given.	Total number.	No. value not given.	Val. given.	Total number.	No. value not given.	Val. given.	Total number.	No. value not given.	Val. given.	Total number.	No. value not given.	Val. given.	Total number.	No. value not given.	Val. given.
Kinderhook,	2	....	$2,500	26	....	$111,850	563	10	$522,725	....	....	....	....	....	....	671	90	$637,075
Livingston,	1	....	1,000	9	....	63,000	318	....	151,457	....	....	....	....	....	....	328	....	215,457
New Lebanon,	....	....	....	7	....	9,800	344	....	271.805	1	....	$50	....	....	....	352	....	281,655
Stockport,	6	....	7,000	9	....	18,600	267	1	113,915	....	....	....	....	....	....	282	1	139,515
Stuyvesant,	6	....	7,115	19	....	44,200	283	....	207,700	3	....	180	5	....	$100	316	....	259,295
Taghkanick,	....	....	....	....	....	....	261	....	84,025	11	....	300	....	....	....	274	2	84,325
Total,	52	....	78,215	388	2	1,130,800	6,665	29	4,449,987	29	....	1,075	20	1	835	7,287	165	5,660,912

CORTLAND COUNTY.

TOWNS.	STONE.			BRICK.			FRAMED.			LOGS.			OTHER DWELLINGS.			TOTAL.		
	Total number.	No. value not given.	Val. given.	Total number.	No. value not given.	Val. given.	Total number.	No. value not given.	Val. given.	Total number.	No. value not given.	Val. given.	Total number.	No. value not given.	Val. given.	Total number.	No. value not given.	Val. given.
Cincinnatus,	....	....	....	1	....	1,500	209	....	102,935	8	....	210	2	....	30	220	....	104,675
Cortlandville,	1	....	6,000	21	....	83,050	789	1	600,134	6	....	125	10	....	960	827	1	690,269
Freetown,	....	....	....	....	....	....	178	....	53,010	8	....	395	1	....	20	188	1	53,425
Harford,	1	....	600	4	....	2,750	119	....	25,955	38	....	1,055	18	....	1,415	180	....	31,775
Homer,	2	....	20,600	11	....	37,500	689	14	506,280	13	....	720	4	....	800	732	27	565,900
Lapeer,	....	....	....	....	....	....	129	....	25,845	13	....	270	....	....	....	142	....	26,115
Marathon,	....	....	....	2	....	500	223	....	115,665	2	....	35	22	....	825	249	....	117,025
Preble,	1	....	1,000	1	....	400	224	....	97,410	13	3	235	1	....	10	240	3	99,055
Scott,	....	....	....	....	....	....	235	....	84,930	12	....	515	....	....	....	247	....	85,445
Solon,	1	....	5,000	....	....	....	182	1	47,535	23	....	1,395	....	....	....	206	1	53,930
Taylor,	....	....	....	....	....	....	182	2	50,030	44	....	1,055	....	....	....	226	2	51,085
Truxton,	2	....	1,100	5	....	5,600	553	1	184,092	73	2	2,049	4	....	105	646	12	192,946
Virgil,	1	....	400	....	....	....	413	4	126,345	18	....	820	14	1	1,005	446	5	129,230
Willet,	....	....	....	....	....	....	151	....	56,005	24	....	605	3	....	250	178	....	56,860
Total,	9	....	34,700	45	....	131,300	4,276	23	2,076,171	295	5	9,484	79	1	6,080	4,727	52	2,257,735

DELAWARE COUNTY.

TOWNS.	STONE.			BRICK.			FRAMED.			LOGS.			OTHER DWELLINGS.			TOTAL.		
	Total number.	No. value not given.	Val. given.	Total number.	No. value not given.	Val. given.	Total number.	No. value not given.	Val. given.	Total number.	No. value not given.	Val. given.	Total number.	No. value not given.	Val. given.	Total number.	No. value not given.	Val. given.
Andes,	4	4	....	....	....	....	360	193	57,535	65	56	187	2	2	....	432	256	57,722
Bovina,	5	....	1,650	....	....	....	198	....	81,133	5	....	125	....	....	....	208	....	82,908
Colchester,	....	....	....	....	....	....	307	1	79,936	96	....	2,943	8	1	235	411	2	83,114
Davenport,	1	....	300	1	....	1,200	351	....	118,260	46	2	1,350	....	....	....	399	2	121,110
Delhi,	2	....	650	....	....	....	401	6	272,033	59	....	3,061	2	1	15	465	8	275,759
Franklin,	3	1	1,300	....	....	....	571	19	273,335	39	1	1,030	1	....	100	618	25	275,765
Hamden,	1	....	700	....	....	....	260	....	103,570	78	....	4,390	....	....	....	339	....	108,660
Hancock,	1	....	200	1	....	600	292	5	117,810	86	49	1,470	50	40	665	430	94	120,745
Harpersfield,	3	....	1,100	1	....	1,500	279	....	124,990	2	....	75	....	....	....	285	....	127,665
Kortright,	9	....	5,600	....	....	....	335	2	154,105	33	....	1,955	2	....	600	380	3	162,260
Masonville,	2	....	400	....	....	....	235	....	74,311	44	....	650	4	....	350	285	....	75,711
Meredith,	3	....	1,350	....	....	....	262	....	102,231	36	....	985	2	....	230	303	....	104,796
Middletown,	1	....	500	....	....	....	460	....	114,045	51	....	1,500	22	....	1,223	534	....	117,268
Roxbury,	6	....	3,500	....	....	....	345	7	104,595	23	7	415	....	....	....	460	100	108,510
Sidney,	....	....	....	....	....	....	297	26	108,000	39	6	925	8	....	300	345	33	109,225
Stamford,	2	....	300	3	....	1,950	280	1	145,070	10	....	405	....	....	....	295	1	147,725
Tompkins,	1	....	350	....	....	....	447	1	229,205	101	....	5,885	42	....	3.985	592	2	239,425
Walton,	....	....	....	2	....	1,050	360	....	160,675	75	....	2,027	19	....	1,170	457	1	164,922
Total,	44	5	17,900	8	....	6,300	6,040	261	2,420,839	888	121	29,378	162	44	8,873	7,238	527	2,483,290

DUTCHESS COUNTY.

TOWNS.	STONE.			BRICK.			FRAMED.			LOGS.			OTHER DWELLINGS.			TOTAL.		
	Total number.	No. value not given.	Val. given.	Total number.	No. value not given.	Val. given.	Total number.	No. value not given.	Val. given.	Total number.	No. value not given.	Val. given.	Total number.	No. value not given.	Val. given.	Total number.	No. value not given.	Val. given.
Amenia,	....	....	....	5	5	....	346	150	122,600	8	2	80	1	....	5	376	173	122,685
Beekman,	3	....	1,800	2	....	2,200	231	....	169,505	6	....	200	....	....	....	242	....	173,705
Clinton,	3	2	125	2	....	650	337	158	77,055	1	1	....	....	....	....	343	161	77,830
Dover,	....	....	....	2	....	4,000	282	2	207,786	4	....	250	1	....	25	289	2	212,061
East Fishkill,	5	....	2,500	6	....	20,500	439	3	278,607	11	....	295	1	....	10	462	3	301,912
Fishkill,	33	9	32,650	54	4	167,875	1,097	94	1,307,564	5	....	435	7	....	1,125	1,205	116	1,509,649
Hyde Park,	20	....	90,550	5	....	49,150	388	2	336,270	....	....	....	2	....	70	415	2	476,040
La Grange,	4	....	2,850	3	....	4,100	321	....	189,350	....	....	....	....	....	....	328	....	196,300
Milan,	7	....	2,700	1	....	1,100	293	1	157,714	2	....	100	....	....	....	203	1	161,614
North East,	1	....	4,000	4	....	2,100	279	....	184,665	5	....	150	2	....	35	291	....	190,950
Pauling,	4	....	700	1	....	3,000	302	....	182.570	12	....	190	5	....	145	324	....	186,605
Pine Plains,	1	....	1,200	....	....	....	274	7	187,565	....	....	....	....	....	....	275	7	188,765
Pleasant Valley,	2	....	50	1	....	4,000	370	8	241,680	....	....	....	....	....	....	374	9	245,730
Poughkeepsie,	18	13	1,350	15	8	11,750	453	219	122,356	....	....	....	....	....	....	502	256	135,456
Poughkeepsie City:																		
1st ward,	2	....	6,000	109	1	259,600	394	....	420,350	....	....	....	....	....	....	505	1	685,950
2d ward,	1	....	1,500	40	....	140,000	303	1	502,300	....	....	....	....	....	....	344	1	643,800
3d ward,	1	....	12,000	63	....	107,400	423	....	397,300	....	....	....	....	....	....	488	1	516,700
4th ward,	1	1	....	91	....	314,900	265	8	414,100	....	....	....	....	....	....	369	21	729,000
Total Poughkeepsie,	5	1	19,500	303	1	821,900	1,385	9	1,734,050	....	....	....	....	....	....	1,706	24	2,575,450
Redhook,	24	....	37,950	18	....	129,500	554	5	588,355	....	....	....	6	....	400	604	7	756,205
Rhinebeck,	45	....	47,100	7	....	17,900	468	....	461,895	....	....	....	5	....	130	525	....	527,025
Stanford,	....	....	....	4	....	1,900	398	2	244,325	....	....	....	1	....	10	403	2	246.235
Union Vale,	1	....	400	....	....	....	253	2	142,790	....	....	....	....	....	....	255	3	143,190
Washington,	1	....	75	1	....	500	477	....	237,530	4	....	85	....	....	....	483	....	238,190
Total,	177	25	245,500	434	18	1,242,125	8,947	662	7,174,232	58	3	1.785	31	....	1,955	9,705	766	8,665,597

ERIE COUNTY.

TOWNS.	STONE.			BRICK.			FRAMED.			LOGS.			OTHER DWELLINGS.			TOTAL.		
	Total number.	No. value not given.	Val. given.	Total number.	No. value not given.	Val. given.	Total number.	No. value not given.	Val. given.	Total number.	No. value not given.	Val. given.	Total number.	No. value not given.	Val. given.	Total number.	No. value not given.	Val. given.
Alden,	1	1	....	3	2	10,020	182	119	74,425	42	42	....	38	38	....	469	405	84,445
Amherst,	33	....	38,550	45	....	44,300	418	....	229,635	341	....	20,381	113	....	21,561	951	1	354,427
Aurora,	1	....	350	9	....	7,150	374	1	183,515	37	2	1,840	311	8	72,260	733	12	265,115
Boston,	1	....	200	....	....	....	202	1	89,775	8	....	775	99	4	26,605	310	5	117,355
Brandt,	....	....	....	....	....	....	143	139	335	17	17	....	34	34	....	196	192	335

ERIE COUNTY.—(CONTINUED.)

TOWNS.	STONE.			BRICK.			FRAMED.			LOGS.			OTHER DWELLINGS.			TOTAL.		
	Total number.	No. value not given.	Val. given.	Total number.	No. value not given.	Val. given.	Total number.	No. value not given.	Val. given.	Total number.	No value not given	Val. given.	Total number	No. value not given	Val. given.	Total number.	No. value not given.	Val. given.
Buffalo city:																		
1st ward,	1	....	$7,000	130	....	$678, 500	462	....	$457, 500	....	....	......	497	....	$226,650	1, 090	....	$1,369, 650
2d ward,	....	....	....	425	7	2, 039, 300	342	4	780, 160	....	....	......	....	....	....	767	11	2, 819, 460
3d ward,	....	....	....	110	....	180, 650	623	....	706, 155	....	....	......	....	....	....	735	2	886, 805
4th ward,	2	....	60, 000	329	....	1, 295, 800	662	....	977, 900	....	....	......	....	....	....	993	....	2, 333, 700
5th ward,	1	....	35, 000	117	1	279, 950	1, 196	5	1, 368, 549	2	....	$1,000	....	....	....	1, 316	6	1, 684, 499
6th ward,	1	....	8, 000	92	2	211, 100	957	3	742, 500	....	....	......	1	1	....	1, 053	8	961, 600
7th ward,	1	....	1, 000	126	3	419, 150	988	3	1, 119, 225	3	....	2, 450	....	....	....	1, 118	6	1, 541, 825
8th ward,	7	1	16, 900	184	....	831, 400	316	....	377, 750	....	....	......	123	....	7, 150	632	3	1, 233, 200
9th ward,	10	....	105, 300	305	....	1, 800, 200	430	2	1, 090, 700	....	....	......	10	....	3, 800	778	25	3, 000, 000
10th ward,	3	....	78, 000	262	3	1, 842, 000	528	1	1, 115, 750	....	....	......	6	....	2, 200	800	5	3, 037, 950
11th ward,	6	....	142, 000	69	....	620, 200	315	....	786, 750	1	....	1, 000	205	....	146, 990	596	....	1, 696, 940
12th ward,	10	....	93, 000	23	....	102, 000	385	4	598, 560	57	1	99, 720	69	1	20, 400	596	58	913, 680
13th ward,	2	....	3, 000	6	....	17, 200	6	....	4, 300	12	....	235	113	....	24, 115	139	....	48, 850
Total Buffalo,	44	1	549, 200	2, 178	16	10, 317, 450	7, 210	22	10, 125, 799	75	1	104405	1024	2	431, 305	10, 613	124	21, 528, 159
Chictawauga,	1	....	400	13	1	10, 700	330	2	95, 915	90	....	7, 970	54	3	4, 290	488	6	119, 275
Clarence,	9	....	8, 700	19	1	24, 500	365	5	161, 825	184	....	14, 185	10	1	690	587	7	209, 900
Colden,	....	....	....	......	....	....	19	6	4, 275	23	23	......	232	148	20, 476	289	192	24, 751
Collins,	....	....	....	2	....	3, 800	314	8	115, 685	30	12	560	14	2	4, 210	362	.24	124, 255
Concord,	1	....	1, 000	8	....	15, 500	457	1	184, 945	28	1	675	36	2	9, 320	531	5	211, 440
East Hamburgh,	....	....	....	3	....	3, 200	59	....	34, 050	40	....	1, 385	272	1	147, 435	374	1	186, 070
Eden,	....	....	....	......	....	....	146	7	24, 971	29	4	308	295	6	98, 510	470	17	123, 789
Evans,	2	....	1, 100	5	....	5, 700	201	1	73, 750	19	4	348	223	17	51, 911	452	24	132, 809
Grand Island,	....	....	....	......	....	....	9	....	3, 250	102	2	7, 825	50	1	9, 310	161	3	20, 385
Hamburgh,	1	....	200	3	....	4, 800	130	4	93, 365	26	1	1, 115	376	3	142, 135	550	22	241, 615
Holland,	....	....	....	1	....	1, 500	146	3	56, 360	24	....	830	93	....	18, 625	265	4	77, 315
Lancaster,	6	....	4, 600	89	2	100, 950	578	19	231, 505	94	32	3, 010	291	74	57, 870	1, 065	134	397, 935
Marilla,	....	....	....	......	....	....	110	....	42, 645	59	....	2, 384	123	....	25, 938	292	....	70, 967
Newstead,	2	....	1, 300	3	....	4, 200	428	2	195, 302	129	86	2, 432	34	9	2, 380	596	97	205, 614
North Collins,	2	....	575	1	....	800	107	26	28, 045	28	15	735	217	111	31, 420	358	155	61, 575
Sardinia,	....	....	....	2	....	3, 000	300	2	85, 165	38	8	375	20	8	735	360	18	89, 275
Tonawanda,	4	....	3, 200	33	....	43, 150	82	....	66, 734	78	....	6, 258	253	....	137, 200	450	....	256, 542
Wales,	3	3	....	1	1	....	292	267	11, 250	26	26	......	1	1	....	336	311	11, 250
West Seneca,	....	....	....	9	....	9, 400	232	....	98, 445	71	....	1, 590	103	....	3, 711	416	1	113, 146
Total,	111	5	609, 375	2, 427	23	10, 610, 120	12, 834	635	12, 310, 966	1638	276	179386	4316	473	1,317,897	21, 674	1760	25, 027, 744

ESSEX COUNTY.

TOWNS.	Stone: Total number.	Stone: No. value not given.	Stone: Val. given.	Brick: Total number.	Brick: No. value not given.	Brick: Val. given.	Framed: Total number.	Framed: No. value not given.	Framed: Val. given.	Logs: Total number.	Logs: No value not given	Logs: Val. given.	Other: Total number	Other: No. value not given	Other: Val. given.	Total: Total number.	Total: No. value not given.	Total: Val. given.
Chesterfield,	8	....	16, 700	25	....	53, 400	454	4	211, 785	72	....	1, 953	....	....	....	559	4	283, 838
Crown Point,	1	....	300	8	....	11, 300	349	3	107, 430	22	....	235	14	1	3, 910	394	4	123, 175
Elizabethtown,	....	....	....	5	....	10, 400	182	1	68, 150	32	....	1, 805	13	....	375	232	1	80, 730
Essex,	5	....	7, 125	36	....	52, 950	298	1	131, 300	17	....	1, 260	3	....	270	359	1	192, 905
Jay,	7	....	5, 400	4	....	3, 100	440	8	121, 842	1	....	100	....	....	....	452	8	130, 442
Keene,	....	....	....	1	....	1, 200	99	....	16, 215	42	....	837	1	....	150	143	....	18, 402
Lewis,	....	....	....	5	....	4, 150	226	3	44, 790	82	1	4, 380	8	1	225	321	5	53, 545
Minerva,	....	....	....	......	....	....	89	....	30, 656	48	....	3, 030	4	....	335	144	3	34, 021
Moriah,	1	....	150	17	....	30, 000	393	....	155, 370	60	....	2, 005	23	....	520	494	....	188, 045
Newcomb,	....	....	....	1	....	1, 000	26	....	7, 650	7	....	750	1	....	150	38	3	9, 550
North Elba,	....	....	....	......	....	....	23	....	6, 390	30	....	1, 512	....	....	....	53	....	7, 902
North Hudson,	....	....	....	......	....	....	54	...	20, 250	18	....	1, 200	8	....	550	80	....	22, 000
St. Armand,	....	....	....	......	....	....	32	1	6, 725	25	....	1, 935	....	....	....	57	1	8, 660
Schroon,	....	....	....	1	....	800	247	1	89, 135	86	....	3, 528	14	....	556	348	1	94, 019
Ticonderoga,	1	....	100	6	....	4, 250	350	1	129, 315	30	....	1, 300	6	....	320	409	17	135, 285
Westport,	2	....	2, 200	26	....	29, 395	285	....	106, 005	30	....	773	16	....	1, 250	396	37	139, 623
Willsboro',	1	....	100	6	....	4, 250	346	1	129, 192	31	....	1, 315	6	....	320	390	1	135, 177
Wilmington,	4	....	3, 300	27	....	29, 675	283	....	102, 220	30	....	773	14	....	745	358	....	136, 713
Total,	30	....	35, 375	168	....	235, 870	4, 176	24	1, 484, 420	663	1	28, 691	131	2	9, 676	5, 227	86	1, 794, 032

FRANKLIN COUNTY.

TOWNS.	Stone: Total number.	Stone: No. value not given.	Stone: Val. given.	Brick: Total number.	Brick: No. value not given.	Brick: Val. given.	Framed: Total number.	Framed: No. value not given.	Framed: Val. given.	Logs: Total number.	Logs: No value not given	Logs: Val. given.	Other: Total number	Other: No. value not given	Other: Val. given.	Total: Total number.	Total: No. value not given.	Total: Val. given.
Bangor,	18	....	11, 900	3	....	2, 500	250	....	71, 100	102	....	2, 163	21	....	1, 120	395	1	88, 783
Belmont,	1	....	800	1	....	1, 500	69	....	22, 865	81	....	3, 655	7	1	1, 725	160	2	30, 545
Bombay,	6	....	6, 200	4	....	4, 650	179	5	94, 465	130	6	7, 296	57	8	4, 015	376	19	116, 626
Brandon,	3	....	1, 640	......	....	....	85	....	16, 140	45	....	2, 259	2	....	26	135	....	20, 065
Burke,	3	....	2, 800	4	....	2, 675	208	....	49, 000	100	....	3, 783	24	....	1, 745	339	....	60, 003
Chateaugay,	6	....	2, 700	11	....	9, 200	249	1	68, 655	170	3	5, 367	29	....	2, 070	466	5	87, 992
Constable,	....	....	....	1	1	....	123	123	....	90	90	......	36	36	....	254	254	....
Dickinson,	4	....	2, 300	......	....	....	140	2	21, 910	82	....	2, 196	2	....	85	230	4	26, 491
Duane,	....	....	....	......	....	....	16	....	4, 440	28	....	1, 065	....	....	....	44	....	5, 505
Fort Covington,	11	....	12, 900	14	....	21, 100	270	....	157, 680	87	....	6, 801	48	....	21, 510	430	....	219, 991
Franklin,	....	....	....	......	....	....	66	....	17, 460	99	....	5, 450	....	....	....	165	....	22, 910
Harrietstown,	....	....	....	......	....	....	17	....	7, 105	40	....	1, 535	....	....	....	58	1	8, 640
Malone,	30	3	34, 400	31	....	39, 450	523	5	371, 506	172	.1	2, 824	114	....	47, 050	871	10	495, 230
Moira,	5	....	3, 900	2	....	3, 000	212	....	75, 125	51	1	1, 651	3	....	150	274	2	83, 826
Westville,	1	....	200	......	....	....	138	2	47, 085	76	2	2, 521	32	....	1, 825	247	4	51, 631
Total,	88	3	79, 740	71	1	84, 075	2, 545	138	1, 024, 536	1353	103	48, 566	375	45	81, 321	4, 444	302	1, 318, 238

FULTON COUNTY.

TOWNS.	Stone: Total number.	Stone: No. value not given.	Stone: Val. given.	Brick: Total number.	Brick: No. value not given.	Brick: Val. given.	Framed: Total number.	Framed: No. value not given.	Framed: Val. given.	Logs: Total number.	Logs: No value not given	Logs: Val. given.	Other: Total number	Other: No. value not given	Other: Val. given.	Total: Total number.	Total: No. value not given.	Total: Val. given.
Bleecker,	....	....	....	......	....	....	79	....	18, 570	80	....	3, 145	14	....	1, 075	173	....	22, 790
Broadalbin,	1	....	600	3	....	5, 200	490	....	193, 390	5	....	150	7	....	3, 012	506	....	202, 352
Caroga,	....	....	....	......	....	....	99	....	19, 920	26	....	1, 785	....	....	....	125	....	21, 705
Ephratah,	....	....	....	......	....	....	356	2	112, 765	18	....	550	....	....	....	375	3	113, 315
Johnstown,	1	....	4, 000	35	8	62, 300	1, 202	225	692, 890	8	2	400	40	4	48, 420	1, 287	240	808, 010
Mayfield,	....	....	....	5	....	3, 900	451	....	118, 715	14	1	730	1	1	....	471	2	123, 345

FULTON COUNTY.—(Continued.)

TOWNS.	STONE.			BRICK			FRAMED.			LOGS.			OTHER DWELLINGS.			TOTAL.		
	Total number.	No. value not given.	Val. given.	Total number.	No. value not given.	Val. given.	Total number.	No. value not given.	Val. given.	Total number.	No. value not given.	Val. given.	Total number.	No. value not given.	Val. given.	Total number.	No. value not given.	Val. given.
Northampton,	....	....	....	4	1	$5, 800	400	....	$138, 580	1	....	$50	1	....	$1,000	406	1	$145, 430
Oppenheim,	....	....	....	......	....	....	399	2	117, 845	33	....	800	3	....	220	436	3	118, 865
Perth,	2	....	....	6	...	7, 900	199	....	94, 325	1	....	100	....	....	......	206	....	102, 325
Stratford,	....	....	....	......	....	....	142	1	23, 985	52	1	1, 162	....	....	......	194	2	25, 147
Total,	2	....	$4, 600	53	9	85, 100	3, 817	230	1, 530, 985	238	4	8, 872	66	5	53, 727	4, 179	251	1, 683, 284

GENESEE COUNTY.

TOWNS.	Stone: Total number.	Stone: No. value not given.	Stone: Val. given.	Brick: Total number.	Brick: No. value not given.	Brick: Val. given.	Framed: Total number.	Framed: No. value not given.	Framed: Val. given.	Logs: Total number.	Logs: No. value not given.	Logs: Val. given.	Other: Total number.	Other: No. value not given.	Other: Val. given.	Total: Total number.	Total: No. value not given.	Total: Val. given.
Alabama,	2	....	2, 000	......	....	....	271	3	151, 335	99	2	2, 695	44	2	2, 900	416	7	158, 930
Alexander,	4	....	2, 700	8	....	11, 650	330	3	144, 100	8	....	525	....	....	......	351	4	158, 975
Batavia,	8	2	9, 250	29	5	138, 600	830	199	647, 115	46	14	2, 658	11	1	1, 200	924	221	798, 823
Bergen,	4	3	100	3	3	....	318	199	83, 420	20	17	395	7	2	700	366	238	84, 615
Bethany,	4	....	4, 200	12	....	9, 300	326	....	140, 550	10	....	320	4	....	40	356	....	154, 410
Byron,	7	....	3, 400	3	....	4, 500	267	....	157, 337	27	....	1, 695	9	....	300	313	....	167, 232
Darien,	1	....	1, 200	8	....	8, 100	383	....	166, 945	9	....	195	17	....	240	418	....	176, 680
Elba,	6	....	5, 650	......	....	....	321	3	194, 960	35	1	1, 325	11	....	1, 048	375	6	202, 983
Le Roy,	16	....	24, 450	22	....	55, 500	624	2	643, 760	32	9	1, 205	22	4	529	716	15	725, 444
Oakfield,	2	1	600	2	1	900	251	134	74, 240	23	21	200	2	2	......	286	165	75, 940
Pavilion,	2	2	....	13	5	11, 400	295	249	34, 340	12	11	300	....	....	......	323	268	46, 040
Pembroke,	2	....	550	2	....	900	419	1	151, 780	81	6	2, 558	42	....	1, 435	549	10	157, 223
Stafford,	2	....	2, 000	5	....	5, 500	341	....	171, 915	6	....	160	6	....	65	360	....	179, 640
Total,	60	8	56, 100	107	14	246, 350	4, 976	793	2, 761, 797	408	81	14, 231	175	11	8, 457	5, 753	934	3, 086, 085

GREENE COUNTY.

TOWNS.	Stone: Total number.	Stone: No. value not given.	Stone: Val. given.	Brick: Total number.	Brick: No. value not given.	Brick: Val. given.	Framed: Total number.	Framed: No. value not given.	Framed: Val. given.	Logs: Total number.	Logs: No. value not given.	Logs: Val. given.	Other: Total number.	Other: No. value not given.	Other: Val. given.	Total: Total number.	Total: No. value not given.	Total: Val. given.
Ashland,	....	....	....	1	1	....	208	159	40, 600	2	2	......	....	....	......	217	168	40, 600
Athens,	22	1	18, 475	49	....	94, 600	361	....	248, 486	6	1	125	....	....	......	438	2	361, 686
Cairo,	3	....	1, 130	11	....	7, 200	424	10	161, 352	6	....	355	1	....	400	448	13	170, 457
Catskill,	38	....	28, 900	55	3	108, 900	828	6	520, 200	2	....	100	5	....	200	930	11	658, 300
Coxsackie,	19	....	12, 400	33	....	64, 500	534	....	854, 805	2	....	75	4	....	70	592	....	431, 850
Dunham,	....	....	....	7	....	8, 700	472	....	215, 070	3	....	105	....	....	......	482	....	223, 875
Greenville,	....	....	....	2	....	4, 000	410	....	172, 275	1	....	25	1	....	100	415	1	176, 400
Halcott,	1	....	500	......	....	....	68	2	15, 050	17	....	795	....	....	......	86	2	16, 345
Hunter,	....	....	....	......	....	....	222	1	54, 735	30	....	1, 305	6	....	285	258	1	56, 325
Jewett,	....	....	....	1	....	1, 500	198	2	30, 775	5	....	80	....	....	......	205	3	32, 355
Lexington,	1	....	300	......	....	....	287	6	90, 805	25	....	590	6	....	470	319	6	92, 165
New Baltimore,	15	....	8, 700	4	....	7, 050	405	....	207, 935	....	....	......	....	....	......	425	1	223, 685
Prattsville,	....	....	....	......	....	....	229	1	100, 555	38	....	1, 265	....	....	......	267	1	101, 820
Windham,	1	....	1, 500	......	....	....	318	....	132, 145	8	....	255	....	....	......	327	....	133, 870
Total,	100	1	71, 925	163	4	296, 450	4, 964	187	2, 344, 788	145	3	5, 045	23	....	1, 525	5, 409	209	2, 719, 733

HAMILTON COUNTY.

TOWNS.	Stone: Total number.	Stone: No. value not given.	Stone: Val. given.	Brick: Total number.	Brick: No. value not given.	Brick: Val. given.	Framed: Total number.	Framed: No. value not given.	Framed: Val. given.	Logs: Total number.	Logs: No. value not given.	Logs: Val. given.	Other: Total number.	Other: No. value not given.	Other: Val. given.	Total: Total number.	Total: No. value not given.	Total: Val. given.
Arietta,	....	....	....	......	....	....	20	1	15, 975	12	....	6, 625	....	....	......	32	1	22, 600
Gilman,	....	....	....	......	....	....	8	....	2, 650	11	....	591	....	....	......	21	2	3, 241
Hope,	1	....	200	......	....	....	111	1	27, 665	21	....	620	1	....	10	135	2	28, 495
Lake Pleasant,	1	1	....	......	....	....	14	14	....	13	12	50	....	....	......	52	51	50
Long Lake,	....	....	....	......	....	....	13	....	2, 300	13	....	455	2	....	270	28	....	3, 025
Morehouse,	....	....	....	......	....	....	23	....	4, 325	29	....	685	3	....	160	56	1	5, 170
Wells,	....	....	....	......	....	....	84	....	17, 965	48	....	1, 370	5	....	875	137	....	20, 210
Total,	2	1	200	......	....	....	273	16	70, 880	147	12	10, 396	11	....	1, 315	461	57	82, 791

HERKIMER COUNTY.

TOWNS.	Stone: Total number.	Stone: No. value not given.	Stone: Val. given.	Brick: Total number.	Brick: No. value not given.	Brick: Val. given.	Framed: Total number.	Framed: No. value not given.	Framed: Val. given.	Logs: Total number.	Logs: No. value not given.	Logs: Val. given.	Other: Total number.	Other: No. value not given.	Other: Val. given.	Total: Total number.	Total: No. value not given.	Total: Val. given.
Columbia,	....	....	....	1	....	4, 000	351	....	140, 645	....	....	......	....	....	......	352	....	144, 645
Danube,	....	....	....	6	....	6, 800	272	41	94, 385	....	....	......	12	1	220	295	47	101, 405
Fairfield,	2	....	2, 700	4	....	4, 600	259	4	198, 075	....	....	......	....	....	......	266	5	205, 375
Frankfort,	3	1	1, 300	7	....	7, 500	566	35	241, 645	4	....	185	1	....	120	658	113	250, 750
German Flats,	4	2	950	43	4	96, 900	673	41	340, 540	1	....	50	2	....	145	725	49	438, 585
Herkimer,	2	1	11. 000	12	3	26, 100	428	116	240, 272	....	....	......	....	....	......	447	125	277, 372
Litchfield,	3	....	5, 600	4	....	7, 400	285	....	119, 460	1	....	15	5	....	3, 250	298	....	135, 725
Little Falls,	15	....	23, 600	53	....	206, 450	647	2	480, 555	1	....	30	8	....	6, 930	726	4	717, 565
Manheim,	1	....	1, 000	5	....	12, 500	295	....	154, 375	1	....	50	2	....	40	304	....	167, 965
Newport,	18	....	131, 150	4	....	9, 500	343	....	208, 065	4	....	150	....	....	......	369	....	348, 865
Norway,	3	3	....	......	....	....	175	140	19, 510	3	3	......	....	....	......	182	147	19, 510
Ohio,	....	....	....	......	....	....	125	2	26, 590	65	1	2, 305	....	....	......	194	7	28, 895
Russia,	5	....	3, 400	3	....	4, 500	381	3	158, 484	31	....	458	2	....	90	424	5	166, 932
Salisbury,	3	....	1, 450	11	1	6, 300	384	5	161, 510	40	....	2, 570	10	....	2, 060	448	6	173, 890
Schuyler,	....	....	....	4	....	5, 350	278	....	95, 390	13	....	525	....	....	......	295	....	101, 265
Stark,	1	....	1, 000	......	....	....	262	19	114, 145	2	1	10	3	1	200	272	25	115, 355
Warren,	2	....	6, 000	2	....	2, 500	331	1	144, 765	....	....	......	....	....	......	335	1	153, 265
Wilmurt,	....	....	....	......	....	....	13	....	1, 765	25	....	1, 055	....	....	......	38	....	2, 820
Winfield,	....	....	....	6	....	6, 700	264	....	142, 865	....	....	......	....	....	......	270	....	149, 565
Total,	62	7	189, 150	165	8	407, 100	6, 332	409	3, 083, 041	191	5	7, 403	45	2	13, 055	6, 898	534	3, 699, 749

JEFFERSON COUNTY.

TOWNS.	Stone: Total number.	Stone: No. value not given.	Stone: Val. given.	Brick: Total number.	Brick: No. value not given.	Brick: Val. given.	Framed: Total number.	Framed: No. value not given.	Framed: Val. given.	Logs: Total number.	Logs: No. value not given.	Logs: Val. given.	Other: Total number.	Other: No. value not given.	Other: Val. given.	Total: Total number.	Total: No. value not given.	Total: Val. given.
Adams,	12	....	11, 375	9	1	10, 150	543	....	389, 688	20	....	655	14	....	360	598	1	412, 228
Alexandria,	15	....	16, 100	1	....	700	388	10	136, 663	186	....	13, 025	10	....	320	602	12	166, 808
Antwerp,	20	....	14, 800	8	....	10, 500	448	15	181, 252	135	2	1, 892	27	....	1, 500	639	18	209, 944
Brownville,	49	....	45, 550	7	....	11, 500	546	....	251, 425	68	....	3, 980	5	....	425	675	....	312, 880
Cape Vincent,	30	....	29, 850	5	....	10, 700	386	1	217, 170	144	....	4, 643	25	1	3, 556	592	4	265, 919

JEFFERSON COUNTY.—(Continued.)

TOWNS.	STONE.			BRICK.			FRAMED.			LOGS.			OTHER DWELLINGS.			TOTAL.		
	Total number.	No. value not given.	Value given	Total number.	No. value not given.	Val. given.	Total number.	No. value not given.	Val. given.	Total number.	No. value not given.	Val. given.	Total number.	No. value not given.	Val. given.	Total number	No. value not given.	Val. given
Champion,	21		$21, 200	4		$2, 700	353	1	$133, 840	6		$220				384	1	$157, 960
Clayton,	11		10, 500				539	1	246, 180	220		6, 638	27		$1,715	797	1	265, 033
Ellisburgh,	9		11, 000	10		6, 200	943	2	444, 710	41		1, 315	14		945	1, 018	3	464, 170
Henderson,	19	1	14, 250	1		700	339	5	192, 215	27		1, 245	6		435	393	7	208, 845
Hounsfield,	30		40, 280	37		54, 400	497	5	221, 815	41	1	2, 375	6		375	620	15	319, 245
Le Ray,	54		45, 500	11		8, 650	475	1	183, 030	55	3	1, 930	8		120	603	4	239, 230
Lorraine,							269	4	91, 315	25		1, 395	1		100	295	4	92, 810
Lyme,	10		12, 900				382	3	140, 850	42	13	1, 100	19	9	2, 305	455	27	157, 155
Orleans,	15	1	30, 050				364	2	131, 050	79		3, 725	14		3, 265	472	3	168, 090
Pamelia,	34	5	31, 000	5		10, 400	369	75	165, 155	9		115	1		100	420	82	206, 770
Philadelphia,	1		1, 000	1		1, 500	279	1	132, 645	28	4	895	5	1	140	315	7	136, 180
Rodman,	3		2, 300	3		3, 700	142		104, 880	3		80	187		58, 125	338		169, 085
Rutland,	16		18, 050	4		4, 800	360	2	155, 220	11	5	120				391	7	178, 190
Theresa,	11		7, 600	20		16, 700	263	1	150, 465	98	2	3, 615	5		2, 025	397	3	180, 405
Watertown,	63	12	135, 700	77	2	253, 000	1, 133		1, 059, 175	6		350	15		2, 225	1, 299	19	1, 450, 450
Wilna,	6		7, 400	5		9, 000	450	11	249, 525	99	19	2, 163	17	4	540	577	34	268, 628
Worth,							66		15, 000	26	1	660	3		75	95	1	15, 735
Total,	429	19	506, 405	208	3	415, 300	9, 534	140	4, 993, 268	1369	50	52, 136	409	15	78, 651	11, 975	253	6, 045, 760

KINGS COUNTY.

TOWNS.	Stone: Total number.	Stone: No. value not given.	Stone: Value given	Brick: Total number.	Brick: No. value not given.	Brick: Val. given.	Framed: Total number.	Framed: No. value not given.	Framed: Val. given.	Logs: Total number.	Logs: No. value not given.	Logs: Val. given.	Other: Total number.	Other: No. value not given.	Other: Val. given.	Total: Total number	Total: No. value not given.	Total: Val. given
Brooklyn city:																		
1st ward,	26		388, 000	381		2, 689, 850	197		714, 900							608	4	3, 792, 750
2d ward,	5		48, 500	227	1	965, 800	505	3	1, 326, 200							739	6	2, 340, 500
3d ward,	112	2	1592, 500	637	3	5, 550, 750	231	1	1, 004, 200							980	6	8, 147, 450
4th ward,	61		576, 000	486		2, 889, 700	779	2	2, 260, 650							1, 326	2	5, 726, 350
5th ward,				357		1, 362, 800	904	4	2, 104, 600							1, 261	4	3, 467, 400
6th ward,	73		678, 000	1, 537	5	7, 384, 700	140		226, 750							1, 751	6	8, 289, 450
7th ward,	15	1	85, 500	373	3	1, 591, 300	1, 239	8	2, 760, 105				151	123	7, 635	1, 783	140	4, 444, 540
8th ward,	6		61, 000	77		270, 200	683		1, 274, 850							793	27	1, 606, 050
9th ward,	10		37, 500	68	1	242, 200	1, 359	6	2, 791, 210							1, 437	7	3, 070, 910
10th ward,	169	1	1080, 700	1, 271	20	5, 433, 850	972	12	1, 897, 870				6	1	450	2, 427	43	8, 412, 870
11th ward,	11		219, 500	782		3, 668, 750	1, 518	2	3, 911, 550							2, 313	4	7, 799, 800
12th ward,	1		5, 000	332		1, 020, 050	335		300, 475				226		22, 600	896	2	1, 348, 125
13th ward,	20		157, 500	769	1	3, 690, 300	894		2, 744, 600				1		500	1, 684	1	6, 592, 900
14th ward,				328		1, 156, 750	862		1, 596, 500				16		13, 100	1, 207	1	2, 766, 350
15th ward,				121	2	372, 450	694	4	1, 268, 220							819	10	1, 640, 670
16th ward,				189		509, 200	1, 308		1, 908, 000							1, 498	1	2, 417, 200
17th ward,				94		308, 600	567	1	1, 133, 800							664	4	1, 442, 400
18th ward,	2		800	10		26, 500	375	2	554, 335							387	2	581, 635
Total Brooklyn,	511	4	4,930,500	8, 039	36	39, 133, 750	13, 562	45	29, 778, 815				400	124	44, 285	22, 573	270	73, 887, 350
Flatbush,				5		350, 000	259	3	644, 700				2		85	266	3	994, 785
Flatlands,							231	2	233, 381							232	3	233, 381
Gravesend,				1		1, 000	198		219, 758				1		25	200		220, 783
New Lots,	2		21, 500	12		23, 900	321		572, 620							335		618, 020
New Utrecht,	2		2, 600	4		18, 000	330	1	553, 225							364	29	573, 825
Total,	515	4	4 954 600	8, 061	36	39, 526, 650	14, 901	51	32, 002, 499				403	124	44, 395	23, 970	305	76, 528, 144

LEWIS COUNTY.

TOWNS.	Stone: Total number.	Stone: No. value not given.	Stone: Value given	Brick: Total number.	Brick: No. value not given.	Brick: Val. given.	Framed: Total number.	Framed: No. value not given.	Framed: Val. given.	Logs: Total number.	Logs: No. value not given.	Logs: Val. given.	Other: Total number.	Other: No. value not given.	Other: Val. given.	Total: Total number	Total: No. value not given.	Total: Val. given
Croghan,							104		21, 630	240		6, 178	10		272	354		28, 080
Denmark,	14		11, 100	1		800	468		184, 345	7		285				490		196, 530
Diana,							80		16, 320	98		2, 937	35		3, 335	222		22, 592
Greig,							179		43, 049	22		539	40		1, 017	241		44, 605
Harrisburgh,							160	160		76	76		3	3		239	239	
High Market,							77		12, 495	102		2, 460	2		37	181		14, 992
Lewis,							97		24, 035	111		5, 883	4		400	212		30, 318
Leyden,	3		3, 600				333		128, 755	6		250	27		551	369		133, 156
Lowville,	7		30, 500	9		15, 000	341		218, 520	1		50				358		264, 070
Martinsburgh,	2		7, 000	6		5, 100	340		148, 830	103		2, 518	1		20	452		163, 468
Montague,							30		3, 650	79		4, 005	7		180	116		7, 835
New Bremen,							189		38, 230	108		2, 606	8		410	305		41, 246
Osceola,							60		9, 719	40		970	4		66	104		10, 755
Pinckney,				1		600	68	22	31, 860	53	53		1		200	123	75	32, 660
Turin,	4		4, 200	1		500	320		120, 435	19		540				344		125, 675
Watson,																173		40, 975
West Turin,	4		5, 100				340		139, 780	29		1, 350	51		771	424		147, 001
Total,	34		61, 500	18		22, 000	3, 195	182	1, 141, 653	1094	129	30, 571	193	3	7, 259	4, 707	314	1, 303, 958

* Wooden houses, kind not stated.

LIVINGSTON COUNTY.

TOWNS.	Stone: Total number.	Stone: No. value not given.	Stone: Value given	Brick: Total number.	Brick: No. value not given.	Brick: Val. given.	Framed: Total number.	Framed: No. value not given.	Framed: Val. given.	Logs: Total number.	Logs: No. value not given.	Logs: Val. given.	Other: Total number.	Other: No. value not given.	Other: Val. given.	Total: Total number	Total: No. value not given.	Total: Val. given
Avon,	1	1		5	4	2, 800	417	237	214, 225	14	14		19	4	2, 888	467	271	219, 913
Caledonia,	20	1	29, 400	12	6	9, 000	343	137	213, 325	33	14	4, 130	45	18	1, 860	453	176	257, 715
Conesus,	2		2, 200				201	6	91, 460	62	1	2, 775	5		120	270	7	96, 555
Geneseo,	7		27, 150	19	3	50, 450	412	25	392, 805	24	11	1, 200	15	7	1, 150	479	48	472, 755
Groveland,	3		3, 700	2		2, 300	208		127, 895	61	2	1, 965	6		330	280	2	136, 190
Leicester,	1		5, 000	3		2, 600	321	4	215, 721	12		3, 675	20		1, 204	357	4	228, 200
Lima,	11		19, 300	18	1	55, 600	593	3	525, 152	15		1, 685	4		35	641	4	601, 772
Livonia,	1		1, 000	12		41, 025	448	2	304, 795	6		1, 216	14		1, 903	401	2	349, 239
Mount Morris,				8		20, 600	462	4	303, 117	45		2, 066	47		2, 565	563	5	328, 348
North Dansville,	2		2, 500	18		61, 705	621	1	511, 305	8		430	44	1	6, 662	695	4	582, 602
Nunda,							415		239, 561	73		3, 765	63		5, 435	552	1	248, 761
Portage,	1		2, 000	2		6, 500	245		127, 154	21		1, 565	33		1, 265	302		138, 484

LIVINGSTON COUNTY.—(Continued.)

TOWNS	STONE.			BRICK.			FRAMED.			LOGS.			OTHER DWELLINGS.			TOTAL.		
	Total number.	No. value not given.	Val. given.	Total number.	No. value not given.	Val. given.	Total number.	No. value not given.	Val. given.	Total number.	No. value not given.	Val. given.	Total number.	No. value not given.	Val. given.	Total number.	No. value not given.	Val. given
Sparta,	4	....	$2,400	....	....	....	175	....	$101,505	45	....	$3,000	7	....	$1,300	232	1	$109,195
Spring Water,	....	....	....	....	....	....	316	1	95,255	106	46	3,630	27	1	1,675	450	49	100,560
West Sparta,	....	....	....	1	....	$1,400	188	....	78,285	57	....	1,475	40	....	5,448	286	....	86,608
York,	4	....	5,800	13	2	20,300	422	6	312,920	26	....	735	14	....	695	482	11	340,450
Total,	57	2	100,450	113	16	274,280	5,787	426	3,854,570	608	88	34,212	403	31	33,835	6,990	585	4,297,347

MADISON COUNTY.

TOWNS	Stone: Total number.	No. value not given.	Val. given.	Brick: Total number.	No. value not given.	Val. given.	Framed: Total number.	No. value not given.	Val. given.	Logs: Total number.	No. value not given.	Val. given.	Other: Total number.	No. value not given.	Val. given.	Total: Total number.	No. value not given.	Val. given
Brookfield,	....	....	....	1	....	750	679	....	329,835	4	2	75	7	....	1,350	692	3	332,010
Cazenovia,	1	....	2,000	9	1	54,000	851	4	543,165	....	....	....	20	....	7,645	890	14	611,810
De Ruyter,	2	....	2,000	2	....	2,000	325	1	173,950	5	....	250	....	....	....	334	1	178,200
Eaton,	6	1	5,400	2	....	4,000	719	3	456,435	....	....	....	....	....	....	727	4	465,835
Fenner,	....	....	....	....	....	....	294	1	105,355	4	....	75	13	....	2,760	311	1	108,190
Georgetown,	1	1	....	....	....	....	265	229	32,795	36	36	....	7	6	10	310	273	32,805
Hamilton,	16	1	32,500	36	....	68,400	645	22	357,897	....	....	....	1	....	100	700	25	458,897
Lebanon,	8	....	9,100	3	....	4,500	296	8	94,855	....	....	....	....	....	....	309	10	108,455
Lenox,	4	....	5,100	28	....	52,700	1,245	8	740,411	58	....	3,425	86	....	8,245	1,422	9	809,881
Madison,	2	....	3,400	5	....	6,000	514	37	249,425	2	....	200	....	....	....	524	38	259,025
Nelson,	....	....	....	....	....	....	360	1	130,225	2	....	75	....	....	....	362	1	130,300
Smithfield,	1	....	600	....	....	....	282	1	133,400	2	1	50	1	1	....	290	7	134,050
Stockbridge,	4	1	3,200	1	....	1,000	369	....	157,830	3	....	80	....	....	....	381	5	162,110
Sullivan,	5	3	4,800	8	....	8,300	844	137	362,732	57	16	1,178	51	14	3,930	969	174	380,940
Total,	50	7	68,100	95	1	201,650	7,688	452	3,873,310	173	55	5,408	186	21	24,040	8,221	565	4,172,508

MONROE COUNTY.

TOWNS	Stone: Total number.	No. value not given.	Val. given.	Brick: Total number.	No. value not given.	Val. given.	Framed: Total number.	No. value not given.	Val. given.	Logs: Total number.	No. value not given.	Val. given.	Other: Total number.	No. value not given.	Val. given.	Total: Total number.	No. value not given.	Val. given
Brighton,	8	2	15,500	67	31	89,350	380	138	148,724	3	3	....	19	....	530	499	196	254,104
Chili,	6	....	12,000	14	....	20,650	293	....	164,075	50	....	2,780	27	....	3,275	390	....	202,780
Clarkson,	18	....	10,850	49	....	74,380	275	....	138,180	38	....	1,660	12	....	635	392	....	225,705
Gates,	8	....	4,750	18	....	33,400	344	....	170,825	32	5	475	21	....	465	423	5	209,915
Greece,	13	....	11,600	13	....	11,400	565	3	313,840	113	....	4,630	95	2	4,335	805	11	345,805
Henrietta,	14	....	17,600	20	....	23,700	339	5	202,252	17	2	955	11	1	270	416	23	244,777
Irondequoit,	12	....	14,800	15	....	23,700	496	10	311,630	46	....	6,630	13	....	510	582	10	357,270
Mendon,	16	....	13,500	7	....	11,000	509	6	249,810	17	17	....	....	....	....	549	23	274,310
Ogden,	9	....	6,950	11	....	12,900	453	1	417,480	33	1	2,535	47	....	3,265	553	2	443,130
Parma,	11	....	10,800	9	....	8,000	454	....	194,330	40	....	805	18	....	1,417	532	....	215,352
Penfield,	14	1	9,200	11	....	17,900	524	8	294,105	32	....	1,172	23	....	1,031	607	12	323,408
Perrinton,	5	....	3,700	9	....	20,400	503	36	319,665	13	3	1,775	40	....	1,287	570	39	346,827
Pittsford,	8	....	12,000	24	....	49,200	331	1	208,719	5	....	190	....	....	....	375	8	270,109
Riga,	7	....	11,100	7	....	4,500	346	1	190,140	14	....	545	10	5	90	384	6	206,375
Rochester City:																		
1st ward,	2	....	13,000	176	2	760,200	139	....	345,230	....	....	....	....	....	....	318	3	1,118,430
2d ward,	4	....	6,600	156	....	733,450	273	....	525,800	....	....	....	....	....	....	433	....	1,265,850
3d ward,	19	....	114,600	203	....	1,066,200	502	....	928,600	....	....	....	4	....	1,800	729	1	2,111,200
4th ward,	4	....	6,450	164	1	627,300	297	2	537,700	....	....	....	....	....	....	469	7	1,171,450
5th ward,	17	....	62,300	141	....	487,900	516	....	660,690	....	....	....	....	....	....	685	11	1,210,890
6th ward,	5	....	6,500	133	....	276,350	781	....	629,300	....	....	....	....	....	....	919	....	912,150
7th ward,	1	....	2,500	104	....	281,800	791	7	829,580	....	....	....	....	....	....	896	7	1,113,880
8th ward,	12	....	26,200	56	....	136,700	664	1	555,900	....	....	....	....	....	....	732	1	718,800
9th ward,	3	....	4,000	97	....	311,075	1,244	....	958,590	....	....	....	....	....	....	1,344	....	1,273,665
10th ward,	12	....	21,050	116	5	352,200	754	4	629,865	1	....	200	....	....	....	883	9	1,003,315
Total Rochester,	79	....	263,200	1,346	8	5,033,175	5,961	14	6,601,255	1	....	200	4	....	1,800	7,408	39	11,899,630
Rush,	9	....	8,500	....	....	....	267	4	176,075	14	1	1,365	10	....	620	301	6	186,560
Sweden,	28	....	26,100	85	....	138,650	543	1	381,705	22	....	1,335	32	....	2,140	712	3	549,930
Union,	9	....	10,200	7	....	9,400	326	3	132,999	73	....	2,752	27	....	1,274	442	3	156,625
Webster,	8	....	7,200	6	....	14,600	415	5	229,835	63	....	1,562	4	....	40	496	5	253,237
Wheatland,	19	....	30,000	42	1	58,400	389	....	260,830	24	3	2,175	5	2	270	480	7	351,675
Total,	301	3	499,550	1,760	40	5,654,705	13,713	236	11,106,474	650	35	33,541	418	10	23,274	16,916	398	17,317,524

MONTGOMERY COUNTY.

TOWNS	Stone: Total number.	No. value not given.	Val. given.	Brick: Total number.	No. value not given.	Val. given.	Framed: Total number.	No. value not given.	Val. given.	Logs: Total number.	No. value not given.	Val. given.	Other: Total number.	No. value not given.	Val. given.	Total: Total number.	No. value not given.	Val. given
Amsterdam,	8	....	19,550	47	....	120,900	689	3	455,980	....	....	....	5	....	2,675	749	3	599,105
Canajoharie,	20	4	46,500	17	1	28,250	569	59	316,985	3	....	45	3	....	830	612	64	392,610
Charleston,	....	....	....	3	....	3,175	351	3	98,930	2	....	30	2	....	80	359	4	102,215
Florida,	2	....	1,000	7	....	18,300	534	2	280,383	....	....	....	1	....	10	544	2	299,693
Glen,	1	....	4,000	9	....	21,400	470	2	279,895	....	....	....	1	....	2,000	483	4	307,295
Minden,	4	....	4,350	43	....	106,950	691	18	374,990	7	....	300	6	....	150	754	21	486,740
Mohawk,	1	....	1,000	7	....	13,500	472	1	359,601	6	....	320	....	....	....	487	2	374,421
Palatine,	15	1	28,300	3	....	5,000	210	6	176,285	3	3	....	....	....	....	231	10	209,585
Root,	5	....	6,625	1	....	1,000	452	....	116,875	2	....	55	4	....	95	464	....	124,650
St. Johnsville,	3	....	5,500	10	....	19,000	262	1	158,985	....	....	....	....	....	....	277	3	183,485
Total,	59	5	116,825	147	1	337,475	4,700	95	2,618,909	23	3	750	22	....	5,840	4,960	113	3,079,799

NEW-YORK COUNTY.

TOWNS	Stone: Total number.	No. value not given.	Val. given.	Brick: Total number.	No. value not given.	Val. given.	Framed: Total number.	No. value not given.	Val. given.	Logs: Total number.	No. value not given.	Val. given.	Other: Total number.	No. value not given.	Val. given.	Total: Total number.	No. value not given.	Val. given
New-York City:																		
1st ward,	1	....	110,000	541	5	7,655,500	10	....	51,800	....	....	....	101	....	236900	660	12	8,054,200
2d ward,	12	....	955,000	228	3	5,174,600	4	1	23,000	....	....	....	....	....	....	256	16	6,152,600
3d ward,	16	....	1,515,000	401	....	10,071,000	....	....	....	....	....	....	1	....	200300	419	1	11,786,000
4th ward,	1	....	27,000	1,036	7	6,565,700	102	1	395,850	....	....	....	19	....	62500	1,162	12	7,051,050
5th ward,	10	....	1,350,000	1,398	8	10,693,400	209	2	981,150	....	....	....	....	....	....	1,620	13	13,024,550
6th ward,	3	1	65,000	870	2	7,661,100	258	....	1,112,650	....	....	....	....	....	....	1,133	5	8,838,750
7th ward,	1	....	500	1,720	11	10,028,000	380	....	1,110,050	....	....	....	....	....	....	2,104	14	11,138,550
8th ward,	6	1	858,000	2,217	4	13,330,416	336	....	1,096,550	....	....	....	....	....	....	2,560	6	15,284,966

NEW-YORK COUNTY.—(CONTINUED.)

TOWNS.	STONE.			BRICK.			FRAMED.			LOGS.			OTHER DWELLINGS.			TOTAL.		
	Total number.	No. value not given.	Val. given.	Total number.	No. value not given.	Val. given.	Total number.	No. value not given.	Val. given.	Total number.	No. value not given.	Val. given.	Total number.	No. value not given.	Val. given.	Total number.	No. value not given.	Val. given.
New-York city:																		
9th ward,	66	....	858700	2,798	17	$14,963,950	508	6	$1,545,914	....	....	......	10	....	22,000	3,339	40	$17,390,564
10th ward,	4	....	142000	1,115	34	6,628,750	590	14	2,265,100	....	....	......	....	....	......	1,713	52	9,035,850
11th ward,	1	....	7000	2,139	5	9,371,200	313	1	754,950	....	....	......	1	....	2,500	2,454	6	10,135,650
12th ward,	3	....	437640	159	1	1,157,090	1,433	13	5,020,280	....	....	......	105	....	30,380	1,700	14	6,645,390
13th ward,	....	....	....	1,178	3	4,955,650	470	1	1,418,650	....	....	......	....	....	......	1,652	8	6,374,300
14th ward,	7	....	1018000	1,123	26	11,104,100	333	13	1,650,950	....	....	......	....	....	......	1,467	43	13,773,050
15th ward,	110	....	2108000	2,014	1	20,452,100	144	1	440,500	....	....	......	....	....	......	2,268	2	23,000,600
16th ward,	163	....	1716000	2,162	20	14,404,300	610	11	1,605,450	....	....	......	....	....	......	2,938	34	17,725,750
17th ward,	73	1	1025000	2,917	16	17,790,350	326	1	811,200	....	....	......	1	1	......	3,340	42	19,626,550
18th ward,	564	1	12221500	1,915	5	17,333,500	119	....	457,700	....	....	......	....	....	......	2,599	7	30,012,700
19th ward,	17	9	55000	363	13	1,639,350	1,185	10	2,056,001	....	....	......	49	45	200300	1,651	114	3,950,651
20th ward,	142	....	1296000	1,910	21	9,849,000	1,176	28	2,489,850	....	....	......	6	....	4,340	3,250	65	13,639,190
21st ward,	389	....	6290500	1,210	....	8,422,050	367	....	1,201,250	....	....	......	....	....	......	1,968	2	15,913,800
22d ward,	28	....	211500	563	1	2,280,700	1,722	....	2,411,900	....	....	......	40	....	23,000	2,355	3	4,927,100
Total, ...	1617	13	32267340	29,977	203	211.531.806	10,595	103	28,900,745	....	....	......	333	46	781920	42,668	511	273,481,811

NIAGARA COUNTY.

TOWNS.	STONE. Total number.	STONE. No. value not given.	STONE. Val. given.	BRICK. Total number.	BRICK. No. value not given.	BRICK. Val. given.	FRAMED. Total number.	FRAMED. No. value not given.	FRAMED. Val. given.	LOGS. Total number.	LOGS. No. value not given.	LOGS. Val. given.	OTHER DWELLINGS. Total number.	OTHER DWELLINGS. No. value not given.	OTHER DWELLINGS. Val. given.	TOTAL. Total number.	TOTAL. No. value not given.	TOTAL. Val. given.
Cambria, ...	21	18	1,300	18	17	900	295	264	18,200	49	47	950	9	9	......	392	355	21,350
Hartland, ...	17	....	16,300	53	....	55,600	226	1	90,735	114	....	5,725	198	1	45,550	608	2	213,910
Lewiston, ...	22	....	33,400	18	....	40,000	303	1	257,650	138	....	9,057	49	....	6,132	530	1	346,239
Lockport, ...	182	4	296,975	75	7	78,190	1,694	17	1,310,108	89	1	6,935	315	66	39,680	2,364	104	1,731,888
Newfane, ...	12	1	8,950	9	....	17,880	454	24	185,920	121	24	10,852	22	3	2,260	618	52	225,862
Niagara, ...	38	....	322,925	38	1	99,000	402	2	584,725	41	....	704	289	101	89,970	808	104	1,097,324
Pendleton, ...	3	....	3,200	3	....	3,600	117	....	38.100	171	....	7,994	80	....	12,043	374	....	64,937
Porter, ...	5	....	16,350	7	....	9,550	375	....	226,913	64	....	6,085	3	....	60	454	....	258,958
Royalton, ...	20	1	19,564	30	....	38,850	587	3	283,720	127	1	8,730	137	....	9,760	905	9	360,624
Somerset, ...	6	....	7,400	11	....	15,100	298	4	119,415	63	14	2,314	1	....	100	379	18	144,329
Wheatfield, ...	15	....	25,400	25	....	38,700	373	1	200,920	167	1	5,940	36	....	7,565	616	2	278,525
Wilson, ...	7	....	7,600	12	1	41,800	237	59	104,585	381	292	7,562	10	2	950	650	357	162,499
Total, ...	348	24	759,364	299	26	439,170	5,361	376	3,420,991	1525	380	72,848	1149	182	214070	8,698	1004	4 906.443

ONEIDA COUNTY.

TOWNS.	STONE. Total number.	STONE. No. value not given.	STONE. Val. given.	BRICK. Total number.	BRICK. No. value not given.	BRICK. Val. given.	FRAMED. Total number.	FRAMED. No. value not given.	FRAMED. Val. given.	LOGS. Total number.	LOGS. No. value not given.	LOGS. Val. given.	OTHER DWELLINGS. Total number.	OTHER DWELLINGS. No. value not given.	OTHER DWELLINGS. Val. given.	TOTAL. Total number.	TOTAL. No. value not given.	TOTAL. Val. given.
Annsville, ...	1	....	300	4	....	1,000	386	4	92,955	69	2	2,250	8	....	410	469	7	96,915
Augusta, ...	3	....	2,400	2	....	2,000	422	2	212,528	1	....	5	....	....	......	428	2	216,933
Ava, ...	2	....	1,800	......	....	....	155	....	36,875	45	1	685	17	....	152	219	1	39,512
Booneville, ...	3	....	15,200	1	....	4,000	584	5	308,790	41	1	1,635	119	16	3,240	748	22	332,865
Bridgewater, ...	1	....	800	2	....	4,000	243	....	112,065	....	....	......	....	....	......	246	....	116,865
Camden, ...	1	....	3,500	2	....	4,200	532	....	269,425	20	....	505	8	....	690	564	1	278,320
Deerfield, ...	....	....	....	7	....	8,100	376	....	170,380	4	....	95	....	....	......	387	....	178,575
Florence, ...	....	....	....	......	....	....	490	1	103,826	....	....	......	....	....	......	490	1	103,826
Floyd, ...	1	....	4,000	2	....	10,500	264	3	82,625	4	....	140	1	....	300	273	4	97,565
Kirkland, ...	3	1	1,500	3	....	1,900	628	8	587,075	1	....	10	....	....	......	635	9	590,485
Lee, ...	8	....	3,500	5	....	6,050	509	....	153,225	27	1	685	6	....	135	555	1	163,595
Marcy, ...	1	....	900	5	....	6,550	311	7	108,055	20	....	1,185	4	....	1,400	342	8	118,090
Marshall, ...	....	....	....	1	....	3,000	381	1	162,880	1	....	20	8	....	805	391	1	166,705
New Hartford, ...	3	....	1,900	26	....	46,500	676	....	469,600	....	....	......	....	....	......	707	2	518,000
Paris, ...	1	....	1,200	2	1	2,000	660	104	289,230	1	1	......	....	....	......	679	121	292,430
Remsen, ...	....	....	....	......	....	....	374	3	175,655	82	1	3,875	21	....	860	478	5	180,390
Rome, ...	3	1	19,100	90	2	470,800	1,431	289	1,002,555	24	21	500	104	51	4,932	1,660	372	1,497,887
Sangerfield, ...	....	....	....	12	....	35,700	434	1	243,600	1	....	25	....	....	......	449	3	279,325
Steuben, ...	3	....	1,850	......	....	....	282	1	38,075	10	....	58	4	....	21	299	1	40,004
Trenton, ...	18	....	21,050	4	....	7,800	600	2	389,848	2	....	20	....	....	......	626	4	418,718
Utica city:																		
1st ward,	....	....	....	63	1	314,400	116	....	145,800	....	....	......	....	....	......	181	3	460,200
2d ward,	....	....	....	74	1	333,700	328	....	342,200	....	....	......	....	....	......	402	1	675,900
3d ward,	....	....	....	93	2	481,800	398	2	567,075	....	....	......	....	....	......	491	4	1,048,875
4th ward,	1	....	400	129	....	628,100	597	....	798,600	....	....	......	....	....	......	727	....	1,427,100
5th ward,	1	....	10,000	41	4	175,500	754	33	738,155	....	....	......	11	2	825	814	46	924,480
6th ward,	2	1	1,300	16	....	26,750	558	2	437,850	....	....	......	2	....	1,650	578	3	467,550
Total Utica city, ..	4	1	11,700	416	8	1,960,250	2,751	37	3,029,680	....	....	......	13	2	2,475	3,193	57	5,004,105
Vernon, ...	....	....	....	4	....	9,000	523	....	272,445	10	1	208	1	....	40	538	1	281,693
Verona, ...	....	....	....	7	....	9,600	11,018	1	433,947	76	3	2,027	104	44	2,833	1,205	48	448,407
Vienna, ...	....	....	....	......	....	....	574	....	170,485	25	3	640	24	....	1,755	623	3	172,880
Western, ...	....	....	....	4	....	3,600	387	1	147,327	27	10	389	44	....	2,046	462	11	153,362
Westmoreland, ...	1	....	400	4	....	5,700	380	....	246,230	1	....	50	2	....	70	389	1	252,450
Whitestown, ...	2	....	1,400	20	2	25,200	691	17	480,050	4	....	250	4	....	360	727	25	507,260
Total, ...	59	3	92,500	623	13	2,627,450	16,062	487	9.789,431	496	45	15,257	492	113	22,524	17,782	711	12,547,162

ONONDAGA COUNTY.

TOWNS.	STONE. Total number.	STONE. No. value not given.	STONE. Val. given.	BRICK. Total number.	BRICK. No. value not given.	BRICK. Val. given.	FRAMED. Total number.	FRAMED. No. value not given.	FRAMED. Val. given.	LOGS. Total number.	LOGS. No. value not given.	LOGS. Val. given.	OTHER DWELLINGS. Total number.	OTHER DWELLINGS. No. value not given.	OTHER DWELLINGS. Val. given.	TOTAL. Total number.	TOTAL. No. value not given.	TOTAL. Val. given.
Camillus, ...	1	....	1,500	10	....	13,600	433	1	226,070	6	....	215	39	....	2,715	489	1	244,100
Cicero, ...	....	....	....	5	....	5,300	490	3	186,710	117	....	5,970	26	....	2,500	642	7	200,480
Clay, ...	....	....	....	8	....	9,600	540	....	222,325	68	....	2,640	22	....	265	638	....	234,830
De Witt, ...	8	....	13,600	12	....	18,300	465	....	222,065	55	....	2,515	34	....	2,325	575	1	258,805
Elbridge, ...	2	....	6,800	34	2	79,500	661	3	447,195	23	....	1,150	81	....	11,845	803	7	545,490
Fabius, ...	2	....	2,700	......	....	....	433	1	188,791	5	1	50	2	....	20	442	2	191,561
Geddes, ...	....	....	....	10	....	32,500	255	1	170,455	1	....	50	100	....	3,028	366	1	206,033
La Fayette, ...	1	....	1,000	5	....	4,200	444	4	148,000	10	....	225	17	....	400	401	8	153,825
Lysander, ...	3	....	1,500	4	....	11,200	803	14	389,146	98	36	1,255	43	11	896	953	63	403,997
Manlius, ...	8	....	5,850	31	....	58,300	1,051	7	532,895	31	....	855	27	....	780	1,148	7	598,680
Marcellus, ...	....	....	....	6	....	13,800	466	....	252,650	3	....	65	13	2	585	488	2	267,100
Onondaga, ...	9	....	18,800	34	....	51,300	829	3	349,205	17	....	410	89	....	2,048	978	3	421,763

ONONDAGA COUNTY.—(Continued.)

TOWNS.	Stone. Total number.	Stone. No. value not given.	Stone. Val. given.	Brick. Total number.	Brick. No. value not given.	Brick. Val. given.	Framed. Total number.	Framed. No. value not given.	Framed. Val. given.	Logs. Total number.	Logs. No. value not given.	Logs. Val. given.	Other dwellings. Total number.	Other dwellings. No. value not given.	Other dwellings. Val. given.	Total. Total number.	Total. No. value not given.	Total. Val. given.
Otisco,	....	....	....	......	....	....	355	1	$125, 112	4	....	$170	3	....	$450	362	1	$125, 732
Pompey,	1	....	$1, 500	3	....	$1, 900	719	....	297, 890	4	....	105	1	....	50	729	1	301, 445
Salina,	10	....	23, 800	15	....	17, 900	333	....	178, 262	21	....	425	36	1	1, 540	417	3	221, 927
Skaneateles,	5	....	3, 500	17	....	43, 900	697	9	504, 748	8	....	935	5	....	700	735	12	553, 783
Spafford,	....	....	....	......	....	....	331	....	120, 926	4	....	45	....	....	......	335	....	120, 971
Syracuse city:																		
1st ward,	1	....	5, 000	21	....	71, 850	511	....	510, 515	....	....	......	4	....	950	537	....	588, 315
2d ward,	3	....	7, 300	28	....	109, 700	445	1	404, 100	....	....	......	....	....	......	476	1	521, 100
3d ward,	....	....	....	45	....	204, 500	176	2	309, 532	....	....	......	20	....	2, 875	241	2	516, 907
4th ward,	3	....	23, 000	88	....	542, 700	459	....	783, 530	....	....	......	27	....	31, 800	577	....	1, 381, 030
5th ward,	....	....	....	35	....	121, 700	322	3	444, 230	....	....	......	36	2	11, 530	393	5	577, 460
6th ward,	3	....	7, 200	150	2	579, 700	254	2	470, 375	....	....	......	1	....	400	418	14	1, 057, 675
7th ward,	....	....	....	140	1	479, 500	508	....	626, 500	....	....	......	7	....	6, 900	655	1	1, 112, 900
8th ward,	....	....	....	50	1	149, 200	344	11	324, 040	....	....	......	....	....	......	394	12	473, 240
Total Syracuse,	10	....	42, 500	557	4	2, 258, 850	3, 019	19	3, 872, 822	....	....	......	95	2	54, 455	3, 691	35	6, 228, 627
Tully,	....	....	....	3	3	....	343	265	62, 950	....	....	......	4	3	200	352	273	63, 150
Van Buren,	....	....	....	8	....	9, 700	508	1	267, 625	23	10	400	51	....	2, 525	591	12	280, 250
Total,	60	....	122, 050	762	9	2, 629, 850	13, 175	332	8, 765, 842	498	47	17, 480	688	19	87, 327	15, 215	439	11, 622, 549

ONTARIO COUNTY.

TOWNS.	Stone. Total number.	Stone. No. value not given.	Stone. Val. given.	Brick. Total number.	Brick. No. value not given.	Brick. Val. given.	Framed. Total number.	Framed. No. value not given.	Framed. Val. given.	Logs. Total number.	Logs. No. value not given.	Logs. Val. given.	Other dwellings. Total number.	Other dwellings. No. value not given.	Other dwellings. Val. given.	Total. Total number.	Total. No. value not given.	Total. Val. given.
Bristol,	2	....	1, 400	1	....	80	292	....	158, 580	38	....	1, 480	1	....	20	334	....	161, 560
Canadice,	....	....	....	......	....	....	140	....	60, 432	45	1	2, 115	....	....	......	185	1	62, 547
Canandaigua,	17	....	41, 400	108	2	408, 900	926	15	974, 680	46	5	4, 900	6	1	26	1, 108	28	1, 424, 906
East Bloomfield,	....	....	....	16	1	19, 600	356	5	209, 255	15	....	675	10	....	245	397	6	229, 775
Farmington,	10	....	12, 900	4	....	7, 900	298	....	168, 430	40	....	2, 770	1	....	50	354	1	192, 050
Gorham,	6	3	5, 400	14	6	8, 500	448	84	173, 713	26	11	701	....	....	......	496	106	188, 314
Hopewell,	4	....	5, 800	3	....	5, 800	283	....	180, 570	12	....	590	3	....	45	305	....	192, 805
Manchester,	13	....	10, 850	5	....	5, 700	492	....	271, 000	21	....	1, 015	2	....	305	533	....	288, 870
Naples,	....	....	....	......	....	....	310	....	192, 695	86	....	3, 115	12	....	920	408	....	196, 730
Phelps,	35	....	50, 900	37	....	65, 450	899	5	537, 860	22	....	1, 130	12	1	3, 000	1, 005	6	658, 340
Richmond,	4	....	3, 700	3	....	2, 125	261	1	167, 240	17	....	525	....	....	......	285	1	173, 590
Seneca,	12	....	26, 000	313	....	694, 900	1, 118	1	829, 000	23	....	1, 360	13	....	17, 750	1, 480	2	1, 569, 010
South Bristol,	....	....	....	......	....	....	141	....	43, 680	84	....	2, 562	....	....	......	225	....	46, 242
Victor,	15	....	19, 900	5	....	11, 300	346	5	239, 330	34	1	683	13	....	349	415	8	271, 562
West Bloomfield,	2	....	1, 400	7	....	5, 450	281	....	147, 955	4	....	120	4	....	155	298	....	155, 080
Total,	120	3	179, 650	516	9	1, 230, 705	6, 591	116	4, 354, 420	513	18	23, 741	77	2	22, 865	7, 828	159	5, 811, 381

ORANGE COUNTY.

TOWNS.	Stone. Total number.	Stone. No. value not given.	Stone. Val. given.	Brick. Total number.	Brick. No. value not given.	Brick. Val. given.	Framed. Total number.	Framed. No. value not given.	Framed. Val. given.	Logs. Total number.	Logs. No. value not given.	Logs. Val. given.	Other dwellings. Total number.	Other dwellings. No. value not given.	Other dwellings. Val. given.	Total. Total number.	Total. No. value not given.	Total. Val. given.
Blooming Grove,	8	....	9, 500	2	....	1, 000	349	....	251, 725	....	....	......	4	1	125	364	2	262, 350
Chester,	1	1	....	7	2	10, 500	255	109	85, 470	....	....	......	12	11	50	277	125	96, 020
Cornwall,	37	2	49, 425	29	....	185, 750	558	5	442, 810	15	....	1, 000	4	....	200	648	12	679, 185
Crawford,	13	....	8, 550	2	....	2, 300	317	....	146, 520	5	....	315	....	....	......	338	1	157, 685
Deerpark,	7	....	7, 400	9	....	26, 100	618	16	579, 950	73	14	3, 915	133	23	16, 725	851	64	634, 090
Goshen,	4	....	7, 300	46	1	66, 100	401	5	400, 720	....	....	......	31	....	1, 520	482	6	475, 640
Greenville,	2	....	1, 400	......	....	....	192	3	113, 485	13	....	475	4	....	120	217	9	115, 480
Hamptonburgh,	6	....	3, 250	2	1	1, 500	201	....	127, 830	1	....	5	2	....	75	212	1	132, 660
Minisink,	1	....	1, 200	1	....	500	224	....	99, 000	5	....	225	....	....	......	231	....	100, 925
Monroe,	6	....	8, 825	2	....	4, 400	560	54	224, 250	152	6	5, 670	12	....	1, 025	737	65	244, 170
Montgomery,	20	5	8, 500	7	2	12, 100	602	160	418, 925	2	....	400	....	....	......	642	178	439, 925
Mount Hope,	1	....	250	4	....	7, 500	271	....	169, 165	7	....	135	35	....	278	318	....	177, 328
Newburgh,	51	3	229, 250	314	3	1, 058, 050	1, 360	14	1, 897, 755	....	....	......	4	....	42	1, 729	20	3, 185, 097
New Windsor,	29	....	26, 675	10	....	43, 300	346	2	317, 025	1	....	75	....	....	......	386	2	387, 075
Wallkill,	19	1	12, 550	25	....	54, 900	838	8	674, 145	16	....	650	15	....	1, 160	915	11	743, 405
Warwick,	23	1	20, 200	9	2	27, 800	720	152	370, 140	115	3	4, 485	3	1	80	875	164	422, 705
Wawayanda,	4	1	3, 800	5	....	5, 300	350	2	211, 880	....	....	......	1	....	25	360	3	221, 005
Total,	232	14	398. 075	474	11	1, 507, 100	8, 162	530	6, 530, 795	405	23	17, 350	260	36	21, 425	9, 582	663	8, 474, 745

ORLEANS COUNTY.

TOWNS.	Stone. Total number.	Stone. No. value not given.	Stone. Val. given.	Brick. Total number.	Brick. No. value not given.	Brick. Val. given.	Framed. Total number.	Framed. No. value not given.	Framed. Val. given.	Logs. Total number.	Logs. No. value not given.	Logs. Val. given.	Other dwellings. Total number.	Other dwellings. No. value not given.	Other dwellings. Val. given.	Total. Total number.	Total. No. value not given.	Total. Val. given.
Barre,	23	9	24, 340	59	4	109, 700	1, 007	193	676, 425	69	24	1, 965	60	25	5, 200	1, 223	260	817, 630
Carlton,	9	1	7, 700	3	....	3, 900	296	....	149, 170	57	23	1, 565	95	2	36, 045	460	26	198, 380
Clarendon,	15	....	12, 050	4	....	4, 000	274	....	129, 345	43	....	3, 185	....	....	......	336	....	148, 580
Gaines,	24	....	35, 450	36	....	44, 900	393	....	228, 525	8	....	795	....	....	......	461	....	309, 670
Kendall,	10	....	10, 500	......	....	....	292	18	129, 340	52	12	1, 905	19	6	1, 825	375	38	143, 570
Murray,	41	....	31, 875	6	....	6, 200	376	2	207, 425	30	....	1, 535	65	....	1, 675	519	3	248, 710
Ridgeway,	38	....	54, 300	13	....	37, 100	668	2	483, 845	32	....	3, 415	182	....	43, 102	933	2	621, 762
Shelby,	17	....	15, 450	4	....	2, 600	449	1	279, 750	33	....	2, 990	90	....	41, 600	593	1	342, 390
Yates,	5	....	5, 100	8	....	6, 750	364	1	171, 510	22	....	1, 195	....	....	......	399	1	184, 555
Total,	182	10	196, 765	133	4	215, 150	4, 119	217	2, 455, 335	346	59	18, 550	511	33	129447	5, 299	331	3, 015, 247

OSWEGO COUNTY.

TOWNS.	Stone. Total number.	Stone. No. value not given.	Stone. Val. given.	Brick. Total number.	Brick. No. value not given.	Brick. Val. given.	Framed. Total number.	Framed. No. value not given.	Framed. Val. given.	Logs. Total number.	Logs. No. value not given.	Logs. Val. given.	Other dwellings. Total number.	Other dwellings. No. value not given.	Other dwellings. Val. given.	Total. Total number.	Total. No. value not given.	Total. Val. given.
Albion,	....	....	....	......	....	....	379	....	110, 405	30	3	600	4	....	85	413	3	111, 090
Amboy,	1	....	400	......	....	....	190	8	38, 585	19	2	355	4	....	75	215	11	39, 415
Boylston,	....	....	....	1	....	200	99	....	17, 710	39	....	1, 557	5	....	115	144	....	19, 582
Constantia,	....	....	....	2	....	2, 600	493	2	243, 125	41	....	1, 440	56	....	4, 030	592	2	251, 195
Granby,	....	....	....	2	1	300	440	284	115, 725	71	65	66	152	80	13, 389	694	459	129, 480
Hannibal,	4	....	1, 800	6	....	4, 050	470	....	110, 350	69	4	909	41	2	860	590	6	117, 969
Hastings,	....	....	....	......	....	....	472	2	154, 195	56	....	1, 495	52	....	3, 335	581	3	159, 025
Mexico,	6	....	10, 800	9	....	14, 450	718	....	352, 290	12	....	420	36	....	6, 075	782	1	384, 035
New Haven	2	....	3, 400	1	....	100	332	2	114, 700	27	....	1, 125	34	....	3, 440	396	2	122, 765

OSWEGO COUNTY.—(Continued.)

TOWNS.	STONE.			BRICK.			FRAMED.			LOGS.			OTHER DWELLINGS.			TOTAL.		
	Total number.	No. value not given.	Val. given.	Total number.	No. value not given.	Val. given.	Total number.	No. value not given.	Val. given.	Total number.	No. value not given.	Val. given.	Total number.	No. value not given.	Val. given.	Total number.	No. value not given.	Val. given.
Orwell,							194	3	$62, 125	32	32		15	5	$850	241	40	$62, 975
Oswego,	5		$3, 800	3		$4, 680	397	1	133, 735	55		$1, 586	63	5	2, 730	523	6	146, 531
Oswego city:																		
1st ward,	21		193, 000	43	1	231, 700	601		765, 325							665	1	1, 190, 025
2d ward,	6		12, 400	7	1	19, 700	371	2	311, 090				72	1	25, 550	460	8	368, 740
3d ward,	5		21, 800	11		62, 500	713	3	745, 935	2		60	25		3, 415	756	3	833, 710
4th ward,	7		46, 000	17	1	161, 100	624	24	675, 850	1	1		87	56	30, 255	737	83	913, 205
Total Oswego city,	39		273, 200	78	3	475, 000	2, 309	29	2, 498, 200	3	1	60	184	57	59, 220	2, 618	95	3, 305, 680
Palermo,							377	2	95, 575	43	3	205	3		50	424	6	95, 830
Parish,	1		300				276		58, 772	41		565	5		115	323		59, 752
Redfield,							115		24, 448	26		770	3		145	144		25, 363
Richland,	6		5, 300	5		7, 300	683	10	293, 225	21	1	720	19		2, 373	735	13	308, 918
Sandy Creek,							394	9	196, 610	19	14	550	1		200	418	27	197, 360
Schroeppel,	1		500				524		269, 181	90		2, 845	71		14, 810	686		287, 336
Scriba,	1		700	1		2, 000	397	2	124, 415	37		550	120		14, 500	558	4	142, 165
Volney,	1		1, 800	22		90, 850	946	2	433. 679	59		1, 495	138		11, 188	1, 166	2	539, 012
West Monroe,				1		500	140		35, 235	26		315	57		6, 695	224		42, 745
Williamstown,							171		48, 775	5		185	5		945	182	1	49, 905
Total,	67		302. 000	131	4	602, 030	10, 516	356	5, 531, 060	821	125	17, 813	1068	150	145225	12, 649	681	6, 598, 128

OTSEGO COUNTY.

TOWNS.	Stone: Total number.	Stone: No. value not given.	Stone: Val. given.	Brick: Total number.	Brick: No. value not given.	Brick: Val. given.	Framed: Total number.	Framed: No. value not given.	Framed: Val. given.	Logs: Total number.	Logs: No. value not given.	Logs: Val. given.	Other: Total number.	Other: No. value not given.	Other: Val. given.	Total: Total number.	Total: No. value not given.	Total: Val. given.
Burlington,	3		3, 000	5		4, 600	333		107, 855							342	1	115, 455
Butternuts,	11	7	9, 600				396	297	79, 020	9	5	195	3	3		427	320	88, 815
Cherry Valley,	2		550	4		12, 000	421	2	257, 455							427	2	270, 005
Decatur,				1		800	164		56, 778	1		40	2		350	168		57, 968
Edmeston,							358		136, 940							358		136, 940
Exeter,	6	6		2	2		274	228	26, 615	2	1	25				284	237	26, 640
Hartwick,	5	5					431	340	46, 220							449	358	46, 220
Laurens,	3		2, 200	1		1, 600	401	1	123, 800	6		110				412	2	127, 710
Maryland,	2		1, 100	1		300	371	1	133, 715	23		565	1		25	398	1	135, 705
Middlefield,	1		1, 000				536	1	190, 600	14		652				551	1	192, 252
Milford,	2		31, 000				420	4	153, 960	25		538				449	6	185, 498
Morris,	7	4	11, 000	3	1	6, 200	344	261	81, 970	13	13					375	287	99, 170
New Lisbon,	3		3, 700	2		2, 000	331	1	154, 920	2		15	1		1, 200	339	1	161, 835
Oneonta,	6		7, 900	1		600	377		166, 105	23	2	230				407	2	174, 835
Otego,	1		800	2		6, 000	363		177, 644	22		715				388		185, 159
Otsego,	16	1	36, 250	17	1	49, 100	695		496, 420	6	1	350	1		1, 500	738	6	583, 620
Pittsfield,							269	269		47	47		1	1		317	317	
Plainfield,	2	1	800	3		7, 000	289	1	189, 135							294	2	196, 935
Richfield,				1	1		250	184	46, 825							252	186	46, 825
Roseboom,	1		1, 000	1		1, 200	337		101, 141	5		75	1		900	345		104, 316
Springfield,	6		13, 450				418	2	241, 540	1		5	1		2, 000	426	3	256, 995
Unadilla,	7		8, 600	4		10, 300	428		216, 260	63		1, 789	14		450	516		237, 399
Westford,							269	1	79, 750	5	3		1		300	275	4	80, 050
Worcester,				2		4, 000	362		123, 050	20		760	3		80	387		127, 890
Total,	84	24	131, 950	50	5	105, 700	8, 837	1594	3, 387, 718	287	72	6, 064	29	4	6, 805	9, 324	1736	3, 638, 237

PUTNAM COUNTY.

TOWNS.	Stone: Total number.	Stone: No. value not given.	Stone: Val. given.	Brick: Total number.	Brick: No. value not given.	Brick: Val. given.	Framed: Total number.	Framed: No. value not given.	Framed: Val. given.	Logs: Total number.	Logs: No. value not given.	Logs: Val. given.	Other: Total number.	Other: No. value not given.	Other: Val. given.	Total: Total number.	Total: No. value not given.	Total: Val. given.
Carmel,							456	302	192, 730	2	2					470	316	192, 730
Kent,				3		4, 500	230	4	86, 390	33		766				275	4	91, 656
Patterson,				2		500	260		116, 520	1		10	1		10	266	2	117, 040
Phillipstown,				41		139, 500	661	1	526, 150	11		478	9		555	722	1	666, 683
Putnam Valley,							282	254	13, 150	16	15	150				298	269	13, 300
South East,	1		200	1		2, 500	372	1	331, 750							374	1	334, 450
Total,	1		200	47		147, 000	2, 270	562	1, 266, 690	63	17	1, 404	10		565	2, 405	593	1, 415, 859

QUEENS COUNTY.

TOWNS.	Stone: Total number.	Stone: No. value not given.	Stone: Val. given.	Brick: Total number.	Brick: No. value not given.	Brick: Val. given.	Framed: Total number.	Framed: No. value not given.	Framed: Val. given.	Logs: Total number.	Logs: No. value not given.	Logs: Val. given.	Other: Total number.	Other: No. value not given.	Other: Val. given.	Total: Total number.	Total: No. value not given.	Total: Val. given.
Flushing,	3		50, 000	11		25, 000	1, 099	2	1, 865, 067							1, 113	2	1, 940, 067
Hempstead,							1, 855	8	1, 377, 167							2, 022	175	1, 377, 167
Jamaica,				7		43, 500	858	8	1, 191, 605							866	9	1, 235, 105
Newtown,	18	2	92, 800	41		199, 600	1, 450	60	2, 511, 900				4		2, 775	1, 518	67	2, 807, 075
North Hempstead,							772	2	874, 961							867	97	874, 961
Oyster Bay,				11	4	14, 200	1, 037	135	791, 115				4		1, 900	1, 510	597	806, 315
Total,	21	2	142, 800	70	4	282, 300	7, 071	215	8, 611, 815				8		4, 675	7, 896	947	9, 041, 590

RENSSELAER COUNTY.

TOWNS.	Stone: Total number.	Stone: No. value not given.	Stone: Val. given.	Brick: Total number.	Brick: No. value not given.	Brick: Val. given.	Framed: Total number.	Framed: No. value not given.	Framed: Val. given.	Logs: Total number.	Logs: No. value not given.	Logs: Val. given.	Other: Total number.	Other: No. value not given.	Other: Val. given.	Total: Total number.	Total: No. value not given.	Total: Val. given.
Berlin,							312		106, 955	76		2, 336	9		735	397		110, 026
Brunswick,	2		1, 600	4		8, 700	493	1	326, 505							499	1	336, 805
Clinton,				21		61, 100	265		156, 400							286		217, 500
Grafton,							289	1	63, 245	43		1, 135	11		2, 255	343	1	66, 635
Greenbush,				49		91, 900	439	1	323, 600				35	33	350	524	35	415, 850
Hoosick,	2		1, 100	24		80, 500	620	4	425, 570	1		25	11		1, 365	658	4	508, 560
Lansingburgh,				162		290, 800	738	5	614, 360				1	1		901	6	905, 160
Nassau,				2	1	2, 000	567	444	96, 535							576	452	98, 535
North Greenbush,	2		600	9		22, 300	297	3	142, 082							309	4	105, 782
Petersburgh,							311	30	90, 225	5		125				316	30	90, 350
Pittstown,				20		17, 250	620		246, 312				11		2, 920	652	1	266, 482
Poestenkill,							370	7	129, 995	29		1, 205				399	7	131, 200
Sand Lake,	2		600	5	1	8, 500	414		232, 540	38		930	6		350	465	1	242, 920
Schaghticoke,				27		50, 400	463	1	291, 467				6		60	498	3	341, 927

RENSSELAER COUNTY.—(CONTINUED.)

TOWNS	STONE. Total number.	STONE. No. value not given.	STONE. Value given	BRICK. Total number.	BRICK. No. value not given.	BRICK. Val. given.	FRAMED. Total number.	FRAMED. No. value not given.	FRAMED. Val. given.	LOGS. Total number.	LOGS. No. value not given.	LOGS. Val given.	OTHER DWELLINGS. Total number.	OTHER DWELLINGS. No. value not given.	OTHER DWELLINGS. Val. given.	TOTAL. Total number.	TOTAL. No. value not given.	TOTAL. Val. given.
Schodack,	2	....	2,300	35	....	$52,300	628	1	381,390	....	....	......	7	....	260	672	1	436,250
Stephentown,	....	....	....	......	....	....	395	7	131,460	11	1	325	....	....	......	431	33	131,785
Troy City:																		
1st ward,	1	....	1,200	146	4	408,000	304	11	325,100	....	....	......	....	....	......	457	21	734,500
2d ward,	2	1	20,000	248	1	928,300	225	....	302,400	....	....	......	....	....	......	475	2	1,250,700
3d ward,	1	....	15,000	145	1	917,700	99	....	191,300	....	....	......	....	....	......	246	2	1,124,000
4th ward,	....	....	....	185	....	773,400	322	....	396,590	....	....	......	....	....	......	507	....	1,169,990
5th ward,	....	....	....	55	1	79,400	184	17	192,400	....	....	......	....	....	......	277	56	271,800
6th ward,	....	....	....	19	....	18,000	306	1	189,280	....	....	......	4	....	220	329	1	207,500
7th ward,	....	....	....	131	1	229,550	255	1	284,750	....	....	......	....	....	......	387	3	514,300
8th ward,	....	....	....	163	....	573,700	194	2	168,300	....	....	......	....	....	......	359	4	742,000
9th ward,	1	....	1,500	72	....	95,160	319	1	296,100	....	....	......	....	....	......	392	1	392,760
10th ward,	1	....	500	37	1	67,700	290	3	267,825	....	....	......	....	....	......	328	4	336,025
Total Troy City,	6	1	38,200	1,201	9	4,090,910	2,498	36	2,614,045	....	....	......	4	....	220	3,757	94	6,743,375
Total,	16	1	44,400	1,559	11	4,776,660	9,719	541	6,373,486	203	1	6,081	101	34	8,515	11,683	673	11,209,142

RICHMOND COUNTY.

TOWNS	STONE. Total number.	STONE. No. value not given.	STONE. Value given	BRICK. Total number.	BRICK. No. value not given.	BRICK. Val. given.	FRAMED. Total number.	FRAMED. No. value not given.	FRAMED. Val. given.	LOGS. Total number.	LOGS. No. value not given.	LOGS. Val given.	OTHER DWELLINGS. Total number.	OTHER DWELLINGS. No. value not given.	OTHER DWELLINGS. Val. given.	TOTAL. Total number.	TOTAL. No. value not given.	TOTAL. Val. given.
Castleton,	24	....	805,900	55	3	844,100	1,075	2	3,068,525	....	....	......	....	....	......	1,154	5	4,718,525
Northfield,	20	....	41,450	14	....	69,800	657	3	958,320	....	....	......	3	....	265	696	5	1,069,835
Southfield,	25	1	715,900	51	....	543,000	682	4	2,492,400	....	....	......	1	....	50	759	5	3,751,350
Westfield,	5	....	8,100	2	....	18,000	604	2	501,250	....	....	......	....	....	......	611	2	527,350
Total,	74	1	1,571,350	122	3	1,474,900	3,018	11	7,020,495	....	....	......	4	....	315	3,220	17	10,067,060

ROCKLAND COUNTY.

TOWNS	STONE. Total number.	STONE. No. value not given.	STONE. Value given	BRICK. Total number.	BRICK. No. value not given.	BRICK. Val. given.	FRAMED. Total number.	FRAMED. No. value not given.	FRAMED. Val. given.	LOGS. Total number.	LOGS. No. value not given.	LOGS. Val given.	OTHER DWELLINGS. Total number.	OTHER DWELLINGS. No. value not given.	OTHER DWELLINGS. Val. given.	TOTAL. Total number.	TOTAL. No. value not given.	TOTAL. Val. given.
Clarkstown,	93	....	52,465	12	1	34,400	535	....	347,700	....	....	......	....	....	......	643	4	434,565
Haverstraw,	2	....	2,400	47	1	139,400	903	....	741,343	19	....	950	2	....	55	974	2	884,148
Orangetown,	86	10	84,500	42	....	85,000	857	12	901,815	....	....	......	1	....	200	986	22	1,071,515
Ramapo,	70	1	31,375	5	....	8,800	480	5	262,530	21	....	685	7	....	310	585	8	303,700
Total,	251	11	170,740	106	2	267,600	2,775	17	2,253,388	40	....	1,635	10	....	565	3,188	36	2,693,928

ST. LAWRENCE COUNTY.

TOWNS	STONE. Total number.	STONE. No. value not given.	STONE. Value given	BRICK. Total number.	BRICK. No. value not given.	BRICK. Val. given.	FRAMED. Total number.	FRAMED. No. value not given.	FRAMED. Val. given.	LOGS. Total number.	LOGS. No. value not given.	LOGS. Val given.	OTHER DWELLINGS. Total number.	OTHER DWELLINGS. No. value not given.	OTHER DWELLINGS. Val. given.	TOTAL. Total number.	TOTAL. No. value not given.	TOTAL. Val. given.
Brasher,	3	....	4,250	1	....	400	247	....	94,695	204	2	5,745	32	....	2,745	487	2	107,835
Canton,	10	....	16,500	12	....	7,900	623	5	338,270	197	....	5,764	24	....	7,555	874	13	375,989
Colton,	....	....	....	......	....	....	149	....	71,700	56	3	2,360	3	....	72	209	4	74,132
De Kalb,	1	....	1,400	......	....	....	274	1	103,895	181	27	4,600	24	7	565	482	37	110,460
De Peyster,	2	....	1,000	......	....	....	123	....	30,440	57	57	......	4	1	500	195	67	31,940
Edwards,	1	....	600	3	....	2,500	133	....	45,830	62	1	2,080	9	....	1,320	208	1	52,330
Fine,	....	....	....	......	....	....	9	....	1,950	41	....	647	2	....	200	57	5	2,797
Fowler,	1	....	7,000	......	....	....	227	5	59,350	51	....	1,555	13	....	765	292	5	68,670
Gouverneur,	1	....	200	18	1	18,300	366	2	119,485	109	1	3,422	3	....	110	498	5	141,517
Hammond,	42	....	81,800	1	....	1,200	185	9	75,625	58	48	715	6	....	540	314	79	159,880
Hermon,	1	....	500	1	....	1,200	181	....	54,040	94	....	1,055	12	....	575	289	....	57,370
Hopkinton,	4	....	3,300	2	....	2,900	191	....	81,885	93	....	4,107	3	....	240	293	....	92,522
Lawrence,	3	....	2,500	......	....	....	365	....	140,620	82	10	2,760	7	....	340	457	10	146,220
Lisbon,	13	....	9,300	6	....	11,600	376	....	144,212	466	2	19,356	45	....	8,800	907	3	193,268
Louisville,	3	....	1,600	9	....	5,300	206	1	33,660	110	110	......	16	8	1,550	345	120	42,110
Macomb,	2	....	1,500	......	....	....	40	....	9,800	181	180	75	36	....	6,315	260	181	17,690
Madrid,	72	....	65,180	32	....	30,250	515	1	258,795	194	2	5,770	31	....	3,015	844	3	363,010
Massena,	8	....	6,200	23	....	23,050	289	....	65,400	126	1	2,116	13	....	1,465	459	1	98,231
Morristown,	20	....	30,800	3	....	4,400	291	....	169,260	83	....	5,340	2	....	200	399	....	210,000
Norfolk,	5	....	4,250	10	....	10,700	249	4	97,195	70	1	2,655	6	....	115	341	6	114,915
Oswegatchie,	53	2	166,050	29	1	92,200	1,220	3	1,201,040	173	10	17,217	180	4	68,273	1,658	23	1,544,780
Parishville,	2	....	3,200	2	....	2,400	288	....	100,335	79	....	2,354	24	....	3,530	395	....	111,819
Pierrepont,	4	....	2,400	4	....	2,150	205	....	67,765	119	....	5,180	16	....	4,335	348	....	81,830
Pitcairn,	1	....	600	......	....	....	50	1	6,235	52	....	1,352	3	....	47	106	1	8,234
Potsdam,	33	....	73,250	8	....	9,500	868	6	596,294	144	10	6,152	71	14	8,545	1,126	32	693,741
Rossie,	18	....	9,600	7	....	5,400	153	1	54,160	69	....	2,070	5	....	378	252	1	71,608
Russell,	2	1	200	2	1	2,000	118	66	32,065	130	120	541	11	10	50	399	334	34,856
Stockholm,	7	....	4,425	3	....	2,900	486	1	138,478	162	1	7,799	38	....	9,915	697	3	163,517
Total,	312	3	497,605	176	3	236,250	8,427	106	4,192,479	3443	586	112,877	639	44	132,060	13,191	936	5,171,271

SARATOGA COUNTY.

TOWNS	STONE. Total number.	STONE. No. value not given.	STONE. Value given	BRICK. Total number.	BRICK. No. value not given.	BRICK. Val. given.	FRAMED. Total number.	FRAMED. No. value not given.	FRAMED. Val. given.	LOGS. Total number.	LOGS. No. value not given.	LOGS. Val given.	OTHER DWELLINGS. Total number.	OTHER DWELLINGS. No. value not given.	OTHER DWELLINGS. Val. given.	TOTAL. Total number.	TOTAL. No. value not given.	TOTAL. Val. given.
Ballston,	2	....	2,300	11	....	30,300	372	....	205,865	....	....	......	....	....	......	385	....	238,465
Charlton,	1	....	100	10	1	14,000	306	1	191,490	....	....	......	....	....	......	318	3	205,590
Clifton Park,	....	....	....	16	....	22,600	413	2	239,525	....	....	......	....	....	......	429	2	262,125
Corinth,	....	....	....	......	....	....	244	....	63,445	25	2	575	24	....	639	296	5	64,659
Day,	....	....	....	......	....	....	141	136	5,300	54	54	......	1	1	......	197	192	5,300
Edinburgh,	....	....	....	2	....	1,300	225	....	58,287	28	1	276	....	....	......	255	1	59,863
Galway,	....	....	....	4	....	3,800	446	....	129,830	....	....	......	....	....	......	451	1	133,630
Greenfield,	2	....	1,300	1	....	1,000	558	....	164,715	12	....	270	5	....	95	579	1	167,380
Hadley,	....	....	....	......	....	....	149	18	32,050	35	....	825	38	1	520	222	19	33,395
Halfmoon,	8	....	3,950	25	2	43,900	568	9	355,405	....	....	......	....	....	......	606	16	403,255
Malta,	....	....	....	3	....	2,700	225	17	96,005	....	....	......	....	....	......	228	17	98,705
Milton,	6	4	1,600	42	2	64,950	703	289	371,485	....	....	......	....	....	......	751	295	438,035
Moreau,	1	....	8,000	9	....	12,750	308	....	154,550	2	....	35	40	....	12,280	360	....	187,615
Northumberland,	....	....	....	4	....	8,800	286	....	113,306	4	....	1,210	4	....	65	300	2	123,381
Providence,	....	....	....	1	....	500	283	....	86,904	....	....	......	2	....	275	286	....	87,679
Saratoga,	....	....	....	41	3	51,800	649	7	340,720	1	....	25	....	....	......	692	11	392,545
Saratoga Springs,	10	2	30,300	117	7	983,450	875	117	1,234,055	....	....	......	....	....	......	1,013	137	2,247,805

SARATOGA COUNTY.—(CONTINUED.)

TOWNS.	STONE.			BRICK.			FRAMED.			LOGS.			OTHER DWELLINGS.			TOTAL.		
	Total number.	No. value not given.	Val. given.	Total number.	No. value not given.	Val. given.	Total number.	No. value not given.	Val. given.	Total number.	No. value not given.	Val. given.	Total number.	No. value not given.	Val. given.	Total number.	No. value not given.	Val. given.
Stillwater,	....	....	$2,000	13	....	$14,200	482	8	$286,725	....	....	......	....	....	......	498	10	$302,925
Waterford,	....	....	....	41	....	113,200	453	1	389,616	....	....	......	....	....	......	498	5	502,816
Wilton,	1	....	400	3	....	2,100	258	....	69,290	2	....	$25	3	....	$75	267	....	71,890
Total,	32	6	49,950	343	15	1,371,350	7,944	605	4,588,568	163	57	3,241	117	2	13,949	8,631	717	6,027,058

SCHENECTADY COUNTY.

TOWNS.	Stone: Total number.	Stone: No. value not given.	Stone: Val. given.	Brick: Total number.	Brick: No. value not given.	Brick: Val. given.	Framed: Total number.	Framed: No. value not given.	Framed: Val. given.	Logs: Total number.	Logs: No. value not given.	Logs: Val. given.	Other: Total number.	Other: No. value not given.	Other: Val. given.	Total: Total number.	Total: No. value not given.	Total: Val. given.
Duanesburgh,	1	....	500	3	....	2,400	524	5	229,720	10	....	395	3	....	4,200	542	6	237,215
Glenville,	3	....	3,300	17	1	23,050	527	24	179,110	1	....	25	5	....	100	556	28	205,585
Niskayuna,	1	....	500	14	....	15,900	179	....	69,425	2	....	45	5	....	80	201	....	85,950
Princetown,	1	....	400	1	....	1,500	164	1	54,275	....	....	......	....	....	......	166	1	56,175
Rotterdam,	7	....	3,055	19	....	18,150	412	4	152,670	1	....	25	1	....	10	440	4	173,910
Schenectady city:																		
1st ward,	1	....	400	128	....	269,300	77	....	71,500	....	....	......	....	....	......	206	....	341,200
2d ward,	1	....	10,000	117	3	271,800	114	8	115,550	....	....	......	....	....	......	233	12	397,350
3d ward,	....	....	....	89	....	116,550	192	....	152,550	....	....	......	....	....	......	281	....	269,100
4th ward,	....	....	....	217	....	375,850	260	....	218,425	....	....	......	3	....	3,000	480	....	597,275
Total Schenectady	2	....	10,400	551	3	1,033,500	643	8	558,025	....	....	......	3	....	3,000	1,200	12	1,604,925
Total,	15	....	18,155	605	4	1,094,500	2,449	42	1,243,225	14	....	490	17	....	7,390	3,105	51	2,363,760

SCHOHARIE COUNTY.

TOWNS.	Stone: Total number.	Stone: No. value not given.	Stone: Val. given.	Brick: Total number.	Brick: No. value not given.	Brick: Val. given.	Framed: Total number.	Framed: No. value not given.	Framed: Val. given.	Logs: Total number.	Logs: No. value not given.	Logs: Val. given.	Other: Total number.	Other: No. value not given.	Other: Val. given.	Total: Total number.	Total: No. value not given.	Total: Val. given.
Blenheim,	....	....	....	....	....	....	182	3	68,430	39	16	810	....	....	......	225	23	69,240
Broome,	....	....	....	....	....	....	383	3	103,365	38	....	855	....	....	......	421	3	104,220
Carlisle,	....	....	....	2	....	5,500	305	....	134,170	2	....	20	2	....	1,300	311	....	140,990
Cobleskill,	....	....	....	1	....	1,500	369	2	218,480	3	....	115	....	....	......	373	2	220,095
Conesville,	....	....	....	1	....	1,200	246	1	88,070	13	....	290	....	....	......	262	3	89,560
Esperance,	....	....	....	2	....	1,600	227	....	101,825	6	....	105	4	....	53	239	....	103,583
Fulton,	....	....	....	1	....	800	389	132	88,835	112	60	1,078	3	1	30	509	197	90,743
Gilboa,	1	....	300	1	....	600	415	....	134,640	60	....	1,240	....	....	......	478	1	136,780
Jefferson,	1	....	500	....	....	....	264	38	97,041	27	23	200	....	....	......	292	61	97,741
Middleburgh,	2	....	150	2	....	1,400	404	126	210,600	64	18	3,650	....	....	......	480	152	215,800
Richmondville,	....	....	....	....	....	....	336	1	198,045	7	....	465	2	....	325	345	1	198,835
Schoharie,	7	....	18,600	13	....	26,400	438	....	254,130	39	1	2,060	1	....	1,200	498	1	302,390
Seward,	....	....	....	3	....	3,200	312	1	163,995	1	1	......	....	....	......	316	2	167,195
Sharon,	1	....	500	4	....	6,000	455	1	264,925	....	....	......	....	....	......	460	1	271,425
Summit,	....	....	....	....	....	....	332	7	116,405	19	....	450	2	....	2,300	354	8	119,155
Wright,	1	....	1,000	1	....	1,000	276	1	105,705	5	....	137	....	....	......	283	1	107,842
Total,	13	....	21,050	31	....	49,200	5,333	316	2,348,661	435	119	11,475	14	1	5,208	5,846	456	2,435,594

SCHUYLER COUNTY.

TOWNS.	Stone: Total number.	Stone: No. value not given.	Stone: Val. given.	Brick: Total number.	Brick: No. value not given.	Brick: Val. given.	Framed: Total number.	Framed: No. value not given.	Framed: Val. given.	Logs: Total number.	Logs: No. value not given.	Logs: Val. given.	Other: Total number.	Other: No. value not given.	Other: Val. given.	Total: Total number.	Total: No. value not given.	Total: Val. given.
Catharines,	....	....	....	2	....	30,600	565	....	363,070	52	....	2,405	50	....	6,010	669	....	402,085
Cayuta,	....	....	....	....	....	....	52	....	26,225	28	....	1,175	38	....	11,750	118	....	39,150
Dix,	....	....	....	10	1	26,000	358	....	182,498	55	....	1,930	121	1	39,922	545	3	250,350
Hector,	1	....	300	1	....	800	784	10	407,700	91	....	4,535	213	3	77,091	1,090	13	490,426
Orange,	1	....	350	....	....	....	311	....	122,025	108	....	3,375	58	...	9,073	485	7	134,823
Reading,	....	....	....	....	....	....	251	....	106,035	15	....	750	....	....	......	266	....	106,785
Tyrone,	....	....	....	....	....	....	313	....	201,960	56	....	1,390	40	....	12,045	409	....	215,395
Total,	2	....	650	13	1	57,400	2,634	10	1,409,513	405	....	15,560	520	4	155891	3,582	23	1,639,014

SENECA COUNTY.

TOWNS.	Stone: Total number.	Stone: No. value not given.	Stone: Val. given.	Brick: Total number.	Brick: No. value not given.	Brick: Val. given.	Framed: Total number.	Framed: No. value not given.	Framed: Val. given.	Logs: Total number.	Logs: No. value not given.	Logs: Val. given.	Other: Total number.	Other: No. value not given.	Other: Val. given.	Total: Total number.	Total: No. value not given.	Total: Val. given.
Covert,	....	....	....	7	....	10,225	374	....	216,625	15	....	610	22	....	2,915	418	....	230,375
Fayette,	11	....	22,000	52	1	63,400	513	1	289,500	34	....	4,325	2	....	425	613	3	379,650
Junius,	13	....	7,450	11	....	8,850	226	1	64,510	18	3	615	....	....	......	269	5	81,425
Lodi,	2	....	3,500	2	1	300	365	33	173,347	20	5	735	12	....	2,500	401	39	180,382
Ovid,	4	....	4,900	6	3	6,900	366	2	255,770	11	....	788	31	....	12,100	424	11	280,458
Romulus,	....	....	....	4	....	7,100	256	....	158,345	41	....	2,554	41	....	27,425	342	....	195,424
Seneca Falls,	2	....	7,200	84	....	277,485	710	5	747,075	9	....	5,270	28	....	4,940	836	8	1,041,970
Tyre,	5	....	7,700	8	....	14,900	215	3	97,400	35	....	1,510	13	1	612	279	7	122,122
Varick,	3	....	2,300	11	....	13,000	259	....	145,030	48	....	2,630	19	....	11,145	340	....	174,105
Waterloo,	1	....	300	82	3	160,975	640	17	459,740	23	....	1,675	....	....	......	747	21	622,690
Total,	41	....	55,350	267	8	563,135	3,924	62	2.607,342	254	8	20,712	168	1	62,062	4,669	94	3,308,601

STEUBEN COUNTY.

TOWNS.	Stone: Total number.	Stone: No. value not given.	Stone: Val. given.	Brick: Total number.	Brick: No. value not given.	Brick: Val. given.	Framed: Total number.	Framed: No. value not given.	Framed: Val. given.	Logs: Total number.	Logs: No. value not given.	Logs: Val. given.	Other: Total number.	Other: No. value not given.	Other: Val. given.	Total: Total number.	Total: No. value not given.	Total: Val. given.
Addison,	....	....	....	....	....	....	385	1	296,945	1	....	100	4	....	215	518	129	297,260
Avoca,	....	....	....	1	....	2,000	287	....	133,980	29	....	1,430	14	....	920	331	....	138,330
Bath,	4	....	9,000	8	....	27,000	845	81	502,480	179	17	6,625	25	4	6,390	1,068	109	551,495
Bradford,	....	....	....	....	....	....	145	2	56,805	85	1	3,365	8	....	620	238	3	60,790
Cameron,	....	....	....	....	....	....	240	....	52,163	75	....	1,682	20	....	474	335	....	54,319
Campbell,	....	....	....	....	....	....	140	....	50,800	60	4	2,345	86	3	4,940	287	8	58,085
Canisteo,	....	....	....	1	....	2,000	286	1	90,105	46	....	1,065	18	....	315	352	2	93,485
Caton,	1	....	800	....	....	....	132	....	35,275	51	....	1,020	90	....	8,950	274	....	46.045
Cohocton,	....	....	....	....	....	....	291	226	50,300	109	108	100	44	....	1,800	444	334	52,200
Corning,	....	....	....	10	1	54,400	647	110	509,610	57	44	775	291	28	35,305	1,037	215	600,090
Dansville,	2	....	2,000	....	....	....	333	....	110,245	42	....	2,470	24	....	5,365	401	....	129,080
Erwin,	....	....	....	....	....	....	246	....	149,710	23	....	1,005	65	....	4,055	334	....	154,770
Fremont,	....	....	....	....	....	....	165	....	48,295	40	....	1,755	16	....	3,675	221	....	53,725
Greenwood,	....	....	....	....	....	....	162	1	48,815	47	....	2,385	28	1	2,875	237	2	54,075
Hartsville,	....	....	....	....	....	....	124	....	24,470	58	....	916	13	....	440	195	....	25,826
Hornby,	2	....	700	....	....	....	156	4	46,550	71	2	1,775	33	4	2,385	262	10	51,410

STEUBEN COUNTY.—(Continued.)

Towns.	Stone. Total number.	Stone. No. value not given.	Stone. Val. given.	Brick. Total number.	Brick. No. value not given.	Brick. Val. given.	Framed. Total number.	Framed. No. value not given.	Framed. Val. given.	Logs. Total number.	Logs. No value not given.	Logs. Val. given.	Other dwellings. Total number.	Other dwellings. No. value not given.	Other dwellings. Val. given.	Total. Total number.	Total. No. value not given.	Total. Val. given
Hornellsville,	2	....	$10, 000	27	....	$68, 900	482	2	$402, 995	46	....	$2, 660	132	1	16, 955	689	3	$501, 510
Howard,	....	....	....	3	....	1, 675	319	3	108, 650	144	75	2, 670	26	....	1, 852	502	88	114, 847
Jasper,	....	....	....	....	....	....	204	....	44, 930	64	....	2, 030	73	....	11, 405	341	....	58, 365
Lindley,	....	....	....	....	....	....	84	....	31, 525	23	....	562	35	....	2, 485	142	....	34, 572
Prattsburgh,	....	....	....	1	....	2, 000	402	1	214, 205	85	....	3, 575	19	....	1, 300	509	3	221, 080
Pultney,	1	....	1, 400	....	....	....	262	....	129, 675	40	1	2, 910	2	....	50	305	1	134, 035
Thurston,	....	....	....	....	....	....	109	1	29, 480	47	2	1, 868	14	1	348	171	5	31, 696
Troupsburgh,	....	....	....	....	....	....	240	73	34, 295	109	29	4, 585	6	1	395	361	109	39, 275
Urbana,	....	....	....	5	....	8, 700	285	....	150, 880	58	....	2, 600	13	....	1, 145	361	....	163, 325
Wayland,	....	....	....	1	....	2, 500	374	....	89, 387	....	....	....	....	....	....	375	....	91, 887
Wayne,	....	....	....	....	....	....	148	1	52, 400	25	....	810	1	....	130	174	1	53, 340
West Union,	....	....	....	....	....	....	105	....	19, 140	106	....	6, 055	3	....	115	214	....	25, 310
Wheeler,	....	....	....	....	....	....	188	2	66, 550	61	8	1, 980	4	....	750	253	10	69, 280
Woodhull,	....	....	....	....	....	....	256	....	70, 659	157	1	7, 215	7	....	95	420	1	77, 969
Total,	12	....	23, 900	57	1	169, 175	8, 042	509	3, 660, 319	1938	292	68, 393	1114	43	115689	11, 351	1033	4, 037, 476

SUFFOLK COUNTY.

Towns.	Stone. Total number.	Stone. No. value not given.	Stone. Val. given.	Brick. Total number.	Brick. No. value not given.	Brick. Val. given.	Framed. Total number.	Framed. No. value not given.	Framed. Val. given.	Logs. Total number.	Logs. No value not given.	Logs. Val. given.	Other dwellings. Total number.	Other dwellings. No. value not given.	Other dwellings. Val. given.	Total. Total number.	Total. No. value not given.	Total. Val. given
Brookhaven,	5	1	5, 900	31	14	29, 000	1, 577	621	872, 610	....	....	....	4	....	453	1, 657	676	907, 963
Easthampton,	....	....	....	2	....	4, 000	399	4	372, 935	....	....	....	....	....	....	402	5	376, 935
Huntington,	....	....	....	3	....	4, 500	1, 349	2	1, 072, 324	....	....	....	....	....	....	1, 356	6	1, 076, 824
Islip,	....	....	....	4	....	1, 900	550	3	355, 690	7	....	215	19	4	5, 717	583	10	363, 522
River Head,	2	....	4, 500	1	....	800	517	2	354, 269	....	....	....	....	....	....	520	2	359, 569
Shelter Island,	....	....	....	....	....	....	85	....	47, 665	....	....	....	....	....	....	85	....	47, 665
Smithtown,	....	....	....	....	....	....	366	....	245, 155	....	....	....	....	....	....	371	5	245, 155
Southampton,	....	....	....	9	....	26, 300	1, 207	2	821, 852	....	....	....	3	....	150	1, 219	2	848, 302
Southold,	2	....	16, 000	6	....	14, 800	1, 039	8	823, 432	....	....	....	....	....	....	1, 048	9	854, 232
Total,	9	1	26, 400	56	14	81, 300	7, 089	642	4, 965, 932	7	....	215	26	4	6, 320	7, 241	715	5, 080, 167

SULLIVAN COUNTY.

Towns.	Stone. Total number.	Stone. No. value not given.	Stone. Val. given.	Brick. Total number.	Brick. No. value not given.	Brick. Val. given.	Framed. Total number.	Framed. No. value not given.	Framed. Val. given.	Logs. Total number.	Logs. No value not given.	Logs. Val. given.	Other dwellings. Total number.	Other dwellings. No. value not given.	Other dwellings. Val. given.	Total. Total number.	Total. No. value not given.	Total. Val. given
Bethel,	1	....	200	....	....	....	511	4	111, 035	56	....	2, 062	1	....	100	569	4	113, 397
Cochecton,	1	....	600	....	....	....	355	36	128, 535	109	....	6, 030	58	17	2, 805	523	53	137, 970
Collicoon,	1	....	400	....	....	....	326	....	78, 375	85	....	3, 620	1	....	10	414	....	82, 405
Fallsburgh,	3	....	5, 800	....	....	....	319	....	84, 324	76	....	2, 265	138	....	38, 491	537	1	130, 880
Forrestburgh,	....	....	....	....	....	....	103	....	28, 910	10	....	585	19	....	1, 290	132	....	30, 785
Fremont,	....	....	....	....	....	....	131	131	....	94	94	....	11	11	....	237	237	....
Highland,	....	....	....	....	....	....	130	....	33, 745	14	....	955	14	....	2, 360	158	....	37, 060
Liberty,	5	....	1, 600	....	....	....	433	3	145, 115	61	....	1, 005	21	....	3, 050	520	3	150, 770
Lumberland,	....	....	....	....	....	....	95	....	23, 575	18	....	725	43	....	1, 660	156	....	25, 960
Mamakating,	3	....	950	....	....	....	665	....	296, 800	66	....	3, 055	14	....	630	748	....	301, 435
Neversink,	....	....	....	....	....	....	342	3	75, 722	50	20	780	21	2	955	413	25	77, 457
Rockland,	....	....	....	....	....	....	174	....	40, 505	47	....	1, 730	6	....	260	227	....	42, 495
Thompson,	....	....	....	....	....	....	568	7	238, 635	35	2	1, 425	11	....	550	619	14	240, 610
Tusten,	1	....	250	....	....	....	78	47	34, 950	36	34	200	3	2	50	151	116	35, 450
Total,	15	....	9, 800	....	....	....	4, 230	231	1, 320, 226	757	150	24, 437	361	32	52, 211	5, 403	453	1, 406, 674

TIOGA COUNTY.

Towns.	Stone. Total number.	Stone. No. value not given.	Stone. Val. given.	Brick. Total number.	Brick. No. value not given.	Brick. Val. given.	Framed. Total number.	Framed. No. value not given.	Framed. Val. given.	Logs. Total number.	Logs. No value not given.	Logs. Val. given.	Other dwellings. Total number.	Other dwellings. No. value not given.	Other dwellings. Val. given.	Total. Total number.	Total. No. value not given.	Total. Val. given
Barton,	....	....	....	5	....	10, 500	661	197	304, 705	80	78	70	24	10	1, 065	770	285	316, 340
Berkshire,	....	....	....	5	....	4, 700	189	....	81, 130	7	....	285	2	....	350	203	....	86, 465
Candor,	....	....	....	5	....	6, 300	628	....	240, 708	76	8	1, 660	35	....	1, 029	744	8	249, 697
Newark,	....	....	....	1	....	2, 500	366	1	157, 240	17	....	445	3	....	125	387	1	160, 310
Nichols,	....	....	....	3	....	2, 700	269	7	118, 550	42	16	1, 550	4	1	225	319	25	123, 025
Owego,	5	....	8, 350	14	....	100, 700	1, 252	....	844, 015	132	....	7, 774	59	....	17, 800	1, 467	5	978, 639
Richford,	....	....	....	1	....	600	195	15	50, 175	29	29	....	2	....	100	231	48	50, 875
Spencer,	....	....	....	1	....	1, 500	327	1	104, 683	26	....	572	3	....	30	357	1	106, 785
Tioga,	....	....	....	....	....	....	464	89	132, 162	74	58	850	33	23	713	571	170	133, 725
Total,	5	....	8, 350	35	....	129, 500	4, 351	310	2, 033, 868	483	189	13, 206	165	34	21, 437	5, 049	543	2, 205, 861

TOMPKINS COUNTY.

Towns.	Stone. Total number.	Stone. No. value not given.	Stone. Val. given.	Brick. Total number.	Brick. No. value not given.	Brick. Val. given.	Framed. Total number.	Framed. No. value not given.	Framed. Val. given.	Logs. Total number.	Logs. No value not given.	Logs. Val. given.	Other dwellings. Total number.	Other dwellings. No. value not given.	Other dwellings. Val. given.	Total. Total number.	Total. No. value not given.	Total. Val. given
Caroline,	....	....	....	....	....	....	378	....	125, 788	17	....	690	82	....	10, 830	477	....	137, 308
Danby,	....	....	....	....	....	....	428	....	172, 100	32	....	886	27	....	4, 040	487	....	177, 026
Dryden,	....	....	....	....	....	....	838	....	430, 765	47	....	2, 080	83	....	14, 125	968	....	446, 970
Enfield,	1	....	1, 500	1	....	1, 000	210	7	137, 410	37	....	1, 307	143	....	54, 825	392	7	196, 042
Groton,	....	....	....	....	....	....	639	....	272, 770	13	....	140	2	....	450	654	....	273, 360
Ithaca,	6	....	27, 500	57	2	118, 350	1, 027	....	1, 089, 225	11	....	300	197	....	71, 600	1, 304	8	1, 306, 975
Lansing,	1	....	6, 000	5	....	4, 800	577	....	208, 237	16	....	645	13	....	300	616	4	219, 982
Newfield,	1	....	150	2	....	2, 000	215	8	85, 360	101	33	3, 985	238	16	56, 530	557	57	148, 025
Ulysses,	....	....	....	12	....	28, 700	559	144	341, 890	13	....	500	12	....	1, 875	596	144	372, 965
Total,	9	....	35, 150	77	2	154, 850	4, 871	159	2, 863, 545	287	33	10, 533	797	16	214575	6, 051	220	3, 278, 653

ULSTER COUNTY.

Towns.	Stone. Total number.	Stone. No. value not given.	Stone. Val. given.	Brick. Total number.	Brick. No. value not given.	Brick. Val. given.	Framed. Total number.	Framed. No. value not given.	Framed. Val. given.	Logs. Total number.	Logs. No value not given.	Logs. Val. given.	Other dwellings. Total number.	Other dwellings. No. value not given.	Other dwellings. Val. given.	Total. Total number.	Total. No. value not given.	Total. Val. given
Denning,	....	....	51, 063	....	....	89, 800	98	1	13, 130	30	....	1, 300	4	....	250	132	1	14, 680
Esopus,	77	....	8, 200	27	....	7, 900	547	....	314, 847	2	....	100	....	....	....	679	26	455, 810
Gardiner,	23	....	22, 110	7	....	1, 500	295	....	115, 280	12	....	490	....	....	....	337	....	131, 870
Hurley,	43	4	370, 550	2	....	460, 600	313	....	86, 276	21	....	820	....	....	....	380	5	110, 706
Kingston,	136	....	16, 562	145	2	6, 800	1, 535	13	1, 957, 435	9	....	2, 675	....	....	....	1, 829	19	2, 791, 260
Lloyd,	38	....	73, 650	3	....	2, 350	336	1	172, 735	2	....	10	....	....	....	379	1	196, 107
Marbletown,	180	2	2, 000	4	....	8, 800	406	3	159, 825	28	....	1, 000	....	....	....	620	7	236, 825
Marlborough,	5	....	18, 950	5	....	15, 600	416	....	338, 110	....	....	....	....	....	....	426	....	348, 910
New Paltz,	39	....	....	8	1	....	254	....	124, 630	15	....	1, 155	1	....	20	317	1	160, 355

ULSTER COUNTY.—(CONTINUED.)

TOWNS.	STONE.			BRICK.			FRAMED.			LOGS.			OTHER DWELLINGS.			TOTAL.		
	Total number.	No. value not given.	Val. given.	Total number.	No. value not given.	Val. given.	Total number.	No. value not given.	Val. given.	Total number.	No value not given	Val. given.	Total number.	No. value not given.	Val. given.	Total number	No. value not given.	Val. given.
Olive,	26	18	3,300				381	164	68,280	76	26	2,525	7	5	150	516	239	74,255
Plattekill,	21	18	1,100	3	3		318	152	80,195	2	2		3		35	348	176	81,330
Rochester,	86	3	37,950	3		2,700	422	2	117,800	106		5,215				617	5	163,665
Rosendale,	34	1	20,190	2		2,100	326	1	150,510	10		550	3		80	375	2	173,430
Saugerties,	118	1	66,550	115		199,600	1,251	1	651,015	1		50	2		210	1,487	2	917,430
Shandaken,	1		150				297	1	60,265	82		2,160	70		17,675	451	2	80,250
Shawangunk,	35		25,200	1		600	401	13	179,600	36		2,640				478	18	208,040
Wawarsing,	38	27	4,050	4		14,700	1,158	323	433,701	121	55	1,465	45		3,866	1,391	430	457,782
Woodstock,	3		2,000				274		59,285	29		565				306		61,850
Total,	903	74	723,580	329	6	813,050	9,028	675	5,082,919	582	83	22,720	135	5	22,286	11,068	934	6,664.555

WARREN COUNTY.

TOWNS.	STONE.			BRICK.			FRAMED.			LOGS.			OTHER DWELLINGS.			TOTAL.		
Bolton,							184		42,288	26		817	6		695	216		43,800
Caldwell,							156		86,740	8		200				164		86,940
Chester,							285		102,605	70		2,375	4		330	359		105,310
Hague,				1	1		80		15,805	13		705	2		200	96	1	16,710
Horicon,							102		29,885	122		5,105	2		250	226		35,240
Johnsburgh,							208		52,815	111		3,420	37		2,630	356		58,865
Luzerne,																265	265	
Queensbury,	6		7,900	89		84,900	1,068		567,595	9		450	10		740	1,182		661,585
Stony Creek,							96	3	20,005	31		985	51	33	1,206	178	36	22,196
Thurman,							62	62		20	20		12	12		238	238	
Warrensburgh,							283		119,491	51		1,720				334		121,211
Total,	6		7,900	90	1	84,900	2,524	65	1,037,229	461	20	15,777	124	45	6,051	3,614	540	1,151,857

WASHINGTON COUNTY.

TOWNS.	STONE.			BRICK.			FRAMED.			LOGS.			OTHER DWELLINGS.			TOTAL.		
Argyle,	1		1,200	22	1	40,100	533	4	220,180	9	1	205	1		500	566	5	262,185
Cambridge,				12		19,850	398	3	196,725	2	1	100	2		250	415	6	216,925
Dresden,							109		23,260	36		845	1		150	146		24,255
Easton,				14		27,600	585		262,154	3		125	4		1,975	559	3	291,854
Fort Ann,	5		5,800	8		10,900	543	9	182,181	45	2	1,327	8	2	515	613	17	200,723
Fort Edward,	1		900	27		43,700	368		246,400	1		25	63		29,340	460		320,365
Granville,				36		49,050	533	4	258,125	5		190	14		1,606	595	11	308,971
Greenwich,				42		94,000	690	4	377,137	3		150	5		550	745	9	471,837
Hampton,				8	1	6,900	138	2	50,300				4		240	161	14	57,440
Hartford,	1		150	6		7,400	381	1	146,497	8		235				396	1	154,282
Hebron,	2		800	6	5	2,500	497	189	120,405							505	194	123,705
Jackson,				6		11,000	316		184,475	1		50				323		195,525
Kingsbury,	3		1,800	7		15,600	540		330,480				2		20	552		347,900
Putnam,	6		4,100	3		2,800	105		36,700	7		85	1		50	122		43,735
Salem,				17		42,500	479		312,695	1		200	9		3,625	506		359,020
White Creek,				14	2	23,800	432		273,895				15		1,685	462	3	299,380
Whitehall,	4		8,300	93	1	185,600	646		404,703	3	1	120				749	5	598,723
Total,	23		23,050	321	10	583,300	7,243	216	3,626,312	124	5	3,657	129	2	40,506	7,875	268	4,276,825

WAYNE COUNTY.

TOWNS.	STONE.			BRICK.			FRAMED.			LOGS.			OTHER DWELLINGS.			TOTAL.		
Arcadia,	17		21,000	64		97,550	853	1	631,775	34		1,850	18		2,390	987	2	754,565
Butler,	4	4		8	7	600	340	269	37,500	52	50	160	10	7	450	414	337	38,710
Galen,	11	1	8,050	27	1	46,800	743	21	420,045	69		5,261	60	5	2,805	924	42	482,961
Huron,	3		2,500				298		96,977	83		2,495	2		50	386		102,022
Lyons,	15		16,800	115		179,300	677	3	448,065	23		935	28	1	3,745	874	20	648,845
Macedon,	9		12,800	5		9,600	425	8	229,545	11	1	515	1		25	453	11	252,485
Marion,	38		30,050	1		600	309		143,625	22		385	12		1,125	382		175,785
Ontario,	14		9,900	3		3,000	347		113,080	63		1,550	24		540	451		128,070
Palmyra,	22		29,150	81		207,900	588	2	533,430	10		1,200	10		600	713	4	772,280
Rose,	6	1	2,500	2		1,800	303	2	88,560	58		850	21		1,030	395	8	94,740
Savannah,	3		3,000	2		1,300	191	4	81,625	120		6,815	27		1,120	343	4	93,860
Sodus,	46		33,600	5		4,400	687	1	282,050	109	2	2,700	60		6,290	908	4	329,040
Walworth,	18		13,850				338		154,355	28		1,140	6		170	390		169,515
Williamson,	42		35,050	7	1	5,250	396	6	168,650	47	1	2,177	2		162	495	9	211,289
Wolcott,	2		2,000	3		6,500	394	2	203,420	130		8,221	64		9,710	593	2	229,851
Total,	250	6	220,250	323	9	564,600	6,889	319	3,632,702	859	54	36,254	345	13	30 212	8,708	443	4,484,018

WESTCHESTER COUNTY.

TOWNS.	STONE.			BRICK.			FRAMED.			LOGS.			OTHER DWELLINGS.			TOTAL.		
Bedford,	4		15,300	1		1,000	610	5	448,465							615	5	464,765
Cortlandt,	2		8,600	91		181,300	1,081	9	1,070,405	3		400	1		50	1,181	12	1,260,755
East Chester,	17		47,350	2		4,500	740	1	849,829				15		1,950	774	1	903,629
Greenburgh,	23		690,700	58	1	441,175	833	8	2,492,016				10		3,900	924	9	3,627,791
Harrison,	13	1	900				205	1	159,475							218	2	160,375
Lewisboro,							338		162,795							338		162,795
Mamaroneck,	1		200	1		15,000	170		173,400							172		188,600
Mount Pleasant,	3		24,600	39		144,900	496	2	608,020							540	4	777,520
New Castle,	1		2,000				316	1	209,145							317	1	211,145
New Rochelle,	12		54,400	2		5,200	483		1,045,725							497		1,105,325
North Castle,	2		800				392		236,425							395	1	237,225
North Salem,							289	1	242,185							289	1	242,185
Ossining,	9	1	357,000	33		108,100	619	1	1,181,150							662	3	1,649,250
Pelham,	7	7		3	2	3,000	107	62	34,650							119	73	37,650
Poundridge,	1		10	1		800	278	5	82,600							281	6	83,410
Rye,	4		27,900	4		30,000	521	1	853,825				2		2,515	531	1	914,240
Scarsdale,	3		16,200				59		68,350							62		84,550
Somers,	1		15,000	6	1	8,300	290	10	205,880							304	18	229,180

WESTCHESTER COUNTY.—(CONTINUED.)

TOWNS.	STONE.			BRICK.			FRAMED.			LOGS.			OTHER DWELLINGS.			TOTAL.		
	Total number.	No. value not given.	Val. given.	Total number.	No. value not given.	Val. given.	Total number.	No. value not given.	Val. given.	Total number.	No. value not given.	Val. given.	Total number.	No. value not given.	Val. given.	Total number.	No. value not given.	Val. given.
Westchester,	20	....	$99, 500	16	....	$61, 800	451	1	$575, 225	....	....	......	6	....	$180	493	1	$736, 705
West Farms,	15	....	193, 500	19	....	55, 300	2, 001	6	3, 847, 975	....	....	......	....	....	......	2, 035	6	4, 096, 775
White Plains,	....	....	....	3	....	28, 000	230	1	368, 875	....	....	......	....	....	......	233	1	396, 875
Yonkers,	20	4	86, 300	190	4	1, 404, 900	1, 126	59	2, 320, 400	....	....	......	....	....	......	1, 368	99	3, 811, 600
Yorktown,	....	....	....	1	....	1, 000	409	....	215, 885	....	....	......	....	....	......	410	....	216, 885
Total,	158	13	1640, 260	470	8	2, 494, 275	12, 044	174	17, 455, 700	3	....	400	34	....	8, 595	12, 758	244	21, 599, 230

WYOMING COUNTY.

TOWNS.	STONE.			BRICK.			FRAMED.			LOGS.			OTHER DWELLINGS.			TOTAL.		
	Total number.	No. value not given.	Val. given.	Total number.	No. value not given.	Val. given.	Total number.	No. value not given.	Val. given.	Total number.	No. value not given.	Val. given.	Total number.	No. value not given.	Val. given.	Total number.	No. value not given.	Val. given.
Attica,	1	....	1, 500	20	....	22, 800	424	....	227, 560	42	....	1, 300	13	....	395	500	....	253, 555
Bennington,	....	....	....	3	....	1, 350	412	....	136, 580	50	....	905	46	....	5, 560	512	1	144, 395
Castile,	2	....	3, 200	......	....	....	402	....	223, 995	60	....	2, 706	8	....	810	472	....	230, 711
China,	....	....	....	......	....	....	247	....	142, 650	95	....	2, 725	1	....	50	345	2	145, 425
Covington,	3	....	5, 000	2	....	4, 000	220	....	169, 430	23	....	3, 125	....	....	......	248	....	181, 555
Eagle,	....	....	....	......	....	....	193	....	62, 125	67	....	1, 210	4	....	170	264	....	63, 505
Gainesville,	....	....	....	1	....	300	309	1	104, 980	28	....	985	12	....	461	350	1	106, 726
Genesee Falls,	....	....	....	......	....	....	169	....	70, 985	5	....	135	44	....	990	218	....	72, 110
Java,	....	....	....	......	....	....	290	17	85, 760	99	85	900	19	9	465	408	111	87, 125
Middlebury,	2	....	2, 100	8	....	8, 800	316	....	198, 962	18	....	795	7	....	460	351	....	211, 117
Orangeville,	....	....	....	......	....	....	234	....	69, 925	17	1	311	....	....	......	251	1	70, 236
Perry,	3	....	3, 400	3	....	2, 400	466	1	380, 770	18	2	825	....	....	......	490	3	387, 395
Pike,	....	....	....	1	1	....	345	207	92, 087	3	3	......	2	2	......	351	213	92, 087
Sheldon,	....	....	....	......	....	....	452	....	102, 880	43	....	1, 305	....	....	......	495	....	104, 185
Warsaw,	....	....	....	12	1	53, 000	486	17	351, 470	5	....	275	6	....	730	510	19	405, 475
Weathersfield,	....	....	....	......	....	....	216	....	76, 025	30	....	590	30	....	2, 725	276	....	79, 340
Totel,	11	....	15, 200	50	2	92, 650	5, 181	243	2, 496, 184	603	91	18, 092	192	11	12, 816	6, 041	351	2, 634, 942

YATES COUNTY.

TOWNS.	STONE.			BRICK.			FRAMED.			LOGS.			OTHER DWELLINGS.			TOTAL.		
	Total number.	No. value not given.	Val. given.	Total number.	No. value not given.	Val. given.	Total number.	No. value not given.	Val. given.	Total number.	No. value not given.	Val. given.	Total number.	No. value not given.	Val. given.	Total number.	No. value not given.	Val. given.
Barrington,	1	....	800	1	....	2, 500	253	....	126, 425	46	....	2, 100	4	....	590	305	....	132, 415
Benton,	4	....	12, 500	2	....	2, 000	445	....	290, 430	34	....	1, 670	2	....	80	487	....	306, 680
Italy,	2	....	1, 200	......	....	....	159	4	54, 230	101	1	2, 100	11	....	320	275	7	57, 850
Jerusalem,	7	....	30, 400	1	....	500	438	6	223, 974	95	16	5, 415	6	1	215	552	28	260, 504
Middlesex,	1	....	500	3	....	2, 800	193	....	89, 980	61	....	4, 420	....	....	......	258	....	97, 700
Milo,	3	....	13, 300	23	....	74, 800	773	4	666, 425	34	....	1, 339	12	....	213	846	5	756, 077
Potter,	1	....	1, 200	13	2	14, 600	336	1	173, 940	43	....	3, 655	3	....	360	402	9	193, 755
Starkey,	2	....	12, 000	5	....	14, 450	460	1	297, 215	22	....	542	12	....	300	501	1	324, 507
Torrey,	4	....	7, 300	4	....	8, 000	218	1	133, 200	16	....	1, 115	5	....	375	247	1	149, 990
Total,	25	....	79, 200	52	2	119, 650	3, 275	17	2, 055, 819	452	17	22, 356	55	1	2, 453	3, 873	51	2, 279, 478

RECAPITULATION OF MATERIAL AND VALUE OF DWELLINGS.

COUNTIES.	STONE.			BRICK.			FRAMED.		
	Total number.	Number value not given.	Value given.	Total number.	Number value not given.	Value given.	Total number.	Number value not given.	Value given.
Albany,	88	22	$424, 725	3, 769	85	$11, 833, 809	9, 385	474	$6, 564, 651
Allegany,	13	....	25, 350	29	....	44, 500	6, 287	389	2, 501, 861
Broome,	4	....	1, 000	82	3	398, 900	5, 529	861	3, 255, 219
Cattaraugus,	5	2	3, 600	9	....	8, 100	4, 942	453	1, 779, 019
Cayuga,	73	7	977, 950	325	6	933, 000	9, 620	104	5, 515, 093
Chautauque,	14	4	12, 100	113	9	298, 400	8, 314	62	4, 336, 028
Chemung,	1	....	3, 500	47	2	546, 800	3, 264	158	2, 701, 364
Chenango,	20	3	25, 450	21	3	47, 900	7, 226	808	3, 722, 359
Clinton,	163	22	145, 950	460	24	635, 570	3, 959	215	1, 472, 319
Columbia,	52	....	78, 215	388	2	1, 130, 800	6, 665	29	4, 449, 987
Cortland,	9	....	34, 700	45	....	131, 300	4, 276	23	2, 076, 171
Delaware,	44	5	17, 900	8	....	6, 300	6, 040	261	2, 420, 839
Dutchess,	177	25	245, 500	434	18	1, 242, 125	8, 947	662	7, 174, 232
Erie,	111	5	609, 375	2, 427	23	10, 610, 120	12, 834	635	12, 310, 966
Essex,	30	....	35, 375	168	....	235, 870	4, 176	24	1, 484, 420
Franklin,	88	3	79, 740	71	1	84, 075	2, 545	138	1, 024, 536
Fulton,	2	....	4, 600	53	9	85, 100	3, 817	230	1, 530, 985
Genesee,	60	8	56, 100	107	14	246, 350	4, 976	793	2, 761, 797
Greene,	100	1	71, 925	163	4	296, 450	4, 964	187	2, 344, 788
Hamilton,	2	1	200	....	....	....	273	16	70, 880
Herkimer,	62	7	189, 150	165	8	407, 100	6, 332	409	3, 083, 041
Jefferson,	429	19	506, 405	208	3	415, 300	9, 534	140	4, 993, 268
Kings,	515	4	4, 954, 600	8, 061	36	39, 526, 650	14, 901	51	32, 002, 499
Lewis,	34	....	61, 500	18	....	22, 000	3, 195	182	1, 141, 653
Livingston,	57	2	100, 450	113	16	274, 280	5, 787	426	3, 854, 570
Madison,	50	7	68, 100	95	1	201, 650	7, 688	452	3, 873, 310
Monroe,	301	3	499, 550	1, 760	40	5, 654, 705	13, 713	236	11, 106, 474
Montgomery,	59	5	116, 825	147	1	337, 475	4, 700	95	2, 618, 909
New-York,	1, 617	13	32, 267, 340	29, 977	203	211, 531, 806	10, 595	103	28, 900, 745
Niagara,	348	24	759, 364	299	26	439, 170	5, 361	376	3, 420, 991
Oneida,	59	3	92, 500	623	13	2, 627, 450	16, 062	487	9, 789, 431
Onondaga,	60	....	122, 050	762	9	2, 629, 850	13, 175	332	8, 765, 842
Ontario,	120	3	179, 650	516	9	1, 230, 705	6, 591	116	4, 354, 420
Orange,	232	14	398, 075	474	11	1, 507, 100	8, 162	530	6, 530, 795
Orleans,	182	10	196, 765	133	4	215, 150	4, 119	217	2, 455, 335
Oswego,	67	....	302, 000	131	4	602, 030	10, 516	356	5, 531, 060
Otsego,	84	24	131, 950	50	5	105, 700	8, 837	1, 594	3, 387, 718
Putnam,	1	....	200	47	....	147, 000	2, 270	562	1, 266, 690
Queens,	21	2	142, 800	70	4	282, 300	7, 071	215	8, 611, 815
Rensselaer,	16	1	44, 400	1, 559	11	4, 776, 660	9, 719	541	6, 373, 486
Richmond,	74	1	1, 571, 350	122	3	1, 474, 900	3, 018	11	7, 020, 495
Rockland,	251	11	170, 740	106	2	267, 600	2, 775	17	2, 253, 388
St. Lawrence,	312	3	497, 605	176	3	236, 250	8, 427	106	4, 192, 479
Saratoga,	32	6	49, 950	343	15	1, 371, 350	7, 944	605	4, 588, 568
Schenectady,	15	....	18, 155	605	4	1, 094, 500	2, 449	42	1, 243, 225
Schoharie,	13	....	21, 050	31	....	49, 200	5, 333	316	2, 348, 661
Schuyler,	2	....	650	13	1	57, 400	2, 634	10	1, 409. 513
Seneca,	41	....	55, 350	267	8	563, 135	3, 924	62	2, 607, 342
Steuben,	12	....	23, 900	57	1	169, 175	8, 042	509	3, 660, 319
Suffolk,	9	1	26, 400	56	14	81, 300	7, 089	642	4, 965, 932
Sullivan,	15	....	9, 800	....	....	....	4, 230	231	1, 320, 226
Tioga,	5	....	8, 350	35	....	129, 500	4, 351	310	2, 033, 368
Tompkins,	9	....	35, 150	77	2	154, 850	4, 871	159	2, 863, 545
Ulster,	903	74	723, 580	329	6	813, 050	9, 028	675	5, 082, 919
Warren,	6	....	7, 900	90	1	84, 900	2, 524	65	1, 037, 229
Washington,	23	....	23, 050	321	10	583, 300	7, 243	216	3, 626, 312
Wayne,	250	6	220, 250	323	9	564, 600	6, 889	319	3, 632, 702
Westchester,	158	13	1, 640, 260	470	8	2, 494, 275	12, 044	174	17, 455, 700
Wyoming,	11	....	15, 200	50	2	92, 650	5, 181	243	2, 496, 184
Yates,	25	....	79, 200	52	2	119, 650	3, 275	17	2, 055, 819
Total,	7, 536	364	$49, 184, 819	57, 450	698	$312, 151, 135	397, 638	18, 671	$297, 453, 492

*

RECAPITULATION.—(Continued.)

COUNTIES.	LOGS.			OTHER DWELLINGS.			Material and value not given.	TOTAL.		
	Total number.	Number value not given.	Value given.	Total number.	Number value not given.	Value given.		Total number.	Number value not given.	Value given.
Albany,	19	7	$193	32	7	$7, 890	298	13, 591	893	$18, 831, 268
Allegany,	966	160	31, 415	806	37	31, 480	91	8, 192	677	2, 634, 606
Broome,	560	120	24, 243	252	32	46, 952	9	6, 436	1, 025	3, 726, 314
Cattaraugus,	1, 252	310	29, 459	1, 270	119	116, 952	37	7, 515	921	1, 937, 130
Cayuga,	475	44	17, 533	385	87	57, 951	38	10, 916	286	7, 501, 527
Chautauque,	639	18	17, 765	866	31	137, 651	42	9, 988	166	4, 801, 944
Chemung,	516	33	19, 400	999	44	207, 971	30	4, 857	267	3, 479, 035
Chenango,	240	49	6, 935	62	9	26, 730	33	7, 602	904	3, 829, 374
Clinton,	1, 988	55	83, 677	408	5	27, 857	16	6, 994	337	2, 365, 373
Columbia,	29	....	1, 075	20	1	835	133	7, 287	165	5, 660, 912
Cortland,	295	5	9, 484	79	1	6, 080	23	4, 727	52	2, 257, 735
Delaware,	888	121	29, 378	162	44	8, 873	96	7, 238	527	2, 483, 290
Dutchess,	58	3	1, 785	31	....	1, 955	58	9, 705	766	8, 665, 597
Erie,	1, 638	276	179, 386	4, 316	473	1, 317, 897	348	21, 674	1, 760	25, 027, 744
Essex,	663	1	28, 091	131	2	9, 676	59	5, 227	86	1, 794, 032
Franklin,	1, 353	103	48, 566	375	45	81, 321	12	4, 444	302	1, 318, 238
Fulton,	238	4	8, 872	66	5	53, 727	3	4, 179	251	1, 683, 284
Genesee,	408	81	14, 231	175	11	8, 457	27	5, 753	934	3, 086, 935
Greene,	145	3	5, 045	23	....	1, 525	14	5, 409	209	2, 719, 733
Hamilton,	147	12	10, 396	11	....	1, 315	28	461	57	82, 791
Herkimer,	191	5	7, 403	45	2	13, 055	103	6, 898	534	3, 699, 749
Jefferson,	1, 369	50	52, 136	409	15	78, 651	26	11, 975	253	6, 045, 760
Kings,	....	....	....	403	124	44, 395	90	23, 970	305	76, 528, 144
Lewis,	1, 094	129	30, 571	193	3	7, 259	....	4, 707	314	1, 303, 958
Livingston,	608	88	34, 212	403	31	33, 835	22	6, 990	585	4, 297, 347
Madison,	173	55	5, 408	186	21	24, 040	29	8, 221	565	4, 172, 508
Monroe,	650	35	33, 541	418	10	23, 274	74	16, 916	398	17, 317, 524
Montgomery,	23	3	750	22	....	5, 840	9	4, 960	113	3, 079. 799
New-York,	....	....	....	333	46	781, 920	146	42, 668	511	273, 481, 811
Niagara,	1, 525	380	72, 848	1, 149	182	214, 070	16	8, 698	1, 004	4, 906, 443
Oneida,	496	45	15, 257	492	113	22, 524	50	17, 782	711	12, 547, 162
Onondaga,	498	47	17, 480	688	19	87, 327	32	15, 215	439	11, 622, 549
Ontario,	513	18	23, 741	77	2	22, 865	11	7, 828	159	5, 811, 381
Orange,	405	23	17, 350	260	36	21, 425	49	9, 582	663	8, 474, 745
Orleans,	346	59	18, 550	511	33	129, 447	8	5, 299	331	3, 015, 247
Oswego,	821	125	17, 813	1, 068	150	145, 225	46	12, 649	681	6, 598, 128
Otsego,	287	72	6, 064	29	4	6, 805	37	9, 324	1, 736	3, 638, 237
Putnam,	63	17	1, 404	10	....	565	14	2, 405	593	1, 415, 859
Queens,	....	....	....	8	....	4, 675	726	7, 896	947	9, 041, 590
Rensselaer,	203	1	6, 081	101	34	8, 515	85	11, 683	673	11, 209, 142
Richmond,	....	....	....	4	....	315	2	3, 220	17	10, 067, 060
Rockland,	40	....	1, 635	10	....	565	6	3, 188	36	2, 693, 928
St. Lawrence,	3, 443	586	112, 877	639	44	132, 060	194	13, 191	936	5, 171, 271
Saratoga,	163	57	3, 241	117	2	13, 949	32	8, 631	717	6, 027, 058
Schenectady,	14	....	490	17	....	7, 390	5	3, 105	51	2, 363, 760
Schoharie,	435	119	11, 475	14	1	5, 208	20	5, 846	456	2, 435, 594
Schuyler,	405	....	15, 560	520	4	155, 891	8	3, 582	23	1, 639, 014
Seneca,	254	8	20, 712	168	1	62, 062	15	4, 669	94	3, 308, 601
Steuben,	1, 938	292	68, 393	1, 114	43	115, 689	188	11, 351	1, 033	4, 037, 476
Suffolk,	7	....	215	26	4	6, 320	54	7, 241	715	5, 080, 167
Sullivan,	757	150	24, 437	361	32	52, 211	40	5, 403	453	1, 406, 674
Tioga,	483	189	13, 206	165	34	21, 437	10	5, 049	543	2, 205, 861
Tompkins,	287	33	10, 533	797	16	214, 575	10	6, 051	220	3, 278, 653
Ulster,	582	83	22, 720	135	5	22, 286	91	11, 068	934	6, 664, 555
Warren,	461	20	15, 777	124	45	6, 051	409	3, 614	540	1, 151, 857
Washington,	124	5	3, 657	129	2	40, 506	35	7, 875	268	4, 276, 825
Wayne,	859	54	36, 254	345	13	30, 212	42	8, 708	443	4, 484, 018
Westchester,	3	....	400	34	....	8, 595	49	12, 758	244	21, 599, 230
Wyoming,	603	91	18, 092	192	11	12, 816	4	6, 041	351	2, 634, 942
Yates,	452	17	22, 356	55	1	2, 453	14	3, 873	51	2, 279, 478
Total,	33, 092	4, 261	$1, 330, 168	22, 240	2, 086	$4, 739, 398	4, 196	522, 325	30, 225	$664, 899, 967

AGRICULTURE.

ALBANY COUNTY.

TOWNS.	ACRES.		CASH VALUE.			Acres plowed the year previous.	Acres in fallow the year previous.	Acres in pasture the year previous.	MEADOW.			SPRING WHEAT.		WINTER WHEAT.
	Improved.	Unimproved.	Of farm.	Of stock.	Of tools and implements				Acres.	Tons of hay.	Bushels of grass seed.	Acres sown.	Bushels harvested.	Acres sown.
Albany, ...	2,958	1,530½	$399,650	$126,539	$10,807	1,179	274	556½	534½	425½	5	......	......	......
Bern, ...	31,171	8,115½	1,005,557	177,170	48,602	11,865	449½	8,400½	7,936	5,311¼	178¼	168½	1,222¼	99
Bethlehem, ...	26,804¾	6,616½	1,849,162	174,561	111,216	9,169½	1,334	8,712	8,627½	8,927½	33½	14½	164	104½
Coeymans, ...	22,563	10,066	1,330,950	113,385	60,139	3,589¼	596½	3,806	6,458½	6,016½	36	19½	88	288
Guilderland, ...	32,590	9,701½	2,402,906	401,176	79,053	11,588½	532	4,828¾	8,400	7,952½	229½	43½	309	182
Knox, ...	21,136	5,115½	791,202	119,701	29,632	8,359¾	375	5,331¼	5,320¼	3,036½	534¾	198¾	1,326	198½
New Scotland, ..	19,012	8,114	1,329,080	106,732	46,189	5,275	1,135	3,533	5,943½	5,738½	102	10	68	231½
Rensselaerville, .	31,501¾	6,603	1,079,725	190,959	42,912	10,254	85	12,346	7,017	4,421	144¼	251¼	1,506	298¾
Watervliet, ...	25,897½	8,193¾	3,007,745	216,641	81,197	10,164	436	5,484	5,302	5,228	12	176	1,933	123
Westerlo, ...	29,101	6,721	1,119,291	150,096	40,351	8,730	257	8,238	8,815	7,522	58	56	311	61
Total, ...	242,735	70,777¼	14,315,268	1,776,960	550,098	80,124	5,474	61,236	64,354¼	54,579¼	1,333¼	938	6,927¼	1,586¼
ALLEGANY COUNTY.														
Alfred, ...	17,733	11,000	558,965	119,139	23,998	3,176	69	8,802	5,370	3,552	106	269	2,395	96
Allen, ...	11,125½	11,514½	432,369	87,229	21,840	2,479	205¼	4,903½	3,424	3,024	52½	198¼	1,722	117½
Alma, ...	925½	22,174	191,079	23,003	2,783	192½	2	203	250½	190½	3¼	7¼	110	39½
Almond, ...	25,249	8,051	675,825	136,678	36,130	4,461¾	1,081	14,423¾	4,102½	3,088½	286½	445	3,756½	697¾
Amity, ...	11,210½	23,032	756,178	109,181	23,706	2,494	454	4,252¾	2,793½	2,439	57¼	240¾	2,296	296½
Andover, ...	10,443½	13,045	428,623	77,002	20,408	2,595½	13	3,737½	2,279½	1,623½	21	161¼	1,425½	21
Angelica, ...	9,417½	18,036½	491,522	73,605	10,656	1,539	162	3,185½	2,440	2,025	11½	144¼	1,400	249
Belfast, ...	9,425¾	13,250¾	532,389	71,180	13,778	1,978¼	468	3,904¼	2,374½	1,943½	41½	263½	1,948	286
Birdsall, ...	7,324	16,754	237,378	52,946	9,685	1,835	251	2,378	2,571	1,919	156	89	717	100
Bolivar, ...	4,203¾	17,736	321,912	36,245	11,263	928¾	38½	1,667	1,192	1,032	37½	44¼	562	24
Burns, ...	8,760¼	7,526½	431,148	67,694	9,909	1,879½	932¾	2,923½	1,815	1,295	146	68	531	881½
Caneadea, ...	6,415	11,784½	539,970	53,382	11,809	1,802½	789¾	1,807½	1,286½	1,458½	2½	86	1,016	453
Centreville, ...	14,488	7,583	464,862	100,336	19,622	2,953¾	63½	7,341½	4,128¼	3,797½	100	475	4,254	59
Clarksville, ...	4,836	17,454	182,359	33,956	9,737	1,483	210	1,518	1,400	1,123	64	140½	1,267	161
Cuba, ...	13,302½	8.911	617,895	109,354	25,478	3,643½	64½	6,247	3,218½	2,851¼	180	599½	5,899	85½
Friendship, ...	11,167	9,958	517,870	84,053	29,705	3,423	....	4,842	2,716	1,937	69	388½	3,383	348
Genesee, ...	3,733¼	15,842	241,335	35,912	11,048	842	248	1,310	1,270½	1,006½	48	54¼	470	25
Granger, ...	8,685	7,380	368,901	61,502	18,364	2,440	497	3,093	2,107½	1,823	73¾	200	2,191	284¾
Grove, ...	6,431¾	11,069	292,424	51,742	12,255	2,083	193	2,078	1,525	1,256	52½	45	395	78½
Hume, ...	12,956½	10,388½	579,713	100,423	21,850	3,303½	533½	4,625	2,888	2,580¾	57¼	450½	4,080½	852¼
Independence, ..	11,912½	9,252	409,305	103,064	21,221	3,441¼	13	5,196	3,270½	925¼	3	195¾	1,074	20
New Hudson, ..	11,282	9,003½	387,540	72,974	15,866	3,038½	135¼	4,165	3,390½	2,573¼	122	573½	3,064	42½
Ossian, ...	10,828	12,720	512,575	57,624	15,440	1,707	1,919	2,919	1,999	1,099	32	97½	740	1,159½
Rushford, ...	13,943½	8,278	588,694	109,151	26,505	2,630¾	62	7,493½	3,670½	3,426¾	21½	469¾	4,130½	41½
Scio, ...	7,223	24,189½	548,214	55,922	14,976	1,624½	345½	2,354¼	1,999¾	1,439¾	64	244½	1,286	60½
West Almond, ..	11,404	10,572	364,286	65,917	15,172	2,406½	214½	5,064½	3,207	2,421½	151½	189¾	1,752	182¾
Willing, ...	3,910¾	7,767	206,655	33,214	10,320	998	51¼	983	1,264	496¾	8½	43¼	303	58
Wirt, ...	12,526½	9,937	472,377	99,310	22,412	3,251½	423¼	5,190½	3,322	2,290	148½	419¼	4,254½	243¾
Total, ...	280,863	354,269¼	12,352,363	2,081,738	575,936	64,631½	9,439½	116,608½	71,276	54,637¾	2,117	6,594¼	56422½	6,964¼
BROOME COUNTY.														
Barker, ...	13,155	9,299	438,660	86,838	15,571	1,935	307	5,564	3,760	3,874	56¾	72½	504	65½
Chenango, ...	29,486	21,040½	1,784,157	253,477	66,591	6,956	630½	10,113½	7,227	7,844	238½	1,523	2,060	539½
Colesville, ...	27,023¼	20,102	1,092,040	165,973	42,173	5,040½	621	10,451½	8,301	7,730½	300½	82½	852	202
Conklin, ...	16,041¾	19,513	1,365,960	131,322	66,490	4,839	575	5,738	4,434	5,205	182	87	1,007	575
Lisle, ...	13,493	10,963	561,155	98,765	17,930	2,450	10½	6,305	4,417	4,162	55	31½	319	34½
Maine, ...	13,879½	17,001½	628,360	88,448	19,789	3,050¼	....	5,007	3,888½	3,774½	75	72	651	111¼
Nanticoke, ...	6,020	8,424	224,810	30,729	11,715	930	194½	2,670	1,920	1,713	37½	1½	24	57½
Sanford, ...	14,350¼	40,509¾	708,400	227,981	21,619	2,363¼	592	5,696	5,084	4,937½	249	24¾	422	21½
Triangle, ...	16,830	8,575	771,220	128,766	27,723	2,242½	95½	8,813½	5,961½	....	19	......	......	12¾
Union, ...	14,167	6,061	2,086,556	87,873	31,799	4,284	409	4,401½	3,630½	3,871½	132	60¾	500½	566¼
Vestal, ...	12,026	13,919	554,993	73,461	20,978	2,569	715	2,953	2,770	2,632	98	67	553	451
Windsor, ...	22,367⅞	29,801	656,086	132,046	30,247	3,866½	785¼	8,840½	6,684¾	7,941	233	131¼	1,229	215¾
Total, ...	198,839⅝	205,208¾	10,872,397	1,505,679	372,625	40,526	4,926¼	76,553½	58,078¼	53,685	1,676¼	2,153¾	8,121½	2,852½
CATTARAUGUS COUNTY.														
Allegany, ...	4,098½	40,677	243,968	28,645	7,582	864½	154½	1,119	1,373	1,187½	31	57¼	579	21½
Ashford, ...	12,138¾	16,423	522,551	103,943	24,580	3,375	279½	4,587½	3,876	2,824½	100¼	501	4,971	79¾
Bucktooth, ...	794	4,617	77,470	10,422	1,920	129	......	224	291	224½	1	......	......	......
Carrolton, ...	1,096¾	22,809⅝	86,920	13,426	3,206	223	7	133	373	283	.....	2	20	......
Cold Spring, ...	2,319½	15,497	160,308	19,435	5,533	530	65	782	686	551½	2	26½	254	8½
Connewango, ...	10,954½	9,512½	470,599	89,420	14,845	2,258½	25	5,088½	3,034	3,086½	79¾	198½	2,195½	24½
Dayton, ...	10,108¾	12,587¼	464,166	70,920	12,386	1,798½	41	4,865	2.663½	2,365½	33½	185⅝	2,221	82½
East Otto, ...	10,753½	11,619	441,464	82,682	17,430	1,824½	5	4,835½	3,352½	2,556	24½	309¼	3,816	26⅞
Ellicottville, ...	9,384⅞	17,722⅝	399,962	55,949	12,527	1,681¾	243	3,224½	2,362	1,569½	96½	132½	1,424	21
Farmersville, ...	19,575¼	13,456¼	699,556	142,053	33,708	3,280	118½	10,202	5,585	4,758	94	230	2,128	62½
Franklinville, ..	13,972	17,401	479,399	101,682	20,862	3,183½	229	6,474	4,047	3,567	238¼	243¾	2,669	121
Freedom, ...	15,874¼	9,398	465,729	109,527	19,927	3,553½	....	7,211	4,527	3,857½	126	348½	3,678	......
Great Valley, ..	4,586¾	26,285	302,583	39,026	7,072	1,157	24	1,224	1,547	1,138½	......	56¼	543	20½
Hinsdale, ...	7,762½	15,232	363,350	60,347	16,110	2,470¼	258½	2,738	2,067	2,041	111½	132½	1,399	119½
Humphrey, ...	10,378¼	6,348	162,818	40,250	7,927	1,361½	60½	2,287½	1,667	1,387½	37½	105½	802	28½
Ischua, ...	7,394	12,566¼	274,855	61,134	13,667	2,121½	58	2,642	2,124	1,903	80¼	176½	1,460½	151
Leon, ...	11,740	9,225⅝	441,588	82,921	16,861	2,318	90	5,250	3,731¾	3,140½	56⅝	234⅝	2,402	105½
Little Valley, ..	5,073⅝	13,213½	259,301	33,212	7,866	872½	69	2,209½	1,450¼	1,030	10¼	38¾	377	17½
Lyndon, ...	10,289¼	9,027	306,308	67,409	16,174	2,352½	116	3,370½	3,386½	2,502	142	259½	2,178½	86
Machias, ...	10,683	9,604½	364,005	70,454	15,836	2,959¾	264	4,170¾	2,605½	1,749	124½	373½	4,631½	45¾
Mansfield, ...	11,301½	11,267½	385,089	74,614	11,881	2,418	54	4,887	3,007½	2,009½	52	124¾	1,282½	32½
Napoli, ...	10,332	11,361¼	416,698	72,249	18,020	2,485	35	4,439	2.871½	2,486	44½	142½	1,700	11

(Continued on page 252.)

ALBANY COUNTY.—(CONTINUED.)

TOWNS.	WINTER WHEAT. Bushels harvested.	OATS. Acres sown.	OATS. Bushels harvested.	RYE. Acres sown.	RYE. Bushels harvested.	BARLEY. Acres sown.	BARLEY. Bushels harvested.	BUCKWHEAT. Acres sown.	BUCKWHEAT. Bushels harvested.	CORN. Acres planted.	CORN. Bushels harvested.	POTATOES. Acres planted.	POTATOES. Bushels harvested.	PEAS. Acres sown.	PEAS. Bushels harvested.
Albany, ...	......	252½	5,063	380	3 714	4	30	71¾	796	185¼	3,428	237¾	15,235	4½	87
Bern, ...	466½	5,861½	56,993½	503½	5,404	387½	3,596½	3,051¼	20,415½	730¾	12,001½	444½	18,875	584¼	5,044
Bethlehem, ...	589	3,396	71,022	2,708	39,321	2	30	769	8,850	1,632½	41,799	1,334	94,585	92½	1,088
Coeymans, ...	1,020	2,267¾	26,259	2,419	24,816	10	139	1,075¼	4,166½	1,419½	11,223	293	9,104	97	654
Guilderland, ...	1,289½	5,494½	102,781	3,469	48,984	1	10	949	6,297	2,453¾	38,792	916⅛	46,929	244¼	2,091
Knox, ...	823	11,830	58,445	386	4,797	100	737	1,686¾	12,261¼	582	9,301	196½	10,530½	164½	1,369½
New Scotland, ..	1,246	2,527	36,068	225½	29,331	......	....	644¾	4,382½	1,281½	18,356	338¼	13,768	157	1,464
Rensselaerville, .	1,261	4,658	40,877	523	4,278	372	3,589	2,925	9,969	1,130	13,347	306½	13,448	272	2,289
Watervliet.....	507	3,437	61,980	1,390	15,552	46	414	660	5,329	1,851	31,148	2,565	143,023	36½	241
Westerlo, ...	222	3,623	35,689	1,033	10,370	75	581	2,890	12,346	1,346	14,296	253	10,157	192½	1,662
Total, ...	7,424	43,347¼	495,177½	15037	186,567	997½	9,126½	14,722¾	84,812¾	12,612¼	193,691½	6,884⅝	375,654½	1,845	15,989½

ALLEGANY COUNTY.—(CONTINUED.)

TOWNS.	WINTER WHEAT. Bushels harvested.	OATS. Acres sown.	OATS. Bushels harvested.	RYE. Acres sown.	RYE. Bushels harvested.	BARLEY. Acres sown.	BARLEY. Bushels harvested.	BUCKWHEAT. Acres sown.	BUCKWHEAT. Bushels harvested.	CORN. Acres planted.	CORN. Bushels harvested.	POTATOES. Acres planted.	POTATOES. Bushels harvested.	PEAS. Acres sown.	PEAS. Bushels harvested.
Alfred, ...	772	1,674	31,008	3	18	72	904	398¾	3,996	326	7,649	156⅜	10,302½	108½	1,537
Allen, ...	1,137	1,488¼	31,544	1	10	202¼	3,014	176½	1,366	122½	3,231	99¾	7,352	73	1,208
Alma, ...	155	140½	3,240	4	29	1	30	11½	203	46¾	1,229	31	2,049	8½	131
Almond, ...	8,999	1,956	30,159½	44	294	189½	2,243	374¾	2,209½	375	12,589	123½	7,299½	303⅜	3,801
Amity, ...	3,425	4,352	28,468	12	122	54½	935	253	2,182	417¼	12,545	138¼	7,825	63	872½
Andover, ...	57	1,783½	34,118	......	....	3¼	19	412¼	3,160¾	231	5,768	191	12,063	57⅝	867½
Angelica, ...	2,562	771¾	16,122	27	271	72¾	1,085	83	789½	169	7,059	75¼	6,350	45½	782
Belfast, ...	3,536	823¼	11,853½	7½	51½	59	710	119¼	499¼	356	10,166	94	5,271½	46½	425½
Birdsall, ...	811	1,200	27,449	10	40	103½	1,465	235¾	2,477	63¼	1,391	89½	5,648	54¾	897
Bolivar, ...	79	609¾	20,649	2	35	10¼	225	62	946½	152½	5,072	73	6,611	17½	440
Burns, ...	8,147	1,017	18,452	49	375	95½	1,191	336	1,824	226	5,508	58⅞	3,953	121½	1,518
Caneadea, ...	7,637	548½	15,348	9½	100	34	754	38¼	345¾	414¾	15,001	74⅛	5,833	29¼	467
Centreville, ...	709	1,617¼	28,220	4½	32	144¾	2,009	71¾	752	279⅝	7,678	133¾	12,005	43	620½
Clarksville, ...	1,052	786½	18,434	15	223	3¼	49	136½	1,093	117	2,994	65	4,354	11½	200
Cuba, ...	647	1,860¾	40,900	15½	103	72¾	1,053	187	1,572	286	7,837	120½	8,481	54½	962
Friendship, ...	3,076	1,568½	28,126	25½	247	142	2,006	213¾	974	336	8,474	156½	6,320	40	431
Genesee, ...	362	446¾	10,530	2	25	1	20	32½	326	156½	5,184	62¼	6,065	7¾	136
Granger, ...	3,369	1,554½	35,586	7	58	129	2,064	54	477	137½	3,357	109½	6,755	82	1,170
Grove, ...	911	1,404½	25,203	26¾	302	68¼	912	186½	1,201	134¾	3,145½	76½	4,201	23	293
Hume, ...	13,345	1,431¼	21,425½	½	7	216¾	2,423	75¼	490½	692	19,295	151⅜	11,540	86	861½
Independence, ..	158	2,316½	21,417½	9	43	3½	31	270½	1,814½	190	3,689	192	11,917½	44½	288½
New Hudson, ..	424	6,748½	28,275	12	57	27	297½	161½	878	222¼	5,296	126¾	7,791	58¾	567
Ossian, ...	15,911	704¼	8,538	10	73	165	1,589	255	2,175	216	4,190	64¾	4,027	62½	659
Rushford, ...	504	1,417¼	24,150	......	....	82¾	1,101	26	167	217⅜	7,964	129½	12,269	46¼	674
Scio, ...	573	761	17,848	12	99	9¾	172	113	1,028½	285¾	7,926	121¼	8,165	31	410
West Almond, ..	1,937	1,598¾	37,915	2	25	80¾	1,185	262	2,776	111½	2,672	111½	8,134	70¼	1,383
Willing, ...	310	510¾	5,280	10	48½	4½	31	166	829	157¼	2,507	96¾	3,450	28	138½
Wirt, ...	2,324	1,753½	45,231	17½	146	53½	937	243¼	2,745½	361	10,172	134½	10,226	70	1,104
Total, ...	82,929	34,845	665,490	338¼	2,834	2,102	28,454½	4,956	39,298¼	6,800½	189,588½	3,057¼	206,258	1,687½	22,844½

BROOME COUNTY.—(CONTINUED.)

TOWNS.	WINTER WHEAT. Bushels harvested.	OATS. Acres sown.	OATS. Bushels harvested.	RYE. Acres sown.	RYE. Bushels harvested.	BARLEY. Acres sown.	BARLEY. Bushels harvested.	BUCKWHEAT. Acres sown.	BUCKWHEAT. Bushels harvested.	CORN. Acres planted.	CORN. Bushels harvested.	POTATOES. Acres planted.	POTATOES. Bushels harvested.	PEAS. Acres sown.	PEAS. Bushels harvested.
Barker, ...	350½	953	22,992	103	1,203	5½	85	254¾	3,277	296½	12,544	110	9,822	4	59
Chenango, ...	2,418½	3,260	86,662	295½	3,666	11	150	979	10,090½	1,326½	34,225	354	25,207	5¾	115
Colesville, ...	314	2,681¼	5,197	356¾	2,824	21¼	329	871	8,929¾	943	23,978	331	20,225½	8½	109
Conklin, ...	3,019	2,114	41,659	1,726	2,163	89	354	817½	7,734	1,079	27,056	198½	11,293	14¾	246
Lisle, ...	285	1,455½	34,016	30	419	41½	853	279½	3,429	461¼	15,998	115½	10,763	2	61
Maine, ...	494	1,540½	31,801	76¼	475	24	278	583½	6,544½	493¼	13,174	201¾	14,557	5⅛	54
Nanticoke, ...	238	612	11,020	64½	689	5¼	72	125¼	2,420	141¾	4,536	68	4,433	5½	94
Sanford, ...	120	908	22,402½	206	2,304	......	....	694½	7,811	222¾	5,565	211½	11,998	1½	44
Triangle, ...	84	996	18,098	42	459	11	151	262¾	2,568	575¾	15,929	160¾	10,552	1	18½
Union, ...	2,950	1,568¾	40,989	265	1,590	2	40	562¼	6,706	1,091½	28,895	235	18,568	2¼	50
Vestal, ...	1,132½	1,122	20,875	149	1,212	......	....	556	5,583	696	14,764	155¾	10,197	2	11
Windsor, ...	521¾	1,689⅜	131,159	376	3,543	4	65	946¾	8,121½	774	18,334	247	12,805	5⅛	71
Total, ...	11927½	18,901⅛	466,870½	3,690	20,546	214½	2,377	6,932¾	73,214¼	8,101¾	214,998	2,388¾	160,420½	57½	932½

CATTARAUGUS COUNTY.—(CONTINUED.)

TOWNS.	WINTER WHEAT. Bushels harvested.	OATS. Acres sown.	OATS. Bushels harvested.	RYE. Acres sown.	RYE. Bushels harvested.	BARLEY. Acres sown.	BARLEY. Bushels harvested.	BUCKWHEAT. Acres sown.	BUCKWHEAT. Bushels harvested.	CORN. Acres planted.	CORN. Bushels harvested.	POTATOES. Acres planted.	POTATOES. Bushels harvested.	PEAS. Acres sown.	PEAS. Bushels harvested.
Allegany, ...	329	514½	13,395	18	181	6½	62	78¾	1,240½	138½	4,849	87⅛	9,327	10½	189
Ashford, ...	952	1,528¼	30,390	5½	69	61	875	111	1,155½	778¼	19,199	235¾	14,679	39¼	529
Bucktooth, ...	......	57	988	2	40	½	6	16	263	65	2,387	28¼	2,540	......	....
Carrolton, ...	......	103¾	2,200	1	10	......	....	22¼	228	88	2,202	53¼	2,866	2½	5
Cold Spring, ...	15	250½	4,939	......	....	......	....	16½	288	157¼	4,515	40½	3,980	4	55
Connewango, ...	292	1,076	25,370	2	22	14¼	228	36¼	457	599⅞	20,028	121½	10,085	38⅜	712
Dayton, ...	864	861	17,627	¼	2	57½	957	27	194½	508¼	14,961	117½	8,591	31¼	456
East Otto, ...	301	687	17,535	1½	22	14¾	228	24	285	531	16,724	119⅝	8,453	11⅞	183
Ellicottville, ...	120	1,066	25,092	8½	89	59⅛	940	131¾	1,703	251⅝	8,582	176¾	14,485¼	25¾	369
Farmersville, ...	620	2,303½	53,824	7	66	51¼	860	85¼	962½	229⅛	7,093	181¾	18,700	56¾	1,051½
Franklinville, ...	1,475	2,046	51,228	34	286	61¾	1,124	136½	1,321	268¼	8,849	174¾	18,021	60⅛	1,013
Freedom, ...	......	2,567¼	45,177	......	....	130¼	1,804	43⅛	312¾	148⅞	3,836	177¼	13,219	78⅝	784
Great Valley, ...	181	690½	13,863	3	25	27¼	318	57¾	681	156¾	5,089	116¾	10,015	2½	41
Hinsdale, ...	837	1,578½	41,765	2	20	6¼	112	213	2,816½	315½	10,781	113¼	10,393	31¾	522
Humphrey, ...	152	799¼	22,274	6	64	4¾	74	136¼	1,617	165½	4,929	95¼	8,635	16¾	308
Ischua, ...	1,573½	1,460	33,749	8¼	151	1¾	32	259¼	2,844	230¼	6,552	99⅜	8,078	36½	582
Leon, ...	1,319	1,107¼	21,721	9¼	27	37¾	630½	39½	400	582¾	17,129	125⅛	10,961	21½	325
Little Valley, ...	185	479⅜	10,224	1	20	2¾	26	25⅛	355	157¼	,302	74⅛	6,421	13	189¾
Lyndon, ...	837	1,671½	31,873	10	72	32¼	385	104¾	1,002½	162½	4,330	144	13,055	39½	539
Machias, ...	522	1,767¾	40,743	12	119	11½	205	105⅞	1,135½	216¾	6,531	140	12,351	132⅛	2,403
Mansfield, ...	215½	1,360	29,944	9½	74½	37½	525	84¾	783	431½	14,747	125½	11,013	8½	108
Napoli, ...	117	1,503¼	37,943	1½	18	9¼	164	72¾	687½	425½	14,093	147	12,068	40⅝	647½

(Continued on page 253.)

ALBANY COUNTY.—(CONTINUED.)

TOWNS	BEANS.		TURNIPS.		FLAX.			HEMP.		HOPS.		TOBACCO.		APPLE ORCHARDS	
	Acres planted.	Bushels harvested.	Acres sown.	Bushels harvested.	Acres sown.	Pounds of lint.	Bushels of seed.	Acres sown.	Tons of hemp.	Acres planted.	Pounds harvested.	Acres planted.	Pounds harvested.	Bushels of apples.	Barrels of cider.
Albany,	5½	80	23	4, 775										786	
Bern,	99¾	569¼	1¼	197	1	90	20½			6	6, 337			22, 016	321
Bethlehem,	8½	92	6½	1, 368								1		16, 239	420
Coeymans,	14½	54	4	668										19, 977	909
Guilderland,	10¾	131	8¼	1, 151	26	686¼	80			6	1, 100			38, 004	1, 297½
Knox,	18½	247	¼	46	17½	1, 243¾	72½							18, 092	388½
New Scotland,	5¼	49	1¼	260										20, 256	1, 142
Rensselaerville,	35¼	203¾	1½	162	6	501	31¼				3			37, 176	461
Watervliet,	28¾	268	57¼	5, 809										17, 273	581
Westerlo,	113	612	1½	260	1¾	154	6							44, 432	518
Total,	339¾	2, 306	104¾	14, 696	52¼	2, 675	210¼			12	7, 440	1		234, 251	6, 038

ALLEGANY COUNTY.—(CONTINUED.)

TOWNS	Beans: Acres planted.	Bushels harvested.	Turnips: Acres sown.	Bushels harvested.	Flax: Acres sown.	Pounds of lint.	Bushels of seed.	Hemp: Acres sown.	Tons of hemp.	Hops: Acres planted.	Pounds harvested.	Tobacco: Acres planted.	Pounds harvested.	Bushels of apples.	Barrels of cider.
Alfred,	33½	445¾	5½	803	2¼	239	8¼					⅛	50½	23, 694	467¼
Allen,	5½	141	⅝	422	5¼	100	32							5, 691	85
Alma,	3¼	36½	7⅛	761										175	
Almond,	15⅛	244½	2¼	346	2½	10	9¼							22, 144	442
Amity,	9¼	187½	5	928	½		1						30	11, 609	173½
Andover,	5¾	90	15	1, 985	⅛	30	1							3, 751	10
Angelica,	3⅜	43½	1	140										3, 780	70
Belfast,	6½	54	¾	45										6, 837	50
Birdsall,	11½	130½	4	553	10		61							2, 527	5
Bolivar,	1¼	53	5½	1, 987										1, 452	3
Burns,	8	99¼	¼	35	6		60							4, 643	68
Caneadea,	4½	67	¾	35										7, 260	158½
Centreville,	7⅜	201½	1⅜	390	1½	200	14			1	500			14, 683	142
Clarksville,			2⅛	425										1, 480	2
Cuba,	6	322½	5¾	1, 515	¼		5							11, 833	68
Friendship,	1½	23	2¼	440	½		3			4	1, 440			9, 009	93
Genesee,	2	19	4¾	981										1, 342	
Granger,	2⅜	44												4, 761	67
Grove,	5	84	5⅜	817	¼									2, 253	17
Hume,	6	84¾	⅞	286									22	15, 721	241½
Independence,	5½	89¼	12⅛	3, 216	¼		¾							7, 315	2½
New Hudson,	7¼	145	3½	872	5	100	4						26	7, 150	7
Ossian,	4⅜	169	2¼	375										2, 865	51
Rushford,	4¾	75	3	391										16, 866	385
Scio,	5¼	90½	8¾	956										4, 684	50½
West Almond,	5⅜	85½	2½	327										4, 480	38
Willing,	3¼	11¼	19⅜	2, 000										816	
Wirt,	8½	138	4⅜	1, 044	½	200	6			2½	828			15, 315	287
Total,	182	3, 174¾	126⅛	22, 075	34⅞	879	205¼			7½	2, 768	⅛	128½	214, 136	2, 983¾

BROOME COUNTY.—(CONTINUED.)

TOWNS	Beans: Acres planted.	Bushels harvested.	Turnips: Acres sown.	Bushels harvested.	Flax: Acres sown.	Pounds of lint.	Bushels of seed.	Hemp: Acres sown.	Tons of hemp.	Hops: Acres planted.	Pounds harvested.	Tobacco: Acres planted.	Pounds harvested.	Bushels of apples.	Barrels of cider.
Barker,	47	43	2½	332	⅛	30	¼						15	19, 154	289
Chenango,	4¾	101⅛	23½	1, 586							100	2	3, 300	28, 023	1, 493
Colesville,	8¼	155	9½	2, 074	4¼		8¾			23¾	14, 050			28, 248	440
Conklin,	4½	156	9½	2, 468						½	600	1	1, 035	17, 474	204
Lisle,		29	¾	158							122	⅛	100	21, 640	216
Maine,	7⅛	114	4½	717	½	20	1					½	100	9, 926	145
Nanticoke,	¾	36½	4	563										4, 955	53
Sanford,	3	54½	11	1, 483	2⅛	327	10							7, 765	30
Triangle,	5	36	2½	152						3	1, 936			22, 286	340
Union,	1¾	68	¼	88	½	55	10			4	1, 500			23, 029	595
Vestal,	2½	20	10	706			3					13	18, 100	9, 899	283
Windsor,	8	136¾	14¼	2, 048	½	46	2½			4	3, 500	¾	1, 000	32, 064	659½
Total,	92⅝	949⅞	92¼	12, 375	8	478	35½			35¼	21, 808	17⅜	23, 650	224, 463	4, 747½

CATTARAUGUS COUNTY.—(CONTINUED.)

TOWNS	Beans: Acres planted.	Bushels harvested.	Turnips: Acres sown.	Bushels harvested.	Flax: Acres sown.	Pounds of lint.	Bushels of seed.	Hemp: Acres sown.	Tons of hemp.	Hops: Acres planted.	Pounds harvested.	Tobacco: Acres planted.	Pounds harvested.	Bushels of apples.	Barrels of cider.
Allegany,	1½	89	8¼	1, 123							21			1, 586½	3
Ashford,	16¼	251½	6¼	819	¼	40	1						20	9, 358	31
Bucktooth,	¾	11	4	525										220	
Carrolton,	1⅞	44	11	1, 762										90	
Cold Spring,	2⅜	56	6½	930										1, 829	25
Connewango,	4	107	3⅜	1, 407										9, 650	27
Dayton,	8⅛	105½	6⅜	1, 202	½	20	5			¾	317			11, 641	80
East Otto,	8⅝	137	4⅞	968	¾	25	3							7, 657	20
Ellicottville,	11⅜	201½	4	1, 093	⅛	500	½					¼	50	2, 518	10
Farmersville,	25⅞	481	5⅛	1, 216						1½				11, 244	74½
Franklinville,	9⅞	230½	10½	1, 968	⅝	200	6							6, 235	14
Freedom,	5½	80½	4¼	972	¼	100	1							7, 356	26
Great Valley,	3¾	27	5½	515										1, 730	9
Hinsdale,	6¼	107	1⅜	205								½	600	5, 665	101
Humphrey,	14	185	12	1, 004	⅜	500								1, 800	
Ischua,	7[illegible]	122½	3⅝	000										5, 488	73
Leon,	10½	143	3¾	1, 170	¼		3½							16, 060	48½
Little Valley,	4⅜	70½	3	386										2, 387	29
Lyndon,	5	172½	2¼	1, 197										3, 647	31
Machias,	19⅞	283	6	824										3, 183	22
Mansfield,	3¾	125	9¼	1, 874	½	50	1							6, 269	31
Napoli,	4¾	115½	4	530	½	100	3							11, 377	120

(Continued on page 254.)

ALBANY COUNTY.—(Continued.)

TOWNS.	MARKET GARDENS. Acres cultivated.	MARKET GARDENS. Value of products.	Pounds of maple sugar made.	Gallons of maple molasses made.	Gallons of wine made.	Pounds of honey collected	Pounds of wax collected.	SILK. Pounds of cocoons.	NEAT CATTLE. Under one year old.	NEAT CATTLE. Over one y'r, exclusive of working oxen & cows.	NEAT CATTLE. Working oxen.	NEAT CATTLE. Cows.	Number of cattle killed for beef.	Pounds of butter.	Pounds of cheese.
Albany,	140½	13,025	......	......	......	405	36	......	26	249	22	540	6,646	7,125	......
Bern,	......	4	1,420	156	......	8,430	539½	......	491	778	249	1,772	250	152,166	4,69
Bethlehem,	252	34,100	45	5	31	5,963	286	......	263	466	198	1,629	780	124,210	10
Coeymans,	......	......	6	1	......	3,563	113	......	468	347	116	699	88	93,252	41
Guilderland,	16	1,565	......	9	37	5,763	355	......	355	604	221	1,691	1,642	165,555	1,28
Knox,	2	......	2,726	116	......	7,360	538	......	285	532	142	1,032	168	90,530	2,66
New Scotland,	......	......	40	3	......	1,105	89	......	177	306	199	966	135	100,050	47
Rensselaerville,	......	100	447	53	......	10,706	799	......	523	686	254	1,632	233	171,440	11,53
Watervliet,	702	48,597	......	......	170	2,415	169	12	204	468	212	1,912	1,341	124,751	6,56
Westerlo,	¼	70	125	15	......	7,940	512	......	392	482	200	1,459	183	144,448	8,79
Total,	1,112¾	97,461	4,809	358	238	53,650	3,436½	12	3,184	4,918	1,813	13,332	11,466	1,173,527	36,52

ALLEGANY COUNTY.—(Continued.)

TOWNS.	Acres cultivated.	Value of products.	Pounds of maple sugar made.	Gallons of maple molasses made.	Gallons of wine made.	Pounds of honey collected	Pounds of wax collected.	Pounds of cocoons.	Under one year old.	Over one y'r, exclusive of working oxen & cows.	Working oxen.	Cows.	Number of cattle killed for beef.	Pounds of butter.	Pounds of cheese.
Alfred,	19¾	1,195	19,980	280	......	7,563	365	......	351	896	141	1,131	151	81,224	176,26
Allen,	......	......	15,613	202	......	2,630	108	......	299	695	158	630	68	63,540	10,17
Alma,	......	......	1,932	28	......	800	15	......	......	248	......	......	3	7,960	34
Almond,	......	......	14,170	238	9	8,031	300½	......	543	1,285	119	997	122	106,930	4,69
Amity,	2	340	6,381	80	......	2,450	121	......	394	614	171	698	78	57,895	15,75
Andover,	......	......	14,580	112	......	4,242	110½	......	364	672	232	777	184	81,430	13,57
Angelica,	......	......	3,450	12	......	1,410	28	......	294	611	91	612	51	43,510	1,83
Belfast,	......	......	2,461	30	......	1,045	57	......	268	647	91	716	54	58,565	14,96
Birdsall,	......	......	8,710	106	......	1,640	74	......	241	584	118	435	33	48,168	1,27
Bolivar,	......	......	4,919	28	......	550	26	......	131	237	120	287	44	35,484	1,23
Burns,	......	......	2,830	47	......	3,780	130	......	241	550	92	478	42	44,420	20,12
Caneadea,	¾	116	650	......	......	690	50	......	230	600	95	544	165	50,901	......
Centreville,	......	......	34,130	345	......	1,640	195	......	417	740	116	1,449	74	103,337	221,07
Clarksville,	......	......	8,113	26	1	1,075	......	......	197	336	131	335	28	29,466	85
Cuba,	......	......	17,643	95	......	2,816	139	......	333	844	113	941	436	105,360	42,84
Friendship,	......	......	7,790	138	......	1,640	118	......	291	642	100	734	119	77,200	10,82
Genesee,	......	250	2,043	92	......	1,616	71	......	131	266	104	293	142	33,715	3,95
Granger,	......	......	10,165	142	......	1,691	116	......	251	551	132	536	61	50,001	4,41
Grove,	......	......	11,474	407	......	2,302	107	......	207	404	112	449	47	49,325	2,52
Hume,	......	......	12,418	126	23	1,351	203½	......	434	847	135	934	119	86,334	12,26
Independence,	......	......	38,615	155	......	2,152	205½	......	413	879	92	705	41	63,505	52,07
New Hudson,	......	......	22,820	117	50	2,866	162½	......	383	735	115	1,043	84	81,530	93,30
Ossian,	......	......	......	......	......	735	31	......	188	332	151	440	74	38,690	1,37
Rushford,	1	71	22,553	219	......	1,805	98	......	333	768	90	1,667	86	96,435	317,95
Scio,	½	50	3,436	70	......	895	29	......	182	333	181	541	88	38,400	2,65
West Almond,	......	......	22,645	162	......	3,117	105	......	350	756	116	661	50	65,350	11,36
Willing,	......	8	6,350	77	......	2,791	103	......	120	260	108	267	21	29,301	41
Wirt,	......	......	16,389	156	20	5,675	253	......	327	686	168	709	85	72,799	6,88
Total,	24	2,030	332,260	3,490	103	68,998	3,321½	......	7,913	17,018	3,392	19,009	2,550	1,700,775	1,044,97

BROOME COUNTY.—(Continued.)

TOWNS.	Acres cultivated.	Value of products.	Pounds of maple sugar made.	Gallons of maple molasses made.	Gallons of wine made.	Pounds of honey collected	Pounds of wax collected.	Pounds of cocoons.	Under one year old.	Over one y'r, exclusive of working oxen & cows.	Working oxen.	Cows.	Number of cattle killed for beef.	Pounds of butter.	Pounds of cheese.
Barker,	......	......	3,156	27	2	2,890	94	......	458	743	178	1,326	263	47,727	5,07
Chenango,	30¼	730	375	6	36	4,971	287	......	805	1,347	507	2,705	115	212,788	1,22
Colesville,	1⅜	85	3,741	79	......	4,690	219	......	795	1,482	461	2,207	126	201,059	7,10
Conklin,	......	......	310	22	34	6,119	210	18	464	935	323	1,233	161	153,514	1,10
Lisle,	......	......	7,375	68	13	3,710	210	......	420	866	156	1,212	62	119,700	5,57
Maine,	......	400	11,848	124	......	4,976	151	......	463	728	330	1,131	97	111,265	2,10
Nanticoke,	......	......	6,675	197	......	927	15	......	212	297	133	570	25	66,000	2,47
Sanford,	1½	80	10,929	188	......	7,512	380½	......	529	731	370	1,067	284	238,350	1,21
Triangle,	......	......	5,396	104	......	1,432	108	......	621	1,053	194	1,745	66	208,177	5,20
Union,	......	......	......	......	17	2,561	114	......	380	706	178	1,260	142	145,251	2,98
Vestal,	......	......	100	45	2	2,480	70	......	257	462	234	644	159	57,562	81
Windsor,	⅛	45	2,403	77½	......	5,112	255	......	806	1,337	467	2,016	119	192,024	6,027
Total,	33¼	1,340	52,308	937½	104	47,380	2,113½	18	6,210	10,687	3,531	17,116	1,619	1,753,417	40,89

CATTARAUGUS COUNTY.—(Continued.)

TOWNS.	Acres cultivated.	Value of products.	Pounds of maple sugar made.	Gallons of maple molasses made.	Gallons of wine made.	Pounds of honey collected	Pounds of wax collected.	Pounds of cocoons.	Under one year old.	Over one y'r, exclusive of working oxen & cows.	Working oxen.	Cows.	Number of cattle killed for beef.	Pounds of butter.	Pounds of cheese.
Allegany,	......	5	4,563	113	......	1,000	54	......	127	233	129	296	68	31,175	1,045
Ashford,	......	......	20,333	156	......	6,863	367	......	559	1,010	235	1,304	67	113,313	144,876
Bucktooth,	......	......	1,085	3	......	235	2	......	37	81	68	94	9	9,805	520
Carrolton,	......	......	530	......	......	500	14	......	52	98	86	137	23	8,995	500
Cold Spring,	......	......	1,400	16	......	510	32	......	74	157	55	170	105	12,813	375
Connewango,	⅛	42¾	27,105	59	......	1,080	83½	......	482	1,574	226	1,019	49	107,988	14,245
Dayton,	......	......	14,480	109	......	2,075	112	......	336	762	143	1,007	46	61,016	113,814
East Otto,	......	......	19,391	45	......	3,279	162	......	444	606	153	1,510	53	86,099	265,000
Ellicottville,	1	10	6,830	20	......	2,183	88	......	330	603	150	591	117	44,845	22,195
Farmersville,	1	30	61,358	361	......	2,772	172	......	692	1,809	164	1,774	107	161,745	151,539
Franklinville,	......	......	22,275	237	7	3,902	245	......	638	1,293	172	999	133	77,870	78,710
Freedom,	......	......	24,067½	149	......	1,586	141	......	593	1,066	90	1,604	70	152,942	37,890
Great Valley,	......	......	2,157	14	......	1,332	75	......	207	282	141	395	131	34,957	240
Hinsdale,	......	......	6,535	92	......	2,085	114	......	285	636	124	624	116	58,200	10,640
Humphrey,	......	......	9,392	16	......	1,030	80	......	272	473	143	422	22	35,464	9,900
Ischua,	......	......	19,188	209	......	3,606	208	......	321	802	154	542	14	44,640	5,870
Leon,	¾	65	18,623	140	......	2,103	119	......	434	823	193	1,021	37	69,314	114,475
Little Valley,	½	25	4,690	73	......	1,345	32	......	185	400	83	238	29	38,635	9,310
Lyndon,	......	......	30,545	122	......	2,620	145	......	459	721	170	826	55	77,700	46,370
Machias,	......	......	23,183	154	......	1,989	82	......	474	728	123	840	55	75,694	10,644
Mansfield,	......	......	6,682	27	......	3,447	148	......	352	692	146	954	50	72,703	199,500
Napoli,	......	......	24,055	105	......	2,275	111	......	405	710	110	790	68	91,775	5,550

(Continued on page 255.)

ALBANY COUNTY.—(Continued.)

TOWNS.	Gallons of milk sold.	Horses.	Mules.	SWINE.		SHEEP.			POULTRY.		DOMESTIC MANUFACTURES.			
				Under 6 months.	Over 6 months.	Number of sheep.	Number of fleeces.	Pounds of wool.	Value of poultry sold.	Value of eggs sold.	Yards of fulled cloth made.	Yards of flannel made.	Yards of linen made.	Yards of cotton and mixed cloth.
Albany,	45, 231	1, 224	20	396	464	144	92	565	198	370	....	....	....	....
Bern,	....	1, 172	....	1, 132	870	6, 686	5, 037	20, 305½	3, 250	4, 837	749½	1, 014	469	474
Bethlehem,	193, 023	1, 155	2	2, 115	1, 478	1, 722	1, 698	6, 575	4, 126	9, 717	393	664	214	284
Coeymans,	....	790	....	1, 277	666	1, 767	1, 372	4, 920	2, 311	4, 521	318	462	130	196
Guilderland,	9, 250	1, 416	....	2, 179	1, 656	2, 824	2, 015	7, 499	3, 020	5, 293	810	1, 263	621	257½
Knox,	....	790	....	615	574	5, 245	3, 695	13, 594½	2, 211	3, 007	723¾	831¾	421	949
New Scotland,	....	749	....	1, 557	1, 006	1, 914	1, 691	6, 420	1, 955	6, 252	697	1, 478	304	....
Rensselaerville,	1, 725	962	....	1, 735	767	12, 003	8, 476	35, 774	2, 767	4, 823	62¾	346	354	112
Watervliet,	253, 765	1, 724	9	1, 194	2, 112	1, 034	943	3, 252	3, 398	3, 847	766	438	214	200
Westerlo,	....	972	....	1, 609	633	3, 715	2, 362	9, 051	3, 078	5, 024	409	723	198	414
Total,	502, 994	10, 954	31	13, 809	10, 226	37, 054	27, 381	107, 956	26, 314	47, 691	4, 929	7, 219¾	2, 925	2, 886½

ALLEGANY COUNTY.—(Continued.)

TOWNS.	Gallons of milk sold.	Horses.	Mules.	Swine under 6 months.	Swine over 6 months.	Number of sheep.	Number of fleeces.	Pounds of wool.	Value of poultry sold.	Value of eggs sold.	Yards of fulled cloth made.	Yards of flannel made.	Yards of linen made.	Yards of cotton and mixed cloth.
Alfred,	2, 129	574	....	240	358	11, 183	8, 700	29, 920	1, 160	799	240	1, 589	498	306
Allen,	....	436	1	154	233	7, 716	5, 619	20, 224	221	451	86	268	73	283
Alma,	....	63	8	......	141	165	81	315	....	55	15	85	....	....
Almond,	1, 425	695	....	435	484	8, 236	7, 161	24, 929	593	1, 026	259	237	280	257
Amity,	101	406	....	210	306	3, 697	2, 443	8, 545	202	570	174½	926	122	476
Andover,	....	355	2	126	357	3, 190	2, 318	7, 254	545	381	190	699	29	736
Angelica,	....	365	....	121	306	4, 219	3, 310	10, 256	212	304	62	349	20	715
Belfast,	680	484	7	161	356	3, 220	2, 004	6, 245	229	493	162	563	150	206
Birdsall,	....	281	4	73	247	1, 581	1, 666	5, 676	123	38	32	142	20	20
Bolivar,	....	167	2	79	137	1, 499	900	2, 936	93	45	35	487	109½	508¼
Burns,	....	400	....	124	299	3, 077	3, 230	12, 149	218	287	155¾	135	78	150
Caneadea,	....	312	....	200	250	1, 484	1, 364	4, 368	13	....	115	323	....	30
Centreville,	....	563	....	128	357	4, 392	3, 781	13, 487	155	857	74	722	564	293
Clarksville,	....	163	....	68	158	2, 518	1, 777	5, 351	7	115	149	469	161	257
Cuba,	....	546	....	224	401	7, 001	4, 501	15, 290	642	668	63	1, 746	188	65
Friendship,	90	490	2	266	296	3, 547	2, 397	8, 120	195	446	40	166	164	1, 972
Genesee,	....	183	....	95	146	2, 207	1, 558	4, 614	45	147	12	442	70	123
Granger,	....	391	1	184	248	3, 716	2, 822	9, 818	175	355	47	278	....	274
Grove,	....	287	5	163	303	2, 067	1, 242	4, 128	213	311	179½	343	161	79
Hume,	....	765	....	331	399	5, 414	4, 539	14, 939	430	993	....	205	264	186
Independence,	....	432	....	180	277	3, 047	3, 347	11, 580	332	360	269¼	504	66	212
New Hudson,	210	509	....	259	351	3, 417	2, 428	8, 195	309	390	167	663	193	222
Ossian,	....	365	....	300	399	2, 646	1, 761	6, 363	16	9	49	175	....	30
Rushford,	....	641	....	213	352	2, 685	1, 973	6, 429	322	313	52	140	179	223
Scio,	6, 066	345	4	120	264	2, 213	1, 500	4, 833	42	207	68	435	....	140
West Almond,	57	395	....	170	244	3, 177	2, 929	9, 737	704	412	116	670	150	244
Willing,	45	153	....	86	165	828	445	1, 375½	102	302	28	236	67	626
Wirt,	....	457	....	253	351	6, 657	4, 620	15, 546	521	884	255	1, 479	447	704½
Total,	10, 803	11, 223	36	4, 963	8, 185	104, 799	80, 416	272, 622½	7, 819	11, 218	3, 095¼	14, 476	4, 053½	9, 337¾

BROOME COUNTY.—(Continued.)

TOWNS.	Gallons of milk sold.	Horses.	Mules.	Swine under 6 months.	Swine over 6 months.	Number of sheep.	Number of fleeces.	Pounds of wool.	Value of poultry sold.	Value of eggs sold.	Yards of fulled cloth made.	Yards of flannel made.	Yards of linen made.	Yards of cotton and mixed cloth.
Barker,	....	284	....	381	360	2, 910	1, 997	6, 051	517	635	259	511	188	432
Chenango,	88, 555	1, 230	....	937	1, 255	7, 116	4, 175	12, 826	14, 663	34, 277	4, 568	576	15	73
Colesville,	....	740	....	630	712	6, 185	3, 637	11, 709	832	1, 419	1, 133½	2, 061	697	544
Conklin,	....	524	....	587	607	4, 526	3, 108	10, 531	1, 229	1, 319	443	725	162	92
Lisle,	....	460	....	246	342	3, 148	2, 127	7, 812	578	1, 237	775	841,	185	146
Maine,	....	396	....	343	399	3, 091	1, 727	5, 627	889	1, 599	401	822	116	245
Nanticoke,	....	173	1	141	145	629	439	1, 528	247	390	100	318	....	77
Sanford,	....	344	6	275	398	2, 366	1, 454	4, 315¼	546	479	621¼	1, 185	387	996
Triangle,	....	503	....	523	399	1, 858	1, 481	4, 999	1, 738	982	441¼	486	99	58
Union,	....	448	....	718	604	2, 240	2, 062	4, 683	843	1, 020	157	269	25	100
Vestal,	....	369	....	435	473	1, 700	1, 707	4, 772	491	314	814	1, 214	412	616
Windsor,	567	527	....	605	636	5, 125	3, 799	11, 471	816	1, 391	835	1, 086	384	560
Total,	89, 122	5, 998	7	5, 821	6, 330	40, 894	27, 713	86, 324¼	23, 389	45, 062	10, 548	10, 094	2, 670	3, 939

CATTARAUGUS COUNTY.—(Continued.)

TOWNS.	Gallons of milk sold.	Horses.	Mules.	Swine under 6 months.	Swine over 6 months.	Number of sheep.	Number of fleeces.	Pounds of wool.	Value of poultry sold.	Value of eggs sold.	Yards of fulled cloth made.	Yards of flannel made.	Yards of linen made.	Yards of cotton and mixed cloth.
Allegany,	....	121	....	52	131	882	488	1, 388	95	287	107	309	53	49
Ashford,	....	475	....	239	485	2, 880	1, 901	6, 410½	621	946	324	1, 239	262	795
Bucktooth,	270	35	....	13	36	136	75	241	94	71	20	30	....	95
Carrolton,	....	36	1	34	60	94	78	241	....	4	9	36	....	30
Cold Spring,	....	104	....	81	81	573	406	1, 002	10	38	54	102	15	287
Connewango,	....	434	....	406	326	1, 922	1, 270	4, 177	705	610	112	513	58	196
Dayton,	....	344	....	153	302	1, 415	947	2, 999½	532	284	238	669	336	465
East Otto,	....	331	....	166	292	1, 381	835	2, 930	195	897	65	573	210	579
Ellicottville,	....	251	5	162	278	2, 040	1, 596	4, 529¾	264	323	46	239	87	45
Farmersville,	....	621	....	270	425	4, 360	3, 095	10, 318½	466	508	167	720	166	997
Franklinville,	....	477	....	257	410	4, 303	2, 457	7, 668¾	327	315	87	418	54	134
Freedom,	....	535	....	198	447	3, 272	2, 271	7, 513½	344	713	253	888	99	946
Great Valley,	....	220	....	110	237	1, 259	755	2, 347	45	101	81	132	....	418
Hinsdale,	....	366	....	229	347	2, 828	1, 472	4, 294	224	371	55	371	....	....
Humphrey,	....	203	....	108	160	1, 822	920	2, 765½	125	69	35	175	46	541
Ischua,	....	306	2	146	340	2, 603	2, 198	5, 960½	271	264	136	648	335	215
Leon,	....	369	....	302	393	2, 314	1, 544	4, 815	635	857	445¼	893½	306	704½
Little Valley,	....	166	....	99	116	698	486	1, 729¾	205	220	62	160	....	41
Lyndon,	....	356	....	191	310	4, 063	3, 177	10, 172	335	419	112½	550	130	156½
Machias,	....	380	....	179	352	3, 446	2, 556	8, 266	626	442	185	797	74	629
Mansfield,	....	312	....	193	228	2, 560	1, 441	4, 898	333	886	75	371	271	500
Napoli,	....	402	....	231	257	2, 155	1, 271	4, 056	359	321	132	764½	105	231

(Continued on page 156.)

CATTARAUGUS COUNTY.

TOWNS.	ACRES.		CASH VALUE.			Acres plowed the year previous.	Acres in fallow the year previous.	Acres in pasture the year previous.	MEADOW.			SPRING WHEAT.		WINTER WHEAT.
	Improved.	Unimproved.	Of farm.	Of stock.	Of tools and implements.				Acres.	Tons of hay.	Bushels of grass seed.	Acres sown.	Bushels harvested.	Acres sown
New Albion, ...	11, 270¾	10, 272¾	$421, 352	$89, 147	$18, 972	2, 462¼	20	5, 302½	3, 093	2, 643	43	162½	1, 799½	47
Olean, ...	2, 518	9, 219	239, 051	28, 120	10, 496	660	135	688	638	634	15	11	136	43
Otto, ...	11, 049½	8, 487¾	431, 809	82, 028	20, 853	2, 002	14	5, 762½	2, 985½	2, 540	60½	232¾	2, 949½	80
Perrysburgh, ...	12, 332⅞	5, 551½	573, 555	99, 188	19, 696	2, 624¼	152	5, 694¼	3, 435	3, 430½	116½	169	2, 042½	317¼
Persia, ...	5, 483⅞	6, 165½	317, 621	48, 823	14, 391	1, 467¼	122½	2, 194½	1, 451¾	1, 460¼	41	154	1, 801½	207¼
Portville, ...	3, 189	18, 823¾	268, 041	35, 282	12, 421	812⅝	101¼	1, 002½	1, 069¼	789	9½	29¼	304	21
Randolph, ...	7, 206⅛	13, 214½	341, 070	68, 619	15, 221	1, 716⅝	44½	2, 412	2, 036	1, 961½	14¼	209⅝	2, 249	33¾
South Valley, ...	1, 714¾	33, 074½	157, 494	17, 955	4, 658	306	137	240	800	613½	3	......	......	31
Yorkshire, ...	11, 059	11, 361	417, 664	73, 716	16, 534	3, 180	56	4, 458½	3, 069	2, 193¾	24	548½	5, 265	77½
Total, ...	266, 435⅝	432. 620⅝	10. 956, 344	1, 972, 598	439, 162	58, 448½	2, 979	109, 719	75, 208½	62, 546¾	1, 812⅝	5, 395⅝	57278½	1, 923⅝

CAYUGA COUNTY.

TOWNS.	Improved.	Unimproved.	Of farm.	Of stock.	Of tools and implements.	Acres plowed the year previous.	Acres in fallow the year previous.	Acres in pasture the year previous.	Meadow acres.	Tons of hay.	Bushels of grass seed.	Spring wheat acres sown.	Bushels harvested.	Winter wheat acres sown
Auburn, ...	4, 427¾	172	277, 245	38, 349	3, 689	645¼	71	600	424	393	4	......	......	75½
Aurelius, ...	18, 003¾	3, 298	1, 239, 964	124, 113	36, 244	5, 786½	651	4, 010	3, 455	3, 117½	318½	69	1, 020	1, 937½
Brutus, ...	9, 395	3, 301	740, 801	85, 253	16, 039	3, 383	196	2, 566	1, 544	2, 073	140	21	18	1, 222
Cato, ...	15, 210¾	5, 159	1, 096, 692	139, 597	38, 779	6, 099½	439	3, 548¼	2, 041¼	2, 618¾	35½	6½	53	2, 213
Conquest, ...	13, 919¾	7, 702	1, 015, 309	128, 214	30, 007	4, 823¼	672	4, 629¾	2, 064	2, 457	63¾	10	78	1, 560¾
Fleming, ...	10, 287½	1, 866	750, 438	73, 112	33, 638	4, 575½	128½	2, 340	1, 631	1, 485	230½	67	837	483
Genoa, ...	19, 951½	6, 710	1, 429, 358	148, 434	38, 123	7, 389	480	6, 043	3, 819½	3. 462¾	91¾	74¾	1, 013	1, 021½
Ira, ...	15. 845	5, 639	966, 315	153, 867	42, 107	5, 014	431½	4, 445	2, 644	2, 900½	70	8½	78	1, 515½
Ledyard, ...	17, 770¼	4, 161½	1, 166, 713	108, 147	28, 318	5, 557½	623½	4, 948½	3, 475½	2, 155	195½	70⅞	704	1, 243½
Locke, ...	11, 466	3, 216	478, 426	75, 075	13, 396	3, 041½	152½	4, 594	2, 943	3, 035	43	198	2, 103½	822½
Mentz, ...	21, 331	6, 197	1, 386, 078	190, 828	52, 381	6, 437¾	1, 471½	5, 865¾	4, 241¾	5, 513¾	206½	26	318	2, 323½
Moravia, ...	11, 994¾	4, 830¼	625, 375	96, 586	18, 795	3, 103	134	4, 184	3, 089½	2, 960½	62	316¼	2, 878	258
Niles, ...	18, 220½	6, 035	991, 889	142, 486	30, 302	6, 513	281¼	5, 672	3, 471½	2, 808½	97½	457¼	5, 208½	606½
Owasco, ...	9, 578	2, 522	689, 445	73, 890	19, 033	3, 419¾	270½	2, 635¼	1, 893½	1, 861¾	93¼	99¾	561	377¼
Scipio, ...	18, 975¼	3, 698	1, 262, 966	133, 294	30, 126	6, 771	925	4, 958	2, 801	1, 970½	286	124½	1, 316	1, 441
Sempronius, ...	11, 278	6, 486	488, 864	83, 203	18, 517	2, 650¾	12	4, 623	2, 986	3, 286	65½	228	3, 322	15
Sennett, ...	17, 453	3, 684	1, 196, 504	137, 275	41, 821	5, 950	94	6, 739¾	3, 533¾	3, 340½	76¼	127	875	905
Springport, ...	11, 313⅛	82; 477½	1, 423, 178	86, 501	31, 288	3, 586¾	791	2, 457	1, 755½	1, 383	178½	34	379	1, 452
Sterling, ...	14, 134	12, 020½	915, 315	139, 352	30, 799	6, 032	460½	3, 741	2, 460	2, 630	93¼	189	2, 255½	621
Summer Hill, ...	10, 941½	5, 678¼	445, 221	81, 548	16, 427	2, 438	11	4, 817¾	3, 225¾	2, 732	82	84⅝	1, 111½	24½
Venice, ...	19, 843½	5, 457	1, 182, 155	154, 980	32, 937	6, 939	379	8, 007	4, 051	3, 105	219	251	2, 995	737
Victory, ...	14, 455½	6, 927½	931, 752	129, 130	33, 748	4, 820	510	3, 724	2, 054	2, 443	94½	22¾	203	1, 085
Total, ...	315, 795⅝	187, 237½	20, 700, 003	2, 523, 234	637, 307	104, 976	9, 184¾	95, 149	59, 604½	57, 732	2, 746¾	2, 485¾	27327	21940½

CHAUTAUQUE COUNTY.

TOWNS.	Improved.	Unimproved.	Of farm.	Of stock.	Of tools and implements.	Acres plowed the year previous.	Acres in fallow the year previous.	Acres in pasture the year previous.	Meadow acres.	Tons of hay.	Bushels of grass seed.	Spring wheat acres sown.	Bushels harvested.	Winter wheat acres sown
Arkwright, ...	12, 256	9, 199	454, 567	86, 230	15, 547	1, 981	7½	7, 097	3, 318	2, 906	11¼	216	2, 523	57
Busti, ...	18, 399	11, 342	840, 953	147, 289	28, 337	3, 541	11	8, 520	5, 869	5, 810	72	410	4, 304	81
Carrol, ...	6, 712	12, 755	442, 336	51, 643	15, 919	1, 484	108	2, 517	2, 558	2, 542	13	192	1, 632	117
Charlotte, ...	12, 696	8, 658	491, 844	99, 748	20, 983	1, 873	....	6, 237	3, 682	3, 339	122½	252	2, 692	8
Chautauque, ...	25, 318	19, 617	1, 144, 999	186, 997	32, 531	3, 506	299½	11, 661	7, 249	8, 250	132¼	282	2, 965	118
Cherry Creek, ..	11, 090	14, 477	348, 645	73, 668	15, 457	1, 908	134	4, 549	2, 988	2, 736	149¼	322¼	3, 689½	58
Clymer, ...	9, 260	13, 965	402, 538	73, 734	13, 099	1, 703	19½	4, 097	2, 232	2, 512	73¼	127¼	1, 114	59¼
Ellery, ...	19, 598½	10, 800	822, 798	149, 223	35, 438	4, 452	103	9, 064	5, 095	4, 985	88¼	503	5, 599	391
Ellicott, ...	9, 951¼	9, 298½	593, 392	76, 827	18, 735	1, 997	219	4, 600	2, 745	2, 697	15	307¾	3, 653½	119¼
Ellington, ...	14, 171	8, 675	576, 480	109, 247	25, 659	3, 302	68¾	6, 681	3, 906	3, 553	47½	393½	4, 990	20
French Creek, ..	6, 668½	16, 448½	304, 292	50, 854	9, 334	1, 219	204	3, 061	1, 812½	1, 745	60	114½	1, 226½	16
Gerry, ...	11. 917	9, 837	505, 899	94, 967	19, 354	2, 169¼	....	6, 034	3, 582	3, 147	36	319½	3, 648	21
Hanover, ...	21, 011	11, 736¾	1, 117, 166	201, 807	47, 514	3, 786¾	407	10, 081¾	5, 829	6, 541½	213½	366½	4, 528¾	790¼
Harmony, ...	28, 728	25, 805	1, 245, 832	224, 196	43, 191	4, 952	252	14, 152	8, 493	8, 586	187¼	477	5, 119½	247
Kiantone, ...	6, 040	4, 234	304, 290	45, 986	9, 465	814	30	2, 875½	2, 041	1, 914	17½	64½	723	38½
Mina, ...	10, 103½	12, 786	347, 058	74, 865	17, 045	1, 629	....	5, 518	2, 863	3, 246	39	101	1, 057	5½
Poland, ...	8, 534½	13, 386	483, 440	67, 410	15, 794	1, 495	130	4, 092	2, 805	2, 921	24½	116	1, 049	55
Pomfret, ...	21, 588½	10, 941¼	2, 092, 233	225, 235	42, 795	4, 003	187½	10, 229	6, 055¼	6, 759½	254	309½	3, 884	479½
Portland, ...	15, 330½	5, 504	848, 959	109, 780	35, 753	2, 897	95	6, 333½	4, 209½	4, 742½	155½	522½	5, 402	485¾
Ripley, ...	16, 696	12, 630	778, 274	131, 435	27, 908	3, 426	99	8, 496	4, 939	5, 371	67½	402¼	4, 838	712¼
Sheridan, ...	15, 559½	6, 719	850, 297	104, 431	30, 880	3, 154¾	95	6, 770½	4, 296	4, 332	268	146	1, 688½	854
Sherman, ...	11, 499	12, 638	476, 381	86, 898	17, 701	1, 727¼	99	6, 156½	3, 474½	3, 614½	67¼	125½	1, 275	25¼
Stockton, ...	16, 028	12, 900½	590, 482	131, 832	22, 548	2, 137	57½	8, 584	4, 535½	4, 418½	8¾	191	2, 460	65
Villenova, ...	12, 759¾	9, 521	54, 639	110, 253	23, 582	2, 199¾	19½	6, 474¾	3, 742½	3, 492	52¾	247	2, 959	28¼
Westfield, ...	18, 194½	10, 272	904, 680	157, 144	25, 991	3, 044¾	161	8, 495	4, 861	5, 511½	110¼	503¼	5, 616	514½
Total, ...	360, 110	294, 145½	17, 022, 474	2, 871, 699	610, 560	64, 401½	2. 806¾	172, 376½	103. 180¾	105, 672	2, 286	7, 011¾	78636¼	5, 366¼

CHEMUNG COUNTY.

TOWNS.	Improved.	Unimproved.	Of farm.	Of stock.	Of tools and implements.	Acres plowed the year previous.	Acres in fallow the year previous.	Acres in pasture the year previous.	Meadow acres.	Tons of hay.	Bushels of grass seed.	Spring wheat acres sown.	Bushels harvested.	Winter wheat acres sown
Big Flats, ...	12, 616½	11, 125	825, 742	89, 730	20, 577	5, 130½	428	3, 216½	2, 130½	2, 654	88	207¾	1, 991	1, 591¼
Catlin, ...	11, 670	9, 316	465, 505	75, 234	23. 054	4, 254	393	2, 792	2, 355	2, 031	217	629	4, 544	653
Chemung, ...	19, 864	20, 364	951, 899	125, 638	33, 956	5, 326	1, 011½	6, 500	4, 363	4, 856	160½	252¾	2, 359¼	1, 251½
Elmira, ...	10, 094¾	6, 425	1, 045, 700	102, 636	20, 363	2, 611	499½	3, 017	2, 420½	2, 461	43	111	1, 103	818½
Erin, ...	9, 638	18, 169	366, 385	59, 710	13, 301	3, 068	356	2, 356	2, 240	1, 898	69	142½	1, 325	371
Horseheads, ...	12, 490	7, 840	805, 110	102, 082	27, 093	3, 482	400	3, 525	2, 481	2, 825½	26	131½	1, 353	1, 439½
Southport, ...	15, 831½	16, 990¼	1, 291, 386	122, 451	33, 957	4, 411½	692	3, 949½	3, 071½	3, 391	69½	198	1, 793	1, 180
Van Etten, ...	12, 689	12, 083	336, 694	57, 028	15, 250	2, 961	524	2, 936	2, 393	1, 868	114	103	820	482
Veteran, ...	15, 326	8, 073	810, 425	107, 042	27, 360	5, 029	344½	4, 946	3, 385½	2, 956½	79	364½	3, 335½	994½
Total, ...	120, 219¾	110, 385¼	6, 898, 846	841, 551	214, 911	36, 273	4, 648½	33, 238	24, 840	24, 941	866	2, 140	18, 624	8, 781¼

CATTARAUGUS COUNTY.—(Continued.)

TOWNS.	Winter Wheat.	Oats.		Rye.		Barley.		Buckwheat.		Corn.		Potatoes.		Peas.	
	Bushels harvested.	Acres sown.	Bushels harvested.	Acres sown.	Bushels harvested.	Acres sown.	Bushels harvested.	Acres sown.	Bushels harvested.	Acres planted.	Bushels harvested.	Acres planted.	Bushels harvested.	Acres sown.	Bushels harvested.
New Albion,....	481	1,278	27,485	6	80	59¼	979	76⅛	811¾	528⅞	16,630	148¾	11,840	41¾	649
Olean,..........	308	341	7,608	7	56	3	60	77	1,235	113	3,567	43	3,905	6	84
Otto, ...	890½	825½	20,219½	......	....	54½	958	57	599	512½	16,573	87⅛	6,686½	23⅜	350
Perrysburgh, ...	3,912	895½	14,811	26¾	367	103¾	1,389½	46⅛	401½	761	20,156	138¼	10,334	7¼	91
Persia,.........	3,659	393¼	8,091	11½	118	32¼	391	27¾	313½	497	14,671	87¾	7,202	18¼	275
Portville,......	158½	350	8,720	1	20	4¼	64	91	1,003½	184¼	6,236	81⅛	9,474	5¼	114
Randolph,......	250	599	9,940	4½	68	17¼	260	50	537	461	14,633	91½	7,479	28⅜	468
South Valley,...	228	133	2,419	14	126	......	....	23	252	88	2,136	31	2,370	2	40
Yorkshire, ...	927	1,504¾	26,513	13	161	40¼	438	45¼	297	517¾	12,452	192¾	13,019	104¼	1,409½
Total, ...	21721	31,798⅜	697,670½	226	2,373½	942⅜	14,095	2,320⅝	26,183	10,271⅜	309,762	3,597⅛	300,245¾	938½	14,492¼

CAYUGA COUNTY.—(Continued.)

TOWNS.	Winter Wheat, bushels harvested.	Oats, acres sown.	Oats, bushels harvested.	Rye, acres sown.	Rye, bushels harvested.	Barley, acres sown.	Barley, bushels harvested.	Buckwheat, acres sown.	Buckwheat, bushels harvested.	Corn, acres planted.	Corn, bushels harvested.	Potatoes, acres planted.	Potatoes, bushels harvested.	Peas, acres sown.	Peas, bushels harvested.
Auburn,........	813	150	2,848	1¼	18	99	2,186	8	180	202	5,835	24¼	2,175	1	50
Aurelius, ...	20342	2,453½	67,706	5	34	841¼	16,993	141½	918	1,781	44,433	107¾	6,260	5½	65
Brutus, ...	9931	1,043	34,158	22	185	406	9,420	70¼	954	1,083½	36,000	132¾	13,886	1	24
Cato, ...	21268½	1,608½	48,508	......	....	1,277	29,382	171⅛	2,530½	1,969¾	66,011	174	17,393	4⅛	70
Conquest, ...	17711	2,080½	68,370	3	40	369	7,367	260¼	3,284	1,848½	54,188	182¼	15,082	11¼	167½
Fleming, ...	3787	1,058½	26,288	180	....	1,011½	21,407½	153¾	1,983	1,133	36,620	73¼	5,848	5¼	66
Genoa,.........	11724	3,101	85,408	4	45	585¼	11,298	348¾	3,769	2,129	60,424	137¾	10,698	8½	130
Ira, ...	12884	1,672¾	47,292	20	109	1,131	23,839	220¾	2,370	1,676	54,645	177½	16,877	15¾	260½
Ledyard,.......	10264	2,231½	49,462	......	....	870½	15,443	146¼	1,103½	1,803¾	39,119	94¾	5,516	3⅞	42
Locke, ...	1405	1,453	34,034	......	....	267	4,150	234¼	2,066	704	19,627	78	5,249	16½	326
Mentz, ...	27171	2,221¼	70,326	......	....	493¼	9,783	297¼	3,746	2,167	66,609	294½	20,905	17¾	296
Moravia, ...	1405	1,090¾	25,023	14½	161	362½	7,007	211¾	2,442	779½	23,900	90⅜	6,627	23⅝	503⅓
Niles,..........	2952	1,395¾	22,933	3	6	2,275½	33,436	371¾	3,698	1,413¼	38,131	117½	8,293⅛	26⅜	327
Owasco,........	2072½	774¾	15,400	1	1¾	898	14,008	214¾	3,020½	854¾	23,480	119½	10,828	40⅛	366½
Scipio, ...	10865	2,423¾	47,372	......	....	1,451	25,449	221¼	2,509	2,090½	50,366	100⅞	8,590	3	37
Sempronius,....	72	963	24,186	......	....	441½	7,943	293½	3,589	388½	13,044	93⅞	10,518	36¼	691
Sennett,........	6104½	1,844	45,366	1	1	1,022	18,536	244½	3,012½	1,679	47,495	320⅛	21,838	43¾	522
Springport, ...	10770	1,366½	35,461	......	....	703	15,240	91	650	1,204	34,050	60¾	4,251	24	207
Sterling, ...	5359	1,625½	43,512	321	4,263	316¼	6,426	371	3,396½	1,818	48,917	375	27,027	60	905
Summer Hill,...	113	1,341	30,809	......	....	196¼	3,788	209½	1,920	357	9,922	103¼	6,942	39¼	775
Venice,.........	6692	2,886	68,606	967	30	893	16,664	246½	3,083	1,585	45,490	128¾	10,077	30½	490
Victory,........	10024	2,274½	63,568	51½	1,438	365¾	8,538	392¾	3,852	1,852	50,237	215	16,838	18	244
Total, ...	193729½	37,059	956,636	1,594¼	6,331¾	16275½	308,303½	4,920⅜	54,076½	30,519	868,543	3,201¾	251,718⅛	435⅝	6,565

CHAUTAUQUE COUNTY.—(Continued.)

TOWNS.	Winter Wheat, bushels harvested.	Oats, acres sown.	Oats, bushels harvested.	Rye, acres sown.	Rye, bushels harvested.	Barley, acres sown.	Barley, bushels harvested.	Buckwheat, acres sown.	Buckwheat, bushels harvested.	Corn, acres planted.	Corn, bushels harvested.	Potatoes, acres planted.	Potatoes, bushels harvested.	Peas, acres sown.	Peas, bushels harvested.
Arkwright,.....	534	830	15,998	¾	11	41	531	23	294	587	17,541	138	10,188	8	109½
Busti, ...	726	1,617	37,858	5	9	59½	921	47	349	993	31,638	190	15,196	20½	299
Carrol,.........	786	499	9,597	58	694	3	32	61	323	462	14,666	91	7,957	4	67
Charlotte, ...	90	1,051	27,690	......	....	37	648	44¼	480	529	14,944	125	10,685	13½	225½
Chautauque,....	1,301	1,668	34,704	7½	155	104	1,814	49	448	1,084	30,677	191	13,703	32¾	428
Cherry Creek, ..	538	764½	16,039	3¾	49½	21¾	330	53	624	629½	18,997	105½	9,088	22¼	268¼
Clymer,........	548½	905¾	17,189	19¾	337	16¼	169	66½	567¾	407¾	8,923	131	12,272	28¼	430
Ellery,.........	5,507	1,751	37,172	7	118	121½	1,994	74	768	1,272	39,751	162	13,091	69	949¾
Ellicott,........	1,452	628	12,801	11½	173½	23½	435	64	437½	765	24,304	118¼	11,274	8½	153½
Ellington,......	245	1,595	38,542	4½	44	20	417	30¾	348½	816	28,244	134	13,574	35½	552
French Creek,...	265	553	9,456	5	62	15¼	195	38	224	43¼	7,019	89¼	6,038	23	306½
Gerry, ...	237	902½	20,017	2¾	45	23	386	14	132	629¼	17,709	201	8,475	14¼	200
Hanover,.......	8,235	1,144	18,110	......	....	89	1,250	45	489½	1,635¾	41,864½	292½	17,706	6½	93
Harmony,......	2,605	2,276	52,907	24½	373	59	1,082	131¼	1,689	1,303	34,403	295	27,642	81½	1,303
Kiantone, ...	387	379½	11,400	......	....	3	54	6	82	247¼	8,105	41	3,532	4½	65
Mina, ...	35	871½	18,353	1	3	65½	858	26½	241½	270	7,224	113¼	9,916	24¾	373
Poland, ...	622	555½	11,944	9	52	5	105	14	221	578½	19,156	102	11,029	10¼	179
Pomfret,... ...	6,936	1,186	21,918	......	....	43¾	1,154	43	271	1,388¼	37,148	228¼	12,870	31	324
Portland, ...	6,832½	675½	12,951	5	40	28½	391	17¾	89½	1,274¾	30,110	134¾	7,411	3½	59½
Ripley,.........	9,858	1,341	21,201	7	200	96½	1,777	58¾	380½	1,071	27,597	125½	7,443	3	59
Sheridan, ...	9,998	887	15,545	2½	12	104	1,509¼	24	88½	1,028¾	23,120	148½	8,288	8¼	94
Sherman, ...	199	962½	20,732	5½	81	42	605	47½	448	329	8,566	118½	11,554	36¼	530
Stockton, ...	435	785	19,840	......	....	81	1,241	17¼	236½	725	23,297	136½	11,243	8¾	176½
Villenova,......	296½	1,018¼	20,892	3½	29	78¼	1,121	34	247½	632¾	18,356	182¾	14,772	20	278½
Westfield,......	7,581	935¾	16,907	17	320	43	637	26¼	184½	1,059½	25,148	129	7,504	18½	169½
Total, ...	66249½	25,782¼	539,763	200½	2,808	1,224¼	19,656¼	1,055¾	9,664¾	19,761¼	558,507½	3,723½	282,451	536¼	7,693

CHEMUNG COUNTY.—(Continued.)

TOWNS.	Winter Wheat, bushels harvested.	Oats, acres sown.	Oats, bushels harvested.	Rye, acres sown.	Rye, bushels harvested.	Barley, acres sown.	Barley, bushels harvested.	Buckwheat, acres sown.	Buckwheat, bushels harvested.	Corn, acres planted.	Corn, bushels harvested.	Potatoes, acres planted.	Potatoes, bushels harvested.	Peas, acres sown.	Peas, bushels harvested.
Big Flats,......	13285½	2,490½	76,622	370	582	251½	7,327	780½	11,259½	969	34,859	127	12,101	¾	32
Catlin,.........	4816	2,226	61,268	10	47	75	1,347	744	7,017	481	8,863	113⅞	9,225	8½	208
Chemung, ...	7509	2,094	51,567	138½	1,074	140	2,849	1,000	14,018	1,493	46,260	164	15,189	1⅜	29½
Elmira, ...	6337	1,064	31,234	66	441	94	1,613	381¼	4,254	760½	37,497½	126⅜	34,842	3¼	58
Erin,...........	2551	1,494	32,747	16	146	24	328	588	7,004	430	10,383	111½	8,947	19½	91
Horseheads, ...	10694½	2,277½	75,558	18	179	175½	3,254	516¼	6,576	859	33,335	118¼	13,741	1½	22
Southport,......	9030	1,502½	42,856	66½	783	181	4,215	549	6,821½	1,057	39,488	171¼	15,625	4¼	81
Van Etten, ...	2437	1,287	23,125	39	271	11¼	194	715	6,997	427½	9,106	100¼	6,936	43⅞	736
Veteran,........	7094	2,814½	78,492	7	35	148¼	2,735	628	5,099½	722½	19,495	149	14,085	6⅜	103
Total,........	63754	17,280	473,469	731	3,558	1,100½	23,862	5,902	69,046½	7,199½	239,285½	1,190½	131,291	89½	1,360½

CATTARAUGUS COUNTY.—(CONTINUED.)

TOWNS.	BEANS. Acres planted.	BEANS. Bushels harvested.	TURNIPS. Acres sown.	TURNIPS. Bushels harvested.	FLAX. Acres sown.	FLAX. Pounds of lint.	FLAX. Bushels of seed.	HEMP. Acres sown.	HEMP. Tons of hemp.	HOPS. Acres planted.	HOPS. Pounds harvested.	TOBACCO. Acres planted.	TOBACCO. Pounds harvested.	APPLE ORCHAR[DS]. Bushels of apples.	APPLE ORCHAR[DS]. Barre[ls] of cid[er].
New Albion, ...	4	201	1⅝	765	½	235	1							4,743	
Olean, ...			2	40										1,426	
Otto, ...	8½	127	2½	311	1⅜	255	11							9,186	
Perrysburgh, ...	18¾	442½	⅞	455	2¼	75	20½			½	150	1	1,100	9,718	12
Persia, ...	4⅝	136	1⅛	289		540	1½							5,260	
Portville, ...	2½	119½	2⅞	1,120										3,069	
Randolph, ...	1⅛	42	1⅝	365										6,200	
South Valley, ...	1	12	2	100										800	
Yorkshire, ...	25⅝	271	1⅝	309	⅛	98	⅜							9,781	1
Total, ...	242¼	4,496½	142½	26,104	8⅜	2,738	58⅜			2¾	488	1¾	1,770	177,173½	1,2

CAYUGA COUNTY.—(CONTINUED.)

TOWNS.	BEANS. Acres planted.	BEANS. Bushels harvested.	TURNIPS. Acres sown.	TURNIPS. Bushels harvested.	FLAX. Acres sown.	FLAX. Pounds of lint.	FLAX. Bushels of seed.	HEMP. Acres sown.	HEMP. Tons of hemp.	HOPS. Acres planted.	HOPS. Pounds harvested.	TOBACCO. Acres planted.	TOBACCO. Pounds harvested.	APPLE ORCHAR[DS]. Bushels of apples.	APPLE ORCHAR[DS]. Barre[ls] of cid[er].
Auburn, ...	3¾	49	⅛	20										1,617	
Aurelius, ...	3¼	52	¼	24										8,880	1
Brutus, ...	8¼	179½	4	417	1	2,000	3					1¼	1,800	22,624	8
Cato, ...	49⅜	955	8⅜	2,347										26,368	7
Conquest, ...	5½	115	7	1,701	1¼	160	4							21,137	4
Fleming, ...	6	62	⅜	85										14,758	2
Genoa, ...	21⅝	271	¾	155	23¼	4,050	161							48,284	5
Ira, ...	28½	571	4	1,776	5½	400	69							44,502	8
Ledyard, ...	13	84	3¾	525	43	8,000	328							10,212	
Locke, ...	7½	88½	1⅜	270										26,190	2
Mentz, ...	14	216	10¼	1,811	¼	500	2					1	1,500	23,568	7
Moravia, ...	23⅜	399½	3½	1,199	¼	25				4	2,000			41,524	2
Niles, ...	70¾	736½	½	55	25¼	2,750	214½			1½	640			31,147	5
Owasco, ...	21	563½	1⅝	165	⅛		3							18,159	5
Scipio, ...	4½	124	¾	175										28,968	2
Sempronius, ...	5½	69	1⅜	333½	37½		371							29,080	1,0
Sennett, ...	16½	317	8¾	1,755										27,430	5
Springport, ...	¼	5												9,134	2
Sterling, ...	16¼	214½	4½	1,825	¼	500								20,086	3
Summer Hill, ...	3¼	33½	3½	772	¼		5½							20,333	1
Venice, ...	6	76			½		5							25,488	6
Victory, ...	30¾	457	11⅜	2,054										23,262	7
Total, ...	359⅛	5,638½	76⅝	17,464½	138⅜	18,385	1,166			5½	2,640	2¼	3,300	522,751	10,3

CHAUTAUQUE COUNTY.—(CONTINUED.)

TOWNS.	BEANS. Acres planted.	BEANS. Bushels harvested.	TURNIPS. Acres sown.	TURNIPS. Bushels harvested.	FLAX. Acres sown.	FLAX. Pounds of lint.	FLAX. Bushels of seed.	HEMP. Acres sown.	HEMP. Tons of hemp.	HOPS. Acres planted.	HOPS. Pounds harvested.	TOBACCO. Acres planted.	TOBACCO. Pounds harvested.	APPLE ORCHAR[DS]. Bushels of apples.	APPLE ORCHAR[DS]. Barre[ls] of cid[er].
Arkwright, ...	8¼	133	3¼	272	1¼		10							11,252	
Busti, ...	13	339	7	1,248	1¼	75	8							20,589	2
Carroll, ...	4½	112	¼	75	½	120	1							7,219	1
Charlotte, ...	4	60½	13	2,400	½	125	4							10,154	
Chautauque, ...	9	154	7½	1,852	½		1½				22		25	26,196	2
Cherry Creek, ...	9¾	295¾	3¾	731	1	183	3¾							12,448	1
Clymer, ...	11¼	186½	4¾	490	2½	372	5¾				7	1	365	3,915	
Ellery, ...	4¼	104	4¼	779	3	590	21							32,104	2
Ellicott, ...	6¼	123	5	859	⅛	10								12,454	1
Ellington, ...	4	200	2¼	1,043	2½	444	16			2½	1,715			22,387	3
French Creek, ...	5½	78½	1¾	80	1	90	2							2,226	
Gerry, ...	4½	66½	2⅜	1,370	¼	60	1½			1	560	½	700	15,567	1
Hanover, ...	17	206½	2¼	273	2	400	13¼			2	100	⅛	300	30,058	4
Harmony, ...	10½	275¾	9¼	3,728	3	605	10							28,352	2
Kiantone, ...	1½	49	½	100										5,742	
Mina, ...	4¼	100	1	313	4		56							6,007	
Poland, ...	5	147	2¼	790	2¼		4							7,098	1
Pomfret, ...	19¾	239	4¾	262										19,037	4
Portland, ...	5	95	2¼	222										12,671	1
Ripley, ...	4⅞	116	¾	155	5¾	375	46							9,016	1
Sheridan, ...	9½	213	1½	400	5¼		58							22,202	4
Sherman, ...	2¾	121	4¼	1,500	2¼	365	13							3,243	
Stockton, ...	10¼	151	4½	903							12			24,300	2
Villenova, ...	17¾	259	1½	120	4	770	27½							14,529	1
Westfield, ...	15¾	213	3¼	395										9,349	1
Total, ...	208⅛	4,038	93⅜	20,360	42⅞	4,584	302¼			5½	2,416	1⅝	1,390	368,115	4,5

CHEMUNG COUNTY.—(CONTINUED.)

TOWNS.	BEANS. Acres planted.	BEANS. Bushels harvested.	TURNIPS. Acres sown.	TURNIPS. Bushels harvested.	FLAX. Acres sown.	FLAX. Pounds of lint.	FLAX. Bushels of seed.	HEMP. Acres sown.	HEMP. Tons of hemp.	HOPS. Acres planted.	HOPS. Pounds harvested.	TOBACCO. Acres planted.	TOBACCO. Pounds harvested.	APPLE ORCHAR[DS]. Bushels of apples.	APPLE ORCHAR[DS]. Barre[ls] of cid[er].
Big Flats, ...	4½	112½	2½	300								28	32,620	16,771	60
Catlin, ...	2½	23	2⅛	286										5,503	6
Chemung, ...	6	903½	5⅜	643	½	10	¼							19,511	55
Elmira, ...	5	54	¼	16								½	700	6,870	25
Erin, ...	7½	82	3	250	5	80	61				2			8,322	13
Horseheads, ...	7¼	164¼	1¾	1,030	½	40	5				100		277	13,916	45
Southport, ...	14⅛	272	2⅛	177										9,513	38
Van Etten, ...	2⅞	78	4	548										8,964	4
Veteran, ...	7	170	5¼	714										17,994	46
Total, ...	56¾	1,859¼	26⅜	3,964	6	130	66¼				102	28½	33,597	107,364	2,9

CATTARAUGUS COUNTY.—(CONTINUED.)

TOWNS.	MARKET GARDENS.		Pounds of maple sugar made.	Gallons of maple molasses made.	Gallons of wine made.	Pounds of honey collected.	Pounds of wax collected.	SILK.	NEAT CATTLE.				Number of cattle killed for beef.	Pounds of butter.	Pounds of cheese.
	Acres cultivated.	Value of products.						Pounds of cocoons.	Under one year old.	Over one y'r, exclusive of working oxen & cows.	Working oxen.	Cows.			
New Albion,	......	......	13,700	75	......	1,458	44	......	496	899	162	1,079	112	90,458	77,166
Olean,	1	$125	......	......	......	385	4	......	83	108	58	286	215	5,310	560
Otto,	......	......	10,312	45	......	3,070	178½	......	369	677	121	1,229	51	77,823	208,476
Perrysburgh,	2⅓	160½	4,667	51	16	3,139	275	......	448	865	152	1,215	45	91,875	128,994
Persia,	1	......	3,570	11	......	1,315	44	......	287	450	88	658	53	42,666	38,666
Portville,	......	......	1,265	......	......	2,193	124	......	113	138	85	323	41	27,983	2,895
Randolph,	......	......	8,595	28	......	500	14	......	386	607	146	647	65	49,090	4,615
South Valley,	......	......	360	3	......	440	15	......	76	145	93	171	33	15,365	......
Yorkshire,	......	......	25,364	26	......	2,169	93	......	401	754	174	868	131	88,925	12,904
Total,	7⅜	463¼	416,300½	2,459	23	62,486	3,378	......	10,417	20,202	4,137	23,633	2,170	1,957,183	1,717,484

CAYUGA COUNTY.—(CONTINUED.)

TOWNS.	Acres cultivated.	Value of products.	Pounds of maple sugar made.	Gallons of maple molasses made.	Gallons of wine made.	Pounds of honey collected.	Pounds of wax collected.	Pounds of cocoons.	Under one year old.	Over one y'r.	Working oxen.	Cows.	Cattle killed for beef.	Pounds of butter.	Pounds of cheese.
Auburn,	18⅝	1,130	......	......	......	......	......	......	37	73	18	123	15	13,550	200
Aurelius,	2½	326	......	......	35	3,522	109	......	336	596	162	977	206	93,290	7,694
Brutus,	......	......	......	......	......	1,030	92	......	350	675	85	656	223	61,088	12,085
Cato,	......	......	310	16	20	1,930	91¼	......	501	1,014	157	1,004	121	93,410	4,411
Conquest,	¾	140	345	19	44	4,658	280	......	406	968	124	998	169	92,992	4,851
Fleming,	......	......	132	......	......	5,555	294	......	147	260	74	441	42	41,690	4,535
Genoa,	......	......	2,975	309	39	4,059	234	......	388	864	119	1,245	148	151,586	9,851
Ira,	½	7,000	1,110	32½	6	3,960	161	......	509	1,090	186	1,227	164	128,399	19,783
Ledyard,	......	200	916	124	......	3,765	130	......	327	535	68	684	204	49,210	8,629
Locke,	......	......	2,035	29	......	2,966	102	......	333	782	97	943	72	105,008	3,976
Mentz,	1	125	12	6	10	5,558	323	......	658	1,475	197	1,629	324	131,564	16,997
Moravia,	......	......	2,809	84	5	3,474	133	......	313	648	101	968	161	124,237	9,519
Niles,	......	......	2,641	140	......	7,653	305	......	441	860	92	1,196	226	145,517	16,273
Owasco,	......	......	825	107¼	......	3,895	153½	......	222	348	79	582	123	62,637	10,470
Scipio,	......	......	30	......	19	3,495	242	......	352	661	118	854	119	72,969	7,139
Sempronius,	......	......	5,008	45	......	3,539	238	......	259	581	82	1,056	162	140,702	5,064
Sennett,	21	960	......	9	16	4,219½	125	......	492	932	159	1,164	134	84,439	29,645
Springport,	......	......	60	......	......	4,480	181	......	229	444	30	2	53	48,630	3,775
Sterling,	4	350	883	55	2	1,412	107	......	433	877	180	1,179	172	112,872	4,917
Summer Hill,	⅛	14	8,930	98	6	3,760	212¾	......	255	581	76	912	69	124,670	5,643
Venice,	......	......	4,905	337	......	4,450	309	......	421	920	182	975	97	101,575	10,640
Victory,	......	......	220	24	......	6,173	343	......	401	856	120	1,007	89	101,987	3,236
Total,	48½	10,245	40,036	1,434¾	202	83,553½	4,165½	......	7,810	16,040	2,506	19,822	3,093	2,082,022	199,33[illegible]

CHAUTAUQUE COUNTY.—(CONTINUED.)

TOWNS.	Acres cultivated.	Value of products.	Pounds of maple sugar made.	Gallons of maple molasses made.	Gallons of wine made.	Pounds of honey collected.	Pounds of wax collected.	Pounds of cocoons.	Under one year old.	Over one y'r.	Working oxen.	Cows.	Cattle killed for beef.	Pounds of butter.	Pounds of cheese.
Arkwright,	2¼	108	8,993	93	......	1,550	42	......	475	789	112	1,348	228	99,029	120,515
Busti,	......	3	33,471	437	......	2,498	758	......	634	1,273	133	1,925	123	195,463	51,780
Carroll,	1½	84	3,886	105	......	1,362	42	......	327	525	187	534	91	50,460	4,700
Charlotte,	......	......	27,111	97	......	1,551	108½	......	564	789	164	1,429	136	139,761	70,280
Chautauque,	2¼	162	24,653	311	......	3,684	250½	......	847	1,305	239	2,799	142	279,574	115,272
Cherry Creek,	......	......	14,416	98	......	2,310	131	......	445	726	196	981	33	10,782	20,580
Clymer,	......	......	24,601	191	......	1,892	100	......	326	759	145	1,012	46	95,669	16,741
Ellery,	3	165	10,164	237	......	1,849	99	......	715	1,113	134	2,033	99	173,569	119,439
Ellicott,	5½	762	1,333	19¼	......	465	30½	......	289	543	122	725	76	64,694	12,884
Ellington,	......	......	28,789	219	......	2,479	223	......	565	925	158	1,168	53	144,717	15,155
French Creek,	......	......	19,059	117	......	2,101	123	......	239	431	118	551	36	58,050	2,218
Gerry,	......	......	16,835	17	......	1,554	61	......	454	789	138	1,155	34	103,685	61,220
Hanover,	4⅓	112	3,461	51	......	5,216	355	......	726	1,555	318	2,305	220	229,772	58,300
Harmony,	......	......	55,549	354	......	3,553	247	......	1,209	2,122	379	3,312	250	332,495	83,172
Kiantone,	......	......	8,083	81	......	485	27	......	228	377	52	613	44	56,530	21,460
Mina,	......	......	17,883	118	......	1,361	114	......	507	849	192	1,002	49	111,065	10,910
Poland,	2	50	10,975	46	......	1,494	108	......	317	711	168	727	145	71,910	6,375
Pomfret,	22¾	1,534	9,476	111	2	2,924	236	......	610	1,271	192	2,748	1,275	175,368	91,509
Portland,	5⅛	540	1,299	94	464½	1,639	189½	......	457	744	226	1,117	238	131,836	8,425
Ripley,	......	......	10,525	219	56	3,375	210	......	548	1,289	232	1,257	85	122,800	17,425
Sheridan,	1	50	1,285	14	13	4,218	320	......	435	1,051	204	1,035	60	105,786	54,706
Sherman,	4¼	179	21,526	177	......	950	72	......	467	606	145	1,260	59	143,745	14,100
Stockton,	⅜	679	34,459	303	......	1,886	120	......	515	707	176	2,299	149	212,926	179,472
Villenova,	......	......	24,000	253	......	1,293	36	......	455	753	160	1,451	52	168,087	36,509
Westfield,	3¼	1,057	8,890	154	89	1,776	139	......	497	1,476	225	1,200	101	112,064	5,214
Total,	57¾	5,485	420,722	3,916¼	624½	53,465	4,142	......	12,851	23,478	4,515	36,046	3,830	3,389,837	1,198,361

CHEMUNG COUNTY.—(CONTINUED.)

TOWNS.	Acres cultivated.	Value of products.	Pounds of maple sugar made.	Gallons of maple molasses made.	Gallons of wine made.	Pounds of honey collected.	Pounds of wax collected.	Pounds of cocoons.	Under one year old.	Over one y'r.	Working oxen.	Cows.	Cattle killed for beef.	Pounds of butter.	Pounds of cheese.
Big Flats,	¼	60	......	......	......	5,083	190	......	414	854	154	959	131	86,702	570
Catlin,	......	......	130	......	......	7,658	224	......	332	543	127	694	58	65,720	......
Chemung,	8	700	545	31	......	8,555	377	......	658	1,069	234	2,183	140	209,735	560
Elmira,	5	3,000	......	6	25	1,640	82	......	208	444	115	938	137	79,767	350
Erin,	......	......	3,090	205	......	5,111	229	......	333	490	202	845	42	72,140	......
Horseheads,	5	500	......	20	......	1,000	......	......	371	663	131	995	340	108,260	2,770
Southport,	7½	688	......	......	7	1,430	78½	......	426	846	201	1,220	919	118,899	......
Van Etten,	......	......	2,653	65	......	4,881	366	......	346	539	191	684	48	57,870	......
Veteran,	......	......	64	36	......	3,833	124	......	408	755	155	1,172	123	125,552	3,611
Total,	25⅜	4,948	6,482	363	32	30,101	1,670½	......	3,496	6,203	1,510	9,690	1,938	924,645	7,861

CATTARAUGUS COUNTY.—(Continued.)

TOWNS.	Gallons of milk sold.	Horses.	Mules.	SWINE. Under 6 months.	SWINE. Over 6 months.	SHEEP. Number of sheep.	SHEEP. Number of fleeces.	SHEEP. Pounds of wool.	POULTRY. Value of poultry sold.	POULTRY. Value of eggs sold.	DOMESTIC MANUFACTURES. Yards of fulled cloth made.	DOMESTIC MANUFACTURES. Yards of flannel made.	DOMESTIC MANUFACTURES. Yards of linen made.	DOMESTIC MANUFACTURES. Yards of cotton and mixed cloths.
New Albion,	....	383	....	262	344	2, 588	1, 530	5, 029¼	$260	$713	238	1. 206	119	391
Olean,	4, 637	155	....	105	221	228	169	483	29	51	46	82	....	....
Otto,	350	335	....	145	307	1, 410	900	3, 051	328	800	132½	290½	632	890
Perrysburgh,	365	425	....	307	406	2, 437	2, 022	6, 844	1, 414	750	382	954	339	372
Persia,	356	240	....	128	196	760	757	2, 512½	349	523	118	360½	66	203
Portville,	72	193	3	151	203	854	464	1, 460	132	233	....	417½	....	169
Randolph,	150	434	....	245	331	1, 253	975	3, 348½	52	699	222	501	167	442
South Valley,	....	88	....	31	105	486	326	920	11	20	23	127	....	89
Yorkshire,	....	400	....	183	332	2, 703	2, 698	8, 625	645	560	177	520	288	1, 049
Total,	6, 200	9, 497	11	5, 376	8, 458	59, 725	41, 080	130, 996½	10, 031	13, 295	4, 139¼	15, 056½	4, 218	11, 659

CAYUGA COUNTY.—(Continued.)

TOWNS.	Gallons of milk sold.	Horses.	Mules.	Under 6 months.	Over 6 months.	Number of sheep.	Number of fleeces.	Pounds of wool.	Value of poultry sold.	Value of eggs sold.	Yards of fulled cloth made.	Yards of flannel made.	Yards of linen made.	Yards of cotton and mixed cloths.
Auburn,	69, 125	377	....	90	294	471	387	1, 272	243	18	18	30	....	100
Aurelius,	10, 592	806	....	761	817	5, 923	5, 663	19, 078	1, 438	11	68	111	....	132
Brutus,	....	527	....	693	719	2, 350	2, 350	8, 125	647	1, 188	43	113	....	....
Cato,	7	854	....	563	816	3, 311	2, 277	8, 409	1, 328	3, 374	119	418	36	60
Conquest,	....	791	....	783	930	5, 374	3, 915	13, 125	1, 052	2, 619	486½	491½	466	499
Fleming,	....	404	....	468	497	3, 483	6, 859	12, 783	1, 394	1, 566	90	41	103	....
Genoa,	....	892	....	878	584	7, 748	8, 827	34, 308	1, 691	4, 799	71	236	110	155
Ira,	....	957	....	1, 077	947	4, 518	2, 979	11, 057	1, 580	3, 455	334	520	213	249
Ledyard,	....	680	....	679	453	9, 696	10, 845	40, 138	2, 286	1, 733	....	....	....	20
Locke,	....	527	....	332	396	1, 901	2, 291	7, 991¼	482	1, 795	149	676	182	133
Mentz,	400	1, 153	2	1, 130	1, 630	5, 348	4, 757	16, 493	2, 036	3, 796	32	213	55	13
Moravia,	270	544	....	510	425	4, 824	3, 978	15, 323	953	1, 183	133	304½	167	120
Niles,	....	833	....	704	720	4, 369	4, 002	15, 204	1, 147	2, 744	502½	975	170	343
Owasco,	2, 185	449	1	501	474	3, 957	3, 283	11, 790½	798	1, 270	105½	417	60	69
Scipio,	....	812	....	636	625	7, 953	8, 481	31, 883	1, 648	2, 521	69	230	125	100
Sempronius,	....	518	....	390	394	1, 517	2, 189	7, 738	715	1, 230	337	610	225	55
Sennett,	1, 400	751	....	765	765	5, 286	3, 716	14, 527½	1, 146	1, 658	143	105	65	25
Springport,	365	566	....	761	617	4, 720	3, 992	14, 693½	824	1, 133	....	....	....	....
Sterling,	....	849	....	762	1, 006	4, 192	2, 818	9, 271½	1, 016	2, 216	334	776½	....	70
Summer Hill,	....	492	1	289	345	2, 752	2, 850	9, 935	679	1, 293	270	337	194	273
Venice,	....	773	....	721	518	10, 257	9, 891	37, 720	2, 030	3, 078	148	370	38	13
Victory,	....	850	....	694	922	3, 681	2, 150	7, 965	1, 283	3, 186	176	776½	161	411
Total,	84, 344	15, 405	4	14, 187	14, 894	103, 631	98, 500	348, 830¼	26, 416	45, 866	3, 628½	7, 751	2, 370	2, 840

CHAUTAUQUE COUNTY.—(Continued.)

TOWNS.	Gallons of milk sold.	Horses.	Mules.	Under 6 months.	Over 6 months.	Number of sheep.	Number of fleeces.	Pounds of wool.	Value of poultry sold.	Value of eggs sold.	Yards of fulled cloth made.	Yards of flannel made.	Yards of linen made.	Yards of cotton and mixed cloths.
Arkwright,	500	391	2	265	382	2, 174	1, 437	4, 853	835	629	373½	588½	152	670
Busti,	....	639	....	353	510	5, 748	3, 919	13, 148	620	468	110	510	253	554
Carrol,	35	266	....	159	221	1, 675	1, 437	4, 376	131	117	366	1, 105	145	149
Charlotte,	....	349	2	263	389	1, 001	894	3, 172½	607	698	74	291	226	190
Chautauque,	100	861	....	620	919	4, 601	3, 286	11, 797	832	1, 056	58	280	232	156
Cherry Creek,	....	375	....	243	328	2, 077	1, 303	4, 204	730	388	92	589	549	482
Clymer,	72	303	2	180	303	1, 624	1, 320	4, 105	149	438	191¾	521	233	986
Ellery,	....	784	....	1, 025	718	3, 813	2, 295	7, 919	1, 783	1, 308	94	766	437	558
Ellicott,	377	413	2	238	224	3, 832	2, 751	7, 854	577	528	46½	99	317	187
Ellington,	200	578	....	377	405	4, 895	3, 564	12, 541	795	970	202½	310½	507	673
French Creek,	....	246	....	107	185	4, 614	1, 206	4, 083¾	209	353	57	358	34	553
Gerry,	....	430	2	270	298	3, 323	1, 982	6, 670	460	184	22	357	156	292
Hanover,	207	898	....	552	1, 112	4, 659	3, 558	12, 670½	1, 427	2, 116	426	956	271	548
Harmony,	....	1, 076	....	850	891	5, 845	3, 295	11, 335	922	1, 187	214	1, 294	947½	1, 485½
Kiantone,	2, 000	168	1	96	139	1, 560	1, 499	5, 365½	65	126	....	10	58	68
Mina,	....	331	2	162	294	2, 101	1, 391	4, 472	240	506	97	629	129	133
Poland,	....	296	....	187	306	1, 941	1, 724	5, 777	113	292	197	418	312	81
Pomfret,	46, 074	1, 139	1	764	1, 132	3, 785	3, 262	11, 105	706	1, 265	167	494	22	165
Portland,	5	510	....	391	492	5, 204	3, 995	12, 684	618	1, 133	136	382	63	414
Ripley,	50	605	....	290	686	8, 740	6, 327	22, 555	1, 122	1, 941	42	426	507	146
Sheridan,	....	481	....	402	461	4, 331	3, 141	10, 830	437	1, 078	148	502	162	807
Sherman,	....	409	....	246	263	2, 135	1, 462	4, 609½	265	551	159	534	256	548
Stockton,	23	457	....	385	405	1, 097	587	1, 887	536	718	109	592	154	390
Villenova,	....	457	....	411	508	3, 285	2, 122	7, 028¼	1, 107	476	681¼	114	826	1, 369½
Westfield,	6, 715	585	1	320	378	6, 094	6, 054	21, 982	341	1, 083	68	117	....	330
Total.	56, 358	13, 047	15	9, 156	11, 949	90, 154	63, 811	217, 024	15, 627	19, 609	4, 131½	12, 243	6, 948½	11, 935

CHEMUNG COUNTY.—(Continued.)

TOWNS.	Gallons of milk sold.	Horses.	Mules.	Under 6 months.	Over 6 months.	Number of sheep.	Number of fleeces.	Pounds of wool.	Value of poultry sold.	Value of eggs sold.	Yards of fulled cloth made.	Yards of flannel made.	Yards of linen made.	Yards of cotton and mixed cloths.
Big Flats,	4, 000	549	....	533	682	3, 009	1, 673	5, 644½	461	1, 048	99	113	40	....
Catlin,	....	503	2	321	488	3, 530	1, 384	4, 389	316	745	457	426	74	376
Chemung,	....	674	....	792	993	2, 482	2, 025	5, 151	594	1, 483	157	626	....	345
Elmira,	28, 682	627	....	454	565	368	277	1, 052	443	650	129	151	....	....
Erin,	....	289	....	239	437	1, 632	1, 270	4, 041	348	378	286	946	240	115
Horseheads,	12, 180	570	....	536	696	2, 496	1, 471	4, 975	370	583	....	193	20	....
Southport,	7, 838	729	2	613	929	1, 408	984	2, 793	272	766	36	48	44	64
Van Etten,	....	348	....	182	407	2, 065	1, 053	3, 092	257	211	307	492	51	520
Veteran,	120	567	2	427	559	4, 374	2, 772	9, 628	741	825	102	320	....	236
Total,	52, 820	4, 856	6	4, 097	5, 756	21, 364	12, 909	40, 765½	3, 802	6, 689	1, 573	3, 315	469	1, 656

CHENANGO COUNTY.

TOWNS.	ACRES.		CASH VALUE.			Acres plowed the year previous.	Acres in fallow the year previous.	Acres in pasture the year previous.	MEADOW.			SPRING WHEAT.		WINTER WHEAT.
	Improved.	Unimproved.	Of farm.	Of stock.	Of tools and implements				Acres.	Tons of hay.	Bushels of grass seed.	Acres sown.	Bushels harvested.	Acres sown.
Bainbridge,	27,680½	20,092	$1,120,135	$192,455	$44,840	5,012	562½	11,636½	7,559½	8,771½	341½	126¾	1,102	369¼
Columbus,	14,319	7,393	589,552	123,840	20,294	2,312	10	8,707	4,926	5,418	85½	93	1,300	.....
Coventry,	21,447	10,605	661,575	119,442	26,223	2,865½	237	10,146	5,599	5,706	196½	111¾	1,420	1
German,	10,663½	6,035½	246,869	65,733	22,051	1,086½	117	4,768	4,576	3,176	37	5½	46	.....
Greene,	28,175¾	14,082½	1,169,774	218,883	39,194	4,437½	438½	14,486	9,040½	9,865½	80¾	51½	444	151½
Guilford,	23,533	10,953	1,048,285	154,811	48,419	2,632½	200	12,562½	7,435½	8,615	126¼	114	973½	114½
Lincklaen,	10,544¾	6,201¼	305,675	68,297	24,911	1,790	....	4,920	3,748¾	3,315½	69½	80½	797	.....
Macdonough,	13,181½	8,619	295,480	85,904	22,170	1,108,	121¾	8,019¼	5,435½	4,448½	44½	20¼	196	.....
New Berlin,	19,942	10,046	734,895	133,934	36,669	2,519¾	36½	9,561¼	5,381¼	6,908	90¾	104¾	1,381½	11
North Norwich,	10,106¼	6,591	695,883	70,693	18,661	1,938	131	4,176¾	3,126	3,243½	76½	34	490	19
Norwich,	19,528¼	6,477½	928,218	179,078	25,217	1,954	129½	10,348	6,258	8,523	53½	80¾	857	6
Otselic,	14,352	9,871	467,108	99,237	25,041	2,467	....	6,692	4,957	4,713½	155	212	1,622½	.....
Oxford,	19,159	12,101	832,865	144,320	29,620	2,845	136	13,688	7,381	7,766	119	118	1,237	32
Pharsalia,	12,794	12,248	415,104	79,056	16,693	1,520	130	5,504	5,216	4,090	37½	18½	210	.....
Pitcher,	13,354⅝	4,395¾	412,796	58,536	23,077	1,654¾	....	6,721	4,375	3,795¾	10	69½	736	4
Plymouth,	15,166	9,671	556,819	115,538	26,065	2,652	54	7,438	5,503	5,246	86	103	1,500	6
Preston,	15,935½	5,361	470,420	107,958	22,258	1,074⅛	27	9,837	4,732¼	4,623	20	18¾	260	.....
Sherburne,	20,702	5,544½	1,039,734	169,867	38,332	4,502¼	71	11,035½	6,095	6,815	216½	196¼	2,507	129
Smithville,	20,341	9,366½	637,260	139,915	41,200	2,352½	466	10,256	7,012	7,131	87	69⅞	974	¾
Smyrna,	16,903½	7,281½	556,005	104,165	18,161	3,415¼	....	7,064¼	5,483½	5,200	105	185½	2,230	53½
Total,	347,828⅜	182,936	13,184,452	2,431,662	569,087	50,138⅝	2,867¾	177,567	113,840½	117,370¾	2,038¼	1,814⅛	20283½	897½

CLINTON COUNTY.

TOWNS.	Improved.	Unimproved.	Of farm.	Of stock.	Of tools and implements	Acres plowed the year previous.	Acres in fallow the year previous.	Acres in pasture the year previous.	Meadow acres.	Tons of hay.	Bushels of grass seed.	Spring wheat acres sown.	Bushels harvested.	Winter wheat acres sown.
Au Sable,	11,067½	10,634	542,507	84,304	17,010	2,489½	15	5,865	3,115	3,126	36	357¾	3402	8¾
Beekmantown,	24,103	13,286½	801,065	145,945	43,243	6,275¼	23	10,379	6,922⅝	7,232	232	846	9980	26½
Black Brook,	5,983¾	69,550¾	212,362	51,927	9,740	1,072¼	11	1,721	1,803½	1,262	5	80½	811	5
Champlain,	18,208	9,035	843,438	100,128	27,251	4,885½	....	8,063	5,163½	6,571	217½	760⅝	8228	3
Chazy,	23,526	56,053	799,783	149,962	37,495	5,958¾	239	8,597¾	6,809	7,645¾	100¾	1,049¼	11909	65½
Clinton,	4,213	24,760	105,332	18,910	3,620	908	169	1,313	1,632½	1,007½	9½	166½	1025½	3
Dannemora,	....	54,919	109,838	....	....	....	....	100	....	....	....	....	....	.....
Ellenburgh,	7,423¾	56,608½	205,080	40,063	15,921	1,707⅝	10	2,089	3,115	1,990¾	101½	222¾	1931¾	9
Mooers,	12,012½	25,308	425,405	69,427	17,385	2,495	36½	4,653	4,209½	4,084½	74	164	1045	5
Peru,	25,050½	19,346½	873,995	151,019	33,385	6,952	53	10,181½	6,839	6,117¾	195½	991½	10179½	41½
Plattsburgh,	14,764½	12,094	655,682	104,038	20,232	4,230	394½	5,182½	5,383¼	4,247¾	59½	463¾	5055	44
Saranac,	11,058¾	39,507¾	292,052	60,451	26,936	2,277¼	877½	3,187¼	3,354	2,331½	1¾	113¼	1008	3
Schuyler Falls,	11,521½	9,984	439,603	71,323	22,508	3,627	106½	4,839	2,826	2,624½	45	334¾	2598	23
Total,	168,932⅝	401,086½	6,306,142	1,047,497	274,726	42,878⅛	1,935	66,171	51,172¾	48,241	1,078	5,550⅜	57172¾	237¼

COLUMBIA COUNTY.

TOWNS.	Improved.	Unimproved.	Of farm.	Of stock.	Of tools and implements	Acres plowed the year previous.	Acres in fallow the year previous.	Acres in pasture the year previous.	Meadow acres.	Tons of hay.	Bushels of grass seed.	Spring wheat acres sown.	Bushels harvested.	Winter wheat acres sown.
Ancram,	21,135	5,784	1,265,780	173,836	22,142	5,426	946	9,056	2,865	3,383	......	......	......	100½
Austerlitz,	22,805	4,987	804,865	103,679	28,158	5,048	286	9,565	4,515	3,698	48	11¾	93	31
Canaan,	16,501	5,218	641,475	73,111	34,279	3,201	399	6,788	3,557	3,078	43	10	118.	100½
Chatham,	26,856	4,381	2,034,000	175,721	50,098	7,425	297	8,167	4,766	4,283	8½	3	14	547
Claverack,	25,055	4,916	1,840,685	136,455	64,638	7,403	23	6,990	6,248	6,050	21½	......	......	173
Clermont,	10,231⅝	2,047	832,029	67,575	31,500	2,548	42	1,894	2,812	3,242	30¼	......	......	243
Copake,	18,343	4,524	1,182,760	141,706	24,367	4,712	39	7,048	3,389	3,011	6	......	......	22
Gallatin,	17,588	6,151	920,574	123,079	32,911	5,118	3,822	5,554	2,637	2,848	104	......	......	57
Germantown,	5,768	573	485,035	47,762	19,522	951	86	1,359	1,988	2,229	87½	40	1	110
Ghent,	22,506	5,420	1,288,835	151,304	44,572	6,664	4,496	4,966	4,529	4,815	20	......	......	557
Greenport,	9,866	1,549	1,118,540	58,010	47,328	1,951	58	1,728	3,375	3,926	34½	2	7½	63¼
Hillsdale,	21,058	5,641	1,125,526	106,313	31,410	5,692	412	9,862	3,796	4,258	25	......	......	60
Hudson,	373	77	52,000	24,445	685	81	4	120	166	178	......	......	......	3
Kinderhook,	15,865	2,811	986,956	84,428	35,781	6,556	272	4,166	2,466	2,802	1	......	......	1,118
Livingston,	20,648	2,055	1,598,540	99,986	39,352	5,302	295	7,526	5,034	4,997	51	......	......	156
New Lebanon,	16,218	3,804	940,369	106,960	42,422	3,220	705	8,516	4,805	4,783	36	27¾	351	14¾
Stockport,	5,650	901	449,810	31,438	20,539	1,172	362	1,294	1,948	1,894	......	1	3	75
Stuyvesant,	10,820	2,448	770,350	66,131	23,760	4,074	36	2,825	2,943	2,934	15	......	......	646
Tagkknick,	16,991	5,968	792,630	86,479	26,985	4,971	157	4,835	2,466	2,694	95	......	......	15
Total,	304,277⅝	69,255	19,130,759	1,858,418	620,449	81,515	12,737	102,259	64,305	65,103	626¼	95½	587½	4,092

CORTLAND COUNTY.

TOWNS.	Improved.	Unimproved.	Of farm.	Of stock.	Of tools and implements	Acres plowed the year previous.	Acres in fallow the year previous.	Acres in pasture the year previous.	Meadow acres.	Tons of hay.	Bushels of grass seed.	Spring wheat acres sown.	Bushels harvested.	Winter wheat acres sown.
Cincinnatus,	10,368	6,015	403,930	75,260	16,290	1,530	22	4,503½	3,480½	3,521	45½	32	311	2½
Cortlandville,	24,150	8,399½	1,467,664	231,114	39,599	5,460¼	49	11,502¾	6,181¾	5,964	119	237¼	3,089	145¼
Freetown,	10,848½	5,159	369,945	72,218	16,974	1,714	....	5,461	3,679	3,289	67	86½	1,153	2
Harford,	7,054½	7,812	212,115	45,690	10,313	1,693	76	2,987	2,125	1,503½	39½	77	827½	72½
Homer,	21,575	11,167⅝	1,170,514	186,046	37,862	4,234	17½	10,036½	6,338¼	5,653½	49⅞	209¾	2,271¼	49½
Lapeer,	9,371	5,654½	323,405	65,157	16,737	1,583½	15	4,611	3,041	2,544	67½	110¼	1,163¾	25½
Marathon,	9,530¾	5,462	400,555	75,133	15,730	1,531½	82½	5,076	2,794¾	2,887	38½	14½	158	6
Preble,	10,713½	5,920	649,705	87,410	27,420	3,487	69	3,746	2,093	2,078	59½	180½	1,327	110½
Scott,	8,772½	5,081	415,256	69,880	18,857	2,415	11	3,495	2,459	2,080	52	192½	2,550½	23
Solon,	10,548¼	7,563	417,325	83,536	19,648	1,606¼	....	5,177	3,574	3,545	37½	104	1,367½	.....
Taylor,	10,244	7,787	345,409	78,016	22,499	1,544	36½	4,727	4,009½	3,643	56½	46¾	457½	1
Truxton,	32,707⅛	21,054¼	1,288,458	283,571	68,679	3,866⅝	....	17,969⅛	10,402	12,712¾	117¼	373⅞	4,453	.....
Virgil,	20,756¼	8,789¾	801,468	155,257	34,948	5,160	98¼	8,505¾	5,999¼	4,721	166½	411¼	5,006	135⅛
Willett,	8,097⅛	7,798⅛	303,922	63,626	12,337	1,113¼	....	3,786	2,795⅛	2,627⅛	42⅛	26¼	226	7
Total,	194,736⅞	113,662⅞	8,569,671	1,571,914	357,893	36,938⅝	476¾	91,583⅝	59,172¼	56,769¼	958⅝	2,102⅝	24361	579⅞

CHENANGO COUNTY.—(Continued.)

TOWNS.	Winter Wheat.	Oats.		Rye.		Barley.		Buckwheat.		Corn.		Potatoes.		Peas.	
	Bushels harvested.	Acres sown.	Bushels harvested	Acres sown.	Bushels harvested.	Acres sown.	Bushels harvested.	Acres sown.	Bushels harvested.	Acres planted.	Bushels harvested.	Acres planted.	Bushels harvested.	Acres sown.	Bushels harvested
Bainbridge, ...	1,163½	2,264¾	52,278	215¾	2,022	24½	361	677	9,476	1,204¾	34,911	325¼	30,609	11⅝	184
Columbus, ...	......	1,400	29,833	10¼	135	75½	973	118	1,166	454½	15,018	174	13,531	9½	139
Coventry, ...	15	1,714¼	36,608	62½	921	1½	25	357	4,545	438¾	14,167	182	15,795	6⅞	110
German, ...	......	718½	10,628	20	286	5	60	197¼	2,238½	135	3,872½	83	5,827	5½	78
Greene, ...	681	2,305¾	50,896	259½	2,591½	2	46	509	5,009	1,012	31,304½	402⅜	22,634	5⅞	154
Guilford, ...	459	1,477⅜	30,980	140¾	1,925	34	621	285⅞	3,284	688½	22,862	167½	15,931	11⅝	120½
Lincklaen, ...	......	1,065	20,414	4½	54	33¾	450	167¼	2,013	211¼	5,991	89⅜	6,160	22	305
Macdonough, ...	......	683	8,981	15	177	4¼	68	174⅜	1,757	260¾	7,125½	116⅜	8,545½	2⅝	39½
New Berlin, ...	82	1,365¼	31,697	31	593½	47¾	1,011	156½	1,958	573¼	19,290	144⅞	12,976	2½	......
North Norwich,	300	929½	23,284	93	1,154	59½	978	142¾	1,674½	548¼	18,705	101¼	13,314	3¼	75
Norwich, ...	45	837¼	19,760	34¾	447	1	14	78	931	553½	24,437	130¾	14,291	3⅜	58
Otselic, ...	......	1,439¾	32,745	6½	21	68½	1,159	126	2,047	321¾	10,017	149½	13,612	38¼	787
Oxford, ...	272	1,474	29.780	124	1,478	5	290	224	2,919	723½	25,288	155½	17,028	......	23
Pharsalia, ...	......	829½	18,023	16	165	12	169	189	2,259	231	5,859	121	9,186	8¾	125
Pitcher, ...	32	1,069¾	17,656	9	96	28½	628	103¾	910¾	307½	9,292	103	8,369	30⅜	439½
Plymouth, ...	44	1,026	22,977	27	535	128	2,284	181	2,180	574	18,622	166½	13,291	13	183
Preston, ...	......	520	11,408	6½	82	23¼	435	81½	964¼	319	11,625	84	9,094½	3	52
Sherburne, ...	986	2,371¾	57,941	33½	615	245½	5,222	138	1,508½	1,125½	43,311	179	15,118	47⅞	898
Smithville, ...	8	1,541⅛	27,140	41¼	576	14	495	229	2,296	381	10,777	152½	11,399	1⅜	37
Smyrna, ...	473	1,672	31,213	36½	655	324¾	6,940	102¾	1,168	681¼	22,006	151¼	13,831	8¾	211
Total, ...	4,560½	26,704½	564,242	1,187¼	14,329	1,138¼	22,229	4,238	50,304½	10,745	354,480	3,179	270,542	236⅛	4,018½

CLINTON COUNTY.—(Continued.)

TOWNS.	Winter Wheat, Bushels harvested.	Oats, Acres sown.	Oats, Bushels harvested	Rye, Acres sown.	Rye, Bushels harvested.	Barley, Acres sown.	Barley, Bushels harvested.	Buckwheat, Acres sown.	Buckwheat, Bushels harvested.	Corn, Acres planted.	Corn, Bushels harvested.	Potatoes, Acres planted.	Potatoes, Bushels harvested.	Peas, Acres sown.	Peas, Bushels harvested
Au Sable, ...	3½	738	12,885	119	951	9½	216	173½	896	551½	9,214	378	25,185	18¼	134
Beekmantown, .	197	2,043½	45,386	85	998	105¾	1,989	914	7,335	818¾	14,063	847¾	52,827	198¾	1,978
Black Brook, ...	50	488¾	4,609	130	618	6	30	87½	574¾	182¾	2,911	313½	18,875	51½	223¾
Champlain, ...	......	2,020½	48,934	9	83	117¼	2,334	350½	3,814¾	414¼	8,974	253⅛	20,106	235½	3,332½
Chazy, ...	659	1,980¼	44,214½	71⅛	1,027	31⅛	516	501½	5,417¼	839¾	13,710½	511⅞	36,552	374⅞	4,338¼
Clinton, ...	13	369½	3,267	11	59½	46¾	305	137	1,078	83¼	834	195¼	12,865	23¼	199
Dannemora, ...	......	....	....	......	....	......	....	....	....	....	....	......	....	......	....
Ellenburgh, ...	84	568½	6,818¼	18½	207	60¼	599½	188½	1,117¾	138½	2,002½	412½	32,019	68¾	514
Mooers, ...	6	887½	7,748	88½	689½	3¼	21	492	1,752⅛	536¾	5,050¾	399¼	14,668	48⅞	336½
Peru, ...	367	2,220¼	49,293	435	3,184	7½	109	657	4,747	1,194	16,323	820¼	58,058	133	1,509½
Plattsburgh, ...	549	1,209½	23,474½	172½	1,453	37½	605	502½	515½	474	8,480	525½	35,224	110¾	1,535
Saranac, ...	7	1,083	12.447	171¾	1,360	7⅛	42½	234	1,461	269⅛	4,057½	503½	28,271	12⅝	124½
Schuyler's Falls,	203	923	17,004	338½	2,443	7	110	368¼	1,942½	629½	6,947½	713¾	50,842	37	320
Total, ...	2,138½	14,532¼	276,080¼	1,649⅞	13,073	439	6,877	4,606¼	30,651⅝	6,132⅛	92,567¾	5,874¼	385,492	1,313⅛	14,545

COLUMBIA COUNTY.—(Continued.)

TOWNS.	Winter Wheat, Bushels harvested.	Oats, Acres sown.	Oats, Bushels harvested	Rye, Acres sown.	Rye, Bushels harvested.	Barley, Acres sown.	Barley, Bushels harvested.	Buckwheat, Acres sown.	Buckwheat, Bushels harvested.	Corn, Acres planted.	Corn, Bushels harvested.	Potatoes, Acres planted.	Potatoes, Bushels harvested.	Peas, Acres sown.	Peas, Bushels harvested
Ancram, ...	548½	2,704	54,558	2,657	21,750	68	1,196	341¼	4,600	2,022	40,786	225	21,006	12	100
Austerlitz, ...	65	1,897	24,764	1,179	12,756	1	4	693¼	6,441	883	16,093	206⅞	17,066	7¾	109
Canaan, ...	187	1,740	31,126	1,125	12,138	9	87	408	5,220	1,054½	24,025	255	18,790	7½	117
Chatham, ...	619	3,577	54,820	3,393	40,225	20	176	553½	4,914	2,955¼	50,338	291¾	17,706	4	69
Claverack, ...	211	3,625	39,221	4,185	48,838	2	5	567½	2,069½	2,462½	27,221	657	23,680	10	98
Clermont, ...	633	1,206	16,118	1,873	14,234	5	67	241½	750	976¾	5,813½	1,530¾	6,499	7	50
Copake, ...	95	2,443	38,157	3,107	40,679	8	68	640	6,070	1,505	26,925	240	20,075	15	220
Gallatin, ...	216	2,758	26,569	3,074	28,215	16	197	639	3,228	1,875	25,238	200	13,084	21	122
Germantown, ..	401	499	5,486	799	5,335	14½	128	137	220	562	2,070	94	2,517	2	15
Ghent, ...	1,017	3,394	35,010	3,955	49,155	4	60	521	2,486	2,491	33,540	348	13,428	2	10
Greenport, ...	179	830	13,502	901	12,145	7	250	160	441	659	5,615	196	6,177	14	97
Hillsdale, ...	436	2,507	38,522	2,436	25,931	4½	80	796	7,382	1,499	27,859	253	19,353	2	40
Hudson, ...	15	23	550	6½	145	2	12	8	81	21	240	9	232½	½	20
Kinderhook, ...	1,501	2,886	61,505	2,768	32,410	18	203	292	2,331	2,398	35,691	430	20,050	......	....
Livingston, ...	263	2,568	35,151	3,245	48,975	10	190	586	2,089	1,849	11,991	274	9,519	5⅝	22¾
New Lebanon, ..	73	1,848	26,230	720	8,736	22½	655	331	2,994	882	20,853	191	15,868	......	....
Stockport, ...	116	589	4,997	250	2,668	6	58	70	252	267	4,438	132	4,114	4	36
Stuyvesant, ...	1,297	1,266	16,192	916	9,255	21	272	158	840	735	10,290	465	21,236	......	....
Taghkanick, ...	100	2,368	20,556	3,275	31,446	13	93	756	1,926	1,342	14,313	201	9,019	24½	211
Total, ...	7,972½	38,728	543,034	39864½	445,036	251½	3,801	7,899	54,334½	26,439¼	383,339½	6,199⅜	259,419½	138⅞	1,336¾

CORTLAND COUNTY.—(Continued.)

TOWNS.	Winter Wheat, Bushels harvested.	Oats, Acres sown.	Oats, Bushels harvested	Rye, Acres sown.	Rye, Bushels harvested.	Barley, Acres sown.	Barley, Bushels harvested.	Buckwheat, Acres sown.	Buckwheat, Bushels harvested.	Corn, Acres planted.	Corn, Bushels harvested.	Potatoes, Acres planted.	Potatoes, Bushels harvested.	Peas, Acres sown.	Peas, Bushels harvested
Cincinnatus, ...	30	734	14,409	52	538	56½	798	168⅝	1,804¼	323⅞	11,436	75⅛	6,560	17½	222½
Cortlandville, ..	1,107¾	2,264	56,005	83½	1,290	403⅝	8,183	236⅞	2,595½	1,579¾	45,974	248¼	21,375	76¾	1,605
Freetown, ...	16	919½	19,041	19	210	108	2,040	204¼	3,201	265	9,142	87⅜	8,414	16¾	347
Harford, ...	757	886½	19,626	53½	549	54¼	882	171½	1,163½	376¾	9,785	81¼	5,260	17¼	288½
Homer, ...	481	2,090½	48,672	5¼	73	178¾	3,376	186¼	1,883¾	1,003½	31,860	250¾	21,500	79⅜	2 139½
Lapeer, ...	192	923¼	19,478	10	61	45½	930	121⅜	1,176½	207¼	6,428	81¾	5,676	12	208
Marathon, ...	31	801	14,598	27	375	107	1,921	146	1,927½	291¾	8,990	86¼	5,937	6¾	107
Preble, ...	764	1,519½	39,993	1	20	462	10,233	179½	2,281½	708	25,750	104⅝	11,411	54	1,043
Scott, ...	174	789½	16,941	3½	32	365	6,219	78⅝	976½	420	16,654	100	9,841	31½	594
Solon, ...	......	830½	16,637	2½	23	33⅛	445	155⅜	1,406½	312	10,051	115⅛	8,537	25¾	457
Taylor, ...	5	811¾	17,025	11¼	164½	26⅝	371	162½	1,930	302	9,343½	104⅜	7,805	31⅜	401
Truxton, ...	......	1,749¾	38,737	......	....	168¼	3,188½	160⅝	1,998	726⅞	28,475	264⅜	25,177	32	550
Virgil, ...	1,082½	2,660¾	52,936	44½	493	370½	6,792½	530⅜	4,490½	729⅜	19,268	182⅛	12,485	97¾	1,464½
Willett, ...	56	518¼	8,688	38¾	343½	23¾	287	122	1,280½	255½	7,547	76¼	5,411	7	100
Total, ...	4,696¼	17,498¾	382,786	351¾	4,172	2,402⅝	45,665½	2,623⅜	28,115½	7,501⅜	240,703½	1,857⅜	155,389	505¾	9,527

CHENANGO COUNTY.—(Continued.)

TOWNS.	BEANS		TURNIPS.		FLAX.			HEMP.		HOPS.		TOBACCO.		APPLE ORCHARDS.	
	Acres planted.	Bushels harvested.	Acres sown.	Bushels harvested.	Acres sown.	Pounds of lint.	Bushels of seed.	Acres sown.	Tons of hemp.	Acres planted.	Pounds harvested.	Acres planted.	Pounds harvested.	Bushels of apples.	Barrels of cider
Bainbridge,	5⅜	99½	20	1,897	½	666	2½			18¼	15,157			40,714	705
Columbus,	8⅜	176	2¾	850	¼		½			39¼	41,883			25,738	182
Coventry,	4⅛	87	1½	249	½	150	4							31,330	355½
German,	1	11	1½	235	½	333				2	1,836			11,616	57
Greene,	6¾	430	5⅝	1,117	⅜	80	½			9½	7,412			41,268	617½
Guilford,	⅞	67½	1¼	351						29¼	15,213			34,093	498
Lincklaen,	13⅝	164¾	3⅞	604	9⅝	11,000	70½			1	440			13,358	84½
Macdonough,	7¼	107	1½	238	¾	135	4½			2	800			16,153	175
New Berlin,	2⅞	52½	1¾	248	¼	35				12¾	8,731			30,227	581½
North Norwich,	1½	85	1¾	152	¼	25	½			8½	7,500			18,162	348½
Norwich,	2¼	389	1⅜	210						5	2,402	½	200	31,889	792
Otselic,	2¼	33	1	20	13¼	1,750	37			16	6,769			11,116	91
Oxford,		86	3½	818						6½	7,205		50	43,924	549
Pharsalia,	3½	29	3	495	2½	284	15					¼	100	11,714	75
Pitcher,	6¼	154	2	500	⅞	500	4			2	1,968			21,582	214½
Plymouth,	10	138	5	535						3	1,238			27,997	209
Preston,	3	52½	¼	150	1	250	6½							35,255	652½
Sherburne,	20⅝	355			1	351	8			37½	29,859			47,115	921
Smithville,	¼	72½	3⅛	775	¼							⅛	200	32,689	266
Smyrna,	2¾	174	½	288	4½	1,077	50			27½	14,919			27,614	185
Total,	102⅝	2,763¼	61¼	9,732	36⅜	16,636	203½			220	163,332	⅞	550	553,554	7,559½

CLINTON COUNTY.—(Continued.)

TOWNS.	Beans, acres planted.	Beans, bushels harvested.	Turnips, acres sown.	Turnips, bushels harvested.	Flax, acres sown.	Flax, pounds of lint.	Flax, bushels of seed.	Hemp, acres sown.	Hemp, tons of hemp.	Hops, acres planted.	Hops, pounds harvested.	Tobacco, acres planted.	Tobacco, pounds harvested.	Bushels of apples.	Barrels of cider
Au Sable,	70	564½	3	645										944	
Beekmantown,	143¾	1,532½	5½	744	¼		2							15,545	241
Black Brook,	9	68	6	841							5			20	
Champlain,	16⅞	302½	⅞	164	36	7,700	234							8,762	93
Chazy,	77¼	1,090	2⅝	534									20	16,704	301½
Clinton,	2¼	14½	½	11						2	1,009			415	4
Dannemora,															
Ellenburgh,	6½	44¾	5⅝	71										210	
Mooers,	25¾	137¾	9½	188½										2,345	2½
Peru,	77⅞	1,981¼	8⅝	842										11,918½	60½
Plattsburgh,	46⅜	458½	2¼	337½										11,967	80
Saranac,	11⅜	84½	4¼	220										1,442	½
Schuyler's Falls,	110⅜	714½	4⅛	716			½							6,664	68½
Total,	597⅜	6,993¼	52⅝	5,314	36¼	7,700	236½			2	1,014		20	76,936½	852½

COLUMBIA COUNTY.—(Continued.)

TOWNS.	Beans, acres planted.	Beans, bushels harvested.	Turnips, acres sown.	Turnips, bushels harvested.	Flax, acres sown.	Flax, pounds of lint.	Flax, bushels of seed.	Hemp, acres sown.	Hemp, tons of hemp.	Hops, acres planted.	Hops, pounds harvested.	Tobacco, acres planted.	Tobacco, pounds harvested.	Bushels of apples.	Barrels of cider
Ancram,	4	34	3	450										14,580	536
Austerlitz,	4½	60	1½	187	¼	50	3						156	12,526	422
Canaan,	9¾	86	11½	325½										14,702	403
Chatham,	7½	67	6¼	372										17,532	1,180
Claverack,	16	87	1	351		25	1½							18,581	1,010
Clermont,	1⅝	8	2	140	2	265	14¼							6,508	340
Copake,		14	5	200										11,671	782
Gallatin,	1	19	4	414	11½	538	20						12	7,662	420
Germantown,														3,959	124
Ghent,	5	26	1	100										7,914	365
Greenport,		3	4¾	1,262										9,493	409
Hillsdale,	5½	45	4¾	335	1¼									26,585	995
Hudson,	3	33	1½	150										270	3
Kinderhook,														7,876	375
Livingston,	¼	3	3½	33	¼	100	2					⅜	250	9,440	503
New Lebanon,	8⅞	212	12¾	1,751										22,436	941
Stockport,	1	2	¼	25										5,170	84
Stuyvesant,	1	25												5,689	222
Taghkanick,	¼	15	4¼	450	3¾	150	14							7,748	336
Total,	69¼	739	67	6,545½	19	1,128	54¾					⅜	418	210,342	9,480

CORTLAND COUNTY.—(Continued.)

TOWNS.	Beans, acres planted.	Beans, bushels harvested.	Turnips, acres sown.	Turnips, bushels harvested.	Flax, acres sown.	Flax, pounds of lint.	Flax, bushels of seed.	Hemp, acres sown.	Hemp, tons of hemp.	Hops, acres planted.	Hops, pounds harvested.	Tobacco, acres planted.	Tobacco, pounds harvested.	Bushels of apples.	Barrels of cider
Cincinnatus,	2	39	⅛	120										14,015	91½
Cortlandville,	15	321	17⅝	3,916	1½	6,250	15			3				54,928	608
Freetown,	1	13	¾	190	⅝	157	7			2	1,100			13,850	40
Harford,	3¾	73½	2	74										10,295	120
Homer,	6½	178¾	9¾	2,661	10	4,000	73			2				55,052	521½
Lapeer,	1½	27	3⅝	490	¼									8,671	85
Marathon,	1⅜	72½	1⅝	367	10	50	85							17,627	62
Preble,	1½	82	⅛	49										24 840	297
Scott,	28¼	382	3½	1,080	201½	45,750	1,917							18,020	205
Solon,	10⅜	143	6⅜	603	¼	45	3						40	21,788	108½
Taylor,	9	112	3⅜	290	2½	615	22			1	933			13,517	75½
Truxton,	7¾	159½	6¾	452	4¾	808	1				4			60,686	1,038
Virgil,	7½	95	4⅜	752	6¼	594	50¾			3½				30,474	404
Willet,	⅝	28	3⅝	680										8,212	82
Total,	96⅝	1,726¼	63⅞	11,724	237⅝	58,269	2,173¾			11½	2,037		40	351,075	3,738

CHENANGO COUNTY.—(Continued.)

TOWNS.	MARKET GARDENS. Acres cultivated.	MARKET GARDENS. Value of products.	Pounds of maple sugar made.	Gallons of maple molasses made.	Gallons of wine made.	Pounds of honey collected.	Pounds of wax collected.	SILK. Pounds of cocoons.	NEAT CATTLE. Under one year old.	NEAT CATTLE. Over one y'r, exclusive of working oxen & cows.	NEAT CATTLE. Working oxen.	NEAT CATTLE. Cows.	Number of cattle killed for beef.	Pounds of butter.	Pounds of cheese.
Bainbridge,	...	...	13,510	82	21	6,586	350	...	919	1,717	510	2,226	195	225,645	14,000
Columbus,	...	...	9,551	118	...	1,910	127	...	293	711	102	1,807	90	107,410	283,019
Coventry,	...	...	14,944	94	...	1,382	84	...	672	878	221	2,140	96	250,270	6,510
German,	...	...	18,365	516½	...	1,060	115	...	281	432	113	1,160	45	123,600	700
Greene,	...	...	6,075	94	3	3,590	290½	...	960	1,479	383	3,603	223	451,433	17,758
Guilford,	...	...	41,225	343	...	3,853	187½	...	955	983	268	2,721	170	344,045	29,226
Lincklaen,	...	...	14,577	104	...	2,762	173½	...	219	468	115	981	60	95,785	19,680
Macdonough,	...	...	16,695	152	...	1,090	157½	...	380	491	138	1,535	96	164,985	1,805
New Berlin,	...	...	6,623	130	...	1,174	102	...	412	803	148	2,439	120	196,839	248,173
North Norwich,	1	57	460	15	5	1,790	158	...	257	623	105	1,061	70	136,381	99,260
Norwich,	...	...	1,264	7	...	780	51	...	515	1,225	193	2,220	147	198,380	107,328
Otselic,	...	...	12,621	50	...	1,672	93	...	336	753	189	1,433	57	141,505	57,300
Oxford,	...	...	12,831	144	...	2,374	122	...	840	1,102	274	1,714	124	289,502	17,100
Pharsalia,	...	...	10,464	17	...	2,492	175	...	263	378	171	1,318	54	114,648	51,450
Pitcher,	...	...	26,046	46	...	2,687	217	...	308	598	116	1,259	57	144,200	13,797
Plymouth,	...	...	17,755	103	...	1,519	105	...	404	833	149	1,531	72	155,663	76,504
Preston,	...	...	10,450	59	...	2,200	221	...	370	757	160	1,497	116	176,953	23,380
Sherburne,	...	...	10,152	377½	...	3,351	213	...	543	1,193	120	2,179	163	208,415	92,708
Smithville,	...	...	19,685	271	...	3,092	243	...	735	930	217	2,620	119	319,695	13,660
Smyrna,	...	...	9,235	112	3	3,338	266	...	500	1,049	195	1,495	102	145,210	39,186
Total,	1	57	272,528	2,835	32	48,702	3,451	...	10,162	17,403	3,887	36,939	2,176	3,990,564	1,212,544

CLINTON COUNTY.—(Continued.)

TOWNS.	Acres cultivated.	Value of products.	Pounds of maple sugar made.	Gallons of maple molasses made.	Gallons of wine made.	Pounds of honey collected.	Pounds of wax collected.	Pounds of cocoons.	Under one year old.	Over one y'r.	Working oxen.	Cows.	Number of cattle killed for beef.	Pounds of butter.	Pounds of cheese.
Au Sable,	2¾	110	...	...	...	2,375	129	...	239	505	70	716	189	38,245	6,475
Beekmantown,	...	...	3,290	78	29	7,548	376	...	771	1,394	100	1,821	512	172,695	17,823
Black Brook,	...	...	250	...	...	700	41	...	150	313	90	554	151	30,091½	600
Champlain,	...	...	7,609	150	...	2,368	91	...	458	910	59	1,096	150	84,210	10,690
Chazy,	...	150	16,351	211	4	7,485	330½	...	728	1,278	193	1,666	151	101,239	14,500
Clinton,	⅛	9	3,515	10	...	324	25	...	94	190	71	371	68	23,560	4,000
Dannemora,	...	...	...	...	...	...	...	...	...	...	...	...	...	...	...
Ellenburgh,	...	...	12,386	265½	...	1,675	168½	...	105	230	104	447	117	39,505	755
Mooers,	...	...	5,454	68	...	4,793	266	...	329	608	320	818	227	81,681	7,505
Peru,	...	139	2,332	24	...	11,122	397½	...	593	1,176	173	1,395	214	111,404	15,696
Plattsburgh,	...	...	1,100	13	...	4,308	151	...	428	758	73	1,016	245	76,350	12,357
Saranac,	...	...	2,245	83	...	5,390	139	...	248	411	163	660	256	57,661	710
Schuyler's Falls,	...	...	1,745	37	14	3,371	124	...	268	603	68	724	105	74,790	14,795
Total,	2⅞	408	56,277	939½	47	51,459	2,238½	...	4,411	8,376	1,484	11,284	2,385	891,431½	105,906

COLUMBIA COUNTY.—(Continued.)

TOWNS.	Acres cultivated.	Value of products.	Pounds of maple sugar made.	Gallons of maple molasses made.	Gallons of wine made.	Pounds of honey collected.	Pounds of wax collected.	Pounds of cocoons.	Under one year old.	Over one y'r.	Working oxen.	Cows.	Number of cattle killed for beef.	Pounds of butter.	Pounds of cheese.
Ancram,	...	...	...	...	...	2,240	142	...	318	564	386	852	91	91,035	300
Austerlitz,	...	9	138	62	362	1,165	34	...	213	383	204	827	135	98,665	8,300
Canaan,	8	980	607	60	...	2,776	101	...	188	319	183	678	107	75,080	12,385
Chatham,	...	...	...	...	213	2,150	83	...	327	572	439	1,452	178	130,875	10,284
Claverack,	27⅛	1,841	1	...	...	1,047	72	...	286	392	286	1,113	160	107,575	1,168
Clermont,	...	...	153	...	10	677	124	...	88	138	63	595	63	42,045	...
Copake,	...	...	70	6	2	1,690	72	...	265	444	272	804	105	72,295	1,220
Gallatin,	5	163	987	37	26	3,019	156	...	335	439	261	837	106	69,075	750
Germantown,	...	...	...	...	24	...	...	...	50	79	60	435	131	33,068	...
Ghent,	...	...	88	12	14	6,927	153	...	306	411	245	981	128	104,023	100
Greenport,	30½	1,500	...	...	22	90	...	...	121	168	77	498	75	45,088	250
Hillsdale,	...	...	60	8	...	1,435	51	...	260	328	278	893	190	98,767	5,061
Hudson,	13	275	...	...	...	...	...	...	...	2	5	118	...	1,700	...
Kinderhook,	...	...	...	...	10	417	16	...	172	277	193	639	92	64,640	626
Livingston,	3	200	44	...	...	1,474	165	...	205	257	135	995	111	90,246	144
New Lebanon,	...	...	8	50	32	1,677	74	...	227	380	226	925	417	84,022	25,794
Stockport,	10	570	...	...	...	425	23	...	82	84	37	327	79	26,173	...
Stuyvesant,	...	...	56	1	...	505	35	4	113	113	121	650	58	45,468	255
Taghkanick,	2	200	567	7	10	3,904	165	...	261	308	230	881	99	67,588	530
Total,	98⅝	5,738	2,779	243	725	31,618	1,466	4	3,817	5,658	3,701	14,500	2,325	1,347,428	67,167

CORTLAND COUNTY.—(Continued.)

TOWNS.	Acres cultivated.	Value of products.	Pounds of maple sugar made.	Gallons of maple molasses made.	Gallons of wine made.	Pounds of honey collected.	Pounds of wax collected.	Pounds of cocoons.	Under one year old.	Over one y'r.	Working oxen.	Cows.	Number of cattle killed for beef.	Pounds of butter.	Pounds of cheese.
Cincinnatus,	...	...	19,165	235	...	825	25	...	363	519	96	1,154	263	118,760	3,070
Cortlandville,	1⅜	190	18,404	551	75	5,767	351	...	625	850	173	2,833	363	319,229	28,021
Freetown,	...	...	17,523	94	...	2,495	200	...	322	498	60	1,233	98	108,690	71,580
Harford,	...	...	2,598	27	...	1,325	54	...	162	279	78	628	36	72,305	16,220
Homer,	...	...	15,593	303½	...	5,083	224½	...	588	1,184	152	2,390	235	279,625	28,622
Lapeer,	...	...	9,546	107	...	1,957	145	...	288	488	108	802	41	76,970	10,520
Marathon,	...	...	6,892	135	...	2,081	145	...	274	508	80	1,068	147	135,009	8,101
Preble,	...	...	5,640	93	...	3,540	202	...	305	571	44	1,032	97	141,030	4,540
Scott,	1½	207	8,120	74	...	3,097	168	...	244	447	84	755	87	91,825	7,604
Solon,	...	...	50,630	402	...	6,000	439	...	255	453	108	1,170	64	140,975	300
Taylor,	...	...	39,385	245	...	4,217	207½	...	347	550	156	1,133	49	151,885	5,835
Truxton,	...	...	44,131	177	6	9,423	809	...	722	1,392	292	4,724	197	416,246	517,281
Virgil,	...	...	13,605	291	...	8,466	512½	...	552	776	121	1,909	149	243,423	4,390
Willett,	...	...	7,745	35	...	1,872	137	...	257	475	157	837	34	83,285	2,595
Total,	2⅞	397	258,977	2,769½	81	56,148	3,619½	...	5,304	8,990	1,709	21,668	1,860	2,379,257	708,679

CHENANGO COUNTY.—(CONTINUED.)

TOWNS.	Gallons of milk sold.	Horses.	Mules.	SWINE. Under 6 months.	SWINE. Over 6 months.	SHEEP. Number of sheep.	SHEEP. Number of fleeces.	SHEEP. Pounds of wool.	POULTRY. Value of poultry sold.	POULTRY. Value of eggs sold.	DOMESTIC MANUFACTURES. Yards of fulled cloth made.	DOMESTIC MANUFACTURES. Yards of flannel made.	DOMESTIC MANUFACTURES. Yards of linen made.	DOMESTIC MANUFACTURES. Yards of cotton and mixed cloths.
Bainbridge,	....	753	....	660	691	6, 438	4, 647	14, 546	978	1, 841	3, 560	1, 646	526	377
Columbus,	....	464	....	443	355	2, 835	2, 455	8, 255	1, 006	1, 255	122	317	605	316
Coventry,	....	534	....	487	534	2, 750	1, 984	6, 926½	784	1, 510	344	747	172	80
German,	....	290	....	141	220	964	859	2, 094	440	432	447	782	559	570
Greene,	862	848	....	781	859	4, 090	2, 923	8, 846¾	714	853	3, 673½	1, 473	113	271
Guilford,	....	697	....	636	660	3, 756	3, 196	10, 616	718	661	273	450	226	160
Lincklaen,	....	376	....	228	258	2, 297	2, 171	7, 534¾	438	221	288½	446	546	302
Macdonough,	....	374	....	263	272	2, 143	1, 697	5, 317	337	655	611¼	1, 013¾	748½	1, 075
New Berlin,	....	645	....	611	436	2, 697	2, 992	9, 669	764	797	461	751	....	86
North Norwich,	60	372	....	450	277	3, 335	2, 884	9, 098	501	680	100	193	42	12
Norwich,	....	632	7	425	578	7, 287	4, 159	14, 319½	6, 932	4, 432	499	601¾	....	88
Otselic,	....	526	....	316	360	2, 562	2, 748	9, 124	599	741	241	377	540	614
Oxford,	1, 200	735	....	765	685	5, 835	3, 452	11, 677	770	738	799	1, 243	120	135
Philadelphia,	....	330	....	265	241	1, 925	1, 625	5, 522	347	442	456	561	479	903
Pitcher,	....	445	....	297	288	4, 487	3, 462	12, 724	570	650	166½	593	281	372
Plymouth,	....	553	....	272	371	4, 413	3, 614	12, 878	600	534	346	505	91	110
Preston,	....	349	....	335	290	6, 793	4, 376	14, 916½	761	559	494¼	561	139	281
Sherburne,	....	841	....	593	596	11, 726	8, 483	28, 833½	1, 559	2, 974	165	179	217	133
Smithville,	....	496	3	604	531	2, 290	2, 146	7, 619¼	623	427	1, 171	1, 585½	94	537
Smyrna,	....	711	....	522	496	7, 300	6, 176	18, 975½	628	1, 379	295½	463	313	1, 417
Total,	2, 122	10, 971	10	9, 094	8, 998	85, 923	66, 049	220, 092¼	20, 069	21, 781	14, 513½	14, 488	5, 811½	7, 839

CLINTON COUNTY.—(CONTINUED.)

TOWNS.	Gallons of milk sold.	Horses.	Mules.	SWINE. Under 6 months.	SWINE. Over 6 months.	SHEEP. Number of sheep.	SHEEP. Number of fleeces.	SHEEP. Pounds of wool.	POULTRY. Value of poultry sold.	POULTRY. Value of eggs sold.	DOMESTIC MANUFACTURES. Yards of fulled cloth made.	DOMESTIC MANUFACTURES. Yards of flannel made.	DOMESTIC MANUFACTURES. Yards of linen made.	DOMESTIC MANUFACTURES. Yards of cotton and mixed cloths.
Au Sable,	300	633	2	175	380	2, 139	1, 605	5, 614	216	314	85	115	....	30
Beekmantown,	1, 000	1, 085	....	469	648	6, 491	4, 000	14, 201	2, 043	2, 084	665	2, 218	56	12
Black Brook,	100	371	25	112	258	486	402	1, 161	8	47	....	....	....	....
Champlain,	2, 000	919	....	260	448	4, 037	3, 664	12, 525¼	473	852	....	....	....	....
Chazy,	....	1, 233	....	370	803	8, 776	5, 924	20, 384½	555	1, 302	204	521½	10	220
Clinton,	....	192	....	89	183	562	423	1, 274	22	3, 164	416	272	....	526
Dannemora,	....	....	....	....	....	....	....	....	....	....	....	....	....	....
Ellenburgh,	....	350	....	69	208	959	888	2, 831½	209	386	....	....	....	....
Mooers,	....	602	....	212	257	1, 581	1, 233	4, 209	266	281	354½	574¾	6	438
Peru,	....	1, 049	....	383	706	5, 528	4, 708	15, 490	984	1, 190	326	1, 056	35	285½
Plattsburgh,	2	1, 005	7	425	431	3, 794	2, 918	10, 342½	304	704	139	180	....	190½
Saranac,	....	511	....	116	334	1, 067	744	2, 579½	40	130	90	145	9	15
Schuylers Falls,	....	494	2	195	337	2, 931	1, 908	6, 521	421	990	290½	614	25	455½
Total,	3, 402	8, 444	36	2, 875	4, 993	38, 351	28, 417	97, 133¼	5, 541	11, 444	2, 570	5, 696¼	141	2, 172½

COLUMBIA COUNTY.—(CONTINUED.)

TOWNS.	Gallons of milk sold.	Horses.	Mules.	SWINE. Under 6 months.	SWINE. Over 6 months.	SHEEP. Number of sheep.	SHEEP. Number of fleeces.	SHEEP. Pounds of wool.	POULTRY. Value of poultry sold.	POULTRY. Value of eggs sold.	DOMESTIC MANUFACTURES. Yards of fulled cloth made.	DOMESTIC MANUFACTURES. Yards of flannel made.	DOMESTIC MANUFACTURES. Yards of linen made.	DOMESTIC MANUFACTURES. Yards of cotton and mixed cloths.
Ancram,	120, 000	510	....	2, 326	1, 509	11, 381	7, 655	24, 959	1, 108	3. 239	20	118	92	....
Austerlitz,	50	514	2	823	370	8, 485	7, 373	24, 311	2, 048	2, 649	18	....	103	30
Canaan,	....	454	....	726	287	8, 711	7, 847	26, 952	1, 400	2, 500	32	629	65	291
Chatham,	7, 522	897	2	2, 163	761	6, 579	6, 183	18, 292	3, 412	4, 016	....	271	15	35
Claverack,	21, 598	841	....	2, 059	829	4, 573	3, 577	10, 554	2, 835	4, 055	168	167	20	167
Clermont,	11, 500	378	....	928	427	2, 539	1, 631	5, 541	2, 190	2, 696	115	283	40	49
Copake,	....	436	....	2, 127	710	7, 211	10, 182	37, 466	1, 328	1, 576	158	118	29	....
Gallatin,	....	520	....	1, 693	837	5, 135	5, 852	18, 148	1, 007	1, 015	398	363	315	132
Germantown,	27, 859	220	....	423	300	243	243	756	503	605	....	....	....	....
Ghent,	24, 267	806	....	1, 640	632	4, 469	4, 107	14, 244	2, 460	2, 963	25	45	....	35
Greenport,	8, 821	346	....	552	373	740	558	1, 743	1, 360	1, 650	8	60	....	....
Hillsdale,	5, 000	538	....	1, 550	636	5, 900	4, 883	16, 278	2, 025	2, 204	60	140	30	6
Hudson,	....	248	....	23	489	....	....	....	25	10	....	....	....	....
Kinderhook,	16, 675	542	2	1, 178	461	3, 865	3, 811	12, 636	1, 422	1, 509	13	....	....	....
Livingston,	27, 227	611	200	1, 283	576	3, 954	2, 907	10, 613	1, 479	3, 168	....	82	37	20
New Lebanon,	....	448	....	657	315	9, 230	9, 817	30, 884	1, 757	2, 171	200	338	553	1, 925
Stockport,	77, 747	133	4	132	118	87	101	359	352	114	....	....	....	....
Stuyvesant,	143, 937	180	....	334	198	1, 442	1, 179	3, 595	466	1, 313	9	30	....	20
Taghkanck,	....	481	1	1, 577	546	3, 005	3, 158	10, 037	1, 624	3, 378	70	351	93	184
Total,	492, 203	9, 103	211	22, 194	10, 374	87, 549	81, 064	267, 368	29, 701	43, 831	1, 294	2, 995	1, 392	2, 894

CORTLAND COUNTY.—(CONTINUED.)

TOWNS.	Gallons of milk sold.	Horses.	Mules.	SWINE. Under 6 months.	SWINE. Over 6 months.	SHEEP. Number of sheep.	SHEEP. Number of fleeces.	SHEEP. Pounds of wool.	POULTRY. Value of poultry sold.	POULTRY. Value of eggs sold.	DOMESTIC MANUFACTURES. Yards of fulled cloth made.	DOMESTIC MANUFACTURES. Yards of flannel made.	DOMESTIC MANUFACTURES. Yards of linen made.	DOMESTIC MANUFACTURES. Yards of cotton and mixed cloths.
Cincinnatus,	....	369	....	266	221	2, 221	1, 883	6, 330	369	378	245	554	14	46
Cortlandville,	9, 440	1, 078	14	938	1, 037	4, 918	3, 409	12, 033	1, 667	2, 727	182¾	746½	165	253
Freetown,	....	363	....	291	235	2, 052	2, 048	6, 466	420	1, 118	307	226	108	330
Harford,	....	227	....	208	172	1, 961	1, 986	6, 473	290	538	242	341½	40	377
Homer,	....	930	....	965	886	3, 438	3, 787	13, 903¼	1, 162	1, 774	83	506	96	218
Lapeer,	....	340	5	246	204	1, 696	1, 540	5, 068¼	348	471	358	787	312	207
Marathon,	723	338	....	328	245	3, 260	3, 472	12, 507	586	752	398	1, 194	276	917
Preble,	....	478	....	519	447	2, 301	1, 741	6, 445	396	1, 621	10	242	38	39
Scott,	2, 920	390	....	193	321	2, 058	2, 048	7, 567	493	838	220	252	666	89
Solon,	....	446	....	286	351	1, 826	1, 407	4, 729½	369	473	278½	425	256	170½
Taylor,	....	328	4	222	280	2, 225	1, 863	6, 492	376	648	373½	764	292	375
Truxton,	50	1, 044	0	768	1, 187	5, 002	4, 962	17, 832	641	1, 556	195	541	367	1, 044½
Virgil,	....	813	1	520	529	6, 800	2, 955	10, 446½	000	3, 188	570¼	1, 395	1, 014	770½
Willett,	....	266	....	250	187	1, 563	1, 369	4, 501	286	400	469	829	160	425
Total,	13, 133	7, 410	27	6, 000	6, 302	41, 321	34, 470	120, 793½	8, 402	16, 482	3, 932	8, 803	3, 804	5, 261½

DELAWARE COUNTY.

TOWNS.	ACRES.		CASH VALUE.			Acres plowed the year previous.	Acres in fallow the year previous.	Acres in pasture the year previous.	MEADOW.			SPRING WHEAT.		WINTER WHEAT.
	Improved.	Unimproved.	Of farm.	Of stock.	Of tools and implements				Acres.	Tons of hay.	Bushels of grass seed.	Acres sown.	Bushels harvested.	Acres sown.
Andes, ...	22, 853	21, 629	$529, 460	$121, 736	$26, 680	3, 406	594	11, 981	7, 883	6, 707	40½	13	105	.....
Bovina, ...	16, 682½	8, 217	440, 699	90, 712	19, 712	2, 010¼	445	8, 943	4, 939	4, 924	26	8¾	47	.....
Colchester, ...	14, 189½	72, 626	465, 203	88, 143	20, 682	2, 600	327½	4, 418	5, 976½	4, 805½	95½	13	90	13
Davenport, ...	19, 220½	14, 844	529, 455	113, 319	25, 045	3, 403	649½	8, 837	5, 865	4, 452	87¾	96½	692	6
Delhi, ...	22, 020¼	16, 273¾	604, 600	147, 841	31, 737	3, 162	1, 034¾	9, 608¾	6, 711	6, 002	18¾	62¼	249½	34½
Franklin, ...	34, 514	14, 499	1, 096, 776	210, 137	54, 324	5, 194½	719½	15, 380¼	10, 690½	9, 476¾	246¼	170¾	1, 327	28¾
Hamden, ...	17, 310	13, 783	486, 323	109, 647	23, 733	3, 058½	732½	9, 128	5, 777	4, 898	124½	39¾	245½	13
Hancock, ...	6, 329	95, 648	384, 210	43, 428	8, 231	838	181½	1, 559½	2, 323½	1, 946	4	......	......	4½
Harpersfield, ...	16, 002½	6, 711	629, 337	127, 919	32, 206	2, 785	171	8, 965	6, 367½	5, 455½	148½	67½	529	21
Kortright, ...	24, 307½	9, 339½	764, 510	170, 212	32, 305	4, 463	447½	14, 297	7, 781½	6, 629	100½	192¾	1, 339½	35
Masonville, ...	13, 519¾	17, 442¾	440, 731	104, 364	19, 782	2, 848½	660½	7, 765¾	5, 250¾	4, 531¼	169¾	49	418½	2
Meredith, ...	21, 194	10, 840¼	554, 555	110, 956	20, 587	3, 184½	284	10, 478½	6, 889½	4, 434½	99½	69½	488½	2½
Middletown, ...	26, 213¾	24, 381½	722, 427	158, 986	32, 542	5, 001	768	11, 507	8, 293½	7, 069	58	12	107	5
Roxbury, ...	34, 635¼	15, 043½	907, 365	189, 728	27, 371	4, 053½	823	18, 644	10, 115½	9, 078	38	132	798	6
Sidney, ...	19, 051	11, 478	641, 955	125, 111	25, 919	3, 031	618½	8, 355	6, 576¾	5, 342½	168¾	122	931¾	69½
Stamford, ...	19, 055¼	9, 522	611, 770	111, 509	30, 613	3, 092	229	7, 836	6, 676	5, 103½	125¼	127¾	740	42¼
Tompkins, ...	18, 721½	40, 314½	867, 541	143, 230	29, 309	3, 466	689½	8, 073½	7, 622½	6, 851	73½	20	153	19¾
Walton, ...	18, 581	35, 859½	568, 339	121, 632	24, 555	2, 612½	702¼	8, 764½	6, 763¼	6, 190¾	116¾	36½	277½	11
Total, ...	364, 400¼	438, 452¼	11, 245, 256	2, 288, 610	485, 333	58, 209¼	10, 077½	174, 541¾	122, 502¼	103, 896¼	1, 741¾	1, 233	8, 538¾	314

DUTCHESS COUNTY.

TOWNS.	Improved.	Unimproved.	Of farm.	Of stock.	Of tools and implements	Acres plowed the year previous.	Acres in fallow the year previous.	Acres in pasture the year previous.	Meadow acres.	Tons of hay.	Bushels of grass seed.	Spring wheat acres sown.	Bushels harvested.	Winter wheat acres sown.
Amenia, ...	17, 709	6, 859	1, 281, 041	143, 438	28, 770	2, 805	58	12, 669	4, 543	5, 109	51	......	......	387
Beekman, ...	13, 003	4, 227	905, 120	105, 794	21, 049	2, 722	121	5, 505	3, 153	3, 422	19½	......	......	697
Clinton, ...	19, 635	4, 429	1, 244, 340	124, 505	44, 549	5, 258	70	7, 573	3, 355	3, 324	18	1	......	542
Dover, ...	17, 482	9, 187	933, 325	124, 820	22, 312	2, 168	26	10, 232	4, 364	4, 464	9	......	......	183
East Fishkill, ...	22, 511	7, 455	1, 537, 535	173, 394	47, 894	4, 092	182	9, 064	5, 488	5, 770	98	......	......	1, 162
Fishkill, ...	25, 672	4, 210	2, 630, 280	233, 655	56, 376	6, 326	1, 112	8, 828	6, 309	7, 003	35	......	......	1, 772
Hyde Park, ...	17, 090	5, 410	2, 127, 734	116, 466	47, 609	4, 543	836	6, 940	3, 959	3, 867	......	12	200	518
La Grange, ...	22, 528½	3, 153	1, 393, 604	145, 903	46, 239	5, 560	134	9, 795	4, 020	4, 242	46	......	......	831
Milan, ...	18, 370½	5, 049	883, 430	121, 847	30, 088	5, 515½	105	7. 446½	3, 165	3, 049	94	2	4	305½
North East, ...	18, 056¼	6, 193½	1, 166, 655	146, 183	32, 392	3, 740¾	1, 123	8, 194¾	4, 225½	3, 475	25	......	......	25½
Pauling, ...	19, 076⅝	9, 773¾	1, 130, 735	122, 030	22, 970	1, 803½	....	11, 046¾	4, 857¾	5, 210	......	......	......	92
Pine Plains, ...	14, 235	3, 941	911, 595	115, 150	22, 700	3, 040	1, 435	4, 971	2, 762	2, 369	......	2	3	228½
Pleasant Valley, .	17, 454½	2, 594	1, 224, 759	119, 937	47, 444	4, 884	77	6, 238	3, 913	3, 720½	65¾	......	......	482
Poughkeepsie, ...	15, 810¾	5, 118	1, 692, 408	192, 245	50, 405	3, 754½	....	3, 982	3, 659½	3, 610	......	......	......	1, 171½
Po'keepsie City, .	1, 176¾	35	293, 800	66, 181	3, 531	284	66½	314	446½	354	5½	6	43	54½
Redhook, ...	19, 423	2, 725	2, 167, 317	137, 562	33, 918	4, 999	214	4, 303	4, 897⅛	5, 729	40	......	......	735¾
Rhinebeck, ...	17, 387¼	4, 379	1, 733, 720	140, 427	36, 598	4, 723	153	5, 267	5, 171	5, 098½	42¾	......	......	875½
Stanford, ...	26, 067	5, 514	1, 619, 268	211, 956	41, 867	6, 081	202	11, 145	5, 071	4, 256	52	......	......	634
Union Vale, ...	12, 000½	2, 875½	584, 385	77, 786	17, 508	2, 922	38	5, 650¼	2, 925½	3, 146½	96	......	......	194
Washington, ...	31, 671	4, 977	2, 001, 994	261, 011	50, 136	7, 012	13	17, 422	6, 816	6, 660	......	......	......	497
Total, ...	366, 359⅝	98, 104¾	27, 463, 045	2, 880, 290	704, 355	82, 233¼	5, 965½	156, 586¼	83, 100⅞	83, 878½	697½	23	250	11614¾

ERIE COUNTY.

TOWNS.	Improved.	Unimproved.	Of farm.	Of stock.	Of tools and implements	Acres plowed the year previous.	Acres in fallow the year previous.	Acres in pasture the year previous.	Meadow acres.	Tons of hay.	Bushels of grass seed.	Spring wheat acres sown.	Bushels harvested.	Winter wheat acres sown.
Alden, ...	11, 721	8, 960	819, 320	84, 487	25, 094	3, 512	138	4, 540	3, 306	3, 547	114	94	933	514
Amherst, ...	17, 298½	12, 003	1, 432, 604	134, 273	31, 654	4, 843¾	1, 629½	2, 292	3, 129½	3, 173	89¼	16	80	2, 353¾
Aurora, ...	19, 363¾	13, 934¾	1, 186, 321	132, 794	38, 901	4, 518½	119¾	7, 623¼	6, 018½	6, 388½	217½	204¾	2, 779	360
Boston, ...	13, 604¼	6, 153	539, 875	77, 530	19, 299	2, 944½	76	5, 469	4, 155½	4, 029½	148½	93	1, 081½	166½
Brandt, ...	7, 666¾	6, 513⅝	434, 510	55, 913	13, 997	1, 854	12½	3, 388	2, 016¾	2, 020¾	33¾	32½	243	172¾
Buffalo, ...	10, 612½	2, 336¼	2, 589, 540	296, 702	31, 179	3, 129¾	1, 930	3, 032	2, 835	4, 184	38	25½	623	421½
Chictawauga, ...	9, 280½	6, 405½	1, 192, 500	66, 442	25, 516	2, 761	345⅞	2, 111½	2, 761	3, 272½	30½	39¾	462	607
Clarence, ...	17, 770	14, 637	1, 461, 090	138, 023	48, 852	4, 346	2, 541	2, 037	2, 827	2, 606	182	695	8, 044	3, 131
Colden, ...	9, 716	12, 702	364, 241	58, 288	16, 276	1, 585	272	3, 302½	2, 708	2, 697	103½	57½	531	83¼
Collins, ...	18, 174	11, 692½	813, 605	140, 094	28, 145	2, 206	140	9, 174¼	5, 227½	5, 905	94	162¼	1, 930	361¼
Concord, ...	23, 950¼	17, 080	1, 034, 619	152, 731	39, 756	5, 313½	138	11, 096½	6, 152½	5, 724½	201¾	1, 093¾	7, 962	170¼
East Hamburgh, .	15, 184¼	8, 170	1, 252, 011	113, 558	44, 609	3, 987¼	59½	5, 203¼	5, 790¼	5, 623½	143¾	83¼	902½	270½
Eden, ...	15, 261¼	7, 814	751, 484	89, 650	35, 351	4, 024½	103	4, 684	4, 374½	4, 312½	312	292	2, 836	353¼
Evans, ...	14, 400¼	10, 977	822, 777	115, 463	35, 445	2, 923¼	184	5, 961½	4, 911	5, 333¾	191½	319¼	3, 587½	149
Grand Island, ...	4, 017	13, 684	374, 345	35, 983	9, 740	741	257½	1, 326	1, 038¼	1, 002	123	11½	127	262
Hamburgh, ...	14, 468¾	8, 183	1, 215, 022	103, 223	34, 659	3, 411	215½	3, 573½	5, 542¼	6, 208	77	204½	2, 206½	172¼
Holland, ...	12, 035¼	9, 369	424, 961	89, 487	20, 399	2, 598	33½	5, 447	3, 423	3, 041	101½	104½	1, 273	63¼
Lancaster, ...	14, 660½	16, 303½	1, 561, 960	115, 481	55, 546	5, 490	633	2, 647½	3, 783	4, 439	159	134¼	1, 815	1, 143¼
Marilla, ...	7, 037½	652	476, 396	58, 792	18, 651	1, 459¾	410½	2, 137	1, 672¾	1, 821¾	79	37½	484½	530¾
Newstead, ...	19, 491	11, 886	1, 461, 374	164, 507	48, 702	4, 719½	2, 923	3, 461	3, 117	3, 322	148	23½	238	3, 451
North Collins, ...	18, 691½	8, 353½	851, 925	158, 700	36, 915	2, 662	133½	7, 788¾	5, 673½	6, 410	491½	75½	577	98
Sardinia, ...	16, 032¼	13, 994	629, 294	106, 740	26, 859	3, 807	154	7, 269	4, 303	3, 401	109	412¼	3, 893½	97
Tonawanda, ...	8, 699½	3, 772½	875, 648	63, 063	17, 679	2, 154½	776¼	1, 348	2, 280½	2, 415	198	15½	266	1, 259½
Wales, ...	14, 538¾	7, 025	619, 623	110, 640	21, 668	3, 382	64	7, 959¾	4, 055¼	4, 336	279¾	126¼	1, 402	397¼
West Seneca, ...	6, 632	11, 743¾	1, 294, 363	55, 480	20, 167	1, 867	43	1, 941½	1, 952	2, 798	54½	152	2, 636	319½
Total, ...	340, 307¼	253, 344⅝	24, 479, 408	2, 718, 053	745, 059	80, 240¾	13, 332⅞	114, 813¾	93, 053½	98, 011¼	3, 720¼	4, 505¾	46913	16907¾

ESSEX COUNTY.

TOWNS.	Improved.	Unimproved.	Of farm.	Of stock.	Of tools and implements	Acres plowed the year previous.	Acres in fallow the year previous.	Acres in pasture the year previous.	Meadow acres.	Tons of hay.	Bushels of grass seed.	Spring wheat acres sown.	Bushels harvested.	Winter wheat acres sown.
Chesterfield, ...	15, 309	21, 897	433, 940	77, 448	15, 641	3, 869	87	7, 485	4, 198	3, 591	30	486½	4, 843	......
Crown Point, ...	17, 489⅛	9, 961	495, 255	119, 831	11, 733	3, 238	....	9, 105	5, 226	3, 991½	104	463¾	5, 271	182
Elizabethtown, ..	9, 487¼	34, 094	228, 580	50, 788	10, 312	1, 976¼	101½	4, 774	2, 793	1, 690½	31	133½	842	10
Essex, ...	14, 857	4, 405	446, 652	95, 484	10, 139	2, 634	35	6, 899	4, 716	3, 969½	265	671½	7, 063	27½
Jay, ...	13, 687	28, 859	280, 616	63, 789	11, 621	4, 011	26	5, 088	4, 117	2, 597	......	556	4, 464	......
Keene, ...	7, 537	79, 165	110, 510	23, 774	5, 412	1, 287½	4	3, 222	2, 523	1, 315	20	180½	1, 115	......
Lewis, ...	14, 068	27, 246	266, 425	74, 265	15, 690	2, 962½	478	6, 638	3, 831	2, 287½	13	298½	1, 854	21
Minerva, ...	5, 329½	143, 215	109, 277	24, 970	6, 018	947	60	1, 871	1, 887	1, 134	2½	6	56	......
Moriah, ...	13, 281	27, 511	357, 435	82, 555	16, 391	2, 308¾	22½	6, 629¼	4, 169¼	3, 253¾	3	232⅜	1, 949	1
Newcomb, ...	950	89, 964	93, 020	4, 940	1, 660	228	....	343	341	204	......	5	47	......
North, Elba, ...	2, 008	88, 912	91, 914	12, 068	3, 943	538½	189	515	662	413	20½	41	510	......

(Continued on page 267.)

DELAWARE COUNTY.—(Continued.)

TOWNS.	Winter Wheat.	Oats.		Rye.		Barley.		Buckwheat.		Corn.		Potatoes.		Peas.	
	Bushels harvested.	Acres sown.	Bushels harvested	Acres sown.	Bushels harvested,	Acres sown.	Bushels harvested.	Acres sown.	Bushels harvested.	Acres planted.	Bushels harvested.	Acres planted.	Bushels harvested.	Acres sown.	Bushels harvested.
Andes, ...	......	1,992½	36,384	374	4,001	1	5	734	5,223½	174½	3,011	226	7,774	2	48
Bovina, ...	......	1,549¾	21,673	371¼	4,029	9	68	359¾	1,574¾	42	887½	128¾	6,109	10	74
Colchester, ...	33½	1,140	11,149	339	3,063	......	....	900½	6,540¼	379⅞	6,667	40	7,168¾	3½	29¼
Davenport, ...	28	1,867	23,565	405½	4,060	6½	92	544½	4,847	426	13,890	237¾	13,926	13½	214
Delhi, ...	67½	2,564	24,442½	228	1,997½	3½	67½	664¼	2,104¾	229	3,534	194⅞	7,847	8¾	123¼
Franklin, ...	110	3,122¼	41,828½	579½	6,284	42¾	669	739¾	6,043¾	650⅝	16,640	392½	26,599	10	119¼
Hampden, ...	132	1,950	19,860	302½	3,300	6½	66	617¾	3,121¼	220	3,326	188¾	7,146	6¾	44
Hancock, ...	42½	502	7,500	153	1,576½	......	....	446	3,559½	265½	5,724	122½	7,489	2¾	41½
Harpersfield, ...	17	1,323½	19,572	196½	1,970	50½	656	592⅛	5,732	191¼	4,634	192½	13,180	42⅜	527
Kortright, ...	52½	2,833	27,818	270	2,504	2	8	552	2,856½	276½	4,458	237¾	9,561	7¾	92
Masonville, ...	20	1,489¾	22,857	242½	2,376	2¼	33½	766	8,033½	204	4,482½	193	14,310½	3⅜	28¼
Meredith, ...	......	2,099¾	26,799	131¼	1,509	6	90	434¼	2,994½	193½	4,309	215½	13,063	7	40
Middletown, ...	30	2,660¼	24,545½	492¾	4,229	½	8	1,167¾	8,764½	371½	6,164½	318¾	14,506½	36½	120½
Roxbury, ...	......	2,332	19,934	596	5,495	19⅛	199	890	3,925	318	5,349	312½	9,786½	29½	235
Sidney, ...	239	1,620	29,229	257	2,649	9	110	466½	5,551	620	18,218	193½	17,441	12⅞	138
Stamford, ...	93	1,927	16,277	234½	1,904	11½	147	434½	2,397½	185½	3,847	190	8,887	14⅜	153½
Tompkins, ...	63½	1,495¼	24,466	207	1,524½	......	....	1,050¾	10,309½	486¾	9,878	257¼	14,526	17⅜	132
Walton, ...	27	1,548¼	18,760	427½	4,056	3	....	610½	2,751¼	309	4,363½	228	10,247	5¾	70
Total, ...	955½	34,016¼	416,659½	5,807¾	56,527½	173⅛	2,219	11,970⅞	86,330	5,543½	119,383	3,869⅞	209,567¼	234⅜	2,229½

DUTCHESS COUNTY.—(Continued.)

TOWNS.	Winter Wheat.	Oats.		Rye.		Barley.		Buckwheat.		Corn.		Potatoes.		Peas.	
	Bushels harvested.	Acres sown.	Bushels harvested	Acres sown.	Bushels harvested,	Acres sown.	Bushels harvested.	Acres sown.	Bushels harvested.	Acres planted.	Bushels harvested.	Acres planted.	Bushels harvested.	Acres sown.	Bushels harvested.
Amenia, ...	1,943	1,437	28,986	224	2,676	2	19	192	2,467	1,223	32,322	167	14,716	......	....
Beekman, ...	4,540	1,222	26,292	453	5,057	......	....	131	817	1,191	21,903	142	7,530	......	....
Clinton, ...	1,934	2,583	35,649	1,792	22,813	......	....	270	2,420	2,223	35,704	184	9,715	......	8
Dover, ...	962	871	15,406	114	1,088	......	....	171	1,436	828	19,235	163	9,632	......	....
East Fishkill, ...	7,794	1,812	37,332	541	5,900	......	....	314	1,868	2,412	35,670	347	12,318	11¾	322
Fishkill, ...	12434	3,096	57,551	790	7,284	10	18	402	3,276	2,775	43,277	219	6,779	4	50
Hyde Park, ...	1,466	1,966	26,695	1,433	15,069	10	46	254	1,575	1,662	20,362	167	5,703	5	114
La Grange, ...	3,177	2,612½	41,246	1,695	20,811	......	....	232	1,064	2,552	31,508½	177½	6,129	......	....
Milan, ...	719	2,602	25,869	2,195½	23,686	4	38	616	3,201	1,715¼	19,126	190⅝	11,486	......	....
North East, ...	992	1,803½	35,126	912½	9,911	76½	1,143	252½	2,710	1,492½	35,784	186	18,273	......	4
Pawling, ...	788	688	14,036	219¾	2,273½	9½	202	151¼	944½	653¼	14,964	269¼	18,099	......	....
Pine Plains, ...	765½	1,608	19,734	1,369⅜	14,149	37	746	153	1,474¼	1,222	24,640	139	11,005	......	....
Pleasant Valley,	1,366	2,105	34,874	1,596	20,121	......	....	147	1,224	1,987½	28,996	133¼	6,942	......	....
Poughkeepsie, ..	5,750	1,991	37,948	373	5,433	5	70	99	965½	1,543½	20,697	113	4,072	½	20
Po'keepsie city, ..	514	133	3,034	6	78	......	....	7	15	79	1,472	37	1,335	2	105
Redhook, ...	1,261	2,299	36,195	1,938	24,041	......	....	320½	2,068	2,126	15,458	230½	10,742	......	....
Rhinebeck, ...	2,522½	2,198	28,206	1,391½	14,633	8	100	454¼	3,210¼	1,701	16,278	217½	9,699	1¼	32
Stamford, ...	2,964	2,906	49,023	1,705	22,650	22½	436	334	3,201	2,496½	56,279	257½	14,503	......	....
Union Vale, ...	737½	1,082	21,158	559	6,801	......	....	279¼	2,472½	881	21,438½	97⅛	6,481	½	15
Washington, ...	1,841	2,571	51,987	1,117	14,589	......	....	485¼	6,715	2,324½	63,194	256¾	20,339	......	....
Total, ...	54470½	37 586	626,347	20424⅞	239,063½	184½	2,818	5,265	43,124¼	33,088	558,308	3,693¾	205,498	25	670

ERIE COUNTY.—(Continued.)

TOWNS.	Winter Wheat.	Oats.		Rye.		Barley.		Buckwheat.		Corn.		Potatoes.		Peas.	
	Bushels harvested.	Acres sown.	Bushels harvested	Acres sown.	Bushels harvested,	Acres sown.	Bushels harvested.	Acres sown.	Bushels harvested.	Acres planted.	Bushels harvested.	Acres planted.	Bushels harvested.	Acres sown.	Bushels harvested.
Alden, ...	7358	1,135	24,376	205	3,198	137	1,705	355	3,360	740	16,212	360	16,412	11	169
Amherst, ...	33041	1,672	38,972	250¾	3,129½	592¾	9,173	168	1,608	1,202	31,188	420	19,496	75	1,465½
Aurora, ...	5755	1,971¾	42,207	16½	179	78	1,264	180¼	1,932¾	1,116¼	28,146	506¼	31,068	59¼	776½
Boston, ...	1824	1,505½	33,254	28	361	59⅛	851	39¼	403½	470¾	12,567	270½	16,107	18⅞	297½
Brandt, ...	1375	568½	9,561	4	46	39¼	318½	89⅝	924	530¼	11,881	177¾	12,860	5¾	77
Buffalo, ...	7108	1,157¾	22,527	32½	508	312½	5,582	21½	165	422⅛	13,367	316¾	22,519	16¾	303
Chictawauga, ...	8441	1,049	26,922	102	1,246	130	2,103	63	622¾	422½	9,854	331⅝	17,271	25½	330
Clarence, ...	41598	1,703	33,463	274	3,873	431	6,403	188	1,838	1,856	49,036	330	17,064	44	719
Colden, ...	1060	840¼	17,585½	20½	237	29½	674	44½	437½	324½	8,081	156	11,710	17⅛	351
Collins, ...	4929	715¾	16,859	13	116	44¼	827	60	693½	731¾	19,449	139⅞	10,691	21½	356
Concord, ...	1666¾	4,699½	47,232	22¼	283	38	518	97½	1,608	1,259⅛	34,841	354⅛	22,566	55¼	651
East Hamburg, .	3637½	1,827	36,268	22¾	162	58	797	80¼	852¾	664½	19,194	500	31,256½	62	943
Eden, ...	4329	1,588¼	31,908	155¼	2,186½	129	1,621	130	1,036	828	20,834	412¼	20,371	39¼	706
Evans, ...	1888½	1,077¾	21,662	25¼	353	83½	1,205	148¾	1,124½	846¼	21,733	235¼	13,922	28¼	391½
Grand Island, ..	4012	328½	9,834	8	35	28	560	19½	364	113¼	4,209	95½	9,928	27	541
Hamburgh, ...	2334½	1,297	28,530	84¾	1,024	144¾	1,959	89½	1,063½	756¼	20,845	376½	21,119	37¼	640½
Holland, ...	921	1,596	31,000	4	36½	33	666	43	315½	432¼	9,862	120½	7,107	16	282½
Lancaster, ...	18828	1,988¾	49,109	240	3,407	208¼	3,809	145¼	1,238	995	27,647	514½	31,934	76½	1 286
Marilla, ...	8978½	540	10,849	46¼	620	56¾	888	11	154¼	545¾	10,303	234	7,779	6	82
Newstead, ...	47479	1,906	47,117	82⅛	1,221	430½	7,339	158¼	1,682½	1,657½	43,428	282½	20,553	37	598
North Collins, ...	781	1,319¼	29,201	65½	651	64¾	678	75¾	906	665¼	13,881	299¾	19,992	24½	381½
Sardinia, ...	1241	2,113	40,742	20¾	243	81½	1,237	94	815½	708	18,853	258	18,811	39¾	542½
Tonawanda, ...	19235	1,074½	25,201	45⅝	583	262½	3,807	43	373	382⅛	13,170	234⅞	8,991	52½	621
Wales, ...	4935	1,635¼	32,926	13½	184	88½	1,339	104	970	689⅝	18,001	264¾	15,431	41½	666½
West Seneca, ...	6057	673¾	17,442	40½	1,097	100¾	1,933	6½	70	269	6,646	261¾	20,392	91⅝	2,144
Total, ...	238812¾	35,983	724,747½	1,822½	24,979½	3,661⅛	57,256½	2,455⅝	24,558¼	18,627½	483,228	7,452¾	445,350½	929⅛	15,321½

ESSEX COUNTY.—(Continued.)

TOWNS.	Winter Wheat.	Oats.		Rye.		Barley.		Buckwheat.		Corn.		Potatoes.		Peas.	
	Bushels harvested.	Acres sown.	Bushels harvested	Acres sown.	Bushels harvested,	Acres sown.	Bushels harvested.	Acres sown.	Bushels harvested.	Acres planted.	Bushels harvested.	Acres planted.	Bushels harvested.	Acres sown.	Bushels harvested.
Chesterfield, ...	2	901	12,800	101	488	9½	100	359	1,657	572	8,121	426¼	25,293	28	144
Crown Point, ...	1,026	1,227	27,741	194½	2,090	13	240½	24¾	140½	725¾	17,226	448½	37,865	101¾	1,228
Elizabethtown, ..	40	730¾	7,107	51½	362	4	55	193½	728	300¼	4,301	222	9,032	52½	271
Essex, ...	213	1,189	22,370	29	120	......	....	77½	377	305	4,880	187½	10,965	143¼	1,776
Jay, ...	......	1,668	22,534	184	1,430	11	109	246	895½	616	11,497	406	32,192	25	95
Keene, ...	......	477½	5,188	29	232½	5	76	143½	1,024½	205½	3,163	184½	11,663	26¼	140
Lewis, ...	86½	939	10,283	419	3,134	½	2	331½	751¾	689¼	9,242	387	19,892	58¼	352¼
Minerva, ...	......	565¼	9,093	25¾	148	......	....	105	930½	92¾	1,655	128¼	10,855	13	196
Moriah, ...	12	920½	16,435	54	639	½	2	17¾	153	467¾	11,070	384¾	26,211	33⅝	328½
Newcomb, ...	......	130	1,985	10	124	2	12	14	147	5	108	55	4,500	3	50
North Elba, ...	......	265	6,244	41½	457	2½	25	14	265	9	265	102½	10,140	10½	138

(Continued on page 268.)

DELAWARE COUNTY.—(CONTINUED.)

TOWNS.	BEANS.		TURNIPS.		FLAX.			HEMP.		HOPS.		TOBACCO.		APPLE ORCHARDS	
	Acres planted.	Bushels harvested.	Acres sown.	Bushels harvested.	Acres sown.	Pounds of lint.	Bushels of seed.	Acres sown.	Tons of hemp.	Acres planted.	Pounds harvested.	Acres planted.	Pounds harvested.	Bushels of apples.	Barrels of cider.
Andes,			5	897										9,737	96
Bovina,	⅛	½	2	465	½	35	1½			2¼				6,966	25
Colchester,	2¼	44¼	31⅞	3,421	¼	6	½							16,165	528
Davenport,	⅞	9	4⅛	925						81½	52,017			9,984	43
Delhi,	3¾	210	5	805	¼	50	1							9,676	72½
Franklin,	3¾	38½	1½	166	¾	50	1½				5,078			29,156	450½
Hamden,	5	28½	6¼	870	½	32	1							7,526	178½
Hancock,	1¾	14	20⅛	2,320										5,835	41
Harpersfield,	4⅛	65½	13⅞	3,423	3⅜	410	5			32½				20,635	188½
Kortright,			⅛	100						1½	700			20,645	149
Masonville,	6⅜	461½	6¼	778	⅜	85	1¾			½	120			13,700	2,871¼
Meredith,	1¾	20	2¼	220	1		1½			11¾	769			11,722	140½
Middletown,	5	55	8¼	896	1	87	4							21,275	173
Roxbury,	3¼	176½	3⅛	266	¼	70	1			11	2,500			21,379	59
Sidney,	4	340	6¼	1,330	¾	58	½			44¼	7,829			17,471	448
Stamford,	2	34	⅛	10		500	2	1	¾	2	15½			11,460	121
Tompkins,	3	103	9¼	2,137										13,205	226
Walton,	3⅝	528	3¼	583	1⅛	94	4½							12,623	107½
Total,	50⅞	2,128¼	129⅜	19,612	10⅜	1,477	25¾	1	¾	187¼	69,028½			259,160	5,918¼
DUTCHESS COUNTY.—(CONTINUED.)															
Amenia,	½	18	7½	2,140								11½	17,467	15,435	431
Beekman,	2	30		1,450										6,868	179
Clinton,		10	76	8,565	½	70	3½							6,184	407
Dover,			9¼	490	⅛	25	1					1	460	4,431	260
East Fishkill,	¾	45	25½	3,310										6,990	282
Fishkill,	9½	185	65	3,345	¼	30	1							3,227	272
Hyde Park,	⅛	1½	138	8,863	¼	50								11,147	467
La Grange,			21	2,168	7½	56								6,156	254
Milan,	½	6½	130	1,719	1½	112	3¾						40	7,716	432½
North East,	8½	172	1½	3,798									500	31,511	1,107
Pauling,			1	465										7,999	212¾
Pine Plains,	⅞	21	2¾	435										6,319	302
Pleasant Valley,	1	3	21¼	380										5,938	159
Poughkeepsie,		30	3¼	750						4	3,100			1,137	54
Po'keepsie City,	½	3												330	
Redhook,			33¾	1,100	½	114	4¼					⅛	40	14,837	503
Rhinebeck,		4	¼	2,355										13,257	610
Stanford,	12	241	277	11,780										24,898	828
Union Vale,	¾	15¾	127⅜	3,064							4			11,392	182½
Washinghton,	¼	2½	6	2,400	½	100	1½							30,821	1,305
Total,	37¼	788¼	946⅜	58,577	11⅛	557	15			4	3,104	12⅜	18,507	216,593	8,247¾
ERIE COUNTY.—(CONTINUED.)															
Alden,	16	135	1½	130	¾	70	4							5,853	483
Amherst,	8	130	4¾	433										8,740	397
Aurora,	34½	506½	14	1,885	20½		192							17,985	127
Boston,	18¼	309	⅝	17										10,997	363
Brandt,	19⅛	217	⅛	95										5,391	82½
Buffalo,	10⅜	149	13⅜	834										2,970	95
Chictawauga,	13¼	139	10½	855½	¼	100	4½							5,743	206½
Clarence,	4	73	5½	735										30,864	1,014
Colden,	1½	138½	3¾	69	1½	20	8½						50	3,819	82
Collins,	12⅞	215½	2¼	630	¼	30	1							16,866	197
Concord,	18	231	3⅞	600	⅛	1,000								17,365½	170
East Hamburgh,	26½	400½	23⅞	3,498										19,254½	243½
Eden,	14½	484½	1¾	92	¼	100	1							14,121	363¾
Evans,	35½	577½	7¼	1,911½							6			11,138	131
Grand Island,	8⅜	210	9	1,291										143	
Hamburgh,	21¼	400½	3	1,095	5½		33							11,170	274
Holland,	4½	248¾	½	345		156				2½	1,656			10,761	286
Lancaster,	3½	60	21½	2,065	1¼	400	4½							13,520	515
Marilla,	5¼	213½	4	835										1,118	
Newstead,	11	275	4½	1,346										20,726	557
North Collins,	14¾	356½	⅝	151	1¾	90	9½							12,506	113½
Sardinia,	19¼	210½	3¼	352	⅛	60	4			1½	1,200			10,266	166
Tonawanda,	4½	61	2½	12										2,179	59
Wales,	16¼	236¼	⅜	60	⅜		4½							12,229	159
West Seneca,	8¾	146	12	1,650	2	3,000	10							470	
Total,	349¾	6,124	154⅜	20,987	34⅝	5,026	276½			4	2,862		50	266,195	6,084¾
ESSEX COUNTY.—(CONTINUED.)															
Chesterfield,	11½	499	1½	170										1,088½	
Crown Point,	25¼	374	⅝	70	1½	50	1½							9,060	174
Elizabethtown,	17¾	120½	8¾	400										3,036	
Essex,	15½	132½												8,812	212½
Jay,	15	54	4	1,000										1,598	
Keene,	18¾	110¼	12	886	⅜	100	2				9			884	1
Lewis,	29¾	188½	4	767	¼		1½							3,599	31
Minerva,	1½	11	2	342										2,171	5
Moriah,	9⅝	110	1½	176	⅛	25	1							4,092	24
Newcomb,	3	11	2	400											
North Elba,			3	700											

(Continued on page 269.)

DELAWARE COUNTY.—(Continued.)

TOWNS.	Market gardens: Acres cultivated.	Market gardens: Value of products.	Pounds of maple sugar made.	Gallons of maple molasses made.	Gallons of wine made.	Pounds of honey collected.	Pounds of wax collected.	Silk: Pounds of cocoons.	Neat cattle: Under one year old.	Neat cattle: Over one y'r, exclusive of working oxen & cows.	Neat cattle: Working oxen.	Neat cattle: Cows.	Number of cattle killed for beef.	Pounds of butter.	Pounds of cheese.
Andes,	......	......	10, 293	376	......	5, 918	257	......	707	939	249	2, 175	99	269, 052	480
Bovina,	......	......	10, 856	231	......	4, 184	306½	......	482	592	70	1, 774	86	223, 490	2, 998
Colchester,	......	......	5, 489	371	......	6, 644	255	......	441	858	426	1, 035	111	97, 572	390
Davenport,	......	......	15, 705	93	......	4, 558	83	......	559	644	179	1, 749	115	192, 860	1, 955
Delhi,	3, 645	$62	9, 517	249	......	2, 703	105	......	518	734	189	2, 051	134	216, 202	1, 080
Franklin,	......	......	22, 466	395	......	7, 590	336	......	890	1, 328	327	3, 195	252	393, 332	12, 249
Hamden,	......	......	16, 992	549	......	4, 154	308	......	619	918	272	1, 682	68	170, 785	1, 146
Hancock,	......	......	1, 130	6	......	4, 150	290½	......	121	298	276	494	65	45, 608	....
Harpersfield,	......	......	53, 346	482	......	4, 100	228	......	549	834	200	1, 775	121	240, 010	3, 364
Kortright,	......	......	34, 041	402	......	5, 140	301	......	934	741	180	2, 385	122	326, 740	1, 310
Masonville,	......	......	7, 818	247	......	7, 751	384¾	......	532	871	300	1, 291	88	124, 252	6, 171
Meredith,	......	......	27, 606	435	10	3, 533	141	......	599	573	164	1, 763	79	221, 217	3, 777
Middletown,	......	7	16, 357	537	......	9, 332	507	......	858	1, 373	379	2, 441	91	261, 611	520
Roxbury,	......	......	10, 594	216	5	6, 172	307	......	858	944	337	3, 817	179	472, 090	2, 115
Sidney,	......	......	4, 739	23	5	3, 156	182	......	561	822	239	1, 756	179	204, 329	7, 880
Stamford,	......	......	16, 649	358	113½	4, 573	342½	......	487	560	158	1, 867	75	245, 658	2. 980
Tompkins,	......	......	6, 442	121	......	13, 316	689	......	730	850	437	1, 616	111	166, 262	11, 500
Walton,	......	......	43, 262	610	......	4, 597	262	......	533	1, 060	398	1, 618	69	155, 505	1, 270
Total,	3, 645	69	313, 302	5, 701	133½	101, 571	5, 285¼	......	10, 978	14, 939	4, 780	34, 484	2, 044	4, 026, 575	61, 185

DUTCHESS COUNTY.—(Continued.)

TOWNS.	Market gardens: Acres cultivated.	Market gardens: Value of products.	Pounds of maple sugar made.	Gallons of maple molasses made.	Gallons of wine made.	Pounds of honey collected.	Pounds of wax collected.	Silk: Pounds of cocoons.	Neat cattle: Under one year old.	Neat cattle: Over one y'r, exclusive of working oxen & cows.	Neat cattle: Working oxen.	Neat cattle: Cows.	Number of cattle killed for beef.	Pounds of butter.	Pounds of cheese.
Amenia,	......	......	20	......	......	2, 551	......	......	327	485	299	1, 592	192	85, 055	9, 866
Beekman,	......	......	....	......	......	1, 213	54	......	246	564	301	796	113	56, 565	5, 497
Clinton,	......	7	386	42	......	2, 158	154	......	171	398	336	1, 359	415	122, 844	636
Dover,	......	......	....	......	......	945	57	......	272	643	368	1, 285	175	55, 951	3, 840
East Fishkill,	......	......	566	15	6	4, 711	203	......	288	882	567	1, 681	297	150, 087	864
Fishkill,	34	3, 365	....	......	12	3, 949	59	......	345	689	257	1, 646	567	105, 548	200
Hyde Park,	3	63	12	4	......	1, 242	130	......	190	300	334	1, 366	292	93, 550	720
La Grange,	......	20	199	......	......	3, 324	222	......	129	345	425	1, 166	207	89, 460	100
Milan,	......	......	49	43½	......	2, 301	139	......	201	426	226	873	105	90, 916	1, 782
North East,	......	37	....	......	......	2, 924	41	......	201	457	344	1, 151	126	62, 825	8, 259
Pauling,	......	......	270	33	......	1, 892	95	......	333	533	402	1, 479	146	89, 460	950
Pine Plains,	......	......	....	......	......	1, 513	87	2	150	309	252	678	75	39, 990	5, 188
Pleasant Valley,	......	......	....	......	......	30	20	......	165	287	246	1, 067	311	106, 785	....
Poughkeepsie,	50½	3, 785	....	......	......	325	75	......	184	250	173	1, 819	357	48, 058	....
Poughkeepsie City,	69¼	5, 450	....	......	......	....	......	......	17	17	14	264	7	1, 350	....
Redhook,	⅛	10	....	......	......	447	38	......	172	278	256	962	102	67, 900	600
Rhinebeck,	1	20	....	2	......	2, 275	131	......	240	344	296	1, 157	229	75, 065	....
Stanford,	......	......	182	14	10	3, 584	146	......	285	577	446	1, 680	175	126, 019	8, 116
Union Vale,	......	......	4	......	7	2, 064	147	......	198	212	192	693	82	57, 614	1, 757
Washington,	½	20	9	6	......	1, 055	32	......	235	934	529	1, 870	286	156, 553	5, 744
Total,	158⅜	12, 777	1, 697	159½	35	38, 503	1, 830	2	4, 349	8, 930	6, 263	24, 584	4, 259	1, 681, 595	54, 119

ERIE COUNTY.—(Continued.)

TOWNS.	Market gardens: Acres cultivated.	Market gardens: Value of products.	Pounds of maple sugar made.	Gallons of maple molasses made.	Gallons of wine made.	Pounds of honey collected.	Pounds of wax collected.	Silk: Pounds of cocoons.	Neat cattle: Under one year old.	Neat cattle: Over one y'r, exclusive of working oxen & cows.	Neat cattle: Working oxen.	Neat cattle: Cows.	Number of cattle killed for beef.	Pounds of butter.	Pounds of cheese.
Alden,	4	3, 010	....	47	......	2, 078	162	......	258	300	198	1, 011	59	55, 424	4, 000
Amherst,	½	50	....	25	20	1, 240	74½	......	286	644	300	1, 294	54	69, 605	100
Aurora,	1	63	4, 343	66	......	4, 291	257	......	318	671	202	1, 236	190	111, 094	15, 095
Boston,	¼	175	3, 532	100	......	920	49	......	233	659	124	1, 165	147	56, 135	115, 545
Brandt,	......	15	775	109	......	2, 347	96	......	216	462	111	817	98	55, 737	82, 282
Buffalo,	137⅝	14, 131	....	......	40	880	90	......	57	242	33	1, 609	3, 039	15, 400	....
Chictawauga,	51½	2, 510	....	4	......	1, 165	79	......	227	268	93	862	31	64, 139	4, 950
Clarence,	5	500	310	65	......	1, 468	......	......	255	536	105	1, 161	53	86, 743	890
Colden,	......	1, 712	8, 099	69	6	1, 399	40½	......	252	381	191	797	59	54, 205	42, 000
Collins,	......	300	7, 284	86	......	1, 500	73	......	497	932	130	2, 764	84	78, 736	586, 384
Concord,	3	85	32, 622	245	......	4, 890	262½	......	618	969	170	2, 461	94	98, 115	460, 881
East Hamburgh,	23⅜	2, 270	1, 302	72	58	2, 828	185	......	257	333	98	1, 368	100	110, 120	38, 500
Eden,	5	370	610	19	......	4, 727	229	......	395	546	208	1, 271	76	112, 660	36, 455
Evans,	4½	535	1, 036	44	16	7, 047	316½	......	357	860	167	1, 467	217	94, 069	27, 625
Grand Island,	5¼	775	....	......	......	1, 750	63	......	143	202	144	250	35	23, 420	40
Hamburgh,	5	375	110	15¼	......	1, 885	111	......	186	302	150	818	127	102, 800	23, 380
Holland,	......	......	9, 840	16	......	3, 325	52	......	357	695	135	780	35	77, 850	7, 907
Lancaster,	188¾	7, 750	230	74	......	1, 908	220	......	384	573	168	1, 176	124	80, 300	3, 130
Marilla,	......	......	7, 382	125	3	1, 314	76	......	168	315	133	487	10	43, 394	2, 904
Newstead,	¾	500	3, 960	161	......	2, 181	117	......	403	674	175	1, 018	64	107, 777	4, 190
North Collins,	......	5	4, 094	129	......	2, 001	173	......	533	879	164	2, 588	182	103, 429	515, 804
Sardinia,	......	......	31, 380	360	......	4, 540	184	......	545	1, 112	217	1, 036	97	95, 645	28, 470
Tonawanda,	5½	184	....	......	......	705	86	......	150	325	59	629	45	26, 920	....
Wales,	......	......	12, 618	65	......	2, 680	164	......	419	931	196	1, 258	89	112, 155	37, 860
West Seneca,	40½	3, 815	100	......	30	590	60	......	110	370	123	508	211	30, 260	....
Total,	481¼	39, 130	129, 627	1, 896¼	173	59, 659	3, 220	......	7, 624	14, 190	3, 794	29, 831	5, 320	1, 866, 132	2, 038, 392

ESSEX COUNTY.—(Continued.)

TOWNS.	Market gardens: Acres cultivated.	Market gardens: Value of products.	Pounds of maple sugar made.	Gallons of maple molasses made.	Gallons of wine made.	Pounds of honey collected.	Pounds of wax collected.	Silk: Pounds of cocoons.	Neat cattle: Under one year old.	Neat cattle: Over one y'r, exclusive of working oxen & cows.	Neat cattle: Working oxen.	Neat cattle: Cows.	Number of cattle killed for beef.	Pounds of butter.	Pounds of cheese.
Chesterfield,	½	71	95	15	......	3, 883	172	......	257	559	86	764	147	46, 929	4, 594
Crown Point,	......	......	1, 342	24	......	1, 384	96	......	525	1, 100	275	842	112	49, 791	9, 266
Elizabethtown,	......	......	475	12	......	3, 275	96¼	......	161	398	131	472	136	28, 020	2, 550
Essex,	......	......	....	......	......	466	33	......	242	797	133	718	92	42, 515	8, 371
Jay,	......	......	1, 700	54	......	2, 255	72	......	550	827	211	735	128	61, 245	6, 390
Keene,	......	......	5, 435	37	......	180	14	......	153	370	102	353	48	21, 257	2, 290
Lewis,	......	......	890	14	......	3, 383	165¾	......	261	644	166	635	72	50, 985	7, 920
Minerva,	......	......	1, 661	32	......	961	66	......	95	187	94	250	31	17, 666	240
Moriah,	......	......	635	8	......	1, 662	106	......	324	671	157	764	248	53, 685	8, 000
Newcomb,	......	......	1, 610	50	......	....	......	......	19	32	25	53	25	3, 065	....
North Elba,	......	......	5, 325	12	......	....	......	......	56	129	49	142	12	7, 856	170

34

(Continued on page 270.)

DELAWARE COUNTY.—(Continued.)

TOWNS.	Gallons of milk sold	Horses.	Mules.	SWINE. Under 6 months	SWINE. Over 6 months.	SHEEP. Number of sheep.	SHEEP. Number of fleeces.	SHEEP. Pounds of wool.	POULTRY. Value of poultry sold.	POULTRY. Value of eggs sold.	DOMESTIC MANUFACTURES. Yards of fulled cloth made.	DOMESTIC MANUFACTURES. Yards of flannel made.	DOMESTIC MANUFACTURES. Yards of linen made.	DOMESTIC MANUFACTURES. Yards of cotton and mixed cloths.
Andes,	....	598	4	346	587	6,710	3,114	11,045½	$372	$276	$961	2,226	....	499
Bovina,	....	414	....	283	423	3,673	1,803	5,966	473	906	435	973	159	846
Colchester,	....	349	....	300	436	3,201	2,037	6,352	180	70	471	1,037	45	330
Davenport,	....	563	....	477	496	3,445	2,218	6,877	382	802	394	1,683	210	326
Delhi,	....	526	....	410	430	4,544	3,089	9,256	766	851	432	593	66	144
Franklin,	....	871	....	752	750	6,930	4,657	13,906¼	979	1,836	290	586	248	130
Hampden,	....	440	....	308	385	5,926	3,049	9,510	419	315	222	917	60	626
Hancock,	....	192	....	150	258	816	561	1,846	4	23	121	293	....	40
Harpersfield,	....	439	....	339	425	2,614	1,339	4,807	957	905	478	1,265	348	373
Kortright,	....	613	....	489	565	3,975	2,623	8,664½	991	1,328	715	1,522	157	175
Masonville,	....	370	....	246	321	3,599	1,746½	5,888	786	655	654	1,114	284	573
Meredith,	....	474	....	432	391	2,826	2,159	7,317	715	881	136½	452	47	31
Middletown,	....	752	....	514	604	4,138	2,619	8,497	905	113	1,367	3,158	247	248
Roxbury,	....	677	....	837	758	3,346	1,987	7,031	1,341	539	715	2,444	91	1,085
Sidney,	....	502	....	363	544	4,449	2,759	9,102	905	1,683	655	705	329½	219½
Stamford,	10	434	....	424	367	3,809	2,549	7,522	607	771	158½	428	28	91
Tompkins,	5,000	490	1	302	434	3,583	2,022	6,249½	381	471	630	877	85	417
Walton,	....	436	....	249	475	3,731	2,168	6,823	363	574	249½	1,015¼	272	355
Total,	5,010	9,140	5	7,221	8,649	71,315	42,499½	·36,659¾	11,526	12,999	9,084½	21,288¼	2,676½	6.508½

DUTCHESS COUNTY.—(Continued.)

TOWNS.	Gallons of milk sold	Horses.	Mules.	Under 6 months	Over 6 months.	Number of sheep.	Number of fleeces.	Pounds of wool.	Value of poultry sold.	Value of eggs sold.	Yards of fulled cloth made.	Yards of flannel made.	Yards of linen made.	Yards of cotton and mixed cloths.
Amenia,	409,195	429	3	1,224	442	4,547	4,010	13,233	2,974	2,206	20	85	....	....
Beekman,	....	317	4	1,208	355	2,027	2,194	7,684	3,202	1,865	....	143	....	40
Clinton,	....	658	....	2,340	763	2,985	2,941	9,692	6,022	6,932	42	133	108	45
Dover,	322,492	283	....	801	475	1,480	1,306	4,087	2,004	799	50	20	10	60
East Fishkill,	....	599	....	1,887	919	2,750	2,626	8,562	4,742	4,287	....	99	....	40
Fishkill,	50,198	1.059	13	1,488	1,183	2,738	2,374	7,400	3,221	4,069	....	....	....	....
Hyde Park,	125,422	642	4	1,526	645	911	744	2,544	2,599	3,344	....	48	....	....
La Grange,	....	552	....	1,548	565	3,418	3,667	11,182	4,671	3,205	....	113	42	....
Milan,	....	506	....	1,610	690	4,916	4,409	14,190¼	2,401	5,169	99	191½	151	65
North East,	201,085	455	....	1,516	561	7,497	7,118	22,284	3,097	2,225	....	....	....	....
Pawling,	314,082	337	....	952	307	2,689	1,670	5,283	1,823	1,302	42	....	30	34
Pine Plains,	3,650	407	....	1,465	652	5,723	5,070	16,172	1,387	2,072	....	....	....	....
Pleasant Valley,	....	476	2	1,374	522	2,142	1,839	5,854	4,488	5,289	....	....	....	....
Poughkeepsie,	60,255	660	....	860	1,469	1,242	1,237	4,047	2,616	3,410	....	....	....	....
Poughkeepsie city,	39,600	439	....	121	383	....	....	....	112	....	....	....	....	....
Redhook,	70,865	654	3	1,271	933	3,151	2,534	8,823	1,993	4,727	37	44	68	....
Rhinebeck,	71,766	652	....	1,374	781	2,141	1,187	3,783	2,683	3,442	185½	358	195	49
Stanford,	149,579	661	....	3,087	1,065	12,116	7,797	26,025	5,785	6,753	36	97	50	....
Union Vale,	14,300	326	....	807	385	3,177	3,169	10,407	2,532	1,224	95	40	46	60
Washington,	137,879	717	....	2,615	817	8,037	7,299	23,891	7,335	6,593	....	27	95	....
Total,	1970,368	10,829	29	29,074	13,912	73,687	63,191	205,143¼	65,687	68,913	606½	1,398½	795	393

ERIE COUNTY.—(Continued.)

TOWNS.	Gallons of milk sold	Horses.	Mules.	Under 6 months	Over 6 months.	Number of sheep.	Number of fleeces.	Pounds of wool.	Value of poultry sold.	Value of eggs sold.	Yards of fulled cloth made.	Yards of flannel made.	Yards of linen made.	Yards of cotton and mixed cloths.
Alden,	187,162	555	....	263	465	2,306	1,997	7,450	671	954	41	208	52	109
Amherst,	4,278	1,004	2	483	1,492	1,568	1,331	4,610½	699	2,815	118½	92	10	90
Aurora,	400	1,033	2	297	936	6,828	5,228	17,812	1,265	944	238	576	43	329
Boston,	....	453	....	210	393	2,431	1,578	5,598	651	496	116	427	25	201
Brandt,	7,713	281	....	169	334	1,326	936	3,020	1,126	639	375	376	....	652
Buffalo,	508,141	2,116	....	291	2,212	56	55	255	1,042	425	....	....	....	....
Chictawauga,	66,571	611	....	186	628	870	237	1,672	334	2,042	477	110	....	94
Clarence,	....	1,073	....	454	1,405	4,844	4,106	13,682	720	3,990	317	567	....	300
Colden,	3,758	337	....	101	271	1,710	920	3,144	2,401	225	329	685	183	365
Collins,	....	618	....	308	468	1,628	1,206	4,158	1,415	1,101	138½	442	87½	873
Concord,	12,360	709	....	310	576	3,329	2,072	6,550	1,533	994	259½	1,123	150	472
East Hamburgh,	204,343	664	....	381	471	4,150	3,166	9,937	1,693	1,308	454¼	681	50	247½
Eden,	2,200	617	....	333	581	2,587	1,812	6,046	1,667	2,527	416	832	275	345
Evans,	131,217	614	3	342	504	3,157	2,191	7,487½	1,867	1,725	187	314	110	364½
Grand Island,	....	129	....	266	513	631	299	1,215	180	203	....	....	....	....
Hamburgh,	22,050	780	....	349	658	1,545	1,031	3,675	679	439	99	328½	145	115
Holland,	....	485	....	251	307	3,604	3,597	11,470	1,434	533	301¾	661	307	868
Lancaster,	5,810	908	....	479	1,015	1,236	714	2,246	686	2,155	12	106	40	112
Marilla,	....	337	....	187	321	1,896	1,728	6,087	763	760	59	234	15	394
Newstead,	100	1,051	....	525	1,143	5,706	4,768	17,012	528	1,139	147	175	....	75
North Collins,	16,764	574	2	281	535	2,464	1,662	5,681	1,338	1,548	261	635	132	1,223
Sardinia,	....	712	....	237	460	6,062	4,688	14,640	1,851	921	443	1,167	129	1,590
Tonawanda,	218	465	....	173	715	346	293	896	192	1,114	50	125	....	....
Wales,	....	575	....	248	440	4,784	3,323	10,350	1,316	1,058	172	359	135	681½
West Seneca,	....	282	1	218	606	21	....	....	212	80	....	30	....	....
Total,	1173,085	16,983	10	7,342	17,449	65,085	48,938	164,694	26,263	30,135	5,011½	10,253½	1,888½	9,500½

ESSEX COUNTY.—(Continued.)

TOWNS.	Gallons of milk sold	Horses.	Mules.	Under 6 months	Over 6 months.	Number of sheep.	Number of fleeces.	Pounds of wool.	Value of poultry sold.	Value of eggs sold.	Yards of fulled cloth made.	Yards of flannel made.	Yards of linen made.	Yards of cotton and mixed cloths.
Chesterfield,	600	537	17	174	318	2,281	2,222	6,768	363	654	....	20	....	23
Crown Point,	....	702	....	407	371	7,589	5,527	20,672	266	220	38	80	....	332
Elizabethtown,	....	304	....	141	156	1,620	1,299	4,366	141	251	32	107	59	....
Essex,	....	528	13	87	369	6,340	5,406	18,543	276	328	....	....	....	....
Jay,	....	401	12	205	352	2,325	2,356	8,910	131	809	176	344	69	....
Keene,	....	162	....	70	131	1,673	1,403	4,413	49	184	270	189	43	615
Lewis,	....	443	....	190	237	4,159	2,871	9,879	235	487	426	311	41	234
Minerva,	....	139	....	58	126	732	401	1,296	13	18	44	260	8	159
Moriah,	300	651	....	128	357	3,316	3,078	10,708½	141	440	....	156	41	210
Newcomb,	....	26	....	5	25	73	74	224	....	....	....	....	....	....
North Elba,	....	57	....	32	44	344	304	925	....	....	14	136	4	32

(Continued on page 271.)

ESSEX COUNTY.—(Continued.)

TOWNS.	ACRES.		CASH VALUE.			Acres plowed the year previous.	Acres in fallow the year previous.	Acres in pasture the year previous.	MEADOW.			SPRING WHEAT.		WINTER WHEAT.
	Improved.	Unimproved.	Of farm.	Of stock.	Of tools and implements				Acres.	Tons of hay.	Bushels of grass seed.	Acres sown.	Bushels harvested.	Acres sown.
North Hudson,	....	....	....	2, 289	....	....	....	....	....	....	......	......	......	......
St. Armand,	1, 107¼	31, 433	$81, 550	6, 380	2, 430	201	....	165	356½	322½	......	52	617	......
Schroon,	15, 712¾	131, 485¾	481, 272	73, 932	21, 264	2, 665	142½	5, 881	5, 601½	3, 121	89¼	193	1, 794¾	7
Ticonderoga,	15, 059	12, 075	367, 678	86, 436	13, 224	2, 551	....	7, 100	5, 203	4, 169	181	323	3, 199	42
Westport,	17, 077½	16, 052	350, 959	70, 765	12, 354	2, 816½	....	8, 080	5, 073½	3, 047½	100	377¾	3, 840¼	15½
Willsborough,	14, 316¼	7, 746½	336, 035	75, 841	16, 666	672	9	5, 445	3, 664	3, 075	149	603	5, 544	9
Wilmington,	8, 168	20, 174	73, 135	24, 659	5, 501	1, 551	179	3, 486	2, 468	958	11	215	1, 000	......
Total,	185, 443⅜	774, 195¼	4, 604, 253	970, 214	179, 999	34, 457	1, 333½	82, 726¼	56, 829¾	39, 139¾	1, 019¼	4, 838⅝	44009¼	315

FRANKLIN COUNTY.

TOWNS.	Improved.	Unimproved.	Of farm.	Of stock.	Of tools and implements	Acres plowed the year previous.	Acres in fallow the year previous.	Acres in pasture the year previous.	Meadow acres.	Tons of hay.	Bushels of grass seed.	Spring wheat acres sown.	Bushels harvested.	Winter wheat acres sown.
Bangor,	13, 931	15, 609	443, 195	79, 266	25, 206	3, 519	27	6, 586	4, 487	3, 156	27¾	783¼	8181½	5½
Belmont,	5, 345	82, 708½	168, 965	29, 619	9, 552	683	419	1, 434	1, 922	1, 334	235	116½	959	......
Bombay,	13, 177¾	9, 889	387, 322	95, 552	28, 968	3, 044	101	6, 092	3, 720	3, 612	73	1, 010½	12568	53
Brandon,	4, 957	177, 890	102, 127	17, 020	5, 935	1, 124	11½	1, 749½	1, 450	771	2	175¾	1990	2
Burke,	9, 175	9, 115	317, 742	62, 347	16, 770	2, 469	....	3, 648	3, 821	2, 938½	......	476¼	3567½	7½
Chateaugay,	13, 840	12, 682	397, 328	66, 315	12, 062	3, 331	....	5, 358	4, 466	3, 385	25	657½	4742	3
Constable,	9, 473¾	11, 005	270, 270	129, 173	17, 495	1, 923½	6	3, 288	2, 678¾	3, 481½	13	240¾	1925	44¼
Dickinson,	8, 651	181, 017	444, 766	49, 964	12, 240	1, 952	4	3, 451	2, 692	1, 755	15	395½	3862	1
Duane,	2, 015	89, 790	32, 725	8, 557	2, 969	596	40	377	568	304	......	82	808	......
Fort Covington,	14, 290	5, 759¾	476, 276	198, 863	21, 990	3, 160¾	67	5, 815½	5, 151	4, 768	108¾	1, 133	13952	23
Franklin,	4, 170	97, 088	217, 074	21, 661	7, 395	1, 088½	178½	554	1, 443½	890	19¼	120¾	1055	2
Harrietstown,	842½	83, 613	75, 945	5, 693	1, 560	259½	....	186	301½	285	7¼	25¾	333	......
Malone,	25, 563	33, 546	963, 072	167, 778	49, 768	5, 742½	74½	10, 828½	7, 685	6, 224	98	1, 069¼	9045½	5
Moira,	11, 031¼	16, 452½	444, 208	61, 425	16, 096	2, 045½	68	4, 593	3, 584	2, 911½	7½	277	2601	5
Westville,	8, 165	8, 800	257, 763	48, 773	15, 329	2, 556	23	3, 464	1, 937	1, 779	31	395	3970	24
Total,	144, 627¼	834, 964¾	4, 998, 778	1, 042, 006	243, 335	33. 494¼	1, 019½	57, 424½	45, 906¾	37, 594½	662½	6, 958¾	69559½	175¼

FULTON COUNTY.

TOWNS.	Improved.	Unimproved.	Of farm.	Of stock.	Of tools and implements	Acres plowed the year previous.	Acres in fallow the year previous.	Acres in pasture the year previous.	Meadow acres.	Tons of hay.	Bushels of grass seed.	Spring wheat acres sown.	Bushels harvested.	Winter wheat acres sown.
Bleecker,	2, 638¾	35, 138	181, 880	15, 408	6, 149	296¾	35	1, 166	735	490	13¾	4¼	40	......
Broadalbin,	17, 413	6, 972	608, 552	113, 199	26, 106	4, 561	23	7, 006½	4, 470	4, 063½	95	122	1, 240	29
Caroga,	2, 306	12, 343	77, 829	15, 700	2, 350	341	16	896	658	506	......	......	......	......
Ephratah,	12, 389½	8, 896	484, 980	84, 966	23, 180	3, 560¾	352	5, 106	2, 820	3, 085	28	29	315	64
Johnstown,	29, 590	10, 751½	1, 325, 010	194, 390	52, 119	9, 556	414	9, 518	7, 053	7, 713	142½	136½	1, 597	211½
Mayfield,	18, 100½	16, 546¼	520, 773	130, 806	27, 373	4, 952	349½	7, 581	4, 098½	4, 131½	39	28	307½	31
Northampton,	12, 932½	5, 308	278, 535	60, 660	19, 081	2, 530	191	5, 986	3, 376½	2, 825	6	98	364	......
Oppenheim,	20, 289¾	11, 760	928, 905	149, 191	33, 166	4, 343	105½	8, 869	6, 299¼	7, 116½	101¾	222½	2, 675	15½
Perth,	12, 505½	3, 993	559, 636	90, 576	25, 923	4, 955½	43	4, 449½	2, 879½	2, 607	81½	86	878	64
Stratford,	5, 250¼	35, 363	137, 531	36, 531	7, 198	1, 134	....	1, 968½	1, 681	1, 365½	12	8	84	......
Total,	133, 415¾	147, 070¾	5, 103, 631	891, 427	222, 645	36, 230	1, 529	52, 546½	34, 070¾	33, 903	519½	734¼	7, 500½	415

GENESEE COUNTY.

TOWNS.	Improved.	Unimproved.	Of farm.	Of stock.	Of tools and implements	Acres plowed the year previous.	Acres in fallow the year previous.	Acres in pasture the year previous.	Meadow acres.	Tons of hay.	Bushels of grass seed.	Spring wheat acres sown.	Bushels harvested.	Winter wheat acres sown.
Alabama,	18, 345½	10, 194¼	1, 271, 692	155, 071	29, 414	3, 538½	4, 492¼	2, 162½	1, 399	1, 821	107	100¼	1, 679	4, 244¼
Alexander,	17, 234	4, 539	1, 022, 152	144, 918	29, 061	3, 068½	2, 002	5, 119½	3, 758½	4, 859	161	104¼	1, 176	2, 019¼
Batavia,	20, 803¾	5, 320½	1, 618, 478	189, 255	42, 321	3, 503½	5, 000	2, 858½	2, 479	3, 684¾	146¼	19¾	344	4, 286
Bergen,	12, 504	4, 126	1, 054, 416	101, 912	26, 909	2, 137	2, 287	2, 209	1, 532	2, 106	58	......	......	2, 568
Bethany,	18, 118	4, 882½	1, 105, 148	134, 694	32, 330	3, 030½	3, 139¼	4, 828½	3, 597	4, 406	264¼	69	718	2, 701¾
Byron,	15, 409	4, 162	1, 332, 870	37, 606	22, 087	2, 715	3, 412	2, 683	1, 701	2, 309	43	......	......	3, 609
Darien,	23, 527	6, 907	1, 232, 819	163, 319	45, 047	1, 225¼	4, 137	7, 990	5, 128	6, 411½	278½	440¾	5, 914	1, 069
Elba,	15, 614	6, 535	1, 239, 131	128, 151	34, 642	2, 925	3, 953	2, 127	1, 819	2, 690	105	7½	100	3, 668
Le Roy,	20, 427	5, 872	1, 895, 220	171, 444	63, 743	2, 876¾	5, 269¼	3, 012¾	2, 403	3, 266½	52	9½	114	5, 396¾
Oakfield,	9, 208½	3, 476¼	613, 394	71, 712	16, 691	1, 756	2, 038	1, 751½	685¾	1, 355	90½	5	68	2, 108
Pavilion,	16, 986¼	4, 322¼	1, 295, 580	144, 435	43, 366	2, 889½	3, 232½	3, 450½	2, 923¾	3, 668	261¾	45	461	3, 159¼
Pembroke,	15, 187¼	12, 297¼	1, 095, 663	129, 089	34, 963	2, 994	2, 466½	3, 879½	2, 589¼	3, 423	135½	36½	411	2, 116¼
Stafford,	15, 648	3, 098	1, 315, 435	104, 024	21, 858	2, 600½	4, 618	1, 270	1, 120½	1, 399	63½	13	169	4, 249
Total,	219, 012¼	75, 732	16, 091, 998	1, 675, 630	442, 702	35, 260	46, 046½	43, 342¼	31, 135¾	41, 398¾	1, 766¼	850½	11154	41194½

GREENE COUNTY.

TOWNS.	Improved.	Unimproved.	Of farm.	Of stock.	Of tools and implements	Acres plowed the year previous.	Acres in fallow the year previous.	Acres in pasture the year previous.	Meadow acres.	Tons of hay.	Bushels of grass seed.	Spring wheat acres sown.	Bushels harvested.	Winter wheat acres sown.
Ashland,	9, 846½	4, 198	277, 700	56, 023	10, 315	2, 110½	102	3, 804	2, 856	2, 344½	12	46	339½	9
Athens,	10, 351½	4, 502½	398, 980	58, 076	20, 379	2, 168¾	128	1, 726	4, 919	4, 493½	10½	29	201	152
Cairo,	22, 541	10, 982	808, 735	110, 197	35, 411	5, 191	797	7, 414	5, 187	4, 350	28	31½	118	182½
Catskill,	19, 146½	17, 613	1, 243, 074	115, 926	43, 215	3, 579½	482	3, 592½	5, 907½	7, 592	7	1	3	362
Coxsackie,	17, 698¼	4, 516	1, 144, 964	97, 566	38, 448	4, 240¾	1, 103	2, 746	8, 257	6, 699	51	57½	266	304½
Durham,	23, 166¼	5, 855	982, 035	148, 458	44, 411	6, 320½	100¼	10, 884¾	6, 205½	3, 998	57	271	1, 291¼	244¾
Greenville,	20, 273¾	5, 535½	936, 900	29, 584	887, 803	4, 998	482	5, 568	6, 059½	6, 067	5½	50½	223½	419
Halcott,	7, 137	4, 007	157, 350	45, 137	8, 137	1, 204	123	3, 519	2, 174	1, 907	12½	1½	24	......
Hunter,	10, 264⅞	40, 456½	129, 000	46, 440	10, 382	712¼	157½	4, 397	4, 011½	2, 495¾	7	1	8	......
Jewett,	15, 167	10, 468¾	277, 456	73, 798	16, 268	1, 162	35	7, 672	5, 629	3, 391	32	7½	36	......
Lexington,	14, 727¾	21, 600	343, 025	80, 691	17, 339	2, 101	368½	5, 305	5, 393¾	4, 468	88¼	26¼	265¼	2
New Baltimore,	18, 279¼	6, 124¼	1, 163, 074	105, 411	41, 711	4, 512¼	1, 282½	5, 367	6, 335	5, 498½	19	39	211	615
Prattsville,	8, 784	4, 854	227, 735	52, 189	9, 020	1, 520	226½	3, 308	2, 708	1, 834	6½	21	63½	2
Windham,	14, 840¼	9, 892	367, 671	73, 464	13, 709	1, 878½	368	5, 827½	5, 753	3, 386	19	25	125½	5
Total,	212, 223⅞	150, 604½	8, 457, 699	1, 092, 900	1,196,548	41, 600	5, 755¼	71, 130¾	71, 395⅛	58, 524¼	355¼	007¼	3, 175½	2, 297¾

ESSEX COUNTY.—(Continued.)

TOWNS.	Winter Wheat.	Oats.		Rye.		Barley.		Buckwheat.		Corn.		Potatoes.		Peas.	
	Bushels harvested.	Acres sown.	Bushels harvested.	Acres sown.	Bushels harvested.	Acres sown.	Bushels harvested.	Acres sown.	Bushels harvested.	Acres planted.	Bushels harvested.	Acres planted.	Bushels harvested.	Acres sown.	Bushels harvested.
North Hudson,..	......	....	....	......	....	......	....	......	....	......	....	......	....	......	....
St. Armand,....	......	137	2,915	9	200	10	228	52	849	11	238	41¼	36,005	2½	46
Schroon,.......	31½	1,062	15,536	51	474	10½	88	371	3,698½	415¼	8,194	311½	23,378	11⅞	129½
Ticonderoga, ...	380	1,347	30,731	106	1,116	15	116	43	258	538	11,357	231	16,513	113	1,548
Westport,.......	15	1,103¾	19,585	33½	166	½	4	55¼	167½	273½	3,562	268⅞	12,999	336¼	3,926
Willsboro',.....	78	1,099	20,768	180½	1,555	1	45	169	1,159	426¼	8,201	270	19,729	117	1,225½
Wilmington,....	......	573	3,631	112	622	1	10	215	500	214	2,289	232	9,989	13	32
Total, ...	2,484	14,334¾	234,946	1,631¼	13,357½	86	1,118½	2,431¾	13,701¾	5,866¾	105,369	4,286⅞	318,021	1,088¾	11,625¾

FRANKLIN COUNTY.—(Continued.)

TOWNS.	Winter Wheat.	Oats.		Rye.		Barley.		Buckwheat.		Corn.		Potatoes.		Peas.	
	Bushels harvested.	Acres sown.	Bushels harvested.	Acres sown.	Bushels harvested.	Acres sown.	Bushels harvested.	Acres sown.	Bushels harvested.	Acres planted.	Bushels harvested.	Acres planted.	Bushels harvested.	Acres sown.	Bushels harvested.
Bangor,........	26¾	852½	13 236	83¾	827	41	539	114¼	962	419¼	9,375	806½	65,963	89½	1,048
Belmont, ...	......	458½	5 881	11½	124	27¾	196	129½	1,006	99¾	1,352	145½	12,631	21	241
Bombay, ...	528½	668	11 766	77½	528	28½	402	102¾	890	391¾	7,156	324¾	21,349	170	2,180
Brandon,.......	13	248½	3,762	42¾	417	6	101	25	221	75¾	925	382¾	33,962	17¾	207
Burke,.........	84	549¼	6,521	145¾	1,203	65½	689	161¼	1,041½	388½	6,102	369	30,221	78	860
Chateaugay,....	33	978	9,188	171	1,260	146	980	265½	1,453	409½	5,412	732½	58,716	115	934
Constable,......	272½	376½	5,085½	370	2,512	20¼	189	151	636	454⅞	5,746	364	28,356	34	336½
Dickinson,......	8	467½	8,643	226	2,465	158¼	89	88	731	392½	6,296	401	29,950	47	561
Duane,.........	......	386	5,836	24	193	12½	131	38¼	476¼	9¾	248	72¼	6,233	½	6
Fort Covington,.	209	710⅞	13,836½	25½	398	75	1,371¾	100⅝	709½	422⅛	9,911	244⅞	18,843	139¼	1,923¼
Franklin,.......	23	569¼	8,033	174	2,368½	1½	30	105½	1,354	25¼	471	192¾	20,559	11	97¼
Harrietstown,...	......	123¾	3,356	3¾	35	10¼	140	54¾	1,063	13⅜	165½	43⅛	6,365	3¼	54
Malone, ...	38	1,845½	29,339	445½	4,657	80¼	1,050	184½	1,868¾	758	13,607	947½	94,772	189⅛	2,604½
Moira, ...	49	614	8,973	156½	1,134	3¾	37	47¾	491	426⅞	8,632½	359	33,581	47½	566
Westville, ...	69	563½	11,161	279	2,070	17	244	137	722	563	8,216	323½	22,924	42	456
Total, ...	1,353¾	9,411⅝	144,617	2,235½	20,191½	693½	6,188¾	1,705⅝	13,625¼	4,850¼	83,615	5,709	484,425	1,004⅞	12,074½

FULTON COUNTY.—(Continued.)

TOWNS.	Winter Wheat.	Oats.		Rye.		Barley.		Buckwheat.		Corn.		Potatoes.		Peas.	
	Bushels harvested.	Acres sown.	Bushels harvested.	Acres sown.	Bushels harvested.	Acres sown.	Bushels harvested.	Acres sown.	Bushels harvested.	Acres planted.	Bushels harvested.	Acres planted.	Bushels harvested.	Acres sown.	Bushels harvested.
Bleecker,.......	......	145	1,770	18	255	13¼	118	29¼	192	20¼	194	110	5,968	1½	3
Broadalbin,.....	260	1,972	39,411	54½	692	166½	2,424	773	8,978	1,029	20,287	367¾	29,938	51	1,041
Caroga, ...	......	183	3,480	5	50	10	149	52½	474	35	710	59½	4,487	4	58
Ephratah,......	658	1,692	29,886	448½	6,951	42	712	620½	7,175	543¾	12,239	239¾	16,998	202½	3,474
Johnstown,.....	1,954½	4,303	98,853	661½	8,409	242¾	4,430	1,501½	21,380	1,967½	50,858	367	38,673	320	6,002
Mayfield,.......	218	2,468¼	47,564	318¾	3,550½	65¼	1,094	835	9,598½	1,157¾	21,324	318¾	24,016	51¾	999
Northampton,...	......	893	18,392	22	268	23	310	462	5,640	617	11,327	232	17,193	11	153
Oppenheim,.....	130	2,190½	39,737	46½	564	137	2,008	525¼	5,113	723¼	16,954	308¼	22,199	69½	1,322
Perth, ...	424	2,795	65,007	127	1,602	186¼	2,745	642¾	10,584	826¼	19,923	163¾	15,601	55½	1,050
Stratford, ...	......	726	11,755	6	42	45¼	714	80¾	624½	93¼	1,917	119¼	7,891	7½	100
Total,........	3,644½	17,367¾	355,855	1,707¾	22,383½	931¼	14,704	5,522¼	69,759	7,013	155,733	2,284	182,964	774¼	14,202

GENESEE COUNTY.—(Continued.)

TOWNS.	Winter Wheat.	Oats.		Rye.		Barley.		Buckwheat.		Corn.		Potatoes.		Peas.	
	Bushels harvested.	Acres sown.	Bushels harvested.	Acres sown.	Bushels harvested.	Acres sown.	Bushels harvested.	Acres sown.	Bushels harvested.	Acres planted.	Bushels harvested.	Acres planted.	Bushels harvested.	Acres sown.	Bushels harvested.
Alabama,.......	76564	947½	31,057	15	10	239	5,402	75¾	750	1,912½	50,999	166½	12,892	19	320
Alexander, ...	39760	1,012	27,108	1	35	334½	6,268	225¾	1,701	961	27,970	197½	11,351	109	1,332
Batavia,........	85828	1,359¼	31,719	6	60	311¾	6,477	212¾	2,278	1,654½	45,687	246⅛	18,350	53	736
Bergen, ...	43805	550½	15,908	......	....	264	5,651	62⅛	333	951½	27,171	95¾	7,052	9	195
Bethany,.......	48063	861¾	19,462	......	....	337¾	5,512	264½	1,681½	1,067	25,316	192	12,991	63¾	791½
Byron,.........	57538	766	24,005	......	....	194	4,701	47	337	1,343	36,567	114¾	8,440	28½	445
Darien,.........	20444	1,410	31,167	47	608	330¼	4,868	274½	2,554	917	23,246	276¾	17,604	76½	1,089
Elba, ...	63564	898	29,985	......	....	217½	5,114	112	832	1,379	39,720	136½	11,567	56½	821
Le Roy,........	112387	647¾	20,456	2	34	208½	4,526	70½	342	1,575	39,361	194⅞	13,142	54½	870
Oakfield,.......	35175	586½	19,098	......	....	70½	1,430	64¾	315	880½	26,451	66	4,834	12½	215
Pavilion,.......	55056	512¼	12,384	2	40	231½	3,729	182¾	1,848½	1,288½	35,998	153⅛	10,448	36½	564
Pembroke, ...	33011	916¼	23,464	6½	62	67	1,082	191½	1,566½	1,351½	34,566	361⅞	25,634	49⅞	646
Stafford, ...	89266	504¾	13,996	20	300	242¾	5,059	46	375	1,005¼	24,000½	182	12,969	53	773
Total,........	760461	10,972½	299,809	99½	1,149	3,049	59,819	1,829⅞	14,913½	16,286¼	437,052½	2,383¾	167,274	621⅛	8,797½

GREENE COUNTY.—(Continued.)

TOWNS.	Winter Wheat.	Oats.		Rye.		Barley.		Buckwheat.		Corn.		Potatoes.		Peas.	
	Bushels harvested.	Acres sown.	Bushels harvested.	Acres sown.	Bushels harvested.	Acres sown.	Bushels harvested.	Acres sown.	Bushels harvested.	Acres planted.	Bushels harvested.	Acres planted.	Bushels harvested.	Acres sown.	Bushels harvested.
Ashland,.......	25	618	4,834	208½	1,910½	40¾	363½	492	2,701½	222	3,806	156¼	7,524	19¾	165½
Athens,........	463½	907¼	11,927½	1,064¾	3,817	8	....	282¼	925	779½	9,954	169½	5,099	32	269
Cairo,..........	558½	1,704	13,153	1,682½	13,246	4	16	1,321½	3,977	1,299½	10,557	381½	8,254	13	83
Catskill,.......	1,132½	1,412	17,089	1,416¼	11,406	16¾	129½	770½	5,340½	1,242½	16,600	278¼	9,245	17¾	156¼
Coxsackie,......	1,013½	1,748¾	18,081	966	7,692	18	83	581	1,582	1,361½	15,998	439¾	17,009	11½	53¼
Dunham,.......	833½	2,532¼	22,698	700½	6,230½	113¼	578	1,294¼	1,448¼	1,446½	8,809	184½	5,821½	38	170½
Greenville,......	1,444½	1,977½	24,060	685	6,221	16	154½	1,394	2,623½	1,433¼	9,897	208	5,679	19½	91
Halcott,........	......	640	8,146	92	830	......	....	386	3,301	61	394	74	1,348	9	52
Hunter,........	......	249½	802	103¾	870	¾	15	243¼	1,896	49¾	807	179¾	8,264	2¾	33
Jewett,.........	......	397¼	3,446	176¾	1,869	16½	124	292¾	1,350¼	159¾	3,842	154½	5,864½	21¾	166½
Lexington, ...	12	923½	6,735	298	2,437	1¾	27	470	2,330½	240	3,657	191⅜	6,902	11	96
New Baltimore,.	1,860	1,841,	22,178	1,443½	11,611½	15½	62	927	2,643	1,163¾	9,871	315	21,789	25⅛	116
Prattsville, ...	3	626	1,751	1,095	2,072	½	4	1,127	975	195½	2,591	140¼	3,536	14¼	60
Windham,......	......	742½	6,007	211¾	2,019½	19½	231	439½	2,820	164¾	2,421	203½	10,536	3¾	20½
Total, ...	7,346	16,319½	160,907½	10144¼	72,232	271¼	1,787½	10,021	33,913⅛	9,819¼	99,204	3,076⅛	116,871	239⅛	1,532½

ESSEX COUNTY.—(Continued.)

Towns.	Beans. Acres planted.	Beans. Bushels harvested.	Turnips. Acres sown.	Turnips. Bushels harvested.	Flax. Acres sown.	Flax. Pounds of lint.	Flax. Bushels of seed.	Hemp. Acres sown.	Hemp. Tons of hemp.	Hops. Acres planted.	Hops. Pounds harvested.	Tobacco. Acres planted.	Tobacco. Pounds harvested.	Apple Orchards. Bushels of apples.	Apple Orchards. Barrels of cider.
North Hudson,															
St. Armand,	¼	8	6⅞	1,280											
Schroon,	7⅜	87¼	10½	1,732	¼		½							3,385	17
Ticonderoga,	1		2	70										7,995	207
Westport,	35½	383	1⅝	370										6,815	31
Willsboro',	89¼	714	1⅝	640	⅛	20				5				10,638	207
Wilmington,	3	15	2	125										1,027	
Total,	284	2,818	64	9,128	2⅝	195	6½			5	9			64,200½	909½

FRANKLIN COUNTY.—(Continued.)

Towns.	Beans. Acres planted.	Beans. Bushels harvested.	Turnips. Acres sown.	Turnips. Bushels harvested.	Flax. Acres sown.	Flax. Pounds of lint.	Flax. Bushels of seed.	Hemp. Acres sown.	Hemp. Tons of hemp.	Hops. Acres planted.	Hops. Pounds harvested.	Tobacco. Acres planted.	Tobacco. Pounds harvested.	Apple Orchards. Bushels of apples.	Apple Orchards. Barrels of cider.
Bangor,	17½	142¼	2¼	342	⅛	500				41	23,782			2,822	24
Belmont,	3½	27½	5¼	95	¾	12	½			1	800			165	
Bombay,	26¼	234¼	1¼	275							142		53	1,054	
Brandon,	4½	75	2¼	115						7	2,700			66	
Burke,	21⅝	221	1	664						6½	2,508			2,626	3½
Chateaugay,	7	51	6	347						20	7,233			2,349	65
Constable,	12¼	100	2	800			1			103½	37,658			4,048	196½
Dickinson,	7¾	76	2⅞	530						1½	44			440	
Duane,			4	570						4¾	4,500				
Fort Covington,	16½	185	1⅛	315						16	7,140	⅛	100	4,042	21
Franklin,	2½	27	9¼	2,198						2	1,369				
Harrietstown,			13⅜	2,180											
Malone,	19	307¼	7⅞	2,945	½	24				208¼	140,441			7,619	67¼
Moira,	16¼	231	5½	968	½	90	1			4¾	2,050			635	
Westville,	20⅛	162	3	748	⅝	78	4			2	850			407	
Total,	174¾	1,839¼	67¼	13,092	2½	704	6½			418¼	231,217	⅛	153	26,273	377¼

FULTON COUNTY.—(Continued.)

Towns.	Beans. Acres planted.	Beans. Bushels harvested.	Turnips. Acres sown.	Turnips. Bushels harvested.	Flax. Acres sown.	Flax. Pounds of lint.	Flax. Bushels of seed.	Hemp. Acres sown.	Hemp. Tons of hemp.	Hops. Acres planted.	Hops. Pounds harvested.	Tobacco. Acres planted.	Tobacco. Pounds harvested.	Apple Orchards. Bushels of apples.	Apple Orchards. Barrels of cider.
Bleecker,	2½	9¼	7¼	233										1,110	4½
Broadalbin,	½	8	2½	245	30¾	42,700	227							11,512	338
Caroga,			4⅜	505						3				490	
Ephratah,	⅛	3	1¼	170						2				4,400	135
Johnstown,	13⅞	375	8	1,222	¾	200	4½							27,844	804
Mayfield,	2	76	6	403	½	250	6			10				18,136	422
Northampton,	1¼	9	1	25										6,441	240
Oppenheim,	4	90	2	320	14¾	1,785	132½			8				15,435	288
Perth,	5⅛	137	1¼	385	94¾	174,035	835½							11,902	420
Stratford,	9¾	54	4½	705	1¾	4,035	10							2,872	19
Total,	39⅛	761¼	38⅛	4,213	143¼	223,005	1,215½			23				100,142	2,670½

GENESEE COUNTY.—(Continued.)

Towns.	Beans. Acres planted.	Beans. Bushels harvested.	Turnips. Acres sown.	Turnips. Bushels harvested.	Flax. Acres sown.	Flax. Pounds of lint.	Flax. Bushels of seed.	Hemp. Acres sown.	Hemp. Tons of hemp.	Hops. Acres planted.	Hops. Pounds harvested.	Tobacco. Acres planted.	Tobacco. Pounds harvested.	Apple Orchards. Bushels of apples.	Apple Orchards. Barrels of cider.
Alabama,	39⅛	837	1¼	238										10,355	217½
Alexander,	28¾	352	3¾	240										33,644	536
Batavia,	9⅞	109	5¼	515	7		26						30	18,436	468
Bergen,	15½	108	6¼	960						2	1,617			15,872	351
Bethany,	59½	720½	1⅜	189	⅛		1			3	1,880	2⅛	2,100	41,912	542
Byron,	48	542								9	6,600			12,366	407
Darien,	113	1,560¼	4¾	727	39	117,500	448½							34,858	498
Elba,	3⅜	44	3	867										29,041	571
Le Roy,	50	589¼	4¾	880	7	1,000	90			7	1,910			26,180	686
Oakfield,	6	66	¼	30										9,818	292
Pavilion,	226¼	2,798	3¾	510	4		30							32,896	517
Pembroke,	22½	367½	2⅞	581										17,585	327½
Stafford,	14	476	4½	909								2	2,000	13,158	354
Total,	635½	8,569½	41¾	6,646	57⅛	118,500	595½			21	12,007	4⅛	4,130	296,121	5,767

GREENE COUNTY.—(Continued.)

Towns.	Beans. Acres planted.	Beans. Bushels harvested.	Turnips. Acres sown.	Turnips. Bushels harvested.	Flax. Acres sown.	Flax. Pounds of lint.	Flax. Bushels of seed.	Hemp. Acres sown.	Hemp. Tons of hemp.	Hops. Acres planted.	Hops. Pounds harvested.	Tobacco. Acres planted.	Tobacco. Pounds harvested.	Apple Orchards. Bushels of apples.	Apple Orchards. Barrels of cider.
Ashland,	3¾	42	8¼	807										11,366	142
Athens,	8½	96½	4⅝	213										10,935	490
Cairo,	21⅛	87	10¼	309	2	10,000				½	26			22,771	511½
Catskill,	3¾	19¼	34¼	1,842	⅜	60						⅛	75	15,153	654
Coxsackie,	3¼	28	1	210	⅛	25								18,318	352
Dunham,	22	92¼	1	141	2	520	14			6				25,805	375
Greenville,	30½	143½	1½	685										25,703	245
Halcott,			½	135										2,490	33
Hunter,	4¼	49	8	957										2,540½	289
Jewett,	5¾	13¾	1¼	97										13,611	64
Lexington,	18	66	2	290	⅛	15	½							13,128	220
New Baltimore,	1¼	12½	1	80										19,361	478½
Prattsville,	9	17	3½	357	⅛					3				3,380	31
Windham,	4¼	26½	4⅜	609½										8,253	69½
Total,	135⅜	693¼	81¾	6,732½	5⅛	10,620	14½			9½	26	⅛	75	192,814½	3,954½

ESSEX COUNTY.—(Continued.)

TOWNS.	MARKET GARDENS. Acres cultivated.	MARKET GARDENS. Value of products.	Pounds of maple sugar made.	Gallons of maple molasses made.	Gallons of wine made.	Pounds of honey collected.	Pounds of wax collected.	SILK. Pounds of cocoons.	NEAT CATTLE. Under one year old.	NEAT CATTLE. Over one y'r, exclusive of working oxen & cows.	NEAT CATTLE. Working oxen.	NEAT CATTLE. Cows.	Number of cattle killed for beef.	Pounds of butter.	Pounds of cheese.
North Hudson,	......	......	....	......	......	....	......	......	7	......	......	21	....	....	....
St. Armand,	......	......	1, 650	49	......	....	......	......	44	40	18	79	30	8, 430	300
Schroon,	......	$55	3, 595	30	......	3, 160	224	......	281	545	241	638	93	55, 980	6, 508
Ticonderoga,	......	......	1, 433	10	......	795	73	......	446	838	64	663	65	56, 126	5, 378
Westport,	......	......	3, 547	51	2	1, 086	71	......	309	603	110	623	317	45, 713	8, 377
Willsborough,	......	......	251	1	7	3, 572	197	......	295	682	110	654	63	50, 718	22, 430
Wilmington,	......	......	200	......	......	1, 280	33	......	165	317	109	343	117	25, 561	810
Total,	½	126	29, 844	399	9	27, 342	1, 419	......	3, 998	8, 739	2, 081	8, 749	1, 736	625, 542	93, 594

FRANKLIN COUNTY.—(Continued.)

TOWNS.	Acres cultivated.	Value of products.	Pounds of maple sugar made.	Gallons of maple molasses made.	Gallons of wine made.	Pounds of honey collected.	Pounds of wax collected.	Pounds of cocoons.	Under one year old.	Over one y'r, exclusive of working oxen & cows.	Working oxen.	Cows.	Number of cattle killed for beef.	Pounds of butter.	Pounds of cheese.
Bangor,	......	......	15, 590	25	......	1, 697	109	......	321	749	179	1, 002	81	80, 438	8, 685
Belmont,	......	......	9, 733	16	......	165	......	......	53	262	113	335	49	29, 550	2, 160
Bombay,	5	525	1, 440	15	......	2, 251	135	......	465	826	170	1, 158	57	258, 671	10, 715
Brandon,	......	......	6, 240	51	......	1, 361	67	......	55	144	113	253	47	17, 883	1, 750
Burke,	......	......	6, 590	20	......	925	35	......	285	554	148	866	....	61, 065	13, 620
Chateaugay,	......	......	13, 028	66	......	1, 208	74	......	291	589	109	990	87	66, 145	4, 752
Constable,	½	55	7, 944	......	......	1, 445	46	......	180	343	97	538	22	46, 885	4, 861
Dickinson,	......	......	14, 865	......	8	2, 130	109	......	171	373	159	652	68	57, 400	12, 344
Duane,	......	......	1, 860	137	......	....	......	......	33	66	60	91	7	7, 448	....
Fort Covington,	⅛	3	6, 360	32	......	1, 205	114	......	451	836	136	1, 422	274	123, 055	2, 849
Franklin,	......	......	3, 245	29	......	....	......	......	79	150	100	251	25	17, 966	440
Harrietstown,	......	......	1, 233	23	......	....	......	......	23	34	35	75	7	5, 010	....
Malone,	......	......	18, 554½	120¼	......	2, 533	134	......	480	1, 174	225	1, 842	462	135, 952	57, 190
Moira,	......	......	14, 463	......	......	3, 145	37	......	282	743	158	872	49	77, 876	22, 430
Westville,	......	......	3, 860	72	......	1, 557	59	......	305	582	57	572	70	64, 696	2, 120
Total,	5⅝	583	125, 005½	606¼	8	19, 622	919	......	3, 474	7, 425	1, 859	10, 919	1, 305	1, 050, 040	143, 916

FULTON COUNTY.—(Continued.)

TOWNS.	Acres cultivated.	Value of products.	Pounds of maple sugar made.	Gallons of maple molasses made.	Gallons of wine made.	Pounds of honey collected.	Pounds of wax collected.	Pounds of cocoons.	Under one year old.	Over one y'r, exclusive of working oxen & cows.	Working oxen.	Cows.	Number of cattle killed for beef.	Pounds of butter.	Pounds of cheese.
Bleecker,	......	......	660	48	10	478	22	......	40	31	65	177	19	12, 670	....
Broadalbin,	......	......	395	18	8	3, 096	236	......	433	811	91	1, 121	309	99, 405	10, 015
Caroga,	......	......	250	5	......	....	......	......	29	63	47	177	9	13, 325	87
Ephratah,	......	670	7, 139	270	......	3, 214	198	......	281	590	85	1, 011	100	83, 525	52, 900
Johnstown,	¼	35	1, 151	47	131	5, 919	307	......	668	1, 126	142	2, 250	580	242, 117	10, 114
Mayfield,	......	......	312	37½	......	4, 635	152	......	470	721	179	1, 287	125	102, 631	27, 306
Northampton,	......	......	1, 426	27	15	2, 048	87	......	261	510	201	509	23	53, 198	6, 045
Oppenheim,	......	......	5, 591	289	10	2, 337	137	......	498	771	183	2, 345	197	127, 741	433, 971
Perth,	......	......	50	17	52	1, 779	155	......	298	600	77	892	115	80, 575	9, 816
Stratford,	......	......	1, 857	62	......	255	6	......	103	177	103	499	32	25, 210	28, 825
Total,	¼	705	18, 831	820½	226	23, 761	1, 300	......	3, 081	5, 400	1, 173	10, 268	1, 509	840, 397	579, 079

GENESEE COUNTY.—(Continued.)

TOWNS.	Acres cultivated.	Value of products.	Pounds of maple sugar made.	Gallons of maple molasses made.	Gallons of wine made.	Pounds of honey collected.	Pounds of wax collected.	Pounds of cocoons.	Under one year old.	Over one y'r, exclusive of working oxen & cows.	Working oxen.	Cows.	Number of cattle killed for beef.	Pounds of butter.	Pounds of cheese.
Alabama,	......	......	3, 050	544	10	3, 435	117	......	372	730	186	927	72	74, 517	12, 248
Alexander,	......	......	2, 875	150	......	2, 650	48	......	371	794	114	781	155	74, 925	12, 385
Batavia,	2⅛	17	2, 279	30	19	1, 293	55	......	400	822	118	1, 240	100	88, 348	4, 825
Bergen,	......	......	2, 500	114	10	1, 625	129	......	315	448	69	589	294	59, 907	4, 686
Bethany,	......	......	27, 016	262	......	5, 495	314	......	360	658	104	832	102	77, 271	16, 179
Byron,	......	......	9, 800	110	......	2, 200	67	......	445	787	82	746	66	62, 820	7, 345
Darien,	1⅝	159	11, 967	142	48½	4, 940	285½	......	387	711	208	1, 095	52	88, 117	11, 528
Elba,	6¼	365	2, 575	44	......	2, 221	71	......	322	599	58	739	63	71, 340	1, 325
Le Roy,	3	100	1, 755	20	7	1, 975	87	......	306	758	91	970	444	89, 247	6, 980
Oakfield,	......	......	430	11	......	805	69	......	196	309	40	329	67	18, 574	1, 293
Pavilion,	......	......	11, 525	268	2	2, 605	168½	......	285	796	124	842	160	80, 087	15, 140
Pembroke,	......	......	1, 670	31	19	1, 855	76	......	328	538	158	888	126	93, 497	8, 438
Stafford,	......	......	2, 614	21	150	1, 260	81	......	211	579	65	563	88	40, 480	3, 501
Total,	13	641	80, 056	1, 747	265½	32, 359	1, 568	......	4. 298	8, 529	1, 417	10, 541	1. 789	919, 130	105, 873

GREENE COUNTY.—(Continued.)

TOWNS.	Acres cultivated.	Value of products.	Pounds of maple sugar made.	Gallons of maple molasses made.	Gallons of wine made.	Pounds of honey collected.	Pounds of wax collected.	Pounds of cocoons.	Under one year old.	Over one y'r, exclusive of working oxen & cows.	Working oxen.	Cows.	Number of cattle killed for beef.	Pounds of butter.	Pounds of cheese.
Ashland,	......	......	1, 510	41	......	3, 847	263	......	327	501	69	727	98	69, 815	1, 025
Athens,	16¾	985	....	......	......	832	57½	......	107	149	93	509	63	42, 776	300
Cairo,	......	......	124	30	......	4, 857	393	......	322	445	231	1, 040	284	96, 675	937
Catskill,	18	1, 330	25	30	......	492	10	......	258	442	210	1, 076	365	90, 720	....
Coxsackie,	21	1, 810	....	......	......	905	137	......	197	237	89	791	161	83, 735	....
Durham,	......	......	149	132	17¼	2, 400	215	......	393	685	221	1, 352	198	121, 917	6, 876
Greenville,	......	......	....	113	......	1, 584	185	......	249	322	170	1, 051	223	109, 906	2, 079
Halcott,	......	......	3, 821	41	......	2, 455	115	......	187	205	104	526	5	60, 916	50
Hunter,	......	......	3, 037	62½	3	1, 345	31	......	280	506	233	605	124	52, 311	130
Jewett,	......	......	21, 660	586	......	1, 975	98¾	......	430	762	209	1, 163	85	113, 520	4, 928
Lexington,	......	......	12, 361	411	......	7, 735	370	......	463	948	246	1, 144	177	105, 290	1, 285
New Baltimore,	¾	49	....	......	......	585	40	......	130	262	125	991	95	90, 589	....
Prattsville,	......	......	1, 049	40	......	3, 146	206	......	193	340	147	750	105	73, 780	50
Windham,	......	......	5, 159	64	......	782	81	......	322	636	202	867	100	79, 980	3, 657
Total,	56½	4, 174	48, 895	1, 550½	20¼	32, 940	2. 202¼	......	3, 858	6 440	2, 349	12, 592	2, 083	1, 191, 930	21, 317

ESSEX COUNTY.—(Continued.)

TOWNS.	Gallons of milk sold.	Horses.	Mules.	SWINE. Under 6 months	Over 6 months.	SHEEP. Number of sheep.	Number of fleeces.	Pounds of wool.	POULTRY. Value of poultry sold.	Value of eggs sold.	DOMESTIC MANUFACTURES Yards of fulled cloth made.	Yards of flannel made.	Yards of linen made.	Yards of cotton and mixed cloths.
North Hudson,	....	15	....	6	12	....	....	....	....	....	....	....	....	....
St. Armand,	....	42	....	84	68	....	....	....	....	....	....	....	....	....
Schroon,	....	426	....	251	320	1,568	1,193	4,421	$122	$343	81	435½	47	229
Ticonderoga,	75	623	....	296	294	4,497	3,735	14,434	701	223	93	40	....	....
Westport,	870	498	....	271	235	5,231	4,054	14,080	571	606	29	136	50	70
Willsboro',	....	448	....	242	314	4,941	3,433	12,743	404	798	68	76	....	50
Wilmington,	....	147	1	128	....	965	802	2,353	47	192	169	374	....	40
Total,	1,845	6,149	43	2,775	3,729	47,654	38,158	134,735½	3,460	5,553	1,440	2,664½	362	1,994

FRANKLIN COUNTY.—(Continued.)

TOWNS.	Gallons of milk sold.	Horses.	Mules.	Swine under 6 months	Swine over 6 months.	Number of sheep.	Number of fleeces.	Pounds of wool.	Value of poultry sold.	Value of eggs sold.	Yards of fulled cloth made.	Yards of flannel made.	Yards of linen made.	Yards of cotton and mixed cloths.
Bangor,	....	558	2	225	353	2,040	1,515	5,325	272	290	177	573	146	844
Belmont,	....	195	1	101	142	692	609	9,950	70	125	129	678	54	361
Bombay,	....	591	....	261	441	2,551	2,680	4,509	239	349	372	210	....	1,900
Brandon,	....	123	....	76	93	706	701	2,221½	54	106	68	481	114	....
Burke,	....	511	....	145	389	1,886	1,405	4,902	147	204	392½	753	18	1,120
Chateaugay,	....	670	....	191	564	2,194	1,785	5,675	223	364	624	841	....	671
Constable,	....	382	....	232	239	1,368	900	3,145½	171	149	8	1,182	204	10
Dickinson,	....	314	....	165	224	1,666	1,318	4,346	103	375	354	1,170	51	717
Duane,	....	66	....	23	62	191	220	541	....	....	43	3	20	26
Fort Covington,	....	634	....	476	635	2,250	2,187	7,275	620	239	312½	1,206	36	392
Franklin,	....	114	....	46	172	179	142	515½	8	99	22	143½	....	....
Harrietstown,	....	24	....	15	44	139	123	394	8	20	18	....	2	38
Malone,	6,300	1,084	....	557	785	4,452	3,814	12,558	442	665	150	747½	63	1,064½
Moira,	....	391	....	133	287	1,548	1,333	4,876	425	286	339	1,313	187	765
Westville,	....	372	....	174	285	2,096	1,383	4,504	353	339	301	250	91	1,459
Total,	6,300	6,029	3	2,820	4,715	23,958	20,175	70,737½	3,135	3,610	3,310	9,551	986	9,367½

FULTON COUNTY.—(Continued.)

TOWNS.	Gallons of milk sold.	Horses.	Mules.	Swine under 6 months	Swine over 6 months.	Number of sheep.	Number of fleeces.	Pounds of wool.	Value of poultry sold.	Value of eggs sold.	Yards of fulled cloth made.	Yards of flannel made.	Yards of linen made.	Yards of cotton and mixed cloths.
Bleecker,	....	95	....	47	66	98	75	292	2,150	2,425	....	61	70	33
Broadalbin,	523	644	....	676	544	2,487	1,467	5,041	2,080	2,766	77	177	87	639
Caroga,	....	115	....	81	105	149	86	280	18	76	155	20	....	46
Ephratah,	....	606	....	614	521	1,374	966	3,591	390	1,351	145	93	118	131
Johnstown,	7,000	1,231	....	1,991	1,365	4,703	3,121	10,473	1,863	1,969	550	666	145	102
Mayfield,	....	1,389	....	601	631	2,601	1,502	5,112½	1,265	1,333	32	65	....	100
Northampton,	100	357	1	295	212	1,764	1,253	4,066	414	372	396	310	20	99
Oppenheim,	....	731	....	713	660	1,501	1,175	4,442	833	1,642	632	698½	307	528
Perth,	470	491	....	691	428	1,965	1,045	3,710	1,204	2,135	66	289	72	47
Stratford,	10	170	....	138	135	327	211	896	72	53	150½	158	76	116
Total,	8,103	5,829	1	5,847	4,667	16,969	10,901	37,903½	10,289	14,122	2,203½	2,537½	895	1,841

GENESEE COUNTY.—(Continued.)

TOWNS.	Gallons of milk sold.	Horses.	Mules.	Swine under 6 months	Swine over 6 months.	Number of sheep.	Number of fleeces.	Pounds of wool.	Value of poultry sold.	Value of eggs sold.	Yards of fulled cloth made.	Yards of flannel made.	Yards of linen made.	Yards of cotton and mixed cloths.
Alabama,	....	1,049	....	921	1,288	8,844	7,693	28,871	589	999	226	493	....	273
Alexander,	250	700	....	337	654	11,530	10,283	40,676	1,130	904	101	280	80	50
Batavia,	20,732	1,229	3	792	1,406	7,802	6,986	26,564	502	672	28	142	30	23
Bergen,	....	683	2	678	634	4,667	4,795	17,575	720	1,009	62½	219	....	14
Bethany,	836	803	5	591	686	9,304	8,035	29,739	985	1,471	....	20	....	....
Byron,	....	970	....	858	894	5,429	7,333	29,793	960	1,689	27	138	....	142
Darien,	134,003	978	....	389	627	14,729	12,833	50,246	1,247	1,213	124	292	99	185
Elba,	125	988	....	866	923	4,618	5,064	19,315	61,300	1,200	131	90	20	91
Le Roy,	670	1,246	1	872	1,100	7,714	6,717	25,679	457	870	24	95	....	40
Oakfield,	....	461	....	393	589	3,007	2,696	10,160	221	316	....	73	....	....
Pavilion,	....	805	....	447	666	11,221	8,922	34,309½	1,879	1,308	60	364½	100	74
Pembroke,	1,198	781	2	384	791	6,594	5,315	20,860	744	1,602	79	237½	55	30
Stafford,	100	702	....	622	865	4,932	4,506	18,216	478	436	....	33	....	....
Total,	157,914	11,395	13	8,150	11,123	100,391	91,178	352,003½	71,212	13,692	862½	2,477	384	922

GREENE COUNTY.—(Continued.)

TOWNS.	Gallons of milk sold.	Horses.	Mules.	Swine under 6 months	Swine over 6 months.	Number of sheep.	Number of fleeces.	Pounds of wool.	Value of poultry sold.	Value of eggs sold.	Yards of fulled cloth made.	Yards of flannel made.	Yards of linen made.	Yards of cotton and mixed cloths.
Ashland,	500	251	....	251	236	962	546	1,907	341	641	111	124	....	48
Athens,	768	393	2	480	406	164	122	482	947	2,052	85½	142	20	15
Cairo,	250	714	5	1,091	572	1,069	670	2,505	1,714	2,337	421	525	168	....
Catskill,	4,000	713	2	992	731	1,615	863	2,882½	1,558	2,057	71	235	181	130
Coxsackie,	66,790	635	....	1,085	480	397	286	991	1,665	3,195	168	287	....	135
Durham,	....	745	....	1,550	694	3,507	3,982	14,757	2,212	3,468	257	261½	121	72
Greenville,	....	698	14	935	508	1,779	1,221	4,311½	2,011	3,499	196	268	32	515
Halcott,	....	152	....	67	133	1,390	775	2,480	340	70	276	582	56	250
Hunter,	350	192	....	90	196	1,205	686	2,297½	366	51	233	265	....	86
Jewett,	....	236	....	203	264	1,869	1,170	4,196	157	138	29	83	34	....
Lexington,	....	354	....	294	297	2,013	772	2,603	405	200	142	405	117	115
New Baltimore,	2,032	610	....	1,009	560	1,248	1,337	4,321½	1,849	3,981	83½	215	41	381
Prattsville,	....	239	....	165	219	608	543	2,180	466	373	98	154	92	41
Windham,	....	271	....	349	217	1,556	1,425	5,056	459	170	20	182	....	42
Total,	74,690	6,203	23	8,561	5,513	19,382	14,398	50,970	14,490	22,232	2,101	3,728½	862	1,830

HAMILTON COUNTY.

TOWNS.	ACRES.		CASH VALUE.			Acres plowed the year previous.	Acres in fallow the year previous.	Acres in pasture the year previous.	MEADOW.			SPRING WHEAT.		WINTER WHEAT.
	Improved.	Unimproved.	Of farm.	Of stock.	Of tools and implements.				Acres.	Tons of hay.	Bushels of grass seed.	Acres sown.	Bushels harvested.	Acres sown.
Arietta, ...	674	197, 760	$25, 850	$5, 267	$1, 336	128	4	181	381½	444	......	2	18	......
Gilman, ...	803	90, 902	94, 331	2, 215	768	111	45	268	360	229	......	......	......	......
Hope, ...	6, 729	56, 168	116, 213	34, 178	7, 470	492	2	2, 473½	2, 474	1, 751½	89½	68½	162	......
Lake Pleasant, ..	2, 737	150, 418	316, 001	9, 460	9, 365	530¾	80	1, 088	940	586	13½	2¾	13	......
Long Lake, ...	744	150, 835	12, 995	2, 821	724	81	....	185	334	141	......	......	......	......
Morehouse, ...	1, 186¼	6, 796½	31, 405	7, 373	2, 053	192¼	6	293¾	602¼	456½	10	......	34	......
Wells, ...	3, 802½	114, 099	160, 209	19, 490	3, 083	599½	3	1, 487½	1, 206	666	1½	3	18	1
Total, ...	16, 675¾	766, 978½	757, 004	80, 804	24, 799	2, 134½	140	5, 976¾	6, 297¾	4, 274	114½	76¼	245	1

HERKIMER COUNTY.

TOWNS.	Improved.	Unimproved.	Of farm.	Of stock.	Of tools and implements.	Acres plowed the year previous.	Acres in fallow the year previous.	Acres in pasture the year previous.	Meadow acres.	Tons of hay.	Bushels of grass seed.	Spring wheat acres sown.	Bushels harvested.	Winter wheat acres sown.
Columbia, ...	15, 668	5, 134½	864, 310	120, 988	39, 158	4, 310¼	9	6, 714½	4, 632¾	4, 500	128½	340½	4, 737½	37
Danube, ...	13, 719	3, 333	834, 626	117, 044	25, 293	4, 181½	22	4, 619½	3, 574½	3, 931½	316	214	2, 541	124½
Fairfield, ...	18, 443½	5, 402	1, 144, 678	177, 566	26, 274	2, 354	23	10, 129	5, 668	6, 982	11	147¾	2, 523½	5
Frankfort, ...	15, 511½	5, 058	849, 593	110, 632	26, 895	4, 423½	173½	6, 060	3, 957	4, 610	30	95½	1, 115	4½
German Flats, ..	14, 406¼	5, 429	793, 830	107, 258	31, 596	4, 370½	283	4, 805	3, 277	3, 649	42¾	190¼	2, 445	26
Herkimer, ...	13, 371	4, 945½	939, 958	129, 269	29, 332	3, 688½	135½	4, 985	3, 489	4, 201	140	162	2, 688	201
Litchfield, ...	13, 329	4, 118	691, 926	105, 255	32, 761	3, 046	....	6, 326	3, 750	3, 880	44	193	3, 097	......
Little Falls, ...	12, 359	3, 686	801, 215	119, 631	18, 855	2, 520	30	6, 737¼	3, 918	4, 939	71½	135½	1, 576½	11¾
Manheim, ...	14, 657	2, 741	1, 054, 343	147, 684	31, 272	2, 009½	10	7, 411½	4, 969	7, 234	128	53½	941	20
Newport, ...	15, 233	4, 289½	742, 056	131, 804	24, 469	2, 367	....	8, 976½	3, 721¼	3, 786	13½	55¼	842	......
Norway, ...	14, 604¼	5, 477¾	537, 565	88, 139	19, 475	1, 512¾	3½	8, 480¼	4, 012½	3, 294½	26½	88	1, 223½	......
Ohio, ...	6, 351¼	14, 201	183, 998	36, 395	10, 732	1, 541	57½	1, 852¼	1, 959¾	1, 149½	18¾	48½	379	......
Russia, ...	20, 360	14, 869	792, 257	142, 848	25, 698	4, 032	5	10, 167	7, 044¾	3, 978	42	242¾	3, 216½	......
Salisbury, ...	17, 218¼	47, 598	736, 028	126, 137	24, 277	2, 713⅜	47½	9, 576⅝	4, 565	5, 283¼	10½	81¼	1, 184½	2½
Schuyler, ...	17, 507	4, 871	1, 018, 200	152, 463	26, 942	5, 042	....	8, 827	3, 550	4, 181	1½	60½	911	71
Stark, ...	14, 187	3, 903	708, 250	94, 180	25, 375	5, 155	97½	4, 204	3, 321	2, 841½	608½	262	3, 037	49
Warren, ...	17, 119½	5, 954¼	998, 590	126, 564	31, 400	4, 329	29	6, 343	4, 845½	5, 306	284	301	3, 978	10
Wilmurt, ...	705	361, 859	377, 351	4, 800	1, 481	227¼	....	222	171½	87½	......	......	......	......
Winfield, ...	12, 665	2, 788	743, 410	95, 580	25, 160	2, 045	12	6, 294	3, 670½	4, 421	26	103¼	1, 713	19
Total, ...	267, 414½	505, 657½	14, 812, 184	2, 134, 237	476, 445	59, 867⅞	938	122, 730⅜	74, 097	78, 254¾	1. 943	2, 774½	38149	581¼

JEFFERSON COUNTY.

TOWNS.	Improved.	Unimproved.	Of farm.	Of stock.	Of tools and implements.	Acres plowed the year previous.	Acres in fallow the year previous.	Acres in pasture the year previous.	Meadow acres.	Tons of hay.	Bushels of grass seed.	Spring wheat acres sown.	Bushels harvested.	Winter wheat acres sown.
Adams, ...	19, 399½	6, 745½	1, 081, 082	132, 493	35, 401	5, 005	99	8, 746½	4, 074½	3, 492½	226¾	489	7091½	778
Alexandria, ...	19, 168	18, 263	692, 040	136, 918	37, 120	4, 600¼	549¼	6, 763½	6, 634½	5, 055½	513	1, 699¾	23463½	163½
Antwerp, ...	41, 099	30, 424	868, 189	175, 521	34, 876	5, 354½	79	16, 068	9, 684	7, 798	280	1, 600	26742	80
Brownville, ...	26, 636	8, 216	1, 013, 172	135, 380	52, 801	7, 858	682	11, 716	6, 635	5, 096	1, 958	2, 523	41053	366½
Cape Vincent, ...	20, 631	10, 561¾	824, 150	115, 416	32, 037	7, 520	239½	7, 126	5, 083	4, 736½	651	2, 892	43365	24
Champion, ...	18, 716½	7, 275.	892, 805	122, 669	35, 232	4, 059	26½	8, 719	5, 572½	2, 949	6	1, 618	8193	72¾
Clayton, ...	29, 257½	19, 986½	106, 290	183, 101	28, 377	7, 327¾	540	11, 395½	8, 414	7, 503	1, 153½	2, 318¼	29731	479¼
Ellisburgh, ...	36, 327¾	12, 242½	2, 256, 887	298, 182	56, 840	10, 257	558	15, 650	7, 085½	6, 386½	943½	1, 069¾	16221	1, 361¾
Henderson, ...	16, 885	6, 616	788, 285	123, 892	32, 621	4, 577	210½	9, 450	3, 632	3, 219½	178	607	9966	500
Hounsfield, ...	21, 622	6, 168¾	1, 013, 513	130, 781	41, 916	7, 545	175	8, 066	4, 387	3, 982	428	1, 198½	21235	624½
Le Ray, ...	38, 264¼	14, 592	1, 162, 050	173, 747	42, 929	7, 316¾	127	11, 961	7, 996½	6, 242	1, 434½	1, 696	21292	403½
Lorraine, ...	13, 192½	6, 678	513, 771	91, 039	21, 899	2, 504	25	6, 317½	3, 982	3, 437	74	330	4839	30½
Lyme, ...	20, 803	8, 109	896, 060	128, 453	40, 135	6, 821	43	6, 539	5, 516	4, 731	2, 849½	3, 606	69634	54¼
Orleans, ...	13, 765½	15, 157	938, 667	162, 036	32, 670	7, 094	252½	8, 212	6, 221½	5, 488	1, 096	2, 040	29368	462
Pamelia, ...	19, 810	3, 836	926, 513	114, 649	26, 613	4, 166½	152	7, 045	5, 184	4, 729	861½	958	14379	248½
Philadelphia, ...	16, 093	5, 747	661, 418	97, 702	26, 093	4, 698	33	6, 378	5, 401	2, 994	371½	1, 325½	16558	48¼
Rodman, ...	15, 749	6, 848	737, 515	135, 456	28, 264	3, 689	....	9, 590	4, 931	3, 972	86	591½	10111	141
Rutland, ...	20, 768½	6, 470	861, 716	120, 977	34, 788	3, 127½	135½	11, 772	5, 569½	4, 206	23	586¼	7877⅛	52½
Theresa, ...	15, 667	9, 937	628, 258	102, 769	26, 813	3, 464	279	7, 068½	4, 705	4, 177½	255	1, 153½	15281	51¼
Watertown, ...	20, 013½	5, 186½	1, 118, 175	180, 356	34, 863	4, 291¼	122	8, 864½	5, 175½	4, 305½	156½	764¾	10586½	327
Wilna, ...	17, 372½	20, 396	631, 473	111, 347	35, 228	4, 282	9½	7, 345½	5, 423½	3, 058½	29½	539	935¾	34½
Worth, ...	3, 981	21, 835½	106, 463	19, 909	5, 894	571½	....	1, 640½	1, 183½	1, 016	27	81½	750	......
Total, ...	465, 222	251. 291	18, 718. 492	2 992, 793	743, 410	116, 129	4, 337¼	196, 434	122, 491	98, 575	13601¾	29687¼	428672⅜	6, 303½

KINGS COUNTY.

TOWNS.	Improved.	Unimproved.	Of farm.	Of stock.	Of tools and implements.	Acres plowed the year previous.	Acres in fallow the year previous.	Acres in pasture the year previous.	Meadow acres.	Tons of hay.	Bushels of grass seed.	Spring wheat acres sown.	Bushels harvested.	Winter wheat acres sown.
Brooklyn, ...	1, 652¼	1, 196¼	4, 765, 450	554, 157	15, 225	1, 258½	72	306	244½	400	......	......	......	41
Flatbush, ...	2, 616	179	1, 089, 025	35, 673	16, 865	1, 282	....	187	768	1, 097	......	......	......	106
Flatlands, ...	3, 235½	1, 950	663, 000	51, 548	28, 265	1, 515	38	390	1, 009	1, 789	6	......	......	181½
Gravesends, ...	2, 506	695	588, 425	32, 815	18, 232	1, 370½	....	269½	441½	683	......	......	......	185
New Lots, ...	1, 862	983½	653, 500	54, 102	13, 231	838	....	131	554	871	......	......	......	164
New Utrecht, ...	3, 999½	591	709, 200	34, 475	25, 525	1, 925	13	258	846	1, 343	......	......	......	209½
Total, ...	15, 871¼	5, 594¾	8, 468, 600	762, 770	117, 343	8, 189	123	1, 541½	3, 863	6, 183	6	......	......	887

LEWIS COUNTY.

TOWNS.	Improved.	Unimproved.	Of farm.	Of stock.	Of tools and implements.	Acres plowed the year previous.	Acres in fallow the year previous.	Acres in pasture the year previous.	Meadow acres.	Tons of hay.	Bushels of grass seed.	Spring wheat acres sown.	Bushels harvested.	Winter wheat acres sown.
Croghan, ...	5, 524	100, 361	407, 238	30, 323	12, 202	1, 782	8	1, 173	2, 017	1, 460	26	205¾	1398	1
Denmark, ...	21, 951½	9, 697½	890, 075	139, 381	26, 156	3, 219¾	36	10, 510¾	6, 052	5, 487	37	762	11256½	79
Diana, ...	5, 747½	84, 953½	132, 269	29, 159	9, 087	1, 517	31	1, 529	1, 930½	836	16	187¼	1073	6½
Greig, ...	4, 854½	81, 481¼	261, 299	37, 221	11, 082	1, 715	34	1, 455½	1, 381½	1, 147½	12¼	51¾	355	3
Harrisburgh, ...	12, 410¾	10, 264	586, 452	73, 417	18, 662	1, 847	....	6, 041½	4, 397½	4, 084	78	452¾	5, 827	......
High Market, ...	7, 718½	28, 966	175, 583	30, 853	5, 947	603¼	....	1, 982	3, 270½	2, 353½	702¾	47¼	525	......
Lewis, ...	4, 099½	14, 538	193, 431	33, 107	5, 047	636¾	....	1, 567½	1, 723½	1, 926	51	2½	24	......
Leyden, ...	13, 670¼	5, 937	661, 595	100, 813	31, 863	2, 140	....	6, 653	4, 670½	5, 565	20½	169¼	2723½	......
Lowville, ...	16, 230½	6, 724	846, 220	121, 790	36, 608	2, 980¼	61½	7, 412¾	5, 212½	4, 555	29½	527	6327	140¼
Martinsburgh, ..	22, 024	20, 716	993, 581	146, 341	34, 920	4, 532½	79	9, 508	7, 436	6, 047½	115	866½	11581	57
Montague, ...	15, 559	9, 999	68, 494	9, 764	3, 586	48	....	81½	582	486½	129½	31	369	......
New Bremen, ..	8, 030	25, 585½	272, 741	39, 599	16, 025	2, 524	1, 321½	2, 617¼	2, 284	1, 385	98½	369¾	2301	11
Osceola, ...	1, 629	61, 992½	141, 704	14, 389	4, 399	483½	....	322	797	730	29½	26¼	269	......

(Continued on page 277.)

HAMILTON COUNTY.—(Continued.)

TOWNS.	Winter Wheat	Oats		Rye.		Barley.		Buckwheat.		Corn.		Potatoes.		Peas.	
	Bushels harvested.	Acres sown.	Bushels harvested	Acres sown.	Bushels harvested.	Acres sown.	Bushels harvested.	Acres sown.	Bushels harvested.	Acres planted	Bushels harvested.	Acres planted.	Bushels harvested.	Acres sown.	Bushels harvested.
Arietta,	......	59	735	1	6	......	......	8½	30	5½	78	68½	1,450	......	......
Gilman,	......	40	425	......	......	......	......	5½	32	8¼	175	12½	1,247	2	20
Hope,	......	504¼	6,760	4½	24	8½	......	210¼	1,561	240¼	3,874	143¼	9,916	4¼	19
Lake Pleasant,	......	180¼	2,379	3	31	2	9	59½	478¾	30	406	45¾	2,641	3	40
Long Lake,	......	59	1,111	16	152	......	......	18½	170	12¼	211	20½	2,226	1	12
Morehouse,	......	119¼	1,628	......	......	......	......	49½	277½	½	5	38	3,188	3¼	30
Wells,	6	226	3,663	8	64	4	33	107¾	364½	139	2,402	77¾	4,589	½	19
Total,	6	1,187¾	16,701	32½	277	14½	42	459½	2,913¾	435¾	7,151	406¼	25,257	14	140

HERKIMER COUNTY.—(Continued.)

TOWNS.	Winter Wheat: Bushels harvested.	Oats: Acres sown.	Oats: Bushels harvested	Rye: Acres sown.	Rye: Bushels harvested.	Barley: Acres sown.	Barley: Bushels harvested.	Buckwheat: Acres sown.	Buckwheat: Bushels harvested.	Corn: Acres planted	Corn: Bushels harvested.	Potatoes: Acres planted.	Potatoes: Bushels harvested.	Peas: Acres sown.	Peas: Bushels harvested.
Columbia,	474	2,244¼	49,982	3½	42	273½	4,376	334¾	4,763	492¾	12,540	234½	18,572	256¾	4,602
Danube,	1,405	1,851¼	41,823	75	1,696	215¼	4,200	284¾	3,359	711	20,911	123	10,794	216¾	3,874
Fairfield,	75	934½	26,442	¾	19	216⅝	5,053	51½	612	339¼	9,862	106⅛	8,609	10¼	312
Frankfort,	32	2,204¼	61,222	63¾	1,271	71¾	1,520	136¾	2,202	856	27,473	283¾	21,008	35⅝	836¼
German Flats,	193	1,898	38,226	332	5,188	173¼	2,542	261½	2,736½	679	16,295	198½	12,053	73½	1,084
Herkimer,	2,046	1,665½	33,103	107	1,757	176	3,471	153	2,259	706½	22,055	123¾	10,338	91	1,580
Litchfield,	......	1,276	32,581	4	60	390½	7,101	70½	1,086	709½	21,915	199¾	18,623	58	1,145
Little Falls,	104	1,205	26,803	76½	1,492	141¾	2,421	175½	1,782	438¼	13,005	150¼	10,412	113⅜	1,919
Manheim,	253	873	21,108	23	320	98½	2,046	41¾	591	442¾	15,073	116¼	11,344	83⅞	1,654
Newport,	......	1,131¼	26,960	31½	505	211¾	4,202¼	91¼	1,391½	599	15,415	115⅝	12,598	17⅞	268
Norway,	......	764¼	15,739	23¾	280	127¾	2,909¼	101	1,562½	208½	5,914	123½	11,751	8⅝	192½
Ohio,	......	1,043	14,738	9¼	92	25	357	157	1,314½	99⅜	2,241	143½	11,101	5¾	105½
Russia,	......	1,856½	44,030	116⅝	1,417	48	874	348¾	3,982½	792¼	21,376	258¾	24,386	12⅜	163
Salisbury,	7	1,837¼	32,369	31¾	180	109⅜	2,043	146	1,379¼	458⅜	11,426	241⅜	16,298	22⅞	328
Schuyler,	524	3,493½	108,680	132	2,376	78	2,404	122	1,788	1,007	30,705	202½	18,370	41	913
Stark,	436½	3,132	65,838	49	805	106	1,485	525¼	6,295	348	7,927	116¾	7,563	331¼	5,639
Warren,	109	2,322½	53,308	......	......	118¼	1,829	408¾	4,743	327½	10,059	202⅛	17,009	172	2,374
Wilmurt,	......	115½	1,855	6	50	......	......	49¾	177	15¾	313	17¾	1,021	½	4
Winfield,	246	915½	29,775	......	......	128	2,606	45¼	852	551¼	19,243	150¾	16,025	35¼	870½
Total,	5,904½	30,763	724,585	1,085⅜	17,550	2,709¼	51,439½	3,505	42,875¾	9,782¼	283,748	3,108½	257,875	1,586⅞	27,864

JEFFERSON COUNTY.—(Continued.)

TOWNS.	Winter Wheat: Bushels harvested.	Oats: Acres sown.	Oats: Bushels harvested	Rye: Acres sown.	Rye: Bushels harvested.	Barley: Acres sown.	Barley: Bushels harvested.	Buckwheat: Acres sown.	Buckwheat: Bushels harvested.	Corn: Acres planted	Corn: Bushels harvested.	Potatoes: Acres planted.	Potatoes: Bushels harvested.	Peas: Acres sown.	Peas: Bushels harvested.
Adams,	9404½	803	19,309	232½	3,092	1233	29,655	14½	155	1,426	23,768	228¼	15,707	105¾	2,001
Alexandria,	1192	778¾	12,152	510	6,646	434	6,926½	36¾	194	397½	4,963	175¾	7,518	337¼	4,130
Antwerp,	857	1,628	38,907	83½	987	504	8,684	29½	201	303½	4,083	263	12,246	564¾	7,631
Brownville,	4199	1,190	29,199	714	9,979	1656	33,848	58	326½	794	13,339	223½	9,663	254½	3,791
Cape Vincent,	257	15,811	7,409	543½	7,635	978	23,427	46⅛	290	554	10,780	243¾	13,107	159¾	2,799
Champion,	864	945¼	16,639	312	3,806	257¼	3,420	71¼	576	921	18,053	318½	23,440	124½	1,484
Clayton,	3802	1,819	25,822	1,311	11,216	986	20,179	45½	195	776	11,373	289½	13,816	274½	4,333½
Ellisburgh,	17356½	1,729¼	47,357	417	5,814	2012	54,094	25	222½	3,886½	92,308	468½	34,662	198	3,985
Henderson,	6057	536½	14,371	89½	1,293	11261	29,330	19½	89	1,095	16,801	182	12,016	67½	963
Hounsfield,	6522½	1,268½	3,406	738	11,164	1687	38,506	60¼	253½	1,302	16,690½	249¾	12,588	263¾	4,066
Le Ray,	5030	1,383¾	25,488	482½	6,969	1399	25,014	83½	634½	697¾	9,841	340¼	16,759	538	5,441
Lorraine,	337	911½	25,380	17½	250	327¼	8,042	22¼	285	588¼	17,589	184½	13,381	63¼	1,110
Lyme,	496	1,050	27,838	314¾	4,810	531½	12,450	25½	124½	478½	8,568	141½	6,870	100¼	1,581
Orleans,	4156	1,616	34,394	633	8,718	1107	21,957	42	217½	810¼	10,146	224	7,531	324½	4,074
Pamelia,	2893	841	18,224	351½	5,992	1090½	21,251	37½	271	276¾	4,545	164¼	7,780	170½	2,307
Philadelphia,	206½	864	10,697	5½	12	345	6,923	54	272	90¼	1,506	136½	5,762	361	5,547
Rodman,	1938	967¼	25,192	6	80	822	18,089	27	226	738	13,857	188¼	11,964	44	710
Rutland,	769	751	13,651	257¼	2,854	423¼	7,923	50	322½	735¼	11,355	255¾	16,832	61¾	840
Theresa,	382	648	10,876	145½	2,045	337¾	6,004	40	248	409¾	4,472	141½	5,057	244	3,052½
Watertown,	3570½	764¾	15,281	330¾	4,452	729	15,195	33¾	225½	1,074¼	12,264½	246½	11,766	115¾	1,485
Wilna,	220	1,727¾	16,788¾	280	1,577½	86¼	977	132¾	471¾	1,083½	14,445	428½	24,983	153¾	1,814
Worth,	......	341¼	8,850	......	......	55¼	790	11¼	109	48¾	1,032	60	5,583	9½	187
Total,	70509½	38,375½	456,230¾	7,775¼	99,391½	28262	392,684½	965⅞	5,909¾	18,486¾	321,779	5,154	289,031	4,536½	63,338

KINGS COUNTY.—(Continued.)

TOWNS.	Winter Wheat: Bushels harvested.	Oats: Acres sown.	Oats: Bushels harvested	Rye: Acres sown.	Rye: Bushels harvested.	Barley: Acres sown.	Barley: Bushels harvested.	Buckwheat: Acres sown.	Buckwheat: Bushels harvested.	Corn: Acres planted	Corn: Bushels harvested.	Potatoes: Acres planted.	Potatoes: Bushels harvested.	Peas: Acres sown.	Peas: Bushels harvested.
Brooklyn,	1,378	38	1,190	20	450	......	......	......	......	205½	8,694	248	28,565	124	14,455
Flatbush,	2,460	121	3,230	8	100	......	......	1	20	327½	9,725	610½	84,822	5	475
Flatlands,	3,626	55	1,425	71	1,353	......	......	......	......	394½	9,955	784½	103,750	18½	......
Gravesend,	2,969	53	1,422	64½	1,213	......	......	......	......	379	7,670	713½	70,595	......	......
New Lots,	3,465	55	1,578	55½	1,021	......	......	18	194	309¾	8,875	262	30,180	......	......
New Utrecht,	4,188	96	2,834	35	723	......	......	2	21	332	9,260	470½	50,325	27	2,000
Total,	18086	418	11,679	254	4,860	......	......	21	235	1,948¼	54,179	3,089	368,243	174½	16,930

LEWIS COUNTY.—(Continued.)

TOWNS.	Winter Wheat: Bushels harvested.	Oats: Acres sown.	Oats: Bushels harvested	Rye: Acres sown.	Rye: Bushels harvested.	Barley: Acres sown.	Barley: Bushels harvested.	Buckwheat: Acres sown.	Buckwheat: Bushels harvested.	Corn: Acres planted	Corn: Bushels harvested.	Potatoes: Acres planted.	Potatoes: Bushels harvested.	Peas: Acres sown.	Peas: Bushels harvested.
Croghan,	2	539½	5,921	365½	3,573	14¾	149	45½	170	315	3,907	308½	14,353	42	425
Denmark,	713¼	893	14,091	48	544	380¾	6,641½	45¾	390	457¼	9,529	237	16,940	175½	2,526
Diana,	10	479	4,170	18	138	13	128	88¾	203	516½	8,529	153½	9,538	59¼	390
Greig,	60	659½	8,731	122¾	962	11	54	117⅝	550	511¾	10,356½	199¾	10,985	31	213
Harrisburgh,	......	899½	18,308	......	......	107¾	1,650½	15¾	184¾	63¼	1,329	161¼	11,029	49	828
High Market,	......	670¼	14,852	13½	141½	9¼	110	218	3,307	6¾	220¼	204½	17,850	6½	87
Lewis,	......	426½	10,592	4½	43	4¼	103	04¼	721	8	246	118	8,011	1¼	38
Leyden,	......	1,346½	39,856	......	......	71½	1,485	29¾	508	233	7,283	225	23,130	8¾	222
Lowville,	2,084	882¾	15,682½	18	125	374½	6,762½	16¾	116	309¾	6,977½	173½	13,047	150⅝	2,558½
Martinsburgh,	798	1,918	40,855	17	180½	394	7,266	57¼	690	482¾	8,792	323¾	25,896	156½	2,848
Montague,	......	257	6,968	4	31	21	352	7½	105	11	246	82	7,599	2¾	52
New Bremen,	31	903¾	8,928	329	3,455½	49¾	307	55½	201½	484	6,111	320	17,271	51½	593
Osceola,	......	271½	5,338	3	40	3½	24	59¾	71½	77	1,632	70½	4,829	......	......

(Continued on page 278.)

HAMILTON COUNTY.—(Continued.)

TOWNS.	BEANS.		TURNIPS.		FLAX.			HEMP.		HOPS.		TOBACCO.		APPLE ORCHARDS	
	Acres planted.	Bushels harvested.	Acres sown.	Bushels harvested	Acres sown.	Pounds of lint.	Bushels of seed.	Acres sown.	Tons of hemp.	Acres planted.	Pounds harvested.	Acres planted.	Pounds harvested.	Bushels of apples.	Barrels of cider.
Arietta,	1	10	2	26											
Gilman,			¼	50										45	
Hope,	2½	99½	6	572	1	6,000								2,326	14
Lake Pleasant,	1¼	22½	1⅛	136										128	
Long Lake,	¾	5	2¾	330											
Morehouse,		2	1⅛	95										7	
Wells,		15½	1½	380										953	4
Total,	5½	154½	14¾	1,589	1	6,000								3,459	18
HERKIMER COUNTY.—(Continued.)															
Columbia,	1¾	13								87	81,068			27,029	483
Danube,	13¼	221			50¼	88,000	631½			31½	30,500			14,416	293
Fairfield,	¼	6½	1	30	13¾	1,950	85							37,772	297½
Frankfort,	9¼	168	1⅜	145						25⅝	17,433		100	21,828	451½
German Flats,	5⅜	106½			38½	23,100	314½			3¾	3,430			17,687	463½
Herkimer,	4½	78			30	20,000	300			1½				20,626	658
Litchfield,	7¾	266		118						16	19,131			36,411	761
Little Falls,	⅞	33	¾	81	5	2,000	1,600			4	6,100			17,515	366
Manheim,	1	15	⅛	50	3	18,500	30			7	7,550			15,174	368
Newport,	8½	148½	2	262	32¾	12,050	322			21	14,581			21,256	321
Norway,	2	56	½	72	14¾					9¼	2,800			8,635	129
Ohio,	1⅜	8½	6⅛	855	½	4.000	1			2	1,200			33	
Russia,	2⅛	37	8¾	214	17	1,700	85			3¾	8,310			17,175	347½
Salisbury,	8⅞	94	5⅛	270	¼	70	2½			¼				9,310	96½
Schuyler,	3¼	109	1⅛	375										14,224	592
Stark,	7¼	88½			103¾	132,550	833			132	127,916		15	16,586	194
Warren,	4⅞	112			2⅞	4,030	34½			240	179,997			19,782	395½
Wilmurt,			½	50	¼	100	2				17				
Winfield,	1¼	55½	¼	57						10	10,000			18,442	229
Total,	83½	1,616	27⅝	2.579	312⅜	308.050	4,241			594⅝	510,033		115	333,901	6,446
JEFFERSON COUNTY.—(Continued.)															
Adams,	31½	325	½	83	40⅞	8,625	333½							17,302	348
Alexandria,	8¼	97¾	3¾	510	1¼	90	4½			4	2,427	⅛	182	932	
Antwerp,	2¾	23½	1	90										1,492	
Brownville,	11¼	246	10½	1,023								¼	120	10,490	60
Cape Vincent,	23⅛	357½	2⅜	139										9,419	108
Champion,	9⅛	146½	½	30	6¾	1,554	62						3,289	10,262	208½
Clayton,	19½	297	2¼	400	⅜	350	1¼			⅛	10			2,770	3
Ellisburgh,	41½	511¾	2¼	309	⅛	190	3					⅛	100	50,656	654½
Henderson,	32	379	⅝	87			12							24,532	500
Hounsfield,	31¼	315½	3½	290	¼	110	4				5			10,147	410½
Le Ray,	15¾	252¼	1	25	1¾	720	60			6½	3,350			7,322	51½
Lorraine,	9	130½	½	150										9,489	188
Lyme,	12	185	¼	30	1⅞	202	8							4,475	32¾
Orleans,	19¾	105	2½	155			1½							1,681	
Pamelia,	9¾	102			1	175	12			2	2,000			1,529	13
Philadelphia,	7¼	38		8	9½		248							83	
Rodman,	5½	98	½	147						2	1,070			12,716	209
Rutland,	26¼	68	5⅛	210										13,943	156
Theresa,	6¾	66½								3½	1,633			640	
Watertown,	24¼	291½	¾	185						19	18,500			25,122	514¾
Wilna,	39¾	172½	2	111½			9½							318	2
Worth,	3¾	72½	1	130	⅛	50	1½							111	
Total,	389½	4.281¼	40⅞	4,112½	64⅛	12,066	760¾			37⅛	28,995	⅛	3,691	215,431	3,459½
KINGS COUNTY.—(Continued.)															
Brooklyn,	65½	6,985	117¼	15,225										50	
Flatbush,	½	12	19½	3,050											
Flatlands,				2,426											
Gravesend,		45	9½	910											
New Lots,			27	4,260											
New Utrecht,			39½	5,130										4	
Total,	66	7,042	212¾	31,001										54	
LEWIS COUNTY.—(Continued.)															
Croghan,	4½	36	1	14			1							40	
Denmark,	8	139	¼	5½	95	20,847	778							8,571	103½
Diana,	12½	140½	8½	497	3	2,000								78	
Greig,	9	164½	1¾	145	¼		1							235	2
Harrisburgh,	1¼	21	½	31	¼	500	1							3,337	64½
High Market,	1½	23	12½	1,262										35	
Lewis,			4¾	750										210	
Leyden,	1⅜	58	½	20	¼	100	5			5				7,600	233
Lowville,	4	94			115⅛	41,835	764			1	400			18,939	381½
Martinsburgh,	8¼	91	1¾	180	2		8			19	8,470			16,088	311
Montague,			5¼	920	2	500									
New Bremen,	⅞	8½	1	65										112	
Osceola,	1½	14½	6¾	1,097										183	

(Continued on page 279.)

HAMILTON COUNTY.—(CONTINUED.)

TOWNS.	MARKET GARDENS. Acres cultivated.	MARKET GARDENS. Value of products.	Pounds of maple sugar made.	Gallons of maple molasses made.	Gallons of wine made.	Pounds of honey collected.	Pounds of wax collected.	SILK. Pounds of cocoons.	NEAT CATTLE. Under one year old.	NEAT CATTLE. Over one y'r, exclusive of working oxen & cows.	NEAT CATTLE. Working oxen.	NEAT CATTLE. Cows.	Number of cattle killed for beef.	Pounds of butter.	Pounds of cheese.
Arietta,			680	25					20	39	33	52	3	3,770	
Gilman,			300	10		80	6		70	24	15	16	3	2,900	
Hope,		$10	4,029	110		3,140	168½		159	290	136	306	50	28,803	1,300
Lake Pleasant,			495	10		480	124		55	96	42	123	15	16,935	670
Long Lake,			1,495	45					12	27	20	36	5	3,622	
Morehouse,			150	11					56	69	50	98	16	8,202	
Wells,			2,358	87		1,910	103		116	211	64	221	35	19,050	800
Total,		10	9,507	298		5,610	401½		488	756	360	852	127	83,282	2,670

HERKIMER COUNTY.—(CONTINUED.)

TOWNS.	Acres cultivated.	Value of products.	Pounds of maple sugar made.	Gallons of maple molasses made.	Gallons of wine made.	Pounds of honey collected.	Pounds of wax collected.	Pounds of cocoons.	Under one year old.	Over one y'r.	Working oxen.	Cows.	Number of cattle killed for beef.	Pounds of butter.	Pounds of cheese.
Columbia,			13,073	469		560	19		333	423	46	1,801	105	79,985	353,309
Danube,			710	26		1,720	123		342	455	43	1,937	70	62,090	343,125
Fairfield,		18	2,813	102	10	3,040	391		272	398	53	3,753	84	76,523	1,238,820
Frankfort,	6	600	441	12	20	4,860	216		329	511	53	1,359	155	111,708	78,365
German Flats,	1	200	4,409	131	45	2.203	152		504	567	24	1,524	254	54,377	285.500
Herkimer,			6,460	356	2	1,017	83		323	364	16	2,266	101	93,541	379,200
Litchfield,			902	11		2,393	139		270	486	76	1,676	211	73,825	395.679
Little Falls,	2	300	2,225	191	35	1,610	57		264	437	10	2,176	261	59,270	587,500
Manheim,			2,265	421		3,150	203		326	379	8	3,320	217	87.533	1,087,200
Newport,		15	2,335	9		2,270	284		180	281	56	2,688	358	70,530	829 989
Norway,			6,498	144		1,193	119		130	233	26	2,137	44	38,145	549,823
Ohio,			6,527	199		435	54		122	206	64	500	53	30,550	58,220
Russia,			10,667	208		3,400	333		240	422	67	2,326	102	94,651	561,425
Salisbury,			2,262	77		1,291	67		255	509	78	1,827	127	65,219	694,500
Schuyler,						1,570	63		293	389	35	2,296	147	76,000	585,450
Stark,			2,235	38		2,238	209½		293	434	15	1,540	103	90,140	140,205
Warren,			7,029	299		4,364	319		305	500	67	1,917	97	83,135	374,299
Wilmurt,			1,302	95					11	13	10	46	4	3,350	700
Winfield,			1.075	855	33	1,033	96		254	329	38	1,564	64	54,805	525,210
Total,	9	1,133	73,228	3,643	145	38,347	2,927½		5.046	7,336	785	36.653	2,557	1.305,377	9.068,519

JEFFERSON COUNTY.—(CONTINUED.)

TOWNS.	Acres cultivated.	Value of products.	Pounds of maple sugar made.	Gallons of maple molasses made.	Gallons of wine made.	Pounds of honey collected.	Pounds of wax collected.	Pounds of cocoons.	Under one year old.	Over one y'r.	Working oxen.	Cows.	Number of cattle killed for beef.	Pounds of butter.	Pounds of cheese.
Adams,	⅝	50	11,492	276		733	55½		422	967	68	1,827	165	99,756	369,109
Alexandria,	1⅜	145	4,546	112	349	2,067	124½		629	885	247	2,200	209	183,209	48,366
Antwerp,			24,945	116		2,390	153		541	1,018	194	4,293	290	379,109	186,215
Brownville,			7,788	454		1,173	40		675	762	56	2,752	242	267,182	118,655
Cape Vincent,	1	30	1,120	24	1	275	10		563	902	128	2,054	136	159,146	24,800
Champion,			69,563	565		1,357	102½		292	620	120	1,941	147	160,596	148,718
Clayton,		30	4,045	48		357	30		818	983	196	3,011	420	206,851	179,475
Ellisburgh,			37,458	671	5	1,256	79		1,077	1,919	316	3,761	286	261,311	342,465
Henderson,	2½	130	8,6 5	121		400	29		521	1,052	48	1,368	119	136,048	36,937
Hounsfield,	10½	510	5.543	44		360	56		456	693	78	1,842	141	148,966	60,118
Le Ray,			18,640	477	42	1,700	102		533	915	80	3,258	229	249,898	257,182
Lorraine,	4½	75	19,804	45		100	15		255	504	84	1,601	34	94,323	211,822
Lyme,			780	16		540	39		518	776	76	1,716	231	120,497	91,716
Orleans,			4,091	93		1,265	105		603	1,073	130	2,662	131	212,975	8,320
Pamelia,	1	150	8,811	258	3	455	81		389	559	58	1,990	313	151,117	192,427
Philadelphia,			8,512	120		580	20		312	447	89	1,729	136	152,784	90,790
Rodman,			12,200	144					401	693	106	2,149	72	181,235	121,325
Rutland,	1	60	52,610	576		115	12		348	512	66	2,643	266	234,065	247,331
Theresa,		530	6,620	49		446	21		316	637	112	1,808	139	163,775	93,780
Watertown,	31	11,080	6,797	159		162	90		374	517	72	2,808	404	222,247	111,240
Wilna,			47,219	253		2,413	126		158	435	138	1,654	108	142,220	47,850
Worth,			5,240	31					70	115	60	405	17	22,298	30,818
Total,	53½	12,790	366,449	4.652	400	18,144	1,290½		10.271	16,984	2,522	49,472	4,235	3,949,608	2,819,459

KINGS COUNTY.—(CONTINUED.)

TOWNS.	Acres cultivated.	Value of products.	Pounds of maple sugar made.	Gallons of maple molasses made.	Gallons of wine made.	Pounds of honey collected.	Pounds of wax collected.	Pounds of cocoons.	Under one year old.	Over one y'r.	Working oxen.	Cows.	Number of cattle killed for beef.	Pounds of butter.	Pounds of cheese.
Brooklyn,	430½	120078			35				3	3	8	1,731	5,195		
Flatbush,		9082							15	7	2	218	157		
Flatlands,	32	3000							35	16	1	258	26		
Gravesend,		4610							55	59	12	223	84	11,030	
New Lots.	378	47067							18	50	16	188	21	6,395	
New Utrecht,	574	89715							34	34	2	216	17		
Total,	1.414½	273552			35				160	169	41	2,834	5,500	17,425	

LEWIS COUNTY.—(CONTINUED.)

TOWNS.	Acres cultivated.	Value of products.	Pounds of maple sugar made.	Gallons of maple molasses made.	Gallons of wine made.	Pounds of honey collected.	Pounds of wax collected.	Pounds of cocoons.	Under one year old.	Over one y'r.	Working oxen.	Cows.	Number of cattle killed for beef.	Pounds of butter.	Pounds of cheese.
Croghan,			17,840	240		350	38		50	314	216	256	72	33,212	
Denmark,			48,225	451		1,080	87		307	559	168	2,160	54	183,849	237,796
Diana,			40,547	326		800	43		63	196	142	387	107	36,900	524
Greig,			9,443	153		1,012	45		67	133	119	425	50	41,240	60,600
Harrisburgh,			18,782	140½		965	74		173	380	78	1,320	43	130,111	147,798
High Market,			500	73		140	5		188	257	163	763	48	54,761	24,200
Lewis,			290			460			84	121	135	505	36	34,824	53,400
Leyden,			6,931	94		780	57		255	383	152	2,164	136	178,566	204,600
Lowville,			22,390	2,006	16	665	40		199	395	70	2,377	81	123,103	497.514
Martinsburgh,	1	100	15,940	304		835	183		307	720	140	2,427	121	104,056	322,327
Montague,	⅛	15	7,635	120					24	74	79	169	29	8,305	
New Bremen,			14,952	165		794	66		89	302	234	642	126	68,437	7,200
Osceola,			2,800	129		541	25		64	148	70	167	19	16,090	

(Continued on page 280.)

HAMILTON COUNTY.—(Continued.)

Towns.	Gallons of milk sold.	Horses.	Mules.	Swine. Under 6 months.	Swine. Over 6 months.	Sheep. Number of sheep.	Sheep. Number of fleeces.	Sheep. Pounds of wool.	Poultry. Value of poultry sold.	Poultry. Value of eggs sold	Domestic manufactures. Yards of fulled cloth made.	Domestic manufactures. Yards of flannel made.	Domestic manufactures. Yards of linen made.	Domestic manufactures. Yards of cotton and mixed cloths.
Arietta,		16		2	25	7	5	36				20		
Gilman,		17		8	8									
Hope,		164		71	134	861	523	1,601½	$341	$70				
Lake Pleasant,		35		34	55	155	99	334	6		25	144		205
Long Lake,		7		4	35	38	39	111				20	20	30
Morehouse,		16		8	17	116	94	320		11	50	65	10	192
Wells,		83		42	67	304	288	849	97	60	108	362		212
Total,		338		169	341	1,481	1,048	3,251½	444	141	183	611	30	639
HERKIMER COUNTY.—(Continued.)														
Columbia,		706		407	486	2,134	1,361	4,978	1,120	982	502	374	208	153
Danube,		539		619	589	1,224	673	2,493	276	921	384	479	63	119
Fairfield,		429		786	699	621	420	1,714¼	663	161	213½	181	69	82
Frankfort,	38,700	679		620	627	1,576	1,189	4,452½	1,341	1,508	264¾	516		222
German Flats,	3,345	667	10	474	530	1,105	754½	2,786	441	534	316	427	16	
Herkimer,	8,925	614		646	741	862	586	2,037	513	506	547	360	237	222
Litchfield,		436		463	467	952	789	3,055	1,335	1,287	72	138		130
Little Falls,	2,480	469		550	721	449	281	1,151	620	643	31	148		25
Manheim,	112	451		736	654	363	297	1,232	220	1,314	362	99	27	117
Newport,	1,198	374		679	584	340	225	896	893	432	121	187	31	281
Norway,	200	257		386	266	154	129	541	286	233		215	15	300
Ohio,		219		80	121	331	207	860	271	140	157	214	123	264
Russia,		525		348	473	1,062	481	1,948	772	638	378	646	55	404
Salisbury,		453		361	373	491	375	1,387	564	289	87	174	62	678
Schuyler,		644		804	657	1,009	410	1,433	910	713	217	404½	17	117
Stark,		603		457	462	1,321	773	2,958	299	579	134	238	95	193
Warren,		673		376	459	2,904	1,735	7,430½	568	534	375	352	241½	190
Wilmurt,		29		5	14	39	28	111	60			40		
Winfield,		331		328	179	769	540½	2,098½	1,337	782				
Total,	54,960	9,098	10	9,125	9,102	17,706	11,254	43,561¼	12,489	12,196	4,161¼	5,192½	1,259½	3,497
JEFFERSON COUNTY.—(Continued.)														
Adams,	17,142	822		532	536	2,452	1,705	6,470⅞	1,979	1,457	361	689	220	519
Alexandria,	6,560	770		453	569	2,689	1,775	5,886	311	524	1,097½	1,135	287	1,384
Antwerp,	15,983	1,085	5	636	810	2,260	1,530	5,355	127	68	430½	356	44	128
Brownville,		1,090		726	640	3,582	2,331	8,554	707	2,035	809	1,044	115	414
Cape Vincent,	1,880	899		561	719	2,050	1,381	5,561½	226	1,405	952½	1,280	269	376
Champion,		649		302	434	1,082	800	2,848	860	671	361½	201½	127	436
Clayton,	1,527	978	8	777	1,005	2,801	2,057	7,284	387	1,124	686	1,640	46	424
Ellisburgh,		1,472		1,165	1,280	4,260	3,749	12,361¼	2,157	2,133	1,089½	1,896	435½	733
Henderson,	50	776		350	488	3,975	2,706	9,254	961	854	354	861	78	268
Hounsfield,	1,352	908	6	468	491	4,021	2,839	9,055	1,316	1,773	606¾	861	193	217
Le Ray,	82,095	998	1	820	710	17,787	1,464	5,401	589	1,454	1,406	1,506	693	707
Lorraine,		395		316	276	1,279	854	2,806	162	432	278	598	290	202
Lyme,	200	857		472	510	2,379	1,609	5,576	119	518	464	496	349	980
Orleans,		909		643	619	2,269	1,599	5,435	285	1,015	1,100	653	141	1,153
Pamelia,	8,046	584		497	394	1,687	1,225	4,747½	607	776	471	666	106	383
Philadelphia,	37,091	564		211	323	1,181	831	2,934	152	344	229	136		326
Rodman,		540		492	404	2,830	1,565	5,054	548	387	620	511	125	923
Rutland,		568		470	458	966	777	2,895	490	828	321	649	180	665
Theresa,		486		397	462	861	850	2,883	130	18	591	597	231	905
Watertown,	20,266	955		499	579	1,499	1,112	4,095½	647	936	275	383	121	38
Wilna,		645		198	515	1,322	1,049	3,572½	585	551	381½	394	187	514
Worth,		109		41	79	169	105	343	3		179	133	143	131
Total,	192,192	17,059	20	11,026	12,301	63,401	33,913	118,372⅝	13,348	19,298	13,063¾	16,685½	4,380½	11,826
KINGS COUNTY.—(Continued.)														
Brooklyn,	2888038	4,750	43	445	1,363				688	262				
Flatbush,	56937	361	11	162	194									
Flatlands,		320	39	187	390									
Gravesends,	3270	300	6	128	250				75	1,130				
New Lots,	82046	268	10	75	241				220	334				
New Utrecht,	3000	315	13	221	308	2	2	7	200	345				
Total,	3033291	6,314	122	1,218	2,746	2	2	7	1,183	2,071				
LEWIS COUNTY.—(Continued.)														
Croghan,		120		75	279	170	160	548	1,257	722	48	126		85
Denmark,		648		326	401	1,791	1,063	4,003	474	114	240½	366½	108½	264½
Diana,	250	179	8	65	162	317	243	729	145	214	245½	279½	14	300
Greig,		223		123	157	188	64	244	39	53	51	82	157	90
Harrisburgh,		365		222	262	684	534	1,852⅝	356	42	238¼	307½	12	323½
High Market,		153		125	152	458	464	1,521½	94	98	178	961½	69	588
Lewis,		117		93	89	88	59	187				104		
Leyden,		446		437	438	944	649	2,240¾	327	93	134½	375	107	134
Lowville,		494		411	396	630	858	3,008	317	226	136	211	158	254
Martinsburgh,		712		460	518	1,365	989	3,815	592	253	266	773	209	190
Montague,		55		13	48	17	11	42	10	21	229		83	125
New Bremen,	125	177		200	291	403	294	956	139	173	85	171	79	308
Osceola,		60	1	39	92	160	72	277	3	118		76		87

(Continued on page 281.)

LEWIS COUNTY.—(CONTINUED.)

TOWNS.	ACRES. Improved.	ACRES. Unimproved.	CASH VALUE. Of farm.	CASH VALUE. Of stock.	CASH VALUE. Of tools and implements	Acres plowed the year previous.	Acres in fallow the year previous.	Acres in pasture the year previous.	MEADOW. Acres.	MEADOW. Tons of hay.	MEADOW. Bushels of grass seed.	SPRING WHEAT. Acres sown.	SPRING WHEAT. Bushels harvested.	WINTER WHEAT. Acres sown.
Pinckney, ...	11,265½	13,150½	$401,751	$65,000	$18,746	1,702¼	....	5,591¾	3,911	4,117½	39	247½	3,785½	......
Turin, ...	13,720	5,642	590,760	92,217	20,545	2,560	5	6,356½	4,983	4,403	26	311¼	4,635	12
Watson, ...	4,705½	8,545	172,959	30,379	9,441	1,830½	65	1,827½	1,311	1,035½	6½	151½	1,381	8
West Turin, ...	15,400½	8,593	722,850	108,829	23,587	2,767½	....	6,867	5,279	6,183	329½	194¼	3,109½	......
Total, ...	184,540½	497,145¾	7,519,002	1,102,582	287,903	32,889¼	1,641	71,496½	57,238½	51,802	1,746½	4,603½	56940	317¾

LIVINGSTON COUNTY.

TOWNS.	ACRES. Improved.	ACRES. Unimproved.	CASH VALUE. Of farm.	CASH VALUE. Of stock.	CASH VALUE. Of tools and implements	Acres plowed the year previous.	Acres in fallow the year previous.	Acres in pasture the year previous.	MEADOW. Acres.	MEADOW. Tons of hay.	MEADOW. Bushels of grass seed.	SPRING WHEAT. Acres sown.	SPRING WHEAT. Bushels harvested.	WINTER WHEAT. Acres sown.
Avon, ...	20,743	5,084	2,092,390	224,355	43,345	8,707	5,230	4,021	2,059½	3,094	5	15	225	5,329
Caledonia, ...	20,602	5,276	2,431,010	216,785	57,677	2,136¾	5,599	3,512	2,249	3,056	19	......	......	5,786
Conesus, ...	13,455½	6,889½	964,746	99,784	20,140	1,910	2,301	3,274	2,002	2,263	60	198	2,998	2,780
Geneseo, ...	22,306¼	6,979	2,088,735	147,038	36,670	3,183½	4,887½	3,959¼	2,331	3,207½	41	1	18	5,209
Groveland, ...	16,479	8,058½	1,560,081	133,374	34,544	2,213½	3,058½	3,482	2,109¼	2,205½	42½	53	626	4,706½
Leicester, ...	17,309¾	3,418	1,343,227	133,373	38,112	2,611½	4,018	2,667½	1,491½	2,128	17½	1	22	5,375¾
Lima, ...	14,410¼	3,342	1,475,160	130,590	39,965	3,038	3,332	2,905	1,944	2,469	126	20	318	3,526
Livonia, ...	19,444¼	3,882½	1,844,948	173,115	38,960	3,556½	4,025	3,468¼	2,808½	3,377	924	253¼	2,836	4,551½
Mount Morris, ..	22,469	5,679	1,902,664	182,900	43,751	3,673½	4,902	4,386	2,824½	2,504½	70	22¾	207	5,972¼
North Dansville,	3,384	1,532	327,955	28,175	5,844	780¾	483	559½	537½	424	4½	33	220	843½
Nunda, ...	12,788¾	5,902½	777,175	109,609	24,325	2,404½	1,220½	2,991½	2,136½	1,828¾	45½	163½	1,204½	2,422¼
Portage, ...	10,361	5,625½	749,038	67,941	22,258	1,870	2,065	1,780	1,293	1,409½	15	167½	1,691	2,357½
Sparta, ...	12,225⅜	8,217	898,225	95,354	34,730	2,293¼	1,576¼	1,974	2,165	1,799½	69	113½	1,112	3,423
Springwater, ...	18,787¼	13,313½	832,424	115,995	25,132	4,850¼	2,104	5,046	3,160¾	2,539½	69½	708	5,339½	2,055¾
West Sparta, ...	12,973⅞	7,085¾	918,301	93,608	21,744	1,735½	2,636	2,423	1,877	1,550¼	43¾	171¼	1,188	2,825¼
York, ...	24,723¼	6,093½	2,200,154	225,388	52,238	3,578	5,496½	4,784	3,691	5,331¾	105	1	20	6,499
Total, ...	262,462½	96,378¼	22,406,233	2,177,384	539,435	48,142½	52,934¼	51,233	34,680	39,187¾	1,657¼	1,922¼	18025	63662½

MADISON COUNTY.

TOWNS.	ACRES. Improved.	ACRES. Unimproved.	CASH VALUE. Of farm.	CASH VALUE. Of stock.	CASH VALUE. Of tools and implements	Acres plowed the year previous.	Acres in fallow the year previous.	Acres in pasture the year previous.	MEADOW. Acres.	MEADOW. Tons of hay.	MEADOW. Bushels of grass seed.	SPRING WHEAT. Acres sown.	SPRING WHEAT. Bushels harvested.	WINTER WHEAT. Acres sown.
Brookfield, ...	30,640⅜	13,564¾	1,237,752	213,672	46,528	5,289¼	49	14,243½	9,591⅝	9,053½	93	300⅛	3,793	5
Cazenovia, ...	23,256½	6,870	1,241,330	186,536	46,057	6,651¾	95	8,692½	5,984½	5,127	62	686	8,548	305½
De Ruyter, ...	12,959	6,859	506,475	95,753	13,710	2,399	....	6,146	3,808	3,756	34½	197¾	2,792	......
Eaton, ...	20,828⅜	8,616½	1,296,951	192,148	35,102	4,042	43½	9,373	5,883	6,284	61¾	261¾	3,286½	30
Fenner, ...	15,021	3,561	722,141	101,835	34,007	5,407	27	5,553	3,218	2,520	22	555¾	6,325	76
Georgetown, ...	11,336½	10,275	346,517	83,801	14,896	1,940½	68¼	4,354	3,403½	3,476½	95¾	117	1,535½	......
Hamilton, ...	19,080¾	5,369½	1,058,757	201,078	32,056	3,249	26	9,273	4,995¼	5,159	3	152½	1,937	31½
Lebanon, ...	19,964⅛	6,171	909,095	183,266	28,833	3,098½	9	8,506½	5,824	6,108	6⅛	164⅜	2,136	......
Lenox, ...	32,206½	16,496½	2,133,250	272,208	59,480	11,866¾	1,182¼	9,570¼	6,069¼	6,201	126½	381¼	4,118½	1,691⅛
Madison, ...	17,468	4,812	960,075	129,640	30,910	3,841	60	7,891	4,579	4,582	89	234½	3,264	143½
Nelson, ...	20,931	6,130⅛	804,126	143,712	26,631	3,213	....	10,442⅜	6,789½	5,594	145½	367	4,520½	1½
Smithfield, ...	11,820	3,426	635,964	119,556	17,941	3,976	34	5,288	2,453	2,423	25	327	3,709	62
Stockbridge, ...	15,512	3,647	841,669	114,973	24,440	5,376	268	5,440½	2,805	2,742	83½	347¾	4,284	740
Sullivan, ...	26,369⅜	15,707	1,659,673	215,684	54,466	8,092⅝	748	8,689⅛	5,142½	5,237½	308	251¾	2,528	1,373
Total, ...	277,393⅜	111,505⅜	14,353,775	2,253,862	465,057	68,442⅛	2,610	113,463	70,545⅞	68,263½	1,155⅝	4,344¾	52777	4,459⅛

MONROE COUNTY.

TOWNS.	ACRES. Improved.	ACRES. Unimproved.	CASH VALUE. Of farm.	CASH VALUE. Of stock.	CASH VALUE. Of tools and implements	Acres plowed the year previous.	Acres in fallow the year previous.	Acres in pasture the year previous.	MEADOW. Acres.	MEADOW. Tons of hay.	MEADOW. Bushels of grass seed.	SPRING WHEAT. Acres sown.	SPRING WHEAT. Bushels harvested.	WINTER WHEAT. Acres sown.
Brighton, ...	12,079¾	1,672	1,787,385	100,425	47,472	3,960½	1,167½	2,194½	2,616	3,388½	61½	19½	349	1,639½
Chili, ...	19,855½	5,172½	1,678,430	172,116	48,776	3,938½	2,906	3,139	3,003	4,239	144½	7¾	77	3,870
Clarkson, ...	15,473	4,626	971,035	126,061	31,370	5,221	1,667	3,969	2,371	3,327	46	10	69	1,882
Gates, ...	10,601	1,935	1,361,815	62,600	27,520	3,143	969½	2,046½	1,885½	2,594	34	14	95	1,458
Greece, ...	24,289	5,770½	2,434,100	218,534	80,628	8,599	2,808	4,828½	3,788	5,289½	143	12½	131½	4,193½
Henrietta, ...	18,527½	3,991	1,901,279	148,026	51,470	4,239	2,155	3,957	2,986	3,939½	118	4⅜	50	4,044
Irondequoit, ...	9,968	3,083½	1,663,565	87,900	27,412	3,087¼	960½	1,475	1,520½	2,074	30	17¾	191	1,731
Mendon, ...	18,931¼	4,412	1,468,910	157,515	39,495	4,940½	3,461	2,739⅜	1,926	2,444	37¼	4½	21	5,048¾
Ogden, ...	18,042	3,631	1,616,045	164,699	67,794	4,355	3,241	3,651	2,633½	3,666½	236	23½	288	3,662⅝
Parma, ...	20,020¾	6,012½	1,521,989	180,355	38,194	6,456½	1,472	4,527	3,059	3,969½	75½	4	25	3,769
Penfield, ...	17,954½	4,962	1,725,424	132,739	54,762	5,382½	1,816½	3,487	2,448½	2,193½	132½	6½	76	2,483½
Perrington, ...	17,295	5,094	1,664,777	185,475	61,390	4,744½	1,694	4,225½	2,564½	3,062¼	78½	15½	297½	2,693
Pittsfield, ...	12,648	2,080½	1,598,208	116,144	39,704	2,894	1,829½	2,472½	1,655	1,586	60	......	......	2,518½
Riga, ...	17,091½	4,000	1,351,625	127,402	40,045	5,749	3,406	2,730	1,982	2,431	162	......	......	4,399½
Rochester, ...	641¾	61½	319,700	151,653	3,765	185¼	....	101½	73	94	......	......	......	......
Rush, ...	14,837	3,556	1,123,366	122,385	26,290	3,080	3,204	2,623	1,576	1,981	42	2	11	3,593
Sweden, ...	17,602¼	4,145½	1,439,701	142,306	28,973	3,608¾	3,141	3,840	2,429	3,057	159½	1	4	3,753½
Union, ...	19,969½	5,706½	1,225,109	146,902	35,926	7,403½	1,070	4,669	2,676½	3,670½	117	3½	77	2,566¾
Webster, ...	15,454	4,703	1,227,946	128,866	34,375	5,783	1,282	3,636	2,672	3,227	38	6	29	2,408
Wheatland, ...	15,559	3,567	1,553,205	152,813	33,342	2,173	2,244	1,848½	1,816	2,505	171½	40	820	3,424
Total, ...	316,840¼	78,182	29,633,614	2,824,916	818,703	88,943¾	40,494½	62,159⅞	45,681	58,738¾	1,886¾	192⅞	2,620	59138⅜

MONTGOMERY COUNTY.

TOWNS.	ACRES. Improved.	ACRES. Unimproved.	CASH VALUE. Of farm.	CASH VALUE. Of stock.	CASH VALUE. Of tools and implements	Acres plowed the year previous.	Acres in fallow the year previous.	Acres in pasture the year previous.	MEADOW. Acres.	MEADOW. Tons of hay.	MEADOW. Bushels of grass seed.	SPRING WHEAT. Acres sown.	SPRING WHEAT. Bushels harvested.	WINTER WHEAT. Acres sown.
Amsterdam, ...	16,065½	3,989	849,812	104,599	31,591	5,729½	216¾	4,116½	3,502¾	3,497	169¼	77½	884	296
Canajoharie, ...	20,596¾	3,701½	1,096,935	158,301	37,425	8,162	246	6,249	4,011	4,208½	296½	250½	2,336	267
Charleston, ...	21,716⅞	4,923	598,692	129,053	25,724	10,331½	64	6,375	4,411	2,905½	743	337	3,081	138¾
Florida, ...	26,053	5,886½	1,352,980	161,777	42,084	11,578½	687	5,499½	5,216	4,937½	1,092½	140½	1,148	745½
Glen, ...	18,731½	4,442¼	943,095	135,707	37,898	9,376	554	4,351	3,523	3,962	652½	95	890	446½
Minden, ...	24,156	5,794½	1,527,304	196,166	45,454	9,256¾	181	7,826¾	5,419	6,461¾	510½	438¾	5,103	363¾
Mohawk, ...	16,517	3,705½	1,262,565	157,845	38,045	7,310	88	5,127	3,633	5,490	334½	49½	548	263
Palatine, ...	19,512½	4,329½	1,238,032	156,480	40,442	6,916⅜	179	6,424¾	4,774½	6,405½	259	82¾	1,176	342½
Root, ...	23,043½	7,372	970,030	141,230	33,114	10,418	185	7,850½	4,466½	3,434½	491½	317½	2,726½	154
St. Johnsville, ..	8,065	2,577	470,247	76,870	17,821	1,876	134	3,139	2,551	3,230	158	109	1,086	07
Total, ...	194,457⅝	46,720¾	10,309,692	1,418,034	358,598	80,955	2,534¾	56,965	41,507¾	44,532¼	4,707¼	1,898	18978½	3,114

LEWIS COUNTY.—(Continued.)

TOWNS.	Winter Wheat.	Oats.		Rye.		Barley.		Buckwheat.		Corn.		Potatoes.		Peas.	
	Bushels harvested.	Acres sown.	Bushels harvested	Acres sown.	Bushels harvested.	Acres sown.	Bushels harvested.	Acres sown.	Bushels harvested.	Acres planted	Bushels harvested	Acres planted.	Bushels harvested.	Acres sown.	Bushels harvested
Pinckney, ...	......	961	27, 236	18½	269	170½	3, 805	33	698	70½	2, 169	148¾	13, 636	22	501
Turin, ...	121	986	22, 581	32	366	243½	5, 939	51¾	603	371	10, 719	145½	11, 694	37¼	758
Watson, ...	26	488¼	6, 740	154½	1, 477	13¾	142	32	89½	529⅛	8, 437	150½	8, 974	33	309½
West Turin, ...	......	1, 456	44, 587	3	38	109½	2, 595	128¾	1, 835	169¾	5, 915	273⅜	29, 059	29⅜	629½
Total, ...	3, 845¼	14, 037½	295, 445½	1, 151¼	11, 383½	1, 992	37, 513½	1, 067⅞	10, 443¼	4, 616⅝	92, 398¼	3, 295⅝	243, 841	856¼	12, 978½

LIVINGSTON COUNTY.—(Continued.)

TOWNS.	Winter Wheat, bushels harvested.	Oats, acres sown.	Oats, bushels harvested.	Rye, acres sown.	Rye, bushels harvested.	Barley, acres sown.	Barley, bushels harvested.	Buckwheat, acres sown.	Buckwheat, bushels harvested.	Corn, acres planted.	Corn, bushels harvested.	Potatoes, acres planted.	Potatoes, bushels harvested.	Peas, acres sown.	Peas, bushels harvested.
Avon, ...	108960	1, 177½	39, 673	11	119	354	7, 481	49¾	223½	1, 369	40, 213	168⅝	10, 389	7	225
Caledonia, ...	134445	476¼	14, 481	......	....	441	9, 899	5	20	1, 115½	29, 348	152½	10, 646	½	12½
Conesus, ...	39409	615	11, 562	4½	95	362	6, 032	118¼	893	556¼	12, 347	74⅞	4, 502	29⅛	322
Geneseo, ...	88643	754	19, 791	......	....	441½	9, 018	38½	1, 045½	1, 146½	34, 803	113¾	6, 714	1½	21
Groveland, ...	70033	502	9, 262	36	298	495½	7, 875	132	813½	826¼	24, 055	76½	5, 180	......	....
Leicester, ...	105579	568½	15, 630	2	45	397¾	7, 298	15	222	1, 552¾	56, 191	95¼	8, 604	3¾	56
Lima, ...	75504	721	26, 696	1	36	508	12, 911	56½	341	1, 070	36, 610	99¾	8, 057	27½	519
Livonia, ...	87779	797½	18, 796	......	....	747¾	14, 459	97¼	596	1, 139½	31, 258½	116⅝	8, 092	33	200½
Mount Morris, ..	85251	933¾	16, 265	6	76	707¾	10, 661	104	808½	1, 509¾	44, 477	124⅝	9, 122	8⅛	133½
North Dansville,	12564	152¼	2, 172	66½	1, 257	78	1, 088	20½	208	258½	5, 852	23	1, 787	½	40
Nunda, ...	32908	819⅝	12, 467	18½	241	214½	2, 828½	223⅛	1, 670	697¼	14, 545	142⅜	9, 723	81⅞	864
Portage, ...	39233	569¾	12, 487	3½	55	232¼	3, 997	47½	510	589	17. 242	136⅝	12, 026	33½	380
Sparta, ...	36495	652	9, 702	156½	1, 083	527	6. 196	272	2, 389	568¾	13, 296	80⅜	5, 948	10	149
Spring Water, ..	18186	2, 004½	27, 082	40	344	380	4, 832	496	3, 204¼	603⅓	12, 291	209⅜	13, 711½	221⅜	2, 641
West Sparta. ...	31243	482½	6, 425	51¼	465	300	3, 491	137½	882	748	17, 878	96⅜	5, 226	17¼	81
York, ...	128547	683¼	19, 499	½	4	790½	15, 189	1¾	9½	1, 422	41, 058	148	12, 529	53¼	754
Total, ...	1094779	11. 909⅜	261, 990	397¼	4, 118	6, 977½	123 255½	1, 814⅜	13, 836¼	15. 172⅞	431. 464½	1, 858⅞	132, 256½	528¼	6, 898½

MADISON COUNTY.—(Continued.)

TOWNS.	Winter Wheat, bushels harvested.	Oats, acres sown.	Oats, bushels harvested.	Rye, acres sown.	Rye, bushels harvested.	Barley, acres sown.	Barley, bushels harvested.	Buckwheat, acres sown.	Buckwheat, bushels harvested.	Corn, acres planted.	Corn, bushels harvested.	Potatoes, acres planted.	Potatoes, bushels harvested.	Peas, acres sown.	Peas, bushels harvested.
Brookfield, ...	48	2, 745¾	52, 887	5	100	257⅝	4, 665	159⅛	1, 869	1, 144⅜	34, 717	352⅝	30, 179	43⅜	685
Cazenovia, ...	1851½	2, 629¼	56, 620	......	....	862¼	13, 862	87¾	1, 306	1, 247¾	40, 949	256¼	20, 669	272¼	5, 405
De Ruyter, ...	......	1, 364½	28, 275	......	....	136	2, 355	118¾	1, 134	257¼	9, 008	108⅞	8, 398	23⅝	492
Eaton, ...	308	1, 330¼	31, 161	......	....	546⅝	10, 800½	46¼	339	940¾	33, 548	216⅞	16, 788½	51¼	911½
Fenner, ...	642	1, 988½	34, 758	......	....	1, 664	21, 888	69¾	730	635¼	17, 117	123⅜	9, 342	89¼	1, 589
Georgetown, ...	......	933½	22, 175	......	....	167	2, 347½	67⅝	657	270⅜	7, 902	150⅝	7, 800	39⅜	483
Hamilton, ...	234	1, 629½	40. 708	7	148	201	4, 028	14	144	744¾	23, 737	149⅞	15, 650	54¾	1, 137
Lebanon, ...	......	1, 424¼	36, 736	......	....	297¾	6, 218	33¾	357	783¼	25, 073	158⅜	11, 453	63	1, 371
Lenox, ...	10976½	3, 489¼	73, 753	55½	904	2, 075	56, 641	313¼	2, 685	3, 401	96, 831	432⅞	25, 627	143⅞	2, 380
Madison, ...	1293	1, 020¾	29, 117	2	20	627½	14, 558	46¼	548	816¼	28, 363	190	16, 856	36	761
Nelson, ...	5	1, 703	30, 332	1¾	42	294¼	4, 363	99⅛	1, 063½	485¼	17, 411	207⅞	17, 367	56¾	776
Smithfield, ...	518	1, 109½	23, 676	12	260	1, 536	22, 376	29	307	658	20, 363	138	9, 590	63	1, 334
Stockbridge, ...	5953½	1, 085½	24, 075	1	3	1, 499	27, 849	13¼	91	1, 172½	32, 764	151½	11, 976	32⅜	692
Sullivan, ...	7491	3, 524¼	87, 364	......	....	292½	5, 280	299	2, 623	2, 364	61, 800	305¾	22, 583	178⅛	2, 957
Total, ...	29320½	25, 977¾	571. 637	84¼	1. 477	10456½	197, 231	1, 396⅞	13, 853½	14. 920¾	449, 583	2, 943½	224, 278½	1, 147	20, 973½

MONROE COUNTY.—(Continued.)

TOWNS.	Winter Wheat, bushels harvested.	Oats, acres sown.	Oats, bushels harvested.	Rye, acres sown.	Rye, bushels harvested.	Barley, acres sown.	Barley, bushels harvested.	Buckwheat, acres sown.	Buckwheat, bushels harvested.	Corn, acres planted.	Corn, bushels harvested.	Potatoes, acres planted.	Potatoes, bushels harvested.	Peas, acres sown.	Peas, bushels harvested.
Brighton, ...	19038	951¼	34, 763	21	266	601½	15, 608	52½	444	912¾	27, 770	422½	34, 815	48⅜	1, 042
Chili, ...	48578	1, 177½	42, 685	29½	496	483½	10, 960	282¼	1, 643½	1, 490½	39, 402	306¾	25, 206	101	1, 386
Clarkson, ...	17338	1, 501	44, 123	9	60	301	7, 130	178	517	1, 780	33, 281	201	13, 542	16	160
Gates, ...	17211	984½	36, 388	1	15	213½	5, 240	142¾	1, 033	988	26, 280	270	22, 952	54½	763
Greece, ...	38043	1, 866	54, 895	41½	513	708½	16, 564	453¼	2, 774¼	2, 545	59. 246	1, 044¾	98, 293	92½	1, 467
Henrietta, ...	54710	3, 464½	59, 296	......	....	407	9, 673	21	176	1, 508½	43, 876	218½	16, 520	119¼	2, 155
Irondequoit, ...	24194	451¾	17, 200	259	3, 615	189¾	4, 288	41¾	404	831¾	21, 172	956¼	87, 633	31¼	573
Mendon, ...	83176	1, 676½	61. 421	18	145	221¼	4, 253	100¾	692½	1, 905¾	50, 065	270	18, 453	65¾	1, 179
Ogden, ...	52168	1, 377¼	47. 188	1½	15	391¼	10, 702	213½	1, 498	1, 443	45, 959	322¾	32, 509	63	1, 403
Parma, ...	24521	2, 028	60, 428	5	81½	438½	10, 416	503	2, 083	2, 543¼	53, 127	386⅜	31, 631	41½	775½
Penfield, ...	34591	2, 031	64, 388	50	725	460⅜	10, 662	258	2, 967½	1, 813	52, 227	736½	57, 044	33¾	515
Perrington, ...	44662½	1, 471½	48, 728	21	281	392¼	8, 525	152¼	1, 591½	1, 583	42, 119	769	62, 150	11½	126
Pittsfield, ...	32178	905	27. 798	13½	165	288½	6, 998	112½	481½	1, 087¾	32, 998	378½	30, 668	76¼	490
Riga, ...	74765	1, 043	34, 825	7	66	463	12, 121	52	214	1, 310½	36, 200	135¾	9, 697	32	649
Rochester, ...	......	25¼	920	9	200	7	200	2	10	29¼	950	16¼	2, 130	3	80
Rush, ...	46998	649	20. 201	3	15	221	4, 610	102	607	1, 458	44, 096	151¾	10, 890	120	2, 085
Sweden, ...	62059	738	24, 556	......	....	552½	12. 918	154¾	805	1, 612¼	43, 962	187	10, 553	7½	131
Union, ...	10669½	2, 025	57, 850	4	96	572½	13, 959	445¾	1, 998	2. 832¼	71, 057	284⅛	27, 899	56	749
Webster, ...	17504	1, 158½	36, 140	157	2, 372	406	8, 461	283	2, 589	1, 698	47, 468	510	42, 586	18	240
Wheatland, ...	107959	497¾	18, 487	2	40	257½	6, 467	18½	95	1, 037	34, 556	161	19. 380	1	60
Total, ...	810363	26, 025¼	792. 370	652	9. 166½	7. 576⅜	179. 755	3. 569½	22. 623¾	30. 409½	805. 811	7. 728¾	654. 551	992⅜	16, 028½

MONTGOMERY COUNTY.—(Continued.)

TOWNS.	Winter Wheat, bushels harvested.	Oats, acres sown.	Oats, bushels harvested.	Rye, acres sown.	Rye, bushels harvested.	Barley, acres sown.	Barley, bushels harvested.	Buckwheat, acres sown.	Buckwheat, bushels harvested.	Corn, acres planted.	Corn, bushels harvested.	Potatoes, acres planted.	Potatoes, bushels harvested.	Peas, acres sown.	Peas, bushels harvested.
Amsterdam, ...	1, 922½	3, 388	78, 364	175½	1, 972	216	4, 374	926	9. 739½	1, 297½	26, 839½	181⅜	14, 207	38½	649
Canajoharie, ...	1, 870	4, 642¾	108, 933	182½	2, 443	402¼	6, 397	961¾	11, 739	899	23, 411	184	14, 367	125	2, 051½
Charleston, ...	611	5, 936½	90, 440	128¼	1, 172	139	1, 285	2, 295	21, 653	541	9, 564	184¼	6, 509	113¾	1, 505
Florida, ...	5, 238½	7, 182	164, 999	332½	5, 001½	136	2, 181	1, 880½	16, 505	1, 520	27, 609	183½	13, 676	46	616½
Glen, ...	3. 414	5, 489	134, 585	474½	7, 055	43½	823	2, 041½	20, 516	948⅜	22, 212	191¾	14, 749	133	2, 375
Minden, ...	3, 373	4, 867¼	129, 084	161	2, 285	484¾	9, 585½	809¾	11, 576	1, 146⅜	32, 265	292¾	24, 923	222	4, 240
Mohawk, ...	2. 532	3, 571	102, 272	559	8, 116	167	3, 063	944¼	16, 413	1, 667	45, 905	241	23, 194	141	2, 904
Palatine, ...	3, 299	3, 203	81, 028	441¼	6, 771	255¾	4, 965	697¼	12, 259	1, 095¾	29. 542	184⅜	14, 824	274½	5, 034
Root, ...	705½	5, 672	96, 484	215½	2, 589	319	3, 674	2, 080	19. 742	952¾	20, 084	206¼	11, 449	236	2, 898½
St. Johnsville, ..	939	536	11, 416	100	1, 708	167	2, 905	161	1, 535	407	10. 085	97	7, 256	38	582
Total, ...	23904½	44. 487½	997. 605	2, 770	39, 112½	2, 330¼	39, 252½	12, 797	141. 677½	10. 494¾	247, 516½	1, 945⅞	145, 154	1, 367¾	22, 855½

LEWIS COUNTY.—(CONTINUED.)

TOWNS.	BEANS.		TURNIPS.		FLAX.			HEMP.		HOPS.		TOBACCO.		APPLE ORCHARDS.	
	Acres planted.	Bushels harvested.	Acres sown.	Bushels harvested.	Acres sown.	Pounds of lint.	Bushels of seed.	Acres sown.	Tons of hemp.	Acres planted.	Pounds harvested.	Acres planted.	Pounds harvested.	Bushels of apples.	Barrels of cider.
Pinckney,	¾	23½												1,202	4½
Turin,	10¾	138	4½	258	1		8							11,013	267
Watson,	4⅞	31												164	
West Turin,	2¾	48	6⅞	586	⅛									4,391	84
Total,	72⅛	1,030½	55⅞	5,830½	219	65,782	1,566			25	8,870			72,198	1,451

LIVINGSTON COUNTY.—(CONTINUED.)

TOWNS.	Beans: Acres planted.	Beans: Bushels harvested.	Turnips: Acres sown.	Turnips: Bushels harvested.	Flax: Acres sown.	Flax: Pounds of lint.	Flax: Bushels of seed.	Hemp: Acres sown.	Hemp: Tons of hemp.	Hops: Acres planted.	Hops: Pounds harvested.	Tobacco: Acres planted.	Tobacco: Pounds harvested.	Apple orchards: Bushels of apples.	Apple orchards: Barrels of cider.
Avon,	2¾	24	1½	110										21,010	572
Caledonia,	6⅞	47												9,350	135
Conesus,	7⅛	71												8,120	216
Geneseo,	4¼	40	1¼	280										25,141	525
Groveland,	½	5	4¼	140										21,302	692
Leicester,	1¼	17	2	600										10,899	235½
Lima,	1¼	47	1½	357										16,654	350
Livonia,	10½	170	3⅜	378						5	4,200		10	29,422	595½
Mount Morris,	5	63½	1⅛	103										11,431	347½
North Dansville,			¼	15						5	10,000			3,345	131½
Nunda,	7½	119½	2⅜	273										10,918	243½
Portage,	11¾	171¼	3¾	931	½	50	½			⅛	55			14,549	324
Sparta,	¾	25	1	10										17,435	696
Springwater,	7¾	86	1¼	250										11,910	74
West Sparta,	5¾	46			⅛	40	3							6,845	251½
York,	8⅝	71	¼	63	1½		10							23,869	539½
Total,	81⅝	1.003¼	23⅞	3.510	2⅛	90	13½			10⅛	14,255		10	242,200	5,928½

MADISON COUNTY.—(CONTINUED.)

TOWNS.	Beans: Acres planted.	Beans: Bushels harvested.	Turnips: Acres sown.	Turnips: Bushels harvested.	Flax: Acres sown.	Flax: Pounds of lint.	Flax: Bushels of seed.	Hemp: Acres sown.	Hemp: Tons of hemp.	Hops: Acres planted.	Hops: Pounds harvested.	Tobacco: Acres planted.	Tobacco: Pounds harvested.	Apple orchards: Bushels of apples.	Apple orchards: Barrels of cider.
Brookfield,	30¾	605½	5⅝	673	3	2,765	19			338½	277,715	⅛	30	53,627	451
Cazenovia,	16⅞	250½	1⅜	57	37½	54,930	367			3	4,000	2½	3,150	49,753	811
De Ruyter,	2¾	52	1¼	20	8½	11,933				32	35,750			28,337	306
Eaton,	31½	519¼	¾	87	½	40	48			336½	320,187	½	600	45,402	712½
Fenner,	11¾	178	⅝	14	13¾	2,150	129			1½	1,534			45,740	418
Georgetown,	9	268	4½	355	1¼	2,500	6½			30¼	24,986			9,509	57½
Hamilton,	13½	329								234¼	182,652			39,152	756
Lebanon,	20	485½		136	1		10			55¼	34,899			31,845	484
Lenox,	16⅝	170½	6⅝	570	¼	80	2½			24	12,846			48,418	1,038
Madison,	67⅛	1,150	⅝	66						309¼	304,504	1	1,200	40,860	500
Nelson,	9⅞	182¼	3⅛	375	5⅞	1,933	47½			16	15,251			60,864	533
Smithfield,	15¼	208								22½	22,504			17,850	274
Stockbridge,	9	214	1	60			14			84¾	73,924	3	5,200	26,166	409
Sullivan,	22⅜	224	3	535	20½	26,250	92			3	1,556	2	3,500	34,154	667½
Total,	276⅜	4,836½	28¼	2,948	92⅛	102,581	735½			1,490¾	1312308	9⅛	13,680	531,677	7,417½

MONROE COUNTY.—(CONTINUED.)

TOWNS.	Beans: Acres planted.	Beans: Bushels harvested.	Turnips: Acres sown.	Turnips: Bushels harvested.	Flax: Acres sown.	Flax: Pounds of lint.	Flax: Bushels of seed.	Hemp: Acres sown.	Hemp: Tons of hemp.	Hops: Acres planted.	Hops: Pounds harvested.	Tobacco: Acres planted.	Tobacco: Pounds harvested.	Apple orchards: Bushels of apples.	Apple orchards: Barrels of cider.
Brighton,	5⅝	101½	13⅛	1,215						9	9,600	3¾	6,700	20,187	454
Chili,	14⅛	134¾	9⅞	1,334										26,819	518
Clarkson,	383	3,575	5	189								8	8,300	27,154	377
Gates,	10½	156	8¾	2,155	3	1,000	45			15	14,000			17,430	268
Greece,	58⅞	607	37⅜	8,430						19½	17,400	¼	200	61,050	526
Henrietta,	2	57	4	427										25,061	866
Irondequoit,	3½	53	20⅜	4,287										12,031	155
Mendon,	4¾	52	3	414										10,670	467½
Ogden,	57½	668½	15¼	3,831							5			40,526	972
Parma,	198¾	1,957	9½	475						½	800			42,509	691
Penfield,	59¾	167½	21	3,183	5		8							38,714	1,001
Perrington,	9½	116	10	1,470						6	1,800	9	9,200	25,729	555
Pittsfield,	14¼	200	10⅜	1,087								39¾	41,250	7,818	814½
Riga,	3½	45½	3⅜	695										23,707	593½
Rochester,	1¼	19	6	165								16	20,000	1,715	13
Rush,	3⅞	28	½	290						1	400			16,790	429
Sweden,	59	623	2	320										30,210	590
Union,	529¼	5,695	1⅛	600	¼		3½				5	⅜	870	20,820	294
Webster,	5	46	8	1,210										33,477	567
Wheatland,	3¼	41	5⅝	730										8,468	160½
Total,	1,427¼	14.342¾	195	32.507	8¼	1,000	56½			51	44,010	77⅛	86,520	491,491	10,312

MONTGOMERY COUNTY.—(CONTINUED.)

TOWNS.	Beans: Acres planted.	Beans: Bushels harvested.	Turnips: Acres sown.	Turnips: Bushels harvested.	Flax: Acres sown.	Flax: Pounds of lint.	Flax: Bushels of seed.	Hemp: Acres sown.	Hemp: Tons of hemp.	Hops: Acres planted.	Hops: Pounds harvested.	Tobacco: Acres planted.	Tobacco: Pounds harvested.	Apple orchards: Bushels of apples.	Apple orchards: Barrels of cider.
Amsterdam,	10⅞	150½	1⅛	321	58½	73,850	525			15½	4,300			16,532	970½
Canajoharie,	73¼	1,076½		5	26½	16,000	239			107½	92,957	⅛	100	11,187	435½
Charleston,	37¾	386½	3	268	271½	118,520	1,344	2		7	10			18,237	468
Florida,	23	275½	½	70	338½	285,730	2,256			3		⅛	50	23,776	623½
Glen	16¼	191½	1⅛	385½	98¼	87,700	636			3	8	⅛	40	15,983	586½
Minden,	9¾	368			216¼	325,500	2,073½			209½	84,251			15,756	482
Mohawk,	11	514		92	2		12			3½				21,024	563
Palatine,	15½	367	1⅛	105	10	12,572	93½			65¾	55,050		10	10,746	679½
Root,	31¼	609½	⅞	86	106½	90,057	566¾			38½	4,800	¼	49	18,070	610
St. Johnsville,		2	¼	19	4	7,000	1			¼	227			4,550	184
Total,	228⅝	3,941	8	1,441½	1,132	1016929	7,746¾	2		453½	241,603	⅝	249	155,861	5,608½

LEWIS COUNTY.—(Continued.)

TOWNS.	MARKET GARDENS. Acres cultivated.	MARKET GARDENS. Value of products.	Pounds of maple sugar made.	Gallons of maple molasses made.	Gallons of wine made.	Pounds of honey collected.	Pounds of wax collected.	SILK. Pounds of cocoons.	NEAT CATTLE. Under one year old.	NEAT CATTLE. Over one y'r, exclusive of working oxen & cows	NEAT CATTLE. Working oxen.	NEAT CATTLE. Cows.	Number of cattle killed for beef.	Pounds of butter.	Pounds of cheese.
Pinckney,	......	......	16, 972	155	......	......	......	......	158	326	126	1, 148	49	109, 480	67, 180
Turin,	......	......	5, 151	74	......	2, 511	96	......	259	446	138	1, 784	91	158, 731	124, 845
Watson,	......	......	4, 845	123	18	461	34	......	52	236	94	402	88	43, 030	25, 600
West Turin,	......	......	3, 675	145	11	518	38	......	344	501	299	2, 055	97	189, 920	113, 157
Total,	1⅓	$115	236, 918	4, 698½	45	11, 912	831	......	2, 683	5, 491	2, 423	19, 151	1, 247	1, 575, 515	1, 896. 741

LIVINGSTON COUNTY.—(Continued.)

TOWNS.	MARKET GARDENS. Acres cultivated.	MARKET GARDENS. Value of products.	Pounds of maple sugar made.	Gallons of maple molasses made.	Gallons of wine made.	Pounds of honey collected.	Pounds of wax collected.	SILK. Pounds of cocoons.	NEAT CATTLE. Under one year old.	NEAT CATTLE. Over one y'r, exclusive of working oxen & cows	NEAT CATTLE. Working oxen.	NEAT CATTLE. Cows.	Number of cattle killed for beef.	Pounds of butter.	Pounds of cheese.
Avon,	3	177½	601	.10	520	2, 955	164	......	365	873	121	676	438	56, 170	4, 670
Caledonia,	......	......	19	10	19	1, 657	206	......	308	1, 200	74	772	162	72, 831	3, 879
Conesus,	......	......	120	100	......	......	......	......	201	674	96	508	63	52, 043	1, 196
Geneseo,	......	......	......	......	17	260	15	......	391	785	101	610	166	43, 392	5, 297½
Groveland,	4	405	......	......	......	1, 626	108	......	343	1, 003	76	837	109	72, 385	1, 364
Leicester,	......	......	880	32	151	1, 419	103½	5	330	864	171	700	67	63, 711	3, 500
Lima,	......	......	2, 725	138	......	1, 625	120	......	266	452	138	606	102	58. 805	10, 025
Livonia,	1	70	175	38	110	2, 370	209	......	368	764	171	586	149	90, 122	15, 529
Mount Morris,	11	350	685	28	......	2, 996	176	......	372	1, 027	147	1, 081	138	95, 250	2, 085
North Dansville,	......	......	......	......	......	460	4½	......	47	83	13	221	912	16, 275	......
Nunda,	......	......	25	8	21	1, 741	177	......	286	621	87	794	298	82, 736	2. 085
Portage,	......	......	......	......	......	547	42	......	194	410	54	486	81	54, 964	3, 590
Sparta,	8¼	62	810	41	89	1, 178	182	......	254	633	80	646	97	57, 749	1, 351
Springwater,	......	......	2, 047	23	......	3, 190	163½	......	337	685	137	831	133	85, 862	6, 173
West Sparta,	......	......	2, 296	57	6	2, 179	106	......	251	581	109	665	117	59, 590	8, 741
York,	½	70	3, 105	54	630	2, 490	174	......	383	1, 301	176	961	197	83, 706	9, 861
Total,	27¾	1, 134½	13, 488	539	1, 563	26, 693	1. 950½	5	4, 696	11, 956	1, 751	10, 980	3, 229	1. 045, 591	79, 346½

MADISON COUNTY.—(Continued.)

TOWNS.	MARKET GARDENS. Acres cultivated.	MARKET GARDENS. Value of products.	Pounds of maple sugar made.	Gallons of maple molasses made.	Gallons of wine made.	Pounds of honey collected.	Pounds of wax collected.	SILK. Pounds of cocoons.	NEAT CATTLE. Under one year old.	NEAT CATTLE. Over one y'r, exclusive of working oxen & cows	NEAT CATTLE. Working oxen.	NEAT CATTLE. Cows.	Number of cattle killed for beef.	Pounds of butter.	Pounds of cheese.
Brookfield,	......	......	9, 491	1, 021	8	5, 982	312	......	532	1, 317	180	2. 435	280	173, 670	250, 146
Cazenovia,	3	215	4, 973½	84	10	3, 775	238	......	515	907	118	2, 157	410	186, 705	186, 356
De Ruyter,	......	......	5, 850	13	......	700	60	......	113	415	110	1, 131	127	76, 975	106, 550
Eaton,	2	110	2, 106	55	41	3, 931	296½	......	521	1, 435	156	2, 147	319	159, 410	290. 775
Fenner,	......	......	2, 738	62	......	4, 179	254	......	320	677	72	974	85	84, 740	62, 705
Georgetown,	......	......	7, 725	120	......	1, 350	167	......	192	326	116	812	66	70, 906	69, 586
Hamilton,	1	66	5, 471	34	......	375	47	......	528	1, 055	96	2, 022	290	118, 423	186, 750
Lebanon,	......	......	5, 531	134	......	3, 695	354½	......	472	1, 046	230	2, 096	75	137, 488	161, 492
Lenox,	7¾	962	1, 449	186	......	7, 568	325	......	822	1, 521	213	2, 765	328	219, 062	75, 965
Madison,	......	......	4, 517	125	......	4, 018	145	......	302	799	126	1, 346	119	113, 045	113, 490
Nelson,	......	......	10, 367	191	......	4, 316	344¼	......	377	833	115	1, 793	117	160, 978	209, 207
Smithfield,	......	......	1, 804	137	......	4, 661	228	......	264	518	74	1, 243	171	96, 414	122, 078
Stockbridge,	......	......	3, 202	361	83	2, 817	215	10	376	867	84	1, 430	158	94, 895	187, 656
Sullivan,	7	457	1, 090	14	66	8, 248	380½	......	572	1. 361	184	1, 716	195	147, 587	64, 838
Total,	20¾	1, 810	66, 314½	2, 537	208	55, 615	3, 366¾	10	5, 906	13, 077	1, 874	24, 067	2, 740	1, 840, 298	2, 087, 594

MONROE COUNTY.—(Continued.)

TOWNS.	MARKET GARDENS. Acres cultivated.	MARKET GARDENS. Value of products.	Pounds of maple sugar made.	Gallons of maple molasses made.	Gallons of wine made.	Pounds of honey collected.	Pounds of wax collected.	SILK. Pounds of cocoons.	NEAT CATTLE. Under one year old.	NEAT CATTLE. Over one y'r, exclusive of working oxen & cows	NEAT CATTLE. Working oxen.	NEAT CATTLE. Cows.	Number of cattle killed for beef.	Pounds of butter.	Pounds of cheese.
Brighton,	43½	5045	......	......	109	1, 117	49	......	189	359	85	561	286	50, 828	1, 480
Chili,	33	3382	440	6	157	2, 237	78	......	474	918	87	966	163	117, 665	4, 360
Clarkson,	......	......	500	10	......	3, 060	59	......	414	679	58	728	85	69, 411	11, 630
Gates,	8	1085	......	......	23	950	25	......	171	332	43	616	293	41, 285	850
Greece,	20½	2180	104	4	55	4, 634	202	......	547	945	175	1, 449	370	159, 985	4, 745
Henrietta,	......	......	1, 750	88	19	3, 614	120	......	341	571	149	822	462	72, 319	7, 873
Irondequoit,	124¾	12580	......	5	30	346	21	......	189	353	88	654	474	45, 512	1, 160
Mendon,	......	......	1, 157	58	......	951	......	......	300	796	126	1, 067	150	96, 020	13, 035
Ogden,	......	25	550	36	78	3. 060	81	......	532	729	82	956	154	110, 217	9, 163
Parma,	⅝	60	350	33	......	4, 372	171¼	......	615	952	88	1, 235	209	150, 751	9, 593
Penfield,	2	162	750	26	42	3, 943	165	......	361	526	140	1, 040	123	94, 318	10, 495
Perrington,	6¾	1189	295	74	......	1, 553	49	......	379	1, 111	116	918	259	81, 868	10. 626
Pittsfield,	......	......	2, 360	10	......	450	16	......	250	447	141	593	193	40, 633	670
Riga,	......	......	1, 850	57	134	2, 628	110	......	374	667	105	745	68	68, 930	10, 425
Rochester,	1¼	629¾	......	......	......	300	......	......	2	20	3	844	46	376	......
Rush,	3	88	1, 370	51	......	2, 380	101	......	274	525	62	686	102	78, 910	4, 400
Sweden,	2	115	3, 211	262	31	1, 458	103	......	512	780	140	1, 002	618	86, 909	12, 600
Union,	......	......	157	16½	11	4, 538	295½	......	639	898	92	968	161	108, 101	7, 011
Webster,	......	......	......	......	......	3, 112	122	......	312	623	90	921	211	126. 350	3, 335
Wheatland,	......	......	500	10	......	1, 335	63	......	281	650	74	793	131	43, 127	7, 802
Total,	245⅝	26540¾	15, 344	746½	689	46, 038	1, 842¾	......	7, 156	12, 881	1, 944	17, 564	4. 558	1. 643, 515	131, 253

MONTGOMERY COUNTY.—(Continued.)

TOWNS.	MARKET GARDENS. Acres cultivated.	MARKET GARDENS. Value of products.	Pounds of maple sugar made.	Gallons of maple molasses made.	Gallons of wine made.	Pounds of honey collected.	Pounds of wax collected.	SILK. Pounds of cocoons.	NEAT CATTLE. Under one year old.	NEAT CATTLE. Over one y'r, exclusive of working oxen & cows	NEAT CATTLE. Working oxen.	NEAT CATTLE. Cows.	Number of cattle killed for beef.	Pounds of butter.	Pounds of cheese.
Amsterdam,	7	550	20	7	110	3, 135	162½	......	311	573	76	1, 059	204	91, 993	1, 320
Canajoharie,	......	......	452	24	29	6, 636	355	......	570	1, 129	80	1, 967	192	140, 765	184, 512
Charleston,	......	......	729	44½	7	7, 401	616	......	467	824	120	1, 204	134	114 398	16, 050
Florida,	......	......	......	10	......	4, 605	398	......	517	991	186	1, 356	289	125, 140	4, 836
Glen,	6¼	785	235	21	157	5, 587	266	......	460	635	104	1, 132	263	105, 410	13, 290
Minden,	5	250	1, 480	118	3	7, 221	563½	......	596	1, 003	92	3, 120	531	187, 345	465, 417
Mohawk,	½	145	1, 447	85	21	5, 760	348	......	545	740	96	1, 558	210	173, 952	13, 490
Palatine,	3	250	7, 952	609	64	9, 274	348	......	578	851	96	2, 676	157	117, 548	494, 923
Root,	2	150	203	11½	17	6, 062	395	......	539	867	143	1, 582	341	120, 124	79, 016
St. Johnsville,	......	......	1, 660	107	......	2, 890	92	......	213	246	53	1, 147	55	34, 710	265, 800
Total,	23¾	2, 130	14. 178	1, 037	408	58, 571	3, 544	......	4, 796	7, 859	1. 046	16, 801	2. 376	1, 211, 385	1, 538, 654

LEWIS COUNTY.—(CONTINUED.)

TOWNS.	Gallons of milk sold.	Horses.	Mules.	SWINE. Under 6 months	Over 6 months.	SHEEP. Number of sheep.	Number of fleeces.	Pounds of wool.	POULTRY. Value of poultry sold.	Value of eggs sold.	DOMESTIC MANUFACTURES. Yards of fulled cloth made.	Yards of flannel made.	Yards of linen made.	Yards of cotton and mixed cloths.
Pinckney,	....	323	....	239	226	884	592	2,011	$134	$78	232½	561	262	....
Turin,	....	412	....	404	399	557	407	1,520	433	273	13	24	....	153
Watson,	20	164	....	149	131	392	305	1,085	169	89	241	358	83	36
West Turin,	6,400	449	....	484	447	1,038	860	3,007	212	104	271	515	191	431
Total,	6.795	5.097	9	3,865	4,488	10,086	7.624	27,046⅞	4,701	2,671	2,609¼	8,291	1,532½	3,369

LIVINGSTON COUNTY.—(CONTINUED.)

TOWNS.	Gallons of milk sold.	Horses.	Mules.	Swine under 6 months	Swine over 6 months	Number of sheep.	Number of fleeces.	Pounds of wool.	Value of poultry sold.	Value of eggs sold.	Yards of fulled cloth made.	Yards of flannel made.	Yards of linen made.	Yards of cotton and mixed cloths.
Avon,	375	838	....	753	754	12,745	12,406	47,574	1,308	657	26	85	....	33
Caledonia,	....	1,101	3	867	942	10,552	10,404	36,666	519	669	52	602	....	30
Conesus,	191	618	....	287	491	8,733	7,187	25,312	484	425	33	60	....	....
Geneseo,	....	616	....	623	648	8,015	8,497	19,574	1,027	652	70	....	....	....
Groveland,	....	892	....	376	659	5,634	5,338	19,329	374	583	482	181½	....	200
Leicester,	150	820	6	520	559	4,487	4,431	16,117	569	740	6	185	75	168
Lima,	1,190	793	....	691	618	8,361	7,025	27,662	816	1,203	....	....	....	....
Livonia,	....	1,034	....	945	800	11,771	11,812	43.801¼	798	1,079	100	330	105	52
Mount Morris,	....	1,058	6	723	1,033	6,934	5,343	18,110	854	968	255	439½	33	172
North Dansville,	5,665	212	....	115	223	1,498	1,056	3,901	15	134	....	30	....	5
Nunda,	896	754	2	468	560	3,516	2,851	10,336½	291	862	282	807	164	99
Portage,	....	474	2	345	406	4,155	3,360	12,180	205	101	169	349½	96	....
Sparta,	....	613	3	378	706	2,173	2,541	8,933	259	797	163	299	43	68
Springwater,	....	903	....	350	813	6,298	7,755	26.551½	473	508	251	360	169½	91
West Sparta,	....	570	1	477	622	3,992	3,703	13.098	493	417	125	414	11	272
York,	358	1,206	24	708	809	13,698	13,130	48,545	236	1,297	107	431	122	302
Total,	8 825	12,502	47	8,632	10,643	112,562	106,839	377.690¼	8,721	11,092	2,121	4,573½	818½	1,492

MADISON COUNTY.—(CONTINUED.)

TOWNS.	Gallons of milk sold.	Horses.	Mules.	Swine under 6 months	Swine over 6 months	Number of sheep.	Number of fleeces.	Pounds of wool.	Value of poultry sold.	Value of eggs sold.	Yards of fulled cloth made.	Yards of flannel made.	Yards of linen made.	Yards of cotton and mixed cloths.
Brookfield,	25	1,055	3	948	762	8,728	7,759	26,925½	2,487	1,645	338½	1,319½	1,090	376½
Cazenovia,	7,500	1,052	....	779	799	4,713	6,513	25,153	1,225	1,898	92	329	61	156
De Ruyter,	....	448	....	277	300	4,943	11,459	22 879	300	313	25	229	161	212
Eaton,	1,891	892	5	540	669	4,606	4,566	16.812	791	1,470	102	449½	151	....
Fenner,	....	631	....	442	433	4,388	4,281	16,880	663	1,429	....	387	102	153
Georgetown,	....	311	....	171	228	2,867	2,947	10,420	510	650	52½	344	191½	143
Hamilton,	....	1,092	....	477	731	3,700	5,203	17,190	601	1,039	261	282	205	138
Lebanon,	....	690	....	589	479	6,423	7,703	28,777	737	1,357	70½	425	61	287½
Lenox,	16,570	1,588	13	1,299	1,378	6,547	5,694	23,495¾	1,887	5,317	199¾	554	162½	335½
Madison,	....	585	....	427	401	4,752	5,674	18.422	1,640	723	90	450½	128	90
Nelson,	....	630	2	517	566	4,586	6,766	24,478½	1,077	1,141	94½	636½	228	2,049
Smithfield,	....	670	1	399	402	2,149	2,199	7,918	756	1,978	9	182	6	18
Stockbridge,	20	681	2	383	470	2,501	2,015	7,384	796	2,316	206	1,001	292	259
Sullivan,	5,020	1,428	6	931	997	5,644	4,131	15,170	984	2,602	446	628	98	806
Total,	31.026	11.753	32	8,179	8.615	66,547	76.910	261,904¾	14,454	23,878	1.986¾	7,217	2,937	5,023½

MONROE COUNTY.—(CONTINUED.)

TOWNS.	Gallons of milk sold.	Horses.	Mules.	Swine under 6 months	Swine over 6 months	Number of sheep.	Number of fleeces.	Pounds of wool.	Value of poultry sold.	Value of eggs sold.	Yards of fulled cloth made.	Yards of flannel made.	Yards of linen made.	Yards of cotton and mixed cloths.
Brighton,	32,800	594	1	431	605	2,110	1,854	6,161	735	954	....	152	....	....
Chili,	....	956	8	917	1,225	8,745	6,952	25,533	1,226	1,145	49	96	42	95
Clarkson,	357	824	....	731	938	7,736	4,929	20,093	765	786	55	112	14	82
Gates,	78,927	600	....	351	476	1,165	667	2,646	428	876	....	20	....	....
Greece,	1,830	1,365	2	1,023	1,986	9,174	5,954	22,323	1,855	2,732	333	951	....	95
Henrietta,	510	867	....	1,028	938	6,055	5,450	19,756	1,383	1,498	40	302	....	30
Irondequoit,	61,622	513	1	360	572	1,167	783	3,231	418	894	23	30	....	....
Mendon,	....	1,155	1	1,102	201	8,658	8,391	30,670	1,530	1,588	....	338	....	....
Ogden,	250	1,009	....	779	1,014	5,690	5,567	23,290	1,280	1,477	93	171	....	25
Parma,	13,125	1,180	....	1,381	1,524	9,626	7,109	26,451	1,186	2,026	269	308	....	154
Penfield,	4,818	1,044	....	960	1,093	4,999	3,026	12,138	1,965	1,817	297¾	260	73	50
Perrington,	81,500	1,000	....	753	923	5,008	3,878	14,268¾	1,320	1,431	....	36	....	108
Pittsfield,	810	831	3	600	607	3,669	3,215	12,403	1,003	1,120	....	....	....	....
Riga,	....	894	....	819	963	7,154	7,048	26,458	479	1,092	....	143	75	....
Rochester,	8,660	1,544	....	16	307	....	....	....	648	12	....	....	....	....
Rush,	360	702	....	1,089	1,013	6,734	5,617	21,102	1,104	2,606	68	56	....	56
Sweden,	840	986	....	674	1,221	5,816	5,105	21,191	772	1,074	75	374	50	186
Union,	....	1,043	....	894	1,504	10,617	6,361	25,376	1,511	1,808	19	289	41	137
Webster,	488	891	....	694	1,037	5,825	3,485	12,961	1,215	768	66	216	69	320
Wheatland,	600	1,015	....	1,039	939	6,869	6,519	24,417	275	588	30	324	....	50
Total,	287,527	18,913	16	15,641	19,086	116.817	91.910	350,468¾	21,098	26,292	1,417¾	4.178	364	1.388

MONTGOMERY COUNTY.—(CONTINUED.)

TOWNS.	Gallons of milk sold.	Horses.	Mules.	Swine under 6 months	Swine over 6 months	Number of sheep.	Number of fleeces.	Pounds of wool.	Value of poultry sold.	Value of eggs sold.	Yards of fulled cloth made.	Yards of flannel made.	Yards of linen made.	Yards of cotton and mixed cloths.
Amsterdam,	40,700	689	....	827	572	2,402	1,280	4,286¾	1,628	2,465	62	67	25	....
Canajoharie,	416	901	....	1,079	928	2,641	1,692	6,184	1,243	2,858	82¼	313½	30	38
Charleston,	....	850	....	642	546	4,855	2,907	10,299	1,395	2,260	593	1,446	540	765
Florida,	465	1,212	1	1,239	811	2,887	2,534	9,103½	1,765	2,448	118	158	30	....
Glen,	3,340	986	....	1,129	904	3,824	3,099	11,243	808	1,826	217	565	243	72
Minden,	11,080	1,074	2	1,406	1,235	2,197	1,855	6,827	885	1,600	213	672	157	409
Mohawk,	4,010	857	....	1,587	1,033	3,818	2,732	10,107	852	2,978	459	703	102	45
Palatine,	....	865	....	1,424	1,033	1,692	1,586	5,904½	742	1,725	748	680	324	77
Root,	5,200	1,036	....	788	840	4,885	2,877	9,222	782	2 251	382	809	598	203
St. Johnsville,	2,960	366	....	489	322	460	363	1,269	413	294	152	179	....	10
Total,	68,171	8,836	3	10,610	8,224	29.661	20,925	74,445¾	10.513	20.705	3.026¼	5,592½	2,049	1 619

NEW-YORK COUNTY.

TOWNS.	ACRES. Improved.	ACRES. Unimproved.	CASH VALUE. Of farm.	CASH VALUE. Of stock.	CASH VALUE. Of tools and implements.	Acres plowed the year previous.	Acres in fallow the year previous.	Acres in pasture the year previous.	MEADOW. Acres.	MEADOW. Tons of hay.	MEADOW. Bushels of grass seed.	SPRING WHEAT. Acres sown.	SPRING WHEAT. Bushels harvested.	WINTER WHEAT. Acres sown.
New-York City,.	1. 050¾	923½	$4, 324, 700	$1,495,212	$11, 395	143½	45	246½	101	157	......	......	......	2

NIAGARA COUNTY.

TOWNS.	ACRES. Improved.	ACRES. Unimproved.	CASH VALUE. Of farm.	CASH VALUE. Of stock.	CASH VALUE. Of tools and implements.	Acres plowed the year previous.	Acres in fallow the year previous.	Acres in pasture the year previous.	MEADOW. Acres.	MEADOW. Tons of hay.	MEADOW. Bushels of grass seed.	SPRING WHEAT. Acres sown.	SPRING WHEAT. Bushels harvested.	WINTER WHEAT. Acres sown.
Cambria, ...	17, 214	5, 767	1, 228, 558	148, 270	60, 108	3, 418	3, 060	3, 122	3, 056	3, 499	226½	15	233	4, 509
Hartland, ...	20, 836¾	9, 600	1, 477, 979	180, 087	37, 849	5, 099	2, 045½	4, 379	2, 910¾	3, 801¼	75	18	133	3, 484¼
Lewiston, ...	15, 812	6, 519¾	1, 350, 100	135, 249	32, 257	6, 739	2, 398	2, 736	2, 850	3, 436	46½	8	120	3, 401½
Lockport, ...	21, 813¼	13, 584½	2, 022, 138	212, 032	59, 518	4, 745½	3, 641	3, 619½	4, 226½	5, 400	269½	17¼	318	4, 464¾
Newfane, ...	22. 268½	10, 173	1, 588, 153	177, 432	58, 862	5, 004¼	3, 392	3, 351	2, 552½	3, 342½	299½	50	681	5, 043
Niagara, ...	6, 754¼	6, 088	974, 145	160, 876	47, 469	1, 465	1, 440	1, 056	1, 582	1, 675½	98	8½	108	1, 408½
Pendleton, ...	9, 843¾	6, 169¼	637, 942	72, 998	23, 175	5, 012¾	1, 739½	1, 526½	1, 472	1, 627	60½	7½	168	2, 124¾
Porter, ...	14, 014	5, 721	1, 177, 807	122, 420	39, 952	2, 288½	3, 287	1, 390	2, 055½	2, 893½	183	19½	187	4, 243½
Royalton, ...	27, 748½	12, 968	2, 011, 986	243, 146	73, 788	6, 762¼	3, 402½	5, 543¾	4, 899⅜	6, 337¾	783½	22¾	409½	4, 843½
Somerset, ...	18, 202	5, 313	1, 119, 742	135, 369	42, 300	3, 472½	3, 364½	3, 311	2, 164	2, 453½	243½	56	958½	4, 186½
Wheatfield, ...	10, 768⅞	10, 937	1, 060, 737	98, 519	32, 771	4, 138⅝	2, 568⅛	1, 590¼	2, 019½	2, 595½	158	12½	185	2, 029½
Wilson, ...	21, 768	8, 269½	1, 672, 062	214, 391	54, 340	4, 399½	3, 883¼	3, 634	2, 732¼	4, 056	235¼	117¾	1, 885	6, 049½
Total, ...	207, 043⅞	101, 110	16, 321, 349	1, 900, 789	562, 389	52, 544⅞	34, 221⅜	35, 259	32, 520⅜	41. 117½	2, 678¾	352¾	5, 386	45788¼

ONEIDA COUNTY.

TOWNS.	ACRES. Improved.	ACRES. Unimproved.	CASH VALUE. Of farm.	CASH VALUE. Of stock.	CASH VALUE. Of tools and implements.	Acres plowed the year previous.	Acres in fallow the year previous.	Acres in pasture the year previous.	MEADOW. Acres.	MEADOW. Tons of hay.	MEADOW. Bushels of grass seed.	SPRING WHEAT. Acres sown.	SPRING WHEAT. Bushels harvested.	WINTER WHEAT. Acres sown.
Annsville, ...	14, 188½	18, 843	538, 072	97, 654	23, 263	3, 775½	4	4, 772½	3, 941	3, 709½	83½	52¼	461	31
Augusta, ...	14, 247½	3, 321½	727, 815	101, 692	22, 632	4, 532½	184½	6, 018	2, 962	2, 401	57	347¾	3, 762	342
Ava, ...	9, 192	13, 295	397, 901	72, 755	17, 612	1, 258½	....	4, 376	3, 385	3, 615	236	9¾	128	......
Boonville, ...	18, 290⅞	21, 810½	1, 019, 838	157, 531	39, 362	3, 122¾	11	9, 514¾	6, 020½	6, 585¼	23¼	94¼	1, 493	145¼
Bridgewater, ...	11, 575½	3, 105½	592, 805	86, 041	13, 772	2, 777½	144	5, 453	3, 039	3, 540	48	173¾	2, 397	64
Camden, ...	13, 421¼	17, 683	649, 422	125, 500	15, 651	2, 776½	116½	5, 756½	4, 002½	3, 233	......	98¾	826	11
Deerfield, ...	16, 990	4, 516	953, 209	122, 736	25, 910	3, 276	....	7, 730	4, 746	4, 199	4½	60	814	15
Florence, ...	13, 131	17, 145	434, 977	89, 034	17, 248	2, 285	193	4, 722	5, 539	4, 001	17¾	47	603	13
Floyd, ...	15, 715¾	5 889	731, 763	105, 302	33, 377	3, 419¼	41½	6, 696	3, 184½	4, 426	24½	63¼	875¼	50
Kirkland, ...	15, 303¼	3, 706	1, 109, 540	117, 107	26, 119	4, 470	82½	6, 622	6, 344⅞	3, 991	63½	195¼	2, 633	191¼
Lee, ...	18, 059	9, 957	895, 420	148, 084	36, 783	4, 322	154	8, 234	5, 323	5, 561½	57	60¼	715	54
Marcy, ...	16, 151	3, 356	946, 650	129, 373	41, 681	3, 751½	35½	7, 609½	4, 342	4, 282½	23½	87½	808	10
Marshall, ...	16, 374	3, 621½	911, 005	125, 207	21, 488	4, 617	17	7, 761	3, 458	3, 869¾	51	185¾	2, 727½	321¾
New Hartford, ..	15, 365¾	2, 630½	1, 229, 730	102, 952	47, 390	3, 547½	30½	5, 945½	4, 432	4, 988	32¼	126¾	1, 512	133¼
Paris, ...	15, 769	3, 609½	974, 046	139, 578	38, 450	4, 342⅝	75½	5, 464¼	3, 930¼	4, 300	134½	258½	4, 115	125¼
Remsen, ...	14, 056¼	57, 687	688, 496	100, 379	21, 965	2, 328½	....	6, 711	197¼	4, 153½	1	219	2, 965	......
Rome, ...	22, 942	19, 326½	1, 633, 010	195, 336	45, 391	6, 020¾	537½	7, 826¾	4, 852¾	5, 495	65	48	404	320½
Sangerfield, ...	14, 810½	3, 803	753, 600	94, 964	18, 988	2, 470¾	35	7, 114	4, 402	4, 006	27½	143¾	2, 026	112½
Steuben, ...	17, 884½	8, 041½	550, 550	131, 900	19, 938	1, 871	....	9, 607¼	5, 743	6, 116½	2½	177⅞	2, 357	......
Trenton, ...	21, 800¼	6, 843½	1, 504, 466	178, 016	48, 482	3, 828	33	10, 296½	7, 092	7, 453	7, 420¼	233	2, 503	3¾
Utica, ...	2 323	292	363, 170	31, 329	8, 462	528	18	708	911	1, 155	37	4	82	3
Vernon, ...	19, 564¾	4, 282½	1, 010, 849	155, 764	28, 949	5, 626½	117½	7, 938½	4, 273	4, 197	65½	289⅞	2, 821	416
Verona, ...	26, 325¼	15, 341½	1, 636, 670	226, 971	42, 043	6, 123¼	130	9, 143½	7, 517¾	8, 931	120¼	65	586½	185
Vienna, ...	13, 595	22, 139	782, 357	107, 094	22, 992	3, 650¼	114	4, 711	3, 436	3, 229	57½	90	704	70
Western, ...	21, 762⅜	9, 292½	891, 418	151, 541	27, 599	3, 756	83	10, 420	7, 293	6, 995½	24	105¾	1, 345	37¾
Westmoreland, .	22, 425¾	4, 242¾	1, 231, 601	178, 541	30, 462	5, 012	115½	11, 335	5, 678½	5, 792¼	18¾	111½	1, 439¾	497
Whitestown, ...	14, 536½	2, 813⅞	1, 136, 501	137, 125	28, 658	3, 533	64½	5, 364¾	3, 699½	4, 707¼	5	48	780¼	25½
Total, ...	435, 800⅜	286, 594¼	24, 294, 881	3, 409, 506	764, 667	97, 022⅛	2, 337½	187, 860¼	119, 745⅝	124, 933½	8, 700½	3, 396⅝	41883¼	3. 177¾

ONONDAGA COUNTY.

TOWNS.	ACRES. Improved.	ACRES. Unimproved.	CASH VALUE. Of farm.	CASH VALUE. Of stock.	CASH VALUE. Of tools and implements.	Acres plowed the year previous.	Acres in fallow the year previous.	Acres in pasture the year previous.	MEADOW. Acres.	MEADOW. Tons of hay.	MEADOW. Bushels of grass seed.	SPRING WHEAT. Acres sown.	SPRING WHEAT. Bushels harvested.	WINTER WHEAT. Acres sown.
Camillus, ...	16, 411	3, 574¼	1, 165, 840	142, 934	35, 583	6, 100¼	556¼	4, 394½	2, 064¾	2, 566	51	31¾	336	2, 085½
Cicero, ...	14, 376⅜	14, 912⅞	1, 145, 868	135, 517	43, 452	5, 063¼	199¼	4, 401¼	3, 161¼	3, 391	204	26¾	298½	461¼
Clay, ...	19, 535¼	10, 681¾	1, 458, 713	171, 212	43, 887	7, 393¼	187	5, 546¾	4, 645	4, 671½	278¼	96½	1025	544½
De Witt, ...	15, 643⅞	6, 294	1, 659, 487	146, 471	46, 404	5, 189¼	463	4, 700	3, 180¼	3, 344	66	88	791½	1, 188
Elbridge, ...	16, 792¼	4, 638	1, 302, 085	164, 722	36, 636	6, 354¼	843	4, 375	2, 586	3, 209	195½	10	62	1, 848½
Fabius, ...	19, 784¼	6, 994½	958, 355	179, 525	35, 251	3, 762	79	9, 635	5, 627¼	5, 205	62¼	431¼	4877	178
Geddes, ...	4, 786	1, 472¾	816, 446	90, 084	15, 464	1, 780⅞	288¼	1, 133¾	899	969¼	3	1½	15½	377
La Fayette, ...	18, 004	5, 982	1, 084, 545	123, 390	38, 357	7, 084¼	252½	5, 171	2, 761¾	2, 528¼	365½	434¼	4642	869½
Lysander, ...	27, 069½	10, 329	1, 777, 046	243, 259	52, 678	8, 924	642	9, 124½	4, 801¾	5, 573½	105¼	106	966	2, 016¾
Manlius, ...	21, 640¼	7, 546⅜	1, 513, 431	173, 079	38, 937	7, 995¾	1, 140	5, 775	3, 544½	3, 423¾	557¼	84¼	824	1, 946½
Marcellus, ...	15, 558¼	3, 319¼	950, 092	132, 534	31, 673	5, 739¾	196	4, 692	2, 695½	2, 736½	117	387¼	5065	766½
Onondaga, ...	33, 001¾	7, 846½	2, 817, 658	272, 247	77, 169	12, 585½	919	8, 500½	5, 439	5, 677½	114	720	9421½	3, 060¾
Otisco, ...	14, 803¼	3, 803	708, 787	106, 409	31, 183	5, 759	93½	4, 882	2, 154½	1, 855½	37½	1, 089¼	12343½	336⅛
Pompey, ...	32, 420¼	8, 286	1, 856, 475	235, 582	75, 358	12, 943½	313	10, 320	5, 889½	5, 238	804	1, 325½	16404	588½
Lima, ...	6, 559¾	2, 219	731, 371	51, 901	12, 438	2, 380½	158¼	1, 755	1, 413	1, 559	4½	51	519	196½
Skaneateles, ...	20, 935½	3, 979	2, 303, 672	154, 320	53, 967	7, 666	149¼	6, 309½	4, 196½	3, 756	341½	466	5735	759½
Stafford, ...	15, 643½	4, 429½	726, 652	115, 088	28, 216	6, 743½	68	5, 320½	2, 661¼	2, 159¼	70½	1, 419	16862	253
Syracuse, ...	1, 992½	293½	456, 650	28, 183	6, 203	653	134	577½	574½	756	4½	3½	22	161½
Tully, ...	12, 269½	3, 996	662, 576	87, 515	23, 662	3, 825	157	3, 826	2, 402¼	1, 797	46¼	371	4243	321¾
Van Buren, ...	17, 301	4, 104	1, 257, 541	149, 537	43, 547	5, 216½	612	4, 557½	2, 496¼	2, 830⅜	66	55	695½	1642
Total, ...	344, 528	114, 701½	25, 353, 290	2, 903, 509	770, 065	123, 159⅜	7, 450¼	104, 997¼	63, 193¾	63, 246⅜	3, 493¾	7, 197¾	85148	19601⅝

ONTARIO COUNTY.

TOWNS.	ACRES. Improved.	ACRES. Unimproved.	CASH VALUE. Of farm.	CASH VALUE. Of stock.	CASH VALUE. Of tools and implements.	Acres plowed the year previous.	Acres in fallow the year previous.	Acres in pasture the year previous.	MEADOW. Acres.	MEADOW. Tons of hay.	MEADOW. Bushels of grass seed.	SPRING WHEAT. Acres sown.	SPRING WHEAT. Bushels harvested.	WINTER WHEAT. Acres sown.
Bristol, ...	17, 023	5, 945½	947, 367	132, 802	31, 448	3, 672¾	957	6, 569	2, 757¼	2, 795¾	188¾	195¼	1663	1,907
Canadice, ...	10, 799	4, 959½	472, 989	68, 676	23, 721	2, 956¼	1, 195	2, 549	1, 439½	1, 263½	1½	1, 206	10754	1, 431
Canandaigua, ...	34, 846½	8, 433	2, 498, 018	257, 638	60, 118	8, 469½	3, 026½	10, 001	6, 010½	5, 344½	561½	472½	3854	4, 032
East Bloomfield,	13, 277	2, 906	1, 040, 941	127, 115	24, 605	3, 104½	1, 265½	4, 408½	1, 791	2, 057½	32½	38½	423	2, 206
Farmington, ...	19, 676½	5, 419	1, 406, 758	188, 781	41, 796	4, 619	1, 579	5, 789½	2, 738	2, 875	140	6	79½	2, 417¾
Gorham, ...	22, 294¼	7, 621¾	1, 473, 065	158, 044	43, 218	7, 081	1, 154½	6, 456	4, 495½	2, 972½	141¼	29	189	2, 121
Hopewell, ...	16, 685	4, 043	986, 891	117, 775	25, 490	5, 427	942	3, 832	2, 726	2, 394	209	4	41	1, 449½
Manchester, ...	18, 085	3, 175½	1, 381, 152	148, 143	40, 553	6, 083	1, 331	4, 695	2, 398½	2, 464½	113¼	8½	68	2, 354¼
Naples, ...	13, 958	10, 117	650, 375	96, 165	19, 610	3, 119	1, 388	4, 576½	2, 190	1, 821	4¼	338½	2079½	2, 200½
Phelps, ...	33, 409½	6, 675	3, 607, 242	277, 057	75, 275	28, 199½	2, 760	7, 098	4, 506	5, 085½	420½	5½	81	3, 764½

(Continued on page 287.)

NEW-YORK COUNTY.—(Continued.)

TOWNS.	Winter Wheat	Oats		Rye.		Barley.		Buckwheat.		Corn.		Potatoes.		Peas.	
	Bushels harvested.	Acres sown.	Bushels harvested	Acres sown.	Bushels harvested.	Acres sown.	Bushels harvested.	Acres sown.	Bushels harvested.	Acres planted.	Bushels harvested.	Acres planted.	Bushels harvested.	Acres sown.	Bushels harvested.
New-York city,	30	19	435	2	25	......	....	....	....	31	1,180	28	1,808	3½	250

NIAGARA COUNTY.—(Continued.)

TOWNS.	Winter Wheat, Bushels harvested.	Oats, Acres sown.	Oats, Bushels harvested	Rye, Acres sown.	Rye, Bushels harvested.	Barley, Acres sown.	Barley, Bushels harvested.	Buckwheat, Acres sown.	Buckwheat, Bushels harvested.	Corn, Acres planted.	Corn, Bushels harvested.	Potatoes, Acres planted.	Potatoes, Bushels harvested.	Peas, Acres sown.	Peas, Bushels harvested.
Cambria,	67561	1,208½	35,824	8	212	351	8,553	145½	1,733	1,254½	42,140	237¼	22,343	41½	1,142
Hartland,	20191	954½	21,431	1	10	275	4,443	396½	4,305	2,209½	54,672	466½	33,865	5	30
Lewiston,	68238	848	21,801	......	....	135⅛	2,786	142¼	1,638	1,018¾	37,105	184¾	18,884	26	419
Lockport,	59280½	1,284¾	40,629	3	40	850½	19,275	174½	1,217	1,476⅛	54,561	340	29,513	203¼	4,199½
Newfane,	56661	681¼	15,673	......	....	176¾	3,929	436½	6,284½	2,408½	66,666	303⅝	29,714	7¼	66
Niagara,	21564	699	25,910	½	73	123½	2,441	84¼	1,335	215½	5,773	87¼	6,905	95	1,544
Pendleton,	28540	1,129½	32,774	......	....	296¾	6,581	139	1,512	635¼	19,085	154	8,526	145¾	2,789
Porter,	69291	460¾	11,975	......	....	30	389	123⅞	1,282	1,174¼	33,363	184¾	18,724	30¼	408½
Royalton,	41442½	2,423¾	73,136	2½	38	1,085¼	22,570	412	3,705	2,122½	68,227	367⅛	30,874½	112	2,027½
Somerset,	38021	624½	13,164	......	....	95	1,455	274¾	2,525	1,773	33,567	276	21,927½	80¾	813½
Wheatfield,	34449	1,399½	40,013	46¼	641	211¼	4,563	120½	1,319	551½	20,573	321½	19,475	84¾	1,506
Wilson,	84672	769	21,068	......	....	151½	2,608	172⅜	2,296	2,457½	73,773	344⅛	34,697	81⅜	1,036
Total,	589911	12,483	353,398	61¼	1,014	3,781⅝	79,593	2,622	29,151½	17,296⅞	509,505	3,266⅞	275,448	913¼	15,981

ONEIDA COUNTY.—(Continued.)

TOWNS.	Winter Wheat, Bushels harvested.	Oats, Acres sown.	Oats, Bushels harvested	Rye, Acres sown.	Rye, Bushels harvested.	Barley, Acres sown.	Barley, Bushels harvested.	Buckwheat, Acres sown.	Buckwheat, Bushels harvested.	Corn, Acres planted.	Corn, Bushels harvested.	Potatoes, Acres planted.	Potatoes, Bushels harvested.	Peas, Acres sown.	Peas, Bushels harvested.
Annsville,	290½	1,784¾	38,515	121¼	1,246½	5⅛	51	396	3,394¾	1,240¾	30,258	262½	20,004	14¼	206½
Augusta,	2,337½	1,114	24,313	......	....	1,418¾	23,762	34¾	434	965¼	21,398	152¼	11,349	29½	515
Ava,	......	827	24,420	6	92	7¾	144	96	1,396	101½	2,615	155	13,182	6¼	138
Boonville,	19	1,817	45.498	30½	304	28¾	496	132¾	1,414	406¼	9,811	396⅝	32,052	12⅞	272
Bridgewater,	727	1,182½	32,920	......	....	371	6,673	25	208	506¾	15,449	166½	15,844	37	924
Camden,	103	888¾	17,777	158	1,367	......	....	197⅞	1,055½	1,016½	19,649	271⅞	15,600	5¼	65¾
Deerfield,	114	1,869	53,880	34	492	96	2,273	76	1,044	755	23,974	363	30,211	3	220
Florence,	110	977½	24,638	277¼	1,809	1½	25	108½	1,215½	405½	10,446	241¼	15,982	¾	13
Floyd,	311	1,499½	40,005	79½	1,197	24½	526	289½	3,308	1,045½	28,754	221⅝	19,888	9⅜	182
Kirkland,	1,754½	1,211⅞	35,527	......	....	688	13,788	92¼	1,344	1,137	36,007	274	25,820	52⅝	1,124½
Lee,	464	1,940½	48,421	172	2,689	2	60	352	4,024	1,525	33,601	322¾	21,675	4	39
Marcy,	40	1,786½	40,069	112	1,676	50½	648	135⅜	1,861	870½	26,521	429⅝	38,846	63½	769
Marshall,	2,787½	1,132¾	30,657	29¾	668	1,136½	22.983	46½	522	1,226¼	39,850	201⅝	20,380	46⅞	913½
New Hartford,	770	1,260½	28,551	2⅛	15	294¼	5,548	108¼	1,493	955	28,129	369¼	27,076	54⅝	1,139
Paris,	1,281¾	1,544	49,316¼	85	....	607	14,088	41½	627	1,101⅝	37,181	330⅝	34,185	50⅞	1,159
Remsen,	......	1,298¾	25,646	75¼	986½	114¼	2,053	37¼	396½	240	6,276	286¾	22,022	11½	141½
Rome,	3,089	2,708	63,595	415¾	5,919	61	1,169	79½	6,256	2,226¾	60,782	568¼	43,757	57⅞	939
Sangerfield,	837	899¾	22,537	6	50	401¾	7,434	58¾	618	648¼	22,954	193¼	19,681	43	858
Steuben,	......	1,124¼	25,636	4	30	59¼	1,182	99½	1.539½	263¼	7,833	200	17,739	8½	196
Trenton,	17	1,586¾	42,569	39	448	50½	992	173½	2,430	1,126	37,758½	306	28,175	16	202
Utica,	......	220	4,810	......	....	27	645	5½	75	146½	4,557	58	5,715	4¾	158
Vernon,	2,456	1,532	33,098	31	178	1,059½	20,957	184½	2,459	1,516¼	43,260	221⅞	17,561	58¼	721¼
Verona,	1,265	2,097¼	57,598	23	244	280¾	4,577	441¼	5,386	2,130¼	58,511	448½	31,306	28¼	395
Vienna,	634	1,188¼	26,531	136	1,448	8	92	350½	2,334⅝	1,445¾	31,317	314⅜	16,876	2½	33¼
Western,	395	1,891½	50,497	140¾	2,652	25½	546	274½	3,703	1,108½	28,838	236½	23,781	16½	258
Westmoreland,	490	2,394¼	56,397	14¾	133	269¼	4,928	253¾	2,756	1,439½	36,762	352½	28,336	41¼	692½
Whitestown,	147	1,393	32,379	28¼	477	96¾	1,790	264¾	3,473½	1,024⅛	29,803	334¼	27,605	33⅜	637¼
Total,	20439¾	39,169⅞	975,800¼	2,021½	24,121	7,185⅛	137,430	4,355½	54,767⅝	26,573½	732,294½	7,678¼	624,648	712	12,912½

ONONDAGA COUNTY.—(Continued.)

TOWNS.	Winter Wheat, Bushels harvested.	Oats, Acres sown.	Oats, Bushels harvested	Rye, Acres sown.	Rye, Bushels harvested.	Barley, Acres sown.	Barley, Bushels harvested.	Buckwheat, Acres sown.	Buckwheat, Bushels harvested.	Corn, Acres planted.	Corn, Bushels harvested.	Potatoes, Acres planted.	Potatoes, Bushels harvested.	Peas, Acres sown.	Peas, Bushels harvested.
Camillus,	10006½	1,980½	59,731	......	....	1,412½	32,969	82¾	588½	1,883¼	58,060	227½	19,857	16½	145
Cicero,	1519½	2,090⅝	59,988	42	400	85¾	1,681½	324¼	3,492½	1,688⅞	44,304	441½	24,842	187⅛	3,504
Clay,	2475½	2,908¼	76,995	177	2,433	505¾	9,794	395	4,075	2,187¼	55,937	419	34,011	128¾	2,314½
De Witt,	3542	1,821½	49,230	2	5	298½	5,740	145½	1,041	1,897	44,580	227¾	14,321	205¼	3,065
Elbridge,	11254	1,700	49,318	34½	520	1,148½	24,263	143¼	1,569	1,991¾	62,324	219⅜	17,670	12¼	197
Fabius,	1239	1,614¼	32,159	......	....	367½	7,599	51⅝	510	778¾	25,736	150½	11,162	111⅝	1,924
Geddes,	1358	770¼	21,151½	......	....	183½	4,256	26¾	92¾	507¼	12,164	124¼	10,834½	27	364
La Fayette,	4862	3,008	58,440	......	....	1,456¾	27,868	97½	985	1,313¼	40,520	190⅛	15,291	96¾	1,373
Lysander,	13534	3,165¾	91,976	104½	1,235½	1,197¾	23,125½	423¾	4,905	3,076⅜	91,623	421¼	38,268	88	1,455
Manlius,	5470¼	3,161¾	72,923	5½	3	524¼	10,051	160¾	1,203½	2,572⅜	61,132	272¾	17,975	184⅛	2,320
Marcellus,	4893½	1,465¼	31,461	1	14	1,437½	23,767	84¾	1,172½	1,409½	40,668	207½	18,220	37	548
Onondaga,	13181¾	4,482¾	111,077	7½	109	2,128	38,443	211½	2,125½	3,230	93,713	520¾	40,518	281⅝	4,226
Otisco,	2271	1,466¾	28,099	......	....	1,682	22,494½	60⅜	683¼	719	20,352	180½	15,620	48¾	598½
Pompey,	2676	4,200	84,332	30	300	2,595½	45,493	227¼	2,033	2,141¾	65,070	356½	25,457	655¾	9,760
Salina,	818	729½	19,928	26	244	118½	2,833	62½	423	801¾	19,919	240¼	15,550	32½	439
Skaneateles,	4264½	1,611¼	36,056	......	....	2,169½	33,806	276⅞	3,137	1,892	50,265	161	13,076	66¼	699
Spafford,	1312½	1,173¼	21,143	4	50	1,917½	28,951	170¼	1,595½	1,044	30,305	133	12,800	83½	951½
Syracuse,	722	280½	7,983	6	15	10½	100	7½	135	196	5,667	43¾	3,663	17½	247
Tully,	1424¾	1,465	29,070	......	....	682¾	10,715	94¼	1,036¼	685¼	20,989	97½	8,059	29⅞	487
Van Buren,	10234	2,414	74,167	¾	12	832¾	17,836	151½	1,650½	2,231¼	64,125	255¾	22,947	15	298
Total,	97058¾	41,509⅛	1015227½	440¾	5,340½	20755¼	371,785½	3,198⅛	32,453¾	32,246⅞	907,453	4,890½	380,141½	2,324⅞	34,915½

ONTARIO COUNTY.—(Continued.)

TOWNS.	Winter Wheat, Bushels harvested.	Oats, Acres sown.	Oats, Bushels harvested	Rye, Acres sown.	Rye, Bushels harvested.	Barley, Acres sown.	Barley, Bushels harvested.	Buckwheat, Acres sown.	Buckwheat, Bushels harvested.	Corn, Acres planted.	Corn, Bushels harvested.	Potatoes, Acres planted.	Potatoes, Bushels harvested.	Peas, Acres sown.	Peas, Bushels harvested.
Bristol,	28066	1,171¾	20,352	20	374	755½	14,119	152⅝	891	1,072	29,742	95	6,454	260½	2,007½
Canadice,	17229	698½	9,370	2	35	199	2,500	316½	1,604	292	5,801	40⅞	3,119	35⅝	284½
Canandaigua,	55099	2,343½	53,708	407	5,645	1,994	36,207	457	2,029¾	2,459½	69,135¼	178½	10,836	356	4,221
East Bloomfield,	40086	951½	31,153	90½	1,360	906½	20,597	32⅝	239	1,102¼	37,018	101½	9,511	34¾	716
Farmington,	30746	1,620½	49,371	49	576	562½	11,150	135	758½	1,909	47,018	200½	11,090	121⅞	1,686
Gorham,	27447½	1,976½	23,844½	18¾	157	2,819½	34,913	281	1,651	1,917¼	36,827	123½	6,034	26¾	312
Hopewell,	20999	1,416	30,685	19¾	402	1,734⅛	28,588	206½	1,418	1,459	35,290	113	9,201	49	499
Manchester,	29142½	1,553	46,152	56	685	1,068½	21,580	228	1,275	2,162½	51,771	193½	14,838	12½	147½
Naples,	16449	814½	7,707	55½	418	381½	3,355	278¼	469½	757	12,385	114	5,472	224½	1,255
Phelps,	63011	3,101	92,828	215	3,178	2,457½	51,483	439¼	3,703	3,927	108,015	596¼	48,284	41½	597

(Continued on page 288.)

NEW-YORK COUNTY.—(CONTINUED.)

TOWNS.	Beans: Acres planted.	Beans: Bushels harvested.	Turnips: Acres sown.	Turnips: Bushels harvested.	Flax: Acres sown.	Flax: Pounds of lint.	Flax: Bushels of seed.	Hemp: Acres sown.	Hemp: Tons of hemp.	Hops: Acres planted.	Hops: Pounds harvested.	Tobacco: Acres planted.	Tobacco: Pounds harvested.	Apple orchards: Bushels of apples.	Apple orchards: Barrels of cider.
New-York city,..	8½	645	27¼	2,060	.....	....	....	.....	.....	.....	....	.....	....	....	....

NIAGARA COUNTY.—(CONTINUED.)

TOWNS.	Beans: Acres planted.	Beans: Bushels harvested.	Turnips: Acres sown.	Turnips: Bushels harvested.	Flax: Acres sown.	Flax: Pounds of lint.	Flax: Bushels of seed.	Hemp: Acres sown.	Hemp: Tons of hemp.	Hops: Acres planted.	Hops: Pounds harvested.	Tobacco: Acres planted.	Tobacco: Pounds harvested.	Apple orchards: Bushels of apples.	Apple orchards: Barrels of cider.
Cambria, ...	10⅛	191	8⅛	1,697	.....	....	....	.....	.....	.....	....	.....	....	35,352	585
Hartland,.......	320	3,110	14⅞	3,018	.....	....	....	.....	.....	.....	....	2¼	4,010	22,514	358
Lewiston,.......	5¼	93	13⅜	1,755	⅜	....	8½	.....	.....	.....	....	.....	....	26,900	556
Lockport,.......	11¾	254	8⅜	1,568	.....	....	....	.....	.....	.....	....	.....	....	30,191	556½
Newfane, ...	78⅛	1,207	15⅝	5,917	.....	....	....	.....	.....	.....	....	.....	....	15,441	193½
Niagara,..... ..	5¾	65½	4	520	.....	....	....	.....	.....	.....	....	.....	....	5,934	211
Pendleton,......	5½	59½	3¼	666	.....	....	....	.....	.....	.....	....	.....	....	6,939	86½
Porter, ...	6⅜	193	10⅜	849	.....	....	....	.....	.....	.....	....	.....	....	19,868	218
Royalton,.......	83⅜	1,205	30	6,067	86½	380	313½	.....	.....	.....	....	.....	....	49,217	963
Somerset,.......	187⅛	2,110½	7	1,194	.....	....	....	.....	.....	.....	....	8⅛	8,000	18,065	223½
Wheatfield, ...	13⅜	146	3¾	153	.....	....	....	.....	.....	.....	....	.....	....	4,629	86
Wilson,.........	48	622	19¼	5,554	.....	....	....	.....	.....	.....	....	½	1,000	20,947	424½
Total, ...	774¾	9,256½	138½	28.958	86⅞	380	322	.....	.....	.....	....	10⅞	13,010	255,997	4,461½

ONEIDA COUNTY.—(CONTINUED.)

TOWNS.	Beans: Acres planted.	Beans: Bushels harvested.	Turnips: Acres sown.	Turnips: Bushels harvested.	Flax: Acres sown.	Flax: Pounds of lint.	Flax: Bushels of seed.	Hemp: Acres sown.	Hemp: Tons of hemp.	Hops: Acres planted.	Hops: Pounds harvested.	Tobacco: Acres planted.	Tobacco: Pounds harvested.	Apple orchards: Bushels of apples.	Apple orchards: Barrels of cider.
Annsville,.......	16⅜	484½	8⅛	1,760	.....	....	....	.....	.....	.....	....	.....	....	8,341	165
Augusta,........	35¼	408	¾	82	.....	....	....	.....	.....	111½	88,727	.....	....	38,135	379
Ava, ...	3	104	7¾	456	1½	337	12	.....	.....	.....	....	.....	....	1,942	11
Boonville,.......	7⅛	67¾	8¼	845	¼	....	3	.....	.....	.....	....	3	6	3,775	23
Bridgewater,....	8	218	....	....	¾	425	9½	.....	.....	13	11,187	.....	....	22,150	210
Camden,........	4	111½	8⅞	2,862	.....	....	....	.....	.....	.....	....	.....	....	23,508	475
Deerfield,.......	....	....	3	300	.....	....	....	.....	.....	.....	....	.....	....	17,330	415
Florence, ...	....	....	3¾	760	.....	....	....	.....	.....	8¾	3,100	4½	1,124	11,770	82
Floyd,..........	7⅜	157	6¼	710	.....	....	....	.....	.....	.....	....	.....	....	18,201	299
Kirkland,.......	64⅛	1,218½	⅞	165	28	....	130	.....	.....	14¼	18,400	.....	....	49,296	732
Lee,............	21¼	205	15	1,695	.....	....	....	.....	.....	1½	1,550	.....	....	22,812	409
Marcy, ...	11⅞	138	12¾	2,342	5	....	40	.....	.....	.....	....	.....	....	19,355	252
Marshall,........	37½	721	....	....	1½	375	17	.....	.....	86½	83,646	1	930	37,309	350¼
New Hartford, ..	11¼	396	5⅞	125	.....	....	....	.....	.....	.....	....	.....	....	52,328	1,237
Paris, ...	18⅝	458	¾	209	2¾	....	40	.....	.....	1⅛	1,600	2	2,700	39,342	687½
Remsen,........	7	60	4¾	152	.....	....	....	.....	.....	1	117	.....	....	1,466	3
Rome,..........	24¼	267	10	1,364	.....	....	1	.....	.....	5	3,700	1	2,000	22,534	549
Sangerfield,.....	25¼	467	¼	6	.....	....	....	.....	.....	364⅝	340,055	22¼	32.435	22,536	579
Steuben,........	2¼	31	3⅜	376	¾	....	11½	.....	.....	.....	....	.....	....	11,057	62½
Trenton,........	7¾	112	3¾	950	98	4,744	961	.....	.....	.....	....	.....	....	28,819	845
Utica, ...	1¼	20	2	550	.....	....	....	.....	.....	.....	....	.....	....	1,242	4
Vernon, ...	78⅛	854	1¼	141	1	200	2	.....	.....	47¼	44,951	.....	....	28,069	1,277
Verona,.........	21¾	315	11	2,200	.....	....	....	.....	.....	20	18,505	.....	....	37,952	1,488¼
Vienna,.........	10⅛	246	28⅝	5,084	⅛	24	¼	.....	.....	.....	....	⅛	25	19,440	342½
Western, ...	8	101	⅝	175	.....	....	....	.....	.....	1¼	500	.....	....	22,713	324
Westmoreland,..	31½	422	¼	10	⅝	280	2¼	.....	.....	.....	....	.....	....	46,596	925
Whitestown,....	9	188½	7¾	1,686	½	250	4	.....	.....	.....	16	.....	....	26,244	609
Total, ...	472¼	7,770¾	155⅝	25,005	140⅝	6,635	1,233½	.....	.....	675¾	616,054	33⅞	39,220	634,262	12,735

ONONDAGA COUNTY.—(CONTINUED.)

TOWNS.	Beans: Acres planted.	Beans: Bushels harvested.	Turnips: Acres sown.	Turnips: Bushels harvested.	Flax: Acres sown.	Flax: Pounds of lint.	Flax: Bushels of seed.	Hemp: Acres sown.	Hemp: Tons of hemp.	Hops: Acres planted.	Hops: Pounds harvested.	Tobacco: Acres planted.	Tobacco: Pounds harvested.	Apple orchards: Bushels of apples.	Apple orchards: Barrels of cider.
Camillus,.......	14¾	233	4⅝	937	.....	....	....	.....	.....	3	2.000	5¾	9,000	30,343	645½
Cicero, ...	19¼	380½	11¼	970½	1½	400	4	.....	.....	.....	....	7¼	9,000	20,131	569
Clay,...........	50⅝	768½	6¾	1,689	2¼	50	24	.....	.....	.....	....	24¾	27,765	27,578	680
De Witt,........	7½	90	5½	72	.....	....	....	.....	.....	.....	....	28¾	32,525	12,564	566
Elbridge, ...	22¾	386¾	11	2,392	.....	....	....	.....	.....	.....	....	11	12,000	26,816	760
Fabius,.........	2⅝	135½	....	70	2¾	587	13	.....	.....	1¾	1,515	.....	....	40,056	294
Geddes,.........	2	55½	6⅝	1,260	.....	....	....	.....	.....	.....	....	9¼	7,563	4,067	57½
La Fayette, ...	8¼	140	⅝	108	.....	....	....	.....	.....	1¾	1,400	1	1,200	36,368	443½
Lysander,.......	173⅝	2,995	16¼	2,676	.....	....	....	.....	.....	.....	....	20½	28,544	48,181	1,373½
Manlius,........	20⅜	233	1¾	110¼	2½	2,750	18½	.....	.....	.....	12	76⅛	75,004	25,176	734½
Marcellus, ...	18½	452	18½	3,273	.....	....	....	.....	.....	.....	....	113	145,310	35,395	756
Onondaga, ...	20	379½	9¼	1,057	.....	....	....	.....	.....	.....	....	21	22,550	73,302½	3,046½
Otisco,..........	6⅛	105	9⅜	1,277	.....	....	....	.....	.....	.....	....	1	1,500	48,715	434¼
Pompey,........	12¾	196	2	220	10	3,500	182½	.....	.....	1¾	2,500	18½	19,793	39,417	800
Salina,..........	14⅝	227	2¼	636	1	2,000	10	.....	.....	.....	....	72	90,883	4,021	107
Skaneateles,.....	52¼	785	5⅝	1,103	7½	1,500	67	.....	.....	.....	....	44¾	48,550	45,658	674
Spafford,........	18¼	563½	1	356	271¼	42,500	2,193	.....	.....	.....	....	.....	....	41,900	572½
Syracuse,.......	¾	22	3¾	180	.....	....	....	.....	.....	.....	....	.....	....	1,251	11
Tully,..........	4¼	85¾	1½	94	20½	4,000	132¾	.....	.....	1	6,000	.....	....	24,465	288½
Van Buren, ...	47¾	750½	2⅜	695	.....	....	....	.....	.....	8	....	16½	23,800	39,141	912
Total, ...	517	8,984	120¼	19,175¾	319¼	57,287	2,644¾	.....	.....	17¼	13,427	471⅛	554,987	624,545½	13,725¼

ONTARIO COUNTY.—(CONTINUED.)

TOWNS.	Beans: Acres planted.	Beans: Bushels harvested.	Turnips: Acres sown.	Turnips: Bushels harvested.	Flax: Acres sown.	Flax: Pounds of lint.	Flax: Bushels of seed.	Hemp: Acres sown.	Hemp: Tons of hemp.	Hops: Acres planted.	Hops: Pounds harvested.	Tobacco: Acres planted.	Tobacco: Pounds harvested.	Apple orchards: Bushels of apples.	Apple orchards: Barrels of cider.
Bristol,.........	11¼	174½	3	381½	¼	....	1½	.....	.....	2	2,160	.....	....	47,339	285½
Canadice,.......	8¾	31¼	¼	....	¾	....	2	.....	.....	.....	....	.....	....	6,543	73
Canandaigua,....	22	210	5½	252	.....	....	....	.....	.....	18	12,000	.....	....	34,331	1,138½
East Bloomfield,.	1¾	68	1¼	163	.....	....	....	.....	.....	6	10,140	.....	....	19,052	631
Farmington,.....	10½	292½	....	1,774	.....	....	....	.....	.....	.....	....	.....	....	30,848	627½
Gorham,........	9⅛	59½	2⅜	475	20	....	92	.....	.....	.....	....	.....	....	22,318	678½
Hopewell, ...	1	98	½	295	12	2,000	60	.....	.....	.....	....	.....	....	31,881	548½
Manchester,.....	5¾	54½	8	871	.....	....	....	.....	.....	.....	....	.....	....	22,729	642
Naples,.........	15¼	97½	2¾	130	.....	....	....	.....	.....	7½	2,500	⅛	30	17,173	106
Phelps,.........	57⅝	864	8⅜	676	½	70	....	.....	.....	.....	5	10	9,150	43,154	1,341½

(Continued on page 289.)

NEW-YORK COUNTY.—(CONTINUED.)

TOWNS.	MARKET GARDENS: Acres cultivated.	MARKET GARDENS: Value of products.	Pounds of maple sugar made.	Gallons of maple molasses made.	Gallons of wine made.	Pounds of honey collected.	Pounds of wax collected.	SILK: Pounds of cocoons.	NEAT CATTLE: Under one year old.	NEAT CATTLE: Over one y'r, exclusive of working oxen & cows.	NEAT CATTLE: Working oxen.	NEAT CATTLE: Cows.	Number of cattle killed for beef.	Pounds of butter.	Pounds of cheese.
New-York City,	157	$66000	......	......	......	......	......	......	4	2,600	......	719	44,405	......	......

NIAGARA COUNTY.—(CONTINUED.)

TOWNS.	Acres cultivated.	Value of products.	Pounds of maple sugar made.	Gallons of maple molasses made.	Gallons of wine made.	Pounds of honey collected.	Pounds of wax collected.	Pounds of cocoons.	Under one year old.	Over one y'r.	Working oxen.	Cows.	Number of cattle killed for beef.	Pounds of butter.	Pounds of cheese.
Cambria,	......	......	170	4	......	1,693	152	......	425	1,209	134	1,018	89	98,077	12,280
Hartland,	¾	90	471	16	3	4,458	187	......	537	1,001	158	1,196	93	110,450	12,353
Lewiston,	3	722	140	2	5	781	18	......	337	604	210	746	134	76,322	405
Lockport,	19	5,050	131	102	2	1,598	153	......	460	958	137	1,540	1,228	124,265	4,170
Newfane,	......	150	1,406	9	......	2,557	88	......	524	1,063	250	1,082	248	91,246	3,460
Niagara,	24	2,600	......	......	......	755	64	......	167	270	98	485	824	22,386	......
Pendleton,	......	......	......	9	......	1,858	71	......	260	401	152	588	77	46,434	1,351
Porter,	⅞	53	......	......	......	2,190	67	......	329	565	160	720	82	66,779	3,697
Royalton,	......	......	520	53	25	4,354	261	......	619	1,081	200	1,479	254	154,271	17,813
Somerset,	......	10	868	25	......	1,501	78	......	469	743	164	816	102	70,063	6,711
Wheatfield,	⅝	56	......	......	5	3,149	140	......	340	509	143	887	142	50,515	820
Wilson,	3⅜	700	75	29	120	2,311	181	......	571	1,030	252	1,151	227	127,499	8,383
Total,	51⅝	9,431	3,781	249	160	27,205	1,460	......	5,038	9,434	2,058	11,708	3,500	1,038,307	71,443

ONEIDA COUNTY.—(CONTINUED.)

TOWNS.	Acres cultivated.	Value of products.	Pounds of maple sugar made.	Gallons of maple molasses made.	Gallons of wine made.	Pounds of honey collected.	Pounds of wax collected.	Pounds of cocoons.	Under one year old.	Over one y'r.	Working oxen.	Cows.	Number of cattle killed for beef.	Pounds of butter.	Pounds of cheese.
Annsville,	......	......	1,815¾	103	18	3,934	87½	......	421	711	341	1,256	88	195,966	3,585
Augusta,	......	......	7,834	797	......	3,173	142	......	234	766	50	1,061	118	107,980	34,330
Ava,	......	......	1,215	288	......	2,194	85	......	215	339	88	1,217	185	81,020	110,200
Boonville,	......	......	6,056	67	......	1,235	43	......	382	495	187	2,612	788	223,525	5,300
Bridgewater,	......	......	990	63	20	1,637	109	......	255	490	64	1,131	82	66,705	146,070
Camden,	......	......	3,437	143	......	3,790	200	......	289	694	167	1,106	101	108,645	15,925
Deerfield,	33½	2,190	306	13	......	1,416	127	......	357	451	58	2,378	5,131	120.170	482,900
Florence,	......	......	650	15	......	940	8	......	158	362	229	1,006	30	124,550	53,350
Floyd,	1¼	325	1,876	64	4	1,957	121	......	349	497	26	2,062	179	120,310	186,400
Kirkland,	......	......	1,464	455	99	3,572	170	......	309	725	97	1,255	118	131,368	37,508
Lee,	......	......	3,819	155	......	5,229	177	......	495	665	127	2,215	1,631	205,859	112 687
Marcy,	57½	7,115	905	24	125	1,130	123	......	373	571	50	1,889	113	160,319	24,907
Marshall,	1	100	1,591	118	......	2,054	97	......	438	1,134	80	1,280	121	103,260	31,372
New Hartford,	16	980	1,406	92	2	3,590	282	......	298	522	115	1,471	361	109,263	67,425
Paris,	2	268	730	77	12	1,948	67	......	338	638	153	1,734	356	148,775	150,155
Remsen,	......	......	3,142	18	......	60	4	......	224	297	118	1,786	217	184,969	116,000
Rome,	10¾	1,005	814	111½	3	4,152	112	......	446	684	209	2,526	1,184	174,296	127.629
Sangerfield,	......	......	6,655	255	3½	1,817	68	......	245	684	79	876	318	71,609	15,080
Steuben,	......	......	1,515	42	......	2,165	87	......	369	596	55	2,764	72	260,800	131,473
Trenton,	......	......	1,640	90	......	5,515	160	......	446	711	88	3,163	460	157,958	539,529
Utica,	103½	2,195	......	......	......	1,120	12	......	32	46	28	497	224	7,712	400
Vernon,	3	150	6,117	109	......	2,637	218	......	394	664	160	2,051	250	136,465	357,375
Verona,	......	20	790	99	......	70,581	264	......	673	1,416	303	2,663	1,332	244,277	176,565
Vienna,	......	7,000	1,631	50	4	3,076	122	......	384	769	250	1,100	264	82,715	25,210
Western,	......	......	3,315	47	......	2,149	146	......	527	656	106	2,989	380	263,090	247,900
Westmoreland,	1	26,200	900	316	13	4,514	212	......	570	856	102	2,411	229	225,012	99,474
Whitestown,	17⅜	1,710	152	3½	......	2,890	212	......	339	563	56	1,295	729	95,558	11,765
Total,	246⅞	49,258	60,765¾	3,615	303½	138,475	3,455½	......	9,560	17,002	3,476	47,794	15,061	3,912,176	3,311,114

ONONDAGA COUNTY.—(CONTINUED.)

TOWNS.	Acres cultivated.	Value of products.	Pounds of maple sugar made.	Gallons of maple molasses made.	Gallons of wine made.	Pounds of honey collected.	Pounds of wax collected.	Pounds of cocoons.	Under one year old.	Over one y'r.	Working oxen.	Cows.	Number of cattle killed for beef.	Pounds of butter.	Pounds of cheese.
Camillus,	......	......	......	......	576	1,194	119	......	435	636	94	1,047	171	110,209	12,470
Cicero,	1	50	467	23½	136	4,148	213½	......	383	769	122	1,324	128	129,140	28,035
Clay,	15½	800	665	40	47	3,677	179½	......	512	1,002	169	1,363	378	120,907	11,535
De Witt,	5¼	385	6	......	......	2,675	108½	......	290	688	190	1,170	82	97,235	13,360
Elbridge,	1	20	14	2	......	4,647	199	......	428	990	141	1,215	297	120,304	17,730
Fabius,	......	......	6,615	746	6	3,685	179	......	357	790	126	2,637	105	143,500	527,770
Geddes,	24¼	2715	......	......	114	2,100	63	......	49	129	23	904	24	40,945	5,150
La Fayette,	......	......	8,898	557	......	10,321	373	......	301	614	79	1,088	97	114,382	6,915
Lysander,	2	350	905	37	196	6,120	336½	......	795	1,677	278	1,949	476	207,813	40,738
Manlius,	¼	50	......	......	2	6,407	267	......	488	941	119	1,365	126	130,077	9,890
Marcellus,	......	......	225	17	15	1,458	39½	......	340	685	92	990	112	95,150	13,073
Onondaga,	180½	11591	2,180	83	117	9,540	446	......	615	1,228	208	2,034	211	223,343	23,139
Otisco,	......	......	8,210	86	3	2,015	124½	......	311	568	119	899	58	83,387	22,613
Pompey,	1½	230	3,321	214	34	6,945	324	......	670	1,207	164	1,894	233	194,815	43,680
Salina,	19⅛	1733	400	50	160	854	31	......	80	260	54	427	149	44,732	400
Skaneateles,	......	10	2,865	41	10	4,787	123	......	483	899	146	1,081	197	90,223	23,286
Spafford,	......	14⅛	4,112	73	......	5,442	388¼	......	364	754	96	906	80	99,575	8,320
Syracuse,	23¾	1295	......	......	153	260	7	......	28	65	16	144	933	6,471	......
Tully,	......	......	5,945	81	......	2,070	171	......	285	458	120	1,102	150	108,654	30,900
Van Buren,	......	......	......	......	14	3,230	165½	......	430	969	98	1,262	262	133,425	21,640
Total,	274⅛	19243⅛	44,828	2,050½	1,583	81,575	3,857¾	......	7,644	15,329	2,454	24,801	4,269	2,294,287	860,644

ONTARIO COUNTY.—(CONTINUED.)

TOWNS.	Acres cultivated.	Value of products.	Pounds of maple sugar made.	Gallons of maple molasses made.	Gallons of wine made.	Pounds of honey collected.	Pounds of wax collected.	Pounds of cocoons.	Under one year old.	Over one y'r.	Working oxen.	Cows.	Number of cattle killed for beef.	Pounds of butter.	Pounds of cheese.
Bristol,	¼	36	1,375	122½	......	3,383	159	......	269	509	147	683	128	60,225	22,724
Canadice,	......	......	135	72	8	3,192	166½	......	209	395	66	424	54	36,625	4,262
Canandaigua,	3½	400	9,723½	312	201½	6,026	439	......	644	1,390	347	1,615	940	146,897	22,901
East Bloomfield,	......	......	7,605	360	25	2,487	75	......	230	522	121	692	97	53,939	8,838
Farmington,	¾	32	2,258	252	......	4,000	178	......	481	900	159	1,130	127	93,258	27,407
Gorham,	⅛	62	4,411	113	......	4,183	193	2	464	817	152	899	128	90,059	10,053
Hopewell,	......	......	389	235	75	6,084	151	......	319	699	54	734	81	60,170	12,522
Manchester,	16	1,810	910	101	28½	2,477	126	......	348	819	148	965	104	79,571	15,293
Naples,	......	20	2,104	61	75	2,920	203	......	332	649	108	708	98	75,160	7,210
Phelps,	28¼	2,175	7,150	162	351½	7,411	191¼	......	715	1,325	160	2,043	356	174,832	33.096

(Continued on page 290.)

NEW-YORK COUNTY.—(Continued.)

TOWNS.	Gallons of milk sold.	Horses.	Mules.	SWINE. Under 6 months.	SWINE. Over 6 months.	SHEEP. Number of sheep.	SHEEP. Number of fleeces.	SHEEP. Pounds of wool.	POULTRY. Value of poultry sold.	POULTRY. Value of eggs sold.	DOMESTIC MANUFACTURES. Yards of fulled cloth made.	DOMESTIC MANUFACTURES. Yards of flannel made.	DOMESTIC MANUFACTURES. Yards of linen made.	DOMESTIC MANUFACTURES. Yards of cotton and mixed cloths.
New-York city,	2,400	14,099	256	178	1,071	....	....	....	....	....	....	....	....	....

NIAGARA COUNTY.—(Continued.)

TOWNS.	Gallons of milk sold.	Horses.	Mules.	SWINE. Under 6 months.	SWINE. Over 6 months.	SHEEP. Number of sheep.	SHEEP. Number of fleeces.	SHEEP. Pounds of wool.	POULTRY. Value of poultry sold.	POULTRY. Value of eggs sold.	DOMESTIC MANUFACTURES. Yards of fulled cloth made.	DOMESTIC MANUFACTURES. Yards of flannel made.	DOMESTIC MANUFACTURES. Yards of linen made.	DOMESTIC MANUFACTURES. Yards of cotton and mixed cloths.
Cambria,	....	946	....	485	884	5,316	4,308	17,445	$1,821	$2,345	23	158	30	....
Hartland,	....	1,301	1	1,059	1,162	9,090	6,123	23,675	1,524	2,620	595	463	165	959
Lewiston,	856	2,798	....	560	858	5,034	3,699	15,141	714	1,158	120	477	....	178
Lockport,	41,021	1,634	....	1,031	2,176	6,834	5,738½	22,398	1,186	2,030	134	341	....	232
Newfane,	....	1,177	....	754	1,277	8,243	6,412	24,663	1,322	1,926	235	766	74	143
Niagara,	16,303	562	1	369	479	800	730	2,719	288	393	56	40	....	36
Pendleton,	455	592	....	302	630	2,111	1,617	5,929¼	509	857	100	339	....	30
Porter,	....	824	....	538	851	5,327	3,063	13,116	631	1,134	12	....	....	....
Royalton,	....	1,635	....	1,125	1,576	12,450	9,194	35,277	1,214	2,291	718½	1,136	135	508½
Somerset,	....	966	....	690	824	9,929	6,124	25,061½	674	948	269	216	16	713½
Wheatfield,	421	606	3	476	1,090	2,028	1,587	6,135	257	1,262	85	252	121	116
Wilson,	123	1,293	....	1,090	1,479	11,197	6,712	28,343½	1,217	2,044	373½	753	....	380
Total,	59,179	14,334	5	8,479	13,286	78,359	55,307½	219,903¼	11,357	19,008	2,721	4,941	541	3,296

ONEIDA COUNTY.—(Continued.)

TOWNS.	Gallons of milk sold.	Horses.	Mules.	SWINE. Under 6 months.	SWINE. Over 6 months.	SHEEP. Number of sheep.	SHEEP. Number of fleeces.	SHEEP. Pounds of wool.	POULTRY. Value of poultry sold.	POULTRY. Value of eggs sold.	DOMESTIC MANUFACTURES. Yards of fulled cloth made.	DOMESTIC MANUFACTURES. Yards of flannel made.	DOMESTIC MANUFACTURES. Yards of linen made.	DOMESTIC MANUFACTURES. Yards of cotton and mixed cloths.
Annsville,	....	537	2	433	642	1,360	874	2,795¾	486	528	192½	556	266	981
Augusta,	980	628	....	417	1,440	2,178	1,737	6,109	871	1,544	267	426	17	93
Ava,	225	287	1	240	230	922	440	1,605	83	99	288	337	310	189
Boonville,	2,225	607	....	538	521	800	410	1,346¾	295	432	159	491	15	308½
Bridgewater,	....	459	....	424	429	2,039	2,338	8,322	866	531	....	111	137	1
Caneadea,	1,920	520	....	368	513	1,878	1,186	3,845	449	756	270	956	34	434
Deerfield,	200	506	....	692	566	874	522	1,896	821	832	325	606	20	368
Florence,	....	299	....	301	509	807	787	2,877	225	274	40	6	....	....
Floyd,	....	636	....	524	562	1,641	1,024	3,444	694	1,183	221	375	....	539
Kirkland,	2,625	697	2	420	565	2,041	1,738	6,056	1,386	1,847	55	199	89	70
Lee,	....	751	....	440	655	2,155	978	3,457½	1,436	742	386	983	....	846
Marcy,	11,680	585	3	575	559	2,068	1,378	4,450	1,056	1,531	86	177	18	461
Marshall,	....	635	....	399	369	1,903	2,488	8,809	958	1,003	55½	443½	45	113
New Hartford,	60,422	746	9	658	603	1,352	1,172	4,390½	1,302	2,618	70	150	....	1,053
Paris,	849	746	8	503	626	2,219	1,825	6,551½	1,292	1,953	120	310	83	137
Remsen,	....	464	....	153	562	852	846	2,714	187	712	456	60	....	734
Rome,	46,791	1,090	....	971	1,398	2,353	1,621	5,706	1,564	1,687	204	639	10	288
Sangerfield,	450	527	....	334	388	5,974	5,498	20,036	352	394	43	239	83	20
Steuben,	....	526	....	300	681	1,267	944	3,172	230	947	527	620	85	1,195
Trenton,	360	778	....	487	723	1,148	791	2,854½	1,075	1,067	305	371	25	158
Utica,	17,925	493	....	294	537	84	84	267	392	213	....	....	....	....
Vernon,	665	835	5	555	609	1,910	1,968	7,155	1,276	1,868	93	369	32	42
Verona,	13,056	1,051	2	1,050	1,041	3,094	2,079	7,421	1,356	2,891	140½	1,005	93	314
Vienna,	56	578	....	522	639	2,253	1,355	4,510	538	1,012	537½	1,027	98	403
Western,	....	774	....	639	726	2,647	1,160	4,005	627	616	193	571	....	972½
Westmoreland,	214	852	....	679	880	3,636	3,010	9,985	1,898	2,915	55	233	63	81
Whitestown,	23,465	791	2	501	838	1,386	962	3,547	1,257	1,628	12	142	77	85
Total,	184,108	17,398	34	13,417	17,811	50,841	39,215	137,327½	22,972	31,823	5,101	11,402½	1,600	9,886

ONONDAGA COUNTY.—(Continued.)

TOWNS.	Gallons of milk sold.	Horses.	Mules.	SWINE. Under 6 months.	SWINE. Over 6 months.	SHEEP. Number of sheep.	SHEEP. Number of fleeces.	SHEEP. Pounds of wool.	POULTRY. Value of poultry sold.	POULTRY. Value of eggs sold.	DOMESTIC MANUFACTURES. Yards of fulled cloth made.	DOMESTIC MANUFACTURES. Yards of flannel made.	DOMESTIC MANUFACTURES. Yards of linen made.	DOMESTIC MANUFACTURES. Yards of cotton and mixed cloths.
Camillus,	....	879	4	1,085	848	5,649	5,137	20,230	1,128	1,457	3	60	....	40
Cicero,	510	901	....	749	803	2,253	1,610	5,544½	1,209	1,627	714½	1,342	120½	727½
Clay,	840	1,177	....	878	1,114	4,292	3,447	12,358	1,212	2,239	739½	1,195	296	1,087
De Witt,	67,856	831	....	728	804	3,686	2,748	10,291	991	2,048	....	36	....	104
Elbridge,	850	879	4	765	1,328	5,325	3,821	13,455	1,166	1,700	69	221	64	20
Fabius,	....	735	....	426	498	2,972	3,336	12,356¾	595	1,383	25	238	81	351
Geddes,	2,515	629	....	240	876	863	603	2,191	452	564	....	41	....	....
La Fayette,	....	811	....	621	761	3,359	3,762	14,470½	1,009	2,753	101	341	79	85
Lysander,	1,598	1,430	....	1,610	1,702	7,494	5,082	19,104	2,431	3,690	601½	1,201	209	459
Manlius,	11,395	1,109	....	799	1,242	4,160	3,790	12,970½	859	2,004	145	255	96	88
Marcellus,	....	780	....	596	618	7,079	6,051	24,353	1,273	1,650	46	79	45	76
Onondaga,	173,830	1,621	....	1,559	1,718	11,660	9,721	36,639¾	3,844	7,509	237	930½	80	116
Otisco,	....	648	....	591	531	5,064	4,835	19,397	686	2,106	76	378	28	218
Pompey,	....	1,427	....	976	1,053	9,338	10,278	38,657	1,651	3,486	14	347	36	67
Salina,	56,740	333	....	354	320	1,557	1,246	4,010½	533	402	18	64	12	....
Skaneateles,	3,000	886	....	729	662	8,937	8,602	32,373	2,614	2,982	51	192½	92	....
Spafford,	....	703	....	520	499	4,430	5,552	21,530	1,376	2,035	155	245	76	234
Syracuse,	11,139	87	....	72	65	756	755	3,000	99	167	....	25	....	....
Tully,	....	562	....	389	374	2,176	1,692	5,918¾	721	1,554	18	116	27	162
Van Buren,	....	902	....	1,040	996	3,152	2,594	9,597	958	2,571	17	66	....	....
Total,	330,273	17,330	8	14,727	16,812	94,202	84,662	318,446¾	24,807	43,927	3,030½	7,373	1,341½	3,834

ONTARIO COUNTY.—(Continued.)

TOWNS.	Gallons of milk sold.	Horses.	Mules.	SWINE. Under 6 months.	SWINE. Over 6 months.	SHEEP. Number of sheep.	SHEEP. Number of fleeces.	SHEEP. Pounds of wool.	POULTRY. Value of poultry sold.	POULTRY. Value of eggs sold.	DOMESTIC MANUFACTURES. Yards of fulled cloth made.	DOMESTIC MANUFACTURES. Yards of flannel made.	DOMESTIC MANUFACTURES. Yards of linen made.	DOMESTIC MANUFACTURES. Yards of cotton and mixed cloths.
Bristol,	....	736	3	711	716	6,949	9,587	130,968	1,734	1,153	15	289½	....	247
Canadice,	....	459	....	298	305	2,770	3,767	13,524	263	265	39	47	44	....
Canandaigua,	28,217	1,506	20	1,853	1,765	15,988	16,506	65,158	3,363	4,305	169½	198	125	178
East Bloomfield,	....	666	2	597	586	7,956	8,189	29,880	870	867	....	....	....	10
Farmington,	142,700	823	....	693	1,055	10,264	8,760	32,660	2,651	2,119	50	181	....	94
Gorham,	....	1,318	....	979	770	10,279	13,354	45,757	1,968	1,600	30	95	20	25
Hopewell,	....	737	1	694	809	5,625	5,671	20,397	1,986	1,546	14	213	20	....
Manchester,	4,200	882	....	866	907	7,419	7,143	28,621	1,540	1,981	....	189	....	....
Naples,	5	643	....	531	590	6,602	7,777	26,034	333	492	319	362	223	172
Phelps,	615	1,710	120	1,537	2,038	13,141	11,061	40,952½	3,160	3,147	25	184	20	128

(Continued on page 291.)

ONTARIO COUNTY.—(Continued.)

TOWNS.	ACRES. Improved.	ACRES. Unimproved.	CASH VALUE. Of farm.	CASH VALUE. Of stock.	CASH VALUE. Of tools and implements	Acres plowed the year previous.	Acres in fallow the year previous.	Acres in pasture the year previous	MEADOW. Acres.	MEADOW. Tons of hay.	MEADOW. Bushels of grass seed.	SPRING WHEAT. Acres sown.	SPRING WHEAT. Bushels harvested.	WINTER WHEAT. Acres sown.
Richmond,......	18, 827	6, 979	$1, 093, 138	$152, 092	$32, 732	3, 054	1, 906	5, 490	3, 026	3, 224	78	576	5, 819	2, 558
Seneca,.........	32, 802	10. 324	2, 516, 285	230, 580	72, 817	11, 639	956	7, 842	5, 850½	4, 863	119	43½	657	2, 233½
South Bristol,...	10, 180	13, 595	434, 661	70, 552	17, 280	1, 668	870	3, 303	1, 862	1, 297	18	168	850	1, 193
Victor,..........	16, 051	3, 969	1, 488, 629	142, 173	59, 936	4, 166	2, 809	3, 999	1, 819½	2, 224	7	4	34	3, 520
West Bloomfield,	12, 726	2, 946½	885, 295	104, 522	23, 156	2, 729	1, 737	2, 886	1, 484	1, 767	98½	82½	1, 067	5, 292½
Total, ...	290, 639¾	97, 108¾	20, 882, 806	2, 272, 115	591, 755	95, 987½	23, 876½	79, 494½	45, 094¼	42, 448¾	2, 133¼	3, 177¾	27659	38680½

ORANGE COUNTY.

TOWNS.	ACRES. Improved.	ACRES. Unimproved.	CASH VALUE. Of farm.	CASH VALUE. Of stock.	CASH VALUE. Of tools and implements	Acres plowed the year previous.	Acres in fallow the year previous.	Acres in pasture the year previous	MEADOW. Acres.	MEADOW. Tons of hay.	MEADOW. Bushels of grass seed.	SPRING WHEAT. Acres sown.	SPRING WHEAT. Bushels harvested.	WINTER WHEAT. Acres sown.
Blooming Grove,	15, 491	5, 549½	1, 157, 075	143, 991	31, 690	1, 671	32½	9, 309½	5, 270½	5, 815½	35½	......	......	275¼
Chester,........	12, 521¼	2, 968	786, 280	127, 687	25, 560	1, 432	12	6, 624½	3, 620	5, 099	15	......	......	125½
Cornwall, ...	10, 874⅜	15, 594	1, 821, 040	153. 693	23, 700	1, 496¼	128½	3, 891	2, 904¼	3, 251	44	......	......	217
Crawford, ...	19, 575	4, 688	939, 780	123, 450	18, 809	2, 865	42	6, 663	4, 885	5, 481	12½	......	......	709
Deerpark, ...	8, 998½	22, 473	607, 755	67, 480	23, 754	2, 129	862¼	2, 653¾	1, 889	2, 149	28½	......	......	263
Goshen, ...	20, 853½	3, 676½	1, 532, 846	190, 183	57, 556	2, 225¼	18	10, 514½	6, 013½	8, 194	39½	......	......	500¼
Greenville,......	12, 675	4, 736	623, 738	102, 162	20, 601	1, 648	92	5, 125	3, 122	4, 076	83	2	11	191
Hamptonburgh,.	14, 519½	2, 184	971, 263	98, 989	27, 815	1, 738	36	6, 748	3, 978	5, 332	9	......	......	421
Minisink,.......	11, 590	2, 497	667, 090	107, 710	20, 347	1, 702¼	933½	5, 991	2, 948½	3, 913	65	1	6	266¾
Monroe,........	19, 959¾	77, 666½	1, 340, 638	159, 190	30, 476	2, 225⅝	485½	9, 166¾	6, 655	6, 650	142¾	......	......	94½
Montgomery, ...	23, 186¼	5, 703	1, 922, 167	223, 242	69, 097	6, 115¾	148	7, 790½	5, 616	7, 481	29	......	......	688¾
Mount Hope,....	12, 070½	3, 890	621, 110	93, 244	23, 422	1, 586	103	5, 943	3. 086¼	3, 344¼	35	......	......	279¾
Newburgh, ...	23, 244¾	4, 078½	1, 904, 630	227, 839	63, 860	6, 057½	190¾	9, 903½	5, 790	6, 792½	12	......	......	464¾
New Windsor, ..	17, 500	3, 371	1, 308, 150	158, 589	40, 247	3, 112	97	7, 047½	4, 923½	6, 053	15	......	......	462¼
Walkill,........	32, 391½	7, 358½	1, 899, 030	271, 354	72, 641	4, 513½	183	15, 807	9, 233½	11, 723½	55¼	......	......	862
Warwick, ...	36, 003¾	20, 326½	2, 473, 238	335, 676	70, 928	6, 586	77½	16, 575½	9, 321	12, 007½	489	2½	10	1, 022¼
Wawayanda, ...	17, 145	2, 855	991, 530	115, 512	18, 722	1, 859	11	8, 358	4, 515	5, 849	1	3	5	233½
Total,........	308, 599⅝	189, 615	21, 567, 360	2, 699, 991	639, 225	48, 962⅛	3, 452½	138, 113	83, 771	103, 211¼	1, 111	8½	32	7, 076½

ORLEANS COUNTY.

TOWNS.	ACRES. Improved.	ACRES. Unimproved.	CASH VALUE. Of farm.	CASH VALUE. Of stock.	CASH VALUE. Of tools and implements	Acres plowed the year previous.	Acres in fallow the year previous.	Acres in pasture the year previous	MEADOW. Acres.	MEADOW. Tons of hay.	MEADOW. Bushels of grass seed.	SPRING WHEAT. Acres sown.	SPRING WHEAT. Bushels harvested.	WINTER WHEAT. Acres sown.
Barre,..........	34, 760¼	13, 893	2, 617, 073	302, 510	84, 404	7, 643¼	6, 231	7, 642¾	5, 034½	6, 696¾	502	22	234	5, 687½
Carlton, ...	21, 330	5, 623½	1, 307, 499	164, 703	46, 115	4, 782½	3, 900	5, 249	2, 565½	3, 532½	64½	3	33	4, 534½
Clarendon,......	15, 080¾	11, 350	826, 695	119, 241	23, 084	2, 958	2, 753	3, 158½	2, 071½	2, 926	82½	5½	50	3, 023½
Gaines,.........	14, 082	3, 845	1, 093, 350	104, 380	39, 412	4, 663	1, 563	2, 930½	2, 131½	3, 270½	227½	10	90	1, 991
Kendall,........	16, 297	4, 940	1, 081, 968	149, 716	41, 387	5, 108	1, 236	4, 496	2, 523	3, 391	129	43½	632	1, 777
Murray, ...	16, 387	4, 786½	1, 026, 486	129, 643	28, 239	4, 025½	1, 769	4, 411	2, 384	3, 176½	75	3	25	2, 310½
Ridgeway, ...	24, 386	6, 798⅝	1, 836, 421	237, 685	65, 814	4, 766	4, 156¼	5, 857	3, 407½	4, 879	158½	4	132	4, 502
Shelby,.........	20, 573¾	6, 913	1, 809, 345	173, 053	53, 025	5, 292¾	3, 725¾	3, 716	2, 801	3, 798½	153½	19¼	391	4, 091¾
Yates,..........	19, 052	4, 177	1, 073, 715	150, 086	42, 386	3, 859	3, 174	3, 703½	2, 232	2, 949½	131½	51¾	619	3, 913
Total,........	181, 948¾	62, 326⅝	12, 672, 552	1, 531, 017	423, 866	43, 098	28, 508	41, 164¼	25, 150½	34. 620¼	1, 524	162	2, 206	31830¾

OSWEGO COUNTY.

TOWNS.	ACRES. Improved.	ACRES. Unimproved.	CASH VALUE. Of farm.	CASH VALUE. Of stock.	CASH VALUE. Of tools and implements	Acres plowed the year previous.	Acres in fallow the year previous.	Acres in pasture the year previous	MEADOW. Acres.	MEADOW. Tons of hay.	MEADOW. Bushels of grass seed.	SPRING WHEAT. Acres sown.	SPRING WHEAT. Bushels harvested.	WINTER WHEAT. Acres sown.
Albion,.........	9, 196¾	16, 109	404, 715	67, 922	20, 235	2, 772¾	992	3, 208½	2, 109½	1, 755½	70	102	1, 070½	117½
Amboy, ...	6, 327½	18, 070¼	244, 609	41, 482	7, 668	1, 517¼	14¼	3, 155½	1, 612½	1, 273½	......	33½	292	......
Boylston,.......	5, 486	17, 379	222, 052	37, 875	9, 179	1, 154	138	2, 662	1, 313	1, 063	112	91½	1, 097	25
Constantia,.....	6, 161	28, 660	510, 417	59, 727	16, 869	2, 133	172	1, 795½	1, 367	1, 208	32	28½	231	44¾
Granby, ...	16, 458	13, 574¾	1, 079, 884	148, 953	38, 287	5, 161½	281	4, 371	3, 561¼	3, 409	121½	80	837	160¾
Hannibal,.......	15, 094⅜	12, 035	856, 273	155, 156	33, 453	4, 913¼	65	5, 255½	3, 282¾	3, 570	58¼	93¾	1, 124	184
Hastings,.......	13, 252½	14, 010	696, 182	104, 672	33, 131	4, 702¼	80½	4, 772	2, 911¼	2, 527¼	64¾	156¼	1, 533½	46
Mexico, ...	20, 206¼	8, 011	1, 029, 682	166, 937	37, 947	5, 008	350¾	9, 234¼	5, 377¼	5, 376	191	472⅝	6, 138	143
New Haven,.....	11, 410¼	7, 603	566, 632	105, 837	26, 083	2, 573½	51¼	4, 223¾	3, 100¾	2, 655½	99½	321⅜	4, 124⅝	44¾
Orwell,.........	8, 537½	17, 345	363, 691	63, 192	17, 337	1, 831	438	3, 203½	2, 436	1, 766	132	121	1, 275	114
Oswego,........	12, 242½	7, 494½	839, 835	105, 515	26, 938	2, 906¼	32½	3, 594½	3, 916½	4, 054	64	138	2, 194	59¼
Oswego city,....	2, 042	783½	353, 450	74, 157	4, 749	342	54½	860½	527	492	......	10¼	93	42½
Palermo, ...	12, 238½	12, 777	640, 758	102. 153	24, 585	3, 943	41½	4, 874½	2, 984	2, 874½	......	170¾	1, 578	48
Parish, ...	9, 010½	15, 921	360, 645	72, 113	20, 226	3, 439½	166	2, 572½	2, 258¾	1, 808¼	43½	97½	699½	30½
Redfield, ...	5, 988½	51, 835	389, 966	39, 589	6, 968	784½	3	2, 318	2, 619½	2, 352	46½	9	145½	......
Richland,.......	19, 632	11, 859	841, 236	158, 368	33, 972	4, 769¼	160½	8, 049	5, 213	5, 077	143½	593	7, 219½	153¾
Sandy Creek,...	16, 738	6, 559½	793, 752	111, 061	22, 371	3, 784¾	....	8, 580	3, 701¾	3, 346½	8	775¼	8, 570½	140¾
Schroeppel,.....	13, 055½	11, 619	864, 977	120, 942	26, 892	4, 243¼	70	4, 505	3, 301	3, 313½	82	129¼	1, 377½	67½
Scriba,.........	14, 398½	8, 936	781, 340	111, 210	33, 286	2, 519½	50½	6, 988¼	4, 394½	3, 756½	40½	132½	1, 855	50¼
Volney, ...	16, 141	12, 521½	1, 017, 583	139, 166	36, 248	4, 213½	147	5, 755	4, 514	4, 367	56½	167	1, 561	48
West Monroe,...	5, 237½	14, 663½	310, 559	43, 083	12, 391	1, 662	29¾	1, 865½	1, 564	1, 403¾	77½	19	187½	17¼
Williamstown,..	5, 271⅛	20, 281½	270, 487	29, 471	7, 714	1, 685½	45½	1, 667½	1, 436¾	689¼	11	171¾	1, 097½	7
Total,........	244, 126	328, 047⅝	13, 438, 725	2, 058, 581	496, 529	66, 059¼	3, 383½	93, 511¾	63, 501½	58, 138	1, 454	3, 914¼	44300⅜	1, 544½

OTSEGO COUNTY.

TOWNS.	ACRES. Improved.	ACRES. Unimproved.	CASH VALUE. Of farm.	CASH VALUE. Of stock.	CASH VALUE. Of tools and implements	Acres plowed the year previous.	Acres in fallow the year previous.	Acres in pasture the year previous	MEADOW. Acres.	MEADOW. Tons of hay.	MEADOW. Bushels of grass seed.	SPRING WHEAT. Acres sown.	SPRING WHEAT. Bushels harvested.	WINTER WHEAT. Acres sown.
Burlington,.....	20, 615½	7, 229½	611, 490	111, 202	28, 904	3, 269¼	29½	11, 771¼	5, 445½	4, 894½	143½	183¾	2, 054½	10½
Butternuts,.....	21, 173	8, 766	756, 248	144, 703	32, 133	3, 114½	228	11, 821½	5, 893¾	5, 977	200	161	1, 772	28
Cherry Valley,..	18, 012	6, 097½	923, 977	130, 547	32, 122	6, 720	184	6, 136½	4, 138	3, 984½	339½	411	4, 554½	111½
Decatur,........	9, 565	3, 617	307, 400	64, 187	15, 634	2, 814	133	3, 836½	2, 772¼	2, 125	221¼	110¼	1, 210½	15½
Edmeston, ...	18, 091½	8, 292	737, 325	124, 706	26, 970	3, 089	15½	9, 237	5, 367½	5, 500½	142¼	135⅛	1, 417	25½
Exeter,.........	14, 135	4, 915	548, 055	93, 417	26. 822	2, 017	41	6, 590	4, 799¼	4, 856	80	171½	2, 185	......
Hartwick, ...	19, 848	5, 583	796, 068	102, 177	22, 870	3, 431½	34	8, 403½	3, 652	3, 170	51½	274¼	3, 306	56¼
Laurens,........	19, 914½	6, 974	698, 950	116, 082	21, 020	3, 645½	88½	9, 959	5, 166	3, 972½	92	199	1, 839	16
Maryland.......	18, 819	13, 541½	823, 205	109, 679	28, 831	5, 230½	396	7, 077	5, 148½	3, 971	213	146¾	1, 195	25½
Middlefield,.....	25, 062	11, 421½	1, 181, 792	162, 080	45, 293	7, 272½	296½	9, 910	6, 207½	5, 712½	100½	332¾	3, 517	187¼
Milford,.........	18, 773¼	9, 466¾	962, 640	114, 761	27, 957	4, 368¼	333¾	8, 241¾	4, 550	3, 879½	129	188	1, 788½	59½
Morris,.........	17, 312	6, 756	624, 355	111, 767	27, 397	2, 529⅛	144	8, 319½	4, 827	5, 087½	109	214	2, 444½	10
New Lisbon,....	20, 025	6, 481	712, 225	106, 227	27, 741	3, 146	33	11, 243½	5, 571	3, 997	43¾	190½	2, 134	1
Oneonta,........	15, 238	7, 303	694, 415	100, 266	29, 847	3, 005⅜	302	7, 700¾	3, 862¾	3, 284	14¾	88½	605½	22
Otego, ...	19, 393⅜	8, 164	1, 146, 825	148, 691	15, 802	3, 066	626¼	8, 878½	5, 315¾	5, 069½	159	237¾	2, 151½	99¼

(Continued on page 292.)

ONTARIO COUNTY.—(Continued.)

TOWNS.	Winter Wheat. Bushels harvested.	Oats. Acres sown.	Oats. Bushels harvested	Rye. Acres sown.	Rye. Bushels harvested.	Barley. Acres sown.	Barley. Bushels harvested.	Buckwheat. Acres sown.	Buckwheat. Bushels harvested.	Corn. Acres planted.	Corn. Bushels harvested.	Potatoes. Acres planted.	Potatoes. Bushels harvested.	Peas. Acres sown.	Peas. Bushels harvested.
Richmond, ...	37675	877	19, 800	24	375	533	10, 128	65¾	393	938	27, 303	66½	4, 172	72½	1, 381
Seneca, ...	30438	2, 791½	56, 577	96⅛	1, 606	3, 849	61, 900	313¾	3, 041	3, 300	83, 576	195¾	12, 514	42	569
South Bristol, ..	10512	376	2, 926	37	263	278	2, 267	107	174	438	4, 854	52	1, 904	113	551
Victor,.........	84181	1, 435	48, 698	41½	642	586	10, 784	18	152	1, 566½	43, 016	359½	33, 892	10¼	178
West Bloomfield,	37407	923½	32, 706	17	291	515	10, 795	62	527	788	24, 839	133	10, 973	49	893
Total, ...	528488	22, 049¾	525, 937½	1, 149⅛	16, 002	18640	320, 375	3, 093	18, 325¾	24, 148	617, 485¼	2, 563⅜	188, 900	1, 449¾	15, 297½

ORANGE COUNTY.—(Continued.)

TOWNS.	Winter Wheat. Bushels harvested.	Oats. Acres sown.	Oats. Bushels harvested	Rye. Acres sown.	Rye. Bushels harvested.	Barley. Acres sown.	Barley. Bushels harvested.	Buckwheat. Acres sown.	Buckwheat. Bushels harvested.	Corn. Acres planted.	Corn. Bushels harvested.	Potatoes. Acres planted.	Potatoes. Bushels harvested.	Peas. Acres sown.	Peas. Bushels harvested.
Blooming Grove,	1, 938	437¾	9, 584	577½	8, 116	......	....	71	333	888½	16, 584	90	4, 363	⅛	30
Chester, ...	1, 141½	407	6, 582	471	6, 904	......	....	100	557	649½	17, 577	164¾	14, 582	......	....
Cornwall,.......	1, 203	364¾	5, 085	476½	5, 158	......	....	176¾	571¼	692¼	8, 051	97¼	2, 649½	2½	47
Crawford, ...	4. 275½	1, 356½	23, 110	1, 039½	9, 551	......	....	234½	1 018	1, 434	20, 595	1, 551½	6, 617	......	....
Deerpark, ...	1, 057	278¼	4, 682	1, 280	9. 491	......	....	443	2, 898	752½	14, 170	240½	12, 304	1	8
Goshen,.........	3. 785½	885¾	22, 801	530½	6, 840	6	70	128	690	1, 100¾	26, 239	138¾	10, 188	2	30
Greenville, ...	814	498	7, 939	811½	6, 094	......	....	397½	1, 857	736	11, 769	50¾	2, 705	......	....
Hamptonburgh,.	2, 715	812½	18, 195	632	9, 104	......	....	45½	292	834	13, 294	66⅜	1, 965	......	....
Minisink, ...	444¾	496½	9. 954	711¾	6, 618½	......	....	286	1, 454	790¾	17, 415	52⅛	2, 828	......	....
Monroe,........	899	455¼	8, 503½	990¾	9, 809	......	3	302	1, 559¼	950¼	23, 580½	150¾	8, 162	......	1
Montgomery,...	5, 163½	2, 093¾	37. 521	2, 279¾	29, 765	9	99	264½	1. 496¼	2, 222¼	31, 418	246½	13, 252	......	....
Mount Hope, ...	988¾	479¼	5, 940	759¼	6, 525	......	....	278	1, 269½	752¼	11, 958	62¼	3, 379½	......	....
Newburgh, ...	3, 871½	1, 721¾	34, 952	2, 038½	28, 649½	......	....	442¾	1, 925½	1, 806¾	33, 984	272¾	10, 758½	3¾	104
New Windsor,..	3, 561	954½	19, 062	1, 122½	13, 485	......	....	220½	1, 398½	1, 378½	25, 138	141	6, 467	¼	8
Walkill,........	5. 838½	1, 742¾	29, 547½	1. 365	14, 715	......	....	416¼	1, 497½	1, 928¾	34, 557	231½	10, 369	......	2
Warwick, ...	4, 465	1, 705	36, 937	2, 234	26, 010	½	7	554½	2. 435½	2, 359	34. 086	171¾	8, 932	......	....
Wawayanda, ...	1, 202	553½	10, 716	540½	5, 466	......	....	286¼	1, 771	685½	17, 075	60¾	4, 030	......	....
Total,.......	43363½	15, 242¾	291, 111	17860½	202, 301	15½	179	4, 647	23, 023¾	19, 961½	357. 490⅛	3, 789½	123, 551½	9⅜	230

ORLEANS COUNTY.—(Continued.)

TOWNS.	Winter Wheat. Bushels harvested.	Oats. Acres sown.	Oats. Bushels harvested	Rye. Acres sown.	Rye. Bushels harvested.	Barley. Acres sown.	Barley. Bushels harvested.	Buckwheat. Acres sown.	Buckwheat. Bushels harvested.	Corn. Acres planted.	Corn. Bushels harvested.	Potatoes. Acres planted.	Potatoes. Bushels harvested.	Peas. Acres sown.	Peas. Bushels harvested.
Barre, ...	90567	8, 532¼	73, 797	1	6	86½	1, 638	288¼	2, 393	3, 382¾	79, 902	464	37, 415	41	598
Carlton, ...	44941	495¼	12, 386	1	13	197½	4, 758	446⅞	1, 928¼	2, 015	46, 416	213	14, 532	14¾	184
Clarendon,......	36649	736½	22, 695	63½	133	97½	1, 951	134	817½	1, 331½	29, 238	162	10, 822	27	346
Gaines, ...	21806½	533¾	16, 562	¼	11	51	1, 110	152½	597¼	1, 199½	32, 080	134¾	12, 295	3¼	65
Kendall,........	8793	879	18, 970	9	75	423	9, 939	252	1, 270½	2. 243½	56, 390	209¼	19, 597	163½	2, 299
Murray, ...	26828	730¼	15, 412	3	35	329	5, 915	325¼	931	1, 928¼	30, 809	168⅛	9, 587	26¼	252
Ridgeway,......	53801	817⅜	20, 586	7	21	138¾	3, 186	257	1, 540	2, 675½	66, 525	308⅝	28, 181	19¾	324
Shelby, ...	58933½	1, 431	38, 447	60	2, 363	150¼	3, 406	193¼	2, 247½	1, 797¼	61, 810	258⅞	23, 955	36	436
Yates, ...	34630	500¾	10, 876	6	120	185¾	4, 168	337¾	1, 169	1, 783	33, 805	193¼	15, 483	79½	967
Total,........	376949	14. 656⅛	229. 731	150¾	2, 777	1. 659¼	36, 071	2, 386⅞	12, 903	18, 356¼	436, 975	2: 111⅝	171, 867	411	5, 471

OSWEGO COUNTY.—(Continued.)

TOWNS.	Winter Wheat. Bushels harvested.	Oats. Acres sown.	Oats. Bushels harvested	Rye. Acres sown.	Rye. Bushels harvested.	Barley. Acres sown.	Barley. Bushels harvested.	Buckwheat. Acres sown.	Buckwheat. Bushels harvested.	Corn. Acres planted.	Corn. Bushels harvested.	Potatoes. Acres planted.	Potatoes. Bushels harvested.	Peas. Acres sown.	Peas. Bushels harvested.
Albion, ...	854	792½	17, 706	272½	3, 495	32	303	157½	1, 457	982	21, 981	277¾	20, 454	7½	113
Amboy,........	......	581¼	10, 741	129	1, 251	3¾	44	113½	589	539	10, 448	121⅛	7, 184	3⅛	48
Boylston, ...	158	444¾	9, 715	56¼	723	35	733	55	372	306½	6. 764	87¼	5, 871	25¼	419
Constantia,.....	435	518⅛	10, 107	183	2, 332	1	25	271¾	1, 578	681¼	15, 840	169¼	9, 000	9¼	126
Granby, ...	1, 554½	1, 999	51, 855	87½	1, 346	117¾	2, 322	324¾	3, 171⅝	1, 727½	48, 850½	404⅜	36, 795	45¼	585
Hannibal, ...	1, 489½	1, 988¼	50, 284	139½	1, 800	105	2, 108	489	4, 393	1, 628½	43, 107	413¼	31, 255	49¾	684
Hastings, ...	331	1, 855¾	39, 666	539½	5, 927	59¼	820	286¼	1, 986½	1, 396¼	25, 401	301	18, 041	95½	1, 221
Mexico, ...	1, 370	1, 896	53, 849	274	3. 344½	154½	2, 934	195⅛	2, 386	1, 446¼	42, 036	565	51, 244	108⅛	1, 912½
New Haven,....	558	891½	22, 026	75½	1, 000½	155⅜	2, 839½	69⅜	545¼	761⅛	17, 085½	280¾	18, 716	42¾	647
Orwell, ...	746	625	16, 229	211	2, 826	7½	158	66½	687	605	17, 186	133	9, 631	5	130
Oswego,........	850	937	22. 342	71¾	870	95¾	2, 401	140¼	1, 032½	934¾	19, 826	346¾	19, 928	17½	253
Oswego city,....	285	104¾	2, 396	1¾	7½	9¼	188	8	56	64¼	1, 517	35⅞	1, 910¼	2½	32
Palermo,.......	471½	1, 268¼	30, 895	361¼	4. 566	37½	685	164¾	1. 274	1, 239¼	29, 122	336	24, 640	36¼	592
Parish, ...	223	924¼	17, 808	174	2. 041	15½	245	325¼	2, 801½	878¼	18, 977	207	14, 350	1½	22
Redfield, ...	......	390¾	9, 155	15	180	16	373	87	772	190	4, 706	76¾	5, 786	2	20
Richland, ...	863	1, 303½	31. 488	109½	1, 396	233¼	4, 160	143	1, 729	1, 732	51, 174	414	30, 962	66¼	1, 045
Sandy Creek,...	1, 143	912¾	20, 156	372¾	4. 643	96¼	2, 115	30¼	313½	1, 412	32, 215	241	14, 370	49	768
Schroeppel,.....	358	1, 730	47, 106	141	1, 885	179¼	3, 188	172½	1, 543½	1, 077½	28, 067	209¼	14, 689	65⅞	1, 362
Scriba,.........	441	786¼	14, 812	176¼	2, 286	108¼	1, 680	172¼	1, 323½	803½	16, 125	369¼	21, 652	23¾	221
Volney,........	291	1, 627¼	36, 407	110¾	1, 395	37	639½	212¼	1, 844½	1, 387¾	35, 177	339	23, 235	35⅜	507
West Monroe, ..	117½	722¼	14, 275½	107¾	1, 066	......	....	170	1, 241⅜	472¾	8, 892	123¾	7, 142	24½	364½
Williamstown,..	57	375	6, 414	124	1, 177	5	93	128¾	508½	653¾	9, 315	132¾	5, 057	3¼	44½
Total, ...	12596	22, 674½	535. 432½	3, 733½	45. 557½	1. 504⅜	28, 054	3, 783¼	31, 605⅝	20 919⅜	503. 812	5, 584⅛	391. 912¼	719½	11. 116½

OTSEGO COUNTY.—(Continued.)

TOWNS.	Winter Wheat. Bushels harvested.	Oats. Acres sown.	Oats. Bushels harvested	Rye. Acres sown.	Rye. Bushels harvested.	Barley. Acres sown.	Barley. Bushels harvested.	Buckwheat. Acres sown.	Buckwheat. Bushels harvested.	Corn. Acres planted.	Corn. Bushels harvested.	Potatoes. Acres planted.	Potatoes. Bushels harvested.	Peas. Acres sown.	Peas. Bushels harvested.
Burlington, ...	68	1, 754	33, 742	8¾	167	102¼	2, 478	226¾	1, 787¾	169⅜	12, 888	237⅜	20, 585	27¼	462
Butternuts, ...	131½	1, 559½	25, 833	102½	1, 195	72¼	1, 002	356½	3, 607	658¾	17, 913	178¼	11, 239	4	70
Cherry Valley,..	597	3, 339	62, 770	60½	701	541¼	8, 527	978¾	10, 593½	390½	9, 610	212¼	17, 380	307¼	5, 205½
Decatur, ...	74½	1, 568	23, 976	78½	990	176½	2. 255	403½	6, 018	164¾	3, 930	150	12, 212	119	1, 821½
Edmeston, ...	156	1, 641¾	34, 043	27	401	80¾	1, 506	104½	954½	538	15, 944	215⅞	18, 790	28¼	429
Exeter, ...	......	761	17, 186	13	190	49¼	791	124	1, 098¾	330¼	9. 659	161⅜	12, 776½	15⅜	288½
Hartwick,......	390¼	1, 620	31, 761	36	535	167¾	2, 085½	218	1, 492	556½	12, 469	183⅛	15, 659	15¾	289
Lawrence,......	16	1, 862¾	29, 595	74½	831	25¾	319	346	3, 010	776½	20, 503	181½	15, 333	6½	101
Maryland,......	144	3, 006¾	52, 297	411⅜	3, 725	89¾	1, 355	811	10, 610	476	11, 444	282¾	24, 611	12⅜	199
Middlefield, ...	712	4, 108	79, 687	310⅛	4, 024	183¾	2, 962	753	7, 390	810¼	20, 137	313	23, 672	189	3, 096
Milford,........	402¾	2, 417½	48, 851	260	2, 735½	48⅝	735	515¼	5, 915½	709⅜	17, 535	222	20, 282	32½	417
Morris, ...	32½	1, 138¾	21, 895	73¼	905	68	1, 156	205¼	1, 800½	493½	15, 454	163½	11, 581	14½	181
New Lisbon,....	3	2, 061¼	33, 458	3¾	51	32¾	443	274	2, 427½	491	12, 478	197⅞	13, 000	9¾	144
Oneonta, ...	80	1, 400¾	14, 725	269⅜	2, 557¼	5½	58	295	2, 611¾	648¾	14, 250	203⅛	16, 272	4½	30⅜
Otego, ...	347½	1, 624¾	26, 187	315	3, 247	26¾	478	350¾	3, 174½	856⅜	25, 866	222¼	19, 115	4	19½

(Continued on page 293.)

ONTARIO COUNTY.—(Continued.)

TOWNS.	BEANS. Acres planted.	BEANS. Bushels harvested.	TURNIPS. Acres sown.	TURNIPS. Bushels harvested.	FLAX. Acres sown.	FLAX. Pounds of lint.	FLAX. Bushels of seed.	HEMP. Acres sown.	HEMP. Tons of hemp.	HOPS. Acres planted.	HOPS. Pounds harvested.	TOBACCO. Acres planted.	TOBACCO. Pounds harvested.	APPLE ORCHARDS. Bushels of apples.	APPLE ORCHARDS. Barrels of cider.
Richmond,	12½	112					12							19,773	160
Seneca,	18	117	6¼	551	7		32			8	4,800			47,753	841
South Bristol,	10	41			1									6,232	47
Victor,	13¼	88	¼	140						1¼	1,146			29,950	486
West Bloomfield,	4⅝	97	⅜	35										18,022	438
Total,	201⅜	2,404¾	39⅜	5,743½	41½	2,070	199½			42¾	32,751	10⅛	9,180	397,098	8,044

ORANGE COUNTY.—(Continued.)

TOWNS.	BEANS. Acres planted.	BEANS. Bushels harvested.	TURNIPS. Acres sown.	TURNIPS. Bushels harvested.	FLAX. Acres sown.	FLAX. Pounds of lint.	FLAX. Bushels of seed.	HEMP. Acres sown.	HEMP. Tons of hemp.	HOPS. Acres planted.	HOPS. Pounds harvested.	TOBACCO. Acres planted.	TOBACCO. Pounds harvested.	APPLE ORCHARDS. Bushels of apples.	APPLE ORCHARDS. Barrels of cider.
Blooming Grove,	1	7½	5¼	950										2,004	61½
Chester,	¼	3½	5¼	1,045										347	26½
Cornwall,	5	66	20⅞	1,530							28			3,179	39
Crawford,			½	150										11,836	399
Deerpark,	4⅜	60	4¾	803										5,505	125
Goshen,	⅛	5	¾	274										921	75
Greenville,			2	300										2,470	117
Hamptonburgh,														2,862	78½
Minisink,	1	10½												3,182	113
Monroe,	2⅛	26	5⅝	1,196										2,173	34
Montgomery,	¼	3	12¾	709										11,671	508½
Mount Hope,	2¾	49¾	3½	570										1,066	107½
Newburgh,	2¾	46	20	1,983										5,601	785½
Windsor,	¼	1	9¾	1,170								1¼	800	5,333	158
Walkill,	2¾	12	11	482	½	30					11			17,510	389½
Warwick,	5¼	50	3	207										3,886½	128
Wawayanda,		8	¼	200										634	43
Total,	27⅞	348¼	105	11,569	½	30					39	1¼	800	80,180½	3,188½

ORLEANS COUNTY.—(Continued.)

TOWNS.	BEANS. Acres planted.	BEANS. Bushels harvested.	TURNIPS. Acres sown.	TURNIPS. Bushels harvested.	FLAX. Acres sown.	FLAX. Pounds of lint.	FLAX. Bushels of seed.	HEMP. Acres sown.	HEMP. Tons of hemp.	HOPS. Acres planted.	HOPS. Pounds harvested.	TOBACCO. Acres planted.	TOBACCO. Pounds harvested.	APPLE ORCHARDS. Bushels of apples.	APPLE ORCHARDS. Barrels of cider.
Barre,	483¼	5,493¼	18	4,325	15	14,000	115							66,000	944
Carlton,	1,042½	10,873	7	869								1¾	3,000	31,092	407
Clarendon,	270	2,940	12¾	1,926										25,966	398½
Gaines,	535¾	5,740	4⅞	780								1¼	1,909	29,372	479½
Kendall,	548	5,728	1¾	400								½	400	16,216	224
Murray,	313¼	2,801	7½	857										19,697	327
Ridgeway,	191	1,491	12	1,220	12½	5,000	75					11⅜	15,440	32,417	700
Shelby,	13½	133½	6¼	803	7	30	35							40,824½	681
Yates,	521	4,986	2½	287	6		60			⅛	16	2	2,122	20,197	373
Total,	3,918¼	40,185¾	72⅜	11,467	40½	19,030	285			⅛	16	17⅜	22,871	281,781½	4,534

OSWEGO COUNTY.—(Continued.)

TOWNS.	BEANS. Acres planted.	BEANS. Bushels harvested.	TURNIPS. Acres sown.	TURNIPS. Bushels harvested.	FLAX. Acres sown.	FLAX. Pounds of lint.	FLAX. Bushels of seed.	HEMP. Acres sown.	HEMP. Tons of hemp.	HOPS. Acres planted.	HOPS. Pounds harvested.	TOBACCO. Acres planted.	TOBACCO. Pounds harvested.	APPLE ORCHARDS. Bushels of apples.	APPLE ORCHARDS. Barrels of cider.
Albion,	10½	86	5	355						10½	5,190			8,020	129
Amboy,	2⅞	31½	2⅛	404	½	130				7¼	1,686			6,248	43½
Boylston,	5	96	2⅛	269	2¾	120	12							2,731	26
Constantia,	3⅛	45	3¼	654	⅛	15							15	5,050	45
Granby,	34	640½	22	3,577	7¾	2,400	52½							25,932	751½
Hannibal,	19¾	295	10¾	2,046	2⅛	140	39							37,664	707½
Hastings,	13⅛	138	1⅜	411						4	2,930			20,016	448
Mexico,	20¾	304½	1½	360	1⅛	390	8½							40,064	859½
New Haven,	7¾	227¼	3½	1,137½	1¼	515								35,141	1,218½
Orwell,	⅞	79	1½	191			100							4,244	45
Oswego,	6¾	134½	10⅜	2,466						1	700			16,830	270
Oswego city,	7⅞	23½	2⅝	1,190										5,225	65½
Palermo,	2¼	65	2½	687	1	246	5			4½	5,150			30.885	653½
Parish,	4⅝	60½	3½	464	1	153	1			5	2,100			16,099	149
Redfield,	3	47	3½	271										327	
Richland,	15¼	304	6¾	2,150	52½	20,500	281½			8¾	7,600			47,315	348
Sandy Creek,	5	69	1½	211	33⅛	12,500	245½			1½	1,654			24,873	60
Schroeppel,	50	904	8½	1,475						3	2,196			13,356	212½
Scriba,	15¾	245	19⅞	2,861			4							33,325	913
Volney,	19⅛	203½	19½	2,897										39,370	883½
West Monroe,	27⅞	289¾	2⅜	488										7,943	163½
Williamstown,	5½	37½	8½	2,088										5,257	113½
Total,	280¾	4,326	142⅝	27,252½	103¼	37,109	749			45½	29,206		15	425,915	8,105½

OTSEGO COUNTY.—(Continued.)

TOWNS.	BEANS. Acres planted.	BEANS. Bushels harvested.	TURNIPS. Acres sown.	TURNIPS. Bushels harvested.	FLAX. Acres sown.	FLAX. Pounds of lint.	FLAX. Bushels of seed.	HEMP. Acres sown.	HEMP. Tons of hemp.	HOPS. Acres planted.	HOPS. Pounds harvested.	TOBACCO. Acres planted.	TOBACCO. Pounds harvested.	APPLE ORCHARDS. Bushels of apples.	APPLE ORCHARDS. Barrels of cider.
Burlington,	14⅝	207¼	2½	673	11	26,000	83½			89¼	61,019		20	38,596	529
Butternuts,	2⅛	123	4⅝	1,129	¼	30	1			14½	9.207			46,420	636
Cherry Valley,	3	134½	1	210	17½	302	84			187¼	176,668½			21,107	356
Decatur,	3⅜	25¾	4¾	676	22¼	3,667	157			30¼	31,692			12,344	213
Edmeston,	15⅞	264	4⅛	706	3⅞	1,247	25			67¾	46,770			33,133	433
Exeter,	3⅝	41	2⅜	315	12⅜	7,138	64			212¾	141,689			30,911	231
Hartwick,	6½	83	¾	135	8½	5,523	65½			191	116,455			26,946	535½
Laurens,	3¼	134		92	1½	275	10			94	48,724			30,460	289
Maryland,	5¼	98	9½	2,161	⅞	175	7½			182¾	141,690			15,800	244
Middlefield,	9	205½	4¾	1,494	4¼	165	23½			279¾	268,197		15	36,608	718
Milford,	5⅜	147¾	2⅜	560						591⅛	305,039	½	400	20,823	413
Morris,	6¼	194	7¼	2,435						59¼	34,693			27,252	358
New Lisbon,	1¼	93½	1½	220	220	⅝	190			36¼	18,165			26,779	340
Oneonta,	1½	28½	3⅛	723		200	3			166¼	77,471			19,990	201
Otego,	2	43½	6⅜	2,173	1⅜	60	3			32	12,495			24,822	488¼

(Continued on page 294.)

ONTARIO COUNTY.—(Continued.)

TOWNS.	MARKET GARDENS. Acres cultivated.	Value of products.	Pounds of maple sugar made.	Gallons of maple molasses made.	Gallons of wine made.	Pounds of honey collected.	Pounds of wax collected.	SILK. Pounds of cocoons.	NEAT CATTLE. Under one year old.	Over one y'r, exclusive of working oxen & cows.	Working oxen.	Cows.	Number of cattle killed for beef.	Pounds of butter.	Pounds of cheese.
Richmond,	......	......	2, 725	84	......	2, 755	204	......	409	890	186	658	77	54, 236	12, 715
Seneca,	19	2, 020	9, 236	504	98	4, 737	215	......	613	1, 204	152	1, 795	280	149, 581	11. 805
South Bristol,	......	......	968	36	......	......	......	......	179	391	121	464	82	55, 548	3 040
Victor,	......	......	425	2	87	1, 905	68	......	400	768	44	820	207	72, 049	5. 370
West Bloomfield,	......	......	5. 060	126	10	1, 575	90	......	247	450	148	579	89	14, 947	8, 685
Total,	67⅞	6, 555	54, 474½	2. 542½	959½	53, 135	2, 458¾	2	5, 859	11, 788	2, 113	14, 202	2, 848	1, 223, 097	205. 921

ORANGE COUNTY.—(Continued.)

TOWNS.	Acres cultivated.	Value of products.	Pounds of maple sugar made.	Gallons of maple molasses made.	Gallons of wine made.	Pounds of honey collected.	Pounds of wax collected.	Pounds of cocoons.	Under one year old.	Over one y'r, exclusive of working oxen & cows.	Working oxen.	Cows.	Number of cattle killed for beef.	Pounds of butter.	Pounds of cheese.
Blooming Grove,	1	74	48	......	1, 605	767	52	......	161	425	252	2, 358	203	95, 060	....
Chester,	1	50	......	......	......	50	10	......	82	269	148	1, 920	194	21, 175	....
Cornwall,	10	1, 755	......	......	400	403	27	......	187	343	205	1, 274	89	77, 844	....
Crawford,	......	......	10	......	......	375	......	......	201	336	261	2, 395	267	252, 020	....
Deerpark,	5	986	77	20	......	3, 000	159	......	200	402	136	726	87	46, 194	....
Goshen,	......	......	......	......	60	1, 350	128½	......	275	679	173	3, 213	373	129, 918	....
Greenville,	......	......	519	13	......	843	77	......	428	465	29	1, 918	132	249, 248	60
Hamptonburgh,	......	......	......	......	......	835	88	......	194	330	138	1, 979	131	177, 820	....
Minisink,	......	......	595	36	......	2, 128	147	......	375	479	40	1, 837	143	243, 749	....
Monroe,	3⅓	331	......	2	10	1, 364	116	......	346	637	357	2, 409	468	98, 270	600
Montgomery,	1	14	98	......	26	485	100	......	273	506	246	2, 859	336	312, 466	....
Mount Hope,	......	......	238	26	......	1, 559	170	......	209	292	38	1, 681	200	141, 146	....
Newburgh,	18⅝	1, 681	1	......	26	2, 762	262	......	345	428	340	2, 456	2, 260	218, 963¾	....
New Windsor,	27⅝	2, 878	......	......	......	2, 555	192	......	343	341	267	2, 169	246	218, 832	....
Walkill,	......	3	275½	38½	39	2, 364	267	......	470	749	256	3, 085	374	365, 843	....
Warwick,	......	150	485	5	......	4, 271	333	......	545	1, 874	517	5, 119	400	416, 494	80, 000
Wawayanda,	......	......	......	......	7	......	......	......	295	442	86	2, 789	272	220, 545	....
Total,	67⅝	7, 922	2, 346½	140½	2, 173	25, 111	2, 128½	......	4, 929	8, 997	3, 489	40, 187	6, 175	3, 285, 587¾	80, 660

ORLEANS COUNTY.—(Continued.)

TOWNS.	Acres cultivated.	Value of products.	Pounds of maple sugar made.	Gallons of maple molasses made.	Gallons of wine made.	Pounds of honey collected.	Pounds of wax collected.	Pounds of cocoons.	Under one year old.	Over one y'r, exclusive of working oxen & cows.	Working oxen.	Cows.	Number of cattle killed for beef.	Pounds of butter.	Pounds of cheese.
Barre,	3¾	375	7, 652	168½	......	4, 575	288	......	892	1, 548	215	1, 845	134	184, 996	31, 116
Carlton,	¼	50	575	24	......	3, 927	189½	......	589	958	126	907	208	93, 261	8, 730
Clarendon,	½	22	4, 375	64	22	2, 981	144	......	378	684	110	872	58	85, 251	10, 687
Gaines,	1	200	......	5½	11	1, 145	78	......	391	627	101	638	51	90, 317	6, 555
Kendall,	......	......	655	4	3	630	14	......	537	900	196	871	151	77, 035	5, 375
Murray,	......	......	203	13	2	1, 956	91	......	402	812	104	731	148	66, 851	8, 942
Ridgeway,	½	50	394	35	48	2, 860	120	......	651	1, 146	126	1, 246	272	115, 124	17, 719
Shelby,	½	117	3, 300	59	17	2, 839	131	......	483	888	112	967	82	112, 570	11, 404
Yates,	......	......	455	49	36	2, 200	96	......	459	982	74	844	190	86, 608	9, 770
Total,	6½	814	17, 609	422	139	23, 113	1, 151½	......	4. 782	8, 545	1, 164	8, 921	1, 294	912. 013	110, 298

OSWEGO COUNTY.—(Continued.)

TOWNS.	Acres cultivated.	Value of products.	Pounds of maple sugar made.	Gallons of maple molasses made.	Gallons of wine made.	Pounds of honey collected.	Pounds of wax collected.	Pounds of cocoons.	Under one year old.	Over one y'r, exclusive of working oxen & cows.	Working oxen.	Cows.	Number of cattle killed for beef.	Pounds of butter.	Pounds of cheese.
Albion,	......	......	3, 000	102	......	2, 265	59	......	249	391	173	769	74	83, 800	10, 550
Amboy,	......	......	1, 685	16	......	1, 491	......	......	98	375	149	464	46	45, 822	1, 314
Boylston,	......	......	3, 287	37	......	65	8	......	86	136	92	570	25	36, 860	70, 522
Constantia,	......	......	505	......	......	1, 204	65	......	156	266	118	457	71	47, 885	1, 050
Granby,	1	50	416	21	10	5, 838	306½	......	398	776	207	1, 120	128	105, 210	3, 201
Hannibal,	......	......	2, 190	44	......	6, 514	312	......	415	900	175	1, 317	444	127, 843	13, 756
Hastings,	......	......	1, 865	23	......	5, 660	258	......	300	676	204	956	162	87, 643	5, 641
Mexico,	1½	15	5, 150	92	49	2, 920	157	......	568	891	197	2, 290	192	204, 992	130, 915
New Haven,	½	43	794	63	......	1, 899	98	......	366	772	112	1, 048	80	133, 550	15, 804
Orwell,	......	......	10, 463	66	......	753	52	......	189	297	94	909	51	105, 324	122, 780
Oswego,	8	418	818	21	......	1, 705	52	......	269	477	138	936	761	97, 306	3, 530
Oswego city,	77¼	10, 346	......	......	10	......	......	......	19	31	3	594	1, 307	3, 400	....
Palermo,	......	......	470	......	......	1, 697	44	......	298	672	176	1, 005	31	107, 315	12, 050
Parish,	......	......	1, 870	52	......	1, 560	109	......	205	460	170	822	60	81, 655	15, 100
Redfield,	......	......	10, 317	119	......	550	25	......	121	213	86	757	49	33, 980	151, 900
Richland,	......	......	4, 710	32	......	2, 635	103	......	551	916	211	2, 244	192	174, 675	123, 970
Sandy Creek,	......	......	3, 640	70	3	157	13	......	346	650	138	1, 583	19	139, 117	167, 575
Schroeppel,	......	80	1, 575	29	......	2, 179	184	......	366	730	179	1, 054	184	81, 222	44, 555
Scriba,	1	30	1, 530	10	4	3, 570	67	......	281	529	121	1, 174	433	159, 514	11, 490
Volney,	4	250	4, 232	107	......	1, 086	45	......	380	530	186	1, 124	227	102, 652	58, 451
West Monroe,	......	......	70	140	3	3, 017	107	......	156	275	88	465	35	47, 609	8, 357
Williamstown,	......	......	955	37	......	935	78	......	116	200	76	325	66	28, 800	2, 950
Total,	93¼	11, 232	59, 542	1, 081	79	47, 700	2, 142½	......	5. 933	11, 163	3, 093	21. 983	4. 637	2, 036, 174	975, 461

OTSEGO COUNTY.—(Continued.)

TOWNS.	Acres cultivated.	Value of products.	Pounds of maple sugar made.	Gallons of maple molasses made.	Gallons of wine made.	Pounds of honey collected.	Pounds of wax collected.	Pounds of cocoons.	Under one year old.	Over one y'r, exclusive of working oxen & cows.	Working oxen.	Cows.	Number of cattle killed for beef.	Pounds of butter.	Pounds of cheese.
Burlington,	......	......	21, 422	273	......	2, 923	257	......	360	701	102	1, 529	118	122, 572	123, 086
Butternuts,	......	......	7, 762	188	......	2, 653	147	......	534	984	140	2, 003	210	173, 046	100, 897
Cherry Valley,	......	30	2, 040	120½	10	5, 409	309	......	353	765	82	1, 250	252	105, 160	22, 218
Decatur,	......	15	7, 018	196	......	2, 411	103	......	212	458	96	855	99	81, 985	12, 435
Edmeston,	......	......	17, 265	173	......	3, 169	208	......	411	892	104	1, 618	145	106, 826	157, 540
Exeter,	......	......	10, 667	380½	......	3, 855	253	......	252	578	76	1, 167	98	85, 235	156, 365
Hartwick,	¼	40	9, 321	245	25	2, 911	135	......	255	740	91	1, 255	142	105, 280	22, 390
Laurens,	......	......	8, 195	191	......	2, 780	185	......	383	664	106	1, 757	126	195, 763	10, 530
Maryland,	......	......	5, 262	276	......	7, 792	285	......	434	819	160	1, 168	173	122, 045	3, 150
Middlefield,	4	250	2, 150	123	......	7, 225	336	......	440	1, 073	144	1, 844	247	153, 130	96, 415
Milford,	......	......	3, 325	57	......	4, 535	210	......	271	731	136	1, 414	191	148, 017	12, 820
Morris,	......	......	11, 449	274	......	1, 760	79	......	391	880	188	1, 531	112	134, 468	53, 625
New Lisbon,	......	......	26, 515	79	......	1, 040	124	......	360	682	90	1, 379	97	144, 600	21, 022
Oneonta,	......	......	542	32	......	4, 289	174	......	381	415	88	1, 335	64	140 935	5, 720
Otego,	......	......	4, 381	204	3	3, 870	194½	......	544	849	195	1, 591	117	179, 195	14, 840

(Continued on page 295.)

ONTARIO COUNTY.—(Continued.)

TOWNS.	Gallons of milk sold.	Horses.	Mules.	SWINE. Under 6 months.	SWINE. Over 6 months.	SHEEP. Number of sheep.	SHEEP. Number of fleeces.	SHEEP. Pounds of wool.	POULTRY. Value of poultry sold.	POULTRY. Value of eggs sold.	DOMESTIC MANUFACTURES. Yards of fulled cloth made.	DOMESTIC MANUFACTURES. Yards of flannel made.	DOMESTIC MANUFACTURES. Yards of linen made.	DOMESTIC MANUFACTURES. Yards of cotton and mixed cloths.
Richmond,	....	719	4	846	567	14, 927	14, 786	52, 945	$393	$382	....	21	....	30
Seneca,	40, 980	1, 556	2	1, 512	1, 380	13, 542	15, 546	58, 433	4, 494	2, 750	30	363	....	180
South Bristol,	....	400	5	337	450	3, 107	3, 348	10, 495½	510	404	76	265	....	89
Victor,	....	902	2	1, 108	667	6, 111	7, 164	28, 320	1, 292	1, 122	15	90	....	....
West Bloomfield,	623	603	....	599	653	48, 045	6, 183	24, 930	571	885	....	....	....	....
Total,	217, 340	13, 660	159	13, 161	13, 258	132, 725	138, 842	609, 075	25, 128	23, 018	782½	2, 497½	452	1, 153

ORANGE COUNTY.—(Continued.)

TOWNS.	Gallons of milk sold.	Horses.	Mules.	Under 6 months.	Over 6 months.	Number of sheep.	Number of fleeces.	Pounds of wool.	Value of poultry sold.	Value of eggs sold.	Yards of fulled cloth made.	Yards of flannel made.	Yards of linen made.	Yards of cotton and mixed cloths.
Blooming Grove,	554, 106	386	6	1, 008	636	2, 467	2, 754	8, 787½	1, 155	1, 048	....	....	....	....
Chester,	637, 426	379	2	332	394	354	454	1, 391	1, 396	1, 257	....	....	....	....
Cornwall,	34, 331	473	....	786	659	846	532	1, 922½	1, 095	1, 379	....	....	....	....
Crawford,	....	570	2	2, 355	1, 145	1, 000	1, 098	3, 599	2, 422	2, 857	199	273	275	....
Deerpark,	36, 845	378	4	415	364	270	243	1, 105	291	351	89	15	14	24
Goshen,	1004, 839	670	....	1, 068	960	2, 474	1, 956	6, 479	890	1, 971	....	....	....	....
Greenville,	....	374	....	777	728	499	321	1, 414	997	674	81	167	30	22
Hamptonburgh,	118, 440	437	....	1, 328	872	2, 403	1, 451	4, 570	1, 360	1, 354	....	....	....	....
Minisink,	8. 537	382	4	955	819	331	244	1, 039	1, 579	1, 084	28	110	....	....
Monroe,	390, 915	541	31	760	812	810	550	1, 791	1, 262	711	20	110	....	....
Montgomery,	500	782	....	2, 886	2, 211	2, 856	2, 378	7, 525	3, 269	4, 558	119	60	....	....
Mount Hope,	261, 403	377	2	538	448	415	324	1, 364	982	876	38	133	....	....
Newburgh,	110, 574	1, 183	5	2, 390	1, 301	973	684	2, 429½	3, 174	3, 212	249	....	....	....
New Windsor,	101, 191	574	....	2, 052	948	1, 199	914	2, 951½	2, 632	2, 415	....	....	....	....
Walkill,	619, 463	921	2	2, 234	1, 544	1, 580	1, 165	4, 199	3, 602	3, 923	124	270½	30	37
Warwick,	350, 584	1, 125	16	3, 130	2, 050	2, 447	1, 865	6, 992	3, 387	4, 055	55	194¾	44	52
Wawayanda,	324, 360	434	....	981	798	453	318	1, 576	1, 201	587	....	65	20	....
Total,	4553, 514	9, 986	74	23, 995	16, 689	21, 377	17, 251	59, 135	30, 694	32, 312	1, 002	1, 398¼	413	135

ORLEANS COUNTY.—(Continued.)

TOWNS.	Gallons of milk sold.	Horses.	Mules.	Under 6 months.	Over 6 months.	Number of sheep.	Number of fleeces.	Pounds of wool.	Value of poultry sold.	Value of eggs sold.	Yards of fulled cloth made.	Yards of flannel made.	Yards of linen made.	Yards of cotton and mixed cloths.
Barre,	9, 514	1, 937	....	1, 651	1, 964	16, 579	12, 068	46, 899½	1, 686	2, 550	266	451	116½	309
Carlton,	12	1, 063	....	567	883	12, 452	7, 610	30, 788	1, 217	986	260½	650	12	185
Clarendon,	....	870	....	450	828	4, 805	3, 491	13, 997	642	1, 369	96	204	....	83
Gaines,	1, 322	639	....	373	599	6, 842	5, 824	22, 374¾	594	1, 007	15	18	16	30
Kendall,	95	798	....	562	897	10, 577	7, 811	31, 570	1, 457	1, 954	282	81	125	398
Murray,	76	807	....	381	698	5, 703	3, 509	13, 915	857	1, 354	41	454	....	291
Ridgeway,	4, 415	1, 538	2	943	1, 201	11, 402	8, 688	31, 663½	1, 004	1, 564	138	56	52½	24
Shelby,	....	1, 058	....	906	1, 186	10, 648	7, 630	30, 012	739	1, 432	189	392½	23	219
Yates,	330	930	....	632	971	12, 277	8, 278	34, 583	895	1, 374	117	373	32	324
Total,	15, 764	9, 640	2	6, 465	9, 227	91, 285	64, 909	255, 802¾	9, 091	13, 590	1, 404½	2, 679½	377	1, 863

OSWEGO COUNTY.—(Continued.)

TOWNS.	Gallons of milk sold.	Horses.	Mules.	Under 6 months.	Over 6 months.	Number of sheep.	Number of fleeces.	Pounds of wool.	Value of poultry sold.	Value of eggs sold.	Yards of fulled cloth made.	Yards of flannel made.	Yards of linen made.	Yards of cotton and mixed cloths.
Albion,	140	429	....	264	441	1, 296	926	3, 290	297	587	308	801	179	533
Amboy,	240	220	....	95	309	854	515	1, 646	88	126	374	502	100	456
Boylston,	....	169	....	143	165	460	336	1, 131	114	69	272	400	208	384
Constantia,	850	392	....	251	403	996	647	2, 068	317	580	194	352	80	211
Granby,	700	903	....	611	989	3, 025	1, 891	7, 027½	1, 186	2, 800	498	815	15	565
Hannibal,	....	1, 097	....	742	1, 145	2, 215	2, 073	7, 028	946	2, 280	304	335½	110	546
Hastings,	....	669	....	510	733	2, 692	1, 446	4, 979¾	899	1, 661	669	1, 291	336	253
Mexico,	2, 790	1, 007	....	883	1, 111	3, 170	1, 503	5, 751	1, 555	2, 425	525½	797	239	509
New Haven,	....	531	....	326	560	1, 878	702	2, 707¼	831	1, 996	215	475½	65	271½
Orwell,	....	278	....	241	229	582	450	1, 642	477	400	172	563	64	253
Oswego,	36, 614	748	....	361	699	1, 934	1, 081	4, 150	697	1, 549	121	132	50	60
Oswego city,	73, 691	596	....	311	893	194	35	144	505	29	....	....	....	....
Palermo,	....	591	....	359	715	2, 331	1, 501	5, 204	509	3, 779	348	547	136	413
Parish,	....	403	22	368	532	1, 263	824	2, 693	444	316	668	774	209	591
Redfield,	....	162	....	66	110	451	270	896	77	134	110	174	....	....
Richland,	....	866	....	716	797	3, 042	1, 838	6, 663	1, 063	1, 257	544	869	209	309
Sandy Creek,	....	557	....	539	600	2, 126	1, 615	5, 928½	589	455	567	684	689	280
Schroeppel,	210	760	....	325	830	2, 768	1, 393	4, 623	650	1, 319	249½	588½	144	105
Scriba,	1, 090	691	....	308	772	1, 302	931	3, 515	620	3, 090	310	267	67	262
Volney,	....	904	1	263	1, 343	2, 185	1, 596	5, 503¼	811	1, 200	420	684	53	194
West Monroe,	....	249	....	157	308	907	545	1, 793	233	396	171½	381	44	319½
Williamstown,	100	176	....	131	182	417	300	1, 063	263	310	126	141	140	225
Total,	116, 425	12, 398	23	7, 970	13, 866	36, 088	22, 418	79, 446¼	13, 161	26, 758	7, 166½	11, 573½	3, 137	6, 740

OTSEGO COUNTY.—(Continued.)

TOWNS.	Gallons of milk sold.	Horses.	Mules.	Under 6 months.	Over 6 months.	Number of sheep.	Number of fleeces.	Pounds of wool.	Value of poultry sold.	Value of eggs sold.	Yards of fulled cloth made.	Yards of flannel made.	Yards of linen made.	Yards of cotton and mixed cloths.
Burlington,	....	565	....	414	426	6, 704	5, 402	16, 705½	2, 477	1, 616	210½	558½	641½	268
Butternuts,	30	605	....	601	551	5, 733	3, 385	11, 669	757	1, 057	318	218	201	55
Cherry Valley,	960	820	2	418	550	2, 480	2, 505	8, 699½	628	1, 704	311	461½	232	172
Decatur,	....	338	....	385	325	2, 551	677	2, 949	659	1, 021	115½	146	314	307
Edmeston,	....	664	....	566	462	6, 355	4, 647	16, 120	1, 543	1, 464	466¾	844	562	1, 274
Exeter,	....	478	....	321	298	5, 239	5, 875	20, 764	1, 049	1, 100	195	451	224	112½
Hartwick,	....	586	....	411	439	3, 728	3, 080	9, 964	994	2, 676	56½	88	545	122
Laurens,	....	581	5	597	511	5, 007	3, 344	10, 699	1, 265	3, 333	220	557	827	194
Maryland,	....	599	....	400	399	4, 105	2, 632	8, 614	780	1, 732	279	597	362	517
Middlefield,	....	933	2	631	653	3, 430	3, 129	10, 363	1, 111	2, 920	174	212	294	45
Milford,	....	662	....	434	533	3, 242	2, 645	8, 771½	668	3, 119	3	12	8	....
Morris,	....	514	....	287	382	3, 719	2, 792	10, 022	575	1, 417	239	306	84	23
New Lisbon,	....	545	....	397	361	7, 035	5, 045	16, 654	1, 810	1, 986	111½	124	331	191
Oneonta,	....	512	....	395	455	3, 956	2, 314	7, 517	889	1, 775	117	579	163	251
Otego,	....	594	....	532	494	8, 453	4, 626	16, 035½	897	2, 489	710¼	675	357	829½

(Continued on page 296.)

OTSEGO COUNTY.—(Continued.)

TOWNS	Acres: Improved.	Acres: Unimproved.	Cash value: Of farm.	Cash value: Of stock.	Cash value: Of tools and implements	Acres plowed the year previous.	Acres in fallow the year previous.	Acres in pasture the year previous.	Meadow: Acres.	Meadow: Tons of hay.	Meadow: Bushels of grass seed.	Spring wheat: Acres sown.	Spring wheat: Bushels harvested.	Winter wheat: Acres sown.
Otsego, ...	20, 374¾	9, 619	$910, 484	$169, 786	$39, 581	4, 536¼	124	9, 367½	6, 806	6, 620½	110¾	366¾	4, 262½	52½
Pittsfield, ...	13, 201¾	7, 072	422, 732	79, 180	23, 630	2, 412¾	125	6, 201	4, 181½	4, 368¼	140¼	90¼	1, 017	4
Plainfield, ...	12, 857¾	4, 103	515, 780	83, 128	11, 489	2, 148⅛	....	6, 962	3, 784⅛	4, 008	51	191¼	2, 861	19¼
Richfield, ...	15, 681	4, 213	776, 700	110, 870	19, 875	2, 422¼	....	8, 330¾	5, 001½	5, 248	77	239¾	3, 746	7½
Roseboom, ...	13, 366¾	6, 730	552, 586	92, 409	21, 822	4, 375¼	198	5, 306¼	3, 366¼	3, 147	140½	224¼	2, 449	72½
Springfield, ...	22, 236½	7, 114½	1, 579, 705	179, 259	40, 452	7, 088½	93¼	8, 668½	5, 926	6, 011	106¾	193¼	2, 394¾	85
Unadilla, ...	20, 543	10, 707½	775, 380	156, 815	39, 444	3, 445	432	9, 789	5, 584	6, 004	173	100½	804½	299¼
Westford, ...	14, 831¾	5, 804	528, 925	80, 415	25, 715	4, 056½	114½	5, 410	3, 465¾	2, 930½	167	220½	2, 497	15½
Worcester, ...	19, 862	9, 588½	731, 735	110, 248	25, 525	5, 514½	553	7, 240	5, 058	4, 251½	246½	133½	1, 240	8
Total, ...	428, 932⅝	179, 550¼	18 318, 997	2, 802, 602	656, 876	92, 717⅝	4, 524¾	196, 401¼	115, 979⅞	108, 069¾	3, 341¾	4, 803⅝	53446¼	1, 231¼

PUTNAM COUNTY.

TOWNS	Acres: Improved.	Acres: Unimproved.	Cash value: Of farm.	Cash value: Of stock.	Cash value: Of tools and implements	Acres plowed the year previous.	Acres in fallow the year previous.	Acres in pasture the year previous.	Meadow: Acres.	Meadow: Tons of hay.	Meadow: Bushels of grass seed.	Spring wheat: Acres sown.	Spring wheat: Bushels harvested.	Winter wheat: Acres sown.
Carmel, ...	19, 300	5, 271¼	1, 599, 155	161, 948	31, 622	2, 513¾	5	1, 069¾	5, 652	6, 040	24½	......	......	97
Kent, ...	15, 241¾	6, 617	678, 485	100, 976	14, 732	1, 620	....	8, 884¾	4, 330½	4, 261	8½	......	......	24
Patterson, ...	13, 789¼	6, 523	864, 995	95, 834	20, 499	1, 206½	....	7, 686	3, 891½	4, 060¼	......	......	......	110½
Phillipstown, ...	11, 505	15, 236	798, 856	92, 067	16, 027	2, 398	519	4, 520	3, 272	3, 370	2	......	......	39
Putnam Valley, .	16, 313	7, 637	679, 750	80, 219	15, 767	2, 399½	10	10, 376	3, 347	3, 443	15½	......	......	64
Southeast, ...	18, 056⅞	3, 163½	1, 527, 608	188, 993	42, 181	1, 677½	447¼	10, 087	5, 698¾	6, 582½	......	......	......	173
Total, ...	94, 205⅞	44, 447¾	6, 148, 849	720, 037	140, 828	11, 815¼	981¼	42, 623½	26, 191¾	27, 756¾	50½	......	......	507½

QUEENS COUNTY.

TOWNS	Acres: Improved.	Acres: Unimproved.	Cash value: Of farm.	Cash value: Of stock.	Cash value: Of tools and implements	Acres plowed the year previous.	Acres in fallow the year previous.	Acres in pasture the year previous.	Meadow: Acres.	Meadow: Tons of hay.	Meadow: Bushels of grass seed.	Spring wheat: Acres sown.	Spring wheat: Bushels harvested.	Winter wheat: Acres sown.
Flushing, ...	11, 083	3, 813	3, 184, 960	183, 865	73, 245	3, 476	80	2, 304	4, 445	7, 105	71	1	28	774
Hempstead, ...	25, 463	14, 888	2, 650, 760	235, 781	113, 886	9, 238	3, 196	4, 479	6, 615	9, 179	45	......	......	1, 026
Jamaica, ...	14, 042½	5, 555	2, 186, 430	128, 791	67, 365	4, 760	619½	1, 651½	5, 125	7, 060	31	......	......	517¾
Newton, ...	10, 288¼	2, 009	3, 146, 600	187, 765	65, 525	3, 882½	86½	753	1, 796¾	2, 655½	3	......	......	374
N'th Hempstead,	23, 150¼	7, 989	2, 534, 400	204, 020	84, 730	6, 729¾	46½	7, 581½	8, 367	11, 101½	192¼	......	......	1, 710½
Oyster Bay, ...	35, 522	22, 950	3, 368, 695	313, 128	107, 641	9, 632	84	7, 460½	11, 285½	14, 294	282	3	20	2, 475¼
Total, ...	119, 549	57, 204	17, 071, 845	1, 253, 350	512, 392	37, 718¼	4, 112½	24, 229½	37, 634¼	51, 395	624¼	4	48	6, 877½

RENSSELAER COUNTY.

TOWNS	Acres: Improved.	Acres: Unimproved.	Cash value: Of farm.	Cash value: Of stock.	Cash value: Of tools and implements	Acres plowed the year previous.	Acres in fallow the year previous.	Acres in pasture the year previous.	Meadow: Acres.	Meadow: Tons of hay.	Meadow: Bushels of grass seed.	Spring wheat: Acres sown.	Spring wheat: Bushels harvested.	Winter wheat: Acres sown.
Berlin, ...	19, 437½	16, 759	476, 578	97, 354	21, 611	2, 004	75½	12, 508	4, 927	3, 280	16	12¾	227	......
Brunswick, ...	23, 512½	4, 264	1, 861, 405	168, 976	65, 004	8, 425	40	6, 073½	5, 698	5, 082½	19	413½	3, 966	27
Clinton, ...	11, 674	2, 789½	1, 170, 920	82, 406	28, 790	4, 548	210	3, 097	3, 337	3, 469	......	45	325	20
Grafton, ...	15, 122½	13, 017½	388, 376	62, 717	13, 893	1, 695½	174½	7, 296	5, 605	3, 461¾	4	31½	369½	4
Greenbush, ...	....	....	....	....	....	....	....	....	....	....	......	......	......	......
Hoosick, ...	31, 341	8, 339	1, 998. 699	246, 351	46, 691	8, 028¾	328	12, 035	7, 159½	6, 356	129	187¼	2, 640½	147¾
Lansingburgh, ..	3, 672½	1, 212½	327, 585	53, 205	7, 932	1, 493	14	918	781	759	......	8¾	103	21
Nassau, ...	20, 281½	5, 754	900, 331	127, 164	48, 819	5, 696¾	264	7, 990	4, 331¼	3, 803½	......	10½	101½	10
North Greenbush	10, 374	2, 181	890, 550	74, 353	32, 561	3, 585	159	2, 130	2, 567	2, 715½	......	69	728	31
Petersburgh, ...	17, 075	7, 388	504, 373	86, 109	18, 456	2, 892	38	9, 613	4, 061	2, 861	48	61	685	......
Pittstown, ...	33, 857⅞	6, 311	2, 140, 598	216, 663	52, 113	9, 572½	1, 944	12, 708	6, 509	6, 630	91	239½	2, 255	176½
Poestenkill, ...	14, 206	4, 247	601, 390	66, 261	24, 145	2, 796	224	3, 515	3, 417	2, 530	2	54	433	8
Sandlake, ...	15, 268½	6, 696	742, 752	84, 832	30, 566	4, 519	154	6, 210	3, 877	3, 224	3	38	329	11
Schaghticoke, ...	21, 979	4, 474	1, 214, 358	144, 937	34, 509	6, 928	77	5, 297	3, 022	3, 247½	22	46	588	98
Schodack, ...	31, 531	8, 039½	2, 308, 760	188, 203	89, 075	13, 221¼	250	8, 564½	6, 606½	6, 097	79½	10	51	105
Stephentown, ...	20, 982	9, 404	599, 920	120, 791	17, 447	2, 738	693	8, 939	6, 197	4, 751	......	34½	514	28
Troy city, ...	1. 898	126½	530, 100	115, 387	8, 836	668	10	758	266	290	21½	4½	68	5
Total, ...	292, 212⅞	101, 002½	16, 656, 695	1, 935, 709	540, 448	78, 810¾	4, 655	107, 652	68, 361¼	58, 557¾	435	1, 265¾	13383½	692¼

RICHMOND COUNTY.

TOWNS	Acres: Improved.	Acres: Unimproved.	Cash value: Of farm.	Cash value: Of stock.	Cash value: Of tools and implements	Acres plowed the year previous.	Acres in fallow the year previous.	Acres in pasture the year previous.	Meadow: Acres.	Meadow: Tons of hay.	Meadow: Bushels of grass seed.	Spring wheat: Acres sown.	Spring wheat: Bushels harvested.	Winter wheat: Acres sown.
Castleton, ...	1, 359	862⅛	1, 108, 000	18, 815	3, 156	316	47	131	373	652	......	9	200	17¼
Northfield, ...	3, 775½	2, 932	1, 179, 325	43, 417	16, 405	1, 216	203	978¼	1, 051½	1, 501	56½	......	......	139
Southfield, ...	2, 752	1, 483	831, 800	35, 530	11, 975	734	3	544	1, 075	1, 586	23	......	......	279
Westfield, ...	7, 185⅞	2, 325	2, 142, 225	75, 263	43, 400	1, 634⅞	589½	1, 353¼	2, 029	3, 293	......	17	375	357
Total, ...	15, 072⅜	7, 602⅛	5, 261, 350	173, 025	74, 936	3, 900⅞	842½	3, 006½	4, 528½	7, 032	79½	26	575	792¼

ROCKLAND COUNTY.

TOWNS	Acres: Improved.	Acres: Unimproved.	Cash value: Of farm.	Cash value: Of stock.	Cash value: Of tools and implements	Acres plowed the year previous.	Acres in fallow the year previous.	Acres in pasture the year previous.	Meadow: Acres.	Meadow: Tons of hay.	Meadow: Bushels of grass seed.	Spring wheat: Acres sown.	Spring wheat: Bushels harvested.	Winter wheat: Acres sown.
Clarkstown, ...	15, 903¼	16, 742½	1, 786, 915	141, 662	53, 595	2, 775	828¾	4, 223	4. 056	4, 824½	4	2½	6	101¼
Haverstraw, ...	7, 151	14, 481	818, 985	250, 851	16, 000	764¼	246¼	1, 823	2, 323¼	2, 585	......	......	......	45½
Orangetown, ...	9, 922	3, 184	955, 675	88, 592	24, 112	1, 727	368	3, 789	2, 566	3, 213	29	......	......	60
Ramapo, ...	13, 505½	16, 445	1, 300, 635	136, 954	34, 623	3, 578¼	720	4, 826½	4, 038¾	4, 205½	17½	......	......	169¼
Total, ...	46, 481¾	50, 852½	4, 862, 210	618, 059	128, 330	8, 844½	2, 163	14, 661½	12, 984	14, 828	50½	2½	6	376

ST. LAWRENCE COUNTY.

TOWNS	Acres: Improved.	Acres: Unimproved.	Cash value: Of farm.	Cash value: Of stock.	Cash value: Of tools and implements	Acres plowed the year previous.	Acres in fallow the year previous.	Acres in pasture the year previous.	Meadow: Acres.	Meadow: Tons of hay.	Meadow: Bushels of grass seed.	Spring wheat: Acres sown.	Spring wheat: Bushels harvested.	Winter wheat: Acres sown.
Brasher, ...	18, 280	40, 725	517, 794	72, 800	18, 173	2, 914	75	6, 567	5, 933	4, 440	59	942	9476	127
Canton, ...	34, 101	29, 593	1, 341, 640	197, 663	39, 339	5, 026	230	15, 112	13, 345	11, 192	329	1, 533	14146	191
Colton, ...	3, 460	127, 293	119, 605	18, 360	4, 481	892	317	966	1, 060	2, 503	31	176	1144	4½
De Kalb, ...	22, 658	26, 616	569, 003	131, 856	28, 930	2, 996	23	9, 507	8, 106	6, 050	106	1, 017	9385	99
De Peyster, ...	12, 334	13, 706	347, 366	81, 719	15, 138	2, 359	38	6, 102	3, 855	2, 556	73	733	8749	110½
Edwards, ...	7, 834	19, 285	240. 162	57, 531	25, 219	2, 073	105	3, 661	2, 814	2, 205	32	556	3237	29
Fine, ...	1, 824	93, 932	108, 772	8, 054	3, 227	454	33	584	633	304	17	76½	242	......
Fowler, ...	15, 732	12, 687	400, 731	109, 319	21, 343	2, 432	....	6, 925	4, 895	4, 353	29½	785	9194	16
Gouverneur, ...	25, 111	12, 157	862, 260	147, 183	25, 168	4, 384	36	11, 721	7, 763	5, 170	100	1, 461	18096	71½
Hammond, ...	15, 701	18, 823	648, 515	106, 262	23, 568	4, 612	29	6, 192	4, 317	3, 665	358	2, 264	31666	192½
Hermon, ...	12, 537	12, 258	393, 145	91, 926	16, 983	1, 929	180	5, 274	4, 450	3, 621	87	640	7284	17
Hopkinton, ...	12, 641	36, 427	621, 117	80, 813	21, 972	1, 928	....	5, 336	4, 275	2, 786	41	597½	5605	5½
Lawrence, ...	17, 338	7, 905	622, 780	94, 898	25, 075	2, 779	....	7, 328	5, 529	4, 776	26	803	8634	12½

(Continued on page 297.)

OTSEGO COUNTY.—(Continued.)

Towns.	Winter Wheat. Bushels harvested.	Oats. Acres sown.	Oats. Bushels harvested.	Rye. Acres sown.	Rye. Bushels harvested.	Barley. Acres sown.	Barley. Bushels harvested.	Buckwheat. Acres sown.	Buckwheat. Bushels harvested.	Corn. Acres planted.	Corn. Bushels harvested.	Potatoes. Acres planted.	Potatoes. Bushels harvested.	Peas. Acres sown.	Peas. Bushels harvested.
Otsego,	383½	2, 694½	55, 690	19½	518	156	2, 309	329½	2, 722	780¼	20, 097	273¾	21, 916	92¼	1, 549
Pittsfield,	40	1, 275¼	26, 680	89½	1, 178	39½	612	154¾	1, 439½	387⅞	13, 557	198	15, 031	11¾	124
Plainfield,	177	946¼	19, 908	2	19	153¼	2, 527	54¾	367½	488¾	15, 125	176⅝	13, 405	17⅝	275½
Richfield,	72	1, 053	22, 075½	3	66	113¾	2, 041	148½	1, 259½	382½	10, 602	129½	10, 825	90¼	1, 565
Roseboom,	284	2, 679	54, 946	92½	974	79¼	1, 034	690½	9, 137	313½	6, 985	228⅛	15, 044	210¾	3, 068
Springfield,	447	3, 970½	78, 914	9	133	331¼	5, 315½	633	10, 388	467⅜	14, 532½	204⅛	21, 586	425⅜	8, 188
Unadilla,	926¼	1, 586	30, 304½	244⅝	2, 985½	6½	130	459¼	5, 473½	825⅝	22, 876	204⅜	19, 488	3	122
Westford,	135	2, 074	37, 908	144½	1, 909	77	962	465¼	6, 612	365¼	9, 312	181	16, 863	44¼	563
Worcester,	58	2, 874	41, 215	382½	4, 181	193¼	2, 808	1, 005⅜	12, 842½	313	7, 004	305½	26, 038	139¼	1, 728
Total,	5, 678	49, 016¼	903, 647	3, 031⅝	34, 218¼	2, 820⅛	43, 889	9, 903⅛	112, 732¾	12, 395	340, 170½	5, 026⅛	412, 703⅓	1, 824¾	29, 935⅞

PUTNAM COUNTY.—(Continued.)

Towns.	Winter Wheat. Bushels harvested.	Oats. Acres sown.	Oats. Bushels harvested.	Rye. Acres sown.	Rye. Bushels harvested.	Barley. Acres sown.	Barley. Bushels harvested.	Buckwheat. Acres sown.	Buckwheat. Bushels harvested.	Corn. Acres planted.	Corn. Bushels harvested.	Potatoes. Acres planted.	Potatoes. Bushels harvested.	Peas. Acres sown.	Peas. Bushels harvested.
Carmel,	811	767½	15, 394	404¼	4, 515	......	....	377¼	3, 705½	926¼	38, 842	230¼	14, 088	......	....
Kent,	194½	522½	10, 390	232	3, 692	......	....	345	1, 732¾	586	13, 145	125¾	5, 866	......	....
Patterson,	826½	395	7, 652	220	2, 322	......	....	112¾	741¾	510¼	13, 850	134½	9, 854	......	....
Phillipstown,	270	854	11, 589	492	5, 123½	......	....	369	1, 116	769	10, 993	237	6, 976	3	48
Putnam Valley,	369	713	10, 779	510	4, 136	......	....	523	1, 789	780	15, 329	350¾	17, 649	......	....
Southeast,	1, 079¾	462½	11, 118	254	3, 102	......	....	164¼	1, 633¼	863¼	27, 760½	120½	10, 071	......	....
Total,	3, 550¾	3, 714½	66, 922	2, 112¼	22, 890½	......	....	1, 891¼	10, 718¼	4, 434¾	119, 919½	1, 198¾	64, 504	3	48

QUEENS COUNTY.—(Continued.)

Towns.	Winter Wheat. Bushels harvested.	Oats. Acres sown.	Oats. Bushels harvested.	Rye. Acres sown.	Rye. Bushels harvested.	Barley. Acres sown.	Barley. Bushels harvested.	Buckwheat. Acres sown.	Buckwheat. Bushels harvested.	Corn. Acres planted.	Corn. Bushels harvested.	Potatoes. Acres planted.	Potatoes. Bushels harvested.	Peas. Acres sown.	Peas. Bushels harvested.
Flushing,	14191	879	20, 763	289	4, 195	24	580	262	1, 864	1, 359¼	42, 476	975⅝	36, 489	......	....
Hempstead,	15500	2, 379	48, 756	2, 787	30, 344	17	239	4, 064	6, 329	3, 644	84, 975	923	63, 082	52¼	3, 551
Jamaica,	10397	327¾	9, 559	755¾	12, 706	......	....	167¾	1, 574	1, 371½	39, 382	623¼	64, 494	8	....
Newtown,	6035	348½	8, 404	74	1, 387	......	....	25	100	687½	27, 655	540¾	53, 983	321	29, 718
No. Hempstead,	22381¾	2, 214½	43, 974	600¾	6, 289	83	1, 229	551	3, 441	2, 935½	62, 304	441⅛	34, 438	1	150
Oyster Bay,	33664½	3, 277½	68, 062	1, 630	16, 098	56	721	1, 229¼	7, 916½	3, 855	80, 893	586⅛	38, 649	1	25
Total,	102169¼	9, 426¼	199, 518	6, 136½	71, 019	180	2. 769	6, 299	21, 224½	13, 852¾	337, 685	4, 089⅞	291. 135	383¼	33, 444

RENSSELAER COUNTY.—(Continued.)

Towns.	Winter Wheat. Bushels harvested.	Oats. Acres sown.	Oats. Bushels harvested.	Rye. Acres sown.	Rye. Bushels harvested.	Barley. Acres sown.	Barley. Bushels harvested.	Buckwheat. Acres sown.	Buckwheat. Bushels harvested.	Corn. Acres planted.	Corn. Bushels harvested.	Potatoes. Acres planted.	Potatoes. Bushels harvested.	Peas. Acres sown.	Peas. Bushels harvested.
Berlin,	......	852	18, 674	49½	760	17¼	229	188	2, 540	606½	16, 557	263	25, 370	......	....
Brunswick,	116	3, 197	58, 263	2, 456	36, 244	40	669	575	6, 054	2, 068½	37, 660	1, 237¼	88, 688	27½	500
Clinton,	105	1, 516	26, 593	1, 416	17, 245	23	281	219½	2, 358	865	17, 510	665¾	48, 361	4	67
Grafton,	50	675¼	11, 179	70½	678	......	....	214¼	1, 761½	306¼	5, 251	409	25, 750	1¼	16
Greenbush,	......	......	......	......	......	......	....	......	......	......	......	......	......	......	....
Hoosick,	675½	2, 542½	63, 981	864½	13, 629½	301	6, 959	471¾	4, 372	2, 616½	52, 160	366	33, 671	17¼	251
Lansingburgh,	200	500½	14, 184	459	8. 239	1	8	37	407	297	5, 496	150¼	9, 605	4	64
Nassau,	5	2, 381	27, 776	2, 174½	22, 237	8½	62	725¾	4, 564	1, 507	24, 300½	385	24, 135	13¼	146
No. Greenbush,	136	1, 229	24, 801	1, 472	19, 653	8	170	114	1, 128	648	13, 342	683	56, 125	8	78
Petersburgh,	......	937	18, 637	44	627	20	334	352	3, 348	803	17, 823	261	22, 643	1	14
Pittstown,	353	3, 756	83, 101	2, 467	34, 651	81½	1, 372	866	7, 717	3, 053	62, 192	636	47, 924	2	70
Poestenkill,	43	954	16, 486	879	10, 195	6	97	208	1, 804	551½	11, 784	503¼	37, 261	7	90
Sand Lake,	39	1, 483	20, 920	1, 447	16, 024	4	77	430	3, 788	846	16, 619	628¼	35, 882	8	107
Schaghticoke,	173	3, 225	91, 221	3, 292	54, 882	81	1, 925	373	4, 873	2, 337	50, 838	825½	61, 860	5	84
Schodack,	272½	4, 952	60, 329	5, 088½	59, 930½	12	155	711¼	4, 269½	3, 020½	41, 096	836¾	43, 224	10½	87
Stephentown,	465	968	18, 652	373	3, 606	13	219	333½	3, 741	884	17, 830	320½	24, 716	......	....
Troy city,	25	127½	3, 580	78	1, 263	13	250	13½	96	123	2, 955	146¾	11, 344	......	....
Total,	2, 658	29, 295¾	558, 377	22630½	299, 864	629¼	12, 807	5, 832½	52, 821	20, 532¾	393, 413½	8, 317¼	590, 559	108¾	1, 574

RICHMOND COUNTY.—(Continued.)

Towns.	Winter Wheat. Bushels harvested.	Oats. Acres sown.	Oats. Bushels harvested.	Rye. Acres sown.	Rye. Bushels harvested.	Barley. Acres sown.	Barley. Bushels harvested.	Buckwheat. Acres sown.	Buckwheat. Bushels harvested.	Corn. Acres planted.	Corn. Bushels harvested.	Potatoes. Acres planted.	Potatoes. Bushels harvested.	Peas. Acres sown.	Peas. Bushels harvested.
Castleton,	246	55¼	1, 420	50	773	......	....	15	509	134¾	3, 512	44¾	4, 077	......	....
Northfield,	1, 993	141¼	2, 567	66¼	1, 200½	......	....	45	563	473¼	12, 801½	113⅜	8, 471	6	410
Southfield,	4, 614	209¼	4, 673	23	356	5	20	8	122	296	8, 095	53¼	2, 972	......	....
Westfield,	4, 482¾	335¾	7, 331½	65½	802	21½	607	11¼	131	651⅝	18, 629	103⅞	6, 219	1	....
Total,	11335¾	741½	15, 991½	204¾	3, 131½	26½	627	79¼	1, 325	1, 555⅝	43, 037½	315½	21, 739	7	410

ROCKLAND COUNTY.—(Continued.)

Towns.	Winter Wheat. Bushels harvested.	Oats. Acres sown.	Oats. Bushels harvested.	Rye. Acres sown.	Rye. Bushels harvested.	Barley. Acres sown.	Barley. Bushels harvested.	Buckwheat. Acres sown.	Buckwheat. Bushels harvested.	Corn. Acres planted.	Corn. Bushels harvested.	Potatoes. Acres planted.	Potatoes. Bushels harvested.	Peas. Acres sown.	Peas. Bushels harvested.
Clarkstown,	736	700	9, 729	1, 077¼	10, 846	2⅝	11	720	3, 152	1, 217½	17, 563	247¼	7, 956½	1	13
Haverstraw,	361½	165½	1, 981	344¼	4, 026	......	....	214¼	633	312½	6, 637	94¾	3, 974	......	....
Orangetown,	512	337½	5, 389	486½	5, 543	......	....	115½	729	582¾	11, 221	355	11, 726	1	36
Ramapo,	1, 336¼	760	11, 069	3, 415¾	11, 185½	½	3	867¼	4, 208¼	1, 345¾	16, 452	526	23, 567	......	....
Total,	2, 945¾	1, 963	28, 168	5, 323¾	31, 600½	3⅛	14	1. 917	8, 722¼	3, 458½	51, 873	1, 223	47, 223½	2	49

ST. LAWRENCE COUNTY.—(Continued.)

Towns.	Winter Wheat. Bushels harvested.	Oats. Acres sown.	Oats. Bushels harvested.	Rye. Acres sown.	Rye. Bushels harvested.	Barley. Acres sown.	Barley. Bushels harvested.	Buckwheat. Acres sown.	Buckwheat. Bushels harvested.	Corn. Acres planted.	Corn. Bushels harvested.	Potatoes. Acres planted.	Potatoes. Bushels harvested.	Peas. Acres sown.	Peas. Bushels harvested.
Brasher,	1, 254	819	12, 366	59	415	11	102	128½	1, 063	549	6, 612	439	26, 317	118	1, 616
Canton,	1, 509	1, 554	28, 689	27	339	172½	2, 469	61	365	670½	11, 079	547	36, 454	309¼	4, 437
Colton,	23	337½	4, 297	58	436	......	....	20½	90	178	2, 442	123½	8, 434	9	121
De Kalb,	833	1, 333	20, 620	20	187	147½	2, 209	14	105½	465	7, 152	288	15, 495	198	2, 390
De Peyster,	550	774½	13, 632	18½	188	74½	1, 270	....	....	118	2, 018	140	7, 985	227	2, 623
Edwards,	21⅓	421½	7, 805	184	1, 509	8½	69	29	248	352	5, 508	161	12, 640	82½	885
Fine,	......	96	904	39½	352	......	....	62	545	119½	2, 008	49½	3, 546	38	50
Fowler,	135	754	15, 236	103	956	46	859	38	351	278	4, 505	66½	9, 988	102½	2, 169
Gouverneur,	585	1, 223	24, 378	85½	948	153½	2, 439	33	280	372	5, 853	279	16, 653	317½	3, 878
Hammond,	1, 332	1, 099	19, 909	19	370	23	3, 698	5	55	224	4, 379	143	6, 576	606	7, 260
Hermon,	111	732	9, 302	13	53	131	2, 132	7½	67	308	5, 557	137	8, 057	144½	1, 757
Hopkinton,	24	294	5, 218	385	3, 232	7	93	72	367	542½	7, 128	362	24, 046	59½	696
Lawrence,	79	561	9, 966	168½	1, 416	10	164	87	643	417	8, 630	662½	50, 285	54½	801

(Continued on page 298.)

OTSEGO COUNTY.—(Continued.)

TOWNS.	BEANS.		TURNIPS.		FLAX.			HEMP.		HOPS.		TOBACCO.		APPLE ORCHARDS	
	Acres planted.	Bushels harvested.	Acres sown.	Bushels harvested.	Acres sown.	Pounds of lint.	Bushels of seed.	Acres sown.	Tons of hemp.	Acres planted.	Pounds harvested.	Acres planted.	Pounds harvested.	Bushels of apples.	Barrels of cider.
Otsego,	6	80	½	50	24½	10, 247	179			611⅝	469, 475			36, 860	457
Pittsfield,	6	105	5	1, 033	3⅝	663	19¼			58½	17, 331			11, 780	171⅜
Plainfield,	13¼	302½	¼	2	¼	500	1½			16	16, 025		8	19, 756	305¾
Richfield,	1¼	64½		41	¼	30				190½	17, 561		100	26, 176	431
Roseboom,	2¼	63½		290	22¼	30	162			127½	123, 807			11, 236	241
Springfield,	3½	110½		23	14¾	39, 050	214			773⅜	880, 828			25, 292	506
Unadilla,	1¾	170¼	⅝	775						15	8, 345			25, 741	385
Westford,	½	10	3⅛	1, 205	13½	2, 987	122			63	56, 040			18, 310	215
Worcester,	2½	82	4⅝	1, 970	3	215	9½			43¼	42, 872			13, 955	183
Total,	119¾	2, 811½	69⅝	19, 091	386⅜	98, 504⅝	1, 424¼			4, 132⅞	3122258½	½	543	601, 196	8. 880

PUTNAM COUNTY.—(Continued.)

TOWNS.	Beans, acres planted.	Beans, bushels harvested.	Turnips, acres sown.	Turnips, bushels harvested.	Flax, acres sown.	Flax, pounds of lint.	Flax, bushels of seed.	Hemp, acres sown.	Hemp, tons of hemp.	Hops, acres planted.	Hops, pounds harvested.	Tobacco, acres planted.	Tobacco, pounds harvested.	Bushels of apples.	Barrels of cider.
Carmel,														8, 616	102½
Kent,		20½	1	483										4, 091	100½
Patterson,	3	8	5¾	885										3, 321	185
Phillipstown,		7	15	1, 447										3, 890	112
Putnam Valley,	7½	175	34⅜	3, 146							20			5, 159	33
South East,	9⅜		46⅜	2, 527										2, 081	281½
Total,	19⅝	210½	102½	8, 488							20			27, 158	814½

QUEENS COUNTY.—(Continued.)

TOWNS.	Beans, acres planted.	Beans, bushels harvested.	Turnips, acres sown.	Turnips, bushels harvested.	Flax, acres sown.	Flax, pounds of lint.	Flax, bushels of seed.	Hemp, acres sown.	Hemp, tons of hemp.	Hops, acres planted.	Hops, pounds harvested.	Tobacco, acres planted.	Tobacco, pounds harvested.	Bushels of apples.	Barrels of cider.
Flushing,	3	60	52	8, 970										955	17
Hempstead,	28½	1, 200½	34	3, 855	½	300	1				9			100	
Jamaica,			76¼	13, 490										51	12
Newtown,	169	20, 800	310½	43, 550										448	
No. Hempstead,	2½	211	55	8, 543							16			1, 205	
Oyster Bay,		11	35	6, 136										587	
Total,	203	22, 282½	562¾	84, 544	½	300	1				25			3, 346	29

RENSSELAER COUNTY.—(Continued.)

TOWNS.	Beans, acres planted.	Beans, bushels harvested.	Turnips, acres sown.	Turnips, bushels harvested.	Flax, acres sown.	Flax, pounds of lint.	Flax, bushels of seed.	Hemp, acres sown.	Hemp, tons of hemp.	Hops, acres planted.	Hops, pounds harvested.	Tobacco, acres planted.	Tobacco, pounds harvested.	Bushels of apples.	Barrels of cider.
Berlin,	7	411	⅞	182	7	935	40							15, 375	429
Brunswick,	20	288	10⅞	1, 826	71	22, 750	575							11, 232	284
Clinton,	¼	100	½	25										4, 990	262
Grafton,	12¾	149	14⅝	1, 453	15½	2, 858	104							4. 780	88
Greenbush,															
Hoosick,	153¾	1, 725	3½	616	954½	266, 050	8. 357½							5, 694	192
Lansingburgh,	1	23	1½	72										1, 550	70
Nassau,	12⅜	160	½	205										12, 634	468
No'th Greenbush,	1	18	6½	1, 700										3, 959	135
Petersburgh,	164	2, 381			238	44, 000	1, 458							10, 338	271
Pittstown,	26½	330	4¼	260	921	266, 120	6, 895							6, 757	174
Poestenkill,	5	47	4	240							15			4, 896	212
Sand Lake,	5¾	44	5⅞	287										10, 593	417
Schaghticoke,			9	1, 425	193	70, 067	1, 837							4, 740	214
Schodack,	9	195	2¾	666						3	1, 600			17, 682	716
Stephentown,	6	78	2¼	1, 035										15, 611	432
Troy city,	¾	30	20	1, 990										410	
Total,	425⅛	5, 979	87½	11, 982	2, 400	672, 780	19, 266½			3	1, 615			131, 241	4, 364

RICHMOND COUNTY.—(Continued.)

TOWNS.	Beans, acres planted.	Beans, bushels harvested.	Turnips, acres sown.	Turnips, bushels harvested.	Flax, acres sown.	Flax, pounds of lint.	Flax, bushels of seed.	Hemp, acres sown.	Hemp, tons of hemp.	Hops, acres planted.	Hops, pounds harvested.	Tobacco, acres planted.	Tobacco, pounds harvested.	Bushels of apples.	Barrels of cider.
Castleton,			5½	448											
Northfield,	¼	25	15¼	1, 243										28	
Southfield,			6	783											
Westfield,	1¼	141¾	12½	2, 007											
Total,	1½	166¾	39¼	4, 481										28	

ROCKLAND COUNTY.—(Continued.)

TOWNS.	Beans, acres planted.	Beans, bushels harvested.	Turnips, acres sown.	Turnips, bushels harvested.	Flax, acres sown.	Flax, pounds of lint.	Flax, bushels of seed.	Hemp, acres sown.	Hemp, tons of hemp.	Hops, acres planted.	Hops, pounds harvested.	Tobacco, acres planted.	Tobacco, pounds harvested.	Bushels of apples.	Barrels of cider.
Clarkstown,	¼	4	16⅝	3, 111							3			1, 015	3½
Haverstraw,			9½	1, 498										65	
Orangetown,	¼	9	8	1, 520										388	1
Ramapo,	5⅜	50	30⅛	4, 663										1, 785	42½
Total,	5⅞	63	64¼	10, 792							3			3, 253	47

ST. LAWRENCE COUNTY.—(Continued.)

TOWNS.	Beans, acres planted.	Beans, bushels harvested.	Turnips, acres sown.	Turnips, bushels harvested.	Flax, acres sown.	Flax, pounds of lint.	Flax, bushels of seed.	Hemp, acres sown.	Hemp, tons of hemp.	Hops, acres planted.	Hops, pounds harvested.	Tobacco, acres planted.	Tobacco, pounds harvested.	Bushels of apples.	Barrels of cider.
Brasher,	13	215	1	434	2	16				2½	1, 200			200	
Canton,	27⅞	340	3⅛	929						16	9, 514			3, 546	2½
Colton,	5	127	⅞	98	¼	1, 000				2	800				
De Kalb,	9½	66	1½	90							200				
De Peyster,	2¼	19	⅜	18						8	4, 450			1, 173	
Edwards,	22	125	¼	30										8	
Fine,	4	27													
Fowler,	2½	17												165	
Gouverneur,	9	128	¾	70						¼	140			410	
Hammond,	4	39								19	5, 831			2, 342	29
Hermon,	11	115	¾	25										832	
Hopkinton,	30½	280	5	1. 349										3, 566	22
Lawrence,	22	268	¼	50						16	7, 050			1, 107	

(Continued on page 299.)

OTSEGO COUNTY.—(Continued.)

TOWNS.	Market Gardens: Acres cultivated.	Market Gardens: Value of products.	Pounds of maple sugar made.	Gallons of maple molasses made.	Gallons of wine made.	Pounds of honey collected.	Pounds of wax collected.	Silk: Pounds of cocoons.	Neat Cattle: Under one year old.	Neat Cattle: Over one y'r, exclusive of working oxen & cows.	Neat Cattle: Working oxen.	Neat Cattle: Cows.	Number of cattle killed for beef.	Pounds of butter.	Pounds of cheese.
Otsego,			8, 279	158		4, 708	297		370	893	132	1, 854	250	134, 801	94, 807
Pittsfield,			9, 260	78		1, 477	75¾		305	649	183	1, 160	69	104, 705	22, 500
Plainfield,			3, 661	147		2, 776	159		139	350	46	1, 223	77	57 755	25, 710
Richfield,		$42	3, 207	91		2, 775	132		282	487	48	1, 745	129	70, 375	451, 700
Roseboom,			9, 400	258		7, 925	414		280	587	138	1, 107	128	115, 160	4, 010
Springfield,		12	2, 935	97		4, 543	238½		449	745	74	1, 673	231	157, 430	173, 479
Unadilla,			2, 116	75		3, 561	143		561	1, 153	340	1, 550	273	143, 184	31, 749
Westford,			7, 974	140		4, 385	76		296	533	80	1, 118	56	109, 780	19, 560
Worcester,	6	50	9, 060	243	5	4, 248	131		448	804	103	1, 587	133	183, 759	1, 925
Total,	10¼	439	193, 206	4, 099	43	93, 020	4, 665¾		8, 711	17, 432	2, 942	34, 713	3, 537	3, 075, 206	1, 638, 493

PUTNAM COUNTY.—(Continued.)

TOWNS.	Acres cultivated.	Value of products.	Pounds of maple sugar made.	Gallons of maple molasses made.	Gallons of wine made.	Pounds of honey collected.	Pounds of wax collected.	Pounds of cocoons.	Under one year old.	Over one y'r.	Working oxen.	Cows.	Number of cattle killed for beef.	Pounds of butter.	Pounds of cheese.
Carmel,	2	504				2, 342	30		222	435	463	2, 113	172	121, 479	
Kent,	¾	60	1, 017	34	5	2, 327	112½		348	512	305	1, 493	208	75, 856	
Patterson,						1, 578½	94		436	302	1, 441		194	61, 400	3, 375
Phillipstown,	2½	210	205	108		2, 310	93		340	539	266	853	450	65, 591	
Putnam Valley,	15	567	2			1, 823	11½		258	491	332	935	125	73, 070	100
Southeast,	1½	125				2, 857	118		144	429	393	2, 457	151	96, 300	
Total,	21¾	1, 466	1, 224	142	5	13, 237½	459		1, 748	2, 708	3, 200	7, 851	1, 300	493, 696	3, 475

QUEENS COUNTY.—(Continued.)

TOWNS.	Acres cultivated.	Value of products.	Pounds of maple sugar made.	Gallons of maple molasses made.	Gallons of wine made.	Pounds of honey collected.	Pounds of wax collected.	Pounds of cocoons.	Under one year old.	Over one y'r.	Working oxen.	Cows.	Number of cattle killed for beef.	Pounds of butter.	Pounds of cheese.
Flushing,	205	17740				888	52		122	117	315	878	287	42, 793	
Hempstead,	7¾	1785				2, 086	106		522	480	381	2, 542	140	155, 048	
Jamaica,	734½	62138				50			75	138	112	852	360	46, 285	
Newton,	2, 222½	255780				40			43	27	89	1, 163	51	17, 416	
North Hemptead,						922	74		237	244	408	1, 611	164	61, 494½	240
Oyster Bay,	17	60	1, 771			2, 003	44		438	717	621	2, 194	212	118, 947	525
Total,	3, 186¾	337503	1, 771			5, 989	276		1, 437	1, 723	1, 926	9, 240	1, 164	441, 983½	765

RENSSELAER COUNTY.—(Continued.)

TOWNS.	Acres cultivated.	Value of products.	Pounds of maple sugar made.	Gallons of maple molasses made.	Gallons of wine made.	Pounds of honey collected.	Pounds of wax collected.	Pounds of cocoons.	Under one year old.	Over one y'r.	Working oxen.	Cows.	Number of cattle killed for beef.	Pounds of butter.	Pounds of cheese.
Berlin,			13, 925	132		5, 343	174		187	386	103	1, 187	167	59, 071	250, 646
Brunswick,	98	9, 657	80	15	14	1, 894	95		269	373	171	1, 538	331	112, 757	125
Clinton,	106	11, 790			28	585	40		106	309	86	1, 101	51	53, 765	
Grafton,			1, 081	102		1, 346	86		223	374	188	734	173	65, 209	4, 070
Greenbush,															
Hoosick,	¾	30	210	71	126	3, 039	203		465	724	266	1, 243	226	69, 325	36, 590
Lansingburg,	2½	1, 000				195	2		25	108	45	290	2, 694	10, 173	
Nassau,	3	103	278	21	431	3, 207	262½		272	628	276	1, 188	226	124, 100	8, 725
North Greenbush,	38	3, 724	1, 025			705	35		90	165	49	999	75	64, 590	
Petersburgh,						892	72		205	483	92	770	116	45, 543	82, 820
Pittstown,				7		5, 360	268		480	676	348	1, 772	467	158, 529	29, 516
Poestenkill,	1	150		6		1, 878	37		191	242	108	667	82	65, 305	2, 780
Sandlake,			233	2	52	2, 277	107		161	339	146	997	347	90, 848	1, 072
Schaghticoke,			25	4	32	2, 670	123		334	642	279	1, 137	283	95, 098	
Schodack,			18	9¼	109	3, 259½	280		201	436	298	1, 575	197	161, 530	3, 563
Stephentown,			1, 080	31		964	56	12	250	654	200	1, 305	254	107, 940	118, 555
Troy city,	125¼	8, 211			10	70			15	20	49	361	2, 021	7, 955	
Total,	374½	34, 665	17, 955	400¼	802	33, 684½	1, 840½	12	3, 474	6, 559	2, 704	16, 864	7, 710	1, 291, 738	538, 462

RICHMOND COUNTY.—(Continued.)

TOWNS.	Acres cultivated.	Value of products.	Pounds of maple sugar made.	Gallons of maple molasses made.	Gallons of wine made.	Pounds of honey collected.	Pounds of wax collected.	Pounds of cocoons.	Under one year old.	Over one y'r.	Working oxen.	Cows.	Number of cattle killed for beef.	Pounds of butter.	Pounds of cheese.
Castleton,	5½	1, 150							51	40	46	132	6	2, 595	
Northfield,	102¾	8, 970				200	13		58	96	76	399	35	12, 525	
Southfield,						275	9		78	98	91	212	50	8, 945	
Westfield,	54	6, 620			64				115	125	187	446	11	300	
Total,	162¼	16, 740			64	475	22		302	359	400	1, 189	102	24, 365	

ROCKLAND COUNTY.—(Continued.)

TOWNS.	Acres cultivated.	Value of products.	Pounds of maple sugar made.	Gallons of maple molasses made.	Gallons of wine made.	Pounds of honey collected.	Pounds of wax collected.	Pounds of cocoons.	Under one year old.	Over one y'r.	Working oxen.	Cows.	Number of cattle killed for beef.	Pounds of butter.	Pounds of cheese.
Clarkstown,						4, 369	53½		187	465	198	1, 111	164	80, 033	2, 500
Haverstraw,	12	1, 500	5		497	235	76		174	242	83	1, 647	53	40, 070	
Orangetown,	9	790				781	19		60	194	96	732	565	35, 328	
Ramapo,	1½	375				3, 282	26		180	415	196	1, 218	203	110, 575	
Total,	22½	2, 665	5		497	8, 667	174½		601	1, 316	573	4, 708	985	266, 006	2, 500

ST. LAWRENCE COUNTY.—(Continued.)

TOWNS.	Acres cultivated.	Value of products.	Pounds of maple sugar made.	Gallons of maple molasses made.	Gallons of wine made.	Pounds of honey collected.	Pounds of wax collected.	Pounds of cocoons.	Under one year old.	Over one y'r.	Working oxen.	Cows.	Number of cattle killed for beef.	Pounds of butter.	Pounds of cheese.
Brasher,			5, 725		40	1, 568	37		481	945	319	1, 633	98	135, 320	24, 982
Canton,			40, 336	142	17	3, 904	192		897	1, 709	385	3, 927	330	30, 840	252, 988
Colton,			59, 145	23		1, 010	51		31	125	62	369	5	10, 340	950
De Kalb,			23, 867	108		1, 816	125		484	1, 155	322	2, 426	301	206, 370	233, 965
De Peyster,			3, 910						289	529	18	1, 442	35	136, 950	12, 200
Edwards,			19, 936	102		1, 134	78		207	582	125	1, 017	82	92, 909	26, 023
Fine,			9, 602	198		90	2		30	69	57	109	21	10, 900	
Fowler,			4, 680	8		2, 265	63		379	753	90	2, 072	60	159, 870	128, 044
Gouverneur,			34, 773	127		1, 727	104		647	764	75	2, 924	143	278, 023	254, 561
Hammond,			5, 464	84		2, 386	129		355	853	58	1, 421	129	112, 821	52, 750
Hermon,			14, 786	254		1, 690	65		320	662	542	1, 753	115	136, 615	155, 500
Hopkinton,			20, 325	95		1, 090	96		268	599	164	948	80	82, 627	15, 190
Lawrence,			24, 660			2, 095	104		449	1, 005	211	1, 621	136	140, 525	31, 725

(Continued on page 300.)

OTSEGO COUNTY.—(Continued.)

TOWNS.	Gallons of milk sold.	Horses.	Mules.	SWINE. Under 6 months	Over 6 months.	SHEEP. Number of sheep.	Number of fleeces.	Pounds of wool.	POULTRY. Value of poultry sold.	Value of eggs sold.	DOMESTIC MANUFACTURES. Yards of fulled cloth made.	Yards of flannel made.	Yards of linen made.	Yards of cotton and mixed cloths.
Otsego,	50	1,009	2	649	820	8,220	6,417	21,615¾	$1,413	$2,041	419	493	170	329
Pittsfield,	....	438	....	438	292	4,576	3,198	9,759	782	1,243	19	153	152	226
Plainfield,	....	410	....	353	312	3,347	3,671	13,033⅓	1,284	705	64	302	95½	229
Richfield,	480	487	....	363	297	2,414	3,971	14,131	695	452	12	104	75	48
Roseboom,	....	528	....	328	448	1,875	1,849	6,331	590	1,569	247	284	448	15
Springfield,	....	1,019	4	564	519	3,425	2,004	8,224½	533	818	79	291½	228	4,639
Unadilla,	1,920	558	2	590	622	7,867	5,345	17,414½	1,244	2,238	192	427	153	327
Westford,	....	534	....	423	457	3,703	2,374	7,159	435	1,561	143	143	333	43
Worcester,	....	673	....	713	552	2,773	1,589	5,490	621	1,268	593	1,242	619	580
Total,	3,440	14,652	17	11,210	11,158	109,937	82,516	278,705¼	23,699	41,304	5,295	9,268½	7,419	10,797
PUTNAM COUNTY.—(Continued.)														
Carmel,	423,536	458	....	1,374	473	2,171	1,396	4,484	2,290	1,618	....	....	....	....
Kent,	312,296	208	....	524	242	1,420	823	3,611	1,991	1,901	31	300	....	219
Patterson,	278,617	268	....	715	256	539	649	2,156	1,661	1,042	....	....	....	....
Phillipstown,	45,808	357	....	710	484	698	314	1,030	2,696	3,331	....	....	....	....
Putnam Valley,	4,800	313	....	769	375	822	790	2,711	1,623	3,723	36	585	20	5
Southeast,	823,853	334	1	598	477	154	108	474¼	1,639	1,104	25	....	....	....
Total,	1888,910	1,938	1	4,690	2,307	5,804	4,080	14,466¼	11.900	12,719	92	885	20	224
QUEENS COUNTY.—(Continued.)														
Flushing,	40,643	989	34	722	1,202	862	499	1,734	4,053	3,000	....	....	....	....
Hempstead,	15,257	1,651	10	1,078	1,841	548	371	1,146	25,152	17,767	....	....	....	....
Jamaica,	55,850	797	35	323	603	....	....	....	3,875	2,309	....	....	....	....
Newton,	70,022	1,397	35	641	568	....	....	....	775	458	....	....	....	....
North Hempstead,	337,949	1,236	43	1,675	1,322	2,777	2,049	6,033⅓	11,608	8,991	....	....	....	....
Oyster Bay,	46,600	1,884	21	2,284	1,969	5,527	4,165	11,679	23,651	12,570	....	....	....	....
Total,	566,321	7,954	178	6,723	7,505	9,714	7,084	20,592½	69,114	45,095	....	....	....	....
RENSSELAER COUNTY.—(Continued.)														
Berlin,	614	449	....	401	364	3,630	2,594	8,527	1,281	924	40	25	111	120
Brunswick,	130,676	973	....	1,595	972	1,269	1,274	4,591	2,020	4,733	180	120	40	114
Clinton,	514,605	492	....	660	468	632	447	1,622	1,125	2,437	103	322	....	109
Grafton,	....	368	....	233	304	1,017	773	2,278½	1,141	681	15	232	67	40
Greenbush,	....	....	....	....	....	....	....	....	....	....	....	....	....	....
Hoosick,	360	863	....	1,664	910	22,394	25,881	84,519	4,186	2,338	79	46	174	....
Lansingburgh,	13,000	314	....	306	384	651	424	1,454	310	383	....	....	....	....
Nassau,	....	644	1	1,283	555	3,458	1,830	5,990	3,035	5,301	380	376	37	185
North Greenbush,	252,085	445	....	429	434	252	182	815	979	3,657	....	....	....	....
Petersburgh,	....	505	....	390	438	5,708	4,783	14,832	2,305	874	....	....	....	....
Pittstown,	540	1,050	....	2,004	979	11,340	9,587	31,805	5,564	3,972	24	83	232	22
Poestenkill,	....	428	....	571	307	804	593	2,141	685	2,393	253	402	....	60
Sandlake,	....	535	....	801	417	742	687	2.618	1,233	3,381	47	98	15	173
Schaghticoke,	....	712	....	2,117	947	5,910	5,669	8,227	1,939	2,522	....	....	....	....
Schodack,	5,900	1,036	....	2,149	962	3,977	2,933	10,434	3,799	8,564	85	318	30	152
Stephentown,	....	472	8	555	401	2,707	1,798	7,493	1,581	1,212	....	15	....	25
Troy city,	108,525	898	1	346	661	118	103	410	257	432	....	....	....	....
Total,	1026,305	10,184	10	15.504	9,503	64,609	59,558	187.756½	31,440	43.804	1,206	2,037	706	1,000
RICHMOND COUNTY.—(Continued.)														
Castleton,	720	101	6	96	87	2	....	....	100	480	....	....	....	....
Northfield,	4,025	229	1	174	222	....	....	....	1,373	3,357	....	....	....	....
Southfield,	15,760	135	5	122	169	25	20	100	289	1,085	....	....	....	....
Westfield,	14,400	380	14	271	585	30	18	60	665	1,530	....	....	....	....
Total,	34,905	845	26	663	1,063	57	38	160	2,427	6,452	....	....	....	....
ROCKLAND COUNTY.—(Continued.)														
Clarkstown,	49,533	677	32	505	371	97	86	317	2,089	3,268	....	....	....	....
Haverstraw,	20,700	1,873	34	282	201	4	3	12	253	371	....	....	....	....
Orangetown,	147,747	418	34	264	251	82	85	273	877	1,372	....	....	....	....
Ramapo,	60,680	747	70	618	693	743	286	983	2,165	2,337	....	....	....	....
Total,	278,660	3,715	170	1.669	1,516	926	460	1,585	5,384	7,348	....	....	....	....
ST. LAWRENCE COUNTY.—(Continued.)														
Brasher,	....	664	....	329	525	2,363	2,191	7,111	199	212	551	533	169	2,115
Canton,	....	1,906	....	902	900	6,165	5,624	20,298	494	1,045	942	2,103	640	829
Colton,	....	135	....	25	106	373	425	1,441	26	4	114	97	....	45
De Kalb,	....	598	....	380	461	1,281	1,269	4,484	46	203	779	687	165	2,258
De Peyster,	....	499	....	233	247	4,334	3,487	10,941	....	....	562	1,061	9	....
Edwards,	....	320	....	180	266	1,490	951	2,806	91	64	492	721	15	1,337
Fine,	....	32	....	25	74	147	126	351	....	....	57	85	26	293
Fowler,	....	529	....	299	339	1,509	1,039	3,786	143	117	141	586	60	140
Gouverneur,	....	679	....	406	424	2,735	2,327	7,582	155	295	461	821	10	584
Hammond,	400	770	....	308	522	3,441	3,156	11,070	89	219	825	650	30	1,002
Hermon,	....	406	....	170	248	998	904	3,019	64	200	561	735	70	767
Hopkinton,	....	450	....	449	296	2,919	2,487	9,671	344	478	192	745	....	337
Lawrence,	....	590	....	250	405	3,328	3,048	9,969	139	654	254	491	137	941

(Continued on page 301.)

ST. LAWRENCE COUNTY.—(Continued.)

TOWNS.	ACRES.		CASH VALUE.			Acres plowed the year previous.	Acres in fallow the year previous.	Acres in pasture the year previous.	MEADOW.			SPRING WHEAT.		WINTER WHEAT.
	Improved.	Unimproved.	Of farm.	Of stock.	Of tools and implements.				Acres.	Tons of hay.	Bushels of grass seed.	Acres sown.	Bushels harvested.	Acres sown.
Lisbon,	36, 959	24, 491	$1, 275, 799	$244, 785	$52, 009	2, 029	344	15, 772	11, 269	10, 681	426	1, 996	22610	223
Louisville,	15, 367	23, 881	452, 295	98, 205	12, 609	3, 314	129	7, 005	4, 557	4. 686	221½	882	11945	172½
Macomb,	10, 435	29, 765	360, 259	63, 821	12, 788	1, 783	79	3, 699	3, 780	2, 536	77	572½	6288	169½
Madrid,	32, 788	28, 551	1, 288, 901	204, 856	50, 490	7, 029	337½	16, 377	10, 636	9, 454	218	1, 775½	18540	129½
Massena,	19, 620	9, 037	500, 540	138, 583	20, 930	3, 016	74	9, 846	5, 943	6, 501	123	924½	13560	237
Morristown,	19, 407	24, 691	1, 007, 985	145, 550	48, 460	4, 860	630½	8, 126	4, 673	5, 133	222½	6, 522½	15882	856
Norfolk,	12, 286	9, 459	423, 735	64, 479	18, 115	2, 101	29	5, 106	4, 091	3, 738	30	569½	5364	37
Oswegatchie,	26, 669	12, 496	1, 263, 327	166, 073	59, 462	5, 663	671½	11, 237	7, 507	7, 704	155½	2, 034	17109	596½
Parishville,	20, 528	42, 602	638, 233	113, 992	36, 150	4, 102	35	9, 309	6, 234	4, 584	69	1, 084½	11505	18
Pierrepont,	10, 339	115, 121	471, 928	64, 508	17, 861	1, 965	27	4, 334	3, 278	2, 466	16½	417	3903	3½
Pitcairn,	3, 900	20, 767	94, 373	20, 005	4, 669	1, 182	6	1, 201	981	554	13	135	736	362
Potsdam,	40, 297	20, 521	1, 835, 515	290, 888	68, 840	5, 692	193½	18, 079	15, 760	13, 397	150½	1, 670	16029	123
Rossie,	8, 482	12, 911	259, 840	60, 472	10, 949	1, 608	131	3, 576	2, 472	2, 055	43	566½	8082	56½
Russell,	12, 080	38, 068	427, 600	86, 680	20, 542	2, 043½	14	5, 365	4, 545	3, 912	101½	592½	5289	24½
Stockholm,	30, 846	21, 763	1, 024, 209	183, 627	48, 947	5, 458	214	12, 678	10, 922	8, 378	65	1, 297	11764	107
Total,	499, 554	885, 531	18, 117, 429	3, 144, 908	751, 437	86, 623½	3, 981	216, 985	163, 623	139, 400	3, 220½	32623	295464	3, 991½

SARATOGA COUNTY.

TOWNS.	Improved.	Unimproved.	Of farm.	Of stock.	Of tools and implements.	Acres plowed the year previous.	Acres in fallow the year previous.	Acres in pasture the year previous.	Meadow acres.	Tons of hay.	Bushels of grass seed.	Spring wheat acres sown.	Bushels harvested.	Winter wheat acres sown.
Ballston,	16, 177	2, 996½	932, 957	106, 421	33, 666	5, 792	18	6, 397	3, 139½	3, 236½	43½	8½	100	515½
Charlton,	15, 166	3, 156	687, 100	84, 950	25, 761	5, 061	....	5, 027	3, 457	3, 113	28½	55½	672½	226
Clifton Park,	23, 541	5, 485	1, 523, 785	138, 651	41, 075	7, 781½	3, 019	5, 764	3, 750	3, 019	110¼	49½	213	353
Corinth,	13, 071	10, 564	277, 795	66, 663	14, 567	2. 680½	....	7, 300	2, 975	1, 885½	96	47¾	216	.....
Day,	7, 017	17, 047	119, 080	40, 906	6, 414	1, 160	98	2, 505	2, 378	1, 706	19	13	30	.....
Edinburgh,	13, 956	25, 028	253, 311	60, 209	8, 442	2, 018¾	9	7, 767¼	3, 927	2, 902	.....	66	760	.....
Galway,	27, 760¼	172	666, 000	115, 770	37, 495	6, 001¼	5	15, 299	7, 054	4, 817	161	71¼	747	156¾
Greenfield,	28, 644½	12, 791½	795, 035	126, 074	44. 790	5, 620½	104	14, 603½	6, 182½	4, 515	205	42½	347½	25
Hadley,	7, 691	13, 498	140, 911	40, 075	6, 962	1, 883	143	3, 121	2, 003	1, 378	17½	26	216	15
Halfmoon,	16, 550	2, 837	975, 700	120, 055	39, 050	4, 690	1, 814	4, 131	2, 659	2, 815½	11	16	187	265
Malta,	14, 434¾	2, 983¾	765, 710	83, 740	15, 706	4, 073¾	1, 578¼	5, 040½	2, 500¼	2, 427¼	33¼	14	93½	232½
Milton,	18, 366½	3, 885	766, 055	138, 041	29, 746	5, 456¼	1, 059½	4, 881	2, 780¾	3, 075	107½	44	272	237
Moreau,	18, 291	6, 304½	648. 089	76, 364	24, 616	6, 026¼	414	6, 456	2, 209¼	2, 018	204½	126	1, 010½	142
Northumberland,	13, 133	5, 925½	736, 435	100, 069	25, 933	5, 466½	336	4, 998	2, 305	2, 632¼	96½	37	559	102½
Providence,	8, 694	5, 401	185, 995	40, 308	13, 940	1, 894	22	4, 653	2, 105	1, 586	2	126¾	1, 163	3
Saratoga,	19, 281½	5, 089½	1, 107, 796	142, 882	41, 519	7, 823½	166	5, 301	3, 555	4, 161	141	16¾	132	455
Saratoga Springs,	11, 740½	6, 386	870, 000	112, 512	27, 197	4, 652	593½	4, 046¾	1, 393¼	1, 599¾	34½	13	98	87½
Stillwater,	22, 401	3, 963	1, 231, 490	151, 013	30, 350	6, 987	511	6, 168	3, 784	3, 544	108½	87½	959	469
Waterford,	3, 523¾	342	353, 490	32, 750	10, 345	1, 020	201	873	660	663	3½	10½	136	41
Wilton,	16, 288½	5, 994	489, 645	64, 973	18, 609	5, 323	592	7, 360	1, 785	1, 650	91	19	162	72
Total,	315, 728¼	139, 849¼	13, 526, 379	1, 842, 426	496, 183	91, 410¾	10, 683¼	121, 692	60, 602½	52, 743¾	1, 514½	890½	8, 074	3, 397¾

SCHENECTADY COUNTY.

TOWNS.	Improved.	Unimproved.	Of farm.	Of stock.	Of tools and implements.	Acres plowed the year previous.	Acres in fallow the year previous.	Acres in pasture the year previous.	Meadow acres.	Tons of hay.	Bushels of grass seed.	Spring wheat acres sown.	Bushels harvested.	Winter wheat acres sown.
Duanesburgh,	33, 911½	10, 827	1, 275, 437	200, 223	49, 893	11, 070½	87	10, 232	7, 654¾	6, 233	552¾	456	3, 613½	80½
Glenville,	22, 341½	7, 159¼	1, 343, 682	158, 759	59, 406	11, 056	271	6, 025½	4, 455½	3, 718	86	185¼	1, 978	300½
Niskayuna,	7, 922	2, 549	579, 323	51, 472	19, 011	2, 852	137	1, 495	1, 638	1, 716	8½	13	130	67
Princetown,	12, 029	3, 421	507, 596	69, 189	20, 924	3, 949	99	2, 942	2, 478	2, 163	83	96	46	147
Rotterdam,	16, 729½	7, 693	1, 136, 290	108, 991	45, 320	8, 025	763	3, 552	2, 314	2, 328	78	65	610	78¾
Schenectady,	515	34	68, 400	8, 102	1, 250	382	10	95	26	27½	.....	.....	.....	.....
Total,	93, 448½	31, 683¼	4, 910, 728	596, 736	195, 804	37, 334½	1, 367	24, 341½	18, 566¼	16, 185½	808¼	815¼	6, 377½	673¾

SCHOHARIE COUNTY.

TOWNS.	Improved.	Unimproved.	Of farm.	Of stock.	Of tools and implements.	Acres plowed the year previous.	Acres in fallow the year previous.	Acres in pasture the year previous.	Meadow acres.	Tons of hay.	Bushels of grass seed.	Spring wheat acres sown.	Bushels harvested.	Winter wheat acres sown.
Blenheim,	9, 864	16, 102	348, 035	74, 027	19, 389	2, 178	568	3, 592	2, 403	1, 940	49½	61	433	253
Broome,	18, 623	8, 375	451, 394	94, 249	24, 044	6, 555	482	6, 631	4, 517	3, 315	177	202	1, 305	35½
Carlisle,	14, 612	6, 243	779, 710	110, 189	26, 663	5, 449½	514	3, 938	3, 366	2, 705	238	215	1, 390	253
Cobleskill,	11, 742	6, 296	728, 010	104, 704	38, 547	4, 963	1, 146	3, 294	2, 697	2, 745	486	130	1, 213	833
Conesville,	12, 907	8, 552	385, 433	78, 119	21, 125	3, 902	235	6, 365	4, 804	3, 130	58	114½	645¼	15½
Esperance,	7, 679½	2, 715¼	386, 845	56, 428	13, 545	3, 810½	78½	2, 119½	1, 719¾	1, 869½	171½	108¼	929½	114½
Fulton,	17, 120½	17, 192	722, 307	140, 271	39, 846	6, 070¼	669	6, 000	3, 863¾	3, 436½	514¼	232½	1, 822	584
Gilboa,	23, 139	13, 398½	578, 955	110, 948	31, 203	5, 529½	679	8, 128½	6, 891	5, 035½	200	187¾	1, 205	80½
Jefferson,	15, 064	8, 045½	530, 127	81, 184	22, 112	3, 093¾	620¾	7, 401½	4, 902½	4, 369	139	211½	1, 319½	95
Middleburgh,	14, 240⅝	11, 609	801, 629	120, 584	34, 422	7, 888½	367	4, 574½	3, 158	2, 819¾	367¾	159¼	1, 242	563½
Richmondville,	14, 207¾	5, 475	585, 940	102, 665	31, 598	5, 253¼	351½	4, 756¾	2, 973	3, 122	272¾	365½	3, 073½	313¾
Schoharie,	9, 401	6, 429	689, 865	82, 288	35, 249	4, 778	242	3, 048	2, 027½	2, 159½	190	72	682	530
Seward,	14, 381	5, 420	816, 295	101, 035	30, 040	5, 109½	607	4, 109	2, 934	3. 213	679½	276	2, 062	379½
Sharon,	19, 297	4, 878	1, 061, 010	128, 440	46, 810	8, 188	639	6, 828	3, 488	2, 881	258	235½	2, 639	619
Summit,	13, 027	6, 040	536, 730	86, 167	20, 277	4, 466	239	4, 988	4, 179	4, 297	185	270¾	1, 914	19
Wright,	12, 599	5, 276	651, 663	87, 391	26, 820	4, 770	419	2, 645	2, 463	1, 737	571	127	1, 200	309
Total,	227, 904⅜	132, 046¼	10, 053, 948	1. 558, 689	461, 690	82, 004¾	7, 856¾	78, 418¾	56, 386½	48, 774¾	4, 557¼	2, 968½	23074¾	4, 997¾

SCHUYLER COUNTY.

TOWNS.	Improved.	Unimproved.	Of farm.	Of stock.	Of tools and implements.	Acres plowed the year previous.	Acres in fallow the year previous.	Acres in pasture the year previous.	Meadow acres.	Tons of hay.	Bushels of grass seed.	Spring wheat acres sown.	Bushels harvested.	Winter wheat acres sown.
Catharines,	18, 160	11, 598	1, 001, 843	132, 992	25, 974	5, 956½	1, 266½	5, 109½	3, 496	2, 737	160½	455¾	4017	1, 566½
Cayuta,	4, 875	7, 168¾	224, 517	36, 656	6, 384	1, 452	231¼	1, 671	1, 218¾	856½	31¾	50¾	426¾	252
Dix,	15, 269	7, 326¾	793, 985	119, 141	32, 927	4, 920	1, 123½	4, 207½	2, 811½	2, 340¾	205	829½	7401½	1, 316
Hector,	45, 904⅛	15, 851	2, 852, 118	336, 670	106, 758	16, 099	2, 071½	11, 931	8, 565	5, 712½	572½	1, 605¼	15516	4, 250¾
Orange,	20, 320¼	11, 304½	755, 104	126, 160	30, 428	7, 342	591½	5, 313	3, 783	3, 075	224½	1, 571	11808	1, 289
Reading,	12, 882½	3, 726½	725, 729	90, 750	21, 302	3, 801	546½	3, 618	2, 185¾	1, 301½	74	409½	2676	1, 228½
Tyrone,	16, 917	6, 023¾	1, 075, 499	131, 989	29, 050	5, 644¾	550½	4, 013⅜	3, 081¾	1, 973	124¼	691	5294	1, 900¼
Total,	134, 336¼	62, 999¼	7, 428, 825	974, 358	252, 823	45, 215¼	6, 381¼	36, 663⅞	25, 141¼	17, 996¼	1, 392½	5, 612¾	33139¼	11803

ST. LAWRENCE COUNTY.—(Continued.)

TOWNS.	Winter Wheat	Oats.		Rye.		Barley.		Buckwheat.		Corn.		Potatoes.		Peas.	
	Bushels harvested.	Acres sown.	Bushels harvested.	Acres sown.	Bushels harvested.	Acres sown.	Bushels harvested.	Acres sown.	Bushels harvested.	Acres planted.	Bushels harvested.	Acres planted.	Bushels harvested.	Acres sown.	Bushels harvested.
Lisbon, ...	940	3, 254	5, 287	66	678	41	760	171	1, 484	769	14, 657	877½	52, 804	423¼	5, 883
Louisville, ...	1, 141	1, 112	20, 531	33	415	27½	430	34	353	446	9, 072	299	18, 053	260½	3, 816
Macomb, ...	1, 388	470	6, 558	15¾	169	71½	786	14½	69	320	2, 584	168	10, 683	167½	1, 801
Madrid, ...	840	3, 095	51, 885	101½	1, 210	22	220	249	2, 205	604	9. 685	681½	46, 055	262	3, 567
Massena, ...	1, 897	869½	19, 201	7	100	15	531	72	466	633½	13, 214	269	20, 542	232½	3, 479
Morristown, ...	3, 208	1, 549	19, 999	63½	946	380½	4, 567	35	154	403½	6, 441	274	9, 811	587½	5, 642
Norfolk, ...	344	604	8, 001	17	112	8	123	54	502	34½	6, 109	252½	16, 968	38	465
Oswegatchie, ...	5, 564	2, 040½	40, 786	33	262	124	1, 699	57	375	448½	9, 177	432	24, 380	375	5, 774
Parishville, ...	125	1, 178	17, 852	354½	3, 854	9½	110	87½	405	895	13, 937	500½	29, 110	78¼	1, 063
Pierrepont, ...	19	479	7, 644	180	2, 081	8	149	29½	120	484	7, 643	195½	12, 328	48	550
Pitcairn, ...	32	338	2, 436	24	114	3	18	41	228	388	8, 068	102	8, 314	25	143
Potsdam, ...	943	1, 596½	23, 906	99	890	75	1, 014	110	712	903½	16, 404	682½	50, 108	33½	3. 011
Rossie, ...	698	502	12, 570	18½	195	45	627	3	25	106	1, 609	112	8, 054	149	2, 357
Russell, ...	229	744½	11, 836	12	114	86½	1, 439	41½	400	563½	10, 513	157½	11, 670	88	1, 268
Stockholm, ...	956	1, 036	16, 227	536½	4, 184	12¾	210	201½	1, 235	1, 162½	18, 609	770½	58, 667	140	1, 521
Total, ...	24780½	28, 866½	437, 041	2, 741¾	25, 725	1, 713¾	28, 187	1, 758	12, 912½	12, 755	220, 593	9, 172	604, 023	5, 234¼	69, 016

SARATOGA COUNTY.—(Continued.)

TOWNS.	Winter Wheat	Oats.		Rye.		Barley.		Buckwheat.		Corn.		Potatoes.		Peas.	
	Bushels harvested.	Acres sown.	Bushels harvested.	Acres sown.	Bushels harvested.	Acres sown.	Bushels harvested.	Acres sown.	Bushels harvested.	Acres planted.	Bushels harvested.	Acres planted.	Bushels harvested.	Acres sown.	Bushels harvested.
Ballston, ...	2, 268	2, 426	58, 928	225½	1, 973	21½	329	707½	6, 601	1, 610	27, 607	337¾	21, 788	21⅝	377
Charlton, ...	1, 574	2, 182	54, 382	93	764	148½	2, 716	813	8, 949½	1, 203½	23, 010	137¾	13, 912	20	442
Clifton Park, ...	1, 129	3, 511	66, 878	2, 573	24, 115	......	....	699	6, 845½	2, 601	38, 617	824	43, 846	13	232
Corinth, ...	......	906½	14, 028	83½	1, 202	3	45	371	2, 425	1, 037	18, 407	307	21, 507	¼	8
Day, ...	......	401	7, 710	33	274	5	31	169	1, 484	421	7, 649	133	11, 292	4	73
Edinburgh, ...	......	790	14, 988	17	214	31	318	307½	2, 918	634½	12, 819	228½	15, 159	3	66
Galway, ...	1, 286	2, 486½	61, 452	105½	1, 047	137	1, 976	947¾	13, 045½	1, 473¾	35, 930	287½	28, 964	10⅛	202
Greenfield, ...	119	2, 122	44, 461	127½	1, 084	......	....	868¼	7, 961	1, 994½	31, 005	556⅛	33, 687	2	18
Hadley, ...	100	665	10, 373	72	618½	......	....	261	1, 671	614	9, 720	177½	10, 531	14½	93
Halfmoon, ...	1, 164	1, 579	47, 562	1, 280	18, 661½	78	1, 103	267	3, 407	1, 368	28, 815	490¾	28, 522	1½	....
Malta, ...	638	1, 731½	36, 840	1, 359	11, 341¾	7	109	596	2, 795	1, 847½	20, 755	377½	19, 083	4¾	44
Milton, ...	2, 371½	1, 940½	44, 050½	571	5, 789	22½	458	1, 105¼	12, 290½	1, 939	31, 184	361	24, 818	53¾	956
Moreau, ...	356	1, 733½	32, 405	912	5, 436	......	....	864½	3, 936½	2, 095½	26, 254	255¾	13, 701	2¼	40
Northumberland	284	2, 474¾	59, 694	631¼	5, 103	5½	52	608⅝	5, 149	1, 787	31, 053	630	39, 589	39½	836
Providence, ...	18	644½	11, 766	2	20	141	1, 319	346½	5, 925	404	10, 985	210	15, 139	......	....
Saratoga, ...	1, 312	2, 567	71, 419	1, 298	16, 357	36	835	860½	8, 938½	1, 814½	38, 813	932	67, 541	75½	1, 759
Saratoga Springs	349	1, 349	13, 621½	724	5, 780	½	5	403¾	3, 270½	1, 360¼	19, 540	379¾	17, 758	17½	245
Stillwater, ...	1, 446	3, 496	41, 753	1, 798	20, 668	21	198	685	5, 338	2, 253	35, 636	575	32, 725	44	625
Waterford, ...	228	501	16, 200	356	3, 931	1	30	66	525	300	6, 250	74½	5, 140	4½	450
Wilton, ...	184	2, 084	35, 709	1, 056	8, 396	......	....	641	5, 407	2, 092	25, 400	470½	22, 970	......	....
Total, ...	14826¼	35, 590½	744. 220	13317¼	132, 774¾	658½	9, 524	11, 588⅛	108, 882½	28, 849¾	479, 449	7, 745½	487. 672	331¼	6, 466

SCHENECTADY COUNTY.—(Continued.)

TOWNS.	Winter Wheat	Oats.		Rye.		Barley.		Buckwheat.		Corn.		Potatoes.		Peas.	
	Bushels harvested.	Acres sown.	Bushels harvested.	Acres sown.	Bushels harvested.	Acres sown.	Bushels harvested.	Acres sown.	Bushels harvested.	Acres planted.	Bushels harvested.	Acres planted.	Bushels harvested.	Acres sown.	Bushels harvested.
Duanesburgh, ..	646½	6, 343	104. 216	177¾	1, 825	225¼	3, 300½	2, 734	20, 870½	926⅜	15, 512	209	10, 826	133⅜	1, 746¼
Glenville, ...	2, 049	3, 976	84, 352	1, 086	13, 275½	94¾	1, 540	1, 466	9, 601½	2, 275½	36, 657	635½	41, 837	99	1, 580
Niskayuna, ...	533	1, 050	21, 107	295	3, 173	13	107	346	2, 244	569	8, 120	390	18, 397	23⅛	390
Princetown, ...	1, 460	2, 451	47, 524	438	5, 831	18	297	591	3, 097	595	9, 259	68	1, 756	62	894
Rotterdam, ...	477	1, 955½	36, 100	1, 820½	19, 968	15	325	831	5, 951	1, 248	21, 003	543	30, 447	71½	941
Schenectady, ...	......	34	469	82	680	......	....	15½	94	76½	1, 728	38½	1, 869	......	....
Total, ...	5, 165½	15, 809½	293, 768	3, 899¼	44. 752½	365½	5, 569½	5, 983½	41, 858	5, 690⅞	92. 279	1. 884	105, 132	389¼	5. 551¼

SCHOHARIE COUNTY.—(Continued.)

TOWNS.	Winter Wheat	Oats.		Rye.		Barley.		Buckwheat.		Corn.		Potatoes.		Peas.	
	Bushels harvested.	Acres sown.	Bushels harvested.	Acres sown.	Bushels harvested.	Acres sown.	Bushels harvested.	Acres sown.	Bushels harvested.	Acres planted.	Bushels harvested.	Acres planted.	Bushels harvested.	Acres sown.	Bushels harvested.
Blenheim, ...	826½	1, 087½	7, 938	385¾	2, 341½	61¾	483½	429	3, 177	277¾	3, 708	148¾	5, 539	32¼	310½
Broome, ...	180	3, 361	29, 891	629	6, 289	146½	1, 244	2, 034	12, 928	372½	4. 948	251¼	7, 270½	279	1, 902½
Carlisle, ...	654	2, 629	29, 703	211	1, 621	298	3, 304	1, 099	12, 244¾	445	10, 529	144	11, 349	355	3, 804½
Cobleskill, ...	2, 562	2, 380	35, 947	425	4, 402	317	2, 695	774	8, 990	531¼	12, 810	152¼	11, 724	217¼	1, 904
Conesville, ...	15½	1, 454	9, 667	418	2, 975½	54¼	395	1, 208½	2, 680½	326¼	3, 178½	204	5, 740	85¾	506¾
Esperance, ...	564	1, 674	27, 627	153½	1, 708	56¾	688	604½	11, 182	354½	8, 505	81⅝	5, 889	36¼	542
Fulton, ...	2, 771½	2, 522	34, 858½	675	7, 234	161¾	2, 163	1, 447¼	16, 238¾	632¼	14, 206½	318¼	18, 926	124½	1, 313
Gilboa, ...	152	2, 211	18, 969	619¼	4, 092½	177	851½	1, 530½	5, 001	489¾	6, 508	330	10, 694	100⅛	769
Jefferson, ...	93½	1, 636	19, 507	210¼	2, 195	64½	615	886½	7, 889	165¾	3, 553	204½	11, 164	30⅝	368
Middleburgh, ...	1, 907	2. 684	32. 813	1, 156½	12, 592	407¼	5, 548	1, 117¾	14, 641	793½	21, 576½	211½	16, 356	142	1, 402
Richmondville, ..	889½	2, 596½	34, 160	447	5, 155	162¾	1, 586	845½	10, 061	470¾	10, 816	186¾	11, 761	201	2, 550
Schoharie, ...	2, 471	1, 950	33, 653	899	17, 087	439	6, 872	770	11, 169	654	19, 682	155¼	16, 754	93¾	1, 327
Seward, ...	1, 650½	2, 875	42, 093	273½	3, 359	158	2, 506	740	11, 468	440¼	11, 505	149	13, 206	203⅞	3, 523
Sharon, ...	2, 180	4, 011	68, 520	228	2, 458	864	12, 763	1, 434	19, 515	662	17. 584	253	16, 925	621	8, 664
Summit, ...	72	2. 223	31, 957	192	2, 079	114	1, 520	910	12, 029	129	2, 656	248	18, 971	130	1, 781
Wright, ...	1, 656	2, 490	32, 760	921	12, 004	90	902	969	9, 864	443	9, 388	126¼	8, 164	236¼	2, 815
Total, ...	18645	37, 784	490, 063½	7, 843¾	87, 592½	3, 572½	44, 136	16, 799½	169, 078	7, 187½	161, 153½	3, 164⅝	190, 432½	2, 888⅝	33, 482¼

SCHUYLER COUNTY.—(Continued.)

TOWNS.	Winter Wheat	Oats.		Rye.		Barley.		Buckwheat.		Corn.		Potatoes.		Peas.	
	Bushels harvested.	Acres sown.	Bushels harvested.	Acres sown.	Bushels harvested.	Acres sown.	Bushels harvested.	Acres sown.	Bushels harvested.	Acres planted.	Bushels harvested.	Acres planted.	Bushels harvested.	Acres sown.	Bushels harvested.
Catharines, ...	11668	2, 295¾	51, 275	56½	462	437¾	5, 624	839	7, 337	824¼	21, 458	153¼	11, 954	10¼	167
Cayuta, ...	1113½	708½	11 664	29½	208	33¼	451	316½	2, 604½	223½	5, 299	41	2, 480	9	118½
Dix, ...	11039½	1, 848¼	48, 241	61	578	326	4, 182	702	6, 836	832¼	19, 493	161	12, 771	29⅝	410
Hector, ...	32514½	5. 941¼	126, 649	260½	2, 563	2, 382	31, 262	2, 538¼	24, 065½	2, 725	65, 093	304¾	22, 829	14⅝	302
Orange, ...	6737	3, 084¼	55, 855	167	1, 270	502	4, 208	1, 089¼	9, 695	681½	13, 316	286¼	20, 460	32¾	384
Reading, ...	7043	1, 553	31. 834	16	86	555½	5, 255	638½	6, 943	632¼	15, 576	115	9, 084	18½	185½
Tyrone, ...	10316	1, 691	31, 729	104	1, 001	826¾	9; 525	1, 119	10, 042	856¼	20, 545½	197¾	1, 528	15⅝	143¼
Total, ...	80431½	17, 122	357, 247	694½	6, 168	5, 063¼	60; 507	7, 242¼	67, 523	6. 775	160. 780½	1. 259	81. 106	129⅞	1, 710¼

ST. LAWRENCE COUNTY.—(CONTINUED.)

TOWNS.	BEANS.		TURNIPS.		FLAX.			HEMP.		HOPS.		TOBACCO.		APPLE ORCHARDS.	
	Acres planted.	Bushels harvested.	Acres sown.	Bushels harvested.	Acres sown.	Pounds of lint.	Bushels of seed.	Acres sown.	Tons of hemp.	Acres planted.	Pounds harvested.	Acres planted.	Pounds harvested.	Bushels of apples.	Barrels of cider.
Lisbon,	28½	207	5	650						8½	5,975			9,693	116
Louisville,	8¾	81	1	123						3	1,900			4,067	39
Macomb,	10¼	139	2½	160						13	4,655			194	
Madrid,	15⅜	336	4½	525	¼	79¼	2½			3½	2,260			8,711	123
Massena,	35	351												4,920	
Morristown,	17½	107½	1⅝	155						114¾	131,860			7,335	37½
Norfolk,	7¾	67	1	40	¼	86	1½			3	2,200			5,798	24½
Oswegatchie,	17	137½	4½	755						32¼	16,251			8,789	141
Parishville,	28	238	5⅜	735										4,377	12
Pierrepont,	17	97								4½	430			2,141	5
Pitcairn,	7	97	⅝	53						2	575				
Potsdam,	24⅜	343	6⅛	649						10	2,480			14,553	149
Rossie,	4	35½	1	62										46	
Russell,	17½	173	4½	262						1	75			2,108	12
Stockholm,	75⅜	955½	19½	634	¼	25¼				½	29			4,416	6½
Total,	475½	5,131	71⅛	7,896	3	1,206½	4			259¾	197,875			90,497	719

SARATOGA COUNTY.—(CONTINUED.)

TOWNS.	Beans, acres planted.	Beans, bushels harvested.	Turnips, acres sown.	Turnips, bushels harvested.	Flax, acres sown.	Flax, pounds of lint.	Flax, bushels of seed.	Hemp, acres sown.	Hemp, tons of hemp.	Hops, acres planted.	Hops, pounds harvested.	Tobacco, acres planted.	Tobacco, pounds harvested.	Bushels of apples.	Barrels of cider.
Ballston,	23	129	19¾	1,691						11¾	12,270			40,710	1,605½
Charlton,				50	25	6,000	211½							23,565	3,036
Clifton Park,	6	26½										½	200	26,038	874
Corinth,	1½	35½	1⅞	330										4,900	72
Day,			1	125										5,761	91
Edinburgh,	¾	24	1¾	470										7,440	234
Galway,	6½	102½	7	1,113	6	2,120	57							31,732	775
Greenfield,	1½	30½	11⅛	1,815							5			26,846	874
Hadley,	11½	47	7½	576										2,595	
Halfmoon,	1	1	¼	152										12,652	482
Malta,	12	58	1¾	322	½		1							19,604	628
Milton,	19½	334	7⅛	1,078	1¼	90	13			6½	6,064			28,810	893½
Moreau,	5¼	29	2¾	360	6	6,000	18							6,131	106
Northumberland,	8⅜	51⅞	12⅜	1,011	3	675	20							5,489	50
Providence,		3	22¼	967										4,538	73
Saratoga,			7	778	20½	200	195							13,842	404
Saratoga Springs,	9⅝	67	7½	616	¼	40	¼				25			4,345	131½
Stillwater,	3	14	3	325										15,734	777
Waterford,	½	7	3½	630										555	2
Wilton,	2½	13	3	400										8,191	278
Total,	112½	972⅞	120¾	12,809	62½	15,125	515¼			18¼	18,364	½	200	289,478	11,386½

SCHENECTADY COUNTY.—(CONTINUED.)

TOWNS.	Beans, acres planted.	Beans, bushels harvested.	Turnips, acres sown.	Turnips, bushels harvested.	Flax, acres sown.	Flax, pounds of lint.	Flax, bushels of seed.	Hemp, acres sown.	Hemp, tons of hemp.	Hops, acres planted.	Hops, pounds harvested.	Tobacco, acres planted.	Tobacco, pounds harvested.	Bushels of apples.	Barrels of cider.
Duanesburgh,	26¾	248½	1¼	85	316¼	175,000	1,688			14	2,600			25,401	480½
Glenville,	30¼	234	13½	2,032	27¼	21,700	193					¼	150	40,628	826
Niscayuna,	10	70	2	662	12	19,000	118							8,309	338
Princetown,	8	43			31	34,500	235							11,826	343
Rotterdam,	12	119	3¾	820	17	10,000	112							19,042	858
Schenectady,			6	550										345	3
Total,	87	714½	26½	4,149	403½	260,200	2,346			14	2,600	¼	150	105,551	2,848½

SCHOHARIE COUNTY.—(CONTINUED.)

TOWNS.	Beans, acres planted.	Beans, bushels harvested.	Turnips, acres sown.	Turnips, bushels harvested.	Flax, acres sown.	Flax, pounds of lint.	Flax, bushels of seed.	Hemp, acres sown.	Hemp, tons of hemp.	Hops, acres planted.	Hops, pounds harvested.	Tobacco, acres planted.	Tobacco, pounds harvested.	Bushels of apples.	Barrels of cider.
Blenheim,	7⅝	59	4¼	492						2½				6,746	116
Broome,	28	144	4½	530	3⅜	301	2½			4½	1,100			10,481	184½
Carlisle,	7⅜	69½	¼	60	6¼	325	20¾			3	1,790			12,992	302½
Cobleskill,	10⅝	112	¼	15	8	1,500	46			12	13,375		15	14,093	242
Conesville,	22⅞	112¾	10¾	1,596	⅝	18								10,686	123½
Esperance,	5⅝	87½	¼	60	26¼	30,200	140½			1	914			7,132	205
Fulton,	29⅞	259	10⅝	1,157	6⅛	600	50	⅛		45½	18,889			11,847	168½
Gilboa,	23⅞	124	3⅝	658	1⅝	88	2½			4½	1,344			13,440	104½
Jefferson,	¾	10	5⅝	2,257						34¼				9,472	81½
Middleburgh,	4⅞	82½	4⅝	530	½	180	8½							11,108	381½
Richmond,	7⅜	107½			4⅛		29			10	11,295			15,261	280
Schoharie,	9⅝	170	¼	100						22	2,000			10,372	235
Seward,	5¾	139½	⅛	64	3⅛	63	36¼			190¾	196,591			18,006	362
Sharon,		80			7¼	400	170½			182¾	188,856			47,182	402
Summit,	2¼	27	5⅛	735	2½	104	14			12½	4,600			12,210	246
Wright,	7⅛	72¼	1⅛	173	2½	137	6¼							11,154	255
Total,	172⅞	1,656½	51⅜	8,427	73½	33,916	526¾	⅛		525¼	440,754		15	222,182	3,689½

SCHUYLER COUNTY.—(CONTINUED.)

TOWNS.	Beans, acres planted.	Beans, bushels harvested.	Turnips, acres sown.	Turnips, bushels harvested.	Flax, acres sown.	Flax, pounds of lint.	Flax, bushels of seed.	Hemp, acres sown.	Hemp, tons of hemp.	Hops, acres planted.	Hops, pounds harvested.	Tobacco, acres planted.	Tobacco, pounds harvested.	Bushels of apples.	Barrels of cider.
Catharines,	13¼	160	4	1,010										21,358	627
Cayuta,	5	43	5	1,298										7,329	153
Dix,	19⅞	188	2¼	237										12,099	346½
Hector,	40¾	604½	6½	820	71⅞	8,028	418				30			57,818	967½
Orange,	43⅝	486	8¾	1,538	½	20	1			1½	700			9,670	314½
Reading,	27¾	253												12,374	196
Tyrone,	18	196½	4⅞	831	1	10	1½					⅛	30	22,581	607½
Total,	176¼	1,931	31⅜	5,734	73⅜	8,058	420½			1½	730	⅛	30	143,229	3,212

ST. LAWRENCE COUNTY.—(Continued.)

TOWNS.	Market gardens: Acres cultivated.	Market gardens: Value of products.	Pounds of maple sugar made.	Gallons of maple molasses made.	Gallons of wine made.	Pounds of honey collected.	Pounds of wax collected.	Silk: Pounds of cocoons.	Neat cattle: Under one year old.	Neat cattle: Over one y'r, exclusive of working oxen & cows.	Neat cattle: Working oxen.	Neat cattle: Cows.	Number of cattle killed for beef.	Pounds of butter.	Pounds of cheese.
Lisbon,	17	$2,854	3,160	65	......	3,898	292	......	1,020	1,839	198	3,507	358	349,863	16,245
Louisville,	......	......	5,210	44	......	515	43	......	629	1,031	191	1,611	98	148,730	4,880
Macomb,	......	......	6,023	136	......	1,594	157	......	283	538	158	981	82	95,850	7,069
Madrid,	1	88	13,539	96	......	3,101	161	......	879	1,740	186	3,693	307	339,082	122,620
Massena,	......	......	11,808	40	......	2,180	59	......	775	1,492	291	1,817	123	148,570	24,940
Morristown,	......	......	6,880	246	......	2,342	167	......	413	934	90	1,850	230	196,289	11,928
Norfolk,	......	......	17,478	20	......	3,145	45	......	296	411	100	1,066	87	87,970	24,845
Oswegatchie,	9¾	880	942	51	......	760	36	......	636	1,520	109	2,616	647	191,901	3,570
Parishville,	......	......	28,432	51	......	......	......	......	354	1,081	258	1,656	119	168,890	58,307
Pierrepont,	3	800	18,955	80	......	957	75	......	153	458	186	978	75	80,643	17,290
Pitcairn,	......	4	11,213	97	......	319	8	......	38	123	78	300	53	3,270	500
Potsdam,	......	......	13,670	400	2	5,506	299½	......	704	1,747	413	4,997	353	452,116	44,608
Rossie,	......	......	5,617	95	......	538	70	......	248	467	56	1,086	104	110,119	14,880
Russell,	½	104	45,374	188	......	1,635	134	......	374	1,173	253	1,518	136	104,170	87,320
Stockholm,	......	......	58,403	320	......	4,350	222	......	764	1,964	575	2,823	235	257,236	45,119
Total,	31¼	4,730	513.913	3,070	59	51,614	2,814½	......	12,403	26,268	5,576	52,161	4,542	4,268,809	1,672,999

SARATOGA COUNTY.—(Continued.)

TOWNS.	Market gardens: Acres cultivated.	Market gardens: Value of products.	Pounds of maple sugar made.	Gallons of maple molasses made.	Gallons of wine made.	Pounds of honey collected.	Pounds of wax collected.	Silk: Pounds of cocoons.	Neat cattle: Under one year old.	Neat cattle: Over one y'r, exclusive of working oxen & cows.	Neat cattle: Working oxen.	Neat cattle: Cows.	Number of cattle killed for beef.	Pounds of butter.	Pounds of cheese.
Ballston,	......	18	......	......	45	2,010	81	......	279	507	126	1,020	207	113,463½	18,428¾
Charlton,	......	......	......	......	......	......	......	......	373	401	108	956	66	65,065	805
Clifton Park,	4	200	......	......	297	1,953½	104	......	238	498	184	1,270	172	101,781	19,285
Corinth,	......	......	597	24	2½	1,232	29	......	252	506	108	602	136	51,580	6,600
Day,	......	......	1,690	40	......	2,070	128	......	228	404	181	380	20	27,775	100
Edinburgh,	......	......	864	27	......	1,850	176	......	380	678	232	614	89	48,495	8,850
Galway,	......	......	175	3	......	2,425	214	......	374	758	188	1,241	110	141,903	12,715
Greenfield,	2½	525	270	9	3	5,285	236	......	437	978	187	1,346	236	106,990	13,865
Hadley,	......	......	730	9	6	2,962	303	......	199	372	162	336	28	30,406	1,400
Halfmoon,	3	700	......	......	......	20	......	......	263	377	145	972	174	79,735	5,090
Malta,	1⅛	188	......	......	31	3,313	180	......	222	441	88	778	159	77,819	13,314
Milton,	3	348	38	6	15	3,710	190½	......	268	545	166	1,170	177	91,657	5,665
Moreau,	8½	435	......	......	30	2,598	152½	......	248	366	41	745	88	67,695	15,270
Northumberland,	⅛	20	15	......	149	4,020	250	......	353	616	88	855	104	84,705	4,857
Providence,	......	......	......	......	......	920	93	......	258	375	160	392	8	39,160	3,970
Saratoga,	1½	80	......	......	80	4,152	150	......	352	634	164	1,217	132	103,922	4,440
Saratoga Springs,	149¼	8,540	20	8	60	1,695	97	......	159	220	78	752	313	55,710	960
Stillwater,	......	......	......	......	15	2,635	76	......	468	641	137	1,259	364	101,935	13,090
Waterford,	74	2,100	......	......	......	140	10	......	32	127	24	248	1,703	16,950	1,250
Wilton,	1	30	......	......	......	2,212	129	......	179	360	58	625	70	61,390	2,947
Total,	248	13.184	4,399	126	733½	45,202½	2,499	......	5,562	9.804	2,625	16,778	4,356	1.468,136½	152,901¾

SCHENECTADY COUNTY.—(Continued.)

TOWNS.	Market gardens: Acres cultivated.	Market gardens: Value of products.	Pounds of maple sugar made.	Gallons of maple molasses made.	Gallons of wine made.	Pounds of honey collected.	Pounds of wax collected.	Silk: Pounds of cocoons.	Neat cattle: Under one year old.	Neat cattle: Over one y'r, exclusive of working oxen & cows.	Neat cattle: Working oxen.	Neat cattle: Cows.	Number of cattle killed for beef.	Pounds of butter.	Pounds of cheese.
Duanesburgh,	......	......	75	16	4	4,791	372½	......	549	1,121	202	1,940	409	194,591	28,684
Glenville,	54	2,700	107	9	10	3,300	156	......	341	779	186	1,482	589	127,599	5,235
Niskayuna,	26	2,830	......	......	17	926	57	......	74	149	48	389	37	34,521	14,500
Princetown,	......	......	25	5	......	3,371	158	......	205	336	88	673	366	53,181	13,800
Rotterdam,	16	1,175	......	......	......	300	39	......	216	431	73	1,065	371	105,770	9,800
Schenectady,	26	1,400	......	......	68	......	......	......	2	46	......	219	432	......	......
Total,	122	8.105	207	30	99	12,688	782½	......	1,387	2,862	597	5,768	2,204	515,662	72,019

SCHOHARIE COUNTY.—(Continued.)

TOWNS.	Market gardens: Acres cultivated.	Market gardens: Value of products.	Pounds of maple sugar made.	Gallons of maple molasses made.	Gallons of wine made.	Pounds of honey collected.	Pounds of wax collected.	Silk: Pounds of cocoons.	Neat cattle: Under one year old.	Neat cattle: Over one y'r, exclusive of working oxen & cows.	Neat cattle: Working oxen.	Neat cattle: Cows.	Number of cattle killed for beef.	Pounds of butter.	Pounds of cheese.
Blenheim,	......	......	1,901	204½	3	6,100	213	16	366	443	106	873	114	86,230	608
Broome,	......	......	532	67	12	12,144	446	......	469	896	221	1,117	95	92,146	2,605
Carlisle,	½	30	2,927	244	13	3,930	233	......	459	757	122	1,078	75	115,586	5,379
Cobleskill,	......	......	2,983	183	......	2,877	223	......	459	679	90	986	121	93,725	6,716
Conesville,	......	......	2,952	46	......	5,835	204¼	......	396	608	234	868	57	95,550	2,640
Esperance,	......	......	40	2	8	3,293	265	......	235	504	62	540	111	53,745	3,025
Fulton,	......	5	2,387	181½	12	10,369	434	......	516	1,037	314	1,492	146	140,939	869
Gilboa,	......	......	5,177	197	2	9,063	480	......	880	750	273	1,927	113	207,265	3,090
Jefferson,	......	......	14,785	37	52	1,355	23	......	520	773	184	1,753	84	183,877	......
Middleburgh,	......	......	50	53	......	4,131	103	......	418	877	203	750	144	93,970	500
Richmondville,	......	......	1,809	113	96	6,580	483½	......	361	689	70	1,009	201	98,580	1,883
Schoharie,	......	......	255	53	......	2,217	140	......	359	752	133	1,006	211	72,060	200
Seward,	......	85	3 675	363	8	2,722	206½	......	399	591	82	1,260	154	136,430	40,661
Sharon,	......	......	1,931	191	......	8,345	489	......	452	770	127	1,201	152	124,965	2,240
Summit,	......	......	5,008	186	4	5,543	235	......	412	585	118	1,530	70	150,815	200
Wright,	......	......	1,407	218	......	5,172	318¼	......	270	436	101	823	194	86,374	400
Total,	½	120	47,819	2,339	210	89,676	4,496½	16	6,971	11,147	2,440	18,213	2,042	1,832,257	71,016

SCHUYLER COUNTY.—(Continued.)

TOWNS.	Market gardens: Acres cultivated.	Market gardens: Value of products.	Pounds of maple sugar made.	Gallons of maple molasses made.	Gallons of wine made.	Pounds of honey collected.	Pounds of wax collected.	Silk: Pounds of cocoons.	Neat cattle: Under one year old.	Neat cattle: Over one y'r, exclusive of working oxen & cows.	Neat cattle: Working oxen.	Neat cattle: Cows.	Number of cattle killed for beef.	Pounds of butter.	Pounds of cheese.
Catharines,	2½	430	10	......	52	5,909	278	......	534	881	167	1,081	300	97,110	8,445
Cayuta,	......	......	1,675	22	......	4,043	192	......	126	291	76	325	36	35,085	1,880
Dix,	3	35	394	20	......	4,183	147	4	494	1,009	121	938	105	89,611	3,381
Hector,	......	......	2,275	124	5½	21,172	857	......	1,151	2,022	339	2,393	338	258,227	8,988
Orange,	......	......	3,938	156	......	7,267	337	......	591	997	212	1,168	118	119,185	2,363
Reading,	......	......	793	17	......	3,325	......	......	393	570	89	702	84	74,087	3,932
Tyrone,	......	......	362	19½	......	6,268	265	......	494	647	124	1,069	145	125,648	3,179
Total,	5½	465	9.447	358½	57½	52,167	2,076	4	3,783	6,417	1,128	7,676	1,126	798,953	32,168

ST. LAWRENCE COUNTY.—(CONTINUED.)

TOWNS.	Gallons of milk sold.	Horses.	Mules.	SWINE. Under 6 months.	SWINE. Over 6 months.	SHEEP. Number of sheep.	SHEEP. Number of fleeces.	SHEEP. Pounds of wool.	POULTRY. Value of poultry sold.	POULTRY. Value of eggs sold.	DOMESTIC MANUFACTURES. Yards of fulled cloth made.	DOMESTIC MANUFACTURES. Yards of flannel made.	DOMESTIC MANUFACTURES. Yards of linen made.	DOMESTIC MANUFACTURES. Yards of cotton and mixed cloths.
Lisbon,	6, 400	1, 717	....	752	1, 152	7, 513	5, 747	20, 742	$1, 371	$2, 417	2, 644	1, 838	180	8, 149
Louisville,	....	724	....	404	545	3, 974	2, 856	10, 614	236	347	929	3, 060	228	244
Macomb,	20	367	20	188	256	1, 250	928	3, 467	88	110	620	265	50	1, 444
Madrid,	75	1, 461	....	874	946	7, 085	5, 243	19, 751	921	2, 456	1, 483	2, 013	504	5, 974
Massena,	530	901	....	607	587	5, 535	4, 063	14, 568	370	237	290	1, 274	348	247
Morristown,	75	1, 032	....	521	559	2, 458	2, 449	8, 402	613	945	1, 162	1, 122	373	2, 735
Norfolk,	....	477	....	332	273	2, 034	1, 245	4. 557	270	182	540	1, 265	195	268
Oswegatchie,	8, 552	1, 409	....	651	968	3, 971	3, 073	11, 286	764	1, 462	1, 345	1, 324	55	2, 590
Parishville,	....	735	....	297	516	5, 389	5, 079	18, 737	525	860	532	1, 285	534	827
Pierrepont,	....	399	....	148	244	1, 203	1, 241	4, 253	209	363	394	893	289	270
Pitcairn,	....	134	....	104	99	258	200	660	26	34	153	274	56	216
Potsdam,	....	1, 505	....	935	1, 019	4, 554	3, 826	12, 890	830	1, 902	854	1, 467	407	1, 715
Rossie,	....	382	....	159	239	1, 290	817	2, 829	20	76	490	270	....	412
Russell,	....	358	....	431	299	2, 046	1, 450	4, 502	254	143	997	1, 583	67	328
Stockholm,	....	1, 082	....	522	690	6, 811	5, 162	16, 896	962	1, 285	738	1, 930	326	573
Total,	16, 052	20, 261	20	10, 881	13, 205	86, 454	70, 413	246, 683	9, 249	16, 310	19, 102	29, 178	4, 943	36, 640
SARATOGA COUNTY.—(CONTINUED.)														
Ballston,	3, 490	654	....	1, 435	603	1, 906	1, 405	4, 841	1, 695	2, 369	59	45	....	....
Charlton,	....	705	....	358	607	2, 276	1, 750	5, 902	1, 404	1, 074	69	73	....	....
Clifton,	5, 990	897	....	1, 483	853	2, 401	2, 388	7, 644	2, 235	4, 056	....	179	....	....
Corinth,	....	421	....	238	270	1, 425	743	2, 333	750	1, 134	137	268	96	103
Day,	....	222	....	149	186	1, 184	797	2, 037	189	67	161	440	114	30
Edinburgh,	....	320	2	205	286	2, 591	1, 318	4, 700	818	403	308	887	138	190
Galway,	....	736	....	742	637	3, 212	1, 991	7, 318	2, 987	3, 374	391	390	90	51
Greenfield,	15, 022	835	....	949	641	3, 032	2, 176	6, 760	2, 637	4, 252	274	526	208	271
Hadley,	....	190	....	178	161	961	450	1, 607	356	408	59	52	....	....
Halfmoon,	200	618	....	1, 035	462	3, 414	1, 698	5, 879	1, 806	2, 716	20	159	....	....
Malta,	5, 400	474	....	885	571	3, 090	1, 751	5, 921	1, 752	2, 590	....	30	15	30
Milton,	4, 300	775	....	925	784	1, 416	1, 326	4, 254½	1, 948	3, 234	84	143	75	....
Moreau,	....	532	....	725	398	2, 350	2, 186	7, 154	1, 215	2, 605	....	....	....	....
Northumberland,	....	581	....	1, 030	488	1, 989	1, 932	6, 531	1, 303	3, 288	49½	68	....	80
Providence,	....	235	....	274	210	900	769	2, 615	1, 467	895	88	149	92	30
Saratoga,	5, 000	832	....	1, 574	720	5, 776	4, 980	17, 582	1, 821	4, 672	20	165	....	....
Saratoga Springs,	16, 790	710	....	620	749	1, 023	745	2, 500¾	749	1, 612	169	193	14	159
Stillwater,	4, 250	862	....	1, 540	772	4, 848	3, 712	11, 859	2, 033	4, 416	88	111	....	....
Waterford,	27, 982	239	....	175	1, 030	462	155	487½	420	484	....	....	....	....
Wilton,	....	455	....	686	369	1, 762	1, 226	3, 844	1, 364	2, 730	....	113	....	....
Total,	88, 424	11, 293	2	15, 206	10, 797	46, 018	33, 498	111, 769¾	28, 949	46, 379	1, 976½	3, 991	842	944
SCHENECTADY COUNTY.—(CONTINUED.)														
Duanesburgh,	....	1, 319	....	1, 266	831	5, 541	3, 472	12, 503½	3, 097	4, 220	297½	656	63	214
Glenville,	54, 430	1, 033	....	1, 183	1, 022	2, 644	1, 563	6, 214	2, 068	5, 184	364	244	62	150
Niskayuna,	5, 040	341	2	254	303	625	420	1, 609	442	769	....	....	....	....
Princetown,	1, 600	404	....	429	355	1, 123	731	2, 832	788	804	271	269	12	114
Rotterdam,	....	731	2	868	792	826	822	3, 250	1, 096	2, 034	133	613	....	....
Schenectady,	12, 000	391	....	208	216	....	....	....	....	....	....	....	....	....
Total,	73, 070	4, 219	4	4, 208	3, 519	10, 759	7, 008	26, 408½	7, 491	13, 011	1, 065½	1, 782	137	478
SCHOHARIE COUNTY.—(CONTINUED.)														
Blenheim,	....	252	....	356	262	1, 388	1, 044	3, 733¾	525	653	310¾	716	581	192½
Broome,	....	608	....	490	472	5, 438	3, 535	13, 774	1, 239	2, 419	530	911	480	171
Carlisle,	625	638	....	653	484	3, 348	2, 045	9, 525	888	2, 912	706	760	423	276
Cobleskill,	....	741	....	702	761	2, 930	1, 964	6, 562	680	2, 478	606½	927	602	582
Conesville,	....	443	....	563	353	3, 460	1, 766	6, 175½	743	1, 078	295¾	303	26	223½
Esperance,	....	379	....	318	300	1, 165	1, 031	3, 530	501	1, 112	150	647	163	179
Fulton,	....	707	....	762	722	3, 520	2, 411	8, 118½	1, 102	2, 367	851½	1, 982¼	1, 032	1, 094
Gilboa,	....	597	....	675	554	3, 385	2, 065	7, 515	1, 601	1, 269	600	1, 128	555	277
Jefferson,	....	452	....	331	460	2, 241	1, 474	4, 953	638	619	437	1, 202½	469	484½
Middleburgh,	....	838	....	935	814	3, 268	2, 479	8, 782	466	658	450	329	270	282
Richmond,	500	601	....	568	525	2, 182	1, 466	5, 195	774	1, 833	718	910	823	402
Schoharie,	....	758	....	956	848	2, 241	1, 489	5, 426	1, 036	1, 561	473	558	188	65
Seward,	....	583	....	732	712	2, 001	1, 601	5, 862	1, 028	3, 082	375¼	673	419	589
Sharon,	2, 600	1, 001	....	654	730	3, 923	2, 238	8, 514	731	3, 867	352	732	517	375
Summit,	6, 500	506	....	478	463	2, 030	1, 128	3, 835	497	1, 310	663	1, 334	590	555
Wright,	....	578	2	738	433	3, 076	2, 130	6, 916	1, 375	1, 979	131	554	238	475
Total,	10, 225	9, 682	2	9. 911	8, 893	45, 596	29, 866	108, 416¾	13, 824	29, 197	7, 649¾	13, 666¾	7, 376	6, 222½
SCHUYLER COUNTY.—(CONTINUED.)														
Catherines,	....	755	2	395	654	6, 216	4, 388	15, 261	802	896	149	353	10	204
Cayuta,	....	176	....	100	203	1, 399	957	3, 075½	250	293	220½	463	147	66½
Dix,	....	661	2	424	595	6, 547	3, 804	21, 444½	894	1, 508	495½	467	158	778
Hector,	25	2, 048	....	1, 790	1, 764	15, 495	16, 907	61, 081	2, 558	2, 971	560	875½	448	1, 609½
Orange,	....	768	....	481	710	6, 213	3, 253	10, 684	1, 058	863	774	700	563	641½
Reading,	....	580	....	379	455	6, 261	5, 278	19, 353	707	834	95½	195	....	68
Tyrone,	100	712	....	802	691	6, 787	6, 202	21, 655¾	904	1, 596	343	479¼	66	410½
Total,	125	5, 700	4	4, 379	5, 072	48. 918	40, 789	152, 554¾	7, 263	8, 961	2, 637½	3, 532¾	1, 392	3, 784

SENECA COUNTY.

TOWNS.	ACRES.		CASH VALUE.			Acres plowed the year previous.	Acres in fallow the year previous.	Acres in pasture the year previous.	MEADOW.			SPRING WHEAT.		WINTER WHEAT
	Improved.	Unimproved.	Of farm.	Of stock.	Of tools and implements				Acres.	Tons of hay.	Bushels of grass seed.	Acres sown.	Bushels harvested.	Acres sown.
Covert,	15, 646¾	3, 27¼	$1, 192, 950	$105, 747	$37, 234	5, 642	1, 068½	3, 368½	2, 022½	1, 551	486½	91½	875½	1, 424⅝
Fayette,	27, 105½	6, 425	1, 824, 187	193, 233	74, 736	9, 471	1, 351	4, 827	4, 210½	4, 145	539	3	25	3, 743½
Junius,	13, 172¾	3, 304	750, 055	79, 300	19, 870	4, 102	325½	2, 644½	2, 090½	2, 049	380	......	......	1, 209½
Lodi,	17, 112	4, 483	1, 084, 783	106, 245	25, 033	7, 351	440	3, 564	2, 703	1, 988	765	948½	8, 791	1, 371
Ovid,	14, 251	3, 812¾	1, 175, 020	107, 788	37, 915	5, 013	949	2, 829½	2, 271½	1, 711½	577½	93½	921	1, 675¾
Romulus,	17, 977⅞	5, 600	1, 276, 923	127, 845	39, 302	6, 974	722	3, 944	3, 075½	2, 160¾	1, 283½	53½	458	1, 057½
Seneca Falls,	11, 781½	2, 316	804, 175	67, 633	21, 962	3, 967½	809½	2, 185	2, 440¼	2, 029½	269	6	38	1, 260
Tyre,	10, 602⅜	8, 438⅛	712, 650	84, 765	29, 916	2, 906¼	398¼	2, 399	1, 941	2, 043½	162	3	30	1, 003¾
Varick,	15, 606½	4, 468	1, 054, 963	111, 273	38, 513	5, 372¾	504½	2, 684	2, 173¼	1, 570½	538	15¼	104½	1, 655
Waterloo,	8, 693½	3, 815	622, 666	55, 718	15, 166	3, 039	135	2, 009¼	1, 732	1, 631	98	15	136	512
Total,	151. 949¾	45, 936⅜	10, 498, 372	1, 039, 547	339. 647	53. 838½	6, 703¼	30, 454¾	24, 660	20, 879¾	5, 098½	1, 229¼	11379	14912⅝

STEUBEN COUNTY.

TOWNS.	Improved.	Unimproved.	Of farm.	Of stock.	Of tools and implements	Acres plowed the year previous.	Acres in fallow the year previous.	Acres in pasture the year previous.	Meadow acres.	Tons of hay.	Bushels of grass seed.	Spring wheat acres sown.	Bushels harvested.	Winter wheat acres sown.
Addison,	9, 375	25, 832	670, 790	71, 776	23, 113	2, 663	570½	2, 288½	1, 950½	2, 037	46	202	1775	512½
Avoca,	13, 011	8, 661	627, 876	92, 112	33, 019	2, 312	894	3, 577	2, 203	2, 044	63½	439	4235	1, 296
Bath,	30. 775	24, 319	1, 601, 406	234. 451	49, 900	9. 535	2, 034½	9, 227½	6, 719	5, 931½	176½	1, 218½	8984	2, 997
Bradford,	7, 264	5, 798	356, 570	57, 794	11, 375	3, 071	313	1, 976	1, 552	1, 354	34	650	5155	752½
Cameron,	10, 871	19, 798	431, 207	70, 517	15, 696	3, 120½	1, 221	2, 823½	2, 390½	1, 952½	45½	257	1692½	1, 894½
Campbell,	8, 242	15, 297	480, 510	75. 834	18, 236	1, 758	291	2, 586	1, 826	2, 241	110	220	2520	470
Canisteo,	9, 184	22, 300	602, 245	66, 698	22, 610	2, 405	843	2, 301	2, 213	1, 884½	7	177	1510	880½
Caton,	7, 712	14, 453	407, 173	66, 455	14, 084	2, 421	294	2, 051½	2, 118½	2, 242	104	180¾	2350	380
Cohocton,	11, 580	14, 441	814, 998	84, 506	32, 607	3, 761	1, 344	3, 596	1, 941	1, 466½	32½	382½	2445	1, 548
Corning,	7, 803	26, 482	527, 330	73, 716	16, 971	2, 395	496½	1, 312½	1, 343	1, 684	19	85½	1036	863½
Dansville,	20, 031	12, 881	984, 201	92, 023	28, 898	4, 993.	3, 044	4, 430	3, 312	2, 064	23	612	3521	2, 983
Erwin,	4, 097	18, 574	720, 689	53, 114	15, 047	1, 267½	507	1, 007¼	920¼	943	40	18	122	523
Fremont,	10, 733	7, 745	446, 470	59, 617	23, 305	4, 330½	696½	2, 856	1, 933	1, 022	10	235	1248	716½
Greenwood,	10, 065	11, 560	358, 885	58, 662	14, 716	2, 670	486	3, 111	2, 157	1, 049	42	124	772	288
Hartsville,	7, 189	13, 632	239, 070	47, 018	9, 075	1, 378	627	2, 948	1, 893	1, 010	6	123	774	462
Hornby,	13, 151	13, 177	524, 450	75, 364	17, 949	3, 961	148½	3, 995	3, 586	4, 203	276	235½	2292½	1, 209
Hornellsville,	8, 745½	9, 216½	713, 204	67, 326	22, 213	2, 477	834½	2, 446	2, 079	1, 786	36½	165	1594½	3, 517
Howard,	20, 534½	17, 657	793, 651	138, 148	38, 100	7, 861	1, 486½	6, 568	3, 665½	2, 476¾	66	657	5041½	1, 240½
Jasper,	13, 227	15, 853	450, 248	84, 989	18, 248	4, 045	348⅛	3, 789	3, 179	2, 011	38¾	355	2489	549
Lindsley,	3, 729	19, 874	426, 495	33, 383	11, 455	1, 206	181	1, 115	628	948	28	16	138	144
Prattsburgh,	23, 136.	11, 858	895, 079	132, 398	36, 602	4, 974	1, 556	6, 950	4, 274	2, 953½	224½	1, 104	10180	1, 744½
Pultney,	15, 730	4, 878½	763, 604	77. 667	39, 414	3, 942	568	3, 769	3, 007	2, 050	121½	491	3133	1, 679
Thurston,	5. 408½	15, 083	319, 239	36, 123	12, 254	1, 515	498	1, 499	1, 231½	1, 231	61½	114½	758	426
Troupsburgh,	16, 545½	17, 947	443, 671	94, 299	17, 767	3, 414	628	5, 596	4, 876	2, 621½	85	372	2516½	477½
Urbana,	17, 126	8, 656	854, 694	105, 535	34, 072	5, 022	742	5, 634	3, 731	2, 252	24	862	4740	1, 743
Wayland,	12, 921½	11, 364½	711, 070	83, 919	30, 539	4, 199	1, 589	2, 809	2, 301½	1, 567½	20	433½	3647	1, 473
Wayne,	9, 813	3, 505	424, 873	56, 432	15, 214	3, 431	242	2, 389	1, 737	1, 098	46	356	1824	830
West Union,	7, 265	14, 268	273, 355	42, 980	10, 575	1, 928	357½	1, 651	1, 755½	721	41	67	347	182½
Wheeler,	14, 334	14, 246	645, 328	83, 348	25, 685	4, 451	1, 039	4, 923	2, 624	1, 440	11½	373	2819	1, 127
Woodhull,	11, 851½	18, 894	486, 249	89, 948	21, 664	3, 166	1, 108	3, 700	3, 254½	2, 465	86	295¾	2354½	859
Total,	361. 450	438, 250½	17, 994, 630	2. 406, 152	680. 403	103, 672½	24, 988⅛	102, 824¾	76, 401¼	58, 749¼	1, 925¼	10821½	82014	33768

SUFFOLK COUNTY.

TOWNS.	Improved.	Unimproved.	Of farm.	Of stock.	Of tools and implements	Acres plowed the year previous.	Acres in fallow the year previous.	Acres in pasture the year previous.	Meadow acres.	Tons of hay.	Bushels of grass seed.	Spring wheat acres sown.	Bushels harvested.	Winter wheat acres sown.
Brookhaven,	33. 696½	90, 723½	2, 306, 555	201, 206	57, 071	6, 718¼	1, 426¾	12, 834¾	5, 830¼	6, 425	185¼	6	34½	1, 547¼
Easthampton,	13, 274	14, 061	645, 135	85, 659	18, 302	1, 037¾	840	6, 789	3, 355	3, 119½	43	......	......	658½
Huntington,	30, 873½	28, 271	2, 505, 914	251, 726	80, 726	7, 109¾	1, 198¾	6, 417¼	7, 454¼	9, 255½	629¼	5	......	1, 937
Islip,	9, 969	35, 757⅛	1. 485, 752	78, 513	26, 341	1, 820½	39	1, 718	2, 671¼	2, 907½	28¾	......	......	431
Riverhead,	12, 883⅜	20, 942¼	1, 079, 915	107, 739	32, 891	3, 602½	535¾	4, 938¾	2, 213	2, 386¾	257	2	25	1, 105
Shelter Island,	4, 889½	3, 181½	173, 575	20, 145	3, 390	715	81½	2, 466	486½	550½	24	......	......	170¾
Smithtown,	12, 545½	17, 645¾	1, 055, 410	92, 155	21, 055	2, 844	....	3, 646	2, 797	3, 091	151	......	......	750¼
Southampton,	24, 447¼	38, 506	1, 598, 956	213, 130	52, 373	6, 050¾	255	8, 725¾	6, 760¾	7, 968	87	......	......	1, 642¾
Southold,	21, 240	11, 482¾	2, 251, 615	221, 375	52, 237	5, 496½	306	8, 901⅜	3, 987½	5, 801½	336	3	70	1, 731
Total,	163, 818⅛	260, 570⅜	13. 102. 827	1, 271, 648	344. 386	35, 395	4, 682¾	56, 436⅞	35, 555½	41, 505¼	1, 741¼	16	129½	9, 973½

SULLIVAN COUNTY.

TOWNS.	Improved.	Unimproved.	Of farm.	Of stock.	Of tools and implements	Acres plowed the year previous.	Acres in fallow the year previous.	Acres in pasture the year previous.	Meadow acres.	Tons of hay.	Bushels of grass seed.	Spring wheat acres sown.	Bushels harvested.	Winter wheat acres sown.
Bethel,	13, 468	38, 855	605, 774	95, 218	23, 385	2, 928½	271	3, 505	4, 400	4, 453	56	......	......	11¾
Cochecton,	7, 596	33, 175	460, 417	65, 601	16, 030	1, 764	150	1, 443	1, 904½	2, 082	359	1½	17	13
Collicoon,	5, 580	121, 475	260, 802	40, 901	9, 830	1, 184	35	1, 188	1, 589	1, 520½	578½	4	44	1¾
Fallsburgh,	18, 651¼	25, 350	702, 896	139, 266	30, 463	3, 293	476½	4, 913¼	6, 603¾	6, 240	418	......	......	......
Forestburgh,	1, 914	25, 049½	251, 845	15, 882	4, 922	265	70	778	618	863½	4¾	......	......	......
Fremont,	3, 170¼	27, 852	270, 654	26, 075	9, 103	804½	435	340	950½	940	192½	......	......	......
Highland,	1, 454¾	7, 449	97, 480	19, 708	3, 511	570¼	20	198	505½	545¼	12	......	......	17
Liberty,	15, 147½	30. 745½	555, 860	114, 550	14, 059	2, 591	439	6, 205¾	5, 054	5, 165½	197½	1⅞	20	1
Lumberland,	1, 714½	34, 415	163, 485	16, 230	3, 400	342½	44¾	229	531½	657½	5	......	......	1
Mamakating,	17, 073½	43, 652½	796, 571	135, 179	27, 530	3, 370	291¼	6, 656½	4, 555½	4, 486½	15½	½	1	284½
Neversink,	14, 366½	24, 176	394, 072	90, 509	18, 580	2, 965	470	4, 957	5, 328	4, 712	52	......	......	......
Rockland,	6, 830	47, 003¾	268, 100	51. 518	9, 681	1. 059	226¾	2, 285½	3, 068¾	2, 474	42	......	......	......
Thompson,	17, 436	28, 303	752, 550	133, 011	26, 370	2, 417½	94	7, 081	6, 362	6, 224½	40	1½	16	½
Tusten,	1, 087	7, 328	74, 815	9, 563	2, 633	53½	....	154	332½	352	......	......	......	3
Total,	125. 489¼	494, 829¼	5, 655, 321	953, 211	199, 497	23, 607¾	3, 023¼	39, 934	41, 803½	40, 716¼	1. 972⅞	9⅜	98	333

TIOGA COUNTY.

TOWNS.	Improved.	Unimproved.	Of farm.	Of stock.	Of tools and implements	Acres plowed the year previous.	Acres in fallow the year previous.	Acres in pasture the year previous.	Meadow acres.	Tons of hay.	Bushels of grass seed.	Spring wheat acres sown.	Bushels harvested.	Winter wheat acres sown.
Barton,	16, 629½	15, 875½	848, 920	127, 659	36, 500	5, 112	1, 273	4, 488	3, 793	4, 093	350½	137	672	1, 245¼
Berkshire,	9, 283	9, 613	396, 243	76, 698	17, 394	1, 492½	115	4, 160½	2, 811	2, 709¼	86	51	711½	23½
Candor,	30, 769	27, 521	1, 438, 077	206, 637	55, 047	8, 964	1, 234½	11, 610	7, 392	6, 758½	289¾	374½	3, 309½	560¾
Newark,	13, 038	16, 182	691, 415	127, 327	22, 490	3, 107½	....	5, 548½	4, 033	4, 108	90	100½	835	46½
Nichols,	12, 050	7, 363½	650, 125	92, 652	21, 485	3, 686¼	207	3, 266	2, 476	2, 907½	1, 021	126	1. 254¼	556
Owego,	33, 801⅛	26, 046½	1, 763, 180	287, 350	66, 670	9, 949¼	883½	10, 338	8, 107½	8, 404	388¾	325¼	2, 861	822¼

(Continued on page 307.)

SENECA COUNTY.—(CONTINUED.)

TOWNS.	WINTER WHEAT	OATS.		RYE.		BARLEY.		BUCKWHEAT.		CORN.		POTATOES.		PEAS.	
	Bushels harvested.	Acres sown.	Bushels harvested	Acres sown.	Bushels harvested.	Acres sown.	Bushels harvested.	Acres sown.	Bushels harvested.	Acres planted.	Bushels harvested.	Acres planted.	Bushels harvested.	Acres sown.	Bushels harvested.
Covert,.........	16975	2, 374½	58, 191	3	15	538	8, 929	399	3, 251½	1, 677½	43, 901	52⅛	3, 197	15	112
Fayette,........	34099	3, 893	106, 833	169	1, 983	1, 080½	18, 543	320	1, 401	3, 039	67, 947	90⅜	5, 205	4	60
Junius,........	16503	1, 472½	45, 292	94	1, 367	826	14, 866	235¼	2, 019	1, 334½	34, 852	190¼	13, 718	9½	93
Lodi,..........	12099	1, 768	45, 047	132	1, 512	1, 047	16, 663	745	4, 252	1, 273	26, 317	71	4, 512	9	109
Ovid,..........	16029	2, 038¼	51, 847	15	100	652¼	11, 174	386½	1, 352	1, 653	36, 497	68¼	3, 549	2⅞	33
Romulus,.......	10479½	3, 133	76, 591	25	203	766¼	12, 548	468	2, 066½	2, 341	52, 013	31⅝	1, 989	1¼	21
Seneca Falls,....	12606½	1, 811	44, 795	12	147	151	2, 310	213½	1, 214	935¼	18, 953	95⅛	4, 759	5½	58
Tyre,..........	13211	1, 451½	44, 039	16¼	322	228	4, 140	194½	2, 300½	1, 084¼	30, 373	159⅜	10, 023	2	25½
Varick,.........	13787	2, 461	57, 189	81	766	770	12, 099	346¼	1, 344	2, 049	41, 441½	38⅝	1, 706	1¼	19
Waterloo,......	5932	1, 027	26, 414	123½	1, 447	221½	3, 584	242¼	2, 236	853	35, 704	294⅛	23, 886	1½	110
Total,........	151721	21, 429¾	556, 238	670¾	7, 862	6, 280½	104, 856	3, 550¼	21, 436½	16, 239¾	387, 998½	1, 091⅜	72, 544	51⅞	640¼

STEUBEN COUNTY.—(CONTINUED.)

TOWNS.	WINTER WHEAT	OATS.		RYE.		BARLEY.		BUCKWHEAT.		CORN.		POTATOES.		PEAS.	
	Bushels harvested.	Acres sown.	Bushels harvested	Acres sown.	Bushels harvested.	Acres sown.	Bushels harvested.	Acres sown.	Bushels harvested.	Acres planted.	Bushels harvested.	Acres planted.	Bushels harvested.	Acres sown.	Bushels harvested.
Addison,.......	5851	774½	17, 820	11½	128	49	1, 026	247	4, 106	395¼	14, 659	108	12, 004	54¾	998
Avoca,..........	12274	1, 674¾	24, 483	30	321	416½	5, 148½	218	1, 543	457½	10, 865	109½	6, 444	226	2, 098
Bath,..........	25315	3, 473	50, 884½	124½	1, 162	1, 438	6, 979½	1, 082¾	5, 332½	1, 584½	27, 330	331¾	14, 379	124⅛	975½
Bradford,.......	3846	953	15, 215	129½	1, 062½	370	3, 839	555½	4, 175½	475½	8, 196	76¼	5, 726	2¾	57
Cameron,.......	3994	4, 134	11, 798	29½	235	225½	2, 135½	460½	1, 422½	337½	4, 620½	97½	3, 864	83	746½
Campbell,.......	5337	696	18, 183	14	162	87	1, 716	204	2, 440	371	15, 278	69	5, 420	15	263
Canisteo,.......	13845½	738½	12, 512	12	67	96¼	1, 414	222½	1, 627	409	10, 862	128¼	6, 964	76	920½
Caton,..........	3414	1, 204½	37, 749	14	149	115¼	2, 392	336½	5, 332	379½	12, 218	158	20, 607	24	454
Cohocton,......	13752	1, 436	22, 188	......	5	505½	4, 202	112¼	832	588	12, 455	155½	7, 531	103½	1, 138
Corning,.......	8240	878½	24, 703	14	200	55¼	1, 126	255½	3, 656	576½	21, 620	93½	10, 309	11⅛	260
Dansville,......	23538	2, 335	25, 076	85	971	366	3, 916	285½	1, 593	580	14, 999	208½	13, 445	157½	1, 115
Erwin,.........	4746	463½	13, 138	2½	20	18	404	196	2, 795½	358	18, 395	68¼	7, 185	29	751
Fremont,.......	4010	2, 909	27, 620	19	162	234½	1, 626	394	1, 625½	283½	4, 724	168½	8, 985	153	1, 079
Greenwood,.....	1538	1, 618	21, 555	30	328	23½	195	485	4, 777	187½	3, 654	119¼	5, 460	65¾	701
Hartsville,......	3706	744	10, 738	5	6	59	596	210	1, 531	183	3, 050	81½	3, 505	66	555
Hornby,........	2519	2, 265	62, 234	86½	729	132	2, 502	526	7, 111	254	8, 108	208	22, 465	46	790
Hornellsville,....	10391	854	11, 865½	9	87	66	514	225	1, 030	388	8, 244	117½	5, 311	71	642½
Howard,.......	6576	4, 579	57, 948	7¾	20	628¼	6, 042½	778½	4, 515½	420½	9, 473	252	13, 539	201¾	1, 799
Jasper,.........	2651	2, 390	33, 397	22½	163	138¾	1, 312	541¾	4, 361	272½	4, 874	149¾	7, 262	174¾	1, 575½
Lindley,.........	1261	446	11, 928	10	65	27	598	174½	3, 239	295	13, 036	47½	6, 933	5	32
Prattsburgh,.....	10124	3, 391	40, 676	20	195½	714½	7, 799	881	2, 294½	440½	7, 129	167	8, 748	251½	2, 045
Pultney,.......	9486	1, 470	19, 947	74	489	420	4, 398	873	3, 813	565½	6, 473	105	5, 268	40¼	365
Thurston,.......	2860½	612	9, 070	8	61	143	1, 616	265½	963	169	2, 818	71	3, 055	15	165
Troupsburgh,...	2477½	1, 722½	21, 002	9	42	27¾	367	512½	3, 907	448	8, 933½	162½	8, 170	213	1, 955
Urbana,........	9590	1, 724	14, 651	166	1, 555	967	6, 591	816	1, 944	673	7, 596	117½	4, 626	9	43½
Wayland,......	11049	1, 212	17, 846	96	1, 203	181½	2, 035	194¾	1, 569	308½	7, 524	172½	11, 604	108¼	1, 043
Wayne,........	3215	1, 292	13, 449	36	139	442	3, 496	694	2, 128	457	8, 018	94½	4, 711	6½	34
West Union,....	1055	1, 233	18, 155	30½	187	8½	47	444	4, 479	177	3, 022	148	7, 878	46¼	261
Wheeler,........	7205	2, 396	25, 783	19	172	303	2, 740	372	1, 404	413	6, 742	91¼	4, 515	164¾	1, 223
Woodhull,......	5723½	1, 551	19, 693	15¾	126	171	2, 100	491¼	4, 444	349	7, 773½	129¾	10, 025	101¾	921½
Total,........	219590	51, 169¾	711, 307	1, 130½	10. 212	8, 429½	78, 873	13, 054¾	89, 990½	12, 796¾	292, 689½	4, 007	255, 938	2, 646¾	25, 006½

SUFFOLK COUNTY.—(CONTINUED.)

TOWNS.	WINTER WHEAT	OATS.		RYE.		BARLEY.		BUCKWHEAT.		CORN.		POTATOES.		PEAS.	
	Bushels harvested.	Acres sown.	Bushels harvested	Acres sown.	Bushels harvested.	Acres sown.	Bushels harvested.	Acres sown.	Bushels harvested.	Acres planted.	Bushels harvested.	Acres planted.	Bushels harvested.	Acres sown.	Bushels harvested.
Brookhaven,....	22092½	2, 038½	44, 953	1, 554¾	13, 083	45¼	961	508	2, 118½	3, 234¾	72, 192	312¾	24, 955	½	8
Easthampton,..	12674½	555	21, 962	56	606	39½	1, 073	1	7½	872¾	31, 556	78¼	8, 973	......	....
Huntington,....	23630½	2, 818¼	55, 655	1, 602⅜	16, 102	91½	1, 571½	1, 587	9, 581½	3, 729¾	74, 248	481½	28, 124½	⅝	55
Islip,...........	7139½	586¾	12, 268	298½	3, 452½	44½	800½	219	1, 661½	816	18, 165	231¼	15, 691	⅛	9
River Head,....	16627½	621	17, 771	468	4, 805	39	830	294⅜	2, 306½	1, 707½	50, 485	656	57, 234	¼	5
Shelter Island,..	2537	239½	6, 727	29	329	8¼	123	4	61	263½	8, 415	59½	4, 840	......	....
Smithtown,.....	8906	1, 199½	24, 243½	371¼	3, 470	32	534	316¾	1, 409	1, 321¾	25, 808	82	3, 695½	......	....
Southampton,...	28264	1, 560¾	55, 509	667⅞	7, 464	161¼	3, 829	86¾	819	2, 937½	116, 805	308⅜	29, 603	......	....
Southold,.......	29649	698	22, 979	237½	2, 901	51	1, 252	68	892	2, 731¾	107, 093	1, 193⅝	130, 947	½	65
Total,........	151520¼	10, 317¼	262, 067½	5, 285¼	52, 212½	512¼	10, 974	3, 085⅛	18, 856½	17, 615¼	504, 767	3, 403¼	304, 063	2	142

SULLIVAN COUNTY.—(CONTINUED.)

TOWNS.	WINTER WHEAT	OATS.		RYE.		BARLEY.		BUCKWHEAT.		CORN.		POTATOES.		PEAS.	
	Bushels harvested.	Acres sown.	Bushels harvested	Acres sown.	Bushels harvested.	Acres sown.	Bushels harvested.	Acres sown.	Bushels harvested.	Acres planted.	Bushels harvested.	Acres planted.	Bushels harvested.	Acres sown.	Bushels harvested.
Bethel,.........	36	1, 141½	18, 297	928	10, 755	......	....	720½	6, 509½	495¾	11, 922	155	8, 783	......	....
Cochecton,......	104	613	9, 618	823½	10 110	45¾	1, 030	500½	5, 862	339	8, 079	179⅜	9, 861	......	2
Collicoon,......	14	510¾	7, 579	486	5, 551	¼	2	293	2, 707	116½	2, 753	147¼	5, 777	1¼	13
Fallsburgh,.....	......	859½	16, 313	545	6, 251½	......	....	813¾	9, 695	401¼	15, 601	171⅜	13, 417	¼	5½
Forestburgh,...	......	53½	685	120	983½	......	....	95½	613½	57¼	1, 009	35¾	2, 503	......	....
Fremont,.......	......	232	4, 096	231½	2, 670	1½	21½	157	1, 775½	57	1, 282	92¾	5, 321	......	29½
Highland,......	59	31½	464	237½	2, 103½	......	....	154¼	1, 570	122⅞	2, 364	67¼	4, 028¾	......	....
Liberty,........	12	946½	16, 401	616¼	7, 479½	......	....	837¼	9, 753	405⅞	10, 209	188⅜	11, 569	1⅛	17½
Lumberland,....	7	23½	363	274	2, 606	......	....	113½	901½	123¾	2, 585	59	3, 818	......	....
Mamakating,...	1, 221½	824½	8, 777	1, 558	11, 665	......	....	692½	2, 469½	1, 261¾	22, 334½	182¼	8, 030	¾	1
Neversink,......	......	659¾	9, 590	1, 060	7, 370	......	....	823	10, 711	372	8, 943	149½	9, 720	......	5
Rockland,......	......	316¼	4, 698	95	1, 049	......	....	503½	5, 333	138	2. 049	123¼	5, 945	2¾	90
Thompson,......	6	712¾	11, 832	445½	5, 210	......	....	619¼	6, 929	451¼	12, 002½	174	12, 314	1	5
Tusten,........	13	79	1, 170	140	1, 349	......	....	80	742	67¼	1, 461	33½	2, 102	......	....
Total,........	1, 472½	7, 004	109, 883	7, 560¼	75, 153	47½	1, 053½	6, 403½	65, 571½	4, 409½	102, 594	1, 759¼	103, 188¾	7⅛	168½

TIOGA COUNTY.—(CONTINUED.)

TOWNS.	WINTER WHEAT	OATS.		RYE.		BARLEY.		BUCKWHEAT.		CORN.		POTATOES.		PEAS.	
	Bushels harvested.	Acres sown.	Bushels harvested	Acres sown.	Bushels harvested.	Acres sown.	Bushels harvested.	Acres sown.	Bushels harvested.	Acres planted.	Bushels harvested.	Acres planted.	Bushels harvested.	Acres sown.	Bushels harvested.
Barton,........	7, 236½	1, 955¼	50, 105	260	2, 202	54¾	915	1, 177	15. 553½	1, 136	34, 354	132⅛	9, 907	19⅛	309
Berkshire,......	130	774½	19, 677	29	296¾	19	410	203¼	2, 290½	326	10, 977	92½	8, 795	9	128
Candor,........	1, 807½	4, 495½	108, 229	377¼	4, 108	87½	1, 051	1, 268¾	17, 669	1, 283¾	36, 560	304½	27, 519	146⅞	1, 115½
Newark,.......	198	1, 724	29, 096	140	577	40¾	490	311	4, 318½	535½	16, 702	182	17, 191	12½	269
Nichols,........	1, 738½	1, 720½	40, 652	435	4, 389	60	949	903½	9, 578	100½	31, 404	117¾	12, 116	⅛	5
Owego,.........	3, 815½	4, 255½	91, 790	819½	8, 537½	46¼	968	1, 655½	20, 899	2, 419¾	68, 072	659	46, 528½	19½	397

(Continued on page 308.)

SENECA COUNTY.—(Continued.)

TOWNS.	BEANS.		TURNIPS.		FLAX.			HEMP.		HOPS.		TOBACCO.		APPLE ORCHARDS	
	Acres planted.	Bushels harvested.	Acres sown.	Bushels harvested.	Acres sown.	Pounds of lint.	Bushels of seed.	Acres sown.	Tons of hemp.	Acres planted.	Pounds harvested.	Acres planted.	Pounds harvested.	Bushels of apples.	Barrels of cider.
Covert,	9⅞	74	⅛	12	40		211							20,648	464
Fayette,	½	11	1⅞	395	131	111,000	1,183							21,622	1,006
Junius,	13	165	⅝	215	43	33,000	277							11,295	576
Lodi,	10½	69	1¼	400	154	16,000	848							17,734	385
Ovid,	2⅝	27	⅝	120	50	3,311	330½							26,718	357½
Romulus,	5½	48	2	30	173	70,500	1,192							20,024	343
Seneca Falls,	6⅛	67¾	2⅛	314	194	184,000	1,344							12,966	338½
Tyre,	5¼	49	5¾	599	15½	32,000	146					⅝	500	20,696	428½
Varick,	5½	49	2¼	97	182½	69,000	1,448½							12,809	517
Waterloo,	1¾	13½	10⅜	2,463	5½	11,000	55					8	16,000	10,766	213½
Total,	60⅝	573¼	27	4,645	988½	529,811	7,035					8⅝	16,500	175,278	4,629

STEUBEN COUNTY.—(Continued.)

TOWNS.	Beans: Acres planted.	Beans: Bushels harvested.	Turnips: Acres sown.	Turnips: Bushels harvested.	Flax: Acres sown.	Flax: Pounds of lint.	Flax: Bushels of seed.	Hemp: Acres sown.	Hemp: Tons of hemp.	Hops: Acres planted.	Hops: Pounds harvested.	Tobacco: Acres planted.	Tobacco: Pounds harvested.	Bushels of apples.	Barrels of cider.
Addison,	¼	30	1¼	90									10	11,235	110
Avoca,	6¾	49	1¾	115										23,412	467
Bath,	40¾	367½	18	3,003	½		3							25,271	628
Bradford,	2¾	36½	3¾	568	4½		22½							8,042	161
Cameron,	6⅝	57	3¼	360						5	1,500			4,644	53
Campbell,	½	12	¼	141									300	11,896	355
Canisteo,	9¼	86	4¼	576										9,893	116
Caton,	10¼	176	3½	493										6,048	18
Cohocton,	6½	74	12½	1,490	⅛	12							3,460	17,095	156½
Corning,	3¼	60	3¾	670						5	4,850	9¾	12,500	8,828	287
Dansville,	11½	105	8	1,134										14,294	132
Erwin,	10⅞	134	1¼	35										3,745	94
Fremont,	3¼	19½	3½	745										14,210	113
Greenwood,	2¾	28	18	1,685							20			3,978	9
Hartsville,	1	10		195										5,525	36
Hornby,	5½	124½	11¾	814							4			14,201	278
Hornellsville,	13¼	111	11½	1,121	¼	80	2							6,217	122½
Howard,	4¼	158	11¾	1,408	15¼	25	85			¾	392			24,461	249½
Jasper,	10½	69½	5	760						2¼	1,880			4,298	84
Lindsley,	4	75	2½	370										5,905	238
Prattsburgh,	31¾	219	11¼	376	59½	1,660	126½							14,790	111
Pultney,	8¼	89	¼	168	13		45							8,347	130
Thurston,	3⅞	26½	18¾	635							3			3,368	22½
Troupsburgh,	13½	213½	3⅜	491										8,518	46
Urbana,	3¼	22	1	105	15		22							12,335	259
Wayland,	6¾	91	¾	63										4,470	23
Wayne,	1	21	¼	14										8,455	141
West Union	4¾	39½	33	4,065										610	
Wheeler,	8⅞	66	3	216										10,024	108
Woodhull,	10¼	116½	5¾	639								1	680	3,174	32
Total,	245¾	2,686½	202⅞	22,545	108⅛	1,777	306			13	8,649	10¾	16,950	297,289	4,580

SUFFOLK COUNTY.—(Continued.)

TOWNS.	Beans: Acres planted.	Beans: Bushels harvested.	Turnips: Acres sown.	Turnips: Bushels harvested.	Flax: Acres sown.	Flax: Pounds of lint.	Flax: Bushels of seed.	Hemp: Acres sown.	Hemp: Tons of hemp.	Hops: Acres planted.	Hops: Pounds harvested.	Tobacco: Acres planted.	Tobacco: Pounds harvested.	Bushels of apples.	Barrels of cider.
Brookhaven,	6¾	144½	59¾	10,503										6,235	185½
Easthampton,	7⅛	194½	5¾	2,616							3			2,690	
Huntington,	2¼	247½	79¾	13,481										1,677	25
Islip,	10⅝	139½	47½	7,073						1⅛	238			1,335	17½
Riverhead,	11	222½	54⅝	9,409							43			6,087	96½
Shelter Island,	2	25½	70¾	14,063										317	
Smithtown,	1	5	60¼	11,323½										680	24
Southampton,	7¾	57½	46¾	5,170							5			2,689	
Southold,	7⅝	345¾	138⅛	30,545							15	½	1,000	6,089	79
Total,	55⅞	1,382¼	563¼	104,183½						1⅛	304	½	1,000	27,799	427½

SULLIVAN COUNTY.—(Continued.)

TOWNS.	Beans: Acres planted.	Beans: Bushels harvested.	Turnips: Acres sown.	Turnips: Bushels harvested.	Flax: Acres sown.	Flax: Pounds of lint.	Flax: Bushels of seed.	Hemp: Acres sown.	Hemp: Tons of hemp.	Hops: Acres planted.	Hops: Pounds harvested.	Tobacco: Acres planted.	Tobacco: Pounds harvested.	Bushels of apples.	Barrels of cider.
Bethel,	½	6	1¾	510						1	100			4,210	94
Cochecton,		28	6½	1,282										2,052	
Collicoon,	5¾	40½	17½	1,411										416	1
Fallsburgh,	4⅝	71½	21¾	5,140½	¼	40	2					¼	40	11,045	124
Forestburgh,			⅛	60										877	15
Fremont,	2½	150½	37	3,743							65			322	
Highland,	¼	11¼	2⅛	454										329	1
Liberty,	6¼	106	20¾	4,423	¼	12	½				6			11,579	221
Lumberland,	1½	16	½	90										37	
Mamakating,	2⅞	35½	3	390½	⅛	40	⅛				5		12	13,543	314
Neversink,		162	1	472										14,545	529
Rockland,	5¾	45	11¼	1,606										4,655	46
Thompson,	2	26	6⅜	820										9,153	344½
Tusten,														535	10
Total,	31½	698¼	129⅝	20,402	⅝	92	2⅝			1	176	¼	52	73,298	1,699¼

TIOGA COUNTY.—(Continued.)

TOWNS.	Beans: Acres planted.	Beans: Bushels harvested.	Turnips: Acres sown.	Turnips: Bushels harvested.	Flax: Acres sown.	Flax: Pounds of lint.	Flax: Bushels of seed.	Hemp: Acres sown.	Hemp: Tons of hemp.	Hops: Acres planted.	Hops: Pounds harvested.	Tobacco: Acres planted.	Tobacco: Pounds harvested.	Bushels of apples.	Barrels of cider.
Barton,	7½	99	3¼	300	13¼	27	98							14,400	358
Berkshire,	2½	140	¾	301	¾	75	6							17,586	238
Candor,	75¼	1,332	6¾	1,093	¾	330	6			1½	800			23,581	935
Newark,	3¼	79	2¼	416	½	125	5						50	16,445	201
Nichols,	½	6½	5¼	611	1¾	120	8							16,896	476½
Owego,	22½	397¾	20¼	3,542	1¼	35	17½			1	400			29,694	709½

(Continued on page 309.)

SENECA COUNTY.—(Continued.)

TOWNS.	Market Gardens: Acres cultivated.	Market Gardens: Value of products	Pounds of maple sugar made.	Gallons of maple molasses made.	Gallons of wine made.	Pounds of honey collected.	Pounds of wax collected.	Silk: Pounds of cocoons.	Neat Cattle: Under one year old.	Neat Cattle: Over one y'r, exclusive of working oxen & cows.	Neat Cattle: Working oxen.	Neat Cattle: Cows.	Number of cattle killed for beef.	Pounds of butter.	Pounds of cheese.
Covert,	......	......	1, 643	113	59	5, 055	144	......	429	714	64	732	188	70, 239	1, 550
Fayette,	......	......	....	11	176	5, 866	179	......	495	1, 011	83	1, 311	228	140, 312	400
Junius,	......	......	50	10	......	1, 890	107	......	289	561	39	727	46	83, 500	5, 290
Lodi,	......	$30	235	55	......	4, 520	130	......	540	574	69	732	127	68, 295	414
Ovid,	......	......	200	57	114	4, 100	215	......	335	576	72	803	118	50, 068	700
Romulus,	......	65	113	......	49	4, 984	174	......	499	366	68	758	141	69, 136	700
Seneca Falls,	¼	40	....	36	2	2, 643	165	......	261	319	51	598	717	63, 095	1, 575
Tyre,	⅝	80	....	4	126	3, 521	149	......	306	511	37	629	124	72, 346	1, 793
Varick,	¼	......	....	25	24	2, 693	225½	......	255	432	30	381	118	52. 457	70
Waterloo,	35	1, 210	....	......	......	2, 277	121	......	202	608	64	465	353	36, 126	1, 320
Total,	36⅛	1. 425	2, 241	311	550	37, 549	1, 609½	......	3, 611	5, 672	577	7, 130	2, 160	705, 574	13, 812

STEUBEN COUNTY.—(Continued.)

TOWNS.	Market Gardens: Acres cultivated.	Market Gardens: Value of products	Pounds of maple sugar made.	Gallons of maple molasses made.	Gallons of wine made.	Pounds of honey collected.	Pounds of wax collected.	Silk: Pounds of cocoons.	Neat Cattle: Under one year old.	Neat Cattle: Over one y'r, exclusive of working oxen & cows.	Neat Cattle: Working oxen.	Neat Cattle: Cows.	Number of cattle killed for beef.	Pounds of butter.	Pounds of cheese.
Addison,	......	......	....	10	46	1, 165	43	......	275	474	188	532	113	56, 550	3, 640
Avoca,	......	......	11, 014	314	......	2, 307	73	6	312	666	96	854	98	77, 063	43, 446
Bath,	1½	66	1, 319	71	39	6, 696	363½	......	780	1, 593	205	2, 042	202	118, 424	13, 630
Bradford,	......	......	20	......	......	1, 338	78	......	192	358	80	501	47	37, 130	450
Cameron,	......	......	2, 262	70½	......	4, 361	271	......	280	603	140	639	192	69, 703	2, 100
Campbell,	......	......	100	......	9	2, 005	74	......	231	556	160	616	74	60, 155	1, 976
Canisteo,	......	82	2, 850	85	......	3, 780	179	......	356	650	186	690	80	52, 040	500
Caton,	......	35	2, 907	61	......	5, 236	149	15	341	584	147	627	103	61, 156	3, 654
Cohocton,	......	200	3, 751	78	......	1, 915	130	......	242	471	282	621	170	67, 245	6, 231
Corning,	24¾	2, 010	....	......	......	3, 311	183	......	164	330	76	678	129	26, 316	500
Dansville,	2	50	3, 350	934	11	3, 270	642	......	386	713	148	980	126	93, 541	18, 539
Erwin,	2	200	....	......	......	1, 735	48	......	127	229	77	385	309	29, 906	6, 000
Fremont,	1¾	36	3, 263	83	......	3, 464	87	......	235	380	68	501	349	50, 075	5, 775
Greenwood,	62½	515	5, 729	160	......	6, 625	311	......	437	606	154	788	64	79, 900	1, 100
Hartsville,	......	......	2, 633	8	......	1, 195	39	......	233	334	119	427	276	37, 045	3, 290
Hornby,	......	......	1, 178	54	......	5, 509	217½	......	306	608	150	663	271	59. 885	1, 915
Hornellsville,	1½	175	405	37	......	3, 440	177	......	222	534	134	530	45	50, 150	1, 204
Howard,	......	......	9, 978	150	......	6, 275	242	15	521	885	220	1, 137	93	129, 746	13, 690
Jasper,	......	......	11, 881	298	5	5, 892	210	......	449	867	137	802	96	93, 168	3, 335
Lindsley,	......	......	....	......	9	2, 137	51	......	174	267	78	327	109	20, 962	100
Prattsburgh,	......	......	4, 287	157	3	5, 510	220	......	439	850	102	929	94	104, 620	7, 717
Pultney,	......	......	981	60	62	5, 127	309	......	460	731	81	755	120	86, 971	5, 419
Thurston,	......	......	838	114	......	2, 728	121	......	107	258	84	295	55	32, 590	665
Troupsburgh,	......	......	16, 953	202	......	9, 025	321½	......	660	1, 072	252	14	32	103, 775	2, 816
Urbana,	5½	255	125	29	3	2, 554	177	......	392	627	98	671	149	62, 350	3, 070
Wayland,	......	25	100	5	......	1, 921	56	......	234	535	262	780	206	55, 200	23, 500
Wayne,	......	......	93	34	......	2, 275	55	......	215	330	38	472	46	55, 345	1, 816
West Union,	......	......	18, 179	351	......	3, 885	200	......	297	431	201	499	56	41, 980	17, 700
Wheeler,	......	......	2, 922	168	......	2, 583	79	......	271	469	99	618	61	50, 693	4, 806
Woodhull,	......	......	5, 169	131	......	6, 389	323	......	577	922	289	911	72	112, 445	4, 745
Total,	101½	3, 649	112, 287	3, 664½	187	113, 653	5, 429½	36	9, 915	17, 933	4. 351	20, 284	3, 837	1, 976. 129	203, 329

SUFFOLK COUNTY.—(Continued.)

TOWNS.	Market Gardens: Acres cultivated.	Market Gardens: Value of products	Pounds of maple sugar made.	Gallons of maple molasses made.	Gallons of wine made.	Pounds of honey collected.	Pounds of wax collected.	Silk: Pounds of cocoons.	Neat Cattle: Under one year old.	Neat Cattle: Over one y'r, exclusive of working oxen & cows.	Neat Cattle: Working oxen.	Neat Cattle: Cows.	Number of cattle killed for beef.	Pounds of butter.	Pounds of cheese.
Brookhaven,	3¼	90	....	......	......	200	17	......	648	1, 139	305	1, 955	292	86, 047	....
Easthampton,	1	150	....	......	6	30	......	......	468	937	75	843	187	37, 621	800
Huntington,	2⅜	388	....	......	......	3, 105	253	......	515	640	267	1, 776	472	114, 558	....
Islip,	6¼	638	....	......	......	291	29	......	247	318	143	695	51	27, 095	650
Riverhead,	3	225	....	......	12	1, 120	42	......	367	494	99	1, 032	99	71, 146	....
Shelter Island,	......	......	....	......	......	....	......	......	113	138	122	154	33	8, 694	30
Smithtown,	......	......	....	......	......	40	2	......	164	368	114	662	82	40, 587	....
Southampton,	9¼	1, 750	....	......	......	1, 102	60	......	1, 078	2, 015	456	2, 037	504	120, 675	100
Southold,	⅛	52	....	......	......	199	11	......	722	1, 005	425	1, 679	458	127, 982	....
Total,	25¾	3, 293	....	......	18	6, 087	414	......	4, 322	7, 054	2. 006	10, 833	2, 238	634, 405	1, 580

SULLIVAN COUNTY.—(Continued.)

TOWNS.	Market Gardens: Acres cultivated.	Market Gardens: Value of products	Pounds of maple sugar made.	Gallons of maple molasses made.	Gallons of wine made.	Pounds of honey collected.	Pounds of wax collected.	Silk: Pounds of cocoons.	Neat Cattle: Under one year old.	Neat Cattle: Over one y'r, exclusive of working oxen & cows.	Neat Cattle: Working oxen.	Neat Cattle: Cows.	Number of cattle killed for beef.	Pounds of butter.	Pounds of cheese.
Bethel,	......	......	....	......	......	2, 538	166	......	604	776	399	1, 042	109	95, 030	....
Cochecton,	......	......	95	5	......	2, 994	173	......	280	537	380	741	74	48, 785	150
Collicoon,	......	......	361	14	......	2, 104	113	......	239	387	306	486	66	24, 589	....
Fallsburgh,	......	......	1, 207	202	......	7, 877	388	......	720	1, 105	623	1, 470	136	126, 329	228
Forestburgh,	......	......	....	......	......	40	5	......	44	67	75	161	30	17, 935	....
Fremont,	......	......	1, 064	48	......	2, 550	173	......	113	152	225	254	38	17, 515	210
Highland,	......	......	5	4½	......	741	50	......	85	120	72	221	41	15, 501	....
Liberty,	½	20	2, 337	139	......	4, 680	308	8	696	1, 201	566	1, 285	173	105, 645	2, 935
Lumberland,	......	......	70	......	......	625	57	......	87	154	80	189	15	14, 155	....
Mamakating,	3⅛	258	996	30	105	2, 079	151	......	310	602	307	1, 553	152	127, 648	....
Neversink,	......	......	2, 409	77	......	5, 668	394	......	572	988	539	989	95	110, 856	150
Rockland,	......	......	4, 006	196	......	4, 992	231	......	303	483	225	559	52	50, 814	675
Thompson,	......	......	....	......	......	4, 058	189½	......	605	974	446	1, 721	149	168, 845	250
Tusten,	......	......	....	......	......	....	......	......	49	53	22	104	25	8, 280	....
Total,	3⅝	278	12, 550	715½	105	40, 946	2, 398½	8	4, 707	7, 599	4, 265	10, 775	1, 155	931, 927	4, 598

SCHUYLER COUNTY.—(Continued.)

TOWNS.	Market Gardens: Acres cultivated.	Market Gardens: Value of products	Pounds of maple sugar made.	Gallons of maple molasses made.	Gallons of wine made.	Pounds of honey collected.	Pounds of wax collected.	Silk: Pounds of cocoons.	Neat Cattle: Under one year old.	Neat Cattle: Over one y'r, exclusive of working oxen & cows.	Neat Cattle: Working oxen.	Neat Cattle: Cows.	Number of cattle killed for beef.	Pounds of butter.	Pounds of cheese.
Barton,	......	......	282	10	......	5, 640	226	......	697	920	233	1, 621	164	167, 685	1, 610
Berkshire,	......	......	6, 179	60	1	3, 113	104	......	377	665	123	949	68	126, 340	14, 209
Candor,	......	8	3, 197	68	15	8, 818	418½	......	907	1, 577	421	2, 303	195	287, 692	15, 996
Newark,	......	......	12, 265	333	57	5, 050	227	......	532	813	213	1, 386	129	145, 189	6, 210
Nichols,	......	......	....	......	......	1, 955	92	......	438	732	202	1, 026	46	102, 185	1, 500
Owego,	2⅛	217	1, 340	25	......	6, 675	258¼	......	1, 073	2, 068	539	2, 813	514	235, 444	4, 644

(Continued on page 310.)

SENECA COUNTY.—(Continued.)

TOWNS.	Gallons of milk sold.	Horses.	Mules.	SWINE.		SHEEP.			POULTRY.		DOMESTIC MANUFACTURES			
				Under 6 months.	Over 6 months.	Number of sheep.	Number of fleeces.	Pounds of wool.	Value of poultry sold.	Value of eggs sold.	Yards of fulled cloth made.	Yards of flannel made.	Yards of linen made.	Yards of cotton and mixed cloths.
Covert,	....	679	....	554	563	3,576	4,142	13,086	$2,244	$1,675	34	91	25	....
Fayette,	180	1,390	....	1,128	2,144	8,290	6,337	21,464	6,307	5,075	31	209	145	300
Junius,	....	731	....	744	666	5,623	3,907	13,857	1,189	967	82	222	22	145
Lodi,	125	763	4	755	856	3,450	3,388	12,247	1,196	662	14	87	....	....
Ovid,	....	688	....	599	568	3,968	3,585	14,241	1,648	2,652	54	103	25	100
Romulus,	204	862	....	665	596	6,134	5,728	21,446¼	1,871	1,089	54	256½	57	95
Seneca Falls,	15,458	560	2	430	3,815	4,042	3,460	11,425	858	1,161	15	84	....	....
Tyre,	1,426	577	....	411	608	4,616	4,609	19,936⅜	1,680	1,838	121	432½	122	72
Varick,	....	755	....	630	720	4,276	3,555	12,973	1,779	1,552	25	126	66	....
Waterloo,	16,888	492	....	346	734	3,559	3,166	10,270	513	652	....	....	....	....
Total,	34,281	7,497	6	6,262	11,270	47,534	41,877	150,946	19,285	17,323	430	1,611	462	712

STEUBEN COUNTY.—(Continued.)

TOWNS.	Gallons of milk sold.	Horses.	Mules.	Under 6 months.	Over 6 months.	Number of sheep.	Number of fleeces.	Pounds of wool.	Value of poultry sold.	Value of eggs sold.	Yards of fulled cloth made.	Yards of flannel made.	Yards of linen made.	Yards of cotton and mixed cloths.
Addison,	....	332	16	340	427	2,448	1,863	6,468	251	378	332	674	....	336
Avoca,	....	600	2	423	664	5,580	3,067	9,310	182	260	240½	367	132	34
Bath,	585	1,368	3	850	1,500	12,169	11,702	38.126	984	1,743	796	1,668	318	287
Bradford,	....	330	....	314	417	3,493	2,178	7,808	272	364	317	578	58	25
Cameron,	75	418	1	159	460	2,847	1,616	5,232½	139	376	311	485	123	267
Campbell,	....	326	....	167	363	2,036	1,219	3,483	239	496	172	434	7	163
Canisteo,	348	377	5	278	538	1,914	1,888	5,589	172	349	642	944	....	90
Caton,	....	341	....	229	381	2,344	1,514	4,870	424	895	72	273	100	291
Cohocton,	....	536	....	280	527	3,255	4,044	14.252	275	562	162	236	178	15
Corning,	3,804	395	8	152	749	828	527	1,516	71	314	12	93	....	....
Dansville,	....	763	....	547	811	5,469	6,219	20,410	417	566	630	465	96	312
Erwin,	803	215	....	215	338	1,495	862	2,991	59	245	....	....	....	....
Fremont,	....	502	....	195	354	1,715	2,129	8,648	965	641	27	25	....	....
Greenwood,	....	300	....	66	354	1,701	1,390	4,598	323	204	187	666	75	125
Hartsville,	....	229	....	135	247	3,007	2,449	9,776	163	128	37	473	88	91
Hornby,	....	382	....	203	371	3,365	1,993	7,519	556	788	285	921	199	56
Hornellsville,	11,695	359	....	276	370	2,522	1,977	6,243	431	565	146	328½	108½	211
Howard,	....	810	2	455	883	6,998	5,346	17,203½	314	727	575	1,030½	176	908
Jasper,	14	496	....	257	469	3,385	3,556	13,370	498	170	330	1,012	279	814
Lindsley,	....	121	....	123	263	967	819	2,700	50	127	....	....	37	....
Prattsburgh,	492	856	....	402	620	8,093	8,877	30,383	446	935	106	912	....	170
Pultney,	40	694	....	625	448	4,968	4,981	16,750	623	953	90	458	180	30
Thurston,	....	170	....	124	207	1,354	1,098	4,405	270	436	308	462	36	342
Troupsburgh,	....	457	....	249	501	5,340	3,243	10,870	484	198	635½	1,774	421	769
Urbana,	900	580	....	499	552	9,946	10,318	29,352	685	633	247	488	70	41
Wayland,	....	504	....	305	700	1,805	1,451	5,987	115	75	354	396	192	346
Wayne,	....	357	....	365	389	3,553	3,289	10,749	417	656	251	298	24	155
West Union,	....	179	....	72	297	1,206	581	1,372	224	266	147	340	243	859½
Wheeler,	....	496	3	311	521	5,220	9,887	31,876	208	313	208	392	100	....
Woodhull,	....	406	....	257	560	2,330	1,401	4,477	379	315	190	710	76	168
Total,	18,756	13,899	40	8,873	15,281	111,353	101,484	336,334	10,636	14,678	7,810	16,903	3,316½	6,905½

SUFFOLK COUNTY.—(Continued.)

TOWNS.	Gallons of milk sold.	Horses.	Mules.	Under 6 months.	Over 6 months.	Number of sheep.	Number of fleeces.	Pounds of wool.	Value of poultry sold.	Value of eggs sold.	Yards of fulled cloth made.	Yards of flannel made.	Yards of linen made.	Yards of cotton and mixed cloths.
Brookhaven,	3,270	1,281	15	1,399	1,994	6,069	4,489	13,894½	5,716	5,965	....	....	204	....
Easthampton,	7,400	568	....	512	564	4,097	3,746	9,161	1,401	3,889	12	113	....	100
Huntington,	3,501	1,583	71	1,385	1,959	5,847	4,324	13,081	19,402	7,839	....	....	....	....
Islip,	1,810	407	32	510	618	610	423	1,239¼	2,204	1,138	....	....	....	....
Riverhead,	12,813	681	5	1,082	974	721	533	1,986½	1,503	7,332	....	50	....	92
Shelter Island,	....	58	....	224	146	2,422	2,148	6,157½	468	864	....	....	....	....
Smithtown,	....	441	28	311	864	3,048	3,234	9,336	2,932	1,391	....	....	22	....
Southampton,	3,080	1,103	5	1,921	2.083	2,986	2,237	6,164½	5,353	11,328	85	89	49	20
Southold,	12,246	989	7	1,682	1,499	2,216	2,044	7,261½	4,420	15,496	....	....	34	....
Total,	44,120	7,111	163	9,026	10,701	28,016	23,178	68,281¾	43,399	55,242	97	252	309	212

SULLIVAN COUNTY.—(Continued.)

TOWNS.	Gallons of milk sold.	Horses.	Mules.	Under 6 months.	Over 6 months.	Number of sheep.	Number of fleeces.	Pounds of wool.	Value of poultry sold.	Value of eggs sold.	Yards of fulled cloth made.	Yards of flannel made.	Yards of linen made.	Yards of cotton and mixed cloths.
Bethel,	....	294	2	495	349	1,171	752	2,530	338	105	260	761	....	57
Cochecton,	....	176	....	184	312	228	172	637½	10	30	....	170	....	65½
Collicoon,	....	78	3	158	205	166	100	357	98	78	10	119	....	....
Fallsburgh,	....	377	9	578	521	1,934	1,201	3,917	456	407	76	139	....	32
Forestburgh,	....	59	6	40	46	140	91	364	35	24	15	58	....	....
Fremont,	....	55	....	30	122	145	107	279	7	38	50	32	....	....
Highland,	182	57	10	80	145	117	57	186½	49	147	12	60	....	....
Liberty,	180	396	5	438	453	2,131	1,088	3,533½	572	124	192½	1,089	72	220½
Lumberland,	....	55	....	83	111	31	31	107	210	810	....	20	....	40
Mamakating,	43,352	587	1	956	795	1,369	964	3,174	1,386	1,719	186	146	....	60
Neversink,	....	344	12	355	339	2,450	1,652	5,421½	403	403	755	2,121	156	527
Rockland,	10	168	5	112	185	1,135	759	2,456	110	47	26	595	....	329
Thompson,	....	440	19	589	506	1,574	1,053	3,659	710	127	292	511	....	181
Tusten,	1,200	6	15	13	31	....	....	....	....	....	....	....	....	....
Total,	44,924	3,092	87	4,111	4,120	12,591	8,027	26,622	4,384	4,059	1,874½	5,821	228	1,512

TIOGA COUNTY.—(Continued.)

TOWNS.	Gallons of milk sold.	Horses.	Mules.	Under 6 months.	Over 6 months.	Number of sheep.	Number of fleeces.	Pounds of wool.	Value of poultry sold.	Value of eggs sold.	Yards of fulled cloth made.	Yards of flannel made.	Yards of linen made.	Yards of cotton and mixed cloths.
Barton,	67	664	6	571	843	3,265	2,300	8,269¼	441	372	266	540	168	16
Berkshire,	....	293	....	334	280	2,230	2,059	7,592½	351	1,162	139	215	145	200
Candor,	500	1,125	....	949	1,070	7,258	5,699	13,574½	864	2,852	899	1,118	557	1,701
Newark,	....	583	....	423	484	3,545	3,400	10,898	886	958	135	683	310	110
Nichols,	....	384	2	538	664	2,776	1,832	6,218	718	850	208	1,054	585	548
Owego,	2,000	1,383	5	1,176	1,661	8,176	4,669	14,657	1,649	2,752	797½	1,197	429	752

(Continued on page 311.)

TIOGA COUNTY.—(Continued.)

TOWNS.	ACRES.		CASH VALUE.			Acres plowed the year previous.	Acres in fallow the year previous.	Acres in pasture the year previous.	MEADOW.			SPRING WHEAT.		WINTER WHEAT.
	Improved.	Unimproved.	Of farm.	Of stock.	Of tools and implements				Acres.	Tons of hay.	Bushels of grass seed.	Acres sown.	Bushels harvested.	Acres sown.
Richford, ...	8, 898	6, 947	$272, 870	$60, 197	$11, 633	2, 064	159	3, 952	2, 292	2, 047	80	83¼	1, 140	44½
Spencer, ...	13, 445	12, 367	506, 841	75, 453	15, 578	3, 428½	80	4, 992½	3, 167	3, 078½	82¼	101	815	365
Tioga, ...	16, 980½	16, 508	1, 025, 893	152, 862	42, 257	5, 006½	428	5, 045	3, 965	4, 296	64½	40¾	340	687½
Total, ...	154, 894⅛	138, 423½	7, 593, 564	1, 206, 835	289. 054	42, 810½	4, 380	53, 400½	38, 036½	38, 401¾	2, 452¾	1, 339¼	11938¼	4, 351¼

TOMPKINS COUNTY.

TOWNS.	Improved.	Unimproved.	Of farm.	Of stock.	Of tools and implements	Acres plowed the year previous.	Acres in fallow the year previous.	Acres in pasture the year previous.	Meadow, Acres.	Tons of hay.	Bushels of grass seed.	Spring wheat, Acres sown.	Bushels harvested.	Winter wheat, Acres sown.
Caroline, ...	20, 120⅓	12, 004	864, 480	143, 258	30, 801	4, 570½	243	6, 698	5, 037½	3, 702¾	259½	466¾	4578½	250
Danby, ...	21, 993½	11, 445	1, 037, 581	151, 846	32, 827	6, 829¼	952½	5, 837	4, 405	3, 453	149	570½	5692	799¼
Dryden, ...	39, 814¾	19, 021¾	2, 161, 829	321, 539	77, 096	12, 850	600½	13, 783½	8, 608	7, 456½	288	534½	6079	1118¾
Enfield, ...	17, 611¾	5, 257	1, 058, 179	127, 744	40, 272	6, 701	613½	3, 995½	3, 325½	2, 380½	548½	226	2342¼	1507
Groton, ...	23, 581¾	7, 981	1, 329, 989	207, 063	37, 883	6, 898½	130	10, 139	4, 881½	4, 714½	126	251¼	3113	279
Ithaca, ...	15, 395	3, 828¼	1, 068, 838	141, 598	33, 475	4, 628	803	3, 595	2, 515	1, 973½	159¾	19	122	1815
Lansing, ...	29, 363	7, 912	1, 778, 353	198, 812	53, 017	12, 164	624	8, 552	4, 120	3, 063½	192½	69¾	570	1691½
Newfield, ...	20, 984¾	14, 040½	1, 006, 059	149, 201	36, 230	7, 572	1, 121½	5, 500	3, 823	3, 022	109¼	1, 043½	10126	1736
Ulysses, ...	16, 752	3, 474½	1, 350, 746	140, 069	38, 034	6, 132	694	4, 592	2, 777½	2, 077½	259	1	20	1843½
Total, ...	205, 616⅝	84, 963¾	11, 656, 054	1, 581, 130	379, 635	68, 345¼	5, 782	62, 692	39, 493	31, 843¾	2, 091½	3, 182¼	32642¾	11040

ULSTER COUNTY.

TOWNS.	Improved.	Unimproved.	Of farm.	Of stock.	Of tools and implements	Acres plowed the year previous.	Acres in fallow the year previous.	Acres in pasture the year previous.	Meadow, Acres.	Tons of hay.	Bushels of grass seed.	Spring wheat, Acres sown.	Bushels harvested.	Winter wheat, Acres sown.
Denning, ...	910	76, 913½	96, 572	15, 975	3, 909	258½	180	238½	622	543	136¾	......	......	......
Esopus, ...	13, 044½	8, 439	1, 271, 890	98, 550	32, 877	3, 795¾	315	3, 046	3, 670¼	3, 282	40	......	......	397
Gardiner, ...	18, 597	7, 281	814, 413	137, 619	37, 835	2, 757	471	8, 096	4, 386	4, 428	77½	......	......	294
Hurley, ...	7, 268¾	9, 858	472, 810	55, 310	21, 213	1, 568	815	1, 763	1, 865	2, 006	......	......	......	182
Kingston, ...	8, 622½	16, 812	1, 603, 220	93, 779	29, 885	1, 756	675½	1, 326	2, 311½	2, 851	69	16¼	803	791
Lloyd, ...	12, 018	6, 513½	918, 035	84, 576	23, 773	2, 840	573½	3, 648	3, 213	3, 868¾	25	¼	5	140½
Marbletown, ...	17, 946¼	14, 787	1, 840, 001	135, 052	48, 219	4, 171½	747½	5, 205¾	4, 289	4, 649½	148	......	......	517
Marlborough, ...	13, 103	2, 874½	1, 015, 660	92, 804	18, 547	3, 145	138	4, 047	3, 291½	3, 835½	10	2	......	147½
New Paltz, ...	14, 428	5, 497½	844, 564	93, 047	39, 149	3, 111¼	203	3, 819	4, 293½	4, 419	123½	......	......	306
Olive, ...	14, 653¼	22, 474	640, 480	91, 034	26, 213	2, 782½	1, 570½	4, 743	3, 844	3, 727½	54	......	......	15
Plattekill, ...	15, 342¾	4, 190½	1, 013, 003	119, 356	32, 702	3, 347½	136	4, 236	3, 726	4, 974½	8	......	......	297
Rochester, ...	18, 087	25, 966½	992, 413	176, 271	44, 995	6, 638	258¼	6, 365½	3, 837¾	178¼	......	......	......	149½
Rosendale, ...	7, 877	3, 371	538, 202	56, 459	24, 463	2, 260	756	2, 130	1, 753	1, 805	41	......	......	111
Saugerties, ...	17, 815½	14, 931¾	1, 351, 125	202, 218	61, 563	3, 536¾	937¾	3, 191	6, 545¾	6, 759	315½	1	7	618
Shandaken, ...	12, 764	79, 891	385, 648	79, 215	15, 786	2, 017	414	3, 246	4, 485	3, 369	48½	......	......	10
Shawangunk, ...	21, 360½	8, 097	965, 950	158, 032	39, 821	5, 244	165	8, 186	4, 437	4, 979	5½	......	......	196
Wawarsing, ...	17, 974¼	46, 052	987, 315	179, 435	47, 338	4, 144	824	6, 030½	6, 041	6, 422	79½	......	......	169½
Woodstock, ...	8, 828¾	24, 253	366, 993	66, 200	16, 484	1, 603	391	3, 546	3, 061	2, 698	20	......	......	49
Total, ...	240, 641	378, 202¾	16, 118, 294	1, 914, 932	564, 772	54, 975¾	9, 571	72, 863¼	65, 672¼	64, 795	1, 201¾	19½	815	4, 390

WARREN COUNTY.

TOWNS.	Improved.	Unimproved.	Of farm.	Of stock.	Of tools and implements	Acres plowed the year previous.	Acres in fallow the year previous.	Acres in pasture the year previous.	Meadow, Acres.	Tons of hay.	Bushels of grass seed.	Spring wheat, Acres sown.	Bushels harvested.	Winter wheat, Acres sown.
Bolton, ...	9, 583⅝	21, 868	192, 560	50, 889	8, 924	1, 552½	90½	4, 630½	2, 966½	2, 445	40¾	55⅞	474½	......
Caldwell, ...	4, 891¾	9, 081	100, 670	26, 264	6, 848	983	186	2, 136	1, 147	767	10½	31	183	19
Chester, ...	16, 498	20, 428	324, 337	76, 075	13, 805	2, 689	14	7, 694	4, 966	2, 778	7	84	660	10
Hague, ...	5, 154½	29, 655½	63, 310	23, 711	4, 225	758¼	42	2, 177	1, 584½	1, 123	27	96¼	927	7½
Horicon, ...	7, 492	28, 555	154, 429	38, 333	10, 011	1, 512	267½	2, 317	2, 758	1, 768	56¼	39	251	......
Johnsburgh, ...	12, 954½	80, 846½	224, 215	59, 003	9, 072	2, 767⅕	29	4, 309	4, 512	2, 962	59	25½	237	......
Luzerne, ...	10, 281⅞	17, 187½	212, 465	44, 505	11, 201	1, 995¼	163½	4, 008	2, 128½	1, 492¼	20¼	22½	122½	6
Queensbury, ...	21, 288⅝	16, 674½	923, 120	134, 601	26, 271	6, 411½	509½	6, 882½	3, 943	3, 720½	118½	60	453½	178
Stony Creek, ...	3, 618	45, 113	62, 561	23, 457	5, 594	667	257	1, 144	1, 324½	998	46	37½	351	......
Thurman, ...	8, 595	41, 922	132, 134	38, 621	7, 885	1, 048	257	3, 233½	2, 718	2, 074	......	34¼	205½	......
Warrensburgh, ...	10, 845	20, 010	214, 445	44, 857	2, 593	1, 470	60	4, 687	3, 086	1, 961	13	55	420	1
Total, ...	111, 202⅝	331, 341	2, 604, 246	560, 316	106, 429	21, 854	1. 876	43, 218½	31, 134	22, 088¼	398¼	540⅞	4, 285	221½

WASHINGTON COUNTY.

TOWNS.	Improved.	Unimproved.	Of farm.	Of stock.	Of tools and implements	Acres plowed the year previous.	Acres in fallow the year previous.	Acres in pasture the year previous.	Meadow, Acres.	Tons of hay.	Bushels of grass seed.	Spring wheat, Acres sown.	Bushels harvested.	Winter wheat, Acres sown.
Argyle, ...	27, 186	8, 350¾	1, 358, 208	200, 781	39, 841	8, 658½	147	9, 052	5, 523	4, 790¼	189	416½	4, 767½	342½
Cambridge, ...	18, 013¼	4, 206	1, 012, 170	123, 340	40, 267	6, 059	....	8, 881	3, 584½	4, 251	79	126¾	1, 555½	151
Dresden, ...	5, 500½	21, 943½	145, 050	31, 278	4, 580	821¼	12	1, 549½	2, 215½	1, 528	19	23¾	257½	7¾
Easton, ...	30, 994¼	6, 936½	1, 829, 710	206, 285	49, 506	9, 036½	120	11, 047¾	5, 783	5, 813½	116	146½	1, 569½	494¼
Fort Ann, ...	22, 619¾	27, 966¾	688, 319	132. 958	18, 682	4, 172¼	612½	9, 248	7, 554¼	5, 626	129½	84½	913	45
Fort Edward, ...	12, 791½	2, 006	510, 013	72, 280	13, 523	3, 477½	50	4, 553	3, 581½	2, 700	101¾	107½	1, 388	51½
Granville, ...	27, 511¼	6, 632	1, 158. 930	153, 717	30, 881	5, 217¼	33	12, 107½	6, 091¼	5, 428½	81½	116¼	1, 459½	66
Greenwich, ...	20, 864½	5, 349	1, 181, 595	159, 506	42, 581	7, 359½	766	7, 178½	3, 516	3, 539	165	103¾	1, 083	258½
Hampton, ...	8, 725	3, 939	287, 500	41, 686	7, 541	1, 541	53	4, 664	2, 351	2, 169	22	21½	242	20
Hartford, ...	21, 978	4, 852¾	1, 039, 390	142, 642	24, 563	5, 525½	5½	10, 291¼	5, 214	4, 326¾	19¼	137	1, 705	51¼
Hebron, ...	25, 515	7, 138	1, 117, 152	151, 239	35, 132	7, 551	200	11, 341	5, 190	4, 796	89½	123¼	1, 584	36
Jackson, ...	17, 981	4, 880	995, 755	121, 186	36, 105	5, 937	....	8, 710	3, 053	3, 316	96	123	1, 612½	134
Kingsbury, ...	18, 440	4, 324½	830, 895	123, 973	27, 284	4, 226½	81	7, 113½	5, 808	4, 717½	89	101¾	926	53½
Putnam, ...	7, 882	12, 423	235, 020	43, 679	7, 848	1, 223	61	4, 526	2, 617	2, 037	93	176	2, 174	84
Salem, ...	25, 104½	7, 976	1, 260, 778	165, 268	37, 577	6, 989½	73	12, 989½	4, 661½	4, 842½	63	107¼	1, 353½	38½
White Creek, ...	22, 683¾	5, 616	945, 413	147, 872	26, 393	4, 585	21	10, 451¼	5, 257¼	4, 591	32	88¼	848½	89¼
Whitehall, ...	19, 240	9, 015	676, 070	128, 674	16, 650	2, 875	49	9, 374½	6, 148	5, 409	44½	31	415	44½
Total, ...	333, 030¼	143, 554¾	15, 271, 968	2. 146, 364	458, 954	85, 255¼	2, 284	143, 078¼	78, 148¾	60, 881	1, 429	2, 034½	23854	1, 968

TIOGA COUNTY.—(Continued.)

TOWNS.	Winter Wheat	Oats.		Rye.		Barley.		Buckwheat.		Corn.		Potatoes.		Peas.	
	Bushels harvested.	Acres sown.	Bushels harvested	Acres sown.	Bushels harvested.	Acres sown.	Bushels harvested.	Acres sown.	Bushels harvested.	Acres planted.	Bushels harvested.	Acres planted.	Bushels harvested.	Acres sown.	Bushels harvested.
Richford, ...	301	1, 048½	26, 567	50½	474	14¼	238	199¼	2, 507	360½	11, 585	86½	6, 009	5½	140
Spencer, ...	2, 195	1, 723½	40, 255	46½	463	26¼	363	439⅞	5, 309	642	19, 921	125½	9, 021	82	1, 332
Tioga, ...	1, 933	1, 796	46, 607	510½	4, 837	28½	541	848	13, 278	1, 035¼	30, 499	143½	13, 432	20¼	297
Total, ...	19. 355	19, 493¼	452, 978	2, 668¼	25, 884¼	377¼	5, 925	7, 006⅛	91, 402½	7, 839¼	260, 074	1, 843⅜	150, 518½	314⅝	3, 992½

TOMPKINS COUNTY.—(Continued.)

TOWNS.	Winter Wheat	Oats.		Rye.		Barley.		Buckwheat.		Corn.		Potatoes.		Peas.	
Caroline, ...	1177½	3, 450	85, 143	108½	1, 155	119	2, 045	844½	7, 672½	1, 174½	34, 973	154⅝	9, 629½	59	750
Danby, ...	4128¾	3, 707½	91, 917	388¼	3, 710	205¾	3, 413	1, 060¾	11, 531	1, 212½	34, 982	190¾	17, 791	73¼	1, 034
Dryden, ...	7506¼	5, 784	154, 037	395½	4, 123	879¼	16, 837	2, 086⅜	15, 217½	2, 735½	70, 086	314½	19, 567	70	1, 044
Enfield, ...	9537	3, 034	81, 930	73	741	598	9, 510	975	9, 411½	1, 256½	37, 232	158½	13, 032	19⅝	292½
Groton, ...	2200	3, 475¾	93, 082	10¼	119	432¾	10, 267	575½	6, 679	1, 644¼	45, 940	209⅛	16, 343	34½	640
Ithaca, ...	15077½	2, 368	49, 988	379½	4, 233	276	4, 613	639½	2, 533½	1, 382	28, 025	140	8, 420½	20⅛	394
Lansing, ...	13074	6, 827	144. 416	64¼	601	431½	6, 694	1, 465¼	7, 801½	2, 287	48, 470	135¾	7, 923	7¼	80
Newfield, ...	10783½	3, 121½	61, 869	286½	2, 645	190½	2, 334	1, 224¾	10, 685	1, 262	33, 719	172⅜	13, 614	25¾	355
Ulysses, ...	20911	2, 374½	50, 601	13½	194	621	9, 582	424¾	2, 773½	1, 783½	38, 775	78½	4, 786	3⅝	70
Total, ...	84395½	34, 142¼	812, 983	1, 719¼	17, 521	3, 753¼	65, 295	9, 296⅜	74, 305	14, 737¾	372, 202	1, 554⅛	111, 106	312⅞	4. 659½

ULSTER COUNTY.—(Continued.)

TOWNS.	Winter Wheat	Oats.		Rye.		Barley.		Buckwheat.		Corn.		Potatoes.		Peas.	
Denning, ...	......	94½	1, 481	73	529	......	....	107¾	1, 295	44⅛	1, 574	37¾	2, 170	4½	2
Esopus, ...	1, 551½	1, 072½	14, 255	1, 212	11, 570½	10	130	412½	3, 170½	1, 060	18, 564	276	11, 662	......	42
Gardiner, ...	1, 069	1, 394	22, 236	1, 423	14, 383	......	....	311½	1, 665¾	1, 408	14, 919	110	3, 850	......	....
Hurley, ...	1, 120	378½	8, 777	1, 659	6, 528	......	....	361	2, 754	618¾	11, 047	139½	8, 324	½	5
Kingston, ...	1, 993½	1, 462	14, 458	1, 500	10, 342	......	....	235¾	2, 176	776	14, 844	254¾	12, 442	3	60
Lloyd, ...	710	987½	13, 500	1, 547¼	18, 999	......	....	405½	1, 733¾	1, 057¼	11, 860	115¾	3, 564	½	9¼
Marbletown, ...	1, 891	1, 630½	24, 133	2, 970½	21, 583½	......	....	979¼	7, 956½	1, 478¾	20, 981	278¼	12, 916	......	....
Marlborough, ..	981½	1, 273	22, 695	1, 622½	19, 325	......	....	277	1, 385	1, 227¼	5, 948	91½	2, 940	1⅛	24
New Paltz, ...	1, 257	1, 301	19, 992	1, 895	18, 552	......	....	469	2, 836	1, 287½	15, 357	122¼	3, 759	1	5
Olive, ...	65	620	7, 214	1, 450	11, 093½	......	....	871½	6, 301½	949	11, 752	223½	7, 469	......	....
Plattekill, ...	1, 245	1, 223½	16, 818	1, 699	19, 759	......	....	601	3, 428	1, 367	16, 183	187¼	8, 559	½	5
Rochester, ...	2, 312½	1, 409½	25, 056	2, 173¾	20, 297½	......	....	949¼	8, 291¾	1, 318½	16, 271	243	8, 943	......	....
Rosendale, ...	370½	521½	6, 702	968	7, 882	......	....	416	2, 726	778½	8, 344	180¼	6, 251	......	....
Saugerties, ...	2, 425¾	1, 365	22, 954	1, 872	12, 224	......	....	616½	3, 135¼	1, 432	15, 390	353½	1, 162½	3	56
Shandaken, ...	......	676	7, 090	427	2, 089	......	....	631	5, 329	278	4, 566	170	8, 000	6	86
Shawangunk, ...	1, 047½	1, 399	26, 130	1, 934¾	19, 095½	......	....	328½	1, 699	1, 577	18, 350	154¾	6, 116	......	....
Wawarsing, ...	1, 145	1, 280½	19, 093	1, 610½	12, 478	......	....	962¾	11, 598	1, 194	28, 593½	356	20, 523	......	....
Woodstock, ...	186	385	5, 521	1, 057	8, 663	......	....	440	3, 195	577½	7, 686	146½	5, 889	¼	2
Total, ...	19370¾	18, 473½	278, 105	27094¼	235, 393½	10	130	9, 375¾	70. 676	18, 429⅛	242, 229½	3. 440½	134, 539½	20⅝	296¼

WARREN COUNTY.—(Continued.)

TOWNS.	Winter Wheat	Oats.		Rye.		Barley.		Buckwheat.		Corn.		Potatoes.		Peas.	
Bolton, ...	......	491¾	8, 362	95½	706	......	....	116½	528½	467¾	10, 248	189¾	12, 416	5⅞	95½
Caldwell, ...	178	216	3, 511	171	694	......	....	165	976	364	5, 915	117	7, 187	4	33
Chester, ...	5	1, 235	16, 333	86	806	......	....	356	3, 069	680	10, 976	342	25, 149	59	662
Hague, ...	48	164½	3, 081	74½	600½	½	9	44¼	235½	241¾	5, 059	108¼	8, 105	16¼	213
Horicon, ...	......	502	7, 274	47½	638	......	....	180¾	1, 056	456¼	11, 746	177	13, 317	41¼	382½
Johnsburgh, ...	......	993	14. 968	93	858½	......	....	392	4, 435	599¾	12, 218	326¼	28, 175	29½	310
Luzerne, ...	35	693½	9, 317	71½	551	......	....	278¼	1, 434	679½	9, 372	190	9, 355	8¼	96
Queensbury, ...	942	2, 048¾	40, 662	733½	5, 231	4	30	935¼	5, 079¼	2, 558	39, 205	682½	35, 405	22⅛	225½
Stony Creek, ...	......	239¾	3, 726	23	189½	......	....	102¾	753½	331¼	5, 135	121¼	9, 437	14½	130½
Thurman, ...	......	377	5, 158	43	330	......	....	162	821	435¼	6, 795	178	11, 847	3½	26
Warrensburgh, ..	4	603	7, 955	38	348	......	....	178	827	455	7, 148	198½	12, 935	16	96½
Total, ...	1, 212	7, 564¼	120, 347	1, 476½	10, 952½	4½	39	2, 910¾	19, 214¾	7, 268½	123, 817	2, 630½	173, 328	220¼	2, 270½

WASHINGTON COUNTY.—(Continued.)

TOWNS.	Winter Wheat	Oats.		Rye.		Barley.		Buckwheat.		Corn.		Potatoes.		Peas.	
Argyle, ...	1, 831½	3, 190½	82, 593	1, 323½	16, 306½	125¼	2, 495½	463½	4, 162	2, 705½	68, 173	1, 184	72, 925	141	1, 698
Cambridge, ...	370	1, 650½	46, 477	990½	14, 397	74	1, 624	195	2, 587	2, 017	45, 940	398½	35, 211	......	....
Dresden, ...	55½	345	9, 204	62	747	......	....	13½	59½	214½	3, 827	105	5, 096	50	511
Easton, ...	1, 170	3, 745½	99, 107	2, 191½	25, 678	234½	4, 032	809½	8, 413	3, 075	69, 722	621½	46, 905	22¼	488
Fort Ann, ...	280	1, 689	35, 405	147	1, 345½	3	44	344¼	2, 238½	1, 320	24, 054	530	27, 451	73¼	945½
Fort Edward, ..	179½	1, 818½	49, 358	193½	2, 108	20	293	236½	1, 432	960	18, 188	205¾	11, 262	58¾	813
Granville, ...	482	1, 889	44, 420	570¼	6, 476	10	189	265¾	2, 174½	1, 482¼	28, 744½	1, 856⅜	107, 972	190½	1, 851
Greenwich, ...	969½	2, 713	76, 633	1, 428	17, 959	15	267	476½	4, 465	2, 306½	57, 042	538	46, 914	25½	450
Hampton, ...	122	559½	12, 523	138½	1, 480	......	....	95	629	442	9, 102	197½	10, 955	25	286
Hartford, ...	363	2, 012	47, 158	321½	3, 921	12½	159	188½	1, 375	1, 307¾	26, 462	1, 681⅜	87, 857	176	1, 593
Hebron, ...	297	2, 575¾	64, 766	421½	4, 679	85½	1, 249	238	2, 464	1, 916½	49, 582	1, 609¼	109, 647	104	1, 152
Jackson, ...	230	1, 962	55, 825	946	14, 051	30	564	188½	1, 940	1, 998	52, 882	588	59, 570	6	122
Kingsbury, ...	427	1, 512	35, 352	93	803	16½	176	369	1, 950	1, 162¼	24, 014	750½	38, 619	51¾	791
Putnam, ...	634	511	11, 649	37	479	......	....	23	166	150	3, 129	94	4. 964	104	1, 378
Salem, ...	176	2, 524	66, 221	562¾	6, 032	97¼	1, 138	325½	3, 246	2, 519¼	61, 974	820¼	61, 934	39	456
White Creek, ...	341½	1, 257¾	33, 625	259½	3, 224	27¼	596	199½	2, 301	1, 470½	30, 823	315⅛	25, 994	¼	4
Whitehall, ...	458½	1, 156	28, 005	222¾	2, 281	9¾	118	112	1, 056	734	16, 020	285¾	14, 009	160⅞	1, 672
Total, ...	8, 387	31, 111	798, 321	9, 908¾	121, 967	760½	12, 944½	4, 543½	40, 658½	25, 781	589. 678½	11780⅞	767, 285	1, 227⅝	14, 210½

TIOGA COUNTY.—(CONTINUED.)

TOWNS.	BEANS.		TURNIPS.		FLAX.			HEMP.		HOPS.		TOBACCO.		APPLE ORCHARDS.	
	Acres planted.	Bushels harvested.	Acres sown.	Bushels harvested.	Acres sown.	Pounds of lint.	Bushels of seed.	Acres sown.	Tons of hemp.	Acres planted.	Pounds harvested.	Acres planted.	Pounds harvested.	Bushels of apples.	Barrels of cider.
Richford,	⅞	31	3	255										10, 927	142
Spencer,	4¾	145	2¾	699										14, 197	311
Tioga,	10⅝	265	⅞	135								½	110	25, 457	898
Total,	127¾	2, 495¼	45⅛	7, 352	18¼	712	140½			2½	1, 200	½	160	169, 183	4, 359

TOMPKINS COUNTY.—(CONTINUED.)

TOWNS.	Beans, acres planted.	Beans, bushels harvested.	Turnips, acres sown.	Turnips, bushels harvested.	Flax, acres sown.	Flax, pounds of lint.	Flax, bushels of seed.	Hemp, acres sown.	Hemp, tons of hemp.	Hops, acres planted.	Hops, pounds harvested.	Tobacco, acres planted.	Tobacco, pounds harvested.	Bushels of apples.	Barrels of cider.
Caroline,	4⅞	69¾	6⅛	196	2	221	18					1	740	33, 834	523½
Danby,	11½	194	7⅜	1, 757	13⅞	773	100½			1¼	838			49, 142	781
Dryden,	34⅛	505	3⅝	1, 242	14⅜	2, 555	139½						50	85, 870	847½
Enfield,	56⅞	606¾	2¼	383	54½	47, 000	497			½	300			31, 721	537
Groton,	13	163	4¼	947	10½	1, 383	96							86, 169	989
Ithaca,	¾	15	¾	46	3	24, 000						20½	26, 300	23, 531	502
Lansing,	1	12		85	59		464							48, 677	675
Newfield,	14½	179	2½	462	16	4, 000	130							29, 758	615
Ulysses,	47¾	356	¼	15	36		261							29, 055	702
Total,	184⅝	2, 100½	27⅛	5, 133	209¼	79, 932	1, 706			1¾	1, 138	21½	27, 090	417, 757	6, 172

ULSTER COUNTY.—(CONTINUED.)

TOWNS.	Beans, acres planted.	Beans, bushels harvested.	Turnips, acres sown.	Turnips, bushels harvested.	Flax, acres sown.	Flax, pounds of lint.	Flax, bushels of seed.	Hemp, acres sown.	Hemp, tons of hemp.	Hops, acres planted.	Hops, pounds harvested.	Tobacco, acres planted.	Tobacco, pounds harvested.	Bushels of apples.	Barrels of cider.
Denning,	5⅛	44½	9	1, 027	¼	20	1							24	
Esopus,	2½	34	24¼	2, 108	1½	106	3½							72, 130	1, 228
Gardiner,					⅝									5, 692	341
Hurley,	¾	6	7½	867	½	80				1	75			3, 315	143
Kingston,	¼	55	7⅛	766	¼	100								4, 460	259
Lloyd,	23½	250½	268½	1, 824	¼	50	1½							4, 864	177½
Marbletown,	2¾	9½	6¼	1, 403	3½	466	20							18, 390	535½
Marlborough,	2¼	13½	33¼	3, 117	¼	25						2	2, 500	4, 782	228
New Paltz,	3	25	¼	100	1	75					75			8, 070	291
Olive,	¼	26	11¼	634	½	500	2							208, 996	547½
Plattekill,			80	2, 499										10, 024	126
Rochester,			4	847	1¼	200	10½						12	3, 051	144
Rosendale,			2½	367	⅛	95							10	5, 455	321
Saugerties,	2¼	14	6	500	7¼	390	39½				10		2	11, 253	389
Shandaken,			23½	2, 692										10, 616	118
Shawangunk,	½	3	⅛	67¼	100									11, 935	122
Wawarsing,	7½	2	25½	4, 882										11, 613	262
Woodstock,	2¾	51	5¾	436						61¼	2, 575			3, 084	374
Total,	53⅜	534	514¾	24, 136¼	117¼	2, 107	78			62¼	2, 735	2	2, 524	397, 754	5, 606½

WARREN COUNTY.—(CONTINUED.)

TOWNS.	Beans, acres planted.	Beans, bushels harvested.	Turnips, acres sown.	Turnips, bushels harvested.	Flax, acres sown.	Flax, pounds of lint.	Flax, bushels of seed.	Hemp, acres sown.	Hemp, tons of hemp.	Hops, acres planted.	Hops, pounds harvested.	Tobacco, acres planted.	Tobacco, pounds harvested.	Bushels of apples.	Barrels of cider.
Bolton,	1¼	12½	3	388							2			6, 592	66
Caldwell,	1¼	65	1¼	170										4, 211	16
Chester,	8	155	14	2, 332							5		10	5, 705	46
Hague,	10¼	76¾	2¾	244										6, 292	80
Horicon,	12¼	78	5¼	585										457¾	
Johnsburgh,	8½	78	16	2, 012										5, 150	5
Luzerne,	3⅝	21	3¾	475										3, 473	58
Queensbury,	28½	253½	13¼	2, 600										20, 744	731
Stony Creek,	11½	69	7¼	1, 036								¼	10	535	
Thurman,	8¼	70	¼	43										3, 511	
Warrensburgh,	1	37	3	320										2, 102	
Total,	94⅛	915¾	69¾	10, 205							7	¼	20	58, 772¾	1, 002

WASHINGTON COUNTY.—(CONTINUED.)

TOWNS.	Beans, acres planted.	Beans, bushels harvested.	Turnips, acres sown.	Turnips, bushels harvested.	Flax, acres sown.	Flax, pounds of lint.	Flax, bushels of seed.	Hemp, acres sown.	Hemp, tons of hemp.	Hops, acres planted.	Hops, pounds harvested.	Tobacco, acres planted.	Tobacco, pounds harvested.	Bushels of apples.	Barrels of cider.
Argyle,	48	557	3⅜	661	57¾	60, 800	397							29, 861	884
Cambridge,	5½	100			648	172, 000	5, 717½							11, 126	473
Dresden,	4¼	17¾	1¾	88										2, 872	
Easton,	3⅞	35½	1½	535	370	136, 000	3, 291½						2, 390	14, 501	519
Fort Ann,	37	307½	3⅝	486	⅛	20					50			6, 812	136
Fort Edward,	11¾	101	¼	46	2	3, 000	15							1, 525	21
Granville,	57¼	1, 182½	¼	209										24, 697	957½
Greenwich,	6¾	139	8¾	645	250	61, 056	2, 024							14, 508	515
Hampton,	16½	168	1¾	165										5, 844	185
Hartford,	138¼	1, 234	3¼	390	14¾	3, 000	114							21, 422	548¾
Hebron,	23	250	3⅛	358	94	5, 100	539							12, 877	296
Jackson,	3¾	42	6	725	342	94, 556	2, 503							8, 621	263
Kingsbury,	17⅛	128	1¾	225										7, 075	245½
Putnam,		11	1⅛	139										4, 652	26
Salem,	49⅝	502	8	1, 495	391	203, 800	2, 962							10, 578	307
White Creek,	14⅞	205½	3⅛	612	689¼	100, 088	5, 440							6, 656	200¾
Whitehall,	6⅝	94½	3¼	739						¼	12			5, 476	232
Total,	444⅛	5, 075¼	50⅞	7, 518	2, 858⅞	830, 420	23, 003			¼	62		2, 390	189, 103	5, 809½

TIOGA COUNTY.—(Continued.)

TOWNS.	MARKET GARDENS: Acres cultivated.	MARKET GARDENS: Value of products.	Pounds of maple sugar made.	Gallons of maple molasses made.	Gallons of wine made.	Pounds of honey collected.	Pounds of wax collected.	SILK: Pounds of cocoons.	NEAT CATTLE: Under one year old.	NEAT CATTLE: Over one y'r, exclusive of working oxen & cows.	NEAT CATTLE: Working oxen.	NEAT CATTLE: Cows.	Number of cattle killed for beef.	Pounds of butter.	Pounds of cheese.
Richford,	......	......	1,390	113	2	1,784	66	......	254	433	96	788	46	84,021	1,625
Spencer,	......	......	702	89	......	3,548	157	......	496	869	243	913	174	90,803	2,200
Tioga,	½	$100	370	25	......	1,795	63	......	523	1,013	253	1,155	103	126,424	2,363
Total,	2⅝	325	25,725	729	75	38,378	1,612¼	......	5,297	9,090	2,323	12,954	1,439	1,365,783	50,357

TOMPKINS COUNTY.—(Continued.)

TOWNS.	Acres cultivated.	Value of products.	Pounds of maple sugar made.	Gallons of maple molasses made.	Gallons of wine made.	Pounds of honey collected.	Pounds of wax collected.	Pounds of cocoons.	Under one year old.	Over one y'r.	Working oxen.	Cows.	Number of cattle killed for beef.	Pounds of butter.	Pounds of cheese.
Caroline,	......	......	4,447	104	......	8,370	377¾	......	546	1,016	203	1,676	136	191,160	5,343
Danby,	......	......	4,100	625	947	8,810	456	......	634	1,059	253	1,342	107	130,978	4,019
Dryden,	......	......	4,528	179	......	12,868	751	......	1,012	1,773	335	3,316	298	390,214	10,094
Enfield,	......	......	1,866	102	14	10,225	411	......	447	909	159	968	139	107,925	495
Groton,	......	52	18,240	349	7	9,518	497	......	628	1,020	85	2,560	212	326,616	36,001
Ithaca,	5	120	....	2	......	5,647	174	37½	374	701	159	871	94	79,625	180
Lansing,	......	......	4,348	151	2	12,851	685	......	528	1,064	114	1,617	162	168,125	1,386
Newfield,	......	......	1,130	25	......	9,400	404	......	598	1,188	238	1,258	173	145,145	1,300
Ulysses,	5	45	1,194	139	1½	5,938	320	......	373	739	120	964	119	106,159	1,310
Total,	10	217	39,853	1,676	971½	83,627	4,075¾	37½	5,140	9,469	1,666	14,572	1,440	1,645,947	60,128

ULSTER COUNTY.—(Continued.)

TOWNS.	Acres cultivated.	Value of products.	Pounds of maple sugar made.	Gallons of maple molasses made.	Gallons of wine made.	Pounds of honey collected.	Pounds of wax collected.	Pounds of cocoons.	Under one year old.	Over one y'r.	Working oxen.	Cows.	Number of cattle killed for beef.	Pounds of butter.	Pounds of cheese.
Denning,	......	......	1,090	64	......	370	28	......	69	129	116	142	12	15,160	....
Esopus,	33½	6,515	1,260	76	13	2,061	104	......	207	299	122	593	138	63,287	....
Gardiner,	......	9	1,737	28	......	1,563	122	......	176	363	279	1,665	188	156,649	....
Hurley,	......	......	371	5	5	1,814	48	21	129	276	160	472	121	39,081	....
Kingston,	2	145	15	4	10	800	106	......	121	215	106	599	1,284	28,752	100
Lloyd,	......	......	321½	16¼	15½	2,631	212	......	178	170	206	649	111	84,534	....
Marbletown,	1	57	4,375	143	8	4,261	329	......	400	651	278	1,432	284	110,870	....
Marlborough,	......	......	....	......	3	1,852	101	......	189	273	222	896	325	99,925	....
New Paltz,	......	......	1,808	88	34	1,890	217½	......	129	289	240	995	249	95,785	....
Olive,	......	......	5,023	257	5	4,734	283	......	331	644	329	944	188	84,955	....
Plattekill,	......	......	50	17	......	1,682	55	......	182	305	280	1,301	163	119,595	....
Rochester,	......	51	2,563	159	17	4,956	350	......	332	703	401	1,295	184	110,773	....
Rosendale,	1	25	667	22	10	860	84	......	117	165	100	534	152	32,715	....
Saugerties,	½	46	7,781	153	......	2,736	228½	......	374	467	230	1,721	198	131,887	....
Shandaken,	......	......	8,002	370	......	8,430	291	......	351	566	335	810	92	53,290	....
Shawangunk,	48	16	1,761	69	1	1,394	215	......	582	451	261	1,027	198	235,000	....
Wawarsing,	......	250	9	......	......	4,984	236	5	568	900	661	1,487	501	152,846	230
Woodstock,	9	......	1,021	31	......	2,880	115	......	328	508	345	770	82	54,527	190
Total,	95	7,114	37,854½	1,502¼	121½	49,898	3,125	26	4,763	7,374	4,671	17,332	4,470	1,669,631	520

WARREN COUNTY.—(Continued.)

TOWNS.	Acres cultivated.	Value of products.	Pounds of maple sugar made.	Gallons of maple molasses made.	Gallons of wine made.	Pounds of honey collected.	Pounds of wax collected.	Pounds of cocoons.	Under one year old.	Over one y'r.	Working oxen.	Cows.	Number of cattle killed for beef.	Pounds of butter.	Pounds of cheese.
Bolton,	¼	10	1,347	53	......	1,639	100	......	280	556	164	588	56	48,606	11,171
Caldwell,	......	......	40	......	......	941	41	......	66	166	56	298	45	27,632	....
Chester,	......	......	1,023	63	......	1,925	98	......	299	569	253	709	91	43,030	4,425
Hague,	......	......	882	25	......	1,410	135	......	194	271	100	269	17	27,300	1,290
Horicon,	......	......	2,268	98	......	1,167	32	......	170	392	166	366	37	44,200	1,290
Johnsburgh,	......	......	5,482	76	......	2,317	114	......	299	579	186	913	103	63,506	5,940
Luzerne,	......	......	322	45	......	1,348	116	......	217	458	102	484	308	40,600	1,800
Queensbury,	2	75	....	......	83	2,009	55½	......	315	605	119	1,363	712	102,982	30,920
Stony Creek,	......	......	3,260	63	......	3,455	152	......	89	176	71	259	52	21,470	658
Thurman,	......	......	3,443	44	......	1,380	104	......	127	283	90	308	22	26,575	4,700
Warrensburgh,	......	......	548	174	5	2,471	114	......	213	374	116	604	54	36,885	2,440
Total,	2¼	85	18,615	641	88	20,062	1,061½	......	2,269	4,429	1,423	6,161	1,497	482,786	64,634

WASHINGTON COUNTY.—(Continued.)

TOWNS.	Acres cultivated.	Value of products.	Pounds of maple sugar made.	Gallons of maple molasses made.	Gallons of wine made.	Pounds of honey collected.	Pounds of wax collected.	Pounds of cocoons.	Under one year old.	Over one y'r.	Working oxen.	Cows.	Number of cattle killed for beef.	Pounds of butter.	Pounds of cheese.
Argyle,	1	18	106	64	......	3,337	232	......	741	1,229	120	1,838	249	163,321	2,875
Cambridge,	6	500	....	......	......	600	82	......	350	532	203	1,071	197	109,204	7,420
Dresden,	1	25	25	12	......	1,728	128	......	198	304	90	300	50	23,323	3,105
Easton,	......	......	8	3	17	4,268	124	......	523	882	263	1,577	137	137,864	42,176
Fort Ann,	......	......	642	6	8½	3,235	200	......	578	923	151	955	41	91,843	44,824
Fort Edward,	3	200	....	......	......	1,360	108	......	320	573	54	667	83	55,014	2,358
Granville,	......	300	1,425	42	......	1,893	185	......	636	827	141	2,023	460	106,160	334,767
Greenwich,	1½	90	....	10	......	1,975	76	......	520	805	153	1,345	225	129,495	17,100
Hampton,	½	12	600	25	......	60	15	......	205	347	50	516	55	36,210	35,632
Hartford,	......	......	....	......	......	925	92	......	420	701	108	1,067	51	104,554	18,109
Hebron,	......	......	1,128	221	15	1,013	76	......	642	890	80	1,567	146	129,987	26,115
Jackson,	......	......	....	......	......	1,435	110	......	321	596	135	1,049	174	106,071	530
Kingsbury,	½	50	115	17	36	1,430	118	......	382	587	88	971	151	94,385	30,542
Putnam,	......	......	600	31	......	335	26	......	357	535	52	468	60	47,490	440
Salem,	......	......	468	80	......	3,195	207	......	549	905	152	1,322	419	143,020	4,635
White Creek,	6	500	101	37	40	2,591	109	......	232	539	180	800	138	67,351	36,150
Whitehall,	2½	415	40	......	......	620	57	......	573	899	80	1,153	358	79,846	27,713
Total,	22	2,110	5,258	548	116½	30,000	1,945	......	7,547	12 074	2,100	18,689	2,994	1,625 138	634,491

TIOGA COUNTY.—(Continued.)

Towns.	Gallons of milk sold.	Horses.	Mules.	Swine. Under 6 months.	Swine. Over 6 months.	Sheep. Number of sheep.	Sheep. Number of fleeces.	Sheep. Pounds of wool.	Poultry. Value of poultry sold.	Poultry. Value of eggs sold.	Domestic manufactures. Yards of fulled cloth made.	Domestic manufactures. Yards of flannel made.	Domestic manufactures. Yards of linen made.	Domestic manufactures. Yards of cotton and mixed cloths.
Richford,	....	284	....	243	202	2, 143	1, 835	4, 627	$494	$552	211	160	94	179
Spencer,	....	426	....	278	395	3, 061	2, 181	6, 590	620	720	105	483	12	362
Tioga,	....	536	....	403	734	3, 698	2, 524	7, 718	467	1, 017	553	1, 067	80	312
Total,	2, 567	5, 678	13	4, 915	6, 333	36, 152	26, 499	80, 144¼	6, 490	11, 235	3, 313½	6, 517	2, 380	4, 180

TOMPKINS COUNTY.—(Continued.)

Towns.	Gallons of milk sold.	Horses.	Mules.	Swine. Under 6 months.	Swine. Over 6 months.	Sheep. Number of sheep.	Sheep. Number of fleeces.	Sheep. Pounds of wool.	Poultry. Value of poultry sold.	Poultry. Value of eggs sold.	Domestic manufactures. Yards of fulled cloth made.	Domestic manufactures. Yards of flannel made.	Domestic manufactures. Yards of linen made.	Domestic manufactures. Yards of cotton and mixed cloths.
Caroline,	185	734	2	798	667	6, 858	5, 172	16, 365½	1, 156	1, 853	1, 208½	1, 212	402	559
Danby,	....	954	....	609	858	7, 051	4, 461	14, 553	1, 657	1, 050	460	665	161	261
Dryden,	....	1, 870	....	1, 233	1, 405	12, 327	9, 225	31, 981½	4, 728	4, 612	830½	2, 376	264	567
Enfield,	....	857	....	736	699	5, 214	3, 826	12, 968	2, 244	1, 525	337	968	63	390
Groton,	....	1, 152	1	880	1, 025	5, 246	4, 062	14, 383	4, 065	14, 219	410	896	244	197
Ithaca,	30, 955	919	....	479	632	4, 494	2, 799	10, 322½	1, 178	967	....	170	....	30
Lansing,	900	1, 270	....	852	995	9, 340	9, 245	31, 001	2, 533	3, 957	236	343	70	82
Newfield,	....	962	....	488	879	5, 373	4, 094	13, 019	1, 150	1, 918	285	828	145	149
Ulysses,	4, 550	725	....	533	590	5, 133	4, 313	16, 241	2, 023	1, 104	....	14	....	24
Total,	36, 590	9, 443	3	6, 608	7, 750	61, 036	47, 197	160, 834½	20, 734	31, 205	3, 767	7, 472	1, 349	2, 259

ULSTER COUNTY.—(Continued.)

Towns.	Gallons of milk sold.	Horses.	Mules.	Swine. Under 6 months.	Swine. Over 6 months.	Sheep. Number of sheep.	Sheep. Number of fleeces.	Sheep. Pounds of wool.	Poultry. Value of poultry sold.	Poultry. Value of eggs sold.	Domestic manufactures. Yards of fulled cloth made.	Domestic manufactures. Yards of flannel made.	Domestic manufactures. Yards of linen made.	Domestic manufactures. Yards of cotton and mixed cloths.
Denning,	....	31	....	21	51	206	119	404	9	....	59½	110	8	10
Esopus,	8, 090	549	4	1, 324	657	453	335	1, 175	1, 626	3, 743	131	224	217	155
Gardiner,	....	504	....	1, 937	1, 011	4, 449	2, 708	7, 866	2, 481	3, 357	....	304	128	27
Hurley,	434	351	....	400	513	387	297	2, 282	776	1, 362	2½	30	15	210
Kingston,	50, 605	1, 018	12	2, 197	780	3, 250	357	1, 253½	1, 212	2, 731	29	192	169	69
Lloyd,	730	636	6	1, 185	598	582	337	1, 196	2, 588	2, 135	28	70	50	60
Marbletown,	10	718	....	1, 829	1, 021	1, 662	1, 077	3, 371	2, 374	3, 103	527	1, 145	710	396½
Marlborough,	60	386	....	1, 333	488	739	414	1, 937	3, 126	2, 328	....	30	....	....
New Paltz,	....	448	....	1, 431	625	1, 991	1, 494	5, 133	2, 414	2, 647	79	285	2	293
Olive,	250	437	....	613	406	1, 147	722	2, 245	515	1, 160	467	920	....	1, 671
Plattekill,	....	518	....	1, 892	786	1, 632	1, 228	3, 917	3, 649	4, 050	....	20	30	40
Rochester,	....	654	5	1, 329	901	2, 055	1, 413	4, 789	1, 790	1, 666	299½	655	174	323¼
Rosendale,	800	317	3	568	401	262	160	566	837	1, 504	116	148	150	33
Saugerties,	15, 825	1, 211	....	811	1, 853	1, 216	808	2, 586	1, 289	3, 051	273	256	598½	478
Shandaken,	....	366	....	204	315	1, 578	983	3, 065	192	68	484	483	25	1, 056
Shawangunk,	20	618	....	2, 541	1, 130	4, 599	2, 307	8, 393	2, 410	3, 848	181	115	....	25
Wawarsing,	12, 063	797	28	938	902	2, 265	1, 813	5, 638	1, 364	2, 164	362	7	....	....
Woodstock,	....	334	....	533	501	1, 368	708	2, 179	285	390	390	453	46	402
Total,	88, 887	9, 893	58	21, 086	12, 939	29, 841	17, 280	57, 995½	28, 937	39, 307	3, 428½	5, 447	2, 322½	5, 248¾

WARREN COUNTY.—(Continued.)

Towns.	Gallons of milk sold.	Horses.	Mules.	Swine. Under 6 months.	Swine. Over 6 months.	Sheep. Number of sheep.	Sheep. Number of fleeces.	Sheep. Pounds of wool.	Poultry. Value of poultry sold.	Poultry. Value of eggs sold.	Domestic manufactures. Yards of fulled cloth made.	Domestic manufactures. Yards of flannel made.	Domestic manufactures. Yards of linen made.	Domestic manufactures. Yards of cotton and mixed cloths.
Bolton,	....	277	....	295	159	2, 065	1, 351	4, 615	380	424	410½	590	265	364
Caldwell,	1, 090	171	....	193	154	856	609	2, 169	333	295	377	442	226	249
Chester,	100	450	....	347	347	2, 270	1, 508	5, 179	105	408	531	593	20	261
Hague,	2	132	....	129	109	501	388	1, 425	72	80	....	26	....	125
Horicon,	200	180	1	171	214	1, 094	752	2, 636	46	219	243	515¾	66	467
Johnsburgh,	....	358	....	369	365	2, 034	1, 410	4, 340	49	227	841	488	....	694
Luzerne,	550	282	2	222	232	930	525	1, 755	502	749	383	154½	....	79
Queensbury,	24, 682	960	....	816	636	3, 154	2, 431	8, 475	1, 438	2, 129	529	611	87	278
Stony Creek,	577	143	....	73	149	601	412	1, 286	61	44	182	319	30	167
Thurman,	....	128	....	83	137	1, 148	904	3, 017	....	623	105	142	....	....
Warrensburgh,	....	260	3	267	236	1, 819	1, 247	4, 104	187	372	142	213	36	183
Total,	27, 201	3. 341	6	2, 965	2, 738	16, 472	11, 546	39, 001	3, 173	5, 570	3, 743½	4, 094¼	730	2, 867

WASHINGTON COUNTY.—(Continued.)

Towns.	Gallons of milk sold.	Horses.	Mules.	Swine. Under 6 months.	Swine. Over 6 months.	Sheep. Number of sheep.	Sheep. Number of fleeces.	Sheep. Pounds of wool.	Poultry. Value of poultry sold.	Poultry. Value of eggs sold.	Domestic manufactures. Yards of fulled cloth made.	Domestic manufactures. Yards of flannel made.	Domestic manufactures. Yards of linen made.	Domestic manufactures. Yards of cotton and mixed cloths.
Argyle,	....	1, 196	....	2, 543	1, 515	4, 567	4, 142	14, 326½	3, 334	8, 095	30	90	70	25
Cambridge,	....	737	....	1, 915	982	9, 715	7, 638	25, 141	5, 336	3, 141	167	303	279	489½
Dresden,	....	150	....	95	117	1, 613	1, 174	4, 228	130	112	34	134	....	235
Easton,	....	1, 030	....	1, 978	1, 050	13, 425	11, 004	35, 411	3, 579	4, 229	464	622	270	179
Fort Ann,	8, 130	797	8	547	580	5, 196	5, 100	16, 998¾	925	784	201	257	43	30
Fort Edward,	3, 380	443	....	549	384	2, 266	1, 857	6, 203½	641	1, 472	....	15	....	25
Granville,	1, 900	855	....	927	654	4, 735	4, 461	15, 196½	1, 822	1, 474	....	164	80	172
Greenwich,	5, 517	913	....	1, 828	862	4, 370	3, 540	11, 764	1, 938	4, 286	107	....	45	60
Hampton,	....	168	....	168	162	4, 432	3, 616	12, 892	428	411	....	....	....	....
Hartford,	465	697	....	872	607	12, 068	9, 229	35, 138¼	1, 619	1, 907	....	86	136	47
Hebron,	....	884	1	1, 543	808	5, 185	3, 983	13, 374½	1, 849	3, 050	15	12	45	....
Jackson,	600	634	....	1, 850	966	6, 817	5, 134	18, 239	2, 194	4, 739	16	40	138	84
Kingsbury,	1, 562	634	....	721	463	5, 931	4, 318	14, 757½	1, 132	1, 629	27	43	74	102
Putnam,	300	240	....	91	123	3, 098	2, 084	7, 266	92	314	32	464	20	135
Salem,	2, 780	888	....	1, 936	1, 027	8, 554	8, 199	27, 025	2, 830	6, 539	....	25	....	20
White Creek,	....	559	2	1, 010	628	18, 905	16, 468	52, 417	2, 582	1, 923	....	....	55	....
Whitehall,	5, 975	882	....	407	397	7, 656	5, 338	20, 488	971	1, 088	40	22	....	30
Total,	30, 609	11, 707	11	18, 980	11, 325	118, 533	97. 285	330, 860½	31, 402	45, 193	1, 133	2, 277	1, 255	1, 633½

WAYNE COUNTY.

TOWNS.	ACRES. Improved.	ACRES. Unimproved.	CASH VALUE. Of farm.	CASH VALUE. Of stock.	CASH VALUE. Of tools and implements.	Acres plowed the year previous.	Acres in fallow the year previous.	Acres in pasture the year previous.	MEADOW. Acres.	MEADOW. Tons of hay.	MEADOW. Bushels of grass seed.	SPRING WHEAT. Acres sown.	SPRING WHEAT. Bushels harvested.	WINTER WHEAT. Acres sown.
Arcadia,........	24,539	5,967¾	$1,919,748	$222,717	$76,867	7,703	1,846½	5,344½	3,532½	4,580	471½	17	151	3,690
Butler,.........	15,316	6,920	966,250	128,745	42,420	5,936	678	3,990	2,184	2,557	90	13	134	1,544
Galen,..........	24,301¼	10,625	1,729,875	216,309	50,795	9,086	1,279	5,642	3,549¾	3,806	210½	10	136	2,625
Huron,..........	12,220½	7,692	765,392	96,050	26,895	5,633½	555½	3,736½	1,859½	1,910	143½	84	732	1,192
Lyons,..........	15,917	5,230	1,314,709	161,246	48,883	5,768½	1,094½	3,862	2,711	3,430	236	9½	172	2,274
Macedon,........	18,674	4,389	1,277,164	162,241	30,211	4,705¼	1,146	4,350	2,904½	3,163	26	6	86	2,254¼
Marion,.........	14,362¼	3,698	838,455	118,114	21,700	4,668	729	3,651¼	2,303⅞	2,683½	256	1	10	1,588½
Ontario,........	13,886⅝	5,978¾	878,312	137,392	28,628	4,108⅞	875½	3,774¼	2,374	2,685½	106	2½	19	1,630½
Palmyra,........	17,099½	4,202¼	1,354,510	156,793	36,253	4,308	1,595	4,034	2,724	3,713	49½	3½	39	2,330½
Rose,...........	13,272⅜	8,577	831,771	125,870	18,091	4,504	566	3,136	1,908½	1,724½	24½	10	138	907½
Savannah,.......	11,250½	7,967¾	814,189	104,036	28,698	4,800½	600	2,906	1,537	1,904	54	......	......	1,245¾
Sodus,..........	29,963⅝	11,697¾	1,616,454	234,992	72,809	10,177⅛	1,977	7,581⅝	4,400	5,072½	156	33	302	3,765¾
Walworth,.......	15,858¾	4,605	1,007,806	128,650	31,484	5,407¼	724¾	4,944½	2,910¼	3,386	44½	7	104	1,521½
Williamson,.....	14,796	5,802	972,828	133,394	34,124	4,455	786	4,546	2,592	2,943	192	25	297	1,498
Wolcott,........	12,995	8,710	749,950	111,876	33,238	4,640	543	2,814½	1,675	1,713½	66	41⅝	367	1,147
Total,........	254,451⅝	102,062¼	17,037,413	2,238,425	581,096	85,901	14,995¾	64,313⅛	39,165⅞	45,271½	2,126	263⅛	2,687	29214¼

WESTCHESTER COUNTY.

TOWNS.	ACRES. Improved.	ACRES. Unimproved.	CASH VALUE. Of farm.	CASH VALUE. Of stock.	CASH VALUE. Of tools and implements.	Acres plowed the year previous.	Acres in fallow the year previous.	Acres in pasture the year previous.	MEADOW. Acres.	MEADOW. Tons of hay.	MEADOW. Bushels of grass seed.	SPRING WHEAT. Acres sown.	SPRING WHEAT. Bushels harvested.	WINTER WHEAT. Acres sown.
Bedford,........	21,243¼	3,473	1,668,553	164,080	49,539	3,759¾	614	10,671⅝	6,114½	8,344	78	5	51	233½
Cortlandt,......	13,614¾	6,966½	1,577,000	153,276	29,278	3,080½	282	5,981	4,490½	5,100½	10	......	......	285½
Eastchester,....	4,506½	13,524	735,050	52,525	11,025	764½	193	1,371½	1,782½	2,572	......	......	......	101½
Greenburgh,....	12,702	2,182¼	3,364,240	104,885	37,785	1,629	342	2,768	2,277	5,127	......	1½	16	125
Harrison,.......	8,616¼	1,676	888,450	72,722	19,088	1,185	29	2,262	2,908½	4,187	4	......	......	308½
Lewisboro',.....	12,840½	4,924	934,515	96,715	24,602	1,640½	39	6,295¼	3,936¾	4,390½	135¼	1	5	184½
Mamaroneck,...	2,831½	1,051	523,700	32,636	6,344	401	34	1,437	926	1,121	......	......	......	30
Mount Pleasant,.	13,396¼	3,130½	1,622,015	110,418	35,144	2,536½	428	5,756	3,798¼	5,797½	13½	167	1,300	217½
New Castle,.....	11,211	2,781	1,009,700	78,360	28,130	1,928½	45	3,902	3,489	4,902	43	......	......	352
New Rochelle,...	3,601	1,562	1,054,200	55,305	15,640	672	143	1,305	1,503	2,471	3	1	25	137
North Castle,....	11,402¼	4,410½	907,900	87,081	27,562	2,060	168	4,654	3,377½	4,600½	107½	......	......	283
North Salem,...	10,970	2,051	888,235	80,209	17,964	1,023	....	5,772½	3,525½	4,590	11½	......	......	150
Ossining,.......	5,891	1,304	1,278,000	70,171	19,925	1,048½	121	962	2,291	3,004	13	......	......	178½
Pelham,........	1,901	1,333	380,500	18,375	12,455	333	43	870	532	968	......	......	......	35
Poundridge,.....	8,214½	3,894¾	480,149	51,322	5,460	1,141¼	71½	3,660½	2,181½	2,303¼	39	......	......	49¾
Rye,...........	6,090	1,251	1,049,050	53,320	17,120	620½	297½	2,058¾	2,410	4,093	4	......	......	176½
Scarsdale,......	2,801¾	1,132½	427,140	41,213	9,881	457½	28½	977	786	1,225	2	7½	78	115
Somers,........	17,234½	3,110	1,396,538	140,383	39,900	2,544¼	183	8,458¼	4,956	6,675	61	......	22	372½
Westchester,....	5,479	2,579½	2,676,340	116,875	22,165	1,051	29	1,740	2,069½	3,174	1,139	......	......	49½
West Farms,....	3,235½	992	2,279,250	93,678	28,185	656	47	737	1,563	2,786	......	......	......	20½
White Plains,...	3,276	9,317	415,750	36,015	11,572	840½	87	1,541	1,619	2,502	15	......	......	146½
Yonkers,.......	9,699	4,267	2,183,400	97,916	23,914	1,850¼	209½	2,805	2,174½	3,327	......	......	......	93½
Yorktown,......	18,389¼	5,035	1,543,495	157,259	45,227	3,424½	1,085½	7,902½	5,598	7,237	83	......	......	576¾
Total,........	209,146¾	81,947½	29,283,170	1,964,739	537,905	34,647½	4,519½	83,890¾	64,309½	90,496⅞	1,761¾	183	1,497	4,222

WYOMING COUNTY.

TOWNS.	ACRES. Improved.	ACRES. Unimproved.	CASH VALUE. Of farm.	CASH VALUE. Of stock.	CASH VALUE. Of tools and implements.	Acres plowed the year previous.	Acres in fallow the year previous.	Acres in pasture the year previous.	MEADOW. Acres.	MEADOW. Tons of hay.	MEADOW. Bushels of grass seed.	SPRING WHEAT. Acres sown.	SPRING WHEAT. Bushels harvested.	WINTER WHEAT. Acres sown.
Attica,.........	16,432	8,628	728,014	117,539	16,920	2,739	469	7,862	5,506	5,205	76	202¾	2,155	513¼
Bennington,.....	22,377	13,110	751,995	147,198	27,575	4,816½	323½	10,255	6,149	6,410	230½	335½	3,640	403¾
Castile,.........	17,970½	5,755	1,218,736	132,167	39,381	3,360¾	3,266	3,919½	2,546½	2,597	65½	135½	1,369	4,121½
China,..........	15,756	13,583	651,831	100,248	24,165	3,354	....	7,049	4,607	4,683½	73	267¼	2,873	335
Covington,......	12,344½	2,980	901,689	101,757	32,570	1,665	3,113	2,194	1,751½	2,130	147	16	190	2,996½
Eagle,..........	12,916	9,923	456,591	90,286	20,575	3,650½	107½	5,087	3,258	2,808	107½	327	3,428	78¾
Gainesville,.....	14,128½	6,290	646,910	94,569	10,073	4,134	136½	4,625½	3,194	2,437	58	184	1,668½	1,211¼
Genesee Falls,...	5,772½	2,925	365,075	34,271	8,305	1,276	847½	1,446	964	934	25	108	920	806
Java,...........	17,996	11,709	699,135	130,187	16,063	4,825	190	7,362	4,689	3,995	64	309½	4,129	212¾
Middlebury,....	15,500	4,603	1,115,724	131,276	40,308	2,692¾	2,217	5,987½	3,579½	4,360	143	234½	3,235	2,400
Orangeville,.....	14,336	6,464	496,935	85,040	16,117	2,150¼	173½	6,934	4,311½	4,605	83	194½	2,462	270
Perry,..........	17,984	4,771	1,300,113	150,888	45,140	2,932¼	3,643½	4,322	2,909½	2,834½	70½	51¼	624½	3,691¼
Pike,...........	11,084	5,930	651,196	97,767	18,052	3,276	381½	5,499½	3,210	2,624	41½	310	2,922	427½
Sheldon,........	17,795	11,656	576,035	109,632	23,136	4,098½	499½	7,241	5,175	5,859	165½	223¾	2,940	172½
Warsaw,.......	16,442	4,782	845,686	125,604	32,854	2,805	1,528	5.945	3,813	4,043	82	125¼	1,208	1,264¾
Wethersfield,...	12,820¼	9,655½	498,152	65,741	22,503	2,998¾	245½	4,467½	3,520½	2,896¼	104¼	275	3,733½	293½
Total,........	241,654¼	122,764½	11,903,817	1,714,170	393,737	50,774¼	17,141½	90,196½	59,184	58,421¼	1,536¼	3,299¾	37497½	19198¼

YATES COUNTY.

TOWNS.	ACRES. Improved.	ACRES. Unimproved.	CASH VALUE. Of farm.	CASH VALUE. Of stock.	CASH VALUE. Of tools and implements.	Acres plowed the year previous.	Acres in fallow the year previous.	Acres in pasture the year previous.	MEADOW. Acres.	MEADOW. Tons of hay.	MEADOW. Bushels of grass seed.	SPRING WHEAT. Acres sown.	SPRING WHEAT. Bushels harvested.	WINTER WHEAT. Acres sown.
Barrington,.....	16,888⅝	5,227	876,259	93,302	28,888	5,526	380½	4,348	2,685	1,378	82	604½	4,715	1,555½
Benton,........	19,496	5,009½	1,666,747	167,118	53,621	7,325	480½	5,036	2,956	2,435½	78½	71	675	1,765
Italy,..........	15,312⅝	10,156½	544,038	78,550	13,844	3,506½	919	4,163	2,608	1,827	35	730¾	4,805¼	1,265¼
Jerusalem,......	26,394½	8,373½	1,422,189	176,064	46,518	6,450½	1,821	7,198½	3,741	2,801	87½	873¾	5,683	3,049¾
Middlesex,......	15,472½	5,172¾	814,085	96,540	25,680	3,746	1,066	5,004¼	2,345½	1,522	1½	61	199¼	2,406½
Milo,..........	18,026½	4,716	1,371,314	153,820	42,849	4,772½	999	4,627	2,456½	1,392	36	145¾	1,161½	2,203
Potter,.........	16,612½	5,599¼	1,050,290	134,625	37,065	4,686¾	607	4,125	2.680	2,046½	26½	84½	506	1,973
Starkey,........	15,858½	4,062½	1,064,203	120,528	30,372	5,261⅝	441½	3,819¼	2,292½	1,422¼	65½	49¼	295	1,901
Torrey,.........	11,481	2,817	882,265	77,896	27,089	3,380	258	2,592	1,608	1,026	37	3½	23	1,468
Total,........	155,542½	51,134	9,691,390	1,098,443	305,926	44,654⅞	6,972½	40,913	23,372½	15,850¼	449½	2,624	18063	17587

WAYNE COUNTY.—(CONTINUED.)

TOWNS.	WINTER WHEAT.	OATS.		RYE.		BARLEY.		BUCKWHEAT.		CORN.		POTATOES.		PEAS.	
	Bushels harvested.	Acres sown.	Bushels harvested	Acres sown.	Bushels harvested.	Acres sown.	Bushels harvested.	Acres sown.	Bushels harvested.	Acres planted.	Bushels harvested.	Acres planted.	Bushels harvested.	Acres sown.	Bushels harvested.
Arcadia,........	43827	2, 380½	73, 470	14¼	205	1, 612¼	34, 444	449	5, 486	2, 583½	63, 634	335½	23, 870	33¾	390
Butler,.........	15284	1, 898½	60, 724	68	1, 178	629	13, 520	218	2, 498	2, 220	63, 487	212½	17, 906	13	210
Galen, ...	30477	3, 337½	106, 511	37¼	701	819	17, 666	345¼	3, 519½	2, 755	70, 074	303⅛	19, 546	40⅞	565
Huron, ...	9055	2, 075	58, 089	120	1, 302	495	11, 646	310¼	2, 411	1, 606	39, 570	209¾	15, 895	14¼	288
Lyons,.........	27075	1, 795¾	56, 234½	30½	282	1, 085¾	24, 975	295½	3, 148¼	2, 008½	49, 040¾	229½	17, 473	17½	897½
Macedon, ...	25665	1, 371½	43, 779	13½	122	813¾	18, 226	130¾	289	1, 991⅞	48, 227	280⅛	16, 777	13¾	110
Marion,........	12301	1, 889⅝	57, 426	16	172	289¾	6, 412	242⅛	1, 748½	1, 743¾	41, 953½	204¾	15, 740	60¼	920
Ontario,........	9386	1, 265	35, 817	9½	124	424	9, 566	150¼	1, 006	1, 689¾	36, 414	229½	15, 272	41¾	636
Palmyra, ...	31022	1, 071¼	36, 500	1	51	1, 180½	27, 481	80½	754	1, 706¼	47, 270	189½	16, 701	10	133
Rose, ...	8893	1, 760½	44, 266	72	885	311	6, 013	310½	3, 270	1, 546½	40, 035	184¾	13, 246	8⅝	156
Savannah,......	15885	1, 506	49, 357	2	40	417	9, 350	182½	2, 753½	1, 554¼	51, 667	157	14, 376	4¾	649
Sodus,.........	24975¾	3, 587¼	101, 291	45¾	420½	1, 088¼	22, 411	756	7, 192	2, 946⅜	74, 803	368⅛	30, 847	70¼	1, 136
Walworth,......	12123	1, 676	51, 590	28	377	522½	11, 566	167⅞	1, 812½	1, 859⅞	48, 314	218½	19, 065	8½	159
Williamson, ...	8475	1, 660	48, 761	37	328	222	4, 877	284	1, 441	1, 616	36, 613	165	13, 835	91	1, 361
Wolcott,........	8031	1, 826	51, 809	80	1, 072	588½	11, 342	298	2, 437	1, 646¼	45, 575	165¼	10, 854	44½	845
Total, ...	282474¾	29, 100⅛	875, 624½	574¾	7, 259½	10498¼	229, 495	4, 220½	39, 766¼	29, 473⅞	756, 677¼	3, 452⅞	261, 403	472¾	8, 455½

WESTCHESTER COUNTY.—(CONTINUED.)

TOWNS.	WINTER WHEAT.	OATS.		RYE.		BARLEY.		BUCKWHEAT.		CORN.		POTATOES.		PEAS.	
	Bushels harvested.	Acres sown.	Bushels harvested	Acres sown.	Bushels harvested.	Acres sown.	Bushels harvested.	Acres sown.	Bushels harvested.	Acres planted.	Bushels harvested.	Acres planted.	Bushels harvested.	Acres sown.	Bushels harvested.
Bedford, ...	1, 666	1, 018	20, 406	781¾	8, 274	......	....	400	3, 246½	1, 227½	38, 124	528¾	31, 432	......	....
Cortlandt,......	2, 185	1, 079	14, 425	489	4, 815	......	....	326	1, 587	995	20, 603	448	18, 944	1½	85
Eastchester, ...	990	187	3, 385	67½	726	......	....	128½	3, 016	314¾	9, 450	89	4, 474	......	10
Greenburgh,....	1, 434½	451	13, 554	234	4, 316	......	....	62½	713	391	20, 079½	177	14, 400	......	....
Harrison, ...	2, 789½	283	4, 713	105½	1, 437	......	....	25	111	569¾	15, 580	191	9, 389	......	....
Lewisboro', ...	1, 235	733½	14, 087	248½	2, 435	......	....	238½	1, 726½	663⅞	21, 168	160⅝	12, 205	......	....
Mamaroneck,...	456	51½	939	13½	168	33	484	7	12	163	4, 141	81½	2, 989	......	....
Mount Pleasant,	2, 044½	924	20, 182	371¼	3, 029	......	....	190	705½	910¾	26, 911	380¼	18, 987	......	....
New Castle, ...	2, 428	665½	11, 752	237½	2, 102½	......	....	126	735½	732	18, 764	178¾	9, 117	......	....
New Rochelle,..	1, 709	154	3, 246	53	631	......	....	6	28	322	8, 210	88	4, 343	......	....
North Castle,...	1, 794½	550¼	9, 594	295½	2, 812	......	....	156¾	863¾	715¾	18, 869	327⅛	17, 783	......	....
North Salem,...	861	292	7, 172	150½	1, 581½	......	....	84¼	708½	504¼	18, 560	83⅜	7, 220	......	....
Ossining,.......	1, 341	240	4, 566	78½	755	......	....	68½	383	339½	19, 881	161	8, 752	......	....
Pelham, ...	518	100½	2, 565	3	45	5	27	....	....	108	3, 005	44¼	2, 203	......	....
Poundridge, ...	262	330½	4, 516	213	1, 924	......	....	200¼	1, 148½	492¼	10, 297	120½	6, 567	......	....
Rye,...........	1, 876	204½	3, 655	41½	560	......	....	11¼	69½	349	11, 998	127¾	7, 523	......	....
Scarsdale,......	967	121½	2, 376	66½	807	2	34	17¼	82	89¾	5, 982	36¾	2, 082	......	....
Somers,........	1, 981	1, 038	20, 505	308½	3, 902	......	....	181½	1, 333	1, 107	36, 091	320	22, 809	......	....
Westchester, ...	645	201¾	4, 480	30	591	......	....	24	95	414½	18, 225	150¾	10, 005	¼	35
West Farms, ...	146	92½	2, 245	7½	84	......	....	14	103	142½	5, 304	86¼	12, 960	1	60
White Plains, ..	1, 517	240½	3, 956	170	870	90	....	37	222	404	13, 355	147	7, 948	......	....
Yonkers,.......	1, 711	350½	9, 581	442½	4, 532	......	....	88	1, 144½	510¼	19, 377	229¾	17, 739	1	40
Yorktown, ...	3, 194½	1, 634½	22, 859	559¾	5, 007	......	....	454	2, 857	1, 372	38, 264	602	36, 378	......	....
Total,........	33751½	10, 943½	204, 759	4, 968¼	51, 404	130	545	2, 846¼	20. 890¾	12, 838⅝	402, 238½	4, 759⅛	286, 249	3¾	230

WYOMING COUNTY.—(CONTINUED.

TOWNS.	WINTER WHEAT.	OATS.		RYE.		BARLEY.		BUCKWHEAT.		CORN.		POTATOES.		PEAS.	
	Bushels harvested.	Acres sown.	Bushels harvested	Acres sown.	Bushels harvested.	Acres sown.	Bushels harvested.	Acres sown.	Bushels harvested.	Acres planted.	Bushels harvested.	Acres planted.	Bushels harvested.	Acres sown.	Bushels harvested.
Attica,.........	10276	999	17, 181	......	....	246½	3, 449	311¼	2, 842½	488¼	12, 029	189½	11, 364	113½	1, 431
Bennington, ...	5372	2, 379½	44, 028	45½	609	358	5, 084	299½	2, 201½	580¼	10, 594	394	15, 261	76	989
Castile, ...	108223½	959	18, 664	2	36	686	12, 356	94½	1, 362	1, 105	34, 186	142¼	13, 027	21¾	287½
China, ...	198	2, 283	53, 657	1½	10	102	1, 420	30½	330	291¼	10, 991	208	15, 724	25¼	494
Covington, ...	60321	344	8, 541	......	....	92½	1, 554	36	398	812½	19, 447	88	5, 782	......	......
Eagle, ...	907	2, 374	53, 484	8	60	234½	3, 550	124½	1, 455½	157½	5, 329	187¼	17, 509	42½	774
Gainesville,.....	17704	2, 254	39, 510	11½	84½	297½	2, 344	133¼	1, 545½	679	16, 553	177¾	13, 806	74¾	793
Genesee Falls, ..	12888	470	9, 855	5	100	119	2, 023	31½	413	401½	11, 583	48	4, 479	12¼	170
Java, ...	3371	2, 880	67, 745	21¾	370	153½	2, 769	57	526	539¼	14, 180	287	16, 520	50¼	720
Middlebury,....	66003½	752½	17. 284	5	75	224½	3, 385	214	2, 003	859	22, 086	194½	9, 153	94½	1, 465
Orangeville, ...	4137	849¾	17, 516	9½	161	228¾	3, 466	92¾	1, 015½	289½	6, 594	164½	10, 902	119½	1, 684
Perry, ...	60580	943½	19, 025	3	45	550¾	12, 069	167½	1, 201	971	27, 096	168½	17, 203	52¾	726
Pike, ...	6347	1, 773½	29, 661	13½	96	290	3, 863	81	725	305	13, 808	156	14, 431	52½	832
Sheldon, ...	2684	2, 108	46, 048	61	927	281½	4. 326	61¼	714½	391	9, 515	315½	12, 940	36	563
Warsaw,.......	18600	1, 004	15, 268	7½	144	177¾	2, 497	331¾	2, 760½	547	13, 102	208½	14, 700	97¾	1, 409
Wethersfield,...	4886½	2, 004	39, 370	17	60	246¾	4, 112	84	784¼	264	6, 913	157½	11, 131	64	989
Total, ...	382498½	24, 377¼	496, 837	211¾	2, 777½	4, 289½	68, 267	2, 150¼	20. 277¾	8, 681	234, 006	3, 086¾	203, 932	933¼	13, 326½

YATES COUNTY.—(CONTINUED.)

TOWNS.	WINTER WHEAT.	OATS.		RYE.		BARLEY.		BUCKWHEAT.		CORN.		POTATOES.		PEAS.	
	Bushels harvested.	Acres sown.	Bushels harvested	Acres sown.	Bushels harvested.	Acres sown.	Bushels harvested.	Acres sown.	Bushels harvested.	Acres planted.	Bushels harvested.	Acres planted.	Bushels harvested.	Acres sown.	Bushels harvested.
Barrington, ...	9366	1, 437	23, 360	342	3, 360	948	11, 424	922¼	5, 269½	872	15, 290	102½	6, 889	5	45
Benton,........	22911	1, 551	31, 314	296	4, 272	2, 471	38, 776	530¼	3, 841	2, 167¼	42, 719	128¾	8, 360	11¾	112
Italy,...... ...	6766½	992¾	7, 533½	35½	295	467	3, 020½	280½	660	473¾	3, 878½	124⅝	5, 311	73	348¾
Jerusalem, ...	28159	2, 045	22, 819	508	5, 395	1, 459½	17, 710	678	2, 149	1, 286	12, 434½	151	7, 879	70	729
Middlesex, ...	22080½	777¾	4, 541	66	502	1, 332½	9, 445	231½	1, 941	1, 154¼	7, 923	89¾	3, 115	14	17½
Milo, ...	23880	1, 349½	18, 430¼	300½	3, 468	1, 345½	15, 121	600	1, 763¼	1, 235	16, 622	121¼	6, 963	10⅛	118
Potter,.........	19664½	925½	10, 003	133	1, 483	1, 778½	20, 408	271¾	1, 021	1, 632⅝	22, 032	96¾	3, 970	3	7
Starkey, ...	16885	1, 558	27, 967	429¼	5, 296	1, 564	19, 659½	657½	6, 456	1, 358¼	30, 344	147¾	11, 585½	4	44
Torrey, ...	19257	843	14, 490	36	446	1, 119½	16, 570	262½	906½	924½	22, 938	56	3, 840	1	23
Total, ...	168969½	11, 479½	160, 457¾	2, 146¼	24, 517	12485½	152, 134	4, 434¼	24, 007¼	11, 103⅝	174, 181	1, 018⅝	57, 912½	191⅞	1, 444

WAYNE COUNTY.—(Continued.)

TOWNS.	BEANS. Acres planted.	BEANS. Bushels harvested.	TURNIPS. Acres sown.	TURNIPS. Bushels harvested.	FLAX. Acres sown.	FLAX. Pounds of lint.	FLAX. Bushels of seed.	HEMP. Acres sown.	HEMP. Tons of hemp.	HOPS. Acres planted.	HOPS. Pounds harvested.	TOBACCO. Acres planted.	TOBACCO. Pounds harvested.	APPLE ORCHARDS. Bushels of apples.	APPLE ORCHARDS. Barrels of cider.
Arcadia	211	2,524	5¾	1,133										38,424	1,004
Butler	2½	58	5	710										51,981	828
Galen	29	621	14⅜	3,183							11	3	3,000	49,588	1,169
Huron	20¼	299	8¼	1,085						1	400			20,361	347½
Lyons	15	284½	3	476	2½		18					1	2,000	51,526	1,129
Macedon	10⅞	182½	6⅛	1,401	¼		2			5				27,949	343½
Marion	20¼	274½	7½	1,045	3½	900	32½							34,035	389½
Ontario	13¾	151¼	5¾	649										17,431	319
Palmyra	2¼	58	2⅛	377						¼	304	20	28,000	33,113	567
Rose	20½	322	12½	3,893							5			28,535	399
Savannah	4⅞	77	2⅜	578	¼	25	½							14,907	310
Sodus	25½	403¾	30⅛	6,873	½	20	4					4⅛	4,900	70,448	910½
Walworth	10	158¾	8⅜	1,477	¼	70	1				17			21,170	494½
Williamson	6	77	5	707	49⅞	21,715	465					½	500	32,702	385
Wolcott	11⅞	375½	6	1,112	¼	530	4½						32	17,456	298
Total	403⅝	5,866¾	122¼	24,699	57⅜	23,260	527½			6¼	737	28⅝	38,432	509,626	8,893½

WESTCHESTER COUNTY.—(Continued.)

TOWNS.	BEANS. Acres planted.	BEANS. Bushels harvested.	TURNIPS. Acres sown.	TURNIPS. Bushels harvested.	FLAX. Acres sown.	FLAX. Pounds of lint.	FLAX. Bushels of seed.	HEMP. Acres sown.	HEMP. Tons of hemp.	HOPS. Acres planted.	HOPS. Pounds harvested.	TOBACCO. Acres planted.	TOBACCO. Pounds harvested.	APPLE ORCHARDS. Bushels of apples.	APPLE ORCHARDS. Barrels of cider.
Bedford	¼	6	140⅜	8,336										3,333	71
Cortlandt	1	30	45½	2,135								½	210	934	14
Eastchester	½	20	12½	1,295										145	2
Greenburgh			60½	6,962							5			430	5
Harrison			9¼	1,065										2,173	33½
Lewisboro'		4	4½	4,413										1,876	211
Mamaroneck			6	280										636	5
Mount Pleasant			7¾	940										1,717	24
New Castle			⅜	90										472	1
New Rochelle	1	10	6½	2,545										156	26
North Castle	½	9	40¼	2,283								2¼	1,540	1,609½	13½
North Salem			1½	515										1,447	97¾
Ossining	2¼	17	39	2,638										510	4½
Pelham			½	50											
Poundridge	½	8	1	230										1,346	46½
Rye			¼	10										1,731	17
Scarsdale			15¾	1,395										493	18½
Somers	¾	19½	66½	2,615										5,765	200½
Westchester			23¾	3,540									2	108	10
West Farms	1¼	130	80	4,780										118	
White Plains			19	2,360										2,243	48
Yonkers	3	20	39⅜	8,902								½	450	29,006	1,406
Yorktown	1	5		3,614										3,889	70½
Total	12	278½	620⅜	60,993							5	3¼	2,202	60,137½	2,325¼

WYOMING COUNTY.—(Continued.)

TOWNS.	BEANS. Acres planted.	BEANS. Bushels harvested.	TURNIPS. Acres sown.	TURNIPS. Bushels harvested.	FLAX. Acres sown.	FLAX. Pounds of lint.	FLAX. Bushels of seed.	HEMP. Acres sown.	HEMP. Tons of hemp.	HOPS. Acres planted.	HOPS. Pounds harvested.	TOBACCO. Acres planted.	TOBACCO. Pounds harvested.	APPLE ORCHARDS. Bushels of apples.	APPLE ORCHARDS. Barrels of cider.
Attica	13⅛	125										⅛	40	40,530	1,028
Bennington	64¾	545½	7	311	2½	122	11	½						20,781	312
Castile	6¾	54	¾	245	¼	10								19,079	421½
China	4½	106½	3	713										6,694	50
Covington	115	1,459												10,735	181
Eagle	4	161	5½	1,585	1	180	4½						75	5,790	
Gainesville	7	80½	13	1,950	13	169	75							24,396	361
Genesee Falls	2	27	1½	205										7,449	171
Java	21¾	289½	72½	1,210						12½	13,400			12,962	101
Middlebury	98½	4,044½	¾	81						5	4,126			35,499	206
Orangeville	10¼	152½	1	299										19,248	226
Perry	15	213½	1½	221										29,524	392
Pike	6½	160	¾	182	1¼		10							21,016	340
Sheldon	4½	70	3¼	160	¼	80								25,649	151½
Warsaw	42½	556	¼	168	1	142	2							33,288	499½
Wethersfield	13	188	2½	397	50¾	5,927	415¾							10,650	77
Total	429⅛	8,232½	113¼	7,727	70	6,630	518¼	½		17½	17,526	⅛	115	323,290	4,517½

YATES COUNTY.—(Continued.)

TOWNS.	BEANS. Acres planted.	BEANS. Bushels harvested.	TURNIPS. Acres sown.	TURNIPS. Bushels harvested.	FLAX. Acres sown.	FLAX. Pounds of lint.	FLAX. Bushels of seed.	HEMP. Acres sown.	HEMP. Tons of hemp.	HOPS. Acres planted.	HOPS. Pounds harvested.	TOBACCO. Acres planted.	TOBACCO. Pounds harvested.	APPLE ORCHARDS. Bushels of apples.	APPLE ORCHARDS. Barrels of cider.
Barrington	3	43½	3¼	250	26	2,500	89							11,509	239
Benton	11	145	1⅜	208	27	33,000	170							34,626	949
Italy	8½	59½	3	139	½		½				5		3	5,903	48½
Jerusalem	10⅛	54	8¼		34	15,500	190							14,814	336½
Middlesex	5¼	21½	1		173¼		214							7,066	114
Milo	4¼	29½	¾	140	58¼	52,000	396½					6	6,000	15,425	685
Potter	17⅜	76½	2⅞	62	8½	500	5½			4	1,600			21,139	586
Starkey	29¼	298¾	5⅛	671	3		10							23,927	572½
Torrey	2¾	17½	¼	30	151¾	141,500	774½							9,364	230
Total	91¾	745¾	25⅞	1,500	482¼	245,000	1,850			4	1,605	6	6,003	143,773	3,760½

WAYNE COUNTY.—(Continued.)

TOWNS.	MARKET GARDENS.		Pounds of maple sugar made.	Gallons of maple molasses made.	Gallons of wine made.	Pounds of honey collected.	Pounds of wax collected.	SILK.	NEAT CATTLE.				Number of cattle killed for beef.	Pounds of butter.	Pounds of cheese.
	Acres cultivated.	Value of products.						Pounds of cocoons.	Under one year old.	Over one y'r, exclusive of working oxen & cows.	Working oxen.	Cows.			
Arcadia,	9½	$1, 100	927	93	12	4, 552	153	......	594	1, 031	110	1, 493	188	140, 054	5, 331
Butler,	......	......	440	266	28	5, 006	143	......	529	1, 100	137	1, 024	119	97, 571	15, 112
Galen,	......	33	573	78	75	5, 885	382	......	694	1, 164	103	1, 649	334	140, 558	16, 278
Huron,	½	59	2, 169	86	......	4, 638	286	......	360	572	159	675	87	59, 850	4, 844
Lyons,	32½	2, 023	169	45	147	4, 272	149	......	436	770	116	1, 610	102	89, 472	4, 128
Macedon,	⅛	310	1, 708	183	85½	2, 350	87½	......	391	806	132	953	106	77, 662	9, 900
Marion,	1¾	285	470	19	......	1, 887	95½	......	331	717	36	974	111	96, 550	18, 763
Ontario,	......	......	300	16	43	2, 650	144	......	480	605	116	923	144	86, 375	17, 400
Palmyra,	......	......	2, 882	99	263	3, 944	119	......	433	802	68	1, 193	534	105, 711	14, 816
Rose,	⅛	8	446	14	15	4, 722	228	......	423	756	107	871	62	66, 330	7, 075
Savannah,	......	......	162	16	......	2, 587	130	......	415	855	78	761	145	69, 216	2, 290
Sodus,	3	265	456	37	12	5, 796	345½	......	785	1, 476	255	1, 846	164	177, 259	9, 755½
Walworth,	......	......	1, 525	151	......	2, 471	63½	......	348	688	112	878	91	68, 464	5, 444
Williamson,	2	100	426	46	......	3, 725	188	......	468	741	69	1, 037	206	91, 822	30, 175
Wolcott,	¼	15	1, 210	91	......	3, 719	306½	70	446	717	164	882	63	79, 186	2, 452
Total,	49¾	4, 198	13, 863	1, 240	680½	58, 204	2, 820½	70	7, 133	12, 800	1, 762	16, 769	2, 456	1, 446, 080	163, 763½
WESTCHESTER COUNTY.—(Continued.)															
Bedford,	......	......	......	......	5	782	26	......	157	314	451	2, 127	353	76, 854	200
Cortlandt,	......	19½	1, 375	......	25	1, 339	61	......	192	376	372	1, 635	272	85, 830	......
Eastchester,	300	......	......	......	......	624	31	......	45	61	132	595	223	19, 732	100
Greenburgh,	⅛	50	......	......	......	1, 402	72	5	235	217	380	858	401	48, 952	......
Harrison,	3	500	......	......	12	479	......	......	188	227	254	766	189	44, 515	100
Lewisboro'	......	......	......	......	......	2, 216	54	......	225	254	302	1, 386	59	62, 767	925
Mamaroneck,	......	......	......	......	30	120	......	......	51	43	60	233	131	16, 957	......
Mount Pleasant,	1½	100	......	......	......	1, 484	59	......	126	344	357	1, 058	215	60, 258	......
New Castle,	......	......	5	......	......	164	......	......	194	234	230	1, 074	609	34, 260	100
New Rochelle,	......	......	......	......	......	150	......	......	99	67	116	343	24	19, 500	......
North Castle,	6	100	......	......	......	944	38¾	......	200	179	268	898	301	92, 036	......
North Salem,	......	......	......	......	......	972	21	......	177	220	237	1, 265	80	77, 376	120
Ossining,	19½	1, 675	30	......	......	35	22	......	142	128	157	685	209	22, 236	......
Pelham,	......	......	......	......	......	......	......	......	17	37	54	126	11	7, 910	......
Poundridge,	......	......	......	......	85	719	17½	......	186	220	201	92	85	66, 029	100
Rye,	......	......	......	......	......	370	16	......	73	117	207	430	64	24, 213	......
Scarsdale,	2¼	520	......	......	......	435	8	......	35	59	68	213	131	17, 339	......
Somers,	......	......	......	......	23	1, 761	60	......	437	313	397	1, 705	302	101, 278	495
Westchester,	27½	3, 325	......	......	10	150	......	......	121	165	160	675	569	20, 955	......
West Farms,	121¾	8, 750	......	......	......	150	20	......	66	59	116	1, 296	21	8, 537	......
White Plains,	......	......	......	......	......	188	16	......	14	61	133	229	48	21, 510	40
Yonkers,	28	3, 415	......	......	......	331	32	......	127	97	279	661	164	37, 644	......
Yorktown,	2	......	......	......	50	2, 767	76	......	368	380	496	1, 728	324	149, 901	......
Total,	511⅝	18454½	1, 410	......	240	17, 592	630¼	5	3, 475	4, 172	5, 427	20, 078	4, 785	1, 116, 589	2, 180
WYOMING COUNTY.—(Continued.)															
Attica,	......	......	6, 610	20	......	2, 285	113	......	364	777	177	1, 354	34	54, 785	145, 950
Bennington,	......	......	15, 274	553	34	5, 079	408	......	517	1, 189	392	1, 355	230	90, 896	14, 618
Castile,	......	......	386	25	48	1, 417	106½	......	354	972	108	887	199	97, 002	7, 171
China,	1½	60	31, 255	29	......	2, 997	109	......	675	1, 301	188	1, 326	354	123, 976	25, 100
Covington,	......	......	2, 550	33	......	615	46	......	179	435	96	488	64	56, 920	3, 945
Eagle,	......	......	30, 284	......	......	1, 780	139	......	417	773	127	832	49	77, 838	16, 986
Gainesville,	......	......	12, 439	88	......	1, 370	71	......	377	776	82	752	79	76, 267	15, 720
Genesee Falls,	......	......	550	3	......	576	27½	......	118	244	42	261	66	14, 485	100
Java,	......	......	17, 095	......	......	2, 395	85	......	646	1, 275	258	1, 470	108	131, 090	42, 050
Middlebury,	1½	177	13, 660	153	45	3, 270	164	......	341	677	150	993	114	81, 770	74, 025
Orangeville,	......	......	9, 919	68	......	1, 952	116	......	341	708	146	1, 584	86	63, 010	273, 150
Perry,	......	......	8, 464	359	......	3, 257	107½	......	355	825	169	899	296	105, 260	15, 718
Pike,	......	......	19, 469	98	......	1, 900	120	......	335	731	45	924	104	73, 887	28, 617
Sheldon,	......	......	11, 962	147	......	985	120	......	607	1, 202	400	1, 602	90	121, 962	67, 310
Warsaw,	......	......	4, 661	85½	......	4, 355	79	......	386	717	134	975	70	88, 076	27, 505
Wethersfield,	......	......	24, 468	146½	......	2, 015	188½	......	339	684	160	1, 035	64	76, 724	65, 140
Total,	3	237	209. 046	1, 808	127	36, 248	2, 000	......	6, 351	13, 286	2, 674	16, 737	2, 007	1, 333, 948	823, 105
YATES COUNTY.—(Continued.)															
Barrington,	......	......	79	11	......	4, 427	238	......	453	519	52	780	89	73, 995	1, 523
Benton,	4½	615	4, 015	89	204	5, 225	227	......	373	773	103	1, 119	660	113, 173	6, 987
Italy,	¼	20	2, 254	76	1	1, 602	90½	......	297	460	98	622	79	65, 540	23, 470
Jerusalem,	......	84	2, 640	167	......	2, 412	141½	......	557	969	113	1, 109	159	106, 673	8, 055
Middlesex,	½	10	440	28	......	2, 090	144	......	303	491	86	598	76	65, 885	8, 062
Milo,	½	25	61	13	118	4, 740	241	......	396	549	63	970	103	92, 705¼	2, 010
Potter,	......	......	7, 836	250	2	2, 298	116	......	340	755	91	686	110	63, 423	5, 147
Starkey,	¼	15	231	79	......	4, 736	256½	......	423	550	88	889	175	91, 299	4, 123
Torrey,	......	......	......	62	35	1, 730	56	......	237	342	48	477	126	44, 566	595
Total,	6	769	17, 556	775	360	29, 260	1, 510½	......	3, 379	5, 408	747	7, 250	1, 577	717, 259¼	59, 972

WAYNE COUNTY.—(Continued.)

TOWNS.	Gallons of milk sold.	Horses.	Mules.	SWINE. Under 6 months	SWINE. Over 6 months.	SHEEP. Number of sheep.	SHEEP. Number of fleeces.	SHEEP. Pounds of wool.	POULTRY. Value of poultry sold.	POULTRY. Value of eggs sold.	DOMESTIC MANUFACTURES. Yards of fulled cloth made.	DOMESTIC MANUFACTURES. Yards of flannel made.	DOMESTIC MANUFACTURES. Yards of linen made.	DOMESTIC MANUFACTURES. Yards of cotton and mixed cloths.
Arcadia,	290	1,453	....	1,415	1,373	10,821	7,631	30,921	$1,980	$3,974	120	363	71	249
Butler,	....	981	....	744	903	4,898	4,586	17,144	1,177	2,835	215	718	154	663
Galen,	7,926	1,373	....	1,273	2,925	8,814	7,390	27,731	2,100	3,438	225	655	51	340
Huron,	....	712	....	579	859	3,716	2,907	10,788	669	2,288	232	713	192	173
Lyons,	7,000	1,320	....	742	1,664	7,722	5,705	20,532	1,357	2,594	15	183	91	71
Macedon,	552	909	4	914	1,010	10,288	7,932	32,196	1,448	1,040	....	....	....	32
Marion,	120	846	...	836	796	3,763	3,700	14,289¼	1,210	2,408	....	46	144	402
Ontario,	....	886	....	441	845	4,020	3,475	13,472½	1,690	1,510	260	768	26	615
Palmyra,	12,660	859	....	763	1,137	7,954	5,484	20,823	1,087	1,910	32	168	68	....
Rose,	50	754	....	486	755	3,727	3,594	11,856	1,050	2,503	134	559	57	95
Savannah,	....	675	....	540	795	4,947	3,299	12,164	749	2,161	227	583	78	478
Sodus,	280	1,616	....	1,454	1,695	15,525	9,989	39,119¼	1,562	4,228	121	450	48	160
Walworth,	....	877	....	662	982	6,845	4,957	17,668	1,417	1,511	43	292	....	....
Williamson,	380	994	1	657	862	7,509	4,224	16,345	935	2,396	9	336	192	308
Wolcott,	65	673	....	669	1,023	4,296	3,063	10,761	807	2,159	352½	407	55	25
Total,	29,323	14,928	5	12,175	17,624	104,845	77,936	295,810	19,238	36,955	1,985½	6,241	1,227	3,611

WESTCHESTER COUNTY.—(Continued.)

TOWNS.	Gallons of milk sold.	Horses.	Mules.	SWINE. Under 6 months	SWINE. Over 6 months.	SHEEP. Number of sheep.	SHEEP. Number of fleeces.	SHEEP. Pounds of wool.	POULTRY. Value of poultry sold.	POULTRY. Value of eggs sold.	DOMESTIC MANUFACTURES. Yards of fulled cloth made.	DOMESTIC MANUFACTURES. Yards of flannel made.	DOMESTIC MANUFACTURES. Yards of linen made.	DOMESTIC MANUFACTURES. Yards of cotton and mixed cloths.
Bedford,	614,814	461	3	843	569	655	546	1,757	5,112	4,162	40	....	....	....
Cortlandt,	88,552	725	....	778	713	302	226	1,139	1,989	2,822	....	....	....	....
Eastchester,	43,888	263	7	302	382	17	11	102	670	791	....	....	....	....
Greenburgh,	79,083	465	13	922	527	1,949	1,726	4,475	1,694	2,563	....	....	....	....
Harrison,	82,302	221	3	586	256	175	169	478	1,627	2,307	....	....	....	....
Lewisboro',	274,536	319	....	595	318	440	561	2,024	2,913	1,852	25	....	....	....
Mamaroneck,	5,900	104	....	195	62	30	21	60	277	280	....	....	....	....
Mount Pleasant,	14,757	389	....	904	565	1,357	1,236	3,659	3,760	3,362	49	86	....	....
New Castle,	258,759	272	2	507	256	476	402	1,354	2,361	2,459	....	....	....	....
New Rochelle,	12,000	166	6	389	56	88	48	145	1,038	1,395	....	....	....	....
North Castle,	77,625	326	2	722	434	136	132	353½	3,921	3,002	....	....	....	....
North Salem,	399,537	230	....	405	201	417	170	632½	1,537	720	....	....	....	....
Ossining,	154,491	338	12	424	407	111	84	285	1,157	1,417	....	....	....	....
Pelham,	....	78	2	76	49	....	....	....	....	....	....	....	....	....
Poundridge,	3,600	157	...	316	267	472	295	1,068	2,496	1,628	....	....	....	....
Rye,	2,240	237	....	353	231	40	34	123	1,227	1,654	....	....	....	....
Scarsdale,	19,540	116	....	245	80	261	175	636	797	1,056	15	....	....	33
Somers,	163,452	394	2	1,220	419	1,695	1,456	5,159	4,479	2,870	78	45	36	50
Westchester,	97,040	375	8	318	249	48	32	203½	559	528	....	....	....	....
West Farms,	52,990	408	....	249	573	24	24	50	2,805	2,050	....	....	....	....
White Plains,	44,810	167	5	348	135	246	246	960	2,818	1,601	....	....	....	....
Yonkers,	60,919	583	8	605	653	705	652	1,657	1,099	1,144	....	....	....	....
Yorktown,	145,576	538	....	1,674	483	1,677	1,027	3,791½	3,568	4,284	....	10	....	20
Total,	2696411	7,332	73	12,976	7,885	11,321	9,273	30,112	47,904	43,947	207	141	36	103

WYOMING COUNTY.—(Continued.)

TOWNS.	Gallons of milk sold.	Horses.	Mules.	SWINE. Under 6 months	SWINE. Over 6 months.	SHEEP. Number of sheep.	SHEEP. Number of fleeces.	SHEEP. Pounds of wool.	POULTRY. Value of poultry sold.	POULTRY. Value of eggs sold.	DOMESTIC MANUFACTURES. Yards of fulled cloth made.	DOMESTIC MANUFACTURES. Yards of flannel made.	DOMESTIC MANUFACTURES. Yards of linen made.	DOMESTIC MANUFACTURES. Yards of cotton and mixed cloths.
Attica,	1,106	592	...	212	532	5,203	6,268	23,215	433	373	52	242	35	17
Bennington,	38,426	806	....	211	488	9,743	7,609	28,108	1,212	1,543	189	798	148	162
Castile,	....	871	....	676	605	6,825	6,632	23,302	489	1,271	279	450	255	201
China,	212	619	....	171	444	4,837	3,828	12,860	367	240	278	777	121	585
Covington,	....	585	....	259	322	7,451	8,451	33,136	368	643	15	216	60	....
Eagle,	....	556	....	168	346	4,708	4,955	17,684	285	619	165	226	228	511
Gainesville,	....	694	....	295	471	7,522	7,024	24,845	584	993	25	67	78	263
Genesee Falls,	400	183	....	137	162	1,832	2,146	6,889	138	416	....	104	....	....
Java,	....	687	....	239	688	6,795	4,884	16,168	1,037	995	951	1,474	508	814
Middlebury,	....	769	6	331	520	11,531	10,545	41,701	682	1,044	15	127	8	14
Orangeville,	....	501	....	177	413	2,303	2,265	7,628	430	481	109	488	30	319
Perry,	....	953	....	498	525	8,551	7,834	32,079	741	1,490	60	245	227	1,413
Pike,	169	602	....	163	405	4,856	8,649	28,167	782	646	38	181	117	....
Sheldon,	....	623	....	210	631	5,607	5,163	16,529½	748	1,339	212	485	90	359
Warsaw,	241	789	....	342	474	2,095	7,120	24,916	1,061	835	14	92	248	102
Wethersfield,	....	528	....	181	378	3,506	3,040	10,746	1,031	387	25	905	896	60
Total,	40,554	10,358	6	4,270	7,404	93,365	96,413	347,973½	10,388	13,315	2,427	6,877	3,049	4,820

YATES COUNTY.—(Continued.)

TOWNS.	Gallons of milk sold.	Horses.	Mules.	SWINE. Under 6 months	SWINE. Over 6 months.	SHEEP. Number of sheep.	SHEEP. Number of fleeces.	SHEEP. Pounds of wool.	POULTRY. Value of poultry sold.	POULTRY. Value of eggs sold.	DOMESTIC MANUFACTURES. Yards of fulled cloth made.	DOMESTIC MANUFACTURES. Yards of flannel made.	DOMESTIC MANUFACTURES. Yards of linen made.	DOMESTIC MANUFACTURES. Yards of cotton and mixed cloths.
Barrington,	....	651	....	574	536	6,351	6,753	24,299	1,349	240	44	141	21	24
Benton,	12,030	924	2	1,086	939	12,381	11,142	41,300½	2,573	2,203	76	145	180	40
Italy,	....	582	....	367	422	3,848	5,497	18,530	532	466	242¾	219¾	96	367
Jerusalem,	....	1,035	....	986	846	9,047	12,413	41,845	1,439	958	22	197	....	35
Middlesex,	....	620	....	575	566	5,918	7,412	25,347	1,063	896	96	151	28	137
Milo,	365	959	....	954	838	5,394	7,266	28,656	1,570	1,133	8	218	50	25
Potter,	....	750	6	666	678	12,203	11,801	42,138½	1,392	1,094	131	581	306	145
Starkey,	....	775	....	862	645	4,999	4,974	17,724	1,479	981	12	33	22	....
Torrey,	200	477	....	596	450	4,686	5,362	19,561	1,157	1,089	....	....	....	....
Total,	12,595	6,773	8	6,666	5,920	64,827	72,620	259,401	12,554	9,060	631¾	1,685¾	703	773

RECAPITULATION OF AGRICULTURAL STATISTICS.

COUNTIES.	Number of persons from whom returns were received.	ACRES.		CASH VALUE.			Acres plowed the year previous.	Acres in fallow the year previous.	Acres in pasture the year previous.
		Improved.	Unimproved.	Of farm.	Of stock.	Of tools and implements.			
Albany,	3, 539	242, 735	70, 777¼	$14, 315, 268	$1, 776, 960	$550, 098	80, 124	5, 474	61, 236
Allegany,	5, 392	280, 863	354, 269¼	12, 352, 363	2, 081, 738	575, 936	64, 631½	9, 439½	116, 608½
Broome,	3, 925	198, 839⅝	205, 208¾	10, 872, 397	1, 505, 679	372, 625	40, 526	4, 926¼	71, 556½
Cattaraugus,	5, 441	266, 435¾	432, 620⅝	10, 956, 344	1, 972, 598	439, 162	58, 448½	2, 979	109, 719
Cayuga,	4, 299	315, 795⅝	187, 237½	20, 700, 003	2, 523, 234	637, 307	104, 976	9, 184¾	95, 149
Chautauque,	6, 547	360, 110	294, 145½	17, 022, 474	2, 871, 699	610, 560	64, 401½	2, 806¾	172, 376½
Chemung,	1, 948	120, 219¾	110, 385¼	6, 898, 846	841, 551	214, 911	36, 273	4, 648½	33, 238
Chenango,	5, 203	347, 828⅝	182, 936	13, 184, 452	2, 431, 662	569, 087	50, 138⅜	2, 867¾	177, 567
Clinton,	3, 551	168, 932⅜	401, 086½	6, 306, 142	1, 047, 497	274, 726	42, 878⅛	1, 935	66, 171
Columbia,	3, 242	304, 277⅝	69, 255	19, 130, 759	1, 858, 418	620, 449	81, 515	12, 737	102, 259
Cortland,	3, 388	194, 736⅞	113, 662⅞	8, 569, 671	1, 571, 914	357, 893	36, 938⅜	476¾	91, 583⅝
Delaware,	5, 458	364, 400¼	438, 452¼	11, 245, 256	2, 288, 610	485, 333	58, 209¼	10, 077½	174, 541¾
Dutchess,	3, 797	366, 359⅜	98, 104¾	27, 463, 045	2, 880, 290	704, 355	82, 233¼	5, 965½	156, 586¼
Erie,	7, 257	340, 307¼	253, 344⅝	24, 479, 408	2, 718, 053	745, 059	80, 240¾	13, 332⅞	114, 813¾
Essex,	2, 715	185, 443⅜	774, 195¼	4, 604, 253	970, 214	179, 999	34, 457	1, 333½	82, 726¼
Franklin,	3, 247	144, 627¼	834, 964¾	4, 998, 778	1, 042, 006	243, 335	33, 494¼	1, 019½	57, 424½
Fulton,	2, 288	133, 415¾	147, 070¾	5, 103, 631	891, 427	222, 645	36, 230	1, 529	52, 546½
Genesee,	3, 063	219, 012¼	75, 732	16, 091, 998	1, 675, 630	442, 702	35, 260	46, 046½	43, 342¼
Greene,	3, 145	212, 223⅞	150, 604½	8, 457, 699	1, 092, 960	1, 196, 548	41, 699	5, 755¼	71, 130¾
Hamilton,	404	16, 675¾	766, 978½	757, 004	80, 804	24. 799	2, 134½	140	5, 976¾
Herkimer,	3, 447	267, 414½	505, 657½	14, 812, 184	2, 134, 237	476, 445	59, 867⅞	938	122, 730⅝
Jefferson,	6, 992	465, 222	251, 291	18, 718, 492	2, 992, 793	743, 410	116, 129	4, 337¼	196, 434
Kings,	398	15, 871¼	5, 594¾	8, 468, 600	762, 770	117, 343	8, 189	123	1, 541½
Lewis,	3, 945	184, 540½	497, 145¾	7, 519, 002	1, 102, 582	287, 903	32, 889¼	1, 641	71, 496½
Livingston,	3, 375	262, 462½	96, 378¼	22, 406, 233	2, 177, 384	539, 435	48, 142½	52, 934¼	51, 233
Madison,	4, 680	277, 393⅝	111, 505⅜	14, 353, 775	2. 253, 862	465, 057	68, 442⅛	2, 610	113, 463
Monroe,	4, 879	216, 840¼	78, 182	29, 633, 614	2, 824, 916	818, 703	88, 943¾	40, 494½	62, 159⅞
Montgomery,	2, 852	194, 457⅝	46, 720¾	10, 309, 692	1, 418, 034	358, 598	80, 955	2, 534¾	56, 965
New-York,	48	1, 050¾	923½	4, 324, 700	1, 495, 212	11, 395	143½	45	246½
Niagara,	3, 968	207, 043⅞	101, 110	16, 321, 349	1, 900, 789	562, 389	52, 544⅞	34, 221⅝	35, 259
Oneida,	8, 315	435, 800⅝	286, 594¼	24, 294, 881	3, 409, 506	764, 667	97, 022⅛	2, 337½	187, 860½
Onondaga,	6, 336	344, 528	114, 701½	25, 353, 290	2, 903, 509	770, 065	123, 159⅜	7, 450¼	104, 997¼
Ontario,	3, 943	290, 639¾	97, 108¾	20, 882, 806	2, 272, 115	591, 755	95, 987½	23, 876½	79, 494½
Orange,	3, 982	308, 599⅜	189, 615	21, 567, 360	2, 699, 991	639, 225	48, 962⅛	3, 452½	138, 113
Orleans,	2, 454	181, 948¾	62, 326⅝	12, 672, 552	1, 531, 017	423, 866	43, 098	28, 508	41, 164½
Oswego,	6, 720	244, 126	328, 047⅝	13, 438, 725	2, 058, 581	496, 529	66, 059¼	3, 383½	93, 511¾
Otsego,	6, 109	428, 932⅝	179, 559¼	18, 318, 997	2, 802, 602	656, 876	92, 717⅜	4, 524¾	196, 401¼
Putnam,	1, 368	94, 205⅞	44, 447¾	6, 148, 849	720, 037	140, 828	11, 815¼	981¼	42, 623½
Queens,	3, 113	119, 549	57, 204	17, 071, 845	1, 253, 350	512, 392	37, 718¼	4, 112½	24, 229½
Rensselaer,	3, 869	292, 212⅞	101, 002½	16, 656, 695	1, 935, 709	540, 448	78, 810¾	4, 655	107, 652
Richmond,	876	15, 072⅜	7, 602⅛	5, 261, 350	173, 025	74, 936	3, 900⅞	842½	3, 006½
Rockland,	1, 221	46, 481¾	50, 852½	4, 862, 210	618, 059	128, 330	8, 844½	2, 163	14, 661½
St. Lawrence,	8, 946	499, 554	885, 531	18, 117, 429	3, 144, 908	751, 437	86, 623½	3, 981	216, 985
Saratoga,	4, 208	315, 728¼	139, 849¼	13, 526, 379	1, 842, 426	496, 183	91, 410¾	10, 683¼	121, 692
Schenectady,	1, 328	93, 448½	31, 683¼	4, 910, 728	596, 736	195, 804	37, 334½	1, 367	24, 341½
Schoharie,	4, 011	227, 904⅜	132, 046¼	10, 053, 948	1, 558, 689	461, 690	82, 004¾	7, 856¾	78, 418¾
Schuyler,	2, 446	134, 336¼	62, 999¼	7, 428, 825	974, 358	252, 823	45, 215¼	6, 381¼	36, 663⅞
Seneca,	2, 238	151, 949¾	45, 936⅜	10, 498, 372	1, 039, 547	339, 647	53, 838½	6, 703¼	30, 454¾
Steuben,	7, 042	361, 450	438, 250½	17, 994, 630	2, 406, 152	680, 403	103, 672½	24, 988½	102, 824¾
Suffolk,	4, 338	163, 818⅞	260. 570⅞	13, 102, 827	1, 271, 648	344, 386	35, 395	4, 682¾	56, 436⅞
Sullivan,	3, 683	125, 489¼	494, 829¼	5, 655, 321	953, 211	199, 497	23, 607¾	3, 023¼	39, 934
Tioga,	3, 088	154, 894⅛	138, 423½	7, 593, 564	1, 206, 835	289, 054	42, 810½	4, 380	53, 400½
Tompkins,	3, 623	205, 616⅝	84, 963¾	11, 656, 054	1, 581, 130	379, 635	68, 345¼	5, 782	62, 692
Ulster,	4, 851	240, 641	378, 202¾	16, 118, 294	1, 914, 932	564, 772	54, 975¾	9, 571	72, 863¼
Warren,	2, 145	111, 202⅝	331, 341	2, 604, 246	560, 316	106, 429	21, 854	1, 876	43, 218½
Washington,	4, 192	333, 030¼	143, 554¾	15, 271, 968	2, 146, 364	458, 954	85, 255¼	2, 284	143, 078¼
Wayne,	4, 767	254, 451⅝	102, 062¼	17, 037, 413	2, 238, 425	581, 096	85, 901	14, 995¾	64, 313⅛
Westchester,	3, 722	209, 146¾	81, 947½	29, 283, 170	1, 964, 739	537, 905	34, 647½	4, 519½	83, 890¼
Wyoming,	4, 131	241, 654¼	122, 764½	11, 903, 817	1, 714, 170	393, 737	50, 774¼	17, 141½	90, 196½
Yates,	2, 242	155, 542½	51, 134	9, 691, 390	1, 098, 443	305, 926	44, 654⅞	6, 972½	40, 913
Total,	231, 740	13, 657, 490¾	13, 100, 692⅜	$799, 355, 367	$103, 776, 053	$26, 927, 502	3, 377, 471	506, 030⅛	4, 984, 114½

RECAPITULATION.—(CONTINUED.)

COUNTIES.	MEADOW.			SPRING WHEAT.		WINTER WHEAT.		OATS.		RYE.	
	Acres.	Tons of hay.	Bushels of grass seed.	Acres sown.	Bushels harvested.	Acres sown.	Bushels harvested	Acres sown.	Bushels harvested.	Acres sown.	Bushels harvested.
Albany,	64, 354¼	54, 579½	1, 333¼	938	6, 927¼	1, 586¼	7, 424	43, 347¼	495, 177½	15, 037	186, 567
Allegany,	76, 273	54, 637¾	2, 117	6, 594¼	56, 422½	6, 964¼	82, 929	34, 845	665, 490	338¼	2, 834
Broome,	58, 078¼	53, 685	1, 676¼	2, 153¾	8, 121½	2, 852½	11, 927½	18, 901⅛	466, 870½	3, 690	20, 546
Cattaraugus,	75, 208½	62, 546¾	1, 812⅜	5, 395⅝	57, 278½	1, 923⅝	21, 721	31, 798⅝	697, 670½	226	2, 373½
Cayuga,	59, 604½	57, 732	2, 746¾	2, 485¾	27, 327	21, 940½	193, 729½	37, 059	956, 636	1, 594½	6, 331¾
Chautauque,	103, 180¾	105, 672	2, 286	7, 011¾	78, 636¼	5, 366¼	66, 249½	25, 782¼	539, 765	200½	2, 808
Chemung,	24, 840	24, 941	866	2, 140	18, 624	8, 781¼	63, 754	17, 280	473, 469	731	3, 558
Chenango,	113, 840½	117, 370¾	2, 038¼	1, 814⅛	20, 283½	897½	4, 560½	26. 704½	564, 242	1, 187¼	14, 329
Clinton,	51, 172¾	48, 241	1, 078	5, 550⅜	57, 172¾	237¼	2, 138½	14, 532¼	276, 080¼	1, 649⅞	13, 073
Columbia,	64, 305	65, 103	626¼	95½	587½	4, 092	7, 972½	38, 728	543, 034	39, 864½	445, 036
Cortland,	59, 172¼	56, 769½	958⅝	2, 102⅜	24, 361	579⅞	4, 696¼	17, 498¾	382, 786	351¾	4, 172
Delaware,	122, 502¼	103, 896¼	1, 741¾	1, 233	8, 538¾	314	955½	34, 016¼	416, 659½	5, 807¾	56, 527½
Dutchess,	83, 100⅞	83, 878½	697½	23	250	11, 614¾	54, 470½	37, 586	626, 347	20, 424⅞	239, 063
Erie,	93, 053½	98, 011½	3, 720¼	4, 505¾	46, 913	16, 907¾	238, 812¾	35, 983	724, 747½	1, 822½	24, 979½
Essex,	56, 829¾	39, 139¾	1, 019¼	4, 838⅝	44, 009¼	315	2, 484	14, 334¾	234, 946	1, 631¼	13, 357½
Franklin,	45, 906¾	37, 594½	662½	6, 958¾	69, 559½	175¼	1, 353¾	9, 411⅛	144, 617	2, 235	20, 191½
Fulton,	34, 070¾	33, 903	5, 192½	734¼	7, 500½	415	3, 644½	17, 367¾	355, 855	1, 707¾	22, 383½
Genesee,	31, 135¾	41, 398¾	1, 766¼	850½	11, 154	41, 194½	760, 461	10, 972½	299, 809	99½	1, 149
Greene,	71, 395¾	58, 524¼	355¼	607¾	3, 175½	2, 297¾	7, 346	16, 319½	160, 907½	10, 144¼	72, 232
Hamilton,	6, 297¾	4, 274	114½	76¼	245	1	6	1, 187¾	16, 701	32½	277
Herkimer,	74, 097	78, 254¾	1, 943	2, 774½	38, 149	581¼	5, 904½	30, 763	724, 585	1, 085⅜	17, 550
Jefferson,	122, 491	98, 575	13, 601¾	29, 687¼	428, 672⅝	6, 303½	70. 509½	38, 375½	456, 230¾	7, 775¼	99, 391½
Kings,	3, 863	6, 183	6	....	....	887	18, 086	418	11, 679	254	4, 860
Lewis,	57, 238½	51, 802	1, 746½	4, 603½	59, 940	317¾	3, 845¼	14, 037½	295, 445½	1, 151¼	11, 383½
Levingston,	34, 680	39, 187¾	1, 657¼	1, 922¼	18, 025	63, 662½	1, 094, 779	11, 909⅝	261, 990	397¼	4, 118
Madison,	70, 545⅞	68, 263½	1, 155⅝	4, 344¾	52, 777	4, 459⅛	29, 320½	25, 977¾	571, 637	84¼	1, 477
Monroe,	45, 681	58, 738¾	1, 886¾	182⅞	2, 620	59, 138⅜	810, 363	26. 025¼	792, 370	652	9, 166½
Montgomery,	41, 507¾	44, 532¼	4, 707¼	1, 898	18, 978½	3, 114	23, 904½	44, 487½	997, 605	2, 770	39, 112½
New-York,	101	157	....	....	....	2	30	19	435	2	25
Niagara,	32, 520⅝	41. 117½	2, 678¾	352¾	5, 386	45, 788¼	589, 911	12, 483	353, 398	61¼	1, 014
Oneida,	119, 745⅝	124, 933½	8, 700½	3, 396⅝	41, 883¼	3, 177¾	20, 439¾	39, 169⅞	975, 800¼	2, 021½	24, 121
Onondaga,	63, 193¾	63, 246⅝	3, 493¾	7, 197¾	85, 148	19, 601⅝	97, 058¾	41, 509⅛	1, 015, 227½	440¾	5, 340½
Ontario,	45, 094½	42, 448¾	2, 133	3, 177¾	27, 659	38, 680½	528, 488	22, 049¾	525, 937½	1, 149⅛	16, 002
Orange,	83, 771	103, 211¼	1, 111	8½	32	7, 076½	43, 363½	15, 242¾	291, 111	17, 860½	202, 301
Orleans,	25, 150½	34, 620¼	1, 524	192	2, 206	31, 830¾	376, 949	14, 656⅛	229, 731	150¾	2, 777
Oswego,	63, 501½	58, 138	1, 454	3, 914¼	44, 300⅞	1, 544½	12, 596	22, 674½	535, 432½	3, 733½	45, 557½
Otsego,	115, 979⅞	108, 069¾	3, 341¾	4, 803⅝	53, 446¼	1, 231¼	5, 678	49, 016¼	903, 647	3, 031⅝	34, 218¾
Putnam,	26, 191¾	27, 756¾	50½	....	....	507½	3, 550¾	3, 714½	66, 922	2, 112¼	22, 890½
Queens,	37, 634¼	51, 395	624¼	4	48	6, 877½	102, 169¼	9, 426¼	199, 518	6, 136½	71, 019
Rensselaer,	68, 361¼	58, 557¾	435	1, 265¾	13, 383½	692¼	2, 658	29, 295¾	558, 377	22, 630⅝	299, 864
Richmond,	4, 528½	7, 032	79½	26	575	792¼	11, 335¾	741½	15, 901½	204¾	3, 131½
Rockland,	12, 984	14, 828	50½	2½	6	376	2, 945¾	1, 963	28, 168	5, 323¾	31, 600½
St. Lawrence,	163, 623	139, 400	3, 220½	32, 623	295, 464	3, 991½	24, 780½	28, 866½	437, 041	2, 741¼	25, 725
Saratoga,	60, 602½	52, 743¾	1, 514½	890½	8, 074	3, 397¾	14, 826¼	35, 590½	744, 220	13, 317¼	132, 774¾
Schenectady,	18, 566¼	16, 185½	808¼	815¼	6, 377½	673¾	5, 165½	15, 809½	293, 768	3, 899¼	44, 752½
Schoharie,	56, 386½	48, 774¾	4, 557¼	2, 968½	23, 074¾	4, 997¾	18, 645	37, 784	490, 063½	7, 843¾	87, 592½
Schuyler,	25, 141¼	17, 996¼	1, 392½	5, 612¾	33, 139¾	11, 803	80, 431½	17, 122	357, 247	694½	6, 168
Seneca,	24, 660	20, 879¾	5, 098½	1, 229¼	11, 379	14, 912⅜	151, 721	21, 429¾	556, 238	670¾	7, 862
Steuben,	76, 401¼	58, 749¼	1, 925¼	10, 821½	82, 014	33, 768	219, 590	51, 169¾	711, 307	1, 130½	10, 212
Suffolk,	35, 555½	41, 505¾	1, 741¼	16	129½	9, 973½	151, 520½	10, 317¼	262, 067½	5, 285¼	52, 212½
Sullivan,	41, 803½	40, 716¼	1, 972¾	9⅜	98	333	1, 472½	7, 004	109, 883	7, 560¼	75, 153
Tioga,	38, 036½	38, 401¾	2, 452¾	1, 339¼	11, 938¼	4, 351¼	19, 355	19, 493¼	452, 978	2, 668¼	25, 884¼
Tompkins,	39, 493	31, 843¾	2, 091½	3, 182¼	32, 642¾	11, 040	84, 395½	34, 142¼	812, 983	1, 719¼	17, 521
Ulster,	65, 672¼	64, 795	1, 201¾	19½	815	4, 390	19, 370¾	18, 473½	278, 105	27, 094¼	235, 993½
Warren,	31, 134	22, 088¾	398¼	540⅞	4. 285	221½	1, 212	7, 564¼	120, 347	1, 476½	10, 952½
Washington,	78, 148¾	69, 881	1, 429	2, 034½	23, 854	1, 968	8, 387	31, 111	798, 321	9, 908¾	121, 967
Wayne,	39, 165⅞	45, 271½	2, 126	263⅛	2, 687	29, 214¼	282, 474¾	29, 100⅛	875, 624½	574¾	7, 259½
Westchester,	64, 309½	90, 496⅞	1, 761¾	183	1, 497	4, 222	33, 751½	10, 943½	204, 759	4, 968¼	51, 404
Wyoming,	59, 184	58, 421¼	1, 536¼	3, 299¾	37, 497½	19, 198¼	382, 498½	24, 377¾	496, 837	211¾	2, 777½
Yates,	23, 372½	15, 850¼	449½	2, 624	18, 063	17, 587	168, 969½	11, 479½	160, 457¾	2, 146¼	24, 517
Total,	3, 384, 440¾	3, 256, 948⅞	120, 866⅝	194, 346⅛	2, 033, 353	601, 141½	7, 059, 049¼	1, 349, 384¼	27, 015, 296	281, 714⅞	3, 039, 438

RECAPITULATION.—(CONTINUED.)

COUNTIES.	BARLEY. Acres sown.	BARLEY. Bushels harvested	BUCKWHEAT. Acres sown.	BUCKWHEAT. Bushels harvested.	CORN. Acres planted.	CORN. Bushels harvested.	POTATOES. Acres planted.	POTATOES. Bushels harvested.	PEAS. Acres sown.	PEAS. Bushels harvested.	BEANS. Acres planted.	BEANS. Bushels harvested
Albany,	997½	9,126½	14,722¾	84,812¾	12,612¼	193,691½	6,884⅝	375,654½	1,845	15,989½	339¾	2,306
Allegany,	2,102	28,454½	4,956	39,298½	6,800½	189,588½	3,057¼	206,258	1,687½	22,844½	182	3,174¾
Broome,	214½	2,337	6,932¾	73,214¼	8,101¾	214,998	2,388¾	160,420½	57½	932½	92⅝	949⅞
Cattaraugus,	942⅝	14,095	2,320⅜	26,183	10,271⅝	309,762	3,597⅛	300,245¾	938½	14,492¼	242¼	4,496½
Cayuga,	16,275½	308,303½	4,920⅜	54,076½	30,519	868,543	3,201¾	251,718⅛	435⅜	6,565	359⅛	5,638½
Chautauque,	1,224½	19,656¼	1,055¾	9,664¾	19,761¾	558,507½	3,723½	282,451	536¼	7,693	208⅛	4,038
Chemung,	1,100½	23,862	5,902	69,046½	7,199½	239,285½	1,190½	131,291	89½	1,360½	56¾	1,859¼
Chenango,	1,138¼	22,229	4,238	50,304½	10,745	354,480	3,179	270,542	236⅛	4,018½	102⅜	2,763¼
Clinton,	439	6,877	4,606¼	30,651⅝	6,132⅛	92,567¾	5,874¼	385,492	1,313⅛	14,545	597⅝	6,993¼
Columbia,	251½	3,801	7,899	54,334½	26,439	383,339½	6,199⅜	259,419½	138⅞	1,336¾	69¼	739
Cortland,	2,402⅝	45,665½	2,623⅜	28,115½	7,501⅝	240,703½	1,857⅞	155,389	505¾	9,527	96⅝	1,726¼
Delaware,	173⅛	2,219	11,970⅞	86,330	5,543½	119,383	3,869¾	209,567¼	234⅜	2,229½	50⅞	2,128¼
Dutchess,	184½	2,818	5,265	43,124¼	33,008	558,308	3,693¾	205,498	25	670	37¼	788¼
Erie,	3,661⅛	57,256½	2,455⅝	24,558½	18,627½	483,228	7,452¾	445,350½	929⅛	15,321½	349¾	6,124
Essex,	86	1,118½	2,431¾	13,701¾	5,866¾	105,369	4,286⅞	318,021	1,088¾	11,625¾	284	2,818
Franklin,	693½	6,188¾	1,705⅜	13,625¼	4,850¼	83,615	5,709	484,425	1,004⅞	12,074½	174¾	1,839¼
Fulton,	931¼	14,704	5,522¼	69,759	7,013	155,733	2,284	182,964	774¼	14,202	39⅛	761¼
Genesee,	3,049	59,819	1,829⅞	14,913½	16,286¼	437,052½	2,383¾	167,274	621⅝	8,797½	635½	8,569½
Greene,	271¼	1,787½	10,021	33,913½	9,819¼	99,204	3,076⅛	116,871	239⅛	1,532½	135⅜	693½
Hamilton,	14½	42	459½	2,913¾	435¾	7,151	406¼	25,257	14	140	5½	154½
Herkimer,	2,709¼	51,439½	3,505	42,875¾	9,782¼	283,748	3,108½	257,875	1,586⅞	27,864	83½	1,616
Jefferson,	28,262	392,684½	965⅞	5,909¾	18,486¾	321,779	5,154	289,031	4,536½	63,338	389½	4,281¼
Kings,	....	....	21	235	1,948½	54,179	3,089	368,243	174½	16,930	66	7,042
Lewis,	1,992	37,513½	1,067⅞	10,443¼	4,616⅝	92,398¼	3,295⅝	243,841	856¼	12,978½	72⅛	1,030½
Livingston,	6,977½	123,255½	1,814⅝	13,836¼	15,172⅞	431,464½	1,858⅞	132,256½	528¼	6,398½	81⅝	1,003¼
Madison,	10,456½	197,231	1,396⅞	13,853½	14,920¾	449,583	2,943½	224,278½	1,147	20,973½	276⅜	4,836½
Monroe,	7,576⅜	179,755	3,569½	22,623¾	30,409⅛	805,811	7,728¾	654,551	992⅜	16,028⅛	1,427¼	14,342¾
Montgomery,	2,330¼	39,252½	12,797	141,677½	10,494¾	247,516½	1,945⅞	145,154	1,367¾	22,855½	228⅝	3,941
New-York,	....	....	....	....	31	1,180	28	1,808	3½	250	8½	645
Niagara,	3,781⅛	79,593	2,622	29,151½	17,296⅞	509,505	3,266⅞	275,448	913¼	15,981	774¾	9,256½
Oneida,	7,185⅛	137,430	4,355½	54,767⅝	26,573½	732,294½	7,678¼	624,648	712	12,912½	472¼	7,770¾
Onondaga,	20,755¼	371,785½	3,198⅛	32,453¾	32,246⅞	907,453	4,890½	380,141½	2,324⅞	34,915½	517	8,984
Ontario,	18,640	320,375	3,093	18,325¾	24,148	617,485¼	2,563⅜	188,900	1,449¾	15,297½	201⅝	2,404¾
Orange,	15½	179	4,647	23,023¾	19,961½	357,490½	3,789½	123,551½	9⅜	230	27⅞	348¼
Orleans,	1,659¼	36,071	2,386⅞	12,903	118,356¼	436,975	2,111⅜	171,867	411	5,471	3,918¼	40,185¾
Oswego,	1,504⅜	28,054	3,783¾	31,605¾	20,919⅝	503,812	5,584⅛	391,912¼	719½	11,116½	280¼	4,326
Otsego,	2,820⅛	43,889	9,903⅛	112,732¾	12,395	340,170½	5,026⅛	412,703½	1,824¾	29,935⅞	119¾	2,811½
Putnam,	....	....	1,891¼	10,718¼	4,434¾	119,919½	1,198¾	64,504	3	48	19⅜	210½
Queens,	180	2,769	6,299	21,224½	13,852¾	337,685	4,089⅞	291,135	383¼	33,444	203	22,282½
Rensselaer,	629¼	12,807	5,832½	52,821	20,532¾	393,413½	8,317¼	596,559	108¼	1,574	425⅛	5,979
Richmond,	26⅛	627	79¼	1,325	1,555⅝	43,037½	315½	21,739	7	410	1½	166¾
Rockland,	3⅜	14	1,917	8,722¼	3,458⅛	51,873	1,223	47,223½	2	49	5⅜	63
St. Lawrence,	1,713¾	28,187	1,758	12,912½	12,755	220,593	9,172	604,023	5,234¾	69,016	475½	5,131
Saratoga,	658⅛	9,524	11,588⅛	108,882½	28,849¾	479,449	7,745½	487,672	331⅜	6,466	112½	972⅞
Schenectady,	365⅛	5,569½	5,983½	41,858	5,690¾	92,279	1,884	105,132	389¼	5,551¼	87	714½
Schoharie,	3,572½	44,136	16,700½	169,078	7,187½	161,153½	3,164⅜	190,432½	2,888⅜	33,482½	172⅞	1,656½
Schuyler,	5,063¼	60,507	7,242¼	67,523	6,775	160,780½	1,259	81,106	129⅞	1,710¼	176½	1,931
Seneca,	6,280½	104,856	3,550¼	21,436½	16,239¾	387,998½	1,091⅜	72,544	51⅞	640¼	60⅝	573¼
Steuben,	8,429½	78,873	13,054¾	89,990½	12,796¾	292,689½	4,007	255,938	2,646¾	25,006½	245¼	2,680½
Suffolk,	512¼	10,974	3,085⅛	18,856½	17,615½	504,767	3,403¼	304,063	2	142	55⅞	1,382¼
Sullivan,	47½	1,053½	6,403½	65,571½	4,409½	102,594	1,759¼	103,188¾	7⅛	168½	31½	698¼
Tioga,	377¼	5,925	7,006⅛	91,402½	7,839¼	260,074	1,843⅜	150,518½	314⅝	3,992½	127¾	2,495¼
Tompkins,	3,753¼	65,295	9,296⅞	74,305	14,737¾	372,202	1,554⅛	111,106	312⅞	4,659½	184⅜	2,100½
Ulster,	10	130	9,375¾	70,676	18,429⅛	242,229½	3,440½	134,539½	20⅜	296¼	53⅜	534
Warren,	4½	39	2,910¾	19,214¾	7,268½	123,817	2,630½	173,328	220¼	2,270½	94⅛	915¾
Washington,	760½	12,944½	4,543½	40,658½	25,781	589,678½	11,780⅞	767,285	1,227⅜	14,210½	444⅛	5,075¼
Wayne,	10,498¼	229,495	4,220½	39,766¼	29,473⅞	756,677¼	3,452⅞	261,403	472¾	8,455½	403⅜	5,866¾
Westchester,	130	545	2,846¼	20,890¾	12,838⅝	402,238½	4,759⅛	286,249	3¾	230	12	278½
Wyoming,	4,289½	68,267	2,150¼	20,277¾	8,681	234,006	3,086¾	203,932	933¼	13,326½	429⅛	8,232½
Yates,	12,485½	152,134	4,434¼	24,007¼	11,103⅜	174,181	1,018⅜	57,912½	191⅞	1,444	91¾	745¾
Total,	212,608⅛	3,563,540	293,233¼	2,481,079¼	917 [illegible]	19,290,691½	220,575¾	15,191,852⅛	48,154¾	705,967⅜	16,917⅜	244,079

RECAPITULATION.—(Continued.)

COUNTIES.	TURNIPS.		FLAX.			HEMP.		HOPS.		TOBACCO.		APPLE ORCHARDS.	
	Acres sown.	Bushels harvested.	Acres sown.	Pounds of lint.	Bushels of seed.	Acres sown.	Tons of hemp.	Acres planted.	Pounds harvested.	Acres planted.	Pounds harvested.	Bushels of apples.	Barrels of cider.
Albany,	104¾	14,696	52¼	2,675	210¼	....	....	12	7,440	1	....	234,251	6,038
Allegany,	126⅛	22,075	34⅞	879	205¼	....	....	7½	2,768	⅛	128½	214,136	2,983
Broome,	92¼	12,375	8	478	35½	....	....	35¼	21,808	17⅜	23,650	224,463	4,747½
Cattaraugus,	142½	26,104	8⅜	2,738	58⅝	....	....	2¾	488	1¾	1,770	177,173½	1,257
Cayuga,	76⅝	17,464½	138⅜	18,385	1,166	....	....	5½	2,640	2¼	3,300	522,751	10,362¼
Chautauque,	93⅜	20,360	42⅞	4,584	302¼	....	....	5½	2,416	1⅝	1,390	368,115	4,524½
Chemung,	26⅜	3,964	6	130	66¼	....	....	......	102	28½	33,597	107,364	2,961
Chenango,	61¼	9,732	36⅜	16,636	203½	....	....	220	163,332	⅞	550	553,554	7,559½
Clinton,	52⅜	5,314	36¼	7,700	236½	....	....	2	1,014	......	20	76,936½	852½
Columbia,	67	6,545½	19	1,128	54¾	....	....	......	....	⅜	418	210,342	9,480
Cortland,	63⅞	11,724	237⅛	58,269	2,173¾	....	....	11½	2,037	......	40	351,975	3,738
Delaware,	129⅜	19,612	10⅜	1,477	25¾	1	¾	187¼	69,028½	......	....	259,160	5,918¼
Dutchess,	946⅜	58,577	11⅛	557	15	....	....	4	3,104	12⅝	18,507	216,593	8,247¾
Erie,	154⅜	20,987	34⅝	5,026	276½	....	....	4	2,862	......	50	266,195	6,084¾
Essex,	64	9,128	2⅝	195	6½	....	....	5	9	......	....	64,200½	909½
Franklin,	67	13,092	2½	704	6½	....	....	418¼	231,217	⅛	153	26,273	377¼
Fulton,	38⅛	4,213	143¼	223,005	1,215½	....	....	23	....	......	....	100,142	2,670½
Genesee,	41¾	6,646	57⅛	118,500	595½	....	....	21	12,007	4⅛	4,130	296,121	5,767
Greene,	81¾	6,732½	5⅛	10,620	14½	....	....	9½	26	⅛	75	192,814½	3,954½
Hamilton,	14¾	1,589	1	6,000	....	....	....	......	....	......	....	3,459	18
Herkimer,	27⅝	2,579	312⅝	308,050	4,241	....	....	594⅝	510,033	......	115	333,901	6,446
Jefferson,	40⅞	4,112½	64⅛	12,066	760¾	....	....	37⅛	28,995	½	3,691	215,431	3,459½
Kings,	212¾	31,001	....	....	....	....	....	......	....	......	....	54	....
Lewis,	55⅞	5,830½	219	65,782	1,566	....	....	25	8,870	......	....	72,198	1,451
Livingston,	23⅞	3,510	2⅛	90	13½	....	....	10⅛	14,255	......	10	242,200	5,928½
Madison,	28¼	2,948	92⅛	102,581	735½	....	....	1,490¾	1,312,308	9⅛	13,680	531,677	7,417½
Monroe,	195	32,507	8¼	1,000	56½	....	....	51	44,010	77⅛	86,520	491,491	10,312
Montgomery,	8	1,441½	1,132	1,016,929	7,746¾	2	....	453½	241,603	⅝	249	155,861	5,608½
New-York,	27¼	2,060	....	....	....	....	....	......	....	......	....	....	....
Niagara,	138½	28,958	86⅞	380	322	....	....	......	....	10⅞	13,010	255,997	4,461½
Oneida,	155⅝	25,005	140⅝	6,635	1,233½	....	....	675¾	616,054	33⅞	39,220	634,262	12,735
Onondaga,	120½	19,175¾	319¼	57,287	2,644¾	....	....	17¼	13,427	471⅛	554,987	624,545½	13,725¼
Ontario,	39⅛	5,743½	41½	2,070	199½	....	....	42¾	32,751	10⅛	9,180	397,098	8,044
Orange,	105	11,569	½	30	....	....	....	......	39	1¼	800	80,180½	3,188½
Orleans,	72⅝	11,467	40½	19,030	285	....	....	⅛	16	17⅛	22,871	281,781½	4,534
Oswego,	142⅞	27,252½	103¼	37,109	749	....	....	45½	29,206	......	15	425,915	8,105½
Otsego,	69⅝	19,091	386⅜	98,504⅝	1,424¼	....	....	4,132⅞	3,122,258½	½	543	601,196	8,880
Putnam,	102½	8,488	....	....	....	....	....	......	20	......	....	27,158	814½
Queens,	562¾	84,544	½	300	1	....	....	......	25	......	....	3,346	29
Rensselaer,	87½	11,982	2,400	672,780	19,266½	....	....	3	1,615	......	....	131,241	4,364
Richmond,	39¼	4,481	....	....	....	....	....	......	....	......	....	28	....
Rockland,	64¼	10,792	....	....	....	....	....	......	3	......	....	3,253	47
St. Lawrence,	71⅛	7,896	3	1,206½	4	....	....	259¾	197,875	......	....	90,497	719
Saratoga,	120¾	12,809	62½	15,125	515¾	....	....	18¼	18,364	½	200	289,478	11,386½
Schenectady,	26½	4,149	403½	260,200	2,346	....	....	14	2,600	¼	150	105,551	2,848½
Schoharie,	51⅞	8,427	73½	13,916	526¾	⅛	....	525¼	440,754	......	15	222,182	3,689½
Schuyler,	31⅝	5,734	73⅜	8,058	420½	....	....	1½	730	⅛	30	143,229	3,212
Seneca,	27	4,645	988½	529,811	7,035	....	....	......	....	8⅝	16,500	175,278	4,629
Steuben,	202⅞	22,545	108⅛	1,777	306	....	....	13	8,649	10¾	16,950	297,289	4,580
Suffolk,	563¼	104,183½	....	....	....	....	....	1⅛	304	½	1,000	27,799	427½
Sullivan,	129⅜	20,402	⅜	92	2⅜	....	....	1	176	¼	52	73,298	1,699¼
Tioga,	45½	7,352	18¼	712	140½	....	....	2½	1,200	½	160	169,183	4,359
Tompkins,	27⅛	5,133	209½	79,932	1,706	....	....	1¾	1,138	21½	27,090	417,757	6,172
Ulster,	514¾	24,136¼	117½	2,107	78	....	....	62¼	2,735	2	2,524	397,754	5,606½
Warren,	69¾	10,205	....	....	....	....	....	......	7	½	20	58,772¾	1,002
Washington,	50⅞	7,518	2,858⅞	839,420	23,003	....	....	¼	62	......	2,390	189,103	5,809½
Wayne,	122¾	24,699	57⅜	23,260	527½	....	....	6¼	737	28⅜	38,432	509,626	8,893½
Westchester,	620⅜	60,993	....	....	....	....	....	......	5	3¼	2,202	60,137½	2,325½
Wyoming,	113¼	7,727	70	6,630	518¼	½	....	17½	17,526	⅛	115	323,290	4,517½
Yates,	25⅞	1,500	482¼	245,000	1,850	....	....	4	1,605	6	6,003	143,773	3,760½
Total,	7,578¼	985,522½	11,764	4,907,556⅝	87,093½	3⅝	¾	9,481¾	7,192,254	786½	946,502½	13,668,830¾	273,639

RECAPITULATION—(Continued.)

COUNTIES.	MARKET GARDENS.		Pounds of maple sugar made.	Gallons of maple molasses made.	Gallons of wine made.	Pounds of honey collected.	Pounds of wax collected.	SILK.	NEAT CATTLE.		
	Acres cultivated.	Value of products.						Pounds of cocoons.	Total number.	Under one year old.	Over one year, exclusive of working oxen and cows.
Albany,	1,112¾	$97,461	4,809	358	238	53,650	3,436½	12	23,247	3,184	4,918
Allegany,	24	2,030	332,260	3,490	103	68,998	3,321½	......	47,332	7,913	17,018
Broome,	33¼	1,340	52,308	937½	104	47,380	2,113½	18	37,544	6,210	10,687
Cattaraugus,	7⅞	463	416,300½	2,459	23	62,486	3,378	......	58,489	10,417	20,202
Cayuga,	48½	10,245	40,036	1,434¾	202	83,553½	4,165½	......	46,178	7,810	16,040
Chautauque,	57¾	5,485	420,722	3,916¼	624½	53,465	4,142	......	76,890	12,851	23,478
Chemung,	25¾	4,948	6,482	363	32	39,191	1,670½	......	20,899	3,496	6,203
Chenango,	1	57	272,528	2,835	32	48,702	3,451	......	68,391	10,162	17,403
Clinton,	2⅞	408	56,277	939½	47	51,459	2,238½	......	25,555	4,411	8,376
Columbia,	98⅝	5,738	2,779	243	725	31,618	1,466	4	27,676	3,817	5,658
Cortland,	2⅞	397	258,977	2,769½	81	56,148	3,619½	......	37,671	5,304	8,990
Delaware,	3,645	69	313,302	5,701	133½	101,571	5,285¼	......	65,181	10,978	14,939
Dutchess,	158⅜	12,777	1,697	159½	35	38,503	1,830	2	44,126	4,349	8,930
Erie,	481¾	39,130	129,627	1,896¼	173	59,659	3,220	......	55,439	7,624	14,190
Essex,	½	126	29,844	399	9	27,342	1,419	......	23,567	3,998	8,739
Franklin,	5⅝	583	125,005½	606¼	8	19,622	919	......	23,677	3,474	7,425
Fulton,	¼	705	18,831	820½	226	23,761	1,300	......	19,922	3,081	5,400
Genesee,	13	641	80,056	1,747	265½	32,359	1,568	......	24,785	4,298	8,529
Greene,	56½	4,174	48,895	1,550	20¼	32,940	2,202¼	......	25,239	3,858	6,440
Hamilton,	....	10	9,507	298	....	5,610	401½	......	2,456	488	756
Herkimer,	9	1,133	73,328	3,643	145	38,347	2,927½	......	49,820	5,046	7,336
Jefferson,	53½	12,790	366,449	4,652	400	18,444	1,290½	......	79,249	10,271	16,984
Kings,	1,414½	273,552	....	....	35	....	....	......	3,204	160	169
Lewis,	1⅛	115	236,918	4,698½	45	11,912	831	......	29,748	2,683	5,491
Livingston,	27¾	1,134	13,488	539	1,563	26,693	1,950½	5	29,383	4,696	11,956
Madison,	20¾	1,810	66,314½	2,537	208	55,615	3,366¾	10	44,924	5,906	13,077
Monroe,	245⅜	26,540	15,344	746½	689	46,038	1,842¾	......	39,545	7,156	12,881
Montgomery,	23¾	2,130	14,178	1,037	408	58,571	3,544	......	30,502	4,796	7,859
New-York,	157	66,000	....	....	....	....	....	......	3,323	4	2,600
Niagara,	51⅜	9,431	3,781	249	160	27,205	1,460	......	28,238	5,038	9,434
Onieda,	246⅞	49,258	60,765¾	3,615	303½	138,475	3,455½	......	77,832	4,560	17,002
Onondaga,	274⅛	19,243	44,828	2,050½	1,583	81,575	3,857¾	......	50,228	7,644	15,329
Ontario,	67⅞	6.555	54,474½	2,542½	959½	53,135	2,458¾	2	33,962	5,859	11,788
Orange,	67⅜	7,922	2,346½	140½	2,173	25,111	2,128½	......	57,602	4,929	8,997
Orleans,	6½	814	17,609	422	139	23,113	1,151½	......	23,412	4,782	8,545
Oswego,	93¼	11,232	59,542	1,081	79	47,700	2,142½	......	42,172	5,933	11,163
Otsego,	10¼	439	193,206	4,099	43	93,020	4,665¾	......	63,798	8,711	17,432
Putnam,	21¾	1,466	1,226	142	5	13,237½	459	......	15,507	1,748	2,708
Queens,	3,186¾	337,503	1,771	....	....	5,989	276	......	14,326	1,437	1,723
Rensselaer,	374½	34,665	17,955	400¼	802	33,684½	1,840½	12	29,601	3,474	6,559
Richmond,	162¼	16,740	....	....	64	475	22	......	2,250	302	359
Rockland,	22½	2,665	5	....	497	8,667	174½	......	7,198	601	1,316
St. Lawrence,	31¼	4,730	513,913	3,070	59	51,614	2,814½	......	96,408	12,403	26,268
Saratoga,	248	13,184	4,399	126	733½	45,202½	2,499	......	34,769	5,562	9,804
Schenectady,	122	8,105	207	30	99	12,688	782½	......	8,614	1,387	2,862
Schoharie,	½	120	47,819	2,330	210	89,676	4,496½	16	38,771	6,971	11,147
Schuyler,	5½	465	9,447	358½	57½	52,167	2,076	1	19,004	3,783	6,417
Seneca,	36⅛	1,425	2,241	311	550	37,549	1,609½	......	16,996	3,611	5,072
Steuben,	101½	3,649	112,287	3,664½	187	113,653	5,429½	36	52,483	9,915	17,933
Suffolk,	25¾	3,293	....	....	18	6,087	414	......	24,215	4,322	7,054
Sullivan,	3⅝	278	12,550	715½	105	40,946	2,398½	8	27,346	4,707	7,599
Tioga,	2⅝	325	25,725	729	75	38,378	1,612¼	......	29,664	5,297	9,090
Tompkins,	10	217	39,853	1,676	971½	83,627	4,075¾	37½	30,847	5,140	9,469
Ulster,	95	7,114	37,854½	1,502¼	121½	49,898	3,125	26	34,140	4,763	7,374
Warren,	2¼	85	18,615	641	88	20,062	1,061½	......	14,282	2,269	4,429
Washington,	22	2,110	5,258	548	116½	30,000	1,945	......	40,410	7,547	12,074
Wayne,	49¾	4,198	13,863	1,280	680½	58,204	2,820½	70	38,464	7,133	12,800
Westchester,	511⅝	18,454	1,410	....	240	17,592	6,370¼	5	33,132	3,475	4,172
Wyoming,	3	237	209,046	1,808	127	36,248	2,000	......	39,048	6,351	13,286
Yates,	6	769	17,556	775	360	29,260	1,510½	......	16,784	3,379	5,408
Total,	12,590⅞	$1,138,682	4,935,815¾	85,091½	18,181¾	2,557,876	138,033½	267½	2,105,465	311,474	577,887

RECAPITULATION.—(Continued.)

COUNTIES.	NEAT CATTLE.		Number of cattle killed for beef.	Pounds of butter.	Pounds of cheese.	Gallons of milk sold.	Number of horses.	Number of mules.	SWINE.	
	Working oxen.	Cows.							Under 6 months.	Over 6 months.
Albany,	1,813	13,332	11,466	1,173,527	36,520	502,994	10,954	31	13,809	10,226
Allegany,	3,392	19,009	2,550	1,700,775	1,044,978	10,803	11,223	36	4,963	8,185
Broome,	3,531	17,116	1.619	1,753,417	40,896	89,122	5,998	7	5,821	6,330
Cattaraugus,	4,137	23,633	2,170	1,957,183	1,717,484	6,200	9,497	11	5,376	8,458
Cayuga,	2,506	19,822	3,093	2,082,022	199,333	84,344	15,405	4	14,187	14,894
Chautauque,	4,515	36,046	3,830	3,389,837	1,198,361	56,358	13,047	15	9,156	11,949
Chemung,	1,510	9,690	1,938	924,645	7,861	52,820	4,856	6	4,097	5,756
Chenango,	3,887	36,939	2,176	3,990,564	1,212,544	2,122	10,971	10	9,094	8,998
Clinton,	1,484	11,284	2,385	891,431½	105,906	3,402	8,444	36	2,875	4,993
Columbia,	3,701	14,500	2,325	1,347,428	67,167	492,203	9,103	211	22,194	10,374
Cortland,	1,709	21,668	1,860	2,379,257	708,679	13,133	7,410	27	6,000	6,302
Delaware,	4,780	34,484	2,044	4,026,575	61,185	5,010	9,140	5	7,221	8,649
Dutchess,	6,263	24,584	4,259	1,681,595	54,119	1,970,368	10,829	29	29,074	13,912
Erie,	3,794	29,831	5,320	1,866,132	2,038,392	1,173,085	16,983	10	7,342	17,449
Essex,	2,081	8,749	1,736	625,542	93,594	1,845	6,149	43	2,775	3,729
Franklin,	1,859	10,919	1,305	1,050,040	143,916	6,300	6,029	3	2,820	4,715
Fulton,	1,173	10,268	1,509	840,397	579,079	8,103	5,829	1	5,847	4,667
Genesee,	1,417	10,541	1,789	919,130	105,873	157,914	11,395	13	8,150	11,123
Greene,	2,349	12,592	2,083	1,191,930	21,317	74,690	6,203	23	8,561	5,513
Hamilton,	360	852	127	83,282	2,670	…	338	…	169	341
Herkimer,	785	36,653	2,557	1,305,377	9,068,519	54,960	9,098	10	9,125	9,102
Jefferson,	2,522	49,472	4,235	3,949,608	2,819,459	192,192	17,059	20	11,026	12,301
Kings,	41	2,834	5,500	17,425	…	3,033,291	6,314	122	1,218	2,746
Lewis,	2,423	19,151	1,247	1,575,515	1,896,741	6,795	5,097	9	3,865	4,488
Livingston,	1,751	10,980	3,229	1,045,591	79,346½	8,825	12,502	47	8,632	10,643
Madison,	1,874	24,067	2,740	1,840,298	2,087.594	31,026	11,753	32	8,179	8,615
Monroe,	1,944	17,564	4,558	1,643,515	131,253	287,527	18,913	16	15,641	19,086
Montgomery,	1,046	16,801	2,376	1,211,385	1,538,654	68,171	8,836	3	10,610	8,224
New-York,	…	719	44,405	…	…	2,400	14,099	256	178	1,071
Niagara,	2,058	11,708	3,500	1,038,307	71,443	59,179	14,334	5	8,479	13,286
Oneida,	3,476	47,794	15,061	2,912,176	3,311,114	184,108	17,398	34	13,417	17,811
Onondaga,	2,454	24,801	4,269	2,294,287	860,644	330,273	17,330	8	14,727	16,812
Ontario,	2,113	14,202	2,848	1,223,097	205,921	217,340	13,660	159	13,161	13.258
Orange,	3,489	40,187	6,175	3,285,587¾	80,660	4,553,514	9,986	74	23,995	16,689
Orleans,	1,164	8,921	1,294	912,013	110,298	15,764	9,640	2	6,465	9,227
Oswego,	3,093	21,983	4,637	2,036,174	975,461	116,425	12,398	23	7,970	13,866
Otsego,	2,942	34,713	3,537	3,075,206	1,638,493	3,440	14,652	17	11,210	11,158
Putnam,	3,200	7,851	1,300	493,696	3,475	1,888,910	1,938	1	4,690	2,307
Queens,	1,926	9,240	1,164	441,983½	765	566,321	7,954	178	6,723	7,505
Rensselaer,	2,704	16,864	7,710	1,291,738	538,462	1,026,305	10,184	10	15,504	9,503
Richmond,	400	1,189	102	24,365	…	34,905	845	26	663	1,063
Rockland,	573	4,708	985	266,006	2,500	278,660	3,715	170	1,669	1,516
St. Lawrence,	5,576	52,161	4,542	4,268,809	1,672,999	16,052	20,261	20	10,881	13,205
Saratoga,	2,625	16,778	4,356	1,468,136½	152,901¾	88,424	11,293	2	15,206	10,797
Schenectady,	597	5,768	2,204	515,662	72,019	73,070	4,219	4	4,208	3,519
Schoharie,	2,440	18,213	2,042	1,832,257	71,016	10,225	9,682	2	9,911	8,893
Schuyler,	1,128	7,676	1,126	798,953	32,168	125	5,700	4	4,379	5,072
Seneca,	577	7,136	2,160	705,574	13,812	34,281	7,497	6	6,262	11,270
Steuben,	4,351	20,284	3,837	1,976,129	203,329	18,756	13,899	40	8,873	15,281
Suffolk,	2,006	10,833	2,238	634,405	1,580	44,120	7,111	163	9,026	10,701
Sullivan,	4,265	10,775	1,155	931,927	4,598	44,924	3,092	87	4,111	4,120
Tioga,	2,323	12,954	1,439	1,365,783	50,357	2,567	5,678	13	4,915	6,333
Tompkins,	1,666	14,572	1,440	1,645,947	60,128	36,590	9,443	3	6,608	7,750
Ulster,	4,671	17,332	4,470	1,669,631	520	88,887	9,893	58	21,086	12,939
Warren,	1,423	6,161	1,497	482,786	64,634	27,201	3,341	6	2,965	2,738
Washington,	2,100	18,689	2,994	1,625,138	634,491	30,609	11,707	11	18,980	11,325
Wayne,	1,762	16,769	2,456	1,446,080	163,763½	29,323	14,928	5	12,175	17,624
Westchester,	5,427	20,078	4,785	1,116,589	2,180	2,696,411	7,332	73	12,976	7,885
Wyoming,	2,674	16,737	2,007	1,333,948	823,105	40,554	10,358	6	4,270	7,404
Yates,	747	7,250	1,577	717,259¼	59,972	12,595	6,773	8	6,666	5,920
Total,	144,597	1,068,427	225.338	90,293,073½	38,944,249¾	20,965,861	579,715	2,254	530,176	539,616

RECAPITULATION.—(Continued.)

COUNTIES	SHEEP.			POULTRY.		CLOTHS OF DOMESTIC MANUFACTURE.			
	Number of sheep.	Number of fleeces shorn.	Pounds of wool.	Value of poultry sold.	Value of eggs sold.	Yards of fulled cloth made.	Yards of flannel made.	Yards of linen made.	Yards of cotton and mixed cloths.
Albany,	37,054	27,381	107,956	$26,314	$47,691	4,929	7,219¾	2,925	2,886½
Allegany,	104,799	80,416	272,622½	7,819	11,218	3,095¼	14,476	4,053½	9,337¾
Broome,	40,894	27,713	86,324¼	23,389	45,062	10,548	10,094	2,670	3,939
Cattaraugus,	59,725	41,080	130,996½	10,031	13,295	4,139¼	15,056½	4,218	11,659
Cayuga,	103,631	98,500	348,830¼	26,416	45,866	3,628½	7,751	2,370	2,840
Chautauque,	90,154	63,811	217,024	15,627	19,609	4,131½	12,243	6,948½	11,935
Chemung,	21,364	12,909	40,765½	3,802	6,689	1,573	3,315	469	1,656
Chenango,	85,923	66,049	220,092¼	20,069	21,781	14,513½	14,488	5,811½	7,839
Clinton,	38,351	28,417	97,133¼	5,541	11,444	2,570	5,696¼	141	2,172½
Columbia,	87,549	81,064	267,368	29,701	43,831	1,294	2,995	1,392	2,894
Cortland,	41,321	34,470	120,793½	8,402	16,482	3,932	8,803	3,804	5,261½
Delaware,	71,315	42,499½	36,659¾	11,526	12,999	9,084½	21,288¼	2,676½	6,508½
Dutchess,	73,687	63,191	205,143¼	65,687	68,913	606½	1,398½	795	393
Erie,	65,085	48,938	164,694	26,263	30,135	5,011½	10,253½	1,888½	9,500½
Essex,	47,654	38,158	134,735½	3,460	5,553	1,440	2,664½	362	1,994
Franklin,	23,958	20,175	70,737¾	3,135	3,610	3,310	9,551	986	9,367½
Fulton,	16,969	10,901	37,903½	10,289	14,122	2,203½	2,537½	895	1,841
Genesee,	100,391	91,178	352,003½	71,212	13,692	352½	2,477	384	922
Greene,	19,382	14,398	50,970	14,490	22,232	2,191	3,728½	862	1,830
Hamilton,	1,481	1,048	3,251½	444	141	183	611	30	639
Herkimer,	17,706	11,254	43,561¾	12,489	12,196	4,161¼	5,192½	1,259½	3,497
Jefferson,	63,401	33,913	118,372⅝	13,348	19,298	13,063¾	16,685½	4,380½	11,826
Kings,	2	2	7	1,183	2,071	....	....	....	....
Lewis,	10,086	7,624	27,046⅞	4,701	2,671	2,609¼	8,291	1,532½	3,369
Livingston,	112,562	106,839	377,690¼	8,721	11,092	2,121	4,573½	818½	1,492
Madison,	66,547	76,910	261,904¾	14,454	23,878	1,986¾	7,217	2,937	5,023½
Monroe,	116,817	91,910	350,468¾	21,098	26,292	1,417¼	4,178	364	1,388
Montgomery,	29,661	20,925	74,445¾	10,513	20,705	3,026¼	5,592½	2,049	1,619
New-York,	....	....	....	....	....	....	....	....	....
Niagara,	78,359	55,307½	219,903¼	11,357	19,008	2,721	4,941	541	3,296
Oneida,	50,841	39,215	137,327½	22,972	31,823	5,101	11,402½	1,600	9,886
Onondaga,	94,202	84,662	318,446¾	24,807	43,927	3,030½	7,373	1,341½	3,834½
Ontario,	132,725	138,842	609,075	25,128	23,018	782½	2,497½	452	1,153
Orange,	21,377	17,251	59,135	30,694	32,312	1,002	1,398¼	413	135
Orleans,	91,285	64,909	255,802¾	9,091	13,590	1,404½	2,679½	377	1,863
Oswego,	36,088	22,418	79,446¼	13,161	26,758	7,166½	11,573½	3,137	6,740
Otsego,	109,937	82,516	278,705¼	23,699	41,304	5,295	9,268½	7,419	10,797
Putnam,	5,804	4,080	14,466¼	11,900	12,719	92	885	20	224
Queens,	9,714	7,084	20,592½	69,114	45,095	....	....	....	....
Rensselaer,	64,609	59,558	187,756½	31,440	43,804	1,206	2,037	706	1,000
Richmond,	57	38	160	2,427	6,452	....	....	....	....
Rockland,	926	460	1,585	5,384	7,348	....	....	....	....
St. Lawrence,	86,454	70,413	246,683	9,249	16,310	19,102	29,178	4,943	36,640
Saratoga,	46,018	33,498	111,769¾	28,949	46,379	1,976½	3,991	842	944
Schenectady,	10,759	7,008	26,408½	7,491	13,011	1,065½	1,782	137	478
Schoharie,	45,596	29,860	108,416¾	13,824	29,197	7,649¾	13,666¾	7,376	6,222⅜
Schuyler,	48,918	40,789	152,554¾	7,263	8,961	2,637½	3,532¾	1,392	3,784
Seneca,	47,534	41,877	150,946	19,285	17,323	430	1,611	402	712
Steuben,	111,353	101,484	336,334	10,636	14,678	7,810	16,903	3,316½	6,905½
Suffolk,	28,016	23,178	68,281¾	43,399	55,242	97	252	309	212
Sullivan,	12,591	8,027	26,622	4,384	4,059	1,874½	5,821	228	1,512
Tioga,	36,152	26,499	80,144¼	6,490	11,235	3,313½	6,517	2,380	4,180
Tompkins,	61,036	47,197	160,834½	20,734	31,205	3,767	7,472	1,349	2,259
Ulster,	29,841	17,280	57,995½	28,937	39,307	3,428½	5,447	2,322½	5,248¾
Warren,	16,472	11,546	39,001	3,173	5,570	3,743½	4,094¼	730	2,867
Washington,	118,533	97,285	330,866½	31,402	45,193	1,133	2,277	1,255	1,633½
Wayne,	104,845	77,936	295,810	19,238	36,955	1,985½	6,241	1,227	3,611
Westchester,	11,321	9,273	30,012	47,904	43,947	207	141	36	103
Wyoming,	93,365	96,413	347,973½	10,388	13,315	2,427	6,877	3,049	4,820
Yates,	64,827	72,620	259,401	12,554	9,060	631¼	1,685¾	703	773
Total,	3,217,024	2,630,203	9,231,959¼	1,076,598	1,360,673	198,203	379,922½	105,086	245,464

MISCELLANEOUS ARTICLES OF FARM PRODUCE.

COUNTIES.	Apricots.		Beets.		Broom Corn.		Cabbages.	Carrots.		Cherries.		Clover Seed.		Cranberries.		Cucumbers.
	Bushels.	Value.	Bushels.	Value.	Tons.	Value.	Value.	Bushels.	Value.	Bushels.	Value.	Pounds.	Value.	Bushels.	Value.	Value.
Albany,	...	...	213	$62	127	$25,080	$12	6,527	$1,893	14	$24	71½	$714	...	...	...
Allegany,	...	...	49	20	...	...	...	9,833	3,051	14	14	1	7	...	...	...
Broome,	...	...	...	...	13½	3,174	...	335	119	40	60	...	...	...	...	...
Cattaraugus,	...	...	103	23	2½	390	...	6,659	2,100	...	...	300	50	...	...	...
Cayuga,	...	...	2,837	1,134	...	371	112	15,872	3,788	1	4	1,325½	9,663	...	...	$75
Chautauque,	...	...	997	272	62	2,138	24	11,741	3,975	62¼	124	10	80	...	...	...
Chemung,	...	...	100	38	¼	52	...	442	180	52½	84	6½	52	...	...	...
Chenango,	...	...	...	...	...	...	...	22,440	5,654	145	138	...	...	...	...	...
Clinton,	...	...	157½	50	...	...	6	11,049	2,950	...	...	...	...	...	...	...
Columbia,	2	$10	...	...	4½	825	...	3,746	1,055	908	284	...	...	...	...	...
Cortland,	...	...	156	19	1	206	...	5,915	2,399	291½	354	6,540	1,090	...	...	...
Delaware,	...	...	385	113	...	...	60	3,288	957	5	8	5	45	...	...	...
Dutchess,	...	...	565	123	...	57	...	1,508	442	...	429	13	121	...	...	...
Erie,	...	...	430	175	...	...	1,891	20,716	5,936	66½	184	1,080	180	...	...	...
Essex,	...	...	...	...	...	...	4	8,547	2,405	...	...	...	...	...	...	...
Franklin,	...	...	15	3	...	...	...	6,403	1,460	...	...	...	...	...	...	...
Fulton,	...	...	166	38	1⅛	130	...	7,025	1,900	...	...	...	...	...	...	...
Genesee,	...	...	887	192	...	...	30	9,421	1,922	4	4	139	1,042	...	...	...
Greene,	2	12	...	...	⅛	18	...	1,230	626	10	36	...	...	...	...	...
Hamilton,	...	...	...	...	...	...	...	99	46	...	...	...	...	...	...	...
Herkimer,	...	...	...	...	25⅛	2,805	...	6,340	1,727	20	20	...	...	...	...	...
Jefferson,	...	...	...	...	...	150	...	7,219	2,918	...	...	...	...	1	$4	...
Kings,	...	...	...	...	...	...	...	...	190	...	...	...	...	...	...	...
Lewis,	...	...	120	30	...	...	48	1,321	894	...	...	...	...	...	...	...
Levingston,	...	...	1,570	389	70½	12,890	...	5,314	1,616	19	20	63	462	...	...	...
Madison,	...	...	15	4	5	704	10	5,029	1,447	125½	131	9	100	...	...	147
Monroe,	...	...	3,810	550	...	...	115	34,859	8,084	12	8	...	...	...	...	...
Montgomery,	...	...	1,122	286	256½	44,846	...	18,313	4,626	3	4	1,250	12,715	...	...	...
New-York,	...	...	...	...	...	...	...	...	...	...	...	...	...	...	...	100
Niagara,	...	...	275	85	4¾	470	60	22,359	5,377	277	222	316¼	2,266	...	...	...
Oneida,	...	...	1,077	274	14¾	2,129	35	18,801	4,757	36	55	4	48	...	...	...
Onondaga,	...	...	2,375	767	...	1,616	86	29,274	7,371	226	260	1,065½	9,146	...	...	389
Ontario,	...	...	1,630	404	...	221	...	4,555	1,560	179	739	257	1,728	...	...	...
Orange,	...	...	1,673	692	...	...	71	2,187	970	90	98	12	94	...	...	...
Orleans,	...	...	680	174	...	260	2	14,400	3,062	24	30	534	5,682	...	...	...
Oswego,	...	...	1,271	339	...	560	64	20,169	5,380	258½	429	...	...	...	...	...
Otsego,	...	...	105	30	...	5	...	10,227	2,611	...	...	447	4,511	...	...	...
Putnam,	...	...	...	...	⅛	30	...	790	395	...	...	...	...	...	...	...
Queens,	...	...	...	...	...	...	8,135	150	80	...	...	...	...	...	...	...
Rensselaer,	...	...	100	37	48	9,745	12	7,430	2,297	89	199	...	...	3	8	...
Richmond,	...	...	...	...	...	...	6,837	...	...	...	25	...	...	30	100	...
Rockland,	...	...	...	...	...	...	...	...	...	...	73	13¾	117	...	...	...
St. Lawrence,	...	...	79	20	...	10	15	25,726	6,718	...	...	...	...	...	...	...
Saratoga,	...	...	655	191	...	1,874	...	10,289	3,380	63	123	2	20	...	...	...
Schenectady,	...	...	1,185	221	727	133,970	20	6,289	1,828	...	...	41	431	...	...	...
Schoharie,	...	...	840	217	134⅜	20,462	...	6,001	1,858	4	4	1,282½	11,602	...	...	...
Schuyler,	...	...	87	28	...	280	41	3,758	1,146	54½	77	628¾	5,191	...	...	...
Seneca,	...	...	680	150	¼	30	...	745	312	393	570	409	2,774	...	...	...
Steuben,	...	...	160	20	...	...	158	1,973	735	91	171	45	274	...	...	...
Suffolk,	...	...	...	...	1	48	500	10,066	3,603	24	32	165	1,311	8	27	...
Sullivan,	...	...	...	5	¼	40	61	18	15	25½	27	...	...	45	135	...
Tioga,	...	...	182	91	...	2,100	150	901	293	...	...	...	...	...	...	...
Tompkins,	...	...	145	37	...	...	...	8,462	2,055	25	41	188¾	1,671	...	...	...
Ulster,	...	...	40	8	...	25	60	30	15	10	5	24	325	...	...	...
Warren,	...	...	...	...	...	...	...	431	36	5	10	...	...	...	...	...
Washington,	...	...	895	216	2½	265	47	9,904	2,617	30	56	...	...	...	...	...
Wayne,	...	...	1,010	244	7½	750	...	12,960	3,248	15	28	369	2,817	...	...	...
Westchester,	...	...	150	15	...	...	2	8,353	3,770	...	61	...	...	...	...	8,908
Wyoming,	...	...	341	98	...	...	...	10,064	2,318	20	22	44	327	...	...	...
Yates,	3	2	...	...	...	...	...	774	205	55	85	...	1,132	...	...	...
Total,	7	24	29,332½	7,884	1,509⅞	268,726	18,668	478,277	132,372	3,787¾	5,372	16,662	77,788	87	274	9,619

MISCELLANEOUS ARTICLES.—(Continued.)

COUNTIES.	Currants.		Feathers.		Fruits. (Not specified.)		Garden Seeds.		Grapes.		Melons.	Millett.		Onions.		Osier Willow.	Peaches.	
	Bushels.	Value.	Pounds.	Value.	Bushels.	Value.	Pounds.	Value.	Bushels.	Value.	Value.	Bushels.	Value.	Bushels.	Value.	Value.	Bushels.	Value.
Albany,					4515½	$7,118		$2,589	155	$168	$110			1½	$1	$100	834½	$2,037
Allegany,	41	$46			41	50						681	$697	345½	430		147	258
Broome,												164	166	20	20		137½	220
Cattaraugus,			15	$9	48	55					219	1,099	1,259	297	298		647½	636
Cayuga,					14	33			8	15				720	397		5,041	3,346
Chautauque,	32	22			172	206		18,420		301	267	157	169	567	446		4,742	3,702
Chemung,	19	17			885	1,041			1	2		2	3	10	10		924	1,053
Chenango,												174	344	20	20			
Clinton,	3	3					480	280				103	98	52	64			
Columbia,	10	18			8459	12,567	20,339	10,945	500	500				2,580	1,381	133	1,999	4,224
Cortland,	13	9			36	27			12	60		35	75	134	96		55	74
Delaware,												82	111	113	106		38½	49
Dutchess,	68	46				4,069				1,837	624	30	30	57	82		1,072	1,538
Erie,	2	3			753	868	192	92		32	1,451	614	399	1,851	2,108		2,616	1,604
Essex,					29	41		50						55	77			
Franklin,												61	61	15	15			
Fulton,	4	4										15	15	79	52			
Genesee,														63	80		3,506	1,229
Greene,					7134½	10,652						15	25				140	142
Hamilton,																		
Herkimer,	20	24									12	36	36	268½	228			
Jefferson,					1175	610					70	53	55	277	228			
Kings,																	15	30
Lewis,												474	128	92	69			
Livingston,					114	113						8	16	93	91		618	490
Madison,					87	158			13	29	13	143½	25	64	54			
Monroe,									23	37	37			441	324		22,134	14,842
Montgomery,	46	48½				15		52		61				74	63			
New-York,														125	100			
Niagara,		51			512	416		2	86	436	20	192	187	850	692		12,378	11,675
Oneida,	10	80					221	125	4	50		150	150	626½	567			
Onondaga,	26½	39				505			50½	148	10	106	170	468	284	18	1,165	1,087
Ontario,					2018½	1,800				1,120	8		15	66	73		3,073	1,785
Orange,	12	12				7,258				154				1,780	1,744		2,705	3,752
Orleans,			37	25	57	68					116			49	54		4,031	2,284
Oswego,	26	26			11311				25¼	74	200	65	88	425½	394		2,244	1,982
Otsego,					2	15		10	2	2		52	52	58½	64		8½	9
Putnam,																		
Queens,							600	150	600	450							111	530
Rensselaer,	31	49½			101½	150		311	28	45				309½	134		392	535
Richmond,						110				42	400							
Rockland,						420								100	100		8	
St. Lawrence,						5		11			60	105	110	105	113			
Saratoga,	38	47				26			30	120	100			83	67			
Schenectady,								375						8	8			
Schoharie,					584	394						19	19	20	17		28	42
Schuyler,	24	24				704						286½	291	5	5		3,195	3,172
Seneca,	57	57									80			15	15		5,777	5,252
Steuben,						1,079				20		302	330	72	75		1,148	1,386
Suffolk,						250				300	150			239	202		1,330	2,469
Sullivan,					20	18		110				514½	553	27½	27		568	797
Tioga,			30	18							95	253	232	204	153		586	865
Tompkins,					175	200						12	12	92	84		1,919	2,871
Ulster,					2420	5,591			10	40	600	60	63	23½	26		1,721	1,950
Warren,														12	12			
Washington,	21	36				31	1,600	5,637	6	32				346	272			
Wayne,					1644	1,194		1,730	26	59		70	130	190	177		25,394	16,174
Westchester,	3	7				1,875				4,975	40			5	10		895	405
Wyoming,					190	234				202		285	279	432	427		397	402
Yates,					576	509			31	57		35	110				1,689	1,390
Total,	506½	669	82	52	43074	60,475	23,432	40,889	1,610¾	11,368	4,682	6,453½	6,503	15026½	12,636	251	115,410½	96,288

MISCELLANEOUS ARTICLES.—(Continued.)

COUNTIES.	Pears.		Plums.		Quinces.		Root Crops. (Miscellaneous.)		Ruta Baga.		Saffron.*		Strawberries.		Value of fruit and ornamental trees.	Miscellaneous.†
	Bushels.	Value.	Bushels.	Value.	Bushels.	Value.	Bushels.	Value.	Bushels.	Value.	Pounds.	Value.	Bushels.	Value.		
Albany,	334½	$304	359	$694	68	$96	191	$22						$1089		$9,670
Allegany,	52	39	1,592½	1,595			658	208	15	$4					$3,120	445
Broome,	11	11	14	18			50	19	20	8						170
Cattaraugus,	39	41	146	115			685	223								130
Cayuga,	395	375	15	34	3¼	3		398			17	$11			1,200	655
Chautauque,	149	92	135½	130	168	228	1,812	557						59	500	3,380
Chemung,	27	26	190	210	3	4										2,177
Chenango,	55	56					30	6							890	32
Clinton,			25	36			360	149							100	10,650
Columbia,	759	532	313	420							249	249	3	75	6,600	16,935
Cortland,	43	29	11	13											250	893
Delaware,	11	8	5	7			130	65						58		55
Dutchess,	278	339	1,780	2,722	720	326	890	411	400	100			4	16	3,969	3,108
Erie,	139	156	207	232			11,772	2,092						1,289	3,415	9,851
Essex,			23	32			140	56								227
Franklin,							3,078	152								267
Fulton,	6	3					1,508	411	140	30						26
Genesee,	267	262			104	104	3,233	2,373					55	220		5,419
Greene,	232	221					28	15								
Hamilton,																
Herkimer,	48	56	10	14											304	758
Jefferson,			121	121			5,751	1,835			797	635			603	3,893
Kings,	115	122						50						3,450		3,115
Lewis,	1	1	1½	3				20						100		2,650
Livingston,	38	31	24	22			2,810	744					28	131	444	1,756
Madison,	485	419	21	26	57	57	24	6					45½	198	15	2,143
Monroe,	240	300	4	4	182½	155							23½	173		273,333
Montgomery,	77	103	125	179	24	30	1,330	316			428	359			9	1,288
New-York,																387
Niagara,	47	50	87	94	52	52	125	31	50					14	25,507	447
Oneida,	468½	760	27	50	63	85	137	46	7	3	50	50			7,291	4,095
Onondaga,	376	402	201	252	33	35	3,932	1,152			185	170		872	18,043	9,276
Ontario,	599	443	265	334			3,498	902						110	9,924	662
Orange,	69	37	146	467	22	34									9,860	5,902
Orleans,	136	132	100	99	26	24	1,909	415							2,519	33
Oswego,	450	432	129½	203	145	117					72	75	5	18		1,814
Otsego,	62½	45	82	133	22	44									300	2,118
Putnam,									1,500	613					2	
Queens,	60	60			5	5								3,774		193,555
Rensselaer,	341	255	341	593			160	65					2	18		630
Richmond,							600	225								3,363
Rockland,			5	5										3,544		15,994
St. Lawrence,			5	2					60	12					500	397
Saratoga,	94	143							710	178				137	10,200	1,303
Schenectady,			312	442												620
Schoharie,	8	4							80	23						18
Schuyler,			630	728			611	172							2,575	
Seneca,	378	289			55	55			10	5					5,000	251
Steuben,	4	4	397	403				164	119	50						407
Suffolk,	91	49	8	10	97	120	2,060	702					205	563		377
Sullivan,	134	103			7	7									1,480	
Tioga,	31	31	22	24											1,300	125
Tompkins,	127	97	4	6			506	115						100	9,800	355
Ulster,	111	84	3	3	7½	9									498	2,358
Warren,			144	113												
Washington,			75	140	1	2		49								407
Wayne,	156	320	5	6	170	104	531	177							14,610	3,127
Westchester,				80			5,368	2,236						254	1,100	3,595
Wyoming,	70	99	212	174			520	124								561
Yates,	15	10	281	244											400	6,194
Total,	7,629½	7,375	8,604	11,232	2,035¼	1,696	54,437	16,703	3,111	1,026	1,798	1,549	371	16,262	142,328	611,397

Total value, ... $1,421,750.

* Dried blossoms of the *Carthamus tinctorius*, used chiefly in dyeing.

† The miscellaneous column includes several very considerable products that were reported together in such a manner that they could not be separated, as "fruits and grain," &c. The following items are included in this column: *Medicinal Herbs*—Albany, $500; Columbia, 59,920 lbs., $13,800. *Pop Corn*—Schenectady, 1,000 bushels, $1,000. *Sweet Corn*—Richmond, $75. *Sweet Potatoes*—Ontario, 11 bushels, $21; Richmond, 90 bushels, $105; Wayne, 6 bushels. *Teasels*—Cattaraugus, $60; Cayuga, $62; Oneida, $928; Onondaga, $6,008. *Tomatoes*—Cayuga, $2; Dutchess, $5; Erie, $200; Kings, $3,115; New-York, $387; Richmond, $3,198, Suffolk, $20. *Woad*—Oneida, 4 tons, $400.

QUANTITY AND VALUE OF SPECIAL MANURES USED.

COUNTIES.	Ashes.		Bone Dust.		Guano.		Gypsum.		Lime.		Phosphate of Lime.		Saline Compounds.		Miscellaneous.*
	Bushels.	Value.	Tons.	Value.	Tons.	Value.	Tons.	Value.	Bushels.	Value.	Tons.	Value.	Bushels.	Value.	Value.
Albany,	200	$20	½	$35	43¾	$2, 172	1, 137⅝	$8, 573	1, 000	$150	1	$56	......	......	$5, 292
Allegany,	50	6	......	......	9	514	422	2, 810	51	15	¾	45	......	......	59
Broome,	500	63	......	......	2	120	837¼	4, 409	43	15	......	......	......	......	......
Cattaraugus,	140	11	......	......	½	30	51¼	526	......	......	......	......	......	......	8
Cayuga,	50	10	......	......	¾	47	1, 591½	5, 027	5, 046	911	......	......	......	......	263
Chautauque,	18	2	⅛	11	......	......	241¼	1, 982	61	24	......	......	......	......	123
Chemung,	......	......	......	......	......	......	926¾	2, 874	160	42	1	55	......	......	......
Chenango,	......	......	......	......	......	......	1, 414¾	6, 129	......	......	⅛	8	......	......	100
Clinton,	200	22	......	......	......	......	268½	2, 189	......	......	......	......	......	......	38
Columbia,	......	20	......	......	19¾	745	1, 337½	11, 837	20	1	1¼	66	......	......	11
Cortland,	121	15	......	2	......	......	528⅞	2, 558	15	3	......	......	......	......	495
Delaware,	......	89	......	5	¼	15	235½	2, 442	237	142	......	......	......	......	......
Dutchess,	1, 002	130	......	......	70	3, 406	2, 630	19, 051	......	......	7	350	......	......	2, 087
Erie,	180	23	......	......	¼	......	545	2, 360	......	400	......	3	......	......	351
Essex,	......	......	......	......	......	......	207	2, 065	......	40	......	......	......	......	63
Franklin,	10	2	......	......	......	......	58½	659	......	......	......	......	......	......	30
Fulton,	70	13	......	......	4	247	477½	2, 508	......	......	⅓	22	......	......	......
Genesee,	40	5	......	......	......	......	1, 197¾	3, 863	159	25	......	......	......	......	122
Greene,	......	......	......	......	⅛	8	217¾	2, 300	......	......	......	......	......	......	1, 194
Hamilton,	......	56	......	......	......	......	1	7	......	......	......	......	......	......	......
Herkimer,	......	90	......	......	1¾	133	2, 076¾	8, 898	815	110	⅜	18	......	......	120
Jefferson,	......	......	......	......	......	......	1, 081	4, 016	......	......	......	......	......	......	95
Kings,	1, 730	173	......	150	45¼	2, 615	......	......	......	......	......	......	......	......	21, 491
Lewis,	......	40	......	......	3	150	157	1, 003	155	21	......	......	......	......	......
Livingston,	......	......	......	......	1⅜	63	2, 459½	10, 335	......	......	......	1	......	......	26
Madison,	1, 997	76	......	......	1	68	1, 618½	5, 816	5, 340	638	......	......	......	$9	101
Monroe,	......	15	......	......	4¼	207	2, 637½	8, 663	500	129	......	......	......	......	2, 429
Montgomery,	......	......	......	......	⅝	36	1, 581	7, 081	......	......	......	......	......	......	363
New-York,	......	......	......	......	......	......	......	......	......	......	......	......	......	......	......
Niagara,	......	......	......	......	......	......	680¼	3, 254	......	......	......	......	......	......	......
Oneida,	2, 170	179	......	42	7¼	546	1, 005½	4, 067	760	124	......	3	30	12	1, 228
Onondaga,	240	20	......	60	½	26	2, 894½	7, 800	248	20	......	......	......	46	16
Ontario,	......	......	......	35	1	53	2, 882	10, 816	......	28	......	......	......	......	148
Orange,	330	38	......	101	27	1, 581	1, 596	12, 504	1, 485	310	......	......	......	......	1, 302
Orleans,	385	48	......	......	......	......	950	5, 325	1, 607	76	......	......	280	94	66
Oswego,	2, 365	217	......	......	⅛	8	497⅞	2, 095	381	74	......	......	......	......	......
Otsego,	......	134	......	......	1	51	1, 920	13, 552	1, 300	349	......	......	......	......	1, 115
Putnam,	200	25	......	85	27¼	1, 122	616	5, 100	300	15	......	......	......	......	95
Queens,	......	......	......	......	1, 206½	60, 274	......	......	......	......	......	......	......	......	......
Rensselaer,	......	35	½	15	14⅛	726	1, 826	12, 370	5, 993	213	⅛	8	......	......	856
Richmond,	......	......	......	60	12⅝	708	......	......	......	......	½	27	......	......	130
Rockland,	......	......	......	......	⅛	5	......	......	5, 300	130	......	......	......	......	4, 437
St. Lawrence,	......	100	......	......	1¼	58	278½	2, 106	125	16	......	......	......	......	10
Saratoga,	2, 362	430	......	......	42	1, 717	2, 188	12, 630	2, 975	366	¼	9	......	......	2, 296
Schenectady,	......	......	......	......	6	291	513⅝	2, 514	......	......	......	......	......	......	290
Schoharie,	......	......	......	......	¼	13	740¾	5, 568	200	50	......	......	......	......	......
Schuyler,	......	......	......	......	......	......	1, 493¼	6, 550	284	73	......	......	......	......	140
Seneca,	1, 061	127	......	......	1¼	78	1, 470	3, 310	2, 263	282	......	......	......	......	386
Steuben,	......	......	......	......	¾	43	2, 540½	12, 226	200	30	......	......	100	432	......
Suffolk,	50, 632	7, 879	......	11, 721	1, 059¼	52, 015	3	16	15, 735	742	21	1, 055	......	......	120, 756
Sullivan,	32	4	......	......	......	......	37	368	45	16	¼	8	......	......	190
Tioga,	20	2	......	......	⅛	6	814¼	3, 987	6	1	......	......	......	......	45
Tompkins,	65	7	......	......	⅛	5	1, 303½	4, 825	546	78	½	15	......	......	352
Ulster,	769	152	......	......	5⅝	258	365¼	2, 524	48, 676	2, 266	25	343	......	......	3, 151
Warren,	......	14	......	......	......	......	357	1, 942	5	2	......	......	......	......	46
Washington,	......	......	......	......	5¼	306	3, 219⅜	19, 401	212	51	3⅜	174	21	8	135
Wayne,	106	12	......	5	1	60	1, 632	5, 727	44	9	......	......	......	......	620
Westchester,	......	...	......	4, 112	172	7, 064	426	2, 374	7, 700	415	8	848	......	......	9, 155
Wyoming,	310	35	......	......	⅛	8	649	3, 400	......	......	......	......	......	......	336
Yates,	143	20	......	......	⅛	9	1, 973½	8, 441	30	7	......	......	......	......	......
Total,	67, 498	10, 359	1⅛	16, 439	2, 800	137, 607	60, 811⅛	304, 773	110, 022	8, 409	70¾	3, 114	431	601	182, 162

Total value of Special Manures, ... $663, 464

* This column embraces such manures as were only mentioned as "miscellaneous," and those that were reported together in such a manner that the quantities and values could not be ascertained separately.

MISCELLANEOUS DOMESTIC MANUFACTURES.

COUNTIES.	Baskets.		Bed Spreads.*		Blankets.		Brooms.		Carpeting.†		Cloth. (Not specified.)		Coverlids.		Currant Wine.		Dried Fruit.	
	Number.	Value.	Number.	Value.	Number.	Value.	Number.	Value.	Yards.	Value.	Yards.	Value.	Number.	Value.	Gallons.	Value.	Bushels.	Value.
Albany,	......	......	21	$10	....	....	......	......	393	$142	......	......	......	......	12	$12	......	......
Allegany,	40	$24	11	68	20	$10	......	......	4,933	2,291	6	......	2	$16	......	......	......	......
Broome,	......	......	......	......	....	....	......	......	......	......	......	......	......	......	......	......	......	......
Cattaraugus,	......	......	5	29	1	6	......	......	4,363¼	2,170	9	$14	22	70	......	......	198½	$492
Cayuga,	......	......	4	21	....	....	1,140	$160	4,899	1,992	19	12	15	112	......	......	8,659	7,339
Chautauque,	......	......	83	337	27	44	......	......	16,547	7,149	161	53	23	74	......	......	222	248
Chemung,	......	......	......	......	42	27	......	......	594	282	30	21	......	......	......	......	......	......
Chenango,	......	......	......	......	24	26	......	......	7,343½	2,770	81	40	......	......	......	......	767	498
Clinton,	......	......	......	......	....	....	......	......	385	248	......	......	......	......	......	......	......	......
Columbia,	3,400	1,700	......	......	....	....	......	......	3,922	1,655	113	89	6	35	......	......	......	......
Cortland,	100	40	1	8	1	3	......	......	5,010	1,662	......	......	16	39	......	......	......	......
Delaware,	......	......	9	53	....	....	......	......	1,761	684	......	......	......	......	......	......	......	......
Dutchess,	......	......	......	......	....	....	......	......	1,735	676	......	......	......	......	......	......	3	11
Erie,	......	......	......	......	2	10	......	......	6,981	2,950	......	......	11	59	......	......	400	516
Essex,	60	30	......	......	....	....	......	......	631	770	......	......	......	......	......	......	......	......
Franklin,	......	......	......	......	....	....	......	......	......	......	......	......	......	......	......	......	......	......
Fulton,	......	......	......	......	....	....	......	......	1,798	659	......	......	2	25	......	......	......	......
Genesee,	......	......	2	2	....	....	......	......	4,025	1,903	......	......	......	......	......	......	50	58
Greene,	......	......	......	......	....	....	......	......	1,990	803	......	......	3	15	29	26	72	117
Hamilton,	......	......	......	......	....	....	......	......	32	12	......	......	......	......	......	......	......	......
Herkimer,	......	......	......	......	....	....	......	......	4,540	2,271	......	......	2	20	......	......	......	......
Jefferson,	160	80	3	30	....	....	......	......	7,072	3,925	......	......	......	......	......	......	......	......
Kings,	......	......	......	......	....	....	......	......	......	......	......	......	......	......	......	......	......	......
Lewis,	......	......	5	38	....	....	......	......	2,027	1,058	......	......	......	......	......	......	......	......
Livingston,	......	......	......	......	....	....	......	......	1,983½	1,042	......	......	9	82	......	......	571	1,074
Madison,	......	......	2	16	70	77	......	......	7,242¾	3,054	......	......	5	41	......	......	56	74
Monroe,	......	......	31	102	....	....	......	......	8,308	3,882	......	......	......	......	......	......	......	800
Montgomery,	......	200	......	......	30	20	......	......	2,615	1,104	......	......	88	54	300	300	......	......
New-York,	......	......	......	......	....	....	......	......	......	......	......	......	......	......	......	......	......	......
Niagara,	......	......	......	......	2	8	......	......	4,520½	2,480	......	......	9	80	......	......	157	404
Oneida,	......	......	......	......	....	....	1,700	320	6,689	2,478	678	422	......	......	......	......	5	7
Onondaga,	100	20	4	84	12	53	350	70	8,390¾	3,240	......	......	8	66	......	......	......	......
Ontario,	......	......	......	......	....	....	700	120	5,636	2,783	......	......	......	......	......	......	490	545
Orange,	......	......	......	......	....	....	......	......	2,708	1,385	......	......	......	......	......	......	32	61
Orleans,	......	......	......	......	25	55	522	97	4,958	2,451	......	......	6	40	......	......	923	1,350
Oswego,	......	......	......	......	3	23	......	......	9,737	4,498	......	......	......	......	......	......	36	42
Otsego,	160	80	4	12	2	20	......	......	6,050	3,289	......	......	6	22	......	......	396	693
Putnam,	......	......	......	......	....	....	......	......	......	......	......	......	......	......	......	......	......	......
Queens,	......	......	......	......	....	....	......	......	......	......	......	......	......	......	......	......	......	150
Rensselaer,	......	......	......	......	18	9	......	......	3,815½	2,028	266	73	3	30	......	......	......	......
Richmond,	......	......	......	......	....	....	......	......	......	......	......	......	......	......	......	......	......	......
Rockland,	54,000	907	......	......	....	....	......	......	......	......	......	......	......	......	......	......	......	......
St. Lawrence,	......	......	10	57	10	28	......	......	3,060	1,184	40	10	13	13	113	113	......	......
Saratoga,	4	3	......	......	....	....	......	......	1,955	865	......	......	1	6	10	10	......	......
Schenectady,	......	......	......	......	....	....	......	......	866	382	......	......	3	15	......	......	......	......
Schoharie,	......	......	......	......	....	....	......	......	2,531	1,236	60	30	14	56	......	......	318	441
Schuyler,	......	......	3	58	....	....	......	......	1,698	756	8	3	2	16	......	......	......	3,163
Seneca,	......	......	......	......	....	....	......	......	2,821	1,365	......	......	2	14	......	......	193½	267
Steuben,	......	......	4	32	....	....	......	......	5,195	2,669	......	......	......	......	......	......	200	242
Suffolk,	......	......	......	......	....	....	300	75	2,592	1,221	......	......	......	......	......	......	......	......
Sullivan,	......	......	......	......	2	3	......	......	1,823	749	......	......	14	56	......	......	26	114
Tioga,	1,000	25	4	30	81	141	......	......	6,114	2,833	23	12	6	34	......	......	......	22
Tompkins,	465	180	......	......	....	....	......	......	2,599	956	......	......	......	......	......	......	19¼	90
Ulster,	......	......	17	63	....	....	......	......	4,186	1,970	15	2	......	......	......	......	......	......
Warren,	......	......	......	......	....	....	......	......	1,315	692	......	......	......	......	......	......	......	......
Washington,	......	......	6	8	....	....	......	......	4,834	1,768	......	......	3	25	......	......	......	......
Wayne,	......	......	......	......	....	....	......	60	9,122	3,574	......	......	5	39	......	......	19,550	22,474
Westchester,	......	......	......	......	4	4	......	......	790	410	......	......	......	......	......	......	......	......
Wyoming,	......	......	8	49	25	20	......	......	3,977	1,776	......	......	......	......	......	......	451	771
Yates,	......	......	......	......	....	....	250	50	4,503½	1,923	......	......	......	......	......	......	697	1,783
Total,	59,489	3,289	237	1,107	401	587	4,962	952	213,617¼	96,115	1,509	781	299	1,154	464	461	34,492¼	43,846

* Including quilts, patchwork and other bed coverings, excepting coverlids.
† Mostly rag carpeting.

MISCELLANEOUS DOMESTIC MANUFACTURES.—(Continued.)

COUNTIES.	Gloves.		Hats.*		Mats.†		Mittens.‡		Oil of Peppermint.		Plaids.		Socks.§		Yarn.‖		Miscellaneous.¶
	Pairs.	Value.	Number.	Value.	Number.	Value.	Pairs.	Value.	Pounds.	Value.	Yards.	Value.	Pairs.	Value.	Pounds.	Value.	
Albany,													5, 239	$1, 314	100	$74	$2, 747
Allegany,	2	$1	211	$61			322	$174					2, 746	936	133	106	470
Broome,																	
Cattaraugus,	60	30	1, 245	308			503	242			11	$5	4, 689	1, 538	38	24	1, 630
Cayuga,							163	73					761	270	196	203	363
Chautauque,			851	272			151	139					2, 595	831	238	185	265
Chemung,													5	2	271	300	13
Chenango,			721	162									2, 382	586	15	12	819
Clinton,			198	67			184	88					11, 483	3, 452	131	131	117
Columbia,					350	$350											3, 945
Cortland,			18	5			141	107					6, 727	1, 775	14	14	252
Delaware,							8	8					5, 232	1, 491	121	114	
Dutchess,													333	120	295	300	118
Erie,	30	21	748	1, 042	70	79	828	301					21, 420	6, 192	542	425	332
Essex,			34	16			52	25					1, 008	439	170	171	307
Franklin,																	
Fulton,							59	35					258	107			275
Genesee,			480	14			138	60					1, 075	422	70	113	212
Greene,			48	10									1, 868	502		6	
Hamilton,													13	6	30	28	
Herkimer,			78	25			683	224					1, 763	499	99	99	
Jefferson,							5	3					2, 258	771	13	13	6, 253
Kings,																	
Lewis,							87	44	672¾	$2, 929			140	52			31
Livingston,							22	45					531	220	167	166	
Madison,	3	2											1, 966	640			206
Monroe,							6	2					1, 040	468			253
Montgomery,											38	24	347	105	70	60	
New-York,																	
Niagara,							1	1					557	229	160½	157	32
Oneida,			30	6			968	548					1, 384	511	300	249	3, 400
Onondaga,				40			381	191					1, 477	594	105	78	317
Ontario,							67	39		296			1, 227	470	42½	33	70
Orange,													149	193	230	255	598
Orleans,	79	90						25					792	300	72	72	
Oswego,			26	10			1, 205	1, 210					3, 768	1, 270	475	473	57
Otsego,			565	137			307	152					10, 078	2, 595	125	123	1, 302
Putnam,																	
Queens,																	
Rensselaer,													229	88			6
Richmond,																	4, 500
Rockland,																	
St. Lawrence,			442	140			53	24					14, 042	3, 861	160	160	1, 036
Saratoga,			77	26			481	372					9, 404	3, 281	27	27	76
Schenectady,													2, 563	683	94	64	
Schoharie,											57	38	4, 997	1, 405	61	39	3
Schuyler,							216	106			20	12	855	438	142	128	186
Seneca,							16	12	40	150			213	90	143	143	30
Steuben,							4	4					3, 498	1, 376	117	123	1, 273
Suffolk,													68	29			
Sullivan,							70	52					1, 362	480	444	424	15
Tioga,				253				76					4, 277	1, 115	20	20	292
Tompkins,			266	68			96	51					8, 657	2, 304	155	153	155
Ulster,											180	116	7	2	25	25	928
Warren,			100	40			401	205					3, 139	1, 036	8	8	72
Washington,													162	54			450
Wayne,			200	80			663	224	2, 399	9, 645			1, 216	426	117	117	48
Westchester,													112	44			
Wyoming,			460	38			220	190					2, 349	615	286	256	2, 740
Yates,							5	2					184	70	48	48	30
Total,	174	144	6, 798	2, 820	420	429	8, 506	5, 054	3, 111¾	13, 020	306	195	152, 645	46, 297	6, 070	5, 719	36, 224

Total value, ... $258,354.

* Chiefly straw, palm leaf and other braided summer hats.
† Sometimes specified as "table" or "floor" mats.
‡ Generally specified as "woolen" or "fringe" mittens, and occasionally as "buckskin" or other materials.
§ Mostly specified as "woolen socks," "hose," &c.
‖ Commonly reported as "woolen yarn," which is believed to be the term intended in nearly every instance.
¶ This class includes those of which the kind and quantity were not given, or which were so reported together that they could not be separated, as "mittens and yarn," &c.

MANUFACTURES.

The returns under this head are arranged under the following Classes:—

CLASS I.—Agricultural Tools and Implements.
" II.—Metallurgy and Manufacture of Metals, and Istruments therefor.
" III.—Manufactures of Fibrous and Textile Substances;—including Machines for preparing the Fibres of Cotton, Silk, Fur, Paper, &c.
" IV.—Chemical Processes, Manufactures and Compounds;—including Medicine, Pharmacy, Dyeing, Coloring and Painting, Baking, Distilling, Brewing, Soap and Candle Making, &c.
" V.—Calorifics;—comprising Lamps, Stoves, Grates, and Apparatus for Cooking, Heating, &c.
" VI.—Steam Engines, Boilers, Locomotives, &c., and parts thereof.
" VII.—Navigation, and Maritime Implements;—comprising Ship Building and Rigging.
" VIII.—Mathematical, Philosophical and Optical Instruments, including Clocks and Watches.
" IX.—Civil Engineering, and Architecture;—comprising Mining, Quarrying, Building, &c.
" X.—Land Conveyance; including Wagons, Carriages, Cars, and other Vehicles, and their parts.
" XI.—Hydraulics and Pneumatics;—including Pumps, Fire Engines, &c.
" XII.—Lever, Screw, and other Mechanical Powers; including Instruments for Weighing, Lifting, &c.
" XIII.—Grinding Mills, Mill Gearing, &c.
" XIV.—Lumber;—including Machines and Tools for Preparing and Manufacturing Wood, and the Trades Connected therewith.
" XV.—Stone, Clay, Cement, Pottery and Glass; including the Making, Dressing and Preparing of Brick and Stone, and the Trades connected therewith.
" XVI.—Leather;—including Tanning and Dressing, the Manufacture of Boots, Shoes, Saddlery, Trunks, Harnesses, &c.
" XVII.—Household Furniture, Machines and Implements for Domestic Purposes;—including Upholstering, Decorating and Furnishing Dwellings.
" XVIII.—Arts, Polite, Fine and Ornamental;—including Music, Painting, Sculpture, Engraving, Books, Stationery, Printing, Binding, Jewelry, &c., and the Trades connected therewith.
" XIX.—Fire Arms, and Implements of War, and Parts thereof;—including the Manufacture of Shot and Powder.
" XX.—Surgical, Medical and Dental Instruments and Apparatus.
" XXI.—Wearing Apparel, Articles for the Toilet, &c.;—including Instruments for Manufacturing, and the Trades connected therewith, &c.
" XXII.—Miscellaneous Manufactures.

CAPITAL INVESTED, VALUE OF RAW MATERIALS AND PRODUCTS, AND NUMBER OF PERSONS EMPLOYED.

CLASS I.—AGRICULTURAL TOOLS AND IMPLEMENTS.

TOWNS.	Number of establishments.	Capital Invested.		Cash Value.		Persons employed.
		In real estate.	In tools and machinery.	Of raw materials used.	Of manufactured articles.	
AGRICULTURAL IMPLEMENTS GENERALLY.						
ALBANY Co.						
Albany, ...	3	$55,000	$27,000	$72,260	$270,075	175
Coeymans,.......	1	800	1,200	1,070	4,000	....
ALLEGANY Co.						
Almond,.........	1	1,000	500	625	7,250	2
BROOME Co.						
Chenango, ...	1	1,600	100	5,080	3,500	2
CATTARAUGUS Co.						
Franklinville,......	1	800	800	1,544	3,000	....
CAYUGA Co.						
Auburn,.........	1	8,000	6,000	7,000	10,000	20
Genoa, ...	2	2,500	550	1,850	6,000	7
CHAUTAUQUE Co.						
Chautauque,......	1	300	1,200	795	7,500	3
COLUMBIA Co.						
Claverack,........	1	3,000	....	1,770	7,350	5
Hudson,.........	1	3,000	4,000	3,000	7,500	10
Kinderhook, ...	1	....	....	7,355	11,000	....
CORTLAND Co.						
Cortlandville, ...	1	....	....	250	3,000	....
Homer,..........	1	....	....	....	480	....
DUTCHESS Co.						
Poughkeepsie city,	2	....	3,300	5,200	20,000	15
ERIE Co.						
Buffalo,..........	3	62,000	21,000	89,675	271,150	159
GENESEE Co.						
Byron,..........	1	....	100	400	800	1
Pavilion, ...	1	300	300	100	2,300	2
HERKIMER Co.						
German Flats,....	1	....	....	....	1,200	....
JEFFERSON Co.						
Pamelia, ...	1	....	300	1 839	6,000	7
KINGS Co.						
Brooklyn, ...	1	7,500	6,000	14,300	28,000	22
LEWIS Co.						
Lowville, ...	1	1,100	1,000	885	1,371	4
LIVINGSTON Co.						
York, ...	1	10,000	10,000	20,220	54,775	55
MADISON Co.						
Cazenovia,........	2	300	1,900	891	6,400	9
MONROE Co.						
Penfield, ...	1	$600	$ 400	$ 4,500	$10,000	6
Rochester,........	2	40,000	17,000	25,179	81,500	58
Sweden, ...	1	7,500	5,500	20,140	61,450	62
NEW-YORK Co.						
New-York, ...	2	62,000	8,500	170,775	295,000	27
ONEIDA Co.						
Paris,............	2	67,000	11,000	70,000	197,000	148
Utica, ...	1	1,000	500	1,200	3,000	4
ONONDAGA Co.						
Fabius,..........	1	700	700	600	2,000	2
ONTARIO Co.						
Canandaigua, ...	1	3,300	800	1,500	3,700	4
East Bloomfield,..	1	3,000	1,500	1,950	9,080	15
ORLEANS Co.						
Barre,...........	1	10,000	6,000	11,500	22,000	20
Ridgeway,........	1	5,000	1,500	6,000	18,000	8
QUEENS Co.						
North Hempstead,	1	2,000	2,000	13,200	24,850	15
RENSSELAER Co.						
Lansingburgh, ...	1	800	1,000	900	2,500	4
North Greenbush,	1	15,000	10,000	50,000	100,000	55
ROCKLAND Co.						
Ramapo, ...	1	2,000	1,000	1,055	2,070	3
STEUBEN Co.						
Bath,............	1	....	25	1,330	3,000	1
TOMPKINS Co.						
Ithaca, ...	1	2,500	200	2,000	2,000	4
ULSTER Co.						
Marlborough, ...	1	....	800	2,500	2,500	4
New Paltz, ...	1	....	50	500	1,200	1
WASHINGTON Co.						
Easton,..........	1	3,000	2,000	9,965	24,000	23
Whitehall,........	1	3,000	2,000	....	....	5
WAYNE Co.						
Arcadia,.........	2	6,500	4,300	....	27,090	23
Macedon, ...	1	5,000	5,000	10,000	25,500	15
WESTCHESTER Co.						
Cortland, ...	1	10,000	5,000	50,900	84,000	54
WYOMING Co.						
Castile,..........	1	1,000	800	975	4,000	4

CLASS I.—(CONTINUED.)

TOWNS.	Number of establishments.	Capital Invested. In real estate.	Capital Invested. In tools and machinery.	Cash Value. Of raw materials used.	Cash Value. Of manufactured articles.	Persons employed.
CHEESE PRESS MANUFACTORIES.						
HERKIMER Co.						
Little Falls, ...	1	$400	$150	$350	$1,350	1
JEFFERSON Co.						
Ellisburgh, ...	1	500	500	200	380	2
CHURN FACTORIES.						
JEFFERSON Co.						
Wilna, ...	1	....	500	6,600	15,000	5
ONEIDA Co.						
Whitestown, ...	2	50	206	1,000	5,250	6
CIDER MILLS.						
CAYUGA Co.						
Mentz, ...	2	350	103	825	1,000	4
CHAUTAUQUE Co.						
Villenovia, ...	1	50	....	100	250	1
CORTLAND Co.						
Cortlandville, ...	1	....	....	....	250	....
DUTCHESS Co.						
Stanford, ...	1	760	1,500	900	1,025	2
GREENE Co.						
Greenville, ...	2	4,600	1,700	1,356	5,061	11
JEFFERSON Co.						
Henderson, ...	1	150	300	400	750	3
LEWIS Co.						
Lowville, ...	1	....	....	1,012	1,200	2
LIVINGSTON Co.						
Caledonia, ...	1	500	....	500	800	2
MADISON Co.						
Madison, ...	1	....	....	2,200	3,122	7
ONEIDA Co.						
Kirkland, ...	1	2,000	1,000	2,000	5,000	3
Paris, ...	1	....	....	....	716	2
Sangerfield, ...	1	....	25	180	300	....
Vernon, ...	1	100	100	500	500	1
ONONDAGA Co.						
Otisco, ...	1	....	....	1,500	1,600	...
ONTARIO Co.						
Phelps, ...	2	600	100	1,170	2,500	8
ORANGE Co.						
Blooming Grove, .	1	500	500	250	500	2
OSWEGO Co.						
Richland, ...	1	700	400	2,170	2,800	8
OTSEGO Co.						
Roseboom, ...	1	....	30	....	100	....
RENSSELAER Co.						
Brunswick, ...	1	....	....	500	1,000	....
SARATOGA Co.						
Milton, ...	1	....	....	1,000	1,500	3
WASHINGTON Co.						
Argyle, ...	2	700	300	125	425	5
WYOMING Co.						
Castile, ...	1	....	250	....	525	....
CLOVER MILLS.						
ALBANY Co.						
Berne, ...	1	1,000	500	....	1,300	1
OTSEGO Co.						
Middlefield, ...	1	....	500	....	100	1
SCHOHARIE Co.						
Cobleskill, ...	1	200	170	....	....	....
Sharon	2	1,400	1,400	....	900	7
Wright, ...	3	3,375	1,125	16,453	17,650	3
SUFFOLK Co.						
Smithtown, ...	1	450	....	870	200	1
ULSTER Co.						
New Paltz, ...	1	300	150	240	280	1
FANNING MILL MANUFACTORIES, ETC.						
CHAUTAUQUE Co.						
Sheridan, ...	1	400	125	509	1,800	3
CHENANGO Co.						
Bainbridge, ...	1	100	100	150	700	2
DUTCHESS Co.						
North East, ...	1	500	500	620	1,400	1
ERIE Co.						
Alden, ...	1	300	100	100	1,495	2
Aurora, ...	2	200	185	700	1,325	6
FRANKLIN Co.						
Westville, ...	1	150	50	430	2,160	3
HERKIMER Co.						
German Flats, ...	1	200	130	100	1,500	2
JEFFERSON Co.						
Orleans, ...	2	200	225	1,228	2,992	3

TOWNS.	Number of establishments.	Capital Invested. In real estate.	Capital Invested. In tools and machinery.	Cash Value. Of raw materials used.	Cash Value. Of manufactured articles.	Persons employed.
LEWIS Co.						
Denmark, ...	1	....	....	$250	$1,500	2
LIVINGSTON Co.						
Leicester, ...	1	$450	$100	225	2,500	3
MONTGOMERY Co.						
Minden, ...	1	450	75	460	1,800	2
ONEIDA Co.						
Trenton, ...	1	200	50	508	966	....
ONONDAGA Co.						
Marcellus, ...	1	50	100	200	1,600	3
Otisco, ...	3	900	900	945	6,080	7
ORANGE Co.						
Mount Hope, ...	1	500	200	600	1,200	2
OTSEGO Co.						
Otsego, ...	2	600	100	162	795	....
RENSSELAER Co.						
Brunswick, ...	1	500	150	60	1,000	6
Schaghticoke, ...	1	7,000	2,000	25,000	29,200	16
ROCKLAND Co.						
Clarkstown, ...	1	300	150	634	1,305	2
ST. LAWRENCE Co.						
Gouverneur, ...	1	200	100	486	2,000	2
Madrid, ...	1	200	50	280	1,200	1
Potsdam, ...	1	1,000	1,200	600	2,450	3
SCHOHARIE Co.						
Esperance, ...	1	300	200	275	1,800	3
WASHINGTON Co.						
Fort Edward, ...	1	....	150	570	4,000	8
WAYNE Co.						
Lyons, ...	1	1,000	700	2,625	7,500	10
WYOMING Co.						
Perry, ...	1	1,000	100	1,548	3,536	5
YATES Co.						
Milo, ...	1	....	200	700	1,815	....
FORK FACTORIES.						
CAYUGA Co.						
Mentz, ...	1	1,000	300	775	3,110	5
CHENANGO Co.						
Pitcher, ...	1	600	800	1,040	2,500	5
MADISON Co.						
Brookfield, ...	1	16,000	7,000	24,000	42,760	50
ONONDAGA Co.						
Skaneateles, ...	1	5,000	....	860	....	6
OTSEGO Co.						
New Lisbon, ...	1	5,000	3,000	7,524	11,500	33
Otsego, ...	1	15,000	4,000	30,334	65,000	40
ST. LAWRENCE Co.						
Brasher, ...	1	4,000	2,000	2,500	13,000	6
SENECA Co.						
Seneca Falls, ...	1	2,000	1,500	16,344	32,000	....
GRAIN CRADLE AND SCYTHE SNATH FACTORIES, ETC.						
CAYUGA Co.						
Mentz, ...	1	2,000	600	550	5,000	6
CHAUTAUQUE Co.						
Ellicott, ...	3	5,800	3,300	7,934	39,900	63
CHEMUNG Co.						
Horseheads, ...	1	....	150	100	....	1
DELAWARE Co.						
Kortright, ...	1	200	100	300	700	2
DUTCHESS Co.						
Stanford, ...	1	100	100	300	1,200	2
JEFFERSON Co.						
Lyme, ...	2	....	....	33	621	....
Rutland, ...	1	250	100	286	759	3
LEWIS Co.						
Lowville, ...	1	700	500	535	2,610	4
LIVINGSTON Co.						
Avon, ...	1	1,000	1,200	120	2,500	4
Caledonia, ...	1	1,500	150	1,857	7,693	4
Groveland, ...	1	30	25	100	675	1
Livonia, ...	1	200	100	1,075	2.400	3
MONROE Co.						
Ogden, ...	2	1,400	250	600	1,100	....
Rochester, ...	1	100	200	100	2,000	2
Webster, ...	1	600	40	20	800	1
ONONDAGA Co.						
Manlius, ...	1	1,600	200	6,610	12,500	8
Onondaga, ...	1	300	150	300	600	1
Van Buren, ...	1	2,000	1,106	264	2,620	2
ORANGE Co.						
Montgomery, ...	1	....	....	70	70	....
Walkill, ...	2	2,000	1,950	1,668	5,000	8
OTSEGO Co.						
Maryland, ...	2	700	350	100	1,400	3
Roseboom, ...	1	500	200	30	400	1

CLASS I.—(Continued.)

TOWNS.	Number of establishments.	Capital Invested. In real estate.	Capital Invested. In tools and machinery.	Cash Value. Of raw materials used.	Cash Value. Of manufactured articles.	Persons employed.
RENSSELAER Co.						
Schaghticoke, ...	2	$2,800	$1,000	....	$12,000	10
SARATOGA Co.						
Providence,.......	1	800	500	$1,200	3,000	4
SCHOHARIE Co.						
Broome,.........	1	2,000	500	197	3,000	5
SCHUYLER Co.						
Catharines, ...	1	300	450	150	600	1
TIOGA Co.						
Newark,.........	1	....	....	25	300	....
STEUBEN Co.						
Bath,............	1	$50	....	$590	$517	1
Hornellsville, ...	1	400	$200	541	1,010	2
WAYNE Co.						
Wolcott,.........	1	500	300	500	1,000	....

GRAIN MEASURE MANUFACTORIES.

TOWNS.	Number of establishments.	In real estate.	In tools and machinery.	Of raw materials used.	Of manufactured articles.	Persons employed.
CHAUTAUQUE Co.						
Ellicott, ...	1	1,000	250	800	1,500	2
FULTON Co.						
Northampton,.....	1	400	300	1,760	2,800	3
SARATOGA Co.						
Providence,.......	2	1,500	800	1,500	5,600	8

HOE MANUFACTORIES.

TOWNS.	Number of establishments.	In real estate.	In tools and machinery.	Of raw materials used.	Of manufactured articles.	Persons employed.
CHENANGO Co.						
Oxford,..........	1	5,000	10,000	13,145	29,099	25
MADISON Co.						
Brookfield, ...	1	8,500	2,100	5,100	....	21
MONTGOMERY Co.						
Amsterdam,......	1	4,400	600	6,960	17,800	13
ONEIDA Co.						
Sangerfield,......	2	1,500	500	5,020	9,900	7
OTSEGO Co.						
Plainfield, ...	1	4,000	2,000	16,425	27,250	20
RENSSELAER Co.						
Nassau,..........	1	500	400	1,225	2,112	2
ST. LAWRENCE Co.						
Potsdam,........	1	4,000	1,000	1,000	4,000	5
SARATOGA Co.						
Milton,..........	2	4,000	1,000	7,500	21,300	20

PLOW AND CULTIVATOR FACTORIES.

TOWNS.	Number of establishments.	In real estate.	In tools and machinery.	Of raw materials used.	Of manufactured articles.	Persons employed.
CATTARAUGUS Co.						
Perrysburgh,.....	1	900	1,600	1,503	2,749	5
Yorkshire,.......	1	....	50	50	500	1
CAYUGA Co.						
Auburn,.........	1	500	200	1,675	2,500	2
Sterling,.........	1	100	400	275	1,500	3
CLINTON Co.						
Beekmantown, ...	1	1,500	1,000	2,500	4,000	3
Champlain, ...	1	....	....	....	1,000	....
COLUMBIA Co.						
Gallatin, ...	1	4,000	500	386	1,200	6
CORTLAND Co.						
Cortlandville, ...	1	6,000	3,000	3,000	6,750	12
Homer,..........	1	....	....	....	992	....
DUTCHESS Co.						
Amenia,.........	1	800	400	230	966	2
FRANKLIN Co.						
Malone,..........	1	....	....	700	900	....
GENESEE Co.						
Bethany, ...	1	300	150	671	1,985	2
GREENE Co.						
Coxsackie,.......	1	1,500	1,000	1,690	4,900	4
LEWIS Co.						
Denmark,........	1	800	....	600	1,200	2
LIVINGSTON Co.						
Avon,...........	2	8,000	6,000	7,020	21,560	20
Mount Morris, ...	1	3,200	1,000	4,513	9,435	4
North Dansville,..	2	1,000	800	1,690	5,550	4
MADISON Co.						
Cazenovia,.......	1	....	25	440	....	1
Stockbridge, ...	1	3,500	1,000	7,507	3,600	14
MONROE Co.						
Chili,............	1	1,000	1,600	450	6,200	4
Greece,..........	1	2,000	1,500	1,800	4,000	4
Henrietta, ...	1	....	....	....	1,500	....
Riga,............	1	500	2,660	1,660	7,340	4
Rochester,.......	3	11,800	2,250	5,430	12,050	10
Rush,............	1	500	250	1,000	3,000	2
Sweden,.........	1	4,000	3,000	6,225	16,425	18
Wheatland,......	1	2,200	200	1,020	3,500	5
MONTGOMERY Co.						
Amsterdam,......	1	4,000	1,000	8,655	19,250	23
ONONDAGA Co.						
Manlius,.........	1	500	75	2,116	3,000	3
ONTARIO Co.						
East Bloomfield,..	2	550	425	4,800	11,200	8
RENSSELAER Co.						
Schodack,........	1	....	....	....	630	....
SCHOHARIE Co.						
Gilboa,..........	1	1,000	300	400	800	2
Seward,.........	1	1,000	500	552	1,225	1

RAKE FACTORIES.

TOWNS.	Number of establishments.	In real estate.	In tools and machinery.	Of raw materials used.	Of manufactured articles.	Persons employed.
ALLEGANY Co.						
Rushford, ...	1	300	50	90	550	1
BROOME Co.						
Colesville,.......	1	500	25	650	1,500	2
Union,..........	2	5,200	1,500	750	3,600	3
CHAUTAUQUE Co.						
Ellicott, ...	1	1,000	1,000	1,100	5,750	8
COLUMBIA Co.						
New Lebanon,....	1	50	200	60	500	2
CORTLAND Co.						
Preble,..........	1	....	....	....	350	....
DELAWARE Co.						
Franklin,........	1	200	10	435	650	1
ERIE Co.						
Aurora,..........	1	....	....	....	400	....
GENESEE Co.						
Le Roy,.........	2	800	300	700	2,600	4
Pavillion,........	1	200	75	....	1,200	2
LEWIS Co.						
Denmark,........	1	....	....	44	500	1
LIVINGSTON Co.						
Springwater,.....	1	1,000	200	95	750	1
MADISON Co.						
Brookfield,.......	2	1,400	500	3,000	13,600	1
De Ruyter,.......	2	1,500	1,500	785	2,450	5
MONROE Co.						
Parma,..........	1	200	1,000	1,125	3,000	5
NIAGARA Co.						
Wilson,.........	1	....	25	716	2,028	1
ONEIDA Co.						
Bridgewater,.....	1	700	200	170	200	3
Camden,.........	3	2,800	800	630	4,000	10
ONTARIO Co.						
Phelps,..........	1	....	....	600	....	....
OSWEGO Co.						
Mexico,.........	1	1,100	300	96	1,745	....
OTSEGO Co.						
Plainfield, ...	5	380	90	883	6,400	....
Roseboom,.......	1	....	....	12	60	....
RENSSELAER Co.						
Schodack,........	1	200	200	300	800	3
ST. LAWRENCE Co.						
Lawrence,........	1	....	150	600	2,000	1
Parishville, ...	1	300	75	195	1,620	5
TIOGA Co.						
Berkshire, ...	2	650	550	260	1,425	4
WASHINGTON Co.						
Hartford,........	1	100	25	15	200	....
WAYNE Co.						
Palmyra,........	1	....	100	600	1,200	1
WYOMING Co.						
Warsaw, ...	1	1,000	800	178	1,200	3

REAPING AND MOWING MACHINE FACTORIES.

TOWNS.	Number of establishments.	In real estate.	In tools and machinery.	Of raw materials used.	Of manufactured articles.	Persons employed.
CAYUGA Co.						
Auburn,.........	1	10,000	5,000	5,000	12,000	12
MONROE Co.						
Chili, ...	1	2,100	1,000	200	10,000	3
Sweden,..........	1	7,000	5,000	14,090	78,000	54
Wheatland,......	1	5,000	2,000	3,490	10,600	8
MONTGOMERY Co.						
Amsterdam, ...	1	2,500	200	8,280	39,000	20
Mohawk, ...	1	2,000	500	1,500	4,500	4
RENSSELAER Co.						
Hoosick,.........	3	15,000	10,250	51,000	165,100	135

SCYTHE FACTORIES, ETC.

TOWNS.	Number of establishments.	In real estate.	In tools and machinery.	Of raw materials used.	Of manufactured articles.	Persons employed.
CAYUGA Co.						
Aurelius,........	1	6,000	1,000	1,680	7,000	6
DUTCHESS Co.						
Pine Plains, ...	1	2,000	3,000	7,000	22,000	11
ERIE Co.						
Collins,..........	1	500	300	300	1,500	3
FRANKLIN Co.						
Malone,..........	1	2,000	500	1,720	3,800	3
RENSSELAER Co.						
Hoosick, ...	2	12,000	2,300	3,647	11,350	13
Troy, ...	1	15,000	1,000	10,648	25,600	25
SARATOGA Co.						
Milton,..........	1	1,200	12,000	58,000	103,000	150

CLASS I.—(Continued.)

TOWNS.	Number of establishments.	Capital Invested. In real estate.	Capital Invested. In tools and machinery.	Cash Value. Of raw materials used.	Cash Value. Of manufactured articles.	Persons employed.
SCYTHE RIFLE MANUFACTORIES.						
Cayuga Co.						
Genoa,	1	$300	$200	$500	$2,000	4
Columbia Co.						
Canaan,	1	2,000	1,150	3,000	6,000	11
Oneida Co.						
Vernon,	1	....	90	752	2,200	5
Rensselaer Co.						
Schodack,	1	250	50	700	2,300	3
Ulster Co.						
Lloyd,	1	40	25	456	1,800	5
SHOVEL MANUFACTORY.						
Westchester Co.						
Rye,	1	6,000	6,000	18,000	30,000	20
TOOL SHOPS.						
Allegany Co.						
Independence,	1	170	200	42	500	2
Cayuga Co.						
Niles,	1	$200	$60	$200	$800	....
Chautauque Co.						
Westfield,	1	4,000	4,000	8,100	23,000	30
Erie Co.						
Buffalo,	1	....	....	....	3,009	....
Jefferson Co.						
Ellisburgh,	1	1,000	150	280	1,200	4
Livingston Co.						
York,	1	....	75	1,400	3,700	3
Monroe Co.						
Rochester,	1	....	1,000	1,300	9,000	5
Onondaga Co.						
Lysander,	1	16,000	500	5,077	12,694	21
THRESHING MACHINE MANUFACTORIES.						
Tompkins Co.						
Groton,	1	500	200	1,365	3,140	6
Yates Co.						
Starkey,	1	1,500	3,000	537	4,200	5

CLASS II.—METALLURGY, AND MANUFACTURE OF METALS AND INSTRUMENTS THEREFOR.

TOWNS.	Number of establishments.	Capital Invested. In real estate.	Capital Invested. In tools and machinery.	Cash Value. Of raw materials used.	Cash Value. Of manufactured articles.	Persons employed.
ANVIL MANUFACTORY.						
Rensselaer Co.						
Troy,	1	5,000	2,000	4,500	15,000	8
AXE AND EDGE TOOL MANUFACTORIES.						
Albany Co.						
Watervliet,	1	30,000	70,000	135,500	280 000	250
Allegany Co.						
Willing,	1	50	100	9,000	15,000	2
Cattaraugus Co.						
Olean,	1	....	....	....	....	....
Chautauque Co.						
Ellicott,	1	200	1,000	6,000	2,100	8
Ellington,	1	500	500	500	1,500	3
Westfield,	1	15,000	5,000	5,250	15,000	25
Chemung Co.						
Elmira,	1	4,000	4,000	63,650	38,000	20
Chenango Co.						
Norwich,	1	7,500	3,500	13,032	52,000	50
Clinton Co.						
Plattsburgh,	1	....	250	200	600	2
Cortland Co.						
Homer,	1	1,100	200	1,000	....	4
Dutchess Co.						
Poughkeepsie city,	1	1,000	1,000	1,600	5,000	5
Stanford,	1	....	1,500	2,335	3,425	6
Erie Co.						
Buffalo,	1	8,000	5,000	8,000	35,000	55
Essex Co.						
Ticonderoga,	1	1,000	500	550	1,000	2
Herkimer Co.						
German Flats,	2	1,500	2,250	3,496	9,600	9
Little Falls,	1	2,000	1,000	1,800	7,000	4
Newport,	1	1,500	150	290	1,000	2
Russia,	2	1,200	400	500	2,000	2
Jefferson Co.						
Watertown,	1	8,000	2,000	6,875	17,472	8
Wilna,	1	....	50	290	1,125	2
Kings Co.						
Brooklyn,	1	2,000	500	4,600	5,500	6
Madison Co.						
Eaton,	1	1,500	20	414	500	2
Hamilton,	1	100	70	250	500	1
Monroe Co.						
Rochester,	2	37,000	62,500	24,143	108,500	97
New-York Co.						
New-York,	6	14,000	6,900	10,079	39,800	52
Niagara Co.						
Lockport,	1	1,000	600	380	1,000	3
Onondaga Co.						
Lysander,	1	2,500	1,000	765	2,500	2
Pompey,	2	2,000	1,800	1,150	3,075	6
Tully,	1	500	500	646	2,100	3
Ontario Co.						
Farmington,	1	1,200	200	30	600	2
Phelps,	1	1,500	1,000	4,000	12,000	10
Oswego Co.						
Volney,	1	5,000	300	2,500	5,000	4
Rensselaer Co.						
Pittstown,	1	4,500	1,500	10,830	22,800	38
Saratoga Co.						
Waterford,	1	4,000	1,000	9,020	30,000	50
Seneca Co.						
Ovid,	1	1,000	500	1,280	1,637	2
Suffolk Co.						
East Hampton,	1	1,000	1,000	1,100	4,000	5
Ulster Co.						
Wawarsing,	1	10,000	12,000	38,180	80,500	82
BELL FOUNDRIES.						
Albany Co.						
Watervliet,	1	25,000	6,000	154,315	175,000	25
Erie Co.						
Boston,	1	800	300	4,972	12,000	6
Buffalo,	1	....	3,000	....	24,000	....
Rensselaer Co.						
Troy,	1	10,000	4,000	72,525	90,000	12
BLACKSMITH SHOPS.						
Albany Co.						
Albany,	7	6,650	4,550	9,962	17,460	26
Bern,	2	....	....	....	....	....
Bethlehem,	1	800	75	201	615	2
Knox,	1	50	70	141	300	....
New Scotland,	2	800	225	600	1,200	4
Rensselaerville,	6	1,000	800	1,630	3,900	12
Watervliet,	6	2,750	900	3.170	8,800	12
Westerlo,	2	300	150	402	1,800	3
Allegany Co.						
Alfred,	3	500	400	531	1,800	4
Allen,	2	150	160	240	950	2
Amity,	6	1,900	1,100	2,085	7,200	13
Andover,	3	750	170	....	....	....
Burns,	4	900	245	725	2,700	7
Cuba,	2	1,000	475	1,100	4,600	5
Friendship,	1	150	50	30	800	2
Hume,	3	525	300	942	3,000	5
Independence,	1	150	800	165	700	2
New Hudson,	2	....	....	90	1,400	....
Ossian,	2	550	175	....	1,600	1
Rushford,	4	1,600	450	1,355	4,000	2
Scio,	3	875	305	1,100	5,736	4
Wirt,	1	500	150	500	1,400	2
Broome Co.						
Chenango,	4	2,600	850	2,233	6,600	10
Colesville,	8	730	600	1,003	4,475	11
Maine,	6	....	....	....	1,250	....
Sandford,	4	1,740	510	1,890	5,100	8
Windsor,	1	400	100	215	800	1
Cattaraugus Co.						
Allegany,	2	1,100	250	760	3,600	4
Conawango,	2	625	80	700	1,700	3
Ellicottville,	3	500	500	1,763	4,600	1
Farmersville,	1	200	100	503	1,500	1
Franklinville,	3	350	285	1,265	4,580	6
Freedom,	4	320	225	850	1,900	4
Hinsdale,	1	300	150	500	1,500	....

CLASS II.—(Continued.)

TOWNS.	Number of establishments.	Capital Invested. In real estate.	Capital Invested. In tools and machinery.	Cash Value. Of raw materials used.	Cash Value. Of manufactured articles.	Persons employed.
Cattaraugus Co.						
Lyndon,.........	1	$100	$100	....	....	1
Mansfield,.......	1	250	50	$900	....	1
New Albion,......	2	500	150	144	$1,400	2
Olean,...........	4	3,850	750	165	4,400	10
Otto,............	2	450	200	989	2,500	6
Perrysburgh,.....	1	700	300	940	3,000	5
Portville,.......	3	200	380	730	3,282	6
Yorkshire,.......	2	200	300	216	1,100	2
Cayuga Co.						
Auburn,..........	5	1,500	300	2,200	3,000	2
Aurelius,........	4	925	275	720	5,100	8
Cato,............	1	100	200	975	2,800	3
Conquest,........	6	830	730	1,267	4,450	10
Genoa,...........	5	1,450	405	411	2,200	5
Ira,.............	4	1,100	280	885	3,100	7
Locke,...........	3	505	240	300	....	3
Mentz,...........	7	1,200	700	1,732	4,400	13
Moravia,.........	2	300	200	162	440	4
Niles,...........	7	1,100	530	1,921	5,200	2
Owasco,..........	3	850	250	965	1,050	5
Sennett,.........	4	1,400	650	881	2,200	5
Summer Hill,.....	1	150	100	62	....	....
Venice,..........	7	1,050	800	....	1,650	....
Chautauque Co.						
Chautauque,......	5	1,700	700	1,100	6,850	9
Cherry Creek,....	4	305	210	501	2,305	5
Clymer,..........	3	230	195	233	940	4
Ellicott,........	5	1,650	675	3,813	4,500	8
Harmony,.........	2	2,800	250	466	2,700	4
Hanover,.........	3	700	275	752	2,600	6
Kiantone,........	1	200	150	210	650	2
Pomfret,.........	6	2,850	1,145	1,997	7,100	12
Portland,........	6	380	380	....	....	....
Sherman,.........	5	....	....	....	2,500	....
Stockton,........	2	....	....	175	500	....
Villenovia,......	1	400	100	302	1,000	2
Chemung Co.						
Chemung,.........	9	400	555	545	4,300	7
Elmira,..........	3	1,700	335	3,050	8,300	9
Southport,.......	1	....	75	300	600	2
Veteran,.........	6	2,080	875	4,583	10,700	10
Chenango Co.						
Bainbridge,......	7	1,300	625	1,422	5,400	39
Coventry,........	2	450	250	300	2,900	....
Greene,..........	2	800	240	253	....	1
New Berlin,......	4	1,350	500	1,065	4,240	6
Norwich,.........	2	1,200	700	1,930	7,750	12
Otselic,.........	4	1,200	325	800	2,805	5
Oxford,..........	6	1,100	555	1,750	7,100	15
Pharsalia,.......	1	50	50	168	650	1
Pitcher,.........	4	240	480	1,836	3,579	5
Plymouth,........	1	700	200	450	1,200	2
Preston,.........	1	300	80	307	600	2
Sherburne,.......	7	1,700	590	687	6,746	11
Clinton Co.						
Ausable,.........	1	1,000	200	600	3,000	4
Beekmantown,.....	6	725	225	1,700	4,600	9
Black Brook,.....	2	300	210	775	3,100	6
Chazy,...........	1	200	100	248	939	....
Ellenburgh,......	3	350	330	365	3,200	5
Peru,............	1	100	150	244	1,800	1
Plattsburgh,.....	2	880	500	450	2,600	3
Saranac,.........	3	475	350	750	1,900	6
Schuyler Falls,...	3	600	300	1,312	4,145	7
Columbia Co.						
Ancram,..........	3	....	350	3,800	6,300	7
Canaan,..........	2	650	200	490	2,000	4
Chatham,.........	5	2,800	265	280	3,500	5
Clermont,........	3	450	375	570	3,600	6
Copake,..........	5	3,100	350	1,140	4,100	2
Germantown,......	3	500	110	....	....	....
Greenport,.......	2	650	175	1,000	....	4
Hillsdale,.......	7	950	406	2,250	5,200	10
Kinderhook,......	9	2,350	1,035	2,060	20,900	18
Livingston,......	3	1,130	475	3,294	5,000	5
New Lebanon,.....	2	1,900	750	600	600	4
Stuyvesant,......	3	400	475	1,600	2,700	3
Cortland Co.						
Cortlandville,....	5	700	550	1,894	4,400	6
Freetown,........	2	350	140	390	1,200	2
Hartford,........	1	150	150	220	800	1
Homer,...........	4	1,900	510	1,614	4,600	6
Preble,..........	2	950	250	599	2,150	4
Scott,...........	1	500	150	400	1,200	2
Solon,...........	2	500	300	600	1,300	3
Taylor,..........	3	700	475	600	2,100	5
Truxton,.........	3	325	315	545	2,250	4
Virgil,..........	3	450	225	377	1,000	4

TOWNS.	Number of establishments.	Capital Invested. In real estate.	Capital Invested. In tools and machinery.	Cash Value. Of raw materials used.	Cash Value. Of manufactured articles.	Persons employed.
Delaware Co.						
Andes,...........	1	$300	$100	$270	$1,200	2
Bovina,..........	4	200	275	1,320	2,137	7
Franklin,........	6	2,180	650	1,685	6,150	14
Hamden,..........	2	1,400	180	616	2,038	3
Harpersfield,.....	5	950	300	1,073	3,810	4
Kortright,.......	3	475	300	1,016	2,524	4
Masonville,......	2	250	275	450	1,800	4
Middletown,......	3	640	300	1,300	3,700	6
Roxbury,.........	3	250	250	1,250	3,100	6
Sidney,..........	2	700	200	257	1,600	2
Dutchess Co.						
Amenia,..........	3	850	183	610	2,300	6
Clinton,.........	3	650	250	660	2,895	3
Dover,...........	2	125	300	1,040	....	6
East Fishkill,....	3	710	200	675	1,800	5
Fishkill,........	4	1,350	375	1,106	3,764	8
Hyde Park,.......	5	100	550	2,440	7,550	10
Lagrange,........	7	5,500	380	1,481	2,350	6
Milan,...........	3	2,800	350	780	3,084	7
Pawling,.........	1	100	100	190	850	2
Poughkeepsie city,	1	600	200	500	1,400	2
Red Hook,........	2	300	190	950	1,500	3
Rhinebeck,.......	5	3,000	350	1,400	4,000	8
Stanford,........	2	4,400	200	350	1,600	6
Washington,......	3	....	130	600	....	....
Erie Co.						
Buffalo,.........	2	1,700	525	1,560	....	9
Collins,.........	1	50	75	300	600	2
East Hamburgh,...	5	800	445	865	2,300	....
Eden,............	2	750	300	475	1,100	1
Evans,...........	2	510	240	1,000	2,395	....
Grand Island,....	2	250	225	608	1,600	3
Hamburgh,........	4	....	300	1,075	1,600	4
Holland,.........	2	550	130	222	1,422	....
Newstead,........	6	400	250	2,050	6,000	2
North Collins,....	1	100	120	1,258	2,000	1
Tonawanda,.......	2	700	350	400	3,600	4
Essex Co.						
Chesterfield,.....	2	1,900	500	1,300	4,000	7
Crown Point,.....	5	1,800	600	1,665	4,500	6
Elizabethtown,....	4	500	650	440	1,500	6
Keene,...........	2	200	175	200	....	1
Lewis,...........	1	100	60	75	500	1
Moriah,..........	6	2,700	650	1,420	8,400	16
North Elba,......	2	50	150	....	....	....
Schroon,.........	4	800	390	740	3,400	6
Willsborough,....	2	600	100	500	1,000	4
Franklin Co.						
Bangor,..........	1	400	100	575	1,200	2
Belmont,.........	1	300	40	....	....	....
Fort Covington,..	3	605	375	1,042	3,600	4
Franklin,........	2	150	200	450	1,500	2
Malone,..........	4	1,700	580	1,546	3,280	3
Westville,.......	4	550	530	453	2,738	7
Fulton Co.						
Bleecker,........	2	200	225	383	930	4
Mayfield,........	2	150	150	375	900	1
Northampton,.....	1	400	200	470	2,400	4
Oppenheim,.......	4	550	270	646	2,300	3
Perth,...........	3	500	1,050	200	2,150	6
Genesee Co.						
Alabama,.........	5	1,191	765	2,595	6,820	14
Alexander,.......	2	400	275	824	2,400	3
Bergen,..........	1	....	....	....	....	....
Byron,...........	5	1,550	580	2,049	4,450	7
Elba,............	2	850	200	850	1,900	4
Le Roy,..........	1	2,000	350	1,400	5,875	7
Oakfield,........	5	10,500	425	2,890	6,650	10
Pavilion,........	4	10,050	310	120	3,500	6
Pembroke,........	2	150	....	600	1,400	2
Stafford,........	6	2,200	470	4,000	5,400	13
Greene Co.						
Athens,..........	3	2,300	550	1,466	5,000	8
Coxsackie,.......	3	2,000	710	2,216	5,900	11
Catskill,........	1	300	100	200	....	2
Durham,..........	3	500	200	750	1,600	3
Greenville,......	4	1,000	450	700	2,800	7
Hunter,..........	2	200	100	....	....	2
New Baltimore,..	1	200	100	483	1,000	2
Windham,.........	2	700	210	385	2,300	....
Herkimer Co.						
Columbia,........	3	250	210	276	2,400	4
Fairfield,.......	2	1,500	212	550	2,600	4
Frankfort,.......	1	200	200	340	1,500	2
German Flats,....	1	400	150	271	1,000	3
Herkimer,........	4	1,650	650	2,280	....	7
Little Falls,.....	4	4,200	775	3,345	7,800	7
Manheim,.........	1	600	100	760	400	1

CLASS II.—(Continued.)

TOWNS.	Number of establishments.	Capital invested. In real estate.	Capital invested. In tools and machinery.	Cash value. Of raw materials used.	Cash value. Of manufactured articles.	Persons employed.
Herkimer Co.						
Newport,	5	$3,450	$1,000	$2,500	$7,100	9
Salisbury,	5	1,950	650	1,879	5,550	11
Stark,	2	250	130	271	1,050	2
Warren,	4	480	385	994	3,300	3
Winfield,	4	925	265	1,400	3,500	6
Jefferson Co.						
Adams,	6	2,225	835	1,174	4,800	12
Alexandria,	2	400	300	1,200	4,000	6
Antwerp,	2	1,200	250	2,050	6,000	6
Cape Vincent,	2	....	....	450	500	....
Ellisburgh,	8	5,350	1,400	3,030	8,360	14
Henderson,	4	1,800	775	540	1,900	6
Hounsfield,	2	700	350	1,500	4,000	4
Le Ray,	1	900	100	600	2,500	3
Lyme,	4	1,100	950	1,563	1,200	3
Orleans,	7	1,550	900	2,822	7,800	13
Pamelia,	3	250	320	500	2,500	5
Philadelphia,	3	1,100	330	1,020	3,500	6
Rutland,	3	300	150	760	2,800	2
Watertown,	5	6,000	850	1,917	9,500	12
Kings Co.						
Brooklyn,	8	12,650	2,490	2,904	4,550	38
Flatbush,	3	1,750	475	....	....	6
Lewis Co.						
Croghan,	1	600	200	....	500	2
Denmark,	2	600	250	350	1,200	3
Lowville,	3	1,700	400	2,383	5,760	10
Martinsburgh,	2	100	90	281	1,200	3
New Bremen,	1	....	80	150	700	1
Livingston Co.						
Avon,	3	950	350	1,450	2,440	4
Caledonia,	5	1,200	590	643	5,000	10
Conesus,	3	275	305	675	1,650	5
Groveland,	7	785	460	1,364	4,280	8
Leicester,	1	15,000	100	160	1,000	2
Lima,	2	150	70	....	900	2
Mount Morris,	4	2,100	550	1,837	5,650	9
Nunda,	3	1,900	750	950	5,400	7
North Dansville,	3	200	375	996	4,000	5
Sparta,	1	500	150	500	....	4
York,	3	3,800	1,360	3,660	12,200	16
Madison Co.						
Brookfield,	2	300	250	250	1,150	4
Cazenovia,	6	950	450	1,725	5,950	11
Fenner,	1	50	80	70	800	1
Georgetown,	1	350	100	240	2,000	2
Hamilton,	3	1,000	750	1,775	5,200	7
Lenox,	5	875	410	613	3,750	7
Nelson,	3	350	195	323	2,100	4
Stockbridge,	1	300	100	400	1,000	1
Sullivan,	5	1,400	750	1,789	6,300	7
Monroe Co.						
Brighton,	4	2,500	700	1,200	5,700	13
Chili,	2	2,200	110	340	2,400	1
Clarkson,	2	1,300	300	1,746	2,600	2
Greece,	1	900	150	160	880	4
Mendon,	9	2,300	1,465	4,275	10,500	20
Ogden,	8	2,025	3,215	2,200	12,200	....
Parma,	4	500	700	1,391	5,239	9
Penfield,	5	1,720	500	660	3,200	3
Perrington,	4	1,625	500	1,807	6,008	6
Pittsford,	4	1,200	630	3,265	5,892	6
Riga,	3	550	250	1,130	2,500	4
Rochester,	6	4,800	825	4,459	10,760	16
Rush,	2	....	....	....	....	....
Sweden,	3	550	400	1,480	5,150	7
Union,	2	900	200	175	2,000	2
Webster,	6	900	455	890	3,543	11
Wheatland,	4	1,250	550	1,435	5,000	9
Montgomery Co.						
Amsterdam,	6	6,700	3,800	2,326	7,272	8
Charleston,	3	450	375	847	3,100	7
Florida,	5	1,250	500	1,000	5,700	10
Glen,	10	12,650	1,295	6,400	16,400	20
Mohawk,	3	2,100	700	4,500	9,000	6
Palatine,	2	600	250	4,250	1,800	6
Root,	10	2,275	1,000	1,990	6,250	5
St. Johnsville,	5	1,900	550	3,423	6,300	11
New-York Co.						
New-York,	53	201,500	30,610	125,826	134,958	263
Niagara Co.						
Hartland,	3	425	294	426	2,700	4
Lewiston,	4	160	725	1,240	4,100	10
Lockport,	5	2,800	900	2,340	6,610	11
Newfane,	6	2,000	1,005	2,280	6,000	11
Porter,	6	3,450	950	1,935	6,700	16
Royalton,	1	400	100	200	600	2
Wheatfield,	4	510	280	110	....	....
Niagara Co.						
Wilson,	3	$1,050	$650	$1,080	$3,100	5
Oneida Co.						
Augusta,	1	600	250	500	1,500	3
Ava,	1	100	190	500	1,200	2
Boonville,	3	1,200	430	625	1,950	6
Bridgewater,	2	1,000	180	680	1,900	4
Deerfield,	2	1,000	250	770	1,900	3
Kirkland,	5	1,750	500	1,278	5,000	7
Lee,	3	900	325	1,160	4,020	2
New Hartford,	1	....	....	....	....	1
Paris,	5	770	600	2,390	4,600	5
Remsen,	2	600	100	....	....	5
Rome,	3	6,500	1,300	5,252	14,275	17
Steuben,	1	50	....	200	500	1
Trenton,	3	375	285	1,727	2,600	3
Utica,	7	4,200	800	6,669	11,800	13
Vernon,	5	1,600	8,000	1,400	44,700	6
Verona,	13	3,500	1,370	3,498	10,750	15
Westmoreland,	2	400	150	319	1,700	3
Whitestown,	6	1,850	600	2,320	8,700	13
Onondaga Co.						
Camillus,	4	200	100	1,000	....	....
Cicero,	4	1,350	500	1,129	3,450	6
Clay,	4	850	285	950	2,500	4
De Witt,	2	600	300	200	1,000	2
Elbridge,	1	....	150	240	1,500	3
Fabius,	3	850	350	880	3,800	6
Geddes,	3	700	395	2,072	4,700	8
La Fayette,	2	200	250	44	1,150	2
Lysander,	4	2,000	630	1,082	4,600	9
Manlius,	3	1,700	450	756	3,300	8
Marcellus,	2	1,215	850	900	2,500	4
Onondaga,	3	250	330	700	2,600	3
Otisco,	1	200	200	700	1,700	3
Pompey,	2	200	150	900	3,000	4
Skaneateles,	1	1,500	200	325	3,000	5
Spafford,	4	450	400	1,025	2,470	7
Syracuse,	8	12,900	2,150	8,567	27,800	20
Tully,	2	1,400	350	654	2,450	6
Ontario Co.						
Bristol,	4	550	590	1,850	5,900	9
Canadice,	1	100	100	300	600	1
Canandaigua,	9	5,450	1,000	2,370	14,200	13
East Bloomfield,	3	1,150	440	1,065	4,850	3
Farmington,	4	1,850	562	500	3,350	7
Gorham,	3	200	235	1,280	3,725	7
Naples,	3	1,050	550	1,015	3,800	5
Phelps,	9	2,440	850	1,450	5,900	12
Richmond,	1	150	100	25	2,000	3
Victor,	2	3,900	1,250	414	....	9
West Bloomfield,	1	1,200	....	585	1,500	3
Orange Co.						
Blooming Grove,	1	50	150	500	800	2
Chester,	1	200	100	850	2,200	3
Hamtonburgh,	1	150	275	1,060	2,600	4
Minisink,	4	400	220	686	2,750	6
Monroe,	5	1,100	425	1,575	4,350	11
Montgomery,	5	400	320	1,588	4,000	4
Mount Hope,	4	1,300	285	2,100	5,300	8
New Windsor,	3	....	350	1,500	3,107	5
Walkill,	10	3,100	1,205	2,854	6,856	13
Warwick,	3	250	100	920	2,400	6
Orleans Co.						
Barre,	8	4,300	860	2,884	5,925	7
Carlton,	7	1,560	875	1,875	5,300	6
Clarendon,	3	1,200	420	1,365	4,800	7
Gaines,	6	1,650	715	1,600	4,800	2
Murray,	5	2,800	900	1,674	7,750	14
Ridgeway,	7	2,675	980	5,351	11,850	19
Shelby,	1	200	100	400	1,300	2
Yates,	1	500	175	430	2,000	....
Oswego Co.						
Granby,	2	1,150	450	100	2,000	2
Hannibal,	2	500	200	785	2,600	5
Hastings,	4	1,000	500	1,656	3,900	2
Mexico,	3	300	225	505	1,200	4
New Haven,	1	100	100	400	900	....
Orwell,	2	250	175	200	1,300	1
Oswego city,	2	3,000	600	1,600	6,000	4
Palermo,	3	500	425	600	2,900	5
Redfield,	1	50	50	1,300	100	2
Richland,	2	750	200	375	1,600	3
Schroeppel,	2	2,000	600	2,996	5,500	6
Scriba,	1	200	60	250	900	1
Volney,	1	1,800	1,000	1,000	3,000	3
Otsego Co.						
Burlington,	5	975	330	344	1,900	5
Butternuts,	2	1,200	500	2,230	6,500	10

CLASS II.—(Continued.)

TOWNS.	Number of establishments.	Capital Invested. In real estate.	Capital Invested. In tools and machinery.	Cash Value. Of raw materials used.	Cash Value. Of manufactured articles.	Persons employed.
Otsego Co.						
Cherry Valley,...	3	$600	$200	$1,000	$3,050	6
Decatur,.........	1	800	100	40	....	....
Edmeston,........	1	200	200	570	2,000	3
Exeter,..........	3	950	250	1,383	4,200	7
Laurens,.........	1	650	100	....	800	....
Maryland,........	5	1,750	500	1,304	5,425	8
Middlefield,......	3	700	250	700	2,700	7
Milford,.........	4	500	360	1,252	3,400	5
New Lisbon,......	3	200	200	697	2,050	....
Otego,...........	5	390	500	851	4,035	7
Plainfield,.......	3	350	265	566	2,100	....
Richfield,........	5	1,350	520	1,335	4,100	7
Roseboom,........	9	715	595	450	4,500	2
Springfield,......	6	7,000	715	4,650	10,450	16
Unadilla,........	2	2,000	500	1,465	5,500	7
Worcester,.......	5	1,000	280	950	3,150	7
Putnam Co.						
Carmel,..........	2	800	300	1,548	5,500	5
Phillipstown,.....	2	950	350	850	5,200	8
Putnam Valley,..	1	1,000	1,200	455	1,750	4
South East,......	1	1,300	300	1,100	2,777	6
Queens Co.						
Hempstead,.......	4	400	160	620	2,750	8
Jamaica,.........	1	400	100	750	2,000	3
Newtown,........	4	1,700	700	2,396	5,000	7
North Hempstead,	2	....	150	500	2,000	5
Oyster Bay,......	3	1,000	290	1,200	2,700	4
Rensselaer Co.						
Berlin,..........	1	200	100	500	1,200	2
Brunswick,.......	6	2,850	1,150	2,055	7,600	11
Clinton,.........	3	500	650	....	....	....
Hoosick,.........	1	600	100	480	1,400	3
Lansingburgh,...	1	1,400	300	700	2,000	3
North Greenbush,	4	1,500	455	2,150	4,200	7
Petersburgh,.....	1	....	....	90	500	2
Pittstown,........	5	775	575	1,600	3,400	6
Poestenkill,......	5	950	350	3,150	1,050	3
Sandlake,........	4	500	215	1,133	3,050	7
Schodack,........	11	3,100	750	1,807	4,750	18
Troy,............	1	300	45	2,000	4,600	....
Richmond Co.						
Northfield,......	4	900	300	2,600	4,800	6
Westfield,........	2	200	100	568	1,800	....
Rockland Co.						
Clarkstown,......	1	500	100	750	3,000	3
Haverstraw,......	4	600	250	....	....	....
Orangetown,......	1	300	100	250	600	1
Ramapo,.........	1	400	100	150	....	....
St. Lawrence Co.						
Brasher,.........	1	1,000	300	1,285	3,740	4
Edwards,........	3	450	325	....	....	....
Gouverneur,......	2	550	250	1,104	2,880	5
Hammond,.......	3	800	280	700	2,250	2
Hermon,.........	1	1,000	220	830	1,800	3
Louisville,.......	3	200	350	550	2,100	5
Madrid,.........	1	2,700	750	1,600	5,500	7
Massena,........	3	275	210	385	2,900	5
Norfolk,.........	2	500	250	300	500	3
Oswegatchie,......	2	750	125	340	2,500	4
Parishville,......	4	1,425	210	1,932	4,500	6
Pierrepont,......	2	600	400	600	2,130	4
Pitcairn,........	1	50	40	175	200	....
Potsdam,........	13	2,705	1,395	3,113	14,700	23
Rossie,..........	1	200	100	640	2,000	3
Russell,.........	2	125	115	400	....	1
Stockholm,.......	3	900	400	700	2,400	5
Saratoga Co.						
Ballston,.........	3	500	250	780	2,680	5
Clifton Park,....	6	2,275	625	3,450	6,800	8
Corinth,.........	1	200	100	150	1,200	2
Edinburgh,......	1	50	100	200	1,000	....
Greenfield,......	3	900	300	540	2,100	4
Halfmoon,.......	1	1,100	325	2,120	3,100	3
Malta,...........	4	525	250	368	2,758	....
Milton,..........	5	1,150	250	879	3,800	9
Moreau,.........	6	1,100	450	1,569	4,800	7
Northumberland,.	4	1,050	310	661	2,781	7
Saratoga,........	2	500	250	1,400	6,500	6
Saratoga Springs,.	6	4,200	975	4,085	14,400	18
Stillwater,.......	5	13,000	500	825	3,350	8
Schenectady Co.						
Duanesburgh,....	4	400	470	965	3,025	3
Glenville,........	3	1,400	650	2,275	5,000	6
Schenectady,.....	1	600	150	200	1,000	1
Schoharie Co.						
Carlisle,.........	2	175	125	370	1,800	3
Esperance,.......	2	575	250	640	2,300	4
Fulton,..........	5	200	325	730	2,600	6
Gilboa,..........	3	275	350	850	2,200	4
Schoharie Co.						
Middleburgh,.....	1	$200	$175	$1,100	$2,200	2
Richmondville,...	5	1,200	420	1,071	3,700	8
Seward,..........	4	2,800	250	325	2,050	6
Sharon,..........	9	1,375	700	1,440	5,750	13
Summit,.........	1	200	225	250	500	1
Wright,..........	2	600	75	366	1,000	3
Schuyler Co.						
Catharines,......	2	400	80	1,600	3,200	4
Cayuta,.........	1	500	150	236	1,200	2
Dix,............	1	....	150	6,500	6,500	....
Hector,..........	10	2,250	1,432	2,878	8,850	14
Orange,.........	5	850	450	565	3,255	6
Reading,.........	1	285	100	24	800	2
Tyrone,.........	3	690	350	770	3,650	6
Seneca Co.						
Fayette,.........	9	1,700	900	3,200	10,000	17
Ovid,............	1	800	100	6,800	....	2
Romulus,........	7	1,400	425	1,232	4,050	8
Seneca Falls,......	1	2,500	1,300	1,200	4,000	6
Varick,..........	3	275	225	400	1,750	5
Waterloo,........	2	2,300	350	1,940	3,500	5
Steuben Co.						
Bath,............	11	3,050	1,060	2,054	10,300	20
Bradford,........	3	390	270	1,050	2,800	4
Canisteo,........	5	960	450	151	....	7
Dansville,........	5	2,250	775	1,663	4,100	12
Erwin,..........	4	1,400	425	2,330	7,000	10
Fremont,........	3	365	390	610	1,620	2
Hornellsville,....	2	350	250	940	1,450	2
Howard,.........	2	800	170	358	1,600	1
Jasper,..........	5	100	300	10	1,900	4
Pultney,.........	2	100	150	120	800	1
Thurston,........	2	125	150	350	800	3
Urbana,.........	5	1,050	350	....	4,100	7
Suffolk Co.						
East Hampton,...	2	400	250	600	2,100	4
Huntington,......	4	650	550	1,550	2,000	9
Islip,............	1	250	50	400	1,300	....
Riverhead,.......	1	400	100	500	1,000	2
Smithtown,......	3	350	150	....	....	3
Southampton,....	4	600	275	800	2,500	7
Southold,........	7	2,375	855	4,175	7,425	12
Sullivan Co.						
Bethel,..........	2	200	200	700	1,900	3
Cochecton,.......	7	1,150	1,090	3,000	9,460	13
Fallsburgh,......	6	400	445	1,579	4,500	6
Mamakating,......	8	1,005	780	1,187	2,900	14
Rockland,........	4	600	245	417	2,500	8
Tusten,..........	2	425	170	1,465	4,175	3
Tioga Co.						
Barton,..........	12	2,000	1,035	1,400	4,075	18
Berkshire,.......	2	500	300	850	2,100	5
Newark,.........	2	500	250	774	2,850	4
Nichols,.........	2	250	250	450	1,700	2
Owego,..........	2	500	250	780	1,640	4
Tompkins Co.						
Caroline,........	7	985	570	1,534	4,880	10
Danby,..........	5	253	335	18	2,563	....
Dryden,.........	7	1,750	705	2,460	4,950	12
Enfield,.........	1	500	100	150	600	1
Groton,.........	7	1,830	810	....	....	....
Ithaca,..........	8	12,250	3,350	8,130	22,700	29
Lansing,.........	5	1,200	285	2,415	5,500	4
Newfield,........	3	700	600	1,275	3,900	5
Ulysses,.........	2	1,000	....	1,100	4,000	6
Ulster Co.						
Esopus,.........	1	500	100	350	800	....
Gardiner,........	1	....	....	250	1,000	2
Hurley,.........	1	700	50	225	800	....
Kingston,........	1	4,000	250	....	....	....
Lloyd,...........	2	250	100	394	950	2
Marbletown,.....	3	370	330	1,110	2,800	4
New Paltz,.......	3	4,800	440	3,000	7,250	7
Olive,...........	1	200	100	864	1,600	2
Plattekill,........	2	....	80	600	1,800	3
Rochester,.......	4	4,200	735	1,950	5,750	10
Saugerties,.......	13	6,275	1,450	6,440	20,878	25
Wawarsing,......	5	1,000	625	1,840	9,000	9
Warren Co.						
Chester,.........	4	700	650	1,272	3,100	8
Johnsburgh,.....	4	200	290	1,050	2,100	5
Queensbury,.....	2	2,800	550	3,150	6,450	6
Stony Creek,.....	2	200	150	170	300	2
Warrensburgh,...	2	1,700	300	1,000	2,800	4
Washington Co.						
Argyle,.........	6	970	450	1,916	5,000	7
Easton,.........	4	1,300	775	2,228	5,500	7
Fort Ann,........	2	450	150	400	1,000	2
Fort Edward,.....	1	500	100	501	1,600	2

CLASS II.—(Continued.)

TOWNS.	Number of establishments.	Capital Invested. In real estate.	Capital Invested. In tools and machinery.	Cash Value. Of raw materials used.	Cash Value. Of manufactured articles.	Persons employed.
WASHINGTON Co.						
Granville,........	6	$550	$345	$1, 765	$3, 400	10
Greenwich, ...	1	400	150	600	600	2
Hartford,.........	4	600	300	1, 161	4, 500	4
Hebron, ...	6	1, 850	510	1, 605	4, 100	12
Kingsbury,.......	3	1, 900	950	2, 700	7, 050	4
Salem,............	4	2, 350	250	1, 517	4, 500	5
White Creek,.....	3	315	350	667	3, 400	6
WAYNE Co.						
Arcadia,.........	5	2, 800	760	3, 347	10, 300	12
Galen,...........	3	500	300	856	1, 100	6
Lyons,...........	3	1, 700	350	1, 590	3, 400	7
Macedon, ...	1	....	125	410	1, 250	....
Marion,..........	6	995	410	970	2, 600	7
Ontario, ...	5	500	450	1, 057	4, 200	6
Palmyra, ...	5	4, 200	1, 275	3, 734	14, 300	8
Sodus, ...	8	1, 450	485	1, 900	6, 100	11
Walworth,.......	3	900	550	1, 775	3, 000	8
Williamson,......	2	300	300	1, 152	3, 000	4
Wolcott, ...	8	2, 400	360	1, 640	8, 900	8
WESTCHESTER Co.						
Bedford,.........	4	1, 250	600	1, 650	4, 400	6
East Chester, ...	1	100	50	300	900	2
Greenburgh,......	1	100	70	150	700	2
Harrison,........	1	800	50	400	2, 000	2
Lewisboro',......	3	400	215	1, 013	2, 250	4
Mount Pleasant,..	2	700	300	100	....	3
North Salem,.....	3	....	275	1, 016	1, 900	1
Rye,.............	1	500	....	....	....	2
White Plains, ...	2	8, 500	900	1, 400	1, 521	6
Yorktown,.......	9	980	775	1, 616	3, 400	10
WYOMING Co.						
Bennington,......	1	300	125	450	1, 200	2
Castile,..........	2	225	175	504	2, 229	5
China,...........	3	1, 300	400	1, 400	2, 200	3
Covington,.......	3	400	450	200	3, 500	5
Genesee Falls,....	1	50	50	400	900	1
Java,............	2	350	200	225	1, 700	3
Middlebury,......	3	1, 200	400	1, 499	5, 300	7
Orangeville,......	2	40	145	230	1, 000	3
Perry,...........	5	1, 700	500	2, 035	6, 600	8
Pike,............	4	850	480	1, 570	4, 500	11
Sheldon,.........	6	1, 325	415	250	2, 500	6
Warsaw,.........	3	1, 650	550	1, 176	5, 200	7
Wethersfield,.....	2	450	300	700	900	2
YATES Co.						
Benton,..........	7	1, 000	625	1, 165	5, 200	10
Jerusalem,.......	3	1, 300	325	1, 500	3, 800	7
Milo,............	2	500	68	1, 100	2, 000	3
Torrey,..........	2	600	150	800	1, 900	3

BOLT MANUFACTORIES.

TOWNS.	Number of establishments.	In real estate.	In tools and machinery.	Of raw materials used.	Of manufactured articles.	Persons employed.
ERIE Co.						
Buffalo, ...	1	....	1, 500	6, 000	12, 500	6
KINGS Co.						
Brooklyn,........	1	800	700	500	1, 500	2
NEW-YORK Co.						
New-York,.......	6	23, 000	12, 000	30, 200	74, 000	71
SARATOGA Co.						
Saratoga Springs,.	1	6, 000	10, 000	1, 280	5, 300	6
SULLIVAN Co.						
Lumberland,......	1	....	200	145	1, 000	3

BRAD AND SPARABLE MANUFACTORY.

TOWNS.	Number of establishments.	In real estate.	In tools and machinery.	Of raw materials used.	Of manufactured articles.	Persons employed.
NEW-YORK Co.						
New-York,.......	1	2, 500	1, 500	1, 800	2, 800	3

BRASS AND COPPER FOUNDRIES.

TOWNS.	Number of establishments.	In real estate.	In tools and machinery.	Of raw materials used.	Of manufactured articles.	Persons employed.
ALBANY Co.						
Albany, ...	3	....	4, 900	22, 000	30, 000	23
DUTCHESS Co.						
Poughkeepsie city,	2	5, 000	4, 500	21, 000	52, 500	31
ERIE Co.						
Buffalo, ...	2	7, 000	4, 000	55, 000	68, 000	32
JEFFERSON Co.						
Watertown,......	1	1, 600	500	2, 130	3, 000	4
KINGS Co.						
Brooklyn,........	4	57, 600	43, 500	208, 008	375, 000	134
LIVINGSTON Co.						
Avon, ...	1	100	200	1, 200	2, 000	3
MONROE Co.						
Brighton,........	1	3, 000	1, 000	250	1, 500	4
NEW-YORK Co.						
New-York,.......	31	173, 600	160, 000	291, 826	754, 740	315
ONEIDA Co.						
Utica, ...	1	800	1, 000	....	5, 000	5
RENSSELAER Co.						
Troy,............	2	2, 000	500	6, 900	13, 560	3

BRASS FINISHING ESTABLISHMENT.

TOWNS.	Number of establishments.	In real estate.	In tools and machinery.	Of raw materials used.	Of manufactured articles.	Persons employed.
MONROE Co.						
Rochester, ...	1	....	$1, 500	$1, 500	$4, 200	4

BRITANNIA WARE AND SILVER PLATING ESTABLISHMENTS.

TOWNS.	Number of establishments.	In real estate.	In tools and machinery.	Of raw materials used.	Of manufactured articles.	Persons employed.
ALBANY Co.						
Albany,..........	2	$4, 000	4, 000	3, 000	12. 000	17
Bethlehem,.......	1	10, 600	15, 000	40, 000	100, 000	92
GENESEE Co.						
Le Roy,..........	1	....	50	....	600	1
KINGS Co.						
Brooklyn,........	1	....	600	500	6, 000	6
NEW-YORK Co.						
New-York,.......	2	600	2, 000	4. 055	10, 500	11
ONEIDA Co.						
Utica, ...	1	....	150	850	2, 400	3
ONTARIO Co.						
Canandaigua,.....	1	500	50	....	600	1
TOMPKINS Co.						
Ithaca,..........	1	500	150	750	700	1

BRONZE CASTING ESTABLISHMENTS.

TOWNS.	Number of establishments.	In real estate.	In tools and machinery.	Of raw materials used.	Of manufactured articles.	Persons employed.
KINGS Co.						
Brooklyn,........	1	....	5, 000	9, 000	25, 000	15
NEW-YORK Co.						
New-York,.......	2	....	2, 500	5, 300	18, 000	16

BUTT AND HINGE FACTORIES.

TOWNS.	Number of establishments.	In real estate.	In tools and machinery.	Of raw materials used.	Of manufactured articles.	Persons employed.
ALBANY Co.						
Watervliet,.......	1	....	10, 000	45, 000	70, 000	90
RENSSELAER Co.						
Lansingburgh,....	3	4, 400	2, 250	25, 660	36, 675	15
Troy,............	1	10, 000	8, 400	24, 223	43, 745	67

CASTOR FRAME MANUFACTORY.

TOWNS.	Number of establishments.	In real estate.	In tools and machinery.	Of raw materials used.	Of manufactured articles.	Persons employed.
NEW-YORK Co.						
New-York,.......	1	....	12, 000	18, 500	29, 400	11

COMPOSITION METAL MANUFACTORIES.

TOWNS.	Number of establishments.	In real estate.	In tools and machinery.	Of raw materials used.	Of manufactured articles.	Persons employed.
ERIE Co.						
Buffalo,..........	1	....	250	3, 000	6. 000	4
RENSSELAER Co.						
Troy,............	1	3, 000	6, 000	4, 500	12. 000	17
WESTCHESTER Co.						
Greenburgh,......	2	3, 000	2, 600	5, 400	10, 600	9

COPPER SMITHING.

TOWNS.	Number of establishments.	In real estate.	In tools and machinery.	Of raw materials used.	Of manufactured articles.	Persons employed.
KINGS Co.						
Brooklyn,........	1	....	150, 000	500, 000	350, 000	102
NEW-YORK Co.						
New-York,.......	14	51, 000	20, 400	304, 528	416, 500	144

CUTLERY MANUFACTORIES.

TOWNS.	Number of establishments.	In real estate.	In tools and machinery.	Of raw materials used.	Of manufactured articles.	Persons employed.
ALBANY Co.						
Albany, ...	1	....	1, 000	....	....	5
CHENANGO Co.						
Greene,..........	1	300	200	360	3, 000	5
CORTLAND Co.						
Willet, ...	1	600	600	836	2, 000	3
DUTCHESS Co.						
Fishkill,..........	1	....	4, 000	4, 202	26, 000	37
NEW-YORK Co.						
New-York, ...	6	14, 000	12. 300	22, 265	60. 000	50

DOOR LATCH MANUFACTORY.

TOWNS.	Number of establishments.	In real estate.	In tools and machinery.	Of raw materials used.	Of manufactured articles.	Persons employed.
GREENE Co.						
Durham, ...	1	....	200	2, 955	11, 000	8

FILE MANUFACTORIES.

TOWNS.	Number of establishments.	In real estate.	In tools and machinery.	Of raw materials used.	Of manufactured articles.	Persons employed.
DUTCHESS Co.						
Fishkill,..........	1	600	2, 000	14, 265	45, 000	55
ROCKLAND Co.						
Ramapo,.........	1	1, 500	200	400	2, 400	6
WESTCHESTER Co.						
Ossining,........	3	20, 000	41, 000	56, 250	238, 000	278

FISH HOOK MANUFACTORY.

TOWNS.	Number of establishments.	In real estate.	In tools and machinery.	Of raw materials used.	Of manufactured articles.	Persons employed.
KINGS Co.						
Brooklyn,........	1	10, 000	700	5, 000	9, 500	13

CLASS II.—(Continued.)

TOWNS.	Number of establishments.	Capital Invested. In real estate.	Capital Invested. In tools and machinery.	Cash Value. Of raw materials used.	Cash Value. Of manufactured articles.	Persons employed.
FORGES.						
Cayuga Co.						
Auburn,	1	$4,000	$6,000	$10,500	$20,000	13
Erie Co.						
Amherst,	1	6,000	4,000	3,850	5,400	3
Buffalo,	2	15,000	50,000	152,000	305,000	130
Essex Co.						
Elizabethtown,	4	17,500	2,700	33,708	62,250	73
Jefferson Co.						
Philadelphia,	1	5,000	100	3,420	6,000	6
Wilna,	1	31,000	1,750	5,205	6,900	32
Monroe Co.						
Rochester,	1	8,000	300	....	....	....
New-York Co.						
New-York,	3	52,000	82,000	95,000	365,000	125
Oneida Co.						
Marshall,	3	2,000	1,200	4,020	7,280	7
Otsego Co.						
Edmeston,	1	800	600	350	1,700	2
St. Lawrence Co.						
Brasher,	3	3,500	1,500	2,665	5,550	7
Ulster Co.						
Wawarsing,	2	18,000	1,000	15,100	40,000	15
Washington Co.						
Fort Ann,	1	2,500	350	1,600	3,700	5
FURNACES.						
Albany Co.						
Albany,	20	344,000	228,500	624,810	1,432,600	1647
Rensselaerville,	1	100	700	400	1,500	3
Watervliet,	4	46,000	59,000	98,000	245,000	124
Allegany Co.						
Cuba,	1	2,000	2,000	1,200	7,000	3
Independence,	1	1,000	400	875	3,500	2
Rushford,	1	800	1,000	585	1,500	1
Scio,	1	10,000	4,000	15,000	20,000	8
Broome Co.						
Windsor,	2	1,000	1,400	1,823	....	4
Cattaraugus Co.						
Olean,	2	6,000	10,500	355	12,270	14
Randolph,	1	1,800	1,800	170	3,000	3
Yorkshire,	1	....	1,000	300	1,500	1
Cayuga Co.						
Auburn,	4	12,500	42,500	31,630	129,500	130
Brutus,	1	8,000	2,500	3,000	7,000	7
Cato,	1	3,000	1,000	739	1,840	....
Ira,	1	2,000	500	900	3,000	2
Mentz,	1	....	....	....	....	....
Moravia,	1	1,500	500	2,725	4,390	6
Venice,	1	1,000	1,000	1,000	1,500	6
Chautauque Co.						
Chautauque,	1	1,000	2,000	1,086	2,372	5
Ellicott,	1	3,000	2,500	4,775	11,000	....
Ellington,	1	800	1,200	400	1,700	2
Hanover,	1	1,500	8,000	5,125	12,480	16
Pomfret,	3	10,000	11,000	16,760	51,848	42
Chemung Co.						
Elmira,	5	40,000	25,950	56,735	100,400	84
Horseheads,	1	3,500	2,000	8,175	14,500	8
Veteran,	1	3,000	200	1,500	4,500	4
Chenango Co.						
Bainbridge,	1	1,000	1,000	375	1,200	2
Greene,	1	3,000	1,500	1,500	4,000	4
Guilford,	1	1,000	2,000	690	4,700	6
Norwich,	1	3,000	5,000	2,000	12,000	17
Oxford,	1	2,000	3,000	2,475	5,000	4
Preston,	9	....	885	....	....	7
Sherburne,	1	300	300	525	2,500	2
Clinton Co.						
Ausable,	1	12,000	15,000	34,595	80,000	63
Champlain,	2	7,000	7,700	11,000	24,000	25
Dannemora,	1	1,000	2,000	17,100	24,000	7
Plattsburgh,	1	15,000	8,000	33,000	75,000	50
Schuyler Falls,	1	2,000	400	1,750	3,600	3
Columbia Co.						
Chatham,	2	7,000	2,000	3,120	8,875	11
Hudson,	1	8,000	6,000	18,500	36,000	20
Taghkanick,	1	1,400	300	1,000	....	5
Cortland Co.						
Homer,	1	4,000	1,000	4,530	5,528	11
Delaware Co.						
Franklin,	1	800	1,500	600	2,175	3
Roxbury,	1	600	800	300	600	1
Stamford,	1	2,000	1,000	....	4,160	5
Dutchess Co.						
Fishkill,	3	165,500	47,500	71,285	79,040	148
Northeast,	1	300	150	200	....	....
Poughkeepsie city,	2	27,000	50,000	31,800	82,000	49
Dutchess Co.						
Rhinebeck,	1	$1,000	$300	$520	$2,080	4
Stanford,	1	300	500	600	1,280	2
Washington,	1	....	500	500	1,000	....
Erie Co.						
Amherst,	1	2,500	100	1,500	3,000	7
Aurora,	1	650	800	400	1,700	4
Buffalo,	2	20,000	30,000	78,300	180,000	175
Collins,	1	1,000	100	3,500	9,400	9
Hamburg,	1	1,000	400	....	500	1
Lancaster,	1	10,000	2,000	4,000	10,000	15
Newstead,	1	2,500	2,500	....	10,000	10
Tonawanda,	1	2,000	1,000	1,500	5,000	4
Essex Co.						
Crown Point,	1	500	500	1,500	3,000	2
Ticonderoga,	1	500	150	1,112	3,080	3
Franklin Co.						
Malone,	1	5,000	3,600	5,184	14,217	17
Genesee Co.						
Alabama,	1	500	1,500	2,000	6,000	2
Byron,	1	500	500	2,900	4,000	4
Le Roy,	1	3,000	1,500	4,050	10,000	8
Oakfield,	1	1,500	700	1,000	1,250	....
Greene Co.						
Catskill,	1	700	300	1,050	2,200	2
Durham,	1	1,600	1,600	855	2,470	5
Prattsville,	1	1,000	3,000	2,400	6,500	4
Windham,	1	2,000	2,500	1,730	10,000	5
Herkimer Co.						
German Flats,	1	3,000	3,000	3,615	86,960	9
Little Falls,	3	11,000	7,700	18,050	35,600	31
Jefferson Co.						
Brownville,	2	8,000	6,000	8,106	19,550	17
Cape Vincent,	1	2,200	1,400	995	2,500	7
Ellisburgh,	1	800	500	395	1,000	1
Hounsfield,	1	1,500	1,200	1,000	3,000	4
Pamelia,	2	16,000	24,000	60,630	130,000	130
Watertown,	1	6,000	2,300	1,640	4,532	9
Wilna,	2	5,500	4,000	7,380	17,750	8
Kings Co.						
Brooklyn,	15	156,000	183,800	472,284	874,940	602
Lewis Co.						
Denmark,	1	2,000	1,000	1,244	2 000	4
Livingston Co.						
Caledonia,	2	500	1,000	1,187	2,587	4
Geneseo,	1	8,000	8,000	2,530	18,800	20
Leicester,	1	5,000	15,000	3,150	....	10
Livonia,	1	1,500	1,200	1,005	3,000	3
Mt. Morris,	1	3,500	3,000	4,046	8,650	9
North Dansville,	2	11,000	3,800	11,230	38,100	22
Nunda,	1	4,000	10,000	15,530	60,250	25
Portage,	1	2,500	1,000	700	3,000	4
Sparta,	1	600	600	1,098	2,400	4
York,	2	4,500	2,000	3,075	7,300	7
Madison Co.						
Brookfield,	1	....	....	1,700	6,000	....
Cazenovia,	2	....	3,200	3,430	6,750	10
De Ruyter,	1	1,000	3,000	3,500	10,000	8
Eaton,	2	5,500	2,700	12,605	18,106	14
Hamilton,	1	1,500	500	1,445	4,000	3
Lenox,	1	2,000	800	870	1,500	6
Sullivan,	1	1,400	5,400	4,400	14,800	7
Monroe Co.						
Mendon,	3	6,150	6,675	10,025	28,000	39
Ogden,	1	1,000	800	....	3,000	....
Penfield,	1	1,600	400	600	1,200	5
Rochester,	6	41,900	40,31[illegible]	104,575	226,600	174
Webster,	1	100	300	500	1,050	3
Montgomery Co.						
Amsterdam,	1	4,000	10,000	4,730	12,000	15
Glen,	1	4,000	400	5,700	9,800	22
Minden,	1	2,000	3,300	3,905	8,500	8
New-York Co.						
New-York,	37	828,900	379,400	695,925	2,146,950	1585
Niagara Co.						
Lockport,	2	2,000	1,500	3,500	8,250	6
Niagara,	1	4,000	500	500	2,000	2
Royalton,	1	1,200	500	1,860	4,500	6
Oneida Co.						
Boonville,	2	3,500	4,000	5,800	13,480	11
Camden,	2	2,500	2,200	3,680	19,225	10
New Hartford,	1	4,000	10,000	7,500	22,000	10
Paris,	2	6,200	2,000	8,800	16,500	19
Rome,	1	10,000	5,000	9,000	18,000	10
Sangerfield,	2	5,000	4,000	20,913	24,200	26
Trenton,	2	3,850	2,000	1,150	3,500	9
Utica,	3	35,000	49,000	63,748	59,000	45
Vernon,	1	8,000	2,000	6,745	13,075	25
Vienna,	1	400	400	260	1,400	1
Westmoreland,	2	15,600	7,500	16,730	58,000	70

CLASS II.—(Continued.)

TOWNS.	Number of establishments.	Capital Invested. In real estate.	Capital Invested. In tools and machinery.	Cash Value. Of raw materials used.	Cash Value. Of manufactured articles.	Persons employed.
ONEIDA Co.						
Whitestown,......	2	$7,000	$4,500	$14,731	$32,440	30
ONONDAGA Co.						
Elbridge,.........	1	4,500	7,000	3,200	9,000	13
Fabius,..........	1	1,200	1,200	700	2,500	5
Lysander, ...	1	4,650	2,200	5,610	9,030	11
Manlius,.........	2	4,500	2,000	2,950	15,200	10
Onondaga, ...	1	500	200	200	1,000	3
Skaneateles,......	2	7,500	3,800	6,275	24,550	14
Spafford,.........	1	600	500	733	2,000	3
Syracuse,........	2	5,000	6,000	46,800	69,000	32
ONTARIO Co.						
Canandaigua,.....	2	3,500	5,500	7,600	15,340	11
East Bloomfield,..	1	350	600	570	1,600	2
Manchester,......	1	.....	600	620	1,600	2
Naples,..........	1	2,000	1,500	1,317	3,200	2
Phelps,..........	1	1,500	1,500	4,800	8,000	5
Richmond,.......	1	1,200	....	791	3,300	8
Victor,..........	1	....	....	....	....	5
ORANGE Co.						
Newburgh, ...	4	17,400	24,500	68,912	141,500	98
ORLEANS Co.						
Barre,...........	2	15,000	5,500	29,822	61,600	41
Murray,.........	1	1,500	1,000	505	1,980	3
Ridgeway,.......	1	5,030	2,000	2,400	5,000	7
Yates,...........	1	1,200	400	375	1,210	....
OSWEGO Co.						
Mexico,.........	1	2,000	1,000	2,000	6,000	3
Oswego city,.....	3	26,500	25,500	29,992	99,540	98
Richland,........	2	5,500	650	972	3,600	3
Sandy Creek,.....	1	1,800	300	400	700	2
Volney,.........	2	13,000	9,000	7,750	35,000	40
OTSEGO Co.						
Butternuts,......	1	1,200	1,500	1,450	12,000	7
Cherry Valley,...	1	1,400	1,200	1,200	3,575	4
Decatur,.........	1	1,500	200	150	480	2
Hartwick,........	1	1,500	3,000	2,800	6,000	6
Morris,..........	1	1,500	1,000	640	3,000	6
Oneonta, ...	3	4,500	3,500	3,005	9,600	10
Otsego,..........	1	3,000	3,000	5,200	8,000	6
PUTNAM Co.						
Phillipstown,.....	1	160,000	60,000	225,000	425,000	530
QUEENS Co.						
Newtown,........	1	20,000	3,000	....	....	5
RENSSELAER Co.						
Greenbush, ...	1	3,000	1,000	1,600	20,000	12
Lansingburgh, ...	1	2,500	50	500	1,500	7
Sand Lake,.......	1	300	1,200	2,915	5,250	4
Troy,............	4	36,300	49,700	90,907	252,280	234
ROCKLAND Co.						
Haverstraw,......	3	22,000	14,000	2,000	....	7
ST. LAWRENCE Co.						
Brasher,.........	1	2,000	2,000	17,825	32,000	24
Canton,..........	1	1,000	1,000	2,452	5,600	4
Edwards,........	1	300	500	....	....	....
Gouverneur,......	1	3,000	1,200	2,090	4,500	8
Oswegatchie,.....	1	....	....	....	....	....
Potsdam,........	2	12,500	5,000	7,000	30,000	20
Stockholm,.......	1	2,000	1,000	1,995	3,750	6
SARATOGA Co.						
Saratoga,........	1	4,000	3,000	8,000	18,000	10
Saratoga Springs,.	1	2,500	3,500	5,500	1,200	7
Waterford, ...	1	15,000	15,000	60,000	100,000	100
SCHENECTADY Co.						
Schenectady,.....	3	18,000	15,700	63,200	80,200	45
SCHOHARIE Co.						
Fulton,..........	1	900	500	300	900	3
Middleburgh, ...	1	300	300	1,150	2,800	2
Richmondville,...	1	1,500	1,500	1,000	4,000	5
Sharon, ...	1	300	300	....	3,000	3
SCHUYLER Co.						
Dix,.............	2	2,700	5,000	3,235	6,100	14
SENECA Co.						
Covert,..........	1	8,000	7,000	7,042	10,300	10
Fayette,.........	1	3,500	6,500	4,500	12,500	15
Ovid,............	1	1,700	1,000	600	2,000	2
Seneca Falls,.....	1	21,000	25,000	42,500	100,000	85
Waterloo,........	1	2,000	2,600	2,295	8,500	5
STEUBEN Co.						
Addison,.........	1	2,000	8,000	14,000	25,000	17
Bath, ...	2	4,200	3,000	7,439	14,000	8
Corning,.........	2	17,000	23,500	100,830	190,000	130
Dansville,........	1	10,500	0,000	2,500	500	10
Erwin,...........	1	12,000	17,000	17,500	34,750	70
Hornellsville,.....	1	1,500	3,500	8,340	14,600	15
Urbana,..........	1	1,000	1,000	1,000	2,000	2
SUFFOLK Co.						
Southold,........	1	2,000	6,900	....	....	18

TOWNS.	Number of establishments.	Capital Invested. In real estate.	Capital Invested. In tools and machinery.	Cash Value. Of raw materials used.	Cash Value. Of manufactured articles.	Persons employed.
SULLIVAN Co.						
Thompson, ...	1	$800	....	$600	$2,000	2
TIOGA Co.						
Barton,..........	1	6,000	$2,000	....	....	4
Candor, ...	1	1,200	1,000	....	4,000	5
TOMPKINS Co.						
Groton,..........	3	4,800	3,700	4,400	8,200	7
Ithaca,..........	2	12,000	19,000	8,900	40,000	42
Lansing,.........	1	300	50	1,500	3,000	3
Ulysses, ...	3	6,500	7,000	6,750	17,000	20
ULSTER Co.						
Kingston,........	2	20,000	22,000	65,000	102,000	44
Marlborough, ...	1	3,200	500	4,000	10,400	9
Saugerties,.......	1	....	3,500	1,535	8,000	8
Wawarsing, ...	1	6,000	8,700	4,302	11,480	11
WASHINGTON Co.						
Granville,........	1	....	....	340	....	....
Kingsbury,.......	2	5,000	3,500	8,114	20,150	15
White Creek,.....	1	1,200	2,000	7,000	20,000	9
Whitehall,.......	1	3,000	5,000	7,000	15,000	18
WAYNE Co.						
Huron,..........	1	100	200	90	1,000	3
Marion,..........	1	2,000	1,500	1,000	2,800	5
Ontario, ...	1	200	200	585	1,600	2
Palmyra, ...	2	8,300	6,800	10,724	40,240	34
Savannah,........	1	1,000	1,200	....	....	4
Sodus, ...	2	3,000	3,000	1,948	3,000	13
Wolcott,.........	2	800	600	910	4,900	5
WESTCHESTER Co.						
Cortland,........	1	10,000	7,500	12,250	30,000	46
Ossining,.........	1	5,000	5,000	13,300	24,000	25
Rye,.............	1	10,000	10,000	32,500	125,000	90
West Farms,.....	1	....	30,000	32,000	60,000	67
Yonkers,.........	1	150,000	40,000	66,000	200,000	250
WYOMING Co.						
Attica,...........	1	600	....	300	1,000	1
Middlebury, ...	1	....	100	670	1,800	....
Perry,...........	2	3,000	4,700	1,781	10,000	7
Pike,............	1	1,000	2,000	390	1,000	4
Warsaw, ...	1	5,000	1,250	8,773	24,000	10
YATES Co.						
Jerusalem,.......	1	1,800	3,200	1,600	5,000	3
Milo, ...	1	3,000	6,000	7,000	15,500	16
Potter, ...	1	1,000	500	700	2,000	3
Starkey,.........	3	3,500	2,600	2,570	6,750	11

GAS FIXTURE MANUFACTORIES.

TOWNS.	Number of establishments.	In real estate.	In tools and machinery.	Of raw materials used.	Of manufactured articles.	Persons employed.
NEW-YORK Co.						
New-York,.......	13	152,500	122,300	473,683	834,300	450
ONEIDA Co.						
Utica, ...	1	....	1,400	10,310	30,000	10

GERMAN SILVER WARE MANUFACTORIES.

TOWNS.	Number of establishments.	In real estate.	In tools and machinery.	Of raw materials used.	Of manufactured articles.	Persons employed.
NEW-YORK Co.						
New-York,.......	1	....	....	12,900	56,000	10
QUEENS Co.						
Flushing,........	1	1,500	200	3,000	5,000	6

GILDING.

TOWNS.	Number of establishments.	In real estate.	In tools and machinery.	Of raw materials used.	Of manufactured articles.	Persons employed.
NEW-YORK Co.						
New-York,.......	7	5,000	5,450	30,000	59,000	69

GOLD LEAF AND FOIL MANUFACTORIES.

TOWNS.	Number of establishments.	In real estate.	In tools and machinery.	Of raw materials used.	Of manufactured articles.	Persons employed.
ERIE Co.						
Buffalo,.........	1	....	1,500	7,200	10,000	6
NEW-YORK Co.						
New-York,.......	7	7,000	10,100	89,560	129,225	88

GOLD AND SILVER PLATING.

TOWNS.	Number of establishments.	In real estate.	In tools and machinery.	Of raw materials used.	Of manufactured articles.	Persons employed.
NEW-YORK Co.						
New-York,.......	13	36,000	10,000	73,645	171,400	171

GOLD AND SILVER REFINING.

TOWNS.	Number of establishments.	In real estate.	In tools and machinery.	Of raw materials used.	Of manufactured articles.	Persons employed.
KINGS Co.						
Brooklyn,........	1	6,000	4,000	200,000	224,000	7
NEW-YORK Co.						
New-York,.......	6	106,000	19,500	1,895,000	1,966,000	73

HAMMER MANUFACTORIES.

TOWNS.	Number of establishments.	In real estate.	In tools and machinery.	Of raw materials used.	Of manufactured articles.	Persons employed.
HERKIMER Co.						
Little Falls,......	1	5,500	3,000	7,000	27,000	15
OTSEGO Co.						
Laurens,.........	1	2,000	300	450	10,000	20
New Lisbon,.....	1	....	....	2,088	10,000	....

CLASS II.—(CONTINUED.)

TOWNS.	Number of establishments.	Capital Invested. In real estate.	Capital Invested. In tools and machinery.	Cash Value. Of raw materials used.	Cash Value. Of manufactured articles.	Persons employed.
HAND IRON MANUFACTORY.						
NEW-YORK CO.						
New-York,	1	$4,500	$1,000	$3,692	$14,000	12
HARDWARE MANUFACTORIES.						
NEW-YORK CO.						
New-York,	1	....	300	60,000	80,000	5
RENSSELAER CO.						
Troy,	1	15,000	5,000	30,000	45,000	44
RICHMOND CO.						
Castleton,	1	500	100	300	1,400	4
HOLLOW WARE MANUFACTORIES.						
ALBANY CO.						
Albany,	1	15,000	10,000	52,500	105,000	75
Watervliet,	1	10,000	3,000	14,275	28,000	43
FRANKLIN CO.						
Malone,	1	....	....	....	1,000	....
SCHENECTADY CO.						
Schenectady,	1	1,200	1,200	9,095	15,000	19
IRON MANUFACTORIES.*						
CLINTON CO.						
Ausable,	4	205,000	27,725	265,400	842,000	1175
Black-Brook,	2	15,000	3,200	97,000	115,000	775
Dannemora,	2	65,000	65,000	100,232	82,020	45
Peru,	2	7,500	5,650	17.830	24,075	23
Plattsburgh,	3	31,000	1,400	37,200	95,000	43
Saranac,	3	4,800	2,000	29,000	62,000	40
Schuyler Falls,	3	11,000	450	33,507	48,895	26
COLUMBIA CO.						
Copake,	1	35,000	10,000	25,000	55,000	40
Hudson,	1	98,000	45,000	96,000	364,000	80
DUTCHESS CO.						
Amenia,	1	5,000	1,500	14,220	16,800	10
Beekman,	1	10,000	1,500	25,000	50,000	80
Dover,	2	17,000	4,500	30,224	39,325	26
East Fishkill,	1	14,000	1,000	14,900	21,000	18
Northeast,	2	17 000	2,000	50,200	79,800	26
Poughkeepsie city,	1	175,000	25,000	173,000	225,000	75
ESSEX CO.						
Crown Point,	1	20,000	2,000	14,000	25,000	30
Elizabethtown,	1	5,000	100	....	....	....
Essex,	1	10.000	200	19.583	30,195	....
Jay,	6	44,000	3,750	99,892	130,900	167
Keene,	1	1,000	600	5,700	8,750	12
Lewis,	2	10,000	900	24,900	55,000	86
Moriah,	1	50,000	2,000	38,000	114,000	60
Newcomb,	1	75,000	1,000	2,500	....	20
North Hudson,	2	25,000	8,000	24,400	42,650	61
Schroon,	1	50,000	8,000	31,875	75,000	20
Westport,	2	25,000	8,000	43,766	86,890	44
Willsborough,	3	14,700	2,280	44.700	62,900	157
Wilmington,	3	6,000	450	18,594	24,170	28
JEFFERSON CO.						
Antwerp,	1	1,000	600	17,817	43.230	13
Philadelphia,	1	2,000	100	18,722	56,662	13
LEWIS CO.						
Diana,	2	86,000	4,200	45,612	45,654	75
ONEIDA CO.						
Annsville,	1	3,000	2,000	10.000	60,000	15
Kirkland,	1	40,000	15,000	65,000	80,000	60
ORANGE CO.						
Monroe,	2	25,000	45,000	117,500	212,000	235
Warwick,	1	40,000	10,000	52,700	157,000	125
OSWEGO CO.						
Constantia,	1	7,000	3,000	27,000	50,000	25
RENSSELAER CO.						
Troy,	3	321,000	150,000	1,029,725	2,436,354	1203
ST. LAWRENCE CO.						
Brasher,	1	3,000	....	8,600	13,200	9
Fowler,	1	22,000	1,500	12,229	23,000	10
Rossie,	2	68,000	6,550	41,380	84,000	94
ULSTER CO.						
Saugerties,	1	25 000	25,000	258,500	360,000	250
Wawarsing,	1	20,000	500	5,500	25.000	15
WASHINGTON CO.						
Fort Ann,	1	....	....	10,975	59,500	28
Fort Edward,	1	55,000	....	....	....	20
WAYNE CO.						
Ontario,	2	9,000	6,500	22,985	61,600	26
Wolcott,	1	4,000	1,500	7,050	13,650	12
IRON PIPE MANUFACTORY.						
NEW-YORK CO.						
New-York,	7	19,000	59.500	186,000	290,000	204
IRON RAILING MANUFACTORIES, ETC.						
ALBANY CO.						
Albany,	1	....	$400	....	....	2
Watervliet,	1	$1,200	350	$3,684	$5,000	4
ERIE CO.						
Buffalo,	1	5,000	3,000	11,200	21,500	12
KINGS CO.						
Brooklyn,	11	79,500	29,050	95,580	345,000	286
MONROE CO.						
Rochester,	2	15,500	23,550	48,400	218,000	46
NEW-YORK CO.						
New-York,	13	167,300	120,900	205,430	807,900	597
ONONDAGA CO.						
Syracuse,	1	3,000	2,000	5,160	16.000	10
SARATOGA CO.						
Saratoga Springs,	1	500	200	500	1,000	1
JAPANED TIN MANUFACTORIES.						
ERIE CO.						
Buffalo,	1	4,000	1,500	5,000	3,000	30
NEW-YORK CO.						
New-York,	4	2,500	850	9,500	21,500	21
LEAD PIPE MANUFACTORIES.						
MONROE CO.						
Rochester,	1	100	1,000	4,500	5,500	2
NEW-YORK CO.						
New-York,	2	70,000	80,000	450,000	400,000	101
LIGHTNING ROD MANUFACTORIES.						
GENESEE CO.						
Le Roy,	1	....	....	960	4,200	6
NEW-YORK CO.						
New-York,	1	....	200	4,510	30,000	2
LOCK MANUFACTORIES.						
ALBANY CO.						
Albany,	1	....	1,500	300	2,000	1
DUTCHESS CO.						
Poughkeepsie city,	1	1,000	500	360	1,625	2
ERIE CO.						
Buffalo,	2	8,800	2,500	4,500	22,000	15
HERKIMER CO.						
Newport,	2	8,000	1,750	1,050	15,500	8
KINGS CO.						
Brooklyn,	1	4,000	500	3,000	3,000	9
MONROE CO.						
Rochester,	3	16,078	12,000	18,302	39,555	25
NEW-YORK CO.						
New-York,	9	34,500	12,450	27,070	88,900	103
WESTCHESTER CO.						
Rye,	1	1,000	500	3,200	4,000	4
MACHINE SHOPS.						
ALBANY CO.						
Albany,	1	1,600	....	1,200	2,000	4
Rensselaerville,	1	300	1,400	140	1,000	2
ALLEGANY CO.						
Angelica,	1	2,000	10,000	15,000	37,000	22
Hume,	1	1,000	1,500	2,450	6,000	9
BROOME CO.						
Chenango,	3	8,000	21,000	20,015	44,500	41
Colesville,	1	600	1,200	9,800	2,000	4
Maine,	1	500	500	....	1,000	1
CATTARAUGUS CO.						
Ellicottville,	1	1,200	1,800	920	2,500	3
CAYUGA CO.						
Auburn,	2	5,000	5,000	2,000	2,000	8
Cato,	1	400	1,400	700	1,300	5
CHAUTAUQUE CO.						
Ellicott,	2	5,500	4,000	3,825	10,770	8
Pomfret,	2	50,000	....	....	....	....
Westfield,	1	3,000	1,000	3,600	6,800	10
CHENANGO CO.						
Sherburne,	1	500	600	350	600	1
CLINTON CO.						
Dannemora,	1	2,000	6,000	25,000	50,000	20
Schuyler Falls,	1	500	1,000	200	1,200	2
COLUMBIA CO.						
Claverack,	1	5,750	3,900	4,500	16,000	16
Hillsdale,	1	1,000	800	500	600	2
CORTLAND CO.						
Cincinnatus,	1	1,200	800	4,850	7,000	4
DELAWARE CO.						
Harpersfield,	1	400	400	234	536	1
Kortright,	1	100	150	150	350	1

* Generally the manufacture of iron from the ore. A few other establishments of a general and miscellaneous class, for the manfacture of iron, thus reported.

CLASS II.—(Continued.)

TOWNS.	Number of establishments.	Capital Invested. In real estate.	Capital Invested. In tools and machinery.	Cash Value. Of raw materials used.	Cash Value. Of manufactured articles.	Persons employed.
Dutchess Co.						
Fishkill, ...	1	$300	$300	$244	$750	2
Poughkeepsie city,	1	....	5,000	6,000	14,000	10
Washington, ...	1	1,500	1,000	200	500	1
Erie Co.						
Buffalo, ...	3	1,200	3,000	1,078	37,250	8
Essex Co.						
Chesterfield, ...	1	15,000	10,000	....	20,000	20
Franklin Co.						
Malone, ...	1	....	....	....	13,000	....
Genesee Co.						
Batavia, ...	1	8,000	9,000	20,000	40,000	30
Greene Co.						
Catskill, ...	1	10,000	8,000	5,595	15,000	16
Durham, ...	1	1,000	250	4,774	7,500	8
Herkimer Co.						
German Flats, ...	2	600	1,100	2,000	4.000	3
Stark, ...	2	2,400	3,900	12,200	17,780	6
Warren, ...	1	2,500	400	400	1,000	2
Jefferson Co.						
Adams, ...	2	3,200	2,300	2,231	9,845	6
Philadelphia, ...	1	1,500	500	500	700	2
Rutland, ...	1	1,500	1,000	1,370	4,788	4
Wilna, ...	2	....	600	300	1,800	3
Kings Co.						
Brooklyn, ...	11	69,300	78,650	96,207	276,000	260
Livingston Co.						
Lima, ...	1	1,000	700	....	....	....
Madison Co.						
Cazenovia, ...	1	....	1,000	250	1,300	3
Eaton, ...	2	3,000	4,000	9,825	19,500	18
Lenox, ...	1	8,000	10,000	7,559	37,400	78
Monroe Co.						
Riga, ...	1	2,000	750	2,420	6,325	12
Rochester, ...	10	130,000	146,216	361,960	594,212	703
New-York Co.						
New-York, ...	36	463,350	243,900	384,659	882,490	1120
Niagara Co.						
Lockport, ...	3	24,000	20,500	21,500	52,000	53
Wilson, ...	1	1,600	300	642	2,293	8
Oneida Co.						
New Hartford, ...	1	9,000	18,000	10,000	23,000	65
Paris, ...	2	400	1,150	1,600	3,800	5
Rome, ...	1	....	6,510	4,950	16,800	15
Sangersfield, ...	1	....	200	500	1 210	2
Utica, ...	2	5,000	13,500	4,800	27,000	33
Onondaga Co.						
Manlius, ...	1	2,500	2,000	6,000	9,000	6
Skaneateles, ...	1	....	2,500	1,300	6,000	4
Syracuse, ...	7	165,500	82,000	151,165	313,000	320
Ontario Co.						
Canandaigua, ...	1	3,000	2,000	5,228	7,721	3
Seneca, ...	2	11,400	3,500	8,120	30,000	40
Orange Co.						
Deerpark, ...	1	....	....	2,100	80,000	25
New Windsor, ...	1	....	10.000	2,084	18,000	22
Walkill, ...	1	8,000	6,000	18,200	28,700	38
Orleans Co.						
Clarendon, ...	1	700	300	1,000	2,900	3
Kendall, ...	1	1,600	200	100	400	2
Oswego Co.						
Oswego city, ...	2	4,000	4,000	5,975	2,800	28
Sandy Creek, ...	1	1,000	200	1,350	2,160	4
Volney, ...	1	2,000	3,000	80	3,000	3
Otsego Co.						
Middlefield, ...	1	600	200	240	2,500	2
Otsego, ...	2	1,500	2,800	3,850	15,860	17
Springville, ...	1	5,000	5,000	13,880	26,000	28
Unadilla, ...	1	3,500	3,000	1,700	10,000	9
Rensselaer Co.						
Schaghticoke, ...	1	4,000	150	....	125	....
Schodack, ...	....	....	....	....	....	....
Troy, ...	5	28,000	25,300	61,700	125,359	65
Rockland Co.						
Haverstraw, ...	1	8,000	2,500	9,400	8,500	17
Ramapo, ...	3	3,000	8,000	13,130	20,720	19
St. Lawrence Co.						
Brasher, ...	2	6,500	3.550	5,369	15,369	16
Edwards, ...	1	1,000	2,000	....	....	....
Oswegatchie, ...	1	8,000	5,000	8,000	14,000	10
Saratoga Co.						
Moreau, ...	1	....	1,500	3,600	6,500	3
Waterford, ...	4	16,000	31,000	40,800	114,000	88
Schenectady Co.						
Schenectady, ...	3	14,000	8,100	26,219	41,900	49
Schoharie Co.						
Carlisle, ...	1	400	300	1,300	4,300	6
Schoharie, ...	1	1,200	1,800	4,600	10,000	10
Schuyler Co.						
Hector, ...	1	2,000	1,500	1,800	3,500	8
Seneca Co.						
Varick, ...	1	$100	$100	$147	$610	1
Tioga Co.						
Owego, ...	1	5,000	2,000	4,320	10,500	7
Tompkins Co.						
Dryden, ...	1	2,000	5,000	1,030	12,000	9
Ulster Co.						
Wawarsing, ...	1	6,000	2,500	2,400	8,000	7
Warren Co.						
Queensbury, ...	1	10,000	4,000	9,500	18,000	15
Washington Co.						
Fort Edward, ...	1	7,000	20,000	6,050	20,000	25
Kingsbury, ...	2	3,000	4,500	11,400	19,200	13
White Creek, ...	1	250	500	500	1,200	2
Wayne Co.						
Arcadia, ...	1	7,000	8,000	6,736	17,758	20
Lyons, ...	1	5,000	5,000	9,750	20,000	25
Westchester Co.						
West Farms, ...	1	15,000	35,000	....	....	....
White Plains, ...	1	15,000	1,100	17,500	36,800	33
Wyoming Co.						
Bennington, ...	1	800	500	552	1,200	3
China, ...	1	2,000	1,000	4,000	....	4

MACHINISTS' TOOL MANUFACTORIES.

TOWNS.	Number of establishments.	In real estate.	In tools and machinery.	Of raw materials used.	Of manufactured articles.	Persons employed.
Monroe Co.						
Rochester, ...	4	25,000	43,000	11,839	79,375	66
New-York Co.						
New-York, ...	1	10,000	7,000	7,500	8,000	10
Rensselaer Co.						
Stephentown, ...	1	500	600	125	....	4

MALLEABLE IRON WORKS.

TOWNS.	Number of establishments.	In real estate.	In tools and machinery.	Of raw materials used.	Of manufactured articles.	Persons employed.
Albany Co.						
Watervliet, ...	1	3,000	2,200	4,500	12,600	10
Greene Co.						
Durham, ...	1	2,500	500	7,850	20,000	26
New-York Co.						
New-York, ...	1	....	2,500	27,000	100,000	50
Oneida Co.						
Westmoreland, ...	1	....	5,100	9,000	20,000	32
Rensselaer Co.						
Troy, ...	1	5,000	5,000	11,000	18,000	20

METALLIC BURIAL CASE MANUFACTORY.

TOWNS.	Number of establishments.	In real estate.	In tools and machinery.	Of raw materials used.	Of manufactured articles.	Persons employed.
Queens Co.						
Newtown, ...	1	7,000	3,500	22,350	80,000	50

METALLIC LIFE BOAT MANUFACTORY.

TOWNS.	Number of establishments.	In real estate.	In tools and machinery.	Of raw materials used.	Of manufactured articles.	Persons employed.
Kings Co.						
Brooklyn, ...	1	55,000	44,200	30,000	80,000	60

PIN MANUFACTORIES.

TOWNS.	Number of establishments.	In real estate.	In tools and machinery.	Of raw materials used.	Of manufactured articles.	Persons employed.
Albany Co.						
Albany, ...	1	....	10,000	560	1,250	9
Dutchess Co.						
Poughkeepsie city,	1	....	....	....	....	....

PLUMBING ESTABLISHMENTS.

TOWNS.	Number of establishments.	In real estate.	In tools and machinery.	Of raw materials used.	Of manufactured articles.	Persons employed.
Albany Co.						
Albany, ...	2	....	5,500	23,000	43,000	23
Erie Co.						
Buffalo, ...	1	10,000	2,000	16,100	25,000	30
Kings Co.						
Brooklyn, ...	3	20,000	900	23,560	31,700	14
New-York Co.						
New-York, ...	22	147,100	11,475	407,095	394,450	235
Queens Co.						
Flushing, ...	1	3,333	325	4,200	7,000	5
Rensselaer Co.						
Troy, ...	1	5,000	7,000	12,000	50,000	30

ROLLING MILL AND NAIL FACTORIES.

TOWNS.	Number of establishments.	In real estate.	In tools and machinery.	Of raw materials used.	Of manufactured articles.	Persons employed.
Essex Co.						
Essex, ...	1	25,000	10,000	75,000	117,000	70
Jay, ...	1	....	....	181,000	267,000	....
Westchester Co.						
Yorktown, ...	1	1.500	5,000	36,840	84,864	23

SAFE MANUFACTORIES.

TOWNS.	Number of establishments.	In real estate.	In tools and machinery.	Of raw materials used.	Of manufactured articles.	Persons employed.
Albany Co.						
Albany	1	15,000	10,000	43,000	200,000	80
Herkimer Co.						
German Flats, ...	1	....	5,000	2,400	10,000	17
Kings Co.						
Brooklyn, ...	2	6,000	21,000	22.960	115,000	60

CLASS II.—(Continued.)

TOWNS.	Number of establishments.	Capital Invested.		Cash Value.		Persons employed.
		In real estate.	In tools and machinery.	Of raw materials used.	Of manufactured articles.	
New York Co.						
New-York, ...	5	$77,000	$57,500	$172,350	$566,000	298
Oneida Co.						
Utica, ...	1	2,750	3,659	7,000	17,031	17
Rensselaer Co.						
Troy, ...	1	15,000	14,000	41,475	168,650	56

SCREW FACTORY.

TOWNS.	Number of establishments.	In real estate.	In tools and machinery.	Of raw materials used.	Of manufactured articles.	Persons employed.
Oneida Co.						
Utica, ...	1	7,000	4,500	10,500	79,950	66

SILVER WARE MANUFACTORIES, &c.

TOWNS.	Number of establishments.	In real estate.	In tools and machinery.	Of raw materials used.	Of manufactured articles.	Persons employed.
Albany Co.						
Albany, ...	6	9,000	9,150	93,500	210,000	49
Allegany Co.						
Rushford, ...	1	300	200	75	900	2
Cayuga Co.						
Brutus, ...	1	....	1,200	....	600	1
Mentz, ...	2	....	1,500	....	....	....
Chautauque Co.						
Pomfret, ...	1	3,000	150	150	1,250	2
Columbia Co.						
Kinderhook, ...	2	700	250	575	1,100	2
Cortland Co.						
Virgil, ...	1	50	50	40	365	1
Dutchess Co.						
Poughkeepsie city, .	4	7,800	2,280	19,360	28,000	13
Rhinebeck, ...	1	200	200	100	500	....
Erie Co.						
Buffalo, ...	2	200	1,600	10,000	15,000	7
Jefferson Co.						
Adams, ...	1	1,000	350	150	900	1
Kings Co.						
Brooklyn, ...	2	4,000	1,930	33,200	54,000	12
Monroe Co.						
Rochester, ...	2	180	700	5,709	9,470	7
New-York Co.						
New-York, ...	83	441,500	271,240	2,111,369	3,809,331	1558
Oneida Co.						
Utica, ...	3	....	1,850	47,730	38,845	42
Whitestown, ...	1	250	100	100	800	1
Onondaga Co.						
Syracuse, ...	3	4,700	5,600	33,862	47,000	27
Orange Co.						
Hamptonburgh, ...	1	1,000	1,500	5,000	8,000	8
Monroe, ...	3	....	260	1,775	3,000	2
Otsego Co.						
Oneonta, ...	1	300	150	....	....	....
Richfield, ...	1	200	75	75	500	2
Queens Co.						
Hempstead, ...	1	....	2,000	2,000	2,400	2
Newtown, ...	1	....	100	....	....	....
Rensselaer Co.						
Troy, ...	2	3,700	1,800	29,500	43,000	9
Rockland Co.						
Clarkstown, ...	1	300	500	10,000	15,000	10
St. Lawrence Co.						
Madrid, ...	1	....	100	200	1,000	1
Oswegatchie, ...	1	7,000	200	500	1,200	3
Seneca Co.						
Seneca Falls, ...	1	200	400	5,000	6,000	2
Steuben Co.						
Bath, ...	2	1,200	400	700	2,300	3
Fremont, ...	1	100	25	150	500	1
Suffolk Co.						
Southold, ...	1	800	100	50	300	....
Tioga Co.						
Barton, ...	2	....	270	200	....	1
Owego, ...	1	....	250	12,000	17,000	6
Tompkins Co.						
Dryden, ...	1	100	50	400	700	1
Ithaca, ...	2	6,300	650	....	4,000	4
Wayne Co.						
Arcadia, ...	1	500	800	300	600	1
Sodus, ...	1	....	25	....	500	1
Westchester Co.						
Eastchester, ...	1	500	100	24,000	28,000	3

SPIKE MANUFACTORY.

TOWNS.	Number of establishments.	In real estate.	In tools and machinery.	Of raw materials used.	Of manufactured articles.	Persons employed.
New-York Co.						
New-York, ...	2	7,000	350	16,720	21,300	9

STEEL SPRING MANUFACTORIES.

TOWNS.	Number of establishments.	In real estate.	In tools and machinery.	Of raw materials used.	Of manufactured articles.	Persons employed.
Rensselaer Co.						
Troy city, ...	1	8,000	4,000	36,000	50,000	30
Seneca Co.						
Seneca Falls, ...	2	2,000	200	3,298	6,000	2

THIMBLE MANUFACTORIES, (GOLD AND SILVER.)

TOWNS.	Number of establishments.	Capital Invested.		Cash Value.		Persons employed.
		In real estate.	In tools and machinery.	Of raw materials used.	Of manufactured articles.	
New-York Co.						
New-York, ...	3	....	$2,350	$44,500	$58,500	16
Suffolk Co.						
Huntington, ...	2	$1,800	1,300	12,000	17,500	11

TIN AND SHEET IRON MANUFACTORIES.

TOWNS.	Number of establishments.	In real estate.	In tools and machinery.	Of raw materials used.	Of manufactured articles.	Persons employed.
Albany Co.						
Albany, ...	3	....	1,350	27,000	65,000	19
Watervliet, ...	2	3,500	1,000	9,436	16,000	11
Westerlo, ...	1	300	150	650	1,500	1
Allegany Co.						
Almond, ...	1	800	200	2,742	5,000	7
Angelica, ...	2	1,600	500	2,358	660	3
Belfast, ...	1	....	250	900	2,200	1
Cuba, ...	1	600	200	500	1,100	1
Friendship, ...	2	1,200	375	300	2,200	3
Rushford, ...	1	700	300	1,200	15,000	1
Broome Co.						
Chenango, ...	4	13,000	4,000	15,645	39,675	25
Colesville, ...	1	....	....	1,500	2,800	2
Sandford, ...	2	2,800	325	1,700	3,700	3
Windsor, ...	1	300	250	500	1,500	1
Cattaraugus Co.						
Allegany, ...	1	500	180	400	500	2
Mansfield, ...	1	250	....	600	....	1
Olean, ...	2	3,300	600	407	5,300	4
Otto, ...	1	300	100	1,500	2,500	....
Perrysburgh, ...	1	....	300	1,600	1,400	1
Cayuga Co.						
Auburn, ...	4	2,000	1,250	4,825	13,400	18
Cato, ...	1	1,000	300	1,600	2,800	2
Genoa, ...	1	2,300	200	2,000	3,000	3
Ledyard, ...	1	500	150	323	430	....
Moravia, ...	1	500	300	1,000	1,500	2
Chautauque Co.						
Chautauque, ...	1	500	425	800	2,000	3
Cherry Creek, ...	1	75	150	328	800	1
Clymer, ...	1	....	200	800	1,500	2
Ellington, ...	1	1,000	400	1,500	4,500	1
Hanover, ...	1	....	150	400	1,500	1
Pomfret, ...	5	10,500	3,550	11,781	20,109	12
Westfield, ...	1	2,500	325	2,190	7,500	8
Chemung Co.						
Chemung, ...	1	700	125	50	600	1
Elmira, ...	7	31,600	2,050	13,408	26,640	24
Vanetten, ...	1	700	300	1,100	2,200	3
Veteran, ...	1	400	150	500	1,000	1
Chenango Co.						
New Berlin, ...	2	1,400	500	1,795	3,570	3
Otselic, ...	1	700	225	300	500	1
Oxford, ...	1	1,500	1,100	4,000	6,000	5
Sherburne, ...	2	900	350	1,577	4,600	4
Smithville, ...	1	250	300	1,000	2,000	3
Clinton Co.						
Ausable, ...	1	....	300	100	2,200	3
Champlain, ...	2	1,000	150	400	1,000	1
Plattsburgh, ...	2	....	500	2,910	4,212	5
Columbia Co.						
Chatham, ...	1	....	4,000	2,000	3,000	1
Hillsdale, ...	1	500	250	1,000	1,600	3
Hudson city, ...	6	12,100	1,475	10,600	19,100	12
Kinderhook, ...	3	1,400	4,580	930	7,050	17
New Lebanon, ...	1	400	300	500	1,200	2
Cortland Co.						
Cincinnatus, ...	1	....	250	600	1,800	2
Cortlandville, ...	2	800	250	1,078	3,200	2
Homer, ...	1	1,400	400	1,600	3,000	1
Scott, ...	1	500	200	700	1,500	2
Truxton, ...	1	500	100	500	800	1
Delaware Co.						
Bovina, ...	1	350	200	482	990	1
Franklin, ...	1	700	450	360	2,300	2
Middletown, ...	1	275	200	600	1,200	2
Roxbury, ...	1	1,300	150	2,200	3,200	2
Walton, ...	1	700	150	698	1,200	....
Dutchess Co.						
Fishkill, ...	4	1,600	1,797	6,274	12,745	9
Hyde Park, ...	1	200	....	500	1,800	2
Poughkeepsie, ...	1	1,200	200	....	600	1
Poughkeepsie city,	7	28,500	2,425	51,480	77,641	6
Red Hook, ...	4	4,650	1,000	18,750	27,500	16
Rhinebeck, ...	1	500	500	1,200	2,400	4
Erie Co.						
Aurora, ...	1	600	200	400	600	2
Buffalo, ...	6	10,500	3,880	26,750	50,850	71
East Hamburgh, ..	1	200	200	400	700	1
Eden	1	....	50	175	400	....

CLASS II.—(CONTINUED.)

TOWNS.	Number of establishments.	Capital Invested. In real estate.	Capital Invested. In tools and machinery.	Cash Value. Of raw materials used.	Cash Value. Of manufactured articles.	Persons employed.
ERIE Co.						
Evans,	1	....	$300	$835	$1,400	....
Holland,	1	....	175	400	800	1
Tonawanda,	2	$5,400	600	2,200	4,000	4
ESSEX Co.						
Chesterfield,	1	....	3,000	3,000	5,000	2
Elizabethtown,	1	100	182	550	1,000	1
Westport,	1	800	300	400	1,000	2
FRANKLIN Co.						
Fort Covington,	2	....	450	3,948	11,000	3
Malone,	3	5,500	800	2,895	4,600	8
FULTON Co.						
Northampton,	1	600	250	540	1,000	1
GENESEE Co.						
Alexander,	1	300	250	875	1,750	1
Batavia,	1	1,000	500	1,725	3,000	3
Bergen,	1	....	....	....	....	....
Le Roy,	2	....	....	6,500	14,000	7
GREENE Co.						
Coxsackie,	1	1,100	....	200	1,120	3
Durham,	1	200	150	1,400	3,000	2
Greenville,	1	750	100	1,350	2,500	2
New Baltimore,	1	200	400	2,850	3,550	2
HERKIMER Co.						
Frankfort,	1	250	200	550	4,000	1
German Flats,	3	1,000	500	5,096	18,640	4
Little Falls,	3	3,200	925	4,450	8,200	8
Newport,	1	450	250	800	1,600	2
JEFFERSON Co.						
Adams,	2	2,400	650	2,998	8,150	7
Alexandria,	1	50	375	400	800	1
Antwerp,	1	400	200	600	2,000	1
Ellisburgh,	2	2,850	700	2,480	4,090	4
Henderson,	1	750	150	765	1,360	1
Hounsfield,	1	4,000	250	600	1,500	1
Le Ray,	1	500	150	1,500	2,500	2
Orleans,	1	200	200	600	1,000	1
Philadelphia,	1	100	150	1,000	1,300	1
Watertown,	5	17,800	3,000	23,549	40,290	14
Wilna,	3	600	525	3,408	5,800	3
KINGS Co.						
Brooklyn,	4	21,000	12,150	63,081	149,200	95
New Lots,	1	600	200	1,700	3,400	2
LEWIS Co.						
Denmark,	1	450	150	600	1,500	1
Lowville,	2	2,000	400	2,529	4,975	6
Turin,	1	700	200	500	1,200	1
LIVINGSTON Co.						
Livonia,	1	500	300	747	2,000	1
Mt. Morris,	1	500	250	3,468	5,000	4
Nunda,	1	300	250	1,000	1,835	1
North Dansville,	1	....	300	1,600	3,000	3
York,	2	300	350	1,569	3,300	2
MADISON Co.						
Cazenovia,	1	1,600	300	6,000	7,000	3
De Ruyter,	1	500	150	900	1,600	1
Eaton,	1	800	225	1,539	1,660	2
Georgetown,	1	1,130	200	820	2,000	1
Hamilton,	1	1,500	400	2,470	4,200	2
Lenox,	2	1,500	400	2,648	5,630	9
Madison,	1	800	200	660	3,700	4
Stockbridge,	1	300	175	1,014	1,875	2
Sullivan,	1	500	100	799	1,222	....
MONROE Co.						
Mendon,	1	600	175	850	1,650	2
Penfield,	1	500	600	1,500	....	3
Perrington,	1	900	300	2,500	5,800	3
Riga,	1	450	250	650	704	2
Rochester,	5	2,300	1,450	22,652	38,550	25
Sweden,	2	....	550	5,630	6,950	4
Webster,	1	700	230	600	900	1
MONTGOMERY Co.						
Amsterdam,	3	5,600	1,070	7,235	10,475	7
Glen,	2	800	200	2,300	2,600	4
Minden,	2	2,500	600	4,000	8,000	4
NEW-YORK Co.						
New-York,	54	141,100	89,030	412,330	953,800	3633
NIAGARA Co.						
Lockport,	1	1,200	450	2,600	6,000	4
Niagara,	3	9,500	1,300	14,000	23,000	13
Wilson,	1	....	200	1,000	2,000	1
ONEIDA Co.						
Boonville,	2	2,400	500	1,712	4,000	5
Camden,	1	1,000	300	2,000	4,000	2
Kirkland,	1	....	300	2,600	3,900	4
Lee,	1	300	150	495	1,000	1
Remsen,	1	2,500	250	200	....	1
Rome,	2	4,000	600	4,452	7,597	11
Sangerfield,	1	500	600	5,000	10,000	5
ONEIDA Co.						
Trenton,	2	$800	$350	$926	$2,391	....
Utica,	5	24,000	3,475	71,592	110,990	46
Vernon,	1	700	200	1,300	2,000	2
Verona,	1	500	200	1,200	2,400	2
Western,	1	1,000	100	1,130	800	3
Whitestown,	2	3,800	550	2,526	10,500	8
ONONDAGA Co.						
Elbridge,	1	2,000	500	500	1,000	1
Fabius,	1	400	250	1,000	1,600	1
Lysander,	1	1,500	250	2,300	3,300	3
Manlius,	2	1,100	475	1,912	3,600	6
Marcellus,	1	600	300	1,000	2,000	4
Onondaga,	1	350	300	400	800	1
Skaneateles,	1	....	300	1,450	2,450	2
Spafford,	1	500	150	1,328	2,600	3
Syracuse,	7	....	3,050	40,500	66,000	23
Tully,	1	....	250	400	850	2
ONTARIO Co.						
Canandaigua,	5	5,100	1,900	6,400	17,400	12
East Bloomfield,	2	450	250	1,625	3,750	4
Naples,	2	700	425	978	1,200	2
Seneca,	3	18,500	1,050	4,100	7,000	5
Victor,	1	....	500	685	....	1
ORANGE Co.						
Blooming Grove,	1	....	450	4,000	5,500	3
Deerpark,	2	3,500	700	1,935	3,750	5
Goshen,	2	6,000	550	12,000	7,500	13
Monroe,	1	300	300	1,200	1,400	2
Walkill,	2	1,800	650	12,500	24,500	13
Warwick,	1	....	....	1,200	2,000	2
ORLEANS Co.						
Barre,	2	4,500	600	4,000	8,000	7
Ridgeway,	3	2,700	400	1,675	3,700	5
Yates,	1	450	350	570	1,000	1
OSWEGO Co.						
Hannibal,	1	....	300	750	1,400	1
Mexico,	2	1,800	400	3,200	5,000	6
Oswego city,	4	24,700	2,071	12,300	24,810	3
Volney,	3	250	....	3,800	7,600	7
OTSEGO Co.						
Laurens,	1	1,200	150	700	1,500	2
Maryland,	1	500	80	595	1,040	2
Middlefield,	1	350	250	1,500	2,500	1
Milford,	1	200	200	873	3,000	1
Morris,	1	1,360	300	1,300	2,400	6
Oneonta,	1	80	180	1,070	1,500	2
Plainfield,	1	400	300	1,200	1,600	....
Richfield,	1	600	300	2,000	3,000	2
Roseboom,	1	400	200	2,000	2,500	1
Springfield,	1	1,500	200	1,200	2,400	2
PUTNAM Co.						
Patterson,	1	500	300	1,670	2,500	3
Phillipstown,	1	4,000	800	3,919	8,000	9
QUEENS Co.						
Flushing,	2	23,000	21,500	82,900	175,000	131
Hempstead,	2	3,000	475	3,100	5,500	6
Jamaica,	2	....	450	....	5,300	6
North Hempstead,	2	3,700	600	4,220	6,400	8
Oyster Bay,	1	3,000	600	4,000	12,000	10
RENSSELAER Co.						
Hoosick,	1	1,500	500	1,000	2,200	3
Lansingburgh,	5	1,500	900	8,162	18,200	14
Troy,	7	15,500	5,200	29,327	47,765	27
RICHMOND Co.						
Westfield,	2	500	600	2,119	6,000	2
ROCKLAND Co.						
Orangetown,	1	3,000	400	5,550	9,600	5
ST. LAWRENCE Co.						
Canton,	1	....	300	1,000	1,500	2
Gouverneur,	1	1,000	450	2,333	3,500	3
Hermon,	1	300	461	1,848	2,848	3
Hopkinton,	1	150	225	100	500	1
Lawrence,	1	800	100	1,000	1,800	....
Madrid,	1	400	200	860	1,350	2
Oswegatchie,	4	13,500	1.250	15,500	23,500	22
Potsdam,	3	4,500	900	5,000	9,400	8
Russell,	1	....	100	100	1,800	....
SARATOGA Co.						
Saratoga,	2	1,500	575	3,400	7,000	6
Saratoga Springs,	3	5,000	1,400	30,200	45,900	13
Waterford,	1	600	500	500	2,500	2
SCHENECTADY Co.						
Schenectady,	2	1,500	1,400	55,000	67,320	29
SCHOHARIE Co.						
Esperance,	1	1,500	200	1,600	3,200	5
Gilboa,	1	400	150	300	800	....
Schoharie,	1	1,500	175	1,500	2,500	2
Sharon,	1	350	20	1,000	2,000	2

CLASS II.—(CONTINUED.)

TOWNS.	Number of establishments.	Capital Invested: In real estate.	Capital Invested: In tools and machinery.	Cash Value: Of raw materials used.	Cash Value: Of manufactured articles.	Persons employed.
SCHOHARIE Co.						
Wright, ...	1	$200	$150	$300	$800	1
SENECA Co.						
Ovid, ...	1	600	200	2,200	....	1
Waterloo, ...	4	10,000	1,080	16,013	21,113	11
STEUBEN Co.						
Bath, ...	4	650	650	5,456	10,820	8
Canisteo, ...	1	500	150	8	1,000	2
Erwin, ...	1	....	300	2,000	3,000	2
Hornellsville, ...	1	3,000	500	4,437	8,514	5
SUFFOLK Co.						
Huntington, ...	2	....	305	2,800	3,550	7
Riverhead, ...	1	2,000	300	4,000	6,000	5
Southampton, ...	1	....	300	800	1,600	3
Southold, ...	1	1,250	400	3,070	4,050	3
SULLIVAN Co.						
Fallsburgh, ...	1	....	400	3,000	7,200	3
Mamakating, ...	2	200	300	765	1,500	4
TIOGA Co.						
Barton, ...	1	3,000	250	120	....	1
Nichols, ...	1	500	300	750	1,250	1
Spencer, ...	1	800	250	1,500	1,800	2
TOMPKINS Co.						
Ithaca, ...	1	6,000	1,500	1,600	18,000	10
Lansing, ...	1	....	200	....	1,200	1
ULSTER Co.						
Marbletown, ...	1	80	150	670	2,270	1
Marlborough, ...	1	....	200	60	600	2
Saugerties, ...	2	1,500	2,000	7,000	16,500	10
Wawarsing, ...	1	1,000	250	826	2,746	1
WARREN Co.						
Queensbury, ...	1	1,200	200	1,430	3,425	2
Warrensburgh, ...	1	600	....	1,000	2,000	2
WASHINGTON Co.						
Argyle, ...	1	400	225	335	600	1
Fort Ann, ...	1	....	300	314	600	1
Granville, ...	1	1,500	350	1,600	7,850	7
Greenwich, ...	1	1,200	250	1,200	2,800	2
WAYNE Co.						
Arcadia, ...	2	1,800	450	2,685	4,770	4
Lyons, ...	2	500	325	2,380	5,400	2
Marion, ...	1	200	200	350	700	2
Palmyra, ...	3	....	1,20[illegible]	8,198	14,188	12
Sodus, ...	1	600	20[illegible]	1,500	3,000	2
Williamson, ...	1	500	25[illegible]	2,050	3,000	2
Wolcott, ...	1	500	200	100	1,000	....
WESTCHESTER Co.						
Bedford, ...	1	300	30[illegible]	620	2,120	1
Eastchester, ...	2	700	600	3,829	6,500	3
Greenburgh, ...	1	....	300	1,708	3,500	3
Lewisboro', ...	1	1,000	350	1,000	1,500	1
North Salem, ...	1	....	300	6,000	8,000	5
Ossining, ...	2	3,000	450	7,350	12,600	6
Rye, ...	2	3,000	1,200	3,500	6,000	6
WYOMING Co.						
Attica, ...	1	$1,000	$300	$830	$1,750	2
Bennington, ...	1	350	200	1,500	2,500	2
Castile, ...	1	2,500	500	2,555	3,366	3
Genesee Falls, ...	1	100	125	650	1,500	1
Middlebury, ...	2	250	290	850	1,500	2
Pike, ...	1	1,000	200	1,200	2,000	2
Warsaw, ...	1	....	250	5,390	10,000	3
YATES Co.						
Jerusalem, ...	1	1,000	250	700	1,200	1
Milo, ...	2	....	300	6,000	....	4
Starkey, ...	1	500	600	1,865	1,290	1
Torrey, ...	1	200	300	400	600	1
TIN FOIL MANUFACTORY.						
NEW-YORK Co.						
New-York, ...	1	5,000	8,000	40,000	50,000	12
TRIP HAMMERS.						
ST. LAWRENCE Co.						
Louisville, ...	2	300	300	350	1,000	2
WIRE WORKS.						
ERIE Co.						
West Seneca, ...	1	....	1,500	200	260	16
NEW-YORK Co.						
New-York, ...	9	....	21,250	101,800	195,500	130
OTSEGO Co.						
Edmeston, ...	1	200	150	800	1,600	2
PUTNAM Co.						
Putnam Valley, ..	1	5,000	3,000	16,000	23,000	9
ULSTER Co.						
Kingston, ...	1	3,000	3,600	2,000	11,500	27
WESTCHESTER Co.						
Cortland, ...	2	7,000	3,500	43,000	109,000	22
Yorktown, ...	1	500	1,000	85	200	6
WIRE RAILING MANUFACTORY.						
NEW-YORK Co.						
New-York, ...	1	14,000	5,000	30,000	125,000	29
WIRE SEIVE MANUFACTORIES.						
KINGS Co.						
Brooklyn, ...	2	6,500	4,300	11,250	23,000	16
ONONDAGA Co.						
Van Buren, ...	1	100	150	700	1,800	5
RENSSELAER Co.						
Troy, ...	1	5,000	1,500	5,000	12,000	8
WAYNE Co.						
Lyons, ...	2	1,700	500	1,861	8,673	3

CLASS III.—MANUFACTURES OF FIBROUS AND TEXTILE SUBSTANCES.

TOWNS.	Number of establishments.	Capital Invested: In real estate.	Capital Invested: In tools and machinery.	Cash Value: Of raw materials used.	Cash Value: Of manufactured articles.	Persons employed.
WNING MANUFACTORY.						
NEW-YORK Co.						
New-York, ...	3	17,000	40	4,000	15,000	20
CARD BOARD MANUFACTORY.						
NEW-YORK Co.						
New-York, ...	2	....	70,000	57,500	120,000	134
CARDING AND CLOTH-DRESSING ESTABLISHMENTS.						
ALBANY Co.						
Berne, ...	1	800	500	4,300	5,150	2
Guilderland, ...	2	6,500	300	2,450	2,920	14
Westerlo, ...	1	1,000	1,500	1,170	1,000	3
ALLEGANY Co.						
Almond, ...	1	....	....	1,820	2,145	....
Andover, ...	1	1,000	500	120	100	1
BROOME Co.						
Colesville, ...	2	100	....	600	600	1
Lisle, ...	2	1,000	1,000	....	....	....
CATTARAUGUS Co.						
Franklinville, ...	1	150	600	3,040	3,500	1
Freedom, ...	1	300	100	1,800	1,800	1
Randolph, ...	1	300	300	....	600	....
CAYUGA Co.						
Brutus, ...	1	800	2,000	....	1,000	3
Locke, ...	1	150	250	....	....	....
Venice, ...	1	500	500	100	....	....
CHAUTAUQUE Co.						
Ellicott, ...	1	1,000	800	....	800	2
Pomfret, ...	1	1,000	800	2,700	4,050	....
Westfield, ...	1	4,000	100	8,000	12,000	21
CHENANGO Co.						
Bainbridge, ...	3	700	1,400	1,950	3,500	4
Otselic, ...	1	1,000	600	3,822	4,750	2
Pitcher, ...	1	....	....	3,250	3,450	....
Preston, ...	1	400	50	....	....	1
Smithville, ...	2	2,000	600	....	1,200	3
CLINTON Co.						
Champlain, ...	2	3,000	200	4,600	5,122	5
Schuyler Falls, ...	1	2,000	500	4,239	33,915	2
COLUMBIA Co.						
Austerlitz, ...	1	150	50	4,000	4,400	1
DELAWARE Co.						
Bovina, ...	2	30	200	3,812	4,754	4
Harpersfield, ...	1	600	400	1,710	2,680	2
Meredith, ...	1	400	300	950	1,150	2
Middletown, ...	1	200	800	10,000	11,000	3
DUTCHESS Co.						
Stanford, ...	1	500	....	....	....	....
ERIE Co.						
Boston, ...	1	....	....	....	1,500	....
Lancaster, ...	1	100	400	150	200	1
ESSEX Co.						
Ticonderoga, ...	1	....	....	600	800	....
FRANKLIN Co.						
Chateaugay, ...	1	500	....	....	....	....

CLASS III.—(Continued.)

TOWNS.	Number of establishments.	Capital Invested. In real estate.	Capital Invested. In tools and machinery.	Cash Value. Of raw materials used.	Cash Value. Of manufactured articles.	Persons employed.
Genesee Co.						
Pavilion,	1	....	$300	$3,000	$230	1
Pembroke,	1	$1,000	500	....	1,500	1
Greene Co.						
Lexington,	1	500	50	1,740	1,390	2
Herkimer Co.						
Russia,	1	800	300	....	600	....
Salisbury,	1	....	....	1,200	1,550	1
Jefferson Co.						
Adams,	1	....	....	1,500	1,800	....
Alexandria,	1	2,000	1,500	....	1,500	2
Ellisburgh,	2	1,200	....	811	1,125	2
Hounsfield,	1	2,000	1,000	4,000	2,480	6
Watertown,	1	1,000	500	....	1,500	3
Wilna,	1	200	300	1,350	1,350	1
Lewis Co.						
Lowville,	1	....	....	1,803	2,393	3
Livingston Co.						
North Dansville,	1	3,000	1,200	142	1,452	1
Madison Co.						
Sullivan,	1	950	900	3,500	3,500	2
Monroe Co.						
Mendon,	2	1,250	35	3,250	9,000	7
Rochester,	1	....	700	6,000	7,220	2
Montgomery Co.						
Canajoharie,	2	600	400	....	180	....
Charleston,	1	3,500	1,000	2,500	4,620	8
Oneida Co.						
Augusta,	2	500	800	2,000	400	2
Lee,	1	2,000	2,000	3,600	1,000	2
Trenton,	1	400	300	300	1,300	....
Onondaga Co.						
De Witt,	1	1,500	400	1,000	2,000	2
Tully,	1	1,500	1,000	....	800	3
Ontario Co.						
Phelps,	1	1,500	600	750	900	2
Orange Co.						
Minisink,	1	500	250	....	....	2
Orleans Co.						
Carlton,	1	2,000	....	....	500	1
Ridgeway,	1	....	1,000	3,000	3,000	2
Oswego Co.						
Granby,	1	1,000	500	2,900	2,400	....
Hannibal,	1	600	400	....	400	2
Hastings,	1	500	500	3,950	5,350	2
Richland,	1	1,000	1,000	3,000	4,000	....
Otsego Co.						
Otego,	1	....	200	750	900	....
Otsego,	1	500	400	....	....	2
Richfield,	1	800	1,000	2,000	2,700	4
Roseboom,	1	500	300	....	450	....
Rensselaer Co.						
Schodack,	1	1,500	300	....	....	5
St. Lawrence Co.						
Edwards,	1	100	250	....	....	1
Hopkinton,	1	150	....	25	300	1
Louisville,	1	200	300	2,500	2,800	2
Oswegatchie,	1	5,000	2,000	3,000	3,500	7
Russell,	1	1,000	300	....	500	....
Schoharie Co.						
Fulton,	1	800	800	2,430	3,450	2
Richmondville,	1	300	635	4,220	3,040	3
Summit,	1	2,000	....	114	225	....
Wright,	2	2,100	1,400	8,601	9,963	3
Schuyler Co.						
Tyrone,	1	600	650	4,502	5,640	6
Seneca Co.						
Seneca Falls,	1	2,000	1,000	....	....	....
Steuben Co.						
Bath,	1	150	500	....	807	2
Troupsburgh,	2	....	....	2,400	300	4
Suffolk Co.						
Smithtown,	1	1,000	1,000	....	....	....
Southampton,	2	2,500	1,000	....	850	2
Sullivan Co.						
Liberty,	1	1,000	....	....	....	....
Neversink,	1	600	100	....	....	1
Tioga Co.						
Nichols,	1	1,000	500	2,700	4,000	1
Tompkins Co.						
Caroline,	1	....	....	3,400	4,220	3
Dryden,	1	100	300	4,173	4,661	1
Ithaca,	1	1,000	1,500	1,575	2,900	....
Ulster Co.						
Olin,	1	1,000	800	2,250	2,550	1
Rochester,	1	1,000	1,500	1,080	275	3
Warren Co.						
Chester,	1	1,650	500	....	....	2
Warrensburgh,	1	1,000	1,200	....	500	1

TOWNS.	Number of establishments.	Capital Invested. In real estate.	Capital Invested. In tools and machinery.	Cash Value. Of raw materials used.	Cash Value. Of manufactured articles.	Persons employed.
Washington Co.						
Argyle,	1	$500	$80	$700	$820	1
Granville,	1	150	50	....	....	....
Wayne Co.						
Huron,	1	750	20	500	600	1
Wolcott,	1	4,000	2,000	4,800	6,000	5
Westchester Co.						
Lewisboro',	1	1,500	500	875	1,500	....
Wyoming Co.						
Java,	1	....	....	....	400	2
Perry,	1	2,000	2,000	4,550	7,175	9
Yates Co.						
Milo,	1	....	....	720	....	....
CARPET MANUFACTORIES.						
Albany Co.						
Albany,	1	2,000	1,500	2,000	5,000	6
Cayuga Co.						
Auburn,	2	30,000	126,000	111,080	375,000	398
Columbia Co.						
Claverack,	1	12,000	4,500	10,450	16,000	40
Dutchess Co.						
Poughkeepsie city,	1	15,000	20,000	70,000	115,000	80
Erie Co.						
North Collins,	1	20	30	....	130	....
Montgomery Co.						
Amsterdam,	2	18,000	29,100	69,000	152,500	121
New-York Co.						
New-York,	3	135,000	170,050	427,075	887,073	780
Oneida Co.						
Vernon,	1	2,000	1,000	3,300	6,000	13
Queens Co.						
Newtown,	1	41,000	9,000	81,950	250,000	145
Westchester Co.						
Mount Pleasant,	1	100	20	440	....	2
Ossining,	2	....	7,500	43,350	93,000	132
West Farms,	2	10,150	25 500	116,100	180,000	172
CARPET YARN MANUFACTORIES.						
Rockland Co.						
Orangetown,	1	5,000	2,000	11,510	19,448	10
Westchester Co.						
North Castle,	1	5,000	2,000	4,690	5,760	8
COTTON FACTORIES.						
Albany Co.						
Watervliet,	4	206,000	341,051	282,144	648,000	827
Cayuga Co.						
Auburn,	1	12,000	6,000	11,250	28,000	56
Moravia,	1	10,000	5,000	15,640	39,000	51
Columbia Co.						
Kinderhook,	7	96,000	148,000	63,260	254,000	413
New Lebanon,	5	110,000	105,000	63,160	146,572	300
Cortland Co.						
Homer,	1	10,000	10,000	17,000	31,350	53
Dutchess Co.						
Fishkill,	4	86,000	154,000	248,506	313,000	782
Pleasant Valley,	1	10,000	10,000	14,487	26,487	60
Poughkeesie,	1	20,000	15,000	10,280	25,000	56
Greene Co.						
Prattsville,	1	10,000	27,650	26,690	50,709	79
Herkimer Co.						
Little Falls,	1	20,000	25,000	12,280	29,175	64
Newport,	1	8,000	10,000	17,500	34,060	63
Stark,	1	9,000	6,000	6,400	15,960	40
Jefferson Co.						
Brownville,	1	15,000	10,000	37,336	56,200	100
Watertown,	1	10,000	5,000	1,500	28,000	47
Madison Co.						
Eaton,	1	15,000	15,000	30,000	50,000	63
Monroe Co.						
Rochester,	2	55,000	95,000	57,000	112,000	240
Montgomery Co.						
Mohawk,	1	5,000	5,000	13,000	25,000	20
New-York Co.						
New-York,	3	29,000	20,000	24,000	162,000	77
Niagara Co.						
Lockport,	1	20,000	20,000	24,750	36,000	95
Oneida Co.						
Kirkland,	1	35,000	35,000	60,730	104,900	186
New Hartford,	5	197,000	260,000	286,755	456,000	820
Paris,	1	25,000	9,000	27,326	48,085	129
Trenton,	1	3,000	3,000	5,000	12,000	27
Utica,	1	60,000	170,000	125,000	250,000	300
Westmoreland,	1	6,000	4,000	32,600	49,000	60
Whitestown,	2	140,000	110,000	225,500	163,000	485

CLASS III.—(CONTINUED.)

TOWNS.	Number of establishments.	Capital Invested. In real estate.	Capital Invested. In tools and machinery.	Cash Value. Of raw materials used.	Cash Value. Of manufactured articles.	Persons employed.
ONONDAGA CO.						
Manlius,	1	$12,000	$4,000	$9,000	$16,000	47
ORANGE CO.						
Blooming Grove,	1	10,000	20,000	15,600	30,000	47
Montgomery,	1	4,000	6,000	18,200	38,000	40
Newburgh,	1	50,000	50,000	65,900	114.984	309
New Windsor,	1	10,000	20,000	14,000	43,000	45
OSWEGO CO.						
Oswego city,	1	25,000	30,000	24,000	55,000	75
OTSEGO CO.						
Hartwick,	2	20,000	18,000	26,000	27,460	82
Laurens,	2	11,350	14,000	20,419	39,431	60
Middlefield,	1	2,000	200	3,360	21,840	34
Morris,	1	18,000	8,000	17,625	30,000	48
Pittsford,	1	5,000	20,000	16,000	25,000	76
RENSSELAER CO.						
Hoosick,	2	39,000	57,000	46,000	102,000	193
Lansingburgh,	1	12,500	15,000	9,500	27,600	56
Pittstown,	2	8,000	4,000	18,600	34,500	60
Schaghticoke,	1	12,000	30,000	31,000	52,000	160
Troy,	2	35,000	30,000	60,450	101,800	386
ROCKLAND CO.						
Clarkstown,	1	4,500	12,000	14,826	37,000	44
SARATOGA CO.						
Halfmoon,	1	....	6,500	11,200	14,500	37
Milton,	2	25,000	60,000	29,300	84,000	168
Saratoga,	1	115,000	310,000	170,000	271,717	426
SCHENECTADY CO.						
Rotterdam,	1	30,000	15,000	13,000	18,000	40
SCHOHARIE CO.						
Gilboa,	1	20,000	30,000	31,000	49,000	90
SENECA CO.						
Waterloo,	1	20,000	20,000	25,600	42,000	75
SUFFOLK CO.						
Southampton	1	15,000	25,000	10,730	26,103	108
TIOGA CO.						
Tioga,	1	....	....	15,000	16,500	3
ULSTER CO.						
Esopus,	2	30,000	21,000	6,125	20,200	60
WASHINGTON CO.						
Greenwich,	1	10,000	6,000	7,000	20,000	44
WESTCHESTER CO.						
New Castle,	1	20,000	10,000	30,000	70,000	26

COTTON BATTING MANUFACTORIES.

TOWNS.	Number of establishments.	In real estate.	In tools and machinery.	Of raw materials used.	Of manufactured articles.	Persons employed.
HERKIMER CO.						
Russia,	1	800	....	1,750	1,852	2
JEFFERSON CO.						
Hounsfield,	1	....	....	720	1,000	2
KINGS CO.						
Brooklyn,	2	16,000	15,000	50,000	70,000	67
LEWIS CO.						
New Bremen,	1	1,000	1,000	940	1,260	2
ONEIDA CO.						
New Hartford,	2	2,000	650	22,004	26,840	16
RENSSELAER CO.						
Brunswick,	1	2,000	2,400	2,000	3,000	5
Stephentown,	1	2,000	3,500	12,100	24,000	11
ROCKLAND CO.						
Ramapo,	1	2,000	800	....	....	....
SARATOGA CO.						
Corinth,	1	1,200	1,000	12,000	16,784	4

COTTON WARP MANUFACTORIES.

TOWNS.	Number of establishments.	In real estate.	In tools and machinery.	Of raw materials used.	Of manufactured articles.	Persons employed.
RENSSELAER CO.						
Sandlake,	1	20,000	10,000	12,000	40,000	38
Schaghticoke,	1	5,000	10,000	11,000	1,800	39
SUFFOLK CO.						
Brookhaven,	2	13,000	15,000	32,500	40,700	40

FELTING AND WADDING MANUFACTORIES.

TOWNS.	Number of establishments.	In real estate.	In tools and machinery.	Of raw materials used.	Of manufactured articles.	Persons employed.
KINGS CO.						
Brooklyn,	1	....	24,000	2,400	5,000	36

FLAX-DRESSING MILLS.

TOWNS.	Number of establishments.	In real estate.	In tools and machinery.	Of raw materials used.	Of manufactured articles.	Persons employed.
CLINTON CO.						
Champlain,	1	1,500	1,500	1,000	2,000	4
CORTLAND CO.						
Scott,	3	1,800	200	5,800	8,500	5
FULTON CO.						
Perth,	2	1,400	700	1,525	2,690	4
HERKIMER CO.						
Fairfield,	1	500	500	1,600	....	12
Little Falls,	1	5,000	1,000	4,800	9,500	17
JEFFERSON CO.						
Ellisburgh,	1	200	....	438	657	3

TOWNS.	Number of establishments.	Capital Invested. In real estate.	Capital Invested. In tools and machinery.	Cash Value. Of raw materials used.	Cash Value. Of manufactured articles.	Persons employed.
KINGS CO.						
Brooklyn,	3	$55,000	$53,000	$347,700	$590,000	98
LEWIS CO.						
Denmark,	1	....	....	1,600	2,500	....
MONTGOMERY CO.						
Amsterdam,	1	1,200	500	3,000	5,660	4
Minden,	1	1,000	1,800	2,800	5,500	7
ONEIDA CO.						
Trenton,	1	300	100	450	675	....
OSWEGO CO.						
Richland,	1	....	....	4,500	6,160	8
RENSSELAER CO.						
Hoosick,	8	1,400	1,100	9,275	11,550	9
Pittstown,	13	10,225	2,600	40,957	43,370	43
Schaghticoke,	2	6,000	12,000	20,000	30,100	50
SCHENECTADY CO.						
Schenectady,	1	....	250	500	1,500	1
SCHOHARIE CO.						
Esperance,	1	1,100	300	2,000	3,515	4
SENECA CO.						
Fayette,	1	2,500	700	2,000	6,000	2
WYOMING CO.						
Gainesville,	1	400	....	1,000	1,200	....
Wethersfield,	1	25	40	530	1,000	1

FRINGE AND TASSEL MANUFACTORIES.

TOWNS.	Number of establishments.	In real estate.	In tools and machinery.	Of raw materials used.	Of manufactured articles.	Persons employed.
ALBANY CO.						
Albany,	1	....	200	5,000	5,000	7
KINGS CO.						
Brooklyn,	2	5,800	2,150	13,000	32,000	55
NEW-YORK CO.						
New-York,	13	66,500	7,900	107,950	243,500	258

FUR-DRESSING ESTABLISHMENTS.

TOWNS.	Number of establishments.	In real estate.	In tools and machinery.	Of raw materials used.	Of manufactured articles.	Persons employed.
ALBANY CO.						
Albany,	1	4,500	1,500	30,000	38,000	15
KINGS CO.						
Brooklyn,	3	4,900	600	10,424	114,700	30
NEW-YORK CO.						
New-York,	11	173,000	2,280	266,400	462,000	169

HAIR CLOTH MANUFACTORIES.

TOWNS.	Number of establishments.	In real estate.	In tools and machinery.	Of raw materials used.	Of manufactured articles.	Persons employed.
NEW-YORK CO.						
New-York,	1	....	500	....	4,000	40
WESTCHESTER CO.						
West Farms,	1	1,200	1,000	400	863	....

LINEN FACTORIES.

TOWNS.	Number of establishments.	In real estate.	In tools and machinery.	Of raw materials used.	Of manufactured articles.	Persons employed.
RENSSELAER CO.						
Pittstown,	1	3,500	3,640	33,500	33,980	37
SARATOGA CO.						
Stillwater,	1	25,000	32,000	30,000	70,000	100

OAKUM MANUFACTORIES.

TOWNS.	Number of establishments.	In real estate.	In tools and machinery.	Of raw materials used.	Of manufactured articles.	Persons employed.
ERIE CO.						
Buffalo,	1	300	200	4,467	7,000	14
NEW-YORK CO.						
New-York,	1	25,000	10,000	46,000	58,000	32

PAPER MILLS.

TOWNS.	Number of establishments.	In real estate.	In tools and machinery.	Of raw materials used.	Of manufactured articles.	Persons employed.
ALBANY CO.						
Coeymans,	2	8,700	18,000	9,950	45,000	38
Rensselaerville,	1	3,000	2,000	....	1,500	3
ALLEGANY CO.						
Angelica,	1	2,900	7,000	....	....	....
BROOME CO.						
Chenango,	1	8,000	7,000	23,460	31,200	12
CAYUGA CO.						
Aurelius,	1	18,000	21,000	48,000	65,000	36
CHAUTAUQUE CO.						
Pomfret,	2	9,000	12,000	23,135	33,500	19
Portland,	1	2,500	1,000	200	525	3
CHENANGO CO.						
New Berlin,	1	5,000	1,000	11,270	17,000	12
COLUMBIA CO.						
Ancram,	1	40,000	15,000	54,000	100,000	62
Canaan,	2	9,600	500	2,686	6,400	6
Chatham,	8	65,630	33,870	35,160	100,800	101
Claverack,	1	9,000	3,000	2,500	5,000	5
Ghent,	1	500	1,000	1,600	5,000	4
Livingston,	1	5,000	3,000	10,690	16,500	15
New Lebanon,	1	10,000	25,000	12,900	18,500	16

CLASS III.—(CONTINUED.)

TOWNS.	Number of establishments.	Capital Invested. In real estate.	Capital Invested. In tools and machinery.	Cash Value. Of raw materials used.	Cash Value. Of manufactured articles.	Persons employed.
CORTLAND Co.						
Cincinnatus,......	1	$400	$200	$2,000	$5,000	4
DELAWARE Co.						
Franklin,........	1	1,000	2,000	1,300	3,250	5
DUTCHESS Co.						
Rhinebeck,.......	1	6,000	2,000	6,100	19,822	8
ESSEX Co.						
Chesterfield,......	1	10,000	4,000	13,080	15,200	13
FULTON Co.						
Broadalbin,......	3	7,000	3,500	8,645	17,125	16
GREENE Co.						
Catskill,........	3	12,000	6,100	15,700	19,000	18
New Baltimore,...	1	3,000	2,000	4,000	5,600	3
HERKIMER Co.						
Frankfort,.......	1	12,000	6,000	5,078	14,040	6
Herkimer,........	1	12,000	16,000	71,224	138,000	130
Little Falls,......	3	27,000	25,200	69,760	104,000	62
JEFFERSON Co.						
Ellisburgh,.......	1	1,000	....	4,560	8,580	11
Watertown,......	1	16,000	4,000	20,626	34,320	14
KINGS Co.						
Brooklyn,........	1	47,000	35,000	12,000	16,000	6
LEWIS Co.						
Greig,...........	1	2,500	1,500	8,050	15,000	10
LIVINGSTON Co.						
Mt. Morris,......	1	4,000	6,000	5,744	11,542	12
North Dansville,..	2	15,000	11,000	48,158	84,163	26
MADISON Co.						
Cazenovia,........	1	5,000	7,000	16,460	20,700	15
Sullivan,.........	1	1,000	1,000	250	1,260	4
MONROE Co.						
Rochester,.......	1	20,000	40,000	73,000	90,000	74
NIAGARA Co.						
Niagara,.........	1	25,000	55,000	109,000	160,000	40
ONEIDA Co.						
Paris,...........	1	20,000	5,000	58,600	70,000	30
Whitestown,.....	2	5,000	5,000	3,575	10,600	9
ONONDAGA Co.						
Manlius,.........	2	15,000	9,000	54,000	77,000	27
Marcellus,........	3	15,000	26,000	32,950	102,300	47
Skaneateles,......	1	10,000	....	3,325	9,000	11
ONTARIO Co.						
Manchester,......	1	1,500	1,500	2,500	5,000	5
Phelps,..........	1	5,000	3,000	9,000	16,500	8
ORANGE Co.						
Blooming Grove,..	1	4,000	1,500	24,000	27,000	9
New Windsor,....	2	55,000	25,000	59,800	120,000	68
ORLEANS Co.						
Shelby,..........	1	12,000	200	4,400	18,000	14
OSWEGO Co.						
Richland,........	1	4,000	....	8,700	19,000	16
Volney,.........	1	10,000	....	12,000	33,000	34
OTSEGO Co.						
Otsego,..........	1	25,000	9,000	28,080	32,200	22
Unadilla,.........	1	1,500	2,400	400	1,600	5
PUTNAM Co.						
Phillipstown,.....	1	4,500	4,500	17,000	30,000	13
QUEENS Co.						
Hempstead,......	4	18,000	9,300	....	....	...
North Hempstead,	2	4,000	2,000	2,225	7,220	9
RENSSELAER Co.						
Hoosick,.........	1	10,000	10,000	16,000	60,000	22
Lansingburgh,....	2	9,000	5,000	6,650	20,100	23
Pittstown,.......	1	7,000	2,500	....	....	...
Schodack,........	1	20,000	15,000	....	85,000	42
Troy,............	3	46,000	36,000	58,200	163,000	69
ST. LAWRENCE Co.						
Madrid,..........	1	3,000	1,000	5,475	6,700	6
Oswegatchie,.....	1	3,000	5,000	10,000	40,000	6
SARATOGA Co.						
Greenfield,.......	2	4,200	8,550	11,139	23,400	14
Milton,..........	4	34,000	27,000	80,530	129,600	75
Stillwater,.......	1	2,000	1,000	8,000	15,000	14
SCHENECTADY Co.						
Rotterdam,.......	1	5,000	5,000	1,200	10,800	13
SCHOHARIE Co.						
Cobleskill,.......	1	100	....	....	....	...
Middleburgh,.....	2	3,000	13,000	26,600	18,000	27
TOMPKINS Co.						
Ithaca,..........	2	15,000	10,000	26,800	26,000	19
ULSTER Co.						
Marlborough,.....	1	1,500	2,000	5,000	9,000	10
Rosendale,.......	1	25,000	5,000	70,000	90,000	48
Saugerties,.......	1	31,500	20,000	85,250	200,000	88
WASHINGTON Co.						
Fort Edward,....	1	5,000	6,000	5,395	35,000	32
Kingsbury,.......	2	11,000	7,000	36,600	51,600	24
WESTCHESTER Co.						
North Salem,.....	2	5,500	4,250	8,044	15,000	7

TOWNS.	Number of establishments.	Capital Invested. In real estate.	Capital Invested. In tools and machinery.	Cash Value. Of raw materials used.	Cash Value. Of manufactured articles.	Persons employed.
PAPER MACHE MANUFACTORY.						
NEW-YORK Co.						
New-York,.......	1	....	$500	$230	$1,000	2
PLAYING CARD MANUFACTORIES.						
NEW-YORK Co.						
New-York,.......	3	$20,000	23,000	65,600	185,000	154
POWER LOOM MANUFACTORIES.						
ALBANY Co.						
Watervliet,......	1	....	2,000	1,550	6,000	5
COLUMBIA Co.						
New Lebanon,....	1	25,000	150,000	21,625	82,500	100
DUTCHESS Co.						
Fishkill,.........	1	5,000	1,000	920	4,000	7
RAG CARPET AND BLANKET MANUFACTORIES.						
DUTCHESS Co.						
Poughkeepsie city,	1	1,000	60	2,300	9,000	4
NEW-YORK Co.						
New-York,.......	1	1,000	55	700	1,920	3
QUEENS Co.						
North Hempstead,	1	....	....	....	935	....
RIBBON FACTORIES.						
KINGS Co.						
New Lots,........	1	....	200	450	900	1
NEW-YORK Co.						
New-York,.......	1	5,000	1,000	10,000	15,000	30
ROPE MANUFACTORIES.						
ALBANY Co.						
Albany,..........	3	3,000	500	11,400	18,500	7
CHENANGO Co.						
Guilford,........	1	150	50	300	520	3
Pharsalia,........	1	200	100	800	2,500	10
DUTCHESS Co.						
Poughkeepsie city,	1	2,000	1,000	40,000	50,000	32
ERIE Co.						
Buffalo,..........	1	....	1,000	2,900	6,300	11
JEFFERSON Co.						
Watertown,......	1	400	100	1,136	1,800	4
KINGS Co.						
Brooklyn,........	10	180,300	246,964	1,407,612	2,205,153	677
NEW-YORK Co.						
New-York,.......	1	4,500	1,200	14,500	28,000	34
ONEIDA Co.						
Utica,............	1	200	100	2,400	4,000	4
OSWEGO Co.						
New Haven,......	1	....	....	55	92	....
Oswego city,.....	1	2,000	2,000	3,600	6,800	9
OTSEGO Co.						
Burlington,......	1	1,500	....	1,120	2,333	4
RENSSELAER Co.						
Lansingburgh,....	1	15,000	15,000	22,086	51,840	34
Pittstown,.......	2	3,700	2,090	10,440	16,800	18
Troy,............	1	700	130	8,500	14,000	8
WAYNE Co.						
Palmyra,........	1	4,000	6,000	22,775	38,000	14
WYOMING Co.						
Gainesville,......	1	....	....	1,000	2,160	3
SEA GRASS MANUFACTORY.						
ERIE Co.						
Tonawanda,......	2	....	....	525	2,340	5
SEWING SILK MANUFACTORIES.						
MADISON Co.						
Eaton,...........	1	6,000	5,000	4,500	5,500	38
NEW-YORK Co.						
New-York,.......	2	....	7,000	65,800	96,000	76
TOMPKINS Co.						
Ithaca,..........	2	4,000	9,000	30,000	40,500	35
WESTCHESTER Co.						
White Plains,....	1	15,000	9,000	38,192	70,000	87
SHAWL AND BLANKET MANUFACTORIES.						
ALBANY Co.						
Watervliet,......	1	15,000	25,000	115,000	275,000	235
ORANGE Co.						
Walkill,.........	1	500	200	3,000	4,500	6
RENSSELAER Co.						
Hoosick,.........	1	10,000	....	....	....	...

CLASS III.—(Continued.)

TOWNS.	Number of establishments.	Capital Invested. In real estate.	Capital Invested. In tools and machinery.	Cash Value. Of raw materials used.	Cash Value. Of manufactured articles.	Persons employed.
SCHENECTADY Co.						
Schenectady,	1	$10,000	$15,000	$54,500	$100,000	90
SENECA Co.						
Waterloo,	1	120,000	30,000	100,488	231,000	176

SHODDY MILLS.

TOWNS.	Number of establishments.	In real estate.	In tools and machinery.	Of raw materials used.	Of manufactured articles.	Persons employed.
ALBANY Co.						
Watervliet,	1	6,000	1,200	5,200	21,840	18
ORANGE Co.						
Newburgh,	2	1,000	1,000	5,000	10,000	15
RENSSELAER Co.						
Troy,	1	2,000	3,000	2,500	8,000	24
ULSTER Co.						
Marlborough,	1	1,500	200	1,200	1,800	1

STRAW PAPER MANUFACTORIES.

TOWNS.	Number of establishments.	In real estate.	In tools and machinery.	Of raw materials used.	Of manufactured articles.	Persons employed.
ALBANY Co.						
Watervliet,	1	7,000	3,000	350	9,000	8
ALLEGANY Co.						
Angelica,	1	2,900	7,000	1,814	....	8
COLUMBIA Co.						
New Lebanon,	1	10,000	7,600	8,330	23,539	18
Stuyvesant,	2	3,000	300	8,876	15,666	15
DELAWARE Co.						
Franklin,	1	3,000	200	640	2,250	3
DUTCHESS Co.						
Poughkeepsie city,	1	3,000	9,000	5,700	19,500	23
Rhinebeck,	1	10,000	500	2,000	6,000	10
Stanford,	3	6,500	1,950	1,395	5,913	10
FULTON Co.						
Broadalbin,	3	....	....	....	....	...
Johnstown,	3	7,500	4,000	4,100	13.500	12
Mayfield,	2	2,400	2,000	3,671	8,700	8
GREENE Co.						
Catskill,	1	7,000	8,000	2,400	15,500	12
Prattsville,	1	2,000	1,000	2,100	8,160	5
Windham,	1	7,500	6,500	600	3,000	7
ONONDAGA Co.						
Manlius,	1	8,000	....	1,500	7,500	8
QUEENS Co.						
Hempstead,	4	18,000	11,300	15,100	28,620	26
RENSSELAER Co.						
Sandlake,	1	6 000	5,000	2,000	16,000	17
SARATOGA Co.						
Milton,	1	2,000	3,000	1,800	8,000	10
SCHOHARIE Co.						
Esperance,	3	10,400	500	3,075	10,370	18
SUFFOLK Co.						
Brookhaven,	1	5,000	1,000	1,860	4,368	4
Huntington,	1	3,000	12,000	1,200	9,000	7
Islip,	1	1,500	1,500	600	2,968	2
WASHINGTON Co.						
Hampton,	1	1,400	5,000	2,500	8,000	12
WYOMING Co.						
Pike,	1	18,000	....	5,000	25,000	11

TAPE AND WEBB MANUFACTORIES.

TOWNS.	Number of establishments.	In real estate.	In tools and machinery.	Of raw materials used.	Of manufactured articles.	Persons employed.
ALBANY Co.						
Albany,	2	2,400	1,500	20,000	24,000	24
CORTLAND Co.						
Virgil,	1	100	100	80	300	1
NEW-YORK Co.						
New-York,	2	....	2,350	18,797	33,600	33
RENSSELAER Co.						
Troy,	1	....	....	627	30,000	2
WESTCHESTER Co.						
Somers,	1	10,000	7,500	14,500	24,000	35

TWINE AND NET MANUFACTORIES.

TOWNS.	Number of establishments.	In real estate.	In tools and machinery.	Of raw materials used.	Of manufactured articles.	Persons employed.
DUTCHESS Co.						
Poughkeepsie city,	1	....	2,000	5,000	7,000	7
KINGS Co.						
Brooklyn,	1	2,000	....	6,000	12,000	9
NEW-YORK Co.						
New-York,	2	4,000	5,900	19,500	26,400	70
ORANGE Co.						
New Windsor,	1	5,000	5,000	7,000	15,000	21
QUEENS Co.						
Hempstead,	1	350	1,500	2,000	3,500	3
Newtown,	4	5,600	1,550	21,238	25,580	25
North Hempstead,	1	....	....	1,000	1,500	....
RENSSELAER Co.						
Lansingburgh,	2	14,000	15,000	43,180	85,000	90
ROCKLAND Co.						
Ramapo,	1	55,000	4,500	34,015	50,000	70
SARATOGA Co.						
Waterford,	1	3,000	3,250	6,000	12,160	10

TOWNS.	Number of establishments	In real estate.	In tools and machinery.	Of raw materials used.	Of manufactured articles.	Persons employed.
SCHENECTADY Co.						
Rotterdam,	1	$14,000	$26,000	$36,000	$55,000	57
ULSTER Co.						
Marlborough,	1	1,000	1,200	4,750	7,200	16
WESTCHESTER Co.						
Somers,	1	1,600	75	875	2,500	4
Yonkers,	2	4,500	1,860	3,140	5,885	13

WOOLEN CLOTH AND YARN FACTORIES.

TOWNS.	Number of establishments	In real estate.	In tools and machinery.	Of raw materials used.	Of manufactured articles.	Persons employed.
ALBANY Co.						
Watervliet,	1	3,000	2,000	11,150	19,020	11
ALLEGANY Co.						
Almond,	1	2,000	1,500	2,028	3,568	9
Rushford,	1	3,500	1,500	4,750	7,200	9
CATTARAUGUS Co.						
Otto,	1	2,000	2,000	360	7,200	13
CAYUGA Co.						
Aurelius,	2	16,500	10,500	30,450	50,600	46
Locke,	1	2,000	1,200	1,500	3,500	5
Mentz,	2	13,000	10,000	21,800	36,250	41
Moravia,	1	1,000	2,000	3,750	7,625	10
CHAUTAUQUE Co.						
Ellicott,	2	16,000	17,000	33,253	53,824	45
Westfield,	1	6,000	2,000	6,500	12,000	....
CHEMUNG Co.						
Elmira,	1	10,000	8,000	68,780	88,227	57
Southport,	1	2,000	2,500	4,200	5,200	7
CHENANGO Co.						
Greene,	1	2,000	1,000	1,050	5,000	6
Guilford,	1	2,000	2,000	3,000	7,000	9
Pitcher,	1	1,500	800	666	1,332	3
Sherburne,	1	225	850	1,040	1,850	3
CLINTON Co.						
Plattsburgh,	1	8,000	3,000	14,935	20,225	20
COLUMBIA Co.						
Claverack,	3	23,000	9,600	37,550	48,950	30
New Lebanon,	2	35,000	22,000	98,100	157,500	109
Stuyvesant,	1	6,000	10,000	27,500	60,000	23
CORTLAND Co.						
Preble,	1	....	....	120	375	....
Truxton,	1	2,000	2,500	4,500	7,920	9
DELAWARE Co.						
Bovina,	1	1,000	3,000	800	1,350	3
Davenport,	1	1,500	500	2,000	1,500	4
Hamden,	1	1,000	1,000	800	1,500	5
Meredith,	1	....	....	1,350	2.500	5
DUTCHESS Co.						
La Grange,	1	8,000	11,000	40,260	46,000	54
Pleasant Valley,	1	2,000	1,000	1,500	1,500	....
Red Hook,	2	8,800	6,000	21,000	29,000	17
Rhinebeck,	1	5,000	1,000	250	1,000	2
Washington,	1	1,200	300	....	....	....
ERIE Co.						
Aurora,	1	1,200	3,000	1,345	2,797	....
Boston,	1	1,000	1,000	615	1,383	2
Buffalo,	1	12,000	6,000	8,509	13,630	29
Collins,	1	4,000	4,000	....	....	....
Concord,	1	4,000	1,000	3,000	5,000	10
Hamburgh,	1	2,000	2,000	2,000	3,000	4
Sardinia,	1	1,000	1,500	1,500	2,500	4
West Seneca,	2	7,500	9,000	16,400	28,320	155
ESSEX Co.						
Chesterfield,	1	5,000	3,000	15,000	24,000	17
Essex,	1	3,000	1,000	1,900	5,000	6
Ticonderoga,	1	1,800	1,500	3,000	5,400	5
FRANKLIN Co.						
Fort Covington,	1	2 000	1,000	4,800	7,000	9
Malone,	1	3,000	1,500	384	660	10
FULTON Co.						
Broadalbin,	1	1,500	700	1,500	3,000	8
Ephratah,	1	3,000	1,500	2,400	4,800	4
GENESEE Co.						
Alexander,	1	4,000	3,000	7,000	14,300	10
Byron,	1	2,500	1,500	7,000	12,000	8
Elba,	1	500	500	300	600	5
GREENE Co.						
Cairo,	1	2,000	1,000	505	925	4
Catskill,	2	22,400	1,000	78,000	143,330	140
Prattsville,	1	5,000	2,000	9,000	10,000	15
Windham,	1	1,000	1,000	2,500	5,000	8
HERKIMER Co.						
Little Falls,	3	42,500	48,000	65,200	136,000	186
JEFFERSON Co.						
Adams,	1	1,000	500	550	1,100	5
Brownville,	1	20,000	4,000	123,000	160,000	85
Watertown,	1	12,000	5,600	69,162	85,255	68
LEWIS Co.						
Lowville,	2	2,000	1,000	1,494	2,125	36
Turin,	1	5,000	3,000	10,400	17,000	18

CLASS III.—(Continued.)

TOWNS.	Number of establishments.	Capital Invested. In real estate.	Capital Invested. In tools and machinery.	Cash Value. Of raw materials used.	Cash Value. Of manufactured articles.	Persons employed.
Livingston Co.						
Livonia, ...	1	$4,000	$2,000	$2,000	$4,300	8
Madison Co.						
Cazenovia, ...	1	15,000	500	32,750	50,000	42
Eaton, ...	3	95,229	20,000	132,899	100,000	236
Lenox, ...	1	1,500	1,500	1,800	3,000	4
Stockbridge, ...	1	7,000	11,000	21,723	127,516	46
Monroe Co.						
Mendon, ...	1	1,000	50	1,350	2,625	4
Rochester, ...	1	....	8,000	27,000	45,000	36
Wheatland, ...	1	800	2,000	5,500	9,200	12
Montgomery Co.						
Amsterdam, ...	1	3,000	3,000	3,720	6,600	5
Canajoharie, ...	1	3,000	2,000	4,000	6,000	5
St. Johnsville, ...	1	2,000	1,500	2,700	5,400	9
Niagara Co.						
Lockport, ...	1	2,000	2,000	1,800	3,600	10
Newfane, ...	1	500	2,500	6,540	8,000	9
Oneida Co.						
Camden, ...	1	4,000	1,000	5,350	12,000	5
Lee, ...	1	2,200	2,000	2,500	4,000	5
Marshall, ...	2	1,625	2,300	14,000	22,500	14
New Hartford, ...	2	39,500	35,200	100,000	160,000	125
Paris, ...	1	50,000	25,000	....	....	3
Sangerfield, ...	1	8,000	....	....	....	....
Utica, ...	1	40,000	85,000	239,300	420,000	244
Vernon, ...	1	1,000	800	355	1,350	3
Whitestown, ...	3	95,000	92,000	82,053	153,752	124
Onondaga Co.						
Camillus, ...	1	7,000	3,000	2,350	6,192	18
Lysander, ...	1	2,000	600	600	775	1
Marcellus, ...	2	16,000	10,000	6,180	15,620	11
Skaneateles, ...	2	36,000	50,800	57,199	86,475	154
Ontario Co.						
Farmington, ...	1	3,500	1,000	600	7,440	10
Manchester, ...	1	2,500	2,000	4,000	7,000	7
Richmond, ...	1	2,000	2,000	400	2,500	4
West Bloomfield, .	1	6,000	....	8,840	14,000	12
Orange Co.						
Cornwall, ...	1	2,000	1,800	1,330	2,017	2
Montgomery, ...	2	31,000	30,000	75,250	134,600	105
Mount Hope, ...	1	3,000	5,000	3,000	5,200	5
Newburgh, ...	1	5,000	4,000	10,500	19,500	10
Walkill, ...	1	600	1,000	4,200	6,720	6
Warwick, ...	1	1,000	5,000	....	600	1
Wawayanda, ...	1	5,000	500	8,000	16,000	8
Oswego Co.						
Mexico, ...	2	2,000	2,500	1,345	2,100	5
Oswego city, ...	1	4,000	1,000	1,500	2,900	8
Schroeppel, ...	1	300	200	....	....	....
Volney, ...	2	14,000	....	1,500	4,000	10
Otsego Co.						
Burlington, ...	2	1,000	1,050	750	2,235	5
Hartwick, ...	1	1,500	1,000	3,000	5,000	7
Laurens, ...	1	1,500	1,500	1,000	2,750	3
Unadilla, ...	1	1,000	1,000	600	1,100	3
Worcester, ...	1	2,000	2,000	2,100	4,800	8
Queens Co.						
North Hempstead,	1	2,000	1,000	1,200	2,250	3
Oyster Bay, ...	2	11,200	12,500	13,300	24,250	23
Rensselaer Co.						
Brunswick, ...	1	3,000	1,500	3,200	8,000	6
Rensselaer Co.						
Pittstown, ...	1	$4,000	$1,500	$4,000	$6,000	7
Sandlake, ...	2	6,500	3,500	23,600	53,460	17
Rockland Co.						
Clarkstown, ...	1	3,800	2,500	8,700	13,500	7
Ramapo, ...	1	2,000	2,500	7,450	11,760	7
St. Lawrence Co.						
Brasher, ...	1	2,000	1,000	6,000	900	14
Madrid, ...	2	5,500	6,000	12,700	21,750	23
Norfolk, ...	1	3,000	2,000	1,966	1,999	8
Rossie, ...	1	9,000	1,000	3,663	6,300	13
Stockholm, ...	2	2,300	2,600	2,700	5,000	14
Saratoga Co.						
Malta, ...	1	1,000	600	2,400	3,430	6
Moreau, ...	1	1,000	500	....	....	....
Providence, ...	2	1,500	1,000	2,900	5,250	10
Schenectady Co.						
Duanesburgh, ...	1	1,500	1,500	700	1,175	2
Glenville, ...	1	3,000	1,500	3,000	4,000	9
Schuyler Co.						
Dix, ...	1	1,500	2,000	3,000	2,500	6
Hector, ...	1	1,500	2,500	1,700	4,000	7
Seneca Co.						
Ovid, ...	1	500	600	400	700	4
Seneca Falls, ...	1	22,810	20,000	64,600	110,000	80
Suffolk Co.						
Brookhaven,*	1	2,000	4,000	....	....	....
Riverhead, ...	1	2,000	300	5,000	10,000	8
Sullivan Co.						
Thompson, ...	1	800	300	1,600	2,300	3
Tioga Co.						
Candor, ...	1	8,000	....	....	6,000	2
Tompkins Co.						
Caroline, ...	1	500	1,500	600	1,500	1
Dryden, ...	1	10,000	5,000	4,500	8,900	9
Newfield, ...	1	2,500	1,600	2,950	4,550	6
Ulster Co.						
Esopus, ...	2	5,400	8,000	7,040	13,600	21
Gardiner, ...	1	1,000	500	700	....	2
Marlborough, ...	1	2,000	2,000	6,000	15,000	14
Warren Co.						
Queensbury, ...	1	3,000	4,000	9,600	16,000	11
Washington Co.						
Argyle, ...	1	1,200	600	1,665	2,850	5
Fort Ann, ...	1	2,000	4,000	30,000	40,000	19
Granville, ...	1	2,000	2,000	12,000	28,000	12
Hampton, ...	1	3,500	1,500	....	....	....
Hartford, ...	1	560	2,000	1,711	2,375	....
Salem, ...	3	5,000	4,000	15,290	23,400	20
Wayne Co.						
Wolcott, ...	1	1,000	2,000	150	1,200	4
Westchester Co.						
North Castle, ...	1	1,000	1,000	2,380	4,160	4
North Salem, ...	1	2,000	1,000	1,120	2,240	5
White Plains, ...	1	1,900	4,500	135	....	4
Wyoming Co.						
China, ...	1	1,500	2,000	7,500	14,000	9
Pike, ...	1	4,000	3,000	9,000	17,500	9
Wethersfield, ...	1	2,500	4,000	2,490	4,200	5
Yates Co.						
Milo, ...	1	2,000	2,000	282	7,200	1
Torrey, ...	1	600	2,000	3,000	4,000	9

CLASS IV.—CHEMICAL PROCESSES, MANUFACTURES, AND COMPOUNDS.

ASHERIES.						
Allegany Co.						
Centreville, ...	2	450	300	2,641	4,270	4
New Hudson, ...	1	100	250	600	800	2
Broome Co.						
Union, ...	1	....	....	....	....	....
Cattaraugus Co.						
Ashford, ...	1	100	....	250	700	1
Randolph, ...	1	100	200	450	1,500	3
Cayuga Co.						
Conquest, ...	1	100	75	1,238	1,700	2
Mentz, ...	1	300	50	35	3,000	3
Venice, ...	1	50	50	....	100	....
Chautauque Co.						
Pomfret, ...	1	150	150	441	750	1
Villenovia, ...	2	560	388	1,460	1,900	2
Chenango Co.						
Plymouth, ...	1	150	80	400	900	1
Smyrna, ...	1	800	100	1,200	2,000	2
Clinton Co.						
Beekmantown, ...	1	200	10	6,000	7,200	2
Chazy, ...	1	250	....	312	750	2
Plattsburgh, ...	2	1,300	400	2,376	3,600	8
Cortland Co.						
Solon, ...	1	200	150	120	2,500	2
Taylor, ...	1	100	400	1,012	1,150	1
Erie Co.						
Buffalo, ...	3	8,000	3,900	24,823	41,595	13
Holland, ...	1	200	200	400	1,000	1
Franklin Co.						
Bombay, ...	1	200	100	600	1,000	1
Burke, ...	1	1,000	500	5,450	7,500	2
Genesee Co.						
Bethany, ...	1	150	323	1,686	2,297	2
Herkimer Co.						
German Flats, ...	1	....	....	764	1,386	....
Jefferson Co.						
Watertown, ...	1	1,000	300	2,350	8,000	....

* Not running.

CLASS IV.—(Continued.)

TOWNS.	Number of establishments.	Capital Invested. In real estate.	Capital Invested. In tools and machinery.	Cash Value. Of raw materials used.	Cash Value. Of manufactured articles.	Persons employed.
Lewis Co.						
Denmark,	1	$400	....	$1,500	$1,500	1
Martinsburgh,	1	25	$100	1,400	2,250	2
Livingston Co.						
Groveland,	1	400	100	937	2,200	2
North Dansville,	1	....	....	1,250	2,050	....
Madison Co.						
De Ruyter,	1	200	100	522	900	1
Nelson,	1	90	100	915	1,200	2
Monroe Co.						
Sweden,	1	150	250	990	1,800	2
Montgomery Co.						
Minden,	1	300	75	400	700	2
Niagara Co.						
Lockport,	1	1,000	500	3,000	4,240	7
Wilson,	1	....	200	500	900	1
Oneida Co.						
Utica,	1	200	300	1,950	2,900	1
Onondaga Co.						
Elbridge,	1	800	450	2,973	4,100	3
Tully,	2	25	300	415	1,500	2
Ontario Co.						
Canandaigua,	1	500	200	888	1,440	1
Phelps,	1	500	125	880	2,205	1
Otsego Co.						
Burlington,	1	500	25	900	1,450	2
St. Lawrence Co.						
De Kalb,	1	300	300	2,800	4,800	2
Edwards,	1	150	750	....	....	....
Gouverneur,	2	2,400	600	3,000	5,200	4
Hammond,	1	300	200	520	1,000	....
Madrid,	1	300	100	1,050	1,300	1
Oswegatchie,	1	500	500	5,800	8,500	3
Potsdam,	1	75	100	850	1,600	1
Seneca Co.						
Romulus,	1	300	400	827	2,064	1
Seneca Falls,	1	1,000	400	13,200	2,575	4
Steuben Co.						
Howard,	1	....	200	240	480	....
Tioga Co.						
Berkshire,	1	250	....	200	400	1
Tompkins Co.						
Caroline,	1	200	75	875	1,400	2
Wayne Co.						
Ontario,	1	300	200	800	1,400	1
Palmyra,	1	....	....	580	1,020	....
Wyoming Co.						
Bennington,	1	400	25	1,805	3,600	2
Java,	2	50	200	1,500	2,400	2
Middlebury,	1	500	150	325	500	1
Pike,	2	400	350	2,081	2,400	2
Wethersfield,	1	350	200	2,646	2,730	1

BAKERIES.

TOWNS.	Number of establishments.	Capital Invested. In real estate.	Capital Invested. In tools and machinery.	Cash Value. Of raw materials used.	Cash Value. Of manufactured articles.	Persons employed.
Albany Co.						
Albany,	15	16,500	6,460	89,145	127,500	57
Allegany Co.						
Rushford,	1	600	400	4,500	24,000	4
Cattaraugus Co.						
Ellicottville,	1	600	300	850	1,400	2
Perrysburgh,	1	350	50	830	1,460	2
Chautauque Co.						
Pomfret,	2	2,550	700	16,732	21,000	8
Chenango Co.						
Oxford,	1	1,500	700	10,000	14,660	6
Clinton Co.						
Plattsburgh,	1	3,000	1,000	10,258	19,344	7
Columbia Co.						
Hudson,	1	6,500	3,030	39,800	51,880	18
Cortland Co.						
Cortlandville,	1	1,200	100	821	1,100	3
Delaware Co.						
Tompkins,	1	300	300	2,120	3,932	4
Dutchess Co.						
Fishkill,	1	400	200	3,600	4,875	4
Hyde Park,	1	....	25	1,250	1,560	....
Poughkeepsie city,	2	3,000	3,300	52,950	3,000	23
Rhinebeck,	2	2,800	650	7,200	8,400	5
Erie Co.						
Buffalo,	14	70,950	6,345	79,158	130,067	54
Tonawanda,	2	....	....	1,288	1,690	2
Franklin Co.						
Fort Covington,	1	600	300	4,000	6,000	4
Malone,	1	....	200	3,250	4,250	3
Genesee Co.						
Alexander,	1	400	50	6,050	8,000	3
Batavia,	1	2,000	1,000	22,000	32,000	4
Herkimer Co.						
German Flats,	1	500	250	1,350	1,700	2
Herkimer Co.						
Little Falls,	2	$2,600	$1,100	$17,910	$22,000	10
Jefferson Co.						
Hounsfield,	1	1,500	250	5,750	8,000	2
Watertown,	3	3,000	1,650	30,241	40,730	16
Kings Co.						
Brooklyn,	9	24,000	4,400	64,510	92,535	49
Lewis Co.						
Lowville,	1	400	15	947	1,500	1
Livingston Co.						
Nunda,	1	400	300	2,300	3,000	2
North Dansville,	1	4,500	600	4,849	6,968	4
Madison Co.						
Lenox,	1	....	450	2,545	3,100	1
Monroe Co.						
Rochester,	8	11,025	2,110	31,813	21,495	24
Montgomery Co.						
Amsterdam,	1	500	....	3,795	4,680	2
Minden,	1	1,000	600	10,500	13,500	6
New-York Co.						
New-York,	54	231,400	525,620	1,416,400	1,727,153	435
Oneida Co.						
Paris,	1	....	17	275	400	1
Rome,	2	12,000	1,150	24,684	34,135	16
Utica,	5	17,000	2,675	87,876	138,920	34
Whitestown,	1	1,000	400	2,520	3,700	3
Onondaga Co.						
Elbridge,	....	....	....	1,000	1,800	2
Syracuse,	1	....	800	1,500	30,000	12
Orange Co.						
Deerpark,	1	1,200	40	20,962	23,000	4
Orleans Co.						
Ridgeway,	2	3,800	600	16,020	19,900	5
Oswego Co.						
Oswego city,	2	9,000	800	57,969	74,411	15
Volney,	1	....	300	5,078	9,000	....
Queens Co.						
Flushing,	5	3,200	1,256	23,320	32,100	12
Rensselaer Co.						
Lansingburgh,	3	3,000	2,310	61,514	100,788	33
Troy,	6	21,000	3,000	108,443	152,452	52
Richmond Co.						
Northfield,	1	1,600	400	10,244	16,656	6
Westfield,	1	1,500	700	2,500	3,700	1
Rockland Co.						
Orangetown,	1	1,500	100	18,934	24,750	....
St. Lawrence Co.						
Oswegatchie,	1	8,000	2,500	25,000	40,000	12
Saratoga Co.						
Saratoga,	1	....	100	1,200	2,000	2
Saratoga Springs,	3	8,300	3,200	26,543	33,138	13
Seneca Co.						
Waterloo,	1	2,500	2,000	10,900	10,900	15
Steuben Co.						
Corning,	1	6,000	5,000	76,200	80,400	20
Hornellsville,	1	1,200	200	2,060	3,000	1
Suffolk Co.						
Huntington,	1	500	400	5,000	5,400	5
Tioga Co.						
Barton,	1	1,100	300	3,500	....	3
Owego,	2	....	900	4,500	8,500	5
Tompkins Co.						
Ithaca,	2	4,500	1,800	21,700	26,000	7
Ulysses,	2	850	100	2,900	4,000	4
Ulster Co.						
Kingston,	1	1,500	200	8,000	10,000	6
Saugerties,	2	1,000	600	14,290	21,500	7
Wayne Co.						
Lyons,	1	500	100	2,360	2,840	2
Westchester Co.						
Eastchester,	3	3,000	350	....	7,800	7
Greenburgh,	2	1,000	20	....	8,700	3
Rye,	1	2,000	300	6,000	5,000	3
Yates Co.						
Milo,	2	5,000	40	6,800	10,000	4

BARILLA MANUFACTURE.

TOWNS.	Number of establishments.	In real estate.	In tools and machinery.	Of raw materials used.	Of manufactured articles.	Persons employed.
Queens Co.						
Oyster Bay,	1	3,000	2,000	24,000	26,250	3

BARYTES MANUFACTURE.

TOWNS.	Number of establishments.	In real estate.	In tools and machinery.	Of raw materials used.	Of manufactured articles.	Persons employed.
Westchester Co.						
Mamaroneck,	1	8,000	5,000	33,850	75,000	18
Rye,	1	2,000	100	6,000	9,000	2

BISCUIT MACHINE MANUFACTORY.

TOWNS.	Number of establishments.	In real estate.	In tools and machinery.	Of raw materials used.	Of manufactured articles.	Persons employed.
Monroe Co.						
Rochester,	1	....	800	1,525	5,250	4

CLASS IV.—(CONTINUED.)

TOWNS.	Number of establishments.	Capital Invested. In real estate.	Capital Invested. In tools and machinery.	Cash Value. Of raw materials used.	Cash Value. Of manufactured articles.	Persons employed.
BLACKING MANUFACTORIES.						
NEW-YORK CO.						
New-York, ……	1	$15,000	$100	$9,500	$15,400	10
WYOMING CO.						
Warsaw, ……	1	1,000	500	6,000	12,000	4
BLACK LEAD MANUFACTORIES.						
ESSEX CO.						
Ticonderoga, ……	2	6,200	1,800	5,300	11,000	9
BLEACHERIES.						
NEW-YORK CO.						
New-York, ……	1	14,000	4,000	26,860	35,000	25
RENSSELAER CO.						
Troy, ……	1	20,000	30,000	……	45,000	24
WETCHESTER CO.						
Somers, ……	1	35,000	10,000	10,841	30,000	46
BREWERIES.						
ALBANY CO.						
Albany, ……	8	331,074	319,900	662,099	931,155	190
Watervliet, ……	1	25,000	19,000	105,200	174,000	40
BROOME CO.						
Chenango, ……	1	7,000	3,000	8,672	12,000	5
CATTARAUGUS CO.						
Ashford, ……	1	600	……	……	……	……
CHAUTAUQUE CO.						
Pomfret, ……	4	2,850	655	3,300	6,120	3
CHEMUNG CO.						
Big Flats, ……	1	1,000	500	1,406	2,000	2
Elmira, ……	1	1,000	4,000	15,800	28,000	6
COLUMBIA CO.						
Hudson, ……	1	30,000	2,000	61,000	90,000	40
DUTCHESS CO.						
Poughkeepsie city,	1	100,000	90,000	144,000	221,000	66
ERIE CO.						
Buffalo, ……	17	187,000	43,000	95,372	188,206	95
Eden, ……	1	1,500	500	2,300	4,100	1
GENESEE CO.						
Alexander, ……	1	1,300	200	500	1,000	1
GREENE CO.						
Catskill, ……	1	2,400	1,000	9,500	18,500	4
HERKIMER CO.						
Little Falls, ……	1	3,500	200	6,000	9,000	3
JEFFERSON CO.						
Watertown, ……	1	4,000	1,850	7,050	13,000	4
KINGS CO.						
Brooklyn, ……	12	65,600	13,800	127,164	157,255	52
LIVINGSTON CO.						
North Dansville, ..	4	1,000	900	6,380	9,822	6
MADISON CO.						
Cazenovia, ……	1	4,500	400	8,755	13,250	6
MONROE CO.						
Rochester, ……	15	86,550	24,700	113,880	198,575	62
Wheatland, ……	1	12,000	5,000	29,800	38,950	4
NEW-YORK CO.						
New-York, ……	19	338,000	109,700	651,080	1,377,292	282
NIAGARA CO.						
Lockport, ……	1	800	800	2,000	3,432	2
ONEIDA CO.						
Rome, ……	3	11,000	5,000	13,650	24,200	12
Utica, ……	4	21,500	10,700	44,105	57,400	26
Whitestown, ……	1	……	400	495	2,100	3
ONONDAGA CO.						
Skaneateles, ……	1	4,000	200	21,950	25,000	……
Syracuse, ……	4	26,000	7,200	30,310	36,125	18
ONTARIO CO.						
Canandaigua, ……	1	10,000	……	55,500	95,750	20
ORANGE CO.						
Deer Park, ……	1	1,000	……	909	3,508	2
Newburgh, ……	1	50,000	25,000	181,050	195,750	37
OTSEGO CO.						
Otsego, ……	1	4,000	500	5,000	7,200	4
RENSSELAER CO.						
Lansingburgh, ……	1	……	……	……	……	……
Troy, ……	7	72,000	42,000	228,500	414,200	100
RICHMOND CO.						
Castleton, ……	1	40,000	……	18,000	36,000	7
ROCKLAND CO.						
Clarkstown, ……	1	4,000	5,000	2,200	5,000	4
ST. LAWRENCE CO.						
Oswegatchie, ……	1	10,000	10,000	12,000	12,000	……
SENECA CO.						
Waterloo, ……	1	7,000	500	5,750	8,000	1
SULLIVAN CO.						
Fremont, ……	1	250	400	350	2,912	1

TOWNS.	Number of establishments.	Capital Invested. In real estate.	Capital Invested. In tools and machinery.	Cash Value. Of raw materials used.	Cash Value. Of manufactured articles.	Persons employed.
WASHINGTON CO.						
Greenwich, ……	1	$200	$500	$1,000	$1,000	2
WAYNE CO.						
Palmyra, ……	1	2,000	500	10,000	12,500	3
WESTCHESTER CO.						
Greenburgh, ……	1	18,000	1,500	5,662	11,200	6
West Farms, ……	1	500	200	700	1,750	2
BRONZE-COLOR MANUFACTORY.						
KINGS CO.						
Brooklyn, ……	1	2,000	2,000	5,000	10,000	70
CAMPHENE DISTILLERY.						
KINGS CO.						
Brooklyn, ……	3	140,500	100,300	1,050,000	1,670,000	85
CHANDLERIES AND SOAP FACTORIES.						
ALBANY CO.						
Albany, ……	4	5,600	7,000	128,133	145,834	12
Watervliet, ……	1	1,200	500	9,000	12,000	7
BROOME CO.						
Chenango, ……	1	3,000	1,000	10,904	17,100	4
CAYUGA CO.						
Auburn, ……	3	5,500	2,625	34,462	39,290	7
CHAUTAUQUE CO.						
Pomfret, ……	1	2,500	6,000	26,520	30,800	2
CHEMUNG CO.						
Elmira, ……	2	6,000	1,500	38,168	45,850	8
COLUMBIA CO.						
Hudson, ……	1	6,000	5,000	……	44,650	5
New Lebanon, ……	1	200	325	3,450	5,030	3
CORTLAND CO.						
Preble, ……	1	50	40	900	1,040	1
DUTCHESS CO.						
Fishkill, ……	1	1,500	500	3,200	4,720	3
Poughkeepsie city,	2	14,500	6,000	20,200	59,300	6
ERIE CO.						
Buffalo, ……	9	29,000	22,300	191,065	554,450	68
FRANKLIN CO.						
Fort Covington, ..	1	……	30	250	360	……
GREENE CO.						
Catskill, ……	1	1,200	1,500	11,475	13,530	4
HERKIMER CO.						
Little Falls, ……	1	2,000	1,000	8,000	9,500	1
JEFFERSON CO.						
Adams, ……	1	500	300	3,233	4,315	1
KINGS CO.						
Brooklyn, ……	2	25,500	11,700	223,830	229,100	64
LIVINGSTON CO.						
North Dansville, ..	2	1,200	1,200	12,633	17,779	7
MADISON CO.						
Cazenovia, ……	2	1,400	650	7,080	8,625	3
De Ruyter, ……	1	400	100	3,260	4,650	1
Lenox, ……	2	700	800	6,990	8,080	2
Nelson, ……	1	250	500	3,236	3,745	2
MONROE CO.						
Mendon, ……	1	60	40	1,750	2,100	1
Rochester, ……	2	5,500	5,000	81,000	42,000	13
NEW-YORK CO.						
New-York, ……	31	264,700	173,500	1,501,571	2,230,927	355
ONEIDA CO.						
New Hartford, ……	1	300	200	……	2,400	2
Rome, ……	1	3,000	500	14,460	18,525	3
Utica, ……	3	13,000	13,800	76,048	94,400	21
Verona, ……	1	1,000	100	625	725	……
ONONDAGA CO.						
Syracuse, ……	2	15,000	3,500	36,750	42,000	7
ONTARIO CO.						
Bristol, ……	1	2,000	700	20,200	24,500	4
ORANGE CO.						
Goshen, ……	1	100	200	1,100	1,200	2
Newburgh, ……	4	29,700	5,200	103,360	152,075	18
QUEENS CO.						
Hempstead, ……	1	200	50	600	750	1
RENSSELAER CO.						
Berlin, ……	1	300	275	1,255	1,530	2
Lansingburgh, ……	1	……	……	……	……	……
Troy, ……	2	9,000	7,000	124,245	138,125	17
RICHMOND CO.						
Westfield, ……	1	170,000	200,000	17,800	24,214	49
SARATOGA CO.						
Saratoga Springs, .	1	1,500	200	……	15,125	2
Waterford, ……	1	1,600	1,500	12,250	16,000	4
SCHENECTADY CO.						
Schenectady, ……	1	3,000	1,500	39,300	80,389	7
SENECA CO.						
Seneca Falls, ……	2	1,000	4,000	……	11,500	……
Waterloo, ……	1	500	300	10,150	11,200	3

CLASS IV.—(Continued.)

TOWNS.	Number of establishments.	Capital Invested. In real estate.	Capital Invested. In tools and machinery.	Cash Value. Of raw materials used.	Cash Value. Of manufactured articles.	Persons employed.
Steuben Co.						
Hornellsville, ...	1	....	....	....	$200	2
Suffolk Co.						
Huntington, ...	1	....	$75	$1,233	1,500	2
Tompkins Co.						
Ithaca, ...	2	$1,900	1,600	8,500	13,600	3
Ulster Co.						
Kingston, ...	1	700	500	6,240	7,000	3
Warren Co.						
Queensbury, ...	1	2,000	600	4,920	5,900	2
Wayne Co.						
Palmyra, ...	1	1,500	700	4,005	5,143	5
Westchester Co.						
Cortland, ...	1	....	500	3,000	29,850	3
Wyoming Co.						
Attica, ...	1	....	100	2,600	3,000	2
Perry, ...	1	....	400	960	1,280	1

CHEMICAL LABORATORIES.

TOWNS.	Number of establishments.	In real estate.	In tools and machinery.	Of raw materials used.	Of manufactured articles.	Persons employed.
Kings Co.						
Brooklyn, ...	6	58,500	24,500	204,260	320,000	42
New-York Co.						
New-York, ...	3	20,000	2,600	13,000	29,000	6

COFFEE, SPICE AND MUSTARD MANUFACTORIES.

TOWNS.	Number of establishments.	In real estate.	In tools and machinery.	Of raw materials used.	Of manufactured articles.	Persons employed.
Albany Co.						
Albany, ...	2	....	5,500	88,000	105,000	21
Kings Co.						
Brooklyn, ...	4	21,000	13,800	49,200	58,640	25
Monroe Co.						
Rochester, ...	1	....	1,200	17,000	25,000	6
New-York Co.						
New-York, ...	14	148,000	29,500	518,950	772,455	165
Oneida Co.						
Utica, ...	1	3,000	2,500	....	30,000	8

CONFECTIONARY MANUFACTORIES.

TOWNS.	Number of establishments.	In real estate.	In tools and machinery.	Of raw materials used.	Of manufactured articles.	Persons employed.
Albany Co.						
Albany, ...	3	2,200	1,300	89,500	145,500	34
Broome Co.						
Chenango, ...	1	4,000	300	4,664	7,000	5
Chenango Co.						
Norwich, ...	1	....	....	3,000	3,600	14
Oxford, ...	1	....	....	....	....	....
Columbia Co.						
Hudson, ...	1	....	....	....	....	....
Dutchess Co.						
Poughkeepsie city,	3	3,000	290	5,900	13,600	7
Erie Co.						
Buffalo, ...	4	20,200	900	22,600	74,000	24
Herkimer Co.						
Little Falls, ...	1	500	300	2,000	3,500	3
Kings Co.						
Brooklyn, ...	2	1,800	25	13,800	15,000	6
Livingston Co.						
Mount Morris, ...	1	2,400	400	15,400	23,000	8
Montgomery Co.						
Amsterdam, ...	1	600	500	3,984	7,800	2
New-York Co.						
New-York, ...	14	65,000	19,000	211,294	490,874	174
Oneida Co.						
Utica, ...	2	....	400	1,500	3,100	4
Onondaga Co.						
Syracuse, ...	1	....	200	1,000	2,000	2
Orleans Co.						
Ridgeway, ...	1	2,000	500	5,200	5,200	2
Putnam Co.						
Carmel, ...	1	....	50	400	1,000	1
Rensselaer Co.						
Lansingburgh, ...	1	600	50	7,195	7,700	4
Troy, ...	4	4,500	3,500	25,000	40,000	23
St. Lawrence Co.						
Oswegatchie, ...	1	....	400	....	20,000	3
Tompkins Co.						
Ithaca, ...	1	2,500	200	12,480	20,000	10
Ulster Co.						
Kingston, ...	1	800	400	10,000	14,000	9
Warren Co.						
Queensbury, ...	1	4,000	500	3,910	5,940	2
Westchester Co.						
Rye, ...	1	1,000	300	2,188	3,419	1

COTTON PRINTING ESTABLISHMENTS.

TOWNS.	Number of establishments.	In real estate.	In tools and machinery.	Of raw materials used.	Of manufactured articles.	Persons employed.
Chenango Co.						
New Berlin, ...	1	7,000	20,000	15,000	182,350	79
Dutchess Co.						
Fishkill, ...	1	19,160	32,968	693,981	748,867	228
Erie Co.						
West Seneca, ...	1	....	....	$6,900	$9,660	10
New-York Co.						
New-York, ...	2	$5,500	$5,000	1,200	12,000	13
Otsego Co.						
Otsego, ...	1	12,000	4,000	....	....	....
Rockland Co.						
Haverstraw, ...	1	50,000	50,000	100,000	1,400,000	180

DISTILLERIES.

TOWNS.	Number of establishments.	In real estate.	In tools and machinery.	Of raw materials used.	Of manufactured articles.	Persons employed.
Albany Co.						
Albany, ...	2	19,200	21,300	80,250	488,500	37
Cayuga Co.						
Auburn, ...	1	8,000	1,000	75,000	83,800	10
Mentz, ...	1	2,000	500	11,520	15,360	4
Niles, ...	1	1,200	....	4,400	9,729	4
Chautauque Co.						
Hanover, ...	1	5,000	7,000	41,950	47,075	7
Chemung Co.						
Horseheads, ...	1	....	....	9,608	16,380	4
Chenango Co.						
Norwich, ...	1	800	1,000	1,200	1,280	2
Columbia Co.						
Hudson, ...	1	1,600	....	10,000	15,000	5
Erie Co.						
Buffalo, ...	2	25,000	15,000	183,300	318,000	23
Genesee Co.						
Elba, ...	1	1,000	500	2,550	5,000	2
Herkimer Co.						
Frankfort, ...	1	2,500	1,500	15,000	17,000	1
Jefferson Co.						
Henderson, ...	1	1,000	1,000	7,000	8,500	3
Pamelia, ...	1	4,000	2,000	76,500	104,600	13
Watertown, ...	1	10,000	1,500	52,175	75,000	8
Kings Co.						
Brooklyn, ...	7	255,000	135,000	1,905,000	2,499,000	215
Livingston Co.						
Leicester, ...	1	600	15,000	50,000	80,000	13
North Dansville, ..	1	2,000	150	8,654	12,001	3
Madison Co.						
Cazenovia, ...	2	1,000	....	101,700	135,750	10
Eaton, ...	3	7,400	2,872	90,966	159,416	16
Madison, ...	2	2,700	2,800	57,264	43,950	13
Sullivan, ...	2	15,075	12,300	77,557	123,320	14
Monroe Co.						
Pittsford, ...	1	6,000	8,000	76,025	108,000	26
Rochester, ...	1	7,000	3,500	27,780	49,684	10
Montgomery Co.						
Canajoharie, ...	1	....	....	....	30,000	....
Florida, ...	1	500	....	3,940	3,900	1
St. Johnsville, ...	1	6,000	2,500	27,000	36,000	6
New-York Co.						
New-York, ...	10	201,000	136,000	1,913,800	2,218,200	134
Niagara Co.						
Lockport, ...	1	4,000	2,000	22,929	27,000	11
Oneida Co.						
Marshall, ...	1	7,000	3,000	138,354	152,727	23
Rome, ...	1	500	100	10,788	13,439	2
Vernon, ...	1	1,000	1,000	16,000	28,100	5
Onondaga Co.						
Elbridge, ...	1	10,000	....	90,000	120,000	12
Marcellus, ...	1	3,000	2,000	45,000	71,900	7
Skaneateles, ...	3	35,000	....	263,125	394,750	21
Ontario Co.						
East Bloomfield, ..	1	300	....	1,639	3,762	2
Phelps, ...	3	9,000	4,000	75,000	133,000	17
Orange Co.						
Montgomery, ...	1	500	1,300	800	2,500	2
Walkill, ...	4	1,925	1,525	2,020	5,480	8
Oswego Co.						
Oswego city, ...	1	18,000	6,000	53,104	102,036	16
Otsego Co.						
Middlefield, ...	1	1,000	1,000	5,000	7,175	2
Oneonta, ...	1	200	300	2,000	4.000	2
Rockland Co.						
Ramapo, ...	2	1,000	1,000	....	....	....
St. Lawrence Co.						
Oswegatchie, ...	1	8,000	2,000	50,000	75,000	20
Saratoga Co.						
Galway, ...	1	....	....	....	....	1
Waterford, ...	1	10,000	500	72,500	75,000	10
Seneca Co.						
Fayette, ...	2	5,400	7,500	15,035	23,695	7
Seneca Falls, ...	1	18,000	8,000	165,500	253,000	18
Waterloo, ...	2	17,500	8,500	118,437	214,279	2
Steuben Co.						
Corning, ...	1	500	500	9,000	10,300	3
Hornellsville, ...	1	600	100	4,500	5,200	1

CLASS IV.—(Continued.)

TOWNS.	Number of establishments.	Capital Invested. In real estate.	Capital Invested. In tools and machinery.	Cash Value. Of raw materials used.	Cash Value. Of manufactured articles.	Persons employed.
Sullivan Co.						
Mamakating,.....	1	$100	$100	....	$300	1
Tioga Co.						
Owego,..........	1	500	1,000	$3,500	8,750	2
Tompkins Co.						
Dryden,.........	1	300	1,000	18,035	22,000	3
Wayne Co.						
Galen,..........	1	14,000	5,000	114,320	121,420	14
Palmyra,........	1	2,500	5,000	61,099	101,728	8
Wyoming Co.						
Attica,.........	1	....	50	....	75	1

DRUG AND MEDICINE MANUFACTORIES.

TOWNS.	Number of establishments.	In real estate.	In tools and machinery.	Of raw materials used.	Of manufactured articles.	Persons employed.
Cattaraugus Co.						
Perrysburgh,.....	1	500	300	1,720	8,482	3
Chautauque Co.						
Chautauque,......	1	600	500	600	3,000	2
Delaware Co.						
Kortright,........	1	200	25	3,435	8,200	8
Erie Co.						
Buffalo,..........	1	7,500	2,500	57,900	80,000	25
Essex Co.						
Chesterfield,......	1	....	....	2,400	10,000	4
Kings Co.						
Brooklyn,.......	4	2,500	....	11,000	14,980	5
Madison Co.						
Cazenovia,........	1	....	5	1,110	2,000	....
Monroe Co.						
Webster,.........	1	200	50	750	7,500	2
New-York Co.						
New-York,......	9	109,500	8,900	107,000	244,000	95
Niagara Co.						
Lockport,........	1	....	....	16,000	41,200	19
Oneida Co.						
Utica,..........	1	....	....	2,000	4,000	2
Onondaga Co.						
Elbridge,........	1	....	....	2,100	6,400	1
Otsego Co.						
Morris,..........	1	300	1,800	1,500	4,000	3
Westchester Co.						
Ossining,........	2	10,000	5,250	40,000	120,000	26

DYEING ESTABLISHMENTS.

TOWNS.	Number of establishments.	In real estate.	In tools and machinery.	Of raw materials used.	Of manufactured articles.	Persons employed.
New-York Co.						
New-York,.......	2	500	1,000	....	....	5
Onondaga Co.						
Syracuse,........	1	....	100	300	800	3
Richmond Co.						
Castleton,.......	2	102,664	84,385	36,939	163,000	313
Westchester Co.						
Mamaroneck,....	1	3,000	2,000	24,720	31,824	20

DYE WOOD MANUFACTORIES.

TOWNS.	Number of establishments.	In real estate.	In tools and machinery.	Of raw materials used.	Of manufactured articles.	Persons employed.
Dutchess Co.						
Poughkeepsie city,	1	15,000	10,000	150,000	180,000	25
Kings Co.						
Gravesend,.......	1	6,000	10,000	104,000	104,000	11
Ulster Co.						
Kingston,........	1	7,000	3,000	600	800	3
Westchester Co.						
West Farms,.....	1	....	....	15,000	20,000	6
White Plains,....	1	35,000	15,000	....	....	....

ELECTROTYPE ESTABLISHMENTS.

TOWNS.	Number of establishments.	In real estate.	In tools and machinery.	Of raw materials used.	Of manufactured articles.	Persons employed.
New-York Co.						
New-York,.......	2	20,000	800	7,000	11,000	10

EMERY, PUMICE STONE AND SAND PAPER MANUFACTORIES.

TOWNS.	Number of establishments.	In real estate.	In tools and machinery.	Of raw materials used.	Of manufactured articles.	Persons employed.
Queens Co.						
Flushing,........	1	3,000	1,500	7,000	37,500	24
Westchester Co.						
Rye,.............	1	....	2,000	9,500	16,000	4

FISH AND WHALE OIL MANUFACTORIES.

TOWNS.	Number of establishments.	In real estate.	In tools and machinery.	Of raw materials used.	Of manufactured articles.	Persons employed.
Kings Co.						
Brooklyn,.......	2	28,000	9,000	141,000	173,000	19
New-York Co.						
New-York,......	7	240,000	74,000	1,296,075	1,729,900	110
Suffolk Co.						
Shelter Island,....	1	300	2,700	....	....	10
Southampton,....	1	1,000	300	1,950	2,000	20

GAS MANUFACTORIES.

TOWNS.	Number of establishments.	In real estate.	In tools and machinery.	Of raw materials used.	Of manufactured articles.	Persons employed.
Albany Co.						
Albany,..........	1	$200,000	....	$235,000	$1,022,200	15
Watervliet,......	1	50,000	$2,000	4,500	9,000	6
Chemung Co.......						
Elmira,..........	1	3,000	4,700	3,990	11,600	4
Columbia Co.						
Hudson,.........	1	14,000	20,000	3,429	6,400	3
Dutchess Co.						
Poughkeepsie city,	1	70,000	5,000	6,150	12,000	5
Erie Co.						
Buffalo,........	1	65,000	625,000	35,850	107,000	60
Herkimer Co.						
Little Falls,......	1	500	5,778	2,660	2,660	2
Jefferson Co.						
Watertown,......	1	3,500	9,000	6,700	8,000	5
Kings Co.						
Brooklyn,........	3	252,200	858,900	154,400	278,000	278
Monroe Co.						
Rochester,........	1	12,000	138,000	14,025	65,109	24
New-York Co.						
New-York,	2	874,675	554,018	928,663	1,625,500	732
Niagara Co.						
Lockport,........	1	10,000	14,200	2,210	9,320	2
Oneida Co.						
Rome,...........	1	5,000	30,000	2,900	10,254	3
Utica,...........	1	13,246	22,753	10,500	24,177	18
Onondaga Co.						
Syracuse,........	1	100,000	5,000	7,906	20,294	5
Orange Co.						
Newburgh,.......	1	60,000	5,000	4,200	11,300	5
Oswego Co.						
Oswego,.........	1	25,000	50,000	5,000	14,000	6
Queens Co.						
Newtown,........	2	28,200	35,000	1,000	2,800	1
Rensselaer Co.						
Troy,............	1	100,000	....	15,500	35,517	25
Tompkins Co.						
Ithaca,..........	1	20,000	1,000	1,200	4,000	3
Ulster Co.						
Kingston,........	1	95,000	3,000	....	....	....
Westchester Co						
White Plains,.....	1	25,000	45,000	....	....	12

GLUE MANUFACTORIES.

TOWNS.	Number of establishments.	In real estate.	In tools and machinery.	Of raw materials used.	Of manufactured articles.	Persons employed.
Albany Co.						
Albany,..........	1	10,000	2,500	4,000	6,000	12
Columbia Co.						
Greenport,.......	1	800	400	3,000	4,000	2
Fulton Co.						
Johnstown,.......	1	2,000	1,000	3,150	5,160	8
Greene Co.						
Athens,.........	1	3,000	1,000	18,765	23,460	12
Kings Co.						
Brooklyn,........	1	25,000	5,000	60,000	150,000	7
Monroe Co.						
Brighton,........	1	2,000	1,000	2,400	5,360	7
Otsego Co.						
Butternuts,......	1	200	30	300	1,000	4
Rensselaer Co.						
Brunswick,.......	1	500	500	....	....	....
Westchester Co.						
Eastchester,......	1	1,000	400	1,200	2,400	3

GUTTA PERCHA MANUFACTORY.

TOWNS.	Number of establishments.	In real estate.	In tools and machinery.	Of raw materials used.	Of manufactured articles.	Persons employed.
New-York Co.						
New-York,......	1	15,000	40,000	95,025	450,000	185

INDIA RUBBER MANUFACTORIES.

TOWNS.	Number of establishments.	In real estate.	In tools and machinery.	Of raw materials used.	Of manufactured articles.	Persons employed.
New-York Co.						
New-York,......	2	115,000	88,000	305,000	610,000	122
Richmond Co.						
Southfield,.......	1	100,000	15,000	15,000	200,000	102
Westchester Co.						
Yonkers,........	1	25,000	5,000	50,000	100,000	50

IVORY BLACK AND BONE MANURE MANUFACTORIES.

TOWNS.	Number of establishments.	In real estate.	In tools and machinery.	Of raw materials used.	Of manufactured articles.	Persons employed.
Albany Co.						
Albany,..........	1	4,000	4,000	500	2,000	8
Kings Co.						
Brooklyn,........	4	7,750	20,525	93,600	106,960	49
Oneida Co.						
Utica,...........	1	....	1,200	850	2,100	6
Queens Co.						
Newtown,........	1	2,000	3,000	20,190	21,200	14

CLASS IV.—(CONTINUED.)

TOWNS.	Number of establishments.	Capital Invested. In real estate.	Capital Invested. In tools and machinery.	Cash Value. Of raw materials used.	Cash Value. Of manufactured articles.	Persons employed.
JAPANED CLOTH MANUFACTORIES.						
KINGS CO.						
Brooklyn, ...	1	$20,000	$5,000	$157,200	$189,600	64
RICHMOND CO.						
Castleton, ...	1	10,000	5,000	20,000	56,160	40
LAMPBLACK MANUFACTORIES.						
KINGS CO.						
Brooklyn, ...	1	25,000	100	3,700	3,700	9
RENSSELAER CO.						
Troy, ...	1	5,000	300	2,000	5,280	4
SARATOGA CO.						
Moreau, ...	1	200	....	30	100	1
STEUBEN CO.						
Corning, ...	1	700	....	800	6,000	4
LARD OIL MANUFACTORIES.						
KINGS CO.						
Brooklyn, ...	1	2,000	4,000	3,000	9,000	4
NEW-YORK CO.						
New-York, ...	6	78,000	33,000	1,510,600	1,839,000	79
RENSSELAER CO.						
Lansingburgh, ...	1	2,000	2,000	43,840	49,840	4
LIQUORICE REFINERY.						
KINGS CO.						
Brooklyn, ...	1	5,000	1,200	49,340	49,340	35
MALT MANUFACTORIES.						
ALBANY CO.						
Albany, ...	8	97,800	6,000	613,318	708,436	84
ERIE CO.						
Buffalo, ...	2	3,500	45,000	53,000	68,000	4
HERKIMER CO.						
German Flats, ...	3	16,500	400	53,000	65,000	10
JEFFERSON CO.						
Adams, ...	1	1,000	....	1,870	2,415	2
Hounsfield, ...	1	4,000	....	6,060	8,253	2
Pamelia, ...	1	600	....	8,800	10,500	2
KINGS CO.						
Brooklyn, ...	1	30,000	1,500	90,000	90,000	12
MONROE CO.						
Rochester, ...	2	14,000	1,000	22,000	33,000	4
MONTGOMERY CO.						
Amsterdam, ...	2	4,500	5,000	20,000	24,050	3
NEW-YORK CO.						
New-York, ...	2	85,000	10,000	193,750	239,000	42
ONTARIO CO.						
Phelps, ...	2	18,500	350	122,000	177,500	25
RENSSELAER CO.						
Lansingburgh, ...	2	88,000	14,500	261,288	323,525	42
Troy, ...	1	10,000	500	37,500	45,000	3
STEUBEN CO.						
Bath, ...	1	5,000	....	21,400	25,000	4
WASHINGTON CO.						
Fort Edward, ...	1	5,000	50	12,350	15,600	2
MATCH MANUFACTORIES.						
ALLEGANY CO.						
Amity, ...	1	1,000	1,250	2,000	11,250	23
CLINTON CO.						
Champlain, ...	1	100	20	60	300	2
Peru, ...	1	125	125	460	1,000	2
HERKIMER CO.						
Frankfort, ...	1	4,000	3,500	8,470	25,000	69
German Flats, ...	1	500	300	1,775	3,275	44
JEFFERSON CO.						
Watertown, ...	1	1,000	700	100	1,000	7
NEW-YORK CO.						
New-York, ...	3	36,000	7,300	12,300	136,500	350
ORANGE CO.						
Montgomery, ...	1	....	1,200	10,000	12,000	2
Walkill, ...	1	1,700	1,000	1,330	16,000	21
OTSEGO CO.						
Hartwick, ...	1	150	300	750	1,200	4
SARATOGA CO.						
Stillwater, ...	1	....	....	1,000	2,400	10
WYOMING CO.						
Gainesville, ...	1	500	....	1,000	4,000	8
YATES CO.						
Starkey, ...	1	1,000	150	885	2,000	6
MEDICINAL HERB AND EXTRACT MANUFACTORIES.						
CATTARAUGUS CO.						
Perrysburgh, ...	1	400	500	1,290	2,850	3
COLUMBIA CO.						
New Lebanon, ...	3	$12,400	$15,800	$25,105	$62,323	49
NEW-YORK CO.						
New-York, ...	1	12,000	100	1,500	3,000	2
MINERAL WATER MANUFACTORIES.						
ALBANY CO.						
Albany, ...	1	....	3,000	2,000	7,000	6
DUTCHESS CO.						
Poughkeepsie city,	2	3,000	4,500	6,500	16,000	21
NEW-YORK CO.						
New-York, ...	16	96,500	23,200	92,650	263,912	329
ONEIDA CO.						
Utica, ...	1	....	6,000	21,000	33,760	7
ORANGE CO.						
Deerpark, ...	1	2,000	1,500	1,455	6,000	7
PUTNAM CO.						
Phillipstown, ...	1	300	1,000	1,800	3,000	6
QUEENS CO.						
Flushing, ...	1	1,000	1,000	1,200	6,750	6
SUFFOLK CO.						
Huntington, ...	2	....	2,200	1,470	3,000	8
WESTCHESTER CO.						
Cortland, ...	1	....	2,000	2,000	8,325	4
OIL CLOTH MANUFACTORIES.						
ALBANY CO.						
Albany, ...	1	1,700	400	5,000	10,000	11
KINGS CO.						
Brooklyn, ...	5	80,500	9,800	115,200	170,250	94
NEW-YORK CO.						
New-York, ...	3	4,000	130	29,854	87,500	143
ONEIDA CO.						
Utica, ...	1	12,000	....	35,000	60,000	25
ORANGE CO.						
Newburgh, ...	1	12,000	1,000	17,085	24,000	16
RENSSELAER CO.						
Lansingburgh, ...	3	25,000	11,500	131,800	154,000	51
SARATOGA CO.						
Milton, ...	1	7,000	3,000	16,700	33,000	17
TOMPKINS CO.						
Ithaca, ...	1	4,000	1,000	3,100	5,000	5
Newfield, ...	1	100	100	150	500	1
OIL MILLS.						
ALBANY CO.						
Albany, ...	1	10,000	8,000	176,200	250,000	20
CHAUTAUQUE CO.						
Pomfret, ...	1	1,200	250	1,500	2,465	1
CORTLAND CO.						
Scott, ...	1	3,000	1,500	3,200	4,325	1
Truxton, ...	1	1,200	800	1,800	3,000	1
FRANKLIN CO.						
Bangor, ...	1	4,000	700	2,800	3,500	2
GENESEE CO.						
Le Roy, ...	1	4,000	....	6,000	9,400	1
HERKIMER CO.						
Manheim, ...	1	1,000	3,500	10,500	13,210	3
JEFFERSON CO.						
Champion, ...	1	2,600	1,000	437	600	1
KINGS CO.						
Brooklyn, ...	2	6,000	13,500	240,000	286,000	36
LEWIS CO.						
Denmark, ...	1	1,400	550	750	1,310	4
Lowville, ...	1	1,000	50	688	1,168	2
MADISON CO.						
Cazenovia, ...	1	1,000	500	1,500	1,875	1
MONROE CO.						
Rochester, ...	1	6,000	2,500	20,000	30,000	2
MONTGOMERY CO.						
Amsterdam, ...	1	8,000	4,000	33,420	38,500	7
NEW-YORK CO.						
New-York, ...	1	60,000	20,000	500,000	550,000	58
ONONDAGA CO.						
Elbridge, ...	1	3,000	2,000	3,575	3,850	1
ORLEANS CO.						
Ridgeway, ...	2	6,000	4,000	8,300	12,640	4
OSWEGO CO.						
Richland, ...	1	4,000	80	2,600	3,600	8
Volney, ...	1	3,000	....	600	924	1
RENSSELAER CO.						
Pittstown, ...	1	20,000	5,000	30,000	41,000	6
SENECA CO.						
Waterloo, ...	1	[illegible] 000	5,300	12,000	17,300	3
STEUBEN CO.						
Dansville, ...	1	300	300	450	900	1

CLASS IV.—(Continued.)

TOWNS.	Number of establishments.	Capital Invested.		Cash Value.		Persons employed.
		In real estate.	In tools and machinery.	Of raw materials used.	Of manufactured articles.	
Tompkins Co.						
Ithaca,	1	$1,000	$1,500	$4,900	$7,810	2
Ulysses,	1	1,500	....	1,200	2,250	1
Yates Co.						
Milo,	1	5,000	200	30,000	31,000	3
PAINT AND COLOR MANUFACTORIES.						
Dutchess Co.						
Poughkeepsie city,	1	5,000	6,000	50,000	100,000	12
Kings Co.						
Brooklyn,	2	10,600	5,100	20,000	50,000	16
Monroe Co.						
Rochester,	1	20,000	14,000	39,900	60,000	20
New-York Co.						
New-York,	3	62,200	24,100	170,500	252,000	58
Oneida Co.						
Sangersfield,	1	2,000	....	....	....	....
Rensselaer Co.						
Grafton,	3	5,100	200	1,370	14,820	8
Richmond Co.						
Northfield,	1	2,000	1,000	8,000	10,000	8
Saratoga Co.						
Halfmoon,	1	1,500	1,500	50	1,500	4
Westchester Co.						
Rye,	1	2,000	500	500	1,350	1
PAINTING AND GLAZING ESTABLISHMENTS.						
Cayuga Co.						
Auburn,	1	3,000	250	3,220	12,000	8
Columbia Co.						
Hudson,	1	500	200	3,000	6,000	5
Kinderhook,	1	400	25	300	550	1
Dutchess Co.						
Hyde Park,	1	....	50	1,600	2,500	4
Erie Co.						
Buffalo,	1	18,000	5,000	39,000	50,000	70
Eden,	1	50	20	150	150	....
Essex Co.						
Willsborough,	1	500	....	....	....	....
Genesee Co.						
Alabama,	1	250	60	475	820	2
Bergen,	2	....	....	....	....	....
Le Roy,	2	....	....	900	4.200	6
Pavilion,	1	....	20	40	900	4
Greene Co.						
Durham,	1	200	50	300	550	1
Herkimer Co.						
Little Falls,	2	1,500	210	2,100	5,200	7
Newport,	1	200	30	170	700	1
Kings Co.						
Brooklyn,	1	....	400	3,000	3,000	15
Livingston Co.						
Lima,	1	....	25	....	....	....
Monroe Co.						
Penfield,	1	300	100	....	500	....
Rochester,	5	4,225	265	7,230	15,515	23
Webster,	2	....	25	....	....	2
Montgomery Co.						
Glen,	1	1,000	100	550	1,500	4
New-York Co.						
New-York,	11	14,650	2,285	30,447	58,800	98
Oneida Co.						
Kirkland,	2	1,000	250	3,070	5,800	8
Utica,	2	....	575	2,250	7,228	9
Ontario Co.						
Canandaigua,	1	2,300	325	4,405	10,300	8
Orange Co.						
Minisink,	1	....	15	322	800	3
Orleans Co.						
Ridgeway,	1	....	200	1,000	2,000	1
Oswego Co.						
Oswego city,	2	2,000	300	2,960	8,000	10
Otsego Co.						
Decatur,	1	....	10	400	600	1
Roseboom,	1	60	75	....	300	....
St. Lawrence Co.						
Madrid,	2	550	108	1,100	2,700	5
Saratoga Co.						
Saratoga Springs,	1	2,000	200	2,520	6,000	4
Ulster Co.						
New Paltz,	1	....	25	100	500	1
Saugerties,	3	500	80	1,330	5,700	8
Wayne Co						
Sodus,	1	....	20	100	150	1
Westchester Co.						
Greenburgh,	2	150	45	40	1,800	5
Wyoming Co.						
Covington,	1	500	100	25	1,750	4

TOWNS.	Number of establishments.	Capital Invested.		Cash Value.		Persons employed
		In real estate.	In tools and machinery.	Of raw materials used.	Of manufactured articles.	
PAINT MILL MANUFACTORY.						
Oneida Co.						
Sangerfield,	1	$2,000	1,500	$1,500	$4,500	3
PAPER STAINING ESTABLISHMENT.						
Richmond Co.						
Castleton,	1	20,000	12,000	26,000	260,000	60
PEARL ASH MANUFACTORIES						
Franklin Co.						
Fort Covington,	1	1,500	200	15,539	22,439	9
Kings Co.						
Brooklyn,	1	3,000	200	200	400	5
St. Lawrence Co.						
Gouverneur,	2	....	....	7,200	10,000	....
Oswegatchie,	1	....	....	180	500	....
PERFUME MANUFACTORIES.						
Albany Co.						
Albany,	1	500	200	1,200	2,500	1
Monroe Co.						
Rochester,	1	4,000	500	9,000	25,000	7
New York Co.						
New-York,	1	....	800	....	9,000	2
PICKLE AND PRESERVE MANUFACTORIES.						
New-York Co.						
New-York,	9	87,000	57,300	217,880	416,000	238
Wetchester Co.						
Eastchester,	1	12,000	....	6,000	30,000	3
Greenburgh,	2	2,400	625	3,540	14,000	2
PRUSSIAN BLUE MANUFACTORY.						
New-York Co.						
New-York,	1	....	600	15,000	20,000	3
PUTTY MANUFACTORY.						
New-York Co.						
New-York,	1	16,000	1,500	20,000	25,000	9
PYROTECHNIC ESTABLISHMENTS.						
Monroe Co.						
Rochester,	1	2,000	300	1,000	3,500	6
Queens Co.						
Newtown,	1	4,000	1,000	5,320	14,000	15
ROSIN OIL FACTORY.						
Kings Co.						
Brooklyn,	5	28,000	34,500	58,250	161,300	46
SALERATUS MANUFACTORIES.						
Allegany Co.						
New Hudson,	1	....	100	3,600	4,800	2
Cattaraugus Co.						
Otto,	1	290	30	192	480	1
Chemung Co.						
Southport,	1	....	....	800	1,600	2
Chenango Co.						
Norwich,	1	300	500	4,000	5,550	7
Franklin Co.						
Fort Covington,	1	500	300	6,000	10,856	2
Jefferson Co.						
Pamelia,	1	500	100	1,400	2,000	1
Kings Co.						
Brooklyn,	2	....	....	37,500	45,500	1
Madison Co.						
Cazenovia,	1	300	50	1,045	1,500	1
Monroe Co.						
Perrington,	1	2,000	400	15,000	21,600	6
New-York Co.						
New-York,	2	26,000	8,000	146,800	175,000	41
Oneida Co.						
Rome,	1	2,400	1,000	2,557	5,000	3
Onondaga Co.						
Syracuse,	1	12,000	3,000	21,800	30,000	10
Rensselaer Co.						
Troy,	1	....	500	8,150	10,000	1
Wyoming Co.						
Wethersfield,	1	200	129	1,260	1,980	1

CLASS IV.—(Continued.)

SALT MANUFACTORIES.

TOWNS.	Number of establishments.	Capital Invested. In real estate.	Capital Invested. In tools and machinery.	Cash Value. Of raw materials used.	Cash Value. Of manufactured articles.	Persons employed.
Cayuga Co.						
Mentz,...........	1	$300	$500	$1,000	$1,063	2
New-York Co.						
New-York, ...	1	7,000	10,000	95,000	110,000	25
Onondaga Co.						
Geddes,..........	32	213,000	2,900	87,590	208,415	130
Salina,...........	32	131,000	2,180	100,159	187,185	157
Syracuse,........	126	756,500	38,695	543,111	972,700	785
Saratoga Co.						
Stillwater, ...	1	....	....	5,400	9,000	....

SALTPETRE REFINERY.

TOWNS.	Number of establishments.	Capital Invested. In real estate.	Capital Invested. In tools and machinery.	Cash Value. Of raw materials used.	Cash Value. Of manufactured articles.	Persons employed.
New-York Co.						
New-York, ...	1	30,000	2,500	180,000	480,000	4

SATINETT PRINTING ESTABLISHMENTS.

TOWNS.	Number of establishments.	Capital Invested. In real estate.	Capital Invested. In tools and machinery.	Cash Value. Of raw materials used.	Cash Value. Of manufactured articles.	Persons employed.
New York Co.						
New-York, ...	1	....	12,000	15,000	18,000	14
Rensselaer Co.						
Lansingburgh,....	1	1,500	600	....	....	....
Troy, ...	1	15,000	10,000	107,049	131,695	37

SILK PRINTING ESTABLISHMENT.

TOWNS.	Number of establishments.	Capital Invested. In real estate.	Capital Invested. In tools and machinery.	Cash Value. Of raw materials used.	Cash Value. Of manufactured articles.	Persons employed.
Richmond Co.						
Castleton,.........	1	25,000	10,000	375,000	465,000	183

STARCH FACTORIES.

TOWNS.	Number of establishments.	Capital Invested. In real estate.	Capital Invested. In tools and machinery.	Cash Value. Of raw materials used.	Cash Value. Of manufactured articles.	Persons employed.
Clinton Co.						
Chazy,...........	1	3,000	....	....	....	....
Ellenburgh,.......	1	3,000	100	2,530	3,000	2
Mooers,..........	1	....	....	....	3,360	....
Plattsburgh,......	2	4,300	265	1,780	2,350	6
Schuyler Falls,...	3	10,000	750	2,485	4,127	7
Erie Co.						
Buffalo,..........	1	1,000	400	750	950	2
Essex Co.						
Chesterfield,......	1	5,000	1 000	5,000	9,400	4
North Elba,......	1	....	800	241	625	3
Franklin Co.						
Bangor,..........	4	6,500	300	8,950	16,050	11
Bombay,..........	1	5,000	25	....	....	....
Brandon, ...	2	4,000	....	3,700	2,670	5
Chateaugay, ...	2	4,000	....	1,250	1,800	3
Constable, ...	1	500	500	1,100	1,800	3
Dickinson, ...	2	3,300	1,600	3,125	3,800	4
Malone, ...	2	1,800	1,000	1,100	1,790	4
Moira,...........	2	1,100	2,100	950	3,043	2
Westville,........	1	1,000	2,500	505	840	2
Herkimer Co.						
Little Falls,......	1	12,000	2,000	....	....	....
Kings Co.						
Brooklyn, ...	1	6,500	1,500	17,250	27,600	7
New-York Co.						
New-York, ...	1	1,400	....	....	....	2
Oneida Co.						
Utica, ...	1	....	....	8,900	12,000	8
Oswego Co.						
Granby,..........	1	4,500	1,000	....	....	....
Oswego city,......	1	100,000	40,000	304,500	460,000	130
Queens Co.						
Newtown,........	1	15,000	4,000	26,300	55,500	14
St. Lawrence Co.						
Hopkinton, ...	2	3,500	800	....	3,700	6
Lawrence,........	2	5,600	100	2,350	4,114	2
Potsdam, ...	1	2,000	500	....	....	....
Stockholm,.......	2	2,000	500	2,000	4,500	4
Washington Co.						
Granville,........	1	8,000	150	150	340	3

SUGAR AND SYRUP REFINERIES.

TOWNS.	Number of establishments.	Capital Invested. In real estate.	Capital Invested. In tools and machinery.	Cash Value. Of raw materials used.	Cash Value. Of manufactured articles.	Persons employed.
New-York Co.						
New-York,.......	14	$1272000	$1257100	$4,507,500	$12167600	1628
Queens Co.						
Newtown,........	1	2000	1000	4,000	7750	3

VARNISH MANUFACTORIES.

TOWNS.	Number of establishments.	Capital Invested. In real estate.	Capital Invested. In tools and machinery.	Cash Value. Of raw materials used.	Cash Value. Of manufactured articles.	Persons employed.
Kings Co.						
Brooklyn,........	3	25,500	2,600	25,300	25,300	10
Monroe Co.						
Rochester,.......	1	....	155	849	1,025	2
New-York Co.						
New-York,.......	5	64,000	9,800	264,520	497,000	73
Rensselaer Co						
Troy,............	1	1,000	500	1,600	20,000	1
Schenectady Co						
Schenectady,......	1	600	....	6,450	8,200	2

VINEGAR MANUFACTORIES.

TOWNS.	Number of establishments.	Capital Invested. In real estate.	Capital Invested. In tools and machinery.	Cash Value. Of raw materials used.	Cash Value. Of manufactured articles.	Persons employed.
Albany Co.						
Albany, ...	1	1,500	2,000	9,000	18,000	4
Columbia Co.						
Hudson,..........	1	....	100	....	3,750	2
Dutchess Co.						
Fishkill,..........	1	800	532	150	1,600	3
Erie Co.						
Buffalo,...........	2	200	2,200	4,250	10,500	4
Greene Co.						
Greenville,.......	1	....	....	....	210	....
Kings Co.						
Brooklyn,........	1	....	1,000	4,728	10,800	5
Monroe Co.						
Rochester,........	2	600	600	3,550	7,250	3
New-York Co.						
New-York,........	1	10,500	8,000	....	....	4
Onondaga Co.						
Syracuse,.........	2	1,000	500	1,650	3,500	3

WAX BLEACHING ESTABLISHMENT.

TOWNS.	Number of establishments.	Capital Invested. In real estate.	Capital Invested. In tools and machinery.	Cash Value. Of raw materials used.	Cash Value. Of manufactured articles.	Persons employed.
New-York Co.						
New-York,.......	1	....	3,000	30,000	35,000	3

WHITE LEAD MANUFACTORIES.

TOWNS.	Number of establishments.	Capital Invested. In real estate.	Capital Invested. In tools and machinery.	Cash Value. Of raw materials used.	Cash Value. Of manufactured articles.	Persons employed.
Erie Co.						
Buffalo,...........	2	45,000	28,000	228,250	295,000	85
Kings Co.						
Brooklyn,........	1	70,000	75,000	395,000	800,000	195
Monroe Co.						
Rochester, ...	1	16,000	2,500	5,747	6,663	2
New-York Co.						
New-York, ...	2	29,000	8,000	24,500	115,000	19
Rensselaer Co.						
Northfield,.......	1	15,000	5,000	166,000	245,000	40
Ulster Co.						
Saugerties,.......	2	46,000	2,200	69,000	81,000	29

WHITING MANUFACTORIES.

TOWNS.	Number of establishments.	Capital Invested. In real estate.	Capital Invested. In tools and machinery.	Cash Value. Of raw materials used.	Cash Value. Of manufactured articles.	Persons employed.
Kings Co.						
Brooklyn,........	1	21,000	3,500	19,300	60,000	17
New-York Co.						
New-York, ...	2	9,000	1,900	12,500	31,500	8

WINTER-GREEN DISTILLERIES.

TOWNS.	Number of establishments.	Capital Invested. In real estate.	Capital Invested. In tools and machinery.	Cash Value. Of raw materials used.	Cash Value. Of manufactured articles.	Persons employed.
Sullivan Co.						
Forrestburgh, ...	1	....	150	1,300	1,600	6
Ulster Co.						
Olive,............	2	....	450	1,650	2,700	2
Wawarsing,......	9	995	....	3,874	5,177	....

CLASS V.—CALORIFICS.

TOWNS.	Number of establishments.	Capital Invested. In real estate.	Capital Invested. In tools and machinery.	Cash Value. Of raw materials used.	Cash Value. Of manufactured articles.	Persons employed.
GRATE MANUFACTORIES.						
Albany Co.						
Albany,	1	....	$1,000	$15,000	$20,000	11
New-York Co.						
New-York,	9	....	25,900	111,000	188,161	122
LAMP AND LANTERN MANUFACTORIES.						
Erie Co.						
Buffalo,	2	4,100	....	11,535	33,500	28
Kings Co.						
Brooklyn,	2	500	5,000	22,255	55,000	36
New-York Co.						
New-York,	5	7,000	34,300	61,800	97,000	77
LOCOMOTIVE LAMP MANUFACTORY.						
Monroe Co.						
Rochester,	3	38,000	4,200	16,558	46,100	20
STOVE MANUFACTORIES.*						
Columbia Co.						
Hudson,	1	10,000	2,000	20,000	75,000	100
Stuyvesant,	1	8,000	2,000	4,350	31,200	17
Dutchess Co.						
Poughkeepsie city,	1	$8,000	$2,000	$18,000	$42,000	15
Erie Co.						
Buffalo,	2	25,500	10,500	111,400	213,000	280
Franklin Co.						
Malone,	1	4,500	5,063	6,280	4,000	14
Kings Co.						
Brooklyn,	2	27,000	3,000	65,000	85,000	82
Monroe Co.						
Rochester,	2	14,000	15,000	30,600	78,000	105
New-York Co.						
New-York,	11	325,000	17,300	129,000	486,350	258
Oneida Co.						
Utica,	3	41,000	22,000	73,050	179,500	103
Rensselaer Co.						
Troy,	4	73,600	33,500	141,400	433,520	430
Saratoga Co.						
Halfmoon,	2	200	15,000	23,500	85,500	75
Stillwater,	1	2,000	600	2,160	5,600	4
Westchester Co.						
Cortland,	4	28,500	3,600	86,247	190,000	155

CLASS VI.—STEAM ENGINES, BOILERS, LOCOMOTIVES, ETC.

TOWNS.	Number of establishments.	Capital Invested. In real estate.	Capital Invested. In tools and machinery.	Cash Value. Of raw materials used.	Cash Value. Of manufactured articles.	Persons employed.
LOCOMOTIVE MANUFACTORIES.						
Albany Co.						
Albany,	1	....	247,500	....	....	171
Erie Co.						
Buffalo,	1	80,000	40,000	54,600	90,000	200
Schenectady Co.						
Schenectady,	1	30,000	70,000	199,825	370,500	450
LOCOMOTIVE SPARK-ARRESTOR MANUFACTORY.						
New-York Co.						
New-York,	1	30,000	1,000	8,250	30,000	9
STEAM ENGINE AND BOILER MANUFACTORIES.†						
Albany Co.						
Albany,	3	35,000	25,700	85,000	138,400	118
Erie Co.						
Buffalo,	4	99,000	45,000	74,362	246,456	169
Kings Co.						
Brooklyn,	1	8,000	1,000	....	75,000	2
New-York Co.						
New-York,	17	1115,500	773,650	1,819,550	3,292,800	3130
Ontario Co.						
Seneca,	1	2,800	6,000	15,700	23,150	25
Orange Co.						
Newburgh,	1	6,000	3,000	17,500	29,500	33
Tioga Co.						
Owego,	1	6,000	6,000	....	16,000	15

CLASS VII.—NAVIGATION AND MARITIME IMPLEMENTS.

TOWNS.	Number of establishments.	Capital Invested. In real estate.	Capital Invested. In tools and machinery.	Cash Value. Of raw materials used.	Cash Value. Of manufactured articles.	Persons employed.
BLOCK MANUFACTORIES.						
Kings Co.						
Brooklyn,	2	30,000	10,000	20,900	70,000	58
New-York Co.						
New-York,	10	10,500	3,300	8,953	37,030	39
Oswego Co.						
Oswego city,	1	10,000	2,000	1.500	10,000	15
BOAT BUILDING.						
Cayuga Co.						
Mentz,	2	4,000	800	960	5,000	8
Chemung Co.						
Big Flats,	1	....	100	1,196	2,500	4
Erie Co.						
Buffalo,	1	500	200	300	1,600	2
Herkimer Co.						
Frankfort,	1	9,000	500	23,000	23,000	15
Livingston Co.						
North Dansville,	2	....	100	3,325	7,100	8
Madison Co.						
Lenox,	1	200	100	1,765	3,900	5
Monroe Co.						
Rochester,	14	57,300	13,050	143,278	341,500	261
Montgomery Co.						
Glen,	1	5,000	100	1,200	6,500	16
New-York Co.						
New-York,	10	85,800	12,395	60,780	127,575	90
Niagara Co.						
Lockport,	2	2,700	725	5,000	7,500	19
Oneida Co.						
Rome,	1	6,000	3,000	18,576	22,400	15
Oneida Co.						
Utica,	3	6,500	3,500	12,528	32,000	34
Verona,	6	5,800	2,300	8,807	23,150	34
Onondaga Co.						
Clay,	1	600	50	800	3,000	6
Elbridge,	2	3,500	250	2,020	7,200	6
Geddes,	1	5,000	500	600	5,000	10
Syracuse,	1	70,000	200	4,000	37,500	50
Orange Co.						
Deerpark,	2	8,000	1,600	2,238	3,425	28
Oswego Co.						
Volney,	2	7,000	1,500	4,500	8,000	18
Saratoga Co.						
Clifton Park,	3	16,000	900	7,700	30,000	38
Seneca Co.						
Seneca Falls,	1	300	200	12,000	23,000	35
Steuben Co.						
Pultney,	1	....	300	1,500	2,850	4
Suffolk Co.						
Easthampton,	1	1,000	300	300	3,000	4
Southold,	1	600	100	800	3,000	3
Sullivan Co.						
Mamakating,	5	6,700	320	15,518	34,750	33
Tompkins Co.						
Ithaca,	4	2,450	1,200	21,706	59,100	43
Lansing,	1	300	100	640	2,150	....
Ulster Co.						
Rochester,	1	1,000	200	4,940	16,000	18
Westchester Co.						
Rye,	1	900	200	1,000	3,000	4
Yates Co.						
Torrey,	1	300	500	2,600	4,000	10

* Those reported under the head of Furnaces, are not here included.

† Those reported under the head of Machine Shops, are not here included.

CLASS VII.—(Continued.)

TOWNS.	Number of establishments.	Capital Invested. In real estate.	Capital Invested. In tools and machinery.	Cash Value. Of raw materials used.	Cash Value. Of manufactured articles.	Persons employed.
CAPSTAN AND WINDLASS MANUFACTORY.						
New-York Co.						
New-York, ...	1	$3,000	$1,500	$10,700	$15,000	4
OAR MANUFACTORY.						
St. Lawrence Co.						
Canton, ...	1	2,500	300	1,000	2,250	3
SAIL MAKING.						
Monroe Co.						
Rochester, ...	1	....	....	5,000	7,500	9
New-York Co.						
New-York, ...	10	86,500	1,120	155,725	181,175	76
Richmond Co.						
Northfield, ...	1	1,000	25	3,310	5,400	5
Suffolk Co.						
Brookhaven, ...	1	....	....	10,600	15,500	6
Southold, ...	1	....	50	8,000	10,000	7
SHIP BUILDING.						
Albany Co.						
Albany, ...	1	4,000	200	15,000	....	28
Watervliet, ...	1	5,000	250	3,550	6,000	13
Broome Co.						
Chenango, ...	1	300	25	200	1,000	3
Dutchess Co.						
Poughkeepsie, ...	1	....	1,000	10,000	41,000	34
Greene Co.						
Athens, ...	1	3,000	200	5,400	22,000	20
Coxsackie, ...	1	6,000	2,000	10,000	22,000	12
New Baltimore, ...	1	1,500	150	5,530	12,000	8
Jefferson Co.						
Clayton, ...	1	2,000	2,200	26,000	50,000	60
Hounsfield, ...	1	....	700	4,000	9,000	20
Kings Co.						
Brooklyn, ...	6	411,000	42,600	579,000	945,000	540
New-York Co.						
New-York, ...	25	673,000	57,300	922,816	2,593,761	1773
Orange Co.						
Newburgh, ...	1	20,000	10,000	37,435	55,500	20
Oswego Co.						
Oswego city, ...	3	28,000	6,000	32,000	151,000	19
Queens Co.						
Newtown, ...	1	45,000	60,000	26,580	130,000	25
Richmond Co.						
Northfield, ...	3	9,500	5,600	6,200	13,400	14
Westfield, ...	2	5,900	3,500	5,950	20,500	20
Rockland Co.						
Clarkstown, ...	1	3,000	500	1,600	1,000	4
Orangetown, ...	2	6,500	300	17,255	39,400	27
St. Lawrence Co.						
Oswegatchie, ...	1	$3,000	$15,000	$7,200	$15,000	40
Suffolk Co.						
Brookhaven, ...	14	16,700	2,655	118,045	281,500	236
Huntington, ...	4	16,000	1,800	51,500	191,000	125
Islip, ...	1	....	2,000	11,702	17,000	18
Smithtown, ...	1	....	500	....	....	....
Southold, ...	5	6,500	4,650	17,000	18,300	40
Sullivan Co.						
Highland, ...	1	5,000	200	345	3,000	9
Ulster Co.						
Kingston, ...	2	7,000	7,000	5,500	5,000	22
Saugerties, ...	1	3,000	30	1,500	3,000	6
Washington Co.						
Whitehall, ...	2	6,000	1,500	4,000	10,450	20
Westchester Co.						
Ossining, ...	1	800	2,000	3,000	8,000	50
SHIP RIGGING.						
New-York Co.						
New-York, ...	2	23,000	5,000	1,040,000	1,700,000	86
SHIP SMITHING.						
Kings Co.						
Brooklyn, ...	2	4,000	550	2,520	5,500	7
New-York Co.						
New-York, ...	26	134,800	34,250	99,230	194,490	168
Oswego Co.						
Oswego city, ...	2	8,000	3,500	5,800	7,000	9
Richmond Co.						
Westfield, ...	1	....	150	1,100	2,900	....
SPAR MANUFACTORIES.						
New-York Co.						
New-York, ...	3	144,000	4,000	200,000	310,000	95
Suffolk Co.						
East Hampton, ...	1	400	200	1,000	2,000	2
Southold, ...	2	300	150	700	1,800	4
STEAMBOAT FINISHING.						
Kings Co.						
Brooklyn, ...	1	17,000	10,000	100,000	150,000	64
TREENAIL FACTORIES.						
Kings Co.						
Brooklyn, ...	1	1,000	....	20,000	21,500	5
Westchester Co.						
North Castle, ...	6	....	....	4,800	5,550	8

CLASS VIII.—MATHEMATICAL PHILOSOPHICAL AND OPTICAL INSTRUMENTS.

TOWNS.	Number of establishments.	Capital Invested. In real estate.	Capital Invested. In tools and machinery.	Cash Value. Of raw materials used.	Cash Value. Of manufactured articles.	Persons employed.
BAROMETER MANUFACTORIES.						
Albany Co.						
Albany, ...	1	400	400	100	700	...
New-York Co.						
New-York, ...	2	....	1,600	4,000	11,000	11
CHRONOMETER MANUFACTORY.						
New-York Co.						
New-York, ...	5	....	16,040	17,300	56,500	49
CLOCK FACTORIES.						
Madison Co.						
Cazenovia, ...	2	3,200	2,200	1,100	4,610	5
New-York Co.						
New-York, ...	5	51,000	9,100	64,000	163,000	87
Suffolk Co.						
Southampton, ...	2	4,500	5,000	4,375	11,000	12
Tompkins Co.						
Ithaca, ...	1	....	500	....	....	4
HYDROMETER MANUFACTORY.						
New-York Co.						
New-York, ...	1	12,000	500	1,000	3,200	2
MATHEMATICAL INSTRUMENT MANUFACTORY.						
New-York Co.						
New-York, ...	10	....	15,100	18,000	101,000	33
NAUTICAL INSTRUMENT MANUFACTORIES.						
New-York Co.						
New-York, ...	3	....	5,300	3,750	16,400	14
Westchester Co.						
Eastchester, ...	1	....	2,000	225	1,400	3
OPTICAL INSTRUMENT MANUFACTORIES.						
Madison Co.						
Lenox, ...	1	1,850	4,000	1,710	12,500	14
New-York Co.						
New-York, ...	3	600	1,550	5,800	18,000	4
PHILOSOPHICAL INSTRUMENT MANUFACTORY.						
New-York Co.						
New-York, ...	1	....	35,000	300	1,800	....
SPECTACLE MANUFACTORY.						
New-York Co.						
New-York, ...	2	10,000	1,000	4,310	19,250	16

CLASS VIII.—(CONTINUED.)

TOWNS.	Number of establishments.	Capital Invested. In real estate.	Capital Invested. In tools and machinery.	Cash Value. Of raw materials used.	Cash Value. Of manufactured articles.	Persons employed.
SURVEYING INSTRUMENT MANUFACTORIES.						
CHENANGO Co.						
Norwich,	1	$250	$1,000	$230	$1,200	2
RENSSELAER Co.						
Troy,	1	8,000	9,000	3,500	28,000	25
TELEGRAPH INSTRUMENT MANUFACTORIES.						
NEW-YORK Co.						
New-York,	2	8,000	10,000	20,550	45,000	21
ONEIDA Co.						
Utica,	1	....	3,200	6,000	19,500	10
RENSSELAER Co.						
Troy,	1	$2,000	$1,500	$1,000	$6,000	8
THERMOMETER MANUFACTORIES.						
COLUMBIA Co.						
New Lebanon,	1	250	350	330	11,450	9
DUTCHESS Co.						
Poughkeepsie city,	1	3,000	700	1,000	4,000	4
KINGS Co.						
Brooklyn,	1	500	400	500	1,500	2

CLASS IX.—CIVIL ENGINEERING AND ARCHITECTURE.

TOWNS.	Number of establishments.	Capital Invested. In real estate.	Capital Invested. In tools and machinery.	Cash Value. Of raw materials used.	Cash Value. Of manufactured articles.	Persons employed.
GYPSUM QUARRY.						
CAYUGA Co.						
Springport,	3	9,500	2,300	12,400	14,200	24
HOUSE BUILDING.						
KINGS Co.						
Brooklyn,	11	82,700	9,300	95,600	254,000	151
MONROE Co.						
Rochester,	3	7,000	3,000	14,000	40,000	103
Rush,	1	....	....	700	1,100	1
NEW-YORK Co.						
New-York,	40	368,600	50,705	194,950	665,000	980
ONEIDA Co.						
Utica,	8	5,680	4,050	13,250	56,000	88
ONONDAGA Co.						
Syracuse,	3	6,000	450	3,300	13,000	16
ONTARIO Co.						
Canandaigua,	1	600	100	1,000	4,000	7
East Bloomfield,	1	800	500	900	2,500	4
Victor,	2	....	250	....	....	8
OSWEGO Co.						
Granby,	1	400	125	100	1,500	2
Oswego,	2	1,700	350	5,200	15,900	19
RICHMOND Co.						
Northfield,	5	1,325	3,175	28,100	68,700	46
SCHUYLER Co.						
Tyrone,	1	400	200	1,856	3,000	5
SUFFOLK Co.						
Huntington,	2	1,325	1,090	8,900	14,000	10
ULSTER Co.						
Saugerties,	4	3,600	825	13,875	36,000	21
WESTCHESTER Co.						
Somers,	3	2,000	3,700	13,800	43,000	45
IRON MINING.						
CLINTON Co.						
Black Brook,	1	....	....	....	45,626	....
Dannemora,	1	108,000	11,000	39,914	52,414	65
Ausable,	1	....	....	750	17,500	50
COLUMBIA Co.						
Copake,	1	10,000	....	....	6,000	....
DUTCHESS Co.						
East Fishkill,	1	5,000	500	1,000	9,000	20
ESSEX Co.						
Moriah,	7	254,000	31,750	....	318,900	443
Schroon,	1	10,000	141	....	6,500	13
JEFFERSON Co.						
Antwerp,	2	8,500	350	....	14,582	33
ONEIDA Co.						
Kirkland,	6	17,500	880	342	41,050	78
Westmoreland,	3	13,000	750	3,850	....	16
ORANGE Co.						
Monroe,	2	9,000	600	....	21,750	43
PUTNAM Co.						
Carmel,	1	2,000	50	....	4,000	4
WAYNE Co.						
Ontario,	2	....	50	....	3,250	21
LEAD MINING.						
ST. LAWRENCE Co.						
Rossie,	1	7,250	14,000	....	8,000	20
MARL AND PEAT BEDS.						
COLUMBIA Co.						
Greenport,	1	....	....	....	400	1
SARATOGA Co.						
Ballston,	1	1,000	10	....	528	....
MASONRY.						
CAYUGA Co.						
Moravia,	1	....	50	....	....	2
CLINTON Co.						
Saranac,	1	....	10	....	600	2
DUTCLESS Co.						
Fishkill,	2	....	109	....	....	14
ERIE Co.						
Buffalo,	1	10,000	200	....	....	20
KINGS Co.						
Brooklyn,	1	....	200	200	2,000	3
MONROE Co.						
Webster,	2	....	6	....	....	[illegible]
MINING MACHINE MANUFACTORY.						
NEW-YORK Co.						
New-York,	1	....	7,000	38,000	50,000	
ORNAMENTAL PLASTERING.						
NEW-YORK Co.						
New-York,	1	....	12,000	50,300	75,000	83
SASH AND BLIND MANUFACTORIES.						
ALBANY Co.						
Albany,	1	2,000	600	4,000	8,000	6
Watervliet,	2	7,000	5,900	2,300	24,200	24
ALLEGANY Co.						
Angelica,	1	1,000	900	455	3,000	3
Belfast,	1	1,000	800	1,075	500	3
Rushford,	2	900	700	410	1,425	3
BROOME Co.						
Chenango,	3	5,100	5,500	10,220	25,190	17
Lisle,	1	500	300	450	1,000	....
CATTARAUGUS Co.						
Allegany,	1	1,000	4,000	2,000	10,600	9
New Albion,	1	2,500	900	360	1,500	2
Olean,	1	1,200	600	....	1,000	12
CAYUGA Co.						
Auburn,	2	....	1,500	1,885	4,611	8
Sterling,	1	400	300	280	1,040	2
CHAUTAUQUE Co.						
Elliot,	3	10,000	17,600	12,700	12,700	17
Mina,	1	200	500	300	600	2
Pomfret,	3	800	975	2,550	6,300	6
CHEMUNG Co.						
Elmira,	1	1,800	2,000	10,275	16,000	10
Veteran,	1	100	400	270	1,000	2
CHENANGO Co.						
Bainbridge,	2	500	1,900	650	2,590	5
Greene,	1	1,800	200	200	....	2
Norwich,	1	2,500	3,000	1,650	1,900	8
Sherburne,	1	2,500	1,000	3,000	8,000	8
CLINTON Co.						
Plattsburgh,	1	....	900	150	430	4
COLUMBIA Co.						
Chatham,	1	400	300	520	1,000	3
Hudson,	1	5,000	2,500	3,700	11,700	11
CORTLAND Co.						
Cortlandville,	1	700	300	625	1,524	2
Truxton,	1	2,000	1,000	2,000	6,000	6
DELAWARE Co.						
Franklin,	1	1,000	500	300	1,000	3
Tompkins,	1	800	500	1,200	5,000	3

CLASS IX.—(CONTINUED.)

TOWNS.	Number of establishments.	Capital Invested. In real estate.	Capital Invested. In tools and machinery.	Cash Value. Of raw materials used.	Cash Value. Of manufactured articles.	Persons employed.
DUTCHESS Co.						
Amenia,	1	$800	$50	$910	$2,160	3
Poughkeepsie city,	3	3,600	2,425	5,250	11,500	13
Rhinebeck,	2	2,500	1,800	1,300	6,200	6
ERIE Co.						
Buffalo,	6	50,800	18,100	3,400	14,000	21
Tonawanda,	1	2,000	1,000	200	1,046	3
ESSEX Co.						
Chesterfield,	1	....	2,000	1,000	3,500	4
Crown Point,	1	3,600	700	400	6,000	6
FRANKLIN Co.						
Constable,	2	500	1,500	1,000	2,800	5
Franklin,	1	150	....	45	150	1
GENESEE Co.						
Alexander,	1	350	700	200	800	1
Batavia,	1	....	100	132	550	1
Elba,	1	200	300	200	800	2
GREENE Co.						
Catskill,	1	3,000	3,000	21,000	40,000	21
HERKIMER Co.						
German Flats,	1	....	2,200	1,200	6,000	9
Little Falls,	1	2,000	1,000	2,000	6,000	4
Newport,	1	500	100	395	900	....
Russia,	1	800	400	600	1,200	1
JEFFERSON Co.						
Adams,	1	1,000	1,100	400	1,300	3
Pamelia,	1	100	700	1,500	3,125	8
Watertown,	1	....	....	390	600	....
Wilna,	1	1,700	800	120	479	3
KINGS Co.						
Brooklyn,	11	25,900	3,800	31,673	102,178	60
LEWIS Co.						
Lowville,	1	700	800	520	4,500	7
LIVINGSTON Co.						
North Dansville,	1	....	300	260	1,500	2
Springwater,	1	500	1,000	4,500	1,500	2
MADISON Co.						
Cazenovia,	1	....	3,500	18,000	28,000	25
Georgetown,	1	1,000	400	1,000	1,500	2
Lenox,	1	1,100	2,000	1,725	3,600	7
Stockbridge,	1	1,000	550	400	775	2
MONROE Co.						
Brighton,	1	2,000	200	300	2,000	4
Perrington,	1	200	800	20	120	2
Rochester,	8	2,856	16,900	24,120	45,875	66
Sweden,	1	600	1,400	800	1,800	4
MONTGOMERY Co.						
Charleston,	1	800	600	530	1,264	2
Glen,	1	....	....	3,050	2,500	....
NEW-YORK Co.						
New-York,	21	75,800	38,550	91,455	210,700	237
NIAGARA Co.						
Lockport,	1	....	....	1,350	5,500	....
Niagara,	2	9,000	1,800	7,250	13,000	18
ONEIDA Co.						
Camden,	1	1,600	....	180	1,800	4
Kirkland,	1	2,000	500	1,140	1,900	3
Lee,	1	1,700	450	730	2,250	4
Rome,	2	3,500	2,000	11,003	24,500	30
ONONDAGA Co.						
De Witt,	1	1,000	1,000	2,200	5,715	3
Fabius,	1	500	100	250	900	2
Manlius,	1	4,000	200	4,400	16,000	8
Skaneateles,	1	400	650	300	500	1
Syracuse,	2	1,350	5,500	5,217	35,785	16
ONTARIO Co.						
Canandaigua,	1	3,000	1,000	450	2,500	3
ORANGE Co.						
Goshen,	1	1,500	150	2,000	3,000	3
Newburgh,	1	4,500	2,300	800	6,000	3
Walkill,	2	1,600	2,000	3,480	5,450	9
ORLEANS Co.						
Ridgeway,	2	1,800	700	1,280	2,500	6
OSWEGO Co.						
Oswego city,	1	....	1,000	2,500	10,000	9
Richland,	1	1,500	1,500	2,200	3,000	11
Volney,	1	....	5,000	10,000	5,100	6
OTSEGO Co.						
Maryland,	1	415	1,000	1,000	1,410	3
Milford,	2	....	350	460	1,850	3
Oneonta,	1	60	125	625	1,200	2
Roseboom,	1	50	100	100	400	....
Unadilla,	1	4,000	1,800	1,200	3,600	7
Westford,	1	400	250	500	1,000	2
Worcester,	1	500	700	100	300	3
QUEENS Co.						
Hempstead,	1	600	100	850	1,500	3
Newtown,	1	1,200	200	1,600	4,500	6
North Hempstead,	1	....	350	525	3,000	6
RICHMOND Co.						
Westfield,	1	$650	$500	$1,330	$2,600	4
ST. LAWRENCE Co.						
Canton,	1	1,000	500	375	1,500	3
Colton,	3	9,500	....	1,400	6,000	10
De Kalb,	1	....	1,000	....	5,000	10
Lawrence,	1	1,200	50	240	200	....
Norfolk,	1	2,000	500	11,200	15,000	15
Oswegatchie,	2	7,000	3,700	3,600	18,000	20
Potsdam,	3	9,000	2,200	8,500	25,900	26
SARATOGA Co.						
Malta,	1	500	350	900	2,000	2
Moreau,	2	....	3,400	8,000	24,000	25
Saratoga,	2	6,200	2,300	3,500	13,000	16
Saratoga Springs,	2	9,000	6,500	37,500	100,000	43
SCHOHARIE Co.						
Schoharie,	1	400	600	700	1,400	3
SCHUYLER Co.						
Catharines,	2	2,700	662	600	3,500	6
Tyrone,	1	200	100	300	800	1
SENECA Co.						
Fayette,	1	1,800	1,000	800	4,000	6
Seneca Falls,	2	14,500	5,300	13,610	44,000	24
STEUBEN Co.						
Addison,	1	5,000	5,000	850	10,000	12
Bath,	1	800	250	1,055	2,200	2
Hornellsville,	2	1,200	2,368	1,175	3,600	4
SUFFOLK Co.						
Huntington,	1	5,000	2,000	3,500	4,300	8
Riverhead,	1	....	50	140	1,000	3
Southampton,	1	1,000	1,500	120	2,000	4
Southold,	2	850	750	1,500	4,000	11
SULLIVAN Co.						
Thompson,	1	500	150	650	1,250	2
TOMPKINS Co.						
Caroline,	1	1,000	1,000	810	1,738	4
Ithaca,	1	1,500	2,000	3,500	6,000	6
ULSTER Co.						
Kingston,	1	2,000	500	900	5,000	3
Saugerties,	1	1,000	1,600	9,300	12,200	13
Wawarsing,	1	600	700	300	1,500	2
WASHINGTON Co.						
Greenwich,	1	700	200	1,500	1,500	3
Hartford,	1	300	200	192	376	....
Kingsbury,	1	200	300	300	1,500	3
WAYNE Co.						
Arcadia,	1	....	....	....	2,000	....
WESTCHESTER Co.						
Eastchester,	3	900	250	1,807	4,400	5
Mount Pleasant,	1	800	150	....	....	2
North Salem,	1	1,500	500	1,100	3,000	1
Ossining,	2	2,200	1,400	1,480	8,500	8
WYOMING Co.						
Castile,	1	800	300	232	1,103	1
China,	2	2,500	400	640	3,500	5
YATES Co.						
Starkey,	1	400	200	465	2,583	....

STAIR-BUILDING ESTABLISHMENTS.

TOWNS.	Number of establishments.	In real estate.	In tools and machinery.	Of raw materials used.	Of manufactured articles.	Persons employed.
NEW-YORK Co.						
New-York,	8	1,700	1,100	4,100	21,900	36

STONE QUARRIES.

TOWNS.	Number of establishments.	In real estate.	In tools and machinery.	Of raw materials used.	Of manufactured articles.	Persons employed.
ALBANY Co.						
Berne,	5	....	....	....	6,560	21
Watervliet,	2	....	900	....	8,000	8
Westerlo,	3	....	52	....	2,040	6
CATTARAUGUS Co.						
Great Valley,	1	700	10	....	300	1
CAYUGA Co.						
Auburn,	1	1,500	50	250	1,200	2
Aurelius,	1	600	100	....	937	3
Springport,	2	11,900	1,000	6,500	8,000	7
CHAUTAUQUE Co.						
Pomfret,	1	300	10	....	375	1
CHENANGO Co.						
Oxford,	2	300	200	....	1,400	7
Plymouth,	1	125	....	....	75	....
CLINTON Co.						
Ausable,	1	250	....	....	....	....
COLUMBIA Co.						
Greenport,	3	5,650	1,865	11,000	11,000	21
Stuyvesant,	1	....	....	....	1,500	2
DUTCHESS Co.						
Dover,	2	3,000	500	5,600	10,200	13
ERIE Co.						
Buffalo,	10	6,600	330	3,515	17,250	54

CLASS IX.—(Continued.)

TOWNS.	Number of establishments.	Capital Invested. In real estate.	Capital Invested. In tools and machinery.	Cash Value. Of raw materials used.	Cash Value. Of manufactured articles.	Persons employed.
Essex Co.						
Willsborough,....	1	$500	$200	$125	$2, 800	....
Franklin Co.						
Malone,..........	2	17, 000	1, 500	....	7, 500	33
Fulton Co.						
Oppenheim,......	1	500	....	165	4, 910	15
Genesee Co.						
Le Roy,..........	4	2, 050	500	1, 350	8, 200	13
Greene Co.						
Athens,..........	4	1, 300	270	....	7, 927	26
Herkimer Co.						
Little Falls,......	1	1, 000	100	....	20, 000	20
Norway,.........	1	....	40	....	250	1
Jefferson Co.						
Lyme,...........	1	....	....	....	10, 000	26
Watertown,......	1	2, 000	40	....	350	3
Lewis Co.						
Lowville, ...	2	200	....	....	735	6
Madison Co.						
Lenox,...........	4	5, 000	465	....	16, 760	43
Monroe Co.						
Mendon,.........	2	800	200	....	3, 900	7
Rochester, ...	2	3, 000	500	....	4, 200	8
Montgomery Co.						
Mohawk,.........	1	....	....	....	20, 000	40
Niagara Co.						
Lockport,........	6	22, 100	6, 500	....	43, 850	241
Oneida Co.						
Bridgewater, ...	1	800	75	....	1, 000	4
New Hartford,....	4	....	....	....	2, 262	6
Paris,............	50	....	....	....	400	....
Verona,..........	2	20, 000	1, 040	....	10, 700	27
Westmoreland,...	1	1, 000	75	240	....	1
Onondaga Co.						
De Witt,.........	1	....	50	1, 795	....	10
Onondaga, ...	3	800	850	950	4, 600	13
Orange Co.						
Deerpark,........	2	$150	$15	$150	150	3
Orleans Co.						
Ridgeway,........	6	35, 400	3, 800	....	43, 100	319
Putnam Co.						
Phillipstown,.....	1	....	200	....	5, 000	5
Rensselaer Co.						
Brunswick, ...	1	....	40	....	1, 600	5
Lansingburgh,....	1	500	150	....	575	....
Troy, ...	4	12, 000	255	....	8, 900	11
St. Lawrence Co.						
Madrid,..........	1	....	100	....	5, 000	16
Potsdam, ...	1	3, 000	200	....	2, 650	6
Saratoga Co.						
Milton, ...	1	....	50	....	1, 500	3
Schenectady Co.						
Schenectady,......	1	500	....	....	500	1
Schoharie Co.						
Sharon, ...	1	1, 000	50	....	600	1
Seneca Co.						
Covert, ...	1	2, 000	....	....	14, 000	30
Fayette, ...	2	....	1, 900	7, 000	8, 000	44
Seneca Falls, ...	1	500	50	....	500	1
Steuben Co.						
Corning,.........	1	....	200	1, 500	1, 500	8
Ulster Co.						
Hurley,..........	1	15, 500	550	....	51, 200	....
Lloyd,...........	1	1, 000	300	....	3, 500	12
Marbletown, ...	2	500	125	....	10, 500	7
Rosendale,........	1	25, 000	500	....	....	30
Saugerties,.......	34	39, 750	3, 632	....	128, 400	368
Woodstock, ...	1	200	....	....	2, 400	9
Washington Co.						
Hampton,........	1	10, 000	200	....	2, 700	15
Hebron,..........	2	4, 000	1, 700	....	2, 000	8
Westchester Co.						
Mount Pleasant,..	1	4, 000	200	....	....	21

CLASS X.—LAND CONVEYANCE.

TOWNS.	Number of establishments.	In real estate.	In tools and machinery.	Of raw materials used.	Of manufactured articles.	Persons employed.
BOW AND FELLOE MANUFACTORIES.						
Herkimer Co.						
Norway,.........	1	100	250	300	974	2
Monroe Co.						
Rochester, ...	2	3, 900	10, 000	9, 500	29, 200	17
St. Lawrence Co.						
Gouverneur,......	1	1, 500	1, 200	850	3, 000	3
Schuyler Co.						
Hector,..........	1	1, 500	300	300	1, 500	2
Ulster Co.						
Lloyd,...........	1	2, 000	1, 500	10, 500	10, 500	6
CAR FACTORIES AND REPAIR SHOPS.						
Albany Co.						
Albany,..........	1	....	4, 000	....	....	54
Allagany Co.						
Amity, ...	1	....	450	1, 200	4, 500	12
Cayuga Co.						
Auburn, ...	1	25, 000	5, 000	10, 876	35, 000	50
Chautauque Co.						
Pomfret,.........	1	4, 000	5, 000	17, 750	27, 000	35
Chemung Co.						
Elmira,..........	1	7, 000	4, 500	4, 060	15, 000	17
Clinton Co.						
Plattsburgh, ...	1	800	10, 000	34, 315	52, 200	50
Erie Co.						
Buffalo, ...	2	39, 000	29, 000	93, 366	163, 100	80
Genesee Co.						
Le Roy, ...	1	24, 000	12, 000	36, 800	68, 650	43
Lewis Co.						
Lowville, ...	1	....	25	412	660	....
Monroe Co.						
Rochester,........	1	17, 000	3, 000	2, 500	32, 500	50
New-York Co.						
New-York, ...	1	....	5, 000	100, 347	204, 000	165
Oneida Co.						
Rome,...........	1	36, 000	6, 000	20, 000	34, 000	40
Utica,...........	2	19, 000	9, 800	53, 000	66, 900	80
Onondaga Co.						
Syracuse,........	1	15, 000	2, 500	....	100, 000	23
Oswego Co.						
Oswego city, ...	1	7, 230	2, 500	1, 650	10, 000	15
Rensselaer Co.						
Greenbush,.......	2	25, 000	51, 000	33 890	169, 000	235
Rockland Co.						
Orangetown, ...	1	125, 000	41, 509	173, 258	173, 258	230
St. Lawrence Co.						
Oswegatchie, ...	1	18, 500	33, 000	45, 650	25, 000	170
Stockholm,.......	1	5, 000	....	....	....	....
Schenectady Co.						
Schenectady,......	1	20, 000	30, 000	41, 000	41, 000	120
Steuben Co.						
Hornellsville,.....	2	12, 500	5, 500	4, 165	28, 000	48
Washington Co.						
Salem,...........	1	20, 000	5, 000	5, 000	25, 000	30
CAR WHEEL FOUNDERIES.						
Albany Co.						
Watervliet,.......	1	28, 000	20, 000	177, 605	247, 500	61
Rensselaer Co.						
Troy, ...	1	....	6, 000	164, 360	200, 000	25
COACH AND WAGON MANUFACTORIES.						
Albany Co.						
Albany, ...	7	50, 500	12, 200	64, 335	156, 300	177
Bethlehem,.......	5	3, 800	785	2, 927	6, 273	14
Coeymans,.......	1	800	350	1, 000	2, 550	5
Knox,...........	1	25	20	50	200	....
New Scotland,....	4	1, 600	320	350	1, 200	3
Rensselaerville,...	2	25	60	225	800	3
Watervliet,.......	8	95, 600	24, 075	123, 204	334, 700	209
Westerlo,........	1	100	300	200	800	1
Allegany Co.						
Alfred,...........	3	1, 000	500	199	1, 350	4
Almond,.........	1	1, 000	500	325	1, 680	....
Amity, ...	2	700	200	600	1, 600	3
Andover, ...	2	650	350	....	....	3
Angelica,.........	2	2, 000	600	2, 355	8, 014	14
Belfast,..........	1	500	100	35	450	2
Burns,...........	2	250	75	135	900	3
Cuba, ...	2	2, 900	525	2, 300	6, 900	7
Friendship, ...	2	1, 400	350	200	1, 800	3
Hume,...........	1	800	500	700	200	4
Independence, ...	1	1, 500	600	350	1, 280	2
Rushford,........	4	1, 800	100	4, 340	14, 571	16
Scio,.............	1	88	75	125	625	....
Broome Co.						
Barker,..........	1	1, 600	300	1, 305	....	10
Chenango,........	4	9, 200	1, 500	4, 412	14, 620	18

CLASS X.—(Continued.)

TOWNS.	Number of establishments.	Capital Invested. In real estate.	Capital Invested. In tools and machinery.	Cash Value. Of raw materials used.	Cash Value. Of manufactured articles.	Persons employed.
Broome Co.						
Colesville,	5	$2,350	$980	$2,350	$6,800	12
Sandford,	2	350	....	600	2,800	4
Windsor,	3	1,200	250	1,160	3,875	1
Cattaraugus Co.						
Ellicottville,	1	700	100	350	2,000	2
Farmersville,	1	300	100	314	944	2
Franklinville,	5	1,300	525	475	2,775	5
Lyndon,	1	....	100	....	....	....
Mansfield,	2	350	250	2,500	....	5
Olean,	2	500	175	100	2,225	4
Otto,	1	400	75	120	730	1
Perrysburgh,	1	350	30	107	680	1
Portville,	1	1,200	250	100	1,000	2
Randolph,	2	1,050	400	2,500	6,400	8
Yorkshire,	1	300	25	25	200	1
Cayuga Co.						
Auburn,	6	8,700	4,500	11,468	36,440	52
Aurelius,	4	1,200	550	900	5,700	12
Cato,	1	500	250	1,100	3,200	8
Genoa,	3	1,100	295	245	1,350	4
Ira,	2	1,200	160	605	3,500	3
Locke,	2	575	75	150	3,000	6
Mentz,	6	2,100	825	4,880	9,450	17
Moravia,	2	450	200	1,162	2,620	3
Niles,	1	400	60	300	800	1
Owasco,	1	2,000	200	667	1,440	3
Sennett,	1	250	200	150	500	2
Summer Hill,	1	350	50	550	400	1
Venice,	1	200	200	....	600	....
Victory,	1	500	100	60	1,500	3
Chautauque Co.						
Chautauque,	3	1,850	1,130	2,550	8,350	8
Cherry Creek,	2	50	35	407	2,618	2
Ellicott,	3	5,500	3,430	5,990	15,270	22
Ellington,	1	400	100	150	700	1
Hanover,	5	900	485	1,300	3,340	6
Harmony,	3	....	....	....	1,500	....
Kiantone,	1	150	65	40	500	1
Pomfret,	7	7,400	2,275	4,110	30,440	26
Sherman,	1	....	....	....	500	....
Stockton,	3	1,500	200	....	3,290	4
Villenovia,	1	300	100	300	1,500	3
Westfield,	1	2,000	100	700	2,700	2
Chemung Co.						
Chemung,	3	500	450	250	1,500	3
Elmira,	4	17,000	4,550	13,490	38,850	46
Horseheads,	1	2,000	1,000	1,200	4,000	17
Veteran,	1	500	450	250	1,500	3
Chenango Co.						
Bainbridge,	1	200	150	50	900	2
Coventry,	1	200	100	30	800	1
Greene,	1	4,000	300	1,500	10,000	14
Guilford,	1	600	100	100	1,000	3
New Berlin,	5	3,450	750	2,842	6,626	8
Norwich,	3	6,700	2,200	13,695	26,500	37
Otselic,	2	600	125	345	1,360	3
Oxford,	4	3,700	650	1,260	7,700	10
Preston,	1	50	25	25	200	1
Sherburne,	1	500	150	945	3,440	6
Smyrna,	1	2,000	500	1,495	9,500	....
Clinton Co.						
Ausable,	2	400	....	400	1,600	4
Beekmantown,	5	1,575	775	785	1,920	8
Black Brook,	3	600	430	1,143	3,650	6
Champlain,	3	3,050	1,200	1,275	5,300	16
Ellenburgh,	1	500	200	400	600	2
Peru,	2	1,200	300	600	4,600	8
Plattsburgh,	1	....	500	1,936	7,750	10
Saranac,	1	1,000	300	550	3,000	8
Schuyler Falls,	2	1,200	330	1,160	3,516	6
Columbia Co.						
Canaan,	4	8,050	450	3,687	16,100	17
Chatham,	8	11,400	1,060	6,625	20,800	25
Clermont,	1	200	300	250	256	1
Copake,	3	4,000	450	1,370	3,900	....
Greenport,	1	200	100	....	....	....
Hillsdale,	3	1,250	575	2,462	5,600	11
Hudson,	2	5,200	1,750	12,750	24,500	25
Kinderhook,	5	5,000	655	510	2,900	3
Livingston,	4	1,350	155	2,621	....	....
New Lebanon,	1	600	175	800	2,500	4
Stuyvesant,	2	1,000	300	500	3,500	5
Cortland Co.						
Cortlandville,	3	3,500	900	1,795	7,920	20
Harford,	1	600	125	....	....	....
Homer,	4	4,200	1,000	5,517	11,350	22
Scott,	2	950	350	500	1,500	3
Truxton,	2	3,000	900	7,272	15,450	17
Cortland Co.						
Virgil,	2	$900	$300	$400	$1,975	3
Willett,	1	500	50	50	500	1
Delaware Co.						
Andes,	2	800	300	1,482	4,185	5
Bovina,	2	250	115	115	592	2
Delhi,	1	600	200	100	2,000	3
Franklin,	5	2,350	850	2,070	13,000	16
Hamden,	2	800	200	560	1,750	5
Harpersfield,	1	1,200	220	3,988	5,760	3
Kortright,	2	360	45	240	721	2
Masonville,	1	75	50	50	500	2
Roxbury,	2	150	125	275	1,200	3
Sidney,	1	500	150	50	500	1
Stamford,	3	400	250	....	2,984	1
Tompkins,	2	1,950	575	985	3,300	4
Walton,	1	1,000	200	685	3,760	4
Dutchess Co.						
Armenia,	2	1,500	525	620	1,790	8
Clinton,	3	1,250	665	350	350	5
Dover,	1	....	50	200	....	3
East Fishkill,	3	625	150	110	1,200	7
Fishkill,	4	1,700	355	3,771	9,145	16
Hyde Park,	2	800	550	1,350	3,000	3
Milan,	3	600	250	220	3,231	5
Pawling,	2	500	100	700	2,200	4
Pleasant Valley,	3	3,000	700	375	10,000	3
Poughkeepsie city,	8	20,400	4,325	54,045	139,800	87
Red Hook,	4	4,200	1,210	4,350	12,300	16
Rhinebeck,	4	2,200	500	4,060	9,800	13
Stanford,	1	3,500	500	200	1,200	2
Erie Co.						
Boston,	2	1,300	200	415	1,300	3
Buffalo,	9	26,600	16,250	16,967	57,050	66
East Hamburgh,	1	1,100	800	770	3,000	6
Eden,	4	550	300	490	2,330	1
Evans,	2	875	375	581	2,040	3
Hamburgh,	1	200	100	450	900	....
Holland,	1	300	100	100	500	1
North Collins,	2	2,000	300	1,294	5,250	9
Sardinia,	3	900	500	950	4,100	7
Tonawanda,	1	250	40	80	600	1
Essex Co.						
Chesterfield,	2	5,500	900	2,000	9,500	11
Crown Point,	2	400	65	200	750	....
Elizabethtown,	1	300	300	200	1,050	2
Essex,	1	250	125	175	500	1
Keene,	1	200	200	200	800	3
Moriah,	3	525	280	300	2,900	7
Schroon,	2	325	240	225	....	....
Ticonderoga,	1	400	100	145	700	2
Westport,	1	800	150	757	2,540	5
Willsborough,	1	1,000	500	1,000	1,500	3
Franklin Co.						
Bombay,	1	350	100	220	941	1
Fort Covington,	3	2,300	1,725	3,785	10,600	11
Franklin,	1	....	35	50	550	1
Malone,	2	1,750	100	1,014	5,127	9
Westville,	1	....	....	30	125	1
Fulton Co.						
Broadalbin,	1	1,000	300	1,720	5,400	8
Johnstown,	3	8,400	1,600	3,700	13,195	19
Mayfield,	1	....	150	30	800	2
Oppenheim,	1	300	200	120	1,000	2
Genesee Co.						
Alabama,	3	750	1,590	770	1,088	4
Alexander,	1	900	200	1,400	3,420	4
Bergen,	1	....	....	....	....	....
Bethany,	1	1,000	200	930	2,000	2
Byron,	2	675	70	80	650	2
Darien,	1	2,000	3,000	4,000	12,000	15
Elba,	2	600	125	625	2,500	4
Le Roy,	3	3,500	1,000	2,410	8,500	14
Oakfield,	5	2,500	1,470	710	8,285	11
Pavilion,	2	2,200	375	600	7,000	16
Pembroke,	1	400	250	650	2,000	5
Stafford,	3	590	135	876	3,400	11
Greene Co.						
Athens,	3	400	150	519	2,000	4
Cairo,	1	500	100	180	568	2
Coxsackie,	2	1,800	550	1,530	4,220	8
Durham,	2	150	175	210	1,125	3
Hamilton Co.						
Wells,	1	50	50	70	845	1
Herkimer Co.						
Fairfield,	1	1,400	100	210	2,000	3
Frankfort,	2	1,500	300	2,634	4,150	9
German Flats,	5	2,400	3,275	1,683	8,220	13
Herkimer,	3	1,000	500	640	2,740	4

CLASS X.—(Continued.)

TOWNS.	Number of establishments.	Capital Invested. In real estate.	Capital Invested. In tools and machinery.	Cash Value. Of raw materials used.	Cash Value. Of manufactured articles.	Persons employed.
Herkimer Co.						
Litchfield,	1	$600	$50	$424	$1,425	4
Little Falls,	3	2,700	450	3,340	10,000	13
Newport,	5	4,400	1,025	3,220	9,844	14
Salisbury,	2	600	665	1,500	4,600	5
Stark,	3	850	325	795	3,358	7
Warren,	2	640	525	235	1,160	5
Jefferson Co.						
Adams,	3	1,450	345	1,457	3,675	7
Alexander,	1	1,000	100	....	800	2
Antwerp,	3	2,500	1,000	2,320	5,200	10
Cape Vincent,	1	....	100	250	620	2
Champion,	1	2,000	800	2,040	5,000	8
Ellisburgh,	4	4,900	1,900	8,700	18,575	25
Henderson,	4	1,400	450	475	2,210	2
Hounsfield,	1	400	150	200	1,200	2
Lyme,	1	200	50	100	880	....
Orleans,	2	175	200	135	954	4
Pamelia,	2	3,000	860	2,125	12,915	16
Philadelphia,	4	2,050	405	575	2,100	4
Rutland,	2	800	200	475	2,300	3
Watertown,	3	9,500	1,300	15,189	27,631	47
Wilna,	1	1,000	100	450	1,350	3
Kings Co.						
Brooklyn,	11	18,300	11,000	25,828	70,550	86
Flatbush,	1	500	200	....	....	2
New Lots,	2	350	225	725	3,250	6
Lewis Co.						
Denmark,	3	3,600	550	2,150	4,300	5
Lowville,	6	3,400	1,100	5,567	17,380	34
Martinsburgh,	1	300	40	88	1,000	4
West Turin,	2	2,500	1,000	625	4,000	10
Livingston Co.						
Avon,	2	3,600	900	3,000	9,000	14
Caledonia,	2	1,700	375	960	3,276	6
Conesus,	1	500	380	1,000	2,500	2
Groveland,	2	500	225	583	2,300	5
Leicester,	1	500	300	300	1,500	3
Lima,	2	1,600	100	150	300	1
Livonia,	2	1,500	500	2,300	6,000	12
Mount Morris,	3	2,600	550	2,136	12,730	11
Nunda,	2	1,200	1,100	1,270	3,544	4
North Dansville,	5	1,680	1,050	8,337	21,684	18
Sparta,	1	1,100	250	2,310	4,500	14
York,	3	1,600	575	1,588	6,375	14
Madison Co.						
Brookfield,	5	$5,600	1,600	9,478	23,320	32
Cazenovia,	5	1,500	800	4,000	14,500	23
Eaton,	1	800	500	1,080	2,430	3
Hamilton,	3	50	200	750	2,600	4
Lenox,	4	8,300	2,200	7,142	15,294	60
Madison,	2	900	300	640	3,380	5
Sullivan,	1	300	200	50	350	1
Monroe Co.						
Chili,	2	1,400	180	360	2,100	3
Clarkson,	3	2,300	750	5,929	17,200	30
Greece,	1	2,000	300	600	990	4
Henrietta,	3	12,800	5,525	10,848	26,690	48
Mendon,	1	....	25	100	1,000	2
Parma,	3	1,150	735	2,554	1,000	9
Penfield,	3	3,300	500	670	5,400	4
Perrington,	4	2,350	2,025	3,975	13,550	20
Pittsford,	1	700	400	1,080	2,421	4
Riga,	2	3,150	850	2,850	18,500	15
Rochester,	13	35,715	7,770	23,434	139,200	166
Rush,	3	4,500	1,600	5,900	13,500	15
Sweden,	1	2,500	300	3,900	9,900	10
Union,	1	500	200	450	1,950	4
Webster,	4	674	380	980	2,255	7
Wheatland,	3	5,800	1,050	4,711	12,500	29
Montgomery Co.						
Amsterdam,	4	2,300	245	300	1,150	....
Charleston,	1	1,000	250	750	1,000	4
Florida,	1	200	100	150	1,000	2
Glen,	1	1,000	50	100	400	1
Minden,	4	9,700	3,800	8,621	23,980	29
Mohawk,	1	1,400	200	100	2,000	2
Palatine,	2	600	130	690	1,700	5
Root,	4	2,100	475	810	3,200	4
St. Johnsville,	3	5,500	650	4,410	8,150	20
New-York Co.						
New-York,	59	415,700	90,510	476,959	1,096,375	1094
Niagara Co.						
Lewiston,	3	610	150	210	2,100	5
Lockport,	6	12,250	1,150	6,777	16,145	28
Newfane,	1	200	75	100	1,125	3
Porter,	4	900	350	750	1,100	12
Royalton,	4	2,850	1,000	1,500	7,700	15
Wheatfield,	3	250	210	350	400	....
Wilson,	3	1,600	300	650	1,950	6

TOWNS.	Number of establishments.	Capital Invested. In real estate.	Capital Invested. In tools and machinery.	Cash Value. Of raw materials used.	Cash Value. Of manufactured articles.	Persons employed.
Oneida Co.						
Annsville,	2	$1,900	$350	$6,800	$4,125	9
Augusta,	1	750	300	200	1,500	3
Boonville,	2	1,700	1,000	2,682	6,500	10
Camden,	1	450	200	377	3,000	5
Deerfield,	2	4,300	650	1,485	11,200	12
Florence,	1	500	200	984	1,600	3
Kirkland,	5	2,700	750	5,437	12,335	16
Lee,	1	1,500	600	1,013	7,220	8
Marcy,	1	1,500	200	45	500	1
Marshall,	1	....	50	200	477	2
New Hartford,	2	8,000	2,500	5,900	5,350	26
Paris,	8	5,850	4,225	3,440	9,080	19
Remsen,	1	....	50	100	500	1
Rome,	5	8,000	1,175	9,573	24,660	43
Sangerfield,	1	1,200	300	800	3,500	5
Trenton,	5	4,100	1,125	3,990	17,121	29
Utica,	10	18,900	22,100	32,514	75,950	112
Vernon,	3	2,200	325	5,204	8,490	22
Verona,	3	450	3,555	225	1,625	3
Westmoreland,	3	1,500	400	1,150	5,290	8
Whitestown,	3	4,200	700	6,335	16,750	20
Onondaga Co.						
Camillus,	2	450	325	135	1,400	....
Cicero,	3	800	275	437	2,300	4
Clay,	4	1,300	165	1,645	3,800	7
De Witt,	2	2,000	900	2,650	7,000	12
Elbridge,	2	1,800	300	380	5,000	8
Geddes,	1	500	300	220	1,000	2
Lafayette,	1	500	250	286	400	1
Lysander,	6	3,900	850	1,736	6,223	12
Manlius,	5	9,300	3,950	7,950	23,500	39
Marcellus,	3	515	190	155	1,930	3
Onondaga,	2	450	250	400	2,100	3
Otisco,	2	350	55	300	1,200	5
Pompey,	1	400	100	150	2,000	4
Skaneateles,	3	7,000	1,900	12,600	43,000	44
Spafford,	1	500	225	410	1,400	2
Syracuse,	6	20,800	4,000	7,600	55,950	66
Tully,	1	2,500	500	5,780	12,900	22
Ontario Co.						
Bristol,	3	1,000	225	500	1,750	5
East Bloomfield,	2	4,600	900	3,560	12,310	15
Farmington,	2	1,300	200	80	1,700	3
Gorham,	3	390	490	1,275	2,990	7
Manchester,	1	2,000	150	300	1,000	2
Phelps,	5	3,700	675	1,591	6,600	19
Seneca,	1	2,000	200	8,000	10,000	12
West Bloomfield,	2	2,800	400	980	4,360	2
Orange Co.						
Blooming Grove,	2	800	400	1,500	3,800	7
Chester,	2	200	65	1,050	2,050	3
Cornwall,	1	300	125	....	....	....
Deerpark,	2	8,000	2,300	6,175	12,400	17
Goshen,	4	3,400	680	1,500	4,310	14
Hamptonburgh,	2	300	110	300	1,250	2
Minisink,	2	900	1,080	1,645	5,635	11
Monroe,	6	4,550	810	3,050	11,700	15
Montgomery,	5	800	330	420	2,237	5
Mount Hope,	2	350	110	750	3,000	5
Newburgh,	1	5,000	250	1,975	4,375	5
New Windsor,	1	....	300	300	900	2
Warwick,	3	250	100	550	4,200	7
Orleans Co.						
Barre,	2	3,000	500	5,700	14,500	16
Carlton,	3	350	190	355	1,245	....
Gaines,	3	750	220	664	2,350	2
Kendall,	1	1,600	200	495	2,460	3
Murray,	2	1,800	250	2,280	4,680	5
Ridgeway,	9	7,575	1,400	6,395	20,495	28
Yates,	1	1,200	300	1,500	3,328	5
Oswego Co.						
Constantia,	4	3,300	1,450	1,829	9,125	12
Granby,	2	2,600	300	2,250	7,000	12
Hannibal,	2	700	350	575	2,500	5
Mexico,	3	1,200	2,900	5,100	16,300	13
Oswego,	4	4,300	925	2,885	9,175	14
Palermo,	1	250	100	500	1,200	2
Richland,	4	4,500	950	5,100	15,500	23
Sandy Creek,	1	800	300	3,000	6,900	7
Otsego Co.						
Burlington,	3	800	650	670	2,150	2
Butternuts,	1	1,500	800	300	6,000	5
Cherry Valley,	2	1,400	100	279	1,912	5
Decatur,	2	2,200	275	700	2,000	5
Edmeston,	1	50	200	500	2,100	3
Exeter,	1	....	75	50	800	1
Laurens,	4	1,600	525	1,955	4,500	7
Maryland,	4	850	340	250	2,475	8
Middlefield,	4	1,500	400	1,150	2,640	5

CLASS X.—(Continued.)

TOWNS.	Number of establishments.	Capital Invested. In real estate.	Capital Invested. In tools and machinery.	Cash Value. Of raw materials used.	Cash Value. Of manufactured articles.	Persons employed.
OTSEGO Co.						
Milford	2	$1,800	$540	$1,000	$4,300	5
Morris	1	2,000	3,000	1,750	7,350	7
New Lisbon	4	275	390	565	1,450	....
Oneonta	1	3,060	700	3,250	16,000	18
Otego	3	2,550	290	2,130	11,348	11
Otsego	4	8,500	1,500	3,977	12,565	11
Plainfield	3	4,300	350	2,710	3,200	5
Roseboom	4	450	175	300	1,600	....
Springfield	5	5,000	780	2,050	7,100	11
Unadilla	2	3,100	3,100	1,670	6,500	10
Westford	1	500	200	250	....	3
Worcester	3	750	275	1,000	2,700	4
PUTNAM Co.						
Carmel	1	500	50	50	500	1
Southeast	1	2,500	400	325	1,000	2
QUEENS Co.						
Flushing	5	9,100	2,050	5,420	19,600	37
Hempstead	3	450	230	1,475	2,800	7
Jamaica	8	14,100	2,200	16,850	46,250	76
Newtown	2	800	200	120	2,000	4
North Hempstead	6	3,800	1,100	3,200	13,086	36
Oyster Bay	2	1,700	800	3,000	10,500	9
RENSSELAER Co.						
Brunswick	3	1,600	400	850	3,200	6
Clinton	1	200	25	....	....	....
Hoosick	1	600	100	480	1,200	3
North Greenbush	3	1,550	400	800	2,600	4
Petersburgh	1	700	100	278	1,121	2
Pittstown	2	1,000	800	1,200	2,800	4
Poestenkill	3	2,000	300	3,150	2,100	11
Sandlake	2	600	100	450	800	3
Schaghticoke	1	....	....	700	800	....
Schodack	6	2,000	750	570	4,600	9
Troy	3	8,500	650	6,050	47,700	50
RICHMOND Co.						
Northfield	1	1,000	350	10,000	17,000	19
Westfield	1	200	30	200	1,000	1
ROCKLAND Co.						
Clarkstown	1	....	200	300	900	2
Haverstraw	4	4,400	1,725	1,000	11,000	13
Orangetown	2	4,700	800	2,300	8,000	11
ST. LAWRENCE Co.						
Canton	2	700	300	900	2,700	7
De Peyster	1	250	100	325	....	2
Gouverneur	2	2,800	750	1,110	2,073	7
Hopkinton	1	75	50	50	600	1
Hermon	2	1,400	600	3,000	6,000	9
Lawrence	1	....	100	200	800	1
Louisville	1	50	50	50	1,500	5
Madrid	2	3,000	800	1,440	8,100	11
Massena	3	450	325	240	3,100	6
Oswegatchie	3	1,900	615	975	4,860	5
Pierrepont	1	....	....	75	400	1
Parishville	2	200	75	105	2,356	3
Potsdam	3	4,625	1,350	3,883	14,000	20
Rossie	2	50	125	125	1,300	2
SARATOGA Co.						
Ballston	2	400	350	515	2,172	8
Clifton Park	2	200	550	150	13,600	....
Corinth	1	1,000	500	200	600	4
Edinburgh	1	1,000	300	200	1,000	1
Greenfield	3	3,300	750	730	5,300	11
Halfmoon	1	1,000	500	1,250	4,060	8
Malta	5	1,500	475	929	3,290	3
Milton	2	500	80	174	1,300	2
Moreau	3	700	235	335	1,300	2
Northumberland	1	45	100	75	870	2
Providence	1	300	160	1,200	22,100	3
Saratoga Springs	3	4,200	650	2,300	7,500	11
Stillwater	3	6,300	650	1,600	4,750	10
Waterford	1	800	250	200	1,000	1
SCHENECTADY Co.						
Duanesburgh	3	500	215	310	1,602	2
Glenville	1	350	100	150	900	2
Schenectady	3	1,100	875	4,132	14,100	19
SCHOHARIE Co.						
Carlisle	3	850	180	280	2,200	5
Cobleskill	1	400	300	....	....	....
Esperance	2	350	70	200	1,100	3
Fulton	3	300	150	350	1,150	5
Gilboa	2	450	300	560	800	2
Richmondville	2	250	125	150	950	2
Seward	2	1,500	125	175	1,200	3
Schoharie	2	4,500	1,200	4,500	21,000	27
Sharon	7	575	370	500	2,550	8
Summit	2	100	135	54	250	....
Wright	1	400	100	105	780	2
SCHUYLER Co.						
Catherines	3	1,300	305	960	2,000	6
SCHUYLER Co.						
Cayuta	1	$150	$60	$100	$600	2
Dix	2	2,000	375	676	5,010	10
Hector	7	2,200	640	669	4,700	10
Orange	1	100	30	51	318	1
Reading	1	200	50	50	400	1
SENECA Co.						
Covert	1	1,000	400	6,000	10,000	10
Fayette	10	7,500	1,550	2,675	13,850	24
Lodi	1	400	400	300	2,775	3
Ovid	1	500	100	450	1,000	3
Romulus	1	50	50	120	500	1
Seneca Falls	1	....	....	350	2,000	3
Varick	3	1,350	....	3,157	17,655	12
Waterloo	1	200	100	100	500	2
STEUBEN Co.						
Addison	1	....	....	100	1,000	1
Avoca	1	150	100	40	750	2
Bath	6	2,400	750	5,221	18,725	22
Bradford	3	475	175	230	2,300	6
Canisteo	1	200	100	130	460	2
Corning	1	100	100	100	1,120	2
Dansville	5	2,250	1,075	389	3,250	12
Erwin	4	1,650	600	750	3,800	8
Fremont	1	100	75	150	600	2
Hornellsville	4	3,450	1,400	4,987	19,564	23
Howard	1	75	200	210	1,000	....
Jasper	2	300	280	260	1,400	5
Pultney	1	700	200	700	1,900	4
Thurston	1	300	150	200	480	2
Urbana	3	5,200	2,000	5,704	21,000	39
Wayne	1	300	100	400	1,200	4
SUFFOLK Co.						
Huntington	5	1,600	400	1,875	6,280	17
Islip	1	200	75	60	500	....
Riverhead	5	3,200	575	940	4,100	8
Southampton	2	400	150	700	1,650	3
Southold	3	485	200	100	500	2
SULLIVAN Co.						
Bethel	1	700	200	400	1,200	2
Cochecton	3	300	150	445	2,300	5
Fallsburgh	1	200	80	300	1,200	1
Highland	1	200	200	160	675	2
Mamakating	6	970	575	965	5,950	9
Thompson	1	1,100	300	875	2,600	5
TIOGA Co.						
Barton	8	2,450	570	400	2,200	10
Berkshire	1	350	50	50	250	1
Nichols	3	2,000	325	750	2,500	4
Owego	4	4,425	1,090	4,143	13,625	17
TOMPKINS Co.						
Caroline	4	390	145	178	1,600	4
Danby	2	400	175	200	850	....
Dryden	4	4,300	775	3,110	12,050	16
Enfield	1	500	200	500	1,000	1
Groton	4	2,800	2,100	8,465	28,600	59
Ithaca	3	3,700	550	2,000	2,500	4
Lansing	5	2,900	565	6,000	11,000	15
Newfield	1	200	100	200	500	1
Ulysses	2	2,700	450	4,100	9,600	12
ULSTER Co.						
Gardiner	2	450	150	160	1,000	2
Kingston	3	6,200	1,100	2,695	42,700	41
Lloyd	2	600	175	290	1,700	4
Marbletown	2	350	150	40	4,700	7
Marlborough	3	2,800	650	1,500	6,800	7
New Paltz	1	....	50	150	1,000	....
Olive	5	1,650	1,215	1,540	7,600	9
Rochester	4	1,400	850	1,050	6,900	11
Saugerties	5	3,450	550	2,250	7,200	8
Shawangunk	1	400	150	400	600	3
Wawarsing	1	2,500	600	600	4,000	4
WARREN Co.						
Chester	2	800	250	310	2,000	3
Queensbury	3	6,900	950	9,626	29,410	41
Warrensburgh	1	2,000	300	1,000	2,500	6
WASHINGTON Co.						
Argyle	5	1,400	425	627	2,725	8
Easton	1	1,500	190	7,290	17,000	8
Fort Ann	3	2,500	700	3,515	5,475	3
Granville	3	2,200	450	1,465	4,000	14
Greenwich	1	1,000	800	4,800	10,000	13
Hartford	4	1,700	415	483	3,650	1
Hebron	2	2,000	110	....	....	2
Kingsbury	4	2,400	1,250	1,550	9,033	14
Salem	2	1,600	450	1,485	6,300	5
WAYNE Co.						
Arcadia	5	3,900	840	2,822	11,152	17
Galen	1	1,200	150	300	4,000	8

CLASS X.—(CONTINUED.)

TOWNS.	Number of establishments.	Capital Invested. In real estate.	Capital Invested. In tools and machinery.	Cash Value. Of raw materials used.	Cash Value. Of manufactured articles.	Persons employed.
WAYNE Co.						
Lyons, ...	2	$1,900	$235	$1,460	$7,216	11
Marion, ...	3	475	185	375	1,600	3
Ontario, ...	2	350	45	125	900	2
Palmyra, ...	3	5,900	1,700	2,800	18,200	23
Sodus, ...	7	2,350	765	3,950	8,000	15
Walworth, ...	2	1,600	100	670	3,100	2
Williamson, ...	1	2,000	200	1,200	3,000	5
Wolcott, ...	3	1,650	950	450	2,700	4
WESTCHESTER Co.						
Bedford, ...	2	1,200	350	2,350	5,600	1
Eastchester, ...	3	1,000	550	2,275	12,500	14
Harrison, ...	1	....	100	400	1,200	2
Lewisboro, ...	3	900	550	870	3,100	7
Mount Pleasant, ..	3	425	75	100	....	2
New Castle, ...	1	....	50	200	300	....
North Castle, ...	2	5,800	1,150	3,590	7,875	10
North Salem, ...	4	3,000	300	615	5,070	9
Ossining, ...	4	12,500	2,000	7,850	17,000	33
Rye, ...	2	2,500	200	1,295	3,300	13
White Plains, ...	2	2,000	150	350	750	4
Yorktown, ...	1	30	30	150	....	1
WYOMING Co.						
Attica, ...	2	1,600	400	1,800	5,920	9
Bennington, ...	3	1,850	375	1,125	10,000	12
Castile, ...	2	6,600	1,950	8,235	27,350	34
China, ...	2	1,400	650	900	4,500	6
Covington, ...	3	300	505	450	2,550	6
Genesee Falls, ...	2	1,900	300	1,850	7,000	7
Java, ...	2	400	50	660	3,000	6
Middlebury, ...	3	510	300	807	3,975	7
Perry, ...	3	900	140	745	4,400	5
Pike, ...	2	500	200	900	2,500	4
Sheldon, ...	2	450	150	250	1,000	2
Warsaw, ...	2	5,800	650	13,269	28,195	28
Wethersfield, ...	2	1,100	325	270	1,900	3
YATES Co.						
Barrington, ...	2	2,200	375	155	2,300	6
Benton, ...	5	3,700	790	1,510	10,600	15
Italy, ...	1	1,200	....	....	....	....
Jerusalem, ...	2	500	400	950	2,500	4
Milo, ...	3	6,200	440	9,000	15,000	13
Starkey, ...	1	2,900	300	4,451	26,000	16
Torrey, ...	1	1,000	150	3,000	6,000	6
HOSE CARRIAGE MANUFACTORY.						
NEW-YORK Co.						
New-York, ...	2	7,000	2,455	3,175	19,200	27
HUB MANUFACTORY.						
SARATOGA Co.						
Moreau, ...	1	....	600	400	9,000	5
PATENT AXLETREE MANUFACTORIES.						
WESTCHESTER Co.						
Eastchester, ...	1	$26,000	$8,000	$14,860	$36,000	35
Greenburgh, ...	1	3,500	1,000	5,000	10,000	12
SPOKE MANUFACTORIES.						
ALLEGANY Co.						
Hume, ...	2	....	250	225	690	2
BROOME Co.						
Chenango, ...	1	225	3,000	720	3,000	5
Colesville, ...	1	....	....	180	800	....
CHEMUNG Co.						
Southport, ...	1	2,000	2,000	700	1,500	4
CHENANGO Co.						
Norwich, ...	1	1,200	1,700	2,400	7,600	7
GREENE Co.						
Catskill, ...	1	....	500	500	2,000	4
LIVINGSTON Co.						
Mount Morris, ...	1	200	400	384	2,000	3
MONROE Co.						
Rochester, ...	1	9,000	2,000	3,125	10,000	21
ONONDAGA Co.						
Van Buren, ...	1	....	600	230	1,750	3
ORANGE Co.						
Blooming Grove, ..	1	3,000	3,000	900	2,500	3
OSWEGO Co.						
Granby, ...	1	500	500	....	....	....
SENECA Co.						
Waterloo, ...	1	....	....	827	2,941	....
ULSTER Co.						
Gardiner, ...	1	....	....	....	....	....
Kingston, ...	1	....	....	2,000	7,000	3
Marlborough, ...	1	5,000	2,000	2,775	10,550	9
WHEELBARROW MANUFACTORIES.						
HERKIMER Co.						
Frankfort, ...	2	1,600	325	225	5,100	5
MONROE Co.						
Rochester, ...	2	....	300	1,758	7,550	4
ONEIDA Co.						
Rome, ...	1	800	260	815	3,000	5
ONONDAGA Co.						
Syracuse, ...	1	12,000	8,000	5,500	20,000	15
ULSTER Co.						
Marlborough, ...	2	5,000	3,200	6,200	32,000	24
WHEEL FACTORIES.						
ALBANY Co.						
Watervliet, ...	1	5,000	2,500	2,800	11,100	10
TOMPKINS Co.						
Ithaca, ...	1	800	1,000	....	....	2

CLASS XI.—HYDRAULICS AND PNEUMATICS.

TOWNS.	Number of establishments.	Capital Invested. In real estate.	Capital Invested. In tools and machinery.	Cash Value. Of raw materials used.	Cash Value. Of manufactured articles.	Persons employed.
BELLOWS MAKING.						
ERIE Co.						
Buffalo, ...	1	2,000	700	11,750	24,000	12
NEW-YORK Co.						
New-York, ...	3	....	200	41,075	53,200	47
FIRE ENGINE MANUFACTORIES.						
MONROE Co.						
Rochester, ...	1	....	300	6,465	15,950	11
NEW-YORK Co.						
New-York, ...	2	13,000	7,500	8,600	40,000	49
SARATOGA Co.						
Waterford, ...	1	6,000	5,000	1,380	40,000	40
PUMP FACTORIES.						
CATTARAUGUS Co.						
Perrysburgh, ...	1	....	150	300	2,000	2
CHAUTAUQUE Co.						
Ellicott, ...	1	500	400	1,900	3,034	3
Portland, ...	1	....	....	....	200	....
CHEMUNG Co.						
Elmira, ...	1	1,600	250	1,945	4,700	5
COLUMBIA Co.						
Chatham, ...	1	1,000	250	....	2,500	2
DUTCHESS Co.						
Poughkeepsie city,	1	1,000	150	2,915	5.250	2
ERIE Co.						
Collins, ...	2	700	300	950	3,475	5
GENESEE Co.						
Batavia, ...	1	....	2,000	6,000	12,000	5
Le Roy, ...	1	....	....	175	800	1
Pavilion, ...	1	60	150	15	200	1
JEFFERSON Co.						
Rutland, ...	1	1,500	1,000	500	1,000	1
KINGS Co.						
Brooklyn, ...	2	6,100	5,300	3,700	15,000	13
LIVINGSTON Co.						
Geneseo, ...	1	1,200	500	50	50	2
MONROE Co.						
Chili, ...	1	....	50	500	1,500	....
Parma, ...	1	100	40	115	700	1
Rochester, ...	2	2,100	900	984	5,400	3
Sweden, ...	2	....	2,000	4,464	17,000	4
ONEIDA Co.						
Utica, ...	2	3,000	325	7,889	23,856	9
OSWEGO Co.						
Granby, ...	1	....	50	900	1,500	....
RENSSELAER Co.						
Troy, ...	1	2,000	100	600	2,000	2
ST. LAWRENCE Co.						
Gouverneur, ...	1	....	....	258	600	1
Potsdam, ...	1	....	50	25	200	....

CLASS XI.—(Continued.)

TOWNS.	Number of establishments.	Capital Invested. In real estate.	Capital Invested. In tools and machinery.	Cash Value. Of raw materials used.	Cash Value. Of manufactured articles.	Persons employed.
Saratoga Co.						
Halfmoon,	1	$800	$50	$1,140	$3,600	3
Warren Co.						
Queensbury,	1	600	400	1,000	2,050	2
Wyoming Co.						
Middlebury,	1	....	50	1,300	3,010	2
Perry,	1	200	100	200	1,000	1
Pike,	1	500	200	150	900	2
STEAM PUMP MANUFACTORIES.						
Kings Co.						
Brooklyn,	1	$20,000	$20,000	$15,000	$60,000	76
Seneca Co.						
Seneca Falls,	3	36,000	31,000	159,441	345,000	214

CLASS XII.—LEVER, SCREW, AND OTHER MECHANICAL POWERS.

TOWNS.	Number of establishments.	In real estate.	In tools and machinery.	Of raw materials used.	Of manufactured articles.	Persons employed.
HOIST WHEEL MANUFACTORY.						
New-York Co.						
New-York,	2	3,000	1,600	2,986	68,000	18
HYDRAULIC JACK MANUFACTORY.						
New-York Co.						
New-York,	1	....	2,000	1,000	6,000	10
JACK SCREW MANUFACTORY.						
New-York Co.						
New-York,	1	....	2,000	1,250	3,800	4
SCALE MANUFACTORIES.						
Monroe Co.						
Rochester,	1	....	3,000	13,500	25,000	10
New-York Co.						
New-York,	5	24,000	4,200	20,560	53,000	35
Oneida Co.						
Verona,	1	150	100	275	850	....
Rensselaer Co.						
Lansingbugh,	1	800	200	1,550	2,050	2

CLASS XIII.—GRINDING MILLS, MILL GEARING, ETC.

TOWNS.	Number of establishments.	In real estate.	In tools and machinery.	Of raw materials used.	Of manufactured articles.	Persons employed.
BAND AND BELTING MANUFACTORIES.						
Dutchess Co.						
Fishkill,	1	1,200	1,000	8,000	10,000	2
Erie Co.						
Buffalo,	1	....	....	....	16,000	....
New-York Co.						
New-York,	1	25,000	2,000	107,700	150,000	25
Oneida Co.						
Utica,	1	....	8,000	10,200	13,300	5
BRAN DUSTER MANUFACTORIES.						
Monroe Co.						
Rochester,	1	....	1,000	1,985	11,250	7
Yates Co.						
Milo,	1	....	400	1,000	2,500	....
FARINA MILL.						
Onondaga Co.						
Manlius,	1	1,200	....	6,000	11,100	2
FEED MILLS.						
Albany Co.						
Albany,	1	14,400	17,000	96,000	108,000	16
Bethlehem,	....	....	....	....	1,590	....
Watervliet,	2	....	1,500	23,800	28,000	4
Cayuga Co.						
Sennett,	2	....	750	....	250	....
Montgomery Co.						
Minden,	1	....	....	2,000	2,300	1
Root,	2	1,000	800	7,100	7,810	....
New-York Co.						
New-York,	1	....	600	175,000	150,000	3
Onondaga Co.						
Onondaga,	1	500	25	2,500	2,800	1
Schoharie Co.						
Richmondville,	1	....	....	1,000	1,100	1
Steuben Co.						
Wheeler,	1	1,000	20	2,450	3,100	1
Washington Co.						
Argyle,	1	500	800	650	700	1
Westchester Co.						
Lewisboro',	1	....	....	....	....	....
GRIST MILLS.						
Albany Co.						
Albany,	1	....	....	315,000	329,940	11
Bern,	3	5,000	5,800	59,000	28,800	4
Bethlehem,	2	12,000	5,800	174,975	191,619	3
Guilderland,	2	10,000	6,000	15,840	17,744	5
Albany Co.						
Knox,	2	2,300	2,000	7,500	7,500	2
New Scotland,	1	8,000	1,000	18,750	20,000	2
Rensselaerville,	4	13,900	2,105	15,900	16,200	7
Watervliet,	5	18,000	28,500	542,000	688,300	27
Westerlo,	3	7,300	60	23,600	26,212	2
Allegany Co.						
Alfred,	1	2,500	80	10,000	13,000	2
Almond,	2	9,500	3,000	23,850	28,030	2
Amity,	2	1,200	....	23,453	26,037	4
Andover,	1	3,000	....	10,800	10,800	2
Angelica,	1	3,000	5,000	28,975	37,055	2
Belfast,	1	9,000	3,000	71,000	97,200	3
Burns,	1	8,000	....	15,750	20,000	1
Cuba,	2	6,000	....	156,000	179,500	3
Friendship,	2	8,000	250	460	32,500	4
Hume,	2	7,500	3,575	71,175	82,510	5
Independence,	2	3,000	1,400	....	1,600	2
Ossian,	1	9,000	....	....	....	1
Rushford,	1	6,000	....	3,000	5,800	2
Scio,	1	4,000	1,500	60,000	....	3
Willing,	1	2,500	....	....	....	1
Wirt,	2	7,350	1,025	36,887	41,200	5
Broome Co.						
Barker,	1	4,000	2,000	2,500	2,500	1
Chenango,	3	9,000	8,550	26,800	30,100	4
Binghamton,	1	15,000	4,500	42,200	79,000	8
Colesville,	4	8,000	2,400	21,350	21,650	4
Conklin,	3	7,000	6,000	32,250	35,455	6
Lisle,	3	3,800	....	12,000	12,000	2
Maine,	2	5,500	....	....	2,000	....
Sanford,	1	10,000	8,000	40,000	46,000	3
Triangle,	1	6,500	1,500	23,475	25,008	4
Union,	5	10,000	4,000	....	....	....
Windsor,	3	2,600	410	....	775	2
Cattaraugus Co.						
Ashford,	2	2,200	....	....	....	2
Coldspring,	1	....	....	11,000	12,450	1
Connewango,	1	3,000	....	23,125	16,500	1
East Otto,	1	500	800	5,500	6,000	1
Ellicottville,	1	3,700	1,000	7,500	9,680	4
Franklinville,	1	3,000	1,500	1,500	16,500	2
Freedom,	2	1,000	2,500	....	....	3
Great Valley,	1	4,000	....	....	1,000	2
Ischua,	1	2,500	....	....	....	....
Mansfield,	1	3,000	300	....	1,000	....
Olean,	1	6,000	600	600	2,000	2
Otto,	1	3,000	....	1,550	3,144	2
Persia,	1	4,000	....	4,500	2,250	....
Perrysburgh,	1	6,000	....	26,000	32,860	2
Portville,	1	2,000	50	3,500	3,850	1
Randolph,	1	4,000	10,000	....	....	2
Yorkshire,	2	7,000	12,000	775	775	1

CLASS XIII.—(Continued.)

TOWNS.	Number of establishments.	Capital Invested. In real estate.	Capital Invested. In tools and machinery.	Cash Value. Of raw materials used.	Cash Value. Of manufactured articles.	Persons employed.
Cayuga Co.						
Auburn,	2	$33,000	$5,000	$124,000	$136,400	12
Aurelius,	1	12,000	....	5,000	8,000	2
Cato,	1	4,000	6,000	12,000	13,450	7
Conquest,	1	5,500	3,800	17,850	18,615	3
Genoa,	4	17,000	1,000	18,621	19,950	9
Ira,	1	300	....	1,800	2,000	1
Locke,	2	4,200	1,000	....	....	....
Ledyard,	2	3,000	1,500	10,824	12,537	....
Mentz,	4	52,500	200	92,675	395,283	24
Moravia,	2	12,000	2,100	18,100	20,525	4
Niles,	2	5,800	....	18,000	27,000	2
Owasco,	1	2,000	2,000	....	1,427	2
Springport,	1	15,000	....	....	....	....
Sterling,	4	7,500	....	....	....	2
Venice,	1	6,000	....	100	1,390	1
Victory,	1	7,000	500	17,000	20,000	5
Chautauque Co.						
Busti,	1	1,000	500	7.045	4,952	1
Chautauque,	5	9,500	525	39,750	40,875	8
Cherry Creek,	1	1,200	2,300	11,715	13,080	1
Clymer,	2	3,350	....	11,000	12,000	2
Ellery,	2	1,800	....	....	1,200	1
Ellicott,	2	23,000	....	42,250	33,220	8
Ellington,	2	3,700	....	3,050	4,475	2
French Creek,	1	1,200	....	....	....	1
Harmony,	1	....	....	....	....	....
Hanover,	3	8,000	4,000	43,750	48,890	3
Mina,	1	2,500	....	....	....	....
Poland,	1	10.000	....	31,000	31,000	1
Pomfret,	4	20,500	8,000	19,584	29,562	6
Portland,	1	3,000	200	3,000	3,700	2
Sherman,	1	4,000	....	1,000	1,500	1
Stockton,	2	3,000	....	....	1,571	....
Villenovia,	1	200	....	2,000	2,200	1
Chemung Co.						
Big Flats,	1	7,000	1,245	8,810	10,035	2
Chemung,	2	10,000	4,500	4,800	4,800	4
Elmira,	5	60,000	6,000	223,604	258,236	19
Horseheads,	2	18,000	2,000	71,150	89,440	5
Southport,	2	13,000	....	35,000	42,000	5
Van Etten,	2	8,000	....	....	....	....
Veteran,	3	12,900	1,800	49,000	50,000	5
Chenango Co.						
Bainbridge,	2	6,100	....	18,000	20,600	2
Greene,	1	3,000	....	15,100	15,100	2
Guilford,	5	12.200	60	21,250	9,212	6
New Berlin,	1	2,000	40	1,500	1,612	2
Norwich,	2	11,500	24	....	5,000	2
Otselic,	2	5,400	6,000	10,150	11,145	3
Oxford,	3	6,500	120	7,000	7,900	3
Pitcher,	3	2,100	....	6,250	6,875	3
Plymouth,	2	4,000	1,520	6,000	6,000	1
Preston,	2	1,000	....	2,600	2,860	2
Sherburne,	4	1,800	805	9,700	11,460	4
Smithville,	1	2,500	....	7,500	7,500	1
Clinton Co.						
Beekmantown,	1	2,000	10	7,000	7,700	1
Champlain,	3	18,000	....	47,500	56,000	6
Chazy,	4	17,000	....	27,069	35,114	4
Ellenburgh,	1	2,000	300	....	....	1
Mooers,	3	9,500	8,800	30,000	39,000	4
Peru,	2	11,500	2,500	83,750	52,750	4
Plattsburgh,	2	40,000	....	209,750	244,300	5
Saranac,	1	2,500	....	800	1,100	2
Schuyler Falls,	2	9,000	30	31,742	36,251	3
Columbia Co.						
Ancram,	1	....	....	....	....	1
Austerlitz,	2	4,700	....	21,050	25,805	....
Canaan,	4	16,700	200	36,200	46,700	7
Chatham,	5	38,000	8,000	124,515	179,977	19
Claverack,	7	42,500	17,000	168,825	184,968	23
Clermont,	1	2,500	1,500	11,220	19,752	3
Gallatin,	2	13,600	4,200	2,200	4,000	2
Ghent,	5	19,900	8,300	72,495	86,648	16
Hillsdale,	4	5,300	2,400	15,005	20,500	7
Kinderhook,	2	10,000	10,000	44,000	84,000	6
Livingston,	4	19,000	4,000	77,031	90,147	7
New Lebanon,	3	5,300	2,816	26,140	26,140	4
Stuyvesant,	2	19,100	21,000	6,162	6,060	2
Taghkanick,	1	10,000	2,000	11,000	12,000	4
Cortland Co.						
Cortlandville,	4	17,000	185	65,731	68,726	7
Harford,	1	4,000	100	17,250	18,000	2
Homer,	5	19,000	1,500	65,000	65,000	4
Preble,	1	4,000	....	....	800	1
Scott,	4	8,800	1,900	17,550	19,230	4
Solon,	1	2,580	200	5,000	6,100	3
Truxton,	4	5,200	3,300	34,315	38,677	5
Virgil,	2	4,500	....	16,000	18,000	2
Cortland Co.						
Willett,	1	$1,000	$100	$2,750	$2,750	1
Delaware Co.						
Bovina,	2	1,400	1,400	620	6,820	2
Colchester,	1	5,000	2,000	10,000	11,000	1
Delhi,	1	800	500	5,000	6,000	1
Franklin,	1	4,000	....	15,000	16,500	2
Hamden,	1	4,000	10	9,162	10,123	1
Harpersfield,	6	8,050	215	38,080	42,964	6
Kortright,	1	2,000	1,000	4,500	450	....
Masonville,	1	4,000	25	7,500	8,300	2
Meredith,	1	500	1,600	2,828	5,132	1
Middletown,	5	6,800	1,780	21,000	22,200	5
Roxbury,	2	4,000	....	16,000	16,103	2
Sidney,	2	8,000	400	9,000	9,900	2
Stamford,	1	3,400	....	....	10,000	1
Tompkins,	1	2,000	....	....	....	1
Dutchess Co.						
Amenia,	1	5,000	500	11,900	15,944	1
Clinton,	5	13,400	....	12,000	16,890	2
Dover,	1	4,000	....	4,000	4,000	....
East Fishkill,	1	6,500	30	20,000	20,000	....
Fishkill,	3	17,000	1.030	7,350	9,350	7
Hyde Park,	1	....	2,000	6,100	6,660	1
La Grange,	5	6,300	11,100	46,500	51,500	8
Milan,	3	9,000	145	23,678	30,350	7
Northeast,	2	4,500	1,000	....	....	2
Pawling,	2	2,500	1,500	10,000	11,000	1
Pine Plains,	2	7,000	2,500	20,000	20,000	....
Poughkeepsie,	1	13,000	9,000	20,000	24,000	5
Poughkeepsie city,	2	32,000	650	31,800	53,000	10
Red Hook,	3	8,500	6,000	224,000	287,000	13
Rhinebeck,	3	17,000	265	44,000	26,500	7
Stanford,	4	13,000	7,800	34,000	18,040	7
Erie Co.						
Alden,	3	9,500	350	31,500	32,674	3
Amherst,	5	54,500	510	168,900	227,000	19
Aurora,	2	6,500	....	9,600	18,310	5
Boston,	3	3,300	1,700	10,017	17,487	2
Buffalo,	8	112,000	90,000	1,465,060	1,524,800	66
Clarence,	2	5,200	4,300	49,378	57,010	3
Collins,	1	8,000	3,000	25,000	27,500	3
Eden,	2	4,500	22	15,900	16,990	1
Evans,	4	10,500	150	15,312	22,115	7
Hamburgh,	2	5,500	1,500	14,000	16,800	5
Holland,	1	2,000	....	6,000	6,600	1
Lancaster,	3	17,000	100	54,700	65,971	8
Marilla,	1	1,600	....	18,000	15,750	1
Newstead,	3	7,000	5,500	....	....	2
Sardinia,	2	4,000	....	....	....	2
West Seneca,	1	3,000	....	....	....	....
Essex Co.						
Chesterfield,	2	23,000	8,000	132,137	150,637	9
Crown Point,	3	11,000	1,950	29,600	32,350	4
Elizabethtown,	3	1,800	50	5,000	5,500	3
Essex,	1	4,500	25	....	....	....
Keene,	1	2,000	100	4,000	4,000	1
Lewis,	1	....	....	3,000	6,000	....
Minerva,	1	....	1,000	4,500	4,500	1
Schroon,	2	2,600	150	12,000	13,500	3
Willsborough,	1	6,000	....	15,000	15,000	2
Wilmington,	1	4,000	2,000	500	500	....
Franklin Co.						
Bombay,	2	7,000	50	8,120	8,685	3
Chateaugay,	2	10,000	....	....	....	....
Constable,	1	2,500	....	8,000	8,000	1
Fort Covington,	2	14,000	1,050	65,000	77,500	5
Malone,	2	15,700	400	50,009	65,159	4
Moira,	1	....	6,000	7,900	8,990	1
Westville,	1	1,500	2,000	17,500	23,350	2
Fulton Co.						
Broadalbin,	3	7,500	4,050	69,488	65,796	5
Ephrata,	3	8,600	2,000	43,000	79,858	4
Mayfield,	2	6,000	100	36,705	39,670	4
Oppenheim,	1	800	300	450	495	2
Genesee Co.						
Alabama,	2	3,000	400	91,000	88,000	6
Alexander,	2	8,000	6,000	22,960	27,600	3
Batavia,	2	9,500	8,000	186,686	213,302	7
Bergen,	1	....	....	....	....	....
Bethany,	1	10,000	50	12,855	33,520	2
Byron,	2	6,000	3,500	58,600	62,000	2
Elba,	1	5,000	6,000	45,000	88,000	5
Le Roy,	4	32,000	15,000	214,250	230,700	12
Oakfield,	2	14,000	....	29,900	38,800	4
Pavilion,	1	6,000	....	....	1,500	1
Pembroke,	3	17,000	1,500	22,900	30,000	4
Stafford,	1	20,000	3,000	200,000	220,000	8
Greene Co.						
Coxsackie,	4	13,000	2,500	55,812	63,414	8

CLASS XIII.—(Continued.)

TOWNS.	Number of establishments.	Capital Invested. In real estate.	Capital Invested. In tools and machinery.	Cash Value. Of raw materials used.	Cash Value. Of manufactured articles.	Persons employed.
GREENE Co.						
Cairo,	2	$2,500	$1,000	$571	$18,305	3
Catskill,	4	14,600	1,300	3,000	12,000	4
Durham,	6	5,300	2,510	32,925	29,470	6
Greenville,	4	10,000	4,200	14,422	15,859	6
Hunter,	1	....	....	....	....	....
Lexington,	2	3,700	35	4,000	4,600	2
New Baltimore,	2	2,500	3,000	24,350	24,840	5
Windham,	2	5,700	....	15,000	15,500	1
HAMILTON Co.						
Morehouse,	1	150	....	....	....	....
HERKIMER Co.						
Columbia,	2	5,000	300	11,900	13,400	2
Frankfort,	1	6,500	2,000	34,750	4,150	4
German Flats,	1	2,500	8,050	16,500	17,240	8
Herkimer,	1	12,000	100	4,500	6,000	2
Little Falls,	2	19,000	2,100	160,000	177,659	8
Newport,	2	....	....	14,085	15,885	....
Russia,	2	3,400	....	4,562	5,900	1
Salisbury,	2	4,000	1,000	25,759	30,073	4
Stark,	2	7,000	....	....	2,200	2
Winfield,	3	8,200	1,970	26,000	47,000	5
JEFFERSON Co.						
Adams,	2	8,600	925	21,750	30,144	4
Alexandria,	2	16,700	300	7,048	14,100	8
Antwerp,	2	2,500	5,500	28,000	30,700	3
Brownville,	2	8,000	5,500	47,400	57,900	5
Champion,	2	18,000	....	79,925	95,900	4
Clayton,	2	10,200	5,000	4,800	7,000	3
Ellisburgh,	7	20,900	....	47,000	51,100	11
Henderson,	4	6,800	5,000	38,035	42,557	5
Hounsfield,	1	8,000	....	37,200	35,000	7
Le Ray,	3	14,000	....	47,337	86,134	5
Lorraine,	3	4,500	....	....	....	....
Lyme,	1	3,000	....	58,150	60,500	3
Orleans,	2	2,100	950	10,000	12,720	3
Pamelia,	3	26,000	4,200	567,423	644,940	17
Philadelphia,	2	7,700	....	20,435	13,993	3
Rutland,	1	4,000	....	6,500	7,500	2
Watertown,	6	39,500	21,000	268,937	353,000	25
Wilna,	3	8,500	1,000	13,500	14,200	7
KINGS Co.						
Brooklyn,	3	85,000	58,000	560,000	635,000	48
New Lots,	2	2,500	1,000	12,200	31,250	3
LEWIS Co.						
Croghan,	1	1,200	200	2,540	2,817	1
Denmark,	1	7,000	4,000	10,400	13,350	1
Greig,	1	3,000	2,000	4,000	4,000	1
Leyden,	1	....	5,000	....	....	....
Lowville,	2	800	1,500	4,250	11,070	4
Martinsburgh,	2	4,500	2,000	13,227	18,314	4
New Bremen,	1	8,000	....	31,500	35,500	3
Turin,	1	5,000	....	11,500	12,625	1
LIVINGSTON Co.						
Avon,	4	15,400	18,700	130,500	170,000	10
Caledonia,	2	10,500	....	21,900	24,460	2
Conesus,	1	10,500	....	20,000	25,000	1
Groveland,	2	13,000	....	103,975	81,950	4
Leicester,	1	8,000	....	35,570	28,950	3
Lima,	2	....	12,000	....	....	....
Livonia,	2	9,225	7,200	8,450	9,900	3
Mount Morris,	3	21,000	16,000	216,639	241,520	7
North Dansville,	4	48,000	....	120,546	153,541	13
Portage,	2	15,000	500	33,450	56,750	5
Springwater,	3	20,250	150	32,243	44,811	3
West Sparta,	1	9,200	....	23,326	25,616	4
York,	2	5,000	5,600	61,600	79,450	3
MADISON Co.						
Brookfield,	2	2,500	50	7,825	9,301	3
Cazenovia,	4	19,000	750	66,726	77,997	9
De Ruyter,	2	6,200	1,300	7,600	8,360	2
Eaton,	1	3,000	200	9,000	10,000	1
Georgetown,	1	13,500	500	4,800	5,800	1
Hamilton,	1	5,000	....	13,950	15,000	1
Lebanon,	1	3,000	100	....	600	1
Lenox,	5	19,000	2,500	13,000	15,400	5
Nelson,	1	....	....	....	....	....
Smithfield,	1	5,000	....	8,850	8,850	....
Sullivan,	3	....	....	20,643	20,643	5
MONROE Co.						
Chili,	2	23,000	1,000	34,000	80,000	3
Greece,	1	2,000	600	6,000	6,000	1
Mendon,	4	29,000	325	305,500	307,000	15
Ogden,	1	200	100	....	2,000	....
Parma,	3	21,000	6,500	100,537	114,150	5
Penfield,	3	32,000	50	77,000	82,000	8
Perrington,	4	33,100	4,775	245,000	257,000	7
Pittsford,	1	7,500	7,500	121,500	144,683	6
Riga,	1	12,000	100	76,098	80,238	3
Rochester,	23	669,300	6,500	5,421,448	5,482,998	180
MONROE Co.						
Rush,	1	$4,500	$450	$75,000	$80,000	4
Sweden,	1	500	3,500	24,475	25,500	3
Webster,	2	5,000	80	20,000	8,000	3
Wheatland,	7	87,000	650	528,426	626,016	28
MONTGOMERY Co.						
Amsterdam,	3	20,700	....	86,151	108,738	2
Canajoharie,	4	26,000	1,400	19,975	19,975	4
Charleston,	1	8,000	....	30,000	3,280	3
Florida,	3	4,500	4,010	19,850	35,235	5
Glen,	3	19,500	13,000	52,200	45,350	25
Minden,	2	17,000	2,800	9,200	12,100	4
Mohawk,	2	11,000	....	43,975	52,150	6
Palatine,	2	5,500	1,025	6,150	1,250	4
Root,	2	1,300	2,100	7,200	8,020	2
St. Johnsville,	2	4,000	6,000	29,700	95,000	5
NEW-YORK Co.						
New-York,	8	102,000	75,700	2,137,200	2,497,719	175
NIAGARA Co.						
Lockport,	4	140,000	19,500	808,500	1,119,800	32
Newfane,	3	20,000	1,800	104,000	120,000	8
Niagara,	2	20,000	10,000	80,000	100,000	7
Porter,	1	15,000	500	130,000	200,600	12
Royalton,	5	36,400	3,000	50,000	69,500	18
Wheatfield,	1	300	3,000	....	....	2
Wilson,	1	6,000	....	32,649	36,337	3
ONEIDA Co.						
Annsville,	1	6,000	3,800	20,125	22,500	4
Augusta,	3	6,200	....	22,175	16,000	3
Boonville,	2	5,200	3,200	16,797	21,784	3
Camden,	1	10,000	....	61,750	64,837	4
Kirkland,	2	10,000	1,100	20,700	22,120	4
Lee,	2	6,500	6,000	72,700	83,293	3
Marshall,	1	4,000	2,000	9,000	1,000	2
New Hartford,	2	18,000	5,000	30,499	39,919	6
Paris,	4	14,800	2,700	47,000	61,560	8
Remsen,	2	6,000	9,500	28,212	34,495	8
Rome,	1	1,000	1,500	40,000	46,010	4
Sangerfield,	3	10,000	100	7,275	10,065	3
Trenton,	4	19,500	1,400	26,240	35,295	14
Utica,	2	12,000	10,000	74,075	90,100	6
Vernon,	3	14,000	9,200	44,500	49,725	10
Verona,	3	15,500	5,200	77,314	97,021	8
Vienna,	3	5,500	3,000	7,720	10,500	5
Western,	1	5,000	500	22,200	46,200	1
Whitestown,	2	13,000	1,050	83,701	102,474	5
ONONDAGA Co.						
Camillus,	3	13,000	12,000	....	....	....
De Witt,	3	17,000	1,000	44,150	48,000	6
Elbridge,	2	28,000	....	27,369	360,000	8
Fabius,	3	9,000	....	24,000	26,200	4
Geddes,	1	5,000	150	6,400	7,062	3
Lysander,	1	7,000	....	2,700	5,160	....
Manlius,	5	39,000	....	155,665	170,338	8
Marcellus,	3	17,000	18,000	87,600	101,000	9
Onondaga,	4	32,000	1,040	94,900	118,381	8
Otisco,	2	7,000	1,000	23,200	23,600	6
Pompey,	1	4,500	50	27,375	34,812	2
Skaneateles,	3	16,000	5,100	29,000	33,340	6
Syracuse,	3	28,500	16,150	337,070	368,275	16
Tully,	1	500	1,500	5,400	6,000	1
Van Buren,	1	10,000	5,000	115,000	118,000	10
ONTARIO Co.						
Bristol,	2	9,000	75	....	1,600	3
East Bloomfield,	6	23,000	7,000	267,675	194 800	7
Farmington,	1	7,500	....	....	3,000	4
Gorham,	3	15,000	3,100	130,500	156,800	7
Hopewell,	2	31,000	14,000	280,000	280,000	39
Manchester,	4	40,000	2,000	44,680	501,243	17
Naples,	4	25,000	1,450	48,992	65,972	4
Phelps,	7	45,600	6,375	131,000	99,240	13
Richmond,	2	6,800	9,200	600	4,000	5
Seneca,	1	3,000	1,500	16,000	1,900	3
South Bristol,	1	800	2,600	9,900	9,900	2
Victor,	3	24,000	1,000	86,000	60,000	6
West Bloomfield,	4	20,000	....	146,000	120,500	8
ORANGE Co.						
Blooming Grove,	3	11,000	4,500	3,000	3,500	6
Chester,	1	300	....	2,000	2,000	1
Cornwall,	2	32,500	1,550	57,293	86,145	8
Deerpark,	4	15,000	200	101,000	134,000	7
Goshen,	1	2,200	2,000	20,000	20,000	1
Hamptonburgh,	1	2,500	....	....	350	1
Minisink,	1	3,000	3,000	1,100	2,600	1
Monroe,	5	10,500	6,700	75,500	77,170	7
Montgomery,	4	26,500	8,500	93,000	140,600	16
Mount Hope,	3	6,000	5,000	22,000	24,200	3
Newburgh,	7	45,200	13,600	136,400	156,280	24
Wallkill,	4	7,800	4,700	15,250	24,070	5
Warwick,	2	6,000	2,000	20,000	22,000	3

CLASS XIII.—(Continued.)

TOWNS.	Number of establishments.	Capital invested. In real estate.	Capital invested. In tools and machinery.	Cash value. Of raw materials used.	Cash value. Of manufactured articles.	Persons employed.
Orleans Co.						
Barre	3	$13,000	$2,100	$25,000	$65,000	16
Carlton	4	25,500	4,000	44,625	51,300	6
Clarendon	1	10,000	2,000	....	2,000	1
Gaines	2	45,000	10,000	588,000	720,000	14
Kendall	2	12,000	1,675	30,310	38,666	3
Murray	3	27,000	600	138,900	175,606	8
Ridgeway	8	82,500	17,200	673,000	1,190,500	30
Shelly	1	35,000	3,000	141,074	139,698	15
Yates	2	9,500	1,003	31,480	20,558	3
Oswego Co.						
Constantia	1	3,000	3,000	12,000	14,000	3
Granby	1	6,000	....	....	1,200	....
Hannibal	1	3,500	....	....	500	1
Mexico	4	10,100	5,600	34,300	37,736	4
New Haven	2	5,600	....	....	....	....
Orwell	1	800	500	....	500	1
Oswego	1	5,000	1,500	10,000	12,500	2
Oswego city	15	423,200	140,000	5,567,422	7,658,724	202
Palermo	2	1,500	....	21,375	24,875	....
Redfield	1	5,000	500	3,000	3,000	1
Richland	4	9,300	8,500	63,700	100,320	6
Sandy Creek	1	4,000	11,050	12,242	16,374	2
Schroeppel	1	600	12,500	27,500	37,375	4
Volney	6	144,000	450	1,071,862	1,539,425	66
Williamstown	1	1,000	....	5,000	5,000	1
Otsego Co.						
Burlington	4	5,240	4,375	....	1,200	5
Butternuts	1	4,000	15,600	....	....	1
Cherry Valley	3	9,000	....	45,750	48,787	4
Edmeston	2	4,000	3,000	....	1,500	3
Laurens	2	1,500	500	....	1,500	2
Maryland	3	4,000	....	15,800	17,400	3
Middlefield	2	2,400	2,400	....	2,400	3
Milford	3	3,800	....	1,875	1,875	1
Oneonta	1	1,200	....	10,000	10,000	2
Otego	2	9,000	....	5,826	5,826	2
Otsego	4	13,000	1,000	18,215	19,380	5
Plainfield	1	3,500	....	....	800	....
Richfield	1	4,000	....	....	....	2
Roseboom	2	8,000	....	....	2,200	2
Springfield	3	4,500	....	....	1,500	1
Westford	1	1,200	2,000	14,000	15,400	2
Worcester	2	8,000	3,000	37,500	41,500	3
Putnam Co.						
Carmel	1	500	1,500	....	....	1
Kent	4	16,700	300	33,000	36,500	6
Phillipstown	1	3,500	750	4,300	5,085	1
Putnam Valley	1	3,500	1,500	10,000	10,000	....
Queens Co.						
Flushing	4	19,000	5,800	71,500	30,700	10
Hempstead	11	36,500	11,400	62,100	76,525	12
Jamaica	2	9,000	1,850	15,750	19,500	2
Newtown	1	7,000	3,000	....	....	1
North Hempstead	2	12,500	3,000	29,375	30,800	2
Oyster Bay	4	39,000	10,500	26,000	24,000	5
Rensselaer Co.						
Brunswick	1	1,000	1,000	5,000	6,000	1
Clinton	1	1,500	300	....	....	....
Greenbush	3	27,000	14,000	49,000	457,000	10
Hoosick	6	20,600	6,500	5,000	5,000	4
Lansingburgh	3	14,500	....	....	....	2
Petersburgh	1	5,600	....	22,625	26,110	1
Pittstown	5	13,250	9,750	116,200	131,784	6
Poestenkill	2	3,000	400	10,000	10,000	2
Sandlake	3	12,000	1,600	50,250	52,700	7
Schaghticoke	1	6,000	....	900	900	2
Schodack	2	3,500	4,000	35,400	22,440	3
Stephentown	1	1,200	1,800	31,000	33,000	2
Troy	5	68,000	12,000	558,733	612,516	38
Richmond Co.						
Northfield	1	8,000	1,000	9,700	12,000	3
Westfield	1	1,000	....	4,000	4,500	....
Rockland Co.						
Clarkstown	2	4 000	1,400	18,000	20,000	3
Haverstraw	1	1,000	....	5,325	6,300	1
Orangetown	4	16,300	2,500	31,055	37,623	2
Ramapo	6	11,100	900	24,825	26,107	2
St. Lawrence Co.						
Brasher	2	8,500	2,000	....	....	1
Canton	3	29,000	2,000	1,800	1,980	5
Colton	1	8,000	....	15,000	16,500	2
Edwards	2	1,000	6,500	....	....	....
Fowler	1	10,000	3,000	....	2,000	1
Gouverneur	1	8,000	44,000	58,000	67,600	2
Hermon	2	4,000	50	20,650	23,850	3
Hopkinton	1	3,000	2,000	180	1,000	1
Lawrence	3	12,000	....	40,437	44,300	3
Louisville	1	1,000	2,000	7,500	8,250	2
Macomb	1	1,000	1,200	11,000	12,100	1
St. Lawrence Co.						
Madrid	2	$4,400	$7,000	$33,788	$17,218	8
Morristown	1	....	....	3,000	3,000	....
Norfolk	1	12,000	....	22,000	20,000	4
Oswegatchie	5	65,000	26,500	336,000	762,000	27
Parishville	1	8,000	50	4,543	5,500	....
Potsdam	3	14,000	5,000	65,575	71,575	....
Rossie	2	16,000	5,100	14,500	34,300	4
Russell	1	10,000	200	11,500	12,500	....
Stockholm	2	5,000	....	4,611	5,411	2
Saratoga Co.						
Charlton	2	5,000	....	....	....	....
Corinth	1	2,000	1,000	10,000	11,000	1
Day	1	500	500	....	....	....
Galway	2	....	....	6,000	6,000	2
Greenfield	1	1,000	400	9,250	10,000	1
Halfmoon	1	9,000	1,200	22,000	29,200	3
Malta	2	4,000	100	2,115	3,420	1
Milton	4	16,000	4,050	31,468	34,900	7
Moreau	3	42,000	....	77,500	92,126	5
Northumberland	1	1,000	5,000	10,050	10,806	1
Providence	3	5,000	1,600	28,000	34,000	6
Saratoga	2	12,000	8,000	29,700	32,500	5
Saratoga Springs	2	8,500	200	10,600	18,200	2
Stillwater	2	15,000	....	38,000	38,000	3
Waterford	5	81,000	2,200	768,168	862,444	28
Wilton	1	1,700	30	7,000	8,300	2
Schenectady Co.						
Duanesburgh	2	13,000	....	5,000	600	4
Rotterdam	3	31,500	9,000	40,000	46,800	7
Schoharie Co.						
Cobleskill	2	1,900	500	500	....	....
Esperance	1	2,000	....	26,250	28,875	2
Fulton	1	1,500	2,000	15,000	15,800	2
Gilboa	3	6,500	7,500	70,000	70,500	2
Jefferson	2	3,000	....	....	....	....
Middleburgh	1	....	....	13,750	13,750	1
Richmondville	3	7,555	155	19,375	21,307	3
Schoharie	2	6,000	....	24,000	26,400	2
Seward	2	10,050	4,100	34,800	41,930	4
Sharon	5	9,600	1,900	3,375	3,375	6
Summit	3	1,900	600	8,250	8,958	2
Wright	2	200	1,600	34,000	37,400	2
Schuyler Co.						
Catharines	5	45,000	1,600	30,250	65,003	16
Cayuta	1	4,000	50	10,000	11,000	1
Dix	3	9,500	100	27,650	33,605	4
Hector	4	16,500	5,500	31,387	17,952	4
Orange	1	1,000	4,000	5,000	15,000	2
Tyrone	1	5,000	5,000	50,000	53,000	2
Seneca Co.						
Fayette	3	18,000	8,000	97,500	112,800	6
Lodi	2	14,000	....	28,977	37,363	4
Ovid	3	5,400	11,000	39,837	74,465	9
Seneca Falls	6	85,150	1,000	25,800	320,905	8
Varick	1	2,500	3,000	12,000	13,000	1
Steuben Co.						
Addison	1	10,000	6,000	....	....	3
Avoca	4	9,000	117	24,450	37,200	4
Bath	5	31,700	500	73,900	97,830	9
Bradford	1	10,000	....	20,000	26,000	2
Cameron	2	8,000	....	16,500	18,205	2
Campbell	1	500	700	2,400	3,000	1
Canisteo	2	6,500	3,000	35,250	35,250	2
Cohocton	2	4,000	13,000	18,800	14,400	2
Corning	1	15,000	1,000	63,000	69,600	3
Dansville	2	1,400	6,300	21,730	46,000	4
Erwin	1	12,000	300	47,000	52,500	3
Fremont	4	13,500	57	23,750	26,200	4
Hornellsville	3	15,500	7,000	120,106	128,293	6
Howard	2	10,075	4,125	....	....	4
Jasper	1	200	500	2,500	2,500	1
Prattsburgh	2	2,000	6,000	38,000	46,000	4
Troupsburgh	2	....	....	11,000	11,410	2
Urbana	2	11,000	8,000	14,000	32,000	4
Wayland	3	3,000	16,000	33,710	33,996	2
Woodhull	1	750	500	....	....	....
Suffolk Co.						
Brookhaven	4	26,200	6,000	14,000	9,230	4
Easthampton	2	....	800	7,500	7,500	....
Huntington	4	13,000	1,000	24,200	25,000	6
Islip	1	10,000	1,500	11,250	13,500	1
Riverhead	1	1,500	500	3,000	3,000	1
Smithtown	5	11,000	50	37,000	40,625	4
Southampton	8	16,100	10,100	68,375	74,660	9
Southold	2	3,000	500	9,765	10,850	1
Sullivan Co.						
Callicoon	2	5,400	2,000	27,600	32,565	4
Cochecton	2	10,000	215	50,000	55,000	3
Fallsburgh	2	3,800	100	20,000	22,000	2

CLASS XIII.—(CONTINUED.)

TOWNS.	Number of establishments.	Capital Invested. In real estate.	Capital Invested. In tools and machinery.	Cash Value. Of raw materials used.	Cash Value. Of manufactured articles.	Persons employed.
SULLIVAN Co.						
Forrestburgh, ...	1	$5,000	$1,100	$5,000	$7,500	2
Highland, ...	1	4,000	....	5,000	2,500	1
Liberty, ...	1	4,000	200	18,300	19,300	2
Mamakating, ...	3	10,500	6,170	84,128	85,401	6
Neversink, ...	2	4,500	150	6,500	6,500	3
Rockland, ...	1	6,000	70	5,322	14,192	2
Thompson, ...	1	4,000	....	6,000	660	2
TIOGA Co.						
Barton, ...	2	800	3,200	1,100	....	1
Berkshire, ...	1	3,000	20,000	....	1,000	1
Candor, ...	3	27,500	2,500	....	67,000	7
Newark, ...	2	4,000	4,000	10,400	19,865	2
Nichols, ...	3	600	1,000	....	2,750	4
Owego, ...	3	13,500	6,000	94,000	106,000	8
Spencer, ...	2	11,800	....	12,531	1,531	2
Tioga, ...	1	5,000	9,000	7,100	7,400	3
TOMPKINS Co.						
Caroline, ...	5	21,700	4,300	88,550	112,249	6
Danby, ...	1	....	6,000	600	1,500	2
Dryden, ...	7	32,500	2,000	69,372	85,594	15
Enfield, ...	1	500	6,000	3,500	4,000	2
Ithaca, ...	4	54,800	15,800	163,000	174,741	16
Lansing, ...	3	32,500	3,000	1,000	1,000	3
Newfield, ...	1	10,000	....	30,600	33,330	3
Ulysses, ...	6	41,500	....	143,500	160,180	10
ULSTER Co.						
Esopus, ...	1	3,000	3,000	13,300	17,145	2
Gardiner, ...	4	11,700	1,000	16,000	33,360	4
Kingston, ...	1	6,000	2,000	8,000	8,000	2
Lloyd, ...	6	16,500	110	90,500	86,684	10
Marbletown, ...	6	17,200	5,100	30,000	45,640	7
Marlborough, ...	6	23,000	....	78,000	87,750	12
Olive, ...	2	4,000	1,500	19,300	21,100	2
Rochester, ...	4	7,500	3,000	36,000	43,000	4
Saugerties, ...	3	5,200	700	55,800	95,800	5
Shawangunk, ...	4	9,000	5,000	5,304	5,304	7
Wawarsing, ...	4	11,200	500	100,100	120,750	5
Woodstock, ...	1	2,100	1,000	5,000	3,200	1
WARREN Co.						
Chester, ...	1	1,700	....	....	1,000	1
Johnsburgh, ...	1	3,000	1,000	7,200	7,200	1
Luzerne, ...	1	1,200	1,800	20,000	22,000	2
Stony Creek, ...	1	2,000	50	5,000	5,500	1
Warrensburgh, ...	1	3,000	1,000	3,500	4,700	2
WASHINGTON Co.						
Argyle, ...	2	7,000	....	35,400	38,990	4
Easton, ...	1	600	....	1,000	1,100	....
Fort Ann, ...	1	3,000	....	6,000	600	1
Granville, ...	6	9,100	1,500	16,000	7,397	3
Greenwich, ...	3	12,000	850	27,000	30,000	6
Salem, ...	2	11,000	2,000	7,827	10,406	4
WAYNE Co.						
Arcadia, ...	2	22,000	150	52,900	63,800	5
Huron, ...	1	4,500	....	27,140	28,140	4
Lyons, ...	3	41,000	100	106,123	116,410	11
Macedon, ...	3	3,000	1,500	12,100	14,500	2
Marion, ...	1	4,000	8,000	25,000	30,000	4
Ontario, ...	2	900	800	8,000	8,850	2
Palmyra, ...	4	9,700	7,000	60,300	68,430	6
Rose, ...	1	3,000	100	....	1,000	2
Sodus, ...	4	15,500	40	79,000	92,500	6
Williamson, ...	1	2,000	2,000	3,300	4,300	1
Wolcott, ...	3	11,500	1,000	12,000	13,800	6
WESTCHESTER Co.						
Bedford, ...	3	9,000	....	23,750	15,100	3
Eastchester, ...	1	1,500	500	....	....	....
Greenburgh, ...	1	10,000	....	17,800	19,680	3
Lewisboro, ...	1	400	700	9,000	10,000	1
Mount Pleasant, ..	3	11,500	500	16,000	19,000	9
New Rochelle, ...	1	7,000	1,000	50,000	50,000	2
North Castle, ...	2	1,200	....	2,600	3,791	1
North Salem, ...	2	5,000	1,500	16,000	17,600	2
Ossining, ...	1	6,000	4,000	20,000	25,000	3
Poundridge, ...	1	2,000	....	....	....	....
WESTCHESTER Co.						
Rye, ...	3	$4,000	$1,500	$41,500	$83,000	3
Somers, ...	3	3,500	850	10,250	10,250	3
West Farms, ...	2	15,000	118,000	110 500	135,200	14
White Plains, ...	2	25,000	7,000	196,000	212,700	10
Yorktown, ...	3	6,100	3,900	54,187	59,173	4
WYOMING Co.						
Attica, ...	3	11,500	150	....	2,900	5
Bennington, ...	2	3,100	3,000	16,000	17,400	4
Castile, ...	2	11,000	....	40,543	62,288	5
China, ...	1	3,000	2,000	....	6,000	2
Covington, ...	3	6,100	4,600	....	1,500	6
Gainesville, ...	1	....	8,000	2,500	8,000	2
Java, ...	1	4,000	....	....	1,200	1
Middlebury, ...	3	9,700	850	2,075	7,300	3
Orangeville, ...	1	1,500	1,500	9,360	9,900	1
Perry, ...	3	27,000	....	81,000	99,000	6
Pike, ...	3	17,800	450	62,600	77,150	6
Sheldon, ...	2	5,000	....	....	1,500	3
Warsaw, ...	3	19,000	3,000	31,000	52,500	6
Wethersfield, ...	2	14,000	6,500	16,100	15,325	2
YATES Co.						
Jerusalem, ...	1	2,000	4,000	15,000	15,000	3
Milo, ...	5	50,000	800	214,500	235,550	10
Potter, ...	1	1,000	200	....	500	1
Starkey, ...	5	15,700	194	26,800	32,016	6
Torrey, ...	3	32,500	800	147.669	177,654	13

MILLSTONE MANUFACTORIES.

TOWNS.	Number of establishments.	Capital Invested. In real estate.	Capital Invested. In tools and machinery.	Cash Value. Of raw materials used.	Cash Value. Of manufactured articles.	Persons employed.
BROOME Co.						
Chenango, ...	1	....	400	4,725	6,400	3
NEW-YORK Co.						
New-York, ...	1	7,000	400	4,000	7,000	12
ONEIDA Co.						
Utica, ...	1	17,000	7,500	21,000	40,000	32
RENSSELAER Co.						
Troy, ...	1	4,500	500	10,000	15,000	14
ULSTER Co.						
Rochester, ...	2	....	110	....	2,800	6

MILLWRIGHT SHOPS.

TOWNS.	Number of establishments.	Capital Invested. In real estate.	Capital Invested. In tools and machinery.	Cash Value. Of raw materials used.	Cash Value. Of manufactured articles.	Persons employed.
HERKIMER Co.						
Salisbury, ...	1	500	350	262	818	1
MONROE Co.						
Chili, ...	1	100	200	....	1,000	....
Rochester, ...	2	6,000	8,100	4,600	21,000	23
OTSEGO Co.						
Decatur, ...	2	400	50	....	450	....
Milford, ...	1	....	25	350	1,080	1
ULSTER Co.						
Marlborough, ...	1	8,000	500	600	225	2
WESTCHESTER Co.						
Mount Pleasant, ..	1	75	150	....	....	....
White Plains, ...	1	4,000	700	225	225	5

PEARL BARLEY MILLS.

TOWNS.	Number of establishments.	Capital Invested. In real estate.	Capital Invested. In tools and machinery.	Cash Value. Of raw materials used.	Cash Value. Of manufactured articles.	Persons employed.
JEFFERSON Co.						
Watertown, ...	1	2,000	1,000	7,000	17,400	4
ONONDAGA Co.						
Manlius, ...	1	6,000	....	7,140	9,270	4

SMUT MACHINE MANUFACTORIES.

TOWNS.	Number of establishments.	Capital Invested. In real estate.	Capital Invested. In tools and machinery.	Cash Value. Of raw materials used.	Cash Value. Of manufactured articles.	Persons employed.
CHENANGO Co.						
Bainbridge, ...	1	1,500	300	1,080	5,600	4
GENESEE Co.						
Darien, ...	1	400	800	1,340	10,000	2
ONEIDA Co.						
Floyd, ...	1	....	....	800	3,000	....
RENSSELAER Co.						
Troy, ...	1	1,500	1,500	2,300	3,000	4

CLASS XIV.—LUMBER, INCLUDING TOOLS AND MACHINES FOR ITS MANUFACTURE.

TOWNS.	Number of establishments.	Capital Invested. In real estate.	Capital Invested. In tools and machinery.	Cash Value. Of raw materials used.	Cash Value. Of manufactured articles.	Persons employed.
AUGER MANUFACTORIES.						
Monroe Co.						
Rochester, ...	1	....	$1,000	$1,710	$4,800	7
Oneida Co.						
Vernon, ...	1	$100	100	106	700	1
Otsego Co.						
Maryland, ...	1	....	....	15	75	1
Rensselaer Co.						
Brunswick, ...	1	10,000	9,000	13,000	65,000	60
BARREL MACHINE MANUFACTORIES.						
Cayuga Co.						
Elmira, ...	1	12,000	10,000	11,050	37,830	31
Cortland Co.						
Cortlandville, ...	1	400	175	255	600	2
BORING MACHINE MANUFACTORY.						
New-York Co.						
New-York, ...	1	....	6,000	3,500	20,000	12
BOX MANUFACTORIES.						
Allegany Co.						
Amity, ...	4	5,000	1,350	39,280	73,805	29
Cattaraugus Co.						
Farmersville, ...	2	....	....	500	1,240	....
Erie Co.						
Buffalo, ...	2	....	13,000	47,800	90,000	73
East Hamburgh, .	1	....	....	2,800	5,000	5
Fulton Co.						
Perth, ...	1	....	....	150	300	8
Kings Co.						
Brooklyn, ...	1	8,000	3,550	3,000	25,000	13
Madison Co.						
Lenox, ...	2	....	50	1,275	2,200	2
Monroe Co.						
Rochester, ...	1	....	800	250	2,500	3
New-York Co.						
New-York, ...	11	56,500	19,400	222,940	321,550	128
Onondaga Co.						
Syracuse, ...	1	....	1,000	7,000	30,000	6
Oneida Co.						
Kirkland, ...	1	500	....	875	1,800	2
Oswego Co.						
Oswego city, ...	1	12,000	9,000	9,650	17,500	22
Rensselaer Co.						
Troy, ...	1	....	....	....	12,000	....
St. Lawrence Co.						
Stockholm, ...	1	3,000	1,000	1,500	4,000	8
Tioga Co.						
Owego, ...	1	....	700	11,000	18,750	14
Westchester Co.						
Ossining, ...	1	....	2,000	80,000	80,000	27
CARPENTER SHOPS.						
Albany Co.						
Albany, ...	7	9,000	2,350	7,500	5,500	77
Rensselaerville, ..	1	150	25	25	100	1
Watervliet, ...	1	1,500	350	3,000	6,000	5
Allegany Co.						
Andover, ...	2	400	325	....	....	....
Cattaraugus Co.						
Freedom, ...	1	....	60	....	....	....
Cayuga Co.						
Auburn, ...	4	2,300	5,300	6,275	20,500	27
Conquest, ...	1	....	50	....	....	....
Mentz, ...	1	....	250	....	....	....
Niles, ...	1	....	....	....	....	4
Chautauque Co.						
Chautauque, ...	1	....	100	....	550	2
Cherry Creek, ...	2	650	565	60	1,000	3
Chemung Co.						
Chemung, ...	4	....	270	....	350	....
Southport, ...	....	....	175	....	550	....
Clinton Co.						
Beekmantown, ...	1	150	75	150	500	1
Columbia Co.						
Hudson, ...	5	3,500	2,550	22,500	48,000	46
Kinderhook, ...	2	700	400	9,800	10,000	10
Cortland Co.						
Cortlandville, ...	1	1,000	3,000	3,500	8,500	6
Dutchess Co.						
Fishkill, ...	1	....	....	....	....	6
Hyde Park, ...	1	....	550	3,500	6,300	16
La Grange, ...	1	200	70	....	....	....
Erie Co.						
Buffalo, ...	2	$4,600	$350	$150	....	6
Grand Island, ...	1	400	70	200	$700	1
Fulton Co.						
Bleecker, ...	7	....	465	....	....	....
Greene Co.						
Athens, ...	3	1,300	350	5,100	7,600	8
Herkimer Co.						
German Flats, ...	2	500	320	1,650	8,500	9
Little Falls, ...	3	2,100	550	1,950	6,000	12
Jefferson Co.						
Pamelia, ...	3	60	330	50	800	2
Kings Co.						
Brooklyn, ...	10	8,000	2,600	5,900	24,900	77
Lewis Co.						
New Bremen, ...	1	....	100	....	1,000	2
Livingston Co.						
Lima, ...	9	....	628	....	....	....
Nunda, ...	1	600	1,200	750	4,000	5
Monroe Co.						
Chili, ...	4	2,700	400	....	2,850	4
Rochester, ...	2	3,500	2,500	16,250	16,250	22
Webster, ...	5	....	225	283	9,800	11
New-York Co.						
New-York, ...	76	232,355	30,050	576,290	1,133,200	810
Niagara Co.						
Porter, ...	1	300	75	....	....	3
Oneida Co.						
Vernon, ...	1	200	100	400	900	2
Onondaga Co.						
Clay, ...	3	....	247	....	....	4
Marcellus, ...	1	....	150	....	500	1
Onondaga, ...	7	2,050	1,710	....	7,950	22
Syracuse, ...	1	....	250	....	....	....
Ontario Co.						
Canandaigua, ...	1	1,000	100	250	4,000	4
Orange Co.						
Minisink, ...	1	....	25	....	....	....
Wallkill, ...	1	1,000	3,000	20,000	30,000	13
Orleans Co.						
Ridgeway, ...	1	500	100	200	500	1
Oswego Co.						
Granby, ...	1	....	50	135	414	2
Otsego Co.						
Decatur, ...	4	400	210	....	1,000	4
Roseboom, ...	7	400	....	....	1,800	3
Putnam Co.						
Carmel, ...	1	....	150	....	....	....
Queens Co.						
Jamaica, ...	2	1,750	1,000	12,000	21,500	16
Richmond Co.						
Westfield, ...	3	1,200	1,400	4,500	31,500	21
Rockland Co.						
Haverstraw, ...	1	200	40	....	....	....
Tompkins Co.						
Caroline, ...	1	....	100	210	633	2
Lansing, ...	1	200	50	250	300	....
Ulysses, ...	1	100	200	200	800	3
Ulster Co.						
Kingston, ...	2	4,000	600	3,000	3,000	13
Warren Co.						
Warrensburgh, ...	1	150	200	300	600	2
Wayne Co.						
Sodus, ...	10	....	970	....	2,645	10
Westchester Co.						
Eastchester, ...	5	1,500	825	13,800	24,500	24
Mount Pleasant, ..	3	100	350	....	....	2
Ossining, ...	1	1,000	100	3,000	6,000	6
Rye, ...	3	4,500	575	4,200	21,000	15
CARPENTERS' TOOL MANUFACTORIES.						
Albany Co.						
Albany, ...	1	....	2,500	5,000	5,000	14
Cayuga Co.						
Auburn, ...	1	....	9,000	27,000	65,000	83
Chemung Co.						
Elmira, ...	1	250	200	400	1,200	1
Columbia Co.						
Austerlitz, ...	1	1,000	1,200	2,000	16,000	13
Erie Co.						
Concord, ...	1	200	150	60	2,000	2
Jefferson Co						
Pamelia, ...	1	5,000	8,000	1,500	4,000	9
Kings Co.						
Brooklyn, ...	1	....	2,000	700	4,000	2
Monroe Co.						
Rochester, ...	2	30,218	10,300	17,000	73,000	84

CLASS XIV.—(Continued.)

TOWNS.	Number of establishments.	Capital Invested. In real estate.	Capital Invested. In tools and machinery.	Cash Value. Of raw materials used.	Cash Value. Of manufactured articles.	Persons employed.
Oneida Co.						
Sangerfield,	1	$2,500	$1,000	$375	$1,800	5
Steuben Co.						
Howard,	1	175	200	200	650	1
CHEESE BOX MANUFACTORIES.						
Allegany Co.						
Alfred,	1	300	200	100	400	1
Rushford,	1	300	200	287	710	2
Cattaraugus Co.						
Ashford,	1	1,000	250	480	1,620	5
Freedom,	1	400	150	300	720	2
Mansfield,	1	1,000	500	700	2,000	6
Otto,	1	1,000	....	1,000	1,800	4
Chautauque Co.						
Pomfret,	1	400	75	230	600	....
Chenango Co.						
Preston,	1	200	60	185	400	1
Sherburne,	1	....	....	....	350	1
Fulton Co.						
Oppenheim,	1	500	300	916	2,700	4
Herkimer Co.						
Columbia,	1	40	80	150	500	1
Fairfield,	2	....	....	....	2,000	....
German Flats,	2	500	300	450	1,460	4
Litchfield,	1	200	200	640	1,125	2
Little Falls,	1	1,400	100	1,120	2,400	3
Manheim,	1	400	600	2,272	4,550	5
Newport,	4	1,200	625	2,674	5,130	7
Norway,	1	1,000	100	340	850	3
Russia,	4	2,900	950	1,650	5,600	10
Salisbury,	4	250	50	680	2,125	1
Winfield,	2	650	175	1,500	2,240	5
Jefferson Co.						
Ellisburgh,	1	....	....	125	280	....
Lorraine,	1	800	....	....	....	....
Philadelphia,	1	900	200	235	1,070	2
Rutland,	1	500	1,500	....	....	8
Watertown,	1	....	900	336	1,500	7
Lewis Co.						
Denmark,	3	1,400	650	1,341	4,225	11
Lowville,	1	....	....	....	117	....
Turin,	1	700	100	264	600	4
Madison Co.						
Brookfield,	1	3,000	1,000	1,200	5,000	8
De Ruyter,	1	1,000	1,000	830	2,400	3
Stockbrige,	1	200	200	180	650	2
Oneida Co.						
Deerfield,	1	2,500	100	600	1,560	4
Marcy,	1	600	100	300	700	2
Trenton,	1	600	....	....	1,000	1
Onondaga Co.						
Geddes,	1	600	40	480	2,500	5
Oswego Co.						
Orwell,	2	300	100	150	980	3
Redfield,	1	....	....	1,250	1,850	....
Otsego Co.						
Exeter,	1	1,400	1,000	40	600	2
Rensselaer Co.						
Berlin,	1	300	75	180	500	1
St. Lawrence Co.						
Canton,	1	1,000	125	375	1,500	3
Washington Co.						
Granville,	4	2,600	1,350	1,595	4,040	10
COOPERS' SHOPS.						
Albany Co.						
Albany,	3	12,200	1,000	16,440	65,500	62
New Scotland,	1	....	50	50	500	1
Rensselaerville,	2	75	250	1,300	3,800	8
Watervliet,	6	12,300	10,825	20,600	44,800	76
Allegany Co.						
Alfred,	2	125	65	58	300	2
New Hudson,	1	200	75	100	650	2
Broome Co.						
Chenango,	1	3,000	300	4,500	22,000	25
Colesville,	4	200	210	825	3,400	....
Sandford,	1	50	75	225	810	1
Windsor,	1	150	30	150	500	1
Cattaraugus Co.						
Franklinville,	3	....	170	110	2,075	4
Freedom,	2	300	300	100	780	2
Otto,	1	150	100	148	800	2
Perrysburgh,	1	50	50	106	688	2
Yorkshire,	1	75	....	75	200	1
Cayuga Co.						
Auburn,	1	7,000	1,000	22,500	35,000	55
Locke,	1	400	500	....	....	....
Moravia,	2	150	100	240	840	4

TOWNS.	Number of establishments.	Capital Invested. In real estate.	Capital Invested. In tools and machinery.	Cash Value. Of raw materials used.	Cash Value. Of manufactured articles.	Persons employed.
Cayuga Co.						
Owasco,	1	$30	$200	$200	$265	1
Summerhill,	4	50	85	1,293	1,326	5
Chautauque Co.						
Chautauque,	3	550	275	450	1,900	5
Cherry Creek,	1	100	77	42	140	1
Clymer,	3	370	145	366	1,033	4
Ellicott,	2	75	140	79	840	....
Hanover,	2	150	150	1,520	4,000	7
Pomfret,	1	200	125	202	1,038	1
Sherman,	2	....	....	....	1,000	....
Stockton,	8	900	150	130	3,433	....
Chemung Co.						
Chemung,	1	....	25	50	300	1
Elmira,	1	1,409	200	2,000	6,000	6
Erin,	1	200	100	50	693	2
Horseheads,	1	....	25	400	1,000	2
Southport,	1	300	50	250	1,000	2
Van Etten,	1	....	....	....	....	....
Veteran,	1	50	50	282	588	2
Chenango Co.						
Bainbridge,	1	925	330	355	2,625	7
Coventry,	1	50	15	136	250	1
Greene,	1	150	75	200	1,000	4
Guilford,	4	730	255	930	3,900	10
New Berlin,	1	600	100	487	600	4
Norwich,	2	750	120	1,100	2,700	5
Pitcher,	1	250	200	2,412	5,724	9
Oxford,	1	400	100	....	....	....
Sherburne,	3	450	230	960	2,350	5
Smyrna,	1	300	80	80	1,000	....
Clinton Co.						
Ausable,	1	....	....	750	2,300	....
Beekmantown,	1	100	50	40	200	1
Champlain,	1	1,000	100	50	160	1
Schuyler Falls,	1	50	50	235	600	1
Columbia Co.						
Chatham,	1	500	....	....	....	....
Cortland Co.						
Cincinnatus,	1	....	20	100	300	....
Cortlandville,	3	50	550	1,390	3,278	6
Freetown,	1	250	65	85	218	1
Harford,	1	100	25	200	216	....
Homer,	1	300	100	252	1,100	2
Truxton,	1	800	500	1,300	4,000	4
Virgil,	1	100	20	150	550	1
Willett,	1	100	25	160	414	1
Delaware Co.						
Davenport,	1	....	40	500	1,400	2
Franklin,	2	125	50	260	960	1
Hamden,	1	100	50	306	752	2
Harpersfield,	2	260	200	605	1,482	4
Kortright,	2	350	115	590	1,612	5
Masonville,	1	200	250	200	900	2
Stamford,	1	25	15	....	100	....
Dutchess Co.						
Fishkill,	1	....	100	570	1,000	2
Hyde Park,	1	....	15	145	750	17
Poughkeepsie city,	4	1,300	650	26,300	59,200	60
Rhinebeck,	1	100	100	200	500	....
Erie Co.						
Aurora,	3	450	250	790	3.600	9
Buffalo,	10	10,250	2,380	22,156	42.197	65
Eden,	1	2,000	1,500	3,700	5,200	16
Lancaster,	1	100	25	50	210	1
Essex Co.						
Chesterfield,	1	....	100	4,800	15,000	3
Crown Point,	1	....	100	330	760	....
Jay,	1	3,500	1,500	2,850	5,847	10
Willsborough,	1	....	....	1,250	2,500	6
Franklin Co.						
Fort Covington,	2	150	125	140	2,000	4
Westville,	1	....	1,000	216	1,585	6
Fulton Co.						
Broadalbin,	6	1,000	1,475	1,239	3,912	10
Johnstown,	2	8,000	150	1,120	2,550	3
Northampton,	2	250	160	1,130	4,000	5
Genesee Co.						
Alabama,	2	300	130	700	1,577	7
Alexander,	2	....	....	385	692	1
Batavia,	1	....	50	900	2,000	6
Bergen,	1	....	....	....	....	....
Bethany,	1	50	15	600	1,475	2
Byron,	1	75	50	100	300	2
Le Roy,	3	1,000	100	1,880	4.900	6
Oakfield,	1	140	20	....	750	1
Pembroke,	4	400	400	3,250	7,200	24
Greene Co.						
Catskill,	2	1,600	350	2,000	5,000	6
Durham,	1	25	30	150	....	....

CLASS XIV.—(Continued.)

TOWNS.	Number of establishments.	Capital invested: In real estate.	Capital invested: In tools and machinery.	Cash value: Of raw materials used.	Cash value: Of manufactured articles.	Persons employed.
GREENE Co.						
Lexington,	1	$400	$100	$400	$1,100	2
HERKIMER Co.						
German Flats,	3	1,600	155	2,598	5,375	9
Herkimer,	1	300	100	500	2,000	2
Little Falls,	3	1,500	675	1,830	4,225	9
Newport,	2	600	150	400	1,500	3
Stark,	2	300	50	210	950	1
JEFFERSON Co.						
Adams,	1	100	75	213	664	1
Ellisburgh,	2	200	150	160	860	2
Henderson,	1	330	100	100	780	1
Le Ray,	1	700	500	150	1,600	2
Lyme,	1	100	75	93	571	....
Pamelia,	1	250	40	....	600	2
Rutland,	2	....	....	175	850	....
Watertown,	1	500	75	....	2,750	4
KINGS Co.						
Brooklyn,	6	19,000	6,900	81,150	127,500	98
LEWIS Co.						
Martinsburgh,	1	50	80	60	200	2
LIVINGSTON Co.						
Conesus,	1	50	65	308	700	2
Groveland,	2	350	25	334	1,740	3
Leicester,	1	....	....	1,260	2,800	5
Lima,	2	....	145	....	....	....
Mount Morris,	2	225	30	1,007	2,600	3
Nunda,	1	200	40	525	1,967	3
North Dansville,	2	325	70	2,450	5,956	9
West Sparta,	1	50	50	655	1,260	3
York,	1	....	50	225	900	2
MADISON Co.						
Brookfield,	1	....	25	100	500	2
Cazenovia,	1	....	20	....	210	1
Georgetown,	1	....	150	210	690	1
Hamilton,	2	150	65	350	1,200	1
Lenox,	2	500	400	728	1,801	3
Sullivan,	2	175	50	732	3,700	2
MONROE Co.						
Chili,	1	200	....	300	1,200	2
Irondequoit,	1	60	50	550	1,020	3
Mendon,	2	200	60	50	700	3
Perrington,	2	250	150	850	22,275	4
Riga,	1	300	....	520	1,200	2
Rochester,	39	46,040	5,090	112,815	225,855	339
Webster,	2	150	90	1,475	2,080	4
Wheatland,	4	2,450	....	11,550	25,400	38
MONTGOMERY Co.						
Mohawk,	2	1,000	70	510	1,399	2
Root,	3	125	40	90	675	....
NEW-YORK Co.						
New-York,	59	113,365	14,165	165,258	346,954	605
NIAGARA Co.						
Lewiston,	1	....	100	280	830	2
Lockport,	5	3,850	1,526	23,375	34,758	75
Newfane,	1	150	150	400	1,300	3
Porter,	2	350	170	3,445	3,720	7
Wilson,	1	200	70	418	1,170	2
ONEIDA Co.						
Ava,	2	200	170	181	825	3
Boonville,	2	1,000	300	832	2,700	8
Deerfield,	1	500	50	74	5,050	3
Kirkland,	1	100	40	145	727	1
Paris,	2	3,000	1,420	1,424	2,646	7
Rome,	3	550	200	648	1,851	6
Utica,	5	600	625	3,203	7,785	17
Vernon,	1	300	15	175	500	1
Verona,	1	50	75	130	500	1
Whitestown,	1	250	75	925	1,800	2
ONONDAGA Co.						
Camillus,	3	1,100	400	1,738	5,850	8
Cicero,	4	645	147	4,672	4,710	7
Elbridge,	1	2,000	2,000	7,000	18,000	20
La Fayette,	2	105	50	195	1,235	3
Lysander,	2	400	600	3,450	9,825	16
Manlius,	3	2,000	255	5,443	9,060	12
Salina,	5	375	375	23,780	35,460	29
Skaneateles,	1	300	30	300	600	2
Spafford,	2	80	75	162	728	2
Syracuse,	12	5,950	1,675	32,550	49,120	72
Van Buren,	3	250	375	1,998	4,193	14
ONTARIO Co.						
Bristol,	2	575	150	400	1,000	5
East Bloomfield,	6	900	100	3,575	7,397	9
Farmington,	1	200	50	100	500	1
Gorham,	1	150	40	340	1,005	2
Phelps,	1	50	25	150	....	....
West Bloomfield,	2	....	....	1,290	2,300	3
ORANGE Co.						
Chester,	1	75	50	50	80	1
Deerpark,	1	$500	$100	$1,600	$3,200	5
Hamptonburgh,	1	100	50	2,000	500	2
Minisink,	1	....	30	211	800	2
Mount Hope,	1	100	100	300	1,200	3
Newburgh,	1	1,500	150	2,400	5,155	4
Walkill,	1	400	50	200	600	2
Warwick,	1	....	....	144	707	2
ORLEANS Co.						
Carlton,	4	590	775	2,762	4,958	8
Gaines,	1	100	75	200	450	2
Ridgeway,	5	450	125	5,100	14,986	15
OSWEGO Co.						
Albion,	4	530	20	1,506	3,880	10
Hannibal,	1	....	....	600	1,000	2
Mexico,	15	110	2,102	4,119	5,235	17
New Haven,	14	3,260	2,559	6,821	25,117	12
Oswego city,	3	4,500	500	8,000	12,436	26
Richland,	4	205	150	9,000	2,900	10
Schroeppel,	1	....	....	975	3,300	5
Scriba,	4	270	115	1,000	8,900	7
Volney,	2	2,550	65	6,380	12,250	19
OTSEGO Co.						
Burlington,	1	150	25	75	500	1
Butternuts,	1	50	75	270	875	2
Decatur,	1	1,000	15	100	250	1
Maryland,	1	200	100	85	450	1
Middlefield,	1	400	400	100	1,000	2
New Lisbon,	3	80	110	185	625	....
Oneonta,	1	150	....	2,325	1,800	3
Otego,	2	115	185	302	1,665	4
Plainfield,	1	150	10	50	150	....
Roseboom,	3	425	200	100	925	1
Unadilla,	2	300	125	672	1,710	4
RENSSELAER Co.						
Grafton,	1	....	100	200	700	4
Greenbush,	1	1,700	800	2,000	14,000	14
Hoosick,	2	300	250	860	2,750	6
Lansingburgh,	2	800	175	4,475	6,549	10
Pittstown,	3	1,600	250	2,300	5,700	12
Schaghticoke,	1	3,500	1,000	3,875	6,500	6
Troy,	2	6,868	350	22,254	33,472	42
ROCKLAND Co.						
Clarkstown,	1	150	30	350	1,200	3
ST. LAWRENCE Co.						
Canton,	1	....	50	40	500	1
Gouverneur,	2	2,075	825	785	1,049	2
Massena,	1	50	25	200	500	1
Parishville,	1	300	50	150	1,225	3
Potsdam,	3	575	75	270	1,325	2
SARATOGA Co.						
Greenfield,	3	625	275	1,976	5,752	10
Northumberland,	1	100	50	117	400	1
Saratoga Springs,	1	250	100	150	600	2
Waterford,	6	4,550	750	38,845	41,780	46
SCHOHARIE Co.						
Conesville,	1	50	10	251	918	4
Fulton,	7	1,100	265	880	4,002	15
Gilboa,	1	75	75	300	750	2
Seward,	2	850	55	50	500	2
Sharon,	1	75	40	100	700	2
Summit,	2	450	125	178	825	1
SCHUYLER Co.						
Hector,	2	250	350	376	900	3
Orange,	3	275	125	295	1,154	4
Tyrone,	2	200	100	300	1,250	2
SENECA Co.						
Fayette,	3	400	880	3,497	8,260	10
Ovid,	1	300	50	407	5,258	....
Seneca Falls,	3	6,400	200	18,140	41,260	66
STEUBEN Co.						
Bath,	1	150	30	140	400	1
Bradford,	2	100	50	133	600	2
Fremont,	2	100	75	115	294	2
Hornellsville,	1	50	100	100	300	1
Jasper,	3	....	127	118	1,050	4
Pultney,	1	250	200	1,916	4,600	3
Troupsburgh,	2	....	....	54	650	3
SUFFOLK Co.						
Huntington,	1	300	200	300	500	2
Southold,	1	1,000	100	1,600	7,500	5
SULLIVAN Co.						
Mamakating,	1	50	20	....	112	1
TIOGA Co.						
Barton,	7	250	295	4,360	11,380	18
Berkshire,	1	25	....	200	450	1
Newark,	1	150	30	183	675	....
Tioga,	1	1,000	200	500	1,000	2
TOMPKINS Co.						
Caroline,	3	450	100	650	2,150	3

CLASS XIV.—(CONTINUED.)

TOWNS.	Number of establishments.	Capital Invested. In real estate.	Capital Invested. In tools and machinery.	Cash Value. Of raw materials used.	Cash Value. Of manufactured articles.	Persons employed.
TOMPKINS Co.						
Dryden,	6	$400	$190	$1,159	$2,878	9
Groton,	2	2,600	1,450	3,400	7,050	10
Ithaca,	1	300	50	500	1,000	3
Lansing,	3	250	115	425	1,100	3
ULSTER Co.						
Lloyd,	15	3,960	855	11,840	27,590	41
Marbletown,	4	760	160	1,634	2,920	6
Marlborough,	3	1,100	1,150	1,360	6,150	10
Olive,	2	850	65	1,762	4,449	17
Rochester,	3	300	50	700	3,130	6
Saugerties,	1	2,000	1,000	1,000	15,000	33
Woodstock,	1	200	300	120	1,000	4
WASHINGTON Co.						
Argyle,	2	350	75	475	2,075	2
Easton,	1	100	30	356	836	2
Greenwich,	1	....	....	5,000	....	....
Putnam,	3	85	....	595	2,325	5
Salem,	1	600	500	200	....	2
WAYNE Co.						
Galen,	1	50	30	168	350	1
Lyons,	1	40	100	200	800	3
Marion,	1	350	100	2,000	4,622	6
Ontario,	4	550	70	860	1,970	5
Palmyra,	3	625	225	4,885	5,950	11
Rose,	1	100	50	425	1,500	3
Sodus,	1	50	150	200	700	2
Walworth,	1	....	20	500	1,020	2
Williamson,	3	1,000	190	2,635	5,207	14
Wolcott,	1	200	100	....	1,500	4
WESTCHESTER Co.						
Yorktown,	1	75	10	60	276	2
WYOMING Co.						
Bennington,	1	100	50	80	500	2
Castile,	2	475	125	200	1,400	3
Genesee Falls,	1	30	50	360	1,500	1
Middlebury,	1	....	....	125	300	1
Pike,	1	100	100	1,050	3,000	4
YATES Co.						
Benton,	1	....	10	150	375	1
Jerusalem,	1	500	75	800	1,500	3
Potter,	4	575	50	2,115	6,425	14
Torrey,	2	500	150	1,550	4,000	7

HEADING MILLS.

TOWNS.	Number of establishments.	In real estate.	In tools and machinery.	Of raw materials used.	Of manufactured articles.	Persons employed.
ONONDAGA Co.						
Cicero,	1	500	....	....	800	1
Lysander,	3	....	....	....	660	....
OSWEGO Co.						
New Haven,	1	200	100	75	100	....
Richland,	1	....	....	50	300	....
Scriba,	1	....	....	100	475	....

HOOP MANUFACTORIES.

TOWNS.	Number of establishments.	In real estate.	In tools and machinery.	Of raw materials used.	Of manufactured articles.	Persons employed.
LEWIS Co.						
Lewis,	1	100	50	1,000	4,000	5
SENECA Co.						
Romulus,	1	....	300	100	1,000	3
ULSTER Co.						
Olive,	1	350	50	1,210	4,143	....

JOINER SHOPS.

TOWNS.	Number of establishments.	In real estate.	In tools and machinery.	Of raw materials used.	Of manufactured articles.	Persons employed.
ALLEGANY Co.						
Alfred,	1	200	850	158	158	1
CAYUGA Co.						
Moravia,	1	50	....	....	....	....
ERIE Co.						
Eden,	2	100	275	400	650	....
Newstead,	1	....	30	....	500	1
MADISON Co.						
Eaton,	1	1,500	1,500	600	1,200	2
ONEIDA Co.						
Camden,	1	1,500	....	300	900	2
Kirkland,	1	400	350	6,500	6,000	5
New Hartford,	1	450	1,000	360	2,000	8
OSWEGO Co.						
Oswego city,	2	....	1,600	2,000	11,000	17
SCHENECTADY Co.						
Duanesburgh,	1	600	200	150	400	....

LADDER AND EAVE SPOUT MANUFACTORIES.

TOWNS.	Number of establishments.	In real estate.	In tools and machinery.	Of raw materials used.	Of manufactured articles.	Persons employed.
NEW-YORK Co.						
New-York,	1	7,000	50	3,800	8,000	7
OSWEGO Co.						
Mexico,	1	....	15	300	720	2
OTSEGO Co.						
New Lisbon,	1	20	10	....	120	....
ST. LAWRENCE Co.						
Hopkinton,	1	100	9,000	700	1,000	1

LATH MANUFACTORIES.

TOWNS.	Number of establishments.	Capital Invested. In real estate.	Capital Invested. In tools and machinery.	Cash Value. Of raw materials used.	Cash Value. Of manufactured articles.	Persons employed.
ALLEGANY Co.						
Amity,	1	....	$1,000	$600	$3,000	8
BROOME Co.						
Chenango,	3	$600	1,150	900	2,640	3
Union,	1	....	....	....	1,200	2
CATTARAUGUS Co.						
Allegany,	1	....	500	....	325	....
Portville,	3	....	400	....	1,168	....
CLINTON Co.						
Plattsburgh,	1	....	....	....	....	....
ERIE Co.						
Aurora,	3	....	135	....	735	....
Eden,	1	200	50	....	75	....
Hamburg,	1	1,000	4,000	2,000	15,000	17
Lancaster,	6	500	....	....	3,549	11
North Collins,	1	....	....	400	350	....
FULTON Co.						
Broadalbin,	1	....	....	60	132	....
Ephrata,	1	....	....	50	150	....
HERKIMER Co.						
Salisbury,	4	....	....	192	1,100	2
LEWIS Co.						
High Market,	1	....	....	250	200	1
Osceola,	1	....	....	15	45	1
LIVINGSTON Co.						
Springwater,	1	....	100	100	350	1
West Sparta,	1	1,000	....	2,000	2,756	3
MADISON Co.						
Cazenovia,	1	....	....	50	50	1
Fenner,	1	....	....	126	140	....
MONTGOMERY Co.						
Mohawk,	2	....	....	550	1,060	....
ONEIDA Co.						
Annsville,	3	175	250	....	1,725	4
Boonville,	1	1,500	200	....	1,562	9
Rome,	1	....	....	10	88	....
Trenton,	1	....	....	....	250	1
ONTARIO Co.						
Phelps,	1	....	....	....	250	1
OSWEGO Co.						
Scriba,	2	....	....	....	200	....
RENSSELAER Co.						
Berlin,	1	....	100	500	1,800	3
Schaghticoke,	1	....	....	187	287	....
SARATOGA Co.						
Milton,	2	....	400	100	169	2
SCHUYLER Co.						
Hector,	1	1,000	....	1,200	1,725	2
SENECA Co.						
Fayette,	1	....	....	....	400	....
SULLIVAN Co.						
Highland,	1	....	....	200	300	....
TIOGA Co.						
Owego,	3	....	450	350	1,225	5
Richford,	1	....	....	....	200	....
TOMPKINS Co.						
Caroline,	2	....	....	....	513	3
Dryden,	4	....	....	20	1,225	....
Newfield,	2	....	....	85	293	1
WARREN Co.						
Queensbury,	3	....	....	....	3,600	....
WYOMING Co.						
Orangeville,	1	500	1,000	....	50	....

MATCH-BOX MANUFACTORIES.

TOWNS.	Number of establishments.	In real estate.	In tools and machinery.	Of raw materials used.	Of manufactured articles.	Persons employed.
TIOGA Co.						
Owego,	2	1,600	1,400	2,100	8,000	11

PATENT MILL-DOG MANUFACTORY.

TOWNS.	Number of establishments.	In real estate.	In tools and machinery.	Of raw materials used.	Of manufactured articles.	Persons employed.
ONEIDA Co.						
Camden,	1	200	50	891	1,620	1

PATTERN MANUFACTORIES.

TOWNS.	Number of establishments.	In real estate.	In tools and machinery.	Of raw materials used.	Of manufactured articles.	Persons employed.
NEW-YORK Co.						
New-York,	2	....	450	2,027	5,000	5
ONONDAGA Co.						
Syracuse,	2	....	300	400	1,700	2
WESTCHESTER Co.						
Cortland,	1	500	500	120	2,160	5

PLANE MANUFACTORIES.

TOWNS.	Number of establishments.	In real estate.	In tools and machinery.	Of raw materials used.	Of manufactured articles.	Persons employed.
NEW-YORK Co.						
New-York,	1	....	2,000	1,500	1,000	2
ONEIDA Co.						
Utica,	1	1,000	800	500	7,000	4

CLASS XIV.—(CONTINUED.)

TOWNS.	Number of establishments.	Capital Invested. In real estate.	Capital Invested. In tools and machinery.	Cash Value. Of raw materials used.	Cash Value. Of manufactured articles.	Persons employed.
TOMPKINS CO.						
Ithaca,	1	....	$300	....	....	2
WESTCHESTER CO.						
Mount Pleasant,	1	$100	150	....	....	....
PLANING MACHINE MANUFACTORY.						
ALBANY CO.						
Albany,	1	....	....	$5,000	$70,000	....
PLANING MILLS.						
ALBANY CO.						
Albany,	1	40,000	20,000	132,000	132,000	8
Watervliet,	3	27,000	25,000	367,000	418,900	154
ALLEGANY CO.						
Amity,	2	....	4,400	8,500	15,314	6
Scio,	1	250	3,500	7,000	....	8
BROOME CO.						
Chenango,	1	5,000	5,000	96,275	130,000	4
CAYUGA CO.						
Auburn,	1	10,000	1,200	....	2,000	3
CHAUTAUQUE CO.						
Ellington,	1	500	500	....	1,000	2
Pomfret,	1	2,000	2,000	3,000	4,000	1
CHEMUNG CO.						
Elmira,	2	19,000	8,500	....	95,000	32
CHENANGO CO.						
Norwich,	1	....	....	....	1,400	....
CLINTON CO.						
Champlain,	1	6,000	6,000	30,000	40,000	15
Plattsburgh,	1	3,000	10,000	8,150	55,000	28
CORTLAND CO.						
Cortlandville,	1	1,200	2,000	....	1,800	2
Homer,	1	2,000	1,500	....	....	....
DUTCHESS CO.						
Poughkeepsie city,	1	....	3,500	....	400	3
ERIE CO.						
Buffalo,	6	30,000	52,300	233,000	389,000	285
East Hamburgh,	1	....	....	90	600	....
GENESEE CO.						
Le Roy,	1	1,500	4,500	26,000	50,000	25
GREENE CO.						
Ashland,	1	800	300	208	208	8
HERKIMER CO.						
German Flats,	1	....	....	8,500	1,000	8
Little Falls,	1	20,000	6,000	20,000	25,000	5
Russia,	1	7,000	5,000	57,000	78,000	13
Salisbury,	2	900	1,600	129,140	152,450	12
JEFFERSON CO.						
Adams,	1	700	850	....	....	3
Watertown,	1	1,500	1,500	6,500	9,000	4
KINGS CO.						
Brooklyn,	6	181,000	40,500	114,400	476,700	153
LEWIS CO.						
New Bremen,	1	....	500	7,700	12,000	2
MONROE CO.						
Rochester,	4	36,000	17,500	117,000	133,000	50
Sweden,	1	1,200	2,300	9,100	11,500	4
MONTGOMERY CO.						
Glen,	1	....	....	3,000	4,200	....
NEW-YORK CO.						
New-York,	4	58,500	44,600	121,500	165,700	100
NIAGARA CO.						
Niagara,	1	6,000	2,500	6,000	8,000	6
ONEIDA CO.						
Rome,	2	8,400	8,400	32,750	53,400	14
Utica,	3	31,000	24,000	70,000	95,000	43
Verona,	1	1,500	2,000	3,000	5,570	5
ONONDAGA CO.						
Syracuse,	2	13,000	5,800	53,491	63,880	22
ONTARIO CO.						
Seneca,	1	1,500	3,000	....	....	5
ORLEANS CO.						
Barre,	1	4,000	7,000	19,000	24,000	10
Ridgeway,	2	6,000	1,500	9,000	16,000	5
Shelly,	1	2,000	2,000	5,000	8,000	3
OSWEGO CO.						
Oswego city,	3	37,000	26,100	91,000	141,000	29
QUEENS CO.						
Flushing,	1	6,000	3,500	15,000	18,000	6
Newtown,	1	6,000	4,000	20,000	25,000	6
RENSSELAER CO.						
Troy,	1	8,000	1,200	10,000	11,000	6
ST. LAWRENCE CO.						
Oswegatchie,	1	2,000	1,500	7,000	9,200	3
SARATOGA CO.						
Saratoga Springs,	1	....	....	11,000	15,300	13
SCHENECTADY CO.						
Schenectady,	1	3,000	3,000	8,000	8,750	2
SCHOHARIE CO.						
Richmondville,	1	1,500	2,000	1,400	3,600	3
SCHUYLER CO.						
Catherine,	1	$7,000	....	....	....	....
SENECA CO.						
Seneca Falls,	1	1,500	$1,500	....	....	2
Waterloo,	1	2,000	3,000	$3,600	$4,650	1
STEUBEN CO.						
Bath,	1	....	1,000	1,500	....	1
Canisteo,	1	2,000	4,000	500	1,200	6
Corning,	1	....	1,500	800	....	4
Hornellsville,	1	3,000	4,000	8,000	12,000	4
TOMPKINS CO.						
Groton,	1	600	1,000	....	....	....
Ithaca,	1	....	....	6,000	7,800	3
WARREN CO.						
Queensburgh,	1	2,800	1,400	4,740	6,700	6
Warrensbury,	1	4,000	3,000	3,000	6,000	6
WASHINGTON CO.						
Granville,	1	300	100	10,000	12,000	3
Kingsbury,	1	4,000	5,000	40,000	46,000	10
Whitehall,	2	11,000	7,000	10,000	40,000	29
WAYNE CO.						
Arcadia,	2	5,000	4,000	15,500	22,000	13
Lyons,	1	700	1,000	2,000	6,000	4
Palmyra,	1	2,000	2,900	6,600	9,075	4
WESTCHESTER CO.						
White Plains,	1	7,000	8,000	125,000	15,500	4
WYOMING CO.						
Warsaw,	1	1,200	2,800	6,000	20,000	12
YATES CO.						
Milo,	1	1,000	3,000	1,500	1,500	2
RULE MANUFACTORIES.						
NEW-YORK CO.						
New-York,	1	....	5,000	8,000	25,000	19
ORANGE CO.						
Walkill,	1	....	200	400	3,000	2
SAW MANUFACTORIES.						
ALBANY CO.						
Albany,	1	....	2,129	....	40,000	22
CHEMUNG CO.						
Elmira,	1	2,650	1,500	2,804	6,600	6
ERIE CO.						
Buffalo,	1	3,000	1,000	5,000	7,500	3
KINGS CO.						
Brooklyn,	1	....	2,500	....	....	17
MONROE CO.						
Rochester,	1	12,000	3,000	20,440	36,000	26
NEW-YORK CO.						
New-York,	2	10,000	10,000	21,000	47,000	29
ORANGE CO.						
Deerpark,	1	4,000	3,000	2,000	25,000	12
Walkill,	1	5,000	4,250	31,100	50,000	37
RICHMOND CO.						
Southfield,	1	2,000	2,000	300	3,500	4
WESTCHESTER CO.						
Ossining,	1	....	3,000	8,050	30,000	100
SAW SET MANUFACTORY.						
HERKIMER CO.						
Russia,	1	1,000	100	575	4,800	5
SCROLL SAWING ESTABLISHMENT.						
NEW-YORK CO.						
New-York,	2	....	4,600	....	4,680	16
SAW MILLS.						
ALBANY CO.						
Albany,	2	3,500	1,200	....	....	4
Bern,	14	5,250	2,250	1,750	3,120	5
Bethlehem,	3	18,500	3,850	6,233	10,748	8
Knox,	5	1,250	450	1,000	1.680	....
New Scotland,	4	5,900	300	4,500	8,500	7
Rensselaerville,	6	1,550	77	150	1,070	6
Watervliet,	4	8,650	3,450	26,200	37,300	14
Westerlo,	5	2,800	580	2,100	3,917	7
ALLEGANY CO.						
Alfred,	1	350	....	250	500	1
Allen,	4	2,800	275	2,550	4,275	7
Alma,	8	55,044	27,500	42,700	104,435	39
Almond,	1	500	....	900	3,000	....
Amity,	19	88,900	2,110	152,275	128,770	137
Andover,	5	5,300	250	10,700	25,000	29
Angelica,	3	19,300	2,100	5,400	20,500	....
Belfast,	8	8,400	9,600	27,412	40,470	60
Birdsall,	2	2,200	60	910	12,000	14
Bolivar,	7	50,190	9,600	21,875	33,975	54
Burns,	8	5,500	5,000	6,460	11,620	15

CLASS XIV.—(Continued.)

TOWNS.	Number of establishments.	Capital Invested. In real estate.	Capital Invested. In tools and machinery.	Cash Value. Of raw materials used.	Cash Value. Of manufactured articles.	Persons employed.
Allegany Co.						
Caneadea,........	5	$5, 250	$6, 675	$18, 507	$26, 195	36
Centreville,.......	6	7, 100	180	5, 950	11, 500	12
Clarksville, ...	7	550	10, 200	15, 800	33, 200	32
Cuba,............	6	6, 000	3, 900	10, 600	17, 460	22
Friendship,.......	6	12, 900	2, 450	3, 950	13, 100	30
Genesee, ...	8	16, 100	1, 425	18, 975	35, 030	21
Hume,...........	7	5, 800	1, 635	8, 400	16, 250	12
Independence, ...	3	1, 800	....	1, 300	2, 550	4
Hew Hudson, ...	8	108, 150	21, 815	20, 800	42, 950	63
Ossian, ...	20	24, 800	3, 700	10, 750	31, 465	49
Rushford,........	4	4, 100	2, 800	9, 125	16, 000	7
Scio,............	24	177, 642	17, 525	124, 652	583, 871	286
Willing, ...	7	8, 200	200	3, 750	1, 750	15
Wirt, ...	6	4, 100	4, 685	13, 500	22, 250	16
Broome Co.						
Barker,..........	4	2, 200	2, 000	2, 350	11, 050	4
Chenango,........	22	45, 000	5, 800	45, 897	90, 515	67
Colesville,........	18	5, 400	4, 800	7, 150	22, 300	19
Conklin,.........	13	16, 800	3, 285	16, 565	31, 040	30
Lisle,............	9	7, 200	....	2, 310	10, 450	5
Maine,...........	15	....	....	1, 125	1, 125	....
Nanticoke,........	8	7, 400	210	3, 100	7, 510	16
Sanford,..........	27	19, 800	275	25, 225	39, 610	38
Triangle,.........	2	700	200	750	1, 700	4
Union,...........	18	10, 800	6, 500	14, 000	37, 750	25
Vestal,...........	6	22, 250	500	13, 100	27, 500	....
Windsor,.........	17	7, 300	510	825	4, 500	15
Cattaraugus Co.						
Allegany, ...	19	54, 750	3, 000	38, 600	65, 260	57
Ashford, ...	12	5, 050	1, 550	....	4, 450	10
Bucktooth, ...	8	37, 000	5, 350	18, 475	29, 000	34
Carrolton, ...	5	10, 500	13, 400	6, 350	12, 800	18
Cold Spring, ...	9	15, 240	5, 800	12, 762	23, 080	28
Connewango,.....	1	400	....	315	1, 000	1
Dayton,..........	5	9, 100	6, 300	300	3, 250	31
East Otto,........	5	2, 500	1, 900	1, 210	3, 897	4
Ellicottville,.......	2	800	....	1, 500	1, 000	2
Farmersville,.....	4	1, 500	1, 000	625	1, 400	5
Franklinville,.....	4	1, 640	2. 900	1, 360	2, 380	7
Freedom, ...	5	2, 300	400	1, 760	3, 510	8
Great Valley,.....	14	24, 900	3, 025	16, 270	24, 375	35
Hinsdale, ...	6	7, 200	375	14, 900	27, 200	19
Ischua, ...	1	2, 000	....	3, 000	3, 000	....
Lyndon,..........	1	300	....	....	....	....
Mansfield,........	3	2, 800	300	1, 200	2, 300	5
New Albion,......	4	3, 740	1, 210	1, 950	4, 350	4
Olean,...........	5	160, 000	25, 800	14, 200	76, 620	26
Otto,............	6	4, 450	38	1, 470	4, 176	7
Persia, ...	4	3, 800	....	2, 750	6, 500	....
Perrysburgh, ...	4	6, 300	100	2, 100	5, 025	7
Portville,.........	12	88, 400	7, 050	58, 700	121, 025	100
Randolph, ...	5	4, 800	3, 225	3, 200	9, 200	10
South Valley, ...	15	17, 000	3, 010	13, 935	31, 040	51
Yorkshire,........	6	3, 980	700	1, 200	3, 300	4
Cayuga Co.						
Auburn, ...	1	3, 000	100	3, 000	6, 000	3
Aurelius,.........	1	....	....	2, 000	5, 000	2
Cato, ...	5	3, 600	1, 840	7, 550	13, 160	12
Conquest,........	3	2, 100	2, 600	5, 625	10, 950	7
Genoa,...........	3	2, 300	150	2, 600	2, 400	6
Ira, ...	7	6, 150	....	2, 384	6, 622	....
Locke,...........	5	3, 600	200	....	....	....
Ledyard,.........	1	400	150	600	750	....
Mentz, ...	5	9, 000	1, 120	4, 900	10, 900	14
Moravia,.........	1	1, 000	60	250	200	1
Niles,............	9	8, 400	....	3, 200	17, 660	8
Owasco, ...	2	5, 500	1, 000	1, 565	2, 835	3
Sennett, ...	2	1, 400	300	....	400	2
Springport, ...	1	3, 500	....	....	....	....
Sterling,.........	13	10, 750	9, 100	....	....	2
Summer Hill,.....	7	3, 727	2, 350	5, 357	5, 391	13
Venice, ...	8	7, 500	....	....	1, 850	....
Victory, ...	5	3, 700	....	....	9, 000	15
Chautauque Co.						
Arkwright,.......	7	5, 250	1, 125	1, 880	4, 350	8
Busti, ...	3	3, 000	1, 750	1, 750	3, 660	5
Carroll,..........	19	....	7, 200	10, 590	25, 108	21
Chautauque,......	10	7, 995	2, 635	4, 220	8, 434	23
Cherry Creek,....	7	3, 750	1, 825	4, 582	8, 479	8
Clymer,..........	4	5, 000	70	4, 525	8, 800	6
Ellery, ...	8	500	....	....	3, 400	....
Ellicott,..........	4	19, 500	300	6, 100	17, 362	20
Ellington, ...	4	2, 200	650	1, 550	3, 650	4
French Creek,....	4	2, 450	90	700	2, 030	4
Gerry,...........	2	1, 700	1, 700	3, 200	4, 000	4
Harmony,........	11	13, 200	500	3, 775	11, 080	9
Hanover,.........	14	9, 150	1, 600	11, 765	27, 200	26
Kiantone,........	3	5, 000	150	3, 000	6, 720	10
Chautauque Co.						
Mina,............	9	$3, 550	....	....	$9, 020	8
Poland,..........	9	16, 500	$3, 800	$10, 130	25, 950	21
Pomfret,.........	17	20, 150	8, 650	9, 000	20, 880	35
Portland, ...	4	4, 000	2, 300	5, 700	8, 900	9
Ripley, ...	3	1, 200	4, 000	1, 625	3, 400	11
Sheridan, ...	9	10, 700	1, 070	9, 800	20, 275	18
Sherman, ...	11	10, 200	360	4, 536	10, 474	12
Stockton, ...	9	8, 250	300	....	5, 595	....
Villenovia, ...	7	4, 100	....	1, 800	4, 530	8
Westfield,........	6	3, 000	....	....	1, 000	12
Chemung Co.						
Big Flats,........	4	33, 524	8, 930	9, 800	14, 200	72
Chemung,........	21	41, 950	17, 100	13, 800	31, 405	43
Elmira,..........	10	8, 700	2, 980	7, 350	25, 740	24
Erin,............	3	550	200	700	1, 380	6
Horseheads,......	8	9, 000	7, 050	15, 550	38, 930	59
Southport,.......	15	17, 100	8, 400	10, 400	35, 970	57
Van Etten,.......	15	....	....	....	....	....
Veteran,..........	23	13, 050	780	16, 215	34, 170	45
Chenango Co.						
Bainbridge,......	7	3, 300	220	4, 155	5, 010	8
Columbus,........	4	1, 650	700	1, 950	3, 000	4
Coventry, ...	3	3, 500	155	2, 000	3, 700	6
Greene, ...	4	3, 000	25	2, 865	30, 000	5
Guilford,.........	3	2, 800	70	1, 750	9, 700	3
New Berlin,......	3	1, 600	105	1, 350	2, 400	2
North Norwich, ..	14	13, 800	1, 500	11, 145	17, 200	13
Norwich,.........	7	3, 800	930	3, 550	9, 505	11
Otselic, ...	7	2, 300	1, 250	2, 540	6, 020	5
Oxford,..........	9	8, 300	530	6, 925	10, 860	14
Pharsalia,........	2	1, 600	50	900	1, 750	4
Pitcher,..........	9	4, 740	....	3, 175	6, 075	9
Plymouth,.......	13	5, 400	855	6, 650	10, 775	18
Preston, ...	7	1, 550	....	1, 850	3, 800	9
Sherburne,.......	12	6, 750	1, 445	5, 675	12, 850	13
Smithville,.......	6	8, 500	525	3, 100	5, 440	7
Clinton Co.						
Ausable,.........	3	12, 000	900	4, 100	5, 220	28
Beekmantown,....	2	1, 200	35	1, 400	2, 600	5
Black Brook,.....	7	65, 400	25, 700	33, 468	85, 660	88
Champlain,.......	18	33, 300	7, 025	28, 993	45, 900	76
Chazy,..........	22	50, 000	....	25, 670	69, 600	96
Clinton,..........	1	500	2, 500	....	1, 000	3
Dannemora,......	1	4, 200	5, 000	10, 000	120, 000	12
Ellenburgh, ...	11	24, 000	2, 100	17, 550	79, 000	63
Mooers,..........	23	41, 450	12, 200	30, 725	76. 000	106
Peru,............	6	7, 300	75	5, 800	37, 400	13
Plattsburgh,......	6	20, 000	1, 535	26, 065	41, 570	•80
Saranac, ...	7	14, 200	4, 400	37, 300	107, 300	102
Schuyler Falls, ...	3	8, 500	115	16, 875	28, 964	14
Columbia Co.						
Austerlitz,.......	2	800	....	310	580	2
Chatham,........	7	5, 400	290	665	2, 860	5
Claverack, ...	3	....	....	780	1, 150	1
Ghent,...........	3	550	75	2, 975	4, 650	3
Hillsdale,.........	2	1, 500	1, 000	1, 900	15, 500	3
New Lebanon,....	3	1, 250	950	....	....	4
Stuyvesant, ...	1	....	....	1, 800	1, 800	2
Cortland Co.						
Cincinnatus,....	1	700	100	300	600	....
Cortlandville, ...	12	11, 600	2, 375	345	3, 030	20
Freetown,........	2	900	35	500	1, 300	2
Harford, ...	7	4. 700	4, 700	2, 200	6, 780	7
Homer,..........	8	4, 550	3, 300	4, 774	8, 775	15
Preble, ...	2	1, 600	200	....	875	4
Scott,............	7	3, 600	590	2, 950	5, 604	7
Solon, ...	3	1, 700	150	1, 150	2, 300	4
Taylor,..........	3	1, 600	650	1, 255	2, 510	3
Truxton,.........	16	8, 350	300	1, 800	7, 440	4
Virgil,...........	2	700	....	350	1, 000	4
Willett,..........	5	2, 800	5	2, 303	3, 723	5
Delaware Co.						
Andes,...........	6	4, 300	125	3, 800	7, 500	15
Bovina,..........	2	600	140	213	877	2
Colchester,.......	45	2, 455	9, 600	23, 060	32, 630	68
Davenport,.......	8	6, 700	800	2, 000	6, 800	13
Delhi, ...	3	1, 500	225	1, 700	2, 400	3
Franklin, ...	11	2, 650	350	4, 928	7, 060	8
Hamden,.........	11	1, 400	30	825	550	5
Hancock,.........	20	18, 500	....	2, 430	5, 850	....
Harpersfield,.....	9	2, 625	130	1, 700	3, 475	9
Kortright, ...	1	500	....	250	500	1
Masonville,.......	11	5, 590	152	4, 700	9, 215	29
Meredith,........	2	7	800	4, 100	4, 600	3
Middletown, ...	27	17. 750	1, 870	15, 092	23, 829	47
Roxbury,........	6	1, 350	....	....	610	6
Sidney,..........	1	1, 000	100	1, 050	1, 400	....
Stamford,........	2	900	150	....	1, 750	2
Tompkins,........	45	24, 900	....	15, 400	37, 400	45

CLASS XIV.—(Continued.)

TOWNS.	Number of establishments.	Capital Invested. In real estate.	Capital Invested. In tools and machinery.	Cash Value. Of raw materials used.	Cash Value. Of manufactured articles.	Persons employed.
Delaware Co.						
Walton,	14	$9,600	$95	$10,375	$16,508	16
Dutchess Co.						
Amenia,	2	900	35	720	1,680	1
Clinton,	1	....	....	120	247	....
Fishkill,	1	4,000	....	4,500	6,000	5
Hyde Park,	1	....	400	266	600	1
La Grange,	1	400	100	....	....	1
Milan,	2	1,500	100	575	850	2
Pawling,	1	300	300	3,500	4,100	1
Poughkeepsie city,	1	....	20	2,800	3,600	1
Stamford,	2	600	200	....	300	1
Erie Co.						
Alden,	9	13,375	665	9,590	17,545	23
Amherst,	5	27,700	950	6,600	12,700	4
Aurora,	6	6,700	150	....	16,350	18
Boston,	3	2,900	600	1,087	2,745	3
Buffalo,	8	21,000	23,400	54,700	150,474	66
Chictawauga,	7	5,600	3,700	7,970	22,440	17
Clarence,	5	7,200	1,800	3,330	9,245	8
Colden,	12	9,200	5,950	5,570	15,620	14
Collins,	8	9,500	800	7,650	13,200	14
Concord,	1	500	200	75	540	1
East Hamburgh,	2	8,500	3,800	3,200	10,900	23
Eden,	9	4,200	198	1,200	2,500	5
Evans,	7	6,850	310	5,767	11,310	9
Hamburgh,	8	10,900	....	....	2,700	....
Holland,	8	6,300	370	3,300	5,695	11
Lancaster,	21	48,300	1,550	38,490	59,150	78
Marilla,	11	8,600	8,700	8,907	17,657	11
Newstead,	4	2,750	3,250	2;512	7,800	2
North Collins,	5	4,400	563	893	2,800	6
Sardinia,	3	10,000	....	....	....	....
Tonawanda,	6	50,600	15,800	28,228	57,140	74
West Seneca,	3	1,800	1,100	2,950	5,900	9
Essex Co.						
Chesterfield,	2	....	1,200	2,300	3,500	6
Crown Point,	7	6,430	737	3,015	5,098	13
Elizabethtown,	10	9,000	610	2,550	3,940	16
Essex,	1	1,000	50	750	1,750	2
Keene,	4	850	115	350	600	2
Lewis,	4	5,700	515	6,600	16,800	11
Minerva,	1	1,000	2,000	920	2,000	4
Moriah,	11	9,450	....	9,025	16,421	45
North Elba,	2	1,400	900	1,600	3,700	5
North Hudson,	3	6,200	3,300	13,500	18,750	33
St. Armand,	2	1,500	150	490	480	2
Schroon,	19	78,900	13,210	49,230	83,090	79
Ticonderoga,	2	5,500	700	16,850	30,100	18
Willsborough,	4	5,000	250	3,050	10,800	5
Wilmington,	1	5,000	1,500	1,500	3,610	10
Franklin Co.						
Bangor,	2	3,000	....	1,500	3,500	4
Belmont,	9	19,900	620	9,625	14,200	38
Bombay,	7	11,300	1,290	9,666	18,947	17
Brandon,	7	5,400	....	5,025	8,050	15
Chateaugay,	15	20,950	....	3,780	9,605	23
Constable,	7	5,100	1,765	2,075	7,460	15
Dickinson,	3	1,000	100	2,000	6,000	5
Duane,	2	10,500	6,200	4,400	7,700	10
Fort Covington,	6	8,800	650	8,925	15,730	11
Franklin,	5	44,900	5,600	25,650	52,300	58
Malone,	10	17,050	1,425	18,825	31,730	28
Moira,	7	3,100	10,000	7,900	20,800	8
Westville,	5	5,000	2,600	10,050	10,250	14
Fulton Co.						
Bleecker,	19	17,300	7,475	13,465	35,556	67
Broadalbin,	7	4,450	1,150	3,615	8,174	14
Caroga,	10	13,900	2,550	13,900	34,800	55
Ephratah,	15	4,250	200	2,000	11,500	2
Mayfield,	5	10,000	350	4,746	10,615	10
Northampton,	3	2,900	1,700	3,517	7,000	10
Oppenheim,	24	10,030	2,555	7,875	12,202	36
Perth,	3	2,050	567	2,000	4,200	6
Stratford,	4	14,000	920	5,830	13,910	10
Genesee Co.						
Alabama,	6	2,800	7,150	7,600	18,540	21
Alexander,	4	3,100	500	2,174	4,320	3
Batavia,	1	....	....	....	692	....
Bergen,	1	....	....	....	....	3
Bethany,	2	1,000	106	750	2,460	3
Byron,	3	6,500	....	....	4,800	5
Darien,	7	1,800	6,100	2,500	6,600	17
Le Roy,	4	2,000	....	3,650	5,600	4
Oakfield,	5	4,200	2,700	3,000	5,300	10
Pavilion,	1	1,400	....	13,500	338	2
Pembroke,	8	20,300	4,550	1,900	17,600	21
Stafford,	4	2,000	15	1,850	3,725	7
Greene Co.						
Coxsackie,	3	2,000	750	1,550	2,490	3

TOWNS.	Number of establishments.	Capital Invested. In real estate.	Capital Invested. In tools and machinery	Cash Value. Of raw materials used.	Cash Value. Of manufactured articles.	Persons employed.
Greene Co.						
Catskill,	5	$2,550	$700	$2,781	$22,350	5
Durham,	3	800	....	1,125	....	....
Greenville,	6	2,300	750	1,355	2,585	10
Hunter,	18	7,700	1,125	....	9,145	27
Jewett,	6	1,500	450	....	2,505	5
Lexington,	11	5,150	165	4,250	6,215	28
New Baltimore,	2	3,000	2,100	8,500	10,500	4
Windham,	8	2,530	2,100	3,625	4,250	20
Hamilton Co.						
Arietta,	4	....	....	4,300	....	....
Gilman,	4	....	....	....	5,100	....
Hope,	10	13,950	7,975	7,800	14,600	30
Morehouse,	2	2,000	1,300	170	490	6
Wells,	3	2,500	280	5,850	9,117	16
Herkimer Co.						
Columbia,	5	2,600	480	3,000	6,500	5
Fairfield,	3	1,400	2,500	....	800	8
Frankfort,	5	5,800	1,100	8,200	25,770	9
German Flats,	6	5,500	750	5,650	8,580	9
Herkimer,	4	9,500	400	8,000	13,715	5
Litchfield,	3	1,200	1,000	2,700	3,900	4
Little Falls,	3	7,000	650	7,325	9,800	5
Manheim,	1	300	1,500	2,500	3,500	2
Newport,	6	3,000	710	3,700	6,904	5
Norway,	2	1,200	900	975	2,025	3
Russia,	15	10,230	325	2,560	7,675	15
Salisbury,	23	35,150	2,480	22,500	41,834	70
Stark,	5	700	....	....	2,250	3
Warren,	6	1,300	....	....	....	....
Winfield,	5	3,500	1,375	1,625	4,200	8
Wilmurt,	2	3,500	450	900	2,150	2
Jefferson Co.						
Adams,	3	7,500	400	2,500	4,992	6
Alexandria,	8	11,000	125	1,681	12,440	14
Antwerp,	7	7,900	10,950	14,625	55,950	55
Cape Vincent,	2	400	1,800	2,200	4,500	5
Champion,	4	8,500	2,650	.6,226	14,114	11
Clayton,	6	2,850	10,200	10,850	22,800	26
Ellisburgh,	11	9,500	190	3,655	8,330	16
Henderson,	4	2,300	525	2,153	4,370	5
Hounsfield,	2	3,000	4,000	9,550	6,450	10
Le Ray,	3	7,900	....	3,500	7,400	8
Lorraine,	6	4,100	800	....	....	....
Lyme,	2	1,000	1,215	700	1,360	5
Orleans,	9	6,450	4,600	6,605	13,760	18
Pamelia,	2	8,000	3,400	11,500	7,300	14
Philadelphia,	7	8,600	1,210	6,370	15,915	8
Rutland,	3	1,100	....	4,900	8,845	10
Watertown,	1	2,000	700	2,400	4,400	3
Wilna,	15	18,650	790	18,760	23,995	30
Worth,	6	5,000	....	....	....	....
Kings Co.						
Brooklyn,	2	36,300	800	4,000	10,800	26
Lewis Co.						
Croghan,	12	9,950	3,425	4,924	7,720	20
Denmark,	5	9,500	150	1,925	9,150	9
Diana,	5	3,300	115	2,925	6,400	10
Greig,	21	54,900	10,340	48,280	60,000	110
High Market,	3	5,300	1,800	2,375	3,500	10
Lewis,	6	8,800	250	2,825	10,400	8
Leyden,	6	....	9,000	....	....	....
Lowville,	5	600	1,610	1,757	3,296	9
Martinsburgh,	6	4,300	1,350	850	1,850	6
New Bremen,	9	11,700	520	8,123	13,575	17
Osceola,	3	900	1,400	350	825	3
Pinckney,	8	5,950	1,100	3,450	8,050	9
Watson,	4	7,100	7,000	....	13,600	13
West Turin,	2	2,200	2,000	2,750	6,500	15
Livingston Co.						
Caledonia,	1	2,000	....	....	3,600	1
Conesus,	3	1,050	1,400	2,300	4,500	4
Groveland,	2	4,600	....	1,500	2,300	3
Livonia,	1	3,500	150	2,400	3,600	4
Mount Morris,	4	7,300	4,300	5,652	14,332	12
North Dansville,	2	1,100	10	679	1,260	2
Portage,	4	22,175	2,500	....	26,091	24
Springwater,	9	12,300	2,800	9,300	30,550	25
West Sparta,	6	800	1,342	11,685	25,991	32
York,	3	3,700	900	200	12,350	5
Madison Co.						
Brookfield,	10	4,500	....	3,655	5,801	....
Cazenovia,	7	4,150	675	5,017	8,540	8
De Ruyter,	9	6,000	4,275	3,800	7,700	9
Eaton,	6	6,200	730	12,900	26,600	8
Fenner,	6	1,600	2,400	3,850	4,570	6
Georgetown,	1	....	....	1,500	2,376	2
Lebanon,	6	1,250	....	....	....	....
Lenox,	14	18,300	1,030	10,444	45,262	26
Madison,	1	1,500	1,500	2,600	2,900	3

CLASS XIV.—(Continued.)

TOWNS.	Number of establishments.	Capital Invested. In real estate.	Capital Invested. In tools and machinery.	Cash Value. Of raw materials used.	Cash Value. Of manufactured articles.	Persons employed.
Madison Co.						
Nelson,	7	$1,005	$2,095	$2,587	$4,769	8
Sullivan,	8	28,000	8,305	16,251	22,300	36
Monroe Co.						
Brighton,	4	8,100	1,415	8,800	13,800	14
Chili,	2	1,000	....	1,500	1,000	7
Greece,	4	7,000	415	2,160	5,000	10
Henrietta,	1	....	....	1,500	1,125	....
Irondequoit,	1	1,000	100	2,000	3,500	2
Mendon,	3	4,100	160	....	1,200	5
Ogden,	3	1,900	400	2,500	6,200	....
Parma,	8	7,700	2,300	4,339	10,260	14
Perrington,	4	5,150	3,300	3,146	13,425	6
Riga,	3	3,500	205	3,560	6,200	5
Rochester,	2	11,000	2,000	50,000	55,600	12
Rush,	4	....	....	925	1,325	....
Sweden,	2	900	1,700	2.700	4,500	5
Union,	6	11,600	1,100	5,990	19,800	11
Webster,	7	3,130	625	3,139	44,080	7
Wheatland,	1	1,500	....	1,600	24,000	2
Montgomery Co.						
Amsterdam,	8	7,800	475	9,800	11,650	4
Canajoharie,	6	2,500	....	....	....	....
Charleston,	4	2,350	46	2,600	2,500	2
Florida,	5	1,900	40	3.510	6,340	7
Glen,	2	2,000	500	11,500	51,800	2
Minden,	2	400	100	150	1,000	1
Mohawk,	4	5,000	930	10,580	15,030	20
Palatine,	6	5,500	485	9,100	7,250	9
Root,	4	2,300	1,675	1,200	2,600	4
St. Johnsville,	2	350	1,250	9,000	18,000	4
New-York Co.						
New-York,	13	537,000	206,100	890,595	1,145,000	278
Niagara Co.						
Hartland,	3	4,800	5,200	6,750	11,000	6
Lewiston,	1	....	3,000	1,500	3,000	3
Lockport,	9	92,000	26,400	115,823	244,631	177
Newfane,	7	11,350	2,275	57,600	126,450	13
Niagara,	5	18,500	5,350	20,925	43,300	23
Porter,	2	900	4,500	6,550	14,300	10
Royalton,	7	18,200	5,100	71,974	112,970	11
Wheatfield,	1	1,000	200	1,200	30,000	2
Wilson,	3	7,300	1,300	4,245	9,971	9
Oneida Co.						
Annsville,	20	12,740	4,040	12,907	24,245	36
Augusta,	5	5.500	400	13,400	9,200	6
Ava,	10	10,700	....	4,790	12,830	12
Boonville,	30	61,800	710	24,582	91,876	104
Bridgewater,	2	1,300	900	750	1,800	3
Camden,	14	22,700	940	12,497	27,019	28
Deerfield,	7	2,125	1,645	....	1,250	....
Florence,	10	13,100	4,625	8,160	16,600	41
Kirkland,	4	12,400	25	7,500	10,500	8
Lee,	7	7,350	1,700	7,400	10,760	10
Marcy,	4	3,200	105	950	4,500	4
Marshall,	5	3,650	750	8,200	13,300	4
New Hartford,	3	7,000	1,500	4,000	1,600	3
Paris,	4	4,400	50	700	2,200	5
Remsen,	18	37,800	25,460	21,770	49,001	53
Rome,	15	8,000	5,295	26,950	42,950	61
Sangerfield,	9	4,430	550	3,471	5,307	8
Steuben,	5	900	1,100	625	1,450	5
Trenton,	7	14,800	6,500	22,100	63,450	97
Utica,	1	400	300	....	105	1
Vernon,	10	7,300	2,900	52,410	14,100	15
Verona,	14	20,500	9,805	17,650	32,745	24
Vienna,	25	32,000	6,180	27,405	48,157	66
Western,	6	8,700	150	2,400	8,200	8
Westmoreland,	4	5,400	680	1,000	5,500	4
Whitestown,	2	3,000	150	1,700	4,400	4
Onondaga Co.						
Camillus,	5	6,200	2,300	1,650	4,000	6
Cicero,	5	9,150	4,160	16,270	26,380	20
Clay,	5	2,450	7,000	6,300	14,000	15
De Witt,	3	2,800	1,550	1,815	4,320	2
Elbridge,	5	11,500	1,720	9,250	18,240	13
Fabius,	8	8,100	500	7,750	17,100	13
Geddes,	1	1,500	150	2,250	3,000	2
Lysander,	9	32,800	1,475	42,990	34,750	37
Manlius,	10	17,300	2,540	17,540	30,175	23
Marcellus,	5	12,000	2,300	9,200	15,400	9
Onondaga,	4	3,000	1,070	5,450	7,000	6
Otisco,	8	2,700	300	3,150	10,061	11
Pompey,	3	1,700	200	800	2,030	4
Skaneateles,	4	5,000	100	15,000	7,700	7
Syracuse,	2	32,000	13,000	17,500	37,500	35
Tully,	2	500	200	....	1,500	2
Van Buren,	2	1,500	1,500	1,240	2,480	4

TOWNS.	Number of establishments.	Capital Invested. In real estate.	Capital Invested. In tools and machinery.	Cash Value. Of raw materials used.	Cash Value. Of manufactured articles.	Persons employed.
Ontario Co.						
Bristol,	4	$2,200	....	....	$1,160	6
Canadice,	3	500	$2,425	$4,200	8,460	8
Canandaigua,	2	4,000	20	4,000	8,000	4
East Bloomfield,	6	4,700	1,300	2,590	5,810	....
Farmington,	2	1,300	35	250	1,300	2
Gorham,	3	1,500	2,000	1,865	3,300	8
Manchester,	1	....	....	1,525	12,125	....
Naples,	14	8,300	241	6,525	14.375	16
Phelps,	7	11,100	545	8,700	8,850	8
Richmond,	1	700	300	100	600	1
South Bristol,	9	7,600	7,700	5,955	18,940	15
West Bloomfield,	2	1,000	....	....	....	....
Orange Co.						
Blooming Grove,	3	2,000	100	800	1,600	3
Deerpark,	5	3,900	345	4,350	8,300	13
Hamptonburgh,	2	1,500	....	....	600	2
Minisink,	1	200	50	200	800	1
Montgomery,	2	2,000	1,000	162,000	164,500	4
Newburgh,	1	30,000	10,000	150,000	200,000	50
Walkill,	5	3,200	1,915	3,700	19,730	8
Warwick,	2	1,400	6,000	900	1,500	2
Orleans Co.						
Barre,	5	3,200	4,300	10,500	16,600	7
Carlton,	7	7,200	3,310	2,355	7,750	11
Clarendon,	2	2,000	500	1,400	5,500	6
Gaines,	4	9,650	2,490	2,300	5,900	9
Kendall,	1	575	40	400	705	1
Murray,	4	2,800	....	2,975	4,330	7
Ridgeway,	8	11,300	6,200	22,550	41,200	15
Shelly,	1	300	....	1,600	4,000	3
Yates,	1	1,600	3	1,200	2,800	2
Oswego Co.						
Albion,	27	31,600	850	24,860	40,920	47
Amboy,	11	3,200	5,050	6,012	14,782	16
Boylston,	4	800	2,800	940	2,400	7
Constantia,	30	86,800	11,560	25,395	64,650	141
Granby,	17	44,900	4,859	14,300	79,350	68
Hannibal,	6	5,200	....	1,650	3,780	11
Hastings,	15	22,800	6,290	14,850	34,785	46
Mexico,	12	18,450	5,585	3,536	10,180	19
New Haven,	8	8,200	150	2,750	9,270	5
Orwell,	7	2,700	1,300	1,400	4,500	6
Oswego,	7	22,500	5,030	30,400	56,300	57
Oswego city,	1	15,000	8,000	15,000	25,000	14
Palermo,	8	8,800	....	4,350	10,000	11
Parish,	4	4,500	450	555	2,575	14
Redfield,	4	1,800	2,300	3,608	7,714	7
Richland,	19	17,750	8,856	14,560	31,680	45
Schroeppel,	5	6,800	4,500	10,100	27,000	26
Scriba,	5	6,300	450	2,200	6,240	10
Volney,	9	15,500	12,000	49,142	96,685	70
West Monroe,	9	3,275	10,400	2,976	13,050	14
Williamstown,	10	12,950	14,750	10,900	23,000	21
Otsego Co.						
Burlington,	11	6,500	75	1,550	5,160	11
Cherry Valley,	4	3,200	60	2,500	5,160	5
Exeter,	1	....	....	500	1,200	1
Laurens,	2	4,300	1,800	1,400	4,000	8
Maryland,	19	11,400	800	10,400	22,085	17
Middlefield,	20	13.925	3,260	18,840	18,840	26
Milford,	12	9,200	75	5,296	10,646	7
Morris,	2	2,300	2,020	2,600	3,425	5
New Lisbon,	4	2,250	....	575	1,550	....
Oneonta,	1	1,000	....	750	1,600	1
Otego,	16	7,600	3,270	5,880	14,530	19
Otsego,	9	3,400	150	1,650	3,190	7
Plainfield,	5	2,625	1,120	2,287	9,150	2
Richfield,	7	2,800	....	....	....	1
Roseboom,	15	7,500	910	....	5,900	3
Springfield,	9	3,960	....	700	1,750	9
Unadilla,	3	1,300	295	1,300	20,500	3
Westford,	1	600	200	300	800	2
Worcester,	1	150	250	150	400	2
Putnam Co.						
Carmel,	2	400	200	1,150	2,200	2
Queens Co.						
Hempstead,	3	5,200	1,450	5,250	6,600	4
Jamaica,	3	9,000	800	3,530	5,000	3
North Hempstead,	1	....	....	8,000	9,000	1
Rensselaer Co.						
Berlin,	7	5,050	9,475	12,436	28,337	20
Brunswick,	1	1.000	300	600	800	2
Clinton,	2	150	140	....	....	....
Grafton,	11	5,200	7,690	1,475	31,983	24
Greenbush,	2	33,000	7,000	22,800	110,000	18
Hoosick,	4	3,600	1,150	2,700	3,800	3
Nassau,	2	1,400	400	1,550	3,185	2
Petersburgh,	2	200	....	976	1,596	....

CLASS XIV.—(Continued.)

TOWNS.	Number of establishments.	Capital invested.		Cash value.		Persons employed.
		In real estate.	In tools and machinery.	Of raw materials used.	Of manufactured articles.	
Rensselaer Co.						
Pittstown,........	16	$12, 550	$37, 050	$9, 338	$15, 060	16
Poestenkill, ...	22	9, 950	3, 195	10, 875	19, 900	21
Sandlake,........	6	5, 250	600	2, 325	5, 275	9
Schaghticoke,.....	1	....	....	1, 600	2, 500	5
Schodack,........	7	5, 800	650	3, 750	6, 450	9
Stephentown,.....	8	4, 500	13, 025	4, 994	7, 274	9
Rockland Co.						
Clarkstown,.......	1	2, 000	50	600	600	....
Haverstraw,......	1	....	....	....	....	....
Orangetown, ...	2	300	50	525	350	1
Ramapo,.........	3	2, 900	500	2, 125	4, 000	3
St. Lawrence Co.						
Brasher,.........	6	12, 000	800	12, 325	39, 293	21
Canton,..........	6	25, 000	775	16, 200	32, 450	26
Colton,...........	4	21, 000	1, 000	49, 375	86, 000	50
De Peyster, ...	2	4, 500	500	3, 250	7, 275	6
De Kalb,.........	1	10, 000	5, 000	800	5, 000	10
Edwards,........	5	4, 250	4, 550	....	....	....
Fine, ...	2	1, 000	15	400	7, 000	2
Fowler,..........	9	26, 000	5, 450	1, 225	3, 050	7
Gouverneur,......	3	8, 000	800	4, 347	9, 251	9
Hammond,.......	2	2, 200	....	637	1, 400	....
Hermon,.........	7	8, 500	895	6, 475	12, 900	14
Hopkinton,.......	6	11, 400	1, 900	3, 750	11, 500	16
Lawrence,........	6	13, 200	....	11, 000	16, 300	18
Louisville,.......	6	2, 900	5, 500	6, 200	14, 100	28
Macomb, ...	4	2, 600	475	2, 400	5, 990	8
Madrid,..........	4	9, 000	6, 850	14, 800	26, 650	18
Massena,.........	3	3, 100	1, 240	1, 625	3, 650	4
Morristown, ...	3	10, 000	5, 500	4, 476	16, 500	9
Norfolk, ...	6	17, 500	1, 550	23, 100	36, 400	32
Oswegatchie, ...	6	18, 350	3, 525	13, 125	35, 640	40
Parishville,.......	6	6, 050	137	7, 110	11, 696	8
Pierpont, ...	5	29, 700	875	6, 350	16, 000	19
Pitcairn,.........	3	3, 000	350	700	2, 007	4
Potsdam, ...	16	150, 600	5, 820	217, 129	332, 280	319
Rossie, ...	6	3, 060	400	3, 855	10, 200	14
Stockholm, ...	11	13, 626	4, 875	8, 209	19, 440	25
Saratoga Co.						
Ballston,.........	3	1, 600	350	3, 000	5, 400	5
Charlton,.........	2	600	....	....	....	....
Clifton Park,.....	5	8, 700	100	6, 100	29, 800	21
Corinth,..........	7	40, 000	720	13, 425	31, 400	39
Greenfield,.......	13	11, 450	485	5, 200	13, 625	16
Hadley,..........	2	11, 000	3, 500	11, 300	19, 800	17
Malta,...........	1	600	25	472	621	....
Milton, ...	7	10, 900	1, 100	4, 900	20, 159	16
Moreau..........	6	82, 000	2, 000	122, 250	184, 450	146
Northumberland, .	1	600	400	750	2, 250	1
Providence, ...	18	11, 900	1, 695	20, 000	23, 300	40
Saratoga, ...	2	5, 500	3, 200	4, 500	6, 000	8
Saratoga Springs,.	1	15, 000	15, 000	1, 000	1, 500	....
Stillwater, ...	3	6, 300	....	8, 500	20, 000	9
Waterford,.......	1	8, 000	200	6, 750	11, 250	10
Wilton,..........	8	7, 500	210	12, 288	19, 024	10
Schenectady Co.						
Duanesburgh, ...	11	6, 850	275	5, 100	9, 000	14
Rotterdam,.......	2	3, 000	400	650	1, 600	3
Schoharie Co.						
Blenheim,........	5	2, 600	1, 200	2, 400	4, 300	9
Carlisle, ...	5	3, 400	....	1, 350	3, 415	8
Cobleskill, ...	4	900	20	....	....	2
Conesville,.......	1	600	400	500	1, 125	4
Esperance, ...	1	500	....	250	450	1
Fulton,..........	18	3, 400	....	2, 575	8, 300	18
Gilboa, ...	5	1, 800	45	2, 250	3, 725	4
Jefferson, ...	8	2, 500	....	....	....	....
Middleburgh, ...	2	5, 900	100	1, 000	2, 060	2
Richmondville, ...	15	7, 800	825	4, 895	9, 673	25
Schoharie, ...	5	6, 200	....	3, 850	7, 325	8
Seward,..........	3	500	200	4, 500	2, 337	5
Sharon, ...	15	13, 100	2, 690	22, 000	22, 000	19
Summit,.........	9	3, 500	550	1, 115	1, 377	....
Wright,..........	22	12, 225	5, 450	10, 057	16, 845	18
Schuyler Co.						
Catharines,.......	10	17, 800	1, 400	13, 775	26, 000	30
Cayuta,..........	7	8, 600	335	6, 600	13, 390	18
Dix,.............	11	10, 100	2, 425	6, 950	11, 960	19
Hector,..........	36	30, 620	5, 675	30, 125	64, 765	56
Orange,..........	11	4, 075	5, 100	5, 331	10, 610	22
Reading,.........	1	1, 500	50	1, 200	3, 100	3
Tyrone, ...	8	2, 050	8, 100	9, 685	16, 830	28
Seneca Co.						
Covert, ...	3	2, 400	3, 100	4, 500	6, 100	6
Fayette, ...	5	7, 100	2, 675	16, 100	21, 400	18
Ovid,............	1	....	....	1, 150	1, 840	....
Seneca Falls,.....	2	8, 000	1, 455	2, 000	4, 255	6
Varick,..........	3	4, 000	200	4, 100	11, 250	6
Waterloo,........	1	6, 000	1, 500	7, 500	11, 000	7
Steuben Co.						
Addison, ...	8	$46, 170	$6, 100	$7, 050	$33, 100	74
Avoca,...........	17	24, 900	182	6, 702	15, 717	30
Bath,............	16	19, 400	5, 380	18, 800	44, 540	35
Bradford,........	2	....	3, 000	10, 500	12, 625	22
Cameron,........	9	17, 800	300	23, 975	38, 150	29
Campbell,........	15	29, 800	1, 900	47, 000	65, 090	71
Canisteo,........	21	25, 900	26, 920	63, 832	100, 300	85
Caton,...........	3	10, 800	4, 000	3, 440	7, 800	19
Cohocton,........	11	20, 000	13, 300	14, 600	42, 750	74
Corning,.........	6	113, 500	11, 100	37, 250	134, 000	78
Dansville,........	11	9, 650	7, 200	13, 231	38, 082	64
Erwin,...........	7	76, 000	11, 350	100, 400	173, 160	102
Fremont,.........	7	6, 000	785	2, 400	5, 450	9
Hornby,.........	5	11, 000	1, 500	5, 000	14, 400	8
Hornellsville, ...	12	36, 600	17, 060	28, 895	111, 200	107
Howard,.........	9	1, 975	8, 000	8, 570	18, 150	21
Jasper, ...	6	1, 260	7, 800	8, 700	12, 550	17
Lindley, ...	6	35, 500	6, 465	57, 400	104, 200	55
Prattsburgh, ...	10	11, 700	1, 175	7, 962	18, 800	13
Pultney,.........	1	2, 000	1, 500	1, 750	2, 800	4
Thurston,........	4	5, 200	4, 475	4, 950	31, 943	35
Troupsburgh, ...	7	2, 100	....	1, 330	2, 210	11
Urbana,..........	3	6, 300	2, 700	4, 700	13, 500	14
Wayland,........	23	12, 540	29, 700	28, 950	49, 425	46
Wayne, ...	1	5, 000	4, 500	4, 250	8, 500	6
West Union,......	4	4, 500	475	12, 000	23, 200	19
Wheeler, ...	7	14, 900	465	12, 700	26, 800	41
Woodhull, ...	7	3, 400	10, 050	7, 150	16, 980	15
Suffolk Co.						
Brookhaven,......	1	....	....	300	450	....
Huntington, ...	2	1, 000	1, 500	250	500	4
Islip,............	1	200	300	1, 000	2, 000	....
Riverhead, ...	1	....	....	....	....	....
Smithtown,.......	2	2, 000	....	....	250	1
Southampton,....	3	1, 200	50	1, 050	2, 150	1
Southold,........	1	1, 500	1, 200	....	....	2
Sullivan Co.						
Bethel,...........	9	21, 350	485	15, 109	270, 805	16
Callicoon,........	8	7, 900	1, 600	5, 150	13, 300	17
Cochecton, ...	17	26, 600	110	11, 550	28, 425	37
Fallsburgh, ...	26	36, 450	8, 492	32, 925	57, 600	40
Forrestburgh, ...	13	81, 800	4, 250	14, 880	31, 314	78
Fremont,.........	7	6, 800	2, 465	6, 017	77, 900	13
Highland,........	9	14. 980	2, 000	5, 675	7, 215	23
Liberty, ...	8	2, 900	....	1, 600	3, 025	2
Mamakating, ...	3	7, 000	125	6, 000	13, 250	8
Neversink, ...	7	7, 613	2, 850	4, 900	9, 200	19
Rockland,........	15	13, 000	685	7, 125	16, 695	39
Thompson, ...	20	28, 500	1, 980	11, 805	29, 965	42
Tusten,..........	3	7, 200	640	2, 050	8, 500	21
Tioga Co.						
Barton,..........	28	22, 800	16, 400	21, 977	58, 725	76
Berkshire,........	6	4, 400	....	1, 950	4, 220	6
Candor,.........	27	33, 800	5, 200	2, 518	87, 604	74
Newark,.........	8	4, 850	3, 275	3, 030	8, 395	13
Nichols, ...	4	12, 400	4, 700	3, 050	8, 100	10
Owego,..........	34	98, 400	12, 250	64, 037	87, 530	90
Richford, ...	10	5, 150	2, 150	7, 650	15, 800	....
Spencer,.........	11	18, 100	1, 100	21, 250	31, 600	34
Tioga,...........	18	25, 700	16, 750	29, 380	53, 400	70
Tompkins Co.						
Caroline, ...	9	8, 100	390	3, 585	8, 420	7
Danby,..........	17	350	5, 075	50	8, 880	26
Dryden, ...	30	26, 300	2, 715	25, 427	43, 167	54
Enfield,..........	5	450	450	1, 200	2, 150	8
Groton, ...	11	1, 900	....	1, 640	2, 850	6
Ithaca, ...	2	4, 000	5, 000	2, 550	5, 300	9
Lansing,.........	9	6, 200	....	6, 500	12, 860	2
Newfield,........	10	10, 150	350	38, 066	109, 240	19
Ulysses, ...	4	7, 100	....	9, 500	14, 000	5
Ulster Co.						
Denning, ...	8	7, 700	565	6, 500	13, 800	23
Esopus,..........	1	500	50	300	750	1
Gardiner,........	7	11, 900	1, 000	2, 850	2, 850	18
Hurley, ...	3	1, 500	3, 725	....	26, 000	3
Lloyd,...........	4	3, 600	470	3, 850	7, 200	6
Marbletown, ...	2	1, 100	100	600	1, 350	3
Marlborough,.....	1	....	20	....	....	....
New Paltz,.......	1	500	25	300	1, 000	2
Olin, ...	23	9, 300	2, 290	4, 300	14, 750	27
Olive,...........	1	600	....	2, 000	3, 000	1
Rochester, ...	8	7, 775	2, 865	6, 600	16, 880	18
Saugerties,.......	2	....	....	1, 500	3, 500	2
Shandaken, ...	6	13, 100	550	4, 250	10, 500	20
Shawangunk,.....	2	2, 000	250	....	800	2
Wawarsing,......	21	35, 100	5, 075	32, 900	48, 600	84
Woodstock,......	5	1, 700	2, 390	2, 650	5, 550	10
Warren Co.						
Bolton,..........	14	9, 000	1, 120	7, 510	14, 280	48

CLASS XIV.—(Continued.)

TOWNS.	Number of establishments.	Capital Invested. In real estate.	Capital Invested. In tools and machinery.	Cash Value. Of raw materials used.	Cash Value. Of manufactured articles.	Persons employed.
Warren Co.						
Caldwell, ...	5	$5,800	$475	$4,200	$4,700	16
Chester, ...	6	3,800	300	2,280	4,800	13
Hague, ...	6	11,400	840	4,700	6,300	10
Johnsburgh, ...	6	6,800	575	5,750	8,500	12
Luzerne, ...	5	3,900	2,800	4,900	7,960	13
Queensbury, ...	6	87,000	14,500	66,600	118,900	124
Strong Creek, ...	11	7,500	325	6,038	9,380	26
Warrensburgh, ...	7	20,200	1,550	26,250	54,100	40
Washington Co.						
Argyle, ...	3	1,200	....	900	1,750	4
Dresden, ...	1	700	....	....	1,450	6
Easton, ...	3	1,700	1,600	1,400	2,000	1
Fort Ann, ...	13	20,600	950	12,020	15,200	17
Fort Edward, ...	3	28,000	....	57,000	97,500	90
Granville, ...	8	5,550	50	70	200	9
Greenwich, ...	3	2,800	775	8,600	12,000	13
Hartford, ...	4	1,050	22	775	1,320	2
Hebron, ...	2	2,000	1,000	1,250	4,750	6
Kingsbury, ...	2	31,050	17,000	94,240	171,500	146
Putnam, ...	4	3,050	....	1,400	2,570	8
Salem, ...	3	3,800	1,300	3,900	6,900	3
Wayne Co.						
Arcadia, ...	9	4,600	5,950	11,110	19,320	9
Galen, ...	1	500	200	210	500	1
Huron, ...	7	7,800	20	2,012	12,975	16
Lyons, ...	4	5,000	900	6,900	13,150	6
Macedon, ...	5	1,500	....	500	750	....
Marion, ...	3	1,100	1,750	2,100	5,400	5
Ontario, ...	17	7,825	6,125	7,275	16,524	23
Palmyra, ...	1	1,200	100	900	2,000	1
Rose, ...	3	650	3,000	3,900	10,170	8
Sodus, ...	12	8,600	2,100	3,965	11,410	15
Walworth, ...	2	700	2,200	1,600	2,925	4
Williamson, ...	8	3,200	6,040	3,193	9,554	32
Wolcott, ...	13	10,650	200	3,450	12,325	20
Westchester Co.						
Bedford, ...	1	....	....	400	650	1
Eastchester, ...	1	42,000	400	1,000	2,500	2
Harrison, ...	2	2,000	300	....	....	....
Lewisboro, ...	5	3,600	....	1,363	2,267	2
New Rochelle, ...	1	5,000	2,000	....	....	....
North Castle, ...	3	4,300	175	657	1,407	4
North Salem, ...	3	....	....	2,675	1,850	1
Poundridge, ...	3	1,500	....	....	....	....
Rye, ...	1	....	....	1,000	2,000	1
Somers, ...	5	1,950	600	1,500	1,700	5
White Plains, ...	1	37,000	13,000	....	....	....
Yorktown, ...	5	4,050	850	2,935	7,025	5
Wyoming Co.						
Attica, ...	8	3,950	....	1,200	3,500	10
Bennington, ...	10	5,750	8,000	6,025	13,950	23
Castile, ...	5	6,250	110	1,100	5,000	5
China, ...	7	5,500	800	900	7,875	10
Covington, ...	3	2,900	250	....	550	3
Eagle, ...	2	4,100	950	2,050	5,000	6
Gainesville, ...	4	....	4,750	230	2,500	7
Genesee Falls, ...	2	13,800	2,050	17,500	33,000	22
Java, ...	5	5,600	2,050	1,875	4,225	10
Middlebury, ...	1	800	11	640	1,860	7
Orangeville, ...	6	1,880	2,000	3,025	3,025	8
Pike, ...	6	8,400	1,135	1,350	8,375	9
Sheldon, ...	7	4,650	390	1,950	3,700	8
Warsaw, ...	3	2,500	800	1,420	2,080	9
Wethersfield, ...	8	11,200	1,190	2,410	4,810	13
Yates Co.						
Barrington, ...	3	30,000	700	3,400	6,400	9
Benton, ...	2	1,850	25	1,100	1,800	4
Milo, ...	5	36,500	4,500	23,200	27,700	21
Potter, ...	6	4,800	2,500	1,000	3,390	10
Starkey, ...	2	5,000	1,100	5,800	8,500	28
Torrey, ...	1	2,000	200	4,000	5,000	1

SHINGLE FACTORIES.

TOWNS.	Number of establishments.	Capital Invested. In real estate.	Capital Invested. In tools and machinery.	Cash Value. Of raw materials used.	Cash Value. Of manufactured articles.	Persons employed.
Allegany Co.						
Allen, ...	1	2,000	75	500	1,500	5
Amity, ...	7	8,000	3,760	27,300	50,240	59
Andover, ...	1	500	....	....	337	1
Belfast, ...	3	3,300	750	2,000	9,000	8
Caneadea, ...	1	900	300	410	1,315	3
Clarksville, ...	3	100	4,300	3,350	8,000	13
Cuba, ...	1	....	500	2,100	4,400	5
Friendship, ...	1	1,500	....	500	5,000	6
Hume, ...	4	....	1,850	3,100	5,500	10
Scio, ...	1	1,200	3,000	5,000	6,000	10
Vestal, ...	2	2,000	50	800	1,200	....
Willing, ...	2	....	1,200	1,500	7,350	14
Wirt, ...	2	300	700	1,200	4,000	9
Cattaraugus Co.						
Allegany, ...	2	$2,300	$500	$1,300	$3,300	7
Cold Spring, ...	2	450	3,300	700	2,800	6
Dayton, ...	4	5,130	2,650	500	1,700	15
Freedom, ...	1	50	70	32	80	1
Perrysburgh, ...	1	....	60	120	100	1
Portville, ...	1	....	200	....	500	....
Randolph, ...	4	1,700	700	....	....	12
Chautauque Co.						
Carroll, ...	2	....	1,500	450	1,400	2
Cherry Creek, ...	2	520	375	362	724	2
Ellicott, ...	1	2,000	200	225	600	3
Poland, ...	5	....	....	710	3,200	4
Chemung Co.						
Erin, ...	3	2,130	700	700	2,590	11
Horseheads, ...	1	300	25	120	440	1
Clinton Co.						
Chazy, ...	2	500	100	50	363	1
Columbia Co.						
Austerlitz, ...	1	200	....	375	750	1
Hillsdale, ...	1	500	10	3,000	4,000	3
Delaware Co.						
Masonville, ...	1	150	5	175	787	1
Sidney, ...	1	150	200	200	450	1
Dutchess Co.						
East Fishkill, ...	1	200	300	150	350	3
Erie Co.						
Aurora, ...	2	300	200	....	2,300	8
Buffalo, ...	1	....	....	7,000	12,000	24
Collins, ...	1	500	1,200	100	200	3
East Hamburgh, ..	1	....	....	....	....	....
Hamburgh, ...	3	700	1,545	1,125	4,300	26
Lancaster, ...	1	800	....	....	2,200	3
North Collins, ...	1	....	200	25	200	....
Tonawanda, ...	1	3,000	800	4,000	8,000	6
Essex Co.						
Elizabethtown, ...	1	300	100	300	400	2
Lewis, ...	2	800	200	....	800	3
Schroon, ...	2	200	350	411	1,275	4
Franklin Co.						
Constable, ...	1	500	500	500	1,500	3
Westville, ...	3	1,400	650	800	2,520	4
Fulton Co.						
Broadalbin, ...	3	700	250	485	975	1
Ephrata, ...	2	....	....	100	350	3
Genesee Co.						
Alexander, ...	1	600	900	180	650	....
Batavia, ...	1	....	100	175	400	3
Pembroke, ...	1	....	....	....	5,000	....
Jefferson Co.						
Cape Vincent, ...	1	100	600	312	1,250	2
Ellisburgh, ...	1	....	....	20	40	....
Henderson, ...	1	....	....	....	....	....
Le Ray, ...	1	500	300	....	1,000	2
Lorraine, ...	2	1,000	....	....	....	....
Wilna, ...	6	....	....	....	880	....
Kings Co.						
Brooklyn, ...	1	3,000	....	8,000	10,000	6
Lewis Co.						
Diana, ...	1	50	....	150	350	2
High Market, ...	1	....	....	600	1,000	2
Madison Co.						
Sullivan, ...	1	....	....	....	1,990	....
Monroe Co.						
Rochester, ...	1	600	1,200	3,318	4,862	8
Sweden, ...	1	1,000	800	865	1,800	4
Montgomery Co.						
Mohawk, ...	2	....	....	500	800	....
Niagara Co.						
Lockport, ...	4	8,250	6,050	12,000	20,950	23
Newfane, ...	1	....	10	450	1,125	1
Porter, ...	1	....	1,000	1,500	3,000	....
Royalton, ...	2	....	....	2,000	3,650	24
Wilson, ...	1	....	....	240	540	....
Oneida Co.						
Annsville, ...	10	1,470	1,160	3,465	9,250	20
Ava, ...	1	....	....	372	1,874	....
Camden, ...	3	2,900	150	1,650	3,870	5
Florence, ...	2	....	....	....	250	....
Vienna, ...	1	....	....	....	11,362	....
Ontario Co.						
South Bristol, ...	1	....	....	400	1,200	2
Orleans Co.						
Barre, ...	1	....	....	333	1,200	....
Clarendon, ...	1	....	....	400	1,400	....
Shelby, ...	1	600	900	1,500	3,000	7
Oswego Co.						
Albion, ...	10	5,500	200	3,180	11,425	18
Constantia, ...	1	700	....	30	524	....

CLASS XIV.—(Continued.)

TOWNS.	Number of establishments.	Capital Invested. In real estate.	Capital Invested. In tools and machinery.	Cash Value. Of raw materials used.	Cash Value. Of manufactured articles.	Persons employed.
Oswego Co.						
Granby,	1	$1,500	....	....	$1,000	2
Orwell,	2	1,000	$600	....	1,100	3
Parish,	1	500	100	$175	600	4
Richland,	5	1,500	1,000	860	2,625	9
Scriba,	2	....	....	....	....	....
Otsego Co.						
Middlefield,	1	500	125	....	1,050	4
Westford,	1	300	300	600	1,600	3
St. Lawrence Co.						
Brasher,	3	300	620	1,600	4,225	8
Canton,	5	3,300	800	3,325	10,400	19
De Kalb,	1	....	....	....	600	....
Fowler,	2	....	400	350	1,175	4
Hopkinton,	3	3,500	800	790	2,600	5
Lawrence,	2	....	....	400	2,200	3
Louisville,	3	400	600	1,750	4,000	6
Macomb,	1	250	200	150	400	2
Madrid,	1	1,500	600	750	1,550	....
Morristown,	1	....	....	340	....	....
Norfolk,	4	5,400	600	3,050	7,600	12
Oswegatchie,	4	7,600	1,500	7,075	24,800	20
Parishville,	1	700	150	187	500	1
Pierrepont,	3	650	550	700	1,375	3
Stockholm,	2	....	150	225	400	2
Saratoga Co.						
Ballston,	1	500	500	800	1,800	2
Milton,	3	350	300	500	2,250	8
Wilton,	1	500	10	150	650	1
Schoharie Co.						
Gilboa,	1	....	15	500	4,000	16
Schuyler Co.						
Cayuta,	3	1,700	400	1,100	2,900	5
Hector,	4	3,780	2,410	7,025	6,250	17
Orange,	1	....	250	500	2,000	2
Tyrone,	2	250	2,200	872	2,550	6
Steuben Co.						
Avoca,	5	....	650	254	1,075	10
Cameron,	1	200	800	550	1,150	3
Caton,	2	....	....	....	8,066	....
Corning,	2	1,000	150	1,365	3,300	2
Dansville,	1	500	100	75	150	3
Erwin,	1	....	2,200	2,000	6,875	4
Howard,	1	....	....	....	600	....
Jasper,	1	600	1,200	3,000	3,000	4
West Union,	1	....	50	200	400	2
Tioga Co.						
Nichols,	1	....	150	400	1,000	....
Owego,	4	1,100	650	720	1,700	6
Richford,	1	....	....	....	125	....
Spencer,	1	....	450	90	300	1
Tompkins Co.						
Caroline,	2	300	....	275	563	....
Dryden,	2	....	....	125	400	....
Enfield,	2	200	300	400	1,200	4
Lansing,	1	2,200	800	500	1,800	4
Washington Co.						
Greenwich,	1	1,500	500	900	2,800	1
Hebron,	1	600	75	500	1,250	2
Westchester Co.						
North Castle,	1	....	....	80	80	....
Wyoming Co.						
Bennington,	1	200	800	200	1,225	5
Genesee Falls,	1	400	600	800	3,840	4
Java,	1	125	500	....	1,000	4
Middlebury,	2	200	100	281	987	2
Orangeville,	1	350	250	....	600	2
Pike,	2	300	500	....	1,250	3
Wethersfield,	2	....	....	300	1,700	....
Yates Co.						
Starkey,	1	1,200	1,500	500	860	3
SHIP TIMBER MANUFACTORIES.						
Erie Co.						
Grand Island,	15	....	....	....	12,979	48
STAVE MANUFACTORIES.						
Broome Co.						
Chenango,	1	2,500	200	2,600	7,500	13
Cayuga Co.						
Victory,	1	200	....	....	600	4
Clinton Co.						
Mooers,	1	800	500	700	2,000	3
Erie Co.						
Amherst,	2	3,800	500	3,200	7,100	13
Aurora,	1	400	50	300	300	2
Buffalo,	2	3,000	3,000	7,000	12,500	30
Essex Co.						
Chesterfield,	1	....	1,500	3,000	6,000	6

TOWNS.	Number of establishments.	Capital Invested. In real estate.	Capital Invested. In tools and machinery.	Cash Value. Of raw materials used.	Cash Value. Of manufactured articles.	Persons employed.
Essex Co.						
Schroon,	1	$500	$300	$650	$1,350	7
Willsborough,	1	200	1,500	675	3,225	6
Franklin Co.						
Bombay,	1	500	100	250	200	3
Chateaugay,	1	1,500	....	750	1,810	5
Fulton Co.						
Caroga,	1	1,000	500	600	4,200	6
Genesee Co.						
Alabama,	1	150	500	600	2,100	7
Alexander,	1	800	800	344	730	1
Pembroke,	1	....	....	....	....	1
Livingston Co.						
Springwater,	1	300	100	150	350	2
Madison Co.						
Lenox,	1	1,000	1,500	600	5,000	5
Monroe Co.						
Greece,	1	500	500	600	1,500	2
Rochester,	1	15,000	3,000	15,000	25,000	25
Webster,	1	....	500	1,250	3,000	10
Niagara Co.						
Lockport,	3	13,500	5,600	12,300	23,100	30
Porter,	1	1,000	2,000	1,500	3,600	14
Wilson,	1	....	1,000	75	180	6
Oneida Co.						
Camden,	1	....	....	250	1,200	1
Onondaga Co.						
Cicero,	2	....	3,200	3,000	5,950	11
Lysander,	1	100	300	150	450	1
Manlius,	1	....	100	262	500	1
Otisco,	1	....	....	....	600	....
Ontario Co.						
East Bloomfield,	1	600	290	850	2,000	18
Orleans Co.						
Carlton,	1	700	1,000	270	945	3
Oswego Co.						
Albion,	2	1,500	50	3,365	8,310	7
Granby,	1	300	....	....	800	....
Hannibal,	1	200	300	1,250	2,000	6
New Haven,	4	700	1,600	3,530	8,600	9
Palermo,	2	300	....	600	1,400	3
Richland,	1	500	200	400	800	5
Schroeppel,	2	1,600	3,700	3,775	7,500	15
Scriba,	1	....	....	....	2,400	....
Volney,	3	2,700	500	2,550	11,200	11
Rensselaer Co.						
Troy,	1	5,000	500	....	6,000	13
St. Lawrence Co.						
Oswegatchie,	1	3,500	250	2,000	30,000	20
Seneca Co.						
Romulus,	1	500	2,000	3,300	8,875	4
Seneca Falls,	1	....	....	....	850	....
Varick,	1	....	....	80	170	....
Waterloo,	1	1,000	2,000	600	1,350	6
Sullivan Co.						
Forrestburgh,	1	600	1,000	1,000	4,000	5
Ulster Co.						
Denning,	1	16,000	20,000	2,400	62,500	28
Marbletown,	1	400	....	100	500	2
Olive,	4	1,550	3,350	300	3,900	7
Warren Co.						
Bolton,	1	400	100	100	300	2
Caldwell,	1	100	100	300	500	2
Queensbury,	1	....	....	....	2,000	....
Rose,	1	....	150	1,500	3,200	2
Wayne Co.						
Williamson,	3	160	530	570	1,310	5
STEEL SQUARE MANUFACTORY.						
Herkimer Co.						
Litchfield,	1	1,000	2,000	1,692	4,500	7
TURNING SHOPS.						
Albany Co.						
Albany,	1	....	1,500	300	1,500	3
Broome Co.						
Maine,	1	600	150	....	500	....
Cattaraugus Co.						
Persia,	1	500	350	200	250	....
Chautauque Co.						
Chautauque,	1	1,000	400	100	500	2
Ellicott,	1	1,000	400	400	4,225	5
Hanover,	2	275	600	950	3,500	5
Pomfret,	3	2,800	1,950	1,430	8,640	6
Chemung Co.						
Elmira,	1	....	100	....	1,000	1
Van Etten,	3	....	....	....	....	....

CLASS XIV.—(Continued.)

TOWNS.	Number of establishments.	Capital Invested. In real estate.	Capital Invested. In tools and machinery.	Cash Value. Of raw materials used.	Cash Value. Of manufactured articles.	Persons employed.
Chenango Co.						
Bainbridge, ...	1	$400	$1,500	$350	$2,500	3
New Berlin, ...	1	....	....	....	600	....
Pitcher, ...	2	200	150	440	1,700	3
Preston, ...	1	....	200	80	250	1
Cortland Co.						
Preble, ...	2	1,500	1,000	1,750	3,750	3
Scott, ...	1	300	100	120	400	1
Delaware Co.						
Delhi, ...	1	100	250	100	800	2
Dutchess Co.						
Poughkeepsie city,	1	....	1,000	1,000	1,500	5
Rhinebeck, ...	1	500	200	150	700	....
Erie Co.						
Buffalo, ...	3	2,600	6,900	12,020	24,030	16
Eden, ...	1	....	....	40	85	....
Newstead, ...	2	1,500	2,150	1,500	5,000	4
Fulton Co.						
Broadalbin, ...	4	1,700	100	1,425	4,170	4
Stratford, ...	1	....	....	1,000	4,500	13
Genesee Co.						
Batavia, ...	1	....	....	....	367	....
Greene Co.						
Catskill, ...	1	....	400	600	3,750	3
Coxsackie, ...	2	500	400	350	1,224	3
Durham, ...	1	....	....	....	300	....
Greenville, ...	1	500	250	200	1,100	1
Lexington, ...	1	300	15	130	200	....
Windham, ...	2	1,000	800	1,400	1,600	4
Hamilton Co.						
Hope, ...	1	....	....	500	2,000	....
Herkimer Co.						
Fairfield, ...	1	....	....	500	1,000	....
German Flats, ...	1	3,000	4,000	3,000	7,000	8
Little Falls, ...	1	3,000	1,000	1,500	5,300	5
Salisbury, ...	3	1,100	520	1,681	5,925	4
Kings Co.						
Brooklyn, ...	1	8,000	3,500	7,000	18,000	20
Lewis Co.						
Diana, ...	1	....	75	56	120	....
Greig, ...	1	300	200	500	500	1
Livingston Co.						
Avon, ...	1	3,500	1,500	1,200	6,000	8
North Dansville, .	1	....	150	....	800	1
Madison Co.						
Fenner, ...	1	100	200	1,000	2,500	2
Sullivan, ...	1	....	....	1,150	1,850	....
Monroe Co.						
Rochester, ...	1	160	300	600	3,000	3
Webster, ...	1	....	200	....	....	1
Montgomery Co.						
Amsterdam, ...	2	1,400	500	1,383	1,665	2
Florida, ...	1	450	30	150	500	2
Root, ...	1	....	100	375	500	1
New-York Co.						
New-York, ...	8	21,700	9,100	12,700	79,750	51
Oneida Co.						
Rome, ...	2	2,500	700	775	1,175	4
Onondaga Co.						
Lysander, ...	1	2,000	300	500	1,500	3
Syracuse, ...	1	3,000	500	1,200	2,400	....
Tully, ...	2	2,300	700	1,400	3,315	5
Ontario Co.						
Phelps, ...	1	1,000	200	1,500	2,000	1
Oswego Co.						
Orwell, ...	1	300	200	....	600	1
Redfield, ...	1	200	600	1,200	2,300	2
Otsego Co.						
Maryland, ...	2	1,300	500	400	907	2
Middlefield, ...	1	200	20	....	150	1
Otego, ...	1	70	200	20	76	1
Roseboom, ...	2	50	75	52	260	....
Queens Co.						
Flushing, ...	1	700	1,400	600	1,500	3
Rensselaer Co.						
Brunswick, ...	1	800	100	150	1,500	3
Stephentown, ...	5	4,400	1,400	348	4,708	13
Saratoga Co.						
Day, ...	1	1,100	250	1,000	....	....
Edinburgh, ...	1	800	100	353	1,272	....
Saratoga Co.						
Providence, ...	1	$800	$100	$1,000	$12,400	3
Saratoga Springs, .	1	....	....	5,000	3,500	....
Wilton, ...	1	400	20	85	424	1
Schenectady Co.						
Rotterdam, ...	1	500	300	10,000	10,000	8
Schoharie Co.						
Conesville, ...	1	50	450	120	288	2
Esperance, ...	1	570	150	500	1,000	1
Fulton, ...	2	650	350	500	2,425	4
Schoharie, ...	1	1,200	....	500	1,100	1
Sharon, ...	1	200	100	300	700	1
Summit, ...	1	30	25	50	200	....
Seneca Co.						
Seneca Falls, ...	1	....	....	....	3,400	....
Steuben Co.						
Urbana, ...	1	400	300	200	500	1
Wheeler, ...	1	500	200	250	600	1
Suffolk Co.						
Southold, ...	1	900	....	....	....	....
Sullivan Co.						
Bethel, ...	1	50	25	200	600	1
Callicoon, ...	1	500	300	400	2,400	2
Fallsburgh, ...	5	1,130	635	1,810	3,133	5
Liberty, ...	1	1,000	....	....	200	....
Rockland, ...	1	....	....	150	300	....
Thompson, ...	3	....	....	1,320	7,000	12
Tompkins Co.						
Ithaca, ...	1	....	1,500	....	....	3
Ulster Co.						
Denning, ...	2	....	....	....	1,965	....
Wawarsing, ...	3	1,900	1,000	1,760	4,500	7
Warren Co.						
Stony Creek, ...	1	600	25	600	2,800	4
Wayne Co.						
Ontario, ...	1	250	600	157	640	2
Westchester Co.						
Yorktown, ...	1	100	150	....	....	1
Wyoming Co.						
Castile, ...	1	350	....	....	300	1
Gainesville, ...	1	....	2,000	800	4,500	4

TRUSS HOOP MANUFACTORY.

TOWNS.	Number of establishments.	In real estate.	In tools and machinery.	Of raw materials used.	Of manufactured articles.	Persons employed.
Monroe Co.						
Rochester, ...	1	1,000	300	3,500	4,290	6

VENEERING MANUFACTORIES.

TOWNS.	Number of establishments.	In real estate.	In tools and machinery.	Of raw materials used.	Of manufactured articles.	Persons employed.
Albany Co.						
Watervliet, ...	1	15,500	5,000	32,615	216,884	15
Chautauque Co.						
Chautauque, ...	1	....	....	....	2,000	3
Gerry, ...	1	150	200	750	3,000	2
Kings Co.						
Brooklyn, ...	1	....	....	15,000	16,000	2

WOOD MOULDING AND CARVING ESTABLISHMENTS.

TOWNS.	Number of establishments.	In real estate.	In tools and machinery.	Of raw materials used.	Of manufactured articles.	Persons employed.
Kings Co.						
Brooklyn, ...	1	500	200	80	1,000	4
New-York Co.						
New-York, ...	13	183,800	18,825	111,420	206,300	185
Oneida Co.						
Utica, ...	1	100	300	200	1,200	1

WOOD MILLS.

TOWNS.	Number of establishments.	In real estate.	In tools and machinery.	Of raw materials used.	Of manufactured articles.	Persons employed.
Erie Co.						
Grand Island, ...	24	....	....	....	25,161	150
Tonawanda, ...	1	....	....	....	4,803	....
Chenango Co.						
Preston, ...	1	50	....	100	500	1
Sherburne, ...	1	....	....	60	240	1
Franklin Co.						
Moira, ...	2	....	....	....	5,000	....
Rensselaer Co.						
Berlin, ...	1	....	....	....	1,000	2

CLASS XV.—STONE, CLAY, POTTERY AND GLASS MANUFACTURES.

BRICK MANUFACTORIES.

TOWNS.	Number of establishments.	Capital Invested. In real estate.	Capital Invested. In tools and machinery.	Cash Value. Of raw materials used.	Cash Value. Of manufactured articles.	Persons employed.
ALBANY Co.						
Albany,	10	$39,425	$24,700	$16,696	$79,900	158
Watervliet,	1	....	300	942	3,600	8
ALLEGANY Co.						
Belfast,	1	....	100	125	225	7
BROOME Co.						
Chenango,	1	4,000	300	....	4,000	11
CATTARAUGUS Co.						
Portville,	1	100	50	63	600	4
CAYUGA Co.						
Springport,	1	400	25	600	....	4
Sterling,	1	600	400	....	2,600	....
CHAUTAUGUE Co.						
Chautauque,	1	....	....	....	600	....
Pomfret,	2	2,100	100	....	2,375	4
CHEMUNG Co.						
Horseheads,	1	3,000	1,000	300	6,000	12
CHENANGO Co.						
Norwich,	1	500	100	....	1,500	3
CLINTON Co.						
Beekmantown,	1	400	50	....	900	5
Champlain,	4	1,400	65	525	5,250	21
Chazy,	1	100	100	150	1,125	5
Mooers,	1	....	....	....	400	....
Plattsburgh,	1	1,000	300	....	2,800	10
Schuyler Falls,	1	500	50	200	800	8
COLUMBIA Co.						
Hudson,	1	9,000	2,000	1,500	15,000	65
Stuyvesant,	1	2,500	1,200	....	2,400	6
CORTLAND Co.						
Cortlandville,	2	....	800	450	2,600	9
DUTCHESS Co.						
Amenia,	1	200	20	63	500	3
Fishkill,	9	57,500	6,800	27,930	65,500	193
Poughkeepsie,	2	6,500	1,800	2,777	10,000	31
Poughkeepsie city,	1	32,000	26,000	1,000	12,000	52
ERIE Co.						
Amherst,	1	150	200	300	1,650	8
Buffalo,	7	33,200	2,570	12,800	30,790	152
Evans,	1	....	40	100	700	4
Lancaster,	1	....	....	....	....	10
Tonawanda,	1	800	200	....	1,520	4
FRANKLIN Co.						
Malone,	1	600	300	200	980	6
FULTON Co.						
Johnstown,	1	1,200	200	70	1,600	7
GENESEE Co.						
Alexander,	1	100	250	360	1,800	3
Le Roy,	1	1,500	500	500	3,600	12
GREENE Co.						
Athens,	6	17,500	7,800	14,451	47,500	192
Coxsackie,	15	43,780	15,400	21,596	85,700	262
Catskill,	1	5,000	2,500	3,200	15,000	36
HERKIMER Co.						
German Flats,	1	....	500	200	2,400	10
JEFFERSON Co.						
Ellisburgh,	1	200	....	100	720	2
Hounsfield,	1	178	10	....	625	3
Watertown,	2	350	450	290	2,825	11
LEWIS Co.						
Lowville,	1	100	200	120	1,000	4
LIVINGSTON Co.						
West Sparta,	1	60	40	72	720	4
MONROE Co.						
Brighton,	3	10,500	22,300	7,500	70,080	121
MONTGOMERY Co.						
Glen,	1	6,000	3,000	1,400	2,300	7
St. Johnsville,	1	500	250	70	1,000	6
NIAGARA Co.						
Lockport,	2	2,400	1,450	....	6,000	18
Niagara,	1	550	230	375	4,500	5
Willson,	2	300	80	205	2,048	8
ONEIDA Co.						
Rome,	3	2,700	330	765	12,900	23
Trenton,	1	....	100	50	550	....
Utica,	1	2,000	250	2,000	3,000	6
ONONDAGA Co.						
Clay,	1	2,400	150	180	2,400	7
Elbridge,	2	350	350	600	10,560	13
Geddes,	5	8,200	1,725	11,625	28,500	66
Skaneateles,	1	1,000	625	106	1,480	5
ONTARIO Co.						
Canandaigua,	2	200	300	575	5,250	17
Seneca,	1	600	50	250	1,400	5
ORANGE Co.						
Deerpark,	1	3,000	400	....	5,000	14
Goshen,	1	100	400	....	6,000	8
ORANGE Co.						
Newburgh,	8	$61,000	$22,000	$21,105	$74,450	215
New Windsor,	4	29,000	4,300	1,500	35,800	91
OSWEGO Co.						
Granby,	1	100	80	....	2,800	8
Hannibal,	1	500	270	180	1,950	6
Mexico,	2	600	390	490	2,000	12
Oswego,	2	500	350	540	3,100	14
Oswego city,	1	1,500	100	842	3,150	8
Richland,	1	700	300	1,800	6,000	12
Volney,	1	70,000	....	....	250	6
OTSEGO Co.						
Morris,	1	36	10	....	500	4
Oneonta,	1	125	25	....	1,000	8
PUTNAM Co.						
Patterson,	1	5,000	500	870	4,500	27
Phillipstown,	1	4,000	200	2,800	12,000	18
QUEENS Co.						
Oyster Bay,	2	550	300	....	2,550	7
RENSSELAER Co.						
Clinton,	1	1,000	200	400	800	....
Lansingburgh,	1	....	1,000	2,000	7,000	20
Troy,	5	25,500	8,800	8,868	43,800	103
RICHMOND Co.						
Northfield,	1	19,000	23,000	18,000	75,000	83
ROCKLAND Co.						
Haverstraw,	33	102,500	105,900	6,500	248,550	757
ST. LAWRENCE Co.						
Canton,	1	200	150	80	800	3
Massena,	1	50	100	....	500	1
Oswegatchie,	2	1,000	200	350	3,500	13
Potsdam,	2	....	375	....	1,705	7
SARATOGA Co.						
Greenfield,	2	1,000	80	1,375	11,700	12
Halfmoon,	1	3,000	150	50	2,400	8
Moreau,	1	....	200	....	3,000	12
SCHENECTADY Co.						
Schenectady,	1	4,000	....	2,000	10,000	40
SENECA Co.						
Seneca Falls,	2	2,500	220	100	1,700	9
Waterloo,	2	3,700	450	200	4,400	12
STEUBEN Co.						
Dansville,	1	1,300	500	100	1,400	6
Hornellsville,	2	600	150	5,400	3,300	14
SUFFOLK Co.						
Brookhaven,	1	....	....	....	1,000	2
Huntington,	3	18,800	5,200	6,960	65,000	115
Southold,	3	6,000	2,100	....	14,892	38
TIOGA Co.						
Candor,	1	200	50	....	1,200	6
TOMPKINS Co.						
Ithaca,	1	600	100	525	2,000	9
ULSTER Co.						
Esopus,	1	6,000	600	400	8,000	20
Saugerties,	10	27,500	3,750	2,410	30,000	76
WARREN Co.						
Queensbury,	1	800	300	1,150	90,000	16
WASHINGTON Co.						
Granville,	1	500	50	....	1,700	3
Greenwich,	1	1,000	100	200	800	2
WAYNE Co.						
Arcadia,	1	1,000	500	600	2,500	5
Lyons,	1	1,000	450	625	3,000	11
WESTCHESTER Co.						
Cortland,	37	10,000	65,400	47,600	337,165	1091
Mount Pleasant,	1	6,000	300	....	10,000	16

BRICK AND TILE MACHINE MANUFACTORIES.

TOWNS.	Number of establishments.	In real estate.	In tools and machinery.	Of raw materials used.	Of manufactured articles.	Persons employed.
GREENE Co.						
Coxsackie,	1	2,000	400	677	3,450	3
ONTARIO Co.						
Canandaigua,	1	1,500	3,000	2,200	9,504	10

ENAMELING FURNACES.

TOWNS.	Number of establishments.	In real estate.	In tools and machinery.	Of raw materials used.	Of manufactured articles.	Persons employed.
NEW-YORK Co.						
New-York,	4	3,000	3,500	16,800	150,500	62

FIRE BRICK MANUFACTORIES.

TOWNS.	Number of establishments.	In real estate.	In tools and machinery.	Of raw materials used.	Of manufactured articles.	Persons employed.
ALBANY Co.						
Albany,	1	25,000	14,000	23,200	23,200	....
KINGS Co.						
Brooklyn,	2	27,000	50,200	21,000	40,000	35
NEW-YORK Co.						
New-York,	2	19,000	30,500	37,110	79,220	40
RENSSELAER Co.						
Troy,	1	5,000	3,000	10,000	28,000	28
WESTCHESTER Co.						
Cortland,	1	4,000	800	1,000	8,000	8

CLASS XV.—(Continued.

GLASS-CUTTING ESTABLISHMENTS.

TOWNS.	Number of establishments.	Capital Invested. In real estate.	Capital Invested. In tools and machinery.	Cash Value. Of raw materials used.	Cash Value. Of manufactured articles.	Persons employed.
New-York Co.						
New-York, ...	7	$64,000	$14,440	$52,685	$131,095	168

GLASS MANUFACTORIES.

TOWNS.	Number of establishments.	Capital Invested. In real estate.	Capital Invested. In tools and machinery.	Cash Value. Of raw materials used.	Cash Value. Of manufactured articles.	Persons employed.
Clinton Co.						
Saranac, ...	1	....	....	4,000	15,000	17
Erie Co.						
Lancaster, ...	1	8,000	1,200	8,530	40,000	60
Jefferson Co.						
Alexandria, ...	1	16,000	3,000	12,900	40,000	30
Kings Co.						
Brooklyn, ...	2	281,200	39,000	119,200	322,000	282
New-York Co.						
New-York, ...	5	36,000	7,000	20,000	45,000	49
Niagara Co.						
Lockport, ...	1	4,250	1,800	7,943	23,000	48
Oneida Co.						
Verona, ...	2	30,500	5,000	30,255	100,000	115
Oswego Co.						
Constantia, ...	4	46,000	5,000	39,197	95,000	119
Saratoga Co.						
Greenfield, ...	1	3,500	500	8,600	25,000	45
Ulster Co.						
Wawarsing, ...	1	37,000	4,000	27,350	100,000	200
Woodstock, ...	1	1,000	1,000	7,353	13,500	32
Wayne Co.						
Galen, ...	1	12,000	3,000	17,300	162,000	75

GLASS-STAINING ESTABLISHMENTS.

TOWNS.	Number of establishments.	Capital Invested. In real estate.	Capital Invested. In tools and machinery.	Cash Value. Of raw materials used.	Cash Value. Of manufactured articles.	Persons employed.
New-York Co.						
New-York, ...	1	80,000	2,000	20,000	50,000	25
Oneida Co.						
Utica, ...	1	600	500	2,700	7,000	10

LIME MANUFACTORIES.

TOWNS.	Number of establishments.	Capital Invested. In real estate.	Capital Invested. In tools and machinery.	Cash Value. Of raw materials used.	Cash Value. Of manufactured articles.	Persons employed.
Albany Co.						
Albany, ...	1	1,500	7,000	12,000	50,000	45
New Scotland, ...	1	1,000	100	400	5,800	9
Watervliet, ...	1	3,000	3,000	5,200	11,000	13
Broome Co.						
Chenango, ...	1	1,000	2,000	3,575	5,250	5
Cattaraugus Co.						
Otto, ...	1	1,000	80	245	500	3
Cayuga Co.						
Aurelius, ...	1	4,000	100	2,650	6,000	6
Ira, ...	1	80	....	112	1,200	2
Chemung Co.						
Elmira, ...	1	3,500	50	3,550	7,260	4
Horseheads, ...	1	2,000	100	1,200	4,000	4
Chenango Co.						
Norwich, ...	1	100	50	1,580	1,750	2
Oxford, ...	1	600	100	1,010	2,000	3
Clinton Co.						
Beekmantown, ...	1	200	15	150	800	2
Chazy, ...	1	600	75	....	1,700	6
Plattsburgh, ...	1	200	....	350	1,100	1
Schuyler Falls, ...	1	1,000	30	700	1,000	1
Cortland Co.						
Cortlandville, ...	3	1,900	152	350	2,300	8
Erie Co.						
Amherst, ...	1	1,000	200	300	5,000	8
Lancaster, ...	2	200	....	200	5,000	2
Essex Co.						
Willsborough, ...	1	2,000	400	1,375	5,000	5
Fulton Co.						
Ephrata, ...	1	....	....	75	600	2
Mayfield, ...	3	....	....	963	1,683	4
Northampton, ...	1	400	200	30	375	1
Genesee Co.						
Batavia, ...	1	....	600	....	936	2
Le Roy, ...	1	1,200	800	400	5,250	8
Greene Co.						
Athens, ...	3	1,650	25	9,100	15,400	19
Coxsackie, ...	1	600	....	1,100	1,290	3
Herkimer Co.						
Litchfield, ...	2	1,700	175	2,025	5,000	3
Jefferson Co.						
Le Ray, ...	1	125	60	200	500	1
Watertown, ...	1	50	800	1,100	1,875	4
Kings Co.						
Brooklyn, ...	3	52,000	5,000	175	11,350	27
Lewis Co.						
Lowville, ...	2	700	55	322	950	2
Madison Co.						
Fenner, ...	1	500	10	1,071	2,900	4
Madison Co.						
Sullivan, ...	1	$500	....	$600	$1,500	2
Monroe Co.						
Penfield, ...	2	....	....	432	1,800	2
Rochester, ...	1	4,000	$800	2,520	5,720	4
Sweden, ...	2	400	50	800	1,250	2
New-York Co.						
New-York, ...	4	49,000	5,600	33,206	61,500	37
Niagara Co.						
Lockport, ...	2	2,800	250	1,850	5,250	7
Niagara, ...	3	1,200	550	2,161	4,430	6
Oneida Co.						
Augusta, ...	1	200	....	1,162	2,160	3
Marshall, ...	1	400	10	375	840	3
Steuben, ...	1	....	....	300	1,200	2
Trenton, ...	2	2,000	....	2,800	8,200	6
Onondaga Co.						
Camillus, ...	1	....	....	....	1,200	3
Fabius, ...	1	....	....	....	2,000	3
Lysander, ...	1	2,000	150	550	1,725	2
Marcellus, ...	1	....	....	2,000	6,000	6
Onondaga, ...	2	3,600	850	2,300	15,350	14
Skaneateles, ...	2	2,200	25	3,100	5,535	8
Ontario Co.						
Phelps, ...	2	900	65	300	1,680	3
Orange Co.						
Deerpark, ...	1	1,000	500	1,000	2,250	5
Rensselaer Co.						
Troy, ...	1	1,000	100	6,500	13,000	8
Rockland Co.						
Haverstraw, ...	1	40,000	2,000	....	35,000	110
St. Lawrence Co.						
De Peyster, ...	1	50	....	100	750	2
Pitcairn, ...	1	100	10	450	600	1
Potsdam, ...	2	4,500	100	838	3,450	2
Saratoga Co.						
Greenfield, ...	1	2,000	20	2,200	5,250	5
Milton, ...	1	....	200	550	1,400	3
Schenectady Co.						
Glenville, ...	1	1,000	800	3,100	5,600	12
Schoharie Co.						
Middleburgh, ...	1	....	....	....	550	....
Seneca Co.						
Fayette, ...	2	300	400	600	2,025	5
Steuben Co.						
Dansville, ...	1	300	50	60	8,750	4
Tompkins Co.						
Ithaca, ...	1	350	10	744	1,650	2
Lansing, ...	1	100	200	100	400	....
Ulster Co.						
Esopus, ...	1	30,000	3,500	....	30,000	45
Kingston, ...	1	2,000	5,000	7,000	31,500	48
Saugerties, ...	1	200	....	....	1,250	2
Warren Co.						
Queensbury, ...	2	17,200	3,000	27,500	83,850	95
Washington Co.						
Greenwich, ...	1	57,000	20,000	15,100	75,000	85
Wayne Co.						
Sodus, ...	4	230	490	....	2,464	8
Westchester Co.						
North Salem, ...	1	1,050	....	200	2,000	....
Yates Co.						
Milo, ...	1	....	....	800	1,500	2

LOOKING-GLASS MANUFACTORIES.

TOWNS.	Number of establishments.	Capital Invested. In real estate.	Capital Invested. In tools and machinery.	Cash Value. Of raw materials used.	Cash Value. Of manufactured articles.	Persons employed.
Albany Co.						
Albany, ...	1	4,000	4,300	27,000	40,000	23
Allegany Co.						
Andover, ...	1	100	....	....	3,600	2
Dutchess Co.						
Poughkeepsie city,	1	2,000	1,000	8,400	19,000	6
New-York Co.						
New-York, ...	14	249,000	23,750	165,500	331,000	267
Onondaga Co.						
Syracuse, ...	1	....	1,500	10,000	20,000	8

MARBLE MANUFACTORIES.

TOWNS.	Number of establishments.	Capital Invested. In real estate.	Capital Invested. In tools and machinery.	Cash Value. Of raw materials used.	Cash Value. Of manufactured articles.	Persons employed.
Albany Co.						
Albany, ...	7	8,000	9,380	37,470	71,400	107
Watervliet, ...	1	600	10	700	1,800	2
Allegany Co.						
Belfast, ...	1	350	50	400	1,500	3
Wirt, ...	1	5	20	350	700	1
Broome Co.						
Chenango, ...	2	14,000	150	6,810	14,000	13
Cayuga Co.						
Brutus, ...	1	700	30	3,000	5,000	5
Mentz, ...	1	600	20	650	2,000	3

CLASS XV.—(Continued.)

TOWNS.	Number of establishments.	Capital Invested. In real estate.	Capital Invested. In tools and machinery.	Cash Value. Of raw materials used.	Cash Value. Of manufactured articles.	Persons employed.
Chautauque Co.						
Ellicott,	1	....	$800	$2,576	$5,146	4
Pomfret,	1	....	550	600	2,500	2
Chemung Co.						
Elmira,	1	$2,000	30	3,000	12,000	5
Veteran,	1	100	25	1,000	2,000	2
Clinton Co.						
Peru,	1	200	20	275	1,000	1
Plattsburgh,	1	150	15	400	1,250	1
Columbia Co.						
Hudson,	1	....	100	....	3,000	2
Kinderhook,	1	500	20	1,500	2,000	1
Cortland Co.						
Cortlandville,	1	150	10	750	1,500	2
Virgil,	1	200	30	750	2,550	2
Delaware Co.						
Walton,	1	550	400	1,500	4,000	3
Dutchess Co.						
Dover,	2	13,000	....	....	5,620	13
Poughkeepsie city,	1	100	....	3,000	5,500	4
Erie Co.						
Buffalo,	2	20,000	10,850	24,800	65,080	48
Franklin Co.						
Malone,	1	....	125	1,125	2,500	3
Genesee Co.						
Batavia,	2	3,000	75	2,900	5,650	1
Le Roy,	1	2,000	650	5,000	10,000	5
Herkimer Co.						
German Flats,	2	800	25	1,600	5,500	5
Little Falls,	1	300	25	500	1,500	1
Jefferson Co.						
Adams,	2	950	65	2,000	6,000	8
Watertown,	2	1,200	45	4,500	8,800	7
Wilna,	1	....	20	800	3,000	2
Kings Co.						
Brooklyn,	6	16,100	7,320	42,000	88,500	100
New Lots,	1	1,400	50	2,650	7,000	7
Livingston Co.						
Nunda,	1	400	50	900	3,000	3
North Dansville,	2	450	390	825	2,607	3
Madison Co.						
Hamilton,	1	700	30	1,600	3,500	5
Lenox,	2	800	325	2,500	6,200	3
Monroe Co.						
Rochester,	2	8,000	500	5,000	14,000	15
Sweden,	1	1,000	25	1,350	2,500	2
Wheatland,	1	....	40	1,600	3,000	3
Montgomery Co.						
Minden,	2	1,000	40	4,000	8,000	6
New-York Co.						
New-York,	32	336,600	76,527	601,230	1,154,500	216
Niagara Co.						
Hartland,	1	25	20	300	1,200	2
Lockport,	1	2,000	10	1,400	5,000	6
Oneida Co.						
Camden,	1	200	20	700	1,450	2
Utica,	1	5,000	3,025	6,750	26,500	31
Onondaga Co.						
Skaneateles,	1	350	10	800	1,800	3
Syracuse,	1	600	25	1,000	6,000	6
Ontario Co.						
Canandaigua,	1	250	20	750	1,800	2
Orleans Co.						
Barre,	1	1,500	50	1,800	5,000	4
Ridgeway,	1	1,000	15	200	2,000	3
Oswego Co.						
Mexico,	1	300	30	1,000	2,000	2
Otsego Co.						
Oneonta,	1	1,250	1,200	4,000	12,000	10
Westford,	1	300	....	1,000	2,000	3
Queens Co.						
Flushing,	1	900	70	840	1,680	2
Jamaica,	1	....	75	2,000	3,000	3
Rensselaer Co.						
Greenbush,	1	1,000	150	2,000	6,000	6
Troy,	2	7,000	3,700	8,000	22,000	18
St. Lawrence Co.						
Madrid,	1	400	50	1,200	3,000	3
Potsdam,	1	50	....	1,000	2,800	2
Saratoga Co.						
Milton,	2	12,500	1,300	1,800	19,500	5
Saratoga Springs,	1	500	15	800	1,800	3
Schoharie Co.						
Schoharie,	1	100	25	1,500	4,000	5
Steuben Co.						
Bath,	1	400	20	1,500	4,000	2
Hornellsville,	1	50	20	500	2,100	4
Suffolk Co.						
Huntington,	1	500	20	250	600	1
Riverhead,	1	900	200	2,500	7,000	4
Tioga Co.						
Barton,	1	$700	....	....	....	2
Tompkins Co.						
Dryden,	1	125	$25	$915	$1,800	3
Ulysses,	1	400	....	1,000	3,000	2
Warren Co.						
Queensbury,	1	....	....	1,000	2,000	....
Washington Co.						
Greenwich,	1	300	200	1,500	3,000	6
Wayne Co.						
Palmyra,	1	1,000	100	1,850	7,500	8
Williamson,	1	....	175	800	2,000	3
Westchester Co.						
Eastchester,	2	28,000	18,000	....	125,000	150
Greenburgh,	1	40,000	5,000	....	30,000	70
North Salem,	1	900	300	4,000	10,000	8
Ossining,	2	7,000	15,700	4,700	6,000	143
Rye,	1	400	15	450	700	4
Wyoming Co.						
Attica,	2	50	25	650	1,250	3
Gainesville,	1	....	60	650	2,500	2
Warsaw,	1	....	10	160	2,535	2

PLASTER MILLS.

TOWNS.	Number of establishments.	Capital Invested. In real estate.	Capital Invested. In tools and machinery.	Cash Value. Of raw materials used.	Cash Value. Of manufactured articles.	Persons employed.
Albany Co.						
Albany,	1	2,000	1,000	2,000	4,000	5
Bethlehem,	1	2,500	100	....	1,750	2
Westerlo,	1	500	5	550	750	1
Broome Co.						
Chenango,	2	9,000	1,000	3,775	5,750	7
Cayuga Co.						
Aurelius,	1	200	....	....	1,000	2
Springport,	3	1,900	....	5,500	5,500	....
Chemung Co.						
Horseheads,	1	1,500	100	1,200	2,500	2
Veteran,	1	800	200	900	1,800	1
Chenango Co.						
Greene,	1	....	....	1,625	2,760	....
North Norwich,	1	....	....	1,484	2,800	....
Oxford,	1	1,000	10	2,500	3,500	2
Sherburne,	2	3,000	150	2,400	4,200	4
Clinton Co.						
Peru,	1	1,000	500	350	502	1
Columbia Co.						
Ghent,	1	....	600	595	1,050	....
Kinderhook,	1	....	200	1,000	1,400	2
Livingston,	2	....	....	875	1,437	2
New Lebanon,	1	1,000	500	600	....	....
Stuyvesant,	1	....	....	600	800	....
Dutchess Co.						
Clinton,	1	100	....	150	425	....
Fishkill,	1	100	....	350	650	....
Milan,	2	....	....	325	400	....
Pawling,	1	....	....	840	1,017	....
Poughkeepsie city,	2	....	....	2,200	4,200	....
Erie Co.						
Newstead,	1	6,000	4,000	562	1,350	....
Essex Co.						
Chesterfield,	1	1,500	400	1,500	2,300	2
Franklin Co.						
Moira,	1	....	....	1,296	2,268	3
Fulton Co.						
Mayfield,	1	1,000	....	1,775	2,500	3
Genesee Co.						
Byron,	1	2,000	....	....	1,050	1
Le Roy,	2	7,000	500	800	1,600	2
Oakfield,	2	6,000	1,000	1,800	9,000	4
Pembroke,	1	300	....	1,050	2,437	2
Stafford,	1	700	....	530	700	2
Greene Co.						
Coxsackie,	1	600	....	625	812	1
Greenville,	1	....	....	672	840	1
New Baltimore,	2	1,000	1,000	772	1,292	2
Herkimer Co.						
German Flats,	2	2,000	....	2,050	3,960	4
Herkimer,	2	4,400	550	4,086	6,100	1
Litchfield,	1	1,000	150	500	700	2
Little Falls,	1	4,500	150	2,100	3,780	4
Jefferson Co.						
Ellisburgh,	1	1,500	....	1,400	2,000	4
Kings Co.						
Brooklyn,	1	15,000	45,000	4,000	4,000	12
Madison Co.						
Lenox,	2	775	180	1,200	2,400	5
Stockbridge,	1	2,000	....	....	1,257	2
Sullivan,	1	....	....	400	800	1
Monroe Co.						
Chili,	1	3,000	50	....	1,800	2
Perrington,	1	1,500	50	1,850	2,550	2

CLASS XV.—(Continued.)

TOWNS.	Number of establishments.	Capital Invested. In real estate.	Capital Invested. In tools and machinery.	Cash Value. Of raw materials used.	Cash Value. Of manufactured articles.	Persons employed.
Monroe Co.						
Riga,	1	$3,000	$50	$500	$1,600	3
Wheatland,	3	12,000	325	10,800	16,200	10
Montgomery Co.						
Amsterdam,	1	600	200	687	1,125	1
Glen,	1	....	....	1,200	2,600	....
Minden,	2	4,000	2,000	1,860	5,120	1
Palatine,	1	200	700	508	....	1
New-York Co.						
New-York,	5	21,700	20,870	34,500	85,675	43
Niagara Co.						
Lockport,	1	5,000	500	4,702	8,000	3
Oneida Co.						
Boonville,	1	1,000	20	400	800	2
Marcy,	1	....	....	225	700	1
New Hartford,	1	1,000	450	1,000	1,750	2
Utica,	1	400	200	440	880	4
Vernon,	2	2,000	650	610	1,450	3
Onondaga Co.						
Camillus,	2	3,000	1,500	838	2,700	5
De Witt,	4	10,300	450	4,284	8,618	9
Lysander,	1	....	....	600	1,080	10
Manlius,	5	15,700	1,000	14,932	19,869	28
Onondaga,	1	1,500	....	600	2,000	....
Ontario Co.						
Manchester,	3	2,000	1,500	1,024	2,617	9
Phelps,	4	24,200	365	1,350	1,125	11
Orange Co.						
Deerpark,	1	1,000	....	1,100	1,700	2
Monroe,	1	....	....	600	800	....
Newburgh,	2	1,000	500	5,100	8,200	3
Orleans Co.						
Ridgeway,	1	1,000	2,000	1,634	2,911	3
Oswego Co.						
Oswego city,	1	20,000	5,000	45,000	75,000	20
Rensselaer Co.						
Hoosick,	1	900	100	7,500	10,000	1
Pittstown,	1	1,000	200	1,020	1,105	3
Schodack,	1	....	....	1,050	....	....
Troy,	2	6,000	1,000	9,000	10,375	1
St. Lawrence Co.						
Madrid,	1	....	....	500	1,500	....
Oswegatchie,	1	3,500	250	1,200	1,800	2
Potsdam,	1	1,000	....	770	1,260	1
Saratoga Co.						
Milton,	1	2,000	300	1,300	1,500	1
Moreau,	1	1,000	700	2,450	3,500	2
Saratoga,	1	1,000	1,000	2,500	5,200	1
Stillwater,	1	6,000	100	12,000	15,000	7
Schuyler Co.						
Dix,	1	....	....	675	1,200	....
Tyrone,	1	200	300	1,500	2,250	2
Seneca Co.						
Covert,	1	800	400	388	843	2
Waterloo,	1	1,500	250	900	1,950	1
Steuben Co.						
Addison,	1	....	....	250	....	3
Bath,	1	2,000	100	3,200	4,000	2
Erwin,	1	1,000	....	2,100	3,325	2
Tioga Co.						
Nichols,	1	....	....	500	1,000	2
Tioga,	1	2,000	300	....	500,000	6
Tompkins Co.						
Caroline,	1	....	25	600	800	2
Ithaca,	1	....	....	1,400	2,000	2
Lansing,	1	800	....	485	937	....
Newfield,	1	....	....	250	525	1
Ulster Co.						
Lloyd,	2	500	....	1,143	2,002	1
Marbletown,	1	1,000	1,000	800	1,400	3
Washington Co.						
Fort Edward,	1	2,500	700	4,000	4,000	1
Greenwich,	1	2,000	50	3,600	1,300	2
Salem,	1	2,000	500	4,200	4,900	2
Wayne Co.						
Lyons,	1	1,500	300	1,200	2,300	3
Westchester Co.						
Mount Pleasant,	2	....	....	380	630	....
North Salem,	1	....	....	1,250	375	....
Yates Co.						
Milo,	2	3,000	....	3,400	4,000	1
Starkey,	1	1,200	15	400	880	2
Torrey,	1	2,500	500	637	1,050	2
PORCELAIN MANUFACTORY.						
Kings Co.						
Brooklyn,	2	60,000	16,000	16,000	90,000	128

TOWNS.	Number of establishments.	Capital Invested. In real estate.	Capital Invested. In tools and machinery.	Cash Value. Of raw materials used.	Cash Value. Of manufactured articles.	Persons employed.
POTTERIES.						
Albany Co.						
Watervliet,	2	$4,500	$30	$6,550	$20,200	21
Broome Co.						
Chenango,	1	2,000	1,000	2,250	9,500	6
Cattaraugus Co.						
Olean,	1	700	100	200	2,164	6
Chenango Co.						
Sherburne,	1	1,500	130	390	2,500	3
Clinton Co.						
Champlain,	1	1,000	100	300	1,000	2
Cortland Co.						
Cortlandville,	1	300	800	1,800	6,000	6
Dutchess Co.						
Poughkeepsie city,	1	....	250	3,000	8,000	11
Erie Co.						
Buffalo,	1	2,000	100	....	500	1
Genesee Co.						
Stafford,	1	300	30	118	1,500	2
Greene Co.						
Athens,	1	6,000	500	2,500	10,000	15
Monroe Co.						
Rochester,	2	9,000	3,000	4,227	12,000	14
New-York Co.						
New-York,	2	60,000	18,500	21,100	71,100	80
Oneida Co.						
Utica,	1	8,000	2,000	11,250	26,000	26
Vienna,	1	650	400	184	1,200	3
Westmoreland,	1	425	25	300	2,500	2
Onondaga Co.						
Elbridge,	1	1,200	700	900	3,000	5
Geddes,	1	3,000	400	3,050	9,360	6
Van Buren,	1	1,000	100	600	3,000	9
Ontario Co.						
West Bloomfield,	2	2,000	475	....	2,200	4
Oswego Co.						
Volney,	1	3,000	100	1,450	5,000	4
Rensselaer Co.						
Lansingburgh,	1	700	100	500	2,500	2
Troy,	1	10,000	1,500	2,000	10,000	8
St. Lawrence Co.						
Oswegatchie,	1	3,500	1,000	1,200	70,000	6
Saratoga Co.						
Moreau,	1	260	....	75	300	1
Schuyler Co.						
Catherine,	1	4,300	700	1,835	11,500	7
Seneca Co.						
Fayette,	1	....	100	100	1,500	2
Suffolk Co.						
Huntington,	1	2,000	500	1,100	3,500	6
Tompkins Co.						
Ithaca,	1	1,800	500	1,637	7,000	6
Ulster Co.						
Wawarsing,	1	1,500	500	1,100	1,500	2
Yates Co.						
Milo,	1	1,000	600	90	5,000	4
ROOFING SLATE MANUFACTORY.						
Washington Co.						
Granville,	5	29,000	1,550	....	70,400	11
SOAP STONE MANUFACTORY.						
New-York Co.						
New-York,	3	4,000	2,100	2,500	17,500	115
STONE CUTTING ESTABLISHMENTS.						
Cayuga Co.						
Auburn,	1	500	100	....	4,000	8
Chenango Co.						
Sherburne,	1	500	25	....	400	1
Dutchess Co.						
Poughkeepsie,	1	....	100	5,000	7,500	11
Erie Co.						
Buffalo,	2	....	200	33,000	71,500	99
North Collins,	1	200	500	25	250	....
Kings Co.						
Brooklyn,	14	100,400	8,450	171,350	256,300	334
Monroe Co.						
Rochester,	1	10,000	900	....	8,000	20
New-York Co.						
New-York,	16	246,200	22,150	167,200	671,500	672
Oneida Co.						
Steuben,	1	....	140	....	1,400	3
Utica,	1	285	50	7,050	11,250	14
Whitestown,	1	200	500	2,800	6,000	10

CLASS XV.—(Continued.)

TOWNS.	Number of establishments.	Capital Invested. In real estate.	Capital Invested. In tools and machinery.	Cash Value. Of raw materials used.	Cash Value. Of manufactured articles.	Persons employed.
Onondaga Co.						
Camillus, ...	1	....	....	....	$600	....
Geddes, ...	1	$20,000	....	....	....	....
Onondaga, ...	3	4,500	$3,050	$4,500	20,500	46
Syracuse, ...	3	3,500	275	2,800	13,500	17
Ontario Co.						
Phelps, ...	1	1,200	25	....	2,000	6
Orange Co.						
Newburgh, ...	1	700	200	1,100	3,000	4
Walkill, ...	1	500	10	400	1,500	2
Rockland Co.						
Orange, ...	1	....	25	300	700	1
Saratoga Co.						
Stillwater, ...	1	....	....	....	....	....
Schenectady Co.						
Schenectady, ...	1	500	50	600	1,400	2
Suffolk Co.						
Southold, ...	1	....	....	1,000	2,000	2
Tioga Co.						
Owego, ...	1	1,400	50	2,500	5,000	3
Ulster Co.						
Saugerties, ...	2	100	2,400	3,740	75,000	150
Warren Co.						
Queensbury, ...	1	500	25	700	2,400	2
Wyoming Co.						
Attica, ...	1	100	....	50	250	1
STONE-CUTTERS' TOOL MANUFACTORY.						
Onondaga Co.						
Onondaga, ...	1	100	80	500	1,200	....
TILE MANUFACTORIES.						
Albany Co.						
Albany, ...	2	6,500	800	1,900	7,500	14
Genesee Co.						
Bethany, ...	1	400	200	93	960	3
Oneida Co.						
Kirkland, ...	1	1,200	300	213	1,400	3
Vernon, ...	1	100	300	....	660	1
Ontario Co.						
Seneca, ...	1	2,900	100	1,000	5,000	4
West Bloomfield, .	2	1,000	200	....	2,300	4
Seneca Co.						
Fayette, ...	2	$1,000	$1,000	$1,000	$5,500	9
Waterloo, ...	1	1,400	300	20	2,500	6
Wayne Co.						
Palmyra, ...	1	2,500	300	675	1,681	3
TOBACCO PIPE MANUFACTORY.						
Albany Co.						
Albany, ...	1	1,300	500	1,000	5,200	9
WATER-LIME MANUFACTORIES.						
Cayuga Co.						
Aurelius, ...	1	1,000	50	425	1,700	4
Erie Co.						
Amherst, ...	1	6,000	500	1,050	3,500	5
Newstead, ...	1	....	....	....	8,000	....
Madison Co.						
Sullivan, ...	1	1,200	300	1,500	3,000	....
Niagara Co.						
Lockport, ...	1	5,000	1,500	1,000	10,000	11
Onondaga Co.						
De Witt, ...	3	6,500	250	3,310	14,337	23
Manlius, ...	7	17,100	920	36,250	49,400	42
Onondaga, ...	1	2,500	4,900	3,925	9,375	18
Syracuse, ...	1	8,000	1,000	4,000	6,000	4
Ontario Co.						
Manchester, ...	1	1,000	150	225	2,000	2
Oswego Co.						
Volney, ...	1	6,500	1,500	9,500	18,180	4
St. Lawrence Co.						
Madrid, ...	1	....	....	500	1,500	....
Schenectady Co.						
Rotterdam, ...	1	9,000	16,000	3,700	8,200	12
Ulster Co.						
Kingston, ...	5	181,500	35,500	42,500	345,710	374
Marbletown, ...	2	45,500	5,300	....	42,500	67
Rosendale, ...	4	135,000	35,000	22,200	197,000	189
WINDOW PLATE MANUFACTORY.						
New-York Co.						
New-York, ...	1	....	2,500	2,000	6,000	4

CLASS XVI.—LEATHER, AND MANUFACTURES THEREFROM.

TOWNS.	Number of establishments.	Capital Invested. In real estate.	Capital Invested. In tools and machinery.	Cash Value. Of raw materials used.	Cash Value. Of manufactured articles.	Persons employed.
BARK MILLS.						
Saratoga Co.						
Greenfield, ...	1	2,500	200	1,000	3,000	1
Ulster Co.						
Wawarsing, ...	1	1,000	500	1,200	1,650	1
BOOT AND SHOE SHOPS.						
Albany Co.						
Albany, ...	9	1,800	2,690	13,986	28,898	47
Bern, ...	4	....	....	....	....	....
Knox, ...	2	100	40	150	375	2
Rensselaerville, ...	5	725	200	2,350	4,755	11
Watervliet, ...	5	3,150	320	14,130	18,600	64
Westerlo, ...	2	150	45	666	1,176	2
Allegany Co.						
Alfred, ...	4	500	150	1,180	2,760	7
Allen, ...	1	200	40	300	600	d
Almond, ...	1	4,000	1,500	24,200	40,000	40
Amity, ...	2	9,000	150	2,000	4,800	7
Andover, ...	2	150	40	....	....	6
Angelica, ...	2	....	....	1,600	4,000	6
Burns, ...	1	....	....	270	600	2
Cuba, ...	1	1,200	300	3,600	8,000	7
Hume, ...	4	600	195	3,215	8,600	13
Rushford, ...	2	950	100	1,975	6,500	9
Scio, ...	1	450	100	3,000	6,075	13
Wirt, ...	2	250	75	1,200	3,200	3
Broome Co.						
Chenango, ...	4	6,800	5,400	20,423	45,000	46
Colesville, ...	6	850	205	2,150	4,300	8
Sandford, ...	2	1,700	130	2,392	5,300	6
Union, ...	1	2,000	....	51	1,200	2
Windsor, ...	3	550	80	850	2,500	4
Cattaraugus Co.						
Allegany, ...	1	600	25	....	1,000	2
Ellicottville, ...	1	....	25	500	1,000	2
Franklinville, ...	2	1,000	100	6,600	13,200	8
Freedom, ...	1	150	25	250	500	1
Hinsdale, ...	1	1,000	....	1,000	2,000	2
New Albion, ...	1	....	100	350	700	....
Olean, ...	1	400	600	....	800	1
Otto, ...	2	....	130	1,867	2,700	5
Perrysburgh, ...	3	700	25	2,868	7,450	6
Portville, ...	2	200	50	443	1,285	2
Yorkshire, ...	1	800	60	300	600	1
Cayuga Co.						
Auburn, ...	6	....	1,750	44,640	18,200	88
Aurelius, ...	2	....	130	924	3,600	7
Brutus, ...	1	....	20	....	200	4
Cato, ...	2	250	200	1,983	4,500	6
Genoa, ...	2	275	55	550	1,150	2
Ira, ...	5	1,450	265	2,160	4,284	10
Ledyard, ...	1	....	100	680	1,860	....
Mentz, ...	6	400	200	1,400	4,700	22
Moravia, ...	4	1,750	130	3,130	6,600	....
Niles, ...	2	....	100	1,050	2,100	1
Owasco, ...	1	200	100	500	1,200	2
Sennett, ...	2	150	50	350	900	1
Summer Hill, ...	2	220	45	974	1,919	3
Chautauque Co.						
Chautauque, ...	3	575	120	720	3,000	5
Cherry Creek, ...	2	310	55	600	1,850	4
Clymer, ...	2	100	35	375	1,000	2
Ellicott, ...	6	900	430	7,400	11,800	23
Gerry, ...	1	300	75	1,200	2,500	3
Hanover, ...	4	1,200	140	4,500	11,600	13
Kiantone, ...	1	....	50	500	1,250	2
Pomfret, ...	9	2,275	555	7,583	24,150	42
Sheridan, ...	1	1,000	200	700	1,200	2
Sherman, ...	3	....	....	....	1,600	....
Stockton, ...	2	....	....	....	1,650	....
Villenovia, ...	2	250	80	700	1,400	4
Westfield, ...	1	600	100	1,400	3,000	5
Chemung Co.						
Chemung, ...	3	150	55	180	1,200	2

CLASS XVI.—(Continued.)

TOWNS.	Number of establishments.	Capital invested. In real estate.	Capital invested. In tools and machinery.	Cash value. Of raw materials used.	Cash value. Of manufactured articles.	Persons employed.
CHEMUNG Co.						
Elmira,	7	$19,400	$1,210	$27,720	$44,268	64
Horseheads,	2	....	125	1,500	3,100	7
Veteran,	3	400	200	2,900	7,550	7
CHENANGO Co.						
Bainbridge,	1	....	10	60	400	2
Columbus,	1	200	50	150	1,000	2
Coventry,	3	700	175	2,000	4,250	10
Greene,	3	93	40	1,340	2,000	3
New Berlin,	5	500	170	3,040	6,800	11
Otselic,	3	400	100	825	1,962	5
Oxford,	2	175	....	3,400	7,200	10
Pharsalia,	1	200	75	800	1,500	2
Pitcher,	2	125	50	750	1,300	2
Preston,	3	270	50	895	1,900	6
Sherburne,	4	1,000	145	3,800	8,700	11
Smyrna,	1	....	15	1,350	2,200	4
CLINTON Co.						
Ausable,	5	....	95	5,710	13,075	19
Beekmantown,	2	275	50	1,050	2,600	3
Peru,	2	120	40	1,700	5,280	2
Plattsburgh,	3	....	420	6,763	21,277	52
Saranac,	2	....	37	450	1,100	4
Schuyler's Falls,	1	....	20	947	1,475	4
COLUMBIA Co.						
Ancram,	2	....	....	....	....	3
Canaan,	4	300	150	1,000	2,500	5
Chatham,	3	2,400	200	2,300	4,700	7
Copake,	7	3,400	220	2,250	4,100	....
Hillsdale,	1	....	25	500	1,000	2
Hudson,	6	2,800	505	16,300	35,050	65
Kinderhook,	5	1,800	220	1,190	8,040	20
Livingston,	1	150	30	1,085	2,225	3
CORTLAND Co.						
Cincinnatus,	3	100	150	5,900	13,000	19
Cortlandville,	3	250	....	8,239	13,600	32
Freetown,	2	150	125	1,400	1,800	5
Harford,	2	200	115	600	1,600	3
Homer,	7	1,350	185	1,700	5,800	8
Preble,	1	200	50	600	1,500	2
Scott,	2	300	125	1,300	2,600	4
Solon,	1	200	50	150	400	1
Taylor,	1	25	30	850	1,475	2
Truxton,	1	400	100	1,000	2,500	4
Virgil,	2	350	55	1,745	3,116	4
Willett,	1	....	40	105	206	2
DELAWARE Co.						
Bovina,	4	200	75	2,102	3,630	8
Franklin,	5	1,425	220	1,470	4,500	7
Hamden,	3	275	125	1,250	2,500	5
Harpersfield,	3	190	65	940	997	6
Kortright,	3	300	90	800	903	....
Meredith,	2	460	75	2,030	4,175	8
Roxbury,	1	100	50	1,200	2,700	3
Sidney,	1	100	30	400	500	....
Stamford,	2	....	150	....	1,200	....
Walton,	2	4,600	1,075	4,575	22,400	4
DUTCHESS Co.						
Fishkill,	13	700	135	6,424	16,680	25
Hyde Park,	3	....	85	2,230	5,000	9
La Grange,	3	700	120	650	1,300	5
Pawling,	1	100	50	400	1,000	2
Poughkeepsie city,	8	10,000	270	10,900	28,150	64
Red Hook,	1	100	50	600	1,200	3
Rhinebeck,	3	1,400	75	2,800	6,956	10
Stanford,	3	450	130	1,300	2,300	5
ERIE Co.						
Amherst,	1	4,000	....	1,950	3,600	6
Aurora,	1	300	40	1,400	3,000	4
Boston,	3	350	75	1,166	2,480	5
Buffalo,	8	2,700	2,410	24,370	54,700	92
Collins,	2	150	90	1,300	2,800	2
East Hamburgh,	1	350	75	1,800	4,200	6
Evans,	2	300	70	1,384	2,984	5
Hamburgh,	2	650	65	1,652	3,900	9
Lancaster,	1	100	70	1,200	1,700	2
Newstead,	3	700	100	1,150	4,100	6
North Collins,	1	30	10	300	600	....
Tonawanda,	6	1,500	....	3,092	11,108	14
ESSEX Co.						
Chesterfield,	1	....	....	1,000	15,000	26
Crown Point,	1	....	....	700	1,500	3
Elizabethtown,	1	300	150	600	2,000	3
Essex,	1	....	....	....	3,000	5
Schroon,	1	100	50	600	1,200	2
Ticonderoga,	2	....	100	2,060	4,720	6
Willsborough,	1	....	75	650	2,125	4
FRANKLIN Co.						
Bangor,	1	....	....	380	1,300	2
Fort Covington,	2	2,000	75	4,845	7,800	6
FRANKLIN Co.						
Malone,	3	....	$255	$3,450	$8,700	16
Westville,	1	$200	20	800	1,157	1
FULTON Co.						
Ephratah,	2	....	....	3,100	6,000	9
Johnstown,	2	1,400	250	5,055	14,357	15
Oppenheim,	1	....	6	100	150	....
Perth,	2	....	15	5	750	1
GENESEE Co.						
Alabama,	2	350	47	1,200	2,400	4
Alexander,	3	550	100	2,465	5,050	7
Batavia,	7	8,500	690	11,560	26,500	42
Bergen,	3	....	....	....	....	....
Bethany,	1	150	50	500	1,000	1
Byron,	3	400	170	2,100	4,400	7
Darien,	2	250	20	200	1,650	3
Elba,	2	400	125	2,150	4,700	6
Le Roy,	4	1,502	250	4,000	9,600	16
Oakfield,	2	850	90	1,700	3,400	7
Pavilion,	5	....	160	850	4,900	11
Stafford,	2	550	85	2,080	4,450	8
GREENE Co.						
Athens,	1	600	50	400	....	2
Coxsackie,	1	....	40	700	2,000	3
Catskill,	2	500	60	1,700	4,400	8
Greenville,	2	500	100	1,950	2,550	6
HERKIMER Co.						
Fairfield,	1	300	30	600	2,000	3
Frankfort,	1	200	40	475	3,000	2
German Flats,	1	2,600	190	5,400	7,600	15
Herkimer,	1	1,400	20	600	2,000	3
Little Falls,	9	8,900	1,120	26,838	55,172	62
Manheim,	5	....	300	946	3,455	5
Newport,	4	1,300	180	2,556	5,263	2
Russia,	1	....	....	....	1,800	2
Salisbury,	4	500	125	1,743	4,404	9
Stark,	3	525	80	725	2,250	5
Winfield,	4	400	375	1,900	2,700	5
JEFFERSON Co.						
Adams,	7	4,975	360	7,808	17,676	24
Antwerp,	6	1,775	255	5,067	12,500	21
Cape Vincent,	2	400	100	1,900	4,600	4
Ellisburgh,	4	1,450	90	2,760	5,400	9
Henderson,	1	....	50	500	1,200	2
Le Ray,	4	825	230	2,950	7,100	19
Orleans,	4	525	90	1,797	3,000	7
Pamelia,	2	250	75	700	2,600	2
Philadelphia,	3	450	95	1,150	2,300	5
Rodman,	1	....	....	500	4,000	8
Rutland,	1	....	....	600	1,350	2
Watertown,	3	3,000	286	13,010	33,970	80
Wilna,	4	....	225	7,800	18,600	15
KINGS Co.						
Brooklyn,	10	12,620	1,305	10,572	46,920	104
LEWIS Co.						
Denmark,	1	....	....	600	1,500	2
Lowville,	3	50	200	1,130	2,930	9
Martinsburgh,	1	....	35	600	....	2
New Bremen,	2	....	15	200	600	1
West Turin,	2	500	140	3,300	4,650	11
LIVINGSTON Co.						
Avon,	1	500	100	50	2,000	3
Caledonia,	1	400	40	2,000	5,000	6
Conesus,	1	100	....	2,000	4,000	2
Groveland,	2	220	50	410	1.200	4
Leicester,	1	570	75	832	2,500	3
Lima,	2	400	20	20	....	....
Livonia,	4	11,000	190	4,250	7,900	13
Mount Morris,	1	700	200	3,662	7,312	....
Nunda,	3	1,600	175	5,628	8,256	14
North Dansville,	8	200	265	17,860	39,963	45
West Sparta,	2	100	75	954	1,620	2
York,	4	850	100	2,763	6,350	12
MADISON Co.						
Brookfield,	2	275	60	900	1,100	3
Cazenovia,	6	4,900	330	8,165	17,800	36
De Ruyter,	2	600	150	1,800	4,000	5
Eaton,	1	400	30	....	2,825	4
Fenner,	1	50	50	1,200	3,000	3
Hamilton,	2	....	70	2,730	7,500	12
Lebanon,	1	50	30	600	1,600	3
Lenox,	9	1,900	600	9,441	15,400	35
Nelson,	2	110	40	171	1,230	2
Smithfield,	1	....	....	....	2,100	....
Stockbridge,	2	200	35	1,960	4,000	2
Sullivan,	1	700	75	1,800	3,600	5
MONROE Co.						
Chili,	2	1,800	55	65	4,000	3
Mendon,	4	840	185	3,100	7,650	11
Ogden,	2	2,375	275	....	8,500	....

CLASS XVI.—(Continued.)

TOWNS.	Number of establishments.	Capital Invested. In real estate.	Capital Invested. In tools and machinery.	Cash Value. Of raw materials used.	Cash Value. Of manufactured articles.	Persons employed.
Monroe Co.						
Parma,	2	$250	$90	$1,005	$1,890	3
Perrington,	3	900	55	3,058	6,625	8
Pittsford,	1	1,200	50	1,000	5,000	4
Riga,	1	....	....	1,989	3,417	5
Rochester,	7	1,210	2,160	138,373	207,476	402
Rush,	3	200	150	2,500	4,100	3
Sweden,	4	2,500	525	6,200	16,850	27
Union,	1	500	50	1,000	3,000	2
Webster,	4	500	61	322	815	5
Montgomery Co.						
Amsterdam,	1	3,500	100	2,500	5,750	10
Charleston,	1	700	25	500	1,200	4
Florida,	4	600	135	1,476	3,425	7
Glen,	3	1,100	155	2,000	4,400	10
Mohawk,	3	950	60	1,140	2,700	8
Root,	7	700	145	2,155	6,300	10
St. Johnsville,	1	....	25	600	900	3
New-York Co.						
New-York,	71	312,300	32,865	588,809	1,839,100	2891
Niagara Co.						
Hartland,	2	650	60	1,320	3,000	5
Lewiston,	2	2,900	150	2,600	5,500	9
Lockport,	10	3,500	240	23,700	53,600	75
Newfane,	4	450	150	1,630	3,270	6
Porter,	3	600	....	....	....	9
Willson,	3	550	130	3,941	6,900	7
Oneida Co.						
Ava,	1	50	50	500	1,000	2
Boonville,	4	1,900	100	4,540	14,300	24
Bridgewater,	2	250	100	1,500	3,000	5
Camden,	2	1,800	....	2,900	5,800	13
Deerfield,	1	50	10	200	350	2
Kirkland,	3	2,800	200	4,909	10,650	12
Lee,	2	600	175	1,600	4,200	6
New Hartford,	3	....	25	170	375	7
Paris,	5	500	155	1,100	2,700	5
Remsen,	1	600	25	2,000	5,000	7
Rome,	6	14,400	1,850	12,191	27,334	35
Sangerfield,	2	1,650	150	2,300	26,000	30
Trenton,	2	1,500	150	2,095	4,350	8
Utica,	18	10,200	980	45,122	92,552	221
Vernon,	2	1,000	100	800	1,950	12
Verona,	7	2,300	330	2,100	8,475	13
Western,	3	500	100	1,975	4,200	6
Westmoreland,	2	....	....	1,225	7,150	11
Whitestown,	6	1,850	3,600	2,180	10,960	20
Onondaga Co.						
Camillus,	2	....	50	700	1,600	1
Cicero,	3	1,350	150	1,910	4,370	7
Clay,	4	150	115	1,700	4,475	5
De Witt,	5	1,400	162	3,625	8,300	11
Elbridge,	1	....	50	500	5,000	3
Fabius,	3	750	55	1,950	4,900	11
Geddes,	2	400	95	2,000	3,800	8
Lafayette,	2	75	35	....	1,450	3
Lysander,	8	1,170	192	5,677	12,228	21
Manlius,	7	3,600	300	10,400	19,325	31
Marcellus,	3	1,550	110	2,535	5,200	6
Onondaga,	1	....	25	200	400	....
Otisco,	2	400	80	650	3,000	4
Pomfrey,	1	100	50	200	500	2
Skaneateles,	2	2,200	100	3,440	7,456	13
Spafford,	1	50	25	200	625	2
Syracuse,	7	2,000	1,655	51,000	148,200	232
Tully,	1	....	30	800	1,850	4
Ontario Co.						
Bristol,	6	430	165	2,465	4,560	7
Canadice,	1	....	40	400	1,000	....
Canandaigua,	4	6,000	260	6,000	6,400	11
East Bloomfield,	5	1,000	675	2,915	9,075	9
Farmington,	3	850	115	85	2,350	3
Gorham,	1	350	20	400	1,118	2
Naples,	2	1,000	50	1,700	3,400	6
Phelps,	2	50	50	1,400	2,800	3
Richmond,	2	1,000	140	300	5,000	8
Seneca,	1	10,000	150	10,000	25,000	26
Victor,	1	500	....	4,000	....	13
West Bloomfield,	1	....	100	2,057	2,500	6
Orange Co.						
Blooming Grove,	2	500	100	1,800	4,000	13
Chester,	2	....	35	455	1,200	3
Cornwall,	2	1,000	125	2,500	4,000	13
Goshen,	2	1,600	475	2,140	5,000	13
Minisink,	3	225	95	1,475	2,220	5
Monroe,	1	....	....	600	1,000	1
Montgomery,	1	50	25	400	1,000	2
Newburgh,	1	....	1,500	50	....	1
New Windsor,	2	....	100	800	1,600	2
Walkill,	2	1,900	140	2,790	5,400	14
Orange Co.						
Warwick,	2	$2,000	$25	$600	$3,700	5
Orleans Co.						
Barre,	4	4,000	400	7,065	13,800	23
Carlton,	6	750	215	2,050	4,110	3
Gaines,	5	900	375	2,650	5,850	7
Murray,	3	1,200	150	2,194	6,240	11
Ridgeway,	7	2,650	470	6,227	13,301	15
Shelby,	1	1,000	100	1,500	3,250	4
Oswego Co.						
Albion,	1	800	50	800	1,275	2
Hannibal,	3	850	230	2,400	5,300	11
Mexico,	5	160	116	1,705	3,650	8
New Haven,	1	....	25	500	1,000	....
Orwell,	1	....	20	200	600	1
Oswego,	1	....	50	350	1,000	2
Oswego city,	9	32,500	950	37,400	77,150	90
Parish,	1	....	....	....	4,000	6
Richland,	2	125	20	2,500	5,600	8
Schroeppel,	1	600	15	500	1,600	2
Volney,	2	....	....	2,500	6,000	10
Willliamstown,	2	600	3,500	800	1,600	5
Otsego Co.						
Burlington,	3	100	110	1,765	3,730	10
Butternuts,	1	250	100	775	2,500	3
Cherry Valley,	1	600	75	950	2,000	5
Decatur,	3	700	47	340	605	3
Edmeston,	2	250	100	850	1,600	2
Exeter,	3	100	140	1,000	2,800	4
Maryland,	8	530	455	1,615	10,150	11
Middlefield,	1	500	50	1,500	3,000	4
Milford,	4	337	68	1,404	2,400	6
Morris,	2	1,700	300	2,500	5,600	13
New Lisbon,	3	90	....	900	2,150	....
Oneonta,	1	50	40	1,200	2,400	7
Otego,	5	810	155	1,295	3,244	7
Otsego,	5	3,900	380	12,422	14,680	51
Plainfield,	1	100	25	600	2,000	3
Richfield,	2	600	40	1,450	3,000	5
Roseboom,	4	300	110	....	3,100	4
Springfield,	2	900	180	2,200	5,100	9
Westford,	1	....	....	300	600	2
Worcester,	2	100	80	1,200	2,300	4
Putnam Co.						
Carmel,	4	3,400	550	6,500	15,000	13
Southeast,	8	3,050	315	13,213	28,131	51
Queens Co.						
Flushing,	5	500	835	3,000	6,700	13
Hempstead,	1	1,000	200	2,500	4,000	8
Jamaica,	1	500	....	500	1,500	3
North Hempstead,	1	1,500	180	1,700	3,625	10
Rensselaer Co.						
Berlin,	2	275	65	750	1,750	4
Brunswick,	1	150	150	25	1,000	2
Hoosick,	2	150	250	1,659	4,625	7
Lansingburgh,	4	....	100	2,650	7,550	15
Sandlake,	4	....	....	2,650	5,550	7
Troy,	12	52,700	5,800	178,921	250,798	355
Richmond Co.						
Northfield,	1	400	75	400	1,000	3
Westfield,	4	100	75	2,040	3,600	1
Rockland Co.						
Clarkstown,	1	1,500	100	1,000	6,582	12
Haverstraw,	1	....	1,500	5,000	....	2
Orangetown,	3	1,500	1,500	52,000	105,300	233
St. Lawrence Co.						
Canton,	3	3,000	575	19,000	40,000	38
Fowler,	1	300	50	1,500	2,500	4
Gouverneur,	1	700	....	5,900	13,000	17
Hammond,	2	200	145	700	1,550	2
Hermon,	1	250	50	1,000	2,500	2
Louisville,	3	500	125	1,700	3,000	7
Madrid,	4	2,240	375	6,400	10,554	25
Massena,	1	50	10	200	700	2
Morristown,	1	400	50	521	1,225	2
Oswegatchie,	5	19,000	600	24,700	70,400	61
Parishville,	1	400	50	990	3,406	4
Pitcairn,	2	50	25	280	550	1
Potsdam,	6	2,200	465	10,960	22,850	22
Rossie,	5	1,250	195	3,001	8,496	8
Stockholm,	1	300	20	300	700	1
Saratoga Co.						
Ballston,	2	125	130	622	1,728	2
Clifton Park,	1	275	60	600	1,200	3
Edinburgh,	1	....	30	185	370	....
Halfmoon,	1	200	50	800	1,700	2
Malta,	4	225	120	918	1,994	....
Milton,	3	2,050	140	2,460	4,800	9
Moreau,	1	....	25	175	358	....
Providence,	1	500	200	1,000	4,000	7

CLASS XVI.—(CONTINUED.)

TOWNS.	Number of establishments.	Capital Invested. In real estate.	Capital Invested. In tools and machinery.	Cash Value. Of raw materials used.	Cash Value. Of manufactured articles.	Persons employed.
SARATOGA Co.						
Saratoga,	2	....	$75	$1,700	$2,624	6
Saratoga Springs,	5	$3,100	480	9,668	20,600	36
Stillwater,	8	....	....	1,950	4,375	11
SCHENECTADY Co.						
Duanesburgh,	3	2,500	570	16,725	28,550	34
Glenville,	2	600	150	4,850	4,750	6
Schenectady,	4	....	220	17,340	31,500	80
SCHOHARIE Co.						
Blenheim,	1	....	50	250	1,400	2
Carlisle,	2	200	100	700	1,600	3
Conesville,	2	200	33	345	693	2
Esperance,	1	1,000	50	330	800	1
Fulton,	4	175	140	900	1,600	4
Richmondville,	1	200	80	420	730	2
Schoharie,	2	350	25	1,800	3,600	8
Seward,	1	600	45	15	400	1
Sharon,	5	400	190	800	2,600	8
Summit,	2	300	110	520	1,000	1
SCHUYLER Co.						
Catharines,	2	1,500	50	1,850	4,700	6
Cayuta,	1	150	30	500	1,500	2
Dix,	1	400	15	400	900	2
Hector,	7	775	230	3,170	7,550	11
Orange,	1	154	75	3,219	6,830	6
Tyrone,	4	1,183	175	2,812	6,700	8
SENECA Co.						
Covert,	1	250	50	600	1,200	5
Fayette,	3	480	125	1,800	4,500	6
Ovid,	2	2,500	150	2,049	4,775	9
Varick,	2	600	150	3,000	5,050	4
Waterloo,	5	4,800	675	8,128	10,953	13
STEUBEN Co.						
Avoca,	1	300	30	300	1,000	2
Bath,	3	2,000	190	4,355	7,400	10
Bradford,	4	630	190	2,900	5,700	9
Canisteo,	1	250	50	1,592	3,000	5
Corning,	4	4,300	250	16,340	12,400	15
Dansville,	3	600	140	1,575	3,500	6
Erwin,	3	280	....	3,900	8,500	11
Fremont,	1	250	30	600	1,000	3
Hornellsville,	4	2,700	225	5,300	13,450	18
Howard,	1	100	75	500	1,500	....
Jasper,	1	....	10	....	200	....
Pultney,	1	75	50	250	1,200	2
Troupsburgh,	1	....	20	....	....	....
SUFFOLK Co.						
Huntington,	6	2,870	627	14,680	22,150	30
Islip,	2	160	30	200	2,500	....
Riverhead,	2	....	50	1,390	2,830	5
Southampton,	6	200	275	6,250	16,800	45
Southold,	2	1,000	......	3,050	6,100	11
SULLIVAN Co.						
Bethel,	1	150	10	250	600	1
Fallsburgh,	2	165	90	800	1,600	1
Highland,	1	....	150	500	900	2
Liberty,	1	....	25	250	550	....
Mamakating,	4	205	65	955	2,500	7
Rockland,	1	100	100	1,000	2,000	2
TIOGA Co.						
Barton,	12	450	325	2,500	4,000	24
Nichols,	1	1,000	100	....	....	....
Owego,	4	5,300	730	18,049	35,331	37
TOMPKINS Co.						
Caroline,	4	400	205	1,512	4,560	8
Danby,	1	....	30	700	1,000	5
Dryden,	8	2,000	315	4,775	11,141	22
Enfield,	1	....	25	300	600	1
Groton,	3	850	....	....	....	....
Ithaca,	9	11,900	1,250	14,180	31,200	39
Lansing,	4	445	80	2,675	5,100	5
Newfield,	2	250	40	860	2,327	4
Ulysses,	2	1,000	110	2,750	5,200	8
ULSTER Co.						
Marlborough,	2	....	50	....	1,000	3
New Paltz,	2	100	75	700	2,000	1
Plattekill,	1	....	50	550	1,000	2
Saugerties,	2	1,000	70	4,000	12,500	26
Wawarsing,	1	....	100	1,360	1,037	5
Woodstock,	1	150	16	1,000	1,050	2
WARREN Co.						
Chester,	1	500	50	1,025	2,500	4
Johnsburgh,	2	....	30	1,960	2,700	4
Queensbury,	1	5,000	50	3,659	10,000	10
Warrensburgh,	3	1,100	50	2,500	3,600	6
WASHINGTON Co.						
Argyle,	4	2,350	200	2,506	5,400	9
Easton,	4	300	190	1,243	2,560	5
Fort Ann,	1	....	30	2,000	5,400	5
Granville,	2	600	90	1,900	4,500	6
WASHINGTON Co.						
Greenwich,	2	$3,800	$1,125	$31,996	$66,500	82
Hartford,	5	550	325	3,643	6,300	6
Hebron,	1	200	60	....	....	1
Kingsbury,	3	725	150	2,600	5,000	11
Salem,	1	3,000	100	3,160	4,000	7
White Creek,	1	1,000	150	2,500	6,000	12
WAYNE Co.						
Arcadia,	5	3,250	400	6,015	15,242	18
Galen,	1	100	85	300	700	2
Lyons,	4	4,575	375	9,484	22,000	40
Marion,	1	600	300	2,000	6,000	15
Ontario,	2	275	80	800	1,810	5
Palmyra,	4	....	665	12,850	18,700	59
Sodus,	4	700	120	3,950	8,100	14
Williamson,	1	400	35	600	1,200	3
WESTCHESTER Co.						
Bedford,	6	1,700	480	9,685	15,023	40
Eastchester,	3	100	....	1,350	4,900	19
Greenburgh,	2	1,550	65	2,500	4,200	8
Harrison,	1	....	....	400	1,200	2
Lewisboro,	5	1,850	550	22,630	62,440	366
Mount Pleasant,	10	1,125	250	22,008	47,720	176
New Castle,	1	....	1,800	800	8,000	40
North Castle,	14	4,250	....	105,839	206,480	406
Ossining,	3	2,200	200	6,500	14,500	48
Rye,	2	4,000	300	2,120	7,040	18
Somers,	1	....	....	250	1,000	1
White Plains,	2	3,700	200	100	3,000	40
Yorktown,	2	125	40	550	1,100	3
WYOMING Co.						
Attica,	2	1,100	250	2,100	4,800	7
Bennington,	3	600	118	1,400	3,550	6
Castile,	2	2,400	95	3,200	7,000	9
China,	3	1,100	110	1,500	3,900	8
Covington,	2	620	70	100	1,900	3
Eagle,	1	....	....	....	1,000	4
Gainesville,	2	....	100	1,400	2,900	5
Genesee Falls,	2	400	80	1,800	4,000	5
Java,	1	100	51	800	2,000	2
Middlebury,	2	700	110	510	2,500	4
Orangeville,	5	140	155	1,300	2,400	6
Perry,	1	2,400	350	6,100	18,100	22
Pike,	5	1,000	375	7,100	13,500	13
Warsaw,	2	....	175	2,545	7,380	15
Wethersfield,	1	75	50	662	1,479	2
YATES Co.						
Benton,	3	....	375	1,570	3,500	5
Jerusalem,	2	800	150	3,100	7,200	13
Milo,	4	100	80	6,929	5,500	18
Potter,	3	....	....	3,900	10,869	19
Starkey,	2	600	110	1,553	3,200	11
Torrey,	1	200	150	500	1,500	3

HAME-TURNING SHOPS.

TOWNS.	Number of establishments.	Capital Invested. In real estate.	Capital Invested. In tools and machinery.	Cash Value. Of raw materials used.	Cash Value. Of manufactured articles.	Persons employed.
ALBANY Co.						
Albany,	1	....	5,000	2,500	3,000	3
CATTARAUGUS Co.						
Perrysburgh,	1	500	250	300	1,200	3
CHENANGO Co.						
Pitcher,	2	220	130	599	1,804	4
LIVINGSTON Co.						
York,	1	700	300	4,820	12,500	14
WESTCHESTER Co.						
Hartford,	1	100	75	150	450	....

HARNESS, SADDLE AND TRUNK MANUFACTORIES.

TOWNS.	Number of establishments.	Capital Invested. In real estate.	Capital Invested. In tools and machinery.	Cash Value. Of raw materials used.	Cash Value. Of manufactured articles.	Persons employed.
ALBANY Co.						
Albany,	3	....	1,900	3,964	61,000	59
Rensselaerville,	2	500	50	2,600	3,700	5
Watervliet,	1	1,000	30	1,000	2,500	2
Westerlo,	1	1,000	125	1,000	1,800	1
ALLEGANY Co.						
Alfred,	1	200	75	600	1,100	2
Allen,	1	50	50	200	750	2
Amity,	1	400	50	500	1,200	2
Andover,	1	500	25	....	....	2
Angelica,	1	....	....	600	1,500	2
Belfast,	1	800	500	1,000	2,000	3
Cuba,	1	800	25	1,500	2,500	2
Friendship,	1	100	75	250	3,000	3
Hume,	1	300	75	2,000	8,000	6
Rushford,	2	600	75	3,100	6,500	6
Willing,	1	....	....	1,000	2,000	3
Wirt,	1	150	50	400	1,500	2
BROOME Co.						
Chenango,	2	2,500	210	2,385	4,050	7
Colesville,	2	230	40	800	2,000	4

CLASS XVI.—(Continued.)

TOWNS.	Number of establishments.	Capital invested. In real estate.	Capital invested. In tools and machinery.	Cash value. Of raw materials used.	Cash value. Of manufactured articles.	Persons employed.
Broome Co.						
Sandford,	1	$1,000	$75	$1,800	$3,500	4
Windsor,	1	200	30	200	350	1
Cattaraugus Co.						
Ashford,	1	25	....	200	300	1
Franklinville,	1	350	20	2,000	1,500	2
Freedom,	1	75	....	600	1,000	2
Mansfield,	1	100	10	200	1,200	....
Olean,	1	1,000	20	55	1,000	2
Otto,	1	400	25	1,100	2,000	2
Perrysburgh,	2	300	70	725	1,493	1
Portville,	1	100	10	200	400	1
Randolph,	1	700	100	....	1,300	6
Cayuga Co.						
Auburn,	1	2,500	100	1,700	6,000	....
Aurelius,	1	200	100	400	1,500	3
Genoa,	3	250	50	1,950	4,050	4
Ira,	2	600	80	1,338	2,500	4
Mentz,	1	....	....	....	....	....
Moravia,	2	900	150	2,500	3,500	5
Niles,	1	200	75	1,000	2,200	2
Sterling,	2	1,200	125	1,150	2,300	1
Chautauque Co.						
Chautauque,	2	150	30	400	2,700	3
Ellicott,	3	1,900	127	4,570	8,825	7
Hanover,	1	....	18	250	550	2
Pomfret,	3	1,400	240	2,658	4,395	7
Stockton,	1	100	....	....	589	....
Westfield,	1	2,500	150	3,500	8,000	5
Chemung Co.						
Elmira,	2	7,000	700	4,469	7,350	12
Horseheads,	1	8,000	50	2,500	4,000	4
Chenango Co.						
Coventry,	1	....	50	500	1,200	2
Guilford,	1	300	10	400	1,000	2
New Berlin,	2	1,000	75	600	1,250	2
Otselic,	1	250	25	600	1,200	2
Oxford,	2	600	10	2,700	5,500	6
Plymouth,	1	100	25	300	500	....
Sherburne,	1	400	100	700	1,500	2
Smyrna,	1	....	15	675	1,200	1
Clinton Co.						
Ausable,	1	800	100	2,000	5,000	4
Black Brook,	1	....	50	400	1,000	1
Peru,	2	600	45	990	2,400	2
Plattsburgh,	2	1,000	100	4,960	4,354	6
Saranac,	2	250	90	1,500	3,200	6
Schuyler's Falls,	1	200	50	506	1,500	2
Columbia Co.						
Chatham,	1	2,000	25	250	700	1
Hudson,	3	5,000	545	3,400	8,700	7
Kinderhook,	1	2,300	400	860	8,000	6
Livingston,	1	....	10	200	481	2
Cortland Co.						
Cincinnatus,	2	150	115	2,225	2,700	....
Cortlandville,	3	1,000	246	3,800	6,200	7
Homer,	1	200	50	3,000	....	3
Preble,	1	250	25	500	1,000	1
Truxton,	1	150	40	300	600	1
Delaware Co.						
Bovina,	2	....	40	405	605	3
Delhi,	2	1,100	150	1,900	3,900	4
Franklin,	3	1,200	95	1,150	3,600	5
Kortright,	1	200	20	600	880	1
Stamford,	1	....	150	....	1,400	1
Walton,	1	300	25	600	1,600	....
Dutchess Co.						
Hyde Park,	1	200	35	1,725	1,407	1
Poughkeepsie city,	3	6,500	175	10,700	28,500	25
Red Hook,	3	850	125	4,300	8,100	8
Rhinebeck,	1	....	50	600	2,000	4
Stanford,	1	200	75	500	1,000	1
Erie Co.						
Alden,	1	60	50	800	1,200	....
Aurora,	1	350	50	900	1,200	2
Boston,	2	300	75	1,350	2,450	4
Buffalo,	6	16,700	1,090	11,925	19,136	25
Collins,	1	300	50	475	784	1
Eden,	1	100	50	150	375	1
Lancaster,	1	350	40	250	600	2
Tonawanda,	1	600	30	1,800	2,200	1
Essex Co						
Crown Point,	1	500	75	600	1,400	2
Moriah,	2	500	90	1,950	4,200	6
Schroon,	1	80	60	150	800	1
Franklin Co.						
Fort Covington,	1	....	50	375	1,000	1
Malone,	2	1,800	150	2,629	7,322	6
Fulton Co.						
Broadalbin,	1	450	100	600	1,200	2
Fulton Co.						
Ephratah,	1	....	....	$700	$1,075	1
Johnstown,	3	$200	$180	2,900	5,696	7
Genesee Co.						
Alabama,	2	240	55	1,000	2,300	3
Alexander,	2	....	45	440	1,090	2
Batavia,	2	9,000	800	4,000	10,500	10
Byron,	1	....	25	600	1,200	2
Elba,	1	500	50	600	1,000	1
Le Roy,	2	75	100	2,100	5,000	5
Oakfield,	1	600	100	1,200	2,500	3
Pavilion,	2	700	75	375	2,500	3
Stafford,	2	400	100	1,372	2,230	4
Greene Co.						
Coxsackie,	1	....	25	1,400	2,000	2
New Baltimore,	1	200	25	120	500	2
Windham,	1	275	60	361	1,250	2
Herkimer Co.						
Frankfort,	1	500	50	200	1,000	1
German Flats,	2	1,050	30	760	1,750	3
Little Falls,	2	900	350	1,600	3,700	4
Newport,	1	600	100	1,500	3,306	3
Salisbury,	2	400	80	1,200	2,050	3
Stark,	1	200	30	600	1,450	2
Warren,	1	250	50	800	2,000	3
Jefferson Co.						
Adams,	1	900	20	1,000	2,000	....
Antwerp,	2	100	75	1,850	4,360	5
Ellisburgh,	4	2,000	195	8,500	17,100	12
Hounsfield,	1	....	30	900	1,800	2
Le Ray,	1	300	50	600	1,500	2
Orleans,	1	50	20	600	1,200	2
Pamelia,	1	100	15	175	1,000	2
Philadelphia,	1	....	25	500	1,200	2
Rutland,	1	....	....	420	1,000	1
Watertown,	2	3,000	300	11,596	15,520	13
Wilna,	2	....	50	675	1,390	4
Kings Co.						
Brooklyn,	5	2,000	640	4,300	9,300	18
Lewis Co.						
Denmark,	1	600	....	600	1,200	2
Lowville,	4	....	135	2,465	6,413	9
Turin,	1	400	....	1,000	2,000	3
Livingston Co.						
Avon,	1	....	50	725	1,500	3
Caledonia,	2	400	100	1,440	2,375	3
Conesus,	1	50	25	200	500	....
Groveland,	1	150	20	275	600	1
Livonia,	1	....	50	829	2,051	3
Mount Morris,	1	600	100	1,200	2,500	3
Nunda,	1	500	150	1,975	3,760	4
North Dansville,	1	1,000	40	1,500	4,000	7
York,	2	200	60	1,050	2,900	3
Madison Co.						
Brookfield,	1	600	50	700	1,776	4
Cazenovia,	4	2,550	350	3,425	7,450	8
De Ruyter,	2	400	120	1,700	2,500	3
Eaton,	1	700	25	800	1,000	2
Hamilton,	2	2,100	80	1,250	2,800	4
Lenox,	3	400	50	1,063	2,360	5
Nelson,	1	150	20	387	825	1
Stockbridge,	1	450	30	500	1,100	2
Sullivan,	1	200	15	570	1,000	2
Monroe Co.						
Chili,	2	725	125	1,525	3,700	3
Henrietta,	1	....	....	200	400	....
Mendon,	2	650	110	1,700	3,500	6
Parma,	3	350	70	900	1,700	4
Penfield,	1	225	225	....	400	....
Perrington,	1	400	75	325	1,650	2
Pittsford,	3	500	200	1,851	4,200	4
Riga,	2	100	40	1,700	2,478	3
Rochester,	4	1,446	250	6,550	25,750	15
Rush,	1	75	25	500	1,000	2
Sweden,	2	1,500	110	4,880	10,200	10
Webster,	2	300	50	1,800	4,900	6
Wheatland,	3	300	165	1,945	2,050	7
Montgomery Co.						
Amsterdam,	2	2,000	200	2,800	6,000	4
Charleston,	1	....	25	300	600	1
Florida,	1	600	50	1,000	2,000	2
Minden,	2	2,500	225	7,200	12,075	9
Mohawk,	1	500	77	950	1,775	2
Root,	2	300	75	775	1,450	1
New-York Co.						
New-York,	32	141,500	20,065	276,147	379,700	293
Niagara Co.						
Lockport,	5	1,800	85	11,300	21,800	24
Newfane,	1	200	50	600	1,000	1
Porter,	2	400	225	2,600	3,500	5

CLASS XVI.—(Continued.)

TOWNS.	Number of establishments.	Capital invested. In real estate.	Capital invested. In tools and machinery.	Cash value. Of raw materials used.	Cash value. Of manufactured articles.	Persons employed.
Niagara Co.						
Royalton,	1	$200	$20	$633	$1,266	3
Wilson,	1	....	100	637	1,400	3
Oneida Co.						
Boonville,	2	600	100	1,700	4,450	5
Camden,	2	....	....	1,400	2,800	3
Kirkland,	2	....	275	1,270	2,550	4
Lee,	1	300	50	300	504	....
Paris,	2	....	550	800	950	3
Remsen,	1	....	10	300	400	1
Rome,	2	8,000	160	5,767	9,100	11
Trenton,	2	100	40	1,393	2,750	2
Utica,	6	700	700	9,870	19,250	28
Vernon,	2	600	150	2,000	4,200	3
Verona,	2	1,200	100	2,700	5,800	6
Western,	1	....	150	550	1,500	2
Whitestown,	1	300	50	1,236	2,050	2
Onondaga Co.						
Camillus,	2	....	15	160	880	....
Cicero,	2	300	65	535	1,400	2
Clay,	1	150	30	500	1,200	1
Elbridge,	1	500	25	300	1,000	2
Fabius,	1	....	....	558	1,629	3
Lysander,	2	650	60	2,550	2,300	4
Manlius,	4	1,900	305	3,100	6,800	10
Marcellus,	1	600	25	1,000	1,800	3
Otisco,	2	300	25	700	1,400	3
Skaneateles,	3	1,150	250	2,628	4,550	9
Syracuse,	6	....	602	11,800	31,500	28
Tully,	1	....	50	325	1,000	2
Ontario Co.						
Bristol,	3	350	290	1,815	3,200	4
Canandaigua,	3	5,000	175	1,950	5,700	6
Farmington,	1	500	50	40	700	1
Naples,	1	300	30	650	900	1
Seneca,	1	1,200	60	1,600	5,000	4
West Bloomfield,	1	....	25	375	750	....
Orange Co.						
Blooming Grove,	1	....	100	800	1,500	4
Chester,	1	....	....	175	983	1
Deerpark,	2	....	30	1,176	2,400	2
Minisink,	2	500	40	1,300	2,500	4
Monroe,	2	550	300	1,300	2,500	4
Montgomery,	1	100	25	630	1,500	2
Mount Hope,	1	....	30	700	1,200	2
Newburgh,	3	10,000	450	3,784	27,200	10
Walkill,	1	500	50	600	1,600	2
Warwick,	1	....	10	160	600	1
Orleans Co.						
Barre,	2	2,000	100	3,700	8,000	7
Gaines,	1	....	50	1,000	2,000	1
Marcy,	1	400	75	1,800	1,750	1
Ridgeway,	2	1,000	220	1,600	3,800	5
Yates,	1	500	50	750	1,800	....
Oswego Co.						
Hannibal,	1	600	....	750	1,400	2
Mexico,	3	1,630	100	1,250	6,452	7
New Haven,	1	....	16	500	1,000	....
Oswego city,	5	10,600	275	5,400	10,575	23
Volney,	2	3,000	....	4,000	9,000	10
Otsego Co.						
Burlington,	1	125	25	900	1,000	1
Butternuts,	1	300	25	125	600	1
Maryland,	2	550	90	782	1,350	3
Middleford,	1	100	30	600	1,200	2
Milford,	1	....	....	....	100	....
Morris,	1	500	50	800	1,200	3
New Lisbon,	1	500	100	800	1,600	....
Otego,	1	1,000	53	725	1,425	2
Otsego,	2	4,500	325	4,838	6,650	11
Plainfield,	1	300	....	1,745	2,100	....
Richfield,	1	200	15	400	700	2
Roseboom,	3	160	110	800	1,600	1
Springfield,	1	600	200	700	2,000	3
Unadilla,	1	....	75	1,000	3,000	4
Worcester,	2	1,300	100	1,600	2,800	3
Putnam Co.						
Carmel,	1	....	15	1,500	2,500	2
Queens Co.						
Flushing,	2	300	50	1,000	4,725	5
Hempstead,	2	1,620	100	2,125	2,500	3
Jamaica,	1	500	50	500	1,000	2
North Hempstead,	1	....	176	1,079	1,000	3
Oyster Bay,	1	600	50	1,500	....	....
Rensselaer Co.						
Berlin,	1	100	25	600	1,000	2
Brunswick,	1	....	50	600	1,000	2
Hoosick,	1	200	30	445	1,430	2
Lansingburgh,	3	....	90	4,400	7,000	9
Troy,	2	2,250	100	6,500	14,500	8

TOWNS.	Number of establishments.	Capital invested. In real estate.	Capital invested. In tools and machinery.	Cash value. Of raw materials used.	Cash value. Of manufactured articles.	Persons employed.
Rockland Co.						
Ramapo,	1	....	$50	$834	$1,800	1
St. Lawrence Co.						
Canton,	2	$3,800	175	3,500	11,000	11
Gouverneur,	2	....	75	2,260	4,800	3
Louisville,	1	....	....	200	400	2
Madrid,	1	200	30	625	1,200	2
Oswegatchie,	3	6,000	475	5,700	10,250	13
Parishville,	1	200	15	625	1,300	2
Potsdam,	2	1,500	50	3,630	7,852	9
Rossie,	2	40	....	1,050	2,300	2
Saratoga Co.						
Ballston,	3	225	60	549	3,225	5
Halfmoon,	2	....	150	3,500	4,800	4
Milton,	2	1,200	105	2,200	3,800	4
Moreau,	1	....	25	640	800	2
Saratoga,	1	....	100	4,000	9,000	4
Saratoga Springs,	1	150	....	4,000	8,000	6
Stillwater,	2	....	....	2,200	3,400	3
Schenectady Co.						
Duanesburgh,	1	....	50	600	2,000	4
Schenectady,	4	....	70	10,700	21,900	13
Schoharie Co.						
Carlisle,	1	100	25	600	1,100	2
Esperance,	2	400	70	1,300	2,400	3
Fulton,	1	....	40	600	1,500	2
Richmondville,	2	550	100	1,172	3,300	5
Sharon,	1	....	25	400	1,000	2
Schuyler Co.						
Catherines,	2	1,100	55	1,800	3,500	2
Dix,	1	300	25	700	1,200	1
Hector,	2	300	80	2,000	3,800	5
Orange,	1	150	20	737	1,375	....
Seneca Co.						
Fayette,	4	1,640	110	1,750	4,900	4
Seneca Falls,	1	2,200	100	3,580	5,000	6
Varick,	1	50	....	275	700	1
Waterloo,	2	4,500	230	1,000	2,500	1
Steuben Co.						
Addison,	2	1,600	200	400	2,200	2
Bath,	4	1,100	210	2,600	4,640	7
Bradford,	1	50	25	250	600	1
Canisteo,	1	100	25	12	750	2
Dansville,	1	100	75	275	360	1
Erwin,	1	500	100	1,600	2,500	3
Fremont,	1	100	50	200	400	1
Hornellsville,	2	570	145	1,555	3,157	2
Howard,	1	....	30	1,000	2,000	....
Jasper,	1	....	30	106	600	2
Suffolk Co.						
Huntington,	3	320	1,025	1,000	2,900	6
Riverhead,	1	600	20	1,200	2,000	2
Southampton,	1	....	50	1,200	2,625	4
Southold,	1	....	20	....	....	....
Sullivan Co.						
Bethel,	1	150	10	250	600	1
Fallsburgh,	1	350	40	300	600	....
Mamakating,	3	160	120	720	2,300	5
Tioga Co.						
Barton,	3	500	80	1,200	1,200	5
Newark,	1	150	50	275	600	1
Nichols,	1	300	40	800	1,600	2
Owego,	3	2,550	300	4,450	9,250	8
Tompkins Co.						
Caroline,	1	150	20	300	530	1
Dryden,	2	1,000	125	1,050	2,000	3
Enfield,	1	....	25	300	600	1
Groton,	1	200	....	1,200	1,720	4
Ithaca,	5	8,500	950	9,150	18,000	22
Lansing,	1	300	20	500	1,000	1
Newfield,	2	400	30	850	1,700	3
Ulysses,	1	800	100	1,200	3,000	3
Ulster Co.						
Gardiner,	1	200	50	200	1,000	2
Marbletown,	2	250	55	3,600	7,600	2
Marlborough,	1	....	40	300	1,200	1
New Paltz,	1	500	50	200	2,000	....
Saugerties,	2	....	70	2,400	6,700	5
Shawangunk,	1	200	175	800	2,000	4
Warren Co.						
Queensbury,	2	3,000	100	1,948	8,075	8
Warrensburgh,	1	600	50	600	1,200	2
Washington Co.						
Argyle,	2	600	95	1,400	2,500	4
Easton,	1	300	30	1,000	2,000	2
Fort Ann,	1	1,200	30	350	1,750	2
Fort Edward,	1	....	25	725	1,600	2
Granville,	2	300	75	825	2,000	4
Hartford,	3	150	200	1,767	3,168	1
Kingsbury,	1	....	300	500	1,000	1

CLASS XVI.—(CONTINUED.)

TOWNS.	Number of establishments.	Capital Invested. In real estate.	Capital Invested. In tools and machinery.	Cash Value. Of raw materials used.	Cash Value. Of manufactured articles.	Persons employed.
WASHINGTON CO.						
Salem,	2	$300	$80	$1,800	$2,500	3
WAYNE CO.						
Arcadia,	3	1,800	115	2,625	5,650	6
Galen,	2	50	2,525	250	700	3
Lyons,	1	....	15	700	2,000	2
Marion,	1	300	25	365	800	2
Palmyra,	3	1,200	200	4,990	10,800	10
Sodus,	2	150	115	1,100	2,700	4
Walworth,	1	....	40	350	700	....
Williamson,	1	....	100	1,700	4,000	2
Wolcott,	1	1,200	....	800	1,200	2
WESTCHESTER CO.						
New Castle,	1	....	10	20	250	....
New Rochelle,	1	3,000	150	1,700	2,000	12
Ossining,	2	2,900	100	1,900	4,500	6
Rye,	2	1,500	350	1,050	2,000	6
Yorktown,	1	....	50	800	1,500	1
WYOMING CO.						
Castile,	1	300	40	450	1,000	2
Java,	1	....	50	660	1,460	2
Middlebury,	1	....	50	195	600	2
Orangeville,	1	....	....	50	75	....
Perry,	2	1,450	160	5,800	10,800	8
Pike,	1	200	55	1,500	3,000	6
Warsaw,	2	....	200	1,160	5,000	8
YATES CO.						
Benton,	1	....	50	400	800	1
Potter,	3	....	....	1,900	3,400	4
Starkey,	1	1,000	25	363	700	1

HOSE MANUFACTORIES.

TOWNS.	Number of establishments.	In real estate.	In tools and machinery.	Of raw materials used.	Of manufactured articles.	Persons employed.
NEW-YORK CO.						
New-York,	2	....	1,100	60,400	77,000	19

LEATHER-SPLITTING GAUGE MANUFACTORY.

TOWNS.	Number of establishments.	In real estate.	In tools and machinery.	Of raw materials used.	Of manufactured articles.	Persons employed.
ONEIDA CO.						
Marshall,	1	300	700	464	4,500	5

MOROCCO FACTORIES.

TOWNS.	Number of establishments.	In real estate.	In tools and machinery.	Of raw materials used.	Of manufactured articles.	Persons employed.
ALBANY CO.						
Albany,	4	18,000	1,700	160,150	212,800	31
CAYUGA CO.						
Auburn,	1	600	600	10,000	15,000	7
JEFFERSON CO.						
Watertown,	2	8,500	1,200	34,645	40,609	16
KINGS CO.						
Brooklyn,	4	79,000	20,200	774,000	2,021,000	141
NEW-YORK CO.						
New-York,	14	48,500	16,600	223,112	481,130	262
NIAGARA CO.						
Lockport,	1	2,000	200	10,000	12,000	4
ORANGE CO.						
Newburgh,	1	5,000	400	20,035	31,000	22
OSWEGO CO.						
Oswego city,	1	15,000	500	48,380	63,000	16
RENSSELAER CO.						
Troy,	1	1,800	500	11,290	11,290	....
ST. LAWRENCE CO.						
Oswegatchie,	1	2,500	500	10.000	12,000	4

MOROCCO CASE MANUFACTORIES.

TOWNS.	Number of establishments.	In real estate.	In tools and machinery.	Of raw materials used.	Of manufactured articles.	Persons employed.
NEW-YORK CO.						
New-York,	4	15,000	6,300	54,150	131,000	94

PARCHMENT AND VELLUM MANUFACTORY.

TOWNS.	Number of establishments.	In real estate.	In tools and machinery.	Of raw materials used.	Of manufactured articles.	Persons employed.
PUTNAM CO.						
Southeast,	1	150	100	1,400	3,050	2

PATENT LEATHER MANUFACTORIES.

TOWNS.	Number of establishments.	In real estate.	In tools and machinery.	Of raw materials used.	Of manufactured articles.	Persons employed.
ERIE CO.						
Lancaster,	1	2,000	500	3,000	6,500	....
KINGS CO.						
Brooklyn,	2	15,000	10,000	55,000	140,000	47
NEW-YORK CO.						
New-York,	1	30,000	500	40,000	50,000	9
RENSSELAER CO.						
Lansingburgh,	1	....	1,000	15,000	30,000	11

POCKET-BOOK AND PORT MONNAIE MANUFACTORIES.

TOWNS.	Number of establishments.	In real estate.	In tools and machinery.	Of raw materials used.	Of manufactured articles.	Persons employed.
NEW-YORK CO.						
New-York,	12	52,500	38,930	128,040	369,000	581

RAZOR STROP MANUFACTORY.

TOWNS.	Number of establishments.	Capital Invested. In real estate.	Capital Invested. In tools and machinery.	Cash Value. Of raw materials used.	Cash Value. Of manufactured articles.	Persons employed.
WASHINGTON CO.						
Kingsbury,	1	$400	$50	$1,792	$14,200	8

SADDLE AND COACH HARDWARE MANUFACTORIES.

TOWNS.	Number of establishments.	In real estate.	In tools and machinery.	Of raw materials used.	Of manufactured articles.	Persons employed.
ALBANY CO.						
Albany,	2	12,000	17,000	17,000	55,000	122
CAYUGA CO.						
Auburn,	1	....	7,000	27,000	50,000	87
ONONDAGA CO.						
Syracuse,	3	16,500	8,300	25,940	57,120	61
WAYNE CO.						
Lyons,	1	3,000	2,000	2,300	12,000	9
WESTCHESTER CO.						
Ossining,	1	....	9,000	20,000	52,000	120

SHOE PEG MANUFACTORIES.

TOWNS.	Number of establishments.	In real estate.	In tools and machinery.	Of raw materials used.	Of manufactured articles.	Persons employed.
ERIE CO.						
Buffalo,	1	800	2,800	2,500	16,000	20
FULTON CO.						
Broadalbin,	2	700	1,750	270	1,890	3
MONROE CO.						
Rochester,	2	600	2,600	2,800	24,400	22
NEW-YORK CO.						
New-York,	6	12,000	3,500	19,900	24,200	46
ONEIDA CO.						
Utica,	2	3,000	120	989	3,882	3
Western,	1	....	....	....	900	3
OTSEGO CO.						
Middlefield,	1	1,000	1,000	100	1,500	2

TANNERIES.

TOWNS.	Number of establishments.	In real estate.	In tools and machinery.	Of raw materials used.	Of manufactured articles.	Persons employed.
ALBANY CO.						
Albany,	1	3,000	50	3,000	4,500	6
Bern,	1	500	200	400	600	1
Bethlehem,	1	1,000	100	1,500	2,500	2
Coeymans,	1	1,200	60	1,105	1,550	2
Knox,	1	800	40	2,226	4,050	1
New Scotland,	1	2,000	50	550	600	2
Rensselaerville,	4	3,600	1,200	60,630	112,200	34
ALLEGANY CO.						
Alfred,	1	1,300	300	1,196	2,000	2
Almond,	2	6,500	6,000	20,970	29,262	8
Amity,	1	600	200	1,125	1,800	2
Andover,	1	1,200	300	1,750	3,450	2
Angelica,	2	2,600	1,600	4,304	14.200	7
Belfast,	1	1,500	1,500	3,585	6,000	4
Bolivar,	1	600	....	600	2,000	3
Cuba,	2	4,500	500	7,000	13,000	6
Rushford,	2	3,500	1,000	2,345	5,050	4
Scio,	2	3,000	400	9,000	....	2
Willing,	1	1,500	....	1,500	....	3
Wirt,	1	1,200	100	700	23,385	3
BROOME CO.						
Chenango,	3	14,000	3,800	16,624	....	14
Colesville,	2	6,000	2,100	33,673	50,634	21
Conklin,	3	3,000	1,500	10,000	16,000	7
Lisle,	1	7,000	3,000	29,700	42,000	20
Maine,	1	5.000	4,000	20,000	35,000	8
Nanticoke,	2	25,000	50	....	183,750	35
Sandford,	2	12,300	5,050	40,750	70,000	23
Triangle,	3	5,500	1,800	19,412	40,424	18
Union,	1	10,000	2,500	....	30,000	15
Windsor,	2	2,500	125	....	....	....
CATTARAUGUS CO.						
Allegany,	1	8,000	....	7,812	9,084	5
Conewango,	1	400	30	250	600	1
Freedom,	1	400	....	300	500	1
New Albion,	1	2,200	500	7,510	10,100	7
Otto,	2	2,100	270	2,130	3,190	4
Persia,	1	4,500	....	5,000	1,000	....
Perrysburgh,	2	7,000	3,040	36,015	45,550	18
Portville,	1	1,000	200	1,300	2,600	2
Randolph,	2	6,000	160	8,700	15,500	7
Yorkshire,	3	6,100	210	5,200	7,200	6
CAYUGA CO.						
Auburn,	2	15,000	8,000	18,300	26,250	13
Conquest,	1	700	50	700	1,000	1
Genoa,	2	900	250	700	1,100	3
Ira,	3	2,100	275	1,260	2,435	1
Locke,	1	100	....	....	....	....
Mentz,	1	4,000	600	13,500	21,500	7
Moravia,	1	2,000	1,000	7,450	15,000	6
Niles,	2	1,450	....	833	4,500	5

CLASS XVI.—(Continued.)

TOWNS.	Number of establishments.	Capital Invested. In real estate.	Capital Invested. In tools and machinery.	Cash Value. Of raw materials used.	Cash Value. Of manufactured articles.	Persons employed.
Cayuga Co.						
Sennett,	1	$1,000	$100	$940	$1,500	2
Sterling,	1	2,500	400	1,800	3,000	3
Summer Hill,	2	520	90	1,323	1,800	3
Victory,	1	300	....	....	500	1
Chautauque Co.						
Busti,	1	500	100	500	1,000	1
Chautauque,	3	6,700	715	4,932	7,811	10
Cherry Creek,	1	100	1,200	3,200	5,450	4
Ellicott,	2	6,700	375	7,948	11,630	3
Ellington,	1	400	200	500	1,000	1
Hanover,	5	6,500	2,160	20,913	32,062	15
Mina,	1	500	200	400	600	....
Pomfret,	4	8,700	4,550	9,690	17,599	14
Ripley,	3	1,500	2,700	4,000	7,900	8
Sherman,	2	1,050	25	720	1,800	2
Stockton,	1	....	....	....	3,000	....
Villenovia,	1	500	20	411	672	1
Chemung Co.						
Chemung,	2	800	90	775	2,512	1
Elmira,	4	10,500	430	7,120	13,350	9
Horseheads,	2	2,000	175	2,250	4,500	4
Southport,	2	12,000	8,000	51,500	68,500	28
Veteran,	1	2,000	25	1,750	3,500	3
Chenango Co.						
Bainbridge,	1	1,200	700	2,400	3,600	2
Columbus,	1	200	175	300	500	1
Coventry,	1	500	450	1,200	2.000	2
Greene,	2	9,000	200	8,250	9,400	4
Guilford,	3	3,500	1,000	15,800	25,749	11
New Berlin,	3	8,500	1,035	26,140	45,423	13
Norwich,	2	8,200	3,100	21.988	26,350	18
Pitcher,	2	500	150	2,880	4,280	3
Preston,	1	700	100	633	900	2
Sherburne,	1	1,000	50	2,000	3.500	2
Clinton Co.						
Ausable,	1	3,000	300	2,000	4,500	4
Beekmantown,	1	1,200	25	630	1,200	2
Black Brook,	1	500	125	700	1,500	2
Champlain,	2	3,000	60	2,650	7,199	5
Chazy,	1	1,000	100	500	3,000	5
Ellenburgh,	1	2,000	100	6,900	9,000	4
Mooers,	1	1,000	2,000	2,000	4,000	2
Peru,	1	1,000	115	1,182	2,000	1
Plattsburgh,	2	8,500	550	10,540	20,900	6
Schuyler's Falls,	2	1,500	50	1,319	2,186	3
Columbia Co.						
Chatham,	1	500	50	500	....	2
Hillsdale,	2	1,800	160	1,800	3,600	2
Hudson,	2	4,500	900	10,900	21,800	9
Kinderhook,	1	1,000	100	3,575	15,000	2
New Lebanon,	2	2,500	812	4,414	7,908	7
Cortland Co.						
Cincinnatus,	2	2.200	800	3,600	6,500	3
Cortlandville,	2	2,400	600	4,301	7,450	5
Harford,	1	500	50	476	1.300	2
Homer,	5	3,650	500	4,600	5,800	3
Preble,	1	1,000	500	1,162	1,525	1
Taylor,	1	250	100	250	500	1
Virgil,	1	400	150	1,184	1,708	2
Delaware Co.						
Andes,	3	12,900	1,000	28,475	38,800	19
Bovina,	1	1,200	20	1,063	1,550	2
Colchester,	2	10,500	3,300	62,744	112,935	28
Davenport,	2	9,000	2,200	82,000	104,000	8
Delhi,	1	1,400	....	750	1,000	2
Franklin,	1	500	100	675	1,350	1
Hamden,	2	4,500	100	11,250	15,490	8
Hancock,	2	65,000	3,500	116,978	161,448	70
Kortright,	1	100	25	300	600	1
Masonville,	1	400	100	300	600	2
Meredith,	2	660	110	1,034	1,560	4
Middletown,	3	18,000	5,500	86,500	140,000	72
Roxbury,	2	2,000	50	1,200	3,000	3
Tompkins,	1	8,000	5,000	55,000	72,000	20
Dutchess Co.						
East Fishkill,	2	900	60	560	2,000	3
Hyde Park,	1	4,000	500	10,020	17,020	7
Northeast,	1	4,000	400	3,500	3,100	2
Milan,	1	2,000	500	1,250	1,300	3
Pine Plains,	1	1,200	250	5,000	....	3
Poughkeepsie city,	1	12,300	2,500	24,650	33,100	21
Rhinebeck,	1	2,500	100	3,800	5,200	4
Erie Co.						
Alden,	1	600	50	1,950	3,900	1
Amherst,	1	1,000	....	16,300	29,000	18
Aurora,	2	2,200	400	13,000	18,050	9
Buffalo,	7	43,500	12,750	396,000	533,363	243
Clarence,	1	400	500	1,055	1,500	3
Colden,	1	400	....	1,100	2,000	1
Erie Co.						
Collins,	3	$3,600	$1,500	$300	$500	1
Concord,	1	1.200	300	1,050	2,800	3
East Hamburgh,	1	3,000	1,500	2,500	4,000	3
Eden,	2	700	1,030	1,100	3,600	5
Evans,	3	6,400	3,115	4,967	8,500	15
Hamburgh,	1	1,200	1,500	700	10,000	18
Holland,	1	2,700	4,000	30,837	45,570	15
Lancaster,	3	20,000	500	89,900	116,730	52
Newstead,	2	1,500	750	800	1,600	1
North Collins,	1	1,200	700	2,700	5,000	4
Sardinia,	1	1,500	1,200	2,500	3,500	3
Wales,	1	1,000	150	1,500	3,000	2
West Seneca,	1	600	1,350	18,750	28,000	15
Essex Co.						
Crown Point,	2	3,000	500	2,551	3,913	2
Elizabethtown,	1	1,000	1,500	1,200	2,000	2
Essex,	1	2,000	500	950	1,800	2
Minerva,	1	10,000	500	34,000	48,000	15
Moriah,	1	2,000	600	2,000	3,000	3
Schroon,	2	9,800	310	32,890	60,500	14
Westport,	1	1,000	100	1,084	3,068	3
Willsborough,	1	600	25	450	800	1
Franklin Co.						
Bangor,	1	800	50	600	1,200	2
Bombay,	1	1,100	....	....	....	....
Fort Covington,	2	2,700	1,200	3,350	5,300	6
Malone,	2	8,000	125	22,361	35,160	8
Fulton Co.						
Bleecker,	3	25,000	6,800	73,870	119,760	45
Broadalbin,	4	3,200	1,400	25,573	32,070	16
Caroga,	1	6,000	3,000	44,000	72,600	35
Ephratah,	2	4,500	1,000	14,200	22,500	11
Johnstown,	5	21,100	100	2,600	4.500	28
Mayfield,	3	8,000	500	14,812	20,400	7
Northampton,	3	4,800	2,550	43,575	54,675	29
Oppenheim,	1	600	100	600	1,000	2
Perth,	1	400	150	700	1,200	4
Stratford,	2	7,000	125	33,600	45,000	8
Genesee Co.						
Alabama,	2	1,700	80	3,025	6,194	3
Alexander,	3	2,300	1,275	9,568	15,650	5
Batavia,	1	2,000	500	1,500	2,700	3
Byron,	1	2,500	300	1,500	3,000	2
Darien,	1	....	....	300	....	....
Oakfield,	1	600	25	800	1,200	2
Greene Co.						
Catskill,	3	4,400	1,600	17,894	27,550	15
Durham,	1	1,000	100	2,512	2,875	4
Hunter,	1	2,500	1,000	3,625	28,000	10
Jewett,	1	350	200	2,400	3,000	3
Lexington,	1	1,000	100	2,200	38,500	16
Windham,	2	4,300	50	16,905	26,371	10
Hamilton Co.						
Hope,	1	5,500	2,000	75,745	99,535	32
Morehouse,	1	350	100	500	1,000	2
Wells,	1	9,000	300	82,505	82,687	28
Herkimer Co.						
Columbia,	1	3,000	300	11,650	23,200	7
Fairfield,	1	500	1,000	....	22,000	8
German Flats,	1	2,000	200	4,000	6,000	1
Herkimer,	1	700	400	4,000	7,200	....
Litchfield,	2	1,400	75	6,830	9,900	5
Little Falls,	2	5,200	1,200	21,800	29,400	9
Manheim,	2	9,000	1,600	105,250	168,580	43
Newport,	1	15,000	500	14,930	17,980	5
Norway,	1	20,000	7,000	80,000	120.000	60
Russia,	4	6,300	1,160	16,510	33,110	15
Salisbury,	3	24,700	2,250	94,389	131,848	47
Warren,	1	6,000	400	27,600	30,000	7
Winfield,	1	1,000	1,000	6,000	14,000	5
Jefferson Co.						
Adams,	2	800	50	714	900	2
Antwerp,	1	1,500	100	1,700	3,000	3
Champion,	2	3,000	930	10,036	13,362	9
Clayton,	1	50	....	600	1,200	2
Ellisburgh,	2	2,700	5	2,752	5,074	5
Henderson,	1	800	200	1,000	1,900	3
Hounsfield,	1	2,500	2,000	2,500	5,000	4
Lorraine,	1	400	30	....	....	....
Lyme,	1	650	12	500	800	....
Orleans,	1	200	60	664	1,034	2
Pamelia,	1	6,000	500	5,275	7,976	4
Philadelphia,	1	1,500	....	1,485	2,800	2
Rodman,	2	1,600	200	4,750	7,600	6
Rutland,	3	1,700	550	6,860	13,300	5
Watertown,	4	11,800	3,800	44,802	62,625	29
Wilna,	1	1,000	200	38,400	57,600	16
Kings Co.						
Brooklyn,	4	6,000	950	18,588	20,776	25

CLASS XVI.—(Continued.)

TOWNS.	Number of establishments.	Capital Invested. In real estate.	Capital Invested. In tools and machinery.	Cash Value. Of raw materials used.	Cash Value. Of manufactured articles.	Persons employed.
Lewis Co.						
Croghan,	1	$3, 000	$1, 000	$16, 402	$19, 000	10
Denmark,	3	3, 400	550	4, 094	8, 200	5
Greig,	4	13, 250	180	72, 796	84, 851	23
Leyden,	1	....	6, 000	14, 049	22, 164	8
Lewis,	1	200	50	250	500	1
Lowville,	1	....	100	332	800	1
Martinsburgh,	1	3, 100	625	2, 604	4, 137	4
New Bremen,	2	4, 400	60	1, 000	2, 000	2
Turin,	1	1, 500	500	3, 598	5, 050	2
Livingston Co.						
Nunda,	1	3, 000	2, 000	5, 950	10, 000	4
North Dansville,	2	3, 100	1, 800	14, 367	21, 884	9
Portage,	2	3, 100	2, 120	5, 650	11, 300	2
Sparta,	1	600	60	1, 387	2, 430	3
Springwater,	1	2, 000	....	....	....	....
Madison Co.						
Brookfield,	1	1, 200	50	3, 030	4, 865	3
Cazenovia,	4	7, 900	1, 530	30, 893	48, 825	17
De Ruyter,	3	5, 700	1, 950	8, 230	14, 200	6
Eaton,	1	5, 000	2, 000	30, 000	20, 000	10
Georgetown,	2	3, 000	200	11, 033	11, 850	4
Hamilton,	3	11, 200	1, 500	47, 425	58, 500	10
Lebanon,	1	200	40	400	500	....
Lenox,	2	1, 700	125	6, 610	10, 000	4
Madison,	2	2, 200	225	1, 500	2, 700	3
Smithfield,	1	1, 500	200	800	1, 600	4
Stockbridge,	1	800	100	1, 355	1, 910	3
Sullivan,	1	1, 000	300	820	1, 300	2
Monroe Co.						
Clarkson,	1	1, 500	500	1, 175	2, 100	4
Ogden,	1	8, 000	4, 000	63, 000	22, 500	18
Parma,	2	4, 500	2, 200	12, 000	17, 800	7
Perrington,	1	1, 000	300	3, 495	5, 280	4
Riga,	1	1, 000	300	1, 438	2, 420	2
Rochester,	4	44, 500	5, 300	89, 637	112, 587	65
Sweden,	1	3, 000	1, 000	12, 000	20, 000	6
Union,	1	1, 000	300	1, 000	2, 400	2
Webster,	2	1, 100	40	2, 675	5, 800	5
Wheatland,	1	1, 500	200	1, 800	2, 900	1
Montgomery Co.						
Amsterdam,	2	1, 200	300	4, 267	5, 820	4
Charleston,	1	700	50	600	750	3
Florida,	2	2, 500	1, 300	6, 670	9, 495	7
Glen,	1	500	50	600	1, 200	....
Minden,	2	6, 200	3, 025	15, 200	19, 500	8
Mohawk,	2	3, 000	300	8, 500	12, 500	6
Palatine,	1	200	40	600	500	3
Root,	3	400	95	370	815	....
St. Johnsville,	1	8, 400	3, 400	42, 100	46, 700	14
New-York Co.						
New-York,	14	119, 500	66, 000	440, 627	808, 810	143
Niagara Co.						
Lewiston,	1	2, 000	50	1, 375	2, 750	3
Lockport,	2	12, 000	2, 300	32, 000	65, 000	20
Royalton,	1	800	50	1, 529	2, 300	2
Oneida Co.						
Annsville,	2	8, 300	1, 100	17, 500	30, 800	7
Ava,	1	1, 500	75	1, 500	2, 200	4
Boonville,	3	30, 300	1, 950	89, 976	131, 091	31
Bridgewater,	1	800	120	2, 100	3, 200	2
Camden,	2	3, 650	....	25, 900	37, 000	11
Florence,	2	17, 000	2, 200	34, 400	56, 500	20
Kirkland,	1	2, 500	250	4, 200	6, 460	3
Lee,	2	2, 400	350	2, 338	4, 440	1
Marcy,	1	5, 000	6, 000	55, 025	56, 000	26
Marshall,	1	5, 000	5, 000	30, 030	38, 400	9
New Hartford,	1	10, 000	1, 200	15, 350	24, 000	14
Paris,	1	3, 500	1, 500	5, 620	7, 600	6
Remsen,	1	2, 000	50	4, 000	6, 000	3
Rome,	2	6, 000	375	4, 042	8, 334	4
Sangerfield,	1	1, 000	150	3, 850	5, 500	4
Steuben,	2	1, 200	130	4, 288	5, 837	4
Trenton,	2	1, 600	150	1, 900	2, 820	2
Utica,	2	5, 000	500	17, 600	28, 000	11
Vernon,	3	4, 100	700	15, 895	21, 300	16
Verona,	2	16, 400	4, 200	67, 800	96, 750	29
Vienna,	2	9, 000	1, 800	12, 047	28, 000	16
Western,	1	1, 000	1, 000	7, 675	12, 000	5
Whitestown,	2	5, 000	2, 500	9, 800	16, 000	7
Onondaga Co.						
Camillus,	1	1, 000	200	4, 500	9, 000	2
Cicero,	1	600	15	1, 400	2, 800	3
Elbridge,	2	2, 500	150	4, 472	5, 700	6
Fabius,	2	2, 800	950	4, 698	10, 000	0
Lysander,	5	8, 900	1, 240	8, 213	44, 750	16
Manlius,	3	4, 800	25	6, 294	9, 700	6
Otisco,	1	300	....	300	560	....
Pompey,	1	150	25	366	702	1
Skaneateles,	1	2, 500	500	1, 500	3, 200	3
Onondago Co.						
Syracuse,	1	$4, 000	$2, 000	$18, 000	$30, 000	20
Tully,	1	500	100	1, 000	2, 000	1
Ontario Co.						
Canandaigua,	1	2, 500	300	17, 300	10, 400	6
East Bloomfield,	1	1, 000	75	2, 811	4, 415	3
Naples,	2	1, 500	55	1, 500	3, 100	3
Phelps,	1	1, 000	200	300	600	1
Orange Co.						
Blooming Grove,	1	2, 500	150	5, 380	8, 600	5
Cornwall,	1	5, 000	1, 000	10, 305	3, 700	10
Deerpark,	1	10, 000	3, 600	25, 000	48, 000	26
Greenville,	1	500	300	3, 094	5, 348	3
Hamptonburgh,	1	200	50	95	300	1
Minisink,	1	800	400	2, 184	3, 562	2
Monroe,	1	3, 000	1, 000	25, 950	29, 750	15
Newburgh,	2	14, 000	4, 000	35, 430	65, 458	24
Walkill,	2	3, 000	325	10, 970	19, 450	8
Warwick,	1	4, 000	1, 000	7, 845	12, 500	3
Orleans Co.						
Barre,	1	....	....	1, 000	....	....
Carlton,	1	2, 500	....	2, 200	2, 440	2
Gaines,	1	3, 000	1, 500	6, 000	12, 000	3
Murray,	1	2, 000	400	5, 000	7, 500	3
Ridgeway,	4	19, 100	6, 590	11, 450	79, 910	26
Shelby,	1	3, 000	100	4, 000	7, 000	4
Yates,	1	700	300	1, 195	1, 195	....
Oswego Co.						
Albion,	2	9, 000	1, 200	41, 750	68, 000	27
Amboy,	2	7, 500	7, 500	43, 285	53, 500	18
Constantia,	2	24, 000	5, 500	93, 000	133, 000	64
Granby,	2	11, 000	4, 000	24, 000	40, 500	10
Hannibal,	3	2, 250	140	2, 225	4, 250	3
Hastings,	2	2, 600	1, 500	8, 800	13, 000	6
Mexico,	4	6, 350	505	4, 973	6, 400	5
New Haven,	1	1, 200	250	500	1, 000	....
Orwell,	2	1, 900	1, 200	11, 900	16, 500	6
Oswego,	1	1, 500	200	980	1, 400	2
Oswego city,	2	22, 000	200	80, 850	108, 600	24
Palermo,	1	600	....	500	1, 000	1
Parish,	1	5, 000	100	5, 000	7, 500	4
Redfield,	1	1, 200	100	1, 800	4, 200	3
Richland,	4	9, 200	1, 380	35, 780	47, 000	14
Sandy Creek,	1	5, 000	....	15, 500	19, 000	4
Schroeppel,	3	7, 400	1, 200	13, 350	21, 000	8
Volney,	2	7, 000	....	20, 450	30, 900	9
Willliamstown,	2	15, 000	75	4, 700	43, 300	12
Otsego Co.						
Burlington,	2	1, 700	10	1, 950	2, 950	3
Butternuts,	1	1, 000	50	995	3, 200	2
Decatur,	1	300	9	200	400	1
Edmeston,	1	100	50	7, 775	8, 200	3
Laurens,	2	1, 400	50	700	1, 200	2
Maryland,	2	9, 000	2, 515	54, 510	68, 444	21
Middlefield,	2	6, 500	4, 500	14, 000	31, 400	13
Milford,	3	5, 200	1, 350	21, 500	26, 500	13
Morris,	2	2, 000	460	5, 036	10, 080	7
New Lisbon,	1	200	200	500	1, 000	....
Oneonta,	1	500	10	1, 000	2, 000	1
Otisco,	1	500	500	700	1, 200	1
Richfield,	1	600	50	600	1, 000	2
Roseboom,	2	4, 000	....	7, 500	14, 000	5
Springfield,	1	2, 000	50	3, 000	5, 000	4
Unadilla,	3	4, 300	450	3, 100	9, 000	9
Putnam Co.						
Phillipstown,	1	700	400	2, 570	3, 500	2
Southeast,	1	700	....	4, 894	7, 200	4
Queens Co.						
Hempstead,	1	1, 500	300	1, 500	3, 000	3
Oyster Bay,	1	1, 000	100	....	....	1
Rensselaer Co.						
Brunswick,	1	1, 500	150	6, 000	9, 000	4
Greenbush,	1	4, 000	1, 000	16, 383	27, 300	10
Nassau,	2	2, 000	500	3, 000	4, 400	4
Poestenkill,	2	4, 000	1, 050	3, 400	6, 800	4
Sandlake,	1	4, 000	2, 000	11, 352	15, 600	5
Stephentown,	1	2, 500	175	3, 200	8, 000	3
Troy,	5	26, 000	10, 600	137, 700	163, 725	112
Rockland Co.						
Orangetown,	1	2, 200	150	500	2, 000	3
Ramapo,	1	100	100	3, 568	4, 800	2
St. Lawrence Co.						
Canton,	1	3, 500	100	6, 900	12, 000	6
Gouverneur,	1	3, 300	100	....	13, 715	6
Hammond,	1	25	....	700	1, 400	....
Hopkinton,	2	2, 200	550	2, 165	8, 395	5
Lawrence,	1	550	25	500	1, 000	1
Louisville,	3	1, 000	550	1, 625	3, 000	6
Madrid,	2	2, 700	700	5, 700	10, 200	9
Massena,	2	1, 150	425	550	1, 000	3

CLASS XVI.—(CONTINUED.)

TOWNS.	Number of establishments.	Capital Invested. In real estate.	Capital Invested. In tools and machinery.	Cash Value. Of raw materials used.	Cash Value. Of manufactured articles.	Persons employed.
ST. LAWRENCE CO.						
Norfolk,	2	$3,000	$400	$2,400	$4,500	4
Oswegatchie,	2	14,000	510	8,500	19,000	10
Parishville,	1	4,000	20	1,703	2,475	2
Pitcairn,	1	50	35	100	200	1
Potsdam,	1	300	100	500	2,000	2
Rossie,	1	150	....	600	1,000	....
Russell,	2	575	100	1,500	1,800	3
Stockholm,	2	2,300	550	2,200	4,700	3
SARATOGA CO.						
Edinburgh,	1	800	100	1,000	2,000	1
Galway,	1	....	....	....	....	2
Hadley,	1	12,000	4,000	93,800	126,000	80
Milton,	2	3,000	2,000	19,200	65,000	8
Providence,	2	4,600	625	4,000	27,000	9
Saratoga Springs,	1	6,000	1,000	8,000	10,000	2
Waterford,	1	1,600	500	6,600	13,000	5
SCHENECTADY CO.						
Schenectady,	1	5,700	....	19,361	20,665	6
SCHOHARIE CO.						
Blenheim,	1	3,000	2,000	6,856	92,747	25
Broome,	2	3,000	2,500	24,107	34,000	15
Carlisle,	1	300	50	400	800	1
Conesville,	1	100	1,000	1,600	2,200	2
Esperance,	1	400	....	915	1,475	1
Fulton,	1	300	150	318	600	....
Gilboa,	1	2,000	200	54,000	83,600	20
Middleburgh,	2	9,000	3,500	49,000	74,000	30
Richmondville,	1	500	....	500	1,000	1
Seward,	2	2,100	300	1,500	2,575	4
Sharon,	3	1,575	250	3,020	6,000	6
Wright,	1	3,000	500	14,750	20,025	....
SCHUYLER CO.						
Catherines,	1	500	50	300	600	....
Cayuta,	1	600	70	800	1,600	3
Dix,	2	1,600	200	1,240	2,700	2
Hector,	4	6,000	850	5,500	10,600	9
Orange,	2	400	3,100	15,586	19,450	6
Tyrone,	3	2,522	1,070	3,413	4,420	3
SENECA CO.						
Fayette,	1	1,000	400	5,625	9,000	6
Junius,	1	2,500	50	3,000	6,000	3
Ovid,	1	900	150	860	1,600	3
Romulus,	1	500	40	1,690	3,382	3
Waterloo,	1	4,700	50	2,349	5,000	....
STEUBEN CO.						
Avoca,	1	1,650	300	4,500	6,400	6
Bath,	2	4,000	250	6,050	4,500	4
Campbell,	1	3,000	12,000	....	....	10
Corning,	1	500	100	3,900	7,800	3
Dansville,	1	600	30	600	1,200	1
Erwin,	1	2,000	150	4,600	8,000	4
Fremont,	2	1,000	125	700	1,400	3
Hornellsville,	2	1,850	680	4,462	7,749	4
Howard,	1	600	40	800	1,500	1
Jasper,	1	150	300	500	1,000	4
Thurston,	1	600	300	575	1,200	1
Urbana,	2	2,000	500	2,000	3,600	4
Wayland,	2	1,600	2,200	6,150	10,300	4
Woodhull,	1	1,000	100	2,000	3,600	2
SUFFOLK CO.						
Huntington,	1	2,000	170	1,886	1,352	3
Islip,	1	1,000	200	500	500	3
Riverhead,	1	....	150	1,200	3,000	2
Southampton,	1	800	325	11,520	13,150	3
SULLIVAN CO.						
Bethel,	3	26,200	2,400	291,267	323,120	110
Callicoon,	3	61,000	11,000	201,556	262,751	90
Cochecton,	5	60,400	700	259,310	259,310	....
Fallsburgh,	3	57,000	7,000	162,150	210,600	82
Forrestburgh,	5	52,000	5,100	105,800	213,000	94
Fremont,	1	4,000	2,500	55,756	84,737	44
Liberty,	2	56,000	4,000	136,050	181,500	57
Mamakating,	6	17,600	1,250	62,334	89,148	23
Neversink,	4	42,000	4,400	206,000	264,000	140
Rockland,	4	20,300	2,200	82,953	110,070	56
Thompson,	3	16,800	1,150	64,575	89,750	26
TIOGA CO.						
Barton,	2	5,000	3,150	5,000	20,000	8
Berkshire,	1	3,000	....	7,000	10,000	5
Canton,	1	13,000	3,000	52,000	78,000	20
Newark,	2	14,000	4,300	52,525	83,420	28
Nichols,	1	....	....	650	2,000	2
Owego,	4	10,600	2,800	48,175	75,500	24

TOWNS.	Number of establishments.	Capital Invested. In real estate.	Capital Invested. In tools and machinery.	Cash Value. Of raw materials used.	Cash Value. Of manufactured articles.	Persons employed.
TIOGA CO.						
Spencer,	1	$1,200	$500	$700	$1,000	2
TOMPKINS CO.						
Caroline,	2	550	125	930	1,800	3
Dryden,	2	2,600	510	5,255	9,200	6
Groton,	4	2,450	100	3,275	6,290	6
Ithaca,	3	12,000	3,100	51,790	431,350	31
Lansing,	1	700	100	200	500	2
Newfield,	1	1,000	200	1,800	3,000	2
Ulysses,	1	1,000	....	1,200	2,400	2
ULSTER CO.						
Denning,	2	15,000	900	48,750	78,941	26
Gardiner,	1	4,500	500	21,400	35,000	14
Hurley,	1	400	500	12,000	17,000	....
Kingston,	1	600	200	6,000	12,000	5
Marbletown,	1	2,000	250	35,000	60,000	2
New Paltz,	1	500	100	650	6,000	2
Olive,	4	45,000	8,000	223,000	473,000	145
Saugerties,	2	5,500	550	17,700	24,250	10
Shandaken,	8	108,500	6,200	353,350	525,000	188
Shawangunk,	1	500	250	50	1,000	1
Wawarsing,	7	60,200	7,340	210,675	327,402	105
Woodstock,	1	5,000	1,500	6,100	48,000	15
WARREN CO.						
Chester,	4	33,000	5 700	160,662	293,000	57
Johnsburgh,	5	61,000	10,200	292,615	577,750	97
Queensbury,	2	800	125	1,700	4,990	2
Stony Creek,	1	6,000	100	30,000	45,000	10
Warrensburgh,	2	7,000	1,500	87,000	121,600	32
WASHINGTON CO.						
Argyle,	1	1,000	50	1,000	2,000	2
Easton,	1	1,000	100	1,674	2,600	2
Fort Ann,	3	4,800	590	7,700	12,700	10
Granville,	2	2,700	400	3,500	4,880	4
Greenwich,	1	2,000	200	1,000	3,310	2
Hartford,	2	1,500	700	1,624	2,550	1
Hebron,	2	4,000	300	3,100	6,250	4
Putnam,	1	100	30	555	905	2
WAYNE CO.						
Arcadia,	5	4,500	1,900	11,705	18,000	10
Lyons,	1	1,500	1,000	2,575	4,200	3
Marion,	1	500	60	125	250	1
Palmyra,	1	2,500	2,600	4,500	7,150	4
Rose,	1	500	25	800	1,600	1
Sodus,	2	1,400	300	3,200	6,400	5
Walworth,	1	500	150	900	1,500	1
Williamson,	1	2,000	200	2,500	3,000	1
Wolcott,	1	6,000	....	13,000	19,000	3
WESTCHESTER CO.						
Cortland,	2	49,000	900	24,800	40,000	16
Greenburgh,	2	2,000	2,500	5,700	10,400	6
New Castle,	1	....	70	300	1,200	1
Rye,	1	1,500	300	5,900	10,000	3
White Plains,	2	15,000	1,150	263,000	952,000	35
Yorktown,	1	800	200	1,060	2,988	3
WYOMING CO.						
Attica,	2	2,000	500	5,118	7,025	5
Bennington,	2	3,000	1,525	4,200	8,500	6
Castile,	1	300	10	823	1,200	1
Covington,	1	800	100	1,000	2,000	2
Eagle,	1	800	200	3,150	5,000	2
Java,	2	3,175	50	5,525	11,050	5
Orangeville,	2	1,800	300	9,050	12,000	8
Perry,	1	2,000	1,000	5,000	9,000	4
Pike,	2	7,200	500	8,500	17,200	8
Wethersfield,	2	1,600	100	2,070	3,100	2
YATES CO.						
Jerusalem,	1	1,500	100	2,000	4,500	4
Milo,	3	3,400	900	6,564	11,550	4
Potter,	1	450	50	60	200	1

WHIP MANUFACTORIES.

TOWNS.	Number of establishments.	Capital Invested. In real estate.	Capital Invested. In tools and machinery.	Cash Value. Of raw materials used.	Cash Value. Of manufactured articles.	Persons employed.
BROOME CO.						
Windsor,	1	200	500	1,000	1,000	....
COLUMBIA CO.						
Hillsdale,	1	....	....	300	1,762	4
MONROE CO.						
Rochester,	2	400	1,800	8,135	20,000	11
NEW-YORK CO.						
New-York,	2	10,000	400	3,800	6,500	4
ONONDAGA CO.						
Syracuse,	1	....	100	2,000	6,000	7
QUEENS CO.						
Hempstead,	1	1,500	500	500	500	2

CLASS XVII.—HOUSEHOLD FURNITURE, MACHINES AND IMPLEMENTS FOR DOMESTIC PURPOSES.

BASKET MANUFACTORIES.

TOWNS.	Number of establishments.	Capital Invested. In real estate.	Capital Invested. In tools and machinery.	Cash Value. Of raw materials used.	Cash Value. Of manufactured articles.	Persons employed.
CORTLAND Co.						
Truxton,	1	....	....	....	$550	....
ERIE Co.						
Tonawanda,	1	....	....	$40	228	2
ESSEX Co.						
Lewis,	1	$125	$10	....	950	2
GREENE Co.						
New Baltimore,	1	....	25	7	75	2
JEFFERSON Co.						
Hounsfield,	1	....	....	....	35	....
NEW-YORK Co.						
New-York,	1	....	25	2,000	3,500	4
ONEIDA Co.						
Verona,	1	1,000	500	900	5,000	16
PUTNAM Co.						
Putnam Valley,	1	....	....	125	1,080	3
ROCKLAND Co.						
Orangetown,	1	100	25	120	1,500	4
SARATOGA Co.						
Greenfield,	1	....	....	....	500	....
WAYNE Co.						
Ontario,	1	20	3	48	400	3
WESTCHESTER Co.						
Lewisboro,	1	....	....	32	600	3

BED, MATTRESS AND COT MANUFACTORIES.

TOWNS.	Number of establishments.	Capital Invested. In real estate.	Capital Invested. In tools and machinery.	Cash Value. Of raw materials used.	Cash Value. Of manufactured articles.	Persons employed.
ALLEGANY Co.						
Amity,	1	....	150	100	240	2
GREENE Co.						
Hunter,	2	1,200	225	540	3,000	6
NEW-YORK Co.						
New-York,	7	7,000	425	50,340	82,000	27
ST. LAWRENCE Co.						
Parishville,	1	800	100	1,000	2,700	4
Stockholm,	1	1,200	500	1,500	3,000	10

BEDSTEAD MANUFACTORIES.

TOWNS.	Number of establishments.	Capital Invested. In real estate.	Capital Invested. In tools and machinery.	Cash Value. Of raw materials used.	Cash Value. Of manufactured articles.	Persons employed.
ALBANY Co.						
Watervliet,	3	33,500	8,000	67,816	105,000	102
CHAUTAUQUE Co.						
Portland,	1	1,000	250	400	1,800	3
CHEMUNG Co.						
Elmira,	1	....	....	....	1,000	....
Veteran,	1	3,000	1,500	6,000	13,000	12
CLINTON Co.						
Ellenburgh,	1	1,000	500	750	1,325	3
CORTLAND Co.						
Cortlandville,	1	....	....	36	125	....
Preble,	1	....	....	....	200	....
Truxton,	1	500	500	200	900	1
DUTCHESS Co.						
Poughkeepsie city,	1	4,000	700	5,400	10,000	12
ERIE Co.						
Lancaster,	1	3,000	1,000	1,500	4,500	7
GREENE Co.						
Hunter,	2	....	1,000	1,250	4,350	6
HERKIMER Co.						
Salisbury,	1	500	250	100	1,200	2
KINGS Co.						
Brooklyn,	1	1,000	50	4,240	8,000	4
MONROE Co.						
Rochester,	3	8,000	3,200	6,486	17,000	9
NEW-YORK Co.						
New-York,	4	....	6,650	13,500	41,000	47
ONEIDA Co.						
Ansville,	1	1,000	200	700	2,100	3
OTSEGO Co.						
Burlington,	1	....	....	250	700	....
RENSSELAER Co.						
Lansingburgh,	1	1,500	2,000	6,500	20,000	10
Troy,	1	....	4,000	5,000	15,000	55
WESTCHESTER Co.						
White Plains,	1	20,000	2,000	930	30,000	65

BILLIARD TABLE MANUFACTORIES.

TOWNS.	Number of establishments.	Capital Invested. In real estate.	Capital Invested. In tools and machinery.	Cash Value. Of raw materials used.	Cash Value. Of manufactured articles.	Persons employed.
NEW-YORK Co.						
New-York,	6	117,000	6,600	38,200	123,500	54

BROOM MANUFACTORIES.

TOWNS.	Number of establishments.	Capital Invested. In real estate.	Capital Invested. In tools and machinery.	Cash Value. Of raw materials used.	Cash Value. Of manufactured articles.	Persons employed.
ALBANY Co.						
Bethlehem,	1	9,000	1,000	8,000	13,000	14
Watervliet,	7	5,300	3,570	32,097	48,005	48
BROOME Co.						
Chenango,	4	6,100	4,170	774	....	4
COLUMBIA Co.						
New Lebanon,	1	....	....	....	....	....
ERIE Co.						
Amherst,	1	....	$300	$7,000	$10,000	14
GENESEE Co.						
Le Roy,	1	$500	....	3,285	6,250	3
Pavilion,	2	150	50	220	2,680	3
GREENE Co.						
New Baltimore,	1	200	60	960	1,680	3
HERKIMER Co.						
German Flats,	2	....	2,000	23,200	40,500	55
MONTGOMERY Co.						
Amsterdam,	2	....	100	6,450	14,250	21
Minden,	2	1,600	380	15,200	22,000	8
Mohawk,	1	700	30	1,120	2,413	3
NEW-YORK Co.						
New-York,	2	6,000	110	10,000	18,000	17
NIAGARA Co.						
Hartland,	1	30	20	557	900	1
Lockport,	1	2,000	1,000	8,000	22,000	24
RENSSELAER Co.						
Hoosick,	2	....	....	....	1,818	....
SCHENECTADY Co.						
Glenville,	11	3,800	6,080	121,891	159,914	138
Rotterdam,	1	....	200	40,000	50,000	30
Schenectady,	3	8,000	575	36,900	57,937	39
SCHOHARIE Co.						
Schoharie,	4	....	320	8,577	13,000	15
SENECA Co.						
Varick,	1	150	25	137	240	1
TIOGA Co.						
Tioga,	1	....	....	....	4,900	....
WAYNE Co.						
Arcadia,	1	....	....	....	....	....
Palmyra,	1	150	....	435	690	1

BRUSH MANUFACTORIES.

TOWNS.	Number of establishments.	Capital Invested. In real estate.	Capital Invested. In tools and machinery.	Cash Value. Of raw materials used.	Cash Value. Of manufactured articles.	Persons employed.
ALBANY Co.						
Albany,	1	....	300	6,500	11,000	6
MONROE Co.						
Rochester,	1	....	150	600	800	6
NEW-YORK Co.						
New-York,	20	49,000	24,000	147,470	283,016	161
ONEIDA Co.						
Utica,	1	8,000	150	1,700	3,000	2
ORANGE Co.						
Newburgh,	1	1,000	500	1,000	2,900	12
RENSSELAER Co.						
Lansingburgh,	13	28,200	15,325	183,585	422,285	949
Troy,	1	30,000	3,000	30,000	60,000	60
WESTCHESTER Co.						
North Castle,	1	2,000	2,000	1,460	1,950	4

CABINET MAKING SHOPS.

TOWNS.	Number of establishments.	Capital Invested. In real estate.	Capital Invested. In tools and machinery.	Cash Value. Of raw materials used.	Cash Value. Of manufactured articles.	Persons employed.
ALBANY Co.						
Albany,	4	5,000	2,500	48,000	71,500	67
New Scotland,	2	400	225	....	1,500	5
Rensselaerville,	2	550	175	950	1,625	5
ALLEGANY Co.						
Almond,	1	2,000	500	1,200	4,000	7
Angelica,	1	1,000	100	2,750	10,000	11
Belfast,	1	400	100	190	1,500	3
Bolivar,	1	600	300	300	3,200	5
Burns,	1	250	50	120	700	1
Cuba,	1	2,000	2,000	1,200	4,500	5
Friendship,	1	500	500	150	1,000	3
Genesee,	1	500	100	60	400	1
Hume,	1	1,500	200	600	1,800	3
Independence,	1	600	225	350	2,100	3
Rushford,	2	1,500	350	430	1,800	3
Scio,	1	1,500	1,500	500	....	....
BROOME Co.						
Chenango,	2	3,000	300	300	2,250	4
Colesville,	1	700	300	95	500	2
Union,	1	3,000	1,000	800	1,500	4
Windsor,	1	300	125	300	2,000	1
CATTARAUGUS Co.						
Allegany,	1	600	150	180	1,000	1
Conewango,	1	500	500	200	700	3
Ellicottville,	2	2,200	350	855	4,200	1
Farmersville,	1	....	300	100	....	1
Franklinville,	2	700	350	270	1,400	1
Freedom,	1	....	70	400	800	1
Olean,	1	....	100	150	....	1
Otto,	1	300	60	375	1,000	3
Persia,	1	550	100	400	1,000	2
Randolph,	3	2,950	1,000	1,683	4,400	6

CLASS XVII.—(Continued.)

TOWNS.	Number of establishments.	Capital Invested. In real estate.	Capital Invested. In tools and machinery.	Cash Value. Of raw materials used.	Cash Value. Of manufactured articles.	Persons employed.
Cattaraugus Co.						
Yorkshire,	1	$2,000	$500	$600	$4,000	6
Cayuga Co.						
Auburn,	4	12,000	8,000	67,800	72,500	113
Brutus,	1	650	200	350	2,000	4
Ira,	1	250	100	150	800	....
Mentz,	1	3,800	6,500	30,000	40,000	15
Moravia,	2	800	125	410	1,000	4
Sterling,	1	200	250	100	700	1
Victory,	1	500	300	100	1,000	2
Chautauque Co.						
Chautauque,	2	375	200	450	1,300	3
Ellicott,	2	3,500	825	1,352	2,700	10
Ellington,	1	800	450	150	800	3
Hanover,	2	1,500	300	1,000	1,500	2
Pomfret,	3	2,850	500	3,486	12,630	14
Sherman,	3	....	....	....	1,500	....
Chemung Co.						
Chemung,	1	300	100	200	200	1
Elmira,	3	1,770	4,397	36,800	61,265	44
Southport,	1	500	100	200	500	....
Veteran,	1	500	150	125	700	1
Chenango Co.						
Columbus,	1	100	75	100	700	2
New Berlin,	1	200	25	120	265	....
Oxford,	1	1,000	1,500	1,000	4,000	5
Pitcher,	1	400	523	243	1,400	2
Sherburne,	1	450	75	400	1,600	2
Smithville,	1	2,000	800	500	3,000	6
Smyrna,	1	8,000	50	96	600	....
Clinton Co.						
Champlain,	3	1,650	500	285	4,500	11
Peru,	1	400	400	825	3,500	3
Plattsburgh,	2	....	1,500	2,727	1,895	12
Columbia Co.						
Hudson,	2	125	375	16,250	29,000	14
Kinderhook,	3	2,550	350	525	3,970	10
Cortland Co.						
Cincinnatus,	1	124	75	250	600	....
Cortlandville,	1	200	1,352	1,000	7,000	9
Freetown,	1	400	225	21	300	1
Homer,	2	3,600	200	4,125	9,000	9
Scott,	1	150	25	150	500	1
Truxton,	1	600	100	300	2,000	2
Delaware Co.						
Andes,	1	600	75	375	800	2
Bovina,	1	....	50	35	205	1
Delhi,	2	675	800	350	2,600	6
Franklin,	2	550	250	850	2,300	4
Kortright,	1	400	100	250	775	2
Roxbury,	1	350	100	250	800	2
Stamford,	1	800	25	....	3,000	2
Dutchess Co.						
Amenia,	1	400	150	350	550	1
Fishkill,	2	2,000	350	723	4,800	8
Poughkeepsie city,	4	10,000	750	5,800	41,000	37
Rhinebeck,	2	3,500	600	800	13,000	9
Erie Co.						
Aurora,	1	500	400	200	900	....
Boston,	1	100	200	75	545	1
Buffalo,	8	105,900	10,200	55,553	237,992	290
Collins,	1	300	400	150	700	....
Hamburgh,	1	500	500	150	600	3
Newstead,	2	700	125	300	1,500	3
North Collins,	3	120	270	600	1,300	3
Tonawanda,	2	500	200	250	1,250	4
Essex Co.						
Chesterfield,	1	4,000	1,500	3,000	8,000	8
Elizabethtown,	1	500	200	100	500	2
Essex,	1	800	350	300	1,500	3
Moriah,	1	500	1,000	270	2,000	....
Schroon,	1	150	50	150	600	1
Franklin Co.						
Constable,	1	....	125	25	800	2
Fort Covington,	2	1,300	1,200	700	4,500	....
Malone,	2	4,700	1,300	535	3,404	4
Fulton Co.						
Broadalbin,	1	1,200	50	200	1,000	2
Northampton,	1	500	300	300	600	2
Genesee Co.						
Alabama,	1	100	50	130	300	1
Bergen,	1	....	....	....	....	....
Byron,	1	....	75	250	900	1
Le Roy,	2	5,300	1,100	5,500	19,000	17
Pavilion,	1	150	25	25	250	1
Greene Co.						
Coxsackie,	1	....	600	200	800	1
Cairo,	1	500	100	1,500	457	2
Durham,	2	650	225	425	2,000	4
Windham,	1	1,500	300	800	2,000	3
Hamilton Co.						
Morehouse,	1	....	$300	$100	$1,000	....
Herkimer Co.						
Fairfield,	1	$100	50	90	400	1
Frankfort,	1	650	100	250	1,000	3
German Flats,	1	750	100	480	1,000	1
Herkimer,	1	500	75	300	2,500	2
Little Falls,	2	2,800	150	2,600	7,000	7
Newport,	1	2,300	200	650	1,500	4
Salisbury,	1	500	150	200	800	1
Stark,	1	800	350	75	500	2
Winfield,	1	500	300	2,500	1,000	2
Jefferson Co.						
Adams,	3	2,800	475	988	2,720	6
Antwerp,	2	1,800	550	750	3,700	4
Brownville,	1	1,000	1,200	5,300	4,250	6
Champion,	1	1,000	500	220	1,200	2
Ellisburgh,	2	1,050	340	800	2,600	4
Hounsfield,	1	250	200	225	1,200	1
Orleans,	1	400	150	220	545	1
Philadelphia,	1	350	100	100	600	1
Rutland,	1	500	50	200	800	1
Watertown,	3	6,400	2,500	7,305	45,000	36
Wilna,	1	5,000	300	600	4,000	4
Kings Co.						
Brooklyn,	16	20,000	16,383	52,511	251,324	149
Lewis Co.						
Greig,	1	150	220	120	400	1
Lowville,	3	500	700	1,105	4,475	8
Martinsburgh,	1	2,000	500	500	3,000	3
Livingston Co.						
Avon,	2	2,000	550	900	4,000	4
Conesus,	1	250	100	245	800	1
Groveland,	1	200	100	60	400	1
Livonia,	1	100	100	250	1,000	1
Nunda,	2	1,800	600	1,076	5,800	7
North Dansville,	3	2,250	675	5,132	13,125	17
Portage,	1	1,000	5,000	300	1,000	2
Madison Co.						
Cazenovia,	3	1,300	150	830	2,900	6
De Ruyter,	1	1,000	2,500	1,450	5,000	6
Eaton,	2	1,700	200	1,400	3,000	6
Georgetown,	1	850	200	100	560	1
Hamilton,	2	6,100	3,150	4,350	13,000	20
Lenox,	2	2,800	200	700	2,500	4
Sullivan,	1	700	100	223	1,400	3
Monroe Co.						
Mendon,	1	450	100	400	1,400	3
Parma,	1	50	125	225	900	1
Perrington,	4	33,100	4,775	....	....	....
Rochester,	6	9,970	5,275	21,472	84,100	114
Sweden,	1	1,500	1,500	4,250	11,000	10
Wheatland,	2	2,600	300	1,079	4,500	7
Montgomery Co.						
Amsterdam,	2	1,300	500	1,500	6,000	4
Glen,	1	800	150	725	925	3
Minden,	2	2,000	200	2,075	3,500	3
Mohawk,	2	2,800	320	1,840	6,100	6
Root,	2	....	25	100	300	....
New-York Co.						
New-York,	98	253,500	225,890	685,143	2,236,794	2116
Niagara Co.						
Hartland,	1	....	500	200	1,000	3
Lewiston,	1	....	7,000	130	1,200	1
Lockport,	2	1,000	2,600	5,500	18,000	33
Niagara,	1	8,000	600	400	10,000	16
Wilson,	1	300	100	105	550	2
Oneida Co.						
Augusta,	2	3,300	2,300	2,385	5,250	16
Boonville,	3	5,100	1,350	1,690	7,115	19
Kirkland,	2	1,100	150	1,688	3,400	7
Rome,	2	3,275	450	1,579	6,120	11
Sangerfield,	1	1,000	650	2,000	5,000	7
Trenton,	1	400	200	150	1,000	3
Utica,	4	16,980	5,250	3,330	113,175	91
Vernon,	2	800	350	800	2,200	3
Westmoreland,	1	1,000	400	370	1,045	2
Whitestown,	3	1,250	420	715	4,300	6
Onondaga Co.						
Camillus,	1	600	500	300	1,000	2
Elbridge,	2	3,500	450	1,120	6,700	10
Fabius,	1	....	....	....	....	....
Lysander,	1	600	....	150	1,500	2
Manlius,	2	2,000	150	810	3,000	6
Pompey,	1	100	200	1,000	2,000	2
Syracuse,	5	6,000	4,250	18,600	117,100	109
Van Buren,	2	1,110	200	634	2,300	4
Ontario Co.						
Bristol,	1	850	350	500	1,500	3
Canandaigua,	2	4,000	200	900	5,000	8

CLASS XVII.—(CONTINUED.)

TOWNS.	Number of establishments.	Capital Invested. In real estate.	Capital Invested. In tools and machinery.	Cash Value. Of raw materials used.	Cash Value. Of manufactured articles.	Persons employed.
ONTARIO Co.						
Naples, ...	2	$2,000	$200	$949	$3,500	4
Richmond, ...	1	500	250	400	2,000	3
Seneca, ...	1	1,600	1,000	10,000	10,000	11
West Bloomfield,.	1	300	25	100	500	....
ORANGE Co.						
Deerpark, ...	1	2,000	500	7,000	9,000	7
Goshen, ...	1	2,000	150	2,000	2,500	5
Minisink, ...	1	250	50	250	800	2
Newburgh, ...	3	4,600	3,050	7,750	22,550	30
Walkill, ...	2	1,100	300	2,000	6,900	6
Warwick, ...	1	800	200	1,000	2,000	3
ORLEANS Co.						
Barre, ...	1	1,500	2,000	3,800	10,000	12
Carlton, ...	1	....	40	50	348	....
Clarendon, ...	1	1,000	250	600	3,000	2
Murray, ...	1	1,000	800	350	1,500	4
Ridgeway, ...	3	2,900	350	1,125	5,000	6
Yates, ...	1	600	150	175	800	2
OSWEGO Co.						
Constantia, ...	1	400	300	220	1,000	2
Hannibal, ...	1	450	100	276	1,000	2
Mexico, ...	3	1,300	475	487	2,600	3
Orwell, ...	1	800	400	....	800	2
Oswego city, ...	4	20,000	4,200	5,787	30,200	51
Richland, ...	2	3,300	900	380	3,400	8
Volney, ...	1	....	300	630	8,000	12
OTSEGO Co.						
Burlington, ...	2	900	700	400	800	4
Butternuts, ...	2	550	2,350	900	6,800	9
Edmeston, ...	1	2,000	1,000	4,000	6,000	8
Laurens, ...	1	500	300	300	3,000	2
Morris, ...	1	1,500	1,000	5,323	5,000	10
Oneonta, ...	2	2,200	1,300	1,000	3,500	7
Otego, ...	1	600	100	220	350	1
Otsego, ...	1	2,000	100	875	3,850	7
Plainfield, ...	1	1,500	500	1,360	2,000	7
Richfield, ...	1	500	300	300	7,000	2
Springfield, ...	1	200	200	500	1,200	3
Unadilla, ...	1	400	50	250	1,000	2
PUTNAM Co.						
Carmel, ...	1	....	100	250	750	1
Southeast, ...	1	1,000	500	2,150	4,000	6
QUEENS Co.						
Flushing, ...	2	4,000	400	1,050	7,000	3
Jamaica, ...	1	2,000	1,000	1,200	2,000	5
North Hempstead,	1	100	100	600	1,500	3
RENSSELAER Co.						
Lansingburgh, ...	4	4,000	950	3,102	18,500	18
Petersburgh, ...	1	400	500	135	445	1
Pittstown, ...	1	300	75	....	....	....
Troy, ...	4	27,000	800	16,500	59,000	46
RICHMOND Co.						
Northfield, ...	1	1,500	500	2,300	6,000	11
ST. LAWRENCE Co.						
Canton, ...	1	5,000	100	1,000	2,500	6
Gouverneur, ...	1	1,000	1,600	1,662	7,800	14
Hermon, ...	1	....	300	700	1,800	3
Lawrence, ...	1	....	50	40	500	2
Madrid, ...	2	1,200	220	360	2,400	3
Oswegatchie, ...	4	8,800	1,700	10,200	25,800	24
Potsdam, ...	1	1,000	300	300	2,500	6
Rossie, ...	1	150	40	92	500	1
SARATOGA Co.						
Edinburgh, ...	1	800	100	125	720	2
Milton, ...	1	300	200	200	1,500	3
Saratoga, ...	1	....	150	900	2,000	4
Saratoga Springs,.	2	1,200	600	5,885	13,000	9
Stillwater, ...	2	....	....	....	....	2
SCHENECTADY Co.						
Duanesburgh, ...	1	....	50	50	191	....
Schenectady, ...	4	3,900	950	12,950	52,000	37
SCHOHARIE Co.						
Middleburgh, ...	1	100	100	950	800	3
Richmondville, ...	1	200	100	150	1,000	2
Schoharie, ...	1	900	1,100	500	1,500	4
Seward, ...	1	1,400	25	300	300	2
Summit, ...	1	50	100	300	600	....
SCHUYLER Co.						
Catherines, ...	1	600	100	800	2,500	2
Dix, ...	1	1,500	....	500	1,500	2
Hector, ...	2	1,300	400	700	2,400	5
SENECA Co						
Ovid, ...	1	....	200	200	2,000	2
Seneca Falls, ...	3	3,900	100	300	5,700	2
Waterloo, ...	1	500	500	2,000	4,000	7
STEUBEN Co.						
Avoca, ...	1	1,000	200	250	800	2
Bath, ...	3	3,500	800	3,200	24,000	12
Bradford, ...	1	300	500	200	700	1
STEUBEN Co.						
Corning, ...	3	$7,400	$3,600	$1,245	$13,867	16
Erwin, ...	1	500	75	160	1,300	2
Fremont, ...	1	500	300	75	755	3
Hornellsville, ...	2	4,500	450	1,775	6,000	9
Jasper, ...	2	250	225	3,600	800	3
Troupsburgh, ...	1	100	25	15	100	1
Urbana, ...	1	1,000	100	800	1,500	1
SUFFOLK Co.						
Huntington, ...	2	400	200	900	1,800	4
Smithtown, ...	1	300	150	....	....	1
Southold, ...	2	3,500	150	700	2,000	6
SULLIVAN Co.						
Liberty, ...	1	300	50	300	1,000	1
Mamakating, ...	3	900	275	125	100	2
Neversink, ...	2	1,000	200	350	500	3
Thompson, ...	1	500	100	375	2,500	3
TIOGA Co.						
Barton, ...	1	1,500	150	250	....	5
Candor, ...	1	2,000	1,000	....	300	4
Nichols, ...	1	300	50	500	1,000	2
Owego, ...	2	800	650	1,080	5,550	6
TOMPKINS Co.						
Caroline, ...	1	400	200	90	1,300	2
Dryden, ...	1	600	200	260	1,800	3
Groton, ...	1	500	75	300	1,000	2
Ithaca, ...	7	8,100	2,000	6,150	15,700	28
Lansing, ...	1	450	100	150	600	1
Newfield, ...	2	400	150	180	1,500	3
Ulysses, ...	3	2,500	750	1,900	5,500	9
ULSTER Co.						
Kingston, ...	4	9,700	740	3,500	19,150	20
Marbletown, ...	1	500	100	120	500	2
Saugerties, ...	2	....	75	860	5,200	6
Wawarsing, ...	1	1,000	150	1,500	3,000	2
WARREN Co.						
Queensbury, ...	2	2,800	1,000	3,455	8,312	9
WASHINGTON Co.						
Argyle, ...	1	600	150	82	291	....
Granville, ...	1	150	150	500	1,500	3
Greenwich, ...	1	800	100	965	3,287	....
Hartford, ...	1	200	250	539	1,626	1
Kingsbury, ...	2	4,150	1,550	1,520	5,900	9
Salem, ...	2	900	300	800	2,000	2
White Creek, ...	1	800	300	500	1,400	6
WAYNE Co.						
Arcadia, ...	1	3,000	1,000	1,540	4,790	6
Marion, ...	1	800	500	1,700	3,000	5
Palmyra, ...	1	5,500	1,800	4,500	15,500	20
Sodus, ...	3	700	500	2,600	5,700	6
Wolcott, ...	2	800	50	500	2,600	3
WESTCHESTER Co.						
Bedford, ...	1	300	200	400	898	....
Greenburgh, ...	2	1,100	400	1,237	2,840	5
North Salem, ...	1	....	100	140	275	....
Ossining, ...	1	....	9,000	9,200	30,000	100
Rye, ...	1	1,000	300	250	2,500	4
White Plains, ...	1	....	100	150	....	2
WYOMING Co.						
Bennington, ...	1	200	250	350	1,300	2
Castile, ...	1	1,000	70	166	1,000	2
China, ...	2	800	600	480	3,500	5
Gainesville, ...	1	....	....	....	500	3
Genesee Falls, ...	1	300	200	250	1,200	....
Java, ...	1	600	50	60	500	2
Middlebury, ...	2	1,100	400	285	1,100	2
Perry, ...	2	1,200	400	2,200	6,300	8
Pike, ...	1	400	25	300	1,000	2
Sheldon, ...	2	800	250	200	800	2
Warsaw, ...	3	3,500	550	1,556	8,070	8
YATES Co.						
Benton, ...	1	300	100	100	800	1
Jerusalem, ...	1	500	200	300	1,000	1
Milo, ...	3	6,000	1,325	2,200	11,000	9
Potter, ...	1	....	....	240	2,000	4

CEDAR WARE MANUFACTORIES.

TOWNS.	Number of establishments.	In real estate.	In tools and machinery.	Of raw materials used.	Of manufactured articles.	Persons employed.
ALBANY Co.						
Albany, ...	1	1,800	500	1,520	3,620	4
NEW-YORK Co.						
New-York, ...	1	....	50	200	4,050	6

CHAIR FACTORIES.

TOWNS.	Number of establishments.	In real estate.	In tools and machinery.	Of raw materials used.	Of manufactured articles.	Persons employed.
ALBANY Co.						
Albany, ...	2	....	1,500	12,000	25,800	....
Watervliet, ...	1	25,000	15,000	27,800	95,000	150
CHAUTAUQUE Co.						
Chautauque, ...	1	....	75	60	600	1

CLASS XVII.—(Continued.)

TOWNS.	Number of establishments.	Capital Invested. In real estate.	Capital Invested. In tools and machinery.	Cash Value. O raw materials used.	Cash Value. Of manufactured articles.	Persons employed.
Chautauque Co.						
Ellicott,	1	$16,000	$360	$2,100	$9,200	13
Sherman,	1	....	....	....	500	....
Chenango Co.						
Norwich,	2	1,600	700	993	3,099	6
Smithville,	1	35	150	60	500	2
Clinton Co.						
Ellenburgh,	1	....	....	250	250	....
Mooers,	1	100	100	7	....	....
Plattsburgh,	1	3,000	200	150	1,500	4
Columbia Co.						
New Lebanon,	1	500	500	2,050	3,000	6
Cortland Co.						
Solon,	1	1,000	150	500	1,500	3
Dutchess Co.						
Poughkeepsie city,	2	8,000	41,500	27,850	116,200	342
Erie Co.						
Newstead,	1	200	25	40	400	1
Essex Co.						
Wilmington,	1	....	500	....	941	....
Fulton Co.						
Johnstown,	1	900	200	300	1,000	4
Genesee Co.						
Alexander,	1	250	60	100	350	1
Greene Co.						
Catskill,	1	800	1,000	3,500	10,000	10
Hunter,	3	4,300	1,600	8,385	18,900	60
Herkimer Co.						
Newport,	1	1,450	350	300	1,200	3
Jefferson Co.						
Ellisburgh,	1	1,000	1,000	1,100	5,000	24
Rutland,	1	1,500	800	2,215	4,000	11
Lewis Co.						
Leyden,	1	....	800	1,275	7,500	12
Osceola,	1	1,000	400	500	1,000	1
Livingston Co.						
Livonia,	1	2,000	200	36	600	1
Madison Co.						
Brookfield,	1	1,400	500	200	1,100	....
Fenner,	1	200	100	100	1,000	2
Hamilton,	1	400	50	225	1,500	3
Monroe Co.						
Rochester,	1	....	5,550	19,100	70,000	250
New-York Co.						
New-York,	27	144,000	15,725	611,772	503,780	455
Oneida Co.						
Annsville,	1	200	50	....	....	1
Boonville,	1	1,000	1,000	5,000	12,000	12
Camden,	1	1,300	1,200	2,000	7,500	12
Lee,	1	700	200	500	2,000	9
Utica,	1	200	50	....	....	4
Onondaga Co.						
Camillus,	2	800	400	50	2,000	3
De Witt,	1	1,000	200	100	500	....
Skaneateles,	1	....	....	3,500	1,000	4
Ontario Co.						
Phelps,	1	1,000	300	600	1,200	4
Orange Co.						
Minisink,	1	150	10	250	800	2
Oswego Co.						
Richland,	1	300	100	180	795	4
Rockland Co.						
Haverstraw,	1	....	400	3,000	4,500	4
Orangetown,	1	....	60	50	500	2
St. Lawrence Co.						
Gouverneur,	1	....	....	300	913	6
Hermon,	1	400	150	150	2,500	2
Potsdam,	1	....	300	375	1,300	2
Providence,	2	800	300	400	2,000	5
Schoharie Co.						
Gilboa,	1	....	25	50	300	1
Steuben Co.						
Bradford,	1	75	50	25	400	1
Sullivan Co.						
Thompson,	1	700	150	300	1,200	3
Tompkins Co.						
Dryden,	1	50	50	25	100	1
Washington Co.						
White Creek,	1	200	600	250	900	1
Wayne Co.						
Wolcott,	1	1,000	....	86	1,250	3
Westchester Co.						
Greenburgh,	1	300	260	700	1,500	5
Wyoming Co.						
China,	1	300	40	50	550	2

COFFEE-MILL MANUFACTORIES.

TOWNS.	Number of establishments.	In real estate.	In tools and machinery.	Of raw materials used.	Of manufactured articles.	Persons employed.
Dutchess Co.						
Washington,	1	1,000	300	500	600	3
Greene Co.						
Durham,	2	2,850	1,500	4,025	12,960	21

FEATHER BRUSH MANUFACTORIES.

TOWNS.	Number of establishments.	Capital Invested. In real estate.	Capital Invested. In tools and machinery.	Cash Value. Of raw materials used.	Cash Value. Of manufactured articles.	Persons employed.
New-York Co.						
New-York,	3	$1,000	$1,000	$19,975	$41,300	51

HOUSE-DECORATING ESTABLISHMENT.

TOWNS.	Number of establishments.	In real estate.	In tools and machinery.	Of raw materials used.	Of manufactured articles.	Persons employed.
New-York Co.						
New-York,	1	....	3,000	1,000	7,000	9

HOUSE-FURNISHING ESTABLISHMENTS.

TOWNS.	Number of establishments.	In real estate.	In tools and machinery.	Of raw materials used.	Of manufactured articles.	Persons employed.
Delaware Co.						
Franklin,	1	200	100	....	550	3
Erie Co.						
Buffalo,	2	....	....	41,000	70,000	6
Jefferson Co.						
Watertown,	1	....	....	3,095	3,095	....
Kings Co.						
Brooklyn,	1	450	20	400	700	2
New-York Co.						
New-York,	10	63,500	5,410	77,300	207,500	121
Oneida Co.						
Utica,	4	....	925	20,095	30,350	22
Onondaga Co.						
Syracuse,	3	....	90	16,200	26,200	20
Oswego Co.						
Oswego city,	1	5,000	500	2,500	5,000	5
Ulster Co.						
Wawarsing,	1	....	800	725	1,665	5

IRON FURNITURE MANUFACTORIES.

TOWNS.	Number of establishments.	In real estate.	In tools and machinery.	Of raw materials used.	Of manufactured articles.	Persons employed.
New-York Co.						
New-York,	3	25,000	21,000	77,700	110,200	78

PAIL MANUFACTORIES.

TOWNS.	Number of establishments.	In real estate.	In tools and machinery.	Of raw materials used.	Of manufactured articles.	Persons employed.
Allegany Co.						
Amity,	2	150	1,200	5,495	9,875	10
Angelica,	1	1,000	1,800	1,840	5,400	5
Chautauque Co.						
Ellicott,	1	1,000	5,000	500	6,000	25
Clinton Co.						
Chazy,	1	1,000	2,000	500	3,720	3
Dutchess Co.						
Poughkeepsie city,	1	200	100	410	1,500	2
Red Hook,	1	800	....	750	1,500	3
Erie Co.						
Aurora,	2	2,000	3,100	2,250	4,950	13
Buffalo,	1	15,000	10,000	19,575	37,900	32
Collins,	1	1,000	2,000	800	5,500	5
Essex Co.						
Crown Point,	1	....	900	2,700	5,400	6
Franklin Co.						
Westville,	1	....	....	355	750	4
Livingston Co.						
North Dansville,	1	2,000	500	2,000	4,000	5
Oneida Co.						
Whitestown,	1	5,000	2,500	3,520	8,000	16
Onondaga Co.						
Skaneateles,	1	3,000	1,000	2,000	10,000	7
Otsego Co.						
Otsego,	1	5,500	300	1,555	4,500	9
Rockland Co.						
Orangetown,	1	7,000	6,500	18,260	33,700	15
St. Lawrence Co.						
Colton,	1	1,400	600	400	1,500	3
Saratoga Co.						
Moreau,	2	....	1,780	10,200	19,000	30
Providence,	1	300	800	1,200	3,500	3
Warren Co.						
Luzerne,	1	300	300	350	2,000	7

PAPER-HANGING MANUFACTORIES.

TOWNS.	Number of establishments.	In real estate.	In tools and machinery.	Of raw materials used.	Of manufactured articles.	Persons employed.
Columbia Co.						
Hudson,	1	5,000	2,000	3,400	6,000	5
Kings Co.						
Brooklyn,	1	9,000	10,000	12,000	30,000	36
New-York Co.						
New-York,	5	101,000	71,000	153,075	428,000	193
Oneida Co.						
Utica,	1	3,000	750	1,400	2,200	7
Richmond Co.						
Castleton,	1	....	....	33,400	37,400	....

RUG AND MAT MANUFACTORIES.

TOWNS.	Number of establishments.	In real estate.	In tools and machinery.	Of raw materials used.	Of manufactured articles.	Persons employed.
Kings Co.						
Brooklyn,	2	7,000	3,700	36,500	87,000	127
New-York Co.						
New-York,	5	185,000	1,700	15,142	81,705	97

CLASS XVII.—(Continued.)

TOWNS.	Number of establishments.	Capital Invested. In real estate.	Capital Invested. In tools and machinery.	Cash Value. Of raw materials used.	Cash Value. Of manufactured articles.	Persons employed.
SOFA AND LOUNGE MANUFACTORIES.						
New-York Co.						
New-York, ...	5	$5,000	$100	$23,710	$181,500	151
WASHING MACHINE MANUFACTORIES.						
Greene Co.						
Coxsackie, ...	1	....	100	300	900	1
New-York Co.						
New-York, ...	1	....	500	2,000	3,500	3
WILLOW WARE MANUFACTORIES.						
New-York Co.						
New-York, ...	4	14,000	15	3,565	11,500	13
Westchester Co.						
Greenburgh, ...	1	300	3,500	190	600	1
WINDOW SHADE MANUFACTORIES.						
Kings Co.						
Brooklyn, ...	1	....	600	25,000	50,000	19
New-York Co.						
New-York, ...	5	13,600	24,150	95,300	252,000	101
Oneida Co.........						
Utica, ...	1	2,000	300	4,000	8,000	2
Onondaga Co.						
Syracuse, ...	1	....	....	400	500	1
Rockland Co.						
Orangetown, ...	1	....	75	2,860	3,600	2
WOODENWARE MANUFACTORIES.						
Greene Co.						
Hunter, ...	2	$1,300	$150	$1,275	$3,350	5
Jefferson Co.						
Adams, ...	1	1,500	1,500	240	3,200	8
Champion, ...	2	2,800	2,700	1,290	7,295	9
Oneida Co.						
Camden, ...	1	....	....	100	550	2
Onondaga Co.						
Elbridge, ...	1	5,000	2,000	5,400	27,000	18
Otsego Co.						
Burlington, ...	1	600	400	400	4,000	12
Morris, ...	1	50	15	50	611	1
Otego, ...	1	....	8	9	57	1
Rensselaer Co.						
Lansingburgh, ...	1	400	100	260	700	1
Saratoga Co.						
Edinburgh, ...	2	11,000	1,600	4,500	25,000	41
Schuyler Co.						
Catherines, ...	1	400	200	200	750	1
Sullivan Co.						
Rockland, ...	1	200	500	720	2,400	6
Tioga Co.						
Nichols, ...	1	350	400	250	2,500	3
Ulster Co.						
Denning, ...	1	1,000	300	800	3,000	8
Warren Co.						
Stony Creek, ...	1	700	250	500	2,000	3
Washington Co.						
Salem, ...	1	300	100	300	1,000	....

CLASS XVIII.—ARTS—POLITE, FINE AND ORNAMENTAL.

TOWNS.	Number of establishments.	Capital Invested. In real estate.	Capital Invested. In tools and machinery.	Cash Value. Of raw materials used.	Cash Value. Of manufactured articles.	Persons employed.
ARTISTS' BRUSH MANUFACTORY.						
New-York Co.						
New-York, ...	1	....	200	1,000	3,000	2
BLOCK LETTER MANUFACTORY.						
New-York Co.						
New-York, ...	1	....	1,000	....	....	3
BOOK BINDERIES.						
Cayuga Co.						
Auburn, ...	1	10,000	22,225	35,650	78,600	54
Chautauque Co.						
Pomfret, ...	1	400	260	370	1,200	2
Dutchess Co.						
Poughkeepsie city,	1	....	800	500	1,600	4
Herkimer Co.						
Little Falls, ...	1	200	200	800	1,600	1
Kings Co.						
Brooklyn, ...	1	....	3,000	2,000	5,350	10
Madison Co.						
Hamilton, ...	1	....	....	60	500	1
New-York Co.						
New-York, ...	32	253,000	170,350	352,860	776,700	1002
Oneida Co.						
Utica, ...	1	....	1,200	1,740	4,800	13
Ontario Co.						
Canandaigua, ...	2	500	550	800	2,800	6
Oswego Co.						
Oswego city, ...	2	12,000	1,150	21,250	7,500	6
St. Lawrence Co.						
Oswegatchie, ...	1	....	800	1,500	4,000	4
Steuben Co.						
Bath, ...	1	....	300	500	1,500	2
Tompkins Co.						
Ithaca, ...	1	....	....	300	300	4
Westchester Co.						
Eastchester, ...	1	....	400	1,500	3,000	5
New Rochelle, ...	1	10,000	1,000	3,750	27,600	16
BOOK BINDERS' TOOL MANUFACTORY.						
New-York Co.						
New-York, ...	1	....	500	600	7,000	17
CAMERA MANUFACTORY.						
New-York Co.						
New-York, ...	1	10,000	700	10,000	40,000	18
DAGUERREOTYPING ESTABLISHMENTS.						
Cayuga Co.						
Auburn, ...	1	....	300	1,000	3,300	1
Moravia, ...	1	100	100	300	1,000	1
Chautauque Co.						
Ellicott, ...	1	....	300	200	1,600	....
Franklin Co.						
Malone, ...	1	700	100	200	600	....
Jefferson Co.						
Watertown, ...	2	....	1,450	2,200	6,000	4
Livingston Co.						
North Dansville, ..	1	300	700	875	2,600	2
Madison Co.						
Lenox, ...	1	....	400	400	1,000	....
New-York Co.						
New-York, ...	10	10,000	30,800	50,500	200,000	182
Onondaga Co.						
Syracuse, ...	3	....	1,650	3,600	7,000	5
Otsego Co.						
Burlington, ...	1	....	250	350	1,000	1
Westchester Co.						
Eastchester, ...	1	....	500	100	1,000	1
Yates Co.						
Milo, ...	2	....	200	1,000	4,000	3
DAGUERREOTYPE CASE MANUFACTORIES.						
Kings Co.						
Brooklyn, ...	1	700	400	1,000	5,000	10
New-York Co.						
New-York.	1	....	2,000	7,000	108,200	54
Orange Co.						
New Windsor, ...	1	10,000	7,000	5,000	20,000	35
ENGRAVING ESTABLISHMENTS.						
Kings Co.						
Brooklyn, ...	1	500	1,000	500	1,500	4
New-York Co.						
New-York, ...	28	50,000	28,500	33,530	179,200	122
Oneida Co.						
Utica, ...	1	....	150	300	1,000	2
ENVELOPE MANUFACTORIES.						
New-York Co.						
New-York, ...	4	50,000	34,000	141,000	240,000	249
GOLD PEN MANUFACTORIES.						
Kings Co.						
Brooklyn, ...	1	6,000	8,000	69,000	112,000	41
New York Co.						
New-York, ...	10	....	88,200	146,650	519,000	163

CLASS XVIII.—(Continued.)

TOWNS.	Number of establishments.	Capital Invested. In real estate.	Capital Invested. In tools and machinery.	Cash Value. Of raw materials used.	Cash Value. Of manufactured articles.	Persons employed.
INK MANUFACTORIES.						
Essex Co.						
Chesterfield,	1	$300	$250	$700	$2,500	4
Wyoming Co.						
Genesee Falls,	1	150	20	500	1,000	....
JEWELRY CASE MANUFACTORY.						
New-York Co.						
New-York,	1	....	250	1,000	5,000	7
LITHOGRAPHING ESTABLISHMENTS.						
New-York Co.						
New-York,	13	70,000	65,050	78,750	260,200	177
MAP COLORING ESTABLISHMENTS.						
New-York Co.						
New-York,	1	....	500	....	12,000	25
MAP PUBLISHING ESTABLISHMENTS.						
New-York Co.						
New-York,	2	....	28,000	30,000	240,000	63
Rensselaer Co.						
Troy,	1	12,000	4,800	8,000	12,000	13
MELODEON MANUFACTORIES.						
New-York Co.						
New-York,	1	28,000	25,000	40,000	190,000	81
Otsego Co.						
Cherry Valley,	2	7,000	4,510	9,450	33,000	35
MUSICAL INSTRUMENT MANUFACTORIES.						
Chautauque Co.						
Harmony,	1	80	160	1,480	4,000	6
Monroe Co.						
Riga,	1	400	500	475	1,000	2
Rochester,	1	800	200	100	425	3
New-York Co.						
New-York,	3	2,100	18,000	14,500	7,500	8
ORGAN BUILDING ESTABLISHMENTS.						
New-York Co.						
New-York,	3	46,200	4,500	61.160	145,000	89
Oneida Co.						
Utica,	1	1,500	1,000	5,065	20,000	18
Steuben Co.						
Pultney,	1	200	50	90	760	2
ORGAN PIPE MANUFACTORY.						
New-York Co.						
New-York,	1	....	300	552	3,000	2
PAPER RULER MANUFACTORY.						
New-York Co......						
New-York,	1	....	300	25	900	3
PIANO FORTE MANUFACTORIES.						
Albany Co.						
Albany,	2	30,000	16,000	30,000	150,000	216
Cayuga Co.						
Auburn,	1	2,500	300	450	2,500	5
Chautauque Co.						
Hanover,	1	400	150	1,000	2,600	3
Chenango Co.						
Norwich,	2	6,100	3,000	15,195	41,750	48
Dutchess Co.						
Poughkeepsie city,	2	5,000	1,400	7,608	21,000	18
Erie Co.						
Buffalo,	5	30,000	8,900	61,171	264,900	208
Genesee Co.						
Bergen,	1	....	....	....	....	....
Jefferson Co.						
Clayton,	1	800	800	1,000	8,000	6
Monroe Co.						
Rochester,	1	37,500	600	2,125	10,000	10
New-York Co.						
New-York,	38	461,557	169,219	481,315	2,000,162	1185
Oneida Co.						
Sangerfield,	1	3,000	1,300	5,000	13,000	10
Utica,	1	150	175	3,287	8,000	8
Onondaga Co.						
Syracuse,	1	....	400	1,730	8,250	8
Orange Co.						
Cornwall,	1	500	800	434	2,500	6
Newburgh,	2	15,000	1,300	7,567	20,000	14
Warwick,	1	4,000	1,000	1,000	3,000	6
Otsego Co.						
Otsego,	1	$1,600	$2,500	$1,000	$3,000	7
Rensselaer Co.						
Schodack,	1	1,000	200	100	1,500	3
Troy,	1	6,000	1,000	8,000	25,000	17
St. Lawrence Co.						
Oswegatchie,	1	4,000	1,000	....	1,500	1
Suffolk Co.						
Brookhaven,	1	1,000	200	2,000	5,000	6
Washington Co.						
Kingsbury,	1	1,500	500	3,000	11,000	9
PIANO TOOL MANUFACTORY.						
New-York Co.						
New-York,	1	....	250	41	585	1
PIANO HARDWARE MANUFACTORIES.						
New-York Co.						
New-York,	2	33,000	33,000	5,920	45,000	32
PIANO STOOL MANUFACTORIES.						
Cayuga Co.						
Auburn,	1	5,500	3,000	800	7,000	6
New-York Co.						
New-York,	1	....	950	1,942	6,000	7
Westchester Co.						
Greenburgh,	1	13,000	1,000	5,095	13,700	16
PICTURE AND MIRROR FRAME MANUFACTORIES.						
Erie Co.						
Buffalo,	3	....	4,200	21,800	36,000	35
Monroe Co.						
Rochester,	2	180	500	400	3,700	5
New-York Co.						
New-York,	8	18,900	23,700	55,600	83,000	72
PRINTERS' INK MANUFACTORIES.						
New York Co.						
New-York,	3	32,000	20,500	36,496	70,000	31
Rensselaer Co.						
Troy,	1	4,000	1,000	3,600	10,000	3
PRINTING OFFICES.						
Albany Co.						
Albany,	3	20,000	45,500	65,500	110,000	171
Cattaraugus Co.						
Olean,	1	1,000	....	150	1,800	2
Cayuga Co.						
Auburn,	5	8,000	75,600	90,200	161,300	108
Cato,	1	....	....	....	....	....
Mentz,	1	1,400	....	1,400	2,500	4
Chautauque Co.						
Pomfret,	3	1,500	3,500	1,468	3,228	5
Chemung Co.						
Elmira,	3	5,500	14,000	5,773	24,920	28
Delaware Co.						
Kortright,	1	600	350	240	1,350	2
Dutchess Co.						
Poughkeepsie city,	4	11,900	21,000	12,401	34,056	35
Erie Co.						
Buffalo,	1	....	4,000	2,000	8,000	10
Herkimer Co.						
German Flats,	1	....	1,000	600	3,500	7
Jefferson Co.						
Adams,	1	600	600	475	1,800	3
Madison Co.						
Hamilton,	2	....	4,500	2,100	6,500	11
Montgomery Co.						
Glen,	1	1,000	1,500	500	500	2
New-York Co.						
New-York,	53	678,000	647,950	798,900	1,545,500	1994
Oneida Co.						
Steuben,	1	....	1,000	600	2,500	5
Utica,	5	....	35,900	27,200	67,475	86
Onondaga Co.						
Syracuse,	5	....	27,500	18,855	65,750	69
Rensselaer Co.						
Troy,	2	12,000	25,000	40,000	206,000	46
St. Lawrence Co.						
Oswegatchie,	2	8,500	15,000	4,225	10,000	17
Saratoga Co.						
Saratoga Springs,	1	2,000	6,000	2,775	10,700	15
Steuben Co.						
Bath,	2	900	4,000	2,450	8,900	10
Ulster Co.						
Saugerties,	1	....	2,000	600	2,500	5
Yates Co.						
Milo,	2	....	4,000	1,130	5,800	9

CLASS XVIII.—(Continued.)

TOWNS.	Number of establishments.	Capital Invested. In real estate.	Capital Invested. In tools and machinery.	Cash Value. Of raw materials used.	Cash Value. Of manufactured articles.	Persons employed.
PRINTING PRESS MANUFACTORIES.						
New-York Co.						
New-York, ...	4	$120,000	$216,000	$216,750	$670,000	492
PRINTERS' ROLLER MANUFACTORY.						
New-York Co.						
New-York, ...	1	....	300	1,450	4,000	1
STATUARY.						
Erie Co.						
Buffalo, ...	1	....	....	1,200	3,000	4
New-York Co.						
New-York, ...	1	2,000	500	1,000	3,000	5

TOWNS.	Number of establishments.	Capital Invested. In real estate.	Capital Invested. In tools and machinery.	Cash Value. Of raw materials used.	Cash Value. Of manufactured articles.	Persons employed.
STEREOTYPING ESTABLISHMENTS.						
New-York Co.						
New-York,.......	12	$31,000	$67,400	$31,980	$121,000	141
TYPE FOUNDERIES.						
Erie Co.						
Buffalo, ...	1	....	3,000	11,340	35,000	39
New-York Co.						
New-York, ...	8	158,000	90,500	120,718	383,000	477
TYPE FOUNDERS' TOOL MANUFACTORY.						
New-York Co.						
New-York, ...	1	....	500	1,500	2,600	2

CLASS XIX.—FIRE ARMS AND IMPLEMENTS OF WAR, MANUFACTURE OF POWDER AND SHOT.

TOWNS.	Number of establishments.	Capital Invested. In real estate.	Capital Invested. In tools and machinery.	Cash Value. Of raw materials used.	Cash Value. Of manufactured articles.	Persons employed.
GUNSMITH SHOPS.						
Albany Co.						
Albany,..........	1	....	500	....	1,500	1
Allegany Co.						
Alfred, ...	1	30	130	98	360	1
Amity, ...	1	150	400	600	1,900	2
Angelica, ...	1	....	200	75	1,000	1
Hume, ...	1	50	400	200	500	1
Cattaraugus Co.						
Franklinville, ...	1	100	100	195	735	2
Olean,...........	1	15	85	505	1,000	2
Cayuga Co.						
Auburn, ...	1	1,000	100	300	1,000	3
Chautauque Co.						
Pomfret,.........	2	250	500	800	2,500	2
Chemung Co.						
Elmira,..........	2	7,500	3,700	1,800	4,500	7
Veteran, ...	1	40	100	138	480	1
Cortland Co.						
Cincinnatus, ...	1	150	350	500	1,200	....
Delaware Co.						
Tompkins, ...	1	150	500	800	3,065	3
Dutchess Co.						
Poughkeepsie city,	1	....	100	200	200	....
Erie Co.						
Buffalo, ...	2	10,000	1,600	375	3,000	4
Essex Co.						
Elizabethtown,...	1	50	50	100	400	1
Franklin Co.						
Westville, ...	1	....	....	90	150	....
Genesee Co.						
Alabama, ...	3	275	200	291	925	7
Alexander,.......	1	....	75	85	490	1
Batavia, ...	1	800	200	500	1,000	2
Herkimer Co.						
German Flats, ...	1	12,000	10,000	7,200	42,700	50
Salisbury, ...	1	500	200	100	200	1
Jefferson Co.						
Hounsfield, ...	1	....	200	200	530	1
Wilna, ...	1	150	300	250	1,200	2
Kings Co.						
Brooklyn, ...	1	3,000	1,000	3,000	7,000	5
Livingston Co.						
North Dansville,..	1	....	1,000	450	2,200	2
Madison Co.						
Lenox, ...	1	800	200	300	600	1
Monroe Co.						
Rochester,........	2	210	700	1,900	5,900	9
New-York Co.						
New-York, ...	6	35,000	68,600	[illegible]8,500	207,500	249
Niagara Co.						
Lockport,........	1	2,000	....	1,000	3,000	5
Oneida Co.........						
Utica, ...	1	200	1,000	....	4,000	5
Onondaga Co.						
Otisco, ...	1	200	200	72	192	1
Syracuse, ...	1	....	500	2,000	7,000	10
Ontario Co.						
Canandaigua,....	2	1,300	450	750	2,800	4
Richmond, ...	1	200	300	237	1,200	3
Seneca, ...	1	300	200	....	....	....
Otsego Co.						
Burlington, ...	1	....	50	....	200	....
Decatur, ...	1	300	100	300	1,300	....
Queens Co.						
Hempstead,......	1	450	300	300	450	1
Rensselaer Co.						
Troy, ...	1	2,000	600	3,000	7,500	6
St. Lawrence Co.						
Potsdam, ...	2	875	800	380	1,000	2
Saratoga Co.						
Saratoga Springs,.	1	600	500	500	751	1
Schoharie Co.						
Gilboa, ...	1	....	....	100	100	....
Schuyler Co.						
Dix, ...	1	1,200	150	200	960	1
Seneca Co.						
Waterloo, ...	1	200	100	500	1,000	1
Steuben Co.						
Bath, ...	1	200	150	250	700	1
Erwin, ...	1	300	150	320	1,000	2
Sullivan Co.						
Cochecton, ...	1	....	300	100	500	1
Mamakating,.....	1	....	100	50	200	1
Tompkins Co.						
Caroline, ...	1	4,000	1,000	1,200	3,000	5
Ithaca, ...	1	500	100	1,200	1,000	2
Yates Co.						
Milo,............	1	300	300	250	600	2
MILITARY ACCOUTREMENT MANUFACTORIES.						
New-York Co.						
New-York, ...	2	300	7,200	....	12,000	11
PERCUSSION CAP MANUFACTORY.						
Rockland Co.						
Haverstraw, ...	1	....	....	35,910	....	30
POWDER MILLS.						
Greene Co.						
Catskill, ...	1	500	1,000	40,000	45,000	10
Monroe Co.						
Brighton, ...	1	5,000	1,000	11,740	20,000	6
Rensselaer Co.						
Schaghticoke, ...	1	20,000	2,000	53,650	76,000	15
Ulster Co.						
Esopus, ...	1	10,000	5,000	6,500	9,000	10
Saugerties,.......	1	2,000	10,000	97,113	122,600	31
Washington Co.						
Hampton, ...	1	4,000	10,000	2,580	2,580	8
SHOT FACTORY.						
New-York Co.						
New-York, ...	1	43,000	5,000	200,000	300,000	23
SHOT-BELT, ETC., MANUFACTORY.						
New-York Co.						
New-York, ...	1	....	600	10,000	25,000	34

CLASS XX.—SURGICAL, MEDICAL AND DENTAL INSTRUMENTS AND APPARATUS.

TOWNS.	Number of establishments.	Capital Invested. In real estate.	Capital Invested. In tools and machinery.	Cash Value. Of raw materials used.	Cash Value. Of manufactured articles.	Persons employed.
BATHING TUB MANUFACTORIES.						
New-York Co.						
New-York,	2	$20,000	$500	$20,100	$27,000	12
DENTAL INSTRUMENT MANUFACTORY.						
New-York Co.						
New-York,	1	....	300	....	....	12
DENTISTS' GOLD MANUFACTORY.						
Kings Co.						
Brooklyn,	1	....	250	10,000	100,000	2
DENTISTRY.						
Albany Co.						
Rensselaerville,	1	....	125	350	1,000	1
Erie Co.						
Eden,	1	400	250	250	700	....
Franklin Co.						
Fort Covington,	1	900	200	900	2,125	....
Genesee Co.						
Le Roy,	1	....	....	1,000	2,500	....
Herkimer Co.						
Newport,	1	350	250	700	1,700	1
Lewis Co.						
Lowville,	1	....	300	1,020	2,800	1
Livingston Co.						
North Dansville,	1	....	1,000	1,500	3,500	2
Madison Co.						
Cazenovia,	1	400	300	1,500	3,500	1
Niagara Co.						
Lockport,	3	500	950	4,500	10,200	5
Oneida Co.						
Bridgewater,	1	200	300	100	1,500	2
Oneida Co.						
Utica,	1	$2,000	$1,500	$1,256	$6,900	4
Onondaga Co.						
Marcellus,	1	....	50	200	600	1
Tully,	1	1,000	500	625	1,400	1
Ontario Co.						
East Bloomfield,	1	....	200	545	1,800	....
Saratoga Co.						
Saratoga Springs,	2	1,500	400	707	3,600	4
Schuyler Co.						
Hector,	1	....	150	500	1,000	1
Steuben Co.						
Avoca,	1	....	400	624	1,800	1
Suffolk Co.						
Southold,	1	1,300	450	....	....	....
Tompkins Co.						
Dryden,	1	200	125	516	1,125	1
Wayne Co.						
Lyons,	1	....	500	950	3,213	2
Yates Co.						
Milo,	1	3,000	200	1,000	3,000	3
SURGICAL INSTRUMENT MANUFACTORIES.						
New-York Co.						
New-York,	4	10,000	2,500	2,700	16,000	54
TEETH MANUFACTORIES.						
New-York Co.						
New-York,	2	50,000	1,800	10,000	24,000	40
TRUSS AND BANDAGE MANUFACTORIES.						
New-York Co.						
New-York,	1	18,000	3,000	10,000	30,000	55
Otsego Co.						
Cherry Valley,	1	1,500	2,500	2,006	5,000	4

CLASS XXI.—WEARING APPAREL, ARTICLES FOR THE TOILET, ETC.

TOWNS.	Number of establishments.	In real estate.	In tools and machinery.	Of raw materials used.	Of manufactured articles.	Persons employed.
BELT CLASP MANUFACTORY.						
Monroe Co.						
Rochester,	1	....	300	990	6,000	3
BUTTON AND COMB MANUFACTORIES.						
Chenango Co.						
Oxford,	1	....	250	....	700	7
Greene Co.						
Windham,	1	2,000	3,000	1,600	12,500	14
Westchester Co.						
Mount Pleasant,	1	1,200	1,000	3,050	9,200	40
CLERICAL ROBE MANUFACTORY.						
New-York Co.						
New-York,	1	....	....	550	850	3
COMB MANUFACTORIES.						
New-York Co.						
New-York,	3	12,000	33,000	33,200	72,000	28
CORSET MANUFACTORY.						
New-York Co.						
New-York,	1	....	200	1,000	4,000	16
DRESS MAKING.						
New-York Co.						
New-York,	12	25,000	9,200	251,400	425,500	1262
Wayne Co.						
Macedon,	1	....	....	1,595	1,963	2
GENTLEMEN'S FURNISHING GOODS MANUFACTORIES.						
New-York Co.						
New-York,	10	14,000	450	367,800	601,000	1871
Yates Co.						
Milo,	1	....	....	10,000	10,000	22
Potter,	2	....	....	3,000	5,300	13
GLOVE AND MITTEN MANUFACTORIES.						
Fulton Co.						
Broadalbin,	3	....	....	12,750	25,840	86
Fulton Co.						
Johnstown,	56	51,600	14,250	711,312	1,122,356	3220
Mayfield,	1	....	....	2,079	2,926	....
Perth,	1	3,000	750	4,000	7,000	6
Lewis Co.						
Watson,	1	....	....	400	1,200	5
New-York Co.						
New-York,	3	....	175	16,000	36,000	21
Otsego Co.						
Otego,	1	50	5	29	58	1
St. Lawrence Co.						
Oswegatchie,	1	2,000	100	1,000	2,000	7
Tioga Co.						
Newark,	1	400	100	1,500	3,500	1
Wayne Co.						
Arcadia,	1	200	....	300	1,200	3
HAIR DRESSING AND WIG MANUFACTORIES.						
New-York Co.						
New-York,	4	35,000	4,300	25,000	67,000	58
Oneida Co.						
Utica,	1	....	50	700	1,600	4
HAT AND CAP MANUFACTORY.						
Albany Co.						
Albany,	8	....	4,250	41,500	187,000	97
Allegany Co.						
Burns,	1	....	40	210	900	1
Cuba,	1	100	150	400	700	1
Broome Co.						
Sandford,	1	....	100	200	500	1
Cayuga Co.						
Auburn,	1	1,900	800	2,250	7,600	10
Chemung Co.						
Elmira,	3	12,000	850	2,988	7,900	4
Columbia Co.						
Hudson,	2	1,200	300	4,560	7,000	8
Kinderhook,	2	900	700	1,450	18,000	13
Cortland Co.						
Homer,	1	100	40	180	683	6
Dutchess Co.						
Poughkeepsie city,	3	....	50	4,300	10,000	7

CLASS XXI.—(CONTINUED.)

TOWNS.	Number of establishments.	Capital Invested. In real estate.	Capital Invested. In tools and machinery.	Cash Value. Of raw materials used.	Cash Value. Of manufactured articles.	Persons employed.
GREENE Co.						
Ashland,	3	$3,600	$3,600	$12,750	$56,000	89
Durham,	1	....	15	350	600	1
Windham,	1	700	500	5,200	12,600	21
JEFFERSON Co.						
Watertown,	2	2,200	350	7,450	14,900	17
KINGS Co.						
Brooklyn,	2	58,400	45,486	782,000	986,000	666
LIVINGSTON Co.						
North Dansville,	1	500	100	700	1,800	2
MADISON Co.						
Cazenovia,	1	1,300	50	626	1,075	3
MONROE Co.						
Rochester,	1	42	30	515	1,200	1
Sweden,	1	....	50	720	1,800	2
NEW-YORK Co.						
New-York,	51	212,800	52,440	1,211,020	2,082,502	1577
NIAGARA Co.						
Lockport,	1	....	300	1,500	3,000	4
ONEIDA Co.						
Rome,	1	3,000	200	2,985	6,900	7
Utica,	4	....	860	51,100	78,000	36
ONONDAGA Co.						
Syracuse,	4	....	450	15,250	32,800	17
ONTARIO Co.						
Phelps,	1	1,600	50	250	600	2
ORANGE Co.						
Walkill,	1	1,500	500	14,000	35,000	26
OSWEGO Co.						
Oswego city,	1	11,000	300	3,800	8,845	10
Volney,	1	....	....	350	500	2
OTSEGO Co.						
New Lisbon,	1	300	25	50	300	....
PUTNAM Co.						
Carmel,	1	150	200	3,000	5,000	3
Patterson,	1	800	800	400	1,200	3
QUEENS Co.						
Newtown,	1	....	300	3,000	12,000	5
RENSSELAER Co.						
Lansingburg,	1	....	150	2,000	3,500	3
RICHMOND Co.						
Southfield,	1	5,000	5,000	....	20,000	63
ST. LAWRENCE Co.						
Canton,	1	4,000	150	250	900	2
Oswegatchie,	2	2,000	50	1,000	2,000	7
STEUBEN Co.						
Hornellsville,	2	2,700	100	800	1,950	3
SUFFOLK Co.						
Huntington,	1	....	200	320	1,300	2
TOMPKINS Co.						
Ithaca,	2	8,000	650	5,000	9,125	24
ULSTER Co.						
Saugerties,	1	....	400	300	1,000	1
WAYNE Co.						
Arcadia,	1	250	50	700	1,200	1
Lyons,	1	800	300	1,300	7,000	3
WESTCHESTER Co.						
Ossining,	1	....	25,000	100,000	140,000	211
White Plains,	1	47,000	11,000	88,480	250,000	218
WYOMING Co.						
Perry,	1	800	100	1,000	2,000	2
YATES Co.						
Milo,	1	....	250	4,000	6,000	3
HAT BLOCK MANUFACTORIES.						
NEW-YORK Co.						
New-York,	3	....	1,900	2,000	6,400	12
HOSIERY MANUFACTORIES.						
ALBANY Co.						
Watervliet,	6	135,000	134,100	292,104	680,850	1241
MADISON Co.						
Eaton,	1	4,000	4,000	2,500	5,000	15
NEW-YORK Co.						
New-York,	1	....	2,000	....	12,000	28
RENSSELAER Co.						
Berlin,	1	2,500	1,500	7,500	18,000	13
SARATOGA Co.						
Milton,	2	18,000	20,000	33,000	60,000	165
WASHINGTON Co.						
Easton,	1	2,000	2,000	1,193	4,200	7
MILLITARY AND FIREMEN'S CAP MANUFACTORY.						
NEW-YORK Co.						
New-York,	1	17,000	....	9,000	900	14
MILLINER SHOPS.						
ALBANY Co.						
Rensselaerville,	2	....	18	1,600	2,000	8
ALBANY Co.						
Westerlo,	1	$200	....	$300	$500	1
ALLEGANY Co.						
Almond,	1	....	....	1,500	2,500	2
BROOME Co.						
Sandford,	2	....	....	2,000	2,900	4
CATTARAUGUS Co.						
Olean,	1	....	....	700	1,100	2
CAYUGA Co.						
Auburn,	3	120	$6,000	6,000	12,000	19
Moravia,	2	650	35	600	1,000	5
Niles,	1	....	....	500	800	2
Sterling,	1	....	....	....	500	5
CHAUTAUQUE Co.						
Pomfret,	3	2,300	90	3,800	5,950	13
CHEMUNG Co.						
Elmira,	1	4,500	150	3,000	4,500	10
CHENANGO Co.						
Otselic,	1	200	....	373	1,082	3
Sheburne,	2	500	....	1,500	2,625	....
DELAWARE Co.						
Bovina,	1	....	....	260	400	2
Kortright,	1	300	....	430	780	2
DUTCHESS Co.						
Amenia,	1	....	30	300	500	2
Fishkill,	4	....	25	2,032	2,675	9
Hyde Park,	1	....	50	600	1,000	1
Rhinebeck,	1	800	....	500	1,000	1
ERIE Co.						
Aurora,	2	1,500	25	1,200	2,100	5
Buffalo,	1	....	....	....	....	2
FRANKLIN Co.						
Malone,	1	200	....	300	800	5
FULTON Co.						
Johnstown,	2	2,000	50	1,500	3,850	8
GENESEE Co.						
Batavia,	1	2,000	30	5,000	8,000	8
Le Roy,	3	3,575	....	4,900	9,900	14
Pavilion,	1	....	....	200	800	2
GREENE Co.						
Coxsackie,	2	....	30	600	1,550	5
HERKIMER Co.						
German Flats,	1	800	25	850	1,000	3
Newport,	2	350	20	1,200	2,100	4
JEFFERSON Co.						
Adams,	3	1,000	100	2,540	2,761	18
Watertown,	4	....	....	9,031	18,886	47
LIVINGSTON Co.						
Groveland,	2	....	....	....	6,108	....
North Dansville,	2	....	....	2,000	3,100	5
MADISON Co.						
Hamilton,	2	1,000	....	8,000	10,000	8
NEW-YORK Co.						
New-York,	12	50,000	15,075	182,945	341,540	634
NIAGARA Co.						
Wilson,	2	....	....	2,400	4,700	5
ONEIDA Co.						
Boonville,	3	1,600	....	4,000	4,500	10
Utica,	10	....	8,700	37,125	56,425	58
Whitestown,	2	500	24	1,500	2,500	8
ONONDAGA Co.						
Elbridge,	1	700	30	1,000	2,500	3
ORANGE Co.						
Walkill,	6	3,000	....	5,000	10,000	30
ORLEANS Co.						
Ridgeway,	4	4,800	325	1,300	6,000	13
OSWEGO Co.						
Mexico,	1	....	....	950	1,425	....
Oswego city,	5	20,000	775	11,000	31,540	36
OTSEGO Co.						
Decatur,	1	....	....	350	550	1
Otego,	3	....	46	445	424	5
Otsego,	1	1,000	....	1,205	2,550	6
PUTNAM Co.						
Carmel,	1	....	....	1,500	2,500	2
QUEENS Co.						
Flushing,	1	3,000	250	800	10,800	16
RENSSELAER Co.						
Troy,	2	4,000	100	15,000	25,000	31
ST. LAWRENCE Co.						
Oswegatchie,	1	....	50	3,000	5,000	5
SCHENECTADY Co.						
Schenectady,	4	2,200	....	10,055	17,200	24
SCHUYLER Co.						
Hector,	1	....	....	500	800	3
Orange,	1	....	40	250	550	1
STEUBEN Co.						
Bath,	3	....	25	3,170	5,050	6
Hornellsville,	1	1,500	3	500	1,250	4

CLASS XXI.—(Continued.)

TOWNS.	Number of establishments.	Capital Invested. In real estate.	Capital Invested. In tools and machinery.	Cash Value. Of raw materials used.	Cash Value. Of manufactured articles.	Persons employed.
SUFFOLK Co.						
Riverhead,	2		$65	$1,600	$4,200	5
Southampton,	1		500	1,200	2,400	13
SULLIVAN Co.						
Mamakating,	2			650	1,600	2
TIOGA Co.						
Newark,	1	$500	10	300	800	3
TOMPKINS Co.						
Dryden,	1	200		100	750	2
Ithaca,	4	6,500	200	6,800	13,800	24
Lansing,	1				50	
ULSTER Co.						
Marbletown,	1	200	5	300	1,200	6
New Paltz,	1		30	400	800	
WARREN Co.						
Chester,	2			1,200	1,651	
WASHINGTON Co.						
Argyle,	1		10	500	600	3
WAYNE Co.						
Palmyra,	2			2,200	3,500	7
Sodus,	3		35	375	850	5
WYOMING Co.						
Attica,	1		40	1,700	3,450	4
YATES Co.						
Jerusalem,	1	50	25	700	1,400	4
Milo,	4		15	4,945	6,000	15

SEWING MACHINE MANUFACTORIES.

TOWNS.	Number of establishments.	In real estate.	In tools and machinery.	Of raw materials used.	Of manufactured articles.	Persons employed.
NEW-YORK Co.						
New-York,	4	10,000	39,200	35,351	245,600	162

SHIRT, BOSOM, AND COLLAR MANUFACTORIES.

TOWNS.	Number of establishments.	In real estate.	In tools and machinery.	Of raw materials used.	Of manufactured articles.	Persons employed.
RENSSELAER Co.						
Berlin,	4	500	2,200	27,140	63,470	169
Grafton,	2		1,600	15,380	20,715	25
Petersburgh,	1		550	15,506	22,736	7
Troy,	14	60,400	56,100	296,632	693,169	2956

STOCK MANUFACTORIES.

TOWNS.	Number of establishments.	In real estate.	In tools and machinery.	Of raw materials used.	Of manufactured articles.	Persons employed.
MONROE Co.						
Penfield,	1			3,000	20,000	32
NEW-YORK Co.						
New-York,	1			12,000	24,000	27

TAILOR SHOPS.

TOWNS.	Number of establishments.	In real estate.	In tools and machinery.	Of raw materials used.	Of manufactured articles.	Persons employed.
ALBANY Co.						
Albany,	24	6,250	655	104,475	184,662	487
Rensselaerville,	1		100	350	100	1
ALLEGANY Co.						
Almond,	1	3,000	100	21,890	67,822	132
Scio,	1	80	5	520	780	
CATTARAUGUS Co.						
Franklinville,	2	450	20	2,000	2,600	2
Olean,	2	1,400	165	200	2,110	8
Otto,	1	200	20	950	3,262	12
Portville,	1	75	10	9,000	10,000	2
CAYUGA Co.						
Auburn,	3	10,000	500	20,000	65,000	227
Moravia,	2	700	60	3,000	4,900	9
Niles,	1	75	40		500	1
CHAUTAUQUE Co.						
Chautauque,	1	300	25	700	2,700	5
Cherry Creek,	1				400	1
Ellicott,	1	500	25	15,800	20,000	55
Kiantone,	1			200	350	1
Pomfret,	4	1,750	25	7,800	16,400	17
CHEMUNG Co.						
Elmira,	6	28,200	1,237	58,200	117,740	304
Veteran,	1	150	30	600	1,500	2
CHENANGO Co.						
Oxford,	1		40		600	3
Sherburne,	1				400	1
COLUMBIA Co.						
Copake,	1	1,500		400	500	1
Hillsdale,	2	3,000	125	800		9
Hudson,	9	6,500	453	48,500	77,500	154
Kinderhook,	1	1,000	25		800	5
CORTLAND Co.						
Homer,	1	1,000	100	4,000	6,000	19
Scott,	1	350	50	10,000	11,000	10
Truxton,	1	600	25	1,500	250	3
Virgil,	2	300	300		350	2
DELAWARE Co.						
Bovina,	1	$100	$10	$1,076	$1,300	2
Franklin,	1	200	50	4,000	8,000	11
Harpersfield,	1	100	10	740	1,100	1
Roxbury,	2	150	114		700	2
DUTCHESS Co.						
Fishkill,	2			4,000	7,100	14
Poughkeepsie city,	17	13,300	1,175	69,750	106,300	155
Rhinebeck,	3	1,800		3,000	6,500	11
Stanford,	1		15		600	2
ERIE Co.						
Buffalo,	2	200	4	50	100	6
East Hamburgh,	1		150	3,000	3,750	11
Lancaster,	1			1,000	1,700	2
Tonawanda,	3	3,200		4,500	8,100	14
ESSEX Co.						
Chesterfield,	1			4,500	15,000	21
Elizabethtown,	1	250	20	900	900	2
FRANKLIN Co.						
Malone,	4	7,200	450	14,600	21,000	27
FULTON Co.						
Johnstown,	1		20	4,300	6,800	5
GENESEE Co.						
Alabama,	3	950	95	4,300	11,050	25
Alexander,	1		10		600	
Le Roy,	2			20,000	30,000	10
Oakfield,	1	600		4,000	12,000	27
Pavilion,	1	100	25		300	1
GREENE Co.						
Durham,	1	300	20	1,500	2,300	4
HERKIMER Co.						
Germah Flats,	2	2,450	20	2,350	8,850	21
Little Falls,	5	5,100	175	11,800	20,600	35
Newport,	3	1,750	85	3,250	5,700	2
Salisbury,	2	400	35	1,950	3,200	5
Stark,	2	200			700	2
JEFFERSON Co.						
Adams,	5	5,750	415	17,336	27,035	44
Cape Vincent,	1			4,500	7,000	13
Ellisburgh,	2	2,350	5	1,800	2,700	2
Henderson,	2	500	40	1,400	2,700	6
Hounsfield,	2	2,200	75	5,000	11,500	13
Watertown,	5	16,500	1,050	125,200	174,000	466
LEWIS Co.						
Lowville,	2	500	175	8,500	13,500	53
LIVINGSTON Co.						
Avon,	3	5,300	355	9,000	25.500	107
Caledonia,	1	700	25	2,535	5,400	8
Conesus,	1	900	25	3,000	6,000	15
North Dansville,	2	130		21,000	32,482	17
York,	1		30	2,000	2,716	1
MADISON Co.						
Cazenovia,	2	2,600	150	3,430	4,885	4
Lenox,	2		275	7,900	12,942	21
Nelson,	1	100	10	1,000	1,250	1
Sullivan,	2	455	100	5,396	8,069	5
MONROE Co.						
Chili,	1		17		400	1
Mendon,	1		20	800	1,500	3
Perrington,	1	600	200	2,250	8,000	10
Riga,	1	200	50	2,500	4,000	7
Sweden,	4		325	33,000	30,800	67
MONTGOMERY Co.						
Amsterdam,	2	2,000	150	12,500	18,000	32
Glen,	1	200	50		2,000	12
NEW-YORK Co.						
New-York,	126	1068,550	50,127	4,317,302	7,592,696	12968
NIAGARA Co.						
Lewiston,	1	1,000	100	1,200	1,800	4
Lockport,	7	1,425		74,000	151,500	246
ONEIDA Co.						
Augusta,	1			1,383	2,320	3
Boonville,	1	1,000	50	4,700	6,300	13
Florence,	1	100	10	300	580	2
Kirkland,	1		150	3,870	2,200	5
Rome,	7	16,400	30	65,800	100,400	160
Utica,	14	39,000	874	825,700	1,122,000	2329
Vernon,	1		150	300	5,000	14
Verona,	1	150	10		500	2
Whitestown,	1	200		1,000	3,500	26
ONONDAGA Co.						
Clay,	1		130	1,200	2,000	3
De Witt,	1	250	100	2,000	2,500	2
Elbridge,	2			11,500	19,500	31
Fabius,	1	300		2,500	3,500	6
Manlius,	1	1.500	120	2,500	4,000	7
Skaneateles,	1	1,000	300	3,000	10,000	23
Syracuse,	3	2,000		60,000	120,000	250
ONTARIO Co.						
Bristol,	3	325	45	5,400	9,600	4

CLASS XXI.—(Continued.)

TOWNS.	Number of establishments.	Capital Invested. In real estate.	Capital Invested. In tools and machinery.	Cash Value. Of raw materials used.	Cash Value. Of manufactured articles.	Persons employed.
Ontario Co.						
Canandaigua,	6	$5, 500	$350	$19, 700	$43, 500	28
East Bloomfield,	2	550	45	4, 800	8, 900	10
Naples,	1	500	75	2, 000	3, 800	8
Seneca,	1	3, 500	100	5, 000	9, 000	37
Victor,	1	....	....	3, 000	....	10
Orange Co.						
Cornwall,	2	1, 400	180	6, 000	20, 500	25
Montgomery,	1	150	5	300	260	1
Newburgh,	1	5, 000	50	10, 000	18, 000	15
Walkill,	3	3, 500	171, 000	39, 400	56, 600	120
Warwick,	2	....	110	750	....	4
Orleans Co.						
Ridgeway,	2	3, 000	200	850	9, 550	46
Oswego Co.						
Mexico,	1	6, 000	....	5, 000	8, 000	8
Oswego city,	9	64, 000	2, 250	154, 000	237, 425	319
Otsego Co.						
Burlington,	2	1, 000	115	9, 512	11, 200	36
Cherry Valley,	2	1, 750	180	6, 910	6, 000	8
Laurens,	1	200	....	....	1, 500	5
Middlefield,	1	100	25	....	500	1
Milford,	2	....	25	....	900	3
Otego,	3	650	144	288	1, 085	5
Otsego,	4	9, 000	110	14, 200	24, 910	38
Roseboom,	1	70	10	....	300	....
Springfield,	1	700	150	1, 200	2, 700	5
Queens Co.						
Flushing,	2	5, 000	225	4, 500	10, 000	19
North Hempstead,	1	250	....	....	2, 000	4
Oyster Bay,	1	....	25	500	1, 800	6
Rensselaer Co.						
Lansingburgh,	2	....	50	11, 000	19, 000	33
Troy,	13	51, 000	....	112, 000	168, 100	232
Rockland Co.						
Haverstraw,	1	....	....	250	3, 000	9
St. Lawrence Co.						
Canton,	1	2, 500	300	7, 000	15, 000	54
Gouverneur,	2	....	200	5, 000	7, 100	17
Madrid,	1	500	20	1, 200	2, 400	6
Oswegatchie,	4	18, 500	300	45, 500	67, 000	167
Potsdam,	3	6, 300	330	17, 500	44, 000	84
Rossie,	1	1, 000	30	6, 000	8, 000	15
Saratoga Co.						
Saratoga,	1	....	100	4, 160	12, 480	13
Saratoga Springs,	3	3, 300	3, 200	20, 900	40, 500	59
Schenectady Co.						
Schenectady,	9	....	....	75, 912	94, 789	182
Schoharie Co.						
Carlisle,	1	300	25	700	1, 400	6
Cobleskill,	1	....	....	....	....	....
Schoharie,	2	1, 150	225	4, 750	10, 000	17
Sharon,	1	....	8	....	500	2
Schuyler Co.						
Dix,	1	800	....	1, 200	1, 600	2
Hector,	2	1, 000	20	....	5, 000	13
Orange,	1	100	5	....	250	....
Schuyler Co.						
Tyrone,	2	$800	$100	$7, 200	$9, 200	11
Seneca Co.						
Fayette,	1	400	....	....	3, 000	4
Waterloo,	5	12, 000	465	22, 914	35, 828	128
Steuben Co.						
Bath,	3	1, 500	304	11, 400	19, 500	30
Corning,	1	1, 200	500	11, 000	....	....
Erwin,	2	....	30	2, 400	3, 800	3
Hornellsville,	2	3, 500	175	17, 000	26, 500	49
Howard,	1	676	15	3, 000	4, 000	8
Suffolk Co.						
Huntington,	3	400	130	11, 000	11, 000	8
Tioga Co.						
Barton,	4	1, 200	50	1, 400	2, 250	15
Owego,	5	8, 000	....	27, 148	42, 287	54
Tioga,	18	....	....	....	....	....
Tompkins Co.						
Dryden,	2	600	185	4, 400	6, 575	8
Groton,	3	425	....	....	....	....
Ithaca,	9	18, 500	1, 200	27, 850	56, 400	87
Ulysses,	1	1, 000	150	4, 000	8, 000	14
Ulster Co.						
Marbletown,	1	300	10	200	....	8
Saugerties,	8	3, 500	190	19, 000	38, 400	60
Warren Co.						
Chester,	1	300	....	900	1, 500	2
Washington Co.						
Argyle,	2	550	35	420	840	3
Salem,	1	....	....	1, 780	2, 250	7
Wayne Co.						
Arcadia,	4	2, 600	300	11, 625	20, 600	32
Lyons,	3	4, 000	35	20, 500	45, 000	81
Palmyra,	2	1, 800	50	12, 400	22, 000	53
Sodus,	1	....	10	700	1, 200	1
Williamson,	1	....	15	8, 500	12, 684	25
Westchester Co.						
Ossining,	1	1, 000	500	3, 750	8, 400	15
Rye,	1	2, 000	....	5, 000	10, 000	20
Wyoming Co.						
Genesee Falls,	1	350	....	1, 800	2, 700	5
Middlebury,	1	....	....	....	200	1
Perry,	2	1, 050	55	6, 900	14, 200	18
Pike,	1	....	150	2, 000	3, 000	5
Yates Co.						
Benton,	2	400	35	750	1, 300	3
Jerusalem,	1	500	50	1, 000	1, 800	11
Milo,	1	....	10	3, 000	5, 000	10
Potter,	1	....	....	....	350	1
Starkey,	1	1, 300	50	2, 545	4, 725	8
Torrey,	1	1, 000	25	600	1, 200	5
UMBRELLA AND PARASOL MANUFACTORIES.						
New-York Co.						
New-York,	20	66, 500	20, 650	732, 348	1, 173, 565	860
Rensselaer Co.						
Troy,	1	1, 300	50	1, 000	2, 500	3

CLASS XXII.—MISCELLANEOUS MANUFACTURES.

TOWNS.	Number of establishments.	In real estate.	In tools and machinery.	Of raw materials used.	Of manufactured articles.	Persons employed.
ALTAR ORNAMENT MANUFACTORY.						
New-York Co.						
New-York,	1	....	600	3, 640	7, 000	12
ARTIFICIAL FLOWER MANUFACTORIES.						
New-York Co.						
New-York,	4	14, 000	2, 200	7, 570	17, 000	96
BANDBOX MANUFACTORIES.						
Erie Co.						
Buffalo,	1	....	100	1, 500	3, 000	4
New-York Co.						
New-York,	2	....	700	9, 262	16, 800	9
Westchester Co.						
White Plains,	1	3, 000	250	2, 200	4, 000	4
BIRD CAGE MANUFACTORIES.						
New-York Co.						
New-York,	3	....	1, 850	4, 750	37, 000	33
Rensselaer Co.						
Troy,	1	....	....	1, 000	3, 000	8
BUTCHER SHOPS.						
Allegany Co.						
Amity,	1	25	10	2, 218	2, 574	1
Cayuga Co.						
Mentz,	1	....	....	....	....	....
Chautauque Co.						
Hanover,	1	1, 000	78	5, 350	6, 550	2
Chenango Co.						
Norwich,	1	1, 500	200	12, 355	12, 355	....
Erie Co.						
Amherst,	1	2, 500	200	10, 000	12, 000	6
Buffalo,	1	....	3, 000	130, 000	130, 000	20
Eden,	1	1, 800	20	800	1, 700	....
Jefferson Co.						
Watertown,	2	....	150	14, 650	16, 415	2
Madison Co.						
Lenox,	1	400	200	32, 000	38, 975	2
Monroe Co.						
Chili,	1	300	170	16, 000	20, 600	....
Rochester,	1	1, 000	10	9, 109	11, 918	2
Montgomery Co.						
Mohawk,	2	300	25	6, 565	8, 510	2
New-York Co.						
New-York,	9	75, 000	11, 500	1, 741, 360	1, 763, 860	138

CLASS XXII.—(Continued.)

TOWNS.	Number of establishments.	Capital Invested. In real estate.	Capital Invested. In tools and machinery.	Cash Value. Of raw materials used.	Cash Value. Of manufactured articles.	Persons employed.
ONEIDA Co.						
Augusta,	1	....	$50	$ 3,750	$5,445	2
Boonville,	1	$80	20	3,044	3,786	2
Camden,	1	....	....	5,376	7,283	1
Kirkland,	1	200	100	2,030	9,400	3
Paris,	1	....	100	2,500	2,400	2
Utica,	5	2,600	309	81,143	112,676	49
Western,	1	400	....	5,600	7,660	....
ONONDAGA Co.						
Cicero,	1	500	100	2,100	3,500	2
Elbridge,	3	2,500	325	11,303	15,886	6
Geddes,	1	3,500	300	47,500	54,025	4
Skaneateles,	1	1,000	30	7,280	8,736	1
Tully,	1	....	....	....	8,750	1
ONTARIO Co.						
Bristol,	1	2,000	10	2,675	34,300	17
Phelps,	1	300	250	6,560	7,560	3
ORANGE Co.						
Deerpark,	1	3,100	150	18,000	20,095	4
Warwick,	1	....	....	2,700	....	....
OSWEGO Co.						
Hastings,	1	200	....	1,500	....	....
OTSEGO Co.						
Butternuts,	1	50	10	6,450	7,475	1
PUTNAM Co.						
Carmel,	1	100	50	1,000	1,750	....
QUEENS Co.						
North Hempstead,	2	1,000	350	31,471	35,389	9
RICHMOND Co.						
Northfield,	1	....	....	15,000	17,000	3
ROCKLAND Co.						
Haverstraw,	1	4,000	300	30,000	30,000	6
ST. LAWRENCE Co.						
Madrid,	1	100	10	800	1,200	2
Potsdam,	2	400	....	6,750	10,000	3
STEUBEN Co.						
Bath,	1	500	200	6,000	7,500	2
SUFFOLK Co.						
Huntington,	1	150	220	7,000	9,000	2
SULLIVAN Co.						
Mamakating,	1	25	15	....	200	1
TIOGA Co.						
Berkshire,	1	....	....	....	....	....
Candor,	1	....	....	2,100	2,100	....
Nichols	1	100	25	3,400	4,750	1
TOMPKINS Co.						
Dryden,	3	99	45	2,649	3,490	3
Groton,	1	....	....	3,000	....	....
Ulysses,	1	400	300	1,000	2,000	2
ULSTER Co.						
Marbletown,	1	500	100	....	8,000	2
Saugerties,	5	1,700	220	8,980	27,050	14
WAYNE Co.						
Arcadia,	2	175	40	5,315	6,015	1
Lyons,	2	1,050	400	7,602	9,249	2
WESTCHESTER Co.						
Bedford,	1	140	20	2,330	3,380	2
Mount Pleasant,	1	3,000	400	....	....	....
North Castle,	1	100	15	1,640	1,940	1
Rye,	3	2,400	175	26,700	28,500	5
Somers,	2	5,200	275	....	20,000	3
Yorktown,	1	50	20	....	....	2
WYOMING Co.						
Attica,	1	950	50	5,716	7,716	3
Warsaw,	1	....	10	2,000	2,500	2

CANE MANUFACTORY.

TOWNS.	Number of establishments.	In real estate.	In tools and machinery.	Of raw materials used.	Of manufactured articles.	Persons employed.
NEW-YORK Co.						
New-York,	1	....	60	1,000	2,000	2

CARPET BAG MANUFACTORY.

TOWNS.	Number of establishments.	In real estate.	In tools and machinery.	Of raw materials used.	Of manufactured articles.	Persons employed.
ORANGE Co.						
Walkill,	1	5,000	4,000	70,000	100,000	1

CHARCOAL MANUFACTORIES.

TOWNS.	Number of establishments.	In real estate.	In tools and machinery.	Of raw materials used.	Of manufactured articles.	Persons employed.
CLINTON Co.						
Ausable,	1	....	....	1,750	8,450	20
Black Brook,	1	....	....	....	73,475	....
Saranac,	18	....	1,570	3,475	30,371	119
ERIE Co.						
Lancaster,	1	150	....	600	2,300	3
Tonawanda,	1	....	....	....	....	....
ESSEX Co.						
Elizabethtown,	1	....	....	....	17,808	55
Keene,	3	....	....	....	2,339	15
Schroon,	1	3,000	1,000	9,375	24,375	50
Westport,	....	....	....	2,700	3,200	....
Willsborough,	1	....	....	300	600	....
ONEIDA Co.						
Ava,	2	....	....	105	280	....
OTSEGO Co.						
Roseboom,	1	$150	....	$75	$250	....
RENSSELAER Co.						
Berlin,	1	....	....	2,000	4,800	13
SULLIVAN Co.						
Fallsburgh,	2	....	....	1,870	3,650	10
ULSTER Co.						
Hurley,	1	....	$400	600	2,400	....
Rochester,	1	....	....	750	2,450	5
Wawarsing,	1	....	....	1,800	4,000	2

CISTERN AND TANK MANUFACTORIES.

TOWNS.	Number of establishments.	In real estate.	In tools and machinery.	Of raw materials used.	Of manufactured articles.	Persons employed.
MONROE Co.						
Rochester,	2	2,500	250	1,015	3,547	3

CORK CUTTING ESTABLISHMENTS.

TOWNS.	Number of establishments.	In real estate.	In tools and machinery.	Of raw materials used.	Of manufactured articles.	Persons employed.
NEW-YORK Co.						
New-York,	2	....	650	3,600	12,000	5

FANCY TURNING ESTABLISHMENTS.

TOWNS.	Number of establishments.	In real estate.	In tools and machinery.	Of raw materials used.	Of manufactured articles.	Persons employed.
MONROE Co.						
Rochester,	1	25	100	150	500	1
NEW-YORK Co.						
New-York,	7	42,000	19,800	53,250	108,000	119

FISHING ROD MANUFACTORIES.

TOWNS.	Number of establishments.	In real estate.	In tools and machinery.	Of raw materials used.	Of manufactured articles.	Persons employed.
MONROE Co.						
Brighton,	1	....	....	100	500	....
NEW-YORK Co.						
New-York,	5	3,600	5,800	3,050	26,200	17

ICE ESTABLISHMENTS.

TOWNS.	Number of establishments.	In real estate.	In tools and machinery.	Of raw materials used.	Of manufactured articles.	Persons employed.
DUTCHESS Co.						
Rhinebeck,	1	20,000	500	....	60,000	80
MONROE Co.						
Rochester,	2	1,800	700	696	8,800	5
NEW-YORK Co.						
New-York,	1	8,000	7,470	10,615	25,000	21
ONEIDA Co.						
Utica,	1	2,000	500	500	3,000	4
ONONDAGA Co.						
Onondaga,	1	400	....	175	800	....
ROCKLAND Co.						
Clarkstown,	1	34,000	34,000	3,865	42,000	102
SUFFOLK Co.						
Southold,	2	1,000	....	100	500	....

PAPER BOX MANUFACTORIES.

TOWNS.	Number of establishments.	In real estate.	In tools and machinery.	Of raw materials used.	Of manufactured articles.	Persons employed.
MADISON Co.						
Lenox,	1	220	235	525	....	23
NEW-YORK Co.						
New-York,	25	31,000	14,200	269,000	464,500	396
RENSSELAER Co.						
Lansingburgh,	1	200	100	840	3,000	3

REFRIGERATOR MANUFACTORIES.

TOWNS.	Number of establishments.	In real estate.	In tools and machinery.	Of raw materials used.	Of manufactured articles.	Persons employed.
MONROE Co.						
Rochester,	1	....	800	3,500	15,000	7
NEW-YORK Co.						
New-York,	1	8,000	5,000	6,500	22,500	9
ULSTER Co.						
Kingston,	1	....	....	3,500	9,350	....

REGALIA MANUFACTORY.

TOWNS.	Number of establishments.	In real estate.	In tools and machinery.	Of raw materials used.	Of manufactured articles.	Persons employed.
ERIE Co.						
Buffalo,	1	....	....	10,000	15,000	18

SAUSAGE MACHINE MANUFACTORY.

TOWNS.	Number of establishments.	In real estate.	In tools and machinery.	Of raw materials used.	Of manufactured articles.	Persons employed.
QUEENS Co.						
Oyster Bay,	1	1,000	500	3,000	6,000	2

SODA FOUNTAIN MANUFACTORIES.

TOWNS.	Number of establishments.	In real estate.	In tools and machinery.	Of raw materials used.	Of manufactured articles.	Persons employed.
MONROE Co.						
Rochester,	1	100	300	348	1,285	2
NEW-YORK Co.						
New-York,	2	20,000	8,000	70,000	85,000	38

TOBACCO AND CIGAR MANUFACTORIES.

TOWNS.	Number of establishments.	In real estate.	In tools and machinery.	Of raw materials used.	Of manufactured articles.	Persons employed.
ALBANY Co.						
Albany,	7	8,000	20,000	65,740	222,900	223
Watervliet,	1	3,000	2,300	18,000	36,288	34
CAYUGA Co.						
Auburn,	3	5,000	1,200	48,668	90,300	81

CLASS XXII.—(Continued.)

Towns.	Number of establishments.	Capital invested: In real estate.	Capital invested: In tools and machinery.	Cash value: Of raw materials used.	Cash value: Of manufactured articles.	Persons employed.
Cayuga Co.						
Mentz,	1	....	....	$50	$6,000	5
Chautauque Co.						
Pomfret,	1	$1,000	....	2,300	6,400	8
Chemung Co.						
Elmira,	1	10,000	$1,600	40,500	60,000	36
Columbia Co.						
Hudson,	1	1,500	400	800	1,400	1
Dutchess Co.						
East Fishkill,	1	500	150	3,000	3,000	6
Fishkill,	3	1,200	2,500	15,800	26,212	43
North East,	1	....	....	600	750	1
Poughkeepsie city,	5	4,000	660	4,100	8,100	15
Red Hook,	1	2,500	4,000	80,000	105,000	59
Rhinebeck,	1	....	25	1,000	2,080	2
Stanford,	1	1,000	350	4,123	6,435	8
Erie Co.						
Buffalo,	5	1,500	1,325	27,325	61,700	65
Fulton Co.						
Mayfield,	1	....	....	290	800	1
Greene Co.						
Lexington,	1	400	800	5,000	6,700	13
Jefferson Co.						
Watertown,	1	1,000	35	10,000	15,000	20
Kings Co.						
Brooklyn,	9	13,000	15,900	47,476	205,620	139
Livingston Co.						
North Dansville,	1	....	....	1,500	3,400	6
Monroe Co.						
Rochester,	4	5,000	5,300	57,453	127,891	96
Montgomery Co.						
Root,	1	....	....	60	300	....
New-York Co.						
New-York,	36	310,000	42,975	428,858	589,840	411
Niagara Co.						
Lockport,	1	....	....	12,000	2,500	2
Oneida Co.						
Rome,	1	5,000	1,200	5,223	7,656	17
Trenton,	1	200	20	5,000	11,000	3
Utica,	4	14,000	8,200	114,690	168,859	214
Onondaga Co.						
Marcellus,	1	500	....	2,000	4,000	6
Syracuse,	3	3,000	2,500	50,000	110,566	99
Van Buren,	1	100	....	400	1,500	3
Orange Co.						
Deerpark,	1	....	....	117	936	1
Montgomery,	2	4,050	1,500	10,800	21,200	22
Newburgh,	1	5,000	300	5,000	9,000	10
Walkill,	2	2,400	200	7,200	11,000	17
Oswego Co.						
Oswego city,	1	4,000	100	3,500	10,000	5
Otsego Co.						
Unadilla,	1	500	....	4,000	9,000	11
Queens Co.						
Flushing,	1	....	100	2,000	3,000	2
Oyster Bay,	1	....	....	800	2,500	4
Rensselaer Co.						
Troy,	3	3,000	....	6,500	20,500	19
Richmond Co.						
Westfield,	2	150	....	2,200	6,000	6
Rockland Co.						
Orangetown,	1	1,500	1,800	8,200	23,500	15
Ramapo,	2	675	290	1,300	2,150	2
St. Lawrence Co.						
Oswegatchie,	1	4,000	50	5,000	10,000	15
Saratoga Co.						
Waterford,	1	....	400	8,337	12,600	14
Steuben Co.						
Hornellsville,	1	48	13	375	1,125	3
Huntington,	1	....	....	300	700	2
Suffolk Co.						
Southampton,	1	....	....	1,500	3,000	2
Southold,	1	....	....	1,500	2,500	7
Sullivan Co.						
Liberty,	2	....	100	2,100	5,552	7
Tioga Co.						
Newark,	1	500	....	500	1,000	....
Richford,	1	300	500	6,500	8,700	....
Tompkins Co.						
Dryden,	1	350	....	800	3,000	6
Ithaca,	5	15,300	4,000	40,100	122,432	76
Ulster Co.						
Kingston,	2	2,200	5	3,500	5,700	6
Saugerties,	1	....	5	1,000	1,500	2
Washington Co.						
Fort Edward,	1	....	....	4,000	6,400	14
Westchester Co.						
Portland,	1	8,000	2,800	61,000	65,400	21
Harrison,	1	....	....	260	400	1
Somers,	1	10,000	4,000	....	....	6
Westchester Co.						
White Plains,	1	$3,000	$1,000	$3,696	$9,538	5
Wyoming Co.						
Attica,	1	....	....	125	560	2

UNDERTAKERS' ESTABLISHMENTS.

Towns.	Number of establishments.	Capital invested: In real estate.	Capital invested: In tools and machinery.	Cash value: Of raw materials used.	Cash value: Of manufactured articles.	Persons employed.
Cayuga Co.						
Auburn,	1	1,000	500	440	1,600	....
Kings Co.						
Brooklyn,	4	825	825	1,874	4,600	4
Monroe Co.						
Rochester,	1	210	50	625	1,350	2
New-York Co.						
New-York,	3	63,000	650	19,500	86,700	53
Onondaga Co.						
Syracuse,	1	....	....	1,200	3,500	....
Orange Co.						
Montgomery,	1	200	50	300	408	1
Oswego Co.						
Oswego city,	2	6,000	200	1,375	11,060	5
Queens Co.						
Flushing,	1	....	....	500	2,107	1
Schenectady Co.						
Schenectady,	1	....	20	490	1,300	2
Schuyler Co.						
Orange,	1	100	300	100	630	1
Suffolk Co.						
Southampton,	1	....	....	200	2,000	....

UNENUMERATED MANUFACTURES.

Towns.	Number of establishments.	Capital invested: In real estate.	Capital invested: In tools and machinery.	Cash value: Of raw materials used.	Cash value: Of manufactured articles.	Persons employed.
Albany Co.						
Watervliet,	1	....	2,000	1,900	6,700	5
Allegany Co.						
Rushford,	2	570	1,000	3,920	6,000	2
Chautauque Co.						
Westfield,	1	....	2,000	....	20,000	30
Columbia Co.						
New Lebanon,	2	2,100	350	350	6,910	10
Dutchess Co.						
Fishkill,	1	5,000	1,000	920	4,000	7
Erie Co.						
Buffalo,	1	100	100	....	....	1
Jefferson Co.						
Le Ray,	1	500	100	144	750	1
Hounsfield,	3	200	363	577	202	6
Lyme,	51	2,800	5,065	....	9,849	58
Kings Co.						
Brooklyn,	13	87,000	24,330	86,820	157,000	180
Madison Co.						
Cazenovia,	1	....	2,500	5,500	10,000	12
Monroe Co.						
Rochester,	1	1,000	400	100	1,500	2
New-York Co.						
New-York,	17	733,400	743,713	804,077	1,275,019	1859
Niagara Co.						
Wilson,	3	....	475	....	950	8
Oneida Co.						
Utica,	1	11,000	6,000	12,000	40,000	50
Onondaga Co.						
Syracuse,	1	1,000	100	1,800	2,500	5
Orleans Co.						
Gaines,	1	200	400	600	950	....
Queens Co.						
Newtown,	1	4,000	....	....	....	66
Rensselaer Co.						
Troy,	1	1,000	2,500	2,500	14,000	12
Richmond Co.						
Westfield,	2	6,000	1,800	4,500	15,000	17
Rockland Co.						
Haverstraw,	1	....	1,000	225	225	5
St. Lawrence Co.						
Macomb,	1	22,000	10,000	....	....	1
Saratoga Co.						
Providence,	1	200	350	800	1,600	1
Suffolk Co.						
Southold,	18	12,400	....	....	20,740	163
Ulster Co.						
Shawangunk,	1	....	600	250	600	....
Wayne Co.						
Wolcott,	1	800	800	512	1,100	2
Wyoming Co.						
Castile,	1	....	250	200	200	....

WHALEBONE MANUFACTORIES.

Towns.	Number of establishments.	Capital invested: In real estate.	Capital invested: In tools and machinery.	Cash value: Of raw materials used.	Cash value: Of manufactured articles.	Persons employed.
New-York Co.						
New-York,	2	10,000	800	90,000	120,000	42
Queens Co.						
Flushing,	1	30,000	40,000	153,500	350,000	....

SUMMARY OF CAPITAL INVESTED, VALUE OF RAW MATERIALS AND PRODUCTS, ETC.

CLASS I.—AGRICULTURAL TOOLS AND IMPLEMENTS.

MANUFACTURES.	Number of establishments.	Persons Employed.					Power Used.		Capital Invested.		Cash Value.	
		Men.	Women.	Boys under 18 years.	Girls under 18 years.	Total.	Establishments using water.	Establishments using steam.	In real estate.	In tools and machinery.	Of raw materials used.	Of manufactured articles.
Agricultural implements generally,	59	1,008	......	57	......	1,065	13	32	$408,100	$172,825	$692,778	$1,738,091
Cheese press manufactories,	2	3	......	......	......	3	1	......	900	650	550	1,730
Churn factories,	3	11	......	......	......	11	1	1	50	706	7,600	17,250
Cider mills,	26	60	......	4	......	64	10	2	11,010	6,308	16,598	30,924
Clover mills,	10	14	......	......	......	14	9	......	6,725	3,845	17,563	20,430
Fanning mill manufactories, etc.,	32	89	......	8	......	97	8	3	16,500	7,940	39,962	85,619
Fork factories,	8	140	......	5	......	145	7	......	48,600	18,600	83,377	172,870
Grain cradle and scythe snath factories, etc.	34	133	......	6	......	139	13	6	26,880	13,221	24,524	109,448
Grain measure manufactories,	4	11	......	2	......	13	4	......	2,900	1,350	4,060	9,900
Hoe manufactories,	10	111	......	2	......	113	9	1	31,900	17,600	56,375	111,461
Plow and cultivator factories,	41	165	......	7	......	172	11	11	62,100	31,385	70,189	163,924
Rake factories,	40	60	......	7	......	67	19	4	19,580	9,675	14,089	60,278
Reaping and mowing machine factories,	9	219	......	17	......	236	6	2	43,600	23,950	83,560	319,200
Scythe factories, etc.,	8	211	......	......	......	211	8	......	38,700	20,100	82,995	174,250
Scythe rifle manufactories,	5	17	6	2	3	28	2	......	2,590	1,515	5,408	14,300
Shovel manufactory,	1	20	......	......	......	20	......	1	6,000	6,000	18,000	30,000
Tool shops,	8	61	......	4	......	65	4	1	21,370	5,985	16,399	53,394
Threshing machine manufactories,	2	10	......	1	......	11	1	1	2,000	3,200	1,902	7,340
Total,	302	2,343	6	122	3	2,474	126	65	749,505	344,855	1,235,929	3,120,409
CLASS II.—METALLURGY AND MANUFACTURE OF METALS AND INSTRUMENTS THEREFOR.												
Anvil manufactory,	1	8	......	......	......	8	1	......	5,000	2,000	4,500	15,000
Axe and edge tool manufactories,	46	798	......	26	......	824	23	13	171,350	179,790	325,182	721,381
Bell founderies,	4	43	......	......	......	43	1	1	35,800	13,600	231,812	301,000
Blacksmith shops,	1,921	3,199	......	115	......	3,314	22	14	878,164	526,392	784,476	2,073,797
Bolt manufactories,	10	82	......	6	......	88	1	4	29,800	24,400	38,125	94,300
Brad and sparable manufactories,	1	2	......	1	......	3	......	1	2,500	1,500	1,800	2,800
Brass and copper founderies,	48	430	......	124	......	554	2	19	250,700	222,100	608,314	1,304,300
Brass finishing establishments,	1	4	......	......	......	4	......	1	....	1,500	1,500	4,200
Britannia ware and silver plating do.,	10	86	11	34	1	132	......	3	16,200	22,000	49,155	132,800
Bronze casting establishments,	3	31	......	......	......	31	......	......	....	7,500	14,300	43,000
Butt and hinge factories,	3	82	......	90	......	172	1	1	14,400	20,650	94,883	150,420
Castor frame manufactory,	1	5	......	6	......	11	......	1	....	12,000	18,500	29,400
Composition metal manufactories,	4	23	1	5	1	30	2	......	6,000	8,250	12,900	28,600
Copper smithing,	15	207	......	39	......	246	......	1	51,000	171,400	804,528	766,500
Cutlery manufactories,	10	91	2	7	......	100	2	5	14,900	18,100	27,663	91,000
Door latch manufactories,	1	7	......	1	......	8	1	......	....	200	2,955	11,000
File manufactories,	5	249	16	74	......	339	2	3	22,100	43,200	70,915	285,400
Fish hook manufactory,	1	8	3	2	......	13	......	......	10,000	700	5,000	9,500
Forges,	24	378	......	40	......	418	16	6	165,300	151,500	327,418	828,780
Furnaces,	388	7,959	......	793	......	8,752	91	198	2,903,350	2,070,025	4,126,127	9,725,775
Gas fixture manufactories,	14	373	25	62	......	460	......	10	152,500	123,700	483,993	864,300
German silver ware manufactories,	2	16	......	......	......	16	......	1	1,500	200	15,900	61,000
Gilding establishments,	7	60	......	9	......	69	......	......	5,000	5,450	30,000	59,000
Gold leaf and foil manufactories,	8	35	25	25	9	94	......	......	7,000	11,600	96,760	139,225
Gold and silver plating establishments,	13	82	74	15	......	171	......	5	36,000	10,000	73,645	171,400
Gold and silver refining establishments,	7	73	......	7	......	80	......	5	112,000	23,500	2,095,000	2,190,000
Hammer manufactories,	3	34	......	1	......	35	2	......	7,500	3,300	9,538	37,000
Handiron manufactories,	1	8	......	4	......	12	......	......	4,500	1,000	3,693	14,000
Hardware manufactories,	3	20	......	33	......	53	2	......	15,500	5,400	90,300	126,400
Hollow-ware manufactories,	4	119	......	18	......	137	......	4	26,200	14,200	75,870	149,000
Iron manufactories,	78	4,829	......	566	......	5,395	61	12	1,777,000	504,655	3,127,909	6,556,220
Iron pipe manufactories,	7	189	......	15	......	204	......	6	19,000	59,500	186,000	290,000
Iron railing manufactories,	31	804	......	154	......	958	......	13	272,000	179,450	369,954	1,224,400
Japanned tin manufactories,	5	28	......	23	......	51	......	......	6,500	2,350	14,500	24,500
Lead pipe manufactories,	3	102	......	1	......	103	......	2	70,100	81,000	454,000	405,500
Lightning rod manufactories,	2	6	......	2	......	8	......	1	....	200	5,470	34,200
Lock manufactories,	19	133	......	28	6	167	3	7	73,378	31,700	57,782	181,580
Machine shops,	189	3,404	......	265	......	3,669	54	110	1,236,450	960,776	1,537,553	3,411,981
Machinists' tool manufactories,	6	72	......	8	......	80	4	1	35,500	50,600	19,454	87,375
Malleable iron works,	5	116	......	22	......	138	......	4	10,500	15,300	59,350	170,600
Metallic burial case manufactory,	1	50	......	......	......	50	......	1	7,000	3,500	22,350	80,000
Metallic life boat manufactory,	1	60	......	......	......	60	......	1	55,000	44,200	30,000	80,000
Pin manufactories,	2	8	1	......	......	9	......	......	....	10,000	560	1,250
Plumbing establishments,	30	260	......	77	......	337	......	1	185,433	27,200	485,955	551,150
Rolling mill and nail factories,	3	93	......	......	......	93	1	......	26,500	15,000	292,840	468,864
Safe manufactories,	11	520	......	8	......	528	1	9	115,750	111,159	289,185	1,076,681
Screw factory,	1	37	9	20	......	66	......	1	7,000	4,500	10,500	79,950
Silverware manufactories,	1,336	107	277	65	......	449	......	25	495,080	307,685	2,447,761	4,322,061
Spike manufactory,	2	9	......	......	......	9	......	......	7,000	350	16,720	21,300
Steel spring manufactories,	3	32	......	......	......	32	3	......	10,000	4,200	39,298	56,000
Thimble manufactories,	5	19	......	8	......	27	......	2	1,800	3,650	56,500	76,000
Tin and sheet iron manufactories,	458	4,767	19	211	12	5,009	......	5	674,750	260,496	1,504,389	3,000,264
Tin foil manufactory,	1	7	......	5	......	12	......	1	5,000	8,000	40,000	50,000
Trip hammers,	2	2	......	......	......	2	2	......	300	300	350	1,000
Wire works,	16	175	11	16	10	212	4	1	15,700	34,000	163,885	341,060
Wire railing manufactory,	1	19	......	10	......	29	......	1	14,000	5,000	30,000	125,000
Wire seive manufactories,	6	24	......	7	1	32	......	......	13,300	6,450	18,811	45,473
Total,	4,783	30,384	474	3,048	40	33,946	302	500	10,078,305	6,426,378	21,806,828	43,192,687

CLASS III.—MANUFACTURES OF FIBROUS AND TEXTILE SUBSTANCES.

MANUFACTURES.	Number of establishments.	Persons Employed. Men.	Women.	Boys under 18 years	Girls under 18 years	Total.	Power Used. Establishments using water.	Establishments using steam.	Capital Invested. In real estate.	In tools and machinery.	Cash Value. Of raw materials used.	Of manufactured articles.
Awning manufactories,	3	12	6	2		20			$17,000	$40	$4,000	$15,000
Card board manufactories,	2	30	100	4		134				70,000	57,500	120,000
Carding and cloth dressing establishments,	264	162	25	29	5	221	84	8	99,480	55,270	174,344	250,552
Carpet manufactories,	18	1,155	556	116	64	1,891	6	4	265,270	394,200	934,745	2,079.703
Carpet yarn manufactories,	2	13		3	2	18	2		10,000	4,000	16,200	25,208
Cotton factories,	86	1,849	3,416	1,501	1,566	8,332	71	31	1,785,350	2,465,401	2,492.531	4,621,133
Cotton batting manufactories	11	48	21	27	13	109	8	2	27,000	24,350	101,514	144,736
Cotton warp manufactories,	4	30	14	28	45	117	4		38,000	35,000	55,500	82,500
Felting and wadding manufactory,	1	6	30			36		1		24,000	2,400	5,000
Flax dressing mills,	45	229	69	93	118	509	30	4	89,550	76,290	451,475	732,077
Fringe and tassel manufactories,	17	55	130	32	103	320		2	72,300	10,250	125,950	280 500
Fur dressing establishments,	15	100	94	5	15	214		1	182,400	4,380	306,824	614,700
Hair cloth manufactories,	2	3	36	1		40			1,200	1,500	400	4,863
Linen factories,	2	40	64	18	15	137	1	1	28,500	35,640	63,500	103,980
Oakum manufactories,	2	20		26		46		2	25,300	10,200	50,467	65,000
Paper mills,	109	922	569	116	67	1,674	86	12	880,030	664,570	1,511,724	2,813,147
Papier mache manufactory,	1	2				2				500	230	1,000
Playing cards manufactories,	3	42	62	12	38	154		3	20,000	23,000	65.600	185,000
Power loom manufactories,	2	102	2	8		112	3		30,000	153,000	24,095	92,500
Rag carpet and blanket manufactories,	3	6	1			7			2,000	115	3,000	11,855
Ribbon factories,	2	3	20	2	6	31		1	5,000	1,200	10,450	15,900
Rope manufactories,	29	399	52	292	129	872	2	7	217,650	276,234	1,550,624	2,448,798
Sea grass manufactories,	2	5				5					525	2,340
Sewing silk manufactories,	6	40	44	24	128	236	1	3	25,000	30,000	138,492	212,000
Shawl manufactories,	5	113	237	42	55	447	1	3	155,500	70,200	272,988	610,500
Shoddy mills,	5	15	17	4	22	58	5		10,500	5,400	13,900	41,640
Straw paper manufactories,	37	209	17	20	6	252	32	5	145,100	90,350	76,611	250,564
Tape and webb manufactories,	7	25	33	19	18	95	1	1	12,500	11,450	54,004	111,900
Twine manufactories,	20	114	96	129	56	395	7	3	110,050	67,835	189,698	308,725
Woolen cloth and yarn factories,	184	1,531	1,014	361	279	3,185	161	9	1,039,949	802,450	2,054,882	3,392,207
Total,	889	7,280	6,725	2,914	2,750	19,669	505	103	5,294,629	5,406,825	10,804,173	19,643,028

CLASS IV.—CHEMICAL PROCESSES, MANUFACTURES AND COMPOUNDS.

MANUFACTURES.	Number of establishments.	Men.	Women.	Boys under 18 years	Girls under 18 years	Total.	Establishments using water.	Establishments using steam.	In real estate.	In tools and machinery.	Of raw materials used.	Of manufactured articles.
Asheries,	68	110				110	2	2	28,325	15,501	113,327	165,302
Bakeries,	196	816	71	145	12	1,044		10	516,825	595,013	2,618,504	3,356,769
Barilla manufactory,	1	3				3	1		3,000	2,000	24,000	26,250
Barytes manufactories,	2	20				20	2	1	10,000	5,100	39,850	84,000
Biscuit machine manufactory,	1	4				4	1			800	1,525	5,250
Blacking manufactories,	2	9	1	3	1	14			16,000	600	15,500	27,400
Black lead manufactories,	2	7		2		9	2		6,200	1,800	5,300	11,000
Bleacheries,	3	82	5	7	1	95	2	1	69,000	44,000	37,701	110,000
Breweries,	128	1,006	12	114	1	1,133	6	39	1,489,024	750,705	2,698,389	4,448,352
Bronze color manufactory,	1	70				70		1	2,000	2,000	5,000	10,000
Camphene distilleries,	3	85				85		2	140,500	100,300	1,050,000	1,670,000
Chandleries, and soap factories,	111	591	15	74	5	685		18	635,810	492,610	2,820.511	4,096,106
Chemical laboratories,	9	40	2	4	2	48		2	78,500	27,100	217,260	349,000
Coffee, spice and mustard manufactories,	22	149	2	69	5	225	1	19	172,000	52,500	673,150	991,075
Confectionary manufactories,	48	242	32	47	17	338		2	115,100	29,515	441,015	906,233
Cotton printing establishments,	7	266	73	91	80	510	3	2	93,660	111,968	817,081	2,352,877
Distilleries,	88	803		2		805	15	39	755,400	432,897	6,267,824	8,681,061
Drug and medicine manufactories,	26	101	55	11	28	195	3	1	131,300	19,330	247,515	553,762
Dyeing establishments,	6	327	3	0	5	341	1	2	106,164	87,485	61,959	195,624
Dye wood manufactories,	5	44		1		45	2	2	63,000	38,000	269,600	304,800
Electrotyping establishments,	2	10				10			20,000	800	7,000	11,000
Emery and pumice stone manufactories,	2	8	5		15	28	2	1	3,000	3,500	16,500	53,500
Fish and whale oil manufactories,	11	144		9	6	159		5	269,300	86,000	1,439,025	1,904,900
Gas manufactories,	26	1,211		3		1,214		4	2,026,321	2,433,349	1,445,783	3,279,131
Glue manufactories,	9	91	1	26		118	1	2	44,500	11.830	92,815	197,380
Gutta percha manufactory,	1	61	114	10		185		1	15,000	40,000	95,025	450,000
India rubber manufactories,	4	99	145	28	15	287	1	2	240,000	108,000	370,000	910,000
Ivory black and bone manure manufactories,	7	73		4		77		5	13,750	28,725	115,140	132,260
Japanned cloth manufactories,	2	95	5	4		104		1	30,000	10,000	177,200	245,760
Lamp black manufactories,	4	15		3		18	1		30,900	400	6,530	15,080
Lard oil manufactories,	8	87				87		5	82,000	39,000	1,557,440	1,897,840
Liquorice refinery,	1	5		30		35		1	5,000	1,200	49,340	49,340
Malt manufactories,	30	241				241	2	10	383,400	84.300	1,516,336	1,835,279
Match manufactories,	15	99	108	158	185	550	3	3	46,075	15,845	40,130	215,925
Medicinal herbs and extract manufactories,	5	42	7	2	3	54	1	2	24,800	16,400	27,895	68,173
Mineral water manufactories,	26	250	9	133	1	393		1	102,800	44,400	130,075	347,747
Oil cloth manufactories,	17	247	40	76		363		5	146,300	26,930	353,889	544,250
Oil mills,	27	159		11		170	18	4	156,200	75,230	1,092,420	1,316,627
Paint and color manufactories,	13	103		24		127	5	3	110,400	52,400	290,320	489,670
Painting and glazing establishments,	61	304		15		319			53,835	11,443	112,104	216,813
Paint mill manufactory,	1	3				3	1		2,000	1,500	1,500	4,500
Paper staining establishment,	1	20	20	10	10	60		1	20,000	12,000	26,000	260,000
Pearl ash manufactories,	5	12		2		14			4,500	400	23,119	33,339
Perfume manufactories,	3	10	13	1	13	37			4,500	1,500	10,200	36,500
Pickle and preserve manufactories,	12	175	50	9	15	249		8	101,400	57,925	227,420	460,000
Prussian blue manufactory,	1	1		2		3				600	15,000	20,000
Putty manufactory,	1	4	1	3	1	9		1	16,000	1,500	20,000	25,000
Pyrotechnic establishments,	2	15		2	4	21			6,000	1,300	6,320	17,500
Rosin oil factories,	5	46				46		5	38,000	34,500	58,250	101,300
Saleratus manufactories,	16	60	13	5	2	80		2	44,490	14,109	250,104	315,866
Salt manufactories,	193	980	99	40	24	1,143	2	4	1,107,800	54,275	832,260	1,488,363
Saltpetre refinery,	1	4				4			30,000	2,500	180,000	480,000
Satinet printing establishments,	3	50	24	10	5	89	2	1	16,500	22,600	122,049	149,695
Silk printing establishment,	1	90	3	60	30	183		1	25,000	10,000	375,000	465,000
Starch factories,	43	234				234	33	4	214,000	61,890	394,916	623,359

CLASS IV.—(CONTINUED.)

MANUFACTURES.	Number of establishments.	Persons Employed. Men.	Women.	Boys under 18 years	Girls under 16 years.	Total.	Power Used. Establishments using water.	Establishments using steam	Capital Invested. In real estate.	In tools and machinery.	Cash Value. Of raw materials used.	Of manufactured articles.
Sugar and syrup refineries,	15	1,613	9	9	.....	1,631	.....	10	$1,274,000	$1,258,100	$4,511,500	12,175,350
Varnish manufactories,	11	78	4	6	.....	88	.....	1	91,100	13,055	298,719	551,525
Vinegar manufactories,	12	26	.....	2	.....	28	.....	.....	14,600	14,932	23,328	55,610
Wax bleeching establishment,	1	3	.....	.....	.....	3	.....	1	.....	3,000	30,000	35,000
White lead manufactories,	9	369	.....	1	.....	370	2	8	221,000	120,700	888,497	1,542,663
Whiting manufactories,	3	24	.....	1	.....	25	.....	1	30,000	5,400	31,800	91,500
Wintergreen distilleries,	12	8	.....	.....	.....	8	.....	.....	995	600	6,824	9,477
Total,	1,351	11,944	941	1,275	486	14,646	115	246	11,497,274	7,591,362	35,692,784	61,527,083

CLASS V.—CALORIFICS.

MANUFACTURES.	Number of establishments.	Men.	Women.	Boys under 18 years	Girls under 16 years.	Total.	Establishments using water.	Establishments using steam	In real estate.	In tools and machinery.	Of raw materials used.	Of manufactured articles.
Grate manufactories,	10	134	.....	9	.....	143	.....	.....	.....	26,900	126,000	208,161
Lamp and lantern manufactories,	9	118	1	21	1	141	.....	5	11,600	39,300	95,590	185,500
Locomotive lamp manufactories,	3	20	.....	.....	.....	20	2	1	38,000	4,200	16,558	46,100
Stove manufactories,	35	1,450	.....	118	.....	1,568	1	22	567,300	131,563	710,987	1,908,670
Total,	57	1,722	1	148	1	1,872	3	28	616,900	201,963	949,135	2,348,431

CLASS VI.—STEAM ENGINES, BOILERS, LOCOMOTIVES, ETC.

MANUFACTURES.	Number of establishments.	Men.	Women.	Boys under 18 years	Girls under 16 years.	Total.	Establishments using water.	Establishments using steam	In real estate.	In tools and machinery.	Of raw materials used.	Of manufactured articles.
Locomotive manufactories,	3	771	.....	50	.....	821	.....	2	110,000	357,500	254,425	460,500
Locomotive spark manufactory,	1	9	.....	.....	.....	9	.....	.....	30,000	1,000	8,250	30,000
Steam engine and boiler manufactories	28	3,338	16	164	.....	3,518	.....	18	1,272,300	860,350	2,012,112	3,841,306
Total,	32	4,118	16	214	.....	4,348	.....	20	1,412,300	1,218,850	2,274,787	4,331,806

CLASS VII.—NAVIGATION AND MARITIME IMPLEMENTS.

MANUFACTURES.	Number of establishments.	Men.	Women.	Boys under 18 years	Girls under 16 years.	Total.	Establishments using water.	Establishments using steam	In real estate.	In tools and machinery.	Of raw materials used.	Of manufactured articles.
Block manufactories,	13	98	.....	21	.....	119	.....	2	50,500	15,300	31,353	117,030
Boat building,	74	780	2	41	.....	823	.....	2	306,450	45,290	363,577	848,700
Capstan and windlass manufactory,	1	4	.....	.....	.....	4	.....	.....	3,000	1,500	10,700	15,000
Oar manufactory,	1	3	.....	.....	.....	3	1	.....	2,500	300	1,000	2,250
Sail-making,	14	82	.....	21	.....	103	.....	.....	87,500	1,195	182,635	219,575
Ship-building,	86	3,066	.....	220	.....	3,286	.....	9	1,287,700	229,860	1,928,308	4,664,811
Ship-rigging,	2	86	.....	.....	.....	86	.....	.....	23,000	5,000	1,040,000	1,700,000
Ship-smithing,	31	158	.....	26	.....	184	.....	.....	146,800	38,450	108,650	209,890
Spar manufactories,	6	91	.....	10	.....	101	.....	.....	144,700	4,350	201,700	313,800
Steamboat finishing,	1	60	.....	4	.....	64	.....	1	17,000	10,000	100,000	150,000
Treenail factories,	7	13	.....	.....	.....	13	.....	.....	1,000	.....	24,800	27,050
Total,	236	4,441	2	343	.....	4,786	1	14	2,070,150	351,245	3,992,723	8,268,106

CLASS VIII.—MATHEMATICAL, PHILOSOPHICAL, AND OPTICAL INSTRUMENTS.

MANUFACTURES.	Number of establishments.	Men.	Women.	Boys under 18 years	Girls under 16 years.	Total.	Establishments using water.	Establishments using steam	In real estate.	In tools and machinery.	Of raw materials used.	Of manufactured articles.
Barometer manufactories,	3	8	.....	3	.....	11	.....	.....	400	2,000	4,100	11,700
Chronometer manufactories,	5	49	.....	.....	.....	49	.....	.....	.....	16,040	17,300	56,500
Clock factories,	10	93	4	10	1	108	2	3	58,700	16,800	69,475	178,610
Hydrometer manufactory,	1	2	.....	.....	.....	2	.....	.....	12,000	500	1,000	3,200
Mathematical instrument manufactories,	10	32	.....	1	.....	33	.....	1	.....	15,100	18,000	101,000
Nautical instrument manufactories,	4	17	.....	.....	.....	17	.....	.....	.....	7,300	3,975	17,800
Optical instrument manufactories,	4	18	.....	.....	.....	18	.....	1	2,450	5,550	7,510	30,500
Philosophical instrument manufactory,	1	2	.....	.....	.....	2	.....	1	.....	35,000	300	1,800
Spectacle manufactories,	2	15	.....	1	.....	16	.....	.....	10,000	1,000	4,310	19,250
Surveying instrument manufactories,	2	26	.....	1	.....	27	.....	1	8,250	10,000	3,730	29,200
Telegraph manufactories,	4	33	2	4	.....	39	.....	2	10,000	14,700	27,550	70,500
Thermometer manufactories,	3	9	5	1	.....	15	.....	.....	3,750	1,450	1,830	16,950
Total,	49	304	11	21	1	337	2	9	105,550	125,440	159,080	537,010

CLASS IX.—CIVIL ENGINEERING AND ARCHITECTURE.

MANUFACTURES.	Number of establishments.	Men.	Women.	Boys under 18 years	Girls under 16 years.	Total.	Establishments using water.	Establishments using steam	In real estate.	In tools and machinery.	Of raw materials used.	Of manufactured articles.
Gypsum quarries,	3	24	.....	.....	.....	24	.....	.....	9,500	2,300	12,400	14,200
House building,	88	1,447	29	20	.....	1,496	1	5	482,130	77,820	395,531	1,217,700
Iron mining,	29	786	.....	.....	.....	786	3	5	437,000	51,471	45,856	540,572
Lead mining,	1	20	.....	.....	.....	20	.....	1	7,250	14,000	.....	8,000
Marl and peat beds,	2	1	.....	.....	.....	1	.....	.....	1,000	10	.....	928
Masonry,	8	43	.....	.....	.....	43	.....	.....	10,000	566	200	2,600
Mining machine manufactory,	1	1	.....	5	.....	6	.....	.....	.....	7,000	38,000	50,000
Ornamental plastering,	1	75	.....	8	.....	83	.....	1	.....	12,000	50,300	75,000
Sash and blind manufactories,	213	1,121	.....	90	.....	1,211	89	50	393,475	245,605	471,281	1,189,042
Stair-building establishments,	8	32	.....	4	.....	36	.....	.....	1,700	1,100	4,100	21,900
Stone quarries,	200	1,599	.....	12	.....	1,611	4	1	263,975	31,639	40,140	533,456
Total,	554	5,149	29	139	.....	5,317	97	63	1,606,030	443,511	1,057,808	3,653,398

CLASS X.—LAND CONVEYANCE.

MANUFACTURES.	Number of establishments.	Men.	Women.	Boys under 18 years	Girls under 16 years.	Total.	Establishments using water.	Establishments using steam	In real estate.	In tools and machinery.	Of raw materials used.	Of manufactured articles.
Bow and felloe manufactories,	6	29	.....	1	.....	30	4	2	9,000	13,250	21,450	45,174
Car factories and repair shops,	26	1,543	.....	4	.....	1,547	1	18	420,030	264,784	679,239	1,274,768
Car-wheel founderies,	2	85	.....	1	.....	86	1	1	28,000	26,000	341,965	447,500
Coach and wagon manufactories,	1,397	6,042	12	328	9	6,391	103	68	1,665,577	471,530	1,712,256	5,005,125
Hose carriage manufactories,	2	26	.....	1	.....	27	.....	1	7,000	2,455	3,175	19,200
Hub manufactory,	1	5	.....	.....	.....	5	.....	.....	.....	600	400	9,000
Patent axletree manufactories,	2	40	.....	7	.....	47	2	.....	29,500	9,000	19,860	46,000
Spoke manufactories,	16	55	.....	9	.....	64	7	7	21,125	15,950	14,960	52,331
Wheelbarrow manufactories,	8	52	.....	1	.....	53	5	2	19,400	12,085	14,498	67,650
Wheel factories,	2	12	.....	.....	.....	12	2	.....	5,800	3,500	2,800	11,100
Total,	1,462	7,889	12	352	9	8,262	125	99	2,205,432	819,154	2,810,609	6,977,848

CLASS XI.—HYDRAULICS AND PNEUMATICS.

MANUFACTURES.	Number of establishments.	Persons Employed.					Power Used.		Capital Invested.		Cash Value.	
		Men.	Women.	Boys under 18 years.	Girls under 18 years.	Total.	Establishments using water.	Establishments using steam.	In real estate.	In tools and machinery.	Of raw materials used.	Of manufactured articles.
Bellows making establishments,	4	57		2		59			$2,000	$900	$52,825	$77,200
Fire engine manufactories,	4	99		1		100	1	1	19,000	12,800	16,445	95,950
Pump factories,	32	62				62	5	3	22,960	14,765	37,975	113,525
Steam pump manufactories,	4	275		15		290	1	1	56,000	51,000	174,441	405,000
Total,	44	493		18		511	7	5	99,960	79,465	281,686	691,675

CLASS XII.—LEVER, SCREW, AND OTHER MECHANICAL POWERS.

MANUFACTURES.	Number of establishments.	Men.	Women.	Boys under 18 years.	Girls under 18 years.	Total.	Establishments using water.	Establishments using steam.	In real estate.	In tools and machinery.	Of raw materials used.	Of manufactured articles.
Hoist wheel manufactories,	2	16		2		18			3,000	1,600	2,986	68,000
Hydraulic jack manufactory,	1	10				10		1		2,000	1,000	6,000
Jack screw manufactory,	1	4				4				2,000	1,250	3,800
Scale manufactories,	8	47				47	1		24,950	7,500	35,885	80,900
Total,	12	77		2		79	1	1	27,950	13,100	41,121	158,700

CLASS XIII.—GRINDING MILLS, MILL GEARING, ETC.

MANUFACTURES.	Number of establishments.	Men.	Women.	Boys under 18 years.	Girls under 18 years.	Total.	Establishments using water.	Establishments using steam.	In real estate.	In tools and machinery.	Of raw materials used.	Of manufactured articles.
Band and belting manufactories,	4	32				32			26,200	11,000	125,900	189,300
Bran duster manufactories,	2	6		1		7	1			1,400	2,985	13,750
Farina mills,	1	2				2	1		1,200		6,000	11,100
Feed mills,	14	28				28	10	1	17,400	21,495	310,500	305,650
Grist mills,	1,475	3,326	6	107	8	3,447	1,154	102	8,056,165	2,117,373	42,345,756	51,531,358
Millstone manufactories,	6	67				67		1	28,500	8,910	39,725	71,200
Millwright shops,	10	26		6	1	33	1	4	19,075	10,075	6,037	24,798
Pearl barley mills,	2	8				8	2		8,000	1,000	14,140	26,670
Smut machine manufactories,	4	10				10	3	1	3,400	2,600	5,520	21,600
Total,	1,518	3,505	6	114	9	3,634	1,172	109	8,159,940	2,173,853	42,856,563	52,195,426

CLASS XIV.—LUMBER, INCLUDING TOOLS AND MACHINES FOR ITS MANUFACTURE.

MANUFACTURES.	Number of establishments.	Men.	Women.	Boys under 18 years.	Girls under 18 years.	Total.	Establishments using water.	Establishments using steam.	In real estate.	In tools and machinery.	Of raw materials used.	Of manufactured articles.
Auger manufactories,	4	67		2		69	2		10,100	10,100	14,831	70,575
Barrel machine manufactories,	2	32		1		33	1	1	12,400	10,175	11,305	38,430
Boring machine establishment,	1	12				12		1		6,000	3,500	20,000
Box manufactories,	32	308		32		340	10	12	85,000	51,850	428,020	685,645
Carpenter's shops,	232	1,272		74		1,346	2	9	295,415	68,980	727,958	1,482,992
Carpenter's tool manufactories,	11	206		8		214	6	2	39,343	29.550	54,235	172,650
Cheese box manufactories,	60	137		6		143	46	2	32,040	13,355	25,155	70,352
Cooper's shops,	661	2.688	2	166	1	2,857	23	10	373,358	97,722	898,635	1,910,489
Heading mills,	7	1				1	2		700	100	225	2,335
Hoop manufactories,	3	6		2		8			450	400	2,310	9,143
Joiner shops,	12	35		1		36	1	3	4,800	5,805	10,468	22,808
Ladder and eave spout manufactories,	4	10				10	1		7,120	9,075	4,800	9,840
Lath manufactories,	68	78		1		79	45	5	6,475	9,735	10,045	49,637
Match box manufactories,	2	9		2		11	2		1,600	1,400	2,100	8,000
Patent mill-dog manufactory,	1	1				1			200	50	891	1,620
Pattern manufactories,	5	11		1		12			500	1,250	2,547	8,860
Plane manufactories,	4	7		1		8		1	1,100	3,250	2,000	8,000
Planing machine manufactory,	1										5,000	70,000
Planing mills,	98	1,065		69		1,134	19	70	647,050	422,250	2,111,744	3,121,297
Rule manufactories,	2	17		4		21		1		5,200	8,400	28,000
Saw manufactories,	11	235		21		256	1	8	38,650	32,379	90,694	245,600
Saw set manufactory,	1	5				5	1		1,000	100	575	4,800
Scroll sawing establishments,	2	10				16		1		4,600		4,680
Saw mills,	4,946	12,906	40	129	3	13,087	3,834	492	7,895,423	1,997,814	7,286,197	14,655.103
Shingle factories,	261	602	4	67	1	674	167	48	118,505	74,250	160,704	407,134
Ship timber manufactories,	15	48				48						12,979
Stave manufactories,	72	327		70		397	27	23	85,060	64,870	84,646	291,455
Steel square manufactory,	1	7				7	1		1,000	2,000	1,692	4,500
Turning shops,	135	291		25		316	81	25	92,785	57,790	94,555	303,739
Truss hoop manufactory,	1	6				6			1,000	300	3,500	4,290
Veneering manufactories,	4	22				22	1		15,650	5,200	48,365	237,884
Wood moulding and carving establishments,	15	176		15		191		6	184,400	19,325	111,700	208,500
Wood mills,	30	154				154	1	2	50		160	36,704
Total,	6,704	20,757	55	697	5	21,514	4,274	722	9,951,174	3,004,875	12,206,957	24.208,041

CLASS XV.—STONE, CLAY, POTTERY AND GLASS MANUFACTURE.

MANUFACTURES.	Number of establishments.	Men.	Women.	Boys under 18 years.	Girls under 18 years.	Total.	Establishments using water.	Establishments using steam.	In real estate.	In tools and machinery.	Of raw materials used.	Of manufactured articles.
Brick manufactories,	269	4,458		242		4,700	31	21	725,104	378,610	269,401	1,719,635
Brick and tile machine manufactories,	2	13				13		1	3,500	3,400	2,877	12,954
Enameling factories,	4	55	5	2		62		1	8,000	3,500	16,800	150,500
Fire brick manufactories,	7	104		11		115		5	80,000	98,500	92,310	178,420
Glass cutting establishments,	7	105	20	38	7	170		7	64,000	14,440	52,685	131,095
Glass manufactories,	21	890	57	100	25	1,072		3	475,450	70,500	302,628	980,500
Glass staining establishments,	2	35		9		44			80,600	2,500	22,700	57,000
Lime manufactories,	100	732		25		757		5	324,886	65,907	172,806	600,384
Looking glass manufactories,	18	254		52		306	1	4	255,100	30,550	210,900	413,600
Marble manufactories,	139	1,737		246		1,983	7	14	555,055	158,617	201,876	1,886,818
Plaster mills,	145	327		4		331	94	7	263,875	103,765	267,719	948,834
Porcelain manufactories,	2	101	6	18	5	130		2	60,000	16,000	16,000	90,000
Potteries,	34	252		19		271		7	131,635	34,240	69,806	310,324
Roofing slate manufactories,	5	115				115			29,000	1,550		70,400
Soap stone manufactories,	3	11				11			4,000	2,100	2,500	17,500
Stone cutting establishments,	60	1,299		108		1,407	1	3	391,285	39,225	404,115	1,165,950
Stone cutters' tool manufactory.	1	2				2			100	80	500	1,200
Tile manufactories,	12	47				47			17,000	3,500	4,901	27,501

CLASS XV.—(CONTINUED.)

MANUFACTURES.	Number of establishments.	Persons Employed.					Power Used.		Capital Invested.		Cash Value.	
		Men.	Women.	Boys under 18 years.	Girls under 18 years.	Total.	Establishments using water.	Establishments using steam.	In real estate.	In tools and machinery.	Of raw materials used.	Of manufactured articles.
Tobacco pipe manufactory,	1	6	2	1	....	9	....	....	$1, 300	$500	$1, 000	$5, 200
Water lime manufactories,	32	745	....	19	....	764	12	10	425, 800	102, 870	130, 085	720, 402
Window plate manufactory,	1	3	....	1	....	4	....	....	....	2, 500	2, 000	6, 000
Total,	865	11, 291	90	895	37	12, 313	146	90	3, 895, 690	1, 132, 854	2, 243, 609	9, 494, 217
CLASS XVI.—LEATHER, AND MANUFACTURES THEREFROM.												
Bark mills,	2	2	....	....	....	2	2	....	3, 500	700	2, 200	4, 650
Boot and shoe shops,	1, 463	7, 792	2, 069	391	120	10, 372	1	....	921, 089	140, 851	2, 628, 554	6, 063, 951
Hame turning shops,	6	24	....	....	....	24	2	1	1, 520	5, 755	8, 369	18, 954
Harness, saddle and trunk manufactories,	594	1, 485	13	114	1	1, 613	....	....	421, 521	60, 050	816, 804	1, 580, 492
Hose manufactories,	2	17	....	2	....	19	....	....	....	1, 000	60, 400	77, 000
Leather-splitting gauge manufactory,	1	4	....	1	....	5	1	....	300	700	464	4, 500
Morocco factories,	30	410	66	27	6	509	4	7	180, 900	42, 400	1, 301, 612	2, 899, 829
Morocco case manufactories,	4	23	....	16	50	89	....	1	15, 000	6, 300	54, 150	131, 000
Parchment and vellum manufactory,	1	2	....	....	....	2	....	....	150	100	1, 400	3, 050
Patent leather manufactories,	5	56	5	6	....	67	....	3	47, 000	12, 000	113, 000	226, 500
Pocket book and port monnaie manufact's,	12	237	4	299	41	581	....	....	52, 500	38, 930	128, 040	369, 000
Razor strop manufactory,	1	1	6	1	....	8	....	....	400	50	1, 792	14, 200
Saddle and coach hardware manufactories,	8	370	2	15	12	399	....	4	31, 500	43, 300	92, 240	226, 120
Shoe peg manufactories,	15	85	4	10	....	99	7	1	18, 100	11, 770	26, 559	72, 772
Tanneries,	863	5, 381	43	99	2	5, 525	418	125	2, 781, 802	585, 211	9, 670, 386	15, 642, 383
Whip manufactories,	8	13	3	7	5	28	3	....	13, 900	7, 800	15, 735	35, 762
Total,	3, 015	15, 902	2, 215	988	237	19, 342	438	142	4, 489, 182	956, 917	14, 921. 705	27, 370, 163
CLASS XVII.—HOUSEHOLD FURNITURE, AND MACHINES AND IMPLEMENTS FOR DOMESTIC PURPOSES.												
Basket manufactories,	12	34	....	4	....	38	1	....	1, 245	593	3, 272	14, 418
Bed, mattrass and cot manufactories,	12	36	10	11	....	57	4	....	10, 200	1, 400	53, 480	90, 940
Bedstead manufactories,	28	316	....	25	....	341	11	3	78, 000	27, 800	121, 028	277, 200
Billiard table manufactories,	6	54	....	....	....	54	....	....	117, 000	6, 600	38, 200	123, 500
Broom manufactories,	54	395	....	53	....	448	1	....	43, 680	19, 990	324, 803	490, 971
Brush manufactories,	39	334	419	238	109	1, 100	1	1	118, 200	46, 125	372, 315	784, 951
Cabinet making shops,	606	4, 369	95	276	6	4, 746	87	44	862, 894	449, 908	1, 371, 919	4, 510, 992
Cedar ware manufactories,	2	10	....	....	....	10	....	....	1, 800	550	1, 720	7, 670
Chair factories,	88	977	122	278	85	1, 462	37	5	225, 110	97, 990	740, 909	931, 078
Coffee mill manufactories,	3	19	....	3	....	22	3	....	3, 850	1, 800	4, 525	13, 560
Feather brush manufactories,	3	33	....	9	9	51	....	....	1, 000	1, 000	19, 975	41, 300
House-decorating establishment,	1	6	....	3	....	9	....	....	....	3, 000	1, 000	7, 000
House-furnishing establishments,	24	97	66	6	15	184	2	1	69, 150	7, 845	161, 315	345, 055
Iron furniture manufactories,	3	70	....	8	....	78	....	2	28, 000	21, 000	77, 700	110, 200
Pail manufactories,	22	176	8	18	....	202	14	5	46, 650	40, 280	74, 660	168, 695
Paper hanging manufactories,	9	112	....	129	....	241	....	5	118, 000	83, 750	203, 275	503, 600
Rug and mat manufactories,	7	113	19	92	....	224	....	....	192, 000	5, 400	51, 642	168, 705
Sofa and lounge manufactories,	5	151	....	....	....	151	....	1	5, 000	100	23, 710	181, 500
Washing machine manufactories,	2	3	....	....	....	3	....	....	....	6, 000	2, 300	4, 400
Willow ware manufactories,	5	13	....	1	....	14	....	....	14, 300	3, 515	3, 755	12, 100
Window shade manufactories,	9	107	4	13	1	125	....	....	15, 600	25, 125	127, 560	314, 100
Woodenware manufactories,	19	68	46	5	....	119	13	....	25, 600	10, 223	16, 294	83, 413
Total,	959	7, 493	789	1, 172	225	9, 679	174	67	1, 977, 279	859, 994	3, 795, 357	9, 185, 348
CLASS XVIII.—ARTS, POLITE, FINE AND ORNAMENTAL.												
Artists' brush manufactory,	1	2	....	....	....	2	....	....	....	200	1, 000	3, 000
Block letter manufactory,	1	3	....	....	....	3	....	....	....	1, 000	....	....
Book binderies,	48	375	449	311	184	1, 319	2	8	286, 100	201, 835	423, 580	917, 050
Book binders' tool manufactory,	1	12	....	5	....	17	....	....	....	500	600	7, 000
Camera manufactory,	1	18	....	....	....	18	....	....	10, 000	700	10, 000	40, 000
Daguerreotyping establishments,	25	107	79	10	4	200	....	....	11, 100	37, 050	60, 725	229, 100
Daguerreotype case manufactories,	3	40	41	16	2	99	....	2	10, 700	9, 400	13, 000	133, 200
Engraving establishments,	30	86	12	10	1	109	....	1	50, 500	29, 650	34, 330	181, 700
Envelope manufactories,	4	28	35	35	151	249	....	1	50, 000	34, 000	141, 000	240, 000
Gold pen manufactories,	11	159	13	33	....	205	....	5	6, 000	96, 200	215, 650	631, 000
Ink manufactories,	2	3	....	1	....	4	....	....	450	270	1, 200	3, 500
Jewelry case manufactories,	1	6	....	1	....	7	....	....	....	250	1, 000	5, 000
Lithographic establishments,	13	177	....	....	....	177	....	....	70, 000	65, 050	78, 750	260, 200
Map-coloring establishments,	1	13	....	5	5	23	....	....	....	500	....	12, 000
Map-publishing establishments,	3	54	7	5	10	76	....	1	12, 000	32, 800	38, 000	252, 000
Melodeon manufactories,	3	34	....	82	....	116	....	1	35, 000	29, 510	49, 450	223, 000
Musical instrument manufactories,	6	18	....	1	....	19	....	1	3, 380	18, 800	16, 555	22, 925
Organ building establishment,	5	107	....	2	....	109	....	....	47, 900	5, 550	66, 315	165, 760
Organ pipe manufactory,	1	2	....	....	....	2	....	....	....	300	552	3, 000
Paper ruler manufactory,	1	1	....	1	1	3	....	....	....	300	25	900
Piano forte manufactories,	67	1, 492	....	102	....	1, 594	2	9	611, 607	38, 744	632, 982	2, 611, 662
Piano tool manufactory,	1	1	....	....	....	1	....	....	....	250	41	585
Piano hardware manufactories,	2	17	....	10	....	27	....	2	33, 000	33, 000	5, 920	45, 000
Piano stool manufactories,	3	28	....	1	....	29	2	....	70, 000	4, 950	7, 837	26, 700
Picture and mirror frame manufactories,	13	89	3	20	....	112	2	6	19, 080	28, 400	77, 800	122, 700
Printers' ink manufactories,	4	31	....	3	....	34	1	3	36, 000	21, 500	40, 096	80, 000
Printing offices,	102	505	518	520	161	1, 704	3	43	752, 900	936, 300	1, 069, 492	895, 579
Printing press manufactories,	4	54	....	....	....	54	....	4	120, 000	216, 000	216, 750	670, 000
Printers' roller manufactory,	1	1	....	....	....	1	....	....	....	300	1, 400	4, 000
Statuary,	2	9	....	....	....	9	....	....	2, 000	500	2, 200	3, 000
Stereotyping establishments,	12	139	....	2	....	141	....	....	31, 000	67, 400	31, 980	121, 000
Type founderies,	9	231	90	73	122	516	....	2	158, 000	93, 500	132, 058	418, 000
Type founders' tool manufactory,	1	1	....	1	....	2	....	....	....	500	1, 500	2, 600
Total,	382	3, 843	1, 247	1, 250	641	6, 981	12	89	2, 426, 717	2, 005, 209	3, 371, 788	8, 331, 161

CLASS XIX.—FIRE ARMS AND IMPLEMENTS OF WAR, MANUFACTURE OF POWDER AND SHOT.

MANUFACTURES.	Number of establishments.	Persons Employed.					Power Used.		Capital Invested.		Cash Value.	
		Men.	Women.	Boys under 18 years.	Girls under 18 years.	Total.	Establishments using water.	Establishments using steam.	In real estate.	In tools and machinery.	Of raw materials used.	Of manufactured articles.
Gun smiths' shops,	65	382	2	31		415	4	2	$87, 345	$98, 840	$132, 261	$379, 888
Military accoutrement manufactories,	2	7	4			11			300	7, 200		12, 000
Percussion cap manufactory,	1	8	2	12	8	30					35, 910	
Powder mills,	6	79	1			80	5	1	41, 500	29, 000	211, 583	275, 180
Shot factory,	1	20		3		23		1	43, 000	5, 000	200, 000	300, 000
Shot belt manufactory, etc.,	1	12		14	8	34		1		600	10, 000	25, 000
Total,	76	508	9	60	16	593	9	5	172, 145	140. 640	589, 754	992, 068

CLASS XX.—SURGICAL, MEDICAL AND DENTAL INSTRUMENTS AND APPARATUS.

MANUFACTURES.	Number of establishments.	Men.	Women.	Boys under 18 years.	Girls under 18 years.	Total.	Establishments using water.	Establishments using steam.	In real estate.	In tools and machinery.	Of raw materials used.	Of manufactured articles.
Bathing tub manufactories,	2	9		3		12		1	20, 000	500	20, 100	27, 000
Dental instrument manufactory,	1	10		2		12		1		300		
Dentists' gold manufactory,	1	2				2				250	10, 000	100, 000
Dentistry,	24	31		1		32			11, 750	8, 150	18, 743	53, 863
Surgical instrument manufactories,	4	51		3		54			10, 000	2, 500	2, 700	16, 000
Teeth manufactories,	2	22		18		40			50, 000	1, 800	10, 000	24, 000
Truss and bandage manufactories,	2	18	40	1		59		1	19, 500	5. 500	12, 006	35, 000
Total,	36	143	40	28		211		3	111, 250	19, 000	73, 549	255, 863

CLASS XXI.—WEARING APPAREL, ARTICLES FOR THE TOILET, ECT.

MANUFACTURES.	Number of establishments.	Men.	Women.	Boys under 18 years.	Girls under 18 years.	Total.	Establishments using water.	Establishments using steam.	In real estate.	In tools and machinery.	Of raw materials used.	Of manufactured articles.
Belt clasp maufactory,	1	1	2			3		1		300	990	6, 000
Button and comb manufactories,	3	20	16	20	5	61	2	1	3, 200	4, 250	4, 650	22, 400
Clerical robe manufactory,	1	3				3					550	850
Comb manufactories,	3	20		5	3	28		2	12, 000	33, 200	31, 200	72, 000
Corset manufactory,	1	2	12	2		16				200	1, 000	4, 000
Dress making establishments,	13	96	799	319	50	1, 264			20, 000	9, 200	252, 995	427, 463
Gentlemen's furnishing goods manufactories,	13	35	1, 741	8	122	1, 906			14, 000	450	380, 800	616, 300
Glove and mitten manufactories,	69	626	2, 670	53	1	3, 350	11	3	57, 250	15, 380	749, 370	1, 202, 080
Hair dressing and wig manufactories,	5	27	30		5	62			35, 000	4, 350	25, 700	68, 600
Hat and cap manufactories,	123	1, 472	637	302	775	3, 186	3	13	384, 642	157, 286	2, 380, 204	4, 029, 780
Hat block manufactories,	3	12				12		1		1, 900	2, 000	6, 400
Hosiery manufactories,	12	179	1, 016	77	197	1, 469	11		161, 500	163, 600	336, 297	780, 050
Military and firemen's cap manufactory,	1	11		3		14			17, 000		300	9, 000
Milliner shops,	153	44	1, 097	13	65	1, 219			122, 545	32, 816	370, 380	691, 622
Sewing machine manufactories,	4	162				162		1	10, 000	39, 200	35, 351	245, 600
Shirt, bosom and collar manufactories,	21	73	3, 084			3, 157			50, 900	60, 450	354, 658	800, 090
Stock manufactories,	2		57		2	59					15, 000	44, 000
Tailor shops,	561	8, 595	12, 484	176	106	21, 361			1, 549, 036	247, 367	6, 981, 322	11, 842, 929
Umbrella and parasol manufactories,	21	103	739	9	12	863			67, 800	21, 700	733, 348	1, 176, 065
Total,	1, 010	11, 481	24. 384	987	1, 343	38, 195	27	22	2, 504. 873	791, 649	12, 656, 115	22, 045, 229

CLASS XXII.—MISCELLANEOUS MANUFACTURES

MANUFACTURES.	Number of establishments.	Men.	Women.	Boys under 18 years.	Girls under 18 years.	Total.	Establishments using water.	Establishments using steam.	In real estate.	In tools and machinery.	Of raw materials used.	Of manufactured articles.
Altar ornament manufactory,	1	6		1	5	12		1		600	3, 640	7, 000
Artificial flower manufactories,	4	3	30	8	55	96			14, 000	2, 200	7, 570	17, 000
Band box manufactories,	4	7		2	8	17			3, 000	1, 050	13, 962	23, 800
Bird cage manufactories,	4	41				41		1		1, 850	5, 750	40, 000
Butchers' shops,	87	342		9		351		2	122, 394	20, 557	2, 355, 371	3, 113, 163
Cane manufactory,	1	2				2				60	1, 000	2, 000
Carpet bag manufactory,	1	10	100	7		117		1	5, 000	4, 000	70, 000	100, 000
Charcoal manufactories,	37	192				192			3, 300	2, 970	25, 400	180, 742
Cistern and tank manufactories,	2	3				3			2, 500	250	1, 015	3, 547
Cork cutting establishments,	2	5				5				650	3, 600	12, 000
Fancy turning establishments,	9	107		5	9	121		2	42, 175	20, 000	53, 710	170, 000
Fishi g rod manufactories,	6	16		1		17		1	3, 600	5, 800	3, 150	26, 700
Ice establishments,	9	209		3		212			67, 200	43, 170	15, 951	140, 100
Paper box manufactories,	27	105	117	11	189	422		1	31, 420	14, 535	270, 325	467, 500
Refrigerator manufactories,	3	14		2		16	1	1	8, 000	5, 800	13, 500	46, 850
Regalia manufactory,	1	3	14		1	18					10, 000	15, 000
Sausage machine manufactory,	1	2				2			1, 000	1, 500	3, 000	6, 000
Soda fountain manufactories,	3	37		3		40		1	20, 100	8, 300	70, 348	86, 285
Tobacco and segar manufactories,	142	1, 134	83	584	119	1, 920	10	19	456, 378	128, 603	1, 244, 166	2, 261, 884
Undertakers' establishments,	17	64	1	4		69		1	71, 335	2, 595	26, 604	115, 248
Unenumerated manufactories,	133	1, 765	374	292	44	2, 475	4	13	891, 270	807, 241	927, 707	1, 595, 815
Whalebone manufactories,	3	25		17		42		1	40, 000	40, 800	243, 500	470, 000
Total,	497	4, 092	719	949	430	6, 190	15	45	1, 782 672	1, 112, 531	5, 369, 269	8, 900, 634
General total,	24, 833	155159	37. 771	15, 736	6, 233	214899	7, 551	2, 444	71, 130, 407	35, 219, 570	178,394,329	317,428,331

DISTRIBUTION OF MANUFACTURING ESTABLISHMENTS AMONG THE SEVERAL COUNTIES.

COUNTIES.	CLASS I.																		CLASS II.							
	Agricultural implements generally.	Cheese press manufactories.	Churn factories.	Cider mills.	Clover mills.	Fanning mill manufactories.	Fork factories.	Grain cradle and scythe snath factories.	Grain measure manufactories.	Hoe manufactories.	Plow and cultivator factories.	Rake factories.	Reaping and mowing machine factories.	Scythe factories, etc.	Scythe rifle manufactories.	Shovel manufactory.	Tool shops.	Thrashing machine manufactories.	Anvil manufactory.	Axe and edge tool manufactories.	Bell founderies	Blacksmith shops.	Bolt manufactories.	Brad and sparable manufactories.	Brass and copper founderies.	Brass finishing establishments.
Albany,	4	....	....	....	1	....	....	....	....	....	....	....	....	....	....	....	....	....	....	1	1	27	....	....	3	....
Allegany,	1	....	....	....	....	....	....	....	....	....	....	1	....	....	....	....	1	....	....	1	....	37	....	....	....	....
Broome,	1	....	....	....	....	....	....	....	....	....	....	3	....	....	....	....	....	....	....	....	....	23	....	....	....	....
Cattaraugus,	1	....	....	....	....	....	....	....	....	....	2	....	....	....	....	....	....	....	....	1	....	32	....	....	....	....
Cayuga,	3	....	....	2	....	....	1	1	....	....	2	....	1	1	1	....	1	....	....	....	....	59	....	....	....	....
Chautauque,	1	....	....	1	....	1	....	3	1	....	....	1	....	....	....	....	1	....	....	3	....	43	....	....	....	....
Chemung,	....	....	....	....	....	....	....	1	....	....	....	....	....	....	....	....	....	....	....	1	....	19	....	....	....	....
Chenango,	....	....	....	....	....	1	1	....	....	1	....	....	....	....	....	....	....	....	....	1	....	41	....	....	....	....
Clinton,	....	....	....	....	....	....	....	....	....	....	2	....	....	....	....	....	....	....	....	1	....	22	....	....	....	....
Columbia,	3	....	....	....	....	....	....	....	....	....	1	1	....	....	1	....	....	....	....	....	....	47	....	....	....	....
Cortland,	2	....	....	1	....	....	....	....	....	....	2	1	....	....	....	....	....	....	....	1	....	26	....	....	....	....
Delaware,	....	....	....	....	....	....	....	1	....	....	....	1	....	....	....	....	....	....	....	....	....	31	....	....	....	....
Dutchess,	2	....	....	1	....	1	....	1	....	....	1	....	....	1	....	....	....	....	....	2	....	44	....	....	2	....
Erie,	3	....	....	....	....	3	....	....	....	....	....	1	....	1	....	....	1	....	....	1	2	29	1	....	2	....
Essex,	....	....	....	....	....	....	....	....	....	....	....	....	....	....	....	....	....	....	....	1	....	28	....	....	....	....
Franklin,	....	....	....	....	....	1	....	....	....	....	1	....	....	1	....	....	....	....	....	....	....	15	....	....	....	....
Fulton,	....	....	....	....	....	....	....	....	1	....	....	....	....	....	....	....	....	....	....	....	....	12	....	....	....	....
Genesee,	2	....	....	....	....	....	....	....	....	....	1	3	....	....	....	....	....	....	....	....	....	33	....	....	....	....
Greene,	....	....	....	2	....	....	....	....	....	....	1	....	....	....	....	....	....	....	....	....	....	19	....	....	....	....
Hamilton,	....	....	....	....	....	....	....	....	....	....	....	....	....	....	....	....	....	....	....	....	....	....	....	....	....	....
Herkimer,	1	1	....	....	....	1	....	....	....	....	....	....	....	....	....	....	....	....	....	6	....	36	....	....	....	....
Jefferson,	1	1	1	1	....	2	....	3	....	....	....	....	....	....	....	....	1	....	....	2	....	52	....	....	1	....
Kings,	1	....	....	....	....	....	....	....	....	....	....	....	....	....	....	....	....	....	....	1	....	11	1	....	4	....
Lewis,	1	....	....	1	....	1	....	1	....	....	1	1	....	....	....	....	....	....	....	....	....	9	....	....	....	....
Livingston,	1	....	....	1	....	1	....	4	....	....	5	1	....	....	....	....	1	....	....	....	....	35	....	....	1	....
Madison,	2	....	....	1	....	....	1	....	....	1	2	4	....	....	....	....	....	....	....	2	....	27	....	....	....	....
Monroe,	4	....	....	....	....	....	....	4	....	....	10	1	3	....	....	....	1	....	....	2	....	69	....	....	1	1
Montgomery,	....	....	....	....	....	1	....	....	....	1	1	....	2	....	....	....	....	....	....	....	....	44	....	....	....	....
New-York,	2	....	....	....	....	....	....	....	....	....	....	....	....	....	....	....	....	....	....	6	....	53	6	1	31	....
Niagara,	....	....	....	....	....	....	....	....	....	....	....	1	....	....	....	....	....	....	....	1	....	32	....	....	....	....
Oneida,	3	....	2	4	....	1	....	....	....	2	....	4	....	....	1	....	....	....	....	....	....	65	....	....	1	....
Onondaga,	1	....	....	1	....	4	1	3	....	....	1	....	....	....	....	....	1	....	....	4	....	53	....	....	....	....
Ontario,	2	....	....	2	....	....	....	....	....	....	2	1	....	....	....	....	....	....	....	2	....	40	....	....	....	....
Orange,	....	....	....	1	....	1	....	3	....	....	....	....	....	....	....	....	....	....	....	....	....	37	....	....	....	....
Orleans,	2	....	....	....	....	....	....	....	....	....	....	....	....	....	....	....	....	....	....	....	....	38	....	....	....	....
Oswego,	....	....	....	1	....	....	....	....	....	....	....	1	....	....	....	....	....	....	....	1	....	26	....	....	....	....
Otsego,	....	....	....	1	1	2	2	3	....	1	....	6	....	....	....	....	....	....	....	....	....	66	....	....	....	....
Putnam,	....	....	....	....	....	....	....	....	....	....	....	....	....	....	....	....	....	....	....	....	....	6	....	....	....	....
Queens,	1	....	....	....	....	....	....	....	....	....	....	....	....	....	....	....	....	....	....	....	....	14	....	....	....	....
Rensselaer,	2	....	....	1	....	2	....	2	....	1	1	1	3	3	1	....	....	....	1	1	1	43	....	....	2	....
Richmond,	....	....	....	....	....	....	....	....	....	....	....	....	....	....	....	....	....	....	....	....	....	6	....	....	....	....
Rockland,	1	....	....	....	....	1	....	....	....	....	....	....	....	....	....	....	....	....	....	....	....	7	....	....	....	....
St. Lawrence,	....	....	....	....	....	3	1	....	....	1	....	2	....	....	....	....	....	....	....	....	....	47	....	....	....	....
Saratoga,	....	....	....	1	....	....	....	1	2	2	....	....	....	1	....	....	....	....	....	1	....	47	1	....	....	....
Schenectady,	....	....	....	....	....	....	....	....	....	....	....	....	....	....	....	....	....	....	....	....	....	8	....	....	....	....
Schoharie,	....	....	....	....	6	1	....	1	....	....	2	....	....	....	....	....	....	....	....	....	....	34	....	....	....	....
Schuyler,	....	....	....	....	....	....	....	1	....	....	....	....	....	....	....	....	....	....	....	....	....	23	....	....	....	....
Seneca,	....	....	....	....	....	....	1	....	....	....	....	....	....	....	....	....	....	....	....	1	....	23	....	....	....	....
Steuben,	1	....	....	....	....	....	....	....	....	....	2	....	....	....	....	....	....	....	....	....	....	49	....	....	....	....
Suffolk,	....	....	....	....	1	....	....	....	....	....	....	....	....	....	....	....	....	....	....	1	....	22	....	....	....	....
Sullivan,	....	....	....	....	....	....	....	....	....	....	....	....	....	....	....	....	....	....	....	....	....	29	1	....	....	....
Tioga,	....	....	....	....	....	....	....	1	....	....	....	2	....	....	....	....	....	....	....	....	....	20	....	....	....	....
Tompkins,	1	....	....	....	....	....	....	....	....	....	....	....	....	....	....	....	....	1	....	....	....	45	....	....	....	....
Ulster,	2	....	....	....	1	....	....	....	....	....	....	....	....	....	1	....	....	....	....	1	....	37	....	....	....	....
Warren,	....	....	....	....	....	....	....	....	....	....	....	....	....	....	....	....	....	....	....	....	....	14	....	....	....	....
Washington,	2	....	....	2	....	1	....	....	....	....	....	1	....	....	....	....	....	....	....	....	....	40	....	....	....	....
Wayne,	3	....	....	....	....	1	....	....	....	....	1	1	....	....	....	....	....	....	....	....	....	49	....	....	....	....
Westchester,	1	....	....	....	....	....	....	....	....	....	....	....	....	....	....	1	....	....	....	....	....	27	....	....	....	....
Wyoming,	1	....	....	1	....	1	....	....	....	....	....	1	....	....	....	....	....	....	....	....	....	37	....	....	....	....
Yates,	....	....	....	....	....	1	....	....	....	....	....	....	....	....	....	....	....	1	....	....	....	14	....	....	....	....
Total,	59	2	3	26	10	32	8	34	4	10	41	40	9	8	5	1	8	2	1	46	4	1,921	10	1	46	1

DISTRIBUTION OF MANUFACTURING ESTABLISHMENTS.—(CONTINUED.)

COUNTIES.	CLASS II.																									
	Britannia ware and silver plating manufactories.	Bronze casting establishments.	Butt and hinge factories.	Castor frame manufactories.	Composition metal manufactories.	Copper smithing.	Cutlery manufactories.	Door latch manufactory.	File manufactories.	Fish hook manufactory.	Forges.	Furnaces	Gas fixture manufactories.	German silver ware manufactories.	Gilding establishments.	Gold leaf and foil manufactories.	Gold and silver plating establishments.	Gold and silver refining establishments.	Hammer manufactories.	Handiron manufactories.	Hardware manufactories.	Hollow-ware manufactories.	Iron manufactories.	Iron pipe manufactories.	Iron railing manufactories.	Japanned tin manufactories.
Albany,	3		1				1					25										2			2	
Allegany,												4														
Broome,												2														
Cattaraugus,												4														
Cayuga,											1	10														
Chautauque,												7														
Chemung,							1					7														
Chenango,												15														
Clinton,												6											19			
Columbia,							1					4											2			
Cortland,												1														
Delaware,							1		1			3														
Dutchess,												9											8			
Erie,					1						3	9				1									1	1
Essex,											4	2											25			
Franklin,												1										1				
Fulton,																										
Genesee,	1											4														
Greene,								1				4														
Hamilton,																										
Herkimer,												4							1							
Jefferson,											2	10											2			
Kings,	1	1				1				1		15						1							11	
Lewis,												1											2			
Livingston,												13														
Madison,												9														
Monroe,											1	12													2	
Montgomery,												3														
New-York,	2	2		1		14	6				3	37	13	1	7	7	13	6		1	1			7	13	4
Niagara,												4														
Oneida,	1										3	21	1										2			
Onondaga,												11													1	
Ontario,	1											8														
Orange,												4											3			
Orleans,												5														
Oswego,												9											1			
Otsego,											1	9							2							
Putnam,												1														
Queens,												1		1												
Rensselaer,			4		1							7									1		3			
Richmond,																					1					
Rockland,									1			3														
St. Lawrence,											3	8											4			
Saratoga,												3													1	
Schenectady,												3										1				
Schoharie,												4														
Schuyler,												2														
Seneca,												5														
Steuben,												9														
Suffolk,												1														
Sullivan,												1														
Tioga,												2														
Tompkins,	1											9														
Ulster,											2	5											2			
Warren,																										
Washington,											1	5											2			
Wayne,												10											3			
Westchester,					2				3			5														
Wyoming,												6														
Yates,												6														
Total,	10	3	5	1	4	15	10	1	5	1	24	388	14	2	7	8	13	7	3	1	3	4	78	7	31	5

DISTRIBUTION OF MANUFACTURING ESTABLISHMENTS—(CONTINUED.)

COUNTIES.	CLASS II.																							CLASS III.		
	Lead pipe manufactories.	Lightning rod manufactories	Lock manufactories.	Machine shops	Machinists' tool manufactories.	Malleable iron works.	Metallic burial case manufactory.	Metallic life boat manufactory.	Pin manufactories.	Plumbing establishments.	Rolling mill and nail factories.	Safe manufactories.	Screw factory.	Silverware manufactories.	Spike manufactories.	Steel spring manufactories.	Thimble manufactories.	Tin and sheet iron manufactories.	Tin foil manufactories.	Trip hammers.	Wire works.	Wire railing manufactory.	Wire seive manufactories.	Awning manufactories.	Card board manufactories.	Carding and cloth dressing estab's.
Albany,			1	2		1			1	2		1		6				5								3
Allegany,				2										1				8								2
Broome,				5														8								4
Cattaraugus,				1														6								3
Cayuga,				3										3				8								3
Chautauque,				5										1				11								3
Chemung,																		10								
Chenango,				1														7								8
Clinton,				2														5								3
Columbia,				2										2				12								1
Cortland,				1										1				6								
Delaware,				2														5								5
Dutchess,			1	3					1					5				18								1
Erie,			2	3						1				2				13			1					2
Essex,				1							2							3								1
Franklln,				1														5								1
Fulton,																		1								
Genesee,		1		1														5								2
Greene,				2		1												4								1
Hamilton,																										
Herkimer,			2	5								1						8								2
Jefferson,				6										1				19								7
Kings,			1	11				1		3		2		2				5					2			
Lewis,																		4								1
Livingston,				1														6								1
Madison,				4														10								1
Monroe,	1		3	11	4									2				12								3
Montgomery,																		7								3
New-York,	2	1	9	36	1	1				22		5		83	2		3	54	1		9	1		3	2	
Niagara,				4														5								
Oneida,				7		1						1	1	4				21								4
Onondaga,				9										3				17					1			2
Ontario,				3														13								1
Orange,				3										4				9								1
Orleans,				2														6								2
Oswego,				4														10								4
Otsego,				5										2				10			1					4
Putnam,																		2			1					
Queens,							1			1				2				9								
Rensselaer,				7	1	1				1		1		2		1		13					1			1
Richmond,																		2								
Rockland,				4										1				1								
St. Lawrence,				4										2				14		2						5
Saratoga,				5														6								
Schenectady,				3														2								
Schoharie,				2														5								5
Schuyler,				1																						1
Seneca,				1										1		2		5								1
Steuben,														3				7								3
Suffolk,														1			2	5								3
Sullivan,																		3								2
Tioga,				1										3				3								1
Tompkins,				1										3				2								3
Ulster,				1														5			1					2
Warren,				1														2								2
Washington,				4														4								2
Wayne,				2										2				11					2			2
Westchester,			1	2							1			1				10			3					1
Wyoming,				2														8								
Yates,																		5								1
Total,	3	2	20	189	6	5	1	1	2	30	3	10	1	143	2	3	5	480	1	2	16	1	6	3	2	114

DISTRIBUTION OF MANUFACTURING ESTABLISHMENTS.—(CONTINUED.)

COUNTIES.	CLASS III.																									
	Carpet manufactories.	Carpet yarn manufactories.	Cotton factories.	Cotton batting manufactories.	Cotton warp manufactories.	Felting and wadding manufactory.	Flax dressing mills.	Fringe and tassel manufactories.	Fur-dressing establishments.	Hair cloth manufactories.	Linen factories.	Oakum manufactories.	Paper mills.	Papier mache manufactory.	Playing cards manufactories.	Power loom manufactories.	Rag carpet and blanket manufactories.	Ribbon factories.	Rope manufactories.	Sea grass manufactories.	Sewing silk manufactories.	Shawl manufactories.	Shoddy mills.	Straw paper manufactories.	Tape and webb manufactories.	Twine manufactories.
Albany,	1		4					1	1				3			1			3			1	1	1	2	
Allegany,													1											1		
Broome,													1													
Cattaraugus,																										
Cayuga,	2		2										1													
Chautauque,													3													
Chemung,																										
Chenango,													1						2							
Clinton,							1																			
Columbia,	1		12										15			1								3		
Cortland,			1				3						1												1	
Delaware,													1											1		
Dutchess,	1		6										1			1	1		1					5		1
Erie,	1											1							1	2						
Essex,													1													
Franklin,																										
Fulton,							2						3											8		
Genesee,																										
Greene,			1										4											3		
Hamilton,																										
Herkimer,			3	1			2						5													
Jefferson,			2	1			1						2						1							
Kings,				2		1	3	2	3				1					1	10							1
Lewis,				1			1						1													
Livingston,													3													
Madison,			1										2								1					
Monroe,			2										1													
Montgomery,	2		1				2																			
New-York,	3		3					13	11	1		1		1	3		1	1	1		2				2	2
Niagara,			1										1													
Oneida,	1		12	2			1						3						1							
Onondaga,			1										6											1		
Ontario,													2													
Orange,			4										3									1	2			1
Orleans,													1													
Oswego,			1				1						2						2							
Otsego,			7										2						1							
Putnam,													1													
Queens,	1												6				1							4		6
Rensselaer,			8	2	2		23				1		8						4			1	1	1	1	2
Richmond,																										
Rockland,		1	1	1																						1
St. Lawrence,													2													
Saratoga,			4	1							1		7											1		1
Schenectady,			1				1						1									1				1
Schoharie,			1				1						3											3		
Schuyler,																										
Seneca,			1				1															1				
Steuben,																										
Suffolk,			1		2																			3		
Sullivan,																										
Tioga,			1																							
Tompkins,													2								2					
Ulster,			2										3										1			1
Warren,																										
Washington,			1										3											1		
Wayne,																			1							
Westchester,	5	1	1							1			2								1				1	3
Wyoming,																			1					1		
Yates,							2																			
Total,	18	2	86	11	4	1	45	16	15	2	2	2	109	1	3	3	3	2	29	2	6	5	5	37	7	20

DISTRIBUTION OF MANUFACTURING ESTABLISHMENTS.—(Continued.)

COUNTIES.	CLASS III	CLASS IV.																								
	Woolen cloth and yarn factories.	Asheries.	Bakeries,	Barilla manufactory.	Barytes manufactories.	Buiscuit machine manufactory.	Blacking manufactories.	Black lead manufactories.	Bleacheries.	Breweries	Bronze color manufactory.	Camphene distilleries.	Chandleries and soap factories.	Chemical laboratories.	Coffee, spice and mustard manufactories.	Confectionary manufactories.	Cotton printing establishments.	Distilleries.	Drug and medicine manufactories.	Dyeing establishments.	Dye wood manufactories.	Electrotyping establishments.	Emery and pumice stone manufactories.	Fish and whale oil manufactories.	Gas manufactories.	Glue manufactories.
Albany,	1		15							9			5		2	3		2							2	1
Allegany,	2	3	1																							
Broome,		1								1			1			1										
Cattaraugus,	1	2	2							1									1							
Cayuga,	6	3											3					3								
Chautauque,	3	3	2							4			1					1	1							
Chemung,	2									2			2					1							1	
Chenango,	4	2	1													2	1	1								
Clinton,	1	4	1																							
Columbia,	6		1							1			2			1		1							1	1
Cortland,	2	2	1										1													
Delaware,	4		1																1							
Dutchess,	6		6							1			3			3	1				1				1	
Erie,	9	4	16							18			9			4	1	2	1						1	
Essex,	3							2											1							
Franklin,	2	2	2										1													
Fulton,	2																									1
Genesee,	3	1	2							1								1								
Greene,	5									1			1													1
Hamilton,																										
Herkimer,	3	1	3							1			1			1		1							1	
Jefferson,	3	1	4							1			1					3							1	
Kings,			9							12	1	3	2	6	4	2		7	4		1			2	3	1
Lewis,	3	2	1																							
Livingston,	1	2	2							4			2			1		2								
Madison,	6	2	1							1			6					9	1							
Monroe,	3	1	8			1				16			3		1			2	1						1	1
Montgomery,	3	1	2													1		3								
New-York,			54				1		1	19			31	3	14	14	2	10	9	2		2		7	2	
Niagara,	2	2								1								1	1						1	
Oneida,	13	1	9							8			6		1	2		3	1						2	
Onondaga,	6	3	1							5			2			1		5	1	1					1	
Ontario,	4	2								1			1					4								
Orange,	8		1							2			5					5							1	
Orleans,			2													1										
Oswego,	6		3															1							1	
Otsego,	6	1								1							1	2	1							1
Putnam,																1										
Queens,	3		5	1									1										1		2	
Rensselaer,	4		9						1	8			4			5									1	1
Richmond,			2							1			1							2						
Rockland,	2		1							1							1	2								
St. Lawrence,	7	8	1							1						1		1								
Saratoga,	4		4										2					2								
Schenectady,	2												1													
Schoharie,																										
Schuyler,	2																									
Seneca,	2	2	1							1			3					5								
Steuben,		1	2										1					2								
Suffolk,	2		1										1											2		
Sullivan,	1									1								1								
Tioga,	1	1	3															1								
Tompkins,	3	1	4										2			1		1							1	
Ulster,	4		3										1			1					1				1	
Warren,	1												1			1										
Washington,	8									1																
Wayne,	1	2	1							1			1					2								
Westchester,	3		6		2				1	2			1			1			2	1	2		1		1	1
Wyoming,	3	7					1						2					1								
Yates,	2		2																							
Total,	184	68	196	1	2	1	2	2	3	128	1	3	111	9	22	48	7	88	26	6	5	2	2	11	26	9

DISTRIBUTION OF MANUFACTURING ESTABLISHMENTS.—(Continued.)

COUNTIES.	CLASS IV.																									
	Gutta percha manufactory.	India rubber manufactory.	Ivory black and bone manure manufactories	Japanned cloth manufactories.	Lamp black manufactories.	Lard oil manufactories.	Liquorice refinery.	Malt manufactories	Match manufactories.	Medicinal herb and extract manufactories.	Mineral water manufactories.	Oil cloth manufactories.	Oil mills.	Paint and color manufactories.	Painting, and glazing establishments.	Paint mill manufactory.	Paper staining establishment.	Pearl ash manufactories.	Perfume manufactories.	Pickle and preserve manufactories.	Prussian blue manufactory.	Putty manufactory.	Pyrotechnic establishments.	Rosin oil factories.	Saleratus manufactories	Salt manufactories.
Albany,	....	....	1	....	....	....	....	8	....	....	1	1	1	....	....	....	....	....	1	....	....	....	....	....	....	....
Allegany,	....	....	....	....	....	....	....	....	1	....	....	....	....	....	....	....	....	....	....	....	....	....	....	....	1	....
Broome,	....	....	....	....	....	....	....	....	....	....	....	....	....	....	....	....	....	....	....	....	....	....	....	....	....	....
Cattaraugus,	....	....	....	....	....	....	....	....	....	1	....	....	....	....	....	....	....	....	....	....	....	....	....	....	1	....
Cayuga,	....	....	....	....	....	....	....	....	....	....	....	....	....	....	1	....	....	....	....	....	....	....	....	....	....	1
Chautauque,	....	....	....	....	....	....	....	....	....	....	....	....	1	....	....	....	....	....	....	....	....	....	....	....	....	....
Chemung,	....	....	....	....	....	....	....	....	....	....	....	....	....	....	....	....	....	....	....	....	....	....	....	....	1	....
Chenango,	....	....	....	....	....	....	....	....	....	....	....	....	....	....	....	....	....	....	....	....	....	....	....	....	1	....
Clinton,	....	....	....	....	....	....	....	....	2	....	....	....	....	....	....	....	....	....	....	....	....	....	....	....	....	....
Columbia,	....	....	....	....	....	....	....	....	....	3	....	....	....	....	2	....	....	....	....	....	....	....	....	....	....	....
Cortland,	....	....	....	....	....	....	....	....	....	....	....	....	2	....	....	....	....	....	....	....	....	....	....	....	....	....
Delaware,	....	....	....	....	....	....	....	....	....	....	....	....	....	....	....	....	....	....	....	....	....	....	....	....	....	....
Dutchess,	....	....	....	....	....	....	....	....	....	....	2	....	....	1	1	....	....	....	....	....	....	....	....	....	....	....
Erie,	....	....	....	....	....	....	....	2	....	....	....	....	....	....	2	....	....	....	....	....	....	....	....	....	....	....
Essex,	....	....	....	....	....	....	....	....	....	....	....	....	....	....	1	....	....	....	....	....	....	....	....	....	....	....
Franklin,	....	....	....	....	....	....	....	....	....	....	....	....	1	....	....	....	....	1	....	....	....	....	....	....	1	....
Fulton,	....	....	....	....	....	....	....	....	....	....	....	....	....	....	....	....	....	....	....	....	....	....	....	....	....	....
Genesee,	....	....	....	....	....	....	....	....	....	....	....	....	1	....	6	....	....	....	....	....	....	....	....	....	....	....
Greene,	....	....	....	....	....	....	....	....	....	....	....	....	....	....	1	....	....	....	....	....	....	....	....	....	....	....
Hamilton,	....	....	....	....	....	....	....	....	....	....	....	....	....	....	....	....	....	....	....	....	....	....	....	....	....	....
Herkimer,	....	....	....	....	....	....	....	3	2	....	....	....	1	....	3	....	....	....	....	....	....	....	....	....	....	....
Jefferson,	....	....	....	....	....	....	....	3	1	....	....	....	1	....	....	....	....	....	....	....	....	....	....	....	1	....
Kings,	....	....	4	1	1	1	1	1	....	....	....	5	2	2	1	....	....	1	....	....	....	....	....	5	2	....
Lewis,	....	....	....	....	....	....	....	....	....	....	....	....	2	....	....	....	....	....	....	....	....	....	....	....	....	....
Livingston,	....	....	....	....	....	....	....	....	....	....	....	....	....	....	1	....	....	....	....	....	....	....	....	....	....	....
Madison,	....	....	....	....	....	....	....	....	....	....	....	....	1	....	....	....	....	....	....	....	....	....	....	....	1	....
Monroe,	....	....	....	....	....	....	....	2	....	....	....	....	1	1	8	....	....	....	1	....	....	....	1	....	1	....
Montgomery,	....	....	....	....	....	....	....	2	....	....	....	....	1	....	1	....	....	....	....	....	....	....	....	....	....	....
New-York,	1	2	....	....	....	6	....	2	3	1	16	3	1	3	11	....	....	....	1	9	1	1	....	....	2	1
Niagara,	....	....	....	....	....	....	....	....	....	....	....	....	....	....	....	....	....	....	....	....	....	....	....	....	....	....
Oneida,	....	....	1	....	....	....	....	....	....	....	1	1	....	1	4	1	....	....	....	....	....	....	....	....	1	....
Onondaga,	....	....	....	....	....	....	....	....	....	....	....	....	1	....	....	....	....	....	....	....	....	....	....	....	1	190
Ontario,	....	....	....	....	....	....	....	2	....	....	....	....	....	....	1	....	....	....	....	....	....	....	....	....	....	....
Orange,	....	....	....	....	....	....	....	....	2	....	1	1	....	....	1	....	....	....	....	....	....	....	....	....	....	....
Orleans,	....	....	....	....	....	....	....	....	....	....	....	....	2	....	1	....	....	....	....	....	....	....	....	....	....	....
Oswego,	....	....	....	....	....	....	....	....	....	....	....	....	2	....	2	....	....	....	....	....	....	....	....	....	....	....
Otsego,	....	....	....	....	....	....	....	....	1	....	....	....	....	....	2	....	....	....	....	....	....	....	....	....	....	....
Putnam,	....	....	....	....	....	....	....	....	....	....	1	....	....	....	....	....	....	....	....	....	....	....	....	....	....	....
Queens,	....	....	1	....	....	....	....	....	....	....	1	....	....	....	....	....	....	....	....	....	....	....	1	....	....	....
Rensselaer,	....	....	....	....	1	1	....	3	....	....	....	3	1	3	....	....	....	....	....	....	....	....	....	....	1	....
Richmond,	....	1	....	1	....	....	....	....	....	....	....	....	....	1	....	....	1	....	....	....	....	....	....	....	....	....
Rockland,	....	....	....	....	....	....	....	....	....	....	....	....	....	....	....	....	....	....	....	....	....	....	....	....	....	....
St. Lawrence,	....	....	....	....	....	....	....	....	....	....	....	....	....	....	2	....	....	3	....	....	....	....	....	....	....	....
Saratoga,	....	....	....	....	1	....	....	....	1	....	....	1	....	1	1	....	....	....	....	....	....	....	....	....	....	1
Schenectady,	....	....	....	....	....	....	....	....	....	....	....	....	....	....	....	....	....	....	....	....	....	....	....	....	....	....
Schoharie,	....	....	....	....	....	....	....	....	....	....	....	....	....	....	....	....	....	....	....	....	....	....	....	....	....	....
Schuyler,	....	....	....	....	....	....	....	....	....	....	....	....	....	....	....	....	....	....	....	....	....	....	....	....	....	....
Seneca,	....	....	....	....	....	....	....	....	....	....	....	....	1	....	....	....	....	....	....	....	....	....	....	....	....	....
Steuben,	....	....	....	....	1	....	....	1	....	....	....	....	1	....	....	....	....	....	....	....	....	....	....	....	....	....
Suffolk,	....	....	....	....	....	....	....	....	....	....	2	....	....	....	....	....	....	....	....	....	....	....	....	....	....	....
Sullivan,	....	....	....	....	....	....	....	....	....	....	....	....	....	....	....	....	....	....	....	....	....	....	....	....	....	....
Tioga,	....	....	....	....	....	....	....	....	....	....	....	....	....	....	....	....	....	....	....	....	....	....	....	....	....	....
Tompkins,	....	....	....	....	....	....	....	....	....	....	....	2	2	....	....	....	....	....	....	....	....	....	....	....	....	....
Ulster,	....	....	....	....	....	....	....	....	....	....	....	....	....	....	4	....	....	....	....	....	....	....	....	....	....	....
Warren,	....	....	....	....	....	....	....	....	....	....	....	....	....	....	....	....	....	....	....	....	....	....	....	....	....	....
Washington,	....	....	....	....	....	....	....	1	....	....	....	....	....	....	....	....	....	....	....	....	....	....	....	....	....	....
Wayne,	....	....	....	....	....	....	....	....	....	....	....	....	....	....	1	....	....	....	....	....	....	....	....	....	....	....
Westchester,	....	1	....	....	....	....	....	....	....	....	1	....	....	1	2	....	....	....	....	3	....	....	....	....	....	....
Wyoming,	....	....	....	....	....	....	....	....	1	....	....	....	....	....	1	....	....	....	....	....	....	....	....	....	1	....
Yates,	....	....	....	....	....	....	....	....	1	....	....	....	1	....	....	....	....	....	....	....	....	....	....	....	....	....
Total,	1	4	7	2	4	8	1	30	15	5	26	17	27	14	61	1	1	5	3	12	1	1	2	5	16	193

DISTRIBUTION OF MANUFACTURING ESTABLISHMENTS—(Continued.)

COUNTIES.	CLASS III.				CLASS IV.							CLASS V.				CLASS VI.			CLASS VII.							
	Saltpetre refinery.	Satinet printing establishments.	Silk printing establishment.	Starch factories.	Sugar and syrup refineries.	Varnish manufactory.	Vinegar manufactories.	Wax bleaching establishments.	White lead manufactories.	Whiting manufactories.	Wintergreen distilleries.	Grate manufactories.	Lamp and lantern manufactories.	Locomotive lamp manufactory.	Stove manufactories.	Locomotive manufactories.	Locomotive spark manufactory.	Steam engine and boiler manufactories.	Block manufactories.	Boat building.	Capstan and windlass manufactory.	Oar manufactory.	Sail-making.	Ship-building.	Ship-rigging.	Ship-smithing.
Albany,							1					1				1		3						2		
Allegany,																										
Broome,																								1		
Cattaraugus,																										
Cayuga,																				2						
Chautauque,																										
Chemung,																				1						
Chenango,																										
Clinton,				8																						
Columbia,							1								2											
Cortland,																										
Delaware,																										
Dutchess,							1								1									1		
Erie,				1			2		2				2		2	1		4		1						
Essex,				2																						
Franklln,				17											1											
Fulton,																										
Genesee,																										
Greene,							1																	3		
Hamilton,																										
Herkimer,				1																1						
Jefferson,																								2		
Kings,				1		3	1		1	1			2		2			1	2					6		2
Lewis,																										
Livingston,																				2						
Madison,																				1						
Monroe,						1	2		1					3	2					14			1			
Montgomery,																				1						
New-York,	1	1		1	14	5	1	1	2	2		9	5		11		1	17	10	10	1		10	25	2	26
Niagara,																				2						
Oneida,				1											3					10						
Onondaga,							2													5						
Ontario,																		1								
Orange,																		1		2				1		
Orleans,																										
Oswego,				2															1	2				3		2
Otsego,																										
Putnam,																										
Queens,				1	1																			1		
Rensselaer,		2				1			1						4											
Richmond,			1																				1	5		1
Rockland,																						1		3		
St. Lawrence,				7																				1		
Saratoga,															3					3						
Schenectady,						1										1										
Schoharie,																										
Schuyler,																										
Seneca,																				1						
Steuben,																				1						
Suffolk,																				2			2	25		
Sullivan,											1									5				1		
Tioga,																		1								
Tompkins,																				5						
Ulster,									2		11									1				3		
Warren,																										
Washington,				1																				2		
Wayne,																										
Westchester,															4					1				1		
Wyoming,																										
Yates,																				1						
Total,	1	3	1	43	15	11	12	1	9	3	12	10	9	3	35	3	1	28	13	74	1	1	14	86	2	31

DISTRIBUTION OF MANUFACTURING ESTABLISHMENTS.—(Continued.)

COUNTIES.	CLASS VII.			CLASS VIII.												CLASS IX.										
	Spar manufactories.	Steamboat finishing.	Treenail factories.	Barometer manufactories.	Chronometer manufactories.	Clock factories.	Hydrometer manufactory.	Mathematical instrument manufactories.	Nautical instrument manufactories.	Optical instrument manufactories.	Philosophical instrument manufactory.	Spectacle manufactories.	Surveying instrument manufactories.	Telegraph instrument manufactories.	Thermometer manufactories.	Gypsum quarries.	House building.	Iron mining.	Lead mining.	Marl and peat beds.	Masonry.	Mining machine manufactory.	Ornamental plastering.	Sash and blind manufactories.	Stair-building establishments.	Stone quarries.
Albany,				1																				10	3	
Allegany,																									4	
Broome,																									4	
Cattaraugus,																								1	3	
Cayuga,																3					1			4	3	
Chautauque,																								1	7	
Chemung,																									2	
Chenango,													1											3	5	
Clinton,																		3			1			1	1	
Columbia,															1			1		1				4	2	
Cortland,																									2	
Delaware,																									2	
Dutchess,															1			1			2			2	6	
Erie,																					1			10	7	
Essex,																		8						1	2	
Franklin,																								2	3	
Fulton,																								1		
Genesee,																								4	3	
Greene,																								4	1	
Hamilton,																										
Herkimer,																								2	4	
Jefferson,																		2						2	4	
Kings,		1	1												1		11				1				11	
Lewis,																								2	1	
Livingston,																									2	
Madison,						2				1														4	4	
Monroe,																	4				2			4	11	
Montgomery,																								1	2	
New-York,	3			2	5	5	1	10	3	3	1	2		2			40					1	1		21	8
Niagara,																								6	3	
Oneida,														1			8	9						58	5	
Onondaga,																	3							4	6	
Ontario,																	4								1	
Orange,																		2						2	4	
Orleans,																								6	2	
Oswego,																	3								3	
Otsego,																									8	
Putnam,																		1						1		
Queens,																									3	
Rensselaer,													1	1										6		
Richmond,																	5								1	
Rockland,																										
St. Lawrence,																			1					2	12	
Saratoga,																				1				1	7	
Schenectady,																								1		
Schoharie,																								1	1	
Schuyler,																	1								3	
Seneca,																								4	3	
Steuben,																								1	4	
Suffolk,	3					2											2								5	
Sullivan,																									1	
Tioga,																										
Tompkins,						1																			2	
Ulster,																	4							40	3	
Warren,																										
Washington,																								3	3	
Wayne,																		2							1	
Westchester,			6						1								3							1	7	
Wyoming,																									3	
Yates,																									1	
Total,	6	1	7	3	5	10	1	10	4	4	1	2	2	4	3	3	88	29	1	2	8	1	1	200	212	8

DISTRIBUTION OF MANUFACTURING ESTABLISHMENTS—(Continued.)

COUNTIES.	CLASS X.										CLASS XI.				CLASS XII.				CLASS XIII.								
	Bow and felloe manufactories.	Car factories and repair shops.	Car wheel founderies.	Coach and wagon manufactories.	Hose carriage manufactories.	Hub manufactories.	Patent axletree manufactories.	Spoke manufactories.	Wheelbarrow manufactories.	Wheel factories.	Bellows making.	Fire engine manufactories.	Pump factories.	Steam pump manufactories.	Hoist wheel manufactories.	Hydraulic jack manufactory.	Jack screw manufactory.	Scale manufactories.	Band and belting manufactories.	Bran duster manufactories.	Farina mill.	Feed mills.	Grist mills.	Millstone manufactories.	Millwright shops.	Pearl barley mills	Smut machine manufactories.
Albany,		1	1	29						1												3	23				
Allegany,		1		24				2															23				
Broome,				15				2															27	1			
Cattaraugus,				18									1										20				
Cayuga,		1		32																		2	30				
Chautauque,		1		31									2										31				
Chemung,		1		9				1					1										17				1
Chenango,				21				1															28				
Clinton,		1		20																			19				
Columbia,				34									1										43				
Cortland,				15																			23				
Delaware,				25																			26				
Dutchess,				40									1										39				
Erie,		2		26							1		2						1				43				
Essex,				15															1				16				
Franklin,				8																			11				
Fulton,				6																			9				
Genesee,		1		25									3										22				[illegible]
Greene,				8				1															27				
Hamilton,				1																			1				
Herkimer,	1			27					2														18		1		
Jefferson,				33									1										48			1	
Kings,				14									2	1									5				
Lewis,		1		12																			10				
Livingston,				26				1					1										29				
Madison,				21																			22				
Monroe,	2	1		48				1	2			2	6					1					54		3		
Montgomery,				21														5				3	24				
New-York,		1		59	2						3	1			2	1	1			1		1	8	1			
Niagara,				24															1		1		17				
Oneida,		3		61					1				2										42	1			[illegible]
Onondaga,		1		45				1	1									1	1			1	36			1	
Ontario,				19																			40				
Orange,				33				1															38				
Orleans,				21																			26				
Oswego,		1		21				1					1										42				
Otsego,				55																			37		3		
Putnam,				2																			7				
Queens,				26																			24				
Rensselaer,		2	1	26									1										34	1			[illegible]
Richmond,				2														1					2				
Rockland,		1		7																			13				
St. Lawrence,		2		26									2										36				
Saratoga,				29		1						1	1										33				
Schenectady,		1		7																			5				
Schoharie,				27																		1	27				
Schuyler,	1			15																			15				
Seneca,				19				1						3									15				
Steuben,		2		36																		1	42				
Suffolk,				16																			27				
Sullivan,				13																			16				
Tioga,				16																			17				
Tompkins,				26						1													28				
Ulster,	1			29				3	2														42	2	1		
Warren,				6									1										5				
Washington,		1		25																		1	15				
Wayne,				29																			25				
Westchester,				28			2															1	29		2		
Wyoming,				30									3										30				
Yates,				15																1			15				
Total,	5	26	2	1,397	2	1	2	16	8	2	4	4	32	4	2	1	1	8	4	2	1	14	1,476	6	10	2	[illegible]

CLASS XXII.—(CONTINUED.)

DISTRIBUTION OF MANUFACTURING ESTABLISHMENTS.—(CONTINUED.)

COUNTIES.	CLASS XIV.																																
	Auger manufactories.	Barrel machine manufactories.	Boring machine manufactories.	Box manufactories.	Carpenters' shops.	Carpenters' tool manufactories.	Cheese box manufactories.	Coopers' shops.	Heading mills.	Hoop manufactories.	Joiner shops.	Ladder and eave spout manufact's.	Lath manufactories.	Match box manufactories.	Patent mill-dog manufactory.	Pattern manufactories.	Plane manufactories.	Planing machine manufactory.	Planing mills.	Rule manufactories.	Saw manufactories.	Saw set manufactory.	Scroll sawing establishments.	Saw mills.	Shingle factories.	Ship timber manufactories.	Stave manufactories.	Steel square manufactory.	Turning shops.	Truss hoop manufactory.	Veneering manufactories.	Wood moulding and carving establishments	Wood mills.
Albany,					9	1		12										1	4		1			43	29				1		1		
Allegany,				4	2		2	3			1		1						3					183									
Broome,								7					4						1					159			1		1				
Cattaraugus,				2	1		4	8			1		4											169	15				1				
Cayuga,		1		3	7	1		9											1					79			1						
Chautauque,					3		1	22											2					184	10				7		2		
Chemung,					4	1		7											2		1			99	4				4				
Chenango,							2	16											1					110					5				2
Clinton,					1			4					1						2					110	2		1						
Columbia,					7	1		1																21	2								
Cortland,		1			1			10											2					68					3				
Delaware,								10																224	2				1				
Dutchess,					3			7											1					12	1				2				
Erie,					3	1		15			3		12						7		1			151	11	15	5		6				25
Essex,								4																73	5		3						
Franklin,								3																85	4		1						2
Fulton,				1	7		1	10					2											90	5		1		5				
Genesee,								16											1					46	3		3		1				
Greene,					3			4											1					62					8				
Hamilton,																								23					1				
Herkimer,					5		23	11					4						5			1		94				1	6				
Jefferson,					3	1	5	10											2					101	12								
Kings,				1	10	1		6											6		1			2	1				1		1	1	
Lewis,					1		5	1		1			2						1					95	2				2				
Livingston,					10			13					2											35			1		2				
Madison,				2			3	9			1		2											75	1		1		2				
Monroe,	1			1	11	2		52											5		1			55	2		3		2	1			
Montgomery,								5								2			1					43	2				4				
New-York,			1	11	76			59				1	2				1		4	1	2		2	13					8			13	
Niagara,					1			10											1					41	9		5						
Oneida,	1			1	1	1	3	19			3		6		1		1		6					238	17		1		2			1	
Onondaga,				1	12		1	38	4							2			2					81			5		4				
Ontario,					1			13					1						1					54	1		1		1				
Orange,					2			8												1	2			21									
Orleans,					1			10											4					33	3		1						
Oswego,				1	1		3	48	3		2	1	2						3					218	22		17		2				
Otsego,	1				11		1	17				1												142	2				6				
Putnam,					1																			2									
Queens,					2														2					7					1				
Rensselaer,	1			1			1	12					2						1					91			1		6				
Richmond,					3																1												
Rockland,					1			1																7									
St. Lawrence,				1			1	8				1							1					138	36		1						
Saratoga,								11					2						1					80	5				5				
Schenectady,											1								1					13					1				
Schoharie,								14											1					118	1				7				
Schuyler,								7					1						1					84	10								
Seneca,								7		1			1						2					15			4		1				
Steuben,						1		12											4					238	15				2				
Suffolk,								2																11					1				
Sullivan,								1					1											145			1		12				
Tioga,				1				10					4	2			1							146	7								
Tompkins,					3			15					8						2					97	7				1				
Ulster,					2			29		1														95			6		5				
Warren,					1								3						2					68			4		1				
Washington,							4	8											4					49	2								
Wayne,					10			17											4					85			3		1				
Westchester,				1	12			1								1	1		1		1			31	1				1				
Wyoming,								6					1						1					77	10				2				
Yates,								8											1					19	1								
Total,	4	2	1	32	232	11	60	666	7	3	12	4	68	2	1	5	4	1	98	2	11	1	2	4948	262	15	71	1	136	1	4	15	29

DISTRIBUTION OF MANUFACTURING ESTABLISHMENTS—(Continued.)

COUNTIES.	CLASS XV.																					CLASS XVI.									
	Brick manufactories.	Brick and tile machine manufactories.	Enameling factories.	Fire brick manufactories.	Glass cutting establishments.	Glass manufactories.	Glass staining establishments.	Lime manufactories.	Looking glass manufactories.	Marble manufactories.	Plaster mills.	Porcelain manufactories.	Potteries.	Roofing slate manufactories.	Soap stone manufactories.	Stone cutting establishments.	Stone cutters' tool manufactory.	Tile manufactories.	Tobacco pipe manufactory.	Water lime manufactories.	Window plate manufactory.	Bark mills.	Boot and shoe shops.	Hame turning shops.	Harness, saddle and trunk manufactories.	Hose manufactories.	Leather-splitting gauge manufactory.	Morocco factories.	Morocco case manufactories.	Parchment and vellum manufactory.	Patent leather manufactories.
Albany,	11			1				3	1	8	3		2					2	1				27	1	7			4			
Allegany,	1								1	2													23		13						
Broome,	1							1		2	2		1										16		6						
Cattaraugus,	1							1					1										16	1	10						
Cayuga,	2							2		2	4					1				1			36		13			1			
Chautauque,	3									2													37		11						
Chemung,	1							2		2	2												15		3						
Chenango,	1							2			5		1			1							28	2	10						
Clinton,	9					1		4		2	1		1										15		9						
Columbia,	2									2	6												29		6						
Cortland,	2							3		2			1										26		8						
Delaware,										1													26		10						
Dutchess,	13								1	3	7		1			1							35		9						
Erie,	11					1		3		2	1		1			3				2			31		14						1
Essex,								1			1												8		4						
Franklin,	1									1	1												7		3						
Fulton,	1							5			1												7		5						
Genesee,	2							2		3	7		1					1					36		15						
Greene,	22	1						4			4		1										6		3						
Hamilton,																															
Herkimer,	1							2		3	6												34		10						
Jefferson,	4					1		2		5	1												42		17			2			
Kings,				2		2		3		7	1	2				14							10		5			4			2
Lewis,	1							2															9		6						
Livingston,	1									3													30	1	11						
Madison,								2		3	4									1			30		16						
Monroe,	3							5		4	6		2			1							34		27						
Montgomery,	2									2	5												20		9						
New-York,			4	2	7	5	1	4	14	32	5		2		3	16					1		71		32	2		14	4		1
Niagara,	5					1		5		2	1									1			24		10			1			
Oneida,	5					2	1	5		2	6		3			3		2					72		26		1				
Onondaga,	9							8	1	2	12		2			8	1			12			53		26						
Ontario,	3	1						2		1	7		2			1		3		1			29		10						
Orange,	14							1			4					2							20		15			1			
Orleans,										2	1												26		7						
Oswego,	9					4				1	1		1							1			29		12			1			
Otsego,	2									2													54		20						
Putnam,	2																						12		1					1	
Queens,	2									2													8		7						
Rensselaer,	7			1				1		3	5		2										25		8			1			1
Richmond,	1																						5								
Rockland,	33							1								1							5		1						
St. Lawrence,	6							4		2	3		1							1		1	37		14			1			
Saratoga,	4					1		2		3	4		1			1							29		12						
Schenectady,	1							1								1				1			9		5						
Schoharie,								1		1													21		7						
Schuyler,											2		1										16		6						
Seneca,	4							2			2		1					3					13		8						
Steuben,	3							1		2	3												28		15						
Suffolk,	7									2			1			1							18		6						
Sullivan,																							10		5						
Tioga,	1									1	2					1							17		8						
Tompkins,	1							2		2	4		1										34		14						
Ulster,	11					2		3			3		1			2				11		1	9		8						
Warren,	1							2		1						1							7		3						
Washington,	2							1		1	3			5									24		13						
Wayne,	2					1		4		2	1							1					22		15						
Westchester,	38			1				1		7	3												52	1	7						
Wyoming,										4						1							34		9						
Yates,								1			4		1										15		5						
Total,	269	2	4	7	7	21	2	101	18	138	144	2	33	5	3	60	1	12	1	32	1	2	1,467	6	595	2	1	30	4	1	5

DISTRIBUTION OF MANUFACTURING ESTABLISHMENTS.—(CONTINUED.)

COUNTIES.	CLASS XVI.						CLASS XVII.																					
	Pocket book and port monnaie manufactories.	Razor strop manufactories.	Saddle and coach hardware manufactories.	Shoe peg manufactories.	Tanneries.	Whip manufactories.	Basket manufactories.	Bed, mattrass and cot manufactories.	Bedstead manufactories.	Billiard table manufactories.	Broom manufactories.	Brush manufactories.	Cabinet making shops.	Cedar ware manufactories.	Chair factories.	Coffee mill manufactories.	Feather brush manufactories.	House-decorating establishment.	House-furnishing establishments.	Iron furniture manufactories.	Pail manufactories.	Paper hanging manufactories.	Rug and mat manufactories.	Sofa and lounge manufactories.	Washing machine manufactories.	Willow ware manufactories.	Window shade manufactories.	Woodenware manufactories.
Albany,			2		10				3		8	1	8	1	3													
Allegany,					17			1					13								3							
Broome,					20	1					4		5															
Cattaraugus,					15								15															
Cayuga,			1		18								11															
Chautauque,					25				1				13		3						1							
Chemung,					11				2				6															
Chenango,					17								7		3													
Clinton,					13				1				6		3						1							
Columbia,					8	1					1		5		1							1						
Cortland,					13		1		3		3		7		1													
Delaware,					24								9						1									
Dutchess,					8				1				9		2	1					2							
Erie,				1	134		1		1		1		19		1				2		4							
Essex,					10		1						5		1						1							
Franklln,					6								5								1							
Fulton,				2	25								2		1													
Genesee,					9						3		6		1													
Greene,					9		1	2	2		1		5		4	2									1			2
Hamilton,					3								1															
Herkimer,					21				1		2		10		1													
Jefferson,					25		1						17		2				1									3
Kings,					4				1				16						1			1	2					
Lewis,					15								5		2												1	
Livingston,					7								11		1						1							
Madison,					22								12		3													
Monroe,				2	15	2			3			1	15		1													
Montgomery,					15						5		9															
New-York,	12			6	14	2	1	7	4	6	2	20	98	1	27		3	1	10	3		5	5	5	1	4	5	
Niagara,					4						2		6															
Oneida,				3	38		1		1			1	21		5				4		1	1					1	1
Onondaga,			3		19	1							15		4				3								1	1
Ontario,					5								8		1						1							
Orange,					12							1	9		1													
Orleans,					10								8															
Oswego,					38								13		1				1									
Otsego,				1	26				1				15								1							3
Putnam,					2		1						2															
Queens,					2	1							4															
Rensselaer,					13				2		2	14	10															1
Richmond,													1									1						
Rockland,					2		1								2						1						1	
St. Lawrence,					25			2					12		5						1							
Saratoga,					9		1						7								3							2
Schenectady,					1						15		5															
Schoharie,					17						4		5		1													
Schuyler,					13								4															1
Seneca,					5						1		5															
Steuben,					19								16		1													
Suffolk,					4								5															
Sullivan,					39								7		1													1
Tioga,					12						1		5															1
Tompkins,					14								16		1													
Ulster,					30								8						1									1
Warren,					14								2															1
Washington,		1			13								9		1													1
Wayne,			1		14		1				2		8		1						1							
Westchester,			1		9		1		1			1	7		1											1		
Wyoming,					16								17		1													
Yates,					5								6															
Total,	12	1	8	15	863	8	12	12	28	6	54	39	616	2	88	3	3	1	24	3	23	9	7	5	2	5	9	19

DISTRIBUTION OF MANUFACTURING ESTABLISHMENTS.—(CONTINUED.)

COUNTIES.	CLASS XVIII.																												
	Artists' brush manufactory.	Block letter manufactory.	Book binderies.	Book binders' tool manufactory.	Camera manufactory.	Daguerreotyping establishments.	Daguerreotype case manufactories.	Engraving establishments.	Envelope manufactories.	Gold pen manufactories.	Ink manufactories.	Jewelry case manufactories.	Lithographic establishments.	Map coloring establishment.	Map publishing establishments.	Melodeon manufactories.	Musical instrument manufactories.	Organ building establishments.	Organ pipe manufactory.	Paper ruler manufactory.	Piano forte manufactories.	Piano tool manufactory.	Piano hardware manufactories.	Piano stool manufactories.	Picture and mirror frame manufactories.	Printers' ink manufactories.	Printing offices.	Printing press manufactories.	Printers' roller manufactory.
Albany,																					2						3		
Allegany,																													
Broome,																													
Cattaraugus,																											1		
Cayuga,			1			2															1			1			7		
Chautauque,			1			1											1				1						3		
Chemung,																											3		
Chenango,																					2								
Clinton,																													
Columbia,																													
Cortland,																													
Delaware,																											1		
Dutchess,			1																		2						4		
Erie,																					5				3		1		
Essex,											1																		
Franklin,						1																							
Fulton,																													
Genesee,																													
Greene,																													
Hamilton,																													
Herkimer,			1																								1		
Jefferson,						2															1						1		
Kings,			1				1	1		1																			
Lewis,																													
Livingston,						1																							
Madison,			1			1																					2		
Monroe,																	2				1				2				
Montgomery,																											1		
New-York,	1	1	32	1	1	10	1	28	4	10		1	13	1	2	1	3	3	1	1	38	1	2	1	8	3	53	4	1
Niagara,																													
Oneida,			1					1										1			2						6		
Onondaga,						3															1						5		
Ontario,			2																										
Orange,							1														4								
Orleans,																													
Oswego,			2																										
Otsego,						1										2					1								
Putnam,																													
Queens,																										1	2		
Rensselaer,															1						2								
Richmond,																													
Rockland,																													
St. Lawrence,			1																		1						2		
Saratoga,																											1		
Schenectady,																													
Schoharie,																													
Schuyler,																													
Seneca,																													
Steuben,			1															1									2		
Suffolk,																					1								
Sullivan,																													
Tioga,																													
Tompkins,			1																										
Ulster,																											1		
Warren,																													
Washington,																					1								
Wayne,																													
Westchester,			2			1																		1					
Wyoming,											1																		
Yates,						2																					2		
Total,	1	1	48	1	1	25	3	30	4	11	2	1	13	1	3	3	6	5	1	1	66	1	2	3	13	4	102	4	1

DISTRIBUTION OF MANUFACTURING ESTABLISHMENTS—(Continued.)

COUNTIES.	CLASS XVIII.				CLASS XIX.						CLASS XX.							CLASS XXI.											
	Statuary.	Stereotyping establishments.	Type founderies.	Type founders' tool manufactory.	Gun smiths' shops.	Military accoutrement manufactories.	Percussion cap manufactory.	Powder mills	Shot manufactory.	Shot belt manufactory, etc.	Bathing tub manufactories.	Dental instrument manufactory.	Dentists' gold manufactory.	Dentistry.	Surgical instrument manufactor's.	Teeth manufactories.	Truss and bandage manufactor's.	Belt clasp manufactory.	Button and comb manufactory.	Clerical robe manufactory.	Comb manufactories.	Corset manufactory.	Dress making establishments.	Gentlemen's furnishing goods manufactories.	Glove and mitten manufactories.	Hair dressing and wig manufactories.	Hat and cap manufactories.	Hat block manufactories.	Hosiery manufactories.
Albany,					1									1													8		6
Allegany,					4																						2		
Broome,																											1		
Cattaraugus,					2																								
Cayuga,					1																						1		
Chautauque,					2																								
Chemung,					3																						3		
Chenango,																			1										
Clinton,																													
Columbia,																											4		
Cortland,					1																						1		
Delaware,					1																								
Dutchess,			1		1																						3		
Erie,	1				2									1															
Essex,					1																								
Franklin,					1									1															
Fulton,																									61				
Genesee,					5									1															
Greene,								1											1								5		
Hamilton,																													
Herkimer,					2									1															
Jefferson,					2																						2		
Kings,					1								1														2		
Lewis,														1											1				
Livingston,					1									1													3		
Madison,					1									1													1		1
Monroe,					2			1										1									2		
Montgomery,																													
New-York,	1	12	8	1	6	2			1	1	2	1			4	2	1			1	3	1	12	10	3	4	51	3	1
Niagara,					1									3													1		
Oneida,					1									2												1	5		
Onondaga,					2									2													4		
Ontario,					4									1													1		
Orange,																											1		
Orleans,																													
Oswego,																											2		
Otsego,					2												1								1		1		
Putnam,																											2		
Queens,					1																						1		
Rensselaer,					1			1																			1		1
Richmond,																											1		
Rockland,							1																						
St. Lawrence,					2																				1		3		
Saratoga,					1									2															2
Schenectady,																													
Schoharie,					1																								
Schuyler,					1									1															
Seneca,					1																								
Steuben,					2									1													2		
Suffolk,														1													1		
Sullivan,					2																								
Tioga,																									1				
Tompkins,					2									1													2		
Ulster,								2																			1		
Warren,																													
Washington,								1																					1
Wayne,														1									1		1		2		
Westchester,																			1								2		
Wyoming,																											1		
Yates,					1									1										3			1		
Total,	2	12	9	1	65	2	1	6	1	1	2	1	1	24	4	2	2	1	3	1	3	1	13	13	69	5	124	3	12

DISTRIBUTION OF MANUFACTURING ESTABLISHMENTS—(Continued.)

COUNTIES.	CLASS XXI.							CLASS XXII.																					
	Military and firemen's cap manufactory.	Milliner shops.	Sewing machine manufactories.	Shirt, bosom and collar manufactories.	Stock manufactories.	Tailor shops.	Umbrella and parasol manufactories.	Altar ornament manufactory.	Artificial flower manufactories.	Band box manufactories.	Bird cage manufactories.	Butchers' shops.	Cane manufactory	Carpet bag manufactory	Charcoal manufactories.	Cistern and tank manufactories.	Cork cutting establishments.	Fancy turning establishments.	Fishing rod manufactories.	Ice establishments.	Paper box manufactories.	Refrigerator manufactories.	Regalia manufactory.	Sausage machine manufactory.	Soda fountain manufactories.	Tobacco and segar manufactories.	Undertakers' establishments.	Unenumerated manufactories.	Whalebone manufactories.
Albany,		3				25																				8		1	
Allegany,		1				2						1																2	
Broome,		2																											
Cattaraugus,		1				6																						1	
Cayuga,		7				6						1														4	1	1	
Chautauque,		3				8						1														1		1	
Chemung,		1				7																				1			
Chenango,		3				2						1																	
Clinton,															20														
Columbia,						13																				1		2	
Cortland,						5																							
Delaware,		2				5																							
Dutchess,		7				23														1						13		1	
Erie,		3				7				1		3			2								1			5		1	
Essex,						2									6														
Franklin,		1				4																							
Fulton,		2				1																				1			
Genesee,		5				8																							
Greene,		2				1																				1			
Hamilton,																													
Herkimer,		3				14																							
Jefferson,		5				17						2														1		55	
Kings,																										9	4	13	
Lewis,						2																							
Livingston,		4				8																				1			
Madison,		2				7						1									1							1	
Monroe,					1	8						2				2		1	1	2		1			1	4	1	1	
Montgomery,						3						2														1			
New-York,	1	12	4		1	126	20	1	4	2	3	9	1				2	7	5	1	25	1			2	36	3	17	2
Niagara,		2				8																				1		3	
Oneida,		15				28						11			2					1						6		1	
Onondaga,		1				10						7								1						5	1	1	
Ontario,						14						2																	
Orange,		6				9						2		1												6	1		
Orleans,		4				2						1																1	
Oswego,		6				10																				2	2		
Otsego,		5				17						1			1														
Putnam,		1										1																	
Queens,		2				4					1	2												1			1	1	1
Rensselaer,		1		21		15	1								1						1					3		2	
Richmond,												1														1		2	
Rockland,						1						1								1						3		1	
St. Lawrence,		1				12						3														1		1	
Saratoga,						4																				1		1	
Schenectady,		4				9																					1		
Schoharie,						4																							
Schuyler,		2				6																					1		
Seneca,						6																							
Steuben,		4				9						1														2			
Suffolk,		3				3						1								2						2	1	18	
Sullivan,		2										1			2											2			
Tioga,		1				27						3														2			
Tompkins,		6				15						5														6			
Ulster,		2				9						6			3							1				3		1	
Warren,		2				1																							
Washington,		1				3																				1			
Wayne,		5				11						4																1	
Westchester,						2				1		9														4			
Wyoming,		1				5						2														1		1	
Yates,		5				7																							
Total,	1	151	4	21	2	560	21	1	4	4	4	87	1	1	37	2	2	8	6	9	27	3	1	1	3	139	17	132	3

QUANTITIES OF RAW MATERIALS AND MANUFACTURED PRODUCTS.

CLASS I.—AGRICULTURAL TOOLS AND IMPLEMENTS.

MATERIALS AND PRODUCTS.	Towns reported.	Quantities.
AGRICULTURAL IMPLEMENTS GENERALLY.		
Lumber, feet of,	23	2,375,000
Iron, tons of,	27	5,713¼
Coal, tons of,	14	1,702
Wood, cords of,	6	1,395
Castings, tons of,	10	2,545
Reaping and mowing machines, number of,	6	2,980
Feed cutters, number of,	5	1,677
Grain threshers, number of,	9	502
Hay pressses, number of,	1	100
Plows, number of,	3	330
Corn planters, number of,	1	25
Corn shellers, number of,	2	75
Cultivators, number of,	1	190
CHEESE PRESS MANUFACTORIES.		
Lumber, feet of,	1	1,000
Iron, tons of,	1	½
Cheese presses, number of,	2	105
CHURN FACTORIES.		
Lumber, feet of,	1	2,000
Iron, tons of,	1	2
Churns, number of,	2	6,800
CIDER MILLS.		
Apples, bushels of,	17	145,460
Cider barrels, number of,	20	16,479
Cider brandy, barrels of,	1	1,000
FANNING MILL MANUFACTORIES, ETC.		
Lumber, feet of,	23	405,000
Castings, pounds of,	6	12,000
" sets of,	2	210
Wire, pounds of,	1	600
Fanning mills, number of,	23	2,985
Other manufactures: 180 churns and 194 pumps.		
FORK FACTORIES.		
Steel, tons of,	8	182
Lumber, feet of,	2	45
Coal, tons of,	3	59
Charcoal, bushels of	1	1,000
Handles, number of,	2	330,000
Hay forks, number of,	7	321,600
Ferules, dozens of,	1	900
GRAIN CRADLE AND SCYTHE SNATH FACTORIES, &C.		
Lumber, feet of,	13	326,000
Iron, tons of,	5	21¾
Coal, tons of,	1	20
Wood, cords of,	2	175
Wire, pounds of,	1	2,000
Varnish, gallons of,	1	62
Scythes, number of,	3	133
Snaths, dozens of,	4	23,120
Cradles, number of,	22	34,786
Other manufactures: forks and rakes 35,096; mop sticks, 400,000; churns, 10,000; horse rakes, 40.		
GRAIN MEASURE MANUFACTORIES.		
Lumber, feet of,	2	135,000
Iron, tons of,	1	2
Measures, sets of,	2	10,500
" number of (in add. to above),	1	49,860
HOE MANUFATTORIES, ETC.		
Lumber, feet of,	2	2,580
HOE MANUFACTORIES, ETC.—(Continued.)		
Iron and steel, tons of,	7	177
Coal, tons of,	4	247½
Hoes, dozens of,	6	9,866½
Forks, dozens of,	2	2,365
Muck hoes, dozens of,	1	70
Ferules, dozens of,	1	30
PLOW AND CULTIVATOR FACTORIES.		
Lumber, feet of,	13	195,000
Iron, tons of,	25	1,091¾
Coal, tons of,	13	299½
Wood, cords of,	5	657
Plows, number of,	23	7,642
Cultivators, number of,	10	1,083
Horse hoes, number of,	1	100
Grain drills, number of,	2	180
Castings, tons of,	13	291
Corn shellers, number of,	1	80
RAKE FACTORIES.		
Lumber, feet of,	17	506,100
Iron, tons of,	3	16
Wire, pounds of,	2	6,200
Horse rakes, number of,	18	15,278
Hand rakes, dozens of,	12	36,694
REAPING AND MOWING MACHINE FACTORIES.		
Lumber, feet of,	4	335,000
Iron, tons of,	4	360
Steel, pounds of,	2	5,000
Coal, tons of,	3	115
Wood, cords of,	1	400
Oil, barrels of,	1	4
Machines, number of,	2	1,450
Mowers, number of,	1	425
Reapers, number of,	3	540
Threshers, number of,	2	60
SCYTHE FACTORIES, ETC.		
Iron, tons of,	7	745
Coal, tons of,	4	1,349
Charcoal, bushels of,	1	1,500
Grindstones, tons of,	1	180
Scythes, number of,	7	99,400
Other manufactures: 12,000 dozen axes, 5,000 dozen other tools.		
SCYTHE RIFLE MANUFACTORIES.		
Lumber, feet of,	3	32,000
Emery, pounds of,	2	6,500
Oil, gallons of,	2	135
Pulverized "crystal," pounds of	1	6,300
Scythe rifles, gross of,	4	2,982
SHOVEL MANUFACTORY.		
Iron, tons of,	1	150
Shovels, dozens of,	1	3,600
TOOL SHOPS.		
Lumber, feet of,	3	40,100
Iron, tons of,	5	39½
Steel, pounds of,	3	20,200
Charcoal, bushels of,	1	3,000
Horse rakes, number of,	2	3,500
Cultivators, number of,	3	2,200
Corn planters, number of,	1	500
Grain drills, number of,	1	40
Grain separators number of,	1	60

CLASS II.—METALLURGY, AND MANUFACTURE OF METALS AND INSTRUMENTS THEREFOR.

MATERIALS AND PRODUCTS.	Towns reported.	Quantities.
ANVIL MANUFACTORY.		
Steel, tons of,	1	150
Anvils, tons of,	1	130
AXE AND EDGE TOOL MANUFACTORIES.		
Lumber, feet of,	2	191,000
Steel, tons of,	19	362
Iron, tons of,	29	1,484
Borax, tons of,	4	13
Coal, tons of,	20	2,348
Wood, cords of,	1	300
Grindstones, tons of,	11	1,039
Axes, number of,	19	224,031
Edge tools, number of,	10	100,000
Hammers, number of,	1	6,868
Harpoons and lances, number of,	1	600
Stocks and bits, number of	1	600
BELL FOUNDRIES.		
Metal, pounds of,	3	980,000
BELL FOUNDRIES—(Continued.)		
Coal, tons of,	2	270
Charcoal, bushels of,	2	12,000
Wood, cords of,	2	100
Bells, pounds of,	3	655,000
" number of,	1	400
BLACKSMITH SHOPS.		
Iron, tons of,	431	4,331½
Coal, tons of,	259	4,536
Charcoal, bushels of,	63	162,727
Miscellaneous articles not specified.		
Wagons, number ironed,	40	1,375
Sleighs, number ironed,	16	189
Miscellaneous products: 30 cultivators, 400 drays and carts, 100 axes, 66 dozen horse shoes—remainder not specified.		
BOLT MANUFACTORIES.		
Iron, tons of,	5	85½

CLASS II.—(CONTINUED.)

MATERIALS AND PRODUCTS.	Towns reported.	Quantities.
BOLT MANUFACTORIES—(Continued.)		
Bolts, tons of,	1	50
Screw bolts, number of,	1	12,000
BRAD AND SPARABLE MANUFACTORY.		
Iron, tons of,	1	20
Brads and sparables, tons of,	1	19
BRASS AND COPPER FOUNDRIES.		
Copper, tons of,	9	1,142½
Coal, tons of,	3	643
Charcoal, bushels of,	1	1,000
Castings, tons of,	4	830½
BRITANNIA WARE AND SILVER PLATING ESTABLISHMENTS.		
Argentine metal, pounds of,	1	90,000
Silver and German silver, ounces of,	3	80,600
Sadlery, coach trimmings, &c., not specified.		
BRONZE CASTING ESTABLISHMENTS.		
Zinc, tons of,	1	10
Metal, tons of,	1	25
Bronze, pounds of,	1	31,600
BUTT AND HINGE FACTORIES, ETC.		
Iron, tons of,	3	1,076
Coal, tons of,	1	113
Hinges, tons of,	1	277½
Butts, number of,	1	83,626
Miscellaneous articles: scales, 2,500; shovels, 2,428.		
CASTOR FRAME MANUFACTORIES.		
Lead, pounds of,	1	50,000
Tin, pounds of,	1	50,000
Castor frames, pounds of,	1	98,000
COMPOSITION METAL MANUFACTORIES.		
Lead, tons of,	1	22
Block tin, pounds of,	1	1,666
Antimony, pounds of,	1	16,666
Composition metal, pounds of,	1	16,000
COPPER SMITHING.		
Copper, tons of,	1	137
Spelter, tons of,	1	10
Tin, tons of,	1	33
Iron, tons of,	1	50
Brass, tons of,	1	55
Still worm, tons of,	1	16½
Other manufactures not specified.		
CUTLERY MANUFACTORIES.		
Iron, tons of,	3	36
Steel, pounds of,	4	2,756
Coal, tons of,	2	17
Butcher and shoe knives,		35,000
Other manufactured products not specified.		
DOOR LATCH MANUFACTORY.		
Metal, tons of,	1	75
Coal, tons of,	1	30
Japan, barrels of,	1	6
Wood, cords of,	1	50
Lumber, feet of,	1	30
Nails, pounds of,	1	600
Door latches, number of,	1	150,000
FILE MANUFACTORIES.		
Steel, tons of,	3	265½
Coal, tons of,	2	1,250
Charcoal, bushels of,	1	1,500
Files, dozens of,	3	151,800
FISH-HOOK MANUFACTORY.		
Wire, tons of,	1	5
Fish-hooks, number of,	1	2,500,000
FORGES.		
Iron, tons of,	10	37,486
Ore, tons of,	2	330
Coal, tons of,	4	2,507½
Charcoal, bushels of,	7	404,800
Wood, cords of,	3	2,750
Wrought iron, tons of,	10	33,798
Nails, tons of,	1	100
Axles, tons of,	1	230
FURNACES.		
Iron, tons of,	192	108,938¼
Steel, tons of,	2	14
Lumber, feet of,	27	523,504
Coal, tons of,	126	33,248
Charcoal, bushels of,	5	13,633
Wood, cords of,	49	1,300
Stoves, number of,	31	81,060
Plows, number of,	35	34,366
Shingle machines, number of,	2	7,358
Steam engines, number of,	15	295
"Mills," number of,	3	214
Castings, tons of,	58	48,605½
GAS FIXTURE MANUFACTORIES.		
Block tin, tons of,	1	12½
Plate tin, boxes of,	1	1,500
Brass, tons of,	1	67
Iron, tons of,	1	18

MATERIALS AND PRODUCTS.	Towns reported.	Quantities.
GAS FIXTURE MANUFACTORIES—(Continued.)		
Copper, tons of,	1	54
Manufactured products not specified.		
GERMAN SILVER WARE MANUFACTORIES.		
Metal, pounds of,	1	2,580
Ware, pieces of,	1	1,540
GOLD LEAF AND FOIL MANUFACTORIES.		
Gold, ounces of,	2	5,688
Leaves of foil,	1	28,800
GOLD AND SILVER PLATING.		
Silver, ounces of,	1	15,000
Manufactured product not stated.		
GOLD AND SILVER REFINING.		
Sweepings, tons of,	1	400
Gold, ounces of,	1	9,000
Silver, ounces of,	1	30,000
HAMMER MANUFACTORIES.		
Steel, pounds of,	2	23,576
Coal, tons of,	2	1,500
Hammers,	2	36,000
HANDIRON MANUFACTORY.		
Copper, pounds of,	1	13,000
Spelter, pounds of,	1	4,333
Iron, tons of,	1	4
Coal, tons of,	1	18
Manufactured product not specified.		
HARDWARE MANUFACTORIES.		
Iron, tons of,	1	2
Manufactured products not specified.		
HOLLOW WARE MANUFACTORIES.		
Iron, tons of,	3	12,566
Varnish, gallons of,	3	750
Coal, tons of,	1	5
Wood, cords of,	1	50
Ware, tons of,	2	550
IRON MANUFACTORIES.		
Ore, tons of,	43	259,047
Coal, tons of,	16	89,276
Wood, cords of,	10	10,125
Charcoal, bushels of	35	12,529,900
Pig iron, tons of,	43	162,748
Rolled iron, tons of,	1	5,250
Nails, tons of,	2	4,121
IRON RAILING MANUFACTORIES, ETC.		
Iron, tons of,	6	3,999
Coal, tons of,	3	517
Lead, tons of,	1	1
Oil, gallons, of,	1	50
Railing, tons of,	3	1,200
Other manufactures: car wheels, 3,500.		
JAPANNED TIN MANUFACTORIES.		
Tin, boxes of,	1	500
Manufactured product not specified.		
LEAD PIPE MANUFACTORIES.		
Lead, tons of,	2	102
Pipe, tons of,	1	25
LIGHTNING ROD MANUFACTORIES.		
Iron, tons of,	2	62
Glass, pounds of,	1	2,500
Lightning rods, tons of,	2	62
LOCK MANUFACTORIES.		
Iron, tons of,	6	23¾
Brass, pounds of,	3	9,200
Copper, pounds of,	2	9,500
Coal, tons of,	3	230
Locks, number of,	5	191,760
Knobs, number of,	1	14,000
MACHINE SHOPS.		
Iron, tons of,	69	22,211¾
Lumber, feet of,	37	3,480,010
Coal, tons of,	33	6,252½
Wood, cords of,	14	3,330
Castings, tons of,	15	6,691¼
Steam engines, number of,	8	80
Horse powers, number of,	5	100
Corn mills, number of,	1	75
Scales, number of,	3	8,070
Axles, tons of,	1	3,000
Trip hammers, number of,	1	12
Safes, number of,	1	334
Printing presses, number of,	1	52
Threshing machines, number of,	1	70
Plows, number of,	1	1,742
Shingle machines, number of,	1	8
MACHINISTS' TOOL MANUFACTORIES.		
Iron, tons of,	3	265
Tools, number of,	1	40
Other manufactures: governor valves, 200; spoke machines, 7; lathes, 156; planing machines, 6; bolt cutters, 6		
MALLEABLE IRON WORKS.		
Pig iron, tons of,	5	1,475
Coal, tons of,	3	400
Wood, cords of,	2	1,000
Malleable castings,	3	255

CLASS II.—(Continued.)

MATERIALS AND PRODUCTS.	Towns reported	Quantities.
MALLEABLE IRON WORKS—(Continued.)		
Other products not specified.		
METALIC BURIAL CASE MANUFACTORY.		
Iron, tons of,	1	600
Coal, tons of,	1	300
Plate glass, feet of,	1	1,500
Oil and varnish, gallons of,	1	500
Burial cases, number of,	1	7,000
PIN MANUFACTORIES.		
Brass wire, pounds of,	2	102,000
Pins, packs of,	1	3,000
Pins, cases of,	1	520
PLUMBING ESTABLISHMENTS.		
Iron, tons of,	2	31½
Plate tin, boxes of,	2	1,700
Lead, tons of,	4	563
Copper and brass, tons of,	2	55½
Pipe, tons of,	2	482
Other products not specified.		
ROLLING MILLS AND NAIL FACTORIES.		
Iron, tons of,	3	6,398
Coal, tons of,	1	1,000
Nails, kegs of,	2	69,000
Bloom iron, tons of,	1	200
Rolled iron, tons of,	1	1,000
Wire and rod, tons of,	1	1,248
SAFE MANUFACTORIES.		
Iron, tons of,	4	3,419
Copper and brass, pounds of,	2	9,300
Cement, barrels of,	1	2,400
Coal, tons of,	1	140
Mahogany, feet of,	1	2,400
Safes, number of,	4	5,550
Other manufactures: number of locks, 850.		
SCREW FACTORY.		
Wire, tons of,	1	131
Screws, gross of,	1	195,000
SILVER WARE MANUFACTORIES, ETC.		
Silver, ounces of,	3	21,794
Gold, ounces of,	3	1,837
Ware, pieces of,	3	69,850
Spoons, dozens of,	1	1,500
SPIKE MANUFACTORY.		
Iron, tons of,	1	230
Coal, tons of,	1	24
Spikes, tons of,	1	225
STEEL SPRING MANUFACTORIES.		
Steel, tons of,	2	326
Coal, tons of,	1	13
Springs, tons of,	1	280
TIN, COPPER AND SHEET IRON MANUFACTORIES.		
Plate tin, boxes of,	159	93,997½
Sheet iron, tons of,	107	5,106¾
Wire, pounds of,	35	118,516
Zinc, pounds of,	2	600
Copper, pounds of,	64	628,865½
Lead, pounds of.	1	3,200
Solder, pounds of,	16	246,485
Block tin, pounds of,	12	3,000
Pans, number of,	4	7,940
Other manufactures not specified.		
WIRE WORKS.		
Iron, tons of,	5	574½
Wire, tons of,	3	558¾
Wire cloth, yards of,	1	3,500
Seives, dozens of,	1	7,000
WIRE RAILING MANUFACTORY.		
Wire, tons of,	1	500
Railing, tons of,	1	460
WIRE SEIVE MANUFACTORIES.		
Wire, pounds of,	4	160,858
Wooden hoops, dozens of,	1	1,000
Seives, dozens of,	1	1,000
Feet of wire cloth,	4	398,910

CLASS III.—MANUFACTURES OF FIBROUS AND TEXTILE SUBSTANCES.

MATERIALS AND PRODUCTS.	Towns reported	Quantities.
AWNING MANUFACTORY.		
Canvas, yards of,	1	50,000
Manufactured product not specified.		
CARDING AND CLOTH DRESSING ESTABLISHMENTS.		
Wool, pounds of,	73	551,019
Cloth, yards of,	27	51,878
Wood, cords of,	1	8
Soap, barrels of,	1	2
Rolls of wool, pounds of,	45	316,638
Fulled cloth, yards of,	35	10,000
Flannel, yards of,	4	6,000
CARPET MANUFACTORIES.		
Wool, pounds of,	9	3,707,500
Worsted and cotton yarn, pounds of,	6	402,000
Dye stuffs, barrels of,	1	100
Dye stuffs, pounds of,	1	150,000
Coal, tons of,	5	2,900
Oil, barrels of,	1	10
Carpeting, yards of,	10	1,820,500
Yarn, pounds of,	1	60,000
Rugs, number of,	1	5,000
CARPET YARN MANUFACTORIES.		
Wool, pounds of,	2	64,500
Rags, pounds of,	1	78,000
Yarn, pounds of,	2	91,600
COTTON FACTORIES.		
Cotton, bales of,	54	59,514
Starch, pounds of,	5	102,200
Oil, gallons of,	6	11,306
Coal, tons of,	6	2,480
Cloth (sheeting and shirting), yards of,	50	67,439,222
Batting and wadding, bales of,	4	100,250
Candle wicking, pounds of,	3	95,837
Bagging, yards of,	1	8,800
Seamless bags, number of,	1	100,000
COTTON BATTING MANUFACTORIES.		
Cotton, pounds of,	8	1,292,400
Wood, cords of,	2	300
Batting, pounds of,	7	659,600
Ropes, pounds of,	1	4,560
COTTON WARP MANUFACTORIES.		
Cotton, pounds of,	3	575,000
Warp, pounds of,	3	435,000
Batts, pounds of,	1	5,000
FELTING AND WADDING MANUFACTORIES.		
Cotton, pounds of,	1	100,000
Felting, bales of,	1	1,500
Wadding, bales of,	1	3,000
FLAX DRESSING MILLS.		
Flax, tons of,	17	4.354½
Dressed flax, tons of,	1	10
Lint, tons of,	13	866½
FLAX DRESSING MILLS—(Continued.)		
Tow, tons of,	2	155
FRINGE AND TASSEL MANUFACTORIES.		
Silk, cotton and worsted, pounds of,	2	28,200
Wool, pounds of,	1	400
Fringe, pieces of,	1	400
Tassels, number of,	1	600
Cord, balls of,	1	1,000
FUR DRESSING ESTABLISHMENTS.		
Skins, number of,	2	68,200
Dressed furs and skins,	2	29,000
HAIR CLOTH MANUFACTORIES.		
Materials used not specified.		
Cloth, yards of,	1	2,300
LINEN FACTORIES.		
Lint, pounds of,	2	334,400
Coarse tow, pounds of,	1	200,000
Fine tow, pounds of,	1	25,000
Hatcheled tow, pounds of,	1	50,000
Linen yarn, pounds of,	1	193,000
Rope yarn, pounds of,	1	118,700
Twine yarn, pounds of,	1	30,500
OAKUM MANUFACTORIES.		
Junk, pounds of,	2	78,250
Coal, tons of,	1	200
Oakum, pounds of,	2	970,942
PAPER MILLS.		
Straw, tons of,	17	6,200
Rags, tons of,	52	19,881½
Lime, bushels of,	21	30,212
Wood, cords of,	25	3,433
Coal, tons of,		
Paper, reams of,	42	2 028,595
Book board, tons of,	14	3,265
Wall paper, tons of,	1	35
Wrapping paper, tons of,	1	87
PAPIER MACHE.		
Paper, pounds of,	1	300
Pearl, pounds of,	1	30
Papier mache goods, pounds of,	1	530
PLAYING CARD MANUFACTORIES.		
Paper, tons of,	1	4,600
Gross of cards,	1	90,200
POWER LOOM MANUFACTORIES.		
Lumber, feet of,	3	101,360
Iron, tons of,	1	300
Looms, number of,	1	12,000
Bobbins, number of,	1	600,000
RAG CARPET AND BLANKET MANUFACTORIES.		
Rags, pounds of,	2	35,000
Cotton, pounds of,	1	4,800
Carpet, yards of,	2	19,000

CLASS III.—(CONTINUED.)

MATERIALS AND PRODUCTS.	Towns reported.	Quantities.
RAG CARPET AND BLANKET MANUFAC'Y.—(Con.)		
Blankets, number of,	1	2, 400
RIBBON FACTORIES.		
Silk, pounds of,	2	2, 040
Cotton, pounds of,	1	100
Ribbon, yards of,	2	16, 200
ROPE MANUFACTORIES.		
Hemp, tons of,	14	8, 650¾
Flax, tons of,	3	165
Tow, tons of,	1	156
Yarn, tons of,	1	889
Oil, barrels of,	1	1, 689
Tar, barrels of,	1	7, 146
Coal, tons of,	2	4, 123
Rope, tons of,	16	6, 902¾
SEA GRASS MANUFACTORY.		
Sea grass, tons of,	1	105
Grass, tons of,	1	90
SEWING SILK MANUFACTORIES.		
Silk, pounds of,	3	27, 556
Silk thread and twist,	4	34, 000
SHAWL AND BLANKET MANUFACTORIES.		
Wool, pounds of,	4	740, 000
Coal, tons of,	1	900
Wood, cords of,	1	75
Long shawls, number of,	3	167, 000
Blankets, yards of,	1	6, 000
SHODDY MILLS.		
Rags, pounds of,	4	550, 000
Shoddy, pounds of,	4	348, 000

MATERIALS AND PRODUCTS.	Towns reported.	Quantities.
STRAW PAPER MANUFACTORIES.		
Straw, tons of,	24	8, 120
Lime, bushels of,	9	11, 765
Oil, gallons of,	3	820
Coal, tons of,	3	950
Wood, cords of,	7	1, 890
Board, tons of,	14	2, 213
Paper, reams of,	8	769, 160
TAPE AND WEBB MANUFACTORIES.		
Yarn, pounds of,	4	77, 398
Lace, yards of,	2	16, 720
Other products, not specified,		
TWINE MANUFACTORIES.		
Linen yarn, pounds of,	3	256, 067
Cotton, pounds of,	4	548, 000
Flax, tons of,	2	170
Twine, pounds of,	2	1, 307, 400
Net pounds of,	1	8, 000
WOOLLEN CLOTH AND YARN FACORIES.		
Wool, pounds of,	40	10, 877, 783
Oil, barrels of,	12	263
Chemicals, pounds of,	5	544, 900
Soap, pounds of,	4	25, 190
Coal, tons of,	3	6
Wood, cords of,	15	13, 825
Cloth, yards of,	111	4, 836, 834
Yarn, pounds of,	24	506, 178½
Knit goods, dozens of,	2	15, 384
Blankets, pairs of,	1	48, 000
Shawls, number of,	1	18, 000

CLASS IV.—CHEMICAL PROCESSES, MANUFACTURES AND COMPOUNDS.

MATERIALS AND PRODUCTS.	Towns reported.	Quantities.
ASHERIES.		
Ashes, bushels of,	54	766, 475
Lime, bushels of,	6	667
Barrels, number of,	5	613
Wood, cords of,	24	4, 558
Potash, tons of,	52	1, 121½
Pearlash, tons of,	2	50
BAKERIES.		
Flour, barrels of,	63	212, 799
Butter and lard, pounds of,	34	630, 030
Sugar, pounds of,	26	1, 073, 303
Wood, cords of,	15	1, 370
Bread, pounds of,	13	6, 495, 960
Crackers, pounds of,	1	240, 000
Confectionery, pounds of,	1	52, 000
BARILLA MANUFACTORY.		
Crude barilla, tons of,	1	800
Manufactured barilla, tons of,	1	750
BARYTES MANUFACTORIES.		
Barytes, tons of,	2	2, 800
Coal, tons of,	1	200
Wood, cords of,	1	100
Ground barytes, tons of,	2	2, 800
BISCUIT MACHINE MANUFACTORIES.		
Iron, tons of,	1	17
Lumber, feet of,	1	3, 000
Cotton duck, yards of,	1	250
Machines,	1	25
BLACKING MANUFACTORIES.		
Black, pounds of,	1	20, 000
Molasses, gallons of,	1	3, 000
Blacking, boxes of,	2	590, 000
BLACK LEAD MANUFACTORIES.		
Graphite, tons of,	1	65
Prepared do, tons of,	1	65
BLEACHERIES.		
Cotton cloth, yards of,	1	260, 000
Coal, tons of,	1	360
Bleached cloth, yards of,	3	3, 340, 000
BREWERIES.		
Barley, bushels of,	34	1, 791, 917
Hops, pounds of,	24	806, 233
Coal, tons of,	10	1, 611
Wood, cords of,	11	2, 837
Beer, barrels of,	29	677, 425
Beer, bottles of,	9	368, 866
Malt, bushels of,	6	174, 702
BRONZE COLOR MANUFACTORY.		
Metal, tons of,	1	2½
Mannfactured products not specified.		
CAMPHENE DISTILLERY.		
Gum, barrels of,	1	10, 000
Camphene, barrels of,	1	10, 000
CHANDLERIES AND SOAP FACTORIES.		
Tallow, pounds of,	47	31, 951, 587
Ashes, bushels of,	15	217, 499
Soda ash, pounds of,	8	2, 398, 000
Wood, cords of,	5	984
Boxes, number of,	4	5, 216

MATERIALS AND PRODUCTS.	Towns reported.	Quantities.
CHANDLERIES AND SOAP FACTORIES.—(Cont'd.)		
Candles, pounds of,	42	8, 005, 138
Soap, pounds of,	27	22, 546, 347
" barrels of,	14	43, 040
Oil, gallons of,	3	1, 011, 575
CHEMICAL LABORATORIES.		
Materials, tons of,	1	295
Chemical products, tons of,	1	180
COFFEE, SPICE AND MUSTARD MANUFACTORIES.		
Coffee and spice, bags of,	3	32, 620
Mustard, pounds of,	1	150, 000
Ground mustard, spice, &c.,		2, 040, 020
CONFECTIONERY MANUFACTORIES.		
Sugar, pounds of,	20	2, 195, 254
Molasses, gallons of,	1	300
Lard, pounds of,	1	300
Drugs, &c., pounds of,	2	121, 200
Coal, tons of,	4	88
Candy, pounds of,	12	2, 399, 754
Confectionery, pounds of,	1	51, 000
COTTON PRINTING ESTABLISHMENTS.		
Cloth, yards of,	3	13, 645, 908
Drugs, tons of,	1	15, 000
Coal, tons of,	1	3, 000
Prints, yards of,	4	19, 355, 908
DISTILLERIES.		
Grain, bushels of,	43	3, 835, 871
Hops, pounds of,	8	18, 830
Apples, bushels of,	1	17, 000
Coal, tons of,	1	1, 450
Wood, cords of,	7	7, 008
Swine, number of,	8	12, 085
Spirits, barrels of,	50	756, 793
Highwines, barrels of,	1	4, 300
Cider brandy, barrels of,	1	1, 415
Pork, barrels of,	6	12, 687
DRUG AND MEDICINE MANUFACTORIES.		
Drugs, pounds of,	2	54, 000
Alcohol, barrels of,	2	77½
Tin, boxes of,	1	10
Glass, boxes of,	1	20
Bottles, number of,	4	68, 988
Vials, gross of,	1	250
Medicine, boxes of,	4	1, 296, 064
" bottles of,	5	190, 193
" barrels of,	2	476
DYEING ESTABLISHMENTS.		
Cloth, pieces of,	1	6, 240
Cloth, pieces printed,	1	6, 240
DYEWOOD MANUFACTORIES.		
Dyewoods, tons of,	4	3, 400
" packages and bbls.,	2	41, 700
EMERY, PUMICE AND SAND STONE MANUFACTORIES.		
Emery, tons of,	1	1, 000
Pumice stone, tons of,	1	50
Sand paper, reams of,	1	25, 000
Emery, tons of,	1	100
Pumice stone, tons of,	1	50

CLASS IV.—(CONTINUED.)

MATERIALS AND PRODUCTS.	Towns reported.	Quantities.
FISH AND WHALE OIL MANUFACTORIES.		
Crude oil, gallons of,	2	6, 078, 375
Fish, number of,	1	195, 000
Refined oil, gallons of,	4	1, 653, 110
Candles, pounds of,	1	766, 500
GAS MANUFACTORIES.		
Coal, tons of,	19	194, 073
Rosin, barrels of,	1	300
Lime, bushels of,	7	209, 589
Gas, feet of,	17	980, 094, 503
Coke, bushels of,	3	134, 808
Coal tar, barrels of,	3	2, 416
GLUE MANUFACTORIES.		
Sizing, tons of,	5	415
Hides, &c., tons of,	2	490
Coal, tons of,	1	10
Glue, pounds of,	8	263, 000
Sizing, pounds of,	1	200, 000
Neats foot oil, gallons of,	1	465
GUTTA PERCHA MANUFACTORY.		
Gutta percha, pounds of,	1	120, 000
Cloth, yards of,	1	300, 000
Manufactured product not specified.		
INDIA RUBBER MANUFACTORIES.		
India rubber, pounds of,	3	745, 000
Manufactured goods, pounds of,	3	865, 000
IVORY BLACK AND BONE MANURE MANUFACT'S.		
Bones, tons of,	4	17, 100
Bone black, tons of,	3	5, 315
Manure, tons of,	2	9, 500
Phosphate of lime, tons of,	1	300
JAPANNED CLOTH MANUFACTORIES.		
Cloth, yards of,	3	813, 200
Japanned cloth, yards of,	3	813, 200
LAMP BLACK MANUFACTORIES.		
Tar, barrels of,	1	3, 700
Rosin, barrels of,	2	1, 300
Lamp black, pounds of,	3	6, 509
LARD OIL MANUFACTORIES.		
Lard, pounds of,	3	2, 362, 000
Lard oil, gallons of,	3	712, 792
Sterine, pounds of,	1	1, 126, 000
LIQUORICE REFINERY.		
Liquorice root, pounds of,	1	219, 000
Gum Arabic, pounds of,	1	73, 000
MALT MANUFACTORIES.		
Barley, bushels of,	15	1, 272, 704
Hops, pounds of,	2	98, 000
Coal, tons of,	3	1, 275
Malt, bushels of,	13	1, 230, 684
MATCH MANUFACTORIES.		
Lumber, feet of,	8	469, 000
Other materials not specified.		
Matches, gross of,	10	582, 500
MEDICINAL HERB AND EXTRACT MANUFACTORIES.		
Slipery elm bark, tons of,	1	10
Roots, tons of,	1	2
Herbs, tons of,	2	293
Prepared herbs, pounds of,	2	126, 290
Extracts, gallons of,	1	1, 762
Medicinal extracts, pounds of,	1	65, 000
MINERAL WATER MANUFACTORIES.		
Soda, pounds of,	1	10, 000
Sugar, barrels of,	2	37, 000
" pounds of,	2	180, 000
Bottles, number of,	2	29, 920
Mineral water, bottles of,	5	2, 603, 000
OIL CLOTH MANUFACTORIES.		
Cloth, yards of,	9	969, 000
Paint, pounds of,	3	1, 256, 000
Oil, barrels of,	6	2, 036
Turpentine, gallons of,	1	17, 400
Oil cloth, yards of,	8	735, 700
OIL MILLS.		
Flax seed, bushels of,	23	661, 100
Coal, tons of,	1	215
Oil, gallons of,	20	1, 280, 665
Oil cake, tons of,	13	7, 069¼
PAINT AND COLOR MANUFACTORIES.		
Chemicals, pounds of,	7	6, 901, 026
Oil, gallons of,	1	8, 000
Cases for packing, number of,	1	20, 000
Kegs, number of,	1	6, 000
Paints, pounds of,	7	8, 184, 000
PAINTING AND GLAZING ESTABLISHMENTS.		
White lead, tons of,	13	179¾
Zinc paint, tons of,	2	41
Oil, gallons of,	9	2, 634
Turpentine, barrels of,	3	89
Product of manufactures not specified.		
PAINT MILL MANUFACTORY.		
Materials used not specified.		
Paint mills, number of,	1	600
PAPER STAINING ESTABLISHMENTS.		
Paper, reams of,	1	10, 400
Stained paper, reams of,	1	10, 400
PEARLASH MANUFACTORIES.		
Ashes, bushels of,	1	36, 923
Black salts, tons of,	3	244
Pearlash, tons of,	3	210
PICKLE AND PRESERVE MANUFACTORIES.		
Vinegar, cider and whiskey, barrels of,	1	5, 150
Molasses, hogsheads of,	1	100
Fruit and vegetables, bushels of,	1	10, 300
Bottles, dozens of,	1	10, 000
Pickles, barrels of,	2	4, 600
Vinegar, barrels of,	1	8, 000
Preserves, &c., bottles,	1	1, 000
PYROTECHNIC ESTABLISHMENTS.		
Nitre, pounds of,	1	5, 000
Sulphur, pounds of,	1	2, 000
Powder, kegs of,	1	400
Charcoal, barrels of,	1	60
Paper, reams of,	1	50
Lumber, feet of,	1	10, 000
Fireworks, pieces of,	1	20, 000
ROSIN OIL MANUFACTORIES.		
Rosin, barrels of,	1	11, 200
Coal, tons of,	1	200
Oil, barrels of,	1	7, 500
SALERATUS MANUFACTORIES.		
Pearlash, tons of,	10	1, 697
Soda ash, tons of,	5	5, 565
Ashes, bushels of,	1	1, 500,
Saleratus, tons of,	13	5, 010¼
Soda, tons of,	1	330
SALT MANUFACTORIES.		
Brine, gallons of,	2	159, 229, 760
Wood, cords of,	4	140, 190
Salt, bushels of,	4	6, 676, 301
" bags of,	4	3, 395, 000
SALTPETRE REFINERY.		
Crude saltpetre,	1	600, 000
Refined saltpetre,	1	600, 000
SATINET PRINTING ESTABLISHMENTS.		
Wool, pounds of,	1	230, 000
Cloth, yards of,	1	247, 705
Satinet, yards of,	1	226, 713
SILK PRINTING ESTABLISHMENT.		
Silk, cases of,	1	1, 500
Handkerchiefs, number of,	1	1, 520, 000
STARCH FACTORIES.		
Wheat, bushels of,	5	377, 600
Potatoes, bushels of,	16	171, 602
Wood, cords of,	2	70
Starch, pounds of,	21	6, 897, 096
SUGAR AND SYRUP REFINERIES.		
Sugar, pounds of,	2	205, 243, 000
Molasses, gallons of,	1	770, 000
Refined sugar, pounds of,	1	102, 260, 000
Syrup, gallons of,	2	2, 927, 500
VARNISH MANUFACTORIES.		
Gum, pounds of,	2	31, 301
Turpentine, gallons of,	2	6, 944
Oil, gallons of,	1	295
Varnish, gallons of,	3	286, 065
VINEGAR MANUFACTORIES.		
Cider, barrels of,	4	2, 900
Apples, bushels of,	1	800
Molasses, gallons of,	1	600
Highwines, barrels of,	4	1, 248
Vinegar, barrels of,	7	149, 170
Cider, barrels of,	1	500
WAX BLEACHING ESTABLISHMENT.		
Wax, pounds of,	1	40, 000
White wax, pounds of,	1	40, 000
WHITE LEAD MANUFACTORIES.		
Lead, pounds of,	6	96, 582, 350
Oil, gallons of,	4	65, 085
White lead, pounds of,	6	283, 840, 050
WHITING MANUFACTORIES.		
Chalk, tons of,	2	5, 500
Oil, gallons of,	1	4, 000
Whiting, tons of,	2	11, 500
Putty, tons of,	1	40
WINTERGREEN DISTILLERIES.		
Wintergreen, pounds of,	3	612, 700
Oil, pounds of,	3	3, 633

CLASS V.—CALORIFICS.

MATERIALS AND PRODUCTS.	Towns reported.	Quantities.	MATERIALS AND PRODUCTS.	Towns reported.	Quantities.
GRATE MANUFACTORIES.			LOCOMOTIVE LAMP MANUFACTORY—(Continued.)		
Iron, tons of,	1	222	Copper, pounds of,	1	6,728
Fenders and grates, number of,	1	4,600	Coal, tons of,	1	400
LAMP AND LANTERN MANUFACTORIES.			Lamps,	1	560
Brass, tons of,	2	7	STOVE MANUFACTORIES.		
Copper, pounds of,	2	26,700	Iron, tons of,	13	13,914
Glass, pounds of,	1	300	Coal, tons of,	7	3,875
Glass, boxes of,	1	200	Wood, cords of,	2	325
Lamps,	1	100	Stoves, number of,	9	54,582
Other products not specified.			Stoves, tons of,	2	2,870
LOCOMOTIVE LAMP MANUFACTORY.			Castings, tons of,	6	5,000
Iron, tons of,	1	12¼	Hollow ware, tons of,	1	15

CLASS VI.—STEAM ENGINES, BOILERS, LOCOMOTIVES, ETC.

MATERIALS AND PRODUCTS.	Towns reported.	Quantities.	MATERIALS AND PRODUCTS.	Towns reported.	Quantities.
LOCOMOTIVE MANUFACTORIES.			LOCOMOTIVE SPARK ARRESTOR MANUF'Y—(Con.)		
Iron, tons of,	2	2,763	Spark arrestors,	1	200
Brass, copper, &c., pounds of,	2	1,665	STEAM ENGINE AND BOILER MANUFACTORIES.		
Lumber, feet of,	1	90	Iron, tons of,	6	33,227
Coal, tons of,	1	1,500	Coal, tons of,	4	3,065
Wood, cords of,	1	500	Charcoal, bushels of,	2	43,000
Locomotives,	1	36	Wood, cords of,	3	1,350
Castings, tons of,	1	1,320	Engines, tons of,	2	2,377
LOCOMOTIVE SPARK ARRESTOR MANUFACTORY.			Boilers, number of,	3	314
Iron, tons of,	1	75	Castings, tons of,	2	10,502

CLASS VII.—NAVIGATION AND MARITIME IMPLEMENTS.

MATERIALS AND PRODUCTS.	Towns reported.	Quantities.	MATERIALS AND PRODUCTS.	Towns reported.	Quantities.
BLOCK MANUFACTORIES.			SHIP BUILDING.		
Lignumvitæ, tons of,	2	226	Lumber, feet of,	16	16,938,000
Iron, tons of,	2	164½	Iron, tons of,	12	1,295
Lumber, feet of,	3	225,000	Oakum, tons of,	1	3¾
Blocks, number of,	1	9,000	Pitch, barrels of,	2	66
BOAT BUILDING.			Copper, tons of,	1	3
Lumber, feet of,	23	7,673,000	Ships and vessels, number of,	12	101
Iron, tons of,	9	373½	SHIP RIGGING.		
Spikes, tons of,	6	173½	Rope, tons of,	1	4,500
Oakum, tons of,	3	9½	Rigging, tons of,	1	4,500
Boats, number of,	20	1,113	SHIP SMITHING.		
Scows, number of,	2	12	Iron, tons of,	4	790
OAR MANUFACTORY.			Coal, tons of,	3	1,081
Lumber, feet of,	1	100,000	Manufactured product, tons of,	2	21
Oars, feet of,	1	75,000	SPAR MANUFACTORIES.		
SAIL MAKING.			Lumber, feet of,	2	1,705,000
Canvas, yards of,	4	306,400	Spars, feet of,	1	1,250,000
Rope, pounds of,	3	21,328	TREENAIL FACTORIES.		
Sails, number of,	2	101	Lumber, feet of,	2	27,000
			Treenails, feet of,	2	27,000

CLASS VIII.—ARTS—POLITE, FINE AND ORNAMENTAL.

MATERIALS AND PRODUCTS.	Towns reported.	Quantities.	MATERIALS AND PRODUCTS.	Towns reported.	Quantities.
BAROMETER MANUFACTORIES.			SPECTACLE MANUFACTORY—(Continued.)		
Quicksilver, pounds of,	1	132	Silver, pounds of,	1	35
Barometers, number of,	1	40	Shell, pounds of,	1	25
CLOCK FACTORIES.			Spectacles, pairs of,	1	3,625
Zinc, pounds of,	1	1,500	SURVEYING INSTRUMENT MANUFACTORIES.		
Clocks, number of,	1	15,600	Brass, pounds of,	2	8,300
Town clocks, number of,	1	18	Steel, pounds of,	1	20
NAUTICAL INSTRUMENT MANUFACTORIES.			Telescopes, number of,	1	12
Brass, pounds of,	1	300	Sets of instruments,	1	800
Instruments, number of,	1	120	TELEGRAPH INSTRUMENT MANUFACTORIES.		
OPTICAL INSTRUMENT MANUFACTORIES.			Iron, pounds of,	1	30,000
Brass, pounds of,	1	2,000	Brass, pounds of,	1	3,000
Glass, pounds of,	1	160	Manufactured products not specified.		
Manufactured products not specified.			THERMOMETER MANUFACTORIES.		
SPECTACLE MANUFACTORY.			Materials used not specified.		
Gold, pounds of,	1	9	Thermometers, number of,	1	18,000

CLASS IX.—CIVIL ENGINEERING AND ARCHITECTURE.

MATERIALS AND PRODUCTS.	Towns reported.	Quantities.	MATERIALS AND PRODUCTS.	Towns reported.	Quantities.
GYPSUM QUARRY.			MARL AND PEAT BED.		
Gypsum, tons raised,	1	9,600	Muck, yards raised,	1	265
HOUSE BUILDING.			SASH AND BLIND MANUFACTORIES.		
Lumber, feet of,	9	5,953,000	Lumber, feet of,	116	11,501,000
Shingles, packages of,	1	29,000	Sash, lights of,	50	2,266,142
Manufactured products not specified.			Blinds, pairs of,	37	55,281
IRON MINING.			Doors, number of,	38	97,160
Coal, tons of,	1	125	STAIR BUILDING ESTABLISHMENTS.		
Powder, kegs of,	1	92	Lumber, feet of,	1	38,000
Ore, tons raised,	13	253,914	Stairs, sets of,	1	175
Ore, tons separated,	1	10,000			

CLASS X.—LAND CONVEYANCE.

MATERIALS AND PRODUCTS.	Towns reported.	Quantities.	MATERIALS AND PRODUCTS.	Towns reported.	Quantities.
BOW AND FELLOE MANUFACTORIES.			HOSE CARRIAGE MANUFACTORY.		
Lumber, feet of,	5	535,000	Lumber, feet of,	1	1,000
Bows, number of,	1	5,344	Iron, tons of,	1	3
Felloes, number of,	2	27,200	Hose carriages, number of,	1	40
Thills, pairs of,	1	5,000	Fire engines, number of,	1	10
CAR FACTORIES AND REPAIR SHOPS.			HUB MANUFACTORIES.		
Lumber, feet of,	10	1,472,000	Elm wood, cords of,	1	100
Iron, tons of,	11	4,730½	Hubs, sets of,	1	5,000
Brass, pounds of,	1	3,200	PATENT AXLETREE MANUFACTORIES.		
Coal, tons of,	4	623	Iron, tons of,	2	183
Cars, number of,	7	580	Coal, tons of,	1	1,000
Repairs, &c., not specified.			Axletrees, sets of,	2	17,000
CAR WHEEL FOUNDERIES.			SPOKE MANUFACTORIES.		
Iron, tons of,	1	3,750	Rough spokes, number of,	9	614,000
Coal, tons of,	2	1,500	Hickory wood, cords of,	1	200
Charcoal, bushels of,	1	5,000	Dressed spokes, number of,	10	594,500
Wood, cords of,	2	190	Axehelves, number of,	2	50,300
Moulding sand, tons of,	1	845	WHEELBARROW MANUFACTORIES.		
Car wheels, number of,	2	27,000	Lumber, feet of,	5	658,000
COACH AND WAGON MANUFACTORIES.			Iron, tons of,	3	46
Lumber, feet of,	352	6,569,200	Wheelbarrows, number of,	5	42,120
Iron, tons of,	181	2,370¼	Scrapers, number of,	1	100
Coal, tons of,	75	1,696¾	WHEEL FACTORIES.		
Spokes, number of,	56	1,115,500	Spokes, number of,	1	20,000
Wagons, number of,	287	33,138	Hubs, sets of,	1	400
Sleighs, number of,	132	3,838	Felloes, number of	1	10,000
			Wheels, sets of,	1	162

CLASS XI.—HYDRAULICS AND PNEUMATICS.

MATERIALS AND PRODUCTS.	Towns reported.	Quantities.	MATERIALS AND PRODUCTS.	Towns reported.	Quantities.
BELLOWS MAKING.			PUMP FACTORIES, ETC.		
Lumber, feet of,	2	235,000	Lumber, feet of,	14	334,000
Cowhides, number of,	2	7,045	Paint, pounds of,	2	5,000
Skins, number of,	1	1,800	Oil, barrels of,	1	10
Nails, pounds of,	1	1,000	Chain, tons of,	4	22¾
Bellows, pairs of,	2	5,200	Castings, tons of,	1	1,900
FIRE ENGINE MANUFACTORIES.			Iron, tons of,	1	5
Iron, tons of,	1	6	Lead, tons of,	1	5
Brass, pounds of,	1	5,000	Pumps, number of,	20	6,898
Copper, pounds of,	1	1,000	Chain pumps, tons of,	1	5
Screws, gross of,	1	100	Lead pipe, tons of,	1	5
Lead, pounds of,	1	18,800	Scales, pairs of,	1	200
Mahogany, feet of,	1	1,000	STEAM PUMP MANUFACTORIES.		
Fire engines,	3	49	Iron, tons of,	2	4,125
Hose, feet of,	1	6,000	Copper, tons of,	2	20
			Steam pumps, number of,	1	200

CLASS XII.—LEVER, SCREW, AND OTHER MECHANICAL POWERS.

MATERIALS AND PRODUCTS.	Towns reported.	Quantities.	MATERIALS AND PRODUCTS.	Towns reported.	Quantities.
HOIST WHEEL MANUFACTORY.			JACK SCREW MANUFACTORY.		
Lumber, feet of,	1	50,000	Lumber, feet of,	1	60,000
Iron, tons of,	1	9	Jack screws, number of,	1	440
Hoist wheels, number of,	1	200	SCALE MANUFACTORIES.		
HYDROSTATIC JACK MANUFACTORY.			Lumber, feet of,	1	12,000
Iron, tons of,	1	¾	Iron, tons of,	4	117
Steel, pounds of,	1	400	Brass, pounds of,	1	600
Brass, pounds of,	1	100	Scales, pairs of,	2	2,230
Hydrostatic jacks, number of,	1	1,000			

CLASS XIII.—GRINDING MILLS, MILL GEARING, ETC.

MATERIALS AND PRODUCTS.	Towns reported.	Quantities.	MATERIALS AND PRODUCTS.	Towns reported.	Quantities.
BAND AND BELTING MANUFACTORIES.			MILL STONE MANUFACTORIES.		
Leather, pounds of,	2	13,200	Burr, blocks of,	3	2,700
Bands and belting, feet of,	2	230,000	Plaster paris, barrels of,	1	200
BRAND DUSTER MANUFACTORIES.			Iron, pounds of,	1	3,000
Lumber, feet of,	1	5,000	Mill stones, pairs of,	2	150
Iron, tons of,	1	9½	Mill stones, tons of,	1	1,100
Wire cloth, yards of,	1	200	MILLWRIGHT SHOPS.		
Bristles, pounds of,	1	150	Lumber, feet of,	1	24,000
Bran dusters, number of,	1	75	Mills, number of,	1	12
FARINA MANUFACTORIES.			PEARL BARLEY MILLS.		
Wheat, bushels of,	1	3,000	Barley, bushels of,	2	14,000
Farina, pounds of,	1	60,000	Peas, bushels of,	1	1,000
FEED MILLS.			Pearl barley, pounds of,	2	214,000
Grain, bushels of,	11	319,600	Feed, tons of,	2	186
Feed, bushels of,	7	234,440	SMUT MACHINE MANUFACTORIES.		
GRIST MILLS.			Lumber, feet of,	1	5,000
Grain, bushels of,	507	29,871,296	Iron, tons of,	1	15
Barrels, number of,	11	1,316,473	Smut machines, number of,	3	248
Flour and meal, hundred weight of,	522	14,578,898			

CLASS XIV.—LUMBER, INCLUDING TOOLS AND MACHINES FOR ITS MANUFACTURE.

MATERIALS AND PRODUCTS.	Towns reported	Quantities.
AUGER MANUFACTORIES, ETC.		
Steel, tons of,	3	208
Coal, tons of,	3	271
Augers, number of,	4	78,400
Traps, number of,	1	1,500
BARREL MACHINE MANUFACTORIES.		
Lumber, feet of,	1	3,000
Iron, tons of,	1	100
Castings, tons of,	1	1½
Wood, cords of,	1	150
Coal, tons of,	1	25
Product of manufacture not specified.		
BOX MANUFACTORIES.		
Lumber, feet of,	13	15,094,000
Nails, pounds of,	4	36,000
Boxes, number of,	16	953,400
CARPENTERS' SHOPS.		
Lumber, feet of,	25	4,102,000
Shingles, thousands of,	1	105
Nails, pounds of,	1	5,600
Products of manufacture not specified.		
CARPENTERS' TOOL MANUFACTORIES.		
Lumber, feet of,	5	580,000
Iron, tons of,	3	153¾
Coal, tons of,	1	200
Planes, number of,	3	103,350
Planing irons, number of,	2	157,200
CHEESE BOX MANUFACTORIES.		
Lumber, feet of,	32	2,775,000
Nails pounds of,	3	1,800
Cheese boxes, number of,	41	540,610
Grain measures, sets of,	1	1,000
Hoops, number of,	1	39,000
COOPERS' SHOPS.		
Staves, thousands of,	188	40,591½
Lumber, feet of,	24	870,850
Timber, feet of,	7	146,500
Hoops, number of,	86	22,113,500
Hoop polls, number of,	30	2,246,000
Hoop iron, tons of,	12	222¼
Heading, feet of,	4	1,978,000
Barrels and casks, number of,	166	3,077,626
Kegs, tubs and firkins, number of,	116	524,728
Churns, number of,	6	2,250
Shooks, number of,	1	600
Fish barrels, number of,	2	5,145
Hoops, number, of,	1	9,879,000
HEADING MILLS.		
Heading timber, cords of,	2	85
Headings, thousands of,	3	200,000
HOOP MANUFACTORIES.		
Timber, feet of,	1	15,000
Poles, number of,	1	325,000
Wood, cords of,	1	500
Hoops, number of,	2	2,781,000
Truss hoops, sets of,	1	500
JOINERS' SHOPS.		
Lumber, feet of,	8	449,000
Wood, cords of,	1	25
Sash, lights of,	1	16,000
Blinds, sets of,	1	105
Doors, number of,	2	940
LADDER AND EAVE SPOUT MANUFACTORIES.		
Lumber, feet of,	3	183,000
Ladders, feet of,	2	14,400
Eave spout, feet of,	1	6,600
LATH MANUFACTORIES.		
Lumber, feet of,	6	2,015,000
Slabs, cords of,	7	2,451
Logs, number of,	3	3,200
Lath, thousands feet of,	19	12,596
Lath, number of,	18	13,370
MATCH BOX MANUFACTORY.		
Lumber, pieces of,	1	300,000
Wood, cords of,	1	250
Boxes, gross of,	1	25,694
PATENT MILL DOG MANUFACTORIES.		
Materials used not specified.		
Mill dogs, sets of,	1	27
PATTERN MANUFACTORIES.		
Lumber, feet of,	2	5,000
Stove patterns, number of,	2	50
PLANE MANUFACTORIES.		
Materials used not specified.		
Planes, dozens of,	2	492
PLANING MACHINE MANUFACTORY.		
Iron, tons of,	1	15
Machines, number of,	1	1,250
PLANING MILLS.		
Lumber, thousands feet of,	50	110,264
Coal, tons of,	1	25
Dressed lumber, feet of,	37	104,000,010
RULE MANUFACTORIES.		
Materials used not specified,		
Rules, dozens of,	1	280
SAW MANUFACTORIES.		
Steel, tons of,	9	617½
Lumber, feet of,	1	19,000
Coal, tons of,	3	252
Saws, number of,	3	34,500
Saws, tons of,	1	75
SAW SET MANUFACTORY.		
Materials used not specified.		
Saw sets, number of,	1	14,000
SAW MILLS.		
Logs, number of,	675	10,167,671
Lumber, feet of,	690	1,368,730,000
Lath, feet of,	1	50,000
SHINGLE FACTORIES.		
Logs, number of,	78	117,455
Butts, cords of,	7	2,687
Shingles, thousands of,	127	161,407
SHIP TIMBER MANUFACTORIES.		
Materials used not specified.		
Oak logs, number of,	1	2,570
Square timber, feet of,	1	6,000
STAVE MANUFACTORIES.		
Timber, feet of,	12	4,334
" cords of,	11	6,385
Bolts, cords of,	18	13,198
Staves, thousands of,	50	31,024
Shooks, number of,	2	1,107,500
STEEL SQUARE MANUFACTORIES.		
Steel, tons of,	1	10
Iron, tons of,	1	9
Grindstones, tons of,	1	6
Squares, dozens of,	1	60
TURNING SHOPS.		
Lumber, thousands feet of,	62	5,472
Mahogany, feet of,	1	126,000
Wood, cords of,	1	888
Broom handles, thousands of,	18	3,010
Fork handles, thousands of,	10	466
Hoe handles, thousands of,	3	83
Table legs, sets of,	4	6,118
Hubs, number of,	7	53,500
Bedstead legs, number of,	7	6,577
Table legs, number of,	4	21,118
Bowls, number of,	1	1,000
TRUSS HOOP MANUFACTORY.		
Wood, cords of,	1	15
Iron, tons of,	1	1¼
Hoops, number, of,	1	8,580
VENEERING MANUFACTORIES.		
Mahogany and cedar, feet of,	2	86,694
Rose wood, feet of,	1	1,500
Satin wood, feet of,	1	10,934
Pine, feet of,	1	50,000
Oak, feet of,	1	5,000
Miscellaneous woods, feet of,	1	5,000
Veneering, feet of,	3	672,328
WOOD MOULDING AND CARVING ESTABLISHMENTS.		
Lumber, thousands feet of,	2	1,810
Carved wood, pieces of,	1	4,155,000
WOOD MILLS.		
Logs, number of,	2	440
Wood, cords of,	6	28,863

CLASS XIV.—STONE, CLAY, POTTERY AND GLASS MANUFACTURES.

MATERIALS AND PRODUCTS.	Towns reported	Quantities.
BRICK MANUFACTORIES.		
Clay, yards of,	17	559,829
Sand, yards of,	1	500
Wood, cords of,	43	25,655
Coal, tons of,	12	4,352
Brick, number of,	100	408,052,000
Tile, number of,	1	70,000
BRICK AND TILE MACHINE MANUFACTORIES.		
Lumber, feet of,	1	8,000
BRICK AND TILE MACHINE MANUFAC'S—(Con.)		
Iron, tons of,	1	1½
Screws, gross of,	1	750
Machines, number of,	1	106
Brick moulds, number of,	1	1,150
ENAMELING FURNACES.		
Coal, tons of,	1	420
Wood, cords of,	1	300
Manufactured products not specified.		

CLASS XV.—(Continued.)

MATERIALS AND PRODUCTS.	Towns reported.	Quantities.
FIRE BRICK MANUFACTORIES.		
Clay, tons of,	5	20, 800
Sand, tons of,	2	2, 300
Coal, tons of,	2	810
Fire brick, number of,	3	1, 850, 000
GLASS CUTTING ESTABLISHMENTS.		
Glass, pieces of,	1	8, 928
Cut glass, pieces of,	1	8, 928
GLASS MANUFACTORIES.		
Soda ash, tons of,	7	1, 325
Potash, tons of,	1	263
Wood, cords of,	8	39, 245
Lime, bushels of,	7	9, 857
Salt, bushels of,	7	2, 950
Lumber, feet of,	5	485, 000
Window glass, boxes of,	5	152, 500
Glass ware, pieces of,	1	500, 000
Bottles, gross of,	1	4, 000
GLASS STAINING ESTABLISHMENT.		
Lead, tons of,	1	5, 000
Products of manufacture not specified.		
LIME MANUFACTORIES.		
Limestone, tons of,	30	67, 400
Limestone, cords of,	9	6, 454
Limestone, bushels of,	1	850
Wood, cords of,	41	29, 977
Coal, tons of,	7	3, 371
Lime, bushels of,	69	4, 214, 025
LOOKING GLASS MANUFACTORIES.		
Lumber, feet of,	2	152, 000
Glass, feet of,	1	18, 000
Gold leaf, packs of,	1	300
Looking glasses, number of,	2	206, 000
Gilt frames,	1	10, 000
MARBLE MANUFACTORIES.		
Marble, feet of,	50	483, 310
Italian marble, feet of,	3	14, 800
Freestone, feet of,	1	425
Monumental slabs, &c., feet of,	34	833, 314
Monumental slabs, &c., sets of,	1	150
Miscellaneous marbles, feet of,	1	3, 725
PLASTER MILLS.		
Gypsum, tons of,	102	190, 517
PLASTER MILLS—(Continued.)		
Ground gypsum, tons of,	89	179, 200
Water lime, tons of,	1	4, 000
PORCELAIN MANUFACTORIES.		
Clay, tons of,	1	300
Coal, tons of,	1	200
Manufactured products not specified.		
POTTERIES.		
Potter's clay, tons of,	21	4, 795
Wood, cords of,	15	7, 030
Coal, tons of,	2	500
Stone ware, pieces of,	3	45, 000
Stone ware, tons of,	2	210
Fire brick, number of,	1	120, 000
ROOFING SLATE MANUFACTORIES.		
Materials used not specified.		
Slate, squares of,	1	26, 600
SOAP STONE MANUFACTORIES.		
Soap stone, tons of,	1	200
Manufactured soap stone, tons of,	1	200
STONE CUTTING ESTABLISHMENTS.		
Rough stone, feet of,	12	3, 160, 447
Dressed stone, feet of,	13	1, 593, 290
STONE CUTTERS' TOOL MANUFACTORY.		
Iron and steel, pounds of,	1	5, 000
Tools, pounds of,	1	4, 000
TILE MANUFACTORIES.		
Clay, tons of,	3	3, 396
Clay, cords of,	1	100
Wood, cords of,	5	751
Drain tile, tons of,	2	896
Drain tile, number of,	6	1, 010, 000
TOBACCO PIPE MANUFACTORY.		
Clay, tons of,	1	50
Pipes, boxes of,	1	5, 200
WATER LIME MANUFACTORIES.		
Stone, tons of,	4	111, 528
Stone, cords of,	1	50
Barrels, number of,	1	2, 500
Wood, cords of,	3	3, 300
Coal, tons of,	1	525
Water lime, barrels of,	14	868, 985

CLASS XVI.—LEATHER AND MANUFACTURES THEREFROM.

MATERIALS AND PRODUCTS.	Towns reported.	Quantities.
BARK MILLS.		
Bark, cords of,	2	600
Ground bark, tons of,	1	150
BOOT AND SHOE SHOPS.		
Leather, pounds of,	305	2, 271, 503
Sides, number of,	17	32, 967
Skins, number of,	20	12, 152
Boots and shoes, pairs of,	260	1, 478, 017
HAME TURNING SHOPS.		
Logs, feet of,	2	64, 000
Iron, tons of,	2	7
Hames, pairs of,	4	71, 400
HARNESS, SADDLE AND TRUNK MANUFACTORIES.		
Leather, pounds of,	207	727, 605
Harness, sets of,	156	13, 663
Trunks, number of,	24	37, 807
Saddles, number of,	7	594
HOSE MANUFACTORIES.		
Leather, sides of,	1	12, 500
Brass, pounds of,	1	2, 000
Manufactured products not specified.		
LEATHER-SPLITTING GAUGE MANUFACTORY.		
Iron, tons of,	1	4
Coal, tons of,	1	2
Gauges, number of,	1	1, 500
MOROCCO FACTORIES.		
Skins, number of,	9	4, 627, 786
Sumach, tons of,	3	95
Oil, barrels of,	1	12
Coal, tons of,	2	65
Dressed skins, number of,	......	838, 795
PARCHMENT AND VELLUM MANUFACTORY.		
Sheep skins, number of,	1	2, 000
Calf skins, number of,	1	2, 000
Goat skins, number of,	1	5, 000
Manufactured product not specified.		
PATENT LEATHER MANUFACTORIES.		
Sheep skins, number of,	3	73, 250
Manufactured products not specified.		
POCKET-BOOK AND PORT MONNAIE MANUFACT'S.		
Materials used not specified.		
Port monnaies, gross of,	......	21, 600
RAZOR STROP MANUFACTORY.		
Leather, sides of,	1	4, 000
Paper, reams of,	1	25
Strops, dozen of,	1	3. 300
SADDLE AND COACH HARDWARE MANUFACTORIES		
Iron, tons of,	4	197
Silver, pounds of,	2	278
Coal, tons of,	2	325
Manufactured products not specified.		
SHOE PEG AND LAST MANUFACTORIES.		
Timber, cords of,	2	640
Lumber, feet of,	2	19, 000
Iron, tons of,	1	5½
Lasts, number of,	5	1, 001, 822
Boot trees, sets of,	3	3, 100
Shoe pegs, bushels of,	4	6, 800
Boot crimps,	2	2, 600
TANNERIES.		
Hides, number of,	437	4, 244, 615
Deer skins, number of,	1	3, 000
Lime, bushels of,	3	600
Oil, gallons of,	89	38, 675
Tallow, pounds of,	51	76, 538
Bark, cords of,	261	268, 442
Wood, cords of,	102	122, 848
Hides tanned, number of,	431	4, 077, 035
WHIP MANUFACTORIES.		
Whalebone, pounds of,	2	1, 000
Rattan, pounds of,	1	1, 000
Manufactured products not specified.		

CLASS XVII.—HOUSEHOLD FURNITURE, AND MACHINES AND IMPLEMENTS FOR DOMESTIC PURPOSES.

MATERIALS AND PRODUCTS.	Towns reported.	Quantities.
BASKET FACTORIES		
Wood, cords of,	3	25
Lumber, feet of,	1	150, 000
Willow, pounds of,	2	500
Baskets, number of,	9	43, 949
BEDDING, COT AND MATTRESS MANUFACTORIES.		
Cloth, yards of,	1	100, 000
Feathers, tons of,	1	150
Hair, pounds of,	1	44, 000
Springs, sets of,	1	8, 000
Beds, tons of,	1	150
Cots, number of,	1	1, 500
Mattresses, number of,	1	1, 500
BEDSTEAD MANUFACTORIES.		
Lumber, feet of,	14	3, 647, 655
Varnish, gallons of,	3	2, 600
Glue, pounds of,	1	1, 500
Castings, pounds of,	1	5, 000
Bedsteads, number of,	15	48, 490
BROOM MANUFACTORIES.		
Brush, tons of,	18	1, 669¼
Handles, number of,	8	888, 300
Twine, pounds of,	4	17, 027
Brooms, number of,	23	1, 562, 422
BRUSH MANUFACTORIES.		
Bristles, pounds of,	4	313, 000
Blocks, feet of,	4	1, 848, 000
Brushes, number of,	2	2, 004, 508
CABINET SHOPS.		
Lumber, thousand feet of,	204	23, 208
Chairs, number of,	22	23, 510
Bedsteads, number of,	25	9, 273
Bureaus, number of,	25	4, 208
Tables, number of,	27	3, 649
Miscellaneous, pieces of,	8	23, 314
CEDAR WARE MANUFACTORIES.		
Staves, number of,	1	10, 000
Hoop iron, tons of,	1	6
Tubs, number of,	1	2, 000
Pails, number of,	1	1, 500
Churns, number of,	1	360
CHAIR FACTORIES.		
Lumber, feet of,	28	5, 168
Varnish, barrels of,	2	53
Paint, pounds of,	2	30, 000
Cane, bales of,	1	400
Cane, pounds of,	1	7, 000
Rattan, tons of,	1	25
Chairs, number of,	36	950, 352
Chair seats, number of,	1	50, 000
Cheese boxes, number of,	1	500
Rakes, number of,	1	3, 000
COFFEE MILL MANUFACTORIES.		
Metal, tons of,	1	75
Lumber, feet of,	1	1, 110
Japan, barrels of,	1	6
Coal, tons of,	1	30
Wood, cords of,	1	50
Coffee mills, number of,	1	90, 000
Coffee mill boxes, number of,	1	16. 000
FEATHER BRUSH MANUFACTORY.		
Materials used, not specified.		
Brushes, number of,	1	14, 750
HOUSE-FURNISHING ESTABLISHMENTS.		
Feathers, pounds of,	1	2, 500
Hair, pounds of,	4	62, 000
Hair seating, yards of,	1	1, 000
Corn husks, pounds of,	1	5, 000
Wire springs, pounds of,	1	4, 500
" " dozens of,	1	400
Ticking, yards of,	1	5, 000
Bass wood, cords of,	1	50
Bedding, pounds of,	1	26, 500
Mattrasses pounds of,	1	32, 000
" number of,	2	2, 605
Sofa chairs, number of,	1	300
IRON FURNITURE MANUFACTORY		
Iron, tons of,	1	524
Iron furniture, tons of,	1	520
PAIL MANUFACTORIES.		
Lumber, feet of,	12	2, 087, 000
Hoop iron, tons of,	8	79
Wire, bales of,	1	70
Pails, number of,	15	501, 928
Tubs, number of,	4	29, 650
PAPER-HANGING MANUFACTORIES.		
Paper, tons of,	5	1, 722
Glue, barrels of,	1	5
Paper, rolls of,	4	762, 000
RUG AND MAT MANUFACTORIES.		
Woolen and linen, pounds of,	1	31, 500
Hemp, pounds of,	1	160, 000
Rugs and mats, number of,	2	120, 794
Matting, pieces of,	1	2, 000
SOFA AND LOUNGE MANUFACTORIES.		
Lumber, feet of,	1	75, 000
Iron springs, dozens of,	1	3, 000
Damask, yards of,	1	6, 000
Sofas, number of,	1	1, 000
Chairs, number of,	1	500
WASHING MACHINE MANUFACTORIES.		
Lumber, feet of,	1	9, 000
Machines, number of,	1	112
WILLOW-WARE MANUFACTORIES.		
Willow, tons of,	1	22
Willow-ware, pieces of,	2	18, 500
WINDOW SHADE MANUFACTORIES.		
Muslin, yards of,	1	5, 000
Oil, gallons of,	1	200
Paint, pounds of,	1	460
Window shades, number of,	2	430, 400
WOODEN-WARE MANUFACTORIES.		
Lumber, feet of,	13	1. 636, 000
Hoop iron, pounds of,	1	2, 500
Sieve hoops, number of,	5	30, 900
Boroles, number of,	1	10, 000
Ladles, dozens of,	2	4, 060
Butter stamps, dozens of,	1	820
Boxes, nests of,	1	20, 000
Trays, number of,	2	16, 000

CLASS XVIII.—ARTS—POLITE, FINE AND ORNAMENTAL.

MATERIALS AND PRODUCTS.	Towns reported.	Quantities.
BOOK BINDERIES.		
Paper, reams of,	2	580
Straw board, tons of,	1	4
Books, number of,	5	1, 061, 100
Ink, pounds of,	1	40, 000
BOOK BINDERS' TOOL MANUFACTORY.		
Brass and iron, pounds of,	1	1, 000
Manufactured product, not specified.		
DAGUERREOTYPING ESTABLISHMENTS.		
Plates, number of,	1	5, 500
Cases, number of,	1	5, 000
Pictures, number of,	3	6, 100
DAGUERREOTYPE CASE MANUFACTORIES.		
Iron, tons of,	1	75
Lumber, feet of,	1	25, 000
Turtle shells, number of,	1	500
Cases, gross of,	2	675
Cases, sets of,	1	200
ENGRAVING ESTABLISHMENTS.		
Metal, pounds of,	1	50
Plates, number of,	1	400
ENVELOPE MANUFACTORY.		
Paper, reams of,	1	20, 000
Envelopes, number of,	1	105, 000, 000
GOLD PEN MANUFACTORIES.		
Gold, ounces of,	1	2, 300
Silver, ounces of,	1	12, 160
Gold pens, ounces of,	1	14, 460
MELODEON MANUFACTORIES.		
Lumber, feet of,	2	150, 000
MELODEON MANUFACTORIES.—(Continued.)		
Melodeons, number of.	2	2, 100
MUSICAL INSTRUMENT MANUFACTORIES.		
Lumber, feet of,	1	10, 000
Musical instruments,	2	524
ORGAN BUILDING ESTABLISHMENTS.		
Lumber, feet of,	2	191, 000
Lead, tons of,	1	4
Block tin, pounds of,	1	3, 500
Organs, number of,	3	146
ORGAN PIPE MANUFACTORY.		
Lumber, feet of,	1	1, 000
Tin, pounds of,	1	2, 000
Zinc, pounds of,	1	200
Organ pipes, number of,	1	14
PIANO FORTE MANUFACTORIES.		
Lumber, thousand feet of,	12	2, 562
Veneering, feet of,	4	58, 600
Buck skins, number of,	1	500
Keys, sets of,	1	600
Coal, tons of,	2	225
Pianos, number of,	18	7, 686
Melodeons, number of,	1	3, 000
PIANO TOOL MANUFACTORY.		
Iron, pounds of,	1	260
Steel, pounds of,	1	100
Tools, number of,	1	210
PIANO HARDWARE MANUFACTORIES.		
Iron, tons of,	1	29
Wire, tons of,	1	12

CLASS XVIII.—(CONTINUED.)

MATERIALS AND PRODUCTS	Towns reported	Quantities.	MATERIALS AND PRODUCTS.	Towns reported.	Quantities.
PIANO HARDWARE MANUFACTORIES—(Con.)			PRINTING OFFICES—(Continued.)............		
Brass, tons of,............................	1	1	Books, volumes of,....................	1	174,000
Hardware, sets of,....................	1	500	PRINTING PRESS MANUFACTORIES.		
PIANO STOOL MANUFACTORIES.			Iron, tons of,............................	1	200
Lumber, feet of,..........................	2	54,000	Copper, tons of,..........................	1	10
Stools, number of,....................	1	3,425	Manufactured product not specified.		
PICTURE FRAME MANUFACTORIES.			PRINTERS' ROLLER MANUFACTORY.		
Lumber, feet of,..........................	3	370,000	Glue, barrels of, ...	1	48
Glass, plates of,..........................	1	20,000	Molasses, barrels of,......................	1	17
Varnish, gallons of, ...	1	100	Manufactured product not specified.		
Glue, pounds of,........................	1	4,000	STATUARY MANUFACTORIES.		
Gold leaf, papers of,......................	1	100	Plaster, pounds of,......................	1	300
Frames, number of,..................	1	20,000	Manufactured product not specified.		
PRINTERS' INK MANUFACTORIES.			STEREOTYPING ESTABLISHMENTS.		
Oil, gallons of,..........................	2	48,540	Metal, pounds of,......................	1	101,000
Rosin, barrels of,..........................	2	3,320	Plates, pounds of,..	1	25,000
Ink, gallons of, ...	2	112,500	TYPE FOUNDRIES.		
Kegs, number of,.....................	1	50,000	Lead, tons of,............................	2	345
PRINTING OFFICES.			Antimony, tons of,........................	1	13
Paper, reams of,..........................	11	11,867	Zinc, tons of,............................	1	1
Ink, barrels of,..........................	1	12	Brass, tons of,............................	1	1¼
Coal, tons of,............................	1	27	Coal, tons of,............................	1	52
Papers, copies of,......................	6	853,800	Type, tons of,......................	1	96

CLASS XIX.—FIRE ARMS AND IMPLEMENTS OF WAR, MANUFACTURE OF POWDER AND SHOT.

MATERIALS AND PRODUCTS	Towns reported	Quantities.	MATERIALS AND PRODUCTS.	Towns reported.	Quantities.
GUN SMITHS' SHOPS.			POWDER MILLS.		
Gun barrels, number of,..................	15	777	Saltpetre, pounds of, ...	1	876,045
Iron and steel, tons of, ...	5	196¾	Brimstone, pounds of,......................	3	147,000
Trimmings, sets of,........................	2	95	Charcoal, tons of,.........................	1	10
Stocks, number of,........................	1	30	Wood, cords of,...........................	2	4,200
Brass, tons of,............................	1	7	Powder, pounds of,..................	5	2,320,000
Guns, number of, ...	24	20,295	SHOT FACTORY.		
PERCUSSION CAP MANUFACTORY.			Lead, tons of,............................	1	2,000
Rolled copper, tons of,.....................	1	47½	Shot pounds of,......................	1	4,000,000
Caps, number of,....................	1	220,500,000			

CLASS XX.—SURGICAL, MEDICAL AND DENTAL INSTRUMENTS AND APPARATUS.

MATERIALS AND PRODUCTS	Towns reported	Quantities.	MATERIALS AND PRODUCTS.	Towns reported.	Quantities.
DENTISTS' GOLD MANUFACTORY.			DENTISTRY—(Continued.)		
Gold, value of,............................	1	$10,000	Teeth, sets of, ...	1	60
Manufactured product not specified.			TRUSS AND BANDAGE MANUFACTORIES.		
DENTISTRY.			Steel and brass, pounds of,................	1	4,300
Gold, ounces of,..........................	4	353	Silk, yards of, ...	1	300
Silver, pounds of,........................	1	5	Trusses and bandages, number of, ...	1	6,000

CLASS XXI.—WEARING APPAREL, ARTICLES FOR THE TOILET, ETC.

MATERIALS AND PRODUCTS	Towns reported	Quantities.	MATERIALS AND PRODUCTS.	Towns reported.	Quantities.
BELT AND CLASP MANUFACTORY.			HOSIERY ESTABLISHMENTS—(Continued.)		
Iron, pounds of, ...	1	1,000	Wool, pounds of, ...	5	675,550
Composition metal, pounds of,.............	1	2,000	Lumber, feet of,..........................	1	111,000
Clasps, number of,......................	1	2,500	Coal, tons of,............................	1	1,250
BUTTON AND COMB MANUFACTORIES.			Shirts and drawers, number of,.........	4	253,600
Lumber, feet of,..........................	1	75,000	Hosiery, pieces of,......................	1	1,800
Bone, tons of,............................	2	26	MILLINERS' SHOPS.		
Buttons, gross of,......................	3	231,500	Silk and ribbons, yards of,................	4	3,455
Combs, gross of,......................	1	2,500	Ribbon and braid, yards of,................	3	8,700
Bone dust, pounds of,..................	1	4,500	Silk ribbon, yards of,......................	5	16,421
COMB MANUFACTORIES.			Straw braid, pieces of,.....................	1	50,000
Shell, pounds of,..........................	1	3,100	Bonnets, number of,......................	1	1,000
Combs, dozens of,......................	1	10,708	Bonnets, number of,..................	25	19,026
DRESS MAKING.			Bonnet frames, number of, ...	1	28,800
Cloth, yards of,..........................	1	3,200	SEWING MACHINE MANUFACTORIES.		
Dresses, number of, ...	1	12,250	Iron and steel, tons of,....................	1	204
GENTLEMEN'S FURNISHING GOODS MANUFACTO-			Machines, number of,................	1	10,000
RIES.			SHIRT, BOSOM AND COLLAR MANUFACTORIES.		
Cloth, yards of,..........................	2	58,000	Linen, yards of,..........................	4	457,168
Shirts and drawers, number of,.........	1	92,000	Muslin, yards of,..........................	2	1,148,190
GLOVE AND MITTEN MANUFACTORIES.			Cotton, dozen spools of, ...	1	600
Skins, number of,..........................	9	345,432	Bosoms, collars and wristbands, doz. of,.	4	448,771
Gloves and mittens, pairs of,...........	8	160,707½	Shirts, dozens of, ...	2	25,865
Whip lashes, dozens of,..............	1	20	STOCK MANUFACTORIES.		
HAIR DRESSING AND WIG MANUFACTORIES.			Silk and satin, yards of, ...	1	4,400
Hair, pounds of,..........................	1	100	Stocks, dozens of......................	1	2,200
Wigs, number of,......................	1	150	TAILOR SHOPS.		
HAT AND CAP MANUFACTORIES.			Cloth, yards of,..........................	85	3,421,642
Furs, pounds of, ...	11	10,593	Garments, number of,................	47	731,348
Silk and plush, yards of,..................	17	42,280	UMBRELLA AND PARASOL MANUFACTORIES.		
Wool, pounds of,..........................	6	367,000	Silk and muslin, yards of,................	1	141,700
Hat bodies, number of, ...	1	3,184	Whalebone, pounds of, ...	1	19,610
Hats, number of,......................	27	305,532	Rattan, pounds of, ...	1	12,000
Caps, number of,......................	6	11,620	Sticks, gross of,..........................	1	625
Furs, number of,......................	1	280	Umbrellas, number of,................	1	52,165
HOSIERY ESTABLISHMENTS.			Parasols, number of,...................	1	36,750
Cotton, pounds of, ...	4	601,950			

CLASS XXII.—MISCELLANEOUS MANUFACTURES.

MATERIALS AND PRODUCTS.	Towns reported.	Quantities.
ALTAR ORNAMENT MANUFACTORY		
Brass, pounds of,	1	2,600
Silver, ounces of,	1	2,080
Altar ornaments, number of,	......	2,760
BANDBOX MANUFACTORIES.		
Paper, tons of,	1	25
Bandboxes, number of,	1	21,000
BIRD CAGE MANUFACTORIES.		
Materials used not specified.		
Cages, number of,	1	2,000
BUTCHERS' SHOPS.		
Beeves, number of,	49	36,322
Calves, number of,	27	5,139
Sheep, number of,	36	46,337
Hogs, number of,	24	14,941
Beef, pounds of,	19	14,991,687
Veal, pounds of,	11	106,895
Mutton, pounds of,	14	435,040
Pork, pounds of,	10	123,100
CARPET BAG MANUFACTORY.		
Carpet, &c., yards of,	1	210,000
Iron, tons of,	1	60
Lumber, feet of,	1	25,000
Carpet bags, number of,	1	180,000
CHARCOAL MANUFACTORIES.		
Wood, cords of,	12	54,195
Coal, tons of,	17	3 164,500
CISTERN AND TANK MANUFACTORIES.		
Lumber, feet of,	1	39,000
Iron, tons of,	1	4¼
Cisterns, number of,	1	109
Tanks, number of,	1	76
FANCY TURNING ESTABLISHMENTS.		
Bone, tons of,	2	1,004
Ivory, pounds of,	1	200
Products of manufacture not specified.		
FISHING ROD MANUFACTORIES.		
Lumber, feet of,	1	10,000
Brass, pounds of,	1	30
Rods, feet of,	1	6,800
ICE ESTABLISHMENTS.		
Materials used not specified.		
Ice, tons of,	6	197,415
PAPER BOX MANUFACTORIES.		
Paste board, tons of,	2	248
Paper, reams of,	1	890
Boxes, number of,	3	2,054,065
REFRIGERATOR MANUFACTORIES.		
Iron, tons of,	2	141
Zinc, tons of,	2	20
Lumber, feet of,	1	100,000
Coal, bushels of,	1	800
Refrigerators, number of,	2	5,300
Meat safes, number of,	1	300
SAUSAGE MACHINE MANUFACTORY.		
Materials used not specified.		
Machines, number of,	1	3,000
SODA FOUNTAIN MANUFACTORIES.		
Metal, tons of,	1	100
Tin, boxes of,	1	500
Brass, pounds of,	1	800
Soda fountains, number of,	1	12
Beer pumps, number of,	1	25
TOBACCO AND SEGAR MANUFACTORIES.		
Tobacco, pounds of,	49	10,286,235
Wood, cords of,	1	50
Cigars, number of,	45	27,370,784
Smoking tobacco, pounds of,	20	4,890,640
Snuff, pounds of,	8	193,084
UNDERTAKERS' ESTABLISHMENTS.		
Lumber, feet of,	9	179,000
Coffins, number of,	8	9,891
Boxes, number of,	2	900
UNENUMERATED MANUFACTURES.		
Lumber, feet of,	1	101,000
Products of manufacture not specified.		
WHALEBONE MANUFACTORIES.		
Whalebone, pounds of	2	450,000
Rattan, pounds of,	1	240,000
Whalebone, pounds of,	1	200,000

INDEX TO MANUFACTURES.

INDEX TO MANUFACTURES.—(Continued.)

INDEX TO MANUFACTURES.—(Continued.)

CHURCHES.

TOWNS.	Number of churches.	Value of church and lot.	Value of other real estate.	Number capable of being seated.	Usual number attending.	Number of communicants.	Salary of clergy, including use of real estate.
BAPTIST CHURCHES.							
ALBANY CO.							
Albany,	6	$117, 000	$5, 000	4, 200	1, 945	1, 586	$7800
Bern,	1	200	......	500	150	70	......
Guilderland,	1	1, 600	......	400	......	10	......
Knox,	1	2, 000	......	350	100	83	......
Rensselaerville,	2	4, 000	200	850	450	345	350
Watervliet,	3	13, 500	3, 000	1, 200	400	261	1650
Westerlo,	1	2, 500	......	400	175	202	500
Total,	15	140, 800	8, 200	7, 900	3, 220	2, 557	10300
ALLEGANY CO.							
Allen,	1	......	......	......	80	45	250
Almond,	1	4, 000	......	300	150	90	400
Amity,	1	3, 000	......	400	150	50	500
Andover,	1	1, 500	......	300	140	78	450
Belfast,	1	2, 000	......	300	150	82	300
Bolivar,	1	1, 800	800	225	150	100	475
Burns,	1	400	......	275	40	40	250
Cuba,	1	1, 000	900	300	200	200	500
Friendship,	1	2, 000	1, 200	500	175	80	500
Hume,	1	800	......	300	125	50	300
Independence,	1	1, 500	......	300	100	60	400
Rushford,	1	3, 500	600	500	200	114	500
Scio,	1	3, 000	......	400	200	65	500
West Almond,	1	1, 000	......	400	100	50	250
Total,	14	25, 500	3, 500	4, 500	1, 960	1, 104	5, 575
BROOME CO.							
Chenango,	2	6, 200	800	1, 100	500	457	1, 300
Colesville,	2	2, 700	200	675	200	202	450
Lisle,	2	5, 000	......	710	300	100	400
Sandford,	1	250	......	275	50	29	150
Triangle,	4	5, 850	885	500	370	184	3, 475
Vestal,	1	600	......	200	70	55	240
Total,	12	20, 600	1, 885	3, 460	1, 490	1, 027	6, 015
CATTARAUGUS CO.							
Allegany,	1	......	......	200	70	51	400
Ashford,	1	2, 000	......	500	120	33	100
Connewango,	1	1, 500	......	400	60	40	200
East Otto,	1	500	......	175	50	28	200
Farmersville,	1	1, 800	......	500	150	60	180
Franklinville,	1	2, 600	......	500	125	100	300
Freedom,	2	1, 500	......	550	350	189	700
Hinsdale,	1	2, 000	......	250	125	119	300
Leon,	1	1, 000	......	300	80	30	225
Olean,	1	1, 500	......	200	150	48	400
Perrysburgh,	1	1, 600	......	......	......	......	......
Randolph,	1	2, 000	......	300	......	......	......
Total,	13	18, 000	......	3, 875	1, 280	707	3, 005
CAYUGA CO.							
Auburn,	1	12, 000	......	800	500	360	900
Brutus,	1	4, 500	......	400	200	225	600
Cato,	1	2, 000	......	500	200	130	700
Fleming,	1	2, 000	......	500	75	60	300
Ira,	1	1, 600	......	300	75	40	450
Locke,	1	2, 500	......	400	100	80	340
Mentz,	3	8, 000	1, 500	1, 250	510	525	1, 050
Niles,	1	1, 500	......	600	......	......	......
Owasco,	1	600	600	300	50	60	450
Scipio,	1	4, 000	1, 000	400	150	100	540
Sempronius,	1	1, 600	......	400	150	74	250
Sennett,	1	5, 000	700	600	150	150	600
Springport,	1	2, 000	......	300	100	60	300
Sterling,	1	2, 500	......	400	200	90	350
Summer Hill,	1	1, 600	......	300	75	80	300
Venice,	1	3, 000	......	320	80	76	225
Victory,	1	1, 700	......	600	70	110	300
Total,	19	56, 100	3, 800	8, 370	2, 685	2, 220	7, 655
CHAUTAUQUE CO.							
Busti,	1	3, 300	400	500	125	150	450
Carroll,	1	1, 500	1, 000	350	200	100	300
Charlotte,	1	1, 400	600	300	100	60	350
Chautauque,	2	3, 200	......	700	150	208	1, 005
Cherry Creek,	2	3, 500	......	225	200	200	......
Clymer,	1	1, 000	350	500	75	70	200
llery,	1	600	400	300	70	30	300
Ellicott,	1	1, 200	800	285	285	200	500
CHAUTAUQUE CO.							
Ellington,	1	$800	......	300	125	70	$250
Hanover,	3	3, 400	$500	950	300	167	950
Harmony,	3	5, 350	300	1, 200	325	385	1, 270
Pomfret,	3	23, 500	......	1, 850	725	300	1, 325
Portland,	2	3, 600	1, 150	750	150	110	525
Sheridan,	1	800	......	300	150	52	300
Sherman,	1	2, 000	......	300	150	70	330
Stockton,	3	3, 000	......	1, 150	450	200	675
Westfield,	1	450	......	500	200	80	500
Total,	28	58, 600	6, 000	10, 730	3, 780	2, 452	9, 230
CHEMUNG CO.							
Big Flats,	1	2, 000	1, 200	300	70	40	400
Chemung,	1	800	......	200	100	45	450
Elmira,	1	14, 000	......	700	450	344	1, 300
Horseheads,	2	3, 600	......	500	200	30	275
Southport,	2	4, 000	400	3, 300	240	120	850
Van Etten,	1	1, 600	......	400	150	60	100
Total,	8	26, 000	1, 600	5, 400	1, 210	639	3, 375
CHENANGO CO.							
Bainbridge,	3	3, 500	......	950	500	227	700
Columbus,	1	1, 000	......	300	40	19	80
Coventry,	1	2, 000	......	300	100	120	300
Greene,	5	10, 900	......	1, 900	800	517	1, 700
Guilford,	2	2, 000	600	700	175	90	450
Lincklaen,	1	500	......	250	50	45	200
Macdonough,	1	1, 500	100	400	100	110	300
New Berlin,	2	2, 800	800	900	450	200	828
North Norwich,	1	1, 500	......	250	70	56	200
Norwich,	1	1, 000	......	1, 000	400	400	900
Otselic,	1	1, 300	......	400	90	30	150
Oxford,	1	2, 000	......	500	200	200	450
Pitcher,	1	2, 000	600	320	180	135	475
Plymouth,	1	1, 600	......	200	100	121	400
Preston,	1	600	......	300	150	64	150
Sherburne,	2	7, 500	......	800	300	208	900
Smithville,	1	1, 500	......	250	100	45	225
Smyrna,	1	2, 400	450	300	150	80	400
Total,	27	45, 600	2, 550	10, 020	3, 955	2, 667	8, 808
CLINTON CO.							
Chazy,	1	100	......	200	60	23	400
Plattsburgh,	1	1, 500	......	400	300	150	450
Total,	2	1, 600	......	600	360	173	850
COLUMBIA CO.							
Canaan,	2	3, 000	400	400	125	105	500
Chatham,	2	2, 800	......	400	250	25	300
Claverack,	1	3, 000	1, 800	330	125	125	500
Hillsdale,	1	3, 000	100	300	120	95	300
Hudson,	1	1, 000	500	500	300	214	600
Kinderhook,	1	2, 000	......	600	......	......	......
New Lebanon,	1	2, 000	......	500	150	50	470
Total,	9	16, 800	2, 800	3, 030	1, 070	614	2, 670
CORTLAND CO.							
Cincinnatus,	1	1, 200	700	500	80	40	220
Cortlandville,	2	6, 200	......	1, 100	600	484	615
Freetown,	1	500	450	200	100	35	275
Homer,	1	6, 000	400	700	500	383	700
Marathon,	1	1, 000	......	500	100	30	......
Solon,	1	1, 000	......	600	100	90	200
Taylor,	1	400	......	150	75	48	150
Truxton,	1	5, 000	800	600	500	290	500
Virgil,	1	2, 500	......	360	75	62	300
Willet,	1	1, 500	......	300	100	35	100
Total,	11	25, 300	2, 350	5, 010	2, 230	1, 497	3, 060
DELAWARE CO.							
Andes,	1	......	......	......	200	......	......
Delhi,	1	2, 500	......	300	......	66	......
Franklin,	2	6, 500	2, 200	650	416	365	900
Hancock,	1	1, 000	......	225	60	29	125
Harpersfield,	1	400	......	350	80	50	200
Masonville,	1	1, 500	150	250	100	90	250
Meredith,	2	2, 500	800	650	300	197	950
Sidney,	1	1, 000	......	250	150	40	60
Tompkins,	3	4, 300	1, 700	750	400	750	550
Total,	13	19, 700	5, 150	3, 425	1, 706	1, 590	3, 035

CHURCHES—(Continued.)

TOWNS.	Number of churches.	Value of church and lot.	Value of other real estate.	Number capable of being seated.	Usual number attending.	Number of communicants.	Salary of clergy, including use of real estate.
Dutchess Co.							
Amenia,	1	4,500	$2,100	280	175	120	$730
Beekman,	1	2,000	750	500	200	91	280
Dover,	2	8,500	......	900	325	147	1,000
East Fishkill,	3	2,650	250	650	215	149	535
Fishkill,	2	13,200	......	900	375	205	1,200
Hyde Park,	1	2,500	......	230	60	25	400
North East,	1	6,000	3,000	500	250	130	700
Pawling,	2	3,700	......	750	150	115	295
Pine Plains,	1	2,000	1,000	350	75	40	600
Pleasant Valley,	1	2,500	1,500	600	175	35	250
Poughkeepsie,	2	27,000	3,000	1,400	650	340	2,100
Red Hook,	1	1,200	......	300	125	34	300
Rhinebeck,	1	2,500	500	200	50	45	300
Stanford,	1	2,500	1,500	500	100	75	100
Total,	20	80,750	13,600	8,060	2,925	1,551	8,790
Erie Co.							
Alden,	1	2,200	......	300	100	74	400
Amherst,	1	5,000	......	600	200	130	475
Aurora,	1	1,800	......	400	250	125	400
Boston,	1	2,000	......	600	100	77	400
Buffalo,	5	54,500	200	2,350	980	553	3,850
Clarence,	1	1,800	......	150	100	120	250
Concord,	1	3,000	......	400	200	182	600
Eden,	1	1,500	300	250	150	85	400
Evans,	1	2,300	700	300	100	133	400
Hamburgh,	1	1,600	......	400	200	100	400
Holland,	1	1,400	......	350	100	51	......
Newstead,	1	3,500	......	350	100	133	400
North Collins,	2	1,800	......	600	150	76	600
Sardinia,	1	1,600	750	500	200	200	500
Wales,	1	1,400	......	500	250	40	400
Total,	20	85,400	1,950	8,050	3,180	2,079	9,475
Essex Co.							
Elizabethtown,	1	2,500	500	350	100	80	450
Essex,	2	3,000	......	500	105	162	......
Jay,	1	2,000	400	300	200	170	400
Minerva,	1	800	......	200	60	70	100
Moriah,	1	2,000	500	450	80	130	310
Schroon,	1	2,000	......	300	60	10	......
Ticonderoga,	1	1,600	......	350	130	75	400
Westport,	1	3,000	......	700	400	100	600
Total,	9	16,900	1,400	3,150	1,135	797	2,260
Franklin Co.							
Burke,	1	1,200	......	300	150	68	300
Chateaugay,	1	200	......	150	......	20	......
Fort Covington,	1	3,000	......	400	250	108	400
Malone,	1	4,000	......	340	300	150	500
Total,	4	8,400	......	1,190	700	346	1,200
Fulton Co.							
Broadalbin,	1	3,000	......	600	300	282	400
Ephratah,	1	1,000	......	500	200	216	350
Johnstown,	1	3,000	......	300	250	170	400
Northampton,	1	1,200	750	300	250	125	550
Total,	4	8,200	750	1,700	1,000	793	1,700
Genesee Co.							
Alabama,	2	6,000	......	600	350	114	850
Batavia,	1	2,500	......	300	200	......	600
Bethany,	1	4,500	......	400	100	25	350
Darien,	1	1,500	500	200	100	40	400
Elba,	1	2,800	......	250	100	95	320
Le Roy,	1	3,000	2,000	400	350	150	800
Pavilion,	1	3,000	......	300	100	150	400
Pembroke,	2	2,200	......	600	250	80	550
Stafford,	1	300	......	300	25	......	......
Total,	11	25,800	2,500	3,350	1,575	654	4,270
Greene Co.							
Athens,	1	2,500	......	300	200	72	400
Cairo,	1	1,500	......	350	......	34	......
Catskill,	1	5,000	......	450	200	158	550
Durham,	1	600	......	200	55	70	100
Greenville,	2	2,150	......	430	270	55	450
Lexington,	1	2,500	......	400	100	75	300
New Baltimore,	1	250	......	200	100	50	200
Total,	8	14,500	......	2,280	925	514	2,000
Hamilton Co.							
Wells,	1	350	......	160	......	......	......
Herkimer Co.							
Frankfort,	1	1,000	200	300	80	40	500
German Flats,	1	1,450	......	200	80	50	200
Litchfield,	1	1,400	300	300	100	55	300
Herkimer Co.							
Little Falls,	1	$5,000	......	500	250	75	$500
Newport,	1	3,000	......	400	250	100	500
Norway,	1	800	$200	450	100	77	300
Salisbury,	1	2,000	500	600	175	94	450
Warren,	1	1,200	......	250	150	50	800
Winfield,	1	2,000	1,000	400	100	80	400
Total,	9	17,850	2,200	3,400	1,285	621	3,950
Jefferson Co.							
Adams,	3	12,000	100	1,450	865	580	1,700
Alexandria,	1	......	......	150	150	35	100
Antwerp,	2	2,000	......	600	150	40	400
Brownville,	1	1,500	50	500	80	......	......
Champion,	1	1,000	......	400	150	89	500
Clayton,	1	2,500	......	350	100	60	500
Ellisburgh,	3	7,500	1,300	1,700	650	556	1,520
Le Ray,	1	1,500	......	400	150	45	350
Lorraine,	1	2,000	......	300	150	69	300
Lyme,	1	1,500	500	300	150	180	450
Orleans,	1	3,000	......	400	150	170	300
Philadelphia,	1	......	......	......	......	36	250
Watertown,	1	10,000	......	700	400	130	800
Wilna,	1	3,500	......	450	75	73	500
Total,	19	48,000	1,950	7,700	3,220	2,063	7,670
Kings Co.							
Brooklyn,	11	255,000	5,000	7,025	4,825	2,278	12,956
Lewis Co.							
Denmark,	1	1,500	......	400	......	......	......
Harrisburgh,	1	600	......	250	100	75	250
Lewis,	1	300	......	175	60	60	200
Leyden,	1	500	......	500	150	111	450
Lowville,	2	5,500	1,500	800	400	183	950
Martinsburgh,	1	1,000	......	......	......	......	......
New Bremen,	1	300	......	200	70	50	......
Total,	8	9,700	1,500	2,325	780	479	1,850
Livingston Co.							
Avon,	1	3,000	1,500	500	150	60	500
Leicester,	1	2,800	50	400	......	80	......
Lima,	1	10,000	2,400	500	300	45	650
Livonia,	3	3,600	800	1,200	350	160	650
Mount Morris,	1	2,500	......	250	200	100	700
North Dansville,	1	4,000	......	300	150	82	500
Nunda,	1	8,000	......	800	300	300	600
Portage,	1	1,000	500	250	100	60	400
Sparta,	1	1,000	......	250	50	30	200
West Sparta,	1	250	300	......	15	......	......
York,	1	4,500	......	500	150	116	500
Total,	13	40,650	5,550	4,950	1,765	1,033	4,700
Madison Co.							
Brookfield,	1	2,200	1,700	330	250	142	400
Cazenovia,	2	9,000	3,000	1,350	500	480	1,200
De Ruyter,	1	1,600	......	200	100	80	......
Eaton,	3	6,000	......	1,300	400	226	1,250
Fenner,	1	1,800	......	350	120	80	400
Georgetown,	1	2,000	......	500	200	112	400
Hamilton,	2	10,500	2,100	1,400	800	400	1,050
Lebanon,	1	1,000	......	375	200	106	300
Lenox,	2	4,000	400	700	275	200	900
Madison,	1	2,500	800	400	150	118	450
Nelson,	1	1,500	......	1,500	100	74	200
Smithfield,	1	1,000	......	500	200	30	500
Stockbridge,	1	1,500	......	300	75	30	......
Sullivan,	3	4,700	......	912	275	126	800
Total,	21	49,300	8,000	10,417	3,645	2,201	7,850
Monroe Co.							
Chili,	2	5,000	......	700	220	233	1,050
Greece,	1	3,000	......	350	250	170	1,650
Henrietta,	2	6,350	2,200	450	160	97	650
Mendon,	1	2,500	......	500	200	110	650
Ogden,	1	4,000	1,000	375	175	140	400
Parma,	2	4,000	500	700	400	260	970
Penfield,	1	4,000	......	400	250	290	600
Perrington,	1	3,000	......	350	200	75	500
Pitsford,	1	3,000	......	400	200	60	400
Riga,	1	3,000	......	400	175	40	400
Rochester,	5	61,000	1,200	2,850	1,550	1,049	3,600
Rush,	1	2,800	......	300	50	45	200
Sweden,	3	9,800	500	1,350	625	311	1,450
Webster,	1	1,000	......	500	250	200	400
Wheatland,	2	6,500	1,200	660	275	165	1,450
Total,	25	118,950	6,600	10,285	4,980	3,245	14,370

CHURCHES—(Continued.)

Towns.	Number of churches.	Value of church and lot.	Value of other real estate.	Number capable of being seated.	Usual number attending.	Number of communicants.	Salary of clergy, including use of real estate.
Montgomery Co.							
Amsterdam,	1	$8,000	......	100	200	198	$500
Charleston,	1	1,500	......	800	300	120	300
Total,	2	9,500	......	900	500	318	800
New-York Co.							
New-York,	26	631,800	$29000	25,900	12,140	7,116	34470
Niagara Co.							
Hartland,	1	3,000	......	500	275	229	500
Lockport,	1	5,000	......	800	200	93	800
Newfane,	1	4,000	......	400	375	260	600
Niagara,	1	4,000	......	225	150	22	600
Porter,	1	2,500	800	350	200	59	350
Royalton,	1	1,000	......	300	250	51	300
Somerset,	2	4,200	1,200	760	350	214	825
Wheatfield,	1	800	......	250	75	15	......
Wilson,	1	3,000	1,000	400	250	159	475
Total,	10	27,500	3,000	3,985	2,125	1,102	4,450
Oneida Co.							
Annsville,	1	300	......	225	200	75	300
Augusta,	1	800	......	400	......	......	......
Boonville,	1	1,500	......	350	75	60	......
Bridgewater,	1	500	......	300	......	25	......
Deerfield,	1	500	......	300	50	......	......
Florence,	1	2,000	......	800	......	......	......
Kirkland,	1	2,000	......	300	100	76	350
Marcy,	2	4,200	......	500	100	130	275
New Hartford,	1	1,000	......	150	75	19	250
Paris,	1	3,500	500	400	300	240	600
Remsen,	2	1,250	......	425	125	140	125
Rome,	2	11,000	......	1,200	450	391	1,650
Sangerfield,	1	3,000	......	400	150	90	300
Steuben,	2	800	700	600	90	52	175
Trenton,	3	5,500	......	800	350	166	750
Utica,	4	26,200	100	2,000	1,000	635	2,324
Vernon,	1	3,500	......	400	120	90	450
Verona,	1	3,000	......	300	150	70	500
Vienna,	1	800	......	300	125	48	250
Westmoreland,	1	1,000	800	350	70	90	400
Whitestown,	2	5,000	1,400	750	440	260	1,000
Total,	31	77,300	3,500	11,250	3,970	2,657	9,699
Onondaga Co.							
Camillus,	1	3,500	......	300	100	65	600
Clay,	1	1,300	100	300	40	48	300
Elbridge,	2	6,000	1,800	750	425	443	1,300
Fabius,	1	3,000	100	600	300	175	450
Lysander,	1	1,500	......	700	75	44	......
Manlius,	2	4,500	......	950	400	370	1,100
Marcellus,	1	1,700	100	230	150	125	400
Onondaga,	1	1,000	......	200	50	56	225
Pompey,	2	1,900	1,000	900	150	70	300
Skaneateles,	1	3,500	......	600	120	120	500
Spafford,	1	1,000	......	400	......	60	......
Syracuse,	1	2,800	......	1,000	400	200	1,200
Tully,	2	4,500	......	600	150	125	360
Van Buren,	2	4,000	100	850	600	171	850
Total,	19	40,200	3,100	8,380	2,960	2,072	7,585
Ontario Co.							
Bristol,	1	4,000	500	600	250	70	550
Canandaigua,	2	7,000	......	1,400	325	185	700
Gorham,	2	5,500	1,550	850	225	35	870
Manchester,	2	5,800	450	750	325	168	1,000
Naples,	1	4,500	......	400	150	100	400
Phelps,	4	8,850	300	1,340	450	225	1,225
Seneca,	1	1,000	......	300	175	90	500
Total,	13	36,650	2,800	5,640	1,900	873	5,245
Orange Co.							
Cornwall,	1	500	......	150	75	35	200
Deerpark,	1	1,500	......	300	150	84	600
Greenville,	1	1,000	......	400	250	52	125
Minisink,	1	3,000	......	375	250	121	500
Newburgh,	1	7,000	......	450	250	167	700
Walkill,	1	3,000	......	400	200	50	500
Total,	6	16,000	......	2,075	1,175	509	2,625
Orleans Co.							
Barre,	1	7,800	2,000	450	350	340	1,000
Carlton,	2	2,500	390	75	84	84	250
Kendall,	1	1,400	......	225	100	50	400
Murray,	2	5,000	800	075	250	174	950
Ridgeway,	1	2,000	......	350	100	100	570
Shelby,	1	500	......	250	150	76	400
Yates,	1	$1,500	$1,800	400	200	180	$500
Total,	9	21,600	4,900	2,125	1,234	1,004	4,070
Oswego Co.							
Albion,	1	1,000	25	200	50	40	200
Amboy,	1	1,000	......	220	75	28	......
Hannibal,	2	2,000	40	450	210	149	775
Hastings,	1	2,000	......	300	175	90	400
Mexico,	2	4,200	......	800	300	165	850
Oswego city,	3	9,500	......	1,400	950	390	2,100
Palermo,	2	1,950	......	450	210	105	250
Richland,	3	4,100	1,300	1,350	450	230	1,150
Sandy Creek,	1	1,500	......	300	100	125	300
Schroeppel,	1	800	......	200	60	46	150
Scriba,	1	......	......	......	......	30	100
Volney,	1	4,000	1,000	400	150	145	700
Total,	19	32,050	1,365	6,070	2,730	1,543	6,975
Otsego Co.							
Burlington,	3	5,100	300	950	350	150	800
Butternuts,	1	2,000	......	500	225	200	400
Decatur,	1	800	......	200	100	26	300
Edmeston,	2	2,600	......	550	200	175	325
Exeter,	1	1,200	......	300	75	52	200
Hartwick,	1	2,700	......	300	150	119	400
Laurens,	1	1,500	......	250	200	134	400
Maryland,	1	1,500	600	500	150	126	530
Middlefield,	2	4,500	700	1,400	400	185	775
Milford,	1	1,500	......	400	200	108	400
Morris,	1	1,200	......	200	100	100	250
New Lisbon,	1	800	......	600	100	110	300
Oneonta,	1	2,000	......	500	180	182	500
Otego,	1	2,500	176	400	70	61	400
Otsego,	1	8,000	......	500	100	88	500
Plainfield,	1	1,600	......	600	90	60	300
Roseboom,	1	1,000	......	500	50	40	......
Springfield,	1	3,000	......	350	200	92	600
Unadilla,	2	3,200	1,000	550	400	151	645
Westford,	2	2,600	......	1,000	1,000	280	725
Worcester,	2	1,300	200	700	200	160	650
Total,	28	50,600	2,976	11,250	4,540	2,599	9,400
Putnam Co.							
Carmel,	2	8,000	500	1,100	500	562	1,100
Kent,	2	5,500	......	800	320	370	370
Patterson,	1	1,200	......	400	200	140	450
Philipstown,	1	3,000	1,000	250	175	105	600
Putnam Valley,	1	1,500	......	400	50	45	......
Total,	7	19,200	1,500	2,950	1,245	1,222	2,520
Queens Co.							
Newtown,	1	12,000	......	200	......	......	......
Oyster Bay,	1	1,000	......	300	50	25	......
Total,	2	13,000	......	500	50	25	......
Rensselaer Co.							
Berlin,	1	3,300	500	550	175	185	400
Grafton,	1	1,600	......	300	100	122	300
Hoosick,	1	1,500	800	650	100	70	450
Lansingburgh,	1	11,000	......	800	350	288	800
Nassau,	1	800	......	350	100	40	350
Pittstown,	1	1,800	......	350	70	60	200
Poestenkill,	1	1,700	......	300	200	45	200
Sand Lake,	1	2,000	1,000	300	100	72	500
Schodack,	1	2,000	......	400	100	50	350
Stephentown,	1	2,000	......	400	150	146	150
Troy,	2	46,000	......	1,800	1,100	950	3,000
Total,	12	73,700	2,300	6,200	2,545	2,028	6,700
Richmond Co.							
Castleton,	1	1,000	......	350	150	40	......
Northfield,	3	9,500	2,000	950	470	310	600
Westfield,	1	1,500	......	400	260	30	400
Total,	5	12,000	2,000	1,700	880	380	1,000
Rockland Co.							
Orangetown,	2	3,000	400	200	125	76	950
Ramapo,	1	1,600	......	250	75	22	400
Total,	3	4,600	400	450	200	98	1,350
St. Lawrence Co.							
Canton,	1	1,000	......	300	200	140	400
De Kalb,	1	3,000	500	350	150	100	450
Edwards,	1	1,400	......	600	250	30	200

CHURCHES.—(Continued.)

TOWNS.	Number of churches.	Value of church and lot.	Value of other real estate.	Number capable of being seated.	Usual number attending.	Number of communicants.	Salary of clergy, including use of real estate.
St. Lawrence Co.							
Fowler,	1	$200	.....	200	100	21	.....
Gouverneur,	1	4,500	$1,200	500	200	208	$500
Hermon,	1	1,200	.....	300	250	80	300
Lawrence,	2	2,900	.....	500	200	115	500
Madrid,	1	1,000	700	400	75	112	500
Massena,	1	300	.....	300	50	50	300
Oswegatchie,	1	5,000	.....	700	200	170	600
Parishville,	1	350	.....	.....	200	160	400
Russell,	1	900	100	300	100	46	300
Stockholm,	1	500	400	200	60	56	250
Total,	14	22,250	2,900	4,650	2,035	1,188	4,700
Saratoga Co.							
Ballston,	1	2,000	1,000	300	175	125	$350
Clifton Park,	1	3,000	900	400	200	185	400
Corinth,	1	800	.....	600	100	25	100
Galway,	2	4,500	100	650	230	218	920
Greenfield,	3	3,200	300	1,000	275	105	625
Halfmoon,	1	1,400	.....	300	120	75	300
Milton,	2	9,500	600	1,400	600	349	1,000
Moreau,	1	700	.....	800	50	50	300
Providence,	1	1,200	.....	300	185	85	300
Saratoga,	1	2,000	1,000	400	200	125	450
Saratoga Springs,	1	8,000	2,000	500	400	300	1,000
Stillwater,	2	4,500	500	650	215	240	1,150
Waterford,	1	4,000	.....	350	100	70	500
Wilton,	1	1,600	.....	225	75	73	235
Total,	19	46,400	6,400	7,875	2,925	2,025	7,630
Schenectady Co.							
Duanesburgh,	1	1,050	.....	400	250	162	300
Glenville,	1	1,000	.....	550	225	95	450
Schenectady,	1	10,000	.....	500	300	173	500
Total,	3	12,050	.....	1,450	775	428	1,250
Schoharie Co.							
Broome,	1	600	.....	200	80	40	.....
Carlisle,	1	200	.....	300	150	200	300
Esperance,	2	2,200	.....	600	330	210	570
Gilboa,	3	700	.....	700	100	122	40
Jefferson,	2	1,200	150	800	300	83	150
Richmondville,	1	1,500	.....	400	150	62	300
Seward,	1	300	.....	450	100	27	585
Sharon,	1	1,200	400	250	160	111	330
Summit,	2	1,600	.....	900	300	129	380
Total,	14	9,500	550	4,600	1,670	984	2,655
Schuyler Co.							
Dix,	3	5,400	150	600	475	211	944
Hector,	3	6,100	1,650	1,100	450	359	1,225
Orange,	2	2,200	.....	500	175	175	550
Reading,	1	800	.....	200	75	35	300
Tyrone,	3	5,700	700	1,075	725	465	1,350
Total,	12	20,200	2,500	3,475	1,900	1,245	4,369
Seneca Co.							
Covert,	2	6,800	1,800	800	325	307	900
Lodi,	1	1,200	1,000	250	150	114	400
Ovid,	1	1,050	600	500	300	110	575
Romulus,	1	3,500	1,900	400	275	185	600
Seneca Falls,	1	3,000	.....	450	300	110	500
Tyre,	1	2,500	700	1,000	140	80	300
Varick,	1	1,200	.....	400	200	36	.....
Total,	8	19,250	6,000	3,800	1,690	942	3,275
Steuben Co.							
Addison,	1	1,000	.....	300	100	60	400
Avoca,	1	2,000	.....	250	150	86	380
Bath,	2	3,700	.....	1,000	400	211	700
Bradford,	1	2,000	50	400	200	107	225
Canton,	1	2,000	.....	350	175	65	350
Corning,	1	3,000	.....	350	250	200	700
Dansville,	2	1,000	.....	1,000	160	42	200
Erwin,	2	1,200	100	300	225	174	650
Hornby,	1	1,400	.....	500	200	130	400
Hornellsville,	1	800	.....	.....	100	35	400
Howard,	2	2,000	.....	620	400	147	800
Jasper,	1	500	.....	400	150	40	500
Prattsburgh,	2	3,600	.....	550	350	192	2,688
Pultney,	2	700	.....	500	400	121	370
Troupsburgh,	2	.....	.....	.....	175	65	375
Urbana,	2	2,600	500	550	400	310	400
Woodhull,	2	2,133	205	300	50	71	.....
Total,	26	29,633	855	7,370	3,885	2,056	9,538

TOWNS.	Number of churches.	Value of church and lot.	Value of other real estate.	Number capable of being seated.	Usual number attending.	Number of communicants.	Salary of clergy, including use of real estate.
Suffolk Co.							
Brookhaven,	1	$1,400	.....	200	80	57	$550
Huntington,	1	1,200	.....	250	150	60	300
Southampton,	1	4,000	.....	500	100	40	500
Southold,	2	5,000	.....	750	500	201	600
Total,	5	11,600	.....	1,700	830	358	1,950
Sullivan Co.							
Liberty,	1	1,500	.....	270	400	160	400
Tusten,	1	500	400	300	60	30	300
Total,	2	2,000	400	570	460	190	700
Tioga Co.							
Barton,	2	3,300	.....	650	230	170	800
Berkshire,	1	1,000	.....	150	100	50	300
Candor,	5	3,700	2,500	1,600	260	304	900
Owego,	1	6,000	2,500	800	450	444	700
Spencer,	1	2,400	1,500	600	200	200	600
Total,	10	16,400	6,500	3,800	1,240	1,168	3,300
Tompkins Co.							
Caroline,	1	200	.....	300	100	68	300
Danby,	2	2,100	.....	1,300	90	80	400
Dryden,	1	1,800	.....	1,000	100	25	.....
Enfield,	1	1,200	.....	500	.....	30	.....
Groton,	2	4,500	.....	700	275	232	550
Ithaca,	1	12,000	.....	500	250	700	700
Lansing,	2	6,000	1,400	700	225	139	700
Newfield,	1	1,000	.....	400	50	82	300
Ulysses,	1	8,000	1,000	600	400	365	800
Total,	12	36,800	2,400	6,000	1,490	1,721	3,750
Ulster Co.							
Kingston,	2	5,000	200	475	290	230	1,100
Marlborough,	1	1,000	.....	400	30	64	250
Olive,	1	600	3,000	300	200	90	500
Rosendale,	1	1,500	.....	250	100	80	300
Saugerties,	1	2,000	.....	300	150	100	500
Wawarsing,	1	1,500	100	225	40	80	.....
Woodstock,	1	500	.....	200	60	38	200
Total,	8	12,100	3,300	2,150	870	682	2,850
Warren Co.							
Chester,	1	1,500	.....	300	200	125	300
Horicon,*	1	.....	.....	140	40	70	150
Johnsburgh,	1	400	.....	150	50	96	250
Luzerne,	1	300	.....	250	.....	.....	.....
Queensbury,	1	4,000	.....	400	300	240	350
Thurman,	1	100	.....	200	100	70	.....
Total,	6	6,300	.....	1,440	690	601	1,050
Washington Co.							
Fort Ann,	2	3,500	300	750	250	271	700
Fort Edward,	2	5,500	.....	750	600	276	600
Granville,	1	3,000	.....	500	200	183	500
Greenwich,	3	8,300	2,300	1,250	800	846	1,350
Hampton,	1	500	.....	500	.....	.....	.....
Hartford,	1	5,000	.....	800	300	380	600
Hebron,	1	2,000	350	250	100	120	400
Kingsbury,	3	7,500	1,200	1,450	450	416	1,285
Salem,	1	1,100	1,200	300	120	121	370
White Creek,	2	3,500	.....	750	250	133	400
Whitehall,	1	5,000	.....	500	125	100	600
Total,	18	44,900	5,350	7,800	3,195	2,846	6,805
Wayne Co.							
Arcadia,	1	5,000	800	300	150	48	600
Butler,	1	2,000	.....	300	150	100	400
Galen,	1	3,000	.....	400	200	190	600
Lyons,	1	2,000	.....	300	100	62	600
Macedon,	1	2,000	.....	400	15	30	.....
Marion,	1	4,000	.....	450	250	260	500
Ontario,	1	700	.....	350	225	85	350
Palmyra,	1	6,000	.....	400	300	200	800
Rose,	1	1,000	.....	350	75	80	300
Sodus,	1	750	800	400	200	43	350
Walworth,	2	4,500	.....	800	400	140	650
Williamson,	1	3,500	.....	350	100	100	400
Wolcott,	2	3,500	.....	748	350	177	650
Total,	15	37,950	1,600	5,548	2,525	1,515	6,200
Westchester Co.							
Bedford,	1	2,000	2,000	300	200	200	600
Cortlandt,	1	4,000	200	300	100	90	600
Eastchester,	1	1,800	.....	100	50	36	.....
Greenburgh,	1	1,500	3,500	275	175	75	1,000

* School house.

CHURCHES.—(Continued.)

TOWNS.	Number of churches.	Value of church and lot.	Value of other real estate.	Number capable of being seated.	Usual number attending.	Number of communicants.	Salary of clergy, including use of real estate.
WESTCHESTER Co.							
Lewisboro',	1	$1,000	1,000	500	100	100	$300
New Rochelle,	1	3,000	......	300	250	42	400
North Salem,	1	300	......	150	......	......	......
Ossining,	1	10,000	5,000	400	250	190	1,050
West Farms,	1	6,000	......	600	350	98	800
Yorktown,	1	5,000	100	500	25	117	......
Total,	10	34,600	11,800	3,425	1,500	948	4,750
WYOMING Co.							
Attica,	1	2,500	......	375	125	127	500
Bennington,	1	100	700	300	125	54	200
Castile,	1	2,500	300	400	250	230	875
China,	1	3,000	700	500	150	120	360
Gainesville,	1	600	300	370	70	40	200
Genesee Falls,	1	1,900	......	300	100	43	400
Middlebury,	2	8,000	1,000	1,300	400	260	950
Orangeville,	1	1,100	......	300	100	61	400
Perry,	2	8,000	1,200	1,250	650	460	1,750
Pike,	1	3,500	......	400	200	189	400
Sheldon,	1	2,000	500	400	150	186	400
Warsaw,	1	4,000	......	500	200	140	800
Wethersfield,	2	800	300	250	200	63	375
Total,	16	38,400	5,000	6,645	2,720	1,973	6,610
YATES Co.							
Barrington,	1	1,000	300	350	200	712	400
Benton,	1	3,500	......	550	250	213	500
Italy,	2	2,200	600	550	150	91	461
Jerusalem,	1	2,000	......	500	60	65	400
Middlesex,	1	3,000	......	300	75	70	330
Milo,	3	13,000	......	2,000	825	575	1,670
Potter,	3	2,900	500	650	300	225	750
Starkey,	1	800	1,700	400	150	125	700
Total,	13	28,400	3,100	5,300	2,010	1,476	5,211

FREE WILL BAPTIST CHURCHES.

TOWNS.	Number of churches.	Value of church and lot.	Value of other real estate.	Number capable of being seated.	Usual number attending.	Number of communicants.	Salary of clergy, including use of real estate.
ALLEGANY Co.							
Hume,	1	200	......	120	50	30	......
BROOME Co.							
Windsor,	1	500	......	250	......	......	......
CATTARAUGUS Co.							
Ashford,	1	2,000	700	500	120	44	180
Dayton,	1	800	......	200	50	40	200
Freedom,	1	800	450	400	150	78	200
Little Valley,	1	600	......	400	100	54	150
Lyndon,	1	1,000	......	250	80	28	100
Randolph,	1	1,400	......	250	......	......	......
Total,	6	6,600	1,150	2,000	500	244	830
CAYUGA Co.							
Summer Hill,	No	house.	......	......	100	47	100
CHAUTAUQUE Co.							
Cherry Creek,	1	1,500	......	225	125	125	......
Chautauque,	1	600	......	300	75	......	......
Ellington,	1	800	......	300	125	70	250
Sherman,	1	1,000	......	250	150	82	370
Villenova,	1	1,100	......	400	75	90	250
Total,	5	5,000	......	1,475	550	367	870
CHEMUNG Co.							
Big Flats,	1	1,600	......	300	100	38	400
Veteran,	1	1,000	400	200	80	48	200
Total,	2	2,600	400	500	180	86	600
CHENANGO Co.							
Columbus,	1	1,200	......	300	150	77	330
New Berlin,	1	500	......	300	50	50	200
Otselic,	1	1,200	......	500	200	50	100
Oxford,	1	1,200	......	300	90	30	250
Pharsalia,	1	1,000	......	250	250	43	100
Plymouth,	1	600	......	300	100	106	200
Preston,	1	......	......	......	100	36	60
Sherburne,	1	900	100	230	75	87	175
Smyrna,	1	500	......	350	75	......	......
Total,	11	8,800	100	3,130	1,230	559	1,865
CORTLAND Co.							
Virgil,	1	800	......	250	100	83	200
DELAWARE Co.							
Davenport,	1	1,000	......	300	100	100	150
Meredith,	1	1,500	......	250	75	30	......
Total,	2	2,500	......	550	175	130	150
ERIE Co.							
Boston,	1	$2,000	......	600	100	77	$400
Collins,	1	200	......	300	40	15	......
Concord,	2	2,000	......	800	250	130	500
Hamburgh,	1	1,200	......	180	......	......	......
Wales,	1	400	......	200	150	40	400
Total,	6	6,400	......	2,080	540	252	1,300
ESSEX Co.							
Chesterfield,	1	8,000	......	500	250	186	700
FRANKLIN Co.							
Fort Covington,	1	3,000	......	400	250	108	400
GENESEE Co.							
Alabama,	1	2,100	$550	400	200	68	353
Bethany,	1	2,000	700	300	175	116	470
Byron,	1	2,300	......	475	150	70	300
Darien,	1	400	......	300	......	......	......
Total,	4	6,800	1,250	1,475	525	254	1,123
HERKIMER Co.							
Columbia,	1	1,000	......	400	300	50	450
German Flats,	1	1,000	......	500	100	30	200
Norway,	1	......	......	......	50	40	300
Total,	3	2,000	......	900	450	120	950
JEFFERSON Co.							
Lyme,	1	1,000	......	250	100	20	100
MONROE Co.							
Parma,	1	1,500	300	300	200	150	400
Penfield,	1	1,500	......	800	200	70	200
Perrington,	1	2,500	......	300	150	50	500
Sweden,	1	2,000	......	250	100	47	450
Union,	1	400	......	500	250	25	150
Total,	5	7,900	300	2,150	900	342	1,700
MONTGOMERY Co.							
Canajoharie,	1	1,800	1,000	500	230	135	300
NEW-YORK Co.							
New-York,	1	10,000	......	500	200	110	1,000
NIAGARA Co.							
Royalton,	1	1,000	......	200	20	6	......
ONONDAGA Co.							
Fabius,	1	1,500	......	300	100	57	300
ONTARIO Co.							
Canandaigua,	1	1,000	......	500	50	50	100
ORLEANS Co.							
Gaines,	1	1,000	......	400	70	40	200
Ridgeway,	1	1,000	......	200	150	35	200
Shelby,	1	1,800	......	300	150	70	350
Total,	3	3,800	......	900	370	145	750
OSWEGO Co.							
Schroeppel,	1	1,000	......	400	150	45	400
OTSEGO Co.							
Oneonta,	1	800	......	400	150	120	300
Otego,	1	1,000	......	200	75	40	100
Plainfield,	2	1,300	700	950	200	159	350
Total,	4	3,100	700	1,550	425	319	750
RENSSELAER Co.							
Poestenkill,	1	200	25	200	100	40	200
Stephentown,	2	2,200	......	800	250	198	200
Total,	3	2,400	25	1,000	350	238	400
ST. LAWRENCE Co.							
Lawrence,	1	800	......	250	100	45	200
SARATOGA Co.							
Hadley,	1	500	......	250	60	30	......
SCHUYLER Co.							
Dix,	1	400	200	300	75	22	135
Orange,	1	600	......	200	75	75	250
Total,	2	1,000	200	500	150	97	385
STEUBEN Co.							
Pultney,	1	400	......	350	100	75	200
Urbana,	1	600	......	175	125	26	300
Total,	2	1,000	......	525	225	101	500
TIOGA Co.							
Owego,	1	1,200	......	400	250	35	100
TOMPKINS Co.							
Caroline,	1	800	300	300	100	30	300

CHURCHES—(Continued.)

TOWNS.	Number of churches.	Value of church and lot.	Value of other real estate.	Number capable of being seated.	Usual number attending.	Number of communicants.	Salary of clergy, including use of real estate.
WARREN Co.							
Johnsburgh, ...	1	$1,200	......	300	100	100	$400
WASHINGTON Co.							
Putnam, ...	1	650	......	184	50	50	150
WAYNE Co.							
Walworth, ...	1	2,500	......	500	200	70	400
WYOMING Co.							
Attica, ...	1	2,500	......	475	125	67	560
Eagle, ...	1	600	......	150	150	30	300
Middlebury, ...	1	2,000	......	550	250	138	551
Sheldon, ...	1	1,000	......	600	100	47	130
Warsaw, ...	1	350	......	250	40	43	275
Total, ...	5	6,450	......	2,025	665	325	1,816
YATES Co.							
Middlesex, ...	1	1,100	......	300	80	7	100

OLD SCHOOL BAPTIST CHURCHES.

TOWNS.	Number of churches.	Value of church and lot.	Value of other real estate.	Number capable of being seated.	Usual number attending.	Number of communicants.	Salary of clergy, including use of real estate.
DELAWARE Co.							
Andes, ...	1	......	......	......	200	......	......
Roxbury, ...	2	6,400	$800	1,100	700	340	500
Total, ...	3	6,400	800	1,100	900	340	500
GREENE Co.							
Halcott, ...	1	600	......	300	50	69	25
Lexington, ...	1	1,800	......	600	250	132	250
Total, ...	2	2,400	......	900	300	201	275
LEWIS Co.							
Turin, ...	1	800	......	300	50	20	......
ONEIDA Co.							
Trenton, ...	1	1,000	......	200	70	40	200
Westmoreland, ...	1	1,000	......	250	100	100	516
Total, ...	2	2,000	......	450	170	140	716
ONONDAGA Co.							
Pompey, ...	1	1,000	......	200	75	25	100
ORANGE Co.							
Walkill, ...	1	1,500	......	400	125	35	100
Warwick, ...	1	3,000	3,000	500	300	98	600
Wawayanda, ...	1	600	......	300	50	30	100
Total, ...	3	5,100	3,000	1,200	475	163	800
ROCKLAND Co.							
Orangetown, ...	1	1,500	1,750	200	150	40	550
Ramapo, ...	1	800	......	200	15	17	125
Total, ...	2	2,300	1,750	400	165	57	675
ST. LAWRENCE Co.							
Fowler, ...	1	1,200	......	400	100	34	......
SCHOHARIE Co.							
Gilboa, ...	1	700	......	400	30	21	100
SCHUYLER Co.							
Hector, ...	1	1,200	......	300	75	40	25
SULLIVAN Co.							
Mamakating, ...	1	2,000	250	500	250	60	......

SEVENTH DAY BAPTIST CHURCHES.

TOWNS.	Number of churches.	Value of church and lot.	Value of other real estate.	Number capable of being seated.	Usual number attending.	Number of communicants.	Salary of clergy, including use of real estate.
ALLEGANY Co.							
Alfred, ...	3	11,500	1,100	1,700	950	1,015	1,100
Friendship, ...	1	1,800	......	300	125	84	100
Genesee, ...	2	2,000	......	500	330	192	504
Independence, ...	1	1,000	400	400	150	150	300
Wirt, ...	1	1,000	......	300	35	35	100
Total, ...	8	17,300	1,500	3,200	1,585	1,476	2,104
CHENANGO Co.							
Lincklaen, ...	1	500	......	250	50	100	300
Preston, ...	1	500	......	150	30	42	......
Total, ...	2	1,000	......	400	80	142	300
CORTLAND Co.							
Scott, ...	1	2,000	......	300	150	143	300
ERIE Co.							
Clarence, ...	1	500	......	250	50	30	200
JEFFERSON Co.							
Adams, ...	2	2,800	5,000	700	530	288	600
Hounsfield, ...	1	700	......	200	40	40	50
Total, ...	3	3,500	5,000	900	570	328	650
MADISON Co.							
Brookfield, ...	2	$3,000	......	900	525	416	$900
De Ruyter, ...	1	2,000	......	200	150	121	350
Total, ...	3	5,000	......	1,100	675	537	1,250
NEW-YORK Co.							
New-York, ...	1	15,000	......	600	100	50	900
ONEIDA Co.							
Verona, ...	2	1,250	......	330	130	92	175
OTSEGO Co.							
Edmeston, ...	1	650	......	200	100	125	220
RENSSELAER Co.							
Berlin, ...	1	3,000	......	375	150	......	......
Petersburgh, ...	1	2,000	......	600	30	100	......
Total, ...	2	5,000	......	975	180	100	......

CHURCHES OF THE CHRISTIAN CONNECTION.

TOWNS.	Number of churches.	Value of church and lot.	Value of other real estate.	Number capable of being seated.	Usual number attending.	Number of communicants.	Salary of clergy, including use of real estate.
ALBANY Co.							
Bern, ...	3	1,700	......	900	350	147	420
Rensselaerville, ...	1	1,400	......	300	200	45	200
Westerlo, ...	1	2,000	......	500	300	75	400
Total, ...	5	5,100	......	1,700	850	267	1,020
CATTARAUGUS Co.							
Machias, ...	1	800	......	500	80	51	300
CAYUGA Co.							
Niles, ...	1	500	......	275	......	......	......
Springport, ...	1	3,000	......	300	200	70	350
Victory, ...	1	1,000	......	300	60	45	300
Total, ...	3	4,500	275	875	260	115	650
CHAUTAUQUE Co.							
Arkwright, ...	1	1,000	100	300	100	60	100
Busti, ...	1	500	......	300	50	12	......
Ellicott, ...	1	1,000	......	300	150	80	225
Ellington, ...	1	600	......	400	......	......	......
Pomfret, ...	1	1,000	......	400	......	......	......
Stockton, ...	1	700	......	350	50	25	100
Total, ...	6	4,800	100	2,050	350	177	425
COLUMBIA Co.							
Austerlitz, ...	1	1,500	......	220	175	60	350
Canaan, ...	1	1,500	......	250	100	75	250
Chatham, ...	1	800	......	200	40	20	300
Hillsdale, ...	1	1,500	......	300	100	18	400
New Lebanon, ...	1	400	......	400	75	35	200
Total, ...	5	5,700	......	1,370	490	208	1,500
CORTLAND Co.							
Cortlandville, ...	1	500	......	300	100	50	300
Hartford, ...	1	400	......	250	75	35	......
Total, ...	2	900	......	550	175	85	300
DELAWARE Co.							
Delhi, ...	1	350	......	180	80	40	50
Hamden, ...	1	1,000	......	200	75	40	250
Kortright, ...	1	400	......	250	......	20	......
Roxbury, ...	1	200	......	150	50	25	......
Total, ...	4	1,950	......	780	205	125	300
DUTCHESS Co.							
Milan, ...	1	2,000	......	700	120	150	375
Stanford, ...	1	1,600	......	320	150	140	300
Union Vale, ...	1	700	......	400	40	40	250
Total, ...	3	4,300	......	1,420	310	330	925
ERIE Co.							
Collins, ...	1	250	......	300	40	38	200
FULTON Co.							
Broadalbin, ...	1	500	......	250	100	72	300
GENESEE Co.							
Pembroke, ...	1	1,000	......	300	150	30	200
Stafford, ...	1	1,400	500	350	200	75	400
Total, ...	2	2,400	500	650	350	105	600
GREENE Co.							
Greenville, ...	1	3,400	......	500	300	300	300
New Baltimore, ...	1	1,200	......	250	200	100	170
Total, ...	2	4,600	......	750	500	400	470
JEFFERSON Co.							
Hounsfield, ...	1	1,200	......	300	60	30	200

CHURCHES.—(Continued.)

TOWNS.	Number of churches.	Value of church and lot.	Value of other real estate.	Number capable of being seated.	Usual number attending.	Number of communicants.	Salary of clergy, including use of real estate.
Livingston Co.							
Lima, ...	1	$1,000	......	300	50	30	$200
Livonia, ...	1	1,500	......	300	200	75	150
Springwater, ...	1	1,000	......	200	100	30	200
Total, ...	3	3,500	......	800	350	135	550
Monroe Co.							
Mendon, ...	1	3,500	......	400	175	40	375
Parma, ...	1	1,500	......	300	200	75	350
Rush, ...	1	1,500	......	300	75	52	150
Total, ...	3	6,500	......	1,000	450	167	875
Montgomery Co.							
Charleston, ...	1	2,000	......	700	350	200	225
Root, ...	1	1,700	......	300	75	......	300
Total, ...	2	3,700	......	1,000	425	200	525
New-York Co.							
New-York, ...	1	....	......	800	250	104	800
Niagara Co.							
Royalton, ...	1	1,800	......	300	100	30	250
Onondaga Co.							
Lysander, ...	1	2,800	......	400	100	70	360
Ontario Co.							
Canandaigua, ...	1	500	......	300	150	50	100
Naples, ...	1	3,000	......	400	150	90	300
West Bloomfield, ...	1	1,200	......	200	75	82	350
Total, ...	3	4,700	......	900	375	222	750
Orleans Co.							
Barre, ...	1	1,300	......	225	40	35	100
Clarendon, ...	1	1,000	......	300	175	70	300
Shelby, ...	1	1,500	......	300	80	20	......
Yates, ...	1	400	......	200	75	20	200
Total, ...	4	4,200	......	1,025	370	145	600
Otsego Co.							
Hartwick, ...	2	2,700	100	500	300	133	400
Laurens, ...	1	1,200	......	250	150	87	250
Milford, ...	1	1,200	......	300	100	60	......
Otego, ...	1	1,200	......	250	150	32	200
Roseboom, ...	1	1,000	800	300	200	40	250
Total, ...	6	7,300	900	1,600	900	352	1,100
Rensselaer Co.							
Berlin, ...	1	2,000	......	350	100	35	250
Pittstown, ...	2	2,500	......	800	120	111	200
Stephentown, ...	1	1,500	100	350	130	86	325
Total, ...	4	6,000	100	1,500	350	232	775
Saratoga Co.							
Ballston, ...	1	500	......	240	30	25	200
Day, ...	1	600	......	460	70	40	100
Galway, ...	1	2,000	......	300	150	75	400
Providence, ...	1	1,400	......	400	180	70	300
Total, ...	4	4,500	......	1,400	430	210	1,000
Schoharie Co.							
Gilboa, ...	1	500	......	200	100	55	120
Richmondville, ...	1	1,000	......	500	250	100	200
Summit, ...	1	1,200	......	1,000	200	130	200
Wright, ...	1	600	......	200	100	40	150
Total, ...	4	3,300	......	1,900	650	325	670
Schuyler Co.							
Hector, ...	1	800	......	250	60	40	100
Steuben Co.							
Cameron, ...	1	800	......	280	70	24	50
Prattsburgh, ...	1	500	......	300	......	......	......
Thurston, ...	1	900	......	250	75	81	150
Total, ...	3	2,200	......	830	145	105	200
Tompkins Co.							
Enfield, ...	1	800	......	500	200	60	200
Wayne Co.							
Arcadia, ...	1	2,500	......	250	150	104	600
Marion, ...	1	600	......	250	300	253	300
Palmyra, ...	1	2,000	......	300	90	54	500
Sodus, ...	1	800	......	300	50	25	200
Total, ...	4	5,900	......	1,100	590	436	1,600
Wyoming Co.							
Castile, ...	1	1,600	125	250	150	74	400
Wethersfield, ...	1	1,500	......	300	50	10	150
Total, ...	2	3,100	125	550	200	84	550

TOWNS.	Number of churches.	Value of church and lot.	Value of other real estate.	Number capable of being seated.	Usual number attending.	Number of communicants.	Salary of clergy, including use of real estate.
Yates Co.							
Starkey, ...	2	$3,600	......	1,600	110	85	$400

CHURCHES OF DISCIPLES OF CHRIST.

TOWNS.	Number of churches.	Value of church and lot.	Value of other real estate.	Number capable of being seated.	Usual number attending.	Number of communicants.	Salary of clergy, including use of real estate.
Albany Co.							
Albany, ...	1	200	......	200	50	50	......
Cayuga Co.							
Auburn, ...	1	1,200	300	150	200	......	......
Cato and Ira, ...	1	2,000	......	350	150	180	400
Mentz, ...	1	1,800	......	250	60	90	......
Total, ...	3	5,000	300	750	410	270	400
Erie Co.							
Amherst, ...	1	1,500	......	400	200	150	500
Lancaster, ...	1	1,000	......	300	50	25	......
Tonawanda, ...	1	800	......	300	50	20	400
Total, ...	3	3,300	......	1,000	300	195	900
New-York Co.							
New-York, ...	1	15,500	......	300	200	100	1,200
Onondaga Co.							
Cicero, ...	2	3,600	160	850	350	200	500
Pompey, ...	1	300	......	300	200	200	300
Tully, ...	1	2,000	......	300	75	140	70
Total, ...	4	5,900	160	1,450	625	540	870
Rensselaer Co.							
Poestenkill, ...	1	600	.....	200	60	50	300
Troy, ...	1	400	......	150	50	40	500
Total, ...	2	1,000	......	350	110	90	800
Seneca Co.							
Waterloo, ...	1	500	......	300	50	35	......
Wayne Co.							
Butler, ...	1	600	......	250	150	160	......

CONGREGATIONAL CHURCHES.

TOWNS.	Number of churches.	Value of church and lot.	Value of other real estate.	Number capable of being seated.	Usual number attending.	Number of communicants.	Salary of clergy, including use of real estate.
Albany Co.							
Albany, ...	1	25,000	......	800	500	200	2,000
Watervliet, ...	1	1,600	......	300	100	20	250
Total, ...	2	26,600	......	1,100	600	220	2,250
Allegany Co.							
Allen, ...	1	300	......	200	50	52	350
Amity, ...	1	1,900	......	250	150	78	700
Andover, ...	1	500	600	200	60	55	400
Belfast, ...	1	....	......	150	18	......	......
Caneadea, ...	1	2,500	110	450	400	28	500
Centreville, ...	1	600	......	175	80	95	100
Friendship, ...	1	2,500	......	300	150	115	640
Hume, ...	1	400	......	300	60	35	300
New Hudson, ...	2	2,200	......	550	160	84	450
Rushford, ...	1	300	......	300	100	73	400
Scio, ...	1	500	......	300	300	50	300
Total, ...	12	11,700	710	3,175	1,528	665	4,140
Broome Co.							
Barker, ...	1	2,500	......	400	150	70	400
Binghamton, ...	1	8,000	......	600	150	115	800
Lisle, ...	2	5,700	750	920	400	154	875
Maine, ...	1	1,500	1,200	400	200	130	450
Triangle, ...	1	2,000	......	500	100	99	450
Total, ...	6	19,700	1,950	2,820	1,000	568	2,975
Cattaraugus Co.							
Allegany, ...	1	2,000	......	300	35	20	500
East Otto, ...	1	300	......	200	100	35	200
Little Valley, ...	1	3,000	......	350	50	35	300
Napoli, ...	1	600	500	300	200	40	300
Randolph, ...	1	3,000	......	400	250	52	500
Total, ...	5	8,900	500	1,550	635	182	1,800
Cayuga Co.							
Genoa, ...	1	2,000	800	300	125	80	400
Moravia, ...	1	3,000	750	600	200	......	500
Sennett, ...	1	5,000	......	400	120	102	700
Summer Hill, ...	1	3,000	1,200	350	115	97	475
Total, ...	4	13,000	2,750	1,650	560	279	2,075
Chautauque Co.							
Busti, ...	1	350	......	300	......	......	......
Charlotte, ...	1	2,000	......	350	150	86	450
Chautauque, ...	1	1,700	......	300	75	13	400
Ellicott, ...	1	2,000	......	470	200	135	500

CHURCHES—(Continued.)

TOWNS.	Number of churches.	Value of church and lot.	Value of other real estate.	Number capable of being seated.	Usual number attending.	Number of communicants.	Salary of clergy, including use of real estate.
Chautauque Co.							
Kiantone,	1	$1,000	$600	300	150	65	$400
Portland,	1	2,000	......	400	100	77	350
Sherman,	1	3,500	......	900	450	200	665
Stockton,	1	500	200	300	100	45	300
Total,	8	14,050	800	3,320	1,225	651	3,065
Chemung Co.							
Elmira,	1	8,000	......	550	500	163	1,200
Chenango Co.							
Columbus,	1	1,000	800	350	75	50	400
Coventry,	2	7,000	......	1,000	350	248	970
Guilford,	2	4,000	550	650	350	225	650
Lincklaen,	1	1,000	......	600	100	30	200
New Berlin,	2	5,000	550	800	200	57	450
Norwich,	1	6,000	2,000	600	200	160	1,000
Pitcher,	2	3,200	900	800	300	171	900
Plymouth,	1	1,000	......	500	......	26	......
Sherburne,	1	3,000	1,000	600	200	125	800
Smyrna,	1	3,000	......	800	150	100	500
Total,	14	34,200	5,800	6,700	1,925	1,192	5,870
Clinton Co.							
Ausable,	1	10,000	......	700	200	330	800
Chazy,	1	2,000	......	550	700	150	500
Mooers,	1	1,500	500	350	50	200	400
Peru,	1	1,500	450	300	100	85	450
Total,	4	15,000	950	1,900	1,050	765	2,150
Columbia Co.							
Austerlitz,	1	1,500	......	400	75	44	400
Canaan,	1	2,000	......	300	150	100	450
Chatham,	1	1,000	......	200	100	80	600
Total,	3	4,500	......	900	325	224	1,450
Cortland Co.							
Cincinnatus,	1	1,500	800	450	150	100	450
Harford,	1	800	......	500	85	5	450
Homer,	1	9,000	1,000	900	700	515	900
Scott,	1	2,000	......	300	100	67	400
Taylor,	1	600	......	200	100	27	150
Virgil,	1	2,000	100	300	100	70	350
Willett,	1	1,600	......	280	50	22	250
Total,	7	17,500	1,900	2,930	1,285	806	2,950
Delaware Co.							
Andes,	1	1,000	300	......	12	......	......
Franklin,	2	7,900	3,200	10,000	525	395	1,600
Hamden,	1	600	......	400	120	......	600
Hancock,	1	2,000	......	300	70	......	400
Meredith,	1	2,000	......	600	70	60	350
Sidney,	2	2,550	......	550	300	88	550
Walton,	2	4,200	1,800	900	640	340	1,255
Total,	10	20,250	5,300	12,750	1,737	883	4,755
Dutchess Co.							
Amenia,	1	3,000	1,500	350	100	45	400
Poughkeepsie,	1	4,000	......	450	225	190	1,000
Northeast,	1	3,500	1,000	400	75	20	500
Total,	3	10,500	2,500	1,200	400	255	1,900
Erie Co.							
Aurora,	1	2,700	1,150	600	215	134	500
Eden,	1	2,000	......	250	80	65	400
Evans,	3	4,100	1,000	900	275	219	1,300
North Collins,	1	1,200	......	300	200	40	400
Total,	6	10,000	2,150	2,050	770	458	2,600
Essex Co.							
Crown Point,	2	3,800	3,500	600	225	150	1,100
Elizabethtown,	1	3,100	1,000	200	75	30	500
Jay,	1	600	250	100	25	......	......
Lewis,	1	3,500	......	650	250	82	500
Ticonderoga,	1	1,300	......	600	100	30	350
Westport,	1	1,000	400	250	75	50	550
Willsborough,	1	3,500	......	300	150	48	500
Wilmington,	1	800	......	300	50	40	200
Total,	9	17,600	5,150	3,000	950	430	3,700
Franklin Co.							
Bangor,	1	200	700	250	125	70	500
Burke,	1	1,350	400	300	150	40	400
Malone,	1	1,000	......	800	400	350	800
Moria,	1	1,400	......	300	50	40	......
Total,	4	3,950	1,100	1,650	725	500	1,700
Fulton Co.							
Johnstown,	1	$1,100	......	600	300	128	$800
Genesee Co.							
Alexander,	1	2,500	1,200	400	150	60	650
Bergen,	2	5,500	1,600	820	400	192	950
Darien,	1	1,000	......	300	50	8	......
Elba,	1	3,000	......	400	158	104	400
Le Roy,	1	3,000	......	300	50	20	500
Stafford,	1	400	......	500	......	......	......
Total,	7	15,400	2,800	2,720	808	380	2,500
Greene Co.							
Durham,	2	6,200	650	800	425	203	590
Herkimer Co.							
Winfield,	1	1,500	......	500	75	72	550
Jefferson Co.							
Adams,	2	5,800	2,500	820	250	170	990
Champion,	2	6,000	500	850	350	194	1,000
Ellisburgh,	2	3,900	......	550	300	90	650
Orleans,	1	2,000	......	280	100	30	......
Rodman,	1	4,500	......	350	240	186	450
Rutland,	1	3,000	2,000	450	300	100	750
Total,	9	25,200	5,000	3,300	1,540	770	3,840
Kings Co.							
Brooklyn,	11	248,000	82,000	9,500	6,645	1 379	16,000
Lewis Co.							
Denmark,	1	1,500	......	350	......	56	......
Leyden,	2	1,600	......	1,100	230	......	700
Total,	3	3,100	......	1,450	230	56	700
Livingston Co.							
York,	1	3,500	......	275	125	44	400
Madison Co.							
Cazenovia,	1	2,500	......	450	150	78	400
Eaton,	1	2,000	......	350	100	68	600
Hamilton,	2	5,600	1,000	1,100	360	130	900
Lebanon,	1	1,200	......	300	150	40	400
Lenox,	1	1,500	......	250	100	30	350
Madison,	1	3,000	300	400	200	180	600
Nelson,	1	1,000	......	200	90	60	90
Stockbridge,	2	1,300	......	700	200	70	700
Sullivan,	1	1,400	......	300	125	34	400
Total,	11	19,500	1,300	4,050	1,475	690	4,440
Monroe Co.							
Brighton,	1	5,000	1,200	400	140	85	700
Clarkson,	1	7,000	......	500	350	150	800
Greece,	1	3,000	......	350	250	170	650
Henrietta,	1	2,500	150	400	90	73	535
Ogden,	1	6,500	......	500	250	134	600
Perrington,	1	3,000	......	350	200	75	500
Riga,	2	6,400	......	700	225	103	1,000
Rochester,	2	65,000	......	1,700	80	70	600
Total,	10	98,400	1,350	4,900	1,585	860	5,385
New-York Co.							
New-York,	9	292,500	2,000	7,450	4,175	905	11,150
Niagara Co.							
Cambria,	1	3,000	1,890	350	175	125	500
Lewiston,	1	2,500	......	300	125	30	400
Lockport,	1	4,000	2,000	275	200	160	800
Niagara,	1	1,000	......	175	130	15	......
Royalton,	1	2,000	......	300	100	25	400
Total,	5	12,500	3,890	1,400	730	355	2,100
Oneida Co.							
Augusta,	2	4,500	500	950	425	278	1,100
Bridgewater,	1	1,800	500	300	150	70	400
Camden,	1	6,000	......	600	400	360	600
Floyd,	1	1,200	......	600	200	40	200
Kirkland,	2	12,200	2,700	1,150	600	230	1,350
Marcy,	2	800	......	350	135	95	150
Marshall,	2	4,700	......	800	175	85	1,050
Paris,	2	3,400	1,000	800	100	58	500
Remsen,	3	2,600	300	700	140	190	276
Sangerfield,	2	3,200	......	650	300	110	500
Steuben,	2	2,000	......	1,000	350	153	300
Trenton,	1	100	......	200	25	18	80
Utica,	1	3,500	500	700	300	256	500
Verona,	1	2,500	1,000	350	250	206	600
Vienna,	1	200	......	150	50	11	......
Whitestown,	1	1,800	......	250	55	12	200
Total,	25	50,500	6,500	9,550	3,655	2,172	7,800

CHURCHES.—(Continued.)

TOWNS.	Number of churches.	Value of church and lot.	Value of other real estate.	Number capable of being seated.	Usual number attending.	Number of communicants.	Salary of clergy, including use of real estate.
ONONDAGA Co							
De Witt, ...	1	$3,000	......	500	75	25	$300
Elbridge, ...	1	5,000	$2,000	700	175	150	700
Fabius, ...	1	1,500	......	500	75	80	400
La Fayette, ...	1	2,000	1,000	400	100	65	550
Onondaga, ...	1	1,000	......	250	60	41	300
Otisco, ...	1	400	......	800	450	222	600
Pompey, ...	1	5,000	......	700	250	235	750
Syracuse, ...	1	2,000	......	500	3,000	115	800
Total, ...	8	19,900	3,000	4,350	4,185	933	4,400
ONTARIO Co.							
Canandaigua, ...	1	10,000	3,500	1,000	800	300	1,350
Bristol, ...	1	5,000	1,100	500	250	60	500
East Bloomfield, ...	1	5,000	3,000	700	350	220	1,000
Gorham, ...	1	2,000	......	300	100	40	450
Richmond, ...	2	2,500	1,000	1,060	290	65	900
Victor, ...	1	3,000	1,500	500	250	150	800
West Bloomfield, ...	1	4,000	1,000	350	200	130	650
Total, ...	8	31,500	11,100	4,410	2,240	965	5,650
ORANGE Co.							
Bloomingrove, ...	2	5,200	2,000	1,150	400	150	600
Walkill, ...	2	3,750	2,500	750	329	360	1,025
Total, ...	4	8,950	4,500	1,900	729	510	1,625
ORLEANS Co.							
Barre, ...	1	2,000	1,000	400	200	155	500
OSWEGO Co.							
Hannibal, ...	1	1,000	......	250	150	99	500
Mexico, ...	1	4,000	2,000	500	250	130	1,000
New Haven, ...	1	2,000	......	350	250	118	500
Richland, ...	1	3,000	1,250	500	250	160	800
Schroeppel, ...	1	1,000	......	300	200	65	400
Volney, ...	1	1,500	800	350	100	50	525
Total, ...	6	12,500	4,050	2,250	1,200	622	3,725
OTSEGO Co.							
Burlington, ...	1	1,000	......	500	......	......	......
Butternuts, ...	1	4,000	1,650	750	300	225	600
Exter, ...	1	500	500	300	100	40	400
New Lisbon, ...	1	1,000	......	500	......	......	......
Otego, ...	1	2,500	200	400	100	37	200
Westford, ...	1	2,000	......	400	100	100	400
Total, ...	6	11,000	2,350	2,850	600	402	1,600
QUEENS Co.							
Flushing, ...	1	1,700	......	250	175	62	800
ST. LAWRENCE Co.							
Canton, ...	2	1,250	......	500	200	65	700
De Kalb, ...	1	700	......	300	100	50	250
De Peyster, ...	1	1,000	......	400	150	30	200
Edwards, ...	1	......	......	......	......	11	......
Gouverneur, ...	1	1,200	......	400	100	70	350
Hopkinton, ...	1	3,000	800	600	100	109	450
Lawrence, ...	2	2,500	......	400	180	60	600
Lisbon, ...	1	1,200	......	300	100	400	400
Madrid, ...	2	8,500	1,000	1,100	350	208	950
Massena, ...	2	4,000	......	750	250	95	1,000
Morristown, ...	1	1,000	......	200	150	35	325
Norfolk, ...	1	2,000	500	1,200	150	125	500
Stockholm, ...	2	2,800	650	950	275	191	870
Oswegatchie, ...	1	800	......	300	185	85	250
Parishville, ...	1	300	......	100	80	80	400
Total, ...	20	30,250	2,950	7,500	2,370	1,614	7,245
SARATOGA Co.							
Greenfield, ...	1	1,000	1,000	300	150	75	400
Malta, ...	1	600	......	250	80	25	80
Moreau, ...	1	1,900	......	200	100	69	600
Waterford, ...	1	3,500	3,900	200	150	60	750
Total, ...	4	7,000	4,900	950	480	229	1,830
STEUBEN Co.							
Prattsburgh, ...	1	3,000	2,000	550	400	397	700
Pultney, ...	1	600	......	300	75	25	100
Total, ...	2	3,600	2,000	850	475	422	800
SUFFOLK Co.							
Brookhaven, ...	4	4,400	500	1,200	835	397	1,250
Islip, ...	1	900	50	125	60	30	100
Riverhead, ...	6	1,550	2,850	1,660	725	463	2,925
Southampton, ...	1	500	......	125	30	30	200
Southold, ...	3	9,100	1,100	435	435	150	1,020
Total, ...	15	22,450	4,500	3,545	2,085	1,070	5,495
SULLIVAN Co.							
Highland, ...	1	$1,500	......	400	200	100	$200
TIOGA Co.							
Berkshire, ...	1	3,500	......	525	225	197	500
Candor, ...	1	3,400	1,500	550	250	190	475
Newark, ...	1	900	1,000	200	50	30	240
Owego, ...	1	8,000	......	700	350	120	800
Spencer, ...	1	3,000	1,000	400	200	111	400
Total, ...	5	18,800	3,500	2,375	1,075	648	2,415
TOMPKINS Co.							
Caroline, ...	1	......	......	......	150	30	250
Danby, ...	1	3,000	......	600	150	100	......
Groton, ...	3	8,000	500	1,200	385	184	1,325
Ithaca, ...	1	500	......	200	100	40	300
Total, ...	6	11,500	500	2,000	785	354	1,875
ULSTER Co.							
Saugerties, ...	1	12,000	......	500	150	45	700
WASHINGTON Co.							
Granville, ...	1	2,500	500	300	150	80	350
Greenwich, ...	1	7,000	2,000	400	150	125	500
Hartford, ...	1	1,000	......	500	......	30	......
Whitehall, ...	1	2,000	......	400	......	......	......
Total, ...	4	12,500	2,500	1,600	300	235	850
WAYNE Co.							
Marion, ...	1	3,000	......	400	200	150	400
Ontario, ...	1	1,500	......	200	100	40	......
Williamson, ...	1	800	......	360	......	50	......
Total, ...	3	5,300	......	960	300	240	400
WESTCHESTER Co.							
West Farms, ...	1	3,500	......	300	100	45	900
Yorktown, ...	1	1,000	500	300	75	50	400
Total, ...	2	4,500	500	600	175	95	1,300
WYOMING Co.							
Castile, ...	1	3,000	......	350	200	133	550
China, ...	1	1,500	......	300	200	90	500
Gainesville, ...	1	2,500	......	500	100	70	500
Java, ...	1	1,200	......	300	100	30	150
Perry, ...	1	3,000	......	550	300	160	650
Pike, ...	1	3,000	......	375	150	70	550
Sheldon, ...	1	800	......	300	80	35	......
Warsaw, ...	1	5,000	......	500	350	190	1,025
Wethersfield, ...	1	400	......	300	......	12	......
Total, ...	9	20,400	......	3,475	1,480	790	3,925
YATES Co.							
Milo, ...	1	5,000	......	500	200	100	600
Potter, ...	1	5,000	500	500	200	100	700
Total, ...	2	10,000	500	1,000	400	200	1,300

EVANGELICAL CHURCHES.

TOWNS.	Number of churches.	Value of church and lot.	Value of other real estate.	Number capable of being seated.	Usual number attending.	Number of communicants.	Salary of clergy, including use of real estate.
ALBANY Co.							
Albany, ...	1	14,000	......	200	50	25	225
ERIE Co.							
Amherst, ...	1	2,500	3,000	300	150	75	340
NIAGARA Co.							
Pendleton, ...	1	1,850	......	300	150	60	125
ONEIDA Co.							
Utica, ...	1	1,500	......	250	150	40	200

EVANGELICAL LUTHERAN CHURCHES.

TOWNS.	Number of churches.	Value of church and lot.	Value of other real estate.	Number capable of being seated.	Usual number attending.	Number of communicants.	Salary of clergy, including use of real estate.
ALBANY Co.							
Albany, ...	2	25,000	......	1,450	900	220	2,200
Bern, ...	1	3,600	1,800	650	350	350	500
Guilderland, ...	1	3,000	2,000	500	350	350	500
Knox, ...	1	2,500	1,000	200	100	80	112
Total, ...	5	34,100	4,800	2,800	1,700	1,000	3,312
COLUMBIA Co.							
Ancram, ...	1	2,000	1,500	300	150	80	400
Claverack, ...	1	4,000	1,500	500	200	400	750
Germantown, ...	1	2,000	......	500	225	200	475
Ghent, ...	1	2,000	1,000	300	150	150	600
Kinderhook, ...	1	3,500	1,600	500	200	180	450
Livingston, ...	1	3,000	......	350	200	195	475
Stuyvesant, ...	1	1,600	......	250	......	......	......
Total, ...	7	18,100	5,600	2,700	1,125	1,205	3,150

CHURCHES.—(CONTINUED.)

TOWNS	Number of churches.	Value of church and lot.	Value of other real estate.	Number capable of being seated.	Usual number attending.	Number of communicants.	Salary of clergy, including use of real estate.
DUTCHESS CO.							
Redhook, ...	2	$10, 800	$3, 000	1, 050	610	290	$1100
Rhinebeck, ...	2	9, 000	4, 700	750	250	220	950
Total, ...	4	19, 800	7, 700	1, 800	860	510	2050
ERIE CO.							
Alden, ...	1	1, 200	......	300	100	80	180
Buffalo, ...	3	24, 500	4, 050	2, 100	1, 350	1, 240	1, 700
Eden, ...	2	2, 250	......	1, 000	350	105	675
Hamburgh, ...	1	1, 250	......	300	100	60	300
Lancaster, ...	1	1, 000	......	300	225	125	350
West Seneca, ...	1	600	......	300	100	75	......
Total, ...	9	30, 800	4, 050	4, 300	2, 225	1, 685	3, 205
FULTON CO.							
Johnstown, ...	1	3, 000	1, 000	450	200	140	500
GREENE CO.							
Athens, ...	1	4, 000	3, 000	350	200	150	500
HAMILTON CO.							
Morehouse, ...	1	......	......	......	28	30	......
HERKIMER CO.							
German Flats, ...	1	600	......	400	30	15	175
Little Falls, ...	1	800	......	160	100	34	......
Ohio, ...	1	300	......	150	40	30	50
Total, ...	3	1, 700	......	710	170	79	225
JEFFERSON CO.							
Henderson, ...	1	......	......	......	40	......	500
Orleans, ...	2	2, 400	......	400	300	170	600
Total, ...	3	2, 400	......	400	340	170	1, 100
KINGS CO.							
Brooklyn, ...	2	11, 300	1, 000	750	550	590	1, 150
New Lots, ...	1	3, 000	......	200	70	......	200
Total, ...	3	14, 300	1, 000	950	620	590	1, 350
LEWIS CO.							
New Bremen, ...	1	800	50	200	50	38	100
LIVINGSTON CO.							
North Dansville, ...	1	5, 000	......	350	250	95	400
MONROE CO.							
Rochester, ...	1	9, 000	800	550	500	400	400
Rush, ...	1	1, 500	......	350	50	30	250
Total, ...	2	10, 500	800	900	550	430	650
MONTGOMERY CO.							
Amsterdam, ...	1	1, 000	......	300	175	80	350
Canajoharie, ...	2	3, 000	......	650	425	136	500
Minden, ...	3	2, 500	1, 000	800	410	115	775
Palatine, ...	2	5, 500	2, 000	800	680	220	550
Total, ...	8	12, 000	3, 000	2, 550	1, 690	551	2, 175
NEW-YORK CO.							
New-York, ...	3	86, 000	5, 000	2, 250	1, 450	1, 620	4, 000
NIAGARA CO.							
Lockport, ...	3	4, 225	......	875	600	270	1, 000
Royalton, ...	1	1, 200	......	200	200	104	300
Wheatfield, ...	4	8, 200	1, 725	1, 750	1, 367	149	1, 260
Total, ...	8	13, 625	1, 725	2, 825	2, 167	1, 423	2, 560
ONEIDA CO.							
Rome, ...	1	2, 000	......	350	130	200	350
Utica, ...	1	4, 000	......	450	350	150	400
Total, ...	2	6, 000	......	800	480	350	750
ONONDAGA CO.							
Clay, ...	1	1, 200	......	300	50	25	100
Salina, ...	1	1, 500	......	300	50	20	100
Syracuse, ...	1	3, 000	......	400	350	300	650
Total, ...	3	5, 700	......	1, 000	450	345	850
OTSEGO CO.							
Hartwick, ...	1	1, 400	......	200	80	51	......
Roseboom, ...	1	1, 000	......	300	200	50	150
Worcester, ...	1	1, 500	......	400	......	40	......
Total, ...	3	3, 900	......	900	280	141	150
RENSSELAER CO.							
Brunswick, ...	1	6, 000	2, 000	500	400	250	835
Pittstown, ...	1	......	......	......	......	85	320
Poestenkill, ...	1	2, 000	......	350	200	80	400
Sandlake, ...	2	7, 500	2, 400	850	400	280	960
Schaghticoke, ...	2	6, 500	1, 800	1, 240	484	192	850
Schodack, ...	1	2, 000	......	300	150	40	450
Total, ...	8	24, 000	6, 200	3, 240	1, 634	927	3, 815

TOWNS.	Number of churches.	Value of church and lot.	Value of other real estate.	Number capable of being seated.	Usual number attending.	Number of communicants.	Salary of clergy, including use of real estate.
RICHMOND CO.							
Northfield, ...	1	$2, 500	$1, 000	450	40	18	$300
ST LAWRENCE CO.							
Morristown, ...	1	1, 100	......	250	100	100	200
SCHOHARIE CO.							
Carlisle, ...	1	1, 000	......	300	250	50	300
Cobleskill, ...	1	2, 000	1, 000	300	150	180	300
Fulton, ...	1	2, 000	......	350	150	100	115
Middleburgh, ...	1	700	1, 200	......	200	70	550
Richmondville, ...	1	1, 000	......	800	125	94	200
Seward, ...	3	6, 500	2, 605	1, 700	700	410	1, 185
Schoharie, ...	2	8, 000	2, 500	1, 150	275	100	750
Sharon, ...	2	2, 700	......	800	500	85	400
Summit, ...	1	1, 000	......	400	150	12	100
Wright, ...	1	1, 985	......	450	350	125	280
Total, ...	14	26, 885	7, 305	6, 250	2, 850	1, 226	4, 180
SENECA CO.							
Fayette, ...	2	3, 500	......	900	375	85	650
STEUBEN CO.							
Wayland, ...	1	1, 100	75	400	300	375	400
SULLIVAN CO.							
Callicoon, ...	1	1, 000	250	300	100	300	225
ULSTER CO.							
Kingston, ...	1	2, 500	......	250	150	120	300
Saugerties, ...	2	2, 000	700	650	300	200	550
Woodstock, ...	1	600	......	300	150	60	......
Total, ...	4	5, 100	700	1, 200	600	380	850
WAYNE CO.							
Lyons, ...	1	5, 000	......	600	450	287	380
YATES CO.							
Potter, ...	1	1, 500	......	250	200	100	90
FRIENDS MEETING HOUSES.							
ALBANY CO.							
Albany, ...	1	6, 000	......	500	180	100	......
Bern, ...	1	225	......	150	......	......	......
New Scotland, ...	1	400	......	200	10	10	......
Rensselaerville, ...	1	800	......	200	40	40	......
Total, ...	4	7, 425	......	1, 050	170	150	......
CAYUGA CO.							
Ledyard, ...	3	4, 500	200	1, 100	180	......	......
Springport, ...	2	2, 800	270	65	79	......	......
Venice, ...	2	2, 500	......	360	100	110	......
Total, ...	7	9, 800	470	1, 525	359	110	......
CHENANGO CO.							
Smyrna, ...	1	500	50	200	80	75	......
CLINTON CO.							
Ausable, ...	2	1, 600	400	530	115	55	......
COLUMBIA CO.							
Ghent, ...	1	700	......	300	25	......	......
Hudson, ...	2	2, 800	500	680	540	77	......
Total, ...	3	3, 500	500	980	565	77	......
DUTCHESS CO.							
Beekman, ...	1	600	300	250	40	38	......
Clinton, ...	2	1, 650	......	475	200	......	......
Dover, ...	1	1, 000	......	200	30	10	......
Hyde Park, ...	1	500	100	200	40	......	......
Pawling, ...	2	2, 000	......	300	30	60	......
Pine Plains, ...	1	200	......	150	30	20	......
Pleasant Valley, ...	1	2, 000	......	400	100	......	......
Poughkeepsie, ...	1	5, 000	500	400	250	......	......
Poughkeepsie city, ...	1	4, 000	......	200	100	100	......
Stanford, ...	2	1, 300	750	40	55	......	......
Union Vale, ...	1	1, 000	......	250	50	......	......
Washington, ...	2	5, 500	21, 500	2, 300	245	275	......
Total, ...	16	24, 750	23, 150	5, 165	1, 170	503	......
ERIE CO.							
Amherst, ...	1	1, 000	200	300	20	......	......
Boston, ...	1	450	......	150	20	......	......
Collins, ...	1	300	......	300	20	30	......
East Hamburgh, ...	2	3, 500	......	1, 000	72	60	......
North Collins, ...	2	1, 400	......	500	80	80	......
Total, ...	7	6, 650	200	2, 250	212	170	......
GREENE CO.							
Athens, ...	1	1, 000	......	150	25	25	......
New Baltimore, ...	3	1, 400	......	1, 000	275	210	......
Total, ...	4	2, 400	......	1, 150	300	235	......

CHURCHES—(CONTINUED.)

TOWNS.	Number of churches.	Value of church and lot.	Value of other real estate.	Number capable of being seated.	Usual number attending.	Number of communicants.	Salary of clergy, including use of real estate.
JEFFERSON Co.							
Le Ray,	1	$1,000	......	300	100	130	......
Philadelphia,	1	600	......	400	30	15	......
Total,	2	1,600	......	700	130	145	......
KINGS Co.							
Brooklyn,	1	12,000	$10000	250	200	275	......
LEWIS Co.							
Lowville,	1	500	......	200	20	......	......
MADISON Co.							
De Ruyter,	2	1,600	......	600	125	109	......
Madison,	1	200	......	75	20	......	......
Total,	3	1,800	......	675	145	109	......
MONROE Co.							
Rochester,	2	7,000	......	500	130	60	......
Wheatland,	2	2,100	......	450	75	105	......
Total,	4	9,100	......	950	205	165	......
NEW-YORK Co.							
New-York,	4	175,000	50,000	5,100	1,700	1,000	......
NIAGARA Co.							
Hartland,	1	1,500	......	400	50	60	......
Lockport,	1	2,000	......	200	30	45	......
Total,	2	3,500	......	600	80	105	......
ONEIDA Co.							
Lee,	1	300	25	300	15	25	......
New Hartford,	1	800	......	100	50	......	......
Verona,	1	500	......	125	25	25	......
Western,	1	810	......	200	70	......	......
Westmoreland,	1	400	......	150	40	40	......
Total,	5	2,810	25	875	200	90	......
ONONDAGA Co.							
Skaneateles,	2	500	......	275	87	55	......
ONTARIO Co.							
Farmington,	3	6,200	800	3,150	575	170	......
ORANGE Co.							
Blooming Grove,	1	1,500	......	200	......	......	......
Cornwall,	2	3,400	500	475	175	......	......
Monroe,	2	1,600	200	300	150	120	......
Total,	5	6,500	700	975	325	120	......
OSWEGO Co.							
Constantia,	1	500	100	300	25	100	......
OTSEGO Co.							
Laurens,	1	250	......	400	30	50	......
Milford,	1	300	......	150	5	......	......
Morris,	1	1,000	400	500	100	100	......
Total,	3	1,550	400	1,050	135	150	......
QUEENS Co.							
Flushing,	2	24,000	......	800	180	......	......
Hempstead,	1	600	200	200	30	......	......
North Hempstead,	3	4,700	......	1,200	190	......	......
Oyster Bay,	4	9,200	600	1,900	330	200	......
Total,	10	38,500	800	4,100	730	200	......
RENSSELAER Co.							
Pittstown,	1	400	100	500	40	50	......
Troy,	1	2,000	1,000	200	20	......	......
Total,	2	2,400	1,100	700	60	50	......
ROCKLAND Co.							
Haverstraw,	1	100	......	120	100	10	......
SARATOGA Co.							
Galway,	1	100	......	150	12	......	......
Greenfield,	2	400	......	350	40	45	......
Halfmoon,	1	300	......	160	12	12	......
Moreau,	1	400	......	150	50	......	......
Saratoga,	1	700	......	600	50	......	......
Total,	6	1,900	......	1,410	164	57	......
SCHUYLER Co.							
Hector,	1	1,000	......	200	50	76	......
SENECA Co.							
Waterloo,	1	1,200	......	300	60	50	......
ULSTER Co.							
Esopus,	1	200	......	200	30	20	......
Marlborough,	2	2,800	......	500	120	......	......
New Paltz,	1	150	......	100	6	......	......
Plattekill,	1	1,500	......	350	50	80	......
Rosendale,	1	1,000	......	300	12	......	......

TOWNS.	Number of churches.	Value of church and lot.	Value of other real estate.	Number capable of being seated.	Usual number attending.	Number of communicants.	Salary of clergy, including use of real estate.
ULSTER Co.							
Wawarsing,	1	$300	......	100	40	25	......
Total,	7	5,950	......	1,550	258	125	......
WARREN Co.							
Queensbury,	2	1,900	......	600	300	300	......
WASHINGTON Co.							
Easton,	2	1,700	$600	740	90	88	......
Granville,	2	2,100	......	450	70	......	......
White Creek,	1	400	......	600	25	......	......
Total,	5	4,200	600	1,790	185	88	......
WAYNE Co.							
Galen,	1	800	......	250	30	50	......
Macedon,	2	2,100	......	600	110	160	......
Palmyra,	1	700	......	300	25	50	......
Total,	4	3,600	......	1,150	165	260	......
WESTCHESTER Co.							
Cortlandt,	3	6,300	......	750	110	85	......
Harrison,	2	4,500	......	800	240	......	......
Lewisboro',	1	1,200	......	500	40	......	......
New Castle,	2	1,400	......	600	190	180	......
North Castle,	1	800	200	500	20	......	......
North Salem,	1	450	......	200	300	......	......
Westchester,	2	5,500	1,000	580	60	......	......
Yorktown,	2	3,500	......	800	150	......	......
Total,	14	23,650	1,200	4,730	1,110	265	......
WYOMING Co.							
Orangeville,	1	300	50	100	6	......	......
GERMAN EVANGELICAL REFORMED CHURCHES.							
CHAUTAUQUE Co.							
Clymer,	1	400	200	150	65	35	$230
ERIE Co.							
Buffalo,	3	8,100	1,000	1,600	1,100	900	1,600
Lancaster,	1	1,000	......	200	100	34	150
Tonawanda,	1	1,800	......	260	180	130	150
Total,	5	10,900	1,000	2,060	1,380	1,064	1,900
LIVINGSTON Co.							
North Dansville,	1	1,500	......	500	60	60	300
Sparta,	1	700	......	300	100	30	125
Total,	2	2,200	......	800	160	90	425
MONROE Co.							
Rochester,	2	8,800	......	750	625	495	750
WAYNE Co.							
Lyons,	1	5,500	......	350	250	200	300
JEWS' SYNAGOGUES.							
ALBANY Co.							
Albany,	3	14,000	......	1,500	850	......	2,400
ERIE Co.							
Buffalo,	1	6,000	1,000	200	40	40	125
KINGS Co.							
Brooklyn,	1	4,000	10,000	200	70	40	200
NEW-YORK Co.							
New-York,	10	177,100	111300	8,575	3,825	1,953	10,500
ONEIDA Co.							
Utica,	1	500	......	70	55	80	240
ONONDAGA Co.							
Syracuse,	2	10,000	800	400	100	75	400
ULSTER Co.							
Kingston,	1	500	......	50	25	......	250
MENEONITES' CHURCHES.							
ERIE Co.							
Amherst,	1	1,000	......	300	200	150	......
Clarence,	3	1,900	......	800	370	230	......
Total,	4	2,900	......	1,100	570	380	......
LIVINGSTON Co.							
Livonia,	1	400	......	150	35	32	......
NIAGARA Co.							
Wheatfield,	1	2,000	......	300	40	30	......
METHODIST EPISCOPAL CHURCHES.							
ALBANY Co.							
Albany,	7	60,300	5,800	4,800	2,335	1,266	5,350
Bern,	4	3,100	......	925	260	130	450

CHURCHES.—(Continued.)

TOWNS.	Number of churches.	Value of church and lot.	Value of other real estate.	Number capable of being seated.	Usual number attending.	Number of communicants.	Salary of clergy, including use of real estate.
Albany Co.							
Bethlehem,	2	$3,500	$500	800	260	75	$450
Coeymans,	3	4,700	2,100	940	350	323	950
Guilderland,	1	2.100	1,300	500	150	100	250
Knox,	3	3,500	1,000	750	430	170	510
New Scotland,	2	1,000	......	800	150	100	......
Rensselaerville,	2	4,000	1,500	675	290	262	775
Watervliet,	7	19,500	8,300	2,350	1,150	769	3010
Westerlo,	2	2,600	......	700	200	80	400
Total,	33	85,300	20,500	13,240	5,575	3.275	12145
Allegany Co.							
Allen,	1	1,000	......	400	100	114	......
Amity,	1	900	......	500	100	50	50
Andover,	1	700	......	300	100	73	518
Angelica,	1	1,500	......	500	......	50	500
Belfast,	1	2,500	600	400	100	400	......
Bolivar,	*2	1,800	1,450	250	150	73	766
Burns,	1	500	......	250	50	35	70
Caneadea,	1	1,500	100	400	125	80	100
Centreville,	1	1,000	700	300	60	100	200
Cuba,	1	1,300	......	300	50	50	135
Friendship,	1	2,000	400	300	200	130	500
Granger,	1	700	350	300	150	100	283
Grove,	1	1,200	......	250	50	21	232
Hume,	1	250	......	300	125	63	350
Independence,	1	1,000	300	275	50	50	250
New Hudson,	2	2,200	......	550	160	125	400
Ossian,	1	600	......	100	40	20	......
Rushford,	1	5,000	1,200	600	300	150	450
Scio,	1	3,500	......	400	150	60	475
Total,	21	29,150	5,100	6,675	2,060	1.744	5,279
Broome Co.							
Barker,	1	1,300	......	250	75	50	450
Chenango,	6	12,400	100	1,900	1,100	688	1,482
Colesville,	4	3,600	600	865	370	411	560
Conklin,	1	2,000	1,200	600	200	218	425
Maine,	2	2,200	......	700	300	266	360
Nanticoke,	1	750	......	300	100	50	360
Sandford,	1	1,200	400	300	100	50	350
Triangle,	2	3,400	......	768	130	78	500
Union,	1	150	......	300	100	......	......
Vestal,	1	2,000	150	400	125	100	375
Windsor,	2	2,300	......	525	250	105	375
Total,	22	31,300	2.450	6,908	2,850	2,016	5,237
Cattaraugus Co.							
Allegany,	1	1,700	1,200	300	100	55	143
Carrolton,	1	....	......	......	75	30	100
Connewango,	1	1,900	600	400	200	80	450
Dayton,	1	1,200	......	350	100	100	230
East Otto,	1	3 500	500	500	150	100	200
Ellicottville,	1	2,500	500	250	50	400	450
Farmersville,	1	1,800	......	500	150	60	180
Hinsdale,	1	1,800	......	300	100	40	125
Leon,	1	500	400	300	100	130	600
Machias,	1	1,100	......	800	150	108	414
Mansfield,	1	1,400	......	350	100	50	320
Olean,	1	4,000	......	450	250	30	500
Otto,	1	3,000	450	350	200	60	350
Perrysburgh,	3	3,500	......	750	225	79	550
Persia,	1	2,500	......	450	150	85	400
Portville,	1	2,000	900	250	130	80	500
Total,	18	32.400	4.550	6,300	2,230	1,487	5,512
Cayuga Co.							
Auburn,	2	19,600	......	1,000	608	308	900
Aurelius,	1	700	......	200	125	75	225
Brutus,	1	4,000	1,000	600	400	300	600
Cato,	1	1,500	......	300	60	30	130
Conquest,	1	2,800	......	370	200	100	500
Fleming,	1	2,000	......	500	70	100	......
Genoa,	2	3,800	100	560	200	110	625
Ira,	2	2,600	600	600	200	130	800
Ledyard,	2	1,600	......	400	230	125	450
Locke,	1	1,600	250	300	90	27	125
Mentz,	3	5,200	1,000	1,230	600	340	900
Moravia,	1	1,200	......	244	200	......	......
Niles,	2	2,200	......	900	250	40	450
Owasco,	1	1,300	......	240	100	45	150
Scipio,	1	1,100	......	200	50	75	250
Springport,	2	3,100	......	700	210	66	245
Sterling,	2	3,150	50	650	100	12	......
Summer Hill,	2	1,000	......	350	163	160	350
Victory,	2	2,500	......	800	135	85	450
Total,	30	60.950	3,000	10.144	3.991	2.128	7,150
Chautauque Co.							
Arkwright,	2	....	......	400	230	70	$90
Busti,	1	$1,500	......	350	60	80	......
Carroll,	1	1,000	......	500	30	30	350
Charlotte,	1	1,300	$500	300	100	40	350
Chautauque,	2	4,250	......	750	150	85	260
Clymer,	2	1,800	......	700	175	92	92
Ellery,	1	150	......	150	50	24	50
Ellicott,	2	4,500	1,150	800	500	277	1,262
Ellington,	1	900	300	400	300	200	400
Gerry,	1	400	......	200	40	12	350
Hanover,	4	5,200	700	1,600	575	225	1,175
Harmony,	5	4,850	1,100	1,600	625	330	1,292
Pomfret,	2	4,500	500	600	325	137	680
Portland,	2	4,800	1,000	850	300	180	487
Ripley,	1	3,000	......	350	150	58	375
Sherman,	1	1,200	......	300	150	85	420
Villenova,	1	800	300	450	75	80	195
Westfield,	2	5,200	......	700	250	61	600
Total,	32	45,350	5,550	11,000	4,085	2,066	7,428
Chemung Co.							
Big Flats,	1	....	......	100	50	20	400
Chemung,	1	2,000	500	400	150	80	600
Elmira,	2	24,000	6,000	1,650	1,100	630	1,880
Erin,	1	1,000	......	350	50	30	......
Horseheads,	2	7,100	900	750	400	250	650
Southport,	2	1,900	600	600	130	70	900
Van Etten,	1	1,400	......	400	30	150	385
Veteran,	2	2,050	800	400	350	200	500
Total,	12	39,450	8,800	4;650	2,310	1,430	5,315
Chenango Co.							
Bainbridge,	3	3,800	......	950	175	125	570
Columbus,	1	800	......	250	100	50	400
Coventry,	2	2,400	......	700	150	54	505
Greene,	2	2,900	......	900	200	180	600
Guilford,	5	7,400	500	2,100	725	370	1,300
Lincklaen,	1	200	......	300	150	50	50
Macdonough,	1	1,600	350	400	150	116	375
New Berlin,	2	4,000	1,300	660	350	248	828
North Norwich,	2	21,000	......	450	150	60	300
Norwich,	1	6,000	1,500	800	500	287	675
Oxford,	1	2.800	600	500	250	166	500
Pitcher,	2	1,800	600	180	180	140	410
Plymouth,	1	1,800	400	250	175	250	510
Sherburne,	2	2.550	750	650	175	200	450
Smithville,	2	1,700	450	175	450	64	1,682
Smyrna,	1	2,000	450	300	150	80	400
Total,	29	62,750	6,900	9,565	4.030	2,440	9 555
Clinton Co.							
Ausable,	2	4,000	......	550	350	195	800
Beekmantown,	3	5.000	875	1,510	540	135	925
Champlain,	1	2,500	600	300	150	70	500
Chazy,	2	5,000	1,800	900	375	215	1,000
Ellenburgh,	1	....	......	......	......	67	......
Mooers,	1	1,200	500	250	75	250	400
Peru,	2	3,000	700	450	280	138	647
Plattsburgh,	1	7,000	3,000	600	300	250	800
Saranac,	1	500	500	150	70	100	500
Schuyler's Falls,	2	5,000	500	570	350	198	400
Total,	16	33,200	8.475	5,280	2,490	1,618	5,972
Columbia Co.							
Ancram,	1	1,000	......	250	75	......	......
Austerlitz,	1	1,500	300	300	160	60	350
Canaan,	2	3,500	500	500	120	70	450
Chatham,	6	11,900	......	2,400	1,100	457	2,170
Copake,	1	3,000	2.000	200	40	15	500
Germantown,	1	1,000	......	250	75	30	120
Hillsdale,	3	7,500	800	850	525	150	925
Hudson,	1	18,000	1,700	800	805	400	1,050
Kinderhook,	2	5,500	......	1,000	550	170	1,200
Livingston,	1	2,350	......	300	100	40	125
New Lebanon,	3	1,400	......	950	130	75	400
Stockport,	1	1,000	......	400	100	70	300
Taghkanick,	1	1,000	600	300	225	100	500
Total,	24	58,650	5,900	8,500	4,000	1,637	8,090
Cortland Co.							
Cincinnatus,	1	1,200	800	450	125	120	400
Cortlandville,	2	6,000	2,000	1,100	575	398	1,100
Freetown,	2	1,600	500	435	200	200	264
Homer,	2	3.800	......	800	250	210	530
Marathon,	1	1,500	1,000	400	300	120	425
Preble,	1	1,500	700	400	150	90	350
Scott,	1	2,000	......	300	150	76	200

* One a school house.

CHURCHES.—(Continued.)

TOWNS.	Number of churches.	Value of church and lot.	Value of other real estate.	Number capable of being seated.	Usual number attending.	Number of communicants.	Salary of clergy, including use of real estate.
CORTLAND CO.							
Taylor,	2	$1,000	$350	350	150	100	$800
Truxton,	2	2,600	150	700	200	133	470
Virgil,	1	1,600	400	300	100	80	300
Total,	15	22,800	5,900	5,235	2,195	1,527	4,339
DELAWARE CO.							
Andes,	1	1,000	......	200	150	80	240
Bovina,	1	1,800	......	300	200	32	200
Colchester,	1	1,000	500	250	50	61	375
Davenport,	3	3,700	......	1,450	600	286	574
Delhi,	1	3,000	......	350	200	127	400
Franklin,	3	4,800	800	7,650	550	519	1,277
Hancock,	3	3,700	......	615	417	146	562
Kortright,	2	1,200	50	1,000	270	165	275
Masonville,	1	1,300	......	250	60	144	350
Middletown,	2	3,100	800	1,600	650	525	950
Roxbury,	3	1,950	......	1,000	500	195	565
Sidney,	2	2,200	......	600	250	65	300
Stamford,	2	3,800	......	800	250	75	450
Tompkins,	2	2,900	1,200	700	200	180	400
Walton,	1	1,500	......	300	65	60	339
Total,	28	36,950	3,350	17,065	4.412	2,660	7,257
DUTCHESS CO.							
Beekman,	1	2,500	1,500	500	200	91	280
Dover,	3	8,400	......	950	310	81	770
East Fishkill,	1	800	......	200	100	16	20
Fishkill,	7	10,500	2,100	2,150	670	465	1,875
Hyde Park,	1	2.000	500	300	75	40	270
Milan,	2	2,800	100	600	225	210	775
Pawling,	2	3,300	......	550	160	64	280
Pine Plains,	1	2,000	1,000	250	200	80	750
Pleasant Valley,	1	500	1,000	500	400	200	700
Poughkeepsie,	3	6.900	3,000	1,000	600	440	1,375
Poughkeepsie city,	3	29.000	......	1,825	1,200	545	2,056
Redhook,	2	3,300	750	400	110	90	900
Rhinebeck,	1	6,000	3,700	300	160	136	800
Stanford,	1	1,000	......	400	50	30	300
Union Vale,	3	5,500	250	1,900	135	110	730
Washington,	1	1,500	......	300	100	55	......
Total,	33	86,000	13,900	12,125	4,695	2,653	11881
ERIE CO.							
Alden,	1	2,200	......	295	70	75	375
Amherst,	1	3,000	550	350	150	100	450
Aurora,	1	1,500	500	350	150	63	400
Boston,	1	700	300	......	125	74	......
Brant,	1	400	......	300	80	30	75
Buffalo,	6	67,000	3,000	3,250	1,900	1,020	4,400
Concord,	1	1,000	......	300	200	200	500
East Hamburgh,	1	1,500	......	300	80	25	100
Eden,	1	500	100	150	75	35	400
Evans,	1	1,800	450	600	100	40	350
Hamburgh,	1	1,350	1.000	300	150	66	450
Lancaster,	4	6,500	1,000	1,100	370	275	860
Newstead,	1	4,000	400	158	158	118	400
North Collins,	2	2,200	......	600	150	76	385
Sardinia,	1	2,000	450	400	125	75	416
Wales,	2	2,200	......	900	450	90	600
Total,	26	97,850	7.750	9.353	4.333	2,362	10161
ESSEX CO.							
Chesterfield,	1	6,000	1,500	500	350	275	425
Crown Point,	1	2.000	400	300	150	170	450
Elizabethtown,	1	3,100	800	300	225	300	425
Essex,	1	2,000	500	200	60	116	400
Jay,	4	4,900	500	750	620	148	1,030
Keene,	1	400	......	300	150	100	150
Minerva,	1	700	......	200	75	50	75
Moriah,	1	1,500	......	300	80	130	310
North Hudson,	1	......	......	125	25	36	300
Schroon,	1	1,600	500	400	75	175	450
Westport,	1	3.000	700	275	175	250	616
Willsborough,	1	3,500	......	350	180	200	450
Wilmington,	1	1,000	50	600	50	50	150
Total,	16	29,700	4.950	4,600	2.215	2,000	5,231
FRANKLIN CO.							
Bombay,	2	3,200	1,700	650	70	142	850
Burke,	1	300	......	......	......	50	......
Chateaugay,	1	1,000	......	400	200	100	400
Constable,	1	250	......	200	260	106	300
Dickinson,	1	400	......	200	25	10	......
Duane,	1	50	......	50	25	10	50
Fort Covington,	1	2,000	800	400	250	108	400
Franklin,	1	......	......	......	125	55	280
Malone,	1	$2,000	$800	400	250	175	350
Total,	10	9,200	3,300	2,300	1,205	756	2,630
FULTON CO.							
Bleecker,	1	......	......	......	50	25	100
Broadalbin,	1	1,200	......	400	200	100	450
Ephratah,	2	1,700	500	750	135	100	400
Johnstown,	2	10,000	1,300	870	550	336	1,100
Mayfield,	1	2,500	......	300	200	80	200
Northampton,	2	3,900	800	550	330	194	430
Oppenheim,	1	1,100	......	200	75	20	65
Total,	10	20,400	2,600	3,070	1,540	855	2,825
GENESEE CO.							
Alabama,	1	1.500	......	300	200	40	350
Alexander,	1	2,000	300	600	150	67	500
Batavia,	1	3,000	......	300	200	100	......
Bergen,	1	2,500	800	320	200	106	500
Bethany,	1	1,200	......	350	50	30	75
Byron,	2	2,700	......	700	200	60	253
Darien,	1	1,600	800	300	100	40	270
Elba,	1	1,600	800	300	80	50	450
Le Roy,	1	6,000	1,500	500	400	200	800
Oakfield,	1	2,000	550	400	175	115	525
Pavilion,	3	5,500	1,000	800	325	183	777
Stafford,	2	4,200	......	400	250	136	850
Total,	16	33,800	5,750	5,270	2,330	1,127	5,350
GREENE CO.							
Ashland,	3	2,200	10	1,150	350	190	470
Cairo,	3	2,950	300	1,050	600	195	420
Catskill,	3	2,900	......	850	325	205	662
Coxsackie,	2	2,700	......	800	400	100	750
Durham,	2	3,300	......	700	210	207	520
Greenville,	2	1,900	......	630	350	141	380
Halcott,	1	600	......	300	125	25	45
Hunter,	1	300	......	200	60	41	350
Jewett,	3	4,500	1,300	1,100	225	120	336
Lexington,	1	1,400	......	250	60	43	120
New Baltimore,	1	1,000	......	300	75	50	40
Prattsville,	1	2,000	700	300	150	55	400
Windham,	1	1,200	......	300	200	320	825
Total,	24	26,950	2,810	7,930	3,130	1,692	5,318
HAMILTON CO.							
Lake Pleasant,	1	200	......	200	30	20	40
Wells,	1	450	......	300	75	40	200
Total,	2	650	......	500	105	60	240
HERKIMER CO.							
Fairfield,	1	1,500	......	600	150	75	350
Frankfort,	4	5,975	150	1,150	400	90	7,800
Herkimer,	2	3,500	......	600	200	100	500
Litchfield,	2	1,200	......	1,300	50	25	60
Little Falls,	1	5,000	500	800	300	184	1,000
Manheim,	2	4,000	1,200	500	200	115	450
Newport,	1	500	......	300	100	70	......
Norway,	1	1,000	700	250	150	58	130
Russia,	1	800	......	400	150	60	60
Salisbury,	2	4,000	......	1,000	350	200	500
Schuyler,	1	2,000	......	500	75	100	500
Stark,	1	800	......	400	100	25	75
Warren,	4	3.800	400	900	550	175	790
Winfield,	1	2,000	1,000	250	125	100	370
Total,	24	36,575	4,950	8,950	2,900	1,377	12,585
JEFFERSON CO.							
Adams,	1	6,000	1,500	450	300	220	500
Alexandria,	1	......	150	150	50	......	100
Antwerp,	1	1,000	......	200	150	50	200
Brownville,	2	2,500	......	525	215	201	609
Champion,	2	2,100	......	650	300	......	184
Clayton,	4	7,400	400	1,050	460	206	1,175
Ellisburgh,	2	4,500	1,300	1,200	450	200	895
Henderson,	2	4,000	......	550	75	50	600
Hounsfield,	1	3,500	......	400	125	129	325
Le Ray,	1	2,000	......	500	300	110	400
Lorraine,	1	500	......	300	100	32	200
Lyme,	2	800	400	400	195	100	510
Orleans,	1	300	......	100	30	25	300
Pamelia,	1	1,450	400	350	250	87	370
Philadelphia,	2	700	......	450	140	65	410
Rodman,	2	2,800	700	400	150	70	500
Rutland,	2	2,000	700	600	210	93	583
Theresa,	1	2,200	400	400	300	219	430
Watertown,	2	19,000	1,000	940	900	462	1,450

CHURCHES.—(Continued.)

TOWNS.	Number of churches.	Value of church and lot.	Value of other real estate.	Number capable of being seated.	Usual number attending.	Number of communicants.	Salary of clergy, includ'ng use of real estate.
JEFFERSON Co.							
Wilna,	1	$4,000	......	400	200	150	$500
Worth,	1	....	......	......	......	35	......
Total,	33	67,050	$6,950	10,015	4,900	2,504	10241
KINGS Co.							
Brooklyn,	27	317,900	41,000	20,500	11,011	4,705	28400
Flatbush,	1	4,000	......	250	100	22	450
Gravesend,	1	700	......	200	75	16	200
New Lots,	1	1,700	......	100	100	......	125
New Utrecht,	1	1,200	......	200	75	20	150
Total,	31	325,500	41,000	21,250	11,361	4,763	29325
LEWIS Co.							
Denmark,	1	1,600	400	300	200	130	400
Lewis,	1	300	200	60	30	......	......
Leyden,	1	200	......	150	......	20	......
Lowville,	1	1,200	2,000	450	200	200	550
Martinsburgh,	2	1,800	300	1,450	200	95	400
New Bremen,	1	1,500	500	400	150	40	450
Pinckney,	1	500	......	400	200	118	......
Turin,	3	3,200	500	1,000	375	115	450
Watson,	1	1,600	......	500	50	20	300
West Turin,	2	1,700	......	450	155	64	200
Total,	14	13,600	3,900	5,160	1,360	802	2,750
LIVINGSTON Co.							
Avon,	2	3,100	......	500	225	180	800
Caledonia,	1	1,500	......	......	......	......	......
Conesus,	1	1,800	300	350	125	40	350
Geneseo,	1	6,000	2,000	600	453	110	650
Groveland,	1	3,000	1,500	500	125	60	450
Leicester,	1	1,200	400	300	100	40	300
Lima,	1	2,000	......	400	350	130	650
Livonia,	1	1,000	......	400	30	44	225
Mount Morris,	2	4,000	800	900	450	137	600
North Dansville,	1	1,200	......	300	250	150	500
Nunda,	1	3,000	600	450	300	125	400
Sparta,	2	1,550	......	600	50	43	120
Springwater,	1	1,500	100	500	100	35	250
West Sparta,	1	1,800	......	300	130	30	250
York,	2	4,500	......	464	140	35	310
Total,	19	37,150	5,700	6,564	2,828	1,159	5,855
MADISON Co.							
Brookfield,	2	850	......	600	175	195	335
Cazenovia,	2	7,500	1,200	500	350	290	850
De Ruyter,	1	1,600	......	200	150	80	280
Eaton,	3	5,400	......	1,400	600	233	815
Fenner,	3	1,950	......	700	335	105	325
Georgetown,	1	....	......	......	75	17	450
Hamilton,	4	8,400	2,200	1,850	760	432	1,364
Lebanon,	1	150	......	200	70	30	100
Lenox,	5	8,000	1,800	1,350	600	375	1,495
Madison,	2	4,600	1,300	700	125	220	900
Nelson,	2	2,200	400	600	300	165	550
Stockbridge,	1	2,500	500	600	350	208	500
Sullivan,	2	3,700	1,000	800	300	200	907
Total,	29	46,850	8,400	9,500	4,190	2,550	9,871
MONROE Co.							
Chili,	2	6,500	1,000	550	200	150	1,102
Clarkson,	2	3,500	......	500	200	70	600
Gates,	1	1,000	......	300	100	60	......
Greece,	2	3,400	......	600	300	66	400
Mendon,	1	2,500	1,000	350	150	95	600
Ogden,	1	3,000	1,000	400	150	59	500
Parma,	2	3,000	500	700	350	209	440
Penfield,	1	4,500	1,000	800	350	124	550
Perrington,	1	800	......	110	40	30	......
Pittsford,	1	2,500	......	300	200	80	300
Riga,	1	1,500	1,200	350	150	56	525
Rochester,	7	53,850	250	3,850	2,450	1,288	5,780
Rush,	2	4,400	1,200	750	150	135	400
Sweden,	2	4,900	1,400	550	290	210	994
Webster,	2	2,500	800	500	350	200	500
Wheatland,	1	2,500	......	400	80	60	550
Total,	29	100,350	9,350	11,010	5,510	2,892	13241
MONTGOMERY Co.							
Amsterdam,	1	100	......	200	100	55	60
Canajoharie,	3	6,450	1,300	1,600	1,000	245	1,025
Charleston,	1	100	......	300	80	50	80
Florida,	1	1,500	1,000	350	100	65	350
Glen,	1	3,000	......	500	250	20	425
Mohawk,	1	3,500	......	500	200	40	500
Minden,	3	6,200	1,000	1,280	650	255	1,200

TOWNS.	Number of churches.	Value of church and lot.	Value of other real estate.	Number capable of being seated.	Usual number attending.	Number of communicants.	Salary of clergy, including use of real estate.
MONTGOMERY Co.							
Root,	1	$1,300	......	300	75	50	$350
Total,	12	22,150	$3,300	5,030	2,455	780	3,990
NEW-YORK Co.							
New-York,	33	582,800	145300	27,030	15,090	8,878	47,900
NIAGARA Co.							
Cambria,	1	3,000	1,000	400	250	162	80
Lewiston,	1	2,500	......	250	60	20	14
Lockport,	4	4,050	100	340	535	217	1,40
Newfane,	2	6,000	550	600	400	148	83
Niagara,	1	5,000	......	300	150	100	30
Pendleton,	1	2,000	......	300	100	70	25
Porter,	3	8,300	700	1,200	500	205	1,10
Royalton,	3	4,800	1,250	1,250	330	250	1,34
Somerset,	1	2,000	350	320	200	101	40
Wheatfield,	1	2,000	......	250	200	100	30
Wilson,	1	3,000	800	475	200	147	65
Total,	19	42,650	4,750	5,685	2,925	1,520	7,51
ONEIDA Co.							
Annsville,	1	800	......	300	50	50	15
Augusta,	1	1,500	500	400	100	135	35
Boonville,	1	2,000	......	450	300	132	32
Camden,	1	4,500	900	500	350	230	60
Florence,	2	900	475	550	200	92	35
Kirkland,	1	2,000	1,200	250	100	80	40
Lee,	2	1,500	......	625	340	68	50
Marcy,	1	1,500	400	500	60	70	47
Marshall,	1	1,600	1,700	400	200	130	40
New Hartford,	1	3,000	......	450	200	120	50
Paris,	2	4,500	1,200	600	400	275	67
Remsen,	2	3,300	600	550	130	33	25
Rome,	2	9,500	......	1,350	450	293	70
Sangerfield,	1	500	50	100	50	......	......
Steuben,	2	2,000	......	450	135	58	1,00
Trenton,	4	4,500	......	1,400	550	164	88
Utica,	3	16,000	4,000	1,600	1,050	635	1,50
Vernon,	2	4,500	1,000	700	350	152	83
Verona,	3	4,700	900	850	500	238	1,29
Vienna,	3	4,800	500	1,600	585	175	80
Western,	3	3,500	500	800	350	150	60
Westmoreland,	3	3,300	1,200	1,170	380	200	96
Whitestown,	3	11,000	1,000	1,300	575	305	50
Total,	45	91,400	16,125	16,895	7,405	3,785	14,05
ONONDAGA Co.							
Camillus,	2	4,400	800	700	230	122	67
Cicero,	2	1,500	1,100	600	140	120	90
Clay,	2	2,200	100	550	300	140	70
De Witt,	3	2,200	500	850	250	125	85
Elbridge,	3	8,200	1,200	950	550	378	1,07
Fabius,	2	2,500	......	450	125	97	75
Geddes,	1	2,500	......	350	200	60	40
La Fayette,	1	800	......	300	170	84	18
Lysander,	4	4,200	1,650	1,700	650	325	1,62
Manlius,	3	4,700	800	895	285	168	9
Marcellus,	1	3,000	800	500	300	110	45
Onondaga,	5	5,400	500	1,380	300	285	62
Otisco,	2	2,000	......	750	300	150	1,40
Pompey,	4	2,300	......	1,000	400	225	77
Salina,	2	950	600	500	335	75	5
Skaneateles,	2	2,750	1,000	490	130	220	49
Spafford,	3	2,900	......	1,000	400	225	77
Syracuse,	4	20,800	1,000	2,450	870	540	1,95
Tully,	2	2,500	......	480	105	82	20
Van Buren,	1	1,000	500	300	80	70	50
Total,	49	76,800	10,550	17,195	6,120	3,601	16,27
ONTARIO Co.							
Bristol,	1	2,200	......	350	125	60	4
Canadice,	1	2,000	......	125	300	50	1
Canandaigua,	2	7,000	1,500	1,600	550	200	1,18
East Bloomfield,	1	1,000	......	208	60	38	14
Gorham,	1	500	......	200	75	30	7
Hopewell,	3	8,100	1,500	1,000	270	96	1,00
Manchester,	3	5,800	1,800	1,000	450	190	1,00
Naples,	1	5,000	700	400	250	200	50
Phelps,	2	2,500	200	950	350	218	69
Seneca,	2	18,000	800	950	600	410	1,20
Victor,	1	1,500	1,000	600	200	150	50
West Bloomfield,	1	1,200	......	200	75	82	3
Total,	19	54,800	7,500	7,583	2,505	1,724	7,1
ORANGE Co.							
Blooming Grove,	4	5,550	......	950	920	110	7
Chester,	2	7,500	1,000	750	400	564	9

CHURCHES.—(Continued.)

TOWNS	Number of churches.	Value of church and lot.	Value of other real estate.	Number capable of being seated.	Usual number attending.	Number of communicants.	Salary of clergy, including use of real estate.
Orange Co.							
Cornwall, ...	4	$6, 550	......	850	405	204	$436
Deerpark, ...	1	1, 000	......	350	200	187	700
Greenville, ...	1	800	......	400	250	52	125
Goshen, ...	2	5, 200	......	800	340	116	670
Minisink, ...	1	800	......	300	50	60	175
Monroe, ...	3	4, 600	$1, 500	1, 050	660	405	985
Montgomery, ...	2	6, 800	1, 400	900	550	205	825
Mount Hope, ...	2	2, 050	......	900	250	110	600
Newburgh, ...	7	22, 400	8, 200	3, 200	1, 900	883	3750
New Windsor, ...	2	4, 100	......	800	350	120	400
Walkill, ...	2	4, 000	1, 000	700	525	540	600
Warwick, ...	6	11, 500	......	1, 950	775	295	895
Wawayanda, ...	1	2, 000	......	300	100	70	......
Total, ...	40	84, 850	13, 100	14, 200	7, 675	3, 921	11926
Orleans Co.							
Barre, ...	2	12, 000	2, 100	950	600	430	1, 100
Carlton, ...	2	3, 400	......	650	270	80	323
Clarendon, ...	1	2, 500	......	300	150	40	300
Gaines, ...	1	2, 000	......	450	150	106	300
Kendall, ...	1	1, 500	800	300	120	150	500
Murray, ...	1	2, 000	800	470	180	70	514
Ridgeway, ...	2	9, 500	400	900	460	230	1, 270
Shelby, ...	4	6, 350	500	900	460	198	1, 250
Yates, ...	2	3, 500	450	750	300	225	125
Total, ...	16	42, 750	5. 050	5, 670	2, 690	1. 529	5, 682
Oswego Co.							
Albion, ...	1	1, 000	25	200	50	40	200
Amboy, ...	1	800	......	270	30	98	328
Constantia, ...	1	1, 000	400	400	100	35	300
Granby, ...	1	450	......	200	100	30	400
Hannibal, ...	1	800	800	250	150	150	475
Hastings, ...	2	1, 750	......	430	205	158	475
Mexico, ...	2	6, 000	1, 000	650	368	368	766
New Haven, ...	1	1, 000	......	350	250	118	500
Orwell, ...	1	1, 000	......	400	150	40	300
Oswego city, ...	3	15, 500	2, 200	1, 550	900	541	1, 550
Palermo, ...	2	1, 050	......	500	225	160	280
Parish, ...	1	1, 000	......	450	75	40	......
Redfield, ...	1	700	......	300	120	70	250
Richland, ...	2	2, 500	1, 100	750	600	325	800
Sandy Creek, ...	1	2, 000	......	400	250	100	350
Schroeppel, ...	2	1, 900	1, 600	900	300	263	600
Scriba, ...	1	2, 000	......	300	200	110	250
Volney, ...	2	7, 000	......	1, 100	400	450	1, 275
Williamstown, ...	1	1, 200	500	250	150	40	325
Total, ...	27	48, 650	7, 825	9, 650	4. 623	3, 136	9, 484
Otsego Co.							
Butternuts, ...	1	1, 500	800	400	150	135	475
Cherry Valley, ...	2	3, 950	800	700	400	175	575
Decatur, ...	1	1, 600	250	600	200	160	300
Edmeston, ...	1	1, 000	......	300	100	85	315
Exeter, ...	2	1, 800	450	800	325	120	300
Hartwick, ...	1	1, 800	......	300	150	100	200
Laurens, ...	2	3, 500	700	550	300	167	750
Maryland, ...	3	2, 800	......	750	350	203	1, 010
Middlefield, ...	1	1, 000	500	400	150	80	410
Milford, ...	2	4, 000	......	500	350	216	540
Morris, ...	1	2, 000	......	300	200	100	400
New Lisbon, ...	1	1, 000	......	400	100	13	75
Oneonta, ...	2	2, 000	400	850	310	229	550
Otego, ...	1	1, 800	110	375	150	113	440
Otsego, ...	3	4, 600	1, 000	1, 100	500	639	850
Richfield, ...	3	2, 000	......	900	100	74	400
Roseboom, ...	2	1, 500	300	650	350	100	400
Springfield, ...	1	2, 000	2, 000	350	300	150	600
Unadilla, ...	2	1, 500	......	300	200	140	335
Westford, ...	2	1, 000	......	1, 000	500	128	700
Worcester, ...	1	1, 000	......	500	100	60	325
Total, ...	35	43, 350	7, 310	8, 025	5, 285	3, 187	9, 950
Putnam Co.							
Carmel, ...	3	7, 000	......	900	275	250	380
Phillipstown, ...	4	7, 100	2, 200	900	665	405	950
Putnam Valley, ...	3	3, 000	700	900	210	220	450
Southeast, ...	1	2, 500	500	500	200	150	280
Total, ...	11	19, 600	3, 400	3, 200	1, 350	1, 025	2, 060
Queens Co.							
Flushing, ...	2	11, 200	1, 500	800	600	130	1, 200
Hempstead, ...	8	21, 000	1, 800	2, 450	1, 550	719	1, 680
Jamaica, ...	2	5, 250	800	725	300	16	860
North Hempstead, ...	2	1, 800	1, 000	600	135	55	525

TOWNS.	Number of churches.	Value of church and lot.	Value of other real estate.	Number capable of being seated.	Usual number attending.	Number of communicants.	Salary of clergy, including use of real estate.
Queens Co.							
Newtown, ...	3	$7, 600	$1, 000	950	260	75	$600
Oyster Bay, ...	4	5, 500	.....	1, 350	925	195	955
Total, ...	21	52, 350	6, 100	6, 875	3, 770	1, 190	5, 820
Rensselaer Co.							
Brunswick, ...	2	2, 800	1, 100	900	190	84	400
Grafton, ...	1	300	......	250	75	50	300
Greenbush, ...	1	4, 000	400	350	225	115	600
Hoosick, ...	2	3. 000	......	450	145	142	700
Lansingburgh, ...	2	9, 500	......	710	400	297	1, 306
Nassau, ...	2	3, 000	200	600	200	101	500
Petersburgh, ...	2	1, 400	......	600	85	130	400
Pittstown, ...	6	10, 800	1, 450	2, 000	420	1, 329	1, 100
Sandlake, ...	2	2, 200	700	530	200	130	750
Schaghticoke, ...	3	1, 525	30	890	255	92	990
Schodack, ...	2	4, 500	1, 100	4, 300	225	130	800
Troy, ...	7	45, 300	3, 000	4, 010	2, 080	1, 330	4, 614
Total, ...	32	88, 325	7, 980	15. 590	4, 500	3, 930	12, 460
Richmond Co.							
Northfield, ...	2	10, 500	3, 000	950	700	290	1, 200
Westfield, ...	2	8, 800	2, 600	1, 200	800	460	1, 300
Total, ...	4	19, 300	5, 600	2, 150	1, 500	750	2, 500
Rockland Co.							
Clarkstown, ...	2	1, 200	......	500	130	80	600
Haverstraw, ...	2	8, 000	3, 000	800	485	385	1, 400
Orangetown, ...	2	6, 000	1, 500	600	350	250	1, 250
Ramapo, ...	2	2, 000	......	800	300	80	600
Total, ...	8	17, 200	4, 500	2, 700	1, 265	795	3, 850
St. Lawrence Co.							
Brasher, ...	2	3, 000	350	700	280	145	350
Canton, ...	2	900	1, 200	600	300	222	300
Colton, ...	1	1, 200	......	375	150	50	250
De Kalb, ...	1	800	......	600	75	15	200
De Peyster, ...	1	......	......	......	......	30	200
Fowler, ...	1	200	......	200	100	21	......
Hammond, ...	1	600	......	450	100	90	375
Hermon, ...	1	1, 350	......	300	200	50	500
Hopkinton, ...	1	1, 300	400	300	175	160	324
Lawrence, ...	2	1, 000	......	175	160	110	500
Lisbon, ...	1	1, 600	300	200	50	200	400
Louisville, ...	1	1, 000	......	600	175	64	400
Macomb, ...	1	200	......	......	......	......	200
Madrid, ...	2	2, 300	......	600	115	78	450
Massena, ...	1	1, 200	......	300	50	100	300
Morristown, ...	2	2, 600	......	400	300	75	395
Norfolk, ...	1	500	300	300	100	125	300
Oswegatchie, ...	3	11, 700	1, 000	1, 600	1, 000	404	1, 700
Parishville, ...	1	1, 350	......	300	150	140	200
Pierrepont, ...	1	2, 000	......	400	150	75	150
Potsdam, ...	3	3, 600	1, 800	1, 000	550	98	536
Rossie, ...	1	1, 100	......	180	80	32	200
Stockholm, ...	1	1, 200	350	350	125	125	450
Total, ...	32	40, 900	5, 700	9, 930	4, 385	2, 399	8, 680
Saratoga Co.							
Charlton, ...	1	1, 500	900	200	75	60	200
Clifton Park, ...	4	10, 400	1, 900	1, 630	481	245	1, 222
Corinth, ...	1	1, 000	......	300	150	40	50
Edinburgh, ...	2	1, 100	......	1, 100	240	100	370
Galway, ...	1	2, 000	1, 000	300	150	85	400
Greenfield, ...	2	2, 500	450	600	125	80	125
Halfmoon, ...	3	5, 600	1, 000	650	270	96	910
Malta, ...	2	2, 200	......	750	175	65	400
Milton, ...	2	5, 800	......	900	325	185	700
Moreau, ...	1	1, 000	......	200	150	120	400
Northumberland, ...	1	1, 200	......	550	150	110	148
Saratoga, ...	3	6, 500	1, 000	1, 050	600	165	700
Saratoga Springs, ...	1	10, 000	600	700	500	320	675
Stillwater, ...	3	7, 300	500	800	440	250	1, 225
Waterford, ...	1	2, 000	1, 000	500	150	100	400
Wilton, ...	1	1, 250	......	250	100	80	125
Total, ...	29	61, 350	8, 350	10, 480	4, 081	2, 101	8, 050
Schenectady Co.							
Glenville, ...	2	3, 200	......	700	450	102	305
Schenectady, ...	2	14, 000	......	1, 050	700	385	1, 300
Total, ...	4	17. 200	......	1, 750	1, 150	487	1. 605
Schoharie Co.							
Blenheim, ...	2	2, 900	......	825	290	87	375
Broome, ...	3	1, 150	15	700	275	100	500
Cobleskill, ...	4	5, 900	......	1, 700	540	210	390
Conesville, ...	2	2, 200	......	800	250	......	155

CHURCHES.—(CONTINUED.)

TOWNS.	Number of churches.	Value of church and lot.	Value of other real estate.	Number capable of being seated.	Usual number attending.	Number of communicants.	Salary of clergy, including use of real estate.
SCHOHARIE CO.							
Esperance,	1	$1,500	......	800	175	100	$460
Gilboa,	2	1,200	......	600	300	70	155
Jefferson,	4	3,750	$50	1,800	600	287	410
Middleburgh,	2	2,150	......	750	245	220	440
Richmondville,	2	1,800	......	700	225	110	625
Seward,	3	2,800	600	1,600	400	230	400
Schoharie,	1	3,300	......	350	150	100	476
Summit,	2	3,400	......	1,300	950	199	285
Wright,	2	1,925	600	550	345	117	476
Total,	30	33,975	1,265	12,475	4,745	1,830	5,146
SCHUYLER CO.							
Catharine,	2	3,600	1,000	450	375	245	1,250
Dix,	3	2,400	......	600	350	120	625
Hector,	7	9,000	1,700	2,025	950	457	2,000
Orange,	1	1,200	800	300	100	......	550
Reading,	1	1,500	......	300	100	25	400
Tyrone,	2	3,625	600	600	325	225	500
Total,	16	21,325	4,100	4,275	2,200	1,072	5,325
SENECA CO.							
Covert,	1	800	......	300	75	100	......
Fayette,	1	1,500	600	350	175	50	250
Lodi,	3	4,900	500	900	480	301	850
Ovid,	2	4,200	1,050	1,150	420	130	900
Seneca Falls,	1	1,200	500	500	250	150	400
Tyre,	1	3,000	......	1,000	200	100	300
Varick,	1	500	......	300	200	170	300
Waterloo,	1	6,000	1,200	350	250	162	420
Total,	11	22,100	3,850	4,850	2,050	1,163	3,420
STEUBEN CO.							
Addison,	1	3,000	......	300	125	80	600
Avoca,	1	2,000	1,000	500	150	100	350
Bath,	2	3,700	......	1,000	400	211	700
Bradford,	1	2,000	50	400	200	107	225
Cameron,	3	2,750	400	850	150	85	400
Campbell,	1	600	......	200	......	20	......
Caton,	1	300	400	250	220	200	440
Cohocton,	3	4,200	700	850	400	400	650
Corning,	2	5,000	......	850	350	100	900
Dansville,	1	1,600	400	800	400	150	530
Erwin,	1	3,000	......	350	150	136	450
Fremont,	1	900	......	400	125	45	100
Hornellsville,	1	2,000	1,500	400	200	110	825
Howard,	1	1,600	600	300	100	44	300
Jasper,	1	1,200	100	400	150	60	400
Prattsburgh,	2	700	......	600	50	28	50
Pultney,	2	200	......	350	200	66	250
Thurston,	3	800	......	650	100	80	455
Troupsburgh,	1	......	700	......	50	100	......
Urbana,	1	2,000	......	300	150	150	400
Wayne,	1	800	......	300	......	......	......
Wheeler,	1	1,000	......	300	100	40	110
Woodhull,	1	1,400	50	300	75	30	400
Total,	33	40,750	5,900	10.650	3,845	2,342	8,535
SUFFOLK CO.							
Brookhaven,	9	11,300	1,150	2,050	1,140	309	2,180
East Hampton,	2	11,000	1,000	1,000	350	220	880
Huntington,	10	12,800	2,050	2,920	1,365	635	2,425
Islip,	3	3,200	50	700	460	225	558
Riverhead,	2	2,400	550	450	175	105	571
Smithtown,	3	3,950	700	1,050	355	102	450
Southampton,	6	7,700	1,500	1,280	568	420	1,950
Southold,	5	3,000	1,475	1,400	650	386	1,995
Total,	40	55,050	8,475	10,850	5,063	2,492	11009
SULLIVAN CO.							
Bethel,	2	500	......	200	100	40	......
Cochecton,	1	1,500	600	200	60	75	450
Fallsburgh,	2	3,100	......	750	225	103	......
Highland,	1	300	......	200	150	50	100
Liberty,	2	3,100	......	900	450	120	400
Lumberland,	1	500	......	200	75	40	50
Mamakating,	6	4,500	......	1,695	685	261	1,040
Neversink,	3	2,300	......	1,000	400	150	900
Rockland,	1	400	......	300	200	30	350
Thompson,	1	1,900	1,000	350	250	122	600
Total,	20	18,100	1,600	5,795	2,595	991	3,890
TIOGA CO.							
Barton,	5	8,550	800	2,000	575	385	1,793
Berkshire,	1	1,500	500	440	100	125	375
Candor,	2	2,400	1,500	550	250	190	475
Newark,	3	3,650	1,200	920	290	233	536
Nichols,	1	2,000	1,000	500	25	150	400
Owego,	4	4,700	1,500	1,550	650	383	1,120
TIOGA CO.							
Spencer,	1	$1,600	......	250	100	75	$300
Tioga,	1	2,500	......	500	180	50	75
Total,	18	26,900	$6,500	6 710	2,170	1,591	4,075
TOMPKINS CO.							
Caroline,	4	5,800	800	1,600	370	233	880
Danby,	3	3,200	600	1,300	350	250	950
Dryden,	5	10,100	2,600	1,450	625	402	1,415
Enfield,	2	2,300	......	700	80	49	270
Groton,	3	4,300	750	726	335	188	1,075
Ithaca,	3	9,400	1,900	1,025	740	487	1,400
Lansing,	4	6,840	......	1,550	450	237	870
Newfield,	1	3,000	600	450	250	270	537
Ulysses,	2	2,500	2,500	1,100	540	350	1,100
Total,	27	47,440	9,750	9,901	3,740	2,466	8,497
ULSTER CO.							
Esopus,	1	1,500	......	500	100	60	100
Hurley,	1	1,000	......	175	60	30	150
Kingston,	4	10,800	3,000	1,850	1,425	783	2,075
Lloyd,	1	2,500	......	500	300	190	500
Marbletown,	1	3,000	800	600	300	......	420
Marlborough,	3	5,500	......	1,050	285	190	730
New Paltz,	1	1,000	......	500	200	100	160
Olive,	1	800	......	250	150	120	350
Plattekill,	3	9,000	......	1,075	431	187	1,200
Rochester,	1	1,500	......	400	200	50	200
Saugerties,	2	3,300	1,800	750	450	211	650
Shandaken,	1	1,500	......	500	100	40	60
Shawangunk,	2	4,500	......	900	400	135	765
Wawarsing,	4	4,850	7,900	1,100	830	360	1,350
Woodstock,	1	1,000	......	400	300	160	500
Total,	27	51,750	13,500	10,550	5,531	2,516	9,210
WARREN CO.							
Bolton,	1	800	......	150	50	20	150
Chester,	3	2,150	......	1,300	230	133	1,150
Horicon,	1	600	......	300	50	50	50
Johnsburgh,	2	2,200	400	600	100	70	350
Luzerne,	1	2,000	800	500	80	140	500
Queensbury,	1	5,500	1,000	500	400	300	500
Warrensburgh,	2	2,800	600	750	110	90	416
Total,	11	16,050	2,800	4,100	1,020	803	3,116
WASHINGTON CO.							
Argyle,	1	600	900	300	150	50	190
Cambridge,	3	1,100	......	900	380	180	675
Easton,	2	1,700	500	450	150	70	525
Fort Ann,	1	3,000	......	400	150	150	400
Fort Edward,	1	10,000	......	600	400	200	400
Granville,	1	2,000	......	250	150	84	426
Greenwich,	3	4,600	2,000	800	300	250	775
Hampton,	1	1,500	......	600	......	......	500
Hartford,	1	1,200	......	300	100	55	400
Hebron,	2	1,900	600	380	235	160	679
Kingsbury,	3	7,000	......	950	500	257	1,000
Salem,	2	2,300	1,000	475	230	120	665
White Creek,	2	5,000	800	500	200	240	600
Whitehall,	2	4,000	......	700	200	125	400
Total,	25	45,900	5,800	7,605	3,140	1,941	7,635
WAYNE CO.							
Arcadia,	2	16,000	1,000	1,150	550	305	1,170
Butler,	2	4,500	300	600	250	220	725
Galen,	2	1,150	1,300	800	350	260	800
Huron,	1	1,000	500	600	100	40	400
Lyons,	2	20,300	1,800	800	450	264	509
Macedon,	1	1,800	......	250	150	52	600
Ontario,	1	400	......	200	75	60	90
Palmyra,	2	6,000	......	675	400	280	990
Rose,	1	1,000	500	400	200	200	325
Sodus,	4	9,750	1,700	1,740	580	410	1,625
Walworth,	1	3,000	1,000	500	300	160	600
Williamson,	1	500	......	300	150	60	......
Wolcott,	2	3,800	400	600	340	275	850
Total,	22	69,200	8,500	8,615	3,895	2,586	8,684
WESTCHESTER CO.							
Bedford,	3	4,500	1,000	950	290	150	1,150
Cortlandt,	3	9,500	200	1,050	590	275	1,300
Eastchester,	3	8,000	1,000	650	390	150	1,450
Greenburgh,	2	7,700	4,700	850	450	320	1,350
Lewisboro,	2	3,000	......	800	300	160	469
Mamaroneck,	1	3,000	......	200	175	110	700
Mount Pleasant,	1	5,000	2,000	500	200	250	575
New Castle,	2	2,150	2,000	550	400	190	800
New Rochelle,	2	7,500	2,500	750	400	150	800
North Castle,	3	3,800	......	1,350	445	300	455

CHURCHES.—(Continued.)

TOWNS.	Number of churches.	Value of church and lot.	Value of other real estate.	Number capable of being seated.	Usual number attending.	Number of communicants.	Salary of clergy, including use of real estate.
Westchester Co.							
North Salem,	2	$4,500	$1,000	900	250	120	$800
Ossining,	1	13,000	1,700	900	500	350	900
Pelham,	1	800	......	100	30	12	......
Poundridge,	1	1,200	1,500	250	100	150	600
Rye,	3	7,000	7,000	920	300	195	1,720
Somers,	2	3,000	......	400	120	82	275
Westchester,	1	2,000	......	200	60	30	325
West Farms,	5	8,500	......	1,410	730	402	2,200
White Plains,	3	11,000	3,100	1,050	450	250	850
Yonkers,	3	4,800	3,000	850	350	165	1,250
Yorktown,	2	4,500	2,700	1,100	300	100	950
Total,	46	114,450	33,400	15,730	6,830	3,911	18919
Wyoming Co.							
Attica,	1	2,500	......	350	80	71	500
Castile,	1	2,500	1,200	310	200	165	475
China,	1	1,200	......	200	150	45	300
Covington,	1	2,500	......	450	150	65	300
Eagle,	1	700	......	250	50	40	300
Gainsville,	2	2,100	500	500	200	135	375
Genesee Falls,	1	2,000	......	400	125	50	250
Java,	1	2,000	400	600	300	80	400
Middleburg,	1	4,000	800	400	150	125	450
Perry,	2	6,200	1,200	625	425	258	850
Pike,	2	4,500	1,000	500	250	180	610
Sheldon,	1	1,200	50	700	100	30	350
Warsaw,	1	6,000	600	600	200	680	......
Wethersfield,	1	400	......	300	......	12	......
Total,	17	37,800	5,750	6,183	2,380	1,936	5,160
Yates Co.							
Barrington,	1	1,200	400	300	140	100	350
Benton,	2	6,100	2,000	300	400	225	1,060
Italy,	1	1,500	......	600	75	80	210
Jerusalem,	1	1,400	300	70	60	60	150
Middlesex,	2	4,500	......	1,150	220	185	450
Milo,	2	7,000	2,000	1,050	950	385	1,510
Potter,	4	8,200	1,050	1,250	750	358	1,010
Starkey,	2	7,000	600	850	300	200	875
Torrey,	1	1,200	300	400	150	40	425
Total,	16	38,100	6,650	6,470	3,045	1,663	6,040

AFRICAN METHODIST EPISCOPAL CHURCHES.

TOWNS.	Number of churches.	Value of church and lot.	Value of other real estate.	Number capable of being seated.	Usual number attending.	Number of communicants.	Salary of clergy, including use of real estate.
Albany Co.							
Albany,	1	3,000	......	500	200	......	500
Cayuga Co.							
Auburn,	1	1,600	......	200	58	8	250
Chemung Co.							
Elmira,	1	2,000	......	400	200	80	250
Dutchess Co.							
Fishkill,	1	500	......	150	50	30	......
Greene Co.							
Coxsackie,	1	1,000	......	275	150	60	......
Herkimer Co.							
Little Falls,	1	450	......	60	30	8	......
Kings Co.							
Brooklyn,	2	14,000	1,000	3,700	900	298	850
Monroe Co.							
Rochester,	2	2,800	150	400	45	10	250
New-York Co.							
New-York,	6	120,000	8,400	4,530	3,005	1,668	2,150
Oneida Co.							
Rome,	1	1,000	......	250	50	9	200
Oswego Co.							
Oswego,	1	900	......	200	30	16	400
Queens Co.							
Flushing,	1	3,000	......	900	300	75	400
Hempstead,	1	150	25	100	40	......	......
North Hempstead,	1	400	30	100	40	30	25
Total,	3	3,550	55	1,100	380	105	425
Rensselaer Co.							
Lansingburgh,	1	600	......	150	120	34	200
Troy,	1	1,200	......	250	100	50	250
Total,	2	1,800	......	400	220	84	450
Richmond Co.							
Westfield,	1	1,000	......	300	50	......	......
Schenectady Co.							
Schenectady,	1	800	......	150	50	......	......
Suffolk Co.							
Brookhaven,	2	700	......	225	75	59	50
Suffolk Co.							
East Hampton,	1	$1,000	......	200	60	35	......
Huntington,	1	600	......	300	200	38	$50
Islip,	2	420	......	180	70	18	30
Total,	6	2,720	......	905	405	150	130
Westchester Co							
Rye,	1	1,000	......	150	50	20	100
Westchester,	1	600	......	100	25	23	134
Total,	2	1,600	......	250	75	43	234

CALVINISTIC METHODIST CHURCHES.

TOWNS	Number of churches.	Value of church and lot.	Value of other real estate.	Number capable of being seated.	Usual number attending.	Number of communicants.	Salary of clergy, including use of real estate.
Cattaraugus Co.							
Freedom,	1	700	......	250	50	30	250
Herkimer Co.							
Newport,	1	250	......	160	20	5	......
Lewis Co.							
Leyden,	1	400	......	150	15	10	......
New-York Co.							
New-York,	1	9,000	......	300	250	100	500
Oneida Co.							
Deerfield,	1	500	......	300	50	......	......
Floyd,	1	300	......	154	100	44	80
Marcy,	1	200	......	300	70	70	150
Remsen,	5	6,200	......	1,350	425	207	526
Rome,	5	8,500	......	1,600	575	262	660
Steuben,	1	500	......	180	188	28	100
Trenton,	1	350	......	150	60	30	80
Utica,	1	3,000	......	900	300	190	300
Western,	1	300	......	150	100	35	100
Whitestown,	1	300	......	100	30	25	50
Total,	18	20,150	......	5,184	1,898	891	2,046

CONGREGATIONAL METHODIST CHURCHES.

TOWNS	Number of churches.	Value of church and lot.	Value of other real estate.	Number capable of being seated.	Usual number attending.	Number of communicants.	Salary of clergy, including use of real estate.
Kings Co.							
Brooklyn,	1	6,000	......	600	300	110	800
Richmond Co.							
Northfield,	1	2,000	......	300	300	60	500
Suffolk Co.							
Islip,	1	600	......	130	80	45	......

EVANGELICAL ASSOCIATION OR GERMAN METHODIST CHURCHES.

TOWNS	Number of churches.	Value of church and lot.	Value of other real estate.	Number capable of being seated.	Usual number attending.	Number of communicants.	Salary of clergy, including use of real estate.
Erie Co.							
Buffalo,	1	3,500	......	300	250	150	250
Fulton Co.							
Bleecker,	1	500	......	300	80	100	100
Herkimer Co.							
Ohio,	1	250	......	125	30	20	25
Lewis Co.							
Croghan,	1	300	......	100	60	40	50
Monroe Co.							
Rochester,	1	4,000	......	300	150	70	300
New-York Co.							
New-York,	4	57,000	$11000	2,600	1,800	2,025	3,450
Oneida Co.							
Rome,	1	200	150	200	60	50	100
Utica,	1	700	......	150	100	60	400
Total,	2	900	150	350	160	110	500
Onondaga Co.							
Syracuse,	1	2,000	......	600	300	100	300
Rensselaer Co.							
Sandlake,	1	300	.....	140	120	80	125
Seneca Co.							
Fayette,	1	600	500	600	175	22	300
Sullivan Co.							
Collicoon,	1	1,500	400	300	40	60	375

METHODIST PROTESTANT CHURCHES.

TOWNS	Number of churches.	Value of church and lot.	Value of other real estate.	Number capable of being seated.	Usual number attending.	Number of communicants.	Salary of clergy, including use of real estate.
Cayuga Co.							
Conquest,	1	2,500	......	300	50	30	150
Moravia,	1	2,500	......	240	150	35	162
Total,	2	5,000	......	540	200	65	312
Chautauque Co.							
Portland,	1	......	......	......	......	60	70

CHURCHES.—(Continued.)

TOWNS.	Number of churches.	Value of church and lot.	Value of other real estate.	Number capable of being seated.	Usual number attending.	Number of communicants.	Salary of clergy, includ'ng use of real estate.
Dutchess Co.							
Fishkill, ...	1	$2,000	.....	300	45	200	$330
Erie Co.							
Boston, ...	1	400	.....	150	25	30	175
Genesee Co.							
Elba, ...	1	2,000	$500	400	150	42	375
Herkimer Co.							
Little Falls, ...	1	1,000	.....	200	125	20	300
Schuyler, ...	1	1,000	300	500	75	30	300
Total, ...	2	2,000	300	700	200	50	600
Jefferson Co.							
Wilna, ...	2	1,510	400	500	190	148	532
Kings Co.							
Brooklyn, ...	1	3,500	.....	200	80	46	.....
Flatlands, ...	2	2,000	.....	550	250	82	600
Gravesend, ...	1	400	.....	125	50	15	800
Total, ...	4	5,900	.....	875	380	143	1,400
Livingston Co.							
Mount Morris, ...	1	4,000	.....	500	150	40	350
Portage, ...	1	1,800	.....	500	60	48	300
Total, ...	2	5,800	.....	1,000	210	88	650
Monroe Co.							
Ogden, ...	1	3,000	.....	400	110	60	250
Rochester, ...	1	1,500	.....	150	100	40	400
Total, ...	2	4,500	.....	550	210	100	650
Niagara Co.							
Hartland, ...	1	550	.....	200	75	16	300
Onondaga Co.							
Manlius, ...	1	800	.....	300	.....	.....	.....
Ontario Co.							
Candice, ...	1	.....	.....	.....	50	12	75
Manchester, ...	2	1,400	.....	550	120	45	105
Richmond, ...	1	1,200	.....	500	75	40	340
Total, ...	4	2,600	.....	1,050	245	97	520
Orange Co.							
Warwick, ...	1	600	.....	20	50	9	.....
Oswego Co.							
Volney, ...	1	2,000	.....	400	60	30	180
Otsego Co.							
Westford, ...	1	1,000	.....	600	80	20	300
Putnam Co.							
Phillipstown, ...	1	250	200	200	50	21	200
Rockland Co.							
Clarkstown, ...	1	500	.....	200	.....	.....	.....
Haverstraw, ...	2	5,500	.....	600	250	90	700
Orangetown, ...	1	800	.....	.....	.....	.....	.....
Total, ...	4	6,800	.....	800	250	90	700
Saratoga Co.							
Malta, ...	1	400	.....	200	50	30	130
Providence, ...	1	600	.....	200	100	30	100
Saratoga Springs, ...	1	500	.....	200	100	36	350
Wilton, ...	1	850	.....	300	75	50	130
Total, ...	4	2,350	.....	900	325	146	710
Schoharie Co.							
Broome, ...	1	1,000	400	300	150	100	350
Suffolk Co.							
Huntington, ...	2	1,400	.....	325	50	.....	30
Southampton, ...	1	1,450	.....	200	100	60	300
Total, ...	3	2,850	.....	525	150	60	330
Washington Co.							
Fort Ann, ...	1	400	.....	200	40	15	.....
Granville, ...	1	100	.....	150	25	.....	.....
Total, ...	2	500	.....	350	65	15	.....
Wayne Co.							
Arcadia, ...	1	1,200	.....	200	100	20	75
Westchester Co.							
Lewisboro, ...	1	500	.....	200	200	15	.....
Poundridge, ...	1	400	.....	250	50	30	300
Total, ...	2	900	.....	450	250	45	300

PRIMITIVE METHODIST CHURCHES.

TOWNS.	Number of churches.	Value of church and lot.	Value of other real estate.	Number capable of being seated.	Usual number attending.	Number of communicants.	Salary of clergy, includ'ng use of real estate.
Kings Co.							
Brooklyn, ...	1	.....	.....	150	30	8	450

TOWNS.	Number of churches.	Value of church and lot.	Value of other real estate.	Number capable of being seated.	Usual number attending.	Number of communicants.	Salary of clergy, including use of real estate.
New-York Co.							
New-York, ...	1	$10,000	.....	900	500	150	$1,500

REFORMED METHODIST CHURCHES.

TOWNS.	Number of churches.	Value of church and lot.	Value of other real estate.	Number capable of being seated.	Usual number attending.	Number of communicants.	Salary of clergy, including use of real estate.
Broome Co.							
Vestal, ...	1	600	.....	200	70	55	240
Windsor, ...	1	600	.....	400	16	.....	.....
Total, ...	2	1,200	.....	600	86	55	240
Cayuga Co.							
Springport, ...	1	2,000	.....	300	200	200	300
Chemung Co.							
Erin, ...	1	700	.....	200	.....	.....	.....
Cortland Co.							
Cortlandville, ...	1	800	.....	250	100	50	115
Dutchess Co.							
Milan, ...	1	900	.....	300	40	15	200
Rockland Co.							
Clarkstown, ...	1	1,100	.....	250	100	15	300
Westchester Co.							
Mount Pleasant, ...	1	2,000	.....	400	250	100	400

WESLEYAN METHODIST CHURCHES.

TOWNS.	Number of churches.	Value of church and lot.	Value of other real estate.	Number capable of being seated.	Usual number attending.	Number of communicants.	Salary of clergy, including use of real estate.
Albany Co.							
Albany, ...	1	3,000	.....	350	150	60	500
Allegany Co.							
Almond, ...	1	600	.....	200	50	17	.....
Granger, ...	1	1,000	.....	300	70	50	200
Hume, ...	1	300	.....	200	50	40	250
Total, ...	3	1,900	.....	700	170	107	450
Broome Co.							
Chenango, ...	1	1,500	.....	400	200	100	150
Binghamton, ...	2	39,000	$2,504	800	900	380	1,600
Total, ...	3	40,500	2,504	1,200	1,100	480	3,100
Cattaraugus Co.							
Lyndon, ...	1	1,200	.....	350	100	80	350
Chautauque Co.							
Sheridan, ...	1	1,000	.....	480	200	32	200
Westfield, ...	1	1,000	.....	300	100	30	400
Total, ...	2	2,000	.....	780	300	62	600
Clinton Co.							
Chazy, ...	1	1,000	900	300	75	65	300
Plattsburgh, ...	1	1,500	.....	350	200	60	100
Total, ...	2	2,500	900	650	275	125	400
Columbia Co.							
Hudson, ...	1	1,000	.....	200	100	40	200
Cortland Co.							
Taylor, ...	1	1,200	300	500	100	35	800
Dutchess Co.							
Fishkill, ...	1	1,000	.....	30	20	18	236
Essex Co.							
Chesterfield, ...	1	800	.....	250	150	80	350
Herkimer Co.							
Litchfield, ...	1	1,500	.....	600	100	25	150
Jefferson Co.							
Antwerp, ...	1	800	.....	200	50	20	.....
Orleans, ...	1	400	.....	200	20	20	100
Watertown, ...	1	3,000	.....	200	50	33	100
Total, ...	3	4,200	.....	600	120	73	200
Madison Co.							
Sullivan, ...	1	600	.....	300	75	20	50
Monroe Co.							
Perrington, ...	2	1,200	.....	600	100	52	192
New-York Co.							
New-York, ...	3	35,000	.....	2,000	2,000	855	4,000
Niagara Co.							
Lockport, ...	1	150	.....	250	100	18	100
Newfane, ...	1	1,400	.....	200	80	18	60
Porter, ...	1	2,500	.....	400	175	50	100
Royalton, ...	1	800	.....	160	150	24	155
Total, ...	4	4,850	.....	1,010	505	110	415
Oneida Co.							
Camden, ...	1	1,200	.....	150	75	45	180
Utica, ...	1	1,200	.....	125	80	62	275
Total, ...	2	2,400	.....	275	155	107	455

CHURCHES.—(Continued.)

TOWNS.	Number of churches.	Value of church and lot.	Value of other real estate.	Number capable of being seated.	Usual number attending.	Number of communicants.	Salary of clergy, including use of real estate.
ONONDAGA CO.							
Manlius, ...	1	$1,000	......	225	100	10	$100
Onondaga, ...	1	1,000	......	260	30	15	......
Syracuse, ...	1	2,500	......	400	150	100	400
Total, ...	3	4,500	......	885	280	125	500
ONTARIO CO.							
Canadice, ...	1	......	......	50	50	20	100
Farmington, ...	1	50	150	500	50	30	50
Hopewell, ...	1	2,000	750	350	100	31	150
Naples, ...	1	1,000	......	500	50	25	......
Richmond, ...	1	300	......	200	75	25	250
Total, ...	5	3,350	900	1,600	325	131	550
ORLEANS CO.							
Gaines, ...	1	1,500	......	350	100	40	350
OSWEGO CO.							
Volney, ...	1	2,000	......	400	150	77	600
ST. LAWRENCE CO.							
Canton, ...	1	800	500	300	100	66	300
Lisbon, ...	1	1,000	500	400	100	40	300
Parishville, ...	1	650	600	200	125	50	245
Stockholm, ...	1	1,235	......	400	100	37	300
Total, ...	4	3,685	1,600	1,300	425	193	1,145
SARATOGA CO.							
Hadley, ...	1	500	......	250	60	30	......
Halfmoon, ...	1	200	......	300	150	80	40
Total, ...	2	700	......	550	210	110	40
SCHUYLER CO.							
Hector, ...	2	1,950	......	600	110	37	110
SENECA CO.							
Junius, ...	2	1,600	......	1,000	400	82	290
Seneca Falls, ...	1	2,500	......	700	200	63	400
Total, ...	3	4,100	......	1,700	600	145	690
TOMPKINS CO.							
Groton, ...	1	600	......	150	80	29	300
ULSTER CO.							
Plattekill, ...	1	1,000	......	450	50	25	200
Woodstock, ...	1	600	......	200	50	36	80
Total, ...	2	1,600	......	650	100	61	280
WARREN CO.							
Warrensburgh, ...	1	800	......	150	30	15	100
WASHINGTON CO.							
Granville, ...	1	......	......	......	......	34	......
WAYNE CO.							
Williamson, ...	1	1,000	......	225	120	48	230
WESTCHESTER CO.							
Cortlandt, ...	2	1,600	......	350	210	72	500
YATES CO.							
Milo, ...	1	4,000	......	400	200	94	400
MORAVIAN CHURCHES.							
KINGS CO.							
Brooklyn, ...	1	12,000	......	150	50	18	500
NEW-YORK CO.							
New-York, ...	1	25,000	22,000	700	200	190	2,000
RICHMOND CO.							
Castleton, ...	1	6,000	......	500	200	60	350
WASHINGTON CO.							
Salem, ...	1	1,000	1,500	200	70	31	270
NEW CHURCH (SWEDENBORGIAN) CHURCHES.							
SUFFOLK CO.							
Riverhead, ...	2	2,800	......	260	95	38	200
TOMPKINS CO.							
Danby, ...	1	1,000	......	500	75	25	300
PRESBYTERIAN CHURCHES—(OLD AND NEW SCHOOL.)							
ALBANY CO.							
Albany, ...	4	213,000	......	4,200	2,500	2,120	8,300
Bethlehem, ...	1	1,200	......	400	60	50	200
Guilderland, ...	1	2,300	......	400	100	50	400
New Scotland, ...	2	4,500	4,000	800	200	160	475
Rensselaerville, ...	1	3,500	1,600	350	150	96	500
Watervliet, ...	2	9,400	......	675	290	112	1,500
Total, ...	11	233,900	5,600	6,825	3,300	2,588	11375

TOWNS.	Number of churches.	Value of church and lot.	Value of other real estate.	Number capable of being seated.	Usual number attending.	Number of communicants.	Salary of clergy, including use of real estate.
ALLEGANY CO.							
Almond, ...	1	$6,000	$1,000	600	350	350	$600
Angelica, ...	1	1,200	......	400	200	80	500
Burns, ...	1	1,500	......	300	125	81	350
Centreville, ...	2	800	500	425	280	140	550
Cuba, ...	1	2,000	......	500	200	180	600
Independence, ...	1	......	1,000	......	......	20	......
Ossian, ...	1	800	......	150	75	45	350
Total, ...	8	12,300	2,500	2,375	1,230	896	2.9 50
BROOME CO.							
Chenango, ...	2	10,750	......	920	900	410	1,300
Colesville, ...	1	2,000	800	270	100	80	450
Conklin, ...	1	2,000	1,000	200	150	40	450
Union, ...	2	7,500	......	600	200	40	400
Windsor, ...	1	2,500	......	400	130	150	400
Total, ...	7	24,750	1,800	2,390	1,480	720	3,000
CATTARAUGUS CO.							
Connewango, ...	1	1,600	......	400	60	40	200
Ellicottville, ...	1	4,000	400	375	110	75	600
Franklinville, ...	1	2,000	......	400	75	25	......
Olean, ...	1	1,500	......	200	150	48	400
Portville, ...	1	3,000	......	300	100	44	600
Total, ...	5	12,100	400	1,675	495	232	1,800
CAYUGA CO.							
Auburn, ...	2	25,000	......	2,500	1,050	590	2,300
Aurelius, ...	1	5,000	......	300	200	130	700
Brutus, ...	1	......	......	......	200	90	400
Cato, ...	1	4,000	......	400	200	130	700
Genoa, ...	2	6,000	1,800	600	175	157	1,100
Ira, ...	1	1,000	......	800	50	27	400
Ledyard, ...	1	6,000	1,400	300	150	75	700
Mentz, ...	1	4,000	2,000	350	300	120	725
Scipio, ...	1	1,500	1,000	400	50	50	430
Springport, ...	1	3,000	......	300	200	70	350
Victory, ...	1	1,500	......	400	75	......	400
Total, ...	13	57,000	6,200	6,350	2,650	1,439	8,205
CHAUTAUQUE CO.							
Ellicott, ...	1	3,500	......	500	300	150	850
Ellington, ...	1	1,200	......	400	150	70	400
Hanover, ...	1	4,500	......	400	250	126	600
Harmony, ...	1	3,000	500	450	150	95	550
Pomfret, ...	2	11,000	......	1,000	460	320	1,500
Ripley, ...	2	8,500	500	900	870	91	1,050
Sheridan, ...	1	300	......	150	......	......	......
Westfield, ...	1	8,000	......	800	400	380	800
Total, ...	10	40,000	1,000	4,600	2,580	1,232	5,750
CHEMUNG CO.							
Big Flats, ...	1	2,000	1,200	300	75	40	400
Elmira, ...	1	12,000	4,000	700	525	433	1,500
Horseheads, ...	1	1,500	1,500	450	175	206	700
Southport, ...	1	1,500	1,000	300	80	60	600
Veteran, ...	1	1,600	......	280	75	25	200
Total, ...	5	18,600	7,700	2,030	930	764	3,400
CHENANGO CO.							
Bainbridge, ...	1	3,000	300	500	150	70	500
Greene, ...	1	3,000	......	500	200	115	500
Guilford, ...	1	1,500	......	600	150	30	175
Macdonough, ...	1	400	100	......	......	......	......
Oxford, ...	1	4,500	......	600	250	130	600
Pharsalia, ...	1	800	80	300	50	32	300
Preston, ...	1	1,000	......	500	50	30	......
Total, ...	7	14,200	480	3,000	850	407	2,075
CLINTON CO.							
Ausable, ...	1	1,600	......	300	50	50	450
Beekmantown, ...	1	4,000	700	800	300	180	500
Champlain, ...	1	7,000	1,500	400	250	250	900
Dannemora,*	1	......	......	300	275	......	600
Mooers, ...	1	1,500	500	350	50	200	500
Plattsburgh, ...	1	4,000	2,000	700	450	300	1,000
Saranac, ...	1	1,000	......	200	80	30	450
Total, ...	7	19,100	4,700	3,050	1,455	1,010	4,400
COLUMBIA CO.							
Ancram, ...	1	1,500	......	300	......	......	......
Austerlitz, ...	1	3,000	......	500	300	100	500
Canaan, ...	1	1,500	500	300	75	75	500
Copake, ...	1	2,500	1,500	500	200	104	450
Hillsdale, ...	1	2,500	......	300	130	73	500
Hudson, ...	1	20,000	......	1,000	600	300	1,250
Kinderhook, ...	1	3,000	1,500	600	250	200	800

* Clinton Prison

CHURCHES.—(Continued.)

TOWNS.	Number of churches.	Value of church and lot.	Value of other real estate.	Number capable of being seated.	Usual number attending.	Number of communicants.	Salary of clergy, including use of real estate.
COLUMBIA CO.							
New Lebanon, ...	1	$2,000	......	600	200	140	$400
Stockport, ...	1	100	......	400	100	12	......
Total, ...	9	36,100	$3,500	4,500	1,855	1,004	4,400
CORTLAND CO.							
Cortlandville, ...	2	7,500	......	1,000	500	378	1,250
Marathon, ...	2	1,500	......	500	150	90	700
Preble, ...	1	1,500	800	600	150	94	400
Truxton, ...	1	7,000	850	600	100	60	500
Total, ...	6	17,500	1,650	2,700	900	622	2,850
DELAWARE CO.							
Andes, ...	1	1,200	......	......	100	14	400
Colchester, ...	1	1,000	......	250	100	90	400
Davenport, ...	1	1,000	......	500	100	25	......
Delhi, ...	2	8,500	1,100	850	500	390	1,500
Hamden, ...	1	6,000	......	400	120	......	600
Harpersfield, ...	1	3,000	......	400	150	50	300
Masonville, ...	1	2,000	2,000	350	100	90	500
Tompkins, ...	2	7,200	2,900	1,350	450	185	1,400
Total, ...	10	29,900	6,000	4,100	1,620	844	5,100
DUTCHESS CO.							
Amenia, ...	2	9,200	2,000	575	250	153	1,290
Clinton, ...	1	1,800	......	250	150	100	400
Fishkill, ...	5	19,000	3,500	2,100	800	366	3,450
La Grange, ...	1	2,500	1,000	400	150	115	600
Pine Plains, ...	1	3,500	500	500	150	60	500
Pleasant Valley, ...	1	11,000	3,000	700	600	1,100	1,000
Poughkeepsie, ...	1	7,000	......	300	250	150	700
Poughkeepsie city, ..	1	20,000	......	800	500	260	1,500
Total, ...	13	74,000	10,000	5,625	2,850	2,304	9,440
ERIE CO.							
Alden, ...	1	2,000	......	300	70	87	400
Aurora, ...	2	3,500	......	800	235	197	1075
Buffalo, ...	8	169,000	33,500	5,250	2,850	1,562	10900
Clarence, ...	1	3,000	1,500	300	200	70	600
Colden, ...	1	1,500	......	300	150	60	400
Collins, ...	1	1,000	......	400	200	86	600
Concord, ...	1	5,000	......	600	200	130	800
Lancaster, ...	1	3,000	1,000	200	40	30	380
Newstead, ...	1	3,500	......	300	125	40	500
Total, ...	17	191 500	36,000	8,450	4,070	2,262	15655
ESSEX CO.							
Chesterfield, ...	1	2,000	......	500	......	10	100
Essex, ...	2	10,500	500	600	150	152	400
Jay, ...	1	1,500	......	300	......	40	......
Moriah, ...	1	5,200	......	300	85	......	......
Schroon, ...	1	2,000	......	300	60	10	......
Total, ...	6	21,200	500	2,000	295	212	500
FRANKLIN CO.							
Chateaugay, ...	1	1,500	700	600	200	70	600
Constable, ...	1	3,000	......	400	150	85	350
Fort Covington, ...	1	4,000	400	500	300	211	450
Total, ...	3	8,500	1,100	1,500	650	366	1,400
FULTON CO.							
Broadalbin, ...	1	4,000	......	800	350	130	500
Johnstown, ...	2	14,000	2,000	1,100	575	286	1,500
Mayfield, ...	1	4,000	......	500	300	125	500
Northampton, ...	2	3,500	......	500	230	70	550
Perth, ...	1	2,500	2,200	550	350	105	630
Total, ...	7	28,000	4,200	3,450	1,805	716	3,680
GENESEE CO.							
Batavia, ...	2	7,000	......	1,000	500	225	1,500
Bergen, ...	1	2,500	800	320	200	106	500
Bethany, ...	2	4,500	......	600	175	117	750
Byron, ...	1	2,500	500	475	110	120	700
Le Roy, ...	1	5,500	......	600	450	300	1,100
Oakfield, ...	1	2,500	......	400	150	70	400
Pavilion, ...	1	2,000	......	250	75	20	400
Pembroke, ...	1	1,500	......	500	250	100	600
Total, ...	10	28,000	1,300	4,145	1,910	1,085	5,950
GREENE CO.							
Ashland, ...	1	2,000	1,000	350	100	30	500
Cairo, ...	1	2,865	800	300	75	65	450
Catskill, ...	1	7,500	500	500	250	179	1,200
Durham, ...	1	1,000	800	250	80	101	490
Greenville, ...	1	3,400	......	400	200	116	570
Hunter, ...	1	700	1,000	300	75	45	500
Jewett, ...	1	3,000	1,300	500	200	120	600
GREENE CO.							
Windham, ...	2	$4,000	1,300	700	300	180	$[illegible]
Total, ...	9	24,465	6,700	3,300	1,280	836	5,[illegible]
HERKIMER CO.							
Fairfield, ...	1	2,000	......	800	150	40	[illegible]
Litchfield, ...	2	3,700	400	800	100	55	[illegible]
Little Falls, ...	1	8,000	2,000	600	500	150	1,[illegible]
Newport, ...	1	2,500	......	400	100	30	[illegible]
Norway, ...	1	600	700	500	......	10	...[illegible]
Russia, ...	1	800	......	300	50	25	[illegible]
Total, ...	7	17,600	3,100	3,400	900	310	2,[illegible]
JEFFERSON CO.							
Alexandria, ...	1	2,000	......	360	125	66	[illegible]
Antwerp, ...	1	3,500	......	600	150	75	[illegible]
Brownville, ...	2	4,800	300	600	200	167	[illegible]
Cape Vincent, ...	1	2,500	2,500	350	150	85	[illegible]
Ellisburgh, ...	1	3,500	......	300	250	70	[illegible]
Hounsfield, ...	1	5,000	1,000	800	200	106	[illegible]
Le Ray, ...	1	2,200	700	400	200	82	[illegible]
Lyme, ...	1	1,800	......	300	200	59	[illegible]
Theresa, ...	1	1,200	......	428	100	94	[illegible]
Watertown, ...	2	29,000	......	1,600	775	430	1,[illegible]
Wilna, ...	2	2,500	225	450	140	72	[illegible]
Total, ...	14	58,000	4,725	6,188	2,490	1,306	7,[illegible]
KINGS CO.							
Brooklyn, ...	13	489,000	9,000	10,975	6,675	3,503	19,[illegible]
LEWIS CO.							
Greig, ...	1	3,000	......	400	50	26	
Lowville, ...	1	3,000	1,500	300	100	124	[illegible]
Martinsburgh, ...	1	100	......	275	170	75	
Turin, ...	2	1,550	400	350	170	90	
Total, ...	5	7,650	1,900	1,325	490	315	2,[illegible]
LIVINGSTON CO.							
Avon, ...	1	2,000	1,500	500	150	60	
Caledonia, ...	1	6,000	......	500	250	90	1,[illegible]
Geneseo, ...	2	11,000	7,000	900	750	320	1,[illegible]
Groveland, ...	1	4,000	1,500	600	100	98	
Leicester, ...	1	3,000	350	600	150	63	[illegible]
Lima, ...	1	......	......	500	300	175	
Livonia, ...	1	3,000	700	450	200	123	[illegible]
Mount Morris, ...	2	12,200	......	1,200	625	209	1,[illegible]
North Dansville, ...	1	4,000	1,200	400	200	150	
Nunda, ...	1	8,000	......	600	300	150	
Portage, ...	1	2,900	......	400	100	49	
Sparta, ...	2	4,200	250	600	130	30	
Springwater, ...	1	1,200	600	250	100	40	
West Sparta, ...	1	1,000	500	500	150	50	...
York, ...	2	5,500	......	664	210	87	
Total, ...	19	68,000	13,600	8,664	3,715	1,694	10,[illegible]
MADISON CO.							
Cazenovia, ...	1	......	......	650	400	263	
De Ruyter, ...	1	2,000	......	500	75	16	
Eaton, ...	1	3,000	......	600	200	65	
Georgetown, ...	1	1,500	500	600	100	40	...
Lenox, ...	5	7,580	3,450	1,570	575	277	2,[illegible]
Smithfield, ...	1	1,400	2,200	600	200	30	
Total, ...	10	15,480	6,150	4,520	1,550	691	4,[illegible]
MONROE CO.							
Chili, ...	1	3,000	1,200	500	200	150	
Gates, ...	1	1,500	......	400	100	50	
Greece, ...	1	3,000	......	275	150	37	
Mendon, ...	2	7,500	3,200	950	255	200	1,[illegible]
Ogden, ...	1	5,000	5,000	450	250	262	
Parma, ...	2	1,150	......	300	120	75	
Penfield, ...	1	2,000	......	1,000	200	60	
Pittsford, ...	1	8,000	......	800	300	170	
Riga, ...	1	300	......	......	......	......	...
Rochester, ...	7	129,400	1,800	5,050	3,290	2,198	9,[illegible]
Sweden, ...	2	15,000	800	1,200	650	320	
Webster, ...	1	3,000	......	300	250	130	
Wheatland, ...	2	9,700	......	1,150	130	158	1,[illegible]
Total, ...	23	188,550	12,000	12,375	5,895	3,810	17,[illegible]
MONTGOMERY CO.							
Amsterdam, ...	3	11,000	3,100	1,400	650	349	1,[illegible]
Canajoharie, ...	1	800	......	500	150	180	
Total, ...	4	11,800	3,100	1,900	800	529	2,[illegible]
NEW-YORK CO.							
New-York, ...	33	1,645500	124700	30,700	17,675	10,643	70,[illegible]

CHURCHES.—(CONTINUED.)

TOWNS.	Number of churches.	Value of church and lot.	Value of other real estate.	Number capable of being seated.	Usual number attending.	Number of communicants.	Salary of clergy, including use of real estate.
NIAGARA Co.							
Lewiston,	1	$2,000	......	300	150	60	$600
Lockport,	2	3,300	......	1,700	700	440	1,500
Niagara,	2	10,000	......	600	325	109	1,300
Pendleton,	1	1,115	......	300	100	50	400
Porter,	1	5,000	$1,500	500	250	300	700
Royalton,	1	2,500	......	350	150	85	425
Somerset,	1	2,000	700	500	150	100	480
Wilson,	1	3,000	1,500	555	275	225	775
Total,	10	28,915	3,700	4,805	2,100	1,369	6,180
ONEIDA Co.							
Annsville,	1	600	400	500	......	......	......
Boonville,	1	......	......	......	......	......	600
New Hartford,	1	7,000	1,600	450	350	208	600
Paris,	1	4,000	1,200	350	150	150	700
Rome,	2	3,500	3,000	1,300	700	470	1400
Sangerfield,	1	4,000	1,200	462	250	127	700
Trenton,	2	6,000	1,000	850	200	215	1070
Utica,	2	100,000	......	2,150	1,250	500	6250
Vernon,	3	10,000	1,300	1,300	425	225	1500
Verona,	1	2,500	......	300	100	50	500
Western,	1	2,500	1,200	350	200	80	650
Whitestown,	3	11,500	1,000	1,500	750	390	2100
Total,	19	151,600	11,900	9,512	4,375	2,415	16070
ONONDAGA Co.							
Camillus,	2	5,000	......	800	290	140	500
Cicero,	1	1,700	600	300	120	60	460
De Witt,	2	3,300	......	600	80	57	600
Elbridge,	1	5,200	......	400	300	208	600
Lysander,	2	5,500	900	1,050	425	290	1250
Manlius,	2	5,000	......	800	300	296	1250
Marcellus,	2	6,800	2,700	950	650	155	650
Onondaga,	2	10,000	......	750	250	111	900
Pompey,	1	1,200	......	300	75	25	200
Salina,	1	3,000	......	500	115	70	600
Skaneateles,	1	5,500	1,500	600	200	159	700
Spafford,	1	2,000	......	300	100	26	......
Syracuse,	3	95,700	......	2,500	1,450	710	4050
Total,	21	149,900	5,700	9,850	4,355	2,307	11760
ONTARIO Co.							
Gorham,	1	3,000	......	300	100	80	500
Hopewell,	1	2,500	......	400	110	35	400
Naples,	1	4,500	......	450	160	90	600
Phelps,	3	10,000	350	1,300	555	276	1,900
Seneca,	2	5,000	2,800	1,400	800	750	1,700
South Bristol,	1	1,000	......	280	50	......	600
Total,	9	26,000	3,150	4,130	1,775	1,231	5,700
ORANGE Co.							
Blooming Grove,	1	3,000	2,400	400	300	57	500
Chester,	1	10,000	1,500	700	500	234	969
Cornwall,	3	8,000	6,000	950	500	309	1950
Crawford,	1	3,500	2,000	700	600	200	850
Deerpark,	1	6,500	......	600	400	70	1000
Goshen,	2	11,000	5,700	800	500	271	1600
Hamptonburgh,	1	2,800	2,000	400	300	100	800
Minisink,	3	7,000	......	1,200	525	303	1100
Monroe,	1	1,500	1,500	2,110	250	63	450
Montgomery,	2	11,500	13,000	1,100	650	294	1350
Mount Hope,	1	2,000	1,150	500	200	100	500
Newburgh,	1	8,000	......	500	400	247	1000
New Windsor,	1	1,800	1,000	250	100	30	700
Walkill,	3	13,500	6,000	1,550	875	668	2450
Warwick,	3	6,000	750	1,200	750	355	1380
Wawayanda,	3	9,700	4,000	1,300	550	276	1800
Total,	28	105,800	47,000	14,260	7,400	3,577	18399
ORLEANS Co.							
Barre,	1	12,000	......	800	450	425	1,000
Carlton,	1	2,000	......	300	175	20	500
Gaines,	2	6,200	1,000	850	290	140	975
Murray,	1	5,000	......	500	200	191	700
Ridgeway,	2	9,000	5,000	1,000	500	450	1,400
Shelby,	1	2,000	600	200	75	82	550
Yates,	1	2,000	......	350	225	90	580
Total,	9	38,200	6,600	4,000	1,915	1,398	5,705
OSWEGO Co.							
Constantia,	1	1,600	......	250	100	21	400
Mexico,	1	1,200	......	500	75	50	......
Oswego city,	2	21,000	......	1,600	1,100	650	2,250
Redfield,	1	1,000	1,200	350	120	27	312
Sandy Creek,	1	2,500	......	350	......	......	500
Volney,	1	6,500	......	600	300	200	950
West Monroe,	1	$900	$175	300	100	20	$80
Williamstown,	1	1,500	......	350	150	50	350
Total,	9	36,200	1,375	4,300	1,945	1,018	4,624
OTSEGO Co.							
Burlington,	1	1,000	......	300	150	109	400
Cherry Valley,	1	14,000	2,000	250	100	75	400
Hartwick,	1	600	700	300	......	......	......
Laurens,	1	2,000	......	300	150	65	400
Middlefield,	1	2,000	1,100	350	150	80	560
Milford,	1	2,500	1,966	350	140	93	500
Oneonta,	1	2,000	......	600	80	65	370
Otsego,	2	6,800	2,300	900	275	325	1,100
Richfield,	1	1,800	......	400	100	35	350
Springfield,	1	1,500	800	300	125	113	600
Unadilla,	1	2,500	......	230	125	60	650
Total,	12	36,700	8,866	4,280	1,395	1,020	5,330
PUTNAM Co.							
Carmel,	2	7,000	3,000	750	290	140	1,175
Patterson,	1	5,000	......	300	200	120	650
Phillipstown,	1	3,000	1,500	350	200	47	700
Southeast,	1	4,000	......	500	200	45	675
Total,	5	19,000	4,500	1,900	890	352	3,200
QUEENS Co.							
Hempstead,	2	14,800	4,000	1,000	550	200	1,400
Jamaica,	1	7,000	7,000	900	700	350	1,300
North Hempstead,	1	2,000	......	60	60	12	150
Newtown,	2	20,000	11,150	675	510	221	2,000
Oyster Bay,	1	2,000	......	300	60	20	400
Total,	7	45,800	22,150	2,935	1,880	803	5,250
RENSSELAER Co.							
Brunswick,	1	1,200	500	600	150	130	350
Greenbush,	1	3,500	......	400	175	118	800
Lansingburgh,	2	6,750	......	1,000	475	373	1,700
Nassau,	2	3,200	1,000	450	200	115	900
Pittstown,	3	3,500	250	320	45	......	......
Sandlake,	1	2,000	......	250	100	52	500
Schaghticoke,	1	4,000	......	350	150	40	450
Stephentown,	1	1,500	500	300	100	70	400
Troy,	7	158,000	5,000	5,750	3,050	2,263	10,350
Total,	19	183,650	7,250	9,420	4,445	3,161	15,450
ROCKLAND Co.							
Clarkstown,	1	1,200	......	200	50	12	550
Haverstraw,	3	11,500	5,100	1,000	370	137	1,500
Orangetown,	2	7,500	2,500	800	250	125	1,050
Ramapo,	2	2,300	2,000	400	200	66	750
Total,	8	22,500	9,600	2,400	870	340	3,850
ST. LAWRENCE Co.							
Brasher,	2	4,500	......	750	200	62	400
Canton,	1	6,000	2,000	500	250	100	700
De Kalb,	1	1,500	......	500	75	20	......
Gouverneur,	1	4,500	1,000	500	250	190	550
Hammond,	1	2,000	......	450	350	142	500
Madrid,	1	1,600	800	500	300	300	550
Morristown,	1	2,000	700	400	150	40	400
Norfolk,	1	4,000	300	1,000	150	100	400
Oswegatchie,	2	15,000	4,300	1,500	1,050	400	1,750
Potsdam,	1	10,000	600	550	350	150	800
Total,	12	51,100	9,700	6,650	3,125	1,504	6,050
SARATOGA Co.							
Ballston,	1	1,800	1,200	500	350	150	600
Corinth,	1	400	......	400	100	15	......
Charlton,	2	6,500	2,700	700	425	246	1,335
Edinburgh,	1	500	650	600	400	60	400
Galway,	1	8,500	......	500	250	190	800
Halfmoon,	1	3,600	......	350	125	60	600
Malta,	1	1,800	800	500	250	60	400
Milton,	2	9,000	2,500	400	200	90	800
Saratoga Springs,	1	11,000	......	800	500	250	1,000
Stillwater,	1	5,000	300	600	350	200	800
Waterford,	1	7,500	3,000	600	300	150	1,000
Total,	13	55,600	11,150	5,950	3,250	1,471	6,735
SCHENECTADY Co.							
Princetown,	1	4,500	......	500	350	180	700
Schenectady,	1	15,000	......	1,200	700	359	1,000
Total,	2	19,500	......	1,700	1,050	539	1,700

CHURCHES.—(Continued.)

TOWNS.	Number of churches.	Value of church and lot.	Value of other real estate.	Number capable of being seated.	Usual number attending	Number of communicants.	Salary of clergy, including use of real estate.
Schoharie Co.							
Broome,	1	$500	$500	800	$50	30	$400
Carlisle,	1	2,000	800	450	250	80	550
Esperance,	1	1,500	......	500	100	40	400
Total,	3	4,000	1,300	1,250	400	150	1,350
Schuyler Co.							
Catharines,	1	2,000	......	300	150	175	700
Dix,	2	2,900	......	900	250	75	1,190
Hector,	3	8,500	2,950	1,300	475	262	1,900
Orange,	1	2,000	800	250	100	100	700
Tyrone,	2	3,500	600	525	270	197	750
Total,	9	18,900	4,350	3,275	1,245	809	5,240
Seneca Co.							
Fayette,	2	3,700	......	800	250	50	875
Junius,	1	1,000	500	800	200	64	......
Ovid,	1	7,000	600	500	300	110	375
Seneca Falls,	1	5,000	700	600	200	......	600
Varick,	1	6,000	1,800	700	400	200	736
Waterloo,	1	2,300	......	700	350	232	925
Total,	7	25,000	3,600	4,100	1,700	656	3,511
Steuben Co.							
Addison,	1	3,000	1,500	400	100	90	600
Bath,	3	5,000	......	800	300	183	800
Cameron,	1	600	500	200	......	19	......
Campbell,	1	800	......	250	100	25	400
Canisteo,	1	1,600	......	290	100	51	1,080
Caton,	1	200	......	150	......	17	......
Cohocton,	1	600	400	200	100	50	450
Corning,	1	4,000	......	400	200	223	700
Dansville,	1	150	......	80	60	......	50
Erwin,	1	1,000	......	300	100	85	500
Hornby,	1	1,200	......	250	75	......	......
Hornellsville,	2	3,600	2,000	800	285	193	1,200
Howard,	1	1,000	700	470	......	......	......
Jasper,	1	600	800	350	100	60	400
Pultney,	1	2,200	2,000	126	160	126	400
Urbana,	1	4,000	1,000	400	200	160	650
Wheeler,	1	300	......	250	50	6	......
Total,	20	29,850	8,900	5,716	1,930	1,287	7,230
Suffolk Co.							
Brookhaven,	8	27,300	8,000	2,500	1,305	396	2,960
East Hampton,	1	3,000	2,000	600	500	361	700
Huntington,	4	13,800	3,800	2,150	1,275	655	2,500
Islip,	1	1,500	......	300	250	30	100
Shelter Island,	1	2,500	......	250	175	111	450
Smithtown,	1	3,500	11,500	350	150	60	500
Southampton,	5	27,500	5,500	2,880	1,475	899	5,200
Southold,	5	12,350	4,300	1,750	1,100	578	3,050
Total,	26	91,450	35,100	10,780	6,230	3,090	15460
Sullivan Co.							
Bethel,	1	2,500	500	350	125	90	550
Cochecton,	1	2,500	......	400	200	40	400
Liberty,	1	2,000	......	700	400	160	400
Rockland,	1	600	......	400	200	12	......
Thompson,	1	3,000	2,500	450	300	172	900
Total,	5	10,600	3,000	2,300	1,225	474	2,250
Tioga Co.							
Newark,	1	2,000	400	500	200	150	500
Owego,	1	1,500	2,000	800	500	240	1,550
Richford,	1	1,800	......	300	100	40	400
Total,	3	5,300	2,400	1,600	800	430	2,450
Tompkins Co.							
Dryden,	2	5,500	1,200	900	300	240	1,000
Enfield,	1	800	......	500	50	30	200
Ithaca,	1	17,500	500	800	500	300	1,000
Lansing,	1	2,000	1,000	400	125	80	550
Newfield,	1	2,000	......	600	75	133	400
Ulysses,	1	12,000	......	550	300	362	900
Total,	7	39,800	2,700	3,750	1,350	1,145	4,050
Ulster Co.							
Kingston,	2	11,900	6,500	1,150	550	260	1,550
Lloyd,	1	3,000	......	500	200	130	550
Marlborough,	2	5,800	1,500	925	600	205	1,100
Plattekill,	1	1,500	......	400	36	20	200
Saugerties,	1	3,000	1,200	200	75	27	600
Total,	7	25,200	9,200	3,175	1,461	642	4,000
Warren Co.							
Bolton,	1	1,200	......	200	40	30	......
Caldwell,	1	3,400	......	300	60	16	300
Chester,	1	$1,200	......	300	60	50	$500
Queensbury,	1	10,000	......	800	300	230	1,000
Warrensburgh,	1	2,500	......	300	80	168	600
Total,	5	18,300	......	1,900	540	494	2,400
Washington Co.							
Fort Edward,	2	3,000	......	450	425	53	400
Granville,	2	7,000	......	650	350	184	926
Hebron,	1	1,800	$1,200	300	90	70	400
Kingsbury,	1	5,000	......	600	300	95	700
Salem,	1	10,000	......	650	300	203	850
White Creek,	1	5,500	1,200	700	400	238	900
Whitehall,	1	13,500	......	900	500	250	1,000
Total,	9	45,800	2,400	4,250	2,365	1,093	5,176
Wayne Co.							
Arcadia,	1	13,000	1,100	700	350	225	1,000
Galen,	1	3,000	......	800	300	160	600
Huron,	1	2,000	1,000	500	150	128	600
Lyons,	1	19,000	5,000	1,000	650	371	1,000
Palmyra,	2	19,500	1,000	1,050	600	405	1,400
Rose,	1	1,000	500	400	200	200	325
Sodus,	2	5,800	......	1,000	300	134	925
Walworth,	1	800	......	200	60	20	300
Williamson,	2	1,200	......	600	150	200	300
Wolcott,	2	8,000	......	748	400	261	1,604
Total,	14	73,300	8,600	6,998	3,160	2,104	8,054
Westchester Co.							
Bedford,	2	4,500	4,600	650	350	219	1,320
Cortlandt,	2	8,500	......	670	500	223	1,500
Lewisboro,	1	3,000	4,800	600	400	190	700
New Rochelle,	1	7,000	......	500	250	65	900
North Salem,	1	3,000	1,800	250	80	55	525
Ossining,	1	12,000	4,000	550	300	150	1,200
Poundridge,	1	2,500	1,200	275	150	90	500
Rye,	2	14,000	3,000	525	200	70	1,220
Somers,	2	4,000	3,500	450	160	80	960
Westchester,	1	9,000	......	300	125	24	.....
West Farms,	2	6,000	......	700	350	113	1,900
White Plains,	1	7,500	1,500	400	250	62	500
Yonkers,	1	30,000	8,000	750	450	135	2,500
Yorktown,	1	5,000	3,000	500	150	66	450
Total,	19	116,000	35,400	7,120	3,715	1,542	14,175
Wyoming Co.							
Attica,	1	3,500	1,300	550	160	113	650
Bennington,	2	1,500	300	325	125	66	300
Covington,	1	1,200	500	400	70	50	350
Genesee Falls,	1	600	......	150	75	40	......
Middlebury,	1	3,000	......	500	150	100	400
Orangeville,	1	1,800	100	300	100	75	400
Perry,	1	6,000	......	500	150	138	800
Sheldon,	1	300	......	150	50	30	100
Warsaw,	1	4,000	2,000	500	150	140	500
Total,	10	21,900	4,200	3,375	1,030	752	3,500
Yates Co.							
Benton,	1	4,000	1,000	400	250	200	650
Italy,	1	1,500	......	600	75	80	210
Jerusalem,	1	3,000	......	300	80	65	600
Milo,	1	8,000	......	600	500	225	1,000
Starkey,	3	4,800	600	1,050	390	737	1,000
Torrey,	1	800	......	200	65	32	450
Total,	8	22,100	1,600	3,150	1,360	1,339	3,910

ASSOCIATE PRESBYTERIAN CHURCHES.

TOWNS.	Number of churches.	Value of church and lot.	Value of other real estate.	Number capable of being seated.	Usual number attending.	Number of communicants.	Salary of clergy, including use of real estate.
Albany Co.							
Albany,	2	8,000	3,000	560	300	270	900
Cattaraugus Co.							
Lyndon,	1	2,000	......	350	100	80	350
Delaware Co.							
Bovina,	1	2,340	......	450	350	179	500
Delhi,	1	1,000	......	300	250	115	400
Hamden,	1	1,200	......	350	150	45	400
Total,	3	4,540	......	1,100	750	339	1,300
Fulton Co.							
Johnstown,	1	3,000	......	340	150	50	500
Kings Co.							
Brooklyn,	1	6,000	......	400	150	60	1,000
Livingston Co.							
York,	1	800	......	......	......	......	450

CHURCHES.—(CONTINUED.)

TOWNS.	Number of churches.	Value of church and lot.	Value of other real estate.	Number capable of being seated.	Usual number attending.	Number of communicants.	Salary of clergy, including use of real estate.
MONTGOMERY CO.							
Florida, ...	1	$2,000	$1,000	500	300	150	$600
NEW-YORK CO.							
New-York, ...	6	378,000	3,000	6,300	3,700	1,708	2,500
WARREN CO.							
Queensbury, ...	1	1,000	......	400	80	40	......
WASHINGTON CO.							
Argyle, ...	2	7,500	4,500	1,190	621	389	1,200
Cambridge, ...	1	6,000	500	600	400	300	900
Greenwich, ...	1	4,000	300	400	200	100	300
Hebron, ...	2	3,000	1,700	850	475	2[illegible]0	950
Putnam, ...	1	200	100	275	275	100	570
Salem, ...	1	2,000	1,500	400	150	80	700
Total, ...	8	22,700	8,600	3,715	2,121	1,199	4,620
WYOMING CO.							
Covington, ...	1	1,200	500	400	70	50	350

ASSOCIATE REFORMED PRESBYTERIAN CHURCHES.

TOWNS.	Number of churches.	Value of church and lot.	Value of other real estate.	Number capable of being seated.	Usual number attending.	Number of communicants.	Salary of clergy, including use of real estate.
CATTARAUGUS CO.							
Lyndon, ...	1	2,000	......	350	100	80	350
CAYUGA CO.							
Sterling, ...	1	2,000	......	450	300	73	......
CHEMUNG CO.							
Erwin, ...	1	700	......	200	......	......	......
DELAWARE CO.							
Andes, ...	2	3,000	......	750	500	215	450
Kortright, ...	3	10,465	......	1,640	825	513	1,530
Middletown, ...	1	1,200	......	200	150	40	400
Stanford, ...	2	5,800	1,000	900	550	229	1,150
Total, ...	8	20,465	1,000	3,490	2,025	997	3,530
FULTON CO.							
Perth, ...	1	3,000	1,500	500	250	165	700
JEFFERSON CO.							
Antwerp, ...	1	2,500	......	300	200	150	500
LIVINGSTON CO.							
Caledonia, ...	1	5,000	500	500	250	208	650
Leicester, ...	1	2,200	550	350	200	60	400
York, ...	1	5,000	3,000	500	300	198	700
Total, ...	3	12,200	4,050	1,350	750	466	1,750
MONROE CO.							
Rochester, ...	1	2,500	......	400	200	140	800
Wheatland, ...	1	2,700	1,500	350	150	50	600
Total, ...	2	5,200	1,500	750	350	190	1,400
NEW-YORK CO.							
New-York, ...	4	98,000	......	3,700	1,950	1,055	7,000
ONTARIO CO.							
Seneca, ...	2	10,500	550	850	400	235	1,000
ORANGE CO.							
Crawford, ...	1	1,600	4,500	300	100	30	650
Hamptonburgh, ...	1	1,000	1,500	500	150	40	600
Newburgh, ...	2	10,000	......	912	600	431	2,000
New Windsor, ...	1	3,000	1,800	460	200	140	600
Total, ...	5	15,600	7,800	2,172	1,050	641	3,850
OSWEGO CO.							
Constantia, ...	1	1,000	......	150	75	35	400
OTSEGO CO.							
Springfield, ...	1	2,000	1,000	350	100	47	600
ST. LAWRENCE CO.							
Lisbon, ...	1	500	1,250	500	200	200	375
SULLIVAN CO.							
Bethel, ...	1	2,500	2,500	350	250	119	700
Mamakating, ...	1	4,000	2,000	500	200	75	550
Total, ...	2	6,500	4,500	850	450	194	1,250
WASHINGTON CO.							
Argyle, ...	1	4,000	......	900	800	465	1,000
Hebron, ...	1	200	1,800	600	400	170	600
Salem, ...	1	10,000	4,000	700	400	221	900
White Creek, ...	1	4,500	1,600	450	150	76	580
Total, ...	4	18,700	7,400	2,650	1,750	932	3,080

REFORMED PRESBYTERIANS OR COVENANTERS' CHURCHES.

TOWNS.	Number of churches.	Value of church and lot.	Value of other real estate.	Number capable of being seated.	Usual number attending.	Number of communicants.	Salary of clergy, including use of real estate.
CAYUGA CO.							
Sterling, ...	1	2,500	......	400	250	75	300

TOWNS.	Number of churches.	Value of church and lot.	Value of other real estate.	Number capable of being seated.	Usual number attending.	Number of communicants.	Salary of clergy, including use of real estate.
DELAWARE CO.							
Bovina, ...	1	$500	......	300	175	30	$280
Kortright, ...	1	2,000	......	400	200	75	300
Total, ...	2	2,500	......	700	375	105	580
KINGS CO.							
Brooklyn, ...	1	......	......	350	250	215	1,400
LIVINGSTON CO.							
York, ...	1	2,000	......	400	250	138	500
MONROE CO.							
Rochester, ...	1	6,500	......	200	200	97	400
NEW-YORK CO.							
New-York, ...	4	71,500	1,000	2,150	1,400	841	25,000
ORANGE CO.							
Montgomery, ...	1	2,500	1,055	400	100	80	350
Newburgh, ...	1	4,000	......	500	480	160	550
Total, ...	2	6,500	1,055	900	580	240	900
ST. LAWRENCE CO.							
Lisbon, ...	2	1,500	......	500	320	170	600
Potsdam, ...	1	1,000	......	500	200	85	450
Total, ...	3	2,500	......	1,000	520	250	1,050
SCHENECTADY CO.							
Duanesburgh, ...	1	3,200	360	600	400	175	675
STEUBEN CO.							
Howard, ...	1	700	250	250	200	43	300
SULLIVAN CO.							
Bethel, ...	1	600	......	250	150	60	400
WASHINGTON CO.							
Argyle, ...	1	1,000	......	400	60	35	100

FRENCH EVANGELIC PRESBYTERIAN CHURCH.

TOWNS.	Number of churches.	Value of church and lot.	Value of other real estate.	Number capable of being seated.	Usual number attending.	Number of communicants.	Salary of clergy, including use of real estate.
FRANKLIN CO.							
Bangor, ...	1	300	......	200	20	18	150

PROTESTANT EPISCOPAL CHURCHES

TOWNS.	Number of churches.	Value of church and lot.	Value of other real estate.	Number capable of being seated.	Usual number attending.	Number of communicants.	Salary of clergy, including use of real estate.
ALBANY CO.							
Albany, ...	5	112,000	3,000	3,050	1,900	565	7,400
Rensselaerville, ...	1	3,000	......	350	70	65	250
Watervliet, ...	2	8,000	4,000	600	350	120	1,425
Total, ...	8	123,000	7,000	3,900	2,320	750	9,075
ALLEGANY CO.							
Angelica, ...	1	4,300	......	325	150	75	500
BROOME CO.							
Binghamton, ...	1	33,000	2,500	800	500	150	1,000
Colesville, ...	1	1,500	1,000	400	70	80	500
Total, ...	2	34,000	3,500	1,200	570	230	1,500
CATTARAUGUS CO.							
Ellicottville, ...	1	3,000	......	350	50	40	600
Olean, ...	1	3,000	......	300	50	25	500
Total, ...	2	6,000	......	650	100	65	1,100
CAYUGA CO.							
Auburn, ...	1	20,000	4,000	800	600	220	2,000
Ledyard, ...	1	1,000	......	200	100	16	550
Total, ...	2	27,000	4,000	1,000	700	236	2,550
CHAUTAUQUE CO.							
Chautauque, ...	1	1,500	......	600	......	20	......
Pomfret, ...	2	8,800	......	600	370	101	1,500
Westfield, ...	1	4,500	......	400	150	45	600
Total, ...	4	14,800	......	1,600	520	166	2,100
CHEMUNG CO.							
Elmira, ...	1	4,000	6,000	250	125	80	1,100
CHENANGO CO.							
Bainbridge, ...	1	4,000	300	......	150	70	500
Greene, ...	1	2,000	......	350	250	100	800
Guilford, ...	1	2,000	1,500	400	175	97	450
New Berlin, ...	1	9,000	1,200	350	300	125	550
Norwich, ...	1	5,000	......	400	100	35	500
Oxford, ...	1	1,000	1,200	300	125	80	800
Sherburne, ...	1	2,000	800	450	175	75	600
Total, ...	7	25,500	5,000	2,250	1,275	582	4,200
CLINTON CO.							
Champlain, ...	1	3,200	......	200	75	22	250
Ellenburgh, ...	1	3,000	......	250	125	15	......

CHURCHES.—(Continued.)

TOWNS.	Number of churches.	Value of church and lot.	Value of other real estate.	Number capable of being seated.	Usual number attending.	Number of communicants.	Salary of clergy, including use of real estate.
Clinton Co.							
Mooers,	1	$550	......	100	50	28	$200
Plattsburgh,	1	12,000	$2,500	600	200	100	750
Total,	4	18,750	2,500	1,150	450	165	1,200
Columbia Co.							
Copake,	1	3,000	2,000	200	40	15	500
Hudson,	1	2,000	......	300	250	150	850
Kinderhook,	1	3,000	......	300	175	50	600
Stockport,	1	11,000	1,800	350	100	20	325
Total,	4	19,000	3,800	1,150	565	235	2,275
Cortland Co.							
Homer,	1	3,500	......	350	100	30	600
Delaware Co.							
Delhi,	1	3,800	......	400	200	......	......
Stanford,	1	2,500	800	350	150	75	385
Walton,	1	3,000	900	450	100	40	210
Total,	3	9,300	1,700	1,200	450	125	595
Dutchess Co.							
Amenia,	1	3,000	......	150	75	25	300
Beekman,	1	2,000	......	200	30	17	300
Clinton,	1	800	......	......	150	......	......
Fishkill,	3	16,500	3,000	1,000	485	220	2,050
Hyde Park,	1	6,000	2,000	250	80	105	800
Pine Plains,	1	200	......	150	30	20	......
Pleasant Valley,	1	1,500	......	200	50	18	50
Poughkeepsie city,	2	27,000	7,000	1,300	850	280	1,900
Red Hook,	4	26,000	4,500	1,000	600	47	2,550
Rhinebeck,	1	5,000	......	300	150	31	960
Washington,	1	2,000	......	300	60	30	......
Total,	17	91,000	16,500	4,850	2,560	793	8,910
Erie Co.							
Buffalo,	4	240,630	13,000	3,450	2,270	840	7,200
Essex Co.							
Chesterfield,	1	2,000	......	140	100	45	650
Franklin Co.							
Malone,	1	3,640	2,000	300	150	56	600
Fulton Co.							
Johnstown,	1	6,000	......	360	180	50	800
Genesee Co.							
Batavia,	1	12,000	3,000	800	400	200	1,200
Le Roy,	1	3,500	2,500	300	250	80	800
Stafford,	1	3,300	......	320	230	78	500
Total,	3	18,800	5,500	1,420	880	358	2,500
Greene Co.							
Athens,	1	5,000	2,500	500	150	50	500
Cairo,	1	2,000	......	250	45	20	250
Catskill,	1	7,000	......	450	200	125	800
Coxsackie,	1	3,600	......	200	70	17	......
Durham,	1	1,500	......	300	75	33	400
Greenville,	1	3,500	......	200	100	35	80
Prattsville,	1	2,000	......	300	100	44	500
Total,	7	24,600	2,500	2,200	740	324	2,530
Herkimer Co.							
Fairfield,	1	100	500	400	100	......	......
Little Falls,	1	6,000	2,500	300	150	50	625
Norway,	1	......	300	......	50	24	400
Total,	3	6,100	3,300	700	300	74	1,025
Jefferson Co.							
Adams,	1	2,800	150	300	90	12	150
Alexandria,	1	1,400	......	200	75	12	200
Brownville,	2	4,800	500	800	250	115	550
Cape Vincent,	1	3,000	1,000	125	100	60	600
Ellisburgh,	1	3,000	1,400	150	60	51	700
Hounsfield,	1	4,000	......	450	100	50	400
Theresa,	1	2,600	......	240	100	21	500
Watertown,	1	18,000	......	700	500	140	1,000
Total,	9	39,600	3,050	2,965	1,275	461	4,100
Kings Co.							
Brooklyn,	22	520,600	8,800	12,200	8,370	4,049	28730
Flatbush,	1	7,000	......	300	100	40	500
New Lots,	1	2,500	......	300	100	15	......
New Utrecht,	2	9,000	......	550	270	55	1600
Total,	26	539,100	8,800	13,350	8,840	4,159	30830
Lewis Co.							
Lowville,	1	2,750	......	200	50	40	450
West Turin,	1	1,200	......	250	75	30	100
Total,	2	3,950	......	450	125	70	550
Livingston Co.							
Avon,	1	$4,000	$1,400	350	150	40	$550
Geneseo,	1	4,500	3,500	275	130	85	1,100
Mount Morris,	1	3,500	......	250	200	92	900
North Dansville,	1	5,000	......	300	150	65	500
Nunda,	1	2,000	......	300	40	20	250
Portage,	1	1,500	......	400	50	50	400
Total,	6	20,500	4,900	1,875	720	352	3,700
Madison Co.							
Cazenovia,	1	3,500	......	275	100	28	300
Fenner,	1	1,500	......	350	......	20	......
Hamilton,	1	4,000	......	300	150	50	600
Total,	3	9,000	......	925	250	98	900
Monroe Co.							
Mendon,	1	3,000	......	350	80	60	500
Pittsford,	1	600	......	150	100	30	263
Rochester,	3	61,650	......	2,300	1,900	853	4,000
Wheatland,	1	400	......	100	......	......	......
Total,	6	65,650	......	2,900	2,080	943	4,763
New-York Co.							
New-York,	43	3,364,500	447900	37,819	21,850	9,006	113397
Niagara Co.							
Lewiston,	1	2,500	......	250	60	60	500
Lockport,	2	27,000	3,000	1,300	450	185	1,500
Niagara,	1	6,000	2,000	400	200	40	850
Total,	4	35,500	5,000	1,950	710	285	2,850
Oneida Co.							
Camden,	1	3,000	800	350	50	60	500
New Hartford,	1	4,000	1,000	500	300	235	600
Paris,	2	8,000	1,000	800	200	58	1,100
Rome,	1	2,000	300	490	250	130	1,100
Sangerfield,	1	4,000	1,000	275	100	40	740
Trenton,	1	1,000	800	300	30	20	350
Utica,	3	21,200	1,000	1,670	1,120	798	2,400
Whitestown,	2	2,900	......	400	108	49	550
Total,	12	46,100	5,900	4,785	2,158	1,390	7,340
Onondaga Co.							
De Witt,	1	1,500	......	250	50	12	300
Elbridge,	1	3,000	......	300	100	60	585
Geddes,	1	1,000	......	275	60	11	......
Manlius,	2	5,000	......	800	300	296	1,250
Marcellus,	1	2,500	......	300	......	......	......
Pompey,	1	500	100	500	......	......	......
Skaneateles,	1	5,500	1,500	350	200	90	500
Syracuse,	2	68,000	10,000	1,100	600	330	2,300
Total,	10	87,000	11,600	3,875	1,310	799	4,935
Ontario Co.							
Canandaigua,	2	5,500	4,000	850	480	225	1,100
East Bloomfield,	1	1,600	1,000	400	60	30	......
Gorham,	1	2,000	550	400	120	......	......
Richmond,	1	500	......	200	25	25	......
Seneca,	2	36,000	......	1,500	275	326	1,400
Total,	7	45,600	5,550	3,350	960	606	2,500
Orange Co.							
Cornwall,	1	6,000	1,500	200	100	69	600
Deerpark,	1	......	......	......	100	20	650
Goshen,	1	13,000	1,500	420	250	67	900
Montgomery,	1	2,000	1,000	400	100	55	500
Newburgh,	1	20,000	4,000	750	600	180	1,200
New Windsor,	1	10,000	5,000	250	100	30	700
Walkill,	1	5,000	......	400	200	25	600
Total,	7	56,000	13,000	2,420	1,450	446	5,150
Orleans Co.							
Barre,	1	3,500	......	300	100	50	600
Ridgeway,	1	6,000	......	400	150	45	700
Total,	2	9,500	......	700	250	95	1,300
Oswego Co.							
Constantia,	1	1,500	500	500	100	10	......
Granby,	1	1,200	1,200	200	55	20	439
Oswego city,	2	27,500	......	1,200	900	260	1,400
Richland,	1	3,000	......	250	75	20	400
Volney,	1	3,000	......	250	100	40	600
Total,	6	36,200	1,700	2,400	1,230	350	2,839
Otsego Co.							
Butternuts,	1	1,600	1,000	400	100	60	550
Cherry Valley,	1	2,000	2,000	600	100	75	400
Morris,	1	5,000	1,400	500	250	184	650
Otego,	1	2,000	......	275	......	12	......
Otsego,	1	6,000	2,000	400	150	110	200

CHURCHES.—(CONTINUED.)

TOWNS.	Number of churches.	Value of church and lot.	Value of other real estate.	Number capable of being seated.	Usual number attending.	Number of communicants.	Salary of clergy, including use of real estate.
OTSEGO CO.							
Richfield, ...	2	$3,700	......	905	75	28	$575
Unadilla, ...	1	3,000	$2,500	330	200	103	900
Westford, ...	1	800	......	300	150	18	......
Total, ...	9	24,100	8,900	3,705	1,125	590	3,775
PUTNAM CO.							
Patterson, ...	1	2,000	......	300	40	24	250
Phillipstown, ...	2	5,000	1,200	450	150	74	1,100
Total, ...	3	7,000	1,200	750	190	98	1,350
QUEENS CO.							
Flushing, ...	2	41,700	50,000	1,200	800	304	1,500
Hempstead, ...	2	14,000	7,850	500	750	140	900
Jamaica, ...	1	12,000	......	500	400	400	600
North Hempstead, ...	1	1,000	2,500	450	150	95	900
Newtown, ...	4	44,000	14,000	1,250	650	185	4,750
Oyster Bay, ...	4	10,100	2,000	1,500	255	115	2,050
Total, ...	14	122,800	76,350	5,400	3,005	1,239	10700
RENSSELAER CO.							
Lansingburgh, ...	1	3,000	4,000	300	400	400	600
Troy, ...	4	106,000	17,000	3,250	2,000	590	7,550
Total, ...	5	109,000	21,000	3,550	2,400	990	8,150
RICHMOND CO.							
Castleton, ...	2	16,000	......	900	500	260	1,900
Northfield, ...	1	80,000	2,000	800	500	250	3,000
Southfield, ...	2	13,000	2,500	800	600	155	2,500
Westfield, ...	1	4,500	2,000	500	150	50	600
Total, ...	6	113,500	6,500	3,000	1,750	715	8,000
ROCKLAND CO.							
Haverstraw, ...	2	5,700	......	350	120	37	......
Orangetown, ...	1	1,500	......	200	60	25	200
Total, ...	3	7,200	......	550	180	62	200
ST. LAWRENCE CO.							
Madrid, ...	1	7,000	3,000	600	100	35	550
Morristown, ...	1	3,000	900	500	200	40	425
Norfolk, ...	1	2,000	......	500	50	25	150
Oswegatchie, ...	1	8,000	2,500	700	500	130	1,200
Potsdam, ...	1	10,000	2,500	300	100	87	750
Total, ...	5	30,000	8,900	2,600	950	317	3,075
SARATOGA CO.							
Ballston, ...	1	2,000	......	200	100	43	350
Charlton, ...	1	1,800	......	200	100	40	200
Milton, ...	1	3,000	2,000	400	250	170	825
Saratoga Springs, ...	1	12,000	......	450	250	130	800
Stillwater, ...	1	2,500	500	350	25	4	550
Waterford, ...	1	3,500	3,900	200	150	60	750
Total, ...	6	24,800	6,400	1,800	875	447	3,475
SCHENECTADY CO.							
Duanesburgh, ...	1	2,500	3,000	300	70	30	700
Schenectady, ...	1	15,000	......	600	400	150	1,300
Total, ...	2	17,500	3,000	900	470	180	2,000
SCHUYLER CO.							
Catharine, ...	2	16,700	400	250	150	50	700
Dix, ...	1	800	......	250	100	12	......
Hector, ...	1	700	......	200	100	34	300
Total, ...	4	18,200	400	700	350	96	1,000
SENECA CO.							
Seneca Falls, ...	1	5,000	......	600	300	110	500
Waterloo, ...	1	4,000	......	350	230	100	650
Total, ...	2	9,000	......	950	530	200	1,150
STEUBEN CO.							
Addison, ...	1	......	......	150	75	26	475
Bath, ...	1	4,000	1,400	450	150	123	800
Corning, ...	1	10,000	......	400	200	54	600
Hornellsville, ...	1	50	......	250	150	16	625
Urbana, ...	1	3,000	......	350	150	50	500
Total, ...	5	17,050	1,400	1,600	725	269	3,000
SUFFOLK CO.							
Brookhaven, ...	2	2,000	......	360	100	36	475
Huntington, ...	1	1,400	......	140	70	28	375
Islip, ...	2	2,900	......	350	80	30	750
Smithtown, ...	1	4,000	400	200	125	12	425
Southampton, ...	1	6,000	......	500	300	50	500
Total, ...	7	16,300	400	1,550	675	156	2,525
SULLIVAN CO.							
Thompson, ...	1	$3,000	......	350	175	70	$500
TIOGA CO.							
Barton, ...	1	2,200	......	300	......	15	......
Candor, ...	1	1,800	......	260	70	37	363
Owego, ...	1	4,000	2,500	400	150	40	800
Total, ...	3	8,000	2,500	960	220	92	1,163
TOMPKINS CO.							
Caroline, ...	1	400	......	200	112	24	300
Danby, ...	1	500	......	600	50	12	100
Groton, ...	1	1,000	......	200	80	40	200
Ithaca, ...	1	4,000	3,000	400	250	100	1,000
Total, ...	4	5,900	3,000	1,400	492	176	1,600
ULSTER CO.							
Esopus, ...	1	4,000	......	120	60	16	500
Kingston, ...	2	6,000	......	440	190	90	800
Marlborough, ...	2	3,500	......	430	175	45	350
Saugerties, ...	1	4,500	1,500	175	100	65	640
Total, ...	6	18,000	1,500	1,165	525	216	2,290
WARREN CO.							
Chester, ...	1	1,000	......	200	30	25	500
Queensbury, ...	1	800	......	200	100	100	400
Total, ...	2	1,800	......	400	130	125	900
WASHINGTON CO.							
Fort Edward, ...	1	5,000	......	400	250	54	325
Granville, ...	1	500	......	......	125	40	600
Hampton, ...	1	500	1,200	300	50	25	500
Kingsbury, ...	1	7,500	......	300	150	53	275
Whitehall, ...	1	13,500	......	250	150	30	500
Total, ...	5	27,000	1,200	1,250	725	202	2,200
WAYNE CO.							
Arcadia, ...	1	4,200	800	225	100	40	750
Galen, ...	1	3,000	......	300	100	43	650
Lyons, ...	1	15,000	1,500	450	300	140	725
Palmyra, ...	1	6,800	2,000	425	225	90	825
Sodus, ...	2	3,900	......	400	15	48	......
Total, ...	6	32,900	4,300	1,800	740	361	2,950
WESTCHESTER CO.							
Bedford, ...	1	4,000	4,000	300	200	100	600
Cortlandt, ...	1	3,000	......	200	100	80	600
Eastchester, ...	1	10,000	4,000	400	100	50	750
Greenburgh, ...	1	9,000	......	275	138	60	500
Lewisboro, ...	1	3,000	......	350	200	13	500
Mamaroneck, ...	1	6,000	3,000	250	160	60	715
Mount Pleasant, ...	1	2,500	......	250	100	......	......
New Castle, ...	1	2,500	......	300	50	12	400
New Rochelle, ...	1	10,000	8,000	450	200	60	1,000
North Castle, ...	3	4,600	300	825	325	70	250
North Salem, ...	1	750	1,200	400	50	27	250
Ossining, ...	1	14,000	6,000	350	200	82	900
Rye, ...	2	20,000	10,000	700	300	120	1,600
Scarsdale, ...	1	6,500	......	211	120	53	800
Somers, ...	1	5,000	......	800	100	25	250
Westchester, ...	1	37,000	50,000	500	200	100	1,800
West Farms, ...	4	9,000	5,500	1,425	800	690	4,800
White Plains, ...	1	5,500	4,000	350	275	80	750
Yonkers, ...	2	37,500	22,500	850	660	296	4,900
Total, ...	26	189,850	118500	9,186	4,278	1,978	21,365
WYOMING CO.							
Warsaw, ...	1	3,200	......	230	125	45	515
Wethersfield, ...	1	2,000	......	500	70	15	150
Total, ...	2	5,200	......	730	195	60	665
YATES CO.							
Milo, ...	1	6,000	......	450	200	......	500

PROTESTANT COMMUNITY OF TRUE INSPIRATION CHURCHES.

TOWNS.	Number of churches.	Value of church and lot.	Value of other real estate.	Number capable of being seated.	Usual number attending.	Number of communicants.	Salary of clergy, including use of real estate.
ERIE CO.							
West Seneca, ...	2	5,000	......	950	820	735	......

PROTESTANT CHURCHES—(MISCELLANEOUS.)

TOWNS.	Number of churches.	Value of church and lot.	Value of other real estate.	Number capable of being seated.	Usual number attending.	Number of communicants.	Salary of clergy, including use of real estate.
ALBANY CO.							
Albany, ...	1	2,300	340	340	200	90	350
ERIE CO.							
Buffalo, ...	2	10,000	......	1,200	800	500	1,100
Lancaster, ...	2	2,000	......	400	230	134	150
Total, ...	4	12,000	......	1,600	1,030	634	1,250

CHURCHES.—(Continued.)

TOWNS.	Number of churches.	Value of church and lot.	Value of other real estate.	Number capable of being seated.	Usual number attending	Number of communicants.	Salary of clergy, including use of real estate.
Lewis Co.							
Lewis,	1	$300	......	200	100	50	$200
Oswego Co.							
Mexico,	1	300	......	150	60	60	......
Seneca Co.							
Fayette,	1	....	......	100	50	25	42

REFORMED PROTESTANT DUTCH CHURCHES.

TOWNS.	Number of churches.	Value of church and lot.	Value of other real estate.	Number capable of being seated.	Usual number attending	Number of communicants.	Salary of clergy, including use of real estate.
Albany Co.							
Albany,	3	111, 200	30, 000	2, 700	1, 950	1, 029	5, 800
Bern,	3	5, 300	5, 000	1, 900	750	190	1, 032
Bethlehem,	2	10, 000	9, 500	1, 500	800	380	1, 500
Coeymans,	1	3, 000	1, 500	450	200	73	500
Guilderland,	1	3, 000	3, 200	650	200	250	600
Knox,	1	1, 200	......	300	100	40	200
New Scotland,	4	9, 700	1, 500	1, 550	430	166	930
Watervliet,	6	32, 200	6, 800	2, 540	1, 980	577	3, 450
Westerlo,	1	2, 500	800	400	200	125	400
Total,	22	178, 100	58, 300	11, 990	6, 610	2, 830	14412
Cayuga Co.							
Fleming,	1	4, 500	......	500	200	130	......
Owasco,	1	3, 000	1, 200	700	250	111	700
Total,	2	7, 500	1, 200	1, 200	450	241	700
Chautauque Co.							
Clymer,	1	800	......	250	100	51	200
Columbia Co.							
Chatham,	1	4, 000	......	370	200	25	650
Claverack,	2	8, 500	3, 000	1, 300	950	409	1, 300
Gallatin,	1	2, 000	400	450	175	150	150
Germantown,	1	3, 000	1, 600	500	200	100	650
Ghent,	2	4, 500	3, 200	825	400	245	1, 300
Greenport,	1	3, 000	2, 000	350	200	75	600
Hudson,	1	15, 000	3, 500	800	400	157	1, 300
Kinderhook,	1	12, 000	......	12, 000	600	300	1, 000
Livingston,	2	16, 000	2, 000	900	550	391	1, 225
Stuyvesant,	1	2, 000	2, 400	400	250	95	525
Total,	13	70, 000	18, 100	17, 895	3, 925	1. 947	8, 700
Delaware Co.							
Roxbury,	2	2, 700	600	500	250	87	850
Dutchess Co.							
East Fishkill,	1	8, 000	3, 500	600	350	100	1, 000
Fishkill,	4	25, 000	14, 000	1, 950	950	483	3, 250
Hyde Park,	1	5, 000	2, 000	250	80	105	800
Poughkeepsie city,	2	40, 000	40, 000	1, 600	800	426	3, 000
Red Hook,	1	4, 000	11, 200	300	200	85	500
Rhinebeck,	1	9, 000	9, 000	700	400	250	1, 500
Total,	10	91, 000	79, 700	5. 400	2, 780	1, 449	10050
Erie Co.							
Buffalo,	1	500	......	200	50	......	1, 200
Fulton Co.							
Caroga,	1	1, 700	......	300	50	......	300
Ephratah,	1	1, 000	500	300	75	75	300
Johnstown,	1	2, 500	......	300	100	30	300
Oppenhein,	1	150	......	100	50	40	100
Total,	4	5, 350	500	1, 000	275	145	1, 000
Greene Co.							
Athens,	2	6, 000	......	900	375	150	750
Catskill,	2	16, 000	2, 000	1, 200	800	300	1, 400
Coxsackie,	2	4, 000	3, 900	1, 200	600	442	2, 100
New Baltimore,	1	2, 000	......	400	100	75	400
Prattsville,	1	3, 000	800	600	300	55	500
Total,	8	31, 000	6, 700	4, 300	2, 175	1, 022	5, 150
Herkimer Co.							
Columbia,	1	2, 000	......	250	75	56	325
Frankfort,	1	2, 000	......	600	70	25	150
German Flats,	2	9, 500	1, 575	2, 500	140	49	820
Herkimer,	1	6, 000	......	600	300	320	800
Manheim,	1	5, 000	......	300	160	60	400
Warren,	1	1, 200	......	250	150	50	800
Total,	7	25, 700	1, 575	4, 500	895	560	3, 295
Jefferson Co.							
Alexandria,	1	3, 000	800	400	150	18	450
Kings Co.							
Brooklyn,	12	297, 300	35, 500	6, 975	2, 705	1, 477	13125
Flatbush,	1	15, 000	25, 000	900	300	130	1500
Flatlands,	1	6, 000	3, 000	400	300	90	1050
Gravesend,	1	6, 000	3, 000	500	200	101	500
New Lots,	2	$13, 000	$8, 000	950	500	126	$2, 00
New Utrecht,	1	6, 000	4, 000	500	300	126	90
Total,	18	343, 300	78, 500	10. 225	4, 305	2, 050	19, 07
Lewis Co.							
Croghan,	1	1, 400	20	200	130	45	42
Livingston Co.							
Mount Morris,	1	1, 200	......	200	20	25	......
Madison Co.							
Sullivan,	1	1, 200	1, 000	3, 000	300	60	60
Monroe Co.							
Rochester,	1	800	175	200	150	154	......
Montgomery Co.							
Amsterdam,	1	2, 200	......	600	100	50	40
Canajoharie,	2	5, 100	200	850	400	145	90
Charleston,	1	500	......	600	275	50	50
Florida,	2	6, 500	......	970	460	195	1, 20
Glen,	2	6, 800	200	1, 050	650	84	1, 15
Mohawk,	1	4, 000	......	800	300	50	60
Minden,	1	6. 000	......	500	300	100	90
Palatine,	1	5, 500	2, 000	600	200	100	45
Root,	1	1, 500	400	400	250	77	40
St. Johnsville,	1	3, 300	1, 500	400	250	100	50
Total,	13	41, 400	4. 300	6, 770	3, 185	951	7, 00
New-York Co.							
New-York,	22	919, 000	157750	21, 650	13, 100	5, 117	39, 80
Oneida Co.							
Utica,	1	15, 000	1, 500	800	300	160	1, 75
Onondaga Co.							
Lysander,	1	2, 500	......	800	50	30	......
Syracuse,	2	22, 000	400	600	800	400	1, 80
Total,	3	24. 500	400	1, 400	850	430	1, 80
Ontario Co.							
Seneca,	1	1, 200	......	600	300	150	80
Orange Co.							
Deerpark,	2	10. 100	......	900	550	171	1, 35
Montgomery,	3	20, 500	17, 600	1, 850	1, 200	555	2, 35
Newburgh,	1	15, 000	......	600	250	180	80
Warwick,	1	3, 000	4, 000	400	375	85	70
Total,	7	48, 600	21, 600	3, 750	2, 375	991	5. 20
Oswego Co.							
Constantia,	1	1, 000	......	150	75	35	40
Queens Co.							
Flushing,	1	15, 000	3, 500	450	300	60	80
Jamaica,	1	10, 000	7, 000	900	550	250	1, 30
North Hempstead,	1	3, 000	2, 500	300	150	43	60
Newtown,	3	34, 000	11, 000	1, 030	650	205	2, 00
Oyster Bay,	1	3, 000	1, 500	500	400	100	50
Total,	7	65, 000	25, 500	3, 180	2, 050	658	5, 20
Rensselaer Co.							
Clinton,	1	4, 000	2, 000	500	350	180	90
Hoosick,	1	3, 000	3, 000	300	175	101	40
Nassau,	1	4, 500	2, 000	500	300	200	72
North Greenbush,	2	9, 000	3, 100	1, 810	300	90	1, 55
Schaghticoke,	1	3, 000	1, 000	300	40	40	40
Schodack,	3	11, 200	2. 400	1, 300	730	460	1, 65
Total,	9	34, 700	13, 500	4, 710	1, 895	1, 071	5, 62
Richmond Co.							
Castleton,	1	13, 000	1, 500	500	250	160	1, 25
Northfield,	1	12, 000	4, 500	800	700	212	1, 35
Southfield,	2	17, 000	3, 000	820	550	440	2, 70
Westfield,	1	4, 000	......	300	50	18	50
Total,	5	46, 000	9, 000	2, 420	1, 550	830	6 80
Rockland Co.							
Clarkstown,	2	9, 000	2, 500	460	350	134	85
Orangetown,	4	24, 500	8, 000	1, 400	900	312	2, 55
Ramapo,	2	2, 500	2, 750	900	275	87	52
Total,	8	36, 000	13, 250	2, 760	1, 525	533	3, 92
Saratoga Co.							
Clifton Park,	1	800	1, 000	350	150	120	60
Day,	1	1, 200	475	860	140	80	50
Northumberland,	2	3, 500	900	800	285	133	75
Saratoga,	1	200	1, 500	425	250	90	50
Waterford,	1	4, 000	3, 000	350	150	82	60
Total,	6	9, 700	6, 875	2, 785	975	505	2, 95

CHURCHES.—(Continued.)

TOWNS.	Number of churches.	Value of church and lot.	Value of other real estate.	Number capable of being seated.	Usual number attending.	Number of communicants.	Salary of clergy, including use of real estate.
SCHENECTADY Co.							
Duanesburgh, ...	1	$16, 000	$600	500	200	35	......
Glenville, ...	2	4, 500	1, 000	1, 300	600	503	$1100
Niskayuna, ...	1	6, 000	1, 200	500	300	160	700
Princetown,........	1	3, 500	......	400	200	70	......
Rotterdam, ...	2	4, 000	4, 200	600	500	140	700
Schenectady, ...	3	31, 500	12, 500	1, 600	1, 030	525	2, 900
Total, ...	10	65, 500	19, 500	4, 900	2, 839	1, 433	5. 400
SCHOHARIE Co.							
Blenheim,..........	1	2, 500	......	325	90	37	300
Cobleskill, ...	2	4, 450	2, 000	575	250	131	470
Fulton, ...	1	2, 000	......	300	150	50	100
Gilboa, ...	1	1, 000	......	500	450	167	600
Middleburgh,.......	1	3, 500	2, 000	700	250	88	650
Seward, ...	1	700	......	300	200	40	150
Schoharie, ...	1	6, 000	2, 500	800	300	100	900
Sharon,............	1	1, 500	1, 000	400	200	120	300
Summit, ...	1	800	......	400	150	12	100
Wright, ...	1	3, 000	500	700	200	70	505
Total, ...	11	25, 450	8, 000	5 000	2, 240	815	4 075
SENECA Co.							
Covert, ...	1	5, 000	1, 500	500	200	140	700
Fayette,...........	1	3, 000	......	500	75	25	......
Lodi, ...	1	7, 000	1, 800	600	400	204	900
Ovid, ...	1	3. 500	......	508	150	46	500
Seneca Falls, ...	1	1, 500	......	......	......	......	......
Tyre,..............	1	1, 600	2, 000	220	130	40	500
Waterloo,..........	1	2, 500	......	500	150	78	......
Total,.............	7	24, 100	5, 300	2, 828	1, 105	533	2. 600
SULLIVAN Co.							
Cochecton,.........	1	1, 500	......	......	......	......	......
Fallsburgh, ...	1	3, 000	......	800	250	116	550
Mamakating, ...	2	5, 900	2, 000	900	525	240	1, 125
Neversink, ...	2	2, 000	......	900	150	130	1, 000
Total, ...	6	12, 400	2, 000	2, 600	925	486	2, 675
TOMPKINS Co.							
Caroline, ...	1	2, 000	600	400	200	50	450
Ithaca,............	1	10, 000	2, 500	600	300	135	800
Total,...........	2	12, 000	3, 100	1, 000	500	185	1. 250
ULSTER Co.							
Esopus,............	3	6, 400	3, 900	630	340	140	900
Gardiner, ...	1	2, 000	1, 200	500	150	82	600
Hurley,............	2	7, 500	......	2, 250	325	145	750
Kingston, ...	2	75, 000	8, 000	2, 200	1, 000	503	2000
Marbletown, ...	3	12, 000	4, 800	1, 525	800	242	1650
New Paltz,.........	1	10, 000	3, 000	800	500	206	850
Olive, ...	2	3, 000	3, 600	800	350	120	950
Plattekill,..........	1	3, 000	2, 500	700	300	120	600
Rochester, ...	1	2, 000	600	600	500	212	500
Rosendale,.........	2	6, 400	1, 600	700	280	230	300
Saugerties, ...	5	25, 500	5, 200	2, 700	1, 450	599	2800
Shandaken, ...	1	1, 000	......	300	50	20	80
Shawangunk, ...	2	4, 200	3, 400	900	700	256	1200
Wawarsing,........	3	13, 500	1, 750	1, 700	800	286	900
Woodstock, ...	1	3, 000	......	500	150	80	......
Total, ...	30	174, 500	39, 550	16, 805	7, 695	3. 241	14080
WASHINGTON Co.							
Fort Edward,.......	1	2, 200	......	400	150	25	......
Easton,............	1	600	......	225	50	50	250
Greenwich, ...	1	5, 600	2, 120	500	250	150	600
Total,...........	3	8, 400	2, 120	1, 125	450	225	850
WAYNE Co.							
Arcadia, ...	1	5, 500	800	300	150	48	600
Williamson,........	1	1, 700	......	600	150	120	321
Wolcott, ...	1	100	......	......	200	42	450
Total, ...	3	7, 300	800	900	500	210	1. 371
WESTCHESTER Co.							
Cortlandt,..........	2	6, 000	600	650	225	95	1, 000
Eastchester,........	2	5, 500	......	500	225	88	1, 200
Greenburgh, ...	2	12, 500	4, 000	700	410	158	1, 100
Mount Pleasant,....	2	19, 000	9, 400	1, 100	500	313	1, 800
West Farms,.......	2	18, 900	......	950	330	120	1, 300
Yonkers,...........	1	12, 000	4, 500	660	420	100	1, 450
Total, ...	11	73, 900	13, 500	4, 560	2, 110	874	7, 850
WYOMING Co.							
Orangeville, ...	1	400	......	100	85	80	180

ROMAN CATHOLIC CHURCHES.

TOWNS.	Number of churches.	Value of church and lot.	Value of other real estate.	Number capable of being seated.	Usual number attending.	Number of communicants.	Salary of clergy, including use of real estate.
ALBANY Co.							
Albany,............	5	$183, 000	$22500	7, 100	13, 000	13, 800	$4, 400
Coeymans,..........	1	1, 200	......	300	150	75	160
Watervliet, ...	3	28, 500	3200	2, 200	3, 700	4, 895	2, 300
Total,............	9	212, 700	25700	9, 600	16, 850	18, 770	6, 860
ALLEGANY Co.							
Angelica, ...	1	1, 000	......	350	200	......	......
Cuba, ...	1	900	300	300	150	150	......
Scio, ...	2	1, 400	......	560	550	200	550
Total, ...	4	2, 300	300	1, 210	900	350	550
BROOME Co.							
Chenango, ...	1	6, 000	2, 000	600	1, 000	1, 000	600
Sandford, ...	1	1, 000	......	168	150	150	......
Total,............	2	7, 000	2, 000	768	1, 150	1, 150	600
CATTARAUGUS Co.							
Allegany, ...	1	800	......	300	100	100	100
Carrolton, ...	1	1, 100	20	800	50	30	......
Ellicottville, ...	1	2, 500	200	250	200	150	700
Olean, ...	1	450	......	150	150	150	350
Total, ...	4	12, 050	220	1, 500	500	430	1, 150
CAYUGA Co.							
Auburn, ...	2	4, 700	1, 200	1, 200	1, 700	3, 000	600
Ledyard, ...	1	350	......	125	60	......	100
Springport,.........	1	2, 000	......	300	200	200	300
Total,............	4	7, 050	1, 200	1, 625	1, 960	3, 200	1, 000
CHAUTAUQUE Co.							
Pomfret,...........	1	20, 000	1, 750	1, 200	1, 200	1, 200	600
CHEMUNG Co.							
Elmira, ...	1	20, 000	3, 000	1, 200	1, 000	1, 000	800
CHENANGO Co.							
Oxford,............	1	800	300	200	150	200	......
CLINTON Co.							
Ausable,...........	1	3, 000	600	650	600	500	600
Black Brook, ...	1	4, 000	100	440	400	800	600
Champlain, ...	1	4, 000	2, 000	800	600	3, 000	600
Peru,..............	1	1, 000	......	400	100	63	200
Plattsburgh, ...	2	10, 000	700	1, 500	1, 550	1, 200	1, 600
Saranac, ...	1	1, 000	500	500	350	......	......
Total, ...	7	23, 000	3, 900	4, 090	3, 600	5, 563	3, 600
COLUMBIA Co.							
Hudson, ...	1	7, 200	......	600	450	1, 000	1, 200
Kinderhook, ...	1	1, 500	......	400	200	100	200
New Lebanon,......	1	1, 200	......	250	200	200	......
Total,............	3	9, 900	......	1, 250	850	1, 300	1, 400
CORTLAND Co.							
Solon, ...	1	1, 000	......	400	100	200	200
DELAWARE Co.							
Hancock, ...	1	500	......	70	50	......	......
DUTCHESS Co.							
Fishkill, ...	1	1, 200	......	......	350	350	600
Hyde Park.	1	1, 000	......	100	50	25	......
Poughkeepsie, ...	2	20, 000	3, 500	1, 450	1, 450	2, 000	750
Total, ...	4	22, 200	3, 500	1, 550	1, 850	2, 375	1, 350
ERIE Co.							
Alden,.............	1	1, 100	......	290	200	200	250
Amherst, ...	2	3, 000	300	700	900	900	950
Aurora,............	1	400	......	120	75	75	100
Buffalo,............	11	275, 080	47, 000	11, 550	10, 250	9, 550	10, 300
Chictawauga,.......	1	700	300	75	25	15	......
Concord,...........	1	5, 000	......	250	75	40	150
Eden, ...	1	2, 000	500	500	500	70	200
Evans, ...	1	850	800	114	80	90	150
Hamburgh, ...	1	1, 000	......	160	300	400	200
Lancaster, ...	1	5, 000	......	400	700	850	400
Marilla,...........	1	825	......	300	100	100	......
North Collins,......	1	600	500	200	250	450	425
Tonawanda, ...	2	3, 200	400	600	250	200	300
West Seneca,.......	1	550	......	350	70	......	......
Total, ...	26	299, 305	49, 800	15, 609	13, 775	12, 990	13, 425
ESSEX Co.							
Chesterfield, ...	1	2, 000	......	500	600	500	500
Minerva,...........	1	500	......	200	100	80	100

CHURCHES.—(Continued.)

TOWNS.	Number of churches.	Value of church and lot.	Value of other real estate.	Number capable of being seated.	Usual number attending.	Number of communicants.	Salary of clergy, including use of real estate.
Essex Co.							
Moriah,	1	$3, 000	......	300	......	130	$500
Ticonderoga,	1	3, 200	......	200	150	150	150
Total,	4	8, 700	......	1, 200	850	860	1, 250
Franklin Co.							
Bombay,	1	1, 500	$1, 200	225	200	200	500
Chateaugay,	1	1, 000	......	200	300	250	400
Fort Covington,	1	3, 500	......	500	350	400	1, 500
Franklin,	1	715	......	200	100	100	100
Malone,	1	1, 500	......	350	1, 000	1, 000	600
Moira,	1	600	......	......	500	500	......
Total,	6	8, 815	1, 200	1, 475	2, 450	2, 450	3, 100
Fulton Co.							
Bleecker,	1	50	......	......	60	100	......
Johnstown,	1	600	......	......	......	......	......
Total,	2	650	......	......	60	100	......
Genesee Co.							
Batavia,	1	3, 000	......	200	200	600	......
Bergen,	1	800	......	100	100	......	......
Le Roy,	1	1, 600	......	240	300	300	300
Total,	3	5, 400	......	540	600	900	300
Greene Co.							
Ashland,	1	200	200	150	40	40	400
Coxsackie,	1	1, 500	......	250	100	150	......
Hunter,	1	500	......	......	......	......	......
Total,	3	2, 200	200	400	140	190	400
Hamilton Co.							
Morehouse,	1	400	......	100	......	......	......
Herkimer Co.							
Little Falls,	1	3, 500	1, 500	600	600	600	......
Newport,	1	1, 700	1, 000	144	144	144	250
Total,	2	5, 200	2, 500	744	744	744	250
Jefferson Co.							
Alexandria,	1	1, 200	......	180	125	125	150
Antwerp,	1	800	......	400	70	......	130
Cape Vincent,	1	600	......	500	300	200	400
Clayton,	1	2, 800	1, 000	350	250	100	400
Le Ray,	1	1, 500	......	300	150	150	100
Orleans,	1	800	......	400	150	170	300
Watertown,	1	2, 500	900	300	1, 500	1, 000	600
Wilna,	1	4, 000	......	400	400	300	300
Total,	8	14, 200	1, 900	2, 830	2. 945	2. 045	2, 380
Kings Co.							
Brooklyn,	15	385, 800	47, 000	22. 860	36, 190	25, 620	16300
Flatbush,	1	3. 000	......	250	200	200	400
New Utrecht,	1	15, 000	......	500	300	400	600
Total,	17	403, 800	47. 000	23, 610	36. 690	26, 220	17300
Lewis Co.							
Croghan,	2	2 900	75	900	350	250	350
Harrisburgh,	1	400	......	200	50	35	200
New Bremen,	1	600	......	250	100	50	100
West Turin,	3	1, 350	300	1, 300	500	620	300
Total,	7	5, 250	375	2, 650	1, 000	955	950
Livingston Co.							
Avon,	1	2, 000	500	250	250	350	600
Geneseo,	1	2, 000	200	320	200	250	200
Lima,	1	2, 500	......	400	400	400	600
Mount Morris,	1	1. 000	......	200	250	......	......
North Dansville,	2	5, 000	500	650	200	295	440
Nunda,	1	500	......	200	100	100	......
Total,	7	13. 000	1. 200	2, 020	1. 400	1, 395	2, 040
Madison Co.							
Cazenovia,	1	3, 000	......	400	300	200	500
Lenox,	1	7, 000	1, 500	400	8, 000	500	600
Total,	2	10. 000	1, 500	800	8, 300	700	1, 100
Monroe Co.							
Greece,	1	1, 800	800	208	175	300	700
Ogden,	1	....	......	200	150	......	......
Rochester,	7	116, 155	1, 000	5, 155	10, 750	10, 300	3, 415
Sweden,	1	3, 000	......	450	375	375	200
Wheatland,	2	6, 600	......	950	750	800	1, 200
Total,	12	127. 555	1, 800	6, 963	12 200	11, 775	5, 515
Montgomery Co.							
Florida,	1	4, 000	......	500	250	700	600
New-York Co.							
New-York,	24	$1610000	$54000	33, 576	100500	78, 488	$31444
Niagara Co.							
Lewiston,	1	1, 000	......	100	200	200	200
Lockport,	1	12, 000	......	800	1, 000	4, 500	600
Niagara,	1	4, 000	......	300	600	550	400
Pendleton,	1	2, 000	800	400	250	250	350
Porter,	1	1, 800	200	200	200	150	200
Total,	5	20, 800	1, 000	1, 800	2, 250	5, 650	1. 750
Oneida Co.							
Annsville,	1	300	......	300	75	50	150
Boonville,	1	300	500	160	100	130	150
Camden,	1	300	......	400	75	......	......
Deerfield,	1	400	500	250	80	35	475
Florida,	1	2, 000	500	1, 000	600	500	600
Kirkland,	1	2, 500	......	250	300	250	300
Rome,	2	7, 500	......	950	1, 000	2, 100	900
Sangerfield,	1	2, 000	......	250	220	200	200
Utica,	3	52, 000	8, 000	3, 000	3, 000	3, 900	2, 850
Verona,	1	800	......	180	100	50	......
Total,	13	68, 100	9. 500	6, 740	5, 550	7. 215	5, 625
Onondaga Co.							
Manlius,	1	1, 000	800	200	100	300	400
Syracuse,	4	57, 500	8, 400	1, 560	4, 260	3, 500	2, 350
Van Buren,	1	2, 000	......	270	200	200	......
Total,	6	60, 500	9, 200	2, 030	4, 560	4, 000	2, 750
Ontario Co.							
Canandaigua,	1	1, 000	4, 000	700	1, 000	2, 000	1, 500
East Bloomfield,	1	1, 200	......	225	250	200	......
Seneca,	1	6, 000	3, 000	460	600	800	600
Total,	3	8, 200	7. 000	1. 385	1, 850	3. 000	2. 100
Orange Co.							
Deerpark,	1	10, 000	......	600	400	1, 500	850
Goshen,	1	2, 000	1, 000	480	700	700	1, 500
Newburgh,	1	15, 000	10, 000	800	700	600	1, 000
Walkill,	1	800	......	300	300	225	1, 000
Total,	4	27, 800	11, 000	2, 180	2, 100	3, 025	4, 350
Orleans Co.							
Barre,	1	1, 800	......	300	150	200	......
Ridgeway,	1	4, 000	......	500	1, 000	700	600
Total,	2	5, 800	......	800	1, 150	900	600
Oswego Co.							
Constantia,	1	1, 000	......	400	300	300	400
Mexico,	1	600	......	150	150	150	......
Oswego,	2	34, 000	......	2, 075	4, 500	4, 000	3, 800
Total,	4	35, 600	......	2, 625	4, 950	4, 450	4, 200
Otsego Co.							
Otsego,	1	1, 200	......	170	170	......	......
Putnam Co.							
Phillipstown,	1	6, 000	......	500	400	200	600
Queens Co.							
Flushing,	1	20, 000	600	1, 000	1, 500	1, 500	1, 000
Hempstead,	2	14, 800	4, 000	1, 000	550	200	1, 400
Jamaica,	1	1, 200	......	500	400	400	60[illegible]
North Hempstead,	1	500	......	300	200	300	30[illegible]
Newtown,	2	7, 000	......	600	325	730	1, 00[illegible]
Total,	7	43, 500	4, 600	3, 400	2. 975	3. 130	4, 30[illegible]
Rensselaer Co.							
Greenbush,	1	900	1, 000	420	600	350	70[illegible]
Hoosick,	1	2, 500	......	250	......	250	30[illegible]
Lansingburgh,	1	3, 000	4, 000	300	400	400	60[illegible]
Schaghticoke,	1	3, 500	2, 500	300	500	400	45[illegible]
Troy,	3	100, 000	12, 000	4, 500	6, 400	6, 400	4, 50[illegible]
Total,	7	109. 900	19, 500	5. 770	7, 900	7. 800	6. 55[illegible]
Richmond Co.							
Castleton,	1	20, 000	1, 000	1, 400	1, 000	......	60[illegible]
Northfield,	1	2, 000	......	400	200	100	......
Southfield,	1	18, 000	5, 000	350	800	1, 200	......
Westfield,	1	2. 500	200	500	300	500	......
Total,	4	42. 500	6, 200	2, 650	2, 300	1. 800	600
Rockland Co.							
Haverstraw,	1	3. 000	3, 000	500	500	300	......
Orangetown,	1	2, 000	......	250	260	300	600
Total,	2	5. 000	3. 000	750	760	600	600

CHURCHES.—(CONTINUED.)

TOWNS.	Number of churches.	Value of church and lot.	Value of other real estate.	Number capable of being seated.	Usual number attending.	Number of communicants.	Salary of clergy, including use of real estate.
ST. LAWRENCE Co.							
Brasher, ...	1	750	......	400	400	400	$300
Canton, ...	1	2, 000	......	280	200	280	500
Madrid, ...	1	4, 000	$1, 000	500	300	1, 000	525
Massena, ...	1	200	......	300	300	300	600
Oswegatchie, ...	1	2, 500	2, 000	1, 200	1, 000	1, 800	700
Potsdam, ...	2	3, 000	1, 500	350	340	50	......
Total, ...	7	$12, 450	4, 500	3, 030	2, 540	3, 830	2, 625
SARATOGA Co.							
Milton, ...	1	1, 000	......	250	200	150	300
Saratoga, ...	1	2, 500	......	625	625	600	1, 000
Saratoga Springs, ...	1	33, 000	......	1, 400	1, 200	1, 200	......
Stillwater, ...	1	4, 000	......	800	700	700	250
Waterford, ...	1	8, 000	......	450	300	300	350
Total, ...	5	48, 500	......	3, 525	3, 025	2, 950	1, 900
SCHENECTADY Co.							
Schenectady, ...	1	9, 500	3, 000	900	600	1, 100	750
SCHUYLER Co.							
Reading, ...	1	1, 000	300	200	100	100	400
SENECA Co.							
Ovid, ...	1	4, 400	......	475	350	300	250
Seneca Falls, ...	1	6, 000	500	500	500	500	800
Total, ...	2	10, 400	500	975	850	800	1, 050
STEUBEN Co.							
Bath, ...	1	1, 500	......	230	100	80	......
Corning, ...	1	4, 500	......	500	400	400	......
Dansville, ...	1	200	150	200	150	150	200
Greenwood, ...	1	1, 000	600	250	100	200	200
Hornellsville, ...	1	1, 000	1, 375	175	200	170	350
Urbana, ...	1	300	......	250	50	30	100
Wayland, ...	1	2, 000	600	300	250	350	400
Total, ...	7	10, 500	2, 125	1, 905	1, 250	1. 380	1. 250
SUFFOLK Co.							
Huntington, ...	1	800	......	300	300	200	500
Southampton, ...	1	1, 000	100	200	200	100	400
Southold, ...	1	....	65	......	90	80	120
Total, ...	3	1, 800	165	500	590	380	1, 020
SULLIVAN Co.							
Mamakating, ...	1	400	......	350	120	60	100
Fremont, ...	1	500	......	224	150	150	100
Total, ...	2	900	......	574	270	210	200
TIOGA Co.							
Barton, ...	1	900	......	156	150	150	422
Owego, ...	1	2, 000	......	400	250	300	600
Total, ...	2	2, 900	......	556	400	450	1, 022
TOMPKINS Co.							
Dryden, ...	1	1, 000	......	200	70	50	150
Ithaca, ...	1	1, 600	......	250	200	......	......
Total, ...	2	2, 600	......	450	270	50	150
ULSTER Co.							
Kingston, ...	2	20, 500	2, 500	1, 550	2, 025	2, 030	1, 350
Rosendale, ...	1	2, 100	......	200	200	200	......
Saugerties, ...	2	5, 600	......	675	900	400	1, 000
Wawarsing, ...	2	3, 600	600	500	355	355	600
Total, ...	7	31, 800	3, 100	2, 925	3, 480	2, 985	2, 950
WARREN Co.							
Queensbury, ...	2	4. 300	......	1, 400	1, 400	1, 400	1, 600
WASHINGTON Co.							
Kingsbury, ...	1	5, 000	......	400	400	300	600
White Creek, ...	1	5, 000	400	500	400	......	......
Whitehall, ...	1	2, 000	......	400	400	700	300
Total, ...	3	12, 000	400	1, 300	1, 200	1, 000	900
WAYNE Co.							
Lyons, ...	1	700	......	150	......	......	......
Palmyra, ...	1	650	......	300	250	250	800
Total, ...	2	1, 350	......	450	250	250	800
WESTCHESTER Co.							
Cortlandt, ...	1	3, 000	1, 500	400	1, 500	470	......
Eastchester, ...	1	....	......	......	200	200	......
Mount Pleasant, ...	1	0, 000	......	500	400	400	720
New Rochelle, ...	1	1, 500	......	240	600	800	600
Rye, ...	1	3, 500	......	360	350	1, 000	600
Westchester, ...	1	4, 000	1, 000	280	300	800	600
West Farms, ...	3	40, 000	2, 000	1, 600	700	550	1, 800
White Plains, ...	1	1, 500	300	250	200	150	250
WESTCHESTER Co.							
Yonkers, ...	1	$20, 000	$1, 000	540	800	800	$1, 200
Total, ...	11	76, 500	5, 800	4, 170	5, 050	5, 170	5, 770
WYOMING Co.							
Attica, ...	1	400	......	......	......	......	......
Bennington, ...	1	230	60	300	250	250	200
China, ...	1	1, 200	200	300	200	300	400
Genesee Falls, ...	1	2, 000	800	400	200	150	300
Java, ...	1	1, 000	600	500	600	650	640
Sheldon, ...	1	2, 500	300	500	400	700	400
Total, ...	6	7, 330	1, 960	2, 000	1, 650	2, 050	1, 940
YATES Co.							
Milo, ...	1	3, 000	1, 200	250	200	100	400
Potter, ...	1	800	200	......	......	......	......
Total, ...	2	3, 800	1, 400	250	200	100	400

SHAKERS' CHURCHES.

TOWNS.	Number of churches.	Value of church and lot.	Value of other real estate.	Number capable of being seated.	Usual number attending.	Number of communicants.	Salary of clergy, including use of real estate.
ALBANY Co.							
Watervliet, ...	1	14, 000	......	800	80	......	......
COLUMBIA Co.							
New Lebanon, ...	1	9, 000	......	1, 000	700	507	......
LIVINGSTON Co.							
Groveland, ...	1	6, 000	......	500	200	135	......

SECOND ADVENT CHURCHES.

TOWNS.	Number of churches.	Value of church and lot.	Value of other real estate.	Number capable of being seated.	Usual number attending.	Number of communicants.	Salary of clergy, including use of real estate.
CAYUGA Co.							
Auburn, ...	1	2, 000	......	200	150	67	600
LEWIS Co.							
Martinsburgh, ...	1	500	......	200	75	30	150
NEW-YORK Co.							
New-York, ...	2	17, 000	......	650	240	90	500
ONTARIO Co.							
Richmond, ...	1	100	......	200	50	20	200
Victor, ...	1	500	......	350	30	15	......
Total, ...	2	600	......	550	80	35	200
WASHINGTON Co.							
Hampton, ...	1	500	......	200	50	30	400
Hebron, ...	1	800	......	200	100	86	200
Total, ...	2	1, 300	......	400	150	116	600

TRUE DUTCH CHURCHES.

TOWNS.	Number of churches.	Value of church and lot.	Value of other real estate.	Number capable of being seated.	Usual number attending.	Number of communicants.	Salary of clergy, including use of real estate.
CAYUGA Co.							
Owasco, ...	1	2, 000	......	500	175	48	400
MONTGOMERY Co.							
Canajoharie, ...	1	500	......	200	50	25	......
Glen, ...	1	2, 000	1, 500	500	200	70	750
Mohawk, ...	1	600	......	200	60	20	100
Total, ...	3	3, 100	1, 500	900	310	115	850
RENSSELAER Co.							
North Greenbush, ...	1	4, 000	......	400	300	40	......
ROCKLAND Co.							
Ramapo, ...	1	1, 000	......	400	150	55	200
SCHOHARIE Co.							
Middlebury, ...	1	800	......	350	70	30	150

BETHELS, FREE AND UNION CHURCHES.

TOWNS.	Number of churches.	Value of church and lot.	Value of other real estate.	Number capable of being seated.	Usual number attending.	Number of communicants.	Salary of clergy, including use of real estate.
ALBANY Co.							
Albany, ...	1	12, 000	......	500	200	......	400
Coeymans, ...	1	1, 000	......	500	100	30	150
Total, ...	2	13, 000	......	1, 000	300	30	550
BROOME Co.							
Chenango, ...	1	625	700	600	75	80	180
Colesville, ...	2	2, 000	600	450	250	257	350
Nanticoke, ...	1	1, 000	......	300	100	80	250
Total, ...	4	3, 625	1, 300	1, 350	425	417	780
CATTARAUGUS Co.							
Machias, ...	1	800	......	500	80	51	300
CAYUGA Co.							
Aurelius, ...	1	1, 000	......	200	100	25	200
CHAUTAUQUE Co.							
Ripley, ...	1	1, 300	100	250	100	50	......
CHEMUNG Co.							
Chemung, ...	2	1. 200	......	300	150	60	650

CHURCHES.—(Continued.)

TOWNS.	Number of churches.	Value of church and lot.	Value of other real estate.	Number capable of being seated.	Usual number attending.	Number of communicants.	Salary of clergy, including use of real estate.
Chenango Co.							
Guilford,	1	$1,000	$500	500	200	80	$400
Macdonough,	1	600	......	300	60	46	100
Norwich,	1	1,300	......	300	100	......	......
Pitcher,	1	2,000	400	400	150	136	500
Sherburne,	1	1,000	......	300	25	30	......
Total,	5	5,900	900	1,800	535	292	1,000
Clinton Co.							
Plattsburgh,	1	1,500	......	400	300	150	450
Columbia Co.							
Clermont,	1	600	......	200	75	......	......
Cortland Co.							
Harford,	1	800	......	500	88	5	450
Virgil,	1	800	......	200	100	......	......
Total,	2	1,600	......	700	188	5	450
Delaware Co.							
Andes,	1	800	......	......	......	15	150
Franklin,	1	200	......	500	......	......	......
Stanford,	1	1,000	......	400	175	120	400
Total,	3	2,000	......	900	175	135	550
Dutchess Co.							
Milan,	1	900	......	300	40	15	200
Pawling,	1	1,000	......	300	60	30	30
Redhook,	1	2,500	......	150	150	......	......
Total,	3	4,400	......	750	250	45	230
Erie Co.							
Buffalo,	3	9,000	4,500	700	340	240	625
Clarence,	1	800	......	200	100	63	200
Collins,	1	600	400	600	200	39	380
East Hamburgh,	1	2,000	......	225	40	30	300
Total,	6	12,400	4,900	1,725	680	372	1,505
Essex Co.							
Crown Point,	1	1,800	......	500	100	......	300
Moriah,	1	2,000	......	300	180	130	500
Schroon,	1	400	......	70	30	25	......
Willsborough,	1	500	......	300	50	......	......
Total,	4	4,700	......	1,170	360	155	800
Franklin Co.							
Bangor,	2	3,600	......	450	......	......	......
Moira,	1	2,000	600	500	450	159	600
Westville,	1	2,000	......	1,000	150	......	......
Total,	4	7,600	600	1,950	600	159	600
Fulton Co.							
Broadalbin,	1	1,000	......	180	150	......	......
Ephrata,	2	1,400	1,300	340	110	40	225
Oppenheim,	2	2,400	......	550	80	45	150
Total,	5	4,800	1,300	1,070	340	85	375
Genesee Co.							
Pavilion,	1	1,500	......	300	50	......	......
Greene Co.							
Cairo,	1	450	......	250	150	......	......
Catskill,	1	700	......	400	100	60	150
Coxsackie,	1	800	......	500	150	......	......
Total,	3	1,950	......	1,150	400	60	150
Herkimer Co.							
Danube,	2	3,700	......	500	150	40	300
German Flats,	1	2,500	......	800	170	30	400
Little Falls,	1	1,000	......	500	60	......	500
Manheim,	2	5,500	......	800	550	60	750
Newport,	1	1,000	......	400	100	72	300
Ohio,	1	800	300	300	150	150	400
Russia,	1	2,000	......	500	75	20	200
Salisbury,	1	2,500	......	700	150	......	......
Stark,	2	2,000	......	800	175	50	200
Total,	13	21,000	300	5,300	1,580	422	3,050
Jefferson Co.							
Antwerp,	1	500	......	200	50	40	200
Brownville,	1	1,800	100	300	80	......	......
Champion,	1	100	......	300	200	......	150
Clayton,	1	2,300	......	300	125	300	......
Ellisburgh,	1	2,400	......	500	200	30	500
Henderson,	1	3,100	......	500	100	350	......
Le Ray,	1	2,000	......	300	100	30	80
Orleans,	1	1,500	......	250	75	50	200
Pamelia,	1	1,450	400	350	250	87	370
Jefferson Co.							
Philadelphia,	1	$2,500	......	400	100	24	$120
Rutland,	2	1,800	......	600	500	170	402
Watertown,	1	3,000	......	500	150	60	210
Total,	13	22,450	$500	4,500	1,930	1,141	2,232
Kings Co.							
Brooklyn,	1	3,000	......	350	220	125	500
Lewis Co.							
Denmark,	2	3,000	......	800	300	57	450
Martinsburgh,	1	1,350	......	300	75	10	100
West Turin,	3	4,000	500	1,100	470	164	900
Total,	6	8,350	500	2,200	845	231	1,450
Livingston Co.							
West Sparta,	1	250	......	200	145	25	100
Madison Co.							
Cazenovia,	1	2,500	......	275	100	28	300
Georgetown,	1	1,500	......	300	100	40	350
Sullivan,	1	2,500	......	400	50	......	200
Total,	3	6,500	......	975	250	68	850
Monroe Co.							
Greece,	1	1,000	......	300	75	......	......
Mendon,	2	1,750	......	575	200	......	......
Ogden,	1	300	400	250	50	40	300
Perrington,	1	500	......	200	80	......	......
Union,	1	500	......	1,000	200	60	200
Total,	6	4,050	400	2,325	605	100	500
Montgomery Co.							
Canajoharie,	1	1,800	1,000	500	230	135	300
Charleston,	1	100	......	300	......	......	......
St. Johnsville,	1	2,800	100	500	80	45	200
Total,	3	4,700	1,100	1,300	310	180	500
New-York Co.							
New-York,	3	11,200	......	1,050	650	455	500
Oneida Co.							
Augusta,	1	1,600	......	......	......	......	......
Boonville,	1	400	......	200	150	23	400
Deerfield,	1	500	......	132	50	100	150
Florence,	2	2,200	100	700	200	......	250
Floyd,	1	1,500	600	250	150	120	370
Lee,	1	1,000	50	500	150	20	350
New Hartford,	1	1,000	......	200	125	......	......
Trenton,	1	1,200	......	300	50	40	200
Verona,	1	1,000	400	250	200	260	360
Whitestown,	1	1,000	......	250	150	......	......
Total,	11	11,400	1,150	2,782	1,225	563	2,080
Onondaga Co.							
Cicero,	1	2,000	......	400	250	75	300
Manlius,	1	1,600	......	200	50	20	300
Spafford,	1	1,500	......	500	75	80	150
Total,	3	5,100	......	1,100	375	175	750
Oswego Co.							
Albion,	1	1,300	300	400	100	50	200
Mexico,	1	800	......	400	100	50	200
Orwell,	1	2,000	......	600	250	60	500
Scriba,	1	1,000	......	250	150	70	300
Total,	4	5,100	300	1,650	600	230	1,200
Otsego Co.							
Exeter,	1	1,000	......	400	......	......	......
Pittsfield,	1	700	......	300	100	50	100
Total,	2	1,700	......	700	100	50	100
Putnam Co.							
Kent,	1	500	......	250	142	25	......
Southeast,	1	2,250	400	500	250	130	600
Total,	2	2,750	400	750	392	155	600
Queens Co.							
Oyster Bay,	1	380	......	80	50	......	......
Rensselaer Co.							
Hoosick,	1	1,000	150	350	......	......	......
Nassau,	1	400	......	100	30	......	......
Pittstown,	1	500	60	300	75	50	......
Total,	3	1,900	210	750	105	50	......
St. Lawrence Co.							
De Kalb,	1	1,200	......	500	75	......	150
Louisville,	1	500	......	400	175	82	300

CHURCHES.—(CONTINUED.)

TOWNS.	Number of churches.	Value of church and lot.	Value of other real estate.	Number capable of being seated.	Usual number attending.	Number of communicants.	Salary of clergy, including use of real estate.
ST. LAWRENCE CO.							
Morristown,	1	$1,200	......	200	75	30	$100
Pierrepont,	1	1,000	......	300	100	80	430
Potsdam,	1	600	......	100	......	9	......
Total,	5	4,500	......	1,500	425	201	980
SARATOGA CO.							
Moreau,	1	700	......	800	50	50	300
Wilton,	1	1,200	......	300	100	56	150
Total,	2	1,900	......	1,100	150	106	450
SCHOHARIE CO.							
Carlisle,	1	900	......	300	200	60	90
Fulton,	3	1,650	......	850	240	91	410
Sharon,	1	1,000	$650	500	300	50	900
Total,	5	3,550	650	1,650	740	201	1,400
SENECA CO.							
Fayette,	1	1,800	......	450	250	325	250
STEUBEN CO.							
Wayland,	2	1,700	150	450	150	200	600
Wayne,	1	600	......	300	......	......	......
Total,	3	2,300	150	750	150	200	600
SUFFOLK CO.							
Huntington,	1	600	......	300	200	38	50
Southampton,	1	4,000	......	500	100	40	500
Total,	2	4,600	......	800	300	78	550
SULLIVAN CO.							
Highland,	1	1,200	......	250	100	60	100
Rockland,	1	500	......	100	50	......	60
Thompson,	1	200	......	150	60	......	......
Total,	3	1,900	......	500	210	60	160
TIOGA CO.							
Candor,	1	2,000	100	600	150	150	250
Nichols,	1	200	......	......	......	......	......
Tioga,	1	3,500	......	700	200	400	850
Total,	3	5,700	100	1,300	350	550	1,100
WARREN CO.							
Luzerne,	1	......	800	250	......	......	......
WASHINGTON CO.							
Dresden,	1	500	......	200	50	45	75
Fort Ann,	1	1,000	......	400	100	25	......
Total,	2	1,500	......	600	150	70	75
WAYNE CO.							
Williamson,	1	1,000	700	300	200	73	600

UNITARIAN CHURCHES.

TOWNS.	Number of churches.	Value of church and lot.	Value of other real estate.	Number capable of being seated.	Usual number attending.	Number of communicants.	Salary of clergy, including use of real estate.
ALBANY CO.							
Albany,	1	8,000	......	400	175	20	1,500
ERIE CO.							
Buffalo,	1	12,000	4,000	600	300	100	2,000
KINGS CO.							
Brooklyn,	2	125,000	1,000	1,650	1,250	400	5,800
NEW-YORK CO.							
New-York,	2	225,000	......	2,500	2,100	310	9,000
ONEIDA CO.							
Trenton,	2	2,700	......	600	200	40	570
Vernon,	1	3,000	......	400	80	......	650
Total,	3	5,700	......	1,000	280	40	1,220
ONONDAGA CO.							
Syracuse,	1	12,000	......	500	500	50	1,200
RENSSELAER CO.							
Troy,	1	2,500	......	300	150	75	700
RICHMOND CO.							
Castleton,	1	10,000	......	300	100	30	1,000
ST. LAWRENCE CO.							
Oswegatchie,	1	......	......	400	300	......	1,000

UNIVERSALIST CHURCHES.

TOWNS.	Number of churches.	Value of church and lot.	Value of other real estate.	Number capable of being seated.	Usual number attending.	Number of communicants.	Salary of clergy, including use of real estate.
ALBANY CO.							
Albany,	1	12,000	......	1,100	300	50	1,000
ALLEGANY CO.							
Amity,	1	800	......	160	50	20	100
Friendship,	1	2,000	......	300	150	50	600
Rushford,	1	1,300	......	250	......	20	......
Total,	3	4,100	......	610	200	90	700
BROOME CO.							
Chenango,	1	$2,000	......	400	200	......	$600
Triangle,	1	1,500	......	500	100	60	250
Total,	2	3,500	......	900	300	60	850
CATTARAUGUS CO.							
Freedom,	1	800	......	250	75	......	200
Mansfield,	1	1,200	......	300	60	......	400
Total,	2	2,000	......	550	135	......	600
CAYUGA CO.							
Auburn,	1	15,000	......	800	400	98	1,000
Genoa,	1	2,500	......	350	75	......	250
Niles,	1	1,500	......	500	......	......	......
Scipio,	1	3,700	......	350	75	......	400
Total,	4	22,700	......	2,000	550	98	1,650
CHAUTAUQUE CO.							
Busti,	1	350	......	300	40	40	......
Charlotte,	1	1,300	$500	300	100	40	350
Ellery,	1	600	......	......	......	......	......
Kiantone,	1	800	......	200	75	20	300
Sherman,	1	1,000	......	175	......	35	......
Westfield,	1	500	......	250	70	26	240
Total,	6	4,550	500	1,225	285	161	890
CHENANGO CO.							
Bainbridge,	1	1,000	......	700	100	75	400
Columbus,	1	1,800	......	450	250	22	400
North Norwich,	1	1,500	......	250	70	40	......
Oxford,	1	3,000	......	500	90	30	......
Preston,	1	500	......	250	50	25	400
Sherburne,	1	400	......	150	60	......	......
Smithville,	1	2,500	......	350	84	46	200
Total,	7	10,700	......	2,650	704	238	1,400
COLUMBIA CO.							
Hudson,	1	6,000	......	500	200	40	750
Stockport,	1	1,000	......	175	50	......	......
Total,	2	7,000	......	675	250	40	750
CORTLAND CO.							
Cortlandville,	1	4,000	......	600	300	260	500
Homer,	1	1,000	......	200	70	40	500
Total,	2	5,000	......	800	370	300	1,000
DUTCHESS CO.							
Poughkeepsie city,	1	10,000	......	450	300	225	600
ERIE CO.							
Aurora,	1	1,500	300	400	......	......	......
Boston,	1	2,000	......	350	60	......	500
Buffalo,	1	1,500	......	600	300	90	1,200
Concord,	1	1,500	......	300	75	......	275
Total,	4	6,500	300	1,650	165	90	1,975
FRANKLIN CO.							
Malone,	1	3,500	......	300	100	50	500
GENESEE CO.							
Alexander,	1	1,500	......	500	150	25	400
Pavilion,	1	2,000	......	300	125	12	500
Stafford,	1	800	......	300	......	......	......
Total,	3	4,300	......	1,100	275	37	900
HERKIMER CO.							
Frankfort,	1	1,600	......	250	75	25	500
German Flats,	1	3,500	......	300	130	......	400
Litchfield,	2	1,900	......	600	250	......	117
Little Falls,	1	4,500	......	400	200	40	550
Newport,	1	2,500	......	600	100	51	300
Russia,	1	1,600	......	300	60	25	150
Total,	7	15.600	......	2,450	815	141	2,017
JEFFERSON CO.							
Brownville,	2	4,300	......	700	100	......	......
Ellisburgh,	1	2,000	......	250	125	30	350
Henderson,	1	2,800	......	600	......	......	......
Watertown,	1	12,000	......	700	400	......	800
Total,	5	21,100	......	2,250	625	30	1,150
KINGS CO.							
Brooklyn,	3	40,500	......	1,050	700	212	3,200
LEWIS CO.							
Denmark,	1	1,000	......	300	75	......	......
LIVINGSTON CO.							
Conesus,	1	1,800	300	350	125	40	350
Lima,	1	1,000	......	300	50	30	200

CHURCHES.—(CONTINUED.)

TOWNS.	Number of churches.	Value of church and lot.	Value of other real estate.	Number capable of being seated.	Usual number attending	Number of communicants.	Salary of clergy, including use of real estate.
LIVINGSTON CO.							
Livonia,	1	$1,000	......	300	200	100	$200
Nunda,	1	2,000	......	300	80	......	250
Total,	4	5,800	$300	1,250	455	170	1,000
MADISON CO.							
Brookfield,	1	2,800	......	300	100	......	300
Cazenovia,	1	2,900	......	400	200	......	350
Hamilton,	1	400	......	250	100	......	400
Lebanon,	1	700	......	300	......	......	......
Madison,	1	1,700	......	325	100	......	400
Nelson,	1	800	......	200	75	30	150
Stockbridge,	1	1,200	......	300	35	30	150
Total,	7	10,500	......	2,075	610	60	1,750
MONROE CO.							
Perrington,	1	2,500	......	325	75	......	250
Riga,	1	2,000	......	200	100	......	300
Webster,	1	2,000	......	300	100	43	492
Total,	3	6,500	......	825	275	43	1,042
MONTGOMERY CO.							
Minden,	2	6,500	350	650	275	50	900
NEW-YORK CO.							
New-York,	4	319,000	......	4,200	3,000	889	8,000
NIAGARA CO.							
Lockport,	1	6,000	......	350	150	40	700
Royalton,	1	3,000	......	400	150	26	500
Total,	2	9,000	......	750	300	66	1,200
ONEIDA CO.							
Bridgewater,	1	2,000	......	500	......	......	......
Kirkland,	1	2,500	......	300	100	......	500
Marshall,	1	600	......	300	75	......	400
Rome,	1	2,000	......	300	100	......	500
Utica,	1	14,000	3,000	600	400	50	800
Total,	5	21,100	3,000	2,000	675	50	2,200
ONONDAGA CO.							
Onondaga,	1	2,000	......	300	100	30	400
Pompey,	1	1,400	......	200	135	......	300
Skaneateles,	1	1,500	......	400	100	12	150
Total,	3	4,900	......	900	335	42	850
ONTARIO CO.							
Bristol,	1	2,000	......	450	150	......	400
Manchester,	1	3,000	......	300	200	30	600
Seneca,	1	5,000	......	300	100	......	500
Victor,	1	1,500	......	500	100	......	......
Total,	4	11,500	......	1,550	550	30	1,500
ORLEANS CO.							
Clarendon,	1	3,500	......	400	200	48	600
Gaines,	1	3,000	......	400	100	40	300
Kendall,	1	2,000	......	400	100	70	300
Ridgeway,	1	2,500	......	300	150	......	300
Total,	4	11,000	......	1,500	550	158	1,500
OSWEGO CO.							
Volney,	1	3,000	......	300	150	50	700
OTSEGO CO.							
Edmeston,	1	2,000	......	300	100	30	440
Morris,	1	1,500	......	400	100	......	400
Otsego,	2	1,900	......	1,150	170	10	700
Richfield,	1	3,000	......	250	50	30	......
Total,	5	8,400	......	2,100	420	70	1,540
RENSSELAER CO.							
Troy,	1	15,000	2,000	500	200	60	1,100
ST. LAWRENCE CO.							
Canton,	1	$5,000	$1,500	450	200	40	600
Colton,	1	1,500	......	300	100	30	500
Edwards,	1	......	......	......	......	......	100
Fowler,	1	1,500	......	500	100	......	......
Hammond,	1	......	......	......	......	......	750
Madrid,	1	3,500	700	500	150	52	500
Oswegatchie,	2	5,000	......	700	600	94	1,850
Potsdam,	1	4,000	1,000	350	175	102	900
Rossie,	1	1,050	......	200	......	......	......
Total,	10	21,550	3,200	3,000	1,325	318	5,200
SARATOGA CO.							
Greenfield,	1	1,000	......	400	......	20	......
Saratoga Springs,	1	3,500	......	300	50	20	......
Total,	2	4,500	......	700	50	40	......
SCHENECTADY CO.							
Duanesburgh,	1	1,500	......	450	80	70	355
Schenectady,	1	1,500	100	250	100	......	500
Total,	2	3,000	100	700	180	70	850
SCHOHARIE CO.							
Carlisle,	1	1,200	......	300	60	......	100
SCHUYLER CO.							
Dix,	1	1,500	200	350	200	57	525
SENECA CO.							
Covert,	1	3,000	......	250	150	80	650
STEUBEN CO.							
Dansville,	1	1,400	50	500	50	30	300
Greenwood,	1	1,500	......	300	150	12	300
Total,	2	2,900	50	800	200	42	600
SUFFOLK CO.							
Huntington,	1	1,200	......	200	75	......	500
Southold,	1	1,800	......	200	80	......	400
Total,	2	3,000	......	400	155	......	900
TOMPKINS CO.							
Caroline,	1	1,000	......	1,000	150	......	125
Groton,	1	1,700	......	200	80	......	250
Total,	2	2,700	......	1,200	230	......	375
WARREN CO.							
Queensbury,	1	4,000	......	400	300	225	500
WASHINGTON CO.							
Hartford,	1	1,200	......	250	80	20	400
WAYNE CO.							
Arcadia,	1	7,000	......	500	300	......	1,000
WESTCHESTER CO.							
North Salem,	1	1,500	2,100	300	70	13	340
Eastchester,	1	......	......	150	100	......	600
Total,	2	1,500	2,100	450	170	13	940
WYOMING CO.							
Bennington,	1	1,500	......	500	75	20	300
Gainesville,	1	300	......	300	75	50	350
Genesee Falls,	1	2,500	......	275	100	25	400
Perry,	1	5,000	......	500	250	50	800
Total,	4	9,300	......	1,575	500	145	1,850
YATES CO.							
Jerusalem,	1	2,800	......	400	90	......	500
Potter,	1	1,500	......	250	30	......	......
Total,	2	4,300	......	650	120	......	500

SUMMARY OF THE STATISTICS OF CHURCHES BY COUNTIES.

COUNTIES	Number of churches.	Value of churches and lots.	Value of other real estate.	Number capable of being seated.	Number usually attending.	Number of communicants or members.	Salaries of clergy, including the use of real estate.
Albany,	129	$1, 138, 585	$133, 440	67, 140	43, 810	32, 982	$78, 674
Allegany,	75	108, 750	13, 610	22, 899	9, 833	6, 537	22, 248
Broome,	63	190, 175	17, 389	21, 846	10, 391	6, 723	24, 297
Cattaraugus,	61	105, 550	6, 820	20, 600	6, 535	3, 839	17, 697
Cayuga,	100	288, 700	22, 920	37, 179	15, 408	10, 729	34, 497
Chautauque,	105	209, 250	16, 000	38, 630	15, 060	8, 730	31, 458
Chemung,	33	129, 250	21, 500	15, 480	6, 605	4, 302	16, 690
Chenango,	111	209, 950	22, 080	39, 915	4, 814	8, 784	35, 073
Clinton,	45	116, 250	21, 725	17, 650	10, 085	9, 624	19, 022
Columbia,	85	259, 250	17, 400	44, 350	15, 895	9, 038	36, 585
Cortland,	51	99, 900	18, 100	19, 975	7, 993	5, 383	17, 164
Delaware,	92	159, 655	23, 900	49, 730	14, 830	8, 359	28, 502
Dutchess,	132	523, 100	170, 550	49, 175	20, 975	13, 256	56, 882
Erie,	155	1, 047, 185	129, 100	64, 427	35, 375	25, 660	75, 041
Essex,	51	109, 600	12, 000	18, 560	8, 155	6, 134	15, 441
Franklin,	35	56, 895	9, 300	11, 265	6, 850	4, 809	12, 280
Fulton,	39	84, 500	11, 850	13, 090	6, 280	3, 399	13, 280
Genesee,	61	144, 200	20, 100	21, 370	9, 453	4, 942	23, 868
Greene,	74	146, 265	22, 060	26, 235	10, 665	5, 949	22, 593
Hamilton,	5	1, 400	....	760	133	91	240
Herkimer,	85	155, 275	18, 225	33, 199	10, 494	4, 628	31, 072
Jefferson,	127	316, 510	30, 275	45, 748	21, 825	13, 752	48, 415
Kings,	149	2, 546, 400	294, 300	104, 960	83, 215	46, 446	160, 986
Lewis,	54	57, 600	8, 245	18, 410	5. 405	3, 141	11, 365
Livingston,	86	227, 700	35, 560	31, 348	13, 431	7, 076	33, 050
Madison,	94	176, 230	26, 350	38, 337	21, 465	7, 787	32, 880
Monroe,	141	769, 805	34, 425	60, 333	37, 065	25, 940	69, 175
Montgomery,	52	122, 650	18, 650	22, 500	7, 730	4, 659	20, 490
New-York,	252	10, 900, 400	1, 192, 350	234, 730	222, 550	135, 406	438, 063
Niagara,	74	206, 140	23, 065	26, 110	14, 277	12, 127	29, 690
Oneida,	201	576, 710	59, 250	84, 148	33, 021	22, 356	73, 117
Onondaga,	142	515, 500	48, 110	55, 390	27, 667	15, 801	55, 989
Ontario,	84	244, 400	39, 330	40, 240	14, 230	9, 519	33, 778
Orange,	112	333, 700	110, 155	46, 052	25, 384	14, 452	54, 825
Orleans,	51	188, 950	39, 650	17, 470	8, 829	5, 569	21, 227
Oswego,	84	218, 000	16, 715	31, 395	18, 058	11, 797	36, 247
Otsego,	117	196, 550	35, 402	46, 330	15, 655	9, 072	34, 715
Putnam,	30	73, 800	11, 200	10, 250	4, 517	3, 070	10, 330
Queens,	73	356, 580	135, 555	27, 740	15, 065	7, 412	32, 495
Rensselaer,	114	665, 575	81, 065	55, 495	27, 464	21, 106	63, 100
Richmond,	29	254, 800	30, 300	13, 770	8, 670	5, 184	21, 050
Rookland,	41	103, 800	32, 500	11, 580	5, 565	2, 655	15, 650
St. Lawrence,	117	222, 785	40, 700	42, 960	18, 900	12, 198	42, 525
Saratoga,	103	269, 900	44, 075	39, 575	17, 200	10, 427	34, 770
Schenectady,	26	147, 750	25, 960	13, 050	7, 514	4, 412	14, 235
Schoharie,	85	110, 360	19, 470	34, 475	13, 605	5, 608	20, 676
Schuyler,	50	87, 075	12, 050	14, 125	5, 440	3, 369	17, 479
Seneca,	48	124, 583	19, 750	22, 103	9, 635	5, 061	17, 588
Steuben,	105	141, 583	19, 855	30, 476	13, 380	8, 779	32, 953
Suffolk,	112	227, 620	50, 640	31, 949	16, 658	7, 917	39, 974
Sullivan,	46	48, 700	11, 300	15, 289	7, 050	3, 255	12, 450
Tioga,	45	85, 200	21, 500	17, 701	6, 505	4, 964	15, 625
Tompkins,	66	161, 940	21, 750	27, 151	9, 312	6, 241	22, 647
Ulster,	100	338, 500	70, 850	40, 720	20, 696	10, 893	38, 470
Warren,	33	54, 450	2, 800	11, 340	4, 590	4, 103	10, 066
Washington,	95	249, 250	37, 870	35, 469	16, 056	10, 132	33, 710
Wayne,	80	248, 300	23, 700	29, 846	12, 445	8, 533	32, 664
Westchester,	148	641, 050	227, 200	33, 391	25, 723	15, 056	76, 503
Wyoming,	74	151, 780	17, 585	27, 158	10, 980	8, 247	26, 546
Yates,	48	121, 400	12, 250	19, 570	7, 725	4, 964	18, 561
Total,	5, 077	$27, 769, 328	$3, 710, 816	2, 141, 159	1, 124, 211	702, 384	$2, 411, 683

COMPARATIVE SUMMARY OF STATISTICS OF CHURCHES IN 1845, 1850, AND 1855.

DENOMINATIONS.	Number of church edifices.*		Value of churches and lots.*	Value of other real estate.		Total value of church property.			Number capable of seating.		Usual attendance.	Number of chur'h memb'rs	Salary of clergy.
	1850	1855.	1855.	1845.	1855.	1845.	1850.	1855.	1850.	1855.	1855.	1855.	1855.
Baptists, (total,)	781	882	$2907483	$537277	$252056	$2441059	2253050	$3159539	335374	350154	143465	89713	$348630
Regular,	....	757	2726283	....	234331	....	....	2960614	....	308335	127480	81796	320101
Free Will,	....	83	104900	....	5425	....	....	110325	....	27414	9775	4823	19239
Old School,	....	18	25100	....	5800	....	....	30900	....	6150	2590	1101	3191
Seventh Day,	....	24	51200	....	6500	....	....	57700	....	8255	3620	2993	6099
Christian Connection,	65	85	101700	....	1725	....	79650	103425	20300	28950	9825	5005	18495
Congregational,	215	301	1260200	125511	184000	813843	779304	1444200	102430	135905	56637	25946	147470
Disciples of Christ,	....	16	32000	....	460	....	....	32460	....	4600	1895	1440	4170
Evangelical,	....	4	19850	....	3000	....	....	22850	....	1050	500	200	890
Evangelical Lutheran,	81	100	336910	....	53255	....	252200	390165	38270	39215	20834	13964	37647
Friends,	133	134	324825	103531	90545	259914	309380	415370	49314	44705	9986	5340	....
German Evangelical Reformed,	1	11	27800	....	1200	....	15000	29000	600	4110	2480	1884	3605
Jews,	14	19	112000	27085	123100	116535	211000	235100	....	10995	4965	2188	14115
Menonites,	4	6	5300	....	....	....	2050	5300	....	1550	648	442	....
Methodists, (total,)	1231	1580	3991105	577508	610224	2482950	2886043	4601329	481270	576960	250995	140196	545179
Episcopal,	....	1391	3514890	....	580565	....	....	4095455	....	515556	225653	127891	498414
African M. E.,	....	33	158720	....	9605	....	....	168325	....	13770	5898	2569	6089
Calvanistic,	....	22	30500	....	....	....	....	30500	....	6044	2233	1036	2796
Congregational,	....	3	8600	....	....	....	....	8600	....	1030	680	215	1300
Evan. Asso. or Ger. M.,	....	15	70850	....	12050	....	....	82900	....	5715	3165	2777	5775
Protestant,	....	45	52510	....	1800	....	....	54310	....	11290	3460	1595	9059
Primitive,	....	2	10000	....	....	....	....	10000	....	1050	530	158	1950
Reformed,	....	8	8700	....	....	....	....	8700	....	2300	716	435	1555
Wesleyan,	....	61	136235	....	6204	....	....	142434	....	20205	8460	3520	18241
Moravians,	3	4	44000	....	23500	....	36000	67500	1500	1550	520	299	3720
New Jerusalem,	2	3	3800	....	....	....	1400	3800	....	764	170	63	500
Presbyterian, (total,)	700	710	5343565	769987	604311	3191777	4356606	5947876	370189	331393	163054	92712	502758
Old and New School,	....	626	4613660	....	554996	....	....	5168656	....	300916	140676	80852	432648
Associate,	....	26	429240	....	16100	....	....	445340	....	4065	7721	3946	12570
Associate Reformed,	....	38	200865	....	30550	....	....	231415	....	18612	9950	5460	25785
Ref. P., or Covenant'rs,	....	19	99500	....	2665	....	....	102165	....	7600	4685	2436	31605
French Evangelical,	....	1	300	....	....	....	....	300	....	200	20	18	150
Protestant Episcopal,	279	346	5854720	721451	849130	2551531	4110824	6703820	140195	157785	78698	32978	320765
Protestant Com. of True Inspiration,	....	1	5000	....	....	....	....	5000	....	950	820	735	....
Protestant, (Miscellaneous,)	....	8	14900	....	340	....	....	15240	....	2390	1440	859	1842
Reformed Protestant Dutch,	233	260	2412600	486261	602515	1778949	3542850	3015115	131025	152254	70093	30197	187683
Roman Catholic,	176	291	3527405	324129	303895	979269	1569875	3831300	126288	176590	272084	242225	156916
Second Advent,	....	8	21400	....	....	....	....	21400	....	2000	695	338	2050
Shakers,	....	3	29000	....	....	....	....	29000	....	2300	980	642	....
True Dutch Church,	....	7	10900	....	1500	....	....	12400	....	2550	1005	288	1600
Union Bethel and Free Churches,	90	152	208455	....	16360	....	139000	224815	32129	50927	17415	7923	34167
Unitarians,	22	16	400200	73958	5000	240027	292075	405200	10225	8750	5155	1025	23420
Universalists,	114	133	676900	66170	12056	354778	327400	688950	55570	49085	18064	4570	56859
Minor Sects,	25	....	....	....	....	....	55500	....	9350	....	....	....	....
Total,	4169	5077	27769328	3852868	3710816	15210632	21219207	31480144	1915179	2141159	1124211	702384	2411683

* The census of 1845 reported the number and value of church edifices as follows:

DENOMINATIONS.	Number.	Value.	DENOMINATIONS.	Number.	Value.
Baptist,	782	$1, 903, 782	Reformed Protestant Dutch,	260	$1, 292, 688
Congregational,	271	648, 332	Roman Catholic,	104	655, 140
Friends,	153	156, 383	Unitarians,	65	166, 069
Jews,	15	89, 450	Universalists,	112	288, 608
Methodist,	1, 123	1, 905, 442			
Presbyterian,	669	2, 421, 790	Total,	3, 822	$11, 357, 764
Protestant Episcopal,	268	1, 830, 080			

SCHOOL HOUSES, HOTELS, STORES AND GROCERIES.

COUNTIES.	SCHOOL HOUSES.												HOTELS AND INNS.	STORES.		GROCERIES.
	NUMBER.						CONDITION.					VALUE.				
	Stone.	Brick.	Framed.	Logs.	Plank.	Total.	Very good.	Good.	Ordinary.	Poor.	Very poor.			Whole-sale.	Retail.	
Albany, ...	6	29	125	......	......	160	4	100	......	42	14	$91, 855	152	151	649	553
Allegany, ...	1	......	246	10	1	258	4	156	6	59	33	53, 580	67	2	146	61
Broome, ...	......	......	171	12	8	191	......	107	17	50	17	31, 973	50	......	144	72
Cattaraugus, ...	1	1	199	18	23	242	2	126	7	87	20	46, 759	38	......	119	46
Cayuga, ...	12	21	202	2	8	245	7	120	11	87	20	78, 265	64	7	118	86
Chautauque, ...	3	5	281	2	7	298	2	155	8	102	31	79, 826	106	9	179	81
Chemung, ...	......	......	104	6	......	110	2	64	2	35	7	29, 597	34	......	112	49
Chenango, ...	3	......	275	1	......	279	1	160	9	96	13	48, 075	63	......	112	54
Clinton, ...	19	34	101	15	......	169	2	86	4	71	6	38, 092	48	......	145	64
Columbia, ...	......	10	170	......	......	180	5	105	14	50	6	57, 889	78	3	203	81
Cortland, ...	4	5	164	5	1	179	1	85	18	65	10	29, 511	32	......	72	23
Delaware, ...	4	......	299	9	2	314	4	186	10	89	25	41, 545	63	......	141	33
Dutchess, ...	1	13	192	......	......	206	15	127	8	49	7	68, 145	70	17	339	133
Erie, ...	5	38	191	10	65	309	2	166	7	108	26	213, 350	143	28	841	711
Essex, ...	4	16	139	13	4	176	......	106	6	50	14	35, 615	35	......	100	26
Franklin, ...	14	4	113	33	3	167	......	85	1	50	31	24, 694	22	......	70	17
Fulton, ...	......	......	107	......	2	109	1	61	7	34	6	21, 235	32	......	81	21
Genesee, ...	27	9	104	3	......	143	1	79	......	47	16	39, 770	32	4	92	41
Greene, ...	5	6	130	......	......	141	4	76	4	51	6	31, 490	68	......	130	67
Hamilton, ...	......	......	23	5	......	28	......	17	......	8	3	3, 450	6	......	7	3
Herkimer, ...	11	11	178	1	......	201	3	122	13	54	9	65, 525	59	......	130	74
Jefferson, ...	60	9	270	23	......	362	6	175	22	134	25	88, 090	97	5	232	131
Kings, ...	......	18	31	......	......	49	2	38	3	4	2	385, 950	466	69	2, 359	1, 120
Lewis, ...	9	4	149	10	2	174	6	97	10	54	7	30, 520	31	......	56	20
Livingston, ...	7	7	159	3	......	176	1	92	5	75	3	72, 226	58	......	179	59
Madison, ...	12	......	215	1	1	229	4	129	5	82	9	55, 000	73	2	121	73
Monroe, ...	41	66	130	2	1	240	3	151	6	69	11	164, 040	113	27	420	290
Montgomery, ...	5	9	102	......	2	118	......	64	4	40	10	36, 735	62	......	106	86
New-York, ...	1	75	5	......	......	81	......	73	......	7	1	1, 519, 100	1, 742	4, 289	9, 617	3, 426
Niagara, ...	41	26	86	4	11	168	......	103	12	45	8	61, 583	67	2	142	142
Oneida, ...	16	15	351	1	3	386	10	217	18	121	20	130, 530	166	50	401	241
Onondaga, ...	40	30	222	......	......	292	6	177	18	80	11	165, 677	120	24	297	232
Ontario, ...	33	29	135	3	......	200	9	117	......	70	4	60, 850	47	......	138	105
Orange, ...	8	12	153	2	......	175	......	113	11	39	12	71, 675	109	12	331	117
Orleans, ...	35	9	81	......	4	129	5	74	4	40	6	62, 836	27	4	99	47
Oswego, ...	10	5	259	7	8	289	3	138	9	121	18	93, 669	99	1	292	186
Otsego, ...	18	1	284	1	1	305	3	140	11	143	8	49, 766	93	......	137	34
Putnam, ...	......	5	51	......	......	56	......	28	......	24	4	37, 530	10	......	50	23
Queens, ...	......	......	74	......	......	74	7	53	4	9	1	56, 915	74	10	152	188
Rensselaer, ...	1	27	170	1	......	199	1	119	14	57	8	109, 400	115	85	513	236
Richmond, ...	1	3	13	......	......	17	1	11	......	4	1	29, 910	68	7	65	55
Rockland, ...	1	2	31	......	......	34	3	23	......	6	2	22, 640	29	......	122	24
St. Lawrence, ...	32	20	307	57	21	437	2	222	10	183	20	86, 810	89	10	231	91
Saratoga, ...	4	26	180	2	3	215	3	117	1	87	7	50, 805	85	......	186	123
Schenectady, ...	2	8	47	......	......	57	......	38	......	15	4	13, 385	49	1	87	76
Schoharie, ...	5	......	187	2	......	194	3	113	1	36	41	35, 155	65	......	112	22
Schuyler, ...	......	......	102	2	14	118	......	52	4	44	18	25, 310	24	......	62	36
Seneca, ...	3	27	66	1	1	98	......	54	8	33	3	35, 002	32	......	94	54
Steuben, ...	1	......	300	27	13	341	10	172	25	117	17	78, 049	87	......	180	66
Suffolk, ...	......	3	143	......	......	146	......	79	9	42	16	41, 210	55	2	221	74
Sullivan, ...	1	......	144	2	6	153	8	93	6	40	6	29, 500	63	......	113	32
Tioga, ...	......	1	140	2	2	145	10	76	8	48	3	28, 441	33	......	85	34
Tompkins, ...	2	4	133	2	20	161	......	95	4	56	6	45, 980	41	3	120	27
Ulster, ...	15	9	179	3	......	206	5	138	10	40	13	70, 055	154	4	314	200
Warren, ...	1	1	118	5	......	125	11	59	13	42	....	29, 151	30	2	81	18
Washington, ...	6	53	174	......	5	238	2	133	2	94	7	56, 549	45	......	150	73
Wayne, ...	63	15	147	......	4	229	6	129	6	74	14	95, 926	42	......	136	74
Westchester, ...	1	9	105	......	......	115	3	52	11	39	10	69, 565	110	4	476	230
Wyoming, ...	3	2	185	3	......	193	1	74	17	89	12	43, 055	48	2	123	37
Yates, ...	3	6	96	2	1	108	1	64	4	39	....	35, 555	25	......	77	23
Total, ...	601	738	9, 238	313	247	11, 137	195	6, 181	447	3, 626	688	$5, 310, 446	6, 025	4, 836	22, 607	10, 421

NEWSPAPERS AND OTHER PERIODICALS

Where published.	Names of Newspapers and Periodicals.	Editors and Publishers.
Albany Co.		
Albany,	Daily Albany Argus,	Calvert Comstock and James I. Johnson, Proprietors,
Albany,	Albany Argus,	Calvert Comstock and James I. Johnson, Proprietors,
Albany,	Weekly Argus,	Calvert Comstock and James I. Johnson, Proprietors,
Albany,	Albany Evening Atlas,	Van Dyck and Cassidy, Editors; H. H. Van Dyck, Publisher,
Albany,	Albany Semi-Weekly Atlas,	Van Dyck and Cassidy, Editors; H. H. Van Dyck, Publisher,
Albany,	Albany Weekly Atlas,	Van Dyck and Cassidy, Editors; H. H. Van Dyck, Publisher,
Albany,	Albany Morning Express,	Carlton Edwards, Editor; Munsell & Co., Publishers,
Albany,	Albany Weekly Express,	Carlton Edwards, Editor; Munsell & Co., Publishers,
Albany,	Albany Evening Journal,	Thurlow Weed, Geo. Dawson, F. W. Seward and J. Ten Eyck,
Albany,	Albany Journal,	Editors; Ten Eyck & Co., Publishers,
Albany,	Albany Weekly Journal,	
Albany,	Albany Daily Knickerbocker,	Hugh J. Hastings,
Albany,	The Weekly Knickerbocker,	Hugh J. Hastings,
Albany,	Albany Daily State Register,	S. H. Hammond, Editor; W. Lacy & Co., Publishers,
Albany,	Albany State Register,	S. H. Hammond, Editor; W. Lacy & Co., Publishers,
Albany,	Albany State Register,	S. H. Hammond, Editor; W. Lacy & Co., Publishers,
Albany,	Albany Evening Transcript,	Cuyler & Henley,
Albany,	Deutsche Freie Blatter,	Henry Binder, Editor; Aug. Miggael, Publisher,
Albany,	American Spectator,	B. F. Romaine,
Albany,	Carson League,	J. T. Hazen and T. L. Carson,
Albany,	The Country Gentleman,	Luther Tucker, Editor and Publisher,
Albany,	Courier and Journal,	Jacob T. Hazen,
Albany,	Family Intelligencer,	Jasper Hazen,
Albany,	Albany Switch,	Edward Leslie,
Albany,	State Police Tribune,	S. H. H. Parsons and R. M. Griffin, Editors,
Albany,	The Youngster,	C. C. Nichols and Sidney Low,
Albany,	The Cultivator,	Luther Tucker, Editor and Publisher,
Albany,	The Journal of the N. Y. State Agricultural Society,	(Official bulletin of the Society,)
Albany,	The Prohibitionist,	Amasa McCoy,
Albany,	New-York Teacher,	Truman H. Bowen,
Albany,	Albany Directory,	Joel Munsell,
Albany,	Annals of Albany,	Joel Munsell,
Albany,	Register of Rural Affairs,	Luther Tucker, Editor aud Publisher,
Albany,	Webster's Almanac,	Joel Munsell,
Watervliet,	Cohoes Cataract,	James H. Masten,
Watervliet,	West Troy Advocate and Watervliet Advertiser,	William Hollands,
Llegany Co.		
Almond,	The Allegany Sentinel,	Pruner & Spencer,
Angelica,	Whig and Advocate,	W. H. Beecher,
Angelica,	Angelica Reporter,	Charles Horton,
Caneadea,	Republican Era, (Oramel)	Horace E. Purdy,
Cuba,	American Banner,	Hatch & Pratt,
Scio,	Genesee Valley Press,	A. N. Cole,
Broome Co.		
Chenango,	The Binghamton Daily Republican,	Wm. Stuart, Editor and Proprietor,
Chenango,	The Broome Republican,	Wm. Stuart, Editor and Proprietor,
Chenango,	Broome County American,	R. Bostwick, Editor; C. S. Williams, Publisher,
Chenango,	Binghamton Democrat,	Dickinson & Lawyer,
Chenango,	Binghamton Standard,	J. Van Valkenburgh, Editor and Proprietor,
Chenango,	Susquehanna Journal,	Wm. H. Pearne, Proprietor,
Union,	The Union News,	Cephas Benedict, Eben M. Betts,
Cattaraugus Co.		
Ellicottville,	Cattaraugus Whig,	Sill & Beecher,
Ellicottville,	Cattaraugus Republican,	Frederick A. Saxton,
Ellicottville,	The Union,	J. T. Henry, Editor; S. Henry, Proprietor,
Olean,	Olean Journal,	Charles Aldrich,
Persia,	Gowanda Chronicle,	Henry M. Morgan,
Randolph,	Randolph Whig,	Benjamin F. & S. J. Morris,
Cayuga Co.		
Auburn,	Auburn Daily Advertiser,	Geo. W. Peck, Editor; O. Knapp, Publisher,
Auburn,	Auburn Weekly Journal,	Geo. W. Peck, Editor; O. Knapp, Publisher,
Auburn,	Auburn Daily American,	J. Stanley Smith, Editor; Wm. J. Moses, Publisher,
Auburn,	Auburn Weekly American,	J. Stanley Smith, Editor; Wm. J. Moses, Publisher,
Auburn,	Cayuga Chief,	Thurlow W. & Emma Brown,
Auburn,	The Cayuga New Era,	William L. Finn,
Auburn,	The Christian Ambassador,	John M. Austin, Editor; Universalist Society, Publisher,
Auburn,	Northern Christian Advocate,	Rev. Wm. Hosmer, Editor; S. C. Coats, F. Reed, D. A. Shepard, A. J. Phelps and P. E. Brown, Publishers,
Mentz,	Port Byron Gazette,	Oliver T. Baird, Editor; Arthur White, Proprietor,
Victory,	The Family Scrap Book,	Peter J. Beecher,
Chautauque Co.		
Chautauque,	Mayville Sentinel,	John F. Phelps,
Ellicott,	The Chautauque Democrat, (Jamestown)	James Parker and Cyrus D. Fletcher,
Ellicott,	Jamestown Journal,	F. W Palmer and E. P. Upham,
Hanover,	Silver Creek Gazette,	Samuel Wilson,
Pomfret,	The Dunkirk Journal,	W. L. Carpenter,
Pomfret,	Fredonia Censor,	W. McKinstry & Co.,
Pomfret,	The Fredonia Advertiser,	Levi L. Pratt,
Westfield,	Westfield Republican,	M. C. Rice & Co.,
Westfield,	The Transcript,	Dennison & Buck,
Chemung Co.		
Elmira,	Elmira Advertiser,	C. G. & S. B. Fairman and M. Ells, Editors,
Elmira,	Elmira Advertiser,	C. G. & S. B. Fairman and M. Ells, Editors,
Elmira,	Elmira Republican,	L. Baldwin and H. E. Lowman,
Elmira,	Elmira Weekly Republican,	L. Baldwin and H. E. Lowman,
Elmira,	Elmira Gazette,	Geo. W. Mason,
Horseheads,	The Philosopher,	Samuel C. Taber,
Chenango Co.		
New Berlin,	The Social Visiter	Joseph K. Fox,

PUBLISHED IN NEW-YORK IN 1855.

To what object devoted.	At what intervals published.	Subscription price per annum.	When established.	Size in inches, and form.
Politics and news,	Daily,	$7 00	1813,	28×42, Folio.
Politics and news,	Semi-weekly,	3 00		28×42, Folio.
Politics and news,	Weekly,	1 00		28×42, Quarto.
Politics and news,	Daily,	6 00	1840,	27×42, Folio.
Politics and news,	Semi-weekly,	2 00		27×42, Folio.
Politics and news,	Weekly,	1 00		27×42, Folio.
News,	Daily,	6 00	1847,	23×36, Folio.
News,	Weekly,	1 00		23×36, Folio.
Politics and news,	Daily,	7 00	1830,	28×42, Folio.
Politics and news,	Semi-weekly,	3 00	1830,	28×42, Folio.
Politics and news,	Weekly,	2 00	1833,	28×42, Folio.
News,	Daily,	3 00	1843,	20×31, Folio.
News,	Weekly,	1 00		20×31, Folio.
Politics and news,	Daily,	7 00	1850,	28×42, Folio.
Politics and news,	Semi-weekly,	3 00		28×42, Folio.
Politics and news,	Weekly,	1 00		28×42, Folio.
Politics and news,	Daily,	4 00	1853,	22×32, Folio.
Politics and news (German),	Tri-weekly,	4 00	1852,	22×32, Folio.
Politics and news,	Weekly,	2 00	1844,	28×42, Folio.
Temperance and news,	Weekly,	1 50	1851,	26×38, Quarto.
Agriculture and horticulture,	Weekly,	2 00	1853,	27×39, (16 pages) Quarto.
Temperance and news,	Weekly,	1 50	1849,	26×38, Quarto.
News,	Weekly,	1 50	1852,	26×38, Quarto.
"Moral reform,"	Weekly,	2 00	1841,	18×25, Folio.
Criminal news,	Weekly,	2 00	July 21, 1855,	26×38, Folio.
Boy's paper,	Semi-monthly,	0 50	1855,	12×19, Folio.
Agriculture,	Monthly,	0 50	1852,	29×43, (32 pages) Octavo.
Agriculture,	Monthly,	....	1849,	14×20, (8 pages) Octavo.
Temperance,	Monthly,	0 50	1854,	25×42, Quarto.
Education,	Monthly,	1 00	1852,	Octavo.
City Directory,	Annually,	1 00	1813,	Duodecimo.
History,	Annually,	1 00	1848.	Duodecimo.
Agriculture, &c.,	Annually,	0 25	1854,	Octavo.
Advertising, &c.,	Annually,	....	1784,	Duodecimo.
News,	Weekly,	1 50	1849,	23×38, Folio.
News,	Weekly,	2 00	1827,	22×32, Folio.
News,	Weekly,	1 50	June 6, 1855,	24×34, Folio.
Politics and news,	Weekly,	1 50	1842,	24×34, Folio.
Politics and news,	Weekly,	1 50	1837,	25×38, Folio.
Politics and news,	Weekly,	1 50	1846,	24×36, Folio.
Politics and news,	Weekly,	1 50	Feb. 28, 1855,	24×34, Folio.
Moral and political reform,	Weekly,	1 50	Jan. 1, 1853,	Folio.
Politics and news,	Daily,	5 00	Feb. 22, 1849,	22×34, Folio.
Politics and news,	Weekly,	1 00	1821,	25×38, Folio.
Politics and news,	Weekly,	1 00	May, 1855,	24×34, Folio.
Politics and news,	Weekly,	1 00	Dec. 15, 1846,	27×42, Folio.
Temperance, news &c.,	Weekly,	1 00	Nov'ber, 1853,	24×35, Folio.
Religion, news, &c.,	Weekly,	1 25	October, 1853,	27×37, Folio.
News,	Weekly,	1 00	1851,	22×32, Folio.
Politics and news,	Weekly,	1 50	1840,	23×35, Folio.
Politics and news,	Weekly,	1 50	1832,	21×36, Folio.
Politics and news,	Weekly,	1 50	1850,	22×32, Folio.
News,	Weekly,	1 50	1852,	22×32, Folio.
News,	Weekly,	1 50	1854,	24×36, Folio.
Politics and news,	Weekly,	1 50	July, 1852,	24×36, Folio.
Politics and news,	Daily,	4 50	1846,	24×32, Folio.
Politics and news,	Weekly,	1 50	1832,	28×44, Folio.
Politics and news,	Daily,	5 00	Feb'ry, 1855,	24×32, Folio
Politics and news,	Weekly,	1 50	Feb'ry, 1855,	28×44, Folio.
Temperance and news,	Weekly,	1 00	Jan. 1, 1849,	24×36, Folio.
Politics and news,	Weekly,	1 50	1847,	28×42, Folio.
Religion and news,	Weekly,	2 00	1850,	25×36, Folio.
Religion and news,	Weekly,	1 00	June, 1844,	26×38, Folio.
News,	Weekly,	1 50	August, 1851,	25×37, Folio.
Miscellaneous,	Monthly,	0 50	1854,	Octavo.
Politics and news,	Weekly,	1 00	1834,	23×34, Folio.
Politics and news,	Weekly,	1 00	Feb'ry, 1853,	25×37, Folio.
Politics and news,	Weekly,	1 00	1826,	25×36, Folio.
Politics and news,	Weekly,	1 50	1853,	24×37, Folio.
Politics and news,	Weekly,	1 00	1850,	24×36, Folio.
Politics and news,	Weekly,	1 50	1821,	27×40, Folio.
Politics and news,	Weekly,	1 50	July 4, 1851,	28×41, Folio.
Politics and news,	Weekly,	1 50	1855,	27×40, Folio.
Politics and news,	Weekly,	1 50	1851,	27×41, Quarto.
Politics and news,	Daily,	4 00	1854,	21×30, Folio.
Politics and news,	Weekly,	1 75		30×42, Quarto.
Politics and news,	Daily,	5 00	1851,	22×32, Folio.
Politics and news,	Weekly,	2 00	1820,	28×42, Folio.
Politics and news,	Weekly,	1 50	1823,	27×42, Folio.
News,	Weekly,	1 50	April 7, 1855,	24×36, Folio.
News,	Weekly,	1 00	1853,	22×33, Folio.

NEWSPAPERS AND OTHER

Where published.	Names of Newspapers and Periodicals.	Editors and Proprietors.
CHENANGO CO.		
Norwich,	The Chenango Union,	Hubbard & Sinclair,
Norwich,	Temperance Advocate,	A. P. Nixon and M. Wright, Editor, J. M. Haight, Publisher,
Norwich,	The Chenango Telegraph,	Francis B. Fisher,
Oxford,	Oxford Times,	Rufus J. Baldwin, Editor, Judson B. Galpin, Publisher,
Sherburne,	Sherburne Transcript,	James M. Scarritt,
CLINTON CO.		
Champlain,	Rouse's Point Advertiser,	David Turner,
Plattsburgh,	American Sentinel,	Brady S. Dewey,
Plattsburgh,	The Clinton County Whig,	Albert G. Carver,
Plattsburgh,	The Plattsburgh Republican,	R. G. Stone,
Plattsburgh,	Nelson's American Lancet,	Horace Nelson, M. D.,
COLUMBIA CO.		
Hudson,	Hudson Daily News,	Richard Van Antwerp,
Hudson,	Hudson Daily Star,	Alexander N. Webb,
Hudson,	Hudson Weekly Star,	Alexander N. Webb,
Hudson,	Columbia Republican,	William Bryan,
Hudson,	Democratic Freeman,	J. B. Langley, Editor, A. N. Webb, Publisher,
Hudson,	Hudson Gazette,	Albertson & Olmsted, Publisher,
Kinderhook,	Rough Notes,	Peter H. Van Vleck,
Kinderhook,	Valatie Weekly Times,	A. N. Hopkins,
CORTLAND CO.		
Cortlandville,	Cortland Democrat,	Henry G. Crouch,
Homer,	The Cortland County Whig,	J. R. Dixon, Editor, Dixon & Case, Publisher,
DELAWARE CO.		
Delhi,	The Delaware Express,	Norwood Bowne,
Delhi,	The Delaware Gazette,	A. M. Paine,
Franklin,	The Weekly Visitor,	Geo. W. Reynolds,
Kortright,	Bloomville Mirror,	S. B. Champion,
Stamford,	Hobart Free Press,	Elbridge B. Fenn,
Tompkins,	Deposit Union Democrat,	Silvester D. Hulse,
DUTCHESS CO.		
Amenia,	Amenia Times,	Joel Benton,
Fishkill,	The Fishkill Journal,	Edward H. Leggett,
Fishkill,	Fishkill Standard,	William R. Addington,
Poughkeepsie city,	Daily City Press,	Nichols, Bush & Co.,
Poughkeepsie city,	Dutchess Democrat,	E. B. Osborne,
Poughkeepsie city,	The Independent Examiner,	H. A. Gould,
Poughkeepsie city,	The Poughkeepsie Eagle,	Isaac Platt and Wm. Schram,
Poughkeepsie city,	The Poughkeepsie Telegraph,	Albert S. Pease, Editor, A. S. P. & Co., Publishers,
Rhinebeck,	American Mechanic and Rhinebeck Gazette,	George W. Clark,
Rhinebeck,	The Rhinebeck Gazette and Dutchess County Advertiser,	William Luff,
ERIE CO.		
Buffalo,	Buffalo Commercial Advertiser,	T. N. Parmelee, Editor, Thomas & Lathrops, Publishers,
Buffalo,	Buffalo Commercial Advertiser,	T. N. Parmelee, Editor, Thomas & Lathrops, Publishers,
Buffalo,	The Morning Advertiser,	C. A. Kellogg and H. C. Gilbert, Eds., Thomas & Lathrops, Pub.,
Buffalo,	Buffalo Patriot and Journal,	T. N. Parmelee, Editor, Thomas & Lathrops, Publishers,
Buffalo,	Buffalo Daily Courier,	William A. Seaver,
Buffalo,	Buffalo Courier,	William A. Seaver,
Buffalo,	Buffalo Weekly Courier,	William A. Seaver,
Buffalo,	The Democracy,	Daniel Wilkinson, Editor, Democracy Printing Association, Pub.,
Buffalo,	The Weekly Democracy,	Daniel Wilkinson, Editor, Democracy Printing Association, Pub.,
Buffalo,	Taghlicher Buffalo Demokrat and Weltburger,	Brunck, Held & Co.,
Buffalo,	Der Weltburger and Buffalo Demokrat,	Brunck, Held & Co.,
Buffalo,	Buffalo Evening Post,	George J. Bryan,
Buffalo,	Buffalo Morning Express,	A. M. Clapp and R. Wheeler,
Buffalo,	Buffalo Express,	A. M. Clapp and R. Wheeler,
Buffalo,	Buffalo Weekly Express,	A. M. Clapp and R. Wheeler,
Buffalo,	Buffalo Daily Republic,	C. C. Bristol and Benj. Welch,
Buffalo,	Buffalo Republic,	C. C. Bristol and Benj. Welch,
Buffalo,	Buffalo Weekly Republic,	C. C. Bristol and Benj. Welch,
Buffalo,	Der Buffalo Telegraph,	Julius Hoffman, Editor, Miller & Bouder, Publishers,
Buffalo,	Der Buffalo Telegraph,	Julius Hoffman, Editor, Miller & Bouder, Publishers,
Buffalo,	Aurora;—Eine Unabhangige Zeitung,	Christian Wieckman & Co.,
Buffalo,	Die Aurora;—Ein Catholisches Wochenblatt,	Christian Wieckman & Co.,
Buffalo,	American Rights,	M. Cadwallader, Editor, Geo. Reese & Co., Publishers,
Buffalo,	Buffalo Christian Advocate,	John E. Robie,
Buffalo,	Buffalo Catholic Sentinel,	Michael Hagen,
Buffalo,	Buffalo Pathfinder,	James Faxon,
Buffalo,	Age of Progress,	Stephen Albro,
Buffalo,	Illustrirte Abend-Schule,	Rev. Diehlman, Editor, H. Fubesing, Publisher,
Buffalo,	Kirchliches Informatorium, (Lutheran,)	J. Andr. A. Grabau,
Buffalo,	Common Sense,	D. P. Stiles,
Buffalo,	Buffalo Medical Journal and Monthly Review of Medical and Surgical Science,	Dr. Austin Flint and Dr. Sandford B. Hunt, Editors, Thomas & Lathrops, Publishers,
Buffalo,	Western Literary Messenger,	Jesse Clement, Editor, Thomas & Lathrops, Publishers,
Buffalo,	The Youth's Casket,	Mrs. H. E. G. Arey, Editor, E. F. Beadle, Publisher,
Buffalo,	Buffalo Directory,	Thomas & Lathrops, Publishers,
Concord,	Springville Herald,	E. D. Webster,
Tonawanda,	Niagara River Pilot,	Silas S. Packard,
ESSEX CO.		
Chesterfield,	The Northern Standard, (Keeseville,)	Wendell Lansing,
Chesterfield,	Essex County Republican, (Keeseville,)	J. W. Reynolds, Editor, J. B. Dickinson, Publisher,
Elizabethtown,	The Elizabethtown Post,	Robert W. Livingston,
FRANKLIN CO.		
Malone,	The Franklin Gazette,	F. D. Flanders, Editor, H. C. Powell,
Malone,	The Frontier Palladium,	J. J. & H. K. Seaver,
FULTON CO.		
Johnstown,	Fulton County Democrat,	Walter N. Clark,
Johnstown,	Fulton County Republican,	George Henry,
GENESEE CO.		
Batavia,	Batavia Democrat,	Henry Todd,
Batavia,	The Republican Advocate,	John H. Kimberly, Editor, Kimberly & Goodrich, Publishers,

PERIODICALS.—(Continued.)

To what object devoted.	At what intervals published	Subscription price per annum.	When established.	Size in inches, and form.
Politics and news,	Weekly,	$1 50	1816,	28×42, Folio.
Temperance and news,	Weekly,	1 25	1855,	24×36, Folio.
News,	Weekly,	1 25	1828,	24×36, Folio.
Politics and news,	Weekly,	1 50	1838,	23×34, Folio.
News,	Weekly,	1 00	July, 1855,	22×32, Folio.
Politics and news,	Weekly,	1 50	January, 1852,	23×32, Folio.
Politics and news,	Weekly,	1 50	January, 1855,	24×37, Folio.
Politics and news,	Weekly,	1 50	1839,	24×38, Folio.
Politics and news,	Weekly,	2 00	1811,	23×38, Folio.
Medical science,	Monthly,	2 00	1850,	Octavo
News,	Daily,	3 00	1855,	19×26, Folio.
Politics and news,	Daily,	4 00	1847,	22×32, Folio.
Politics and news,	Weekly,	1 00	1841,	24×37, Folio.
Politics and news,	Weekly,	1 50	August, 1818,	24×38, Folio.
Politics and news,	Weekly,	1 50	1848,	24×37, Folio.
Politics and news,	Weekly,	1 50	1824,	24×38, Folio.
News,	Weekly,	1 50	1853,	22×32, Folio.
Politics and news,	Weekly,	1 50	July, 1853,	24×38, Folio.
Politics and news,	Weekly,	1 50	1840,	24×36, Folio.
Politics and news,	Weekly,	1 50	1824,	27×37, Folio.
Politics and news,	Weekly,	1 50	1839,	24×32, Folio.
Politics and news,	Weekly,	1 50	1819,	24×36, Folio.
Politics and news,	Weekly,	1 50	April 14, 1855,	24×38, Folio.
News,	Weekly,	0 50	1851,	12×18, Folio.
News,	Weekly,	0 50	January, 1855,	13×18, Folio.
News,	Weekly,	1 50	1853,	24×36, Folio.
News,	Weekly,	1 00	1852,	23×29, Folio.
News,	Weekly,	1 50	1854,	22×32, Folio.
News,	Weekly,	1 50	1842,	24×36, Folio.
News,	Daily,	3 25	1852,	20×27, Folio.
Politics and news,	Weekly,	1 50	1845,	28×40, Folio.
Temperance and news,	Weekly,	1 50	January, 1855,	24×38, Folio.
Politics and news,	Weekly,	2 00	1785	28×42, Folio.
Politics and news,	Weekly,	1 50	1824,	28×41, Folio.
Politics and news,	Weekly,	1 50	1846,	22×32, Folio.
News,	Weekly,	1 50	1849,	24×36, Folio.
Politics and news,	Daily,	8 00	1835,	28×42, Folio.
Politics and news,	Tri-weekly,	5 00	1835,	28×42, Folio.
Politics and news,	Daily,	5 00	1855,	23×34, Folio.
Politics and news,	Weekly,	1 00	1815,	27×42, Folio.
Politics and news,	Daily,	6 00	1835,	27×42, Folio.
Politics and news,	Tri-weekly,	3 00	1835,	27×42, Folio.
Politics and news,	Weekly,	1 00		26×42, Folio.
Politics and news,	Daily,	6 00	1854,	26×42, Folio.
Politics and news,	Weekly,	1 50	1854,	Folio.
Politics and news,	Daily,	4 00	1837,	22×32, Folio.
Politics and news,	Weekly,	2 00	1837,	27×42, Folio.
Politics and news,	Daily,	3 00	1850,	21×28, Folio.
Politics and news,	Daily,	6 00	1846,	28×42, Folio.
Politics and news,	Tri-weekly,	3 00	1846,	28×42, Folio.
Politics and news,	Weekly,	1 00	1846,	28×42, Folio.
Politics and news,	Daily,	0 00	1848,	28×42, Folio.
Politics and news,	Tri-weekly,	4 00	1848,	28×42, Folio.
Politics and news,	Weekly,	1 50	1848,	28×42, Folio
Politics and news,	Daily,	3 00	1845,	21×28, Folio.
Politics and news,	Weekly,	1 00	1845,	24×36, Folio.
News, religion, &c.,	Tri-weekly,	3 00	1853,	22×32, Folio.
News, religion, &c.,	Weekly,	2 00	1853,	24×36, Quarto.
Politics and news,	Weekly,	1 50	1854,	21×28, Folio.
Religion and news,	Weekly,	1 50	1850,	27×40, Folio.
Religion and news,	Weekly,	2 00	Jan'y 4, 1843,	26×36, Folio.
Advertising,	Weekly,	Gratis.	1850,	21×28, Folio.
Spiritual manifestations,	Weekly,	2 00	1854,	(16 pages,) Quarto.
Evening schools, &c.,	Semi-monthly,	0 75	1854,	16×24, (8 pages,) Octavo.
Religion,	Semi-monthly,	1 00	1850,	19×24, Quarto.
Insurance,	Monthly,	0 50	1855,	22×28, Quarto.
Medical science,	Monthly,	2 50	1845,	Octavo.
Literature,	Monthly,	1 50	1845,	Octavo.
Juvenile literature,	Monthly,	0 50	1852,	Octavo.
City Directory,	Annually,	1 50		Octavo.
Politics and news,	Weekly,	1 50	1850,	23×32, Folio.
News,	Weekly,	2 00	1853,	24×38, Folio.
Politics and news,	Weekly,	1 50	1854,	23×34, Folio.
Politics and news,	Weekly,	1 00	1839,	23×34, Folio.
News,	Weekly,	1 00	1851,	26×38, Folio.
Politics and news,	Weekly,	1 00	1838,	Folio.
Politics and news,	Weekly,	1 50	1835,	24×37, Folio.
Politics and news,	Weekly,	1 50	1839,	24×36, Folio.
Politics and news,	Weekly,	1 00	1838,	22×32, Folio.
Politics and news,	Weekly,	1 50	Decemb'r, 1852,	24×36, Folio.
Politics and news,	Weekly,	2 00	1811,	24×36, Folio.

NEWSPAPERS AND OTHER

Where published.	Names of Newspapers and Periodicals.	Editors and Proprietors.
GENESEE Co.		
Batavia,	Spirit of the Times,	Charles S. Harley,
Le Roy,	Genesee Herald,	William C. Grammon,
Le Roy,	The Le Roy Gazette,	Charles B. Thompson,
GREENE Co.		
Catskill,	American Eagle,	Henry Baker,
Catskill,	Greene County Whig,	Trowbridge & Gunn,
Catskill,	Recorder and Democrat,	Joseph Josebury,
Coxsackie,	The Coxsackie Union,	Hoffman & Van Bergen,
Prattsville,	Prattsville Advocate,	William R. Steele,
HAMILTON Co.		
Lake Pleasant,	Hamilton County Sentinel,	John C. Holmes & Co.,
HERKIMER Co.		
German Flats,	Ilion Independent,	George W. Bungay,
German Flats,	The Mohawk Valley Sentinel,	L. W. Peters,
Herkimer,	Herkimer Democrat,	C. C. Witherstine and Jacob S. Hayes,
Little Falls,	Eclectic Bulletin,	T. Squires,
Little Falls,	Herkimer County Journal,	D. Ayer,
Little Falls,	Mohawk Courier,	H. N. Johnson and A. W. Eaton,
JEFFERSON Co.		
Adams,	Jefferson County Democrat,	Elijah J. Clark,
Watertown,	The Jefferson Union,	Elon Comstock,
Watertown,	The New-York Reformer,	L. Ingalls and L. M. Stowell,
Watertown,	Northern New-York Journal,	A. W. Clark and John Fayel,
Watertown,	Almanac,	A. H. Hall,
Watertown,	Directory,	—— Huntington,
KINGS Co.		
Brooklyn,	The Brooklyn Daily Eagle,	I. Van Anden,
Brooklyn,	Saturday Evening Miscellany,	I. Van Anden,
Brooklyn,	Brooklyn Evening Star,	E. B. Spooner,
Brooklyn,	The Long Island Star,	E. B. Spooner,
Brooklyn,	Daily Independent Press,	G. W. Bishop and J. A. F. Kelly,
Brooklyn,	Brooklyn Morning Journal,	J. Weston Heighway, Editor, Hogan & Heighway, Publisher,
Brooklyn,	The Brooklyn Daily Times,	Bennett & Smith,
Brooklyn,	Long Island Anzeiger,	Edward Rohr,
Brooklyn,	Triangel,	Edward Rohr,
Brooklyn,	The Union Ark,	J. Schnebly,
Brooklyn,	Brooklyn City Directory,	Wm. H. Smith,
Brooklyn,	Brooklyn City and Kings Co. Record,	Wm. H. Smith,
LEWIS Co.		
Lowville,	Northern Journal,	Cordial Storrs, Jr.,
Martinsburgh,	The Lewis County Republican,	Daniel S. Bailey,
West Turin,	Northern Blade, (Constableville,)	Fairchild & Eames,
LIVINGSTON Co.		
Geneseo,	The Geneseo Democrat,	George A. Saunders & Co.,
Geneseo,	Livingston Republican,	James T. Norton,
Lima,	Genesee Valley Gazette,	S. M. Raymond,
Mount Morris,	The Livingston Union,	Hugh Harding,
North Dansville,	Dansville Herald,	H. L. & L. H. Rann,
Nunda,	The Young American,	David B. Galley,
MADISON Co.		
Eaton,	Madison Observer (Morrisville,)	J. & E. Norton,
Hamilton,	Democratic Reflector,	G. R. Waldron & Co.,
Hamilton,	Madison County Journal,	Thomas L. James and W. W. Chubbuck,
Hamilton,	New-York State Radii,	Levi S. Backus,
Lenox,	Oneida Sachem,	Ira D. Brown, Editor, John Crawford, Publisher,
Cazenovia,	Cazenovia Republican,	Seneca Lake,
Cazenovia,	Madison County Whig,	H. A. Coolidge,
Sullivan,	Chittenango Herald,	Sanford J. Cobb,
MONROE Co.		
Rochester,	Rochester Daily Advertiser,	H. Bumphrey, Editor, Rochester Dem. Pr. Association, J. D. Halsted, Secretary and Agent,
Rochester,	Rochester Advertiser,	
Rochester,	Rochester Republican,	
Rochester,	Rochester Daily American,	Daniel Lee, Alexander Mann, and C. P. Dewey,
Rochester,	Rochester American,	Daniel Lee, Alexander Mann, and C. P. Dewey,
Rochester,	Rochester Weekly American,	Daniel Lee, Alexander Mann, and C. P. Dewey,
Rochester,	Rochester Daily Democrat,	S. P. Allen and Fr. S. Rew, Editors, A. Strong & Co., Publish's,
Rochester,	Rochester Democrat,	S. P. Allen and Fr. S. Rew, Editors, A. Strong & Co., Publish's,
Rochester,	The Monroe Weekly Democrat,	S. P. Allen and Fr. S. Rew, Editors, A. Strong & Co., Publish's,
Rochester,	The Rochester Daily Union,	Isaac Butts, Editor, Curtis & Butts, Publishers,
Rochester,	The Rochester Union,	Isaac Butts, Editor, Curtis & Butts, Publishers,
Rochester,	The Rochester Weekly Union,	Isaac Butts, Editor, Curtis & Butts, Publishers,
Rochester,	Anzeiger des Nordens,	Louis Hurtz,
Rochester,	Frederick Douglass' Paper,	Frederick Douglass,
Rochester,	The Genesee Evangelist,	Rev. R. W. Hill,
Rochester,	Moore's Rural New-Yorker,	D. D. T. Moore and others,
Rochester,	Prophetic Expositor and Bible Advocate,	Joseph Marsh,
Rochester,	The Advent Review and Sabbath Herald,	James White, Editor,
Rochester,	The Genesee Farmer,	D. Lee and James Vick, Editors, J. Vick, Publisher,
Rochester,	The Wool Grower and Stock Register,	D. D. T. Moore and others,
Rochester,	Youth's Instructor,	James White,
Rochester,	Rochester City Directory,	D. M. Dewey, Publisher,
MONTGOMERY Co.		
Amsterdam,	Amsterdam Recorder,	X. Haywood,
Glen,	Montgomery County Whig, (Fultonville,)	Thomas R. Horton,
Minden,	Mohawk Valley Register, (Fort Plain,)	D. S. Kellogg and W. C. Kendall,
Mohawk,	The American Star, (Fonda,)	Wm. S. Hawley,
Mohawk,	The Fonda Sentinel,	Clark & Thayer,
NEW-YORK Co.		
New-York,	New-York Commercial Advertiser,	Francis Hall & Co., Publishers,
New-York,	New-York Spectator,	Francis Hall & Co., Publishers,
New York,	Morning Courier and New-York Enquirer,	J. Watson Webb,
New-York,	Semi-Weekly Courier and New-York Enquirer,	J. Watson Webb,
New-York,	The New-York Family Courier,	J. Watson Webb,

PERIODICALS.—(Continued.)

To what object devoted.	At what intervals published.	Subscription price per annum.	When established.	Size in inches, and form.
Politics and news,	Weekly,	$2 00	Feb'ry, 1819,	25×36, Folio.
News,	Weekly,	2 00	May, 1854,	28×40, Folio.
Politics and news,	Weekly,	2 00	1827,	25×36, Folio.
Politics and news,	Weekly,	1 00	1854,	23×30, Folio.
Politics and news,	Weekly,	1 25	1831,	25×36, Folio.
Politics and news,	Weekly,	1 50	1801,	25×37, Folio.
Politics and news,	Weekly,	1 25	1851,	24×36, Folio.
News,	Weekly,	1 00	1855,	19×26, Folio.
Politics and news,	Weekly,	2 00		Folio.
News,	Weekly,	1 00	1855,	23×32, Folio.
Politics and news,	Weekly,	1 50	1855,	22×32, Folio.
Politics and news,	Weekly,	1 50	1841,	24×36, Folio.
News,	Tri-weekly,	1 25	1855,	12×18, Folio.
Politics and news,	Weekly,	1 50	1839,	24×36, Folio.
Politics and news,	Weekly,	1 50	1833,	24×36, Folio.
Politics and news,	Weekly,	1 25	1843,	24×36, Folio.
Politics and news,	Weekly,	1 50	October, 1854,	28×42, Folio.
Reform, news, &c.,	Weekly,	1 00	1850,	26×38, Folio.
Politics and news,	Weekly,	1 50	1848,	26×40, Folio.
	Annually,			Duodecimo.
	Annually,			Duodecimo.
News,	Daily,	3 25	1841,	22×32, Folio.
News,	Weekly,	2 00	1855,	26×38, Folio.
News,	Daily,	3 25	1841,	24×36, Folio.
News,	Weekly,	1 50	1809,	24×36, Folio.
News,	Daily,	3 25	July 16, 1850,	23×32, Folio.
News,	Daily,	3 00	1851,	22×34, Folio.
News,	Daily,	3 25	July, 1848,	23×30, Folio.
News, (German)	Weekly,	1 50	Sept. 2, 1854,	19×24, Folio.
Free Masonry, (German)	Semi-weekly,	3 00	April 7, 1855,	18×24, Quarto.
Temperance,	Monthly,	1 00	1851,	24×36, (16 pages,) Quarto.
City Directory,	Annually,	1 50		Duodecimo.
Annual Register,	Annually,	0 75	1855,	Duodecimo.
Politics and news,	Weekly,	1 50	1837,	25×37, Folio.
Politics and news,	Weekly,	1 50	1830,	26×37, Folio.
News,	Weekly,	1 00	1855,	21×25, Quarto.
News,	Weekly,	1 50	April 4, 1855,	24×35, Folio.
News,	Weekly,	1 50	1837,	24×34, Folio.
	Weekly,	1 50	1854,	25×36, Quarto.
Politics and news,	Weekly,	1 50	1834,	22×32, Folio.
News,	Weekly,	1 50	1849,	25×36, Folio.
News,	Weekly,	1 50	Nov'ber, 1854,	21×31, Folio.
Politics and news,	Weekly,	1 50	1822,	23×32, Folio.
Politics and news,	Weekly,	1 50	1842,	26×38, Folio.
Politics and news,	Weekly,	1 50	1849,	24×33, Folio.
News,	Weekly,	1 50	1840,	25×37, Folio.
News,	Weekly,	1 00	1854,	24×34, Folio.
Politics and news,	Weekly,	1 50	May, 1854,	23×32, Folio.
Politics and news,	Weekly,	1 50	1844,	24×34, Folio.
Politics and news,	Weekly,	1 50	1854,	22×32, Folio.
Politics and news,	Daily,	5 00	1826,	25×36, Folio.
Politics and news,	Tri-weekly,	3 00	1826,	25×36, Folio.
Politics and news,	Weekly,	1 50	1826,	30×47, Folio.
Politics and news,	Daily,	6 00	1845,	28×42, Folio.
Politics and news,	Tri-weekly,	4 00	1845,	28×42, Folio.
Politics and news,	Weekly,	1 00	1845,	30×46, Folio.
Politics and news,	Daily,	6 00	1828,	28×42, Folio.
Politics and news,	Tri-weekly,	4 00	1828,	28×42, Folio.
Politics and news,	Weekly,	2 00	1828,	30×46, Folio.
Politics and news,	Daily,	6 00	1852,	25×36, Folio.
Politics and news,	Tri-weekly,	3 50	1852,	Folio.
Politics and news,	Weekly,	1 50	1852,	28×42, Folio.
Politics and news,	Tri-weekly,	3 00	1854,	21×29, Folio.
Anti-Slavery and news,	Weekly,	2 00	1847,	26×38, Folio.
Religion and news,	Weekly,	1 50	1845,	26×37, Folio.
Agriculture and Horticulture,	Weekly,	2 00	1850,	28×40, Quarto.
Religious,	Semi-weekly,	2 00	1844,	(32 pages,) Octavo.
Religious,	Semi-weekly,	1 00	Novem'r, 1850,	20×28, Quarto.
Agriculture,	Monthly,	0 50	1829,	(32 pages,) Octavo.
Agriculture,	Monthly,	0 50	1850,	(32 pages,) Octavo.
Religious,	Monthly,	0 25	August, 1852,	(8 pages,) Octavo.
City Directory,	Annually,	1 50		Duodecimo
Politics and news,	Weekly,	1 50	May, 1854,	23×33, Folio.
Politics and news,	Weekly,	1 00	1839,	22×32, Folio.
News,	Weekly,	1 25	1853,	24×36, Folio.
Politics and news,	Weekly,	1 00	1855,	28×42, Folio.
Politics and news,	Weekly,	1 50	1847,	25×36, Folio.
Commercial intelligence and news,	Daily,	10 00		30×46, Folio.
Commercial intelligence and news,	Semi-weekly,	4 00		30×45, Folio.
Commercial intelligence and news,	Daily,	9 00	1829,	33×56, Folio.
Commercial intelligence and news,	Semi-weekly,	4 00		30×46, Folio.
News,	Weekly,	2 00		30×52, Folio.

NEWSPAPERS AND OTHER

Where published.	Names of Newspapers and Periodicals.	Editors and Publishers.
NEW-YORK CO.		
New-York,	Courier des Etats-Unis,	Ch. Lasalle,
New-York,	Le Courier des Etats-Unis,	Ch. Lasalle,
New-York,	New-York Day Book,	N. R. Stimson,
New-York,	New-York Weekly Day Book,	N. R. Stimson,
New-York,	New-Yorker Demokrat,	Wm. Schluter,
New-York,	New-Yorker Demokrat,	Wm. Schluter,
New-York,	Dye's Bank Bulletin,	John S. Dye,
New-York,	New-York Express,	James and Erastus Brooks,
New-York,	New-York Express,	James and Erastus Brooks,
New-York,	New-York Express,	James and Erastus Brooks,
New-York,	The New-York Herald,	James Gordon Bennett,
New-York,	The Weekly Herald,	James Gordon Bennett,
New-York,	The New-York Journal of Commerce,	Hallock, Butler & Hale,
New-York.	Journal of Commerce,	Hallock, Butler & Hale,
New-York,	Weekly Journal of Commerce,	Hallock, Butler & Hale,
New-York,	Journal of Commerce, Jr.,	Hallock, Butler & Hale,
New-York,	The Evening Mirror,	Hiram Fuller,
New-York,	The New-York Weekly Mirror,	Hiram Fuller,
New-York,	New-York Daily News,	G. J. Tucker, Editor, McIntyre & Parsons, Publishers,
New-York,	New-York National Democrat,	G. J. Tucker, Editor, McIntyre & Parsons, Publishers,
New-York,	New-Yorker Abend Zeitung,	Friedrich Rauchfast, Publisher, Heman Raster, Editor,
New-York,	Atlantische Blatter,	Friedrich Rauchfast, Publisher, Heman Raster, Editor,
New-York,	New-Yorker Staats-Zeitung,	Anna Uhl,
New-York,	New-Yorker Staats-Zeitung,	Anna Uhl,
New-York,	Sonntagsblatt der N. Y. Staats-Zeitung,	Anna Uhl,
New-York,	The Evening Post,	Wm. C. Bryant and John Bigelow,
New-York,	Semi-Weekly Evening Post,	Wm. C. Bryant and John Bigelow,
New-York,	Weekly Evening Post,	Wm. C. Bryant and John Bigelow,
New-York,	Le Progres,	J. Heilman, Proprietor,
New-York,	The Sun,	Moses S. Beach,
New-York,	The Weekly Sun,	Moses S. Beach,
New-York,	New-York Daily Times,	Raymond, Harper & Co.,
New-York,	New-York Semi-Weekly Times,	Raymond, Harper & Co.,
New-York,	New-York Weekly Times,	Raymond, Harper & Co.,
New-York,	New-York Times for California, &c.,	Raymond, Harper & Co.,
New-York,	New-York Daily Tribune,	Greeley & McElrath,
New-York,	New-York Semi-Weekly Tribune,	Greeley & McElrath,
New-York,	New-York Weekly Tribune,	Greeley & McElrath,
New-York,	New-York Tribune for California, &c.,	Greeley & McElrath,
New-York,	The New-York Mercantile Journal,	Lyon & Hillyer,
New-York,	Shipping and Commercial List and N. Y. Prices Current,	Autens & Bourne,
New-York,	The Albion,	W. Young & Co., Publishers,
New-York,	American Agriculturist,	Allen & Co., Publishers,
New-York,	American Celt,	McGee & Mitchell,
New-York,	The American Mining Chronicle,	M. B. Monck & Co.,
New-York,	America's Own,	E. B. Childs, Editor, Childs Brothers, Publishers,
New-York,	The New-York Atlas,	Herrick & Ropes,
New-York,	American Railroad Journal,	Henry V. Poor, Editor, J. W. Schultz & Co., Publishers,
New-York,	Der New-Yorker Beobachter,	Wm. Schluter,
New-York,	Brother Jonathan,	Benj. H. Day,
New-York,	Christian Advocate and Journal,	Thomas E. Bond & Carlton Philips,
New-York,	The Christian Intelligencer,	Rev. Elbert S. Porter, Editor,
New-York,	Christian Spiritualist,	
New-York,	The Churchman,	John Hecker,
New-York,	The Church Journal,	Rev. John Henry Hopkins, Jr.,
New-York,	The Asmonean,	Robert Lyon, Editor,
New-York,	The Citizen,	John McClanahan,
New-York,	New-York Clipper,	Frank Queen,
New-York,	Carrington's Commissionaire,	J. S. Penn, Editor, Jno. W. Carrington, Proprietor,
New-York,	The Crayon,	W. J. Stillman and J. Durand,
New-York,	New-York Weekly Critic,	Cleveland & McElrath,
New-York,	Criminal Zeitung,	Rudolph Lexow,
New-York,	The New-York Chronicle,	Holman & Gray, Publishers,
New-York,	The New-York Crusader,	G. F. Secchi de Casali,
New-York,	New-York Courier,	James L. Smith & Co.,
New-York,	Y Cymbro Americaidd, (Cambro-American,)	John M. Jones,
New-York,	Deutch Amerikanisches Gewerbe-Blatt,	Heinrich Geyer,
New-York,	Y Drych a'r Gwyliedydd, (Mirror and Watchman,)	Richards & Jones, Publishers,
New-York,	New-York Dispatch,	A. J. Williamson,
New-York,	New-York Dutchman,	E. Weston & Co.,
New-York,	L' Eco d'Italia,	G. F. Secchi de Casali,
New-York,	New-York Evangelist,	Wm. Bradford and H. M. Field, Editors,
New-York,	The Express Messenger,	A. L. Stimson,
New-York,	New-York Freeman's Journal and Catholic Register,	James A. McMaster,
New-York,	The Examiner,	Edw. Bright & Co.,
New-York,	The Home Journal,	Geo. P. Morris and N. P. Willis,
New-York,	The Honest Truth,	M. Doheny, Editor, R. Walsh, Publisher,
New-York,	The Independent,	L. Bacon, R. S. Storrs, Jr., and G. P. Thompson, Editors,
New-York,	The Irish American,	P. Lynch and W. L. Cole,
New-York,	New-York Weekly Leader,	Cleveland & McElrath,
New-York,	New-York Ledger,	R. Bonner,
New-York,	Leonori's New-York Bank Note List,	L. J. Leonori,
New-York,	Mercantile Guide and Family Journal,	Wm. E. Blakeney,
New-York,	Life Illustrated,	Fowler & Wells,
New-York,	Mirror of Fashion,	Genio C. Scott,
New-York,	The Mormon,	John Taylor,
New-York,	Musical World,	R. S. Willis,
New-York,	National Anti-Slavery Standard,	Am. Anti-Slavery Society,
New-York,	National Police Gazette,	Robert A Seymour,
New-York,	New-York Observer,	Sidney E. Morse & Co.,
New-York,	New-York Path Finder,	John F. Whitney,
New-York,	New-York Peoples' Organ,	James Mackean,
New-York,	New-York Family Herald,	James Warnock,

PERIODICALS.—(CONTINUED.)

To what object devoted.	At what intervals published.	Subscription price per annum.	When established.	Size in inches, and form.
Literature and news,	Daily,	$8 00	1828,	21×30, Folio.
Literature and news,	Weekly,	4 00		(16 pages,) Quarto.
Politics and news,	Daily,	6 00	1849,	22×32, Folio.
Politics and news,	Weekly,	2 00	1849,	Quarto.
Politics and news,	Daily,	5 00	1847,	24×38, Folio.
Politics and news,	Weekly,	2 50	1847,	38×48, Quarto.
Broken bank detector,	Daily,	5 00	1855,	26×37, Folio.
Commerce and politics,	Daily,	7 00	1855,	Folio.
Commerce and politics,	Semi-weekly,	......	1855,	Folio.
Commerce and politics,	Weekly,	......	1855,	Folio.
News,	Daily,	7 00	1835,	32×45, Quarto.
News,	Weekly,	3 00	1837,	32×45, Quarto.
News, commerce, &c.,	Daily,	10 00	1827,	32×52, Folio.
News, commerce, &c.,	Semi-weekly,	4 00	1827,	32×52, Folio.
News, commerce, &c.,	Weekly,	2 00	1827,	32×52, Folio.
News, commerce, &c.,	Daily,	5 00		24×34, Folio.
News, &c.,	Daily,	6 00	1844,	23×31, Folio.
Literature and Politics,	Weekly,	1 00	1828,	25×38, Folio.
News, &c.,	Daily,	4 00	1855,	23×31, Folio.
Politics and news,	Weekly,	1 50	1855,	31×46, Quarto
News,	Daily,	5 00		28×38, Folio.
News,	Weekly,	1 00		19×26, Folio.
Political,	Daily,	5 00	1834,	Folio.
Political,	Weekly,	2 50	1834,	28×40, Folio.
News,	Weekly,	1 00	1848,	23×30, Folio.
General news,	Daily,	10 00	1802,	31×46, Folio.
General news,	Semi-weekly,	3 00	1802,	31×46, Folio.
General news,	Weekly,	2 00	1802,	31×46, Folio.
Literature and news,	Daily,	8 00	1853,	21×29, Folio.
News,	Daily,	3 00	1833,	24×35, Folio.
News,	Weekly,	0 75	1836,	24×35, Folio.
Politics and news,	Daily,	6 00	1851,	34×44, Quarto
Politics and news,	Semi-weekly,	3 00	1851,	34×44, Quarto
Politics and news,	Weekly,	2 00	1851,	34×44, Quarto
Politics and news,	Semi-monthly,	2 00	1851,	34×44, Quarto
Politics and news,	Daily,	6 00	1841,	34×44, Quarto
Politics and news,	Semi-weekly,	3 00	1842,	34×44, Quarto
Politics and news,	Weekly,	2 00	1841,	34×44, Quarto
Politics and news,	Semi-monthly,	1 50	1849,	34×44, Quarto
Commercial news,	Tri-weekly,	5 00		25×38, Folio.
Commercial news,	Semi-weekly,	7 00	1798,	29×44, Quarto
British news and literature,	Weekly,	6 00	1822,	Page 13×18, (12 pages,) Quarto
Agriculture,	Weekly,	2 00		Page 9×13, (16 pages,) Quarto
Politics and religion,	Weekly,	2 00	1850,	Folio.
Mining and iron manufacture,	Weekly,	3 00		25×36, Quarto
News, &c.,	Weekly,	2 00	1849,	Folio.
News, Literature, &c.,	Weekly,	2 00	1836,	30×46, Folio.
Railroads, &c.,	Weekly,	5 00	1831,	Page 9×11, (28 pages,) Quarto.
General miscellany,	Weekly,	1 50		25×34, Folio.
General miscellany,	Weekly,	1 00		27×38, Folio.
Religion and morals,	Weekly,	1 25	1826,	Folio.
Religion and morals,	Weekly,	2 00	1830,	28×44, Folio.
Spiritualism,	Weekly,	2 00	1854,	24×36, Folio.
Religion,	Weekly,	3 00	1832,	35×46, Quarto.
Religion,	Weekly,	3 00	1853,	26×38, Quarto.
Jewish interests,	Weekly,	3 00		24×38, Quarto.
Irish American news,	Weekly,	3 00	1854,	32×48, (16 pages,) Quarto.
Sporting intelligence,	Weekly,	1 50	1853,	24×36, Folio.
General literature,	Weekly,	......	1855,	12×20, Quarto.
Fine arts,	Weekly,	3 00	1855,	Page 9×11, (16 pages,) Quarto.
News and literature,	Weekly,	2 00	1855,	26×38, Folio.
Criminal intelligence,	Weekly,	3 50	1851,	Folio.
Religious intelligence,	Weekly,	......		29×44, Folio.
Anti-Jesuitical,	Weekly,	2 00	1853,	24×32, Folio.
News, &c.,	Weekly,	2 00		32×45, Folio.
News, (English and Welch,)	Weekly,	1 00	1855,	21×26, Folio.
Mechanics,	Weekly,	2 00	1855,	18×26, Quarto.
Religion,	Weekly,	1 50	1854,	26×36, Folio.
Literature and general news,	Weekly,	2 00	1846,	36×54, Quarto.
General news,	Weekly,	2 00	1848,	28×40, Folio.
Italian politics and news,	Weekly,	4 00	1849,	19×26, Folio.
Religious intelligence,	Weekly,	2 00	1830,	28×44, Folio.
General literature,	Weekly,	1 25		24×34, Folio.
Religion,	Weekly,	2 50	1839,	32×50, Quarto.
Religious intelligence,	Weekly,	2 00		28×40, Folio.
Literature and news,	Weekly,	2 00	1846,	26×36, Folio.
Irish American news,	Weekly,	1 50	1855,	24×32, Quarto.
Religious intelligence,	Weekly,	2 00	1848,	34×50, Quarto.
Politics, literature and news,	Weekly,	1 50	1849,	26×38, Folio.
General news,	Weekly,	2 00	1853,	26×38, Folio.
News,	Weekly,	1 00	1846,	28×42, Folio.
Counterfeit detector,	Weekly,	2 50	1850,	Page 8×12, (24 pages,) Quarto.
Mercantile news,	Weekly,	1 00	1852,	26×38, Folio.
Literature and news,	Weekly,	2 00		24×36, Quarto.
Fashions,	Weekly,	3 00	1840,	Quarto.
Mormonism and politics,	Weekly,	2 00	1855,	26×40, Folio.
Music,	Weekly,	......		Page 9×11, (16 pages,) Quarto.
Anti-slavery,	Weekly,	2 00	1840,	Folio.
Criminal reports, &c.,	Weekly,	2 00	1845,	26×40, Folio.
Religious intelligence,	Weekly,	2 50	1823,	36×48, Quarto.
Railroads, &c.,	Weekly,	1 00	1847,	23×32, Folio.
Temperance,	Weekly,	1 00	1842,	20×28, Quarto.
General literature,	Weekly,	......		Page 8×12, (16 pages,) Quarto.

NEWSPAPERS AND OTHER

Where published.	Names of Newspapers and Periodicals.	Editors and Proprietors
New-York Co.		
New-York,	New-York Picayune,	Wm. H. Levison,
New-York,	New-York Recorder and Register,	E. Bright, Jr., & L. S. Cutting,
New-York,	New-York Sunday Courier,	J. F. Smith & Co.,
New-York,	The Sunday Leader,	Ingraham & Sweet,
New-York,	Protestant Churchman,	H. Anthon, S. H. Tyng, and E. H. Canfield,
New-York,	El Pueblo,	Francis Aquero Estrata,
New-York,	Real Estate Gazette,	Joseph Barlow,
New-York,	Sabbath Recorder,	G. B. Utter, Editor,
New-York,	Scientific American,	Munn & Co.,
New-York,	Spirit of the Times,	Wm. T. Porter, Editor, John Richards, Publisher,
New-York,	Spiritual Telegraph,	Partridge & Britton,
New-York,	Sunday Mercury,	Krauth & Caldwell,
New-York,	Sunday Times and Noah's Weekly Messenger,	Noah, Deans & Howard,
New-York	Thompson's Bank Note and Commercial Reporter,	J. F. Thompson,
New-York,	True American,	Wm. E. Blackeny,
New-York,	United States Economist,	T. P. Kettell, Editor,
New-York,	United States Military and Naval Argus,	John Crawley, Editor,
New-York,	The United States Mining Journal,	Lyon & Hillyer,
New-York,	La Verdad,	P. Santacilia, Editor,
New-York,	Advocate and Family Guardian,	Mrs. Sarah Bennett,
New-York,	Bible Examiner,	George Storrs,
New-York,	Dye's Bank Mirror,	John S. Dye,
New-York,	Der Lutherische Herold,	Henry Ludwig,
New-York,	New-York Musical Review and Gazette,	Mason Brothers,
New-York,	Sunday School Advocate,	D. P. Kidder,
New-York,	Sunday School Journal,	F. A. Packard,
New-York,	Youth's Penny Gazette,	F. A. Packard,
New-York,	Americanischer Botschafter,	Rev. W. A. Halleck,
New-York,	American Messenger,	Am. Tract Society,
New-York,	American and Foreign Christian Union,	Am. and F. C. U.,
New-York,	American Journal of Photography,	Charles A. Seeley, Editor and Proprietor,
New-York,	American Medical Monthly,	E. H. Parker, Editor, E. P. Allen, Publisher,
New-York,	American Medical Gazette,	E. Meredith Reese, Editor, J. A. Dix, Publisher,
New-York,	American National Preacher,	E. Carpenter,
New-York,	American Missionary,	Am. Missionary Association,
New-York,	American Phrenological Journal,	Fowler & Wells,
New-York,	The Banker's Magazine and Statistical Register,	J. Smith Homans,
New-York,	The Bible Union Reporter,	Wm. H. Wyckoff and C. A. Buckbee,
New-York,	Blackwood's Edinburgh Magazine,	L. Scott, Publisher, (re-print,)
New-York,	The Carrier Dove,	Com. of Board Missions P. E. Church,
New-York,	Chamber's Journal,	Bunce & Bro., Publishers, (re-print,)
New-York,	The Child's Paper,	Am. Tract Society,
New-York,	The Children's Magazine,	P. E. S. S. Union,
New-York,	The Christian Diadem,	Z. Patten Hatch, Editor and Proprietor,
New-York,	Churchmen's Monthly Magazine,	Rev. B. T. Onderdonk, Editor,
New-York,	New-York Colonization Journal,	Rev. J. B. Pinney,
New-York,	The New Charitable Monthly,	W. C. Conant, Editor,
New-York,	Commercial Register,	Franklin Woods,
New-York,	Y Cylchgrawn Cenedlaethol,	John M. Jones,
New-York,	The Dime,	Leland, Clay & Co.,
New-York,	New-York Dental Recorder,	Charles W. Ballard,
New-York,	Dinsmore's Railway Guide,	Dinsmore & Co.,
New-York,	Disturnel's Railroad Guide,	J. Disturnel,
New-York,	The Dressmakers' and Milliners' Guide,	S. T. Taylor, Publisher,
New-York,	The Eclectic Magazine,	W. H. Bidwell,
New-York,	The Foreign Missionary,	Board F. M. of Presbyterian Ch.,
New-York,	Frank Leslie's New-York Journal	Frank Leslie,
New-York,	Frank Leslie's Gazette of Fashions,	Frank Leslie,
New-York,	Hall's Journal of Health,	W. W. Hall, Editor,
New-York,	Harpers' New Monthly Magazine,	Harper & Brothers,
New-York,	Harpers' Story Book,	Harper & Brothers,
New-York,	The Home Missionary,	Am. Home Missionary Soc.,
New-York,	Home Mission Record,	Am. Baptist H. M. Soc.,
New-York,	The Home Circle,	Garret & Co.,
New-York,	Hunt's Merchants' Magazine and Commercial Review,	Freeman Hunt,
New-York,	Humphrey's Journal,	S. D. Humphrey,
New-York,	The Insurance Monitor,	F. Jones, Jr.,
New-York,	The Jewish Chronicle,	R. E. McGregor,
New-York,	Journal of the American Temperance Union,	Rev. J. Marsh, Editor,
New-York,	The Journal of Medical Reform,	J. M. Comings, Editor,
New-York,	The N. Y. Journal of Medicine and Collateral Science,	S. S. Purple, and S. Smith, Editors,
New-York,	The Knickerbocker Monthly Magazine,	L. G. Clark, Editor, S. Heuston, Publisher,
New-York,	Ladies' Keepsake and Home Library,	Burdick & Scovill,
New-York,	The Ladies' Repository,	D. W. Clark, Editor,
New-York,	Ladies' Wreath and Parlor Annual,	Burdick & Scovill,
New-York,	Livingston's Monthly Law Magazine,	John Livingston,
New-York,	The London Lancet,	Stringer & Townsend, Publishers, (re-print,)
New-York,	The Masonic Register and Union,	J. F. Adams, Editor,
New-York,	New-York Medical Times,	H. D. Bulkley, Editor,
New-York,	Merry's Museum and Parley's Magazine,	S. T. Allen & Co., Publishers,
New-York,	Mining Magazine,	Wm. J. Tenney,
New-York,	Missionary Advocate,	J. P. Durbin,
New-York,	The Missionary Herald,	Board of Missions,
New-York,	Monthly Record of Prison Association,	Com. of Prison Association,
New-York,	Monthly Trade Gazette,	G. S. Wells,
New-York,	The Mother's Magazine and Family Monitor,	S. T. Allen,
New-York,	Musical Pioneer,	J. P. Woodbury,
New-York,	National Magazine,	Abel Stevens, Editor,
New-York,	Nichols' Monthly,	Tho. L. Nichols,
New-York,	The Parish Visitor,	Rev. C. W. Adams,
New-York,	The Plow, the Loom and the Anvil,	Moses P. Parish,
New-York,	Putnam's Monthly,	Dix & Edwards, Publishers,
New-York,	Reports of Practice Cases in New-York Courts,	Abbott Brothers, Editors,

PERIODICALS.—(CONTINUED.)

To what object devoted.	At what intervals published.	Subscription price per annum.	When established.	Size in inches, and form.
Comic illustrations, &c.,	Weekly,	$1 00	1849,	23×32, Folio.
Religious intelligence,	Weekly,	2 00	1845,	Folio.
General news,	Weekly,	2 00	1845,	Folio.
General news,	Weekly,	1 00	1855,	Folio
Religious intelligence,	Weekly,	2 50		26×40, Quarto.
Liberty in general,	Weekly,	......	1855,	Quarto.
Real estate,	Weekly,	2 00	1855,	Quarto.
Religious intelligence,	Weekly,	2 00	1844,	24×34, Folio.
Science and mechanics,	Weekly,	2 00	1845,	24×32, Quarto.
The turf, and sporting literature,	Weekly,	5 00	1831,	Page 13×19, (12 pages,) Quarto.
Spiritualism,	Weekly,	2 00		24×36, Folio.
General news,	Weekly,	1 00	1839,	29×42, Folio.
General literature,	Weekly,	1 00	1840,	Folio.
Bank note list, and commercial news,	Weekly,	2 50	1840,	Page 8×11, (40 pages,) Quarto.
Politics and news,	Weekly,	2 00	1853,	Folio.
Commercial news,	Weekly,	5 00	1852,	30×44, Folio.
Military intelligence,	Weekly,	2 00	1838,	26×38, Folio.
Mining intelligence,	Weekly,	3 00		24×38, Quarto.
Spanish news,	Weekly,	Gratis.		19×38, Folio.
Home of the friendless,	Semi-monthly,	1 00	1834,	20×28, Quarto.
Religion,	Semi-monthly,	1 00	1844,	Octavo.
Bank note list,	Semi-monthly,	2 00		Page 7×11, (32 pages,) Quarto.
Religious intelligence,	Semi-monthly,	1 00	1850,	24×38, Quarto.
Music,	Semi-monthly,	1 00		Page 9×12, (16 pages,) Quarto.
Sunday schools,	Semi-monthly,	30	1841,	Page 10×13, (8 pages,) Quarto.
Sunday schools,	Semi-monthly,	25	1829,	Page 9×11, (8 pages,) Quarto.
Sunday schools,	Semi-monthly,	25	1843,	Page 10×13, (4 pages,) Quarto.
Religious intelligence,	Monthly,	25	1847,	Folio.
Religious intelligence,	Monthly,	25	1843,	22×30, Folio.
Religious intelligence,	Monthly,	1 00		Octavo.
Photography,	Monthly,	1 00		Octavo.
Medical science,	Monthly,	3 00	1854,	Octavo.
Medical science,	Monthly,	2 00		Octavo.
Sermons,	Monthly,	1 00	1826,	Octavo.
Missions,	Monthly,	......		18×36, Quarto.
Phrenology,	Monthly,	1 00		Page 9×12, (24 pages,) Quarto.
Banking,	Monthly,	5 00		Octavo.
Religious intelligence,	Monthly,	1 00		Octavo.
Literature,	Monthly,	3 00	1816,	Octavo.
Missions,	Monthly,	25		Page 10×14, (4 pages,) Quarto.
Literature,	Monthly,	1 50		Octavo.
Juvenile anecdotes, &c.,	Monthly,	10	1852,	Page 10×14, (4 pages,) Quarto.
Sunday schools,	Monthly,	37		18mo.
Religious intelligence,	Monthly,	1 10		Octavo.
Missions,	Monthly,	2 00	1824,	Octavo.
Colonization,	Monthly,	50	1832,	31×42, Folio.
Five Points Mission,	Monthly,	50		Octavo.
Commerce and agriculture,	Monthly,	50	1855,	36×54, Quarto.
Commerce and agriculture,	Monthly,	......		Octavo.
Illustrated family paper,	Monthly,	1 00	1854,	Octavo.
Dental science,	Monthly,	2 00		Octavo.
Railroad guide,	Monthly,	1 50		18mo.
Railroad guide,	Monthly,	1 50		18mo.
Fashions,	Monthly,	5 00	1842,	Page 9×11, Quarto.
Literature,	Monthly,	5 00	1841,	Octavo.
Foreign missions,	Monthly,	50		Octavo.
Literature,	Monthly,	2 00		Page 9×13, Quarto.
Fashions,	Monthly,	3 00	1853,	Page 10×13, Quarto.
Medicine and hygiene,	Monthly,	1 00	1854,	Octavo.
General literature,	Monthly,	3 00		Octavo.
Stories for children,	Monthly,	3 00	1850,	12mo.
Home missions,	Monthly,	1 50	1854,	Octavo.
Home missions,	Monthly,	25	1826,	20×24, Folio.
Literature,	Monthly,	25		25×36, Folio.
Commerce and trade,	Monthly,	5 00	1854,	Octavo.
Photography,	Monthly,	2 00	1839,	Octavo.
Insurance,	Monthly,	1 00		Page 9×12, Quarto.
Missions to Jews,	Monthly,	1 00		Octavo.
Temperance,	Monthly,	1 00	1844,	Quarto.
Medical reform,	Monthly,	1 00		Octavo.
Medical science,	Monthly,	3 00		Octavo.
Literature,	Monthly,	5 00		Octavo.
Literature,	Monthly,	1 00		Octavo.
Literature and religion,	Monthly,	2 00	1851,	Octavo.
Literature,	Monthly,	1 00		Octavo.
Law,	Monthly,	3 00	1846,	Octavo.
Medical science,	Monthly,	5 00	1845,	Octavo.
Free masonry,	Monthly,	2 00		Octavo.
Medical science,	Monthly,	2 00		Octavo.
Juvenile literature,	Monthly,	1 00	1841,	Octavo.
Mining,	Monthly,	5 00	1853,	Quarto.
Missions,	Monthly,	10	1845,	Quarto.
Foreign missions,	Monthly,	1 00		Octavo.
Prisons,	Monthly,	......		Octavo.
Trade,	Monthly,	50	1855,	Page 9×12, Quarto.
Home education,	Monthly,	1 00	1833,	Octavo.
Music,	Monthly,	50	1855,	Octavo.
Literature and religion,	Monthly,	2 00	1852,	Octavo.
Social science and progressive literature,	Monthly,	1 00	1855,	12mo.
Religious intelligence,	Monthly,	25	1852,	22×32, Folio.
Agriculture,	Monthly,	3 00	1848,	Octavo
Art and literature,	Monthly,	3 00	1853,	Octavo
Law cases,	Monthly,	6 00		Octavo

NEWSPAPERS AND OTHER

Where published.	Names of Newspapers and Periodicals.	Editors and Publishers
NEW-YORK CO.		
New-York,	Republic der Arbeiter,	Wm. Weitting,
New-York,	Reviser,	Rev. Silas E. Shepherd,
New-York,	Sabbath School Visitor,	Seventh Day Baptist Soc.,
New-York,	The School Fellow,	J. S. Dickerson,
New-York,	The School Mate,	A. R. Phippen,
New-York,	The Sailor's Magazine,	Am. Seamen's Friend Soc.,
New-York,	The Sacred Circle,	Judge Edmonds, Dr. Dexter and O. G. Warren,
New-York,	The Spirit of Missions,	Missionary Com. of P. E. Ch. M.,
New-York,	The Standard Bearer,	Rev. H. Dyer,
New-York,	United States Insurance Gazette and Magazine,	G. E. Currie,
New-York,	United States Journal,	J. M. Emmerson & Co.,
New-York,	United States Magazine,	J. M. Emmerson & Co.,
New-York,	United States Nautical Magazine and Naval Journal,	Griffiths, Bates & Co.,
New-York,	United States Review, "Democracy,"	Lloyd & Campbell,
New-York,	The Water Cure Journal,	Fowler & Wells,
New-York,	Mrs. Whittlesey's Magazine,	A. G. Whittlesey, Editor, Z. P. Hatch, Publisher,
New-York,	Woodworth's Youth's Cabinet,	Francis C. Woodworth, Editor,
New-York,	Working Farmer,	J. J. Mapes, Editor, F. McCready, Publisher,
New-York,	Yankee Notions,	Thomas W. Strong,
New-York,	The Young Christian,	
New-York,	Youth's Temperance Advocate,	Am. Temp. Union,
New-York,	The British Medico-Chirugical Review,	S. S. & W. Wood, Publishers, (re-print,)
New-York,	Christian Review,	James Woolsly,
New-York,	The Edinburgh Review,	L. Scott, Publisher, (re-print,)
New-York,	The Forcep,	N. Y. Teeth Manufac. Co., Publishers,
New York,	The London Quarterly Review,	L. Scott, Publisher, (re-print,)
New-York,	Methodist Quarterly Review,	J. McClintock, Editor,
New-York,	The New-York Quarterly,	Jas. G. Reed, Publisher,
New-York,	The North American Homœopathic Journal,	Wm. Radde, Publisher,
New-York,	The North British Review,	L. Scott, Publisher, (re-print,)
New-York,	Periodical Paper of Am. and F. Bible Soc.,	Am. and F. Bible Soc.,
New-York,	The Protestant Episcopal Quarterly Review,	H. Dyer, Publisher,
New-York,	The Scalpel,	Edward H. Dixon, Editor,
New-York,	The Westminster Review,	L. Scott, Publisher, (re-print,)
New-York,	Braithwaite's Retrospect of Practical Medicine and Surg'y,	Stringer & Townsend, Publishers, (re-print,)
New-York,	Scott's Report of Fashions,	Genio C. Scott,
New-York,	American Portrait Gallery,	J. M. Emmerson & Co.,
New-York,	American Turf Register,	John Richards, Publisher,
New-York,	New-York City Directory,	John F. Trow,
NIAGARA CO.		
Lockport,	Lockport Daily Advertiser,	A. S. Prentiss,
Lockport,	Lockport Daily Courier,	Pomeroy & Fox,
Lockport,	The Niagara Courier,	Pomeroy & Fox,
Lockport,	Lockport Daily Journal,	M. C. Richardson,
Lockport,	The Lockport Journal,	M. C. Richardson,
Lockport,	The Niagara Democrat,	John Campbell,
Niagara,	Niagara Falls Gazette,	Wm. Pool and Benj. F. Sleeper,
ONEIDA CO		
Boonville,	Black River Herald,	L. C. Childs,
Kirkland,	Oneida Chief, (Clinton,)	F. E. Merritt,
Kirkland,	The Northern Farmer, (Clinton,)	T. B. Miner,
Rome,	Y Cyfaill, [The Friend—Welch,]	Wm. Rowland and Thomas Jenkins,
Rome,	The Rome Excelsior,	O. B. & E. W. Pierce,
Rome,	The Roman Citizen,	Alfred Sandford,
Rome,	The Daily Sentinel,	Wager & Rowley,
Rome,	The Rome Sentinel,	Wager & Rowley,
Sangerfield,	Waterville Journal,	C. B. Wilkinson, Editor, N. Whitney, Publisher,
Steuben,	Y Cenhadwr Americanidd,	Rev. Robert Everett,
Utica,	Utica Morning Herald,	Ellis H. Roberts,
Utica,	Oneida Weekly Herald,	Ellis H. Roberts,
Utica,	Utica Daily Observer,	De Witt C. Grove, Publisher,
Utica,	Observer and Democrat,	De Witt C. Grove, Publisher,
Utica,	Utica Evening Telegraph,	Thomas R. McQuade & Co.,
Utica,	The American Baptist,	Wareham Walker, Editor,
Utica,	The Gospel Messenger and Church Record of Western New-York,	Rev. Wm. A. Mattoon, Editor, De Witt C. Grove, Publisher,
Utica,	The Utica Teetotaler,	Wesley Bailey, Editor,
Utica,	The Opal,	Inmates of State Lunatic Asylum,
Utica,	Journal of Insanity,	Officers of Lunatic Asylum,
Utica,	Utica City Directory,	William E. Richards,
Vernon,	The Circular, (Oneida,)	George W. Noyes, Editor,
Vernon,	Vernon Transcript,	John R. Howlett,
ONONDAGA CO.		
Elbridge,	The Jordan Transcript,	Nathan Burrell, Jr.,
Lysander,	Onondaga Gazette, (Baldwinsville,)	C. M. Hosmer and J. M. Clark,
Skaneateles,	Skaneateles Democrat,	Harrison B. Dodge,
Syracuse,	Syracuse Evening Chronicle,	S. G. Arnold, Editor, S. H. Clark, Publisher,
Syracuse,	The Weekly Chronicle,	S. G. Arnold, Editor, S. H. Clark, Publisher,
Syracuse,	Syracuse Daily Journal,	Andrew Shuman, Editor, J. G. K. Truair, Publisher,
Syracuse,	Syracuse Weekly Journal,	Andrew Shuman, Editor, J. G. K. Truair, Publisher,
Syracuse,	Syracuse Daily Standard,	Agan & Summers,
Syracuse,	Onondaga Standard,	Agan & Summers,
Syracuse,	Onondaga Demokrat, (German,)	Geo. Saul and Charles Hoffendahl,
Syracuse,	Syracuser Zeitung, (German,)	Otto Reventlow,
Syracuse,	The Syracusean and United States Review,	William H. Moseley,
Syracuse,	The Wesleyan,	Lucius C. Matlock, Editor and Agent,
Syracuse,	The Unionist,	Prime & Stickney,
Syracuse,	The Reformer,	Prime & Stickney, Editors, S. H. Clark, Publishers,
Syracuse,	The World's Advocate,	Ross & Gurneer,
Syracuse,	The American Medical and Surgical Journal,	S. H. Potter and E. H. Stockwell,
Syracuse,	Juvenile Instructor,	L. C. Matlack,
Syracuse,	Syracuse City Directory,	

PERIODICALS.—(Continued.)

To what object devoted.	At what intervals published.	Subscription price per annum.	When established.	Size in inches, and form.
Reform,	Monthly,	$2 00	1850,	Octavo.
Notes on the Bible,	Monthly,	1 00	1854,	Octavo.
Religious intelligence,	Monthly,	0 25	1850,	Page 10×13, (4 pages,) ... Quarto.
Education,	Monthly,	1 00		12mo.
Education,	Monthly,	1 00	1850,	12mo.
Moral improvement of seamen,	Monthly,	1 00		Octavo.
Spiritualism,	Mouthly,	2 00		Octavo.
Missions,	Monthly,	1 00	1836,	Octavo.
Juvenile religious anecdotes, &c.,	Monthly,	0 25	1852,	18mo.
Insurance,	Monthly,	3 00		Octavo,
General news,	Monthly,	0 25	1849,	36×50, Quarto.
Arts, manufactures, &c.,	Monthly,	1 00	1854,	Page 9×12, (32 pages,) Quarto.
Nautical intelligence and science,	Monthly,	5 00		Octavo.
Literature and Politics,	Monthly,	5 00		Octavo.
Hydropathy, physiology, &c.,	Monthly,	1 00		Page 9×12, (12 pages,) Quarto.
Literature and education,	Monthly	1 00		Octavo.
Instruction and amusement,	Monthly,	1 00	1839,	12mo.
Agriculture,	Monthly,	1 00	1849,	Quarto.
Comic illustrations,	Monthly,	1 25	1852,	Quarto.
Religion,	Monthly	......		Page 10×13, (4 pages,) Quarto.
Temperance,	Monthly,	0 25		Page 9×12, (4 pages.) Quarto.
Practical medicine and surgery,	Quarterly,	3 00		Octavo.
Religious literature,	Quarterly,	3 00	1835,	Octavo.
Literature,	Quarterly,	3 00	1804,	Octavo.
Dentistry,	Quarterly,	1 00		Octavo.
Literature,	Quarterly,	3 00	1807,	Octavo.
Literature,	Quarterly,	2 00	1818,	Octavo.
Literature,	Quarterly,	3 00		Octavo.
Homœopathy,	Quarterly,	2 00		Octavo.
Literature,	Quarterly,	3 00		Octavo.
Bible cause,	Quarterly,	......	1838,	Octavo.
Literature,	Quarterly,	3 00		Octavo.
Laws of health, &c.,	Quarterly,	1 00		Octavo.
Literature,	Quarterly,	3 00		Octavo.
Medical science,	Semi-annually,	2 00	1840,	Octavo.
Fashions,	Semi-annually,	3 00	1825,	Octavo.
Biography, &c.,	Annually,	......	1852,	Octovo.
Sporting, &c.,	Annually,	1 00	1829,	Octavo.
City Directory,	Annually,	2 50	1852,	Octavo.
Advertising,	Daily,	Gratis.	1854,	10×16, Folio.
Politics and news,	Daily,	5 00	1840,	22×32, Folio.
Politics and news,	Weekly,	1 50	1828,	27×42, Folio.
Politics and news,	Daily,	5 00	1852,	22×32, Folio.
Politics and news,	Weekly,	1 50	1851,	28×42, Folio.
Politics and news,	Weekly,	1 50	1821,	24×36, Folio.
News,	Weekly,	1 50	1854,	23×34, Folio.
Politics and news,	Weekly,	1 50	1851,	23×32, Folio.
News,	Weekly,	1 00	1851,	22×32, Folio.
Agriculture,	Monthly,	1 00	1851,	(48 pages,) Octavo.
Religion,	Monthly,	1 50	1838,	(36 pages,) Octavo.
Temperance and freedom,	Weekly,	1 25	1852,	Folio.
Politics and news,	Weekly,	1 75	1840,	28×40, Folio.
Politics and news,	Daily,	5 00	1852,	24×36, Folio.
Politics and news,	Weekly,	1 50	1837,	28×42, Folio.
News,	Weekly,	1 25	January, 1855,	Folio.
Religion,	Monthly,	1 50	1840,	(40 pages,) Octavo.
Politics and news,	Daily,	5 00	Nov'ber, 1851,	26×38, Folio.
Politics and news,	Weekly,	1 50	Nov'ber, 1851,	28×42, Folio.
Politics and news,	Daily,	5 00	1848,	24×36, Folio.
Politics and news,	Weekly,	1 25	1816,	26×36, Folio.
News,	Daily,	3 50	1853,	21×31, Folio.
Religion and news,	Weekly,	1 50	1854,	26×38, Folio.
Religion and news,	Weekly,	2 00	1825,	24×36, Folio.
Temperance and news,	Weekly,	1 00	1849,	24×36, Folio
Miscellaneous,	Weekly,	1 00		Octavo.
Insanity,	Quarterly,	3 00		Octavo.
City Directory,	Annually,	1 00	1817,	12mo.
Socialism,	Weekly,	1 00	1851,	18×24, Folio.
News,	Weekly,	1 00	1850,	23×32, Quarto.
News,	Weekly,	1 25	January, 1853,	22×30, Folio.
Politics and news,	Weekly,	1 00	1846,	22×32, Folio.
Politics and news,	Weekly,	1 50	1840,	24×36, Folio.
Politics and news,	Daily,	5 00	1854,	24×36, Folio.
Politics and news,	Weekly,	1 00	1854,	25×37, Folio.
Politics and news,	Daily,	5 00	1844,	25×37, Folio.
Politics and news,	Weekly,	1 25	1839,	25×37, Folio.
Politics and news,	Daily,	5 00	1850,	24×36, Folio.
Politics and news,	Weekly,	1 50	1825,	28×42, Folio.
Politics and news,	Weekly,	2 00	1852,	22×32, Folio.
Politics and news,	Weekly,	2 00	Aug. 15, 1855,	22×33, Folio.
News,	Monthly,	1 00	1848,	20×27, Folio.
Religious intelligence,	Weekly,	1 50	1843,	26×37, Folio.
Religious intelligence,	Monthly,	0 25	1854,	(Discontinued,) Folio.
Religious intelligence,	Weekly,	1 50	1854,	26×37, Folio.
Medical advertisements,	Semi-monthly,	0 25	1855,	Folio.
Medical,	Monthly,	2 00	1853,	(40 pages,) Octavo.
Religion,	Semi-monthly,	0 25	1843,	12×19, Folio
Religion,	Annually,	......		12mo.

NEWSPAPERS AND OTHER

Where published.	Names of Newspapers and Periodicals.	Editors and Proprietors.
ONTARIO Co.		
Canandaigua,	The Ontario Messenger,	Jacob J. Mattison,
Canandaigua,	The Ontario Repository,	George L. Whitney,
Canandaigua,	The Ontario Times,	Wilson Miller,
Phelps,	The Western Atlas,	Washington Shaw,
Seneca,	Geneva Courier,	William Johnson,
Seneca,	The Geneva Gazette,	Stephen H. Parker and Geo. M. Horton,
Seneca,	Geneva Independent and Fireman's Gazette,	William K. Fowle,
ORANGE Co.		
Deerpark,	The Tri-States Union, (Port Jervis,)	James H. Norton,
Goshen,	Independent Republican,	James J. McNally,
Goshen,	Goshen Democrat and Whig,	Mead & Webb,
Newburgh,	Highland Courier,	William E. Smiley,
Newburgh,	The Newburgh American,	R. P. L. Shafer & Co.,
Newburgh,	Newburgh Gazette,	William L. Allison,
Newburgh,	Newburgh Telegraph,	Ed. M. Ruttenber,
Newburgh,	Literary Scrap Book,	R. Denton,
Wallkill,	Banner of Liberty, (Middletown,)	Gilbert Judson Beebee,
Wallkill,	The Whig Press, (Middletown,)	John W. Hasbrouck,
Wallkill,	Signs of the Times, (Middletown,)	Gilbert Beebee,
Wallkill,	The Separate American or Quarterly Review, (Middlet'n,)	David James,
ORLEANS Co.		
Barre,	Orleans American, (Albion,)	S. A. Andrews and E. R. Reynolds,
Barre,	The Orleans Republican, (Albion,)	J. O. Willsea and C. G. Beach,
Barre,	Spirit of Seventy-Six, (Albion,)	J. O. Nickerson and Miss M. A. Barnum, Eds., J. O. Nickerson, Pub.
Ridgeway,	The Medina Tribune,	Harvey A. Smith,
Ridgeway,	The People's Journal,	J. W. Swan, Editor,
OSWEGO Co.		
Oswego city,	Oswego Daily Palladium,	W. N. Oswell and Z. P. Ottaway, Publisher, D. Farling and W.
Oswego city,	Oswego Weekly Palladium,	N. Oswell, Editors,
Oswego city,	Oswego Times and Journal,	Winchester & Ferguson, Publishers, C. Hull, Editor,
Oswego city,	Weekly Times and Journal,	Winchester & Ferguson, Publishers, C. Hull, Editor,
Richland,	The Pulaski Democrat,	J. C. Hatch,
Schroeppel,	American Banner and Oswego Co. Organ, (Phœnix,)	James H. Field,
Volney,	Oswego County Gazette,	George E. Williams,
Volney,	Fulton Patriot, (Fulton,)	T. S. Brigham,
OTSEGO Co.		
Morris,	The Village Advertiser,	H. S. Avery,
Oneonta,	The Oneonta Herald,	L. P. Carpenter,
Otsego,	The Freeman's Journal, (Cooperstown,)	S. M. Shaw,
Otsego,	The Otsego Democrat, (Cooperstown,)	James I. Hendryx,
Otsego,	Otsego Examiner, (Cooperstown,)	B. W. Burditt,
Otsego,	Otsego Republican, (Cooperstown,)	A. M. Barber,
Cherry Valley,	Cherry Valley Gazette,	Amos Botsford,
PUTNAM Co.		
Carmel,	Putnam County Courier,	James D. Little,
QUEENS Co.		
Flushing,	Flushing Journal,	Charles R. Lincoln,
Flushing,	The Long Island Times,	Wm. R. Burling & Co.,
Hempstead,	The Hempstead Inquirer,	Morris Snedeker,
Jamaica,	Long Island Democrat,	James J. Brenton,
Jamaica,	The Long Island Farmer, and Queens Co. Advertiser,	Charles Walling, Publisher,
RENSSELAER Co.		
Lansingburgh,	Lansingburgh Democrat,	Wm. J. Lamb,
Lansingburgh,	Lansingburgh Gazette,	Alexander Kirkpatrick,
Troy,	The Northern Budget,	C. L. McArthur,
Troy,	Budget,	C. L. McArthur,
Troy,	The Troy Daily Times,	John M. Francis,
Troy,	Troy Daily Traveller,	Wm. L. Avery, Editor, Fisk & Avery, Publishers,
Troy,	Troy Weekly Traveller,	Wm. L. Avery, Editor, Fisk & Avery, Publishers,
Troy,	Troy Daily Whig,	Charles D. Brigham, Editor,
Troy,	The Troy Whig,	Charles D. Brigham, Editor,
Troy,	New-York Family Journal,	A. A. Fisk, Publisher,
Troy,	City Directory,	C. L. McArthur,
RICHMOND Co.		
Southfield,	Staten Islander,	F. L. Hagedorn,
Southfield,	Der Deutche Staten Islander,	August Fries,
ROCKLAND Co.		
Haverstraw,	Rockland County Messenger,	Robert Smith,
Orangetown,	Rockland County Journal, (Nyack,)	Wm. G. Haeselbarth,
ST. LAWRENCE Co.		
Canton,	The St. Lawrence Democrat,	Henry C. Simpson,
Gouverneur,	The Progressive Age,	G. Dickson Greenleaf,
Oswegatchie,	The Ogdensburgh Sentinel,	Stillman Foote,
Oswegatchie,	St. Lawrence American,	W. H. Yeaton and E. Holbrook,
Oswegatchie,	St. Lawrence Free Press,	G. K. Lyman,
Oswegatchie,	St. Lawrence Republican,	Hitchcock, Tillotson & Haddock,
Oswegatchie,	The Boys' Daily Journal,	H. R. James, J. W. Hopkins and C. Foster,
Oswegatchie,	The Boys' Journal,	H. R. James, J. W. Hopkins and C. Foster,
Potsdam,	Potsdam Courier and Journal,	Harvy C. Fay,
SARATOGA Co.		
Milton,	Ballston Democrat,	Seymour Chase,
Milton,	Ballston Democratic Whig Journal,	Albert A. Moor,
Saratoga,	Battle Ground Herald,	Richard N. Atwell & Co.,
Saratoga Springs,	The Saratoga Daily News,	E. J. Huling and G. C. Rice,
Saratoga Springs,	The Saratoga Whig,	E. J. Huling and G. C. Rice,
Saratoga Springs,	Saratogean,	B. F. Judson & Co.,
Saratoga Springs,	Temperance Helper,	B. F. Judson & Co.,
Saratoga Springs,	The Daily Republican,	Thomas G. Young,
Saratoga Springs,	Saratoga Weekly Republican,	Thomas G. Young,
Saratoga Springs,	Saratoga Sentinel,	Clark & Thayer,
Saratoga Springs,	The Old Settler,	Anson H. Allen,
Saratoga Springs,	The Morning Star, (Mechanicsville,)	C. Smith & Co.,

PERIODICALS.—(Continued.)

To what object devoted.	At what intervals published	Subscription price per annum.	When established.	Size in inches, and form.
Politics and news,	Weekly,	$1 50	1803,	24×34, Folio
Politics and news,	Weekly,	1 50	1802,	26×38, Folio.
Politics and news,	Weekly,	1 50	1852,	26×38, Folio.
News,	Weekly,	1 50	1854,	23×32, Folio.
Politics and news,	Weekly,	1 50	1830,	24×36, Folio.
Politics and news,	Weekly,	1 50	1810,	24×36, Folio.
News,	Weekly,	1 00	1851,	22×26, Folio.
Politics and news,	Weekly,	1 50	1851,	24×36, Folio.
Politics and news,	Weekly,	1 00	1800,	27×36, Folio.
Politics and news,	Weekly,	1 00	1830,	25×36, Folio.
Politics and news,	Weekly,	1 00	1843,	24×36, Folio.
Politics and news,	Weekly,	1 50	Aug. 24, 1855,	24×36, Folio.
Politics and news,	Weekly,	1 50	1822,	28×42, Folio.
Politics and news,	Weekly,	1 00	1829,	26×38, Folio.
Literature,	Monthly,	1 00		Octavo.
News,	Weekly,	1 00	August, 1848,	22×32, Quarto.
Politics and news,	Weekly,	1 50	Nov'ber, 1851,	24×36, Folio.
Religion, (Old School Baptist,)	Semi-monthly,	1 50	October, 1832,	24×34, Quarto.
Anti-Slavery and Sep. American Church, (colored,)	Quarterly,	0 25	1851,	15×20, Folio.
Politics and news,	Weekly,	1 50	1822,	25×37, Folio.
Politics and news,	Weekly,	1 50	1829,	27×39, Folio.
Politics and news,	Weekly,	1 00	1853,	25×36, Folio.
Politics and news,	Weekly,	1 00	1852,	25×36, Folio.
News,	Monthly,	0 25	1855,	22×32, Folio.
Politics and news,	Daily,	6 00	1850,	22×32, Folio
Politics and news,	Weekly,	1 50	1820,	24×36, Folio
News,	Daily,	6 00	1846,	24×36, Folio
News,	Weekly,	1 50	1847,	25×37, Folio
News,	Weekly,	1 25	1850,	24×36, Folio
News,	Weekly,	1 00	April, 1855,	22×32, Folio
Politics and news,	Weekly,	1 25	1853,	22×32, Folio
News,	Weekly,	1 50	1844,	Folio
News,	Quarterly,	0 12	1851,	12×18, Folio
News,	Weekly,	1 00	Feb'y 9, 1853,	22×32, Folio
Politics and news,	Weekly,	1 50	1808,	27×42, Folio.
Politics and news,	Weekly,	1 00	1847,	25×38, Folio.
Politics and news,	Weekly,	1 50	1854,	28×42, Folio
Politics and news,	Weekly,	1 50	1808,	24×36, Folio
News,	Weekly,	1 50	1824,	22×32, Folio
Politics and news,	Weekly,	1 50	1814,	24×38, Folio
News,	Weekly,	2 00	1842,	23×33, Folio
News,	Weekly,	2 00	1855,	23×33, Folio.
News,	Weekly,	1 50	1831,	22×32, Folio.
Politics and news,	Weekly,	2 00	1835,	22×32, Folio.
Agriculture and news,	Weekly,	2 00	1819,	23×33, Folio.
Politics and news,	Weekly,	2 00	1838,	24×36, Folio.
Politics and news,	Weekly,	2 00	1798,	24×36, Folio.
Politics and news,	Daily,	7 00	1840,	24×36, Folio.
Politics and news,	Weekly,	1 00	1792,	Folio.
Politics and news,	Daily,	4 50	1851,	24×36. Folio.
Politics and news,	Daily,	4 50	1846,	24×36, Folio.
Politics and news,	Weekly,	1 00	1846,	24×36, Folio.
Politics and news,	Daily,	8 00	1835,	26×38, Folio.
Politics and news,	Weekly,	1 00	1835,	26×38, Folio.
Miscellany,	Weekly,	1 50	1844,	26×38, Quarto.
Directory,	Annually,	1 00	1828,	12mo.
News,	Semi-weekly,	3 00	1840,	Quarto.
News,	Weekly,	1 50	1855,	Quarto.
News,	Weekly,	1 50	May, 1846,	23×32, Folio.
News,	Weekly,	1 50	1850,	24×37, Folio.
Politics and news,	Weekly,	1 00	1855,	24×36, Folio.
News,	Weekly,	1 00	1855,	24×36, Quarto.
Politics and news,	Weekly,	1 00	1844,	26×40, Folio.
Politics and news,	Weekly,	1 00	1855,	30×46, Folio.
News,	Weekly,	1 00	1855,	21×30, Folio.
Politics and news,	Weekly,	1 00	1816,	30×46, Folio.
News,	Daily,	3 00	August, 1854,	12×14, Folio.
News,	Weekly,	1 00	1854,	15×23, Folio.
News,	Weekly,	1 00	1852,	24×36, Folio.
Politics and news,	Weekly,	1 50	1844,	24×36, Folio.
Politics and news,	Weekly,	1 50	1851,	24×35, Folio.
News,	Weekly,	1 50	August, 1853,	Folio.
News,	Daily,	$1, season.	1855,	20×29, Folio.
Politics and news,	Weekly,	1 50	1838,	25×36, Folio.
Temperance and news,	Daily,	......	1855,	Folio.
Temperance and news.	Weekly,	1 00	1855,	24×36, Folio.
News,	Daily,	$1, season.	1843,	21×28, Folio.
News,	Weekly,	1 50	1843,	24×38, Folio.
News,	Weekly,	1 50	1854,	24×36, Folio.
Literature,	Monthly,	0 50	1849,	21×27, Folio.
News,	Weekly,	1 00	1854,	12×18, Folio.

NEWSPAPERS AND OTHER

Where published.	Names of Newspapers and Periodicals.	Editors and Publishers
SCHENECTADY Co.		
Schenectady,	Morning Star,	Clark & Colborne,
Schenectady,	Schenectady Democrat,	Clark & Colborne,
Schenectady,	The Schenectady Cabinet,	S. S. Riggs,
Schenectady,	Schenectady Reflector,	A. A. Keyser,
SCHOHARIE Co.		
Cobleskill,	Cobleskill Journal,	John Brown,
Schoharie,	The Democratic Republican,	Rosseter & Hall,
Schoharie,	Schoharie Patriot,	Peter Mix,
Schoharie,	The Oasis,	Students of Schoharie Academy,
SCHUYLER Co.		
Havana,	Havana Journal,	J. B. Look,
Havana,	The Schuyler County Democrat,	Averill & Baxter,
Watkins,	The Watkins Republican,	S. M. Taylor,
SENECA Co.		
Ovid,	The Ovid Bee,	Congdon Fairchild,
Seneca Falls,	American Reveille,	Gilbert Wilcoxen, Editor, Sherman Baker, Publisher,
Seneca Falls,	Seneca County Courier,	Isaac Fuller,
Waterloo,	The Seneca Observer,	Charles Sentell,
STEUBEN Co.		
Addison,	Voice of the Nation,	Anthony L. Underhill,
Bath,	The Steuben Courier,	Henry H. Hull,
Bath,	Steuben Farmers' Advocate,	William C. Rhoades,
Bath,	Temperance Gem,	Jenny and Caroline Rumsey,
Corning,	The Corning Journal,	Geo. W. Pratt, Editor and Publisher, J. M. Packer, Printer,
Corning and Elmira,	Elmira Southern Tier Farmer and Corning Sun,	Ira Brown,
Hornellsville,	Hornellsville Tribune,	Edwin Hough,
SUFFOLK Co.		
Huntington,	Long Islander,	George H. Shepard,
Huntington,	The Suffolk Democrat,	Wm. D. McGregor,
Southampton,	The Corrector, (Sag Harbor,)	Henry W. Hunt,
Southold,	Republican Watchman, (Greenport,)	Samuel Phillips,
Riverhead,	The Suffolk County Gazette,	John Hancock,
SULLIVAN Co.		
Mamakating,	Sullivan County Whig, (Bloomingburgh,)	John Waller, Jr.,
Thompson,	Republican Watchman, (Monticello,)	James E. Quinlan,
Thompson,	The Union Democrat, (Monticello,)	Frederick A. De Voe,
TIOGA Co.		
Barton,	The Waverly Advocate,	Baldwin & Polleys,
Owego,	The Owego Gazette,	Hiram A. Beebe,
Owego,	Owego Times,	William Smyth,
Owego,	Southern Tier Times,	
TOMPKINS Co.		
Ithaca,	The American Citizen,	A. E. Barnaby,
Ithaca,	Ithaca Chronicle,	Anson Spencer,
Ithaca,	Ithaca Journal and Advertiser,	J. H. Selkreg,
Ithaca,	Templar and Watchman,	Myron S. Barnes,
ULSTER Co.		
Kingston,	Kingston Democratic Journal,	Wm. H. Romeyn and H. L. Tobey,
Kingston,	The Peoples' Press,	Daniel Bradbury,
Kingston,	The Ulster Democrat,	S. R. Harlow,
Kingston,	The Ulster Republican,	Solomon S. Hommell,
Kingston,	Rondout Courier,	J. P. Hageman,
Saugerties,	Saugerties Telegraph,	William Hull,
Wawarsing,	Ellenville Journal,	R. B. Taylor,
WARREN Co.		
Chester,	The Star of Destiny,	A. D. Milne,
Queensbury,	Glens Falls Free Press,	Zabina Ellis,
Queensbury,	Glens Falls Republican,	Hall & Little,
WASHINGTON Co.		
Fort Edward,	Public Ledger,	H. T. Blanchard,
Granville,	Granville Telegraph,	Marcellus Strong,
Greenwich,	Washington County People's Journal,	John W. Curtiss,
Kingsbury,	The Sandy Hill Herald,	E. D. Baker,
Salem,	The Salem Press,	William B. Harkness,
White Creek,	Washington County Post,	R. K. Crocker,
Whitehall,	The American Sentinel,	John E. Watkins,
Whitehall,	Whitehall Chronicle,	B. B. Smith,
Whitehall,	The Whitehall Democrat,	G. H. Dudley and J. B. Wilkins,
WAYNE Co.		
Arcadia,	The Newark Whig,	Geo. D. A. Bridgman,
Galen,	The Clyde Times,	Joseph A. Paine,
Lyons,	Lyons Gazette,	William Van Camp,
Lyons,	Wayne County Whig,	Rodney L. Adams,
Palmyra,	The Palmyra American,	Edwin S. Averill,
Palmyra,	The Wayne Sentinel,	Andrew A. Matthewson,
WESTCHESTER Co.		
Cortlandt,	The Highland Eagle, (Peekskill,)	John W. Spaight,
Cortlandt,	Peekskill Republican,	M. F. Rowe,
Eastchester,	The Mount Vernon Gazette,	Egbert S. Manning,
Ossining,	Hudson River Chronicle, (Sing Sing,)	William C. Howe,
Ossining,	The Westchester Herald, (Sing Sing,)	Caleb Roscoe,
West Farms,	Westchester Gazette,	Henry D. Hill,
West Farms,	Westchester County Journal,	James Stillman,
White Plains,	Eastern State Journal,	Edmund G. Sutherland,
Yonkers,	The Yonkers Herald,	Thomas Smith,
Yonkers,	The Westchester News,	W. B. Hudgins,
WYOMING Co.		
Attica,	Attica Atlas,	Silas Folsom,
Perry,	Wyoming Times,	Truman S. Gillett,
Warsaw,	Western New-Yorker,	H. A. Dudley,
Warsaw,	Wyoming County Mirror,	Babbitt & Lewis,

PERIODICALS.—(CONTINUED.)

To what object devoted.	At what intervals published.	Subscription price per annum.	When established.	Size in inches, and form.
News,	Daily,	$4 00	February, 1855,	20×30, Folio.
Politics and news,	Weekly,	1 50	October, 1854,	24×36, Folio.
Politics and news,	Weekly,	1 50	1809,	24×36, Folio
Politics and news,	Weekly,	1 50	January, 1834,	23×35, Folio.
News,	Weekly,	1 50	May, 1855,	24×36, Folio.
Politics and news,	Weekly,	1 00	1820,	24×38, Folio.
Politics and news,	Weekly,	1 50	1838,	22×32, Folio.
Literature,	Semi-monthly,	0 75	1855,	12×18, Folio.
Politics and news,	Weekly,	1 00	April 16, 1853,	23×32, Folio.
Politics and news,	Weekly,	1 00	April 25, 1855,	24×36, Folio.
Politics and news,	Weekly,	1 00	June, 1854,	22×32, Folio.
News,	Weekly,	1 50	1838,	22×32, Folio.
Politics and news,	Weekly,	1 50	1855,	Folio.
Politics and news,	Weekly,	1 50	1835,	23×35, Folio.
Politics and news,	Weekly,	1 50	1824,	24×36, Folio.
Politics and news,	Weekly,	1 50	Jan'y 1, 1855,	Folio.
Politics and news,	Weekly,	1 50	1843,	24×38, Folio.
Politics and news,	Weekly,	1 50	1815,	25×38, Folio.
Temperance and literature,	Weekly,	0 50	1854,	Folio.
Politics and news,	Weekly,	1 50	1846,	24×32, Folio.
Agriculture,	Weekly,	1 50	1854,	22×32, Quarto
News,	Weekly,	1 50	Nov. 19, 1852,	24×36, Folio.
Temperance and news,	Weekly,	1 50	1840,	22×32, Folio.
News,	Weekly,	1 50	1847,	23×32, Folio.
Politics and news,	Semi-weekly,	2 00	August 3, 1822,	22×28, Folio.
Politics and news,	Weekly,	1 50	Septem. 1826,	22×32, Folio.
Politics and news,	Weekly,	1 50	1849,	22×31, Folio.
Politics and news,	Weekly,	1 50	1844,	24×36, Folio.
Politics and news,	Weekly,	1 00	1828,	24×36, Folio.
Politics and news,	Weekly,	1 00	1854,	24×36, Folio.
News,	Weekly,	1 50	1852,	24×36, Folio.
News,	Weekly,	1 00	1812,	24×37, Folio.
News,	Weekly,	1 50	1836,	26×38, Folio.
News,	Weekly,	1 50	1853,	26×38, Folio.
Politics and news,	Weekly,	1 50	1855,	26×38, Folio.
Politics and news,	Weekly,	1 50	1828,	Folio.
Politics and news,	Weekly,	1 00	July 4, 1815,	25×37, Folio.
Temperance,	Weekly,	1 00	1853,	24×34, Folio.
Politics and news,	Weekly,	2 00	1837,	28×42, Folio.
Politics and news,	Weekly,	1 50	1853,	22×37, Folio.
Politics and news,	Weekly,	1 25	1846,	25×37, Folio.
Politics and news,	Weekly,	1 50	1837,	30×42, Folio.
News,	Weekly,	1 50	1847,	Folio.
News,	Weekly,	1 50	1847,	28×42, Folio.
News,	Weekly,	1 50	1849,	Folio.
Religion,	Weekly,	1 00	July, 1855,	(32 pages,) Octavo.
Politics and news,	Weekly,	1 50	1828,	24×36, Folio.
News,	Weekly,	1 50	1854,	Folio.
Politics and news,	Weekly,	1 00	1854,	24×36, Folio.
News,	Weekly,	1 00	1848,	Folio.
Politics and news,	Weekly,	1 00	1842,	24×36, Folio.
Politics and news,	Weekly,	1 00	1821,	22×32, Folio.
Politics and news,	Weekly,	1 00	1850,	24×36, Folio.
Politics and news,	Weekly,	1 00	1788,	24×36, Folio.
Politics and news,	Weekly,	1 00	June 7, 1855,	24×36, Folio.
Politics and news,	Weekly,	1 00	1838,	23×34, Folio.
Politics and news,	Weekly,	1 00	1843,	22×29, Folio.
Politics and news,	Weekly,	1 50	1854,	23×32, Folio.
Politics and news,	Weekly,	1 00	1850,	23×32, Folio.
Politics and news,	Weekly,	1 50	1849,	23×33, Folio.
Politics and news,	Weekly,	1 50	1838,	25×38, Folio.
Politics and news,	Weekly,	1 00	1855,	24×34, Folio.
Politics and news,	Weekly,	1 50	1823,	23×33, Folio.
News,	Weekly,	1 50	1851,	24×38, Folio.
News,	Weekly,	1 00	1830,	24×36, Folio.
News,	Weekly,	2 00	1854,	24×36, Folio.
Politics and news,	Weekly,	2 00	1837,	24×36, Folio.
News,	Weekly,	2 00	1817,	24×36, Folio.
News,	Weekly,	2 00	1849,	Folio.
News,	Weekly,	1 50	1852,	Folio.
Politics and news,	Weekly,	2 00	1845,	24×37, Folio.
News,	Weekly,	1 00	1852,	23×32, Folio.
News,	Weekly,	2 00	1853,	24×36, Folio.
Politics and news,	Weekly,	1 00	January, 1851,	22×32, Folio.
News,	Weekly,	1 50	May 9, 1855,	23×33, Folio.
Politics and news,	Weekly,	1 50	1841,	24×36, Folio.
Politics and news,	Weekly,	1 50	1848,	24×36, Folio.

NEWSPAPERS AND OTHE

Where published.	Names of Newspapers and Periodicals.	Editors and Proprietors.
YATES Co.		
Milo,	Yates County Whig, (Penn Yan,)	Stafford S. Cleveland,
Milo,	The Penn Yan Democrat,	Spicer & Stanton,
Starkey,	The Dundee Record,	John J. Diefendorf,

SUMMARY OF NEWSPAPER

COUNTIES.	TOTAL NUMBER.		FORM.				INTERVALS OF PUBLICATION.								
	News-papers.	Other periodicals.	Folio.	Quarto.	Octavo.	12mo. and 18mo.	Daily.	Tri-weekly.	Semi-weekly.	Weekly.	Semi-monthly.	Monthly.	Quarterly.	Semi-annually.	Annually.
Albany,*	29	7	23	6	4	3	7	1	4	15	1	4			
Allegany,	6		6							6					
Broome,	7		7				1			6					
Cattaraugus,	6		6							6					
Cayuga,	9	1	9		1		2			7		1			
Chautauque,	9		8	1						9					
Chemung,	6		5	1			2			4					
Chenango,†	6		6							6					
Clinton,	4	1	4		1					4		1			
Columbia,	8		8				2			6					
Cortland,	2		2							2					
Delaware,	6		6							6					
Dutchess,	10		10				1			9					
Erie,‡	31	5	27	4	5		9	5		15	2	4			
Essex,	3		3							3					
Franklin,	2		2							2					
Fulton,	2		2							2					
Genesee,	5		5							5					
Greene,†	5		5							5					
Hamilton,†	1		1							1					
Herkimer,	6		6					1		5					
Jefferson,§	4	2	5			2				4					
Kings,¶	10	2	8	2		2	5		1	3		1			
Lewis,	3		2	1						3					
Livingston,	6		5	1						6					
Madison,	8		8							8					
Monroe,‖	17	5	15	2	4	1	4	5		7	2	3			
Montgomery,	5		5							5					
New-York,**	145	78	80	65	69	9	19	1	8	87	10	87	13	2	
Niagara,‖	7		7				3			4					
Oneida,	17	6	16	1	5	1	4			13		4	1		
Onondaga,‡	16	2	16		2	1	3		1	9	1	3			
Ontario,	7		7							7					
Orange,††	11	1	9	2	1					9	1	1	1		
Orleans,	5		5							4		1			
Oswego,	8		8				2			6					
Otsego,	7		7							6			1		
Putnam,	1		1							1					
Queens,	5		5							5					
Rensselaer,	10	1	9	1		1	4			6					
Richmond,	2			2					1	1					
Rockland,	2		2							2					
St. Lawrence,	9		8	1			1			8					
Saratoga,§§	12		12				3			8		1			
Schenectady,	4		4				1			3					
Schoharie,	4		4							3	1				
Schuyler,	3		3							3					
Seneca,	4		4							4					
Steuben,	7		6	1						6		1			
Suffolk,†	5		5						1	4					
Sullivan,	3		3							3					
Tioga,†	4		4							4					
Tompkins,†	4		4							4					
Ulster,	7		7							7					
Warren,‡‡	2	1	2		1					2		1			
Washington,	9		9							9					
Wayne,	6		6							6					
Westchester,	10		10							10					
Wyoming,	4		4							4					
Yates,	3		3							3					
Total,	559	112	469	91	93	20	73	13	16	411	18	113	16	2	1

* The circulation of 2 dailies, 3 semi-weeklies, 3 weeklies, 1 semi-monthly, and 1 monthly not reported.
† The circulation of 1 weekly not reported.
‡ The circulation of 1 daily, 2 tri-weeklies, 5 weeklies, 1 semi-monthly, and 1 annual not reported.
§ The circulation of 1 annual not reported.
¶ The crculation of 1 daily not reported.
‖ The circulation of 1 monthly and 1 annual not reported.
** The form of 7 periodicals, and the circulation of 4 dailies, 1 tri-weekly, 3 semi-weeklies, 38 weeklies, 6 semi-monthlies, 45 monthlies, and 5 quarterlies, not reported.
†† The circulation of 1 monthly and 1 quarterly not reported.
‡‡ The circulation of 1 monthly not reported.
§§ The circulation of 2 dailies not reported.

PERIODICALS.—(CONTINUED.)

To what object devoted.	At what intervals published.	Subscription price per annum.	When established.	Size in inches, and form.
Politics and news,	Weekly,	$1 50	1836,	25×40, Folio.
Politics and news,	Weekly,	1 00	1818,	24×37, Folio.
Politics and news,	Weekly,	1 00	1843,	24×36, Folio.

AND OTHER PERIODICALS.

TO WHAT OBJECTS DEVOTED.											CIRCULATION OF EACH EDITION SO FAR AS REPORTED								
Politics.	Religion.	Agriculture.	Education.	Science and arts.	Temperance.	Medicine.	Law.	Literary.	Juvenile.	Miscellaneous.	Daily.	Tri-weekly.	Semi-weekly.	Weekly.	Semi-monthly.	Monthly.	Quarterly.	Semi-annual.	Annual.
17		4	1		2				1	11	19, 676	500	2, 796	38, 521		42, 000			61, 400
6														4, 175					
4	1				1					1	250			5, 080					
4										2				3, 904					
5	2				1					2	950			16, 700		200			
9														7, 502					
5										1	1, 100			3, 400					
2					1					3				4, 112					
4						1								2, 558		1, 800			
6										2	1, 150			4, 600					
2														1, 578					
3										3				5, 150					
4					1					5	1, 300			12, 950					
22	5		2			1		1	1	4	9, 400	2, 700		14, 640	1, 900	8, 200			
2										1				2, 625					
2														1, 325					
2														900					
4										1				4, 300					
4										1				2, 400					
1																			
4										2				3, 580					
3										3				7, 700					15, 000
....					1					11	8, 040			10, 800	800	2, 000			6, 500
2										1				2, 400					
1										5				3, 830					
6										2				5, 570					
14	4	3								1	6, 700	5, 200		50, 000	1, 500	8, 800			
2										3				2, 560					
21	45	3	7	9	3	13	3	31	9	86	48, 107		24, 291	912, 980	253, 850	1,200, 700	31, 600	11, 000	13, 000
5										2	1, 350			4, 300					
8	4	1			2	1				7	4, 960			37, 160		14, 200			450
10	4					2				2	2, 700		12, 000	12, 184	1, 500	3, 850			
4										3				5, 250					
8	1							1		2				17, 356	4, 800		150		
4										1				3, 000		1, 900			
3										4	1, 100			4, 325					
4										3				6, 500			200		
1														800					
1		1								3				2, 915					
9										2	4, 900			5, 110					600
....										2			700	250					
....										2				1, 000					
3									2	4	200			7, 650					
3						1		1		7	300			6, 425		2, 000			
3										1	700			1, 430					
2								1		1				1, 800	250				
3														1, 800					
3										1				2, 802					
4		1			1					1				5, 250		2, 000			
3					1					1			600	1, 500					
3														3, 144					
....										4				2, 900					
3					1									3, 600					
4										3				6, 588					
1	1									1				750					
8										1				4, 973					
6														3, 205					
2										8				8, 270					
3										1				2, 235					
2										1				3, 025					
274	67	13	10	9	15	19	3	35	13	219	312, 783	8, 400	40, 387	1, 294, 340	264, 600	1,287, 650	31, 950	11, 000	96, 950

APPENDIX.

CENSUS OF THE INDIANS RESIDING ON RESERVATIONS.*

The present, census of the Indians of New-York, is the second that has been officially reported, these people having been uniformly omitted in all previous enumerations, excepting for the special purposes of distributing annuities, or carrying into effect treaties for the cession and surrender of their lands on their final emigration from the State.

In 1845, a separate census of Indians was taken under the direction of Henry R. Schoolcraft, Esq.,† the leading numerical results of which, are combined with those of the present census in the following tables. The novelty of this measure, and its supposed infringement upon their ancient and still cherished independence, and especially a jealousy lest these inquiries into their condition and property, might have connection with some designs against their lands, on that occasion, embarrassed the operations of those appointed to obtain it, and led to much discussion and difficulty. In the present case, fewer objections were raised, and the principal obstacle was found in their ignorance of the facts concerning which the inquiries were made. Unaccustomed to the measuring of land or its products, the answers to inquiries concerning agriculture, like those relating to ages, and other details, were frequently guess-work and, as often left to the judgment of the marshal. So far as practicable, educated natives were appointed to take this census, and in cases were this could not be done, the services of resident interpreters familiar with the affairs of the several reservations were obtained, and care was taken to explain the objects of the enumeration, and remove any jealousies which might have been excited by its inquiries.

Although many details of the history of the native tribes of the State, since its colonization by Europeans, have been preserved, we have few definite estimates by which to compare the numbers at different periods, and the rate of their diminution from a numerous and powerful, to a few and feeble people. In 1698, Governor Bellomont estimated that the Five Nations and the River Indians, had been reduced by war in nine years from 2,800 to 1,320, these numbers being probably those of fighting men.‡ In 1763, Sir William Johnson, reported the number of men among the several tribes of the Iroquois Confederacy, and others residing within or on the borders of New-York as follows: §

Mohawks, - - - -	160	Onondagas, - - - -	150	Oswegatchies, - - -	80
Oneidas, - - - -	250	Cayugas, - - - -	200	Tuscaroras, - - -	140
Senecas, - - -	1,050	Emigrants from southward, on the Susquehanna, - - -			200

Of the Oswegatchies a part resided in Canada, and of the last named some may have lived in Pennsylvania.

In 1774, it was estimated that there were of the scattered River Indians, 300; of the Mohawks, 406; of Oneidas, 500; and of all the nations about 2,000 fighting men, and 10,000 souls. The Senecas were much the most numerous being nearly half the whole number.

Such other statistics as have been obtained concerning these tribes, will be given in connection with the remarks upon each.

---

* In addition to those thus returned, there were reported 235 Indians, (102 males and 133 females,) not residing on reservations, which are enumerated with the population of the towns in which they live. They were distributed as follows: Allegany, 2; Broome, 3; Cattaraugus, 2; Chautauque, 1; Chemung, 1; Chenango, 4; Clinton, 3; Cortland, 1; Delaware, 10; Dutchess, 4; Erie, 11; Essex, 2; Greene, 2; Hamilton, 1; Herkimer, 1; Jefferson, 9; Kings, 8; Madison, 11; Monroe, 1; New-York, 11; Niagara, 2; Oneida, 4; Onondaga, 5; Ontario, 2; Orange, 2; Queens, 7; St. Lawrence, 33; Saratoga, 1; Schoharie, 18; Steuben, 1; Suffolk, 50; Warren, 17; and Westchester, 5.

† Senate document, 1846, Vol. I., No. 24.

‡ Colonial History of New-York, iv., page 337.

§ Colonial History of New-York, vii., page 582.

COMPARATIVE POPULATION OF INDIAN RESERVATIONS IN 1845 AND 1855.

RESERVATIONS.	WHERE LOCATED.	TOTAL.		SEX.				MARRIAGES YEAR PREVIOUS.		BIRTHS YEAR PREVIOUS.	
				Males.		Females.					
		1845.	1855.	1845.	1855.	1845.	1855.	1845.	1855.	1845.	1855.
Allegany, *a* ...	South Valley, Cold Spring, Bucktooth, Great Valley and Carrolton, Cattaraugus Co.,......	783	754	390	376	393	378	6	.....	19	20
Buffalo, *b*.....	Lancaster, Erie Co.,..........................	446	......	200	....	246	....	3	.....	10	......
Cattaraugus, *c*.	Perrysburgh, Cattaraugus Co., Collins, Erie Co., and Hanover, Chautauque Co.,..............	922	1,179	449	575	473	604	12	.....	33	21
Oneida, *d*	Lenox, Madison Co., and Vernon, Oneida Co.,..	157	161	71	88	86	73	.....	.....	13	6
Onondaga,....	Fayette and Onondaga, Onondaga Co.,..........	368	349	173	173	195	176	5	.....	16	10
St. Regis, *e*....	Bombay, Franklin Co.,........................	260	413	126	206	134	207	.....	*	7	17
Shinecock, *f*...	Southampton, Suffolk Co.,....................	......	160	....	89	....	71	.....	.....	.....	......
Tonawanda, *g*.	Pembroke and Alabama, Genesee Co., Newstead, Erie Co., and Royalton, Niagara Co., ...	505	602	224	290	281	312	4	7	13	10
Tuscarora, ...	Lewiston, Niagara Co.,.......................	312	316	148	150	164	166	6	6	10	16
Total,......	....	3,753	3,934	1,781	1,947	1,972	1,987	36	.....	121	100

RESERVATIONS.	1845.			1855.						PLACE OF BIRTH, 1845.			PLACE OF BIRTH, 1855.		
				CIVIL CONDITION											
	Married females under forty-five.	Unmarried females, sixteen to forty-five.	Unmarried females, under sixteen.	Single.	Married.	Widowers.	Widows.	Number of families.	Average number in each family.	State of New York.	Other States of the United States.	British Provinces.	State of New-York.	Other States of the United States.	British Provinces.
Allegany, ...	393	127	33	473	246	11	24	138	5.5	752	35	.....	709	44	1
Buffalo,...............	73	47	61	.. ....	....	....	....	.....	.....	433	1	6	.....	.....	......
Cattaraugus, *h*.........	105	46	35	747	370	16	46	228	5.1	903	.....	7	.....	.....	......
Oneida, *h*	24	3	47	129	29	....	3	21	7.1	155	1	1	.....	.....	......
Onondaga, *h*	63	19	73	260	78	3	8	57	6.1	364	.....	1	.....	.....	......
St. Regis, ...	134	44	5	247	153	3	10	87	4.7	125	.....	135	212	.....	201
Shinecock,.............	....	....	....	109	44	3	4	32	5.0	.....	.....	.....	159	1	......
Tonawanda, ...	281	101	45	333	225	12	32	106	5.7	496	.....	11	554	45	3
Tuscarora, ...	18	10	11	199	98	5	14	66	4.8	286	.....	30	309	1	6
Total,................	555	208	531	2,497	1,243	53	141	735	5.3	3,514	37	191	.....	.....	......
Per centage of total Indian population,......	14.78	.5.44	14.15	63.47	31.59	1.35	3.59	.....	.....	.....	.....	.....	.....	.....	......
Per cent. of similar classes throughout State,....	8.85	6.19	18.84	60.08	36.15	1.02	2.75	.....	.....	.....	.....	.....	.....	.....	......

RESERVATIONS.	AGES, 1855.																	
	Under 1 year.		1 and under 5.		5 and under 10.		10 and under 15.		15 and under 20.		20 and under 25.		25 and under 30.		30 and under 35.		35 and under 40.	
	Male	Fem.	Male.	Fem.	Male.	Fem	Male.	Fem	Male.	Fem.	Male.	Fem.	Male.	Fem.	Male.	Fem.	Male.	Fem.
Allegany, ...	7	13	29	44	64	57	51	54	55	52	36	34	31	19	14	17	23	23
Cattaraugus, ...	11	10	67	75	94	106	71	60	39	56	61	52	42	42	42	49	39	37
Oneida, ...	5	1	6	7	11	12	16	9	11	10	7	4	3	5	7	4	1	6
Onondaga,...	6	4	24	22	17	12	20	22	18	18	16	13	11	14	14	11	12	12
St. Regis,..	6	11	32	32	32	29	20	32	27	27	16	11	18	12	11	13	8	4
Shinecock, ...	....	....	8	5	15	12	13	12	11	5	7	5	6	3	5	8	7	7
Tonawanda,..	7	3	25	30	39	39	31	37	32	32	26	26	11	24	18	15	24	21
Tuscarora, ...	8	8	14	23	19	25	24	19	15	22	15	21	14	10	11	7	9	6
Total, ...	50	50	205	238	291	292	246	245	208	222	184	166	136	129	122	124	123	116
Percentage of total Indian population, ...	1.77	1.77	5.20	6.05	7.40	7.40	6.25	6.24	5.28	5.05	4.67	4.22	3.44	3.27	3.10	3.16	3.14	2.94

a Of those residing on the Allegany reservation, 63 were Onondagas, 1 Cayuga, and the rest Senecas.

b This settlement has been broken up by the removal of its former occupants, and sale of the reservation.

c The number reported in 1855, was, from the negligence of the marshal, too small. In May, 1855, 1,388 were returned as entitled to share in annuities, viz: 1,230 Senecas, 34 Onondagas, living with Senecas, 100 Cayugas, and 24 Munsees. 1,021 reside in Erie, 138 in Cattaraugus, and 20 in Chautauque county.

d Of those reported in 1855, 101 reside in Madison, and 60 in Oneida counties. The returns of civil condition, in this and Onondaga, are too indefinite to be relied upon

e The largest part of this village is in Canada. The official census of Canada, in 1851, '52, showed in this part, 1,069 inhabitants, of whom 4 were of English or Welch, 3 of Scotch, 3 of Irish, 209 of French, 4 of United States, and 845 of native origin. 549 were males, and 520 females.—*Census of Canada*, 1851, '52, i. 322.

f These Indians were not reported separately in 1845.

g In this reservation the pagan party very reluctantly afforded any information, and in some instances refused to answer the inquiries. Of the above, 76 reside in Erie, 28 in Niagara, and 498 in Genesee county.

* Four marriages were contracted the year previous, at St. Regis, but as the ceremony was performed at the church, in Canada, they are not noted above.

h Place of birth not reported in 1855.

CENSUS OF INDIAN RESERVATIONS.—(CONTINUED.)

RESERVATIONS.	AGES, 1855.																	
	40 and under 45.		45 and under 50.		50 and under 60.		60 and under 70.		70 and under 80.		80 and under 90.		90 and under 100.		100 and over.*		Unknown.	
	Male.	Fem	Male.	Fem	Male	Fem.	Male.	Fem.	Male	Fem.	Male	Fem	Male.	Fem	Male	Fem	Male.	Fem
Allegany,	17	16	15	13	10	20	12	9	7	3	2	1	1	2	2	....	....	1
Cattaraugus,	28	25	23	24	33	34	10	18	9	10	3	2	2	3	1	1	....	....
Oneida,	4	6	5	1	7	3	2	2	....	1	....	1	....	....	....	....	3	1
Onondaga,	8	13	8	9	6	7	6	7	4	3	1	4	....	....	....	....	2	5
St. Regis,	9	12	7	6	12	8	7	4	....	5	2	....	....	....	....	....	....	....
Shinecock,	4	....	3	2	8	6	2	3	....	1	....	2	....	....	....	....	....	....
Tonawanda,	14	16	4	15	18	11	10	10	5	4	3	4	2	1	....	3	21	21
Tuscarora,	6	5	3	5	3	9	4	4	1	....	3	2	....	....	....	....	1	....
Total,	90	93	68	75	97	98	53	57	26	27	14	16	5	6	3	4	27	28
Percentage of total Indian population,	2.29	2.36	1.73	1.90	2.46	2.49	1.35	1.45	0.66	0.68	0.22	0.23	0.13	0.14	0.08	0.10	0.68	0.69

RESERVATIONS.	SCHOOLS.		CHILDREN BETWEEN 5 AND 16.		CHILDREN ATTENDING SCHOOLS.		Number over 21 who cannot read or write.	CHURCHES.		No who adhere to native religion, 1845	Church members of all sects, 1855.	Number pledged to temperance, 1845.
	1845.	1855.	1845.	1855.	1845.	1855.		1845.	1855.			
Allegany,	2	*e*5	227	242	162	100	*f*	1	*d*2	603	117	158
Buffalo,	2	....	117	....	57	....	....	1	....	436	*a*5	28
Cattaraugus,	5	*o*6	142	200	100	200	*h*396	1	*g*2	865	56	90
Oneida,	1	*p*2	59	52	20	80	....	1	1	133	31	35
Onondaga,	1	*1	169	73	40	50	11	1	*c*1	330	38	128
St. Regis,	....	*n*2	81	132	....	*k*34	*m*89	....	*l*1	....	....	....
Shinecock,	....	1	....	54	....	....	....	....	*b*1	....	....	....
Tonawanda,	1	*u*2	126	153	40	....	*r*244	1	*v*1	465	40	200
Tuscarora,	2	*t*2	63	91	43	....	*q*62	2	*s*1	249	63	231
Total,	14	21	984	997	462	464	....	8	10	3,081	350	870

RESERVATIONS	DEATHS THE YEAR PREVIOUS, 1845.		DEATHS DURING THE YEAR PREVIOUS, 1855.**															
			Total number.	Males.	Females.	Native countries.			Season.				Cause of death.					
	Male.	Fem.				New-York.	Other states.	British poss'ns.	Spring.	Summer.	Autumn.	Winter	Cholera	Consumpti'n.	Fevers.	Hooping cough.	Inflammation.	Other causes.
Allegany,*	13	13	......	......	......	......	......	......	......	......	......	......	......	......	......	......	......	......
Buffalo,	14	7	......	......	......	......	......	......	......	......	......	......	......	......	......	......	......	......
Cattaraugus,*	14	16	......	......	......	......	......	......	......	......	......	......	......	......	......	......	......	......
Oneida,*	1	......	......	......	......	......	......	......	......	......	......	......	......	......	......	......	......	......
Onondaga,	11	12	14	......	......	......	......	......	......	......	......	......	......	......	......	......	......	......
St. Regis,	5	3	3	2	1	1	......	2	1	1	1	......	......	......	1	......	......	2
Shinecock,	......	......	......	......	......	......	......	......	......	......	......	......	......	......	......	......	......	......
Tonawanda,	4	3	7	4	3	7	......	......	3	......	......	4	......	......	2	1	2	2
Tuscarora,	1	3	12	6	6	12	......	......	1	5	3	3	3	1	3	......	1	4
Total,	63	57	36	12	10	20	......	2	5	6	4	7	3	1	6	1	3	8

* The ages of these persons were as follows : *Allegany*, 100 and 107; *Cattaraugus*, 101 and 100; *Tonawanda*, 104, 100 and 101.

a Incomplete.

b Congregational, not incorporated. The same house used for school purposes. House capable of seating 160. Usually attending 60. Communicants 30.

c Methodist Mission church, worth $700. Capable of seating 400, usually attending 60.

* Average attendance 22. Studies taught, spelling, writing, geography, arithmetic, &c.

d Of these churches one belongs to the A. B. C. F. Missions, (Presbyterian,) is valued at $400, is capable of seating 200, usually attending 100, and number of communicants 60. The other belongs to the Baptist Missionary Society; is valued at $300, is capable of seating 150; usually attending 80, and number of communicants 46.

e These school houses are all built of plank, are in good condition and nearly new. One cost $300, and the others about $200 each. These schools are mission schools, and there are no other schools on the reservation. Number of children between the ages of 6 and 18 who attend school 100, and of those between the same ages who do *not* attend, 150.

f There are on the Allegany reservation 30 Indians who can read English, 60 who can read Seneca, 25 who can write English, and 36 who can write Seneca. Three newspapers are taken on the reservation.

g One of these churches belongs to the American Board, (Presbyterian,) is valued at $400, seats 400, and has 145 communicants. The other belongs to the Methodists, cost $2,000, and has 40 communicants. The Baptists claim 30 communicants on this reservation.

h On the Cattaraugus reservation 78 are reported as capable of reading, and 45 of reading and writing.

k At St. Regis 108 children do *not* attend school.

l Of the St. Regis Indians, 338 are reported as Catholics, 48 as Methodist, and 8 as Episcopal. The Canada census of 1851–2 reported of those including whites, living north of the provincial line, 978 Catholic, 21 Episcopal, 56 Presbyterian, 9 Baptists, and 5 of no creed. The church above noted belongs to the Methodists, and is situated at the edge of the reservation, near the village of Hogansburgh. The Catholic church of this village is in Canada.

m 63 persons were reported as capable of reading the Mohawk dialect of the Iroquois. The Catholic service of the church is printed and used in this language at St. Regis.

n Of these school houses, one, in very good condition, valued at $400, is situated on the reservation, near the village of St. Regis, but is poorly attended. The other, a very poor building, valued at $80, is on the road from Hogansburgh to Fort Covington, and the attendance at this school is also very small. The English government sustains a school in St. Regis village, but the attendance at this is also small. Of children between 4 and 21, (unmarried,) 43 attended school during the year previous, and 89 did not. Of persons over 21 years of age 117 could not read or write, and 65 could read Iroquois.

o Five of these schools are under the care of missionaries. The average attendance is 150. The state school, under the superintendence of Marius B. Pierce, has 34 scholars, with an average of 25.

p The *Windfall School*, among the Oneidas, in Madison Co., has 40 scholars, with an average of 15. Studies pursued, reading, writing, spelling, arithmetic, geography, English grammar, drawing, and book-keeping. Mrs. H. A. E. Hall, teacher. The *Orchard School*, in Oneida, commenced about five months since, has 40 scholars, with an average of 20. Studies, reading, writing, spelling, arithmetic and geography. Miss R. M. Allen, teacher.

q On the Tuscarora reservation 34 can read but not write.

r On the Tonawanda reservation 11 can read but not write, and 5 can read Seneca.

s This Church belongs to the A. B. C. F. Missions, is valued at $450, with $1,600 of other real estate, can seat 150, usual attendance 80, and number of communicants 88. The same society have a female boarding school valued at $1,400.

t These school houses are of wood, in fair condition, and valued at $150 each.

u These are very poor. One is valued at $100. New school houses are very much needed.

v Belongs to the Baptists, valued at $300, capable of seating 150, usually attending 40, number of communicants 25.

** Returns in 1855 incomplete.

CENSUS OF INDIAN RESERVATIONS.—(CONTINUED.)

RESERVATIONS.	ACRES OF IMPROVED LAND.		CASH VALUE, 1855.		WHEAT.				OATS.				RYE.				BARLEY.			
					Acres sown.		Bushels harvested.		Acres sown.		Bushels harvested.		Acres sown.		Bushels harvested.		Acres sown.		Bushels harvested.	
	1845.	1855.	Of stock.	Of tools.	1845.	1855.	1845.	1855.	1845.	1855.	1845.	1855.	1845.	1855.	1845.	1855.	1845.	1855.	1845.	1855.
Allegany,	2, 163½	1, 714	$14, 155	$3, 152	46	10	503	142	212¼	2*	4, 366	1, 951		9		90	6		35	
Buffalo,	1, 914								115½		4, 251									
Cattaraugus,	2, 439	3, 032½	27, 121	8, 151	184	10*	2, 032	3, 603	88	4*	10, 544½	5, 147		*		40	96¼	4*	1, 300	690
Oneida,	421	354¾	2, 106	1, 056½	14	21½	325	417	28½	48	720	707					10	4	200	419
Onondaga,	2, 043¼	2, 063½	6, 969¾	8, 942¼	87¾	76	1, 156	221	107	75½	2, 110	2, 076½					2½		70	
St. Regis,	591¼	1, 425½	9, 503	2, 676	42½	82¾	195	938	51	63½	290	642					¾			
Shinecock,			1, 050	215		2½		71		5		150								
Tonawanda,	2, 216	2, 515	15, 526	2, 999	200	126	2, 400	1, 715	100	87½	2, 500	2, 811	4		60		42		550	
Tuscarora,	2, 079½	3, 092	17, 004	5, 781	405½	745	4, 897	8, 041	205½	193	4, 085	5, 216					20	3	430	60
Total,	13, 867½	14, 197¼	$93, 434¾	$32, 973	979¾	1, 073¾	11, 508	15, 148	907	478½	28, 866½	18, 700½	4	9	60	130	177¾	11	2, 585	1, 169

RESERVATIONS.	BUCKWHEAT.				CORN.				POTATOES.				PEAS.			
	Acres sown.		Bushels harvested.		Acres planted.		Bushels harvested.		Acres planted.		Bushels harvested.		Acres sown.		Bushels harvested.	
	1845.	1855.	1845.	1855.	1845.	1855.	1845.	1855.	1845.	1855.	1845.	1855.	1845.	1855.	1845.	1855.
Allegany,	18¼	18*		1, 706	407		8, 565	5, 534	146½		3, 638	3, 966	18¼		90	26
Buffalo,	3				163½		2, 925		33		1, 444		18½			
Cattaraugus,	6½	8*	647	358	535¾	22*	9, 936	16, 272	91¾	2*	7, 192	7, 355		*	324	43
Oneida,					60½	55½	1, 458	1, 160	32¼	2½	841	126	3½		35	60
Onondaga,	2½		50		189½	188½	4, 492	3, 473	21	20¼	840	868¼	7¾	6½	91	29¾
St. Regis,	8	4½		30	65½	98¾	658½	902	20⅝	43⅜	410	2, 094	27	30½	105	336½
Shinecock,						39		1, 530		7		388				
Tonawanda,	5		112		170	159	3, 950	3, 725	40	15¾	1, 150	1, 179	30	5	200	44
Tuscarora,	18	20½	245	128	152	228½	3, 515	7, 225	31	47	1, 166	2, 665	5		65	
Total,	61¼	51	1, 054	2, 222	1, 743¾	791¼	35, 499½	39, 821	416⅛	137⅝	16, 681	18, 641¼	110	42	910	539¼

RESERVATIONS.	BEANS.				TURNIPS.				APPLE ORCHARD		MEADOW.				Acres plowed year previous.	Acres in fallow year previous.	Acres in pasture year previous.	Pounds of maple sugar.	Gallons of maple molasses.	Lbs. of honey.	Lbs. of wax.
	Acres planted.		Bushels harvested.		Acres sown.		Bushels harvested.		Bushels of apples.	Bbls. of cider.	Acres		Tons of hay.	Bush. of seed.							
	1845.	1855.	1845	1855.	1845.	1855.	1845.	1855.	1855.	1855.	1845.	1855.	1855.	1855.	1855.	1855.	1855.	1855.	1855.	1855	1855.
Allegany,				209	25¾		29	120	3, 570		416½	144	290					806	7		
Buffalo,											174½										
Cattaraugus,		*¼		528	5½	*	179	110	860	34	251	*4	246		*17			1, 770	52	280	10
Oneida,	3¼	3⅛	11	84¼					40		17	42	40½				16	60	70		
Onondaga,					¾		30		1, 798		116¼	84¾	93½	80	578½	9	126½	431	21½		
St. Regis,	11	¾	18	11	13–16			2				414½	387		68		†	340	5		
Shinecock,		1½		13		¼		30				½	1		57¼						
Tonawanda,	1	¾	15	11	3	¼	60	15	2, 071		180	145¾	248¾		76	27	14	7, 555	14		
Tuscarora,				123	2½		55		636		195	283	238		388	485	578	1, 702	35	170	10
Total,	15¼	6⅝	44	979¼	38.5-16	½	353	277	8, 975	34	1, 350¼	1, 118½	1, 504¾	80							

RESERVATIONS.	DOMESTIC ANIMALS.															
	Number of neat cattle.		Neat cattle under one year.		Neat cattle over one year old.		Working oxen.	Number of cows milked.		Number of horses.		Number of sheep.		Number of swine.	
	1845.	1855.	1845.	1855.	1845.	1855.	1855.	1845.	1855.	1845.	1855.	1845.	1855.	1845	1855.
Allegany,	585	389		104		285	84	169	119	149	96	79	9	627	526
Buffalo,	270							87		123		41		369	
Cattaraugus,	450	729		153		576	154	209	235	262	197	405	91	991	1, 054
Oneida,	50	43		1		42		28	20	17	18			46	36
Onondaga,	189	141		33		108	9	82	40	64	42	49	44	327	142
St. Regis,	90	161	17	30	16	131	29	42	66	50	108			112	142
Shinecock,		16		2		14	4		10		6				32
Tonawanda,	305	261		45		216	49	88	95	130	97	50		390	409
Tuscarora,	336	349		62		287	68	98	112	153	109	215	92	596	464
Total,	2, 275	2, 089	17	430	16	1, 659	397	803	697	948	673	839	236	3, 458	2, 805

* Returns incomplete.

† The pasture of both parties of the St. Regis Indians, is in common, embracing an unenclosed field of about 2,000 acres.

CENSUS OF INDIAN RESERVATIONS.—(Continued.)

Reservations.	Pounds of butter.		Value of unenumerated farm products, 1855.	Domestic manufactures, 1855.					
	1845.	1855.		Axe helves, whips, &c.	Baskets and brooms.	Bead work.	Clothing.	Socks.	Miscellaneous.
Allegany,	....	1,740	$131	$50	$170	....	....	....	$100
Buffalo,	4,888	....	....	....	....	....	....	....	....
Cattaraugus,	2,426	2,271	....	....	....	$40	....	$3	....
Oneida,	1,140	....	....	....	....	530	....	....	....
Onondaga,	1,150	....	489	....	....	564	....	....	....
St. Regis,	....	3,540	....	....	400	885	$90	....	....
Shinecock,	....	410	....	....	....	....	....	....	....
Tonawanda,	3,200	9,540	....	....	....	....	....	....	....
Tuscarora,	7,537	6,988	190	....	15	10	....	....	110
Total,	20,341	24,489	$810	$50	$585	$2,029	$90	$3	$210

Occupations.

Allegany, 1 carpenter, 22 farmers, 12 hunters, 1 Indian doctor, 4 lumbermen, 1 miller, 1 minister, 1 pilot, and 1 student.

Cattaraugus, 3 carpenters, and 1 blacksmith.

Onondaga, 1 wagon maker.

St. Regis, 1 clerk, 58 farmers, 2 hunters, and 9 laborers. A considerable number reported as farmers, devote a part of the summer to rafting timber on the St. Lawrence.

Shinecock, 1 farmer, 18 fishermen, and 33 mariners.

Tonawanda, 2 broom-makers, 2 carpenters, 87 farmers, 1 interpreter, 7 laborers, 1 lawyer and engineer, 1 mason, 1 physician, 2 preachers, and 1 teacher. A saw mill, valued at $700, is owned by an Indian family on this reservation.

Tuscarora, 22 bead-workers, (females,) 1 carpenter, 4 "corn planters," 1 doctor, 26 farmers, 14 laborers, 10 musicians, and 1 wagon-maker.

Inns, Stores, and Groceries.

Allegany, 2 inns and 1 retail store kept by whites; 1 grocery kept by an Indian.

St. Regis, 2 groceries kept by whites.

NOTES RELATING TO THE SEVERAL INDIAN TRIBES.

Cayugas.—These Indians have now no separate reservation, being scattered among other tribes. A considerable number removed to beyond the Mississippi river many years since, and in 1831 the annuities due from the State, amounting to $2,300, were divided; the sum of $1,700, being allowed to those west of the Mississippi, and $600 to those in New-York. Of the 550 Sandusky Cayugas who had thus removed, nearly all died. In 1847, 25 returned to New-York, and in 1849 the legislature appropriated $600 from their annuity to bring back the few survivors who wished to return. A treaty was held June 7, 1850, between the Cayugas and the Commissioners of the Land Office, which provided that a periodical census should be taken by their chiefs. The first of these, dated March, 1855, is as follows:

CENSUS OF CAYUGAS, 1855.

Residence.	Heads of families.	Men.	Women.	Children.	Total.
In the State of New-York,	48	29	37	77	143 } 201
West of Mississippi river,	10	....	....	....	58 }

Oneidas and Onondagas.—Mr. Nathaniel T. Strong, an educated Seneca, living in Chautauque county, was appointed to take the census of these tribes. His report was accompanied by the following letter, which commends itself to a careful perusal:

"Cattaraugus Reservation, *Irving*, *Nov.* 10, 1855.

To the Honorable Secretary of State:

Sir.—After receiving your commission, and the instructions to take the census of the Indians residing upon the Onondaga Reservation, in the county of Onondaga, and the Oneida 'Indian Settlement,'* in the counties of Madison and Oneida, in June last, I proceeded to Onondaga Castle, the remnants of the Onondagas first claiming my attention. On my arrival, I communicated to some of the leading chiefs the object of my visit. The chiefs thereupon called a council, to which I made known the requirements of the Constitution of the State, and the provisions of the present law, authorizing the census to be taken of the inhabitants once in every ten years, in obedience to the Constitution. I was asked whether this census, and the

* There is, at present, no reservation belonging to the Oneidas.—H.

statistical information to be obtained, had not reference to some kind of taxation? I replied, that the present law did not contemplate any such object, and I further assured them, that the State probably would not impose upon them any kind of taxation, so long as they remained in their present condition as Indians in tribal capacities, and governed by their own peculiar laws; but whenever they shall have changed that condition and become citizens of the State, then a law would most likely be enacted to meet their then condition. The chiefs then informed me that I might go on and take the census.

"I accordingly commenced my labors, making use of the blanks furnished me so far as they were applicable to the Onondagas and the Oneidas. On the third day of my labors, some mischievous persons having circulated a story to the effect, that the census I was taking actually had reference to some kind of taxation, a large council was called and I was notified to attend, which I felt it my duty to do.

"The council was opened, and, after the usual preliminary forms observed by the Indians, I was requested, with great politeness, to re-state to the council my official instructions, with which I very cheerfully complied, repeating substantially the printed instructions, and stating what I supposed was the object of the State, &c., after which I withdrew from the council, that the assembled chiefs might deliberate on this to them momentous question; after several hours spent in agitating the subject, I was re-called to the council. Upon taking my seat, I was informed that the council had been deliberating on the subject of my mission among them, and had come to the conclusion not to interfere with me, but allow me to finish my labors unmolested.

"I was highly pleased with the Onondaga people, on account of the politeness and courtesy shown me whilst I was among them, especially on the part of the old chiefs, the head of whom is the venerable Harry Webster. In the progress of my mission when I came to the house of this interesting relict of the old-time aboriginal chieftains, for the purpose of taking the census, and enquired his age, he arose and went into an adjoining room whence he returned with a square pine stick, perhaps four feet long, thickly covered with notches in parallel rows. These he deliberately commenced to count, on numbering one row he declared his age to be seventy-six years, and the same number as that of his wife, whom he had buried but the day previous. He had carefully preserved the ages of every other member of his family, numbering sixteen, on this wooden chronometer. This is a vestige of the ancient method of chronology among the aborigines.

"The Onondagas are now few in number, as the census herewith returned will show. With deep regret I am constrained to say, that the unmixed Onondagas are gradually dwindling away, but the cross of the Onondagas with the Oneidas are increasing in number. The Onondaga Reservation is understood to contain seven thousand acres of land, rich and fertile as any in the State of New-York; three thousand four hundred acres are in a state of cultivation, say two thousand acres are in the *highest state* of cultivation.

"The Onondagas are gradually advancing toward civilization. The almost unconquerable prejudices against the civilization of the white man, are giving away in the mind of the Onondaga. As this prejudice melts away progress in civilization is more perceptible. Like some of the stupendous floods in nature warring against strong obstructions and barriers, as fast as the barriers of error yield the tide of civilization sweeps onward, overwhelming in ruin the old land marks of barbarism, but scattering fertility and the seeds of a new life in its resistless course. But the white man is delaying and interfering with the eventual civilization of the Onondaga. How does he interfere? is the natural question. In this way: The rich men of Syracuse and its vicinity, come to the Onondaga Indian, and say to him, 'Here you have one or two hundred acres of land, I will give two or three, or five hundred dollars cash down for the use of this land for four or five years, and when I leave, the land will be greatly improved and enhanced in value.' The sum thus offered seems large to the uncalculating Indian, and accordingly is generally accepted. Many hundred acres of land are leased in this way for less than one dollar per acre, and the amount paid, I am told, is often times spent in less than a month. In this way, a continual indolence, disastrous to the hopes of the philanthropist, is fostered. If the Onondagas are to be benefited in the possession of their fertile lands, the leasing system is either to be forbidden by law or regulated in some proper manner by the State; otherwise, the present mode of leasing lands which has become so general, must eventually prove their ruin. I refer to the statistical returns made of this people, in which many hundred acres of their land are reported as being improved, and how little it has been cultivated by the Indian proprietors. Comparatively speaking, they have scarcely raised grain enough for their own consumption. I felt some reluctance in refering to this subject, but I regard it to be of vital importance to the future well being of the Onondagas. It is with that view that I have presented it for the information of the Secretary of State.

"The estimates of the value of the Onondaga lands, I am aware, are pretty high, as the basis from which it is formed is the value of the lands adjoining them belonging to the whites. Two-thirds of all the cultivated lands belonging to the Onondagas, amounting to three thousand and odd acres, are in the possession of the whites by lease, and, therefore, I can see no reason why I should put the value of the Indian lands lower than that of the whites.

"As regards the statistical information, I obtained it just so far as it was possible, after no inconsiderable trouble and labor, and was obliged to employ assistance to accomplish the desired object, notwithstanding, I confess it is imperfect and unsatisfactory in some respects.

"The Onondagas have but one school, under the direction of a teacher employed, I believe, by Rev. Sam'l J. May, of Syracuse, as agent for the State. There are but few scholars who attend regularly, and no one of the Indians appears to take any interest in its success. There appear to be no regulations in the school, the children are dismissed from study for almost every trifling cause in order to conciliate them.

"The parents do not really of themselves know whether the children attend the school; all they know is, that the children start for the school, and as to whether they ever get there is a matter of no concern to them. A majority of the Onondagas are conscientiously opposed to their children being taught in schools, because they believe that they are absolutely distinct from the whites, and that their future destiny is as different and as wide apart as the distinctions of complexion, habits, thoughts and feelings now prevailing between the two races. They believe the Great Spirit never designed that the red man should be taught to learn books.

"To show the many devices employed to keep the people from sending their children to school, I will relate the following anecdote, communicated to me by the venerable and distinguished pagan chief, Governor Black Snake, of Allegany. He said that soon after the commencement of schools on the Allegany reservation, the prophet communicated to the 'keepers of the faith,' that the Great Spirit was displeased with them because they sent their children to school, which was one of the devices of the evil spirit to lead them astray; that it was his will that they should at once discontinue sending their children to schools. The 'keepers of the faith' heard the message with dismay, and on consultation among themselves came to the conclusion that they would refer the whole matter to the venerable chief, Governor Black Snake, and be guided by his decision, little doubting, however, that he would decide that the children should be kept from school. A committee was accordingly appointed from their number to wait upon the Chief, and they did so, and were received by him with the usual urbanity of that famous Chief of the American forest. After hearing the revelations of the prophet relative to the schools, and being informed of the deep concern of the 'keepers of the faith' thereat, but that nevertheless they had resolved to be guided by his decision. The venerable chief replied, that he was deeply sensible of the honor which the 'keepers of the faith' had done him, and that he had listened to the narrative of the committee with great attention.

"'Now,' said he, 'listen to my decision. I decide that the children shall be kept in school, notwithstanding the revelation of the prophet, and if the Great Spirit is displeased with his red children for this act, the evil spirit will torment the children themselves in hell, and *not us*, old people!'

"The 'keepers of the faith' left the chief disappointed, but did not dare to disregard his decision. Thus, he said, the schools were continued.

"The Onondaga school requires careful attention, and by persons who take a decided interest in this noble but fading race, aside from the emolument received for instructing and superintending the school. The parents need to be taught, also, and be made sensible that the education of their children is the last hope of their race, and that unless the children are educated, they must be overwhelmed by the irresistible tide of progress and civilization, sweeping them down with its relentless current into the gulf of oblivion, whose waters will settle over them forever. It is very desirable that the State should devise some permanent and feasible plan for the education of the Onondaga children in a more efficient manner. The Onondagas proper have been gradually decreasing for the last century. The reasons are, I think, obvious, and can be accounted for in this way. They have been strict in not mixing with the other portions of the Five Nations, although there was no rule against intermarriages, but the descent being through the female line, in part produced this result. As a general rule, when a woman intermarries, she goes and resides with her husband, and amongst his Nation and friends, and her children are accounted to belong to the mother's Nation and clan. The consequence is they are regarded as strangers, having no permanent interest with the people and Nation with whom they are residing, and this custom operated as a prohibition against intermarriages.

"The Onondagas kept themselves united, and this system enabled them to keep themselves a distinct community for many years, notwithstanding their proximity to the other people of the Five Nations. This, undoubtedly, is one of the true causes which operated against them in lessening their numbers, and this is generally its effect on small communities. For since the last large sale to the State of the Oneida lands, and their removal out of the State, some two hundred of them remained behind as stragglers, and were compelled by necessity to claim the hospitality of their Onondaga friends; since this period the Onondagas and Oneidas have amalgamated, and the population has increased rapidly. While there is a ray of light in the path of the red man, will not the State do something more than it has ever yet done to rescue the remnants of this noble race, by giving them the means of educating their children for a few years, until they shall become a self-sustaining people? Will not the statesmen and philanthropists of this noble State join hands in the christian enterprise of rescuing from impending extinction the remnant of the Onondagas? Let the associations, the thronging memories of the past plead for them. The story of their wrongs and sorrows is familiar to all, and its recital by one little versed in any but the lore of the woods cannot enhance its interests, or clothe it with additional power to stir your sympathies. O let your hearts be moved with pity toward them! Though their pride and stoicism are traditional, be assured they have warm hearts, and are keenly sensitive to their degradation and fallen State. The warlike Iroquois, once styled the 'Romans of the West,' whose fathers welcomed yours to their shores, cherished them when *theirs* was the power to oppress and destroy; whose bones lie mingled with your fathers' on many a battle-field, who were ever loyal, even to heroism, toward your race, regardless of the alluring voice of that powerful rival, whose fortifications frowned down upon you from the opposite banks of the St. Lawrence and Niagara, and who would have wrested this fair territory from you but for the Iroquois, this people, once united, once numerous, once powerful, once giving such rich promise of a speedy civilization, are reduced to a broken, feeble, dispirited band. But this remnant can be saved if efforts are made in time. If neglected, they will soon pass away, and the shadows of the grave will hide the wronged and sorrowing race from your sight forever. No monuments will then perpetuate their memory, save the mountains and rivers whose names they gave, and no records will do justice to their rude virtues and sad history, but the imperishable records of a just and avenging God!

"After having got through with the Onondagas, I then repaired to the 'Oneida Indian Settlement.' On my arrival, I found they were in two settlements called the 'Windfall' and the 'Orchard' parties. I called upon the leading men of the 'Windfall' party, in Madison county first, and to them I made known the object of my visit. They were not able to agree whether I should take the enumeration or not, as they were fearful that it was in some way connected with taxation, as they were before taxed by the action of the county in which they lived. I explained the law to them, and upon the next day it was deemed proper to adjourn the deliberation to the seats of the 'Orchard' party, in Oneida county. It was then decided that I should take the census, which I proceeded to do, the people gathering in one place and giving me all the information I required without calling at their houses; as I had every confidence in the men who arranged this matter, I did not hesitate to adopt this course. They were men known to me, so that the statistical information of 'Oneida Indian Settlement,' has been obtained without calling at a single house. It will be seen that the Oneidas own but a few acres of land, which is the property of a few individuals, and their friends are residing with them who have no lands.

"This interesting people are now but few in number in this State, as the census returns show. They still cling with great tenacity to the homes and haunts of their ancestors. They have two good schools, and the children have made a commendable progress. I was pleased with their appearance. These people have embraced the Christian religion. They have one missionary among them, who spends part of his time with them and is doing much good, but they are poor and need the aid and sympathy of the humane and the fostering care of the State.

"In relation to this people, a solemn question arises as to what is to become of them. Their land is reduced to a few acres, and emphatically the words of a distinguished Seneca orator would apply to them, 'They have hardly land enough to spread a blanket upon!' They are increasing in numbers, and every year increases their difficulties. A few years more, if they remain in the same friendless condition, they will have become uprooted and dispersed, the sad end of the Oneidas of New-York, a people who have ever proved themselves the steadfast friends of the people of this State. In the Revolution, when four of the Five Nations took up the tomahawk in behalf of the British King and against the Colonies, they alone remained loyal to the colony of New-York, and shared with her all her trials and dangers during that memorable struggle. Their lands are now in the possession of the people of the State, and the Oneidas are as aliens in the land of their fathers. Will not the recollection of the early trials and common dangers shared by the fathers of the State, create a generous emotion in the hearts of their sons, and induce them in their greatness and wealth, to extend their aid to the children of those generous warriors who defended their firesides in the times which tried men's souls? It has become imperative that their children receive a useful education and learn the arts as a means of livelihood, as their lands are now gone from them. There has occurred no death among this people for two years, and at the time of my visit there was not a single case of sickness among them.

"The subject of the reclamation of the Red man is one of deep and absorbing interest. There are now four thousand members of the six nations residing in the State of New-York. In many repects they have become assimilated to the condition of the dense white population which surrounds them. Necessity has compelled them to resign the arrow and spear for the plow, and the fertile soil now yields that sustenance which they but recently sought in the pathless forests and prolific streams. Reluctantly diverted from the exciting chase and perilous war-path, the mind of the young warrior now seeks another aliment and is quickened by new aspirations. He sees a new field opened before him, with pressing inducements to enter and emulate his white brethren in the friendly contest for the triumphs of industry and civilization. Hereditary pride, the prejudice of complexion, and it may be, the rememberance of past indignities and wrongs, have hitherto prevented him from relaxing his tenacious grasp on the customs and memories of his fathers, and initiating himself into a new and better life. But a change has been gradually wrought in his condition, mode of life and habits of thought, which gives a flattering promise for the future.

"It is conceded that there are but two means of rescuing the Indian from his impending destiny, these are education and Christianity. The question arises, who has accomplished the most in the work of civilization for the Red man in this State? The answer is, the missionaries; the Red man is mainly indebted to them for what has been accomplished for him and his children, in education and in the knowledge of Christianity. The faithful and self-denying missionaries have labored among the New-York Indians for many years, relying partially upon their own inadequate means in carrying on their arduous labors. The consequences have been slow, but whatever has been done is chiefly due to them and to the denominations of Christians they represented. The State of New-York has expended large sums of money of late years, to aid the Red man in his civilization, which have done much good. But I am inclined to the opinion, that much of this money has been expended injudiciously, which, in proper hands, and with a better management, could have accomplished much greater good. Often times money has been placed in the hands of men who scarcely knew the Indians, men who have never been in nor seen an Indian school, they were selected to superintend the schools and the funds for the payment of teachers, without consulting their qualifications for furthering the progress of Indian civilization, and they had no interest in its success any further than the emolument that is attached to the superintendency.

"I respectfully suggest, therefore, for the consideration of the Secretary, that the future appropriations by the State for the benefit of the Red man, that this *sacred trust* be committed into the hands of the missionaries, who are able to make the most judicious use of the means for civilizing and ameliorating the condition of the Indian population of the State of New-York.

Respectfully submitted,

HON-NON-DEUH, or,

NATH'L T. STRONG."

By an act passed in 1847, a census of the Onondagas is taken annually, and reported to the Comptroller, as the basis of distribution of annuities. The results of these enumerations have been as follows:

YEARS.	On the Onondaga reservation.	On the Allegany reservation.	On the Cattaraugus reservation	On the Tonawanda reservation.	On the Tuscarora reservation.	Total.
1847,	a269	88	32	6	22	417
1848,	310	94	40	11	21	476
1849,	b333	89	43	11	24	500
1850,	309	90	39	13	25	476
1851,	314	87	25	12	28	466
1852,	321	92	41	....	27	481
1853,	330	c	c	c	c	505
1854,	304	92	33	6	29	464
1855,	309	93	35	9	32	478
1856,	302	c	c	c	c	462

St. Regis.—The Indian village of St. Regis,*d* on the south bank of the river St. Lawrence, where it is intersected by the 45th degree of north latitude, was founded about the year 1760, or a little before, by a colony from Caughnawaga, near Montreal, under Father Anthony Gordon, a Jesuit priest of that mission.

A tradition is preserved at St. Regis, that in the early part of the last century, two little boys of the name of Tarbell were stolen by the Indians, while at play, in the town of Groton, Massachusetts, and

a Of these 160 are reported as old settlers, and 109 as returned emigrants.

b Ten deaths occurred on this reservation during the preceding year. Of the number reported in 1849, 210 were of the resident, and 123 of the emigrant party. The latter, had been somewhat increased by removals from Cattaraugus.

c Reported together.

d The natives call their village Ak-wis-sas-ne, "where the partridge drums" alluding, not as would appear, to the abundance of this game, but to a peculiar rumbling noise heard in winter, occasioned by the passage of masses of ice from the rapids above under the solid ice opposite the village. In extremely cold weather ice dams form occasionally very suddenly, causing a destructive overflow of the river and much injury to property along the banks. St. Regis is named from Jean François Regis, a native of Languedoc, who joined the Jesuit order and spent several years in zealous missionary labors among the poor in France. He died in 1640, and was canonized in 1737. His festival occurs on the 16th of June.

adopted and reared among the natives at Caughnawaga, acquiring their habits, language and manners. Upon reaching manhood, they married daughters of the chiefs; but from a difference of race, or other causes, a series of petty quarrels ensued between the young men and Indians of their age, which was finally quieted by their removal with their families to the site of the present village of St. Regis, where they were residing at the time of Gordon's arrival. The descendants of these Tarbells have ever since resided at St. Regis, and several have been distinguished as chiefs and head men of the tribe. One of them, named Lesor Tarbell, was a prominent chief about fifty years since, and was very much esteemed by the whites for his prudence, candor, and great worth of character. The name occurs repeatedly in treaties and other negotiations which these people have held with the State of New-York.

The settlement at St. Regis was increased on the breaking up of the mission at Fort Presentation, (now Ogdensburgh) in 1760, and the removal of a part of the Oswegatchies, although the latter did not finally abandon their settlement until 1806. Both of these sources of emigration were originally formed by the removal of Indians from New-York to Canada, through the influence of the French, and the language at St. Regis at the present time, is the Mohawk dialect of the Iroquois. This emigration from New-York, was encouraged by the French, with the double view of securing the Indian trade, and of attaching the natives to the Catholic religion, which has since been sustained among them.* These people retain none of the festivals and ceremonies of their ancestors, but the ancient distinction of bands has been transmitted in the female line to the present time, the number in June 1855, on the American side of the line being as follows: Wolf, (Okawaho), 195; Plover, (Rotinesiio), 89; Little Turtle, (Rotisennakehte), 41; Big Turtle, (Ratiniaten), 33; Bear, (Okwari), 21; not known, 41.

The St. Regis Indians formerly claimed the title of the islands in the St. Lawrence above their village, as far as French Creek, and in the early settlement of St. Lawrence county, serious difficulties were apprehended between the grantees under the Indians, and the patentees under the State. Within a few years, considerable sums have been paid by the State, for the right which these Indians had lost in the transfer of their lands by the location of the national boundary. They also claimed an undefined territory in the northern part of the State, besides a large tract in Canada. By a treaty held in May, 1796, the "Seven Nations of Canada"† surrendered to New-York all their title to land, with the exception of six miles square at St. Regis, one mile square on Salmon river, at the present village of Fort Covington, one mile square at the mills on Grass river below the present village of Massena, and the natural meadows on Grass river. These reservations have since been reduced by successive sales, to a tract of about 14,030 acres, a part of which is leased to whites for a term of years, by virtue of an act passed in 1841. The American party received from the State of New-York for the lands ceded an annuity of $2,131.66, which is equally divided among them per capita, by an agent appointed by the Comptroller.

The lands of these people in Canada have been mostly sold, or leased, the rents of which amount to about $2 per head to the British party. In addition to this, the English government gives presents of blankets and pilot cloth to each person, of a value proportioned to their age. Powder, shot and guns are also given, but it is understood that these presents are to be hereafter discontinued.

To increase these slender revenues, which are often anticipated by the sale of certificates to whites at a great discount before payment is due, most families cultivate small patches of land, while a considerable number of the young men are employed, during the early months of summer, in conducting rafts down the rapids of the St. Lawrence. Some go out to labor among the farmers in harvest, and a few resort to the primitive mode of hunting and fishing for subsistence.‡ There are a few good farmers among these people, who manage their affairs with ability and success, but the greater number exhibit an indolence and apathy that promises little in the way of improvement, without a radical change in their circumstances, a practical education of the young in the language and arts of civilized life, and at a proper period, the division of the common lands into individual rights. An examination of the accompanying tables, will show an unusual proportion of children, and the enumerations annually made for the distribution of annuities indicate a gradual increase in numbers among them. This growth has been repeatedly checked

---

* At St. Regis, the succession of Catholic missionaries has been as follows: Anthony Gordon, 1760 to 1775, after which the mission was without a priest for four or five years. Fathers Denaut, (afterwards Bishop of Quebec,) Lebrun and L'Archambault, occasionally visited the place in this interval. In December, 1785, Roderick McDonnell succeeded and remained until his death. He has been followed by Fathers Rinfret in 1806, Jean B. Roupe in 1807, Joseph Marcoux in 1812, Nicholas Dufresne in 1819, Joseph Vallé in 1825, and Francis X. Marcoux, the present incumbent, in 1832. The number reporting themselves as belonging to the several religions in 1855, was: Catholics, 339; Methodist, 48; Episcopalians, 8. The Canada census of 1852, gave 978 Catholics, 21 Episcopalians, 56 Presbyterians and 8 Baptists, as residing in the Canadian portion of the village, including both whites and Indians. A Methodist mission was established at Hogansburgh, on the border of the Reservation, in 1847, '48.

† Of the settlements composing these seven nations, only that at Caughnawaga ever participated in the treaties with New-York or shared in the annuities paid under them. A further account of these treaties will be given under the head of "Cessions of land by the Iroquois."

‡ These people seldom or never become chargeable to the town or county in which they live.

by the ravages of epidemics,* to which their habits of life particularly expose them. Were it not for these unusual causes, their numbers would have ere this exceeded the capacity of their reservation for comfortable agricultural support.

Previous to the war of 1812, the whole tribe was governed by twelve chiefs, chosen for life, after their ancient custom, and the annuities and presents of both governments were shared equally among them. Upon the declaration of war, it was agreed with these people, that they should remain neutral, but in violation of this engagement, a company of about eighty warriors was raised for the British army, who served during the war. Several of the tribe afterwards joined the American army, among the most efficient of whom was Col. Louis Cook, or Atiatonharonkwen, who had held a commission from the Commander in Chief, as lieutenant colonel in the army of the Revolution, and whose wonderful native sagacity and energy of character, had given him a commanding influence with the Indian tribes.

The war created parties among the St. Regis people, which have continued till the present time. It also led to a change in the form of government, the British party retaining the old system of chiefs, with the number reduced to seven. This mode was continued until June, 1855, when it was abolished on account of the misconduct of those who had held the office many years, and it was ordered that in future there should be an annual appointment of chiefs by the English government. The American party are required by a law of the State, to elect three trustees annually, who have the general charge of public affairs. The election of these officers is often conducted with much spirit, the American Indians being divided into parties, chiefly on the policy of leasing their lands.

The distinction of party, which originated in the war, has been continued by hereditary descent on the fathers' side to the present time. By the consent of the chiefs, or trustees, a man can be transferred from one to the other, or Indians from other places may be admitted to the rights of either, but this is seldom done.† A woman loses her rights in one party, by marrying a member of the other, but acquires for herself and children the rights of her husband. A white woman upon marrying an Indian, gains for herself and children a right to the same annuities or presents that her husband receives, but a white man on marrying an Indian woman acquires no right, nor does the woman, or her children, lose their right as Indians if they remain on the reservation. The presents of the British government are divided among British Indians only, and the amount varies with the age of the person. The annuities paid by the State of New-York, are shared equally among the American Indians without reference to age. The lands of both parties are held in common, and families of either party may reside in the territory of their own or the other government without losing their rights.‡ Although the law recognizes no individual rights to the soil, custom has sanctioned the holding of land for the exclusive benefit of families, and these rights are bought and sold among themselves. A white person marrying and living with the Indians, is sometimes allowed to acquire this conventional title to land. Formerly it was held, that upon the death of a father, the house and furniture belonged to the daughters and the right of land to the sons, but the children now share equally in the division of property.

Any Indian may appropriate for cultivation so much as he pleases of the woodlands on the reservation, provided he clears and occupies it, and the improvements on the land so assumed may be sold to others of the tribe. Indians may pasture upon the commons as many cattle as they please, there being no regulation as to the number to which any person shall be limited. Whites frequently hire the privileges of the common, by paying the chiefs, or trustees, a price agreed upon, which is usually an eighth of a dollar a week or two dollars for the season per head. Woodlands are held as common property, and every Indian has the right of cutting wood wherever he pleases, either for his own use or for sale.§ It is evident that these regulations could only exist among an indolent and semi-barbarous people, and that with the least enterprise or emulation in the acquirement of property, their reservation would soon be appropriated altogether, by individuals and conflicting claims would quickly lead to discord and confusion. This community of landed interest is undoubtedly a bar to further improvement, and until it is changed, there can be little prospect of advancement in civilization. The State of New-York has maintained for several

* In the spring of 1829, the small pox swept off great numbers. On the 29th of June, 1832, the cholera broke out among them, accompanied by a typhus fever, and about 340 cases occurred, of which 134 were fatal. In 1849 the cholera again appeared, destroying 29, and the same year about 500 cases of small pox occurred, proving fatal to 30. In 1850 typhus fever prevailed the whole summer.

† The nativities of those living on the American side in 1855 were as follows: St. Regis, Canada side, 179; ditto, American side, 201; Lake of the Two Mountains 13; Caughnawaga 9; Northwestern country 2; St. Francis 1; Oneida 1.

‡ In June, 1855, there were 375 American and 38 British Indians living in the State of New-York. The number of American Indians living in Canada was 160. The whole number of Indians drawing annuities from New-York was 535, and of those receiving rents and presents from the British government 643. The number of the American party during several years has been as follows: 1846, 452;—1847, 465;—1848, 495;—1849, 487;—1851, 498;—1852, 497;—1853, 470.

§ Within a few years large quantities of wood have been taken from the reservation. An intelligent citizen of Hogansburgh estimates that between four and five thousand cords were taken off within the last year. It is mostly sold at Montreal. The destruction of timber has since been rapid, and promises soon to lead to serious altercations and difficulties.

years two schools upon the reservation, but these are very poorly attended, and little or no benefit is now derived from them.

The Tuscaroras.—This once powerful tribe was adopted by the Iroquois and became the sixth member of their confederacy in 1712. They came originally from the country of the Neuse and Tar rivers, in North Carolina, where, in 1708, they counted fifteen towns and twelve hundred warriors. Mr. William Mount Pleasant, an intelligent native chief, was appointed to take the census of the Tuscaroras residing on their reservation in Lewiston, Niagara county, but being prevented by an accident, his son Silas acted as marshal. The returns were accompanied by a letter from the person first appointed, which embraces many interesting facts concerning the history and present condition of these people.

After stating the rudeness and barbarism of their primitive condition,—"Their council fire still burning and the smoke from their earthen pipes ascending up toward heaven—their state house constructed of bark and poles, their palaces their wigwams, and their grist mill—two small stones for cracking corn to make their samp—their Savior, the Thar-on-ya-wa-go, that is to say, the holder of the heavens who killed their enemies, their time of Pentecost the ripening of their corn," he adds: "They were, nevertheless, happy in their estimation, until the pale faces from the other side of the great waters came and commenced their agressions upon their lands. They were aggrieved and wronged in the onset. Their neighbors, the trespassers upon their territory, were not of a character to have a very nice sense of right and wrong. They commenced surveying and parceling out, without their consent, the lands which they had held from time immemorial. These extraordinary proceedings gave rise to a rupture between the native born inhabitants and the aliens, which terminated in the almost total destruction of the Tuscaroras, by combining the forces of North and South Carolina with the Cherokees, Creeks, Catawbas, Yamases and Ashley Indians. Their council fire was extinguished by the blood of Tuscaroras, and the prisoners, eight hundred in number, were carried off to South Carolina where they were sold for slaves, which was worse than death to them. Thus defeated and persecuted, driven from their lands and homes by the adverse results of a contest provoked by wrong aggression, soon after the fall of fort Na-ha-ru-ke, in 1713, the Tuscaroras found themselves unable to sustain their nationality, and were obliged to move northward to seek an asylum among their brethren in New-York. They came to Oneida, a portion of them lived with the Oneidas, and a part of them settled at Gu-da-nea-ka, now Chittenango. At this period the Tuscaroras began to scatter, some settled at O-nea-ho-qu-ga, others at Cha-nan-ke, now Chenango, some at Can-nea-so-ra-ka, some at Kan-nan-tats and some at Geneseo with Senecas, not as tenants in common, but as tenants at will or by sufferance. Although the Tuscaroras were adopted into the Five Nations, who thus became six, they had no independent territory which they could call their own. Such was their condition previous to the Revolution. At the commencement of hostilities a portion of the Tuscaroras espoused the American cause, several of them becoming trustworthy officers who held commissions in the United States service during the war. Such of them as had fallen under the influence of the English, through the Johnson family, as the political horizon became darkened around them in 1780, embarked in canoes upon Oneida lake, passed down the Oswego river and coasted along Lake Ontario to Fort Niagara, where they encamped in the winter of 1780, near the garrison, drawing a portion of their subsistence in the form of rations. The change of their diet caused a great mortality, and many of them died on the banks of the Niagara. In the spring the whole party left the banks for the east, on the Indian trail that leads to Tonawanda, Cannanwagas in Avon, to Canandaigua, &c. They came to a place on the site of an old Indian fort and mounds—a beautiful common, where was once an ancient Indian village. The party stopped for the night, and in the morning one of their number was sick with fever. A part of them proceeded on their way to the Seneca settlements at Geneseo, and the rest of them remained. The spring being advaneed, the party concluded to plant their corn which they received at Fort Niagara, and they thus became permanent settlers in the Niagara country.

"After the war those of the Tuscaroras who lived to the east, as already stated, removed from time to time to this place, until all settled in one locality. They had no better title than they had at the east, and were merely squatters upon the territory of another distinct nation. At Herkimer or Mohawk, in June, 1785, a treaty was held with the Oneidas and Tuscaroras, by George Clinton and other commissioners,* at which, for a consideration of $11,500, these nations ceded to the State of New-York the lands lying between the Unadilla and Chenango rivers, south of a line drawn east and west between these streams and north of the Pennsylvania line. The Oneidas were the principal negociators, the Tuscaroras merely acting as a party on account of the rights secured to them by the treaty of Fort Stanwix, in 1784, for in fact, they had no claim to the territory so ceded but were merely as guests.

---

* Treaty of Fort Herkimer, June 28, 1785. See *Indian Deeds and Treaties*, ii, page 147, Secretary's office.

"In 1797 a treaty was held at Geneseo, on the Genesee river,* between the Seneca Nation and Robert Morris, at which Jeremiah Wadsworth attended as commissioner for the United States, and William Shepard as agent for Massachusetts. The Senecas then ceded all their lands to the latter party, with the exception of certain reservations, among which was that occupied by the Tuscaroras, commonly called the Seneca Grant, containing one square mile, and the Holland company afterwards donated to them two square miles adjoining their first reservation. By these grants the Tuscaroras were relieved from serious apprehensions of being left without homes between the banks of the Niagara and the Hudson.

"The leading chiefs wishing still more land, and having no money to purchase, thought of the country they had left in North Carolina ninety years before, but considered their chances of recovering any pay for it very poor. After several councils, it was agreed to send a delegation to that State, and money was loaned by individuals who depended upon the success of the measure for repayment. Upon their arrival, the delegation found their proofs insufficient, and it was necessary to send back to Lewiston, and to Grand River in Canada, where some Tuscaroras lived who had recently emigrated from North Carolina, and were well acquainted with the rivers and country. The claim was at last established, and the avails of the lands were placed in the United States treasury in trust for them.

"In 1804 the Tuscaroras purchased for $13,722, of the Holland Company, 4,329 acres, making the total amount of the tract 6,249 acres. This purchase was made by Gen. Dearborn, then Secretary of War, with the fund received from North Carolina. Thus after they had gone through various vicissitudes and a severe ordeal for the space of ninety-one years, they finally rested in the possession of a quiet and peaceable, but moderate possession under the protection and fostering care of the Empire State, for which the Tuscaroras are truly grateful."

Mr. Mount Pleasant communicated with his report a detailed statement of the transactions of the New-York Indians with the Menomees of Green Bay and the general government, and after specifying the manner in which each of the New-York tribes have been paid for their interest in the purchase, he adds: "But alas for the Tuscaroras, they have not received their interest in these lands as yet. No reservation was made for them at Green Bay, and no money has been paid to us at our homes as was contemplated in the beginning. It is very clear that our rights are just as good as those of the St. Regis and Oneidas in New-York. The payments of the said sums have been made at their respective reservations, as a remuneration for moneys laid out by the said tribes, and for services rendered by their chiefs and agent in securing the title to the Green Bay land. We are talking about building a church in the centre of our reservation. The old meeting-house stands on one side of the reservation, and very inconvenient to a portion of the inhabitants; besides it is much decayed, and requires great expense to be repaired. Should the money be obtained from the government of the United States,—the sum of $3,000 which we certainly ought to have, it would come handy to apply in building a House of God, or some other public improvement of which we stand in need. We are like a fox crossing a creek on a log with a piece of meat in his mouth. He looked down below and saw a shadow of his meat in his mouth, and let go at once and jumped to catch a shadow, supposing it to be a substance. The shadow disappeared, and he coolly made to the shore, and on sober reflection he began to lecture himself with this exclamation: 'O how foolish I am to let the substance go for the sake of catching a shadow. The substance is gone and the shadow has disappeared and I remain in want.'"

The following account is given of the origin and condition of their schools and other public improvements of the reservation:

"Missionary labors were commenced among the Tuscaroras about the year 1805,† at which period the people were merged in paganism, superstition and ignorance. A school was established with a few scholars, and a meeting-house was built by the Board of Missions. In the war of 1812–15, this, with the village, was burnt by the British Indians in retaliation; as the Tuscaroras had previously scoured the Canada frontier and forests when Gen. Dearborn was encamped at Fort George. Soon after the war missionary operations were resumed, a meeting-house was built, mostly at the expense of the Indians, and a school was opened. In 1831 the first framed school-house (22 by 24) was built by the chiefs at the expense of Indians having an interest in the cause of education. At this period agriculture began to advance slowly, and an attempt was made to establish a boarding-school for boys among them; but this and another attempt since

---

* This treaty was held Sept. 15, 1797. See *American State Papers; Indian Affairs*, i., p. 620.

† From an address of the Tuscarora chiefs to the directors of the Northern Missionary Society, dated Oct. 6, 1800, it appears the Rev. Elkanah Holmes had visited this settlement, and gained the confidence of the Indians to such a degree that they made an earnest appeal for the establishment of schools, and other means of improvement. But two of the natives could then read.—*New-York Missionary Magazine*, ii., p. 64.

made, both failed for want of means.* By the united effort of the chiefs and John Elliot, then missionary, a temperance society of about one hundred members was formed in 1831, and this number has since been considerably increased. About 1849, a second framed school house (18×30) was built by the Indians, to accommodate the south eastern portion of the reservation. Subsequently another building (24×30) was erected for a boarding school, adjoining the new school house, partly at the expense of the Indians and partly by the aid of Miss Thayer, the teacher.

"The nation holds meetings every two or three months during the year for the furtherance of temperance, purity of morals, education and industry, under the direction of the chiefs; the brass band always in attendance with their music.† At these meetings speeches are made for the promotion of these objects, and the council house is found too small to accommodate all who wish to attend, for which reason the chiefs have decided to enlarge it. Religion is reserved for the minister to promulgate on the Sabbath, and his meetings are generally well attended, the number of church members being eighty-eight. There is no pagan party here, all having the historical not evangelical faith. They have a small library and also a society denominated the 'Tuscarora Mutual Improvement Society,' which, during the winter months, holds meetings, at which they make reports upon the condition of the world as far as they know, debate upon different questions and make stump speeches on a variety of subjects. These are often very interesting times. They hold an annual feast on New-Year's day, and after the dinner they assemble in the council house and devote the day to discussions on the general welfare. In 1841, they enacted a Maine law, prohibiting the introduction of liquors into their territory under the penalty of forfeiture. In 1847, they abolished dancing of every kind as detrimental to the morals of the young. Agriculture is the sole dependence of our people, some part of their lands being leased out at two dollars per acre. In 1816, the first framed building was built after the pattern of the pale faces, and in 1829, the first framed barn was erected. There are now twenty-seven framed barns, thirteen framed dwelling houses, one stone house and one stone store house on the reservation, besides the council house (23×30), and meeting house (26×36) with a steeple and bell, built about thirty-three years ago.

"The following is the original stock of Indians residing on the reservations:

Catawbas, whose grand mother was taken prisoner in the wars between the Tuscaroras and Catawbas of Carolina before 1708, and was adopted among them, - - - - - - - - - - 13
Delawares, who were also adopted by the Tuscaroras, - - - - - - - - - - - - - 54
Mohegans, also adopted, who came originally from North Carolina, - - - - - - - - 4
Onondagas, who retain their tribe and draw the Onondaga annuities; they are not adopted, and are a part of the Six Nations, - - - - - - - - - - - - - - - - - - - 28
Oneidas, not adopted for the same reason; they do not draw annuities from the State, - - - 4

"There are among the Tuscaroras, one wagon maker, two joiners, two carpenters and two doctors.

"In estimating the value of each farm, the soil was not included nor the wild lands, for the reason that the soil is owned by the nation jointly, under the care of the chiefs who act as trustees. It only includes what improvement has been made upon the state of nature, in clearing, buildings and fruit trees. The columns headed 'voters' and 'aliens' were left blank, for the reason that we are neither voters nor aliens, but natural born Americans."

CESSIONS OF LAND IN THE STATE OF NEW-YORK BY THE IROQUOIS.

The intimate connection of this subject with the history, condition and prospects of these people, gives especial interest to statistics concerning it. To facilitate reference to these transactions, the following memoranda have been prepared from the official records in the Secretary's office:

In 1777, when New-York became an independent State, the native owners of Long Island and the country bordering upon the Hudson and Mohawk rivers, had mostly conveyed their title to the Crown of England, or to persons or associations authorized by the Colonial government to acquire it.

Under the English government it was not customary to grant patents for land, until the aboriginal title was extinguished by purchase. The practice was, to apply for a license to purchase in the King's name, and the deed being obtained and annexed to a second petition, the Governor issued a warrant to the Surveyor-General to cause a survey to be made of the quantity purchased. The Attorney-General was then directed to prepare a draft of a patent which was laid before the council, and if approved, was engrossed, recorded, sealed and issued. In the earlier periods less formality was observed, and the frauds and abuses practiced, led, in several instances to the annulling of extensive purchases, and to the

* There were at the time of making this report, two schools in operation, the teachers being paid by the State, under an act of 1854. Average attendance in the winter months, 60. The boarding school for girls numbered 18 scholars, with a fair prospect of doing much good. There was one Sabbath school on the reservation.

† This band, ten in number, was organized by a constitution in 1846, for the purpose of promoting temperance among the people, their instruments costing about $200. There is also a choir of singers who practice in the winter season.

introduction of checks to prevent the recurrence of these frauds. The practice of requiring an actual survey by the Surveyor-General, or his deputies, was introduced in 1736.

The Iroquois had ceded but comparatively a small part of their lands at the time of the Revolution, and the hostile course which most but the Oneidas and Tuscaroras pursued during the war, placed them in an unfavorable position with regard to their claims upon the return of peace. Popular hatred, sustained by the recollection of recent horrors of Indian warfare, to some extent found expression in the councils of the new government, and while the latter appeared anxious to reward those who had lately been their allies, or who had remained neutral, by liberal concessions, it evinced a not less fixed determination of holding the hostile portion responsible for the policy they had adopted.

The first law of the State government on this subject was enacted Oct. 23, 1779, in which, after reciting the mischief done by the Indians, and their infidelity and abuse of former favors, naming especially the Mohawks, Onondagas, Cayugas and Senecas, it empowered the Governor and four commissioners* to execute if possible, a treaty of pacification, and to ask, demand, and by every way and means in their power to obtain an engagement, not only for securing the State and its subjects from further hostilities, but for indemnifying the public from injuries already committed, by exacting such compensation and retribution as might be deemed proper. These commissioners were to act in behalf of the State, in any treaty which the United States might hold, and their proceedings were to be reported to the Legislature.

On the 25th of March, 1783, the Governor and council of appointment were authorized to appoint three Commissioners of Indian Affairs,† to superintend the business of the Indians generally, and to examine into and ascertain the territorial claims of the Oneidas and Tuscaroras, with the view of adopting such measures as might secure their contentment and tranquility.

The first general treaty with the Six Nations after the war was made at Fort Stanwix, October 22, 1784, by Oliver Wolcott, Richard Butler, and Arthur Lee, commissioners plenipotentiary, appointed by Congress for at purpose. It required, under the pledge of hostages, the immediate surrender of all prisoners, and secured to the Oneidas and Tuscaroras the quiet possession of their lands. The Six Nations ceded all their lands west of a line from Lake Ontario, four miles east of the Niagara river, to Buffalo creek, and thence south to Pennsylvania; thence west to the end of Pennsylvania, and thence south along the west bounds of that State, to the Ohio river. The stipulations of this treaty were renewed at Fort Hamar, on the 9th of January, 1789, and the Six Nations secured in their possession east of the line above-mentioned, excepting a reservation six miles square at Oswego. The Mohawks took no part in this treaty.‡

A general treaty was also held at Canandaigua, November 11, 1794, under the direction of Timothy Pickering, at which the separate treaties which had been made by the Oneidas, Onondagas, and Cayugas, with the State of New-York, were confirmed, and goods to the value of $10,000 were delivered to the Indians, besides the annual sum of $3,000, in addition to the $1,500 previously allowed.§

The original constitution of New-York‖ restricted the right of purchasing lands from the Indians to the State, in its sovereign capacity, and an act passed March 18, 1788, imposed a penalty of $250, and further punishment by fine and imprisonment, at the discretion of the courts, for violation of this provision. It also adopted measures for preventing intrusion, and protecting the rights of the natives. These, or similar restrictions, have been continued till the present time, and all treaties for the purchase of Indian lands, until a recent period, have been made by the Governor, or commissioners, authorized by special acts for the purpose. On the 25th of May, 1841, the Commissioners of the Land Office were authorized, with the consent of the Governor, to treat with the Indians for the purchase of lands, and to pay off the principal of the annuities of certain tribes at their discretion. With the exception of a few of the earlier treaties, each tribe has negotiated separately with the State in the cession of its lands, and in more recent periods sectional and local parties acted independently in these negotiations.

Mohawks.—This tribe was particularly involved in the hostile operations of the British in the revolution, and removed near the close of the War to Grand river, in Upper Canada. By a treaty held at Albany with the federal government, March 29, 1797, they surrendered their right to the soil of New-York for $1,000, to be distributed among the tribe, and $600 to be paid to the deputies who attended the treaty. They were parties to the treaty at Buffalo creek in 1788.

Oneidas.—From an original memorandum preserved in the office of the State Engineer and Surveyor, it appears that the Oneidas, towards the close of the colonial period of New-York, claimed "from the 'Line

* Anthony Van Schaick, Levi Pawling, Peter Schuyler, and Col. Jacob Klock, were named commissioners.

† Abram Cuyler, Peter Schuyler, and Henry Glen, were appointed to this office June 27, 1783. On the 6th of April, 1784, the Governor was authorized to associate with this commission such other persons as he might deem proper.

‡ American State Papers, Indian Affairs, i., 5–10.

§ President Washington, on the 23d of April, 1792, recommended a plan, which was confirmed by the Senate, in which the Senecas, Oneidas, (and Stockbridges incorporated with them), the Tuscaroras, Cayugas, and Onondagas, were to receive annually $1,500, to be expended in purchasing clothing, domestic animals, and implements of husbandry, and for encouraging artificers to reside in their villages Ib., p. 225.

‖ Section 37.

of Property' reversed, and continued from the Canada creek, till it comes to a certain mountain, called *Esoiade*, or the Ice Mountain, under which mountain that Canada creek, opposite to the Old Fort Hendrick heads;* from thence running westerly to an old fort which stood on the creek, called *Weteringhra Guentere*,† and which empties into the River St. Lawrence, about twelve miles below Carleton, or Buck's Island, and which fort the Oneidas took from their enemies a long time ago; from thence running southerly to a rift upon the Onondaga river called Ogontenagea, or Aguegonteneagea (a place remarkable for eels), about five miles from where the river empties out of Oneyda lake." This somewhat ambiguous boundary would probably include the whole of Madison, Oneida, Herkimer, Lewis, and parts of Jefferson and Oswego counties.

In 1785, June 28, a treaty was made at Fort Herkimer, with the Oneidas and Tuscaroras, by Governor Clinton and the Commissioners of Indian affairs, in which the former ceded the country between Unadilla and Chenango river, for $11,500 in goods and money.

In 1788, Sept. 12, a treaty was held at Fort Schuyler with the Oneidas, by Governor Clinton, William Floyd, Ezra L'Hommedieu, Richard Varick, Samuel Jones, Egbert Benson and Peter Gansevoort, Jr.,‡ on the part of New-York, at which the former ceded all their lands to the State, excepting certain reservations for their own use and that of their friends, the Stockbridges and Brothertown Indians, with a tract ten miles square reserved for Peter Penet, located near the St. Lawrence, and another ten miles square to John Francis Perache. The sum paid by the State was $2,000 in money, $2,000 in clothing, $1,000 in provisions, $500 for a grist mill and an annuity of $600.

In 1795, Sept. 15, a treaty was held with the authorised deputies of the Oneidas, by Philip Schuyler, John Cantine and David Brooks, on the part of the State, by which the former ceded part of their former reservation for the sum of $2,952, an annuity of $2,952, with the conditional sale of other parts at the rate of $3 annually per 100 acres.

In 1798, June 1, a treaty was held with the Oneidas, at their village, before Joseph Hopkinson, United States Commissioner, by Egbert Benson, Ezra L'Hommedieu and John Tayler, agents of the State, in which the former ceded a part of their reservation for the sum of $200, and an annuity of $700. This was ratified by the President, February 21, 1799.

In 1802, March 5, an agreement was entered into at Albany between Governor Clinton, Ezra L'Hommedieu nd Simeon DeWitt, agents for the State, and the Oneidas, in which a further cession was made of several parcels of land for $900, and an annuity of $300. In 1802, June 4, the above agreement was ratified before John Tayler, United States Commissioner.

In 1805, March 21, an agreement of partition was executed between the Christian, or Skanendo's,§ and the Pagan, or Cornelius'¶ parties of the Oneidas.

In 1807, March 13, the Christian party of the Oneidas quit-claimed a part of their tract, for an annual rent of the interest at six per cent. at seventy-five cents per acre, on the land conveyed. The sum of $600 was advanced on the rents thus secured.

In 1809, February 16, the Christian party of the Oneidas, sold the remaining part of their Fish Creek reservation (7,500 acres) only reserving 300 acres to Abraham Van Eps and the right of fishing to themselves. The terms were $600 in cash, $1,000 to be paid in June after, and an annuity of six per cent. interest on $2,000. Certain Indian families residing east of the creek, had liberty to retain land to the extent of 640 acres while they continued to reside upon it. A tract of 400 acres was reserved for Angel De Ferrier.

In 1809, February 21, the Pagan party of the Oneidas, sold their lands east of Oneida creek, and extending from Oneida lake to Mud creek, which empties into Oneida creek to the southward of the Seneca turnpike, for the annual interest at six per cent., at fifty-six cents per acre, of the land sold. The sum of $1,000 was advanced in part payment. Reservations for particular families, were made in this and most subsequent cessions.

In 1810, March 3, and 1811, February 27, treaties were made by which the Christian party of the Oneidas, sold to the State parts of their reservations, at the rate of fifty cents per acre, receiving a part of this sum, and agreeing that on the remainder they would receive annual interest at the rate of six per cent.

In 1811, July 20, the Oneidas released to the State their claim to lands held by the Stockbridge and Brothertown Indians, as described in the certificate of Guy Johnson, dated October 4, 1774. For this they received $200, and a further sum of $1,000 in November following.

* Now known as East Canada creek.(?)
† French Creek, at the present village of Clayton.
‡ These commissioners were appointed by an act passed March, 1788.
§ Skanendo, a distinguished chief of the Oneidas, embraced Christianity under the preaching of Rev. Samuel Kirkland, at an early period in his mission, and ever after remained his warm personal friend. The ascendency which the latter acquired with this tribe, was in no small degree due to the aid and influence of this chief. He died March 11, 1816, aged about 110 years.
¶ Cornelius Doxtater, who subsequently became a party to several treaties with the State.

In 1815, March 3, the Christian party released to the State several lots in their reservation at the rate of $1 per acre, receiving a part of the money at the time of making the sale. The lands were to be surveyed and appraised, and persons owning improvements were to receive their value.

In 1817, March 27, the second Christian (heretofore Pagan) party of the Oneidas,* released a part of their lands, with reservations to individuals. Six hundred acres were to be sold for the purpose of erecting a church upon their tract. They received at the rate of $2 per acre for the lands conveyed.

In 1824, August 26; 1829, February 13; 1829, October 8; and 1833, April 5, the first Christian party conveyed to the State portions of their reservation, receiving a part of the sums due at the time of the treaties, with an agreement for such further sums as might be found due upon survey and appraisement.

In 1826, February 21, the second Christian (late Pagan) party of the Oneidas released certain lands for $3 per acre, receiving $1,000 down, the remainder to be paid in June following, or when the Governor might be satisfied that they were about to remove to Green Bay.

In 1827, February 2; 1830, April 3; 1834, February 6; and 1837, February 4, the Orchard party of the Oneidas conveyed to the State parts of their reservation, receiving a portion of the sums due at the time of the treaties, and in most cases with an agreement for such further sums as might be found due upon survey and appraisement.

In 1838, an act was passed, directing the payment of half of the principal of the annuities due to the Oneidas residing in Wisconsin. The total amount then annually paid by virtue of the several treaties made previous to this, was as follows:

Treaty of 1788, September 22,	$600 00	Due to all parties of the Oneidas. After the partition of March 21, 1807, each party drew separate annuities for sales made in their land reservations.
" 1795, June 1,	3,269 28	
" 1798, June 1,	700 00	
" 1802, March 5,	300 00	
" 1802, June 4,	300 00	
" 1807, March 13,	644 86	Due to the Christian party.
" 1809, February 16,	120 00	
" 1811, February 21,	332 48	Due to the Pagan party.
" 1811, February 27,	71 82	Due to the Christian party.
" 1817, March 27,	120 85	Due to the second Christian party.
" 1824, August 26,	240 00	Due to the "Green Bay" port'n of the Christ'n party.
	60 00	Due to the "Detroit" portion of the Christian party.

The principal of the above at 6 per cent., owned by the	whole nation, was	$86,154 66
" " "	Christian party, treaties of 1807–9,	17,040 50
" " "	First Christian party,	4,000 00
" " "	Pagan, second Christ'n, or Orchard part's,	7,555 50
Total owned by all parties,		$114,750 66

In carrying into effect the act of 1838, it was found that there were then living at Duck, or Green Bay, 578, and in New-York 706, Oneidas. The sum of $27,965.14 being the amount due to the former, was paid in the summer of 1838.

By an act passed in 1839, the Commissioners of the Land Office were required to pay to the Oneidas all surplus moneys arising from the sale of lands above their appraised value. This excess in 1843 amounted to $48,722.14.

In 1840, June 19, the First and Second Christian Parties of the Oneidas, to accommodate those who were desirous of removing to Upper Canada, or elsewhere, beyond the limits of the State, in accordance with an act passed March 8, 1839, executed a treaty, by which they ceded to the State all their lands held in common in Oneida and Madison counties. There remained of these lands about 4,509 acres, to which 578 persons were entitled to an equal share. The improvements, subsequently found to amount to $14,285, were declared the property of the families or individuals who had made them, and were ordered to be sold for their benefit.

* In 1816 Bishop Hobart, of the Protestant Episcopal Church, established a mission at Oneida, and appointed Mr. Eleazer Williams as a catechist, lay reader and school teacher, to reside with them. Such was the success of this measure that in January, 1817, a memorial adopted in council and signed by eleven chiefs and head men, was addressed to the Governor, in which they requested henceforth to be known as the Second Christian Party of the Oneida Nation. There were confirmed by Bishop Hobart in 1818, 89; in 1819, 56, and in all, during the continuance of the mission, upwards of 500 persons. The Church above mentioned was consecrated September 21, 1819, as St. Peter's Church. In 1840 the edifice was sold, removed to Vernon, and re-erected by the Unitarian Society. Mr. Solomon Davis succeeded Williams in 1822, the latter having removed to Green Bay, with a part of the tribe. (See *Clarke's Onondaga*, i., 230; *Jones' Oneida*, 862.)

A Methodist Mission Church was formed at Oneida in 1829, by the Rev. Dan Barnes. The success of the enterprise was for several years quite small, but since 1841 it has been more prosperous.

In 1841, March 8, a portion of the first and second Christian party of the Oneidas, hitherto known as the "Home party," ceded about 275 acres. It was subsequently ascertained, that the value of the lands thus sold was $7,220.50, and of the improvements $638.75, to which seven families were entitled proportional shares. The sum of $2,160, was advanced the May following, to assist thirty-six persons to remove to Canada.

In 1841, March 13, an emigrating portion of the Orchard party of the Oneidas, ceded a tract of 217 1-2 acres, subsequently found to be worth $5,297.57, exclusive of improvements to the value of $1,510.75, to which three families were entitled proportional shares. The sum of $2,640, was advanced on this in May, to assist them in removing to Canada.

In 1842, May 23, June 25, the Orchard party of the Oneidas, in the town of Vernon, released to the State all their remaining lands, on conditions similar to those acquiesced in by the first and second Christian parties, June 19, 1840. There were found sixteen persons proposing to emigrate to Canada, and forty who intended to remain.

In 1846, February 6, all parties of the Oneidas agreed by treaty, to release to the State the missionary lot in Westmoreland, containing 331¼ acres, which had been granted in 1786, to the Rev. Samuel Kirkland, in trust for the use of the missionary or minister whom the Oneidas might engage to reside with them. It was subsequently found that the following number of persons were entitled to share in the payment made under the purchase:

At Duck Creek, in Wisconsin, - - -	786	persons, who received - -	$866 72
Canada West, - - - - - - -	491	" - - -	541 42
New-York, - - - - - - -	225	" - -	248 11
Total number of Oneidas in 1846, -	1,502	" - -	$1,636 25

Stockbridge Indians.—A remnant of the Mohegan, or Muhhekanock tribe, settled near the Oneida in 1783-88, under the pastoral care of the Rev. John Sargent, who came to reside permanently among them in 1796, and remained there till his death, September 8, 1824. In the Oneidas' treaty of 1788, a tract six miles square, in the present towns of Augusta, Oneida county, and Stockbridge, Madison county, was secured to them by the State. These people numbered about 420 in 1785, and 438 in 1818. In the year last named, about one-fourth of the Stockbridges went to settle on lands that had been given them on the White river, in Indiana, many years previous, but before their arrival these lands had been sold by the native proprietors.

In 1821, with other Indians of New-York, they purchased of the Menominees and Winnebagoes, a tract of land on the Wisconsin and Fox rivers, in Wisconsin. A great part of the tribe removed the next year, and the remainder have since followed. The Stockbridge Indians have held the following treaties with the State:

In 1818, July 14, they sold to the State a tract of 4,500 acres, excepting 50 acres leased for the benefit of their poor, and two other tracts of 890 and 250 acres, for which they received $5,380, and an annuity of $282.49.

1822, February 23; 1822, August 28; 1823, September 16; 1825, June 21; 1825, October 1; 1826, June 29; 1827, February 26; 1829, March 21; 1829, April 25; 1829, September 8; and 1830, April 30, treaties were held, by which the Stockbridge Indians in Oneida and Madison counties, sold to the State portions of their reservations, usually receiving a part of the sum due at the time of the treaty, the remainder to be paid subsequently under conditions agreed upon.

In 1842, July 20, and 1847, September 24, agreements were executed between the Commissioners of the Land Office and the Stockbridge Indians, of Wisconsin, relative to certain lots in New Stockbridge.

The State having in 1848 and 1850 (in consideration of the profits arising on the re-sale of certain lands heretofore sold by the Stockbridge Indians) provided a fund of $36,000, the interest of which was to be paid annually to them; and a misunderstanding having arisen between these Indians, and a portion of the tribe known as the "Citizen party," in relation to the said fund, an agreement was executed February 6, 1852, regulating its division and payment.

Brothertown.—Previous to the Revelutionary war, arrangements had been made for the removal of the remnants of Indian tribes in New Jersey, Connecticut, Rhode Island, Massachusetts, and the southern part of New-York, to the Oneida country. A settlement was formed near Oriskany, and in 1786, the Rev. Samson Occum, a Mohegan, with 192 emigrants, removed thither. In the treaty of 1788, the Oneidas reserved to the New England Indians, consisting of Mohegan, Montagues, Stoningtons, and Narragansets, the Pequots of Groton, and the Nahantics of Farmington, a tract two miles in length by three in breadth, in the present town of Marshall, Oneida county, which was subsequently secured to them by law. Having no common language, they adopted the English, and they received the common appellation of "Brothertown

Indians." Their affairs were managed by superintendents appointed for the purpose, and considerable advance was made by them in civilization.* In 1822, having purchased a tract of land in Wisconsin, a part of them removed thither. In 1827 the superintendents were authorized to sell the lands of the tribe. In 1831 another emigration occurred, and about 1849, the last of these Indians removed west.

The following contracts and agreements have been executed between these Indians and the State:

1841, June 8. A contract and arrangement were made between the Commissioners of the Land Office and the Brothertown Indians, by which the sum of $14,249.29, belonging to that portion of the tribe residing in Oneida county, was divided between those intending to remain, in all 98 persons, and those intending to remove to Wisconsin, 50 in number. To those that emigrated, the balance, over the cost of removal, was to be paid on their arrival at their destination, and to those that remained the interest was to be paid as formerly.

1843, April 13. A second agreement was made between the same parties, by which the State paid the principal of the fund, belonging to the tribe, to the superintendents for distribution among its several members.

St. Regis.—In 1796, May 31, the "Seven Nations of Canada"† held a treaty at the city of New-York, before Abraham Ogden, United States commissioner, with the agents of the State of New-York, and of the patentees of Macomb's purchase, by which they ceded all their lands in this State, excepting a tract equal to six miles square at the village of St. Regis, a mile square on Salmon river, embracing the present village of Fort Covington, and a mile square at the lower mills on Grass river, with the natural meadows below them. For this cession they were to receive £1,233 6s. 8d., and an annuity of £213 6s. 8d., New-York currency.

In 1816, March 15, the St. Regis Indians ceded to the State the mile square on Salmon river, and 5,000 acres on the east end of their principal reservation. To this was added February 20th, 1818, 2,000 acres adjoining the first cession.

In 1824, March 16, they released their interest to the mile square on Grass river. On the 29th of June, and December 14th following, they released several tracts at and near the village of Hogansburgh, amounting to 1,144 acres, and on the 23d of September, 1825, another tract of 840 acres on the east side of St. Regis river, near Hogansburgh.

In 1845, February 21, they sold to the State the meadows on Grass river, ascertained to embrace about 210 acres. These cessions, and the consideration paid for them, may be summed up as follows:

---

* The following statement of the condition of these and other Indians in the central part of the State, was presented in the State Senate, March 12, 1819, by the Society of Friends, who had been directing their efforts towards the social improvement of these people:

"A STATISTICAL ACCOUNT OF THE BROTHERTOWN, STOCKBRIDGE, SOUTH SETTLEMENT OF THE ONEIDA AND ONONDAGA TRIBES OF INDIANS, TAKEN IN THE YEAR 1813.

"The Brothertown tribe consists of 302 persons, these having about 2,000 acres of land cleared and in cultivation. They are considerably advanced in agricultural knowledge, and have 90 cows, 30 horses, 16 yoke of oxen, 93 young cattle, 88 sheep, and a great number of swine. They have a grist mill, 2 saw mills, 16 framed houses, and 18 framed barns; 21 plows, 17 sleds, 3 carts and 3 wagons. Four of them are carpenters, 2 blacksmiths, 4 shoemakers, 2 tailors, and 5 weavers. Their manufactures the last year were 320 yards woolen, and 600 linen cloth, and their produce was about 11,300 bushels of grain of various kinds, and 3,400 bushels of potatoes.

"The Stockbridge tribe consists of 475 persons. They have about 1,200 acres of land cleared; they have a grist mill, 2 saw mills, 8 framed houses, 7 framed barns, 26 horses, 20 pair of oxen, 54 milch cows, 44 young cattle, 56 sheep, and 50 swine; and their produce, 2,500 bushels of grain.

"The south settlement of the Oneida tribe, (being that part of the tribe to which the attention of Friends has been especially directed,) consists of 440 persons. They have 500 acres of land improved, 6 framed houses, 1 saw mill, 2 wagons, 10 plows, 25 horses, 24 oxen, 33 cows, 118 young cattle, 40 sheep, and 100 swine; their produce 3,000 bushels of grain.

"The Onondaga tribe consists of 250 persons. They have about 500 acres of land cleared and in cultivation; they have 6 pair of oxen, 10 cows, some young cattle, and their produce was 1,850 bushels of grain. This settlement has distinguished itself for its sobriety, there being but *few* of its numbers that have been known to be intoxicated for a considerable time past.

"Since the above account was made out, these people have improved considerably in agriculture and mechanical knowledge. A saw mill has been erected in the Onondaga settlement, and a great improvement has been made by the women of the Stockbridge and Oneida south settlement in spinning and weaving. In 1817 the Oneida women manufactured 280 yards of cloth, and those of Stockbridge 410 yards and 30 coverlids, and had 260 runs of yarn on hand. Their progress in manufactures has been much facilitated by spinning schools which have been taught in Oneida and Stockbridge, and one has been more recently opened in Onondaga which is likely to produce the same beneficial result."—(*Memorial of Friends, Assem. Papers, Indian Affairs*, xli., p. 89. Secretary's Office.)

The extent of the several Indian reservations and number of inhabitants in each, in 1819, was stated by a Legislative committee, in their report upon a part of the Governor's message of that year as follows:

RESERVATIONS.	Tribes.	Population.	Acres in reserv'n.
Allegany river,	Seneca,	597	30,469
Buffalo,	Seneca,	686	83,557
Cattaraugus,	Seneca,	389	26,880
Genesee River, (5 res.)	Seneca,	456	31,648
Oil Spring,	Seneca,	.....	640
Oneida,	Oneida,	1,031	20,000
Onondaga,	Onondaga,	300	7,000
St. Regis,	St. Regis,	400	10,000
Stockbridge,	Stockbridge,	438	13,000
Tonawanda,	Seneca,	365	46,209
Tuscarora,	Tuscarora,*	314	1,920
Total,		4,976	271,323

* Erroneously stated as "Seneca," in the report.

The committee estimated the average value of these lands at $6 per acre.—(*Assembly Papers, Indian Affairs*, xli., page 143. Secretary's Office.)

† By this term several settlements of domiciliated Indians, formed by Catholic missionaries under the French government in Canada, and mostly made up of parties induced to emigrate from the Iroquois, of New-York, have been known. The seven villages, it is said, originally consisted of an Iroquois, an Algonquin and a Nipesing branch, at the Lake of Two Mountains, an Iroquois branch at Caughnawaga, near Montreal, and another at Oswegatchie, a colony of Hurons at Lorette, and of Abnaquies, at St. François. The St. Regis mission, formed about the time of the breaking up of that at Oswegatchie, took the place of the latter. The Caughnawaga shared equally with the St. Regis Indians, in the annuities paid under the treaty of 1796, (except a few years during and after the war of 1812–15), until by an order of the Commissioners of the Land Office of May 16, 1844, under authority of an act passed May 25, 1841, the former were paid $4,444.44, in full for the principal of their share. The Indians of St. Regis have acted independently in all negotiations with New-York since 1796. Their present annuity from the State amounts to $2,131.66.

DATE OF TREATY.	Acres conveyed.	Amount paid down.	Annuity
1796, May 31,	......	$3,197 96	$533 33
1816, March 15,	5,640	....	1,300 00
1818, February 20,	2,000	....	200 00
1824, March 16,	640	1,920 00	....
1824, June 29,	1,000	1,750 00	60 00
1824, December 14,	144	1 00	305 00
1825, September 23,	840	2,100 00	....
1845, February 21,	210	621 20	....
Total,	10,474	$9,581 17	$2,398 33

The amount of land remaining to this tribe in the State, is about 14,030 acres, a part of which is leased to whites for a term of years.

Onondagas.—In 1788, September 12, a treaty was held at Fort Schuyler, by which this tribe ceded to the State all their lands, excepting a tract at the south end of Onondaga lake and the right of making salt in common with the State. For this cession they received 1,000 French crowns ($1,090), clothing to the value of $500, and an annuity of $500. This treaty was confirmed at Fort Stanwix, June 16th, 1790, for the further sum of $500.

In 1793, November 18, a treaty was held at Onondaga, by which a part of their former reservation was released for $410 paid at the time, $218 in June following, and an annuity of $410. This treaty was confirmed July 28th, 1795, at Cayuga Ferry, and the annuity increased to $800, to date from 1793. They at this time released their common right to the salt springs, the land around Onondaga lake, and a strip half a mile on each side of the creek north of their reservation, for $700, and 100 bushels of salt annually.

In 1817, February 25, a treaty was held at Albany, by which the Onondagas sold a part of their former reservation for $1,000 paid down, and a further annual payment of $430, and 50 bushels of salt.

In 1822, February 11, another treaty was held at Albany, at which they sold 800 acres of their lands for $1,700.

In 1829, February 28, an agreement was made at Albany with the Onondagas living at Buffalo, changing the mode of paying their annuities.

Cayugas.—In 1789, February 25, a treaty was held at Albany, by which the Cayugas ceded all of their lands east of the Massachusetts pre-emption line, excepting a reservation equal to 100 square miles on both sides of Cayuga lake, a small tract on the Seneca river, and a mile square at Cayuga ferry. The consideration agreed upon was $500 in silver at the time of the treaty, $1,625 in June following and an annuity of $500. On the 22d of June, 1790, the Cayugas, for a gratuity of $1,000, confirmed this treaty at Fort Stanwix.

In 1795, July 27, a treaty was held at Cayuga ferry, at which they ceded their reservation on Cayuga lake and the lands at Scawyace and elsewhere, excepting the individual reservation of one mile square at Cannogai,* to their chief Fish Carrier, (to be leased for his benefit), and a common reservation of two miles square for the tribe. They received for this cession $1,800, and an addition to their annuity of $1,800.

In 1807, May 13, the Cayugas released to the State, for the sum of $4,800, their right to last remaining reservations belonging to the tribe within the State.

In 1829, February 28, a treaty was held with the Cayugas of Sandusky, changing the mode of paying their annuities, and providing that they might be drawn by drafts, or bills of exchange, signed by four chiefs.

Senecas.—The transactions of this tribe in regard to the sale of their lands, have mostly been with persons acting under the authority of Massachusetts, the only portion for which they have negotiated with New-York being the islands in the Niagara river, and the lands along its border.

The charters granted to the Plymouth Company in 1620, and to Massachusetts in 1691, included the territory between certain limits on the Atlantic coast westward to the South Sea. The grant of the territory since known as New-York, made in 1664 to the Duke of York, included the territory from a line twenty miles east of the Hudson river westwardly without limit, and from the Atlantic coast to Canada.

The conflicting claims thus occasioned were finally adjusted by commissioners appointed by the two states, who met at Hartford, and on the 16th of December, 1786, entered into a convention, or treaty, by which the State of New-York retained the sovereignty and jurisdiction of the territory in controversy, and surrendered to the commonwealth of Massachusetts the right of pre-emption of the soil from the native Indians. The territory thus conveyed embraced all the land from one mile east of the Niagara river to a

* Canoga, on the west side of Cayuga lake, in the present towns of Fayette, Seneca county.

line running from a point in the north line of Pennsylvania, 82 miles west of the Delaware river, northward through Seneca lake to Lake Ontario, and amounted to about six millions of acres.

In 1788, July 8, a treaty was held at Buffalo creek, between the Five Nations, and Oliver Phelps, and Nathaniel Gorham, acting under authority derived from Massachusetts, at which the natives ceded, without reservation, about 2,600,000 acres in the eastern part of the Massachusetts lands, since known as the Phelps and Gorham purchase. This purchase was bounded west by a line beginning at a point in the north line of Pennsylvania, due south of the confluence of the Canaseraga creek with the Genesee river; thence north to the Genesee, and along that river to a point two miles north of Cannewagus village; thence west twelve miles, and thence northwardly twelve miles from the Genesee river to Lake Ontario. The consideration paid was £2,100, ($5,250), and an annuity of $5,000.* A quit claim of this conveyance was executed in the name of the Mohawks, Oneidas, Cayugas and Tuscaroras, at Canandaigua, August 4, 1789. The country thus ceded was exclusively occupied by the Cayugas and Senecas.

On the 15th of September, 1797, Robert Morris, of Philadelphia, who had purchased from Massachusetts the pre-emptive title to the remaining lands claimed by that state within the limits of New-York, since known as the "Holland Land Company's Purchase," obtained a treaty with the Senecas, at Geneseo, before Jeremiah Wadsworth, United States commissioner, and William Shepard, appointed by Massachusetts, by which these Indians sold their title to these lands, excepting certain reservations for $100,000, to be vested in the stock of the bank of the United States, and held in the name of the President of the United States, for the use and benefit of their nation. This treaty was confirmed by the President, April 11, 1798. The following reservations were made:

A tract at Canawagus, (near Avon), two miles square, to be laid out in such a manner as to include the village, extending in breadth one mile along the river.

A tract at Big Tree, two square miles at the village to be laid out in like manner.

A tract at Little Beardstown, two square miles at the village, to be laid out in like manner. Ceded by treaty at Buffalo creek, June 30, 1802, to Oliver Phelps, Isaac Bronson, and Horatio Jones, for $1,200.

A tract at Squawky Hill, of two square miles, of which one mile was to be laid off on the river, to include the village, and the other directly west thereof and contiguous thereto.

A tract at Gardeau, on both sides of the Genesee river, since known as the "Mary Jemison Tract."

A tract at Kaounadeau, extending eight miles along the Genesee river, and two miles in breadth.

A tract on Cattaraugus creek and along Lake Erie to the Eighteen Mile creek, and another tract between Cattaraugus and Connonduweyea creek. These were exchanged with the Holland Land Company at a treaty held at Buffalo creek, June 30, 1802, for a tract on Cattaraugus creek, at the present Cattaraugus reservation.

A tract of forty-two square miles at or near the Allegany river, being the present Allegany reservation.

A tract of two hundred square miles, to be laid off partly at the Buffalo and partly at the Tonnawanta creeks.

Several reservations have since been purchased by parties holding the pre-emptive right. The Senecas have held treaties with the State for the cession of lands reserved in the settlement with Massachusetts, as follows:

In 1802, August 20, at Albany, before John Tyler, United States commissioner, by which they ceded their right to the mile strip along the Niagara river, from Buffalo creek to Stedman's farm. For this they received $200 down, $5,300 payable at Albany, and $500 in chintz, calico, and other goods suitable for women. They retained the right of passing the ferry at Black Rock free of toll, and stipulated the gift of a mile square each to Horatio Jones and Jasper Parrish.

In 1815, September 12, at Buffalo, they ceded the Islands in Niagara river within the limits of the State, for $7,000, and an annuity of $500.

* Bitter complaints were subsequently made by the Indians, in regard to this treaty. The following extract from a speech by Red Jacket, at Tioga Point, before Timothy Pickering, Mr. Street, a person then connected with the Indian Department, and others being present, November 21, 1790, will give an idea of their grievances.

After stating the preliminary negotiations of the treaty, he added: "And last summer, a year ago, we came to Canandaigua, expecting to receive ten thousand dollars, but then we found that we had but five thousand to receive. When we discovered the fraud we had a mind to apply to Congress, to see if the matter could not be rectified; for when we took the money and shared it, every one here knows, that we had but about a dollar apiece for all that country. Mr. Street! you very well know, that all our lands came to, was but the price of a few hogsheads of tobacco. Gentlemen who stand by, (looking around and addressing himself to the white people who were present,) do not think hard of what has been said. At the time of the treaty, twenty broaches would not buy half a loaf of bread, so that when we returned home there was not a bright spot of silver about us."—*American State Papers, Indian Affairs*, i., page 214.

EXPLANATION OF THE PLATES.

The principle upon which the several diagrams accompanying this work are constructed, is similar in all. The surface of each figure is divided horizontally into spaces representing *numbers, or proportions*, which are reckoned upwards from the bottom line, and their amount indicated by a scale engraved upon the left hand margin. It is also divided vertically into spaces denoting *time*, corresponding with the intervals between the years along the top of the diagram. Upon the vertical lines, points are taken, at distances from the bottom corresponding with the numbers to be exhibited. These points are then connected by continuous or dotted lines, which by their rise or fall, as followed from left to right, exhibit the progressive increase or decrease of the numbers they represent.

PLATE I:

Upon this plate are exhibited the changes in the population of each county in the state since 1790, as given on page xxxiii of the Introduction. As it was impracticable to draw in one diagram, as many lines as there are counties, seven separate figures were constructed upon an uniform scale, one of which was extended to double the height of the others, to embrace those counties which exhibit the largest increase in numbers. Even upon this, it was found necessary to carry back the line for New-York city twice, thus extending it three times the length of the page. Several features of these diagrams deserve notice. The descent between 1810 and 1814, in some counties, and corresponding rise in others, was in part due to the numbers who retired from the frontiers to the interior, on account of the war with Great Britain. The falling off in population of Montgomery and other counties along the state canals, between 1840 and 1845, was chiefly from the removal of transient persons on the suspension of labor upon the canal enlargement. The nearly stationary, or in some cases decreasing numbers in several of the counties, during the last few years, is supposed to be mainly due to emigration to the western states, and removal to the large cities. As each inflection of these lines is produced by some general or local cause of prosperity or decline, these diagrams may be considered as concise exponents of our history.

PLATE II:

Fig. 1. *Comparative population of the Colony of New-York at different periods.*—Upon this figure the lines marked "Total Blacks" and "Total Population," respectively represent by their distances from the bottom line their relative numbers at different times. The comparative areas of the spaces designated "White Males," "White Females," "Black Males" and "Black Females" are proportioned to their relative numbers, as given on page xiv of the Introduction.

Fig. 2. *Total increase of population in the State and comparative numbers by sexes and colors.*—This figure is constructed upon the same principle as Fig. 1, and embraces the period between 1790 to 1855.

Fig. 3. *Irregularities in the return of ages by single years, and the equalizing effect of arrangement in groups of five years, as illustrated by the census of France in* 1851.—The number of all classes, and of single, married and widowed, were classified in the census referred to by single years. From the tendency to report ages in round numbers, the result exhibited the inequalities shown by the five zig zag lines, while the same numbers, reduced to averages in periods of five years, produced the regular curved lines passing through the former. The space between the line of "Total Population," and "Sum of Married and Widowed," represents the comparative number of single persons at different ages.

PLATE III:

Fig. 1. *Comparative number of electors under the first State Constitution.*—The aggregate number of electors, as given on page x of the Introduction, is shown in this figure by the upper curved line, and the number belonging to each class, by the comparative areas of the spaces in which they are designated.

Fig. 2. *Voters and Aliens under the late and present State Constitution.*—The number of these classes are shown by the lines designated "Voters," and "Aliens," respectively. The date of two prominent events tending to increase the number of the former, by extending the elective franchise, are given upon this figure.

Fig. 3. *Comparative number of Slaves in New-York from* 1698 *until their final emancipation.*—This figure is constructed upon the numbers given on pages vii, xi and xiii, of the Introduction. Under the act of 1817, most of the slaves held in the state became free on the 5th day of July 1828. Those of advanced age continued the property of their former owners, who were responsible for their support without public charge. The number of slaves by sexes, between 1786 and 1820, was not reported.

FIG. 4. *Comparative quantities of Cereal Grains.*—The number of bushels of grain reported under this head, since 1840, is shown by lines bearing the names of the crops they represent. The drouth of 1854, was a very prominent cause of the decline in the quantity of wheat, as compared with other years.

FIG. 5. *Comparative number of Domestic Animals.*—The construction of this figure is upon the same principle as the last.

FIG. 6. *Number livng in New-York, and in several cities and countries at different perio ds, compared to each* 1,000 *persons in* 1855. Unlike the preceding figures, this exhibits the relative, instead of the absolute increase of population. The height of each curve above the bottom line, bears the same relation to the height of the figure, that the population of the city or country it represents, has borne at different times, to its present numbers. This figure is constructed upon the numbers given on page xxxv of the Introduction.

INDEX.

[In most instances in which two pages are noted upon one line, the first refers to the beginning of the arrangement by counties and towns, and the second, to the summary of the preceding by counties. The paging of the Introduction being in Roman, and the body of the work in Arabic numerals, rendered the use of both of these systems necessary in the Index. To facilitate reference, the same subject is often placed under several heads.]

DIAGRAM,

Illustrating the Comparative changes of population in the several Counties of New York, from 1790 to 1855

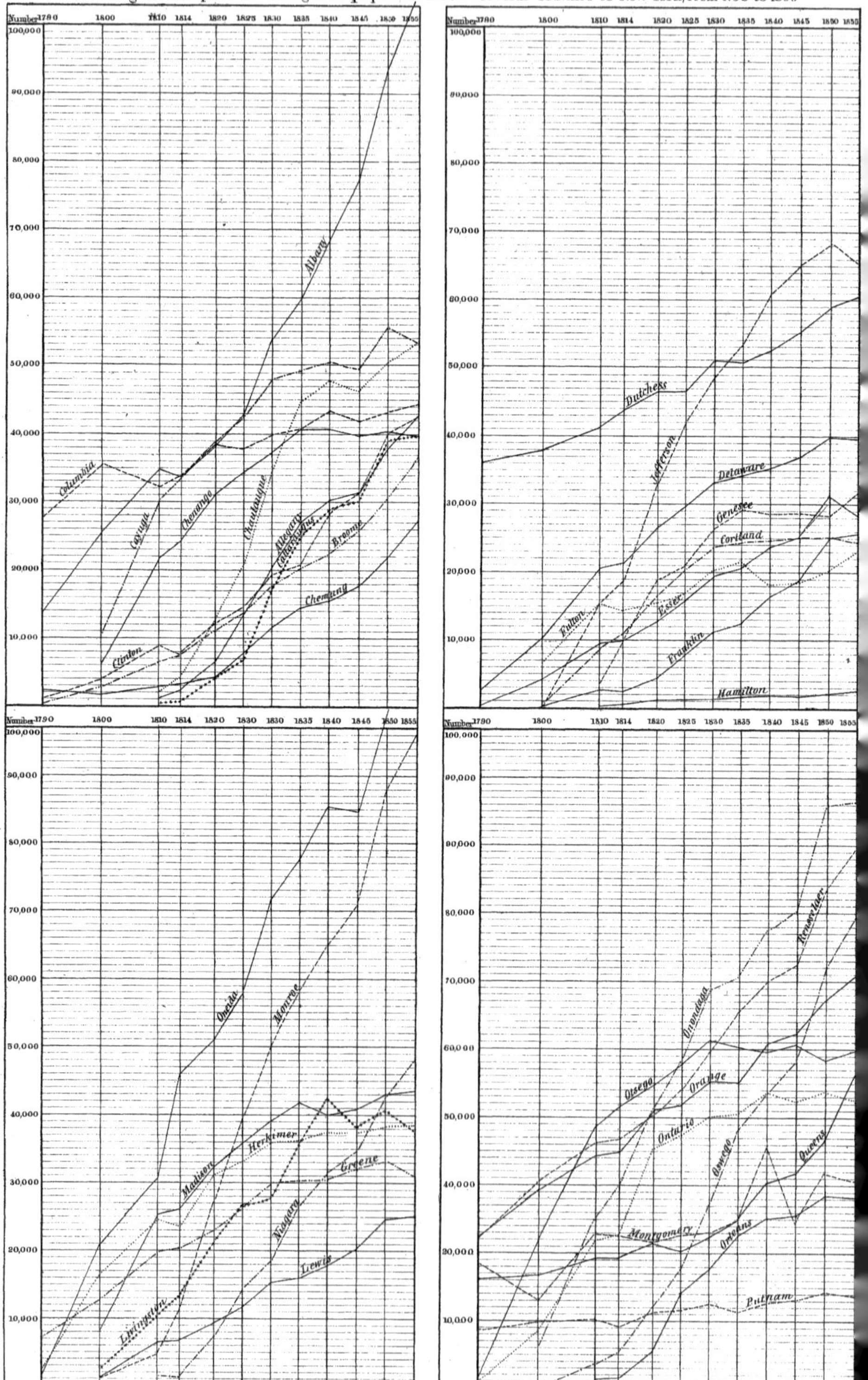
Number 1790 1800 1810 1814 1820 1825 1830 1835 1840 1845 1850 1855
100,000
90,000
80,000
70,000
60,000
50,000
40,000
30,000
20,000
10,000
Albany
Columbia
Cayuga
Chenango
Chautauque
Allegany
Cattaraugus
Broome
Chemung
Clinton
Dutchess
Jefferson
Delaware
Genesee
Cortland
Fulton
Essex
Franklin
Hamilton
Oneida
Monroe
Herkimer
Madison
Greene
Niagara
Lewis
Livingston
Rensselaer
Onondaga
Otsego
Orange
Ontario
Oswego
Queens
Montgomery
Orleans
Putnam
Drawn by F.B. Hough

DIAGRAM, PL. I.

Illustrating the Comparative changes of population in the several Counties of New York, from 1790 to 1855

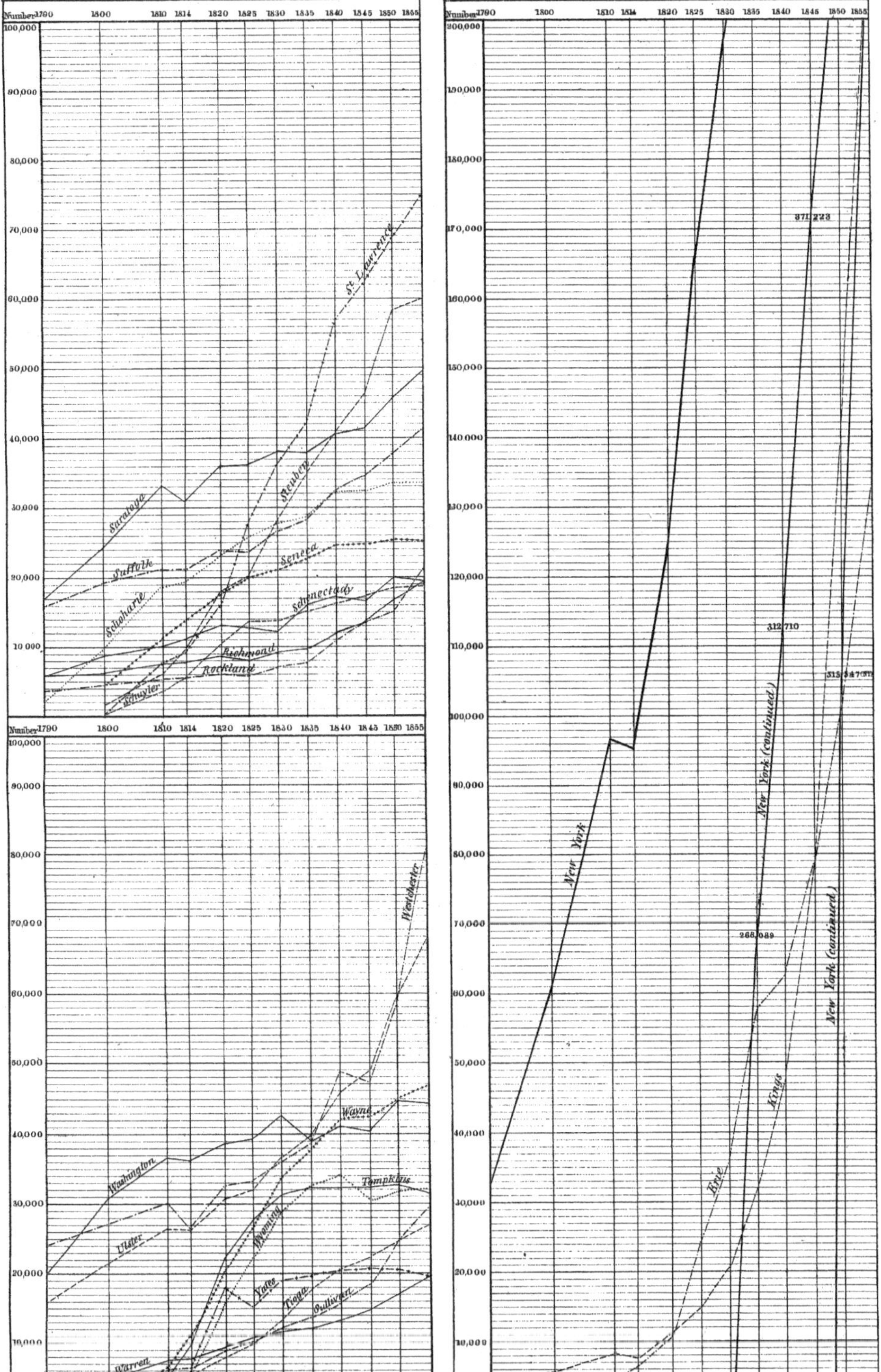

C. Van Benthuysen, Albany, N. Y.

www.ingramcontent.com/pod-product-compliance
Lightning Source LLC
LaVergne TN
LVHW021218110826
845150LV00002B/200